International Dictionary of Theatre-1
PLAYS

International Dictionary of Theatre-1

Volume 1
PLAYS

Volume 2
PLAYWRIGHTS

Volume 3
ACTORS, DIRECTORS AND DESIGNERS

International Dictionary of Theatre-1

PLAYS

EDITOR
MARK HAWKINS-DADY

PICTURE EDITOR
LEANDA SHRIMPTON

St J

St James Press

Chicago and London

Front cover – *The Spanish Tragedy,* National Theatre, London 1982
(© Donald Cooper)

© 1992 by St. James Press

All rights reserved. For information, write to:
ST. JAMES PRESS
233 East Ontario Street
Chicago, Illinois 60611, U.S.A.
or
2-6 Boundary Row
London SE1 8HP

British Library Cataloguing in Publication Data
International dictionary of theatre.
    Vol.1: Plays.
    I. Hawkins-Dady, Mark
    792.0321

    ISBN 1-55862-095-8

CONTENTS

EDITOR'S NOTE

The *International Dictionary of Theatre* is in three volumes: *Plays* (Volume 1), *Playwrights* (Volume 2), and *Actors, Directors and Designers* (Volume 3).

The selection of people and plays appearing in the Dictionary is based on the recommendations of the advisors listed on page ix, and its focus, as the titles of the individual volumes suggest, is primarily on the various genres of drama (both as literature and as performance) as distinct from the other performing arts such as opera, dance, mime, the musical, performance-art, and folk, ritual, and community theatre.

The scope of the Dictionary is historical (ranging from the theatre of Ancient Greece to that of the present day) and international, covering plays of some 20 languages, and playwrights, actors, directors, and designers of many nationalities. Many entries are illustrated with photographs of productions, designs, portraits, or engravings.

VOLUME 1: Plays

Volume 1 contains entries on over 620 notable plays. Many have become acknowledged "classics" through study and performance. Some are rarely performed now, but have historical significance. Others, and particularly those from the last 20 years, represent the work of recently established writers and those with emerging reputations.

In the case of plays written in languages other than English, we have made a selection of those works which, through study, performance, or reputation, have become highly regarded and well known in the English-speaking world.

A NOTE ON THE ENTRIES

Entries are in alphabetical order of title. Plays in languages other than English are generally placed according to their most familiar English translation; full cross-referencing of titles will, however, enable the reader to locate a play by its original title or by alternative translations of that title.

Every entry contains, where known, the date and location of first publication and first production; a chronological list of books and articles about the play; and a critical essay on the play by one of the Dictionary's contributors. For plays published and/or produced before the 20th century, a chronological list of modern editions is provided. For plays written in languages other than English, a chronological list of modern translations is given.

In the lists of translations and editions, an author's "complete works" have generally been omitted; these are listed in the relevant author's entry in Volume 2 (*Playwrights*). In all listings, the publication dates and places are the first or earliest known.

The Criticism Section

The books and articles listed in this section are in chronological order of publication. They concentrate on critical interest over the last 25 years (since the mid-1960's), although, in many cases, earlier material is also cited.

For reasons of space, and to avoid repetition, it has been the general policy to exclude the following categories from the lists of criticism:

    (a) General works on dramatic periods, movements, and genres.

    (b) Monographs, essay collections, and articles dealing more broadly with an author's work; since the vast majority of the authors represented in Volume 1 are included in Volume 2 (*Playwrights*), in each relevant entry in *Plays,* the reader is referred to the appropriate entry in *Playwrights*.

    (c) Articles of less than five pages in length.

In three cases — Goethe's *Faust*, Rojas' *Celestina*, and Shakespeare's works — the sheer quantity of critical material is impossible to list here. Therefore, in these three entries only book-length studies are listed, and the reader is referred to appropriate bibliographies for further information on articles.

The criticism section cites books and articles in the major European languages (notably French, German, Italian, and Spanish) as well as in English. Books and articles in the less familiar East-European languages and in languages using non-Roman alphabets are not cited.

ACKNOWLEDGEMENTS

I should like to thank the following for their help in this project: all the advisers and contributors; the late Jim Vinson, for laying the foundations in the initial stages; John and Barbara Cavanagh; the staff of the British Library, the much-missed British Theatre Association, London University Library, Queen Mary and Westfield College Library, and Royal Holloway and Bedford New College Library; Martha Bremser; Warren Cheshire; Tracy Chevalier; Michèle Hore; Daniel Kirkpatrick; Vicky Linklater; Brian Pearce; and my colleagues and friends at St. James.

ADVISERS

Arnold Aronson
Martin Banham
Eugene Benson
Michael Billington
David Bradby
James Brandon
Jarka M. Burian
Marvin Carlson
John Russell Brown
Ruby Cohn
Tish Dace
Daniel Gerould
Vera Gottlieb
Peter Holland
William D. Howarth

Christopher Innes
Bruce King
Felicia Hardison Londré
Frederick J. Marker
Walter J. Meserve
Michael Patterson
Kenneth Richards
Laurence Senelick
Peter Thomson
Stanley Wells
George E. Wellwarth
Margaret Williams
George Woodyard
Katharine Worth

CONTRIBUTORS

Asbjørn Aarseth
Gunilla Anderman
Richard Andrews
Frank Ardolino
Arthur Ballet
Chris Banfield
Martin Banham
Judith E. Barlow
Gene A. Barnett
Susan Bassnett
Richard C. Beacham
Joss Bennathon
Susan Bennett
Eugene Benson
Renate Benson
Günter Berghaus
Michael Bertin
Michael Billington
George Bisztray
Franz G. Blaha
Michael R. Booth
Roy Booth
David Bradby
George W. Brandt
Anthony Brennan
Peter Brigg
Anthony D.P. Briggs
Christina Britzolakis
John Russell Brown
Molly Brown
John Bull
Jarka M. Burian
Mark Thornton Burnett
Rob Burns
Martin Butler
Denis Calandra
David Carnegie
Dennis Carroll
Anthony J. Cascardi

Janet Clare
Janet Clarke
Katharine Cockin
L.W. Connolly
Thomas F. Connolly
Philip S. Cook
Brian Corman
W.A. Coupe
Karen Cronacher
Brian Crow
Eugene Current-Garcia
Tish Dace
Clifford Davidson
Peter Davison
Barbara Day
William Dolby
Leonard E. Doucette
Tony Dunn
Margaret Eddershaw
Gwynne Edwards
Stanislaw Eile
Peter Falckenberg
Peter Fitzpatrick
Kathy Fletcher
Verna A. Foster
Richard Foulkes
Antonio Franceschetti
Steven H. Gale
David George
Daniel Gerould
C.J. Gianakaris
Colin Gibson
Richard B. Gidez
Donald Gilman
S.E. Gontarski
John Goodliffe
Robert Gordon
Lynn Carbón Gorell
Christopher Gossip

Anthony Graham-White
Frances Gray
Michael Grosvenor Myer
Valerie Grosvenor Myer
James Hansford
Michael Hattaway
Mark Hawkins-Dady
Roger W. Herzel
Juan Carlos Hidalgo Ciudad
Graham Holderness
Marion Peter Holt
Mark Anthony Houlahan
Jane House
William D. Howarth
Derek Hughes
Hugh Hunt
John D. Hurrell
R.D.S. Jack
Robert Jordan
Brian Keith-Smith
Veronica Kelly
Dennis Kennedy
Adele King
Bruce King
Pamela M. King
Laurence Kitchin
H. Gustav Klaus
Margaret M. Knapp
A.V. Knowles
Manfred K. Kremer
Rosette C. Lamont
Bernd-Peter Lange
Paul Lawley
Ramón Layera
Robert Leach
M.A. Levene
Peter Lewis
Tim Lewis
Felicia Hardison Londré
N.J. Lowe
James MacDonald
Ann L. MacKenzie
Colin Mackerras
G. Jonathon Mallinson
Eivor Martinus
Paul McGillick
Howard McNaughton
Gordon McVay
Anthony Meech
Walter J. Meserve
Patrick Miles
Christian H. Moe
Mary Pat Mombourquette
Margery Morgan
Marcia K. Morrison
J.R. Mulryne
Steve Nicholson
Kirsten F. Nigro
John Osborne
Malcolm Page
D. Keith Peacock
Brian Pearce
Andy Piasecki
Donald Pirie

Ludvika Popenhagen
Raphael Portillo
Rosemary Pountney
Jennifer Preston
Roger Prior
Leonard C. Pronko
Colin Radford
Margaret Loftus Ranald
Donald Rayfield
Leslie du S. Read
Bonnie Hildebrand Reynolds
Francesca H.A. Richards
Kenneth Richards
Laura Richards
Hugh Rorrison
Nicholas Round
Donald Roy
Glendyr Sacks
Robert K. Sarlós
Claude Schumacher
Irene Scobbie
Lesley Sharpe
Robert Silvester
James Simmons
G. Singh
Robert Skloot
Peter Skrine
Maya Slater
Irene Slatter
Christopher Smith
James L. Smith
Roger Sorkin
Lesley Anne Soule
Jane Spencer
Alexander Stillmark
Ronald W. Strang
Elizabeth Swain
Diana Taylor
George Taylor
Val Taylor
Philip Thody
Andrew T. Tsubaki
Elaine Turner
Meg Twycross
Joanna Udall
Gary Vena
Colin Wills Visser
Carla Waal
Anthony Waine
Peter Walcot
David H. Walker
J. Michael Walton
Alan G. Waring
Daniel J. Watermeier
Dennis Welland
David Whitton
Margaret Williams
Simon Williams
Peter Womack
Claudia Woolgar
Katharine Worth
W.E. Yates
Phyllis Zatlin
Hersh Zeifman

International Dictionary of Theatre-1

PLAYS

A-Z LIST OF PLAYS

Absurd Person Singular (Alan Ayckbourn)
Accidental Death of an Anarchist (Dario Fo)
The Adding Machine (Elmer Rice)
The Admirable Crichton (J.M. Barrie)
After Haggerty (David Mercer)
After the Fall (Arthur Miller)
Ajax (Sophocles)
Alcestis (Euripides)
The Alchemist (Ben Jonson)
All For Love (John Dryden)
All My Sons (Arthur Miller)
All's Well That Ends Well (William Shakespeare)
American Buffalo (David Mamet)
Aminta (Torquato Tasso)
Andromache (Jean Racine)
Antigone (Sophocles)
Antigone (Jean Anouilh)
Antony (Alexandre Dumas *père*)
Antony and Cleopatra (William Shakespeare)
The Architect and Emperor of Assyria (Fernando Arrabal)
Arden of Faversham (Anonymous)
As You Like It (William Shakespeare)
The Ascent of F6 (W.H. Auden and Christopher Isherwood)
At the Hawk's Well (W.B. Yeats)
The Atheist's Tragedy (Cyril Tourneur)
Awake and Sing! (Clifford Odets)

Baal (Bertolt Brecht)
The Bacchae (Euripides)
Back to Methuselah (G.B. Shaw)
The Bad-Tempered Old Man (Menander)
The Balcony (Jean Genet)
The Bald Prima Donna (Eugène Ionesco)
The Barber of Seville (Pierre-Augustin Caron de Beaumarchais)
Bartholemew Fair (Ben Jonson)
The Basic Training of Pavlo Hummel (David Rabe)
The Battles of Coxinga (Chikamatsu Monzaemon)
The Beaux' Stratagem (George Farquhar)
The Bedbug (Vladimir Mayakovsky)
Before Dawn (Gerhart Hauptmann)
The Beggar (Reinhard Sorge)
The Beggar's Opera (John Gay)
The Bells (Leopold Lewis)
Benkei in the Boat (Kanze Kojirō Nobumitsu)
Berenice (Jean Racine)
Beyond Human Power (Bjørnstjerne Bjørnson)
Bingo (Edward Bond)
The Birds (Aristophanes)
The Birthday Party (Harold Pinter)
Black-Eyed Susan (Douglas Jerrold)
The Blacks (Jean Genet)
Blood Relations (Sharon Pollock)
Blood Wedding (Federico García Lorca)
The Blue Bird (Maurice Maeterlinck)
Boesman and Lena (Athol Fugard)
Bonds of Interest (Jacinto Benavente y Martínez)
Boris Godunov (Alexander Pushkin)
The Braggart Soldier (Titus Maccius Plautus)
Brand (Henrik Ibsen)
Break of Noon (Paul Claudel)
Brighton Beach Memoirs (Neil Simon)
Britannicus (Jean Racine)

The Broken Heart (John Ford)
The Broken Jug (Heinrich von Kleist)
The Brothers (Terence)
The Brothers Menaechmus (Titus Maccius Plautus)
The Browning Version (Terence Rattigan)
Burn This (Lanford Wilson)
Bussy D'Ambois (George Chapman)
Butley (Simon Gray)

Caligula (Albert Camus)
Candida (G.B. Shaw)
The Candle-Bearer (Giordano Bruno)
The Captain of Köpenick (Carl Zuckmayer)
The Caretaker (Harold Pinter)
Caritas (Arnold Wesker)
Caste (T.W. Robertson)
The Castle of Perseverance (Anonymous)
Cat on a Hot Tin Roof (Tennessee Williams)
Cato (Joseph Addison)
The Caucasian Chalk Circle (Bertolt Brecht)
Celestina (Fernando de Rojas)
El Cepillo de Dientes (Jorge Díaz)
The Chairs (Eugène Ionesco)
The Chalk Circle (Li Xingfu)
The Changeling (Thomas Middleton and William Rowley)
The Chapel Perilous (Dorothy Hewett)
A Chaste Maid in Cheapside (Thomas Middleton)
Chatterton (Alfred de Vigny)
The Cherry Orchard (Anton Chekhov)
The Chest (Lodovico Ariosto)
The Chester Cycle (Anonymous)
The Cheviot, The Stag, and the Black, Black Oil (John McGrath)
Children of a Lesser God (Mark Medoff)
The Children's Hour (Lillian Hellman)
The Churchill Play (Howard Brenton)
El Cid (Pierre Corneille)
Cinna (Pierre Corneille)
The Clandestine Marriage (David Garrick and George Colman the Elder)
Cloud Nine (Caryl Churchill)
The Clouds (Aristophanes)
Cock-a-Doodle-Dandy (Sean O'Casey)
The Cocktail Party (T.S. Eliot)
Coelina (René Charles Guilbert de Pixérécourt)
Come Back Little Sheba (Willam Inge)
Comedians (Trevor Griffiths)
The Comedy of Errors (William Shakespeare)
Comedy, Satire, Irony and Deeper Meaning (Christian Dietrich Grabbe)
The Conquest of Granada, Parts One and Two (John Dryden)
The Conscious Lovers (Sir Richard Steele)
The Contractor (David Storey)
Coriolanus (William Shakespeare)
The Corn Is Green (Emlyn Williams)
Corruption in the Palace of Justice (Ugo Betti)
The Country Wife (William Wycherley)
The Criminals (José Triana)
The Critic (Richard Brinsley Sheridan)
Cross Purpose (Albert Camus)
The Crucible (Arthur Miller)
Cymbeline (William Shakespeare)
Cyrano de Bergerac (Edmond Rostand)

xvi

LIST OF PLAYS BY AUTHOR

Accademia degli Intronati di Siena
The Deceived

Arthur Adamov
Professor Taranne

Joseph Addison
Cato

Aeschylus
The Oresteia
The Persians
Prometheus Bound
Seven Against Thebes
The Suppliants

Edward Albee
A Delicate Balance
Tiny Alice
Who's Afraid of Virginia Woolf?
The Zoo Story

Vittorio Alfieri
Oreste

Maxwell Anderson
What Price Glory?
Winterset

Leonid Andreyev
He Who Gets Slapped
The Life of Man

Anonymous
Arden of Faversham
The Castle of Perseverance
The Chester Cycle
Everyman
Gammer Gurton's Needle
Mankind
Maria Marten
Master Peter Pathelin
N-Town Plays
La Venexiana
The York Cycle

Jean Anouilh
Antigone
Ring Round the Moon

An-sky
The Dybbuk

John Arden
Serjeant Musgrave's Dance
The Workhouse Donkey

Lodovico Ariosto
The Chest

Aristophanes
The Birds
The Clouds
The Frogs
Lysistrata

Roberto Arlt
Saverio El Cruel

Fernando Arrabal
The Architect and Emperor of Assyria

W.H. Auden
The Ascent of F6

Alan Ayckbourn
Absurd Person Singular
The Norman Conquests

Imamu Amiri Baraka (LeRoi Jones)
Dutchman

Howard Barker
Victory

Peter Barnes
The Ruling Class

J.M. Barrie
The Admiral Crichton
Peter Pan

Philip Barry
The Philadephia Story

Pierre-Augustin Caron de Beaumarchais
The Barber of Seville
The Marriage of Figaro

Francis Beaumont
The Knight of the Burning Pestle
The Maid's Tragedy
Philaster

Samuel Beckett
Endgame
Happy Days
Krapp's Last Tape
Not I
Play
Waiting For Godot

Henry Becque
The Vultures

Brendan Behan
The Hostage
The Quare Fellow

Aphra Behn
The Rover

Jacinto Benavente y Martínez
Bonds of Interest

Alan Bennet
Forty Years On

Steven Berkoff
East

Thomas Bernhard
The Force of Habit

Ugo Betti
Corruption in the Palace of Justice

Bjørnstjerne Bjørnson
Beyond Human Power

Alexander Blok
The Puppet Show

George Henry Boker
Francesca da Rimini

Robert Bolt
A Man For All Seasons

Edward Bond
Bingo
Lear
Saved

Dion Boucicault
London Assurance
The Shaughraun

Bertolt Brecht
Baal
The Caucasian Chalk Circle
The Good Person of Setzuan
Life of Galileo
Man Equals Man
The Measures Taken
Mother Courage and Her Children
The Resistable Rise of Arturo Ui
The Threepenny Opera

Howard Brenton
The Churchill Play
The Romans in Britain

Giordano Bruno
The Candle-Bearer

Georg Büchner
Danton's Death
Woyzeck

Antonio Buero Vallejo
The Sleep of Reason

Mikhail Bulgakov
The White Guard

Edward Bulwer-Lytton
Money

Alexander Buzo
Norm and Ahmed

Pedro Calderón de la Barca
The Great Theatre of the World
Life is a Dream
The Mayor of Zalamea

Albert Camus
Caligula
Cross-Purpose

Cao Yu
Thunderstorm

Josef Čapek
The Insect Play

Karel Čapek
The Insect Play
R.U.R.

Emilio Carballido
I, Too, Speak of the Rose

Paul Vincent Carroll
Shadow and Substance

Aimé Césaire
A Season in the Congo

George Chapman
Bussy D'Ambois
Eastward Ho!

Anton Chekhov
The Cherry Orchard
Ivanov
The Seagull
The Three Sisters
Uncle Vanya

Luigi Chiarelli
The Mask and the Face

Chikamatsu Monzaemon
The Battles of Coxinga

Alice Childress
Wedding Band

Caryl Churchill
Cloud Nine
Top Girls

Colley Cibber
Love's Last Shift

Paul Claudel
Break of Noon
The Satin Slipper

Jean Cocteau
The Infernal Machine

George Colman the Elder
The Clandestine Marriage

William Congreve
The Double-Dealer
Love For Love
The Way of the World

Marc Connelly
The Green Pastures

Michael Cook
Jacob's Wake

Pierre Corneille
El Cid
Cinna
Horatius
The Theatrical Illusion

John Coulter
The Riel Trilogy

Noël Coward
Design For Living
Hay Fever
Private Lives

Fernand Crommelynck
The Magnificent Cuckhold

Rachel Crothers
He and She

Richard Cumberland
The West Indian

Gabriele D'Annunzio
Francesca da Rimini

Augustin Daly
Under the Gaslight

Alma De Groen
The Rivers of China

Eduardo De Filippo
Saturday, Sunday, Monday

Thomas Dekker
The Shoemaker's Holiday
The Witch of Edmonton

Shelagh Delaney
A Taste of Honey

Jorge Díaz
El Cepillo de Dientes

John Dryden
All For Love
The Conquest of Granada, Parts One and Two
Marriage à-la-Mode

Marcel Dubé
The White Geese

Alexandre Dumas *fils*
The Lady of the Camelias

Alexandre Dumas *pére*
Antony

Friedrich Dürrenmatt
The Physicists
The Visit

David Edgar
Destiny

T.S. Eliot
The Cocktail Party
The Family Reunion
Murder in the Cathedral

Nikolai Erdman
The Suicide

Sir George Etherege
The Man of Mode
She Would if She Could

Euripides
Alcestis
The Bacchae
Electra
Hippolytus
Iphigenia in Tauris
Medea
The Trojan Women

George Farquhar
The Beaux' Stratagem
The Recruiting Officer

Georges Feydeau
A Flea in Her Ear

Henry Fielding
Tom Thumb

Harvey Fierstein
Torch Song Trilogy

John Fletcher
The Maid's Trilogy
Philaster
The Two Noble Kinsmen

Dario Fo
Accidental Death of an Anarchist

Denis Fonvizin
The Minor

John Ford
The Broken Heart
'Tis Pity She's a Whore
The Witch of Edmonton

David French
Leaving Home

Brian Friel
Philadelphia, Here I Come!
Translations

Max Frisch
The Fire Raisers

Christopher Fry
The Lady's Not For Burning

Athol Fugard
Boesman and Lena
The Island
''Master Harold''... and the Boys
Sizwe Bansi is Dead

Charles Fuller
A Soldier's Play

John Galsworthy
Justice
Strife

Griselda Gambaro
Los Siameses

Federico García Lorca
Blood Wedding
The House of Bernarda Alba
Yerma

David Garrick
The Clandestine Marriage

John Gay
The Beggar's Opera

Gratien Gélinas
Tit-Coq

Jean Genet
The Balcony
The Blacks
The Maids

Priest Genne-Hōin
Suehirogari

Jean Giraudoux
The Trojan War Will Not Take Place

Susan Glaspell
The Verge

Johann Wolfgang von Goethe
Faust
Götz von Berlichingen mit der eisernen Hand

Nikolai Gogol
The Government Inspector

Carlo Goldoni
The Mistress of the Inn
The Servant of Two Masters

Oliver Goldsmith
She Stoops to Conquer

Witold Gombrowicz
Marriage

Maxim Gorky
The Lower Depths
Summerfolk

Carlo Gozzi
Turandot

Christian Dietrich Grabbe
Comedy, Satire, Irony and Deeper Meaning

Harley Granville-Barker
The Madras House
The Voysey Inheritance

Günter Grass
The Plebeians Rehearse the Uprising

Simon Gray
Butley

Paul Green
In Abraham's Bosom
Johnny Johnson

Robert Greene
Friar Bacon and Friar Bungay

Alexander Griboyedov
The Misfortune of Being Clever

Trevor Griffiths
Comedians

John Guare
The House of Blue Leaves

Giovanni Battista Guarini
The Faithful Shepherd

Christopher Hampton
The Philanthropist

Peter Handke
Kaspar
Offending the Audience

Lorraine Hansberry
A Raisin in the Sun

David Hare
Plenty
Pravda
Teeth 'n' Smiles

Moss Hart
Once in a Lifetime
You Can't Take It With You

Walter Hasenclever
Der Sohn

Gerhart Hauptmann
Before Dawn
The Weavers

Václav Havel
The Memorandum

Sidney Kingsley
Dead End

Heiner Kipphardt
In the Matter of J. Robert Oppenheimer

Heinrich von Kleist
The Broken Jug
Penthesilea
The Prince of Homburg

Oskar Kokoschka
Murderer, Hope of Women

Kong Shangren
Peach Blossom Fan

Arthur Kopit
Indians
Oh Dad, Poor Dad, Mamma's Hung You in the Closet and
I'm Feeling so Sad

Zygmunt Krasiński
The Undivine Comedy

Franz Xaver Kroetz
Farmyard

Thomas Kyd
The Spanish Tragedy

Eugène Labiche
An Italian Straw Hat

Pär Lagerqvist
The Hangman

Lao She
Teahouse

Ray Lawler
The Doll Trilogy

Jacob Michael Reinhold Lenz
The Soldiers
The Tutor

Hugh Leonard
Da

Mikhail Lermontov
Masquerade

Alain-René Lesage
Turcaret

Gotthold Ephraim Lessing
Emilia Galotti
Minna von Barnhelm

Leopold Lewis
The Bells

Li Xingfu
The Chalk Circle

Georg Lillo
The London Merchant

Sir David Lindsay
A Satire of the Three Estates

John Howard Lawson
Processional

John Lyly
Endimion

Charles MacArthur
The Front Page

Niccolò Machiavelli
Mandragola

Imre Madách
The Tragedy of Man

Maurice Maeterlinck
The Blue Bird
Pélleas and Mélisande

Antonine Maillet
La Sagouine

David Mamet
American Buffalo
Glengarry Glen Ross

Pierre Carlet de Chamblain de Marivaux
The Double Inconstancy
The Game of Love and Chance

Christopher Marlowe
Doctor Faustus
Edward II
The Jew of Malta
Tamburlaine the Great, Parts One and Two

René Marqués
Los Soles Truncos

John Marston
Eastward Ho!
The Malcontent

Bruce Mason
The Pohutukawa Tree

Philip Massinger
A New Way to Pay Old Debts

Somerset Maugham
For Services Rendered

Vladimir Mayakovsky
The Bedbug
Mystery Bouffe

Greg McGee
Foreskin's Lament

John McGrath
The Cheviot, the Stag, and the Black, Black Oil

Mark Medoff
Children of a Lesser God

Henry Medwall
Fulgens and Lucrece

Menander
The Bad-Tempered Old Man

David Mercer
After Haggerty

Adam Mickiewicz
Forefathers' Eve

Thomas Middleton
The Changeling
A Chaste Maid in Cheapside
The Revenger's Tragedy (possibly by Tourneur)
Women Beware Women

Arthur Miller
After the Fall
All My Sons
The Crucible
Death of a Salesman
A View From the Bridge

Langdon Mitchell
The New York Idea

Molière
Don Juan
The Imaginary Invalid
The Learned Ladies
The Misanthrope
The Miser
The Pretentious Young Ladies
The School For Wives
Tartuffe
The Would-Be Gentleman

Tirso de Molina
The Trickster of Seville

Ferenc Molnár
Liliom

Henry de Montherlant
Queen After Death

William Vaughn Moody
The Great Divide

Anna Cora Mowatt
Fashion

Sławomir Mrożek
Tango

John Murrell
Waiting for the Parade

Alfred de Musset
Lorenzaccio

Peter Nichols
A Day in the Death of Joe Egg

Thomas Norton
Gorboduc

Louis Nowra
The Golden Age

Winston Ntshona
The Island
Sizwe Bansi is Dead

Sean O'Casey
Cock-a-Doodle Dandy
Juno and the Paycock
The Plough and the Stars
The Silver Tassie

John O'Keeffe
Wild Oats

Eugene O'Neill
Desire Under the Elms
The Emperor Jones
The Great God Brown
The Hairy Ape
The Iceman Cometh
Long Day's Journey Into Night
Mourning Becomes Electra

Clifford Odets
Awake and Sing!
Waiting for Lefty

Joe Orton
Entertaining Mr. Sloane
What the Butler Saw

John Osborne
The Entertainer
Look Back in Anger

Alexander Ostrovsky
The Forest
The Storm

Thomas Otway
Venice Preserved

George Peele
The Old Wives Tale

Arthur Wing Pinero
The Magistrate
The Second Mrs. Tranqueray

Harold Pinter
The Birthday Party
The Caretaker
The Homecoming
No Man's Land
Old Times

Luigi Pirandello
Henry IV
Right You Are (If You Think You Are)
Six Characters in Search of an Author

René Charles Guilbert de Pixérécourt
Coelina

José Triana
The Criminals

Tsurya Nanboku IV
The Scarlet Princess of Edo

Ivan Turgenev
A Month in the Country

Nicholas Udall
Ralph Roister Doister

Rodolfo Usigli
El Gesticulador

Ramón del Valle-Inclan
Lights of Bohemia

Alexander Vampilov
Duck Hunting

John Van Druten
The Voice of the Turtle

John Vanbrugh
The Provoked Wife
The Relapse

Lope de Vega Carpio
Fuenteovejuna
Justice Without Revenge
Peribáñez and the Comendador of Ocaña

Boris Vian
The Empire Builders

Alfred de Vigny
Chatterton

George Villiers, Duke of Buckingham
The Rehearsal

Voltaire
Zaïre

Derek Walcott
Dream on Monkey Mountain

John Walker
The Factory Lad

Martin Walser
Home Front

John Webster
The Duchess of Malfi
The White Devil

Frank Wedekind
The Lulu Plays
Spring's Awakening

Othmar Weiss (and others)
The Oberammergau Passion Play

Peter Weiss
The Investigation
Marat/Sade

Arnold Wesker
Caritas
The Wesker Trilogy

Patrick White
The Season at Sarsaparilla

John Whiting
The Devils

Oscar Wilde
The Importance of Being Earnest
Lady Windemere's Fan
Salomé

Thornton Wilder
Our Town
The Skin of Our Teeth

Emlyn Williams
The Corn is Green

Tennessee Williams
Cat on a Hot Tin Roof
The Glass Menagerie
The Night of the Iguana
A Streetcar Named Desire

David Williamson
The Removalists
Travelling North

August Wilson
Fences

Lanford Wilson
Burn This

Stanisław Ignacy Witkiewicz
The Water Hen

Charles Wood
Dingo

William Wycherley
The Country Wife
The Plain Dealer

Stanisław Wyspiański
The Wedding

W.B. Yeats
At the Hawk's Well
The Death of Cuchulain
On Baile's Strand
Purgatory

Émile Zola
Thérèse Raquin

Carl Zuckmayer
The Captain of Köpenick

A

ABSURD PERSON SINGULAR
by Alan Ayckbourn

First Publication: In *Three Plays*, London, 1977.
First Production: Library Theatre, Scarborough, 26 June
          1972.

*   *   *

Set in three different kitchens on three successive Christmas
Eves, *Absurd Person Singular* depicts social and professional
reversals of fortune. The first-act hosts are Sidney and Jane
Hopcroft: he is pushy and domineering, she is nervously
house–proud, and together they run a general store. Their
guests (apart from a hearty, unseen pair of teachers) are their
bank manager, Ronald Brewster-Wright and his loftily
patronising wife, Marion, plus a womanizing architect,
Geoffrey Jackson, and his pill-popping spouse, Eva. Sidney
and Geoffrey both look to Ronald for business patronage: the
former needs a loan for a property-development scheme, and
the latter needs support for his design of a new shopping
complex. The second act is set in the Jacksons' kitchen. Their
marriage is on the rocks; Geoffrey's design for a "Super
Shopperdrome" is way over budget; and Eva's desire to kill
herself is met with genial, kindly misunderstanding. Only the
jaunty, up-and-coming Sidney Hopcroft remains the life and
soul of the party. The third act shifts to the Brewster-Wrights'
gloomy, underheated Victorian kitchen. He and his alcoholic
wife, now sunk in a permanent alcoholic stupor, barely
communicate. The roof has literally fallen in on Geoffrey's
Shopperdrome. But the Hopcrofts are thriving and, when they
arrive with direly unsuitable presents, they force everyone to
play party games and dance to their tune.

This was a vital transitional play for Ayckbourn, one that
proved he was a sharp social commentator as well as a shrewd
observer of English domestic rituals. Indeed, with the passage
of time, the play has come to seem uncannily prophetic, for
what it clearly shows is the rise of the go-getting, opportunistic
little entrepreneur at the expense of the lazy, incompetent
professional and managerial middle-classes. When the play
was revived by Ayckbourn himself in 1990, it became apparent
that it had intuitively anticipated the era of Thatcherism: it was
not simply a well-oiled comic machine but a document for our
times. Even the device of labelling the acts "Last Christmas",
"This Christmas", and "Next Christmas" implied that the
future belonged to the kind of ruthless, dynamic capitalist
adventurer personified by Sidney Hopcroft.

In the broadest sense of the word, *Absurd Person Singular* is
a political play. But Ayckbourn also writes, with penetrating
insight, about differing attitudes to marriage. For Sidney, a
wife is an extension of his own power: in the first act he
callously berates Jane for the social gaffe of locking herself out
of her own kitchen and by the end of the play has transformed
her into the perfect acolyte. For the compulsively philandering
Geoffrey, a wife is simply convenient domestic security. It is
fascinating, however, to note that by the third act he has
become totally dependent on Eva to rescue his shattered
architectural career. For the hazy, twice-married, upper-
middle-class Ronald, women in general and wives, in particular, are, as he says, "a completely closed book": we deduce, in
fact, that it is his amiable negligence that has driven Marion
into gin-swilling isolation. Ayckbourn has always been an
instinctive feminist, and he here pins down, with mordant
accuracy, the selfishness, cruelty, and incomprehension with
which English men treat their wives.

But Ayckbourn's forte is for writing a specific kind of tragicomedy which manages to reduce the audience to helpless
laughter while filling them with a retrospective sense of guilt:
something embodied to perfection in this play's central act. Its
whole dynamic comes from watching Eva attempt to kill
herself by running at a kitchen-knife, putting her head in the
gas-oven, swallowing pills and paint-stripper, and hanging
herself from the light flex. Each attempt at suicide is thwarted
by one of the other characters who re-interprets it in his or her
terms—ovens to the bustlingly domestic Jane, for instance, are
things to be cleaned ferociously. Ayckbourn brilliantly demonstrates the way people are cocooned inside their own egos so
that they cannot even recognise despair. But the scene also
works unnervingly on the audience who roar with laughter and
then pull back in slightly shame-faced horror.

Power, class, sex, despair: these are the ingredients of
Ayckbourn's durable, ground-breaking comedy. He is sometimes accused of a manipulative coldness towards his characters but that seems to me untrue: he shows genuine compassion
for the play's abused women and reserves whatever bile he has
for Sidney Hopcroft and his particular brand of armour-plated
materialism. But what is finally remarkable about the play is
how much of England it puts on the stage and how it warns us
that entrepreneurial capitalism, when devoid of any social
conscience, is both dangerous and destructive. This is
Ayckbourn the comic moralist at his best.

—Michael Billington

1

ACCIDENTAL DEATH OF AN ANARCHIST
(Morte accidentale di un anarchico)
by Dario Fo

First Publication: Verona, 1970; revised edition, Turin, 1974.
First Production: Via Colletta Milan (La Comune), 10
        December 1970.

Translations
Accidental Death of an Anarchist, translated by S. Cowan, in
    Theatre, vol. 10 no. 2, 1979.
Accidental Death of an Anarchist, translated by Gillian Hanna,
    adapted by Gavin Richards, London, 1980.

Criticism
(For general works on the author, see *Playwrights* volume)

Articles:
Suzanne Cowan, "Dario Fo, Politics and Satire: An Introduc-
    tion to *Accidental Death of an Anarchist*", in *Theatre*, vol. 10
    no. 2, 1979.
Pina Piccolo, " Farce as the Mirror of Bourgeois Politics:
    Morte accidentale di un anarchico", in *Forum Italicum*, 20,
    1986.
Joylynn Wing, "The Performance of Power and the Power of
    Performance: Rewriting the Police State in Dario Fo's
    Accidental Death of an Anarchist", in *Modern Drama*, 33,
    1990.

*   *   *

The setting of the play is a Milan police station, where a
political activist has fallen to his death from a window while
being interrogated about terrorist bomb attacks in the city. A
zany visitor, who carries disguises about with him and claims to
be a "Maniac", wanders into the police station, rouses the
suspicions of the police and, in order to evade them, pretends
to be the examining magistrate who has arrived to conduct an
enquiry into the anarchist's death. As he attempts to pursue
the "truth" of the matter in a reasonable way, he mercilessly
pulls apart the police statements, exposing them as a tissue of
distortions and fabrications. As the police stumble in to ever
greater confusion and contradiction they expose the fascistic
arbitrariness of their conduct. The "Maniac" proposes they
devise a new theory to account for what actually happened: the
police, he suggests, were just chatting and laughing with the
anarchist in order to cheer him up when inexplicably he
jumped out of the window.

Accidental Death is rooted in the actual, and for all its rich,
farcical inventiveness is, in a sense, a political documentary,
that much the more incisive for the grotesquerie of its action. It
is based on actual events which followed a terrorist bomb
attack on a branch of the Banca Nazionale dell'Agricoltura in
Milan in December, 1969, when a certain Giuseppe Pinelli, an
anarchist railway worker, was arrested on a charge of planting
the bomb, and while under interrogation fell to his death from
the window of a police station. The subsequent official
enquiry, police statements to the media, and the final official
report, all contained many inconsistencies and contradictions,
leaving the suspicion that little of the truth of the matter had
actually been sought, let alone brought out. Fo puts this
situation to brilliant comic account thanks, not least, to the
central comic device of having a "Maniac" serve as a judicial
investigator: this turns the supposedly rational world of the
police station on its head and, as the comic incidents accumulate, the "madman" emerges as apparently sane, and the sane
as apparently mad.

As the device of the "Maniac" indicates, and Fo himself has
acknowledged, the play was "cast in a grotesque style", the
distinctly farcical action, and the extravagantly comic types
who people it, serving to keep the audience a certain distance,
both engaged and detached, and therefore able to observe the
situation critically and appreciate the political thrust of the
satire. Fo has a distinct, comic preference for the vigorous,
anarchic world of farce, and he sees farce as manifestly of the
popular meridian, carrying a corrosive satirical force relished
by working class audiences: the extravagances of farce are a
time-honoured strategy by means of which the oppressed seek
to subvert by comic ridicule the power of their class masters.
Accidental Death of an Anarchist is cast in just such a
vigorously ridiculing vein; it is a wildly inventive farce, the
action of which is driven along at an impressive pace. Indeed
much of the acid power of the play derives from the manner in
which it exposes the moral rottenness beneath the state's
smooth facade of rectitude and legality. As the investigator
"madman" goes about his task the play builds its indictment of
a political system that traffics in bare-faced lies, empty
sentiments, and hypocritical expressions of moral concern,
while at the same time maintaining a veneer of order and
legality. The play corrosively exposes, too, the ways in which
the social democratic state can turn even a scandalous example
of establishment ruthlessness to its own ends.

Like so much of Fo's work, however, *Accidental Death* is not
a piece that easily transfers culturally, nor does it translate
readily from Italian to another language. Certainly the play's
London success turned much more upon the sheer farcical brio
of the stage orchestration than upon any elements of meaningful political satire left in the piece after it had been put into
English, and rough English equivalents found for its many
targets. These difficulties indicate how firmly rooted the play is
in its own social, political and cultural milieu; it requires, for its
full appreciation, an understanding of peculiarly Italian issues
and historical situations, like the vestigial fascist relationships
embedded in some sectors of society; the "strategy of tension"
the Christian Democratic government was accused of pursuing
in the late 1960's and early 1970's; and the far left's acutely
hostile view of the Communist Party, reflected here in the
satirical treatment accorded the figure of a Communist Party
journalist from *Unita*, possibly based on a real life reporter.
Broad matters of this kind, as well as innumerable local
references, are inevitably lost in the processes of translation
and adaptation. Yet, paradoxically, *Accidental Death of an
Anarchist* is unquestionably the most widely performed of Fo's
plays outside Italy.

—Laura Richards

THE ADDING MACHINE
by Elmer Rice

First Publication: New York, 1923 (without scene 5); in *Plays*,
        London, 1933 (complete).
First Production: Garrick Theatre (The Theatre Guild), New
        York, 19 March 1923.

Criticism
(For general works on the author, see *Playwrights* volume)

Articles:

Richard A. Weaver, "*The Adding Machine*: Exemplar of the Ludicrous", in *Players*, 49, 1974.

Loren L. Zeller, "The Two Expressionistic Interpretations of Dehumanization: Rice's *The Adding Machine* and Muñiz's *El tintero*", in *Essays in Literature*, 2, 1975.

Russell E. Brown, "Names and Numbers in *The Adding Machine*", in *Names*, 34, 1986.

*   *   *

The Adding Machine tells the story of Mr. Zero, "a failure. A waste product. A slave to a contraption of steel and iron", as Charles tells him in the last of the play's eight scenes.

The action is set forth in eight stylized scenes. In the first, Mrs. Zero taunts her husband, in a long monologue, about the fact that it has been seven years since he had a rise in pay, and that he dare not ask for one. At the office, Zero and Daisy are working together: she calls out figures which Zero adds up. At the same time each is wondering (in interior monolgues) if they would be better off married to each other. Then the boss enters and brutally tells Zero that, far from any rise he might hope for, he is to be replaced by an adding machine. That evening, Zero is late arriving at a meagre party his wife has arranged, at which the guests are simply given numbers. Following the arrival of a policeman (expected by Zero), Zero announces "I killed the boss this afternoon" as he is led away. At a "Place of Justice," Zero is found guilty following a trial in which he tells, with relish, of the lynching of a "dirty nigger" in Georgia.

He is found guilty and is imprisoned in a cage-like structure (akin to that in O'Neill's *The Hairy Ape*), where his wife visits him and he is prepared for execution. The last three scenes are set in "A Graveyard", "A Pleasant Place (Elysium)", and "Another Office",—"a sort of cosmic laundry" where those such as Zero are given a superficial refit to prepare them for another life of service. Zero makes his final exit vainly chasing what he believes to be a beautiful young woman—Hope.

In notes he wrote for Dudley Digges, who played Zero in the first production, Rice explained:

> What we must convey. . .is a subjective picture of a man who is at once an individual and a type . . . . In the realistic play, we look at the character from the outside. We see him in terms of action and of actuality. But in the expressionist play we subordinate and even discard objective reality and seek to express the character in terms of his own inner life. An X-ray photograph bears no resemblance to the object as it presents itself to our vision, but it reveals the inner mechanism of the object as no mere photographic likeness can.

The Adding Machine was almost wholly novel in the American theatre at the time—Rice had heard of expressionism but had not read or seen any of the plays of Georg Kaiser, Walter Hasenclever, or Ernst Toller, though he had possibly come across Theodore Dreiser's expressionist one-acters in *Plays of the Natural and Supernatural*, 1916; yet he achieved a remarkably mature result.

Quite apart from its undoubted theatricalism, very unusual in English-language expressionist drama—perhaps only the expressionist section of O'Casey's *The Silver Tassie* approaches it—*The Adding Machine* is important in the development of American drama. Its opening scene may have been influenced by O'Neill's *Before Breakfast* (which itself looks back to Strindberg's *The Stronger*), and it points forward to the use of this monologue technique in, for example, Pinter's *The Room* and Albee's *Zoo Story*. There is a striking similarity of tone, as well as specific action (e.g., the interview of "hero" and boss) between *The Adding Machine* and Miller's *Death of a Salesman*. The expressionist and non-realistic techniques—the depersonalisation, the voicing of what is being thought by one character but unheard by another (compare O'Neill's *Strange Interlude*), the stylised action and dialogue of the party scene, the setting and Zero's monologue in the trial scene—all look forward to drama of the future, yet we are never conscious of a "pack of techniques". The clue to Rice's success is to be found in his use of humour and its unifying effect.

Zero's story, and the implications of the play as a whole, are intensely depressing. It is Rice's particular achievement to create a dramatic effect that enables that depressing message to be understood and enjoyed. The play is suffused with humour of various kinds—sometimes savage, often ironic, frequently hitting off natural characteristics, occasionally gentle, as in Daisy's delight in the flowers of Elysium when she and Zero meet: "Look at the flowers! Ain't they just perfect! Why, you'd think they was artificial, wouldn't you?". There is also a good line of gallows humour in the graveyard scene; this is in part provided by the aborted attempt of Judy O'Grady to make love on Zero's grave, and partly by the dialogue Zero shares with Shrdlu (the confused letters of his name suggest the way a badly controlled mechanism—a typewriter—depersonalises humankind) when they rise from their graves. When their talking disturbs the other dead, one of them, The Head, cries out in exasperation: "Are you going to beat it or not? [*He calls into the grave*]: Hey, Bill, lend me your head a minute", and Bill's skull is thrown at Zero and Shrdlu. Rice's achievement is better understood by contrasting his graveyard scene with that which opens Hasenclever's expressionist drama, *Humanity*.

—Peter Davison

ADELPHI. See **THE BROTHERS.**

ADELPHOE. See **THE BROTHERS.**

THE ADMIRABLE CRICHTON
by J.M. Barrie

First Publication: 1914 (private printing); London, 1918.
First Production: Duke of York's Theatre, London, 4 November, 1902.

Criticism
(For general works on the author, see *Playwrights* volume)

Articles:

Grace A. Lamacchia, "Textual Variations for Act IV of *The Admirable Crichton*", in *Modern Drama*, 13, 1970.

*   *   *

The Admirable Crichton: Duke of York's Theatre, London, 1902 (first production)

In *The Admirable Crichton* Lord Loam seeks to prove his radical democratic views by inviting servants and family to tea on grounds of apparent equality. His daughters and butler, Crichton, oppose his views. The latter upholds that nature teaches the law of domination, although different circumstances may create different hierarchies and leaders. A shipwreck later deposits the leading players on a desert island, where Crichton's contentions are proved. He becomes Governor, while Loam contentedly plays a concertina and the other aristocrats serve their former butler. Crichton begins to have kingly longings and is about to marry Loam's eldest daughter, Lady Mary, when a ship is sighted. He chooses to give the warning, using one of his many practical inventions to shoot a flare. He thus dooms himself to return to the manor house. Soon the old order re-establishes itself. Loam's nephew, the Hon. Ernest Woolley, "re-writes" the shipwreck story with himself as hero and Crichton a footnote; Lady Mary marries another aristocrat. In the Definitive Edition, the drama concludes with Crichton leaving the Loams, praising England, and redefining Lady Mary's claim that he is the "best man among us" with the rejoinder, "On an island, my lady, perhaps".

The Admirable Crichton breaks with Barrie's established dramatic practice in three major ways. His apprenticeship plays were adaptations of earlier prose works for the stage; *Crichton* may have originated from Conan Doyle's suggestion that the shipwrecking of a king and a sailor might be an interesting plot or from the much publicised radical practices of the Countess of Carlisle, but it has no link with Barrie's earlier fiction. Until *Crichton*, the evolution of ideas for any theatrical production had been a slow and gradual one, traced through Barrie's notebooks; but in this case, a full drafting suddenly appears, giving MacKail grounds for his claim that "Barrie saw the whole story and the whole shape in one lightning glance". Thirdly, the main plot directly conveys a theme of some philosophical significance, inviting critical comparison with Rousseau and Nietzsche; this is a departure from Barrie's habit of using a superficial, romantic, surface text to convey deeper and darker ideas indirectly.

A circular romance structure drawn from the past, in particular, *The Tempest*, joined with extravagant theatricality, pushed advances in Edwardian stagecraft to their limits. The sets were magnificent, the demands on lighting extreme, and Barrie chose to experiment with electricity with a daring almost as great as that of Crichton in the fantasy. The carpenters went on strike prior to the first performance which thus became one of the longest nights out at the theatre on record. Despite their tiredness, almost all of the critics present celebrated the work as Barrie's first successful, serious drama. They recognised the ironic skills which controlled the opening scene—with Loam praising democracy but protecting his own aristocratic comforts and the strongest support for hierarchy coming from the servants. They appreciated the parodic characterisation of Wilde via the epigrammatic posturing of the Hon. Ernest Woolley. Some even noted the more severe satire directed against a society where birth rather than merit conferred power, and they linked it with Barrie's Scottish roots in a more democratic, educational tradition. Beerbohm accepted this but still regretted the "bitter taste" left when the Loams were revealed to be liars as well as fools.

There *is* a cruel line to *The Admirable Crichton* for Barrie is considering life as a battle for power in Darwinian terms. For that reason, he removes his characters from a civilised society into a more primitive one. His central thesis, that Nature will determine who rules and define the limits of their power, is reflected in the alternative title—*Circumstances Alter Cases*. The many different endings devised for the play should also be related to argument rather than authorial uncertainty. As early as *The Little Minister*, Barrie discovered that the author's desire to conclude might lead to oversimplification. Then, he had provided a harsh draft ending with the hero threatening to cane the heroine but withdrew it in favour of kisses and rose trees. In *Crichton*, depending on the text you consult, the butler does or does not marry a lower servant; does or does not set himself up in a public house (named or not named "The Case is Altered"); praises or does not praise England; argues with Lady Mary, agrees with her, laughs with her or remains darkly silent. The crucial constant is Crichton's dissociation of himself and his fate from that of the Loams. As befits a Waiter-hero who accepts the dictates of Nature and hierarchy, he foresees that the days of gentility are numbered. As yet the revolution has not come, however, and his scope for power is limited to variations on strategy. He must be in the best possible position of readiness. When World War I came and Barrie made Crichton the warrior hero, he was blamed for commercial opportunism. In fact, he may simply have been celebrating external confirmation of fictive prophecy, for then the case was *actually* altered and Crichton's waiting over.

—R.D.S. Jack

THE AFFECTED YOUNG LADIES. See **THE PRETEN-TIOUS YOUNG LADIES.**

AFTER HAGGERTY
by David Mercer

First Publication: London, 1970.
First Production: Aldwych Theatre, London (Royal Shakespeare Company), 26 February 1970.

*   *   *

The flat which drama critic, Bernard Link, has leased from a man called James Haggerty is invaded by Claire, Haggerty's aggressive American girlfriend, and their infant Raskolnikov. As the flat is gradually decorated the three begin to create a temporary family. Bernard's father arrives, sparking off guilty wranglings about Bernard's Yorkshire, working-class origins. He has rehearsed all this to himself in earlier political scenes which flashback to him lecturing at all the key places in Left–wing, post-war history: Budapest, Moscow, Havana, Paris and Prague. Claire's history as 1960's activist similarly counter-points domesticity in Act Two.

In Act II, Scene Two, Bernard returns home, drunk, at four in the morning after a fraught evening with The Living Theatre. His father, censorious, is waiting up for him. The baby howls off-stage and Claire enters in her housecoat. Bernard kisses her, then spreads his arms wide in a gesture of ironic inclusion. "Here we are at last", he says. "Our heterogeneous little family. All under one roof. At last". He continues: "Welcome home, *all* you strangers". This is the heart of the play, and a summary of the obsession of the new drama in the 1950's and 1960's. The family and the home are juxtaposed with heterogeneity and alienation. International radicalism cohabits with provincial puritanism. Bernard does his best to lead the life of the rootless metropolitan. But we never hear more than a few lines of his lecture in Prague or wherever before he slides into an internal dialogue with his father where his sophistication is powerless against grim, Yorkshire common-sense. But when Bernard's father actually turns up at the end of Act I, Claire is surprised. She doesn't connect Bernard with distinct, social origins. "He never mentioned his parents", she tells Mr. Link.

The visual motif of the play is the gradual domestication of the flat's bare interior. The decorating is done by strangers and one of them is homosexual so his family interest is minimal. But by the end of Act I a family of sorts is living in it. The father is not the father, the mother doesn't want to be a mother and the grandfather has no blood-relationship to the child. In this skewed version of the nuclear family, the post-war generation has been forced into roles, rather than freely choosing to create relationships. They want to be free but the outlines of conventions and traditions still mould them. Flashbacks of Claire's life in Act II deliberately parallel Bernard's in Act I. The daughter of a wealthy American she was radicalised by Haggerty's charm and the 1960's counter-culture. She recounts, in a series of clipped images, the demonstrations, the meetings, the travelling, the politics of the period. But she has a father whose money she can't escape and a child whose demands she can't deny. She is obsessed with Haggerty since he epitomises that icon of freedom, the "Outsider", but she does mention her own gesture of autonomy in her first, long, internal dialogue. "Haggerty, I *told* you. I *invented* the way I speak. It is calculated to negate my background and suggest whorish undertones".

This is minimal creativity to pit against the mythical force of Haggerty or the rigid contours of tradition, but Claire has at least retained a personal dynamism that overwhelms Bernard's lethargy. She sums him up very accurately in the opening lines of the play: "It's obvious at once your mind is kind of sluggish. And mine is *fast*". Yet by the end she is ready to sink into a kind of platonic marriage with him. It seems improbable, even in 1970, that she would settle for such a passive character. Mercer has, in Bernard, reproduced too faithfully a stereotype of English fiction—the sensitive, self-loathing intellectual who nonetheless gets the girl. This is a hero overfamiliar from the campus fiction of Amis and Bradbury, and detectable in later, more radical, drama such as Brenton and Hare's *Pravda* and Edgar's *Maydays*.

Haggerty, however, counters him. Like his child, Haggerty never appears on stage. While Bernard fights through his Oedipal inheritance with his father, the next generation of fathers and sons seems to be beyond that complex. Haggerty rejects patriarchy by, simply, not being there. He maintains a presence through telegrams but at the end, after Mr. Link leaves, his empty coffin is delivered to the flat. He has been killed as a guerilla in Africa. He is a construct, evoked by his wife through memory, and by himself, through telegrams. He is the free, self-produced man whom Bernard would like to be and whom Claire resents but is obsessed by. He is a myth and dies a mythical, 1960's death as a guerilla in Africa. But mythical heroes die in order to be reborne. Following *After Haggerty* there was a long sequence of investigations, in plays of the 1970's and 1980's, of the links between politics, sex and the family. In these, as it were, Haggerty is forced to "come home", to show himself, and he meets a new woman, the angry heroine, in the plays of Caryl Churchill and Pam Gems. Structurally and thematically the play sums up with great accuracy a moment of transition between one distinctive tradition of political radicalism and its successor.

—Tony Dunn

AFTER THE FALL
by Arthur Miller

First Publication: New York, 1964.
First Production: Washington Square Theatre, New York
(American National Theatre Association),
23 January, 1964.

Criticism
(For general works on the author, see *Playwrights* volume)

Articles:
Paul T. Nolan, "Two Memory Plays: *The Glass Menagerie* and *After the Fall*", in *McNeese Review*, 17, 1966.
John J. Stinson, "Structure in *After the Fall*: The Relevance of the Maggie Episodes to the Main Themes and the Christian Symbolism", in *Modern Drama*, 10, 1967.
Rolf K. Högel, "The Manipulation of Time in Miller's *After the Fall*", in *Literatur in Wissenschaft und Unterricht*, 7, 1974.
Clinton S. Burhans, "Eden and the Idiot Child: Arthur Miller's *After the Fall*", in *Ball State University Forum*, vol.20 no.2, 1979.
Steven R. Centola, "The Monomyth of Arthur Miller's *After the Fall*", in *Studies in American Drama*, 1, 1986.

*   *   *

After the Fall is an expressionistic play, representing in two acts of more than 40 loosely defined episodes the memories of Quentin, a twice-divorced lawyer in his forties, with all the distortion, questionable reliability, and selective focus that are the psychological traits of memory. Quentin is poised between relationships with two women: Maggie, who died about 15 months previously, and Holga, whose capacity for hope encapsulates Quentin's future. Memory retrieves the circumstances of Quentin's first marriage, to Louise, his previous sexual adventures, and his image of his father and of his mother who died four or five months before. Quentin's quest is the retrieval of lost innocence, a journey which takes him through the Depression experiences of his parents and family, Holga's knowledge of the European concentration camps, and the disintegration of his own friendships in the face of American investigations into the communist movement. Within such contexts, Maggie stands out initially to Quentin as a defenseless ingénue, an illusory gateway to a lost Eden, although her moral flaccidity is very clear to the audience. The

second act has a chronological, narrative cohesion that is rare in expressionism, basically following the development and collapse of the relationship with Maggie. Quentin comes to see the irony in his first perception of her as the epitome of truth and morality, but rationalises her appeal as exercising his desire for power through the exhibition of her helplessness. The final episode shows her disintegration under alcohol and drug abuse and Quentin moving through an image of Auschwitz to align himself with Holga as the post-Fall companion in a world of guilt and self-awareness.

Quentin articulates the "Fall" of the title as alluding to the loss of Edenic innocence, as embodied in Maggie; this makes Quentin a modern Adam, falling in both moral and intellectual terms, but he more frequently identifies with the Cain myth. For the audience, however, the first association is probably with the dominant element in the set, the "fallen", "blasted stone tower of a German concentration camp", which is explicitly connected with a post-Edenic loss of innocence in a century in which corruption has escalated. As the play develops, there are hints that the title may also allude to mental collapse, to the winter of the soul, and to the stock market slump of the Depression, an economic environment which had a severe impact on Quentin and his parents.

The suggestiveness of the title, and the tentative way it is interpreted, draw attention to the unreliability of the play's narrative. A definition of psycho-expressionism popular earlier in the century presented it as "the dynamic projection of a disordered mind", and the dreamers of Strindberg, Toller, and O'Neill had abandoned the mimesis of surface reality and established grotesque distortion as a commonplace within the movement. Quentin's troubled mind is the primary factor that is presented as controlling stage representation throughout the play, but, as is common in expressionism, there is frequent uncertainty about the degree of choice he has in generating memory or reconstructing it. A key element is the figure of the Listener, "sitting just beyond the edge of the stage itself", whom Quentin often addresses but whose voice is not heard by the audience. Functionally, the Listener is a catalyst for self-disclosure, but he may be taken either as an external confessor/interrogator figure or as an internal function of Quentin's mind, objectified on the stage. When a new character appears, Quentin can tell the Listener, "I'm not sure why I bring her up", indicating that he has control over his memory, an impression often supported elsewhere, as when he "drops his arms, aborting the image", and the character in question accordingly exits. But at other points, particularly in the second act, memory characters surprise, anger, or dominate Quentin, so that his presidency over the inner drama is questioned.

Since its premiere, the reception of *After the Fall* has been dominated by the belief that in the play Miller was fictionalising his own life, and in particular his marriage to Marilyn Monroe. The publicity that that relationship generated meant that all of Miller's subsequent writings would inevitably be subjected to scrutiny by the prurient, but this dimension of response was greatly augmented by Elia Kazan's direction of the first production, in which Maggie appeared closely to resemble Monroe, who had recently commited suicide. A number of magazine interviews by Miller focussed on this aspect of the play, and the resultant critical stand-off pivoted on the appropriateness of writers marketing their private lives. By the end of the 1980's, however, it has been accepted as axiomatic that all autobiography involves fictionalisation, and vice versa, so that the play can now be accepted as perhaps the most technically audacious work by an author who has never written anything that is not in some sense experimental, and as a major contribution to the development of the rich tradition of American dramatic expressionism, standing there beside the major works of O'Neill, Williams, Albee, Terry, and Shepard.

—Howard McNaughton

AGAMEMNON.   See THE ORESTEIA.

AIAS.   See AJAX.

AJAX (Aias)
by Sophocles

First Production: c. 441 BC?

Editions
The Ajax, edited by Sir Richard Jebb, Cambridge, 1896 (with English translation)
Ajax, in *Sophocles:2*, edited by F. Storr, London, 1913 (Loeb Classical Library; with English translation).
Ajax, edited by W.B. Stanford, London and New York, 1963.
Ajax, in *Sophoclis Tragediae 1*, edited by R.D. Dawe, Leipzig, 1984.
Ajax, in *Sophoclis: Fabulae*, edited by H. Lloyd Jones and N.G. Wilson, Oxford, 1990 (Oxford Classical Texts).

Translations
Ajax, in *Electra and Other Plays*, translated by E.F. Watling, Harmondsworth, 1953.
Ajax, translated by John Moore in *Sophocles II*, Chicago and London, 1957 (Complete Greek Tragedies Series).
Ajax, in *Four Plays by Sophocles*, translated by Theodore Howard Banks, New York, 1966.
Ajax, translated by Robert Cannon, in *Sophocles: Plays, Two*, edited by J. Michael Walton, London, 1990.

Criticism
(For general works on the author, see *Playwrights* volume)

Books:
J.C. Kamerbeek, *The Plays of Sophocles; Commentaries, Part One—The "Ajax"*, Leiden, The Netherlands.
Joe Park Poe, *Genre and Meaning in Sophocles' "Ajax"*, Frankfurt, 1987.

Articles:
S.M. Adams, "The *Ajax* of Sophocles", in *Phoenix*, 9, 1955.
B.M.W. Knox, "The *Ajax* of Sophocles", in *Harvard Studies in Classical Philology*, 65, 1961.
M.W. Wigodsky, "The 'Salvation' of Ajax", in *Hermes*, 90, 1962.
W.E. Brown, Sophocles' *Ajax* and Homer's Hector", in *Classical Journal*, 61, 1965.
P. Biggs, "Disease Theme in Sophocles' *Ajax*, *Philoctetes*, and *Trachiniae*", in *Classical Philology*, 61, 1966.

M. Simpson, "Sophocles' Ajax: His Madness and Transformation", in *Areth*, 2, 1969.
J. Ferguson, "Ambiguity in *Ajax*", in *Dioniso*, 44, 1970.
P. Burian, "Supplication and Hero Cult in Sophocles' *Ajax*", in *Greek, Roman and Byzantine Studies*, 13, 1972.
V. Leinieks, "Aias and the Day of Wrath", in *Classical Journal*, 69, 1974.
J.F. Davidson, "The Parados of Sophocles' *Ajax*", in *Bulletin of the Institute of Classical Studies*, 22, 1975.
V.J. Rosivach, "Sophocles' *Ajax*", in *Classical Journal*, 72, 1976.
M. Sicherl, "The Tragic Issue in Sophocles' *Ajax*", in *Yale Classical Studies*, 12, 1977.
D. Cohen, "Imagery of Sophocles: A Study of Ajax's Suicide", in *Greece and Rome*, 25, 1978.
Philip Holt, "The Debate Scenes in the *Ajax*", in *American Journal of Philology*, 102, 1981.

*   *   *

After the death of Achilles in the war against Troy, the Greek hero's arms were awarded to Odysseus rather than to Ajax who believed he had deserved them. Intent on revenge for the slight, Ajax is diverted from his purpose by the goddess Athena who drives him mad so that he kills and tortures sheep and cattle, seeing them as his Greek enemies. When he returns to sanity, shame at what he has done impels him to commit suicide. Odysseus pleads with Agamemnon and Menelaus for Ajax to be treated with the respect due to a hero and eventually wins his point.

Ajax is the only Sophocles play, with the arguable exception of *Philoctetes*, in which a god or goddess appears. Traditionally a devout man, Sophocles proposes a theological standpoint which is more complex than it is sometimes painted. Ajax may have been planning a dire revenge against his former friends, when he believes himself cheated of his due, but the way in which the goddess Athena gloats over the state to which she has reduced him looks forward to the savage Dionysus of Euripides' *Bacchae* rather than back to the wise patron-goddess of Athens who solves the problems in Aeschylus' *Oresteia*.

Applying modern standards to a Greek attitude towards friends and enemies is, of course, risky. Turning the other cheek would have seemed as contrary to the nature of the Greek hero as turning his back. Nevertheless, there is in *Ajax* a sense of moral argument which suggests that man is progressing beyond the simple rules of programmed response. Odysseus is not only the soldier who defeated Ajax in the award of arms but is also traditionally a crafty and untrustworthy man whose eye is always to the main chance. So he appears in Sophocles's later play *Philoctetes*, where his machinations to persuade the eponymous hero to go to Troy are so Machiavellian as to be self-defeating. In *Ajax* this is the sort of man Athena is expecting when she invites Odysseus to witness Ajax' humiliation. Instead of pleasure at the downfall of an enemy, Odysseus shows himself instinctively compassionate.

The tone of the play is established in the first scene. All the later characters to appear reveal predictable attitudes. Ajax' half-brother, Teucer, defends him as best he may, but he is only half-hero as well as half-brother. Tecmessa, mother of Ajax' son Eurysaces, is loyal and loving but utterly without influence in such a male world. Agamemnon and Menelaus, respectively commander-in-chief of the Greek forces at Troy, and husband of Helen, the cause of the war, are angry savages for whom the only response to what Ajax has done is the ultimate insult: deprivation of burial. Odysseus stands up to them and wins for Ajax the honour due to what the man was when he was a friend, not what he became when thwarted and deranged. If the play's moral dimension is its paramount feature, there is little sense of *Ajax* degenerating into a tract. The appearance of Athena in the prologue is literally above the action where Odysseus cannot see her. Such an awareness of stage space, a principal factor of Sophocles' stagecraft in all his surviving plays, is given an unusual twist in the handling of both location and chorus.

Changes of scene are rare in surviving Greek tragedy and appear to have become more so, with tragedy moving towards realism at the same time as comedy, in the hands of Aristophanes, moves to a world of fantasy where anything can happen anywhere. The initial setting of *Ajax* is outside Ajax's tent, over which Athena appears (presumably, in the original production, with the help of the stage-crane). After Athena has departed and Ajax has returned to sanity, his sailors, who form the chorus, and Tecmessa with his baby attempt to save him from despair at the carnage he has perpetrated. For a time it seems that they have been successful. Ajax emerges from his tent calm and apparently reconciled to what he has done. He departs for the beach to cleanse himself.

News arrives that this is to prove a crucial day in Ajax's fortunes and the chorus and Tecmessa leave the scene to look for him. Ajax now appears at the sea-shore and carefully prepares his own death, before falling on the sword given to him in battle by the Trojan Hector. The sense of isolation is emphasised both by the place where the action is now unfolding and by the absence of the chorus who habitually accompany on-stage action, from their first entrance through to a play's conclusion. Physical use of the resources of the Athenian theatre and the expectations of the audience are consciously manipulated by Sophocles to draw attention to the man's loneliness and to the unusual sight on the Greek stage of someone committing suicide.

Ajax is a touching play and a heartening one for ending on a note of hope, if not reconciliation. Life may present atrocities and heroes may perpetrate them, but a case can be made for human decency which allows some rules and some rights for even the major sinner.

—J. Michael Walton.

EL ALCALDE DE ZALAMEA. See **THE MAYOR OF ZALAMEA.**

ALCESTIS (Alkestis)
by Euripides

First Production: Athens, 438 B.C.

Editions
Alcestis, edited by W. S. Hadley, Cambridge, 1896.
Alcestis, edited by E. H. Blakeney, London, 1899; revised edition, 1933.
Alcestis in *Euripides, 4*, edited by Arthur S. Way, London, 1912 (Loeb Classical Library; with translation).
Alcestis in *Euripides: Selected Plays 1*, edited by D. F. W. van Lennep, Leiden, The Netherlands, 1949.
Alcestis, edited by A. M. Dale, Oxford, 1954; revised edition, 1978.
Alcestis in *Euripides: Fabulae 1*, edited by J. Diggle, Oxford, 1984 (Oxford Classical Texts).

Translations
Alcestis, translated by H. Kynaston, Oxford, 1906.
Alcestis, translated by Gilbert Murray, London, 1915.
Alcestis, translated by Richard Aldington, London, 1930.
Alcestis, translated by D. W. Lucas, 1951.
Alcestis in *Euripides: Three Plays*, translated by Philip Vellacott, Harmondsworth, 1953; revised version, in *Three Plays*, Harmondsworth, 1974.
Alcestis, translated by Richmond Lattimore in *Euripides I*, Chicago and London, 1955 (Complete Greek Tragedies Series).
Alcestis, translated by Alistair Elliott, San Francisco, 1965.
Alcestis, translated by William Arrowsmith, New York and London, 1974.

Criticism
(For general works on the author, see *Playwrights* volume)

Books:
John R. Wilson (ed.), *Twentieth Century Interpretations of "Alcestis"*, Englewood Cliffs, New Jersey, 1968.
Gustav Adolf Seeck, *Unaristotelische Untersuchungen zu Euripides: Ein Motivanalytischer Kommentar zur "Alkestis"*, Heidelberg, 1985.

Articles:
J. T. Sheppard, "Admetus, Verrall, and Professor Myres" in *Journal of Hellenic Studies*, 39, 1919.
D. M. Jones, "Euripides' *Alcestis*: Certain Features of Dramatic Importance in the Composition of the Play", in *Classical Review*, 62, 1948.
Thomas G. Rosenmayer, "*Alcestis*: Character and Death" his in *The Masks of Tragedy*, Austin, Texas, 1963.
Anne Pippin Burnett, "The Virtues of Admetus" in *Classical Philology*, 60, 1965.
L. Golden, "Euripides' *Alcestis*: Structure and Theme", in *Classical Journal*, 66, 1971.
N. P. Gross, "*Alcestis* and the Rhetoric of Departure", in *Quarterly Journal of Speech*, 60, 1974.
R. M. Nielson, "*Alcestis*: A Paradox of Dying", in *Ramus*, 5, 1976.
Victor Castellani, "Notes on the Structure of Euripides' *Alcestis*", in *American Journal of Philology*, 100, 1979.
Michael Lloyd, "Euripides' *Alcestis*", in *Greece and Rome* (second series), vol. 32 no. 2, 1985.

*   *   *

Alcestis is generally agreed to be the earliest of Euripides' surviving plays. As by the time of writing he was over 40 years old and well into his career as a playwright, there can be no apologies, if such be necessary, for the play as a fledgling effort. It is a mature work. That it should be necessary to state this is a mark of the unease that the play has provoked among classical critics both for its form and its content.

The action is simple enough. Admetus had treated the god Apollo with magnanimity when Apollo was forced to serve a sentence as a herdsman for killing the Cyclopes. Apollo had in return bestowed on Admetus the benefit of cheating death if he could find a surrogate. Alcestis, the wife of Admetus, is the only one who will agree to die in his place. The play opens with Apollo confronting Death who has arrived to remove his victim. Death claims his due but, before the funeral is complete, Admetus' friend Heracles arrives at the palace. Admetus' decision not to reveal what has happened, but to pass off the state of mourning as for someone of little importance, is an ambivalent one. He is known as a hospitable man and Heracles would never stay if he knew what had really happened. At the same time, there is more than a suggestion that Admetus is embarrassed at the prospect of having to admit to allowing his wife to die instead of him. Heracles gets drunk, finds out the truth and, suddenly sobered, departs to fight with Death for Alcestis. When he reappears with the veiled figure of Alcestis, he puts Admetus through a searching test to see whether he truly deserves to have his wife back, before leaving with the enjoinder to Admetus to show more respect to his guests in future.

This apparently trite message gives some indication of the perplexing nature of a drama of constant appeal but unusual style. That this difficulty is not a new one seems indicated by the fact that the play was presented fourth in Euripides' submission, a position normally reserved for a satyr play. The satyr play was a short, farcical afterpiece to three tragedies, treating a strand of the story, or one of the themes from the preceding plays, probably combining parody, fantasy, and sheer vulgarity in about equal measure, but lacking any tragic potential. *Alcestis*, if not tragic in tone, has at least the potential for tragedy within it and is best classified as a romance.

Eager to foster the satyric formula, critics have pointed to Heracles' drunken entrance and drawn parallels to Silenus, leader of the satyrs, and to the happy ending. Others have responded by pointing to the fact that Heracles' bad behaviour lasts for no more than 40 lines, while the mourning lament of the chorus and the savagery of Admetus' row with his father, who had declined to sacrifice himself, argue for a high seriousness.

A modern audience, less inclined than that of other periods of the theatre to offer every play a label, is unlikely to find the mixture of tragic and comic elements difficult to reconcile. Clearly Euripides was writing an experimental piece, for which the Great Dionysia provided no obvious outlet. Such a spirit of experiment in the text gives encouragement for the play to receive a comparable treatment in performance. The best-known modern version is that directed by Robert Wilson for the American Repertory Theatre in 1986, noted for being highly theatrical and highly controversial.

The power of the play resides in the questions Euripides appears to ask, arising from a series of strong and moving scenes; most importantly, what sort of a boon is it that Apollo has bestowed on Admetus? Beyond that, what sort of a man must Admetus be to have agreed so readily to his wife's sacrifice of herself on his behalf? While Heracles is away confronting Death, Admetus is occupied blaming his father for failing to offer himself as a victim when he has so few years left. In terms of survival of the clan Admetus may have a point, but Euripides clearly suggests Admetus's instinctive selfishness. It may be that the pangs of guilt are already reaching out to Admetus and the scene with his father is crucial to the change of heart he exhibits in the finale.

Returning with the veiled figure of Alcestis, Heracles tests Admetus to see whether or not he deserves to have his wife back. By this time Admetus' grief, that has hitherto made no more than a token appearance, well larded with concern about what people will think of him, has given way to genuine contrition. Greek heroes learn by suffering. Usually it is too late for them. "Tragic time", as Peter Thomson wrote, "has no nick". For Admetus there is a nick. He gets a second chance and will probably be the better for it. The Athenians may have been uneasy about where *Alcestis* belonged in the dramatic programme, but our understanding of tragedy and comedy would be diminished had it not survived.

—J. Michael Walton

THE ALCHEMIST
by Ben Jonson

First Publication: London, 1612; revised version in *Works*, London, 1616.
First Production: Globe Theatre, London, 1610.

Editions

The Alchemist, edited by Douglas Brown, London, 1966 (New Mermaid Series).
The Alchemist in *Ben Jonson: Three Plays*, edited by Michael Jamieson, Harmondsworth, 1966.
The Alchemist, edited by J.B. Bamborough, London, 1967.
The Alchemist, edited by F. H. Mares, London, 1967 (Revels Plays).
The Alchemist, edited by J. B. Steane, Cambridge, 1967.
The Alchemist, edited by S. Musgrove, Edinburgh, 1968.
The Alchemist, edited by Arthur Sale, London, 1969.
The Alchemist, edited by Alvin B. Kernan, New Haven, Connecticut, and London, 1974 (Yale Ben Jonson).
The Alchemist in *The Selected Plays of Ben Jonson, 2*, edited by Martin Butler, Cambridge, 1989.
The Alchemist, edited by Peter Bement, London, 1987.

Criticism
(For general works on the author, see *Playwrights* volume)

Books:
R. V. Holdsworth (ed.), *"Everyman in His Humour" and "The Alchemist": A Casebook*, London, 1978.

Articles:
Edgar Hill Duncan, "Jonson's *Alchemist* and the Literature of Alchemy", in *Publications of the Modern Language Association*, 61, 1946.
Joseph T. McCullen Jr., "Conference with the Queen of Fairies: A Study of Jonson's Workmanship in *The Alchemist*", in *Studia Neophilologica*, 23, 1950.
Maurice Hussey, "Ananias the Deacon: A Study of Religion in Jonson's *The Alchemist*", in *English*, 9, 1953.
Calvin G. Thayer, "Theme and Structure in *The Alchemist*", in *English Literary History*, 26, 1959.
Robert E. Knoll, "How to Read *The Alchemist*", in *College English*, 21, 1960.
Barry Targan, "The Dramatic Structure of *The Alchemist*", in *Discourse*, 6, 1963.
Alan C. Dessen, "*The Alchemist*: Jonson's 'Estates' Play", in *Renaissance Drama*, 7, 1964.
William Blissett, "The Venter Tripartite in *The Alchemist*", in *Studies in English Literature*, 8, 1968.
James V. Holleran, "Character Transmutation in *The Alchemist*", in *CLA Journal*, 11, 1968.
Judd Arnold, "Lovewit's Triumph and Jonsonian Morality: A Reading of *The Alchemist*", in *Criticism*, 11, 1969.

The Alchemist: Theatre Royal, Drury Lane, 1743 (engraving after painting by Zoffany)

Myrddin Jones, "Sir Epicure Mammon: A Study in 'Spiritual Fornication'", in *Renaissance Quarterly*, 22, 1969.

William Empson, "*The Alchemist*", in *Hudson Review*, 22, 1969–70.

Robertson Davies, "Ben Jonson and Alchemy" in *Stratford Papers, 1968–69*, edited by B. A. W. Jackson, Shannon, 1972.

Richard Levin, "'No Laughing Matter': Some New Readings of *The Alchemist*", in *Studies in the Literary Imagination*, 6, 1973.

Malcolm H. South, "The 'Uncleane Birds, in Seventy-Seven': *The Alchemist*", in *Studies in English Literature, 1500–1900*, 13, 1973.

R. Dutton, "*Volpone* and *The Alchemist*: A Comparison in Satiric Technique" in *Renaissance and Modern Studies*, vol. 18, 1974.

R. L. Smallwood, "'Here, in the Friars': Immediacy and Theatricality in *The Alchemist*" in *Review of English Studies*, vol. 32, 1981.

Geraldo U. de Sousa, "Boundaries of Genre in Ben Jonson's *Volpone* and *The Alchemist*" in *Essays in Theatre*, May 1986.

Robert N. Watson, "*The Alchemist* and Jonson's Conversion of Comedy" in *Renaissance Genres: Essays on Theory, History, and Interpretation*, edited by Barbara Kiefer Lewalski, Cambridge, Massachusetts, 1986.

Ruth Evans Netscher, "The Moral Vision of *The Alchemist*: Tricks, Psycotherapy and Personality Traits" in *Literature and Medicine*, 7, 1988.

*   *   *

Subtle and Dol, a con-man and a whore, set up in business in the house of Lovewit, who has retreated to the country to escape the plague in London. In league with Lovewit's servant, Face, they attract victims from a wide cross-section of English society, their only common characteristic being their gullibility in believing that the alleged alchemist can indeed transform base metals into gold. Only Surly—companion of the con-artists' most extravagant victim, Sir Epicure Mammon—sees through their deceptions and uses their own weapon of self-transformation to try to expose them. But he is unsuccessful; so fixed are the gulls in their obsessive pursuit of what they desire—and their belief that Subtle can deliver it—that they take no heed of Surly's warnings. The conning is only curtailed with the return of the master of the house to London, to discover from his neighbours that there have been strange goings-on in his absence. Face, restored to his original identity as Jeremy the butler, tries to lie his way out of trouble but as the victims of his trickery converge on the house he is finally forced to tell the truth to his indulgent master. Lovewit's forgiveness is rewarded, in a final act of transformation stage-managed by Face, by his marriage to the comely Dame Pliant, sister of one of the gulls. The play ends with the latter realising the extent of their gullibility, Subtle and Dol double-crossed by their former accomplice, and Face triumphant, though now once again brought under the control of his respectable master Lovewit.

As in Jonson's other masterpieces, *Volpone* and *Bartholomew Fair*, the dramatis personae of *The Alchemist* are divided into two groups: the con-artists and their victims. What distinguishes them is not so much their moral qualities—the victims are no more virtuous than the crooks—but their relative skills as actors. Subtle, Dol, and Face, like Volpone and Mosca, are brilliantly versatile performers, able to present themselves convincingly in a bewildering array of roles, and to switch from one role to another at a moment's notice. Thus endowed, they are able, at least for a while, to achieve their own acquisitive ends, fleecing those who are no less greedy but lacking the theatrical skills of their predators. If gold and the Fair are the central images of acquisitiveness and its formidable energies in the other two plays, in this it is alchemy, the contemporary pseudo-science of transforming base metals into gold.

Jonson's attitude to alchemy and alchemists was one of undisguised scorn, as was his feeling about much of the theatre of his day. The two responses were linked, at least to the extent that both involve a repugnance to what the dramatist evidently considered illegitimate pretence and illicit images of transformation. The context for both the popularity of alchemy and theatre, and for Jonson's feelings about them, was a society that was witnessing the rapid expansion of economic activity and, along with it, what must have seemed to many the overturning of traditional values and customs, and the growing difficulty of unmistakably interpreting individual identity and motive from outward appearances. In this general "loosening-up" of traditional modes of behaviour, English society seemed to be assuming a new theatricality, a growing freedom to present new and multiple images of the self that was itself a product and expression of a developing market economy. As Jonson, viewing the matter conservatively and pessimistically, put it in *Discoveries*: "our whole life is like a *Play*: wherein every man, forgetfull of himselfe, is in travaile with expression of another. Nay, wee so insist in imitating others, as wee cannot (when it is necessary) returne to our selves . . . . "

The Alchemist, serving what Jonson considered to be theatre's proper, high moral function, uses alchemy to show the grotesque folly of contemporary acquisitiveness. But the pursuit of wealth is not the whole story, for Subtle and his accomplices exploit a wide range of dreams and delusions. Dapper wants a charm to make him a successful gambler; Drugger seeks guidance on how to set up his new shop; Kastril, the "Angry Boy", isn't interested in financial gain—he merely wants Subtle to transform him into a successful man-about-town. Each in his own way is pursuing a dream of personal success, in which money is only one ingredient. This is even more true of Subtle and Face's more egregious victims: Sir Epicure Mammon and the Anabaptists named Tribulation and Ananias. For them, Subtle holds out the promise of the "stone" itself, the means to transform base metals into gold. For Tribulation and Ananias this promises not just endless wealth but the power that goes with it. And though his name suggests his obsession with untold riches, Mammon is not simply greedy; he dreams of a bizarre utopia in which he will use his wealth to make everyone else rich too, and fantasizes that alchemy will restore him to perpetual youth and endow him with unlimited sexual potency.

The alchemist's victims dream of money but, even more so, of transforming themselves and their lives through the power of alchemy. But they are deceived by those whose powers of transformation, of creating persuasive but deceptive illusions, is much greater than their own. If the play is a warning against alchemy it is also implicitly a cautionary demonstration of the power of the theatrical, not just on the stage, but in everyday social life. Jonson's attitude to theatre, on the evidence of this and his other major plays, seems to have been deeply ambivalent: it may educate but, all too often, it merely deludes and debases. *The Alchemist* was evidently written to flay folly and vice; but in doing so it explored the dynamic power of a theatricality which extends beyond the walls of the playhouse and which was able to fascinate and even partially seduce its author, in spite of himself.

—Brian Crow

ALKESTIS.   See ALCESTIS.

ALL FOR LOVE; or, The World Well Lost
by John Dryden

First Publication: London, 1678.
First Production: Theatre Royal, Drury Lane, London
December, 1677.

Editions

All for Love, edited by Arthur Sale, London, 1961.
All for Love, edited by Benjamin Griffith, Great Neck, New York, 1961.
All for Love, edited by R. J. Kaufmann, San Francisco, 1962.
All for Love, edited by John J. Eynck, New York, 1966.
All for Love, in *John Dryden: Four Tragedies*, edited by L.A. Beaurline, Chicago and London, 1967.
All for Love, edited by David Vieth, Lincoln, Nebraska, 1972 (Regents Restoration Drama Series).
All for Love, edited by N.J. Andrew, London and New York, 1975.

Criticism

(For general works on the author, see *Playwrights* volume)

Books:
Bruce King (ed.), *Twentieth Century Interpretations of "All For Love"*, Englewood Cliffs, New Jersey, 1968.

Articles:
R.J. Kaufmann, "On the Poetics of Terminal Tragedy: Dryden's *All For Love*" in *Dryden*, edited by Bernard Schilling, Englewood Cliffs, New Jersey, 1963.
Peter Nazareth, "*All For Love*: Dryden's Hybrid Play", in *English studies in Africa*, 6, 1963.

D.W. Jefferson, "The Significance of Dryden's Heroic Plays" in *Restoration Dramatists*, edited by Earl Minor, Englewood Cliffs, New Jersey, 1966.

Eugene M. Wraith, "*All For Love*", in *Restoration Dramatists*, edited by Earl Minor, Englewood Cliffs, New Jersey, 1966.

Howard D. Weinbrot, "Alexas in *All For Love*: His Geneology and Function", in *Studies in Philology*, 64, 1967.

Derek W. Hughes, "The Significance of *All For Love*" in *Journal of English Literary History*, 37, 1970.

F.J. Kearful, "'Tis Past Recovery': Tragic Consciousness in *All For Love*", in *Modern Language Quarterly*, 34, 1973.

John A. Vance, "Antony Bound: Fragmentation and Insecurity in *All for Love*", in *Studies in English Literature, 1500–1900*, Summer 1986.

J.M. Armistead, "Egypt in the Restoration: A Perspective on *All for Love*", in *Papers on Language and Literature*, Spring 1986.

Robert L. King, "*Res et Verba*: The Reform of Language in Dryden's *All for Love*", in *English Literary History*, Spring 1987.

*   *   *

All for Love begins with Egyptian priests warning of a coming disaster. Conquests and imperial politics belong to the past; the focus is on the doomed lovers in their last days. With Caesar hovering in the background waiting to finish off Antony and Cleopatra, they must choose between their love, their suspicions of each other, and their doubtful options for personal survival. Antony, passive and melancholic, dreams of the past. Cleopatra still adores him and fears his departure. The play is a series of confrontations between Antony and representatives of the duties he has abandoned. Each time he is won over to duty but soon is brought back to the primacy of his love for Cleopatra. First Ventidius, "his General", urges him to return to the glories of warfare. Then he is confronted by his Roman wife Octavia (Caesar's sister) and their two children. Next he banishes his best friend Dollabella, who is also attracted to Cleopatra. Alexas, the Queen's eunuch, attempts to restore Antony's love for Cleopatra by falsely reporting that she has killed herself. Antony commits suicide, believing that he has nothing left for which to live. Cleopatra, finding him dying, kills herself, to be worthy of Antony and to prevent Caesar's triumph.

While usually regarded as Dryden's best play, *All for Love* is often unfavourably contrasted to the greater range of themes, interests, and psychology of Shakespeare's *Antony and Cleopatra*. Restoration notions of decorum, including the demand that a hero and heroine should be blameless, meant that Dryden had to shift the complex motivations of power, politics, and sexuality from Antony and Cleopatra to minor characters, such as Alexas, or delete them from the play, so that his two central characters could be seen as a pattern for ideal lovers. The play concludes "And Fame to late Posterity, shall tell, / No Lovers liv'd so great, or dy'd so well". Such classicizing, idealizing, and universalizing (even in its imagery of Mars and Venus) is characteristic of this play. Yet the play is very much of its period and its assumptions reflect the Restoration court's libertinism and often expressed complaints that duty interferes with the pleasures of love. Many scenes are basically lovers' quarrels followed by reconciliation as the immediate source of jealousy or fear of desertion is removed and the lovers are reunited, each convinced that the other is still sincere and true.

Antony is a strangely introverted, withdrawn character for a great warrior or lover. He is often melancholic, lethargic, passive, dreamy. He is put into motion only by the stimulation

ALL FOR LOVE.

M.ʳˢ YATES as CLEOPATRA.
I'll die, I will not bear it, you may hold me.
Act V. Scene 1.

Published March 22.ᵈ 1777 by T. Lowndes & Partners.

All for Love: Theatre Royal, Drury Lane, 1766

of others, either through their urging him to duty or through the attractions of Cleopatra. While his depression might be the result of political losses to Octavius Caesar, it seems part of his inability to decide between duty and love. Cleopatra can at times sound vulgarly shrewish in her complaints and her jealousy but she is so deeply in love that she has even less instinct for survival than Antony. By the values of the play any manipulative strategy for survival is seen as morally demeaning. This is a play in which the main characters are "softies". Rather than Shakespeare's fascinating, experienced bitch-goddess, this Cleopatra appears to be virgin to the ways of the world. Even Dollabella, Antony's friend and confidant, is made of soft stuff: "Nature has cast me in so soft a mould, / That but to hear a story feign'd for pleasure / Of some sad Lover's death, moistens my eyes, / And robs me of my Manhood".

All for Love is part of a change in Restoration drama away from the high artifice of the heroic play with its compressed epic plot, undefeatable heroes, scenes of admiration and wonder, and rhymed verse. Instead there is a new focus on character, pathos, sentiment, and compassion expressed through blank verse. The aim of the tragedy is to raise pity and compassion for such lovers. To achieve this, Dryden concentrates on the last days of Antony and Cleoptra; the drama benefits from the psychological intensity that results from observing the classical unities of time, place, and a single story. Dryden also imitates the style of Shakespeare's tragic period by using metaphors and verbal pictures and by pointing to the response he wants from the audience: "See, see how the Lovers sit in State together, / As they were giving Laws to half Mankind". To make certain the audience does not miss the point, it is expanded the way a metaphor is developed into a "conceit": "Th' impression of a smile left in her face, / Shows she dy'd pleas'd with him, for whom she liv'd, / And went to charm him in another World". Whereas Dryden previously assumed that surprising events, extraordinary incidents, and a cleverly designed plot are the heart of tragedy, he now felt that the speeches, especially as they raise passion, are the most significant part of this new, affective theatre. Shakespeare's verbal pictures were a way to show two lovers so sincerely bonded to each other that they have given "all for love". This is more often a subject for poetry than drama; the lyric is the normal place to show and explore such emotions. *All for Love* at times seems more an illustration, a series of lyrical pictures, than a drama of conflict.

The emotional scene between Antony and Octavia and the confrontation between Octavia and Cleopatra bring out the main conflicts. Octavia is Antony's legal Roman wife and she regards Cleopatra as little more than a trollop who has misled her husband from virtue; but Octavia is shown to be cold, frigid, dignified, but passionless, the voice of established society. By contrast Cleopatra often seems a long loved, now unprotected, mistress on the verge of being discarded without means to save herself. Part of her charm is an innocence, more appropriate to inexperienced youth, that Dryden wrote into her character. *All for Love* was written at a time when French and English critics were moving towards moral didacticism and public taste was reacting to the aggressive libertinism of the Restoration court by a renewed concern with morals and manners; Dryden is careful not to make his hero and heroine victims of sexuality and lust, and rarely touches on such emotions.

—Bruce King

ALL MY SONS
by Arthur Miller

First Publication: New York, 1947.
First Production: Coronet Theatre, New York, 29 January, 1947.

Criticism
(For general works on the author, see *Playwrights* volume)

Articles:
Barry E. Gross, "*All My Sons* and the Larger Context", in *Modern Drama*, 18, 1975.
Arvin R. Wells, "The Living and the Dead in *All My Sons*", in *Modern Drama*, 18, 1975.

S.K. Bhatia, "Father and Son Relationship in *All My Sons* and *Death of a Salesman*", in *Rajasthan Journal of English Studies*, 4–5, 1976–77.

*   *   *

All My Sons, Arthur Miller's first Broadway success, centres on the Keller family: father Joe, mother Kate, son Chris. A manufacturer of military airplane parts during World War II, Joe Keller was convicted (but later exonerated on appeal) of knowingly shipping out defective cylinder heads, resulting in the deaths of 21 American P-40 pilots. The catalyst for the play's action is Chris's startling announcement that he intends to marry Ann Deever, the daughter of Joe's former business partner (on whom Joe had placed the blame for his war-time crime and who is currently serving a jail sentence) and the fiancée of Chris's younger brother, Larry, an air-force pilot who has been missing in action for three years. Kate, unable to accept Larry's death, is adamant that Chris and Ann never marry. As the play progresses, a series of long-buried secrets is gradually brought to light: Chris discovers that Joe is guilty of the crime of which he stood accused; all three Kellers discover that Larry is dead, having committed suicide out of shame over his father's treachery; and, most crucially, Joe discovers that there is something more important than the financial well-being of his immediate family (his reason for committing the crime)—a discovery that ultimately leads to his own suicide.

Structurally and thematically, *All My Sons* is heavily indebted to the plays of Henrik Ibsen, a major influence on all Miller's work. The intense Ibsenite realism of *All My Sons*, where the ghosts of the past return both to haunt the present and to shape its future, is immediately evidenced in the minutely detailed setting of the Kellers' back garden—a setting which remains constant throughout all three acts. Miller obeys every possible unity in this early play. Thus the events of the play unfold during the course of a single August Sunday: one long day's journey into night. And to complete this neo-classical rigour, there is also unity of action: as in Ibsen, the play dramatizes a central ideological struggle, a literally life-and-death struggle of ethics and values. As Miller has commented: "Joe Keller's trouble. . .is not that he cannot tell right from wrong but that his cast of mind cannot admit that he, personally, has any viable connection with his world, his universe, or his society . . . . The fortress which *All My Sons* lays siege to is the fortress of unrelatedness".

The spokesman in the play for "relatedness," for a connection with the larger "family" of humanity, is Chris. As his name suggests, Chris is a metaphoric Christ, a secular "saint" espousing universal love for all God's children. "Chris, a man can't be a Jesus in this world", Joe cries out in anguished self-defence at the play's climax. But that is precisely what the idealist Chris demands. Joe's justification for his crime is the primacy of family: "I'm his father and he's my son", he says of Chris, "and if there's something bigger than that I'll put a bullet in my head!". For Chris, of course, there *is* something bigger than that; to believe otherwise is to abandon civilization to the beasts, to ethical chaos. However much he chooses to rationalize his crime, Joe is not divorced from his society, from the world at large: he has responsibilities to that world, to himself as a social (and therefore a *human*) being. "What the hell are you?", Chris demands of his father at the height of their confrontation: the key question in all of Miller's plays. Joe's ultimate answer is to walk off stage and put a bullet in his head, thereby both acknowledging his guilt and conceding the validity of Chris's (and Larry's) moral vision: Larry killed himself because the pilots Joe sent to their deaths were, in a larger context, *all* his "sons".

All My Sons: Wyndhams Theatre, London, 1981

The debt to Ibsenite realism undoubtedly accounts for much of the power of *All My Sons*: once caught up in its intricate and relentless plot, an audience finds itself inevitably swept along by the play's urgency and moral passion. At the same time, however, Miller's relative immaturity as a playwright occasionally betrays itself. For many critics, the play's sometimes creaky contrivances—a climactic letter from beyond the grave; the denouement propelled by a slip of the tongue; the sudden blurting out of long-buried truths for maximum dramatic effect—smack of the worst excesses of the well-made play, of soap opera. Further, while the play painstakingly spells out Joe Keller's guilt, what about *Chris's* "guilt"? Miller has shamelessly stacked the deck, allowing Chris to hold all the moral cards and to exult in playing them. This makes Chris, despite his status as Miller's alter ego and the play's ethical *raisonneur*, in many ways a difficult character to admire: his idealism can so easily come across as smug self-righteousness, as adolescent whining.

Still, for all its shortcomings, *All My Sons* is an important play. In its focus both on the family and on the debunking of the materialism and "success-at-any-price" aspects of a spiritually debased American Dream, it is typical not only of much American drama in general but of the entire body of Arthur Miller's theatrical work in particular. However much they may vary stylistically, all Miller's plays explore the same thematic ground: the conflict between, on the one hand, individual identity and integrity (who are you? what do you believe? what

should you believe?), and, on the other, the beliefs and values of American society at large—a conflict Miller first dramatized successfully, and rivetingly, here in *All My Sons*.

—Hersh Zeifman

ALL'S WELL THAT ENDS WELL
by William Shakespeare

First Publication: London, c. 1602.
First Production: London, 1623.

Editions

All's Well That Ends Well, edited by Arthur Quiller-Couch and John Dover Wilson, Cambridge, 1929 (The New Shakespeare).
All's Well That Ends Well, edited by G.K. Hunter, London, 1959 (3rd edition); corrected edition, London, 1962 (The Arden Shakespeare).
All's Well That Ends Well, edited by Jonas A. Barish,

Harmondsworth, 1964; revised edition, 1980 (Pelican Shakespeare).

All's Well That Ends Well, edited by Sylvan Barnet, New York, Toronto, and London, 1965 (Signet Classic Shakespeare).

All's Well That Ends Well, edited by Barbara Everett, Harmondsworth, 1970; revised edition, 1978 (New Penguin Shakespeare).

All's Well That Ends Well, edited by Russell Fraser, Cambridge, 1985 (New Cambridge Shakespeare).

Criticism

(For general works on the author, see *Playwrights* volume)

Books:

Joseph G. Price, *The Unfortunate Comedy: A Study of "All's Well That Ends Well" and its Critics*, Toronto, 1968.

Howard C. Cole, *The "All's Well" Story from Boccaccio to Shakespeare*, Urbana, Illinois, 1981.

J.L. Styan, *All's Well That Ends Well*, Manchester, 1984.

Jean Fuzier and François Laroque, *"All's Well That Ends Well": Nouvelles Perspectives critiques*, Montpellier, 1985.

Mark Scott (ed.), *"All's Well That Ends Well"* in *Shakespearean Criticism, 7*, Detroit, Illinois, 1988 (anthology of criticism).

Articles:

For information on the many articles about *All's Well That Ends Well*, see the bibliographies listed in the *Playwrights* volume, and the annual Shakespeare Bibliography in *Shakespeare Quarterly*, published by the Folger Shakespeare Library, Washington D.C. (1950–).

*   *   *

Helena, daughter of a famous physician, loves Bertram, the son of the Countess of Rossillion. In Paris she cures the French king of a severe illness and wins Bertram as her husband in reward from the king. Bertram considers her his social inferior and abandons her immediately after the wedding to seek, with his frivolous companion Parolles, honour and fame in a war in Italy. He informs Helena by letter that she can never call him husband unless she gets a ring from his finger and is made pregnant by him. Helena fulfils both conditions when, unknown to him, she becomes his bed-partner in place of Diana, a girl he has wooed in Florence. Parolles, who has made a foolish boast that he will capture an enemy drum, is ambushed by his own men and, when blindfolded and interrogated, slanders them all, which brings him shame when the trick is revealed. Believing Helena to have died, his elders are willing to forgive Bertram and match him in marriage to one of his own class. Helena arrives in time to reveal that she has fulfilled the conditions Bertram demanded and he consents now, amid shame about his uncovered deceptions, to accept her as his wife.

Based on a story from Painter's translation of *The Palace of Pleasure* the play contains dark elements that have led some critics to consider it a problem comedy. It is one of the few Shakespeare comedies which countenances the possibility of a marriage across class lines. The aristocracy of France is

All's Well That Ends Well: Stratford-Upon-Avon, 1989 (Royal Shakespeare Company)

decayed, forcibly imaged in the king's sickness, and needs an infusion of fresh blood. Helena, an almost saint-like figure with miraculous skills, is allowed to pursue and win the Count who needs all the help he can get to achieve redemption from a life of frivolous and feckless selfishness. The play shows us a world of once solid, firmly rooted values in decline and being eclipsed by a newer world of opportunists willing to pay only lip-service to older ideals. In pursuing the bubble, reputation, figures such as Bertram and Parolles cannot afford the kind of honour, courtesy, and honesty for which the old Count Rossillion was celebrated. In their restless energy they become slaves of the time and victims to fashion.

Helena is the only member of the younger generation who has strong, continuing links with an older system of values, and, as child of Gerard de Narbon, is inheritor of his healing skills. The king has no faith in the skill of his doctors but is recovered not merely to health but to youthful vigour by Helena's cure. Her faith in her father's skill and her willingness to wager her life on the efficacy of his cure brings her the reward of Bertram. Bertram is one of the least likeable of Shakespeare's suitors. A shallow, young Renaissance buck, he bobs along in the tide of fashion incapable of seeing through his ill-angel, the transparent Parolles, who fools scarcely anyone else with his pretensions. Bertram is little better than Parolles who seeks to fake an honourable triumph in battle. But Parolles under cross-examination helps us to see that the companions who torment him are not as noble as they pretend. Some of the mud he throws in his slanderous characterization of them sticks, for they are captives of the tyrant, appetite. Just as Parolles is tricked and kept in the dark so, too, is Bertram, by Helena's bed-trick of substituting herself for Diana. In what he believes is a feckless despoiling of virginity, Bertram seals himself to the bargain he made with his wife and so performs, not a soldier's indulgence, but a husband's duty. Talk of virginity and honour sealed by rings echoes through the play as Bertram seeks to betray his honour undetected and the women co-operate to make him true to it against his will and knowledge.

The comedy is unusual in that the old are not obstructive figures in the way of the fertile renewal that youth promises to their wintry world but are, instead, allies of Helena, for she wins the support of the Countess and Lafew, as well as the king. She rescues them from mere doting nostalgia for the old, aristocratic world and offers them hope for some vigorous common-sense in the newer more frivolous world displacing the old values. She is not a born aristocrat; but the infusion of her noble spirit offers hope for the redemption of the declining world.

The old figures falter towards the end of the play, unaware that Bertram is not worthy of the compassionate forgiveness they bestow on him. The ease with which they forget Helena, whom they believe has died, indicates how quickly they can revert to dotage. The king is a dangerously crotchety and unstable figure quite capable of punishing the innocent and forgiving the guilty. In the unseemly haste of reverting to type to seal up the usual alliance of noble households they uncover, in the evidence of the ring, the dark deed of Bertram's past. Critics have often thought Helena too active in her own cause but in such a dangerously disturbed society it is evident that someone sensible is required to push matters in a healthy direction. Helena's recovery of the king did not ensure a renewed society. She is required to effect another miracle. She must come back from the dead to claim her own; her blood must revive this decaying stock. She is an amalgam of both old and new and combines her father's skills—his sense of faith and sacrifice—with a pragmatic ability to get what she wants. We accept her opportunism because she is the only character in the play who exerts any energy to stop a bad situation getting worse and to save a world which, at times, seems almost beyond renewal.

—Anthony Brennan

AMERICAN BUFFALO
by David Mamet

First Publication: New York, 1977.
First Production: Goodman Theatre Stage Two, Chicago, 23 November 1975.

Criticism
(For general works on the author, see *Playwrights* volume)

Articles:
June Schlueter and Elizabeth Forsyth, "America as Junkshop: The Business Ethic in David Mamet's *American Buffalo*", in *Modern Drama*, 26, 1983.

*   *   *

American Buffalo is set in a junk shop run by Don Dubrow, a man in his late 40's. In the first act, Don and his young friend, Bobby, prepare to steal a coin collection from a man who, a week earlier, bought a buffalo-head nickel from Don. Angered by the man's condescension and a suspicion that the coin was worth much more than he was paid, Don has arranged a heist with Bobby as the one to do the actual robbery. Teach, a "friend and associate", convinces Don to take him on as a partner instead and to cut Bobby out of the deal. In Act II, tension runs high as Don and Teach wait for Fletcher, another friend Don has insisted on taking into the partnership. When Bobby appears with a buffalo nickel to sell and the story that Fletch is in the hospital, Teach becomes suspicious and convinces Don that they have been betrayed, and Bobby and Fletch have stolen the coin collection themselves. When Bobby cannot answer their questions satisfactorily, Teach viciously bashes him on the side of the head with a heavy object. A phone call corroborates Bobby's story; a fight erupts between Don and Teach, and Teach goes berserk, trashing the junk shop. After the emotional storm has passed, the three men awkwardly make peace with one another and leave to take Bobby to the hospital.

As is typical of Mamet's work, *American Buffalo* depicts a very specific segment of society, but raises issues of more general concern about the American way of life. Don, Teach, and Bobby inhabit an urban world of resident hotels, cheap diners, and pawn shops. They are petty crooks without the intelligence or forethought necessary actually to carry out the robbery they plan, but the projected heist serves to illuminate the values of the characters and to focus attention on their relationships. Don serves as a father or mentor figure to the inept Bobby, and early in the play, he tries to explain the difference between "business", which he sees as "People taking care of themselves", and friendship: "When you walk around you *hear* a lot of things, and what you got to do is keep clear who your friends are, and who treated you like what. Or else the rest is garbage, Bob, because I want to tell you something . . . . Things are not always what they seem to be". The garrulous Teach, who fancies himself a profound thinker,

American Buffalo: National Theatre, London, 1978

is obsessed by the need for loyalty among friends, yet he has little trouble convincing Don to dump Bobby from their financial deal or to believe that the boy's inarticulateness and Fletcher's absence are proof of a double-cross. Teach rewrites his code of ethics and behavior at a moment's notice in order to follow the most crucial of his objectives, which is to look out for his own economic interests, even at the cost of someone else. Having internalized a warped notion of the traditional American value of independence, Teach defines "free enterprise" as "The freedom. . .Of the *Individual*. . .To Embark on Any Fucking Course that he sees fit. . .In order to secure his honest chance to make a profit".

The junk shop full of discarded merchandise becomes a metaphor for this morally bankrupt world as the characters continually contradict their own empty profession of ethics in the absence of any objective standard. The buffalo-head nickel, the central image of the play, is, significantly, a coin whose sliding value depends upon circumstances and the knowledge of its beholder. Characteristic of Mamet in its poetic manipulation of rhythm, the language of the play reflects the inner emptiness of the characters. Their limited vocabulary, omission of words, tortured grammar, and reliance on profanity reflect a lack of command over their lives and emotions. In a world devoid of guiding principles, the men are always perilously close to chaos, as shown by the eruption of violence at the play's end, yet in the midst of their moral confusion, they long for the humane interaction which their own actions constantly subvert. Bobby reveals that he lied about a crucial detail of the robbery and purchased the second buffalo nickel in an effort to please Don and gain his approval.

As Teach ransacks his friend's shop with an instrument formerly used to drain the blood from a slaughtered pig, he voices his own perception of reality: "The Whole Entire World./There Is No Law./There Is No Right And Wrong./The World Is Lies./There Is No Friendship./Every Fucking Thing . . . . Every God-forsaken Thing . . . . We all live like the cavemen". The final, ineffectual groping of the men toward a reconciliation is a sad illustration of their need and their essential isolation.

Mamet's characters are both funny and pathetic in their evasions, manipulations, and excesses. The halting rhythms of the dialogue are designed to provoke both laughter and thought. In performance, the violence of the play's conclusion is disturbing, but it is a fitting image for the author's depiction of a society in which the pursuit of personal monetary gain has supplanted or perverted all other patterns of behavior.

—Kathy Fletcher

AMINTA
by Torquato Tasso

First Publication: Venice, 1581.
First Production: Palace of Belvedere, Belvedere Island, Po River, Italy, 31 July, 1573.

Editions

Aminta [with translation], edited and translated by Ernest Grillo, London and Toronto, 1924.

Aminta, edited by A. Solerti, Turin, 1926.

Aminta, edited by L. Fassio, Florence, 1948.

Aminta, edited by Paul Renucci, Paris, 1952.

Aminta, edited by B.T. Sozzi, Padua, 1957.

Aminta, edited by Claudio Varese, Urbino, 1961.

Aminta, edited by Giorgio Barbieri Squarotti, Padua, 1968.

Aminta, edited by C.E.J. Griffiths, Manchester, 1972 (based on Sozzi's edition).

Aminta, edited by Giorgio Cerbani Baiardi, Urbino, 1976.

Translations

Amyntas, translated by F. Whitmore, Penzance, Cornwall, 1900.

Amynta [John Oldmixon's 17-century translation] in *A Renaissance Treasury*, Garden City, NY, 1953.

Aminta, in *The Genius of the Italian Theatre*, edited by Eric Bentley, New York, 1964.

Torquato Tasso's "Aminta" Englished: The Henry Reynolds Translation, edited by Clifford Davidson, Fennimore, Wisconsin, 1972.

Criticism

(For general works on the author, see *Playwrights* volume)

Books:

A. Corsaro, *Su "L'Aminta" di Torquato Tasso*, Naples, 1930.

M. Sansone, *"L'Aminta" di Torquato Tasso*, Milan, 1941.

G. Citanna, *Gioventi, amore, vita cortigiane nell' "Aminta"*, nd.

G. Bonalumi, *Introduzione all' "Aminta"*, Bologna, 1958.

M. Fubini, *Introduzione all' "Aminta"*, 1967.

Richard Cody, *The Landscape of the Mind: Pastoralism and Platonic Theory in Tasso's "Aminta" and Shakespeare's Early Comedies*, Oxford, 1969.

Isida Cremona, *L'Influence de l'"Aminta" sur la pastorale dramatique française*, Paris, 1977.

Giovanni Da Pozzo, *L'ambigua armonia: studio sull' "Aminta" del Tasso*, Florence, 1983.

Articles:

D. Vittorini, "Realistic Elements in Tasso's *Aminta*: A Revision", in *Italia*, 25, 1948.

B.T. Sozzi, "Saggio sull' *Aminta*" in *Studi sul Tasso*, Pisa, 1954.

M. Fittoni, "Intorno all'ordito classico dell' *Aminta*" in *Convivium*, 29, 1961.

C. Varese, "*L'Aminta*" in *Pascoli politico, Tasso e altri saggi*, Milan, 1962.

Mario Fubini, "*L'Aminta* intermezzo alla tragedia della *Liberata*", in *Giornale storico della litteratura italiana*, 145, 1968.

B.T. Sozzi, "Di un'edizione cinquecentesca dell' *Aminta*", in *Studi Tassiani*, 18, 1968.

Vittorio Mora, "*L'Aminta* del Tasso e la traduzione in dialetto bergamasco di Giuseppe Cavagnari", in *Studi Tassiani*, 23, 1973.

Giovanni Iorio, "Soluzione musicale e soluzione teatrale: Un trentannio di studi sull' *Aminta*", in *Cultura e scuola*, 69, 1979.

David R. Shore, "The Shepherd and the Court: Pastoral Poetics in Spenser's *Colin Clout* and Tasso's *Aminta*", in *Canadian Review of Comparative Literature*, vol.7 no.4, 1980.

Daniela Dalla Valle, "Aspects de l'influence de l'*Aminta* en France: Les Relations entre la pièce, son public et son milieu", in *L'Age d'or du mécénet*, edited by Roland Mousnier, Paris, 1985.

* * *

In *A Dialogue: The Speakers John Milton and Torquato Tasso* (London, 1762), Milton tells his Italian predecessor: "I honoured your memory when living" and *Comus* "is on as respectable a footing with my countrymen as is the *Aminta* with yours. There is, however, this difference: you had followers in this, I had none"; which tells us about the privileged position of *Aminta* in Italian literature and of the unique position of Milton's *Comus* in English.

Aminta came out in 1573. It is the most famous pastoral play in Italian and deals with the shepherd Aminta's love for the nymph Silvia. Although a pastoral play, there is much of the courtly world in *Aminta*, and it may well be regarded as an idealization of courtly love. While bringing to the fore Tasso's dramatic mastery, *Aminta* also exemplifies his lyric power.

A jewel of poetic elegance, structural harmony and linguistic exquisiteness, *Aminta*'s dramatic character as a pastoral play is closely tied up with, if not altogether subordinate to, its poetic character. Both the plot and the action are not so much dramatically enacted as narrated, and Tasso is not so much interested in probing into the psychology of his characters as in using them as both agents and mouthpieces of the sentiments of love and courtship, yearning and tenderness, uncertainty and fulfilment. The play teems with echoes from classical writers such as Theocritus, Anacreonte, Ovid and Virgil, and from Tasso's immediate predecessors such as G.B. Cinthio, author of *Egle* (1545), Agostino Beccari, author of *Il sacrificio* (1554), and Agostino Argenti, author of *Lo sfortunato* (1567).

Tasso's familiarity with court life—with its pressures, intrigues and corruption on the one hand, and with its urbanity, sophistication, and magnificence on the other—made him yearn for something utterly different, something his heart and imagination could turn to and thereby experience a joy and a satisfaction the world of reality could not give him. Thus he creates an Arcadian dream world in *Aminta*, with its nymphs and shepherds, sylvan beauty and tranquillity, nature and romance. The young shepherd Aminta and the nymph Silvia are the main protagonists of the play. The other characters are Dafne (Silvia's companion), Tirsi (Aminta's companion), Satyr (who loves Silvia), Nerina (the messenger), Ergasto (the nuncio), and Elpino (the shepherd). There is also a personification of Love, and a Chorus of the shepherds.

In the Prologue, Love appears in a pastoral garb and declares its nature and character as being, among the gods, "il più potente" (the most powerful), and its intent being that of inspiring "nobil sensi a' rozzi petti" (noble sentiments in rough hearts). Aminta is in love with Silvia, but she is only interested in hunting, and this in spite of Dafne's efforts to persuade her to taste "le gioie / che gusta un cor amato riamando" ("the joys the loved heart experiences by loving in return"). Aminta, on the other hand, is love-sick and desolately cries his heart out to the rocks and the waves which feel pity for him, but Silvia, "crudele e bella" ("cruel and beautiful"), has no compassion for him, much less any love. His despair has reached such a point that he feels close to death, while hoping that after his death Silvia, "commossa da tarda pietate, / piangesse morto che già vivo uccise" ("moved by late pity might / weep for him when he is dead, having killed him while he was alive").

interested in him even less than in Aminta. And yet his love for her is expressed in an even more poignant way and with a greater poetical efficacy than Aminta's. However, at a certain point, the satyr attacks Silvia who is opportunely freed from him by Aminta. Nevertheless she still doesn't reciprocate Aminta's love and he is resolved to kill himself. One day Nerina, Silvia's hunting companion, tells her that she found wolves hovering upon Aminta's blood-stained garments, which convinces Silvia of Aminta's death; she bursts into tears, runs to the supposedly dead body of Aminta and throws herself on it while confessing her love for him. But, as luck would have it, Aminta wasn't really dead, only wounded. Thus they are both happy, find their dream of love fulfilled, and get married which brings the story to a happy ending, both Aminta and Silvia realizing what the Chorus calls "questa beatitudine maggiore" ("this utmost bliss")—namely, love.

—G. Singh

AMYNTAS. See **AMINTA.**

ANDROMACHE (Andromaque)
by Jean Racine

First Publication: Paris, 1668.
First Production: Théâtre de l'Hôtel de Bourgogne, Paris, 1667.

Editions

Andromaque, edited by Yves Brunswick and Paul Ginestier, London, 1958.
Andromaque, edited by Denise P.-Cogny and Pierre Cogny, Paris, 1961; revised edition, Paris, 1985.
Andromaque, edited by Anne Ubersfeld, Paris, 1961.
Andromaque, edited by Bernard Lalade, 1965.
Andromaque, edited by Jean-Paul Bannes, Paris, 1965.
Andromaque, edited by Daniel Mornet, Paris, 1966.
Andromaque, edited by Philip Koch, Englewood Cliffs, New Jersey, 1970.
Andromaque, edited by R.C. Knight and H.T. Barnwell, Geneva, 1977.

Translations

Andromache, in *The Best Plays of Racine*, translated by Lacy Lockert, Princeton, New Jersey, 1936.
Andromaque in *Jean Racine: Five Plays*, translated by Kenneth Muir, London, 1960.
Andromaque in *Three Plays of Racine: "Andromaque"; "Britannicus"; "Phaedra"*, translated by George Dillon, Chicago and London, 1961.
Andromaque in *The Complete Plays of Jean Racine* (2 vols.), translated by Samuel Solomon, New York, 1967.
Andromache in *"Andromache" and Other Plays*, translated by John Cairncross, Harmondsworth, 1967.

Bibliography

June Moravcevich, *Jean Racine's "Andromaque": An Annotated Bibliography*, Paris, Seattle, and Tübingen (Papers on Seventeenth Century Literature—Bibliography 17).

Criticism

(For general works on the author, see *Playwrights* volume)

Books:
G. Grimmer, *"Andromaque" de Racine*, Paris, 1955.
Jean Pommier, *Tradition littéraire et modèles vivants dans l'Andromaque de Racine*, Cambridge, 1962.
Peter France, *Racine: "Andromaque"*, London, 1977.

Articles:
R.C. Knight, "*Andromaque* et l'ironie de Corneille", in *Actes du Premier Congrès International Racinian*, 1962.
R.C. Knight, "Emprints et souvenirs dans *Andromaque*", in *Jeunesse de Racine*, April–June 1962.
André Lebois, "*Andromaque* ou la hautise de la nuit", in *Dix-septième siècle: Recherches et portraits*, Paris, 1966.
Steen Jansen, "L'Unité d'action dans *Andromaque* et dans *Lorenzaccio*", in *Revue Romane*, 3, 1968.
Pierre Han, "Racine's Use of the Concept of Myth in *Andromaque*", in *Romance Notes*, 11, 1969.
Robert W. Hartle, "Symmetry and Irony in Racine's *Andromaque*", in *Paths to Freedom: Studies in French Classicism in Honor of E.B.O. Borgerhoff, L'Esprit Créateur*, vol. 2 no. 2, 1971.
H. Gastan Hall, "Pastoral, Epic and Dynastic Dénouement in Racine's *Andromaque*", in *Modern Language Review*, 69, 1974.
William A. Mould, "The 'Innocent Stratagème' of Racine's *Andromaque*", in *French Review*, 48, 1975.
D. Shaw, "The Function of Baroque Elements in *Andromaque*", in *Forum for Modern Language Studies*, vol. 11 no. 3, 1975.
June Moravcevich, "Racine's *Andromaque* and the Rhetoric of Naming", in *Papers on Language and Literature*, 12, 1976.
Reinhard Kuhn, "The Palace of Broken Words: Reflections on Racine's *Andromaque*", in *Romanic Review*, 70, 1979.
Miloard Mergitic, "*Andromaque* ou la lecture des signes: Étude de l'ironie tragique", in *Papers on French Seventeenth Century Literature*, 11, 1979.

*   *   *

In the aftermath of the Trojan War Pyrrhus has brought back Andromaque, the widow of the slain warrior Hector. He keeps Andromaque and her son Astyanax captives in his palace in Epirus. Oreste is sent there by the Greeks as an ambassador to obtain young Astyanax, last of the royal line of Troy. But the emissary has other plans: he wants the hand of the Greek princess Hermione, currently betrothed to Pyrrhus, who in turn is besotted by his Trojan prisoner. By Act IV Andromaque has devised a plan to escape Pyrrhus's blackmail (marry me, or I will deliver your son to the Greeks): she will marry Pyrrhus, who she believes will protect Astyanax, but then kill herself, thus remaining faithful to her dead husband Hector. Now spurned by Pyrrhus, Hermione orders the ever-hopeful Oreste to kill the king during the wedding ceremony. The assassination is carried out (Oreste himself arrives too late to take part) but Hermione then turns on Oreste and goes out to commit suicide over Pyrrhus's body. Oreste goes temporarily mad and power passes into the hands of Andromaque and her son.

With *Andromaque*, Racine achieved lasting renown at the age of only 28. It confirmed his mastery of Greek subject-matter, his skill as a poet in the Alexandrine verse-form, and his total command of the form and dramatic devices of a five-act tragedy. Perhaps the best constructed of all French 17th-century plays, it depends for much of its effect on the linear pattern of unreciprocated passions, so different from the conventional "eternal triangle" pattern of much serious drama

Andromache: Old Vic Theatre, London, 1988

of the period and one found regularly elsewhere in Racine. At the beginning of the chain is Oreste, besotted with Hermione, who hopes desperately that Pyrrhus will return her passion. But Pyrrhus, in turn, has eyes only for his captive Andromaque, the fourth and last of the principal characters on stage. Yet she, too, can reject his advances because she is still loyal to the memory of her dead husband, Hector, and to the prospect that the line, and hence the fame, of Troy will survive through Astyanax, their son.

The plot, however, is not a straightforward progression, because of repeated, consistent rejection by characters of the advances of others. What injects suspense and tension into *Andromaque* and makes it a gripping as well as a profound stage experience are the hesitations, the changes of mind and reversals of fortune, the frustrated hopes and the apparent, but shortlived, successes. By his position on the chain it is inevitably Oreste who nurses the greatest illusions. There is no-one to his left, as it were, on whom he may fall back if Hermione fails to show the interest he yearns for. He arrives with expectations, is soon disillusioned and yet persists with his quest, even when he sees with unexpected clarity that Hermione's murmurings of love are but a superficial disguise for her jealousy in being rebuffed by Pyrrhus. This dogged determination is what keeps his hopes alive, despite the presence of what he calls fate, what we might perceive as bad luck or bad timing. His plight is self-inflicted, the product of passion but not one in which the Gods have a hand.

Hermione, formally betrothed to Pyrrhus, has much more of a case for complaint. As the suspicious and eventually spurned woman, she can turn not just on the king but also on Andromaque who, she believes, is leading him astray. With two persons to attack and her self-pity to keep nourished, she has even less time for Oreste than he might reasonably have expected. Where Racine's skill shows through is in the scenes where Hermione is neither downcast nor triumphant but torn with doubts, unsure of whether Pyrrhus will return to her and, if so, what she would do then. When, in Act III, she believes that he is about to marry her, she interprets this as proof of his undying affection. Yet this moment of naive hope is followed by a scene in which she tells Andromaque that there is no-one who can influence Pyrrhus more easily than she, the captive Trojan. Behind the ironic jibe lies more than a hint of Hermione's insecurity, and soon confirmation that Pyrrhus is only interested in Andromaque leads to her fateful commission to Oreste.

The emotional pendulum, swinging between hope and despair, serves to disguise a pattern of constant loves. Pyrrhus, like Oreste and Hermione, keeps his eye firmly on his desired goal: by threats and cajoling he hopes to win Andromaque's hand. Blackmailing her with none-too-subtle threats against Astyanax is the dominant approach; precious play on words, where he makes Hermione the captive and Andromaque the queen (of his heart), is another, adopted simultaneously in scenes which prove doubly disconcerting to his prisoner. For Andromaque, the main aim is resistance at any cost, through unswerving loyalty to her late husband and the name of Troy. Pyrrhus's use of Astyanax as a pawn causes her to despair at times, and in her first meeting with Pyrrhus she frostily rejects his offer to act as the young boy's father if she will submit. But by the end of Act III, unaffected by the changing fortunes of

Hermione, or by the desires of Oreste (whom she never meets), Andromaque, in a memorable scene evoking the death of Hector, is forced into a corner. Her solution is to accede to Pyrrhus's wishes but then salve her conscience by committing suicide. To do this she has to take on trust his earlier promise to look after Astyanax and his interests. Pyrrhus, she declares, is "violent but sincere"—a perhaps naive judgement which, in the end, is not put to the test, for Pyrrhus dies at the altar at the hands of the Greeks, in fulfilment of what the jealous Hermione believes she wishes and only later comes to realise is the very opposite of that.

The plot's seemingly linear pattern is thus deceptive, disguising a host of back-and-forward movements which help to give *Andromaque* a depth and realism which transcend the apparently trite storyline. It is the weakest of the principal characters, the captive Andromaque, who holds all the best cards and dictates the way the game will go, although she is largely unaware of her dominant position. Along with the forceful but irrational Hermione, she contributes to the gallery of great Racinian tragic heroines. Her present plight, and that of her son, is the basic plot of the action. But the play is dominated by the past, evoked in a series of memorable descriptions of the fall of Troy and of characters' roles in it. And where Racine achieves near-perfection is in adding a haunting future perspective, by the survival of Andromaque and Astyanax. What, we ask, lies in store for these remnants of Troy? Their honour is intact and was perhaps worth fighting for during the five acts, but the outlook is bleak or at best uncertain. Will life for them be more fulfilling than assassination for Pyrrhus, or suicide for Hermione?

—Christopher Gossip

ANDROMAQUE. See **ANDROMACHE.**

ANE SATYRE OF THE THRIEE ESTAITIS. See **A SATIRE OF THE THREE ESTATES.**

ANTIGONE
by Sophocles

First Production: Athens, c.441 B.C.

Editions

The Antigone, edited by Sir Richard Jebb, Cambridge, 1900.
Antigone, in *Sophocles:1*, edited by F. Storr, London, 1912 (Loeb Classical Library; with translation).
Antigone, in *Sophoclis Fabulae 2*, edited by A. Colonna, Turin, 1978.
Antigone, in *Sophoclis Tragoediae 2*, edited by R.D. Dawe, Leipzig, 1979.
Antigone, edited and translated by Andrew Brown, Warminster, Wiltshire, 1987 (with translation).
Antigone, in *Sophoclis Fabulae*, edited by H. Lloyd-Jones and N.G. Wilson, Oxford, 1990 (Oxford Classical Texts).

Translations

Antigone, translated by Elizabeth Wyckoff in *Sophocles, 1*, Chicago, 1954 (Complete Greek Tragedies Series).
Antigone in *Three Theban Plays*, translated by T.H. Banks, New York, 1956.
Antigone, translated by Paul Roche, in *The Oedipus Plays of Sophocles*, New York, 1958.
Antigone, in *Three Tragedies: "Antigone"; "Oedipus the King"; "Electra"*, translated by H.D.F Kitto, Oxford and New York, 1962.
Antigone, in *Four Greek Plays*, translated by Kenneth McLeish, London, 1964.
Antigone, in *The Theban Plays*, translated by E.F. Watling, Harmondsworth, 1967.
Antigone, translated by Richard Emil Braun, New York, 1973.
Antigone, in *The Three Theban Plays*, translated by Robert Fagles, New York and London, 1982.
Antigone, in *The Theban Plays*, translated by Don Taylor, London, 1986.
Antigone, in *The Three Theban Plays*, translated by C.A. Trypanis, Warminster, Wiltshire, 1986.

Criticism

(For general works on the author, see *Playwrights* volume)

Books:
R.F. Goheen, *The Imagery of Sophocles' "Antigone"*, Princeton, 1951.
I.M. Linforth, *Antigone and Creon*, Berkeley, California, 1961.
Gerald F. Else, *The Madness of Antigone*, Heidelberg, 1976.
Harald Patzer, *Hauptperson und Tragischer Held in Sophokles' "Antigone"*, Wiesbaden, 1978.
Joan V. O'Brien, *Guide to Sophocles' "Antigone"*, Carbondale, Illinois, 1978.
George Steiner, *Antigones*, Oxford, 1984.
Th.C.W. Oudemans and A.P.M.H. Lardinois, *Tragic Ambiguity: Anthropology, Philosophy and Sophocles' "Antigone"*, Leiden, 1987.
John Wilkins, *"Antigone" and "Oedipus the King"*, Bristol, 1987 (companion to Fagles' translation)

Articles:
E. Messemer, "The Double Burial of Polynices", in *Classical Journal*, 37, 1942.
I.M. Linforth, "Antigone and Creon" in *University of California Publications in Classical Philology*, 15, 1954–61.
H. Lloyd-Jones, "Notes on Sophocles' *Antigone*" in *The Classical Quarterly*, 7, 1957.
J. Halthorn, "Sophocles' *Antigone*: Eras in Politics", in *Classical Journal*, 54, 1958.
A.T. von S. Bradshaw, "The Watchman Scenes in the *Antigone*" in *The Classical Quarterly*, 12, 1962.
L. Mackay, "*Antigone, Coriolanus*, and Hegel", in *Transactions and Proceedings of the American Philological Association [TAPA]*, 93, 1962.
J.H. Kelly, "Problems of Interpretation in the *Antigone*" in *Bulletin of the Institute of Classical Studies* (London), 10, 1963.
C.S. Levy, "Antigone's Motives: A Suggested Interpretation" in *Transactions of the American Philological Association [TAPA]*, 94, 1963.
C. Segal, "Sophocles's Praise of Man and the Conflicts of *Antigone*", in *Arion*, vol. 3 no. 2, 1964.
E.J. Daly, "Three Keys to the *Antigone*", in *Thought*, 42, 1967.

Antigone: National Theatre, London, 1984

W.M. Calder, "Sophocles' Political Tragedy, *Antigone*" in *Greek, Roman and Byzantine Studies*, 9, 1968.

J.S. Margon, "The First Burial of Polyneices", in *Classical Journal*, 64, 1969.

Thomas F. Holey, "Inversion in the *Antigone*: A Note", in *Arion*, 9, 1970.

R. Coleman, "The Role of the Chorus in Sophocles' *Antigone*", in *Proceedings of the Cambridge Philological Society* (new series), 18, 1972.

J.C. Hogan, "The Protagonists of the *Antigone*", in *Arethusa*, 5, 1972.

M. McCall, "Divine and Human Action in Sophocles: The Two Burials of the *Antigone*", in *Yale Classical Studies*, 22, 1972.

A.S. McDevitt, "Sophocles' Praise of Man in the *Antigone*", in *Ramus*, 1, 1972.

J.S. Margon, "The Second Burial of Polyneices", in *Classical Journal*, 68, 1972.

S. Bernadete, "A Reading of Sophocles' *Antigone*", in *Interpretation*, 4–5, 1975

Joan V. O'Brien, "Sophocles's Ode on Man and Paul's Hymn on Love: A Comparative Study", in *Classical Journal*, 71, 1975–76.

S.F. Wiltshire, "Antigone's Disobedience", in *Areth*, 9, 1976.

H. Petersmann, "Mythos and Gestaltung in Sophokles' *Antigone*" in *Wiener Studien*, 91, 1978.

J.F. Davidson, "The Parados of the *Antigone*: A Poetic Study", in *Bulletin of the Institute of Classical Studies* (London), 30, 1983.

O. Taplin, "The Place of Antigone" in *Omnibus*, 7, 1984.

Sheila Murnaghan, "*Antigone* 904–920 and the Institution of Marriage", in *American Journal of Philology*, 107, 1986.

*   *   *

The sons of Oedipus, Eteocles and Polyneices, have killed each other in single combat. Because Polyneices had attacked his own city, Thebes, its ruler Creon has ordered that his body be left unburied. The play opens as Antigone and Ismene, the sisters of the dead men, discuss Creon's proclamation. Antigone vows to bury Polyneices herself when Ismene hesitates to help her. After her departure, the chorus enters, followed by Creon who defends his action. A guard rushes in to announce that someone has buried the body. Sent away, he soon returns with Antigone, whom he has caught in the act of attempting a second burial. She confesses and defends the moral basis for her action. Ismene too is brought in, and asks to share the blame. Creon condemns both to death. When the sisters have been taken away, Creon's son Haemon who is betrothed to Antigone, enters to argue with his father, and threaten that he will die with her. Ismene has been reprieved, but Antigone is to be walled up alive to starve. After she is led away, the blind prophet Teiresias arrives to denounce Creon's action, and warn of retribution. Once the prophet has left, Creon changes his mind and hurries away to have Antigone released. Too late: Antigone has hanged herself, and Haemon, after first attempting to kill his father, takes his own life with a sword. After hearing the messenger's dire account of these events, Eurydice, Creon's wife, exits into the palace. Creon re-enters with the body of Haemon, whereupon the mesenger returns to announce that Eurydice too has committed suicide. Her body is revealed from inside the palace, and the play ends with Creon and the chorus in bitter lamentation.

Antigone is in one sense a play of conflicting moral principles in which both sides can marshall strong arguments in their support. Creon insists on the necessity of civil order and the primacy of the rule of law; Antigone claims allegiance to a higher law, that of religious and familial duty, which must, she insists, outweigh the demands of the state. Tragedy is inherent (as the philosopher Hegel pointed out) in the irreconcilable conflict between two absolute moral imperatives each of which may be thought of as "right".

Sophocles however, embodies these principles in individual characters, and in doing so greatly complicates the argument between them. In the course of the play the purity of Creon's position is compromised, and yet, paradoxically, he gains thereby in tragic depth and the sympathy he may command from an audience. In the end he bases his case less on moral principle than on expediency and protecting his own position and authority, and seems more stubborn than high-minded. But, having implicitly already abandoned the moral high ground, when told of his error by Teiresias, he is quick to reverse himself and to seek to make amends. The damage however, is done, and Sophocles takes particular care in his stagecraft to emphasize the pathos of Creon's fate to us, while giving relatively less weight to that of Antigone, defiant heroine that she is. Creon loses both son and wife; his family is destroyed, and we witness his suffering. By contrast, Antigone is never given an opportunity to show much concern for her intended husband (the two are never brought together on stage), nor does she linger in the spectators' presence, or consequently in their sympathy, in marked contrast to Creon who probably is meant to remain on stage from his first entrance until he leaves to rescue Antigone. Similarly, at the conclusion of the play, it is the corpses of Creon's wife and son that are brought on stage; not that of Antigone.

In performance, therefore, the emotional balance of the play shifts from what one might feel in reading it. It becomes Creon's play. Antigone may be conceived—indeed, often has been—as an admirable symbol of personal integrity who courageously stands up to the brute power of an impersonal state. Yet in terms of what Sophocles chooses to show us in performance, the greater tragedy is more readily seen to be Creon's. Antigone's moral choice and her steadfast adherance to it may be interpreted as right and noble, but her loyalty to her conscience is very costly and destructive in its consequences, and renders her, in dramaturgical terms, not so much subject to fate as the agent through which others (some innocent) are made to suffer their fate. This is not to suggest that Sophocles must be thought of as asserting that opposition to authority (particularly when authority is exercised in a tyrannical manner) is wrong; only that the play is less straightforward in meaning, and more ambiguous in its moral position, than it is sometimes claimed to be. It is, perhaps, owing to this quality that few Greek tragedies have held the stage more securely, or been subject to more adaptations. The figure of Antigone has been seen as everything from a frail but courageous saint, nobly confronting oppression, to a neurotic egoist, perversely pursuing martyrdom. *Antigone* is a troubling and provocative work, precisely because it seeks to explore the greatest of all political questions: the conflict between the individual and society.

—Richard C. Beacham

―――――――――

ANTIGONE
by Jean Anouilh

First Publication: In *Nouvelles pièces noires*, Paris, 1946.
First Production: Théâtre de l'Atelier, Paris, 4 February 1944.

Translations
Antigone, in *Antigone and Eurydice*, translated by Lewis Galantière, London, 1951.

Criticism
(For general works on the author, see *Playwrights* volume)

Books:
Etienne Frois, *"Antigone": Analyse critique*, Paris, 1972.
W.D. Howarth, *Anouilh: "Antigone"*, London, 1983.

Articles:
P. Conradie, "The *Antigone* of Sophocles and Anouilh—A Comparison", in *Acta Classica*, 2, 1959.
William Calin, "Patterns of Imagery in Anouilh's *Antigone*", in *French Review*, 41, 1967.
W.N. Ince, "Prologue and Chorus in Anouilh's *Antigone*", in *Forum for Modern Language Studies*, 4, 1968.
Walter Albert, "Structures of Revolt in Giraudoux's *Electre* and Anouilh's *Antigone*", in *Texas Studies in Literature and Language*, 12, 1970.
Carolyn Asp, "Two Views of Tragedy: Sophocles and Anouilh", in *Barat Review*, 5, 1970.
Dolore M. Burdick, "Antigone Grows Middle-Aged: Evolution of Anouilh's Hero", in *Michigan Academician*, 7, 1974.
Michael Spingler, "Anouilh's Little Antigone: Tragedy, Theatricalism, and the Romantic Self", in *Comparative Drama*, 8, 1974.
Richard Hewitson, "Anouilh's *Antigone*: A Coherent Structure", in *Australian Journal of French Studies*, 17, 1980.
Redmond O'Hanlon, "Metatragedy in Anouilh's *Antigone*", in *Modern Language Review*, 75, 1980.

*   *   *

A bold and impressive re-interpretation of the legend in the tragedies of Sophocles and Aeschylus, Anouilh's play concentrates on the period following the discovery by Oedipus that he had killed his father and married his own mother. Jocasta had immediately committed suicide and Oedipus, her son and her husband, having first blinded himself, had subsequently died in exile. Of their four children, Antigone, the youngest, and her sister Ismène had witnessed the struggle for power between their two brothers, Eteocles and Polynices. In the battle for the control of Thebes, both brothers had died in single combat and, as the play begins, their uncle Créon, now Regent, has just granted Eteocles the dignity of a state funeral. Polynices' corpse has been left to rot outside the city gates. Any attempt to give the traitor's body ritual burial will be punishable by death.

This background is explained in the long opening speech of the Chorus, another element which Anouilh has retained from the tragedies of Ancient Greece. And yet, from these opening lines, it is already clear that Anouilh's treatment will be fundamentally different in form, tone, and outlook from all earlier versions.

For a start, the Chorus consists, not of a group of Theban citizens who comment on, and share in, the action, but of one detached observer whose diction and manner make the character more like a modern cabaret compère, introducing the other characters as actors destined to play their part; to enact a pre-ordained event. The legendary figures are no longer victims of the gods, but prisoners of a form of theatrical destiny, fated for all time to play their allotted role.

The action begins at dawn with Antigone's return to the royal palace. She has defied Créon: using a child's seaside spade, she has performed a token burial. In the opening scenes (of a play which, in fact, has no formal division into acts or scenes), first with her aging nurse, then with her sister and subsequently her fiancé, Antigone shows all the frailty, courage, determination, and vulnerability of the traditional heroine, but expressing herself in a modern idiom which continues the anachronistic tone of the prologue.

Many critics were appalled by an Antigone who asks for coffee and talks of childhood games and her pet dog. These objections were fuelled by later scenes: Antigone is arrested by guards whose mundane preoccupations are expressed in barrack room slang; and she is interrogated by Créon who talks of her dolls, her brothers' fast sports cars and their visits to night clubs. Furthermore, in the long exchange between the heroine and the Regent which lasts for approximately one quarter of the entire play, Antigone's defiance is not inspired by such traditional motives as religious principle or a quest for justice.

Other critics objected to the topical, World War II interpretation of the play which Barsacq's production did much to encourage: for a Parisian audience during the German occupation, the guards' leather trench coats would have been a reminder of the Gestapo, and Créon in shirt sleeves, as he interrogates Antigone, would have had similarly harrowing associations.

Anouilh has been much criticised for degrading the legend, for cheapening the significance of his subject, for turning the heroine into a stubborn, wilful adolescent. And yet, despite these criticisms, *Antigone* has been an immense success. The first production ran for 475 performances; the play has since been translated and performed worldwide. Even the sternest critics do not deny its intensely moving and powerfully dramatic qualities. Anouilh's theatrical craftsmanship is particularly remarkable in two scenes: the central conflict with the tyrant, and the daring last scene in which Antigone is denied permission to write a farewell letter to her fiancé Hémon and has to dictate her message to the semi-literate thug who is on guard before her execution.

Antigone is an outstanding example of Anouilh's unerring technical skill. As in many of his other plays, there is the characteristic blend of humour and pathos (of pink and black, to use Anouilh's own terms); there is a re-examination of such recurrent themes as childhood and happiness; like Thérèse in *La Sauvage*, and other Anouilh heroines, Antigone represents youth, purity, and integrity in opposition to mediocre convention, conformity, and crabbed age; and the sustained use of dramatic imagery recalls Anouilh's major preoccupation with the theatricality of life and the blurred distinction between reality and illusion.

Antigone is particularly important for two further reasons; it marks a significant development in the dramatist's personal philosophy; and by a lengthy comparison of tragedy and drama half way through the play, the Chorus provides an interesting and rare insight into Anouilh's dramatic theory.

By refusing the values of the traditional heroine and by spurning the base satisfactions of mortal life, Antigone joins the lineage of Anouilh's early heroines—and heroes—who say "No" to happiness and even to life itself for reasons that are obscure or, as she herself admits, absurd. However, Créon's acceptance of life and convention, when divorced from the purely topical, wartime interpretation, is given a force and a cogency that mark an evolution in Anouilh's outlook. It is

inadequate to give a purely technical explanation for Créon's strength. Certainly, the contestants need to be evenly matched for the "prize fight" at the centre of the evening's entertainment to be convincing. Créon's acceptance marks a turning point in Anouilh's attitude which is all the clearer when *Antigone* is contrasted with two other plays which Anouilh based on subjects from antiquity: *Eurydice* (1942) and *Médée* (1946). Whereas the audience is sympathetic to Eurydice's refusal and death, the behaviour of Médée is so detestable that sympathy goes to those, like Jason, who say "Yes". *Antigone* has to be viewed as a transitional play, which one critic has interpreted as a double tragedy: the tragedy of those who, like the heroine, confront death and accept the consequences, and simultaneously the tragedy of those, like Créon, who have the courage to confront life with its own inevitable degradations.

Such a thesis is far removed from the focus of classical tragedy with which Anouilh deliberately invites comparison through the Chorus's provocative definitions of tragedy and drama. For those prepared to discard tradition and accept Anouilh's success in modernising, transposing and humanising the legend, the Chorus's intervention adds to the play by making *Antigone* both the theory and the practice of tragedy. For the traditionalist, the classification of tragedy is unwarranted. One solution is to describe *Antigone* as "tragedy in the process of re-definition", but the invention of a label is merely an academic exercise. The essential point is the problem itself for which here, as elsewhere, Anouilh pointedly offers no solution. He leaves his audience to opt for tragedy or drama, to side with Créon or Antigone. His refusal to impose a view leads to confusion: indeed, far from seeing Antigone as a symbol of the French Resistance, some critics in 1944 interpreted Anouilh's portrayal of Créon as sympathy for the occupying army, and he was accused of fascist tendencies. Invariably, Anouilh chooses to present problems rather than supply answers. On one point there is universal agreement: tragedy or not, like it or not, *Antigone* is generally accepted as a masterpiece by a theatrical craftsman at the height of his powers. It is a permanent landmark in 20th-century French theatre.

—Colin Radford

ANTONY
by Alexandre Dumas *père*

First Publication: Paris, 1831.
First Production: Théâtre de la Porte-Saint-Martin, Paris, 1831.

Editions
Antony, edited by Maurice Baudin, Oxford, 1929.

*   *   *

Adèle, the heroine, has married Colonel d'Hervey after a brief but intense love-affair with the mysterious Antony, which had come to an end when he suddenly disappeared from her life. The play opens as she learns that he has returned to Paris; and although she does her best to avoid him, her feelings prove stronger than ever. She tries to escape to join her husband, but Antony pursues her, and she finally becomes his mistress.

Broken by the struggle between her guilty love for Antony and her duty towards her husband and child, she cannot face her husband; and as he arrives back in Paris she implores her lover to save her honour. As the Colonel batters at the door, Antony takes her in his arms and stabs her to death with the famous curtain-line: "Yes, she is dead: she resisted me, so I killed her!"

Like Vigny's *Chatterton* four years later, this is a play of ideas on a contemporary subject in the domestic manner; but Dumas's dramatic idiom is very different from Vigny's. Dumas excels in the *coup de théâtre* and the melodramatic curtain-line. In Act I, Adèle has heard of Antony's return to Paris and leaves the house, resolved not to risk seeing him again. Her horses bolt, and she is saved by the heroism of a stranger, who is brought in injured: it is of course Antony. On her insistence that he must leave as soon as he is out of danger, he tears the bandage from his injury, crying: "An excuse, is that all I need? Now surely you will let me stay?" Similarly, at the end of Act III, when Adèle is travelling to Strasbourg to join her husband, Antony overtakes her and sends on the post-horses from the next staging-post. Adèle has no choice but to stay the night, and the two available rooms have a connecting balcony. Antony breaks a window, opens her door, and takes her in his arms: "Don't make a sound! It is I, Antony!"; the curtain falls as he carries her into the bedroom.

This is the stagecraft of melodrama, but of all Dumas's plays set in the contemporary world, *Antony* is the furthest removed from that popular genre. The impulsiveness, the violence, are very much in character with the hero—as are the repeated expressions of an extravagant Byronism ("You expect me to hesitate over committing another crime? To lose my soul for such a trifle? That would be doing Satan's job for him!")—and they stand out in sharp contrast to the civilised life-style of the rest of the characters. Adèle and her friends—the members of upper-class Paris society whom we meet in Acts II and IV—represent an ordered world, with its conventions, its compromises, and its hypocrisies: a world against which Antony stands opposed as an outsider, a man of mystery. *Antony* is a play of ideas because Dumas has set out to challenge this world of appearances; but that does not necessarily mean that he endorses the destructive, anti-social activity of his central character. The embryonic Byrons in the audience of 1831 no doubt did identify with Antony, but we are at liberty to look on him with greater detachment, as a pathological case of someone acting out an artificial pose. In any case, the social message is conveyed less through what Antony himself says and does, than through the personality of Adèle. When she falls victim to Antony's seductive powers, Adèle has offended against the formal moral conventions of the society she belongs to, but she remains an "honnête femme", and retains our sympathy throughout, compared with the women who manage to preserve their reputation simply by making the right sort of compromise. There can be no doubt of the heroine's "authenticity"—to use a modern term—by the side of the other representatives of society whose care is all for appearances; and contemporary spectators must have been led to reflect, as are today's readers, that the integrity of the individual personality is worth more than a conventional virtue that merely consists of lip-service to a social code. Adèle's position, torn between the claims of virtue and the force of passion, is a banal one in all conscience; and the fact that her suffering is so credible, and that she makes such a strong appeal to our sympathy, is a real tribute to the sincerity of Dumas's writing.

More specifically, the play propounds a positive thesis with regard to the position of the illegitimate in the society of Dumas's day: a thesis all the more eloquently presented in that it is not argued directly by a lay figure as spokesman for the author, but is allowed to emerge indirectly as Adèle guesses the reason for Antony's sudden departure and his mysterious behaviour. In Dumas's eyes, the anti-social posturings of this particular Romantic hero are explained, if not fully justified, by the ostracism invoked against those who have no name: "So, you see, the anathema is pronounced: those who suffer must continue to suffer", Indeed, compared both with Diderot's *The Natural Son* and with the younger Dumas's play of the same name, neither of which lives up to the claim suggested by this title to be considered as a serious play of ideas on the subject of illegitimacy, *Antony* succeeds in marrying thesis and plot in a stimulating challenge to the prejudices of society.

Antony was one of the most successful plays of the 1830's. Originally accepted by the Théâtre-Français, it was shelved for various reasons, including the lukewarm attitude of leading actors, until Dumas withdrew it and offered it to the Porte-Saint-Martin. The reception of the play benefited enormously from this transfer to a *boulevard* theatre. Marie Dorval and Bocage were much more sympathetic, and their style of acting much more appropriate, than would have been the case with their counterparts at the Théâtre-Français; and the first night has passed into legend alongside that of Hugo's *Hernani*: Dumas's memoirs describe the frenzied reception, which culminated in his being mobbed as he took a curtain-call, and his coat being pulled from his back and torn to shreds by playgoers eager for a memento of the occasion.

—William D. Howarth

ANTONY AND CLEOPATRA
by William Shakespeare

First Publication: London, 1623.
First Production: London, c.1606.

Editions
Antony and Cleopatra, edited by John Dover Wilson, Cambridge, 1950 (The New Shakespeare).
Antony and Cleopatra, edited by M.R. Ridley, London, 1954 (Arden Shakespeare).
Antony and Cleopatra, edited by R.E.C. Houghton, Oxford, 1962.
Antony and Cleopatra, edited by Stanley Gardner, London, 1963.
Antony and Cleopatra, edited by Maynard Mack, Harmondsworth; revised edition, Baltimore, 1970 (Pelican Shakespeare).
Antony and Cleopatra, edited by Barbara Everett, New York, Scarborough, and London, 1964 (Signet Classic Shakespeare).
Antony and Cleopatra, edited by Emrys Jones, Harmondsworth, 1977 (New Penguin Shakespeare).

Criticism
(For general works on the author, see *Playwrights* volume)

Books:
John Russell Brown (ed.), *"Antony and Cleopatra": A Casebook*, London, 1968.

Antony and Cleopatra: National Theatre, London 1987

Julian Markels, *The Pillar of the World: "Antony and Cleopatra" in Shakespeare's Development*, Columbus, Ohio, 1968.

A.P. Riemer, *A Reading of Shakespeare's "Antony and Cleopatra"*, Sydney, 1968.

Philip J. Traci, *The Love Play of "Antony and Cleopatra": A Critical Study of Shakespeare's Play*, The Hague, 1970.

E.A.M. Coleman, *The Structure of Shakespeare's "Antony and Cleopatra"*, Sydney, 1972.

Janet Adelman, *The Common Liar: An Essay on "Antony and Cleopatra"*, New Haven, Connecticut, 1974.

Marilyn L. Williamson, *Infinite Variety: Antony and Cleopatra in Renaissance Drama and Earlier Tradition*, Mystic, Connecticut, 1974.

Mark Rose (ed.), *Twentieth Century Interpretations of "Antony and Cleopatra"*, Englewood Cliffs, New Jersey, 1976.

Margaret Lamb, *"Antony and Cleopatra" on the English Stage*, Rutherford (New Jersey) and London, 1980.

Michael Steppat, *The Critical Reception of Shakespeare's "Antony and Cleopatra" from 1607 to 1905*, Amsterdam, 1980.

Michael Scott, *Antony and Cleopatra*, London, 1983 (Text and Performance Series).

J. Leeds Barroll, *Shakespearian Tragedy: Genre, Tradition, and Change in "Antony and Cleopatra"*, Washington, D.C., 1984.

David A. Male, *Antony and Cleopatra*, Cambridge, 1984 (Shakespeare on Stage Series).

Kenneth Muir, *Antony and Cleopatra*, Harmondsworth, 1987.

Mark W. Scott (ed.), *"Antony and Cleopatra"* in *Shakespearian Criticism, 6*, Detroit, Illinois, 1987 (anthology of criticism).

Harold Bloom (ed.), *William Shakespeare's "Antony and Cleopatra"*, New York, 1988 (Modern Critical Interpretation).

Articles:

For information on the many articles about *Antony and Cleopatra*, see the bibliographies listed in the *Playwrights* volume, and the annual Shakespeare Bibliography in *Shakespeare Quarterly*, published by the Folger Shakespeare Library, Washington D.C. (1950–).

*   *   *

Antony, a truant in Egypt, receives news of his wife's death and determines to return to Rome to mend political fences, a plan to which Cleopatra only reluctantly accedes. He makes his peace with Octavius (who believes Antony has been derelict in his duties) by agreeing to a political marriage to Octavia, Caesar's sister. When Antony abandons Octavia to return to his "Egyptian dish", Caesar makes war on him. Antony makes a series of disastrous military decisions, deferring to Cleopatra in spite of objections by his followers. Humiliated by defeat in battle Antony believes Cleopatra to be conspiring with Caesar. To stem his anger Cleopatra has a report sent to Antony that she has died. Instantly Antony resolves to join her in death. After botching his suicide he is told that she still lives and, carried to the monument, he dies in her arms. Cleopatra, captured by Caesar and aware that she will be humiliated as chief exhibit in a parade of captives, plots to outwit him. With the aid of an asp smuggled in by a countryman she kills herself, and, in a tableau dressed as triumphant queen, she leaves Caesar "a great ass unpolicied".

Shakespeare acknowledges in the views of the Roman soldiers at the outset the common view of these lovers as degraded figures, a drunkard and his whore. Around key selected events from Plutarch's extensive account Shakespeare certainly emphasizes the decline in Antony's soldiership but he also questions the low esteem in which the lovers were often held. It is the most episodic play in the canon but it is firmly organized around the central issue of where Antony belongs. The play relentlessly examines the issue of who the real Antony is and shows him being torn apart as the forces of empire and love vie for his allegiance. The lovers, being great actors, are imbued with a constant awareness of their own greatness and their need to live up to their reputations and self-images. Their mutual attraction drives them to folly and defeat, but also to vitality; generosity, and a careless indifference to the ruthless calculations required to retain power. Like theatrical stars they compete for domination of the stage but they aim to stand up peerless together, the envy of all. Enobarbus's vivid account of their first meeting on the Cydnus indicates that they have been upstaging each other since the inception of their relationship. For both of them, acting is not disguise but heightened self-realization, a living up to what they owe to their position, and so a world without storm and passion is intolerable to them, which is why the calm, submissive Octavia has no power to bind Antony to her. In the 3023 lines of the play only a little more than a sixth is given over to the vivid sequences in which they share the stage together. After Antony first leaves Egypt over 40% of the play passes before they share the stage together again. They share the stage in 11 scenes but only on three occasions do they share it for more than 50 lines and their longest interaction is only 110 lines long. Because the characters know each other so well their short sequences have a remarkable impact. Most of their meetings are stormy and conducted at boiling point and their rare moments of harmony are sublimely moving because they are so hard won.

The play is polarized between the languorous, sensual atmosphere of Egypt and the cold, brisk world of Rome, usually heavily emphasized by stage decor in production. The prodigality of the lovers is contrasted throughout to the dry, cold calculations of Caesar, a shrewd politician who achieves "success" but is totally without charisma. Antony inspires affection among his followers and the cyclic movements from despair to gaiety in his camp are keyed entirely to his moods. Caesar has no comparable ability as a leader. In his decline Antony is increasingly forced into a role which is a combination of player-king and stage-braggart, a change registered in Enobarbus' commentary. Invoked by Antony's wayward folly this bluff soldier eventually deserts to Caesar. Despite the shrewdness of a move governed by his head the heart of Enobarbus rebels and he dies in a ditch in despair at his abandonment of Antony. Anyone prone to dismiss Antony as merely a "strumpet's fool" is invited to consider the fate of Enobarbus with care.

What both of the lovers fear in defeat is that they will become mere actors in Caesar's humiliating parade of captives to mock their former greatness. Antony, hearing of Cleopatra's death embraces death like a smug bridegroom. The scene at the monument with its improvised, laborious heaving aloft of Antony, though it audaciously borders on comedy, is very moving. It sets up by contrast Cleopatra's death which is staged with such deliberate dramatic precision. She, who destroyed her man of men by pretending to be dead destroys her oppressor by pretending to want life. She is again for Cydnus and gives a final performance to mock destiny and the demeaning role Caesar has prepared for her. Like Antony she is relieved to be able to undertake an action which brings down the curtain on the stumbling drama of accommodating unwelcome roles. She fights, in a performance that can only be given once, to achieve the tragic end with which the audience is already familiar from history. The great skill of the play is in its mingled yarn, the grandeur and terrifying power of its central figures juxtaposed to their thoroughly human weaknesses. It is the mixture of pettiness, folly, greatness, generosity, demeaning trickery, and flashes of harmony in constant oscillation which compels attention.

—Anthony Brennan

THE ARCHITECT AND EMPEROR OF ASSYRIA
(l'Architecte et l'Empereur d'Assyrie)
by Fernando Arrabal

First Publication: In *Théâtre Panique: L'Architecte et l'Empereur d'Assyrie*, Bourgeois, 1967.
First Production: Théâtre Montparnasse, Paris, 1967.

Translations
The Architect and Emperor of Assyria, translated by E. d'Harnancourt and A. Shank, New York, 1969.
Architect and Emperor of Assyria, in *Arrabal: Plays 3*, translated by Jean Benedetti and John Calder, London, 1970.

Criticism
(For general works on the author, see *Playwrights* volume)

Articles:
Charles R. Lyons, "The Psychological Base of Arrabal's *L'Architecte et l'Empereur d'Assyrie*", in *French Review*, 45, 1972.
Renée Geen, "Arrabal's *The Architect and Emperor of Assyria*", in *Romance Notes*, 19, 1978.

*   *   *

A Freudian black comedy in two acts, the play dramatises the fantasies, obsessions, and secret desires of two men marooned together on a desert island. The Emperor, the sole survivor of a plane crash, parachutes on to the island where he meets the aboriginal inhabitant who commands the forces of nature. He designates him "Architect", teaches him language, and educates him in Western thought and philosophy. In the succession of games and role-play which make up the action, it is slowly revealed that the self-styled Emperor and master of civilisation is a compulsive mythomaniac who in reality was only an inadequate little man haunted by guilt and failure. He tells the Architect that he murdered his mother and demands the supreme penalty. In the final scene the Architect devours his corpse and in so doing transforms himself into the Emperor, whereupon a new plane crash brings a new survivor to the island and the cycle recommences.

The Architect and Emperor of Assyria: Old Vic Theatre, London, 1971 (National Theatre Company)

Arrabal calls this play a "panic ceremony", after the movement he founded in 1962 with Jodorowsky, Topor, and Sternberg. Panic, named after the god Pan, was conceived by Arrabal as "a way of life governed by confusion, humour, terror, chance, and euphoria". Theatrically, it implied a form of delirious fiesta expressing the fundamental irrationality and confusion of life, but underpinned by a precise mathematical construction. According to Arrabal, the play's rhythms and patterns are based on principles derived from set theory. Theatrically, its strength lies in the combination of a simple formula—two characters inventing roles for themselves—and the kaleidoscopic renewal of surprising images that are generated by their free-flowing relationship.

The combination of ritual and cruelty has led critics to detect an Artaudian influence in the play. It seems likely, however, that the work springs from more subjective, less metaphysical concerns than Artaud's theatre of cruelty. Like all Arrabal's works, which have been likened to a gallery of private obsessions, the play has an autobiographical basis. The sado-masochistic images, the neurotic obsessions (notably the oppressive image of a castratory mother-figure), the erotic fantasies, and the sense of voyeurism are recurrent elements in Arrabal's theatre. To that extent, the play could easily appear as self-indulgent exhibitionism, a charge often levelled against Arrabal's theatre. In *The Architect and the Emperor of Assyria*, however, the subject attains an exemplary and mythic dimension which is often lacking in Arrabal's more introverted dramas. The colonial relationship between natural man and civilised man suggests a 20th-century Robinson Crusoe / Man Friday theme which some productions have used to highlight the individual's alienation in a modern, consumer society.

Allegorical themes aside, the play's principal interest rests in its highly theatrical exploration of identity and human relationships. In their role-playing the two characters enact the archetypal human relations: mother-child, master-slave, teacher-pupil, doctor-patient, penitent-confessor, executioner-victim. These permutations provide some of the most striking modern theatrical images of the instability of human relations based on domination and submission.

The perpetual transformation of role leads initially to a fragmentation of identity, but the unifying thread which is progressively revealed is the Emperor's pursuit of the Self. The quest for identity appears as a process of stripping away successive layers of fantasy to arrive at a core of residual truth when the Emperor finally confronts the naked truth about himself. The underlying motive which propels the action is an urge to confess and expiate the past. In this sense the play comes close to envisaging a liberation from the past, but the final twist whereby the action returns to its starting point makes it an ultimately pessimistic play.

A non-naturalistic play which depends on a mechanism of excess, it requires uninhibited performers and a director with a strong sense of the baroque to wrest stage images from the text. It has been best served by the Argentinian directors of the "Ecole Latine" who share Arrabal's sense of sacred ceremony. Two major productions, very different in their approach to the play, but both of them benchmarks of sorts, were by Jorge Lavelli (Théâtre Montparnasse, Paris, 1967) and Victor Garcia (National Theatre, London, 1971). Lavelli, who directed the play's première, played it as a precise and sombre ritual, highlighting the essential loneliness of man and the mythic encounter between the elemental forces of nature and Western civilisation. Garcia's more strident production was a frenzied psycho-drama, a quest for identity in which raw emotion was laid bare. Unlike Lavelli's production, which held the two characters in a finely balanced see-saw relationship, Garcia's was hugely dominated by the neurotic guilt of the Emperor

(played by Anthony Hopkins) and his urge to be judged.

Arrabal presents the subject as a theatrical game, a set of variations on the "permitted lie" of theatre in which one presumed reality constantly yields to another. In this way the action generates a succession of provocative images. Although its discourse may be somewhat narrow for some tastes, the combination of Arrabal's imagistic style and capacity for sustained myth-making make it a powerful projection of the author's inner world and, along with *The Car Cemetery*, his most impressive work.

—David Whitton

L'ARCHITECTE ET L'EMPEREUR D'ASSYRIE. See **THE ARCHITECT AND EMPEROR OF ASSYRIA.**

ARDEN OF FAVERSHAM
Anonymous

First Publication: London, 1592.
First Production: Probably before 1592.

Editions
Arden of Faversham in *Three Elizabethan Domestic Tragedies*, edited by Keith Sturgess, Harmondsworth, 1969.
The Tragedy of Master Arden of Faversham, edited by M.L. Wine, London, 1973 (Revels Plays).
The Tragedy of Master Arden of Faversham, edited by Martin White, London, 1982 (New Mermaid Series).

Criticism
(For general works on the author, see *Playwrights* volume)

Books:
Anita Holt, "*Arden of Faversham*: A Study of the Play first Published in 1592", Faversham, Kent, 1970 (Faversham Papers Series).

Articles:
Sarah Youngblood, "Theme and Imagery in *Arden of Faversham*", in *Studies in English Literature 1500–1900*, vol. 3 no. 2, 1963.
Michael T. Marsden, "The Otherworld of *Arden of Faversham*", in *Southern Folklore Quarterly*, 36, 1972.
Eugene P. Walz, "*Arden of Faversham* as Tragic Satire", in *Massachusetts Studies in English*, vol. 4 no. 2, 1973.
Ian and Heather D. Ousby, "Art and Language in *Arden of Faversham*", in *Durham University Journal*, 37, 1976.
Sybil Truchet, "Alice Arden and the Religion of Love", in *Caliban*, 17, 1980.
Catherine Belsey, "Alice Arden's Crime", in *Renaissance Drama*, 13, 1982.
Lena Cowen Orlin, "Man's House as his Castle in *Arden of Faversham*", in *Medieval and Renaissance Drama in England*, 2, 1985.

*   *   *

The play, based on real events, depicts the repeated

attempts to kill Thomas Arden by his wife, her lover and others, then his murder, and the incrimination, arrest and sentence of his killers. The dramatist found in Holinshed's *Chronicle* material ideally suited to the public playhouse: a multiplicity of characters and sensational incidents, with a satisfactory moral to apply at the end.

The play avoids the inception and negotiation of the crime by Alice Arden and her lover; the affair has begun and murder been decided upon from the start. This decision, attributed to powerful forces of exterior evil is generically typical: *A Warning for Fair Women* (1599) gives over a similar decision to an allegorical dumb show, and in *The Witch of Edmonton* (Dekker, Ford and Rowley, 1621), Frank conceives his murder when the devil in the form of a black dog rubs against his leg. The 16th century was interested in a different "why?" — the role of providence in allowing and punishing crime.

Arden's murder was remarkable for the number of attempts needed, and the play depicts them all. The motivator is Alice, the dramatist's most remarkable character, whose passions dwarf their object. Co-conspirators with Alice and Mosby are Michael and Clarke, both for love of Mosby's sister, Susan, who also assists. A tenant forced off his land by Arden suggests the hire of two assassins, Black Will and Shakebag, presented as villains of the blackest theatrical dye.

Amidst heady talk about undetectable poisoning, Alice rashly tries poisoned broth, in which Arden detects an unwholesome taste. Black Will and Shakebag try: in London, a shop shutter drops on Black Will's head as he lies in ambush, later Michael fails the conspiracy, waking his master, who locks doors left open. At Rainham Down, Arden, going home to Kent, meets other travellers as Shakebag prepares to shoot. He escapes again as a mist leaves Black Will and Shakebag blundering, the latter falling into a ditch. Alice provokes a quarrel between Mosby and Arden, the hit-and-miss men taking Mosby's side, but Arden and a friend beat them off. Interspersed are scenes in which the intended victim, unsurprisingly, reports a bad dream, and Mosby and Alice quarrel, Alice sensationally tearing up a prayer book to prove her devotion to him alone. Several characters are given long soliloquies, Michael revealing his horror, Mosby his distrust of Alice, there being no tight dramatic focus.

At Rainham Down, discharging his pistol at the sky, Shakebag expresses astonishment at Arden's "wondrous holy luck". Arden, a hard businessman throughout, alienates heaven in Scene 8, denying help to a desperate petitioner, Reede, who curses Arden for unjustly holding land from him: "that plot of ground which thou detains from me. . .Be ruinous and fatal unto thee". After this, Arden is finally murdered, and his body dumped, as the epilogue solemnly informs the audience, "in that plot of ground / Which he by force and violence held from Reede".

After the frustration of Arden's escapes, the conspirators kill in group hysteria, which is effectively conveyed: the ill-conceived crime is committed collectively, as Arden, playing backgammon, is set upon by his entire household. The macabre comedy of Black Will and Shakebag's thwarted attempts is not excluded: the former creeps between Michael's legs to approach Arden unseen.

Arden's blood, once the conspirators finally have shed it, proves supernaturally resistant to removal. If Providence finally left the unmerciful Arden to his fate, it also exposes the murderers: as the body is being disposed of, snow stops falling, leaving footprints. One detail is unassimilable to a demonstration of heavenly justice: an innocent man (Bradshaw) is sentenced with the others, and the repentant Alice will not do enough to save him. At least part of providential purpose remains enigmatic.

The action suggests the primitive "suspense by delay" plotting of Thomas Kyd. Kyd's influence on the writer can be seen in the verse, which has purple passages and stray classical references, and relishes soliloquy. But the writer was not able to deploy Kyd's more elaborate rhetorical devices, or to imitate his tautly effective stichomythia. Kyd may have had a hand in the play. Shakespeare was the other dramatist connected with Pembroke's men: some consider this play (like the similar *Yorkshire Tragedy*) for the Shakespeare Apocrypha.

—Roy Booth

ARLECCHINO SERVITORE DI DUE PADRONI. See **THE SERVANT OF TWO MASTERS.**

AS YOU LIKE IT
by William Shakespeare

First Publication: London, 1623.
First Production: c.1599;   earliest   recorded   production, Wilton House, Wiltshire, 1603.

Editions
As You Like It, edited by Isabel J. Bisson, Oxford, 1941.
As You Like It, edited by S.C. Boorman, London, 1959.
As You Like It, edited by Ralph M. Sargent, Baltimore, 1959; revised edition, 1970 (Pelican Shakespeare).
As You Like It, edited by Albert Gilman, New York, 1963; revised edition, 1987 (Signet Classic Shakespeare).
As You Like It, edited by J.H. Oliver, Harmondsworth, 1968 (New Penguin Shakespeare).
As You Like It, edited by Agnes Latham, London, 1975 (Arden Shakespeare).
As You Like It, edited by Richard Knowles, New York, 1977 (New Varorium edition).
As You Like It, edited by Joseph Mattern, Modern Language Association of America, 1977.

Bibliography
Jay L. Halio and Barbara C. Millard (eds.), *"As You Like It": An Annotated Bibliography, 1940–1980*, New York, 1985 (Garland Shakespeare Bibliographies).

Criticism
(For general works on the author, see *Playwrights* volume)

Books:
Jay L. Halio (ed.), *Twentieth Century Interpretations of "As You Like It"*, Englewood Cliffs, New Jersey, 1968.
Mark W. Scott (ed.) *"As You Like It"* in *Shakespearian Criticism, 5*, Detroit, Illinois, 1987 (anthology of criticism).
Harold Bloom (ed.), *As You Like It*, New York, 1988.
John Harold Baker, *Comments on Shakespeare's "As You Like It"*, Reading (no date).

Articles:
For information on the many articles about *As You Like It*, see

Painted by W. Hamilton.   Engrav'd by I. Schiavonetti

SHAKSPEARE.

Ros. To you I give myself, for I am yours.   As you like it?   Orl. If there be truth in sight, you are my Rosalind

ACT V. SCENE IV.

As You Like It: Act V, Scene IV, engraving after painting by William Hamilton, late 18th century

Halio and Millard's bibliography and the annual Shakespeare Bibliography in *Shakespeare Quarterly*, published by The Folger Shakespeare Library, Washington D.C. (1950–).

*   *   *

Orlando is humiliated and denied his patrimony by his brother Oliver. He challenges and defeats a wrestler in the service of Frederick, the usurping duke, and falls in love with Rosalind, daughter of the exiled Duke Senior. His defeat of Charles brings him Frederick's enmity and he flees from court. Rosalind is forced to flee in disguise to the forest of Arden, too, by the Duke's unjust banishment and is accompanied by her cousin Celia and the jester, Touchstone. In the forest Orlando meets the exiled Duke who leads a band of merry outlaws among whom is the melancholy philosopher, Jaques. Orlando meets Rosalind now disguised as a young shepherd, Ganymede, and, to practice his wooing, agrees to pretend that Ganymede is Rosalind. A young shepherdess, Phebe, disdains her swain and falls in love with Ganymede. Touchstone pursues and marries Audrey, a country girl. Oliver, who has

been sent to capture his brother, has his life saved by Orlando, abandons his enmity, and falls in love with Celia. Rosalind abandons her role as Ganymede and marries Orlando. Her father is restored to his dukedom, and pastoral sojourn is ended.

The play, which focuses on a number of figures forced into exile, has a good deal to say about sudden reversals of fortune. Like most comedies, it presents us with characters subject to the whirligig of fortune's wheel, in favour and out of favour, subject to sudden whims of temper or to sudden repentance in figures such as Oliver and Frederick, or to sudden passions as in Orlando, Rosalind, Audrey, Touchstone, Celia, and Phebe. All of these changes are set against the framework of Jaques' speech on the seven ages of man which characterizes life as that of an actor shuffling through the inevitable sequence of roles that the process of aging brings. The play alternates the dark, brooding, mean-spirited, world of the court with the sunny, benign, pastoral retreat of Arden. There is a contrast, too, between the unreasoning acts of malice perpetrated by blood relatives and the unexpected civility and generosity of strangers which helps to illuminate a complex study in the play of what is "natural". All of the acts of capricious malignity are confined to the first half of the play and are displaced by the genial holiday spirit of the woodland world. Arden is a kind of democratic crossing place where figures of all classes submit to love's folly in a serene, unshadowed world where trees are soon blooming with Orlando's verses of praise to Rosalind.

Jaques' resistance to, and mockery of, love is a salt that adds savour to the antics of the various pairs caught in the toils of love. He and Touchstone are complete inventions of Shakespeare and crucial additions as commentators. Their astringent remarks never become dominant but they remind us that the artifice of the pastoral world is only a temporary accommodation, that Arden is a special, almost magical, place. Touchstone asserts that "we ripe and ripe and rot and rot", but the play indicates that it is not cause for melancholy brooding. The emphasis is on ripening rather than decay, for we must mock fortune and get on with the business of Nature, bask in the sun while we have the chance, as the characters do in Arden, retaining always, of course, a sense of proportion, as Rosalind does. Though she may be many fathoms deep in love she retains a realist's clear-eyed vision that extravagant, romantic declarations are, like everything else, subject to mutability.

Shakespeare transforms the rambling source story, Thomas Lodge's *Rosalynde*, with remarkable discipline and shrewd economy into a multi-layered account of the benefits which love brings, despite the folly it induces, in redeeming a world disordered by selfish cruelty. The confessions caused by disguise never threaten to get out of hand as in some of Shakespeare's other comedies. Rosalind dominates the plot and manipulates events but she is exempted from any imputation of cruel superiority by her vulnerability to her womanly emotions concealed behind her masculine attire. The action ripens at a relaxed pace with the frequent infusion of songs. Even the melancholy Jaques can retire to a contemplative life without casting any cloud over the harmony of the ending.

—Anthony Brennan

THE ASCENT OF F6
by W.H. Auden and Christopher Isherwood

First Publication: London, 1937
First Production: Mercury Theatre, London, 23 February 1937.

Criticism
(For general works on the author, see *Playwrights* volume)

Articles:
Ronald Maken, "Power and Conflict in *The Ascent of F6*", in *Discourse: A Review of Liberal Arts*, vol. 7 no. 3, 1964.
Forrest E. Hazard, "*The Ascent of F6*: A New Interpretation", in *Tennessee Studies in Literature*, 15, 1970.
Douglas B. Kurdys, "*The Ascent of F6* and *For the Time Being*, by W.H. Auden: The Play of Theme", in *Form in the Modern Verse Drama*, Salzburg, 1972.
Eric Salmon, "*The Ascent of F6*", in *Is the Theatre Still Dying?*, Greenwood, Connecticut, 1985.

*   *   *

Michael Ransom heads a mountaineering expedition to F6, a peak situated on the frontier between British Sudoland and Ostnian Sudoland. For Ransom, the ascent of F6 is a heroic ideal, but for the authorities, who, headed by his brother Sir James Ransom, persuade him to undertake the adventure, it is a manoeuvre for imperialist ascendancy. A rumour has been spread amongst the colonial subjects that whichever of the two rival powers scales the peak will control both territories. Though Michael Ransom despises his brother's world, he agrees to climb the mountain at the urging of his mother. To the rapt attention of the national media, the members of the group perish one by one in the final stages, excepting Ransom who dies when he reaches the summit.

The Ascent of F6 is a deeply topical play in its involvement with the characteristic concerns of 1930's left-wing, literary intellectuals: the anatomizing of a decadent and oppressive social order; the conception of heroism; and the vexed relationship between knowledge and action, artistic creativity and politics. It is also an experimental poetic drama which draws on Modernist techniques but attempts to bridge the Modernist gap between artist and audience.

The plot of *The Ascent of F6* is filtered through at least four different, juxtaposed, narrative frames; a deliberate fragmentation of perspective which is reflected in the miscellany of styles, from highly crafted prose and Shakespearian blank verse to doggerel rhymes; from tragic soliloquy to music-hall farce. Perhaps the most obvious narrative frame is the boys' adventure story, a favourite vehicle for the "Auden generation" which used it to explore its own ambivalence about commitment to the Marxist cause. The climber, like the airman, was very much the hero of 1930's *reportage*; Ransom was based in part on T. E. Lawrence, who seemed to many a model of "the Truly Strong Man". The appeal to this species of naive realism is, however, undermined by a parodic use of myth and fable. The mountain labelled "F6" by the colonial authority is known to the subject races as Chormopuloda, the haunted mountain, and their superstition of the Demon that must be conquered by the climber is realized in the phantasmagoric final scene, which dramatizes the fevered consciousness of the dying hero.

Another level on which the play works is that of political allegory. The other side of Ransom's "heroism" is a propaganda stunt organized by an alliance of government minister, general, newspaper magnate, and colonial aristocrat. F6 is a symbol of imperial power, and its meanings are shown to have social consequences. In one stage-box the representatives of state power comment chorically on the action through the mass media which they control; the opposite stage-box is inhabited by representatives of the people on the receiving end of this "information", Mr. and Mrs. A., an anonymous suburban couple. Though they are initially cynical about political speeches ("Talk about treaties, talk about honour, mad dogs quarrelling over a bone"), only the voice of the gramophone gives a semblance of meaning to their barren, alienated existence, and they are soon captivated by the news story of the ascent of F6. It acts as a palliative or anodyne for their resentment and inspires them to go on a holiday they cannot afford. The alleged disinterestedness of the climbers provides highly effective ideological bait, so that after hearing Lord Stagmantle, the newspaper magnate, hail the climbers as representatives of "England's honour" and "the spirit of Man", Mr. and Mrs. A. are convinced that all "can read of these actions and know them great". But the form of the play itself, with its competing stories and discourses, gives the lie to any notion of a universal or objective truth free from ideology.

The third perspective available on the action is tragic and focuses on the conflict of motive in the character of the hero which leads to his death on the summit of F6. The play begins with Ransom meditating in Hamlet-like vein on the illusori-

The Ascent of F6: Mercury Theatre, London, 1937 (first production)

ness of virtue and knowledge. He is the complex, sensitive, self-conscious man who wants to believe that his motive for agreeing to climb F6 is pure, or "disinterested", valour, and who can know himself fully only when it is too late. Ransom's need to occupy the moral high ground becomes a means of self-deception. When he looks into the monks' crystal he sees that his desire to be a saviour of mankind is actually a desire for mass adulation. The implication is that tragedy's cult of heroic individualism, which ties in with the "great men" narrative of history, tends to foster a Fascist style of thought. Ransom is urged by the abbot to relinquish his mission and choose the way of self-abnegation, thus eluding the Demon or will to power, and refuses. In fact he sacrifices the other members of the group to his spiritual pride; in another parodic allusion to *Hamlet* he addresses a skull rhetorically at the very moment that one of his comrades is being killed by an avalanche.

Entangled with the political and tragic plots is a Freudian one, suggested by Ransom's remark that "a mountain is a mother" and which reads his heroic action as inspired by Oedipal desire and sibling rivalry. In the dreamlike final episode the terrors of the unconscious are projected onto the stage and the doppelgänger relation between Michael Ransom and his brother James is exposed. They confront each other as enemies and play a deadly chess contest using the other

characters as pawns. James dies confessing that "It was not Virtue—it was not Knowledge—it was Power!". Michael dies after the identity of the Demon, the veiled figure on the summit controlling the action, is revealed as that of his mother.

This is a highly ambiguous conclusion which precludes any direct political message, for if action is always tainted by a "wicked secret", and knowledge inseparably bound up with the will to power, the prognosis for social transformation is not hopeful. What the play does do, by refusing to offer a single, unitary "master-narrative" to the audience, is to estrange and undermine the myths on which social oppression feeds.

—Christina Britzolakis

AT THE HAWK'S WELL
by W.B. Yeats

First Publication: In *The Wild Swans at Coole; Other Verses; and A Play in Verse*, 1917.
First Production: Lady Cunard's drawing room, Cavendish Square, London, 2 April 1916.

Criticism
(For general works on the author, see *Playwrights* volume)

Articles:
Anthony Thwaite, "Yeats and the Noh", in *Twentieth Century*, 162, September 1957.
Klaus P.S. Jochum, "W.B. Yeats's *At the Hawk's Well* and the Dialectic of Tragedy", in *Vishabharati Quarterly*, 31, 1965–66.
Halbert A. Reeves, "Dramatic Effectiveness of the Imagery in Yeats's *At the Hawk's Well*", in *McNeese Review*, 19, 1968.
Edna G. Sharoni, "*At the Hawk's Well*: Yeats's Unresolved Conflict Between Language and Silence", in *Comparative Drama*, 7, 1973.
F.C. McGrath, "*At the Hawk's Well*: Unified Form in Yeats's Drama", in *Canadian Journal of Irish Studies*, 3, 1977.
Natalie C. Schmitt, "Intimations of Immortality: W.B. Yeats's *At the Hawk's Well*", in *Theatre Journal*, 31, 1979.
Bettina L. Knapp, "Yeats (1865–1939): *At the Hawk's Well*: An Unintegrated Anima Shapes a Hero's Destiny", in *A Jungian Approach to Literature*, Carbondale, Illinois, 1984.
William B. Worthen, "The Discipline of the Theatrical Sense: *At the Hawk's Well* and the Rhetoric of the Stage", in *Modern Drama*, 30, 1987.

*　　*　　*

Time—the Irish Heroic Age. At a desolate place with a bare tree and a dry well watched over by a mysterious Guardian, an Old Man waits, as he has done for 50 years, for the waters of immortality to flow. A Young Man—the mythical hero Cuchulain—joins him; they argue as to who shall first drink the water when it comes. The Guardian of the Well, possessed by supernatural powers, begins a magical dance; the Old Man falls asleep and Cuchulain pursues her offstage. On returning he finds that the water has come and gone: both men have missed it. Cuchulain departs on a career of violent and tragic adventure.

Such a summary of this poetic drama with a running-time of a mere 25 minutes or so, the first of Yeats's *Plays for Dancers*, hardly does justice to it. Its haunting form is at least as important as its story. In this one-act play without scenery, three Musicians with faces made up to resemble masks unfold and fold up again a curtain which defines the "magical" acting space behind it. Playing drum, zither, and gong, they recite or sing the lines that conjure up the imaginary scene, and they comment on the action. The dance of the mute Guardian of the Well, also made up in masklike fashion, is the play's theatrical climax. The Young Man and the Old Man, creatures of legend, wear masks.

Yeats' inspiration for the form of *At the Hawk's Well* came from Japanese noh drama, though in fact it differs from the latter in several ways. Noh, which does use masks, features no painted faces. Noh has a chorus of eight or ten singers and a separate group of musicians (a flute-player and two or three drummers); here both these functions are combined. In noh the climactic dance is performed by the principal player; here it is a mute character that dances. Noh draws on well-known stories from Japanese literature or mythology; Yeats invented

At the Hawk's Well: Design by Edmund Dulac for the Guardian of the Well, 1916

his plot for the hero Cuchulain. Nevertheless similarities abound. In particular, Yeats adopted noh's building a whole play around some key metaphors, visual or verbal. Hawk, bare tree, and dry well recur as images in an elemental setting of sea, rock, wind and fire.

When the play was first performed on 2 April 1916 in the intimate atmosphere of Lady Cunard's drawing-room in London, Yeats was delighted. When it was done a few days later for a larger semi-public gathering, he was less happy. His wish to restrict the audience to "personal friends and a few score people of good taste" defines the inherent limits of the play's appeal.

At the Hawk's Well projects a pessimistic view of life: both questers are balked. Different critics have perceived different meanings in the play, but aesthetically it achieves the hypnotic, dreamlike effect typical of noh. When it was translated into Japanese, fully adapted to noh conventions, and performed in Tokyo in 1949 by the Kita School (one of the five traditional noh companies), it must have seemed as much at home in the East as ever it had done in the West.

—G.W.Brandt

THE ATHEIST'S TRAGEDY; or, The Honest Man's Revenge by Cyril Tourneur

First Publication: London, 1611.
First Production: London, c.1607–1611.

Editions
The Atheist's Tragedy, in *John Webster and Cyril Tourneur: Four Plays*, New York, 1956.
The Atheist's Tragedy, edited by Irving Ribner, London, 1964 (Revels Plays).
The Atheist's Tragedy, edited by Brian Morris and Roma Gill, London and New York, 1976 (New Mermaid Series).
The Atheist's Tragedy, in *The Plays of Cyril Tourneur*, edited by George Parfitt, Cambridge, 1978.

Criticism
(For general works on the author, see *Playwrights* volume)

Articles:
Clifford Leech, "*The Atheist's Tragedy* as a Dramatic Comment on Chapman's *Bussy* Plays", in *Journal of English and Germanic Philology*, vol. 52 no. 1, 1953.
Robert Ornstein, "*The Atheist's Tragedy* and Renaissance Naturalism", in *Studies in Philology*, vol. 51 no. 2, 1954.
Glen A. Love, "Morality and Style in *The Atheist's Tragedy*", in *Humanities Association Bulletin*, vol. 5 no. 1, 1964.
R.J. Kaufmann, "Theodicy, Tragedy, and the Psalmists: Tourneur's *Atheist's Tragedy*", in *Drama in the Renaissance: Comparative and Critical Essays*, edited by Clifford Davidson, C.J. Gianakaris, and John H. Stroupe, New York, 1986.

*   *   *

D'Amville, an atheist, worshipping only wealth and status, murders his brother Lord Montferrers, and having declared falsely that Montferrers' son Charlemont has been killed in the wars succeeds to the title. To advance his family further he marries off his sickly, elder son Rousard to Castabella, who is in love with Charlemont. Informed by Montferrers' ghost, Charlemont returns but is thrown into prison after quarrelling and fighting with Sebastian, D'Amville's second son, whose life he spares when restrained by a second appearance of Montferrers' ghost. Sebastian recovers Charlemont from prison and a feigned reconciliation is effected between Charlemont and D'Amville. D'Amville plots to have Charlemont murdered, but in self-defence Charlemont kills the assassin and is again imprisoned. Here he is joined by Castabella whom he had earlier rescued from rape by D'Amville who was desperately attempting to sire an heir himself on his daughter-in-law. Vengeance finally overtakes D'Amville: His elder son dies, his younger son is killed in a sexual scuffle, he himself "*runs distract*". He spectacularly interrupts the trial of Charlemont, and when the death sentence is pronounced, D'Amville, over-anxious to dispose of his long-suffering nephew, seizes the executioner's axe and in his haste to behead *Charlemont, "strikes out his own brains"*. Before expiring he confesses everything. Charlemont recovers his inheritance and is reunited with Castabella, declaring: ". . .Now I see / That patience is the honest man's revenge". The play is subtitled *The Honest Man's Revenge* and belongs to the genre known as revenge tragedy. Therein lies its major interest to the academic, for to the modern reader much of the action is grotesquely melodramatic.

The play has all the attributes of a typical revenge tragedy: a villainous unprovoked attack on an innocent victim, ghosts,

madness, a reminder to leave vengeance to God, counter-plots of violence, and a ritually enacted finale in which justice is eventually obtained. But, unlike earlier plays in this genre (Kyd's *The Spanish Tragedy* and its imitators), in this play the villain takes centre-stage, and the revenger becomes a passive bystander. He listens to the ghost's warning:

> Return to France, for thy old father's dead,
> And thou by murder disinherited.
> Attend with patience the success of things,
> But leave revenge unto the King of kings.

He duly returns but it requires a second appearance of the ghost to make him heed the full warning. Charlemont then does what all previous revengers had failed to do; although greatly provoked he waits patiently for God to intervene on his behalf. God does so but only at the most protracted eleventh hour imaginable.

As a declared atheist, D'Amville in 17th-century terms would have been considered a terrible figure. Released from the fear of Hell and divine retribution he could commit appalling crimes with immunity. He remarks at the end of the play's first scene: "Let all men lose, so I increase my gain / I have no feeling of another's pain". It is salutary therefore that by the end of the play his belief in himself is shattered and he lapses into madness; picking up the axe to rid himself once and for all of Charlemont he destroys himself instead, recognising as he does so the hand of God: "......But yon power that struck me knew the judgement I deserved And gave it". Charlemont confirms the role of divine intervention: "Only to Heaven I attribute the work / Whose gracious motives made me still forbear / To be mine own revenger".

Throughout the play, D'Amville has persistently reflected on human nature, denying the existence of an overall providential order, a power modifying the force of nature. God to the atheist is but a superstitious credulity. At the trial scene D'Amville begs the body of Charlemont "for an anatomy". Like Lear, he would discover via dissection "The efficient cause of a contented mind": Charlemont's calm acceptance of death, if that is what God intends, puzzles the atheist.

This philosophical discussion running throughout the play and expressed in ringing declamatory terms is at once the play's strength and it's weakness. Such lengthy ruminations, especially when indulged in at violent and emotional climaxes, may have transfixed a Jacobean audience but will hardly interest many of today's theatre-goers. Yet Tourneur clearly intended his play to be such a polemic, introducing, to enhance his argument, supportive images of water and wine, death's heads and charnel houses, which, to the modern mind, have lost their symbolic significance and simply appear macabre.

Unfortunately, too, it is the minor characters in the play that Tourneur imbues with dramatic life; his major figures remain personified abstractions. The portrait of D'Amville has some dramatic and psychological truth in the final act, but he remains a monstrous, melodramatic figure. On the other hand, Sebastian, his loose-humoured rebel son, has instant stage charisma; he is an irresistible charmer in pursuit of life and sex. Levidulcia, the sexually voracious mother of Castabella, is also vividly created, pursuing her victims (willing or unwilling) with silky assurance and stunning aplomb.

The play is of enormous academic interest but it would be a brave company today who chose to include it in its repertory.

—Philip S.Cook

AU RETOUR DES OIES BLANCHES. See **THE WHITE GEESE.**

DER AUFHALTAME AUFSTIEG DES ARTURO UI. See **THE RESISTABLE RISE OF ARTURO UI.**

AUS DEM BÜRGERLICHEN HELDENLEBEN. See **SCENES FROM THE HEROIC LIFE OF THE MIDDLE CLASSES.**

L'AVARE. See **THE MISER.**

AVES. See **THE BIRDS.**

AWAKE AND SING!
by Clifford Odets

First Publication: In *Odets: Three Plays*, New York, 1935.
First Production: Belasco Theatre (Group Theatre), New York, 19 February 1935.

Criticism
(For general works on the author, see *Playwrights* volume)

Articles:
Richard Pearce, "[Faulkner's] *Pylon, Awake and Sing!* and the Apocalyptic Imagination of the 30's", in *Criticism*, 13, 1970.
Kshamanidhi Mishra, "Clifford Odets' *Awake and Sing!*: A Leftist Play", in *Punjab University Research Bulletin: Arts*.

* * *

Five flights up is the Bronx apartment of Bessie Berger. She dominates the family and determines what goes: light shall be shut out, the shades pulled down ("I like my house to look respectable"), telephone calls from her son's girl shall be censored, father shall be ordered out into the snow to walk the dog, and phonograph records promising a new Eden for America shall be smashed.

No one can raise his voice in this house because "they'll hear you down the dumbwaiter". Bessie ironically offers to serve "a special blue plate supper in the garden", but there is no garden; there's no patch of green to escape to. The roof offers two options; you can go there to walk the dog, or you can go there to jump off. Threats of self-elimination abound. The proud beauty of a daughter, Hennie, is burdened with a pregnancy by a stranger she can't trace; the father is someone "from out of town", the true New Yorker's phrase for the rest of the world beyond one's neighborhood. She says she'll "jump out the window" if they don't lay off the pressure for her to find a marital stand-in to mask her disgrace. It's the heart of

the Depression, and many choose the same escape route: "Still jumping off the high buildings like flies—the big shots who lost all their cocoanuts". In Bessie's waking nightmare, she too ends up on the streets, but not from self-propelled velocity: "They threw out a family on Dawson Street today. All the furniture on the sidewalk. A fine old woman with gray hair". She's determined nobody will do that to her. She grabs onto her options to feed her family and keep them together. Like Brecht's Mother Courage, she earns our grudging admiration for her wit and her competency.

Competing visions of Paradise are presented. For Moe, street-wise but not lucky enough to emerge from the Great War with both legs, "Par-a-dise" is Hennie. His campaign is for her to escape: "Sure, kids you'll have, gold teeth, get fat, big in the tangerines. . .Cut your throat, sweetheart. Save time". He offers, instead, a moonlit cruise to Yama Yama land.

Jacob, the patriarch of the Berger family, clings to a vision of Paradise he's sure the workers of the world can attain. It's part Edenic myth fed by the voice of Caruso ("From *L'Africana*. . .a big explorer comes on a new land. . .'Oh paradise on earth! Oh blue sky, oh fragrant air—'") and part Old Testament prophesy ("Awake and sing, ye that dwell in dust"). Though Jacob can spout Isaiah and quote from *Exodus* in Hebrew, he has, in fact, rejected God and taken Marxism as his new religion. His hopes are pinned on a future for his grandson Ralph.

In the play's climax, key deceptions the family lives with are revealed. At this juncture, Odets audaciously yokes together Bessie scolding her father to walk the dog with her father's evocation of Judaism's central patriarchal tenet, faith in one master of the universe:

> *Bessie*: Don't stand around Poppa! Take Tootsie on the roof. And don't let her go under the water tank.
> *Jacob*: Schmah Yisroael. Behold!

With stunning understatement, Jacob exits into the snow with, "Tootsie is my favorite lady in the house". He's never heard from again. We're given this report from the immigrant janitor: "He shlipped maybe in the snow. . .Your fadder fell off de roof".

What is Jacob's legacy, besides the $3,000 insurance policy he leaves to Ralph? Jacob was an out-of-work barber who claimed, "I'm studying from books a whole lifetime"; but when Ralph inherits his leftist library, he discovers that "the pages ain't cut in half of them". As in Ibsen's *Wild Duck*, as in Miller's *Death of a Salesman*, we're left to assess the value of the big talk, the shock of the human sacrifice. Will Jacob's vision lead to revolution or must we agree with his more modest self-portrait—"Look on this failure and see for seventy years he talked. . .A man who had golden opportunities but drank instead a glass tea".

Odets' original title was not the affirmation of Isaiah about dwellers in the dust arising to a new world. The original title was from a line of Hennie's, *I Got the Blues*. In that version, Moe is picked up for bookmaking; therefore, Hennie does not get to desert her child and her deceived husband to join Moe (if ever so temporarily) in Yama Yama land. Odets had both Bessie and Ralph withhold much needed money from the family. Harold Clurman insisted that Odets' original conclusion was "almost masochistically pessimistic", and the leverage of the stage director altered the shape the playwright had crafted.

And so we're presented with Ralph abruptly abandoning his pursuit of his girl. His grandfather died to provide him with a means of escape from this family, but suddenly Ralph feels no need for the inheritance, no need for his much awaited declaration of independence. Instead, he's content to move into Jacob's old room, cut the pages of those books, and become a labor organizer.

Odets is an important link between the European pioneers of realism and America's own theatrical flourishing after World War II. He has an unerring ear for self-depracating humor, the Yiddish inflection of urban American speech. One factor that might be holding back a full appreciation of this, his best-realized play, is the patched together jolt of the optimistic ending Clurman helped to impose.

—Roger Sorkin

B

BAAL
by Bertolt Brecht

First Publication: Potsdam, 1922; revised edition, 1955; alternative version (of 1926 production) as *Lebenslauf dese Mannes Baal*, in *Baal: Drei Fassungen*, Berlin, 1966.
First Production: Altes Theater, Leipzig, 8 December 1923; alternative "stage version": Deutsches Theater, Berlin, 14 February, 1926.

Translations
Baal, translated by Peter Tegel in *Bertolt Brecht: Collected Plays, 1*, edited by John Willett and Ralph Manheim, London, 1970.

Criticism
(For general works on the author, see *Playwrights* volume)

Books:
Dieter Schmidt, *"Baal" und der junge Brecht: Eine Textkritische Untersuchung zur Entwicklung des Früwerks*, Stuttgart, 1966.
Dieter Schmidt (ed.), *Baal: Der böse Baal der asoziale: Texten, Varianten und Materialen*, Frankfurt, 1968.
Paula Rothstein, *Brechts "Baal" und die moderne Aggressionsforschung*, Ann Arbor, Michigan, 1978.

Articles:
Bluma Goldstein, "Bertolt Brecht's *Baal*: A Poetic Existence", in *Festschrift für Bernhard Blume: Aufsätze zur deutschen und europäischen Literatur*, edited by Egon Schwarz and others, Göttingen, 1967.
Paul K. Kurz, "*Baal* und der junge Brecht", in *Stimmen der Zeit*, 181, 1968.
Phillip Blumberg, "The Crisis of Association: Brecht's *Baal*", in *Yale / Theatre*, vol. 6 no. 2, 1975.
Robert C. Conard, "The Hidden Structure of Brecht's *Baal*", in *Studies in Language and Literature*, edited by Charles Nelson, Richmond, Kentucky, 1976.
Michel Vanhelleputte, "*Baal* et l'hédonisme du jeune Brecht", in *Théâtre de toujours d'Aristote à Kalisky*, edited by Gilbert Debusscher and Alain Van Crugten, Brussels, 1983.
David Bathrick, "Patricide or Re-generation?: Brecht's *Baal* and *Roundheads* in the GDR", in *Theatre Journal*, 39, 1987.

*   *   *

Baal, the bohemian lyric poet, is lionised by businessmen and their wives while he gorges himself at a buffet. Baal rejects their patronage and takes to the life of a vagabond. In a loosely structured chronicle format, the play follows Baal's career and his relationships, which culminate in the murder of his male lover, before he dies alone, on the run from the police, in the forest.

In 1918 Brecht wrote to his friend Caspar Neher that he wanted to write a play on the life of François Villon, the "murderer, street-robber and ballad writter". In the event, Brecht's full-length play *Baal* was written quickly as a reaction to Hanns Johst's play *Der Einsame (The Lonely One)*, on the life and death of the poet and playwright Grabbe, which Brecht felt gave an inaccurate and over-romanticised view of the experience of being a poet.

At its premiere *Baal* gained a notoriety which it has maintained over the years. Baal's sexual exploits with two sisters, his callous rejection of a woman impregnated by him, his homosexual relationship with Ekart, and Ekart's murder have led critics to picture Baal as a selfish hedonist and immoralist. Brecht himself in the "stage version" of the play *Lebenslauf des Mannes Baal (Life Story of the Man Baal*, 1926), pointed up the moral objections to Baal's behaviour in scene headings such as: "Baal misuses his power over a woman", and, writing later in life of his early plays, stressed the antisocial aspect of Baal. *Baal* was certainly conceived and first written at a time when Brecht liked to see himself as the scourge of the Bavarian bourgeois sensibility, but Baal as a character is more than simply a negative role model, and the play is considerably greater than a cautionary tale, or an attempt merely to shock.

Baal's aim in life is more than to "épater les bourgeois" and bite their hands as they jostle to feed him. The first scene, in which we see Baal behaving like an "enfant terrible", is written in a grotesque style quite out of keeping with the rest of the play. It serves as a prologue to the main argument of the drama. Baal rejects this false, easy world and sets out into an altogether harder, but genuine world of experience, which provides material for his poetry. He cannot accept the narrowness of the life as "court poet" to the circle of bourgeois patrons who are titillated by his offensive behaviour. Baal must be open to every experience if his poetry is not to be limited in its expression and relevance. Baal cannot restrict his receptivity to caring for Sophie, nor to any *one* woman, or man. What seems like irresponsibility is in fact a particular kind of integrity. The life Baal chooses is hardly to be envied; it is a difficult one, often uncomfortable, always uncompromising, and leading to a lonely death in the forest.

Brecht's play has a number of links with Johst's. Baal's seduction of the fiancée is borrowed directly, but the character of Hans Eckardt in *The Lonely One* is split by Brecht into his Johannes, the innocent and naive, unable to comprehend Baal, and Ekart, the musician and Baal's lover. Brecht's reworking of the character of Ekart allows him to show to what lengths Baal is driven in pursuit of his art—beyond the bounds of the socially acceptable, even to murder. However, the principal differences between the plays highlight Brecht's early clarity of vision. The atmosphere in Johst's play is one of tragedy, and his poet is predictably melancholic. In *Baal*, on the other hand, Brecht shows evidence of his prodigious gifts as a theatre poet. Lyricism pervades the play, with haunting descriptions of nature in the mouth of Baal the poet, above all in the songs he sings, as Brecht himself did, to his own guitar accompaniment. The lyricism is vital and assertive, mirroring the individual tone of Brecht's lyric poetry of his time in Augsburg.

Baal is not a generalised image of the Romantic suffering artist. He suffers and dies, as the fulfilment of a demanding contract he has entered into freely with the natural world, to realise his destiny as a poet.

In this cool presentation of sensational and offensive images on stage, we can already detect the beginnings of Brecht's ideas on the role of the theatre. In a diary entry for February 1922, Brecht claims that he had hoped in *Baal* to avoid a great error observed in other art: "its attempt to carry the spectator away with it". Already in *Baal*, despite the nature of the material, Brecht has the intention of distancing the audience from the action on stage, of not violating the audience's "splendid isolation", of encouraging a critical attitude in them and of discouraging them from over-identification with the characters in the play. Thus *Baal*, while reflecting the bohemian life-style Brecht was attempting to lead at the time, also adumbrates concerns and techniques which were to be central to Brecht's writing for the rest of his life.

—Anthony Meech

THE BACCHAE (Bakchai)
by Euripides

First Production: Athens, c. 405 B.C.

Editions
Bacchae, edited by A.H. Cruikshank, Oxford, 1893; second edition, 1934.
Bacchae, edited by E.R. Dodds, Oxford, 1944, 2nd edition 1960.
Bacchae, edited by E. Christian Knopff, 1982.

Translations
The Bacchae, translated by Margaret Kinmont Tennant, London, 1926.
The Bacchae, in *"The Bacchae" and Other Plays*, translated by Philip Vellacott, Harmondsworth, 1954.
The Bacchae, translated by Henry Birkhead, 1957.
The Bacchae, translated by William Arrowsmith, in *Euripides 5*, Chicago and London, 1959 (Complete Greek Tragedies Series).
The Bacchae, translated by G.S. Kirk, New York, 1970.
The Bacchae in *The Trojan Women; Helen; The Bacchae*, translated by Neil Curry, Cambridge, 1981.
The Bacchae in *Euripides: Plays One*, translated and edited by Michael J. Walton, London and New York, 1988.

Criticism
(For general works on the author, see *Playwrights* volume)

Books:
R.P. Winnington-Ingram, *Euripides and Dionysus: An Interpretation of "The Bacchae"*, Cambridge, 1948.
W. Sale, *Existentialism and Euripides: Sickness, Tragedy and Divinity in the "Medea", the "Hippolytus" and the "Bacchae"*, Berwick, Victoria, 1977.
Charles Segal, *Dionysiac Poetics and Euripides' Bacchae*, Princeton, New Jersey, 1982.
Hans Oranje, *Euripides' "Bacchae": The Play and Its Audience*, Leiden, 1984.
Arthur Evans, *The God of Ecstasy: Sex-roles and the Madness of Dionysus*, New York, 1988.

Articles:
G.M.A. Grube, "Dionysus in the *Bacchae*", in *Transactions and Proceedings of the American Philological Association* [*TAPA*], 66, 1935.
E.R. Dodds, "Maenadism in the *Bacchae*" in *Harvard Theological Review*, vol. 33 no. 3, 1940.
L.M. Mead, "Euripides and The Puritan Movement. A Study of the *Bacchae*", in *Greece and Rome* (second series), 10, 1940.
R. Schechner, "*The Bacchae*: A City Sacrificed to a Jealous God", in *Tulane Drama Review*, vol. 5 no. 4, 1961.
Robert Dyer, "Image and Symbol: The Link Between the Two Worlds of The *Bacchae*", in *AUMLA Journal*, 21, 1964.
E. Savage, "The *Bacchae* as Theatre of Spectacle", in *Drama Survey*, vol. 3 no.4, 1964.
William Arrowsmith, "The *Bacchae*: From Four Sides", in *Yale / Theater*, vol.1 no.1, 1968.
J.A. Larue, "Prurience Uncovered: The Psychology of Euripides' Pentheus", in *Classical Journal*, 63, 1968.
A.P. Burnett, "Pentheus and Dionysus: Host Guest", in *Classical Philology*, 65, 1970.
G. Deverux, "The Psychotherapy Scene in Euripides' *Bacchae*", in *Journal of Hellenic Studies*, 90, 1970.
M. Arthur, "The Choral Odes of the *Bacchae* of Euripides", in *Yale Classical Studies*, 22, 1972.
W. Sale, "The Psychoanalysis of Pentheus in the *Bacchae* of Euripides", in *Yale Classical Studies*, 22, 1972.
W.F. Lynch, "Euripides' Bacchae: The Mind in Prison", in *Cross Currents*, Summer 1975.
W.C. Scott, "Two Suns Over Thebes: Imagery and Stage Effects in the *Bacchae*", in *Transactions and Proceedings of the American Philological Association* [*TAPA*], 105, 1975.
V. Castellani, "That Troubled House of Pentheus in Euripides' *Bacchae*", in *Transactions and Proceedings of the American Philological Association* [*TAPA*], 106, 1976.
B. Seidensticker, "Comic Elements in Euripides' *Bacchae*", in *American Journal of Philology*, 99, 1978.
R. Seaford, "Dionysiac Drama and The Dionysiac Mysteries", in *Classical Quarterly* (new series), 31, 1981.
Justina Gregory, "Some Aspects of Seeing in Euripides' *Bacchae*", in *Greece and Rome* (second series), vol. 32 no.1, 1985.
Christine M. Kalke, "The Making of a Thrysus: The Transformation of Pentheus in Euripides' *Bacchae*", in *American Journal of Philology*, 106, 1985.
J.-P. Vernant, "Le Dionysos masqué des Bacchants d'Euripide", in *L'Homme*, 93, 1985.
Jennifer R. Marsh, "Euripides' Bakchai: A Reconsideration in the Light of Vase-Paintings", in *Bulletin of the Institute of Classical Studies* (London), 36, 1989.

* * *

The god Dionysus returns in disguise to Thebes where he

The Bacchae: Mermaid Theatre, London, 1964

was born. Rejected by his family, he is now set on punishing his cousin Pentheus, king of Thebes, for denying his divinity. Pentheus has Dionysus imprisoned but he escapes and persuades the king to dress up as a woman so as to witness the Dionysiac rites. Pentheus's mother, Agave, and the other women tear Pentheus to pieces believing him to be a lion. Cadmus, the grandfather of both Pentheus and Dionysus, restores Agave to sanity while Dionysus looks on unrepentant.

Euripides went to live in Macedon for the final years of his life. *The Bacchae* was written there and performed posthumously in Athens in 405 B.C. The play revolves around the clash between a traditional culture in the person of Pentheus, and a foreign invasion in the figure of Dionysus, the god intent on introducing his religion to Thebes. Dionysus opens the play with a prologue, disguised as a man, in which he outlines his progress through Asia with his chorus of Bacchae before returning to his birthplace. The son of Zeus and Semele, he is both an individual and a representative of a religion of freedom and mystical powers. Introduced primarily as a religion for the women of Thebes, this religion has claimed Cadmus, founder of Thebes, and the prophet Teiresias among its converts. The young Pentheus sees his authority under threat when, under the influence of the god, the women of Thebes abandon the city and roam the mountains, apparently performing miracles.

Whether or not such miracles occur in the play is an open question. When Dionysus and Pentheus meet face to face, it soon becomes apparent that Dionysus's power is related to his ability to confuse and delude. This is how he escapes from imprisonment. It is never quite clear whether an earthquake, which the chorus "see" destroy the palace, really takes place.

When Dionysus begins to exert his influence over Pentheus he persuades him to dress in women's clothes, believing these will serve as a disguise. He is torn apart by women who think he is a lion, his head returned on a Bacchic wand brandished by his mother. Cadmus, now freed from Dionysus's influence, has the task of bringing his daughter to see what she has done. At the end of the play Dionysus reveals himself as a god and Cadmus and Agave depart into exile.

A bloodthirsty enough story, the play is pervaded by a sense of theatrical power. For the Greeks, Dionysus was the god of ecstasy, as well as the god of wine. He was also the god of illusion and the god of the theatre. The play is full illusions: Dionysus is in disguise; Cadmus and Teiresias deck themselves out as Bacchants; Pentheus dresses up; a messenger reports remarkable events he claims to have witnessed—milk pouring from the earth, women unharmed by weapons that bounce off them, superhuman strength, snakes licking blood off human faces.

This world beyond reason is one with which Pentheus is ill-equipped to cope, but his clash with Dionysus is not a simple meeting of rational and irrational. Pentheus is no Apollo-figure for all his claims that he stands for order in a world that threatens to become chaotic. Dionysus destroys Pentheus by locating the Dionysiac elements in him: his conceit, his childishness, his prurience, turning him into a voyeur who contributes to his own destruction. Dionysus does so in the name of his religion which he claims as benign and beneficial except when opposed. Yet his motives are personal. Half-god, but from a mortal mother, he resents as a human being that he is excluded from his human family. As a god he has divine power to execute a revenge that is fearsome in its callousness.

This ambiguity about where an audience's, or indeed the author's, sympathies may lie, has led to widely divergent interpretations and productions. For some, Dionysus is a destructive force whose cat-and-mouse cruelty disqualifies him from any claims to approval. At least one rationalist critic refused to believe him a god at all, but a sinister con-man with skill as a hypnotist. His defenders regard Pentheus as a "fascist" dictator in opposition to the life-force. Popular in the 1960's, this view led to bizarre adaptations like the Performance Group's *Dionysus in '69.*

The play can stand a variety of treatments but functions best as a warning against excess of any kind, thus linking it to Euripides' earlier *Hippolytus*. The power that Dionysus represents, and of which the chorus of Bacchae serve as a living manifestation, is both formidable and mysterious. It exists and, whether the story is seen primarily at a literal or at a figurative level, the implications are the same. There are aspects of the individual and of the collective which transcend reason and should be recognised. Pentheus, in trying to maintain order in Thebes, is suppressing not only the instinctive desire of the women to escape from the constant drudgery of their everyday lives, but also those aspects of himself which are part of the feminine side to his nature. Dionysus, who wins all the arguments and all the battles, does so at the expense of both humanity and compassion. To an audience of any age such a sacrifice is likely to seem too great.

—J. Michael Walton

BACK TO METHUSELAH
by George Bernard Shaw

First Publication: London, 1921.
First Production: Garrick Theatre, New York (Theatre Guild), in three parts, on 27 February, 6 March, and 13 March, 1922.

Criticism
(For general works on the author, see *Playwrights* volume)

Articles:

R. Hamilton, "Philosophy of Bernard Shaw: A Study of *Back to Methuselah*", in *London Quarterly Review*, July 1945.

H.D. Rankin, "Plato and Bernard Shaw, Their Ideal Communities", in *Hermathena*, 93, 1959.

Margery M. Morgan, *"Back to Methuselah": The Poet and the City*, in *Essays and Studies by Members of the English Association*, 13, 1960.

Daniel Leary and Richard Foster, "Adam and Eve: Evolving Archetypes in *Back to Methuselah*", in *Shaw Review*, 4, 1961.

Rüdiger Reitemeier, "Sündenfall und Ubermensch in G.B. Shaws *Back to Methuselah*", in *Germanisch-Romanische Monatsschrift*, 16, 1966.

Harry M. Geduld, "*Back to Methuselah*: Textual Problems in Shaw", in *Art and Error: Modern Textual Editing*, edited by Ronald Gottesman and Scott Bennett, Bloomington, Indiana, 1970.

Kenneth Lawrence, "Bernard Shaw: The Career of the Life Forces", in *Modern Drama*, 15, 1972.

Raymond S. Nelson, "*Back to Methuselah*: Shaw's Modern Bible", in *Costerus*, 5, 1972.

Eugene Tanzy, "Contrasting Views of Man and the Evolutionary Process: *Back to Methuselah* and *Childhood's End*", in *Arthur C. Clarke*, edited by Joseph D. Olander and Martin H. Greenberg, New York, 1977.

Warren S. Smith, "Serendipity or Life Force? The Darwinians, Teilhard de Chardin and *Back to Methuselah*", in *Teilhard Review*, 14, 1979.

Daniel Armstrong, "*Back to Methuselah*: Shaw's Debt to Swift", in *Cahiers Victoriens & Edouardiens*, 21, 1985.

Frederick P.W. McDowell, "Some Reflections on *Back to Methuselah* in Performance", in *SHAW*, 8, 1988.

*   *   *

Back to Methuselah is a cycle of five plays. The first, *In the Beginning*, consists of two sections: a kind of overture to the cycle based on the Genesis story of Adam and Eve and the Serpent, followed by Act II, in which Cain, the first murderer, is the central character. The second play, *The Gospel of the Brothers Barnabas*, has a post-war setting, contemporary with Shaw's writing of the work: thinly disguised caricatures of Asquith and Lloyd George, supposed to be the Prime Minister and the Leader of the Opposition, call at the home of Franklyn Barnabas, an intellectual in public life, to hear him and his biologist brother expound their theory of the necessity for a prolongation of the span of human life. The title of the third play, *The Thing Happens*, does not give away the surprise that the first pair to whom it happens are the Barnabas parlour-maid and the curate who was in love with Franklyn's daughter Savvy. When their actual ages are discovered, in a Britain of the 22nd century, governed largely—and efficiently—by Blacks and Chinese, he is Archbishop of York and she is a Cabinet Minister. The fourth play, *Tragedy of an Elderly Gentleman*, contrasts the interests and attitudes of the Long-Livers, who inhabit an area near Galway Bay, with those of a party of Short (to us, normal)-Livers who have come to consult the Oracle on the best time to call a general election. The fifth play, *As Far as Thought Can Reach*, is set in an Arcadian glade where a company of Youths and Maidens, born fully-grown from huge eggs, pass through all the stages of life to mental and emotional maturity in four short years. Two Ancients, devoted to contemplation and wisdom, represent the condition to which the youngsters then progress. One of the youths, Pygmalion, plays at experimental science and invents two human automata. The group watches a play-within-a-play, in which the automata recapitulate human progress from the primitive condition of twentieth-century newspaper readers to the acquisition of a soul and the discovery of altruistic love,— though the Woman murders her maker by the way. The glade fades from view, and out of the darkness come the voices from Eden, joined by the voice of Lilith, the divine mother and principle of continuous, unceasing creation. Her combined warning and promise of an inconceivable infinity of life is the main element in a finale which balances the overture and rounds off the cycle as an aesthetic unity.

Back to Methuselah is Shaw's most ambitious and sustained work in dramatic form. His description of the whole as a "Metabiological Pentateuch", or "Bible of Creative Evolution", is alarmingly pretentious, even though half joking. It suggests that he wished here to work out his philosophy as completely as possible; yet the play is not a dogmatic work, it moves through a variety of styles, and a motive it never forsakes is the indictment of politics and politicians for chronic shortsightedness in vision and action limited by electoral considerations. A letter he wrote to Granville Barker (who, as a producer, had established Shaw as the leading modern British dramatist) reveals that Wagnerian music drama, the

Back to Methuselah: Birmingham Repertory Theatre, 1923

great cycle of *The Ring of the Nibelungs* in particular, was another precedent he had in mind, not least for its technique of unifying a large work with many interrelated themes: "I may have to disregard the boredom of the spectator who has not mastered all the motifs, as Wagner had to do". He was demanding unusual and unremitting closeness of attention, perhaps supplemented by study of the text, to ensure maximum understanding and pleasure from a performance. Writ-

ing at a period of his life when he had no clear prospect of any staging of the new work (for the war had destroyed the conditions in which serious new drama could be produced in London, and the general public might not have forgiven him for publishing *Commonsense about the War*, 1914), he seems to have cared less than usual about the exigencies of the theatre. In particular, the immensely long speeches exchanged between the Elderly Gentleman and Zoo are largely actionless and devoid of visual interest, though they are fascinating and often moving to read and might be equally effective on radio.

What is, perhaps, most remarkable about the cycle is how the structures of thought find expression in what can only be called musical structures, so that each of the parts is intricately linked with the others, and a tremendous range of tone, feeling and thought is patterned through repetition and variation into a subtle and complex whole, from the first sounding of dominant themes in the sparely written first scene to the rich polyphonic prose of Part IV. The chronologically developed, science-fiction fable is counterbalanced by a philosophic drama of recurrence and changing perspectives. The contrast between short livers and long livers is a variant on Swift's device of the opposition of small to large, to produce a satirically clashing, double vision (Gulliver in Laputa among the inventors and Gulliver among the Houyhnhnms, especially, have contributed to the form of plays within the cycle). Instead of employing a single unifying hero, Shaw challenges the sense of onward-flowing time by exploiting correspondences between characters in the different parts, which easily arise through practical need for one company of actors to fill the roles in five plays. At each stage there is something familiar about the people: Savvy Barnabas is Eve in a new costume, turning up again as Zoo and then the Newly Born; the professional politicians recur, though individual personalities, like names, sometimes combine into one; Cain returns as Napoleon, Emperor of Turania, as the theme of murder returns with the killing of Pygmalion in Part V; some quality of the self-renewing Serpent, who initiates the action of the cycle, is recalled by eternal Lilith, who closes it.

Through setting, costume, the names of characters, and the music of flutes, Shaw identifies the remote future Utopia of Part V with the ancient Greek Utopia of Plato's *Republic* (having anticipated this by staging Plato's metaphor of the Cave in the business with the Oracle in Part IV). G.K. Chesterton condemned Shaw's puritanism for coming up with a chilling dream of an ascetic and loveless future for mankind; but *Back to Methuselah* does not depart from the dramatist's consistent attitude: Utopias are only speculative, ideals only provisional—to be scrapped when their usefulness is past. Though *Back to Methuselah*, which even brings St. Paul on the spiritual mysteries into the argument, is prime evidence in support of Shaw's claim to a religious consciousness, the whole fulfils its purpose as an exercise in philosophic thinking which may do something to correct the crass and destructive pragmatism of everyday politics.

—Margery Morgan

THE BAD-TEMPERED OLD MAN (Dyskolos / Dyscolos) by Menander

First Production: Lenaean Festival, Athens, c. 316 B.C.

Editions
Dyscolos, edited by Jean Bingen, Leiden, 1960.
Menandri Dyscolos, edited by H. Lloyd-Jones, Oxford, 1960.
The Dyskolos of Menander, edited by E.W. Handley, London, 1965.
Dyscolos, in *Menandri Reliquae Selectae*, edited by F.H. Sandbach, Oxford, 1972; revised edition, 1990.
Papyrus Bodmer 4: Ménandre: "Le Dyscolos", edited by Victor Martin, Geneva, n.d.

Translations
Menander's "Duskolos"; or, The Man Who Didn't Like People, translated by W.G. Arnott, London, 1960.
The Bad-Tempered Old Man, or, The Misanthrope, translated by Philip Vellacott, Oxford, 1960.
Feast of Pan, translated by R.N. Benton, Louth, Lincolnshire, 1977; second edition, 1984.
The Dyskolos, translated by Carroll Moulton, New York, 1977.
Old Cantankerous, in *Menander: Plays and Fragments*, translated by Norma Miller, Harmondsworth, 1987.

Criticism
(For general works on the author, see *Playwrights* volume)

Articles:
R.A. Pack, "On the Plot of Menander's *Dyscolus*", in *Classical Philology*, 30, 1935.
P.J. Photiades, "Pan's Prologue to the *Dyskolos* of Menander", in *Greece and Rome* (second series) 5, 1958.
W.E. Blake, "Menander's *Dyskolos*: Restorations and Emendations", in *Classical Philology*, 55, 1960.
J.G. Griffith, "The Distribution of Parts in Menander's *Dyskolus*", in *Classical Quarterly* (new series), 10, 1960.
K. Lever, "The *Dyskolus* and Menander's Reputation", in *Classical Journal*, 55, 1960.
L.A. Post, "Virtue Promoted in Menander's *Dyscolus*", in *Transactions and Proceedings of the American Philological Association* [*TAPA*], 91, 1960.
K.J. Reckford, "*Dyskolos* of Menander", in *Studies in Philology*, 58, 1961.
Walther Kraus, "Menanders *Dyskolos*: Forschungsbericht", in *Anzeiger für doie Altertumswissenschaft*, 15, 1962.
L.A. Post, "Some Subtleties in Menander's *Dyscolus*", in *American Journal of Philology*, 84, 1963.
E.S. Ramage, "City and Country in Menander's *Dyskolos*", in *Philologus*, 110, 1966.
E. Keuls, "Mystery Elements in Menander's *Dyskolus*", in *Transactions and Proceedings of the American Philological Association* [*TAPA*], 100, 1969.
M. Anderson, "Knemon's Hamartia", in *Greece and Rome* (second series), 17, 1970.
David Wiles, "Menander's *Dyskolos* and Demetrios of Phaleron's Dilemma", in *Greece and Rome* (second series), vol.31 no.2, 1984.
N.J. Lowe, "Tragic Space and Comic Timing in Menander's *Dyskolos*", in *Bulletin of the Institute of Classical Studies* (London), 34, 1987.
Christina Dedoussi, "The Borrowing Play in *Dyskolos* 891–930", in *Bulletin of the Institute of Classical Studies* (London), 35, 1988.

*   *   *

The *Dyskolos* (*Bad-Tempered Old Man*) won first prize when presented by Menander at the Athenian Lenaean festival in January 316 B.C. It was only in the late 1950's that this example of Greek New Comedy became known once again, having been recovered from a papyrus text dating back to the 3rd century A.D.. The "bad-tempered old man" of the title is the farmer Cnemon, a misanthrope who mistakenly believes that he has no need of others and, therefore, lives alone except for his daughter and an aged woman servant. The god Pan causes a young man about town, Sostratos, to fall in love with the girl, and Sostratos, having won the support of Cnemon's stepson Gorgias, eventually joins Gorgias in rescuing Cnemon from a well. This experience convinces Cnemon of the folly of his way of life and he proceeds to entrust his daughter to Gorgias, who chooses his new friend as her husband; Sostratos, in turn, persuades his own father to marry his sister to Gorgias. A party which celebrates the betrothals concludes the action. A division into five acts and the replacement of choral song by musical interlude are noticeable features of the *Dyskolos*.

New Comedy typically exploits the theme of romantic love, and here it is Sostratos who is totally enamoured, so much so, in fact, that he speaks of falling in love at first sight and dying if he fails to win the girl. Sentiments so extravagant strike us as being amusing and would have been absolutely hilarious to the Greeks for whom an arranged marriage was the norm. But at the same time, an audience, whether ancient or modern, tends throughout to laugh *with* rather than *at* Sostratos. The presentation of Cnemon poses a particular problem; his character must be clearly established, but he can himself appear on stage only in short snatches—otherwise, he would fail to live up to his reputation as a loner. Menander solves this problem by having the slave Pyrrhias, the step-son Gorgias, and even the god Pan comment on Cnemon's awkwardness. Cnemon's absence highlights his important speech, when rescued from the well—a speech which is more "ethical" than "psychological"; that is, it tells us nothing about Cnemon's emotions but stresses how we all need the help of our fellow men. The *Dyskolos* is conventional in that it features the stock characters to be seen in New Comedy (e.g., the cook who, is always forgetting the tools of his trade and has to borrow them). But the fifth act's riotous party, when Cnemon is savagely teased and made to dance, reveals an aspect of Menander's art not previously suspected.

Neatness of motivation and naturalism were considered characteristic of Menander by the ancient critics, and both are illustrated in the *Dyskolos*. The action of the comedy is set in the Attic countryside beside a shrine of the god Pan and the Nymphs, and this allows a prologue to be delivered by Pan which functions as the equivalent of a modern theatre programme, detailing the setting, characters, and basic plot. Cnemon, his daughter, and Gorgias live in the vicinity, and Sostratos is drawn there by love. But how are Sostratos's family also to assemble at the same spot and preparations for the concluding party to be made? We learn at the end of Act II: Sostratos's mother has dreamt that Pan has fettered her son and then set him to work on the land by the god's shrine, and so the mother organizes a sacrifice there to ensure a happy outcome. Of course, Pan *has* "fettered" the young man, but with chains of love, and Sostratos is currently digging away (at Gorgias's suggestion) so that Cnemon might be led to believe him a farmer. And the trick pays off, for Gorgias is able to tell his father that Sostratos is no idler, while expressing a personal admiration for the man who, having "lived soft", is willing to toil. The audience can also enjoy a quiet chuckle when Sostratos returns to the stage complaining as he rubs an aching back.

Sostratos is a townsman whereas Gorgias represents the country. Each excels in his own way: Sostratos with words, so that he persuades his father to accept the "pauper" Gorgias as son-in-law; Gorgias with action, so that he, "a veritable Atlas", extricates Cnemon from the well while Sostratos gazes adoringly on the girl. But both engage in moralizing and preach from very much the same text: in Act II Gorgias warns that luck changes and the rich can be corrupted—you must deserve your prosperity; in Act V Sostratos tells his father that fortune may transfer its favour to another—if you have money, it is a good idea to be generous in case you are ever in need yourself. Moral sentiments of this kind are commonly expressed in New Comedy which is very much the equivalent of modern situation comedy: Menander's comedy is concerned with the life and problems of the upper middle-class in an Athens whose comedy has lost its political, satirical, and coarser elements. Horseplay is now restricted, and knock-about comedy is associated with just the lower classes, slaves, and cooks. Comedy is no longer local, but universal—a fact which explains the abiding influence of Menander.

—Peter Walcot

———

BAKCHAI.   See THE BACCHAE.

———

BALAGANCHIK.   See THE PUPPET SHOW.

———

THE BALCONY (Le Balcon)
by Jean Genet

First Publication: Paris, 1956; revised version, 1962.
First Production: Théâtre du Gymnase, Paris, 18 May 1960.

Translations
The Balcony, translated by Bernard Frechtman, London, 1958; revised edition, 1966.

Criticism
(For general works on the author, see *Playwrights* volume)

Articles:
Rima D. Reck, "Appearance and Reality in Genet's *Le Balcon*", in *Yale French Studies*, 29, 1962.
Benjamin Nelson, "*The Balcony* and Parisian Existentialism", in *Tulane Drama Review*, vol. 7 no. 3, 1963.
Harry E. Stewart, "Jean Genet's Saintly Preoccupation in *Le Balcon*", in *Drama Survey*, 6, 1967.
Harry E. Stewart, "Jean Genet's Mirror Images in *Le Balcon*", in *Modern Drama*, 12, 1969.
Françoise Clabecq and Jean Blairon, "*Le Balcon*: Autour de quelques objets", in *Obliques*, 2, 1972.
Michèle Piemme, "Espace scénique et illusion dramatique dans *Le Balcon*", in *Obliques*, 2, 1972.
Dina Sherzer, "Les appellatifs dans *Le Balcon* de Genet", in *French Review*, 48, 1974.
Gisèle Feal, "*Le Balcon* de Genet ou le culte matriarchal: Une Interprétation mythique", in *French Review*, 48, 1975.
Albert Bermel, "Society as a Brothel: Genet's Satire in *The Balcony*", in *Modern Drama*, 19, 1976.
Yvette Went-Daoust, "Objets et lieux dans *Le Balcon* de Jean Genet", in *Neophilologus*, 63, 1979.
Martin A. Bertman, "A Metaphysical Analysis of Genet's *Le Balcon*", in *Agora*, 4, 1979–80.
Christiane V. Jacquemont, "The Essence of the Game and Its Locus in Jean Genet's *Le Balcon*", in *French Review*, 53, 1980.
David H. Walker, "Revolution and Revisions in Genet's *Le Balcon*", in *Modern Language Review*, 79, 1984.
Maria Shevtsova, "The Consumption of Empty Signs: Jean Genet's *The Balcony*", in *Modern Drama*, 30, 1987.

The Balcony: Aldwych Theatre, London, 1971 (Royal Shakespeare Company)

The Balcony was first published in 1956, after some years of silence and self-examination on Genet's part, apparently provoked by his reading of Sartre's monumental analysis of his life and work, *Saint-Genet, Comédien et Martyr*, 1952. The play betrays a new sureness of theatrical vision on Genet's part. In particular it foreshadows the treatment of public (rather than purely personal) themes, the choice of a more episodic structure and the use of an open stage that mark his subsequent plays.

The Balcony deals with the relationship between political power and the human imagination. It is set largely within the "maison close" which gives the play its name and where these two forces meet. In French slang, a brothel is frequently termed a "house of illusions", a sobriquet which Irma, the madame of this particular establishment, is proud to acknowledge. In the first three scenes her clients are seen acting out fantasies of power, in which they play figures of authority: a bishop, a judge, and a general. A fourth scene, in which a client impersonates a lice-ridden beggar, appears to be offered as a sardonic counterpoint, perhaps indicating the lot of the common man. But the events that take place inside the Grand Balcony are intimately linked to the progress and the failure of a revolution taking place outside. The rebels succeed in killing the heads of the church, of the judiciary and of the army. The functions of the latter are then assumed by Irma's three clients, while she herself assumes that of the late Queen, who has perished in an explosion which has destroyed the royal palace. Together they ensure the continuance of the *status quo*.

Genet's point seems to be, quite simply, that illusion is vastly more powerful than reality. Everything in the play seems to emanate from and return to Irma's house of illusions. Significantly, of the rebel leaders, the only two who are identified by name are Roger, the brothel's former plumber, and Chantal, once one of Irma's whores. The action of the play finds its climax—the defeat of the rebels—in the killing of Chantal, who has been manipulated into serving as a revolutionary symbol. Its denouement is provided by Roger's return to the brothel, a recognition perhaps of his powerlessness to change reality and of his need for illusion. Even those who seem genuinely powerful in the world of *The Balcony* are as preoccupied with conquering the minds of the masses as with defeating them physically. George, the Chief of Police and Irma's lover and master, feels that his power will be absolute only when he has joined the Bishop, the Judge, and the General in the pantheon of those whom her clients come to emulate. This view seems to be vindicated in the last scene of the play, when Roger expresses the wish to act out the fantasy of lying in state in the Chief of Police's mausoleum. Even Roger's subsequent attempt to nullify the power of the Chief of Police in an act of sympathetic magic, by castrating himself, is seen to be self-defeating. George responds by ostentatiously reassuring himself that his virile parts are still intact.

Despite the furore aroused by *The Balcony* on its publication, Genet denies that the play has any specific satirical import. Instead he claims that it is "the glorification of Image and Reflexion". Only if played in this way will the work's meaning—satirical or not—become manifest. In fact, *The Balcony* is a double-edged work. From a left-wing perspective it has been read as an exposé of the techniques applied in modern society to the repression of mass revolutionary consciousness. From the right it has been seen as a pessimistic critique of the illusoriness of all political (and specifically of revolutionary) action.

Genet himself offers no clue to the appropriateness or otherwise of these readings. *The Balcony* does contain some historical allusions, one of which is a reference to Franco's massive monument to the Nationalist dead of the Spanish Civil War, the "Valley of the Fallen". Genet also suggested that Roger's self-mutilation represented the attitude displayed by the Spanish Republicans in acknowledging their defeat. But the analogy is partial at best, since the Civil War was not a revolutionary one, but resulted from a right-wing military putsch. And the Chief of Police's aspiration to a personality cult centred on his mausoleum is more reminiscent of Lenin than of Franco. Ultimately the play's power to endure lies precisely in its ambivalence. For while the play demonstrates the ineffectiveness of political action, it also exposes the emptiness of political power. In no character is this more evident than in the Queen's Envoy, the cynical emissary of a monarch who no longer exists (and whose essence was absence when she did). Equally, the Chief of Police's domination of the collective consciousness (like that of the false Bishop, Judge, and General) is purchased at the price of an impotence no less real than Roger's self-inflicted mutilation. To maintain his prestige as image, he withdraws from the world of action, from life. For the commercially-minded Irma, he has become an expensive luxury. The play concludes when, outside the Grand Balcony, the revolution can be heard beginning again.

The Balcony was deemed too scandalous and subversive to be staged in 1950's France. Its world premiere took place in London in 1957. But Genet distanced himself violently from Peter Zadek's English production, which he saw as parochializing his concerns. Nor has he endorsed any subsequent production of the play. After a French premiere of *The Balcony* was made possible by the success of *The Blacks* (1959), a revised version of the play (in 9 rather than 15 scenes) was staged by Peter Brook at the *Théâtre du Gymnase* in May 1960. And for Erwin Piscator's Frankfurt production of 1962, Genet produced what was then described as a final version of *The Balcony*, accompanied by instructions on its staging. This is the basis of Bernard Frechtman's English translation. But the text of the play that was published in volume four of Genet's *Oeuvres complètes* in 1968 contains further substantial revisions.

—Tim Lewis

THE BALD PRIMA DONNA (La Cantatrice chauve)
by Eugène Ionesco

First Publication: Paris, 1954.
First Production: Théâtre des Noctambules, Paris, 11 May 1950.

Translations
The Bald Prima Donna, translated by Donald Watson, London, 1961; revised edition (with additional scene), London, 1966.

Criticism
(For general works on the author, see *Playwrights* volume)

Books:
Pascal Charvet, *"La Cantatrice chauve" d'Eugène Ionesco*, Paris, 1977.

Articles:
Eugène Ionesco, "The Tragedy of Language: How an English Primer Became My First Play", in *Tulane Drama Review*, vol. 4 no. 3, March 1960.

Theodore Messenger, "'Who was that lady. . .?' The Problem of Identity in the *Bald Soprano* of Eugène Ionesco", in *North Dakota Quarterly*, vol. 36 no. 2, 1968.

Olga and Isaak Revzine, "Expérimentation sémiotique chez Eugène Ionesco: *La Cantatrice chauve* et *La Leçon*", in *Semiotica*, 4, 1971.

John T. Dorsey, "Plays on Words: Language in Ionesco's *La Cantatrice chauve* and Handke's *Kaspar*", in *Journal of the College of International Relations*, 1981.

*   *   *

The curtain rises on a middle-class English couple, Mr. and Mrs. Smith: the wife is a non-stop chatterbox who has nothing to say beyond praising the cooking of their maid, Mary, while Mr. Smith is content with clicking his tongue from behind his opened newspaper. He is busy scanning the obituary page where a notice appears about the death of one Bobby Watson. Confusion pervades the exchange between husband and wife as to the gender of the dead person since both husband and wife were called Bobby. The clock strikes seven, three, then five, as Mrs. Smith wonders when the two Bobby Watsons plan to get married. The time is definitely "out of joint". These speculations, which also include the little Bobby Watsons, are interrupted by Mary who comes in to announce the arrival of Mr. and Mrs. Martin. As the Smiths rush out to change, their guests settle in the vacant armchairs. Although Mr. and Mrs. Martin have come down on the same train from Manchester, they do not seem at first to know one another. Step by step they reconstruct their lives, becoming convinced that they are man and wife. Mary, the self-proclaimed "Sherlock Holmes" of the play, blows up their pyramid of evidence by stating that the little girl they assume to be their child cannot be their offspring: ". . .whereas it's the right eye of Donald's child that's red and the left eye that's white, it's the left eye of Elizabeth's child that's red and the right eye that's white". There are no certainties in Ionesco's world. With the unexpected arival of the Captain of the Fire Brigade, the maid's erstwhile lover, matters disintegrate further. The Fireman's absurdist tales unleash a kind of madness. The play ends with the Smiths and Martins dancing round and round like cannibals, hurling invectives or hissing syllables at one another. At the end, the Martins and Smiths trade roles and places. Everything starts all over again.

When *The Bald Prima Donna* was presented by Nicolas Bataille in 1950 on the tiny stage of the now defunct Théâtre des Noctambules, the one-act sketch was received as a witty prank, the kind of show one might expect to see in a cabaret. The title appeared to be a joke since no bald diva was seen on the stage. The audience was unaware that the Fire Chief had slipped up in rhearsal, substituting the words "bald prima donna" for another group of nonsense terms, and as a result Ionesco decided that this chance twist of the tongue would determine the play's title. Such a solution was in keeping with the tradition of Dadaism, a school whose own title came from flipping open a dictionary and choosing a word at random. Ionesco, the admitted heir of Tristan Tzara, welcomed the intrusion of chance as an element of his aesthetic.

Ionesco likes to say that in composing *The Bald Prima Donna* he was not quite certain of what he had produced. He assumed that it was "something like the tragedy of language", and was therefore amazed to hear the audience laughing. Later, when he had had time to reflect upon this non-psychological, apolitical work, he came to see it as pure structure, like a musical composition or an architectural construction. Although Ionesco claimed the text of the play was "dictated" to him by the characters from a conversation book, *English Made Easy*, a careful analysis reveals that it is crafted with minute precision, that the rhythm of the play gathers momentum and reaches a crescendo. Although Ionesco sub-titles this sketch an "anti-play", pointing out its parodic intent, it must be seen as a lampoon that plays homage to the genre it mocks.

Most French critics made the mistake of considering this comedy to be social satire, a way of poking fun at bourgeois French society by means of a cartoon version of the British middle class. However, Ionesco is quick to declare: "I'm a good bourgeois myself!". If any joke was intended, it was at the expense of boulevard melodrama in the style of Henri Bernstein. Nicolas Bataille claims to have imitated this style in directing his actors, just as he ordered his set designer to recreate the decor of *Hedda Gabler*. Ionesco suggests that his play must be understood to be the satire of bourgeois mentality, not bourgeois customs. He says that he makes fun of a universal petite-bourgeoisie, of men of fixed ideals, who live by slogans, using mechanical language without ever questioning it.

There are six characters in the *Bald Prima Donna*. The Smiths and the Martins are interchangeable, and in the end they do change places. The Maid and the Fire Chief, her erstwhile lover, are no less indistinct, but they are colorful rather than gray. Ionesco's Mary is the Bacchante of Dionysus / The Fire Chief whom she celebrates by reciting a paean to fire. Of course the Fire Chief is enchanted with this celebration of his "conception of the world". It seems that being worshipped in this manner frees his own creative impulses; he manifests a gift for story telling. Both Mary's paean and her lover's surrealist fables constitute the dynamite charge that brings down the walls of convention. The play's rhythm intensifies, grows delirious. What becomes obvious is that the flat, cartoon-like characters are made of words, not of flesh and blood.

Ionesco's first play is still his favorite because of its simple abstract quality. It has been running at the Théâtre de La Huchette in the Latin Quarter for over 35 years. It is also widely performed in university campuses in the United States. The *Bald Prima Donna* has ushered in the leading dramatic form of the second half of the 20th century, the metaphysical farce.

—Rosette C. Lamont

———

THE BALD SOPRANO.   See THE BALD PRIMA DONNA.

———

THE BARBER OF SEVILLE; or, The Useless Precaution (Le Barbier de Séville; ou, La Précaution inutile) by Pierre-Augustin Caron de Beaumarchais

First Publication: Paris, 1775.
First Production: Comédie-Française, Paris, 23 February 1775.

Editions
Le Barbier de Séville, edited by Louis Allen, London, 1951; revised edition, 1978.

Le Barbier de Séville in *Théâtre de Beaumarchais*, edited by
Maurice Rat, Paris, 1956.
Le Barbier de Séville, edited by Léon Lejeable, London, 1961.
Le Barbier de Séville, edited by Georges Bonneville, Paris,
1962.
Le Barbier de Séville, edited by E.J. Arnould, Oxford, 1963.
La Genèse du "Barbier de Séville", edited by E.J. Arnould,
Dublin and Paris, 1965 (includes texts of the different
manuscripts).
Le Barbier de Séville, in *Théâtre: Beaumarchais*, edited by
Jean-Pierre de Beaumarchais, Paris, 1980.
Le Barbier de Séville, edited by Fabienne Buton, Paris, 1989.

Translations
The Barber of Seville, in *The Genius of French Theater*,
translated and edited by A. Bermel, New York, 1961.
The Barber of Seville, in *Classical French Drama*, translated
and edited by W. Fowlie, New York, 1962.
The Barber of Seville, in *"The Barber of Seville" and "The
Marriage of Figaro"*, translated by John Wood, Harmo-
ndsworth, 1964.

Criticism
(For general works on the author, see *Playwrights* volume)

Books:
Robert Niklaus, *Beaumarchais: "Le Barbier de Séville"*,
London, 1968.
Sylvie and Jacques Dauvin, *"Le Barbier de Séville" de
Beaumarchais*, Paris, 1981.

Articles:
Émile Jules François Arnould, *"Le Barbier de Séville* et la
critique"*, in *French Studies*, 16, 1962.
Sallie J. Hall, *"'Amour sans repos': Some Literary Ancestors
of *The Barber of Seville* and *The Marriage of Figaro"*, in
Comparatist, May 1988.

*   *   *

Captivated at first sight by Rosine's beauty, Count Almaviva
has followed her from Madrid to Séville where she is confined
under lock and key by her suspicious guardian, Dr. Bartholo,
who intends to make the young heiress his wife. One evening,
as he waits beneath her window for a glimpse of her, Almaviva
encounters Figaro, his former valet, now a barber in the city,
and taking advantage of Bartholo's temporary absence, he
improvises a song of love to Rosine in the guise of a penniless
suitor called Lindor, whereupon Figaro agrees to help him foil
the old man's plan and marry her. As Bartholo's barber,
Figaro gains admittance to the household, puts the servants
out of action and makes contact with Rosine before the Count
presents himself as a drunken soldier with a billeting order and
manages to pass a letter to Rosine. Donning yet another
disguise, he returns later claiming to be a pupil of Don Bazile,
Rosine's music master, and in Bartholo's presence the couple
contrive a mutual expression of love in the form of a singing
lesson before the pretence is rumbled. Finally, under cover of a
stormy night, the house is re-entered with a key filched by
Figaro and a wedding contract between the Count and Rosine
is ratified by the same notary Bartholo had summoned for this
purpose, with Figaro and a bemused (and bribed) Bazile acting
as witnesses. Bartholo arrives with a magistrate to apprehend
the intruders only to discover that he has lost a bride but may
keep her dowry in exchange.
Beaumarchais' own synopsis of the plot—"A doting old man
aims to marry his ward tomorrow; a quicker-witted young

lover forestalls him and makes her his wife the same day, under
the guardian's very nose and roof"—not only has the virtue of
brevity but situates the play firmly in the tradition of the
comedy of intrigue inherited from Plautus and Terence and,
more particularly, shows its affinity with *commedia dell'arte*. In
essence, the action is little more than a tissue of devices drawn
from Italian comedy: disguises, concealments, stealthy passing
of letters, slapstick, audible sotto voce, elaborate dramatic
irony, etc. It is as if Beaumarchais had consciously resolved to
put together an anthology of tried and trusted techniques for
raising a laugh; indeed, a comment in the preface to the
published version ("I offer you today an exceedingly gay
comedy") virtually suggests as much. What is remarkable, in
his first full-length comedy, is the sheer fluency and apparent
ease with which he keeps so many balls in the air at once and
contrives to make it consistently amusing and compelling.
In part this is attributable to the urgency of the action—the
fact that Bartholo intends to marry Rosine the following day,
then brings the ceremony forward to the same night—which
generates that sense of pace so necessary in farcical comedy
and enables Beaumarchais to create set pieces of spiralling
hilarity, like the sequence in Act III where everyone on stage is
anxious (for different reasons) to see the back of Bazile and an
epidemic of asides and whispering leads to a universal concern
for his health culminating in a chorus of "Good nights". There
are also some deft touches of theatrically self-referential
comedy, as in Almaviva's suggestion that his music-master
disguise is too conventionally stagey, and in his overhearing of
an "inaudible" stage whisper.
Superficially, the principal characters are also strongly
reminiscent of *commedia* types. Bartholo is clearly based on
Pantalone, Figaro on Arlecchino, while Almaviva and Rosine
correspond to the figures of the lovers. But there are palpable
differences. The Count has the headstrong swagger of a
hidalgo as well as a ready tongue and, significantly, he at first
proposes a seduction of Rosine, believing her to be already
married; Rosine herself is unusually mettlesome and out-
spokenly critical of her guardian's repressiveness; Bartholo is
far more astute than his *commedia* forbear, almost a match for
Figaro, and an 18th-century reactionary to boot; and Figaro,
while resourcefully aiding young love to outwit aged authority
in the accepted tradition, shows an independence of outlook
and spirit which leaves no room for deference towards his
erstwhile master. In other words, each is given a greater depth
and individuality in ways which Beaumarchais will go on to
develop in *The Marriage of Figaro* and *The Guilty Mother* and
which support the notion that he intended the three Figaro
plays to constitute an organic trilogy.
He had, after all, begun his theatrical career as a disciple of
Diderot, and his first two plays (a success and a relative failure
respectively) were serious, sentimental "drames" in the
Diderot vein. In regretting these past "errors" his preface to
The Barber of Seville is manifestly tongue-in-cheek and he
does indeed add that its chief protagonists could offer suitable
material for any kind of play. This is precisely what the trilogy
demonstrates, moving from comedy of intrigue in the first play
to "drame" in the third via a transitional piece containing
elements of both genres. It is achieved with the same central
characters, appropriately evolved, and confirms Beaumarchais's abiding loyalty to (and perhaps preference for) the
"drame".
The première of *The Barber of Seville* proved something of a
disaster, overburdened as it was with thinly veiled polemic
concerning Beaumarchais's personal affairs. (Autobiographical touches are still present in the parallel between Figaro's
theatrical career and Beaumarchais's own, and possibly even
in his name—a suggested corruption of "fils Caron," the

author's family name.) Reverting substantially to a shorter version accepted and rehearsed for production two years earlier, he quickly reworked the script in time for the second performance three days later, when it was a triumph, and the play has continued to be regularly performed ever since—1200 times to date at the Comédie-Française alone, where the entire trilogy was specially re-staged in 1989/90 to accompany the bicentenary celebrations of the Revolution.

—Donald Roy

LE BARBIER DE SÉVILLE. See **THE BARBER OF SEVILLE.**

BARTHOLOMEW FAIR
by Ben Jonson

First Publication: London, 1631.
First Production: Hope Theatre, London, 31 October 1614.

Editions
Bartholemew Fair, edited by E.A. Horsman, Cambridge, Massachusetts, 1960.
Bartholemew Fair, edited by Eugene M. Waith, New Haven, Connecticut, 1963.
Bartholemew Fair, edited by Edward B. Partridge, Lincoln, Nebraska, 1964 (Regents Renaissance Drama Series).
Bartholemew Fair, in *Ben Jonson: Three Comedies*, edited by Michael Jamieson, Harmondsworth, 1966.
Bartholemew Fair, edited by Douglas Duncan, Berkeley, California, 1972.
Bartholemew Fair, edited by G.R. Hibbard, London, 1977 (New Mermaid Series).
Bartholemew Fair in *The Complete Plays of Ben Jonson 4*, edited by G.A. Wilkes, Oxford, 1982.
Bartholemew Fair in *The Selected Plays of Ben Jonson, 1*, edited by Johanna Procter, Cambridge, 1989.

Criticism
(For general works on the author, see *Playwrights* volume)

Books:
Freda L. Townsend, *Apologie for "Bartholemew Fair": The Art of Jonson's Comedies*, New York, 1947.
Francis Teague, *The Curious History of "Bartholemew Fair"*, Lewisburg, Pennsylvania, 1985.

Articles:
J.A. Barish, "*Bartholemew Fair* and Its Puppets", in *Modern Language Quarterly*, 20, 1959.
James E. Robinson, "*Bartholemew Fair*: Comedy of Vapours", in *Studies in English Literature 1500–1900*, vol.1 no.2, 1961.
Eugene M. Wraith, "The Staging of *Bartholemew Fair*", in *Studies in English Literature 1500–1900*, vol.2 no.2, 1962.
Jackson I. Cope, "*Bartholemew Fair* as Blasphemy", in *Renaissance Drama*, 8, 1965.
Richard Levin, "The Structure of *Bartholemew Fair*", in *Publications of the Modern Language Association [PMLA]*, 80, 1965.

Barry Targan, "The Moral Structure of *Bartholemew Fair*", in *Discourse*, 8, 1965.
Lee Umphrey, "Jonson's *Bartholemew Fair* and the Popular Dramatic Tradition", in *Louisburg College Journal of Arts and Sciences*, June 1967.
Don Mager, "The Paradox of Tone in *Bartholemew Fayre*", in *Thoth*, 9, 1968.
John M. Potter, "Old Comedy in *Bartholemew Fair*", in *Criticism*, 10, 1968.
Joel H. Kaplan, "Dramatic and Moral Energy in Ben Jonson's *Bartholemew Fair*", in *Renaissance Drama* (new series), 1970.
R.B. Parker, "The Themes and Staging of *Bartholemew Fair*", in *University of Toronto Quarterly*, 39, 1970.
Vincent F. Petronella, "Jonson's *Bartholemew Fair*: A Study in Baroque Style", in *Discourse*, 13, 1970.
Calvin C. Smith, "*Bartholemew Fair*: Cold Decorum", in *South Atlantic Quarterly*, 71, 1972.
Guy Hamel, "Order and Judgement in *Bartholemew Fair*", in *University of Toronto Quarterly*, 43, 1973.
William Blissett, "Your Majesty Is Welcome to a Fair", in *The Elizabethan Theatre 4*, edited by G.R. Hibbard, Toronto, 1974.
David McPherson, "The Origins of Overdo: A Study in Jonsonian Invention", in *Modern Language Quarterly*, 37, 1976.
John Scott Colley, "*Bartholemew Fair*: Ben Jonson's 'A Midsummer Night's Dream'", in *Comparative Drama*, 11, 1977.
R. Juneja, "Eve's Flesh and Blood in Jonson's *Bartholemew Fair*", in *Comparative Drama*, vol.12 no.4, 1978–79.
J. Haynes, "Festivity and The Dramatic Economy of Jonson's *Bartholemew Fair*", in *English Literary History*, vol.51 no.4, 1984.

*   *   *

When *Bartholomew Fair* opened at the Hope Theatre on Bankside on 31 October 1614, Ben Jonson was already a playwright and masque writer of reputation, successful in the public theatre with major plays for the King's Men such as *Volpone* and *The Alchemist*, and for the Children's companies, plays such as *Poetaster* and *Epicoene*. The second night of *Bartholomew Fair* was staged before King James at court, where Jonson was well-known as the author of spectacular masques in productions by Inigo Jones. The Hope was a new theatre, used for bear-baiting as well as plays, with a demountable stage that could be taken away to accommodate blood sports; it was already, according to Jonson's Induction "as dirty as Smithfield, and as stinking every whit". The social and aesthetic distance from here to the Court represents an appropriate image for this play, where Jonson offers the widest spectrum of Stuart humanity any of his plays attempt, and where his imagination ranges freely from classical allusion to the bric-a-brac of the everyday. Jonson had many years of playwriting left to him, but in several respects *Bartholomew Fair* represents the culmination of his career, the most ambitious piece, theatrically, he ever wrote, the most diverse linguistically, and the most serious in terms of self-enquiry. If the play satirises self-confident judgements, and ridicules Puritan sentiment and anti-theatrical prejudice, it also exposes the flimsiness of theatre itself, impermant as the stage of the Hope, and an artifice, no more, in comparison with human needs, and the untidy competitiveness of the human ego. The play leaves us with an impression of the author's mind preoccupied with the density and the diversity of the world (the text is crammed with references to *things*; a production

Bartholomew Fair: Edinburgh Festival, 1951

demands a vast number of hand props), and the impossibility of charting an intellectually-defensible path through the world's ways. Such an impression sits closer to the core of Jonson's imagination, it could be argued, than the stereotyped image of the classically-learned savant and censor of morals.

The theatrical image that makes possible the heterogeneous diversity of the play, its precarious, barely-contained energies, is Bartholomew Fair itself. The Fair, established in Smithfield since 1120, and by this date an annual event, swarms in Jonson's play with no fewer than 31 characters, not counting minor figures, of whom 19 could reasonably be called principals. Such profligacy, even with intricate doubling, mimics the sprawling activity of the real Fair, and mirrors the untidy complex of competing interests that make up early Stuart society. To the Fair come visitors such as clerk-of-the-court John Littlewit and his pregnant wife Win-the-Fight; Bartholomew Cokes, a country gentleman, and his guardian Humphrey Wasp; Quarlous and Winwife, young men about town; and Zeal-of-the-Land Busy and Dame Purecraft, ardent Puritans. All come to see and judge, and in the last case to censor; but all come also to enjoy and indulge. Even Justice Adam Overdo, magistrate of Pie-Powders, and nominal overlord of the Fair, is taken in by its wiles, despite a command of the languages of authority, legal, biblical and classical. The denizens of the Fair, among them Lantern Leatherhead the hobbyhorse-seller, Joan Trash the gingerbread-woman, Jordan Knockem the horse-courser, and Punk Alice the "mistress o' the game", have a raw energy, and an absence of moral scruple, that give them the better of the naive if privileged visitors. At the core of the Fair stands the Booth of Ursula, the pig-woman, a central attraction of fleshly pursuits, "the very womb and bed of enormity" according to Overdo, where characters eat, fornicate and urinate. The physicality of the action carries through into a carnality of language that extends the visual image of Ursula's own grossness. When the play moves towards its close with a puppet-play that parodies the classical myths of Hero and Leander, the ideal lovers, and Damon and Pythias, the ideal friends, and draws attention to the fictionality of playing, we find ourselves suspended between carnival delight and a sense of the flimsiness of human reason and human society.

Bartholomew Fair is a wonderfully theatrical piece revelling in the variety of human utterance—each character has an identifying and idiosyncratic dialect—of human appearance—the Fair is crammed with costumes, disguises, trade clothes of all kinds—and of human bodily characteristics, from the slightness of Mooncalf, through Win-the-Fight's pregnancy to the vast physique of Ursula. To stage it requires huge resources, great directorial skill, adaptability and energy on the part of the actors, and an alert and understanding audience such as Jonson solicits in his Induction. The game, though, is worth the expense.

—J.R. Mulryne

THE BASIC TRAINING OF PAVLO HUMMEL
by David Rabe

First Publication: New York, 1972.
First Production: Newman Theater of the Public Theater, New York, 20 May 1971.

Criticism
(For general works on the author, see *Playwrights* volume)

Articles:
Bonnie Marranca, "David Rabe's Vietnam Trilogy", in *Canadian Theatre Review*, 14, 1977.
Barbara Hurrell, "American Self-Image in David Rabe's Vietnam Trilogy", in *Journal of American Culture*, 4, 1981.

*   *   *

In a Vietnamese brothel, Pavlo Hummel is blown apart by a grenade thrown in the window. Then the black soldier Ardell, an alter ego, appears and prompts a replay for the dying Pavlo of his army life, and this forms the fractured action of the play. In the Georgia boot-camp, Pavlo emerges as a friendless young man desperate to "belong". His quirky need to be "individual", including his way of telling tall stories to "show-boat", gets him into trouble with the other recruits. But with his inner voice of Ardell, he survives the motory brutality of basic training, and masters its physical skills. After training, he briefly re-visits his dysfunctional "family" of mother and half-brother. When he is posted to Vietnam as a medic, he experiences his first sex with a prostitute and his first real intimations of mortality when tending a human "stump". When he urgently opts for combat duty, he is wounded three times; on Ardell's prompting, he applies for a transfer back home, but instead is given the award of the Purple Heart. Then the action comes full circle—and we learn that the fatal grenade was lobbed by a fellow soldier, an older man he squabbled with over the prostitute's favors. At the end, he is goaded by Ardell to say what he now thinks of "the cause"; he repeatedly screams that it is "Shit" before Ardell slams his coffin shut.

David Rabe's *The Basic Training of Pavlo Hummel* was the first American play of stature to deal with the Vietnam war experience, by a playwright who had served there. Its first major professional production by Joseph Papp was well received and Rabe followed it with another play, *Sticks and Bones*, dealing with the return of a blind Vietnam veteran to his uncomprehending and stereotypical middle-class family. But *The Basic Training of Pavlo Hummel*, partly because it is less contrived in its technique, and partly because it presents the war directly, is the more powerful play of the two.

Rabe himself emphasises that *Pavlo Hummel* is not an "anti-war" play in the political sense, and his attitude to some of the values and skills the army inculcates seems ambivalent. Martin Gottfried (in the *New York Post*) perceptively commented in his review of the 1977 production that "Rabe has treated military basic training as an American rite . . . . [He] captures the rite uncannily and elevates it to mythic stature. And he takes the metaphor of basic training one stop further, making it a ritual that must conclude with death, whether in the army or out of it".

But the U.S. Army and its treatment of Pavlo is also a metaphor for Rabe's deeper thematic concern: the coercive power of an institution on the individual. For Pavlo finds that his "rite of passage" is a journey to nowhere, and that the army has not fostered either his individuality or his manhood. Neither does it act as a surrogate "family". At the end of Act I,

it re-fashions him into a killing mask in dress-uniform and dark glasses, and the kind of resilience it gives him accrues almost totally from his military function. In Act II, he finally begins to realise both what he has missed and what his possibilities are. But by then the institutional trap has closed and he is swallowed whole, denied even a "heroic" end in the field. Several critics felt that Pavlo remains an uncomprehending cipher, and that this weakens the play. It is true that he never achieves self-realisation and that his talent is for "leaping into the fire"; but if played resourcefully, as he was by William Atherton in the first New York production and later by Pacino on Broadway, Pavlo can be touching in his eagerness for individuality and for street-wisdom. He is an archetype for all those who lack the means within themselves to develop an identity and a sense of belonging, who look to an external "system" to provide those needs, and who are betrayed.

Two dramaturgical devices serve to "characterise" Pavlo in this way and to stress the pathos of his "incompleteness", as well as depict a potential in him that is never realised. The first is the language that Rabe uses, for it clearly establishes differences between the institutionalized, "societal" idioms of the military, and the more fractured, inchoate, and personalized talk of Pavlo himself. His co-option by military values is signalled partly by his taking over more of this imposed idiom in the later scenes of the play. The other device is more problematic: Ardell, the "invisible" black alter ego, draws Pavlo out, establishes his confusions, and forms a conduit for Pavlo's "inner self" to be manifested. But Ardell's functions are too varied, and the values of his different personae too inconsistent—conscience, devil's advocate, mentor, teacher, surrogate sergeant, "angel of death"—for the device to come into focus for the audience and register as a strong, discrete theatrical element in its own right. But this flaw does not fatally compromise the play, and the shifting functions for Ardell have their own fascination.

The scenography forms an ideal trampoline for characterisation and structure—and the structure is a perfect embodiment of the violence of the training ritual as well as that of the field, and an apt analogue for Pavlo's "progress". The training tower in the back suggests the impersonal power of the system that dominates Pavlo; and the indeterminate and fluid locations of the downstage areas, together with the area lighting, emphasise the evanescence and instability of memory and the fact that Pavlo has no clearly defined "private space" to grow in.

The Basic Training of Pavlo Hummel will surely remain one of the classic dramatic treatments of the Vietnam war, but also an enduring treatment of the theme of the individual vainly searching for sustenance and development within an indifferent institutional structure.

—Dennis Carroll

———

LES BÂTISSEURS D'EMPIRE. See **THE EMPIRE BUILDERS.**

———

BATRACHOI.   See **THE FROGS.**

———

THE BATTLES OF COXINGA (Kokusenya Kassen)
by Chikamatsu Monzaemon

First Production: Tekemoto Puppet Theatre, Osaka, 26
November 1715.

Translations
The Battles of Coxinga, in *Major Plays of Chikamatsu*,
translated by Donald Keene, New York, 1961.

*　　*　　*

The category of the play is "Jidai-mono" (History Plays)
with *Aragoto* (Rough or Bravura) style acting. It was first
performed on November 26, 1715, at the Tekemoto (Puppet)
Theatre in Osaka, destined to mark the puppet theatre's
longest, continuous performance record of all time, with a
seventeen-month long run. Revived frequently thereafter, the
play is recognized as the most popular work of Chikamatsu. It
was originally written for the puppet theatre but was almost
instantaneously adapted for Kabuki, presenting a number of
successful performances at theatres such as the Mandayū in
Kyoto (1716), and the Nakamura and Ichikawa Theatres in
Edo (Tokyo) (1717). The Edo performances represented the
first adaptation of a puppet play into the Edo Kabuki form,
which prided itself for more manly plays in contrast to Osaka
Kabuki, which did well with plays of a more gentle genre. The
earliest known dramatization, as a puppet play, of the same
historical incident was *Kokusenya Tegara Nikki* (The Diary of
Kokusenya's Successful Campaign), staged around 1703 at the
Shinanojō Theatre.

Tei Seikō (in Chikamatsu's play he appears as Watōnai,
under his Japanese name) accompanies his father, Tei Shiryū,
who was a political refugee from Ming China, to fight against
the Tartars to restore the power of the Ming Dynasty.
However, his venture was unsuccessful, and Tei Seikō retreated to Taiwan. He finally died there in 1662. Because of the
proximity of the two countries and the fact that Tei Seikō was a
half Japanese who became a famed warrior noted for bravery,
the Japanese public was well informed about the Tei Seikō
expedition and had shown considerable interest in what had
happened during his adventures. Chikamatsu's dramatization
of the story was reflective of such a time.

In Chikamatsu's play, Tei Shiryū, learning about the
downfall of the Ming Dynasty under the hands of the Tartars,
decides to go back to China with his son, Watōnai (Tei Seikō),
and his Japanese wife, to render any help he can to restore
Ming rule. They come to see Kanki, a Chinese general and the
husband of Kinshōjo, Shiryū's daughter by his Chinese wife, to
seek his help in fighting against the Tartars. But Kanki is now
an important general in service to the Tartar King, and he
refuses to cooperate on the basis that he cannot sever his
association with his lord just because he is requested to side
with his wife's relatives. But upon Kinshōjo's suicide to
eliminate that crucial obstacle to his commitment to noble
action, he decides to join his forces with Watōnai. Kanki
bestows on Watōnai the name of "Kokusenya", to signify the
honor of sharing the Emperor's name for one's distinctive
service. The mighty forces of the threesome succeed in driving
out the Tartar hordes after a great battle.

As a puppet drama, the play has a well-structured and
extensive plot of incomparable scale, comprising five acts and
twelve scenes, while as a Kabuki play, only the following
scenes of Act III are performed: "Before the Castle of Kanki",
"a Room in the Castle", "Beneath the Castle Wall" (in which
Watōnai's *aragoto* acting is famous), and the "Same Room in
the Castle".

In earlier puppet theatre practice, a humorous puppet scene
(commonly called "noroma" after the name of the puppeteer
who specialized in presenting intermission scenes) was inter-
posed between acts, following the pattern of Nō performances,
which presented a Kyōgen comedy between two Nō plays. The
puppet *entr'acte* entertainment seemed to provide a means to
cover the shortcomings of the rather brief story of the main
puppet drama as well as present an unrelated but humorous
scene to entertain the audience. *Kokusenya Kassen*, however,
was endowed with such an extensive story with fully developed
characters, that Chikamatsu dropped the relief act altogether
in order to hold the audience's attention undisturbed. It is
believed that other puppet theatres quickly followed suit, and
the interim scene was soon dropped completely. Thus,
Chikamatsu and *Kokusenya Kassen* revolutionalized the performance conventions of the puppet theatre.

Dealing with unfamiliar Chinese situations and characters
certainly presented difficult problems for Chikamatsu to
handle, but he met the challenge brilliantly and, reflecting his
extensive learning, free flowing imagination and rich skill in
providing colorful language, he was able to produce a masterpiece for all time. The play also responded sensitively to the
rising conscience of the populace about their unity as Japanese
people and their collective recognition of its proud heritage as
one unified nation.

The intricate relationships between characters created a
complex web of situations exemplifying how to live one's life in
a manner which would satisfy one's obligation to society (*giri*)
and at the same time allow one to fully express one's warmth as
a human being (*ninjō*). The instances of Kanki refusing to join
Watōnai because of his belief in unwavering loyalty to his
Master as a condition of manhood (*giri*), Kinshōjo's suicide to
eliminate the obstacle which was preventing Kanki's alliance
with Watōnai (*giri*), and the suicide of Kinshōjo's stepmother
in order to die with her stepdaughter (*giri* as well as *ninjō*), are
a few of the intricately woven threads comprising the human
fabric of feudalistic times. Watōnai's larger-than-life acting
requirements (*aragoto* style) skillfully heightens the dramatic
effect, emphasizing the clarity of social values and magnifying
the righteous deeds of brave men and women, thus enhancing
the enjoyment as an audience witnesses the unfolding of his
drama of idealism.

It is quite common for the puppet theatre and Kabuki to
share masterpieces with each other, adapting them to the
unique production style of each. *Kokusenya Kassen* is an
eloquent example of this common practice.

—Andrew T. Tsubaki

THE BEAUX' STRATAGEM
by George Farquhar

First Publication: London, 1707.
First Production: Theatre Royal, Haymarket, London, 8
March 1707.

Editions
The Beaux' Stratagem, in *George Farquhar*, edited by William
Archer, London, 1906.
The Beaux' Stratagem, edited by Bonamy Dobrée, Bristol,
1929.

The Beaux' Stratagem: Engraving after a painting by Samuel De Wilde, 1804

The Beaux' Stratagem, edited by Vincent F. Hopper and Gerald B. Lahey, Great Neck, New York, 1963.

The Beaux' Stratagem, edited by Eric Rothstein, New York, 1967.

The Beaux' Stratagem, edited by Michael Cordner, London, 1976 (New Mermaid Series).

The Beaux' Stratagem, edited by Charles N. Fifer, Lincoln, Nebraska, 1977 (Regents Restoration Drama Series).

Criticism
(For general works on the author, see *Playwrights* volume)

Books:
Raymond A. Anselment (ed.), *"The Recruiting Officer" and "The Beaux' Stratagem": A Casebook*, London, 1977.

Articles:
Martin A. Lawson, "The Influence of Milton's Divorce Tracts on Farquhar's *Beaux' Stratagem*", in *Publications of the Modern Language Association* [*PMLA*], 39, 1924.

Garland J. Gravitt, "A Primer of Pleasure: Neo-Epicurianism in Farquhar's *The Beaux' Stratagem*", in *Thoth*, 12, 1972.

Barry N. Olshen, "*Beaux' Stratagem* on the 19th Century London Stage", in *Theatre Notebook*, vol. 28 no.2, 1974.

*   *   *

The beaux, Aimwell and Archer, have spent all their money in London, and their stratagem is to descend on a provincial town, one of them posing as a peer and the other as his servant, secure a lucrative marriage, and split the proceeds. The play shows this operation in Lichfield, where the richest household, that of Lady Bountiful, also contains her unmarried and well-endowed daughter Dorinda, her descriptively named son Squire Sullen, and his stylish and discontented wife. Aimwell courts Dorinda, according to plan, but rapidly starts to fall in love with her for real, while Archer embarks on a frankly libertine courtship of Mrs. Sullen.

This "genteel comedy" scenario is complemented by a set of sub-plots featuring a cast of "humours" characters from further down the social scale: at least two of these—Sullen's manservant Scrub and the innkeeper Boniface—became star roles when the play was immediately (and lastingly) successful. The below-stairs writing has a weight and idiosyncrasy unusual in Restoration comedy; we see the gentry household from the point of view of those who serve it, live round it, or try to rob it, as well as those who own it. Indirectly, as he did directly in *The Recruiting Officer*, Farquhar is using his own military experience: arriving at the inn, chatting up the local girls, scouting around for prospects, the two strategists are behaving very like a recruiting party, and their interests coincide similarly with those of the comedy, in that their expedition is a deliberate performance which works like an exploratory drilling, exposing the different strata of the local society.

If its social amplitude is one reason to regard the play as giving a realistic turn to its genre, there's another in its exceptionally serious treatment of unhappy marriage. That wedlock is an accursed state is of course an iron convention of Restoration comedy, if only as the indispensable condition of guilt-free adultery. But Farquhar here concentrates the guerrilla raids of the rake-hero into an official campaign: the Sullens live in a state of mutual detestation, though neither has committed any actionable, marital offences, and in proposing that they ought to be allowed to separate by mutal consent, Farquhar is both domesticating the constitutionalism of the post-1688 political world, and drawing directly on that very unlibertine authority, Milton. Although Mrs. Sullen's husband is a boor whose manners depress even the local highwayman, the play accepts, with characteristic liberalism, that the Squire's hunting-and-drinking lifestyle is fairly harmless, and that if it's what he likes, it's hard on him that he's shackled to a woman whose lively elegance prevents him from enjoying it in peace.

However, critics and directors who embrace the play as an instance of social realism emerging from the shell of an artificial comic convention seem to be missing the distinctive artificiality of Farquhar's own comic technique. Towards the end of the play, the highwayman, Gibbet, breaks into Mrs. Sullen's bedroom and Archer, who is there, for dishonourable reasons, claps a pistol to his head.

Archer: Come, rogue, if you have a short prayer, say it.

Gibbet: Sir, I have no prayer at all; the government has provided a chaplain to say prayers for us on these occasions.

Archer's line is conventional; he is acting the hero to impress Mrs. Sullen. Gibbet's reply is then funny because of the way it suggests a whole alternative conventionality—its tranquil, somewhat bureaucratic register places the possibility of being instantly shot in a known class of eventualities for which there is a proper procedure. It is a glimpse of life from the highwayman's perspective in a way; an extension to

Gibbet, you could say, of the good-nature with which Far-quhar enters into the points of view of both the Sullens. But it doesn't do that realistically; rather, the shift of viewpoint is a conceit, in that it attributes to Gibbet's terms of reference exactly the same *normality* as it does to those of the law-abiding characters. Something really quite analogous is happening when Archer, in his role as manservant, claims the right to suffer from the spleen, an exclusively upper-class disorder:

> Madam, like all other fashions it wears out, and so descends to their servants: though in a great many of us, I believe, it proceeds from some melancholy particles in the blood, occasioned by the stagnation of wages.

The two-pronged witticism (servants are infected with melancholy by their employers on the level of affectation, but also on that of reality) is mordantly class-conscious. But once again, it isn't realistically "the voice" of the servant class: Archer-the-servant is taking over not only the hypochondria of his betters, but also their normative and universalising discourse. The identification is not experiential, but relaxed, intellectual, "let's-pretend"—the case is of course exceptionally clear here because Archer isn't really a servant, but is playing at it, and faking an autobiography to fit his role.

It's this playfulness which gives the script its friendliness and temperate euphoria on the stage. In its jokes, and in its more extended set-pieces of misunderstanding and deception, it's constantly constructing arbitrary normalities which hang in the air for a little as if the law of gravity had been temporarily suspended. The effect is at once farcical, whimsical, and elusively satiric—not so much recalling Farquhar's Restoration predecessors as anticipating his later countryman Wilde.

The most notable prize of this sophisticated theatricality is the ending. A blatant *deus ex machina* appears in the shape of Mrs. Sullen's wealthy and enlightened brother, who not only announces that Aimwell's elder brother has arbitrarily died, so that Aimwell really is the peer he was pretending to be, but also, apparently on his own responsibility, dissolves the Sullens' marriage. The show ends with a dance in which the two couples celebrate, respectively, their wedding and their divorce, and a choric reassurance that "Consent is law enough to set you free". This is, of course, not quite true even now, and in 1707 it wasn't true at all. It's the most impudent of the play's vindications of the space it's been exploring all along: the theatre as an enclave where reality is at the disposal of inventiveness. The inventive freedom has a real beauty, and only the crass chauvinism of the French and Irish stereotypes, which disfigures the margins of the plot, discloses its basis (explicit in the prologue) in the rather ugly imperial self-confidence of the aftermath of Blenheim and Ramillies.

—Peter Womack

THE BEDBUG (Klop)
by Vladimir Mayakovsky

First Publication: Moscow, 1929.
First Production: Meyerhold Theatre, Moscow, 13 February, 1929.

Translations
The Bedbug, translated by Max Hayward, in *"The Bedbug"*

and Selected Poetry, edited by Patricia Blake, New York, 1960.
The Bedbug, in *The Complete Plays of Vladimir Mayakovsky*, translated by G. Daniels, New York, 1968.

Criticism
(For general works on the author, see *Playwrights* volume)

Articles:
V.A. Lavrov, "Mayakovsky's Satirical Comedy *The Bedbug*", in *Soviet Studies in Literature*, vol. 2 no. 2, 1967.
Svetlana le Fleming, "An Approach to the Understanding of Mayakovsky's *Klop*", in *Journal of Russian Studies*, 30, 1975.
T. Menetrey, "The Relationship of the Fantastic Future to the Present in Mayakovsky's *Klop* and *Bania*", in *Melbourne Slavic Studies*, 17, 1983.

* * *

"The theatre is not a reflecting mirror, but a magnifying glass", wrote Vladimir Mayakovsky, thus taking issue with Hamlet in a typically daring formulation. His words are most remarkably exemplified in *The Bedbug*, a linguistically dazzling, riotously comic, satirical masterpiece.

The play concerns Ivan Prisypkin, a thorough-going proletarian, who having supported the revolution through his trade union activities, now wishes to rise in status by marrying a manicurist. This entails betraying his working-class girl friend, but even her apparent suicide leaves him unruffled and he goes to his wedding, with his friend and mentor in upward mobility, Oleg Bayan. The wedding feast degenerates into drunkenness, the stove is overturned and the place goes up in flames. By the time the fire brigade arrives, all the guests are dead, though one body cannot be accounted for.

50 years later, in a technological Utopia, the preserved body of a worker has been discovered frozen in a block of ice. It is Prisypkin, trapped in the fireman's hosed water ever since that freezing wedding night. The Institute for Human Resurrection asks the world what should be done with the find: they vote to resurrect him. But in the desiccated world of 50 years hence, in which his former girl friend, for instance, is a scientist who recalls "love" as an outlandish phenomenon, Prisypkin has no place. He is dirty, smelly, he smokes, drinks, plays the guitar, and is even infested with a bedbug, the like of which has been eradicated decades before. After a series of adventures, it is decided that the only way forward is to put him and his bedbug in the zoo. From his cage, Prisypkin sees us in the auditorium, recognizes us as fellow-creatures, appeals to us. . .but the zoo director shuts him up, apologises to us, and calls for music.

As written, the play seems hardly more than a series of sketches, and the full flavour and impact can only be obtained from a production. The point is important, because the very sketchiness of the text has led literary commentators to mistake its import. There has been much argument, for instance, about the meaning of the future as presented in the play, with apologists for communism arguing that the aridity of the fantasy shows that Mayakovsky is presenting us with Prisypkin's mistaken vision of the Soviet future, and apologists for capitalism calling it Mayakovsky's horrified vision of Soviet reality.

In fact, it is neither, being rather a thoroughly theatrical device (a magnifying glass) which aims to provide a perspective on the present. Precisely what the future might or would be like is not a subject which engages Mayakovsky here; it is simply designed to "alienate" the present which is the subject of the play. The point is that Prisypkin, and those like him,

The Bedbug: Meyerhold Theatre, Moscow, 1929 (first production)

have no place in the future, whatever that future may be, for Prisypkin is a type, not a real character; a type which Mayakovsky saw becoming more prevalent as the fervour of the revolution withered away. "There are no situations in my play which are not based on dozens of actual instances", he wrote, referring particularly to articles *Komsomolskaya Pravda* had published. The overweening and self-consciously working class proletarian, who no longer needed to respect his fellow citizens, vulgar in habits and self-indulgent in behaviour, was one of the least attractive phenomena created by the revolution. He was the target of Mayakovsky's barbs.

Thus, Oleg Bayan was created from a real poet whom Mayakovsky thought was teaching the youth of the day to adopt petit-bourgeois attitudes. His name is that of a musical instrument, as is Prisypkin's new designation—Pierre Skripkin; Pierre to match his fiancée's high falutin Elzivera Renaissance, and Skripkin, meaning a violin. Yet these comic, repulsive, complacent would-be gentlemen are frighteningly like too many of us, even today and even in societies most unlike the young Soviet Union.

The relevance of the satire is achieved in large measure through the highly original theatrical techniques, described by Eisenstein as a "montage of attractions". The attractions are presented almost as turns complete in themselves—the lascivious dance at the wedding feast, the firemen's entry and song, the science fiction-like awakening of Prisypkin in the the future. Mayakovsky insisted that the actors must indulge in "no psychologising", and Vladimir Lyutse, director of the first

Leningrad production in 1929, noted that "the actor's performance is created through the solving of a series of physical problems". This style is often thought of as a poster technique, because it sets a series of bright, brilliant images, each of which uses spare but appropriate language, side by side. Each self-contained theatrical image thus created then collides with the next to develop meaning through juxta-positioning. Thus, the image of the raucous pedlars in the auditorium is set beside that of the *soi-disant* refinement of Prisypkin and his mother-in-law-to-be, and immediately we are at the heart of the play.

This theatricality allows full scope to the inherent ambiguities: Prisypkin may be revolting, but his position as protagonist, and recipient of the dehumanised future people's emotionless treatment, certainly elicits sympathy. Is his resurrection serious or comic? Is the fire at the wedding a symbolically necessary cleansing? Why must it be put out? The action asks such questions. A major reason this play provoked the Stalinist apparatchiks to fury is precisely because it asks questions, and refrains from providing glib, predetermined answers. Its magnifying glass scrutiny revealed flaws and problems which a more conventional dramatic technique might have missed, and it did it by unexpected theatricality.

—Robert Leach

BEFORE DAWN (Vor Sonnenaufgang)
by Gerhart Hauptmann

First Publication: Berlin, 1889.
First Production: Lessingtheater, Berlin, 20 October 1889.

Editions
Vor Sonnenaufgang, edited by Brigitte E. Schatzky, Oxford, 1964.

Translations
Before Dawn, in *The Dramatic Works of Gerhart Hauptmann, 1*, London and New York, 1916.
Before Dawn, translated by Richard Newnham in *Three German Plays*, London, 1963.
Before Daybreak, translated by Peter Bauland, Chapel Hill, North Carolina, 1978.
Before Sunrise, translated by James Joyce, edited by Jill Perkins, Huntington Library, San Marino, California, 1978.

Criticism
(For general works on the author, see *Playwrights* volume)

Books:
Reiner Poppe, *Gerhart Hauptmann: "Vor Sonnenaufgang"; "Die Weber"; "Der Biberpelz": soziales Engagement und politisches Theater*, Hollfeld, 1978.

Articles:
Gerhard Schulz, "Gerhart Hauptmanns *Vor Sonnenaufgang*", in *Germanisch-Romanische Monatsschrift*, 14, 1964.
Halina Filipowicz, "Dream and Death in Gerhart Hauptmann's *Vor Sonnenaufgang* and Eugene O'Neill's *Beyond the Horizon*", in *Acta Universitatis Wratislaviensis*, 233, 1974.
Rüdiger Bernhardt, "Gerhart Hauptmanns *Vor Sonnenaufgang*", in *Weimarer Beiträge*, 30, 1984.
John Osborne, "Gerhart Hauptmanns *Vor Sonnenaufgang*: zwischen Tradition und Moderne", in *Deutschunterricht*, vol. 40 no. 2, 1988.
Raleigh Whitinger, "Gerhart Hauptmann's *Vor Sonnenaufgang*: On Alcohol and Poetry in German Naturalist Drama", in *German Quarterly*, 63, 1990.

*   *   *

Alfred Loth, a young Berlin economist with strongly-held views on eugenics and alcoholism, arrives in Witzdorf to research the impact of new industry on the community. He looks up a former student associate, Hoffmann, now managing a mining company and married to the daughter of Krause, a local farmer. Loth's personality and refreshingly new ideas attract Helene Krause, Hoffmann's sister-in-law, and a love affair develops. When, thanks partly to the intervention of the local doctor, the stark truth dawns on Loth that he has joined a family of alcoholics, he leaves Witzdorf precipitately. Helene kills herself in despair.

Alcoholism is ostensibly the central concern of Hauptmann's first play right from the initial drink which Hoffmann offers and Loth refuses. Its physical and psychological effects were a burning issue in 1889, and Hauptmann skilfully combines it with the Ibsenesque technique of the outsider arriving to spark off a ripe situation in this pioneering example of Naturalist drama in Germany. Ibsen, Fontane and the Berlin director Otto Brahm hailed the play as an exciting artistic breakthrough, and its turbulent premiere at a matinee performance given by the Berlin *Frei Bühne* (Free Stage Society) is remembered as a landmark in German theatrical history. It was certainly a bold stroke to take a typical representative of the new scientifically educated and sociologically aware generation and make him the unwitting agent of a tragic exposure of a sick society; in doing so Hauptmann adapted the classical technique of *Oedipus* to a situation symptomatic of the capitalist industrial age. But *Before Dawn* is also a drama deeply concerned with human beings and their vulnerability to the multiple pressures exerted upon them and within them by modern life; it gives dramatic expression to their need for understanding and affection, and conveys their longing to escape the limitations of their social circumstances: Helene demonstrates this need in her urgent love for Loth; Hoffmann reveals it in his desire to make money; old Krause demonstrates it in his addiction to drink. Hauptmann's indictment of the impact of industry on an agrarian society is harsh, but his satire is offset by a greater compassion for a set of characters who are powerless to resist the momentum of a socio-economic change, graphically conveyed, as the curtain goes up on Act I, by the setting, a modernized farmhouse; "urban affluence grafted onto rural poverty", says the stage direction.

The Naturalist tenets (heredity, environment and the pressure of the moment) are all firmly adhered to in the drama, yet their presence is for the most part unobtrusive since the tragic human implications transcend physical dimensions. Admired by many early spectators as a brave act, Loth's abandonment of Helene for the sake of his principles is now generally seen as an implicit condemnation of the one who got away: it is perhaps significant that Hauptmann modelled this problematic character with his rigid views on a contemporary who later became a prominent Nazi racial theorist. It is characteristic of the deeper allusiveness of Hauptmann's apparently colloquial, realistic text that Loth flees depraved, benighted Witzdorf as his biblical namesake Lot fled Sodom and Gomorrah. The play is rich in subtle textual and visual detail of this kind, most notably the extended opening to Act II during which nothing happens on stage apart from the fact that dawn gradually breaks over the Witzdorf countryside: the detailed stage directions here heralded a revolution in theatrical production and stage lighting which the original producer Otto Brahm responded to with sensitivity and technical innovation.

—Peter Skrine

_____

BEFORE DAYBREAK.   See **BEFORE DAWN.**

_____

BEFORE SUNRISE.   See **BEFORE DAWN.**

_____

THE BEGGAR (Der Bettler)
by Reinhard Sorge

First Publication: Berlin, 1912.
First Production: Deutsches Theater, Berlin, 23 December 1917.

Criticism

(For general works on the author, see *Playwrights* volume)

Books:

Martin Rockenbach, *"R.J. Sorge: Studien zu Sorges kunstlerischen Schaffen Berücksichtigung der dramatischen Sendung "Der Bettler"*, Leipzig, 1923.

Articles:

Stephen Shearier, "Modernist Consciousness and Mass Culture: Alienation in *Der Bettler* by Reinhard Sorge", in *German Studies Review*, 11, 1988.

*   *   *

The action of this five act play, subtitled *Eine dramatische Sendung (A Dramatic Mission)*, takes place in Berlin; it traces the spiritual and psychological development of a young man in his various roles as Poet, Son and Lover. The Poet strives to realize his "holy" vocation, that is, to transform a decadent society into a nobler one; for this he must first undertake a pilgrimage into the mystical realms of poetic vision. As Son and Youth (Lover) he must overcome the dominance of his parents—which he does, symbolically, in the killing of both—and return the love of the Young Girl, in order to achieve manhood. He finally allows his beloved to join him in a twofold role: as mother of their future child, and as his "pilgrim's staff" on his spiritual journey. Biological renewal thus parallels a mystical renewal: "I want to take the world onto my shoulders and carry it to the sun with songs of praise".

Sorge understood the title *Der Bettler* to be symbolic of his "yearning hunger and prayer to Heaven" at a time when he had not yet "found God". (He converted to Roman Catholicism in 1913). The first full-length expressionist play to appear in book form—apart from Kokoschka's ten-page sketch *Murderer, Hope of Women*—it established the key features of expressionist drama. Although the play's division into five acts suggests a traditional form, its intrinsic structure of seemingly loosely-connected scenes with alternating realistic and dream episodes reveals, in fact, a *Stationendrama* which depicts the transformation theme already found in August Stindberg's *To Damascus*, and developed later by Georg Kaiser, August Stramm, and Ernst Toller.

Because the *dramatis personae* of *Der Bettler* are nameless types the audience is reminded that they are an expression of the author's vision rather then a realistic representation of individual characters. Another aspect typical of expressionist drama is the play's inherent criticism of outlived tradition; in this case Sorge, through the voice of the Critics, attacks neoromantic drama, especially that of Ernst Hardt and Gerhart Hauptmann. The new poet proclaimed in *Der Bettler* also distances himself from the elitist character of art championed by the George circle. His art is meant to be universal in order to reach all mankind. The Poet, therefore, asks his mentor to finance a new mass-theatre for the purpose of fulfilling his vision. But, typically, he is neither understood by his mentor, nor by the Friend (Botho Graef) whom he leaves. The Poet realizes that his role is that of an outsider who must pursue his visionary mission alone.

Like *To Damascus, Der Bettler* belongs to the genre of *Ich-Drama* because of its many autobiographical elements. The protagonist, the Poet, is Sorge himself, as are the Son and the Youth; he is also the poet in the play within the play. In this highly complex dramatic structure, Sorge has the Poet declare *Der Bettler* to be his manuscript which he just finished, thus doubling as author and main character. However, after this statement the Poet slips back into his original role. Like Sorge at that time, the Poet expresses the need for a transcendental experience which will enable him to find a new symbolic language with which to express the unspeakable and the eternal which he perceives as the essence of art. Only then can he fulfill his mission: to "renew mankind through the spirit". Although Sorge does not speak of the "New Man", his protagonist is quite clearly a forerunner of this figure so prominent in German expressionist drama.

Other autobiographical events relate to Sorge's father, a master builder, who died in a mental institution; the Father of the play is grotesquely mad, drumming away on a child's drum, stabbing a young bird with his pen to use its blood for colouring his useless drawings, and designing bizarre machines which—in his megalomanic vision—would be at once beneficial for mankind while being capable of destroying it. The Son poisons the Father (and inadvertently the Mother) in order to free him from his mental anguish; but underlying the Son's motive is the desire to liberate himself from an overpowering, traditional father-figure who has stifled his psychological and spiritual development; furthermore, the Father symbolizes the threat of a new technology which will run amok if not stopped. This episode represents the climax of the Son's deliberate severance from the external world; his only ally is the Young Girl, but she cannot be considered an equal partner since her love and admiration for him are so unconditional—she is even willing to forsake her child by another man—that she, in effect, effaces herself. The Young Girl is modelled after Suzanne Hendewerk, Sorge's future wife; in the play's family episode she is even called Susanne by the Son.

Like many young writers, Sorge attempted to incorporate into this work too much private experience and ecstatic, even romantic, visions of his art; the play lacks restraint and discipline and its style is uneven. Yet the artistic novelty of *Der Bettler* outweighs its weaknesses. What Sorge possessed undisputedly was a truly ingenious instinct for theatricality. He introduced, for example, simultaneous scenes, special lighting effects (spot-lights, fade-ins, black-outs), and an imaginative use of curtains and staircases. In Act I he also documents, in "staccato" fashion, the easy pleasures of the mindlessly decadent society of pre-War Berlin. Sorge's stage directions—contrary to those of a number of expressionist dramas—are completely performance-oriented and effective. Thus *Der Bettler*'s successful premiere under Max Reinhardt was due largely to Sorge's grasp and display of modern stage techniques, all contributing to the play's importance as a document of early expressionist drama.

—Renate Benson

THE BEGGAR'S OPERA
by John Gay

First Publication: London, 1728.
First Production: Lincoln's Inn Fields, London, 1728.

Editions

The Beggar's Opera, edited by F.W. Bateman, London, 1934.
The Beggar's Opera, edited by Edgar V. Roberts and Edward Smith, Lincoln, Nebraska, 1968 (Regents Restoration Drama Series).
The Beggar's Opera, edited by Peter Elfed Lewis, Edinburgh, 1973.

The Beggar's Opera: Haymarket Theatre, London, 1940

The Beggar's Opera in *John Gay: Dramatic Works*, edited by John Fuller, Oxford, 1983 (2 vols.).

The Beggar's Opera, edited by Bryan Loughrey and T.O. Treadwell, Harmondsworth, 1986.

Criticism
(For general works on the author, see *Playwrights* volume)

Books:

Charles E. Pearce, *"Polly Peachum," Being the Story of Lavinia Fenton (Duchess of Bolton) and "The Beggar's Opera"*, London, 1913.

Frank Kidson, *"The Beggar's Opera": Its Predecessors and Successors*, Cambridge, 1922.

Charles E. Pearce, *"Polly Peachum. The Story of Polly" and "The Beggar's Opera"*, London, 1923.

David Harrison Stevens, *Some Immediate Effects of "The Beggar's Opera"*, Chicago, 1923.

William Eben Schultz, *Gay's "Beggar's Opera": Its Content, History and Influence*, New Haven, Connecticut, 1923.

Yvonne Noble (ed.), *Twentieth-Century Interpretations of "The Beggar's Opera"*, Englewood Cliffs, New Jersey, 1975.

Peter Lewis, *The Beggar's Opera*, London, 1976.

Harold Bloom (ed.), *John Gay: "The Beggar's Opera"*, New York, 1988 (Modern Critical Interpretations).

Articles:

S. Goulding, "Eighteenth Century French Taste and *The Beggar's Opera*", in *Modern Language Review*, July, 1929.

A.V. Berger, "*The Beggar's Opera*, the Burlesque, and the Italian Opera", in *Music and Letters*, 17, 1936.

Bertrand H. Bronson, "*The Beggar's Opera*", in *University of California Publications in English*, vol.8 no.2, 1941; also in *Restoration Drama: Modern Essays in Criticism*, edited by John Loftis, New York, 1966.

C.F. Burgess, "The Genesis of *The Beggar's Opera*", in *Cithara*, 2, 1962.

M. Goberman, "Mr. John Gay's *The Beggar's Opera*", in *Music Review*, February 1963.

M. Goberman, "Political Satire: John Gay's *The Beggar's Opera*" in *Midwest Quarterly*, 6, 1965.

J. Preston, "Ironic Mode: A Comparison of *Jonathon Wild* and *The Beggar's Opera*", in *Essays in Criticism*, 16, 1966.

R.M. Wardler, "Hazlitt on *The Beggar's Opera*", in *South Atlantic Quarterly*, Spring 1971.

William A. McIntosh, "Handel, Walpole and Gay; The Aims of *The Beggar's Opera*", in *Eighteenth Century Studies*, 7, 1974.

Dieter Schulz, "Zur Funktion der Songs in John Gays *Beggar's Opera*", in *Deutsche Vierteljahrsschrift für Literatur-wissenschaft und Geistesgeschichte*, 49, 1975.

J.T. Klein, "Satire in a New Key: The Dramatic Function of the Lyrics of *The Beggar's Opera*", in *Michigan Academician*, 9, 1977.

Carolyn Kephardt, "An Unnoticed Forerunner of *The Beggar's Opera*", in *Music and Letters*, vol.61 nos. 3–4, 1980.

Peter E. Lewis, "The Uncertainty Principle in *The Beggar's Opera*", in *Durham University Journal*, 72, 1980.

Lowell Lindgren, "*Camilla* and *The Beggar's Opera*", in *Philological Quarterly*, vol.59 no.1, 1980.

Richard J. Salmon, "Two Operas for Beggars: A Political Reading", in *Theoria*, 57, 1981.

Michael Denning, "Beggars and Thieves", in *Literature and History*, Spring 1982.

Yvonne Noble and Nicholas Temperley, "*The Beggar's Opera* (1953 and 1983)" [comparison of film and television versions], in *Eighteenth-Century Life*, vol.10 no.2, 1986.

*   *   *

To the theatregoing public, John Gay and *The Beggar's Opera* are virtually synonymous. This highly original work, the first ballad opera, is his masterpiece, and is one of the very few 18th-century plays that have survived in the theatre to become classics of English drama. First staged by John Rich at the Lincoln's Inn Fields theatre which he managed, *The Beggar's Opera* has gone down in theatre history as the play that made "Rich gay and Gay rich". Following its unprecedentedly successful opening run in 1728, it exerted a powerful influence during the following decades, creating a vogue for ballad operas and ballad farces, but it has also had an impact on the 20th century via Bertolt Brecht. Exactly 200 years after its initial production, Brecht closely modelled his *Die Dreigroschenoper* (*The Threepenny Opera*) on Gay's ballad opera, combining words and music in a similar way to produce an entertaining yet satirically provocative piece of music-theatre.

Although *The Beggar's Opera* overshadows Gay's other dramatic work, it is by no means unprecedented in his output for the theatre. In his first play, *The Mohocks*, he explores the potential of dramatic burlesque and parody, something he does more fully and successfully in *The What D'Ye Call It*, a popular afterpiece in the 18th century. The controversial *Three Hours after Marriage* (1717), in which Gay was aided by two other members of the Scriblerus Club, Pope and Arbuthnot, contains some burlesque elements, but is really an amusing and caustic Scriblerian satire in the guise of a farcical comedy. Gay's great achievement in *The Beggar's Opera* is to integrate such disparate ingredients as dramatic burlesque (mainly of Italian opera), Scriblerian social and political satire, and attacks on individuals (chiefly the Prime Minister, Sir Robert Walpole) by developing the ironic methods he experimented with in *The Mohocks* and especially *The What D'Ye Call It*.

In 1728 *The Beggar's Opera* was a daring satire as well as a radically new departure in opera because of its use of popular tunes and of "low" subject matter. Indeed it is partly a burlesque of the dominant operatic form of the time, Italian opera, and Gay's attribution of an "opera" to a "beggar" would have seemed disorientating and even paradoxical. *The Beggar's Opera* can also be seen as a lively and humorous comedy with unconventional characters and an unusual setting—"a Newgate pastoral, among the whores and thieves there" (a prophetic phrase used by Swift in a letter to Pope in 1716, in which he suggests that Gay should write such a work). At the same time it is the love story of the promiscuous but engaging rogue, Macheath, and the comparatively innocent and utterly devoted Polly—a love story that appeals to the emotions and at times achieves genuine pathos. But if the play is, in one way, a low-life romance with Macheath as hero and Polly as heroine, it is simultaneously an anti-romance with Macheath as anti-hero and Polly as anti-heroine, ridiculing the sentimentality and spurious heroics of much serious, contemporary drama and opera. The characters exist at two levels: as anti-types at the burlesque level, and in their own right at the non-burlesque level. *The Beggar's Opera* is plainly a most complex work in which Gay achieves a delicate balance between comedy and pathos, thus avoiding both cynicism and sentimentality. Such textual instability and uncertainty are also typical of Gay's best poetry.

Today Gay's burlesque of Italian opera can be appreciated only by stretching the historical imagination, but if he had not been intent on devising an antidote to this immensely popular foreign import, he would not have revitalized English opera by creating the new form of the ballad opera, alternating speech and songs. As a music lover, Gay did not object to all-sung Italian opera as such, only to the snobbish vogue it enjoyed with fashionable London audiences. With the exception of an overture to reinforce the burlesque resemblance to Italian opera, none of the music for *The Beggar's Opera* was specially composed. Gay wrote the words for all 69 airs with well-known tunes in mind, many being ballads—hence the name given to the new form. While pretending to offer a conventional opera, even adhering to the three-act structure of operas rather than the five-act form of regular plays, he turns the operatic world upside-down, substituting a cross-section of the contemporary London underworld for the expected mythological or courtly settings and characters. Instead of noble actions, dignified emotions, and refined language, Gay provides crime, double-dealing, lechery, and the argot of highwaymen. In doing so, he drew on the careers of the two best-known criminals of the 1720s, Jack Sheppard and Jonathan Wild, both of whom were hanged shortly before Gay wrote the play. Polly's father, Peachum, is closely modelled on Wild, a particularly accomplished exponent of organised crime.

In a couple of earlier plays, Gay shows how burlesque can be transmuted into ironic social and political satire, but does not exploit this technique. In *The Beggar's Opera*, however, he systematically adapts his mock-heroic reversals for satirical purposes, using such burlesque inversions as Macheath's role as an "operatic" hero in order to expose the corrupt values of high society and Walpole's Government. Although the descriptions of Macheath as a "Gentleman" and a "great Man" are in one sense deeply ironic, he proves to be just as deserving of such labels as many of those in the beau monde, Parliament, and the army to whom they are applied. Gay uses this two-way irony to suggest that the behaviour of outwardly respectable men of position and power is often morally indistinguishable from that of criminals. *The Beggar's Opera* therefore provides a panoramic survey of the distorted moral values and perverted human relationships produced at all social levels by urban life. For Gay, self-interest and greed are the main driving forces of urban society, from the aristocracy to the underworld, and money is both the the principal goal aimed at and the standard for measuring success. To convey a world dominated by Hobbesian "interest", Gay appropriately constructs a plot based on a series of betrayals, deceptions, and reversals, including the totally unexpected burlesque reversal at the end when Macheath is reprieved in order to secure the happy ending obligatory in opera, no matter how arbitrarily it is imposed.

The comic surface of *The Beggar's Opera* does not mask Gay's underlying seriousness, but his approach is never portentous, and his satire is so successful because of the wit and vitality with which it is presented in a most enjoyable and brilliantly theatrical play. Perhaps what is of most lasting value is the almost anarchic spirit in which Gay questions conventional assumptions and subverts orthodox social values and prejudices. By creating a topsy-turvy world in which a highwayman is a hero and criminals are shown to be less reprehensible than politicians and lawyers, Gay exposes the sandy foundations on which the status quo of public morality is established. He also subjects words like "honesty", "friendship", and "duty" to a penetrating scrutiny that reveals the way in which they are often abused and rendered meaningless. Like most great works of art, *The Beggar's Opera* can be appreciated at many levels.

—Peter Lewis

LES BELLES-SOEURS.   See **THE SISTERS-IN-LAW.**

THE BELLS
by Leopold Lewis

First Publication: London, 1871.
First Production: Royal Lyceum Theatre, London, 25 November 1871.

Editions
The Bells, in *Nineteenth Century Plays*, edited by George Rowell, London, 1953; second edition, London, 1972.
The Bells, in *Hiss the Villain*, edited by Michael R. Booth, London, 1964.
The Bells, in *Nineteenth Century British Drama*, edited by L.R.N. Ashley, Glenview, Illinois, 1967.

Criticism
(For general works on the author, see *Playwrights* volume)

Books:
David Mayer (ed.), *Henry Irving and The Bells*, Manchester, 1980 (Irving's script, with original music and memoir).

*   *   *

Adapted from a French play, *Le Juif polonais* by Erckmann-Chatrien, *The Bells* is a melodrama in three acts. On Christmas Eve, exactly 15 years after the unsolved mystery of the murder of a Polish Jew near the village, the story of which is told early in Act I, the prosperous burgomaster and innkeeper Mathias is troubled by the sound of sleigh bells, which nobody else in the room can hear. After the company has departed, Mathias hears the bells again and is terrified to see a vision of snow-covered country, the Jew in his sleigh, and a man with an axe following the sleigh. The Jew fixes his eyes on Mathias, who falls senseless as the act ends. In Act II the convalescent burgomaster is determined to hurry on the marriage of his daughter Annette with Christian, the gendarme of the village. He reflects on his cunning in arranging this marriage and upon his prosperity, which dates from the murder of the Polish Jew and the disappearance of his money belt weighted with gold. The bells ring again, but Mathias defies them. In Act III the revellers celebrating the signing of the marriage contract retire from Mathias's bedroom. A Court of Justice materialises mysteriously on the stage, and Mathias, accused before it of the murder of the Jew, is hypnotised by a Court-appointed mesmerist into a detailed re-enactment of his crime. The Court condemns Mathias to death; the stage lights go down, and the wedding party enters in the morning only to discover a haggard Mathias trying to tear an imaginary rope from his neck. As he falls dead, the sound of bells ceases.

Although *The Bells* is one of the best-known melodramas of the 19th century, in several respects it fits uneasily into this category. The central character, Mathias, is hardly a hero, but despite his past crime is not really a villain either. Christian, whose youth is appropriate to melodramatic heroism, is a nullity of a character, matching in insignificance the nominal heroine, Annette. There is almost no action and certainly no happy ending, although it might be said that virtue triumphs (ultimately) in the death of Mathias. Indeed, we call *The Bells* a melodrama for want of a better word. The play was ahead of its time as a psychological drama, reflecting the intense interest of mid- and late Victorians in the complexities of the human mind, symptoms of this interest including a fascination with mesmerism, automatic writing, spiritualism, and the like. The conflict in *The Bells* is between Mathias's fear of exposure and his unshakeable respectability in the village. Notwithstanding conventional views of the play, Mathias shows no signs of conscience, and is only concerned lest his crime should be found out. The weirdness and supernatural quality of the phantom Court of Justice that convicts him is not psychologically modern, however, but quite in the long melodramatic tradition of spectres and the horrifically abnormal.

The Bells is notable in two other respects. In terms of staging, the vision of the Polish Jew in his sleigh which Mathias sees at the end of Act I is an excellent example of a standard feature of Victorian stage machinery, the "rise and sink", in which the back scene, in this case the wall of a room in an inn, is constructed in two halves, the top half then rising into the flies and the bottom sinking through the stage to reveal a fully set and painted tableau behind. The Court scene in Act III was the result of another common feature of contemporary staging, the painting of a scene—the wall of Mathias's bedroom—on a gauze, which illuminated from the front resembled the prosaic wall it was supposed to be. Lit from behind, however, the wall disappeared and the Court was revealed, the gauze remaining down to give the scene a suitably misty and eerie appearance. Such a method was adopted for the revelation of visions in dreams and in stressful moments of waking life. *The Bells* is also notable in that it made the creator of Mathias on the English stage, Henry Irving, into a star, after 15 years of acting with provincial companies and in several London theatres. Mathias was Irving's most popular part with the public, and he played it over 800 times.

—Michael R. Booth

The Bells: Royal Lyceum Theatre, London, 1871 (first production)

BENKEI IN THE BOAT (Funa-Benkei)
by Kanze Kojirō Nobumitsu

First Production: Unknown

Translations

Benkei in the Boat, in *The Noh Drama: Ten Plays from the Japanese*, translated by Nippon Gakajutsu Shinokai, Tokyo, 1960.

*   *   *

The Category of the Play is V, Kiri Nō (Program Concluding Play) with a designation of "hataraki-mono" (war-dance piece), in two acts. There is no record of any early performance. There is an entry dated April 2 of 1595 in the *Record of Lord Genkyo*, which deals with an annotation on the play. The source of the play is an incident of a youthful general, Minamoto no Yoshitsune (1159–1189), leaving Kyoto to flee from the pursuit of his half-brother, Yoritomo (1147–1199), which appeared in several records, such as *Azuma Kagami* (as an incident of November 6, 1185); *Gempei Seisuiki*, Vol. 46; *Heike Monogatari*, Vol. 12. However, none mentions Yoshit-

sune's parting from his mistress, Shizuka, nor his tempestuous encounter with the ghost of Taira-no-Tomomori. Thus these two important elements of the play are believed to have been added by the playwright. In Act. I, Yoshitsune has contributed brilliantly to the victory of the Minamoto clan over the Taira after a series of battles which finally ended in 1185. The relationship of Yoshitsune to his half-brother, Yoritomo, the Commander in Chief of the Clan, deteriorated quickly afterwards due to an over-jealous report by Yoritomo's lieutenant that Yoshitsune was plotting to overthrow Yoritomo. Yoshitsune has vacated his position in the capital (Kyoto) as his brother's deputy chief and fled to the beach of Daimotsu (in today's Osaka Prefecture) to embark on a trip to Western Japan to seek out a protector. Yoshitsune was accompanied only by several of his loyal retainers and his mistress, Lady Shizuka. Accepting the advice of his top retainer, Benkei, Yoshitsune bids farewell to Lady Shizuka before the group leaves on a boat trip. Shizuka dances Chū-no-mai (or sometimes Jo-no-mai), dance steps accompanied only by instrumental music, without choral chanting, after she expresses her encouragement with her dance and accompanying choral chant for a restoration of the friendly union between the brothers.

In Act II, with the help of a boatman, the group sets off on a sea voyage. Despite a calm sea at the outset, Yoshitsune's trip is disrupted by an intense storm caused by the appearance of the ghosts of the lost warriors of the Taira Clan. They are led by General Taira-no-Tomomori, who repeatedly and viciously attacks Yoshitsune with the dance movement known as *hataraki*. However, the determined defense by Yoshitsune, supported by Benkei, who offers a furious prayer, successfully vanquishes the ghost of Tomomori, and it eventually vanishes among the waves.

This is one of the most popular Nō plays due to the diverse dramatic elements contained in a single play. The *shite*, the lead actor, will play both the roles of Shizuka and Tomomori: a great challenge for an actor to play two dramatically different characters within a play. Benkei, who is the *waki*, the secondary actor, has more than the usual amount of participation in the play, as he performs a pivotal function in Yoshitsune's action. *Ai-Kyōgen*, the boatman, played by a Kyōgen actor, will be involved in a dialogue with Benkei while rowing the boat. The sequence indicates an advanced stage in the development of the *Ai-Kyōgen* as a useful character to enrich a dramatic situation, just as Sophocles successfully integrated the second actor and the chorus to strengthen his tragedies.

The role of Yoshitsune is played by a boy between the ages of 10 and 14 who has already accumulated a considerable experience as a young Nō actor. Having a child (*ko-kata*) play the role of such an illustrious character as Yoshitsune (or an emperor) is due to three significant reasons. The first is a matter of the aesthetic distance. Nō tries to avoid too realistic a portrayal of a character whose identity could be misconstrued as that of the actor himself. A child playing an adult will ensure such a confusion is not created. The second reason is simply to give an opportunity for a talented child actor to expand his acting experience, and the third is the fact that a child actor tends to have what Zeami calls "the flower of a beginner", which elicits from the audience a gentle, warm and natural admiration for a not too overly contrived performances of a *ko-kata*.

Utilizing an historical situation, Nobumitsu created a truly dramatic story, encompassing the sorrow of parting, the courage of youth, and the intense vengeance of a fallen general, all in a single play.

—Andrew T. Tsubaki

BERENICE (Bérénice)
by Jean Racine

First Publication: Paris, 1671.
First Production: Théâtre de l'Hôtel de Bourgogne, Paris, 21 November, 1670.

Editions
Bérénice, edited by Robert Edward Pellisier, New York, 1915.
Bérénice, edited by W.S. Maguinness, Manchester, 1929.
Bérénice, edited by Daniel Mornet, Paris, 1934.
Bérénice, edited by C.L. Walton, 1965.
Bérénice, edited by Magdeleine Jacques-Benoist, Paris, 1966.

Translations
Bérénice, in *Jean Racine: Five Plays*, translated by Kenneth Muir, London and New York, 1960.
Bérénice, in *The Complete Plays of Jean Racine* (2 vols.), translated by Samuel Solomon, New York, 1967.
Berenice, in *"Andromache" and other plays*, translated by John Cairncross, Harmondsworth, 1967.

Criticism
(For general works on the author, see *Playwrights* volume)

Books:
G. Michaut, *La "Bérénice" de Racine*, Paris, 1907.
James J. Supple, *Racine: Bérénice*, London, 1986.
Jacques Morel, *Racine: La Romaine, la Turque et la Juive: Regards sur "Bérénice", "Bajazet", "Athalie"*, Aix-en-Provence, 1986.

Articles:
Lacy Lockert, "Racine's *Bérénice*", in *Romanic Review*, 30, 1939.
F. Fergusson, "Action as Rational: Racine's *Bérénice*", in *Hudson Review*, vol. 1 no. 2, 1948.
Sylvie Chevalley, "Les Deux *Bérénice*", in *Revue d'histoire du théâtre*, 22, 1970.
Pierre Han, "'Vraisement' and 'Decorum': A Note on the Baroque in *Samson and Agonistes* and *Bérénice*", in *Seventeenth Century News*, 1971.
Sandra Soares, "Time in *Bérénice*", in *Romance Notes*, 15, 1973.
William M. Evans, "Does Titus Really Love Bérénice?", in *Romance Notes*, 15, 1974.
Martin Mueller, "The Truest Daughter of Dido: Racine's *Bérénice*", in *Canadian Review of Comparative Literature*, 1, 1974.
J. Whatley, "L'Orient Desert: *Bérénice* and *Antony and Cleopatra*", in *University of Toronto Quarterly*, 44, 1975.
Robert Emory, "*Bérénice* and the Language of Sight", in *Romance Notes*, 19, 1978.
J.A. Dainard, "The Power of the Spoken Word in *Bérénice*", in *Romance Review*, 67, 1976.
Noémi Hepp, "Le Personage de Titus dans *Bérénice*: Essai de mise au point", in *Travaux de linguistique et de littérature* (Strasbourg), 18, 1979.
Marie-Odile Sweetser, "Néron et Titus vis par Racine", in *French Literature Series*, 8, 1981.
Pierre Hans, "Adieu: *Raison d'état* as Dramatic Motivation in *Bérénice*", in *Nottingham French Studies*, vol. 22 no. 1, 1983.
Jessica Muns, "Thomas Otway's *Titus and Berenice* and Racine's *Bérénice*", in *Restoration*, vol. 7 no. 2, 1983.

*   *   *

Antiochus, King of Comagène, has for five years secretly loved Bérénice, Queen of Palestine. She loves, and has been brought to Rome by, the Emperor Titus who wishes to marry her. But Titus hesitates in the face of the disapproval of the Roman Senate, and Bérénice is perturbed at his apparent change in feelings. Titus finally decides to send Bérénice back to Palestine. He asks Antiochus to inform the Queen of his decision, who does so, abandoning all hope of a successful outcome for himself. Bérénice is surprised and indignant, and insists on hearing her fate from Titus in person. He gives as his reason the interests of Rome, but Bérénice by her pleas succeeds in shaking his resolve. Titus is called away to the Senate. When he returns he finds the Queen threatening to commit suicide, causing him to envisage taking his own life also. Antiochus reveals his love for Bérénice to Titus and announces his departure from Rome. Moved by the example of the two men, Bérénice finds the strength for her own renunciation, and the play concludes with the three main characters aware that they will never see each other again.

The composition and production of *Bérénice* was the occasion of the final confrontation between the past master of classical tragedy, Pierre Corneille, and his young challenger, Racine. The latter's play was first performed at the Hôtel de Bourgogne in Paris on 21 November 1670, and just a week later Corneille's *Tite et Bérénice* was given by Molière's troupe at the Palais Royal. The subject of *Bérénice* was probably suggested to Racine by Henriette d'Angleterre, Louis XIV's sister-in-law, who may have wished to remind the King of a past romance between them. It has also been suggested that Bérénice's line to Titus—"You are the Emperor, Lord, and yet you weep"—is reminiscent of the remark made to the King by Marie Manicini when he was forced to leave her: "You weep and yet you are the master".

The confrontation between Corneille and Racine may also have been inspired by Henriette d'Angleterre, but there is no real evidence, and it would seem more likely that Corneille himself decided to challenge his young rival. In the event, he would probably have done better to refrain, for if the success of his play was honourable, it was far outstripped by that of Racine's which, in the author's own words, attracted as many people to its 30th performance as it had to its first.

But Racine, too, would seem to have been working with Corneille in mind. Indeed, he challenges the old master on his own territory, for *Bérénice* is the most Cornelian of all his works, with a setting taken from Roman history and a plot devoted to the conflict between personal desires and duty to the State. There the resemblance ends, however, and in his preface Racine states explicitly how his conception of tragic dramaturgy differs from that of certain of his comtemporaries—a clear allusion to Corneille. Whereas they criticized his work for its lack of incident, Racine advocates simplicity, and claims that true skill in writing tragedy lies not in the manipulation of an unrealistically complicated plot, but in the constructing of "something out of nothing" which will grip the spectators by nothing more than "a simple action sustained by violent passions, beautiful sentiments, and elegant expression".

In *Bérénice* Racine attempted to push this to the limit. Whereas Corneille's version has two pairs of lovers, he settles for a trio of characters, together with their respective confidants. Thus, he neglected the historical Domitian and Domitia picked up by Corneille, and instead invented the character of Antiochus, who, by functioning as a go-between despite his own feelings, serves to increase the general atmosphere of suffering, and who also acts as a moral exemplar to the main protagonists in his own self-abnegation and renunciation.

There is simplicity, too, in the play's setting, which consists of an ante-chamber between the apartments of Titus and Bérénice where they have been accustomed to meet. It is decorated with their entwined initials—a symbol of their former unity—which now serve to mock them. This decor also demonstrates spatially the conflict facing Titus, as when he wishes to follow the distressed Queen, but is obliged to leave in the opposite direction when summoned by the Senate. And surrounding this erstwhile haven and even intruding into it in the form of the shouts of its populace, are the constantly evoked power and splendour of Rome against which even the Emperor Titus is impotent. This glory, as described, for example, in the account of the deification of Titus's father, Vespasian, is in marked contrast to the desolation of the defeated East from which both Bérénice and Antiochus come and to which they will return.

The plight of the characters drew tears from a contemporary audience who delighted in such dilemmas, but no less a critic than Voltaire subsequently expressed the view that the spectacle of the separation of a lover and his mistress did not constitute a tragedy. Racine foresaw this criticism and attempted to counter it in his preface, where he claims that blood and death are not essential in a tragedy, where it is enough that the action should be elevated, the actors heroic and passions aroused. He adds that a tragedy above all should express the "majestic sadness" which he considers the chief attraction of the genre.

Thus *Bérénice* has been considered variously, and not altogether unjustly, as a somewhat unsuccessful dramatic experiment, or an overly refined tragic elegy. This is not to do the play full justice, however, and if modern audiences are less prone to tears than those of the 17th century, there is still a great deal to recommend *Bérénice*, in its poignant and true descriptions of the pain of love and separation, as when the Queen accuses Titus of not considering her feelings or in desperation begs for the means to end her life, or when Titus finds it impossible to break his silence before her; the whole culminating in Antiochus's final, heart-broken "Alas!".

—Janet Clarke

DER BESUCH DER ALTEN DAME. See **THE VISIT.**

DER BETTLER. See **THE BEGGAR.**

BEYOND HUMAN POWER, Parts One and Two
  (Over Ævne I; Over Ævne II)
by Bjørnstjerne Bjørnson

First Publication: Copenhagen, 1883
First Production: *Over Ævne I*: New Theatre (Nya Teatret), Stockholm, 3 January, 1886; *Over Ævne II*: Christiana Theatre, Christiana, 23 December 1895.

Translations
Pastor Sang [*Over Ævne 1*], translated by William Wilson, London, 1893.
Beyond Our Power in *Bjørnstjerne Bjørnson: Plays*, translated by Edwin Björkman, London, 1913.
Beyond Our Might, in *Bjørnstjerne Bjørnson: Plays* (series 2), translated by Edwin Björkman, London, 1914.
Beyond Our Power, translated by L. Hollander, in *Chief Continental Plays*, edited by T.H. Dickinson, Boston, Massachusetts, 1915.

Criticism
(For general works on the author, see *Playwrights* volume)

Books:
J. Nome, *Bjørnsons Dikterproblem: Studier omkring "Over Ævne"-ideen*, Oslo, 1934.

Articles:
B. Madson, "Bjørstjerne Bjørnson's *Beyond Human Power* and Kaj Munk's *The Word*", in *Modern Drama*, vol. 3 no. 1, 1960–61.
Aldo Keel, "Zum Aufbau von Bjørnsons *Over Ævne I*", in *Edda*, 84, 1984.

*   *   *

Towards the end of the 1870's Bjørnson was planning a series of plays based on the theme of overexertion. Only two plays were written, with an interval of 12 years. Although he gave them a common title, and although four characters from *Part One* reappear in *Part Two*, the two parts should be regarded as independent plays. *Part One* is a two-act play with the action set in a modest vicarage in northern Norway. The vicar's wife, who is suffering from long term sleeplessness and paralysis, is ill in bed. Her husband, the Reverend Adolf Sang, who is renowned for his alleged powers as a supernatural healer, has asked their two children, Rakel and Elias, to return home and join him in a collective effort of praying in order to restore their mother's health. Mrs Sang does not share her husband's uncomplicated, strong faith in the reality of miracles, and it turns out that the children, too, have lost their religious belief. The vicar decides to start praying for the miracle all by himself, in the nearby church. In the second act, on the afternoon of the following day, people are gathering outside, and a group of clergymen enter the stage and start deliberations concerning which position to adopt on the importance of miracles in the Christian religion. In the meantime the patient has fallen asleep, and on awakening she gets up, leaves the bed and approaches her husband as he returns from the church. They embrace, but she is unable to remain standing, and sinks to the ground in his arms, dying. The vicar utters his final words—"But this was not the intention—? Or—?. . .Or—?" and dies of a heart attack.

Beyond Human Power, Part One is generally regarded as Bjørnson's most powerful drama. It contains a rich variety of emotions and attitudes considering religious faith and the central question of miracle. It also consists of a number of cleverly conceived characters, especially among the gathered clergy. What might have become an abstract discussion of theological dogma is made into an existential test where several among the characters express their personal commitment, waiting to see with their own eyes whether the superhuman healing will take place. The pathetic suspense dominating the second act, with Pastor Sang praying and singing off-stage, is effectively balanced by elements of comic relief represented by the group of hungry and somewhat confused clergymen gathering around their bishop. Various stages of belief and miracle expectancy are presented, and the scene shows a skilful dramatization of the options available to Lutheran ministers facing possible evidence of superhuman healing.

The dramatic effect of the action is heightened by references to the extraodinary qualities of the surrounding scenery: heavy rain is followed by bright sunshine, the smell of bird cherry is sensed intensely by the patient, and, as the Pastor at the end of Act I starts praying and ringing the church bells, a dangerous rockslide is loosened in the steep mountain-side, for a moment threatening both the church and the vicarage. The danger is fended off as if by the spiritual power of the Pastor. The end of Act II shows a corresponding effect; amidst hallelujahs by Pastor Sang, echoed by the group of clergy, the miracle is on the verge of manifesting itself but turns out to be abortive in the end. The limits of human power is overstepped and the result is fatal. The final comments indicate the tragic discrepancy between the will of man and the ruling power of God.

In *Beyond Human Power, Part Two* Bjørnson turned towards the question of socialism, investigating the destructiveness inherent in certain, anarchistic attitudes in the class struggle. The first of the four acts presents the difficult social conditions of workers on strike, such as poverty, hunger, alcoholism, frustration, and class hatred. On the side of the workers we find Elias Sang, who is willing to go very far in demolishing the power of the factory owners, and Pastor Bratt, who lost his faith in Christianity when the miracle test failed. A more compromising and conciliatory spirit is Pastor Falk, another one of the clergymen of *Part One*. A confrontation between spokesmen for the workers on strike and Holger, their unflinching employer, takes place in the second act, which also presents the altruistic Rakel Sang, who is taking a mediating position expressing love and care for the needy ones. The third act is set in a great hall, showing a convention of factory owners and investors discussing the formation of an employers' union, in order to protect their interests. The castle has been undermined, and this is revealed to the participants by Elias who is present, disguised as a servant. In the ensuing turmoil Elias is shot by Holger, and the explosives are detonated, killing everyone except Holger. In the final act the crippled Holger is nursed by Rakel in an institution which he earlier had donated to her. Another one of her patients is Pastor Bratt, who is now insane. Rakel is joined by Credo and Spera, children of Holger's sister, with positive visions for a future where the class struggle is replaced by a spirit of foregiveness and where discontent and frustration is defeated through the technological development which will make life easier for everyone.

The two first acts show considerable dramatic qualities; the high number of characters is well motivated in the need for a broad picture of the labour conflict. The violent outcome of the third act, with only one survivor, exceeds somehow the logic of dramatic catastrophe. The destruction of the castle and the industrialists is beyond humanity, not in the sense of being superhuman, but in the sense of being inhuman. Elias is sanguine like his father was, easy to influence, and going to extremes with the best of intentions.

The final part of the last act is devoted to an optimistic presentation of a possible future, seen through the allegorical eyes of Credo (Faith), Spera (Hope) and Rakel (representing Love). Bjørnson here expresses his own version of utopian socialism, his idealistic belief in man's ability to overcome the social problems generated by modern industrialisation. This element of preaching affects the dramatic tension of the play. *Part Two* is artistically less successful than *Part One*, where the action is more tightly constructed and where the suspense is maintained right on to the end.

—Asbjørn Aarseth

BEYOND OUR MIGHT.   See **BEYOND HUMAN POWER.**

BEYOND OUR POWER.   See **BEYOND HUMAN POWER.**

BIALE MALŻEŃSTWO.   See MARIAGE BLANC.

BIEDERMANN UND DIE BRANDSTIFTER.   See THE FIRERAISERS.

BINGO: SCENES OF MONEY AND DEATH (AND PASSION)
by Edward Bond

First Publication: In *"Bingo" and "The Sea"*, London, 1974.
First Production: Northcott Theatre, Exeter, Devon, 14 November 1973.

Criticism
(For general works on the author, see *Playwrights* volume)

Articles:

Christy L. Brown, "Edward Bond's *Bingo*: Shakespeare and the Ideology of Genius", in *Iowa State Journal of Research*, 60, 1986.

Lou Lappin, "The Artist in Society: Bond, Shakespeare, and *Bingo*", in *Before His Eyes: Essays in Honor of Stanley Kauffmann*, edited by Bert Cardullo, Lanham, Maryland, 1986.

Jenny Spencer, "Edward Bond's *Bingo*: History, Politics and Subjectivity", in *Historical Drama*, Cambridge, 1986 (Themes in Drama Series).

* * *

Shakespeare, in the last days of his life, is persuaded by William Combe, a Stratford farmer and magistrate, not to oppose the enclosure of common land from which Shakespeare derives rent-revenues. The playwright, however, tries to help a young, female vagrant, despite her having sex with the half-senile husband of his oldest servant. Combe has her whipped and, when she later returns and commits arson, she is hanged from a public gibbet. Shakespeare and Ben Jonson meet and quarrel about art and money in a local tavern, the Golden Cross. Shakespeare gets drunk, lends Jonson some money and gets a bottle of poison in return. At an adjoining table a group of labourers, led by the millenarian son of Shakespeare's servant, discusses drastic measures to prevent Combe's enclosing. Combe overhears them and threatens them with the full rigour of the law. Later Shakespeare is found wandering over the snow-covered fields by his daughter Judith. The rear-stage rush of figures and the gunshot are revealed, in the last scene, to have been another attempt on Combe's enclosures. An old man had been accidentally shot by his son. Shakespeare keeps to his bed, slips his will under the door to Judith who is battering to be let in, and dies from Jonson's poison.

Bond aims to create a Shakespeare who is imprisoned by the social values of his period and, at the same time, released by his imaginative use of language. "Enclosure" operates as both a political practice and as a metaphor for containment. Structurally the play, following the seasons from autumn to winter, enacts a journey out from Shakespeare's garden, via hill and tavern, to a snow-covered field. But the playwright is too old and, now, too implicated in local affairs to escape the domestic clichés of house and family. He dies in his bed but, as a final gesture of independence, the door is locked against Judith and his wife. The last people he talks to are the son who shot his father and destroyed a family and Combe who will destroy the old community. But they are voices of the future. The son speaks the imagery and phraseology, brilliantly recreated by Bond, of millenarian Christianity: "Let me be free", he cries. "Liberty. Where no-one stand 'tween me an' my god, no one listen when I raise the song a praise, an' I walk by god's side with curtsey an' fear nothin', as candid loike a child". He foreshadows such radical religious groups as the Diggers and the Fifth Monarchists who helped turn the world upside down during and after the Civil War. Combe speaks the new discourse of capitalist agriculture where profit cuts up land-ownership and its traditional rights and responsibilities. "Stay in your garden", he advises Shakespeare in the first scene, "I'll pay for that". Shakespeare doesn't stay but he now has no other base from which to interpret the world. The further he moves from home the more richly imaginative his language becomes. But his only audience is a hanged girl, a simple old woman, or, in a soliloquy across the snowy fields in Scene 6, himself.

Yet in the central Scene 4, with Ben Jonson, he hardly speaks. Jonson represents the forum, the London theatre, where Shakespeare had a platform. His first question is about the burning of his theatre and when Jonson asks him what he is writing he replies "Nothing". Jonson, walking to Scotland because there "might be a book in it", is the truly mobile, rootless artist. He is garrulous, witty and broke. Bond gives him some realistically sardonic asides—"I helped to uncover the gunpowder plot. Keep in with the top". But he also pours out his hatred and envy for Shakespeare's "serenity" and New Place respectability. In a shrewd juxtaposition of life and art, while Combe warns the labourers off filling in his ditches, Jonson rhapsodises about the quiet fields and cool, mossy graves of country life. This is rural reality versus pastoral artifice and Shakespeare, as Jonson knows, had dramatised this debate throughout his career. But Shakespeare has no more arguments. He has sided with Combe, and anyway he is dead drunk.

Shakespeare does speak, at length, in Scenes 3 and 4, in a carefully contrived diction in which realistic detail and image never quite coalesce into the metaphorical discourse that is the genius of Shakespeare's own writing. This is a clever device which avoids all the dangers of cod Elizabethan and incorporates the stark monosyllabics which are such a feature of Bond's own style. At the end of scene three, under the gibbet, Shakespeare is deliberately made incapable of achieving fully his characteristic poetry: ". . .a swan flew by me up the river. On a straight line just over the water. A woman in a white dress running along an empty street". It is as if Bond, as a modernist, leaves it to the reader to supply the "like" and make the simile, but also portrays a Shakespeare in decline since he would certainly have given his reader the full simile. Bond is showing us the *process* of metaphorising, not the metaphor completed. The more Shakespeare isolates himself, the less his literary sensibility can achieve this completion. He observes and he speaks but the observations will not transform themselves into images: "The dream. The wolves. The iron teeth. The snow. The wind. My voice. A dream that leads to sleep". Here, as if laid out on an instrument-table, are all the items that could make up one of those intricate coagulations of language we find so frequently in *Antony and Cleopatra* or *The Winter's Tale*. But the artist can no longer fit them together, in part because the snow and the wolves and the wind are a reality he is suffering and not images in the study, in part because the world in which such organic connection was unselfconscious is passing. Bond displays history in the syntax of the poet. Shakespeare is already speaking in the atomistic manner of the late seventeenth century.

At the end Shakespeare wants reassurance about his past: "Was anything done?" is the question that agonises him to near-hysteria in the last scenes. "Nothing", which is Judith's stage-reply to her question about his new will, is really the reply to Shakespeare's own question. Combine the two and you have a skilful variant on the opening line of *Waiting for Godot*: "Nothing to be done". Bond, as a Marxist, has always resisted the nihilism of the Absurdists. His Introduction to *Bingo* asserts his belief in a rational, just society. Shakespeare's society was neither, yet it produced the greatest genius of the language. The play wrestles with this conundrum and, unlike agit-prop work of the 1970's, pays due respect to both aesthetics and politics. Bond is an artist himself and has known, more than most, the vicious constraints that society has tried to impose upon his talent.

—Tony Dunn

THE BIRDS (Ornithes / Aves)
by Aristophanes

First Production: Great Dionysia Festival, Athens, 414 B.C.

Editions

Aves, edited by H.M. Blaydes, London, 1882.
Aves, edited by J. van Leeuwen, 1902; second edition, Leiden, 1968.
"The Birds" of Aristophanes, edited by Benjamin Bickley Rogers, London, 1908 (with translation).
Birds, edited and translated by Alan H. Sommerstein, Warminster, Wiltshire, 1987 (with translation).

Translations

The Birds, translated by B.H. Kennedy, London, 1908.
The Birds, translated by Benjamin Bickley Rogers, London, 1920.
The Birds, in *"The Birds" and "The Frogs"*, translated by Marshall McGregor, London, 1927.
The Birds, translated by Gilbert Murray, London, 1950.
The Birds, translated by William Arrowsmith, Ann Arbor, Michigan, 1961 (Complete Greek Comedy Series).
The Birds, translated by Kenneth McLeish, in *"The Frogs" and Other Greek Plays*, London, 1970.
The Birds, translated by David Barrett, in *The Knights; The Birds; The Assemblywomen; Wealth*, translated by David Barrett and Alan H. Sommerstein, Harmondsworth, 1978.
The Birds, in *Four Plays of Aristophanes*, translated by James Martinband, 1983.

Criticism

(For general works on the author, see *Playwrights* volume)

Articles:

C.N. Jackson, "Decree-seller in the *Birds* and the Professional Politicians at Athens", in *Harvard Studies in Classical Philology*, 30, 1919.
T.F. Higham, "Two Notes on Aristophanes' *Birds*", in *Classical Quarterly* (new series), 26, 1932.

R.E. Wycherley, "Aristophanes' *Birds*, 995–1009", in *Classical Quarterly* (new series), 31, 1937.
L.B. Lawler, "Four Dances in the *Birds* of Aristophanes", in *Transactions of the American Philological Association* [*TAPA*], 73, 1942.
W.E. Blake, "The Aristophanic Bird Chorus—A Riddle", in *American Journal of Philology*, 64, 1943.
J.R.T. Pollard, "*Birds* of Aristophanes—A Source Book for Old Beliefs", in *American Journal of Philology*, 69, 1948.
E.M. Blaiklock, "Walking Away from the News: An Autobiographical Interpretation of Aristophanes' *Birds*", in *Classical Review* (new series), 17, 1967.
T.G. Rosenmeyer, "Notes on Aristophanes' *Birds*", in *American Journal of Philology*, 93, 1972.
W. Arrowsmith, "Aristophanes's *Birds*: The Fantasy Politics of Eros", in *Arion* (new series), 1, 1973.
F. Schreiber, "Double-Barreled Joke: Aristophanes' *Birds*", in *American Journal of Philology*, 95, 1974.
T. Gelzer, "Some Aspects of Aristophanes' Dramatic Art in the *Birds*", in *Bulletin of the Institute of Classical Studies*, 23, 1976.
B.R. Katz, "*The Birds* of Aristophanes and Politics", in *Athanaeum*, 54, 1976.

* * *

The *Birds* was written by Aristophanes at a time when the mood in Athens was one of buoyant optimism, and this happiness is reflected throughout the comedy. The Athenians had just launched a great expedition against Sicily, and confidently expected to bring the whole of that island rapidly under their total control and thereby secure a winning advantage in the long-standing struggle with Sparta. The comedy won second prize.

The plot of the *Birds* is pure fantasy. It opens with two elderly Athenians, Peisetaerus and Euelpides, seeking peace and quiet and, therefore, consulting Tereus, once a mortal but now transformed into a hoopoe and, as a bird, likely to know somewhere "nice and fleecy". In the end it is decided to found an entirely new city, and Peisetaerus demonstrates the force of his name ("Persuader of Companions") by convincing the chorus of birds that, degraded though they presently may be, they can regain their previous power by building a city of the birds in mid-air and, thereby cutting the gods off from earth. Nephelokokkygia (Cloudcuckooland) is founded and a series of dubious characters—priest, poet, oracle-monger, the architect Meton, inspector from Athens, decree-seller—appears only to receive short shrift and to be sent packing. Others visit the city in pursuit of wings, a young man who wants to throttle his father, the poet Cinesias and an informer, and then deities intervene, Prometheus, Poseidon, Heracles and a Triballian or barbarian god, the last three in order to negotiate a settlement of the birds' blockage of heaven. The outcome is a surrender of power by the gods, symbolized by marriage between Peisetaerus and Basileia (or "Sovereignty").

The *Birds* is a typical Aristophanic comedy in which a crazy idea is suggested and then its merits discussed; in the end the idea is implemented and its consequences illustrated by a rapid succession of farcical scenes; joyous celebration brings the action to a close. Although the sequence of events may seem simple, the *Birds* is characterized by a wealth of variety and invention: thus it boasts a total of 22 adult speaking parts, all managed by just three players; its prologue takes the audience from surprise to even greater surprise. In it, two tired men are wandering lost in a wilderness; one carries on his wrist a jackdaw and the other a crow, and they are also weighed down with ritual paraphernalia: a bucket, pot and myrtle wreaths.

They knock, not at a door, but at a rock and this is opened, not by a slave, but a slave-bird and one with a massively gaping beak. The bird's master turns out to be Tereus, a savage tyrant but now not merely changed into a hoopoe, but a hoopoe devoid of plumage, so that terror inspired by the slave becomes laughter prompted by the master.

The chorus of 24 birds, each one carefully identified, offers great scope both for colourful display of costume and for song imitating the sounds of nature; suspecting betrayal, the birds advance threateningly on the two humans as if they were heavily armoured infantrymen of Athens; but peace is restored and in parody of military orders the birds are instructed by their leader to "ground their spirit. . .like a hoplite". Parody can be detected again when the birds outline a theogony which stresses their own importance in the scheme of things, while the chorus-leader's assessment of the advantages of possessing wings happily associates the audience in the action of the comedy—if you've got wings and get fed up watching the tragedies, you can fly home, have a bite to eat, and then come back for the afternoon's comedy!

The different visitors to Cloudcuckooland all contribute in their own way to the general hilarity: the poet cannot be silenced; the oracle-monger is hoist with his own petard when Peisetaerus produces his personal book of predictions; Meton is a coward; the inspector is assaulted and the decree-seller chased away. The would-be parricide wants to exploit the "law of nature", believing the birds throttle and peck their parents; Cinesias, a frequent butt of comic humour, was notorious for his musical innovations, and here he supports his wish to become a nightingale with appropriate song; the informer, or "sycophant", is shameless in his desire for wings so that he can serve summonses more easily, but is driven running from the stage. The divine callers provide a fitting climax: Prometheus is desperate not to be spotted by Zeus and so cowers beneath a parasol; Poseidon proves to be an incompetent ambassador, Heracles is a glutton and fool, while the Triballian's attempt at speaking Greek produces sheer nonsense. Throughout the comedy the humour inherent in an ever changing succession of music-hall-type sketches more than compensates for a modern audience's difficulty in appreciating jokes intelligible only in the context of 5th-century Athens. The *Birds* must be rated as the happiest example of an Aristophanic extravaganza.

—Peter Walcot

THE BIRTHDAY PARTY
by Harold Pinter

First Publication: London, 1959; revised edition, London, 1965.
First Production: Arts Theatre, Cambridge, 28 April 1958; revised version, Aldwych Theatre (Royal Shakespeare Company), London, 18 June 1964.

Criticism
(For general works on the author, see *Playwrights* volume)

Books:
Michael Scott (ed.), *Harold Pinter: "The Birthday Party", "The Caretaker", "The Homecoming"*, London, 1986.

Ronald Knowles, *"The Birthday Party" and "The Caretaker"*, London, 1988 (Text and Performance Series).

Articles:
Simon O. Lesser, "Reflections on Pinter's *The Birthday Party*", in *Contemporary Literature*, 13, 1972.
Michael W. Kaufman, "Actions That a Man Might Play: Pinter's *The Birthday Party*", in *Modern Drama*, 16, 1973.
Charles A. Carpenter, "'What have I seen, the scum or the essence?' Symbolic Fallout in Pinter's *Birthday Party*", in *Modern Drama*, 17, 1974; revised article, in *Harold Pinter: You Never Heard Such Silence*, edited by Alan Bold, London, 1984.
Andreas Fischer, "Poetry and Drama: Pinter's Play *The Birthday Party* in the Light of His Poem 'A View of the Party'", in *English Studies*, 60, 1979.
Richard A. Andretta, "The Chicken That Crossed the Road: A Study of Harold Pinter's *The Birthday Party*", in *Journal of English*, 8, 1980.
Bert Cardullo, "Pinter as Painter-Poet: Notes, Mostly on *The Birthday Party*", in *McNeese Review*, 31, 1984–86.

*　　*　　*

The Birthday Party, Pinter's first full-length play, takes place at the home of Meg and Petey Boles and concerns their lodger, Stanley, whose past is obscure, though he fantasises about having been a concert pianist. Meg gives Stanley a drum for his birthday, which he plays as though possessed as the first act closes. In Act II Stanley tries to get rid of some new lodgers, Goldberg and McCann, but they respond by subjecting Stanley to rapid-fire interrogation, until he is reduced to speechlessness. The act culminates in Stanley's birthday party, in which McCann breaks Stanley's glasses during a game of blind man's buff, the lights go out and, in a sinister climax, Stanley (encumbered by the drum, into which he has stumbled) begins to strangle Meg and is bent giggling over a young girl, Lulu, when the curtain falls. Act III comes full circle with Meg and Petey at breakfast, as at the opening of the play. Stanley is brought down a changed man, still speechless ("Uh-gug-ug-gug-eeehhh-gag"). Goldberg and McCann leave, taking Stanley "to Monty" and threaten Petey when he tries to stop them. Meg at the end of the play has understood nothing and fails to register Stanley has gone.

The initial lack of success of *The Birthday Party* in the late 1950's is not surprising. Pinter had yet to create a market for the particular brand of menace that is the signature of his early plays, such as *The Room* and *The Dumb Waiter* (also 1957), where, like Stanley, the protoganists are sequestered in a room and are threatened by intruders into their womb-like privacy. Critics, such as Milton Shulman, were puzzled: "The world of Harold Pinter is shadowy, obsessed, guilt-ridden, claustrophobic and, above all, private. You are expected to find your way through it without signposts, clues or milestones".

Pinter is even said to have received the following enquiry from an audience member:

I would be obliged if you would kindly explain to me the meaning of your play *The Birthday Party*. These are the points which I do not understand. 1) Who are the two men? 2) Where did Stanley come from? 3) Were they all supposed to be normal? You will appreciate that without the answers to my questions I cannot fully understand your play.

Pinter's reputed response ("1) Who are you? 2) Where do you come from?", etc.) naturally ignored such strictures—and

The Birthday Party: Shaw Theatre, London, 1975

audiences gradually became increasingly fascinated, hooked into the plays by their ambiguities, a technique Pinter had learned from Samuel Beckett. (Pinter warmly acknowledges a debt to Beckett since first discovering his writing in 1949.)

One of the major pleasures of Pinter's drama is his use of language, ranging from jargon used as a protective shield to prevent intruders seeing what is underneath, to a characteristic use of pauses of varying lengths, so that a work is virtually orchestrated by silence, and meaning accrues in the subtext—in what is *not* said. At the opening of *The Birthday Party* it is as though Pinter had produced a tape recording of the inanities we actually speak, as opposed to the shapely sentences often given to stage figures by earlier dramatists. In using such dialogue onstage, Pinter not only introduces a rich vein of humour, but allows an audience to recognise the realism of stating the obvious. Many a breakfast-time conversation is based on similar emptiness:

Meg: Is that you Petey? (*Pause*) Petey, is that you?
Petey: What?
Meg: Is that you?
Petey: Yes, it's me.
Meg: What? (*She opens the hatch and looks through.*) Are you back?
Petey: Yes.

The Birthday Party also demonstrates a use of language as a weapon, as Goldberg and McCann, by their quick-fire questioning of Stanley (a known technique in brainwashing, designed to fluster and confuse) reduce him to inarticulacy:

Goldberg: Which came first?

McCann: Chicken? Egg? Which came first?
Goldberg: Which came first? Which came first? which came first?
(*Stanley screams*)

Stanley's subsequent silence marks the disintegration of his personality. Following Goldberg and McCann's ministrations he does indeed "need special treatment"—for which the two men are "taking him to Monty" as Goldberg ominously informs Petey. Goldberg and McCann seem in a sense to be projections or manifestations of Stanley's strongly-developed sense of guilt and fear of pursuit—of which we are made aware before he encounters the two men. At the same time Goldberg and McCann are frighteningly real. The barrage of words with which they crush Stanley, their vitality and comic vulgarity, the swagger and aggression, and the rhythms of their language have a richness that comes straight out of the Jewish idiom of Pinter's family background as well as the regional influence of London's East End. For audiences unused to the Jewish idiom, the disturbing power of Pinter's writing owes a good deal to the strangeness of this mixture of the unfamiliar with the familiar.

The ambiguities in *The Birthday Party* are integral to the play's impact. We never know precisely who Goldberg and McCann are, or what (if anything) Stanley has done, that they seem to be pursuing him. We are left with a sense of genuine unease, as though indescribable evil really were stalking outside the door of even the most ordinary of homes, awaiting its chance to enter.

—Rosemary Pountney

BLACK-EYED SUSAN
by Douglas Jerrold

First Publication: London, 1829.
First Production: Royal Surrey Theatre, London, 8 June
          1829.

Editions

Black-Eyed Susan, in *Nineteenth Century Plays*, edited by
   George Rowell, London, 1953.
Black-Eyed Susan, in *English Plays of the Nineteenth Century
   1*, edited by Michael R. Booth, Oxford, 1969.

Criticism

(For general works on the author, see *Playwrights* volume)

Articles:
Paula M. Morgan, "E.L. Davenport and *Black Eyed Susan*: A
   Musical Episode in Nineteenth-Century Theatre", in *Prin-
   ceton University Library Chronicle*, Autumn 1986.

*   *   *

Black-Eyed Susan lives with her mother, Dame Hatley, in a
cottage the rent of which is greatly in arrears owing to the long
absence at sea of her husband, William. Captain Hatchet (his
punning name is intended to be noticed by the audience)
hatches a plot with Raker to persuade Susan that William is
dead, offering then to marry Susan and, if refused, leave Susan
and her mother to face the threat of eviction. Raker's response
to this plot well sums up the pseudo-maritime language of this
nautical melodrama (a characteristic all such plays exploited):

> Slack your fore-sheet, Captain Hatchet; if you must spin
> such galley yarns, let it be to the marines, or the landlady
> of the Ship; but see that you don't again bring tears into
> an old sailor's eyes, and laugh at him for hoisting an
> answering pendant to signals of distress. You marry
> Susan? Now belay, belay the joke.

At the end of the scene, Raker is left alone and tells the
audience that despite appearances he'll take care to keep his
heart the right colour. A bailiff is called in but, in the nick of
time, Hatchet arrives and pays the outstanding rent intending
to return on the next day to propose. William, returning with
the other sailors, interrupts Hatchet telling Susan he is dead,
and their subsequent fighting is curtailed at a critical moment
(marked "Tableau") when Lieutenant Pike and the Marines
arrive to arrest Hatchet and Raker for smuggling. However,
William gets into another fight and strikes Captain Crosstree;
the act ends with another tableau and slow music. In Act II,
William is found guilty of striking an officer, and he has a
chance to display his fortitude (in extravagant nautical language) and makes a magnificent procession to the scaffold (a
favourite melodramatic device). In the surprise denouement, a
gunshot rings out, and Captain Crosstree rushes in with a
document retrieved from the victim's body which declares that
villainy had kept back William's release from the Navy, so that
when he struck Crosstree, William "was not the King's sailor".
The Admiral frees him, the sailors cheer, and William and
Susan are united.

This lengthy plot summary serves to show the many twists of
fortune essential to good melodrama, and also gives a taste of
the language. What cannot be done is represent the music—
the "melo" so essential to this drama. In this play, the theme
song is the ballad "Black-Eyed Susan" but, in addition to other

songs, the music from the pit would, long before Wagner,
provide *leitmotivs* for the various characters, probably associating them with particular instruments—flute for the heroine, trumpet for the hero, double-bass for the villains,
bassoons for the comics. At its surface level, the play—which
was a great hit in its own day, and revived throughout the
century—provided excitement, comedy, sentiment, and
music. It had that essential quality found also in such songs as
"Villikins and His Dinah" of switching from side-splitting
comedy to heart-rending pathos and back with great speed, a
characteristic known as "Robsonianism", much admired by
Sir Henry Irving. If the audience sat back it would not doubt
that all would prove well for William and Susan. Jerrold's skill
lay in screwing them up to suspend their disbelief doubly—that
they were not simply in a theatre witnessing a fiction, but also
that Susan and William were not endangered. This he did
triumphantly: the play was one of the first to exceed a run of
100 nights, eventually running for 400, and T.P. Cook, as the
first William, had one of his greatest hits.

It is true the melodrama far too easily shows that good
triumphs; in fact the good are too good and the bad unremittingly wicked; the characterisation is sterotyped, the language
exaggerated, the tunes trite; but at bottom it is an intensely
loyal play. True virtue lies in those who are true blue, in this
context a colour associated with the Royal Navy, and there is a
special virtue associated with seamen. In fact, we have to
consider the play as a social, as well as a dramatic, document.

Black Eyed Susan sees virtue in the "ordinary seaman", in
ordinary people. The eviction of the poor and the seduction of
the innocent were real enough. It is the officers and their like

Black-Eyed Susan: Royal Surrey Theatre, London, 1829 (first production)

who are criminal. It is chance that permits William to escape hanging, not justice. We are never in any doubt wherein goodness lies—in such as Susan and William. That is not to say all the officers are evil. It is Lt. Pike whom William charges with ensuring that when William is "in dock" (i.e. in his coffin) that his locket containing Susan's hair is buried with him. For many audiences, experiencing little justice themselves and subject to poverty, this drama (and many like it) was simultaneously subversive in showing the ordinary people as virtuous and their masters as the source of wickedness, yet preaching loyalty and the triumph of goodness. The implications of repeated productions of such plays in the century before World War I are worth pondering on. Also worth consideration is the complexity of the language. It is easy to find the exaggerated navalese ridiculous, but it is also surprisingly demanding of an audience. Like so many music-hall songs and acts of the period, it made sophisticated demands on relatively uneducated audiences.

—Peter Davison

THE BLACKS (Les Nègres)
by Jean Genet

First Publication: Paris, 1958.
First Production: Théâtre de Lutèce, Paris, 28 October 1959.

Translations
The Blacks, translated by Bernard Frechtman, London, 1960.

Criticism
(For general works on the author, see *Playwrights* volume)

Articles:
Susan Tubes, "The White Mask Falls", in *Tulane Drama Review*, 7, 1963.
Homer D. Swander, "Shakespeare and the Harlem Clowns: Illusion and Comic Form in Genet's *The Blacks*", in *Yale Review*, 55, 1965.
Anthony Graham-White, "Jean Genet and the Psychology of Colonialism," in *Comparative Drama*, 4, 1970.
Albert C. Chesneau, "Idée de révolution et principe de réversibilité dans *Le Balcon* et *Les Nègres* de Jean Genet", in *Publications of the Modern Language Association [PMLA]*, 88, 1973.
Anne C. Murch, "Je mime donc je suis: *Les Nègres*, de Jean Genet", in *Revue des Sciences Humaines*, 150, 1973.
Jeannette L. Savona, "*The Blacks* by Jean Genet: A Dimensional Approach", in *Australian Journal of French Studies*, 10, 1973.
Robert Fraser, "What's Happening in *The Blacks*? Speculations on the Dramatic Art of Jean Genet", in *Asemka*, vol. 1 no. 2, 1974.
Graham D. Martin, "Racism in Genet's *Les Nègres*", in *Modern Language Review*, 70, 1975.
Neal Oxenhandler, "Can Genet Be Saved? Remarks on *The Blacks*", in *Contemporary Literature*, 16, 1975.
Wolfgang F. Sohlich, "Genet's *The Blacks* and *The Screens*: Dialectic of Refusal and Revolutionary Consciousness", in *Comparative Drama*, 10, 1976.
Jeanne M. Baude, "*Les Nègres* de Jean Genet, tragédie grecque?", in *Travaux de Linguistique et de Littérature*, vol. 17 no. 2, 1979.
Richard C. Webb, "Ritual, Theatre, and Jean Genet's *The Blacks*", in *Theatre Journal*, 31, 1979.
Pierre Brunel, "Tentation et refus de l'opéra: *Les Nègres* de Jean Genet", in *Travaux de Linguistique et de Littérature*, vol. 18 no. 2, 1980.
Loren Kruger, "Ritual into Myth: Ceremony and Communication in *The Blacks*", in *Critical Arts*, vol. 1 no. 3, 1980.
Keith Q. Warner, "*Les Nègres*: A Look at Genet's Excursion into Black Consciousness", in *CLA Journal*, 26, 1982.
Una Chaudhuri, "The Politics of Theater: Play, Deceit, and Threat in Genet's *The Blacks*", in *Modern Drama*, 28, 1985.

* * *

The action of *The Blacks* is set in colonial Africa. Three strands of action are interwoven, though it is questionable whether any of them amounts to a plot. At its most overt level the play consists of the re-enactment, by a group of black actors, of the rape and murder of a white woman. Juxtaposed with this is the developing relationship between Village, the young black man who plays the killer, and Virtue, a young black woman who has been used as a whore by the whites. Meanwhile, offstage, a traitor to the black cause is tried and executed, while a new black leader is acclaimed and takes up the cudgels.

As Genet's sub-title, *A Clown Show*, indicates, the most overt level of action is self-consciously bogus. Thus the catafalque which has been said to contain the body of the white victim is revealed to be as empty as the phantasm it incarnates. Genet's focus at this level is less on black reality (his title significantly is not *Les Noirs* but the white term *Les Nègres*) than on the stereotypes imposed on black people by white culture. The roles played by the actors are crude, ill-fitting caricatures of the images of blackness nurtured by the white audiences for whom Genet asserts that the play is intended. But the actors also have an onstage audience in the ambiguously styled "Court", which comprises five further black actors wearing partial, white masks. The Court, which initially holds sway from a high platform stage left, embodies various aspects—military, legal, political and religious—of colonialism. But its attempt to penalize the perpetrator of the crime acted out before it founders for lack of a victim. And the punitive expedition that it then mounts is thwarted by drink, fatigue and the jungle. Finally the Court dies, leaving behind religion, in the derisory shape of the black clergyman Diouf, who remains alone on the platform it has vacated. From the skirts of Diouf too, in his role as the victim of Village's crime are born several small dolls, each in the shape of a member of the Court, which appear to represent the lingering menace of neo-colonialism.

In stark contrast to their roles as actors, the task taken on by Village and Virtue in their own persons is that of casting off the sexual stereotypes—rampant black stud and submissive black whore—imposed upon them by white culture. Their aim instead is to forge a genuinely new kind of black love, undistorted by the white concepts of romance and chivalry. The play's conclusion deals precisely with their aspiration towards this egalitarian ideal. This seems an admirable, but arduous endeavour. The likelihood of their realizing it is shrouded in ambiguity. At the end of the play, Village and Virtue symbolically turn their backs on the white audience. But the strains which accompany this triumphal tableau—the "opening measures of the minuet from *Don Giovanni*"—are an insidious reminder of the persistence of white stereotypes. This is also the tune to which the black actors have danced at the beginning of the play, so its repeated use here sounds a pessimistic note.

An even more pronounced ambiguity pervades the political action of the play, which takes place offstage. It is largely reported by Newport News, whose barefoot integrity is expressed in his refusal to sport the inept approximation of evening dress that is *de rigueur* for the rest of the troupe. Genet pointedly juxtaposes the white thirst for vengeance and the black desire for justice. But it is nonetheless arguable that black justice is summary at best. From the moment the traitor has been apprehended, his fate is sealed. And this is a matter for serious debate between the authoritative figure of Archibald, the master of ceremonies, and Newport News. Ambiguites also surround the status and the role of the new black leader evoked by Newport News. If much, at this level of the play, is left unresolved, it is presumably because Genet saw that the forging of black nationhood would be a painful and perilous enterprise.

Genet wrote *The Blacks* in 1957, after an actor had asked him to write a play for an all-black cast. It was first staged by Roger Blin, with a black amateur company, *Les Griots*, at the Théâtre de Lutèce on 28th October 1959. Unusually, Genet gave this *mise en scène* his wholehearted endorsement. For twenty years, from 1960, he would permit the French text of the play—a revised version of the 1957 text—to be published only in a version illustrated by 33 still photographs of Blin's production. *The Blacks* has been staged with repeated success in the United States, where it has had a particular resonance for Afro-American audiences. To the extent that its central theme is racism rather than colonialism, it is to be assumed that its resonance will be enduring.

—Tim Lewis

BLOOD RELATIONS
by Sharon Pollock

First Publication: In *Blood Relations and Other Plays*, Edmonton, Alberta, 1981.
First Production: As *My Name Is Lisbeth*, New Westminster, British Columbia, 1976; as *Blood Relations*, Theatre 3, Edmonton, Alberta, 1980.

Criticism
(For general works on the author, see *Playwrights* volume)

Articles:
Susan Blackburn-Stone, "Feminism and Metadrama: Role-playing in *Blood Relations*", in *Canadian Drama*, 15, 1989.

* * *

Since its premiere, Sharon Pollock's play has been produced extensively across Canada and the United States. Acclaimed by Canadian critics as Pollock's most theatrically intricate and lyrical play, *Blood Relations* won the first Governor General's Award for Drama in 1981.

Like several of Pollock's plays, *Blood Relations* focuses on an actual historical event—the Borden murders that took place in Fall River, Massachusetts, in 1892. Unlike her earlier work, however, this play goes beyond documentary realism in creating a world of its own on stage. In *Blood Relations* Pollock

uses the medium of theatre not only as a vehicle for examining issues, but as a social institution, which by its very nature is paradigmatic of the society in which we live. The play reveals that the world on stage, which both actor and spectator have brought into being, is granted authenticity only when it mirrors the ideology of the society within which it is confined.

The play opens and closes in Lizzie Borden's parlour, ten years after the grisly axe-murder of her parents. Act I begins with Lizzie entertaining her guest and probable lover, the Actress, who is based on the historical character of Nance O'Neill. The Actress urges Miss Lizzie to confess, either to being a murderer or a "pretentious small-town spinster". In answer to the Actress's prodding, Miss Lizzie draws the Actress into another world by challenging her to play the role of Lizzie.

The challenge is picked up by the Actress in a play-within-the-play, which takes the characters back to 1892, where they become participants in events within the Borden household. Miss Lizzie assumes the role of Bridget, the maid, while the Actress becomes Lizzie. As figures from the past enter the "dream thesis", the fabric of the Bordens' family history begins to unravel. Miss Lizzie/Bridget acts as Actress/Lizzie's guide through the pattern of dependence and servitude that has been Miss Lizzie's experience of life within the Borden family. Through Miss Lizzie/Bridget's manipulations, Actress/Lizzie becomes caught up in the hostility and fear that permeate the home and, in this vulnerable position, she is open to subtle suggestions from Miss Lizzie/Bridget that offer hope of freedom through death, either her own or her family's.

In Act II, as Actress/Lizzie becomes more involved in the family's pathology, the dividing line between Lizzie and Miss Lizzie becomes harder to discern. As Miss Lizzie watches Actress/Lizzie absorb her ideology through Miss Lizzie/Bridget's manipulations, she comes to the realization that she too has been acting out the aspirations of her older, and conventional, sister, Emma. Miss Lizzie now perceives herself as a "puppet", acting not autonomously, but with Emma's desires controlling her every move.

The ending of the play is shrouded in mystery; while it establishes that Actress/Lizzie is capable of murder, it does not conclusively confirm Miss Lizzie's guilt. It veils culpability behind a myraid of characters. If Miss Lizzie did wield the hatchet, it was a hatchet forged by the heat of passion that arose from the greed of Mrs. Borden and her brother, the dehumanizing effect of Mr. Borden's insensitivity, and the manipulations of Emma. Even the audience is refused the position of the innocent bystander when Miss Lizzie "*looks to the hatchet—then to the audience*" and accuses them.

Pollock denies the spectator the right to sit passively and judge the reality on stage. Instead she demands that the audience acknowledge that the act of judging makes them active participants in the theatrical event. It is the audience's standards, beliefs, and prejudices—their ideology—that allow them to perceive, understand, and grant authenticity to the reality portrayed on stage. Through Miss Lizzie, Pollock turns the spectators' ideology back on themselves by making them examine their beliefs in the context of their ability to understand and credit the reality that *Blood Relations* illuminates.

The feminine perspective in *Blood Relations* does not merely point to the evolution of the women's movement from the horrific conditions women were subject to in the 19th century. Pollock goes beyond the obvious social statement to examine how the personal becomes political. Within the confines of the play, questions of personal identity are illuminated. The audience watches Lizzie's identity being created on stage and they are compelled to recognize the forces that go into creating that identity. The play's ambiguous ending is sustained by the spectators, who have come to the realization that these forces must take some responsibility for the actions of the character they have created.

—Mary Pat Mombourquette

BLOOD WEDDING (Bodas de sangre)
by Federico García Lorca

First Publication: Madrid, 1935.
First Production: Teatro Beatriz, Madrid, 8 March 1933.

Translations
Blood Wedding, in *From Lorca's Theatre: Five Plays*, translated by James Graham-Luján and Richard L. O'Connell, New York, 1941.
Blood Wedding, translated by Gwynne Edwards in *Federico García Lorca: Three Plays*, edited by Gwynne Edwards, London, 1988.

Criticism
(For general works on the author, see *Playwrights* volume)

Books:
Rupert C. Allen, *Psyche and Symbol in the Theater of Federico García Lorca: "Perlimplin"; "Yerma"; "Blood Wedding"*, Austin, Texas, 1974.
C.B. Morris, *García Lorca: "Bodas de sangre"*, London, 1980.

Articles:
Rubert C. Allen, "The Fusion of Poetry and Drama in *Blood Wedding*", in *Modern Drama*, 2, 1959.
R. Dickson, "Archetypal Symbolism in Lorca's *Bodas de Sangre*", in *Literature and Psychology*, vol. 10 no. 2, 1960.
Ronald Gaskell, "Theme and Form: Lorca's *Blood Wedding*", in *Modern Drama*, 5, 1963.
Eva K. Touster, "Thematic Patterns in Lorca's *Blood Wedding*", in *Modern Drama*, 7, 1964.
Julian Palley, "Archetypal Symbols in *Bodas de Sangre*", in *Hispania*, 50, 1967.
Juan Villegas, "El Leitmotiv del Caballo en *Bodas de Sangre*", in *Hispanófila*, 29, 1967.
Charles L. Halliburton, "García Lorca, the Tragedian: An Aristotelian Analysis of *Bodas de sangre*", in *Revista de Estudios hispánicos*, 2, 1968.
Rose A. Zimbardo, "The Mythic Pattern in Lorca's *Blood Wedding*", in *Modern Drama*, 10, 1968.
Fernando Cuadra Pinto, "Para un analisis de *Bodas de Sangre*", in *Revista Signos de Valparaiso*, 3, 1969.
Luis Gonzalez-del-Valle, "*Bodas de sangre* y Sus Elementos Tragicos", in *Archivum*, 21, 1971.
Luis Gonzalez-del-valle, "Justica Poetica en *Bodas de sangre*", in *Romance Notes*, 14, 1972.
Norma L. Hutman, "Inside the Circle: On Rereading *Blood Wedding*", in *Modern Drama*, 16, 1973.
John T.H. Timm, "Some Critical Observations on García Lorca's *Bodas de sangre*", in *Revista de estudios hispánicos*, 7, 1973.
Reed Anderson, "The Idea of Tragedy in García Lorca's *Bodas de sangre*", in *Revista hispánica moderna*, 38, 1974–75.

Grace Álvarez-Altman, "*Blood Wedding*: A Literary Onomastic Interpretation", in *García Lorca Review*, 8, 1980.
C. Christopher Soufas, "Interpretation in/of *Bodas de sangre*", in *García Lorca Review*, 11, 1983.
Wendy L. Rolph, "Lorca/Gades/Saura: Modes of Adaptation in *Bodas de sangre*", in *Anales de la literatura española contemporánea*, 11, 1986.
Norman C. Miller, "Lullaby, Wedding Song, and Funeral Chant in García Lorca's *Bodas de sangre*", in *Gestos*, 5, 1988.

*   *   *

Blood Wedding (*Bodas de sangre*), set in a rural community in southern Spain, is the story of the Bride who, on the day of her wedding, elopes with a former lover, Leonardo Félix, and of the Bridegroom's pursuit, which ends in his own and Leonardo's deaths. Act I reveals, in its three scenes, the Bridegroom's mother's grief for her husband and her elder son, both killed in a feud with the Félix family, and her fear for the Bridegroom, intent on marrying a girl previously associated with Leonardo Félix; Leonardo's unhappy marriage; the arrangements for the marriage of the Bridegroom and the Bride, and her continuing passion for Leonardo. Act II develops existing tensions: in its first scene a bitter confrontation between the Bride and Leonardo gives way to the joy of the wedding-guests, celebrated in song and dancing; in the second scene the animation of the wedding-reception is progressively darkened by the Bride's agitation, the Mother's fears, Leonardo's disturbing presence, and his final escape with the Bride. Act III introduces mysterious and frightening figures: the Moon, Death (an old beggar-woman), and three woodcutters. Moon and Death arrange between them the fight in which Leonardo and the Bridegroom kill each other. In the final scene the Mother, Leonardo's widow and the Bride lament both their loss and the tragic events which have taken place.

The immediate source for the play was a newspaper account of 1928 describing the flight in Almería of a newly married woman with a former lover and their pursuit by the bridegroom's family. Literary sources and influences included, above all, J. M. Synge's *Riders to the Sea*, known to Lorca in a Spanish translation, and, more generally, Ibsen's *Peer Gynt* (Peer Gynt abducts Ingrid) and Shakespeare's *Romeo and Juliet* in which irresistible love and family feud are combined. The themes of Lorca's play are, however, those of his earlier poetry and theatre, rooted in his personal circumstances and in particular in his homosexuality: love, frustration, passing time and death, the preoccupations of his earlier "serious" theatre as well as of his comic pieces. His increasing turning to tragedy from 1930 onwards can be explained in several ways, the most important, no doubt, being a deep-seated sense of personal unhappiness. But interwoven with this was Lorca's Andalusian awareness of the crucial role of fate in human lives, deeply ingrained in the Spanish mentality. And a third influential factor was undoubtedly the presentation in the early 1930's, in various Spanish cities, including Madrid, of such outstanding Greek tragedies as *Medea* and *Electra*.

Although it is set in rural Spain and its characters are people of the countryside, *Blood Wedding* is one of Lorca's least realistic plays. Though differentiated from each other, the characters have a symbolic and archetypal quality implicit in their names: the Mother, the Father, the Bride, the Bridegroom, etc. Even the apparently realistic name of Leonardo is an amalgam of the leonine power and the ardent passion which constitute his nature. The characters are, moreover, consis-

Blood Wedding: Donmar Warehouse, London, 1988 (Communicado Theatre Company)

tently linked to the world of nature—the Mother to Mother Earth: the heat and force of human passion to the blazing sun and rushing rivers—in a way which suggests not only that they feel very strongly, but that their lives are ruled by forces as irresistible as those which move the tides and determine the succession of the seasons. In Act III such forces manifest themselves in the non-human figures of Moon and Death whose manipulation of the human characters underlines their smallness and insignificance.

The symbolic resonances of the action are enhanced by Lorca's theatrical style, at the opposite pole from naturalism. Stage directions stylize and simplify, omitting detail and creating images which both mirror the predominant mood of a scene and extend its implications, as in Act I, Scene One where the room—"*a room painted yellow*"—is an exteriorization of the Mother's bitterness as well as an image of the anguish of suffering woman at large. Throughout the play the settings perform a similar function and are matched in that respect by every other aspect of stage-performance, true to the spirit of Craig, Appia, Maeterlinck, and, in Spain, Valle-Inclán. In terms of movement, the still, despairing, seated figure of the Mother in Act I. Scene One, has its opposite in the lively movement of the wedding-guests in Act II, or the restlessly pacing Leonardo at different moments in the play. Similarly, the lighting of the stage is at every point expressive of mood, from the darkness that accompanies and underpins the chaotic passions of the bride and Leonardo at the beginning of Act II, Scene One, to the flood of sunlight which heralds the wedding

later in the scene, and the icy blue light which announces the approach of Moon and Death in Act III. Language, too, is vital in this respect. The celebratory songs of Act II have a surging momentum expressive of joy and creativity, and the lament which ends the play has the heaviness of inescapable sorrow. The style of *Blood Wedding*, integrating setting, movement, lighting, speech, and music, communicates the tensions to which its characters are exposed and suggests, through its marked stylization, the extent to which their experience is universal. As J. L. Styan has observed, in *Modern Drama in Theory and Practice* (1961), "He worked outside the mainstream of European symbolist drama, but his contribution to this genre is in many ways the most accomplished and exciting we have . . . . "

The tragic power of *Blood Wedding*, perhaps more intense than that of any other 20th-century play, has been compared to that of the tragedies of Sophocles or Euripides. On the other hand, Lorca experienced in his own time the anguish of the individual, frustrated and tragically crushed by implacable rules—social and religious. Given his genius, his passionate nature, and the particular culture from which he came, it is not surprising that he should have written a tragedy as powerful, and as ancient and modern, as *Blood Wedding*.

—Gwynne Edwards

THE BLOOMERS.   See **SCENES FROM THE HEROIC LIFE OF THE MIDDLE CLASSES.**

THE BLUE BIRD (L'Oiseau bleu)
by Maurice Maeterlinck

First Publication: Paris, 1909.
First Production: Moscow Art Theatre, Moscow, 30 September 1908.

Translations
The Bluebird, translated by Alexander Teixeira de Mattos, London, 1909.
Maurice Maeterlinck's "Blue Bird", adapted by Brian Wildsmith, Oxford, 1977.

Criticism
(For general works on the author, see *Playwrights* volume)

Books:
Henry Rose, *Maeterlinck's Symbolism: "The Blue Bird" and Other Essays*, London, 1910.
Florence G. Fidler, *The Bird that is Blue. A Study of Maeterlinck's Two Fairy Plays*, 1928.

On Christmas Eve a poor wood-cutter's children, Tyltyl and his sister, Mytyl, dream that an aged crone (with a strong resemblance to their neighbour) enters their bedroom and asks them to bring her the blue bird of happiness to cure her sick child. She transforms herself into the Fairy Berylune and with the aid of a magic diamond opens the children's eyes to the spiritual essence behind mundane appearances. The "souls" of Dog and Cat materialise, along with those of Milk, Bread, Sugar, Water, Fire, and the pure spirit, Light. They accompany the children on their quest which takes them from the Fairy Berylune's palace through the Land of Memory (where they meet their dead grandparents) the Palace of Night, and the Kingdom of the Unborn. They have a terrifying encounter with embittered trees and animals, and realise, in a graveyard, that death is an illusion. Each time they capture a blue bird it changes colour, escapes or in some way evades them. The dream ends, and Tyltyl offers their old neighbour's ailing child the bird that has been there all the time, his own caged dove. The girl is cured, but the bird flies away: the blue bird of happiness remains an elusive figment.

The Blue Bird was the one play of Maeterlinck's to enjoy an enormous popular success. It kept its place in the theatrical repertory often as a Christmas play, till long after his more intense, symbolist plays of the 1890's had suffered a (temporary) eclipse. It has also been made into a film, a ballet, and a musical play. Its optimism contrasted sharply with the dark mood of earlier plays like *The Death of Tintagiles* (1895) in

The Blue Bird: Haymarket Theatre, London, 1910

which, as Maeterlinck said "the riddle of existence was answered only by the enigma of annihilation". Whereas the child, Tintagiles, was snatched from his sisters by death in the form of a monstrous Queen, for the brother and sister in *The Blue Bird*, the dreaded graveyard becomes a beautiful garden.

Another new feature of *The Blue Bird* was its genial, if grotesque, humour. Sugar breaks off his long sugar-stick fingers and Bread cuts slices off his stomach with his Turkish scimitar to feed the children when they are hungry. Colloquial notes are struck in the midst of grand fantasy. Night, awesomely clad in black, complains fretfully in Act III to her ally, the Cat, that humankind's invasion of her territory is making her Terrors afraid to leave the house: most of her Sicknesses have become ill. The mystical graveyard scene is preceded by a comical picture of general fright, with the Dog shaking like a leaf and Milk feeling herself about to "turn".

Like most of Maeterlinck's plays, *The Blue Bird* made a strong appeal to artists. Stanislavsky used all the resources of the Moscow Art Theatre to make the premiere a thrilling visual event. Vladimir Egorov created exquisitely stylised sets ("delicate as lace" Stanislavsky had stipulated) which Maeterlinck admired so much he wanted them used again for the London and Paris productions. In the event the production at the Haymarket Theatre, London (8 December 1909) had designs by Cayley Robinson which were equally effective in a decorative style owing much to English pantomime tradition. Tyltyl (played by a young actress) was a gamin Dick Whittington figure, Mytyl, in her scarlet cloak, a type of Red Riding Hood; the grandparents' cottage in the Land of Memory was a cosy place, with roses round the door, as in a child's picture book.

Contemporary English reviewers tended to see the play as a "transcendental pantomime", complete with talking animals and magical transformation scenes. Maeterlinck acknowledged affinities with the English Christmas play when he paid a tribute to J.M. Barrie as "father of Peter Pan, grandfather of the Blue Bird". But Stanislavsky pleased him by his insistence on the play's visionary quality. The Russian actors were instructed to prepare their roles with the same seriousness they would bring to characters of Chekhov; they were to find parallels in real life, study the behaviour of some animal, make friends with children and try to enter their imaginative world. Each country put its own stamp on the play; according to Georgette Leblanc, who co-directed it in Paris, the character of Light changed radically from being a saint in Moscow to a nurse in London, and in her own production, a pagan statue.

For its early audiences the play offered a congenial and hopeful moral lesson, with the emphasis on Tyltyl's realisation that the blue bird of happiness is not to be owned by anyone, the act of giving is what brings it within reach. Modern audiences and readers might be more aware of the darker, enigmatic aspects of the play, the quality usually thought of as "Maeterlinckian". In a Belgian production of 1980, for example, the grandparents' house was no cosy cottage but a box on wheels into which they stepped, to be wheeled away, the moment the children turned from them. Scenes like those in the graveyard or the land of the unborn embody Maeterlinck's belief that consciousness extends far beyond our normal awareness. The forces of light may prevail in the play but there are intimations of a more sombre perspective, as when one of the embryos shrinks from the thought of earth ("I don't want to be born") or the trees and animals savagely bear down on the children, seeking revenge for the cruelty men have practised on them. The horror is dispersed when Light reminds Tyltyl to turn the magic diamond but it has not gone away: the peacefully grazing cows and quiet trees still contain a terrible potential for violence. Light's warning seems

especially apt for today's "green" age of anxiety about man's treatment of his environment.

—Katharine Worth

————

BODAS DE SANGRE.   See **BLOOD WEDDING.**

————

BÖDELN.   See **THE HANGMAN.**

————

BOESMAN AND LENA
by Athol Fugard

First Publication: Cape Town, 1969.
First Production: Rhodes University Little Theatre, Grahamstown, South Africa, 10 July 1969; revised version, Circle in The Square Theatre, New York, 22 June 1970.

Criticism
(For general works on the author, see *Playwrights* volume)

Articles:
Frank Levy, "Fugard's *Boesman and Lena*: Physical and Metaphysical Exhaustion", in *Yale / Theatre*, vol. 4 no. 1, 1973.
Derek Cohen, "Athol Fugard's *Boesman and Lena*", in *Journal of Commonwealth Literature*, vol. 12 no. 3, 1978.
Barrie Hough, "Fugard's *Boesman and Lena* in Perspective", in *CRUX*, vol. 13 no. 1, 1979.

*   *   *

Boesman and Lena are a Coloured couple who have spent most of their lives on the road. As the play begins, they enter carrying all their worldly possessions, their *pondok* having been bulldozed to the ground by the White authorities that morning. There is little physical action in the play. Boesman and Lena argue and reminisce. An old African appears out of the darkness, an image of age and decrepitude, and while Boesman wants nothing to do with him, Lena talks to him, recounting the story of her life with Boesman, even though he can't understand her or she him. The old man dies, silently, in the darkness. In a fury, Boesman beats the corpse, and then, fearing arrest for murder, insists that they once again pick up their burdens and resume their endless tramping of the roads.

Athol Fugard has described writing for the theatre as a way of bearing witness to South African social and political realities, but his *Notebooks* also demonstrate his desire to deal with "metaphysical" experience on the stage, influenced by his reading of writers such as Camus, Beckett, and R.D. Laing. *Boesman and Lena* is a play that invites audiences to engage at these two levels simultaneously, offering an image both of the pain and degradation engendered by the *apartheid* system and of the inescapable suffering of existence itself. The spectator should emerge from a successful performance having under-

Boesman and Lena: Hampstead Theatre, London, 1984

gone an experience which is rooted in the specific oppressions of the South African system but which also has immediate existential resonances, not dissimilar perhaps to those created by *Waiting for Godot*.

For Boesman and Lena, who have spent so much of their time together on the road, the overall shape and significance of life is closely bound up with the sequence of their travels and the events and emotions associated with them. For Lena, especially, it is crucial to impose some kind of order by knowing the exact sequence of their wanderings. At first she is confused, but she continues worrying about the correct order until she thinks she has it right: "It's coming! Korsten. Empties, and the dog. *Hond*! How was it now? Redhouse—Swartkops—Veeplas—Korsten. Then this morning the bull-dozers. . .and then . . . . [*Pause.*] Here! I've got there!". But her elation is short-lived. Boesman enjoys pointing out that she is wrong and confusing her further. One day, he suggests, she will even have to ask him who she is: "What about Rosie? Nice name Rose. Maria. Anna. Or Sannie! Sannie who? *Sommer* Sannie Somebody".

For the audience, their wanderings become more than the evocation of physical displacement caused by the racism of *apartheid*; they give dramatic expression to the ancient motif of life as a journey, the elemental passage of everyman and everywoman through existence, and the struggle to make sense of it by identifying landmarks on the way. As Lena puts it:

I meet the memory of myself on the old roads. Sometimes young. Sometimes old. Is she coming or going? From where to where? All mixed-up. The right time on the wrong road, the right road leading to the wrong place.

The third character of the play, Outa, the old black man, says not a word but his presence and relationship with Lena are crucial for the meanings which *Boesman and Lena* can generate. Lena insists that someone must bear witness to her life. She tells the uncomprehending Outa the story of the dog that she fed when Boesman wasn't looking and which rewarded her by coming at night and, as Boesman slept, sat and watched her:

All the things I did—making the fire, cooking, counting bottles or bruises, even just sitting, you know, when it's too much. . .he saw it. *Hond*! I called him *Hond*. But any name, he'd wag his tail if you said it nice. I'll tell you what it is. Eyes, *Outa*. Another pair of eyes. Something to see you.

Like the dog, the old man is the instrument, however humble, of a demand of which Lena is eventually fully conscious—the demand that her life be *seen*, witnessed by another. The victim of the *apartheid* system, the victim of Boesman's violence (itself the product of his humiliation as a poor Coloured in South Africa), Lena nevertheless refuses to allow her existence to pass away unnoticed in another consciousness, even if it is that of the "lowest of the low"—a dog or the old, dying man. It is an image with affinities both to existentialist thought and to Fugard's conviction that one of the main functions of his theatre is to bear witness to the lives of people who may otherwise be unnoticed and forgotten.

—Brian Crow

BONDS OF INTEREST (Los intereses creados)
by Jacinto Benavente y Martínez

First Publication: In *Benavente: Teatro 16*, Madrid, 1908.
First Production: Teatro de Lara, Madrid, 9 December 1907.

Translations
Bonds of Interest, in *Plays*, edited and translated by J.G. Underhill, New York, 1923. (4 vols.).

Criticism
(For general works on the author, see *Playwrights* volume)

Books:
Eduardo Galán Font, *Claves para la lectura de "Los intereses creados" de Jacinto Benavente*, Madrid, Barcelona, and Mexico, 1986.

Articles:
Erasmo Buceta, "En torno de *Los intereses creados*", in *Hispania*, 4, 1921.
Dámaso Alonso, "De *El Caballero de Ellescas* a *Los Intereses Creados*", in *Revista de filología espagñola*, 50, 1970.
José Vila Selma, "Notas en torna a *Los intereses creados* y sus posibles fuentes", in *Cuadernos hispanoamericanos*, 241–43, 1970.
Robert J. Young, "Unpredictable Features in the Style of Benavente's *Los intereses creados*", in *Language & Style*, 9, 1976.
Fernando Lázaro Carreter (ed.), [introduction to] *Los intereses creados* by Jacinto Benavente, Madrid, fifth edition, 1979.
Gérard Dufour, "Note sur le personnage de 'Leandro' dans *Los intereses creados* de Jacinto Benavente", in *Cahiers d'études Romanes*, 7, 1982.
Arnold M. Penuel, "Form, Function, and Freud in Benavente's *Los intereses creados*", in *Hispanófila*, 84, 1985.

*   *   *

The setting for this *commedia dell'arte* "puppet" farce, in a prologue and two acts, is an imaginary country at the beginning of the 17th century. Two penniless adventurers, Leandro and Crispin, arrive at an inn. Casting Leandro in the role of noble master and himself as servant, Crispin hoodwinks the innkeeper into giving them free lodging and food, as well as extending credit to the poet Arlequin and the Captain. He then manoeuvers the impoverished matchmaker Doña Sirena and her maid Colombina into setting a romantic stage for Leandro and Silvia, daughter of the wealthy Polichinela. Forming alliances based on vested interests, Crispin succeeds in outwitting Pantalón and the representatives of justice, who come pursuing him, and overcomes Polichinela's opposition to the marriage of the young couple, who have fallen in love.

The play is generally considered the Nobel Prize winner's most "universal"; along with his tragedy *La Malquerida* (*The Passion Flower*), it continues to be performed internationally. *Bonds of Interest* is an elaborate example of metatheatre. At the level of the frame play, the characters respond to their anticipated roles from the *commedia dell'arte* and all the concomitant devices of classic farce. Crispin, however, also functions as a would-be dramatist-within-the-play who creates a text for himself and Leandro. Once Leandro has adopted his role-within-the-role of noble master, he enters into a romantic comedy with Silvia. In the meantime, Crispin, in his role as servant, plays out a variety of intrigues in which he manipulates the others by their greed and vanity. Nor is the role-playing limited to the two "picaros." Polichinela's affluence hides his past as Crispin's fellow galley slave. Doña Sirena earns her way in the world by exploiting surface appearances. Silvia, true to the models of classic farce, readily enters the game in order to trick her father into approving her marriage. The Doctor, administering a flexible justice, executes a rapid role reversal when Crispin offers monetary incentives.

Benavente exploits the subversive potential of metatheatre to satirize the external reality of the spectators. His characters, whose actions are motivated by self-interest, serve as a mirror to human foibles and to bourgeois society's materialism and hypocrisy. But the playwright also cleverly incorporates two opposing messages in his text, allowing spectators to eschew Crispin's cynicism and accept, instead, Silvia's final comforting words that love conquers all.

Bonds of Interest begins with a theatricalist prologue in which Crispin informs the audience of the antecedents to the farce and assures them that what they are about to see is not real and therefore should not be taken seriously: the characters are puppets, not people (Benavente himself delivered the prologue on some occasions). However dramatically effective the introductory monologue may be, Crispin is hardly a reliable narrator. The marionettes he announces are, in fact, flesh and blood actors. Even overlooking that discrepancy as a metaphorical allusion, the spectator is left with the instruction to ignore what follows, including, presumably, Silvia's idealistic praise of love as an ennobling force. By deciding to take Silvia at face value, as audiences have often done, the spectator is thereby duped into accepting Leandro, the softer of the two "picaros", as romantic hero, and Silvia, the disobedient daughter who deceives her old father, as romantic heroine. That acceptance of Leandro is further complicated by a tradition, starting with the original production, of having the role played by an actress. In short, one may either believe, as the play-title indicates, that it is human nature to engage in farce in order to protect self-interest, or smile and accept the romance that results from role-playing within the role (with or without cross-gender acting) as an ideal to live by.

It is Crispin, the manipulator par excellence, who delivers an oft-quoted speech about the division in human nature; because he has assumed the baser, materialistic aspects, Leandro is free to encarnate man's loftier qualities. That Leandro's noble character is merely a role Crispin has created for him may slip by unnoticed unless one focuses on the theme of appearance versus reality underscored by the metatheatrical games. In a 1978 revival, Francisco Nieva's design, consistent with Benavente's stage directions, highlighted this theme by calling attention to the fact that the buildings were mere facades. The inn is not really an inn, nor is Doña Sirena's pavillion really a pavillion. If nothing in the dramatic world is real, then Leandro and Silvia's love at first sight is just as suspect as the Doctor's justice and Polichinela's past. The final touch of irony in Benavente's satirical text lies in the audience's willingness to suspend disbelief and accept the facade of true love as a transcendental message.

—Phyllis Zatlin

LES BONNES. See **THE MAIDS.**

BORIS GODUNOV (Boris Godunov)
by Alexander Pushkin

First Publication: 1831.
First Production: Maryinsky Theatre, St. Petersburg, 17 September 1870.

Editions
Boris Godunov (second edition), edited by Louis Segal, London, 1938.
Boris Godunov, edited and translated by Philip L. Barbour, New York, 1953 (with translation).

Translations
Boris Godunov, translated by A. Hayes, London, 1918.
Boris Godunov, translated by F.D. Reeve in *Anthology of Russian Plays 1*, New York, 1961.
Boris Godunov, translated and adapted by D.M. Thomas, Leamington Spa, Warwickshire, 1985.

Criticism
(For general works on the author, see *Playwrights* volume)

Articles:
Kevin Moss, "The Last Word in Fiction: On Significant Lies in *Boris Gudunov*", in *Slavic and East European Journal*, Summer 1988.

* * *

Performance of *Boris Godunov* was delayed by censorship problems for almost half a century until the play was finally staged at the Maryinsky Theatre, St. Petersburg, in 1870. Although still in the Russian repertory it is not often performed because of technical difficulties and some artistic shortcomings (in fact, it is much better known as the operatic version by Mussorgsky). The play covers the career of Boris Godunov from 1598 to 1605, the period of his regency. Pushkin accepts the historically uncertain suggestion that Boris had previously arranged the murder of the tsarevich Dimitry in boyhood; in the play much is made of the agonies of conscience which he suffers as a result. Godunov proves to be a wise, considerate, but unpopular ruler who is blamed by the people for every last misfortune suffered by the country. He also has to take account of a pretender to the throne, a "False Dimitry", who is really a runaway novice, Grigory Otrepev, the same age as the dead tsarevich. Grigory has learned about Dimitry from Pimen, an old monk who is an assiduous chronicler of Russian history. Escaping to Lithuania, the pretender raises an army and marches on Russia. After several successes he is routed on the battlefield but at that very time Boris is struck down and dies, on stage, after reporting his crimes and entrusting the government of the country to his young son, Fyodor. Meanwhile, the pretender recovers, advances, and assumes power himself. Fyodor's death is announced to the people and a shout of triumph is called for. A famous concluding stage direction informs us that, "The people remain silent".

The Shakespearean resonances in *Boris Godunov* are many and well documented. Perhaps in an effort to distance himself from Shakespeare Pushkin decided not to break up his play into the usual acts and scenes, though an underlying five-act structure may still be discerned. The normal list of *dramatis personae* is also omitted. The result is an apparent collage of loosely connected scenes and a wide range of characters, some of whom appear only once. Thus the play has gained a reputation for diffuseness which is, ironically, all too justified by the coherence and brilliance of some of the individual scenes. It also suffers from the structural shortcoming that the two adversaries, who never met in real life, cannot be brought into confrontation on stage.

Nevertheless, the merits of this play are considerable. Its characterization was something quite new for the Russian theatre. Real historical figures rub shoulders with invented ones; they range in age from the very young to the very old and cover the entire spectrum of society from royalty, to poor townsfolk, and an idiot boy. They are depicted with the kind of roundness, subtlety, and sympathy which creates a sense of truth. The play also presents a majestic impression of Russian history and institutions. Above all, it contains some of Pushkin's finest poetry. Once again departing from Shakespeare, Pushkin opted not for the free-ranging English pentameter but for the French variant, which insists on a second-foot caesura in every line. This curious constraint—which goes right against the poet's normal proclivities—turns out well; the slight sense of formality enhances the dignity of several famous scenes. The Russian language is heard at its noblest in a series of memorable monologues—by Pimen, by the Patriarch of the Russian Orthodox Church, and, on more than one occasion, by Boris himself. The quality of the language in *Boris Godunov* can never be satisfactorily translated, and without it the value of the play is much diminished. Translations do exist, though, and the first of them, by Alfred Hayes, was produced in 1925 by the Birmingham University Dramatic Society supported by Granville Bantock and Adrian Boult. Since then, performances abroad have been rare and even in the Soviet Union a new production is hailed as adventurous. The latent qualities of *Boris Godunov* are, however, so substantial that even in translation this play should be regarded as producible.

—Anthony D.P. Briggs

LE BOURGEOIS GENTILHOMME.　See **THE WOULD-BE GENTLEMAN.**

THE BOURGEOIS GENTLEMAN.　See **THE WOULD-BE GENTLEMAN.**

THE BRAGGART SOLDIER (Miles Gloriosus)
by Titus Maccius Plautus

First Production: Probably before 200 B.C.

Editions
Miles Gloriosus, edited by Robert Y. Tyrrell, London, 1881; third edition, 1899.
Miles Gloriosus, in *Plautus: Comoediae, 2*, edited by Wallace M. Lindsay, Oxford, 1903 (Oxford Classical Texts).
The Braggart Warrior [with translation], in *Plautus, 3*, Cambridge, Massachusetts and London, 1924 (Loeb Classical Library).
Miles Gloriosus, edited by Mason Hammond, Arthur M. Mack, and Walter Moskalew, Cambridge, Massachusetts, 1963; revised edition, 1976.

Translations
The Swaggering Soldier, in *"The Pot of Gold" and Other Plays*,
translated by E.F. Watling, Harmondsworth, 1965.
The Braggart Soldier, in *Plautus: Three Comedies*, translated
by Erich Segal, New York, 1969.

Criticism
(For general works on the author, see *Playwrights* volume)

Articles:
R. Haywood, "On the Unity of *Miles Gloriosus*", in *American
Journal of Philology*, 65, 1944.
J. Hason, "The Gloriosus Military", in *Roman Drama*, edited
by T. Dorey, New York, 1964.
G. Williams, "Evidence for Plautus's Workmanship in the
Miles Gloriosus", in *Hermes*, 86, 1958.
V.J. Cleary, "Monkey Business in the *Miles Gloriosus*", in
Classical Journal, 67, 1972.

*   *   *

Pyrgopolynices, megalomaniac mercenary and insatiable womaniser, has kidnapped Pleusicles's mistress, Philocomasium, from Athens and brought her home with him to Ephesus. Shortly afterwards, Pleusicles' loyal slave Palaestrio is captured by pirates while trying to warn him of this treachery, and coincidentally has been sold to Pyrgopolynices himself. Now, by Palaestrio's doing, Pleusicles has secretly established himself next door in the house of the elderly bachelor Periplectomenus, and has access to Philocomasium by a hidden passage between the two houses. When the soldier's second slave Sceledrus sees the lovers together, Palaestrio persuades him the girl he has seen is Philocomasium's identical twin sister, and by using the secret passage Philocomasium is able to appear in both roles. Next, Palaestrio persuades Pyrgopolynices that Periplectomenus has a beautiful young wife who is secretly in love with the soldier, and engages a luscious impostor to play the role. Smitten, Pyrgopolynices dismisses Philocomasium to go home with her "sister" while he turns his sexual attentions to the "wife," Acroteleutium. Caught in the act, he is beaten and threatened with public castration; blubbering and humiliated, he buys his way out with a fine, and discovers too late the nature of Palaestrio's trick.

Plautus's longest play may also be the first complete work of Latin literature we have. The unique absence of lyric *cantica* seems to argue for an early date, and a late writer refers the obscure topical joke at line 211 to the scarcely less mysterious punishment of the poet Naevius, suggesting a date before 200 BC. Of the Greek play it adapts nothing is known beyond the title, *Alazon* (*Bigmouth*).

Like the later *Pseudolus* and Terence's *Eunuch*, the *Miles* presents the systematic humiliation of a blustering, military *machisto* by a resourceful slave–hero, who reverses their roles by hijacking his martial language and imagery, and traps him in an elaborate impersonation to cheat him of his money, his sexual fulfilment, and his credibility. In the other plays mentioned, this theme is secondary, but the *Miles* treats it centrally—despite the strangely redundant twins ploy of the first half, in which Pyrgopolynices is not involved and which is scarcely mentioned again. Structural interference with the Greek source has been suspected, but the evidence is uncertain; and the two halves are perhaps more thematically connected than has been recognised.

The key to the play's unity lies in the close relationship in New Comedy between the house, the household, and the person. The citizen's house, as much as his cloak and tunic, is part of his uniform as a free man. It is his sphere of exclusive power, whose contents (including guests, women, and slaves) are under his full control. Like the late *Casina*, the *Miles* traces the degradation of a free citizen by violation of house, clothing, and body; in both the crime is confusion of the categories of legitimate sexual access, and the fatal rendezvous takes place in a neighbour's house and spills out into the public space of the street. In the *Miles*, even more overtly, violation of the house (via the secret door) and violation of the body are stages of a single development: the transfer of power over Pyrgopolynices's social and corporal person away from himself to Periplectomenus.

Thus despite an undeniable leisureliness over plot detail in the first half, the stage space and characters are actually used with considerable economy. As the opening scene establishes, Pyrgopolynices lives in a fantasy world of epic heroism and irresistibility to women. Palaestrio's trick disguises the characters of the play as roles within that fantasy, and in doing so lures the soldier deeper into the self-delusion of his inner world while the outer is gradually taken from him. His house, his mistress, his slave, and finally his very masculinity fall one by one into the power of his enemies, by progressive leakage of each across the boundary from his own house and control to that of Periplectomenus. The love-hero Pleusicles, as an alien in Ephesus, is necessarily a secondary figure, which suits Plautus's taste well; citizen lovers are not for him figures of large dramatic interest in the way they are for Terence. But his role is still important: in Ephesus, his status is precarious (that of a powerless *xenos*) but at home in Athens (whither he, Philocomasium, and Palaestrio embark at the end of the play, and which is evoked on stage by the use of the harbour exit) he can resume his status as a free citizen immune to any retaliation.

For a play so founded on sex, violence, and the subversion of regular orders, it is striking how careful the *Miles* is with its moral and legal pretexts. Most readers hear a note of preposterous, Plautine mischief in the stern finger-wagging moral of the soldier's closing words. But Plautus has been more deliberate than we might expect in preparing the ground for this last-minute surge of unlikely piety. Pyrgopolynices has violated codes of ownership while a stranger in Athens, by abducting Philocomasium (apparently a freeborn *meretrix*, not a slave) from her mother; the form of Pleusicles's retaliation is thus morally as well as symmetrically apt. Pyrgopolynices acknowledges the dangers of surrendering licit sex for illicit, to the extent of expressing last-minute qualms over Acroteleutium's marital status, and only walks into the trap because Palaestrio convinces him she is newly divorced—a significant glimpse of the soldier's moral awareness of his actions. And even Periplectomenus's long didactic gag routine on the pleasures of bachelor old age serves a thematic function, in banishing the motif of legitimate marriage firmly from the world of this play, and deflecting any hint of the adultery plot's threatening anyone but its victim.

But it would be wrong to emphasise thematic coherence over comic. The energy and influence of the *Miles* lie in the quintessentially Plautine deployment of comic language, imagery, and types in his favourite pattern of elaborate, ludic impersonation under the direction of the dramaturgic slave. The figure of the braggart soldier this play has bequeathed to the dramatic tradition was, ironically, by no means a Plautine invention. But it does foreshadow much that is best, and most characteristic, in his own mature work.

—N.J. Lowe

BRAND
by Henrik Ibsen

First Publication: Copenhagen, 1866.
First Production: Nya Teatret [New Theatre], Stockholm, 24
March 1885.

Translations
Brand, translated by C.H. Herford, London.
Brand, translated by F.E. Garrett, London, 1915.
Brand, translated by Miles Menander Dawson, Boston, 1916.
Brand, translated by Michael Meyer, London, 1967 (condensed version).
Brand, translated by James Kirkup with J.W. MacFarlane, in
The Oxford Ibsen, 3, edited by James Walter McFarlane,
Oxford, 1972.
Brand, translated by Theodore Jorgenson, Northfield, 1962.
Brand, translated by G.M. Gathome-Hardy, London, 1966.
Brand, translated by Inga-Stina Ewbank, Minneapolis, 1981.

Criticism
(For general works on the author, see *Playwrights* volume)

Books:
P.G. La Chenais, *"Brand" d'Ibsen: Étude et analyse*, Paris,
1933.
H.W. Freihow, *Henrik Ibsen's "Brand"*, Oslo, 1936.
Finn Thorn, *Lov og evangelium: tanker om Henrik Ibsens
"Brand"*, Oslo, 1951.
Åse H. Lervik, *Ibsens verskunst i Brand*, Oslo, 1969.
Bjorn Hemmer, *"Brand"; "Kongsemnerne"; "Peer Gynt": En
Studie i Ibsens romantiske diktning*, Oslo, 1972.

Articles:
Julius E. Olson, "Gerd, the Hawk, and the Ice-Church in
Ibsen's *Brand*", in *Scandinavian Studies and Notes*, 6, 1920–
21.
B.M. Kinck, "Dramaet *Brand*", in *Edda*, 30, 1930.
S. Svensson, "*Brand* och den svenska göticismen", in *Edda*,
30, 1930.
D. Haakonsen, "Henrik Ibsen's *Brand*", in *Edda*, 41, 1941.
Harald Beyer, "Ibsen's *Brand*", in *The Norseman*, 8, 1950.
C.E.W. Dahlström, "Brand—Ibsen's Bigot", in *Scandinavian
Studies and Notes*, 22, 1950.
Pavel Fraenkel, "Ibsen's *Brand* og europeisk titanisme", in
Edda, 56, 1956.
Victor Hellern, "*Brand*: symboler og tolkninger", in *Edda*, 56,
1956.
John Hems, "Abraham and Brand", in *Philosophy*, 39, 1964.
Irving Deer, "Ibsen's *Brand*: Paradox and the Symbolic
Hero", in *Lock Haven Bulletin*, vol. 1 no. 3, 1961; reprinted
in *Ibsen: A Collection of Critical Essays*, edited by Rolf
Fjelde, Englewood Cliffs, New Jersey 1965.
Abdalla A. Metwally, "Brand: Ibsen's Enigmatic Character",
in *Studies in Modern Drama*, 1, Beirut, 1971.
Sandra E. Saari, "Ibsen's *Brand*: The Nineteenth-Century
Play and the 1978 British National Theatre Production", in
Scandinavian Studies, 51, 1979.
Inga-Stina Ewbank, "*Brand*: the Play and the Translation", in
Ibsen: "Brand", Minneapolis, 1981.
John E. Bellquist, "Ibsen's *Brand* and *Når vi dode vågner*:
Tragedy, Romanticism, Apocalypse", in *Scandinavian
Studies*, 55, 1983.
Wolfgang Sohlich, "Ibsen's *Brand*: Drama of the Fatherless
Society", in *Journal of Dramatic Theory and Criticism*, vol.
3 no. 2, 1989.

* * *

On his way across the mountains of western Norway to take
up his position as a curate of a fjord parish, Brand encounters a
young painter, Einar, and his fiancée, Agnes. The young
couple are happy and playful, whereas Brand is devoted to a
great mission: he wants to teach his fellow men truthfulness to
their convictions. Brand's God demands consistency of mind
and actions: "Be what you have to be/Wholly and completely. . .". Agnes is impressed by Brand, and becomes his
wife. Gerd, a mad girl, scorns him; she prefers the huge "ice
church" in the mountains to the small church by the fjord. The
moral standards Brand preaches are absolute, and apply to
himself and his kin as well as to his parishioners. His mother is
attached to her worldly goods, and her deathbed request for
absolution is rejected by him since she is unwilling to let go of
them. The doctor strongly recommends a change of climate for
Brand's and Agnes's little weak son; Brand falters, but cannot
relinquish his mission. After the death of the son, Agnes clings
to his memory, but Brand persuades her to give his clothes to a
gipsy woman with a baby. These losses sap the strength of
Agnes, and she dies. Using his maternal inheritance, Brand
completes the building of a bigger church. The civil servants of
the region want to ensure his loyalty to the state, but Brand
realizes that even this new church is too small. He sets out for
the "ice church" in the mountains, followed by his parishioners. The hardship makes them turn against him,
however, and he continues alone. At the "ice church" (a big,
hanging glacier), Gerd is hunting for a hawk with a rifle, and
the shot releases an avalanche. Perishing with her under the
ice, Brand cries out his final question: does not the will of man
contribute at all to salvation? The answer comes from a voice
heard through the roll of thunder: "God is Love!".

Ibsen originally intended *Brand* as an epic poem, but the
composition went slowly. He decided to leave the epic, and
write in the form of a dramatic poem. The five-act drama in
rhymed verse was a burst of energy following Ibsen's disgust at
the decision of the governments in Norway and Sweden to
leave Denmark alone in its fight against Prussia, in spite of the
rhetoric of Scandinavian brotherhood, particularly in academic circles. Brand is turning against his people for their lack
of moral courage, and the poet was to a great extent giving vent
to his own feelings at the time through the urgent appeals of the
prophet-like character. Shortly after the completion of the
poem, Ibsen wrote a letter to Charles XV, King of Sweden and
Norway, asking for a grant and stating what he saw as his life's
task: ". . .the work of arousing the people of our nation and
urging them to think great thoughts".

An issue much debated is the question of how to judge
Brand. He seems so extreme in his religious zeal, so inhuman
in his demands for "All or Nothing" that it becomes impossible
to accept his message *and* survive. Should he be considered an
impressive spiritual leader in an age of moral apathy? Or is he
an excessive idealist whose tragic mistakes the dramatist does
his best to unmask? There was in contemporary philosophy
and poetry a certain trend of Romantic heroism opposing all
kinds of institutional endeavour and the spirit of compromise it
generally entailed. Behind it are the writings of Søren
Kierkegaard and his passionate individualism—an attitude
which attracted the young Ibsen, and which he never completely abandoned in his writings and views; Ibsen's admiration for strong and uncompromising minds, men who paid little
attention to considerations of convenience, is well
documented.

Brand is not representing the same affirmative position all
through the text. On the surface his conviction seems firm
enough except for the very end, when he questions his central
belief in the saving power of the will. He is in doubt on several
occasions, however, struggling with his own conscience

regarding the way he treats his mother and his son.

Still, Brand's speeches carry a certain amount of persuasive power. This is more than one can say of most of his opponents. The Doctor is a sympathetic humanitarian. According to him, the ancient law of God and man does not apply to the present generation: "Its first commandment is: 'Thou shalt be humane!'" Brand's response is a rejection of "that wishy-washy word". He does not recognize a change of the law. The others speak with little spiritual authority; indeed they are the targets of satire. The Mayor tries to influence Brand by congratulating him and offering the possibility of a knighthood. He has no objection to "a thundering great sermon" in the new church; the effect of its acoustics is amazing. The Dean wants to promote a collective Christendom, a kind of herd religion, as opposed to Brand's insistence on the individual's responsibility before God. The Dean's message is anti-individualist: "Each man must subjugate his own peculiar gifts, / Neither advancing nor raising himself unduly, / But humbly hiding himself among the masses". This is of course contrary to Ibsen's Romantic concept of the Self.

In worldly terms Brand is no doubt a loser. Through a paradoxical statement concluding Act IV he sees his loss as a victory, however, "The loss of *All* brought everything to you. . . / Only what is lost can be possessed for ever!". The question of his soul's salvation is left unanswered at the moment of his death. The concluding message from the voice, "God is Love!", is ambiguous. Has Brand been a false teacher all the time with his emphasis on the will of the individual, and is the voice from above reproaching him, since he did not understand the true nature of God? Or is the voice saying that the divine grace is all-embracing, and Brand forgiven? The question may sound theological, but should be studied in aesthetic terms. The tragic end can in no way deny the greatness of the hero. Ibsen's *Brand* is a brilliant instance of the titanic idealism inherent in the Romantic age.

—Asbjørn Aarseth

BREAK OF NOON (Partage de Midi)
by Paul Claudel

First Publication: Paris, 1906; revised edition, 1948; further revised edition, 1949.
First Production: Théâtre Marigny, Paris, 16 December 1948.

Translations
Break of Noon, translated by W. Fowlie, in *"Break of Noon" and "The Tidings Brought to Mary"*, Chicago, 1960.
Break of Noon, translated by Jonathon Griffin, Ipswich, c. 1990.

Criticism
(For general works on the author, see *Playwrights* volume)

Books:
Anne Ubersfeld, *Claudel: Autobiographie et histoire—"Partage de midi"*, Paris, 1981.

Articles:
V. Lee, "The Revising of *Partage de midi*", in *French Review*, vol. 38 no. 3, 1965.

Moriaki Watanabé, "Le 'don' ou la logique dramatique de *Partage de midi*", in *Revue des lettres modernes*, 180–182, 1968.
Mildred Deuel, "A Study of the Dramatic Structure of *Partage de midi* from 1905–1949", in *French Review*, 45, 1972.
Harold A. Waters, "Claudel's *Partage* desacralized", in *Espirt Créateur*, 13, 1973.
Michel Lioure, "Ombre et lumière dans *Partage de midi* de Paul Claudel", in *Travaux de linguistique et de littérature*, vol. 13 no. 2, 1975.
Valentini P. Brady, "The Blazing Firmament: The Symbolic Substructure of *Partage de midi*", in *Claudel Studies*, vol. 3 no. 2, 1976.
Michael Gillespie, "*Partage de midi*: From the Page to the Stage", in *Claudel Studies*, vol. 3 no. 2, 1976.
Moses M. Nagy, "Revolt and Reconciliation in *Partage de midi*", in *Claudel Studies*, vol. 3 no. 2, 1976.
M.J. Whitaker, "Les vingt partages de *Partage de midi*", in *Claudel Studies*, vol. 3 no. 1, 1976.
Bettina L. Knapp, "*Break of Noon*: A Cosmic Awakening", in *Theatre and Alchemy*, Detroit, 1980.
Michael Autrand, "La mise en spectacle de l'amour-passion dans *Partage de midi*", in *Information littéraire*, 37, 1985.
Pierre Brunel, "*Partage de midi* et le mythe de Tristan", in *Revue des lettres modernes*, 747–52, 1985.
Antoinette Weber-Caflisch, "*Partage de midi*: mythe et auto-biographie" in *Revue des lettres modernes*, 747–52, 1985.
Marie F. Etienne, "'Co-naissance' and 'Regard' in *Partage de midi*", in *Claudel Studies*, 12, 1985.
Gérard Peylet, "La transcendance de l'espace et la négation du temps à l'heure de *Partage de midi*", in *Bulletin de la Société Paul Claudel*, 101, 1986.
Antoinette Weber-Caflish, "'Le nom de son rival': Essai sur l'histoire du texte de *Partage de midi*", in *Cahiers de textologie*, 1, 1986.
Marie J. Whitaker, "Temps et mouvement dans *Partage de midi*", in *Revue d'histoire littéraire de la France*, 87, 1987.
Ann Bugliani, "Sexual Ambiguity in *Partage de midi*", in *Claudel Studies*, vol. 15 no. 1, 1988.
Charles Long, "Joyce's 'missymissy', Cocteau's 'eternal cycle', and Claudel's 'Ysé'", in *Claudel Studies*, vol. 15 no. 1, 1988.
Mitchell Shackleton, "Métaphore et métonymie dans *Partage de midi*", in *French Studies in Southern Africa*, 17, 1988.

*   *   *

Break of Noon is a three-act play written in non-rhyming Claudelian verse. Act I is set on a steamship bound for China. There are four passengers: the morose and taciturn Mesa; the virile, dominant male, Amalric; the weak, shiftless adventurer, De Ciz; and his beautiful wife, Ysé. In her youth, Ysé refused to marry Amalric, who insists he will possess her yet. She is drawn to Mesa, despite his apparent disapproval. He too recognises that they are intended for each other, but after confessing this they draw back, frightened of the consequences. Act II takes place in a Hong Kong cemetery. De Ciz intends to depart on a dangerous mission leaving Ysé behind. She begs him not go, but immediately afterwards agrees to live with Mesa, and asks him to ensure her husband's departure. Act III is set in a besieged and semi-ruined house where Ysé is living with Amalric and her child by Mesa. A bomb is set to explode to avoid them falling into the hands of the Chinese. Mesa appears and asks Ysé for an explanation of her departure and her failure to answer his letters. She does not reply. Amalric returns, the two men fight and Mesa is crippled. At Ysé's suggestion, Amalric searches his pockets and finds a pass allowing them to escape. They leave Mesa

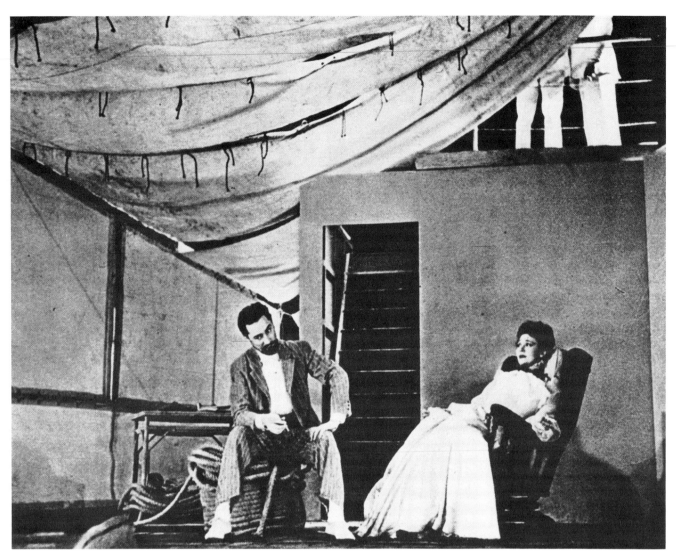

Break of Noon: Théâtre Marigny, Paris, 1948 (first production)

behind to certain death, together with his son, murdered by Ysé. In a moment of supreme revelation, Mesa speaks to God, declaring that at last he understands the divine purpose of his relationship with Ysé. That she was the means of breaking through the egotism which made him incapable of giving himself to God. Finally, Mesa is rejoined by Ysé, and in their last moments they are united in a dream reconciliation, achieving immortality by mutual consent to a mystic marriage in the eyes of God.

Break of Noon is the most immediately autobiographical of Claudel's works. In 1900, Claudel experienced a conflict of vocations between his diplomatic and literary careers and his religious convictions. He returned to France from China to go on monastic retreat, but, whether because of his lack of aptitude, or else because of the Boxer rebellion in China, his superiors decided he should return there. Claudel perceived this as a rejection by God, but felt he had no option but to obey. On the boat back to China, he began an affair with a married woman with four children. She lived with Claudel for four years, finally leaving him, pregnant with his daughter, to marry another man. *Break of Noon* was written the following year with an almost therapeutic purpose, but the crisis it represents was only fully resolved some twenty years later in

The Satin Slipper. More than just the events of this period, *Break of Noon* recreates the bitterness and distress provoked by Claudel's religious crisis, as well as the his loneliness abroad. Yet he was able to distance himself enough to criticize his own egotism in the character of Mesa. He later, however, condemned the play's "erotic frenzy".

Break of Noon is an excellent example of the Beatrician aspect of Claudel's works, whereby a woman is the means of bringing a man to God. Claudel begins with the premise that each individual has a divinely intended mate, exploring the consequences of an insuperable barrier to their union. Mesa and Ysé meet at noon at a point between East and West—the turning point in their lives. The Claudelian definition of divine grace is that of an opportunity in time. Mesa's sin is that he fails to recognize that the moment of grace has come. He is obsessed by his recent rejection by God. And instead of merely breaching Mesa's egotism by making him aware of the need of the other, Ysé initially goes too far and fills the breach she has created. Inevitably he comes to hate and resent her, and it is only her final departure in Act III that creates the conditions necessary for his communion with God. Thus, the play also illustrates the Augustinian thesis that even sin can be beneficial in bringing a man to God. Yet if Ysé too is saved, it is almost coincidental, since in a male dominated society she exists only in order to be of service to Mesa. And although she is depicted with warmth and affection as a strong, beautiful, mature woman, her tragedy is seen to be that she has chosen a weak man as her husband, rather than one strong enough to dominate her and provide her with the security Claudel believes all women crave.

Break of Noon, with its resonances of Tristan and Ysolde, and David and Bathsheba, has been described as one of the most effective of 20th-century tragedies. The construction is almost classical in its simplicity, with its focus on a small group of characters and their emotional development over a comparatively short period of time. The characters work on two levels, illustrating the metaphysical thesis, while being at the same time fully-developed and psychologically credible, and their language, while maintaining the tone of mystical lyricism common to Claudel's plays, is closer to the speech patterns of everyday conversation. Similarly, the settings of the play are the most realistic imagined by Claudel up to this point, whilst not neglecting the use of certain stylized symbolic effects.

Break of Noon was never intended to be performed, yet Claudel wrote to Gide in 1909 that it was the only one of his plays then capable of being given. Even so, it was not until 1948, after years of obdurate refusal, that Claudel allowed Jean-Louis Barrault to direct the work. Claudel and Barrault worked together closely on this production, which starred Barrault as Mesa and Edwige Feuillère as Ysé. Claudel was inspired to reconsider and revise his work, adding new stage directions, breaking up monologues, making the expression more colloquial, altering characterization (Ysé in Act III now abuses Mesa and accuses him of having mistreated her), and above all clarifying the conclusion. Barrault, however, prevailed upon Claudel to restore some of the original ending. The resulting text of 1948 is, therefore, a compromise, not entirely to Claudel's taste, so that the following year he produced a third "new stage version" of *Break of Noon*, exaggerating the changes in characterization and excluding still more of the lyrical imagery.

—Janet Clarke

BRIGHTON BEACH MEMOIRS
by Neil Simon

First Publication: New York and London, 1984.
First Production: Abmanson Theatre, Los Angeles,
10 December 1982.

Criticism
(For general works on the author, see *Playwrights* volume)

Articles:
Dan Walden, "Neil Simon's Jewish-Style Comedies", in *From Hester Street to Hollywood: The Jewish American Stage and Screen*, Bloomington, Indiana, 1983.

*   *   *

Brighton Beach Memoirs is an autobiographical play depicting a series of family crises in the Jerome family of the Brighton Beach section of Brooklyn in September 1937. The play is set against the Depression and the approaching war in Europe. By

the time the play ends all the family problems—career decisions, illnesses, finances, sibling rivalry, family relationships—are resolved, and the Jeromes look forward with dignity and unity to the future and to the arrival of refugee relatives from Hitler's Europe.

The first in a trilogy (the other two are *Biloxi Blues* and *Broadway Bound*), *Brighton Beach Memoirs* is Simon's *Remembrance of Things Past*, a look back at his adolescence. Like Tennessee Williams' *The Glass Menagerie*, *Brighton Beach Memoirs* is a memory play; it reaches back into the family past with more affection than Williams' play, but with less lyricism. Like Williams' play, it employs the perspective of a single character to provide exposition, move the action ahead, and comment on characters and situations. In *Brighton Beach Memoirs*, this character is 15-year-old Eugene Morris Jerome. Composition book in hand, Eugene is an ideal narrator for he hopes to be a writer some day. The family crises he records will become the matter for his writing as did Simon's family and situations become the matter of his own plays.

Certainly there is enough material in the Jerome family saga for several plays. As Jack, the father, points out, "If you didn't have a problem, you wouldn't live in this house". Eugene's immediate ambition is to tryout for the Yankees, but he would be willing to give up both baseball and writing "if I could see a naked girl while I was eating ice cream". His older brother Stanley—"either I worshiped the ground he walked on or I hated him so much I wanted to kill him"—is in danger of losing his job; later, he gambles away the family's food money. Jack—"a real hard worker. He was born at the age of 42"— holds down two jobs to make ends meet and in Act II is felled by a heart attack. Big-hearted though she is, Kate, the mother, lays guilt upon her family, and over the years has built up resentment against her widowed sister, Blanche, who lives with the Jeromes: "I was the workhorse and you were the pretty one". Blanche has two daughters: Laurie suffers from asthma, and Nora wants to quit school for a career on the stage. Then there are concerns over the fate of numerous relatives in Europe.

Eugene, the audience's guide to the world of the Jeromes, is a much put-upon youngster, forever setting the table or running for groceries—"Next year I'm entering the Grocery Store Olympics"—forever being blamed for minor household mishaps. For all problems, big or small, Eugene has a wisecrack; he is able to look with humor at what life deals out. He also has most of the play's funniest lines; as filtered through Eugene's perceptive and gently ironic consciousness, the soap opera situations seem less calamitous and clichéd. But as guide, commentator, and Greek chorus, Eugene is less a character in a play than an observer. His is the central consciousness, yet he is on the periphery of the action rather than at its center. Although he comments, "How am I going to become a writer if I don't know how to suffer", he suffers little: liver and cabbage for dinner ("a Jewish medieval torture" is his description of it) and the frustrations of puberty.

One can fault the play for its too many plot lines. Some dovetail, commenting on each other; others, like that dealing with Blanche's aborted date with an eligible Irish bachelor, could easily have been dropped. There is also an excess of similar scenes. Act II has a shrill quarrel and reconciliation between Blanche and Nora, and an even shriller quarrel and reconciliation between Blanche and Kate. Moreover, problems are too neatly wrapped up, the rough edges of family relationships too easily sanded.

Still, the play's strengths more than compensate for its weaknesses. Simon skillfully combines the comic and the serious without taking away from either. The one-liners, the hallmark of Simon's earlier plays, give way here to humor that comes naturally from character and situation, not from some joke book. The quiet conversations between Jack and Stanley are genuinely effective in their understatement. The scene in which Nora tells Laurie how she realized their father really was dead—when she put her hand in his overcoat pocket "and everything was emptied and dry-cleaned and it felt cold"—is movingly poignant. The exchange between Eugene and Stanley about masturbation is both hilariously funny and in good taste. These scenes and others have an honest ring to them. Although *Brighton Beach Memoirs* at times settles too easily for happy endings and the easy laugh, it is a play that looks back with honest affection and humor at all our family pasts, and reminds us of our common humanity.

—Richard B. Gidez

BRITANNICUS (Britannicus)
by Jean Racine

First Publication: Paris, 1670.
First Production: Théâtre de l'Hotel de Bourgogne, Paris, 13 December 1669.

Editions
Britannicus, edited by H.J. Chaytor, Cambridge, 1928.
Britannicus, edited by Daniel Mornet, Paris, 1934.
Britannicus, edited by H.R. Roach, London, 1952.
Britannicus, edited by Maurice Rat, Paris, 1962.
Britannicus, edited by Philip Butler, Cambridge, 1967.

Translations
Britannicus, in *Jean Racine: Five Plays*, translated by Kenneth Muir, New York, 1960.
Britannicus, in *Three Plays of Racine*, translated by George Dillon, Chicago and London, 1961.
Britannicus, in *"Andromache" and Other Plays*, translated by John Cairncross, Harmondsworth, 1967.
Britannicus, in *The Complete Plays of Jean Racine*, translated by Samuel Solomon, New York, 1967 (2 vols.).
Britannicus, in *Britannicus; Phaedra; Athaliah*, translated by C.H. Sisson, Oxford, 1987.

Criticism
(For general works on the author, see *Playwrights* volume)

Books:
W.G. Moore, *Racine: "Britannicus"*, London, 1960.

Articles:
H. Ault. "The Tragic Protagonist and the Tragic Subject in Racine's *Britannicus*", in *French Studies*, 9, 1955.
J. Brody "'Les yeux de César': the Language of Vision in *Britannicus*", in *Studies in Seventeenth Century French Literature*, Ithaca, New York, 1962.
Ralph Albanese Jr., "Patterns of Irony in *Britannicus*", in *Australian Journal of French Studies*, 14, 1976.
Ingrid Birman-Heyndels, "Le *Non-dir* dans *Britannicus* de Jean Racine", in *Revue des langues vivantes*, 43, 1977.
Serge Doubrovsky, "L'Arrivée de Junie dans *Britannicus*: La Tragédie d'une scène à l'autre", in *Papers on French Seventeenth Century Literature*, 1978.

John Campbell, "The Tragedy of *Britannicus*", in *French Studies*, vol. 37 no. 4, 1983.
Guy McAuley, "The Spatial Dynamics of *Britannicus*: Text and Performance", in *Australian Journal of French Studies*, vol. 20 no. 3, 1983.
Ronald W. Tobin, "Néron et Junie: Fantasme et tragédie", in *Papers on French Seventeenth Century Literature*, 10, 1983.

* * *

Set in Imperial Rome, *Britannicus* depicts the first crime perpetrated by the Emperor Nero. Racine himself described the play as the story of "the birth of a monster". After three years' exemplary reign, Nero, tiring of virtue, has decided to shake off the influence of his domineering mother, Agrippina, and to liberate himself from his resentment and fear of his stepbrother, Britannicus, the rightful heir to the Empire. His first act is to abduct a young noblewoman, Junia. This gesture of defiance against his mother, who protects her, is also an assault on Britannicus, who is in love with her. Unfortunately for Britannicus and Junia, Nero no sooner sets eyes on Junia than he falls in love with her. His jealousy of Britannicus reaches fever-pitch when the two rivals confront each other, and Nero orders his guards to seize Britannicus. Agrippina attempts to intercede. In a central scene she invokes all her past authority over him, and all the hideous crimes she has committed in the past in order to secure the throne for him: she married her own uncle, the Emperor Claudius, then murdered him. Nero dare not oppose her openly, and it is left uncertain whether he will choose good or evil. Finally he arranges a banquet of reconciliation with Britannicus. The banquet, which takes place offstage, is described in detail. Nero invites Britannicus to drink to their reconciliation; his evil counsellor Narcissus pours the poisoned wine; and Nero watches his step-brother die without a flicker of emotion. In the Emperor's presence Agrippina foretells his future crimes, and predicts that he will go so far as to kill her.

This tragedy is noteworthy for its use of history. The feeling of impending doom essential to tragedy is much enhanced by the fact that it is common knowledge that Nero was the most monstrously evil of the Roman Emperors. We realize that he is bound to stop being virtuous; the question, and the interest of the play, is just how this is to happen.

In describing the court and the main characters Racine reproduces much of the atmosphere of Tacitus and Suetonius with remarkable fidelity. The character of the young noblewoman Junia is, however, invented. Her presence polarizes the rivalry between the two brothers, and helps make Britannicus into a poignant figure, a virtuous prince and faithful lover who is destroyed in spite of his merits (the real Britannicus, unlike Racine's character, was only 14 years-old when he died). But the main focus of the play is the relationship between the Emperor and his domineering mother, Agrippina. Nero is torn between obedience and rebelliousness. His only means of shaking off his mother's influence seems to be to resort to evil behind her back.

This is a play about power. Nero has absolute power in theory, but does not feel free to indulge his whims while his mother is there to judge him. Agrippina assumes that she has earned the right to rule her son. Because it is she who won him the throne, she fully intends to remain the power behind it. Mother and son fight a decisive battle for power and Nero wins by tricking her: he pretends to give in, then secretly plots the murder. Her failure to appreciate his potential for evil is a result of her overconfident personality: she simply fails to realize that, albeit by surreptitious means, her son has become capable of having his own way at last.

This power-struggle is contrasted with the sufferings of two characters who are completely powerless. Britannicus is the only son of the Emperor Claudius; but he is nothing more than a prisoner at Nero's court. Destined to die, he is marked out as a victim from the start. Even his secret thoughts are betrayed by his closest confidant, Narcissus, who is Nero's secret agent. Britannicus's love for Junia, too, is controlled by Nero, who keeps the couple apart until in a scene of supreme voyeuristic cruelty he orders Junia to reject Britannicus: "Hidden near this spot, I will be watching you . . . . / His death will inevitably follow / If you let a loving gesture or a sigh escape you". Junia too is helpless. Nero imprisons her, spies on her and revels in her suffering with sadistic relish: "I loved the very tears I made her weep". Her undoubted virtue and good sense cannot save her from misfortune; but at least she finally escapes death and dishonour by fleeing to the temple of the Vestal Virgins after her lover has been murdered.

The Roman setting reinforces this atmosphere of tormentors and victims. Although the rules of classical French tragedy mean that there are no crowd scenes onstage, Racine manages to convey the impression of a court full of silent watchers; and guards wait offstage to seize Nero's victims. "These walls have eyes," Junia says in dread. In the end, we learn that the silent crowd has risen up and lynched the evil Narcissus; but the Emperor in his greatness is beyond their reach.

One of the strengths of the play is the tension between the evil and violent passions that form the subject-matter, and the formal, classical French structure (the play is written in rhyming couplets according to a strict five-act pattern). This contrast reinforces the portrayal of this corrupt court: just as its opulence and ceremony cover monstrous crimes, so the elegance and formality of the play's structure clash with the horror of the subject-matter to produce a powerful and brutal tragedy.

—Maya Slater

THE BROKEN HEART
by John Ford

First Publication: London, 1633.
First Production: Blackfriars Theatre, London, c. 1629.

Editions

The Broken Heart, in *Ford's 'Tis Pity She's a Whore and The Broken Heart*, edited by S.P. Sherman, Boston, 1915.
The Broken Heart, edited by Brian Morris, London, 1965 (New Mermaid Series).
The Broken Heart, edited by Donald K. Anderson, Jr., Lincoln, Nebraska, 1968 (Regents Renaissance Drama Series).
The Broken Heart, in *John Ford: Three Plays*, edited by Keith Sturgess, Harmondsworth, 1970.
The Broken Heart, edited by T.J.B. Spencer, London, 1980 (Revels Plays).
The Broken Heart in *The Selected Plays of John Ford*, edited by Colin Gibson, Cambridge, 1986.

Criticism

(For general works on the author, see *Playwrights* volume)

Articles:
S.P. Sherman, "Stella and *The Broken Heart*", in *Publications of the Modern Language Association* [*PMLA*], vol. 24, no. 17, 1909.
G.H. Blayney, "Convention, Plot, and Structure in *The Broken Heart*", in *Modern Philology*, 56, 1958.
M. Carsaniga, "Truth in John Ford's *The Broken Heart*", in *Comparative Literature*, 10, 1958.
Charles O. McDonald, "The Design of John Ford's *The Broken Heart*", in *Studies in Philology*, 59, 1962.
Donald K. Anderson Jr., "The Heart and the Banquet: Imagery in Ford's '*Tis Pity* and *The Broken Heart*", in *Studies in English Literature 1500–1990*, 2, 1962.
R.T. Burbridge, "Moral Vision of Ford's *The Broken Heart*", in *Studies in English Literature 1500–1990*, 10, 1970.
R.J. Kaufmann, "Ford's *Wasteland: The Broken Heart*", in *Renaissance Drama* (new series), 3, 1970.
T.N. Greenfield, "Languages of Process in Ford's *The Broken Heart*", in *Publications of the Modern Language Association* [*PMLA*], May 1972.
Arthur L Kistner and M.K. Kistner, "The Dramatic Functions of Love in the Tragedies of John Ford", in *Studies in Philology*, 70, 1973.
David Malouf, "The Dramatist as Critic: John Ford and *The Broken Heart*", in *Southern Review: An Australian Journal of Literary Studies*, 5, 1979.
A. Barton, "Oxymoron and The Structure of Ford's *The Broken Heart*", in *Essays and Studies*, 33, 1980.
Michael Neil, "Ford's Unbroken Art: The Moral Design of *The Broken Heart*, 1980.
Carol A. Burns, "*The Broken Heart* 'Piec'd up Again'", in *Ball State University Forum*, vol. 24 no. 4, 1985.
Marie L. Kessel, "*The Broken Heart*: An Allegorical Reading", in *Medieval and Renaissance Drama in England*, 3, 1986.
Phoebe S. Spinrad, "Ceremonies of Complement: The Symbolic Marriage in Ford's *The Broken Heart*", in *Philological Quarterly*, Winter 1986.
Verna Ann Foster and Stephen Foster, "Structure and History in *The Broken Heart*: Sparta, England, and the 'Truth'", in *English Literary Renaissance*, Spring 1988.

* * *

Ithocles, a young Spartan noble, has forced his sister Penthea into an unhappy marriage with a wealthy and jealous old man, Bassanes, breaking her betrothal to Orgilus. He returns in triumph from war, is honoured by King Amyclas, and falls in love with the king's daughter, Calantha; she then rejects Nearchus, Prince of Argos, for him. Orgilus requires his own sister, Euphrania, to accept his choice of marriage partner, then gives out that he has gone to Athens. However, disguised as a student of the philosopher Tecnicus, he spies on her growing affection for Prophilus, Ithocles's friend, and reveals his presence to Penthea who rejects him, vowing fidelity to her old husband Bassanes. Orgilus abandons his disguise, and returns to court where he gives his blessing to Euphrania's marriage and professes reconciliation with Ithocles. Ithocles visits his sister Penthea, filled with remorse at her suffering; Bassanes, discovering the pair together, wildly accuses them of incest. Penthea despairs, and shortly after commending her brother to Calantha, loses her wits and starves herself to death. At this, Orgilus traps Ithocles and murders him. At the marriage feast for Prophilus and Euphrania, Calantha (apparently unmoved) learns of the death of her father, Orgilus, and Penthea. She condemns Orgilus, who chooses to bleed to death. After seeing to the future administration of her kingdom, and claiming the dead Ithocles as her husband, Calantha dies of a broken heart.

Although the origins of Ford's plot probably lie both in classical history (the world of antiquity, as the 17th century knew it, is recreated with some care) and in the contemporary forced marriage of Penelope Devereux, Lady Essex (to whom the dramatist dedicated his first published work), *The Broken Heart* is essentially an original creation, a deliberate and highly wrought work of art. Despite its praise by critics from Charles Lamb onwards, it has an uncertain place in the theatre; it was not revived until 1898 and has received only four British productions over the last 30 years. Lawrence Olivier's Bassanes dominated the single professional production, at the Chichester Festival, in 1962; there was little in it of what Lamb found in the play, "sublimity. . .in the actions and sufferings of the greatest minds".

The human response to emotional and physical suffering and death is Ford's tragic theme in *The Broken Heart*, displayed by an almost exemplary group of characters, in the setting of an ancient community famous for its code of stoical endurance and the suppression of open emotion. Throughout the play powerful dramatic tensions arise from the opposition of unbearably rigid standards of conduct and outbursts of strong natural feeling, seen equally in Penthea's demand that Orgilus, her too passionate lover bursting in on her from the past, should "set [his] wits in a less wild proportion", Bassanes' unavailing, almost comic efforts to control his desperation at the madness of his wife, and the "silent griefs" which at last "cut the heartstrings" of Calantha.

Characteristic of this play are effects of pity and admiration as the audience watches men and women fight for self-control or lose the unequal struggle. Penthea's noble and self-denying support for her brother's love for Calantha is set against her pitiable collapse into madness, in which, freed from the iron restraints of honour and reason, she can express her agonising sense of all she has lost in her enforced marriage to Bassanes; Orgilus's passion for revenge (compared to a raging sea and a violent blast of wind) finds its complement in the steady courage of his death (appropriately figured as the drying up of the fountain of life, the icing over of a heart no heat will ever thaw).

In the manner of a Greek tragedy, the action is set in train by a single prior act of "rash spleen" on the part of Ithocles. Its consequences are worked out among a closely knit group of aristocrats and rulers, none of whom, finally, behaves basely or villainously; even Bassanes achieves a measure of self-control and is rewarded with the marshalship of Sparta, while Orgilus's entrapment of Ithocles is motivated by anguish for his sufferings and becomes a competition in honour with his courageous victim. The fall of Ithocles comes unexpectedly at the moment of keenest remorse for what he has done to Penthea and the height of his happiness in the love of Calantha. Calantha, in turn, experiences a similar sudden reversal of fortune, and the metaphoric imagery of the play insists on the fall of "colossic greatness". Behind the action stands the mysterious will of the gods, expressed in an ominous series of Delphic oracles.

The experiences and the behaviour of Ford's characters are enlarged by the poetic texture and the dramaturgy of the play. Life is represented as a general journey towards the grave, signified not only in the deaths through age, grief, and violence of five of the leading characters, but also in a solemn and stately poetry of mortality, drawing on images of the failure of natural phenomena, dissolution, sleep and dreams. Ford's language invests even his most sensational incidents with a symbolic gravity: the stately measure which Calantha continues to lead as messages of disaster throng in on her at once

personifies "the soul in tune, at whose sweet music all our actions dance" and the heart-breaking code of Spartan fortitude. Orgilus, bleeding to death as he stands propped on two staves, sees himself as "feeble man. . .bending to his mother, the dust he was first framed on". Elegiac songs, music, and spectacular ceremonies, such as the enthroned body of Penthea, and the funeral procession of Ithocles, perfectly enact the sad solemnity which gives *The Broken Heart* its special tragic character.

Of all of Ford's plays, *The Broken Heart* offers the richest and most poetic sense of the operation and conflict of life-creating and life-destroying forces at work in nature, as it does of the "death-braving" potential of men and women.

—Colin Gibson

THE BROKEN JUG (Der zerbrochene Krug)
by Heinrich von Kleist

First Publication: Berlin, 1811.
First Production: Weimar, 2 March 1808.

Editions
Der zerbrochene Krug, edited by R.H. Samuel, London, 1950; second edition, 1968.
Der zerbrochene Krug, Stuttgart, 1957.

Translations
The Broken Jug, translated by P.R. Lawrence, in *Four Continental Plays*, edited by John P. Allen, 1964.
The Broken Pitcher, translated by Bayard Quincy Morgan, Chapel Hill, North Carolina, 1961.
The Broken Jug, translated by Roger Jones, Manchester, 1977.
The Broken Jug, in *Heinrich von Kleist: Five Plays*, translated by Martin Greenberg, New Haven, Connecticut, 1988.

Criticism
(For general works on the author, see *Playwrights* volume)

Books:
C. Birk, *Heinrich von Kleist: "Der zerbrochene Krug". Ein Beitrag zur Inszenierung des Lustspiels*, 1910.
Helmut Sembdner, *"Der Zerbrochene Krug": Erläuterungen und Dokumente*, Stuttgart, 1973.
Gernot Müller, *Kommentar zu Kleists "Der zerbrochene Krug"*, Lund, 1975.

Articles:
S. Atkins, "Some Notes to Kleist's *Der zerbrochene Krug*", in *Philological Quarterly*, 22, 1943.
J. Krampelmann, "Kleist's *Krug* and Shakespeare's *Measure For Measure*", in *Germanic Review*, 26, 1951.
J. Krampelmann, "Shakespeare's Falstaff Dramas and Kleist's *zerbrochene Krug*", in *Modern Language Quarterly*, 12, 1951.
A. Neumann, "Goethe and Kleist's *Der zerbrochene Krug*", in *Modern Language Quarterly*, 13, 1952.
Ilse Graham, "The Broken Pitcher: Hero of Kleist's Comedy", in *Modern Language Quarterly*, 16, 1955.
R. Nicholls, "Kleist's *Der zerbrochene Krug*, Oedipus, and The Comic Tradition", in *Theatre Annual*, 21, 1964.

The Broken Jug: Theatre Royal, Stratford East, London, 1986

Fritz Martini, "*Der zerbrochene Krug*: Bauformen des Lustspiels", in *Jahrbuch der deutschen Schillergesellschaft*, 9, 1965.

Manfred Schunicht, "Heinrich von Kleist: *Der zerbrochene Krug*", in *Zeitschrift für deutsche Philologie*, vol. 84 no. 4, 1965.

Oskar Seidlin, "What the Bell Tolls in Kleist's *Der zerbrochene Krug*", in *Deutsche Vierteljahrsschrift für Literaturwissenschaft und Geistesgeschichte*, 51, 1977.

Diethelm Brügemann, "Kleist's *Der zerbrochene Krug*: Ein Satyrspiel zu Goethe's *Faust*", in *Faust Blätter*, 37, 1979.

Mark G. Ward, "Kleist's *Der zerbrochene Krug* and Romanticism", in *Orbis Litterarum*, 35, 1979.

Wolfgang Wittkowski, "*Der zerbrochene Krug*: Gaukelspiel der Autorität, oder Kleist's Kunst, Autoritätskritik durch Komödie zu verschleiern", in *Sprachkunst*, vol. 12 no. 1, 1981.

W.C. Reeve, "Ein dunkles Licht: The Court Secretary in Kleist's *Der zerbrochene Krug*", In *Germanic Review*, vol. 58 no. 2, 1983.

Dirk Grathoff, "Der Fall der *Krug*: Zum geschichtlichen Gehalt von Kleist's Lustspiel", in *Kleist-Jahrbuch*, 1984.

Alexander Stillmark, "Kleist's *Der zerbrochene Krug* and Gogol's *The Inspector General*: A Comparative View", in *New Comparison*, 3, 1987.

*   *   *

Every picture tells a story, and there is nothing especially remarkable in the fact that Heinrich von Kleist should have followed a practice which had become quite firmly established in the final decades of the eighteenth century and should have chosen to base a play on an engraving which he chanced to see while on his travels in Switzerland in 1803. What is more surprising is that so serious-minded a writer developed the rather sentimental, pictorial material into what has come to be recognised as one of the finest of German comedies, and what is truly astounding is that *The Broken Jug* should at one and the same time be both hilariously funny and extremely pessimistic.

The picture in question (an engraving by Jean-Jacques Leveau of a painting by Louis-Philibert Debucourt, entitled *The Broken Jug*) portrays a peasant woman standing before a somewhat non-plussed village judge and demanding to know who had been responsible for smashing a decorated old jug that she, apparently, inherited and had cherished for years. This typical scene, which other sources in fact prefer to identify with the better-known work of Jean-Baptiste Greuze, presents, so to speak, a "still" from a rural drama; we are implicitly invited to reflect on the circumstances of the case and speculate on the possible outcome in the light of our interpretation of the characters of the major participants and of the onlookers whose poses are expressive of a variety of attitudes. Kleist's response was to present, in the seemingly cosy environment of a village near Utrecht in the good old days, the tale of a judge Adam who, as we soon realise, had smashed that fine jug as he was making an unceremonious exit from that peasant woman's home where he had, despite his age and status, been paying court to her attractive young daughter Eve.

We see him first in the early morning trying to find ways of explaining to his clerk how he has come to lose his wig, that *sine qua non* of judicial dignity, and why his body is covered with bruises and scratches. His unease is compounded when it is announced that a court inspector of notorious severity will arrive shortly to check on the way Adam conducts the cases submitted to him for judgement. Shortly afterwards Frau Marthe arrives to present with peasant volubility her complaint about the smashing of the jug. The chief suspect is young Ruprecht, a sturdy peasant lad, and it is not long before we come to realise that what is really at stake is not so much the broken jug as Eve's shattered reputation. Adam shifts and squirms, dilly-dallies and prevaricates, but, of course, in the end the truth comes out.

At one level this is a droll comedy of country ways, with the plot developing with all the unstoppable inevitability of farce at its best. There is apparently nothing too serious at stake either, for, as we quickly appreciate, Frau Marthe is making much ado about nothing of any particular value when she involves a law court in so trivial a domestic misfortune as the breaking of a jug. As for Eve, she is knowing enough to cope with a little *contre-temps* like this without besmirching her fair name. The tone of the conclusion is, moreover, considerably lightened when at the end of his day of growing discomfiture, the judge is, in fact, let off pretty well scot-free.

All the same, like many other comedies, *The Broken Jug*, has its serious side. The names given to the characters themselves suggest this seriousness. The inspecting judge is called Walter, meaning "ruler", and the peasant woman who can't leave well alone when a little more patience would serve better is Marthe, with obvious Gospel echoes. More pertinently still, the judge who sins and tries to cloak his guilt is Adam, and the young woman who leads him into temptation is Eve. The central image of the breaking of crockery is potent in sexual symbolism. Moreover, as Kleist himself remarked, the action and spirit of this entertaining comedy has marked affinities with *Œdipus Rex*, Sophocles' exemplary portrayal of man's inability to employ his intellect effectively to escape from, or even just to cope with, the misfortunes that beset him. After recognising this link it is only a short step to make the connection between *The Broken Jug* and the issue that haunted Kleist throughout his tragic existence, namely the attack made on the powers of human rationality by the German philosopher Immanuel Kant. For the Enlightenment, reason was reckoned to be capable of dealing with all human predicaments, if only prejudice was not allowed to intervene and warp men's judgements. Kant had destroyed such facile optimism, and *The Broken Jug* may safely be interepreted as an imaginative response, in comic guise, to Kant's *Critique of the Power of Judgement* of 1790.

When first performed in Weimar in 1808 the play was not well received. Kleist attributed the failure to Goethe who did not understand that this verse-comedy, whose action, in a single setting, represents a single episode in Adam's day, should be performed in a single act. Goethe unnecessarily split it into three. Since then, however, *The Broken Jug* has won recognition as one of the finest of German comedies, no doubt precisely because it combines fun and philosophy in such a convincing fashion.

—Christopher Smith

THE BROKEN PITCHER. See **THE BROKEN JUG.**

THE BROTHERS (Adelphoe)
by Terence

First Production: At the Funeral Games for L. Aemilius Paullus, Rome, 160 B.C.

Editions
Adelphi, in *The Comedies of Terence*, edited by S.G. Ashmore, New York, 1908.
Adelphi, in *Terence*, London, 1912 (2 vols.; with translation; Loeb Classical Library)
Adelphi, in *P. Terenti Afri Comoediae*, edited by Robert Kauer and Wallace M. Lindsay, Oxford, 1926.
Adelphi in *The Plays of Terence*, edited and translated by William Ritchie, London, 1927 (with translation).
Adelphoe, edited by R.H. Martin, Cambridge, 1976.
The Brothers, edited and translated by A.S. Gratwick, Warminster, Wiltshire, 1987 (with translation).

Translations
The Brothers, in *The Comedies of Terence*, translated by F. Perry, 1929.
The Brothers, in *The Comedies of Terence*, Chicago, 1962 (Lawrence Eachard's 17th century translation).
The Brothers, in *Roman Drama*, translated by Samuel Lieberman, New York, 1964.
The Brothers in *"The Brothers" and Other Plays*, translated by Betty Radice, Harmondsworth, 1965.

Criticism
(For general works on the author, see *Playwrights* volume)

Books:
Otto Rieth, *Die Kunst Menanders in den "Adelphen" des Terenz*, 1964.
Viktor Pöschl, *Das Problem der "Adelphen" des Terenz*, Heidelberg, 1975.

Articles:
W.G. Arnott, "The End of Terence's *Adelphoe*: A Postscript", in *Greece and Rome*, 10, 1963.
John N. Grant, "The Role of Canthara in Terence's *Adelphi*", in *Philologus: Zeitschrift für das klassische Altertum*, 117, 1973.
W.E. Forehand, "Syrus' Role in Terence's *Adelphoe*", in *Classical Journal*, 69, 1973.
Hugh Lloyd-Jones, "Terentian Technique in the *Adelphi* and the *Eunuchus*", in *Classical Quarterly* (new series), 23, 1973.
J.N. Grant, "The Ending of Terence's *Adelphoe* and the Menandrian Original", in *American Journal of Philology*, 96, 1975.
J.N. Grant, "Three Passages in Terence's *Adelphoe*", in *American Journal of Philology*, 97, 1976.
F.H. Sandbach, "Donatus' Use of the Name Terentius and the End of Terence's *Adelphoe*", in *Bulletin of the Institute of Classical Studies* (London), 25, 1978.

* * *

Micio, an easy-going old bachelor, adopted Aeschinus, the

son of his brother, the strict Demea. Demea has continued to raise his other son, Ctesphio, himself. Aeschinus steals a music girl, Bacchis, from a pimp, apparently to enjoy as his mistress. Micio, who views Aeschinus' action relatively lightly, is reproached by the boy's true father, Demea, for this indulgence. Both are unaware that in fact Bacchis has been abducted by Aeschinus on behalf of his brother Ctesphio, who is Demea's responsibility. Aeschinus however, is not entirely blameless himself; he has seduced Pamphila, a poor but virtuous Athenian girl, but is afraid of admitting this to Micio. Sostrata, the mother of Pamphila, misconstrues Aeschinus' action, assuming that he has taken the courtesan for himself, abandoning Pamphila, whom he had earlier promised to marry, and who is about to have his child. Although upset by this, Aeschinus is unwilling to betray his brother by revealing the truth. Micio, however, learns of Sostrata's unhappiness and Pamphila's plight, and after getting Aeschinus to confess, agrees that he may marry Pamphila. Meanwhile, Demea has discovered the truth about his son Ctesphio's affair with the music girl, blames Micio, but later acknowledges that his own stern methods have failed. He now treats everyone generously, at Micio's expense, allows Ctesphio to marry the courtesan, and persuades Micio to take Sostrata for his wife.

Terence's last work is also widely regarded as his greatest. The opening scene efficiently lays out the central ethical conflict which motivates the action of the play. Micio argues for generosity and lenience in raising a child: this will assure the development of a good, open, and honest nature. Demea's position is diametrically opposed: he advocates frugality, strict discipline, and obedience. The curiosity of the audience is immediately engaged in its desire to see how these two contrasting views will be reflected in the action of the play and which will be shown to be superior. The basic plot is logically presented, without digressions or inconsistency, as Terence sustains interest not through complication but through shifts in pacing and tone and a variety of different types of exchanges and confrontations between the characters. Despite its underlying didacticism, the work succeeds as theatrical entertainment through its skilful use of characterisation, visual humour, farce, irony, and, in the end, reversal and surprise.

The four central characters are strongly drawn. The differing psychologies of Micio and Demea are vividly represented, as is the marked contrast between the personalities of the two sons, Aeschinus and Ctesphio. A good deal of pathos is aroused by the depiction of the plight of Pamphila and her mother. The scene in which Micio gradually extracts the truth from Aeschinus about his affair with Pamphila is highly realistic and the two characters superbly individualised. The overall impression which the play conveys is of genial good sense and moderation, with justice and harmony achieved in the end. Even the pimp is dealt with fairly in this most amiable and enlightened of Roman comedies.

The most memorable aspect of the play, and one that makes it particularly effective in performance, is the subtle trickery practised upon the audience. In the beginning we are led to believe that Aeschinus really does love the girl he abducted, and are told nothing of Pamphila, whose existence comes as a surprise. Terence later contrives a more fundamental deception in that the action of the play and the presentation of its characters encourage the audience, from the first, to sympathize strongly with Micio and to support his position on the question of child-rearing. This preference appears to be finally confirmed when the stern Demea evidently undergoes total (and unexpected) conversion, confesses the error of his ways, and resolves in the future to be more open and generous. He then, however, swiftly reduces Micio's tolerant and apparently wise principles to absurdity. Demea as a father has become an

object of ridicule (in a manner which may well have discomfited the Roman sense of propriety) but he now takes subtle and appropriate revenge, turning the tables on Micio in a final hilarious scene in which he takes, and gives, delight in exploring the possibilities in his newly adopted persona. The formerly harsh and puritanical curmudgeon turns generous and easy-going to a fault, making everyone happy at the expense of Micio, to whom he presents a series of increasingly outrageous requests. Micio, trapped by his own principles, is powerless to resist these calls upon his generosity, and in the end, even agrees as an act of kindness to take Sostrata for his wife.

The play thus compels the audience to think again, to recognise that a middle path is best, and that abstract principles must be tested in action and evaluated according to particular circumstances and personalties. The message of the play, and the answer it gives, to the ethical questions placed before the audience arise naturally and are distilled in an entertaining, and ultimately plausible, manner from the personalties and circumstances of its characters.

—Richard C. Beacham

THE BROTHERS MENAECHMUS (Menaechmi)
by Titus Maccius Plautus

First Production: Unknown

Editions
The Two Menaechmuses [with translation], in *Plautus, 2*, edited by P. Nixon, Cambridge, Massachusetts, and London, 1917 (Loeb Classical Library).
Menaechmi, edited by P. Thoresby Jones, Oxford, 1918.
Menaechmi, edited by Clara M. Knight, Cambridge, 1919.
Menaechmi, edited by Nicholas Moseley and Mason Hammond, Cambridge, Massachusetts, 1933.
Menaechmi, edited by Gilbert Lawall and Betty Nye Quinn, with Eugene Fawcett, Chicago, 1978; second edition, 1980.

Translations
The Twin Brothers, in *Plautus: Five of His Plays*, translated by Sir Robert Allison, London, 1914.
The Twins, translated by Barrett H. Clark, New York, 1914.
The Menaechmi, translated by Richard W. Hyde and Edward C. Weist, Cambridge, Massachusetts, 1930.
Menaechmi, translated by Frank O. Copley, New York, 1949.
The Twins, in *Plautus: Six Plays*, translated by Lionel Casson, Garden City, New York, 1963.
The Menaechmi Twins, in *Roman Drama*, translated by Samuel Liebermann, New York, 1964.
The Brothers Menaechmus, in *"The Pot of Gold" and Other Plays*, translated by E.F. Watling, Harmondsworth, 1965.
Menaechmi, in *Plautus: Three Comedies*, translated by Erich Segal, New York, 1969.

Criticism
(For general works on the author, see *Playwrights* volume)

Articles:
W. Connely, "When Plautus is Greater than Shakespeare: Imprints of *Menaechmi* on *Comedy of Errors*", in *Classical Journal*, 19, 1924, and 20, 1925.

P.G. Moorhead, "The Distribution of Roles in Plautus' *Menaechmi*", in *Classical Journal*, 49, 1953.

J. Arthos, "Shakespeare's Transformation of Plautus", in *Comparative Drama*, vol.1 no.4, 1967–68.

E. Fantham, "Act IV of the *Menaechmi*: Plautus and his Original", in *Classical Philology*, 63, 1968.

E.W. Leach, "*Meam Quom Formam Noscito*: Language and Character in the *Menaechmi*", in *Arethusa*, 2, 1969.

J. Woodruff, "Mythological Notes in the *Menaechmi*", in *Classical Bulletin*, 51, 1974.

*   *   *

Twin brothers were parted as children. Now grown up, and both known as Menaechmus, one has arrived in Epidamnus looking for the other. All kinds of confusion is caused when they are mistaken for one another before they eventually meet and misunderstandings are resolved.

Plautus's plays were all adaptations of Greek originals from up to a hundred and fifty years before he wrote. *Menaechmi* was certainly not the first "comedy of errors" to be written but, together with his *Amphitryon*, represents the original of a long series of mistaken identity plays which have propped up a whole corner of European comedy.

Menaechmi sees plot at its most straightforward and least sophisticated. The background is initially spelled out to the audience in a prologue to ensure that, however confused the characters get, the audience are always at least one step ahead. The first character to appear after the prologue is the local Menaechmus, who is in the process of stealing his wife's dress to give it to his mistress, who conveniently lives next door. He is hampered by the constant attentions of a parasite, Peniculus, but manages to deliver the dress and order dinner before leaving for town. The arrival of his twin brother together with a slave Messenio, triggers off the misunderstandings, enhanced by the foreign brother's eye for the main chance when he is offered a free dinner with a pretty girl. A maid with a gold bracelet to be taken to the jeweller's, the wife of his brother, and then her father add to the complications. A comic doctor diagnoses the local Menaechmus mad but is helped out by his brother's slave.

There is no doubt that *Menaechmi* was one of Shakespeare's main sources for *The Comedy of Errors*, but the Plautus play is not entirely overshadowed by the later piece and does possess a number of features which suggest that it is still eminently playable. The "error" itself, though confined to the two brothers (whereas Shakespeare contrives twin slaves in addition) is fully exploited. The foreign Menaechmus is mistaken for the local Menaechmus by everyone in the play who knows him—parasite, mistress, maid, wife and father-in-law. In the case of the Doctor, who has never met either of them, the actions of the one are taken as the basis for a medical examination of the other, thus confusing his diagnosis. The changes are carefully rung.

There is one fundamental difference between *Menaechmi* and *The Comedy of Errors* that derives from the two plays' settings and emphasis. *Menaechmi* introduces first the local Menaechmus. He has a larger role than his brother and gets into trouble largely because of his cheating nature. The play takes place in Epidamnus. The Latin word *damnum* means "loss of money" and most of the characters' problems relate to a loss of what they think are their dues. In contrast, Shakespeare has the foreign Menaechmus as his major character, and sets the play in Ephesus, a centre of witchcraft, causing the visitor to credit all the confusion to the supernatural and the sinister.

Plautus's play is cunningly geared to stretching plausibility to the limit, but not too far, bearing in mind the holiday audience for which he was writing. The local Menaechmus has to provide the central focus because the foreign one has arrived in the town expressly to look for someone who looks like him. He has no distractions. Were he regularly the victim of the error, he would have to be so stupid as to defy even stage logic. As it is, the recognition-scene between the two brothers is sometimes felt to be over-prolonged, but if the gag will hold for the rest of the play, it can certainly take a lengthy denouement. Everything depends on the playing, and for the masked players of the Plautine stage such elaboration was perfectly acceptable.

The world that Plautus creates is consciously a stage world in which the lax morality belongs much more to the Greece of his original sources than to the Rome of his own time. There is little to be gleaned from *Menaechmi* about Plautus's audience beyond their taste in theatrical performance. Even this is diluted by the loss of the musical dimension which is thought to have been important enough in productions of Plautus's plays for them sometimes to be described not as Roman comedy but as Roman opera.

The sense of an actor's text is strong, however,—particularly a text for an actor in a mask. The comic unreality contributes to a general goodwill which overshadows the shady morality of the leading characters. There is no social comment but the play is fun and funny, if never deep. Nobody gets hurt for long. The stagiest of plays, *Menaechmi* derives most of its humour and much of its charm from consciously acknowledging precisely how and where it is set.

—J. Michael Walton

THE BROWNING VERSION
by Terence Rattigan

First Publication: London, 1949.
First Production: Phoenix Theatre, London, 8 September 1948.

*   *   *

The plot of this play focuses on Andrew Crocker-Harris, a classics master at an English public school, who is retiring prematurely because of ill-health, and who is confronted by his wife's infidelity and his failure in his chosen profession. Like much of Rattigan's work, *The Browning Version* is drawn from his own experience; in this case as a pupil at Harrow School. The prototype for Crocker-Harris was one of Rattigan's teachers, Mr. Coke Norris, and the central incident of the pupil, Taplow, presenting Crocker-Harris with a copy of Browning's translation of the *Agamemnon* of Aeschylus is based on fact (although there is some doubt as to whether Rattigan himself was the boy involved). Certainly Taplow's interest in cricket and golf reflect Rattigan's enthusiasm for those games.

The action of *The Browning Version* is set in the Crocker-Harris's sitting-room, replete with a stained-glass door leading to the garden as well as an internal door, concealed by a screen. Appropriately, in view of its classical associations, the play observes the unities of time, place, and action demonstrating Rattigan's renowned craftsmanship at its best. Although the dialogue is characteristically everyday (with Taplow's school-

The Browning Version: Phoenix Theatre, London, 1948 (first production)

boy slang) Rattigan imbues Crocker-Harris with a distinctive turn of speech (reflecting his classical education) and an articulateness, enabling him to comment upon his predicament (though not to express his feelings), which are consistent with naturalistic drama.

As the title implies, Rattigan seeks to establish parallels between his play and its classical source, thus Taplow remarks to Frank Hunter, a science master and Muriel Crocker-Harris's current lover: "It's rather a good plot, really, a wife murdering her husband and having a lover and all that . . . . " Of course, Crocker-Harris's fate is not the (literal) blood-bath which awaited Agamemnon on his return from the Trojan War, but Mrs. Crocker-Harris uses the no less deadening battery of psychological warfare as she relentlessly humiliates and degrades her husband. In terms of exploration of character and motive *The Browning Version* is closer to Euripides and his treatment of that other archetypal triangle (Theseus, Phaedra, and Hippolytus) in *Hippolytus* than to Aeschylus's bloody chain of murder and revenge.

The eternal triangle was a favourite formula for Rattigan. Although the central character, torn between two lovers, is usually a woman, it has been suggested that Rattigan on occasion depicted homosexual relationships under the guise of heterosexual ones. For Rattigan, the essence of a triangular relationship was that it enabled him to polarise the conflict between two types of love—on the one hand, the "higher love" (social and intellectual companionship and compatibility) and on the other, merely sexual gratification. Thus Muriel Crocker-Harris is caught between her 18-year-long, increasingly arid, marriage and her passionate affair (one of many) with Frank Hunter, in which she is the helpless and undignified pursuer. Crocker-Harris's classical knowledge facilitates Rattigan's exploration of what Plato in *The Symposium* characterised as "the two Aphrodites. . .common love and the other Heavenly love". He does this with an erudition which makes the following speech central not only to this play but to Rattigan's work as a whole:

> Two kinds of love. Hers and mine. Worlds apart, as I know now, though when I married her I didn't think they were incompatible. In those days I hadn't thought that the kind of love—the love she requires and which I was unable to give her—was so important that it's absence would drive out the other kind of love—the kind of love that I require and which I thought, in my folly, was by far the greater part of love . . . .

Although this exploration of the two loves is the major theme of *The Browning Version*, there are others. Alongside the emotional repression of his marriage Crocker-Harris has sought the popularity of his pupils—"by pandering to their delight in his mannerisms and tricks of speech he has tried to compensate for his lack of natural ability to make himself liked" (Michael Darlow and Gillian Hodson, *Terence Rattigan*, 1979). This might be seen as a reflection of Rattigan's willingness as a dramatist to court popular success in the form of the endorsement of Aunt Edna the "nice, respectable, middle-class, middle-aged, maiden lady", who made her debut as Rattigan's representative playgoer in his Preface to Volume Two of his *Complete Plays* (in which *The Browning Version* appears). Such an identification of author and character would imply a sense of failure on Rattigan's part even at this, the most commercially and critically successful period of his career.

Rattigan was taken to task for flinching from unhappy endings to his plays, preferring to send theatregoers home in a reassured state of mind. *The Deep Blue Sea* is susceptible to this criticism, but not so *The Browning Version*. Rattigan contemplated a tragic outcome (probably Crocker-Harris's death from his heart condition), but instead left his protagonist facing an uncertain future both professionally (at a crammer's) and matrimonially (will Muriel accompany him?). Crocker-Harris does, however, assert his right to make his valedictory speech at the end of the next day's prize-giving. In the film version, Rattigan's old friend Anthony Asquith prevailed upon him to open up the action of the play and to extend it to conclude with Crocker-Harris (Michael Redgrave) making his speech. The film thus finishes on a sentimental, "Mr. Chips" note which betrays the integrity of the original play.

Lasting about 80 minutes in the theatre, *The Browning Version* required a companion piece for which Rattigan provided one of his most ebullient comedies *Harlequinade*, about a performance of *Romeo and Juliet* in a midland town. As a double-bill the two plays provide opportunities for the actors to demonstrate their versatility. Although John Gielgud (rather tactlessly) turned down Rattigan's invitation to create the part of Crocker-Harris it has since become one of the recognised classic roles of the modern stage, drawing fine performances from Eric Portman (1948), Nigel Stock (1976), Alec McCowan (1980), and Paul Eddington (1987).

—Richard Foulkes

––––––––––

DIE BÜCHSE DER PANDORA.   See **THE LULU PLAYS.**

––––––––––

BÜRGER SCHIPPEL.   See **SCENES FROM THE HEROIC LIFE OF THE MIDDLE CLASSES.**

––––––––––

EL BURLADOR DE SEVILLA Y CONVIVADO DE PIEDRA.   See **THE TRICKSTER OF SEVILLE.**

––––––––––

BURN THIS
by Lanford Wilson

First Publication: New York, 1987.
First Production: Mark Taper Forum, Los Angeles, 22 January 1987.

Criticism
(For general works on the author, see *Playwrights* volume)

Daniel J. Watermeier, "Lanford Wilson's *Liebestod*: Character, Archetype, and Myth in *Burn This*", in *A Lanford Wilson Casebook*, edited by Jackson Bryer, New York, 1990.

*   *   *

Burn This is essentially a contemporary, romantic comedy concerned with how and why an unlikely pair "fall in love"; an ironic, sometimes uncomfortable, love story with a resolution

Burn This: New York, 1987

that is only tentatively happy. Wilson himself has described the romantic passion at the core of his play as "a juggernaut that just knocks down everything in front of it".

Set in a loft apartment in Manhattan, the action centers on Anna, a modern dancer and aspiring choreographer. At the opening, Anna is bereft by the death of her gay room-mate Robbie, also a dancer and choreographer, who has been killed in a boating accident. Anna is consoled by Larry, a second room-mate, and her boyfriend Burton, a successful screenwriter.

In the second scene, Robbie's older brother Pale visits Anna to collect Robbie's things. Pale's behavior is loutish, but Anna perceives that his behavior masks an innate sensitivity and feelings of personal loss and anger. When Pale finally breaks down weeping, Anna takes him to her bed, succumbing to what she calls "the bird-with-the-broken-wing syndrome". On the morning after, however, Pale abruptly departs.

Some months later on New Year's Eve, Pale drunkenly reappears at Anna's apartment. Following a violent confrontation between Pale and Burton, Anna rejects Burton and once again goes to bed with Pale. But the next day, she confesses that she is afraid of becoming emotionally involved with Pale and asks him to leave. He does so reluctantly but without argument. Anna, however, has clearly fallen in love with Pale. She tries to forget him through work, by choreographing a new dance.

In the final scene, Larry has arranged for Pale to see the premiere of this dance without Anna's knowledge and then afterwards, by means of a note, conspired to bring them

together alone in the apartment. Although both Pale and Anna half-heartedly protest that they don't want to fall in love, they concede, as Pale says, that they "never felt nothin' like this". In the final moments of the play, Anna puts Larry's note in an ashtray and, as Larry directed, burns it. While the ashtray fire flickers, the lovers embrace and the curtain drops.

Although contemporary in style, Wilson achieves a certain universality in *Burn This* by grounding his present-day characters against particular archetypes, and their situation against a mythic, principally Teutonic, past. Thus, various verbal and scenic allusions associate Anna and Pale with such legendary lovers as Wagner's *Flying Dutchman* characters, Vanderdecken and Senta, and *Siegfried* characters, Seigfried and Brunnhilde. There are also a number of references to the world of gothic horror stories. Indeed, the action of *Burn This* is not only romantic but also Romantic in tone or temperament; Pale is in many respects an absorbing fusion of Romantic hero and modern anti-hero; while Anna is a synthesis of the mythic, nurturing-mother archetype, Romantic heroine, and modern, "liberated" woman.

In this context, *Burn This* explores the nature of *eros* in contemporary American culture, its relationship to death and to renewal and creativity in both life and art. It is to date Wilson's most complex, sophisticated, and daring play.

—Daniel J. Watermeier

BUSSY D'AMBOIS
by George Chapman

First Publication: London, 1607; revised edition, 1641.
First Publication: London (St. Paul's Boys), 1604.

Editions

Bussy D'Ambois, in "*Bussy D'Ambois*" and "*The Revenge of Bussy D'Ambois*", edited by F.S. Boas, Boston and London, 1905.
Bussy D'Ambois, in *The Tragedies of George Chapman*, edited by T.M. Parrott, London, 1918.
Bussy D'Ambois, edited by Jean Jacquot, Paris, 1960.
Bussy D'Ambois, edited by N.S. Brooke, London, 1964 (Revels Plays).
Bussy D'Ambois, edited by Robert J. Lordi, Lincoln, Nebraska, 1964 (Regents Renaissance Drama Series).
Bussy D'Ambois, edited by Maurice Evans, London, 1965 (New Mermaid Series).

Criticism

(For general works on the author, see *Playwrights* volume)

Books:

Gunilla Florby, *The Painful Passage to Virtue: A Study of Chapman's "The Tragedy of Bussy D'Ambois"*, Lund, The Netherlands, 1982.

Articles:

Richard H. Perkinson, "Nature and the Tragic Hero in Chapman's *Bussy D'Ambois*", in *Modern Language Quarterly*, 3, 1942.
Michael H. Higgins, "The Development of the 'Senecal Man': Chapman's *Bussy D'Ambois* and Some Precursors", in *Review of English Studies*, 23, 1947.
William G. McCollom, "The Tragic Hero and Chapman's *Bussy D'Ambois*", in *University of Toronto Quarterly*, 18, 1949.
Peter Ure, "Chapman's *Tragedy of Bussy D'Ambois*: Problems of the Revised Quarto", in *Modern Language Review*, 48, 1953.
Elias Schwartz, "Seneca, Homer, and Chapman's *Bussy D'Ambois*, in *Journal of English and Germanic Philology*, 56, 1957.
Irving Ribner, "Character and Theme in Chapman's *Bussy D'Ambois*", in *English Literary History*, 26, 1959.
C.L. Barber, "The Ambivalence of *Bussy D'Ambois*", in *Review of English Literature*, 2, 1961.
Robert P. Adams, "Critical Myths and Chapman's Original *Bussy D'Ambois*", in *Renaissance Drama*, 9, 1966.
P. Bement, "The Imagery of Darkness and of Light in Chapman's *Bussy D'Ambois*,", in *Studies in Philology*, 64, 1967.
Raymond B. Waddington, "Prometheus and Hercules: The Dialectic of *Bussy D'Ambois*", in *English Literary History*, 34, 1967.
John Freehafer, "The Contention for *Bussy D'Ambois*, 1622–41", in *Theatre Notebook*, 23, 1968.
Linwood E. Orange, "*Bussy D'Ambois*: The Web of Pretense", in *The Southern Quarterly*, 8, 1969.
Roger T. Burbridge, "Speech and Action in Chapman's *Bussy D'Ambois*", in *Tennessee Studies in Literature*, 17, 1972.
Albert H. Tricomi, "The Revised *Bussy D'Ambois* and *The Revenge of Bussy D'Ambois*: Joint Performance in Thematic Counterpoint", in *English Language Notes*, 9, 1972.
William Dean, "Chapman's *Bussy D'Ambois*: A Case for the Aesthetic and Moral Priority of the 1607 version", in *Journal of the Australasian Universities Language and Literature Association*, 38, 1972.
Albert H. Tricomi, "The Revised Version of Chapman's *Bussy D'Ambois*: A Shift in Point of View", in *Studies in Philology*, 70, 1973.
R. Corballis, "*Bussy D'Ambois*: The Textual Problem Once More", in *AUMLA Journal*, 45, 1976.
P. Dean and J. Johnson, "Structure in the *Bussy* Plays of Chapman", in *English Studies*, vol. 61 no. 2, 1980.
Deborah Montuori, "The Confusion of Self and Role in Chapman's *Bussy D'Ambois*", in *Studies in English Literature 1500–1900*, Spring 1988.

*   *   *

The play is set in the reign of Henri III of France. It opens with Bussy alone and in reduced circumstances contemplating the rule of Fortune. Monsieur, the King's brother, conscious of the "thread" between himself and a crown, and of the service that a man of spirit "beyond the reach of fear" might be able to render him, offers Bussy his protection and introduces him to the court where, as a parvenu, he encounters much contempt and antagonism, to which he responds in kind, without respect for rank. Duels follow in which Bussy is the sole survivor of six combatants; but with the support of Monsieur he secures the King's forgiveness. Subsequently, Tamyra, the wife of the Count of Montsurry repels the amorous advances of Monsieur; but, then with the assistance of a friar, she is visited by Bussy, now her lover. Meanwhile, Bussy has risen in the King's favour and is regarded by Henri as an "Eagle" who will be his protector. Monsieur and the Duke of Guise, now united in hatred and envy of Bussy, plan to reveal his adultery to Montsurry. Monsieur eventually shows an incriminating letter to Montsurry who, now convinced of his wife's guilt, tortures her, forcing her to write to Bussy summoning him to a rendezvous where a trap is set. The friar, who had tried to help Bussy and Tamyra by raising a spirit to intercept the letter, witnesses the torture and dies from the shock. Montsurry, disguised as the dead friar, lures Bussy to his hired murderers where, after heroic resistance, Bussy is mortally wounded and, standing "like a Roman statue", delivers a great speech with words of pardon for his murderers and a plea to Montsurry to forgive his "matchless wife". He declares that neither Fate nor his murderers can claim "any glory" in his death, but that his heart is broken by the sight of Tamyra's wounds. In a final exchange Montsurry yields to his wife's appeal for forgiveness but says that their love is at an end. The play closes with the friar's ghost proclaiming that, like Hercules, Bussy has become a star which will "th'aged skie, Chere with new sparkes of old humanity".

There has been much discussion of Bussy's character and the moral or philosophical basis of his behaviour. In a speech after the King has pardoned him, Bussy makes the remarkable claim that he is not subject to the ordinary rule of law: "When I am wrong'd and that law failes to right me, Let me be King my selfe (as man was made) And doe a justice that exceeds the law". Earlier Monsieur, noting his spirited response to hostile courtiers, says in an aside: "His great heart will not downe, 'tis like the Sea". Viewed according to a moral perspective, he has been condemned as arrogant and subversive, governed by selfish passions, but perhaps it would be more in keeping with the spirit of the play to describe him in terms of magnificent effrontery, and a number of critics have noted Chapman's affinity with Marlowe. Bussy's assertions of autonomy and his assumption of a political role independent of court factions inevitably represent a potential danger to the state, but also make him vulnerable to personal jealousies and antagonisms. There are also elements of the Stoicism which was to become important in Chapman's later work; although it has been suggested that the play is the better for not being dominated by this ethical tradition, Chapman's awareness of it is very evident and there are stoic elements in Bussy's final speech.

The metaphysical character of Chapman's language makes him exceptionally difficult in comparison with other dramatists of this period; yet the impact of the verse is extraordinarily powerful and in this respect he has been seen as a worthy descendant of Marlowe. Swinburne, one of his most eloquent admirers, referred to his "constant energy and intensity of expression" and noted that "with all its tumid and turbid exuberance of speech, the action of this play never halts or flags". Bussy's dramatic presence is matched by that of Tamyra, whose speeches express with remarkable effect the plight of a woman overcome with guilty passion and poignantly aware of her condition. Also dramatically impressive is the relationship between Monsieur and Bussy, which takes on a somewhat enigmatic quality. One of the most brilliant and pungent passages in the play, and an example of Chapman's formidable wit, is their lengthy dialogue which has the formal character of a flying, an agreed exchange of vituperation. Monsieur taxes Bussy with a multitude of crimes and absurdities, everything "but killing of the king", to which Bussy relies with a recital of Monsieur's scandalous treacheries—he never does good but to do ill—closing with an expression of gratitude for all he has done for himself but "only in royall hope to kill the king".

Throughout the play the court world into which Bussy has been introduced is depicted as one of peculiar cynicism and depravity. In Jonathan Miller's production at the Old Vic, London, in 1988, the court scenes were notable for their palpable atmosphere of intrigue and jealousy, particularly engendered by the activities of the intelligencer. The sinister sound of disembodied whispers anticipating the King's comment in Act IV, "here's naught but whispering with us", was a device which marked the opening of the production and which was repeated before subsequent episodes of plotting and betrayal. Pillars provided advantageous positions for the spying activities of Maffe, Monsieur's servant. Factions of courtiers hunched menacingly together. Although Bussy claims that he regards ambition as subordinate to honesty and declares that he intends "to rise in Court with vertue", his tragedy, ultimately, is that he is unable to remain immune from the pernicious effects of the power that he once disdained.

—Janet Clare

BUTLEY
by Simon Gray

First Publication: London 1971.
First Production: Criterion Theatre, London, 1971.

Criticism
(For general works on the author, see *Playwrights* volume)

Articles:
Sophia B. Blaydes, "Literary Allusion as Satire in Simon Gray's *Butley*", in *Midwest Quarterly*, 18, 1977.

*   *   *

Butley is Simon Gray's best and most popular drama to date. The play depicts a day in the life of Ben Butley, who teaches English at a college of London University. The two-act play is set in Butley's office, which he shares with Joseph (Joey) Keyston. As Act I opens we see Butley avoiding a telephone conversation with the head of his department by pretending that he is in the midst of a tutorial with a student. Moments later a student appears at his door for a tutorial, but Butley refuses to see him, saying that he is too involved in administrative matters to do so at this time. Joey enters and tells Butley about spending the weekend with a friend, Reg Nuttall. Miss Heasman, another student, appears and asks to set a time for her tutorial. Butley manages to delay her, again pleading "administrative tangles". Later, Anne, Butley's ex-wife, visits the office and informs her former husband that she is going to get remarried.

Act II opens during Miss Heasman's tutorial. While Joey is teaching a class, Reg comes calling for him. It turns out that Joey, a former student of Butley's and his current lover and housemate, is leaving Butley for Reg; Joey returns to the office, and after a confrontation with Butley, leaves with Reg. At the conclusion of the play Gardner, a student with a reputation for being difficult, turns up for a meeting with Butley. However, Butley decides that he does not want to start another personal relationship, so he sends Gardner away. The play ends with Butley alone in his office.

Essentially, *Butley* depicts the character of the protagonist, Ben Butley, an ego-centered, selfish, insensitive man. The strength of the play derives first from this characterization and second from the devices that Gray employs to reveal Butley's nature. Interestingly, Gray's academic career is reflected in both of these elements. He taught at Trinity College, Cambridge, and has been on the faculty at Queen Mary College of the University of London since 1965. Clearly, this educational background was important to him. As he has said, "I went to university when I was seventeen and I never left".

From the beginning of the play it is obvious what kind of a person Butley is. His desk is described, for example, as "*a chaos of paper, books, detritus*". The state of his office reflects the disordered nature of his life. Furthermore, his egocentrism and the tactics that he uses to isolate himself from others and from his responsibilities are evident in his very first speech. Throughout the rest of the play Gray expands upon and refines Butley's nature as revealed in that first telephone conversation with his department head. Because the play is concerned with the protagonist's character, there is no action and no traditional plot, as word games, wit, literary allusions, and cruelty are utilized to reveal Butley's character. He emerges as a tragic, lonely man who wants some sort of relationship with someone, but who is so self-centered that he is incapable of giving enough of himself or accepting enough from anyone else to allow them to penetrate his sarcasm to create a truly emotional relationship. In an attempt to create a defense mechanism that will allow him to avoid any emotional connections, Butley creates a wall of sterile intellectualism that he hides behind and which serves to reinforce the self-directed defeat that he generates.

While the unappealing and sorrowful character that Gray portrays is interesting in itself, Gray's depiction of that character saves both the character and the play from being completely unsympathetic. Indeed, while Butley is consistently sarcastic and offensive with other people and is extremely capable of making his victims suffer because he knows where they are most vulnerable, at the same time he is very witty. His self-deprecating jokes about homosexuality, frequent use of *double entendres* and literary allusions simultaneously provide further insight into Butley himself and establish a tone of humorous stylishness in the play. There is no doubt that these intellectual elements are outgrowths of Gray's academic life. Finally, Butley is, as he suggests, surrounded by foolish people, but he cannot see beyond their flaws to their common humanity, and by rejecting them he has doomed himself to a life of loneliness, a victim of his own image of himself as an individual isolated by his feelings of superiority to those who surround him.

—Steven H. Gale

———

BYGMESTER SOLNESS.   See **THE MASTER BUILDER.**

———

CALIGULA (Caligula)
by Albert Camus

First Publication: In *"Caligula" and "Le Malentendu"*, Paris, 1944; revised edition, 1947; further revised edition, 1958.
First Production: Théâtre Hébertot, Paris, 26 September 1945 (revised version); Petit Théâtre de Paris, 1958 (further revised version).

Translations
Caligula, translated by S.R. Gilbert in *"Caligula" and "Cross Purpose"*, London, 1948.

Criticism
(For general works on the author, see *Playwrights* volume)

Articles:
G. Bree, "Camus' *Caligula*: Evolution of a Play", in *Symposium*, 2, 1958.
André Alter, "De *Caligula* aux *Justes*: De l'Absurde à la justice", in *Revue d'histoire du théâtre*, 12, 1960.
R.W.B. Lewis, "*Caligula*: Or the Realm of the Impossible", in *Yale French Studies*, 25, 1960.
L.Z. Hammer, "Impossible Freedom in Camus' *Caligula*", in *Personalist*, 44, 1963.
I.H. Walker, "The Composition of *Caligula*", in *Symposium*, 20, 1966.
Grahame C. Jones, "Camus's Caligula: The Method in His Madness", in *Essays in French Literature*, 5, 1968.
Janine Rattared, "Points de vue sur *Caligula*", in *Praxis*, 15, 1968.
L.B. Rosenfeld, "The Absurd in Camus' *Caligula*", in *New Theatre Magazine*, 8, 1968.
Emilien Carassus, "Le *Caligula* de Camus de 1937 à 1958: Notes sur la genèse et les variantes", in *Littératures: Annales publiées par l'Université de Toulouse*, 7, 1971.
A. James Arnold, "Camus' Dionysian Hero: *Caligula* in 1938", in *South Atlantic Bulletin*, 38, 1973.
Kenneth Marrow, "*Caligula*, a Study in Aesthetic Despair", in *Contemporary Literature*, 14, 1973.
Janine Gilles, "*Caligula*: de Suétone à Camus", in *Etudes classiques*, 42, 1974.
George H. Bauer, "*Caligula*, portrait de l'artiste ou rien", in *Revue des lettres modernes*, 419–24, 1975.
Alfred Cismaru, "*Caligula* Revisited", in *Francia*, 41, 1982.
James A. Arnold, "La Poétique du premier *Caligula*", in *Caligula: Version de 1941*, by Albert Camus, Paris, 1984.
Robert Wexelblatt, "Camus' *Caligula* and Nietzsche", in *Lamar Journal of the Humanities*, vol.13 no.1, 1987.

* * *

The flamboyant, young Emperor Caligula has reacted violently to first perceptions of an absurb confrontation of man's desires and the nature of the universe; an awareness triggered by the death of Drusilla, his sister and mistress. He discovers that "men die and they are not happy". After his revelation, Caligula tells his faithful servant to find him the moon, since if this were possible, it would be a sign that the universe is not hostile to individual desires. He also decides to force others to see reality by acting, himself, as a "logical" scourge. His first action is to require the patricians of Rome to write testaments leaving all their money to the state; he can then execute them when the state needs funds. Acts II through IV take place three years later, and include a series of scenes illustrating how Caligula destroys the moral values of the patricians, their personal integrity, and their belief in reason. Caligula forces the families of his victims to laugh, he capriciously kills men, he arbitrarily closes the country's granaries, and declares a famine. He does not, however, try to protect his own life, and accepts his coming death. Just before he is killed by a patrician uprising, he realises that he has failed to reach his goal: "I have chosen a wrong path, a path that leads to nothing. My freedom isn't the right one".

Caligula, Camus's first play, and often considered his best, was written in 1938 when he was 25. It was not performed until 1945, in a memorable production with Gérard Philipe (then an unknown young actor) in the title role. For the 1947 text Camus made changes, including the addition of several scenes. The definitive text is the 1958 edition, used for production at the Petit Théâtre de Paris.

The play is based in part on Suetonius's portrait of Caligula, from which Camus takes several incidents to show Caligula's "madness". He adds, however, a metaphysical cause for Caligula's behaviour, the recognition of the meaninglessness of the world.

Caligula is highly dramatic; the emperor is an actor and a director producing a tragic farce on the stage of Rome, a play to illustrate his understanding of the universe. In Act II he stages a banquet in which he drags a wife from her husband and rapes her; in Act III he performs as Venus, forcing the patricians to worship him with such litanies as "Teach us the truth of this world, which is not to have any". In Act IV, he stages a poetry competition in which the unsuccessful poets (who write standard romantic verse on the stated theme of death) are required to lick their slates with their tongues.

The structure of the play is rather fragmented. Each act is a series of set scenes—either Caligula's dramatic portrayals of the absurd, or his conversations with one of his entourage. Since the basis for the emperor's actions is established from the beginning, there is little forward movement. The patricians plan to revolt at the beginning of Act II, but do not act until the final scene. The power of the play is not in plot or character development but rather in the theatrical tableaux Caligula devises, and in the language. The diction is elevated; Indeed the eloquence and poetry of Caligula's speech occasionally form an ironic contrast with his actions.

The play rests largely upon the characterization of the emperor, who, in spite of his decision to use his power against others, is in many ways more admirable and idealistic than those who surround him. The patricians are, like the bourgeoisie of Algiers in *The Outsider*, blind to the absurd nature of the world. They are, as well, cowardly, self-serving, hypocritical. Caligula's accomplices—Caesonia, his mistress who still loves him, and Helicon, an ex-slave trying to better himself—are also unaware of why the emperor acts as he does. Only two characters understand the seriousness of Caligula's desires: Scipion, a young poet who loves Caligula even after his father is killed by the emperor; Cherea, an older statesman who has recognized the nature of the "absurd" ("seeing the sense of life disappear is unbearable") but has decided that revolt against the universe cannot be accompanied by revolt against other human beings. *Caligula* poses a question to which Camus returns frequently in his later work: In a world with no transcendent meaning, what arguments can be advanced for respecting human life? Cherea's opposition to Caligula is the closest the play comes to an explanation of why the emperor's path is wrong. For Cherea, "some actions are more beautiful than others"; for Caligula, "all actions are equal" in a world without meaning.

As Camus himself said in a commentary on the play, Caligula is a tragic hero because, in spite of the dangerous errors of his position, he has realized that man must recognize the absurd and revolt against it. He is also a hero in consenting to his own death. His error is to deny other individuals. Although written before what are often considered Camus's most "absurd" works, in which rebellion is essentially individual (*The Outsider*, *The Myth of Sisyphus*), *Caligula* already contains the theme of solidarity that Camus was to develop in such later works as *The Rebel*: "I revolt, therefore we are".

Camus denied, however, that the play was "philosophical". It is, for him, "a tragedy of the intelligence"; the tragic recognition of the "absurd" leads, however, not to intellectual debate, but rather to a series of passionate actions. In the forceful portrayal of its hero, *Caligula* is the most theatrically successful of Camus's plays.

—Adele King

CAMILLE. See THE LADY OF THE CAMELIAS.

IL CANDELAIO. See THE CANDLE BEARER.

CANDIDA
by George Bernard Shaw

First Publication: In *Plays Pleasant and Unpleasant*, London, 1898; revised version in *Collected Plays*, London, 1930.
First Production: Her Majesty's Theatre, Aberdeen, 30 July 1897.

Criticism
(For general works on the author, see *Playwrights* volume)

Books:
Robert Wittman, *Candida; or, What Shaw Really Meant*, Hicksville, New York, 1974.

Articles:
Arthur H. Nethercot, "The Truth about Candida", in *Publications of the Modern Language Association* [*PMLA*], 64, 1949.
Walter N. King, "The Rhetoric of *Candida*", in *Modern Drama*, vol. 2 no. 2, 1959.
Jacob Adler, "Ibsen, Shaw and *Candida*" in *Journal of English and Germanic Philology*, 59, 1960.
Paul L. Lauter, "*Candida* and *Pygmalion*: Shaw's Subversion of Stereotypes", in *Shaw Review*, 3, 1960.
Charles L. Holt, "*Candida*: The Music of Ideas", in *Shaw Review*, 9, 1966.
Terry Otten, "Candida and Henry Higgins: Shaw's Mentors to the Human Spirit", in *Discourse*, 11, 1968.
Herbert Bergman, "Comedy in *Candida*", in *Shavian*, vol. 4 no. 5, 1972.
Charles A. Berst, "The Craft of *Candida*", in *College Literature*, 1, 1974.
Walter Lazenby, "Love and 'Vitality' in *Candida*", in *Modern Drama*, 20, 1977.
Betsy C. Yarrison, "Marchbanks as 'albatros': An Interpretation of *Candida*", in *Shaw Review*, 20, 1977.
Bert Cardullo, "The Mystery of *Candida*", in *SHAW*, 6, 1986.

*   *   *

In Shaw's *Candida* we have a situation which was common among European writers both before and after Shaw—that of an eternal triangle, two men loving one woman, who is usually married to one of them. But in true Shavian style what was normally the story of a weak and fickle unfaithful wife is turned around. Candida is a faithful wife, and she is far stronger than any other character in the play. Her husband, the Reverend James Morell, is a Christian Socialist clergyman in Hackney, London. Although apparently a strong man able to direct the hearts and souls of men through his mastery of rhetoric, Morell's faith in himself is smashed aside by the young, shy Eugene Marchbanks, the rival to his wife's affection. As Morell's weakness is revealed, so, paradoxically, is Marchbanks' strength. Candida is asked to choose between the two, and though Morell is her choice, she remains the enigma at the centre of the play, the "new woman" who is both saint and sinner. *Candida* is truly a play of its time, and firmly bears witness to Shaw's support for sexual equality.

Until Shaw began writing for the theatre, there had been no modern, British dramatist who had seen contemporary political, social, and religious issues as fitting subjects for the stage. Looking to Norway at what Ibsen had been doing since the 1870's, Shaw decided to do the same; that is, tackle the issue of how the everyday lives of people were affected by external affairs, and more specifically the growing force of the feminist movement.

Candida was written as a response to Ibsen's *A Doll's House*, but the relationship between Candida and Morell is a reversal of that between Nora and Torvald Helmer. Ibsen tells the story of a "doll" who finally comes to life and slams the door on her husband and child. Shaw alters Ibsen's story, since he shows a seemingly strong, living man to be, in reality, a "doll". *Candida* is not the best or most important of Shaw's plays, but it has always been popular, and is an interesting

Candida: Globe Theatre, 1937

example of Shaw's early work. Its reversal of the roles of the sexes is one of the most famous in Shavian dramas, and, in addition to reflecting Shaw's support for the feminist movement, it also stays true to his comment that all superior women are masculine, and all superior men are feminine.

The very title of the play reflects one of Shaw's maxims. He did not choose to use a common name, but instead formed his heroine's name from the adjective "candid". Just as being frank and truthful—and as a result often shocking his audiences—was an aim running throughout Shaw's work, so Candida shows these qualities when dealing with her husband and Marchbanks. The original title of the play was *Candida: A Mystery*, and this has been interpreted by come critics to refer to Marchbanks as the apparently weak and dependent poet proving to be far stronger than the confident, self-assured clergyman. While this is clearly an element within the play, the very clarity of this theme implies that it is not the mystery referred to in the original title. In the final "auction" scene, Morell offers his strength for his wife's defence, but Candida recognises this strength for what it is—totally dependent on her love and support, for its continuation. Marchbanks, on the other hand, has spent his life in spiritual isolation, and has therefore learnt self-dependence, and so, too, learnt to live

without the support of another's love. Morell, recognising his weakness, actually says to his wife, "What I am you have made me with the labour of your hands and the love of your heart". The axis of *Candida* so clearly revolves around weakness and strength, that it cannot be the mystery Shaw refers to.

A far greater mystery is Candida herself. She is, and remains, the faithful wife, and yet she still allows Marchbanks, knowing that he loves her, to lay his hands on her lap (a specific stage instruction) and to utter her name, adoringly, over and over again. The question must be asked: is this the action of a totally virtuous woman? And earlier Candida said to her husband, "Ah, James, how little you understand me, to talk of your confidence in my goodness and purity. I would give them both to Eugene as willingly as I would give a shawl to a beggar dying of cold . . . . "

It is interesting to note what Shaw himself said about Candida, viz. that she was a "very immoral female. . .who, without brains and strength of mind. . .would be a wretched slattern or voluptuary". Candida enjoys the slave-like adoration Marchbanks lavishes upon her, and she allows herself to enjoy it openly and physically. But she is never more than passively unfaithful to her husband. She knows he is weak, and she knows that Marchbanks' poetic, romantic temperament could not exist shuttered up within the confines of the domestic world she inhabits. This is the mystery of the play, since Candida is both immoral and respectable at the same time.

One of the main weaknesses of *Candida* is the absence of a convincing impression of life for the characters outside the play. There are references to a wider life—Morell's preaching; Candida's father, Burgess, and his pay disputes with his workers; the typist, Miss Proserpine, being one of many previous typists to have loved Morell—but the characters and their actions within the play form a world in themselves. They seem enclosed in their domestic domain and there is little real sense of a wider, spontaneous life in which they live and move as individuals. As Nora slams the door at the end of *A Doll's House*, we feel that she is opening a door to something else, but when Marchbanks leaves at the end of *Candida* we ask, to what?

What this makes evident is that *Candida* is one of Shaw's early plays. Later in his writing Shaw was to develop an ability to live with his characters in a far closer sense, so that he seemed to know what they were doing outside of the world he had created for them on the stage. Rather then existing in a self-contained world like *Candida* they also inhabited the wider and greater dimension of real life. So it is that when *Candida* ends, and the heroine reaches down to her husband to love and support him, we cannot be sure that Morell, though wiser about himself, is any wiser about the mystery which is his wife.

—Claudia Woolgar

———————

THE CANDLE BEARER (Il Candelaio)
by Giordano Bruno

First Publication: Paris, 1582.
First Production: Unknown; possibly not performed until
                  1968.

Editions
Candelaio in *Opere italiene de Giordano Bruno, 3*, Bari, 1909.
Candelaio in *Opere*, edited by Augusto Guzzi and Rosario
   Amerio, Milan-Naples, 1956.
Candelaio, edited by Isa Guerrini Angrisani, Milan, 1976.
Candelaio in *Il teatro italiano 2: La Commedia del Cinque-
   cento, 3*, edited by Guido Davico Bonino, Turin, 1978.

Translations
The Candle Bearer, translated by J.R. Hale, in *The Genius of
   the Italian Theatre*, edited by Eric Bentley, New York, 1964.

Criticism
(For general works on the author, see *Playwrights* volume)

Articles:
R. Tissoni, "Saggio di un commento stilistico al *Candelaio*", in
   Giornale storico dell letteratura italiana, 137, 1960.
S. Ferrane, "*Il Candelaio*: scienza e letteratura", in *Ital-
   ianistica*, 2, 1973.

*   *   *

Three well-established middle-aged citizens—Bonifacio, Bartolomeo, and Manfurio—are gulled by a loose-knit alliance of rogues. Bonifacio, despite having a beautiful young wife, lusts after Vittoria and is being bled of his money by their go-betweens. Bartolomeo, a miser, has fallen for the alchemical spiel of a confidence-trickster, and thereby neglects his wife's sexual needs, which she satisfies, as opportunity offers, with one of the rogues. Manfurio, a pedantic schoolteacher, is not in active pursuit of a particular sin or folly, and so for much of the play the scenes that display his pomposity seem to serve as interludes between those that advance the other two plots.

By the end of the complex interweaving of the plot strands, the rogues have disguised themselves as the watch and give each of the three gulls his come-uppance. Manfurio loses not only his money but even his clothes. Bonifacio, through the "bed-trick", has gone to bed not with Vittoria but with his own wife; furthermore, he went to the tryst disguised in the clothes of one of the rogues, who now accuses him of having "stolen my person and gone about committing villainies under cover of it". The "watch" sends him to prison, leaving his wife free to pursue her own pleasurable revenge with the rogue whose clothes her husband wore. The schoolteacher, who has inflicted his whimsically twisted Latin on everyone throughout the play, ends up being cross-examined by "the watch", who wilfully misunderstand his Latin tags and conclude that "you try to show us what your art consists of, and we find it's the art of buggering small boys!" He suffers a beating in the style he has himself so often inflicted on his pupils.

"We live in terms of those who piss and crap, though we direct our prayers and requests to pictures and statues", Vittoria declares at the mid-point of the play. The plot's focus on the gulls' self-delusion and lack of self-knowledge is balanced by a cheerful acknowledgment of the senses, from the phallic candle of the title, to women's need for sexual intercourse because "nature abhors a vacuum". Giordano Bruno calls the play:

A comedy by Bruno Nolano
Academician of no Academy
Called the world-weary

and cites the Latin tag meaning "In sadness laughter, in laughter, sadness". A prologue promises us

puposeless purposes, feeble plots, trivial thoughts, idle hopes, bursting hearts, bared breasts, false surmises, alienation of wits, poetic furies, clouding of the senses, perturbations of the imagination, wanderings of the intellect, pervervid faith, senseless anxieties, dubious studies, untimely germinations, and the glorious fruits of madness.

This prologue is sandwiched between an antiprologue, in which the speaker laments the total unreadines of the players and his own incomprehension of the play's befuddling complexites, and the appearance of a beadle to re-introduce the play: "Whoever saw a comedy open with a beadle? To which I answer: Rot you!". This Mannerist self-consciousness continues throughout. The play sparkles with paradoxes, anecdotes, and rhetorical set-pieces, often bawdy. Bruno makes extravagant extrapolations from the characters' fumblings to produce often outrageous, general rules of human conduct.

Is it only coincidence that the best Italian comedy of the preceding generation, *The Mandrake*, was by Machiavelli, whose political handbook, *The Prince*, shocked by its worldly realism, and that *The Candle Bearer* is by a man who, being burned for heresy, averted his gaze from the crucifix? Not altogether. Dedicating his play, Bruno claimed that "the dust clouds raised by the absurd. . .nourished my understanding".

As the first substantial speech of his comedy says, "Everything is open to doubt, and as far as love is concerned we see proof of that remark every day". Satiric comedy is of course skeptical and cynical, and both Machiavelli's and Bruno's comedies use traditional characters and plot situations; the world is turned upside down only within established conventions. Nevertheless, the free play of analytical and empirical minds gives a bite that sets these comedies apart and, particularly in *The Candle Bearer*, there are incidental, verbal thrusts that, if we were given time to consider them, threaten to tear the conventions apart.

—Anthony Graham-White

LA CANTATRICE CHAUVE. See **THE BALD PRIMA DONNA.**

THE CAPTAIN OF KÖPENICK
(Der Hauptmann von Köpenick)
by Carl Zuckmayer

First Publication: Berlin, 1930.
First Production: Deutsches Theater, Berlin, 5 March 1931.

Translations
The Captain of Köpenick, translated by David Portman, London, 1932.

Criticism
(For general works on the author, see *Playwrights* volume)

Books:
Hartmut Schieble (ed.), "*Der Hauptmann von Köpenick: Erläuterungen und Dokumente*, Stuttgart, 1977.
Winfried Löschburg, *Ohne Glanz und Gloria: die Geschichte des Hauptmanns von Köpenick*, Berlin, 1978.
Hans Gehrke, *Carl Zuckmayer, "Der Hauptmann von Köpenick": Interpretation und Materialien*, Hollfeld, 1983.

Articles:
E. Speidel, "The Stage as Metaphysical Institution: Zuckmayer's Dramas *Schinderhannes* and *Der Hauptmann von Köpenick*", in *Modern Language Review*, 63, 1968.
Lore Lucas, in *Textsorte: Drama: Analysen, Lernziele, Methoden*, Bochum, 1977.
Charles W. Hoffman, "Zuckmayer's *Hauptmann von Köpenick*: Of Laughter, Uniforms, and the Basement", in *West Virginia University Philological Papers*, 29, 1983.
Gerald P.R. Martin (ed.), "Die 'Affaire' von Köpenick—heute auf der Bühne: Kritiker äussern sich zu Aufführungen in Berlin, München un Mainz", in *Blätter der Carl-Zuckmayer-Gesellschaft*, 10, 1984.

*   *   *

The Captain of Köpenick is a vivid, and often very funny, portrayal of Imperial Germany in 1910. Based on a police report of 1906, it gives the background to, and eventual description of, Wilhelm Voigt, a down-and-out, who, on release from prison, disguises himself as an army Captain, besieges a local town hall to steal a pass card, arrests the Mayor, and makes off with the municipal funds, before his success comes to an end.

Voigt, who dominates the play partly because he is almost the only character who tries to resist the insidious influence of the Imperial regime, gains in stature because Zuckmayer altered the self-centred, criminal, nationalistic features of the original model into a champion of human rights, sympathetic to others who suffer, respectful of those in authority who are humane, a rebel rather than a revolutionary. His sentence of 15 years in prison for falsifying a post-office form has put him beyond the pale; poverty led him to petty crime and, now released, he is not eligible for a work permit, because he has not worked for several years. Worst of all, because he has not served in the army he gets no sympathy from potential employers. The strict, social structuring of Berlin society is a direct offshoot of the military system, for, as Wormser the tailor remarks: "I agree with the great Herr Darwin. Other ranks still have prehensile tails. Homo Sapiens begins with a Lieutenant!". The Jewish tailor carves out a living, and a status, by making uniforms in a society that encourages hierarchical divisions and rewards, and where the correct uniform exercises power; the distance on clothing between purely decorative posterior buttons is used to ridicule those who believe in their importance.

Voigt refuses to be stifled within such a society, and his search for an escape from it leads him to reflect on his situation, when one day he will stand before his Creator and have to answer for what he has done with his life. His simple, fearful faith provides him with the impetus to apply every ounce of shrewdness he can muster to beat the system and make himself respectable. He contrasts with all the supporting characters in turn, often representing a purer form of honesty, patriotism, concern or optimism. Only by using the very means by which the regime protects itself, in order to procure illegally what he needs, does he almost succeed in his limited objective. That he fails is partly due to chance—Köpenick town hall does not administer passes—but also because he does not understand enough the hierarchical patterns of the regime. His presence in uniform is enough, however, to test the gullibility of those he meets—first the soldiers outside the station toilet when he makes his first entry as a fully-garbed Captain, then when he musters his detachment of soldiers, finally when he first enters the town hall. His brother-in-law, Hoprecht, recognises through him just how vulnerable the regime is when he states: "The man's positively dangerous!"—a comment ironically parallel to one made about Adolf Hitler by the Professor of Architecture of Vienna University when rejecting him as a potential student. Voigt's importance as a warning is tempered, however, by the splendid final scene when he is invited by the Chief of Police to put on the uniform once more for his pleasure. Standing before the mirror Voigt laughs at himself until he cries; a deeper, human laughter develops and with it one final mocking judgement on himself with the word: "Impossible!".

This was Zuckmayer's sixth drama, written in 1930, and first performed in Berlin 1931—an immediate success. It was not difficult to spot the parallel between Wilhelmine militarism and its reincarnated national socialist form. The subtitle—"A German Fairytale"—emphasises the more universal theme of the poor man achieving riches and power for one day with an individual scoring a limited triumph over authority. Most of the play was written in various levels of Berlin dialect, reproducing rich strata of social irony and interchanges almost impossible to translate successfully. The play thus lends itself to interpretation firstly as a local, historically-bound realistic account of mainly petty bourgeois, Berlin suburban life, then

The Captain of Köpenick: Old Vic Theatre, London, 1971 (National Theatre Company)

as the universal, type-setting symbolism of a unique character instantly recognisable within a tradition of fools and picaros. In a preface to the new English edition (Methuen 1971) Zuckmayer emphasises the double-track character of the original play:

> The basic construction—or better, the composition—of the original play moves along two tracks: the story of the hapless man, slowly waking up to the use of his wits, and the story of the uniform's slow degradation. And it begins—a warning signal for the Germany of 1931—with the birth and idolatry of the Uniform, while the man looking for work is thrown out as a beggar. These two threads are interwoven in the way of musical themes or motifs—which, of course, slows down the pace of the action—more like an epic tale than a fast-moving plot—each of the short scenes serving as a link in the chain. For the German mind and the German theatre, it is just this slowness that creates a special kind of tension—since everybody in the audience knows beforehand where the tracks will lead—the hoax of Köpenick being generally known and remembered. The later this hoax comes, the longer it is held back, the more it is enjoyed—and its point appreciated—by the German public.

Zuckmayer also points out that Voigt's quest for work as a cobbler was a deliberate choice within the fairytale tradition of the cobbler as "a man with a witty and whimsical sense of imagination—the man who *outwits the devil*".

The original play is extremely carefully structured using maximum fore-shadowing and recall techniques to elicit reflection and laughter. The three-act, "classical", thesis-antithesis-synthesis form is counterpointed with the interplay of the two major themes of Voigt's development, and the rise and fall of the influence of the uniform. Appearance and reality form a further dimension played out on different levels to give the whole action a particular and a symbolic level of reference. Much of this underlying complexity has been lost in the two-act English version where "a man's quest for a bit of paper to establish his identity" (John Mortimer) becomes the main purpose of the play, and where the central part was re-written with the actor Paul Scofield in mind.

—Brian Keith-Smith

THE CARETAKER
by Harold Pinter

First Publication: London, 1960.
First Production: Arts Theatre Club, London, 27 April 1960.

Criticism
(For general works on the author, see *Playwrights* volume)

Books:

Michael Scott (ed.), *Harold Pinter: "The Birthday Party"; "The Caretaker"; "The Homecoming"*, London, 1986.

Ronald Knowles, *"The Birthday Party" and "The Caretaker"*, London, 1988 (Text and Performance Series).

Articles:

Kent G. Gallagher, "Harold Pinter's Dramaturgy", in *Quarterly Journal of Speech*, 52, 1966.

David Cook and Harold F. Brooks, "A Room with Three Views: Harold Pinter's *The Caretaker*", in *Komos*, 1, 1967.

A. Callen, "Comedy and Passion in the Plays of Harold Pinter", in *Forum for Modern Language Studies*, 4, 1968.

Robert P. Murphy, "Non-Verbal Communication and the Overlooked Action in Pinter's *The Caretaker*", in *Quarterly Journal of Speech*, 58, 1972.

Errol Durbach, "*The Caretaker*: Text and Subtext", in *English Studies in Africa*, 18, 1975.

Gerald M. Berkowitz, "Pinter's Revision of *The Caretaker*", in *Journal of Modern Literature*, 5, 1976.

Charles A. Carpenter, "A Quicksand in Pinterland: *The Caretaker*", in *Arizona Quarterly*, 33, 1977.

Ricki Morgan, "The Multiple Nature of Reality in Pinter's *The Caretaker*", in *Quarterly Journal of Speech*, 64, 1978.

Ronald Knowles, "*The Caretaker* and the 'Point' of Laughter", in *Journal of Beckett Studies*, 5, 1979.

Surendra Sahai, "Pinter's *The Caretaker*: A Treatise on Urbanization", in *Indian Journal of English Studies*, 19, 1979.

Graham Woodroffe, "Taking Care of the 'Coloureds': The Political Metaphor of Harold Pinter's *The Caretaker*", in *Theatre Journal*, 40, 1988.

* * *

The action of *The Caretaker* takes place in, and is concerned with the occupancy of, a single West London room. The room is dilapidated, leaking, and cluttered with junk; it resembles a chaotic store-room rather than a living space. There is only one object that seems out of place: a statue of Buddha. Into this room the slow, hesitant Aston brings a shambling and garrulous Welsh tramp called Davies, having just rescued him from a punch-up in a "caff". Aston lives in the room (the Buddha is his) but it belongs to his younger brother Mick. Indeed, in an extended silent preface to the action we see Mick, a threatening figure, alone and leather-jacketed, laying visual claim to the room and its contents. The broad outline of the action, which involves only these three, and which is conducted largely in a series of duet-scenes, is easily traced. Having been taken in by the trusting Aston, Davies ingratiates himself, first with his host and then with Mick (who had begun by terrorising him), to the extent that each brother, indepen-

The Caretaker: National Theatre, London, 1980

dently of the other, offers him the position of caretaker on the premises. The shifty tramp then attempts to displace his host by playing one brother off against the other. But he is out of his depth in this particular game, and he is finally rejected decisively by both brothers. Their mutual understanding—if indeed they have one—is indicated by nothing more than a single faint smile ("I think it's a smile that they love each other", remarked Pinter on one occasion).

This plot seems most conveniently viewed in terms of game and strategy: Davies' opportunistic tactics are trumped by the lethal overarching intention(s) of the brothers. As usual in Pinter, language itself becomes a matrix of strategies; words (and silence) are modes of attack and defence within the fields of interpersonal negotiation and struggle between characters. Language is pared down to function, its truth-value fades, and almost every area of the play is ultimately infected by indeterminacy. We are compelled to attend closely to the minutiae of verbal manners—Mick's slick Cockney with its odd changes of register; Davies' Welsh rhythms and improvisatory loquacity; Aston's painful ponderousness of utterance. The overall effect is (in a famous phrase) the "comedy of menace" which we identify with the term "pinteresque". *The Caretaker*, as its author has affirmed, "is funny. But only up to a point".

A territorial imperative is the condition of the action, and strategic manipulation its substance, but the central dynamic of the play concerns individual identity. It finds its focus in Aston's narrative (referred to by Davies as a "long chat") at the end of the second of the play's three acts. Aston tells of how a visionary clarity and quietness to which he had access in his youth, and which set him apart from others, was shattered by the institutionalized torture of Electro-Convulsive Therapy (1960's irrationalism and anti-psychiatry are both foreshadowed here). The story may not be true, but the horror it articulates, of a socially sanctioned penetration of self which results in a kind of deadness, is genuine enough (and familiar in Pinter: it recalls Stanley's experience in *The Birthday Party*). It accounts for Aston's constant preoccupations, as well as for his manner. He is a do-it-yourselfer, a getter-together of materials, and a repairer of things: he spends much of the time "poking" the broken plug of a toaster (a mordantly ironic detail, given his previous experience of electricity). The end of his story associates the reconstruction of his own identity with his cherished plan to build a garden shed. The investment of his desire for a reconstructed identity in the shed-workshop, and in what it will enable him to do, is enormous ("I can work with my hands . . . . That's one thing I can do"). Yet it is also comically circular: "I've got that shed to get up. If I don't get it up now it'll never go up. Until it's up I can't get started". The shed is, as it were, *suspended* as a permanent object of desire, an idea.

Mick's declared, personal imperative, though very different from his brother's, is similarly impossible to satisfy. In his final "passionate" outburst against Davies, he reveals an obsession in his "business" interests not with an object but with a dynamic: "I got to think about expanding. . .in all directions. I don't stand still. I'm moving about, all the time". Not expanding *into*, or moving *towards*, but simply expanding and moving: there can be no limit, no fulfilment. The exercise of power over people seems to be Mick's substitute activity, providing as it does a practicable way of "expanding"—in several, if not all, directions.

Davies repeatedly and comically claims that the "papers" which will ratify his identity ("they tell you who I am") are in Sidcup, and he invents ludicrous reasons for not going to get them. Yet the very means by which he buys time to root himself in the room—the permanent deferral of definite

"official" identity—make him a suitably pliant subject for casting and manipulation in the brothers' play of identity. Davies as caretaker—in his incongruous uniform of velvet smoking-jacket—is useful, even necessary, for as long as he complies with his role. When he ceases to comply, he is ejected, a pathetic non-person.

When Mick finally rejects Davies, he hurls Aston's Buddha "against the gas stove. It breaks". The implied association of the eastern statue with the stinking vagrant, both of them "picked up" by Aston nearby, is a comic one. Indeed, with its qualities of stillness, quietness, poise, and inner harmony, the Buddha is the very antithesis not only of Davies, but of the perpetual mover, Mick. But if the room itself is a metaphor for Aston's chaotic consciousness, the Buddha on the gas stove embodies his desire to regain the visionary clarity and quietness of which, he claims, the electric torture in hospital deprived him. Mick's act of destruction can be read as an act of love: the attempt to release his brother from the toils of a delusion. Their shared, faint smile notwithstanding, it is not clear that he is successful. The statue broken, the brief chilling game is over, and as Davies crumbles pathetically, bereft of the verbal facility which was his only sure possession, Aston gazes out of the window and resumes his dream of the garden shed.

—Paul Lawley

CARITAS
by Arnold Wesker

First Publication: London, 1981.
First Production: National Theatre, London, 7 October 1981.

*   *   *

Late in the 14th century, the bondsmen to Henry, Bishop of Norfolk, grow restive. Their rebellions take several forms: fuming over frequent tax collections; attempted escape from servitude; a futile request for permission to learn to read; joining Wat Tyler's rebellion; even a priest's challenge to church authority. These male modes of resisting oppression, however, merely parallel the central revolution, as Christine Carpenter, an anchoress immured in the church wall, asks to be released from her vows.

As he often does elsewhere, Arnold Wesker in *Caritas* expresses universal human concerns by dramatizing the dilemma of an unusual female protagonist. On a tri-partite set consisting of the church interior, the window and part of the exterior wall of Christine's cell anchored to that church, and her father's carpentry workshop, Wesker first unfolds the theatrically charged events leading to Christine's change of heart. At 16 she vows canonical obedience, dons her habit, and prostrates herself before the altar, in the religious ceremony for enclosing an anchoress. We smell the incense, hear the church liturgy—spoken, chanted, and sung—as well as the misgivings expressed by Christine's parents and, most poignantly, by her fiancé, Robert, who agonizes over her renunciation of their life together: "She's seen blue skies, she won't forget that. She's seen mares mate, she won't forget that. She's seen lambs skip, the calves suck, the settin' sun, the rivers run, and once she's seen me naked, touched me once, an' she won't forget that".

Eventually it is revealed how correctly Robert prophesies,

but first there is a chilling spectacle as the hole in the wall, through which Christine has passed to her new life, is sealed up by huge stones. Like Edgar Allan Poe's doomed Fortunato in "The Cask of Amontillado", Christine will never more emerge from the wall alive, and, also like Montresor's victim, when entombed alive, she goes mad, but much more slowly.

Since Christine has "freely" chosen her fate, she must first, over a three-year period, come to regret her decision. The development from the 16-year-old anchoress calmly singing of forsaking all for God to the moment when the Bishop of Norfolk refuses, at the end of Act I, to release Christine, is punctuated by a children's chant which includes the taunt "Had a vision, had a word, had a revelation yet?" The town gossip, Matilde, likewise challenges Christine to observe signs from God by recounting outside her barred window tales of saints. Hearing of these martyrs—or masochists—prompts Christine to implore her priest for haircloth and chains, and to beg God for "a showing". Bred to admire and to wish to emulate mortification of the flesh, she starves and flagellates herself until, triumphantly, she hallucinates, but the priest kills her joy by warning against visions from Satan. Small wonder Christine's resolve, after three years' incarceration and manipulation, cracks, and she shrieks for her release. After the Bishop refuses to breach her cell—"a vow is a vow"—the walls revolve, revealing a dirty, terrified Christine.

For the play's second act, Christine is seen in her cramped cell, confined not only by her physical immurement but by the mental manacles which the rigid church hierarchy will not loosen. Despite her devout prayers to God and her fervent pleas to the church, Christine cannot obtain her freedom, not even when she blasphemes, not even when her grip on sanity recedes. The play concludes with her touching her dungeon's narrow boundaries, mumbling "This is a wall, an' this is a wall, an' this is a wall, an' this is a wall, an' this is a wall, an' this is . . . . ''

That the tragedy extends beyond Christine's own fate the first act's epic scope clearly establishes. Yet it is the claustrophobic pity and fear which is evoked by the young anchoress in Act II which endows *Caritas* with its extraordinary dramatic power. Some reviewers of the play's premiere at the National Theatre, London, were enraged by the poetic license which combines events from two different parts of the 14th century, moves the action from Surrey to Norfolk, and eliminates the real Christine's escape and return to her prison. Such criticism ignores the potency Wesker achieved, in part by making these changes. Wesker substitutes the failed flight of Robert's father for Christine's own attempt at freedom, an economy of plot construction which helps forge links between his tale's two parts as well as build unbroken anguish over the woman's disintegrating spirit.

Wesker's typical themes include the free spirit defying authority, the individual opposing a puissant church or state, injustice, alienation (societal and domestic), idealism, and the primacy of knowledge and education. All these can be discerned in *Caritas*. A parable of the destruction of the human spirit, *Caritas* can be interpreted—and more importantly, experienced emotionally—on many levels: political, religious, professional, and personal. Clearly the fetters of dogma shackle Christine, and church and state are one. Thus, anyone enmeshed in political or religious oppression, untempered by *caritas* (compassion), will identify strongly with this young hero who rebels against her bonds—in her case against a particularly patriarchal culture—and rage against oppressive forces. We may even find this 1981 play prescient in its application to events in Europe at the end of that decade. Yet the play's potent metaphor extends also to any ultimately entrapping situation—a job, familial obligations, a moribund

relationship, an obsolete commitment, someone else's expectations for us. Whatever the pressures in our lives which appear forever unyielding, stultifying, coercive, and confining, Christine's defeat compels tears and horror.

—Tish Dace

LA CASA DE BERNARDA ALBA.   See **THE HOUSE OF BERNARDA ALBA**.

LA CASSARIA.   See **THE CHEST**.

CASTE
by T.W. Robertson

First Publication: London, 1868.
First Production: Prince of Wales's Theatre, London, 6 April 1867.

Editions

Caste, in *The Principal Dramatic Works of Tom William Robertson*, London, 1889 (2 vols.).
Caste, in *"Society" and "Caste"*, edited by T. Edgar Pemberton, Boston and London, 1905.
Caste, in *Representative British Drama: Victorian and Modern*, edited by Montrose J. Moses, Boston, 1913; revised edition, 1931.
Caste, in *Nineteenth Century British Drama: An Anthology of Representative Plays*, edited by Leonard Ashley, Glenview, Illinois, 1967.
Caste, in *Nineteenth Century Plays*, edited by George Rowell, London 1953; second edition, 1972.
Caste, in *Plays by Tom Robertson*, edited by William Tydeman, Cambridge, 1982.

*   *   *

The best of a series of domestic comedies by Tom Robertson presented at the Prince of Wales Theatre, London, under the management of Squire and Marie Bancroft, *Caste* opened in April 1867 with Bancroft as Captain Hawtree and his wife (Marie Wilton) as Polly Eccles. Described by Bancroft as a "truthful representation of life and manners as they really are", *Caste* is customarily credited with leading the reaction against the artificiality of mid-Victorian drama by proving the merit of realistic set construction, properties, and furnishings in the English theatre, as well as by convincingly establishing the importance of careful stage direction and subtle character representation in theatrical practice. While the distinction of *Caste* in these respects deserves recognition, its reputation in theatre history has sometimes overshadowed its intrinsic dramatic merits.

The plot and structure of *Caste* are straightforward. The Hon. George D'Alroy, an army officer, falls in love with and marries an actress, Esther Eccles, despite the cautions of his

Caste: John Hare & George Honey, Prince of Wales Theatre, London, 1871

convention, but the play falls far short of espousing radical revision of values in class structure. "Caste's all right", George concludes. "Caste is a good thing if it's not carried too far. It shuts the door on the pretentious and the vulgar: but it should open the door very wide for exceptional merit. Let brains break through its barriers, and what brains can break through love may leap over". The likes of Sam Gerridge and Eccles, however, should know their place and stay there.

But this is to over-simplify. For while Robertson's social ethic may be restrained, his dramatic imagination happily complicates matters. The Marquise, for example, the strongest exponent of caste in the play, is consistently ridiculed. In attempting to buy Esther's child she is also morally repugnant. Eccles, too, is morally repugnant. He irresponsibly squanders his daughter's meagre resources, he steals jewellery from his grandson's neck, and he is constantly self-serving. Yet he is also the wittiest, most colourful, and most engaging character in the play, displaying a resistance and roguish self-sufficiency that transcend class barriers.

This complexity of theme and characterization is enhanced by Robertson's skills and experimentation with language. George D'Alroy is given a lisp; Polly takes delight in mimicking Hawtree's upper-class accent; the Marquise pompously recites Froissart in Chaucerian English; and the speech of both Eccles and Gerridge is rich in colloquial vocabulary and imagery. There are, as well, moments of brilliant comedy. In Act II George is enduring the unbridled wrath of his mother as he discloses that he is married (having unsuccessfully tried to hide his wife in a closet) when Eccles unexpectedly and, for George, calamitously, arrives and is introduced to the Marquise: "Eccles! Eccles! There never was an Eccles. He don't exist", she responds in a line worthy of Wilde.

Against these undoubted strengths one must balance the contrivances of George's presumed death and timely reappearance, and some awkward and discordant changes of mood. The humour of some of Eccles's conversations and soliloquies in Act II sits uncomfortably with revelations that he beat and oppressed Esther as a child. And D'Alroy's indifference to having murdered a sepoy in India—together with Polly and Sam subsequently joking about it—is offensive.

—L. W. Conolly

———

EL CASTIGO SIN VENGANZA. See **JUSTICE WITHOUT REVENGE.**

———

THE CASTLE OF PERSEVERANCE
Anonymous

Composition: 1400–1425.
First Production: No record of professional production. First non-professional production possibly at Culham College, Abingdon, 1974.

Editions

The Castle of Perseverance, in *The Macro Plays*, edited by Mark Eccles for The Early English Text Society, London, 1969 (facsimile and transcription).

friend Hawtree and the opposition of his mother, the Marquise de St. Maur, both of whom are class (or caste) conscious. Shortly after the marriage, George is posted to India on active service. By the opening of Act III (which, according to Marie Bancroft, played for the unusually long time of one hour and twenty minutes in the original production), Esther has a child, George is missing in action (presumed dead) and Esther's father has drunk and gambled away the money provided by George to support Esther during his absence. She survives only with the quiet support of Hawtree, spurning efforts by the Marquise to buy her child from her. George, however, has only been captured, not killed; he escapes from his captors, returns to England, and is reunited with friends and family. Eccles is sent off to Jersey ("where spirits are cheap") on an allowance of two pounds a week "to drink yourself to death in a year", and the Marquise reconciles herself to having a former actress as a daughter-in-law. The only other two characters in *Caste* (with the exception of George's servant) are Polly Eccles (Esther's sister) and Sam Gerridge, a mechanic and tradesman who also believes in "caste". By the end of the play Polly and Sam are engaged to be married, and the future for George and Esther looks equally assured.

Innovative in its approach to design and stage direction (which is extremely detailed throughout the text), *Caste* also dallies with the socially sensitive issue of class distinction and barriers in Victorian England. George and Esther defy

The Castle of Preseverance, in *English Morality Plays and Moral Interludes*, edited by Schell and Shuchter, New York, 1969.

The Castle of Perseverance, in *The Macro Plays*, edited by David Bevington, New York, 1972.

The Castle of Perseverance, in *Medieval Theatre*, edited by David Bevington, Boston, 1975.

The Castle of Perseverance, in *Medieval English Drama*, edited by B. Stone and J. Purkis, 1977.

The Castle of Perseverance, in *Four Morality Plays*, edited by Peter Happé, Harmondsworth, 1979.

Criticism

Books:

Richard Southern, *The Medieval Theatre in the Round: A Study of the Staging of "Castle of Perseverance" and Related Matters*, London, (2nd edition), 1957.

Articles:

Walter K. Smart, "The Castle of Perseverance; Place, Date and a Source", in *The Manly Anniversary Studies*, Chicago, 1923.

J. Wilson McCutchan, "Covetousness in *The Castle of Perseverance*", in *University of Virginia Studies*, 4, 1951.

J. Willis, "Stage Directions in *The Castle of Perseverance*", in *Modern Language Review* 51, 1956.

J. Bennett, "The Castle of Perseverance; Redactions, Place and Date", in *Medieval Studies*, 24, 1962.

Edgar T. Schell, "On the Imitation of Life's Pilgrimage in *The Castle of Perseverance*", in *Journal of English and Germanic Philology*, 67, 1968.

Natalie Schmitt, "Was There a Medieval Theatre in the Round?", in *Theatre Notebook*, 23, 1969.

Catherine Belsey, "The Stage Plan of *The Castle of Perseverance*", in *Theatre Notebook*, vol. 28, 1974.

Alan J. Fletcher, "'Coveytyse Copbord Schal Be at the Ende of the Castel Be the Beddys Feet': Staging the Death of Mankind in *The Castle of Perseverance*", in *English Studies*, August 1987.

S.E. Holbrook, "Covetousness, Contrition, and the Town in the *Castle of Perseverance*", in *Fifteenth-Century Studies*, vol. 13, 1988.

* * *

The play is a late medieval, religious morality, with a cast list of personified abstractions in opposing, balanced groups. It opens with the World (Mundus), the Devil (Belyal), and Flesh (Caro), each in turn on his own booth-stage, boasting of his powers and of his determination to destroy Mankind (Humanum Genus). Mankind is "born"—naked and weak, wavering between the contradictory paths of advice given to him by the Good and Bad Angels. He eventually opts to follow the Bad Angel who introduces him to Pleasure (Voluptas) and Folly (Stulticia), they quickly lead him to World and, in return for giving total allegiance to worldly ways, Mankind is sumptuously dressed and then passed to Covetous (Avaricia) to be briefed on how to acquire worldly wealth, and then to the rest of the Seven Deadly Sins.

Meanwhile, the Seven Virtues agree to help the Good Angel part Mankind from the Deadly Sins; they lead him to safety in the Castle of Perseverance. War is declared, six of the Deadly Sins attack the Castle, and the Virtues hurl down scalding ammunition—roses, symbolic of Christ's passion. The forces of good seem to be winning, but Covetous quietly circles the Castle and, with honeyed, silken words, wheedles Mankind

out of the Castle by pointing out that he needs money in his old age (Mankind ages throughout the play). The Virtues are powerless to prevent Mankind's departure from the Castle; he has free will and cannot be constrained. Death (Mors) then appears, kills Mankind, and the Bad Angel carries off his soul, after his unsuccessful appeals to the Good Angel.

The Four Daughters of God now appear. Mercy (Misericordia) has heard her name called and with her sisters Peace (Pax), Truth (Veritas), and Justice (Justicia), has come to investigate. They debate the fate of Mankind's soul but cannot come to an agreement, so decide to place their case before God the Father whose booth-stage now opens, revealing him sitting in majesty. After listening to the Daughters, God declares in favour of Mercy and orders Mankind's soul to be retrieved from Hell; his soul is brought up to share God's heavenly abode. The play closes with the actor playing God stepping out of his role saying: "Thus endeth out games. / To save you from sinning, / Ever at the beginning / Think on your last ending", and the action is completed with a *Te Deum*.

This play is the most complete, surviving, early religious English Morality play (*The Pride of Life* pre-dates it but is seriously incomplete). Although two leaves of the unique manuscript of *Castle* are missing (with a consequent loss of some 200 lines) this is not a serious lapse in a play of 3,649 lines, especially when a quite detailed plot is given in its Banns (even though it is thought these Banns are a later addition to the play and do not quite square with the play itself; the Banns indicate that Mankind's soul is saved through the intercession of the Blessed Virgin Mary).

With typical personified abstractions as characters, and with the usual morality structure of fall and redemption, this play is of the "full scope" morality genre depicting the birth, life, death, and salvation of its protagonist, Mankind. It promotes the sacraments of the Church, extols the way of Christian virtue, comments on the unexpected and inexorable advent of Death, and emphasises that God's mercy is infinite. Although undeniably verbose, the play is theatrically entertaining, by turns amusing and serious, didactic, and spectacular.

The manuscript contains notes and a sketch depicting the play's staging, which constitutes a valuable addition to our understanding of the production of medieval theatre. The play was written to be performed in a circular, open space with five perimeter stages and a central stage (representing the Castle built high on stilts). The audience is located between the stages on the perimeter and kept out of the central acting area (the "place" or *platea*). The action flows between these six stages across and around the "place". The cast is large, with 33 speaking characters, and minimal opportunities for doubling up. The play is a very active one with lots of opportunities for colourful costume, spectacle, and pyrotechnics.

Like all medieval drama the play is written in verse of strong rhythm and abundant alliteration but of surprising flexibility. Its main form is a 13-line stanza: *abababababcdddc*, which is particularly effective even though characters never speak less than a full stanza. The language (Middle English) is a variety of East Midlands dialect possibly of Norfolk. Stage directions and names of characters are in Latin. Although there are a number of female characters, in accordance with medieval theatre practice all parts would have been played by males. There is no evidence as to who originally created or performed the play which in presentation would have lasted up to four hours. From the Banns it is evident that the play was expected to be played at different locations in the region, although to achieve this a large, affluent company with a high degree of organisation would have been necessary.

In the 20th century the play (in a reduced form) has been produced occasionally, although not professionally, and not until 1974 was it given a full-scale open air performance in accordance with the original staging plan—at Culham College, Abingdon. In 1979 it was also staged in Canada on the campus at Toronto University. Both productions proved beyond question the play's highly effective, theatrical potential. It is to be regretted that the scale of the play, calling for a large cast and considerable resources, militates against frequent revival of this ambitious but exceptionally fine morality play. It deserves to be better known.

—Philip S. Cook

CAT ON A HOT TIN ROOF
by Tennessee Williams

First Publication: New York, 1955; revised edition, New York, 1975.
First Production: Morosco Theatre, New York, 24 March 1955; revised version, American Shakespeare Theatre, Stratford, Connecticut, 1974.

Criticism
(For general works on the author, see *Playwrights* volume)

Articles:
William Sacksteder, "The Three *Cats*: A Study in Dramatic Structure", in *Drama Survey*, 5, 1966–67.
Tom S. Reck, "The First *Cat on a Hot Tin Roof*: Williams' 'Three Players'", in *University Review*, 34, 1968.
James R. Blackwelder, "The Human Extremities of Emotion in *Cat on a Hot Tin Roof*", in *Research Studies*, 38, 1970.
R.M. Mansur, "The Two 'Cats' on the Tin Roof: A Study of Tennessee Williams's *Cat on a Hot Tin Roof*", in *Journal of the Karnatak University: Humanities*, 14, 1970.
Susan N. Mayberry, "A Study of Illusion and the Grotesque in Tennessee Williams' *Cat on a Hot Tin Roof*", in *Southern Studies*, 22, 1983.

* * *

The play takes place on one afternoon in a bed-sitting-room of a plantation mansion somewhere in the southeastern United States. The story concerns the members of "Big Daddy" Pollitt's family and their attempts to secure for themselves his cotton plantation before he dies. Brick Pollitt, an alcoholic ex-football star, and his wife Margaret ("Maggie the Cat") struggle with each other and with Brick's older brother Gooper and his wife Mae to take control of "twenty-eight thousand acres of the richest land this side of the valley Nile". Brick, sodden with alcohol and disgusted with life, is totally indifferent to the estate and to his wife Maggie who hopes never again to face the humiliating poverty of her childhood. In the course of their rancorous arguing, Brick discloses to his father that the old man is dying of cancer, and Maggie, hoping to earn Bid Daddy's approval and frustrate the others, lies that she and Brick are expecting a child. The play concludes with no resolution to the question of who will inherit the plantation and no answer to the question as to whether Brick and Maggie will ever again resume their sexual relationship, although that seems highly unlikely.

Cat, along with *The Glass Menagerie* and *A Streetcar Named Desire*, is counted among Williams's most popular and impor-

Cat on a Hot Tin Roof: Laurence Olivier as Big Daddy and Robert Wagner as Brick, 1976 (production filmed for television)

tant dramatic achievements (though the other two are much superior to it). It has been frequently revived since its premiere. In fact, the strength of the play lies especially in its *three* finely drawn characters, each rich enough to attract the great actors of the day. Ben Gazzara played the original Brick to Barbara Bel Geddes's Maggie; the roles were assumed in the 1958 film of the play by Paul Newman and Elizabeth Taylor. Big Daddy was played by Burl Ives on both stage and screen; Lawrence Olivier played the part in a 1976 television version.

Cat shows many of the themes which Williams wrote about for his entire creative life: the pain of physical, social, and economic ostracism (Maggie's poverty and Brick's broken ankle and fear of homosexuality), the heartbreak of unrequited love (Maggie's rejection by Brick), the worthiness of the most vulnerable and abused people (even the slovenly, corpulent Big Mama has a moment of dignity when "she almost stops being fat"), and the destruction of beauty through age, drugs, alcohol, or the cruelty of others. Williams's special genius was to bring a kind of poetic longing to the theatre (skillfully employing stage lighting to emphasize this), and to present the image of life as a fierce and usually doomed struggle for even a single moment of truth and wholeness. In *Cat*, it is Brick who is disillusioned to the point of dysfunction with the "mendacity" of the world he is trying to hobble away from, and Maggie who carries the procreative force which determines the continuity of life, even in a depraved world. Typical in its reflection of Williams's love of language and his deeply felt Southern heritage, *Cat* only suggests the violence and decadence which was to characterize the themes and form of Williams's later work. By the end of the 1950's, some critics have argued, the decline of his artistry was already clearly in evidence.

Concerning *Cat*, the great strength of the play rests in its powerful second act, in the confrontation scene between Big Daddy and Brick. With brilliantly orchestrated interruptions of their encounter increasing the intensity of their mutual regard and mutual resentment, the scene holds the audience tightly until the emotional grip is broken by the double revelation of the two secrets Williams keeps from his characters (Big Daddy's knowledge of his cancer and Brick's knowledge of his ambiguous relationship to his dead friend Skipper). After the secrets are revealed, little remains for the play except to finish the nasty dispute over the ambiguous legacy of the plantation, a problem Williams never completely solved.

At the urging of *Cat*'s first director and Williams' long-time collaborator Elia Kazan, Williams altered the third act of *Cat* at its premiere to accommodate Kazan's three objections: that more needs to be seen of Big Daddy (who disappears at the end of Act Two in the original text), that more needs to be known about Brick after his confrontation with his father, and that more sympathy needs to be shown for Maggie before the play ends. The "new" act three was seen by most directors and critics as inferior to the "old" unproduced one (though it ran on Broadway longer than any other Williams play), and Williams tinkered with the script yet again for a 1974 production by the American Shakespeare Theatre. Nonetheless, though the changes tell us much about Williams's own insecurity, the play's strengths lie outside the specific versions of the text, in the three powerful character portrayals and the "broken world" (in Esther Jackson's phrase) that embodies what Williams calls in the second act of the play "the truth of human experience".

—Robert Skloot

CATO
by Joseph Addison

First Publication: London, 1713.
First Production: Theatre Royal, Drury Lane, London, April 1713.

Editions

Cato, in *British Dramatists from Dryden to Sheridan*, edited by G.H. Nettleton and A.E. Case, Boston, 1939.
Cato, in *Eighteenth Century Plays*, edited by R. Quintana, New York, 1952.

Criticism

(For general works on the author, see *Playwrights* volume)

Articles:
F.E. Novak, *Die bürgerlichen Züge in Addison's "Cato"*, Berlin, 1940.
Robert Halsband, "Addison's *Cato* and Lady Mary Wortley Montagu", in *Publications of the Modern Language Association* [*PMLA*], 65, 1950.
M.M. Kelsall, "The Meaning of Addison's *Cato*", in *Review of English Studies*, 17, 1966.

F.M. Litto, "Addison's *Cato* in the Colonies", in *William and Mary Quarterly*, 23, 1966.
Franz Zaic, "Joseph Addison's *Cato*", in *Das englische Drama im 18 und 19 Jahrhundert*, edited by Heinz Kosok, 1976.

*   *   *

The historical context of Addison's five-act tragedy presents the most famous of Roman stoics trapped at Utica with the army he is leading to resist the forces of the emergent dictator, Julius Caesar. With Cato are his sons Portius and Marcus, who in the first scene reveal that they are both in love with Lucia, daughter of the senator Lucius. This situation is paralleled in rival suits for Cato's daughter Marcia by the Numidian prince Juba and the senator Sempronius. In the second act, Cato's senate at Utica is sitting and is addressed by an ambassador from Caesar. Caesar himself does not appear in the play, and his personality is sketched only briefly, although it is approximated in the figure of Sempronius, who shocks Juba by offering to abduct Marcia for him. A third-act coup against Cato by Sempronius and the Numidian general Syphax is not immediately successful, and the next act begins with an absurd situational drama in which Sempronius disguises himself as Juba to coax Marcia away, but is killed, leaving a corpse for Marcia to mistake, in a scene reminiscent of *Cymbeline*, for that of her preferred lover. The act ends with Cato's sublimely stoical response to the death of Marcus at the hands of Syphax's troops, leaving the final act for Cato's own suicide, facilitated by a reading of Plato's *Immortality of the Soul*.

Addison's play has been seen as a terminal point in the development of English heroic drama, a projection of the sub-genre which had flourished within the context of imported French neoclassicism in the early period of the Restoration. Many features of heroic drama remain in *Cato*, including what may, from the perspective of classical philosophy, be regarded as a happy ending to a play that Addison termed a tragedy. However, the dramaturgic audacity of the play lies in the very constricted range of character types at the core of the action, and the issue of their essential appropriateness to drama at all.

Dennis's famous objection that "I should be apt to think, that a nest of Stoicks could supply us, with no more proper persons for an excellent Tragedy, than a Nest of Fools can do for an excellent Comedy" has frequently been taken as grounds for an indictment of the play as a whole, asserting that stoicism is inherently undramatic. However, Dennis's phrasing—possibly inadvertently—draws attention to the fact that although the title character is a stoic saint most of the rest of the cast are at best aspirant stoics who have not attained any absolute state and are in continuous danger of being seduced from their professed ideals. Cato is their constant mentor, but in the probability of their failure according to his yardstick there is an obvious potential for tragedy.

Cato's first entrance to the stage is delayed until the second act. In part, this is to give him the grand entrance that all leading actors relish, and it also establishes the tentative nature of the other characters' ethical positions. But in addition it allows Cato's stoicism to be presented in the abstract, particularly in terms of an ascetic apatheia, "severely bent against himself; renouncing sleep, and rest, and food, and ease", looking "down on pleasures, and the baits of sense". His "rigid virtue" is the product of "reason", and determines his behaviour throughout the play, including his suicide. This accords with the writings of Cicero and Seneca from which the characterisation is derived. Less clearly sketched, however, is the way in which Cato's apatheia has been circumvented on the political front; the origins of his commitment to action are not presented, beyond the fact that Caesar represents a polarised

Cato: Engraving, 1713

antithesis to his own character type, and there is no vision of cosmic or social harmony as an objective for the military action, apart from the implications of natural imagery of storms, seas, and mountains.

The imperturbability of the title character seems almost absolute; only once does his mastery falter, when Portius attempts to prevent his suicide, but he distances his emotions, and controls his only personal crisis in the play, within a dozen lines. Apart from this, he shows none of the capacity for dilemma, dividedness, miscalculation, or hubris that tragic theory would expect. For this reason, the sub-plot, which has traditionally been regarded as a tangential effort to generate conventional dramatic action, acquires a peculiar importance. In the main plot, there is a frequent contrast between Cato's emotional containment and Numidian impetuousness, which is very similar to that of Caesar and Sempronius. For them, impetuous action is almost an index to manhood, and it is even argued that the privations of their military service parallel Cato's self-abnegation. In the younger generation, however, apatheia is a constant ideal, and the acknowledgement of love is itself a deviation from that ideal. Apart from the issue of congestion, the love-matches are ostensibly delayed only because the younger characters have a sense of priority in the face of civil war; yet a latent suspense is generated because their passion is fundamentally in conflict with stoicism.

Cato is unquestionably a work of great importance in terms of its expression of the literary and ethical idealism of Augustan England. Voltaire praised it as the first "*tragédie raisonnable*" in English, and William Guthrie wrote a long comparison with Hamlet, finding that Cato's "is the speech of pre-determined resolution, and not of human infirmity; it is the language of uncertainty, not of perturbation; it is the language of doubting; but of such doubts, as the speaker is prepared to cut asunder if he cannot resolve them". Guthrie's analysis works from an initial stance of admiration eventually to echo points which Dennis had argued several decades earlier, and most of Dennis's attack on Addison's stagecraft must be accepted as valid, especially his comments on the presentation of the suicide: that Cato should "give himself the mortal Wound in his Bed-chamber; and then be brought back into that Hall to expire, purely to shew his good Breeding, and save his Friends the trouble of coming up to his Bed-chamber; all this appears to me to be improbable, incredible, impossible". For all that, *Cato* must command attention as a play which challenges traditional assumptions about the dramaturgic tractability of various character types, and about the nature of drama itself.

—Howard McNaughton

THE CAUCASIAN CHALK CIRCLE
(Der kaukasische Kreidekreis)
by Bertolt Brecht

First Publication: As *The Caucasian Chalk Circle*, in *Two Parables*, Minneapolis, Minnesota, 1948.; In *Sonderheft, Sinn und Form*, Potsdam, 1949; in book form, Berlin, 1954.
First Production: Nourse Little Theatre, Northfield, Minnesota, May 1948 (in English); Theater am Schiffbauerdam, Berlin, June 1954 (in German).

Translations
The Caucasian Chalk Circle, translated by Eric and Maja Bentley in *Two Parables for the Theatre*, Minnesota, 1948; revised edition, Harmondsworth, 1966.
The Caucasian Chalk Circle, translated by James and Tania Stern, with W.H. Auden, in *Brecht: Collected Plays, Volume 7*, edited by John Willett and Ralph Mannheim, London, 1960.

Criticism
(For general works on the author, see *Playwrights* volume)

Books:
Werner Hecht (ed.), *Materialien zu Brechts "Der kaukasische Kreidekreis"*, Frankfurt, 1966.
J.M. Ritchie, *Brecht, "Der kaukasische Kreidekreis"*, London, 1976.

Articles:
H. Bunge, "Brecht Probiert: Notizen und Gedanken zu Proben in Bertolt Brechts Stück *Der kaukasische Kreidekreis*", in *Sinn und Form*, 9, 1957.

H. Bunge, "The Dispute Over The Valley", in *Tulane Drama Review*, vol. 4 no. 2, 1959.

M. Alter, "The Technique of Alienation in Bertolt Brecht's *Caucasian Chalk Circle*, in *CLA Journal*, 8, 1964.

Keith M. Sagar, "Brecht in Neverneverland: *The Caucasian Chalk Circle*", in *Modern Drama*, 9, 1966.

Bertold Brecht, "The Prologue to *The Caucasian Chalk Circle*", translated by Hugo Schmidt and Jerome Clegg, in *Tulane Drama Review*, vol. 12 no. 1, 1967.

Ronald Gaskell, "The Form of *The Caucasian Chalk Circle*", in *Modern Drama*, 10, 1967.

W.A.J. Steer, "The Thematic Unity of Brecht's *Der kaukasische Kreidekreis*", in *German Life & Letters*, 21, 1967.

Surab Tscharchalaschili, "*Der kaukasische Kreidekreis*: Seine Geschichte und die Verfremdungstheorie von Bertolt Brecht", in *Weimarer Beitrage*, Heft S., 1968.

Louis Blenkner, "Redemption in Chaos: Brecht's *Caucasian Chalk Circle*", in *American Benedictine Review*, 21, 1970.

Edward M. Berckman, "The Function of Hope in Brecht's Pre-revoluntionary Theater", in *Brecht Heute*, 1, 1971.

John Fuegi, "*The Caucasian Chalk Circle* in Performance", in *Brecht Heute*, 1, 1971.

Robert Spaethling, "Zum Verständnis der Grusche in Brechts *Der kaukasische Kreidekreis*", in *Unterrichtspraxis for the Teaching of German*, vol. 4 no. 2, 1971.

G.H.S. Mueller, "The Narrator in Brecht's *Der kaukasische Kreidekreis*", in *Furman Studies*, vol. 21 no. 2, 1974.

John Ditsky, "Brecht's Judging Jesus: *The Caucasian Chalk Circle*", in *New Laurel Review*, vol. 7 no. 1, 1977.

T.N. Holmes, "Descrying the Dialectic: A Heterodox Line on the Prologue to Brecht's *Der kaukasische Kreidekreis*", in *Journal of European Studies*, 7, 1977.

Sammy K. McLean, "Messianism in Bertolt Brecht's *Der gute Mensch von Sezuan* and *Der kaukasische Kreidekreis*", in *Seminar: A Journal of Germanic Studies*, 14, 1978.

Linda Hill, "The Love of Life, Justice, and Scandal: Azdak in Brecht's *Der kaukasische Kreidekreis*", in *German Studies Review*, 2, 1979.

Pankaj Khanna, "Structural Unity in Brecht's *The Caucasian Chalk Circle*", in *Literary Criterion*, vol. 14 no. 3, 1979.

Thomas John DiNapoli, "Bertolt Brecht's *Der kaukasische Kreidekries*: A Study of Form and Context", in *Literatur in Wissenschaft und Unterricht*, vol. 14 no. 4, 1981.

Helen M. Whall, "Future Imperfect: The Pastoral Tense of Bertolt Brecht's *The Caucasian Chalk Circle*", in *Studies in the Humanities* (Indiana), 9, 1981.

*   *   *

The Caucasian Chalk Circle is the last of the great plays Brecht wrote in exile, and the first to look beyond the Nazis and World War II to the future. It is a composite play. Two groups of peasants with conflicting proposals for restoring agriculture after the retreat of Hitler's armies from Soviet Georgia decide to stage a play. The first part of it tells the story of Grusha, a servant girl in ancient Grusinia who saves the Governor's baby son during a palace revolution and rears him selflessly in hazardous times until a counter-revolution enables his natural mother to claim him back. The second part tells how, by a set of curious chances, Azdak, an anarchic village scribe, becomes Judge in the capital Nukha and pronounces a Solomonic verdict when the case of the mother versus the foster mother is brought before him. The play over, the peasant players decide that as the child was given to the more maternal claimant, so the valley should be given to the irrigators whose plan is more socially beneficial. The frame-work with its utopian vision of collective decision-taking is sometimes cut, of which neither Brecht nor any hard-line Brechtian could approve.

The play has in Grusha and Azdak two plum parts. It was written as a vehicle for Luise Rainer, an Austrian actress who had won two Oscars, but she found Grusha, indeed the entire play, too unglamourous, and yet another of Brecht's attempts to get a play on Broadway was frustrated. Grusha is a carefully structured character. She is, at the outset, slow on the uptake and one of nature's victims. As the city burns and the Governor's head is spiked on the gate, she watches over, and eventually steals off with, his abandoned son. She has no lines at this point. The Singer describes her thoughts and finally comments, "Terrible is the temptation to do good". Moving as it is, all sentiment is eliminated from this situation and the pathos is carefully controlled. Grusha, who got engaged as the upheaval started, now has to fend for herself in a competitive society. As she flees to the Northern Mountains she is overcharged by a peasant, sneered at by aristocrats, and let down by a promising foster-mother. She has to club a pursuing Ironshirt unconscious and cross a dangerous rope bridge, and by the end of their shared dangers she is bonded to the child. By the time her soldier fiancé, Simon, comes back, years later, from the wars, she has had to marry a draft-dodger to secure the child's future. It is a part that Brecht reworked as soon as he had written it to play down the initial humanitarian gesture as servile and pig-headed and show the development of her character; that is, the maternal bonding and her acquisition of class-consciousness, as a process determined by her exposure to society. By the end of the play she is the salt of the earth, which she was not at the beginning.

Azdak is a thief and a poacher, and a covert revolutionary from the start. When a fugitive stumbles into his hovel he automatically conceals him from the law, only later discovering that it was the Grand Duke. Thinking he has betrayed the revolution he turns himself in, to discover that there has merely been a coup. But his effrontery gets him appointed judge and having saved the Grand Duke a second time, his wit and lack of scruple enable him to subvert the law and oversee a brief golden age of justice. Brecht contrives all this with great wit and sarcasm. For example, a rich farmer accuses his stable-boy of raping his daughter; Azdak observes her walk, and fines her for assaulting the boy with a dangerous backside. A sequence of farcical episodes like this establish Azdak as a great comic figure, an alter ego of his Mephistophelian creator.

In the middle of the play there is a time-shift as the Azdak action begins on the same Easter Day on which Grusha encumbered herself with the child. The two stories converge in the trial scene in which the mothers are invited to pull the child out of a chalk circle. The biblical Solomon and the Prince in the 13th century Chinese *Chalk Circle* use the test to determine the biological mother as the obvious real mother in the societies of their day, but in Brecht's version the Governor's widow only wants her son so she can claim her inheritance, whereas the "proletarian" Grusha has sacrificed all for the boy. It is Grusha who lets go in the tug-of-war with the boy, and it is to her that Azdak awards him. The motivation is clearly ideological, but none the less convincing for that. This, as Brecht says in the epilogue, is a play about the change, about laws having to be scrutinized to ensure they have retained their validity.

The Caucasian Chalk Circle is a classic example of epic theatre. It does not develop an integrated conflict in terms of character, but tells two separate, exotic tales to illuminate a problem posed in the prologue. There are large jumps between the separate narrative blocks which make up this "montage". The Grusha and Azdak components are themselves built up from short episodes which illuminate aspects of their characters respective interaction with society, and the episodes are linked by the Singer, who functions as narrator and commentator. The constant alternation between two modes of presentation—the multi-character episodes and the solo narrative—forces the audience to retune at regular intervals, and inhibits the suspension of disbelief which Brecht considered to be death to the critical faculties. To this purpose there is also much music and song. Brecht's marxist message is laboured in the collective farmers' scenes, but otherwise it is effortlessly integrated into the structure of the play which comes across as an entertaining exploration of social justice.

—Hugh Rorrison

CELESTINA (La Celestina)
by Fernando de Rojas

First Publication: As *Comedia de Calisto y Melibea*, 1499; revised and expanded as *Tragicomedia de Calisto y Melibea*, c. 1502.

Editions
La Celestina, edited by Javier Costa Clavell, Barcelona, 1969.
La Celestina: Tragicomedia de Calisto y Melibea, edited by Dorothy S. Severin, Madrid, 1974.
Comedia o tragicomedia de Calisto y Melibea. . ., edited by Miguel Marciales, Mérida, Venezuela, 1977.
Celestina, edited by Dorothy S. Severin, Warminster, Wiltshire, 1987 (with James Mabbe's 1631 translation).

Translations
The Celestina: A Novel in Dialogue, translated by L. B. Simpson, Berkeley, California, 1955.
La Celestina, translated by M. H. Singleton, Madison, Wisconsin, 1958.
La Celestina, translated by P. Hartnoll, London and New York, 1959.
La Celestina, translated by J. M. Cohen, New York, 1964.
The Spanish Bawd, translated by James Mabbe (1631), edited by Guadalupe Martínez Lacalle, London, 1972.

Bibliographies
Adrienne Schizzano Mandel, "*La Celestina*" *Studies: A Thematic Survey and Bibliography, 1824–1970*, Metuchen, New Jersey, 1971.
Joseph T. Snow, "*Celestina*" *by Fernando de Rojas: An Annotated Bibliography of World Interest, 1930–1985*, Madison, Wisconsin, 1985.

Criticism
(For general works on the author, see *Playwrights* volume)

Books:
Stephen Gilman, *The Art of La Celestina*, London, 1956.
Alan D. Deyermond, *The Petrarchan Sources of La Celestina*, London, 1961.
Dorothy S. Severin, *Two Spanish Masterpieces: "The Book of Good Love" and the "Celestina"*, London, 1970.
Jose Muñoz Garrigos, *Contribucion al Estudio del Lexico de "La Celestina"*, Murcia, 1974.
Espenza Gurza, *Lectura existencialista de "La Celestina"*, Madrid, 1977.

Juan Alcina, *Fernando de Rojas: La Celestina*, Barcelona, 1983.
Ciriaco Morón Arroyo, *Sentido y forma de "La Celestina"*, Madrid, 1984.
D. W. McPheeters, *Estudios humanísticos sobre "La Celestina"*, Potomac, Maryland, 1985.
Louise Fothergill-Payne, *Seneca and "Celestina"*, Cambridge, 1988.
Dorothy Sherman Severin, *Tragicomedy and Novelistic Discourse in "Celestina"*, Cambridge, 1989.
Charles A. Fraker, *Celestina*, 1990.

Articles:
See Mandel's and Snow's bibliographies and the journal *Celestinesca* (also edited by Snow).

*   *   *

A young gentleman, Calisto, falls sick with love for the noble and wealthy Melibea. His servant, Sempronio, advises calling in the procuress Celestina (in whose house his own mistress, Elicia, lives). A younger servant, Pármeno, protests but is overruled. Celestina corrupts Pármeno, offering him sex with the prostitute Areúsa, and persuades Melibea, using a blend of plausible argument and black magic. Calisto, granted an interview with his beloved, secures her promise to meet him again by night in her garden. Meanwhile Celestina and the servants quarrel over the gold chain she has wheedled out of Calisto; they murder her and are summarily executed. Calisto keeps his rendezvous and seduces Melibea. Here the two versions—*Comedia* and *Tragicomedia*—diverge. The former has Calisto, leaving the walled garden that same night, fall from his ladder to his death. In the longer version of the *Tragicomedia* a full month of secret lovemaking intervenes, during which Celestina's two prostitutes conspire with the braggart Centurio to avenge the old bawd's murder. Calisto hears the scuffle as his servants are attacked in the street, hastens down the ladder, falls, and is killed. Melibea, despairing, flings herself off a tower; her mother dies of grief; her father is left to mourn alone.

Celestina is an inexhaustibly problematic text. The author of the *Comedia* disclaims credit for its long first act, but does not state who wrote it or when. Nor do we know how much he contributed to the *Tragicomedia*: most critics favour a theory of homogeneous authorship, but this has been fiercely contested. At least this author names himself: he is Fernando de Rojas, a Salamanca law-graduate from Puebla de Montalbán, near Toledo. It is known that the Rojas family were converted Jews (but not how recently-converted, or how residually Jewish). In the 1520's the Inquisitors investigated his father-in-law, but Rojas survived until 1541, the much-respected sometime mayor of Talavera de la Reina.

It remains unclear how far the harsh historical experiences of Spanish *conversos* inform Rojas' uncompromising irony and pessimism. In *Celestina*, values are named only to be betrayed; moral advice becomes a tool of argument for time-servers; the yearnings of idealistic love yield perfunctorily to the quick fix of the bawd. Religion is accorded the most cursory of lip-service; few even try to live well, and by doing so they escape no element of suffering or despair. Fate and selfishness rule; there are, as one critic writes "no recipes to live by". Is this merely "the world" as seen by an ultra-ascetic Christian moralism, such as the original *Celestina* overtly purports to convey? Or is it the world as imagined after one religious system has collapsed under persecution, and its triumphant persecutor is known only as a vehicle of tyranny and hypoc-

Celestina: Compania Nacional de Teatro Clasico, Madrid, 1988

risy? These alternatives open a whole gamut of divergent interpretations.

Celestina can be taken as an orthodox and exemplary sermon against lust and greed, or as an earthy lampoon against pretentious courtly love-rhetoric. We may choose to stress its roots in comic tradition: Rojas himself called it a "Terentian work", and its closest analogues are in Renaissance Latin comedy. Its social satire may reflect a general disintegration of medieval certainties, with the shift towards an urban, secular society where values and loyalties are displaced by money and material advantage. Even on this view, Rojas' *converso* experience would prevent his idealizing older social forms. It may have done much more, promoting a wholly negative and corrosive vision of actual Christian society. *Celestina*, interpreted in this light, would prefigure much 20th-century writing: root-and-branch social protest; subversive celebration of repressed sexual licence; nihilistic existential despair. All these readings, though, would need to accomodate Rojas' extraordinary powers of characterization—Calisto's fatuity; Melibea's passion; Pármeno's shiftiness and insecurity; above all, Celestina, demonic, garrulous, and grotesque—and the vitality of his language.

These qualities in *Celestina* greatly influenced the handling of erotic episodes—and especially of the go-between—in pre-Lopean Spanish drama from Encina to Torres Naharro and beyond. Lope de Vega himself drew on Rojas' example in plays like *El caballero de Olmedo* (*The Knight of Olmedo*), as well as his own dialogue, *Dorotea*. The tradition continues in Salazar y Torres' Celestinesque *El encanto es la hermosura* (*The Charm is Beauty*, 1675), remodelled by Solís in 1818. In this century, Rojas' influence is apparent in Valle-Inclán and Sastre. Abroad, the English *Interlude of Calisto and Melibea* (1525) responds directly to *Celestina*: so too, arguably, do Machiavelli's *Mandragola*, the Portuguese António Ferreira's *Bristo* (1562), *Romeo and Juliet*, and even *Othello*. *Celestina* also helped to shape the realist tradition in Dutch theatre.

The history of *Celestina* itself on stage belongs to the present century, and it is impressive. Fernández Villegas' version (1909) has had over twenty successors in Spanish: noteworthy are those of Alvaro Custodio in the 1950's, Alejandro Casona, in the 1960's, Camilo José Cela in the 1970's, and Angel Facio and Gonzalo Torrente Ballester in the 1980's.

English stage versions include Ashley Dukes' loose imitation *Match-maker's Arms* (1951), and a dozen others, equally divided between independent renderings—mainly for American campus theatres—and adaptations of James Mabbe's translation (*The Spanish Bawd*, 1631). Joan Littlewood (Stratford East, London 1958), Charles Lewsen (Sheffield, 1978), and Robert David Macdonald (Glasgow, 1986) have all produced versions of the piece. Notable among a similar number of French adaptations are versions by Jacques Copeau (unperformed), Albert Camus, Paul Achard, and Jeanne

Moreau has appeared memorably as Celestina (Paris, 1989). *Celestina* has also inspired operas, a musical, a ballet, and film and television versions.

—Nicholas G. Round

EL CEPILLO DE DIENTES; o, Náufragos en el parque de atracciones
by Jorge Díaz

First Publication: In *La víspera de degöello*, Madrid, 1967.
First Production: Sla Talía, Santiago [one-act version], 1961; two act version, Teatro Valle-Inclán, Madrid, 1966.

Criticism
(For general works on the author, see *Playwrights* volume)

Articles:
María A. Salgado, "*El cepillo de dientes* and *El apartamiento*: Two Opposing Views of Alienated Man", in *Romance Notes*, vol. 27 no. 3, 1977.
Diógenes Fajardo, "Aspecto mítico-ritual en dos obras de Jorge Díaz", in *Texto crítico*, 22-23, 1981.
Ronald D. Burgess, "*El Cepillo de dientes*: Empty Words, Empty Games?", in *Estreno: Cuadernos del teatro español contemporáneo*, vol. 9 no. 2, 1983.
Leon F. Lyday, "Inversion in the Absurdist Plays of Jorge Díaz", in *Romance Notes*, vol. 27 no. 1, 1986.
Daniel Zalacaín, "*El cepillo de dientes* y el humorismo en el teatro absurdista hispanoamericano", in *Symposium*, 42, 1988.

*   *   *

Act I consists of the strange and nonsensical breakfast conversation between Him and Her. They speak in clichés and recite advertisement jingles; they complain about each other's tastes in music and furniture; she gets hysterical about the brand of cigarettes he smokes; he is so much distraught because she has used his toothbrush to clean her shoes that he strangles her. He then calmly sits down to read about his crime in the morning paper.

In Act II the dead wife enters as Antona, the maid. When she discovers the body, he offers absurd reasons for committing the crime. Overcome with passion, they begin to make love wildly, destroying everything that gets in their way. Suddenly Antona is the wife again; exhausted by their physical exertions, they both wonder if all this is really necessary just to have good sex. They begin to fight over trivialities; she kills him with a fork, but he comes back to life. All the lights go out, the stage scenery disappears, leaving them alone, to meditate on how they can possibly survive their overwhelming love for each other.

The Toothbrush (*El cepillo de dientes*) is generally recognized as one of the most accomplished examples of Latin-American absurdist theatre. Written while the playwright Jorge Díaz was working closely with Ictus, then the foremost experimental theatre in Santiago, Chile, *The Toothbrush* is clearly reminiscent of European absurdism, especially of the works of Ionesco. Like these, Díaz's play has no traditional plot line; rather, the action is circular, ending where it began. The characters have no psychology and undergo no noticeable character development. What they say and do seems illogical and wholly spontaneous. The believable dialogue of stage realism is totally absent here and in its place are strings of clichés, *non sequiturs*, bits and pieces of unconnected conversation. As in most absurdist theatre, language here suffers a devaluation, as it serves to show how little we do in fact communicate, despite the time and effort we spend talking. Thus the breakfast scene between Him and Her is not so very unrealistic, for by parodying the way husbands and wives talk past (not with or even at) each other while reading the morning paper, Díaz underscores the degree to which language, in its general everyday usage, can be alienating rather than binding. The humorous use of advertising jargon and jingles, of lyrics from popular music (particularly the Argentinian tango) and from film, point to the intentional deformation or manipulation of language to sell products or imagery in an eager consumer society.

The Toothbrush also shares with other absurdist drama a fascination with games and role-playing. For Him and Her, life together is like being in an amusement park. They are like children whose imagination lets them play out their fantasies, and experience the thrill of killing each other, but who have the security of it all as make-believe. Their games are rituals, repeated day after day, as a way of filling an otherwise vacuous existence and, oddly enough, of bringing them together in a shared experience. Therefore the ludic structure of *The Toothbrush* has a deeper meaning than the obvious one of people indulging in apparently silly and perverse games just to pass the time or to give sexual zest to an otherwise flat marriage.

The theatre of the absurd has been closely associated with the philosophy of existentialism and with the pessimism of post-World-War-II Europe. In Latin America, however, neither phenomenon was experienced first-hand, so it is not surprising that absurdism there should take on its own particular traits. In *The Toothbrush* this development is perhaps most patent in its appropriation of the mechanics of absurdist drama, but not of its philosophical implications. Some commentators therefore have considered it to be excessively imitative and too interested in comic effect at the expense of intellectual content. When staged, this is indeed an extraordinarily funny play, farcical in its pace and continuously surprising for its verbal wit. And although at times Díaz seems to be carried away by his own sense of the ridiculous, *The Toothbrush* is not theatrical fluff. Considered within the context of the 1960's in Latin America and Spain, its irreverence towards theatrical form and middle-class values was shocking if not threatening to many audience members. For actors it demanded a new approach to their craft, which at that time still suffered from the legacy of a rather melodramatic and romantic tradition. With a play like *The Toothbrush*, actors and directors were forced totally to rethink notions of characterization and verisimilitude. Díaz's creative use of stage space and the set, which inverts itself by 180 degrees between Act I and Act II, helped in the process of eliminating the invisible fourth wall of proscenium theatre. And although much of the humorous effect can be traced to the comic antics in plays by Ionesco and Beckett, and these in turn to vaudeville, circus, and silent film, much of the fun in *The Toothbrush* also has roots in the traditions of local humor and of the Hispanic stand-up comic.

Because *The Toothbrush* does not, apparently, combine notions of the absurd with political protest, as did many of the absurdist plays written by Latin-American playwrights in the 1960's, it has been criticized by some as being élitist and, despite its theatrical innovations, ideologically reactionary. Díaz himself has admitted that at the time of writing this play, he, as well as many other Chilean and Latin-American dramatists, were much influenced by the pressure (then very strong) to make Latin American art universal, that is, palatable and interesting to foreign, particularly European, audiences. This notwithstanding, *The Toothbrush* does have a Latin-American texture to it. In their obsession with gadgets and fancy consumer products, most if not all of them imported from the United States, and in their penchant for speaking like characters in movies or announcers for television commercials, He and She are clearly symbols of Third World economic and cultural dependency. Given that this dependency is still very much an issue for many Spanish-speaking nations, *The Toothbrush* retains a significant place in the repertory of modern Latin-American drama.

—Kirsten F. Nigro

CHAGUAN.   See TEAHOUSE.

CH'A-KUAN.   See TEAHOUSE.

CHAIKA.   See THE SEAGULL.

THE CHAIRS (Les Chaises)
by Eugène Ionesco

First Publication: Paris, 1954.
First Production: Théâtre Lancry, Paris, 22 April 1952.

Translations
The Chairs, in *Ionesco: Plays One*, translated by Donald Watson, London, 1958.

Criticism
(For general works on the author, see *Playwrights* volume)

Articles:
R. Schechner, "The Enactment of the 'Not' in *Les Chaises* of Eugene Ionesco", in *Yale French Studies*, 29, 1962.
Marian Tolpin, "Eugène Ionesco's *The Chairs* and the Theater of the Absurd", in *American Imago*, 25, 1968.
Edith W. Williams, "God's Share: A Mythic Interpretation of *The Chairs*", in *Modern Drama*, 12, 1969.
Maria Majewska, "*Les Chaises*: structure et son aspect théâtral", in *Acta Universitatis Wratislaviensis*, 265, 1975.
J.P. Little, "Form and the Void: Beckett's *Fin de partie* and Ionesco's *Les Chaises*", in *French Studies*, 32, 1978.
Ingrid H. Coleman, "Memory into 'Message': The Forgetting of the Myth of Origins in Ionesco's *Les Chaises*", in *Perspectives on Contemporary Literature*, 9, 1983.

*   *   *

In an auditorium on an unnamed island, an Old Man and an Old Woman are awaiting the important guests they have invited to spend the evening with them. The Old Man, a caretaker, laments the eminent career he might have had. While his wife consoles him as a mother might, he behaves like a child, sitting on her lap or toddling around the stage. The first two guests—a Lady and a Colonel—arrive. To the audience they are invisible. Their presence is conveyed purely by the reactions of the two visible characters. They are followed by two more invisible guests, Mrs. Lovely and her Photographer husband. The Old Man discovers in Mrs. Lovely a long lost sweetheart, while his wife makes a grotesque attempt to seduce the Photographer. They appear to be acting out repressed desires, or aspirations long since discarded as unbefitting persons of their age. But the Old Man claims to have put his energies into philosophy, with the result that he now has a message to convey to the world. The old couple evoke memories of their family. Each contradicts the other's story. Each tells a tale of guilt and loss. They are joined by more invisible characters. A group of journalists and gradually a whole crowd, complete with a small child, fills the room. At last the Emperor arrives. The Old Man fawns on him, complains about life's vicissitudes and describes, in a bizarre yet banal way, the circumstances in which he was granted the revelation which those present have come to share. Eventually a visible character, the Orator, appears. His strategy appearance—his dress is that of a 19th-century artist—makes him seem less real even than the invisible characters. His task is to convey the Old Man's message. Confident that the truth will now be told, the couple throw themselves out of the window in a joint suicide bid. But the Orator turns out to be mute. On the blackboard provided for him he writes the suggestive but meaningless word "ANGELBREAD" and follows this with a line of letters. Then dissatisfied, he replaces this with the words "ADIEU DIEU APA" and leaves. Now for the first time clearly audible noises emanate from the invisible crowd. This is an important moment. To the play's first director, Sylvain Dhomme, Ionesco wrote: "This is. . .the ending I had in mind when I wrote the play, it was written *for* this ending, an ending I had envisaged before I started".

Several of Ionesco's recurrent preoccupations are voiced in *The Chairs*. One of the central motifs of the play is the couple. To Claude Bonnefoy, Ionesco explained:

> The couple is the world itself, it's man and woman, Adam and Eve, the two halves of humanity who love one another, find one another, who are sick and tired of loving one another; who, in spite of everything, cannot not love one another, who cannot exist except together

The old couple of *The Chairs* seem afflicted by a kind of affective degeneracy. They do not share an adult relationship. Instead each provides a kind of surrogate fulfilment of the emotional needs of the other. The Old Man finds in his wife the mother he has lost, while the Old Woman treats her husband like the son she possibly never had. Linked to this central motif are the Ionescian constants of time, death, and childhood. To some extent, *The Chairs* may also be viewed as a self-conscious work, dealing with the situation of the dramatist and the nature of the theatrical experience itself. However, Ionesco identifies his most fundamental concern in *The Chairs* as absence, or the ontological void. The last moment of the play expresses this. In Ionesco's words:

> The chairs remain empty because there's no one there. And at the end, the curtain falls to the accompanying noises of a crowd, while all there is on the stage is empty

chairs, curtains fluttering in the wind, etc . . . . and there's nothing. The world doesn't really exist. The subject of the play was nothingness, not failure. It was total absence, chairs without people. The world does not exist because in the future it will stop being, everything dies, you know.

The basic tone of *The Chairs* is that of bathos. The accelerating rhythm with which the guests arrive creates a sense of expectation that is deflated by the Orator's muteness and the incomprehensibility of his written message. In categorizing the play as a "tragic farce", the author of *The Chairs* is clearly conscious of his distinctive contribution to 20th-century theatre.

—Tim Lewis

———

LES CHAISES.   See THE CHAIRS.

———

THE CHALK CIRCLE (Hui-Lan Ji)
by Li Xingfu (also known as Li Hsing-tao or Hwuy-lan-ke)

First Publication: Unknown. Earliest surviving edition, 1614.
First Production: Probably late 13th century or early 14th century.

Translations
The Circle of Chalk (Klabund's translation) in an English version by James Laver, 1929, London.
The Chalk Circle, translated by Ethel van der Veer, in *World Drama*, New York, 1933.
The Story of The Circle of Chalk, translated by Frances Hume, London, 1953.

Criticism
E. Ludowyk, "The Chalk Circle: A Legend in Four Centuries", in *Comparative Literature*, 1, 1960.

*   *   *

The pretty young singing-girl Chang Cherry-Apple marries wealthy Squire Ma as his secondary wife. She loves him and is happy. When her son by him, Shoulang, is five years old, however, the Squire's number one Wife, with the help of her paramour, Chao the Court Clerk, poisons Squire Ma, and accuses Cherry-Apple of the murder, pretending in the process that Shoulang is her own son. A venal magistrate cruelly beats a confession out of Cherry-Apple, and she is sent to Kaifeng prefectural court, a harrowing journey through a snowstorm, for confirmation of sentence. There, her brother Chang Lin, a constable of the court, pleads for her, and Judge Bao re-examines the evidence. He tests the veracity of the two women by placing Shoulang within a chalk-drawn circle (literally "enclosure" or "pen"), and ordering the two women to compete in trying to drag the little boy out of it. Cherry-Apple refuses to try too hard in case she hurts her son, and through her feelings, the Judge is able to ascertain that she is, indeed, the true flesh-and-blood mother. This helps resolve the other aspects of the case, and punishments and rewards are issued.

In the first act of Bertolt Brecht's play *The Caucasian Chalk Circle*, an old peasant asks the singer, who is about to organise a play within the play, "Will it be one of the old plays?", and the singer replies: "Yes, a very old one. It's called *The Chalk Circle*, and derives from a Chinese original." The Chinese origin is, of course, Li Xingfu's play.

Other version's of Li Xingfu's name are Li Xingdao and Li Qianfu. He came from Jiangzhou, in present Xinjiang county, in Jiangxi province. At some point in his life, he was, perhaps, a recluse, turning his back on the mandarin and literate society. He died some time before AD 1330. This is the only play now attributed to him. The play is one of the Variety Play (*zaju*) genre that first flourished in Northern China around ancient Peking, and that was indeed China's first mature form of drama. It is in the standard four acts, and contains the optional "wedge act" used to provide extra space for short episodes. It only survives in editions from the early seventeenth century, and only in its backbone of song can we place any trust as being of pristine 13th or 14th-century origin.

This is one of a number of "Judge Bao" plays. Judge Bao, more so than the Judge Dee celebrated by Van Gulik's books and the television versions of them, is famed in China as the judicial wizard or "judge-cum-detective". His literary personality is based, however remotely at times, on the real-life, eminent judge and administrator, the harsh minister Bao Zheng (999–1062), transmogrified by literature, legend and entertainments into a noble-minded champion of justice, the star of many a drama, story and comic-strip. The play's theme is the most renowned of the Judge Bao tales, using as it does a gripping theme common to other ancient traditions of the world, Indian, Greek, Roman and biblical among them.

A summary does little justice to this drama of more than mere justice. It's packed with twists and turns of plot, and plentiful tensions and explosions of action. In the typical, traditional Chinese manner it also refreshes audience powers of reception by comic episodes: the ludicrous bias of the Magistrate, a free-for-all punch-up between Chang Lin and the escort constables, a hard-done-by inn-keeper's decision to abandon his trade after one day's profitless hassle, and so on. There is much beautiful poetry in its songs, and Cherry-Apple is a delightful, suffering heroine. The good and bad are both highlighted with pleasing extremism, and the audience would never have been allowed to lose the thread or have a dull moment. Above all, there's the theme of the chalk circle, the proclaiming of the victory of flesh-and-blood emotions, a topic that Brecht very deliberately stood on its head, giving the stepmother the victory, but which is actually beyond either simplification, and will always be debated. Li Xingfu focuses on one side of the argument with consummate deftness of plot-manipulation and much first-rate poetry.

The west has long had an acquaintance with Li Xingfu's play. As well as appearing in translation, it has received a number of productions in the 20th century (including one starring Lawrence Olivier), and has been broadcast on radio.

—William Dolby

———

THE CHANGELING
by Thomas Middleton and William Rowley

First Publication: London, 1653.
First Production: Phoenix Theatre, London, 1622.

Editions

The Changeling, edited by N.W. Bawcutt, London, 1953; revised edition, 1963 (Revels Plays Series).

The Changeling, edited by P. Thomson, London, 1964 (New Mermaid Series); second edition, edited by Joost Daalder, 1990.

The Changeling, edited by G.W. Williams, Lincoln, Nebraska, 1966 (Regents Renaissance Drama Series).

The Changeling, edited by M.W. Black, Philadelphia, Pennsylvania, 1966.

The Changeling, in *Three Jacobean Tragedies*, edited by Gāmini Salgādo, Harmondsworth (revised edition) 1969.

The Changeling, in *Thomas Middleton. Three Plays*, edited by Kenneth Muir, London and Totowa, New Jersey, 1975.

The Changeling, in *The Selected Plays of Thomas Middleton*, edited by David L. Frost, Cambridge, 1978.

The Changeling, in *Middleton: Five Plays*, edited by Brian Loughrey and Neil Taylor, Harmondsworth, 1988.

Criticism

(For general works on Middleton, see *Playwrights* volume)

Books:

R.V. Holdsworth (ed.), *Three Jacobean Revenge Tragedies: A Casebook*, London, 1990.

Articles:

Ernst. G. Mathews, "The Murdered Substitute Tale", in *Modern Language Quarterly*, 6, 1945.

Karl J. Holzknecht, "The Dramatic Structure of *The Changeling*", in *Renaissance Papers*, 1954.

Christopher Ricks, "The Moral and Poetical Structure of *The Changeling*", in *Essays in Criticism*, 10, 1960.

Robert G. Lawrence, "A Bibliographical Study of Middleton's and Rowley's *The Changeling*", in *The Library*, 16, 1961.

E. Engleberg, "Tragic Blindness in *The Changeling* and *Women Beware Women*", in *Modern Language Quarterly*, 23, 1962.

T.B. Tomlinson, "Poetic Naturalism—*The Changeling*", in *Journal of English and Germanic Philology*, 63, 1964.

Dorothy M. Farr, "*The Changeling*", in *Modern Language Review*, 62, 1967.

Thomas L. Berger, "The Petrarchan Fortress of *The Changeling*", in *Renaissance Papers*, 1969.

J. Chesley Taylor, "Metaphors of the Moral World: Structure in *The Changeling*", in *Tulane Studies in English*, 20, 1972.

Penelope B.R. Doob, "A Reading of *The Changeling*", in *English Literary Renaissance*, 3, 1973.

Joseph M. Duffy, "Madhouse Optics: *The Changeling*", in *Comparative Drama*, 8, 1974.

H.E. Jacobs, "Constancy of Change: Character and Perspective in *The Changeling*, in *Texas Studies in Literature and Language*, 16, 1975.

Raymond J. Pentzell, "*The Changeling*: Notes on Mannerism in Dramatic Form", in *Comparative Drama*, 9, 1975.

Mohammad Kowsar, "Middleton and Rowley's *The Changeling*: The Besieged Temple", in *Criticism*, Spring 1986.

Dale B.J. Randall, "Some New Perspectives on the Spanish Setting of *The Changeling* and Its Source", in *Medieval and Renaissance Drama in England, 1500–1900*, 3, 1986.

Joost Daalder, "Folly and Madness in *The Changeling*", in *Essays in Criticism*, January 1988.

*   *   *

The Changeling concerns a spoiled young girl, Beatrice-Joanna, about to marry her father's choice of suitors, Alonzo de Piracquo, when she falls in love for the first time—with a nobleman, Alsemero, who proposes to her after seeing her in the temple. Alsemero offers to challenge Piracquo, but Beatrice fears for his safety. Since she cannot disobey her father and marry the man she loves, she resorts to murder by proxy, removing the deed from herself by employing as murderer a man she loathes, her father's servant De Flores, who is obsessed by her. De Flores kills Piracquo, but demands Beatrice as his reward. She is forced to submit to De Flores and, no longer a virgin, must substitute her maid Diaphanta in her bed when she marries Alsemero. This is a supreme irony: it is the bed Beatrice had caused a murder to possess, but she cannot enjoy it. Moreover when Diaphanta endangers the subterfuge by remaining too long in bed, De Flores murders her also. Thus Beatrice becomes inextricably entangled in a web of guilt, culminating in De Flores' killing of them both, when the truth comes out.

In the style of the period, the main plot alternates throughout with a subplot. The subplot explores an unequal match between young Isabella and her jealous, elderly doctor-husband, Alibius, who locks her in his madhouse in his absence, watched over by his servant Lollio. In an attempt to woo Isabella, two potential suitors—Antonio and Franciscus—cozen their way into the asylum. The main plot is generally attributed to Middleton and the subplot to Rowley. This is not a wholly satisfactory attribution, since the differences in style and tone that operate when shifting from main to subplot might well be seen as differences inherent in tragic and comic *writing*, and thus potentially attributable to either dramatist. The two plots are linked by ideas such as love being a madness that can seize its victim, a transforming power that can turn innocence into evil. Its victims are seen to be subject to illusion: Isabella reveals the hollowness of her suitors' affections; Beatrice is not what Alsemero thinks her to be.

The play is remarkable for the psychological depth of the Beatrice / De Flores relationship. At the outset Beatrice is self-willed and self-deceiving. Used to having her own way, she sees Piracquo merely as an obstacle to be removed, connecting the murder only with her repulsion for De Flores: "I shall rid myself / Of two inveterate loathings at one time". When De Flores confronts her with the dead man's finger with her betrothal ring upon it, she is genuinely shocked ("Bless me! What hast thou done?") and tries to pay him with the ring. When she realises she, herself, must become his payment, she is as horrified as though she were innocent ("Why, 'tis impossible thou canst be so wicked"). But De Flores forces home her implication in the crime ("A woman dipt in blood and talk of modesty?") and Beatrice has to capitulate. Her submission in having to cross the stage into his arms is particularly powerful, because her repulsion for De Flores has been evident throughout. She cannot bear even to touch a dropped glove he returns to her, and her language when speaking of him is full of imagery of poison. The play is strangely modern in that the repulsion is also a fascination, like a subconscious need ("This ominous ill-fac'd fellow more disturbs me, / Than all my other passions"). Once De Flores has made Beatrice face the fact that, in their guilt, they "should stick together", he becomes essential to her. Unlike Alsemero he sees her as she is, while he is the only person with whom she needs no mask. When Diaphanta endangers their scheme by dallying almost until dawn with Alsemero, Beatrice is forced to admire De Flores' prompt action: "Here's a man worth loving".

Middleton reveals Beatrice's dilemma with precision and insight. At first there is her natural selfishness, unused to being thwarted. From her perspective the incitement to murder is

The Changeling: Aldwych Theatre, London, 1978 (Royal Shakespeare Company)

not so much a crime as a sudden inspiration to prevent the man she loves either being killed, or having to flee the country. She sees these as fitting fates for De Flores, however, and sacrifices both him and her fiancé without a qualm, only to have her guilt brought home to her by her chosen instrument, to whom she must now give herself. That Middleton even has flashes of sympathy for Beatrice is evident in some of her asides: ("This [Alsemero] was the man was meant me, that he should come / So near his time, and miss it!") and in her *cris de coeur*: "I'm in a labyrinth" and: "I must trust somebody". Before the cold-blooded, second murder she has capitulated entirely to her seducer: "do what thou wilt now."

De Flores is shown as entirely amoral and unscrupulous, with a blackly comic enjoyment of his evil that is again, curiously modern. Beatrice was right in her instinctive flinching from him. He is clear-sighted, where she is not, and is thus able to make full use of his one opportunity to gain power over her, while, ironically, she thinks *she* has the whip hand. This is the first of three vital errors of judgement made by Beatrice. She also fails to anticipate the extent of Diaphanta's lust, and, finally, she acknowledges to Alsemero that she has murdered for his sake.

The language of the play is highly charged, with particular emphasis on such words as "change", "will", "judgement", and "service", and with a typically 17th-century enjoyment of *doubles entendres*. The very word "changeling", while ostensibly referring to Antonio, also embraces the amorality of De Flores. The idea of transformation, though mainly concerned with madness and love, is also carried through in the substitution of Diaphanta for Beatrice and in the physical changes induced by Alsemero's unpleasant chastity test. Above all it is pinpointed in the changed relations between Beatrice-Joanna and De Flores, and in the change in Alsemero's perception of Beatrice from idealisation to horror: "Oh thou art all deform'd".

—Rosemary Pountney

CH'ANG-SHENG TIEN.   See THE PALACE OF ETERNAL YOUTH.

CHANGSHENG DIAN.   See THE PALACE OF ETERNAL YOUTH.

UN CHAPEAU DE PAILLE D'ITALIE.   See AN ITALIAN STRAW HAT.

THE CHAPEL PERILOUS; or, The Perilous Adventures of Sally Banner
by Dorothy Hewett

First Publication: Sydney, 1972; revised edition, 1977.
First Production: New Fortune Theatre, Perth, Western Australia, January 1971.

Criticism
(For general works on the author, see *Playwrights* volume)

Articles:
Jean Whitehead, "Ordeal by Freedom: A Carve up of Sally or Society?", in *Westerly*, 1, 1971.
Reba Gostand, "Quest or Question? Perilous Journey to the Chapel", in *Bards, Bohemians and Bookmen*, edited by Leon Cantrell, St. Lucia, Queensland, 1976.
Judith Barbour, "Privileged, Authentic, Transcendent, Arcane: The Limits of Naturalism in Some Contemporary Australian Plays", in *Southerly*, 1977.
Carla Dente Beschiera, "Dramatic Conventions and Techniques in *The Chapel Perilous* by Dorothy Hewett", in *Linguistica e letteratura*, 8, 1983.

*   *   *

The Chapel Perilous, a musical play in two acts, and Dorothy Hewett's best-known work, chronicles the life of its central figure, the gifted and rebellious poet, Sally Banner, from her schooldays in the 1930's to late middle age. The prologue is set in Sally's school, a conservative, religious institution where she is a brilliant but disturbing pupil, whose rebelliousness against adult hypocrisy and conservatism is expressed in her iconoclastic climbing of the chapel tower and her refusal to bow to the altar. In Act I Sally seeks the independence of spirit which she craves through sexual freedom, first with her teenage lover, Michael, and later with her husband David and the political activist Saul. But in Act II, her disillusion with all these relationships sees her turn to left-wing politics for fulfilment, a commitment which ultimately proves as sterile as romantic love. Both her quests, through personal relationships in Act I and impersonal social commitment in Act II, lead to desperate losses in human terms, including estrangement from her family and lovers, isolation from her contemporaries, and, cruellest of all, the death of her child. The play's climactic scene—a surreal trial in which they all return to accuse her—brings her to a point of existential self-understanding from which she is able to return to the school chapel as a middle-aged celebrity, and bow to the altar which was once the focus of her schoolgirl rebellion. The ending, however, is far from Sally's submission to a conventional society. The occasion of her return to the school is her presentation of a stained-glass window of herself to the chapel in which she always refused to bow; the illumination of the window at the end of the play signals Sally's reclaiming of the chapel tower she once climbed as a schoolgirl, as well as her acceptance of herself and her contemporaries.

The play is a large-scale, even sprawling, epic work, written for an open stage, with a chorus which refracts into individual characters, multiple roles for many of the performers (excluding Sally and her lover Michael), a succession of briefly sketched scenes moving rapidly through place and time, sudden, and often ironic, changes in style and mood, and moments of music, song, and spoken poetry. The set is dominated by three, huge, totem-like "authority figures" from which emerge the significant figures in Sally's life, with some characters further refracted through disembodied voices played over an amplifier. The language ranges from often comic colloquialism to more elevated, poetic language and verse (from other writers as well as Hewett herself), while the music includes both popular ditties, such as the bawdy "Good Ship Venus", sung by the chorus on Sally's disappointing wedding night, and more lyrical and reflective songs. The eclecticism of the play's style makes for an extremely dense and rich work, though it is arguable that at times, as in much of

Hewett's work, it is too densely written to be readily accessible in performance. Similarly, the doubling and trebling of roles according to a schema signifying the authority that various characters exert over Sally's development, which the author states is essential to the play's meaning, may not always communicate its significance to a theatre audience.

Sally's personal quest for artistic, sexual, and political freedom is given a much wider, idealistic context in the dominating image of the chapel and in the schoolgirl's chanting of the legendary quest for the Holy Grail (hence the "Chapel Perilous" of the title), and at times the language and quotations from literature appear to elevate the action to a quasi-symbolic level. But Sally's particular story also takes place in a specifically Australian, historical context from the 1930's to the 1960's. Through the songs and dances of various decades, performed by the chorus, and the representative figures into which the chorus refracts, *The Chapel Perilous* evokes a vivid sense of Australian society over several decades, often with a good deal of humour and ironic undercutting. In particular, the thumbnail sketches of Sally's conservative, but opinionated, parents; her hypocritical teachers; and minor characters such as the gushing Miss Funt, who conducts a culture program on national radio; all display an almost malicious wit at the expense of provincialism and pretension. This recreation of Australia's emergence from pre-war provincialism to a more aware, if less picturesque, society is one of the play's real achievements, often overlooked in the other issues *The Chapel Perilous* has tended to raise.

Although now accepted as an contemporary Australian, classic, and often studied by secondary-school students, the play retains something of its initial reputation as an "immoral" piece. It shares with all of Hewett's work the qualities which have often polarised critical and audience responses to her—an affirmation of female sexuality, an iconoclastic attitude towards received authority and morality, and a free-wheeling, even apparently wayward, dramatic form. The character of Sally has also aroused both passionate identification and intense dislike; both views, however, overlook the ironically amused, and at times even savage, scrutiny of the central character, whose mistakes and gaucheries are as vividly portrayed as her courage and idealism. A taxing role for a performer, ranging as it does from adolescent precocity to middle-aged disillusion and acceptance, Sally Banner is one of the most memorable characters in Australian drama.

—Margaret Williams

A CHASTE MAID IN CHEAPSIDE
by Thomas Middleton

First Publication: London, 1630.
First Production: Swan Theatre, London, c.1611–1613.

Editions
A Chaste Maid in Cheapside, edited by A. Brissenden, London, 1968 (New Mermaid Series).
A Chaste Maid in Cheapside, edited by C. Barber, 1969.
A Chaste Maid in Cheapside, edited by R. B. Parker, London, 1969 (Revels Plays).
A Chaste Maid in Cheapside, in *Thomas Middleton: Three Plays*, edited by Kenneth Muir, London and Totowa, New Jersey, 1975.
A Chaste Maid in Cheapside, in *The Selected Plays of Thomas Middleton*, edited by David L. Frost, Cambridge, 1978.
A Chaste Maid in Cheapside, in *Thomas Middleton: Five Plays*, edited by Bryan Loughrey and Neil Taylor, Harmondsworth, 1988.

Criticism
(For general works on the author, see *Playwrights* volume)

Articles:
Richard Levin, "The Four Plots of *A Chaste Maid in Cheapside*", in *Review of English Studies*, 16, 1965.
Charles A. Hallett, "Middleton's Allwit: The Urban Cynic", in *Modern Language Quarterly*, 30, 1969.
Arthur F. Marotti, "Fertility and Comic Form in *A Chaste Maid in Cheapside*, in *Comparative Drama*, Spring 1969.
Robert I Williams, "Machiavelli's *Mandragola*, Touchwood Senior, and the Comedy of *A Chaste Maid in Cheapside*", in *Studies in English Literature 1500–1900*, 10, 1970.
Joanne Altieri, "Against Moralizing Jacobean Comedy: Middleton's *Chaste Maid*", in *Criticism*, Spring 1988.

*   *   *

In Middleton's *A Chaste Maid in Cheapside* adulterers, acquiescent cuckolds, and whores move around London in almost totally careless celebration of their immorality. No family unit is exempt from sexual promiscuity, and even married couples who love each other are unfaithful. Set during Lent, with its ban on the consumption of meat, the word "flesh" offers the opportunity for one *double entendre* after another as gentry sexually enjoy citizens comply, and citizens comply, content in the security of financial support. The plot works out triangular relationships, so that sexual and financial desires are happily resolved, and the play offers a vivid interpretation of early 17th-century London life.

With more specific time and locality references than are found in any of Middleton's other plays, *A Chaste Maid in Cheapside* is a city comedy, described by one critic as "the richest and most typical of Middleton's comedies". The play assumes a detailed knowledge of contemporary London in its audience, and almost every name has ironic, symbolic value, as can be seen from the title itself since the usual women "chased" in Cheapside were prostitutes.

Una Ellis-Fermor described *A Chaste Maid* as a play in which we get a "microcosm of that immense range that characterizes Middleton's work", and it is for this very reason that the play is much used as a text in schools and universities. It is self-contained, and yet also hints at themes which Middleton was to work out at greater length in his later plays—most notably in its brief passages dealing with remorse and spiritual collapse—themes which later appear in *The Changeling* and *Women Beware Women*.

The structure of the play is very carefully worked out, although the overall impression is one of chaotic life and sexual competition. The plot is built around two triangular relationships, each between two men and a woman, the intrigues of which could be classified as sub-plots developed to rival the central lovers' plot (that involving Moll Yellowhammer and Touchwood Junior) in importance. *A Chaste Maid* is therefore a non-classical mixture of plots and episodes forming parallels and balanced contrasts. All this interweaving makes the play confusing to read, but a comic delight to watch.

The language Middleton uses is rich in sexual *doubles entendres*, as we discover in the opening act, when Maudline Yellowhammer (the goldsmith's wife) is talking to Moll, her daughter, about the dancing lessons she had in her youth.

Referring to her dance teacher Maudline remembers, "He missed me not a night; I was kept at it;/ I took delight to learn, and he to teach me." Scarcely a line does not include a lewd innuendo, and the result is a cheapening of sex, criticising it through excessive exaggeration. And yet, curiously, one does not judge and condemn the adulterers, cuckolds, whores, and financial profiteers. They obviously enjoy the lives they are leading, and Middleton's careful structure of the plot means that they use and manipulate sexual relations to support and create families. *A Chaste Maid in Cheapside* is Middleton's greatest celebration of vivacity and the strength of human nature to overcome obstacles—and it is this which we delight in rather than condemning the immorality outright. Some have criticised this inability to reach a simple, moral interpretation of the play, but this is not what Middleton wanted. He never intended more than entertainment in his comedies, and this is supported by the final solution to *A Chaste Maid* being worked out through a theatrical trick—the "resurrection" of Moll and Touchwood Junior—rather than a moral denouement.

Throughout the play sexual relations are reduced to terms of mercantile advantage, as marriage is viewed as a business contract, and fertility and chastity as commodities. There is, therefore, much reference to numbers, and many business phrases, and materialism is shown as a cause of class conflict. And yet, despite this perversion of family relationships, we cannot condemn Touchwood Senior and his wife who separate temporarily to avoid having more children they cannot afford, and are then able to reunite after Touchwood Senior has personally ensured that Lady Kix will produce an heir, and Sir Oliver Kix, eternally grateful for the "potion" which has cured his wife's infertility, offers Touchwood and his wife a house and a living in his own home. However, immoral his behaviour, Touchwood Senior has been true to his word: "The feast of marriage is not lust, but love, / And care of the estate." Middleton so convincingly reverses normal moral standards that we come to accept the world of Cheapside, and the satire is so upside down that we hardly notice when Sir Walter Whorehound jealously accuses a husband of daring to sleep with his own wife. This joyfully irreverent world is given its greatest stamp of authenticity by the accuracy of Middleton's setting, and it is this physical world which, externally, unifies the chaos of the society living within.

—Claudia Woolgar

CHATSKY.   See THE MISFORTUNE OF BEING CLEVER.

CHATTERTON
by Alfred de Vigny

First Publication: Paris, 1835.
First Production: Comédie-Française, Paris, 12 February 1835.

Editions
Chatterton, edited by Watson Bain, London, 1925.
Chatterton, edited by Liano Petroni, Bologna, 1962.
Chatterton, edited by Jean Delume, Paris, 1964.

Chatterton, edited by Jean-Pierre Barricelli, Englewood Cliffs, New Jersey, 1967.
Chatterton, edited by A.H. Diverres, London, 1967.
Chatterton, edited by Martin B. Friedman, Paris, 1967.
Chatterton, in *Chatterton; Quitte pour la peur*, edited by F. Germain, Paris, 1968.
Chatterton, edited by Jean Delume, Paris, 1969.

Criticism
(For general works on the author, see *Playwrights* volume)

Books:
C. Wesley Bird, *Vigny's "Chatterton": A Study of Its Genesis and Sources*, Los Angeles, 1941.
P. Moreau, *Stello; Daphne; Chatterton*, Paris, 1949.
Robin Buss, *Vigny: "Chatterton"*, London, 1984.

Articles:
R. Dale, "*Chatterton* is the Essential Romantic Drama", in *L'Esprit Createur*, vol. 5 no. 3, 1965.
Georges Lamoine, "Thomas Chatterton dans l'oeuvre de Vigny et dans l'histoire", in *Dix-huitième siècle*, 3, 1970.
Barry V. Daniels, "An Exemplary French Romantic Production: Alfred de Vigny's *Chatterton*", in *Theatre Survey*, 16, 1975.
Carol Wootton, "The Deaths of Goethe's Werther and de Vigny's Chatterton", in *Revue de littérature comparée*, 50, 1976.
Jean Jourdheuil, "Les Enjeux de *Chatterton*", in *Europe*, 589, 1978.
Barbara T. Cooper, "Exploitation of the Body in Vigny's *Chatterton*: The Economy of Drama and The Drama of Economics", in *Theatre Journal*, vol. 34 no. 1, 1982.
Jean Jourdheuil, "L'Escalier de *Chatterton*", in *Romantisme*, 12, 1982.
Robert T. Denommé, "*Chatterton* ou le dilemme du héros dans un monde non héroïque", in *Cahiers de l'Association Internationale des Etudes Françaises*, 35, 1983.

*   *   *

Chatterton, the young Bristol poet, lodges in London in the house of the industrialist John Bell and his wife Kitty. He keeps himself to himself, shunning the company of former friends, and only the elderly Quaker, a fellow-lodger, recognises the gravity of his unstable mental condition, as well as his precarious financial situation; though the tender-hearted Kitty and he have developed a mutual, though unacknowledged, love. Chatterton has made a last appeal for support by writing to Beckford, the Lord Mayor. When Beckford's response comes, offering him a post as a footman, Chatterton kills himself. This is immediately followed by Kitty Bell's death of a broken heart.

The simplicity and sparseness of the plot and action (which takes place, with a concentration worthy of Racine, in less than a day) are what first strike the reader or spectator. Vigny himself called the play "the story of a man who having written a letter in the morning, waits for a reply until the evening. When it arrives, it kills him". A contemporary defined the three-act structure even more neatly: "Act I: Shall I kill myself? Act II: I'm going to kill myself. Act III: I do kill myself"! Vigny's originality is to have married this classical economy of structure to a content which is that of the domestic drama on a modern subject and in a contemporary idiom. The characters surrounding the young poet are recognisably those of the spectator's own world: John Bell the self-made factory owner, striking a hard bargain and expecting others to be equally

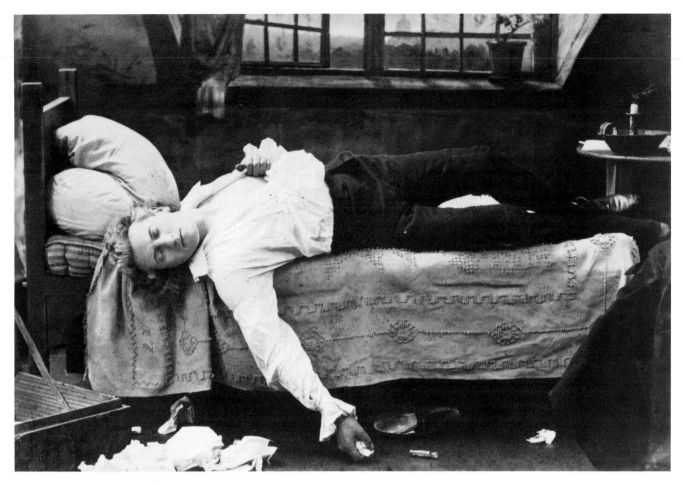

Chatterton: Wilson Barrett as Chatterton, Princess's Theatre, London, 1984

ruthless; Beckford, the successful man in a similar mould, with little time for the self-absorption of the young intellectual; Kitty the self-effacing wife and mother, much younger than her husband and totally dominated by him, guiltily conscious of her growing interest in her young lodger. The Quaker stands somewhat apart from the action, though he is constantly present to comment on it: it is not so much that he is implausible, as that his role is too obviously a functional one. He is the author's mouthpiece, and though he does not express the authorial viewpoint in a dogmatic or dictatorial manner, his curtain-line—"Into Thy bosom, Lord, into Thy bosom receive these two martyrs!"—is a clear indication of the author's sympathies, and a pointer to the reaction expected from the audience.

The play was accompanied on publication by a prefatory letter in which Vigny chose to distance himself from the other Romantic dramatists of the 1830's, expressing a scarcely veiled criticism of the colourful historical dramas of Hugo and Dumas by referring to the "entertainment of the public by visual spectacle and childish surprises", and stating that the time was now ripe for what he called a "drama of ideas". His play, he said, was "a plea on behalf of unknown sufferers. . .my object was to show the man of spiritual values suffocating in a society of materialistic values, where calculating greed mercilessly exploits intelligence and hard work". More particularly, the play and its preface address the problem of suicide among young intellectuals, and its causes: "I do not seek to justify these desperate acts, but merely to raise a cry of protest against

society's indifference which drives these unfortunates to take their lives". There had been a significant number of suicides, particularly among young writers and artists, in the years leading up to the appearance of *Chatterton*: "Can you not hear the lonely pistol-shots?", cried Vigny; and his play was provocative as well as timely. Some contemporary politicians and journalists alleged that it was an "apologia for suicide", and during its highly successful run (first at the Comédie-Française, then at the Odéon, where it had an enthusiastic reception from students) there was another well-publicised suicide of a young writer. What Vigny was appealing for was an enlightened society in which the budding creative writer should be subsidised: "guaranteeing just a few years of material existence to anyone who has given a single proof of the divine spark". But whatever contemporary support such a thesis might hope to command, its dramatic expression surely suffers because of its one-sidedness. John Bell, though convincing enough, is a totally unsympathetic representative of the materialistic outlook, and even Beckford is presented as lacking in understanding and sympathy—though his offer of employment, which Chatterton sees as so humiliating, might be regarded from an objective point of view as not ungenerous.

Of Chatterton himself Vigny wrote: "The Poet was everything for me: Chatterton was merely a name to attach to him". This suggests a certain symbolic abstraction, and indeed the central character is a rather shadowy figure. His origins and background remain enigmatic, and he lacks the credibility that might have been provided by even the most rudimentary *curriculum vitae.* He is too obviously based on a Romantic cliché, that of a youth still in his teens whom life has already turned into a mature cynic. The death-wish, the conviction that he is persecuted by a malevolent fate, are traits shared with a whole generation of literary figures; what is lacking are traits characterising him as an individual. This is compounded by the nature of his calling. Whereas a banker or a businessman can establish credibility by his actions, poetic genius has to be taken on trust. The true Chatterton, the precocious talent who really did die at 17, lent himself well enough to idealisation as Wordsworth's "marvellous boy", but the realistic idiom of domestic drama requires a character of flesh and blood. Vigny's concept of a drama of ideas was a noble one, but in practice *Chatterton* depends too much on the audience being able to share certain assumptions with the playwright. Once the anti-bourgeois fervour of the young Romantics was gone, the play was too dated; and though the Comédie-Française has revived it in our own day, we tend to prefer our drama of ideas to be based on the give-and-take of debate rather than on fervently held conviction.

—William D. Howarth

———

CHAYKA. See THE SEAGULL.

———

THE CHERRY ORCHARD (Vishnevy sad)
by Anton Chekhov

First Publication: Moscow, 1904.
First Production: Moscow Art Theatre, January 1904.

Editions
Vishnevy sad, edited by Donald R. Hitchcock, Letchworth, 1978.

Translations
The Cherry Orchard: A Comedy in Four Acts, translated by S, Mandell, New Haven, Connecticut, 1908.
The Cherry Orchard, translated by C.C. Daniels and G.R. Noyes in *Masterpieces of the Russian Drama*, edited by G.R. Noyes, New York, 1933.
The Cherry Orchard, translated by Hubert Butler, London 1934.
The Cherry Orchard, translated by S.S. Koteliansky, Harmondsworth and New York, 1940.
The Cherry Orchard, translated by Stark Young, New York 1947.
The Cherry Orchard, translated by Elisaveta Fen in *Three Plays: "The Cherry Orchard"; "Three Sisters"; "Ivanov"*, 1951; reprinted in *Chekhov, Plays*, Harmondsworth, 1959
The Cherry Orchard in *The Oxford Chekhov, 3*, edited and translated by Ronald Hingley, London, 1964.
The Cherry Orchard, translated by David Magarshack, in *Anton Chekhov: Four Plays*, London, 1969.
The Cherry Orchard, translated by Laurence Senelick, Arlington Heights, Illinois, 1977.
The Cherry Orchard, translated by Michael Frayn, London, 1978.

Criticism
(For general works on the author, see *Playwrights* volume)

Books:
Louis V. Talento, *Anton Chekhov: "The Three Sisters"; "The Cherry Orchard"*; New York, 1970.

Articles:
Daniel Charles Gerould, "*The Cherry Orchard* as a Comedy", in *Journal of General Education*, 11, 1958.
Jacqueline E.M. Latham, "*The Cherry Orchard* as Comedy", in *Educational Theatre Journal*, 10, 1958.
Norman Silverstein, "Chekhov's Comic Spirit and *The Cherry Orchard*", in *Modern Drama*, 1, 1958.
P. Warner, "The Axe in Springtime (*Cherry Orchard*)", in *Theoria*, 10, 1958.
L. Goldberg, "Chekhov's Comedy *The Cherry Orchard*", in *Scripta Hierosolymitana*, 19, 1967.
Dorothea Krook, "Tragic and Comic: Chekhov's *The Seagull* and *The Cherry Orchard*", in *Elements of Tragedy*, New Haven, Connecticut, 1969.
Beverly Hahn, "Chekhov's *The Cherry Orchard*", in *Critical Review*, 16, 1973.
Herta Schmid, *Strukturalistische Dramentheorie: Semantische Analyse von Cechows "Ivanov" und "Der Kirschgarten"*, Kronberg, 1973.
Jean P. Barricelli, "Counterpoint of the Snapping String: Chekhov's *The Cherry Orchard*", in *California Slavic Studies*, 10, 1977.
Clayton A. and Joanna T. Hubbs, "The Goddess of Love and the Tree of Knowledge: Some Elements of Myth and Folklore in Chekhov's *The Cherry Orchard*", in *South Carolina Review*, vol. 14 no. 2., 1982.
Karl D. Kramer, "Love and Comic Instability in *The Cherry Orchard*", in *Russian Literature and American Critics*, edited by Kenneth N. Brostrom, Ann Arbor, Michigan, 1984.
Verna A. Foster, "The Dramaturgy of Mood in *Twelfth Night* and *The Cherry Orchard*", in *Modern Language Quarterly*, 48, 1987.

*   *   *

The play was written in 1903 and when first performed was directed by Stanislavsky and designed by Simov. Stanislavsky himself played Gaev, his actress wife Lilina played Anya, while Chekhov's wife, the actress Olga Knipper, played Ranevskaya.

As always in Chekhov's major dramatic works, there is little plot as such, but the action of the play centres on the fate of the cherry orchard (beautiful but no longer productive) and the characters who live on and around the estate. Lack of money, a *leitmotif* in Chekhov's literary and dramatic works, means that Ranevskaya, the owner of the estate, can no longer afford to keep the estate and her childhood home. Warm, generous, and feckless, she is unable to face the reality of losing the cherry orchard, and rejects the compromise offered by Lopakhin (son of a former serf) to cut down the orchard, build holiday homes—and save her home. As a result of her inability to compromise and face the economic realities, she loses the whole estate, and Lopakhin, the new "capitalist" and business man, becomes the owner.

The play draws an interesting sociological picture of Russia at the beginning of the 20th century. The old aristocracy and land-owning gentry were becoming impoverished and many proved unable to cope with the changes taking place. Chekhov's dramatic treatment of Ranevskaya and her brother

The Cherry Orchard: Theatre Royal Haymarket, London, 1983

Gaev is compassionate but objective: they are both sad and comic. As always, Chekhov avoids stereotypes: Lopakhin is presented as a decent, honourable man whose affection for Ranevskaya motivates his attempt to help her. But time is running out (Lopakhin is, effectively, the "time-keeper" in the play). Providing a thematic and structural balance to Lopakhin is the "eternal student", Trofimov (suspended from university for political activities) who passionately articulates the desire for a better, more equal Russia, and points up the symbolism of the cherry orchard: "All of Russia is our orchard".

From his letters it is clear that Chekhov wanted to write a comedy, and on 15 September 1903 he wrote to Stanislavsky's wife, Lilina: "My play is not a drama, but a comedy, in places even a farce", and the play's subtitle is "A Comedy in Four Acts". The play is a unique blend of farce and irony, symbolism and realism. Difficulties have arisen in production, given the essentially serious nature of the play: Chekhov had major problems trying to persuade Stanislavsky and the Moscow Art Theatre company that the play was not a tragedy, and to this day relatively few productions capture the nature of the comedy. There are many comic characters and moments in the play: Gaev proclaiming a great speech—to a bookcase: Simeonov-Pishchik ("Squeaker") swallowing a complete bottle of Ranevskaya's pills with a glass of beer, and his claim that he is a descendant of the horse Caligula declared "a senator"; even the serious Trofimov, who cannot grow a proper beard, and declares himself "above love". After a row with Ranevskaya, Trofimov makes a dignified exit—only to fall down the stairs off-stage. Characteristic of much of Chekhov's

work, the use of comedy heightens the poignancy and real feelings of his characters: Chekhov ensures our sympathy for Ranevskaya and Gaev in the loss of the estate—when he was 16, he had lost his own home and knew from personal experience the unhappiness that results.

Another frequent misconception in the interpretation of the play relates to the character of Lopakhin. In many productions he has been portrayed as a greedy capitalist—boorish, rude, and insensitive. But, as Chekhov wrote to Stanislavsky: "Lopakhin is a decent man, in every sense of the word. He must behave with decorum and intelligence . . . . You mustn't lose sight of the fact that Lopakhin is loved by Varya, a serious and religious girl. She wouldn't have fallen in love with a grasping peasant". Chekhov uses both Lopakhin and Trofimov to articulate different political solutions for Russia, but neither Chekhov nor the play suggest "an answer", though the need for change, and the inevitability of change, are evident throughout the play.

Chekhov's settings and sound effects (as in the twice-repeated, famous, "breaking string" sound effect) illustrate the relationship between realism and symbolism. The setting for Act II, for example, illustrates both the past (the old shrine) and the present and future—the telegraph poles and the outline of a town on the horizon suggesting the encroaching industrialisation. Equally, the sudden entrance of the tramp in Act II brings the "outside world" into the domestic and familial situation.

Productions of the play are too numerous to mention but it has been regularly staged by some of the greatest directors, actors, and designers throughout Europe, (such as Peter Brook and Jean-Louis Barrault). The play's appeal is timeless despite its context in Russia at the turn of the century. With compassion and irony, Chekhov exposes our inability to face reality, and he deals with the ordinary, banal, and often trivial details of everyday life in an extraordinary way. As Trevor Griffiths has said: "The play is objectively comic and subjectively painful"—we identify with the characters and yet appraise them. The relationship between text and subtext is fascinating in the play, as in the scene in which Varya and Lopakhin talk about the weather and other trivia instead of the marriage proposal which really preoccupies both of them; or in the conversation between Anya and Dunyasha—the latter talking about her proposal of marriage whilst Anya, not listening, expresses her joy at her home-coming. Equally, Chekhov captures the comic unhappiness of so-called "minor" characters—such as the eccentric governess, Charlotte Ivanovna, and the unfortunate Yepikhodov (nicknamed Twenty-Two Misfortunes) whose farcical mishaps amount to a metaphor for his situation. The enduring qualities of the play—its treatment of ordinary people leading ordinary lives, and its power and depth in performance—will no doubt ensure a continued place in the repertory of world theatre.

—Irene Slatter

THE CHEST (La Cassaria)
by Lodovico Ariosto

First Publication: prose version, Florence, 1509; verse version, Venice, 1546.
First Production: Teatro Ducale at the Court of the d'Este Family, Ferrara, 5 March 1508 (prose version); Teatro Ducale, Ferrara, 29 February 1531 (verse version).

Editions
La Cassaria (prose and verse versions), in *Ariosto: Commedie, 3*, edited by A. Casella, G. Ronchi, and E. Varasi, Milan, 1974.

Translations
The Coffer, in *The Comedies of Ariosto*, translated by E.M. Beaume and L.G. Sbrocchi, Chicago and London, 1975.

Criticism
(For general works on the author, see *Playwrights* volume)

Articles:
A. Gisolfi, "Ariosto's Delightful Prologue to *La Cassaria*", in *Theatre Annual*, 22, 1965–66.
D. Clouet, "Empirisme ou égotisme: la politique dans *La Cassaria* et les *Suppositi* de l'Arioste", in *Les Écrivains et le pouvoir en Italie à l'époque de la Renaissance*: (second series), 3, Paris, 1974.

*   *   *

The Chest is the first of the five extant plays by Ludovico Ariosto, better known as the author of *Orlando Furioso*, the masterpiece of Italian Renaissance chivalric literature. The action takes place in the city of Mytilene (Sibaris in the second version). Two young men are helped by their servants to take the two slave-girls they love from a pander, cheating him with the pledge of a chest full of gold which belongs to the rich father of one of them. Even if characters and plot clearly derive from the comedies of Plautus and, even more, Terence, *The Chest* is one of the first original plays of the Italian Renaissance. Starting with the last decade of the 15th century and during the course of the 16th, the interest of both public and authors in the theatre was particularly widespread and very fashionable, not only in Ferrara at the court of the Estate family, but also in several other Italian cities; it led first to numerous performances of the classical plays in the original or in Italian translations, and subsequently to a series of attempts to imitate them in new, modern contexts (the so-called "erudite comedy"). *The Chest* rates among the earliest examples of a text which mixes classical elements with the reality of contemporary life, and its first performance in 1508 (with the effective stage set designed by Pellegrino da Udine, one of the regular painters employed by the Este family) marked an immediate success.

Ariosto displays in this work a great talent and mastery in creating a sequence of situations and intrigues which capture the attention throughout the well-balanced five acts. A succession of familiar characters appears naturally and unaffectedly on the stage: the young penniless lover, who tries his best to conquer his beloved without hurting his father's feelings and financial resources too much; the rich old man, who looks after his money more energetically than he does his son's happiness, and expects from him a behaviour impossible at his age; the pander, dishonest and full of vices, who can easily be tricked while he attempts to deceive the others; the cunning servant, who manages to help his young master without jeopardizing his position with the old one; and so on. All these situations and characters, and many of the things they say, are reminiscent of the classical comedies; but Ariosto added several references to contemporary life (e. g., Mytilene is no longer only a city of ancient Greece, but also the modern one dominated by the Turks), satirizing social abuses and habits of the Spanish, the Roman court, and the Ferrarese people.

The play observes Aristotle's three unities: the action takes place within 24 hours, on a square or large street in front of the houses of the rich old man and the pander. The plot centers on the trick performed by one of the servants against the latter with the chest of gold of the former (from which the play derives its title). However, it is important to note that there is not only one protagonist or leading figure who controls the action through the five acts. As often happens in Renaissance literature, the trick devised by the servant is only partially successful, and he, himself, runs into troubles with his old master—until another servant comes to his rescue, conceiving a stratagem which removes all difficulties and ensures the happy ending with the triumph of the lovers, the defeat of the pander, and no major financial burden for the father. So, Ariosto's vision of human life and his attitude towards man, as reflected in the *Furioso*, is evident also in this play: all characters are, in turns, deceivers and deceived, nobody transcends the others in astuteness and intelligence, and no-one is portrayed as totally stupid and a victim of the others' abuse.

—Antonio Franceschetti

THE CHESTER CYCLE
Anonymous

Composition: Late 14th Century; earliest surviving, complete manuscript, 1591.
First Production: Chester, late 14th century.

Editions
The Chester Mystery Plays edited by Godfrey W. Matthews, Liverpool, Liverpool, 1925.
The Chester Mystery Plays (selection), edited by Maurice Hussey, London, 1957.
The Chester Mystery Cycle, edited by R.M. Lumiansky and D. Mills, Early English Text Society, 1974.

Criticism
(For general works on the author, see *Playwrights* volume)

Books:
Hans Utesch, *Die Quellen der Chester-Plays*, Kiel, 1909.
Walter Wilson Greg and Frederick Millet Salter (eds.), *The Trial and Flagellation with Other Studies in the Chester Cycle*, Oxford, 1935.
Brother Linus Urban Lucken, *Antichrist and the Prophets of Antichrist in the Chester Cycle*, Washington, D.C., 1940.
F.M. Salter, *Medieval Drama in Chester*, Toronto, 1955.
Peter W. Travis, *Dramatic Design in the Chester Cycle*, Chicago, 1982.
R.M. Lumiansky and David Mills, *The Chester Mystery Cycle: Essays and Documents*, Chapel Hill, North Carolina, 1983.
David Mills (ed.), *Staging the Chester Cycle: Lectures Given on the Occasion of the Production of the Cycle at Leeds in 1983*, Leeds, 1985.
Steven E. Hart and Margaret M. Knapp, *"The Aunchant and Famous Cittie": David Rogers and the Chester Mystery Plays*, New York, 1988.

Articles:
Albert C. Baugh, "The Chester Plays and French Influence", in *Schelling Anniversary Papers*, 1923.
S.F. Crocker, "The Production of the Chester Plays", in West Virginia University Philological Studies, 1, 1936.
F.M. salter, "The Banns of the Chester Plays", in *Review of English Studies*, 15, 1939.
J.B. Severs, "The Relationship Between the Brome and Chester Plays of *Abraham and Isaac*", in *Modern Philology*, 62, 1945.
Arthur Brown, "A Tradition of the Chester Plays", In *London Mediaeval Studies*, vol. 2 Part 1, 1951.
R.M. Lumiansky, "Comedy and Theme in the Chester *Harrowing of Hell*", in *Tulane Studies in English*, 10, 1960.
Nan Cooke Carpenter, "Music in the Chester Plays", in *Papers on English Language and Literature*, 1, 1965.
Bernice F. Coffee, "The Chester Play of *Balaam and Balak*", in *Wisconsin Studies in Literature*, 4, 1967.
Theo Stemmler, "Zur Datierung der *Chester Plays*", in *Germanisch-Romanische Monatsschrift*, July 1968.
Oscar L. Brownstein, "Revision in the *Deluge* of the Chester Cycle", in *Speech Monographs*, 36, 1969.
Phillip McCaffrey, "The Didactic Structure of the Chester *Sacrifice of Isaac*", in *Comitatus*, 2, 1971.
Leslie H. Martin, "Comic Eschatology in the Chester *Coming of Antichrist*", in *Comparative Drama*, 5, 1971.
Joseph Candido, "Language and Gesture in the Chester *Sacrifice of Isaac*", in *Comitatus*, 3, 1972.
Harry N. Langdon, "The Staging of the Ascension in the Chester Cycle", in *Theatre Notebook*, 26, 1972.

Lawrence M. Clopper, "The Chester Plays: Frequency of Performance", in *Theatre Survey*, vol. 14 no. 3, 1973.
Ruth B. Davis, "The Scheduling of the Chester Cycle Plays", in *Theatre Notebook*, 27, 1973.
Hans-Jürgen Diller, "The Composition of the Chester Cycle Plays", in *Theatre Notebook*, 27, 1973.
Lawrence M. Clopper, "The Rogers' Description of the Chester Plays", in *Leeds Studies in English*, 1973–74.
Bennett A. Brockman, "Cain and Abel in the Chester *Creation*: Narrative Tradition and Dramatic Potential", in *Medievalia et Humanistica*, 5, 1974.
Peter W. Travis, "The Dramatic Strategies of Chester's Passion Pagina", in *Comparative Drama*, 8, 1974.
Kevin J. Harty, "The Chester *Fall of Lucifer*", in *McNeese Review*, 22, 1975–76.
Kevin J. Harty, "The Unity and Structure of the Chester Mystery Cycle", in *Mediaevalia*, 2, 1976.
Peter W. Travis, "The Credal Design of the Chester Cycle", in *Modern Philology*, 73, 1976.
Kathleen M. Ashley, "Divine Power in the Chester Cycle and Late Medieval Thought, in *Journal of the History of Ideas*, 39, 1978.
Lawrence M. Clopper, "The History and Development of the Chester Cycle" in *Modern Philology*, 75, 1978.
Kevin J. Harty, " 'And Sheepe Will I Keepe no More': Birth and Rebirth in the Chester *Adoration of the Shepherds*, in *American Benedictine Review*, 1978.
Lawrence M. Clopper, "The Principle of Selection of the Chester Old Testament Plays", in *Chaucer Review*, 13, 1979.
Phillip Zarilli, "From Destruction to Conservation in the Chester *Noah* Play", in *Theatre Journal*, 31, 1979.
John J. McGavin, "Sign and Transition: The *Purification* Play in Chester", in *Leeds Studies in English*, 11, 1980.
Lorrayne Baird, " 'Cockes Face' and the Problem of *Poydrace* in the *Passion*", in *Comparative Drama*, vol. 16 no. 3, 1982.
Kevin J. Harty, "Adam's Dream and the First Three Chester Plays", in *Cahiers études*, 21, 1982.
Ruth M. Keane, "Kingship in the Chester Nativity Play", in *Leeds Studies in English*, 13, 1982.
Lawrence M. Clopper, "Arnewaye, Higden and the Origin of the Chester Plays", in *Records of Early English Drama Newsletter*, 8, 1983.
George Ovitt, "Christian Eschatology and the Chester Judgement", in *Essays in Literature* (Macomb, Illinois), vol. 10 no. 1, 1983.
Karl Tamburr, "The Dethroning of Satan in the Chester Cycle", in *Neuphilologische Mitteilungen*, vol. 85 no. 3, 1984.
Joseph E. Grennen, "Tudd, Tibbys Sonne, and Trowle the Trewe: Dramatic Complexities in the Chester Shepherds' Pageant", in *Studia Neophilologica*, vol. 57 no. 2, 1985.
Norma Kroll, "Cosmic Characters and the Human Form: Dramatic Interaction and Conflict in the Chester Cycle *Fall of Lucifer*", in *Medieval and Renaissance Drama in England*, 2, 1985.
David Mills, " 'In This Storye Consisthe Oure Chefe Faithe': The Problems of Chester's Play(s) of Passion", in *Leeds Studies in English*, 16, 1985.
Martin William Walsh, "Demon or Deluded Messiah? The Characterization of Antichrist in the Chester Cycle", in *Medieval English Theatre*, 7, 1985.
Norma Kroll, "Equality and Hierarchy in the Chester Cycle Play of Man's Fall", in *Journal of English and Germanic Philology*, April 1987.
Rosalba Spinalbelli, "The Eschatological Scene of the *Last Judgement*", in *Fifteenth-Century Studies*, 13, 1988.

The Chester cycle of mystery plays is the only complete cycle to survive in more than one source manuscript. The extant cycle is made up of 25 plays. Their topics are most clearly described by the list of titles ascribed to them by their most recent editors in the Early English Text Society, which also indicates the guild responsible for the performance of each one: *The Fall of Lucifer* (Tanners); *Adam and Eve; Cain and Abel* (Drapers); *Noah's Flood* (Waterleaders and Drawers of Dee); *Abraham, Lot and Melchysedeck; Abraham and Isaac* (Barbers); *Moses and the Law; Balaack and Balaam* (Cappers); *The Annunciation* and the *Nativity* (Wrights); *The Shepherds* (Painters); *The Three Kings* (Vintners); *The Offerings of the Three Kings* (Mercers); *The Slaughter of the Innocents* (Goldsmiths); *The Purification; Christ and the Doctors* (Blacksmiths); *The Temptation; the Woman taken in Adultery* (Butchers); *The Blind Chelidonian; The Raising of Lazarus* (Glovers); *Christ at the House of Simon the Leper; Christ and the Moneylenders; Judas' Plot* (Corvisers); *The Last Supper; The Betrayal of Christ* (Bakers); *The Trial and Flagellation* (Fletchers, Bowyers, Coopers and Stringers); *The Passion* (Ironmongers); *The Harrowing of Hell* (Cooks); *The Resurrection* (Skinners); *Christ on the Road to Emmaus; Doubting Thomas* (Saddlers); *The Ascension* (Taylors); *Pentecost* (Fishmongers); *The Prophets of Antichrist* (Clothworkers); *Antichrist* (Dyers); *The Last Judgement* (Websters).

Five manuscripts survive of the complete cycle, ranging from 1591 to 1607. There are also three manuscripts which contain fragments: one, possibly 14th-century, containing part of *The Resurrection*, another containing the *Antichrist* from around 1500, and a third, from 1599, which contains *The Trial and Flagellation of Christ*. Although the cycle has a very rich textual tradition, all the major texts are later in date than the last recorded performance in Chester which was at Midsummer 1575. None of the texts has the status of a producer's working copy, therefore, or of an authoritative, civic version of the plays.

Two of the later versions of the full cycle contain versions of the so-called *Banns*, the proclamation or description of the plays which precedes the text. Banns are also included in independent manuscripts, including one from the pre-Reformation period, which indicates that the "wives" of the city produced the *Assumption of the Virgin Mary*. Although mystery play cycles are commonly associated with the feast of Corpus Christi, those from Chester were separated from the feast, and from single day performance, early in the 16th century, were expanded and played on the Monday, Tuesday, and Wednesday of Whit week. Modifications were made to the cycle in the Reformation period, after which their performance record becomes more patchy. In 1575 the plays were moved to Midsummer's Day, to coincide with the city's other major public festival, in an attempt to staunch archiepiscopal disapproval of their performance, but, except for a performance of the Shepherds' play in 1577–78, the cycle ceased production at that date.

In addition to its rich textual tradition, Chester has, in the form of David Rogers' *Breviary* of 1608–9, the only description by a contemporary of mystery play performance. Rogers describes processional performance at a variety of stations, or stopping places, around the city, as well as the actual pageant vehicles:

> These pagiantes or carige was a highe place made like a howse with 2 rowmes beinge open on the tope, the lower rowme they apparrelled and dressed them selves, and the higher rowme they played, and they stoode upon vi wheeles. And when they had donne with one cariage in one place thay wheled the same from one streete to another . . . .

The somewhat surprising assertion that these vehicles had six wheels is not conclusively borne out by guild accounts which suggest the more usual four.

The evidence of the late texts of the Chester cycle suggests a remarkable degree of coherence in both physical and thematic elements. The eight-line stanza, rhyming *aaab aaab*, is used throughout, and the whole has a tonal evenness indicative, if not of a single author, at least of heavy editorial control. Thematically, too, the cycle conforms to broad patterns which dictate its relationship with its audience. The whole of Christian history is treated as a pattern of prophesy and fulfillment. There is no attempt in this to create sustained dramatic illusion; both the symbolic significance of events and the imitative nature of performance are consistently highlighted. Actions are seen in terms of a divine plan, as the voice of God consistently commands and instigates. All action by other individual characters has an antiphonal pattern, as it conforms to, or impotently resists, the demands of providence.

Complementary to God is the figure of the Expositor who controls action at a different level, explaining the significance of events to the audience, ordering and hurrying the plays along. Events are constantly held up for examination as object-lessons of wider significance for the audience. In keeping with this, the Chester cycle contains a comparatively large number of characters who represent contemporary society, thereby integrating the narrative function and didactic function of the plays. Hence, when Hell has been harrowed, the audience is treated to a diatribe by a dishonest alewife who has been left there on the departure of the prophets and patriarchs to endure perpetual punishment for watering her ale.

To ensure a clear demonstrative effect, the visual aspect of performance was very important. The cycle's stage directions, predominantly in Latin, do not so much elucidate how a particular action was to be achieved from a practical point of view, but what, at a given significant moment, had to take place in order that that significance was clearly apparent. For example, the opening direction to the *Harrowing of Hell* play clearly serves a function other than that of giving practical information to a director: "*Et primo fiat lux in inferno materialis aliqua subtilitate / machinata et postea dicat Adam*" [And first a light, subtly contrived, is made of some matter in hell, and afterwards Adam says]". All action is presented as demonstration and all episodes as having a signifying force beyond their status as unique historical events.

—Pamela M. King.

THE CHEVIOT, THE STAG, AND THE BLACK, BLACK OIL
by John McGrath

First Publication: Kyleakin, Isle of Skye, Scotland 1973; revised version, 1975; further revised version, London, 1981.
First Production: At the "What Kind of Theatre" conference, Edinburgh, 31 March 1973; publicly, at Aberdeen Arts Centre, 24 April 1973.

* * *

The Cheviot, The Stag, and the Black, Black Oil dramatises the history of the Scottish Highlands from the time of the

Clearances in the early 19th century until the 1970's, using an episodic format and a wide variety of theatrical devices to show the continuing battle between the indigenous people and outsiders exploiting the land for their own wealth. The story is presented from a specifically socialist viewpoint and draws a particularly strong link between the exploitation by 19th-century entrepreneurs, who appropriated land for grazing when they introduced the Cheviot sheep, and that of the oil companies in the 1970's. It is as critical of the Highlands and Islands Tourist Board who view oil rigs as a tourist attraction, as of 19th-century Lords who ignored the needs of families and sold their tracts of land for profit. Beneath its setting and detail, *The Cheviot* is also a direct attack on the ethos of capitalism, and though it acknowledges the potential benefits of the oil, it exposes the way profits are used to make individuals rich rather than shared by the community.

The form of the play and the freedom of its performance are as important as the story itself. In some respects *The Cheviot* is in the documentary tradition of the "Living Newspapers" of the 1930's and *Oh What a Lovely War*, although it relies on performers' skills rather than technology to make its points. It is designed both as a teaching play and an entertainment, using witty and inventive techniques to uncover aspects of a forgotten or ignored history, and highlighting facts above story or character. The style works best where information and entertainment exist side by side, less well when, as perhaps happens occasionally, the entertainment becomes a sugar coating on the pill of instruction.

The Cheviot also adapts familiar and theatrical forms and devices for a new political use: and the whole work resembles a traditional Scottish *ceilidh*. The diversity of style allows Queen Victoria to be played by a man singing in falsetto about "her" Scottish mountains, Texas Jim to sing in Country and Western style about his plans to make money from the oil ("Screw your landscape, screw your bays/I'll screw you in a hundred ways"), and Whitehall to be embodied by a single actor operating a government overseer with puppet strings, while singing to a well-known hymn tune, "Oil, oil, underneath the sea,/I am the Lord of the Oil said he . . . . " It also allows performers to step out of character and address the audience directly with crucial factual information, comments on the action, or at one point, to read straight forwardly from historical accounts a list of the injuries inflicted by the forces of law and order on women resisting attempts to evict them.

McGrath consciously tries to avoid the familiar trap and tradition of merely lamenting what has happened; to justify its retelling, the history needs a meaning for the present, inspiring through example people's continuing resistance against similar enemies. Thus in the first performance, by the 7:84 theatre company, armies were shown being turned back or humiliated, officers were thrown into the water by the Highlanders they had come to evict, men refused to be bribed into joining the British Army to fight against the Russians, and the Duke of Sutherland was told that the despotic Tsar could hardly rule more brutally than *his* family had done. If no contemporary victories against the oppressors are shown, then this is because the audience must themselves apply the lessons from the past to their own society. According to McGrath: "For every defeat, we would also celebrate a victory. . .for every oppression, a way to fight back. At the end, the audience left knowing they must choose, and that now, of all times, they must have confidence in their ability to unite and win."

The nature of the audience was crucial to the project. *The Cheviot* was the first production by the Scottish branch of the 7:84 company which determinedly avoided established theatres and middle-class audiences. It was performed to local people in town halls and villages, with the company mingling with audiences to collect further information and stories or discuss the politics of the show. The play itself was followed by a dance for which members provided live, traditional music. Throughout, the action was punctuated by traditional songs and dances (and the audience encouraged to join in). It was also fundamental to the ethos of the company that all members contributed to the research and collection of material, which the writer then shaped for performance. A play such as *The Cheviot* depends for its success on the atmosphere of live performance—the relationship developed between performers and audience. However a television version of this production was made and shown in 1974.

—Steve J. Nicholson

CHICKEN SOUP WITH BARLEY. See THE WESKER TRILOGY.

CHILDREN OF A LESSER GOD
by Mark Medoff

First Publication: New York, 1980.
First Production: Mark Taper Forum (Center Theatre Group), Los Angeles, 25 October 1979.

Criticism

Articles:
Barbara Horn, "Speech vs. Language: An Overview of Communication", in *Essays in Arts and Sciences*, May 1988.

*   *   *

The action of *Children of a Lesser God* "takes place in the mind of James Leeds". Time is fluid in the play, as characters "step from his memory for anything from a full scene to several lines", and place changes rapidly on the stage which holds "only a few benches and a blackboard". James is a speech teacher, aged "thirtyish", at a State School for the Deaf. Upon his arrival at the school, he encounters Sarah Norman, a former student, now in her mid-20's, who has been deaf from birth. Sarah lives and works at the school as a maid, and has steadfastly refused to try to speak, or read lips. James is immediately attracted to this bright, abrasive young woman, and is determined to break through her wall of resistance and lead her into interaction with the larger world. The action of the play follows their problematic courtship, marriage, and finally separation, as Sarah comes to the realization of her own need for independence.

While the love affair of Sarah and James gives the play a particular human interest, the importance of the work lies in its depiction of two separate cultures—hearing and deaf—and the difficulties encountered by those who try to bridge the two. Mr. Franklin, the supervising teacher at the school, prohibits the love affair and then questions the marriage, warning James that "Whether you intend it or not, you're about to uproot Sarah from the only home she's ever known . . . . You're asking Sarah to step away from the community of the deaf". The second act begins with Sarah's first card party—a test of how completely she has been integrated into the middle-class

Children of a Lesser God: New York, 1980

hearing world. While she turns in a splendid performance designed to impress both Franklin and her newly reconciled mother, Sarah later confesses to James, "I feel split down the middle, caught between two worlds". James soon becomes exhausted serving as translator for Sarah. He finds it impossible to enjoy music, one of his great loves, because his wife cannot share it, and he is constantly frustrated in his attempts to comprehend fully the experience of a world without sound.

The deaf and hearing cultures of the play are characterized by separate languages. Sarah, who is profoundly deaf, communicates totally in sign language, but variations in communication methods within the deaf community are represented by Orin and Lydia, both students at the school, who have some residual hearing, read lips, and speak as well as use sign language. Sarah, however, refuses to do anything she cannot do well, and late in the play argues for the acceptance of her own language: "my hands are my voice; and my language, my speech, my ability to communicate is as great as yours. Greater, maybe, because I can communicate to you in one image an idea more complex than you can speak to each other in fifty words". Medoff solves the problem of a hearing audience's unfamiliarity with sign language by having James translate Sarah's side of their conversations as if for his own benefit, and much of the play's visual interest in performance comes from the beauty of this physical language.

The personal difficulties of Sarah and James become more obviously connected to political issues when Orin enlists Sarah's help in a campaign to charge the school with discrimination for not hiring enough deaf teachers. Many of the misconceptions and mistakes made by well-meaning people from the hearing community are illustrated by Edna Klein, a lawyer brought in to help in the challenge. Sarah comes to realize that, as Miss Klein wishes to speak for all deaf people, James wants to speak for her, and in the process of trying to articulate her feelings in a speech to be given before a committee, Sarah explains that she has always been devalued as somehow defective because "everyone was supposed to hear but I couldn't and that was bad". Everyone has assumed that she could not understand and could not speak for herself. The very integrity of her own identity as a separate person has been ignored: "Until you let me be an individual, an *I*, just as you are, you will never truly be able to come inside my silence and know me. And until you do that, I will never let myself know you. Until that time, we cannot be joined. We cannot share a relationship".

After a climactic argument in which James forces Sarah to try to speak, she leaves him, and, despite his remorse and awakening understanding of her position, she refuses to return: "I'm afraid I would just go on trying to change you. We would have to meet in another place; not in silence or in sound but somewhere else. I don't know where that is now. I have to go it alone". While the play does not minimize their difficulties, it ends with the hope of reconciliation as James dreams of her returning so they can be joined once again.

Written especially for the actress Phyllis Frelich, *Children of a Lesser God* is important historically as a play for the hearing theatre which includes a part for a deaf performer. The simplicity and directness of its style emphasize the beauty of its two languages, and the presentation of prejudice and misunderstanding give the play a valuable social function. Its emotional appeal, however, comes from the sensitive handling of the story of two people who struggle to understand, and to love, amidst enormous difficulties.

—Kathy Fletcher

THE CHILDREN'S HOUR
by Lillian Hellman

First Publication: New York, 1934.
First Production: Maxine Elliott Theatre, New York, 20 November 1934.

Criticism
(For general works on the author, see *Playwrights* volume)

Articles:
Philip M. Armato, "'Good and evil' in Lillian Hellman's *The Children's Hour*", in *Educational Theatre Journal*, 25, 1973.
Philip Williams, "Homage to Lillian Hellman: Notes on *The Children's Hour*", in *Doshisha Studies in English*, 28, 1982.
Carol S. Tufts, "Who's Lying? The Issue of Lesbianism in Lillian Hellman's *The Children's Hour*", in *Minnesota Review*, 33, 1989.

*   *   *

Karen Wright and Martha Dobie run a girls' school in a small New England town. Their relationship, Wright's imminent marriage, and the future of the school are threatened when a neurotically vindictive pupil publicly accuses the headmistresses of lesbianism. The child's grandmother forces the parents to withdraw their children, Wright and Dobie sue for damages, and a scandal erupts. The incriminating testimony is subsequently exposed as bogus and the lawsuit is paid in full, but not before Dobie commits suicide and Wright breaks off her engagement. The play ends with a stinging indictment of the criminally indulgent grandmother.

Hellman marked her playwriting debut in 1934 with this searing examination of good and evil, taken from an actual case in 19th-century Scotland, which was suggested to her by her close companion, the crime novelist Dashiell Hammett. The play's boldness was distinguished by more than the intrigue of sexual deviation. There is genuine malevolence in the portrayal of Mary Tilford, the disturbed, adolescent informer, which transcends most of the American plays of the period, and which prefigures much of Hellman's writing for the next three decades. Time and again her characters threaten with the chilling aplomb of this precocious prototype. Mary bullies the timid and flatters the vain with the perverse vehemence of a changeling.

The central target, however, is a petty, narrow community eager to act on circumstantial evidence, resulting in the eventual destruction of the accusers and the innocent alike. The title, as such, is acutely ironic. For Hellman, above all, is an adult dramatist, revealing precisely how far people will manipulate others to advantage. In this respect, a film version, written by Hellman and released in 1936, lost little in transforming the intrigue into adulterous betrayal. The blackmail is worked just as convincingly as in the original, the indictment as strong. The theme of scare-mongering gives the play a political dimension which made its revival in 1952 particularly apposite (Hellman was called to testify before a House Un-American Activities Committee, and was later prevented from working in Hollywood; Hammett was actually imprisoned.)

Hellman was often accused of admitting a melodramatic strain into her writing. There is evidence of it here in the final confrontation between Wright and Mrs. Tilford. The author recognized that she may have been, as she said, a bit too much "on the nose" in her meting out of justice. The focus is perhaps too slight to bear such tragically formal retribution. "It's over for me", Wright says, "but it will never be over for you", in the closing moments. It is probably sufficient for the audience to see for themselves the damaging effects of the gossip. In a national drama corn-fed on palliatives, however, Hellman's bald assertion against the status quo is, to some extent, justified. It will be remembered that *The Children's Hour* opened on Broadway in the same season as Odets's *Awake and Sing!* and Sherwood's *The Petrified Forest*—three harbingers of cultural revolution. Hellman's attack was the more invidious. With 691 performances, too, it proved to be her greatest commercial success. And although she consistently dealt with themes of abiding social moment, never again did she confront so directly the theme of the public lie. Brought into new focus by her victimisation at the hands of McCarthy witch-hunters, this play established her as a controversial, American spokesperson for the next half century.

—James MacDonald

CHOEPHORI. See **THE ORESTEIA.**

CHOEPHOROI. See **THE ORESTEIA.**

THE CHURCHILL PLAY; As it Will be Performed in the Winter of 1984 by the Internees of Churchill Camp Somewhere in England.
by Howard Brenton

First Publication: London, 1974; revised version, in *Brenton: Plays, One*, London, 1986.
First Production: Nottingham Playhouse, Nottingham, 8 May 1974; revised version, The Other Place (Royal Shakespeare Company), Stratford-Upon-Avon, 1978; further revised version, Barbican Theatre (Royal Shakespeare Company), London, November 1988.

*   *   *

The play opens in Westminster Palace on January 1965; a group of service-men are guarding the coffin containing the body of Sir Winston Churchill. They pass the time arguing and joshing each other until they hear a noise. Slowly the figure of the "great man" rises from his box and speaks: "On m'way to Bladon Churchyard. Choc-box last resting-place for the old man. Bloody sentimentality. Dogpiss on my grave more like". As he accepts a light for his cigar, military commands are heard off-stage and full lighting goes up on an amateur-looking set. We have in fact been watching a rehearsal for a play not in 1965, nor even in 1974 the year of the play's first performance, but in 1984. Furthermore, it transpires that we are not in a theatre at all but in Camp Churchill, one of 28 internment prisons for political detainees.

The Churchill Play: Barbican Theatre, London, 1988 (Royal Shakespeare Company)

This later information we only acquire by degrees. What is at first important is the way in which Brenton's stunning *coup de théâtre* works to jerk the audience away from the kind of sentimentally patriotic piece they had been lulled into expecting—and many at the first night at Nottingham were indeed expecting—into a subversive re-slanting of the material: Churchill not as hero but as villain, and his name on a political prison an appropriate epitaph to the legacy he has left the world.

The play being rehearsed is for a visiting Parliamentary Commission, sponsored by the liberal Captain Thompson, a doctor who has no remedies for the real problems of the country's malaise, as symbolised by conditions in the camp. Early on we learn that an Irish prisoner has been killed on his way to the camp, and shortly afterwards the prisoners are told that another inmate has been "dumped", making a total of three that month. In a heated exchange with the Captain the more conventionally right-wing Sergeant fills in the more immediate political context. "Ten years down Ulster streets. Then the late seventies and the laws against industrial unrest . . . . The British Army's got politicised, y'see". Despite its then futuristic dating, the basic premises for the play derive from the army's occupation of Ireland and the industrial troubles culminating in the miners' strike and the "three-day week" of 1973.

The prisoners' offences are mostly trivial, and the punishment, (unlimited imprisonment, brutality, and a strong chance of being "dumped") is out of all proportion. Only Mike McCullough and the Irishman, Convery, who is murdered before he arrives at the camp, can be thought of as possessing any potential for real political action. And significantly, after the prisoners rehearse the Yalta Conference scene of the play in a tin bath—"What's the bath symbolic of then? Europe. Europe, sat upon by 'bums a Super Powers"—it is Mike, previously reluctant to become involved, who ends the first half of the play by declaring "Breakout".

The second half of the play is dominated by the prisoners' play-within-a-play, a remarkable piece that moves rapidly between the polarities of naturalism and political cabaret, gradually revealing the accumulated anger that will lead to action. In part its function is simply to offend the status quo by its attack on Churchill, the "great man" who helped carve up the modern world and the man on whose ideological legacy the foundations of the camp have been built. But if the prisoners' play offers the deconstruction of the hero, it also demonstrates convincingly the continuing strength of his successors.

After a slightly altered reprise of the opening of *The Churchill Play*, the prisoners take the two audiences, that of the Commission and that in the theatre, "back through history", offering a re-reading of post-1939 history as a gradual decline into the present barbarism. The famous incident at Peckham, for instance, when a man is supposed to have shouted to Churchill, "We can take it. Give it 'em back", is altered to, "We can take it. But we just might give it back to you one day". Churchill's medical decline is paralleled with the decline of the nation, just as the Sergeant has earlier informed the guilt-ridden and drunken Labour peer: "What do you do with a slobbering, rabid dog?. . . Y'take it out and shoot it, don't you Sir? Like we did in Ireland".

The entertainment is, then, an act of defiance in itself, and will act as the cover for a greater act, an attempted breakout of the prisoners as projected by Mike. Although the mindlessly anarchic Jimmy—self-confessed "neo-Luddite, Leeds chapter"—is technically responsible for fouling up the break, it is always evident that it could never have succeeded for, as Mike says in his last speech of the play, "Nowhere to break out to, is there. They'll concrete the whole world over any moment now."

And what do we do? Survive. Survive. In the cracks. Either side of the wire. Be alive". And on that note the play ends, the small hope of survival, and of continuing to struggle, set against the metaphorical image of the nation as one vast, policed camp, rotting away. It is an image that, for many, has come to seem even more resonant long past its supposed "sell-by" date of 1984.

—John Bull

EL CID (Le Cid)
by Pierre Corneille

First Publication: Paris, 1637; revised edition, 1682.
First Production: Théâtre du Marais, Paris, December 1636 / January 1637

Editions
Le Cid (1637 text), edited by Maurice Cauchie, Paris, 1946.
Le Cid, edited by N. Scarlyn Wilson, London, 1949.
Le Cid, edited by Paul Ginestier and Yves Brunswick, 1961.
Le Cid (1682 text), edited by G. Griffe, Paris, 1962.
Le Cid, edited by G. Chappon, Oxford, 1968.
Le Cid (1637 text), edited by Peter H. Nurse, London, 1978.

Translations
El Cid, in *Six Plays by Corneille*, edited and translated by Paul Ladis, New York, 1931.
El Cid, in *Classical French Drama*, edited and translated by W. Fowlie, New York, 1962.
The Cid in *The Cid; Cinna; The Theatrical Illusion*, translated by John Cairncross, Harmondsworth, 1975.
Le Cid, translated by Vincent J. Cheng, Newark, New Jersey, and London, 1987.

Criticism
(For general works on the author, see *Playwrights* volume)

Books:
Henry Lyonnet, *"Le Cid" de Corneille*, Paris, 1928.
G. Reynier, *"Le Cid" de Corneille: Étude et analyse*, Paris, 1929.
B. Matulka, *The Cid as a Courtly Hero from the "Amadis" to Corneille*, New York, 1929.
G. Mony (ed.), *"Corneille: "Le Cid", "La Chanson de Rodrigue": Explication and Commentaire*, Paris, 1964.
M.R. Margitic, *Essai sur la mythologie du Cid*, Mississippi, 1976 (Romance Monographs).
W.D. Howarth, *Corneille: "Le Cid"*, London, 1988.
Gabriel Mony, *La Chanson de Rodrigue: Explication et commentaire de la piéce "Le Cid" de Pierre Corneille*, Draguignan, 1988.

Articles:
H. Ault, "The Denouement of *Le Cid*", in *Modern Language Review*, 48, 1953.
M. Sedgwick, "Richelieu and the 'Querelle du *Cid*'", in *Modern Language Review*, 48, 1953.
P.J. Yarrow, "The Denouement of *Le Cid*", in *Modern Language Review*, 50, 1955.
Robert J. Nelson, "The Denouement of *Le Cid*", in *French Studies*, 14, 1960.

A.S. Gerard, "Baroque and the Order of Love: Structural Parallelism in Corneille's *Le Cid* and Vondel's *Jeptha*", in *Neophilologus*, 1965.

A.D. Sellstrom, "The Rôle of Corneille's Infante", in *French Review*, 39, 1965–66.

J.A. Dainard, "The Motif of Hope in *Le Cid*", in *French Review*, 44, 1970–71.

R. Pintard, "De la tragicomédie à la tragédie: L'Example du *Cid*", in *Missions et Démarches de la Critique*, Paris, 1973.

W.O. Goode, "Hand, Heart and Mind: The Complexity of the Heroic Quest in *Le Cid*", in *Publications of the Modern Language Association* [*PMLA*], 1976.

C.J. Gossip, "The Denouement of *Le Cid*, Yet Again", in *Modern Language Review*, 75, 1980.

Patrice Pavis, "Dire et faire au théâtre: L'Action parlée dans les stances du *Cid*", in *Etudes littéraires*, vol.13 no.3, 1980.

Phillippe Sellier, "*Le Cid* et le modéle Théâtre héroïque de l'imagination", in *Stanford French Review*, vol.5 no.1, 1981.

Mohammed Kowsar, "In Defense of Desire: Chimène's Role in *Le Cid* Reconsidered", in *Theatre Journal*, vol.34 no.3, 1982.

Madeleine Bertaud, "Rodrigue et Chimène: La Formation d'un couple héroïque", in *Papers on French Seventeenth Century Literature*, 11, 1984.

Milorad R. Margitic, "Les Deux *Cid*: De la Tragi-comédie baroque à la pseudo-tragédie classique", in *Papers on French Seventeenth Century Literature*, 11, 1984.

C.B. Kerr, "*Le Cid* de face et de profil", in *Revue d'histoire du théâtre*, vol.39 no.2, 1987.

*   *   *

The play is set in Seville. Rodrigue and Chimène love each other and their marriage is planned, but a quarrel between their two fathers disrupts this promise of happiness. Rodrigue is called on by his father, Don Diègue, to avenge in a duel an insult by Chimène's father to their family honour; this he does, and the count is killed. Chimène seeks Rodrigue's life from the king in retribution, but when Rodrigue offers himself to her, she will not kill him. Meanwhile, a Moorish fleet threatens Seville. Rodrigue quickly gathers an army, repels the invaders and captures their two kings, who hail him "Le Cid" (the Lord). In spite of this, Chimène continues to demand his punishment. The king reluctantly consents to a single combat between Rodrigue and a champion of Chimène, but on condition that they agree to marry the victor. Rodrigue again offers her his life and again she refuses, urging him to fight, if only to save her from his rival. Rodrigue disarms his opponent, but spares his life. Chimène is deceived into thinking that Rodrigue is dead, and confesses her continued love for him; and yet, when the truth comes to light, she still cannot reconcile herself to the thought of marriage with him. The king insists on the union, but agrees to a delay; he sends Rodrigue to command his armies against the Moors, trusting that time will heal all wounds.

As this brief summary reveals, the action of the play is complex. First designated a *tragi-comédie*, *Le Cid* situated itself in a tradition of plays immensely popular in the 1630's, whose plots were full of suspense and excitement, and which invariably ended happily. The originality of this play, though, lies in its focus not on such events themselves, but on the moral dilemmas they pose for the protagonists; not on external, but on internal action. The major occurences, such as the two duels and the battle against the Moors, take place offstage, and dramatic attention is turned instead to the confrontation of characters with each other or with themselves.

Both hero and heroine are seen in the grip of a problem

El Cid: Engraving, 1762

which necessitates moral compromise. After the insult to his family name, Rodrigue is faced not so much with a difficult choice between love for Chimène and duty to his father, but with the inevitability of a single course of action which is both desired and yet unsatisfactory. The hero cannot accept a stain on his name, which defiles his integrity as a lover and a nobleman, and yet, paradoxically, the satisfaction of reasserting his honour through revenge is undermined by the realisation that Chimène is then herself dishonoured. The intensity of this dilemma is doubled by the fact that Chimène recognises and fully participates in it, and Corneille portrays in them a shared acknowledgement of the cruel logic which dictates their action: love, as much as duty, impells them to do each other harm. Both are uncompromisingly lucid in their assessment of the tragic situation, but they are not presented as superhuman; beneath their facade of resolve, Corneille suggests human frailty and weariness. Rodrigue performs heroic deeds, and yet he longs only for death; Chimène speaks constantly of revenge, and yet she cannot take it when the opportunity is given.

The denouement of the play was—and remains—the subject of considerable debate. In some ways, it is characteristic of the tragi-comic genre in so far as it appears to offer a happy resolution of conflict: Rodrigue has distinguished himself in battle, and is said to have brought back to life through such deeds the valiant count whose life he took. For 17th-century critics, the prospect of marriage in these circumstances was quite unacceptable, and seemed to imply that the heroine had lost all concern for her honour. It is clear, though, that Chimène remains conscious of the moral and personal problems which face her, as insoluble now, as earlier, and her final words in the play suggest the tragic loneliness of a character who desires, but fails, to rewrite the past. Rodrigue's new identity of "Le Cid" makes him all the more worthy of her love, but cannot eradicate his old identity as her father's killer; he may resurrect Don Gomès metaphorically, but he cannot do so literally. The impetus for the reconciliation, though, comes from the king and has its own particular political implications. As Chimène herself realises, the rights of the individual are subordinate to the demands of the state, and her moral scruples are overridden by the king's more pressing need to reward the one to whom he owes the defence of his authority.

Of all Corneille's plays, this is certainly the best known and most frequently performed. It was a huge success with audiences of the time, who delighted in this touching tale of lovers struggling in the face of insuperable obstacles to their happiness; in its subtle and compelling portrayal of heroic conflict with an ineluctable destiny it marks the birth of French classical tragedy. And yet it was also very unpopular with Corneille's rivals and critics. The dramatist was accused of plagiarising a Spanish play based on the same theme, of breaking conventions of theatrical regularity by attempting to fit too much action into the represented 24 hours, and above all of immorality. The critics regarded his subject, although attested in history, as presenting moral dilemmas unsuitable for the stage. Corneille, though, argued that the essential pleasure and force of tragedy was to be found precisely in those historical events whose very exceptional circumstances give rise to unique pressures and conflicts; and throughout his career, he remained unrepentant.

—G. Jonathon Mallinson

LE CID. See **EL CID.**

CINNA; or, The Clemency of Augustus
  (Cinna; ou, la Clémence d'Auguste)
by Pierre Corneille

First Publication: Paris, 1643.
First Production: Théâtre de l'Hôtel de Bourgogne, Paris, 1642.

Editions
Cinna, edited by Robert Lejeune, Paris, 1933.
Cinna, edited by Laurence Melville Riddle, New York, 1934.
Cinna, edited by N. Scarlyn Wilson, London, 1951.
Cinna, edited by Marcel Barral, Paris, 1962.
Cinna, edited by D.A. Watts, London, 1964.
Cinna, edited by Ian McFarlane, Paris, 1965.
Cinna, edited by Hélène and Daniel Martha, Paris, 1976.

Translations
Cinna, in *The Cid; Cinna; The Theatrical Illusion*, translated by John Cairncross, Harmondsworth, 1975.

Criticism
(For general works on the author, see *Playwrights* volume)

Books:
François Lasserre, *Corneille de 1638 à 1642: La Crise technique d'"Horace", "Cinna" et "Polyeucte"*, Paris, 1990.

Articles:
G.L. Van Roosbroeck, "Corneille's *Cinna* and the *Conspiration des Dames*", in *Modern Philology*, 20, 1922.
Serge Doubrovsky, "*Cinna* et la dialectique du monarque", in *La Table ronde*, 164, 1961.
Louis Herland, "Le Pardon d'Auguste dans *Cinna*", in *La Table ronde*, 158, 1961.
D.R. Clarke, "Heroic Prudence and Reason in the 17th Century: August's Pardon of Cinna", in *Forum for Modern Language Studies*, 1, 1965.
Robert J. Nelson, "Kinship and Kingship in *Cinna*", in *Forum for Modern Language Studies*, 1, 1965.
Jacques Ehrmann, "Les Structures de l'echange dans *Cinna*", in *Temps modernes*, 1966; translated as "Structures of Exchange in *Cinna*", in *Yale French Studies*, 36/37.
E. Stell, "The Role of 'connaissance' in the Voluntary Action of Auguste in *Cinna*", in *Romance Notes*, vol.11 no.2, 1969–70.
André Georges, "L'Evolution morale d'Auguste dans *Cinna*", in *L'Information littéraire*, vol.34 no.2, 1982.
Odette de Morgues, "Coherence and Incoherence in *Cinna*", in *Form and Meaning: Aesthetic Coherence in Seventeenth Century French Drama*, edited by W.D. Howarth, Ian McFarlane, and Margaret McGowan, Amersham, England, 1982.
Gerhard C. Gerhardt, "Ökonomie und Machtpolitik in Corneille's *Cid*", in *Romanische Forschungen*, 95, 1983.
Andrée Georges, "La Pensée politique de Cinna", in *Romanic Review*, vol.74 no.4, 1983.
P.J. Yarrow, "Réflexions sur le dénouement de *Cinna*", in *Papers on French Seventeenth Century Literature*, 11, 1984.
Catherine J. Spencer, "*Cinna*: 'Un Crayon imparfait. . .?'", in *Romanic Review*, November 1987.
A. Georges, "Importance et signification du rôle de Livie dans *Cinna* de P. Corneille", in *Romanic Review*, vol.79 no.2, 1988.

*   *   *

Octave-César Auguste, the Roman emperor, has put Emilie's father to death but has then brought her up virtually as his own daughter. She now engages her lover Cinna to lead a conspiracy against Auguste, with the sole aim of avenging her father. Cinna and a fellow-plotter, Maxime, are summoned by the emperor, who discusses with these, until now his close advisers and friends, whether, and indeed how, to abdicate. Maxime argues in favour of Auguste stepping down, but Cinna, paradoxically, persuades him to retain power, since he knows that Emilie's vengeance requires assassination of a reigning tyrant. Cinna's mounting hesitations are brushed aside by Emilie, but the conspiracy is betrayed through Maxime, a rival for her hand. Distraught yet indignant, Auguste ponders execution and possible suicide. Cinna, Emilie and Maxime are brought before him in turn; unexpectedly, perhaps, each is pardoned and Emilie accepts that her former enmity has vanished.

First performed in Paris in the summer of 1642, *Cinna* shows Corneille's talents at their height. He takes a well-known Roman figure, Augustus Caesar, and sheds fresh light on his complex character by staging a historical event but giving it an unhistorical though plausible motive, through the creation of Emilie, instigator of the conspiracy. Her personal hatred of the emperor and singleminded desire that he be seen to die for her (if not by her hand) dominate the opening scenes. But others soon question whether Auguste has not changed his spots, while she herself admits to being torn between her call for assassination and a continuing, deep love for the chief conspirator. This dichotomy makes her final acceptance of clemency at least psychologically credible. Cinna's naive early enthusiasm to please his beloved is dampened by Auguste's unexpected desire to abdicate: the central act of the play shows Cinna's torment and his grudging agreement to continue with Emilie's plans. Maxime's decision to reveal the plot through a servant removes this dilemma and leaves Cinna to come to terms with a man he has long admired. From protagonist and eloquent exponent of the republican ideal (his is the longest part), Cinna becomes increasingly passive, acted upon rather than active in the second half of the play.

The tragedy deals with the "Cinna episode" in the life of Auguste, who can be seen as the most interesting, if not the most forceful character. Before curtain-up he has shed his bloodthirsty past, when he was known as the tyrant Octave, and his present world-weariness comes as a surprise to the two conspirators from whom he seeks advice in Act 2. News of the plot leaves him feeling betrayed, vengeful at times, yet also insecure, dissatisfied with supreme power, and conscious of his own past behaviour which was no more humane than that of Cinna now. To find Emilie and also Maxime, his "only friend", among the conspirators will add greatly to his distress. The small part which Corneille gives to Auguste's wife Livie late on in the play is crucial. She advocates pardon, but one designed to enhance her husband's long-term political reputation. Auguste rejects her proposal as inappropriate, but it lies dormant in his mind and perhaps serves to trigger the magnanimous clemency which emerges, almost to his surprise, only moments after threats of execution have crossed his lips. This inspired solution, effectively neutralising all opposition and giving the emperor a fresh perspective and a new wind, provides a "happy ending" to a play without any deaths.

As well as being a writer of forceful, rhetorical verse, Corneille is an accomplished creator of political and emotional conflict and a master of suspense, raising end-of-act tension in a plot which unobtrusively observes the unities of time, place (two locations, but conceivably within the same imperial palace) and—most importantly—action. His three principal characters, united by friendship and quasi-familial ties, all evolve, although at different speeds and along paths of different lengths, and thus add verisimilitude to historical truth, which the dramatist was prepared to accept as the main criterion for dramatic success. There is no blood shed, on the stage or even in the wings, but entrenched beliefs, prejudices, desires and illusions die, past and unwanted characteristics disappear, old skins are sloughed off and the play ends, not with unbecoming humiliation or whimpers of inevitable acceptance, but with resounding statements from the conspirators about the glory of imperial power and, from Auguste, the conviction that the past is past, that there will, for all, be a better tomorrow, that he has achieved his long-sought peace of mind. In Corneille's idiosyncratic view, tragedy can encompass a storyline in which characters fight against the odds, facing enormous risks, doing their utmost, but being prevented from carrying out their chosen designs by figures or powers beyond their control. It is just such a conjunction of circum-stances which endows *Cinna* with what Corneille, if not all modern critics, would see as its genuinely tragic aura.

—Christopher Gossip

THE CIRCLE OF CHALK. See **THE CHALK CIRCLE.**

THE CLANDESTINE MARRIAGE
by David Garrick and George Colman the Elder

First Publication: London, 1766.
First Production: Theatre Royal, Drury Lane, London, February 1766.

Editions
The Clandestine Marriage, in *The Plays of David Garrick, 1*, edited by Harry William Pedicord and Frederick Louis Bermann, Carbondale, Illinois, 1980.
The Clandestine Marriage, in *The Plays of David Garrick, 1*, edited by Gerald M. Berkowitz, New York, 1981.
The Clandestine Marriage, in *Plays by David Garrick and George Colman the Elder*, edited by E.R. Wood, Cambridge, 1982.

Criticism
(For general works on the authors, see other volumes)

Articles:
Joseph M. Beatty Jr., "Garrick, Colman and *The Clandestine Marriage*", in *Modern Language Notes*, 36, 1921.
Frederick L. Bergmann, "David Garrick and *The Clandestine Marriage*", in *Publications of the Modern Language Association* [*PMLA*], 67, 1952.
Helmut E. Gerber, "*The Clandestine Marriage* and Its Hogarthian Associations", in *Modern Language Notes*, 72, 1957.

*   *   *

Fanny, youngest daughter of Sterling, a rich "parvenu" merchant, has married her father's clerk, Lovewell, a man of honour but with no prospects. Since Sterling is trying to buy his way into the ranks of the gentry by marrying his daughters off to poor aristocrats, there is no hope that he will approve a match with someone of lower station than himself. Lovewell's only hope is that Lord Ogleby will intercede on his behalf and so secure the match with Fanny. Meanwhile Sterling's eldest daughter, Betsy, is promised to Sir John Melvil. However, he too succumbs to Fanny's charms, and offers himself as *her* husband. So smitten is he with her charms that he is prepared to take £50,000 as dowry rather than the £80,000 promised on behalf of Sterling's eldest daughter. Thus Fanny acquires a suitor as well as a "clandestine" husband. She appeals to Lord Ogleby for help in extricating herself from this conundrum; he mistakes the appeal for a declaration of interest in him, and so becomes a second rival suitor. Finally Fanny and Lovewell's marriage is declared in public; Lord Ogleby gives his approval, and so Sterling and Mrs. Heidelberg, Fanny's aunt, assent to

The Clandestine Marriage: William Farren as Lord Ogleby, Covent Garden Theatre, London, 1818, (painting by Samuel De Wilde)

the match, since Ogleby's word marks the marriage with the sign of the "qualaty" which they crave.

As actor, manager, and playwright, Garrick was the presiding genius of London theatre in the mid-18th century. In *The Clandestine Marriage* he exploited to the hilt his unrivalled knowledge of stagecraft he had learnt as an actor, the grasp of the repertory he needed to survive as a manager who had to know, on a daily basis, what plots and what plays would fill the seats of the Theatre Royal; and finally, in writing the play in collaboration with George Colman, he tailored the parts to suit the capabilities of the actors in his company.

This last is most obvious in the case of Lord Ogleby, written to be played by Garrick himself, and who thus seems like a series of variations on Garrick's own comic stage "turns"; as alternately coxcomb, lecher, and drunkard, charmingly convinced as he dresses and scents himself each day for the "lists of love" that he is still in his prime, and that for him to pursue Fanny is not simply grotesque. His attentions to her are elaborately charming and geriatric but not threatening. In the last act he is transformed from ardent lover into wish-fulfilling godfather; his assent magically makes Fanny's "clandestine" marriage possible. So the part requires winsome hilarity coupled with charisma, a combination well suited to Garrick's "mercurial" comic style.

Garrick, however, eventually declined to play "his" part in the piece; it was initiated instead by Tom King. Garrick's refusal to play Ogleby led to his quarreling with his co-author and good friend, George Colman, for Colman feared that without Garrick the play might not triumph. On that score he need not have been anxious, for the play was a hit, performed 19 times in its first season, and 68 in the following decade. The play text went through three editions in the six weeks after it was first published.

The quarrel initiated a long-running squabble as to who exactly was responsible for which parts of the play, until Bergmann's study of the play's manuscripts proved that Garrick was responsible for at least half the play, including the character of Ogleby, as well as the fifth act, which expertly engineers false discovery upon false discovery in Sterling's house; the discoveries increase the audience's anxiety until the clandestine marriage (of which they have been aware since the first scene) is finally revealed to the assembled cast. The act demonstrates Garrick's grasp of stagecraft: its arrivals and exits are nicely calculated to keep the audience in a state of delighted surprise. This delight complements the bustle of the first act, which energetically involves the audience in the plot as well as the world of the play.

That energy inevitably means the absence of a rich verbal texture, for the play was written to be performed and not to be read as a closet drama. Consequently, though it has been produced several times in the 20th century, it has not received the attention granted to the comedies of Sheridan and Goldsmith, though its initial commercial success was as great as their "hits".

The play's scenario was taken from the first plate of Hogarth's "Marriage-à-la-Mode" series; Garrick and Colman's characters thus serve as dramatic proof of the "novelistic" manner in which Hogarth's portraits were read. Garrick and Colman transpose into theatrical space the rich merchant (Sterling) contracting with a decrepit nobleman (Ogleby) for the hand in marriage of the merchant's daughter (Fanny). Garrick's prologue calls attention to the play's descent from Hogarth, as well as its demonstration of Horace's tag (so obsessively reworked by 18th-century artists) "ut pictura poesis"; or rather here "ut pictura comoedia". Like Hogarth's pictures and Horace's urban poems, Garrick's play mines a rich vein of satiric "realism". Its targets would have been readily identifiable to the original audience, though exaggerated for comic effect.

Sterling, as his name suggests, cares for nothing but money and position. It is inconceivable to him that Lovewell should marry his daughter, since Lovewell has "no stuff in the case, no money". He is excessively fond of parading visitors around his own estate, so "improved", as he thinks, in the "approved" new style. For Sterling, Mrs. Heidelberg and Betsy, indifference in a marriage is fine, so long as you have a coach and six to ride in. Fanny, true to her "bourgeois" upbringing, wants the coach and six as well as the man she loves. She gains the latter and keeps the former. In the process she herself is laughed out of the excesses of sentiment to which she is prone, and which Garrick later attacked in his prologue to Goldsmith's *She Stoops to Conquer*.

Four years after the first performance of *The Clandestine Marriage*, Garrick called for a "Comedy of Character" calculated to make an audience "laugh [not] cry". His call was not simply a theoretical corrective, for here, in *The Clandestine Marriage*, which contains some of his best comic writing (including a brilliant ensemble epilogue) he and Colman devised an exuberant demonstration of "Genuine Comedy & Vis Comica".

—Mark Anthony Houlahan

CLOUD NINE
by Caryl Churchill

First Publication: London, 1979.
First Production: Dartington Hall College of Arts (Joint Stock Theatre Company), Devon, 14 February 1979.

Criticism

(For general works on the author, see *Playwrights* volume)

Articles:
Elizabeth Russell, "Caryl Churchill: Sexual Politics and *Cloud Nine*", in *Revista Canaria de estudos ingleses*, 12, 1986.
Joanne Klein, "Seeing Double: Theatrical Conceits in *Cloud Nine*", in *Journal of Dramatic Theory and Criticism*, vol.1 no.2, 1987.
Margaret and David Buchbinder, "Having It Both Ways: Cross-Dressing in Orton's *What the Butler Saw* and Churchill's *Cloud Nine*", in *Journal of Dramatic Theory and Criticism*, vol.2 no.1, 1987.

*   *   *

The first of the two thematically and chronologically related (but sharply dissimilar) acts of Churchill's play is set in the heyday of British imperialism in Victorian Africa. It gives a wildly satiric picture of the sexual confusions and entanglements of a colonial household presided over by Clive and his wife Betty. Its scenes reveal a chasm between social norms all characters subscribe to and try to keep up, and disruptive forces in their own natures manifesting themselves in adultery, homosexuality, and pederasty. The rigid code of behaviour required for their repression or concealment also obtains in the treatment of the native African population. The second act transposes the main characters of the first act (Clive and his family) into a contemporary metropolitan setting in London. The enforced unity of Victorian morality is dissipating in the main characters' attempts at personal emancipation, however partial and contradictory.

The play connects the theme of sexual politics with a perspective on the social conditions they presuppose or reinforce. The play's tone shifts from a wildly satirical view of Victorian people not meant to be more than caricatures, to a much more empathetic portrait of people struggling to liberate themselves from past and present oppression. In the first act the patriarchal system of the British Empire is mirrored in the upper middle-class family of Clive, his wife, and their children, Victoria and Edward. All are shown as victims of a rigid regime forcing them, at least outwardly, to conform to conventional role-patterns of a middle-class family. Any stability in this pattern is pre-empted by both personal and political realities. Clive has a violent affair with a visiting neighbour, Mrs. Saunders; his wife Betty falls in love with his best friend, the colonial explorer Harry; Harry is a homosexual who has taken up relations with Edward and his head servant Joshua, and even makes a mistaken attempt at the scandalized Clive; Betty, in her turn, is passionately loved by her servant Ellen. The marriage between Harry and Ellen, arranged to save appearances, is as unlikely to hold as any other relationship between people estranged from their real natures. Similarly, and for related reasons, the native African rebellion that Clive's colonial duty it is to quash eventually threatens to subvert his very household. The final scene in the first act has the Uncle-Tom figure of the servant Joshua overcome his alienation from his tribe and family and take aim at Clive, with Edward looking on unconcernedly, to indicate loyalties being dissolved from within as from outside.

Between the first and second acts 100 years of historical time have been compressed into just 25 years of the main characters' life-time. In many important respects Betty and her children have achieved their emancipation from the classical middle-class role-models. Betty is finally leaving her husband and is tentatively but determinedly trying to lead an independent life. Edward has come out in a gay ménage in which he soon adopts some traits typically ascribed to women, and Victoria, who in Act I had a fitting symbolical representation as a puppet, has to reconcile marriage, motherhood, and a lesbian attachment to the working-class mother Lin. While not all tension is removed from the characters' lives, the resulting changes in behaviour are such as to make a bemused Clive—whose only brief reappearance occurs at the very end of the second act—yearn nostalgically for the lost certainties of the colonial past.

The play's major innovative device of syncopating individual and historical time inscribes political themes into personal development. While Act I gives a deliberately stereotyped view of a patriarchal, Victorian family that only allows some flexibility in a few of the portraits of the system's victims (the adult women, the son), Act II allows more pyschological depth to its panorama of contemporary confusions and present lifestyles. Churchill enters a lot more into her characters' minds here, without, however, getting stuck in psychological realism since it is people's public behaviour that serves as a connecting link between the two acts. This insistence on the social dimension of the action is emphasized neatly by the device that has become important for some contemporary, feminist playwrights: cross-casting. By this means the boundaries separating male and female roles, children and adults, black and white, are symbolically transgressed to allow the audience more than the usual detachment from conventional processes of identification.

In its critical picture of Victorian upper-class life with its rigidly enforced codes, its double standards of morality, and excruciating conformist pressures, the play often utilizes farce to bring home general cultural points. Both the obvious unhappiness caused by suppressing people's identities and the idea of human happiness that the play's title ironically refers to, underpin a mischievous social system. However, at the end of the first act, the farcical props are removed to reveal naked aggression and force as a corollary of imperialist hegemony that can be turned against the aggressors as well as the victims. The second act of *Cloud Nine* has a much less unified dynamic because it tries to spell out the process of personal liberation as one involving difficult and even painful choices, as in Betty's separation from her uncomprehending husband, Clive, and in Victoria's gradual coming to terms with her social and sexual conditioning, and the resultant choices in her everyday life in which an equally tentative emancipation is recorded. It has rightly been said that the straightforward and seemingly didactic energy of Act I is replaced by a much less certain and more experimental dramaturgy in Act II. While there is an unmistakeable narrowing in the play's analytic connection of personal and social levels—only a hint at British involvement in Northern Ireland reminds us of the continuing legacy of the colonialist past—this shift in Churchill's preoccupations makes the play a much more intimate document of contemporary life and the plurality of possible lifestyles in it. The feminist perspective accordingly moves from larger political formations—in which a trace of the origins of the play in the workshop methods of the Joint Stock Theatre Company that first produced it can still be detected—to the level of day-to-day concerns. This change of emphasis was certainly in line with the impact of feminism on plays by women (and some men) in the late 1970's.

—Bernd-Peter Lange.

THE CLOUDS (Nephelai / Nubes)
by Aristophanes

First Production: City Dionysia Festival, Athens, 423 B.C.

Editions
Nubes, edited by Frederick H.M. Blaydes, London, 1890.
The Clouds, edited and translated by W.J.M. Starkie, London, 1911 (with translation).
Nubes, edited by J. Van Leeuwen, Leiden 1898; reprinted, 1968.
Clouds, edited by K.J. Dover, Oxford, 1968.
The Clouds, edited and translated by Alan H. Sommerstein, Warminster, Wiltshire, 1982 (with translation).

Translations
The Clouds, translated by William Arrowsmith, Ann Arbor, Michigan, 1962 (Complete Greek Comedy Series).
The Clouds, translated by Frank K. Wilson, Bath, 1966.
The Clouds, in *Lysistrata; The Acharnians; The Clouds*, translated by Alan H. Sommerstein, Harmondsworth, 1973.
Clouds, in *Clouds; Women in Power; Knights*, translated by Kenneth McLeish, Cambridge, 1979.
The Clouds, in *Four Plays of Aristophanes*, translated by James H. Martinband, 1983.

Criticism

(For general works on the author, see *Playwrights* volume)

Books:
Raymond K. Fisher, *Aristophanes' "Clouds": Purpose and Technique*, Amsterdam, 1984.

Articles:
N.N. Dracoulides, "Aristophanes' *The Clouds* and *The Wasps*", in *American Imago*, Spring 1966.
G. Lazier, "A Comic View of the Sophists: Aristophanes' *Clouds*", in *Western Speech*, vol.30 no.3, 1966.
C. Segal, "Aristophanes' Cloud Chorus", in *Aret*, 2, 1969.
J.W.H. Adkins, "Clouds, Mysteries, Socrates and Plato", in *Antiochthon*, 4, 1970.
E.A. Havelock, "The Socratic Self as It Is Parodied in Aristophanes' *Clouds*", in *Yale Classical Studies*, 22, 1972.
R.S. Brumbaugh, "Scientific Apparatus on Stage in 423 B.C.", in *Yale Classical Studies*, 22, 1972.
P. Karavites, "Socrates in the Clouds", in *The Classical Bulletin*, 50, 1974.
R.A. Anselment, "Socrates and *The Clouds*: Shaftesbury and a Socratic Tradition", in *Journal of the History of Ideas*, 39, 1978.
H. Tarrant, "Midwifery and the *Clouds*", in *Classical Quarterly* (new series), vol.38 no.1, 1988.

*   *   *

The *Clouds* was awarded only the third prize at the City Dionysia festival of 423 B.C., and a last place was clearly a great disappointment to the playwright. Aristophanes subsequently modified the *Clouds*, though the revised version appears never to have been presented on the stage at Athens. The text we possess today represents this revision in which the chorus of Clouds indignantly proclaims in the parabasis that this, the best of Aristophanes' efforts, failed undeservedly at the hands of an unintelligent audience because it refused to exploit crude, coarse jokes but attempted something new and subtle.

The "hero" of the comedy is Strepsiades or "Twister", a prosperous farmer married to an aristocratic lady who has encouraged their son in wild extravagance. Now the farmer, desperate to foil his creditors, tries to persuade the son Pheidippides to enter Socrates' "school" so that he may learn how to argue and thus avoid paying his debts. But the son, horrified by the school and its students, refuses and the father, who does join the school and meets the chorus of Clouds, proves to be the most stupid of pupils, unable to cope with measures, rhythms, or the use of words. On witnessing, however, the "agon", or verbal contest, between the personified abstracts Right and Wrong, Pheidippides is induced by the victory of Wrong to study the art of rhetoric under the guidance of Socrates and turns out to be an adroit pupil, easily able to make a complete fool of Strepsiades in debate and, furthermore, to beat his father up. The comedy ends not with the standard celebration but with the outraged parent applying a torch to Socrates' establishment, thus taking comic advantage of a type of boisterous action on stage already denounced in the parabasis.

Strepsiades and Pheidippides offer a strong contrast between the old and the young, illustrating a standard conflict between the generations. The son is very much the man about town, conscious of his social status and with marked aristocratic pretensions, whereas the father prefers the country and is a total boor. The villain of the piece, however, is the Athenian philosopher Socrates, who is here depicted as a representative of the new "sophistic" education; an equivalent of the modern guru, yet no spiritual teacher but someone dirty, unkempt, a thief and charlatan concerned with the acquisition of money and little else. Aristophanes' Socrates is in need of everything, including scruples. The result is a gross caricature which undoubtedly caused Socrates much harm, as he himself asserted at his trial in 399 B.C. when he was condemned for corrupting the youth, and for impiety.

The picture of Plato's teacher presented here is unfair— Socrates did not charge fees, operate any kind of school, or teach rhetoric and the means by which the weaker argument might be made to seem stronger—but there are occasional touches of the authentic Socrates in, for example, the method of argumentation and the use of homely illustration. But Aristophanes was not bothered with fairness but with mounting an attack on a new breed of intellectuals undermining, in the opinion of the average person, conventional morality and values at a time, moreover, when Athens was engaged in a devastating war. The notoriously ugly Socrates, who went around in the company of considerably younger men and made a habit of asking stupid questions of his fellow citizens whose perfectly sensible answers he then exposed as being sadly inadequate, offered an obvious target whereby the philistinism of many in the audience might be reinforced.

The *Clouds* met with a comparative lack of success in spite of popular resentment aimed at Socrates, a remarkable range of humour extending from linguistic subtleties to cracks at the expense of notorious gays and select members of the audience, and some quite devastating stage effects such as the initial appearance of Socrates suspended high above the actual stage so that his thoughts might not be "corrupted" by too close a contact with the moisture-attracting earth. Why was the play unsuccessful? Perhaps the answer is to be found in the clash between Right and Wrong as they urge the merits of their different types of education, the old and the new. The former stresses physical endurance, the value of traditional music and poetry, acceptance of conventional opinions and beliefs, the need for moderation and respect for those older, but the latter stresses the absolute reverse and it is Wrong who wins the argument and so secures the allegiance of Pheidippides. And Wrong does this by violent attack, by misrepresentation, by ignoring the main issues, and by identifying the whole audience as sodomites. Could all this have been altogether too much for Athenians already inclined to sympathize with the roughly 60-year-old Strepsiades, and so explain the disappointing reception afforded the *Clouds*? At the same time a concentration on Socrates and the techniques of the sophists does give the *Clouds* an appeal which the humour at the expense of others (well known in their time but mere names today) will never inspire.

—Peter Walcot

COCK-A-DOODLE-DANDY
by Sean O'Casey

First Publication: London, 1949.
First Production: People's Theatre, Newcastle-Upon-Tyne, 10 December 1949.

Criticism

(For general works on the author, see *Playwrights* volume)

Articles:
Bobby L. Smith, "Satire in O'Casey's *Cock-a-Doodle Dandy*", in *Renascence*, 19, 1967.
Walter C. Daniel, "The False Pattern in Sean O'Casey's *Cock-a-Doodle Dandy*", in *College Language Association Journal*, 13, 1969.
Ronald G. Rollins, "Ritual to Romance in *Within the Gates* and *Cock-a-Doodle Dandy*", in *Modern Drama*, 17, 1974.
Christopher Murray, "Two More Allusions in *Cock-a-Doodle Dandy*", in *Sean O'Casey Review*, 4, 1977.
Violet M. O'Valle, "Melville, O'Casey, and *Cock-a-Doodle Dandy*", in *O'Casey Annual*, 1982.

*   *   *

The entire action of O'Casey's allegorical farce takes place outside the home of Marthraun, who has become rich through ownership of the local bog. Though a capitalist, he is also steeped in Irish puritanism, and currently troubled by the return of Loreleen, a daughter from his first marriage who has been brought up in England free from her father's commercial and ethical values. Much of the action is expressionistic, representing the anxieties, absurdities, phobias, superstitions, and obsessions of Marthraun and his society, and the catalyst for this is Loreleen's carefree disregard for local totem and taboo. Marthraun's arguing with Mahan about freight payments is dominated by complaints about Loreleen, whose entrance reveals casualness and an intelligent cynicism which eludes the men completely. A couple of labourers flirt with her, and as she brushes them off they see her transmute into "a fancy-bred fowl". The rest of the action is bound together with society's persecution of Loreleen, sometimes represented on stage as "the demonised Cock" and sometimes as the woman herself. The cock invades the house and pecks at the holy pictures, the old man Shanaar tries to exorcise it by yelling pidgin Latin at it, but the cock meekly allows itself to be led away by the gentle and tolerant messenger Robin Adair. The first scene ends with Father Domineer leading the parish in bidding farewell to the dying Julia, who is going to Lourdes. In the second scene, the characters' grotesque image of Loreleen escalates to a higher pitch of absurdity, with the aid of alcohol, and the comic mood persists even to the end, when Domineer, demanding the sacking of a man who is living in sin, accidentally kills him. Much of the final scene is also comic, with Domineer exorcising the house and Loreleen defying him, but it suddenly turns sour when she is dragged in, having been brutalised by the villagers for being found in an intimate context with the (married) Mahan. Loreleen leaves town, with most of the women accompanying her, but the play finds yet another level of bitterness for its end, where the (uncured) Julia returns from Lourdes and the Messenger proclaims his uncompromising verdict on Marthraun as an archetype of Irish citizenry: "Die. There is little else left useful for the likes of you to do".

Every commentator on this play seems to have devised a new hybrid genre to account for it; "allegorical farce" is as good as any, but it only partially indicates the mature O'Casey's masterly skill at blending numerous dramatic modes while retaining every conceivable unity. As well as modulations in the level of seriousness, which had existed from his earliest full-length plays, there are also sharply contrasting modes of representation. The consequent diversity would lead most playwrights into structural chaos, but this play increasingly sharpens its focus in the final scene, so that the ending leaves no possibility of relief or ambiguity. Moreover, the dramatic strategy finally targets responses which the play itself has generated and in which the audience has colluded. In early O'Casey, the mingling of laughter and tears meant that light-hearted foolery could be taken as an antidote to the unpalatable severities of contemporary Ireland. The unprincipled buffoons are the survivors. Here, the pernicious potential of buffoons is revealed, and they are given the death sentence.

Almost every element of the play is in some sense satire, but O'Casey's broad strategy of indictment consists in transposing the Horatian into the Juvenalian. From the start, it is clear that the men are the satirical targets, but they are so pathetic and credulous that our laughter at them can be almost affectionate: their rhetorical athleticism, their cowardice, their duplicity (particularly in sexual attitudes), and their very occasional charm mean that if the audience does not find them admirable nor does it find them contemptible. But when these qualities are later politicised, they become lethal, and the potential for a witch-hunt is exposed in every opinionated boor.

In many respects, the play resembles an Irish version of Euripides' *Bacchae*, particularly in the mobilisation of gender, the persecution of the "other", the element of possession and alleged possession, the invasion of an alien ideology, and the liberating potential of dance, alcohol, and love. The entrenched sexism of the men exposes them as hypocrites from the start, hypocrites in their attitudes to women as much as in their attitudes to their workers. By contrast, the women develop a receptivity to Loreleen's "English" ethos, and reject the sexual and economic oppression epitomised in Marthraun. But O'Casey's naming, which is rarely subtle, directs us to the greater figure of institutionalised oppression in Father Domineer, unparalleled in terms of heroic hypocrisy in his response to killing the worker he only meant to curse, and cementing the union of church and capitalism. O'Casey's play is ultimately bleaker than Euripides', because if Adair survives the play, so too does Domineer: to end the play differently would be to misrepresent the troubles of O'Casey's vision of Ireland—where it did not achieve professional production until 1975.

—Howard McNaughton

THE COCKTAIL PARTY
by T.S. Eliot

First Publication: London, 1950.
First Production: Edinburgh Festival, 22 August 1949.

Criticism
(For general works on the author, see *Playwrights* volume)

Books:
E. Martin Browne, *The Making of a Play: T.S. Eliot's "The Cocktail Party"*, Cambridge, 1966.
William Tydeman, *"Murder in the Cathedral" and "The Cocktail Party"* London, 1988 (Text and Performance Series).

Articles:
P. Munz, "Devil's Journal or *The Cocktail Party*", in *Hibbert Journal*, 49, 1951.
N.A. Scott, "T.S. Eliot's *The Cocktail Party*: Of Redemption and Vocation", in *Religion in Life*, vol. 20 no. 2, 1951.
Ulrich Weisstein, *The Cocktail Party*: An Attempt at Interpretation on Mythological Grounds", in *Western Review*, 16, 1952.

The Cocktail Party: Royal Lyceum Theatre, Edinburgh 1949

Robert B. Heilman, "*Alcestis* and *The Cocktail Party*", in *Comparative Drama*, 5, 1953.

E. Schwartz, "Eliot's *Cocktail Party* and the New Humanism", in *Philological Quarterly*, 32, 1953.

R.A. Colby, "The Three Worlds of *The Cocktail Party*: The Wit of T.S. Eliot", in *University of Toronto Quarterly*, 24, 1954.

Jack Winter, "'Prufrockism' in *The Cocktail Party*", in *Modern Language Quarterly*, 22, 1961.

Newby Toms, "Eliot's *The Cocktail Party*: Salvation and the Common Routine", in *Christian Scholar*, 47, 1964.

Richard P. Hovey, "Psychiatrist and Saint in *The Cocktail Party*", in *Hidden Patterns: Studies in Psychoanalytic Literary Criticism*, edited by Leonard F. and Eleanor B. Manheim, New York, 1966.

Arthur K. Oberg, "*The Cocktail Party* and the Illusion of Autonomy", in *Modern Drama*, 11, 1968.

Lois G. Thrash, "A Source for the Redemption Theme in *The Cocktail Party*", in *Texas Studies in Literature and Languages*, 9, 1968.

M.J. Lightfoot, "Uncommon Cocktail Party", in *Modern Drama*, 11, 1969.

Vinod Sena, "The Ambivalence of *The Cocktail Party*", in *Modern Drama*, 14, 1972.

Gary T. Davenport, "Eliot's *The Cocktail Party*: Comic Perspective as Salvation", in *Modern Drama*, 17, 1974.

S. Jaret McKinstry, "Mixed Meanings: Role-Calling in T.S. Eliot's *The Cocktail Party*", in *Rackham Journal of the Arts & Humanities*, 2, 1982.

Stephen Wade, "The Orchestration of Monologues: *The Cocktail Party* and a Developing Genre", in *Agenda*, 23, 1985–86.

Michael Selmon, "Logician, Heal Thy Self: Poetry and Drama in Eliot's *The Cocktail Party*", in *Modern Drama*, December 1988.

*   *   *

The social gathering of the title takes place in the drawing room of Edward Chamberlayne, whose wife, Lavinia, has suddenly left him, and who is in the embarrassing situation of having to play host at a pre-arranged cocktail party. After some desultory and trivial conversation, the small group of guests disperses, though two of them, Alex and Julia, continue to harrass Edward with unwanted attentions, and an uninvited guest stays behind to offer some gnomic advice on his marriage. The rest of the play discloses and unravels the tangled relationships between the Chamberlaynes and their party guests. Edward, it emerges, has had a secret extramarital affair with Celia, as has Lavinia with Peter, who is, however, secretly in love with Celia. The uninvited stranger together with his assistants, Julia and Alex are the agents of comic reconciliation. The stranger is revealed in the second act to be Henry Harcourt-Reilly, an eminent psychiatrist, in whose consulting room the Chamberlaynes decide to remain together and Celia recognizes that she has a spiritual vocation. The play ends with another cocktail party, given by the Chamberlaynes two years later. Edward and Lavinia have saved their marriage, Peter has become a successful film-maker, and the absent Celia, it is revealed, has become a nun and has died a martyr in colonial territory.

T.S. Eliot's project in this verse play was a dual one: to restore the poetic drama to the modern stage as an effective vehicle of communication, and to accommodate religious themes within the secular terms of modern, theatrical convention. *The Cocktail Party* represents a turning-point in his career as a dramatist; it was the first of the plays specifically addressed to a popular audience. After the experimental, highly stylized, poetic dramas *Sweeney Agonistes, Murder in the Cathedral*, and *The Family Reunion*, all of which, it could be argued, contain elements of tragedy, he turned towards the fashionable mode of his time, the drawing-room comedy of manners as exemplified by Noel Coward. The action of *The Cocktail Party* takes place on two discrete yet simultaneous levels: firstly that of a frivolous entertainment revolving around marital infidelity and romantic misalliances within polite society, and secondly that of a metaphysical and ultimately transcendental meditation on the nature of the good life. This doubleness of purpose requires a poetry muted, and restrained, by the demands of conversational dialogue, yet capable of emotional intensity at critical moments, so that (as Eliot explained elsewhere) it should work its effects on the audience without their being aware of it.

In *The Cocktail Party*, the minor and eccentric "character" roles of comedy which typically provide "light relief" have an utterly serious purpose. The avuncular psychiatrist (Sir Henry), the garrulous society matron (Lady Julia), and the fussy, well-meaning friend (Alex) turn out to be the Guardians, or agents of divine providence. In the first act, Alex and Julia appear to be unconscious butts of humour as Edward tries to keep them from finding out his domestic situation: in the second act all three are revealed as conscious not only in a literal, but also in a deeper, analogical or spiritual sense of what has gone wrong, and as having a secret power to influence the course of events. In one sense they are the Community of Christians as described in Eliot's *The Idea of a Christian Society*, the select, enlightened minority which acts as the conscience of the masses. Edward, after his puzzling encounter with the "stranger", tells Celia:

The self that can say "I want this—or want that"—
The self that wills—he is a feeble creature;
He has to come to terms in the end
With the obstinate, the tougher self; who dies not speak
Who never talks, who cannot argue;
And who in some men may be the *guardian*—
But in men like me, the dull, the implacable,
The indomitable spirit of mediocrity.
The willing self can contrive the disaster
Of this unwilling partnership—but can only flourish
In submission to the rule of the stronger partner.

The division between the personality or passional self and a deeper psychic principle or guardian spirit forms the comic plot of *The Cocktail Party*. The Romantic desire for ecstatic communion with an earthly object is firmly rejected, as is the existentialist impatience with constraints on the freedom of consciousness. For most of us, then, the good life consists in resignation to the way things are. Sir Henry leads the patients to cure themselves by showing them the necessity of their own natures. Edward and Lavinia are reunited when they choose to accept the banality and limitation of married life. Celia, however, has had a vision of the ultimate falsity of all worldly appearances. Having lost the illusion of romantic love, she becomes aware of a deeper disillusion with secular life itself, "an awareness of solitude" and "a sense of sin". Sir Henry prescribes a trip to an unknown "sanatorium" which turns out to be the religious life, the way of saintliness.

Celia's fate is exceptional; it differs from the average lot of "indomitable mediocrity" and is therefore played out offstage, beyond the comic world of the play. In the fourth act, which brings the cocktail party round again, the Chamberlaynes have, as advised, made the best of a bad job and are seen in a state of somewhat tepid, married contentment. Celia has been crucified on an anthill, and the news of her martyrdom casts a tragic shadow over the party talk, moving her former lover Peter to reassess his life.

The spectacularly horrible manner of Celia's death, which in the original version of the play was dwelt upon in even greater detail, led some critics to complain of a jarring disproportion. The Guardians view this as a happy death, a triumphant self-fulfilment in the love of God; but the undeniable, masochistic tinge, so characteristic of Eliot's poetic sensibility, would seem to violate the comic mode. Celia's extremity of suffering is, of course, supposed to redeem the mediocrity of the average existence. The cocktail party, an impoverished substitute for the possibility of human love, continues, but it is doubtful whether the play's ruling metaphor is adequate to the breadth of the "human condition" which it claims to represent.

—Christina Britzolakis

LE COCU MAGNIFIQUE. See **THE MAGNIFICENT CUCKOLD.**

COELINA; or, The Child of Mystery
  (Coelina; ou, l'Enfant du mystère)
by Guilbert de Pixérécourt

First Publication: Paris, 1800; revised edition, Paris 1841.
First Production: Théâtre de l'Ambigu-Comique, Paris, 2 September 1800.

Editions
Coelina, ou L'Enfant du mystère, edited by Norma Perry, Exeter, Devon, 1972.

Translations
Coelina; or, A Tale of Mystery, translated by John Wallace, London, 1802.

Criticism
(For general works on the author, see *Playwrights* volume)

Articles:
Norma Perry, [introduction in] *Coelina, ou L'Enfant du mystère*, Exeter, Devon, 1972.

*   *   *

The heiress Coelina has two uncles: M. Dufour her guardian, whose son Stéphany she loves and hopes to marry, and M. Truguelin, who wants to marry her to his own son for her money. A dumb beggar, Francisque, has recently been given shelter at Dufour's house. We are told that eight years earlier he was found nearby with his tongue cut out. He declines to reveal the identity of the perpetrators of the crime, but hints that they are not unknown to Dufour. Truguelin arrives and recoils in horror at the sight of Francisque, but is himself recognized by Dr. Andrevon who had found and treated the latter after the attack. Coelina overhears Truguelin and his servant plotting to kill Francisque and intervenes to save him.

Dufour decides that Coelina and Stéphany should be married as soon as possible.

Act 2, set in Dufour's garden, opens with an entertainment to celebrate the engagement of the two lovers. It is interrupted by a messenger from Truguelin denouncing Coelina as the illegitimate daughter of Francisque. Dufour, ignoring his son's pleas, turns them both out of the house. Andrevon has, however, denounced Truguelin to the police. The spectacular decor for the last act consists of a mountainside mill and millrace. After a chase during which an unfortunate guard is hurled from a bridge into the torrent below, Truguelin is captured. Francisque is proved to have been secretly married to Coelina's mother, thus removing the stain of illegitimacy. Stéphany is now set to inherit the family wealth and his father agrees that the marriage can proceed.

This work, one of the first and most successful of melodramas, was adapted by Pixérécourt from Ducray-Duminil's novel *Coelina* (1798). It was an immediate success, performed 387 times in Paris alone. Certain critics have seen in melodrama the decadence of tragedy. It is more likely, however, that the genre had as its source the popular boulevard genre of heroic pantomime. There the emphasis was on spectacle, and its influence can be seen in *Coelina* in the importance accorded to decor, tableaux and episodes of music and dancing, as well as in the role of Francisque, who is called upon to express in mime such complicated sentiments as his inability to lie, or his fears that Coelina will come to regret the wealth she has lost for his sake. However, as a welcome relief from pantomime, which had latterly come to contain a somewhat unhealthy supernatural element, *Coelina* was particularly praised by contemporaries for its sustained plot, its depiction of character, and the naturalness of its dialogues. There are several plot and character inconsistencies, but in the play's defence it must be said that the plot is vigorously handled and that the pomposity common in tragedy of the period is mercifully absent.

Coelina is a melodrama *par excellence* in that it exploits two of the themes most fundamental to the genre: the persecution of innocence by evil, and the call of the blood (as when Coelina is instinctively drawn to and defends her father even though ignorant of his true identity). In this work, however, innocence is personified in the form of two mistreated characters: Coelina and Francisque. Other characters typical of melodrama also appear: the good man led to believe false appearances (Dufour), the innocent booby (Michaud), and, above all, the dastardly villain (Truguelin).

Coelina is typical, too, in its settings and structures: melodramas frequently feature an enclosed space, often a garden, which is the preserve of virtue, and into which the troubler of innocence will intrude, and here it is Dufour's house and garden which have become a refuge for both Coelina and Francisque. Again, the villain is frequently driven out temporarily, as when Dufour reacts to Truguelin's plot to murder Francisque, only to return triumphant, here in the person of Truguelin's agent bringing Coelina's birth certificate. The fact that this occurs in the midst of a celebration and results in the expulsion of innocence from the enchanted domain is also typical. Innocence's recovery of its rightful position in the world depends on the persons by whom it has been judged, in this case Dufour, recognising that they are in error. It is a characteristic of virtue, however, that it cannot protest to clear its name, but merely passively resist, so that it is not by their own efforts, but rather as a result of external circumstances that the victims' true natures are recognised— here by Andrevon's denunciation to the police.

The third act of a melodrama, in what is, in effect, a version of tragic catharsis, usually consists of a highly spectacular, physical acting out of virtue's liberation from the oppressive efforts of evil. *Coelina* is no exception, with its confrontation between Francisque and Truguelin, and the latter's struggle with a band of guards and final defeat by a group of peasants. An interesting feature of the play is, however, the villain's vigorous expression of his remorse in the midst of a violent thunderstorm. Typically, the melodrama ends with the public recognition of where evil and virtue truly lie, with the one being eradicated as Truguelin is led away in chains, and the other rewarded with the renewed promise of the marriage between Coelina and Stéphany.

—Janet Clarke

THE COFFER.   See THE CHEST.

COME BACK, LITTLE SHEBA
by William Inge

First Publication: New York, 1950.
First Production: Booth Theatre, New York (Theatre Guild),
                15 February 1950.

Criticism
(For general works on the author, see *Playwrights* volume)

Articles:
Steven R. Centola, "Compromise as Bad Faith: Arthur
    Miller's *A View from the Bridge* and William Inge's *Come
    Back, Little Sheba*", in *Midwest Quarterly*, 28, 1986.

*   *   *

Set in the American middle west, the play is focused on Lola, a slatternly wife, who yearns to find her lost dog, Sheba, and on her husband, Doc, a man who hoped to one day become a medical doctor but instead ended up a chiropractor, who had had to marry Lola, because she was expecting a child. Doc goes on a destructive drunken binge but eventually tries to remain sober through Alcoholics Anonymous. Lola has a roomer, Marie, to help ends meet and this young lady, a student, is occasionally and quite casually having an affair with Turk, a javelin thrower and fellow student. This affair excites both the lust and the jealous moralist in Doc, who then gets very drunk and savagely threatens his slovenly wife. Eventually Doc goes to a hospital, sobers up, and returns home to his ineffectual wife.

Originally staged on Broadway in 1950, *Come Back, Little Sheba* was a star vehicle for Shirley Booth as the hapless and hopeless Lola, and for Sydney Blackmer as Doc, whose disappointed dreams and human errors turn him to drink and eventually to the point of murdering Lola—the symbol of his frustrations. Concurrently, Sheba, the lost puppy for whom Lola wails and whimpers and calls out, is a fairly obvious substitute for lost youth, lost hopes, and, finally, lost love: "Little Sheba should have stayed young forever".

Inge explores the workings of Alcoholics Anonymous in this play, which in its time, was both shocking and a revelation to the general public. At another level, the play concerns Marie's affair with Turk, a hunk with a one-track mind, and this stratum of *Come Back, Little Sheba* also proved shocking to audiences in its time. If Sheba is a blatant symbol of the lost years, Turk's javelin is almost an embarrassing symbol of virility and sexual acrobatics.

Lola is as bored with her life as Doc is trapped by his. Their indiscretion as youngsters has ensnared them in what today seems as quite an unnecessary relationship. When she isn't calling Sheba, Lola flirts with the mail-man and the milk-man, tries to talk to uninterested neighbors, and listens to the radio. But she is very curious about Turk and probably would not mind enjoying his favors, if he would be so obliging. And Doc secretly yearns for Marie. Both Lola and Doc are old dogs "playing old tricks". There isn't much that is subtle about the text or the sub-text of the play. Piling on the symbolism, Inge brings in lilacs which "don't last long" and neither does youth, Little Sheba, Doc's abstinence, Turk's sexual interests, and Lola's understanding of what's going on around her.

As the play progresses, the tension of Lola's whining and of Marie and Turk bedding down drive Doc to drink. Psychologically, as well as theatrically, it's all too unsubtle nowadays, but it was certainly attention-getting in the 1950's, partly because of the star performances and partly because of the racey subject matter. It was moving, exciting, and even thought-provoking and full of theatrical images. In the ending, Doc and Lola are stuck with each other. They are all they have: and to put an end to the hopes, and the play, Lola tells Doc that Little Sheba is dead and will never come back.

—Arthur Ballet

LA COMEDIA DE CALISTO Y MELIBEA. See
CELESTINA.

COMEDIANS
by Trevor Griffiths

First Publication: London, 1976; revised edition, London,
                1979.
First Production: Nottingham Playhouse, Nottingham, 20
                February 1975.

Criticism
(For general works on the author, see *Playwrights* volume)

Articles:
Craig Clinton, "Politics and Compromise: Trevor Griffiths'
    Comedians", in *Theatre Annual*, 35, 1980.
Manfred Beyer, "Trevor Griffiths' *Comedians*: Der Komiker
    als Wahrer der Menschlichkeit", in *Sprachkunst*, 20, 1989.

*   *   *

The structure of *Comedians* is that of every backstage movie of the 1930's: setting up the show (in this case, a club night that provides the culmination of a Workers Educational Association course in standup comedy), doing the show, and responses to the show that will launch some of its members to stardom.

Here, however, the structure also interrogates the politics of laughter, and through them the dialectic between reform and revolution. The course tutor, Eddie Waters, is an old-fashioned, Northern comedian who teaches humanist, comic values: "We work *through* laughter, not *for* it . . . . A true joke, a comedian's joke, has to do more than release tension, it has to *liberate* the will and the desire, it has to *change the situation*". He steers his class away from the racist and sexist stereotypes of the club comic. The group comprises several of these potential stereotypes—two Irishmen (from North and South), a Jew, a milkman. The comic style Eddie teaches them helps them to celebrate their ethnic roots and personal individuality. Faced with the chance of performing in front of Bert Challenor, a manager with the entrée to the professional, showbiz world, some of them sell out, slipping into the timeworn routine of jokes about Pakistanis and smutty innuendo, with varying degrees of confidence and success, while Mick Connor, the Irishman, sticks to his gently ironic routine about being an Irishman abroad and is told by Challenor that "people don't learn, they don't want to, and if they did, they won't look to the likes of us to teach 'em".

The play is not a straightforward confrontation between Eddie's values and Challenor's, however. There is a third way, personified in the act of Eddie's most brilliant and wayward pupil, Gethin Price. Dressed as a combination of skinhead and whiteface clown, he performs a series of complx Kung Fu exercises punctuated by football chants and finally confronts a pair of expensively dressed dummies with an aggression that grows ever greater with his frustration at their continuing silence. "You can laugh, you know, I don't mind you laughing. . .I'm *talking* to you. . .there's people who'd call this *envy*, you know, it's not, it's hate". He ends with an attack on the female dummy, pinning a flower on her which slowly forms a dark, red stain spreading over her. Challenor, predictably, dismisses this in seconds, but the subsequent debate between Eddie and Gethin is at the centre of the third act. Eddie accuses Gethin of "drowning in hate", although he admits that the act was "brilliant". Gethin accuses Eddie of forgetting his roots in the class war that made him a great comedian in the first place: "We're still caged, expoloited, prodded and pulled at, milked, fattened, slaughtered, cut up, fed out. We still don't belong to ourselves. Nothing's changed. You've just forgotten, that's all". Eddie can only counter this with a story of his personal failure as a comedian: after visiting a concentration camp just after the war he found there were "no jokes left"; he also admits that "I got an erection in that place", an admission whose implications neither he nor Gethin seems fully to understand.

The frequent stage directions describing Price's delivery as "perfect"—he's the only one who can manage the loaded tonguetwister "The Traitor Distrusts Truth"—his ability to anticipate Eddie's points in class, his slick parody of him, and his final exit, in which he declares his intention to "wait for it to happen", suggest that Griffiths' sympathies lie with his revolutionary energy. There is, however, a deeply disturbing sexism about Gethin which is never fully articulated. At the beginning of the play he improvises an obscene limerick that sparks off Eddie's sermon on stereotypes. At the end of his act he talks across, not to, the female dummy before literally "penetrating" her. If Eddie has gone soft on old-style revolution, Gethin remains true to its failure to question gender roles. Interesting dynamics were created by an all woman version of *Comedians* at the Liverpool Festival of Comedy in 1985, devised by Griffiths and a group of experienced female comedians. Gethin / Glenys' act remained much the same, but its meaning altered simply by virtue of her sex; the obscenities became a measure of a sexual consciousness only partially

raised; her attack on the male dummy became not an act of rape but the revenge of a flower-seller, a member not just of an oppressed class but of a sex relegated to the bottom of that class.

—Frances Gray

THE COMEDY OF ERRORS
by William Shakespeare

First Publication: London, 1623.
First Production: London, c. 1591–1594; first recorded production, Gray's Inn, December 1594.

Editions
The Comedy of Errors, edited by Sir Arthur Quiller Couch and John Dover Wilson, Cambridge, 1962 (The New Shakespeare).
The Comedy of Errors, edited by R.A. Foakes, London, 1962 (The Arden Shakespeare).
The Comedy of Errors, edited by Paul A. Jorgensen, Baltimore, Maryland, 1964 (Pelican Shakespeare).
The Comedy of Errors, edited by Harry Levin, New York and London, 1965 (Signet Classic Shakespeare).
The Comedy of Errors, edited by Stanley Wells, Harmondsworth, 1972 (New Penguin Shakespeare).
The Comedy of Errors, edited by T.S. Dorsch, Cambridge, 1988 (New Cambridge Shakespeare).

Criticism
(For general works on the author, see *Playwrights* volume)

Books:
T.W. Baldwin, *On the Compositional Genetics of "The Comedy of Errors"*, Urbana, Illinois, 1965.
Laurie L. Harris (ed.), *"The Comedy of Errors"*, in *Shakespearian Criticism 1*, Detroit, Illinois, 1984 (anthology of criticism).

Articles:
For information on articles about *The Comedy of Errors*, see the bibliographies listed in the *Playwrights* volume and the annual Shakespeare Bibliography in *Shakespeare Quarterly*, published by the Folger Shakespeare Library, Washington D.C. (1950–).

*   *   *

Based on Plautus' *Menaechmi*, Shakespeare's early comedy improves on its source by fielding not one, but two, sets of identical twins, a feature possibly derived from another play by Plautus, *Amphitruo*. One pair, both called Dromio, had been bought from a poor woman to be reared as servants to the other pair, both called Antipholus. During a shipwreck while the four were still infants, each pair of brothers was divided so that one Antipholus and one Dromio were left with Antipholus's father, Egeon, while the other two were apparently lost with Egeon's wife, Aemilia.

The play is set in the city of Ephesus where an Antipholus (of Syracuse) and his attendant Dromio arrive, unaware that their twins are living there. They are immediately mistaken for the

The Comedy of Errors: Stratford-Upon-Avon, 1990 (Royal Shakespeare Company)

resident pair, and confusions multiply as masters and servants begin to identify each other wrongly. The unremarkable, social arrangements of Antipholus of Ephesus (a disgruntled wife, a friendly Courtesan, a transaction with a goldsmith) become the focus of extraordinary passion and anxiety as the unwitting visitors encounter the natives.

The play is predominantly a farce: mistaken identity is the apparently inexhaustible source of comic confusion, and characterization is basic. But it is also a romance, at least in the action of the framing story, based on Gower's tale of *Apollonius of Tyre*: Egeon, looking in vain for the Syracusian twins who have set out to find their other halves, arrives at Ephesus and falls foul of a law against merchants from Syracuse. He will lose his life unless a large forfeit is paid. Our knowledge of the twins' history comes from his speech of explanation to the Duke of Ephesus, and it is a masterpiece of tragi-comic writing, subtly designed to guide our responses to the rest of the play, at once satisfying our reason with factual detail, while stretching our credulity with preposterous coincidences. "A heavier task could not have been imposed / Than I to speak my griefs unspeakable", says Egeon, warming to his theme, and apparently innocent of the self-contradictory pun. With loving detail he describes the fastening of the mixed pairs of babies to opposite ends of a spare mast, the breaking of the mast against a rock which resulted in the exact division of his family, and the appearance of two rescuing ships which then completed the work of Fortune and compounded this "unjust divorce". The prophecy of a happy ending is latent in Egeon's account: all the indicators suggesting a romance are there, ones which Shakespeare was to use again, more fully, in

Pericles, when he returned to Gower's tale and allowed Pericles, like Egeon, to find his long-lost wife in a religious order in Ephesus.

Before the family can be reunited, domestic and social situations involving the twins demonstrate how an individual's sense of identity is rooted in his relationships: if you know who your husband / wife / master / servant is, then you know who you are. If doubt is cast on these certainties, the play implies, the state totters. In Ephesus, financial transactions too confirm identity. Egeon must pay 1,000 marks to preserve his life there; the first anxiety of Antipholus of Syracuse (the result of a conversation with the wrong Dromio) is that his gold has been misappropriated; later, Antipholus of Ephesus is arrested for debt when his money is mistakenly given to his brother. Possession of money is the barometer of well-being, just as the whereabouts of a gold chain indicates the state of Antipholus of Ephesus's marriage: the chain was intended as a gift for his wife Adriana but, doubting her fidelity (she is unknowingly entertaining his brother), he offers it instead to the Courtesan, and confirms this substitute relationship by taking a ring from her.

Displacement is one of the governing principles of the action and the focusing of the audience's visual attention on two pairs of twins makes the interplay clear. The new, strange, or unaccountable must either occupy the space belonging to the known, or be excluded by it. Much of the comedy arises from characters' attempts to make what they see tally with what they think they know so that the familiar pattern of life will be preserved. The most usual recourse is to accuse others who are behaving aberrantly of madness or satanic possession, and the visitors can only account for their reception by regarding Ephesus (perhaps in the light of its biblical reputation) as a place of sorcery and enchantment, full of false appearances.

To the characters in this play illusion is threatening, and its potential as a means of access to a new kind of truth (as in, perhaps, *A Midsummer Night's Dream*, or *The Winter's Tale*) is limited to a brief moment in Antipholus of Syracuse's wooing of Luciana, Adriana's sister, when he, instead of rejecting her mistaken view of him, offers himself for transformation: "Are you a god? Would you create me new?". But the moment passes, and in the rest of the play, love is presented as an uneasy compromise between freedom and possession in marriage. Adriana's jealousy when she thinks herself supplanted, and her unwillingness to accept what she assumes is her husband's divided attention, reflects the whole city's problems with the duality of the twins. Only a rigid insistence on the single and individual seems to be able to preserve this world from chaos. The Duke, seeing the brothers together for the first time, can only accept the reality of one: "One of these men is *genius* to the other; /. . .which is the natural man, / And which the spirit?". The Dromios alone offer the radical solution and point the way out of farce into romance. They accept their doubleness and choose to leave the stage together: "We came into the world like brother and brother, / And now lets go hand in hand, not one before another".

—Joanna Udall

COMEDY, SATIRE, IRONY AND DEEPER MEANING
(Scherz, Satire, Ironie, und tiefere Bedeutung)
by Christian Dietrich Grabbe

First Publication: in *Dramatische Dichtungen von Grabbe*, Frankfurt, 1827.
First Production: Akademietheater, Vienna, December 1876 (private performance); Schauspielhaus, Munich, May 1907 (public performance).

Editions
Scherz, Satire, Ironie, und tiefere Bedeutung, in *Hannibal; Napoleon oder die hundert Tage; Scherz, Satire, Ironie, und tiefere Bedeutung*, Stuttgart, 1943.
Scherz, Satire, Ironie, und tiefere Bedeutung, in *Werke*, edited by Roy C. Cowen, Munich, 1975–77 (3 vols.).

Translations
Comedy, Satire, Irony and Deeper Meaning, translated by Barbara Wright, London, 1955.

*   *   *

Comedy, Satire, Irony and Deeper Meaning (*Scherz, Satire, Ironie und tiefere Bedeutung*) by Christian Dietrich Grabbe takes us through a chaotic but essentially slight action in three acts. Liddy, niece of Baron von Haldungen, and fiancée of Baron Wernthal, attracts the attentions of the rascally Freiherr von Mordax. Wernthal is prepared to solve his financial problems by throwing Liddy into the arms of Mordax in exchange for a consideration, but the threatened and betrayed heroine is rescued by the upright, though physically repulsive Mollfels, whom she finally marries.

Such a summary scarcely does justice to the sheer exuberance and pace of Grabbe's play and perhaps more important than this trite and unremarkable central action are the numerous scenes given over to minor characters, such as the scheming and bibulous local schoolmaster, the poet Rattengift (Ratsbane), the Devil, the Devil's grandmother, and Grabbe himself, who as a wellknown drunkard, arrives in time to participate in the final booze-up. These are the scenes which are informed by Grabbe's puckish sense of fun and his love of the incongruous, and constitute vehicles for his often whimsical, but often very bitter, satire and irony.

The unconventional nature of the play, written in 1822 and published in 1827, is probably its most striking feature. Not surprisingly, the predilection for grotesque and absurd effects ensured that no producer dared risk putting it on the stage, and it had to wait until 1907 to be performed. The title indicates the various levels of humour embodied in the main action and the sub-plots. Occasionally these are characterised by a rather juvenile desire to *épater les bourgeois* (the Devil, for instance, is captured by the local schoolmaster in a trap baited with condoms). Often they are genuinely funny: the Devil has left Hell to escape the spring-cleaning and now passes himself off as a high-ranking Lutheran pastor by the name of Dr. Theophilus Teufel. Finding it cold on earth, he surprises the assembly on one occasion by going and sitting in the lighted stove. His oaths invert the normal ones: "God take him", or "Go to God", and he amazes the local smith when he requests him to shoe his cloven hoof. ("Horse's foot" in German usage). Other scenes startle in their incongruity or absurdity: in exchange for the Devil's help in winning Liddy, Mordax ("Murderex") has to promise to allow his son to study philosophy and to kill 13 journeyman tailors, a task he duly carries out in a scene entirely free of dialogue (Act III, scene 2). But it is the satirical element that predominates. Grabbe never tires of mocking the stupidity of the academic establishment and the insipidity of contemporary cultural and literary life. His "typical" poet, Rattengift, spends most of the play trying to write a poem, but never gets beyond the first line, which runs: "I sat at my table and chewed pens". Nor does he

Comedy, Satire, Irony and Deeper Meaning: Woodcut by Karl Thylmann, c. 1915 (published in edition of play, Munich 1915)

spare classical German literature, which is well-known in Hell: Schiller's Posa has opened a pub there called the Queen Elizabeth Arms and does a nice side-line as a procurer (a very palpable hit at *Don Carlos*). But Grabbe's real *bêtes noires* are contemporary female writers such as Elise von Hohenhausen or Louise Brachmann, the latter being a lady, we are told, to whom the local fishmonger is deeply indebted, since her works provide paper to wrap herrings in. Ironically, it is Grabbe's satire that has preserved the names of these literary ladies from the oblivion that would otherwise have been their fate.

Amusing and effective though such sallies are, it is the play's anticipation of many future developments in the theatre that makes it remarkable. In an age that still saw classicism as the apogee of cultural achievement, Grabbe wrote a play in which non-reality and absurdity are central, and which foreshadows the Expressionists in its readiness to break the illusion of the stage. For example Mordax and Wernthal escape their just punishment by pointing out that actors have no legal powers and climbing into the orchestra, where they have friends amongst the musicians. In much the same way, Grabbe's own appearance as a character on the stage is intended to destroy the illusion, while the monstrous ugliness of Mollfels as the gallant lover mocks all the accepted conventions of the stage and produces a sort of alienation effect. Grabbe does not seek to create characters, but satirical caricatures who correspond, in their grotesqueness, to the grotesque quality of the action. Caricature and satire are, of course, as old as drama itself, but Grabbe is remote from established concepts such as *castigo ridendo mores*, and the butts of his satire are not merely the traditional deluded and abnormal types who exist in an essentially normal and sane world. As Grabbe remarked to his publisher, behind the comedy and absurdity, his play makes the same point as his nihilistic tragedy, *Herzog Theodor von Gothland* (a youthful conflation of influences deriving from Schiller's *The Robbers, Titus Andronicus*, and Kleist's *Family Schroffenstein*) and his satire is far from affirming the world as we know it by castigating aberrations from the norm. Rather he takes us into a nihilistic, bedlamite world where everyone and everything is, to a greater or lesser degree, absurd or mad. Sense, reason, the normal processes of logic are lost. The whole world is unhinged. There is neither morality nor immorality. Reality is, at worst, meaningless, at best, incapable of comprehension, and the way out of the dilemma posed by an insane world is not to seek to understand it, but to laugh at it. The "deeper meaning" behind the jest, the satire, and the irony, is that the world is a pointless joke in bad taste from which only alcohol can procure temporary relief. It is the confession of a man who sought meaning in the world and could find none and whose very laughter is thus a cry of despair.

—W. A. Coupe

THE CONQUEST OF GRANADA, BY THE SPANISH, Parts One and Two
by John Dryden

Part One
First Publication: London, 1672.
First Production: Theatre Royal, Bridges Street, London, c. December 1670.

Part Two
First Production: London, 1672.
First Production: Theatre Royal, Bridges Street, London, January 1671.

Editions
The Conquest of Granada, in *John Dryden*, edited by George Saintsbury, New York, 1904 (2 vols.).
The Conquest of Granada, in *Selected Dramas of John Dryden, with "The Rehearsal" by George Villiers*, edited by George R. Noyes, Chicago, 1910.
The Conquest of Granada (Parts One and Two) in *John Dryden. Dramatic Works*, edited by Montague Summers, London, (6 vols.) 1931–32.

Criticism
(For general works on the author, see *Playwrights* volume)

Books:
Eugene M. Waith, *The Herculean Hero in Marlowe, Shakespeare, and Dryden*, London and New York, 1962.

Articles:
Jean Gagen, "Love and Honour in Dryden's Heroic Plays", in *Publications of the Modern Language Association* [*PMLA*], 77, 1962.

*   *   *

The play has a historical setting: Granada in the period of its reconquest by the Spaniards in the 15th century. The Moorish King of Granada, Boabdelin, sees his power disintegrate in the quarrel between two factions at his court, the Zegrys and the Abencerrages. The main plot deals with the heroic feats of the noble stranger Almanzor who brings victory to whichever side he supports. He falls in love with Almahide who has promised to marry Boabdelin, but agrees to the union with Almanzor after the Moorish king's death and the victory of the Spaniards. Almanzor turns out to be descended from Spanish noble parentage. Two subsidiary plots concern the rivalry of Abdallah and Abdelmelech for the love of the ambitious schemer Lyndaraxa and the love of a noble couple from the warring Moorish factions, Ozmyn and Benzayda.

Dryden's double play, two five-act pieces that were first produced separately, but as one heroic drama in all productions after 1671, marks the culminating point in the short flowering of the heroic play in England. It is an idealized variant of the definition of a play that Dryden had formulated in his *Of Dramatic Poesy* (1668): "A just and lively image of human nature, representing its passions and humours, and the changes of fortune to which it is subject, for the delight and instruction of mankind". The "Essay of Heroic Plays" with which Dryden prefaced the first book edition of 1672, in the dedication to the Duke of York, qualified Dryden's Aristotelean standpoint by specifying "ideal imitation" as the new genre's object, by pointing to the heroic poem as his literary model, stressing the imagination as its creative mode, and also by justifying the reproduction of a courtly setting and larger-than-life characters. Besides having all these characteristics, *The Conquest of Granada* uses the model of heroic poetry to paint a broad, epic canvas into which the exalted rulers and two contrasting noble couples function as the main sources of "admiration" (i.e., "wonder"). This Dryden saw as the dominant effect the writers of heroic plays were aiming at since Sir William Davenant introduced the form to the English stage after the Restoration.

The play's complex narrative allows Dryden to combine a number of individual fates with the opposing forces in the Spanish reconquest of Granada. The setting alternates unevenly between the Moorish and the Christian camps and their factions. Perhaps surprisingly, the perspective is almost entirely on the Arab kingdom, not on the Spanish court of Ferdinand and Isabella. The scenes involving the noble lovers, Benzayda and Ozmyn, from the warring factions of the Zegrys and the Abencerrages give a distinct echo of the Romeo and Juliet motif, and these characters finally bring about the reconciliation of their families. Similarly, the central pair of lovers, Almanzor and Almahide, re-enact, in their final union, the arrival of a liberal, Christian rule over Granada. But as in most epic-type drama, historical movement is not completely absorbed in individual lives. There is a broader process of decadence and dissension in the Arab kingdom of Granada only incompletely synchronized with the stratagems of the potential usurper, Prince Abdalla, King Boabdelin's brother, and the ambitious plans of his female antagonist, Lyndaraxa.

Dryden's contemporaries were aware of the analogies of the historical action to their own time. The heroic, military exploits of the almost superhuman Almanzor express an extended eulogy on the King's brother, the Duke of York. The strange reversal of roles between the opposing Moorish factions—the intolerant Muslim Zegrys actually doing more for the downfall of the kingdom than the Abencerrages in their humane pro-Christian attitudes—points to a polemical contrast between English Puritans and loyal Roman Catholics under Charles II. At a deeper thematic level, Dryden uses the historical scenes as an illustration of a teleology of historical change. Justice is brought about by the doing of lawless and ambitious men, who unwittingly do God's work by making the virtuous prevail and by destroying the unjust. This idealistic trust in a superior logic behind human agency—which is close to legitimistic, political theory of Restoration thinkers like Sir Robert Filmer—is responsible for the optimistic outcome of Dryden's heroic plays. At the end of *The Conquest of Granada* the path is clear for Almanzor's and Queen Almahide's love, and for—harmony between the vanquished Moors and the Christian Spaniards incorporating them in their benevolent regime.

The play's salient, formal qualities accentuate the idealist transcendence over realistic representation. Before Dryden changed his mind about rhyme in plays, he used rhymed heroic couplets in his heroic drama. The characterization leaves little scope for psychology, but adheres to a melodramatic system of black and white stereotyping. Therefore, Almanzor's central conflict between love and honour, obviously based on the French *tragédie classique* and Mlle. de Scudéry's prose romances, makes for splendid, rhetorical elaboration rather than any realistic, psychological grounding. In some of the long monologues this rhetoric descends into plain rant and stretches the suspension of disbelief beyond most later audiences' limits.

The transformation of the play's high pathos into melodrama, the rhetorical stylization of the dialogues—both point to the difficulties Dryden encountered in legitimating the heroic in an essentially unheroic period. The result is an almost operatic quality in this play, as in most heroic plays. Dryden shared with the then new form of the opera the reliance on the effect of "admiration". His attempt at a reconstruction of the heroic can only describe an idealized, social hierarchy by employing a less than exclusive rhetorical mode. It was no accident that the burlesque of Dryden's heroic plays that followed soon after *The Conquest of Granada* (and in the same theatre where Nell Gwynne had been playing Almahide) should have come from within the courtly élite (in the Duke of

Buckingham's *The Rehearsal*). Later on, the German dramatist Lessing voiced a bourgeois aesthetic by calling "admiration" the effect appropriate to the rabble. It was in this historical conjuncture that Dryden's finely constructed, sophisticatedly-rhymed, heroic play fell into theatrical, if not academic, oblivion.

—Bernd-Peter Lange

THE CONSCIOUS LOVERS
by Sir Richard Steele

First Publication: London, 1723.
First Production: Theatre Royal, Drury Lane, c. 8 November, 1722.

Editions

The Conscious Lovers, in *Richard Steele*, edited by G.A. Aitken, London, 1903.
The Conscious Lovers, in *Eighteenth Century Comedy*, edited by W.D. Taylor, London, 1929.
The Conscious Lovers, edited by Shirley Strum Kenny, Lincoln, Nebraska, 1967 (Regents Restoration Drama Series).
The Conscious Lovers, in *The Plays of Sir Richard Steele*, edited by Shirley Strum Kenny, Oxford, 1971.

Criticism

(For general works on the author, see *Playwrights* volume)

Articles:
Rodney M. Baine, "The Publication of Steele's *Conscious Lovers*", in *Studies in Bibliography*, 2, 1949–50.
John Loftis, "The Genesis of Steele's *The Conscious Lovers*", in *Essays Critical and Historical Dedicated to Lily B. Campbell*, Berkeley and Los Angeles, 1950.
Dieter Schultz, "Richard Steele—*The Conscious Lovers*", in *Das Englische Drama im 18 und 19. Jahrhundert*, 1976.
W. Gerald Marshall, "'Joy too exquisite for laughter': A Re-Evaluation of Steele's *The Conscious Lovers*", in *Literature and Belief*, 4, 1984.

*   *   *

This play was first performed at the Drury Lane Theatre, London, in 1722, but the author had begun to write it as early as 1713. This was Steele's fourth and last play and it was also the one which brought him the most fame and money. He took the plot from Terence's *Andria* although he made a few changes to adapt it to his own idea of what the "new" English comedy should be. Colley Cibber contributed to this adaptation and he also participated in both the final writing of the script and in its production.

The action of the comedy begins on the day when the hero, Bevil Junior, is to marry Lucinda, thereby complying with the wishes of his father, Sir John Bevil. But Bevil Junior is, in fact, in love with a poor, unknown lady called Indiana, and Lucinda's father (Mr. Sealand, a wealthy merchant) knowing this, is suspicious although keen on the match. Bevil Junior's best friend, Myrtle, is in love with Lucinda, who returns his love. In order to achieve their goals without arousing suspicion, Bevil and Lucinda make use of their respective servants, Tom and Phillis, (without doubt the most comic characters in the whole play and in love with each other). The plot becomes complicated when Mrs. Sealand, Lucinda's mother, plans to marry her with Cimberton, a ridiculous character, the typical coxcomb of 17th-century English comedy, and a member of the aristocracy.

The young couples strive to overcome the obstacles which stand in the way of their unions, while their fathers negotiate the financial terms of the marriage contract. After a series of incidents in which Myrtle disguises himself twice and he and Bevil Junior almost fight a duel caused by unfounded jealousy, the problems are resolved by the discovery that Indiana is Sealand's long-lost daughter from a previous marriage and is therefore acceptable in the eyes of Sir John Bevil. Now Myrtle can marry Lucinda, especially as Cimberton decides he no longer wants her when he finds out she will have to share her dowry with her newly found half-sister.

The play was a great success, so much so that it was performed 18 times in succession (something unusual then) and republished many times in the 18th century. This success was largely due to the quality of the production—the chronicles of the time gave praise to the lavish costumes and scenery and to the performers—but above all to the fact that the playwright fully satisfied the audience's expectations. One must bear in mind that at this time the theatre attracted mainly a bourgeois audience who wished to see situations on stage which corresponded to their own lives. Steele had already published his ideas about a new type of comedy which combined humour with pathos and presented virtuous characters, edifying customs, and a refined language, all with a didactic aim. In short, *The Conscious Lovers* was the model for what was called "genteel drama" which later became known as "sentimental comedy". This play is not the first work of this genre but it is the best representative of it.

The humour in this play lies mainly in the role of the servants, while their superiors are the protagonists of the complications in the plot. Some of them tend to be highly sentimental, for instance, as in the scene which halts the duel and saves the friendship of both Bevil Jr. and Myrtle. The very last scene, when Sealand discovers his long-lost daughter, produces a very emotive situation between Sealand, Isabella (his sister), and Indiana. Terence's capricious ending—the result of an accumulation of coincidences—becomes in Steele's comedy a scene of great pathos where the virtuous behaviour of his characters is rewarded.

The author, in putting his theoretical ideas into practice, was also defending his own political sympathies: on the one hand, he put an end to the social satire and the crude language of Restoration drama, and on the other hand, he exalted the merchant class through the character of Sealand—his name itself is significant—as an emblem of the power of the bourgeoisie. The continuous references to the business world, to the sentimental aspects of life, and to the virtuous behaviour of the characters correspond perfectly with the whig ideology of the author.

The two outstanding aspects in this play are the comic subplot with the servants Tom and Phillis—they try to imitate, ironically, the customs of their superiors—and the author's attempt at psychological characterization. This play represents a significant move away from Restoration drama, although a few traits of this period are evident in the caricatures of Cimberton and Mrs. Sealand. Today, interest in *The Conscious Lovers* is mainly historical due to the great influence it exerted over the English theatre of the time.

—Rafael Portillo and Juan Carlos Hidalgo Cuidad

THE CONTRACTOR
by David Storey

First Publication: London, 1970.
First Production: Royal Court Theatre, London, 20 October 1969.

Criticism
(For general works on the author, see *Playwrights* volume)

Articles:
James E. Porter, "*The Contractor*: David Storey's Static Drama", in *University of Windsor Review*, 15, 1979–80.

*   *   *

The main action of *The Contractor* is the realistic erection, decoration, and subsequent dismantling of a marquee used to celebrate the main event of the play—a wedding that takes place offstage between Act II and Act III. Four workmen and their foreman put up the tent and are ordered about, cajoled, and sometimes helped by the contractor himself, Ewbank. His daughter, Claire, is the bride-to-be. Completing the cast of characters are the bridegroom, who is a young doctor, Ewbank's son Paul, Ewbank's wife, and his elderly parents. As the marquee is constructed and dismantled the characters' interaction creates a portrait of British society with its class and generational differences, while also posing questions about work, family, art, progress, and human relations.

Storey provides little in the way of plot, conflict, or character development, but the physical task of putting up the tent instantly compels. How will it be done? Will it work? His structure is Chekhovian in that his focus is on a group of characters whose comings and goings build up atmosphere and texture through a welter of social detail: characters are defined through language, the observance of social rituals, consumption of food, and jokes—particularly about work and social relationships. The music-like structure of Chekhov is also apparent in the blending and repetition of themes and phrases, the fluid transitions from duet to quartet to ensemble and so on, and the orchestration of characters.

Ewbank, for no given reasons other than cheapness employs social misfits whom no-one else will hire. The foreman, Kay, has served time for embezzlement, and Mrs. Ewbank comments, "They've been had up for a lot of things. The men that work for you". The two Irishmen, Fitzpatrick and Marshall are the liveliest; their bickering on occasion borders on a stand-up comedy routine. Denny is mentally disabled, but despite some rough teasing is ultimately protected by his workmates. Ewbank favors him with extra treats: a bun, a second piece of wedding-cake. Bennett is a chronic complainer, but it turns out his wife has just left him. Other snippets about the characters' lives emerge through their banter, petty altercations, and teasing, and it is clear that there is little personal trust between them. However, what unites them is work, accomplished with ease, co-operation, and efficiency, led by Ewbank whose pride in the art of tentmaking tempers his general irascibility. They are misfits in the outside world but a functioning unit in their work.

The workmen are not the only misfits. Ewbank has risen from artisan to management and has become wealthy, but he seems dislocated, spending most of the play unnecessarily hovering over his workers and neglecting the wedding guests arriving in his house. His son is even more dislocated. His father's success has bought him a university education but he is as ill-at-ease with his doctor brother-in-law as with his family or the workmen. He wanders in and out, hands in his pockets, sometimes joining the men at work. Old Ewbank has become senile and lives in the past when he was a rope-maker. He roams about clutching his bits of rope, cursing progress and machines: "If I had my time again I'd burn the bloody lot."

Class structure emphasizes the dislocation of the characters. Most obviously it separates those who put up the tent from those who use it. Of Ewbank it is said, "He never really found his proper station in life". That he is more at ease with the workers points up that money does not erase class roots, nor, in Paul's case, does education. Yet they uphold the form and emphasize the surface barriers through the cursory ritual of offering the workers a quick drink and piece of cake after the work is completed. Storey also shows barriers between generations. Old Ewbank understands little of his son or his grandchildren and has escaped into madness. Ewbank bewails the modern world to Kay: "It's left you and me behind". He does not understand his children, and his usefulness to them has been reduced to money.

The idea of usefulness is inherent in the title of the play. Contracts establish terms of use. Ewbank is, by profession, a contractor, and has contracted with his men to put up the marquee. The central, though unseen, event of the play is the signing of a marriage contract. Other social contracts are at issue in the play, defined by family and class relationships. While the most meaningful contract seems to be the work contract, bringing temporary harmony to the workers, the social contracts are shakier, the terms vaguer.

Work brings people together in Storey's world. On the other hand what remains after work are a few holes in the perfectly manicured lawn. The creative act, work, is followed by use, resultant chaos, dismantling, and final disappearance. Is Storey suggesting a pessimistic metaphor for life? For art? For human achievement? Storey's play certainly functions on a polyvalent, metaphorical level and while the ultimate message may have little cheery to say beyond the healing capabilities of work and community, *The Contractor* has a vibrant comedic energy. The tape-recorder accuracy of the language, with its spectrum of accents from Yorkshire to Irish, working class to upper class, is a key factor in the comic energy, as is Storey's skillful juxtaposition of character and character detail, such as Denny's insatiable hunger and his unfailing good humor, Ewbank's outbursts of irritability and his repeated condolences to Kay for having four daughters.

Through the central action of putting-up a tent, Storey creates a richly textured play. It is naturalistic in some of its detail, particularly its accordance of real and stage time, its language, its implication of the power of heredity and environment, but *The Contractor* is just as much a play of poetry and metaphor which explores implications of class, social, and work contracts and the whole nature of human endeavor.

—Elizabeth Swain

THE CORAL. See **THE GAS TRILOGY.**

LES CORBEAUX. See **THE VULTURES.**

CORIOLANUS
by William Shakespeare

First Publication: London, 1623.
First Production: London, probably c.1607–1610.

Editions

Coriolanus, edited by H.H. Furness Jr., Philadelphia, 1928 (New Variorum Shakespeare).
Coriolanus, edited by Harry Levin, Baltimore, 1956 (Pelican Shakespeare).
The Tragedy of Coriolanus, edited by John Dover Wilson, Cambridge, 1960 (The New Shakespeare).
Coriolanus, edited by Reuben Brower, New York, Scarborough (Ontario), and London, 1966 (Signet Classic Shakespeare); revised edition, 1987.
Coriolanus, edited by G.R. Hibbard, Harmondsworth, 1967 (New Penguin Shakespeare).
Coriolanus, edited by Maurice Harmon, Dublin, 1972 (Malone Shakespeare).
Coriolanus, edited by Philip Brockbank, London and New York, 1976 (Arden Shakespeare).

Criticism
(For general works on the author, see *Playwrights* volume)

Books:
James E. Phillips (ed.), *Twentieth Century Interpretations of "Coriolanus"*, Englewood Cliffs, New Jersey, 1970.
Clifford C. Huffman, *"Coriolanus" in Context*, Lewisburg, Pennsylvania, 1971.
Leigh Holt, *From Man to Dragon: A Study of Shakespeare's "Coriolanus"*, Salzburg, 1976.
Brian Vickers (ed.), *Coriolanus*, London, 1976.
Bennett A. Brockman (ed.), *Shakespeare's "Coriolanus": A Casebook*, London, 1977 (anthology of criticism).
Jean-Paul Debax and Yves Peyré (eds.), *"Coriolan": Théâtre et politique*, Toulouse, 1984.
Harold Bloom (ed.), *William Shakespeare's "Coriolanus"*, New York, 1988.
Bruce King, *Coriolanus*, London, 1989.
Mark W. Scott and Sandra L. Williamson (eds.), *"Coriolanus"* in *Shakespearian Criticism 9*, Detroit, Illinois, 1989 (anthology of criticism).

Articles:
For information on the many articles about *Coriolanus*, see the bibliographies listed in the *Playwrights* volume and the annual Shakespeare Bibliography in *Shakespeare Quarterly*, published by the Folger Shakespeare Library, Washington D.C. (1950–).

* * *

Coriolanus was Shakespeare's last tragedy. He adapted the story of the Roman warrior who was unable to accommodate himself to the rituals of civic office from Thomas North's translation of Plutarch's *Lives of the Noble Grecians and Romans*, 1579.

Caius Martius wins a great victory over the Volscians at Corioli, from which city he takes his cognomen, Coriolanus, awarded as a testament to his valour. On his return to Rome he is persuaded to seek the office of consul, but his testy behaviour towards the plebeians, who had suffered not only from war but from famine, enables their tribunes to procure his banishment. He leaves Rome and seeks refuge at the house of

Coriolanus: Ian McKellen as Coriolanus, National Theatre, London, 1984

Aufidius, general of the Volscians and his erstwhile enemy, and then leads a Volscian army back towards Rome to exact a revenge on his city. His mother Volumnia, at the head of a delegation, which also includes his wife and son, persuades him to turn back. After withdrawing to Antium, a Volscian town, he is publicly murdered by a faction of conspirators led by Aufidius.

This austere play has seemed to some commentators to be more of a debate than a tragedy; Bernard Shaw, responding to the way there are no characters with whom an audience might easily empathize, thought it Shakespeare's best *comedy*. The verse is spare and functional, the action is studded with the clamour of battle, and although the family of Coriolanus plays an important role in the play, the hero displays an inability to form easy relationships with anyone. Like many of the later tragic heroes, Coriolanus withdraws from his society, thus increasing his isolation. Human interest, however, is to be found not only in men's private lives, and like so many other Shakespearean texts, *Coriolanus* addresses itself to hard political questions: should valour, in a post-feudal age, be the basis of honour? Is a charismatic military leader necessarily the best head of the body politic? Patricians are set against plebeians, and when, in a set piece, Meninius Agrippa friend to Coriolanus, attempts to defend patrician authority and privilege by a parable which purports to vindicate the domi-nance of the belly (symbol for the patriciate), an audience might be aware more of mutual dependence and the special pleading of a humorous old man. The writing of the play may have been catalysed by English grain riots in 1607, yet it is impossible from the text to locate Shakespeare's own opinions concerning aristocracy and democracy. There are no obvious ways of legitimising either political order.

At the beginning of the 19th century Hazlitt had some fine things to say about the "insolence of power" displayed by Coriolanus, and Bertolt Brecht, who made a notable adaptation of the play, pointed out that Coriolanus seems to have much more in common with the enemy of his nation, Aufidius, than with his fellow citizens. The plebeians do not deserve the vilification cast upon them and their suffering might be brought out in a production of the play, but, on the other hand, they are ill served by their representatives, the Tribunes Sicinius Velutus and Junius Brutus, who, it might seem, procure the banishment of Coriolanus mainly because they fear their own political eclipse.

The play also focuses on the effects of the political rites of passage on the personality of Coriolanus. In performance, audiences may be aware of a contrast between the hero's bravura actions and the poetic presentations of him as an aristocratic, Herculean hero on the one hand, and his emotional restrictedness and immaturity on the other. His image seems studied, and audiences suspect, with the First Citizen, that his patriotism may derive from a compulsive attempt to please his mother, and that in his love of war is a substitute for emotions and feelings. The effects of his upbringing at Volumnia's hands seem to have disqualified him for family life: he compliments his wife Virgilia as his "gracious silence" and we have glimpses of single-minded savagery in his son. There is, however, no key to his personality, as Shakespeare brings out at the end of Act 4 where Aufidius is given a long and important speech which sceptically offers a catalogue of alternative "readings" of the hero. The death of Coriolanus is sudden and brutal, the hero is given little to indicate that he has won through adversity to tragic recognition. But earlier we have glimpses that he is no mere automaton as when, for example, he cryptically and paradoxically admits: "I play the man I am".

The play was not a preferred vehicle for the great Shakespeareans of the 18th century, and in the 19th century productions tended to be notable for their scenic grandeur rather than their political insight. Mrs. Siddons, however, played Volumnia in 1806 with her brother John Kemble who, as Coriolanus, seemed to contemporaries to have created his finest performance in a glorious incarnation of "Roman manliness". In our times Olivier shone in the role, at the Old Vic in 1938 and again in 1959 in a production directed by Peter Hall. Ian Richardson, Ian Hogg, Nicol Williamson, and Alan Howard have been notable Coriolanuses at Stratford-Upon-Avon. The play's problematizing of militarism has spawned a long series of productions and adaptations in Germany, the most notable of which is the unfinished adaptation by Bertolt Brecht which concedes the usefulness of Coriolanus as a machine for war but demonstrates how a state might grow out of the need for such heroes, having taken away from the text many of the passages which celebrate heroism. *The Plebeians Rehearse the Uprising* by Günter Grass (1966) suggests that Brecht had in fact become more interested in revolt in the theatre than revolution in the streets.

—Michael Hattaway

THE CORN IS GREEN
by Emlyn Williams

First Publication: London, 1938.
First Production: Duchess Theatre, London, 20 September 1938.

*　　*　　*

For its first audience, in the midst of economic depression, *The Corn Is Green* was an offbeat fairy tale. Miss Moffatt, a middle-aged woman of tremendous energy, founds a school in the Welsh valleys in the teeth of local opposition and discovers an untutored genius, Morgan Evans, whom she manages, at last, to send to Oxford. It gave Sybil Thorndike and countless actresses after her a rich and original character to play, a spinster of intellect and power who was neither a figure of fun nor tragically crossed in love, and explored, as few plays had previously, the complexities of the teacher-pupil relationship with all its subtle shifts of power. What strikes one today, however, is less the Cinderella aspects of the tale than the ambiguities and contradictions raised by the interplay between the play's novel collection of characters and its conventional three-act structure. Williams provides the staple necessity of the well-made plays—a strong "curtain" at the end of the second act. Just as Miss Moffatt is organising Morgan's vital examination she is interrupted by the housekeeper's daughter who announces that Morgan has made her pregnant and demanding marriage. Miss Moffatt manages to prevent Morgan from overhearing and the curtain falls as he is quietly writing his answers—but of course we know that after the interval he will discover the truth.

Williams wraps up the question neatly with a bittersweet conclusion. Miss Moffatt persuades Morgan to take the scholarship which he has, of course, won, and takes on the upbringing of his child herself. For her, this is both painful, because it means that they can never meet again ("It would be madness for you to come into contact with the child")—and an opportunity for a new kind of life. When Morgan protests she points out to him that this is a solution for the mature man he must suddenly become, not a romantic boy, and that he owes it to her and himself to go on "to become a great statesman of our country"—a prospect which makes "Bessie Watty and her baby seem a little unimportant":

It seems we are to accept Miss Moffatt's reading of the situation. Indeed it seems that this is Williams' own position as he struggles to set up Bessie as "Wicked Witch" to Miss Moffatt's "Fairy Godmother", cumbering her with an exit line like "My friend gave me this buckle, isn't it nice? He offered me a tiny one, real, but I think the false is prettier, don't you?". However, Bessie also has space to justify herself: "When I'm your age I'll love the idea of a baby, but life hasn't yet begun for me". Such lines only mark her as villainess rather than a troubled girl if one believes that biology is destiny: easier to accept in the 1930's perhaps—but the vital presence of Miss Moffatt in the play serves to undermine the notion. And if Miss Moffatt has the right to control her own life, why is Bessie condemned for refusing to sacrifice herself to Morgan Evans' career? The question is intensified because our belief in Evans as a potential statesman has to be taken on trust. He occupies a complicated position in the social hierarchy—financed by the local squire, nourished by Miss Moffatt's belief in him as an individual, shaped by a world run by an alien nation (Welsh is his first language) and brought up in abject poverty—and at no point does he make any attempt to comment on it; in fact he never makes anything resembling a political statement. Nor is it ever clear whether "our country" is England or Wales,

The Corn is Green: Duchess Theatre, London 1938 (first production)

though Williams makes great play with the distinction and the fact that the former is in an essentially exploitative relationship to the latter. Our only touchstone is in the area of sexual politics—and if he agrees with Miss Moffatt that beside his own self-advancement his responsibility to a working-class girl and her illegitimate baby is "unimportant" one might ask what he would consider "important". The question is not posed until it is too late to explore it; thus Morgan and Miss Moffatt seem to be endorsing the sexual double standard that has all too often disfigured British politics. It is a tribute to the energy of Williams' characterisation that one is so disappointed; he has shown the development of a genius, enjoyably and convincingly; and to make a strong curtain has shown that genius at the outset of his career meekly bowing to the *status quo*.

—Frances Gray

CORRUPTION IN THE PALACE OF JUSTICE
   (Corruzione al palazzo di giustizia)
by Ugo Betti

First Publication: In *Sipario*, vol.4 no.35, March 1949; in book form, in *Il Teatro di Ugo Betti*, Milan, 1953.
First Production: Teatro delle Arti, Rome, 7 January, 1949.

Translations
Corruption in the Palace of Justice, in *Ugo Betti: Three Plays*, translated by H. Reed, New York, 1958; also in *The New Theatre of Europe*, edited by Robert Corrigan, New York, 1962.

Criticism
(For general works on the author, see *Playwrights* volume)

Articles:
Ugo Betti, "Notes for the *Corruption at The Palace of Justice*", in *Tulane Drama Review*, vol.8 no.3, 1964.
Federico Doglio, "Preface" to *Corruzione al palazzo di giustizia*, Bologna, 1966.
G. Cimino, "Un'opera tra le piu significative di Betti: *Corruzione al palazzo di giustizia*", in *Il Ridotto*, vol.3 no.9.
Giuliana Stentella, "L'officina di Ugo Betti: *Corruzione al palazzo di giustizia*", in *Esperienze letterarie*, vol.7 no.3, 1982.
Esther Sánchez-Grey Alba, "The Purifying Agony of [Usigli's] *El Niño y la niebla* and *Corruzione al palazzo di giustizia*", in *Papers on Romance Literary Relations*, 1983.

*   *   *

The scene throughout is a stark council chamber in the Palace of Justice in an unspecified country. Ludvi-Pol, a man who is suspected of wielding vast power by bribing a high court judge, is found dead in the Palace. Councillor Erzi is ordered to root out the traitor in the court. Suspicion falls on the aged President Vanan, but all may be involved and essential evidence has disappeared. Elena, the adolescent daughter of Vanan, is an innocent in the murky Palace environment. Judge Cust, the real culprit, is strangely stirred by her fragility and innocence, but in order to save himself he completely destroys her pure image of her father. Her spirit crushed, she commits suicide. Chief Justice Croz collapses from a heart attack and declares himself to be the criminal. With the road to power open before him, Cust is, however, unable to absolve himself. Memories of Elena obsess him and compel him to confess the truth. The play ends as he slowly ascends a long staircase to see the Lord High Chancellor.

Corruption in the Palace of Justice was finished in 1945 but not produced until 1949. It is often considered Betti's most representative play and the format of the investigation is typical of much of his dramatic output. The material outline of the plot is not as clearly defined as it would be in a realistic style of writing. As Silvio D'Amico has pointed out, Betti "proceeds by hints, allusions, sudden outbursts and lightning bolts"; it is not the plot that matters most but "its tragic and lyric vibrations". The play has symbolic overtones and a mysterious atmosphere of dream and nightmare.

While the subject is corruption, guilt, and justice, this is no courtroom drama or a murder-mystery play but rather a drama of self-exploration on philosophical and metaphysical levels. Betti explores the question of man's basic nature, the concepts of free will, innocence, conscience, human and divine justice.

The world of *Corruption* hovers between the real and the metaphysical in this play of ideas. It is a world suffering from moral and physical decay. Outside the Palace, the city is filthy, diseased, and full of fear. The inhabitants are thirsting for a sacrificial victim. Inside, the Palace has become a rogue's paradise. Judges are venerated here for their power over the destiny of others, but they are as venal as the man in the street; the evil abounding in the city has infiltrated the labyrinthine halls of justice. There is not enough light or air to see and breathe properly. Images of death and decay abound: a man, Ludvi-Pol, lies dead offstage; Vanan is described as a corpse, and Croz is dying; a record clerk with his trolley piled high with documents for the archives is compared to an undertaker who unloads dead bodies from the hearse into the graveyard. An expert in language, Betti applies metaphors of disease: malicious gossip is gangrenous, and corruption a red pustule that forms leprous scabs on human bodies.

In this terrible environment, it is the dynamism of power that tempts and that corrupts. Those who judge are lonely rocks who are endlessly buffeted by the "implacable interests" and "boundless wealth" of "savage, irresistible, ferocious" men. This is a Hobbesian vision where man stands against man.

Tha battle for power is waged in the council chamber where the investigation is underway. Although all the judges are intelligent and eloquent, they have all been corrupted to different degrees in their struggle to get to the top. The corruption of Judges Persius, Bata, and Maveri—pompous, self-satisfied, hypocritical toadies—is unrefined compared to the malignancy of Croz and the subtle craft of Cust. Nobody trusts anyone. While the dying Croz is so utterly cynical that he passes on his mantle of power to one he knows is corrupt, it is Cust who is guilty of the most evil. He is attracted by the innocent, fragile beauty of Elena and fantasizes that she is his daughter, wife, and mother all at once. In her innocence he sees the "radiance of justice herself". But while he longs for innocence and an all-encompassing love, in his own self-interest he acts, paradoxically to destroy them.

But out of this viciousness comes Cust's growing conscious-

ness of guilt and his attempt at absolution. He cannot drown out Elena's dying scream in his ears or wash her innocent blood from his hands. And it is that innocent blood that ultimately redeems him. As Silvio D'Amico said, Betti is a poet "of our time" who depicts man's nostalgia for a forgotten innocence and his search for expiation in a world of horror and corruption. The play is a strong indication that Betti believes that man can only find redemption in a power higher than a secular court of justice. It is up to each individual to find his route to that power.

Some critics see *Corruption* as a direct comment on the political atmosphere and purges in Italy after the fall of Mussolini. It has been suggested that the influential Ludvi-Pol represents Mussolini whose body was mangled by the populace. Such an interpretation, however, gives much too narrow a reading to a play that transcends any particular situation.

—Jane House

CORRUZIONE AL PALAZZO DI GIUSTIZIA.
See CORRUPTION IN THE PALACE OF JUSTICE.

THE COUNTRY WIFE
by William Wycherley

First Publication: London, 1675.
First Production: Theatre Royal, Drury Lane, January 1675.

Editions

The Country Wife, edited by Thomas H. Fujimura, Lincoln, Nebraska, 1965 (Regents Restoration Drama Series).
The Country Wife, in *Three Restoration Comedies*, edited by Gāmini Salgādo, Harmondsworth, 1968.
The Country Wife, in *Restoration Comedies*, edited by Dennis Davison, London, 1970.
The Country Wife, edited by John Dixon Hunt, London, 1973 (New Mermaid Series).
The Country Wife, edited by David Cook and John Swannell, London, 1975 (Revels Plays).
The Country Wife in *The Plays of William Wycherley*, edited by Peter Holland, Cambridge, 1981.

Criticism
(For general works on the author, see *Playwrights* volume)

Articles:
Emmett L. Avery, "*The Country Wife* in the Eighteenth Century", in *Research Studies of the State College of Washington*, 10, 1942.
Ronald Berman, "The Ethic of *The Country Wife*", in *Texas Studies in Literature and Language*, 9, 1967.
Roy S. Wolper, "The Temper of *The Country Wife*", in *Humanities Association Bulletin*, 18, 1967.
J. Peter Verdurmen, "Grasping for Permanence: Ideal Couples in *The Country Wife* and *Aurung Zebe*", in *Huntington Library Quarterly*, 42, 1979.
Derek Cohen, "The Revenger's Comedy: Female Hegemony in *The Country Wife*", in *Atlantis*, vol.5 no.2, 1980.
Douglas Duncan, "Mythic Parody in *The Country Wife*", in *Essays in Criticism*, vol. 31 no.4, 1981.

The Country Wife: Old Vic Theatre, London, 1936 (Tyrone Guthrie's production designed by Oliver Messel)

H.W. Matalene, "What Happens in *The Country Wife*", in *Studies in English Literature 1500–1900*, vol.22 no.3, 1982.

James Thompson, "Providence and Verbal Irony in *The Country Wife*", in *Southern Review*, vol.47 no.4, 1982.

Harold Weber, "Horner and His 'Women of Honour': The Dinner Party in *The Country Wife*", in *Modern Language Quarterly*, vol.43 no.2, 1982.

Harold Love, "The Theatrical Geography of *The Country Wife*", in *Southern Review*, vol.16 no.3, 1983.

Deborah C. Payne, "Reading the Signs in *The Country Wife*", in *Studies in English Literature 1500–1900*, Summer 1986.

Michael Neill, "Horned Beasts and China Oranges: Reading the Signs in *The Country Wife*", in *Eighteenth-Century Life*, May 1988.

Helen M. Burke, "Wycherley's 'Tendentious Joke': The Discourse of Alterity in *The Country Wife*", in *The Eighteenth Century*, Fall 1988.

*   *   *

In Wycherley's third comedy the main plot concerns Horner, a London libertine, who initiates a rumour that he is impotent and by this ploy secures for himself sexual access to three women in succession: Mrs. Squeamish, Lady Fidget, and Margery Pinchwife, the eponymous heroine. Margery is also the connecting link to the second line of the plot in which the former rake Mr. Pinchwife, who married her thinking her ignorance would secure her fidelity, is promptly cuckolded by her and Horner when he takes her to London into the society of his friends of old times. The third strand in the action develops around the rivalry between the fop Sparkish and the true gallant, Harcourt, for the hand of the heiress Alithea. In the play's denouement there is a strong contrast between the happy end to Harcourt's and Alithea's courtship, and Pinchwife's resigned acquiescene to the fate of a cuckold, the play's naive heroine having learned her lesson in polite society. Even at the end, Horner's stratagem remains undetected by all except those women he has enjoyed.

The three interconnected plots in *The Country Wife* carry divergent dramatic weight. There is a striking disparity between the rather predictable courtship of Harcourt and Alithea, the positive models of a fine couple, in which Sparkish, as Harcourt's rival, is never sufficiently attractive to cast serious doubt on the outcome of a very subdued love affair, and the other two plots, which are much livelier. Margery Pinchwife is Wycherley's novel contribution to an otherwise well-established, character hierarchy of the Restoration comedy of manners: wits, fops, lecherous older women and accessible younger women, all present in this play. Margery is a "natural", a libidinous, noble savage whose naivety makes her an easy prey to Horner's seduction, but who actually gains in independence and self-assurance in the process. The urban culture of fashionable, London society subjects her to a learning process in which her initial, marital subjection is reversed. Equally improbable and projective is the main plot with which the play begins and ends, Horner's successful feigning of impotence, a motif borrowed from Terence's *Eunuch*. Horner turns into a kind of sexual superman who manages to convert Sir Jasper Fidget's and, by the end of the play, Pinchwife's initial distrust and jealousy into a mistaken reliance on his harmlessness. In the course of the play, Wycherley transforms the traditional pattern of the love chase. From being a predatory seducer of women, Horner more and more turns into an object of their pursuit. Margery falls in love with him, and in the brilliantly indecent "China scene" (Act IV, Scene 3) both Mrs Squeamish and Lady Fidget follow each other in their sexual encounters (off-stage) with Horner, who briefly abducts them from the scene ostensibly to view his collection of precious china.

The gradual reversal of roles between rake and the fine ladies in the play affects the dominant character of Horner who is much more in the centre of interest than the comedy's ostensible heroine. The reading of the play very much depends on the interpretation of Horner's character. From the early performances of *The Country Wife* on the London stage, and throughout the critical discussion of the comedy, there have been conflicting responses to its central, male character. Everything hinges on a choice between viewing Horner as a Hobbesian libertine, flouting accepted morality in a more blatant way than other rakes in Wycherley's comedies, or viewing him as a "satirist"; a satirical tool used by the author to expose the one universal vice ascribed to most female characters in fashionable society: hypocrisy. Only Alithea, who is a pale figure anyway, and Margery Pinchwife, who never reaches civilized standards until the end of the play, are exempt from this vice. As in Wycherley's treatment of his hero, Manly, in his last play, *The Plain-Dealer*, the author seems uncertain about principal character's function in the moral framework of the comedy. Horner never grows into a sympathetic character, but his victims certainly deserve all they get, and indeed want, from him. The indecision matters dramatically because of the relative off-handedness of the exemplary couple's (Alithea and Harcourt's) courtship, and the avoidance of any moralistic register in the treatment of Margery where there is a similar antithesis of two equally problematic moral stances: jealous domination and amoral hedonism. The play's discourse establishes a standard of morality in one plot line only to deconstruct it in another, so that the epithet "moral Wycherley" became, in the comedy's stage career, a strategic defence against moralistic attacks.

The dramatic texture affords little evidence for interpretation of its perspective as a moralistic one. The only admission to didacticism can be detected in the deliberate exposure of the three society women and their hypocritical behaviour. All other characteristics of *The Country Wife* elaborate upon the established formulae of the Restoration comedy of manners: witty repartee as the epitome of brilliant dialogue; the setting, in genteel, contemporary society; the flights of comic fantasy; and the elegant manipulation of stock character types. Wycherley's special mark here is the tightly controlled plotting that never seems strained in spite of the improbability of its basic motif. The moralistic reinterpretations of Wycherley's finest play give evidence of an attempt on the part of the

audience in 18th century England to reappropriate some aristocratic libertinism for the literary canon. For this purpose the play had to be revised. It survived for a long time in purged adaptations that omitted most of the comedy's undoubted obscenity. After the positive re-evaluation of Restoration comedy in the early 20th century, *The Country-Wife* has kept the stage in its original text.

—Bernd–Peter Lange

THE CRIME OF LOUIS RIEL.   See **THE RIEL TRILOGY.**

THE CRIMINALS (La noche de los asesinos)
by José Triana

First Publication: Havana, 1965.
First Production: Sixth Festival of Latin American Theatre, Havana, Cuba, 1966.

Translations
The Criminals, translated by Pablo Armando Fernández and Michael Kustow, in *The Modern Stage in Latin America: Six Plays*, edited by George Woodyard, New York, 1971.

Criticism
(For general works on the author, see *Playwrights* volume)

Articles:
Julio Ortega, "*La noche de los asesinos*", in *Cuadernos Americanos*, 164, 1969.
Ann Murch, "Genet, Triana, Kopit: Ritual as *danse macabre*", in *Modern Drama*, vol.15 no. 4, 1973.
Kirsten F. Nigro, "*La noche de los asesinos*: Playscript and Stage Enactment", in *Latin American Theatre Review*, 11, 1977.
Erminio G. Neglia, "El asedio a la casa: un estudio del decorado en *La noche de los asesinos*", in *Revista Iberoamericana*, 110–111, 1980.
Martha O'Nan, "The 1967 French Critical Reception of José Triana's *La noche de los asesinos*", in *Festschrift José Cid Pérez*, edited by Alberto Gutiérrez de la Solana and Elio Alba-Buffill, New York, 1981.
Priscilla Meléndez, "El espacio dramático como signo: *La noche de los asesinos* de José Triana", in *Latin American Theatre Review*, 17, 1983.
Isabel Alvarez-Borland and David George, "*La noche de los asesinos*: Text, Staging and Audience", in *Latin American Theatre Review*, 20, 1986.
Teresinka Pereira, "La distribución, disposición y orden de los personajes en los ejercicios o juegos de actuación en *La noche de los asesinos* de José Triana", in *Confluencia*, vol.4 no. 1, 1988.

*   *   *

La noche de los asesinos, an example of non-illusionistic theatre, posits the theme of man's estrangement from himself. Because he finds communication difficult, he resorts to game playing, hoping through re-enactment to break down the barriers that prevent his social interaction. The play begins with three supposedly adolescent characters, Lalo, Beba, and Cuca, who instantly embark on a series of savage games wherein they replay the "murder" of their parents, adopting multiple roles as the parents, the police, the neighbors, and other relatives. It is clear from the outset that the re-enactment takes place every day, as if they wished to purge themselves of an oppressive world which suffocates them.

Frequently described as a play which falls within the "Theatre of the Absurd", *La noche de los asesinos* shares the characteristic of turning its back on traditional theatre. Whereas in the latter the audience is clearly separated from the action unfolding before it, in viewing *Noche*, the audience is forced to be an active participant. The sparse setting of the play and the unfolding ritual draw the audience into a world where the boundaries between illusion and reality are constantly shifting.

The play begins on a jarring note, as the characters talk about the murder. The audience is thus immediately brought into the action, as it realizes that the representation is one of an ongoing occurrence. Furthermore, it is jolted by both the substance of the game playing and the underlying theme it exposes. Lalo dominates the action in Act I, trying to assert his control over the game the three have agreed to play. Act I is the preparatory set-up of the ritualized murder. In interchanging roles, Lalo, Beba, and Cuca adopt the roles of the parents, presenting the various family arguments which have lead them to their feelings of imprisonment. Lalo-Father mocks Cuca-Mother, and the audience realizes that his speeches represent both his way of thinking and that of his father's. The children's rebellion is focused against their parents, alternating between Lalo's outright hatred and Cuca's conciliatory suggestions for accepting them and their world. It is Beba who is caught between the two; she is the most indecisive of the three, and the one who reacts with physical unrest to their game–playing. As they begin another "game" within the re-enactment, Beba takes on the role of a neighbor, describing the murder, the blood, and the lingering horror of death. The scene quickly shifts to a recounting of what led them to this moment, wherein Beba-Father and Cuca-Mother mock and punish the adolescents. The games continue, with Lalo as the mother recounting the pain of her marriage and pregnancy, leading to miscommunication with the father and the children. It is clear that all of Act I has served as a rehearsal for the changes the children hope to realize. In enacting the ritual murder of their parents, the children are trying to control their fictive world because they have failed to control their real one.

In Act II, the audience sees the game–playing taking place after the "murder" has been committed. It consists mainly of the police investigation of the murder. Whereas in Act I Lalo dominated the games, it is in Act II that Cuca takes control, setting in motion a trial scene that completely demoralizes Lalo. In ever-changing triangles of control, the children re-enact various scenes which purportedly explain the domestic strife. The re-enactments serve as their minds' view of the daily submission to their parents' tyranny, yet also show the parents' submission to a larger, more devastating force outside all of their control. The play becomes a microcosm of society, of the world at large. By telling us about Lalo's, Beba's, and Cuca's inability to change the world they live in, the play speaks of the broader issues of repression and unchanging social problems.

In the play, the words and actions of the multiple characters reinforce the feeling of hostility shown towards the children. They, in play-acting these other members of their immediate world (parents, relatives, neighbors, police), do so to establish the perceived oppression of the established powers. Because

they feel trapped, repressed, they lash out in vitriolic accusations against all the obstacles they believe prevent them from asserting their own power. Because their actions are based on illusions and more importantly, *delusions*, the children cannot hope to break out of their imprisonment. The ritual of enactment must thus begin again, for the childrens' perceptions cannot but implode into their real world. The delusions are fed by the play-acting, which, in turn, depends wholly on their subjective view of a confrontational society. There can be no resolution to the conflict. Unlike rites of passage, where the individual moves into and then out of the sacred world to become incorporated into his society as a contributing member of it, in *Noche* the ritual is self-perpetuating. The children, who indeed perceive themselves as separated from the group, never become assimilated with the group again. They are prisoners of their own delusions, within walls of their own making. They repeat the ritual, not because it is a fantasy, but because they need to purge themselves of their own fears and their perceived attitudes towards a society that they believe restricts them.

—Lynn Carbon Gorell

THE CRITIC; or, A Tragedy Rehearsed
by Richard Brinsley Sheridan

First Publication: London, 1781.
First Production: Theatre Royal, Drury Lane, 30 October 1779.

Editions
The Critic; or, A Tragedy Rehearsed, New Haven, Connecticut, 1908.
The Critic, edited by W.H. Low and A.S. Collins, London, 1927.
The Critic, edited by Robert Herring, London, 1935.
The Critic, edited by James Brodie, London, 1939.
The Critic, edited by J.C. Trewin, London, 1949.
The Critic, edited by David Crane, London, 1989 (New Mermaid Series)

Criticism
(For general works on the author, see *Playwrights* volume)

Articles:
Dane Farsworth Smith, "*The Critic*, its Sources and its Satire", in *The Critics in the Audience of the London Theatre from Buckingham to Sheridan*, Albuquerque, 1953.
Robert F. Williamson Jr., "*The Critic* and Theatrical Decline", in *Their Form Confounded: Studies in the Burlesque Play from Udall to Sheridan*, The Hague, 1975.

*   *   *

Mr. and Mrs. Dangle are discovered at breakfast "*reading Newspapers*". She criticizes her husband for his involvement in trivial theatrical affairs. Mr. Sneer enters and directs his sarcasm upon the next arrival, Sir Fretful Plagiary. Sir Fretful rejects the criticism the others offer of his "execrable" tragedy. Mr. Sneer fabricates a devastating newspaper attack on Sir

The Critic: Thomas King as Puff, Theatre Royal, Drury Lane, London, 1779 (engraving after a painting by Zoffany)

Fretful's playwriting, which Sir Fretful pretends to meet with amusement and indifference. A family of Italian performers enters to provide linguistic mayhem and a musical interlude. Mr. Puff follows immediately after and demonstrates his skills in the fabrication of flattering reports. Dangle and Sneer leave to attend a dress rehearsal of Mr. Puff's tragedy, *The Spanish Armada*, at the Drury Lane theatre.

In the second act, Dangle, Puff, and Sneer comment upon Puff's tragedy and intervene in the rehearsal. The tragedy deals with the ill-starred relationship between Tilburina, the daughter of the Governor of Tilbury Fort, and Don Ferolo Whiskerandos, the captive son of the Spanish Admiral. Act 3 introduces a subplot in which the Justice and his lady discover their long lost son, and adds a complication to the main plot when the nieces of Sir Walter Raleigh and Sir Christopher Hatton are discovered also to be in love with Don Whiskerandos. Whiskerandos is killed by a jealous Beefeater, and Tilburina and her confidant make their entrance: "*mad, according to custom*". Puff's tragedy concludes with a masque and a spectacular patriotic representation of the defeat of the Armada.

On October 2, 1779, the *Morning Chronicle* announced that, "Mr. Sheridan's new farce, which is said to be a piece of ridicule against news-paper puffing, in the very articles that serve as puffs for it, we now hear will not be ready this fortnight". This would suggest that the initial conception might well have been confined to the first act; the burlesque in Acts 2 and 3 was an afterthought.

Certainly Sheridan seems to have taken particular care over the opening scenes, and he is reputed to have said that "he valued the first Act more than anything he wrote". In it he satirizes a succession of false critics: Dangle, the theatrical hanger-on; Sneer, who is scathingly sarcastic; and Puff, who unabashedly praises work he is paid to promote. In Sir Fretful Plagiary, Sheridan skewers the sensitive and vain playwright who is unable to tolerate the slightest criticism. This cruel and hilarious portrait Sheridan himself confessed was based in part on the playwright Richard Cumberland.

Sheridan's audience could identify these figures with specific contemporaries. But Sheridan was also exposing his own experiences as a playwright and theatre manager: like Dangle he was compelled to entertain theatrical riff-raff; like Puff he had written to promote his own productions; like Sir Fretful he was sensitive to criticism.

The burlesque tragedy that occupies Acts II and III was inspired by contemporary political events. In June of 1779, Spain declared war on England, and in August of the same year the Spanish and French fleets were in the Channel, threatening an invasion. The parallel with the earlier Armada was obvious. The theatres were quick to exploit the event. In August, Sadler's Wells presented a musical entertainment, *The Prophecy; or, Queen Elizabeth at Tilbury*, which was probably devised by its manager, Thomas King. This was the same Thomas King who created the role of puff in *The Critic*, and this, no doubt, is one of the reasons why it is Puff and not Sir Wilful Plagiary who is the author of *The Spanish Armada*.

Burlesque was a well established tradition in the English theatre. A number of antecedents can be cited for Sheridan's brilliant essay in the form, of which the most obvious is Buckingham's *The Rehearsal* (1671). From it, Sheridan took the central device of presenting a play in rehearsal. In Buckingham's burlesque Smith and Johnson comment on the proceedings and express a normative point of view. Sheridan both unifies his play and creates an ironic perspective by carrying over Dangle and Sneer as observers, and by making Puff the author of the ridiculous tragedy. The heroic play had been burlesqued in *The Rehearsal*; it is still ridiculed in *The Critic*, but the criticism is extended to include the affective, or sentimental, drama that had succeeded the heroic play.

The Spanish Armada, however, is not so much a parody of specific plays as a burlesque of all that is potentially absurd in the theatre, and as such its comedy is undiminished by time. The excesses of actors are ridiculed. This could take the form of parodying contemporary actors. John Bannister, for instance, as Whiskerandos sent up "Gentleman" Smith's impersonation of Richard III. Miss Pope, as Tilburina, parodied the celebrated mad scenes of Mrs Crawford. The necessity of understanding the technical limitations of the theatre are exposed as the Under Prompter informs Puff that he must have "some business put in here before the drop, [or] they shan't have time to clear away the fort, or sink Gravesend and the river". These limitations are triumphantly overcome at the conclusion of the play by de Loutherbourg's astounding scenic inventions, which create a false spectacle capable of arousing true patriotism in the audience.

Sheridan's burlesque demonstrates, finally, the pitfalls of playwriting, which, again, are not confined to a particular genre or period. The dangers of clumsy exposition are revealed as Sir Walter Raleigh, for the benefit of the audience, tells Sir Christopher Hatton nothing he does not already know. The necessity of finding a sign that can adequately convey intended meaning is demonstrated when Lord Burleigh enters, sits down, comes forward and shakes his head and exits. Puff attributes to this action a complex meaning. "The devil!" Sneer exclaims. "Did he mean all that by shaking his head?".

It is not surprising that *The Critic* came entirely to supplant *The Rehearsal* as the most popular burlesque on the English stage. Its scope is comprehensive, exposing as it does the limitations of critics, playwrights, theatre practitioners, and the theatrical medium itself.

—Colin Wills Visser

CROSS PURPOSE (Le Malentendu)
by Albert Camus

First Publication: In *Le Malentendu*; *Caligula*, Paris, 1944; revised version, in *Le Malentendu*; *Caligula*, Paris, 1958.
First Production: Théâtre des Mathurins, Paris, 1944.

Translations
Cross Purpose, in "*Caligula*" and "*Cross Purpose*", translated by Stuart Gilbert, London, 1948.

Criticism
(For general works on the author, see *Playwrights* volume)

Articles:
Reino Virtanen, "Camus' *Le Malentendu* and Some Analogues", in *Comparative Literature*, 10, 1958.
Ralph Behrens, "Existential 'Character-Ideas' in Camus' *The Misunderstanding*", in *Modern Drama*, 7, 1964.
N.C. Chase, "Images of Man: *Le Malentendu* and *En Attendant Godot*", in *Wisconsin Studies in Contemporary Literature*, 7, 1966.
D.M. Church, "*Le Malentendu*: Search for Modern Tragedy", in *French Studies*, 20, 1966.

Heinz Moenkemeyer, "The Son's Fatal Homecoming in Werner and Camus", in *Modern Language Quarterly*, 27, 1966.

R. Bruce Dutton, "Une Tragédie classique au vingtième siècle: Une Étude structurale de *Malentendu* d'Albert Camus", in *Proceedings of the Pacific Northwest Conference on Foreign Languages*, 20, 1969.

Henry Amer, "Une Source du *Malentendu*", in *Revue d'histoire littéraire de la France*, 70, 1970.

Herbert Knust, "Camus' *Le Malentendu* and Doderer's *Zwei Lügen*", in *Archiv für das Studium der neueren Sprachen und Literaturen*, 208, 1971.

Beverly M. Matherne, "Hope in Camus' *The Misunderstanding*", in *Western Speech*, 35, 1971.

Mary A. F. Witt, "Imprisonment in Camus' 'Modern Tragedies': *Les Justes, Requiem pour une nonne, Le Malentendu*", in *Comparative Drama*, 5, 1971.

Raphael A. Cancel, "Camus' *Le Malentendu*: The Riddle of the Sphinx", in *Revista da ietras* (University of Puerto Rico), 4, 1972.

Curtis Whittington Jr., "The Earned Vision: Robert Penn Warren's *The Ballad of Billie Potts* and Albert Camus' *Le Malentendu*", in *Four Quarters*, 21, 1972.

Charles P. Marie, "A Re-Examination of 'Form and Meaning' in Camus' *Le Malentendu*", in *Nottingham French Studies*, vol.17 no.2, 1978.

Elwyn F. Sterling, "*Le Malentendu*: A Misunderstanding in the English Version", in *Romance Notes*, 19, 1978.

Patricia M. Hopkins, "The Failure of Language in *Les Mouches* and *Le Malentendu*", in *Francia*, 33, 1980.

Norman Stokle, "Camus' *Le Malentendu*: An Exercise in Modern Tragedy", in *Laurels*, 51, 1980–81.

Mary A. Witt, "[Buzatti's] *Un caso clinico* and *Le Malentendu*: Theatres of Transition, Tragedies of Space", in *Comparatist*, 6, 1982.

David B. Parsell, "Aspects of Comedy in Camus' *Le Malentendu*", in *Symposium*, 37, 1983–84.

Patricia Hopkins, "Camus' Failed Survivor: *Le Malentendu*", in *Rocky Mountain Review of Language and Literature*, 39, 1985.

*   *   *

At a remote inn somewhere in Bohemia, a woman and her daughter have taken to robbing and assassinating their guests. By this means they hope to accumulate sufficient money to leave their gloomy country and start a new life in a new land. The woman's son, who left home many years before, returns unrecognized and puts up at the hotel without declaring his identity in order to get to know his family again before surprising them and disclosing the truth about himself. He is murdered by his mother and sister who are subsequently driven to despair and suicide when his wife, anxious about his disappearance, arrives and reveals to them what they have done.

The plot of this play appears to derive from a folk legend. Camus' early working title was *Budejovice*, which makes explicit its Czechoslovakian antecedents. The hero of Camus' novel *The Outsider* finds the story in a newspaper cutting under the mattress in his prison cell. He reads it to help pass the time, concluding that looked at in one way it is improbable while from another point of view it is perfectly natural. In any event, he affirms, it shows the folly of playing tricks. In Camus' play the story serves to illustrate the absurdist world-view. Human beings cannot count on circumstances to serve their interests: the horrible coincidence which *Cross Purpose* relates is at bottom a perfectly normal occurrence in a universe governed by random forces. A specifically Camusian theme is that of exile. The Mother and her daughter, Martha, hunger for escape from the claustrophobic world they inhabit, dream of a homeland where their desires and aspirations will be realised: but there is no escape from the universe to which human beings are confined. At another level, Camus constructs his play around the opposition between a landlocked northern Europe of clouds, miasma and depression, and a Mediterranean ideal of sun, seascapes and clarity. Mother and daughter have been contaminated by the atmosphere in which they have had to live, so that in a sense their crime is an illustration of the moral confusion into which humans can sink as a reaction to the world's indifference. Part of the play's aim is to convey the intense, disquieting unreason which poses as conviction in the mind of Martha. It is she who drives her mother on when the latter falters in her resolve, wearying of bloodshed and fearful that they are, after all, tempting fate. Martha's bitter consolation is that they are merely hastening the normal train of events for their victims; she compares the signs of torment on the corpses of those who have fallen by accident into the river with the lesser degree of suffering undergone by those whom they help on their way.

Camus' aim was to create a modern tragedy of the absurd on the classical theme of destiny. The play is indeed faithful to the conventional tenets of the genre. It depicts the urge to find happiness defeated by a combination of human presumption and the ironies of fate, and its essential theme of non-communication culminates in a profoundly tragic anagnorisis. Moreover, in accordance with the author's metaphysical preoccupations, the psychology of the characters is less important than their fate. The plot is stark, the setting simple, the development austere and unrelenting. The key incidents which perpetuate the misunderstanding and precipitate the brother's death all involve excruciating ironies which audiences sometimes find difficult to accept. During a conversation with Jan, her as yet unrecognized brother, Martha's determination to kill him begins to weaken until he, thinking to convey something of his reasons for returning, speaks of the urge to find a homeland, which, in turn, provokes her to do away with him and escape in pursuit of her own utopia. Similarly, drugged tea (the first phase of the murder plot) is served to Jan on the basis of a misunderstood message from the aged servant; and when the mother finally recoils from killing and decides to halt the murder it is just too late. The revelation of the drugged victim's identity is delayed when his passport falls from his pocket and falls behind the bed while the women are preparing to carry him outside and drop him in the river. Such incidents complement dialogue which is constantly at cross-purposes because the speakers are implying something other than what they say and the protagonists are too wrapped up in their private dreams, fears and aspirations to infer the interlocutor's meaning. As Camus once remarked, all the misfortune of humans stems from their failure to use clear language. Certainly the dramatic tone of the play is characterized by allusive, elliptical statements and enigmatic actions shot through with allegorical overtones.

Throughout, the play traces an arduous line between the extremes of banality and melodrama. Camus' point is that the absurd *is* humdrum, that tragedy *does* arise from trivial pretexts and misjudgements, and that chance remarks and coincidental clashes of purpose are the stuff of everyday life. But in spite of his success in creating the fraught, highly-strung and claustrophobic atmosphere which characterizes the work, it is debatable whether his text rises to the level of dramatic significance he sought to sustain. He strove to forge a new language for drama, far removed from casual naturalism, capable of realizing a pared-down lyricism that could impart a classical dignity to his material. In general it is felt that this play does not achieve that ideal in a workable form, but that paradoxically Camus, the philosopher and rationalist, hit upon a visceral expression of the irrational, nightmarish suffocation that was later to be associated with the "Theatre of the Absurd".

—David H. Walker

THE CROWS.   See **THE VULTURES.**

THE CRUCIBLE
by Arthur Miller

First Publication: New York, 1953; revised edition, 1954.
First Production: Martin Beck Theatre, New York, 22 January 1953.

Criticism
(For general works on the author, see *Playwrights* volume)

Books:
C.J. Partridge, *The Crucible*, Oxford, 1971.
John H. Ferres (ed.), *Twentieth-Century Interpretations of "The Crucible"*, Englewood Cliffs, New Jersey, 1972.
Leonard Smith, *The Crucible*, London, 1986.
Bernard F. Dukore, *"Death of a Salesman" and "The Crucible"*, London, 1989 (Text and Performance Series).

Articles:
Henry Popkin, "Arthur Miller's *The Crucible*", in *College English*, vol.26 no.2, 1964.
David M. Bergeron, "Arthur Miller's *The Crucible* and Nathaniel Hawthorne: Some Parallels", in *English Journal*, 58, 1969.
John H. Ferres, "Still in the Present Tense: *The Crucible Today*", in *University College Quarterly*, vol.17 no.4, 1972.
N. Joseph Calarco, "Production as Criticism: Miller's *The Crucible*", in *Educational Theatre Journal*, 29, 1977.
Robert A. Martin, "Arthur Miller's *The Crucible*: Background and Sources", in *Modern Drama*, 20, 1977.
John Ditsky, "Stone, Fire and Light: Approaches to *The Crucible*", in *North Dakota Quarterly*, vol.46 no.2, 1978.
E. Miller Budick, "History and Other Spectres in Arthur Miller's *The Crucible*", in *Modern Drama*, 28, 1985.
Edmund S. Morgan, "Arthur Miller's *The Crucible* and the Salem Witch Trials: A Historian's View", in *The Golden and the Brazen World: Papers in Literature and History, 1650–1800*, edited by John M. Wallace, Berkeley, California, 1985.

*   *   *

The play is set in Salem, Massachusetts, 1692, when very real witch hunts took place in America. John Proctor and his wife, Elizabeth, are trapped and eventually destroyed by hysterical young girls who are frightened and who discover the power of unverified accusations and vicious lies. Caught by the Reverend Parris in a night prank in a forest in which they try to "kill" Elizabeth because Abigail lusts for John, the girls fear the punishment that they might receive and so they declare that they have been bewitched by Tituba, a black servant who has invoked the Devil. To save their hides, the girls declare that some of the citizens of Salem have been in the service of the Devil, leading church and civil courts to damn these innocent folks to being hung unless they confess and recant. A young minister, John Hale, sees through the hypocrisy and lies but he is powerless against a court which has committed itself to searching out the "truth" and eliminating "the devil" from the Commonwealth. Greed, stupidity, fear are all fed by the girls until Proctor is damned to die and the girls, fearing exposure, flee, leaving a society that has almost completely torn itself apart.

The Crucible is Arthur Miller's angry, powerful, eloquent response to the fear-filled days of the 1950's when Congressional committees searched for and witlessly accused a wide range of people of being "communists". It is particularly a metaphor for the Senator McCarthy witchhunt after World War II, which, in time, spread fear throughout the country, resulting in artists, teachers, "common folk" being declared subversive, losing their jobs, and being ostracized from American society. Substitute the maniacal zeal of the Senator for the absolute certainty of the clerics and the courts in *The Crucible* and the play's implications are clear. In order to save their necks, the girls play on the suspicions and jealousies of the community: in the 1950's, as in the 17th century, people were ever eager to testify to the wickedness of neighbors, friends, colleagues, in order to save their jobs and "names". In the play ignorant, irrational gossip becomes accusation, revenge, false testimony and faked evidence until the community is on a rampage against its fellows. Foreigners are automatically suspect, as is Tituba.

Early mis-steps, such as Proctor's relations with Abigail, become full-fledged sins in the eyes of the hysterical. But even Abigail realizes the horror of what is happening and frankly says, ". . .what pretense Salem was. . .the lying lessons. . .taught by all those Christian women and their covenanted men!". Everyone has some misdeed to rue, but such errors can become cause for hangings and pilloring in a world ruled by un-reason and bent on salvation. Once let loose, the fire will run its course: Mrs. Proctor says that the ". . .town's gone wild", and Miller clearly means that the "town" symbolizes Washington, where jack-courts and pompous committees demanded confessions. Driven by fear, if one must hang for merely denying guilt, one will ". . .swear to anything".

Ironically, when Proctor counts on his wife's truthfulness the most, she waffles and so damns her husband to death. Fear leads to uncertainty and compromise. Proctor can only be saved if he will confess, although it will be a false confession. But Proctor cannot ". . .live without his name". He will not, cannot, live a lie. Like Miller before a Congressional committee, Proctor will not sell out his friends. He goes to be hanged leaving his wife and children and history to honor his name.

Miller's own position before Congressional committees was one which would not betray his friends and co-artists although he might have saved himself. He watched otherwise distinguished and talented theater people slip into supplication, begging for exoneration and wildly pointing fingers. The split in the artistic community was to be deep, distrusting, and harmful. With *The Crucible*, Miller dramatized, and perhaps explained, a dreadful era in American life. If the play is overwrought, there is a therapy and a wisdom in putting events at arm's length. For Miller the stage is the perfect platform. While *The Crucible* has its most obvious, and best documented, parallel with McCarthyism, the play's lessons are for

The Crucible: Royal Shakespeare Company tour, 1984

all forms of doctrinaire self-righteousness. The modern Fundamentalist insistence in "purifying" the arts, the schools, the bedchambers of modern America seems a particularly apt contemporary parallel for the themes dealt with in *The Crucible*. The play is, and probably always will be, "relevant" for audiences grown distrustful of authority, of governments, of theologies, of people who are absolute, hysterical, unreasonable, and unreasoning. It is a frightening play and a powerful testament.

—Arthur Ballet

CYMBELINE
by William Shakespeare

First Publication: London, 1623.
First Production: London, probably c. 1610.

Editions
The Tragedie of Cymbeline, edited by Horace Howard Furness Jr., Philadelphia and London, 1913 (New Variorum Edition).
Cymbeline, edited by G. Boas, London, 1935.

Cymbeline, edited by J.M. Nosworthy, London, 1955 (Arden Shakespeare).
Cymbeline, edited by J.C. Maxwell, Cambridge, 1960 (The New Shakespeare).
Cymbeline, edited by Robert B. Heilman, Baltimore, 1964 (Pelican Shakespeare).
Cymbeline, edited by Richard Hosley, New York, 1968 (Signet Classic Shakespeare).

Bibliography
Henry E. Jacobs (ed.), *Cymbeline*, New York, 1982 (Garland Shakespeare Bibliographies).

Criticism
(For general works on the author, see *Playwrights* volume)

Books:
Derick R.C. Marsh, *The Recurring Miracle: A Study of "Cymbeline" and the Last Plays*, Pietermaritzburg, South Africa, 1962.
Mark W. Scott (ed.), *"Cymbeline"* in *Shakespearian Criticism*, Detroit, Illinois, 1987 (anthology of criticism).
Roger Warren, *Cymbeline*, Manchester, 1989 (Shakespeare in Performance Series).

Articles:
For information on the many articles about *Cymbeline*, see Jacob's bibliography, the bibliographies listed in the *Playwrights* volume, and the annual Shakespeare Bibliography

Cymbeline: Engraved frontispiece from Nicholas Rowe's 1709 edition

in *Shakespeare Quarterly*, published by the Folger Shakespeare Library, Washington D.C. (1950–).

*   *   *

In *General Observations on the Plays of Shakespeare* (1756), the neoclassical critic, Samuel Johnson attacked the late romance *Cymbeline* for "the folly of the fiction, the absurdity of the conduct . . . . and the impossibility of the events in any system of life . . . . " A straightforward summary of the plot would make the play sound as implausible and absurd as Johnson maintained, but an analysis of the various plot threads, and the dominant motifs which emerge from them, would serve to show how Shakespeare expertly balances and mixes various levels of language and staging to produce a complex drama that is united on psychological, social, dynastic, and nationalistic levels. When judged from the perspective of real life, the events of *Cymbeline* may seem "unresisting imbecility", as Johnson put it, but when evaluated as a fictive world, the play reveals a well-modulated plot which, as the romantic critic William Hazlitt asserted, "moves forward with increasing rapidity at every step, its various ramifications are drawn from the most distant points to the same centre;. . .and the fate of almost every person. . .is made to depend on the

solution of a single circumstance—the answer of Iachimo to the question of Imogen respecting the obtaining of the ring from Posthumous".

The most cogent way to discuss the involved plot of *Cymbeline* is to divide it into three connected strands in the order of their importance: (1) the marital plot which concerns the tortuous relationship between the young lovers Posthumous and Imogen; (2) the dynastic plot involving King Cymbeline, his daughter Imogen, his stepson Cloten, his evil second wife, and his "lost" sons Guiderius and Arviragus; (3) the nationalistic plot which results from the war between Britain and Rome over the unpaid tribute. Shakespeare interweaves these skeins, emphasizing one, then the other, providing links between them, and finally coalescing and unravelling them in a climactic revelation.

Interwoven among the central plot strands are the two dominant dramatic motifs of *Cymbeline*: discrepant awareness and divided loyalties and identities. These motifs convey the sense of Ovidian metamorphosis which is at the heart of the play. The statements, motivations, and actions of the characters are deceptive, shifting, and fallible. Deceit, intrigue, hypocrisy, and violence dominate, but in the midst of this flux we sense a moral and providential order being effected because some of the characters, although ignorant of many important facts concerning their lives and identities, demonstrate admirable traits. As a confirmation of the audience's expectations in the penultimate scene of the play, Jupiter descends and promises a beneficial denouement.

No other play of Shakespeare has such a developed sense of dramatic irony in which the audience repeatedly knows more than the characters do; they are swept along by events whose significance they do not begin to understand. Imogen, the plucky heroine, is unaware of almost all of the forces arrayed against her. When Posthumous orders Pisanio to kill her, the loyal servant refuses to obey his master, advising her to disguise herself as a man and become a servant to Caius Lucius. However, at Milford Haven she is "adopted" by her real brothers who say they love her like brothers, which is more true then they realize. When she becomes ill and takes the drug given to her by Pisanio for medicinal purposes, it induces a comatose state, as we knew it would having heard the physician Cornelius describe its effect. After Cloten's headless body is placed next to her in the tomb built by her brothers who believe she has died, she awakens and imagines that the disguised corpse is Posthumous killed by the treacherous Pisanio. But, of course, the audience knows otherwise.

The second motif invokes divided loyalties and identities. Characters are alienated in their external relations and within themselves. Posthumous provides the best example of this motif, because for most of the play he remains the excluded and disenfranchised man, looking for a settled place and identity. His marginality is indicated initially by his name which refers to his being born after the death of his immediate family. As a result of his family's valiant martial service, he becomes a ward of Cymbeline, but is banished when he marries Imogen. After having ordered the death of his wife for her seeming lack of virtue, he repents and returns to England with the Roman invasion. But he dons humble British garb and serves his former country bravely; however, after this service, he changes back to Roman dress in the hope of being arrested and executed as a traitor. While awaiting his execution, his family members appear in a dream and berate Jupiter for his continuing bad treatment of the deserving Leonati clan. Jupiter promises a benevolent unravelling of their problems, and his prediction is fulfilled as Posthumous's divided loyalties and identities are resolved when he is reunited with Imogen at Cymbeline's court. Although each thought the other was dead, they are now "resurrected" and back where they started out, but with great differences in their self-awareness and understanding of the world around them.

Cymbeline is a richly Ovidian play in its depiction of the mercurial, deceptive, and complex nature of human personality. Iachimo, the shape-changer, emerges from the trunk and proceeds to act out a figurative version of Ovid's tale of the rape of Philomela by Tereus, which Imogen had been reading at bedtime. Shakespeare physically delineates Posthumous's shifting identities by means of the different clothes he wears. As James Siemon remarks: "That he [Posthumous] is unable to relate his role. . .to any stable costume indicates his deep. . .confusion:. . .confusion over one's proper dress is an appropriate expression for confusion over one's true nature . . . ." What stands out after the numerous disguises, the merging and shifting identities, the reversals and restorations, and the dramatic ironies and final revelations is Shakespeare's infinite variety as the master shape-changer and circus master who is able to show us his complete repertory of dramatic stock engaged in unendingly various but significant and coherent, action.

—Frank Ardolino

CYRANO DE BERGERAC
by Edmond Rostand

First Publication: Paris, 1898.
First Production: Théâtre de la Porte-Saint-Martin, December, 1897.

Editions
Cyrano de Bergerac, edited by Oscar Kuhns, New York, 1968.
Cyrano de Bergerac, edited by Jacques Truchet, Paris, 1983.
Cyrano de Bergerac, edited by Edward A. Bird.

Translations
Cyrano de Bergerac, in *Plays*, translated by H.D. Norman, New York, (2 vols.), 1921.
Cyrano de Bergerac, translated by Brian Hooker, London, 1924.
Cyrano de Bergerac, translated by Humbert Wolfe, London, 1937.
Cyrano de Bergerac, translated by Christopher Fry, London, 1975.

Criticism
(For general works on the author, see *Playwrights* volume)

Books:
Mary L. Engel, *Edmond Rostand: "Cyrano de Bergerac"*, New York, 1969.

Articles:
C. Brenner, "Rostand's *Cyrano de Bergerac*: An Interpretation", in *Studies in Philology*, 46, 1949.
M. Butler, "The Historical Cyrano de Bergerac as a Basis for Rostand's Play", in *Educational Theatre Journal*, 6, 1954
M. Butler, "Sources of Plot Ideas in *Cyrano de Bergerac*", in *Western Speech*, vol. 19 no.2, 1955.

Paul Vernois, "Architecture et écriture théâtrales dans *Cyrano de Bergerac*", in *Travaux de linguistique et de littérature*, vol.4 no.2, 1966.
Ann B. Dobie, "*Cyrano de Bergerac*: A Reconsideration of Romanticism and Realism", in *Southern Speech Journal*, 26, 1971.
Patricia E. Williams, "Some Classical Aspects of *Cyrano de Bergerac*", in *Nineteenth-Century French Studies*, 1, 1973.
William D. Howarth, "*Cyrano de Bergerac*, or the Triumph of Romantic Drama", in *Sublime and Grotesque: A Study of French Romantic Drama*, London, 1975.
Jacques Truchet, "Le *Cyrano* de Rostand: Aspects politiques d'un triomphe théâtral", in *Commentaire*, 6, 1983.

* * *

The eponymous hero, an outstanding swordsman and a versatile poet, possesses an enormous, grotesque nose; and his ugliness is an obstacle to the fulfilment of a secret love for his cousin Roxane, a beautiful bluestocking. Discovering she loves the handsome Christian, a fellow-officer in the Cadets de Gascogne, he generously devotes himself to the furthering of this love-affair. Since Christian has no imagination or wit, Cyrano writes repeated love letters on his behalf full of poetry and passion. The couple marry, to the chagrin of Roxane's powerful suitor the Comte de Guiche who, as commander of the Cadets, sends them to fight at the siege of Arras. Christian, by now aware that Roxane loves him less for his physical attractions than for the intellectual and imaginative qualities that belong to Cyrano, seeks death in battle. As he is killed, Cyrano, who was about to sound out Roxane's real feelings, chivalrously remains silent; and the secret is kept until the day of his own death, 15 years later, when, mortally wounded in a cowardly ambush, he confesses the truth to Roxane. She admits that it was for Cyrano's qualities that she had loved Christian, and as he hears this declaration that his love is reciprocated, Cyrano dies.

A principal reason for the play's remarkable success, in 1897 and with audiences ever since, is its astonishing verbal virtuosity—the picturesque vocabulary, the audacious rhymes, the varying moods and rhythms, the puns and plays on words—which creates such an impression of life and vigorous movement. But *Cyrano* is not merely the work of a skilled literary craftsman: the tirades, the swaggering outbursts, the poetic flights of fancy, come across not as so many set pieces by the author, but rather as virtuoso performances by a character who is not only a swashbuckling Gascon, but also a skilled juggler with words: the Poet as Hero, in an art form which depends on the act of poetic creation, provides a rare match between character and the dramatic vehicle in which the character is presented. Cyrano is larger than life, but we accept him as a convincing embodiment of genius because the historical figure he is based on left behind a rich stock of anecdotes testifying to life lived to excess, in a period—the France of Louis XIII and Richelieu—in which we can readily believe such excess to have flourished. In fact, historical research since Rostand's day has shown that Cyrano was not a Gascon, and that Bergerac was the name of a small property near Paris; however, the central character, and many of the supporting characters too, are convincingly based on 17th-century source materials, and references to Cyrano's own writings and his celebrated exploits make this an exceptionally well authenticated portrait. Nevertheless, literary display is seldom for its own sake; and the most memorable examples are of poetic invention accompanied by action, and furthering the plot. For instance, the famous ballad in Act I, composed while fighting a duel, with the refrain "As I end the poem, I'll make

Cyrano de Bergerac: Wyndhams Theatre, London, 1900 (Sir Charles Wyndham as Cyrano)

my hit!''; the fantasy on the theme of space-travel by which Cyrano delays Guiche so that Christian and Roxane can marry: and the closing scene in which Cyrano, reading aloud Christian's last letter, which he knows by heart, betrays to Roxane the fact that he was its author. Rostand's ability to move, amuse, or entertain us with words is supported throughout by spectacle and action: perhaps the best example of this is Act IV where the Cadets, starving at the siege of Arras, are joined by Roxane in a carriage full of food and drink. (The whole play has indeed been called by a modern editor a "gastronomic fantasy".)

70 years on from the publication of the *Preface to Cromwell, Cyrano de Bergerac* provides the triumphant vindication of Victor Hugo's formula for the new Romantic drama: a historical play in verse, giving a colourful, lively portrayal of the period chosen, mixing the serious and the lighthearted, with a central character based on the antithetical opposition of sublime and grotesque. In Cyrano's case, this is by no means limited to the obvious contrast between an unprepossessing physical exterior and the exalted imagination of a poet. More than that, the hero's grotesque appearance symbolises the earthbound reality which, according to Romantic metaphysics, constantly frustrates and defeats the human spirit—and not only that of the poet and would-be lover—in its aspiration towards the ideal. Despite his extravagance, Cyrano is a human character with whom spectators and readers find it by no means impossible to reach the necessary degree of sympathetic identification: not because we ourselves aspire to the same sort of heroics, but because he expresses a Romantic idealism, a nostalgia for absolute values, latent in us all. It does not matter that he is not a successful lover: indeed, it is essential his ideal should remain unfulfilled, and that he should die at the very moment that his dream is about to become reality, so that the purity of the dream may be preserved. It is the steadfast pursuit of the ideal, the unwavering belief in the dream, that counts; and Rostand's hero embodies Romantic aspirations that are certainly not limited to 17th- (or to 19th-) century France.

Some part of the play's success with its first spectators was no doubt due to the sort of jingoistic bravado that was welcome to French ears just when national pride badly needed a boost; but time has shown that its appeal is less parochial and less superficial than this, and it has never lost its popularity with actors and audiences. Written with one of the outstanding actors of the day, Constant Coquelin, in mind for the part of Cyrano (Sarah Bernhardt joined him to play Roxane, though she did not create the role), the play has continued to be associated with the Coquelin family: Constant's son Jean played the pastry–cook, Ragueneau, alongside his father and then succeeded him in the title-role, while Jean-Paul Coquelin, Jean's son, was awarded a prize for his recording of the part in 1955.

—William D. Howarth

DA
by Hugh Leonard

First Publication: Newark, Delaware, 1976; revised edition, London and New York, 1978.
First Production: Olney Theatre, Olney, Maryland, 7 August 1973.

* * *

Hugh Leonard's best known and most successful play, *Da*, is set in 1968 in the Dublin suburb of Dalkey. Charlie, an adopted son (and the autobiographical stand-in for the playwright), has returned to his boyhood home for the funeral of his father, Nick Tynan—his "da." He is clearing out his father's personal effects before taking the evening plane back to London where he is a successful writer. Since *Da* is a "memory play" (somewhat like Tennessee Williams' *The Glass Menagerie*), about 90 per–cent of it takes place in the mind and memory of Charlie. Thus, the action is cinematic, free-flowing through time and space. The first and last scenes of the play take place on the day of Da's funeral. The rest of the play is composed of gracefully connected flashbacks which occur over the previous 35 years. These scenes involve, besides Charlie and his dead parents, Young Charlie, an earlier teenage version of himself, and four other characters: Oliver, a friend of his youth; Mr. Drumm, a civil servant; Mrs. Prynn, an elderly, Quaker lady; and Mary Tate, a local girl. However, Da and the older Charlie (42) dominate the play. Da is an ignorant, foolish, and irritating man, and so an embarrassment to his son and sometimes to his wife. However his love and compassion for the boy create a sense of guilt in Charlie, who would like to put his life with Da behind him, but he is haunted by the memories of a father who gave him so much. At the end of the play, Charlie leaves for the airport, locking the front door and throwing away the key. He immediately discovers, however, that he cannot leave behind his memories of Da who "has walked out through the fourth wall" (stage direction) and will cheerfully follow him to London.

Thematically, the play develops along three related lines. The first of these, involving only Charlie, is the sobering advent of middle-age with its intimations of mortality that come to most people following the death of a parent. "Now we are both parentless", Charlie tells Oliver. "We've gone to the head of the queue". As if to emphasize this, he is confronted with Young Charlie, who both amuses and disgusts him. A second and more important theme involves a son's guilty attempt to come to terms with the past via a confrontation with the memories of his father. "The shame of being ashamed of them [his parents] was the worst part", Charlie recalls. His

flight from home and even from Ireland was not just an attempt to build a better life independently but also an admission of guilt. Da is "the enemy", Mr. Drumm tells Charlie; "The dangerous ones are those who amuse us. There are millions like him: inoffensive, stupid, and not a damn bit of good. They've never said no in their lives. . .If you have any sense, you'll learn to be frightened of him". Drumm is trying to teach Charlie to reject the mediocrity of his father's world in order to find self-respect in his own. And yet, having made a place for himself in England, Charlie wonders, "How could I belong there if I belonged here?". The third theme, the most important and universal, is paternal love and sacrifice. "It was a long time before I realized that love turned upside down is love for all that", Charlie admits at the end of Act I. In the last scene of the play, he is surprised to learn that his father left a will giving him £135 "with more to come". Over the last few years, Da had hoarded the money Charlie sent him from England. Now, after his death, he proudly returns it to his son as a modest legacy. For as long as he can remember, Da has been *giving* to him, Charlie recalls: "Here's. . .a shilling for the pictures, a new suit for the job. Here's a life". When did I ever get a chance to pay it back, to get out from under, to be quit of you?" *Da* was written "to pay off a debt to my father", Leonard said in 1980. "But the play made me successful as a writer and since I couldn't have written it without my father, the debt's now greater than ever". Writing the play helped him realize that "for all the indecent haste to bury my childhood like a dead cat, there was an ache of loss".

Da is a great role, a stage character of the dimensions of a top-notch O'Casey creation, and altogether a very funny man. However, it is Charlie who has the sharpest, funniest lines of the play. The other characters are well developed, and each has at least one good scene. Mag (for Margaret), Da's often shrewish wife and Charlie's fretful mother, is a proud martyr to her own maternal benevolence, with her constant harping on the dangers of rearing an adopted child. Oliver, a self-improvement addict who placed all his faith in Dale Carnegie, is a slightly acidulous portrait of a youthful friend. Mary Tate, known as the "Yellow Peril", is a local girl whom Young Charley awkwardly attempts to seduce. Mrs. Prynn, Da's employer, gives him as a memento of his 54 years of service, not the cash bonus he expects, but a relic of the 1906 San Francisco Earthquake Fire. Mr. Drumm, a dour, acerbic civil servant in the Land Commission office, successfully recommended Charlie for his first job, even as he warned him against accepting it. (Mr. Drumm gets his own turn in the spotlight in Leonard's play called *A Life*, 1979.)

Leonard acknowledged not long after the Off-Broadway opening of *Da* in 1978 that the play is "pretty nearly totally autobiographical". In 1979, he published a memoir, *Home Before Night*, in which he covered with vitality and humour

Da: Olympic Theatre, Dublin, 1973

and in much greater detail the events dramatized in *Da*, and in 1989, a sequel, *Out after Dark*.

—Gene A. Barnett

DACHNIKI.   See **SUMMERFOLK.**

DACHNIKY.   See **SUMMERFOLK.**

DAKGHAR.   See **THE POST OFFICE.**

LA DAME AUX CAMÉLIAS.   See **THE LADY OF THE CAMELIAS.**

THE DANCE OF DEATH, Parts One and Two
   (Dödsdansen, fürstelen; Dödsdansen, andra delen)
by August Strindberg

First Publication: Stockholm, 1901 (both parts).
First Production: Residenztheater, Cologne, September 1905
             (in German); Intimate Theatre, Stockholm,
             1909 (in Swedish).

Translations
The Dance of Death, in *Five Plays of Strindberg*, translated by
   Elizabeth Sprigge, Garden City, New York, 1960.
The Dance of Death, in *Dramas of Testimony by August
   Strindberg*, translated by Walter Johnson, Seattle and
   London, 1975 (The Washington Strindberg).

The Dance of Death, in *Strindberg: Plays, 2*, translated by Michael Meyer, London, 1975.
The Dance of Death, in *Five Plays by August Strindberg*, translated by Harry G. Carlson, Berkeley, California, and London, 1983.

Criticism
(For general works on the author, see *Playwrights* volume)

Articles:
Karl-Ivar Hildeman, "Strindberg, *The Dance of Death* and Revenge", in *Scandinavian Studies*, 35, 1963.
Marion A. Taylor, "Edward Albee and August Strindberg: Some Parallels Between *The Dance of Death* and *Who's Afraid of Virginia Woolf?*", in *Papers on Language and Literature*, 1, 1965.
David Bronsen, "*The Dance of Death* and the Possibility of Laughter", in *Drama Survey*, 6, 1967.
Orley I. Holtan, "The Absurd World of Strindberg's *The Dance of Death*", in *Comparative Drama*, 1, 1967.
M.G. Robinson, "Prisoners at Play: Form and Meaning in Strindberg's *The Dance of Death* and Beckett's *Endgame*", in *Journal of European Studies*, vol.15 no.1, 1985.

*   *   *

The Dance of Death has undoubtedly coloured the prevalent view, in the Anglo-Saxon countries at least, of Strindberg as a misogynist and a misanthrope. The play is about a marriage which has survived several storms and struggles and is now settling uncomfortably into its last desolate stage before death puts a definite end to it.

Edgar and Alice, the main protagonists, are suffering their 25th year of married life in a symbolically circular room in a military fortress where Edgar is serving as an artillery officer. He has one year left until retirement and he feels great resentment about the fact that he never made it to the rank of Major. He is a man who has been "passed over". Another source of strife is Alice's abandoned career as an actress, something which the two laurel wreaths hanging in a prominent position on the wall are a poignant reminder of.

Alice, ten years younger than her husband, gave up her career when she married, and now feels cheated and frustrated, locked in a love-hate relationship without wealth or social position and spurned by the other officers' wives. Alice and Edgar are obliged to create their own entertainment with card-playing, piano music, and the captain's dance. Overfamiliarity has led to boredom and that in turn twists into cruel taunting when their communication comes to a stand-still.

The couple's two grown-up children have left the "prison" on the island for the city life on the mainland. Occasionally, there is a reminder of their existence in the messages transmitted through the telegraph apparatus on the captain's table. This contraption is also a messenger from the "other world" as it is constantly threatening to break into and shatter their world.

During the course of the play, Kurt, an old friend of the family arrives to take up his post as Master of Quarantine, but because of his gentle sympathetic nature he is soon seduced into becoming a catalyst for the two warring partners. Reluctantly, he is drawn into a whirlpool of lust and hate, lies and recriminations and his presence almost manages to upset the status quo. The couple's mutual feelings of hate and disappointment are momentarily diverted and Kurt's friendship is sought by both husband and wife in a vampire-like fashion.

The grotesque dance alluded to in the title of the play refers to the medieval "danse macabre" and more particularly perhaps to a Hungarian dance which the captain loves to perform in spite of his weak heart. The dance also serves as a metaphor for the human predicament in its absurdity.

Once, when Edgar dances to Alice's accompaniment and in Kurt's presence, he collapses on the floor. The prospect of his imminent death unleashes new seams of cruelty in their relationship. Alice rejoices prematurely, Kurt is sexually attracted to Alice to the point of intoxication and obsession and for a moment when Kurt bites Alice's throat, vampire-like, there seems to be a real possibility of a new "dance of death", a new doomed partnership. However, Edgar recovers, and eventually the couple come to the realisation that they are imprisoned in their marriage in the same way as they are symbolically imprisoned in their circular room in the fortress. They turn to Kurt for the last time and appeal for his understanding, beg him to deliver them from their personal hell, but Kurt knows that whoever he chooses to help will pull him down as well. Edgar and Alice are like two drowning persons, hanging on to him with all their strength and in order to survive he has to leave them. Edgar and Alice have no more illusions about their marriage, but their cynicism possesses a great deal of gallows' humour which relieves the tension both for them and for the audience.

At first sight this play appears to be a sequel to Strindberg's naturalistic dramas *Miss Julie* and *The Father*, written about 12 years previously. All these three plays depict the battle of the sexes, they all take place in one room and there is an important outdoor area immediately outside the confined playing space in all the three plays: the garden with the midsummer dance and the rising sun in *Miss Julie*, the snowscape and the fast night-ride by horse in *The Father* and the sea with the strong wind in *The Dance of Death*. But whereas Strindberg has taken great pains to create an entirely naturalistic setting in the two earlier plays, *The Dance of Death* is an altogether more symbolic piece. The audience is never allowed to forget the claustrophobia of the room especially as the two doors at the back open out to the fresh air and the sound of the sea as a contrast. The doors with their glass panes serve as a dividing line between the couple's personal hell and the outside world. Down by the water, the ferry departs for the mainland. That journey, that escape across the water surely has more than a passing resemblance to Charon's ferry trip across the Stygian river—the passage to and from the land of the dead.

The second part was added as a palliative to *Part I* and has a different tone altogether. The three main characters from the First Part have been joined by two members of the younger generation: Judith (Edgar's and Alice's daughter) and Allan (Kurt's son who has been sent to the island on Edgar's instigation). The oppressive room of the First Part has been replaced by Kurt's light, airy drawing-room with elegant furniture and a peaceful view over the sea.

The story is a tale of role-reversal and parasitical exploitation. The opening of *Part II* also contrasts greatly with that of *Part I*. Judith arrives in the drawing-room like a conventional ingenue with a short summer frock and a tennis racket in one hand in uncharacteristic Strindbergian fashion. Her target is Allan, a studious young man who appears to be immune to her bold advances. Judith attacks him with flattery, flirtatiousness, and a good portion of self-confidence. Her behaviour defies the laws of decorum and throughout the play Judith is the one who takes the initiative. With her passionate and strong-willed nature she dominates the men around her and skilfully avoids being pushed about by her authoritarian father who tries to marry her off to a 60-year-old colonel.

At the beginning of *Part II* Kurt is installed as Master of Quarantine on the island and Edgar views his beautiful home with envy. Gradually Kurt is stripped of all his belongings due to a financial miscalculation prompted by Edgar who gleefully watches Kurt's collapse. The Captain has deceived Kurt, ousted him from his home, lied to him, taken charge of his son, and robbed him of his chances to stand for Parliament. The captain's "vampirism" is without any redeeming features. He is a tyrant of colossal dimensions and his fatal stroke, which is a direct result of his daughter's defiant stance when she refuses to marry the person that he has selected for her, can be seen as a kind of Divine Justice. Nevertheless, at last Alice manages to summon up some compassion for him. Despite Edgar's interference and firm plans for his daughter, Judith and Allan are drawn to each other and their passionate love blossoms in the second half of the play and manages to neutralize the acrimonious atmosphere in the house. Strindberg makes us acutely aware of the danger ahead when Judith throws herself in Allan's arms. Everything is obviously going to repeat itself and Judith and Alan are carrying on the family tradition in sexual politics. Twenty years hence we can presume that they will have reached the same stage as that which Edgar and Alice had arrived at in *Part I*.

The best written character in *Part II* is undoubtedly Judith who comes across as an amazingly liberated, forthright young woman who conquers with a lethal combination of strength, intelligence and passion. Her sweeping, seductive powers reduce the young men in her circle to whimpering youths who either throw themselves on the sofa with a lace handkerchief pressed to their mouth, or walk in the woods, crying. Maybe these young men serve as a warning to those who are ready to succumb to a woman's charms. When Allan kneels in front of Judith and kisses her foot in total submission, she dismisses him with a prosaic remark about him getting black shoe polish on his mouth. Judith has wit, humour, and a sense of fun, and she is devastatingly attractive.

Alice lacks the strength and venom she had in *Part I*, and Kurt's humble acceptance of the disasters that befall him tend to weaken the play. Kurt remains stoical and forgiving throughout and reminds one of a latter-day Job.

The plot is rather improbable and with its loose construction it is not difficult to see why this play is performed so rarely on its own. A shortened version has appeared as an adjunct to the main play on some occasions and could serve as an interesting echo to the burnt-out marriage in *Part I* and as a reminder of the inescapable nature of human love: the blind overture in the initial stages of a love affair, the awakening passion in the young people and then the consuming nature of their love as when Allan points out that he feels like a log at the bottom of the pile waiting to be burnt. After the fire we get the smouldering ashes of a past passion represented by Alice and Edgar.

—Eivor Martinus

DANTON'S DEATH (Dantons Tod)
by Georg Büchner

First Publication: Frankfurt, 1835 (abridged version); complete version in *Nachgelassene Schriften*, 1850.
First Production: Belle-Alliance Theater, Berlin, 5 January 1902.

Editions
Dantons Tod, in *"Dantons Tod" and "Woyzeck"*, edited by Margaret Jacobs, Manchester, 1954; second edition, 1963; third edition, 1971.
Dantons Tod, in *Dantons Tod; Leonce and Lena; Woyzeck*, edited by Fritz Bergermann, Frankfurt, 1963.

Translations
Danton's Death, translated by S. Spender and G. Rees, London, 1939.
Danton's Death, translated by J. Holmstrom in *The Modern Theatre 5*, edited by Eric Bentley, Garden City, New York, 1955–60.
Danton's Death, in *Classical German Drama*, edited and translated by T.H. Lustig, New York, 1963.
Danton's Death, translated by James Maxwell, London, 1968; revised edition, 1969.
Danton's Death in *The Plays of Georg Büchner*, translated by Victor Price, Oxford, 1971.
Danton's Death, translated by Jane Fry, adapted by Howard Brenton, London, 1982; also in *Büchner: The Complete Plays*, edited by Michael Patterson, London, 1987.

Criticism
(For general works on the author, see *Playwrights* volume)

Books:
Wolfram Viehweg, *Georg Büchner's "Dantons Tod" auf dem deutschen Theater*, 1964.
Josef Jansen (ed.), *"Dantons Tod": Erläuterungen und Dokumente*, Stuttgart, 1969.
Louis F. Helbig, *Das Geschichtsdrama Georg Büchners: Zitatprobleme und historische Wahrheit in "Dantons Tod"*, Bern and Frankfurt, 1973.
Jürgen Siess, *Zitat und Kontext bei Georg Büchner: eine Studie zun den Dramen "Dantons Tod" und "Leonce und Lena"*, Göppingen, 1975.
Alfred Behrmann and Joachim Wohlleben, *Büchner, "Dantons Tod": eine Dramenanalyse*, Stuttgart, 1980.
Heinrich Pingel, *Georg Büchner's "Dantons Tod"*, 1981.
William H. Rey, *Georg Büchners "Dantons Tod": Revolutionstragödie und Mysterienspiel*, Bern, 1982.
Dorothy James, *Büchner's "Dantons Tod": A Reappraisal*, London, 1982.
Peter von Becker (ed.), *Georg Büchner's "Dantons Tod": kritische Studienausgabe des Originals mit Quellen, Aufsätzen und Materialen*, Frankfurt, 1985.
Matthew H. Wikander, *The Play of Truth and State: Historical Drama from Shakespeare to Brecht*, Baltimore, Maryland, 1986.
Herbert Wender, *Georg Büchners Bild der Grossen Revolution: zu den Quellen von Dantons Tod*, Frankfurt, 1988.

Articles:
Lee Baxandall, "Georg Büchner's *Danton's Death*, in *Tulane Drama Review*, 6, 1962.
E.M. Fleissner, "Revolutions as Theatre: *Danton's Death* and *Marat/Sade*", in *Massachusetts Review*, 7, 1966.
Douglas Milburn Jr., "Social Conscience and Social Reform: The Political Paradox of *Danton's Death*", in *Rice University Studies*, 53, 1967.
Richard Beacham, "Büchner's Use of Sources in *Danton's Death*, in *Yale/Theatre*, 3, 1972.
T.M. Holmes, "The Ideology of the Moderates in Büchner's *Danton's Death*", in *German Life and Letters*, 27, 1974.
Peter B. Waldeck, "Georg Büchner's *Dantons Tod*: Dramatic Structure and Individual Necessity", in *Susquehanna University Studies*, 9, 1974.

Danton's Death: National Theatre, London, 1982

Reinhold Grimm, "*Dantons Tod*: ein Gegenentwurf zu Goethes *Egmont*?", in *Germanische-Romanische Monatsschrift*, 33, 1983.

Christine Heiss, "Die Rezeption von *Dantons Tod* durch die deutschamerikanische Arbeiterbewegung im 19. Jahrhundert", in *Georg Büchner Jahrbuch*, 4, 1984.

Mohammad Kowsar, "Analytics of Schizophrenia: A Deleuze-Guattarian Consideration of Büchner's *Dantons Tod* and Weiss's *Marat / Sade*", in *Modern Drama*, 27, 1984.

Elke H. Rockwell, "Todesthematik und Kontextstruktur in Georg Büchners Drama *Dantons Tod*", in *Colloquia Germanica*, 18, 1985.

Gerhard P. Knapp, "*Dantons Tod*: die Tragödie des Jakobinismus: Ansätze einer Deutung", in *Diskussion Deutsche*, 92, 1986.

Rodney Taylor, "The Convergence of Individual Will and Historic Necessity in Büchner's *Danton*", in *Neue Germanistik*, Spring 1986.

Timothy J. Chamberlain, "Signs of Friendship: The Function of Hérault in *Dantons Tod*", in *Monatshefte*, 80, 1988.

David Horton, "'Die gliederlösende, böse Liebe': Observations on the Erotic Theme in Büchner's *Dantons Tod*", in *Deutsche Vierteljahrsschrift für Literaturwissenschaft und Geistesgeschichte*, June 1988.

Margarete Kohlenbach, "Puppen und Helden: Zum Fatalismusglauben in Georg Büchners Revolutionsdrama", in *Germanisch-Romanische Monatsschrift*, vol.38 no.4, 1988.

Rodney Taylor, "History and the Transcendence of Subjectivity in Büchner's Robespierre", in *Neophilologus*, 72, 1988.

Alain Cozic, "Danton face à Robespierre dans *Dantons Tod* de Büchner", in *Littératures*, 20, 1989.

Paul Levesque, "The Sentence of Death and the Execution of Wit in Georg Büchner's *Dantons Tod*", in *German Quarterly*, 62, 1989.

*   *   *

This four-act (*not* three-act as some hand-books have it) play focuses on the final weeks of Danton's life in 1794. It is the year after the execution of the king in the French Revolution. The revolutionary fervour to which Danton had contributed so much has given way to a dangerous phase of stagnation during which the confrontation between the radicals and the moderates is heading for the final show-down. In this situation Danton refuses to speak to the Convent. Instead he regales his friends with witticisms about life and death and lives a life of luxury while Robespierre preaches the gospel of virtue and terror in the Jacobine club. A final conversation between Robespierre and Danton only drives them further apart. While Danton declines to take any action, Robespierre and St. Just plan his destruction. Convinced that his enemies would not dare to arrest him, Danton hesitates until it is too late. He faces his accusers with a brilliant speech in his own defence. By turning his harsh words against him, and by using a street rebellion in his support as a pretext, Danton's enemies quickly send him to the guillotine. In stoic resolve he faces death along with his supporters, among them his closest friend Camille Desmoulins whose wife closes the play by provoking her own execution.

Büchner wrote the play at the age of 21 and like his *Woyzeck* it was completely unlike contemporary drama. In the same way in which *Woyzeck* is often seen as a precursor of German expressionist theater, *Danton's Death* should receive credit for being the first *realistic* play in German literature. But as was the case with *Woyzeck*, his contemporaries were not ready for Büchner's modernity. Not only would the all-pervasive censorship have prevented a performance (as late as 1891 the editors of *Vorwärts* went to jail for reprinting the play), but the German stage, still bound by illusionary concepts, was hardly ready for the hectic change of short scenes, and the fractured nature of the play. The major problem, however, would have been that Büchner presented what has since become known as anti-heroes at a time when audiences were accustomed to see on stage heroes and heroines of the calibre of Schiller's Mary Stuart.

When Büchner wrote the play he was influenced by his failed political and revolutionary activities—his *Hessian Courier* was published in July 1834 and he was forced to flee Germany in March 1835—and also by his studies of the French revolution. The latter, in particular, had a profound impact on him. Two letters written at that time reflect his reaction; the first, to his fiancée ("Ich fühle mich wie zernichtet unter dem grässlichen Fatalismus der Geschichte"), expresses his feelings of utter destruction by the "terrible fatalism" of history, and the second, in February 1834 to his parents, said: "nobody can determine not to become a fool or a criminal—because if our circumstances were the same we should surely all become the same" (this last letter is usually referred to as the "fatalism letter"). It is in the light of these two autobiographical remarks that *Danton's Death* has to be understood. The play is a historical drama; in view of the fact that Büchner quotes directly from historical documents he had studied, it might even be called a documentary drama. In accordance with his own conviction that it is the playwright's duty to get as close to historical events as possible, he lifts some of the speeches before the Convent directly from his historical sources. In order to give a true portrayal of history he masterfully crafts mass scenes in the streets and mixes them with the encounters of his dramatis personae. At the center of the action are Danton and his opponent Robespierre. Danton at the height of his career has been overtaken by his fatalism, even nihilism. He is tired of the revolution and of life itself. No longer willing to act in self-defense, he hides behind his conviction that "they would not dare". That he no longer believes in the social revolution, whose protagonist he had once been, is symbolized by his indulgence in sensuous pleasures. Juxtaposed with "immoral" Danton is "virtuous" Robespierre, the "incorruptible". He is portrayed as a fanatic missionary who, in his arrogance, believes he has to force people into freedom, brotherhood, and equality by murdering thousands in the name of the state. He goes so far as to elevate himself above Christ by stating: "He had the ecstasy of pain. I have the torment of the executioner. Who denies himself the more, he or I?". From Büchner's historical viewpoint, both Danton and Robespierre can be seen as instruments of history who fulfil their pre-determined roles while they believe they are acting to advance humanity. Danton at least has recognized the futility of it all and goes to the guillotine in a fatalistic mood proclaiming that it is better to end life as an "epigram" than as an "epic poem". But it is Danton's contempt ("The world is chaos. It will give birth to a God called Nothingness") that deflects attention from the fate of individuals towards society as a whole.

Despite some Marxist critics' claims that *Danton's Death* is directly connected to the *Hessian Courier* and in itself is a depiction of class struggle, the play conveys, more than even *Woyzeck*, Büchner's pessimistic acceptance of determinism. His concept of determinism goes far beyond the protest against social structures that might be changed by man. His Danton symbolizes the human condition that, in the absence of a transcendent point of reference, can only lead to fatalism and boredom; as the protagonist himself says: "You put on your shirt, then your trousers. . . .You put one foot in front of the other. Sad. There is absolutely no vision of any other way of doing it: millions have always done it like that, millions always will. . . .It's all very boring and very, very sad".

—Manfred K. Kremer

DANTONS TOD.   See **DANTON'S DEATH.**

A DAY IN THE DEATH OF JOE EGG
by Peter Nichols

First Publication: London, 1967.
First Production: Citizens Theatre, Glasgow, 9 May 1967.

*   *   *

The title character of *A Day in the Death of Joe Egg*, Peter Nichols's first London stage play, is a severely spastic ten-year-old girl whose father, mimicking a doctor with a music-hall German accent, aptly but cruelly terms a "wegetable". *Joe Egg* has very little plot as such. The first act is in effect a two-hander, focusing on Joe's parents, Bri and Sheila, with Joe and the audience as essentially silent (but constantly addressed) spectators. We learn a great deal about the couple in this act: their personality quirks, the fragile state of their marriage, and, especially, the various stratagems they have devised in order to bear the appalling tragedy of Joe. Act II opens up the action with the introduction of the couple's friends Freddie and his wife Pam, and then later Bri's mother Grace, all of whom (however caricatured) have definite opinions about the best way to deal with Joe. The play ends with Bri, having failed in a half-hearted attempt at euthanasia, packing up his bags and running out on Sheila (who remains oblivious to his departure) and on Joe (who is always oblivious) in a denouement left deliberately ambiguous—either an act of supreme cowardice, or a brave bid to achieve salvation.

Like almost all of Nichols' plays, *Joe Egg* is specifically rooted in autobiography: the dramatic situation, though obviously transmuted into art, mirrors Peter and Thelma Nichols' experience with their eldest child Abigail. Out of this personal pain Nichols has forged a play that is not only intensely moving, as might be expected, but also—unexpected and, to some critics, unacceptable—wildly funny. *Joe Egg*, again like almost all of Nichols' plays, is written in what the author has termed a "comic-strip style", a style greatly influenced by Thornton Wilder's *The Skin of Our Teeth* and closely related to English music-hall or American vaudeville.

A Day in the Death of Joe Egg: Comedy Theatre, London, 1967

Like music-hall performers, the characters in *Joe Egg* are constantly breaking the fourth wall—by repeated direct address to the audience, by self-conscious acknowledgements that they are in a theatre (when Bri calls Freddie "a pain in the arse", Grace mutters "I hate a play with language"), or, most frequent of all, by stepping out of character to do a comic routine, like Bri's German doctor or his impersonation of a staggeringly inept vicar. Nichols' original title for the play— and one he now wishes he had kept—was "Funny Turns", simultaneously evoking both Joe's spastic fits, graphically dramatized for us throughout the play, and Bri's and Sheila's way of responding to those fits and to their pain generally, through the anodyne of the music-hall performer's comic acts.

This breaking of the proscenium functions as a kind of "alienation" technique for the audience, although Nichols claims it is the opposite of Brecht's: "[my] alienation techniques. . .are supposed to involve you, draw you in, make the

experience more intense". The specific example he cites is the Act I curtain, in which the actress playing Joe suddenly skips on stage and announces the intermission, blissfully healthy and "normal". This is indeed an intensely moving moment, the "magical" fulfillment of her parents' dream ("Wouldn't she be lovely if she was running about?"). But it also provides the audience with an important release, a surprisingly necessary reminder that Joe is not a *real* spastic child but an actor, and therefore "alienates" us in the Brechtian sense as well. An audience needs that Brechtian distancing; it allows us to be sufficiently detached from the horror of Joe's plight so that we can permit ourselves to laugh without guilt at Nichols' comic treatment of her. And it further allows us, again as in Brecht, to be sufficiently detached so that we can *think*, form opinions, make judgments about the "problem" of Joe, for when the play's characters address us directly, they are often attempting to "appeal" to us as in a courtroom, to persuade us of the morality of their views concerning Joe; the audience is being cast as "jury", expected to ponder issues of "right" and "wrong". Nor is it only the audience who requires such Brechtian distancing. Nichols' characters similarly need it, especially Bri and Sheila: breaking through the fourth wall by breaking into music-hall "funny turns" is their way of coping with their pain.

A Day in the Death of Joe Egg raises some highly relevant social issues. Perhaps humour used as an "anaesthetic", is ultimately dangerous. "Isn't that the whole fallacy of the sick joke?", Freddie wonders. "It kills the pain but leaves the situation just as it was?". How, then, do we alter the situation? Bri argues for euthanasia, and on one level Nichols' play is a lively debate about the merits of that particular solution (among others). But on another level, the play is not primarily about Joe at all: Joe becomes a metaphor for the "illness" of Bri and Sheila's marriage, the prism through which we see reflected the character flaws each brings to the relationship. The name "Joe Egg" can thus be read as symbolizing the state of their marriage, which the full title of the play informs us is a "death"; maybe Bri is therefore justified in seeking to escape. For all its thematic interest, however, the importance of *Joe Egg* rests ultimately on its stylistic innovations. Nichols took an enormous risk in dramatizing this sad saga of a profoundly disabled child as a comedy: might not audiences feel they were being encouraged to laugh *at* Joe? The play constantly walks a very thin tightrope, but the risk pays off. *Joe Egg* is black humour at its blackest but also its most redemptive.

—Hersh Zeifman

THE DAYS OF THE TURBINS.   See THE WHITE GUARD.

DEAD END
by Sidney Kingsley

First Publication: New York, 1936.
First Production: Belasco Theatre, New York, 1935.

*   *   *

Public Enemy Babyface Martin returns to his boyhood home in a New York City slum to see his mother and his former girlfriend. His mother repudiates him, and his girl has been forced into prostitution and is riddled with venereal disease. To save a neighbourhood delinquent from following in Martin's criminal path, a boyhood friend informs on Martin and uses the reward to get the boy out of the slum. Martin dies in a bloody gun battle with police, but there is some hope for the boy if he can escape the "dead end" of inner-city decay.

Few plays in American history have had the social impact of Kingsley's naturalistic masterpiece. Not only did it initiate a Congressional campaign of slum clearance but its depiction of juvenile delinquency (recreated in a film version scripted by Lillian Hellman) inspired a series of "Dead End Kid" films which represented the Depression era to millions.

The play's 1936 production featured Norman Bel Geddes's landmark set of a vast cityscape juxtaposing opulent tower

Dead End: Set design by Norman Bel Geddes, 1935

block and insect-ridden slum. This set reflected the panoramic sweep of the action. Nearly half a dozen stories are interrelated to support the thesis of environmental decay. No single character dominates, but the stories are compelling enough in their realism to create the impression of a mini-world.

The gang's portrayal is perhaps most memorable as the first of its kind in American drama. Kingsley's reproduction of demotic street speech, hard to decipher on the page, established a precedent in dramatic verisimilitude, and very little of the adolescents' dialogue seems toned down for commercial appeal. Their casual cruelty is quite amoral and encompasses racism and victimisation of the weak with unsparing candour.

The rest of the action, by contrast, is less vivid largely through its familiarity. But charges of sentimentality and caricature do not withstand close examination. The authorial voice of a would-be architect crippled with rickets is humanised by his final appearance as a police informer. The "romance" between him and the mistress of a tycoon avoids sentimentality because of her ultimate decision to accept the softer option of financial security, and because the architect stops short of settling for a poorer candidate.

There is scant moralising outside the narrative, and the theme is pervasive enough to enable the main characters to have fully-wrought presence, from the prostitute to the politically militant sister of the gang's leader injured in a street demonstration.

The original production achieved one of the longest runs in Broadway history (687 performances). The play has been unfairly ignored for major revival, despite its contemporary impact. The panoramic focus lends itself admirably to anti-realistic, "epic" interpretation, with particular advantages for present-day group-orientated companies. Ever the craftsman, Kingsley made his reputation with *Dead End*, and the play, surviving in history as the most memorable of its era, deserves a major revival.

—James MacDonald

THE DEATH AND RESURRECTION OF MR. ROCHE
by Thomas Kilroy

First Publication: London and New York, 1969.
First Production: Olympia Theatre, Dublin, 7 October 1968.

*   *   *

The Death and Resurrection of Mr. Roche is an example of a play that utilizes a late night drinking party (cf. Albee's *Who's Afraid of Virginia Woolf?*) as a laboratory for an examination of the minds, morals, and souls of both host(s) and guests. After an evening in Murray's Pub, six Dublin men, five of whom are still single, collect around midnight in Kelly's drab apartment to continue drinking and talking. Mr. Roche, a known homosexual and the last to arrive, is teased in a friendly way and locked into the small bathroom with Kevin, a student. When he is released, he explains that he is claustrophobic. Kelly increasingly resents Roche and picks a quarrel with him; this time they force him into a small, basement-like area called the "holy-hole". When they pull him out after a few minutes, Doc, a perennial medical student, pronounces him dead. Kelly frantically and foolishly prevails on Doc and Kevin to try to dispose of the body by leaving it on a park bench. When Kelly and Seamus, who have known each other for a long time, are left alone in the apartment, Kelly reveals that he and Roche have had a brief homosexual encounter. Very early the next morning, Doc, Kevin, and Mr. Roche return to Kelly's apartment in high good humour, explaining that Roche had been revived in the rain as they tried to dispose of him. As the group breaks up, Kelly is fearful that Roche will try to blackmail him, but the older man cheerfully claims to have no recollection that anything happened between them.

The play, of course, is not really about Mr. Roche but about Kelly, a 36-year-old civil servant who looks longingly back at his peasant rearing in a cottage which, unlike his Dublin flat ("Flats isn't a house"), was a "natural place to live in". He has the peasant's love of living and working on the land ("what I'd prefer if I was given the free choice"), and he evokes not only the fertility of a life-style but also of the soil as he describes harvesting vegetables "with the roots black and wet, lovely to the touch, like silk". However, he had been a "bright hair-oil scholarship boy" who had gone off to Dublin to become "the success of my family". Although he proudly announces that he has no "complexes about myself", he is lonely and aware of ageing, finding consolation only in the "sameness" of everything (anticipating his friend Seamus's complaint). He sentimentalizes the years in Dublin and his very tenuous friendships. He boasts loudly of having principles, "if others haven't", and is forceful in his denunciation of Roche for his homosexuality, all of which might suggest he has something to hide. When the man is thought to be dead, Kelly is concerned only about the bad publicity which will focus on him.

Kelly's soul-baring scene with Seamus begins with a sad confession that he has not visited his home and family for a long time. Although he is lonely, he cannot abide the "skittering and giggling" of females, and he wonders if there is "something up" with him. Gradually the extent of his relationship with Roche unfolds: the occasional drink, the overnight visit, and finally the brief confession that "God forgive me. I let him handle me. . . ." At this point, Kelly appears to be thoroughly awash in equal parts of misery, hypocrisy, and self-deception. Withal, however, he remains comically concerned for his reputation: "Prison I can take. It's the bad name that leaves me wake at the knees". He realizes that he has given himself away to an old friend and that Seamus must now live

with his secret. It is left to conjecture just how this will affect their friendship.

If *Death and Resurrection* is principally about Kelly, it is, to some extent, also about Seamus, a teacher, who is only two years married but already disillusioned by the "sameness" of married life. His wife "surrounds me with the same things", he complains; "her sameness is beginning to drive me mad". Nor is Kelly's romanticizing of the past any good, either. "What was healthy then is sick now", he says; "you're all sick. . . . Why haven't you changed even a little?". Kelly is in "the same situation" as when he came to Dublin several years ago, and although married, he himself is not much better off. Sadly he concludes, "I'm as happy as ever I'll be". Kelly and Seamus, taken together, are judgments on the sterility of contemporary life—and not just in Ireland.

The phoenix-like Mr. Roche has a symbolic function and also seems to speak for the playwright. Being homosexual, he is an outsider and a threat to their masculinity and at the same time a compassionate truth-bringer who exposes the spiritual sterility of their lives and for this he is, Christ-like, put into the tomb, the "holy-hole". "Jesus," Kelly exclaims at first sight of the revived, "resurrected" man, who then provides an apocalyptic-like description of the dawn he had just witnessed which was "like the beginning of life again". He denounces the "withering, joylessness" of their lives in Act I as they systematically reduce themselves to the animal level with alcohol, damning their pretensions to dignity and self-respect. At the end of the play, he tells Kelly, "We all need sympathy now and again. Everybody needs sympathy". As some of them leave for early mass, he admonishes them to pray "for all the dead and the living dead". Roche the Revelator is the most humane character in the play.

Death and Resurrection is not a play about homosexuality; it is a play about the waste of mediocre, mis-spent lives; about the price of "success" and alienation from family and roots; and most importantly, about the need for compassion, tolerance, sympathy, and understanding. It is a play that is peculiarly Irish in some respects but which has reverberations that are recognizable both East and West of Ireland.

—Gene A. Barnett

DEATH AND THE KING'S HORSEMAN
by Wole Soyinka

First Publication: London, 1975.
First Production: Ife-Ife, Nigeria, 1976.

Criticism
(For general works on the author, see *Playwrights* volume)

Articles:

André Lefevre, "Soyinka's *Death and the King's Horseman*", in *AVRUG Bulletin*, vol.9 nos.2–3, 1982.

Adetokunbo Pearse, "Myth and Meaning in *Death and the King's Horseman*", in *Lore & Language*, 8, 1983.

David Richards, "Òwe l'esin òrò: Proverbs like Horses: Wole Soyinka's *Death and the King's Horseman*", in *Journal of Commonwealth Literature*, vol.19 no.1, 1984.

Julius Ogu, "Thematic Imagery and Dramaturgical Accent in Soyinka's *Death and the King's Horseman*", in *Nigerian Theatre Journal*, 2, 1985.

Jacques Leclaire, "The Universality of Wole Soyinka's *Death and the King's Horseman*", in *Nouvelles du sud*, 2, 1985–86.

Jasbir Jain, "The Unfolding of a Text: Soyinka's *Death and the King's Horseman*", in *Research in African Literatures*, 17, 1986.

James Booth, "Self-Sacrifice and Human Sacrifice in Soyinka's *Death and the King's Horseman*", in *Research in African Literatures*, 19, 1988.

Richard M. Ready, "Through the Intricacies of 'the fourth stage' to an Apprehension of *Death and the King's Horseman*", in *Black American Literature Forum*, 22, 1988.

* * *

The play opens in the marketplace of the ancient town of Oyo, in western Nigeria. Elesin Oba, accompanied by his drummers and praise-singers, is on his way to die so as to accompany his dead lord, the Alafin of Oyo, to the spirit-world in accordance with Yoruba tradition. But he sees and desires a beautiful young woman, the betrothed of the son of the market-woman Iyaloja, who agrees reluctantly to Elesin's marriage to her son's intended bride before his ritual suicide. When Pilkings, the young District Officer learns of the intended death he orders the arrest of Elesin. But the market-women, led by Iyaloja, prevent the soldiers reaching him and the marriage is consummated. Elesin enters a deep trance, as he prepares to die. But death does not come soon enough. Scene four ends with the arrival of Elesin in hand cuffs, arrested before he has been able to complete his ritual obligation to his people. He is rejected by his son Olunde, whose conversation with Pilkings' wife Jane at a European fancy-dress ball reveals much about white attitudes to the people they have colonized as well as the fact that Pilkings has once before intervened in the life of Elesin's family, by sending Olunde off to medical school in England to train as a doctor. Olunde has returned in anticipation of his father's successful execution of his duty, but the final scene reveals that he is prepared to make up for Elesin's failure by performing the act himself. His body is brought in to the singing of a dirge and Elesin, in a last desperate act, finally succeeds in killing himself and belatedly embarking on the journey to the ancestors.

Death and the King's Horseman, written during Soyinka's stay in England in the 1970's, has proved to be one of his more popular plays, at least outside Nigeria. This may be partly because it gives vivid theatrical expression to the richness and, for Western readers and audiences, fascinating strangeness of his native Yoruba culture, while being more accessible than some of his other major drama. It may also be because this play, more than his others, has stronger resonances for Western audiences because of its depiction of colonialism in Africa—an historical experience which in recent years has been extensively treated in literature and drama.

The British in Africa, in this version, are not a pretty sight. They are presented as contemptible in their ignorance of and insensitivity to African culture. Pilkings and his wife are first seen in *egungun* masquerade costumes which they are to wear at a fancy-dress ball in honour of a visit by the Prince of Wales. It doesn't occur to them that they are committing sacrilege, in the eyes of local people, by dressing as the spirits of the dead. Culturally tunnel-visioned, Pilkings and his kind cannot see that ritual suicide of the kind Elesin Oba proposes to commit is not barbaric, however strange and incomprehensible it may legitimately appear to a European, but a necessary ritual act of the greatest significance in this community, the disruption of which is a cultural catastrophe. The point about barbarism is forcibly driven home by Olunde in his conversation with Jane Pilkings, when he comments on the mass, and the involuntary

slaughter which is going on in Europe. (Soyinka takes the poetic liberty of setting the action during the World War II, though it is based on events which occurred in 1946.)

In a note prefixing the published version of the play, however, Soyinka has insisted that the colonial issue is not truly central but merely "a catalytic incident"; the main confrontation of *Death and the King's Horseman* "is largely metaphysical". The religious and cultural import of the ritual suicide which Elesin so belatedly commits is articulated by Iyaloja towards the end of the play: "He [Elesin] knows the meaning of a king's passage.. . .He knows he has condemned our king to wander in the void of evil with beings who are enemies of life". Elesin's failure to ensure the smooth transition of the spirit of the king to the world of the dead, there to be reunited with the ancestral spirits, endangers—and perhaps worse than endangers—the harmonious relations between the living, the dead and the unborn, upon which the health of society depends. Though his son sacrifices himself—like so many of Soyinka's protagonists—for his people's sake, his action may have come too late. Elesin himself recognizes that his failure was not only due to the intervention of the white man but was also the product of "a weight of longing on my earth-held limbs". Consequently, he commits a "blasphemy of thought", and as his praise-singer points out, "What the end will be, we are not gods to tell". The only hope lies in the unborn, in the child Elesin's young bride may have in her womb.

—Brian Crow

DEATH OF A SALESMAN: Certain Private Conversations in Two Acts and a Requiem
by Arthur Miller

First Publication: New York, 1949.
First Production: Morosco Theatre, New York, 10 February 1949.

Criticism
(For general works on the author, see *Playwrights* volume)

Books:

Gerald Weales (ed.), *Arthur Miller: "Death of a Salesman": Text and Criticism*, New York, 1967.

C.J. Partridge, *Death of a Salesman*, Oxford, 1969.

Walter J. Meserve (ed.), *Studies in "Death of a Salesman"*, Columbus, Ohio, 1972.

Helene Wickham Koon (ed.), *Twentieth-Century Interpretations of "Death of a Salesman"*, Englewood Cliffs, New Jersey, 1983.

Bernard F. Dukore, *"Death of a Salesman" and "The Crucible"*, London, 1989 (Text and Performance Series).

Harold Bloom (ed), *Arthur Miller's "Death of a Salesman"*, New York, 1988 (Modern Critical Interpretations).

Articles:

R. Brian Parker, "Point of View in Arthur Miller's *Death of a Salesman*", in *University of Toronto Quarterly*, 35, 1966.

Arthur K. Oberg, "*Death of a Salesman* and Arthur Miller's Search for Style", in *Criticism*, 9, 1967.

Death of A Salesman: National Theatre, London, 1979

Barclay W. Bates, "The Lost Past in *Death of a Salesman*", in *Modern Drama*, 11, 1968.

Thomas E. Porter, "Acres of Diamonds: *Death of a Salesman*", in *Myth and Modern American Drama*, Detroit, 1969.

Irving F. Jacobson, "Family Dreams in *Death of a Salesman*", in *American Literature*, 47, 1975.

William Aarnes, "Tragic Form and the Possibility of Meaning in *Death of a Salesman*", in *Furman Studies*, 29, 1983.

Richard T. Brucher, "Willy Loman and *The Soul of a New Machine*: Technology and the Common Man", in *Journal of American Studies*, 17, 1983.

M.C. Anderson, "*Death of a Salesman*: A Consideration of Willy Loman's Role in Twentieth-Century Tragedy", in *CRUX*, vol.20 no.2, 1986.

Eugene R. August, "*Death of a Salesman*: A Men's Studies Approach", in *Western Ohio Journal*, vol.7 no.1, 1986.

Steve Vineberg, "Willy Loman and the Method", in *Journal of Dramatic Theory and Criticism*, vol.1 no.2, 1987.

Peter J. Burgard, "Two Parts Ibsen, One Part American Dream: On Derivation and Originality in Arthur Miller's *Death of a Salesman*", in *Orbis Litterarum*, 43, 1988.

Leah Hadomi, "Fantasy and Reality: Dramatic Rhythm in *Death of a Salesman*", in *Modern Drama*, 31, 1988.

*   *   *

Willy Loman, the hero—or anti-hero—of *Death of a Salesman* is said by his elder son, Biff, to have had "all the wrong dreams. All, all wrong. He never knew who he was". The play tells through flashbacks intercut into present-day action, of the false aims, degradation, and final decline of a salesman who believes he is "vital in New England" but who, in reality, is a failure—as salesman, as father, and, in Biff's eyes, as husband. The two-act play has a sub-title, "Certain Private Conversations in Two Acts and a Requiem". At first this seems a trifle portentous, but it accurately describes the behind-the-scenes life of the public salesman. One thread of the story shows an aging Willy Loman (he has a Jonsonian-style symbolic name), disappointed in his children (Biff and Happy), with failing car and worn-out fridge, less and less able to cope with his daily round, despite the support of his faithful wife, Linda. He is failing to sell, and when he calls on his boss, Howard Wagner, to request to be transferred to New York, he discovers he is not wanted, and is fired. Even his little patch of garden grows nothing. The second act ends with the sound of Willy driving off at high speed to commit suicide. His funeral takes place on the very day the house is paid off. "We're free and clear. . . .We're free. . .", says Linda, as the curtain falls, "And there'll be nobody home".

The play's original title was "The Inside of His Head" and that aptly described both the delusions Willy has about himself and his sons and the world of memories which are enacted within the main action. Biff, a fine athlete, fails to win a college place and calls at Willy's hotel in Boston unexpectedly to persuade Willy to see his teacher, "Because if he saw the kind of man you are, and you just talked to him in your [salesman] way. . .I'm sure he'd come through for you". Then a woman appears through the bathroom door, dressed only in a black slip, and there is a brilliant moment of humiliation for all three expressed in the most economical dramatic terms. This exposure of Willy's infidelity to his son comes almost at the end of the play but, chronologically, years earlier. We have had a subtle hint that Willy took women companions on his sales-trips early in the play when the voices of Linda and an unnamed woman overlap, but Willy's deception of his wife and its revelation to Biff are deliberately placed much later. Miller has adapted Ibsen's technique of retrospective exposition—the technique whereby the events that led to the present are only fully revealed at the climax of the present. Shortly after the scene in the Boston hotel room, Biff confronts Willy with a length of hose that he suspects Willy intended to use to commit suicide by gassing himself. He reveals that his father was no more than an assistant to an assistant salesman, and that he, Biff, is a wastrel who has spent three months in gaol for stealing a suit in Kansas City. He has now just stolen a valuable pen from the desk of the man from whom he hoped to get a good job. He realises, as he tells his father, "I'm a dime a dozen, and so are you!". Almost comically, yet pathetically, Willy," in an uncontrolled outburst", breaks out, "I am not a dime a dozen! I am Willy Loman, and you are Biff Loman!". Biff has to be restrained from attacking his father and sums up their common failures:

> I am not a leader of men, Willy, and neither are you. You were never anything but a hard-working drummer who landed in the ash can like all the rest of them! I'm one dollar an hour, Willy! I tried seven states and couldn't raise it. A buck an hour! Do you gather my meaning?

It would be wrong to dismiss Willy as a mean, rather pathetic, hypocrite. It is easy, and not wholly incorrect, to see him as epitomising a society in which money and sales—talk count for more than human values. Willy's values, like those of his society, are false, but the tragedy for Willy is that they are rooted in a genuine love for his wife, even though loneliness and failure draw him to seek consolation in passing women, and he has a real desire to build something worthwhile for his family and to provide his children with a good start in life. His dream world is, perhaps not wholly convincing, further dramatised by his conversations with Ben who beckons to a world out there where fortunes are to be made—to the riches of Africa or the timberlands of Alaska—but the deception he has worked on Linda makes her dissuade him: "Why must everybody conquer the world? You're well liked, and the boys love you, and someday. . .[you'll] be a member of the firm. . .".

Death of a Salesman could easily be a depressing story of failure, but it has much humour. Often scenes begin with lightness, even joy and hope, and the comic and melodramatic are juxtaposed so that the overall effect can reasonably claim to be a tragedy of the common man (upon which subject Miller has written perceptively). It is a cliché to say that *Death of a Salesman* dramatises the failure of the American Dream; but it is also true that not many salesmen are driven to Willy's end. The tragedy is Willy's tragedy, our tragedy, not specifically America's.

—Peter Davison

THE DEATH OF CUCHULAIN
by W.B. Yeats

First Publication: In *Last Poems and Two Plays*, Dublin, 1939.
First Production: Abbey Theatre, Dublin, 1945.

Criticism
(For general works on the author, see *Playwrights* volume)

Books:
Reg Skene, *The Cuchulain Plays of W.B. Yeats: A Study*, London, 1974.

Articles:
John R. Moore, "Cuchulain, Christ, and the Queen of Love: Aspects of Yeatsian Drama", in *Tulane Drama Review*, vol.6 no.3, 1962.
Phillip L. Marcus, "Myth and Meaning in Yeats's *The Death of Cuchulain*", in *Irish University Review*, 2, 1972.
Phillip L. Marcus, " 'Remembered Tragedies': The Evolution of the Lyric in Yeats's *The Death of Cuchulain*", in *Irish University Review*, 6, 1976.
Phillip L. Marcus, " 'I make the Truth': Vision and Revision in Yeats's *The Death of Cuchulain*", in *Colby Library Quarterly*, 12, 1976.
Richard Londraville, "W.B. Yeats's Anti-Theatre and Its Analogs in Chinese Drama: The Staging of the Cuchulain Cycle", in *Asian Culture Quarterly*, vol.2 no.3, 1983.

* * *

Yeats's last play shows him still at the height of his powers, bold, personal, in touch with a lifetime's work, wild, jokey, challenging. It also has characteristic failures; his fascination with the material of the Irish sagas never directly produced a great poem or play. It was a sort of patriotic lumber he carried in his head, and only when he acknowledges this does his work seem truly of its time: "Players and painted stage took all my love, / and not those things that they were emblems of". He works from this position in the first long speech of the play, spoken by an Old Man who is the Yeats of *On the Boiler*—bitter, bad-tempered, and good fun: "I have been selected because I am out of fashion and out of date like the antiquated romantic stuff the thing is made of". One can see why people invoke Yeats as a precursor of Beckett. This idea relates as well to one of his last poems, also about Cuchulain, in which the dead man of violence is obliged to study the gentle art of sewing. Both works have bird imagery. The Old Man parades many of Yeats's prejudices, against commercial drama and Book Societies, etc. As elsewhere in Yeats it is hard to separate a defensible conservatism from a foolish snobbery, yet he brings it off more or less by overtopping himself: "I spit! I spit! I spit!".

The play then moves from dynamic prose into fairly conventional blank verse as Eithne Inguba confronts the dying Cuchulain. In so far as Yeats uses sources he relies on the dubious, but influential, Standish O'Grady. Yeats never has Shakespeare's way with mythological material, but he uses history as well as anybody.

The blank verse is fairly tired, like the substance of his plot, Eithne speaks one message, but has a letter in her hand that contradicts it. He "must face odds no man can face and live". The introduction of symbolic figures like The Morrigu, a war goddess, adds very little. Yeats touches on some mysteries of the human heart, of how love can be mixed with hate; but only specialists could claim it has any dramatic interest.

Aoife, the mother of the son he killed in *On Baile's Strand*, turns up; but this confrontation is dissipated in slack verse and a melodramatic conception of character: "Maeve parted ranks that she might let you through. / You have the right to kill me". By many clever touches the ageing artist pumps life into these charades; Aoife winds a magic scarf about him and he objects: "There was no reason so to spoil your veil: / I am weak from loss of blood" and he says of her son, "Age makes more skilful but not better men". Well put and touching, but for the discriminating audience Yeats demanded their discourse has to be recognised as a second hand summary of old themes. Aoife hears The Blind Man approach, and leaves the stage, her important questions unasked, because a really dramatic event is going to happen. She never returns. The cynical, wily, but limited Blind Man of *On Baile's Strand* comes on to cut the hero's throat. Because the idea has substance the verse gains poise: "Somebody said that I was in Maeve's tent, / And somebody else, a big man by his voice, / That if I brought Cuchulain's head in a bag / I would be given twelve pennies. . .".

Every production of a Yeats play has to cope with difficult problems. Yeats had committed himself to a drama of masks and dances for which the literary critic can hardly speak, so much depends on the designer and the dancer. But that is not a mistake: it shows a courage and generosity that have been justified by recent developments in Irish and, no doubt, in world drama.

The final passage in this short play is spoken by The Singer in ballad metre. It has something of the Crazy Jane poems, and a great many odds and ends from the later poems, chiefly a bold but inappropriate connecting of Pearse at The Post Office in 1916 and the death of Cuchulain. Pearse was certainly obsessed by Cuchulain, but he had invented his own Cuchulain most unlike Yeats's world-weary, sexually sophisticated figure. Yet Yeats's final imaginings will always be fascinating to his admirers though never fully part of the world repertory.

—James Simmons

THE DECEIVED (Gl'Ingannati)
by the Accademi degli Intronati di Siena

First Publication: Venice, 1537.
First Production: Carnival, Siena, 1532.

Editions
Gl'Ingannati, edited by I. Sanesi and G. Laterza, 1912.
Gl'Ingannati, in *Commedie del Cinquecento 1*, edited by Nino Borsellino, Milan, 1962.
Gli Ingannati, edited by F. Cerreta, Florence, 1980.

Translations
The Deceived, translated by Thomas Love Peacock in *The Genius of The Italian Theater*, edited by Eric Bentley, New York, 1964.
The Deceived, translated by Bruce Penman, in *Five Italian Renaissance Comedies*, edited by Bruce Penman, Harmondsworth, 1978.

Criticism

Books:
L. Petracchi Constantini, *L'Accademia degli Intronati e una sua commedia*, Siena, 1928.

Articles:
G. Cavazzuti, "Ludovico Castelvetro e la commedia *Gl'Ingannati*", in *Giornale storico della letteratura italiana*, 40, 1902.
R. Andrews, "*Gli Ingannati* as a Text for Performance", in *Italian Studies*, 37, 1982.

*   *   *

A young girl, Lelia, takes service disguised as a page boy with Flamminio, the man she loves, and is employed by him to carry messages to his new love-object Isabella—who falls for the "male" go-between instead. The arrival in town of Lelia's twin brother Fabrizio causes confusion, but eventually brings harmony when Isabella marries Fabrizio and Flamminio marries the unmasked Lelia; so far, so familiar. But there are more differences than similarities with Shakespeare, in terms of plot, tone, style and supporting characters. Unlike the loyal Viola, Lelia deliberately exploits her position to deceive Isabella and Flamminio alike. Both heroines are living with (or trying to avoid) their elderly fathers, who play a major part in the plot—indeed Lelia's father is trying to marry her off to Isabella's father. Thus, like almost all classical comedies, this is a story of families in a city, not of free wanderers in Illyria or in a forest. The passions expressed by the lovers are blatantly sexual, and both marriages are secured by previous fornications (off stage, but only just), which are exploited for bawdy fun and comment. The protagonists are surrounded not only by comic servant figures, but by caricatures of a Pedant and a Spanish braggart soldier, both figures anticipating masks in the *commedia dell'arte* which was to emerge in the second half of the century.

One of the liveliest and most performable of 16th-century Italian comedies, and recognized as a plot source for *Twelfth Night*, this play risks being overlooked in drama history just because of its lack of an identifiable author. It was put on at the end of Carnival in 1532 (1531 "Sienese style") by the Accademia degli Intronati. It was probably their first dramatic production, and initiated the Academy's influential role over the next decades in setting models for structured, gentlemanly social occasions (*veglie senesi*, "Sienese evenings").

There are various features which make this more of a performers' play, and less of an imitative literary exercise, than some "erudite comedies" from Italy in this period. The dialogue is remarkably smooth, lively and unfussy, allowing itself just one element of expressionism in making the soldier speak Spanish (of a sort) throughout. The authors show a good instinct for the inconsequential backchat and jokes which keep an audience amused, there is a good variety of comic antagonisms between characters, and a well-judged amount of local and topical colour. Most of all, the clear invitation to have the twins played by the same person (they never appear together, not even in a final reunion) shifts the emphasis away from potential emotional pathos towards a game of performed virtuosity with which the audience can collude. In the end everyone has been "deceived", and all are humiliated to some degree. A discreet element of symbolism suggests that this is a true Carnival play, in which actors and audience (originally all members of the Academy) are invited to wear the fool's cap for a day.

—Richard Andrews

A DELICATE BALANCE
by Edward Albee

First Publication: New York, 1966.
First Production: Martin Beck Theatre, New York, 12 September 1966.

Criticism
(For general works on the author, see *Playwrights* volume)

Articles:

Robert M. Post, "Fear Itself: Edward Albee's *A Delicate Balance*", in *CLA Journal*, 13, 1969.

Terence Brown, "Harmonia Discord and Stochastic Process: Edward Albee's *A Delicate Balance*", in *Re: Artes Liberales*, vol.3 no.2, 1970.

John J. Von Szeliski, "Albee: A Rare *Balance*", in *Twentieth Century Literature*, 16, 1970.

Charles R. Bachman, "Albee's *A Delicate Balance*: Parable as Nightmare", in *Revue des langues vivantes*, 38, 1972.

M. Gilbert Porter, "Toby's Last Stand: The Evanescence of Commitment in *A Delicate Balance*", in *Theatre Journal*, 31, 1979.

Benu Mohanlal, "Theme of Disorientation in Albee's *A Delicate Balance*", in *Indian Journal of American Studies*, vol.12 no.1, 1982.

Gene A. Plunka, "Edward Albee's *A Delicate Balance*: A Rite of Passage from Sterility to Tranquility", in *Journal of Evolutionary Psychology*, 9, 1988.

Helge N. Nilsen, "Responsibility, Adulthood and the Void: A Comment on Edward Albee's *A Delicate Balance*", in *Neophilologus*, 73, 1989.

*   *   *

After the physical violence of Edward Albee's First Play, the one-act *Zoo Story*, and the verbal violence of his commercial success, *Who's Afraid of Virginia Woolf?*, *A Delicate Balance* surprised audiences with its elegant drawing-room manners—manners and servants, even unseen ones, being virtually unheard of in the modern American theater. Yet the unspecified affluence and upper-crust *politesse* and wit do not undermine Albee's seriousness of purpose, a meditation on the definition of "home". The men and women on stage debate the privileges and obligations of this cherished institution much as Robert Frost's farmer and his wife do in "Death of the Hired Man", the husband asserting that "home is the place where, when you have to go there, / They have to take you in", the wife preferring to call home "something you somehow haven't to deserve". Albee does not directly allude to Frost's poem, but he does continually ask about each of the characters whether the householders "have to take you in" and who "deserves" to find a place there.

The suburban home of Tobias and Agnes is hardly on the scale of the robber baron "cottages" in turn-of-the-century Newport. But like those seaside imitations of Versailles, this house has no room for guests. They can easily provide visitors with an anisette or a cognac; the real test comes when someone requires a room of his own. Best friends of 40-years standing arrive unannounced, unexpectedly. They baffle Tobias and Agnes by asking to stay. Claire, the clear-sighted sister-in-law of the house, is less startled and pronounces with equanimity, "I was wondering when it would begin. . . when it would start". She might be referring to the beginning of the unraveling of settled complacency.

At the center of the play is Claire's analysis of the American character. Alcohol and bachelorhood have conspired to keep her in the home of Tobias and Agnes. Here she is challenging the rights of her niece Julia—36, her fourth divorce imminent—to return to the nest once again:

> Are you home forever, back from the world? To the sadness *and* the reassurance of your parents? Have you come to take my place? . . .
> You're laying claim to the cave! Well, I don't know how they'll take to that. We're not a communal nation, dear; giving, but not sharing, outgoing, but not friendly.

Claire makes us question how long rights to a place in the family nest can be assumed. Despite the collectivist experiments of the time, Claire told the play's 1960's audience that "we're not a communal nation". One extra person—a sister-in-law, a prodigal daughter, a best friend and his wife—can unsettle the delicate balance of the bourgeois home. There is never a lack of material sustenance here, but there is a finite quantity of emotional sustenance. The play asks how thin we dare to stretch the elastic of emotional ties before they snap.

Julia has come knocking at the parental door before. Her father notes that each time she has felt betrayed by one of her husbands (as they turn to gambling, to boys, to other women, to nihilism) she returns. This time, to her agitated dismay, "THERE IS A HOUSE FULL OF PEOPLE!. . .I have no place to put my things. . . ." Only a true householder should be allowed to fix himself a drink, and she is appalled at Harry's presumption ("I'll do it; don't trouble yourself, Julia"). Defeated at the bar, Julia returns with her father's pistol. Ignoring the improbable vaudeville of her Aunt Claire discombobulating the high-toned guests with a lowly accordion, Julia insists, "Get them out of here, Daddy, getthemoutofheregetthemoutofheregetthemoutofheregetthemoutofhere. . . ."

Will Tobias cave in? Will he discard his oldest friend in the world and that friend's wife? Albee calls Tobias's big set speech of decision "an aria" performed by "a man who kept his emotions under control too long". The unspecified angst that made the bourgeois comfort of Harry and Edna's own home suddenly intolerable to them is identified only as: "There was nothing. . .but we were very scared." Artaud has compared what great theater can do to an audience with what plague can do to a city. Here Albee has called the nameless *anomie* of Harry and Edna a plague, a terror that could be fatally contagious. Nonetheless, Tobias faces that threat of contagion with saint-like acceptance:

> I HAVE BUILT THIS HOUSE! I WANT YOU IN IT!
> I WANT YOUR PLAGUE! YOU'VE GOT SOME TERROR WITH YOU? BRING IT IN!. . .
> I find my liking you has limits. . .
> BUT THOSE ARE MY LIMITS! NOT YOURS!. . .
> I DON'T WANT YOU HERE! I DON'T LOVE YOU!
> BUT BY GOD. . .YOU STAY!

Before Tobias's "aria", Harry admitted that if the situation had been reversed and the angst-ridden Tobias and Agnes had arrived at his door-step to move in and be comforted, "I wouldn't take them in. . .they don't. . .they don't have any right". When the aria is complete, Edna's gesture shows that she and Harry have no intention of accepting the offer to stay; their bags are packed; she asks for them to be brought down.

Tobias strives to extend the bourgeois definition of home. This heroic attempt to go beyond his own emotional capacities is cut short by his friends' unwillingness to stay. But Agnes is ready to accept the conventional limits of friendship with the pat response "Yes; well, don't be strangers." The chilling rejoinder is, "Oh, good Lord, how could we be? Our lives are. . .the same". The play ends with the delicate balance only temporarily restored. Like Claire at the end of Act One, the audience at the conclusion of the play is left "wondering when it would begin. . .when it would start" to unravel again.

—Roger Sorkin

THE DEPUTY.   See THE REPRESENTATIVE.

DESIGN FOR LIVING
by Noel Coward

First Publication: London, 1933.
First Production: Cleveland, Ohio, 2 January 1933; transferred to Ethel Barrymore Theatre, New York, 24 January 1933.

*   *   *

Gilda loves Otto. Leo comes home. Gilda loves Leo. Otto goes. Otto comes home. Gilda loves Otto. Gilda goes. Otto and Leo fall into each other's arms. They get Gilda back. The curtain falls as they howl with laughter, twined in an unbreakable threefold embrace.

"When all three of us had become stars of sufficient magnitude. . .we would meet and act triumphantly together". Coward had always intended to write a play for himself and his friends, Alfred Lunt and Lynne Fontanne; their longstanding friendship was founded on shared ambition, on dreams of success discussed in "shabby, uncongenial rooms. . .over potato salad and dill pickles". This, perhaps, made inevitable not just the three starring roles but the subject of the play—success and the public face. The play had other links with the Lunts, too; some years before Coward had watched Fontanne in O'Neill's *Strange Interlude*, a play about a woman torn between two men. He was not impressed with the play, but in *Design for Living* he echoed the triangular situation; if his treatment of it was less theatrically adventurous than O'Neill's, his exploration of the issues raised was perhaps less conventional, and this led to the fact that, as he always lamented, the play was never "sufficiently loved". The 1930's did not care for *Design for Living*, perhaps taking its title too literally, and the general verdict was that it was "unpleasant". Coward, however, was less concerned with prescribing modes of sexual conduct than with exploring the way in which private and public faces interact. All three protagonists are sexually attractive and they use this to market themselves to the public—Leo as a writer, Otto as a painter, and Gilda as a designer. All three have to integrate this fact into their personal relationships. Success can cut across their affection, their mutual loyalty, and it can also trap them into playing conventionalised sex-roles. Both Leo and Gilda, for instance, after a stolen night, feel guiltily that they have been acting out stereotypes: "New spring model, with a few extra flounces", says Leo of himself, while Gilda condemns herself for "squirming with archness, being aloof and desirable, consciously alluring, snatching and grabbing". Success, as Gilda remarks,

is an aphrodisiac, but it also removes from their relationship the element of need; they have to find a new foundation for love when all the struggles are over.

Need, passion, and jealousy were taken for granted in *Strange Interlude*. O'Neill treats them as if they were as inevitable as a forest fire and the only question remaining is how much destruction they can wreak. Coward shows them as problems to be faced; he does not offer solutions but implies that destructiveness can be transcended in shared laughter. Desire is not inevitable but one of the weapons in charm's armoury, which can be used or controlled at will; jealousy is a conventional response which an unconventional lover can learn to transcend in laughter: both Leo and Otto strut and rage at each other, but when Gilda leaves them both they form a mutual alliance which explodes the stereotype and leaves them free to win her back; they intrude on her successful but dull married life and use all their charm to draw her ineluctably into an anarchic game, forcing her through shared jokes to join them in defining their tight, little group against the rest of the world.

One never sees them operating as a threesome, and this does raise the question as to whether the "design" at the end is really a possible one. However, Coward makes it seem inevitable by the relentless comic symmetry of his stage patterns. These have the smooth mechanism of farce, but with one difference—while, in farce, characters hide under beds and in wardrobes in symmetrical patterns, here the movement is towards disclosure. Characters hide in bedrooms, but only temporarily. Invariably they emerge to admit to each shift in their relationship, to face the emotional consequences, but also to think them through: this frankness imbues the trio with a tenderness that counterpoints their go-to-hell stance towards the bourgeois world. It is, in fact, an antifarce, using a farce structure to play merry hell with the sexual stereotypes on which farce depends.

—Frances Gray

DESIRE UNDER THE ELMS
by Eugene O'Neill

First Publication: In *Complete Works 2*, New York, 1924.
First Production: Greenwich Village Theatre, New York, 11 November 1924.

Criticism
(For general works on the author, see *Playwrights* volume)

Articles:
Mathew T. Conlin, "The Tragic Effect in *Autumn Fire* and *Desire Under The Elms*", in *Modern Drama*, February 1959.
Sophus Kenneth Winther, "*Desire Under The Elms*: A Modern Tragedy", in *Modern Drama*, December 1960.
Murray Hartman, "*Desire Under The Elms* in The Light of Strindberg's Influence", in *American Literature*, 33, 1961.
William R. Reardon, "The Path of a Classic: *Desire Under the Elms*", in *Southern Speech Journal*, 31, 1966.
Michael Hinden, "*Desire Under the Elms*: O'Neill and the American Romance", in *Forum*, vol.15 no.1, 1977.
Patrick J. Nolan, "*Desire Under the Elms*: Characters by Jung", in *Eugene O'Neill Newsletter*, vol.5, no.2, 1979.

Preston Fambrough, "The Tragic Cosmology of O'Neill's *Desire Under the Elms*", in *Eugene O'Neill Newsletter*, vol.10 no.2, 1986.

Michael Mikos and David Mulroy, "Reymont's *The Peasants*: A Probable Influence on *Desire Under the Elms*", in *Eugene O'Neill Newsletter*, vol.10 no.1, 1986.

Bette Mandl, "Family Ties: Landscape and Gender in *Desire Under the Elms*", in *Eugene O'Neill Newsletter*, vol.2 no.2, 1987.

*   *   *

The setting of *Desire Under the Elms* is "in, and immediately outside the Cabot family farmhouse in New England" in Spring, 1850. The title refers to the two giant elms which brood oppressively over the house. Ephraim Cabot, a crusty, twice-widowed 75-year-old patriarch, already the father of three sons, brings home a new wife, the buxom, 35-year-old Abbie Putnam, who has married the old man solely to gain possession of this hardscrabble farm. She finds him physically repulsive, and seduces his 25-year-old youngest son Eben, who had aided the older boys to decamp to California after stealing their father's hidden savings. Significantly, the seduction takes place in the parlour, formerly haunted by Eben's mother's ghost. The following Spring Abbie bears Eben's son, with whose birth the young man loses succession to the farm. The aged Ephraim accepts the child as his, celebrating with Dionysian revelry though neighbors suspect the truth. Abbie and Eben quarrel so violently that she smothers the child believing that this is the only way she can keep his love. In grief and rage Eben goes to inform the Sheriff, while Abbie reveals the child's paternity to Ephraim. Eben returns to face Ephraim's disinheritance, but he no longer cares, having decided to share Abbie's guilt by claiming to be a co-conspirator. The two lovers walk out of the door hand in hand into the rising sun as the Sheriff comments "It's a jim-dandy farm, no denyin'. Wished I owned it".

Banned in Boston and refused public performance in England until 1940 because of its themes of incest and infanticide, this play established Eugene O'Neill as the preeminent serious American dramatist of his time. Language, locale, and imaginative conflation of myths come together here in a play which evokes the timeless irony of human existence.

The language is spare, colloquial, apt for those who are basically inarticulate. By contrast, in moments of intense passion, Ephraim turns to the basic book of his world, the *King James Bible*. The religious sensuality of the *Song of Solomon* contrasts with the stony farm and rigid New England Puritanism. This is part of American mythology, but O'Neill has superimposed it upon the ancient myths of Greek drama, most notably those of Phaedra, Oedipus, and Medea. In addition, he has also included ideas and concepts drawn from Nietzsche and Freud. These disparate elements are melded into a unique whole which produces an ironic, perhaps melodramatic, equivalent to Aristotelian pity and fear.

The Oedipal competition between the puritanical father and his three sons in farming and in sex is made clear from the beginning, while Eben's love for his dead mother and the farm Ephraim filched from her is central. Abbie is portrayed as a combination of Phaedra / Medea in her seduction of a stepson, and as a murderess who wishes she had killed her husband. At the same time she shares with Eben a romantic primitivism, a response to nature that is also present in Ephraim. For this theme O'Neill went to Nietzsche for that contrast between the Apollonian and the Dionysiac. Ephraim's guiding maxim has always been "God's hard, not easy", so he returned from the midwest, where the crops grew too easily, to fight nature in the land of flint and stone. His sensuality returns in the spring as an enemy to a puritan ethic he battles to maintain, and his grotesque caperings at the baby's birthday party signify the repressed Dionysiac tendencies to which he capitulated in marrying Abbie. Ephraim, Eben, and Abbie are destructively bound together in their kinship with the land, with nature itself. Possession of land, fertility, crops, and identification with the seasonal cycle of nature drive these tortured folk toward a fate pre-ordained by Ephraim's punitive deity.

Despite its careful construction and powerful theatricality, *Desire under the Elms* has had its greatest successes in the university, non—commercial, and regional theatre. Notable productions include the one designed by Alexander Tairov at the Kamerny Theatre, Moscow (1927) which O'Neill himself saw in May 1929 when it toured France. He praised the company for its imaginative production of both *Desire* and *Mourning Becomes Electra*. The play has remained popular in both Russia and Eastern Europe, possibly for political reasons. In the United States it has been performed almost yearly, the 1963 Circle in the Square production, with Colleen Dewhurst, George C. Scott, and Rip Torn, being the most successful production to date. The film, with alterations to suit the Italian accent of Sophia Loren, was over-long, and the opera by Edward Thomas, even though revised, has not yet garnered great praise.

—Margaret Loftus Ranald

DESTINY
by David Edgar

First Publication: London, 1976; revised edition, London, 1978; further revised edition, in *Plays One*, 1987.

First Production: The Other Place (Royal Shakespeare Company), Stratford-Upon-Avon, 22 September 1976; revised version, London, 1985.

Criticism
(For general works on the author, see *Playwrights* volume)

Articles:

Michelene Wandor, "The British Left: *Destiny* and *Maydays* by David Edgar", in *Look Back in Gender: Sexuality and the Family in Post-War British Drama*, London, 1987.

*   *   *

Destiny opens in 1947 in a British army barracks in India on the occasion of Indian independence, and follows the characters from there back to England, to a Midlands by-election some 25 years later. It is the death of the British Colonel which causes the by-election, at which his son stands to continue the tradition of old-fashioned, paternalistic Conservatism. Sergeant Turner becomes the candidate for the extreme right-wing Nation Forward Party (NF) after losing his antique business, as he mistakenly thinks to entrepreneurial immigrants. Major Rolfe becomes a successful business man who promises financial support to the NF after his son is murdered by the IRA, though it is actually his multi-national company which has destroyed Turner's business. Finally, Khera, the

Indian servant, becomes a shop steward leading a factory strike over working conditions, which becomes the focus for the NF to mobilise support. Through a series of debates, discussions, and political meetings, the play charts the events of the by-election, and more particularly the development of the right from the Conservative M.P. Enoch Powell's famous 1968 "Rivers of Blood" speech onwards. Though the Conservative wins the election and the Labour Party comes second, the NF wins a quarter of the votes to demonstrate its potential as a serious political threat in the future—particularly with the promise of financial support from sections of the business community which regard the Conservatives as weak and ineffective.

Edgar's play was the result of careful research carried out through reading and interviews, and is essentially an analysis of the nature of the extreme right in Britain in the 1970's, and the different types of people attracted to it. He has no interest in scoring easy points by simply dismissing the Right's supporters as mere jackbooted fascists, but makes an almost unique attempt as a left-wing playwright to understand rather than caricature the Right, starting from the premise that only by understanding its attraction can it be defeated. Edgar sets out to challenge his audience by asking them, in his own words: "How far are you really away from this?. . .Have you ever felt like this?", and he ends the play with the voice of Adolf Hitler proclaiming that only by understanding and destroying the Nazis at the beginning could their rise have been prevented.

Part of the threat explored in *Destiny* is the way in which a movement which at first seems obscure, pathetic, and laughably inept, grows to a position of power; when we first see the NF at meetings they are struggling to collect contributions to pay for the hall, their Union Jack is displayed upside down, their microphone doesn't work, and their supporters have views so diverse that it seems impossible to unite them. The party is initially given to the unpleasant but pointless wearing of Nazi paraphernalia for ritualistic celebrations of Hitler's birthday, and their election candidate, Turner, appears to be totally incompetent in trying to learn, parrot fashion, the answers to probable questions, being chiefly obsessed with the idea that immigrants are spreading parasitic worms. Then, in a theatrical coup, Edgar jumps to a meeting at which Turner addresses the theatre audience as his supporters, and repeats the speech at which we previously laughed; this time he is radio-mixed, his manner is "cool, assured, professional", and his voice "echoes round the theatre". Suddenly, he is chillingly impressive.

Stylistically, the play is an interesting mixture of the agit-prop, in which Edgar had had considerable experience, and a more rounded and realistic naturalism. It permits direct address to transmit information—occasionally in rhyming verse—and scenes which are organised on a schematic basis. However, the fact that Edgar wrote the different types of NF follower from a chart, or that scenes were written around a previously decided list of points, only becomes obvious through careful analysis rather than during performance. The characters are not simply caricatures; though their personal backgrounds are not explored, they embody specific and complex political stances. The play therefore implicitly argues that our behaviour is dictated by politics rather than by psychology.

Destiny questions simplistic left-wing mythology about the extreme Right. When the Labour candidate suggests after the election that the Conservative success was due to the level of support for the NF candidate, it is pointed out that this is true only if the NF took its votes from former Labour supporters; the place of Socialism alongside Nationalism in the policy of a Party which takes Hitler's National Socialists as its inspiration

is frequently discussed, and apart from a section attacking foreigners, one NF election statement could, we are told, have come from *Tribune*, the Labour newspaper. Even the Labour candidate's wife, who is employed on a local Community project with working-class people worried about their housing and employment prospects at a time of high immigration, resents the easy statements of her husband and the automatic posturing of the Left which denies the existence of problems and dismisses all opponents as fascists: "You make your great bloody statements about unrestricted immigration and institutional racism", she tells him, "Well, you can afford to". However, in case he should seem to suggest that there is a valid connection between the far right and Socialism, Edgar shows the eventual purging from the NF of those leaders sympathetic to the Socialist side of the manifesto.

Although one might argue that *Destiny* raised an unnecessary and false alarm since, to date, the right-wing National Front has not become a serious political force in Britain since the play was written, Edgar claims that what he failed to predict was the major shift to the right by the Conservative Party—including its attitude to racial issues—which has made the growth of a separate fascist party unnecessary.

—Steve Nicholson

THE DEVILS
by John Whiting

First Publication: London, 1961.
First Production: Aldwych Theatre (Royal Shakespeare Company), London, 20 February 1961.

Criticism
(For general works on the author, see *Playwrights* volume)

Articles:
John Ditsky, "Whiting's Self-Possessed: *The Devils*", in *The Onstage Christ: Studies in the Persistence of a Theme*, London, 1980.
E.T. Kirby, "Demonic Possession and the 'religious game' in John Whiting's *The Devils*", in *Proceedings of Asclepius at Syracuse: Thomas Szasz, Libertarian Humanist*, Albany, New York, 1980.

*   *   *

The action of *The Devils* takes place predominantly in or near the town of Loudun in central France between the years 1623 and 1634. The play charts the downfall of Urbain Grandier, a handsome, ambitious, and lecherous young priest. The instigator of his downfall is Sister Jeanne of the Angels, the hunchbacked young prioress of a local convent whom Grandier has never met but who, having heard of his amorous exploits, and following his rebuttal of her invitation to him to act as the convent's confessor, becomes so obsessed with him that she claims that he is an agent of the devil and is causing her to experience diabolical visitations. Sister Jeanne's satanic "possession" soon infects the nuns in her charge who, when confronted by the church's exorcists, cry out scurrilously in demonic voices and perform grotesque and obscene antics.

The Devils: The Pit, Barbican Centre, London, 1984 (Royal Shakespeare Company)

These displays of evident diabolical possession are soon employed by Grandier's enemies in the town, church and state to discredit him and, in spite of the fact that a member of the royal family, Prince Henri de Condé, is able to reveal by a clever trick that the nuns are not really possessed but are either in the grip of sexual hysteria or merely play-acting, Grandier is accused of being an agent of Satan, horrifically tortured, declared guilty, and ultimately burnt at the stake.

The Devils was Whiting's last full-length play. It was commissioned by Peter Hall to open the Royal Shakespeare Company's first season at the Aldwych Theatre, London. Unlike most of Whiting's earlier plays it was critically acclaimed, T.C. Worsley, for example, describing it in the *Financial Times* as a "masterpiece". The play was based upon Aldous Huxley's *The Devils of Loudun* (1952) whose documentary-style narrative Whiting attempted to integrate with themes which he had been exploring throughout his career. One feature of Huxley's book which paralleled Whiting's own concerns was its discussion of upward, horizontal, and downward self-transcendence as the means by which humanity attempts to come to terms with its existence. By Huxley's definition, upward self-transcendence involved saintliness, martyrdom, or extreme piety; horizontal self-transcendence meant seeking meaning in good works, politics, or through a relationship with another human being; while downward self-transcendence signified a descent into beastliness through sensual gratification. Whiting attempted to mould the historical narrative in order to bring out these features in his characterisation of Grandier but was unfortunately forced to compromise his favoured themes. Early in the play Grandier

confesses to God that hitherto he has filled his life with such characteristics of downward self-transcendance as selfish pride, sensual luxury, and lust. Having discovered that this is merely an evasion of his existential dilemma, Grandier then attempts, as do many of the heroes of Whiting's earlier plays, to find salvation through another human being, the young girl Phillipe, whom he seduces and secretly marries but abandons as soon as she becomes pregnant. Now so disgusted with existence that he is almost in despair, Grandier ultimately attempts to achieve martyrdom by embracing the threats posed by Sister Jeanne's accusations and by courting the disapproval of the state (represented by Cardinal Richelieu) for his support of Loudun's Governor D'Armagnac's stand against the demolition of the city-walls. The God whom Grandier wishes to reach proves, however, to be merely an extension of himself. "I created God", he declares to the sewerman, who acts in the play as Grandier's confessor and as the embodiment of base physicality. Subsequently imprisoned by the church authorities, and faced with the threat of pain, Grandier nevertheless soon admits to himself that his creation of God was "a trick of the sun, some fatigue of the body". His existential journey concludes rather disappointingly, however, with his all too easy acceptance of the innocent and unworldy Father Ambrose's suggestion that he should not act but should surrender himself to the will of God. "Let Him take me as I am", concludes Grandier "There is meaning, after all. I am a sinful man and I can be accepted". At the close of the play, his legs broken by torture and his hair and moustache shorn off, Grandier is carried through the streets, "a ridiculous, hairless, shattered doll",—a disturbing image of what Jeanne has described earlier "as the purpose of man: loneliness and death".

The Devils has been criticised for being structurally disjointed. Indeed, the plots involving Grandier and Jeanne are only tenuously linked and, other than providing the vehicle by which Grandier is ultimately brought face to face with his own mortality, Jeanne and her nuns' exhibition of demonic possession, while being extremely theatrical, is somewhat irrelevant to his existential dilemma.

The play's pseudo-epic structure, which appears to lay importance upon the public context of its action, has also been considered to be at odds with its exploration of Grandier's inner struggle. In his earlier plays Whiting had, however, characteristically employed setting not so much as a material or social environment but as an extension of the state of mind of his central character. This applies similarly to *The Devils* where the world surrounding Grandier is gradually revealed as one of hanging corpses, sewers, malformed creatures in bottles, a hunchbacked prioress, and her grotesquely cavorting nuns, and, finally, after Grandier's death, an apocalyptic world in which "the town seems to be on fire" and "a church gapes like a sulphurous mouth". This is not the materialistic world of the epic but is closer to the visionary world of Expressionism and as such is the ideal context for Grandier's existential struggle. Owing to its compromise between Whiting's favourite themes and the demands of historical drama, *The Devils* may not be a fully integrated play, but nevertheless in its undoubted theatrical power it stands as a flawed masterpiece written by a much underestimated dramatist.

—D. Keith Peacock

DIADIA VANIA. See **UNCLE VANYA.**

THE DIFFICULT MAN (Der Schwierige)
by Hugo von Hofmannsthal

First Publication: Berlin, 1921.
First Production: Residenztheater, Munich, 8 November 1921.

Translations
The Difficult Man, in *Hofmannsthal: Selected Writings 3*, translated by Willa Muir, New York, 1963.

Criticism
(For general works on the author, see *Playwrights* volume)

Books:
Heike Söhnlein, *Gesellschaftliche und private Interaktionen: Dialoganalysen zu Hofmannsthals "Der Schwierige" und Schnitzlers "Das weite Land"*, Tübingen, 1986.

Articles:
R.C. Norton, "Hugo von Hofmannsthal's *Der Schwierige* and Granville Barker's *Waste*", in *Comparative Literature*, 14, 1962.

R.C. Norton, "Inception of Hofmannsthal's *Der Schwierige* and Goethe's *Torquato Tasso*", in *Publications of the English Goethe Society*, 33, 1963.

T.E. Carter, "Structure in Hofmannsthals Lustspiel *Der Schwierige*", in *German Life and Letters*, 18, 1964.

Douglas A. Joyce, "Some Uses of Irony in Hofmannsthal's *Der Schwierige*", in *Modern Language Quarterly*, 30, 1969.

P. Manger, "Once More 'Praeexistenz-Tyche-Existenz' in Hofmannsthal's *Der Schwierige*", in *Seminar: A Journal of Germanic Studies*, 6, 1970.

Horst Wittmann, "Hofmannsthals *Der Schwierige*: die Potentialität des Leichten", in *Seminar: A Journal of Germanic Studies*, 10, 1974.

Benjamin Bennett, "Missed Meetings in Hofmannsthal's *Der Schwierige*", in *Forum for Modern Languages Studies*, 12, 1976.

Jürgen Rothenberg, "'Durchs Reden kommt ja alles auf der Welt zustande': sum Aspekt des Komischen in Hugo von Hofmannsthals Lustspiel *Der Schwierige*", in *Jahrbuch der Deutschen Schillergesellschaft*, 21, 1977.

W.E. Yates, "*Der Schwierige*: The Comedy of Discretion", in *Modern Austrian Literature*, vol.10 no.1, 1977.

Wolfgang Frühwald, "Die sprechende Zahl: Datensymbolismus in Hugo von Hofmannsthals Lustspiel *Der Schwierige*", in *Jahrbuch der Deutschen Schillergesellschaft*, 22, 1978.

Thomas Heine, "The Force of Gestures", in *German Quarterly*, 1983.

Carol Wootton, "Hofmannsthal and Eliot: The Problem of Lack of Communication as Revealed in Two Plays, *Der Schwierige* and *The Cocktail Party*", in *Selective Affinities: Comparative Essays from Goethe to Arden*, New York, 1983.

Herbert Gamper, "Hofmannsthal und Bauernfeld: ein wahrscheinliches Vorbild zum *Schwierigen*", in *Hofmannsthal-Forschungen*, 8, 1985.

Frederick A. Lubich, "Hugo von Hofmannsthals *Der Schwierige*: Hans Karl Bühl und Antoinette Hechingen unter Aspekte der Sprache und Moral", in *Monatshefte*, 77, 1985.

Hans Weigel, "Triumph der Wortlosigkeit: ein Versuch über Hugo von Hofmannsthals Lustspiel *Der Schwierige*", in *Nach wie vor Wörter: literarische Zustimmungen, Ablehnungen, Irrtümer*, Graz, 1985.

Bernhard Greiner, "Die Rede des Unbewussten als Komödie: Hofmannsthals Lustspiel *Der Schwierige*", in *German Quarterly*, 59, 1986.

Jean Wilson, "'Ein Genre kopieren': Convention and Conversion in Hofmannsthal's *Der Schwierige*", in *Seminar: Journal of Germanic Studies*, 23, 1987.

*   *   *

The elegant Count Hans Karl Bühl, now nearly 40, has returned to Vienna from the war, his view of life altered by a visionary experience when a trench collapsed over him. He has become aware of higher values that are beyond words and has come to sense "that it is impossible to open one's mouth without causing the most hopeless confusion". Doubtful of his ability to communicate, he has become hesitant in making any commitments. Hence his role as a "difficult man", though the force of the title *Der Schwierige* would in fact be better rendered as "hard to please": he is not awkward but fastidious. His elder sister, Crescence, persuades him to go to a soirée at the salon of aristocratic friends, the Altenwyls, to plead on behalf of her son Stani for the hand of the daughter of the house, Helene. Once there, he tells Helene of his admiration for a circus clown, Furlani, who creates confusion on all sides, but always with style and elegance. Hans Karl tries to say a formal farewell to Helene and also to bring about a reconciliation between Antoinette Hechingen, a married woman with whom he has had an affair in the past, and her husband, whose qualities he has learnt to value during the war. First Helene and then Antoinette are wooed by the pushy, North German Baron Neuhoff, but he is rebuffed by both of them. When Hans Karl returns to the salon in Act III, Helene proposes to him; then, since Hans Karl is unwilling to face her father's request that he make a speech in the Upper House of the Austrian parliament, they leave together, so that when the final curtain falls the traditional tableau of young lovers is conspicuously lacking—a consequence, Stani says, of their "bizarre" character.

The form of the play is that of the society comedy ("Konversations-stück") cultivated in the Burgtheater in Vienna in the 19th century, especially in the works of Eduard von Bauernfeld, and adopted also by Hofmannsthal's friend Schnitzler. Indeed, with his past as an amorous "adventurer", Hans Karl shares some of the qualities of Schnitzler's Anatol. Hofmannsthal was also influenced by his long devotion to Molière; one work that in a sense functioned as a preparatory study for *Der Schwierige* was a one-act comedy *Die Lästigen* (1916) written to be produced by Max Reinhardt and based loosely on Molière's *Les Fâcheux*.

The action of *Der Schwierige* seems to take place after the end of the World War I, which is always referred to in the past tense; but that impression is offset by the references to the Upper House, which did not meet after the end of the monarchy in October 1918. The apparent contradiction is, no doubt, partly the result of the protracted genesis of the play. The first notes on it go back to 1908; most of the writing was done in 1917; and the final revision was not complete until 1920–21. The final effect, however, is surely deliberate: that of an imagined post-war world that never in fact existed, in which the society of pre-1914 Vienna lives on.

In this setting, Hofmannsthal treats one of the central themes of his whole work—the moral development of the individual. This is associated in Hans Karl's case with an acute sensitivity towards nuances of language—a theme that links the play with Hofmannsthal's celebrated "Chandos Letter" of 1902. Hans Karl, whose social elegance conceals what is essentially an artistic temperament, is out of sympathy with the trivial conversation at the soirée; he is keenly aware that the important things are inexpressible. The problematic quality of language as a medium of communication is comically represented in a telephone call that he makes to Hechingen at the end of Act I, in which everything he says is misunderstood; it is precisely with the misunderstandings of verbal communication that he admiringly contrasts the silent mime of the clown Furlani.

The play has a further layer of significance as an idealised portrait of a vanishing, aristocratic society. A letter written to Schnitzler in November 1918 shows that Hofmannsthal himself felt that he had captured the "charm and quality" of that society at the very moment of its dissolution. The "old" and the "new" stand in contrast, as for example in the very names Altenwyl and Neuhoff. Another example is the contrast between Hans Karl's loyal and sympathetic old retainer, Lukas, and a bumptious new servant, Vinzenz, who counts on ruling the roost but is in fact dismissed. This opposition of old and new, to the disadvantage of the new, ties in with Hofmannsthal's post-war devotion to the idea of a "conservative revolution", a salvaging of cultural values threatened in the political and social upheaval of modern Europe. So too does the contrast between Hans Karl and the wordy Neuhoff,

who at the soirée expresses his contempt for Viennese high society (especially as represented in Hans Karl), cut off as it is, he says, from the real "intellectual crises" of the times. That the decorous Austrian Hans Karl, and not the would-be-masterful Prussian, wins the hand of Helene clearly has symbolical overtones: a wishful reversal of the decline of Austria on the political map and a triumph of the old order in parallel to the defeat of the ironically-named Vinzenz.

Rejected by the Burgtheater under the direction of Anton Wildgans (at least partly because of Wildgans's hostility to Max Reinhardt, with whom Hofmannsthal was closely associated), *Der Schwierige* is widely acknowledged to be Hofmannsthal's masterpiece and probably the most sophisticated example of high comedy in the German language. It requires skilful balance in performance, in that the elegance of the social milieu must not be sacrificed to crude comic effect, while the comic effect in turn must not be sacrificed to the need in the central part for what Hans Karl calls "discretion"; but it is precisely that balance that the best productions succeed in achieving. That by Max Reinhardt formed one of the highlights of his first season at the Theater in der Josefstadt in Vienna in 1924: Gustav Waldau played the title role that he had created in Munich, with Helene Thimig as Helene Altenwyl (a part played in Munich by Elisabeth Bergner). "Discretion" is a word used by Hans Karl himself, about Furlani, and Hofmannsthal, writing to Leopold von Andrian in October 1917, described his task in the play as reconciling that very effect with the "demands of such an indiscreet form as comedy".

—W.E. Yates

DINGO
by Charles Wood

First Publication: London, 1969.
First Production: Royal Court Theatre, London, 15 November, 1967.

Criticism
(For general works on the author, see *Playwrights* volume)

Articles:
Malcolm Page, "Charles Wood: *How I Won the War* and *Dingo*", in *Literature / Film Quarterly*, 1, 1973.

*   *   *

The two acts of *Dingo* give equally desolate views of World War II. The first is set in a desert emplacement during the north African campaign. Various soldiers drop in on its two occupants, Dingo and Mogg, most notably the Comic who attempts to entertain the troops. Some of the same characters are in the internment camp of the second act, including the Comic. This time he functions as Master of Ceremonies for a camp entertainment (in both senses) that provides cover for an escape by the officers. The play ends with the liberation of the camp; even Churchill arrives, to "urinate on the West Wall of Hitler's Germany".

The incidents themselves are less important than the sometimes phantasmagoric vision of the horrors of war.

Almost all Charles Wood's plays deal with war and they can be seen as so many variations on the presentation of war, not only in theatrical terms, but also in terms of public image. In *Dingo* its grim reality is all the more horrific for being constantly counterpointed against culturally approved and sanitized images of war. The mix is evident within a few lines of the play's opening, with two soldiers whose faces are "burned, bloated, splashed with gentian violet" as medication for desert sores, idly talking to each other and the audience:

Dingo: I shall shortly piss gentian violet.
Mogg: Then piss some over me.
Dingo: The thing about fighting a desert war. . .
Mogg: We agreed not to talk about it.
Dingo: I must state it for them.
Mogg: Piss some over me because my sores are lifting up their flaming lips.
Dingo: The thing about fighting in the desert is that it is a clean war—without brutality. And clean limbed—without dishonourable actions on either side.
Mogg: They say.

The contrast between image and reality is emphasized at the end of the play when Tanky—whose screams as he burns to death in his tank have come right after the opening dialogue of the play, and whose charred, seated form has been carried around like a ventriloquist's dummy by his mate—keeps repeating "He killed me" through the camp's liberation and the beginning of the glorification of the now finished war. While the stubborn fact of the phrase and the charred corpse are unchanging, "he" seems to shift reference from N.C.O. to officer to Churchill, so that the simple statement seems to become an indictment of a system. The phrase, thrice repeated, is the last line of the play. It is appropriate that the dead should have the last word.

The upper-class officers have internalized the traditional heroics of war. Wood's view is that of the eponymous Dingo, the professional soldier, the swaddie. He and the draftee, Mogg, direct an officer through a minefield and Dingo bets "the next one to scream is clean, dry and slightly upper class white English". By the end of the play an officer's corpse is slung on the ropes of a boxing ring that represents the barbed wire around the camp. Killed during the great escape while dressed as a chorus girl, he wears a costume implying the unreality of his attitudes. War to him is like a cricket match and even in death he wants a medal. Beside him, Tanky's charred corpse stubbornly insists, visually and verbally, on the simple reality of death. The presentational style allows Wood to go beyond the microcosms of the play: for example, the Comic can sit on a lavatory with Churchill and Eisenhower puppets arguing about Arnhem, a flash-forward can show us Churchill campaigning in the 1945 election, the dead can speak.

—Anthony Graham-White

DNI TURBINYKH.   See **THE WHITE GUARD.**

DOCTOR FAUSTUS
by Christopher Marlowe

First Publication: "A" text, London, 1604; "B" text, London, 1616.
First Production: London, c. 1588; earliest recorded performance, Rose Theatre, London, 1594.

Editions
The Tragical History of Doctor Faustus, edited by Frederick S. Boas, London, 1932.
The Tragical History of Doctor Faustus, edited by Russell H. Robbins, Woodbury, New York, 1948.
Marlowe's "Doctor Faustus", 1604–1616: Parallel Texts, edited by W.W. Greg, Oxford, 1950.
Doctor Faustus, edited by John D. Jump, London, 1962 (Revels Plays).
Doctor Faustus, edited by Roma Gill, London, 1965 (New Mermaid Series); second edition (using "A" Text), 1989.
Doctor Faustus, in *Christopher Marlowe: The Complete Plays*, edited by J.B. Steane, Harmondsworth, 1969.
Doctor Faustus: The A Text, edited by David Ormerod and Christopher Wortham, Nedlands, Western Australia, 1985.
Doctor Faustus, edited by Roma Gill, Oxford, 1990 (The Complete Works, 2).

Criticism
(For general works on the author, see *Playwrights* volume)

Books:
Philip Brockbank, *Marlowe: "Doctor Faustus"*, London and Great Neck, New York, 1962.
Willard Farnham (ed.), *Twentieth Century Interpretations of "Doctor Faustus"*, Englewood Cliffs, New Jersey, 1969.
Nigel Alexander, *The Performance of Christopher Marlowe's "Doctor Faustus"*, London, 1971.
J.H. Birringer, *Marlowe's "Doctor Faustus" and "Tamburlaine": Theological and Theatrical Perspectives*, Frankfurt, 1984.
William Tydeman, *Doctor Faustus*, London, 1984 (Text and Performance Series).
William Empson, *Faustus and the Censor: The English Faust-Book and Marlowe's "Doctor Faustus"*, Oxford, 1987.
Roy T. Erikson, *The Forme of Faustus Fortunes: A Study of "The Tragedie of Doctor Faustus" (1616)*, Oslo, 1987.

Articles:
L. Kirschbaum, "Marlowe's *Faustus*: A Reconsideration", in *Review of English Studies*, 19, 1943.
W.W. Greg, "The Damnation of Faustus", in *Modern Language Review*, 41, 1946.
Nicholas Brooke, "The Moral Tragedy of *Doctor Faustus*", in *Cambridge Journal*, 7, 1952.
L.B. Campbell, "*Doctor Faustus*: A Case of Conscience", in *Publications of the Modern Language Association [PMLA]*, 67, 1952.
Robert Ornstein, "The Comic Synthesis in *Doctor Faustus*", in *English Literary Renaissance*, 22, 1955.
Joseph T. McCullen, "Dr. Faustus and Renaissance Learning", in *Modern Language Review*, 51, 1956.
Clifford Davidson, "Doctor Faustus of Wittenberg", in *Studies in Philology*, 59, 1962.
C.L. Barber, "The Form of Faustus' Fortunes Good or Bad", in *Tulane Drama Review*, vol.8 no.4, 1964.
G.K. Hunter, "The Five-Act Structure in *Doctor Faustus*", in *Tulane Drama Review*, vol.8 no.4, 1964.

Doctor Faustus: Aldwych Theatre, London, 1974 (Royal Shakespeare Company)

Sherman Hawkins, "The Education of Faustus", in *Studies in English Literature*, 6, 1966.

T. McAlindon, "Classical Mythology and Christian Tradition in Marlowe's *Doctor Faustus*", in *Publications of the Modern Language Association [PMLA]*, 81, 1966.

Kenneth Muir, "Marlowe's *Doctor Faustus*", in *Philologica Praegensia*, 9, 1966.

Erich Kahler, "Doctor Faustus from Adam to Sartre", in *Comparative Drama*, 1, 1967.

Gerald Morgan, "Harlequin Faustus: Marlowe's Comedy of Hell", in *Humanities Association Bulletin*, vol.18 no.1, 1967.

F. Manley, "The Nature of Faustus", in *Modern Philology*, 66, 1968–69.

A.L. French, "The Philosophy of *Dr. Faustus*", in *Essays in Criticism*, 20, 1970.

Russell and Clare Goldfarb, "The Seven Deadly Sins in *Doctor Faustus*", in *College Language Association Journal*, 13, 1970.

Michael Hattaway, "The Theology of Marlowe's *Doctor Faustus*", in *Renaissance Drama*, 3, 1970.

N. Alexander, "The Performance of Christopher Marlowe's *Dr. Faustus*", in *Proceedings of the British Academy*, 57, 1971.

Thomas B. Stroupe, "*Doctor Faustus* and *Hamlet*: Contrasting Kinds of Christian Tragedy", in *Comparative Drama*, 5, 1971.

Kurt Tetzel van Rosador, "*Doctor Faustus*: 1604 and 1616", in *Anglia*, 90, 1972.

F. Bowers, "Marlowe's *Doctor Faustus*: The 1602 Additions", in *Studies in Bibliography*, 26, 1973.

Gerald H. Cox, "Marlowe's Doctor Faustus and 'Sin Against the Holy Ghost'", in *Huntington Library Quarterly*, 36, 1973.

R.H. West, "The Impatient Magic of Doctor Faustus", in *English Literary Renaissance*, 4, 1974.

N. Kiessling, "Doctor Faustus and the Sin of Demoniality", in *Studies in English Literature, 1500–1900*, 15, 1975.

C.B. Kuriyama, "Dr, Greg and *Doctor Faustus*: The Supposed Originality of the 1616 Text", in *English Language Review*, 5, 1975.

Sara M. Deats, "*Doctor Faustus*: From Chapbook to Tragedy", in *Essays in Literature*, vol.3 no.1, 1976.

J. Reynolds, "Faustus' Flawed Learning", in *English Studies*, 57, 1976.

A.N. Okerlund, "The Intellectual Folly of Doctor Faustus", in *Studies in Philology*, 74, 1977.

Edward A. Snow, "Marlowe's *Doctor Faustus* and the Ends of Desire", in *Two Renaissance Mythmakers: Christopher Marlowe and Ben Jonson*, edited by Alvin Kernan, Baltimore and London, 1977.

William Blackburn, "'Heavenly Words': Marlowe's Faustus as a Renaissance Magician", in *English Studies in Canada*, vol.4 no.1, 1978.

M.L. Warren, "*Doctor Faustus*: The Old Man and the Text", in *English Literary Renaissance*, 11, 1981.

Phoebe S. Conrad, "The Dilettante's Lie in *Doctor Faustus*", in *Texas Studies in Literature and Language*, vol.24 no.3, 1982.

Lorraine Kochanske Stock, "Medieval *Gula* in Marlowe's *Doctor Faustus*", in *Bulletin of Research in Humanities*, vol.85 no.4, 1982.

Michael H. Keefer, "Verbal Magic and The Problem of The A and B Texts of *Doctor Faustus*", in *Journal of English and Germanic Philology*, vol.82 no.3, 1983.

Johannes H. Birringer, "Between Body and Language: 'Writing' The Damnation of Faust", in *Theatre Journal*, vol.36 no.3, 1984.

Patrick Cheyney, "Love and Magic in *Doctor Faustus*: Marlowe's Indictment of Spenserian Idealism", in *Mosaic*, vol.17 no.4, 1984.

Malcolm Pittock, "God's Mercy is Infinite: Faustus's Last Soliloquy", in *English Studies*, vol.65 no.4, 1984.

Kenneth L. Golden, "Myth, Psychology, and Marlowe's *Doctor Faustus*", in *College Literature*, vol.12 no.3, 1985.

Stephen E. Rayburn, "Marlowe's *Doctor Faustus* and Medieval Judgement Day Drama", in *Publications of The Mississippi Philological Association*, 1985.

Christopher Ricks, "*Doctor Faustus* and Hell on Earth", in *Essays in Criticism*, vol.35 no.2, 1985.

Hilary Gatti, "Bruno's Heroic Searcher and Marlowe's *Doctor Faustus*", in *Rinascimento*, 26, 1986.

Rowland Wymer, "'When I behold the Heavens': A Reading of *Doctor Faustus*", in *English Studies*, vol.67 no.6, 1986.

Michael H. Keefer, "History and the Canon: The Case of *Doctor Faustus*", in *University of Toronto Quarterly*, vol.56 no.4, 1987.

John S. Mebane, "Metadrama and The Visionary Imagination in *Doctor Faustus* and *The Tempest*", in *South Atlantic Review*, vol.53 no.2, 1988.

*   *   *

In Marlowe's play, Dr. Faustus, sitting in his study at the University of Wittenberg, surveys the range of his learning. He finds Divinity, Logic, Philosophy, and Medicine wanting, though each is dismissed on faulty grounds. He resolves to try the forbidden arts—"Negromanticke books are heavenly", he persuades himself. "A sound Magician is a demi-god" (or "a mighty god" according to the corrupt 1604 text). Having laid himself open to temptation, he is duly tempted. Mephistophilis promises much but Faustus's dreams of knowledge and power are unrealised. In the sub-plot, his man, Wagner, and the Clown mock the bargain he has made. In the 24 years Mephistophilis serves him, Faustus performs mainly trivial tricks but he does raise spirits (ie. devils) including those in the form of Alexander and his Paramour and, finally, despite the warnings of a symbolic Old Man, puts himself beyond hope of salvation by raising a spirit representing Helen of Troy. He kisses her, so escaping this world's limits, but also damning himself eternally: "Her lips such forth my soul, see where it flies". In a final speech during his last hour on earth, he pleads for mercy and blames others for his fate; at the last moment he concedes he must curse himself and Lucifer "That hath deprived me of the joys of heaven"—and is dragged off to Hell.

Doctor Faustus presents a number of difficulties. Its textual problems are complex; Marlowe wrote it with one or more collaborators whose identities are uncertain. Cold analysis suggests Faustus's credibility is undermined from the outset; the moment of damnation (though it might not trouble a secular audience) is ambiguous, and for those brought up on Goethe, it can seem trivial. Yet it can offer an exciting and moving dramatic experience and it has some wonderful poetry.

Understanding Faustus's first speech is important. It is a mixture of obscure learning and the obvious which ought to warn the audience not to take Faustus at face value. However, what was obvious at the end of Elizabeth I's reign is not so now. Divinity is dismissed on grounds which would be patently wanting to a 16th-century audience: "If we say we have no sin, / We deceive ourselves and the truth is not in us". "Why then, belike, / We must sin, and so consequently die. . . .". But even the most unlettered of the audience would spot Faustus's glib error—the omission of the saving grace, "But if we confess our sins, he is faithful and just to forgive us our sins"—so we must *not* consequently die, as Faustus says. The play is liberally sprinkled with clues to Faustus's self-deception, especially found in the way the meanings of words are inverted or falsely linked: "magic" and "miracle", "conjure" and "canonize". Faust even uses Christ's last words on the cross, "Consummatum est", to mark his signing, in his blood, of the deed of gift of his soul to Lucifer.

The play is full of such devices. The Good and Evil Angels are more complex than those of *Everyman*. The Good Angel may be theologically sound but would inhibit scientific endeavour; the Evil Angel encourages the latter, but for selfish ends. Faustus ought to be capable of judging good from evil, but he fails the test. Although Faustus's bargain is so empty—he admits that what he learns amounts to no more than "slender trifles"—he has his moment of triumph. In tune with the play as a whole, it is also the moment of damnation (at least in dramatic terms for it can be argued that theologically Faustus is damned from the moment he signs his compact with the devil). When Faustus raises devils to represent Alexander and his paramour, he warns the Emperor not to speak to the spirits and when the Emperor moves to embrace them, Faustus intervenes. Verbal or physical intercourse with spirits is unforgivable. And Faustus warns the Scholars not to address Helen, "for danger is in words". Yet, he embraces Helen, a succuba. There, embedded in one of the most famous speeches in English drama—"Was this the face that launched a thousand ships?" (note the ambiguity)—is the evidence that his fate is sealed: his soul has been sucked forth (which has sexual and theological implications). Faustus has triumphed in going beyond man's terrestrial limits, but he has been simultaneously dammed and it is as a damned soul that he will be "eternized". To drive home that this is so, Marlowe places speeches by an Old Man before and after the appearance of Helen. Prior to her appearance he tells Faustus that an Angel hovers over his head "with a vial full of precious grace"—salvation is still possible if he will go no further—but after Faustus's intercourse with Helen (the kiss) the Old Man cries out, "Accursed Faustus, miserable man, / That from thy soul excludest the grace of heaven". Faustus's last hour is dramatised in language as moving as any Marlowe wrote, a passage that stands comparison with the mature, tragic Shakespeare: "The stars move still, time runs, the clock will strike, / The devil will come, and Faustus must be damned. . . ."

—Peter Davison

————————

DÖDSDANSEN, I-II.   See **THE DANCE OF DEATH.**

————————

THE DOLL TRILOGY
   Kid Stakes
   Other Times
   Summer of the Seventeenth Doll
by Ray Lawler

The Trilogy
First Publication: Sydney, 1978.
First Production: Russell Street Theatre (Melbourne Theatre
   Company), 1977.

Summer of the Seventeenth Doll
First Publication: Sydney, 1957; revised edition, Sydney,
   1978.
First Production: Union Theatre, Melbourne, 28 November
   1955.

Kid Stakes
First Publication: In *The Doll Trilogy*, Sydney, 1978.
First Production: Russell Street Theatre, Melbourne, 2
   December 1975.

Other Times
First Publication: In *The Doll Trilogy*, Sydney 1978.
First Production: Russell Street Theatre, Melbourne, 14
   December 1976.

Criticism
(For general works on the author, see *Playwrights* volume)

Articles:
S. Ramaswamy, "An Australian *Doll's House*: Ray Lawler's
   Summer of the Seventeenth Doll", in *Indian Journal of
   English Studies*, 12, 1971.
Chris Johnson, "Is That Us? Ray Lawler's *Summer of the
   Seventeenth Doll* and David French's *Leaving Home*", in
   Canadian Drama, 6, 1980.
Nadia Fletcher, "Humour in *The Doll Trilogy*", in *Australian
   Drama Studies*, 7, 1985.
John McCallum, "The *Doll* and the Legend", in *Australian
   Drama Studies*, vol.3 no.2, 1985.
Joy Hooton, "Lawler's Demythologizing of the *Doll: Kid
   Stakes* and *Other Times*", in *Australian Literary Studies*, 12,
   1986.

*   *   *

When Ray Lawler's *Summer of the Seventeenth Doll* was
premiered in Melbourne, it marked the coming of age of the
Australian theatre. Three themes marked it out as one of those
plays in which a writer exploits the myths and realities of his
native land in order to help his countrymen to see more
accurately what they are like.

The Doll Trilogy: Summer of the Seventeenth Doll,   Elizabethan Theatre, Sydney, 1956

The first of these themes was the contrast between the city, where jobs were dull but the fun intense, and the country, where men were men, where real money and genuine prestige were earned by the exercise of physical toughness, leadership, and strength under appalling physical conditions, but where the passage of youth marked the end of the only life worth living. The second theme was mateship. The harshness of the Australian climate, coupled with the dependence of the Australian economy on activities which required men to be absent for long periods from their homes, meant that the most important relationships were between men. The dependence of the itinerant labourer on his mate, a relationship from which any tinge of homosexuality was so automatically excluded as to make the very mention of it unthinkable, emphasised the relegation of Australian women who had a far more subordinate role than her American or British counterpart.

In the United States, often the wife accompanied her husband as they set off for the conquest of the new territories: she sat next to him on the covered wagon, shared the perils and excitement of the building of the log cabin, the raising of children in what had only recently been a wilderness, and made her own distinctive contribution to the slow establishment of civilisation through the churches and the township. It was dangerous and difficult, but it meant that women were necessary, and therefore equal partners to the men. In Australia women stayed at home. The confinement of the Australian woman to a purely domestic role was the third theme in *Summer of the Seventeenth Doll*, more fully elaborated in the two other plays in the Trilogy, *Kid Stakes* and *Other Times*.

The plot of the first, and best known, of the three plays, *Summer of the Seventeenth Doll*, reveals how the two mates, Barney and Roo (short for Reuben) come down, apparently as usual, to spend their five-month lay-off period in Melbourne, resting when the sun is too hot even for them from the back-breaking work of cutting cane under the blistering heat north of Cairns. But something has changed. For the first time for 17 years, Barney and Roo will not be making a foursome with Nancy and Olive. Nancy has decided, after 16 years as Barney's mistress (although not directly acknowledged there is no doubt that the two have been sleeping together every lay-off since 1937), to marry a bookseller: stable, reliable, but by the Australian macho ethos which is the tragic preoccupation of the trilogy, unbearably dull. Her place is to be taken, theoretically at any rate, by the sceptically-minded widow, Pearl, whose suspicious and disbelieving glance heightens the collapse of the dream in which the four have been living. This dream is symbolised by the kewpie doll, to the alert spectator as well as the convinced Freudian, an obvious baby substitute, which Roo has been in the habit of bringing to Olive as a symbol of the good times they have always had together. But everything has changed, and Nancy has got out just in time. Roo is now over 40, no longer the leader of the pack. His failure to adjust to this change is the second element, after the departure of Nancy, that puts an end to paradise. It leads to the collapse of his relationship not only with Olive but also with his mate, Barney. The wrecking of Olive's life is symbolised by her own destruction of the doll he has brought her and the tearing down of the decorations which Pearl has seen from the beginning as tawdry, but which have, for seventeen years, symbolised glamour, happiness and love. The play caused an understandable sensation in Australia itself by its exploitation of Australian speech habits, its direct confrontation of Australian myths, and its total freedom from feelings of cultural inferiority cringe which had, until then, required Australian writers to imitate English models instead of seeking out their own idiom in the way that Australian landscape painters had.

Twenty years later, *Kid Stakes* examined the beginning of the relationship, and made clear that marriage was out of the question because of the impossibility of the girls following the men to their work place, because Barney had already—at the age of 18—sired two bastards from different women in the space of two months in his home town, and because Olive refused to tie Roo down and bring up children for most of the time by herself. *Other Times* looked at the return of Roo and Barney from active service in World War II and offered a highly accurate analysis of Australian attitudes to authority. Roo, a natural leader, has consistently refused to accept promotion, partly because this would have separated him from the slower and less intelligent Barney, and partly because of a characteristically Australian vision of authority, (dating back to the beginning of the country as a penal colony) as a force that exploits and oppresses. Although successfully produced in an expressionist style by Jean Mignon at the Anthill Theatre, Melbourne, in 1983, the plays are essentially the triumph of naturalism. The justified assumption throughout is that this is really happening to real people, and that Alice's reply to the Red King's mournful question "You don't imagine that those are real tears?" is an undoubted and unequivocal "Yes".

—Philip Thody

A DOLL'S HOUSE (Et Dukkehjem)
by Henrik Ibsen

First Publication: Copenhagen, 1879.
First Production: Royal Theatre, Copenhagen, December 1879.

Translations
A Doll's House, translated by William Archer, in *Ibsen's Prose Dramas 1*, edited by William Archer, London, 1890.
A Doll's House, translated by R. Farquharson Sharp and Mrs. E. Marx-Aveling, 1910.
A Doll's House, translated by Norman Ginsbury, London, 1950.
A Doll's House, in *Ibsen: Six Plays*, translated by Eva Le Gallienne, New York, 1957.
A Doll's House, translated by James Walter McFarlane in *The Oxford Ibsen, 5*, London, 1961.
A Doll's House, in *Ibsen: Four Major Plays*, translated by Rolf Fjelde, New York, 1965.
A Doll's House, translated by Michael Meyer, London, 1965; corrected version in *Ibsen: Plays 2*, London, 1980.
A Doll's House, in *Ibsen: Plays*, translated by Peter Watts, Harmondsworth, 1965.

Criticism
(For general works on the author, see *Playwrights* volume)

Books:
Yvonne Shafer (ed.), *Approaches to Teaching Ibsen's "A Doll's House"*, New York, 1985.

Articles:
Marvin Rosenberg, "Ibsen vs. Ibsen, or: Two Versions of *A Doll's House*", in *Modern Drama*, 12, 1969.

ET DUKKEHJEM
af Henrik Ibsen

Scene af 2den Akt.

Rank (Hr. Jerndorff) sætter sig ved Pianoet og spiller | ninger til hende; hun synes ikke at høre det; hendes Haar
en Tarantella.   Nora (Fru Hennings) danser med stigende | løsnes og falder ud over Skuldrene; hun ænser det ikke,
Vildhed.   Helmer (Hr. Emil Poulsen) har stillet sig ved | men vedbliver at danse. Fru Linde (Frøken Dehn) kommer
Ovnen og henvender jævnlig under Dansen rettende Bemærk- | ind og bliver forbavset staaende ved Døren.

A Doll's House: Royal Theatre, Copenhagen, 1879 (first production)

Elaine H. Baruch, "Ibsen's *Doll's House*: A Myth for Our Time", in *Yale Review*, 69, 1980.

Austin E. Quigley, "*A Doll's House* Revisited", in *Modern Drama*, 27, 1984.

Yvonne Shafer, "Complexity and Ambiguity in Ibsen's *A Doll's House*", in *Literature in Performance*, vol.5 no.2, 1985.

Carol S. Tufts, "Recasting *A Doll's House*: Narcissism as Character Motivation in Ibsen's Play", in *Comparative Drama*, 20, 1986.

Joan Templeton, "The Doll House Backlash: Criticism, Feminism, and Ibsen", in *Publications of the Modern Language Association* [*PMLA*], 104, 1989.

*   *   *

A Doll's House explores a young mother's realisation that her life has been spent in a paternalistic environment, passed, like a doll, from her father's house to her husband's, encouraged to be helpless, rather than to think for herself. The one opportunity she has had to demonstrate her native intelligence and resourcefulness she must conceal from her husband, Torvald. Informed when Torvald was gravely ill that the only way of saving his life was a holiday in the sun (which her husband would not afford) Nora borrowed the money from a moneylender, Krogstad, pretending it came from her father. Her father's signature was necessary as surety for the loan, but since he was dying Nora determined not to worry him and forged the requisite signature after his death. Torvald recovered on holiday, but Nora had to save from her housekeeping to repay Krogstad *and* endure Torvald's reproaches for extravagance. Krogstad uses his knowledge of the forgery to try to regain his job at the bank when Torvald (newly-appointed as manager) gives it to Nora's school friend, Christine Linde. A subtle interweaving of plot and subplot highlights Nora's situation in relation to that of Christine, as well as Krogstad's social disgrace in relation to the impending discovery of Nora's forgery. Torvald's reactions when he learns the truth are the opposite of Nora's expectation, leading to her realisation that she has never really known her husband and that her overriding responsibility now is to educate herself and understand the world she inhabits before she is fit to bring up children; thus the play ends with her leaving home.

The sound of the door closing behind Nora re-echoed

around Europe, causing shock waves of scandal and debate. Victorian opinion predictably was with the husband and Nora was disapproved of as a "bolter". *The Daily Telegraph* commented after the first London performance of the play in 1889:

> We do not honestly believe that these ideas as expressed in *The Doll's House* (sic) would find favour with the great body of English play goers. How could Torvald Helmer at any possibility have treated his restless, illogical, fractious and babyish little wife otherwise than he did?

Ibsen was claimed by the rising suffragette movement, although he disavowed any intention of encouraging female emancipation. Contemporary critics clung to this as to a lifeline; even a generation later, when editing the 1910 Everyman edition of the play, R. Farquharson Sharp could write:

> It must be remembered to his credit that Ibsen, in spite of his enthusiastic advocacy of a woman's right to the development of her own individuality, would never give any countenance to the self-styled "emancipated" woman. He had no patience with those whose idea of self-development seems to consist chiefly in the abandonment of the sphere in which woman is pre-eminent and the invasion of spheres for which she is organically unsuited.

Nora's changing point of view is symbolised in the play by the tarantella. Not only is Nora contemplating suicide at the time rather than let Torvald take the blame for her action, so that her dance (accompanied by the dying Dr. Rank) is an embryo dance of death, but her uncontrolled movement forecasts her breaking free from Torvald:

> Torvald: I could never have believed it. You have forgotten everything I taught you.

When Nora finally sees her husband as he is, her insights are devastating. Torvald informs her that "no man would sacrifice his honour for the one he loves", to which she responds: ". . .thousands of women have. . ." Her response to the law is similarly refreshing: "According to it a woman has no right to spare her old dying father, or to save her husband's life. I can't believe that". Her decision: "to see if I can make out who is right, the world or I" is one we can still recognise—women's response to male-dominated institutions. The play has not dated. Moreover the final glimpse Nora allows Torvald of marriage as an equal partnership—"a real wedlock"—is an idea that is only beginning to find expression a century later. What we now recognise as blindly chauvinist attitudes reveal Torvald also as a victim of 19th-century conditioning, which made domestic autocrats of husbands.

The overriding necessity of education for women is perhaps what emerges most strongly from the play. Nora's leaving home is intended as a positive step, but what opportunities were open to an untrained woman (especially one bearing the social stigma of having left her husband and family)? It is worth remembering that Bernard Shaw, himself inspired by the work of Ibsen to begin writing his own social dramas, pointed out in *Mrs Warren's Profession* (1893) how few openings existed; what drudgery for pitiful wages awaited women in factories, for example.

Ibsen signalled what might be called the start of Modernism in a letter to Georg Brandes (1870):

How the ideas tumble about us now! And indeed it is time. All that we have been living on until now is but scraps from the table of the last century's revolution. Liberty, Equality and Fraternity are no longer the same as they were in the days of the guillotine. These politicians only want individual revolutions, external revolutions, or political revolutions. But all that is just small change. What matters is the revolution of the spirit.

It is a "revolution of the spirit" that, nine years later, Ibsen gave to Nora in *A Doll's House*, bringing about what is often described as a turning-point in the history of European drama.

—Rosemary Pountney

DOM JUAN.   See DON JUAN.

DON JUAN; or, The Feast with the Statue
(Dom Juan; ou, Le Festin de pierre)
by Molière

First Publication: Paris, 1682; with additions, Amsterdam, 1683.
First Production: Théâtre du Palais-Royal, Paris, 15 February 1665.

Editions
Dom Juan, edited by Robert Jouanney, Paris, 1957.
Dom Juan, edited by W.D. Howarth, Oxford, 1958.
Dom Juan, edited by Guy Leclerc, Paris, 1960.
Dom Juan, edited by Anne-Marie and Henri Marel, Paris, 1963.
Dom Juan, edited by Léon Lejealle, Paris, 1965.
Dom Juan, edited by Phillippe Sellier, London, 1969.

Translations
Don Juan, in *Molière: Five Plays*, translated by John Wood, Harmondsworth, 1953; retitled as *"The Miser" and Other Plays*, 1960.
Don Juan, in *Don Juan; Forced to be a Doctor*, translated by George Graveley, St. Albans, Hertfordshire, 1954.
Don Juan; or, The Libertine [John Ozzell's 1665 translation, revised by Oscar Mandel], in *The Theatre of Don Juan*, edited by Oscar Mandel, 1963.
Don Juan; or, The Statue at the Banquet, translated by Wallace Fowlie, Great Neck, New York, 1964.
Don Juan, in *"Tartuffe" and Other Plays*, translated by Donald M. Frame, New York, 1967.

Criticism
(For general works on the author, see *Playwrights* volume)

Books:
Felix Gaiffe, *Dom Juan*, Paris, 1935.
André Villiers, *Le "Dom Juan" de Molière: Un Problème de mise en scène*, Paris, 1947.
J. Arnavon, *Le "Dom Juan" de Molière*, Copenhagen, 1947.

Oscar Mandel, *The Theatre of Don Juan: A Collection of Plays and Views*, Lincoln, Nebraska, 1963.

Jacques Scherer, *Sur le "Dom Juan" de Molière*, Paris, 1967.

Jean-Marie Teyssier, *Réflexions sur "Dom Juan" de Molière*, Paris, 1970.

Robert Horville, *"Dom Juan" de Molière: Une Dramaturgie de rupture*, Paris, 1972.

Christine Geray, *Molière: "Dom Juan"*, Paris, 1974.

Janine Krauss, *Le "Dom Juan" de Molière: Une Libération*, Paris, 1978.

Anne-Marie Mathiot (ed.), *Lectures de "Dom Juan" de Molière*, Paris, 1981.

Serafino Pizzari, *Le Mythe de Dom Juan et la comédie de Molière*, Paris, 1986.

Articles:

Constant Coquelin, "Le *Dom Juan* de Molière", in *Revue de Paris*, vol.11 no.2, 1904; translated as "*Dom Juan* of Molière", in *International Quarterly*, 8, 1903.

James Brander Mathews, "Molière's *Don Juan*", in *Sewanee Review*, 18, 1910.

Robert V. Merrill, "Molière's Exposition of a Courtly Character in *Don Juan*", in *Modern Philology*, 19, 1921–22.

Francis Baumal, "*Dom Juan*, comédie d'actualité", in *Belles-Lettres*, 4, 1922.

J. Doolittle, "Humanity of Molière's *Dom Juan*", in *Publications of the Modern Language Association* [*PMLA*], 68, 1953.

R. Grimes, "The Don Juan Theme in Molière and Kierkegaard", in *Comparative Literature*, 6, 1954.

W.G. Moore, "*Don Juan* Reconsidered", in *Modern Language Review*, 52, 1957.

H.G. Hall, "Comic *Dom Juan*", in *Yale French Studies*, 23, 1959.

Hallam Walker, "The Self-Creating Hero in *Don Juan*", in *French Review*, 36, 1962.

Richard N. Coe, "The Ambiguity of Don Juan", in *Australian Journal of French Studies*, 1, 1964.

Francis L. Lawrence, "The Ironic Commentator in Molière's *Don Juan*", in *Studi francesi*, 12, 1968.

Jules Brody, "*Dom Juan* and *Le Misanthrope* or The Esthetics of Individualism in Molière", in *Publications of the Modern Language Association* [*PMLA*], 84, 1969.

I. Singer, "Shadow of Don Juan in Molière", in *Modern Language Notes*, 85, December 1970.

I. Singer, "Molière's *Dom Juan*", in *Hudson Review*, 24, 1971.

William O. Goode, "Dom Juan and Heaven's Spokesman", in *French Review*, 45, 1972.

Philip Stewart, "An Analysis of the Plot in *Dom Juan*", in *French Review*, 45, 1972.

J-J. Pelous, "Les Problèmes du temps dans le *Dom Juan* de Molière", in *Revue des sciences humaines*, 152, 1973.

Joseph Pineau, "Dom Juan 'mauvais élève'", in *Revue des sciences humaines*, 152, 1973.

Constant Venesoen, "*Dom Juan* ou la conversion manquée", in *Revue belge de philologie et d'histoire*, 51, 1973.

Nathan Gross, "The Dialectic of Obligation in Molière's *Dom Juan*", in *Romanic Review*, 65, 1974.

G. Defaux, "*Dom Juan* ou la comédie foudroyée", in *Travaux de linguistique et de littérature* (Strasbourg), vol.15 no.2, 1977.

Jean-Pierre Dens, "*Dom Juan*: Héroïsme et désir", in *French Review*, 50, 1977.

David Shaw, "Egoism and Society: A Secular Interpretation of Molière's *Dom Juan*", in *Modern Languages*, 59, 1978.

Thérèse Malachy, "Le Carnaval solitaire de *Dom Juan*", in *Les Lettres romanes*, 35, 1981.

G.F. McCarthy, "Characterisation in Molière: The Case of *Dom Juan*", in *Modern Languages*, Vol. 62 no.1, 1981.

Barbara Woshinsky, "The Discourse of Disbelief in Molière's *Dom Juan*", in *Romanic Review*, vol.72 no.4, 1981.

David Ball and Frank H. Ellis, "Molière's *Dom Juan*: Form, Meaning, Audience", in *Modern Philology*, vol. 81 no.2, 1983.

Charlotte Schapira, "La Séduction face au ciel dans *Dom Juan* de Molière", in *Neohelicon*, 11, 1984.

Franco Tonelli, "Molière's *Dom Juan* and the Space of the *Commedia dell'arte*", in *Theatre Journal*, December 1985.

Larry W. Riggs, "The Issues of Nobility and Identity in *Dom Juan* and *Le Bourgeois Gentilhomme*", in *French Review*, February 1986.

G.F. McCarthy, "Role and Rhythm in Molière's *Dom Juan*", in *Australian Journal of French Studies*, vol.24 no.1, 1987.

Noël A. Peacock, "*Dom Juan*: ou, le libertin imaginaire", in *Forum for Modern Language Studies*, October 1988.

*   *   *

In Act I, Dom Juan has induced Doña Elvire to leave a convent and marry him, and has now abandoned her; she is coming in search of him. His valet, Sganarelle, explains to Doña Elvire's valet that Dom Juan is an unprincipled seducer and that the marriage was a sham, one of many that he has contracted. Sganarelle remonstrates ineffectually with Dom Juan over the immorality of his life; Doña Elvire confronts him, he hypocritically pretends to religious scruples about their marriage, and goes off to attempt the abduction of another woman. In Act II, Dom Juan's boat has capsized in the course of this attempted abduction and he has been rescued from drowning by a peasant. He attempts to seduce the peasant's fiancée and another peasant woman simultaneously but is interrupted by word that armed men are searching for him.

In Act III, Sganarelle and Dom Juan have disguised themselves and are hiding in a forest. Sganarelle attempts again to persuade his master of the dangers of an immoral life. They encounter a beggar; Dom Juan attempts to persuade him to abandon his pious scruples. Dom Juan chivalrously rescues a man from robbers, who is revealed to be Dom Carlos, Elvire's brother; Carlos insists to his retinue that, since Dom Juan has rescued him, they must wait until another time to avenge his sister's honor. Sganarelle and Dom Juan find themselves before a tomb; it opens to reveal the statue of the Commander, whom Dom Juan had killed. Dom Juan jestingly invites the statue to dine, it nods its head, and they flee. In his lodgings, Dom Juan gets rid of a creditor; his father berates him for disgracing the family honor; Doña Elvire, who has decided to re-enter the convent, implores him to save his soul; the Statue appears. In Act V, Dom Juan tells his father that he has reformed, but reveals to Sganarelle that he has adopted religious hypocrisy as the most expedient mask for a licentious life. Finally The Statue appears and leads Dom Juan off to hell, while Sganarelle cries out for his lost wages.

Dom Juan has always been Molière's most controversial play. Its initial run drew very large audiences, and drew also heated charges of blasphemy and atheism; the outrage of Molière's attackers seems to have focussed on his performance in the rôle of Sganarelle, rather than on the script itself. After 15 performances, the play vanished abruptly from the repertory, and was not revived in its original form until the mid-19th Century.

The summary of the action given above demonstrates the feature of the play that has most troubled the critics: the absence (uncharacteristic for Molière) of a clear plot-line, and the episodic, almost disjointed nature of the sequence of scenes—many of which are highly developed in themselves but introduce characters who never appear in the play again. For a long time it was believed that Molière could not have intended to produce such a loosely-constructed script and that he must therefore have thrown it together in great haste. This theory was demolished by the discovery in 1963 of a scene-painters' contract dated more than ten weeks before the opening of the play, showing that the development of the script was already far advanced at that point and that the lack of continuity must have been deliberate.

This contract is also of interest in showing how integral the visual production was to Molière's conception of this puzzling play. It was a "machine play", but unlike other examples of that popular seventeenth-century genre it exploited a constant ironic tension between the visual splendors of the setting and the deflating references to it in the speeches of Sganarelle. Even the spectacle of hellfire at the end must have been subverted by the buffoonish Sganarelle, leaving the impression not of an edifying moral lesson but of a self-mockingly stagy presentation of superstitious myth—sufficient cause, certainly, for the outrage of a portion of Molière's original audience.

—Roger Herzel

THE DONNELLY PLAYS
    Sticks and Stones
    The St. Nicholas Hotel
    Handcuffs
by James Reaney

The Trilogy
First Publication: Erin, Ontario, 1983.

Sticks and Stones
First Publication: Erin, Ontario, 1975.
First Production: Tarragon Theatre, Toronto, November 1973.

The St. Nicholas Hotel
First Publication: Erin, Ontario, 1976.
First Production: Tarragon Theatre, November 1974.

Handcuffs
First Publication: Erin, Ontario, 1977.
First Production: Tarragon Theatre, Toronto, March 1975.

Criticism
(For general works on the author, see *Playwrights* volume)

Articles:
Gerald Parker, " 'History, story and story-style': James Reaney's *The Donnellys*", in *Canadian Drama*, 4, 1978.
Eric Roberts, "*Sticks and Stones*: History, Play, and Myth", in *Canadian Drama*, 4, 1978.
D. Bessai, "Documentary Theatre in Canada: An Investigation into Questions and Backgrounds", in *Canadian Drama*, 6, 1980.
Manina Jones, " 'The Collage in Motion': Staging the Document in Reaney's *Sticks and Stones*", in *Canadian Drama*, 16, 1990.

The *Donnelly* plays are based on fact, and the facts, though dramatised, are closely related in word and spirit to the events of 1844–80 in and around Biddulph Township (near London, Ontario). The Donnelly parents emigrated from Ireland in 1844 and their seven sons and one daughter were born in Canada. They lived in a community rife with Catholic and Prostestant rivalry, made more complex by events going back to Tipperary in 1766. *Sticks and Stones* takes the events to 1867 by when, despite much violence on both sides, including murder and barn and factory burning, the Donnellys had gained an awesome reputation. The father had served seven years for murder, and the play ends with the Donnellys' barn being burnt down and their water-pump destroyed; nevertheless, they vow never to leave Biddulph. Part II of the trilogy centres on the stage-coach line run by the Donnelly family, still outsiders. Their rivals oppose them with tollgates, and finally at the end of the play, Michael Donnelly is murdered. It is by then 1879 and one brother has died of TB and another has been sentenced to two years' imprisonment for assault. In Part III, the time-span of the play is much shorter. It is concerned with the murder, by a "Vigilante Committee", of four Donnellys— the parents, two sons, and a cousin, Bridget, in 1880. It concludes with the leader of the vigilantes, James Carroll, being found "not guilty" of the murders. This "trial", highly stylised, represents two historical trials, both of which failed to convict anyone, and is set, as a stage direction explains, in the early 1970's in the graveyard of St. Patrick's, Biddulph. Here, public myth and literal documentary are merged: "On the anniversary of the murder it is the custom for crowds of people in cars to come up, park and wait for a possible ghostly appearance at the Donnelly grave". The act opens with the ghosts of Mr. and Mrs. Donnelly standing behind two cloths representing their first and second gravestones. A car radio can be heard blaring out "At the Hop", a chorus sets the scene, and the voices of tourists can be heard as they seek cheap "entertainment".

Reaney's conclusion not only dramatises the way the bloody and violent events associated with the Donnellys and their enemies have entered the public consciousness, but also the way they had almost invariably been trivialised. It also hints at the kinds of techniques Reaney draws on to tell his story. Few plays sustain over such a long period of stage-time the fluidity of techniques, the imaginative use of limited resources—so that the limitations are a virtue, not a restricting influence— and the varieties of dialogue as does the *Donnelly* trilogy. When Part I was First Presented, Ross Woodman wrote, "it is not only the best Canadian play yet written, it is among the best poetic dramas ever written, better, for example, than any of the plays of Yeats, Eliot and Fry. Reaney conjures from a vicious and, at root, sordid and brutal story a drama that can genuinely claim to be a modern tragedy. What is more, he sustains this over nine acts.

Reaney does not only use time shifts at the end of the final play. For example, in *St. Nicholas Hotel*, though the historical time is 1873, a Chorus in "a drifting voice" recalls other events that occurred in 1875, 1881–97, 1891, and 1925. His use of props is also both economical and imaginative. Great play is made with a number of ladders in *Sticks and Stones*, and the stagecoach dispute is enacted in a way that anticipates the technique used in the Royal Shakespeare Company's *Nicholas Nickleby* (1980): "*The convention for the stage wagons should involve at least one wheel each and a solid block of actors 'inside' the coach; other actors are the sides of the road and move against the coaches to give the illusion of a journey. . . . The drivers hitch up horses [imaginary] and check wheels and parcels; passengers.*" Reaney makes considerable use of sound—clapping and stamping in *Handcuffs*, for

The Donnelly Plays: Sticks and Stones, Tarragon Theatre, Toronto, 1973

example—and music and song; there is even a brief horn and fiddle contest in *St. Nicholas Hotel*. There is inventive deployment of chorus with varieties of speech—poetic, colloquial, stylised. The stagecoach rivalry that leads to the crash that runs Donnelly off the road in 1875 is occasionally reminiscent of Auden's commentary for the film *Night Mail* (1935).

It is sad that this remarkable trilogy should have been neglected by the English theatre. Few contemporary plays are more deserving of a major full-scale production.

—Peter Davison

THE DOUBLE-DEALER
by William Congreve

First Publication: London, 1694.
First Production: Theatre Royal, Drury Lane, c. November 1693.

Editions
The Double-Dealer, in *Complete Plays*, edited by Herbert J. Davis, Chicago and London, 1967 (2 vols.).

The Double-Dealer, in *The Comedies of William Congreve*, edited by Anthony J. Henderson, Cambridge, 1977.
The Double-Dealer, edited by J.C. Ross, London and New York, 1981 (New Mermaid Series).

Criticism
(For general works on the author, see *Playwrights* volume)

Articles:
Anthony Goose, "Plot and Character in Congreve's *Double-Dealer*", in *Modern Language Quarterly*, 29, 1968.
John Barnard, "Passion, 'Poetical Justice', and Dramatic Law in *The Double-Dealer* and *The Way of the World*", in *William Congreve*, edited by Brian Morris, London, 1972.
Brian Corman, "The Mixed Way of Comedy: Congreve's *The Double Dealer*", in *Modern Philology*, 71, 1974.

*   *   *

The Double-Dealer was Congreve's least well-received play, and the least popular of his plays throughout the 18th century. It is also the most highly experimental of his comedies, a likely explanation for its relative lack of popularity. It was perhaps especially confusing to its audience because the plot at first seemed so conventional. The setting is Lord Touchwood's house on the eve of the marriage of his witty, young nephew Mellefont to Cynthia, the daughter of Sir Paul Plyant. The two are in love and eager to marry; the only apparent obstacle is Lady Touchwood, who is also in love with Mellefont. But rather than being a typically ineffective, comic, blocking parent, Lady Touchwood is more than equal to her task. And she is assisted by the title character, her lover Maskwell, who has insinuated himself into Lord Touchwood's household and Mellefont's trusted friendship. The play traces the villains' attempts to stop the marriage.

Lady Touchwood and Maskwell resemble the rogues of Ben Jonson's comedies, most notably Volpone and Mosca, in that it is they, rather than Mellefont and Cynthia, who are the cleverest people in the play and the initiators of most of the action. The more passive lovers are usually placed in the position of responding to the schemes of the villains. And like Jonson's rogues, Congreve's villains elicit an ambivalent response from the audience: it is especially difficult to condemn outright Maskwell's bare-faced, forthright manipulation of his victims. Even when he tells them what he is like, they refuse to believe him. What finally defeats the villains (again, like Volpone and Mosca) is themselves: Maskwell attempts to deceive Lady Touchwood in order to win Cynthia for himself. When she finds out, they quarrel and are overheard by Cynthia and the injured Lord Touchwood. Their villainy exposed, they are no longer able to prevent the marriage of Cynthia and Mellefont.

The comic tone of the play is provided by two additional cuckolding actions. In the first, Mellefont's friend, the libertine wit Careless, seduces the willing Lady Plyant, whose husband seems the only man who does not interest her. Much of the humour here depends on the contrast between Lady Plyant's eager foray into adultery and the aggressive chastity she shows her husband, who is swaddled in blankets 364 nights each year. In the other action, the poetaster Lady Froth indulges in an affair with the fop Brisk that is based primarily on mutual flattery: he admires her poetic powers, as evidenced by her verse-epic *The Sillibub*; she in turn admires his wit. Lady Froth's self-consciously aristocratic Lord is too proud and too self-satisfied to believe himself a cuckold, an interesting contrast to the uxorious and self-effacing Sir Paul. These two near-farcical triangles help modulate the seriousness and intensity of the main action—an intensity enhanced by Congreve's decision (stated in the Dedication) "to preserve the three unities of the drama. . .to the utmost severity". But they also offer a bitterly ironic contrast to the Maskell-Lady Touchwood-Lord Touchwood triangle, as the near universal adultery tends to level the more serious characters and the fools. As a result, the virtuous Cynthia and Mellefont are the more isolated in a society made up largely of knaves and fools. True love and moral decency are rare qualities in the world of the *The Double-Dealer*; their scarcity and their vulnerability make them all the more precious. And love's triumphs in Congreve's plays are rarer still, all the more reason to treasure them.

The Double-Dealer was written with the leading actors of the United Company in mind. Thomas Betterton played the title role, one of a line of Iagolike, clever villains he developed late in his career. Elizabeth Barry was the obvious Lady Touchwood; Anne Bracegirdle the perfect Cynthia. Its host of comic humours characters provided rich roles for the Company. Despite a strong cast and the support of the likes of Dryden, however, *The Double-Dealer* did not repeat the success of *The Old Batchelour*. Congreve's defensive dedication addresses a number of objections: the use of soliloquy, satire of women, bawdy language, and, most centrally, that "the Hero of the Play. . .is a Gull, and made a Fool and cheated". But an eloquent defense and Dryden's fine poem "To My Dear Friend Mr. Congreve, On His Comedy Called The Double-Dealer", were not enough to overcome the lukewarm response of the audience.

The Double-Dealer: Engraved frontispiece from 1777 edition

The Double-Dealer was revived in this century by the Stage Society in 1916 and has benefitted more recently from important productions by Michael Benthall at the Old Vic, William Gaskill at the Royal Court, and Peter Wood at London's National Theatre. The critical success of these last two productions suggests that the curious generic hybrid that so perplexed earlier audiences is more welcome in the late 20th Century than ever before.

—Brian Corman

LA DOUBLE INCONSTANCE.   See **THE DOUBLE INCONSTANCY.**

THE DOUBLE INCONSTANCY (La Double Inconstance)
by Pierre Carlet de Chamblain de Marivaux

First Publication: Paris, 1724.
First Production: Comédie-Italienne, Paris, April 1723.

Editions
La Double Inconstance, in *Théâtre complet*, edited by Frédéric Deloffre, Paris, 1968 (2 vols.).

Translations
Double Infidelity, in *Seven Comedies by Marivaux*, translated by Oscar and Adrienne S. Mandel, Ithaca, New York, 1968.
Infidelities, translated by David Cohen, in *The Game of Love and Chance; Infidelities; Up From The Country*, edited by David Cohen, Harmondsworth, 1980.
The Double Inconstancy, translated by Nicholas Wright, in *Marivaux: Plays*, edited by Donald Roy, London, 1988.

Criticism
(For general works on the author, see *Playwrights* volume)

Articles:
Janet Whatley, "*Le Double Inconstance*: Marivaux and The Comedy of Manipulation", in *Eighteenth Century Studies*, 10, 1977.
Jean Rousset, "Une Dramaturge dans la comédie: La Flaminia de *La Double Inconstance*", in *Revista di letterature moderne e comparate*, vol. 41 no. 2, 1988.
Michael Moriarty, "Identity and its Vicissitudes in *La Double Inconstance*", in *French Studies*, vol. 43 no. 3, 1989.

* * *

La Double Inconstance is one of Marivaux's earliest comedies of love. A prince is obliged by the laws of his country to marry one of his subjects, but without coercing her. He has fallen in love with a country girl, Silvia, and seeks, with the help of Flaminia, to win her away from her beloved Arlequin. The Prince conceals his true identity from Silvia and courts her as a simple *officier*; Flaminia befriends Arlequin, beguiles him with good food and wine, and awakens his love. The plot is successful and at the end of the play Silvia and Arlequin give themselves over to their new loves.

As is often the case in Marivaux, this play has little external action, but focuses instead on the shifting relationships between characters and the transformation of their feelings. At one level, the comedy seems to trace the dawn of "true" love in Silvia and Arlequin as each is confronted with hitherto unknown emotions. What each thought to be love, deep and permanent, is slowly revealed to be quite superficial when compared with what they begin to feel for their new partners. It is as if the characters attain a form of self-realisation in a controlled and painless way, carefully led by the Prince and Flaminia who direct and monitor every stage in the process. The stylization of comic form, with its beautifully orchestrated changes of affection, combines here with discreet insight into the human heart to form the kind of theatrical entertainment often associated with this dramatist. It was of this play that an early reviewer coined the term "*métaphysique du coeur*", applied, often disparagingly by his contemporaries, to the delicacy of analysis contained in so many of them.

This blend of the artificial and the natural which characterises Marivaux's conception of the play is an essential part, too, of its thematic structure. In his depiction of the Prince's love for Silvia, the dramatist brings together the courtly and the rustic and he exploits the comic potential of this juxtaposition of two quite different modes of life. The sophistication and intelligence of Flaminia serves to highlight the naivety of the two country lovers, who are slowly but surely manipulated and transformed. Conversely, Arlequin, a figure traditional in the *commedia dell'arte*, has the witty non-conformism to cut through the artifice of courtly customs and traditions, revealing the absurdity of ceremony and honour. The contrast, though, does not end here and Marivaux lends to this traditional comic figure a further thematic function, as he casts a critical light not only on the particular courtly environment, but also on the moral basis of the play's action, namely the Prince's plan to separate two perfectly happy lovers simply in the name of love. From the outset he refuses to see the purpose or justification of such a scheme: love may be its motive, but can that justify what in other contexts would appear merely as the abuse of power? The prince himself has no answer to offer.

The Prince's intrigue is seen to have other flaws, too. It may be the unaffected innocence of Silvia which first appeals to him, and yet in order to persuade her to love him, he has to have her educated in the ways of the court. Flaminia's strategy is to awaken in Silvia the desire to outshine all her rivals by telling her that more sophisticated ladies regard her beauty and its effect on the prince as merely ephemeral; her determination to love is fuelled by these attacks on her self-respect. The natural spontaneity so highly prized by the Prince can only be won if it is first merged with vanity and defiance; to capture innocence is also, paradoxically, to contaminate it.

Indeed the very nature of the plot raises further questions about the interaction of nature and artifice. The play may seem to suggest that what happens to Silvia and Arlequin is already latent in them, and that they slowly realise their full potential. And yet the context into which they are placed actually determines this sequence of events as much as it witnesses them. The situation is wholly contrived and the audience is left in doubt as to the stability of the feelings thus aroused. The prince courts in disguise, and the love he awakens in Silvia is love for this particular image of him, rather than for the person himself. As for Flaminia, the consummate actress, Marivaux never makes clear how far her words correspond to the strategic role she plays in courting Arlequin and how far they reflect her feelings; the character remains opaque, a mysterious confusion of the spontaneous and the contrived. Both Silvia and Arlequin trust her implicitly, and yet neither ever learns of her role in the play. The mechanism of deception which animates the plot remains to the last a significant component of its meaning.

The final scenes subtly evoke something of this complexity, as both Silvia and Arlequin express confusion as much as delight at the events which have befallen them. All certainty has been removed from them and they are faced with the unpredictability of feelings once held to be so sure. They have been taken over completely and cannot understand why they act as they do. The comedy may offer the promise of a new order, but it is one based not simply on the power of love, but as the play's title suggests, on its frailty and unreliability, on a "double inconstance," the ending is as unstable as the love which creates it. Beneath the apparent simplicity of form, Marivaux juxtaposes, in a suggestive tension, order and chaos, artifice and nature; it is one of the strengths of this comedy and of his work as a whole.

—G. Jonathon Mallinson.

DOUBLE INFIDELITY.   See **THE DOUBLE INCONSTANCY.**

DR. FAUSTUS.   See **DOCTOR FAUSTUS.**

THE DRAGON (Drakon)
by Evgeny Schwartz

Composition: 1943.
First Publication: Moscow, 1960.
First Production: Leningrad   Comedy   Theatre,   Moscow,
          1944.

Translations
The Dragon, in *The Naked King; The Shadow; The Dragon*,
    translated by Elisaveta Fen, London, 1976.

Criticism
(For general works on the author, see *Playwrights* volume)

Articles:
Claudine Amiard-Chevrel, "*Le Dragon* d'Eugène Schwarz",
    in *Les voies de la création théâtrale*, vol.3, edited by Jean
    Jacquot and Denis Bablet, Paris, 1970–79.

*   *   *

The Dragon by Evgeny Schwartz was given just one performance in its author's lifetime, a "tryout" on tour in Moscow by the Leningrad Comedy Theatre under the direction of Nikolai Akimov in 1944. It apparently proved too difficult for the authorities, however, and was not performed again in the U.S.S.R. until the 1960's, by which time its author was dead. Abroad, however, the play has been Schwartz's most popular, and at home, too, now, there are signs that it is beginning to be fairly assessed. Its mixture of fantasy, grotesquerie, and overt theatricality makes it modernist and challenging, in spite of its apparent simplicity.

The story seems initially merely a fairy tale. A town under the tyrannical domination of an evil dragon, who demands a young maiden as a sacrifice each year, is visited by Lancelot, a knight errant. Despite the resignation to her fate of the latest chosen victim, Elsa, Lancelot determines to challenge the dragon. The mayor, and his loathesome son, Heinrich, who protests his love for Elsa, try to persuade her to murder Lancelot, but she refuses. Lancelot, meanwhile, with some magical help, joins battle with the three-headed monster and, watched by the towns-people, defeats it. Mortally wounded, he is carried away from the town—and Elsa—for ever. A year later, the mayor, proclaiming he is the dragon's conqueror, has installed himself as a new dictator. The people are required to praise him; those who refuse are jailed. The only sign of rebellion is a repeated piece of graffiti—the letter "L"—chalked on walls throughout the town, and Elsa's refusal to marry the mayor. Unexpectedly, magically, Lancelot returns. Disappointed by the people's submission, he has the mayor and his son carted off to gaol, takes Elsa for himself and starts out on the task of making everyone happy.

The exhilerating ending may contain of hint of horror: is the benevolent Lancelot, too, about to turn into a dragon? On the face of it, apparently not, for the play clearly partakes of the atmosphere of a dramatic fairy tale. The author's unselfconscious understanding of the fairy tale world, with talking animals, magic carpets, horrid dragons, and so on, lends the play an attractive charm, and allows it to appear morally concerned but never bombastic. Indeed, by employing fairy tale motifs within an apparently real framework, Schwartz here almost solves that most difficult literary and theatrical problem—how to create goodness without sentimentality. The "happy ending" seems fitting and just.

But in performance the play is less straightforward. If the acting is sincere and the motivation of the characters understandable (unlike in fairy tales, when it is frequently arbitrary) and if the details of the production are true to life, then fantasy and theatrical surprises may produce in an audience a frisson of doubt rather than simply contented acceptance.

Critics, sensing this insecurity, have suggested that the play is an allegory which they have then tried to unravel. Some (including Schwartz's friend and producer, Nikolai Akimov) have suggested that the dragon is Hitler and the mayor the victorious allies who took advantage of the exhausted Soviets after the war, and others, particularly in the west, that the dragon is Stalin. Others again have argued that the dragon is tsarism, and the mayor, bolshevism. Perhaps, then, Lancelot represents Lenin and the mysterious letter "L" reveals a desire to return to the true spirit of Leninism. All or any thesis may largely fit, which is one reason why such literalness is unlikely to be the whole answer. It is probably best to regard the play as presenting images of the way dictatorship works rather than a coded description of any one, specific dictator. Such an interpretation would explain why Lancelot's final lines, seemingly so kind, are actually so ominous: "I love all of you, my friends," he insists. "Otherwise, why should I go to all this trouble over you?" (Just such a question any dictator might ask). "And if I love you, everything will be fine. And all of us after long trials and tribulations [meaning, perhaps, show trials and concentration camps] will be happy, very happy at last!". The velvet glove fails to conceal wholly the iron fist.

Schwartz spent three years writing *The Dragon*, and its subtle construction is easily overlooked. The comedy, for instance, comes not simply through the jokes, but through thoroughly theatrical devices, such as the presentation of the mayor and his son as a comedy double act, or the choral unity of the two drivers who provide Lancelot with the magic carpet. The depressed townspeople are a means of focusing the theme, comparable to a Greek chorus: they are not just "a crowd", but have a specific influence on the development of the events. Their importance as a group helps to isolate Lancelot, whose "aloneness" is part of his status. It is notable, however, that unlike so many plays which present "character" as something static, most of the persons in this drama change and develop as the action progresses: this is as true of Lancelot, who evolves from deliverer to judge, as it is of Elsa, who only gradually turns to an acceptance of Lancelot.

Finally, what makes this play memorable is its "futurist" orientation. "We *will* be happy, very happy", protests Lancelot at the end. Though never a self-proclaimed Futurist, Schwartz shares with Mayakovsky and others a concern not simply to analyse the present, but to relate it to the future. This gives an apparently naive fairy tale surprising modernity and strength.

—Robert Leach

DRAKON. See **THE DRAGON.**

DREAM ON MONKEY MOUNTAIN
by Derek Walcott

First Publication: In *"Dream on Monkey Mountain" and Other Plays*, New York, 1970.
First Production: Central Library Theatre, Toronto, 12 August 1967.

Criticism
(For general works on the author, see *Playwrights* volume)

Articles:
Sybil L. James, "Aspects of Symbolism in Derek Walcott's *Dream on Monkey Mountain*", in *Literary Half-Yearly*, vol.26 no.1, 1985.
Jan R. Uhrbach, "A Note on Language and Naming in *Dream on Monkey Mountain*", in *Callaloo*, 29, 1986.

*   *   *

Dream on Monkey Mountain is set in a jail on the island of St. Lucia. Most of the action takes place within the dreams of Makak, a black peasant charcoal-burner, during a night when he has been imprisoned for his own self-protection, after being violently drunk and destructive in the local market. He had a vision of a white woman, an apparition variously called the white goddess, muse, and the moon, who tells him to return to Africa. The jailer (Corporal Lestrade) and the criminals at first speak approvingly or ambivalently about the white man's law while Makak hates himself for being black. Makak dreams of leading the local black people back to Africa where, in one of many transformations within his dream, he becomes a famous warrior. His jailer becomes one of his followers. Makak, after a reversal of historical white-black power relations (he is sent a "floral tribute of lilies from the Ku Klux Klan") ritualistically beheads the white goddess. This frees him from his love-hate obsession with whiteness, he wakes and for the first time in the play says his real name, Felix Hobain. He resolves to return to his home on Monkey Mountain which is compared to Eden, paradise, a new begining, and is symbolic of the New World.

Dream on Monkey Mountain has been acted in many versions including the New York Negro Ensemble production of 1970 which, while winning the 1971 Obie, is known to have disturbed Walcott for its strong anti-white emphasis. As in most of Walcott's plays a conflict between two opposing strengths leads to resolution. Here, as in most of Walcott's writing of this period, the resolution is the rediscovery of the West Indian black that he belongs in the New World and that the islands, which could be paradise despite their history and poverty, are a new beginning. The play sees genesis in the greenery of St. Lucia and not in Africa from which the New World black has become distinct. This means accepting a mixing of cultures and races, recognizing that a new society and culture has been and is being, created, rather than being obsessed with the Manichaean polarities of white and black and the burden of past injustices.

An advantage of using a dream for most of the play is the rapid transformations of scene and character. The play is swift-moving and full of surprises, disguises, and powerful scenes. In the dream, Makak's friend Moustique, like a hanger-on or parasite of Roman comedy, becomes a con-man and hopes to get money by impersonating his buddy Makak as leader of a back-to-Africa movement. He is unmasked and killed. At the beginning of Part Two there is a scene in the jail which seems like a return to reality but is a dream within the dream and initiates a secondary plot as the two characters Tigre and Souris decide to escape and pretend to become followers of Makak so as to rob him of money they foolishly assume he has hidden. From now on the dream exists on two levels, part of Makak's psychosis, as he imagines he is returning to Africa while the others in the dream think he is deluded and are humouring him while going to Monkey Mountain. Increasingly the play becomes violent with contradictory plots eliding into each other. Then there is the shock of the beheading on stage of the white goddess, immediately followed by a return to the jail where Makak wakes surrounded by a sympathetic, helpful jailor and Moustique.

Walcott moves his themes and symbols through various layers of significance. These include Walcott's coming to terms with his own half-white family background, his love of the English language and its poetry (the muse or white goddess), and the relationship of the English culture of the St. Lucian brown, protestant, middle class to the francophonic Catholicism and Vodunism of the St. Lucian black majority with its patois. Walcott's "A Note on Production" invites us to see Makak's dream as a part of the author's own psyche. Indeed the various characters in the play and their transformations—such as Corporal Lestrade's change from a strong defender of white law to the most violent exponent of black racial assertion—should probably be seen as conflicting aspects of both the author's feelings and of the West Indian personality. It is the Mimic Men, those most filled with self-hate and in love with whiteness, who become the most violent converts to an inverted racism in which white is evil.

Walcott's quotations prefacing parts of *Dream on Monkey Mountain* and various allusions within the play show that Frantz Fanon's *The Wretched of the Earth* is one of the influences. Fanon's play examines the way white dominance in colonialism makes blacks want to become whites. A sense of inferiority turns to self-hate and then seeks an outlet through the reversal of roles and a liberating violence against the white oppressor. According to Fanon this is the only way to create a new national culture in contrast to imitation of the colonizer, or nostalgic idealization of the past. Makak's self-hatred, belief that he is ugly, drunkeness and his dream follow Fanon's pattern. After the fantasy of returning to Africa Makak must liberate himself from his obsession with whiteness, especially as represented by white women, through violence. But unlike the radical culture born out of destruction and blood that Fanon assumes, Walcott suggests that this is a dream, a fantasy, and that the future must be built on oneself, on the various contradictions and influences, including the European heritage, that are part of the West Indies.

While the racial and cultural themes are obvious and shaped by the plot, the play also concerns West Indian theatre. It has strong folk elements, such as a black peasant as the main character, the use of song and dance, and various forms of English and French. Some characters have such symbolic names as Moustique, Tigre, Souris and Lestrade. As in a fable, or in Walcott's earlier *Ti-Jean and His Brothers*, the plot is illustrative. From fable the play develops into ritual drama like that of Genet and Soyinka. But, as Walcott observes in "What the Twilight Says: An Overture" prefacing *Dream on Monkey Mountain and Other Plays*, when the Trinidad Theatre Workshop produced Soyinka's *The Road*, the kind of possession by the god Ogun that the play demanded from an actor was impossible for the West Indian, Afro-Christian. "We could pretend to enter his power but he would never possess us. . . .The actor's approach could not be catatonic but rational; expository, not receptive". If the plot of Walcott's play is a racial and cultural allegory, it is also an allegory of West Indian theatre and acting. The influences, like Caribbean culture, range broadly. As with Walcott's poetry of the period the play gives classical European form—its European sources are probably as much in Roman drama and Ben Jonson, as in Strindberg and Genet—to folk culture in which its use of West Indian speech and culture is part of its meaning, its return to genesis, and not merely local colour, in contrast to the confused melange of Africanisms in the African scenes. The mixture of verse and prose, music, drumming, dance, switching of roles, dialect, plays within plays, trials, apparitions and the contrast between the apparently impoverished characters and the rich, grand themes contained within themselves make the play extraordinarily effective theatre.

—Bruce King

A DREAM PLAY (Ett Drömspel)
by August Strindberg

First Publication: Stockholm, 1902.
First Production: Svenska Teatern [Swedish Theatre], Stockholm, 17 April 1907.

Translations
A Dream Play, translated by Arvid Paulson, in *Strindberg: Eight Expressionist Plays*, edited by John Gassner, New York, 1945.
A Dream Play, in *"A Dream Play" and Four Chamber Plays*, translated by Walter Johnson, Seattle, Washington, 1973 (The Washington Strindberg).
A Dream Play, in *Strindberg: Plays 2*, translated by Michael Meyer, London, 1975.
Dreamplay, in *Strindberg: Three Experimental Plays*, translated by F.R. Southerington, Charlottesville, Virginia, 1975.
A Dream Play, in *Five Plays by August Strindberg*, translated by Harry G. Carlson, Berkeley, California, and London, 1983.

Criticism
(For general works on the author, see *Playwrights* volume)

Articles:
Evert Sprinchorn, "The Logic of *A Dream Play*", in *Modern Drama*, 3, 1962.
Walter Johnson, "*A Dream Play*: Plans and Fulfillment", in *Scandinavica*, 10, 1971.
Raymond Jarvi, "*Ett Drömspel*: A Symphony for the Stage", in *Scandinavian Studies*, 44, 1972.
Tomas Alldahl, "*Ett Drömspel* och *Spöksonaten*: Det konkreta språkets teater", in *Meddelanden från Strindbergssällskapet*, 53–54, 1974.
Stephen R. Lawson, "Strindberg's *Dream Play* and *Ghost Sonata*", in *Yale Theatre*, 5, 1974.
Jocelyn Powell, "Demons That Live in Sunlight: Problems in Staging Strindberg", in *Yearbook of English Studies*, 9, 1979.
Austin E. Quigley, "*A Dream Play*", in *The Modern Stage and Other Worlds*, New York, 1985.

A Dream Play: Harriet Bosse, Svenska Teatern, Stockholm, 1907
(first production)

Tamás Bécsy, "*A Dream Play*: Is It a Drama Indeed?", in *Strindbergiana*, 2, 1987.

*   *   *

"I'm writing *The Rising Castle*," August Strindberg wrote to Harriet Bosse, his third wife, in September 1901. And a month later—"Come and read about the Corridor Man, it'll be finished today." The Corridor Man was the Officer waiting in vain at the theatre for Victoria, his fiancée who never comes. Originally conceived as the main theme, the Corridor drama was reduced to a subplot in the final version of what was eventually to be named *A Dream Play*.

Inspired by his wife's oriental looks and the teachings of Indian religions, Strindberg provides the God Indra with a daughter, Agnes, unknown to Indian mythology. She descends to earth, sent by her father, in order to experience the sufferings of ordinary mortals. The world, according to Buddhist doctrines is but an illusion, the result of Brahma, the divine Primary Force being seduced by Maya or the impulse of Procreation. Thus, the world is a dream, existing only through sin. *A Dream Play*, in other words, is a picture of life and its ordeals.

Throughout, Indra's daughter comments on the human condition—"Poor humans". Everyone she encounters bears witness to the truth of this observation. The Officer who waits in vain at the theatre is also forced to return to his school days and is humiliated by the stern teacher when he fails to remember his tables. The Lawyer who becomes Agnes's husband has the laurel wreath snatched from his brow as high academic honour is about to be bestowed on him, in spite of his life-long dedication to the cause of the poor. "The judiciary", he is told, "is everyone's servant, except the servant's". The Bill-sticker who spends his life dreaming about a green fishing net discovers, when he finally gets one, that he does not like it as much as he thought he would. And the futility of it all is graphically illustrated when the mysterious door with the four-leafed clover is finally, in the presence of the four university faculties, shown to lead to nowhere. "Nothing there! The mystery of life, it's all about nothing", concludes, significantly, the representative of the theological faculty. Finally, before Agnes returns to her father, she also meets the Poet and in Fingal's cave she interprets for him what he, as a mortal, is unable to hear or to understand.

A Dream Play "is about you, of course—Agnes, who is going to free the prisoner in the castle", wrote the 52-year-old Strindberg to his young wife. The Rising Castle, functioning as a frame for the whole play, clearly symbolizes life on this earth—beautiful from the outside but full of naked rooms where everyone inside feels imprisoned. It is not difficult to see that the author must have seen his young wife as a life-line, a liberating force. Indeed, with the men she encounters—the Officer, the Lawyer, and the Poet—Agnes evokes different women—mother, sexual partner, and intellectual companion.

Not only was Strindberg interested in dreams and their interpretations; he was also a day-dreamer and indeed most frequently viewed life as a somewhat confused dream. As in *To Damascus* and *The Ghost Sonata* he tried, in his own words, "to capture the inconsistent yet ostensibly logical structure of a dream. Everything can happen.. . . . Time and Place do not exist". In order to achieve this he retains an underlying structure while at the same time allowing individual parts of the set to undergo functional transformations with the shifting of the scenes. The gate leading to the theatre changes to become the entrance to the Lawyer's office, the tree bereft of its leaves turns into a coat hanger and the locked door with the four-leafed clover becomes the front of a filing cabinet.

Equally dream-like is the unpredictability of the sequence of events. Indra's daughter frees the Officer from his imprisonment in the Rising Castle. In the following scene we find him waiting for Victoria, carrying a bunch of roses. He wants to know what is concealed behind the mysterious door and sends for a blacksmith. Instead the glazier arrives but before he has had a chance to get on with the job the police burst on to the stage and prevent the door from being opened. The Officer, now furious, goes to see the Lawyer to take legal action in order to get the door open. But when he is finally granted an audience he does not remember what brought him there in the First Place. "I just wondered. Has Miss Victoria left?". The Lawyer calms him down and having tried the door again, now part of the filing cabinet, he leaves to prepare for his graduation ceremony. In the scenes that now follow, the Lawyer takes over as lead player, a role which he in turn later passes on to the Poet.

In those symbolic or expressionistic plays written after his so-called Inferno crisis, Strindberg pioneered the exploration of the border-line between reality and fantasy. Giving dramatic form to our innermost dreams and fears he does not make it easy for us: often we can't tell if what is taking place on stage is real or imagined. In this respect, as in many others, he was a true innovator in the theatre.

—Gunilla Anderman

DIE DREIGROSCHENOPER. See **THE THREEPENNY OPERA.**

ETT DRÖMSPEL. See **A DREAM PLAY.**

THE DUCHESS OF MALFI
by John Webster

First Publication: London, 1623.
First Production: Blackfriars Theatre, London, c.1613.

Editions
The Duchess of Malfi, edited by Elizabeth M. Brennan, London, 1964 (New Mermaid Series); second edition, 1983.
The Duchess of Malfi, in *John Webster: Three Plays*, edited by D.C. Gunby, Harmondsworth, 1972.
The Duchess of Malfi, edited by Clive Hart, Edinburgh, 1972.
The Duchess of Malfi, edited by John Russell Brown, London, 1974 (Revels Plays).
The Duchess of Malfi, in *The Selected Plays of John Webster*, edited by Jonathon Dollimore and Alan Sinfield, Cambridge, 1983.

Criticism
(For general works on the author, see *Playwrights* volume)

Books:
Gunnar Boklund, *"The Duchess of Malfi": Sources, Themes, Characters*, Cambridge, Massachusetts, 1962.
Clifford Leech, *John Webster—"The Duchess of Malfi"*, London, 1963.
Norman Rabkin (ed.), *Twentieth Century Interpretations of "The Duchess of Malfi"*, Englewood Cliffs, New Jersey, 1968.
R. V. Holdsworth (ed.), *"The White Devil" and "The Duchess of Malfi": A Casebook*, London, 1975.
Joyce E. Peterson, *Curs'd Example: "The Duchess of Malfi" and Commonweal Tragedy*, Columbia, Missouri, 1978.
Valerie A. Moffett (ed.), *Notes on Webster's "The White Devil" and "The Duchess of Malfi"*, London, 1979.
Richard Allen Cave, *"The White Devil" and "The Duchess of Malfi"*, London, 1988 (Text and Performance Series).
Dympna Callaghan, *Woman and Gender in Renaissance Tragedy: Study of "King Lear," "Othello," "The Duchess of Malfi", and "The White Devil"*, New York, 1989.
Kathleen McLuskie and Jennifer Uglow, *The Duchess of Malfi*, Bristol, 1989 (Plays in Performance Series).

Articles:
C.W. Davies, "The Structure of *The Duchess of Malfi*: An Approach", in *English*, 12, 1958.
J.L. Calderwood, "*The Duchess of Malfi*: Styles of Ceremony", in *Essays in Criticism*, 12, 1962.
Alexander W. Allison, "Ethical Themes in *Duchess of Malfi*", in *Studies in English Literature 1500–1900* 4, 1964.
Jane Marie Luecke, "*The Duchess of Malfi*: Comic and Satiric Confusion in a Tragedy", in *Studies in English Literature, 1500–1900* 4, 1964.
J.G. Riewald, "Shakespeare Burlesque in John Webster's *The Duchess of Malfi*", in *English Studies* (supplement), 45, 1964.

The Duchess of Malfi: National Theatre, London, 1985

Frank B. Fieler, "The Eight Madmen in *The Duchess of Malfi*", in *Studies in English Literature 1500–1900*, 7, 1967.

R.R. Waddington and James P. Driscoll, "Integrity of Life in *The Duchess of Malfi*", in *Drama Survey*, 6, 1967.

Frank W. Wadsworth, "Some Nineteenth Century Revivals of *The Duchess of Malfi*", in *Theatre Survey*, 8, 1967.

G. Wilson Knight, "*The Duchess of Malfi*", in *Malahat Review*, 4, 1967.

Louis G. Giannetti, "A Contemporary View of *The Duchess of Malfi*", in *Comparative Drama*, 3, Winter 1969–70.

David Luisi, "The Function of Bosola in *The Duchess of Malfi*", in *English Studies*, 53, 1972.

S.W. Sullivan, "The Tendency to Rationalize in *The White Devil* and *The Duchess of Malfi*", in *Yearbook of English Studies*, 4, 1974.

Ellen R. Belton, "The Function of Antonio in *The Duchess of Malfi*", in *Texas Studies in Literature and Language*, 18, 1976.

Joan M. Lord, "*The Duchess of Malfi*: 'The Spirit of Greatness' and 'of Wisdom' ", in *Studies in English Literature*, 16, 1976.

Marianne Nordfors, "Science and Realism in John Webster's *The Duchess of Malfi*", in *Studia Neophilologica*, 49, 1977.

David M. Bergeron, "The Wax Figures in *The Duchess of Malfi*", in *Studies in English Literature*, 18, 1978.

R.B. Graves, "*The Duchess of Malfi* at the Globe and Blackfriars", in *Renaissance Drama*, 9, 1979.

Charlotte Spivack, "*The Duchess of Malfi*: A Fearful Madness", in *Journal of Women's Studies in Literature*, 1, 1979.

Susan C. Baker, "The Static Protagonist in *The Duchess of Malfi*", in *Texas Studies in Literature and Language*, 22, 1980.

Catherine Belsey, "Emblem and Antithesis in *The Duchess of Malfi*", in *Renaissance Drama*, 11, 1980.

Bettie Anne Doebler, "Continuity in The Art of Dying: *The Duchess of Malfi*", in *Comparative Drama*, 14, 1980.

F.H. Langham, "Truth and Effect in *The Duchess of Malfi*", in *Sydney Studies in English*, 6, 1980.

Phoebe S. Spinrad, "Coping with Uncertainty in *The Duchess of Malfi*", in *Explorations in Renaissance Culture*, 6, 1980.

Anat Feinberg, "Observation and Theatricality in Webster's *The Duchess of Malfi*", in *Theatre Research International*, 6, 1980–81.

John L. Selzer, "Merit and Degree in Webster's *The Duchess of Malfi*", in *English Language Review*, 2, 1981.

Charles Wilkinson, "Twin Structures in John Webster's *The Duchess of Malfi*", in *Literature and Psychology*, vol.31 no.2, 1981.

John Loftis, "Lope de Vega's and Webster's Amalfi Plays", in *Comparative Drama*, 16, 1982.

Margaret Mikesell, "Catholic and Protestant Widows in *The Duchess of Malfi*", in *Renaissance and Reformation*, 7, 1983.

Kathleen McLuskie, "Drama and Sexual Politics: The Case of Webster's Duchess", in *Drama, Sex and Politics*, edited by James Redmond, Cambridge, 1984 (*Themes in Drama 7*).

Frank Whigham, "Sexual and Social Mobility in *The Duchess of Malfi*", in *Publications of the Modern Language Association* [*PMLA*], 100, 1985.

*   *   *

The central action of *The Duchess of Malfi* is strange but comparatively simple: a noble young widow proposes to Antonio, the Steward of her household, and keeps the subsequent marriage secret; when children are born this becomes increasingly difficult. The Duchess's brothers, one a Cardinal and the other, Ferdinand, Duke of Calabria and the Duchess's twin, have paid Bosola, the Provisor of Horse, to spy on his mistress, and so news from the court soon reaches them in Rome. The brothers vow revenge for the marriage. The Duchess flees but, when overtaken by a troop of armed men, Antonio escapes with the children and she is captured and imprisoned. Ferdinand visits his sister and torments her by coming in the dark and leaving a dead man's hand in hers, so that she believes it to be Antonio restored to her; then he has wax effigies of Antonio and the children presented, so that she belives them to be dead; then he looses madmen into her cell to babble about lechery and ambition; then he sends Bosola to her disguised as an Old Man; then a coffin, cords, and a bell; and finally, on his orders, the Duchess is strangled.

This story is only the core of the play, and it is complete before the end of Act IV. After she has fallen dead, the Duchess comes alive again (Shakespeare had worked such a trick in *Othello*) and, on being told that Antonio is alive, calls out "Mercy!" and dies. This has such an effect on Bosola that he calls out on "sacred innocence", weeps, and vows to "do good" before it is too late. The consequences are shown in Act V, when Bosola's efforts go so wrong that his confrontation with the Cardinal results only in the death of Julia, the Cardinal's mistress; later he kills Antonio by mistake in the dark. Bosola does manage to kill Ferdinand, but only after the prince has given him his death-wound and—"in the scuffle"—has killed his own brother. Before they die, both brothers go mad, Ferdinand thinking he is a wolf and the Cardinal haunted by "a thing armed with a rake" that seems to strike at him from the depths of his fishpond. When all the principals lie dead or dying, Delio (Antonio's friend and confidant) arrives with the Duchess's son; the boy does not say a word, but the survivors are asked to acknowledge him as the new Duke.

The complications of the fourth and fifth acts are matched by strands woven into the early narrative. Various incidents show the Duchess's court to be a place of intrigue, ambition, and superstition. At Rome the Cardinal welcomes his mistress, whom Delio has followed to woo with money. Ferdinand shows his sister their father's dagger, to threaten the absent husband, and tells a story about Reputation, Love, and Death. On one occasion the Cardinal is seen divesting himself of ecclesiastical robes to fight as a soldier in the field of battle.

Webster's portrait of the young and beautiful Duchess is at the centre of this complicated "tragedy of blood" and she holds the closest attention as she tries to follow her own instincts and learns to face madness and death with courage—"I am Duchess of Malfi still"—and also with humility: ". . .Heaven-gates are not so highly arch'd / As princes' palaces, they that enter there / Must go upon their knees". After her death she not only inspires Bosola's attempted reparation, but appears to Antonio as a vision from her tomb as an echo urges him to fly his fate.

But Bosola's part is the longest and in the first edition his name was placed at the head of the list of characters where the names of princes are normally placed. His story is told fully, so that the audience hears of his service for 11 years in the galleys as a criminal. He first appears as "the only court gall", dissatisfied with his fortune and castigating corruption and injustice. While he serves his secret pay-masters, his sympathies are drawn towards the Duchess and, when she begins to confide in him, the deep concern apparent in his replies leads her to tell him everything and take his advice about how to escape Ferdinand's anger. In Act V Bosola strives to be a witness for other values than those by which he has lived: "Let worthy minds ne'er stagger in distrust / To suffer death, or shame for what is just—/ Mine is another voyage".

Webster organized the complicated action of *The Duchess of Malfi* in five distinct acts, and between each an interval of time elapses and the action moves ahead, altering appearances each time. These acts have carefully judged climaxes, so that step by step the net of consequences widens to include new representations of an ambitious, egotistical, and insecure world. Yet this structure is almost hidden by the subtlety of Webster's detail which gives a remarkable impression of teeming imagination and flickering clarity. As if to hold the shifting images still for the audience's attention, a string of rhymed couplets and self-conscious aphorisms are introduced to the dialogue. Some feelings are never wholly articulate—notably Ferdinand's incestuous lust for his sister and Antonio's callow egotism—but the audience is alerted to fleeting impressions as the action drives forward through all its subterfuges and complications. Ferdinand himself warns Bosola in Act I: "Your darkest actions—nay, your privat'st thoughts—/ Will come to light". Through formal splendours, elaborate digressions, night alarms, domestic incidents, delicate fantasies, cynical hypo-crisies, and horrendous tortures, Webster seems intent on illuminating the most secret sources of human action and on provoking moral judgements.

—John Russell Brown

DUCK HUNTING (Utinoi Okhoty)
by Alexander Vampilov

First Publication: In *Angara*, 6, 1970.
First Production: A. Upit State Academy Theatre of Latvia, Riga, 25 April 1976.

Translations
Duck Hunting, translated by Alma H. Law, New York, 1980.

Criticism
(For general works on the author, see *Playwrights* volume)

Books:
Elena Streletsova, *Plen "Utinoi Okhoty"*, Moscow, 1991.

Articles:
Rudolf Neuhäuser, "Wampilow: *Die Entenjagd*", in *Das russische Drama*, Düsseldorf, 1986.

*   *   *

The play opens with Zilov, the main character, alone in his flat waiting for the weather to clear so that he can leave with his friend Dima on his long-awaited, annual duck-shooting holiday. A funeral wreath is delivered inscribed to Zilov by his friends; this triggers a dream sequence of them discussing him dead, and a flash-back to when he and his wife moved into their first flat. We see Zilov's dying relationship with his wife, his alcoholism, his obsession with the annual duck-shoot, an attempt to fob off his mistress onto his boss, the beginnings of an affair with a pretty 18 year old (Irina), and a criminal falsification of facts by him in the course of his job. In Act II, his wife reveals that she has had a lunchtime abortion of their child, and a row develops nearly ending in her rape. The falsification at work is uncovered and Zilov narrowly escapes sacking. His father dies. Instead of leaving on the long journey to the funeral, Zilov is observed by his wife dallying with Irina. Subsequently his wife leaves him and a flash to the present

reveals Irina has too. In Act III he insults all his friends at a drunken celebration of the start of his shooting holiday and they plan the wreath. Now in the present, he calls off the duck-shoot and prepares to commit suicide, but is prevented. Left alone, he becomes "completely calm" and rings Dima to say he is ready to leave for the shoot after all.

This play is generally considered Vampilov's masterpiece and can claim to be the most complex piece of Russian theatre since Chekhov. An outline of the plot may, to the western reader, suggest melodrama. It is a very painful play, but the intensity of the action is thoroughly true to Soviet life and each event is presented with such a subtle range of mood and perspective as to be deeply engaging and convincing. It is, in fact, not Vampilov's handling of time and events that is problematical, but the moral interpretation of the hero and the whole concept of "duck hunting".

Zilov is a very familiar type of Soviet male—so much so that some critics see the play as a Soviet update of *Ivanov* (the young Vampilov was steeped in Chekhov) and others have called the disintegration of Zilov's personality socially "prophetic". All the vices are present and clearly there is poetic justice in Zilov's friends calling him a corpse. However, an element of chance constantly creeps into Zilov's decline, which makes his moral responsibility tantalisingly ambiguous. If, for instance, his wife had not sprung the question of a child on him at the end of the housewarming party he might have been more capable of showing his (apparently genuine) enthusiasm. When she rings him at work to confirm that she is pregnant, she catches him just after he has met Irina for the first time, and again misconstrues his tone: she instantly decides on the abortion, which deeply outrages Zilov. Most poignant of all, in Act II, Zilov addresses a passionately sincere confession of his own guilt, and call to start life afresh, to his wife through the door that she has just succeeded in locking to prevent him beating her; but unbeknownst to him his wife has already slipped quietly out of the flat and out of his life.

The ending is particularly ambiguous. After deciding not to kill himself, Zilov throws himself face down on the bed, his body heaves for some time, but "*whether he has been crying or laughing it is impossible to tell*". The phrase is repeated when, after lying motionless for an even longer time, he "*gets up and we see his calm face*". He has undergone a catharsis, but it is desperately difficult to tell whether the calm he has achieved is one of new resolution or utter resignation. Has he, in fact, finally succumbed to the spiritual emptiness of the man he is now going duck-shooting with?

The character Dima is an equally recognisable type of Soviet Russian. He is honest, hard-working, but has the brutal efficiency of a KGB man. Other characters are vaguely afraid of him and he is the only one consistently referred to not by surname but function: "The Waiter". He is, in Zilov's words, a "giant" of duck-hunting; but he is interested only in the killing. Zilov, however, is a hopeless shot (it is implied that he has not yet killed a bird) and is evidently obsessed with the shooting but by the beauty and tranquillity of the Siberian lakes and forest. "Only there", he says through the door to his absent wife, "do you feel yourself to be a person". Through his exploration of the symbol of "duck-hunting" itself, Vampilov favourably compares Zilov with this *alter ego*, just as he portrays Zilov's affair with Irina as springing not from philandering but from a deep desire to "return" to purity and innocence. A case can be made, then, for Zilov being a man still possessing positive values, and the play being "dedicated to the transformation, and in the final analysis rebirth . . . of a person" (Streletsova).

The range of character, emotion, pace, style and theatrical focus make *Duck Hunting* an immensely difficult but rewarding play for actors and directors. For many years it suffered from the Soviet censorship. In 1986, however, a fine television version created a sensation in post-Brezhnev Russia. This production suggested that the sheer length of the play, and its experimental merging of realism with poetic and dream drama, are perhaps, more amenable to the camera than the theatre; there appear to have been no really successful Russian or western stage performances to date.

—Patrick Miles

ET DUKKEHJEM.   See A DOLL'S HOUSE.

DUTCHMAN
by Imamu Amiri Baraka [LeRoi Jones]

First Publication: In *Dutchman and The Slave*, New York, 1964.
First Production: Cherry Lane Theatre, New York, 24 March 1964.

Criticism
(For general works on the author, see *Playwrights* volume)

Articles:
Hugh Nelson, "LeRoi Jones' *Dutchman*: A Brief Ride on a Doomed Ship", in *Educational Theatre Journal*, 20, 1968.
Tom S. Reck, "Archetypes in LeRoi Jones' *Dutchman*", in *Studies in Black Literature*, 1, 1970.
George R. Adams, "'My Christ' in *Dutchman*", in *CLA Journal*, 15, 1971.
John Ferguson, "*Dutchman* and *The Slave*", in *Modern Drama*, 13, 1971.
Julian C. Rice, "LeRoi Jones' *Dutchman*: A Reading", in *Contemporary Literature*, 12, 1971.
Albert Bermel, "The Poet as Solipsist: *Dutchman*", in *Arts in Society*, 9, 1972.
Albert Bermel, "*Dutchman*, or The Black Stranger in America", in *Arts in Society*, 9, 1972.
Diane H. Weisgram, "LeRoi Jones' *Dutchman*: Inter-racial Ritual of Sexual Violence", in *American Imago*, 29, 1972.
Jerome Klinkowitz, "Leroi Jones: *Dutchman* as Drama", in *Negro American Literature Forum*, 7, 1974.
Willene P. Taylor, "The Fall of Man in Imamu Amiri Baraka's *Dutchman*", in *Negro American Literature Forum*, 7, 1974.
George A. Levesque, "LeRoi Jones' *Dutchman*: Myth and Allegory", in *Obsidian*, vol.5 no.3, 1979.
Louis J. Casimir, "*Dutchman*: The Price of Culture Is a Lie", in *The Binding of Proteus: Perspectives on Myth and the Literary Process*, edited by Marjorie W. McCune and others, Lewisburg, Pennsylvania, 1980.
Helene Keyssar, "Lost Illusions, New Visions: Imamu Amiri Baraka's *Dutchman*", in *The Curtain and the Veil: Strategies in Black Drama*, New York, 1981.
B.T. Seetha, "Tension between Art and Ideology: *Dutchman* and *The Slave*", in *Osmania Journal of English Studies*, 22, 1986.

*   *   *

On a hot summer's day in New York City, Clay, a young Negro, rides the subway to a friend's party. A white woman, Lula, boards the train, having previously observed Clay; she engages him in conversation, at first desultory and flirtatious, then increasingly abusive and threatening. Provoked, Clay finally explodes in anger, assaulting both Lula and a drunk watched silently throughout by other white travellers. In an abrupt reversal, Lula stabs Clay, killing him; then she orders the other passengers to throw his body from the car, covering up the murder. As the play ends, another young black man boards the train, attracting Lula's attention; her approach is delayed by the arrival of an old black conductor, but as he leaves the now almost empty car, Lula turns her gaze back to her likely next victim.

Dutchman played first at the Cherry Lane Theatre in Greenwich Village, New York, in 1964, winning an Obie award; it later transfered to the Black Arts Repertory Theatre in Harlem, a theatre founded by Jones himself, with an exclusively black audience. Essentially a two-hander, this one-act piece is extraordinarily compressed and controlled: full of powerful anger, resonant far beyond the confines of its apparently simple situation. It should properly be viewed in the context of 1960's America, for it was First Produced in the year following the assassination of John F. Kennedy, and the first American troop involvement in Vietnam; and against the backdrop of the rise of the Civil Rights movement and the Black Power initiative, following in the wake of the school bombing in Birmingham, Alabama, and the burning of Watts, a black section of Los Angeles. Jones, later to change his name to Amiri Baraka—a more overtly African name—saw his plays as interventions in the political struggle, addressing a particular issue: black pride and self-image.

The play is therefore primarily addressed to a black audience, though it did not truly find its audience until Jones moved it to the Harlem theatre. Its success off-Broadway—during the explosion of fringe theatre in New York in the 1960's—derives not only from its vibrant language and tight structure but also from its central issue, which offered some resonances also to white audiences. American writing at this time was preoccupied with questions of personal identity and the problematic relationship between the individual and society, in particular, with the compromises and questionable choices with which the individual is confronted. For the American black population at this time, such questions were formulated in terms of assimilation and colonisation, and were of immediate political and social import, but for many in the white audiences, the questions were also urgent and immediate.

Dutchman's ability to address both constituencies resides in Jones' use of a mythic structure, both ancient and modern. The title recalls the myth of the Flying Dutchman, condemned forever to sail with his undead crew as punishment for an offence against the natural order. The "loop" structure of the play, which suggests an ongoing cycle of black/white, male/female, violent aggression echoes the Dutchman's eternal voyage. But more contemporary myths are also addressed, the myths of black existence in late 20th-century America: myths which underpin and propel the black struggle. Jones offers an uncompromising confrontation with these and with black history.

Clay, his 20-year-old male protagonist, is offered as an articulate and pleasant character at the outset. Provoked by the louche and sexually predatory Lula, he is, by turns, amused and exasperated by her insistence; he tries to placate her with civility, imitating her tone and manner, seemingly both attracted and also unnerved by her. But the more he maintains this approach, refusing to be baited by her racial gibes and slurs, the more aggressive Lula becomes, dominating him in an inexorable fashion. Clay prides himself upon his articulacy, using language to defend himself, to deflect the offensiveness of her underlying attitude. When he is ultimately pushed beyond the limits of tolerance—and of his linguistic evasions—Jones gives him both a physical action, the attack upon the drunk, and also a verbal assault upon all the white passengers including Lula. It is a stream of pungently expressed invective, chilling in its statement of the impossibility of reconciliation and cohabitation between black and white. It is a speech of great impact, stripping away the codes of black culture which Clay—and Jones—claims whites utterly misread, and attempt to appropriate.

Lula's identification of Clay's attempted assimilation into the dominant white culture—traceable in the very articulacy and civility upon which he prides himself—is the source of her contempt and ultimate violence. Lula offers an emblematic representation of the white position, from the black viewpoint and from a male viewpoint; the ritual action of *Dutchman*, as well as being viewed within the context of the Black movement, can also be read against another 1960's socio-political phenomenon the Women's Liberation initiative. As the repository of the negative aspects of the play, Lula is also very much a female stereotype; she is irrational, emotionally unstable, sexually confrontational, and homicidally violent. Her verbal attacks upon Clay can also be read as a form of castration, continually denigrating his masculinity. Yet there are possibilities of exploring the boundaries of the stereotype, too; for she is as trapped and oppressed by the ritual action as is Clay. Both are betrayed, and betraying. It is this openness of the text that renders it accessible to the white audience also; *Dutchman*, set in the subway *"heaped in modern myth"* as Jones' stage direction claims, is a human, rather than simply a black, play.

—Val Taylor

DYADYA VANYA.   See UNCLE VANYA.

THE DYBBUK; or, Between Two Worlds (Dybbuk) by An-sky [Solomon Rappaport]

First Production: Warsaw (Vilna Troupe), 1920.

Translations
Between Two Worlds—The Dybbuk, translated by Alice Lewisohn Crowley, 1925?
The Dybbuk, translated by Henry G. Alsberg and Winifred Katzin, New York, 1926.
The Dybbuk, translated by S. Morris von Engel, Winnipeg, Manitoba, 1953.

Criticism
(For general works on the author, see *Playwrights* volume)

Articles:
Robert Lima, "Rite of Passage: Metempsychosis, Possession, and Exorcism in S. An-Sky's *The Dybbuk*", in *Literature and the Occult*, edited by Luanne Frank, Arlington, Texas, 1977.

Bettina L. Knapp, "*The Dybbuk*: The Spagyric Marriage", in *Journal of Altered States of Consciousness*, 4, 1978–79.
Pearl Fishman, "Vakhtangov's *The Dybbuk*", in *Tulane Drama Review*, vol.24 no.3, 1980.

*   *   *

In a small Jewish village in Eastern Europe at the turn of the century, Channon, a brilliant Hassidic student is drawn to fellow students' talk of miracle-working Rabbis. He, himself, has been studying the forbidden Kabala. He admits his love for Leah, daughter of Sender, a wealthy merchant, vowing if he cannot obtain the necessary wealth we will use "unholy powers" to have her. When news comes that Sender has finally arranged a marriage, Channon dies. Leah dances at her wedding feast, but is troubled by what happens to souls which died before their time. When she goes with her grandmother to invite her dead mother to her wedding, she invites Channon. At the ceremony, Channon's spirit—the dybbuk—takes possession of Leah. Holy Reb Asrael invites the City Rabbi Shem to assist him in exorcising the dybbuk. Reb Shem summons the spirit of Nissin ben Rifke, Channon's father, who has entreated him in dreams. Ben Rifke tells how he and Sender as boyhood friends pledged their children in marriage before they were born. He claims Sender rejected Channon because of poverty. The court rules that Sender should give half his wealth to the poor and orders the dybbuk to leave Leah's body. But only under excommunication does the dybbuk agree to leave. When Leah is alone, Channon calls to her, "I have left your body—I will come to your soul". Leah leaves the magic circle and merges with her destined lover.

The great popularity of this apparently insular play arguably owes much to the context in which that story takes place. *The Dybbuk* is not a personalized love story, but one which calls into question theological and existential questions regarding man's place in the universe.

The Dybbuk, after all, is a Yiddish play, its source and life set in the sub-society of Eastern European Jewry. An-sky, himself a folklorist, uses Jewish folklore to establish for a "foreign" audience the fundamental elements of Jewish consciousness which both inform and necessitate the drama. This fabric of intellectual debate and emotional response creates, through the love story, an experience of spirit which is, arguably, the purpose and power of the play.

The play opens in a synagogue, implying the presence of God in the lives of man. The conversations between the students center on Biblical and Talmudic references, traditional tales which consider man's relationship to the Creator, the boundaries of life and death, the power of the soul. The language uses images of light and flame to reflect both the Creator and the life of man. Thus a moral and metaphysical context is established within which the action and central issues are fundamentally bonded. The love story is the crisis through which the interpretation of the relationships between Man, God, and other Man in a tightly bonded universe is debated.

Through these discussions, too, the fundamental assumptions that inform the moral context are established. Man here, in contrast to the Christian concept of Original Sin, is assumed to be essentially good. As the possessor of free choice, he has total responsibility for his actions. Though he may sin, he is always redeemable through further action. Thus, the activity of man is a dialogue with God; his actions effect God's universe as God's will affect him.

Reb Shem: Every sin and every wrong that a man commits brings the destruction of the world

The Dybbuk: Almeida Theatre, London, 1986

Both this active relationship with God and the gift of free choice inevitably place obligations on the individual. The love story functions as a catalyst and focuses on the tension between two basic, but immutable obligations: the obligation to revere, protect and continue God's gift of Life:

> *Reb Asrael:* Leave the body of this girl in that a living branch of the eternal tree of Israel may not wither and die

And the obligation to God to fulfill one's destiny

> *Channon:* I am her destined bridegroom

The students' talk in the synagogue considers the problems of man's existence through references ranging from the Torah to superstition. In this tightly integrated world, magic and practicality, superstition and faith, folk tales and doctrine, ghosts and the living, spirit and flesh—all cohabit and co-mingle. All discussion, all actions refer back to the opening chant:

> Wherefore, wherefore
> Did the soul
> From its exhalted heights
> Fall into abysmal depths?
> Within the fall the power lies
> To rise again

Only in such a context, where the power of the invisible is raised to an active, motivating force, could one accept Channon's death, the self-willed overcoming of body by spirit. This proof of the strength of his spirit allows him to become a dybbuk and inhabit Leah's body.

An-sky carefully refrains from developing detailed personalities for his characters. Leah and Channon, though fatally bound, seem barely to know each other; this gives more power to their "destined" roles. There are neither heroes nor villains here; all are treated with usual fairness. Sender, for example, though he has put earthly wealth before spiritual value, is presented as one who has lost his way.

The setting of Act II presents a perfect visual image of the play's action: on one side, the synagogue; across, Sender's house, the wedding party and the feast for the poor representing not only the process of individual life but man's obligation to the community; between them, the grave of the martyred bride and bridegroom.

Act III is the mundane counterpart to Act I: not God's house, but the house of the holy man Reb Asrael. He doubts his reputation as "the Messenger of God"; it is not for man, as we know from the Book of Job, to second-guess the Almighty. Reb Shem begins a second round of telling tales. These, however, create a vision of a vast, cosmic interactive network, a series of heirarchies which simultaneously confirms man's rightful place in the universe and implies his obligations within it. The existence and power of the soul are presented as undeniable facts that give meaning to existence and provides a touchstone for mundane reality. Indeed, we have already *seen* proof in the death of Channon and Leah's possession by the dybbuk. As Reb Shem says: "If a man were to develop his soul as carefully as he develops his body, what deep abyss might his soul not cross on the slender cord of life," and the known limits to the physical world might be traversed. The physical occupation of Leah's body by the dybbuk (the most difficult production problem) confronts both the characters and the audience with an immediate experience of metaphysical forces in mundane existence. Only the dybbuk, tormented by the denial of Destiny, forced to cross the barriers of time, space, and moral law, takes physical form to embody the relationship between body and spirit, between choice and destiny, between man's obligations to man, and those to God.

In responding to this play, the passionate absoluteness of the lovers and the power of spirit that traversed all boundaries wrench the heart, but the horror of the control of the living by the spirit of the dead cannot be condoned. The conflict between the two, essential, moral obligations—to fulfill one's convenant with destiny and to preserve and perpetuate life—must somehow be resolved, and only man can resolve it. Although the court denies the obligation of the marriage pledge on grounds that it can not apply after death, Channon cannot be forced, even under excommunication, to leave Leah's body. Ultimately, he must choose to do so, and albeit under duress, he leaves of his own will. Thus, she is "herself" when he calls from beyond the grave, and joins him of her own free will, merging into his light.

The invisible, the power of destiny and the soul itself, are made visible on the stage, taking active and moral place in the physical world. Unexpectedly, the physical death of the lovers is overpowered by the surging life of the spirit and sense of completion. An audience, engaged in the process, may not only be party to a folk tale and a love story, but also a participant in a spiritual experience.

—Elaine Turner

DYSCOLOS. See **THE BAD-TEMPERED OLD MAN.**

DYSKOLOS. See **THE BAD-TEMPERED OLD MAN.**

DZIADY. See **FOREFATHERS' EVE.**

EARTH SPIRIT. See **THE LULU PLAYS.**

EAST
by Steven Berkoff

First Publication: In *East; Agamemnon; The Fall of the House of Usher*, London, 1977; revised edition, London, 1978.
First Production: Traverse Theatre, Edinburgh, 1975; revised version, Greenwich Theatre, London, 1976.

* * *

Berkoff has written of *East* that it "takes place within my personal memory and experience and is less a biographical text than an outburst of revolt against the sloth of my youth and a desire to turn a welter of undirected passion and frustration into a positive form".

The "positive form" Berkoff chose is that of a highly stylised theatre piece, more a series of vignettes and monologues than a play in the traditional sense. It combines several disparate elements, from music hall and mime to Shakespeare and Classical Greek drama. The acting, according to Berkoff, "has to be loose and smacking of danger", which is also a perfect description of the play itself.

East opens with the stage completely bare except for five empty chairs and a large screen across the back. (This bare stage is typical of Berkoff. He has written that by "eliminating the junk of sets" and "freeing the stage and giving it space", the spectator becomes more involved because his own imagination and interpretation become a necessary part of the production.) As images of the real East End are projected onto the screen the five characters, Mike, Les, Sylv, Mum, and Dad, enter and take their seats. Then, accompanied by an off-stage piano, they launch into a chaotic rendition of "My Old Man Says Follow the Van".

In the curious mix of Shakespearian allusion and Cockney argot that characterises much of the speech throughout the play, Mike and Les explain to the audience that though they are now the best of friends, the first time they met they nearly killed each other in a fight over Mike's girlfriend, Sylv. This is followed by a gruesome description of the actual fight: Mike tells about his "raziory which danced about his face like fireflies. . ." and rhapsodises about "that soft thud, thwat, as knife hits flesh. . .". The two men relate how they made their way together to hospital, finally "thick as tealeaves in a pot

that's stewed too long", and united in their mutual hatred of the girl they were just fighting over.

Time continually moves backwards and forwards in *East*; one moment we are in the present, the next we are reliving some moment from the past—many of these time-changes are brought about by one character telling a story directly to the audience, while the others act as chorus.

Following a flashback to her first sexual encounter with Mike, Sylv bemoans the fact that she wasn't born a man, able to enjoy sexual freedom without being referred to as "an old scrubber-slag-head". A similar sentiment is echoed by Mum during her recollection of an incident in a cinema where, in the darkness, she engaged in mutual masturbation with a stranger only to discover, when the lights went up, that he was her son.

Les speaks with great bitterness about the time he worked in a clothing store, "that charnel house of gabardine and worsted hell", and was arrested for rape. In another monologue he tells of a bus ride during which he ogled a beautiful woman and came to the realisation that he would never have the nerve to speak to her. He will spend his life with what he calls "dirty scrubbers", because of his own low self-image: ". . .it tumbled then—it dropped—the dirty penny—that we get what we ARE".

East concludes with two speeches of resolution; one spoken by Mike and Les in unison, the other a monologue by Sylv. The men speak of anger: "I'm sick of my house, I'm sick of my family, in fact they make me sick". They fantasise about a life of crime: "We'll threaten and murder, connive and rob, the law's on our side, we'll pay the slobs.. . .We'll get fat, we'll kill and we'll knife. I hate you pseudo bastards, I hate you with my life".

Sylv's speech concerns the indignity of poverty: ". . .fill in forms at dole queues and stand behind the sacks of skin that are called men and women, translated into numbers crushed in endless files. . .waiting, while ma and pa makes little noughts and crosses upon coupons called hope—or—death. . .". Sylv's final words are her resolution: "We will not end our days like this".

However, it doesn't seem likely that Sylv's resolution will be realized. *East* ends as it began, with Les and Mike repeating their first three lines, word for word. The implication is that no matter what they resolve and no matter what they try, for these characters, trapped by their poverty and lack of education, nothing will ever change. Like the Red Queen in *Through the Looking Glass*, they will continue to run and run as fast as they can just so they can stay in the same place.

—Molly Brown

Eastward Ho!: Mermaid Theatre, London, 1981

EASTWARD HO!
by George Chapman, Ben Jonson, and John Marston

First Publication: London, 1605.
First Production: Blackfriars Theatre, London, 1605.

Editions
Eastward Ho, in *The Plays and Poems of George Chapman: The Comedies*, edited by Thomas Marc Parrot, London and New York, 1914.
Eastward Ho, edited by Julia Hamlet Harris, New Haven, Connecticut, 1926.
Eastward Ho!, edited by C.F. Brooke and N. Paradise in *English Drama, 1580–1642*, Boston, 1933.
Eastward Ho!, edited by C.G. Petter, London, 1973 (New Mermaid Series).

Criticism
(For general works on the author, see *Playwrights* volume)

Articles:
R.E. Brettle, "*Eastward Ho*, 1605, by Chapman, Jonson and Marston: Bibliography and Circumstances of Production", in *Library* (fourth series), 9, 1929.
J.Q. Adams, "*Eastward Ho* and its Satire Against the Scots", in *Studies in Philology*, vol. 28, 1931.
Percy Simpson, "The Problem of Authorship of *Eastward Ho!*", in *Publications of the Modern Language Association* [*PMLA*], 59, 1944.

Richard Horwich, "*Hamlet* and *Eastward Ho*", in *Studies in English Literature 1500–1900*, 11, 1971.
Ralph A. Cohen, "The Function of Setting in *Eastward Ho*", in *Renaissance Papers*, 1973.
D.J. Lake, "*Eastward Ho!*: Linguistic Evidence for Authorship", in *Notes and Queries*, April 1981.

* * *

The two strands of the main plot, as in some Tudor morality plays, follow the rise and fall of contrasting good and bad characters, Touchstone's apprentices Golding and Quicksilver. The latter lives a prodigal life with dissolute gentry and abets Sir Petronel Flash in his marriage to Touchstone's affected daughter Gertrude, whose one ambition is to be a lady. He also helps Sir Petronel to cheat Gertrude of some land she inherited to finance his trip to an idyllic Virginia— Eastward ho down the Thames—while he sends her East too in a coach to his non-existent castle. Meanwhile, Touchstone marries his other daughter to Golding, who wishes that "the superfluity and cold meat left at their nuptials will, with bounty, furnish ours". In a farcical subplot Sir Petronel steals away the young wife of the old usurer who is his financier, with the usurer enthusiastically aiding in his own cuckoldry because he believes the woman in question is a colleague's wife.

A storm spills all the bad characters, including those from the subplot, into the Thames. Sir Petronel and Quicksilver are arrested at Touchstone's charge and brought before Golding, whose miraculous rise has, in a day, brought him the powers of a magistrate. Imprisoned, both are repentant (Quicksilver playing the penitent as assiduously as he played the spendthrift before), and Golding skilfully effects a general reconciliation.

Despite the fact that the authors of *Eastward Ho* were essentially cashing in on the popularity of what was in 1605 a new sub-genre, city comedy, they achieved a seamless collaboration, probably because they were parodying the dramatic conventions they employed. Touchstone spouts more wise saws and proverbs than any other character in British drama, which Quicksilver occasionally tosses back in his teeth; at the end Quicksilver sings a long ballad of repentance for the edification of his fellow-prisoners. The parody of dramatic and literary conventions leaves the authors' moral stance ambiguous: is the audience supposed to endorse Golding's thrifty plans for a wedding feast, as Touchstone does? How true a "touchstone" for us is that character? How genuine are the final repentances? Or consider Quicksilver's whore, whose name is Sindefy but whom everyone calls Sin, who speaks more down-to-earth sense than anyone else in the play, and to whom Quicksilver is married off at the end—is it the reward of mock-repentance to marry Sin or does true repentance lead him to "sin defy"? Yet if such ambiguities distinguish *Eastward Ho* from late morality plays, neither is it just a satire of city types, as its immediate predecessors *Westward Ho* and *Northward Ho* were; the characters do seem to learn and develop—and not only the foolish and bad ones, but the priggish Golding too. All, finally, is wrapped in a genial tolerance centered on Touchstone, who will indulge his wife's and daughter's disastrous marriage plans, and who, even while prosecuting Quicksilver for his large thefts from him with Sir Petronel as accesory, knows that his own good nature will lead him to forgive them.

One senses the authors' delight in the world as it is, and its potentialities, and this energizes and individualizes the characters—whether it be in giving a sea-captain a vision of a golden Virginia or in giving Quicksilver the argument that because he helps gentlemen to spend their money "I am a good member of the City, if I were well considered"; or in Touchstone's account of his rise: "I hired me a little shop, fought low, took small gain, kept no debt book, garnished my shop, for want of plate, with good wholesome sentences [proverbs]". Even the usurer is allowed to compare himself favorably with merchants who "expose other men's substances to the mercy of the winds,. . .all for greedy desire to enrich themselves with unconscionable gain. . .where I, and such other honest men as live by lending money, are content with moderate profit". As the various quotations suggest, the authors delight in ironic contrast: the characters' own claims reveal their limitations and liabilities. More generally, too, geniality is tinged with irony, sometimes with wryness. Touchstone comforts the usurer, "If you be a cuckold, it's an argument you have a beautiful woman to your wife", and forgives his own wife in a less than whole-hearted manner: "she has been my cross these thirty years, and now I'll keep her to fright away sprites, i' faith". *Eastward Ho* gives a sense that the vigour of the play derives directly from the thriving times it represents.

—Anthony Graham-White

L'ÉCOLE DES FEMMES. See **THE SCHOOL FOR WIVES.**

THE ECSTASY OF RITA JOE
by George Ryga

First Publication: Vancouver, 1970.
First Production: Playhouse Theatre, Vancouver, 23 November 1967.

Criticism
(For general works on the author, see *Playwrights* volume)

Articles:
Neil Carson, "George Ryga and The Lost Country", in *Canadian Literature*, 45, 1970.
David Watson, "Political Mythologies. An Interview with George Ryga", in *Canadian Drama*, 5, 1979.
Gary Boire, "The Train of Thought in George Ryga's *The Ecstasy of Rita Joe*", in *Canadian Literature*, 113–14, 1987.

*   *   *

George Ryga's *The Ecstasy of Rita Joe*, a landmark in Canadian theatre history, is one of the best known Canadian plays. At a time when there was very little in the way of original Canadian drama, Malcolm Black, then artistic director of the Vancouver Playhouse, commissioned Ryga to write a play based on a newspaper report of the murder of a Native girl on Vancouver's skid row. *The Ecstasy of Rita Joe* opened at the Playhouse in 1967 with Frances Hyland as Rita Joe. The play was re-mounted in 1969, with some changes, at Ottawa's National Arts Centre with the same actors in the lead roles, directed by David Gardner, and has since been produced in Britain and the USA, and has formed the basis for a ballet.

The Ecstasy of Rita Joe is the story of a young native girl who leaves her reserve and comes to the city but cannot survive the cultural changes that are forced upon her. The story ranges from her childhood on the reserve to her struggles to adapt to life in the city. Over the course of the play she is on trial for various crimes, including vagrancy, shoplifting, and prostitution, of which she may or may not be guilty. Finally, she is brutally raped and murdered. The play is also Jaimie Paul's story, embodying the frustrations and anger of the native youth who recognizes that the past way of life is gone, yet for whom there is no future with which to replace it. He too is killed at the play's ending. David Joe represents the older generation of native people and a way of life that is dying, as well as a desperate hope that the future will somehow heal itself. White society is dramatized through the figures of the magistrate (law and justice), the priest (church), the teacher (education), Mr. Homer (social service), and the folk singer (white, liberal culture). Each of these characters, and by implication the institutions they represent, fail to understand Rita Joe and thereby contribute to her inevitable demise.

While Ryga has been criticized for the stereotypical nature of his characters, this is both a deliberate and necessary strategy, for *Rita Joe* is more than the sum of individual and isolated experiences and events—it captures the common scenario in any society where the oppressor and oppressed live side by side.

The play probes the total lack of understanding between the dominant white culture in Canada and the oppressed peoples of the First Nations. Ryga exposes the blatant, racist attitudes of white society towards Native people. *The Ecstasy of Rita Joe* offers no easy solutions; Ryga presents the problems, the devastating realities of this cultural clash, but the play makes it abundantly clear that what is needed to fight against racism is understanding and respect for different cultures.

The Ecstasy of Rita Joe shocked its initial audiences partly because of the raw and brutal action of the play, but also because racism towards Canada's Native people was rarely acknowledged and certainly not challenged in white middle-class theatres such as the Vancouver Playhouse and the National Arts Centre. For centuries the dominant Euro-Canadian society, supported by government policy, had worked towards annexation and assimilation of Native culture. The deaths of Rita Joe and Jaimie Paul reflect the pessimism of this situation, though there are some grounds for believing that over the last twenty years there has been some progress towards acknowledging Native rights.

The structure of the play is episodic (Ryga called it a ballad play) consisting of a series of flashbacks to events in Rita Joe's memory. This structure—where past and present are interwoven—was emphasized by Charles Evans's set design for the original production, which consisted of a circular ramp ranging from two feet above the stage at its highest point to below stage level at the front.

—Jennifer Preston

———

EDWARD II; The Troublesome Reign and Lamentable Death of Edward II
by Christopher Marlowe

First Publication: London, 1594.
First Production: London, probably by Pembroke's Men, c. 1592.

Editions
Edward II, edited by Osborne William Tancock, Oxford, 1942.
Edward II, edited by J.E. Morpurgo, London, 1949.
Edward II, edited by W. Moelwyn Merchant, London, 1967 (New Mermaid Series).
Edward II, edited by Roma Gill, London, 1967.
Edward II, edited by J.B. Steane in *Christopher Marlowe. The Complete Plays*, edited by J.B. Steane, Harmondsworth, 1969.
Christopher Marlowe's "Edward II": Text and Major Criticism, edited by Irving Ribner, New York, 1970.
Edward II, in *The Plays of Christopher Marlowe*, edited by Roma Gill, London, 1971.

Criticism
(For general works on the author, see *Playwrights* volume)

Books:
Lawrence Michael Benaquist, *The Tripartite Structure of Christopher Marlowe's Tamburlaine Plays and "Edward II"*, Salzburg, 1975.

Articles:
L.J. Mills, "The Meaning of *Edward II*", in *Modern Philology*, 32, 1934.
Robert Fricker, "The Dramatic Structure of *Edward II*", in *English Studies*, 34, 1953.
Irving Ribner, "Marlowe's *Edward II* and the Tudor History Play", in *English Literary History*, 22, 1955.

Clifford Leech, "Marlowe's *Edward II*: Power and Suffering", in *Critical Quarterly*, 1, 1959.
Leonora Brodwin Leet, "*Edward II*: Marlowe's Culminating Treatment of Love", in *English Literary History*, 31, 1964.
Yuichi Wada, "Edward II as Tragic Hero", in *Studies in English Literature* (Tokyo), 41, 1964.
Eugene M. Waith, "*Edward II*: The Shadow of Action", in *Tulane Drama Review*, vol.8 no.4, 1964.
Takashi Kurokawa, "*De Casibus* Theme and Machiavellianism—In Connection with the Theme of *Edward II*", in *Shakespeare Studies* (Japan), 7, 1968–69.
R.A. Watson, "*Edward II*: A Study in Evil", in *Durham University Journal*, 68, 1976.
Shoji Sasaki, "'If Words Will Not Serve': Marlowe's Provocative History Play", in *Shakespeare Studies* (Tokyo), 19, 1980–81.
Sara Munson Deats, "*Edward II*: A Study in Androgyny", in *Ball State University Forum*, vol.22 no.1, 1981.
S. Viswanathan, "King Edward II's 'Two Bodies': A Perspective on Marlowe's Play", in *The Literary Criterion* (India), vol.16 no.4, 1981.
James Voss, "*Edward II*: Marlowe's Historical Tragedy", in *English Studies*, vol.63 no.6, 1982.
Mark J. Lidman, "Marlowe's *Edward II*: A Study in Kingship", in *Publications of the Mississippi Philological Association*, 1984.
John F. McElroy, "Repetition, Contrariety, and Individualization in *Edward II*", in *Studies in English Literature, 1500–1900*, vol.24 no.2, 1984.
Sharon Tyler, "Bedfellows Make Strange Politics: Christopher Marlowe's *Edward II*", in *Drama, Sex, and Politics*, edited by James Redmond, Cambridge, 1985 (*Themes in Drama*).
Mathew N. Proser, "Edward's Perils: Masochism and Marlowe's Suffering King", in *Literature and Psychology*, vol.34 no.1, 1988.

*   *   *

In *Edward II*, arguably his last play, Marlowe departs from the foreign and exotic landscapes of earlier drama and turns to English history to write a *de casibus* political tragedy. The King's infatuation with the young Piers de Gaveston leads to growing opposition from the barons, spearheaded by the Earls of Lancaster and Warwick, Mortimer, and his nephew, young Mortimer, who becomes the principal antagonist. Resentment of Edward's culpable neglect is fuelled by Gaveston's lowly origins; he is dismissed scornfully by Mortimer as "one so base and obscure". Edward greets such hostility with defiance but the barons are powerful enough to coerce the King into agreeing to Gaveston's banishment. However, they then work to have him recalled so that they can discredit Edward further in the eyes of the House of Commons. Gaveston returns and is treated contemptuously by the earls, who blame Edward's infatuation for the deterioration in national morale and in international status. This erosion of royal authority, coupled with the Mortimers' personal grievance at Edward's refusal to ransom their kinsman, leads to threats of rebellion and deposition. Gaveston tries to escape, but is captured and eventually executed. Edward's expression of grief—"O shall I speak or shall I sigh and die?"—is followed by avowals of revenge and the adoption of a new favourite, Young Spencer. The ambitious Mortimer is imprisoned in the Tower, but he escapes to France and creates a faction around the Queen and her son, the young Prince Edward.

As Mortimer gains ascendancy, Edward's fall appears imminent. The Queen and Mortimer, now lovers, land in

Edward II: Stratford-Upon-Avon, 1990 (Royal Shakespeare Company)

England and gather support. Edward is taken captive and, having relinquished his power and craving death, he is passed between jailers until he arrives at Kenilworth Castle. In a scene of hideous cruelty, he is pierced with a burning spit and murdered by Mortimer's agent, Lightborn. Mortimer's triumph is short-lived: the newly crowned Edward III accuses him of treason and orders his death. The final tableau reveals Mortimer's head proffered to Edward's hearse as the young King dons his mourning robes.

Edward II explores the tragic effects of infatuation; in this context Edward is typical of the intemperate Marlovian figure consumed by an overriding desire. But there is little evidence of nobility in the wilful king who squanders his Kingdom because Gaveston is more important to him: "Ere my sweet Gaveston shall part from me / This isle shall fleet upon the ocean / And wander to the unfrequented Inde". The barons, however, do not act from moral outrage, but because they see in Gaveston a threat to their privileges. They loathe Gaveston because of his lowly birth and because of his foreign and effeminate ways. Gaveston, for his part, despises their uncouthness and hereditary privileges: "Base leaden earls, that glory in your birth, / Go sit at home and eat your tenants' beef". Edward can only respond to this conflict by helplessly following his self-destructive passion, steadfastly believing that Gaveston loves him "more than all the world". Whether this trust is justly founded, or whether Gaveston is motivated by social ambition, remains uncertain.

The play is structured as a series of careers of individuals who scale the summit of their ambition and are destroyed by it. Baldock reminds his friend Spencer that "all rise to fall". Spencer's career as the King's favourite does, indeed, mirror (albeit less spectacularly) that of Gaveston. But it is Mortimer whose ambitions exemplify most fully the *de casibus* motif. He boasts of his authority which he believes to be unassailable, only to realize that it is unwise to presume upon Fortune's perpetual goodwill: "Base Fortune / now I see that in thy wheel / There is a point to which when men aspire / They tumble headlong down; that point I touched, / and seeing there was no place to mount up higher".

Marlowe's language in *Edward II* is uncharacteristically lean, pared of most of the evocative imagery and sensuousness of *Tamburlaine* and *Doctor Faustus*. This comparative austerity is relieved by Gaveston's expressions of sensual hedonism and by Edward's pitiful laments, which must have influenced Shakespeare in his portrayal of the deposition of Richard II. In the early scenes Isabella's language too is emotionally affecting, but as she aligns with Mortimer it acquires a plainness and loses the passion which underscored her earlier distress.

—Janet Clare

EDWARD THE SECOND. See EDWARD II.

ELCKERLIJK. See EVERYMAN.

ELECTRA (Elektra)
by Euripides

First Production: Athens, c. 422 B.C.–416 B.C.

Editions
The "Elektra" of Euripides, edited by C.H. Keene, London, 1893.
Electra, in *Euripides 2* [with translation], edited by Arthur S. Way, London, 1919.
Electra, edited by J.D. Denniston, Oxford, 1939.
Electra, edited and translated by M.J. Cropp, Warminster, Wiltshire, 1988 (with translation).

Translations
Electra, translated by Gilbert Murray, London, 1905.
Electra, translated by D.W. Lucas, London, 1951.
Electra, translated by Emily Townsend, in *Euripides, 5*, Chicago, 1959 (Complete Greek Tragedies Series).
Electra, in *"Medea" and Other Plays*, translated by Philip Vellacott, Harmondsworth, 1963.
Electra, translated by Moses Hadas, Indianapolis, Indiana, 1964.
Electra, translated by David Thompson, Old Woking, 1964.

Criticism
(For general works on the author, see *Playwrights* volume)

Articles:
T. England, "The *Electra* of Euripides", in *Classical Review*, 40, 1926.
H. Lloyd-Jones, "Some Alleged Interpolations in Aeschylus' *Choephori* and Euripides' *Electra*", in *Classical Quarterly*, 11, 1961.
M.J. O'Brien, "Orestes and the Gorgon: Euripides *Electra*", in *American Journal of Philology*, 85, 1964.
M. Kubo, "The Norm of Myth: Euripides' *Electra*", in *Harvard Studies in Classical Philology*, 71, 1966.
G.H. Gellie, "Tragedy and Euripides' *Electra*", in *Bulletin of the Institute of Classical Studies* (London), 28, 1970.
F. Zeitlin, "The Argive Festival of Hera and Euripides' *Electra*", in *Transactions and Proceedings of the American Philological Association* [*TAPA*], 101, 1970.
G.W. Bond, "Euripides' Parody of Aeschylus", in *Hermathena*, 118, 1974.
D. Bain, "*Electra* 518–44", in *Bulletin of the Institute of Classical Studies* (London), 24, 1977.
V. Rosivach, "'The 'Golden Lamb' Ode in Euripides' *Electra*", in *Classical Philology*, 73, 1979.
Giuseppina Basta Donzelli, "Euripide, *Elettra*", in *Bulletin of the Institute of Classical Studies* (London), 27, 1980.
K.C. King, "The Force of Tradition: The Achilles Ode in Euripides' *Electra*", in *Transactions and Proceedings of the American Philological Association* [*TAPA*], 110, 1980.
G. Arnott, "Double the Vision: A Reading of Euripides' *Electra*", in *Greece and Rome* (second series), 28, 1981.
J.H.W. Morwood, "The Pattern of the Euripides *Electra*", in *American Journal of Philology*, 102, 1981.
David Kovacs, "Castor in Euripides' *Electra*", in *Classical Philology* (new series), vol.35 no.1, 1985.
David Kovacs, "Euripides, *Electra* 518–44: Further Doubts About Genuineness", in *Bulletin of the Institute of Classical Studies* (London), 36, 1989.

*   *   *

Before the *Electra* opens, King Agamemnon has been murdered by his wife Clytemnestra and her lover Aegisthus; the son Orestes has been sent into exile and the daughter Electra married to a farmer in an attempt to prevent her having children likely to threaten the new rulers. But now Orestes returns home with a friend Pylades, brother and sister are reunited, and the murderers are, in their turn, ruthlessly cut down. The play ends with the appearance of the gods Castor and Polydeuces who proceed to marry the still virgin Electra to Pylades and to order Orestes to Athens, promising acquittal from the charge of matricide.

There has been endless debate as critics have attempted to establish the precise relationship between the two *Electra*s, that is, Sophocles' and Euripides' similar treatment of this revenge theme. Almost the only firm fact known is that the *Choephori (Libation-Bearers)*, Aeschylus's version of the same myth, is some 40 years earlier in date than either, and is quite clearly referred to by Euripides who has introduced into the basic myth one startling innovation: he has married Electra to a poor farmer, a marriage which violates the norm of 5th century Athenian society where an arranged marriage between those of equal wealth and status is the rule. Euripides makes his Electra marry someone well beneath her and it is not surprising perhaps that she assumes the role of "nagging wife"; the husband is simple but honest and has never touched the princess, a hardly convincing scenario; Orestes himself is far from being a heroic figure, proving tortured, indecisive, and always on the lookout for a means of retreat; there appears to be little affection between brother and sister. In brief, Euripides strikes a new note of "realism" but it is realism of a special kind of which, essentially, stresses the unheroic. Thus, as the play begins Electra appears making her way to fetch water; she looks like a slave with her shorn head and tattered dress and, most devastating of all, she carries poised on her head a jar: much play is made of this simple but effective prop. Her husband urges her to take things more easily but she refuses, revelling in her humiliation. This is characteristic of Euripides the realist, so often condemned by his contemporaries for departing from accepted standards.

Equally remarkable is the "recognition scene" when Electra and Orestes are reunited, and here we see a riposte to the corresponding episode in Aeschylus's *Libation-Bearers* and it is a criticism of Aeschylus's indifference to realism: an old man appears bringing a lamb and cheese so that Electra and her husband may entertain the newly arrived guests, who are actually Orestes and Pylades; the old man tells Electra that he has seen offerings at the grave of Agamemnon and wonders whether Orestes may have secretly crept back home. He asks Electra to compare a lock of hair dedicated at the tomb with her own hair. Such a comparison is ridiculed by the woman—many share similar hair although they are in no way related. Measure your foot-print with foot-prints at the grave, he next proposes, and Electra is quick to point out that rocky ground does not yield prints, and, furthermore, the female sex has smaller feet. The old man persists: if you should encounter Orestes, you will be able to recognise his clothes, a suggestion which Electra finds equally absurd. When Orestes does then appear, Electra, who has already met him and been told that he is still alive, fails to recognise him; the old man stares at Orestes and excitement mounts, but Electra is not convinced until she sees on her brother's brow a scar he once received "chasing a fawn" with her, a recognition token which also serves as a symbol for their subsequent pursuit of their father's murderers.

Recognition is delayed and the same technique—whereby expectations are deliberately disappointed—is followed when a messenger reports the death of Aegisthus at the hands of Orestes: Aegisthus meets the strangers and invites them to join a sacrifice, not being willing to brook any refusal; his bodyguards put down their arms; Aegisthus invites Orestes to cut up the sacrifice, handing over to him a knife; Orestes does this but, even when he exchanges one knife for another more suitable one, does not strike his enemy; and then, when it seems that nothing is going to happen, Orestes, quite abruptly, rises on his toes and shatters Aegisthus's spine.

But it is Electra who feels for her dead father and initiates action: she gloats over the body of Aegisthus; she shows herself to be unremittingly blood-thirsty in urging her mother's death; Clytemnestra visits Electra, ironically believing her daughter to have borne a son, and the two women engage in a bitter debate in which Electra denounces the sisters Helen and Clytemnestra and accuses her mother of preferring her lover to her children. Clytemnestra in reply makes the telling point that it has always been Electra's nature to love her father. The slight signs of remorse that Electra shows immediately after her mother's death seem simply conventional, and are not compelling enough to modify an appraisal of a woman driven by extreme grief and humiliation to extract a revenge whose emotional intensity sustains the drama, and which can only be resolved by the intervention of a divine authority. It was not by chance that Freud coined the term "Electra Complex".

—Peter Walcot

ELECTRA (Elektra)
by Sophocles

First Production: Unknown.

Editions
Electra, edited by F.A. Paley, Cambridge, 1887.
The "Elektra" of Sophocles, edited by M.A. Bayfield, London, 1901.
Electra, in *Sophoclis Fabulae*, edited by A.C. Pearson, Oxford, 1924; corrected edition, 1964.
"Electra" of Sophocles Together With the First Part of the "Peace" of Aristophanes, edited and translated by J.T. Sheppard, Cambridge, 1927 (with translation).
Electra, edited by J.H. Kells, Cambridge, 1973.

Translations
Electra, translated by Francis Fergusson, New York, 1938.
Electra, in *"Electra" and Other Plays*, translated by E.F. Watling, Harmondsworth, 1953.
Electra, in *Sophocles: Three Tragedies*, translated by H.D.F Kitto, London, 1962.
Electra, in *Four Plays by Sophocles*, translated by Theodore Howard Banks, New York, 1966.
Electra, translated by W. Sale, Englewood Cliffs, New Jersey, 1973.
Electra, in *Electra; Antigone; Philoctetes*, translated by Kenneth McLeish, Cambridge, 1979.

Criticism
(For general works on the author, see *Playwrights* volume)

Books:
I.M. Linforth, *Electra's Day in the Tragedy of Sophocles*, Berkeley, California, 1963.

Electra (Sophocles):   The Pit, Barbican Centre, 1988 (Royal Shakespeare Company)

Peter Klimpe, *Die "Elektra" des Sophokles und Euripides' "Iphigenie bei den Tuarern": Ein Beitrag zur Diskussion über das Aufführungsjahr von Sophokles' "Elektra"*, Göppingen, 1970.

J.C. Kamerbeek (ed.), *The Plays of Sophocles, Commentaries: Part 5, "Electra"*, Leiden, 1974.

Articles:

G.M. Kirkwood, "Two Structural Features of Sophocles' *Electra*", in *Transactions and Proceedings of the American Philological Association* [*TAPA*], 73, 1942.

V.E.G. Kenna, "The Return of Orestes", in *Journal of Hellenic Studies*, 81, 1961.

C.P. Segal, "The *Electra* of Sophocles", in *Transactions and Proceedings of the American Philological Association* [*TAPA*], 97, 1966.

P.T. Stevens, "Sophocles: Electra, Doom or Triumph?", in *Greece and Rome* (second series), 25, 1978.

J.F. Davidson, "Homer and Sophocles *Electra*", in *Bulletin of the Institute of Classical Studies* (London), 35, 1988.

*   *   *

Orestes, son of Agamemnon and Clytemnestra, arrives back in Argos from exile to avenge the murder of his father by his mother. A plot is hatched which leads to the death of Clytemnestra and her lover Aegisthus, but the play centres on the character of Electra, Orestes' sister, and her sufferings at the hands of Clytemnestra.

The Electra plays of Sophocles and Euripides share plot and main characters, if not title, with *Libation-Bearers*, the middle play of Aeschylus's *Oresteia*. The relationship between the two *Electra* plays is a subject of constant debate, as no firm date can be assigned to either. The approach is so different that a case can be made for either *Electra* having been written as a riposte to the other. What is not in doubt is that at the time of writing his *Electra* Sophocles and Euripides each knew Aeschylus's *Libation-Bearers* and could be confident that their audience did too.

Sophocles declares his independence from any previous version in the opening scene with the arrival back in Argos of Orestes and Pylades with Orestes' Servant or Tutor, a new character in the story, who is to play a major role in carrying out Orestes' revenge on Clytemnestra and Aegisthus. When Orestes has announced his intentions, the Tutor persuades him to leave before the entrance of Electra. The rest of the play is effectively Electra's; she remains on stage, a picture of mounting desperation, as she continues to mourn her father despite her mother's plans to have her put away. She loses her last hope with the news that Orestes has been killed in a chariot-race. She resolves to take action herself, with or without the help of her sister Chrysothemis. With no more than a quarter of the play to run, she finds herself confronting the urn containing her brother's ashes.

But his death is, in fact, only supposition. The audience know that her brother is alive and holding the urn himself. It was the Tutor who told the story of the fatal race. It is all part of the plot, and only Electra's passionate grief weakens Orestes' resolve to keep her in the dark until he has succeeded in his revenge. Electra's plight runs parallel to Orestes's return, but until late in the play has no effect upon it. Indeed, when brother and sister are reunited their extravagant behaviour almost sabotages the plot.

The recognition scene, which Aeschylus placed early in his *Libation-Bearers*, is delayed by Sophocles so as to provide an emotional climax that the violent end of Clytemnestra and Aegisthus barely matches. The use of a stage-property, in this case the urn, is a device used elsewhere by Sophocles to concentrate and externalise an issue; Ajax's sword in *Ajax*, and the bow of Heracles in *Philoctetes* offer similar examples of the stage power residing in an object. The urn has the extra dimension of being both a mechanism in the plot and a trigger to the release of Electra from her captivity.

The powerful emphasis on Electra's character is at the expense of the moral dilemma of Orestes. Aeschylus based the *Oresteia* on the paradox inherent in the demand of a God that a son avenge his father, when to do so involves the killing of his mother. Euripides in his *Electra* stresses the horror of the act of matricide with an Orestes driven reluctantly to commit an unnatural act. For both of these playwrights the climax was the murder of Clytemnestra—with Aegisthus killed first in order not to distract from the mother and son confrontation.

Sophocles reverses the order of the murders. Aegisthus is away from the palace when the Tutor tells of the chariot-race and when Orestes introduces the urn to confirm the story. Clytemnestra's death is simply an appropriate act accompanied by neither the threat of the Furies which hounded Aeschylus's Orestes, nor the conscience and revulsion which torment him in Euripides' version. For Sophocles, Apollo has authorised Clytemnestra's death and that is enough. When Aegisthus does appear, Clytemnestra is already dead, a sheeted figure he takes for the body of Orestes. The revelation that it is Clytemnestra offers as macabre a moment as any in Sophocles and leads rapidly to the conclusion of the play. Though Orestes and Electra are now united, her oppressors dead, her story continues to run parallel to that of her brother without the two truly overlapping.

By consciously bypassing the issue of matricide Sophocles returns to a Homeric notion of justice. In the *Odyssey* Orestes had been held up as a model of filial behaviour with no questions raised about the rightness of his actions. But in Homer Aegisthus was the principal villain and there was no Electra. Aeschylus had added the moral dimension with the clash between Apollo, demanding that Orestes avenge his father, and the Furies demanding their due for the murder of a mother. Sophocles does not dodge this issue. He deflects it, by introducing new characters and a novel dramatic structure, in order to point to Electra herself. Few Greek plays are as single-minded in their presentation of the individual.

—J. Michael Walton

———

ELEKTRA (Euripides). See **ELECTRA.**

———

ELEKTRA (Sophocles). See **ELECTRA.**

———

AZ EMBER TRAGÉDIÁJA. See **THE TRAGEDY OF MAN.**

———

EMILIA GALOTTI
by Gotthold Lessing

First Publication: Berlin, 1772.
First Production: Hoftheater, Brunswick, March 1772.

Editions
Emilia Galotti, edited by E.L. Stahl, Oxford, 1946.

Translations
Emilia Galotti, New York, 1959.
Emilia Galotti, in *Five German Tragedies*, translated by F.J. Lamport, London, 1969.
Emilia Galotti, translated by Edward Dvoretzky, New York, 1979.

Criticism
(For general works on the author, see *Playwrights* volume)

Books:
Reinhart Meyer, *Hamburgische Dramaturgie und Emilia Galotti*, Frankfurt, 1933.
Edward Dvoretzky, *The Reception of Lessing's "Emilia Galotti" (1772–1900)*, Cambridge, Massachusetts, 1959.
Edward Dvoretzky, *The Enigma of Emilia Galotti*, 1963.
Edward Dvoretzky, *The Eighteenth-Century Translations of "Emilia Galotti"*, Houston, Texas, 1966.
Joachim Schmitt-Sasse, *Das Opfer der Tugend: zu Lessings "Emilia Galotti" und einer Literaturgeschichte der 'Vorstellungskomplexe' im 18. Jahrhundert*, Bonn, 1983.

Articles:
Ernst Feisse, "Lessing's *Emilia Galotti* and Goethe's *Werther*", in *Modern Philology*, 15, 1917.
Robert T. Ittner, "*Werther* and *Emilia Galotti*", in *Journal of English and Germanic Philology*, 41, 1942.
Leonard Forster, "Werther's Reading of *Emilia Galotti*", in *Publications of the English Goethe Society* (new series), 27, 1958.
Ilse Appelbaum-Graham, "Minds Without Medium: Reflections on *Emilia Galotti* and *Werthers Leiden*", in *Euphorion*, vol.56 no.4, 1962.
Edward Dvoretzky, "Goethe's *Werther* and Lessing's *Emilia Galotti*", in *German Life and Letters* (new series), 16, 1962.
Roy C. Cowen, "On the Dictates of Logic in Lessing's *Emilia Galotti*", in *German Quarterly*, 42, 1969.
Manfred Durzak, "Das Gesellschaftsbild in Lessings *Emilia Galotti*", in *Lessing Yearbook*, 1, 1969.
Klaus-Detlef Müller, "Das Erbe der Komödie im bürgerlichen Trauerspiel: Lessings *Emilia Galotti* und die *Commedia dell'arte*", in *Deutsche Vierteljahrsschrift für Literatur und Geistesgeschichte*.
Frank G. Ryder, "Emilia Galotti", in *German Quarterly*, 45, 1972.
Leonard P. Wessell Jr., "The Function of Odoardo in Lessing's *Emilia Galotti*", in *Germanic Review*, 47, 1972.
Alois Wierlacher, "Das Haus der Freude oder warum stirbt Emilia Galotti?", in *Lessing Yearbook*, 5, 1973.
Michael M. Metzger, "Soziale und dramatische Struktur in Lessings *Emilia Galotti*", in *Jahrbuch für internationale Germanistik*, vol.2 no.3 (series A), 1976.
John D. Pointer, "The Pearls of *Emilia Galotti*", in *Lessing Yearbook*, 9, 1977.
Clark S. Muenzer, "Virginity and Tragic Structure: Patterns of Continuity and Change in *Emilia Galotti, Iphigenie auf Tauris* and *Die Jungrau von Orleans*", in *Monatshefte*, 71, 1979.

Peter Schäblin, "*Emilia Galotti*: Die Szenen V, 6 und 7 im Kontext", in *Sprachkunst*, vol.12 no.1, 1981.
Gloria Flaherty, "Emilia Galotti's Italian Heritage", in *Modern Language Notes*, vol.97 no.3, 1982.
Hans-Georg Werner and Gotthard Lerchner, "Lessings *Emilia Galotti*: Prolegomena zu einer Interpretation", in *Zeitschrift für Germanistik*, vol.3 no.1, 1982.
Gloria Flaherty, "*Emilia Galotti* in Fact and Fiction", in *Lessing Yearbook*, 15, 1983.
Gerhard Kaiser, "Krise der Familie: Eine Perspektive auf Lessings *Emilia Galotti* und Schillers *Kabale und Liebe*", in *Recherches Germaniques*, 14, 1984.
E.O. McInnes, "'Eine bürgerliche Virginia'? Lessing's *Emilia Galotti* and the Development of the Bürgerliches Trauerspiel", in *Orbis Litterarum*, vol.39 no.4, 1984.
Laurence A. Rickels, "Deception, Exchange, and Revenge: Metaphors of Language in *Emilia Galotti*", in Lessing Yearbook, 16, 1984.
G.A. Wells, "What is Wrong With *Emilia Galotti*?", in *German Language and Literature*, vol.37 no.3, 1984.
Christian Brown, "'Der widerwärtige Missbrauch der Macht' oder 'Die Verwandlung der Leidenschaften in tugendhafte Fertigkeiten', in Lessings *Emilia Galotti*", in *Lessing Yearbook*, 17, 1985.
Albert M. Reh, "*Emilia Galotti*: 'Grosses Exempel der dramatischen Algebra' oder 'Algebra der Ambivalenz'", in *Lessing Yearbook*, 17, 1985.
John Whiton, "Why Does Emilia Galotti Want to Die?", in *Seminar*, vol.21 no.4, 1985.
Wolfgang Wittkowski, "Bürgerfreiheit oder—feigheit? Die Metaphor des 'langen Weges' als Schlüssel zum Koordinatensystem in Lessings politischen Trauerspiel *Emilia Galotti*", in *Lessing Yearbook*, 17, 1985; translated as "Emancipation or Capitulation of the Middle Class? The Metaphor of the 'Long Path' as a Key to Lessing's Political Tragedy *Emilia Galotti*", in *Lessing and The Enlightenment*, edited by Alexej Ugrinsky, New York, 1986.
Ingrid Haag, "Les Silences d'Emilia: A propos d'*Emilia Galotti*, tragédie bourgeoise de G.E. Lessing", in *Cahiers d'Etudes Germaniques*, 10, 1986.
Martin Schenkel, "'Wer über gewisse Dinge den Verstand nicht verlieret, der hat keinen zu verlieren': Zur Dialektik der bürgerlichen Aufklärung in Lessings *Emilia Galotti*", in *Zeitschrift für deutsche Philologie*, vol.105 no.2, 1986.
Iris Denneler, "'Das einzige Wort!'—'Buchstabieren Sie es zusammen!': Ein Versuch *Emilia Galotti* neu zu lesen", in *Germanisch-Romanische Monatsschrift*, vol.37 no.1, 1987.
John Stickler, "Lessing and Aura of Censorship: Implications for *Emilia Galotti*", in *Lessing Yearbook*, 19, 1987.
Arnd Bohm, "Gottsched's *Sterbender Cato* as a Pretext for Lessing's *Emilia Galotti*", in *Seminar*, vol.24 no.1, 1988.
Colin Walker, "'So tief liess mich die Gnade nicht sinken': On the Absence of Divine Grace in *Emilia Galotti*", in *Publications of the English Goethe Society*, 57, 1988.

*   *   *

Set in the fictional Italian state of Guastalla, *Emilia Galotti* concerns the attempt of the ruling Prince to seduce Emilia Galotti, the beautiful daughter of a middle-class family politically opposed to him. He makes unsuccessful overtures toward her in church and then gives permission to his secretary Marinelli to abduct Emilia on her way to her marriage with Count Appiani. The Count is killed and Emilia, in the company of her mother, is sequestered in the Prince's hunting lodge, where she successfully resists his advances. Her father Odoardo arrives to save her. Encountering first the Prince's cast-off mistress, Countess Orsina, he learns of the danger his daughter is in; Orsina gives him a dagger. When he is eventually allowed to see his daughter, she, terrified at remaining in the Prince's power, persuades her father to kill her. Rather than be exposed to the sexual temptations of a corrupt aristocratic life, Emilia prefers death.

Emilia Galotti was one of the first bourgeois tragedies to find a permanent and central place in the German repertory. The play is notable for the tautness of its action, for its sustained suspense, and its economical, realistic dialogue that effectively represents the emotional turmoil of the characters. Nevertheless, despite the excitement generated by the action, the spectator consistently maintains an ironic perception of all the characters involved. It is not at all fanciful to argue that the dramaturgical technique of Ibsen's prose plays is prefigured in Lessing's drama.

Given the relatively oppressive, political conditions of Germany in the latter half of the 18th century, *Emilia Galotti* has often been considered a drama of protest. Some of Lessing's contemporaries interpreted Guastalla as the petty principality so characteristic of Germany at that time—in particular the Duchy of Brunswick where Lessing was employed as librarian to the Duke's court, at Wolfenbüttel. But Lessing denied such an interpretation, partly, no doubt, because to acknowledge it may well have jeopardised his position. But his denial was motivated to a greater degree by his sense of the artistic quality of his play.

What is perhaps most distinctive about *Emilia Galotti* is the way in which Lessing constantly avoids melodrama. The action has melodramatic features: the abduction of Emilia, masterminded by the intriguer Marinelli and executed by the cloak-and-dagger highwayman Angelo, being a prime example. But the melodrama is constantly tempered. The abduction, for example, is a botched affair, bringing the Prince no closer to the satisfaction of his desires and compromising him politically; its failure is central to much of the action.

However, Lessing's power of characterization is the main guarantor that the action never slips into melodrama. Additionally, it allows him to fulfil what, in the *Hamburgische Dramaturgie* (*Hamburg Dramaturgy*), he had defined as one of the prime purposes of drama: the leading of audiences to understand the humanity of others regardless of their public position. He noted: "if we pity kings, we pity them as human beings, not as kings". The Prince in *Emilia Galotti*, far from being an out-and-out villain, is a figure for whom audiences and readers feel sympathy. While he allows personal desires to prevail over public responsibility, he is aware of this failing and frequently betrays what seems to be a deep-seated respect for the values of his opponents. Furthermore, while he is all too subject to the machinations of Marinelli, who *is* an unmitigated villain, he becomes increasingly aware of his secretary's venality and of the absurdity of his own predicament.

While Lessing's perception of petty royalist rule is modified by his understanding of the human motives behind absolutist gestures, he does not represent his middle-class characters in a consistently sympathetic vein. Emilia's mother, Claudia, is all too easily attracted by the glamour of aristocratic life, while her husband Odoardo is honest but, crucially, lacks intelligence. Even Count Appiani, in the one appearance he makes, seems an acute depressive. But the most intriguing character is Emilia herself. Her death has been the central theme of much of the considerable critical literature the play has generated. In killing off his heroine, Lessing was following the classical story of Virginia, well known to his contemporaries and not infrequently dramatised. As if to emphasise this, he has Emilia refer to the classical source just before Odoardo stabs her. Given the realistic milieu of the action, the speech

containing this reference sounds inflated, even pompous, a tone that is aggravated by what seems to be insufficient motive for her death, namely her fear of living in aristocratic luxury. The problem is that Lessing, who until this point has had Emilia only appear twice, has not given himself sufficient opportunity to develop her character. On her first appearance she is virtually hysterical after hearing the Prince's advances to her in church, on her second, after the abduction, she is more under control; afterwards, we hear reports of her being coolly distant with the Prince. On the fairly scant evidence available, it would appear that Emilia, sensing the presence of sexual desire within herself, responds to her fear that she might succumb with various forms of repression. Her suicide is therefore the most extreme manifestation of this repression. But whatever its cause, the death of Emilia Galotti is a devastating example of the waste caused by absolutist power once it has devolved into a process that is beyond the capacity of a single human being to control.

—Simon Williams

THE EMPEROR. See **HENRY IV (Pirandello).**

THE EMPEROR JONES
by Eugene O'Neill

First Publication: In *The Emperor Jones; Diff'rent; The Straw*, New York, 1921.
First Production: Playwright's Theatre, New York, 1 November 1920.

Criticism
(For general works on the author, see *Playwrights* volume)

Articles:
Emil Roy, "Eugene O'Neill's *The Emperor Jones* and *The Hairy Ape* as Mirror Plays", in *Comparative Drama*, 2, 1968.
Robert R. Findlay, "*The Emperor Jones*: O'Neill as Scene Designer", in *Players Magazine*, 45, 1969.
Ruby Cohn, "Black Power on Stage: *Emperor Jones* and *King Christophe*", in *Yale French Studies*, 46, 1971.
John R. Cooley, "*The Emperor Jones* and the Harlem Renaissance", in *Studies in the Literary Imagination*, vol.7 no.2, 1974.
Madeline Smith, "*The Emperor Jones* and Confession", in *Bulletin of The West Virginia Association of College English Teachers*, 8, 1983.
Donald P. Duclos, "A Plank in Faulkner's 'lumber room': *The Emperor Jones* and *Light in August*", in *Eugene O'Neill Newsletter*, vol.11, no.2, 1987.

*   *   *

In eight expressionistic scenes, this play follows the descent of Brutus Jones, former Pullman porter, from "civilized" power as emperor of a Caribbean island through tribal pursuit to "primitive" death. At first, Jones treats the natives, as well

The Emperor Jones: Paul Robeson, Ambassador's Theatre, London, 1925

as his cockney lieutenant, Smithers, with contempt. Strangely, however, when the drumbeat begins, it is Smithers who first senses its ominous portent. Jones is overconfident, and even when he becomes aware of the "bush niggers" rebellion against him, he believes himself to be impervious to overthrow. Nevertheless, he becomes easy prey to the power of magic, yet unable to use it himself. As his "collective unconscious" (or racial memory) awakens in him—expressed in scenes of a tribal ritual, a slave-ship, an auction, and a chaingang—and, pursued by "little formless fears", one by one he uses up his silver bullets, without which (he had announced) he cannot be killed. But the natives have cast one for him.

Often discussed as a treatment of the question of race, in reality this play deals with the dichotomy of human nature: its inherent savagery and the superimposed veneer of civilization. It also represented his boldest use so far of sensual, kinesthetic, theatrical means in the representation of symbolic manifestations of unconscious and supernatural forces aroused by rituals—at odds with the prevailing "realism", which has also characterized his own work as well. The drumbeat, specified in its rhythmic correspondence to the pulse, and the illusion of "pure space" (rendered on the tiny stage in Macdougal Street with the European scenic device known as a "plasterdome") were the culmination of a series of radical experiments aimed at creating realistic depictions of hallucination. *The Emperor Jones'* performance resulted in a sensational success for the then unheard-of amateur group, the Provincetown Players, their black star, Charles Gilpin, propelling the production to Broadway, and eventually to London. Although the author's identification of the "primitive force" within homo sapiens with an Afro-American ex-slave is rooted in the prevailing atmosphere of racial prejudice, it must also be remembered that Brutus Jones was the first "straight" leading role played on the American stage by a black man in a white company.

—Robert K. Sarlós

THE EMPIRE BUILDERS (Les Bâtisseurs d'empire)
by Boris Vian

First Publication: Paris, 1959.
First Production: Théâtre Recamier (Théâtre Nationale Populaire), Paris, 22 December 1959.

Translations
The Empire Builders, translated by Simon Watson Taylor, New York, 1967.

Criticism
(For general works on the author, see *Playwrights* volume)

Articles:
François Billetdoux, "Boris Vian et le 'Schmürz'", in *Obliques*, 8–9, 1976.
Anna D. Amelung, "De la quête du moi à l'univers socialisé: une étude des structures de *L'Arrache-coeur* et des *Bâtisseurs d'empire*", in *Chimères*, vol.11 no.2, 1978.
Martha O'Nan, "Names in Boris Vian's *Les Bâtisseurs d'empire*", in *Literary Onomastics Studies*, 7, 1980.
Alfo Finco, "Dino Buzzati's *Un caso clinico* and Boris Vian's *Les Bâtisseurs d'empire*: a comparison", in *Francia*, 41, 1982.

Gert Pinkernell, "Boris Vians Tragigroteske *Les Bâtisseurs d'empire* als Chronik der Ära Mollet (1956/57)", in *Romanistische Zeitschrift für Literaturgeschichte*, 8, 1984.
Grant Crichfield, "'La Carte n'est pas la territoire' ou l'Espace 'patafantastique' des *Bâtisseurs d'empire* de Boris Vian", in *Degré Second*, 9, 1985.
Charles J. Stivale, "Of 'Schmürz' and men: Boris Vian's *Les Bâtisseurs d'empire*", in *Romance Studies*, 7, 1988.

* * *

One characteristic of the post-World-War-II French antitheater, dubbed by critic Martin Esslin *The Theater of the Absurd*, is a central enigma, often associated with an absent or inexplicable character, as in Samuel Beckett's *Waiting for Godot* and Eugène Ionesco's *The Bald Prima Donna*. Boris Vian offers us a set of variations on this theme in *The Empire Builders* in the form of the omnipresent but unexplained *Schmürz* (a name derived from the German word for pain, *Schmerz*), and the equally enigmatic but malevolent Noise, "frightening to hear but difficult to describe". They drive a family from floor to floor, to progressively smaller living quarters, as the family's ideals and possessions dwindle.

The play features a family (Father, Mother, and daughter, Zenobia), their maid, Mug, a Neighbor (who, like the family, is being driven from apartment to apartment by the Noise), and the *Schmürz*, who is waiting in a corner when the family stumbles on stage amid confusion and uncertainty, loaded down with what is left of its possessions.

Living in a world of inexplicable forces, the family refuses to accept or even confront irrationality and uncertainty. Its members, save Zenobia, even ignore the needs of the limp, bandaged, bleeding, zombie-like figure of the *Schmürz* (but thoughtlessly Father and Mother repeatedly whip, beat, kick, stab and even shoot it throughout the play, almost as a psychological release from their frustrations and concealed anxieties), and although they flee from it, the family also refuses to explore the meaning of the Noise, which apparently also follows them from apartment to apartment.

The hasty removal from the apartment below, which opens the play, is apparently not the family's first flight, and each movement upwards in the building signals a decline in the family's fortunes, a fact recognized only by Zenobia, who alone tries to confront the reality of the family's plight:

> It's going to be just like before, only a little worse.
> We'll be a little worse off. . . .The nights will pass, the days will be like the nights, and then suddenly we'll hear the noise, we'll climb the stairs, we'll leave something behind by mistake. . .and we'll only have a single room. . .with someone [the *Schmürz*] already in it.

In Act II we learn that the neighbor's son, Xavier, has mysteriously died, and the maid, who speaks in strings of synonyms, abandons the family. When Zenobia is coaxed to cross the hall to ask the Neighbor for Xavier's bed, she discovers that the neighbor's door, like the one to the family's second room, is mysteriously sealed, and as she returns to her own apartment she is locked out by the mysterious force associated with the noise. The family hastily flees to the attic-apartment without her, but as Act III opens the Mother emits "a blood curdling scream" and has apparently fallen victim to the force associated with the Noise.

Act III is the Father's monologue. He is alone in the attic-apartment with no exit and where, stripped of family responsibility, he begins to confront the Noise: "At one time I pretended not to hear it when it began to echo. Yes. . .setting an example. . .in front of the family". To fight the malign force the Father dresses in his military uniform and deals with the crisis of his own identity by taking inventory of his bodily organs. His attempts to reason through his existence repeatedly lead him only to the impasse of tautology or to triviality. As the Noise and a sound of knocking at the door increase, the father totters towards the balcony where he slips. Vian's French wording allows a central ambiguity in the climax which forces a director either to have the Father fall back onto the floor of the apartment or have him sucked out of the window. In *The Empire Builders* the choice was made by the translator, "*He slips and falls to the floor, screaming*", although the Royal Shakespeare Company followed the Vilar production and had the Father fall out of the window. The first ending is obviously less theatrical but the second may recall too vividly the climax of Ionesco's *The Chairs*.

The threats (real or imagined) surrounding the family remain enigmatic nor is much exposition offered to explain this family except for a clichéd re-creation of the parents' courtship and marriage in mine, so *The Empire Builders* is a work firmly within the irrationalist tradition of the "Theater of the Absurd". It seems, however, to have lasted less well than other examples of this genre. The reason may be the strongly derivative nature of the play, or perhaps that the symbols of the irrational, (*Schmürz* and the Noise) are less compelling than, say, the absentee Godot or the Rhinoceros of Ionesco's play of that name. Although Vian's dialogue is inventive, the banality of family dialogue is more adroitly handled in *The Bald Prima Donna*, where, as in *The Empire Builders*, Ionesco offered us a set of multiple endings. Vian's closing stage directions are in that tradition: "*And perhaps the door opens, and perhaps schmürzes enter, vague outlines in the dark. . .*". Finally, the threats to bourgeois domestic security (our personal empire) and even an image like the *Schmürz* itself may have been handled more memorably and integrated more tightly into the fabric of the drama in the work of Harold Pinter, as with the vagabond Matchseller of *A Slight Ache*.

—S.E. Gontarski

EN ATTENDANT GODOT.   See **WAITING FOR GODOT.**

ENDGAME (Fin de Partie)
by Samuel Beckett

First Publication: In French, in *Fin de Partie: suivi de Acte sans paroles*, Paris, 1967; as *Endgame* in *Endgame: A Play in One Act; Followed by Act Without words: A Mime for One Player*, New York and London, 1958.
First Production: In French, as *Fin de Partie*, Royal Court Theatre, London, 3 April 1957; as *Endgame*, Cherry Lane Theatre, New York, 28 January 1958.

Criticism
(For general works on the author, see *Playwrights* volume)

Books:
Clancy Sigal et al (eds), *Materialen zu Becketts "Endspiel"*, Frankfurt, 1968.
Bell G. Chevigny (ed.), *Twentieth Century Interpretations of "Endgame"*, Englewood Cliffs, New Jersey, 1969.
Vincenzo Romano, *La fine di un inizio: interpretazione dell' "Endgame" di Samuel Beckett*, Bari, 1975.
Harold Bloom (ed.), *Samuel Beckett's "Endgame"*, New York, 1988.

Articles:
Anthony Easthope, "Hamm, Clov, and Dramatic method in *Endgame*", *Modern Drama*, 10, 1968.
Konrad Schoell, "The Chain and the Circle; A Structural Comparison of *Waiting For Godot* and *Endgame*", in *Modern Drama*, 11, 1968.
Anne C. Murch, "Les Indications scéniques dans le nouveau théâtre: *Fin de partie*, de Samuel Beckett", in *Australian Journal of French Studies*, 6, 1969.
Maria J. Wolber, "Beckett's *Endspiel*: Versuch einer gesellschaftskritischen Deutung", in *Deutschunterricht*, vol. 25 no.2, 1973.
Thomas D. Eisele, "The Apocalypse of Beckett's *Endgame*", in *Cross Currents*, 26, 1976.
Robert J. Nelson, "Three Orders in *En attendant Godot* and *Fin de partie*: A Pascalian Interpretation of Beckett", in *French Forum*, 1, 1976.
Patricia Merivale, "*Endgame* and the Dialogue of King and Fool in the Monarchical Metadrama", in *Modern Drama*, 21, 1978.
Simone Guers-Martynuk, "L'Alchemie du théâtre de Beckett dans *Fin de partie*", in *Chimères*, vol.12 no.2, 1979.
Helene Keyssar, "Theatre Games, Language Games, and *Endgame*", in *Theatre Journal*, 31, 1979.
Paul Lawley, "Symbolic Structure and Creative Obligation in *Endgame*", in *Journal of Beckett Studies*, 5, 1979.
Thomas Metscher, "Beckett and Tragedy: A Note on *Endgame*", in *Gulliver*, 5, 1979.
Dina Sherzer, "Beckett's *Endgame*, or what talk can do", in *Modern Drama*, 22, 1979.
Robert Wilcher, "The Museum of Tragedy: *Endgame* and *Rosencrantz and Guildenstern Are Dead*", in *Journal of Beckett Studies*, 4, 1979.
James Acheson, "Chess With the Audience: Samuel Beckett's *Endgame*", in *Critical Quarterly*, vol.22 no.2, 1980.
Seán Golden, "Familiars in a ruinstrewn land: *Endgame* as political allegory", in *Contemporary Literature*, 22, 1981.
Stephani P. Smith, "Beckett's Absent Children: A Reading of *Fin de partie*", in *Nigerian Journal of French Studies*, 1, 1981.
Theodor W. Adorno, "Trying to Understand *Endgame*", in *New German Critique*, 26, 1982 (translation of 1961 article).
Richard K. Simon, "Dialectical Laughter: A Study of *Endgame*", in *Modern Drama*, 25, 1982.
Rei Noguchi, "Style and Strategy in *Endgame*", in *Journal of Beckett Studies*, 9, 1984.
Gabriele Schwab, "On the Dialectic of Closing and Opening in Samuel Beckett's *Endgame*", in *Yale French Studies*, 67, 1984.
Sylvie D. Henning, "Samuel Beckett's *Fin de partie*: variations on the hermeneutic theme", in *Boundary 2*, 12, 1985.
Emmanuel Jacquart, "L'Archétype bourreau-victime dans *Fin de partie*", in *Travaux de linguistique et de littérature*, vol. 23 no.2, 1985.
M.G. Robinson, "Prisoners at Play: Form and Meaning in Strindberg's *The Dance of Death* and Beckett's *Endgame*", in *Journal of European Studies*, vol.15 no.1, 1985.

Endgame: Young Vic Theatre, London, 1980 (San Quentin Drama Workshop)

Sharon K. O'Dair, " 'The contentless passion of an unfruitful wind': Irony and laughter in *Endgame*", in *Criticism*, 28, 1986.

Estelle M. Thaler, "Apocalyptic Vision in *Heartbreak House* and *Endgame*: the Metaphor of Change", in *Zeitschrift für Anglistik und Amerikanistik*, 34, 1986.

Paul Lawley, "Adoption in *Endgame*", in *Modern Drama*, 31, 1988.

Frederick F. McGlynn, "Self, Language, and Being in Beckett's Trilogy and *Endgame*", in *Williamette Journal of the Liberal Arts*, vol.4 no.1, 1988–89.

* * *

If Samuel Beckett had not already written *Waiting for Godot* there can be little doubt that *Endgame* would have made him famous for an enigmatic style of drama which delights those who are prepared to accept the challenge of its rare combinations of intellectual complexity and overtly artificial theatricality, of pervading deep metaphysical pessimism and moments of irrepressible hilarity. Some complained of obscurity but in the years since its first production, under the direction of Roger Blin, at the Royal Court Theatre the play has become a modern classic.

Beckett originally conceived the play in French, calling it *Fin de partie*. He was himself also responsible for the English version. Though he made a number of changes which merit attention, *Endgame* may be regarded primarily as a translation of the original, and it is a fascinating study to examine the renderings that Beckett adopted for some of his more problematic and more idiomatic passages.

The title of the play, whether in French or English, appears to refer to the final phase of a game of chess, the endgame when all the exciting manœuvering with the pawns and the more mobile pieces is over and we settle down to the last, absolutely inevitable fatal stroke that will trap the king. "Checkmate" is generally interpreted as meaning "the king is dead". Beckett does not develop possible allegories derived from chess; indeed, in that famous ironic dictum "no symbols where none intended" he warns us all against those attempts to find some facile re-expression of the precise meaning which critics used to be certain was lurking in his plays but which, for some reason, he never seemed able to make explicit for himself. To some, the chilly setting of a bare room with just two small curtained windows high up in the walls suggested a hide-out where the last survivors of a nuclear holocaust are living out their last days. The interpretation makes some sense, but really there is nothing in the text to warrant anything so specific.

What we certainly do witness is a portrayal of the sense of an inevitable and irreversible decline in humanity. The mood is all the more sombre because memories of the past, far from assuaging present unhappiness, add to its pain. There is, moreover, no question of seeking comfort in this predicament, as many a classical tragic hero does in his, by seeking out explanations of present misfortunes and finding consolation in the realisation that there exists some chain of causality which makes sense of experience. In other circumstances the will, even the malevolence, of the deity might be evoked so that mankind might, in its suffering, at least grasp at this last straw of comfort, a guarantee that there was a divine plan even if its fulfilment demanded human suffering. But that possibility is ruled out too. Worse still, there is the conviction that God, like everything else except what we see on stage, is dead; this adds to the feeling of abandonment, of disappointment, of the terrible loneliness that is each individual's ultimate fate. The theme is not perhaps a new one, and with an author like Beckett who spent long years in France and knew French literature intimately, it is especially tempting to refer to the harrowing portrayal of the "wretchedness of man without God" that is given by Blaise Pascal, the seventeenth-century Jansenist apologist, in his famous *Pensées*, but it is presented with uncommon force in *Endgame*.

Hamm, crippled, blind and in need of a catheter, sits throughout the play in an armchair fitted with castors. Occasionally his servant, Clov, wheels him around the set, and once or twice he strains to try to propel himself about, using a gaff like a punt pole. More significant than his movements is his insistence on being placed precisely in the centre of the stage. He demands to know what is going on outside, generally receiving the answer that there is nothing to be seen, and he reflects, enraged for most of the time, on his predicament. Again and again he refers to the fact that things are coming to an end; most devastatingly of all, he declares that his punishment cannot go on much longer, and, since no precise explanation can be given, we realise that his crime is nothing other than the fact of existence itself. He longs for the time when next he will be able to have another painkiller, a "calmant" as it is called in the French, a "sedative", which it is tempting to think might be an "opiate" with all that it would imply in a France that knows its Marxism.

Nagg and Nell, Hamm's parents, we see only in a pair of dustbins. Their lives are virtually over, and Nell dies before the play ends. They too are mutilated, immobile, with thoughts of the past which cannot beguile their present sufferings. In their son there is no affection; he, like Job, can only curse those who ventured on the irresponsibility of giving him life. The relation between Hamm and his servant Clov, who is at least mobile to some degree though not able-bodied, is also oddly strained. The two have no affection for one another, yet they do not part. From early on there are suggestions that it is only self-interest that keeps the servant there. He needs food, and only his master knows the number on the combination lock to the larder, but we soon come to appreciate there must be more to it than this. When Clov does go, his departure marks a decisive downturn, and the end of the play follows after a final soliloquy by Hamm.

The action of *Endgame* provokes a lot of laughter, not all uneasy and in a play that places much stress on things coming to a stop, there is more movement on stage than might be expected. The language, spiced with colloquialisms, is full of literary and Scriptural allusions. It demands attention, and if there is some difficulty in following Hamm's thread of thought through the maze of consciousness, that plainly conveys his own insoluble predicament.

—Christopher Smith

ENDIMION; the Man in the Moon
by John Lyly

First Publication: London, 1591.
First Production: (Children of St. Pauls) Greenwich, London, c. 2 February 1588.

Editions
Endimion, in *Minor Elizabethan Drama, 2*, London, 1910.
Endimion, in *The Plays of John Lyly*, edited by Carter A. Daniel, Lewisburg, Pennsylvania, London and Toronto, 1988.

Criticism
(For general works on the author, see *Playwrights* volume)

Articles:
J.W. Bennett, "Oxford and *Endimion*", in *Publications of the Modern Language Association [PMLA]*, 57, 1942.
Bernard F. Huppé, "The Allegory of Love in Lyly's Court Comedies", in *English Literary History*, 14, 1947.
J.A. Bryant, "The Nature of the Allegory in Lyly's *Endymion*", in *Renaissance Papers*, 1956.
Peter Weltner, "The Antinomic Vision of Lyly's *Endymion*", in *English Literary Renaissance*, 3, 1973.
Sallie Bond, "John Lyly's *Endimion*", in *Studies in English Literature 1500–1900*, 14, 1974.
Sara Deats, "The Disarming of the Knight: Comic Parody in Lyly's *Endymion*", in *South Atlantic Bulletin*, 1975.
Peter Saccio, "The Oddity of Lyly's *Endimion*", in *The Elizabethan Theatre, 5*, 1975.
C.C. Gannon, "Lyly's *Endimion*: From Myth to Allegory", in *English Literary Renaissance*, 6, 1976.
Robert S. Knapp, "The Monarchy of Love in Lyly's *Endimion*", in *Modern Philology*, 73, 1976.
Carol Lenz, "The Allegory of Wisdom in Lyly's *Endimion*", in *Comparative Drama*, 10, 1976.
Maurice Charney, "Female Roles and the Children's Companies: Lyly's Pandora in *The Woman in the Moon*", in *Research Opportunities in Renaissance Drama*, 22, 1979.

*   *   *

Freely invented around the Endimion myth, Lyly's play is court art, its strengths the product of the special context for the main performance: a comedy of sensibility, refined even in its inoffensive "low" humour (Sir Tophas and his page require an audience who remember having had an education), but also a play interestingly nervous of larger, offensive meaning, nuanced yet evasive, torn between a safe, firm hold on unreality and the desire to suggest inside knowledge ("we hope. . .none will apply pastimes"—The Prologue).

Endimion secretly loves Cynthia, the unattainable chaste moon; his more reasonable friend Eumenides loves Semele, her sharp-tongued lady-in-waiting. Tellus, jealous of his love, and angered by his using her as a cloak for his affections, employs a witch to cast Endimion into a 20-year sleep (which passes between Act III, Scenes 3 and 4). Eumenides is granted one wish at a well whose waters will only clear at the tears of a constant lover. After typical Lylyian self-debate, and advice from an older character, he chooses to seek the release of Endimion rather than the attainment of Semele: the adverse critic of Endimion's "sotted" love is moved to an act of self-transcendence. The play passes on smoothly to the release of Endimion through Cynthia's kiss, the predictable reward of Eumenides, and a definition agreed upon between Cynthia and a rejuvenated Endimion ("this honorable respect of thine shall be christened love in thee, and my reward for it favor"); all this despite the central moral choice of the play being a reasoned preference of male friendship to "vain love". Semele, as soon as she is released from Cynthia's earlier sentence to hold her tongue for a year, or lose it, has wit enough to point out the anomaly.

A comic sub-action shadows Endimion's story: Sir Tophas (a part evidently written for an adult actor among the boy players) announces his sudden love for the witch, praises her in burlesque displacements of qualities appropriate to a lover's admiration, and sleeps in emulation of Endimion. There are also the lower ranks of pages ("Now our masters are in love up to the ears, what have we to do but to be in knavery up to the crowns?"), servant girls, and two philosophers brought in, as is usual in Lyly, to learn true wisdom in the only place it can be got: the court, and from the monarch.

The play is in prose, Lyly's notorious Euphuism, with its insistent patternings of sound and sense, as deployed in his fiction *Euphues: The Anatomy of Wit*, emerging from the solvent requirement of drama as an instrument of some liveliness and precision. Unusually for an Elizabethan play, this is dramatic writing in which the importance of prose fiction (that is, Lyly's own) can be felt: as with 18th-century sentimental comedy, the wordy self-analysis by the main characters, often given in the form of monologue, suggests a transplanting to the stage of the kind of attention to feeling prose fiction can readily give. R. Y. Turner (in *English Literary History*, 1962) notes that "unless we speak loosely, we cannot say that English comedies dramatized love before Lyly began writing plays". The new subject requires thorough "anatomy", part of which is to subject it to parody and down-grading: Lyly's dialogue must be fervent and high-flown for Endimion, funny for Tophas and his page ("Doth Dipsas stoop? Will she yield? Will she bend?—Master, she is bent, I warrant you") and emphatic in adverse comment ("The love of men to women is a thing common, and of course; the friendship of man to man infinite, and immortal").

Lyly's scenic art is over-regular, and (except in the dramatisation of Eumenides' dilemma) the voices and attitudes in his play do not interact dramatically: not for him the confrontation of servant and master, lady and clown. Each act has its comic scene. The scenes themselves often fall into a pattern: entry by a soliloquist, who then observes and comments on another character arriving ("But here cometh. . ."), their dialogue, and separate exits ("But I will after him. . ."). The stage is cleared at the end of each scene, rather than presenting a character remaining on stage to be joined by new personnel. The scenes do not vary much in length. It is probable that Lyly wanted to give his boy-players plenty of respite from being on stage in front of the Queen herself, which must have been nerve-wracking for them—and him!

The first audience for this play could enjoy the titillating possibility of "application". Direct, contemporary allusion is no longer believed after the excesses of Bond's edition, but the play does align with the "Petrarchan politics" of Elizabeth's court: a discontented Endimion, despairing in his hopes of favour, slackening in his love (for this is how the witch presents Endimion's sleep), finally advanced through the intercession of his friend; these aspects would have been understood by every aspirant for place at the performance, or at the semi-public rehearsals by which Lyly seems actually to have earned money for his company.

—Roy Booth

ENDYMION. See **ENDIMION.**

AN ENEMY OF THE PEOPLE (En Folkefiende)
by Henrik Ibsen

First Publication: Copenhagen, 1882.
First Production: Christiana Theatre, Christiana, Norway, 13 January 1883.

Editions
En Folkefiende, Oslo, 1935.

Translations
An Enemy of the People, translated by Jenny Covan, London, 1924.
An Enemy of the People, translated by Norman Ginsbury, London, 1946.
An Enemy of the People, in *The Oxford Ibsen*, 6, edited and translated by James W. MacFarlane, London, 1960.
An Enemy of the People, in *Henrik Ibsen: The Complete Major Prose Plays*, translated by Rolf Fjelde, New York, 1978.
An Enemy of the People, translated by Michael Meyer, London, 1963; corrected version in *Ibsen: Plays, 2*, London, 1980.

Criticism
(For general works on the author, see *Playwrights* volume)

Books:
Peter Kramer, *Henrik Ibsen: "Ein Volksfiend" und "Die Wildente": die Wandlung der dramatischen Anlage und des Persönlichkeitsbildes in ihrer Bedeutung für Erziehung und Unterricht*, Bern, 1985.

Articles:
A. Lepke, "Who is Doctor Stockmann?", in *Scandinavian Studies*, 32, 1960.
Martha I. Halsey, "The Rebel Protagonist: Ibsen's *An Enemy of the People* and Buero's *Un soñador para un pueblo*", in *Comparative Literature Studies*, 1969.
Jorgen Haugen, "Aktivismens bevissthetsform med saerlig henblikk på Ibsen, Brandes og *En folkefiende*", in *Kritik*, 39, 1976.
Brian Johnston, "The Poetry of *An Enemy of the People*", in *Scandinavica*, 18, 1979.
Jeffrey B. Berlin, "The Concept of Truth in Ibsen's *An Enemy of the People*", in *Ibsenforbundet: Årbok*, 1981–82.

*   *   *

Compared with *Ghosts* (1881), which had fewer characters than the average Ibsen play, the eleven named characters of *An Enemy of the People* suggest an effort to represent every social sector of the small Norwegian spa resort where the whole action is set, especially as three of those characters have media connections. The town's economy depends on the spa, which has been developed largely through the efforts of Dr. Stockmann, the brother of the Mayor and son-in-law of Kiil, a local tannery owner. In the first act, however, Stockmann discovers that the water supply is polluted, to the extent of causing typhoid among those who visit the baths, and with the naïveté of a single-minded, scientific researcher he is about to publish his "great discovery" and address the problem. It seems straightforward, and at first most of the citizenry regards him as a civic hero. However, people gradually realise that the process of improving the baths would wreck the town's economy and reputation. There is a public meeting, in which opinion turns against Stockmann, he is denounced as a public enemy, and he announces that the polluted water supply is symbolic of the contamination of a society in which "the majority has a monopoly of the truth". In the last act, his house is stoned, he loses his job, his daughter is dismissed, his younger children are sent away from school, and he finally observes that "the strongest man in the world is the man who stands alone".

Ibsen's preoccupation with the dangers inherent in a quest for truth, which would reach its full articulation in the notion of the "life-lie" in *The Wild Duck*, is fundamental to the dramatic position of Stockmann. Whereas other Ibsen protagonists such as Nora (in *A Doll's House*) and Mrs Alving (in *Ghosts*) find a degree of liberation in confronting a "guilty secret" on an interpersonal plane, Stockmann's truth has an existence completely independent of him, and has been verified in the most clinical sense possible—in a laboratory. Moreover, the truth about the pollution has a dynamic of its own, and its public impact will continue regardless of the position that Stockmann takes in relation to it. Publicly, Stockmann's martyrdom is an absurdity, since his self-sacrifice will have little impact in the domain of public health, and if *An Enemy of the People* were a simple, thesis play his gesture would be an irrelevance. However, as the play develops, public health becomes rather less the issue than personal integrity, so that Stockmann becomes the site for an Hegelian conflict of moral imperatives. The status of individuality as opposed to the collective is the point at which the action finally rests, but this has been anticipated early, in the prominence that has been accorded to the publication of opinion through the media. In such a context, every piece of behaviour or private propensity is subject to politicisation.

An Enemy of the People is a remarkably stark play for Ibsen, especially in its language and use of symbolism. Building projects very often have symbolic properties in the plays of his maturity, and that is clearly the case with the baths in this play. But there is little complexity in this otherwise characteristic, environmental symbol; its interpretation is not really questioned or debated, by any of the characters, so that it almost acquires an objectivity in its status, without any mystical or poetic dimension. To an extent, this obviously reflects the fact that the central character is a scientist, but in the last two acts Stockmann's rhetoric does introduce numerous, animal analogues to express his view of the general public. A long speech against mob rule dwells on the superiority of pedigree animals over mongrels, and recurrent references to dogs and wolves emphasise that Stockmann's stand is against herd or pack thinking. The Darwinistic argument of Hovstad, the newspaper editor, that "every animal must fight for survival" is accepted as a challenge by Stockmann, who tries to throw him out of the window.

Stockmann, like all the male characters in the play, has a civic status, and this is brought into conflict with his domestic responsibilities. His ideological stance dictates that when society is improved, then his children will have better lives, but he also comes to see that the aetiology of the present "moral scurvy" can be traced back through several generations—the "sins-of-the-fathers" principle of biological determinism which emerges in most of Ibsen's plays of this period. In the last act, Kiil has been buying up shares in the Baths, which have become very cheap, with money he had intended to leave to Stockmann's children, and his revelation of this is tantamount to blackmail. The doctor's assertion that most of the pollution comes from the tannery leads Kiil to the inference that "my grandfather, and my father before me, to say nothing of myself, have been slowly poisoning the town all these years", and he retaliates by financially challenging Stockmann's image of himself as a "decent father". The appeal to quality of parenthood is a recurrent motif in Ibsen's plays, but Stockmann's resistance is exemplary.

Though there is evidence that Ibsen had been thinking of this play for some years—and possibly as early as *Pillars of Society*—it is generally accepted that the formative drafting of the play occurred within the context of the journalistic furore over *Ghosts*, a furore which is fictionalised in *An Enemy of the People*. Much critical opinion concurred that *Ghosts* resembled an "open sewer", and it is easy to see the next play as essentially a dramatisation of that metaphor. A consequent reading of Stockmann as autobiographical, though a truism at one level (and acknowledged by Ibsen in his correspondence), is a severe over-simplification of Ibsen's dramatic strategy, although it is noteworthy that Stanislavsky found the character a reflection of the author's childishness and short-sightedness. However, the play's ending does have a mischievous ambivalence, especially as Stockmann gives up his notion of emigrating to the New World and toys with the idea of educating the juvenile "mongrels" to try to produce the type of citizens that might constitute the society he wants. Thus a work that seems to have reverted to the tradition of the well-made play retrieves some of the "technical novelty" that Shaw termed the "discussion play", and the wryly ironic ending of a play which Ibsen perceived as a comedy shows that, if autobiography it is, the author was still capable of self-effacing laughter.

—Howard McNaughton

ENRICO IV.   See HENRY IV (Pirandello).

THE ENTERTAINER
by John Osborne

First Publication: London, 1957.
First Production: Royal Court Theatre, London, 10 April
              1957.

Criticism
(For general works on the author, see *Playwrights* volume)

Articles:

Michael Raab, "*The Entertainer*: Die Music Hall als Symbol für England", in "*The Music Hall is Dying*": *Die Thematisierung der Unterhaltungsindustrie im englischen Gegenwartsdrama*, Tübingen, 1989.

*   *   *

In an English seaside town in the mid-1950's, Archie Rice, a second-rate music-hall comedian, struggles to sustain his act and livelihood in the fast-changing climate of mass media entertainment. At home, his father, Billy, a former music-hall star, his second wife, Phoebe, his daughter Jean, just visiting from her work with handicapped children in London, and his son, Frank, a former conscientious objector, wait for news of his son, Mick, a soldier taken prisoner in Cyprus. Eventually, Mick is killed. Archie's desperate struggle for survival drives him to including nudes in his show and even to consider marrying a young woman whose family might invest in his show. Billy's reward for putting paid to this last arrangement is an appearance in Archie's show, during which he dies. The taxman is also after Archie. His audience is unsympathetic. Phoebe is calling for him to follow his successful brother, Bill, and run a hotel in Canada. Jean decides to continue teaching. Frank goes to Canada. But Archie decides to stay and "'ave a go".

The play presents Archie's home life interspersed with scenes of his music-hall act. Indeed, the play is treated as a music-hall evening, each scene announced by an advertisement sheet with the appropriate number. The play takes "theatris mundi" literally; this theatre is, indeed, the world. The metaphor on which the play depends extends to the theatre building itself and the audience within it, forming an inextricable relationship between the stage action and its implications, and the audience.

Although a music-hall board stands on stage announcing the homey, "realistic" scene between Jean and Billy which opens the play as "Number One", it is certainly possible to ignore this hint and take the scene at face value. However, when Archie comes on stage, confronting the audience directly, it suddenly finds itself transformed into Archie's music-hall audience. This change requires a conscious adjustment on the part of the audience. The poverty of Archie's material makes an audience self-conscious. Archie's material and the family scenes inform on each other making Archie's plight, his attempt to find a foothold in a changing world, less personal than social. The changing social milieu, the lack of values, the marginalisation of the individual, are isolated in bitterness and despair in Archie's act. "I feel sorry for you people", says Billy. "You don't know what its really like. You haven't lived most of you. . .you don't know what life can be". And Archie sings to his audience: "Why should I care/Why should I let it touch me. . ./If they see you're blue, they'll—look down on you/So why should I bother to care? (Thank God I'm normal)".

The individual becomes an example of the social malaise. The pretence to international influence and power Britain no longer has is centralized in Mick, a British conscript taken prisoner in a police action who, despite governmental objections, is killed, simply another dispensible cog in the machinery. "We're all right, all of us" replies Jean ironically to Billy's outburst of patriotism. "*We*'re all right. God save the Queen." Archie's act quickly follows: "I've played in front of them all. 'The Queen', 'The Duke of Edinborough', 'The Prince of Wales' and the—what's the name of that, other pub?''; and then he sings "We're All Out for Number One".

The music-hall becomes a metaphor for the positive qualities of the society in which it's flourished, the qualities which are being discarded in this social change. Billy's reminiscences assist in creating a picture of, and an emotional attachment to, the music hall, establishing the values of taste, classless entertainment, externally acknowledged standards of excellence, community, and genuine appreciation. But the criteria of the "New World" are elaborated in Archie's songs: rampant, calloused individualism ("Why Should I care", "We're All Out for Number One") combined with conformity ("Thank God I'm Normal").

However, the more that is revealed of Archie's life, the less one can enjoy his act. "The wife" is the pathetic Phoebe and there is an increasing desperation that creeps on stage with him, as well as callousness and pathos. Yet, at the same time,

the play builds a strong identification in the audience with those values of the music hall and its imminent demise that transcends attachment to any of the individual characters. Archie himself is hardly an attractive character, but he attracts greater sympathy as he becomes the living representative of all that the music-hall suggests.

Archie's last performance is a masterly piece of writing. Every care has been taken to prevent even a giggle escaping the audience. He slanders his family. He repeats jokes barely humorous the first time he told them. He is awkward and desperate. The audience knows it is his last chance and yearns for Archie and the music-hall to survive. The embarrassment of watching a truly bad act calls attention to the fact that his success depends on his audience's reception of his performance.

Associations of theatrical performance provide the visual imagery of the final scene. In the single spotlight on the dark stage, inseparable from romantic and ironic implications and intimations of life and death, Archie directly confronts his audience, the theatrical terms indistinguishable from their social implications: "You've been a good audience. Very good. A very *good* audience. Let me know where you're working tomorrow night—and I'll come and see YOU". Through the extension of the theatrical metaphor, *The Entertainer* pushes further than the nostalgic reminiscences and generalised jabs at society often attributed to Osborne. In a disturbingly emotional manner, the play reinstates the audience as responsible members of society with the ability, indeed, the obligation, to make choices and take action. That formless mass, "society", that inadvertently victimises so many hapless heroes of social realism, is defined and experienced as a collection of individuals who, like Archie, are not only its products but its producers.

—Elaine Turner

ENTERTAINING MR. SLOANE
by Joe Orton

First Publication: London, 1964.
First Production: New Arts Theatre, London, 6 May 1964.

Criticism
(For general works on the author, see *Playwrights* volume)

Articles:
Maurice Charney, "Occulted Discourse and Threatening Nonsense in Joe Orton's *Entertaining Mr. Sloane*", in *New York Literary Forum*, 4, 1980.

*   *   *

Entertaining Mr. Sloane was Joe Orton's first full-length play, and, like the earlier *Ruffian on the Stair*, it borrows heavily from the "invaded room" model as developed, in particular, by Harold Pinter. As in Pinter's *The Caretaker*, a newcomer attempts to manipulate, and is manipulated by, the current inhabitants of the house. Kath takes pity on a young man down on his luck and offers him temporary shelter. Sloane soon becomes Kath's lover and starts to act as chauffeur for her brother Ed, a rich, homosexual wheeler-dealer who develops a

Entertaining Mr. Sloane: Beryl Reid as Kath and Malcolm McDowell as Sloane, Royal Court Theatre, London 1975

strong sexual interest in Sloane. Securely installed in the house, and with the prospect of a moneyed future, Sloane sets about playing sister off against brother. However, he has previously murdered a photographer who had taken some compromising photographs of him; the connection is made by Kath's father who threatens to tell the police, and Sloane murders him, too. Here, as elsewhere in the play, Orton displays no moral interest in the situation, and the plot is concluded with Sloane's manipulation of brother and sister being turned around, so that it is he who is blackmailed into remaining there, effectively as a sexual prisoner.

It soon becomes apparent that Orton is not much concerned with the complexities of psychological motivation. This play is all about surface and not about depths, about the linguistic games that Orton can play with the varied and frequently contradictory forms of language deployed by the characters. We are invited to enjoy the games but never to feel sympathy for the players. Orton's interest lies in the way the characters express themselves, and not in the why. The characters in *Entertaining Mr. Sloane* do not possess the degree of self-knowledge that, indeed, might allow them to ask such questions of themselves. Our laughter is a superior laughter, born of an awareness that the characters on stage do not understand what it is about their language that is amusing: this is in stark contrast to the characters in an Oscar Wilde comedy, for example, who are only too aware of their own wit. Kath finds herself able to accept the murder of her father and the sharing of the murderer's sexual favours with her brother because she can find a form of words that will gloss over, rather than question, the state of her relationship with Sloane. "See,

Ed, he hasn't lost respect for me": as if, with all the vagueness the term "respect" brings with it from a world of genteel discourse, the loss of it had anything to do with it.

Furthermore, Orton seems as little interested in developing much beyond the bare mechanics of plot. His fascination with the devious potentiality of human behaviour overrides any concern with plausible, narrative closure. There *is* a plot in *Entertaining Mr. Sloane*, and as such it must be resolved, but it really does not matter much what the conclusion is—an ending with Sloane regaining an upper hand over the pair, for instance, would make no essential difference to the play—as long as it brings the particular events to a point of *stasis*. Orton does not wish us to see the play as possessing a moral structure, still less to see it in terms of a process of discovery about the characters and their motivations. The plot is here simply a convenient peg on which to hang his own obsessions.

What these obsessions are is fairly apparent both in the conflicting offers of straight and homosexual sex offered to Sloane, and in the setting—a macabre version of the ordinary domestic household—in which the offers are made. What Ed has to offer Sloane is a kind of more elevated version of the world Orton was then living in, a consciously aggressive affront to the suburban decencies of his Leicester youth. Thus, although the play's structure is derived from a tradition of farce, and the insistently witty banter from that of a comedy of manners, the main interest of *Entertaining Mr. Sloane* comes from the interplay between past and present in quasi-biographical terms; between the repressions and hypocrisies of Orton's own early years, and the hedonistic possibilities of a newer liberated self in the London *demi-monde* of the 1960's.

It is both an epitaph to Orton's past and an ambiguous signpost pointing in the direction in which his future seemed to lie.

During her initial seduction of Sloane, Kath feels a certain maternal propriety is in order. "I don't think the fastening on this thing I'm wearing will last much longer. . .you should wear more clothes, Mr. Sloane. . .I believe you're as naked as me. And there's no excuse for it. . .I'll be your mamma. I need to be loved. Gently. Oh! I shall be so ashamed in the morning", she says as the stage direction reinforces the need for modesty with the cue that she "*switches off the light*". The confusion of sexual energy and working-class niceties that characterises Kath was familiar to Orton's sister when she first saw the play in 1975: "That's my mum! That's her! Its like seeing a ghost". And in a sense she is a ghost, the ghost of a past that Orton spent most of his short dramatic career trying to exorcise. Kath acts both as mother and as lover to Sloane—"Baby, my little boy. Mamma forgives you". In *Entertaining Mr. Sloane*, Orton created a role for himself in a rearranged "family", first killing off the unwanted "Dadda", and then being willingly coerced into servicing both the handsome Ed of the new world and his sister's peculiar mixture of spinsterly lust and maternal coyness, of the old.

—John Bull

EPICOENE; or, The Silent Woman
by Ben Jonson

First Publication: In *The Workes of Benjamin Jonson*, London, 1616.
First Production: Whitefriars Theatre (The Children of the Queen's Revels), London, 1609.

Editions
Epicoene; or, The Silent Woman, edited by Aurelia Henry, New York, 1906.
Epicoene, edited by W.R. Macklin, London, 1926.
Epicoene in *Jonson: Three Plays*, edited by Brinsley Sheridan and C.H. Herford, New York, 1957.
Epicoene; or The Silent Woman, edited by L.A. Beaurline, Lincoln, Nebraska, 1966 (Regents Renaissance Drama Series).
Epicoene, edited by Edward Partridge, New Haven, Connecticut, 1971 (The Yale Ben Jonson).
Epicoene; or, The Silent Woman, edited by R.V. Holdsworth, London, 1979 (New Mermaid Series).
Epicoene; or, The Silent Woman, in *The Selected Plays of Ben Jonson*, *1* edited by Johanna Procter, Cambridge, 1989.

Criticism
(For general works on the author, see *Playwrights* volume)

Articles:
Oscar James Campbell, "The Relation of *Epicoene* to Aretino's *Il Marescalco*", in *Publications of the Modern Language Association* [*PMLA*], 46, 1931.
Edward B. Partridge, "The Allusiveness of *Epicoene*", in *English Literary History*, vol. 22 no.2, 1955.
Jonas A. Barish, "Ovid, Juvenal and *The Silent Woman*", in *Publications of the Modern Language Association* [*PMLA*], vol. 71 no. 1, 1956.

Thomas Kranidas, "Possible Revisions or Additions in Jonson's *Epicoene*", in *Anglia*, 83, 1965.
Ian Donaldson, "'A Martyr's Resolution': Jonson's *Epicoene*", in *Review of English Studies*, 18, 1967.
L.G. Salingar, "Farce and Fashion in *The Silent Woman*", in *Essays in Theatre* (new series), 20, 1967.
Michael Taylor, "Jonson's *Epicoene*: Art For Nature's Sake", in *Humanities Association Bulletin*, 20, 1969.
Mark A. Anderson, "The Successful Unity of *Epicoene*: A Defense of Ben Jonson", in *Studies in English Literature 1500–1900*, 10, 1970.
John Ferns, "Ovid, Juvenal, and *The Silent Woman*: A Reconsideration", in *Modern Language Review*, 65, 1970.
William E. Slights, "*Epicoene* and the Prose Paradox", in *Philological Quarterly*, 49, 1970.
Michael Shapiro, "Audience vs. Dramatist in Jonson's *Epicoene* and Other Plays of the Children's Troupes", in *English Language Review*, 3, 1973.
W. David Kay, "Jonson's Urbane Gallants: Humanistic Contexts for *Epicoene*", in *Huntington Library Quarterly*, 39, 1976.
Alexander Leggatt, "Morose and His Tormentors", in *University of Toronto Quarterly*, 45, 1976.
Huston D. Hallahan, "Silence, Eloquence, and Chatter in Jonson's *Epicoene*", in *Huntington Library Quarterly*, 40, 1977.
Emrys James, "The First West End Comedy", in *Proceedings of the British Academy*, 68, 1982.
Michael Flachmann, "*Epicoene*: A Comic Hell For a Comic Sinner", in *Medieval and Renaissance Drama in England*, 1, 1984.
Barbara C. Millard, "'An Acceptable Violence': Sexual Contest in Jonson's *Epicoene*", in *Medieval and Renaissance Drama in England*, 1, 1984.
Julita Rydlewska, "*Epicoene* and the Craft of Comedy", in *Studia Anglica Posnaniensa*, 18, 1986.
P.K. Ayers, "Dreams of the City: The Urban and the Urbane in Jonson's *Epicoene*", in *Philological Quarterly*, 66, 1987.
Philip Mirabelli, "Silence, Wit, and Wisdom in *The Silent Woman*", in *Studies in English Literature 1500–1900*, vol. 29 no.2, 1989.
Karen Newman, "City Talk: Women and Commodification in Jonson's *Epicoene*", in *English Literary History*, vol. 56 no. 3, 1989.

*   *   *

Ben Jonson's comedy *Epicoene* (1609) followed his brilliant satire *Volpone* by three years and preceded his equally dazzling farce *The Alchemist* by one. Though *Epicoene* does not represent as stunning a dramatic achievement as either of those works, it nonetheless cultivates distinctly fresh territory in human behaviour from which to draw laughter.

The plot follows a "theme and variations" format. Morose, a wealthy gentleman of London, detests all loud sounds and so has insulated his home with bizarre padding devices to muffle even ordinary house noises. Unmarried and without offspring of his own, Morose has only his nephew Sir Dauphine Eugenie as heir. But Sir Dauphine is something of a playboy, surrounded by other merry (and loud) young men about town (Clerimont and Truewit), so that Morose is uneasy about bequeathing all his goods to him. Then, when particularly annoyed with Sir Dauphine, Morose determines to marry and produce offspring of his own to inherit his wealth. Sir Dauphine apparently goes along with his uncle's decision and offers to help find a suitable wife—that is, a demure woman who speaks very little (*Epicoene* is sub-titled *the Silent*

Woman). With his nephew's "help", Morose locates a young girl named Epicoene who apparently fulfills his requirements. A marriage ceremony is conducted and Morose looks forward to outmanoeuvring his dilettante nephew. But Epicoene immediately changes her manner, becoming an outspoken feminist who surrounds herself with gossipy society women. Morose's home suddenly overflows with gallants and ladies, coming and going to be entertained by Epicoene. Morose rues his decision to marry Epicoene and when Morose declares he can stand the situation no longer and begs to be divorced on his very wedding day, Sir Dauphine again offers to help. In return for working out a guaranteed easy divorce for his uncle, Sir Dauphine is to be reinstated as Morose's sole heir. Finally, Sir Dauphine then pulls off Epicoene's disguise to reveal that "she" actually is a young boy—hence the marriage is invalidated and Sir Dauphine is new master of the house.

The characteristics of classical New Comedy can be discerned in the play. A grumpy older, richer character (*senex iratus*) tries to compete with a young man (*adulescens*) in the arena of love, only to be outwitted and defeated. In the process of losing the love battle, the older man also loses his wealth to the youth, to precipitate a new society mirroring the values of the younger generation. There is also another technique found in Jonson's other works. Jonson is well known for popularising the theory of "humours" as a comic device in drama. That theory claims that an imbalance in one's bodily fluids (humours) leads to a corresponding imbalance in one's personality. For Jonson any form of erratic conduct is an appropriate target for laughter. Morose ranks his prospective brides according to how quiet they remain, revealing idiosyncracy. Moreover, Jonson plumbs the full humour of Morose's eccentricity by describing the old man's attempts to maintain silence in his home. First, he has all his floors padded, and stuffed pillows strapped to all the stairs. He places barriers at one end of his street to inhibit carriage or wagon traffic past his house. And when his wife, Epicoene, invites noisy bedlam into his home, he climbs to the attic where he is described as being perched on a rafter like an owl, with pillows covering his ears.

Epicoene includes novel as well as familiar features. When first staged at Whitefriars, the comedy was performed by the Children of the Queen's Revels, an all-boy troupe. The title *Epicoene* therefore resonates with comic irony, as does the disguise of a boy playing a girl. And, of course, *all* the female roles in the play were then performed by boys. One important women's club in the play is comprised of Lady Haughty, Lady Centaur, and Mistress Mavis who call themselves the Ladies Collegiates. The members are loud, aggressive, bossy, and concerned only with arranging sexual trysts with handsome young men in their society circuit. Their meetings—some of which are depicted in the play—are devoted to identifying new, good-looking men in town, devising how to gain their company, and how to avoid pregnancy by using contraceptive means. The men in *Epicoene*, in contrast, tend to seem demasculinised. Sir John Daw and Sir Amorous La Foole are braggarts from classical comedy, insisting that they have enjoyed love affairs with all the important women in London. In the course of the play, Dauphine and his friends arrange to show up these boasters for what they are, mere talkers with no conquests whatsoever. And even Dauphine and his colleagues Clerimont and Truewit appear strangely asexual. Their ultra-refined tastes and senses of humour reflect no gender, just pure intellect. As a consequence, *Epicoene* is a rare work for the theatre that generates an atmosphere of total androgyny throughout—ironically in keeping with the boys' company.

Epicoene is set in an aristocratic London household, not the middle-class shops of *Every Man in His Humour*, or the upper middle-class dwelling of Lovewit in *The Alchemist*, or the palazzo of a grandee like Volpone. Jonson implies that folly reigns among the rich as well as among the modest. As usual with Jonson, his language is masterful, and he creates character through apt diction and speech rhythms. But *Epicoene* can seem laboured in parts because of some excessively long passages, usually written in prose. When Jonson takes too much delight in his command of rhetoric, he is subject to overwriting. Despite its excessive length, though, *Epicoene* has many fresh images of human nonsense to show its audiences.

—C.J. Gianakaris

EQUUS
by Peter Shaffer

First Publication: London, 1973.
First Production: Old Vic Theatre (National Theatre Company), London, July 1973.

Criticism
(For general works on the author, see *Playwrights* volume)

Articles:
J. Alexis Burland, "Discussion of Papers on *Equus*", in *International Journal of Psychoanalytic Psychotherapy*, 5, 1976.
Sanford Gifford, " 'Pop' Psychoanalysis, *Kitsch*, and the 'as if' Theater: Further notes on Peter Shaffer's *Equus*", in *International Journal of Psychoanalytic Psychotherapy*, 5, 1976.
Jules Glenn, "Alan Strang as an Adolescent: A Discussion of Peter Shaffer's *Equus*", in *International Journal of Psychoanalytic Psychotherapy*, 5, 1976.
Jacob E. Slutzky, "*Equus* and the Psychotherapy of Passion", in *International Journal of Psychoanalytic Psychotherapy*, 5, 1976.
James R. Stacy, "The Sun and the Horse: Peter Shaffer's Search for Worship", in *Educational Theatre Journal*, 28, 1976.
Julian L. Stamm, "Peter Shaffer's *Equus*—A Psychoanalytic Exploration", in *International Journal Of Psychoanalytic Psychotherapy*", 5, 1976.
John Corbally, "The *Equus* Ethic", in *New Laurel Review*, vol. 7 no.2, 1977.
Barbara Lounsberry, " 'God-Hunting': The Chaos of Worship in Peter Shaffer's *Equus* and *Royal Hunt of the Sun*", in *Modern Drama*, vol.21 no.1, 1978.
Hélène M. Baldwin, "*Equus*: Theater of Cruelty or Theater of Sensationalism?", in *West Virginia University Philological Papers*, 25, 1979.
Jeffrey Berman, "*Equus*: 'After such little forgiveness what knowledge?' ", in *Psychoanalytic Review*, vol.66 no.3, 1979.
James W. Hamilton, "*Equus* and the Creative Process", in *Journal of the Philadelphia Association for Psychoanalysis*, 6, 1979.
Neil Timm, "*Equus* as a Modern Tragedy", in *West Virginia University Philological Papers*, 25, 1979.
Barry B. Whitman, "The Anger in *Equus*", in *Modern Drama*, vol.22 no.1, 1979.
Margaret A. Emelson, "A Horse of a Different Color: A Critique of Peter Shaffer's *Equus*", in *Journal of Evolutionary Psychology*, vol.1, no.2, 1980.

Equus: National Theatre, London, 1976

Gene A. Plunka, "The Existential Ritual: Peter Shaffer's *Equus*", in *Kansas Quarterly*, 12, 1980.

I. Dean Ebner, "The Double Crisis of Sexuality and Worship in Shaffer's *Equus*", in *Christianity and Literature*, 31, 1982.

Dennis A. Klein, "Peter Shaffer's *Equus* as a Modern Aristotelian Tragedy", in *Studies in Iconography*, 9, 1983.

Una Chaudhuri, "The Spectator in Drama/Drama in the Spectator", in *Modern Drama*, 27, 1984.

Doyle M. Walls, "*Equus*: Shaffer, Nietzsche, and the Neuroses of Health", in *Modern Drama*, 27, 1984.

Anthony V. Corello, "*Equus*: The Ritual Sacrifice of the Male Child", in *Psychoanalytic Review*, 73, 1986.

*   *   *

A chance remark by a friend at the BBC led Peter Shaffer to write *Equus* (1973). The friend recounted a news story about a youth in a provincial town outside London who, seemingly without cause, struck out the eyes of several horses in a stable. From that sketchy account, the author had the skeletal plot for what has become a modern classic. Two discrete but intertwined stories make up the plot. At the surface is the puzzle involving Alan Strang, an apparently unexceptional youth, who has been ordered to a psychiatric hospital in southern England because of a heinous crime: the blinding of six horses at the stables where he worked. The courts could determine no justifiable reason for the abhorrent deed; so it becomes the task of the psychiatrists to figure out—and treat—the cause. Hesther Salomon, a magistrate and confidante, asks Martin Dysart to take on young Strang since the other doctors are too repulsed by the boy's act to provide him with objective care. Against his better judgement, Dysart agrees.

Most of the 21 scenes which comprise the first act are given over to Dr. Dysart's investigation of the conflicts that led to the incident. Shaffer's earlier predilection for detective tales is evident here, because in any overview *Equus* closely resembles the suspense thriller. Dysart is the sleuth who tracks down, step by step, those factors in Alan Strang's life that eventually led him to destroy the animals. Through hypnosis, abreaction, and alleged "truth drugs", Dysart ultimately isolates the psychic sources for Alan's aberrant behaviour, a form of psychosexual disfunction: and the shorter second act (14 scenes) embodies the psychiatrist's regimen—a carefully staged abreaction—which relieves the boy of his problem. In Shaffer's dramatic construct, however, concurrent with his discovering Alan's underlying problems, Dysart comes to realise his own dilemma—the second story in the plot. The psychiatrist is undergoing a crisis of conscience growing out of disillusionment with himself, his profession, and contemporary society. Despite his reservations, Dysart does "cure" Alan as the play ends. Yet it is obvious that ridding the boy of his mental conflicts only reverts them onto Dysart himself. *Equus* ends with Shaffer's patented resolution—that is, no resolution in a rudderless universe.

Equus does not enjoy the large cast and multiple plots of some of Shaffer's other important works such as *Royal Hunt of the Sun* and *Amadeus*. But a new conciseness and tight focus are gained. The central theme of *Equus* concerns Shaffer's favourite subject, man's aspiring to reach a knowable god whose existence implies a universal order. As is typical with Shaffer, the full story in the plot requires at least two, conflicting protagonists, and in fact, here, there are three. Alan Strang is the nominal center of the story since it is the diagnosis and curing of his psychological problems that constitute the main action of the play. Yet a greater drama arises in the soul of Dr. Dysart whose spiritual anguish is even greater than Alan's. Shaffer frames a three-part puzzle at the play's outset. On stage, in the background, stands a living tableau of a teenage boy nuzzling a horse-figure; in the foreground sits Dysart at his desk in a hospital. Dysart points to the pair behind him, noting that the boy, not the horse, holds the key to Dysart's own dilemma. Dysart directly addresses the audience: "I'm lost. . .I'm desperate. . .In a way, it has nothing to do with this boy. The doubts have been there for years". From the play's first lines, the playwright establishes that the play involves the interlocked lives of these three figures—the ailing boy, the purportedly healing physician, and the mysterious horse-deity.

Dysart's investigations show that part of Alan's mental aberration concerns a bizarre personal worship he initiates with a horse—Equus—as god. Alan's father is a confirmed agnostic who undercuts the Christian religious beliefs which Dora, the boy's mother, insists on. At the same time, the youth's first horse ride proved sexually stimulating to him. In a primitive, natural fashion, Alan fuses the two chief forces in his life—worship and sex—into a single figure: the god Equus. By sneaking horseback rides at night in the nude, Alan ritualises his adoration of the horse-god while also experiencing a form of auto-eroticism. The curtain scene for the first act depicts Strang's amazing form of religio-sexual worship when Dysart gets the boy, in hypnosis, to expose his hidden desires. In highly stylised fashion, Alan—naked—rides on the shoulders of the "horse"—actually an actor wearing a metallic headpiece denoting a horse's head. As "horse" and rider frenetically circle the stage space, Alan cries out in religious and sexual ecstacy at the moment of climax.

Dysart then understands the basis for the boy's strange behaviour. Now the dilemma begins to be a professional one for the doctor: whether to permit Alan his personal form of worship or to destroy his home-made religion in order to return him to society's conventions. Moreover, Dysart begins to see how tepid his own life is compared to Alan's. Dysart tells Hesther, "Without worship you shrink, it's as brutal as that. . .I shrank my *own* life. No one can do it for you. I settled for being pallid and provincial, out of my own eternal timidity. . . .But that boy has known a passion more ferocious than I have felt in any second of my life. And let me tell you something: I envy it". But Hesther convinces Dysart to do his professional duty. As a paid agent of society, he is expected to mend his patients's minds and souls, allowing them to live in harmony with society. A final scene of abreaction near the end of *Equus* shows Alan stabbing out the eyes of the stylised horse figures; the boy thereby purges himself of his nightmares for good. For freeing Alan from his self-made spiritual world, however, Dysart is forced into a life of self-doubt. The gripping drama ends with the doctor announcing to the audience in horror, "There is now, in my mouth, this sharp chain. And it never comes out".

Equus marks the perfecting of Shaffer's use of narrative frame in his dramas. Dysart plays a dual-role as participant in the inner story concerning Alan's psychological conundrum but is also a narrator who can step outside the plot's action to address playgoers directly. The prime benefit of such a dual-level format is its flexibility in moving the plot through space and time. Even more urgent in *Equus* is the perfecting of Shaffer's concept of Apollonian and Dionysian characteristics in human nature. Alan Strang epitomises the Dionysian—that which is creative, intuitive, inspirational. Dysart is the Apollonian—ordered, premeditated, systematic. Like Shaffer's other major works, *Equus* provides audiences with provocative themes and gripping theatrical images on stage.

—C. J. Gianakaris

DER ERDGEIST.   See **THE LULU PLAYS.**

DIE ERMITTLUNG.   See **THE INVESTIGATION.**

EUMENIDES.   See **THE ORESTEIA.**

EVERY MAN IN HIS HUMOUR
by Ben Jonson

First Publication: London, 1601; revised version in *The Workes of Benjamin Jonson*, London, 1616.
First Production: London (Lord Chamberlain's Men), c. September 1598; revised version, Court of James I, London, February 1605.

Editions
Every Man in His Humour, edited by Percy Simpson, Oxford, 1919.
Every Man in His Humour, edited by Henry Holland Carter, New Haven, Connecticut, 1921.
Every Man in His Humour, edited by R.S. Knox, London, 1923; second edition, 1949.
Every Man in His Humour, edited by G.B Harrison, London, 1926.
Every Man in His Humour, edited by Arthur Sale, London, 1941; second edition, 1949.
Every Man in His Humour, edited by Martin Seymour-Smith, London, 1966 (New Mermaid Series).
Every Man in His Humour, edited by Gabriele Bernhard Jackson, New Haven, Connecticut, and London, 1969.
Every Man in His Humour, edited by J.W. Lever, Lincoln, Nebraska, 1971 (Regents Renaissance Drama Series).
Every Man in His Humour: A Parallel Edition of the 1601 Quarto and the 1616 Folio, edited by J.W. Lever, London, 1972.

Criticism
(For general works on the author, see *Playwrights* volume)

Articles:
Sallie Sewell, "The Relation Between *The Merry Wives of Windsor* and Jonson's *Every Man in His Humour*", in *South Atlantic Bulletin*, 16, 1941.
Martin Kallich, "Unity of Time in *Every Man in his Humour* and *Cynthia's Revels*", in *Modern Language Notes*, 57, 1942.
Henry L. Smuggs, "The Comic Humours: A New Interpretation", in *Publications of Modern Language Association* [*PMLA*], vol.62 no.1, 1947.
J.A. Bryant, "Jonson's Revision of *Every Man in His Humour*", in *Studies in Philology*, 59, 1962.
O.B. Hardison, "Three Types of Renaissance Catharsis", in *Renaissance Drama* (new series), 2, 1969.
Lawrence L. Levin, "Clement Justice in *Every Man in His Humour*", in *Studies in English Literature 1500–1900*, 12, 1972.
John S. Colley, "Opinion, Poetry, and Folly in *Every Man in His Humour*", in *South Atlantic Bulletin*, 39, 1974.
A. Richard Dutton, "The Significance of Jonson's Revision of *Every Man in His Humour*", in *Modern Language Review*, 69, 1974.
P. Hyland, "A Possible Source of Jonson's *Every Man in His Humour* (1601)", in *Notes and Queries*, vol.26, no.2, 1979.
D. Heyward Brook, "Ben Jonson's Humor Plays and the Dramatic Adaptation of Pastoral", in *English Miscellany*, 28–29, 1979–80.

*   *   *

This is an Elizabethan city comedy, orchestrating a dozen sharply delineated types in a centreless network of interlinked plots. The structure can be traced back, somewhat arbitrarily, to the figure of Wellbred, a witty young gentleman without responsibilities who disrupts the orderly life of the city by leading the mildly scandalous life of a "gallant" while staying in the house of Kitely, his tensely respectable, citizen brother-in-law. He invites his like-minded friend Edward Kno'well, and they amuse themselves by entertaining a retinue of fools and would-be gentlemen, including the grotesque fake-soldier, Bobadill. The presence of this motley gathering affects all the members of the household: Kitely becomes insanely fearful for his wife's chastity; Wellbred's rustic brother Squire Downright is intolerably provoked by the fools and gets in a

Every Man in His Humour: Charles Dickens as Captain Bobadil, St James's Theatre, London, 1845 (amateur production)

fight with them; and Kitely's sister Bridget makes a runaway marriage with Edward. Meanwhile, Edward's father, fearing that his son is being drawn into evil ways, pursues him to the city, where he spends the whole of the play failing to catch up with him because of the machinations of his servant Brainworm, a trickster and disguise-artist in the manner of Roman comedy, who has decided to throw in his lot with the son rather than the father. Eventually the entire cast assembles at the house of Justice Clement, accurately described in the *dramatis personae* as "an old merry magistrate", who presides over the unravelling of the accumulated misunderstandings and the reconciliation of everybody.

Jonson's title identifies, with characteristic critical self-awareness, the play's comic method. "Humour" is a theory which links behaviour to the balance of fluids in the body; it thus introduces into dramatic characterisation a principle which is at once arbitrary and unlimited. Downright's aggression, and Kitely's jealousy, are unstoppable because of the sense in which they are not responses to circumstances, but irreducible personal drives. The effect in Kitely's case (the most serious part of the text psychologically) is farcical and pathetic at the same time: he isn't a fool, and he can see how irrational suspicions are distorting his vision, but there's nothing he can do about it. Bobadill is a different version of the

same paradox: it's perfectly obvious that he's a cowardly scrounger, but in projecting himself as a world-beating duellist he isn't exactly lying—rather, his fantasy of absolute, gladiatorial mastery is a role which he lives. It's not surprising that Charles Dickens played the part with great enthusiasm and success; its tone is oddly proleptic of Dickens's own ultimately innocent monomaniacs.

The social matrix of all this gratuitous self-expression is the same in Dickens and Jonson: both are, in both senses, writers of London. (The first version of *Every Man* was formally set in Florence, but when Jonson revised it a decade or so later and anglicised it, he was only bringing it home to what had evidently been its real setting all along.) The city of the play is full of the institutions and habits—smoking, fashion, publishing, "buzz-words", pawnbrokers, water-carriers, suburbs, restaurants, voluntary societies, municipal law enforcement, the Royal Exchange—which, taken together, constitute at once a new urban environment and the necessary conditions of the plot. Within this environment—and within this plot—social contact is not so much a matter of relationships within a shared communal or hierarchical framework as a random sequence of collisions between nonconformable identities and codes. People bump into one another, mistake each other's meanings, invade each other's space. To an extraordinary extent, the action depends on multiplying situations in which one character doesn't know where—or often who—another character is. London appears as a place which offers unlimited opportunities for getting lost, literally or culturally, and also for deception, since the general unfixedness of social roles renders individuals uncheckable. Brainworm, despite a fairly marginal function in the plot, is thematically central as the virtuoso of this last possibility: for him, the streets are liberating because, "translated thus from a poor creature to a creator", he can be anyone he chooses. In short, the city is anarchically individuating, which is miserable for those who are seeking to confirm some kind of natural authority (such as Old Kno'well over his son, or Kitely over his wife), but enjoyable for those who adopt social space as "a mart, / A theatre, a public receptacle / For giddy humour"—that is, the knowing fantasists (the wits), the unknowing fantasists (the fools), and, by implication, the audience. We all make ourselves up, shopping around for the phrases, clothes and companions we like, every man in his humour. Every *man*, it should be added, because the common receptacle of humours is always a latently violent place: when the wandering identities do collide, one is usually gulling, humiliating, threatening or beating another. A "man" is, or rather ought to be, someone who can take care of himself, verbally and physically; it's a masculine conception of individuality; the women's roles in the play are small and indistinct.

The subtlest version of humour is the anti-humourist with whom the play begins, Old Kno'well. Perhaps because of his own ambivalence about the mores Old Kno'well disapproves of, Jonson doesn't simply make him the easily derided old man (*senex*) of Plautine or Italian comedy. Rather, he fits him into that dramatic position (he is gulled, he fights a losing battle against the natural vitality of his heir, he is at last forced to consent to a marriage which took place without his knowledge, etc.), but then *writes* the role as an anthology of skilfully worked imitations from Juvenal, so that the old man's strictures on "the age" are both energetic and authoritative. The effect is curiously dislocated, as the discursive forcefulness of Old Kno'well's first few scenes tails out into practical ineffectuality once the plot gets under way. This is again an example of London's "randomising" of relationships. The dramatic condition of Old Kno'well's rhetorical authority has been his status as the head of an out-of-town household, his humanist Latinity that of a paterfamilias. As such, his disapproval of Edward's way of life carries weight. But once he has come to London, Wellbred can dismiss him: "an' our wits be so wretchedly dull that one old plodding brain can outstrip us all, would we were e'en press'd, to make porters of; and serve out the rest of our days in Thames Street". This explicitly urban frame of reference is competitive rather than hierarchical, and makes status depend on quick-wittedness rather than either seniority or wisdom, so that while Old Kno'well's values are not exactly overturned, they are deprived of influence; his speeches are no longer a form of truth, but merely reflect the way he happens to see things—his humour.

It's clear that despite its physiological basis, "humour" is, as one minor character comments, "bred in the special gallantry of our time". In the revised version of the play especially, the individual humours are neatly differentiated socially: the imagery of Kitely's jealousy connects it with his merchant's terror of being over-reached and losing his credit; the squire's "downrightness" is at once "choler" and a country impatience with metropolitan affectation; the fool's determination to be melancholy is a panicky reaction to the way style seems to be supplanting birth as the most important criterion of gentility. The play might be seen as a rather early, "bourgeois" comedy of individual character, were it not for the fact that Jonson's conservatism identifies individuality as both socially determined and inherently funny.

—Peter Womack

EVERYMAN
Anonymous

First Publication: England, probably c. 1520; earliest surviving edition, c.1528–29.
First Production: Unknown

Editions
"Elckerlijk", A Fifteenth Century Dutch Morality and "Everyman", edited by H. Logeman, 1892.
Everyman, in *Three Medieval Plays*, edited by John Allen, London, 1953.
Everyman, in *Everyman and Medieval Miracle Plays*, edited by A.C. Cawley, London and New York, 1956.
Everyman, in *Mystery and Morality Plays*, edited by Martin E. Browne, New York, 1960.
Everyman, edited by A.C. Cawley, Manchester, 1961 (Old and Middle English Texts); second edition, 1977.
The Summoning of Everyman, edited by Geoffrey Cooper and Christopher Wortham, Nedlands, Western Australia, 1980.
Everyman, in *Three Late Medieval Morality Plays*, edited by G.A. Lester, London and New York, 1981. (New Mermaid Series).

Criticism

Books:
Henry de Vocht, *"Everyman": A Comparative Study of Texts and Sources*, Louvain, 1947.
Jozef Van Mierlo, *De Prioriteit van "Elckerlyck" tegenover "Everyman" gebandhaafd*, Antwerp, 1948.
Genji Takahashi, *A Study of "Everyman" with Special Reference to its Plot*, Tokyo, 1953.
Donald Gilman (ed.), *"Everyman" and Company*, 1989.

Articles:
Francis A. Wood, "*Elckerlyc-Everyman*: The Question of Priority", in *Modern Philology*, 8, 1910.
E.R. Tigg, "Is *Elckerlijc* Prior to *Everyman*?", in *Journal of English and Germanic Philology*, 38, 1939.
R.W. Zandvoort, "*Everyman-Elckerlijc*", in *Etudes anglaises*, 6, 1953.
Helen Adolf, "From *Everyman* to *Elckerlijc* to Hofmannsthal and Kafka", in *Comparative Literature*, 9, 1957.
Lawrence V. Ryan, "Doctrine and Dramatic Structure in *Everyman*", in *Speculum*, 32, 1957.
David Kaula, "Time and The Timeless in *Everyman* and *Dr. Faustus*", in *College English*, 22, 1960.
Helen S. Thomas, "The Meaning of the Character 'Knowledge' in *Everyman*", in *Mississippi Quarterly*, 14, 1961.
Helen S. Thomas, "Some Analogues of *Everyman*", in *Mississippi Quarterly*, 16, 1963.
Thomas F. Van Laan, "*Everyman*: A Structural Analysis", in *Publications of the Modern Language Association [PMLA]*, 78, 1963.
John Conley, "The Doctrine of Friendship in *Everyman*", in *Speculum*, 44, 1969.

Allen D. Goldhamer, "*Everyman*: A Dramatization of Death", in *Classica et Mediaevalia*, 30, 1969.

Dennis V. Moran, "The Life of Everyman", in *Neophilologus*, 56, 1972.

Michael J. Warren, "*Everyman*: Knowledge Once More", in *Dalhousie Review*, 54, 1974.

Earl G. Schreiber, "*Everyman* in America", in *Comparative Drama*, 9, 1975.

Thomas J. Jambeck, "*Everyman* and the Implications of Bernardine Humanism in the Character of 'Knowledge'", in *Medievalia et Humanistica*, 8, 1977.

Cheryl Frost, "*Everyman* in Performance", in *Literature in North Queensland*, 6, 1978.

Shirley Kossock, "The Morality Play: *Everyman*", in *Communique* (Pietersburg), vol.5 no.1, 1980.

C.J. Wortham, "*Everyman* and the Reformation", in *Parergon*, 29, 1981.

Donald F. Duclow, "*Everyman* and the *Ars Moriendi*: Fifteenth Century Ceremonies of Dying", in *Fifteenth-Century Studies*, 6, 1983.

Richard Hillman, "*Everyman* and the Energies of Stasis", in *Florilegium*, 7, 1985.

Willie Manson, "Knowing and Doing in *Everyman*", in *The Chaucer Review*, vol.19 no.3, 1985.

Phoebe S. Spinrad, "The Last Temptation of *Everyman*", in *Philological Quarterly*, vol.64 no.2, 1985.

Stanton B. Garner Jr., "Theatricality in *Mankind* and *Everyman*", in *Studies in Philology*, 84, 1987.

John Cunningham, "Comedic and Liturgical Restoration in *Everyman*", in *Comparative Drama*, 22, 1988.

*   *   *

Everyman follows the Dutch *Elckerlijc*, from which it is translated, but adds a prologue that introduces the action and announces the moral emphasis on the ending of life at which time all men (and women) will be brought to "a generall rekeninge". God then speaks—a character that made this play problematic early in the 20th century when William Poel produced it, since the deity was at that time forbidden by law to appear on the English stage—to complain of mankind's unhappy condition, which leads him to announce that consequently humans will face a reckoning and he calls up Death to be his messenger. As in the Dance of Death scenes in late medieval art Death comes to Everyman to announce that on this day his life is to be terminated and that he will be accountable for the way in which he has lived his life. Everyman, who is unready, first requests Fellowship, and then Kindred and Cousin to accompany him—requests that will not be honored—while Goods, whom he has loved inordinately, advises him that he cannot come with him—and if he did, he would be the cause of more harm than good. On the other hand, Good Deeds, though too weak to be of assistance, has a sister, Knowledge, who offers hope by taking Everyman to Confession and giving him the scourge of penance. Everyman will now put on the garment of contrition, and thereupon his Good Deeds will be revived and made strong. Everyman will also receive the help of Beauty, Discretion, Strength, and Five Wits, and will go to a clergyman (offstage) for Holy Communion. However, in the end all desert him except Good Deeds as he commits his soul to God with the assurance that he will be welcomed into heaven by angels.

Elckerlijc, the source of *Everyman*, is an example of *Rederijker* drama produced by the Dutch Rhetoricians (nearly 600 extant plays of this type have been reported). The play is based on the legend of Barlaam and Josaphat as it appears in the collection of Christian saints' lives known as *The Golden Legend*. Derived from a Buddhist parable of a man who has been summoned before a king (i.e. God), the story tells of three friends whom he has asked to accompany him—friends who are identified as Riches, Kindred, and Good Works. Only Good Works will be faithful to him on his journey.

As a morality play, *Everyman* presents a lively picture of humanity when staged that differentiates it from the anaemic abstractions that are often associated with this kind of allegorical drama. Part of the difficulty comes from a crucial misunderstanding of *allegory* in post-18th-century thought, since in fact a drama such as *Everyman* (like the 15th-century English moralities, *The Castle of Perseverance* and *Mankind*) can be seen to embody real human experience when played by live actors on stage. This was the discovery that came with Poel's highly successful production—a production that later became celebrated in America as well as in England. This production influenced George Bernard Shaw and also inspired the writing by Hugo von Hofmannsthal of *Jedermann* (*Everyman*), a modern adaptation that was produced by Max Reinhardt in the cathedral square at Salzburg. The staging suggested by the text of *Everyman* has also been a strong influence on the structure of many modern theaters, which have tended to offer a more flexible acting space than the 19th century proscenium-arch stage would allow.

Everyman is a product of the 15th– and early 16th–century social and religious context. Death was much emphasized in the religious art and sermons of the time, as well it might be since mortality rates were then exceptionally high. Such themes emphasizing death need to be seen in part as a deterrent to self-indulgence and as an argument for the holy life. Death, as in the play, is often pictured as a cadaver holding a dart or spear, which will be used to stab the man chosen to die; this also happens in *The Castle of Perseverance*.

The dramatic structure evident in *Everyman* is that of life triumphing over death especially through the assistance of Knowledge, Good Deeds, and Discretion as well as the Sacraments of the Church. These testify to a rather heavy Catholic emphasis as well as to the stress on charity as necessary activity for men and women of means during the period when the play was written. However, the universality of the play and its flexibility have been demonstrated in Poel's production in which Everyman was played by a woman, and in Robert Benedetti's production for the 1974–75 season at the Guthrie Theater in Minneapolis in which the actors in the drama took turns playing him. The play appeals to audiences because of its fine use of language and because of its optimistic confrontation with the ultimate reality of human life— the fact of death.

—Clifford Davidson

THE FACTORY LAD
by John Walker

First Publication: In *Duncombe's British Theatre 11*.
First Production: Surrey Theatre, London, 15 October 1832.

Editions

The Factory Lad, in *English Plays of The Nineteenth Century, 1*, edited by Michael R. Booth, London, 1969.
The Factory Lad, in *"The Magistrate" and Other Nineteenth Century Plays*, edited by Michael R. Booth, 1974.

* * *

The Factory Lad is a melodrama in two acts. A group of workmen in a northern cotton mill are dismissed by their new employer, Westwood, because he is installing steam-powered looms. The desperate workmen, afraid of poverty and starvation, conspire to revenge themselves on Westwood, break into his premises, smash the machinery, and set the mill on fire. They are led by a half-crazed poacher and outcast, Will Rushton, who has suffered under the injustices of the Poor Laws. The arsonists are hunted down by soldiers and caught; the suffering wife of the nominal hero, George Allen, goes mad. The arrested men are brought before a corrupt justice of the peace, Bias. He is denounced by Rushton, who then shoots Westwood dead after the latter has spurned the frantic pleas of Jane Allen for mercy.

The Factory Lad is a notable example, the first of its kind, of the drama of industrial conflict, a sub-genre which has stretched from this play through John Galsworthy's *Strife* to Howard Brenton's *Weapons of Happiness* and much television drama. The play antedates the novel of industrial misery and struggle by several years. Frances Trollope's *Michael Armstrong, the Factory Boy* was not published until 1840, and Disraeli's *Sybil* and Mrs Gaskell's *Mary Barton* followed in the same decade. Like much socially radical, domestic melodrama, *The Factory Lad* treats events of some years before: the Luddites began smashing power looms in 1811 and again after 1815, but class hostility, a feature of industrial relations as well as of melodrama throughout the century, was a social theme of great importance throughout the pre-Victorian and Victorian periods. The enmity between master and worker in industrial melodrama echoes that between peer and commoner, or squire and peasant in other domestic melodrama, and *The Factory Lad* is typical of the melodrama of class conflict.

The villain of *The Factory Lad* is therefore a factory owner, and the hero a humble workman: character stereotypes quite appropriate to melodrama. Westwood is not only ruthless to his employees, despite the fact that his father (from whom he has just inherited the factory) was a good, kind master, but is also awaiting the arrival of a French chef for his household, a sign of heartless self-indulgence, while his former employees and their families go without bread. Without employment, their only recourse is the sort of meagre and grudging parish charity meted out to poor Will Rushton, a recourse angrily rejected by the men and by George Allen, whose wife and two small children function to enhance the predicament of his poverty and introduce a strong note of pathos. Yet although Westwood is a villain, his economic arguments command respect: an owner must survive bad times by retrenchment and increasing productivity—thus the use of machinery. In melodrama, however, where social good and evil are always personalised and made manifest through individual behaviour, economic questions and larger social issues are always subordinated to the actual struggle between good and bad characters, and here there is no question where the sympathy of the audience and reader should lie—with Allen and his workmates, not with the cost-efficiency minded Westwood.

Certain essential characteristics of melodrama are however, missing from *The Factory Lad*. There is no comic relief and no happy ending, and nothing is left for the workmen and Rushton at the end of the play but the gallows or transportation. Indeed, the play can be seen as more a tragedy than a domestic melodrama, and is written with considerable power and a feeling for the industrial working class. Furthermore, *The Factory Lad* is unusual in the development of melodrama in that the "hero" is not really George Allen but a collective—the group of five dismissed workmen.

—Michael R. Booth

———

FADREN. See **THE FATHER.**

———

THE FAIRGROUND BOOTH. See **THE PUPPET SHOW.**

———

THE FAIR MAID OF THE WEST; or, A Girl Worth Gold,
   Parts One and Two
by Thomas Heywood

Part One
First Publication: London, 1631.
First Production: London, before 1610.

Part Two
First Publication: London, 1631.
First Production: London, c. 1597–1610.

Editions
The Fair Maid of the West, in "*A Woman Killed with Kindness*"
   and "The Fair Maid of the West" [Part One only], edited by
   Katharine Lee Bates, Boston, New York, and Chicago,
   1917.
The Fair Maid of the West [Parts One and Two], edited by
   Robert K. Turner Jr., Lincoln, Nebraska, 1968 (Regents
   Renaissance Drama Series).
The Fair Maid of the West, Part 1, edited by Brownell
   Salomon, Salzburg, 1975.

Criticism
(For general works on the author, see *Playwrights* volume)

Articles:
W.E. Roberts, "Ballad Themes in *The Fair Maid of the West*",
   in *Journal of American Folklore*, 68, 1955.

*   *   *

The heroine of the title, Bess Bridges, a virtuous tavern
maid, is in love with Spencer, a gentleman, but they are
prevented from joining in marriage. When Spencer kills a
gallant in a brawl, he is forced to flee to the Azores where he is
wounded in a duel. His servant, Goodlack, charged with
returning to England and testing Bess's chastity, is won over by
her and enters her service. The lovers are finally reunited at the
court of Mullisheg, King of Fez. In *Part Two* the marriage is
once again thwarted as Mullisheg decides that he wants Bess
for himself. With the aid of their servants, Clem, Goodlack
and Roughman, Bess and Spencer foil Mullisheg's plans but
are separated in the process. After adventures in Italy and the
dissolution of a promise that disallows Spencer from acknowledging Bess, the lovers are reconciled and harmony is
restored.

A play of adventure and romance, *The Fair Maid of the West*
is a product of the euphoria that swept England in the late
Elizabethan period in the wake of The Earl of Essex's
successful military campaigns. Gallants anxious for military
glory flock the streets of Plymouth at the start of the play, and a
mood of patriotic fervour prevails. These nationalistic sentiments show themselves in admiring remarks made by the non-
English characters about English daring, valour and fortitude.
They are suggested, too, in unflattering reflections (from the
English characters) upon Spanish perfidity, Moorish incivility
and the Italian predilection for vengeance.

In keeping with the play's patriotic tone, a desire for honour
emerges as the dominant thematic interest. But it is not a
single, unitary definition of honour that Heywood explores.
The urge to gain renown, a need to denigrate personal
achievement, the will to preserve the Christian faith and the
thirst for admiration and respect come to be associated with
the drive to be perceived as honourable, and every character

understands honour according to his or her own requirements.
Materialistic language is given equal dramatic emphasis, and
monetary metaphors are insistently repeated. Jewels are the
subject of constant allusion and word-play as they connote
variously the gems themselves, Bess's chaste attachment to
Spencer, a treasured possession, and Clem's testicles. Booty
takes the form of gold in the imaginations of the English
gallants, but it quickly becomes apparent that Bess is of greater
value; she is worth more than gold, she outshines and outlasts
the deceptive glitter of bullion.

Alone, however, honour and gold do not account for the
separation of Bess and Spencer and their subsequent troubles.
Treated in detail in the play is a deeply-rooted suspicion of
women and the conviction that eventually they will prove fickle
and disloyal. This is the belief that prompts Spencer to enjoin
Goodlack to tempt Bess, that lies behind a series of misogynis-
tic comments upon women, and impels doubting male characters never to trust a woman's word. Part of Bess's achievement
is that she manages to challenge such assumptions and to
remain resilient in the face of masculine hostilities.

The position of women in the play is further complicated by
a series of oaths or promises made by the male characters
which constrains independent action and prohibits the spontaneous expression of emotions. Quick to form a contractual
agreement with another party, Spencer pledges to observe the
most rigorous kinds of deprivation in the cause of his
reputation and name. He is keen to be bound by oaths and,
when they are undertaken, to obey their stringent restrictions.
Thus he is forced to separate himself from Bess on numerous
occasions and to postpone repeatedly their union. By contrast,
Bess does not need to assert herself in such formal terms and
waits patiently until her lover's complications have been
resolved.

It is possible that Heywood, through Spencer, is mocking
the code of honour to which all of the male characters clamour
to subscribe. Certainly Spencer falls short of the typical,
Renaissance lover in several respects: he is first presented as a
gambler; he cannot contain himself from entering into affrays;
he flees from justice; he *actively* seeks to bring renown upon
himself; and he is intrigued by the prospect of meeting the
Duke of Florence's beautiful mistress. Hollow and illusory
appear the principles adopted by the male characters when set
against Bess's strength, fidelity and courage.

An ironic commentary upon Spencer is offered in Clem,
Bess's apprentice. He also labours under obligations, but they
are manifested in the terms of his apprenticeship contract.
Although he courts honour, this does not bring about an
improvement in his circumstances; such is his enthusiasm to
advance himself, he unwittingly manages to be castrated, and
the end of the second part of the play shows him as a
crestfallen, emasculated creature.

Bess rises above the difficulties experienced by the male
characters, and it is through her that Heywood communicates
royal compliments and his nationalistic allegiance. Dressed as
a page and a captain, Bess is able to perform valiantly in the
wars and receives praise for her military exploits. Being
elevated to positions of authority in foreign courts permits her
to free imprisoned Christians and to make charitable endow-
ments. Explicit associations with Elizabeth I are made by
several of the characters, and Heywood's eulogistic attitude
towards monarchal institutions is revealed.

But the play is not monotonous in its investigation of matters
of national importance. It abounds in witty exchanges, scenes
of low comedy, dumb shows and a variety of dramatic devices.
The characters develop and grow in complexity, entertaining
grand ambitions, falling prey to temptations, and recovering
their moral integrity. Unity is achieved in the kisses that

punctuate the beginnings and endings of both parts: Bess provocatively kisses the Duke of Florence at the end of the play, and Spencer is propelled into declaring his identity, into abandoning his vows, and into bringing his relations with his lover to a successful close.

—Mark Thornton Burnett

THE FAIR PENITENT
by Nicholas Rowe

First Publication: London, 1703.
First Production: Lincoln's Inn Fields, Spring 1703.

Editions
The Fair Penitent, edited by Sophie Chantal Hart, Boston, 1904.
The Fair Penitent, in *Three Plays by Nicholas Rowe*, edited by James R. Sutherland, London, 1929.
The Fair Penitent, in *Plays of The Restoration and Eighteenth Century*, New York, 1931.
The Fair Penitent, edited by J.H. Wilson, Boston, 1963.
The Fair Penitent, edited by Malcolm Goldstein, Lincoln (Nebraska) and London, 1969 (Regents Restoration Drama Series).

Criticism
(For general works on the author, see *Playwrights* volume)

Books:
Alfred Behrend, *"The Fair Penitent": A Contribution to Literary Analysis with a Side-Reference to Richard Beer-Hofmann, "Der Graf von Charolais"*, Bern, 1907.

Articles:
Donald B. Clark, "An Eighteenth-Century Adaptation of Massinger", in *Modern Language Quarterly*, 13, 1952.
Lindlay A. Wyman, "The Tradition of The Formal Meditation in Rowe's *The Fair Penitent*", in *Philological Quarterly*, 42, 1963.
Frank J. Kearful, "The Nature of Tragedy in Rowe's *The Fair Penitent*", in *Papers on Language and Literature*, 2, 1966.
J.M. Armistead, "Calista and the 'Equal Empire' of Her 'Sacred Sex'", in *Studies in Eighteenth-Century Culture*, 15, 1986.

*   *   *

Calista (the Fair Penitent) is given in marriage by her father, Sciolto, to his protégé, Altamont. She has, however, already been seduced by Lothario, with whom she is still infatuated. Calista sends a note to Lothario requesting a final meeting, but Lothario drops the letter, which is found by Horatio, who is married to Lavinia, Altamont's sister. Calista, confronted with the letter, tears it to shreds, and Altamont refuses to believe Horatio's accusations, provoking a breach between them. Altamont is disabused, however, when he discovers Calista and Lothario together. He kills Lothario in the ensuing duel. Calista in the final act is discovered grieving beside the body of Lothario. The stoic Sciolto encourages Calista to commit suicide which she finally does after her father has been mortally

The Fair Penitent: Engraving, 1827

wounded in the disturbances that follow Lothario's death.

The Fair Penitent was one of the most frequently performed tragedies of the 18th century. It influenced the development of continental, domestic tragedy and the English novel— Lothario is the inspiration for Lovelace in Samuel Richardson's *Clarissa*. Its appeal was partly due to the fact that Rowe had written his play with specific actors in mind. Calista was created for Elizabeth Barry, and Lavinia for Anne Bracegirdle. Elizabeth Barry had enjoyed her greatest successes in the plays of Thomas Otway, in which she perfected the ability to move the audience to tears that Rowe then exploited in this tragedy. Otway's plays were themselves an important influence on Rowe's work too.

Nicholas Rowe based his play on an earlier tragedy, *The Fatal Dowry*, by Philip Massinger and Nathan Field, which he adapted to the tastes of his audience by imposing a neo-classical simplicity on his material, reducing the number of characters from 21 to 8, and limiting the action to a single, fateful day. He rendered the tragedy domestic by rejecting, as he says in his prologue, the traditional subject matter of tragedy, "the fate of kings and empires", and substituting for it "a melancholy tale of private woe". He also accommodated the female component of his audience by making the protagonist a woman, Calista. This was the first of his three "she-tragedies".

The play is heavily moralistic. Lavinia is the exemplification of feminine docility. Her husband, Horatio, is given the concluding couplet, "If you would have the nuptial union last, / Let virtue be the bond that ties it fast". But this did not prevent Anne Bracegirdle, as Lavinia, from appearing in a bantering epilogue in which she castigated the male propensity to "huff and domineer by right divine".

A subsidiary concern in the play is the friendship of Altamont and Horatio, which is severely strained by Altamont's refusal to believe in Calista's perfidy, but is finally restored when Horatio cannot be indifferent to Altamont's anguish: "A flood of tenderness comes o'er my soul; / I cannot speak! I love, forgive, and pity thee!". The male quarrel and reconciliation scene had been very effectively developed by Dryden in the encounter between Antony and Ventidius in *All for Love* (1677). A similar episode occurs later with the quarrel between Bevill and Myrtle in Sir Richard Steele's *The Conscious Lovers* (1722).

Altamont himself is a curiously ineffectual character, possibly because he is demoted from being the central figure that he is in the source play, *The Fatal Dowry*. Much of the action concerning him in the earlier play is here reduced to narrative exposition. It was remarked at the time that Altamont is both insipid and difficult to play convincingly. Lothario, on the other hand, is remarkably attractive. He seems to descend directly from the libertine heroes of Restoration comedy, and like Dorimant in *The Man of Mode* still has something of "the angel undefiled" in him. Dr Johnson found this attractiveness disquieting, remarking that "Lothario, with gaiety which cannot be hated, and bravery which cannot be despised, retains too much of the spectator's kindness".

The entrance of the central character, Calista, is delayed until the opening of the second act. Fatally attracted to Lothario, she remains indifferent to Altamont. To his cheerful comment, "O, then let my Calista bless this day, / And set it down for happy" she bitterly replies, "'Tis the day / In which my father gave my hand to Altamont; / And as such I will remember it forever". Calista can also reproach her father directly for disposing of her hand without consulting her, and her great outcry in the third act of the play—"How hard is the condition of our sex. / Through every state of life the slaves of man!" marks her as a proto-feminist and is clearly directed to the women in the audience.

Calista's destruction of the incriminating letter, her brazen denial of Horatio's accusations, and her willingness to deceive Altamont were all ill-received at the time, but Rowe remarks in the prologue to the play that not all his characters are exemplary:

Let no nice taste the poet's art arraign,
If some frail, vicious characters he feign;
Who writes should still let nature be his care,
Mix shade with lights, and not paint all things fair,
But show you men and women as they are.

However, in the final act, although she rejects the paraphernalia of penitence imposed upon her, Calista confronts her action and its consequences, responding to her father's question, "Why didst thou turn to folly, then, and curse me?" with the wonderfully incisive response, "It was because I loved, and was a woman". Recognizing her affinities with her father, she accepts his proffered dagger.

Pity, Rowe wrote in his dedication of his play to the Duchess of Ormond, "is one of the main designs of tragedy". In *The Fair Penitent* Rowe's main objective was to move his audience to pity for the unfortunate Calista. In this he succeeded. Rowe's tragedy achieves its effects through exploiting the emotional responses of the audience, a characteristic of the "affective tragedies" of the Augustan period.

—Colin Wills Visser

THE FAITHFUL SHEPHERD (Il pastor fido)
by Giovanni Battista Guarini

First Publication: Venice, 1589 (but with "1590" on title page).
First Production: Crema, 1595.

Editions

"Il pastor fido" e il Compendio della poesia tragicomica, edited by Gioachino Brognoligo, Bari, 1914.
Il pastor fido, edited by Luigi Fasso, Turin, 1976.
Il pastor fido (with Sir Richard Fanshawe's translation), edited by J.H. Whitfield, Edinburgh, 1976.
Il pastor fido, edited by Ettore Bonora, Milan, 1977.

Translations

The Faithful Shepherd, translated by Richard Fanshawe, London, 1647; in a critical edition, edited by Walter F. Staton and William E. Simeone, Oxford, 1964; reprinted at Austin, Texas, 1976; also in *Five Italian Renaissance Comedies*, edited by Bruce Penman, Harmondsworth, 1978.
The Faithful Shepherd, translated by William Grove, London, 1782.
A Translation of Battista Guarini's "Il pastor fido" by Dr. Thomas Sheridan, edited by Robert Hogan and Edward A Nickerson, Newark, Delaware, 1989.

Criticism

Books:
Vittorio Rossi, *Battista Guarini e il "Pastor fido"*, Turin, 1886.
A. Scupa, *Studio critico sul "Pastor fido" di G. Battista Guarini*, Norcia, Tonti, 1892.
Giovanni Sannino, *La drammatica pastorale: "L'Aminta" e il "Pastor fido"*, Naples, 1906.
Luigi Ammirati, *Una serata di gala a Nola nel Cinquecento: La prima rappresentazione del "Pastor fido" con il Prologo di G.B. Marino*, Nola, 1962.
Nicoletta Neri, *"Il pastor fido" in Inghilterra*, Turin, 1963.
Nicolas J. Perella, *"The Critical Fortune of Battista Guarini's "Il pastor fido"*, Florence, 1973.
Daniela Dalla Valle, *Pastorale barocca. Forme e contenuti dal "Pastor fido" al dramma pastorale francese*, Ravenna, 1973.

Articles:
Charles Dejob, "Sur Guarini et son *Pastor fido*", in *Bulletin italien*, 7, 1907.
Chandler Beall, "A Quaint Conceit from Guarini to Dryden", in *Modern Language Notes*, 64, 1949.
Ferruccio Ulivi, "La poetica del Guarini e il *pastor fido*", in *Humanitas*, 6, 1951.
Marie Z. Wellington, "La constante Amarillis and its Italian Pastoral Sources", in *Philological Quarterly*, 34, 1955.
Geoffrey Bullough, "Sir Richard Fanshawe and Guarini", in *Studies in English Language and Literature Presented to Karl Brunner*, edited by S. Korninger, Vienna-Stuttgart, 1957.

Matteo Cerini, "L'ombra di un capolavoro: *Il pastor fido* del Guarini", in *Letterature moderne*, 7, 1957.

D. Petrini, "Guarini e il *Pastor fido*", in *Dal Barocco al Decadentismo*, 1, Florence, 1957.

N.J. Perella, "Fate, Blindness and Illusion in the *Pastor fido*", in *Romanic Review*, 49, 1958.

N.J. Perella, "Amarilli's Dilemma: The *Pastor fido* and Some English Authors", in *Comparative Literature*, 12, 1960.

Daniela Dalla Valle, "La fortunata francese del *pastor fido*", in *Studi francesi*, 8, 1964.

J.H. Whitfield, "Sir Richard Fanshawe and *The Faithful Shepherd*", in *Italian Studies*, 19, 1964.

Deanna Battaglin, "Leonardo Salviati e le *Osservazione al pastor fido* del Guarini", in *Atti e memorie dell'Accademia Patavina di scienze, lettere ed arti*, 67, 1964–65.

Domenico Ortisi, "La poesia del *Pastor fido* del Guarini", in *Convivium*, 35, 1967.

Norbert Jonard, "Le Baroquisme du *Pastor fido*", in *Studi secenteschi*, 10, 1969.

Judith Popovich Aikin, "Guarini's *Il pastor fido* in Germany: Allegorical and Figural Aspects", in *Studi Germanici*, 16, 1978.

Lee Bliss, "Defending Fletcher's Shepherds", in *Studies in English Literature 1500–1900*, vol. 23 no. 2, 1983.

James J. Yoch, "The Renaissance Dramatization of Temperance: The Italian Revival of Tragicomedy and *The Faithful Shepherdess*", in *Renaissance Tragedy: Explorations in Genre and Politics*, edited by Nancy Klein Maguire, New York, 1987.

*　　*　　*

Hardly less famous or less widely translated and imitated than Tasso's *Aminta*, is *Il pastor fido* (1590), a verse drama in five acts, with a chorus at the end of each one of them, by Giambattista Guarini (1538–1612), Tasso's contemporary and rival. It constitutes the author's sole claim to fame, although he wrote some poems, a comedy and numerous literary and political tracts as well.

The main characters in the play—Mirtillo and Amarilli (Milton's "Amaryllis in the shade")—have a tragic grandeur about them and are caught in a rich web of passions and sentiments, adventures and hazards. Mirtillo and Amarilli are in love with each other, but there are insurmountable difficulties in their way: Amarilli is engaged to Silvio, who is, however, loved by Dorinda. But Silvio is so engrossed in hunting that he has no time for either Amarilli or Dorinda. Mirtillo, is loved by Amarilli *and* Corsica, a wanton nymph who, in turn, is loved by Coridon. Corsica embodies all that is sensuous, voluptuous and hedonistic in life, coupled with an unbridled instinct to make the most of it so long as it lasts. It is chiefly her character and conduct that Francesco De Sanctis had in mind in describing *Pastor fido*, rather unjustly, as "the poetry of lust". Through deceitful means Corsica manages to have Mirtillo and her rival, Amarilli, condemned to death. And Silvio, through a mishap, wounds Dorinda, mistaking her for a wolf. When he realizes his mistake he is so repentant that he decides to marry her. However, there is another turn in the story: Mirtillo turns out to *be* Silvio who was engaged to Amarilli. Hence he marries her without any impediment.

The play ends with the chorus greeting the "happy couple" (Mirtillo and Amarilli) who have "sown in Tears" what they can now reap "in Comfort", thereby illustrating the moral that "true joy is a thing / That springs from vertue after suffering".

Essentially a pastoral play, *Il pastor fido* was translated into English for the first time by John Dymock in 1602, and was imitated by John Fletcher in his pastoral play *The Faithful Shepherdess*. Together with Tasso's play, it also inspired Thomas Randolph's pastoral *Amyntas, or the Fatal Dowry* (1638), and there are traces of its influence on Milton's choruses in *Samson Agonistes*. In 1647 Sir Richard Fanshawe offered what is considered to be the best translation of *Il pastor fido*. It represents a fusion of the tragic and the comic, and is rich not so much in action as in monologues, narrative descriptions and above all lyricism (even though Guarini did not profess to be a poet)—factors which made A.W. Schlegel think of it as a precursor of modern drama. In what may be regarded as a sort of apology to his *Compendio della poesia tragicomica* (1601), Guarini sets out to explain his aim and intention in *Il pastor fido*—to entertain rather than to instruct, and to assert the predominance of the natural, the sensual, and the idyllic in human life. Love and pity, youth and beauty are dealt with as things to be experienced for their own sake rather than contemplated in the abstract or analysed, or diagnosed, at a psychological or spiritual level. This explains both the immense popularity of *Pastor fido*, and the extremely moving character of some of the scenes in it which so impressed Voltaire, and which he explained by observing that "ce qui touche le coeur se grave dans la mémoire".

—G. Singh

THE FAMILY REUNION
by T.S. Eliot

First Publication: London, 1939.
First Production: Westminster Theatre, London, 21 March 1939.

Criticism
(For general works on the author, see *Playwrights* volume)

Books:

Maria Clotilde Rezzano, *"The Family Reunion": A Study*, Buenos Aries, 1942.

Articles:

Roy Battenhouse, "Eliot's *The Family Reunion* as Christian Prophecy", in *Christendom*, 10, 1945.

Anne Ward, "Speculations on Eliot's Time World: An Analysis of *The Family Reunion* in Relation to Hulme and Bergson", in *American Literature*, 21, 1949.

Donald Carne-Ross, "The Position of *The Family Reunion* in the Work of T.S. Eliot", in *Revue des Lettres modernes* (new series), vol.1 no.2, 1950.

Ronald Gaskell, "*The Family Reunion*", in *Essays in Criticism*, 12, 1962.

Richard E. Palmer, "Existentialism in T.S. Eliot's *The Family Reunion*", in *Modern Drama*, 5, 1962.

Marjorie J. Lightfoot, "*Purgatory* and *The Family Reunion*: In Pursuit of Prosodic Description", in *Modern Drama*, 7, 1964.

Jennifer I. Isaacs, "Eliot the Poet-Playwright as Seen in *The Family Reunion*", in *English*, 16, 1966.

Vinod Sena, "Eliot's *The Family Reunion*: A Study in Disintegration", in *Southern Review*, 3, 1967.

J. Guhathakurta, "The Use of Myth in Eliot's Plays: *The Family Reunion*", in *Dacca University Studies*, 16, 1968.

The Family Reunion: Westminster Theatre, London, 1939 (first production)

H.Z. Maccoby, "Difficulties in the Plot of *The Family Reunion*", in *Notes and Queries*, 15, 1968.

Leo Hamalian, "The Figures in the Window: Design in T.S. Eliot's *The Family Reunion*", in *College Literature*, 4, 1977.

Michael T. Beehler, "Troping the Topic: Dis-closing the Circle of *The Family Reunion*", in *Boundary 2*, vol.8 no.3, 1980.

Theresa M. Towner, "From Romance to Ritual: The Evidence of *The Family Reunion*", in *South Central Review*, vol.6 no.1, 1989.

*   *   *

Harry, Lord Monchensey, returns after a long absence to the family seat, Wishwood, where his aged mother, Amy, is to celebrate her birthday. Also assembled are other relations including Amy's sisters. The special guests are a Chorus—an updating of the Greek Eumenides—whom only Harry can see, and who embody his guilt about the death of his wife whom, he is convinced, he has killed. Only Agatha, one of Harry's aunts appreciates Harry's visions because she has her own secret, an affair with his father many years before. Harry finally leaves, to do unspecified good works, relinquishing the title to his brother John. His mother dies and, in a last scene of ritual expiation, Agatha and Mary (Harry's intended) circle her birthday cake and blow out the candles.

Although considered a puzzling example of the "new" verse drama when first produced in 1939, *The Family Reunion* can now be read as a variant on that quintessential genre of the 1930s, the country-house "whodunit". Secrets revealed in the library, a civilised manservant, an obsequious local policeman, and an upper-class family that closes ranks against outsiders—all these elements are familiar props of popular narrative in the inter-war years. Eliot's twist is that it is not secular but divine law that delivers judgement. Aunt Agatha rightly remarks in the second scene of Part II: "What we have written is not a story of detection, / Of crime and punishment, but of sin and expiation". We never discover whether Harry did kill his wife, not only for reasons of dramatic suspense, but also because this is a minor issue in Eliot's Christian, detective story. The primal crimes have been committed before the play begins. They are the disobedience in Eden and the murder of Christ. The only question to be answered is how, and how much, must this criminal pay in expiation. Harry therefore suffers neurosis, hallucination, and a permanent state of "outsiderdom". When he abandons his inheritance at the end Agatha presumes he will become a missionary. He denies this and his future is left obscure, but Eliot once observed to Michael Redgrave: "I think he and the chauffeur go off to get jobs in the East End". The play can therefore be seen to fit squarely into the continuum of Eliot's spiritual concerns since the 1920s and was written at a time (1936–8) when he was living in personal and spiritual isolation. No family, not even a family in Christ, could console him.

As drama, *The Family Reunion* is static. Across two interior sets, drawing-room and library, a set of upper-class stereotypes move and converse. Amy is the implacable matriarch, Charles the middle-aged conservative, Mary the "sensitive" poor relation, Downing the discreetly intelligent manservant. The moments of ritual—the Eumenides revealed behind the drawing-room curtains, the incantation around Amy's birthday-cake—are impressive but incompatible with the commonsensical conventions of the country-house drama. The deliberate references to Henry James are clear evidence of the influence of that other New England expatriate on Eliot; but prose fiction allows James to explore the hypocrisies and velleities of the English aristocracy with a psychological subtlety that Eliot's awkward mixture of humdrum verse and symbolist poetry does not. Eliot wanted a form of verse in which "everything can be said that has to be said", but the highly accented idiolect of the gentry reads parodically now, although, as recent successful revivals indicate, there is still an audience for it. What is exciting in the language is that trick of social symbolism that Eliot had developed from *The Love Song of J. Alfred Prufrock* onwards and that Auden utilised so effectively. "Go south!", exclaims Amy's sister Violet, in horror: "to the English circulating libraries, / To the military widows and the English chaplains, / To the chilly deck-chair and the strong, cold tea. . .". Agatha speculates on how Harry must have remembered his childhood at Wishwood: "The nursery tea, the school holiday / The daring feats on the old pony", and as in *Four Quartets*, childhood is a moment, but only a moment, of magical release:

I only looked through the little door
When the sun was shining on the rose-garden:
And heard in the distance tiny voices
And then a black raven flew over.

But when the symbols become ritualistic or religious they blur and sound portentous. The antiphony between Mary and Harry about the ambiguities of Spring is a good example. Mary talks of the "ache in the moving root / The agony in the dark" and we have lost even the earlier precision of her analysis of Harry: "You attach yourself to loathing / As others do to loving". But the clarity of Eliot at his symbolic best suddenly emerges at the end of the passage: "The aconite under the snow / And the snowdrop crying for a moment in the wood".

We live in an age of revived interest in religion and, in Britain at least, of total confusion about the future of the family. There is therefore every reason to believe that Eliot's Calvinistic dissection of this primary, social unit will continue to fascinate audiences. As codes of speech and dress become even more detached from social class, it is equally probable that the gentry speaking poetry could be part of a new naturalism. Eliot's illiberalism would also seem to be consonant with the politics of today. *The Family Reunion* articulates some of his most private obsessions, and can most usefully be read with the poetry of *The Wasteland* and *Four Quartets*. For someone unfamiliar with his work this play presents a powerful dramatisation of the problems of guilt in the modern world.

—Tony Dunn

THE FANLIGHTS. See **LOS SOLES TRUNCOS.**

LA FARCE DE MAÎTRE PIERRE PATHELIN. See **MASTER PETER PATHELIN.**

THE FARCE OF MASTER PETER PATHELIN. See **MASTER PETER PATHELIN.**

FARMYARD (Stallerhof)
by Franz Xaver Kroetz

First Publication: In *Theater heute*, 1971; in book form, in *Vier Stücke*, Frankfurt, 1972.
First Production: Deutsches Schauspielhaus, Hamburg, 1972.

Translations
Farmyard, translated by Michael Roloff, in *"Farmyard" and Other Plays*, edited by Richard Gilman, New York, 1976.
Stallerhof, in [*Rainer Werner Fassbinder's*] *Shakespeare the Sadist*; [*Rainer Werner Fassbinder's*] *Wolgang Bauer, Bremer Coffee*; [*Peter Handke's*] *My Foot My Tutor*; [*Franz Xaver Kroetz's*] *Stallerhof*, London, 1977.

Criticism
(For general works on the author, see *Playwrights* volume)

Articles:
Kurt Lüthi, "Sprachnot: ein Kommentar zu F.X. Kroetz *Stallerhof* im Grenzgebiet zwischen Literatur und Theologie", in *Prophetische Diakonie*, edited by H. Erharter and others, Vienna, 1977.
John Lutterbie, "Subjects of Silence", in *Theatre Journal*, 40, 1988.

*   *   *

Farmyard is set in rural Bavaria. A farmer, his wife, and Sepp, a hired hand in his mid-fifties, eke out a living for themselves and for the couple's daughter, Beppi, a retarded girl in her early teens. After establishing the depressed domestic scene, Kroetz focuses on the development of the unlikely relationship between Sepp and Beppi. In Act One they interact at work on the farm, then he takes her to a county fair and "deflowers her". Act Two shows them enjoying a modicum of happiness until Beppi becomes pregnant and her irate parents dismiss Sepp. In Act Three Beppi's mother and father consider keeping the child (it might be a boy), but decide abortion is the wiser choice. At the last moment, however, the mother can't go through with it. As the play ends we hear Beppi crying out to her parents through her labor pains.

The first two scenes of *Farmyard* can serve as a model for Kroetz's technique throughout. In the first scene while her mother is working in the kitchen, Beppi struggles to read the message on a postcard from her aunt. The sheer effort she makes to enunciate the words, and her sense of accomplishment once she succeeds, signal an important theme in the play.

Self-confidence, fulfillment and social power are linked to a command of language. This theme is present in numerous Kroetz plays, though here with the focus on a handicapped girl it is immediately apparent. Beppi's mother slaps her face and sharply criticizes her for stumbling over the words, then when the girl triumphantly reads the note loudly and clearly, the only response is a barked order to "dry the dishes at once". The mother has communicated all too well herself: articulation is one thing, real power another. The last utterance of the final act of *Farmyard* nicely sums up the irony as the new life inside of Beppi causes her to cry out "Mama, Papa".

In the second scene of *Farmyard* Kroetz further explores the idea of communication and dependency. Beppi milks a cow and Sepp shovels manure while he tells her a story about a white Captain who selects as his mate an Indian maiden considered to be taboo by her tribe. The "happy ending" story, directly out of pulp fiction or the movies, has significance not just for the effect it might have on an impressionable teenager, an outsider herself, but also for the fact that the tone of the scene is very different from the aggression which opens the play. On the surface of it, two people at work are pleasantly interacting. But the complexity of communication obviously encompasses much more than just words. As things turn out, Sepp's story of a white Captain "rescuing" an Indian maiden suggests something other than innocent, avuncular concern. The older man does indeed "take" Beppi, yet by the end of the play one has the impression that the gentler moments between them is the best one can hope for in this particular world.

The story in Scene Two functions in other ways typical for Kroetz. A diminished level of cultural awareness among the characters leaves very little common ground in conversation beyond the Bible, or pulp fiction, or ubiquitous, proverbial expressions. The adults in the play repeatedly indulge in clichés of the "God helps those who help themselves" sort whenever problems arise. The received cultural wisdom is a mechanism of control, inhibiting inquiry or thought. Characters are further hemmed in by the societal roles they have been assigned, such as employee, parent, or female sex partner. Each seems to come with a fixed mode of expression and behavior. In *Farmyard* to a large degree, and certainly by the end of the sequel, *Ghost Train*, there seems to be greater hope for the deformed and inarticulate Beppi to be able to communicate freely and directly than for anyone else around her. She occasionally even brings life to the set phrases. There is something unusually poignant, for instance, about *her* use of "do unto others" immediately after painful intercourse with Sepp. His response is silence.

In the *Ghost Train* sequel, Beppi asserts her independence by breaking from her parents and keeping the child. A key scene shows her responding to their criticism with a simple emphatic "I", to which the father says "We're not talking about you". Towards the end she receives a letter from the authorities in brutally cold, bureacratic language ordering her to surrender her child. Her response is to smother the baby lovingly and prepare a box to transport it, complete with "breathing holes", as she would for her pet hamster. Ironically, the mutual dependency with the child defines her state of freedom; then, that is made impossible.

The strength of Kroetz's early plays in performance owes much to his attention to minute details. He prefaces *Farmyard* with notes calling for a sparse setting; a real dog, which must be female; an attention to dialect; and a precise observation of pauses. He wants to evoke the environment and the characters as they shape each other, in the tradition of stage naturalism. A challenge in production is to establish performance values which resist sacrificing the ordinary humanity and charm of Kroetz's "little people", as they have been called, to the

tabloid sensationalism of the story line. For example, in one scene Beppi has an accident on the ghost train ride at the county fair. After Sepp wipes the diarrhea from her leg, the stage directions indicate he "*takes her and deflowers her*". Another scene, the one which follows the white Captain and Indian maiden story, reads in its entirety: "*Sepp sits on the toilet taking a shit. He masturbates*". Kroetz has on occasion expressed the hope that audiences will look beyond the repulsive acts on stage, will contemplate their causes. This takes careful direction in the theatre.

In the premiere of *Farmyard* at the Deutsches Schauspielhaus in Hamburg, director Ulrich Heising created what was referred to at the time as a kind of "radical realism" with choices such as a full one minute pause in the beer garden scene (Act III, scene 3) after Sepp contemplates retirement to the city with the line, "Then I'm a free man. No one's gonna tell me what to do, no way". Sepp yearns for a secure freedom and Beppi is terrified that he might be leaving her. A minute's silence can seem an eternity on stage, but the choice seems right for Kroetz's play. An audience ponders in actual time what the characters must be thinking about.

Further details which become clear only in production would be the very simple but brutal acts, such as Sepp drowning kittens in front of Beppi because he feels she betrayed him; or the murder of Sepp's dog by the "wronged" farmer. In the absence of adequate language, violence becomes the means of communication. When one considers the sequence of events from *Farmyard* through *Ghost Train*, virtually beginning in the cow stall and ending up with Beppi preparing a "hamster cage" for her dead child it becomes clear that the references to animals—the tenderness with which Sepp feeds his dog, the horror with which Beppi watches the drowning kittens—are very important. This is a matter of production no less crucial than the words on the page. An actor and director himself, Kroetz writes plays with deceptively simple language, but which contain a richness of theatrical possibility.

—Dennis Calandra

FASHION; or, Life in New York
by Anna Cora Mowatt (Ritchie)

First Publication: London, 1850.
First Production: Park Theatre, New York, 24 March 1845.

Editions

Fashion, in *American Plays*, edited by Allan G. Halline, New York, 1935.
Fashion, in *Representative American Plays* (seventh edition), edited by Arthur Hobson Quinn, New York, 1953.
Fashion, in *Dramas From the American Theatre, 1762–1909*, edited by Richard Moody, New York, 1966.
Fashion, in *"The Black Crook" and Other Nineteenth-Century American Plays*, New York, 1967.
Fashion, in *Six Early American Plays, 1798–1900*, edited by William Coyle and Harry G. Damaser, Columbus, Ohio, 1968.

Criticism

(For general works on the author, see *Playwrights* volume)

Articles:
Daniel F. Havens, "Cultural Maturity and the Flowering of Native American Social Comedy: Mowatt's *Fashion* (1845)", in his *The Columbian Muse of Comedy: The Development of a Native Tradition in Early American Social Comedy, 1787–1845*, Carbondale, Illinois, 1973.

* * *

Fashion begins as a typical drawing-room comedy. Zeke, the new Negro servant in the Tiffany household, meets Millinette, the French maid, and asks her a standard question, although in his own style: "What I wants to know is your publicated opinion, privately expressed, ob de domestic circle". Actions, however, immediately overshadow opinions. Aping foreign cultures and worshipping fashion, Mrs. Tiffany is trying to marry her daughter, Seraphina, to Count Jolimaitre. Adam Trueman, a rich Yankee and the catalyst of all actions in the plot, has no patience with fashion or foreigners or Mrs. Tiffany and her pretensions. By Act III all of the conflicts of the plot have been carefully prepared: an extravagant Mrs. Tiffany versus a financially beleaguered Mr. Tiffany; Mr. Tiffany versus Snobson, his blackmailing clerk; Count Jolimaitre versus Seraphina and Gertrude, the governess he outrageously opportunes. In an attempt to discredit Jolimaitre, Gertrude is caught in an embarrassing situation which momentarily confuses Trueman's belief in her goodness, but a fifth act rights all wrongs and joins the proper hands. Snobson is charged with forgery; Jolimaitre and Millinette, an old flame, will marry; Gertrude and Colonel Howard, a stalwart American soldier, will marry; and the Tiffanys, at Trueman's insistence, will go to the country to learn "economy, true independence, and home virtues, instead of foreign follies" (Act V, scene 1).

Opening on 24 March 1845, *Fashion; or, Life in New York* ran for 18 performances and proved to be a commercial success. After the puffing prior to opening night, however, even some of the indulgent reviewers showed that they had reservations, although most critics touched on the idea that here was a play that might stimulate American theatre. Edgar Allan Poe reviewed *Fashion* twice in *The Broadway Journal*, at first finding the play "theatrical but not dramatic" but also seeing it as "in many respects. . .superior to any American play", although not representative of high dramatic art. His interest, however, either in Mrs. Mowatt as a performer in her play or in the play itself, was such that in his second review he admitted to having seen every performance to date.

The idea of fashion is the true center of the wit and enterprise in the play. "A woman of fashion *never* grows old", says Mrs. Tiffany; "Age is always out of fashion". Fashion, according to Trueman, is "an agreement between certain persons to live without using their souls! To substitute etiquette for virtue—decorum for purity—manners for morals!". Trueman also provides the clear moral of the piece: don't be led astray by dreams of wealth or deceived by false fashions. Such views, presented within the popular framework of "life in New York" and with a wit that was not generally practiced among American dramatists, were particularly attractive to mid–19th–century, American audiences. Other dramatists tried to imitate Mrs. Mowatt's work, but without her success, and she herself did not write another play of comparable effect.

With caution and moderation, or extravagant flamboyance, many reviewers tried to see *Fashion* as a key to the future of American dramatic literature. The times, however, were not right; nor was the play a sufficient exemplum. Rather than providing a key to the future, *Fashion*, as Poe pointed out, merely suggested that there was hope. By chance, *Fashion* caught the wandering attention of thoughtful reviewers, and it has since become a focal point for modern historians. Like all of her peer playwrights, however, Mowatt wrote *Fashion* to succeed on stage, not in the library. Even by design, it would not meet the vague standards for drama determined by contemporary magazine editors and literary critics.

A fusion of melodrama and farce exhibiting the follies of fashionable life in New York City, *Fashion* held something for everyone—moral commentary, a nationalistic theme, a city-versus-country conflict, love episodes, a melodramatic villain, society caricatures, witty epigrams, a country Yankee, an American hero, a Negro servant, patriotic sentiments, a temperance issue, a French count and a French maid, and satire throughout. For what *Fashion* lacked in spectacle—although there is a ballroom scene—a variety of action, style and characters compensated. Clearly, the play satisfied the desire for theatrical entertainment sought by a great many people, while Mrs. Mowatt's fashionable reputation substantially helped its reception. A number of other playwrights had also written plays that stimulated critics to raise again the popular cry for meaningful American drama but it was this strange and alluring mixture of nationalism and snobbery permeating America at the time that gave *Fashion* its status.

—Walter J. Meserve

THE FATHER (Fadren)
by August Strindberg

First Publication: Helsingborg, 1887.
First Production: Casino Theatre, Copenhagen, 14 November 1887.

Editions
Fadren, Stockholm, 1921.

Translations
The Father, in *Strindberg: Plays, 5*, translated by Edwin Björkman, New York, 1916.
The Father, in *Strindberg: Six Plays*, translated by Elizabeth Sprigge, Garden City, New York, 1955.
The Father, in *Strindberg: Three Plays*, translated by Peter Watts, Harmondsworth and Baltimore, 1958.
The Father, in *Strindberg: Seven Plays*, translated by Arvid Paulsen, New York, 1960.
The Father, in *Strindberg: Plays, 1*, translated by Michael Meyer, London, 1964; revised version in *The Father; Miss Julie; The Ghost Sonata*, London, 1976.
The Father, in *Pre-Inferno Plays*, translated by Walter Johnson, Seattle and London, 1970 (The Washington Strindberg).
The Father, in *Strindberg: Five Plays*, translated by Harry G. Carlson, Berkeley, California, and London 1983.

Criticism
(For general works on the author, see *Playwrights* volume)

Articles:
C.E.W.L. Dahlström, "Is Strindberg's *Fadren* Naturalistic?", in *Scandinavian Studies*, 15, 1939.

The Father: Dramaten, Stockholm, 1968

C.E.W.L. Dahlström, "Strindberg's *Fadren* as Expressionist Drama", in *Scandinavian Studies*, 16, 1940.

C.E.W.L. Dahlström, "Strindberg's *Fadren* as Tragedy", in *Scandinavian Studies*, 27, 1955.

Charles Lyons, "The Archetypal Action of Male Submission in Strindberg's *The Father*", in *Scandinavian Studies*, 36, 1964.

Albert Bermel, "The Child as Husband: *The Father*", in *Contradictory Characters: An Interpretation of the Modern Theatre*, New York, 1973.

Vivi Edström, "Spelet om dorrern i Strindbergs *Fadren*", in *Svenskläraföreningens: Årsskrift*, 1975.

John E. Bellquist, "Strindberg's *Father*: Symbolism, Nihilism, Myth", in *Modern Drama*, 29, 1986.

Gail Finney, "The Devil in the House?: Strindberg's *The Father*", in *Women in Modern Drama: Freud, Feminism, and European Theater at the Turn of the Century*, Ithaca, New York, 1989.

*   *   *

In *The Father*, as in the later *Miss Julie*, the central theme is the conflict of the sexes, a conflict informed, at least in part, by the traumas of Strindberg's marriage to the actress Siri von Essen.

The plot has the inevitability, coolness and cohesion of a Greek tragedy. The action takes place in a single room, the Captain's study, while the time of actual performance, with short intervals between acts, closely mirrors the time of the action. The play begins with the Captain and his brother-in-law, the Pastor, discussing whether or not the servant, Nöjd, can be held responsible for the kitchenmaid's pregnancy. When questioned, Nöjd argues that he should not have to provide for the child as there is no way of telling whether he is the father. This idea—the fact that a man can never know if he's truly a child's father—first occurs almost incidentally within a discussion between the Captain and the Pastor about the future of the Captain's own Daughter, Bertha, and it becomes the central theme of the play and the main obsession of the Captain.

The play is a study of madness. The Captain, Adolf Lassen, is an amateur scientist. He is an impulsive, authorative man, a misogynist, with a deep subconscious fear of women. He is also an enormously vital and creative individual, domineering, childlike and strangely sympathetic—a complex, multifaceted character, at once prejudiced and self-aware. The play dramatises the conflict between him and his cunning, yet apparently all-too-sane wife, Laura, who manages to bring his sanity into question, finally reducing him to a pathetic figure in a straight-jacket, who suffers a stroke.

Throughout the play, Bertha is the focus of the marital conflict, Laura and Adolf both wishing to assert their rights over her, as if the child becomes a projection of their own desires, aspirations, and needs. In the first act, the Captain tells Margaret, the nurse, that "it isn't enough for me to have given the child life. I want to give it my soul too". However, Adolf wishes his child to be educated and independent, and his main concern is to get her away from the house, away from the influence of Laura and her sinister mother whose voice is heard even though she never appears.

Adolf unwittingly suggests the idea that one can never know who is a child's father which Laura uses to lead him to defeat. "Then how can a father have all these rights over her child?", she asks. Later she suggests to him that he may not be Bertha's father at all, suspicions which begin to obsess him, but which she finally, maliciously, reveals to be completely unfounded.

In her efforts to free herself from the burden of Adolf's domination, Laura suggests to the new doctor that her husband is mentally unstable. There are two possible ways of playing Dr. Östermark: either as a literalistic man of science misled by a clever woman, or as a willing dupe, ironically playing his part, flirtatiously engaged in a complex double-game with Laura, easily submitting to her charm. As evidence of her husband's mental condition, she tells him about his delusions: "Can you imagine—he even asked if he was the father of his child!".

The second act concludes with the long, emotionally charged, argument between Laura and Adolf, in which he begs to be told for certain that he is *not* the father, to relieve him of his doubts. This is probably the most remarkable scene in the play, its mood fluctuating unpredictably between tenderness and sudden passion or violence. At one point Adolf reaches towards a state of dreamlike perception: "When women grow old and cease to be women, they get beards on their chins. . . We who greeted the dawn were no longer cocks but capons, and the hens answered our false call, so that when the sun should have risen we found ourselves sitting in moonlight among ruins, just like in the good old days. It had only been a fretful slumber, a wild dream. It was no awakening". With almost careless, sadistic abandon, Laura reveals her intentions of having him certified, a revelation which provokes him to fling a lighted lamp—a moment of horrific, nightmarish effect.

In the final act, Adolf, now regarded as a dangerous lunatic, takes down his revolver from the wall, apparently intending to kill his daughter, yet the cartridges have been removed. Is he really as dangerous as they think, or is he only self-destructive? Does he really intend to kill Bertha, or is he simply playing a part, knowing that he is being observed?

The play superbly dramatises a sane man's absolutely credible descent into insanity. Yet who is "sane" in this play? Laura is revealed as an unscrupulous, self-righteous villain, the doctor as a physical coward, entirely subjective in his assessment of Adolf's condition, the Pastor as a moral coward, while both Margaret and Nöjd can be seen as traitors, unwilling to support Adolf. Even Bertha finally betrays him and comes under Laura's influence.

Adolf may be "insane", but only because he is judged to be so by other characters in the play, characters whose judgements are either flawed or self-motivated. He remains the most sympathetic, engaging, eccentric character in the play, and an audience might well be left preferring his idiosyncracies and fallibility to the moralistic "infallibility" of those who present themselves as mentally stable. To what extent is his destruction self-willed? While he lies helpless in his straight-jacket, Laura tells him, "I didn't plot any of this—it just glided forward on rails which you laid yourself—and before God and my conscience, I feel that I'm innocent, even if I'm not". Does he actually provoke his own downfall, much as Miss Julie provokes hers? This is just one of the questions which would face an actor trying to come to terms with this role. The play, stylistically composite, bringing together elements of melodrama, naturalism, and symbolism, while anticipating Strindberg's later expressionistic style, is also enormously challenging for the director. Does the play occur entirely within the Captain's own mind, the other characters simply figments of his imagination, or is he a projection of their imaginations? It is a play which leaves one with questions not answers, and its power to compel, challenge and disturb is remarkable.

—Brian Pearce

FAUST
Faust, Part One (Faust: Der Tragödie erster Teil)
Faust, Part Two (Faust: Der Tragödie, zweiter Teil)
by Johann Wolfgang von Goethe

Faust (Both Parts)
First Production: Hoftheater, Weimar, 6–7 May 1876.

Part One (Erster Teil)
First Publication: In *Werke, 8*, Tübingen, 1808.
First Production: National Theatre, Brunswick, 19 January 1829 (first complete performance).

Part Two (Zweiter Teil)
First Publication: In *Werke: Ausgabe letzte Hand, 4*, Stuttgart and Tübingen, 1827 (fragments: lines 8488–10038); lines 4613–6036 published 1828; Part Two complete in *Werke: Ausgabe letzte Hand, 41*, Stuttgart and Tübingen, 1832
First Production: Schauspielhaus, Hamburg, 4 April 1854.

Urfaust [early manuscript]
Composition: c. 1772–75.
First Publication: As *Goethe's Faust in ursprünglicher Gestalt nach der hochhausenschen Abschrift*, edited by Erich Schmidt, Weimar, 1887; revised by Schmidt, in *Weimarer Ausgabe, 39*, 1897.

Faust, A Fragment (Faust, Ein Fragment)
First Publication: In *Schriften, 7*, Leipzig, 1790.

Editions
Faust, der Tragödie erster Teil [including *Faust, Ein Fragment* and *Urfaust*], edited by Hans Lebede, Berlin, 1912.
Faust I and II (2 vols.), edited by W. Schröer, Leipzig, 1915–17.
"Urfaust" and "Faust, Ein Fragment", edited by L.A. Willoughby, Oxford, 1943.
Faust I and II (2 vols.), edited by Carl Enders, Basle, 1949.
Faust—Part I; Part II; Urfaust (seventh edition), edited by Erich Trunz, Hamburg, 1949.
Faust (2 vols.), edited by R.-M.S. Heffner, Helmut Rehder, and W.F. Twaddell, Madison, Wisconsin, 1950.
Urfaust, edited by R.H. Samuel, London, 1958.
Faust I, edited by W.H. Bruford, London, 1968.
Faust: Der Tragödie erster Teil, edited by L.J. Scheithauer, Stuttgart, 1971.
Faust, Munich, 1978 (Goldmann Klassiker).
Faust (2 vols.), Leipzig, 1982 (Reclam edition).

Translations
Faust I and II, translated by Anna Swanwick, London, 1905.
Faust I and II [including *Urfaust*], translated by W.H. Van der Smissen, London, 1926.
Faust, translated by Bayard Taylor, London, 1949.
Faust, Part I, translated by Philip Wayne, Harmondsworth, 1949.

Faust: Woodcut showing production at the Lyceum Theatre, London, 1885

The Urfaust, translated by Douglas M. Scott, Woodbury, New York, c.1958.

Faust, Part II, translated by Philip Wayne, Harmondsworth, 1959.

Faust, translated by Barker Fairley, Toronto, 1970.

"Faust": A Tragedy: Background and Sources; The Author on the Drama; Contemporary Reactions; Modern Criticism, edited by Cyrus Hamlin, translated by Walter Arndt, New York, 1976.

Faust, Part I, translated by Randall Jarrell, New York, 1976.

Faust, in *Goethe's Plays*, translated by Charles E. Passage, London, 1980.

Faust, translated by John Amster, London, 1985.

Faust, Part One, translated by David Luke, Oxford, 1987.

Faust, Parts One and Two ("performing version"), translated by Robert David MacDonald, Birmingham, 1988.

Dr. Henry Faust: The Tragedy's First and Second Parts, translated by John A. Roth, Lanham (Maryland) and London, c.1988.

Criticism
(For general works on the author, see *Playwrights* volume)

Books:

F. Melian Stawell and G. Lowes Dickinson, *Goethe and "Faust"*, London, 1928.

Heinrich Rickert, *Goethe's "Faust"*, Tübingen, 1932.

Alexander Gillies, *Goethe's "Faust": An Interpretation*, Oxford and New York, 1957.

Hermann E. Hinderks, *Goethe's "Faust" and the Crisis of Modern Man*, Belfast, 1957 [lecture text].

Stuart Atkins, *Goethe's "Faust": A Literary Analysis*, Cambridge, Massachusetts, 1958.

Alfred Dieck (ed.), *Goethe über den "Faust"*, Güttingen, 1958; second edition, 1963.

Theodor Friedrich and Lothar Johannes Scheithauer, *Kommentar zu Goethe's "Faust"*, Stuttgart, 1959.

Franz Ulbrich, *Das Inszenierungsproblem des "Faust II. Teil"*, Kassel, 1960.

Hans Schwerte, *"Faust" und die Faustische: Ein Kapitelideologie*, Stuttgart, 1962.

Theodor Friedrich, *Goethes "Faust" erläutert*, Leipzig, 1963.

Reinhard Buchwald, *Führer durch Goethes Faustdichtung: Erklärung des Werkes und Geschichte seiner Entstehung* (seventh edition) 1964.

Wilhelm Emrich, *Die Symbolik von "Faust II": Sinn und Formen* (third edition), Frankfurt, 1964.

Dorothea B. Spada, *"Faust, Parts I and II": A Scene by Scene Analysis*, New York, 1964.

Fritz Stich, *Goethes "Faust"*, Bern, 1964.

Eudo C. Mason, *Goethe's "Faust": Its Genesis and Purport*, Berkeley, California, 1967.

Valters Nollendorfs, *Der Streit um den "Urfaust"*, The Hague, 1967.

W.H. Bruford, *Goethe's "Faust I" Scene by Scene*, London, 1968.

Helgard Reich, *Die Entstehung der ersten fünf Szenen des Goetheschen "Urfaust"*, Munich, 1968.

Georg G. Wieszner, *Goethe's "Faust": Ein geistiger Überblick*, Nuremburg, 1968.

Hermann Reske, *"Faust": Eine Einführung*, Stuttgart, Berlin, Cologne, and Mainz, 1971.

Liselotte Dieckmann, *Goethe's "Faust": A Critical Reading*, Englewood Cliffs, New Jersey, 1972.

Joachim Müller, *Zur Motivstruktur von Goethe's "Faust"*, Berlin, 1972.

Paul Requadt, *Goethe's "Faust I": Leitmotivik und Architektur*, Munich, 1972.

W. Resenhöfft, *Goethe's Rätseldichtungen im "Faust"*, Bern, 1972.

Gottfried Richter, *"Faust": Ein christliches Mysterium*, Stuttgart, 1973.

T. Friedrich and L.J. Scheithauer, *Kommentar zu Goethe's "Faust"*, Stuttgart, 1974.

Werner Keller (ed.), *Aufsätze zu Goethe's "Faust I"*, Darmstadt, 1974 [anthology of criticism].

Dorothea Lohmeyer, *Fund die Welt: Der zweite Teil der Dichtung: Eine Anleitung zum Lesen des Textes*, Munich, 1975.

Wilhelm Resenhöft, *Goethe's "Faust": Gleichnis schöpferischer Sinnerfassung*, Bern, 1975.

Alan P. Cottrell, *Goethe's "Faust": Seven Essays*, Chapel Hill, North Carolina, 1976.

Heinz Hamm, *Goethe's "Faust": Werkgeschichte und Textanalyse*, Berlin, 1978.

Harold Jantz, *The Form of "Faust": The Work of Art and Its Intrinsic Structure*, Baltimore, Maryland, 1978.

H. Kobligk, *Faust I*, Frankfurt, 1978.

Nabil Mesh-Hadi, *Die Entschätzung der Alchemie in Faust-Deutungen*, Frankfurt, 1979.

Joachim Müller, *Die dramatische Funktion von Mephistos Monolog in Goethe's "Faust I": "Verachte nur Vernunft und Wissenschaft. . .",* Berlin, 1980.

I.A. White, *Names and Nomenclature in Goethe's "Faust"*, London, 1980.

John Gearey, *Goethe's "Faust": The Making of Part I*, New Haven, Connecticut, 1981.

Friedrich Oberklager, *"Faust I and II": Werkbesprechung und geisteswissenschaftliche Erläuterungen* (2 vols.), Schaffhausen, 1981–82.

Hans Arens, *Kommentar zu Goethe's "Faust I"*, Heidelberg, 1982.

Günther Mahal, *Faust-Rezeption in Russland und in der Sowjeunion*, Knittlingen (Faust Museum), 1983.

Rüdiger Scholz, *Goethe's "Faust": Ein einführender Forschungsbericht*, Rheinfelden, 1983.

Jens Krause, *Der Tanz ser Zeichen: Poetische Struktur und Geschichte in Goethe's "Faust II"*, Königstein, 1985.

Jane K. Brown, *Goethe's "Faust": The German Tragedy*, Ithaca, New York, 1986.

Douglas J. McMillan (ed.), *Approaches to Teaching Goethe's "Faust"*, New York, 1987.

John R. Williams, *Goethe's "Faust"*, London, 1987.

Edward Jamosky, *The Reconciliation of Opposites in Goethe's "Faust" and William Blake's "Marriage of Heaven and Hell"*, Des Moines, Idaho, 1988.

Hans Arens, *Kommentar zu Goethes "Faust II"*, Heidelberg, 1989.

Sidney Johnson (ed.), *Faust Through Four Centuries: Retrospect and Analysis*, Tübingen, 1989.

Articles:

For information on the numerous articles about *Faust*, see the bibliographies listed under Goethe in the *Playwrights* volume.

* * *

After a dedicatory poem and two preliminary scenes we find Faust in his study, despairing of penetrating through learning to the deeper realities of life. Summoning up the Earth Spirit, the amoral force which moves all nature, Faust is mocked and rejected and is close to suicide. The next day he is followed home by Mephistopheles in the form of a black poodle. The two conclude a wager that if Faust should ever bid the fleeting moment stay Mephistopheles can take him. Rejuvenated by a magic potion, Faust enters into a tragic affair with an innocent girl, Gretchen, whose involvement with Faust makes her indirectly responsible for the deaths of her brother and her mother. The first part closes with Gretchen awaiting execution for the murder of her child. In *Part Two* Faust awakens from a healing sleep. At the Emperor's court he and Mephistopheles summon up the shadows of Paris and Helen of Troy. In Act II Faust sets off to the Classical Witches' Sabbath to reclaim Helen from Persephone. In Act III they are united, a symbolic union of the classical and medieval worlds. A son, Euphorion, symbol of poetry, is born to them. After Euphorion's early death Helen returns to Persephone, leaving only her garments which change into a cloud and bear Faust away. In Act IV Faust helps the Emperor by supernatural means to defeat a rival and receives as a reward a strip of coastline for a land reclamation project. Faust, blind and a hundred years old, utters a provisional satisfaction in the words of the wager, falls dead and though claimed by Mephistopheles is borne up to heaven.

The Faust story passed into German literature through the publication by Spiess in 1587 of the *History of D. Johann Faust.* Marlowe quickly took up the material for his play, *Doctor Faustus,* which crossed back to Germany through the visits of wandering English players and became well known as a puppet play. Lessing was the first German dramatist to consider giving the material serious literary treatment, while the turbulent seeker after boundless knowledge and experience attracted the "Storm and Stress" writers Müller the Painter and F. M. Klinger, as well as Goethe himself. Goethe's treatment is far removed from the moralising tone and vicarious thrills offered by the subliterary versions. He was originally drawn to the titanic energy and restlessness of the Faust figure but came later to treat, through him, more universal human problems. Though making use of Christian symbolism, Goethe's vision is secular, and though Faust is "saved", that salvation is not to be understood in Christian terms but as an affirmation of what is of enduring value in human existence.

Faust was Goethe's life's work. He began it in the early 1770's, from which period dates the *Urfaust* fragment. The next stage was the somewhat augmented *Faust. A Fragment* of 1790. In the late 1790's Goethe again took up the work, encouraged by his friend and ally Friedrich Schiller. From this period dates the decision to divide the work into two parts, the beginnings of the Helen of Troy section and the addition of the framing and wager scenes. After the publication of *Part One* in 1808, Goethe again put the work aside until the last years of his life, completing *Part Two* between 1824 and 1831.

One of the central critical problems raised by a work written over such a protracted period of time is that of unity. The Nordic world of the original legend was often far from Goethe's preoccupations in his classical and post-classical phases. He himself frequently stressed in later years that the scenes of *Faust* were separate worlds, only loosely linked to each other. The work has clear discontinuities and shows an indifference to the causal relationships normally associated with the dramatic form. From the first the Gretchen tragedy, perhaps the only truly dramatic sequence in the work, dominated the *Urfaust,* moving the focus of attention away from Faust. Later additions and adjustments were designed to correct this, but within *Part One* its poetic force resists total integration. Act II and III of *Part Two* take place on a different plane from the rest of the action, to which Faust returns in Act IV. The figures of Faust and Mephistopheles undergo metamorphoses in the course of the action and the nature of their relationship changes also. Faust's rejuvenation in the Witch's Kitchen in *Part One* disrupts any psychological coherence to the character. At the start of *Part Two* his sleep of forgetfulness warns us that *Part Two* will not be a sequel to *Part One,* for now Faust is a mythical figure who provides the focus for an exploration of a vast range of themes—mythology, tradition, scientific experiment, the natural world, the poet's experience, political upheaval, the abuse of power—that reflect not only Goethe's intellectual world but also his engagement with his times. The wager struck by Faust and Mephistopheles is of doubtful dramatic importance even in the Gretchen tragedy. In *Part Two* it disappears altogether for long stretches, as does the sparring relationship between the two figures we knew in *Part One.* Mephistopheles indeed finds himself something of an alien being in the Classical Witches' Sabbath and has to assume the form of ugliness within a world of beauty. The framework also lacks consistency, the "stagey" heaven dominated by the Lord in the "Prologue in Heaven" giving way, in the final scene, to the structured heaven ascending to the Mater Gloriosa.

Yet amid these apparent discontinuities, there are many themes, symbols and parallel elements that link the various worlds of the play and, by a technique of mirroring, enrich their significance. Most notably perhaps, a key female figure appears in each part—Gretchen and Helen, and with each of them Faust enters into a union which is both erotic and spiritual. Each imparts to Faust a vital experience: love in the case of Gretchen and beauty in the case of Helen. Arguably these are what save Faust; these are the experiences of supreme value that bring human beings in touch with the divine. A penitent once called Gretchen is interceding for Faust as his spirit is borne up to heaven. Between the two Parts there are the obviously parallel worlds of the traditional Witches' Sabbath and Goethe's ironic invention, the Classical Witches' Sabbath, while the masquerade of Act I of *Part Two* contrasts in its tamed mythology with the classical world in the Classical Witches' Sabbath, particularly with the Triumph of Galatea. The theme of striving, of restless activity, runs through the work, from the Lord's confidence that a man errs as long as he strives to the angels' assurance, and at the end that anyone who ceaselessly strives is open to redemption. Yet this is also an ambiguous theme, and critics disagree over whether Faust's restless activity contributes to his salvation or results in any moral improvement.

The unity in diversity of *Faust* is exemplified not only by thematic richness but also by the virtuosity of Goethe's use of widely varying verse forms, from the doggerel known as "Knittelvers" in the opening of "Night" to the serene trimeter of the Helen tragedy. Madrigal verse, blank verse, free verse and songs are all to be found in *Part One,* as well as a small amount of prose. *Part Two* shows equal diversity, including passages in *terza rima* and alexandrines.

—Lesley Sharpe

THE FEAST OF PAN. See **THE BAD-TEMPERED OLD MAN.**

LES FEMMES SAVANTES. See **THE LEARNED LADIES.**

FENCES
by August Wilson

First Publication: New York, 1986
First Production: Yale Repertory Theatre, New Haven, Connecticut, 30 April 1985.

Criticism
(For general works on the author, see *Playwrights* volume)

Articles:
Heather Henderson, "Building *Fences*: An Interview with Mary Alica and James Earl Jones", in *Theatre*, vol.16 no.3, 1985.

* * *

As he runs from his home in the American south, Troy Maxson, the son of a black sharecropper, is borne north by the great migration of his people searching for the promised land. Unskilled and unwanted, he searches the streets of distant cities until the day he kills a man to stay alive. He learns how to play baseball in jail, rises to prominence in the Negro leagues, but is barred from playing in the major leagues because of the color of his skin. He was great before the game was fair, and the game will "never, never, never, never, never" come again. "There ought not never have been no time called too early" is how he puts it, as he tries to understand why his father beat him as a child.

Fences is a play about a national, American pastime. The greatest white baseball player, Babe Ruth, died at 53 years of age; Troy is 53 as the play begins, and a comparison of Troy and Ruth is both compelling and to the point. Babe Ruth was everything Troy is: large-spirited, a drinker, and womanizer, physically imposing, and a slugger. It suits Wilson's purpose, perhaps, to imply their divergent destinies. If Yankee Stadium is, by repute, linked with Ruth, then Troy gives rise to a quite different set of associations: a back-alley of Pittsburgh, the life his family leads on his garbage collector's pay, the rag ball he hits with a dusty bat.

The era which Wilson describes—the late 1950's and the dawn of the civil rights movement—enables a bitter experience of the past to clash with the awakening hope of the future. Troy, distrustful of his own experience, consequently fails to understand his son's aspirations. Troy, a responsible man belittled by an irresponsible society and its racism, needs the strength beyond endurance to accommodate his wasted potential. Under the pressure, he becomes irresponsible, hurting family and friends. His personality conspires with his victimization in a horrific image of the self-inflicted wound of racism. Many questions are raised. With more greatness in him, Troy has more to lose; he is more bitter as a consequence. But with greatness in him, he also has it in him to change. And yet he is beaten down; he even beats himself—"Hallelujah! I can't taste nothing no more!".

With the negative response to oppression so much in evidence, it is nevertheless important to note that Wilson is not fashioning a martyr. If Troy is a victim of racism, not all victims of racism become like Troy. How deeply Wilson explores the race issue is a question. He kills Troy before the end, with the final word being spoken over his grave. He thereby avoids an issue and misses an opportunity. What happened to Troy in the missing intervening years between the final scenes? Did he come to understand why his father beat him as a child? Did he come to understand his son? These questions are left open.

—Michael Bertin

FIN DE PARTIE.   See ENDGAME.

———

THE FIRE RAISERS (Biedermann und die Brandstifter)
by Max Frisch

First Publication: As *Herr Biedermann und die Brandstifter*, 1955 (radio version); Frankfurt, 1958 (stage / television version).
First Production: On Bayerischer Rundfunk, 26 March 1953 (radio version); Schauspielhaus, Zürich, 29 March 1958 (stage version).

Translations
The Fire Raisers, in *Three Plays*, translated by Michael Bullock, London, 1962; also in a single edition, 1962.

Criticism
(For general works on the author, see *Playwrights* volume)

Books:
Sybille Heidenreich, *Andorra; Biedermann und die Brandstifter*, Hollfeld, 1974.
Ingo Springmann (ed.), *Max Frisch, "Biedermann und die Brandstifter": Erläuterungen und Dokumente*, Stuttgart, 1975.
Renate and Reinhard Meurer, *Max Frisch: "Biedermann und die Brandstifter": Interpretation*, Munich, 1983.

Articles:
Dennis Davison, "Max Frisch's *The Fire Raisers*", in *Komos*, 1, 1968.
Philip G. Hill, "A Reading of *The Firebugs*", in *Modern Drama*, 13, 1970.
Dietrich Meinert, "Das Absurde als Mittel der Verfremdung in Frischs *Biedermann und die Brandstifter*", in *Acta Germanica*, 5, 1970.
John T. Brewer, "Max Frisch's *Biedermann und die Brandstifter* as the Documentation of an Author's Frustration", in *Germanic Review*, 46, 1971.
Rajendra Padture, "*Biedermann und die Brandstifter: Ein Lehrstück ohne Lehre* (1953): die Skepsis von Max Frisch", in *German Studies in India*, 12, 1988.

* * *

An unspecified city in Europe has been the scene of a spate of arson attacks, all of which have been carried out by a group of men whose strategy for each new attack remains the same. The newspapers report amost daily on the wave of fires and "good citizens" like the play's main character, Gottlieb Biedermann, can be heard in their local pubs telling each other what ought to be done with the arsonists once they are caught. Then Biedermann's own home becomes a target, as first one fireraiser, Schmitz, thinly disguised as a vagrant pedlar, then another, Eisenring, in a head waiter's uniform, and finally a revolutionary intellectual all inveigle Biedermann into giving them shelter. Within a day the drums of petrol are being stored in the attic and despite suspecting from the very beginning that he and his wife may be the next victims of the fireraisers, Biedermann fails to take action. On the contrary he invites them to a dinner party and even provides them with the matches to light the ignition fuse—the over-confident arsonists have forgotten theirs!

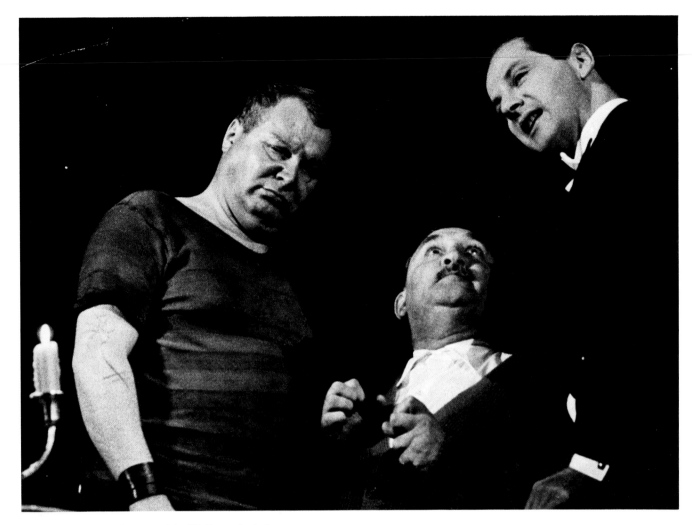

The Fireraisers: Schauspielhaus, Zurich, 1958 (first production)

The Fireraisers is both a satire and an allegory. On the satirical level Frisch's intended audience are his fellow Swiss and himself, for, as critical of human weaknesses as Frisch may be, he is a writer who has never deluded himself about his own fallibility. The Swiss people, around 1950, (when Frisch first had the idea for the play) were feeling particularly pleased with themselves as they looked around at their immediate European neighbours and beyond. They saw states ravaged by war, societies divided by ideology, systems being undermined from within, and from without by external military or political pressures. Switzerland, on the other hand, thanks to its deep-seated traditions of democracy and liberalism and by virtue of its political neutrality—quite apart from its firm financial and economic foundations—appeared to be immune to such crises and catastrophes.

Frisch, sceptical and vigilant, set out to shatter such illusions. He wanted to show how conservatism and complacency were just as dangerous, and ultimately self-destructive, as the more traditional and visible forces of violence and anarchy. These forces are presented in the comically stylised yet menacing figures of the three fireraisers, especially Schmitz and Eisenring. While the latter may not be instantly recognisable as Swiss types, Gottlieb Biedermann and his wife certainly do conform to many of the values and attitudes we associate with that highly successful and survival-conscious nation in the heart of Europe. He is a self-made man, thanks to a hair tonic

he manufactures; an individualist who believes the state should keep out of his life; a proud, class-conscious member of the bourgeoisie; a conspicuous consumer of the products of the affluent society; and, finally, as his name suggests, a God loving man.

Yet *The Fireraisers* would never have been the world-wide success it was, attracting such politically-minded directors as Erwin Piscator and Lindsay Anderson, if its message had been restricted to provincial, Swiss life. Frisch has broadened its validity to make a universal statement. His use of fire as the play's central symbol is one means to this end. We associate this element with almost every major, historical event and development in this century, from the artillery battles of World War I and the aerial bombardments of the following war—resulting in the conflagrations of Dresden and Hamburg—to the mass incinerators of Auschwitz and, finally and inexorably, to the atomic mushroom that hung over Hiroshima. Indeed, some productions have drawn parallels between the storing of petrol drums in Biedermann's attic and the stockpiling of nuclear missiles in the very heart of the civilised nations. And Frisch's allegory exposes furthermore our ability to deceive ourselves that they are not really there at all and anyway would never be deployed, or at least not so as to bring harm to ourselves.

Our almost innate capacity for self-deceptions of this kind is highlighted in the play by another technique which lifts *The*

Fireraisers into the plane of allegorical theatre. A pseudo-Greek chorus of firemen is stationed ever ready on the stage in order to deal with the fire once it occurs. But its critical function is to encourage the audience to think about the real causes of so-called tragedies. The chorus voices Frisch's own view that many tragedies are in fact avoidable, if only individuals would use their powers of reasoning to add two and two together. Furthermore it bemoans our all too human tendency to avoid our social responsibilities and bewails our comforting, but irrational, belief in fate being to blame for our tragedies, rather than human folly.

We should therefore understand the sub-title of *The Fireraisers, A Morality Without a Moral*, partly as a gesture of despair by Frisch at man's congenital refusal to learn from past errors and partly as an ironic and provocative challenge to an audience finally to read the writing on the wall, before it really is too late. At the same time the sub-title is an insider's joke directed towards (the spirit of) Frisch's former mentor Brecht, the great writer of morality plays *with* a moral. Frisch cannot share the latter's unswerving faith in man's common sense nor his conviction that the theatre really can effect change. For that reason, Frisch's plays remain ultimately no more than "plays" or, in the case of Biedermann's playing with fire, very black farces.

—Anthony Waine

A FLEA IN HER EAR (La Puce à l'oreille)
by Georges Feydeau

First Publication: Paris, 1909.
First Production: Théâtre des Nouveautés, 2 March 1907.

Translations
A Flea in Her Ear, translated by Barnett Shaw, London and New York, 1966.
A Flea in Her Ear, translated by John Mortimer, London and New York, 1968.

Criticism
(For general works on the author, see *Playwrights* volume)

Articles:
W. Joseph Stell, "Twin Comedy", in *Southern Theatre*, vol.24 no.2, 1981.

*   *   *

By the time he wrote *La Puce à l'oreille* Feydeau was the king of the light French farce known as *vaudeville*, and had mastered all the techniques of that form. With dazzling skill and tireless energy he concocts a story of incredible complexity. Chandebise confides to his friend, Dr. Finache, that he has recently become impotent. Almost at the same time his wife Raymonde expresses to her old friend Lucienne doubts regarding her husband's fidelity, since he no longer makes love to her. Moreover she has just discovered the suspenders she embroidered for him returned from a shady hotel known as Le Minet Galant (in one translation known as the Pretty Pussy Inn); the suspenders we later discover were left at the hotel by her nephew Camille, who adds confusions by registering under the same family name as her husband. Raymonde convinces

Lucienne to write a passionate, unsigned letter to Chandebise, asking him for a rendezvous at the hotel, intending to turn up herself and accuse him of infidelity. Chandebise, astonished that anyone should have conceived such a passion for him, assumes that it was intended for his best friend Tournel and hands the letter to him. Tournel, unknown to Chandebise, has been pursuing Raymonde for some time. The plot in Act I is complicated further by the raging jealousy of Lucienne's Latin American husband who accidentally reads the letter addressed to Chandebise and recognizes his wife's handwriting. He sets off to the hotel, and Chandebise's lusty young nephew Camille runs off to warn Tournel, whom he knows has replaced Chandebise, but Camille has a cleft palate and speaks a gibberish that is incomprehensible to most people.

The rest of the farce plays out the multiple possibilities of this scenario, further complicated in Act II by the appearance of a hotel porter, Poche, who is the double of Chandebise (both roles are played by the same actor). At the hotel all hell breaks loose, as unexpected and unwished-for encounters take place. Without exception all the characters from Act I arrive at the hotel, including the chamber-maid who comes to dally with Camille, and her husband, the butler, who comes to check up on her. The many strands of the piece are finally unravelled when Chandebise discovers his wife's ruse, the jealous husband of Lucienne discovers her innocence, and all discover that Chandebise and Poche are as alike as two peas in a pod.

Such a plot, with several important strands and the perplexing resemblance of Chandebise/Poche, suggests infinite possibilities of confusion, connection and surprise, and Feydeau seems to take advantage of them all. With the almost insane inventiveness that is his hallmark, at a vertiginous rate he brings character after character into collision at the hotel.

Like many of Feydeau's plays, *A Flea in Her Ear*, begins much like a comedy of manners, as we are introduced into the family life of a well-off, middle-class household. To be sure, there is the riotously funny speech of Camille, misunderstood by the amazed visitors who take him for a foreigner or an idiot. By and large, however, the first act is a skillfully constructed, highly amusing exposition, preparing for the complications that will proliferate in Act II. In standard Feydeau fashion, Act II shows the nightmarish encounter of all those who would rather not meet, played at manic speed, and punctuated by the cries of the victims, "What a night, my God, what a night!". Act III is necessarily long and involved to enable the plots to unravel. Unlike some of Feydeau's less successful third acts, however, there is no languishing of interest, no slowing down of the frantic pace, for the identities of Chandebise and Poche remain a puzzle for the characters until almost the end, and the madly jealous Latin husband, Homénides, loose with a gun, adds excitement and intensity as he pursues his wife's alleged lover.

The double role of Chandebise/Poche offers a challenge to a virtuoso actor, for it demands the ability to depict widely differing character types, one an invariably drunk, not-too-bright hotel porter, and the other the picture of bourgeois respectability. It also requires a certain athleticism in order to effect the rapid changes backstage, for in Acts II and III Poche disappears at one side of the stage, and Chandebise enters within a minute from the other side. Feydeau, always the master theatre director, gives ample notes in his text advising the actor how best to effect the costume changes.

Although Feydeau dismissed Naturalism as untheatrical and uninteresting, it is noteworthy that many of the major themes of the naturalists are treated—although with a much lighter hand than most earnest naturalists were capable of—in this masterly farce with strong realistic underpinnings. Indeed, one might argue that *A Flea in Her Ear* presents a general tableau

A Flea in her Ear: Old Vic Theatre, London, 1989

of sexual orientations, treating, in a comic key, problems that one could well treat seriously. Feydeau himself asserted that the comic playwright chose subjects that would make an undertaker shiver, and showed them in a comic perspective. The four married couples we see in the farce play out four different variations on marriage: Raymonde and Chandebise have reached a crisis because the husband is unable to satisfy his wife; Lucienne, on the other hand, complains of precisely the opposite problem—she wishes her husband would give her a little rest; the maid Antoinette, the spirited wife of the butler Etienne, attempts to betray him with the frisky young Camille; the fourth married couple is made up of Ferraillon, the hotel proprietor, and his wife, Olympe, a former cocotte. Ferraillon, an ex-army sergeant, enjoys kicking and beating his wife, and she, in turn, adores these attentions—as does Poche who is roundly kicked in the seat of the pants by his boss. The unmarried characters round out the picture, including: the playboy Camille; Dr. Finache who, it is suggested, misses the recently dismissed, handsome, young hotel porter; and an Englishman who is waiting for anyone who might show up.

The situations give rise to dialogue that treats sexual problems in piquant detail, often amusingly expressed, as when Raymonde describes her husband as a raging torrent that has suddenly run dry, or when the young wife, Raymonde, protests that she is willing to be Tournel's mistress, but doesn't want to go to bed with him. Some fundamental feminine and masculine attitudes towards sex, at least as Feydeau understood them, are made unabashedly clear.

The "alcohol problem" also puts in an appearance and adds

to the picture of the seamy side of life, but always portrayed with an eye for comic possibilities. Poche is rarely sober and the hotel proprietor's old uncle, Baptistin, is kept in a special bed in one room, where he is instructed to complain of his stomach ache—although he apparently spends much of his time drinking.

Baptistin is lying in a revolving bed—one of Feydeau's most clever mechanical contrivances. Should clients in the room we see onstage wish to disappear suddenly (say, upon the arrival of an unexpected spouse), they have only to push a button and the bed turns into the next room, bringing Uncle Baptistin into the onstage room. Some of the most hilarious and nightmarish moments in the play arise from the functioning of this bed. When Tournel finds himself alone with Raymonde in the hotel, he prepares to leap into bed with her. Frightened, she pushes what she thinks is a bell to summon help; instead the bed turns and Tournel finds himself inexplicably in the lap of old Uncle Baptistin. This inconceivable event offers an impressive example of the nightmarish atmosphere Feydeau succeeds in creating for his characters, lost in a world that seems to have gone mad. It is not surprising that absurdist writers like Ionesco looked back to Feydeau as a forerunner, and that post-World-War-II critics found in him a metaphysical dimension that his contemporaries would never have suspected.

—Leonard C. Pronko

THE FLIES (Les Mouches)
by Jean-Paul Sartre

First Publication: Paris, 1943.
First Production: Théâtre de la Cité, Paris, 3 June 1943.

Translations
The Flies, in *Sartre: Two Plays*, translated by Stuart Gilbert,
London, 1946.

Criticism
(For general works on the author, see *Playwrights* volume)

Books:
Keith O. Gore, *"La Nausée" and "Les Mouches"*, London,
1970.
Peter Royle, *Sartre: l'Enfer et la liberté: Étude de "Huis clos" et
des "Mouches"*, Quebec, 1973.
Pierre Brunel, *Les Mouches*, Paris, 1974.

Articles:
Theophil Spoerri, "*Les Mouches* de Jean-Paul Sartre", in
Lettres, vol.3 no.1, 1945.
Ludwig W. Kahn, "Freedom: An Existentialist and an Idealist
View", in *Publications of the Modern Language Association*
[*PMLA*], vol.44 no.1, 1949.
Rudolph Stamm, "The Orestes Theme in Three Plays by
Eugene O'Neill, T.S. Eliot, and Jean-Paul Sartre", in
English Studies, 30, 1949.
D.J. Conacher, "Orestes as Existentialist Hero", in *Philologi-
cal Quarterly*, 33, 1954.
George Ross Ridge, "Meaningful Choice in Sartre's Drama",
in *French Review*, 30, 1956.
Dolores M. Burdick, "The Concept of Character in
Giraudoux's *Electre* and Sartre's *Les Mouches*", in *French
Review*, December 1959.
Michael J. Buckley, "*Les Mouches*: Antinomies Within Athe-
istic Humanism", in *Cithara*, November 1963.
François Van Laere, "La Liberté sur le vif: Sartre et *Les
Mouches* aujourd'hui", in *Synthèses*, 256–57, 1967.
Angela Belli, "Jean-Paul Sartre: *Les Mouches*", in *Ancient
Greek Myths and Modern Drama: A Study in Continuity*,
New York and London, 1968.
Gilbert Debusscher, "Modern Masks of Orestes: *The Flies* and
[Jack Richardson's] *The Prodigal*", in *Modern Drama*, 12,
1969.
Donald J. Freeze, "Zeus, Orestes, and Sartre: An Interpreta-
tion of *The Flies*", in *New Scholasticism*, 44, 1970.
Jean Sarrochi, "Sartre dramaturge: *Les Mouches* et *Les
Séquestrés d'Altona*" in *Travaux de linguistique et de littéra-
ture*, vol.8 no.2, 1970.
Richard Israel, "The Tragedy of Human Existence in Sartre's
The Flies", in *Utah Academy of Sciences, Arts and Letters*,
1970–71.
Robert W. Artinian, "Foul Winds in Argos: Sartre's *Les
Mouches*", in *Romance Notes*, Autumn 1972.
Peter Royle, "The Ontological Significance of *Les Mouches*",
in *French Studies*, 26, 1972.
Marcus Allen, "Character Development in the *Oreste* of
Voltaire and *Les Mouches* of Jean-Paul Sartre", in *CLA
Journal*, September 1974.
David G. Burnett, "Movement and Stasis in *The Flies* of Jean-
Paul Sartre", in *Perspectives on Contemporary Literature*,
vol.4 no.2, 1978.
Patricia M. Hopkins, "The Failure of Language in *Les
Mouches* and *Le Malentendu*", in *Francia*, 33, 1980.

Jacqueline Viswanathan, "*Les Mouches* au-delà de l'existen-
tialisme", in *Incidences*, vol.6 no.1–2, 1982.
Ingrid Galster, "*Les Mouches*, pièce résistante?", in *Lende-
mains*, 42, 1986.

*   *   *

The Flies is a grim and sombre re-interpretation of a Greek
myth dramatised originally by Aeschylus, Sophocles and
Euripides. On his return from the Trojan wars, King Agamemnon of Argos was murdered by his wife Clytemnestra and her
lover Aegisthus. Sartre's play begins when, years later,
Agamemnon's son, Orestes, returns from exile and decides to
join with his sister Electra in avenging their father. They are
not deterred by the advice and threats of Jupiter who,
disguised as a traveller, has observed Orestes and his tutor
throughout their journey along the Gulf of Corinth. Together,
they murder the royal couple; but Electra repents, whereas
Orestes, having freed the population of Argos from the
usurper's tyranny, refuses the throne to which he is the rightful
heir and moves on, taking with him the swarms of flies that
have plagued the city ever since Agamemnon's death.

Sartre's version of the legend, his first play to be performed
professionally, emphasises the themes of liberty and oppression in ways quite unlike those of his predecessors. While a
prisoner of war in Stalag 12 at the start of World War II, he had
written a play *Bariona*, supposedly to entertain his fellow
prisoners at Christmas, but in fact to stimulate their flagging
morale with a message of resistance. This bizarre experience of
a Christmas play written by an atheist had shown him how to
evade German censorship by cloaking his subject in antiquity.
On his release and return to Paris, he used the same device for
The Flies, this time using Greek rather than biblical antiquity.
Interpreted on a topical and political level, the subject
provided Sartre with a means of appealing to the inner liberty
and spirit of resistance in his Parisian audience. Every one of
the central characters has a symbolical value beyond their
legendary persona. Aegisthus represents the German invader,
and Clytemnestra, the French collaborator; Electra and
Orestes are, respectively, the French Resistance movement
and the Free French Army.

It is inadequate to see *The Flies* merely as an ingenious
political allegory. 1943 was also the year in which Sartre
published his major philosophical essay, *L'Etre et le néant*
(*Being and Nothingness*); so it is far from surprising that he
uses the play to examine not only the immediate, political
problem in occupied France, but also the more general
problems of responsibility, choice, commitment, and human
liberty which are central tenets of Existentialism. In fact, no
play by Sartre gives such a clear, almost mathematical
exposition of his philosophy, as we follow the parallel developments of Orestes, the legendary hero, murdering Aegisthus,
and Orestes, the uncommitted traveller who ultimately
assumes responsibility for the liberty of his fellow men.

There are clearly defined stages or stations in what can be
seen as the Existentialist education of the central character.
The drab, deserted streets of Argos when Orestes and his tutor
arrive, and the drab clothing of its fearful occupants are, on the
political level, references to wartime rationing and curfews.
On a philosophical level, Sartre is criticising all who are
prepared to abdicate personal liberty and responsibility. The
people of Argos—like the Vichy government—were content
to accept their fate. The visitors are joined by their fellow
traveller, Jupiter, who attempts to dissuade Orestes from
staying and intervening in the affairs of Argos, but Orestes'
humanist education makes him reluctant to accept conventional religion. Indeed, he denounces both religion and

humanism, leaving himself detached, empty and aimlessly drifting. At this realisation of his own being and his nothingness, his first reaction is to abdicate his liberty, to avoid commitment and to leave.

Faced with a totally gratuitous existence in a world devoid of divine guidance and acceptable yardsticks, everyone is, like Orestes, obliged to create personal values. These, says Sartre, are to be measured not in terms of the traditional moral standards of good and evil, but by their authenticity, their contribution to human liberty. After a meeting with his sister, Orestes rejects the solutions to his dilemma to be found in escape and in the slow, painstaking process of education. He opts for the swift, violent solution of murder as a means of liberating the people of Argos. Together, Orestes and Electra commit the murders, but for each of them the outcome is different. Unlike Orestes, who accepts responsibility for an authentic act undertaken in the interests of human liberty, Electra is overcome with remorse. For years she had dreamed of vengeance, but failed to act; now, when she has shared in the murder, repentance turns her action into an empty gesture prompted by ill faith, and she quickly surrenders her individual liberty to the comfortable authority of Jupiter.

The play was not particularly well received by Parisian audiences in 1943 or at the 1951 revival. As Sartre himself later admitted, it is not entirely satisfactory from the philosophical point of view. Orestes' decision to leave Argos after the double murder creates an unfortunate ambiguity: certainly, if he were to stay and rule, it could appear that one tyranny has merely replaced another; but doubt must be cast on the authenticity of the hero's choice and action once he decides not to stay and share with his fellow Argosites the consequences of the new situation which his murders have created.

For those not concerned with its philosophical and political implications, *The Flies* has shortcomings of a purely dramatic variety. The play is long, and the dialogue lacks theatrical crispness. A recent and fervent convert to the theatre, with a background of fiction and philosophy, Sartre lacked dramatic intuition and the technical skill which a combination of experience and his acute intelligence were to bring to some of his plays. Seeing in theatre "a great, collective religious phenomenon", he made the mistake of preaching. *The Flies* was nevertheless a brave attempt, most successful on the topical and immediately political plane.

—Colin Radford

THE FLOATING WORLD
by John Romeril

First Publication: Sydney, 1975.
First Production: The Pram Factory, Melbourne, August 1974.

* * *

Australian playwright John Romeril's drama focuses on an ordinary, middle-aged couple on board a 1975 cut-rate "*Woman's Weekly* Cherry Blossom Cruise", after embarkation from Australia sailing to Japan. The Husband, Les Harding, the drama's protagonist, is a survivor of a World-War-II Japanese prison camp. He boozes moodily while his prattling wife flirts and plays the typical tourist. As the cruise

progresses, the veteran's prison camp memories increasingly engulf his mind. He confuses a Malaysian waiter with a Japanese officer, and a cabin mate with a dying prison comrade accusing him of betrayal in returning to the enemy's land. Other shipboard passengers take on roles in the inward reality of the protagonist's past, which increasingly intrudes upon the outward reality of the present to the point of merger. The veteran's fragmented memories ultimately propel him insanely to attack Japanese citizens upon his arrival in Yokohama. Harding ends up in a strait jacket babbling to the long-dead, wartime mates of his memory that he has avenged their deaths. Initially considered to have merely strange behavior by his wife and those around him, he has gone progressively mad, reliving his experiences as a prisoner of war on the infamous Burma-Thailand railway. Ironically, in his final state of insanity, Harding proclaims that he is "well again" and is able to describe the crisis of his war imprisonment when he arduously achieved the physical recovery from beriberi marking his survival. Paradoxically, his "restoration" has been into mental illness.

Romeril's comic but ultimately tragic drama probes the phenomenon of Australian xenophobia and what may be termed "colonial mentality" along with some of its major historical and political causes. Such causes are related to aspects of Australia's involvement in the two World Wars as seen through the eyes of Harding as he goes insane. Harding is introduced as a vulgar, working-class Australian male, or "ocker", who represents the characteristic prejudices and behavior-patterns of his type. He is the native of a country until very recently fearful of being an isolated white colony dangerously surrounded by yellow Asia. As a World War II veteran, he harbors the national dread of the Japanese, a fear climaxed by experiences of 15,000 Australian soldiers captured and held as prisoners of war after the fall of Singapore in 1942, of whom 5,000 died. Harding also shares with his countrymen a distrust of the British, a belief that they betrayed Australian troops at Gallipoli (in World War I) and Singapore, alongside a concomitant feeling of subservience ingrained from a Depression-impoverished childhood. When a retired Royal Navy officer on the cruise becomes friendly towards him and his wife, Harding is suspicious as to why a British officer would fraternize with him. During his immersions in past reality, Harding sees him as one of the disliked and snobbish British officers in command of Australian soldiers in the prison camp. As a working-class Australian, Harding's sense of being a second-class citizen to British, or yellow Asiatic, masters, or any authority figures, rankles strongly.

At first Harding conceals his xenophobia and insecurity beneath uncouth behavior and a mask of rudely aggressive self-assertion marked by boozing and braggadocio. In its first half, the play sets up comic incidents relating to Harding's social mask; and the action follows the comic rituals of a package holiday tour. The cruise's comic trenchantly entertains with a surfeit of tasteless repartee and organizes pointless games. The ship's waiter becomes a Japanese businessman delivering incomprehensible instructions while hawking a mechanical toy. Mrs. Harding basks in the sun and in the friendship of the British Navy officer while spouting banalities gleaned from women's magazines, as her husband disturbs her show of false sophistication with bawdy poems. Coming to focus amidst the comedic kaleidoscope of the culture and the cruise activities, however, is a portrait of disintegration. As the ship nears its destination, the protagonist's past consumes him, and the audience is forcefully shown the frightened insecurity underlying the social mask that Harding has created for himself. Romeril effectively presents the paradox of the crude, brazen Australian, which is illusion, as opposed to the vulnerable, insecure man behind the mask, which is the reality.

Contained in twenty scenes (each given a Brechtian caption in the play's published version), the action is designed to flow easily from one scene to another. The scenes utilize both realistic and expressionistic styles to present a reality as seen by the protagonist which cumulatively builds in emotional tension as Harding's inner reality takes over. The characters are successfully drawn, ranging from the Hardings to the six other characters who take on multiple identities. These figures reflect aspects of contemporary society as well as the objectification of antagonists in "the floating world" of Harding's subconscious.

Romeril has written a theatrical and thoroughly stageworthy play which allows flexibility in production approach. In a 1975 production at Sydney's Nimrod Theatre, a white-platformed setting on a thrust stage furnished an effective space for the fluidity of the play's many scenes, while lighting, sound, and all other production elements adeptly collaborated to facilitate the progressively intense transitions between expressionistic memory sequences and present reality.

An antipodean *Woyzeck, The Floating World* is a major work of Australian theatre meriting attention. In this work as well as his others, Romeril makes significant social, political and artistic statements in a manner that is accessible to a wide-ranging audience. He is one of several Australian dramatists whose energetic work should not be ignored on the western side of the world.

—Christian H. Moe

EN FOLKEFIENDE.   See **AN ENEMY OF THE PEOPLE.**

———————

LA FOLLE JOURNÉ.   See **THE MARRIAGE OF FIGARO.**

———————

FOOL FOR LOVE
by Sam Shepard

First Publication: In *"Fool for Love" and "The Sad Lament of Pecos Bill on The Eve of Killing His Wife"*, San Francisco, 1983.
First Production: Magic Theatre, San Francisco, 9 February 1983.

Criticism
(For general works on the author, see *Playwrights* volume)

Articles:
Peter L. Podol, "Dimensions of Violence in the Theatre of Sam Shepard: *True West* and *Fool for Love*", in *Essays in Theatre*, 7, 1989.
Allen Ramsey, "The Boundaries of Illusion in *Fool for Love*", in *Notes on Contemporary Literature*, vol. 19 no. 4, 1989.

*   *   *

Fool For Love: National Theatre, London, 1984

Eddie and May are lovers; nevertheless they hate each other. The lonesome cowboy and sexy cook of Sam Shepard's *Fool For Love* just love to fool for it, and their 15-year erotic extravaganza is best described as a game of hide-and-seek.

With gallant bravado and with his horses in tow, our hero hits the road again and searches the great Southwest of America for the woman of his dreams. And he finds her, sitting on a four-poster bed in a motel room on the edge of the Mojave Desert. She is not in a dreaming mood, however; she's in a dreadful fit over his suspected affair with a volatile Countess, for while Eddie has been searching for May, the Countess has been searching for him.

If *Fool For Love* opens with a cliché, it certainly doesn't end with one. Shepard's elaboration of the love triangle creates a mythic iconography of the American imagination, and the extra dimension, the deepening of the action, comes through a character called the Old Man. This seedy presence sits to the side of the stage and actually talks, but "he exists only in the minds of May and Eddie". Why do they share an inner voice? It turns out the "Old Man" is their father, although they are his children by different women; it seems the Old Man was trapped in his own game of hide-and-seek with their mothers, and the rules of this game are open to interpretation.

In a manner of speaking, then, *Fool For Love* is a double-decker triangle; its action, through a neat dramaturgical trick, being the simultaneous presentation of two affairs. As the play unfolds, we delve deeper into the past, and discover the past *is* the present. We hear the Old Man's lyrical lay of yesteryear as we discover the fraud of the Old Man's lyrical lie; and we experience the discordant note of Eddie and May's romantic quest as Eddie and May thrash through to a lyricism all their own. Since the phantasm of love is highly confusing in all its familiar manifestations, Shepard provides May with a comic date, Martin, and he becomes our surrogate in his sense of amazement.

A very American play in its restlessness, *Fool For Love* is shaped by the fevered elegance of classicism. With its saddles, shotguns, and tequila sex, the play is a country-western variation on the theme of obsessive love; and, though the comparison may seem surprising, one Racine may have cherished. The quarrel of Eddie and May is a test which confirms them as an inbred breed apart, and their love is raised to the condition of fate by the entanglements of incest.

Shepard limits his use of time, place, and action to a single day, room, and even a single mania. Their blood boiling in a pressure-cooker space, Eddie and May suffer the sheer claustrophobia of love. The proud declamations of the French classical stage become here body punches to the groin; our laid-back hero receives his while his up-front sweetheart is screaming "don't you touch me!". And as the sound of banging heads fades in the West, the echo is gently amplified by the microphones Shepard indicates should be placed in the walls of his set. The end is an erotic conflagration, but it has its tender moments. Eddie walks out on May, but May follows him out.

—Michael Bertin

FOR COLORED GIRLS WHO HAVE CONSIDERED SUICIDE WHEN THE RAINBOW IS ENUF
by Ntozake Shange

First Publication: San Lorenzo, California, 1976; revised version, New York, 1977.
First Production: "Bacchanal" (a women's bar), Berkeley, California 1974; revised version, Studio Rivbea, 7 July, 1975.

Criticism
(For general works on the author, see *Playwrights* volume)

Articles:
Erskine Peters, "Some Tragic Propensities of Ourselves: The Occasion of Ntozake Shange's *For Colored Girls Who Have Considered Suicide When the Rainbow is Enuf*", in *Journal of Ethnic Studies*, vol. 6 no. 1, 1978.
Sandra Hollins Flowers, "*Colored Girls*: Textbook for the Eighties", in *Black American Literature Forum*, vol. 15 no. 2, 1981.
Andrea Benton Rushing, "*For Colored Girls*: Suicide or Struggle", in *Massachusetts Review*, 22, 1981.
Tobe Levin and Gwendolyn Flowers, "Black Feminism in *For Colored Girls Who Have Considered Suicide When the Rainbow is Enuf*", in *History and Tradition in Afro-American Culture*, edited by Gunter Lenz, Frankfurt, 1984.
Carolyn Mitchell, " 'A Laying On of Hands': Transcending the City on Ntozake Shange's *For Colored Girls Who Have Considered Suicide When the Rainbow is Enuf*", in *Women Writers and the City: Essays in Feminist Literary Criticism*, edited by Susan Merrill Squier, Knoxville, Tennessee, 1984.

*   *   *

For Colored Girls Who Have Considered Suicide / When The Rainbow Is Enuf consists of twenty "choreopoems that" express different, complex experiences of African–American women in vibrant, explosive poetry punctuated by music and dance. The play established the importance of the choreopoem, a collection of related poems combined with song and dance, as a uniquely African–American form of performance. Seven African–American actresses, identified by the colors of their dresses (brown, yellow, orange, red, blue, purple, green), sing, dance, and recite poems that fuse personal, political, and spiritual concerns. The poems explore the personal torment of women victimized by both racism and sexism through addressing issues such as: the silencing of the African–American women's voice, feminine sexuality, date rape, abortion, life in Harlem, loneliness, the glory of the African heritage, wife-battering, and solidarity among African–American women. The women in the play struggle to affirm their heritage, race, and gender, for "bein alive & bein a woman & bein colored is a metaphysical dilemma". The gravity of this dilemma is dramatically realized in the climactic poem, "A Night with Beau Willie Brown". This poem describes the relationship of a psychically-damaged, Vietnam veteran with his young lover, Crystal. Shell-shocked and unable to work, Beau Willie vents his frustration on the racist country he served by brutalizing his wife and children. When Crystal refuses to marry him, he drops their two children from a fifth story window. The women in the play survive and transcend the devastating realities resulting from class, race, and gender difference. In the final scene of the play, "a laying on of hands", the women participate in a healing process by expressing collective solidarity and self-affirmation: "I found god in myself / & i loved her / i loved her fiercely".

For Colored Girls Who Have Considered Suicide...: New York, 1976

The play portrays conflicting stories that represent a spectrum of women's experiences, rather than subsuming the different voices of African-American women beneath one definitive image, or myth, of the African-American experience. Shange is attentive to the differences among women, and the variety of their emotional responses to social, economic, and political constraints. In the first poem, the Lady in Brown celebrates music which expresses discontinuity, rather than the unity symbolizing the suppression of differences: "Half-notes scattered / without rhythm / no tune. . .it's funny / it's hysterical / the melody-less-ness of her dance". As the individual notes are not harmonized into one melody, so the different women are not localized into one space, but are disparate, free to express regional differences: "I'm outside chicago / i'm outside detroit / i'm outside houston. . .".

In the second poem, the women each express different views of their sexuality. One woman reveals in her graduation / sexual initiation night: "WOW / by daybreak / I just cdnt stop grinnin", while another woman admits, "i never did like to grind". In another poem, a woman's sexuality is revealed as a masquerade of "orange butterflies and aqua sequins" which wash away in the bath: "Laying in water / she became herself / ordinary". She has no desire of her own, but is only the object of desire: "she glittered honestly / delighted she was desired". Her sexuality is revealed as a social construction, subject to patriarchal structures, rather than as a "natural", expressive reality.

Shange's play is also distinguished by its formal, structural and linguistic innovations. The choreopoem form was influenced by the works of Sonia Sanchez, Beah Richards, Alexis De Veaux, and Judy Grahn. The choreopoem allows the different women in the play to express their material, historical situation in an emotional, lyrical, dynamic performance. The choreopoem breaks down the distinctions between the material and the spiritual, objective reality and subjective reality, psychological realism and Brechtian alienation. The subjective state of the performer is politicized, as the effects of history are played out as personal emotional experience.

Emotional experience is expressed not only in poetry and song, but also in dance. As a component of the choreopoem, dance challenges the opposition between interiority and exteriority, as the subjective world is expressed through bodily experience. When Shange played the part of the lady in orange in the Broadway production, she created a uniquely African–American grammar of gestures and strides to accompany the African–American dialect of the poems.

Shange's text is written in lower-case letters, contractions, and abbreviations, expressions of her rebellion against the colonizer's English. Shange's writing reflects her conscious war against the symbolic order, the pre-constituted, colonizing representational system which already informs African-American experience. Her "mutilations" of the written word suggest the brandings and markings the American colonizers inflicted upon African flesh. Shange uses language as a visual register of historical effects.

The choreopoem resists the rationality and empiricism of the well-made play, the colonizer's aesthetic; instead, Shange's play reflects the spirituality of the African tradition. Within the African tradition, language, music, and dance are *mojos*, spiritual force-fields of energy which allow the individual to transcend material reality and experience wholeness. Shange's choreopoem form, with its emphasis upon *mojos*, is her response to a Western, Eurocentric system of aesthetics which gives priority to the spoken word.

For Colored Girls Who Have Considered Suicide / When The Rainbow Is Enuf appeared as a controversial challenge to the predominantly white feminist movement and the predominantly male black power movement of the 1970s. The play's success helped both movements to question their exclusion of African–American women, to question their own complicity in racism and sexism.

—Karen Cronacher

FOR SERVICES RENDERED
by Somerset Maugham

First Publication: London, 1932.
First Production: Globe Theatre, London, 1 November 1932.

* * *

This play charts the decline of the Ardsleys, a middle-class family located in a small country town in Kent in Southern England. It ends with one of the three daughters still glumly married to a tenant farmer of lower status, another certifiably insane, the youngest about to elope with an unprincipled businessman old enough to be her father, and their mother suffering from a terminal illness. Her only son, blinded in battle, is immobilized, and a close friend of the family commits suicide.

A few months before Hitler came to power West End audiences, and indeed most of the nation, were scarcely ready to tolerate one of the finest plays of the interwar years, though the cast included Cedric Hardwicke, Ralph Richardson and Flora Robson. Reactions to a revival were vitiated by a change of fashion which resented the "well-made play" connotations of french windows, social tennis, and frequent servings of tea. In fact the stock responses aroused only get in the way of Maugham's deeper concerns. On a basis of severely func-

For Services Rendered: Globe Theatre, London, 1932 (first production)

tional, but now and then limp, dialogue, what he offers is an indictment not only of one family and its bankrupt values, but of the anxiety and self-deluding complacency of England, much of it still applicable today.

In order to justify this high estimate of what at first might seem little more than tired naturalism in an outmoded stage idiom, devoid of the sparkle typical of Coward, Maugham's contemporary, a close look at Maugham's construction is called for. To begin with, his theme, indicated by the title, both frames the action and runs through it. It is the ingratitude and condescension of English society towards armed forces survivors of World War I. Tied in with that theme is money, whether it be expressed in the hard life of a woman married to a tenant farmer risen from the ranks, or in the bankruptcy of a naval officer unable to adapt to a civilian career. Past heroism may be viewed as a handicap, the decorations earned now faded into a background of failure.

With the author's savage indignation—two of his characters excepted—kept rigidly in check, Maugham's indictment is made through the Ardsley family, crisply brought to life as an all too credible group. Their maid is a part of it, minimally involved but not exploited as a comic figure, and so is the local doctor, partner in episodes of great sensitivity with the stoical mother, who is morally superior to everyone. She sounds a note at once within and beyond other concerns and is worthy of Chekhov. The rest inhabit a jungle of frustration, none more explicitly than the prettiest daughter, Lois, in a conflict between urgent sexuality and unsuitable outlets for it. With a choice of predators in the shape of a farmer, crudely aware of her needs, and an ageing tycoon given to soppy romanticism, Lois takes a calculated risk based on what has been shown of a third alternative, her family and this provincial backwater.

That Lois is hard but not unsympathetic is a tribute to Maugham's psychological insight. The same applies to her elder sister Eva, brought relentlessly, by way of the loss of her fiancé in the war and the suicide now of a man she yearns for, to a shattering breakdown in what was perhaps Flora Robson's finest performance.

However, the play has imperfections where Maugham's bold message rides clear from the action into polemic. The first, not out of character, is the outburst of the blind son Sydney against the "vanity, greed and stupidity" to which he and the other war casualties were sacrificed. The second is Ardsley himself, a monster of hypocrisy, complacency, and conformism, blissfully unaware of the suffering on his own doorstep. With too facile irony on Maugham's part, Ardsley embodies the main theme, but he is living proof of his son's contention that those in power have learnt nothing from the war and are set to "muddle on" into another.

—Laurence Kitchin

THE FORCE OF HABIT (Die Macht der Gewohnheit)
by Thomas Bernhard

First Publication: Frankfurt, 1974.
First Production: Salzburg Festival, 27 July 1974.

Translations
The Force of Habit, translated by Neville and Thomas Plaice, London, 1976.

Criticism
(For general works on the author, see *Playwrights* volume)

Articles:
Alfred Barthofer, "Das Cello und die Peitsche: Beobachtungen zu Thomas Bernhards *Die Macht der Gewohnheit*", in *Sprachkunst: Beiträge zur Literaturwissenschaft*, 7, 1976.
Ernst Grohotolsky, "*Die Macht der Gewohnheit*, oder: die Komödie der *Dialektik der Aufklärung*", in *In Sachen Thomas Bernhard*, edited by Kurt Bartsch and others, Königstein, 1983.

*   *   *

The Force of Habit takes place entirely in the caravan of Caribaldi, director and owner of a small, travelling circus. As he has done everyday for the last 22 years, Caribaldi is looking forward to rehearsing Franz Schubert's *Forellenquintett* with his granddaughter, the Juggler, the Clown, and his nephew, the Lion Tamer, all of them reluctant or rebellious musicians. As always, the rehearsal is unsuccessful: the Lion Tamer cannot play with his arm in a bandage (it is possible that he simulates his injury to sabotage the rehearsal) and finally begins to batter his piano with his head and fists. A discouraged Caribaldi throws the mutinous ensemble-members out of his caravan and prepares himself for another abortive performance and rehearsal in Augsburg, their next stop, as the radio plays the first few bars of the *Forellenquintett*.

The Force of Habit, Bernhard's fourth play, is the comedy of a neurotic obsession with achieving artistic perfection in an imperfect world. Caribaldi's dream of "making a habit out of precision" cannot be achieved in the dusty and windy microcosm of his caravan moving on to progressively more sordid places. The phrase "Morgen Augsburg", the incessantly reiterated *leitmotif* of the play, is symptomatic of this deteriorating, existential condition that makes the fantasy of a perfect performance of the Schubert quintet an absurd mirage. In the end, it is less important to achieve the desired perfection than to persist in the attempt; just as continuing to wait becomes the existential *raison d'être* for Samuel Beckett's characters, so continuing the abortive rehearsals becomes Caribaldi's shield from the abyss of hopelessness into which he glimpses every day.

On a more topical level, *The Force of Habit* illustrates Bernhard's negative attitude towards matters German, particularly in the realm of the arts. Caribaldi speaks contemptuously of Germany—represented by Augsburg which is called a "dirty cesspool"—and praises everything Romanic: Pablo Casals, his Italian instruments; even his own name is a reference to Garibaldi, the Italian freedom fighter. In Germany, where his circus goes on tour, the atmosphere is not conducive to great art; the public flocks to the circus performances of a troupe of grotesque misfits. When the mayor of Augsburg threatened to take Bernhard to court for the defamation of his city's character, the playwright diffidently wrote back: "From my vantage point here in Lisbon I see Augsburg as even more fundamentally repulsive than in my new play. My pity for all Augsburgers and those in Europe who think of themselves as Augsburgers is immense, boundless, and absolute".

The structure of the play follows that of the *Forellenquintett*: the lively "allegro" of Scene I is followed by a quieter middle-part, in which Caribaldi is for the most part alone with his granddaughter. These first two scenes run parallel to the circus performance; the last scene with its cacophonic breaking up of the rehearsal and the concurrent destruction of Caribaldi's fantasy of the perfect performance takes place as the circus folds its tents to prepare for the trip to Augsburg and the next, indubitably unsuccessful, rehearsal.

The Force of Habit strictly follows the Aristotelian unities, thus creating the illusion of reason and order. Embedded into this structure is a technique Bernhard has employed in all three of his preceding plays: the play within the play. While the external structure—the travelling circus troupe and their performances—perseveres on in its monotonous, rigorous progression to ever more sordid places, the doomed rehearsals of the Schubert piece present a dramatic counterimage. Caribaldi wields almost absolute power (*Macht*) over the other four characters in the course of their daily lives: they depend on him for their livelihood. In the rehearsals the situation is reversed: in order to realize his ideal of a perfect performance of Schubert, Caribaldi depends on the goodwill and co-operation of the very people he has coerced to become musicians, creating the same mutual dependency the Lion Tamer recognizes between himself and the animals he forces to perform tricks. Where both art and circus performance are reduced to the same level of repetitiveness and nonsense, tedium and disgust become the dominant forces: "We do not want life/but it must be lived/we hate the *Forellenquintett*/but it has to be played".

In a world populated by sick, mutilated, oppressed people, true art is no longer possible; a dusty, windy caravan or the cesspool, Augsburg, are not fertile soil for great art—Caribaldi's Italian cellos don't sound right in the northern climate. The only defense against the feeling of despair, the only vitalization of an otherwise hopeless existence, is to raise the act of rehearsing to the level of art, hoping against hope that the process will one day miraculously bear fruit. "Morgen Augsburg" is thus both a motif of resignation and of hope: it is a pitiful station in the circus's progress but also the locus for the next rehearsal.

—Franz G. Blaha

FOREFATHERS' EVE (Dziady)
by Adam Mickiewicz

First Publication: Parts I (sketch), II, and IV in *Poezji, 2* [*Early Poems, 2*], Vilnius [Wilno], Lithuania, 1823; Part III, with poem *Ustęp* [*Digression*], Paris, 1832.
First Production: Cracow, 1848 (fragments); Lvov, 1889 (fragments); Cracow, 1901 (complete).

Editions
Dziady, Warsaw, 1947.
Dziady, Czesc I [*Part I*], Wroclaw, 1971.

Translations
Forefathers' Eve, translated by D.P.L Radin and G.R. Noyes, in *Slavonic Review*, 3–4, 1924–25.
The Forefathers, Parts I and II, translated by Count Wladyslaw Potocki of Montalk, London, 1944.
Forefathers' Eve, Part III: The Great Improvisation, translated by L. Varèse, New York, 1956.

Forefathers' Eve, Part III, translated by "various hands", edited by G.R. Noyes, revised by Harold B. Segel, in *Polish Romantic Drama*, edited by Harold B. Segel, Ithaca (New York), and London, 1977.

Criticism

Articles:
Abraham G. Duker, "Some Cabbalist and Frankist Elements in Adam Mickiewicz's *Dziady*", in *Studies in Polish Civilization*, edited by Damian Wandycz, New York, 1966.
Gerald E. Darring, "Structural Unity in *Forefathers' Eve, Part III*", in *Zagadniena Rodajów Literackich: Woprosy Literaturnych Zanrov / Les Problèmes des genres littéraires*, vol.14 no.2, 1972.
Helen N. Fagin, "Adam Mickiewicz: Poland's Romantic Poet", in *South Atlantic Bulletin*, vol.42 no.4, 1977.
Karol Sauerland, "Zwischen Irrationalem und Rationalem oder die *Totenfieier* von Mickiewicz und der *Kordian* von Slowacki", in *Parallelen und Kontraste: Studien zu literarischen Wechselbeziehungen in Europa zwischen 1750 und 1850*, edited by Hans-Dietrich Dahnke and others, Berlin, 1983.
Rolf Fieguth, "Erinnerungszwang als dramatische Form über Adam Mickiewiczs frühe szenische Dichtung *Dziady* (1823)", in *Wiener slawistischer Almanach*, 16, 1985.

* * *

Forefathers' Eve (*Dziady*) by Adam Mickiewicz consists of four loosely connected parts, which in reference to the time and place of their writing are divided into the Vilnius (*Parts I, II*, and *IV*) and the Dresden *Forefathers' Eve* (*Part III*). With *Parts II, III*, and *IV* subtitled "poems", and *Part I* "spectacle", this drama in verse is generally regarded as the most innovative and outstanding work of the Polish Romantic theatre. The unusual, seemingly broken form without dramatic plot and tension, the inclusion of lyrical and epic passages (and even full, independent poems) and the introduction of crowd scenes, made *Forefathers' Eve* unacceptable to the 19th-century men of theatre. Therefore the drama was not staged until 1901. Although already regarded as an inspired poem by its contemporaries, it has achieved its full theatrical triumph in 20th-century Poland.

Mickiewicz never finished *Part I* (Existing fragments were published posthumously), but with a typical Romantic defiance and nonchalance decided to include *Parts II* and *IV* in the second volume of his early poems (1823). Different in form and character, they are both connected with the old Byelorussian rite of "Dziady" (Forefathers), which involves calling upon the dead and offering them food on All Souls' Day. In this way the poet kept to his own principle that national literature should look for inspiration in local folklore instead of imitating ancient classics. There was also an implied opposition against recognized, "dead" truths, represented by the official culture, in favour of unrecognized, "living" truths cherished by the common people, the peasants.

Part II portrays the sacred ceremony of the Forefathers' Eve, where peasants gathered in a remote chapel to witness the appearance of ghosts. It contains three parallel episodes, each one initiated by incantations, centered on the description of a spectre and his/her story, and closed by a moral admonition, repeated by the crowd. The message is simple and not specifically Romantic: life should be experienced in its fullness, which includes pain and sorrow, love and pity.

The solemnity of choral recitations and the mystery of

Forefathers' Eve: Narodowy Theatre, Warsaw, 1967

waiting for the supernatural in Part II is followed by the tension and vehemence of contradictory feelings in Part IV. This consists of a long monologue by an unhappy lover, Gustaw, because his only partner, the old priest, not only speaks very little but can be also regarded as a voice within the protagonist's tormented self. In fact, even Gustaw's own ontological status looks uncertain: is he a ghost who only recreates the story of his unrequited love, ending in suicide, in order to warn the living? Or is he a Romantic madman whose frenzy is really followed by self-inflicted death? This mystery of the Forefathers' Eve remains purposely unsolved and coincides with a very ambiguous message. Gustaw's stream of feelings, where direct confessions turn into vivid reminiscences of his past affection, has been placed within the frames of subjective and objective points of view. The speaker, like Don Quixote a man inspired by reading, creates the appealing images of a passionate love to an idealized woman, but his powers appear adversely affected by ecstasy and illusion when confronted with the sober words of the listening priest and the recalled opinions of others. Consequently the adoration of love is followed by its partial deconstruction. The great passion has eventually disclosed its inner side: that of illusion, self-deception and madness.

Part III, published much later (1832), belongs among the most important and most influential works of Polish literature. Written in Dresden and stimulated by the recent defeat of a national uprising against Russia, the drama portrays events from the poet's life eight years previously. It concerns the trial of Vilnius's patriotic youth, carried out by the Russian authorities in 1824. This rather minor incident is transformed into a national drama, with the personal mythology acquiring a universal dimension. As a result, *Forefathers' Eve, Part III*, has become a leading patriotic poem. Its description of national martyrdom and its vision of the future of Poland has exerted a powerful impact on the Polish mind, its appeal still in force today.

Part III is linked with the previous parts by the final scene at a cemetery on Forefathers' Eve, and by the mystical transformation of Gustaw, the lover from *Part IV*, into Konrad, a national leader. The existing drama actually forms the first act of an unfinished work and contains a prologue, nine scenes, and an epic supplement which is a cycle of poems about Russia. Chronologically it follows *Parts II* and *IV*, but apart from symbolic links between Gustaw and Konrad, it has little in common with them. Critics usually distinguish in *Part III* the historical episodes, set in contemporary Poland, from the spiritual drama, located in the sphere of religious and national mythology. The former are represented by Scene 1, set in a Vilnius prison, the portrayal of the Polish establishment in a Warsaw salon (Scene 7), and the episodes in the Russian Senator's house (Scene 8). The latter includes the prologue, where Gustaw turns into Konrad, Konrad's long monologue called the Improvisation (Scene 2), the exorcisms carried out on Konrad by Father Peter (Scene 3), the dream of an innocent girl, Eve (Scene 4), Father Peter's vision of the future of Poland (Scene 5), the Senator's dream (Scene 6), and the final scene in a cemetery (Scene 9).

Actually, the mythological sphere permeates the realistic one and both are subordinated to the structure of a morality play which is founded on the battle between the forces of good and evil, externalized from the human soul (in particular, Konrad's) into a universal struggle. The clear-cut division between good and evil embraces not only angels and devils, whose presence accompanies the events, but also the human world. Accordingly, the Vilnius trial is raised to the symbolic level of Herod's Massacre of the Innocents, with its echo of the martyrdom of Christ himself. When Mickiewicz proudly stated in his preface to the drama that Poland's sufferings and devotion in the previous 50 years "were unparalleled since the times of the persecution of Christianity", he elevated the Polish–Russian conflict to the divine plane of a struggle between right and wrong. Here the tsar is identified with the Prince of Darkness, while his servants, including Polish traitors, are the functionaries of Hell. Thus the political conflict appears as a moral one, and the three partitions of Poland in the 18th-Century are likened to the crucifixion of Christ in Scene 5. The idea of Poland as "the Christ of nations" paved the way for a national Messianism, shared by many Poles in the 19th Century.

Despite his predominantly critical assessment of Russia and the Russians, Mickiewicz was far from advocating the anti-Christian idea of violence. The tones of revenge, present in the drama, are eventually replaced by Christian forgiveness, and punishment is left to God. His thunderbolt kills one of the Polish traitors, and Father Peter announces the inevitable advent of divine justice. The last of the epic poems added to the drama contains the ominous picture of a flood afflicting St Petersburg. In much the same way, Konrad in the course of events, undergoes another transformation. In the first episodes, including his powerful Improvisation, he combines Byronic pride and scorn for commoners with the Promethean struggle with God on behalf of humanity. But his vision of a poet-creator, equal in his power to the Almighty, is eventually deconstructed, like Gustaw's illusions about Romantic love. Moreover, this time the protagonist is misled not by books, but by vulgar and grotesque devils, later exorcised by Father Peter. A reborn person, he seems destined to play the role of a national Messiah, foreseen by Father Peter.

Part III represents even more challenging proposals for stage production than the previous parts. Combining realism with poetic fantasy, lyrical monologues and dreams with group scenes, dialogues with music and dance, it can achieve outstanding theatrical results, as it did in Konrad Swinarski's production (1973). The particularly Polish nature of *Forefathers' Eve* probably accounts for its rather negligible interest outside Poland, George Sand's study *Essai sur le drame fantastique. Goethe—Byron—Mickiewicz* (1839) being an exception.

—Stanislaw Eile

FORESKIN'S LAMENT
by Greg McGee

First Publication: Wellington, New Zealand, 1981.
First Production: By Theatre Corporate, Auckland, New Zealand, 30 October 1980.

Criticism
(For general works on the author, see *Playwrights* volume)

Articles:
Gareth Cordery, "*Tom Brown's Schooldays* and *Foreskin's Lament*: The Alpha and Omega of Rugby Football", in *Journal of Popular Culture*, vol. 19 no. 2, 1985.
David Carnegie, "The Metamorphoses of *Foreskin's Lament*", in *Australasian Drama Studies*, 17, 1990.

* * *

Foreskin's Lament is ostensibly a play about rugby players in a small New Zealand town in the 1970's. Act I is set in a changing shed after the mid-week practice, amidst crude and often very funny team banter. However, the fullback Foreskin (all the players are principally known by nicknames) learns that Clean may have deliberately kicked and concussed the team captain in order to obtain the captaincy himself. In Act II, at the after-match party on the Saturday night, knowing that Clean has injured their captain again, this time fatally, Foreskin challenges his team-mates and the audience to recognize the hollowness of the myths and conformist values by which New Zealand society has judged itself for a century and more.

The extraordinary force of the first productions of *Foreskin's Lament* in 1980 and 1981 lay in the correspondence between the play's analysis of New Zealand society and the experience of the audience. The association of rugby with New Zealand was clear. When the old-fashioned coach, Tupper, berates Foreskin for raising unpleasant doubts ("This is a team game, son, and the town is the team. It's the town's honour at stake when the team plays"), he is defining ideals of rugby, and of New Zealand, in terms of consensus, loyalty, and male comradeship. There is no difficulty in identifying models of behaviour. The heroic legends are of rugby or war, either of which will straighten out errant youngsters like Foreskin who question traditional codes. Two characters in particular represent challenges to this view. The brutal Clean has returned from Vietnam with a cynical version of American individualism (very different from Tupper's World-War-II romanticism): "You stick it to them, that's their philosophy. Right up the arse....Everything's there for the taking, not the asking". Clean pays lip-service to traditions of mateship and loyalty, but in fact uses them as a cover for his naked aggression and ambition. The other challenge comes from Foreskin's liberal, lawyer girlfriend, Moira, who recognizes, as Foreskin himself does, that New Zealand society, in almost a mirror image of rugby values, achieves its smug consensus without thought for the violence it breeds, for the simplifying and brutalizing of all sensitivity, and for the oppressive marginalizing of outsiders—women, homosexuals, even intellectuals like Foreskin. Tupper's chivalric myths are less than half the truth. Moira demands Foreskin make a choice: "Me. As opposed to the imbecilic Tupper, or the moronic Clean". But what Foreskin sees, as none of the others does, is that "it's not a competition". He tells her, "their smell is your smell, it's they who decide for us which road, what speed, how far, and who drives". Moira doesn't believe it. Foreskin insists, "I've always believed it. But it used to be quite comforting. Perhaps that's what I'm mourning". In other words, he recognizes the rite of passage of himself and the country. Like circumcision (hence *Foreskin's Lament*), New Zealand's post-colonial coming of age involves pain and loss of innocence. The apparent harmony of the past, New Zealand as a classless consensus society, God's Own Country, are revealed as illusions, and the divisions of the present have no obvious solution in the future.

Part of the enormous popularity of the play when it first appeared was undoubtedly the uninhibited, locker–room humour and the comic acting potential of many of the parts. In several productions the "old bull" Tupper, incorrigible traditionalist, blinkered but warm-hearted, has nearly stolen the show. Tupper's eventual realisation of the evil to which he has been so blind, that Clean has killed his own teammate and called it an accident, is an awakening of almost tragic agony that goes near to making him the central character. Foreskin, however, sees most clearly and feels most deeply. Like an Elizabethan tragic hero, he is singled out as the anguished observer of a corrupt society. His liberal ideas, his defence of the weak, his independent thinking, comic wit and verbal virtuosity, establish him for the audience as the principal character just as much as his central position in the play's structure. When, near the end of the play, he breaks out of the naturalist fourth-wall convention in order to address the audience direct with the long monologue which is the "lament" of the title, the move seems an inevitable extension of his impossible dilemma, made dramaturgically possible by the close identification of the audience with his anger, sorrow, and anguish.

Audiences and readers alike have recognized the play as a theatrical and literary milestone. It anatomizes New Zealand society, through the metaphor of rugby, as no play has done before. And through its rough humour, and the painful intensity of Foreskin's dilemma and lament, it does this without rancour or bitterness; only with a deep sense of loss.

—David Carnegie

THE FOREST (Les)
by Alexander Ostrovsky

First Publication: In *Otechestvennye zapiski* [*Annals of the Fatherland*], 1871.
First Production: Alexandrinsky Theatre, St. Petersburg, 1 November 1871.

Editions
Les, in *Groza; Les; Bespridannitsa*, edited by E. Kalmanovskogo, Leningrad 1977.

Translations
The Forest, translated by C. Winslow and G.R., Noyes, New York, 1926.
The Forest, in *Five Plays of Alexander Ostrovsky*, translated by E.K. Bristow, New York, 1969.
The Forest, in *Ostrovsky: Plays*, translated by Margaret Wettlin, Moscow, 1974.

Criticism
(For general works on the author, see *Playwrights* volume)

Articles:
Irene Zohrab, "Problems of Style in the Plays of A.N. Ostrovsky", in *Melbourne Slavonic Studies*, 12, 1977.
Irene Zohrab, "Problems of Translation: The Plays of A.N. Ostrovsky in English", in *Melbourne Slavic Studies*, 16, 1982.

*   *   *

Written in 1870 and first produced the following year, *The Forest* has perhaps equal claims with *The Storm* to being Ostrovsky's best play. It concerns the despicable landowner and petty tyrant Gurmyzhskaya who is selling her forests to Vosmibratov the former peasant, now businessman (a character-type who was not to appear again for some 30 years until Chekhov's *The Cherry Orchard*), in an attempt to disinherit her nephew of the land which should be his. She intends that her ward, Aksyusha, should marry the young nincompoop Bulanov. Vosmibratov cheats Gurmyzhskaya out of some of the money he owes her for the forests and suggests that she give Aksyusha a sizeable sum as a dowry so that she can marry his own son Petr.

The nephew who has been trying to make his own way in the world has taken up the profession of tragic acting under the name of Neschastlivtsev (The Unhappy One). He returns to his aunt's home accompanied by a comic actor, Arkashka (or Schastlivtsev, The Happy One) and pretends to be an army officer, while he makes Arkashka play the part of his valet. He recovers for Gurmyzhskaya the money Vosmibratov had swindled out of her. However, then Arkashka overhears her giving the money to Bulanov and tells Neschastlivtsev; but Neschastlivtsev has too much respect for his aunt to believe him. Upset by this treatment Arkashka reveals their true identity which leads to their nearly being driven out of the house. Aksyusha then asks Neschastlivtsev for 2,000 roubles which is the amount Vosmibratov will accept as her dowry; but he is actually penniless. So, he extracts from his aunt a payment of 1,000 roubles as the price for giving up his inheritance. Neschastlivtsev then hears his aunt announce her own engagement to Bulanov and refuse to give Aksyusha a kopeck, whereon he gives Aksyusha 1,000 roubles, which Vosmibratov is now happy to accept, and the two actors depart.

After establishing himself as the leading playwright of his day, Ostrovsky was accused, after the emancipation of the peasants in 1861, of having run out of ideas. This was put down to the fact that the world of merchants he had portrayed so well (the "Kingdom of Darkness" as it was known), and on which his fame rested, was fast disappearing and that he had little understanding of the new social conditions. However a series of plays in the 1860's and 1870's soon contradicted such suspicions. *Enough Simplicity in Every Wise Man* (or *The Scoundrel* as it is usually known in English) with its witty satire on high society in the new Russia; *A Warm Heart* with its wonderful portrayal of a young girl protesting at the stifling atmosphere in which she is forced to live; and *Easy Money*

The Forest: The Other Place, Stratford-Upon-Avon, (Royal Shakespeare Company)

which deals with the contrasts between the *nouveau riche* and the now impoverished, former landowning class are all ample proof of this. It is, however, *The Forest* which is the best of Ostrovsky's later plays.

Classical in form, with its five acts, its observance of the three unities, and the symbolic names of some of its characters, it is concerned with the ill effects of money and the cupidity and selfishness it causes. Its leading character, Gurmyzhskaya, is another representation of the tyrannical, self-centred woman, the *samodur*, which had its most fearsome portrayal in Kabanova in *The Storm*, but here the character-type's methods are different. While her predecessors wielded power for its own sake, Gurmyzhskaya uses it to forward her own ignoble fancies, which are based on the accumulation of capital and a lack of concern for anyone else; this is the prime purpose of her selling the forest to her equally grasping counterpart, Vosmibratov. The forest itself can, of course, be seen as symbolizing the shield around the old patriarchal estates which is now to be removed, letting in the blasts from the new age. It is into this world that the two actors unwarily intrude. The greed, egoism, and hypocrisy of most of the other characters are thrown into sharp relief by the genuine nobility of these two, especially the tragic Neschastlivtsev, and they have been, not without some justification, compared to Don Quixote and

Sancho Panza. Despite its adverse comments on capitalism, *The Forest* is also a play about the more positive sides of human nature and its ability to rise above the pettiness of life's concerns. This is epitomized in Neschastlivtsev's final speech where he defends himself and Arkashka from Gurmyzhskaya's taunts that they are only clowns:

No, we are the actors, and you are the clowns; we love, we quarrel, we fight, and we help our brothers with our last, hard-earned kopeck. And you? All your life you've talked about the welfare of society and the love of man. But what have you actually done? Whom have you fed? Whom have you comforted? Only your-selves. . .You are the clowns, not us.

Ostrovsky, nothing if not realistic, has given us in *The Forest* a number of unlikable, cynical, selfish and domineering charac-ters, but he has also championed the essential goodness of the human spirit.

—A. V. Knowles

FORTY YEARS ON
by Alan Bennett

First Publication: London, 1969.
First Production: Apollo Theatre, 31 October 1968.

*   *   *

Bennett's play is set in a minor English public school, Albion House, where staff and pupils are presenting the end of term play, "Speak for England, Arthur", a chronological revue of British political and cultural history from the turn of the century to the end of World War II. The revue comprises readings from actual and fictional literary memoirs, historic radio broadcasts, poems, parodic sketches, slide lectures and songs, most of which are filtered through the memories of Hugh, an upper-class, Conservative Member of Parliament, and his wife, Moggie (suggested by the real-life partnership of Harold Nicolson and Vita Sackville-West). With Nursie, their elderly nanny, they reminisce, grumble, and comment on the conduct of war from the safety of their refuge in the basement of Claridge's Hotel. The play-within-the-play marks the occasion of the Headmaster's retirement and the transfer of office to his senior housemaster, Franklin. The parts in the school entertainment are taken variously by the Headmaster, Franklin, a junior housemaster Tempest, the bursar's secretary Miss Nisbitt, and Matron. Other parts are played by the boys of Albion House who also sing and provide musical accompaniment.

Bennett's first stage play owes much to his experience as writer and performer of cabaret, revue, and television satirical comedy. What started as a stockpile of sketches for a projected revue became in turn a radio play (unproduced) and, with the addition of the school framework, the stage play which enjoyed great success when first produced in 1968 with Sir John Gielgud as the Headmaster and Bennett himself as Tempest. Bennett has disarmingly described his comedy as "an elaborate life-support system for the preservation of old jokes".

The location of *Forty Years On* undoubtedly allows the dramatist to recycle and renew some stock jokes and routines—the many disasters attending amateur performance, schoolboy mayhem, the peculiar language of educational and moral control, and the clichés of an (almost) all-male institution. Bennett seizes these opportunities gleefully and unashamedly, furnishing the Albion House scenes with ripe examples of schoolboy humour and schoolmaster sarcasm with an added undercurrent of homosexual jokes. A Confirmation Class, for example, slides inexorably into a sex lesson conducted too eagerly by a master with roving hands. Elsewhere, Tempest delivers the old joke, "I wish I could put my hands on the choir's parts". The historical and cultural snippets of "Speak for England, Arthur" not only provide fuel for a running battle between Franklin and the Headmaster, who views the former's production with deep suspicion as a radical departure from the past successes of *Samson Agonistes* and *Dear Octopus*, but allow Bennett scope for a range of comic forms. The loose structure easily accomodates set pieces of literary parody, as in the sketch on the Abdication Crisis in the style of "Sapper" or John Buchan. A grotesque romantic encounter on Primrose Hill between Bertrand Russell and Lady Ottoline Morrell, the latter impersonated as a giantess by two boys in outrageous costume, verges on pantomime, while a mock memoir of T. E. Lawrence, whose girlish giggle is said to have earned him the nickname Tee Hee Lawrence, is gloriously silly.

Bennett's characteristically diffident estimate of the play, however, does scant justice to his technical abilities, his precise mimicry of speech styles or to the delicate balance he achieves of low comedy, sharp satire and affectionate homage to a British past which, by 1968, seemed thoroughly outdated and yet still exercised a strong nostalgic pull.

Bennett's method of provoking laughter is best exemplified by the Headmaster's opening address. His high-minded speech is constantly interrupted and subverted by inopportune aircraft noises, coughs, nose blowings and schoolboy misdemeanours, or by his own sudden swoops into prayer. This interruptive technique becomes Bennett's main comic tactic throughout the play. The entertainment, episodic by nature, is further punctuated by the Headmaster's policing for smut, by unscheduled eruptions of the victorious rugby team into the performance, and by the on-stage presentation of the interval of "Speak for England, Arthur". Bennett consistently generates a double laughter: that which savours the exactness of language, character and situation (both in the school scenes and the parodic re-creations), and that which greets the bathos occasioned by the mundane or ludicrous interruption.

This comic strategy, modulating erratically in tone from the touching to the absurd, the noble to the crass, suffuses the play and gives life to Bennett's overall metaphor of the school as post-war Britain. Albion House, "this little huddle of buildings in a fold of the downs", exhibits in microcosm the symptoms of Britain's 20th-century decline. Poised on the verge of bankruptcy, ripe for change but still clinging to the old values of privilege, order and gentlemanliness, it mounts a public performance in a "gloomy Victorian Gothic" hall in celebration of the past. (In a typically double-edged image Bennett has the old Headmaster being made up swathed in a prop Union Jack.) The performance, however, is barely under control and is in any case being subverted from within by the new man, Franklin.

The conceit is by no means novel, and in the hands of Brenton or Hare has been more abrasively pursued, but Bennett has the courage to play it for all it is worth, granting equal weight to nostalgic evocation and to ridicule. In the original production Gielgud lent genuine dignity to the Headmaster's fading world, employing his lyrical voice in sly awareness of its potential for grandeur as well as triteness, in contrast to the more waspish notes of Bennett's own Tempest. The play defies interpretation along narrow, ideological lines; rather it encourages an amused observation of the British and their institutions, noting their hypocrisy, amateurishness, and philistinism as well as their innocence, idealism, and love of tradition.

—Ronald W. Strang

———

THE FOSSIL. See **SCENES FROM THE HEROIC LIFE OF THE MIDDLE CLASSES.**

———

FRANCESCA DA RIMINI
by George Henry Boker

First Publication: In *Plays and Poems*, New York, 1856 (2 vols.).
First Production: Broadway Theatre, New York, 26 September 1855.

Francesca da Rimini: Lawrence Barrett as Lanciotto, 1882

Editions
Francesca da Rimini, in *Dramas From the American Theatre 1762–1909*, edited by Richard Moody, Boston, 1966.

Criticism
(For general works on the author, see *Playwrights* volume)

Articles:
Gertrude Urban, "Paolo and Francesca in History and Literature", in *Critic*, 40, 1902.
Archibald Henderson, "The Rimini Story in Modern Drama", in *Arena*, 39, 1908.
John C. Metcalfe, "An Old Romantic Triangle: Francesca da Rimini in Three Dramas", in *Sewanee Review*, 29, 1921.
Paul C. Sherr, "George Henry Boker's *Francesca da Rimini*: A Justification for the Literary Historian", in *Pennsylvania History*, 34, 1967.
Paul D. Voelker, "George Henry Boker's *Francesca da Rimini*: An Interpretation and an Evaluation", in *Educational Theatre Journal*, 24, 1972.
Jules Zanger, "Boker's *Francesca da Rimini*: The Brothers' Tragedy", in *Educational Theatre Journal*, 25, 1973.
Kent G. Gallagher, "The Tragedies of George Henry Boker: The Measure of American Romantic Drama", in *Emerson Society Quarterly*, 20, 1974.
Claude R. Flory, "Boker, Barrett and the Francesca Theme in Drama", in *Players*, 50, 1975.

*   *   *

Boker's *Francesca da Rimini* deals with an old story—that of Paolo and Francesca, depicted first by Dante in the fifth canto of the *Inferno*. To satisfy a power struggle between the city states of Ravenna and Rimini, a marriage is arranged between Lanciotto, a soldier of considerable stature, and Francesca, daughter of Guido da Palenta of Ravenna. Because Lanciotto is physically deformed, his handsome brother Paolo is sent in his stead to go through a proxy marriage. Francesca, however, is kept ignorant of the substitution, and her emotions are aroused by Paolo. Later, Francesca and Paolo, through the maliciousness of a servant, are discovered by Lanciotto, who takes his revenge. Of those who had dramatized the story, George Henry Boker was the first to write a play in English. His contributions lie not wholly in the dramatic quality he found in the story but in his portrayal of character and the tangled lives he imagined with such sympathy and passion.

Boker worked with great care to tell the familiar story in terms of his admiration for the character he must have considered his protagonist. Act I is essentially exposition. The arranged wedding is ridiculed by Pepe, the king's fool, whose complicated character reveals Boker's interest in contrasting good and evil and exposing the quality of society that corrupts. There is genuine brotherly affection between Paolo and Lanciotto, and it is agreed that Paolo will go to Ravenna and speak to Francesca of Lanciotto, "not as I ought to be, but as I am". When Pepe basely taunts the extremely self-conscious Lanciotto for his physical deformity, he receives a blow for his insolence, and for that blow demands "your life!". Foreshadowing throughout the play is adroitly managed; irony is plentiful; humor lightens the heavy theme; spectacle provides a change of pace, as do contrasting scenes of joy and sorrow. Superstition and fate are carefully introduced to suggest destinies beyond man's understanding or control.

Act II belongs to Francesca whose girlish charm and filial devotion are displayed in counterpoint to the suberterfuge being practiced by her father and by Paolo until, by the end of the act, her innocence is shattered and the depth of her character is revealed in her mature acknowledgement of the cruel game being played. In Act III the betrothed pair meet for the first time, and Boker shows his skill and perception in dramatizing the great irony so feared by Paolo who, better than anyone, knows the truly sensitive and beautiful person of Lanciotto existing within the mis-shapen body. Full of joy because a woman loves him, Lanciotto suddenly feels that he can love, but Francesca, shaken by her first view of Lanciotto, turns aside to whisper to herself: "Thus I begin the practice of deceit". Although fearful that he may "have duped myself", Lanciotto enjoys a lover's dream as Act IV begins. Later, his true sentiments bared to the world, he questions his vision. Showing anger and frustration, and in thoughts dramatically parallel to those of Francesca in Act II, Lanciotto attempts to make light of his love and regain control of his life as an approaching battle allows him to escape from Rimini.

Paolo's reading of the story of Lancelot and Genevra to Francesca eventually inspires them to declare their love. Pepe, the malcontent, ever watchful, bears this information to Lanciotto and produces Paolo's dagger to suggest a deeper calculated crime before Lanciotto silences him forever. In the final scene, poignantly dramatic but overdone in the tradition of romantic tragedy, Lanciotto discovers the lovers together and begs them to lie and make unnecessary the act of honor and revenge he must commit.

In terms of the play's structure, the main character is Lanciotto. Forced into a situation he does not want, he enlists the aid of his brother and deceives himself into thinking that love can be his, until he recognizes Francesca's feelings and is forced by Pepe to see the truth and bring death to all. Fate lends a hand; malignant society is introduced into his world through Pepe, but Lanciotto determines the major actions of the play. Yet Boker called his play *Francesca da Rimini* and evidently had in mind for his heroine the actress Julia Dean for whom he had written *Leonor de Guzman*. Francesca's presence does motivate others, but although she struggles with herself through four acts of the play, she makes no discovery after Act II and does little to change the direction of the play. In the final scene she becomes only a means to "honor" for Lanciotto. One could ask: "Whose tragedy is it?".

The answer lies in Boker's major problem for the 1855 production of *Francesca da Rimini*: the fact that the theatre of the 1850's exploited the star performer. Boker, however, wrote a play with four great parts and two leading characters. Francesca is an excellent role. Her delightful determination to please her father by falling in love with a stranger is soon contrasted with her patently false confession, after she understands what has happened, that "I'm glad I kept my heart safe, after all" and her bitter realization that she can leave her home "with no regret". Paolo is more than a handsome playboy. Sensitive to his brother's problems and feelings, he suffers the remorse of the fallen while insisting that Lanciotto satisfy his honor. More than a clever fool who hides behind his coxcomb, Pepe is a complex individual—a foil to Lanciotto in appearance and beliefs, and idealist with thoughts about social reform, a sadist who delights in torturing Lanciotto, a man who understands the "democracy of death" and is bitter about the life he is destined to lead.

The leading actor, Edwin Forrest, would never have accepted this play, and E. L. Davenport did not excel in his 1855 performance. No actor or actress at this time saw in *Francesca da Rimini* a vehicle for success. Consequently, the play languished until acting conditions began to change and one actor, with the help of the critic William Winter, envisioned the potential of this play for his future. When Lawrence Barrett revived *Francesca da Rimini* in 1882, the star system in the theatre still existed, but there were modifications to it as well as a growing core of actors and actresses who could provide distinguished supporting roles for a leading performer. It is revealing, of course, that an actor rather than an actress revived the play. Thirty years after the play's disappointing first reception, the *New York Tribune* could announce on 24 January 1885 the 100th performance of Barrett's production in New York.

—Walter J. Meserve

FRANCESCA DA RIMINI
by Gabriele D'Annunzio

First Publication: Milan, 1903.
First Production: Teatro Costanzi, Rome, 9 December 1901.

Translations
Francesca da Rimini, translated by Arthur Symons, New York and London, 1902.
Francesca da Rimini, translated by G. Martinelli, in *Continental Plays*, edited by T.H Dickinson, New York, 1923.

Criticism
(For general works on the author, see *Playwrights* volume)
Articles:
Emilio Mariano, "La *Francesca da Rimini* e i suoi significati", in *Quaderni del vittoriale*, 24, 1980.

*   *   *

Francesca da Rimini was the first play of a proposed trilogy on the Malatestas. The second, *Parisina*, was performed in 1913, but the third, *Sigismondo Malatesta*, never appeared. The story of Francesca da Rimini was extremely familiar to Italian audiences, since it was immortalized by Dante in the *Divine Comedy*.

Dante placed the doomed lovers, Paolo and Francesca, in Hell, but also conveyed his own strong sense of sympathy for their plight. Their appearance, in Canto V of the *Inferno*, is one of the most powerful episodes of the *Divine Comedy*, and echoes of Dante can be found throughout D'Annunzio's play. Both Paolo and Francesca were historical personages, but through Dante they have become archetypes, along with other mythical adulterers such as Tristan and Isolde, and Launcelot and Guinevere. D'Annunzio focusses attention on Francesca, showing how she is sold into marriage with the deformed Gianciotto by her vicious brother, and misled into giving her consent because she believes that she is going to marry Gianciotto's handsome brother, Paolo. Like Tristan and Isolde, Paolo and Francesca fall in love when he comes to escort her back to Rimini to her new husband, and that love is too strong for them to resist. They are betrayed by another brother, the young Malatestino, who desires Francesca himself and so tells Gianciotto of her adultery with Paolo. In a dramatic climax, Gianciotto bursts into Francesca's chamber and stabs her and Paolo to death.

D'Annunzio develops this well-known story-line in various ways, most strikingly in his depiction of Paolo's brothers, Gianciotto and Malatestino. His depiction of Gianciotto arouses considerable sympathy, for despite his tyrannical reputation and deformed body, he is shown as a man genuinely in love with his wife and close to his brother. His tragedy is to be betrayed by the two people that he trusts and cares for the most. The villain in D'Annunzio's version is not the husband but the youngest brother, the demonic Malatestino, who first appears in Act II, badly wounded in the ongoing battle. He loses an eye through his injuries, but insists on struggling back into combat, telling Francesca that he is incapable of feeling pain. Later, it becomes apparent that he is also incapable of feeling love or affection, and that he is an incarnation of evil. Interestingly, in the first production the part of Malatestino was played by a woman, Emilia Varini.

Francesca da Rimini was written for Eleonora Duse, who, at 43 years of age, was at the height of her fame in 1901. Her relationship with D'Annunzio, which lasted from 1897 to 1904, when it collapsed in bitterness and recrimination, was as much an artistic collaboration as a love affair. D'Annunzio wanted to create a new, Italian, lyric theatre, while Duse wanted to extend what she perceived as the narrow repertoire of plays available to Italian actors. *Francesca da Rimini* became their special project, and after the mixed response to their earlier collaboration on *La città morta* (March, 1901), no effort was spared in trying to make the play a success. Adelaide Ristori, the grand old lady of the Italian theatre, wrote to her son that Duse had virtually ruined herself financially by the vast amount of money that she had put into *Francesca da Rimini*. Both Duse and D'Annunzio wanted the production to be spectacular, and so specialist advisors were employed to work on costumes and sets to ensure authentic, medieval splendour, an elaborate reconstruction of medieval siege weaponry was designed for the military sequence in Act II, Mariano Fortuny was brought in as designer (though he resigned two months before the opening) and the costumes were made of expensive silks and brocades. Rehearsals ran for two months prior to the opening, and D'Annunzio took on the tasks of director, designer and choreographer, despite his lack of practical theatre experience. Tension in rehearsals ran high, and such was D'Annunzio's inexperience as a director that the performance on the opening night lasted six hours, part of the scenery collapsed, the battle scenes filled the theatre with choking black smoke and Luigi Pirandello, who was in the audience, was moved to comment that he had "never suffered so much in a theatre" as he did on that occasion. The tour was a financial disaster, though audience response was mixed, with opinion divided as to the aesthetic qualities of the production and the play itself. After the opening night D'Annunzio made radical cuts to the text, thereby reducing the playing time to a more acceptable length.

D'Annunzio's intention of creating a major spectacular piece of theatre is both the strength and the weakness of the play. His structuring highlighted the visual aspect, and so the five acts presented a series of elaborately designed interiors in which the actors appeared like performers in a pageant. Act I is set in the home of Francesca and her family, with a split-level design that allowed maximum effect when Duse made her first entrance in Scene 5, walking through the loggia and descending the great staircase. Act II takes place in the castle of the Malatestas during a battle, and opens with two soldiers preparing a cauldron of boiling Greek fire. Francesca's experiment with the Greek fire, when she lights a torch and soliloquizes on the splendour of the flame is one of the great set-pieces of the play. For Act III, a medieval bedroom was lavishly constructed, that would also be used in Act V, whilst the set for Act IV consisted of an octagonal armoury. The four sets alternated between the femininity of the rose garden and the boudoir, and the masculinity of the armoury and tower, but making considerable use of split levels, staircases and rooms-within-rooms. The vastness of the sets, as some critics noted, dwarfed the actors completely. D'Annunzio's staging, along with his conception of theatre, used the actor more or less as a prop.

There is very little characterization in the play. Paolo and Francesca are archetypes rather than characters, and the evil brothers (Francesca's own brother Ostasio and Paolo's brother Malatestino) are also stock figures. There is some attempt at characterization with Gianciotto, but not much, and Francesca's women function as a chorus. Smaragdi, the slave girl, serves as Francesca's confidante but is never developed as a character. For D'Annunzio, what mattered was the function of a personage in the development of the plot and his or her placing in the *tableaux vivants* of which the play consists. The stage directions give precise details for the staging of these tableaux, and the final sequence in which Francesca and Paolo die in one another's arms is minutely described.

Francesca da Rimini is a period piece. It belongs to the era of grandiose stagings and large casts and is theatrical but in a very literary way. Like most of D'Annunzio's plays, it has fallen into obscurity, but is nevertheless a fine example of *fin-de-siècle* theatre and shows the extremes to which a writer like D'Annunzio was prepared to go in his endeavours to revitalize the Italian lyric tradition.

—Susan Bassnett

FRIAR BACON AND FRIAR BUNGAY
by Robert Greene

First Publication: London, 1594.
First Production: London, c. 1589; earliest recorded production, by Strange's Men, 19 February 1592.

Editions

Friar Bacon and Friar Bungay, in *The Plays and Poems of Robert Greene*, edited by John Churton Collins, Oxford, 1905.
Friar Bacon and Friar Bungay, in *Minor Elizabethan Drama*, London, 1910.
Friar Bacon and Friar Bungay, edited by Daniel Seltzer, Lincoln, Nebraska, 1963 (Regents Renaissance Drama Series).
Friar Bacon and Frair Bungay, edited by J.A. Levin, London, 1969 (New Mermaid Series).

Criticism

(For general works on the author, see *Playwrights* volume)

Books:
Kerstin Assarsson-Rizzi, *"Friar Bacon and Friar Bungay": A Structural and Thematic Analysis of Robert Greene's Play*, Lund, 1972.

Articles:
J.D. McCallum, "Greene's *Friar Bacon and Friar Bungay*", in *Modern Language Notes*, 35, 1920.
Percy Z. Round, "Greene's Materials for *Friar Bacon and Friar Bungay*", in *Modern Language Notes*, 21, 1926.
Walden F. McNeir, "Traditional Elements in the Character of Greene's *Friar Bacon*", in *Studies in Philology*, 45, 1948.

A.H. MacLaire, "Greene's Borrowings from His Own Prose Fiction in *Bacon and Bungay* and *James IV*", in *Philological Quarterly*, 30, 1951.
Frank Towne, "White Magic in *Friar Bacon and Friar Bungay*", in *Modern Language Notes*, 67, 1952.
Peter Mortenson, "*Friar Bacon and Friar Bungay*: Festive Comedy and 'Three-Form'd Luna'", in *English Literary Renaissance*, 2, 1972.
Albert Wertheim, "The Presentation of Sin in *Friar Bacon and Friar Bungay*", in *Criticism*, 16, 1974.
Paul Dean, "*Friar Bacon and Friar Bungay* and *John of Bordeaux*: A Dramatic Diptych", in *English Language Notes*, vol.18 no.4, 1981.
Charles Hieatt, "A New Source of *Friar Bacon and Friar Bungay*", in *Review of English Studies*, 32, 1981.
Joseph R. Stodder, "Magus and Maiden: Archetypal Roles in Greene's *Friar Bacon and Friar Bungay*", in *Journal of Evolutionary Psychology*, vol.4, nos. 1–2, 1983.
Frank Ardolino, "'Thus Glories England over all the West': Setting as National Encomium in Robert Greene's *Friar Bacon and Friar Bungay*", in *Journal of Evolutionary Psychology*, vol. 9 nos. 3–4, 1988.

*   *   *

Out hunting, Prince Edward is smitten with "country Margaret". She, however, falls in love with his emissary, Lacy, the Earl of Lincoln, who is posing as a farmer, and he with her. With the help of Friar Bacon's magic, Edward sees their wooing and prevents Friar Bungay from marrying them. Eventually, however, Lacy persuades Edward to prize honor and friendship above lust and jealousy. In the over-plot the King negotiates the marriage of Prince Edward to "lovely Elinor", princess of Castile, who, enamored of the prince's portrait, "dar'd for Edward's sake cut through the seas" in pursuit of the match. The play ends with a double wedding of the two couples.

The comic sub-plot concerns Friar Bacon's efforts to make a brazen head that will answer philosophical questions and enable him "to compass England with a wall of brass". He is a Faustian figure, thinking of the great deeds magic will allow him to achieve, but in fact serving the whims of his rulers—most notably in a competition in which he defeats his rivals, Bungay and the Emperor's magician, in an interlude halfway through the play. Later on, Bacon renounces magic:

> . . . Bacon must be damn'd
> For using devils to countervail his God.
> Yet, Bacon, cheer thee; drown not in despair:
> Sins have their salves, repentance can do much;
> Think Mercy sits where Justice holds her seat.

Marlowe, writing *Dr. Faustus* some three years after 1589, the probable date of Greene's play, seems to have borrowed some details from it. Appropriately for a comedy, Friar Bacon has faith in repentance and mercy where Faustus can only despair. Like Margaret, he will give up the rest of his life to prayer. But there remains the natural magic, of love, an "enchantment" of which the characters often speak. Lacy confronts Margaret: "God or Lord Lacy. Which contents you best,/To be a nun or else Lord Lacy's wife?". To this she replies:

> The flesh is frail; my Lord doth know it well,
> That when he comes with his enchanting face,
> Whatso'er betide, I cannot say him nay.
> Off goes the habit of a maiden's heart,

And, seeing fortune will, fair Framlingham,
And all the show of holy nuns, farewell!
Lacy for me, if he will be my lord.

Her spirit has led one critic to call her the first notable woman of Elizabethan drama, the prototype of Shakespeare's romantic heroines. For his part, having won her, Lacy's thoughts switch to what he might get for breakfast. Greene's characters have healthy appetites for all the physical pleasures.

The formulae of romantic comedy as Shakespeare practiced it were first put together in *Friar Bacon and Friar Bungay*. Here we find dramatized the contrast between court and country, the nobility of nurture and the nobility of nature, the parallel loves of different classes. This, for example, is Prince Edward's description of how Margaret caught his eye:

Whenas she swept like Venus through the house,
And in her shape fast folded up my thoughts,
Into the milkhouse went I with the maid,
And there amongst the cream bowls she did shine
As Pallas 'mongst her princely huswifery.
She turned her smock over her lily arms,
And dived them into milk to run her cheese;
But, whiter than the milk, her crystal skin,
Checked with lines of azure, made her blush
That art or nature durst bring for compare.

Although the speech ends ominously with the Prince suggesting that he would "with Tarquin, hazard Rome and all / To win the lovely maid of Fressingfield", there is something almost ingenuous in his impulsiveness, as the invocation of Venus, Pallas and Lucrece to describe a girl making cheese suggests. These references remind us of the incongruities between the Prince's world and Margaret's and that the "frolic courtiers" are, in intention, only playing holiday. But the play is also about the different definitions of love—as lust, as enchantment, as fidelity—and the play moves from one to another as it proceeds.

We sense in Greene a joyous and healthy respect for the pastoral but everyday world: for the sensuous gestures of Margaret making cheese, "lusty frolic bucks" to hunt, or "kine with fair and burnish'd heads, / With strouting dugs that paggle to the ground". It is a world whose natural impulses no one can escape. To the double wedding of the last scene Bacon contributes a prophecy of an idyllic England under the rule of Edward's descendants. Such serious stuff acknowledged, the play ends with—what else?—an invitation to let "hearts be frolic" and to feast.

—Anthony Graham-White

THE FROGS (Batrachoi / Ranae)
by Aristophanes

First Production: Lenea Festival, Athens, 405 B.C.

Editions

The Frogs (fourth edition), edited by W.W. Merry, Oxford, 1884; sixth edition, 1952.
Ranae, edited by Frederick H.M. Blaydes, London, 1889.
Ranae, edited by J. van Leeuwen, 1896; second edition, Leiden, 1968.

The Frogs, edited by F.G. Plaistowe, London, 1896.
The Frogs, edited by T.G. Tucker, London, 1906.
The Frogs, edited by W.B. Stanford, London, 1958; second edition, 1963.

Translations

The Frogs, translated by Gilbert Murray, London, 1908.
The Frogs, in *"The Birds" and "The Frogs"*, translated by Marshall McGregor, London, 1927.
The Frogs, in *Aristophanes: Four Comedies*, translated by Dudley Fitts, New York, 1962.
The Frogs, translated by Richmond Lattimore, Ann Arbor, Michigan, 1962.
The Frogs, in *Three Greek Plays*, translated by Peter D. Arnott, Bloomington, Indiana, 1964.
The Frogs, in *"The Frogs" and Other Plays*, translated by David Barrett, Harmondsworth, 1964.
The Frogs, in *"The Frogs" and Other Greek Plays*, translated by Kenneth McLeish, 1970.
The Frogs in *Aristophanes: Plays, 2*, translated by Patric Dickinson, London, 1976.

Criticism
(For general works on the author, see *Playwrights* volume)

Books:
D.J. Littlefield (ed.), *Twentieth Century Interpretations of "The Frogs"*, Englewood Cliffs, New Jersey, 1968.

Articles:
J.D. Denniston, "Technical Terms in *The Frogs* of Aristophanes", in *Classical Quarterly*, 21, 1927.
A.M. Young, "The *Frogs* of Aristophanes as a Type of Play", in *Classical Journal*, 29, 1933.
R.E. Wycherley, "Aristophanes' *Frogs*", in *Classical Review*, 59, 1945.
G.T.W. Hooker, "The Topography of the *Frogs*", in *Journal of Hellenic Studies*, 80, 1960.
C.P. Segal, "The Character and Cults of Dionysus and the Unity of the *Frogs*", in *Harvard Studies in Classical Philology*, 66, 1961.
James Redfield, "Die *Frösche* des Aristophanes: Komödie und Tragödie als Spiegel der Politik", in *Antaios*, 4, 1963.
C.F. Russo, "The Revision of Aristophanes' *Frogs*", in *Greece and Rome* (second series), 13, 1966.
E.K. Borthwick, "Seeing Weasals: The Superstitious Background of the Empusa Scene in the *Frogs*", in *Classical Quarterly* (new series), 18, 1968.
C.W. Dearden, "What Happened to the Donkey? Aristophanes' *Frogs*", in *Classical Philology*, 65, 1970.
Nancy Demand, "The Identity of the *Frogs*", in *Classical Philology*, 65, 1970.
A. Hurst, "Aeschylus or Euripides", in *Hermes*, 99, 1971.
J. Henderson, "The *Lekythos* and the *Frogs* 1200–1248", in *Harvard Studies in Classical Philology*, 76, 1972.
A.H. Sommerstein, "Aristophanes' *Frogs*", in *Classical Quarterly* (new series), 24, 1974.
W.E. Higgins, "A Passage to Hades: *The Frogs* of Aristophanes", in *Ramus*, 6, 1977.
Rose A. Zimbardo, "Comic Mockery of the Sacred: *The Frogs* and *The Second Shepherd's Play*", in *Educational Theatre Journal*, 30, 1978.
Richard H. Allison, "Amphibian Ambiguities: Aristophanes and his Frogs", in *Greece and Rome* (second series), vol. 30 no.1, 1983.

* * *

January 405 B.C., and Athens is months away from historic collapse in the naval débâcle of Aegospotami. Dionysus, patron god of drama, embarks on a perilous quest to the underworld to revive the dying *polis* by a miracle: the resurrection of tragedy, in the person of Euripides, who died in Macedon the previous spring. Arriving after many embarrassments and trials, the feckless god is invited to judge an artistic debate between the ghosts of Euripides and Aeschylus (the theatrical giant of the previous generation) for the infernal chair of poetry. Aeschylus wins, and returns to life in Euripides' place.

The *Frogs* is a landmark text for four quite separate reasons. First, it was its author's, and Old Comedy's, supreme achievement, the only 5th-century play known in any genre to have been granted a repeat production by acclaim. Second, it is the sole, contemporary analysis of one of the turning-points in European history: the crisis of democratic Athens in the last months of empire and the final, fatal throes of the Peloponnesian War. Third, it is our single most important document about the production and reception of tragedy in its heyday; and fourth, it is the earliest, sustained work of Western literary criticism, the first (and in some ways the most acute) stage in a debate about the nature and function of art that sets the agenda for Plato and Aristotle.

The *Frogs* attempts nothing less than an analysis of the moral, political, and cultural crisis of *fin-de-siècle* Athens, under the central metaphor of the death of tragedy. The figures of Aeschylus and Euripides in the play are made spokesmen for their respective generations: Aeschylus's is the generation that made Athens great, that saved Greece from the Persians, founded the empire, and saw the first great flowering of the arts; Euripides's is the generation that brought Athens to its knees, that lost the war, that threw away the empire, and allowed its arts to succumb to the avant-garde. With deft disingenuousness and wit, Aristophanes turns each of the two poets' theatrical trademarks into symptoms of the spirit of his age. The resulting caricatures are necessarily bizarre: the politically radical, theatrically flamboyant Aeschylus becomes a reactionary gentleman militarist, while the humane and complex Euripides appears in the by-now familiar disguise, already exercised in the *Thesmophoriazusae*, of atheist, misogynist, and amoral, ultra-democrat opportunist.

Even so, the *Frogs* is packed with shrewd insights into the dramatic quirks of both tragedians: Aeschylus's distinctive use of silence and immobility, baroque language and imagery, and bold music-theatre effects; Euripides' strange prologues, musical and choreographic avant-gardisms, kitchen-sink plots, and quicksilver intellectual and verbal legerdemain. Even more valuably, we learn something of how late 5th-century audience taste responded to these diametrically contrasting artists: the archaic opacity and immobility of Aeschylus tempered by dazzling poetry and Homeric dignity of action; Euripidean theatre's controversial pursuit of sensational, sceptical, and technically experimental novelties.

But the play's most striking intellectual theme is the playful, yet astonishingly sophisticated, exploration of contemporary literary thought. In common with Plato and Aristotle, the *Frogs* argues powerfully that art must justify itself by its social utility, by educating or otherwise improving its audience. But it goes beyond either of its great successors in demanding *how* poetry can improve its audience, and demolishing naive solutions by brilliant *reductio ad absurdum*. To defend the line that the didactic role of poetry lies in its factual content, Aeschylus begins (not unreasonably) from the claim that Hesiod is of value as an early agricultural handbook, and leads (preposterously) to the conclusion that the *Iliad* is of value purely as a manual of military instruction. The enduring myth of the artist's superior wisdom is put to the practical test of asking each poet for practical advice on headline, political issues of the day; the responses are sublimely impractical, even incomprehensible. The Platonic view of the media as purveyors of behavioural role-models ludicrously turns *Persians* and *Seven against Thebes* into martial propaganda, and *Hippolytus* into an invitation to incest. Only once, when Euripides claims to have "taught the audience to think for themselves, by putting logic into my plays, and asking questions", is no effective refutation offered. Dionysus misunderstands the point, diverts it into a joke, and further discussion is curtailed by a lyric. The modernity of the proposal should not be exaggerated—it is less a general claim that art can "ask questions", more a comment on the intellectual rhetoric of Euripidean dialogue. But it is still one of the most profound, and overlooked, ancient remarks on the use of art.

Inevitably, the debate on tragedy dominates modern attention; but the first half of the play is bravura comic writing. The double-act of Dionysus and his slave Xanthias is the prototype of the great master/servant duos of later comic fiction, in and out of the theatre; and the montage of sketches along the road to Hell is the last and finest exploitation of the fluid, anti-illusionistic use of space and set in comedy, shortly to succumb to the rigid "naturalism" of tragedy. Aristophanes' characteristically rich layering of levels of humour generates the usual conceptual acrobatics and jokes about jokes, and the running gag of an underworld much like the upper one is milked with great elegance and invention. If the play as a whole seems darker and more elegiac than is usual in Old Comedy, it is less for its setting than its theme. With hindsight, we know that imperial Athens and the great age of tragedy were already extinct—though great things lay ahead in the afterlife. Aristophanes himself survived, to see his city revive and his chosen art enter a new and spectacular lease of creativity, in which he himself was a leading pioneer. But some things stayed dead, and for us at least Greek tragedy was one of them.

—N.J. Lowe

FRÖKEN JULIE.   See **MISS JULIE.**

FROM MORN TO MIDNIGHT.   See **FROM MORNING TO MIDNIGHT.**

FROM MORNING TO MIDNIGHT
(Von morgens bis mitternachts)
by Georg Kaiser

First Publication: Berlin, 1916.
First Production: Kammerspiele, Munich, 28 April 1917.

Translations
From Morn to Midnight, translated by A. Dukes, in *Poet Lore*, 21, 1920; also in *Introduction to Drama*, edited by R.C. Roby and B. Ulanov, New York, 1962.

From Morn to Midnight, translated by Ulrich Weisstein in *Plays for the Theatre: An Anthology of World Drama*, edited by Oscar G. and L Brockett, New York, 1967.

From Morning to Midnight, in *Georg Kaiser: Five Plays*, translated by J.M. Ritchie, Rex Last, and B.J. Kenworthy, London, 1971.

Criticism

(For general works on the author, see *Playwrights* volume)

Books:

Ernst Schürer (ed.), *Georg Kaiser, "Von morgens bis mitternachts": Erläuterungen und Dokumente*, Stuttgart, 1975.

Articles:

Wilfried Adling, "Georg Kaiser's *Von morgens bis mitternachts* und die Zersetzung des dramatischen Stils", in *Weimarer Beiträge*, 5, 1959.

R. Koester, "*Von morgens bis mitternachts* and Hesse's *Klein und Wagner*", in *Orbis Litterarum*, 24, 1969.

Leroy R. Shaw, "The Strategy of Exchange: Georg Kaiser's *Von morgens bis mitternachts*", in *The Playwright and Historical Change: Dramatic Strategies in Brecht, Hauptmann, Kaiser, and Wedekind*, Madison, Wisconsin, 1970.

Denis Calandra, "Georg Kaiser's *From Morn to Midnight*: The Nature of Expressionist Performance", in *Theatre Quarterly*, 21, 1976.

Steven P. Scher, "Georg Kaiser's *Von morgens bis mitternachts*: Isolation as Theme and Artistic Method", in *Theatrum Mundi: Essays on German Drama and Literature*, edited by Edward R. Haymes, Munich, 1980.

Michael Patterson, "Kaiser's *Von morgens bis mitternachts* in Performance (1917 Onwards)", in *The Revolution in German Theatre 1900–1933*, London, 1981.

H.J. Schueler, "The Symbolism of Paradise in Georg Kaiser's *Von morgens bis mitternachts*", in *Neophilologus*, 68, 1984.

Ulrich Weisstein, "Was noch kein Auge je gesehen: A Spurious Cranach in Georg Kaiser's *Von morgens bis mitternachts*", in *The Comparative Perspective on Literature: Approaches to Theory and Practice*, edited by Clayton Koelb and Susan Noakes, Ithaca, New York, 1988.

Rhys W. Williams, "Culture and Anarchy in Georg Kaiser's *Von morgens bis mitternachts*", in *Modern Language Review*, 83, 1988.

*   *   *

From Morning to Midnight (Von morgens bis mitternachts) depicts a day in the life of a small-town cashier who robs his bank of 60,000 marks in the mistaken belief that money will buy him an exciting new life. He flees his narrow-minded, bourgeois family and, after a series of disappointing experiences in Berlin, is brought to the Salvation Army by a girl who seems to be the answer to his search for a meaningful life; when she betrays him in order to receive the reward offered for his arrest he realizes that "Not all the money from all the banks in the world can buy anything of real value. You always get less than you pay for". Disillusioned, he commits suicide.

By 1912 when Kaiser wrote *From Morning to Midnight* he had already more than twenty plays to his credit, but none had been performed publicly and only two of them, *Die jüdische Witwe* (*The Jewish Widow*) and *König Hahnrei* (*King Cuckold*) are noteworthy. With *From Morning to Midnight*, Kaiser began his expressionist period which catapulted him into fame and turned him into Germany's most successful and widely performed dramatist until 1933. The play, among the

earliest German expressionist *Stationendrama*, is the best example of its kind. It consists of two parts containing seven stations which depict a day in the life of the Cashier; in characteristic expressionist fashion they are only loosely linked and their action takes place in different localities. The characters named only after their functions are abstract types devoid of all individuality. The motivating agent of *From Morning to Midnight* is money which determines the Cashier's fate after his break-out from his daily, mindless routine, driving him from one "station" to another in his attempt to buy something of value and to create a meaningful existence for himself. Typical of all Kaiser's expressionist plays is the theme of the possible renewal of man. It can be said that Kaiser, in fact, created the figure of the "New Man" who would always be associated with expressionist drama; he also was the first one to realize that this figure was nothing but an idealistic chimera unable to survive in society. In *From Morning to Midnight* Kaiser tests the idea of regeneration through wealth: can one buy the essence of life? However, from the very beginning of his new venture the Cashier discovers to his horror that money does not reveal the truth but, on the contrary, hides or distorts it. What was originally meant to be a carefree adventure with a woman of easy virtue turns into a nightmarish journey where nothing and nobody are what they seem to be; this is already demonstrated at the beginning of the play where the Lady who causes him to commit a criminal act turns out to be an honest character, while the Salvation Army Girl who preaches unselfish love and forgiveness reveals herself, at the end, as nothing more than a greedy hypocrite. The sixth station depicts most graphically the distorted world encountered by the Cashier; in seeking erotic diversion with various, apparently beautiful, masked girls he finds out that their masks only cover their ugliness; they are symbolic of the grotesque discrepancy between reality and appearance. Instead of revelation and transformation the Cashier finds betrayal.

Closely related to the question of what values money can buy, is the problem of how to determine life's quintessence, a theme integral to Kaiser's work. In *From Morning to Midnight*, the Cashier discusses the question and its relation to Death in the visionary snowfield scene whose eerie atmosphere bears apocalyptic traits. This scene, which forms the climax and end of Part One, is the best in the play, and one of the most effective in expressionist theatre. Having effaced his tracks in the snow the Cashier takes a comfortable seat in the bare branches of a tree; he suddenly finds himself in the midst of a wild, forboding storm: "The hurricane has lashed the snow from the branches. Remnants stick in the crown and form a human face with grinning jaws. A skeleton hand holds the hat". Its dynamic, and increasingly ecstatic, style conveys effectively the Cashier's state of fear and excitement about his future. Death is depicted as the "policeman of man's existence" which is readily accepted by the Cashier: "I believe you are even part of myself". But like many of Kaiser's protagonists who are gamblers he rejects Death at this point: "Ring me again at midnight". In another powerful scene at the play's close, Death, formed by the wires of the Salvation Army's chandelier, is finally revealed to be the answer to the Cashier's frenzied but frustrating race from station to station—the last station is Death: "His beckoning finger shows the way out— where to?". In a surprising move Kaiser associates the dying Cashier with Christ, an aspect more fully and more logically developed by him in the depiction of future characters who represent the "New Man".

The ending has two aspects: on the one hand, it underlines man's loss of values and ensuing disillusionment as well as his inability to become truly regenerate; on the other hand it is the first statement of Kaiser's growing conviction that humanity even as pure as Christ's is not realizable in a world in which existence is, *per se*, tragic.

—Renate Benson

THE FRONT PAGE
by Ben Hecht with Charles MacArthur

First Publication: New York, 1928.
First Production: Times Square Theatre, New York, 14 August 1928.

*   *   *

The Press Room of the Chicago Criminal Courts Building, where all three acts are set, is crowded with journalists covering a hanging which is to take place early the next morning. The execution (of Earl Williams, the murderer of a black policeman) has been twice postponed so that it will have maximum effect just before an imminent election, where the black vote and the law-and-order platform will be pivotal; factors which the world-weary cynicism of the newspapermen dwells on expansively in intervals in their gambling and talk about women. Also on their mind, however, is a rumour that Hildy Johnson is retiring from court reporting after 15 years to leave town and get married. This is confirmed by Hildy on his arrival, with the additional news that he is going into the comfortable world of advertising, where his pay will more than double. Hildy is booked on a train with his fiancée, Peggy, and prospective mother-in-law that night, and he takes advantage of the situation to make a last abusive telephone call to Walter Burns, his boss. The rest of the action involves the hour-by-hour deferral of these plans, as the mayor and sheriff collude in concealing a reprieve, the condemned man escapes, a hunt takes most of the reporters across the city, and the escaper crashes in through the window to give himself up to Hildy, who immediately becomes immersed in the best scoop of his career. The resolution has dimensions of melodrama, with the release of the handcuffed Hildy and Burns after the general exposure of corruption and blackmail, and the couple departing to take a later train, though—in a final wry twist to the plot—Burns ensures that Hildy will be arrested on arrival in New York.

Initially, the authors intended to reflect their "intellectual disdain of and superiority to the Newspaper", but in writing the play found they were "not so much dramatists or intellectuals as two reporters in exile". Thus, despite its "oaths and realisms" the work became "a Valentine thrown to the past, a Ballad full of *Heimweh* and Love". The managing editor, however, is emphatically excluded from the Valentine when he is described in a stage direction as "*that product of thoughtless, pointless, nerve-drumming unmorality* [sic] *that is the Boss Journalist—the licensed eavesdropper, trouble-maker, bombinator and Town Snitch, misnamed The Press*". Inasmuch as other factors of disdain remain in the play, they are directed at local government, which unfolds as a maze of nepotism, self-advancement, and other corruption. A secondary—and much lighter—filament of satire focusses on the emergent vogue for popular psychoanalysis, picking as targets a policeman who analyses Williams as a "dual personality", a reporter who has a phobic obsession with dirt, and a psychiatrist who, assessing Williams' sanity, gets him to re-enact the crime with the gun he uses to escape.

Though *The Front Page* has often been termed a "comic melodrama", it is, in fact, closer to a farcical comedy, with a complicated and implausible pattern of intrigue, concealment, coincidence, and situational absurdity maximising the resource value of every door, window, and even desk on stage. What keeps the play beyond pure farce is the depth of its societal and personal portraiture, the characters' capacity for pain, sadism, childishness, and emotional closure providing a subtext to every laugh. The studied insensitivity of most of the journalists is tested through the catalyst of minor characters such as Mollie Malloy, a prostitute who comforted Williams when she found him in a disturbed state the day before the murder and thus became a key witness. The reporters, however, have sensationalised her connection with the condemned man well beyond the point of exaggeration, and their brutal baiting of her, which will result in her attempt at suicide in the second act, emphatically registers how out of touch with her humanism they are. When, with "*a scream of terror and exultation*" she throws herself through the upper window, the journalists are mostly "*awed and astonished*", and even Hildy seems to have forgotten her a little later; this contrasts strongly with the response of the sole policeman present, who is "*sick at heart*", his body "*doubled up with pain*". Emotional cauterisation seems an essential precondition for journalism, and in the first act this is registered through the regular sound of the gallows being exercised, with a "*whirr and crash*" indicating that sandbags are being used to test the equipment.

That journalism is an arena in which manhood is proven is asserted throughout the play. When a reporter's wife appears, we are told "If she is a bit acidulated, tight-lipped and sharp-spoken, no one can blame her, least of all these bravos of the press room, who have small respect for themselves or each other as husbands, fathers and lovers". She expresses her reservations about Hildy's marriage, and another reporter comments: "If I was married to that dame I'd kick her humpbacked". At the end of the second act, Hildy's "tortured male spirit takes refuge in hysteria", and he rejects his fiancée, declaiming "God damn it—I'm a newspaper man", which throws her into retreat, "*her sobs filling the room and corridor*". Hildy's remorse consists in observing that he treated her "like she was some waitress", but Burns consoles him by telling him that he "acted like a man for the first time in [his] life!'. Burns' belief that women are murderers or "Borgias" is scarcely substantiated by the conduct of Mollie or Peggy, but the fundamental misogyny of the play's tribute to the newspaper world echoes through Peggy's final acceptance of Hildy's insistence on his marriage to journalism: "Peggy will always remember that she said this and always forget that she didn't mean it". Yet, early in the second act, we have been told: "In her unconscious and highly noble efforts to make what the female world calls 'a man' out of Hildy, Peggy has neither the sympathy nor acclaim of the authors, Yet—regarded superficially, she is a very sweet and satisfying heroine".

—Howard McNaughton

FRUEN FRA HAVET. See **THE LADY FROM THE SEA.**

THE FRUITS OF CULTURE. See **THE FRUITS OF ENLIGHTENMENT.**

THE FRUITS OF ENLIGHTENMENT
(Plody Prosveshcheniya)
by Leo Tolstoy

First Publication: 1891.
First Production: Yasnaya Polyana [Tolstoy's Estate], 30 December 1889 [amateur production].

Translations
The Fruits of Culture, translated by G. Schuman, Boston, 1891.
The Fruits of Enlightenment, translated by E.J. Dillon, London, 1891.
The Fruits of Culture, in *Plays*, translated by A. and L. Maude, London, 1905.
The Fruits of Enlightenment, in *The Dramatic Works of Tolstoy*, translated by N. Dole, New York, 1923.
The Fruits of Enlightenment, translated by Michael Frayn, London, 1979.

Criticism
(For general works on the author, see *Playwrights* volume)

Articles:
Richard Freeborn, "Tolstoy's 'Upstairs, Downstairs': Some Thoughts on his Comedy *The Fruits of Enlightenment*", in *Journal of Russian Studies*, 40, 1980.

*   *   *

The play is based on a real incident, a seance that Tolstoy had watched when visiting a friend in Moscow. Confined to bed in 1886, Tolstoy started to write this comedy on Spiritualists, but did not complete it. In 1889 he finished it when his daughter Tanya and the other children needed something for an amateur production on the family estate. Friends, neighbours and the whole family were involved in rehearsals during which Tolstoy revised and rewrote the play. It was finally given its first performance on 30 December 1889.

In April 1890 the play was performed for the Tsar who disliked the play, and decided it was unsuitable for professional (and hence censored) production, but that it would be allowed for performance by amateurs. The objection to the comedy was political: the play pokes fun at the nobility, and several members of the aristocracy were offended by it. As the critic B.V. Vameke put it, Tolstoy showed: "The two-faced aspect of old Russia: on the one hand, the Russia of the nobility with spiritualistic seances and bourgeois liberalism—the Russia with silk lining; and on the other, the Russia shivering under a straw roof, the Russia ruled by darkness". Stanislavsky put on a private performance of the play at the Hunters' Club in Moscow (with Vera Komissarzhevskaya in the role of Betsy) in 1891, and from then on it became part of the repertoire. The comedy was then performed at the Alexandrinsky Theatre on 26 September 1891, and on 12 December of the same year at the Maly Theatre. It has subsequently become a classic of the Russian comedy repertory, but has scarcely received a proper professional production in Britain.

The plot is uncomplicated: three peasants want to buy the land on which they work from their landowner. Each of the three is clearly differentiated: the first peasant is confident that he can deal with the nobility; the second (the father of Semyon, the pantry-boy) is pragmatic and sensible; while the third peasant is always tense and worried. The previous summer their master had promised that they could buy the land from him and pay it off in instalments, but he then changes his mind and wants all the money immediately or the deal is off. Using

The Fruits of Enlightenment: Maly Theatre, St Petersburg, 1891

the fact that the master and his friends are believers in Spiritualism, Tanya the chambermaid gets him to change his mind and revert to the original promise so that she and Semyon can marry and go off and live in the country.

The comedy deals with two separate problems. First, it shows the nobility at its most idle, indulging in Spiritualist seances and far more affected by superstition and fear than are their so-called "ignorant" servants. Thus, for example, the mistress is terrified that the peasants will carry infection from a diphtheria epidemic, and she orders that anywhere they might have been (particularily the kitchen) must be scrubbed down and disinfected. The doctor reinforces her anxieties by agreeing with her. The point is made in a conversation in Act III between two servants: the nobility are so terrified of infection that they will let their children die alone rather than risk contamination. The second "theme" of the play is that of the problem of ownership of the land, a long-standing preoccupation of Tolstoy's. At Yasnaya Polyana Tolstoy had tried to introduce reforms and improve the condition of the peasants (by, for example, opening schools), but was met with considerable distrust and suspicion from them. It is significant that none of the peasants in *The Fruits of Enlightenment* are like those who in reality gave Tolstoy such a difficult time. The comedy, typically, is partly aimed at "instruction"—as Tolstoy said, drama "is probably the most influential province of art".

Many of the characters of the play were based on friends and acquaintances of Tolstoy's, and they recognised themselves in the characters on stage; the model for the professor wrote Tolstoy an offended letter. The Stout Lady resembled the wife of the poet Fet, while some of the servants (Yakov the butler, Fyodor the valet) are based on their real-life counterparts in the Tolstoy household. Significantly, Tolstoy's characterisation of the servants is stronger and more interesting than that of the aristocrats, and the servants make it clear that they feel equal to their masters. As Grigory, the footman, says in Act III: "We are people, aren't we? It's them that think we understand nothing. . . but I can understand them alright. You talk about the difference between us and them—there is no difference". Tolstoy reinforces this by portraying Tanya, the chambermaid, as resourceful and intelligent in using the seance to get the master to sign the paper selling the land to the peasants. The servants, of peasant stock, are proud of the noble house in which they work and yet their first loyalty is to the peasants on the estate, and it is to the countryside that they wish to return. Even Yakov the butler is only working in the house in order to help his family in the country. Tolstoy mocks the self-opinionated aristocracy (their use of French, and generally the characters of the Master, the minister Sakhatov, the Stout Lady and the Professor), and the result is a comedy with witty dialogue and sharp satire.

—Irene Slatter

FUENTE OVEJUNA. See **FUENTEOVEJUNA.**

FUENTEOVEJUNA
by Lope de Vega Carpio

First Publication: 1619.
First Production: Unknown.

Editions
Fuente Ovejuna, edited by Américo Castro, Madrid and Barcelona, 1919.
Fuenteovejuna, edited by William Michael Smith, London, 1948.
Fuenteovejuna, in *Fuenteovejuna; Peribáñez, El comendador de Ocaña* (second edition), edited by Francisco García Pavón, Madrid, 1967.
Fuente Ovejuna, in *Fuenteovejuna; El mejor alcalde*, edited by Lidio Nieto Jiménez, Madrid, 1972.
Fuente Ovejuna, edited by Maria Grazia Pofeti, Madrid, 1978.
Fuente Ovejuna, edited by Juan M. Marín, Madrid, 1981.
Fuente Ovejuna, edited and translated by Victor Dixon, Warminster, Wiltshire, 1989 (includes translation).

Translations
Fuente Ovejuna, in *Lope de Vega: Four Plays*, translated by John Garrett Underhill, New York, 1936.
Fuente Ovejuna, translated by A. Flores and M. Kittel, in *A Treasury of The Theatre* (revised edition), edited by John Gassner, New York, 1951.
Fuente Ovejuna, translated by R. Campbell, in *The Classic Theatre, 3*, edited by Eric Bentley, Garden City, New York, 1959.
Fuente Ovejuna, in *Lope de Vega: Five Plays*, translated by Jill Booty, edited by R.D.F. Pring-Mill, New York, 1961.
Fuente Ovejuna, translated by William E. Colford, New York, 1969.

Criticism
(For general works on the author, see *Playwrights* volume)

Books:
J.E. Varey, *La Inversión de valores en "Fuenteovejuna"*, 1976.
Teresa J. Kirschner, *El protagonista colectivo en "Fuenteovejuna"*, Salamanca, 1979.
J.B. Hall, *Lope de Vega: "Fuenteovejuna"*, London, 1985.

Articles:
C.E. Annibal, "The Historical Elements of Lope de Vega's *Fuenteovejuna*", in *Publications of the Modern Language Association* [*PMLA*], 49, 1934.
Inez I. MacDonald, "An Interpretation of *Fuente Ovejuna*", in *Babel*, 1, 1940.
Joaquín Casalduero, "*Fuenteovejuna*", in *Revista de filología hispánica*, 5, 1943; also in *Estudios sobre el teatro español*, Madrid, 1962.
G.W. Ribbans, "The Meaning and Structure of Lope's *Fuenteovejuna*", in *Bulletin of Hispanic Studies*, 31, 1954.
Leo Spitzer, "A Central Theme and its Structural Equivalent in Lope's *Fuenteovejuna*", in *Hispanic Review*, 23, 1955.
Bruce W. Wardropper, "*Fuente Ovejuna: el gusto* and *el justo*", in *Studies in Philology*, 53, 1956.
William C. McCrary, "*Fuenteovejuna*: its Platonic Vision and Execution", in *Studies in Philology*, 58, 1961.
R.D.F Pring-Mill, "Sententiousness in *Fuente Ovejuna*", in *Tulane Drama Review*, 7, 1962.
Francisco López Estrada, "*Fuente Ovejuna* en al teatro de Lope y de Monroy (Consideración crítica de ambas obras)", in *Anales de la Universidad Hispalense*, 26, 1965.
Robert L. Fiore, "Natural Law in the Central Ideological Theme of *Fuenteovejuna*", in *Hispania* (Los Angeles), 49, 1966; revised version in *Drama and Ethos: Natural-Law Ethics in Spanish Golden Age Theater*, Lexington, Kentucky, 1975.
Francisco López Estrada, "Los villanos filosóficos politicos (La configuración de *Fuente Ovejuna* a través de los

Fuenteovejuna: National Theatre, London, 1989

nombres y 'apellidos')", in *Cuadernos hispanoamericanos*, 238–40, 1969.

Everett W. Hesse, "Los conceptos del amour en *Fuenteovejuna*", in *Revista de archivos, bibliotecas y museos*, 75, 1969–72.

Javier Herrero, "The New Monarchy: A Structural Reinterpretation of *Fuenteovejuna*", in *Revista hispánica moderna*, 36, 1970–71.

Carlos Serrano, "Métaphore et idéologie: sur le tyran de *Fuenteovejuna* de Lope de Vega", in *Les Langues néo-Latines*, 4, 1971.

Eduardo Forastieri Braschi, "*Fuenteovejuna* y la justificación", in *Revista de estudios hispánicos* (Puerto Rico), 1–4, 1972.

J.B. Hall, "Theme and Structure in Lope's *Fuenteovejuna*", in *Forum for Modern Language Studies*, 10, 1974.

Teresa J. Kirschner, "Sobrevivencia de una comedia: historia de la difusión de *Fuenteovejuna*", in *Revista canadiense de estudios hispánicos*, 1, 1976–77.

Robin Carter, "*Fuenteovejuna* and Tyranny: Some Problems of Linking Drama with Political Theory", in *Forum for Modern Language Studies*, 13 1977.

Teresa J. Kirschner, "Evolucíon de la crítica de *Fuenteovejuna* de Lope de Vega, en el siglo XX", in *Cuadernos hispanoamericanos*, 320–21, 1977.

Jaime Moll, "Correciones en pensa y crítica textual: A propósito de *Fuente Ovejuna*", in *Bolétin de la real academia espagñola*, 62, 1982.

Angus McKay, "The Crowd in Theater and the Crowd in History: *Fuenteovejuna*", in *Renaissance Drama*, 17, 1986.

Victor Dixon, " 'Su majestad habla, en fin, como quien tanto ha acertado': La conclusión ejemplar de *Fuente Ovejuna*", in *Criticón*, 17, 1988.

Bernal Montero Herrera, "*Fuenteovejuna* de Lope de Vega y el maquievalismo" in *Criticón*, 45, 1989.

*　　*　　*

The action of *Fuenteovejuna* takes place in and around the year 1476 and centers on three interrelated, historical subjects which Lope de Vega combines into a single action in the play. The first is the uprising of the town of Fuenteovejuna against Fernán Gómez de Guzmán, the Commander of the military Order of Calatrava in the year 1476; the second is the attempt by the Order of Calatrava, against the efforts of the Catholic monarchs Ferdinand and Isabela of Spain, to seize the strategic town of Ciudad Real in that same year; the third is the larger conflict between the Catholic monarchs of Spain and Alfonso and Doña Juana of Portugal. Lope centers the principal action of the play upon the Commander's depredations in the town of Fuenteovejuna and their consequences, while the secondary action revolves around the Commander's treason against Ferdinand and Isabela. These two actions are portrayed against the backdrop of life in a village characterized as an innocent and harmonious pastoral paradise. In Act I, the Commander attempts violently to assert himself over the townspeople and to interrupt the planned wedding of two of its members, Laurencia and Frondoso. In the second act the villagers confront the fact of the apparent inability of any one of their members to confront the Commander and demand justice against him. In Act III the townspeople collectively rise up against the Commander and behead him in an act of nearly ritualistic violence. The conclusion of the play turns on the attempt by the Catholic rulers to locate the perpetrators of the crime against the Commander. In response to the inquest and attempts at torture by the agents of the Crown, the townspeople claim collective responsibility for what they have done and express their unity with the cry "All together: Fuenteovejuna did it!" ("!Todos a una Fuenteovejuna lo hizo!"). When confronted with this response, the rulers decide that they can only pardon the townspeople; the village is placed directly under the jurisdiction of the Crown, and the alliance between the people and the monarchy is triumphantly restored.

Lope draws his historical information about the events of *Fuenteovejuna* from the chronicle by Rades y Andrada (the *Crónica de las tres órdenes militares*, 1572), as well as from traditional ballads, some of which also depend on Rades' text. This is a history play, but one in which Lope adapts the details of historical events to larger "poetic" purposes. In its overall structure, *Fuenteovejuna* resembles a literary romance. The action moves from a moment of harmony, through a period of trial, to the reconstruction of a more perfect world. As in romance, an idyllic land is placed in danger by a demonic figure and is then rescued from his threats. But unlike the typical romance, the tyrant-monster of this play is not defeated by any alien or mysterious knight. Rather, he is routed by the peasants themselves, who act *en masse* to slay him. *Fuenteovejuna* is in this sense a collective play, and its true hero is the entire town. The popular uprising, the revenge slaying of the Commander, the cleansing of the villagers' honor, and their defiance of the authorities who come to extract a confession from them, are all collective actions, as are several ritual moments in the play—the celebratory entrance of the Commander in Act I, the celebration prompted by the wedding of Laurencia and Frondoso, the ritual slaying of the Commander, and the ceremonial recognition of the villagers by the rulers at the close of the play. Through the incorporation of such ritual moments *Fuenteovejuna* itself served to gather people together so that they could celebrate, in communion with each other, those ideals and values concerning honor that they held in common.

In addition, *Fuenteovejuna* may be seen as one of the many plays in which Lope de Vega recognizes that the concept of honor does not apply only to those noble enough to claim it by birth, but may extend to the peasants of society as well. In *Fuenteovejuna*, Lope's belief in the potential nobility of the peasants is buttressed by a Platonic notion of ideal love. This love is represented in amorous terms in the relationship between Laurencia and Frondoso and is shown to be superior to "natural" love or desire. At a more general, interpersonal level the principle of love is revealed to be at work in the relationship among all the people of the town as a principle of mutual respect. Thus it is Mengo, one of the humblest among the villagers, who, before the play's close, comes to demonstrate his solidarity with the group, to gain their respect, and to recognize the superiority of Platonic over natural love.

During the historical course of its interpretation and reception, *Fuenteovejuna* has been taken as a revolutionary play, and has been seen as a symbol of popular freedom and independence. To be sure, *Fuenteovejuna* attempts to re-imagine social relationships along more just lines, but despite its depiction of mob violence it is a decidedly pre-revolutionary play, and recent studies have cast doubts on the plausibility of attempts to read it as a revolutionary drama. Lope attempts to imagine a purer or more perfect image of the relationship between peasants and monarchs, not to overturn that relationship in favor of the independence or equality of all members of society. Lope reaffirms the alliance of the monarchy and the people against their common enemy, the feudal nobility.

—Anthony J. Cascardi

FULGENS AND LUCRECE
by Henry Medwall

First Publication: London, c.1512–16.
First Production: Unknown.

Editions

"Fulgens and Lucrece": A Fifteenth-Century Secular Play, edited by Frederick S. Boas and Arthur W. Reed, Oxford, 1926.
Fulgens and Lucrece, in *Five Pre-Shakespearian Comedies*, edited by Frederick S. Boas, London, 1934.
Fulgens and Lucrece, in *English Moral Interludes*, edited by Glynne W. Wickham, London, 1976.
Fulgens and Lucrece, in *The Plays of Henry Medwall*, edited by Alan H. Nelson, Cambridge and Totowa, New Jersey, 1980.
Fulgens and Lucrece, edited by Peter Meredith, Leeds, 1981.

Criticism

Articles:
Charles R. Baskervill, "Conventional Features of Medwall's *Fulgens and Lucrece*", in *Modern Philology*, 24, 1927.
James K. Lowers, "High Comedy Elements in Medwall's *Fulgens and Lucrece*", in *English Literary History*, 8, 1941.
Robert C. Jones, "The Stage World and the 'Real' World in Medwall's *Fulgens and Lucrece*", in *Modern Language Quarterly*, 32, 1971.
John Scott Colley, "*Fulgens and Lucrece*: Politics and Aesthetics", in *Zeitschrift für Anglistik und Amerikanistik*, 23, 1975.
Hiroshi Ozawa, "The Structural Innovation of the More Circle Dramatists", in *Shakespeare Studies* (Japan), 19, 1980–81.
Peter Meredith and Meg Twycross, "'Farte Pryke in Cule' and Cock-Fighting" in *Medieval English Theatre*, vol.6 no.1, 1984.
Thomas Pettitt, "Tudor Interludes and the Winter Revels", in *Medieval English Theatre*, vol.6 no.1, 1984.

* * *

Fulgens, senator of Rome, permits his daughter Lucres to decide which of her two suitors she will marry: Publius Cornelius (Scipio), a wastrel and arrogant patrician, or Gaius Flaminius, an intelligent and virtuous public servant, though a plebeian. She declares that she intends to choose "hym whiche is moste honurable". The suitors meet to plead their respective cases in a set-piece debate before Lucres. She defers judgement, but afterwards confides in the audience that she will choose Gaius, "For in this case I do hym commend / As the more noble man, sith he thys wyse / By meane of hys vertue to honoure doth aryse". Comic complications are added by A and B, two members of the audience who volunteer themselves as servants to the two suitors, carry misleading messages, and spend most of their time courting Lucres' maid, Joan. She leads them on through a series of competitions for her favours until, getting them trussed up and helpless, she beats them soundly and declares that she is engaged to someone else.

The play is divided into two parts, the first to be played at dinner and the second "in the evening, about supper" during the Christmas festivities (possibly on Twelfth Night) in a late medieval Great Hall. It acts as a showcase for a whole repertoire of Christmas games and competitions: singing, wrestling, a mock-joust called "fart-prick in cule" with the participants trussed up like chickens, and the more elegant entertainment of a court disguising, an elaborate masked and costumed dance which was the forerunner of the court masque.

The original title of the play was probably not *Fulgens and Lucres*. The (?)1512 titlepage calls it "a godely interlude of Fulgens Cenatoure of Rome. Lucres his doughter. Gayus flaminius. & Publius Cornelius. of *the disputacyon of noblenes*". The main plot is a dramatisation of *The Declamation of Noblesse*, a free translation by John Tiptoft, Earl of Worcester (made c. 1460, published by Caxton 1480) of the *De Vera Nobilitate* ("Concerning True Nobility") of Buonaccorsa da Montemagno (written in Latin c.1428). There was a long tradition of debate over the nature of true nobility or *gentilesse*: did it belong solely to those of noble birth, or was it a more personal, individual quality, "virtue not blood", and therefore available to anyone with the intelligence and innate qualities to cultivate it? In the 1490's, this was a more than academic question. The court of Henry VII had replaced the old aristocracy of the Wars of the Roses with "new men", bureaucrats of no great birth who had worked their way to power and wealth by public service, like Edmund Dudley, the Sussex lawyer who became Henry's righthand man, and who "used his title of king's councillor as proudly as any peerage". Gaius Flaminius claims Lucres despite his low birth because of his character and his achievements. But he is not a homespun revolutionary: he aspires to become part of the establishment, and one who will himself become an ancestor of a noble family. Even though it may have been written for Medwall's patron, Cardinal Morton, himself a "new man", the play is politically circumspect: Cornelius has to be painted as a bully and a wastrel, for as Lucres points out in her summing-up, if he had been virtuous as well as nobly born there would have been no contest: he must have won.

Fulgens and Lucrece may be the earliest surviving script of a secular English play, but it juggles with the conventions of staging and actor-audience relations with a sophistication and assurance which suggests a long tradition behind it. The subplot (which is played out in the first half) is Medwall's own invention, though it uses several folk-motifs such as the mock-wooing also found in a contemporary popular song called "Joan quoth John". It provides a down-to-earth mirror image of the aristocratic rivalry in the main plot.

The play has been called "the first romantic comedy in English", but this is due more to the delineation of the characters and liveliness of the dialogue than any complexity of plot. The comic scenes consist of an ingeniously contrived series of running gags, made hilarious by the ebullient and inventive personalities of A and B. The suitors are no mere mouthpieces for the debate, but subtly characterised. Lucres herself is often hailed as a Shakespearean heroine: her poise and humour show her completely in control of her two suitors and of the debate. She and her maid Joan would of course have been played by boys.

Nothing is known about the original production of *Fulgens and Lucrece*. Suggestions that it may have been played before Cardinal Morton at Lambeth Palace are pure speculation, as are the suggested occasions on which this might have happened. It might equally have been meant for a college hall, or for an Inn of Court. In the 20th century it has been revived by university groups.

—Meg Twycross

FUNA-BENKEI.   See BENKEI IN THE BOAT.

FUNNYHOUSE OF A NEGRO
by Adrienne Kennedy

First Publication: New York, 1969.
First Production: The Circle in the Square Theatre, New York, 14 January 1962.

Criticism
(For general works on the author, see *Playwrights* volume)

Articles:

Lorraine A. Brown, " 'For the characters are myself': Adrienne Kennedy's *Funnyhouse of a Negro*", in *Negro American Literature Forum*, 9, 1975.

Rosemary K. Curb, "Fragmented Selves in Adrienne Kennedy's *Funnyhouse of a Negro* and *The Owl Answers*", in *Theatre Journal*, 32, 1980.

Philip C. Kolin, "From the Zoo to the Funnyhouse: A Comparison of Edward Albee's *The Zoo Story* with Adrienne Kennedy's *Funnyhouse of a Negro*", in *Theatre Southwest*, vol. 16 no. 1, 1989.

*   *   *

Before the curtain opens, a faceless, mumbling, female figure sleep-walks across the forestage carrying a bald head, and establishes that this is a nightmare play. The central action has a fluid texture, with time and place stretching and dissolving, defying conventional notions of cause and effect in behaviour, and substituting elements of associative linking between the brief scenes that are suggested. A number of these involve bedrooms, constantly reinforcing the dream motif, but the bedroom is not always obviously that of Sarah, the title character. In the opening scene it is, in fact, Queen Victoria and the Duchess of Hapsburg who are standing beside the bed, though their dialogue and identical, masked appearance immediately unsettle notions of identity. Victoria even refers to her father as a "black Negro" who, though dead, keeps returning to her. In a long monologue, the title character explains that Victoria, the Duchess, Jesus, and Patrice Lumumba are parts of herself and that the rooms on stage are "the places myselves exist in." None of these secondary characters has more than a trace of historical, individualising detail; blackness is important to Lumumba, though also to the others, and the bond with his father is important to Jesus—as well as to the others. The murder of the father, by all of the sub-characters, is followed by Sarah hanging herself, and the play ends with brief, relatively objective, dialogue between a Funnyman and a Funnylady indicating that Sarah was out of touch with reality.

As a psycho-expressionistic, one-act play, *Funnyhouse of a Negro* stands by itself as its own statement: it simply represents the hallucinatory texture of a dream in which the tormented self is fragmented and recomposed with agonising conjunctions, to the point of annihilation. Like any staged dream, it challenges the audience's instinct towards interpretation, and this may follow any dream theory from the Strindbergian to the biological and the early Freudian notion of masochistic wish-fulfilment. But Kennedy's dramatic strategy subverts logic and interpretation in numerous ways. Not only are sub-characters, like Jesus, divorced from their received identity, but they collide and merge with one another so that they cannot even be taken as Sarah's distorted perception of them. Moreover, their constant merging makes troublesome any attempt to identify them as discrete parts of Sarah's psyche, so that even the term "alter ego" is unsatisfactory.

Two parts of the play introduce a somewhat incongruous element of objectivity. Sarah's early monologue presents her as a self-conscious narrator apparently offering a rationale of the action. Firstly, a quantity of mundane detail links her to Kennedy's own life as a student, and the noose around her neck hints that the entire action may represent her last thoughts at the point of suicide. On the other hand, her historical and geographical indeterminacy is also emphasised, and her "ancient" appearance suggests that she may be an archetype. Secondly, the two characters who clumsily diagnose her as psychotic at the end appear to be looking at her from outside, but because they are given some qualities of figures from a carnival funnyhouse there is the possibility that theirs is a mirroring function, reflecting Sarah's dislocated sense of identity.

Feminist criticism has produced some provocative approaches to this play. Kennedy wrote it shortly after living for a period in Ghana, which is clearly the source of the image of Jesus as a white, male colonizer. Yet Jesus also shares the constraints of living under a patriarchy, a phobic bondage which does not dissolve with the murder of the father. Sarah's dominant self constructs images of otherness in the form of masculinity and blackness, a construction which seems to be related to the rape of her mother by her (black) father. The opening scene (which taxes hard the resources of stagecraft) involves "great black ravens" flying over Victoria's bed, while Jesus's colonising mission has recurrent imagery of white doves and white stallions. Sarah's preferred self-image is that of Victoria who, like the Duchess, underscores her whiteness by being dressed in white satin and wearing an alabaster mask, all of it picked out by "strong white light". Sarah claims that she killed her father by bludgeoning his head with an "ebony mask" such as Lumumba carries through most of the play. Sarah's only "glaring negroid feature" is her "kinky hair"; on her first appearance, she is partially bald, and all the sub-characters lose their hair in prodigious quantities. In these terms of Sarah's frenzied aspiration to whiteness, the play is almost a literal illustration of a leading argument in Fanon's *Black Skin, White Masks*.

Disfigurement, self-effacement, and head mutilation recur throughout the play, from the severed head carried emblematically by the sleep-walker to the masks which constitute detached heads, and to the details of the father's death. Lumumba's head "appears to be split in two with blood and tissue in eyes". That this is Artaudian "theatre of cruelty" few would dispute, but the sensory aggression is nowhere gratuitous: it all contributes to the expression of the agony of a self that cannot accept her self.

—Howard McNaughton.

THE FURIES.   See THE ORESTEIA.

G

GALILEO. See **LIFE OF GALILEO.**

THE GAME OF LOVE AND CHANCE
(Le Jeu de l'amour et du hasard)
by Pierre Carlet de Chamblain de Marivaux

First Publication: Paris, 1730.
First Production: Comédie-Italienne, Paris, 23 January 1730.

Editions

Le Jeu de l'amour et du hasard, London, 1912.
Le Jeu de l'amour et du hasard, edited by M. Shackleton, London, 1954.
Le Jeu de l'amour et du hasard, edited by Pierre Michel, Paris, 1963.
Le Jeu de l'amour et du hasard, edited by J.B. Ratermanis, Englewood Cliffs, New Jersey, 1967.
Le Jeu de l'amour et du hasard, edited by Raymond Laubreaux, Brussels, 1971.

Translations

Love in Livery, translated by Harriet Ford and Marie Louise le Verrier, New York, 1907.
The Game of Love and Chance, in *French Comedies of The Eighteenth Century*, translated by Richard Aldington, London, 1923.
The Game of Love and Chance, in *Classical French Drama*, translated by Wallace Fowlie, New York, 1962.
The Game of Love and Chance, in *Seven Comedies by Marivaux*, translated by Oscar and A. S. Mandel, Ithaca, New York, 1968.
The Game of Love and Chance, translated by David Cohen, in *Up From The Country; Infidelities; The Game of Love and Chance*, edited by David Cohen, Harmondsworth, 1980.
The Game of Love and Chance, translated by John Walters, in *Marivaux: Plays*, edited by Claude Schumacher, London, 1988.

Criticism
(For general works on the author, see *Playwrights* volume)

Books:
Graham E. Rodmell, *Marivaux: "Le Jeu de l'amour et du hasard" and "Les Fausses Confidences"*, London, 1982.

Articles:
Albert Barrera-Vidal, "Les différents niveaux de langue dans le *Jeu de l'amour et du hasard* de Marivaux", in *Die neueren Sprachen*, 15, 1966.

Robert J. Nelson, "The Trials of Love in Marivaux's Theatre", in *University of Toronto Quarterly*, 36, 1967.
James S. Munro, "The Moral Significance of Marivaux's 'comédies d'amour'", in *Forum for Modern Language Studies*, 14, 1978.
Robert Halsband, "The First English Version of Marivaux's *Le Jeu de l'amour et du hasard*", in *Modern Philology*, vol. 79 no.1, 1981.
Thomas F. Carr, "Marivaux's *Jeu de l'amour* et 'de la raison'", in *Australian Journal of French Studies*, vol. 21 no. 1, 1984.

*   *   *

In Act I, Silvia's father, M. Orgon, has arranged her marriage with a very suitable young man, Dorante, on condition that the young people like each other when they meet and both freely consent to the match. Nevertheless Silvia is alarmed, fearing that the artificial circumstances of the interview will not allow her to judge her suitor's true character or their affinity for each other. Lisette, Silvia's maid, cannot understand these refined scruples. Silvia conceives the idea of changing places with Lisette, so that she can observe Dorante unobserved. Her father consents to this disguise, then reveals to Mario, Silvia's brother, that Dorante has had the identical idea. Dorante arrives, disguised as a valet; he and Silvia are immediately thrown together, under the watchful eyes of M. Orgon and Mario, on the informal terms appropriate to their assumed identity as servants. Mario even insists that they address each other with the familiar "*tu*", form used by servants and also by lovers. Each is strongly attracted to the other, and each finds the other superior to his or her social station. Arlequin enters, disguised as Dorante, and plays the role of master crudely and with great enjoyment.

In Act II, Lisette warns M. Orgon that "Dorante" (in reality Arlequin) is falling in love with her; M. Orgon gives her permission to marry him. As for the other couple, Lisette reports that he sighs and she blushes. Arlequin declares his love for Lisette (each, of course, thinking that the other is of a higher station). Dorante declares his love for Silvia, who is confused and distraught by feelings which she cannot acknowledge. Dorante returns and reveals his true identity; Silvia instantly recognizes that what she has felt was love. She decides, however, to continue her disguise as a servant.

In Act III, Silvia resolves that Dorante must be willing to sacrifice rank, fortune, and father's approval to marry her. Lisette and Arlequin agree to marry, then reveal their true status to each other without resentment or disappointment. Dorante proposes to Silvia and she accepts, then reveals that she is, after all, the bride chosen for him by his father and hers. Dorante is delighted that he has given proof of the genuineness of his love.

The Game of Love and Chance is, of Marivaux's plays, the

The Game of Love and Chance: as *Successful Strategies,* Lyric Studio, London, 1983

best-known and most frequently produced in France, and the one that best survives translation into English. It is a fascinating fusion of the values of the emerging, bourgeois, realistic drama with those of the *commedia dell'arte*: the play was written for the actors of the Comédie Italienne and owed much to their style of performance. To this older tradition belong the devices of disguising and exchange of social roles which form the permise of the play; if the audience is willing to accept the inherent artificiality of this premise (and many in the original audience were not), then the psychological reactions of the characters caught in this situation of their own making will seem realistic, fresh, and natural.

The perfect symmetry of the double disguising provides a frame within which the contrasts of class and gender can be explored. The servants have a much greater degree of emotional freedom than their masters and can recognize and accept their feelings without difficulty: thus the first time we see them on stage together it is already established that they are in love. Silvia and Dorante, in contrast, are inhibited in their emotional lives because of the obligation to choose wisely—an obligation that is imposed on them not only by their social position but also because, in a striking departure from the standard convention of comedy, their fathers have given them the freedom to approve or disapprove the proposed marriage. For Dorante, this means an agonizing struggle between his love for a supposed servant and his duty to his social class. For Silvia the situation is even more painful:

because she is a woman, she cannot acknowledge even to herself that she is attracted to a man of a lower class; thus her distress and her near breakdown in Act II before she discovers that Dorante is in fact a man to whom she can permissibly be attracted.

The characters work out these problems through speech: they discover what they feel through listening to what they say. The language is tentative, subtle, often ambiguous; and until quite recently Marivaux's reputation was tied to an ethereal, super-refined image of 18th-century sensibility. Contemporary directors have done much to revise this view of Marivaux by bringing out a disquieting and thoroughly modern, psychological consciousness in his plays. But this revisionism has for the most part bypassed *The Game of Love and Chance*, his acknowledged masterpiece, even though Silvia can plausibly be charged with vanity and cruelty in her treatment of Dorante and one might question the motives of both of the lovers in conceiving the plan to spy on each other. These darker perspectives are valid for those who choose to look beneath the surface of the play, but it is not obligatory to do so: the surface itself presents a fully rewarding experience of innocence and charm.

—Roger Herzel

GAMMER GURTON'S NEEDLE
Anonymous (perhaps by William Stevenson)

First Publication: London, possibly as *Dyccon of Bedlam*, c. 1562–63; only surviving 16th-century edition (as *Gammer Gurton's Needle*), London, 1575.
First Production: Christ's College, Cambridge, before 1575.

Editions

Gammer Gurton's Needle, edited by Henry Bradley, in *Representative English Comedies from the Beginnings to Shakespeare*, edited by Charles Mills Gayley, 1903.
Gammer Gurton's Needle, in *Anonymous Plays* (third series), edited by John S. Farmer, 1906.
Gammer Gurton's Needle, in *Chief Pre-Shakespearian Dramas*, edited by Joseph Quincy Adams, London, 1924.
Gammer Gurton's Needle, in *Elizabethan and Stuart Plays*, edited by C.R. Baskervill, V.B. Heltzel, and A.H. Nethercot, New York, 1934.
Gammer Gurton's Needle, in *Five Pre-Shakespearian Dramas*, edited by F.S. Boas, 1934.
Gammer Gurton's Needle, in *Tudor Plays*, edited by Edmund Creeth, New York, 1966.
Gammer Gurton's Needle, in *Three Sixteenth-Century Comedies*, edited by Charles Whitworth Jr., London and New York, 1984 (New Mermaid Series).

Criticism

Articles:
Charles W. Roberts, "The Authorship of *Gammer Gurton's Needle*", in *Philological Quarterly*, 19, 1940.
Homer A. Watt, "The Staging of *Gammer Gurton's Needle*", in *Elizabethan Essays in Honor of George F. Reynolds*, 1945.
Reginald W. Ingram, "*Gammer Gurton's Needle*: Comedy Not Quite of the Lowest Order?", in *Studies in English Literature 1500–1900*, 7, 1967.
William B. Toole III, "The Aesthetics of Scatology in *Gammer Gurton's Needle*", in *English Language Notes*, 10, 1973.
Anthony Graham-White, "Elizabethan Punctuation and the Actor: *Gammer Gurton's Needle*", in *Theatre Journal*, vol.34 no.1, 1982.
N. Lindsay McFadye, "What Was Really Lost in *Gammer Gurton's Needle*?", in *Renaissance Papers*, 1982.
John W. Velz, "Scatology and Moral Meaning in Two English Renaissance Plays", in *South Central Review*, vol.1 nos.1–2, 1984.
Douglas Duncan, "*Gammer Gurton's Needle* and the Concept of Human Parody", in *Studies in English Literature 1500–1900*, vol.27 no.2, 1987.
Stanley J. Kozikowski, "Comedy Ecclesiastical and Otherwise in *Gammer Gurton's Needle*", in *Greyfriar*, 18, 1987.
C.H. Ross, "The Authorship of *Gammer Gurton's Needle*", in *Anglia*, 19, 1987.

*   *   *

Gammer Gurton has lost her needle. Diccon gets her to believe that her neighbour, Dame Chat, has stolen it while, he also persuades Dame Chat that she is accused by Gammer Gurton of stealing and stewing her rooster. When the village priest, Doctor Rat, is called upon to resolve the resulting imbroglio, Diccon persuades him that he can catch Dame Chat using the needle if he crawls through a hole into her house.

Since he has just warned Dame Chat that Gammer Gurton's husband, Hodge, has sworn to break in and kill all her chickens, she has set a pan of scalding water inside the hole and Rat gets a hot reception—although for some time she persists in believing that it is Hodge she has beaten. The Bailiff sorts everything out and metes out a mock sentence to Diccon, the conditions of which he must swear to on Hodge's backside. When Diccon slaps Hodge on the rump, the needle is painfully found, still in Hodge's recently repaired breeches. All leave to drink together.

Gammer Gurton's Needle and Nicholas Udall's *Ralph Roister Doister*, are the first surviving English comedies to borrow the five-act form and the setting between two houses from Roman comedies. But while the derivation of Udall's characters from their Roman counterparts is clear, those of *Gammer Gurton's Needle* have been thoroughly anglicized. This naturalization of the Roman model is achieved in two ways: by the use of a native dramatic tradition and by the vigorously colloquial language. Diccon, who sets all the other characters at loggerheads, is a close relative of the Vice character of the Morality plays. The prologue refers to him as Diccon the Bedlam, a mentally unstable discharged patient now begging his way through life, but he is the most astute character in the play. Bedlam is, rather, what he creates. Like the Vice, he is an outsider, begins the action by confiding his dishonest nature to the audience, and has delight in the prowess of his own glib tongue as his only motive for the mischief he causes. It is appropriate to his role as a Vice character that the person who actually suffers from his conniving is the parish priest.

The language has a colloquial vigour that points the way to the Cheapside scenes of Shakespeare's *Henry IV* plays. The author's freedom of language and imagination invigorate the tumbling rhythms and rhyming couplets. The play, attributed on the title page to "Mr. S", was most probably written by William Stevenson, a Fellow at Christ's College, Cambridge. Sometimes one can sense the college man making fun of country people, as in the *double entendre* of Hodge's explanation of his wife's loss: ". . . her needle, man! 'Tis neither flesh nor fish; / A little thing with an hole in the end, as bright as any siller, / Small, long, sharp at the point, and straight as any pillar". And we are aware of the author's artifice when a fanciful metaphor contributes an unlikely rhyme: "My guts they yawl-crawl and all my belly rumbleth, / The puddings [entrails] cannot lie still, each one over other tumbleth: / By Gog's heart, cham so vexed and in my belly penn'd [pain'd] / Could one piece were at the spitalhouse, another at the castle end". Similarly, we are conscious that certain speeches are intended as set-pieces, such as a description of Hodge blowing at the household cat's eyes, mistaking them for sparks in the dead fire, and scaring her up into the roof. Much of the time, though, one responds directly to the vividness of the language—to hearing, for example, of Tom Tankard's cow careering around "as though there had been in her arse a swarm of bees"—and especially so during the passages of flyting when the scurrilous and scatological exchanges achieve an Aristophanic zest. This linguistic zest, the gleeful ingenuity of Diccon, and the cheerful goodheartedness of Hodge allow *Gammer Gurton's Needle* to succeed on the stage today.

—Anthony Graham-White

GAS, I-II. See **THE GAS TRILOGY**.

_____

THE GAS TRILOGY
The Coral (Die Koralle)
Gas I
Gas II
by Georg Kaiser

The Coral (Die Koralle)
First Publication: Berlin, 1917.
First Production: Neues Theater, Frankfurt, 27 October
1917.

Gas I
First Publication: Berlin, 1918.
First Production: Neues Theater, Frankfurt, and
Schauspielhaus, Düsseldorf, 28 November
1918.

Gas II
First Publication: Potsdam, 1920.
First Production: Vereinigte Deutsches Theater, Brünn
[Brno], Czechoslovakia, 29 October 1920.

Translations
Gas I, translated by H. Scheffauer, London, 1925; also in
Twenty-Five Modern Plays, edited by S.M. Tucker and A.S.
Downer, New York, 1953.
The Coral, translated by Winifred Katzin, New York, 1963.
Gas II, translated by Winifred Katzin, New York, 1963.
Georg Kaiser: Five Plays [includes *The Coral, Gas I, Gas II*],
translated by B.J. Kenworthy, R. Last, and J.M. Ritchie,
London, 1971.

Criticism
(For general works on the author, see *Playwrights* volume)

Books:
Heinrich Breloer, *Georg Kaisers Drama "Die Koralle":*
Persönliche Erfahrung und ästhetische Abstraktion, Ham-
burg, 1977.
Peter Schlapp, *Georg Kaisers "Gas I": Textanalyse und*
Konzept einer szenischen Realisation, Frankfurt, 1983.

Articles:
Robert Kauf, "Georg Kaiser's Social Tetralogy and the Social
Ideas of Walter Rathenau", in *Publications of the Modern*
Language Association [*PMLA*], 77, 1962.
Nicholas V. Galichenko, "Twentieth-Century Vistas of Peace
and War: Some Parallels in Georg Kaiser's *Gas II* and
Mikhail Bulgakov's *Adam and Eve*", in *Germano-Slavica*,
2, 1977.

*   *   *

Georg Kaiser's three plays *The Coral, Gas I* and *Gas II*
illustrate the expressionist ideal of the "New Man" against a
background of class struggle in increasingly futuristic settings.
The Coral (first performance Frankfurt 1917), although usually accepted as the first part, is a complete 5-act account of a
millionaire industrialist whose tragic parental origins he seeks
to overcome by making money and by sparing his son similar
hardships. His wish to fashion his son's life is thwarted when
the son becomes a stoker on a cargo-boat while the father
entertains guests on his private yacht. Shattered by his son's
revolt (which is paralleled by an explosion in his main factory)
the millionaire, instead of shooting himself with the gun left by
his son after failed patricide, kills his secretary. The secretary
(the millionaire's double who often represented him) carries a
piece of coral for final identification. The millionaire takes the
coral, is arrested for murdering his "employer", and can only
accept the son's offer to identify him as the millionaire
provided the son renounces his revolt. The millionaire is led off
to execution seeing his ideals carried on by the "Man in Grey"
who has recognised in the first act how the millionaire has
formed his own "inner Doppelgänger" in his son.

The play is full of ironic twists that not only demonstrate that
the New Man concept will remain a vision, but also relativise
all genuine efforts to break down social differences and ease
human suffering. Physical suffering caused by poverty or
exploitation is counterbalanced by inner uncertainties. The
millionaire, through an act of violence and deception, theoretically overcomes the arrogant demands of his will and
reaches a higher state of awareness where, like a piece of coral,
he can drift on the tides of life and death. He no longer needs a
subservient "Doppelgänger", for the coral has given him the
open-eyed wonder of the childhood he was never able to
enjoy. In becoming inwardly certain he must die as Millionaire
and, as the judges insist, as Secretary.

Gas I (first performance in Düsseldorf, 1918) in 5 acts shows
the millionaire's son who now controls his father's former huge
gas factory. He has innovated worker participation in a form of
socialist part-ownership where success depends on ever-
increasing achievements and productivity, and the individual is
only of value as a skilled mechanical operator. Gas has become
the state's prime industrial power source, so that its failure
would spell economic disaster. Unexpectedly, the safety
mechanisms cannot prevent an explosion that destroys the
works, the workers no longer able to master the latest
technology used. Appalled by this, the owner refuses to
rebuild and start production again. Instead he tries to persuade
the survivors to construct an ideal garden city and develop a
community independent of advanced industrial processes. The
workers, however, do not wish to become "human", but
continue as wealth-earning, affluent automata. They elect the
Chief Engineer to replace the owner and rebuild the factory to
answer demands of the state and other industries profiting
from rearmament. The factory is nationalised, and the state
has to protect the owner from his workers' revenge. In parallel
to the end of Shaw's *Man and Superman*, the owner's daughter
looks forward to giving birth to a New Man—the first of a more
hopeful and human generation.

In the three-act *Gas II* Kaiser explores his ideas further in a
vision of the future with a new factory with gas held in reserve
for an expected war, the Chief Engineer in charge, and the
workers divided into coloured teams operating control and
information systems that are removed from the actual production of gas and demand endlessly repetitive responses. A
struggle ensues between strikers who call for freedom from
their machine-controlled existence and those who fear invasion. The "Blue" control-figures are quickly overrun by enemy
"Yellow" figures who force renewed production of gas with no
shared profits. Act III repeats the opening situation, but when
production falls, the "Yellow" forces surround the factory and
threaten to destroy it. In the ensuing confrontation between
the Chief Engineer, the so-called "Millionaire Worker", and
the masses, a new invention, poison gas, is offered as a means
of regaining power over the "Yellow" forces. The "Millionaire
Worker" tries to persuade them to undertake a new spiritual
way that would free them from dependence on material gain.

The Gas Trilogy: Gas I, Staatstheater, Berlin, 1928

The masses opt for the poison gas, and as the Chief Engineer throws his phial into the air, the enemy begins to open fire. Workers and enemy forces alike are hideously destroyed in the final holocaust.

Where *Gas I* depicts the end of the individual voice, *Gas II* extends this to predict, in dramatic form, the end of the world. The final result depends on the gullibility of the masses and their inability to support various utopian solutions proposed. Kaiser's repeated and balancing devices in the plays' structures, individual speech patterns, colour symbolism, and growing abstractionism and foreshortening of language establish a growing feeling of inevitability. None of the characters act freely, and the crowd-scenes are marked by the power of rhetoric to produce propagandist visions of futures either under totalitarian regimes or as garden-city utopias. Central ideas are unfolded with deliberate control, thus making the two plays prime examples of Kaiser's so-called "Denkspiele" (thought-plays). Huge swings of opinion responding to clear and compressed speeches, especially in Act IV of *Gas I*, represent the climax of expressionist dramatic art and mark growing interest in the problems and fate of man in the mass rather, than the isolated individual. Gas, as the central focus of these two plays, is a symbol perhaps of the power of man to

wring from nature a product to ease his own existence and provide the means to economic progress; but it also poses a threat. Not only technical skill, but also correct emotional and ethical attitudes are needed by those who exploit and use such a commodity. Lack of proportion and the ruthless exploitation of the production formula and the control mechanisms to their utmost limits cause the explosion. Just as the machines become unpredictable when overworked, humans, when reduced to automata, can be equally self-destructive.

As with other examples of expressionist drama, the text is only one factor within a total theatrical experience. The *Gas* trilogy is a *Gesamtkunstwerk* ("total work of art") where a variety of technical devices combine to produce an intense experience. Spatially, Kaiser used abstract, geometric forms in the stage-settings, in the constellations of characters, and in the representative use of a sliding roof to reveal the vault of the sky or a fore-shortened mechanical reproduction of it. Structurally the scenes in both plays are paralleled, and within each pair of scenes numbers and pairings of working figures emphasise the fatal repeat mechanism from *Gas I* to *Gas II*. The timing of the first performances of the plays thus supports an overall interpretation that they are meant as a warning to man not to repeat the catastrophe of World War I and the industrial processes that led to its outbreak. Rhetorical use of language, using compressed, repetitive speech-rhythms, especially in the crowd-scenes, suggests an emotional response to the ideas expressed rather than a reasoned reaction to them. Above all, clipped, emphatic phrases and stichomythia produce an intensifying effect that heightens the sense of unavoidable, head-on clashes and eventual catastrophe.

—Brian Keith-Smith

GENGANGERE. See **GHOSTS.**

GESCHICHTEN AUS DEM WIENER WALD. See **TALES FROM THE VIENNA WOODS.**

EL GESTICULADOR
by Rodolfo Usigli

First Publication: In *El hijo pródigo*, Mexico City, 1948
First Production: Palacio de Bellas Artes, Mexico City, 17 May 1947.

Criticism
(For general works on the author, see *Playwrights* volume)

Articles:

Daniel Meyran, "Approximación a *El gesticulador* de Rodolfo Usigli", in *Communidad*, 58, 1976.
Donald L. Shaw, "Dramatic Technique in Usigli's *El gesticulador*", in *Theatre Research International*, 1, 1976.
John W. Kronik, "Usigli's *El gesticulador* and the Fiction of Truth", in *Latin American Theatre Review*, 11, 1977.
Marianna Merritt Matteson, "On the Function of the Imposter in the Plays of Rodolfo Usigli", in *Selecta*, 2, 1983.
Pedro Bravo-Elizondo, "El concepto de la revolución de lo mexicano en *El gesticulador*", in *Texto critico*, 10, 1984.
Daniel Zalacaín and Esther P. Mocega-González, "El ciclo vital heróico en *El gesticulador*", in *Language Quarterly*, vol. 22 nos. 3–4, 1984.
Catherine Larson, "No conoces el precio de las palabras: Language and Meaning in Usigli's *El gesticulador*", in *Latin American Theatre Review*, 20, 1986.
Arthur A. Natella Jr., "Christological Symbolism in Rodolfo Usigli's *El gesticulador*", in *Discurso literario*, 5, 1988.
Laura R. Scarano, "Correspondencias estructurales y semánticas entre *El gesticulador* y *Corona de sombra*", in *Latin American Theatre Review*, 22, 1988.
Mabel Morana, "Historicismo y legitimación del poder en *El gesticulador* de Rodolfo Usigli", in *Revista iberoamericana*, 55, 1989.

*   *   *

Set vaguely in the 1930's, *El Gesticulador* is a play about political demagoguery and the relative value of personal and collective truth in post-revolutionary Mexico. César Rubio, a failed and disillusioned history professor has taken his family back to his home town in northern Mexico where he hopes to capitalize on his extensive knowledge about the history of the Revolution to further his personal career. Quite fortuitously Oliver Bolton, a Harvard historian doing research on the revolutionary process, arrives at Rubio's house. While staying there, Bolton is duped into believing that his host is none other than César Rubio a legendary populist general supposedly murdered during one of the last battles of the revolution. Rubio even manages to sell Bolton bogus documentation to substantiate his claim. Following Bolton's unauthorized newspaper reports about his supposed major discovery, Rubio is quite unexpectedly hurled into the political limelight much to the surprise and disbelief of his wife and children. His son, in particular, who is very suspicious about his father's sudden ascent into power, watches, in amazement, the swarm of national party officials, local politicians and enthusiastic supporters who come to pledge their allegiance to their new leader. Lionized by his daughter and his supporters and fully convinced of the legitimacy of his messianic project, Rubio assumes his new identity and proceeds to challenge the party leadership and in particular, General Navarro, the regional strongman. Ironically, impersonating a dead man, that is, living a lie, assures César Rubio and his family the respect and the security he could not attain through lawful means. Ultimately, however, his imposture will cost him his life as Navarro, the man who had actually murdered the original General Rubio, has Rubio, the professor assassinated. Thus, the obscure history professor transcends the limitations of his mundane and uninspiring existence; fulfilling his wish for a more heroic and meaningful personal destiny he dies a violent death but his fictional identity lives on. The institutionalized revolutionary party adds yet another mythologized name to its pantheon of fallen heroes.

History and myth, honesty and duplicity, truth and falsehood, authenticity and imposture are the ingredients of this artistically complex and culturally rich play. Variously interpreted as a realistic representation of contemporary Mexican values and institutions, an indictment of the inherent weaknesses of the Mexican character, a universal statement on basic human flaws, the play has also been celebrated for its ambiguity and its obvious metatheatrical, self-referential qualities. Considered by literary historians as the play that signaled the start of modern Mexican drama, *El Gesticulador* had an enormous popular success when it was first put on stage in 1947. Regarded by some as a none too subtle attack on the Revolution and on the government it lasted only two tumultuous weeks before it was cancelled under pressure by the authorities and organized labor. Still viewed, both locally and internationally, as a classic and as one of the most valid and powerful statements on the nature of Mexico's social and political institutions, this play continues to enjoy great popularity both as theatre and socio-political commentary.

—Ramon Layera

DER GESTIEFELTE KATER. See **PUSS IN BOOTS.**

THE GHOST SONATA (Spöksonaten)
by August Strindberg

First Publication: Stockholm, 1907.
First Production: Intimate Theatre, Stockholm, 21 January
1908.

Translations
The Spook Sonata, in *Plays, 4*, translated by Edwin Björkman,
New York, 1916.
The Ghost Sonata, translated by Elizabeth Sprigge, in *The
Play: A Critical Anthology*, New York, 1951; also in *Six
Plays of Strindberg*, Garden City, New York, 1955.
The Ghost Sonata, in *The Chamber Plays*, translated by Evert
Sprinchorn and others, New York, 1962.
The Ghost Sonata, in *Strindberg: Plays, 1*, translated by
Michael Meyer, London, 1964.
The Ghost Sonata, in *Eight Expressionistic Plays*, translated by
Arvid Paulsen, New York, 1965.
The Ghost Sonata, in *"A Dream Play" and "The Ghost
Sonata"*, translated by Carl Richard Mueller, San Francisco,
1966.
The Ghost Sonata, in *"A Dream Play" and Four Chamber
Plays*, translated by Walter Johnson, Seattle and London,
1973 (The Washington Strindberg).
The Ghost Sonata, in *Strindberg: Five Plays*, translated by
Harry G. Carlson, Berkeley, California, 1983.

Criticism
(For general works on the author, see *Playwrights* volume)

Books:
Egil Törnqvist, *Bergman och Strindberg: "Spöksonaten"—
drama och iscensättning; dramaten 1973*, Stockholm, 1973.

Articles:
Milton A. Mays, "Strindberg's *Ghost Sonata*: Parodied Fairy
Tale on Original Sin", in *Modern Drama*, 10, 1967.
Stephen C. Bandy, "Strindberg's Biblical Sources for *The
Ghost Sonata*", in *Scandinavian Studies*, 40, 1968.
Egil Törnqvist, "*Hamlet* and *The Ghost Sonata*", in *Drama
Survey*, 7, 1968–69.
Egil Törnqvist, "Sein und schein in Strindbergs *Spooksonate*",
in *Maatstaf*, 17, 1970.
Raymond Jarvi, "Strindberg's *The Ghost Sonata* and Sonata
Form", in *Mosaic*, vol.5 no.4, 1972.
Gerald Parker, "The Spectator Seized by the Theatre: Strind-
berg's *The Ghost Sonata*", in *Modern Drama*, 14, 1972.
Stephen R. Lawson, "Strindberg's *Dream Play* and *Ghost
Sonata*", in *Yale / Theatre*, vol. 5 no.3, 1974.
Göran Stockenström, " 'The journey from the isle of life to the
isle of death': The Idea of Reconciliation in *The Ghost
Sonata*", in *Scandinavian Studies*, 50, 1978.
Brian Spittles, "Arkenholz Discovering Beulah: Strindberg's
Blakean Vision in *Spöksonaten*", in *Scandinavica*, 20, 1981.
Bert Cardullo, "Ingmar Bergman's Concept for His 1973
Production of *The Ghost Sonata*: A Dramaturg's
Response", in *Essays in Arts & Sciences*, 14, 1985.

*   *   *

This is a symbolist play in three scenes which approximate to
three movements in a musical composition (Strindberg alluded
to Beethoven's Piano Sonata in D minor, opus 31, no.2). The
first scene, set in a Stockholm square on a bright Sunday
morning, is mainly exposition: after a brief demonstration that

The Ghost Sonata: Dramaten, Stockholm, 1942

this world is stranger than it seems, it concentrates on the
encounter between a Student and an old man in a wheelchair,
"Boss" Hummel, who undertakes to get him entry into the fine
house before them, home of the beautiful Young Lady the
Student so admires. Scene 2—mainly dramatic in effect, the
scene of a "ghost supper", bringing together a group of old
people whose past lives are intricately intertwined—and Scene
3—predominantly lyrical, a prolonged, though comically
interrupted, duet between the Young Lady and the Student in
the Hyacinth Room—could represent simultaneous actions
arranged in sequence. Each closes with the singing of a passage
from the medieval, Icelandic Hymn to the Sun, and the play
ends with a back projection of Böcklin's painting, "The Isle of
the Dead".

Ghost Sonata is one of the final group of plays Strindberg
wrote for The Intimate Theatre opened in Stockholm in 1907
by the young actor, August Falck, in collaboration with the
dramatist, as a show-case for Strindberg's work. The
auditorium seated just over 100 persons, and the stage was
tiny. Appropriately, Strindberg planned his new pieces as
"chamber plays", having in mind the recently founded studio
theatres elsewhere in Europe, especially Max Reinhardt's
Kammerspielhaus in Berlin, but also suggesting an analogy
with chamber music. *Ghost Sonata* was the most revolutionary
of the new works in its form: enough plot material for more
than one long play is compressed and abstracted into a
collection of motifs, and a large cast of characters is similarly
given the compressed intensity of symbolic figures. As in a
medieval morality play, the (modern) house acquires the
general significance of a house of life, specifically a house of
guilty secrets. The Student functions as audience-surrogate
within the drama: the veils of illusion fall from his eyes and he
beholds the hidden nature of human life.

The resources of the Falck–Strindberg theatre were very
limited, and this play had to wait for its production by
Reinhardt in 1916, in Berlin, for the sensational success which
established it as the unique classic it has remained. In effect,
Strindberg had invented a new kind of theatre, widening the

range of possibilities for later playwrights. His truest follower, who nevertheless denied specific influence, was Samuel Beckett.

Ghost Sonata marks a coming into its own of the specific art of the theatre which Gordon Craig had foretold in England in 1905. It is not a literary text to be interpreted on stage so much as a prompt book for the deployment of all the means of theatre: visual spectacle and a succession of striking and imaginatively potent stage images, the placing of objects in space, the movement of figures, the interplay of sounds, speech and silence, mime and dialogue, actual music, an actual painting to affect mood; and the core of drama in the interaction of well-defined characters, the radical changing of relationships between them, including a turning of the wheel of fate, surprise, intensity, and release, and a variety of passionate and more diffused emotions, with a grotesque humour darting through the whole.

Strindberg thought of giving this play the secondary title, "Kama-Loka", a theosophical term for a spirit realm extending to the threshold of the peace of death. In addition, he seems to have borrowed the Student's family name (Arkenholz) from Swedenborg. There is no doubt that mystical concepts contributed to the form taken by *Ghost Sonata*, but the dramatist's practice is eclectic (he shared his generation's interest in comparative mythology): as the Hymn to the Sun is evidently a Christianised version of old pagan material, so the Christian values of sin, atonement, and redemption, realised in Scene 2, are balanced by the figure of the Buddha holding an allium in full flower, presiding over the unstable paradise of the Hyacinth Room in Scene 3. All are images to convey a provisional understanding of the nature of life and death.

The selection of characters and the stories encapsulated in each bring a number of contrasted motifs into focus: age and youth, guilt and innocence, beauty and grotesque horror, tyranny and servitude, pretension and humiliation, sin and redemption, love and death. Yet everything remains actual and substantial. Although Strindberg plays tricks with time, the location is always a 20th-century city with telephones and electric light; and one of the legs of the writing-desk in the Hyacinth Room is irritatingly shorter than the others. Even ghosts are at home there: the Milk Girl at the fountain, who washes the Student's eyes, has a wire crate full of bottles. Moments of humour abound, and the supernatural is not insulated against it: so the corpse in its winding-sheet comes out to count the wreaths at the funeral. A caricaturist's technique gives vividness to characters, as with the mummified old woman who talks like a parrot, or Hummel, a cripple standing in his wheelchair, drawn like a tyrant in his chariot by a crowd of silent, spectral beggars.

The "ghost supper" of aged sinners is a variation on the banquet which occurs in several of Strindberg's long plays (e.g. *To Damascus*). Exposure and reversal are regular features of the scene; the climax here is the exposure and disposal of the self-appointed judge, the Mummy's deed of mercy to the rest. The counterpointed scene of the young couple moves unexpectedly away from happiness in the speeded-up decline of love into bitterness familiar from the dramatist's earlier work. The treatment here is tender and resigned. Worn-away by imperfection, poisoned by food, and stifled by the air of this world, the Student's dream girl fades into death. The Böcklin painting, at the end, restores a serene beauty, but with the chill of an unchanging world, empty of people.

—Margery Morgan

GHOSTS (Gengangere)
by Henrik Ibsen

First Publication: Copenhagen, 1881.
First Production: Aurora Turner Hall, Chicago (in Norwegian), 20 May, 1882.

Translations

Ghosts, translated by William Archer in *"The Pillars of Society" and Other Plays*, edited by Havelock Ellis, London, 1888.

Ghosts, translated by Norman Ginsbury, London, 1938.

Ghosts, translated by Bjørn Koefoed, New York, 1952.

Ghosts, in *Ibsen: Six Plays*, translated by Eva Le Gallienne, New York, 1957.

Ghosts, in *The Oxford Ibsen*, 5, translated and edited by James Walter McFarlane, London, 1961.

Ghosts, translated by Michael Meyer, London, 1962; corrected version in *Ibsen: Plays One*, London, 1980.

Ghosts, in *Ibsen: Four Major Plays*, 2 translated by Rolf Fjelde, New York, 1970.

Criticism
(For general works on the author, see *Playwrights* volume)

Books:

Asbjørn Aarseth, *"Peer Gynt" and "Ghosts"*, London, 1989 (Text and Performance Series).

Articles:

C.A Swanson, "Ibsen's *Ghosts* at the Théâtre Libre", in *Scandinavian Studies*, 16, 1941.

Irving Deer, "Ibsen's Aim and Achievement in *Ghosts*", in *Speech Monographs* 24, 1957.

Eleazer Lecky, "*Ghosts* and *Mourning Becomes Electra*: Two Versions of Fate", in *Arizona Quarterly*, 13, 1957.

Robert W. Corrigan, "Ibsen's *Ghosts* as Tragedy", in *Educational Theatre Journal*, 1959.

J.B. Sanders, "Ibsen's Introduction to France: *Ghosts*", in *French Studies*, 18, 1964.

Walter Stern, "No Need of this Hypothesis: *Ghosts* and the Death of God", in *Critical Quarterly*, 9, 1967.

Brian Johnston, "Archetypal Repetition in *Ghosts*", in *Scandinavian Studies*, 41, 1969.

B.S. Field Jr., "Ibsen's *Ghosts*: Repetitions and Repetitions", in *Papers on Language And Literature*, 8 (supplement), 1972.

John Northam, "Some Uses of Rhetoric in *Ghosts*", in *Ibsenforbundet: Årbok*, 1972.

Odd I Langholm, " 'Kammerherre Alvings asyl': en ironisk dimensjon i Ibsens *Gengangere*", in *Kirke og Kultur*, 78, 1973.

Charles W. Leland, "*Ghosts* Seen from an Existential Aspect", in *Ibsenforbundet: Årbok*, 1974.

David Thomas, "Patterns of Interaction in Ibsen's *Ghosts*", in *Ibsenforbundet: Årbok*, 1974.

John S. Chamberlain, "*Gengangere* and 'Emigrantlitteraturen' ", in *Scandinavica*, 16, 1977.

K.S. Misra and Assia M. Elsoffary, "Ibsen's *Ghosts*", in *Journal of English*, 4, 1977.

Errol Durbach, "The Dramatic Poetry of Ibsen's *Ghosts*", in *Mosaic*, vol.11 no.4, 1978.

Charles W. Leland, "In Defense of Pastor Manders", in *Modern Drama*, 21, 1978.

Evert Sprinchorn, "Science and Poetry in *Ghosts*: A Study in Ibsen's Craftsmanship", in *Scandinavian Studies*, 51, 1979.

Ghosts: Young Vic, London, 1986

Bert Cardullo, "The Form That 'can no longer paint': *Ghosts* and Osvald", in *New Orleans Review*, 8, 1981.

Egil Törnqvist, "Hur inleds Ibsens *Gengangere*? Kring drama-receptionens metodologi", in *Tijdschrift voor Skandinavistiek*, vol.4 no.1, 1983.

*   *   *

Mrs. Alving, widow of Captain Alving, has built an orphanage in his memory, to be dedicated by Pastor Manders. Her son Osvald, an artist living in Paris, has returned for the ceremony. Captain Alving was dissolute and debauched; Regina, a servant in the household, is his daughter by a maid. Thus Mrs. Alving and Manders are horrified to hear Osvald speaking of love to Regina. Osvald tells his mother that he is suffering from a mental disorder; since he thinks his father was a virtuous man, Osvald has rejected a medical explanation that his illness is a result of his father's venereal disease. Mrs. Alving decides to tell Regina and Osvald the truth about their father but she is interrupted by a fire that destroys the orphanage. Jakob Engstrand, Regina's supposed father, cleverly persuades Manders that the fire was caused by a candle the Pastor threw away and offers to take the blame himself. When Osvald enters, exhausted from trying to fight the fire, Mrs. Alving tells him that her husband's "joy of living" was frustrated by his life in provincial society and by her own puritanical attitudes. Learning that Osvald is ill, and that marriage to him would be incestuous, Regina leaves to start her own life. Osvald tells his mother that his brain will soon rot

and forces her to promise to poison him when this happens. As the sun rises, Osvald's mind suddenly unbalances. Mrs. Alving is left in terror, unable to decide whether to comply with Osvald's wishes.

The action of *Ghosts* is essentially the gradual unveiling of the secrets of the past and the effect of this unveiling on the characters, all of whom are self-centred and incapable of understanding the point of view of others. None is interested in the truth for its own sake; even Osvald is motivated only by a desire to understand his illness. Manders and Engstrand are products of a society in which appearance counts more than truth. Mrs. Alving, because of her religious upbringing, is the initial cause of the tragedy. She in effect blackmails her husband into allowing her complete control of the household, in order to keep his behaviour from causing a public scandal.

Ghosts is a drama about free will and determinism. Is the individual free or is conduct determined by heredity and environment? Ibsen presents the problem but does not attempt to resolve it. Mrs. Alving wants to be free from the constraints of her society and has rejected intellectually many of its tenets. She is unable emotionally, however, to break with the traditional life she has led; at best she can hope to find liberation through her son. Then hereditary determinism mocks all her plans, and she is defeated. *Ghosts* suggests that in spite of our striving for freedom, it can never be achieved and that life will always thwart mankind's hopes. Osvald's hereditary disease is a modern equivalent of the Greek concept of fate, and of the Judaeo-Christian concept of original sin. If he rejects a theological concept of sin, Ibsen remains haunted by a feeling of man's moral limitations. The tension between moral shortcomings and the desire for happiness gives *Ghosts* great dramatic power.

The play has a closely organised structure. It observes the classical unities of time and place: all the action occurs within less than 24 hours and is set in one room in Mrs. Alving's house. The play is divided into three acts, each of which begins with a conversation introducing the main motifs and each of which ends in a moment of dramatic suspense. The play is primarily the story of Mrs. Alving—her attempts to impose her own pattern of the life on the household, and her failure. A second story is that of Engstrand's schemes to get money from Pastor Manders for his Seamen's Home (in reality a brothel). While the primary story is a tragedy, the story of Engstrand's schemes is rather a comic satire about the deception of a gullible man by a clever hypocrite. The two stories are connected by various thematic parallels. Both are concerned with the primacy of appearance over truth in society. Both treat of the rights and duties of parents and children. The home Engstrand wishes to establish is a satiric inversion of the orphanage Mrs. Alving has built. It is a measure of the bitterness of Ibsen's view of mankind that the scoundrel, Engstrand, flourishes while Mrs. Alving is defeated.

In *Ghosts* Ibsen creates a scene that visually reinforces the themes of the play. All the action takes place in Mrs. Alving's "garden-room". It is a room that opens to the outside, so that an immediate contrast is apparent between the ordered life she has established for herself and the violent forces outside that impinge on her security. Ibsen indicates in his stage directions the continued presence of the rain, which provides an image both of the gloom of provincial Norwegian society and of the fates beyond our control which influence human life. There is also, as part of the setting, a conservatory, which seems less formal than the main room. It is associated with youth and beauty. Towards the end of the play Mrs. Alving moves into the conservatory for the first time, a movement that suggests she has discarded the conventional order she tried to maintain. Then, ironically, the sun—which would seem to promise happiness and fulfilment—rises, as Osvald loses his sanity.

—Adele King

AN GIALL.   See **THE HOSTAGE**.

THE GLASS MENAGERIE
by Tennessee Williams

First Publication: New York, 1948.
First Production: Civic Theatre, Chicago, 26 December 1944.

Criticism
(For general works on the author, see *Playwrights* volume)

Books:
R. Brian Parker (ed.), *"The Glass Menagerie": A Collection of Critical Essays*, Englewood Cliffs, New Jersey, 1983.
Harold Bloom (ed.), *Tennessee Williams's "The Glass Menagerie"*, New York, 1988 (Modern Critical Interpretations).
Delma E. Presley, *"The Glass Menagerie": An American Memory*, Boston, 1990.

Articles:
Nilda G. Joven, "Illusion and Reality in Tennessee Williams' *The Glass Menagerie*", in *Diliman Review*, 14, 1966.
Elmo Howell, "The Function of Gentlemen Callers: A Note on Tennessee Williams' *The Glass Menagerie*", in *Notes on Mississippi Writers*, 2, 1970.
Glenn Man, "Memory as Technique and Theme in *The Glass Menagerie* and *Death of a Salesman*", in *Notre Dame English Journal*, vol. 5 no. 2, 1970.
Thomas L. King, "Irony and Distance in *The Glass Menagerie*", in *Educational Theatre Journal*, 25, 1973.
Edmund A. Napieralski, "Tennessee Williams' *The Glass Menagerie*: The Dramatic Metaphor", in *Southern Quarterly*, 16, 1977.
R. Brian Parker, "The Composition of *The Glass Menagerie*: An Argument for Complexity", in *Modern Drama*, 25, 1982.
Rajshekhar Mansur, "The Emissary in Tennessee Williams' *The Glass Menagerie*: A Study of the Role of Jim O'Connor", in *Journal of the Karnatak University*, 28, 1984.
R. Brian Parker, "The Circle Closed: A Psychological Reading of *The Glass Menagerie* and *The Two Character Play*", in *Modern Drama*, 28, 1985.
John H. Jones, "The Missing Link: The Father in *The Glass Menagerie*", in *Notes on Mississippi Writers*, 20, 1988.
Elianne B. Berutti, "*The Glass Menagerie*: Escapism as a way out of Fragmentation", in *Estudos anglo-americanos*, 12–13, 1988–89.

*   *   *

Tom Wingfield, a merchant seaman in World War II, recalls his youth in St. Louis during the depression of the 1930s, when he lived at home with his mother, Amanda, and his sister, Laura. A sensitive, imaginative young man who compensates for a menial job and the drabness of his life by seeking adventure vicariously through movies, Tom eventually finds himself torn between his obligations at home and his need for excitement and change. The action moves toward a crisis as Amanda, who holds on to vestiges of her youth as a genteel southern belle, insists that Tom bring a "gentleman caller" home to Laura, a withdrawn, delicate figure who is extremely self-conscious because of a slight physical handicap. Tom invites a co-worker, Jim O'Connor, home for dinner one evening. Jim and Laura, who were casually acquainted in high school, hit it off remarkably well, but expectation gives way to despair when Jim reveals he is already engaged. Tom flees to a life at sea, but cannot escape his guilt-impacted memories of Laura, who is left alone with a disconsolate but not defeated Amanda.

Perhaps Tennessee Williams's most lyrical and autobiographical play, *The Glass Menagerie* is rich in bitter-sweet nostalgia for a past and for relationships that may have been sources of pain but also provided great emotional involvement and a sense of belonging. Dealing with characters and a situation that could have drifted into sentimental banality, Tennessee Williams instead created a masterpiece of compassionate insight and distinctive theatrical vitality.

The play is effective in alternating scenes from the past with Tom's solo reflections in a war-torn present. With delicacy but also with considerable ironic humor, Williams reveals the hopes and fears, tensions and love, that coexist within a tight family unit very much like his own. As Tom disarmingly tells us, it is a "memory play", rich in atmosphere, at times frankly sentimental. Amanda, Laura, and Tom disappoint and exasperate each other, but that in itself also signals their profound love and dependency on each other. Stifled by their environ-

The Glass Menagerie: New York, 1945 (Laurette Taylor & Julie Haydon)

ment, forced into embarassing, sometimes humiliating postures, each has a secret life and dream that inherently has little likelihood of actualization. The focal point of the play, the visit of the gentleman caller, crystalizes their longings and frustrations: great happiness seems imminent, but galling disappointment is the result.

The Glass Menagerie is an early exploration of one of Williams' recurrent themes, which also happens to be one of the great 20th-century themes: the increasingly acute need for illusion to compensate for essentially alienated lives. Amanda, stuck in a life of petty domestic discontent, compulsively recalls, as through a golden haze, her life as a young woman besieged by gentlemen callers. Laura subsists on her fragile collection of glass and on memories of an unattainable high school hero. Tom, who of the three is most unflinching in facing reality, has his own dream of bold adventure in the larger world. By the end of the play, Amanda and Laura may have retreated to another level of illusion, but in a powerfully affecting final speech Tom reveals the rootlessness and emptiness that have been his since cutting the ties that bound him to a place and a situation he could no longer endure.

Offsetting the pathos and sentiment inherent in these lives is a strain of wry irony and sometimes broad humor. Moreover,

the characterizations are complex enough to accomodate lifelike incongruities. Amanda is given to a nostalgia that borders on fantasy but she is also tough-minded and inclined to shrewishness; part fool, part tragic figure, she is also a survivor and fiercely devoted to her children. Tom is not only an impatient, rebellious son, but one who is deeply affected by his mother's and sister's plight. Laura, perhaps the least complex of the family, is not merely a pathetic victim. She has streaks of stubborn independence, innate tact, and courage that are genuinely affecting. Williams also provides the play with an effective antidote to sentimentality that involves several Brechtian elements—not really surprising in view of Williams' participation in the early 1940's in the Dramatic Workshop of the New School, headed by Erwin Piscator, one of Brecht's mentors in Germany. Especially noteworthy is the extensive use of a narrator who not only establishes the *theatrical* reality of the action by simultaneously functioning as a character and a stage manager, but also consistently conveys the gritty, background reality of world and national events of the 1930s; against which the personal family drama of the Wingfields acquires a special poignancy that is, of course, very un-Brechtian. Williams' use of captions for each scene, another Brechtian touch, is also effective in offsetting an audience's incipient emotional involvement. Such elements distance the action and either place it in a historical, socio-political context, or let us view it from a perspective that is at least partially ironic.

In effect, Williams manages to blend elements of psychological naturalism, Brechtian dramaturgy and stagecraft, and a distinctive poetry not only of language but also of theatre. Such theatre poetry is best exemplified in the final moment of the play, when Williams creates a powerfully expressive tableau that juxtaposes Tom's final psychological farewell, expressed in the present, with Amanda's mute but supremely compassionate consoling of Laura in the past.

Preferring "truth, in the pleasant disguise of illusion" to "illusion that has the appearance of truth", Williams presents a truth from which have been filtered the crueller, harsher, even grotesque realities that often came to mark his subsequent major plays. *The Glass Menagerie* reflects the vulnerability of Tennessee Williams before he tasted fame and was forced to deal with its corrosive distractions.

—Jarka M. Burian

THE GLASS OF WATER; or, Causes and Effects
 (Le Verre d'eau, ou les effets et les causes)
by Eugène Scribe

First Publication: Paris, 1840
First Production: Théâtre Français, 17 November 1840.

Translations
The Glass of Water, in *Nineteenth-Century French Plays*, edited by J.L. Borgerhoff, New York, 1931.
The Glass of Water, translated by D. Bodee, in *"Camille" and Other Plays*, edited by S.S. Stanton.

*   *   *

Scribe's five-act comedy takes place in 18th-century London at the palace of Queen Anne. The complication-filled plot revolves around the conflicting efforts of two adversaries to influence the monarch to support disparate political policy toward war with France. Bolingbroke, the play's protagonist, is a Member of Parliament whose party supports the cause of peace and is opposed by the Duchess of Marlborough, whose strong influence over the Queen perpetuates her husband's interests (as a successful general now fighting abroad) in delaying peace negotiations. She has denied French envoys access to the Queen and her ministers. Impeded from reaching Queen Anne to promote his cause, Bolingbroke undertakes a series of strategies to break the Duchess's power, every one of which is met by a counter-attack from his adversary. Important pawns in the main struggle are a young couple for whom Bolingbroke acts as protector: Masham, a guardsman, and his beloved Abigail, a shop-girl favored by the Queen but blocked by the Duchess from a court appointment (which she eventually wins owing to a plan of Bolingbroke's). While the Duchess progressively executes effective counter-schemes reversing successful schemes of her adversary, Bolingbroke learns that both the Queen and the Duchess desire Masham with neither being aware of the other's longing. In a climactic masterstroke to discredit the Duchess, the protagonist instigates the revelation to both women that each is a rival for

Masham. The secret is exposed by means of a glass of water requested at a court party. Behaving impertinently, the jealous Duchess angers Queen Anne, who forces her favorite's resignation. Subsequent failed attempts by the Duchess to regain power facilitate a resolution in which Bolingbroke is made a minister at court, a peace treaty with France is to be signed, and the long-desired but long-denied marriage of the lovers will be permitted, thus ensuring their happiness. Final events have been initiated by a simple glass of water.

While a historical situation with some factual foundation is employed as the basis for the plot, it serves less as an accurate portrait of the time than as a framework for Scribe's formula for dramatic construction. *The Glass of Water* offers a prime example of the *pièce bien faite*, or "well-made play", a form created by the author which significantly influenced dramatic structure in modern drama. A major feature of the structure is the primacy of a plot which bears a pattern of intensifying action and suspense, carefully prepared by exposition, and assisted by contrived entrances and exits of the characters, and which is characterized by a series of high and low points in a sympathetic hero's fortunes in which success and reversal alternate from scene to scene. Also the Scribean plot is commonly dependent on a secret known to the audience but not to certain characters until its revelation in a climactic scene restores the hero, often a youthful figure whose interests are represented by a worldly protector, to good fortune.

Typical of Scribe's method and orchestration of characters, the play's largely expository first act introduces its major figures, essential situation, and the issues that will generate impending conflict. Bolingbroke, who faces obstacles to his political objectives and his personal status, serves as the protector of the youthful hero Masham, whose problems encompass threatened reprisal for killing a venomous noble in a duel and the complication of being desired by three women. Two of the latter are older and influential women (the Queen who employs him and the Duchess of Marlborough, who controls the Queen) and both are able to thwart his wish to marry Abigail, whom he loves. The Duchess emerges as the formidable adversary of the equally clever Bolingbroke and the young couple he defends. To accomplish his aims, Bolingbroke engages in a battle of wits with his antagonist, which begins the action near the end of the first act and progressively intensifies in a see-saw contest, with one side and then the other mastering the situation. The conflict drives the action to the *scène à faire*, or climactic "obligatory scene" anticipated by the audience, marking the lowest and highest point in the fortunes of Bolingbroke and Masham, and culminating in the disclosure of a secret: the identities of two high-born rivals for the young guardsman are made known to each. Masham's wish to marry Abigail seems hopelessly blocked by the two powerful women who admire him. Bolingbroke restores his cause and that of Masham by manipulating the revelation of "the secret", which forces the Duchess's dismissal and fall from power, thus elevating him to influence, and forces the Queen to allow the lovers to marry in order to save embarrassment. Moreover, the play's resolution is a logical consequence of the dramatic action, skillfully preparing the audience to anticipate and accept it.

In *The Glass of Water*, the prominence of the intricately constructed plot renders theme and character less important. The characters, while theatrical, lively, and well-contrasted, tend to be one-dimensional puppets of the dramatic action. The play's theme is expressed in Bolingbroke's belief that small actions bring great events. A simple glass of water has resulted in a shift of political power, a peace treaty with France, and the happiness of young lovers. Yet the drama's strength and focus lie in the structure of its plot.

While Scribe's play, with its unrealistic contrivances, appears old-fashioned today, the historical influence of its "well-made" structure on modern drama through Ibsen and beyond cannot be denied. Modern drama owes a debt to Scribe, and his theatrical craftsmanship must be admired.

—Christian H. Moe

GLENGARRY GLEN ROSS
by David Mamet

First Publication: New York and London, 1984.
First Production: National Theatre, London, 21 September 1983; first US production, at Goodman Theatre, Chicago, 6 February 1984.

Criticism
(For general works on the author, see *Playwrights* volume)

Articles:
Mathew C. Roudané, "Public Issues, Private Tensions: David Mamet's *Glengarry Glen Ross*", in *South Carolina Review*, vol.19 no.1, 1986.
Peter Hasenberg, "'Always be Closing': Struktur und Thema von David Mamets *Glengarry Glen Ross*", in *Anglistik und Englischunterricht*, 35, 1988.

Philip C. Kohn, "Mitch and Murray in David Mamet's *Glengarry Glen Ross*", in *Notes on Contemporary Literature*, vol.18, no.2, 1988.

* * *

"*We are in a real estate office. There is a sales contest near its end. The four salesmen have only several more days to establish their position on the sales graph. . .The top man wins a Cadillac, the second man wins a set of steak knives, the bottom two men get fired*". Mamet's own scene-setting note on *Glengarry Glen Ross* (the title refers to the useless areas of land being sold) leaves no doubt about the character of its dramatic world. It is one in which money and competition obliterate all other considerations. "To me", Mamet has said, "the play is about a society based on business. . . a society with only one bottom line: How much money you make". It is also—more specifically—about language as power in this commercial-competitive context.

The play has two, very different, acts. In its three scenes, the first act offers three variations, each cast in duet-form, on the theme of persuasion. The setting is a Chinese restaurant in Chicago. In the first scene, Shelly "the Machine" Levene, once a star salesman but now fading badly, tries with increasing desperation to get the cool Williamson to give him the best "leads" (appointments with prospective customers)—resorting eventually to bribery. In the second scene, the gestures of mutual consolation made by the frustrated no-hoper Moss with the already-defeated Aaronow turn out to be a tactic designed to compromise Aaronow by involving him in Moss's plan to rob the real estate office and sell the "hot" leads. The third

Glengarry Glen Ross: National Theatre, London, 1983 (first production)

scene also involves deception. Richard Roma, the current star salesman and "ruler" of the office, first hypnotizes a man called Lingk with some unbuttoned philosophizing, then pounces. Lingk has become a prospective customer; Roma seemed to be relaxing, but in fact he was doing his job. The Cadillac is almost his.

Act II harnesses and combines the dynamic energy of these three encounters in a conventional plot-structure. It is the next morning and the office has been ransacked. Throughout the act the salesmen are called into an adjoining room to be questioned. Levene bursts into the office to celebrate and recount his "closure" of a big sale, but this is later revealed to be a dud. Then Lingk arrives to cancel Roma's sale to him. Roma stalls, but when Williamson mentions that the check is already cashed, Lingk rushes out and the sale is doomed. Williamson is abusively berated, first by Roma and then by Levene, but when the latter lets slip that he knows Williamson was lying about the leads, he betrays his own guilt for the robbery. Only the thief could have known. Williamson reports Levene. Roma resumes his predatory quest for the Cadillac.

An account of the plot barely hints at the linguistic virtuosity of the writing. As Jack Shepherd (the original Roma) put it: "The rhythms are slick, fast, syncopated, like a drum solo. . .What's missing is the tune". The effect is dazzling and, at first, very funny. There is a rich orchestration of voices, sounding the whirling idiom of sales-speak—"leads", "sits", "closes", "boards", "streaks"—which is rhythmically sustained by a constant stream of highly expressive obscenities. The very opacity of the writing makes us aware of speech as *act*, as something that functions rhetorically rather than as a lucid medium of transmission. Whatever the words used, the pace, the rhythms, the tones, the pauses, are designed to bully, to cajole, to persuade, to advance, to retreat, to seduce, to impress. "High-speed Pinter" said one reviewer, and Pinter is the play's dedicatee. But in Mamet there is a *professional* imperative: the salesman is a rhetorician; his job hinges on the power of speech, the *act* of utterance. As Mamet has said, recalling his own experience working in a real estate office, "the salesmen were primarily performers. They went into people's living rooms and performed their play about the investment properties". They are intrinsically theatrical.

It is hardly surprising, then, that the salesmen's relations to their customers are structured by fictions. When the expert Roma engages Lingk in the final scene of Act I, he does so through a rather sophisticated fiction—a "philosophy" cast in the form of an implied narrative within which the product represents the opportunity for the buyer to affirm his essential, authentic being through the existential act undertaken at the awesome moment of purchase. When Lingk arrives in Act II in the attempt to withdraw from the purchase, he is again inducted into a fiction. This time it takes the form of an improvised scene between Roma and Levene in which the latter plays the part of a high-ranking American Express executive and intimate of Roma's—they both make themselves out to be in a terrible hurry to get away. And, ironically, Lingk is finally sent off by a fiction from Williamson: the lie about the check that eventually brings about Levene's self-betrayal. Thus the customer Lingk's connections with the salesmen are fashioned entirely out of fictions, one following another.

The salesmen also keep a fiction "in play" among themselves. This is the idea of the "frontier ethic", which demands the energy and initiative of the rugged individualist, but which also requires partnership, dependability, male fellowship. We glimpse shades of Willy Loman when Levene, flushed with apparent success, asserts that "a man's his job": "I was born for a salesman. And now I'm back, and I got my *balls* back". It

is a vocation—one for Real Men. The salesman who does not conform is a "fairy" or a "cocksucker". And yet, as Mamet himself has pointed out, the frontier ethic "was always something for nothing": "take the land from the Indians and give it to the railroad". The predatory individualism of the men introduces an inevitable, irremediable contradiction into the frontier ethic, which then becomes a potential vehicle of domination within relationships ultimately structured by competitive power. The plot energetically plays out the ironic implications of this ethical contradiction.

Speaking *ex cathedra* about his plays, Mamet is apt to sound a moral note. Yet he has referred to this play as a "gang comedy", and we do well to recognize that—not for the first time in Mamet's work—its energies are exhilaratingly complicit with those of the professional performers it represents. If the con-man has become a recurrent focus of literary and theatrical fascination in this century, it is because it enables the writer to reflect on his own relation to his audience's needs and desires. *Glengarry Glen Ross* reflects on the culture, and the pleasure, we share with these Chicago salesmen.

—Paul Lawley

THE GOLDEN AGE
by Louis Nowra

First Publication: Sydney, 1985; revised edition, Sydney, 1988.
First Production: Studio Theatre, Melbourne, 8 February 1985.

Criticism
(For general works on the author, see *Playwrights* volume)

Articles:
Peter Fitzpatrick, "*The Golden Age*", in *Australian Drama Studies*, October 1985.
Veronica Kelly, "Apocalypse and After: Historical Visions in Some Recent Australian Drama", in *Kunapipi*, vol. 9 no. 3, 1987.
Gerry Turcotte, "'The circle is burst': Eschatological Discourse in Louis Nowra's *Sunrise* and *The Golden Age*", in *Australasian Drama Studies*, 11, 1987.
Veronica Kelly, "'Nowt More Outcastin': Utopian Myth in Louis Nowra's *The Golden Age*", in *A Sense of Exile: Essays in the Literature of the Asia-Pacific Region*, edited by Bruce Bennett, Perth, Western Australia, 1988.

*   *   *

Set in Tasmania during World War II, the play shows the discovery of an isolated family of inbred descendents of 19th-century convicts and gold-seekers living in the depths of the South-West forests speaking a syncretic patois made up of archaic, British, regional dialects. Their young discoverers, Francis and Peter, are variously fascinated and repelled by these people, whose chances of reproduction, despite the erotic energy particularly of Betsheb, appear to be problematic. Hence the group's martriarch, Queenie Ayre, resolves that they return to "civilisation". On their arrival in Hobart they become the objects of amused indulgence and scientific curiosity, but political expediency soon dictates that they are incarcerated for the duration of the war in a lunatic asylum lest their physical degeneration be used as evidence supporting Nazi racist propaganda. Only Betsheb survives to be reunited eventually with her lover, the working-class soldier Francis, who has been brutalised and alienated by his experiences in the European conflict. They return to the forest to make what future they can.

A mythic and highly poetic play loosely based on an incident in Tasmanian history, *The Golden Age* deals with problems of definition of culture and civilisation, and with the broad patterns of Australian, and more generally post-colonial, history. The play foregrounds the generic choice of romance, rather than tragedy, and alludes to the myths of Utopia, of Eden (with the ambivalent, cultural resonances this holds for colonised, invader societies) and of Orestes. Its main theme concerns exile and homecoming, formally signalled by the use of two embedded playlets where reunions occur after long exiles: Euripides' *Iphigenia in Tauris* and the happy-ending version of *King Lear*.

The lost people are the descendents of the original white outcasts of the penal colony of Van Diemen's Land and bear with them memories and physical traces of the savage past in the society of "rack 'n' cat". Their genetic entropy suggests that their culture too is endangered. Their contemporaries, the cultivated Archer family, are in their own way inheritors of an historic alienation. The two principal characters, Betsheb and Francis, can be read as separated halves of an entity who strive for union to heal a rift both psychic and cultural. Francis, the working-class boy, is differentiated from his middle-class friend Peter, and the play contains ample social comedy as their worlds come into contact, and later when they themselves encounter the powerful, oral culture of the forest people. But by the time he has endured, and been complicit in, the nightmare of European "civilisation", imprisoned for an ambiguous crime, and "transported" to Australia, Francis has relived the historical paradigm of the convict experience also implicit in the fate of the lost people. His final reunion with Betsheb in the forest is a suspended ending, in that their love attempts to close an historical cycle without necessarily charting the shape of its successor. But for Betsheb at least it is a homecoming, and in the final words of the play she promises "Nowt more outcastin".

Combining earthy wit and concreteness of observation with folklore motifs and ambitious fabulation, *The Golden Age* alludes not only to white migrant and refugee experiences in a multi-cultural society, but also to Aboriginal history—Tasmania being the island where genocide by the British came closest to complete success. Nowra gives the outcast group vitality, spirituality, a highly theatricalised physicality and intense mutual devotion; all signs of a concealed Aboriginality. The presence through absence in the play of Aboriginal experience expresses the group's impact upon the white Australian consciousness: as "other" the Aborigines cannot be directly appropriated for representation but may be alluded to obliquely. In performance the lost "tribe" presents challenges for vocal and mimetic skills. The tribe's condensed but expressive language and crippled, intense, bodily presence demand energy and invention from the actors, and in Betsheb Nowra has created one of the most charismatic and demanding female roles in modern theatre.

—Veronica Kelly

THE GOOD HOPE (Op Hoop van Zegen)
by Herman Heijermans

First Publication: Amsterdam, 1901.
First Production: Hollandsche Schouwburg, Amsterdam, 24 December 1900.

Translations
The Good Hope, translated by L. Saunders and C. Heijermans-Houwink, New York, 1928.

* * *

Simon, the shipwright, informs the shipowner, Bos, that the timbers of the fishing vessel, The Good Hope, are rotten; but in spite of this it is put to sea and sinks, with the loss of many fishermen, including Barend and Geert, the two sons of Kniertje.

The Good Hope, Heijermans' four-act "play of the sea", is his most famous play, warmly received, especially in Germany but also produced all over the world and interpreted in Dutch film and opera. The Good Hope is just one example of the many fishing boats heavily insured and sent out in all weathers by the shipowner prepared to put others' lives at risk while his capital is secure. As the play reveals, the fishermen are far from secure, enduring a hard life of few rewards, with danger at sea and poverty at home. Most of the characters are tragically resigned to their lot, seeking comfort in God or in drink; the play presents little hope for change. Heijermans drew on his own fishing-village experience, of a time before the merchant shipping act of 1909 protected workers in the Dutch fishing industry. Heijermans exposed the inequalities of life in his writings, and his socialism is represented in this and other plays, including the companion piece to *The Good Hope, Ora et Labora* (*Pray and Work*), his "play of the land", about the Frisian peasants.

Typical of naturalistic plays, dialogue is used to render the wider social determinants of the action. The scenes are set in rooms, while the sea and The Good Hope are never presented on stage. The first three acts of the play are set in Kniertje's cottage. She is the mother of the two young men, Barend and Geert, who, like Eelke in *Pray and Work*, are rebellious instead of submissive. In the first act, Barend's justified fear of drowning results in his refusal to go to sea and he is rejected by the villagers as a coward. Heijermans' anti-militarist ideas, developed in *The Suit of Armor* and in this play, are explored in the character of Geert who returns from prison, having been charged with insubordination and thrown out of the navy. Courage and hard work are valued in the community, while fear, particularly of death, is ever present and articulated by the fishermen in their superstitions. Heijermans ensures that our sympathies lie with the exploited fishermen but examines also the contribution of religion and conservatism in their continued exploitation. Kniertje's tragedy is that she chastises both her sons, urging them to obedience and respect for authority. This proves ultimately to be misguided, for those in authority are seen to have only their own interests at heart. Memorable performances of Kniertje include those by Ellen Terry (in 1907 and 1912) and Eva le Gallienne (in 1927).

The second act opens ominously with the drunken shipwright's warning that *The Good Hope* is not seaworthy, but no one listens in the midst of Kniertje's birthday celebrations. The shipowner, Bos, interrupts their singing of the "Marseillaise" at the height of the party, to call the men to board *The Good Hope*, which prompts an argument between Geert and Bos, providing the only moment of direct confrontation in the play.

The moment of danger passes. Although Geert's criticisms of Bos are fair, his challenge to the shipowner's authority results only in Kniertje losing her much-needed cleaning job at Bos's house. The men leave to board, except for Barend, who has run away after learning from Simon, the shipwright, that the ship is not seaworthy. He seeks refuge in his mother's cottage, and the act ends with the police's attempts to force him on board *The Good Hope*.

The third act of the play is dominated by story telling, as the women gather at Kniertje's cottage to wait to hear of the return of the fishermen. They talk of their experiences of the sea, that they "pay dear for the fish" in the many deaths of their relatives drowned at sea. Clementine, the shipowner's daughter, is included in this group, although her family are responsible for the hard lives of these women. Like Gaaike and Dobbe in *The Seventh Commandment*, Clementine is more enlightened and sympathetic than her father, and presents an example of Heijermans' skilful portrayal of even minor characters. She is accepted by all except Jo, Kniertje's niece, who angrily articulates this class conflict. Kniertje asserts that prayer is their only comfort and refuses to blame the shipowners. However, she does express a sense of injustice that the burgomaster should be comfortably eating shellfish while The Good Hope is missing. Jo's admission to Kniertje that she is Geert's lover is met with criticism for the sin but also comfort. The act ends with Kniertje reading her prayer book, while Jo cries and the storm howls outside.

One of Heijermans' strengths as a playwright is demonstrated in the subtle accumulation of scenes which help to develop the dramatic tension; the connections between the scenes are apparent only towards the end of the play. Setting the fourth act in the shipowner's office reveals the very different preoccupations of the shipowner, Bos, and his wife, Mathilde. Mathilde is busy launching an appeal to repair the church clock when news arrives that The Good Hope is sunk and Barend has been washed ashore. Simon, the shipwright, accuses Bos of murder by his negligence which Clementine refuses to corroborate. While the act is punctuated by concerned relatives inquiring about their fishermen, Bos's response is merely that one must submit to the will of God and that business is business. He refuses to pay for Jo to bring back Barend's body for burial but is not presented simply as a villain; he began as a poor fisherman. His hypocrisy in appropriating religion for maintaining a sense of resignation in the suffering working classes is revealed when Bos learns that Jo is expecting Geert's child. He informs Kniertje that the appeal fund, designated only for those leading a moral life, cannot provide Jo with any money.

While the play, ending with Kniertje's submissive resignation, exposes the exploitation of those working in the fishing industry, it does not present any easy solutions. The shipowner's concern for his ship rather than for human life is demonstrated, but the play also examines the resigned acceptance of suffering of the fishing community, from the submissive Kniertje to the hard-working old fishermen, Cobus and Daantje.

—Katharine Cockin

———————

THE GOOD PERSON OF SETZUAN
(Der gute Mensch von Sezuan)
by Bertolt Brecht (with R. Berlau and M. Steffin; music by Paul Dessau)

First Publication: As *The Good Woman of Setzuan*, in *Parables For The Theatre*, translated by Eric Bentley, Minneapolis, Minnesota, 1948; in *Versuche, 12*, Frankfurt, 1953 (in German); revised edition, 1958.
First Production: Schauspielhaus, Zürich, 4 February 1943.

Translations
The Good Woman of Setzuan, in *Parables For the Theatre*, translated by Eric Bentley, Minneapolis, Minnesota, 1948; revised version, Harmondsworth, 1966.
The Good Person of Setzuan, translated by John Willet in *Plays Two*, London, 1962.
The Good Person of Sichuan, translated by Michael Hofmann, London, 1989.

Criticism
(For general works on the author, see *Playwrights* volume)

Books:
Kurt Bräuttigam, *Bertolt Brecht: "Der gute Mensch von Sezuan"*, Munich, 1966.
Werner Hecht (ed.), *Materialien zu Brechts "Der gute Mensch von Sezuan"*, Frankfurt, 1968.

Articles:
Wilhelm Fahlbusch, "Der entfremdete Mensch. Eine Studie zu Bert Brecht *Der gute Mensch von Sezuan*", in *Monatshefte für Pastoral-Theologie*, 48, 1959.
E. Loeb, "Sartre's *No Exit* and Brecht's *The Good Woman of Setzuan*: A Comparison", in *Modern Language Quarterly*, 22, 1961.
Franz Lau, "Bertolt Brecht und Luther: Ein Versuch der Interpretation des *Guten Mensch von Sezuan*", in *Luther-Jahrbuch*, 29, 1962.
Edward M. Berckman, "The Function of Hope in Brecht's Pre-revolutionary Theater", in *Brecht heute*, 1, 1971.
Peter Ruppert, "Brecht's *Der gute Mensch von Sezuan*: Dialectic Toward Utopia", in *South Atlantic Bulletin*, vol. 41, no. 4, 1976.
Elizabeth Boa, "Marxist Maths: Brecht's *Der gute Mensch von Sezuan*", in *Modern Languages*, 59, 1978.
Sammy K. McLean, "Messianism in Bertolt Brecht's *Der gute Mensch von Sezuan* and *Der Kaukasische Kreidekreis*", in *Seminar*, 14, 1978.
Janet K. Swaffar, "The Ethics of Exploitation: Brecht's *Der gute Mensch von Sezuan*", in *University of Dayton Review*, vol. 13 no. 3, 1979.
Zsuzsanna Ozsvath, "Brecht's *The Rise and Fall of the City of Mahagonny* and *The Good Woman of Setzuan*: Beyond Marxism", in *Studies in Literature*, 13, 1981.
Johannes Goldhahn, "Brechts *Der gute Mensch von Sezuan*: eine realistische Parabel", in *Weimarer Beiträge*, 30, 1984.
Hubert Zapf, "Two Concepts of Society in Drama: Bertolt Brecht's *The Good Woman of Setzuan* and Edward Bond's *Lear*", in *Modern Drama*, 31, 1988.

*   *   *

Three gods, as yet unsuccessful in their search for a good person, arrive in Setzuan. Wang, the waterseller (and narra-

The Good Person of Setzuan: National Theatre, London, 1989

tor) can only find them accommodation with the prostitute Shen Te. The next day, feeling they have succeeded in their quest, the gods give Shen Te 1000 silver dollars, with which she buys a tobacco shop. She is inundated with human parasites and creditors. The only way to keep her shop solvent seems to be to invent a stern male cousin, Shui Ta. Shen Te borrows money and prepares to sell the shop to allow her lover (Sun) to bribe his way into a job as a pilot in Peking. He abandons her when she does not give him the money, after she has discovered his plan to go there alone. Shui Ta, however, sets up a flourishing tobacco factory and employs Sun as a harsh overseer. Shen Te is pregnant by Sun, and spends so much time as Shui Ta that she is accused of Shen Te's murder. At the trial (where the gods are the judges), Shen Te reveals her secret. The gods depart, and the play ends with Shen Te's problems unresolved.

The various themes of *The Good Person of Setzuan*, came together slowly over a period of ten years. As early as 1928 Brecht had outlined a play in which a whore dressed as a man and ran a flourishing cigar factory. In this outline Brecht presents prostitution as the ultimate self-alienation produced by the capitalist system (an idea that was to recur frequently in his work), as well as an escape route for the victim through the adoption of a mask to gain invulnerability. The three wandering gods can be traced back to a visit made by Brecht, Döblin, and Bronnen to Dresden. Brecht punishes the town for the shabby treatment they received there in a poem in which his three gods destroy a town in which they were not well received. The idea of a search for a good person Brecht himself traces back to the Bible story of Sodom and Gommorah.

The Good Person of Setzuan, was eventually finished in January 1941, having been written, with frequent interruptions, in a number of European countries during Brecht's exile from Germany. It was first performed in Zurich in February 1943, but in Germany not until November 1952. Brecht confessed that, of all his plays, it had given him the most trouble. Indeed, much of the peculiar interest of the play lies in Brecht's unwillingness (or inability) to resolve the contradictions it contains. Of all of Brecht's plays it is the most open-ended. The intention of the "Dialectical Theatre" of Brecht's later writing is that the audience will itself discover the synthesis emerging from the theatrical dialectic presented by the action on stage. It is not Brecht's intention that his plays be seen as complete when they finish, nor that all the problems posed be resolved, but the difficulties with which Shen Te comes to terms, by recourse to her *alter ego*, Shui Ta, are dwarfed by those she would have to face after the birth of her child, given the limitation imposed by the gods on her invoking of her cousin.

The gods escape from the real world on their pink cloud—a parody of the traditional entrance of the *deus ex machina* to resolve the insuperable problems of the action. The three gods in the play have shown themselves to be far from omniscient (they have to rely on progress reports from Wang), and they explicitly state that they are not omnipotent (they did not cause the collapse of the dam). Their greatest weakness is their perceived irrelevance to the contemporary community. Nobody needs to believe in them as they no longer have any real power to affect the course of events. Their aim in the play is to validate their normative view of good and evil. In finding Shen Te—one good person—they are satisfied, and in refusing to countenance her problems at the end of the play they save themselves from having to contemplate changing their thinking. The first god reports the atheists as saying that the world must be changed because no-one can *be* good and *stay* good. In Shen Te they convince themselves they have found their good person, and they reward her with the gift of money, to help her

to continue to do good.

Brecht had already rejected a normative view of morality—as a result of his reading both of Marx and of Chinese philosophy—in favour of a concept of good and evil determined by social conditions, and in this play, in the "heightened antithesis" of the characters of Shen Te and Shui Ta, he makes one of his most striking theatrical statements on the relation between good and evil. The fundamental paradox in the character of Shen Te is caused not by a psychological flaw, but by the irresistible economic and social forces working upon her. The unwilling split in Shen Te, to produce Shui Ta, graphically shows how socio-economic forces compel goodness to embrace evil in order to survive in the system in which she finds herself. Shen Te herself in the court says. "It has torn me in two". The irony is that the instinct for survival (strengthened by her pregnancy), gives increasing dominance to Shui Ta, until the gods impose their limitation.

In the epilogue written later to explain the apparently unsatisfactory ending of the play, an actor calls on the audience to look for a way for people to be able to do good and survive. But it would be possible to see the play as convincing an argument for the oriental concept of the necessary balance of assertive "masculine" strength and "feminine" caring in personality, as it would be to see the play as a naïve call for a Marxist Utopia.

—Anthony Meech

THE GOOD PERSON OF SICHUAN.   See **THE GOOD PERSON OF SETZUAN.**

THE GOOD WOMAN OF SETZUAN.   See **THE GOOD PERSON OF SETZUAN.**

GORBODUC; or, The Tragedy of Ferrex and Porrex by Thomas Norton and Thomas Sackville

First Publication: London, 1565.
First Production: Inner Temple Hall, London, 1 January 1561 or 1562.

Editions

Gorboduc, in *Minor Elizabethan Drama, 1*, London, 1910.
Gorboduc, in *Early English Classical Tragedies*, edited by John W. Cunliffe, Oxford, 1912.
Gorboduc, in *Five Elizabethan Tragedies*, edited by A.K. McIlwraith, 1938.
Gorboduc, edited by Irby B. Cauthen Jr., Lincoln, Nebraska, 1970 (Regents Renaissance Drama Series).
Gorboduc, in *Minor Elizabethan Tragedy*, edited by T.W. Craik, London, 1974.

Criticism

Books:

Howard Baker, *Introduction to Tragedy: A Study in Development of Form in "Gorboduc", "The Spanish Tragedy" and "Titus Andronicus"*, 1939.

Articles:

Homer A. Watt, *"Gorboduc; or, Ferrex and Porrex"*, Madison, 1910.

S.A. Small, "The Political Import of the Norton Half of *Gorboduc*", in *Publications of the Modern Language Association [PMLA]*, 46, 1931.

Sarah R. Watson, "*Gorboduc* and the Theory of Tyrannicide", in *Modern Language Review*, 34, 1939.

Marvin T. Herrick, "Senecan Influence in *Gorboduc*", in *Studies in Speech and Drama in Honor of Alexander M. Drummond*, Ithaca, New York, 1944.

Barbara H.C. De Mendonca, "The Influence of *Gorboduc* on *King Lear*", in *Shakespeare Survey*, 13, 1960.

Robert Y. Turner, "Pathos and the *Gorboduc* Tradition", in *Huntington Library Quarterly*, 25, 1962.

Ernest W. Talbot, "The Political Import of the First Two Audiences of *Gorboduc*", in *Studies in Honor of DeWitt T. Starnes*, Austin, Texas, 1967.

Philip Dust, "The Theme of 'Kinde' in *Gorboduc*", in *Salzburg Studies in English Literature*, 12, 1973.

Mark Breitenberg, "Reading Elizabethan Iconicity: *Gorboduc* and the Semiotics of Reform", in *English Literary Renaissance*, vol. 18 no. 2, 1988.

*   *   *

The plot of the play is conveniently given in its "Argument":

> Gorboduc, King of Britain, divided his realm in his life time to his sons, Ferrex and Porrex. The sons fell to dissension. The younger killed the elder. The mother, that more dearly loved the elder, for revenge killed the younger. The people, moved with the cruelty of the fact, rose in rebellion and slew both father and mother. The nobility assembled, and most terribly destroyed the rebels; and afterwards, for want of issue of the Prince, whereby the succession of the crown became uncertain, they fell to civil war, in which both they and many issues were slain, and the land for a long time almost desolate and miserably wasted.

Regarded as the first extant, English, "regular" tragedy, *Gorboduc* is an example of Tudor "academic drama" i.e., a play not written for public presentation by professional performers (the first Elizabethan playhouse not being built until 1576). The term "regular" draws attention to its decidedly structured nature which is that of ancient classical drama. The play is divided into five acts, each act apart from the last being followed by a Chorus commenting on its action and significance. Such action is violent and destructive, not to say sensational, yet all action occurs off-stage and is described in graphic, reported speech. The dialogue has little give and take; long speeches are endemic. The language of the play is not prose but heightened verse of a decidedly rhetorical nature. Allegory, symbolism, and classical allusion litter the text. It is by no means a naturalistic play. All this is not to say it follows slavishly the so-called dramatic rule of the classical unities—those of time, place, and action.

Other noteworthy features include the fact that the play (apart from the Chorus) is written entirely in blank verse—the first extant English example—and that each act is preceded by an elaborate dumb show accompanied by music. The tragedy moreover is not that of its protagonist, King Gorboduc, but of his country, "Britain realm". The play's clear didactic intent focuses on the fate of a country where no Prince exists to succeed to the crown and where the succession is left open and unnamed. The play indicates that in such a situation, a "princely state (is) open prey to greedy lust and to usurping power" where "all right and law shall cease"—a situation in which civil war and anarchy will ensue. At the time of the play's presentation, Elizabeth was unmarried and the succession was unsecured.

The subject-matter of the play—the story of King Gorboduc of "Britain realm"—comes from legend and can be traced back to Geoffrey of Monmouth, who first declared that the rulers of Britain were descended from Brute, great grandson of Aeneas the founder of New Troy. The plot also echoes that of King Lear (the tenth descendant), another ancient British monarch who unwisely divided his realm during his lifetime.

Many commentators claim the influence of Seneca on the play, because of its accent on violence and the spilling of blood. But many typical Senecan features do not appear in the play—there is no supernatural element (there are no ghosts), and although Queen Videna avenges the murder of her favourite son, the play has no emphasis on a revenge-theme as such. Neither is there any reflection of the Senecan doctrine of fate or Stoicism. The play's other so-called Senecan features, such as its five-act structure, use of chorus, rhetorical style, and sententia can be more precisely identified as classical, dramatic elements—but of Greece, not Rome.

Little attention has been given to the play's theatrical potential which is considerable, not in naturalistic, but in formal terms. Of particular interest are the five dumb shows which preface each act. These are carefully constructed to include a musical accompaniment of rising shrillness and cacophany, echoing the growing tension in the kingdom. Designed to be performed with appropriate, ritual formality, these "shows" are theatrically and effectively devised. Characterisation in the play is also formal; the roles are simple representations of various opinions. Little movement on stage is called for; the primary requisites are a clear, well-modulated speaking voice and appropriate gesture. The play calls for no scenery (it is played on the typical Elizabethan unlocalised stage), with a consequent emphasis on costume. All in all, the play has the typical ingredients of stylised Tudor drama.

The blank verse in which most of the play (except the chorus's rhymed stanzas) is written betrays its early composition; there is none of the variety and effectiveness wielded by the later Marlowe and Shakespeare. The style is consistent and grave, the verse mainly end-stopped, and occasionally pedestrian. It is, however, less archaic than the language in which its "argument" is couched and with competent delivery (in the Inns of Court students practised drama to better their skills at public speaking) would no doubt have proved effective. As the first regular, blank verse, English tragedy the play merits and rewards study.

—Philip S. Cook

GORE OT UMA. See **THE MISFORTUNE OF BEING CLEVER.**

GÖTZ VON BERLICHINGEN, WITH THE IRON HAND
(Götz von Berlichingen mit der eisernen Hand)
by Johann Wolfgang von Goethe

First Publication: Darmstadt, 1773.
First Production: Berlin, 12 April 1774.

Editions
"Adalbert von Weislingen" [Part one of the 1819 Weimar stage-version], edited by Eugen Kilian, Leipzig, 1919.
Götz von Berlichingen, edited by James M. Clark, London and Edinburgh, 1961.
Götz von Berlichingen, edited by Klaus Lindemann, Munich, Vienna and Zurich, 1980.

Translations
Ironhand, translated by John Arden, London, 1965.
Götz von Berlichingen, in *Goethe: Plays*, translated by Charles E. Passage, London, 1980

Criticism
(For general works on the author, see *Playwrights* volume)

Books:
Reinhold Pallmann, *Der historische Götz von Berlichingen mit der eisernen Hand und Goethes Schauspiel über ihn: Eine Quellenstudie*, Berlin, 1894.
Paul Hagenbring, *Goethes "Götz von Berlichingen": Erläuterungen und literarhistorische Würdigung*, Halle, 1911.
Hans Schregle, *Goethes Gottfried von Berlichingen*, Halle, 1923.
Heinrich Meyer-Benfrey, *Goethes "Götz von Berlichingen"*, Weimar, 1929.
Hermann Blumenthal (ed.), *Zeitgenössische Rezensionen und Urteile über "Götz" und "Werther"*, Berlin, 1935.
Karl Walter, *Schiller's erster "Wallenstein"-Darsteller und Goethes "Götz" (Neufassung von 1804) in Weimar*, Münster, 1939.

Articles:
John Albrecht Walz, "Goethe's *Goetz von Berlichingen* and Lillo's *History of George Barnwell*", in *Modern Philology*, 3, 1906.
Franz Skutsch, "Zur *Geschichte Gottfriedens von Berlichingen dramatisiert*", in *Festschrift zur Jahrhundertfeier der Königl. Universität zu Breslau*, Breslau, 1911.
H.W. Nordmeyer, "Eine amerikanische Übersetzung von Goethes *Götz*", in *Journal of English and Germanic Philology*, 16, 1917.
James Taft Hatfield, "*Götz von Berlichingen* in America", in *Germanic Review*, 24, 1949.
Detlev W. Schumann, "Goethe and Friedrich Carl von Möser: A Contribution to the Study of *Götz von Berlichingen*", in *Journal of English and Germanic Philology*, 53, 1954.
Ilse Applebaum Graham, "Götz von Berlichingen's Right Hand", in *German Life and Letters*, 16, 1963.
Frank G. Ryder, "Toward a Re-evaluation of Goethe's *Goetz*: Features of Recurrence", in *Publications of the Modern Language Association* [*PMLA*], 79, 1964.
H.G. Haile, "'Herr, er will uns fressen': The Spirit of *Götz*", in *Journal of English and Germanic Philology*, 64, 1965.
David R. Couch, "A Theatrical Evaluation of Goethe's Abridged Stage Adaptation of *Götz*", in *German Quarterly*, 41, 1968.
Christa Fell, "Justus Möser's Social Ideas as Mirrored in

Goethe's *Götz von Berlichingen*", in *Germanic Review*, 54, 1979.
Volker Neuhaus, "Johann Wolfgang Goethe: *Götz von Berlichingen*", in *Geschichte als Schauspiel: Deutsche Geschichtsdramen*, edited by Walter Hinck, Frankfurt, 1981.
Arlene Akiko Teroaka, "Submerged Symmetry and Surface Chaos: The Structure of *Götz von Berlichingen*", in *Goethe Yearbook*, 2, 1984.
Benjamin Bennet, "Prometheus and Saturn: The Three Versions of *Götz von Berlichingen*", in *German Quarterly*, vol.58 no.3, 1985.
Alan Menhennet, "Historical Ambivalence in Goethe and Scott", in *New German Studies*, vol.13 no.3, 1985.
Fränk Göttmann, "*Götz von Berlichingen*: Überlebter Stauchritter oder moderner Raubunternehmer?", in *Jahrbuch für fränkische Landesforschung*, vol.46 no.1, 1986.
Hans Reiser, "Goethe, Möser, and the *Aufklärung*: The Holy Roman Empire in *Götz von Berlichingen* and *Egmont*", in *Deutsche Vierteljahrsschrift für Literaturwissenschaft und Geistesgeschichte*, vol.60 no.4, 1986.
Kenneth D. Weisinger, "*Götz von Berlichingen*: History Writing Itself", in *German Studies Review*, vol.9 no.2, 1986.
Frank M. Fowler, "Regularity Without Rules: The Formal Structure of Goethe's *Götz von Berlichingen*", in *German Life and Letters*, vol.51 no.1, 1987.
Peter Möller, "Aber die Geschichte schweigt nicht: Goethes *Geschichte Gottfriedens von Berlichingen und der eisernen Hand dramatisiert* als Beginn der deutschen Geschichtsdramatik", in *Zeitschrift für Germanistik*, vol.8 no.2, 1987.
G.A. Wells, "*Götz von Berlichingen*: History, Drama, and Dramatic Effectiveness", in *Publications of the English Goethe Society* [*PEGS*], 56, 1987.
Wolfgang Wittkowski, "Homo Homini Lupus, Homo Homini Deus: *Götz von Berlichingen mit der eisernen Hand* als Tragödie und als Drama gesellschaftlicher Aufklärung", in *Colloquia Germanica*, vol.20 no.4, 1987.

*   *   *

Götz, a free knight of the Empire, is in conflict with the Bishop of Bamberg, whose lieutenant, Weislingen, Götz has captured. Weislingen becomes engaged to Maria, Götz's sister, and is allowed to return to Bamberg. While there, Weislingen falls under the spell of Adelheid von Walldorf, a court adventuress, and marries her. Weislingen is sent by the Bishop to arrest Götz, now besieged in his castle with his faithful friends Lerse and Sickingen (Sickingen has married the deserted Maria). Götz is tricked into leaving his castle and is captured; but while on trial in Heilbronn, he is rescued by Sickingen. Götz returns to live quietly in his castle, but agrees to lead the Peasants' Revolt. Weislingen is poisoned on the orders of Adelheid, who is herself condemned by the secret court of the Fehmgericht. Götz is wounded and captured, and dies in prison with the word "freedom" on his lips.

Götz von Berlichingen was Goethe's first large scale work for the theatre. It was first published in 1773, and staged by the Koch company in 1774 in Berlin, where it enjoyed unprecedented success and ran for 14 performances. This revolutionary play was quickly recognised as a model by the new literary movement of the *Sturm und Drang* ("Storm and Stress"). The play was the result of Goethe's friendship with Herder and their discussions during the winter of 1770, when Herder introduced Goethe to Shakespeare, Ossian, folksongs, and the Gothic in the search for a truly representative German voice in literature and the theatre to replace the culture dominant in

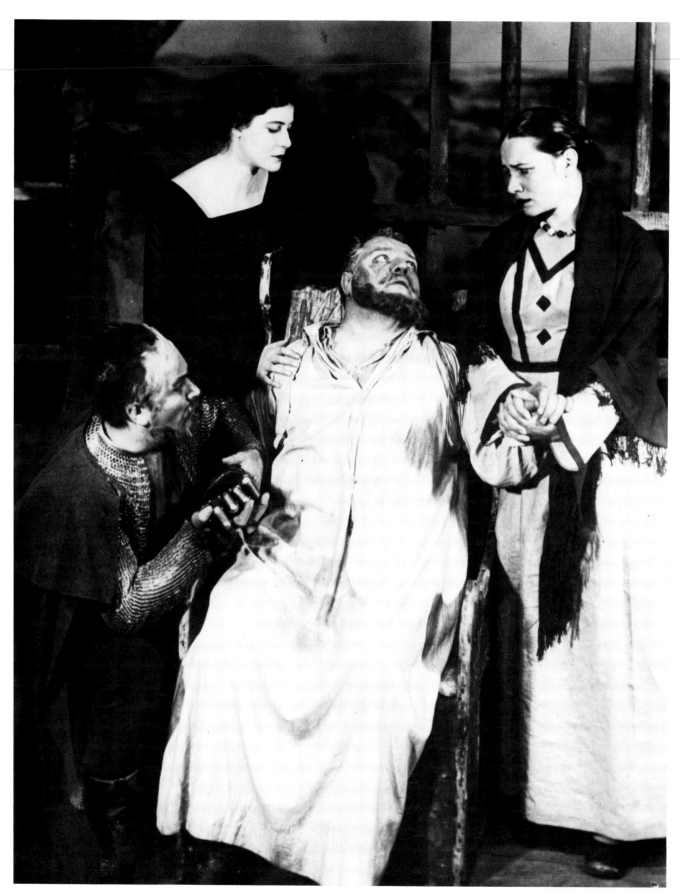

Götz von Berlichingen: Staatstheater, Berlin, 1930

Germany at the time (in particular in the Leipzig of Goethe's student days), which under the tutelage of Gottsched, sought to emulate French neo-classicism.

Götz von Berlichingen represented a decisive break with the traditions of the Enlightenment and neo-classicism, both for the drama and the theatre, in its theme, content, structure, and language. In imitation of Shakespeare's history plays, Goethe chose as his hero a 16th-century German free knight of the Empire (dramatising his life story from his autobiography). In doing so, he opened up the previously disregarded, teutonic past as a subject for theatrical treatment, and instituted German historical drama. In the structure of the play Goethe followed what he understood as Shakespeare's freedom of construction. Adopting an epic, chronicle style, he rejected the classical unities, allowing the action to cover decades in Götz's life, to change scene no less than 56 times (22 times in the third act alone), and to build up a composite picture of the character of Götz by means of scenes which function as "snapshots", rather than by way of a traditionally constructed plot. Goethe freed himself from the artificiality of the alexandrine verse-form customarily employed by writers aping the French neo-classical style (as he himself had done in his earlier anacreontic dramas), and chose to write the play in a muscular prose, expertly tailored to suit the speaker, and ranging from language appropriate to the judges of the Fehmgericht and the court to Götz's infamous: "Er kann mich am Arsch lecken" ("He can kiss my arse"). The songs in the play are written in an unaffected style reminiscent of the folk songs which Herder had described as the "voice of the people".

The most important and revolutionary development was, however, in the depiction of the character of Götz himself. Lessing, describing the play as a "beautiful monstrosity" maintained that Goethe had simply: "put a man's life story into dialogue and was proclaiming it as a drama". This was precisely Goethe's intention, to portray "one of the noblest of Germans, and to rescue the memory of a worthy man". Götz is shown as the outstanding example of the *Kraftmensch* (strong, free man), admired and portrayed by the writers of the *Sturm und Drang* movement; a man who is not constrained by the artificial rules of an effete society which the writers of the new movement saw all around them. A figure reminiscent of the heroes of Homer, Götz is presented as a man of transparent honesty. He is loyal, a defender of the poor and the underprivileged, and, above all, a man of action rather than reflection. He loves simple food and simple pleasures, distrusts book learning and the educated, preferring the honesty of nature to the corruption of the court of Bamberg and the institution of the church. He is a man of his word, and does not shirk responsibility for his actions. He is defeated by the morally equivocal forces of a new and more complex age in which his teutonic virtues are an anachronism. There is a deal of false nostalgia for a man who is bound to fail, but will fail with the word "freedom" on his lips. Indeed, yearning for the unattainable is one of the features of the writing of the new movement. But what freedom does Götz seek? It is the freedom to exercise *Faustrecht*, the right to plunder passing merchants. This is the freedom of anarchy, a freedom which certainly does not extend to his wife and sister, whose lives are bounded by marriage and the kitchen. Such questions are ignored by Goethe in the limited characterisation of the figures in the play other than Götz.

Despite these faults *Götz von Berlichingen* has remained a popular play, both with readers and with audiences. Götz was a powerful figure of freedom and integrity to a generation of pre-Romantic writers from the bourgeoisie who felt themselves trapped in a Germany divided into 300 petty, autocratic states. The play was an important influence on Walter Scott

and Alexandre Dumas, as well as spawning a genre of *Ritterstücke* (plays about knights) in Germany, which themselves formed an important source for later writers of English Gothic melodrama. In Germany Götz remains a symbol of German national identity.

—Anthony Meech

THE GOVERNMENT INSPECTOR (Revizor)
by Nikolai Gogol

First Publication: St. Petersburg, 1836; revised edition, 1841; further revised edition, in *Works of Nikolai Gogol*, 1842.
First Production: Alexandrinsky Theatre, St. Petersburg, 19 April 1836.

Editions
Revizor / The Inspector General (second edition) edited by D. Bondar, London, 1945.
Revizor, Moscow, 1952.
Revizor, edited by W. Harrison, Letchworth, Hertfordshire, 1964.

Translations
The Inspector General, translated by T. Seltzer, New York, 1916.
The Government Inspector, in *"The Government Inspector" and Other Plays*, translated by Constance Garnett, London, 1926.
The Inspector General, translated by J. Doleman Jr. and B. Rothberg, Boston, 1937.
The Government Inspector, translated by D. Campbell, London, 1947.
The Government Inspector, in *"The Storm" and Other Russian Plays*, translated by D. Magarshack, New York, 1960.
The Government Inspector, translated by Edward O'Marsh and Jeremy Brooks, London, 1968.
The Inspector, in *Four Russian Plays*, translated by Joshua Cooper, Harmondsworth, 1972.
The Government Inspector, in *The Theater of Nikolay Gogol*, translated by Milton Ehre and Fruma Gottschalk, Chicago and London, 1980.

Criticism
(For general works on the author, see *Playwrights* volume)

Articles:
Jostein Börtnes, "Gogol's *Revizor*: A Study in the Grotesque", in *Scando-Slavica* (Copenhagen), 15, 1969.
Simon Karlinsky, "The Alogical and Absurdist Aspects of Russian Realist Drama", in *Comparative Drama*, 3, 1969.
Bodo Zelinsky, "Gogol's *Revizor*: Eine Tragödie", in *Russian Literature Triquarterly*, 36, 1971.
Ruth Sobel, "A Soviet Actor and Director Looks at Gogol and *The Government Inspector*", in *Journal of Russian Studies*, 35, 1978 [interview with Oleg Tabakov].
Jan Kott, "Eating of *The Inspector General*", in *Theatre Quarterly*, 5, 1975.
Goldie Blankoff-Scarr, "The Use of Person in Gogol's *Revizor*", in *Equivalences*, vol.10 nos.1–2, 1979.

The Government Inspector: National Theatre, London, 1985

Milton Ehre, "Laughing through the Apocalypse: The Comic Structure of Gogol's *Government Inspector*", in *Russian Review*, 39, 1980.

Christa Ebert, "Die Rolle Gogols im Streit um ein neues Kunstverständnis: Die Kontroverse um Meyerholds *Revisor*-Inszenierung", in *Erbe und Erben: Traditionsbeziehungen sowjetischer Schriftsteller*, edited by Edward Kowalski and Georgi I. Lomidse, Berlin, 1982.

Per-Arne Bodin, "The Silent Scene in Nikolaj Gogol's *The Inspector General*", in *Scando-Slavica* (Copenhagen), 33, 1987.

*   *   *

In October 1835, Gogol asked Pushkin for "some anecdote" because he was "itching to write a comedy". Pushkin obliged with what became the plot of *The Government Inspector*, which received its premiere on 19 April 1836 in the presence of the Tsar and most of his ministers and courtiers. It caused a sensation, some members of the audience cheering and clapping, others booing and hissing. The relish and delight the play provoked then has continued ever since, and stimulated a vast number of productions, to make this perhaps the most famous of all Russian plays.

The corrupt mayor of a small Russian town learns from the postmaster (who steams open letters) that a government inspector is coming incognito to the town. There is a penniless ne'er-do-well, Khlestakov, who is staying at the inn, unable to leave—or even to order meals—because he has no money to pay his bill, having lost it all at cards. The mayor and his equally corrupt town officials believe Khlestakov is the government inspector. They make much of him, give him vast sums of money as bribes, the mayor even promising him his daughter in marriage (while the mayor's wife tries desperately to win his heart for herself). Khlestakov gets all he can out of the situation, then leaves town, just before the postmaster steams open one of his letters to a friend. The truth is revealed. As the mayor and his companions writhe in agony, a message is brought summoning them to meet the Tsar's government inspector.

After the first performance, Gogol wrote that the play had struck him as "bizarre and repellant", and he spent years rewriting it. Its grotesque fairy-tale world, comical and frightening, remained stubbornly the same, however. In it, characters often bump into each other, or fall over one another or through doorways. Pyotr Ivanovich Bobchinsky, for instance (not to be confused with Pyotr Ivanovich Dobchinsky, naturally) falls on his nose and appears in the following scene with a big red plaster on it. Characters who tumble about and have red noses are, of course, clowns, and other characters have similar theatrical pedigrees—the mayor's wife is a coquette, her daughter an *ingénue*, and Khlestakov a braggart or trickster. The Mayor himself, though he seems at first glance to be a bumbling father figure, in fact has the rapacity and fear of Pantalone.

The plot also hinges on an apparently age-old theatrical

device—mistaken identity. But whereas in most plays the "unmasking" leads to some sort of reconciliation or resolution, the ending to this play has quite the opposite effect: the fear referred to above is intensified, and the characters are left on stage caught in its icy grip. In a stunning *coup de théâtre*, all the characters who hear the final summons to the government inspector's presence freeze in grotesque attitudes for "almost a minute and a half" before the curtain finally falls. The moment still has immense theatrical power.

There are other factors, too, which give this play an unsettling potency. For instance, the comedy carries no overt "message" or "moral". Nor is there any of the traditional sentimentality of comedy, which would have the play end with a happy couple getting married. Nor is there the kind of "intrigue" one expects from comedy, but rather there are characters who desperately try to improvise their way out of a string of disconcerting predicaments.

The air of desperate improvisation lends the play a feeling of urgent spontaneity, which is reinforced by the fact that it almost conforms to the three unities—its action is swift without deviation or subplot; it all happens in little over 24 hours; and apart from one scene in the inn, everything takes place in the mayor's parlour. This gives pace and focus to the action, which is characterised by almost self-contained episodes rather than the more usual unfolding of a plot. The structure is surprisingly symmetrical and static: in Act I the Mayor plans his dishonesties; in Act II he visits Khlestakov; in Act III Khlestakov visits the Mayor; in Act IV Khlestakov puts into practice his own dishonesties. The last act is a sort of coda—the consequences of what has happened—though far from the conventional happy ending of comedy.

Gogol later said that in this play he had tried to gather "everything that was rotten" in Russia into a pile, and then to laugh at it, and this attitude may be another factor which makes the play seem "repellant". But the fact that no-one is redeemed is probably its most original feature. Meredith held that comedy "strips folly to the skin, displays the imposture of the creature, and is content to offer her better clothing". Gogol refuses to offer any "better clothing", in the sense of an antidote to the grotesque "rottenness" presented. This is highly unusual. Where Jonson presents a similar rottenness in *Volpone*, for instance, he counterbalances the evil with "good" characters like Bonario and Celia. Where Molière is motivated by a similar contempt in, say, *The Misanthrope*, his elegance and wit provide an implicit positive for us to cling to.

Gogol presents a raw and twisted image of tsarist corruption, and at the end the mayor asks the audience directly: "What are you laughing at?", answering, "You're laughing at yourselves!". Nevertheless that laughter is crucially important to the way in which we apprehend the play. We can acknowledge Gogol's fury, share his contempt, understand his amazement; the most telling thing Gogol does, however, is to make us join in his laughter. We laugh uproariously, repeatedly, delightedly: and this is what makes this comedy so rich and satisfying.

—Robert Leach

EL GRAN TEATRO DEL MUNDO. See **THE GREAT THEATRE OF THE WORLD.**

THE GREAT DIVIDE
by William Vaughn Moody

First Publication: New York, 1909.
First Production: As *The Sabine Women*, Garrick Theatre, Chicago, 12 April 1906; as *The Great Divide*, Princess Theatre, New York, 3 October 1906.

*   *   *

The Great Divide owes its inception, and much of its symbolic imagery, to Moody's travels in the American west in the early 1900's. The title refers not only to the geographical, continental divide, but to the cultural clash in *fin-de-siècle* America between the primitive, but more "natural", open and dynamic west, and the more civilized, but tradition-bound, inhibited, east. This contrast is embodied in the two leading characters; Ruth Jordan, a scion of the puritanical, eastern establishment and Stephen Ghent, an independent, freer-thinking westerner. Although essentially realistic in style and a play of ideas, the fairly complicated plot of *The Great Divide* is in the tradition of the standard 19th-century romance play.

Act I is set in a cabin in the Arizona desert where 19 year old Ruth has been living with her older brother, Philip, and his wife, Polly. Left alone while Philip takes Polly to the train station, Ruth is attacked by three half-drunken men, intent on raping her. Ruth offers herself to Ghent if he will save her from his more brutish companions. He agrees, buying off one with a string of gold nuggets and wounding the other in "a square stand-up shoot-out". Although Ruth urges Ghent to "go away now", he holds her to her promise and takes her off to his gold mine in the Cordilleras.

Act II takes place about a year later. Ghent is now a rich man and seemingly has been a model husband. But Ruth cannot forgive Ghent for buying her. Refusing to spend any of his money on herself, except for necessities, she has been secretly weaving Indian-style rugs and baskets and selling them to the tourists at a nearby hotel. There she is discovered by Philip and Polly who have been trying to track her down. With the money she has earned, Ruth has bought back the string of gold nuggets. Although she confesses to Ghent that she's pregnant, throwing the string at him (a detested symbol of their bargain), she departs with her brother for New England.

The final act takes place in the Jordan home six months later. Ruth with her newborn son is living as a tormented, virtual recluse, unable to accept either Ghent's sincerity and devotion or her love for him. The faltering family business, has been saved by a mysterious "benevolent uncle" who is Ghent himself. He has followed Ruth east and has been secretly giving her mother money. Ghent finally appears and reveals his generosity to Ruth and Philip, but Ruth counters by telling her family for the first time the actual circumstances of their "marriage". Philip is outraged, but his mother urges him to leave Ruth and Ghent alone to work out the "dreadful trouble" between them. In the conversation that follows, Ruth and Ghent gradually concede their differences, but also their love and their potential for happiness, for a truly "good life". Ruth, in particular, realizes that Ghent has risen to "a wholly new existence which flooded the present and the future with brightness. . .and reached back into our past and. . .made of all of it something to cherish!" and she urges Ghent to teach her, and especially their son, how to take the good aspects of both their lives and grow strong and happy. The child, it is implied, will be a synthesis of the best in both cultures.

The Great Divide utilizes many of the conventional, dramaturgical techniques of the period and its dialogue is sometimes too literary or poetic. The resolution, moreover, depends, as Alan Downer acutely observes less on an intellectual transcendence than on "the power of love to conquer all obstacles, however mountainous" (in *Fifty Years of American Drama 1900–1950*, 1951). But Ruth and Ghent are fully and believably developed as both dramatic characters and cultural archetypes. Moody's explorations of cultural conflict, ethical ambiguity, and gender relationships are, furthermore, distinctly modern. Balancing thematic seriousness with theatrical effectiveness, *The Great Divide* clearly stands above most American drama of its era. It was, moreover, a critical and commercial success. The New York production ran for two years and was followed by a successful national tour and production in London. Two films were also made of *The Great Divide*—a silent version in 1917 and a "talking" version in 1924.

—Daniel J. Watermeier

THE GREAT GOD BROWN
by Eugene O'Neill

First Publication: In *The Great God Brown; The Moon of the Caribbees; And Other Plays*, New York, 1926.
First Production: Greenwich Village Theatre, New York, 23 January 1926.

Criticism
(For general works on the author, see *Playwrights* volume)

Articles:
R. Skene, "The *Bacchae* of Euripides and *The Great God Brown*", in *Manitoba Arts Review*, 10, 1956.
Robert Berkelman, "O'Neill's Everyman", in *South Atlantic Quarterly*, 58, 1959.
Mardi Valgemae, "Eugene O'Neill's Preface to *The Great God Brown*", in *Yale University Library Gazette*, 43, 1968.
Kenneth M. Rosen, "O'Neill's Brown and Wilde's Gray", in *Modern Drama*, 13, 1971.
Frank R. Cunningham, "*The Great God Brown* and O'Neill's Romantic Vision", in *Ball State University Forum*, vol.14 no.3, 1973.

*   *   *

At the graduation dance, Billy Brown agrees to go into his father's building business. His friend Dion, however, must put aside his desire to be an artist; donning a cynical, uncaring mask (literally and figuratively), he agrees to go into business to please his mother and placate his father. Seven years later, Dion is working for Brown, his drawings the root of Brown's success. He is also married to Margaret, the girl they both loved, but Margaret is in love not with Dion but with his mask, and she yearns for Brown's wealth and social position. Dion finds solace with Cybil, a prostitute, and drowns his money in drink. He suffers beneath his dissipated life until he dies. When Dion dies, Brown dons his mask and thus acquires Margaret. But he cannot withstand the anarchism of Dion's spirit, get Margaret to love him for himself, nor achieve Dion's artistic gift. Unable to keep up the pressure of the dual personalities, Brown, too, dies.

The tangled complexities of the plot of *The Great God Brown* make even a synopsis difficult. Although important in the context of O'Neill's consistent experimentation within the theatre, especially his attempts to blend Expressionism with the realist tradition, the play's exposition is often laborious, and its machinations appear needlessly complex. The action, for example, demands a time span that, in itself, seems to reduce both the narrative and dramatic movement of the play: seven years between the prologue and the first act; seven years, again, between Acts I and II; and following, a few months and then a few weeks to finish off the play. Constant changes of scene, as well, do not assist in developing a strong dramatic through-line, especially when the assumed realistic base demands these changes of scenery! The structure, too, is confusing. Although entitled *The Great God Brown*, the play concentrates on Dion. He is the focus and the play appears to be dealing with his elaborate inner struggle until suddenly he dies and Brown moves into his place, a readjustment one is unprepared for except by the title.

Nor does the play lend itself easily to intellectual analysis and theory. The action is dependent upon the use of masks; yet the setting is mundane, suggesting the use of masks might be purely illustrative. However, as one examines the play in detail, this illustrative approach defies logic. Yet, although in many ways ponderous, the play, even in reading, can be extremely, enigmatically, powerful.

The emotional impact of *The Great God Brown* is unlikely to be the result of the tortuous logic superimposed on the fairly undramatic plot, nor the clichéd ideas reiterated through the dialogue. Arguably, the elusive power of the play depends less on its ponderous logic than on its creator's consummate skill in creating a complex, sensual theatrical experience where impact and significance are transmitted through sound and visual image.

The "problem" of the play focuses on the use of masks. The interpretive tendency is to explain their use literally, as a direct illustration of the individualist concept of the separation between the inner/outer man, the "real" person set against the public self. To a point, this approach works quite well. Dion dons his cynical mask to "mask" his artistic, sensitive, spiritual self from his parents and the world. Margaret falls in love with his mask and shuns his "real self". Unable to expand, trapped by the mask, his inner self suffers and is seen to be purified through that suffering. The inner and outer self appear to have separate existences. At the same time, the two personas intrinsically affect each other. Dion's inner soul is purified by the suffering imposed by the necessity of the mask and the life it leads. Also, although the weight of the suffering eventually causes his death, there is no indication in the play that unity between the selves was genuinely possible. After all, everyone, including Cybil, has a mask. Nor is it implied that the spiritual perfection in which Dion dies could have been reached had he not been "forced" to wear the mask. Merged, then, with the images of the divided self are suggestions regarding spiritual experience in a materialist world, as if one were almost dependent on the other. Dion's story follows a kind of "imitation of Christ" where spiritual transcendence is dependent on the suffering imposed by material values and excess.

To make matters more complicated, when Brown puts on the mask he is taken to be Dion. Margaret, mistaking Brown in Dion's mask for her husband, finds total fulfilment in a partner combining Dion's persona and Brown's financial success. On the simplest level, perhaps, the mask implies not only the divided self and self-imposed personas but those projected by others.

The plot is also an anguish of unrequited love. Margaret loves Dion's mask and is repelled by his true self. Dion is in love with Margaret but cannot therefore reveal it to her. His mask mistreats both the self and her, thus she has to wear a public mask. Brown also loves Margaret. Attracted to his business prowess, her happiness is complete when Brown wears Dion's mask, but is based on deceit. Since she cannot love Brown for himself, as she could not love Dion, she consumes him as he consumes Dion. Brown himself is destroyed because even with Dion's mask, he cannot be Dion. Dion's artistic skill and originality, the inspiration of his spirit, do not come with the mask. Brown's "possession" of Dion brings not fulfilment but anguish.

There is not a little of Nietzsche's theories running through the play. The name Dion suggests Greek culture, implying artistic purity. At the same time, it is blatantly a shortened form of "Dionysius". His surname, Anthony, suggesting "St Anthony" completes the dichotomy. The mask's irresponsible, crass behavior and compulsive drinking provides the Bacchanalian opposite through which the Apollonion spirit is purified. The material acquisition and greed by which the others live are also misplaced Dionysian traits. In these terms, the anguish of the play rests in the unresolvability of these opposites. The suggestion is that this resolution is prevented by the demands of the materialist society where neither force can gain genuine expression and thus, instead of compatible interaction, each is pushed to its extreme. One might argue that much of the impact of the play rests in the tension between these extreme forces and their impossible striving to unite.

The use of masks also creates a visual context which releases language from the demands of the explanatory and the informative, allowing emotional expression of almost operatic force. Indeed, as in opera, the very sounds of the words, often reinforced through repetition, rhythm, and alliteration, takes precedence over their meaning. Released from literalness, the dialogue can also unembarrassingly explode into excessiveness, the purpose of which is arguably not to transmit information but to transmit the raw extremity of emotion. A line like: "No! I'm a man! I am a lonely man! I can't go back! I have conceived myself!" is certainly worthy of any Victorian melodrama. One could argue that this very excess is endemic to the final effect of the play. The very sound of the language combined with the vivid but complex visual action created by the masks strives to create an intense emotional field through which the extremity of the characters' struggles, suffering, and despair may be transferred, raw, to the audience.

Although hardly the most fully integrated of O'Neill's dramas, *The Great God Brown* is an important step in his own struggle to explore the communicative capacities of the stage. This attempt to extend a story through visual and aural experience to the point where the emotional content becomes the main vehicle of communication may be long-winded, erratic, and over-complex, but its force, for all that, not only pays tribute to O'Neill's skills of stagecraft but also calls attention to the power of the sensual elements of the theatre.

—Elaine Turner

THE GREAT STAGE OF THE WORLD. See **THE GREAT THEATRE OF THE WORLD.**

THE GREAT THEATRE OF THE WORLD
(El gran teatro del mundo)
by Pedro Calderón de la Barca

Composition: Probably c. 1633–35.
First Publication: 1655.
First Production: Probably c. 1649.

Editions
El gran teatro del mundo, edited by Eugenio Frutos Cortés, Salamanca, 1958.
El gran teatro del mundo, in *Pedro Calderón de la Barca: Autos Sacramentales*, edited by D.F. Plaza y Janés, Buenos Aries, Barcelona, Mexico, 1961.
El gran teatro del mundo, in *El gran teatro del mundo; El alcalde de Zalamea*, edited by C. Rivas-Xerif, 1965.
El gran teatro del mundo, in *El gran teatro del mundo; El alcalde de Zalamea*, edited by A. Isasi, Angulo, 1968.
El gran teatro del mundo, edited by Domingo Ynduráin, Madrid, 1973.

Translations
The Great Theatre of the World, translated by Richard C. Trench, in *The Life and Genius of Calderón*, London, 1856; revised by John G. Underhill, in *Twenty One Non-Royalty One-Act Classics*, edited by Margaret Mayorga, New York, 1944.
The Great World-Theatre, translated by Francis E. Sipman, Einsiedeln, Switzerland, 1955.
The Great Theater of the World, translated by Maynard Mack, in *Masterpieces of the Spanish Golden Age*, edited by Angel Flores, New York, 1957.
The Great Stage of the World, translated by George W. Brandt, Manchester, 1976.

Criticism
(For general works on the author, see *Playwrights* volume)

Books:
Eugenio Frutos Cortés, *El gran teatro del mundo; El gran mercado del mundo*, Madrid, 1987.

Articles:
Georges Cirot, "*El gran teatro del mundo*", in *Bulletin hispanique*, 43, 1941.
A. Vilanova, "El tema de *El gran teatro del mundo*", in *Boletín de la Real Academia de Buenas Letras*, Barcelona, 23, 1950.
Federica de Ritter, "*El gran teatro del mundo* (la historia de una metáfora)", in *Revista nacional de cultura* (Caracas), 14, 1952.
Everett W. Hesse, "La dialéctica y el casuismo en Calderón", in *Estudios*, vol. 9 no. 27, 1953.
J. Jacquot, "*Le Théâtre du monde* de Shakespeare à Calderón", in *Revue de littérature comparée*, 31, 1957.
Sebastián Bartina, "La *Biblia* y Calderón. Contenido bíblico en *El gran teatro del mundo*", in *Razón y Fe*, 158 and 160, 1958–59; reprinted in book form, Barcelona, 1958.
William A. Hunter, "Toward a More Authentic Text of Calderón's *El gran teatro del mundo*", in *Hispanic Review*, 29, 1961.
Louis C. Pérez, "Preceptiva dramática en *El gran teatro del mundo*", in *Hispanófila*, vol. 10 no.30, 1967.
Robert L. Fiore, "Calderón's *El gran teatro del mundo*: An Ethical Interpretation", in *Hispanic Review*, 40, 1972.
V.V. Valembois, "Calderón, desempolvado: Estudio comparativo entre *El gran teatro del mundo* y *A puerta cerrada*", in *Cuadernos hispanoamericanos* (Madrid), 295, 1975.

The Great Theatre of the World: Granada, Spain, 1935

Harold G. Jones, "Calderón's *El gran teatro del mundo*: Two Possible Sources", in *Journal of Hispanic Philology*, 1, 1976.

Robert W. Felkel, "*El gran teatro del mundo* of Pedro Calderón de la Barca and the Centrality of Grace", in *Bulletin of the Comediantes*, 31, 1979.

Ignacio Elizalde, "El problema social en dos obras dramáticas de Calderón" in *Letras de Deusto*, vol. 11 no. 22, 1981.

N.D. Shergold, "Calderón and *Theatrum Mundi*", in *Arts du Spectacle et histoire des idées*, edited by Jean-Michel Vaccaro, Tours, 1984.

*   *   *

The Great Theatre of the World is one of Calderón's many *autos sacramentales*. These are one-act dramatic compositions in verse, generally allegorical in nature, which always refer to some aspect of the Christian Eucharist and often incorporate a Eucharistic celebration. Many *autos*, including this one, were written specifically for the celebration of the feast of Corpus Christi. The *autos* have a liturgical and didactic function, and dramatize fundamental theological or doctrinal issues in a forthrightly allegorical manner.

The Great Theatre of the World begins with the appearance of the Author, who creates the stage setting and the characters who will figure in the work and summons the World to appear on stage. World explains the history of man on earth according to a salvationist narrative. The first epoch of human history contains the story of existence from creation to the time of the great flood, and goes on to include man's salvation from the flood, and the covenant of peace, to the institution of natural law. The second epoch of human life corresponds to the period of the written law (i.e. to the Old Testament), and the third to the law of grace or of Christian salvation.

After the scene has been made ready, the characters themselves appear on stage. Author once again speaks, and creates the allegorical characters of Rich Man, Worker, Poor Man, King, Beauty, and Discretion. Before these characters are fashioned they lack free will and so are unable to choose their roles in life; but afterwards it is up to them to choose to do good or evil according to their free will. They will be rewarded according to the way in which they exercise their capacity for choice. Calderón affirms that the social and material differences among men may be radically contingent; the distinctions of social status are not arbitrary creations of men but correspond to the needs of social life. But it is essential to do good works regardless of one's station in life: "Do good, for God is God" ("*Obrar bien, que Dios es Dios*"). Each man who plays one of the assigned parts thus also has an individual purpose—to gain his own salvation.

As the play proceeds Author watches the theatre-like actions or "representation" of the various characters he has created. He himself intervenes on only two occasions: at the beginning, in order to indicate his transcendent position with respect to his characters and to warn them that what they do will be seen from on high; and later in order to remind them that they can mend their ways but must always act in accordance with their freedom of will. In the representation itself the characters are associated in terms of contrasting groups: Discretion and Beauty, Poor Man / Worker, and Rich Man. When World declares the representation concluded, and when the celestial globe is closed, he asks each one what they have done. All are required to return the gifts with which they were endowed at the opening of the representation, except Child and Poor Man, who had nothing to begin with. The characters seek out the banquet of rewards promised by the Author to all those who played their roles well. This is the Eucharistic moment of the *auto*, when the celestial orb is once again revealed, along with the chalice and host, and the Author is seated on his throne. Discretion and Poor Man are called directly to share in the glory of the Eucharist, while King and Worker are sent to Purgatory. But since King assisted Religion in its time of need, he is pardoned and allowed to share directly in the Eucharistic reward.

The Great Theatre of the World must first be understood as a theological and allegorical work, one that is fully informed by Calderón's knowledge of theology through his Jesuit education. Its teachings are those of post-Tridentine Spain, and are heavily influenced by Calderón's Christian neo-scholasticism. At the same time, the play cannot be isolated from its social and political context and represents an alliance of three important spheres of culture in Golden Age Spain: religion, theatre, and state power. The work is representative of Spanish culture in the declining years of the Golden Age, when the influence of the Council of Trent was still indirectly felt, yet when the theocratic State had gained ideological control of the means of representation.

The Great Theatre of the World stands out from among Calderón's *autos* as the one that is simplest in its diction and most straightforward in its execution. And yet the play is not without its internal complexities. *The Great Theatre of the World* is one of the most important examples of Calderonian metatheatre. Theatre and the allied, moral concept of role serve as the vehicles of a theological allegory, which teaches a Christianized version of the moral lesson to be drawn from the awareness that the world is a stage and that men are but actors on it. Yet Calderón's representation of the play within a play also displays a high degree of artistic self-consciousness, and the *auto* must be appreciated for the sheer brilliance of its language and the elegance of its allegorical construction as well as for its doctrinal lessons.

—Anthony J. Cascardi

THE GREEN PASTURES
by Marc Connelly

First Publication: New York, 1930.
First Production: Mansfield Theatre, New York, 26 February 1930.

Criticism
(For general works on the author, see *Playwrights* volume)

Articles:
Robert Withington, "Notes on the Corpus Christi Plays and *The Green Pastures*", in *South Atlantic Bulletin*, 9, 1934.
John T. Krumpelmann, "Marc Connelly's *The Green Pastures* and Goethe's *Faust*", in *Studies in Comparative Literature*, edited by W.F. McNeir, Baton Rouge, Louisiana, 1962.
Walter C. Daniel, "*The Green Pastures*: American Religiosity in the Theatre", in *Journal of American Culture*, vol.5 no.1, 1982.

*   *   *

The Green Pastures is now considered a historical curiosity, but in its day the success of the play was phenomenal. Premiered on Broadway in 1931, garlanded with praise and a Pulitzer Prize, the original production toured continuously for five years before returning for an extended run on the New York stage. A mere 15 years later, the play was triumphantly revived on Broadway. What was the appeal of a down-home dialect play where an all Black cast recreate Bible stories?

Part of the appeal was the apparent novelty of the piece. Marc Connelly simply but ingeniously combined three traditions. There is the miracle or mystery play: religion made local. There is the oral tradition of stroytelling (in this case the fables of the Deep South collected by Roark Bradford in his book *Ol' Man Adam and His Chillun*). Most significantly, *The Green Pastures* appropriates all the razzmatazz and reassuring familiarity of the negro minstrel show.

In the wake of the Wall Street Crash, and its disruptive implications for the natural order of things, *The Green Pastures* opened with the comforting image of a Sunday school bible class. After this, the images become a little more exotic, but the moral uplift offered continues unabated. Heaven is represented as a Deep South fish fry. Babylon resembles nothing so much as an illegal Harlem drinking club during prohibition. Mankind sins, mankind suffers, but even De Lawd (a majestic but approachable preacher) realises that he must suffer too. As yet another spiritual swells, the curtain falls.

The premise may have been simple but the execution was lavish. The play requires a cast of 75 adults, ten children and a choir of 50 people. 17 different scenes are specified, and two revolving stages, a treadmill, and an everchanging cyclorama are required.

The economic impossibility of full-scale productions is doubtless one reason why *The Green Pastures* is seldom performed today. But the problem is that *The Green Pastures* offers a white man's version of black people, written for a white audience. A contemporary reviewer described the play as "a region of gentleness, this in contrast to the harsh demand of our day". To relieve the anxieties of the Depression, White people can watch happy black folk gambol in a mythical version of the Deep South. The real South offered Black people illiteracy, poverty, no vote, and the Klu Klux Klan. Under the circumstances, Langston Hughes's 1935 description of the play as "a naïve dialect play about a quaint funny heaven full of niggers" is appropriate.

The Green Pastures: Mansfield Theatre, New York, 1930 (first production)

By utilising the old minstrel show conception of black people as unsophisticated, good-natured, and easily duped, Connelly reinforces the images depicted in 19th-century, American drama and fiction. No doubt such symbols of docility and comic ineptitude endeared in uncertain times. In *The Green Pastures* good black people, from Adam through to Hezdrel, are simple, respectful, rural folk who know their places. Bad black people live uptown, talk dirty, dress flash, and carry knives. How reassuring to urban white audiences to see such threatening characters drowned nightly in the Flood.

While *The Green Pastures* ostensibly celebrates what Connelly calls "the living religion of thousands of negroes in the Deep South", the play tends to offer caricatured and oppressive images. The language of Connelly's introduction and of contemporary reviews is unintentionally patronising. Black people are "untutored", "unburdened by the differences of more educated theologians". They are "simple" but redeemed by "humility and purity" and "the simple truth it (the play) puts into the mouths of its children". Traditional power relationships and prejudices are confirmed, and it is not surprising that the play's 1950 revival was cited by the Committee for the Negro in the Arts as an example of "the refusal of Broadway producers to present a true and honest picture of Negro life".

—Joss Bennathan

GROZA. See **THE STORM.**

LA GUERRE DE TROIS N'AURA PAS LIEU. See **THE TROJAN WAR WILL NOT TAKE PLACE.**

GUEST OF REALITY. See **THE HANGMAN.**

DER GUTE MENSCH VON SEZUAN. See **THE GOOD PERSON OF SETZUAN.**

THE HAIRY APE
by Eugene O'Neill

First Publication: In *The Hairy Ape; The First Man; Anna Christie*, New York, 1922.
First Production: Playwright's Theatre, New York, 9 March 1922.

Criticism

(For general works on the author, see *Playwrights* volume)

Articles:
Bernard Baum, "*The Tempest* and *The Hairy Ape*", in *Modern Language Quarterly*, 14, 1953.
Marden J. Clark, "Tragic Effect in *The Hairy Ape*", in *Modern Drama*, 10, 1968.
Prabhat N. Das, "Expressionism and *The Hairy Ape*", in *Indian Journal of English Studies*, 9, 1968.
Emil Roy, "Eugene O'Neill's *The Emperor Jones* and *The Hairy Ape* as Mirror Plays", in *Comparative Drama*, 2, 1968.
Prabhat N. Das, "The Alienated Ape", in *Literary Half-Yearly*, vol. 11 no. 1, 1970.
Thakur Guruprasad, "Experimentation with Dramatic Technique in O'Neill's *The Hairy Ape*", in *Indian Journal of English Studies*, 14, 1973.
Abdulaziz Y. Saqqaf, "The Nature of Conflict in *The Hairy Ape*", in *Journal of English*, 1, 1975.
"Focus on *The Hairy Ape*", in *Eugene O'Neill Newsletter*, vol. 1 no. 3, 1978.
Péter Egri, " 'Belonging' Lost: Alienation and Dramatic Form in Eugene O'Neill's *The Hairy Ape*", in *Acta Litteraria Academiae Scientiarum Hungaricae*, 24, 1982.
Michael Whitlach, "Eugene O'Neill and Class Consciousness in *The Hairy Ape*", in *Zeitschrift für Anglistik und Amerikanistik*, 35, 1987.
Marilyn Jurich, "Men of Iron, Beasts of Clay: The Confluence of Folk-tale and Drama in 'Joe Magarac' and *The Hairy Ape*", in *Eugene O'Neill Newsletter*, vol. 12 no. 2, 1988.
Ann Massa, "Intention and Effect in *The Hairy Ape*", in *Modern Drama*, 31, 1988.
Hubert Zapf, "O'Neill's *Hairy Ape* and the Reversal of Hegelian Dialectics" in *Modern Drama*, 31, 1988.

*   *   *

The author's second expressionist play is (as *The Emperor Jones*) in eight scenes, and likewise deals with the duality of human nature, this time in the urban jungle of "man-eating" machines. The action begins in a steamship's fo'c'sle, reminiscent of O'Neill's early sea-plays, with silent Yank sitting among his noisy and inarticulate animal-like mates in the position of Rodin's "The Thinker" (a recurring stage direction). A contrasting scene shows the first-class deck, with Mildred, the millionaire ship-owner's bored, spoiled daughter. There is a confrontation: she looks down into the stoke-hole (an archetypal image of machine-age hell), sees Yank shovelling coal into the gaping maw of the furnace, recoils with horror

The Hairy Ape: National Theatre, London, 1987 (Berlin Schaubühne production)

and calls him a hairy ape. Yank's brutal anger stems from the conviction that "I belong, she don't",—referring both to the surrounding Sea Mother, and to the Machine Age—but her exclamation has raised existential doubts in him, which he pursues in the following scenes without finding answers. In New York, on Fifth Avenue, he encounters a series of puppet-like parvenues with mask-like faces, in an I.W.W. office a couple of bureacratized labor leaders, in jail the jeering and compassionless underclass, and at the zoo the eponymous, silent, but powerful, gorilla who, Yank believes, also belongs. He breaks into the cage thinking he has found the answer, embraces the gorilla and falls lifeless.

Like *The Emperor Jones, The Hairy Ape* has been misinterpreted; the play has been seen as a simple indictment of capitalism and an angry incitement to revolution. But O'Neill probes deeper: Yank rejects, and is rejected by, the workers' movement as much as by the upper classes. He is the embodiment not so much of the industrial proletariat as of the anguished and alienated human being, Everyman trying to find his place in a world transformed without his conscious participation. Again, O'Neill makes use of anti-realistic, theatrical devices, this time specifying the need for "expressionist" scenes—supplied by Robert Edmond Jones. But the repeated choruses of guttural sounds, the clangor, the eerie light of the stokehole, the suggestion of lifelessness in the mask-like faces on Fifth Avenue, the parallel between the prison's and the zoo's cells, the towering figure of the gorilla, all were here employed before plays using similar techniques such as Elmer Rice's *Adding Machine* and before (according to an O'Neill letter) the dramatist had read or seen Kaiser's *Massenmensch*.

—Robert K. Sarlós

HAMLET
by William Shakespeare

First Publication: London, 1603 ("bad" first quarto); with variants, 1604 ("good" second quarto); with variants, in the First Folio, 1623.

First Production: London, c. 1599–1601.

Editions
Hamlet (2 vols.), edited by H.H. Furness, London, 1879 (New Variorum Edition).

Hamlet, edited by John Dover Wilson, Cambridge, 1934; second edition, with corrections, 1954. (The New Shakespeare).

Hamlet, edited by George Lyman Kittredge, 1939; revised edition, edited by Irving Ribner, 1967.

Hamlet, edited by Cyrus Hoy, New York, 1963 (Norton Critical Editions).

Hamlet, edited by Edward Hubler, New York, 1963; second edition, 1987 (Signet Classic Shakespeare).

"The Tragedy of Hamlet": A Critical Edition of the Second Quarto, 1600, edited by T.M. Parrott and Hardin Craig, New York, 1976.

Hamlet, edited by T.J.B. Spencer, Harmondsworth, 1980 (New Penguin Shakespeare).

Hamlet, edited by Harold Jenkins, London, 1982 (Arden Shakespeare).

Hamlet, edited by Philip Edwards, Cambridge, 1985 (New Cambridge Shakespeare).

Hamlet, edited by G.R. Hibbard, Oxford, 1987 (Oxford Shakespeare).

Bibliographies
Anton A. Raven, *A "Hamlet" Bibliography and Reference Guide, 1877–1935*, Chicago, 1936.

Glen D. Hunter, "Shakespeare's *Hamlet*: A Comprehensive Bibliography of Editions and Paraphrases in English, 1876–1981", in *Bulletin of Bibliography*, 38, 1981.

Rand F. Robinson (ed.), *"Hamlet" in the 1950's: An Annotated Bibliography*, New York and London, 1984 (Garland Shakespeare Bibliographies).

Criticism
(For general works on the author, see *Playwrights* volume)

Books:
Elmer Edgar Stoll, *"Hamlet": An Historical and Comparative Study*, Minneapolis, Minnesota, 1919.

Lilian Winstanley, *"Hamlet" and the Scottish Succession*, Cambridge, 1921.

John Dover Wilson, *The Manuscript of Shakespeare's "Hamlet" and the Problems of its Transmission*, 1934.

John Dover Wilson, *What Happens in "Hamlet"*, Cambridge, 1935.

John W. Draper, *The "Hamlet" of Shakespeare's Audience*, Durham, North Carolina, 1938.

George Ian Duthie, *The "Bad" Quarto of "Hamlet"*, 1941.

Paul S. Conklin, *A History of "Hamlet" Criticism, 1601–1821*, New York, 1947.

Ernest Jones, *Hamlet and Oedipus*, London, 1949.

Claude C.H. Williamson (ed.), *Readings on the Character of Hamlet, 1661–1947*, London, 1950.

D.G. James, *The Dream of Learning: An Essay on "The Advancement of Learning", "Hamlet", and "King Lear"*, Oxford, 1951.

Peter Alexander, *Hamlet: Father and Son*, London, 1955.

Harry Levin, *The Question of "Hamlet"*, New York, 1959.

L.C. Knights, *An Approach to "Hamlet"*, London, 1960.

John Russell Brown and Bernard Harris (ed.), *Hamlet*, London, 1963 (Stratford-Upon-Avon Studies).

Morris Weitz, *Hamlet and the Philosophy of Literary Criticism*, London, 1965.

Eleanor Prosser, *Hamlet and Revenge*, Stanford, California, 1967.

David Bevington (ed.), *Twentieth Century Interpretations of "Hamlet"*, Englewood Cliffs, New Jersey, 1968.

John D. Jump (ed.), *"Hamlet": A Casebook*, London, 1968.

Maurice Charney, *Style in "Hamlet"*, Princeton, New Jersey, 1969.

Nigel Alexander, *Poison, Play and Duel: A Study in "Hamlet"*, London, 1971.

Harold Fisch, *Hamlet and the Word: The Covenant Pattern in Shakespeare*, New York, 1971.

Paul Gottschalk, *The Meaning of "Hamlet": Modes of Literary Interpretation Since Bradley*, Albuquerque, New Mexico, 1972.

Lee Sheridan Cox, *Figurative Design in "Hamlet"*, Columbus, Ohio, 1973.

William G. Holzberger and Peter B. Waldeck (eds.), *Perspectives on "Hamlet"*, Lewisburg, Pennsylvania, 1975.

Eleanor Rowe, *"Hamlet": A Window on Russia*, New York, 1976.

P.J. Adams, *Mousetrap: Structure and Meaning in "Hamlet"*, Toronto, and Buffalo, New York, 1977.

Hamlet: Royal Court Theatre, London, 1980

Jagodish Purkayastha, *The Tragic Vision of Life in "Hamlet" and "King Lear"*, Salzburg, 1977.

Avi Erlich, *Hamlet's Absent Father*, Princeton, New Jersey, 1978.

Andrew Gurr, *"Hamlet" and the Distracted Globe*, Edinburgh, 1978.

L.C. Knights, *"Hamlet" and Other Shakespearian Essays*, London, 1979.

Kenneth Muir and Stanley Wells (eds.), *Aspects of "Hamlet"*, Cambridge and New York, 1979.

Robert Marks, *"Hamlet": Another Interpretation*, Mahoney City, Pennsylvania, 1980.

Martin Scofield, *The Ghosts of "Hamlet": The Play and Modern Writers*, Cambridge and New York, 1980.

Walter N. King, *Hamlet's Search for Meaning*, Athens, Georgia, 1982.

James L. Calderwood, *To Be And Not to Be: Negation and Metadrama in "Hamlet"*, New York and London, 1983.

Gunnar Sjögren, *Hamlet the Dane: Ten Essays*, Lund, 1983.

Peter Davison, *Hamlet*, London, 1984 (Text and Performance Series).

Roland M. Frye, *The Renaissance Hamlet: Issues and Responses in 1600*, Princeton, New Jersey, 1984.

Laurie Lanzen Harris and Mark W. Scott (eds.), *"Hamlet"*, in *Shakespearian Criticism, 1*, Detroit, Illinois, 1984 [anthology of criticism].

Martin Dodsworth, *Hamlet Closely Observed*, London, 1985.

John A. Mills, *"Hamlet" on Stage*, Westport, Connecticut, and London, 1985.

Harold Bloom (ed.), *William Shakespeare's "Hamlet"*, New York, New Haven, Connecticut, and Philadelphia, 1986 (Modern Critical Interpretations).

Michael Hattaway, *Hamlet*, London, 1987 (The Critics Debate Series).

Arthur McGee, *The Elizabethan "Hamlet"*, New Haven, Connecticut, and London, 1987.

Peter Mercer, *"Hamlet" and the Acting of Revenge*, London, 1987.

Maurice Charney, *Hamlet's Fictions*, New York and London, 1988.

S.C. Sen Gupta, *"Hamlet" Once More*, Calcutta, 1988.

Cedric Watts, *Hamlet*, Boston, 1988 (Twayne's New Critical Introductions to Shakespeare).

Articles:

For information on the many articles about *Hamlet*, see the bibliographies listed above, the bibliographies listed in the *Playwrights* volume, and the annual Shakespeare Bibliography in *Shakespeare Quarterly*, published by the Folger Shakespeare Library, Washington D.C. (1950–).

*   *   *

The Tragedy of Hamlet, Prince of Denmark is a play about revenge, like other Elizabethan tragedies, like Seneca's (which had been translated from Latin into robust English), and like many of the Greek tragedies which came before them. Hamlet returns to the court at Elsinore for his mother's marriage to his uncle, Claudius, who is now King of Denmark in his father's place. Less than two months before, Hamlet senior had been alive and now his Ghost seeks out "young Hamlet" to reveal that he had been murdered by Claudius and to demand revenge. The rest of the play sees that brought about, and in the process Gertrude, the Queen, is killed, as is Hamlet himself. Laertes who has tried to kill Hamlet on Claudius's instructions is also killed; he is son of Polonius (a counsellor whom Hamlet kills believing him to be the king spying on him) and brother of Ophelia whom Hamlet had loved and then, in the play, rejects so that she goes mad and dies. Complicating the action still more, the Norwegian prince, Fortinbras, brings an army to Denmark on the way to fight for a small plot of land in Poland and it is he who arrives at the end of the play to claim the Danish throne; Hamlet's dynasty leaves no survivor.

Unlike the revenge tragedies on which it was modelled, *Hamlet* has been performed in every age since it was written. Its central role is acknowledged, world-wide, as an actor's greatest challenge and opportunity; for Hamlet does not turn to violence, like his predecessors, without passing through a series of crises which demand a wide range of reaction and cause him to question the world in which he lives and his own deepest thoughts and instincts. He is for ever on the brink of new understanding and truer feelings. He does not kill until it seems to him a necessary and inevitable act; and even then, Hamlet feels his task unfinished and begs Horatio, a fellow student, to "Report me and my cause aright/To the unsatisfied".

Above all, perhaps, Hamlet is a play which presents a quest for the truth about a corrupt world and never yields a simple answer. To its "young. . .noble. . .gentle. . .loving" prince— "the expectancy and rose of the fair state" as Ophelia calls him—Shakespeare has given both intelligence and passion. He feigns madness to conceal his mission as revenger, but that madness becomes a means of revealing his own nature, to himself and to the audience: impulsive, insecure, idealistic, sceptical, and tortured by love for his father and mother and for the young Ophelia. He has been a student at the University of Wittenberg: with Horatio, and with Rosencrantz and Guildenstern, two other "schoolfellows" who are set to spy on him, he is drawn to show his need for a "man that is not passion's slave" and to see himself as someone who can take no delight in man or woman. To Ophelia he likens himself to "a fellow. . .crawling between earth and heaven".

To find out whether Claudius is indeed guilty of murder—for Hamlet's scepticism distrusts even the words of the Ghost— Hamlet uses some actors who are visiting Elsinore to perform a play which is very like the circumstances of his father's death. In scenes with these players, Hamlet behaves like an actor and like an audience, and is trapped, as it were, in his own device to reveal the truth about the world: why should "this player here" thrive in a "dream of passion", while he finds that he can do "nothing"?

Scene by scene, Hamlet is tested as a son, a student, a lover, a politician, an actor, and a man. The funeral of Ophelia and the imagined darkess of the battlements of Elsinore where the Ghost walks bring the play, based on primitive story and myth, into relationship with the Christian beliefs in which Shakespeare and his audience were brought up. The concluding scene tests Hamlet's courage.

Perhaps the most extraordinary quality of this (literally) outstanding play is that it seems actor-proof and director-proof. However Hamlet is cast, and even when the play is greatly cut or set visually in an unlikely or mundane world, the action takes hold of an audience and the words that are spoken, however imperfectly, come alive in their minds. Shakespeare's dramatic structure is strong and inherently exciting, and his writing is endlessly inventive and sensitive. For no other play did he coin so many new words—this is susceptible to quantitative proof—or so compose that the words of the text seem to arise instinctively from the inner consciousness of each speaker and from passionate commitment. The many characters of the play are brilliantly and distinctly imagined; each is presented from his or her own point of view and is seldom merely a foil to Hamlet or the other principals.

—John Russell Brown

HANDCUFFS.   See THE DONNELLY PLAYS.

HANDS AROUND.   See LA RONDE.

THE HANDS OF GOD (Las manos de Dios)
by Carlos Solórzano

First Publication: Mexico City, 1957.
First Production: Teatro del Seguro Social, Mexico City, 1956.

Translations
The Hands of God, translated by Keith Leonard and Mario Soria, Hirham, Ohio, 1968.

Criticism
(For general works on the author, see *Playwrights* volume)

Articles:
Frank Dauster, "The Drama of Carlos Solórzano", in *Modern Drama*, 7, 1964.
Peter J. Schoenbach, "La libertad en *Las manos de Dios*", in *Latin American Theatre Review*, vol.3 no.2, 1970.
David Foster, "The Image of Language in Solórzano's *Las manos de Dios*: The Degradation and Subversion of Communication", in *Mester*, vol.8 no.1, 1979.
John R. Rosenberg, "The Ritual of Solórzano's *Las manos de Dios*", in *Latin American Theatre Review*, vol.17 no.2, 1984.

*   *   *

This three-act play is set in the plaza of a rural town in Latin America. Groups of silent, impoverished townsfolk are walking about slowly, when suddenly a peasant runs in. He tells of a man dressed in black, who appeared mysteriously out of nowhere and who seemed to know everything about all of them. The stranger turns out to be the Devil, visible only to those who question and rebel against their oppressors. The local priest threatens the townsfolk with damnation should they give in to any of Lucifer's temptations, but the young girl Beatriz refuses to accept her lot and that of her brother, who has been imprisoned only because he dared to stand up to the all-powerful owner of the town and surrounding farms. The

Devil convinces Beatriz that the only way to free her brother is to bribe his jailer. Having no money, she is forced to steal the jewels that adorn the right hand of the church's icon of the Holy Father. The Devil assures her that God will understand, but when she is caught stealing, Beatriz pays with her life. The play closes with the Devil wondering when he will win his struggle to help people make themselves free.

The Hands of God is essentially a contemporary rendition of a medieval Spanish *auto-da-fé*, an allegorical play in the vein of *Everyman*, where good and evil enter into debate or combat, and the dogma of the Church is triumphant. However, Solórzano inverts traditional beliefs by having the Devil symbolize a positive force, as opposed to the negative, conservative one of the Church, which outlaws all independent thinking and which has allied itself in Latin America all too often with oppresive, civil authority. Solórzano also inverts other traditional religious beliefs by his creative use of a Mexican theatrical form called *la quema de Judas*, or "the burning of Judas". Part of the Easter celebration, these are plays with life-size puppets or papier-mâché dolls, which end with the public burning of the Judas figure. In *The Hands of God* the angry townspeople kill Beatriz, accusing her of being a traitor to them and to God; it is clear to the audience, however, that Solórzano presents her as an innocent victim, the first (it is to be hoped) of many courageous individuals who will dare to directly confront their oppressors.

Solórzano not only borrows from the Catholic, Hispanic theatrical tradition, but from the Attic one as well. He represents the townspeople as a chorus of men and women, all dressed in typical peasant clothes, their backs hunched over under the heavy burden they carry. Throughout most of the play they are spectators, silently pantomiming their reactions of alarm and fear to what they witness. They are unable to see the Devil in their midst, a blindness that symbolizes their acceptance of the way things are. However, during Act III, when the Devil and the priest enter into debate, the chorus gains sight and voice—it begins to think for itself and is nearly convinced to side with Beatriz; unfortunately, the priest manages to work it into such a frenzy that it ends up as little more than an angry mob.

The pitting of the individual against society in *The Hands of God*, and the message that each one of us is the maker of his or her own freedom, are typical of Solórzano's theatre. After 1945, many intellectuals and artists in Latin America felt the impact of European post-war philosophy, and were particularly attracted by the notion of personal and collective responsibility developed in Sartrean existentialism. Solórzano is the one playwright most identified with this tendency, and he has been rightly praised for giving an essentially imported philosophy a quite original, and Latin American, theatrical expression. In *The Hands of God* he uses motifs from popular folklore and religion. The stage setting evokes a very Latin American world; the social and economic forces at work there are endemic to the whole region, and thus Solórzano indicates that this town could be anywhere in Hispanic America. He manages, in this way, to be specific and literal, while at the same time suggestive and figurative.

In the context of Latin American playwriting, *The Hands of God* was an important experiment at a time when many dramatists were still debating the question of how national their theatre should be. Many were anxious to break with the old traditions of realism which tended heavily towards illusionism and the folkloric. At the same time, many shared a belief that the theatre in countries plagued by political unrest and social inequities should in some way reflect as well as condemn these realities. Some playwrights ultimately found the way to do this by emulating the epic theatre of Brecht; others adapted the theatre of the absurd and the so-called theatre of cruelty to a specifically Latin American context. Still others, like Solórzano in *The Hands of God*, used the anti-illusionistic techniques of traditional, popular theatre and storytelling to comment on contemporary conditions in their countries. This is the period when Enrique Buenaventura, the internationally acclaimed Colombian playwright and director, wrote the first versions of his *In the Right Hand of God the Father*, which bears many similarities in technique and purpose to Solórzano's play. Although the latter has not enjoyed the continued stage success of Buenaventura's play, *The Hands of God* is a fine example of what could be called the hybridism of Latin American drama in its mixing of the old and the new, of the European and the American, in a theatre aimed at both artistic and social reform.

—Kirsten F. Nigro

THE HANGMAN (Bödeln)
by Pär Lagerkvist

First Publication: As prose work, Stockholm, 1933; as play, in *Dramatik*, Stockholm, 1946.
First Production: National Theatre, Bergen (in Norwegian); first Swedish production, at the Vasa Theatre, Stockholm, 28 December 1934.

Translations
Guest of Reality, translated by E. Mesterton and D.W. Harding, London, 1936.
The Hangman, in *Pär Lagerkvist: The Modern Theatre: Seven Plays and an Essay*, translated by Thomas R. Buckman, Lincoln, Nebraska, 1966.

Criticism
(For general works on the author, see *Playwrights* volume)

Articles:
A. Paulson, "*The Hangman*: Criticism", in *Theatre Arts*, 19, 1935.
Eric O. Johannesson, "Pär Lagerkvist and the Art of Rebellion", in *Scandinavian Studies*, 30, 1958.
Arne Hannevik, "Pär Lagerkvist's Drama *Bödeln*", in *Edda*, 51, 1964.

*   *   *

This one-act play by the Swedish writer Pär Lagerkvist was first published as a prose work, for Lagerkvist saw little prospect, at the time, of having his plays performed. However his friend Per Lindberg, the brilliant Swedish producer, persuaded him to dramatise it and collaborated closely with him when mounting it.

The play is in two parts, with the Hangman, dressed in blood-red and on stage throughout, as a unifying factor. In a medieval tavern the rude superstitious tradesmen are in awe of the silent Hangman. As they sit carousing they first call him the embodiment of evil but then remember occasions when he had helped people. The grotesque "Gallows-Lasse", who has already been mutilated by the Hangman as punishment for crimes, rounds off Part One with a defiant account, frightening

The Hangman: Vasa Theatre, Stockholm, 1935 (Gösta Ekman in title role)

Øverland, with Kolbjørn Buøen in the title role. Much of the scenery was then sent to the Vasa Theatre, Stockholm, where the first Swedish performance took place on December 28, 1934 with Gösta Ekman as the Hangman. A similar production opened at the National Theatre in Oslo with August Oddvar in the part on March 3, 1935. Lindberg successfully integrated the expressionistic and symbolic elements in the play and while contrasting the two eras also realised Lagerkvist's additional cosmic dimension. The flickering shadows in the medieval tavern were "like projections of the darkfilled souls of craftsmen". In the modern setting he employed similar effects to those in his 1928 production of Toller's *Hoppla, wir leben!*: amplified martial music by Honegger, a clip from a film of Remarque's *Im Western Nichts Neues* (*All Quiet on the Western Front*), and jazz played by Duke Ellington and his Cotton Club Orchestra. The contrapuntal use of class representatives (decadent rich, prostitutes, officers, proletariat) reinforced with strident music is Brechtian. When, after the frenzied cacophony and his monologue, the Hangman exits into a grey dawn, accompanied by distant drum rolls, the cosmic dimension is again evident.

In Norway the play received great acclaim, especially from the many anti-Quislings, while in Stockholm it was badly received; but in both countries it was interpreted as a *political* play. It is still a powerful dramatic work but as such has two difficulties: the central figure has to sit silently on stage for all but the last few minutes of the play; and there is always the danger of the symbolism finally becoming too metaphysical for the theatre.

—Irene Scobbie

in its intensity, of how he pulled up a mandrake in the shadow of the gallows to assist him in even more infamous practices; he, surely, and not the Hangman, is the embodiment of evil in Man.

The medieval tavern fades, to reveal a modern restaurant where customers include representatives of the champagne-drinking upper class and the sausage- and beer-consuming lower class. The *lumpenproletariat* are also depicted in mime. Whereas the medieval carousers kept a respectful distance from the Hangman, their modern counterparts are pleased to approach him. They propound their theories about the superiority of the Aryan race and the splendour of war. A great crescendo is reached when the armed public turn on the negro jazzband players for daring to eat in their presence. Some are shot dead, others beaten up, and the remainder are forced to start playing again, which they do in frenzied manner. A euphoric man praising order, discipline, and victory gives the Nazi salute and awaits the Hangman's reaction. This leads to the climax of the play. For the first time the Hangman speaks. His long monologue proves him to be the immortal representative of man's spirit and a sacrifice to man's blood lust. Evil has broken out again and, sickened though he is of man's cruelty, he is obliged to take up his duties again, like Christ taking up the cross. For most of the play a young woman dressed in rags, but with a halo of light, has sat beside the Hangman. In his monologue the Hangman states that her solicitude has enabled him to continue to perform his duties. Goodness as well as evil would seem to form an eternal part of the human condition.

Per Lindberg produced the play four times. The first performance was at the National Theatre in Bergen on October 23 1934 in a Norwegian translation by Arnulf

HAPPY DAYS (Oh Les Beaux Jours)
by Samuel Beckett

Happy Days
First Publication: New York, 1961.
First Production: Cherry Lane Theâtre, New York, 17 September 1961.

Oh Les Beaux Jours
First Publication: Paris, 1963.
First Production: Théâtre de France, Paris, September 1963.

Criticism
(For general works on the author, see *Playwrights* volume)

Books:
J. Knowlson (ed.), *Samuel Beckett's Production Notebook: Happy Days*, London, 1985.
Katharine Worth, *"Waiting for Godot" and "Happy Days"*, London, 1990 (Text and Performance Series).

Articles:
David J. Alpaugh, "Negative Definition in Samuel Beckett's *Happy Days*", in *Twentieth Century Literature*, 11, 1966.
Ruby Cohn, "Beckett Directs *Happy Days*", in *Performance*, vol.1 no.2, 1972.
Yves Bridel, "Sur le temps et l'espace dans le théâtre de S. Beckett: *En attendant Godot—Oh les beaux jours*", in *Étude des Lettres*, vol.6 no.2, 1973.

Happy Days: Peggy Ashcroft as Winnie, Old Vic Theatre, London, 1975 (National Theatre Company)

Jürgen Hoegl, "Die Krise der Verständigung: Becketts *Happy Days*", in *Sprache im Technischen Zeitalter*, 57, 1976.

Anne M. Drew, "A Sigh into a Looking Glass: The Trickster in *The Winter's Tale* and *Happy Days*", in *Comparative Literature Studies*, 26, 1989.

*   *   *

Happy Days presents one of the most memorable stage-pictures even Beckett ever created. It is certainly his most surrealistic, with its bizarre dislocation and relocation of the normal. Amidst the *"blazing light"* of a *"hellish sun"*, and against a *"very pompier trompe l'œil backcloth"* of a desert plain, we see, embedded above her waist in a mound of scorched grass, Winnie: *"about fifty, well-preserved, blonde for preference, plump, arms and shoulders bare, low bodice, big bosom, pearl necklace"*. To her right, at least partially hidden by the mound for much of the play, sits her husband Willie, with his bald head and boater. Woken by a bell that *"hurts like a knife. . .A gouge"*, Winnie talks and talks, until finally it is time for her song. She gets minimal, often merely monosyllabic, help from Willie. His chief preoccupation is his newspaper, from which he reads out the odd resonant phrase ("Wanted bright boy"!). Winnie's babble is apparently indefatigable, though not merely empty, and its function soon becomes clear. The dense fabric of memories, observations and allusions which goes to make up any ordinary domestic existence is here made to serve the absurd—yet heroic—

purpose of survival in an extraordinary, entirely non-domestic environment. "Sorrow keeps breaking in" on Winnie, but the surface holds, and the poignant comedy of desperation that is characteristic of Beckett's greatest drama becomes richly evident.

In Act I (this is the only Beckett play apart from *Waiting for Godot* to have more than one act) Winnie has to hand as her main resource a *"capacious black bag, shopping variety"*, from which she can ritually unload a range of ordinary everyday objects: toothbrush, mirror, spectacles, brush, lipstick, medicine, hat, comb, nail-file, musical-box, together with an extraordinary one—a revolver. Things happen too: her parasol catches fire, and the appearance of an ant occasions genuine excitement. But in Act II she is bereft of even these objects and events. Now she is embedded up to the neck and she *"faces front motionless"*. All she can do is take visual stock of what remains to her—chiefly her own features. The environment is stranger now: there are no events, but instead only eerily indefinable sounds. Words remain, but her rhythms are now more desperate, and her optimism even more touchingly ludicrous: "Oh this *is* a happy day, this will have been another happy day! (*Pause.*) After all. (*Pause.*) So far". Finally something does happen. Willie appears from behind the mound and crawls towards Winnie. Clad in top hat and tails, he is, the stage direction informs us, *"dressed to kill"*, and the revolver is *"conspicuous to her right"* on the mound. But the song she sings is of romantic love (it is the *Merry Widow* waltz duet), and he might merely want to kiss her. Willie's crawl is never completed; the final tableau leaves the enigma unresolved, and the play ends in a unique blend of the pathetic and the grotesque.

The role of Winnie demands a virtuoso performance, calling as it does for a remarkable degree of discipline, energy and resourcefulness. Notable—and very different—Winnies have been Madeleine Renaud, Peggy Ashcroft and Billie Whitelaw, the last-named under Beckett's own direction. It is hardly surprising that the qualities demanded of the player should be identical with those manifested by the character herself, for Winnie is a quintessentially *theatrical* being. She speaks of a "strange feeling that someone is looking at me" and takes great care to order and regulate the doings and happenings that are under her control, as though continuously improvising her script and action: the day cannot go by without the hoisting of the parasol, and it must end with the song and the prayer. Her whole performance is bounded, prompted, *required* by a theatrical signal: the bell. And Willie is finally necessary because he is her audience, the performer's ultimate guarantee of identity.

But if the performer needs the audience, she also loathes it. Winnie recounts her "memory" of the "last human kind—to stray this way", a Mr. and Mrs. "Shower—or Cooker" (German: *schauen*, to look; *gucken*, to peep). The man made the characteristic audience-demand: "What does it mean? he says—What's it meant to mean?". But the woman defended Winnie against his interpretative prurience ("Has she anything on underneath? he says") and finally demanded release from her partner: "Let go of me. . .Drop dead". The very vehemence of Winnie's narration suggests that the story is a complex fictional projection of her own simultaneous need for an audience and desire for release from all performance whatever. Such is her determination to maintain her quotidian optimism that the contrary desire can achieve expression only in displaced form, through a memory/fiction. Her other story, which images the womb-regression of a child called Milly, seems to articulate similar impulses. Here a grotesque, sexual violation of the girl by a mouse echoes Winnie's own experience of the gouge-like bell; Beckett's own description of Winnie as a "child-woman" lends force to this speculation. The play thus registers the profound ambivalence of its central character towards the very medium of her existence by sexualising, in a disturbing way, the relationship between performer and audience.

If Beckett spoke of Winnie as "an interrupted being", it is not only because she constantly interrupts her own stream of language, but because her very identity is imperfect, unfinished. Accordingly, her concern with her appearance is much more than merely cosmetic. She is engaged in *making herself up* in a radical sense: she strives to construct an identity even as she is being progressively swallowed up by the earth. That her heroically absurd project should follow the contours of the theatrical medium itself is a feature entirely characteristic of her creator's drama as a whole.

—Paul Lawley

DER HAUPTMAN VON KÖPENICK. See **THE CAPTAIN OF KÖPENICK.**

HAY FEVER
by Noël Coward

First Publication: London, 1925.
First Production: Ambassador's Theatre, London, 8 June 1925.

Criticism
(For general works on the author, see *Playwrights* volume)

Articles:
C.R. Yaravintelimath, "Noël Coward's *Hay Fever*: A Study", in *Journal of the Karnatak University*, 18, 1974.

* * *

The Bliss family has invited four intimate friends down to their place in Cookham, meaning to seduce their guests. However the Blisses end up abandoning them. The Blisses live in their own world, a realm which has precious little to do with external reality and the visitors to it are so completely bewildered that they end up seriously pondering whether they actually will be served tea at "teatime". Driven to starvation by their hosts' indifference and to distraction by their antics the guests unceremoniously depart. "How very rude!" exclaims Mrs. Bliss on hearing that they have done so.

Nothing is supposed to happen over a weekend and in this play Coward takes this social dictum to absurdly comic levels. A retired actress, Judith Bliss, will have absolutely nothing to do with the care and feeding of her guests, the only things that seem to interest her are a word game of her own creation called "Adverbs" and the replaying of scenes from her old stage vehicles over and over again. Coward's choice of a word game whose rules are incommunicable artfully telegraphs the point of his play: one cannot learn the rules of life; one must simply have them. The Bliss menage creates its own milieu through a family code whose idiom is basically theatrical. Even though her children appear to loathe their mother's self-indulgent theatrics, they effortlessly feed her her "lines", practically on cue.

In its way the comedy is a sort of social reportage. Coward has identified the source of *Hay Fever* as being the evenings he spent at the Riverside Drive apartment of the actress Laurette Taylor in New York City, during which Miss Taylor subjected her guests to frenzied parlor games.

Thus on one level, *Hay Fever* presents us with an ancient and even severe situation: the observance of the laws of hospitality. Granted that in the beau-monde context of the play the laws of hospitality have degenerated into mere social graces, but rarely has the gracious living of high society been shown to be as graceless as it is in *Hay Fever*. For what we see and hear in this play is the merest lip service to courtesy, indeed the laws of hospitality are flagrantly flouted, decorum is ignored, etiquette non-existent. No one is adequately or even inadequately introduced; no provisions are made for the feeding of guests; people wander in and out indiscriminately; conversations are interrupted and there is hardly a trace of civility. The Blisses do not even go through the motions of wanting to be polite; they are so staggeringly self-obsessed as to be completely incapable of legitimate social exchange. They treat everyone else as supernumeraries in the theatrical extravaganza of their lives.

One of Coward's cleverer devices is the bedroom controversy that develops among the Bliss family when each member finally realizes that the other has invited someone down for the weekend. Something called "The Japanese Room" is the coveted sleeping chamber and each member of the family

Hay Fever: Criterion Theatre, London, 1932

desires it for his or her own particular guest. Each tries to palm off a place called "Little Hell" on the other's chosen companion. We become privy to this information during a dialogue between Judith Bliss and her brother Simon—with their mother presiding—which elegantly limns the barbarous nature of their way of life. Coward sets up the discussion as a sort of apologia for indecency. We learn that the Blisses are quite proud of their ways and believe themselves to be a breed apart.

It is this "otherness" that reflects Coward's own feelings about the way of the world in the early 20th century. John Lahr has said that Coward's comedies focus on a "talentocracy" whose self-awareness stems from its feeling of difference from, and indifference to, the traditional aristocracy's modes. In *Hay Fever* Coward shows how this self-conscious differentiation becomes self-propelling. As Sorel says of her parents, they have: "spent their lives cultivating their arts and not devoting any time to ordinary conventions and manners and things"— note that "arts" is modified with a possessive.

The playwright himself was the first person to admit that *Hay Fever* is awfully short on plot development or even action. In his introduction to *Hay Fever* (*Play Parade, 1*) Coward goes so far as to call it "one of the most difficult plays to perform that I have encountered". He goes on to posit that the work is wholly dependent upon "the expert technique" of its performers. If the dialogue is delivered with any archness—for example should the actress playing Myra Arundel indicate in the slightest that she *knows* beforehand that her "haddock is disgusting"—the play will become insufferable. The characters must never revel in their "upper-class ellipticalness" (to use Robert Kiernan's phrase). They must simply take it for granted.

Coward's tenets for comic playwriting are most cogently illustrated by *Hay Fever*. It does not achieve its effects via epigrammatic flourishes, but rather by simple phrases being delivered in very complicated situations. Taken out of context

the "laugh lines" are vacuous, but within the dramatic situation of the play they are hilarious.

In 1964 the National Theatre chose this play to be the first work that it presented by a living English dramatist. Coward directed the revival himself and its success started a tremendous renewal of interest in his works.

—Thomas F. Connolly

HE AND SHE
by Rachel Crothers

First Publication: In *Representative American Plays*, New York, 1917; revised version in *Representative American Plays*, second edition, New York, 1925.
First Production: Poughkeepsie, New York, October 1911.

Criticism
(For general works on the author, see *Playwrights* volume)

Articles:
Lois C. Gottlieb, "Obstacles to Feminism in the Early Plays of Rachel Crothers", in *University of Michigan Papers in Women's Studies*, June 1975.
Lois C. Gottlieb, "Looking to Women: Rachel Crothers and the Feminist Heroine", in *Women in the American Theatre* (revised edition), edited by Helen Krich Chinoy and Linda Walsh Jenkins, New York, 1987.

*   *   *

Ann and Tom are a married couple, both of whom are sculptors. Tom is supportive of Ann's career—which is clearly subordinate to his—until she wins a first prize of $100,000 in a competition they have both entered (Tom is placed second). Initially Tom seems pleased but then begins to complain that fulfilling the prize commission will interfere with Ann's family obligations. A bitter argument ensues in which Tom asks, then demands, that she renounce the commission. The fight is interrupted by the appearance of their teenage daughter, Millicent, who has come home unexpectedly from boarding school. Millicent announces that she became engaged to a chauffeur when she was forced to spend a vacation at school while Ann worked on her models. Horrified, Ann determines that she must devote all her time to dissuading Millicent from her planned marriage. She asks Tom to execute the frieze for her, and he agrees.

Woven through the main story is a subplot involving Tom's assistant Keith McKenzie, Ann's friend Ruth Creel, and Tom's sister Daisy. Keith and Ruth are engaged, but Ruth breaks the engagement when Keith, who believes all wives should stay at home, balks at her accepting a career advancement she covets. With the help of Ann's father, Dr. Remington, Keith begins a romance with the far more domestic Daisy.

He and She has had a rocky stage history. No fewer than three productions of the drama (which was renamed *The Herfords* during its 1912 run but then reverted to its original title) were mounted before a fourth production finally arrived in New York City in 1920, this time with Crothers herself in the starring role. Despite mixed reviews, *He and She* had a run of only 28 performances. The play was first published in Quinn's *Representative American Plays* in 1917, but the more familiar version is the revised one, which Crothers prepared for later editions of the anthology and which reflects changes made for the 1920 production.

He and She is one of Crothers' most complex and provocative works, and it continues to intrigue scholars and directors. A play in which action and even character development are subservient to the presentation of varying points of view, *He and She* shows the influence of both Ibsen and Shaw. Most reviewers of the 1920 production saw Ann's giving up of her sculpting commission as Crothers' assertion that women belong in the home, not in the career world. Some critics applauded this apparently very conservative stance, while others expressed dismay. One reviewer was pleased that "Miss Crothers. . .wisely puts the task of wife and mother in the first place", but Heywood Broun complained, "We have always found that the soup tastes just the same whether it is opened with loving care or by the hired help. Nor are we convinced that young daughters tend to become entangled in unfortunate love affairs the instant a mother begins to paint a picture or deliver a series of lectures". There is much merit to Broun's objection, of course; it never occurs to the characters in the play—as it rarely occurred to anyone in the early part of the century—that someone other than a mother could care for a 16-year-old girl. In an interview Crothers claimed that "a profession need not necessarily upset a woman's home life", but *He and She* suggests the likelihood of conflict if the home life includes children. The climax of the work was particularly disappointing to those who admired her immediately preceding play, *A Man's World*, whose heroine is an outspoken defender of equality between the sexes.

Still, *He and She* is a more subtle and complicated drama than this debate would suggest. As the playwright herself once pointed out, Ann renounces the commission not because of her husband's desire but because of her daughter's perceived need: Tom's wishes are given no more validity than Ann's. Crothers also makes very clear that Ann will often, in future, regret the choice she has made. The playwright obviously considered this an important point, for she added a speech to the conclusion of the revised version in which Ann tells Tom: "And I'll hate you because you're doing it [the frieze]—and I'll hate myself because I gave it up—and I'll almost—hate—her". Like many of her generation Crothers had difficulty envisioning women with both successful careers and marriages, but she was sensitive enough to portray the painful decisions involved.

Moreover, the play does suggest that the home is not the "natural" place for all women, and that women artists are at least equal in talent to their male counterparts. Even the thoroughly misogynist Dr. Remington acknowledges that Keith has no right to ask Ruth to give up her promising career in journalism, and Ann wins a highly competitive contest, defeating both her husband and a (presumably) large number of other, prominent, male sculptors. Early in the play Tom dismisses Ann's work as not in "this class", but her victory proves him wrong.

For the most part Crothers keeps the dialogue lively and engrossing—no mean feat in a play so heavily dependent on discussion. Even if she sometimes sacrifices dramatic probability and character consistency to the demands of the debates, *He and She* remains an absorbing contribution to the genre of the problem play in America. And those debates themselves—about women's talents, rights and obligations—continue to occupy us 80 years after Crothers put them on stage.

—Judith E. Barlow

HE WHO GETS SLAPPED (Tot Kto Polyuchayet Poschechiny) by Leonid Andreyev

First Publication: Moscow, 1915.
First Production: Dramatic Theatre, Moscow, 27 October 1915.

Translations
He, The One Who Gets Slapped, translated by Gregory Zilborg, New York, 1921.
He Who Gets Slapped, translated by G. Carlin, New York, 1925.

Criticism
(For general works on the author, see *Playwrights* volume)

Articles:
Sonia Ketchian, "On the Semantic Structure of Andreev's *Tot, kto polucaet posceciny*", in *Russian Language Journal*, 114, 1979.

*   *   *

A middle-aged man, who has obviously seen better days, comes to a small circus seeking employment. Asked to invent his own act, he becomes "He Who Gets Slapped", a clown whose feat will be to receive the blows and abuses of others. The charm and beauty of Consuela, the bareback rider, awakens love and protectiveness in the character He. Consuela, presumably the daughter of Count Mancini, an impoverished aristocrat who lives off her earnings and is preparing to sell her in marriage to The Baron, it later transpires is a Corsican peasant of unknown parentage, fashioned by Mancini for his profit. Unconsciously, Consuela loves her partner, the young Bazano, and he would love her, to the desperation of the fiery lion tamer and the manager's common law wife, Zinida, who loves Bazano to desperation. The character He is visited by a gentleman, a Prince, who, having abducted He's wife and confiscated his work and ideas, vulgarizing them in a book which has made the Prince a household name, begs He to return to society, for his absence is haunting the Prince's life. He refuses, and tries to woo Consuela and warn her against Mancini and the Baron, but she pays no attention. After Consuela's benefit performance, He poisons a glass of water which he offers to Consuela. She drinks half; He drinks the other half. The Baron shoots himself.

Although *He Who Gets Slapped* does not conform to expectations of social realism in Russian turn-of-the-century drama, it does seem oddly familiar. It fits comfortably into the tradition of neo-Gothic romances, like *Phantom Of The Opera* and *Trilby*, relying on some of the same conventions for the development of its plot and characters and its emotional effect.

Although neither as physically repellent as the Phantom, nor as evil as Svengali, He still depends for his position in the play, as well as the audience's sympathy, on grotesquerie, encapsulated by his voluntary persona as "He Who Gets Slapped". A fine conglomerate of a hero, he is physically unattractive; although not so ugly as to have to wear a mask, his unattractiveness, by convention, both denies him romantic fulfilment and allows a depth of sensitivity and desire which encourages the audience's trust and compassion. No longer young enough to be entitled, by convention, to simple romantic success, he is not so old that his love for Consuela might appear absurd. He, too, has been wronged: mystery and suffering cloud his past.

Part of He's attraction lies in the tension between his wilful detachment from the chaos of human desire by joining the circus and becoming the lowliest of the clowns and his embroilment through his unwilling love for Consuela. His ambiguities contribute to the dramatic effect of the play, for his actions, too have ambivalent effect. His abandonment of his own life for the circus and his rejection of the Prince's appeals arouse both feelings of criticism for his stubborn absoluteness and admiration for its personal heroism. We can be apalled by his poisoning of Consuela and at the same time be grateful for his saving her from the possession of Mancini and the Baron, and for retaining her purity.

The wounded grotesque, the "mentor" figure of The Phantom and Svengali, is divided between He and Mancini. Their relationships with Consuela create the Romantic divide between body and spirit, between material existence and inner truth that sets the moral and emotional tone of the drama. It is Mancini who has "made" Consuela. She has been so long under his spell that her childhood as a peasant is forgotten. Her memories of simple, free, "natural" life, even consciousness of her own "nature", have become merely vague intimations of a dream, a pastoral myth. So, one might infer, the "natural" man is detached from his true self by the machinations of social power and material greed.

It is to this myth that He addresses himself as he talks to her about "the gods". His tales express the depth of his love for her, suggesting the justification of destiny. They also call forth images of pastoral perfection, of pure ideals which create a moral basis in which "love" and the inner spirit are superior to profit and social control. Consuela considers herself Mancini's daughter and values the exchange that will make her the Baron's wife, unable to see she is merely a commodity passed between them for their own gain. He's struggle is to "unmake" her, to wake her and restore her to her "natural" self. Failing this, he is forced to kill her to preserve her beauty and purity.

Even as He implores her to wake, he knows that should she wake, she would find herself in love with Bazano. Bazano, too, is asleep, prevented from recognition of his own feelings by the chimera of class. Since this is self-imposed, Bazano is presented as less worthy of Consuela.

The setting of the play, like that of *The Phantom* and *Trilby* is crucial to its action. The central image in all three is "performance". The theatrical performance sets up a dichotomy between "real life" and fantasy which easily accomodates and re-enforces the thematic separation between the physical and the spiritual, and the moral implications of the contrived versus the natural. Through the isolation of the performer, the artist becomes a heightened representative of human kind. The demand for excellence, the exposure of the performer to the criticism of the faceless multitude, and the hidden private pain behind the glamorous act, as well as the very act itself, all contribute to the image of the performer as the embodiment of the human condition.

However, whilst *Phantom* and *Trilby* rely on the dazzling, luxurious world of opera, Andreyev sets his play in the circus. Opera suggests, along with wealth, privilege and class, socially acknowledged tradition and standards of excellence. The circus, however, suggests a world of anarchic independence, somewhere on the fringes of society where little boys go when they run away from home; a domestic foreign legion romantically assumed to be full of misfits with dark secrets hiding behind anonymity. In contrast to the ordered wealth and elegance of the opera, the circus is the very epitome of romantic tawdriness. Circus skills do not gain the social praise of the trained voice nor the justification of traditional standards of the opera. They are essentially anarchic, private obsessions through which each individual confronts a singular,

human limitation. Though they have no purpose beyond their enactment, they involve risk and danger. The circus performer pursues not a universally acknowledged idea but a personal demon, an illusion significant only to himself which takes form in his performance.

These connotations inform the action and emotional content of the play. He merges into a self-created role he sees as the exact embodiment of his experience and sets himself to extend it to its utmost limits. The obsessive quest that motivates the circus act becomes an active metaphor for the internal lives of the characters. The dedication to manifest the dream beyond the physical limits in order to free and manifest the spirit in form becomes a positive ideal. Thus the members of the circus troupe become the guardians of purity of soul and imply a heroism that makes Mancini and the Baron appear crass, shabby, and soulless. The clear morality devalues wealth and power in comparison with purity of spirit and the energetic passion of dreams.

—Elaine Turner

HEARTBREAK HOUSE
by George Bernard Shaw

First Publication: In *Heartbreak House; Great Catharine; and Playlets of the War*, New York, 1919.
First Production: Garrick Theatre, New York, 10 November 1920.

Criticism
(For general works on the author, see *Playwrights* volume)

Articles:
Frederick P.W. McDowell, "Technique, Symbol and Theme in *Heartbreak House*" in *Publications of the Modern Language Association* [*PMLA*], 68, 1953.
John Jordan, "Shaw's *Heartbreak House*", in *Threshold*, vol.1 no.1, 1957.
Robert Corrigan, "*Heartbreak House*: Shaw's Elegy for Europe", in *Shaw Review*, 2, 1959.
Robert R. Reed, "Boss Mangan, Peer Gynt and *Heartbreak House*", in *Shaw Review*, 2, 1959.
Michael J. Mendelsohn, "The Heartbreak Houses of Shaw and Chekhov", in *Shaw Review*, 6, 1963.
D.C. Coleman, "Fun and Games: Two Pictures of *Heartbreak House*", in *Drama Survey*, 5, 1966–67.
Richard Hornby, "The Symbolic Action of *Heartbreak House*", in *Drama Survey*, 7, 1968–69.
Michael W. Kaufman, "The Dissonance of Dialectic: Shaw's *Heartbreak House*", in *Shaw Review*, 13, 1970.
Roger B. Wilkenfeld, "Perpetual Motion in *Heartbreak House*", in *Texas Studies in Literature and Language*, 13, 1971.
Daniel J. Leary, "Shaw's Blakean Vision: A Dialectic Approach to *Heartbreak House*", in *Modern Drama*, 15, 1972.
Stanley Weintraub, "*Heartbreak House*: Shaw's *Lear*", in *Modern Drama*, 15, 1972.
Joseph Frank, "Internal vs. External Combustion: Dickens' *Bleak House* and Shaw's *Major Barbara* and *Heartbreak House*", in *Shaw Review*, 20, 1977.

Heartbreak House: Court Theatre, London, 1921

Martin Quinn, "The Dickensian Presence in *Heartbreak House*", in *Shaw Review*, 20, 1977.

Rhoda B. Nathan, "The 'daimons' of *Heartbreak House*", in *Modern Drama*, 21, 1978.

Sally P. Vogt, "*Heartbreak House*: Shaw's Ship of Fools", in *Modern Drama*, 21, 1978.

Anne Wright, "Shaw's Burglars: *Heartbreak House* and *Too True to Be Good*", in *Shaw Review*, 23, 1980.

James Woodfield, "Ellie in Wonderland: Dream and Madness in *Heartbreak House*", in *English Studies in Canada*, 11, 1985.

Estelle M. Thaler, "Apocalyptic Vision in *Heartbreak House* and *Endgame*: The Metaphor of Change", in *Zeitschrift für Anglistik und Amerikanistik*, 34, 1986.

Axel Kruse, "Bernard Shaw's *Heartbreak House*: The War in 'Neverland'", in *Sydney Studies in English*, 13, 1987.

Rhoda B. Nathan, "The *House* with No Exit: The Existential Shaw", in *Independent Shavian*, 25, 1987.

Joseph Hynes, "*Heartbreak House*: Between Modernism and Postmodernism", in *Independent Shavian*, 26, 1988.

Marilyn Throne, "The Social Value of the Privileged Class: A Comparison of Shaw's *Heartbreak House* and Friel's *Aristocrats*", in *Colby Library Quarterly*, 24, 1988.

* * *

Heartbreak House is set on one September afternoon and evening in Sussex in a country house which resembles a ship. A girl, Ellie, enters and falls asleep, and the whole play can be seen as her dream. Seven more main characters, middle and upper-middle-class, enter one by one in the first act, providing social comedy of mistaken identity. The main plot-line, such as it is, involves Ellie being in love with Hector, who proves to be the husband of her friend, Hesione. So Ellie decides, cold-bloodedly, to marry Boss Mangan for his money, symbolising her dominance by hypnotising him. Then she discovers a new serenity through love for 88-year-old Captain Shotover, sometimes half-insane and sometimes a visionary. A few minutes from the end, without warning, bombs start to fall. The characters expect to die, welcoming the excitement and the sound of the engines in the air which are like Beethoven. A bomb falls nearby, killing only Mangan and a burglar.

Shaw subtitles his play "a fantasia in the Russian manner". "Fantasia" means both the absence of formal construction and a debt to existing themes; "Russian" refers to Chekhov and to Tolstoy's *Fruits of Enlightenment*. Ellie reads Shakespeare at the start and *Heartbreak House* may be seen as deconstructions successively of *Othello, Midsummer Night's Dream* and *King Lear*.

Three levels may be seen in *Heartbreak House*. The surface layer is a society comedy which, as in a play like *Major Barbara*, shifts increasingly to serious debate as the piece unfolds. The comedy is of the tangles of idle, bored, upper-middle-class people, for whom falling in and out of love is a pastime. Because of the preoccupation with personal relations, the ship of state is drifting.

The second level is an allegory of the moral and political failure of the European leisure class, as Shaw emphasises in an untypically solemn, indeed bitter, preface. Shotover represents a traditional spirit of adventure and enterprise, but now he is very old—distracted, absent-minded, drunk. One daughter, Ariadne, has married a colonial administrator who keeps order with bamboo canes, a type Shaw labels "Horseback Hall"; while Hesione is an artistic, Bloomsbury type. Ellie's father, Mazzini Dunn, personifies ineffectual idealism, so running Britain devolves on the capitalist, Mangan. Hence the unexpected bombs at the end: the outbreak of World War I.

The third and strangest level is about uncertainty and inconsistency. This is shown most clearly through Shotover's constantly mistaking identity—yet he may only be pretending not to know who Ariadne or Mazzini are. Characters have basic contradictions. Hector, for example, though a liar and braggart, is courageous but keeps it secret. Shotover is a richly comic character, yet he also seeks to unify power and wisdom, and has sought experience, not fearing death. He is referred to as "supernatural" and as "the Ancient Mariner"; he married a black witch and there are hints of Faust and a Superman. He is, in his own words, one of those "so sufficient to themselves that they are only happy when they are stripped of everything, even of hope".

Shaw was writing while shocked by the war: the common-sense, Fabian reforms he had preached for many years had had little effect and barbarism had replaced progress. Shaw asks here: Why did the war happen? and what English shortcomings allowed a drift to it? "What then is to be done?" asks Shotover in Lenin's words in the first act, and near the end he finally gives advice: "Learn your business as an Englishman. . . .Navigation. Learn it and live; or leave it and be damned". Perhaps there is still time for good people (for it is the turn of a woman, Ellie) to begin to steer the ship of state.

The drama has been described as a heartbroken socialist's view of the future of England. The end is ambiguous. Ellie reverts to calling Hector "Marcus" and hopes the bombs return the next night. Does she mean by this that she wants destruction and death? Or does she mean that facing death is a challenge, a way of living fully, as Shotover did when he was at the wheel of his ship in a typhoon? Or does she want to hear the sound again, the drumming in the air that is like Beethoven? The tone is ambiguous.

The play is finally about heartbreak. The condition of England and of the world in 1916 (when Shaw did all or most of the writing) was heartbreaking. Hector lists six of them as heartbroken in the last act, though the kind Randall experiences is not serious. Ellie, learning that Hector is married, says: "I have a horrible fear that my heart is broken, but that heartbreak is not like what I thought it must be". Soon she discovers "it is the end of happiness and the beginning of peace", and realises "I feel now as if there was nothing I could not do, because I want nothing". So "there is a blessing on my broken heart". As with Major Barbara and Vivie in *Mrs Warren's Profession*, a young woman suffers and comes through. Heartbreak leads to serenity, salvation, even a readiness to act.

—Malcolm Page

HEDDA GABLER
by Henrik Ibsen

First Publication: Copenhagen and Christiana, 1890.
First Production: Hoftheater, Munich, 31 January 1891; in Norwegian, Christiania, 26 February 1891.

Translations
Hedda Gabler, translated by William Archer, in *Ibsen's Prose Dramas, 5*, London, 1891; revised version in *Collected Works, 10*, London, 1907.

Hedda Gabler, translated by Michael Meyer, London 1962; revised edition, 1974; corrected version in *Ibsen: Plays, 2*, London, 1980.
Hedda Gabler, in *The Last Plays of Henrik Ibsen*, translated by Arvid Paulsen, New York, 1962.
Hedda Gabler, translated by Otto Reinert, New York, 1962.
Hedda Gabler, in *"Hedda Gabler" and Other Plays*, translated by Una Ellis-Fermor, Harmondsworth, 1964.
Hedda Gabler, in *Ibsen: Four Major Plays, 1*, translated by Rolf Fjelde, New York, 1965.
Hedda Gabler, translated by Jens Arup, in *The Oxford Ibsen, 7*, edited by James Walter McFarlane, London, 1966.
Hedda Gabler, translated by Max Faber, London, 1966.
Hedda Gabler, translated by Eva Le Gallienne, London, 1953.
Hedda Gabler, translated by Alan S. Downer, New York, 1961.

Criticism
(For general works on the author, see *Playwrights* volume)

Books:
Else Høst, *"Hedda Gabler"*, Oslo, 1958.
Kari Fjørtoft, *"Hedda Gabler" i samtid og ettertid: Den Norske Kritikartradisjonen i Kvinneperspektiv*, Oslo, 1986.

Articles:
C.W. Mayerson, "Thematic Symbols in *Hedda Gabler*", in *Scandinavian Studies and Notes*, 22, 1950.
Herbert Blau, "*Hedda Gabler*: The Irony of Decadence", in *Educational Theatre Journal*, 5, 1953.
Jens Arup, "On *Hedda Gabler*", in *Orbis Litterarum*, 12, 1957.
Halvdan Koht, "Hedda Gabler: Forhistorie og symbol", in *Nordisk Tidskrift*, 34, 1958.
Peter Simonen, "Om *Hedda Gabler, Lille Eyolf*, og Lord Byron", in *Edda*, 62, 1962.
John R. Northam, "*Hedda Gabler*", in *Ibsenforbundet: Årbok*, 1968–69.
Ola Moe, "*Hedda Gabler* og den moderne tragedies dilemma", in *Edda*, 72, 1972.
Gerd E. Rieger, "*Hedda Gabler*: Satisfaktion wird nicht gegeben", in *Skandinavistik*, 6, 1976.
Sandra E. Saari, "*Hedda Gabler*: The Past Recaptured", in *Modern Drama*, 20, 1977.
Beverly M. Matherne, "A Kierkegaardian Study of *Hedda Gabler*", in *Western Journal of Speech Communication*, 42, 1978.
Yvonne L. Sandstroem, "Problems of Identity in *Hedda Gabler*", in *Scandinavian Studies*, 51, 1979.
Toril Moi, "Narcissisme som forsvar: Ibsens *Hedda Gabler*", in *Eigenproduksjon*, 18, 1983.
Theoharis C. Theoharis, "*Hedda Gabler* and 'The Dead'", in *English Literary History*, 50, 1983.
Patricia F. Behrendt, "The Narcissus Paradigm in *Hedda Gabler*", in *Journal of Evolutionary Psychology*, 6, 1985.
Elinor Fuchs, "Mythic Structure in *Hedda Gabler*: The Mask Behind the Face", in *Comparative Drama*, 19, 1985.
Joanne E. Gates, "Elizabeth Robins and the 1891 Production of *Hedda Gabler*", in *Modern Drama*, 28, 1985.
Stein H. Olsen, "Why Does Hedda Gabler Marry Jorgen Tesman?", in *Modern Drama*, 28, 1985.

*   *   *

First produced in Munich in 1891, *Hedda Gabler* is one of Ibsen's sharply critical analyses of contemporary European bourgeois society; but it is also one of his major tragedies.

Hedda Gabler: Aldwych Theatre, London, 1975 (Royal Shakespeare Company)

Hedda (known by her maiden rather than her married name), the daughter of a general, is the wife of a tepid and domesticated academic, George Tesman. The opening scenes show her bored with her husband, alienated from her domestic and family context, simmering with frustrated aspiration and inhibited energy. Her brittle security is shattered by the arrival of an old school friend, Thea Elvsted, who has left her husband in order to act as muse to a dissolute, brilliant writer, Eilert Lovborg, who in turn once harboured a passion for Hedda. Challenged by the romantic idealism of Thea and Eilert, Hedda directs her energies towards destroying them: she encourages Eilert into a drunken oblivion during which he loses the irreplaceable manuscript of his new book; she conceals the fact that Tesman has found it; and she gives him a pistol with which to commit a romantic suicide. She then burns the manuscript, fantasising that she is sacrificing Eilert's and Thea's "child". Eilert does shoot himself, but accidentally, in a grotesque fashion, and in the sordid circumstances of a brothel. Hedda's romantic desires continually turn to the cynical disillusionment of black farce: "Everything I touch becomes ludicrous and despicable". She finds herself stranded between her husband and Thea, who begin to reassemble Eilert's book from his notes; and the opportunistic advances of Judge Brack, who identifies Hedda's pistol, guesses at the truth, and makes it apparent that he intends to blackmail her into sexual submission. Trapped more tightly and irrevocably in the results of her own actions than she was to begin with in the conventional bourgeois marriage, Hedda shoots herself in the head.

The play's title places firmly at the centre of the drama the figure of a complex, difficult, intractable, unappeasable woman. The life and death of Ibsen's heroine are shot through with psychological and social contradictions. A woman of aristocratic prejudices and expectations (as General Gabler's daughter) she has compromised with bourgeois society by marrying a vacuous, careerist academic. Hungry for life and sensation, Hedda yet has a powerful, emotional aversion to human contact. Her acute dissatisfaction with the boredom and triviality of domestic life co-exists with a neurotic fear of risk and danger. The assumption of superiority she cherishes is confirmed and supported by her social station, but then subverted by the genuinely courageous behaviour of the timid Thea, who has abandoned her husband, and by the creative genius of Eilert, the lover she had formerly rejected. Hedda is acutely aware of the immense gulf dividing the ideal possibilities of life—passion, adventure, heroic action, creative achievement—and the petty preoccupations of the respectable, middle-class family. Yet her attempts to bridge that separation take the form of minor social games—attempting to manipulate the lives of others, or playing with her father's pistols—which ultimately turn savagely, and tragically, wrong. Beneath the apparently secure and placid surface of bourgeois life, Ibsen depicts the stirrings of violent and anarchic energies, which occasionally break through in a mythical and symbolic, dramatic language—when Hedda burns the mansuscript, imagining it to be a child, or when she imagines Eilert as Dionysus, sacrificing himself to the principles of beauty and power. The attempt to reconcile these contradictions, if only by destructive interference, is what makes Hedda Gabler a tragic heroine.

The tragic arena is no longer a cosmic struggle between moral contraries as in Greek drama, or an epic conflict between opposed historical ideas as in the drama of the Renaissance; tragedy is now enacted in the cramped space of a 19th-century drawing-room. Yet the tragic conflict is in many ways the same as in the tragedies of earlier theatres: though she challenges no gods and kills no kings, Hedda Gabler yet succeeds in prising open the sealed illusions of her society, seizes on their central contradictions, and reveals, by demonstrating the impossibility of their reconciliation, the self-divisions of the age. Hedda is contaminated by her civilisation, and yet transcends it by disclosing its deep alienation: "A woman" Ibsen wrote in 1878, "cannot be herself in modern society".

—Graham Holderness

HEIMAT. See **MAGDA**.

HENRY IV (Enrico IV)
by Luigi Pirandello

First Publication: In *Maschere nude, 4*, Florence, 1922.
First Production: Teatro Manzoni (Ruggeri Company), Milan, 24 February 1922.

Translations
Henry IV, translated by Edward Storer, in *Pirandello: Three Plays*, New York, 1922.
Henry IV, translated by Frederick May, in *"Right If You Think You Are" and Other Plays*, edited by E. Martin Browne, London, 1962.
The Emperor, translated by Eric Bentley, in *The Genius of the Italian Theatre*, edited by Eric Bentley, New York, 1964.
Henry IV, translated by Julian Mitchell, London, 1979.
Henry IV, translated by Robert Rietty and John Wardle, in *Collected Plays, 1*, edited by Robert Rietty, London, 1987.

Criticism
(For general works on the author, see *Playwrights* volume)

Articles:
Maurizio Del Ministro, "Interpretazione di *Enrico IV*", in *Rassegna della letteratura italiana*, 73, 1969.
Ross Chambers, "*Enrico IV* (1921): la comédie de la folie", in *La Comédie au chateau: contribution à la poétique du théâtre*, Paris, 1971.
Federico Doglio, "Appunti per una lettura dell'*Enrico IV* di Pirandello", in *Istituto di studi Pirandelliani, quaderni*, 1, 1973.
Elena J. Conte, "Lettura scenografica dell'*Enrico IV*", in *Rapporti*, December 1976.
Alan Roland and Gino Rizzo, "Psychoanalysis in Search of Pirandello: *Six Characters* and *Henry IV*", in *Psychoanalytic Review*, 64, 1977.
Henning Mehnert, "Pirandellos *Enrico IV* und das Problem der multiplen Persönlichkeit", in *Germanisch-Romanische Monatsschrift*, 28, 1978.

M. Candida Toaldo, "L'*Enrico IV* e il 'pirandellismo' ", in *Humanitas*, 33, 1978.
Umberto Mariani, "*Enrico IV*, o della 'logica potente e profonda' ", in *Rivista di studi Pirandelliani*, 6, 1980.
Michael Caesar, "Enrico's Foil: The Function of Belcredi in *Enrico IV*", in *Yearbook of the British Pirandello Society*, 2, 1982.
Michael Patterson, " 'Laingian' Reading of Pirandello's *Henry IV*", in *Modern Drama*, 27, 1984.
Guiliana Sanguinetti Katz, "La pazzia di Enrico IV", in *Yearbook of the British Pirandello Society*, 6, 1986.
Halina Sawecka, "Proposition d'une relecture de *Henry IV* de Pirandello sous l'angle des rapports entre le théâtre et la folie", in *Acta Universitatis Wratislaviensis*, 895, 1986.
Douglas Biow, "Psychoanalysis, History, Marginality: A Study of Violence and Disease in Pirandello's *Enrico IV*", in *Italica*, 66, 1989.

* * *

Henry IV is the most frequently performed of Pirandello's plays in Italian and in English. It is one of only three plays that he wrote and designated as tragedies, the other two being *Diana e la Tuda* (*Diana and Tuda*) and *La vita che ti diedi* (*The Life I Gave You*), and has often been described by critics as "Shakespearean" in its intensity. The play offers a strong central role for a virtuoso actor and was originally written in 1921 for Ruggero Ruggeri, shortly after the successful run of *Six Characters in Search of An Author*. In the letter to Ruggeri offering him the play, Pirandello describes *Henry IV* as "one of my most original works". Generations of audiences have subsequently come to share his view.

Before the play begins, an event has taken place that determines the circumstances of the action that follows. 20 years previously, a group of wealthy young people took part in a masquerade, each one disguised as a character from history. The man playing the medieval Emperor, Henry IV, fell off his horse, hit his head and was then shut away for the next two decades with brain damage. The fall has left him with the delusion that he is indeed Henry IV, and he lives in a secure house decorated to look like a medieval castle, cared for by servants in period costume. When the play begins, a new servant, Bertoldo, has just been hired, but is wearing the wrong clothes, since he has confused the medieval Henry IV with the Renaissance king of the same name. After this comic start, a group of visitors arrive: the Countess Matilde, the woman Henry had been in love with twenty years earlier; her daughter Frida who looks exactly like her mother; the Marquis Di Nolli, Frida's fiancé, who is Henry's nephew; Belcredi, Matilde's lover, who had also taken part in the ill-fated masquerade; and a psychiatrist. Matilde hopes that Henry can still be cured of his madness, a view that Belcredi looks upon with utter cynicism. When Henry finally appears, he is a pathetic, painted, clown-like figure, but gradually through his language and the games he plays, we begin to suspect that he is more intelligent than he appears. In the second act, in a spectacular *coup de théâtre*, Henry reveals that he is not mad at all; he recovered some years earlier but has continued to play out the role of a madman. Matilde and her party, unaware of this, decide to try and shock Henry back into sanity. They arrange for Frida and Di Nolli to stand in the frames that previously held life-size portraits of Matilde and Henry as young people, in the hope that this stark contrast between art and reality will make Henry realize what time he is living in. But the plan misfires; Henry is so shocked that he is almost driven back into madness, and when Belcredi accuses him of play-acting, Henry reveals that Belcredi had been responsible

Henry IV: Her Majesty's Theatre, London, 1974

for making the horse rear and throw him in the first place, because both men were rivals for the love of Matilde. Henry takes his revenge and stabs Belcredi to death. Ironically, by this gesture Henry appears to the world to be truly mad, though the audience, like the dying Belcredi, recognize that he has in fact committed an entirely logical, sane act of vindication. The play ends with Henry realizing that he is now trapped in the role of the mad emperor for ever.

The structure of *Henry IV* follows the conventional three act pattern; Pirandello does not attempt to experiment with theatre form in the way he had done with *Six Characters*. . .and would do later with many of his other plays. The protagonist, Henry IV, is the focal point of the play, and although his first appearance is delayed, thereby creating an intensely theatrical moment when he does finally enter, he dominates the action that follows.

The play takes up a familiar Pirandellian theme: the impossibility of determining what are the boundaries between sanity and madness. It has been pointed out that Pirandello may have been drawn to the problem of the relativity of madness through his own personal life history—his wife, Antonietta, was committed to a mental hospital in 1918. The particular form of her mental illness also fuels speculation about another key Pirandellian theme, again apparent in *Henry IV*: excessive, sexual jealousy. Henry accuses Belcredi of having deliberately caused his accident 20 years earlier so as to have the way clear to Matilde, and whatever the truth of this accusation (and Pirandello constantly reminds us that all truth is relative, and dependent on individual perspective) the motif of sexual rivalry between the two middle-aged men is power-

fully depicted and provides opportunity for a good deal of ironic humour.

It has often been stated that *Henry IV* is a play about illusion and reality, about the impossibility of defining (or curing) madness. But it is also a play about growing old, about the inevitability of the passing of time. Henry's painted cheeks, Matilde's dyed hair are crude indicators of a desperate attempt to stop time and hold on to youth. When Henry sees Frida in the picture frame, for a moment he believes that time has indeed stopped, perhaps even turned backwards, and that he is seeing Matilde as she was 20 years before. The horror of this possibility brings him back to the brink of madness.

Reviews of the original production and of the revival—directed by Pirandello himself—that toured Europe in 1925, praised the power of Ruggeri's acting, noting how brilliantly he was able to play the many shifts of mood and emphasis that the role demands. Later, Lamberto Picasso became the second great Italian interpreter of a role that has been revived by a range of international actors, including Rex Harrison (1974) and Richard Harris (1990). Although written in the early years of his playwriting career, *Henry IV* may be considered as Pirandello's equivalent to *King Lear*, and there are times when the play comes second to none in its tragic intensity and power to move an audience.

—Susan Bassnett

HENRY IV
Henry IV, Part One
Henry IV, Part Two
by William Shakespeare

Henry IV, Part One

First Publication: London, 1598.
First Production: London, c.1596–98; earliest recorded production, by the Lord Chamberlain's Men, March 1600.

Editions

Henry IV, Part One, edited by S.B. Hemingway, Philadelphia, 1936 (New Variorum Edition).
King Henry IV, Part One, edited by A.R. Humphreys, London, 1960 (Arden Shakespeare).
Henry IV, Part One, edited by Maynard Mack, New York, 1965; second edition, 1987 (Signet Classic Shakespeare).
Henry IV, Part One, edited by P.H. Davison, Harmondsworth, 1968 (New Penguin Shakespeare).
Henry IV, Part One, edited by David Bevington, Oxford, 1987 (Oxford Shakespeare).

Henry IV, Part Two

First Publication: London, 1600.
First Production: London, c.1597–98; earliest recorded production, at Court, 1612.

Editions

Henry IV, Part Two, edited by Matthias Shaaber, Philadelphia, 1940 (New Variorum Edition).
Henry IV, Part Two, edited by Norman L. Holland, New York, 1965; second edition, 1988 (Signet Classic Shakespeare).
Henry IV, Part Two, edited by A.R. Humphreys, London, 1966 (Arden Shakespeare).
Henry IV, Part Two, edited by P.H. Davison, Harmondsworth, 1977 (New Penguin Shakespeare).
The Second Part of "King Henry IV", edited by Giorgio Melchiori, Cambridge, 1989 (New Cambridge Shakespeare).

Bibliographies

Michael Kiernan (ed.), *"Henry the Fourth, Part One": A Bibliography to Supplement the New Variorum Edition of 1936 and the Supplement of 1956*, New York, 1977.
M.A. Shaaber (ed.), *"Henry the Fourth, Part Two": A Bibliography to Supplement the New Variorum Edition of 1940*, New York, 1977.

Criticism

(For general works on the author, see *Playwrights* volume)

Books:
Harold Jenkins, *The Structural Problem in Shakespeare's "Henry IV"*, London, 1956.
David P. Young (ed.), *Twentieth Century Interpretations of "Henry IV, Part Two"*, Englewood Cliffs, New Jersey, 1968.
George. K. Hunter (ed.), *"Henry IV, Parts One and Two": A Casebook*, London, 1970.
Keiji Aoki, *Shakespeare's "Henry IV" and "Henry V": Hal's Heroic Character and the Sun-Cloud Theme*, Kyoto, 1973.

T.F. Wharton, *Henry the Fourth, Parts One and Two*, London, 1983 (Text and Performance Series).
Laurie Lanzen Harris and Mark W. Scott, *"Henry IV, Parts One and Two"*, in *Shakespearian Criticism, 1*, Detroit, 1984.
David Bevington (ed.), *"Henry the Fourth", Parts One and Two: Critical Essays*, New York, 1986.
Harold Bloom (ed.), *William Shakespeare's "Henry IV, Part One"*, New York, New Haven, Connecticut, and Philadelphia, 1987 (Modern Critical Interpretations).

Articles:
For information on the many articles about *Henry IV, Parts One and Two*, see the bibliographies listed above, the bibliographies listed in the *Playwrights* volume, and the annual Shakespeare Bibliography in *Shakespeare Quarterly*, published by the Folger Shakespeare Library, Washington D.C. (1950–).

*   *   *

The outline of the first and second parts of *Henry IV* can be sketched in a single sentence: the conversion of a young man described by his father in *Richard II* as "unthrifty", a "young wanton, and effeminate boy" to a king fit to rule and to become capable of winning a glorious victory at Agincourt against all odds. Another way to describe the plays is as a dramatic study of the nature of authority. In *Part 1* Prince Hal is seen drinking and robbing with Sir John Falstaff and his common associates whilst his father struggles to put down challenges from the Percies of Northumberland, Glendower of Wales, Lord Mortimer, and Earl Douglas of Scotland, to the throne he has usurped. At the Battle of Shrewsbury, at which the rebels are vanquished, Prince Hal puts Douglas to flight and kills the younger Percy, Henry Hotspur. Though he has redeemed himself in his father's eyes, in *Part 2* it is as if he has to repeat the process. However, he is now shown much less closely associated with his low companions of *Part 1* and Falstaff has lost some of his vivacity. After the Battle of Gaultree Forest—a shabby victory (at which the Prince is not present) won by Hal's brother, John of Lancaster—and the death of Henry IV, Falstaff is formally rejected by Hal, now enthroned as Henry V—a fate he had promised Falstaff early in *Part 1*. Hal's mentor is no longer Falstaff but the Lord Chief Justice, with whom, early in the story, Hal and Falstaff had quarrelled; Hal's "education" is thus shown to be completed and he can worthily assume the authority of kingship.

It is reasonable to suppose that when he embarked on *Richard II*, Shakespeare had in mind carrying the story through to Agincourt, especially as he had already dramatised the reigns of Henry VI and Edward IV and the accession of Henry VII. There is much interrelation of material in the tetralogy but, more importantly, the historical sweep is continuous. Further precedent for Hal's conversion and his victory at Agincourt existed in a crude, anonymous play, *The Famous Victories of Henry the Fifth*, which Shakespeare must have known about even if he had not read the manuscript. What is a matter of dispute is whether Shakespeare had in mind a trilogy—*Richard II, Henry IV*, and *Henry V*—or a tetralogy. A trilogy seems more probable, the second part of *Henry IV* then being an immediate outcome of the great success of *Part 1*. The similarity of pattern shared by each part, especially Hal's need to redeem himself twice in his father's eyes (even if that may be explained as the kind of repetition appropriate to myth) hardly points to advance planning. However, if there are outward similarities, Shakespeare makes the two parts distinct in tone. The cliché that the two

Henry IV, Part Two: Barbican Theatre, London, 1982 (Royal Shakespeare Company)

parts are as the two sides of the same coin has a certain validity, but *Part 2* is, in fact, much more than the obverse of *Part 1*. The second part has never been as successful as the first. Whereas *Part 1* was published in a number of editions before its inclusion in the First Folio of 1623, *Part 2* appeared only in 1600 and it is still, today, less of a theatrical draw than *Part 1*, chiefly because a much less sympathetic Falstaff is not quite compensated for by the delightful justices, Shallow and Swallow. Yet in some ways, *Part 2* is a more interesting, even more satisfying, drama, denser in texture and showing greater insight into its characters.

Prince Hal is enigmatic. His engaging waywardness in *Part 1*, his youthful follies, his need for a father figure in Falstaff in place of his own cold and suspect father—whose act of usurpation and disposal of Richard are never allowed to drop out of mind, being recalled even on the eve of Agincourt in *Henry V*—are all appealing (and fruitful material for psycho-analytic study). There is pleasure in his achievement at Shrewsbury in *Part 1* (largely unhistorical—he was wounded but did not kill Hotspur), but in *Part 2*, much concern (largely misplaced) at his rejection of Falstaff. Whereas Shakespeare distances Hal from his father, and also from his equally cold and calculating brother, John of Lancaster, he does make a particular point of hinting that Hal comes from the same stock. Early in *Part 1* Hal, when he sets about planning his conversion, is shown to be as calculating as was his father in his protestation of allegiance to Richard II:

So when this loose behaviour I throw off,
. . . like bright metal on a sullen ground,

My reformation, glittering o'er my fault,
Shall show more goodly, and attract more eyes
Than that which hath no foil to set it off.
I'll so offend, to make offence a skill,
Redeeming time when men think least I will.

This speech has been taken as a sort of "chorus-speech" to be understood out of character, designed to explain to the audience that the irresponsible Hal will in time become the hero they know. As, however, the "myth of Hal's conversion" was well known, the audience hardly needed warning by such a sophisticated device. It is better to take the speech in character: that this *is* cold calculation and appropriate to Hal's callow youth, but that the influence of those with whom he associates will play a part in developing a warmer-hearted Hal—the hero of Agincourt. It is noticeable that Shakespeare characterises Hal as devoid of the kind of natural wit that is so abundant in Falstaff. The opening of *Part 1*, Act II, Scene 4 shows Hal teasing the young potboy, Francis. It is a curiously ineffective game, so much so that at its end, Poins asks Hal, "Come, what's the issue?". It is also significant that whereas Hotspur is shown with one of Shakespeare's most attractive female characters, his wife Kate, Hal is never thus shown until, at the end of *Henry V*, he woos Katherine, daughter of the French king, in a scene that at its conclusion borders on rape. The relationship of Hal to Hotspur and to Falstaff is a key to understanding what is at issue in *Part 1*.

In a morality play such as *Everyman*, the principal character is given advice by Good and Evil Angels, and Everyman begins by following evil ways but eventually takes the Good Angel's advice. Shakespeare takes this further: in *Part 1* Hal is positioned in between Hotspur (whom his father would rather have as his son) and Falstaff, who acts as a father-figure to him and, in the play-within-the play at the end of Act II, scene 4, takes on the role of father *and* king. Hotspur espouses an outmoded concept of honour, whereas Falstaff dismisses honour in his last speech in Act V, Scene 1. It is just too easy in a modern production to respond to a sympathetic Falstaff's attitude uncritically. Hal must follow neither the outmoded Hotspur nor the nihilistic Falstaff. Falstaff's rejection, prefigured in Hal's last line of the play-within-the-play (when he speaks "as King"), is enacted in *Part 1* when he also rejects Falstaff's attitude to honour (hence his unease in Falstaff's company in *Part 2*). What Hal must do is find his own concept of "honour" and if we call that honour "integrity" we shall, in the late 20th century, possibly find this more comfortable. Hal must learn to exercise authority with integrity. In *Part 1*, this is the path Hal successfully finds for himself, on the way losing nothing in his admiration for Hotspur's shining example and learning something of the warmth of humanity from Falstaff and his cronies. The first part of the Prince's "education" is thus completed.

In *Part 2*, Hal is seen much less with Falstaff; he is kept apart from the trickery of his brother at Gaultree; his relations with his father remain cold and, when he places the crown on his head before his father is dead, he can well be rebuked that he hides a thousand daggers in his thoughts. Whereas in *Part 1* Hal is shown successful in battle, in *Part 2* he (and Shakespeare) face a more difficult task: the rejection of Falstaff and what he stands for. Shakespeare made things more difficult by creating Falstaff as such an attractive character. But he is not just an engaging buffoon. In the play-within-the-play of *Part 1* Hal (again acting the role of King) accurately describes him as "that reverend Vice, that grey Iniquity, that Father Ruffian [Devil], that Vanity in years". These are all "characters" that in a morality drama would have to be whipped from the stage. Too much sentiment is often wasted on Falstaff. Put another way: with Richard II in mind (the young wanton, and effeminate boy), would the throne be better entrusted to a Hal with Falstaff or to a Hal with the Lord Chief Justice (who has had the courage—the integrity—not to be intimidated by Prince Hal)? Certainly there was no doubt in the 16th Century. As Tyndale, the translator of the Bible put it in 1536, "It is better to have a tyrant unto a king than a shadow. . . a king that is soft as silk and effeminate. . . shall be much more grievous unto the realm than a right tyrant". Sad it is, but Falstaff must be rejected so that Hal can rule with integrity and purpose.

—Peter Davison

HENRY V
by William Shakespeare

First Publication: London, 1600 ("bad" first quarto); "authoritative" version in First Folio, 1623.
First Production: London, c. 1598–99; earliest recorded production, at Court, January 1605.

Editions
Henry V, edited by John Dover Wilson, Cambridge, 1947 (The New Shakespeare).
King Henry V, edited by John H. Walter, London, 1954 (Arden Shakespeare).
Henry V, edited by John Russell Brown, New York, 1965 (Signet Classic Shakespeare).
Henry V, edited by Alfred Harbage, Baltimore, Maryland, 1967 (Pelican Shakespeare).
Henry V, edited by Gary Taylor, Oxford, 1982 (Oxford Shakespeare).

Bibliography
Joseph Candido and Charles R. Forker (eds.), *"Henry V": An Annotated Bibliography*, New York and London, 1983 (Garland Shakespeare Bibliographies).

Criticism
(For general works on the author, see *Playwrights* volume)

Books:
Ronald Berman (ed.), *Twentieth Century Interpretations of "Henry V"*, Englewood Cliffs, New Jersey, 1968.
Michael Quinn (ed.), *"Henry V": A Casebook*, London, 1969.
Keiji Aoki, *Shakespeare's "Henry IV" and "Henry V": Hal's Heroic Character and the Sun-Cloud Theme*, Kyoto, 1973.
Peter Davison, *"Henry V" in the Context of the Popular Dramatic Tradition*, Winchester, Hampshire, 1981.
Mark W. Scott (ed.), *"Henry V"*, in *Shakespearian Criticism*, 5, Detroit, Illinois, 1987 [anthology of criticism].
Harold Bloom (ed.), *William Shakespeare's "Henry V"*, New York, New Haven (Connecticut) and Philadelphia, 1988 (Modern Critical Interpretations).

Articles:
For information on the many articles about *Henry V*, see Candido and Forker's bibliography, the bibliographies listed in the *Playwrights* volume, and the annual Shakespeare Bibliography in *Shakespeare Quarterly*, published by the Folger Shakespeare Library, Washington D.C. (1950–).

*   *   *

The action of *The Life of Henry the Fifth* starts soon after the beginning of Henry's reign, before he has proved himself as king. He is shown raising money, dealing with disrespect and treachery, and leading an army across the English Channel in pursuit of a claim to the throne of France. The city of Harfleur is captured, but soon the small English army is engaged in a forced march in bad weather across enemy territory. The French army is mustered in great strength and gives battle at Agincourt. Henry has the victory and the play ends with a peace treaty and the betrothal of the young English king to Katharine, princess of France.

This outline suggests that *Henry V* was written to glorify leadership and conquest, and Shakespeare has provided a chorus to speak very much in this vein. He calls Henry "the mirror of all Christian kings". In an epilogue he directs attention to a "full course of. . .glory" in which "this star of England" most greatly lived: "Fortune made his sword / By which the world's best garden he achieved / And of it left his son imperial lord". But these sentiments do not apply to the whole play. In the Epilogue, the Chorus continues to speak of Henry's death which left his successor a mere child who lived to see the loss of France and the consequent suffering of his realm; and all this is implicit in the five acts that have gone before—victory is not shown to be complete.

Henry V: Richard Burton, Stratford-Upon-Avon, 1951

The play has rousing calls to battle: "Once more into the breach, dear friends, once more" and "He that outlives this day, and comes safe home, / Will stand a-tiptoe when this day is named, / And rouse him at the name of Crispian". But in searing self-examination and prayer before battle, Henry likens himself to a "wretched slave" and reveals deep-seated fears; he knows that "all that I can do is nothing worth" to appease his guilt for succeeding to the English throne as a consequence of his father's murder of Richard II. The foreign war had been undertaken on his father's advice as a means of deflecting attention from his own uncertain authority at home.

The play can be produced as a pageant of the famous victories of the plucky English against the effete and over-confident French—and a version of this interpretation is seen in the film in which Laurence Olivier starred during World War II, when the British were again at odds with parts of Europe. But Shakespeare has provided many occasions to show the cruelty and suffering which war entailed, and when these are accentuated in production the impact changes and *Henry V* becomes an anti-heroic and anti-war drama—this was the emphasis of Kenneth Branagh's film version of 1989.

Pistol, Bardolph and Nym, Henry's companions from the two Henry IV plays (written immediately before *Henry V*), are shown to be cowards in battle; Bardolph is subsequently hanged for stealing, and Pistol decides to return to London to boast of wounds he never suffered and earn a livelihood as "bawd" and "cutpurse". Moreover the English army is seen to open the "vasty jaws" of hungry war and its commanders in the field quarrel among themselves about how to wage war and about their own importance. Henry threatens Harfleur with "heady murder, spoil and villany", and at the glorious battle of Agincourt, quite against the rules of war, he orders the throats of his prisoners to be cut: "And not a man of them that we shall take / Shall taste our mercy". A strain of anger and domineering insensitivity runs strongly in Henry and can be accentuated in performance. It is mastered only by the "witchcraft" of Kate, princess of France, whom he woos either at cunning length or with shamefaced clumsiness.

Henry V is a political play in that it can make an audience acutely aware of the consequences of power, leadership and conflict. But it is also moral and affecting in that it brings a careful focus to bear on the strength and difficulties of trust between men and women. The scene in which Henry woos Kate and that in which Kate tries (or pretends to try) to polish up her English in preparation for this assault, are gentle and mocking examples of this—Kate's dialogue is too lively and fresh to play her as a mere pawn in a political wrangle between her superiors. More broadly humorous, and yet strongly motivated, is the quarrel between Fluellen, a Welsh Captain, and Williams, an English soldier, the result of misunderstandings which Henry himself has instigated; this strand of the play's action leads to all three acknowledging each other's worth.

Earlier in the play, while its action is still located in England, Mrs. Quickly, Hostess of a London tavern and another character from the Henry IV plays, tells how Falstaff will "yield the crow a pudding one of these days; the King has killed his heart"; and soon she returns, the play still on the brink of its main action, and tells of the old knight's death, fumbling with sheets, crying out for sack, and "in some sort, indeed", speaking of women and the Whore of Babylon. This still moment is funny and even grotesque, but also sensitive and affecting; it makes an inescapable mark, as military and political matters gather momentum, and causes an audience to reflect that Henry has renounced the friends of his youth and to question whether the only judgement on political life is "it must be as it may".

Henry V centres on its titular hero, but a large cast of varied characters, French and English, privileged and under-privileged, is deployed so that the story of his progress is counterpointed by other lives and issues. Viewing the play as a whole, an audience must count the costs of conquest and question the strength of every "heart".

—John Russell Brown

HENRY VI
   Henry VI, Part One
   Henry VI, Part Two
   Henry VI, Part Three
by William Shakespeare

Henry VI, Part One
First Publication: In the First Folio, London, 1623.
First Production: London, c.1589–91; earliest recorded production, Rose Theatre (King's Men), March 1592.

Editions
The First Part of King Henry VI, edited by John Dover Wilson, Cambridge, 1952 (New Shakespeare).
The First Part of King Henry VI, edited by Andrew S. Cairncross, London, 1962 (Arden Shakespeare).
The First Part of King Henry the Sixth, edited by David Bevington, Baltimore, Maryland, 1966 (Pelican Shakespeare).
Henry VI, Part One, edited by L.V. Ryan, New York, 1967 (Signet Classic Shakespeare).
Henry VI, Part One, edited by Norman Sanders, Harmondsworth, 1981 (New Penguin Shakespeare).
Henry VI, Part One, edited by Michael Hattaway, Cambridge, 1990 (New Cambridge Shakespeare).

Henry VI, Part Two
First Publication: As *The First Part of the Contention Betwixt the Two Famous Houses of Yorke and Lancaster*, London, 1594 ("bad" first quarto); "authoritative" version in the First Folio, 1623.
First Production: London, probably c.1590–92.

Editions
The Second Part of King Henry VI, edited by John Dover Wilson, Cambridge, 1952 (New Shakespeare).
The Second Part of King Henry VI, edited by Andrew S. Cairncross, London, 1957 (Arden Shakespeare).
Henry VI, Part Two, edited by Arthur Freeman, New York, 1967 (Signet Classic Shakespeare).
The Second and Third Parts of King Henry VI, edited by Robert K. Turner and George W. Williams, Baltimore, Maryland, 1967 (Pelican Shakespeare).
Henry VI, Part Two, edited by Norman Sanders, Harmondsworth, 1981 (New Penguin Shakespeare).

Henry VI, Part Three
First Publication: London, 1595 ("bad" first quarto); Combined with *Part Two* as *The Whole Contention Betweene Two Famous Houses, Lancaster and Yorke*, 1619; "authoritative" version in First Folio, London, 1623.
First Production: London, before 1592 (probably c. 1590–91).

Editions
The Third Part of King Henry VI, edited by John Dover Wilson, Cambridge, 1952 (New Shakespeare).
The Third Part of King Henry VI, edited by Andrew S. Cairncross, London, 1964 (Arden Shakespeare).
The Second and Third Parts of King Henry VI, edited by Robert K, Turner and George W. Williams, Baltimore, Maryland, 1967 (Pelican Shakespeare).
Henry VI, Part Three, edited by Milton Crane, New York, 1968 (Signet Classic Shakespeare).
Henry VI, Part Three, edited by Norman Sanders, Harmondsworth, 1981 (New Penguin Shakespeare).

Bibliography
Judith Hinchcliffe (ed.), *"King Henry VI, Parts One, Two, and Three": An Annotated Bibliography*, New York and London, 1984 (Garland Shakespeare Bibliographies).

Criticism
(For general works on the author, see *Playwrights* volume)

Books:
David Riggs, *Shakespeare's Heroical Histories: "Henry VI" and Its Literary Tradition*, Cambridge, Massachusetts, 1971.
Peter Kleine, *Zur Figurencharakteristik in Shakespeares "Henry VI": Ein Vergleich mit den Quellen unter Berücksichtigung der Textüberlieferung und der Konzeption moderner Historik*, Munich, 1980.
Regina Dombrowa, *Strukturen in Shakespeares "King Henry the Sixth"*, Amsterdam, 1985.
Laurie Lanzen Harris and Mark W. Scott (eds.), *"Henry VI, Parts One, Two, and Three"*, in *Shakespearian Criticism, 3*, Detroit, Illinois, 1986 [anthology of criticism].

Articles:
For information about articles on *Henry IV, Parts One, Two, and Three*, see Hinchcliffe's bibliography, the bibliographies listed in the *Playwrights* volume, and the annual Shakespeare Bibliography in *Shakespeare Quarterly*, published by the Folger Shakespeare Library, Washington D.C. (1950–).

*   *   *

Part One: At Henry V's funeral, the English nobility squabbles while territory he won in France is lost. The French forces are repulsed by Salisbury outside Orleans but the Dauphin is inspired by Joan le Pucelle to return to the attack and raise the siege. Gloucester's and Winchester's men brawl outside the Tower of London even as Salisbury is killed and Orleans lost. The national hero, Talbot, swiftly recaptures the city, routs the enemy, and resists the machinations of a French countess. The nation, however, cannot resist factionalism: the white rose of York against the red rose of Lancaster, the Lord Protector and the State versus Winchester and Rome. The young Henry VI attempts to reconcile these factions. After Rouen is "lost and recovered in a day" by Talbot, Joan persuades Burgundy to forsake the English. Henry is crowned in Paris and sends Talbot to chastise the deserter. The dissension between York and Somerset leaves Talbot without aid at Bordeaux, and he and his son die fighting valiantly against the odds. The victorious French are only defeated when the English army at last unites in battle. In the action, York overcomes Joan and condemns her to the stake, while Suffolk (a Lancastrian) captures Margaret of Anjou and, enchanted by her beauty, woos her in Henry's name.

In *Part Two*, Henry marries Margaret on terms arranged by Suffolk. The giving of hard-won territories in France to her father angers Gloucester. Others share his anger, but for factional gain conspire to discredit Gloucester. His wife is accused of witchcraft. York convinces Warwick and Salisbury of his right to the throne then leaves to serve Henry in Ireland, having encouraged Jack Cade to lead an insurrection while he is out of the country. Gloucester's wife is punished and banished. He is then arrested for high treason and, against Henry's better judgement, is imprisoned. Winchester and Suffolk have Gloucester murdered, but popular reaction to the crime is so strong that Suffolk is banished. He bids farewell to Queen Margaret who pledges him her heart. Winchester dies, maddened by guilt, and Suffolk is killed by pirates on the Kent coast. Cade incites a popular uprising which is successful until Clifford persuades the mob to turn against their leader. Cade flees, to be discovered and killed by a Kentish gentleman in his English garden. York returns from Ireland and marches on London. Henry attempts to appease him, but the long-standing antagonism between the houses of York and Lancaster erupts in the battle of St Albans. York, aided by his sons and by Salisbury and Warwick, is victorious and rushes to reach London and Parliament before the King.

Part Three: York has control in Parliament when Henry arrives. The King attempts to secure peace by yielding succession to York's sons in return for York's loyalty during his lifetime. He appoints York as Protector and Warwick as Chancellor. Margaret is enraged by Henry disinheriting their son and raises an army to attack York's faction near Wakefield. Clifford murders the defenceless boy Rutland, York's youngest son. York, himself, is captured and taunted by Margaret with a mock-coronation on a mole-hill and then killed. Warwick joins forces with York's other sons and defeats the Lancastrians in a battle where father kills son and son father while the King of England sits helpless on a mole-hill. With victory for the house of York, Edward is proclaimed King and his younger brothers, Richard and George, are made Dukes of Gloucester and Clarence. Warwick is entrusted to arrange a marriage between Edward and the King of France's daughter. Henry, having fled to Scotland, returns to England in disguise and is captured by royal gamekeepers, loyal now to the new King, while Edward falls in love with a widow, Elizabeth Grey, and woos. Margaret, with her son, seeks the protection and help of the King of France, just as Warwick appears to negotiate the royal marriage. In the midst of the tense politics that ensue, a messenger arrives with the news that Edward has married Lady Grey. Warwick joins forces with Margaret and the King of France, and finds a temporary ally in the Duke of Clarence. Edward is overthrown and Henry restored to the throne; but Richard engineers his brother's release and annihilates Warwick. The three sons of York then defeat Margaret and kill her son before her eyes. Richard murders Henry VI in the Tower. So Edward and Lady Grey as King and Queen, with their new-born son, rejoice that all opposition to the House of York has been destroyed, while Richard—with menacing asides—indicates his own ambition to wear the crown.

These plays are the product of a robust popular theatre. What can appear a mishmash of styles is on stage—as a number of fine productions during the last thirty years have shown—a deliberate and purposeful diversity. Abrupt contrasts create an immediacy which invigorates the formal groupings, symmetrical images and parallel actions stressing that the montage of moments from the past, as an interrogation of structures of power, is as much about now as then. The episodic form of these early histories is not shaped by any sense of resolution. At the end of each part, the play of power progresses unabated. It is in the repetitions and juxtapositions that both questions and answers are formulated. Paired scenes use some similarity to emphasize difference: antithetical scenes use difference to point to complicities.

Throughout the trilogy, the stress on disorder raises issues of order. What constitutes good government, social stability and justice? How important are community ties and responsibilities? The shifting patterns and energies of the stagecraft define the scope of an audience's questions and, although the plays deal with a continuous story and articulate common concerns, this scope is different in each of them. The opening scene of each part prefigures the particular manner in which social disintegration is to be explored and our sense of community is to be addressed. In *Part One*, Henry V's corpse fathers a line of corpses on stage (Salisbury, Mortimer, Bedford) marking the passing of a felt ideal of unity and action which terminates in the death of Talbot and his son. Even as chivalry and solidarity are mourned and mythologized around the late king's coffin, dissension and inaction is seen to accumulate loss and betrayal. The funeral is interrupted, as are subsequent state occasions, and the appeal to patriotism throughout is as curtailed and incomplete as these ceremonies. In *Part Two*, the royal marriage is the first of many an alliance contracted in the play with little care for anything but personal gain. It is, like its progeny, a partnership that carries no conviction (as Suffolk's terms make clear), an association that commands no sense of allegiance. When the three closest to the contract exit, new coalitions are sought and, as numbers on the stage progressively dwindle, a series of associations are defined only to be derided by those left on stage. By the end of the scene, York is left alone to demonstrate how alliance is an expedient mask for an individual ambitious for power. This devaluation of alliance affects all levels of society as Cade ruefully observes later in the play: "Was ever feather so lightly blown to and fro as this multitude?". In *Part Three*, Henry's abdication in parliament of hereditary obligations is immediately explored in terms of the family unit, stressing the destruction and rejection of familial ties and values. It is a context invoked throughout the play as father kills son, son kills father, and "sweet Ned" is slaughtered before his mother's eyes. The grim atmosphere of the celebrations in the final scene is not solely dependent on Richard of Gloucester's machiavellian asides. It springs from the references that cluster around the "happy family unit" of Edward, Lady Grey, and their baby prince, "Young Ned".

The plays are among Shakespeare's earliest work. His authorship has been questioned, and a variety of hands have been detected. It is possible that there may have been collaboration or reworking of earlier material in places but, in recent years, there has been a growing conviction among critics that there is a unity of conception and execution for which Shakespeare is responsible. This unity not only embraces this trilogy; it includes *Richard III*, a play in which many of the themes are seen to culminate and which is clearly anticipated in the remarkable development of Richard's character from *Part Three*, Act III, Scene 2 onwards. Although much of their early stage history must remain conjectural, all three plays were written by 1592. They were immensely popular, and an understanding of their stagecraft gives us an insight into those vital formative years for the English stage from the days of the Armada to Alleyn's outstanding season at the Rose in 1591/2.

—Leslie du S. Read

HENRY VIII,
by William Shakespeare (possibly with John Fletcher)

First Publication: In the First Folio, London, 1623.
First Production: London, 1612; earliest recorded production, 29 June, 1613.

Editions
Henry VIII, edited by R.A. Foakes, London, 1957 (Arden Shakespeare).
Henry VIII, edited by J.C. Maxwell, Cambridge, 1962 (The New Shakespeare).
Henry VIII, edited by F.D. Hoeniger, Baltimore, Maryland, 1966 (Pelican Shakespeare).
Henry VIII, edited by A.R. Humphreys, Harmondsworth, 1971 (New Penguin Shakespeare).
King Henry VIII, edited by J. Margeson, Cambridge, 1990 (New Cambridge Shakespeare).

Bibliography
Linda McJ. Micheli, *"Henry VIII": An Annotated Bibliography*, New York and London, 1988 (Garland Shakespeare Bibliographies).

Criticism
(For general works on the author, see *Playwrights* volume)

Books:
Cumberland Clark, *A Study of Shakespeare's "Henry VIII"*, London, 1931.
A.C. Partridge, *The Problem of "Henry VII" Reopened*, Cambridge, 1949.
Laurie Lanzen Harris and Mark W. Scott (eds.), *"Henry VIII"*, in *Shakespearian Criticism, 2*, Detroit, Illinois, 1985 [anthology of criticism].
Francis A. Shirley (ed.), *"King John" and "King Henry VIII": Critical Essays*, New York and London, 1988.

Articles:
For information on articles about *Henry VIII*, see Micheli's bibliography, the bibliographies listed in the *Playwrights* volume, and the annual Shakespeare Bibliography in *Shakespeare Quarterly*, published by the Folger Shakespeare Library, Washington D.C. (1950–).

Since it appears in the Folio of 1623, and can be assigned with confidence to 1613, *Henry VIII* is, officially, Shakespeare's last play. It's a surprise ending—Shakespeare abandoning the mythic and magical forms of what are usually called the "last plays" and returning to a genre he hadn't touched since 1599. And since 1850 it has been persistently argued, on internal evidence, that the play is not solely his, but was a collaboration with John Fletcher. The authorship debate is lengthy and still unresolved; on the whole, as usual with Shakespeare, the critics who admire the play tend to argue for him as sole author, while those who are unhappy with its lack of unity and consistency resort to the "disintegrationist" theory. On the whole, the effect of the uncertainty has been to safeguard the 19th-century romance of *The Tempest* (1611) as Shakespeare's culminating "farewell to the stage" by defining *Henry VIII* as hack work, as a *pièce d'occasion* (the occasion being Princess Elizabeth's marriage to the Elector Palatine in February 1613), and as the pretext for a lot of spectacular pageantry—which is how it has traditionally been staged.

At first sight, the shape of the play appears to support this verdict. An early spectator described it as "representing some principal pieces of the reign of Henry 8", and "pieces" there are: the trial of the Duke of Buckingham, the king's divorce from Katharine of Aragon and his marriage to Anne Boleyn, the fall of Wolsey, the Catholic hierarchy's unsuccessful attempt to impeach Cranmer, and the birth of the future Queen Elizabeth. The diversity of events is reflected in the stylistic heterogeneity which prompted the theories of collaboration: besides the political narrative and citizen comment recognisable from Elizabethan chronicle drama, there are elements of satire, tragedy, romantic comedy, masque and antimasque. If the play *is* by Shakespeare, it's a strange anthology of his earlier modes of writing. And there are at least four major spectacles of state: a masque at Wolsey's palace, the formal hearing of the divorce case, the coronation of Anne, and the christening of Elizabeth. The stage directions for some of these are among the most elaborate in Shakespeare; it is clear on both internal and external evidence that the play's first production was notable for its lavish costumes and attention to ceremonial detail.

However, if the play is a miscellany, this is clearly not because it is inertly following the linear sequence of a chronicle. In fact it treats its sources with at least as free a hand as Shakespeare did in the tetralogies. Take for example Anne's coronation in Act IV, scene 1: crowned, with pearls in her hair, she passes over the stage in the midst of a procession of lords and ladies in gold coronets. Then, Act IV, scene 2 shows the last illness of Katharine, the queen she has supplanted. Katharine sleeps briefly, and sees a vision of "six personages, clad in white robes, wearing on their heads garlands of bays, and golden vizards on their faces", who dance ceremoniously about her, and repeatedly hold an extra garland over her head. The realistically presented coronation is followed by a dream crowning which echoes and attenuates its imagery: excluded from the royal celebrations, Katharine is invited to a feast in Heaven. Interestingly, her vision also recalls medieval presentations of the Assumption of the Blessed Virgin; in what is, historically, the moment of the English Reformation, the Catholic queen becomes, as it were, a defeated saint. In the same scene, she hears how her old enemy, Wolsey, also destroyed by the events surrounding the rise of Anne, has died repentant at Leicester Abbey. Thus the whole structure of Act IV, while taking the spectacle of state as its central event, elegiacally orchestrates it with the death of Catholic England—by the spiritual peace of their departure, Katharine and Wolsey, the two great obstacles to Protestant monarchy, are made to confer a paradoxical blessing on what would otherwise be the vapid triumphalism of the coronation. The point about the dramaturgy here is that the orchestration is deliberate. In reality, Wolsey died in 1530, Anne was crowned in 1533, and Katharine died in 1536: the stage simultaneity of the three events is powerfully symbolic and, in its dissolution of conflict, ideologically adroit. The attendant juxtaposition of divergent dramatic levels is the sign, not of an opportunistic cobbling together, but of a thoroughly intentional unity.

The Prologue speaks as if the fall of greatness were the main theme, and much of the play's dynamism comes from the paired tragedies of Katharine and Wolsey. But it's a contained dynamism. Wolsey's fall, in particular, occupies one scene, travelling from arrogant prosperity through anxiety, struggle, defiance and despair to a strange, achieved patience, in a single, masterful set piece. This really does seem like "late" writing, relaxed and powerful within the successive familiar *topoi*. However, the structure which contains these all but casual tragedies is not tragic, but historical and providential. In one sense, everything is plotted around the birth of Elizabeth, which is the occasion of a radiant prophecy of the splendours of her reign. Anne, her mother, meets the king in Act I, is made a Marchioness in Act II, marries him in Act III, is crowned in Act IV, and gives birth in Act V; in romance fashion, all the attendant "falls" and compromises are healed by their having helped to prepare for the arrival of the redemptive child. But it isn't at all a play about Anne, who after the second act is entirely silent, and seen only at her coronation. Her rise is a disappearance into the personality of the king; the teleology is brutal in this respect; she is strategic only as the instrument for the production of his heir. The play's story is, after all, that of its eponymous hero.

What Katharine's replacement by Anne means for the play of forces on the stage is that a strong wife, with a latently heroic degree of autonomy, gives way to one who is wholly the king's creation. The move from Wolsey to Cranmer has exactly the same logic: Wolsey is the model of an over-mighty subject, both because of his personal ascendancy and because of his independent power-base in a supra-national church, whereas Cranmer is Henry's own archbishop, Protestant, loyal, meek, and entirely dependent on royal support for his survival. In the play's most delicately written scene, Henry, guilty, experienced, and shrewd, meets Cranmer at one in the morning on the eve of a crucial council meeting and, with a dictator's capricious irony, explains to him how he must defend himself against his enemies if he is to avoid the fate of his heavenly master. Cranmer is overcome with gratitude; Henry is at once touched, amused, and exasperated by his saintly protegé's political cluelessness. Deftly and almost naturalistically, the scene sketches the way that each of them, the tyrant and the martyr, needs the other to produce the happy ending.

Thus the play could be summarised as chronicling the king's emergence from a compromised Catholic polity into a Protestant position of absolute sovereignty, a transition which it endorses without idealising. At the end of the subsequent council meeting, having whipped his dissident magnates into line, Henry says: "As I have made ye one lords, one remain:/So I grow stronger, you more honour gain". That slightly dubious combination of national-unity idealism and autocratic threat seems to be more or less where the play levels out. The figure of reconciliation is taken up from the "last plays" and restored to English royal history; it survives in its new and unfriendly context, but not unscathed.

—Peter Womack

HENRY THE EIGHTH. See **HENRY VIII.**

HENRY THE FIFTH. See **HENRY V.**

HENRY THE FOURTH, I-II. See **HENRY IV.**

HENRY THE SIXTH, I-III. See **HENRY VI.**

HEPTI EPI THEBAS. See **SEVEN AGAINST THEBES.**

HERNANI
by Victor Hugo

First Publication: Paris, 1830.
First Production: Comédie Française, Paris, 25 February 1830.

Editions
Hernani, edited by C. Kemshead, Oxford, 1906.
Hernani, edited by G. Sablayrolles, Paris, 1971.
Hernani, in *Théâtre, 1*, edited by Raymond Pouilliart, Paris, 1979.

Translations
Hernani, translated by R.F. Sharp, London, 1898.
Hernani, in *French Romantic Plays*, edited by W.W. Comfort, New York, c.1933.
Hernani, in *Chief French Plays of the Nineteenth Century*, edited by E.M. Grant, New York, 1934.
Hernani, translated by Linda Asher, in *The Genius of The French Theater*, edited by A. Bermel, New York, 1961.
Hernani, translated by H.F. Collins, New York, 1968.

Criticism
(For general works on the author, see *Playwrights* volume)

Books:
Reinhold Frick, *Hernani als litterarischer Typus*, Plieningen, 1903.
G. Lote, *En Préface à "Hernani"*, Paris, 1930.
Keith Wren, *Hugo: "Hernani" and "Ruy Blas"*, London, 1982.

Articles:
Jacques Duval, "Un *Cinna* romantique: *Hernani*", in *La Revue Latine*, 3, 1904.
James D. Brunner, "The Characters in Victor Hugo's *Hernani*", in *Sewanee Review*, 13, 1905.
Léon Guillot de Saix, "Le Manuscrit de *Hernani*. 19 août–24 sept. 1829", in *L'Ami du lettre*, Paris, 1929.

John A. Hess, "Goethe's *Egmont* as a Possible Source of Hugo's *Hernani*", in *Modern Philology*, 27, 1929.

René Jasinski, "La Bataille d'*Hernani*", in *La Nouvelle Revue des jeunes*, 10 May 1930.

Maurice Souriau, "La Bataille d'*Hernani*", in *La Vie intellectuelle*, January 1930.

Erwin Schneider, "Victor Hugos *Hernani* in der Kritik eines Jahrhunderts (1830–1930)", in *Romanische Forschungen*, 47, 1933.

Madame Dussane, "Le Centenaire d'*Hernani*", in *La Revue Hebdomadaire*, May 1939.

Michel Achard, "*Hernani*", in *Conferencia*, 54, 1949.

Jean-Jacques Bernard, "La Nouvelle Bataille d'*Hernani*", in *Adam International Review*, 19, 1952.

M.A. Williams, "A Precursor of *Hernani*", in *French Studies*, 13, 1959.

Malcolm D. McLean, "The Historical Accuracy of Hugo's *Hernani*", in *South Central Review*, 22, 1962.

Pierre Halbwachs, "A Propos de la 'Bataille d'*Hernani*' ", in *Romanticisme et politique, 1815–1851*, Paris, 1969.

Leonard Stocker, "Hugo's *Hernani* and Verdi's *Ernani*", in *Southern Quarterly*, 8, 1970.

Henri Maillet, "Structure d'un drame romantique: *Hernani*", in *L'Information littéraire*, 23, 1971.

Scott Stringham, "Giuseppe Verdi and Victor Hugo: Some Notes on the Transformation of *Hernani* into *Ernani*", in *West Virginia University Philological Papers*, 18, 1971.

J.R.B. Clark, "*Hernani* Reconsidered or Don Carlos Vindicatus", in *Modern Languages*, 53, 1972.

Maryse Jeuland-Meynaud, "De l'*Hernani* de Hugo à l'*Ernani* de Giuseppe Verdi", in *Cahiers d'Etudes Romanes*, 3, 1977.

Jean Gaudon, "Sur *Hernani*", in *Cahiers de l'Association Internationale des Etudes Françaises*, 35, 1983.

Fernande Bassan, "La Réception critique d'*Hernani* de Victor Hugo", in *Revue d'histoire du théâtre*, vol.36 no.1, 1984.

Jean Gaudon, "En marge de la bataille d'*Hernani*", in *Europe*, March 1985.

Yves le Hir, "Aspects du vers ternaire dans *Hernani*", in *La Revue des lettres modernes*, 1988.

*   *   *

The heroine, Doña Sol, is loved by three men: her elderly guardian, Ruy Gomez, whom she is due to marry; the King of Spain, Don Carlos; and the bandit leader Hernani, whose love she returns. Hernani is motivated by the desire for vengeance on the King; Carlos by his ambition to become Emperor; all three men by jealousy, at the same time as by their strong sense of honour. In Act I Carlos saves Hernani from detection by Ruy Gomez; in Act II Hernani spares Carlos's life; in Act III Ruy Gomez refuses to hand Hernani over to Carlos, who abducts Doña Sol instead. Hernani accepts that his life is forfeit to Ruy Gomez, but demands a chance to avenge himself on Carlos: he will then lay down his life when Ruy Gomez claims it. Act IV takes us from Spain to Aix-la-Chapelle, where Carlos is proclaimed Emperor. He pardons the conspirators who have been plotting against him (including Hernani and Ruy Gomez), reinstates Hernani in his rank and titles as Duke of Aragon, and bestows Doña Sol on him. Act V opens with the marriage celebrations. But Ruy Gomez appears, reminding Hernani of his promise, and claiming his life. The lovers die together; Ruy Gomez kills himself.

Hernani was the first of Hugo's verse dramas to be performed after the publication of *Cromwell* (1827) and its celebrated *Préface*, which had contained the blueprint for a new form of historical drama, abandoning the rigid construction and the linguistic idiom of neo-classical tragedy in

favour of a freer, more comprehensive, and more colourful style. The production had been well publicised in advance, and was to be the occasion of a sustained confrontation between the conservative supporters of the classical tradition and the enthusiastic young partisans of change (Hugo had replaced the customary paid "claque" with his own hand-picked team of young painters, poets and musicians led by such figures as Théophile Gautier and Gérard de Nerval). This noisy and disruptive "Battle of *Hernani*" lasted through the first few performances; the hostility of many of the actors lasted longer than this, and although finally the play broke box-office records with a run of 39 performances, the "victory"—the conquest of the Théâtre-Français as the citadel of reactionary opposition—proved rather a hollow one. Both dramatists and actors were wary of repeating the experience, and for the most part, the history of French Romantic drama was to be made in other theatres.

The brief summary given above, while it reveals well enough the melodramatic absurdities of the plot, cannot begin to suggest the play's positive qualities. Despite Hugo's protestations, *Hernani* has little value as dramatised history, and the historical setting (16th-century Spain) is merely there to provide colour and atmosphere. The play's subtitle, "Castilian Honour", indicates the theme which underlies the plot, unifying the action; the sub-plot of Carlos's election as Emperor is acceptable as a subsidiary development entirely compatible with this principal theme. Hernani as hero can be seen to illustrate Hugo's approach to character, set out in the *Préface* to "*Cromwell*", as the antithetical juxtaposition of "sublime" and "grotesque". As a bandit and outlaw, governed by an overriding desire for vengeance on the King, Hernani is nevertheless the Romantic lover, capable of the most exalted feelings—though the fact that the two terms of the antithesis are in this case by no means incompatible makes the character a good deal easier to accept than some of Hugo's later protagonists. Hernani, as a Romantic hero, is very much in the Byronic mould, brooding and fatalistic; but above all Hernani and Doña Sol together provide the paradigm of the Romantic pair of lovers, doomed to be defeated by the forces representing the society they live in, with its tyrannies and its injustices, able to consummate their union only in death. Such is Hugo's dramatic and poetic skill that, forgetting the manifest absurdity of the plot at this point, we are able to accept the absolute rightness of the lovers' voluntary death together. The inability of an exceptional love between twin souls, seeking an ideal union, to survive in a less than perfect world was to become the great theme of 19th-century Romantic tragedy and it was *Hernani* which successfully embodied the first notable treatment of the theme.

That it did so is a tribute to the imaginative insight with which this young poet (Hugo was aged 28 at the time of writing *Hernani*) conceived a totally new form of verse drama, and the vision with which the new formula was implemented. "Vision" seems a more fitting term than "skill", for detailed craftsmanship was not Hugo's forte as a playwright; some of his detailed effects (such as the King hiding in a cupboard at the beginning of the play) can be irritatingly inappropriate, and he had a very cavalier attitude to the details of dramaturgical logic (for instance, the whole of Act IV is set in Charlemagne's tomb). There are, it is true, features of his verse dialogue that can be equally irritating: the frequent lapses into banality, and some at least of the extravagant rhymes; but nobody could fault the sureness of touch which determined the placing, and the execution, of the lyrical set pieces: Ruy Gomez's elegiac lament on old age in Act III, Hernani's self-abasement when he has wronged Doña Sol by his jealousy, later in the same act, and above all the lovers' closing duet. In these, and other, cases, it is quite proper to regard the structure of *Hernani* in the same way as that of a 19th-century opera: a dramatic framework for a series of static, lyrical passages on the eternal themes of love, jealousy, old age, ambition, and death. In taking Hugo's *Le Roi s'amuse* (1832) as the basis of his *Rigoletto*, Verdi unquestionably improved on the original; the same cannot be said of his adaptation of *Hernani*, not so much because *Ernani* is a poorer opera, as because Hugo had already succeeded so well in creating a lyrical masterpiece.

—William D. Howarth

HINDLE WAKES
by Stanley Houghton

First Publication: London, 1912.
First Production: Aldwych Theatre, London, 16 June 1912.

*   *   *

In essence this play is a study of two families in the English north country town of Hindle: the Hawthorns, employees in a local cotton mill, and the Jeffcotes, former mill hands who have risen to be mill owners. The action opens in the combined living-room kitchen of the rented home of mill worker Christopher Hawthorn and his family, and the first scene establishes the relationship between the Hawthorns and the Jeffcotes about which all the action turns. The Hawthorn's daughter, Fanny, a girl in her 20's, has been away from home for several days, and Christopher and his wife are anxious as to where she has been. When she returns she says she has been with a friend, Mary, in Blackpool, but this catches her out in a lie, for during the weekend Mary has been drowned. In fact Fanny has spent the weekend not in Blackpool with Mary, but in Llandudno with Alan Jeffcote, the son of the mill owner, Nat Jeffcote. Scandal threatens, and Christopher and his wife are convinced the only honourable solution is for Alan to marry Fanny: when he hears the tale of the weekend in Landudno, Nat Jeffcote reluctantly agrees. Much of the play indeed consists in discussions between the two families of the moral and social implications of the "weekend", and the proper way to proceed if an unacceptable situation is to be saved. Alan, who is engaged to marry Beatrice Farrar, the daughter of another self-made Hindle man, Sir Timothy Farrar, is reluctant to give her up for Fanny; but by the end of Act II, and notwithstanding his mother's conviction that marriage to Fanny would be a misalliance, under pressure from his father, he feels impelled by propriety to do so. Beatrice in turn acknowledges she must renounce Alan to a woman who has a greater claim upon him. No one is happy with this solution apparently required by social convention and notions of respectability, but all accept there is no alternative. All, that is, save Fanny herself. To everyone's astonishment she declines Alan, regarding him as no more than a casual flirtation, a pick-up for the weekend, and she affirms her determination to lead her own life in her own way, to the bewildered satisfaction or regret of the members of the two families.

Hindle Wakes: Aldwych Theatre, London, 1912, (first production)

Hindle Wakes is generally thought to be the most successful of the plays of the so-called Manchester school of dramatists that also included Harold Brighouse and Allan Monkhouse. All three, and several lesser writers too, were largely discovered thanks to the activities of the Repertory Theatre Company, established by Annie Horniman at Manchester's Gaiety Theatre. Under the direction of the Gaiety's then artistic manager, Lewis Casson, *Hindle Wakes* however opened in London and was an instant success, transferring to the Playhouse Theatre, and then to the Court Theatre in Sloane Square. It finally opened in Manchester in November 1912, where it broke all box-office records, subsequently toured widely in England, (and more particularly in the north), and was later staged in New York, Chicago and elsewhere in the United States. So considerable was the London success of the play that it encouraged theatre managements in the capital to hire some of the Gaiety's best actors and actresses, a poaching that in the longer run weakened the Manchester repertory.

Although the subject matter of *Hindle Wakes* seems now quite innocuous, in 1912 it was another matter. Even before the London production the play had been turned down by the Liverpool Repertory Theatre, its subject being thought too daring and controversial. The questions raised became distinctly teasing debates for the times: How independent could a young female afford to be? How far was she tied by conventional notions of respectability? Was a loveless marriage a necessary fate for a woman whose honour was compromised in the eyes of society? What constituted right morality in female conduct? Was it right and proper there should be one standard for men, and another for women? None of these questions were of course new in drama; they had been asked in "Society drama" since the 1890's. What was new was the social level at which they were being asked, and the firmly confident voice in which they were being asked. That Houghton did not simply stumble by accident on an engagingly controversial subject seems clear from references in the dialogue to women's independence, votes for women and the freedom women could enjoy by being economically independent. The play became a talking point, rather as Ibsen's *A Doll's House* had been. It was, for its time, laudibly affirmative of the rights of working class women to determine their own lives, unrestrained by the pressures of narrow and unexamined assumptions.

The play's success is altogether understandable. Not only was its subject timely, but the manner of its execution was impressive: the dialogue was fluent, plausible and idiomatic, the treatment of character sharp and ironic, and the naturalistic depiction of the north country, small-town world alert to local detail. The whole had an authentic ring to it. Of course in important respects it both simplified and sentimentalised its subject, for it does not really confront the reality of the position of early 20th-century working class women in a male world; Fanny's assertion of independence smacks more of fiction than felt life: its implausibility can be seen if we compare it with the predicament of the heroines in the somewhat later novels of Jean Rhys. But the play spoke up with commendable vigour for female freedoms, and at a time when such support was needed. Indeed, *Hindle Wakes* remains a fresh and engaging play, persuasive in its characterisation and in its handling of a milieu that in 1912 had been little seen on the English stage. It was revived in London in 1949 with some success, and has been televised very successfully.

—Kenneth Richards

HIPPOLYTOS.   See HIPPOLYTUS.

HIPPOLYTUS (Hippolytos)
by Euripides

First Production: Athens, 428 B.C.

Editions
Hippolytus, edited by J.P. Mahaffy and J.B. Bury, London, 1881.
The "Hippolytus" of Euripides, edited by W.S. Hadley, London, 1889.
Hippolytus, edited by Gilbert Murray, Oxford, 1902.
Hippolytus, in *Euripides, 4* [with translation], edited by Arthur S. Way, London 1912, (Loeb Classical Library).
Hippolytus, edited by W.S. Barrett, Oxford, 1964.
Hippolytus, edited by John Fergusson, Bristol, 1984.

Translations
Hippolytus, translated by Gilbert Murray, 1900.
Hippolytus, in *Three Greek Tragedies*, translated by David Grene, Chicago, 1942.
Hippolytus, translated by Rex Warner, London, 1949.
Hippolytus, translated by E.P. Coleridge, in *Three Great Greek Plays*, Lymon Bryson, 1960.
Hippolytus, translated by Donald Sutherland, in *Hippolytus in Drama and Myth*, Lincoln, Nebraska, 1960.
Hippolytus, translated by Kenneth Cavandar, San Francisco, 1962.
Hippolytus, translated by Robert Bragg, New York and London, 1974.
Hippolytus, in *Euripides: Three Plays*, translated by Philip Vellacott, Harmondsworth, 1953; second edition, 1974.
Hippolytus: A Companion with Translation, translated by Gilbert and Sarah Lawall, Bristol, 1986.

Criticism
(For general works on the author, see *Playwrights* volume)

Books:
W. Sale, *Existentialism and Euripides: Sickness, Tragedy and Divinity in the "Medea", the "Hippolytus" and the "Bacchae"*, Berwick, Victoria, 1977.

Articles:
I. M. Linforth, "Hippolytus and Humanism", in *Transactions and Proceedings of the American Philological Association* [*TAPA*], 45, 1914.
J.A. Spranger, "The Art of Euripides in *Hippolytus*", in *Classical Review*, 33, 1919.
J.A. Spranger, "The Meaning of the *Hippolytus* of Euripides", in *Classical Quarterly*, 21, 1927.
S. Flygt, "Treatment of Character in Euripides and Seneca: The *Hippolytus*", in *Classical Journal*, 29, 1934.
D. Grene, "The Interpretation of *Hippolytus* of Euripides", in *Classical Philology*, 34, 1939.
H. Herter, "Theseus and Hippolytus", in *Rheinisches Museum für Philologie*, 89, 1940.
W.B. Stanford, "The *Hippolytus* of Euripides", in *Hermathena*, 63, 1944.
B.M.W. Knox, "The *Hippolytus* of Euripides", in *Yale Classical Studies*, 13, 1952.

Richmond Yancey Hathorn, "Rationalism and Irrationalism in Euripides' *Hippolytus*", in *Classical Journal*, 52, 1957.

R.P. Winnington-Ingram, "*Hippolytus*: A Study in Causation", in *Entretiens sur l'antiquité classique*, 6, 1960.

D.J. Conacher, "A Problem in Euripides' *Hippolytus*", in *Transactions and Proceedings of the American Philological Association* [*TAPA*], 92, 1961.

L.G. Crocker, "On Interpreting *Hippolytus*", in *Philologus*, 101, 1961.

Richmond Lattimore, "Phaedra and Hippolytus", in *Arion*, 13, 1962.

Charles Segal, "The Tragedy of the *Hippolytus*: The Waters of the Ocean and the Untouched Meadow", in *Harvard Studies in Classical Philology*, 70, 1965.

C.W. Willink, "Some Problems in *Hippolytus*", in *Classical Quarterly*, 18, 1968.

Bernard D. Frischer, "Concordia Discors and Characterization in Euripides' *Hippolytus*", in *Greek, Roman, and Byzantine Studies*, 11, 1970.

Charles Segal, "Shame and Purity in Euripides' *Hippolytus*", in *Hermes*, 98, 1970.

J. Whitaker, "Hypothesis of Euripides' *Hippolytus*", in *Classical Review* (new series), 21, 1971.

K.J. Reckford, "Phaethon, Hippolytus, and Aphrodite", in *Transactions and Proceedings of the American Philological Association* [*TAPA*], 103, 1972.

Charles Segal, "Curse and Oath in Euripides' *Hippolytus*", in *Ramus*, 1, 1972.

Gisela Berns, "Nomos and Physis. An Interpretation of Euripides' *Hippolytos*", in *Hermes: Zeitschrift für klassische Philologie*, 101, 1973.

G.J. Fitzgerald, "Misconception, Hypocrisy, and the Structure of Euripides' *Hippolytus*", in *Ramus*, 2, 1973.

Evelyne Meron, "De L' *Hippolyte* d'Euripide à la *Phèdre* de Racine: Deux Conceptions du tragique", in *Dix-septième Siècle*, 100, 1973.

D. Edwards, "*Tess of the D'Urbervilles* and *Hippolytus*", in *Midwest Quarterly*, 15, 1974.

R. Padel, "Imagery of the Elsewhere: Two Choral Odes of Euripides", in *Classical Quarterly*, 24, 1974.

A.V. Rankin, "Euripides' *Hippolytus*: A Psychopathological Hero", in *Arethusa*, 7, 1974.

K.J. Reckford, "Phaedra and Pasiphae: The Pull Backward", in *Transactions and Proceedings of the American Philological Association* [*TAPA*], 104, 1974

J. Moline, "Euripides, Socrates and Virtue", in *Hermes*, 103, 1975.

J.J. Smoot, "Hippolytus as Narcissus, An Amplification", in *Arethusa*, 9, 1976.

G.E. Dimock, "Euripides' *Hippolytus*, or Virtue Rewarded", in *Yale Classical Studies*, 25, 1977.

C.A.E. Luschnig, "The Value of Ignorance in the *Hippolytus*", in *American Journal of Philology*, 104, 1983.

Alan H. Sommerstein, "Notes on Euripides' *Hippolytos*", in *Bulletin of the Institute of Classical Studies* (London), 35, 1988.

*   *   *

In a prologue, Aphrodite, goddess of love, voices her resentment of Hippolytus, the son of Theseus (ruler in Troezen) because the youth fails to honour her, devoting himself instead entirely to Artemis, goddess of chastity and hunting. Aphrodite declares her intention to punish Hippolytus by having his stepmother Phaedra fall in love with him, which the goddess will disclose to Theseus and thereby cause him to curse his son. The plot follows this course. Hippolytus is seen expressing contempt for love and refusing to pay respect to Aphrodite. Phaedra, sick with her love, confesses the passion she holds for her stepson to her nurse, who first consoles her and later in a well-meaning but disastrous act, informs Hippolytus. Enraged, he doesn't believe her, and curses all women. Phaedra withdraws to the palace to commit suicide. Theseus now arrives, is informed of Phaedra's death, and, subsequently grieving over her body, finds a note in her hand, written by her, falsely accusing Hippolytus of rape. Confronted, Hippolytus vigorously denies the charge, but is banished by Theseus, who calls upon the god Poseidon to punish him.

After a choral interlude, a messenger arrives to relate how Hippolytus has suffered a grave accident caused by the sea-god. Before the youth can be carried in, Artemis appears, reveals the truth, and condemns Theseus for his rash curse, while placing the ultimate blame upon Aphrodite. Hippolytus is brought in, and is reconciled with Theseus before dying, mourned by the King and chorus.

The play is, except for the *Bacchae*, the only work by Euripides in which a god is represented as an integral motivating force in the action. However, although ostensibly the result of divine action, and framed at beginning and end by the appearance of a goddess, *Hippolytus* also functions as a purely human drama, in which the goddesses may be seen to represent natural forces as well as conflicting aspects of human psychology. It is one of the earliest tragedies to make love its central issue. Indeed, it is partly on the basis of *Hippolytus* that Euripides is frequently credited with laying the foundation for modern, psychological drama. Apart from their symbolic significance, the goddesses also serve important dramatic functions: Aphrodite provides the audience with plot exposition; Artemis is used efficiently to convince Theseus, beyond all doubt, of the truth. Significantly, even she cannot, in the end, rescue Hippolytus from the consequences of having offended Aphrodite (that is to say, of ignoring an essential aspect of life).

The "agent" of Aphrodite's divine revenge is the utterly plausible and mundane figure of the nurse, who gives what she thinks is practical and sensible advice to Phaedra, but disastrously miscalculates Hippolytus' reaction. Similarly, Phaedra's vicious revenge upon Hippolytus can be seen as an act of human, not divine perfidy. Euripides ensnares his spectators in moral ambiguity. They first feel a certain sympathy for Phaedra who struggles against herself, but later must condemn her deceit. Similarly they are likely to be critical of Hippolytus for his smug chastity (which a Greek audience would certainly have viewed as excessive if not perverse), but later are moved by the injustice of the disproportionate punishment he suffers.

Thus the play resists being resolved into any clear-cut moral statement. The audience cannot take comfort in identifying crime and punishment since the ultimate "message" of the play (if it is not simply that gods can be dangerous and capricious) is that human beings are vulnerable to passions that are not subject to rational control and can easily destroy them.

Although the plot and outcome are delineated in the prologue, the play does not devolve into simply a "case history" for the edification of a dispassionate audience. The careful construction and modulation of the work itself compels attention, as Euripides traces and balances the tragic potential of three conflicting personalities brought together: the well-meaning but credulous Theseus, the righteous and self-absorbed Hippolytus, and Phaedra gripped by her unnatural passion. The playwright further works upon his audience, using a number of skilfully employed, dramatic devices. Hippolytus reacts to the nurse's disclosure with Phaedra herself present on stage. Her silent figure, as she hears

Hippolytus's crushing denunciation, is eloquent and affecting. Later, a sense of tension and suspense is engendered by the failure of the chorus (who have been sympathetic to Phaedra's plight, and in their ode "see" her hang herself) to intervene and save her when the nurse calls frantically from within the palace for help. Of course, following convention, the chorus *cannot* act, but in performance the scene is intensified by the spectators' half-imagining that they might. A similar, imaginative intensity is achieved by the messenger's highly charged and moving account of Hippolytus's accident, caught in the reins when his horses are frightened by a bull sent from the sea by Poseidon. When his broken body is brought on and Hippolytus confronts and then forgives Theseus, the audience witness a deeply moving scene of pathos and human suffering. This is underscored and given greater poignance by the moral ambiguity that Euripides has placed before them. His characters are simultaneously victimised by their own psychology and exposed to the callous manipulation of the jealous goddesses.

—Richard C. Beacham

* * *

DER HOFMEISTER. See **THE TUTOR.**

* * *

HOME
by David Storey

First Publication: London, 1970
First Production: Royal Court Theatre, London, 17 June 1970.

Criticism
(For general works on the author, see *Playwrights* volume)

Articles:
Helmut Papajewski, "Unbestimmtheit als struktureller Grundzug von David Storeys *Home*", in *Literatur in Wissenschaft und Unterricht*, 4, 1975.
Carol Rosen, "Symbolic Naturalism in David Storey's *Home*", in *Modern Drama*, 22, 1979.
Steven Joyce, "A Study in Dramatic Dialogue: A Structural Approach to David Storey's *Home*", in *Theatre Annual*, 38, 1983.

* * *

From the inconsequential yet worldly conversations between two middle-aged men, Harry and Jack, and then the earthy and innuendo-laden exchanges between two women, Marjorie and Kathleen, it gradually emerges that all four are in a mental home. Manoeuvring for chairs round the metal garden-table, the men and women meet up and tentatively pair up. Albert, a younger inmate, shows off to the others by lifting up a chair, then the table, with one hand. The women mock him and the men are unimpressed. Harry and Jack repeat, with subtle variations, their opening conversation, but finish the play in tears.

Home forces us, because of its minimal action, to pay great attention to the dialogue. Clichés, isolated by skilful pauses, or emphasised by repetition, acquire a resonance and even a metaphorical force. "Well", "still", "mind", "really" are the small-change of ordinary conversation. As the "home" of the title is gradually shown to be a mental institution, these innocent language-counters become charged with deeper meanings. Questions about health, calmness, mental stability and reality itself are being posed. Harry and Jack, however, until challenged by the women, refuse to move beyond cliché. Well-dressed and, apparently, fit and well, they present themselves as the epitomes of two gentlemen of the world in the early years of retirement. Jack, in particular, recalls a wide range of incidents and acquaintances in his life and provides sage reflections on politics. "The ideals of life, liberty, freedom could never have been the same—democracy—well, if we'd been living on the Continent, for example". Harry is more the appreciative listener and prompter. His cliché is "oh, yes", which remains a simple positive until the end when he switches to "oh, no", then begins weeping. World War II is a focal point for shared experience:

> Harry: Ah, yes. . .Couldn't have got far, in our job, I can tell you, without the Royal Air Force.
> Jack: No. No.
> Harry: Britannia rules the waves. . .and rules the skies, too. I shouldn't wonder.

Families provide opportunities for anecdote and reflection, jobs for display of technical expertise. The whole first act reads like a dramatisation of Flaubert's *Dictionnaire des idées reçues*, and the women demolish these pretensions in Act II. But Storey's point is that, in or out of home, this is how men of a certain age and class speak. Language is a shield, not a probe. Madness should be kept at bay by ritual and convention. The style seems Pinteresque but the ethic derives from Hemingway.

"You all right?" is the cliché of Marjorie and Kathleen, which they ask everyone and which contrasts in its mutuality and wholeness with the staccato conversations of the men. They hate secrets and are realistic about where they are and why they are there. Marjorie and Kathleen are compulsive exhibitionists. In a central exchange between Marjorie and Jack it is the working-class woman's realism that counters the gentleman's fantasy. "Home tomorrow" explains Jack enthusiastically. "Set up here for good" states Marjorie flatly. They have no regrets about incarceration since their real home-lives are unbearable. " 'S not like home" states Marjorie. Kathleen responds, "Thank Gawd". The women are vulgar and body-centered, finding sexual innuendo in everything the two men say on their first encounter and asking quite bluntly "What you in for?". Marjorie stands no nonsense from Arthur, for whom coherent language has been reduced to idiotic gestures of physical strength. She challenges him to a mock-fight and, in a baby-like exchange of "won't" and "will", language signifies no more than primitive power. The women are much more conscious than the men of the imagistic possibilities of speech. Kathleen goes into uncontrollable screeches as, discussing the film *Up the Amazon*, Jack remarks: "The canoe, now, was not unlike my own little boat". But the women's referential range—sex, food, the body—is much more limited and their view of "home" is stripped of any fantasy. Their earthy realism is, in fact, as stereotypical as the men's bufferish sophistication. They are cockney "girls", killing themselves with laughter at men and work. They are as desperate as Jack and Harry and, for all four of them, home is not a place where you can be yourself, but a theatre for games of language.

Storey combines naturalist and absurdist techniques in this play as if trying to test the strengths of the two conventions against each other at a time (1970) when each had produced a significant body of post-war work, and in a theatre, the Royal

Home: Ralph Richardson as Jack and John Gielgud as Harry, Royal Court Theatre, London, 1970 (first production)

Court, which had staged much of the best of such work. The distinguished cast for the first production—Richardson, John Gielgud, Dandy Nichols, and Mona Washbourne—ensured comic timing of vicious hilarity and a projection of the theatricality of it all. Storey has explored at length, in subsequent works of fiction and drama, the revolt of the imagination against the constraints of domesticity. He never dramatised the theme with such wit and concentration as in *Home*.

—Tony Dunn

HOME FRONT (Zimmerschlacht)
by Martin Walser

First Publication: In *Der Abstecher; Die Zimmerschlacht; Übungsstück*, Frankfurt, 1967.
First Production: Kammerspiele, Munich, 7 December 1967.

Translations
Home Front, in *The Contemporary German Theatre*, New York, 1972.

*   *   *

The plot of *Home Front* begins with Felix Fuerst, a geography and history teacher at the local grammar school, hatching his own plot. Felix and Trude, a middle-aged and middle-class married couple, have been invited to a party thrown by their friend Benno who has recently married a stunningly beautiful young woman, aged 24. Felix, jealous of his friend's success, seeks to sabotage the party by organising a boycott together with the other invited guests. Forced by Felix's action to spend the evening at home, the couple's ability to sustain their unity and morale, using only their own resources, gradually collapses. Eventually they decide to go to the party after all, where all the other guests have long since arrived.

Home Front took audiences and critics alike by surprise, for Walser's three previous plays had concerned themselves with contemporary public issues, such as the West German middle-class's moral failure to digest the lessons of its fascist past and to show any real sympathy for its unfortunate victims in *Eine deutsche Chronik* (*The Rabbit Race*); the consumer mentality which the so-called "economic miracle" had engendered in all classes of society *Überlebensgross Herr Krott* (*Larger Than Life Mr. Krott*); and the failure of the younger and older generations to establish an honest dialogue about the recent German past *Der schwarze Schwan* (*The Black Swan*). Walser, in dealing now with the very private issue of marriage, appeared to be turning his back on society and abrogating his social responsibility as a dramatist, a role which German writers of the 1960's seemed predestined to perform.

In fact Walser's portrait of a marriage under strain reveals as much about the wider society in which that particular institution is embedded as it does about the individual, psychological mechanisms which stem from the marital partners' innate make-up. For example, when Felix confesses to his wife the real reason why he does not wish to go along to the party—namely his sense of inadequacy *vis-à-vis* the friend who has ditched his first wife and "acquired" a much younger "model"—he repeatedly refers to her as Benno's "property". The values of the market place have been internalised and are applied to human relationships. Felix's sense of inferiority is further compounded by the fact that his main teaching subject at school, geography, does not carry the status of other more prestigious subjects, which, if pupils fail them, necessitate them repeating the year.

Felix's sagging identity as a successful member of the male species, let alone of bourgeois society, comes under further attack from his frustrated wife Trude whose own perception of men betrays many signs of social conditioning. Thus she compares her husband's lack of hair with Benno's greater success (symbolizing male virility) in this area. She secretly enjoys hearing her husband's tales of implicit, marital infidelity when they are in bed, and is angry with him when he claims during the long evening at home that the stories are invented. She taunts Felix about his cowardice in disposing of a mouse which is loose in the house, and she also encourages him to tell her (fictitious) stories of his bravery as a fighter pilot in the war.

Under the guise of a comedy Walser skilfully reveals the male ego to be a sensitive and vulnerable object. But equally, and this no doubt also explains why *Home Front* soon became the most frequently performed modern German play for several years, he lays bare the psyche of the female partner. Trude is shown, particularly in the area of her sexuality, to be living a life of frustration, unfulfilled fantasies and charades. She finally gives vent to her real feelings and longings in a monologue which is one of the most powerful written by a male writer in the modern German theatre. It is her moment of truth, and of Felix's too, as their marital rituals, verbal games, and mental masquerades dry up and they finally confront one another and themselves as they really are. An almost existential sense of alienation pervades the stage, before business as normal is resumed and the couple retreat back into their role playing, paradoxically a more "natural" and secure reality.

If, in the earlier parables about the shortcomings of his society, Walser's characters and fables are conceived mainly in order to evoke and expose social reality, in *Home Front* this is only partly the case. For now Walser discovers how the reality of the theatre itself can be harnessed to enable characters to express themselves more fully, especially when the dramatic subject is a marriage built upon fictions rather than feelings, driven by routines and habits rather than by needs and desires, and oscillating uneasily between tragedy and farce. It must have been the instinctive feeling for the intrinsic theatricality of the situation which first attracted the interest of the great veteran German director, Fritz Kortner, who had heard it in its original form as a radio play. He directed the premiere at the Munich Kammerspiele, highlighting as one critic put it, the "Chaplinesque qualities" and the "clown's face of a marriage" and thus helped to launch *Home Front* as one of the German theatre's rare examples of entertaining, psychological theatre.

—Anthony Waine

THE HOMECOMING
by Harold Pinter

First Publication: London, 1965; revised edition, 1968.
First Production: Aldwych Theatre (Royal Shakespeare Company), London, 3 June, 1967.

Criticism
(For general works on the author, see *Playwrights* volume)

Books:
Michael Scott (ed.), *The Birthday Party; The Caretaker; The Homecoming: A Casebook*, London, 1986.

Articles:
Bert O. States, "Pinter's *Homecoming*: The Shock of Non-recognition", in *Hudson Review*, 21, 1968.
Herbert Goldstone, "Not So Puzzling Pinter: *The Homecoming*", in *Theatre Annual*, 25, 1969.
John D. Dawick, "'Punctuation' and Patterning in *The Homecoming*", in *Modern Drama*, 14, 1971.
Ricki Morgan, "What Max and Teddy Come Home to in *The Homecoming*", in *Educational Theatre Journal*, 25, 1973.
Vera M. Jiji, "Pinter's Four Dimensional House: *The Homecoming*", in *Modern Drama*, 17, 1974.
Rosette C. Lamont, "Pinter's *The Homecoming*: The Contest of the Gods", in *Far-Western Forum*, 1, 1974.
Alan Roland, "Pinter's *Homecoming*: Images in Dramatic Action", in *Psychoanalytic Review*, 61, 1974.
Richard M. Coe, "Logic, Paradox, and Pinter's *Homecoming*", in *Educational Theatre Journal*, 27, 1975.
Krystyna Napiórkowska, "Language as an Aspect of the Search for Identity in Harold Pinter's *The Homecoming*", in *Studia Anglica Posnaniensia*, 8, 1976.
Penelope Prentice, "Ruth: Pinter's *The Homecoming* Revisited", in *Twentieth Century Literature*, 26, 1980.
Charles A. Carpenter, "'Victims of Duty'? The Critics, Absurdity, and *The Homecoming*", in *Modern Drama*, 25, 1982.
Michael Hinden, "To Verify a Proposition in *The Homecoming*", in *Theatre Journal*, 34, 1982.
Bert Cardullo, "Life in the Foreground: Dramatic Method in *The Homecoming*", in *Ariel*, vol.18 no.3, 1987.
Deborah A. Sarbin, "'I Decided She Was': Representation of Women in *The Homecoming*", in *Pinter Review*, 3, 1989.

* * *

The playwright himself has said that *The Homecoming* is the only one of his plays that comes "near to a structural entity which satisfies me". Yet of Pinter's major plays, this is the one that has provoked the sharpest critical disagreements. It is perhaps not surprising that claim and counter-claim should surround a play that so persistently and disturbingly thwarts the naturalistic expectations that its domestic setting and familial subject habitually raise. The briefest account of the action will serve to suggest the play's potential to generate heated debate.

The setting is "an old house in North London" which is the home of an all-male family. Its patriarch is an irascible retired butcher called Max. With him are his benign brother Sam, who is a chauffeur, and his sons Lenny and Joey—the former apparently a pimp, the latter a demolition man by day and an aspiring boxer by night. A third son, the academic philosopher and teacher Teddy, returns to the house from America after six years' absence, bringing with him his (English) wife Ruth, who

The Homecoming: Watford Palace Theatre, 1969, (Harold Pinter as Lennie, right)

is a stranger to the family. Having, in the first act, been viciously tested by Lenny and abusively received by Max, Ruth is, in the second act, claimed by the men of the house in an explicitly sexual fashion, and, as Teddy prepares to leave again for America, they plan—and negotiate with Ruth herself—to set her up as a prostitute. Uncle Sam protests but drops down dead. Teddy leaves. Ruth stays. The action has spanned just 24 hours.

For its most forceful detractor, Simon Trussler, *The Homecoming* is a "modishly intellectualized melodrama", "a succession of isolated effects", complete with "a yawning probability gap", arrived at by "imposing a formula upon a form". "Pinter's enterprise is sick" and "the writing is becoming automatic". The points are well made. It is easy to feel that the characteristic Pinter manner, in which language becomes strategy, a mode of attack and defence within the ebb-and-flow of subtextual hostilities, has here become mannerism; that the typically high level of indeterminacy is enabling legitimate questions of plausibility to be sidestepped. This *locus classicus* of the Pinteresque is certainly open to the charge of self-parody. Helpful points of reference for a more positive evaluation of the play might be the drama of Strindberg or the films of Buñuel. *The Homecoming*, with its sudden violent juxtapositions, verbal and visual, and its frequent, almost surreal grotesquerie, readily calls to mind their stylistic modes. All three artists, in their different ways, provoke naturalistic expectations only to violate them. And each does so in his attempt to address the issues of power and sexuality within the domestic–familial context. If *The Homecoming* reveals—as

has been claimed—"the naked animal", it is with this central purpose.

Ruth claims to have been "a photographic model for the body". When she is introduced into the male household she is perceived as a sexual threat—and rightly so, for firmly defined conceptions of gender and sexuality are at the foundation of existing power-relations in the house. The blustering Max attempts to maintain intimidatory sway over his family by persistently invoking memories of "real" men—either his erstwhile friend, the omnicompetent, Aberdonian street-fighter "Mac", or his father, "a number one butcher" ("I commemorated his name in blood"). In comparison with these sanguineous paragons, Lenny, Sam and Teddy are all "bitches", and Sam a queer, a "tit" and a "wet wick". Yet Max is also anxious to assign to himself the role of biological mother: "I gave birth to three grown men. All on my own bat"; "I suffered the pain, I've still got the pangs". Although he commemorates his dead wife Jessie as an ideal mother, he routinely refers to her as a "slutbitch" and a whore, and when he resolves to take his new daughter-in-law into his house, it is within a projected scenario involving the same dual role for her. The potential domestic power of the woman as matriarch is to be cancelled out by her economic subjection as whore.

But the enigmatic Ruth subverts the intention. When the disturbing sexual power with which she had countered Lenny's verbal intimidation in Act I seems finally to have been harnessed by the prostitution-scheme, she shows cold efficiency in the negotiations concerning her "professional" position, and in the play's closing moments assumes the attitude and absolute authority of a matriarch. As her husband leaves, she sits "relaxed on her chair", the head of the pathetic Joey cradled in her lap and the crumbled, stammering Max kneeling at her feet. The displaced patriarch seems to be entering second childhood.

Max has in any case only ever been the nominal head of the household. The real controlling figure has been Lenny. His verbal dexterity and confidence—apparent in his fierce subtextual onslaughts on Max, Ruth and Teddy—mark him out as such. Yet, paradoxically, it is as a silent watcher of the others, as bearer of a controlling gaze, that his status is most potently established. In the concerted finales of both acts the activity comes from Max, and Ruth is the centre of attention, but it is the silent observing presence of Lenny that matters. The text's final stage direction is "Lenny stands, watching".

Yet the enigma of the play will not easily yield to the model of pimp-son controlling whore-matriarch and through her the whole household. Although the gaze of power is Lenny's, the claim to knowledge-through-seeing comes, odd as it may seem, from Teddy, the strangely acquiescent victim. Asserting, in self-defence, the inaccessibility of his "critical works" to the family, he says: "It's a question of how far you can operate on things and not in things. . .To see, to be able to *see*! I'm the one who can see. . . I can observe it. . . But you're lost in it". The *émigré*'s position of *exteriority* is simultaneously his weakness and his strength. Ruth rules the house, and Lenny rules Ruth. But, with Ruth as his agent, Teddy may now be the real power-holder—the outsider *in*. As the play's first director, Peter Hall, put it: "the biggest bastard in a house full of bastards is actually the man who at first sight appears to be the victim". That the text licenses such a perceptual peripeteia without ever permitting confirmation of its truth only serves to underline the indeterminacy of *The Homecoming*.

—Paul Lawley

HOPPLA! (Hoppla, wir leben!)
by Ernst Toller

First Publication: Potsdam, 1927.
First Production: Kammerspiele, Hamburg, 1 September 1927; revised version, Theater am Nollendorfplatz, Berlin, 3 September 1927.

Translations
Hoppla!, translated by Hermon Ould, London, 1928; also in *Ernst Toller: Seven Plays*, London, 1935, and in *Masters of the Modern Theatre*, edited by B. Ulanov, New York, 1961.

Criticism
(For general works on the author, see *Playwrights* volume)

Articles:
Hugh Rorrison, "Piscator's Production of *Hoppla, wir leben, 1927*", in *Theatre Quarterly*, 37, 1980.
Wolfgang Rothe, "Ernst Toller: *Hoppla, wir leben!*", in his *Deutsche Revolutions-Dramatik seit Goethe*, Darmstadt, 1989.

* * *

Hoppla, wir leben!, a five act play with prologue, depicts the life of a former revolutionary, Karl Thomas, in Berlin society of 1927. Having spent eight years in an asylum, Thomas discovers that the world is run by corrupt industrialists, bankers, and politicians; accordingly he joins his former friends in their fight against the capitalist system. Wrongly accused of the murder of a minister he and his friends are imprisonned, but unable to stand this "madhouse of a world" any longer, Thomas hangs himself.

Hoppla, wir leben! began Toller's second phase as a dramatist after his release from prison in 1924. In 1919 he had been sentenced to five years imprisonment for his role in the short-lived, Bavarian, soviet-like Republic. The performance that same year of his first play, *Die Wandlung (Transfiguration)*, an expressionist *Stationendrama*, made Toller famous overnight. During his years in prison he was extraordinarily productive, writing, among other works, three full-length plays (including *Masse Mensch*) which were at once produced by Germany's most brilliant young directors, designers, and actors, receiving international acclaim. All these plays were written against the backdrop of Toller's war experience, his political activities in 1918/1919, and his concern for the proletariat. In the years between 1924 and 1927 he devoted much of his time to political activity and travel. His experience and newly gained insight, combined once more with autobiographical events from his short political career in 1918/19, form the basis of *Hoppla, wir leben!*.

The play offers a satirical and profoundly pessimistic picture of German society in a Weimar Republic whose political and industrial interests are dominated principally by a lust for wealth and power. As in his earlier plays, Toller sympathizes with the ordinary people who lead a futile struggle against an economic and political apparatus which exploits and abuses them. In *Hoppla, wir leben!*, Toller has almost completely abandoned his former expressionist style in which he dramatized his vision of a united mankind in favor of a more realistic analysis of what was wrong with society and why; the play is, in fact, one of the best of *aktuelles Theater* (political theatre) of the 1920's.

In his attempt to begin a "normal" life, Karl Thomas is confronted with a variety of people and situations, including a former revolutionary, Kilman, who has turned into a decadent minister of state riding with the tide, and a mad psychiatrist who—in a grotesque scene—makes Thomas realise that the politicians and their military agents are far more dangerous to mankind than the patients in the asylum. Karl Thomas recognizes that the Republic has, in fact, been betrayed and that the struggle of his working-class friends is in vain. Almost the whole of Act III takes place in the Grand Hotel where Toller, in a rapid succession of scenes, unmasks the moral decline and the growth of political forces which contributed to the demise of the Weimar Republic. However, despite his newly gained insight, Karl Thomas continues dreaming about reforms, unwilling and unable to confront reality. He abandons his plan to shoot Kilman—and thus his fight for the working poor—since he believes that Kilman's death would not bring about any positive changes. In fact, Thomas chooses to resign. The characterization of this protagonist as an anti-hero is a good illustration of how Toller's earlier idealism has been tempered by time and experience. Like *Masse Mensch*, where the ethical conviction and idealistic, futurist vision of Sonia is opposed and refuted by the realistic logic of the Nameless One, Karl Thomas's original, optimistic belief is quickly set straight by reality and his ideals are bluntly rejected, even ridiculed by his friends. For example his proposal, to his lover, Eva Berg, now a dedicated feminist, to escape with him to a "saner" world because he is, by now,

Hoppla, wir Leben!: Theater am Nollendorfplatz, Berlin, 1927 (Piscator's production)

disgusted with politics, is scorned by her: "Do you imagine that a southern sun, palm trees, elephants, coloured clothes, would make you forget the way mankind really lives? The paradise you dream about does not exist". *Hoppla, wir leben!* demonstrates once more Toller's acute political awareness which manifests itself in all his *oeuvre*. The play's original, four-act version, has Karl Thomas returning voluntarily to the mental asylum in order to escape the "madhouse" of the "real" world. However, in a change of mind, he decides to join his fellow-workers and fight their cause, but is forced to remain in the hospital because the psychiatrist realizes that Thomas now represents a true enemy of the state. This ending, although also tragic, has the figure of Karl Thomas bear, once more, witness to Toller's unyielding belief in mankind and the possibility of achieving a new and better social order. Toller was always both an idealistic dreamer and a prescient, political observer. The closing of this version is particularly cynical, befitting the play's message better than the later one written for the Piscator production.

Hoppla, wir leben! as produced by Erwin Piscator on 3 September 1927 in Berlin was, in fact, the result of a close collaboration between the two men. Not only was the ending changed but a number of new scenes were introduced to allow for the use of modern media and stage techniques. For example, Toller wrote a number of film sequences depicting political and social events relevant to the play's message, and also had Walter Mehring write a political song highlighting the decadence of a doomed society. Finally, he wrote stage directions which were obviously meant for the Piscator production and which had the entire play take place on a mobile, tiered scaffold, which was divided into various rooms allowing for simultaneous staging. This particular production made theatre history; apart from establishing Piscator as Germany's leading director of political theatre, it also represented the culmination of Toller's fame on stage.

—Renate Benson

HOPPLA, WIR LEBEN! See **HOPPLA!**

HORACE. See **HORATIUS.**

HORATIUS (Horace)
by Pierre Corneille

First Publication: Paris, 1641.
First Production: Théâtre de l'Hôtel de Bourgogne, Paris, before March 1640.

Editions
Horace, edited by Will G. Moore, Oxford, 1953.
Horace, edited by P.J. Yarrow, London and New York, 1967.

Translations

Horace, in *The Chief Plays of Corneille*, translated by Lacy Lockert, Princeton, New Jersey, 1952; revised edition, 1956.

Horace, translated by Albert Bermel, San Francisco, 1962.

Criticism

(For general works on the author, see *Playwrights* volume)

Books:
R.C. Knight, *Horace*, London, 1981.

Articles:
B. Mathews, "*Cid* and *Horace*", in *International Quarterly*, 7, 1903.

W. Moore, "Corneille's *Horace* and the Interpretation of French Classical Drama", in *Modern Language Review*, 34, 1939.

W.G. Moore, "*Horace* et *Wilhelm Tell*", in *Revue de littérature comparée*, 19, 1939.

W.H. Barber, "Patriotism and *Gloire* in Corneille's *Horace*", in *Modern Language Review*, 46, 1951.

W.A. Nitze, "*Vertu* as Patriotism in Corneille's *Horace*", in *Publications of the Modern Language Association* [*PMLA*], 67, 1952.

Carlo R. François, "En Résiliant *Horace* ou les objections de la conscience", in *French Review*, 28, 1955.

Peter Newmark, "A New View of *Horace*", in *French Studies*, 10, 1956.

J.W. Scott, "The 'Irony' of *Horace*", in *French Studies*, 12, 1959.

J. Morel, "A Propos du Plaidoyer d'Horace: Réflexions sur le sens de la vocation historique dans le théâtre de Corneille", in *Romanic Review*, 51, 1960.

D.G. Charlton, "Corneille's Dramatic Theories and the 'Didacticism' of *Horace*", in *French Studies*, 15, 1961.

Laurence E. Harvey, "Corneille's *Horace*: A Study in Tragic and Artistic Ambivalence", in *Studies in Seventeenth-Century French Literature*, 33, 1963.

Richard A. Mazzara, "More on Unity of Character and Action in *Horace*", in *French Review*, 36, 1963.

Elliott M. Grant, "Reflections on Corneille's *Horace*", in *French Review*, 37, 1964.

P. Bouvet, "La Tendresse dans *Horace*", in *L'Information littéraire*, 17, 1965.

Albert Walter, "The Metaphor of Origins in *Horace*", in *French Review*, 40, 1966.

Elliott Forsyth, "The Tragic Dilemma in *Horace*", in *Australian Journal of French Studies*, 4, 1967.

Charles G. Whiting, "The Ambiguity of the Hero in Corneille's *Horace*", in *Symposium*, 23, 1969.

Dain A. Tafton, "On Corneille's *Horace*", in *Interpretation: A Journal of Political Philosophy*, 2, 1972.

W. Victor Wortley, "Horace's *crime passionel*", in *Romance Notes*, 14, 1972.

William Cloonan, "Women in *Horace*", in *Romance Notes*, 16, 1975.

Christopher J. Gossip, "Tragedy and Moral Order in Corneille's *Horace*", in *Forum for Modern Language Studies*, 11, 1975.

James M. Symons, "Structural Clues to Corneille's Meaning in *Horatius*", in *Theatre Journal*, 31, 1979.

Bettina L. Knapp, "Pierre Corneille's *Horace*: Heroism? Sacrifice?—The Power Hungry", in *Classical and Modern Literature* (Terre Haute, Indiana), vol.1 no.2, 1981.

Mitchello Greenberg, "*Horace*, Classicism and Female Trouble", in *Romanic Review*, vol.74 no.3, 1983.

Susan Tiefenbaum, "Blood and Water in *Horace*: A Feminist Reading", in *Papers on French Seventeenth-Century Literature*, vol.10 no.19, 1983.

Philip Koch, "*Horace*: Réponse cornélienne à la querelle du *Cid*", in *Romanic Review*, vol.76 no.2, 1985.

Barbara Woshinsky, "'Aimer un bras': Metonymic Mutilation in Corneille's *Horace*", in *Papers on French Seventeenth-Century Literature*, vol.12 no.22, 1985.

W.J. Dickson, "Corneille's Use of Judicial Rhetoric: The Last Act of *Horace*", in *Seventeenth Century French Studies*, 10, 1988.

Diane R. Fourny, "'A quoi bon me défendre?': *Horace* and Psychoanalysis", in *Romanic Review*, vol.79 no.2, 1988.

André Georges, "Les Croyances et la foi religieuses des personnages dans *Horace* de Pierre Corneille", in *Les Lettres romaines*, vol.42 no.3, 1988.

*   *   *

Rome is at war with its neighbouring city Alba. To avoid general bloodshed, each side agrees to nominate three warriors to fight a representative combat. During the intervals between Acts I and II, Rome chooses Horace and his two brothers, while early in Act II the Albans appoint Curiace, also one of triplets. While Curiace is betrothed to Horace's sister, Horace himself is married to Curiace's sister Sabine. Battle is engaged, and first reports suggest to Horace's father that his three sons have been defeated ignominiously. It is then learned that, left as the sole Roman combatant, Horace has retreated but only in order to kill each of the Curiaces in turn. His sister Camille, bemoaning the death of her lover and attacking the Roman ideals, is stabbed to death by Horace, who expresses no remorse. Act V is devoted to the judging of the victor-killer. The King of Rome, having listened to pleas from various interested parties and admitted that the the stabbing was a crime, decides against punishment, as Horace's usefulness to the state outweighs his personal guilt.

The first in a series of Roman tragedies by Corneille, *Horace* has been much criticised, in particular for its apparent lack of unity of action and for the unfeeling (and hence, it is said, untragic) nature of the play's protagonist. 20th-century commentators have helped to soften Horace's image, but the nuancing of his character, while legitimate and necessary, still leaves him, in the end, an isolated figure. The main contrast which Corneille seeks to set up is with Curiace, the Alban representative (none of the other brothers on either side appears on stage). Nominated later than Horace, more sensitive than him, and not yet settled into marriage, Curiace is depicted as resigned to defeat, worked on by his sister and his lover. Yet Corneille is at pains to stress his valour, a military record equal to Horace's, his obedience to orders, and a potential for victory denied by his innate humanity.

Both of the women exert pressure, notably at the end of Act II (when only the chance arrival of Horace's father saves the day) in an argument in which the men's determination and pride is opposed to the ironical jibes of Sabine, whose sarcastic play on the terms "firmness", "worth", "glory", and "sacrifice" is so effective that even Horace admits to have been shaken by her verbal attack. The women present the arguments of love, seen from the different standpoints of marriage and betrothal. Neither woman is a passive victim, since each is prepared to die for the cause she defends. But their influence on the representative combat, and hence on the central action of the tragedy, is minimal. In the main, first part of the play their points of view, however humane and legitimate, are overruled by the elder and younger Horace. The older man's devotion to the state, and to the honour of his family as symbolic of that service, is entire; he cannot contemplate the apparent defeat of Horace and his brothers and is intolerant of all the women's emotions and fears.

But Corneille was correct to call his play *Horace* and not *Les Horaces*, for the plot is dominated by this one, combative warrior. It is easy to judge his outspoken devotion to Rome as blindly insensitive and to reduce the character to a one-dimensional, cardboard cut-out or patriotic brute. The stance he adopts is, indeed, inflexible, but external factors impinge on his behaviour and influence it to some extent. The women's pleas may only serve to strengthen his resolve in battle and, paradoxically, ensure the victory they fear. But with Curiace in Act II his virile determination cannot hide admissions of affection and an awareness that his present commission must call for a determination and courage unique to the two families, which goes beyond the norm and will test their resolve to the uttermost. Unlike Curiace he accepts military commands "blindly", that is, unquestioningly; can we not say that that is the correct as well as the opportune attitude in the circumstances? His sister's quite deliberate provocation of him in Act IV coincides with his return from the battlefield. Still intoxicated with victory after a difficult combat and irrational as a result, he acts not coolly but instinctively to restore the very name of Rome which she vilifies and to "forget" the lover with whose death she reproaches him.

Moral order can only be restored by an independent figure, divorced from the close network of family ties which Corneille has constructed. King Tulle listens in turn to Horace senior, to Valère—who has been seeking Camille's hand—, to Sabine, and to Horace himself. The latter defends his actions and offers to die, not for killing Camille, but in order to protect his *gloire*, that is, both his public reputation and his inner, personal satisfaction and peace of mind. Tulle, as dependent on Horace as the King in *Le Cid* is on Rodrigue, places his self-interest (or Rome's interest) and Horace's strength of purpose (*vertu*) above the latter's guilt and orders the young warrior to live on in order to serve the state.

The tragedy of *Horace* lies not in the deaths of five of the six combatants or even in the murder of Camille, but in the survival of the title-character, pardoned, even praised, yet isolated, committed to a public role which leaves unresolved his relationships with others, in particular with the grieving Sabine—a constant reminder to him of Alba and its defeat. The play is not broken-backed, with a secondary action or second "danger" disturbing its unity. The death of Camille is as inevitable as the victory of Horace; it is part and parcel of the same endeavour and Corneille, despite his later self-criticism, was quite right to push the plot that far and on into the final act of judgement. In the end Horace is seen as an outsider, a man with human traits, certainly, but also with an almost superhuman (or subhuman?) ability to suppress them in the name of a patriotic ideal. This is the innate flaw of character which makes the play—and Corneille's and our attitudes to it—so interestingly ambivalent.

—Christopher Gossip

THE HOSTAGE (An Giall)
by Brendan Behan (with Joan Littlewood)

An Giall [Gaelic version]
First Publication: In *Poems and a Play in Irish*, Dublin, 1981.
First Production: Gaelic League, Dublin, 1958.

The Hostage [in collaboration with Joan Littlewood]
First Publication: London, 1958; revised edition, 1962.
First Production: Theatre Royal, Stratford East (Theatre Workshop), London, 14 October 1958; revised version, Théâtre des Nations Festival, Paris, 11 June 1969.

Criticism
(For general works on the author, see *Playwrights* volume)

Articles:
Gordon M. Wickstrom, "The Heroic Dimension in Brendan Behan's *The Hostage*", in *Educational Theatre Journal*, 22, 1970.
Johannes Kleinstück, "Brendan Behan's *The Hostage*", in *Essays and Studies by Members of the English Association*, 24, 1971.
Paul M. Levitt, "Hostages to History: Title as Dramatic Metaphor in *The Hostage*", in *Neueren Sprachen*, 5, 1975.
Richard Wall, "*An Giall* and *The Hostage* Compared", in *Modern Drama*, 18, 1975.
Johan Hendricks, "The 'theatre of fun': In defence of Brendan Behan's *The Hostage*", in *Anglo-Irish Studies*, 3, 1977.

*   *   *

The play is set in a seedy, Dublin lodging-house-cum-brothel owned by Monsewer, a dotty, Oxford-educated Englishman who has adopted an outlandish Irish nationality, complete with bagpipes. The house is run by Patrick, lame veteran of the Irish Rebellion, and his as-good-as-wife, Meg. These two preside over the *outré* and lunatic occupants like indulgent parents. A British soldier has been kidnapped and is to be brought to the house as a hostage; he will be killed if the Belfast execution of an Irish youth convicted of an IRA bombing is carried out. When the young, English soldier arrives he is liked and looked after, especially by the servant girl Teresa. The two 19-year-olds fall in love, but the soldier's hopes that Teresa will help him escape are thwarted when, tipped off by one of the occupants, the police raid the house to free the hostage. Caught in the crossfire, the soldier is killed.

Such a plot summary conveys only a small part of the action, for the play is constructed on the lines of music hall entertainment. Scenes are interrupted by characters breaking into song or dance, ranging from Irish jigs and ballads to deliberately shocking, mock-cabaret numbers such as "We're here because we're queer/Because we're queer because we're here", performed by a collection of male homosexual prostitutes. The audience is regularly addressed from the stage and characters frequently digress into story-telling, at which times the rest of the characters often drift on stage to listen.

The play's ending epitomises its mixture of styles. As the police attack the house, a highly theatricalized battle erupts on the stage, full of shots, screams, drum-rolls, smoke, and hurtling bodies. When the air clears, the hostage lies dead. The servant girl, mourning, kneels to give him her forlorn blessing. There is a pause, then sudden green light on the soldier, who rises and sings raucously:

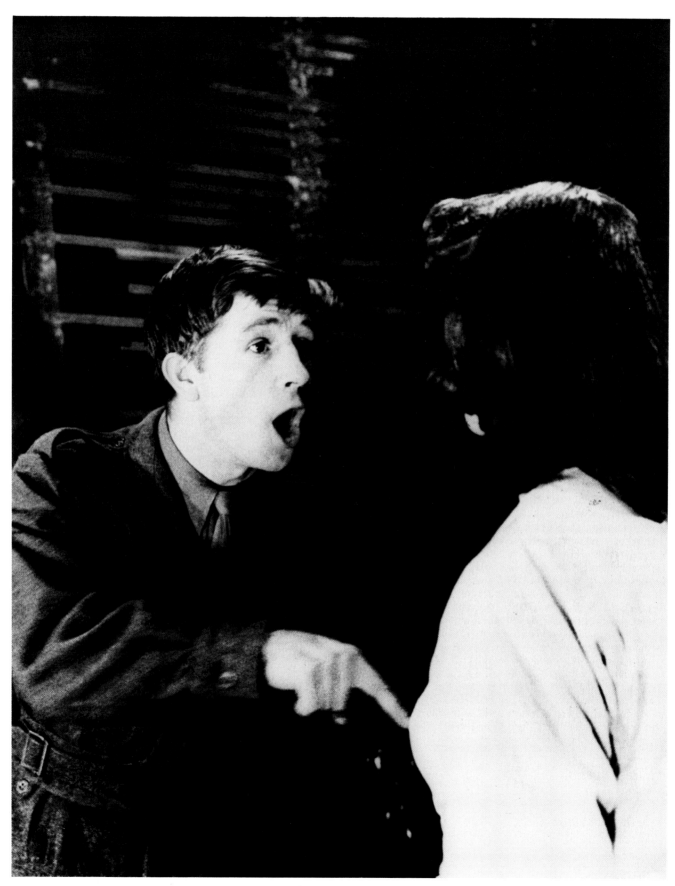

The Hostage: Wyndhams Theatre, London, 1959

The bells of hell,
Go ting-a-ling-a-ling,
For you but not for me.
Oh death, where is thy sting-a-ling-a-ling?
Or grave thy victory?

The stage brightens and the entire cast sing the refrain to the audience.

The play as we have it is the product of a collaboration between Behan and Joan Littlewood, the remarkable director of The Theatre Workshop in London. Behan's earlier *The Quare Fellow* had been staged straightforwardly by the same company. In 1958, Behan agreed to write a piece for an Irish language group using a small, Dublin theatre. This play, *An Giall*, written in Gaelic, is the early version of *The Hostage*. Littlewood asked for a translation, which Behan promised but delivered only intermittently and incompletely. Meanwhile, creation of the play proceeded in rehearsals. Through this process, a simple, realistic drama was transformed into a multi-layered piece of theatre. This was Joan Littlewood's method. "Joan took a play to pieces and she put it back together again with actor's inserts, ad libs and catch phrases". Behan was a willing collaborator. "Joan Littlewood has the same views on the theatre that I have", he later wrote, "which is that music hall is the thing to aim at. . . .While they were laughing their heads off, you could be up to any bloody thing behind their backs".

What Behan was up to behind their backs is not entirely what was expected of a playwright born and bred into the IRA and who had spent time in jail for it. For all the play's professional Irish charm, it is less a celebration of Irish nationalism than might appear. The serious scenes point up sharply differing attitudes towards the cause. The sentimental fanaticism of the elders is contrasted with the political disengagement of the young lovers, who are the victims in the end. And when Monsewer spouts Gaelic, Pat turns to the audience and says, "Do you hear that? That's Irish. It's a great thing, an Oxford education! Me, I'm only a poor Dublin man. I wouldn't understand a word of it". Yet the sympathy for those who believe and suffer for the freedom of Ireland still works in the play.

One critic called Behan "more a player than a playwright". Certainly the huge success of *The Hostage* was greatly assisted by unpredicted appearances of the author on stage to joke and sing with the actors. His style owes much to the time he spent in various pubs and prisons. Nonetheless, he was a serious writer who admired, and frankly emulated, O'Casey, just as Joan Littlewood learned much from Brecht. *The Hostage* contains many echoes of *Juno and the Paycock* and *The Threepenny Opera*. More importantly, however, it is a genuine attempt to combine the power of realism with that of political cabaret. The critic who remarked, "it's magnificent, but it isn't drama" was right. It is a piece of theatre, one of the few works of the post-war period that truly brought text and performance into collaboration and confrontation.

—Lesley Anne Soule

THE HOUSE OF BERNARDA ALBA (La casa de Bernarda Alba)
by Federico García Lorca

First Publication: Buenos Aries, 1945.
First Production: Teatro Avenida, Buenos Aires, March 1945.

Translations
The House of Bernarda Alba, translated by James Graham-Luján and Richard L. O'Connell, New York, 1941.
The House of Bernarda Alba, in *Three Tragedies of Federico García Lorca*, translated by Sue Bradbury, London, 1977.

Criticism
(For general works on the author, see *Playwrights* volume)

Books:
Ricardo Doménech (ed.), *"La casa de Bernarda Alba" y el teatro de García Lorca*, Madrid, 1985.

Articles:
Miguel A. Martínez, "Realidad y símbolo en *La casa de Bernarda Alba*", in *Revista de estudios hispánicos*, 4, 1970.
Grace Alvarez-Altman, "Charactonyms in García Lorca's *House of Bernarda Alba*: Sexual Nihilism Within the Typology of Literary Onomastics", in *Onomastica Canadiana*, 46, 1973.
Carole Slade, "The Hell of Bernarda's House", in *García Lorca Review*, vol.3 no.2, 1975.
Wilma Newberry, "Patterns of Negation in *La casa de Bernarda Alba*", in *Hispania*, 59, 1976.
Nina M. Scott, "Sight and Insight in *La casa de Bernarda Alba*", in *Revista de estudios hispánicos*, 10, 1976.
Farris Anderson, "*La casa de Bernarda Alba*: Problems in Act One", in *García Lorca Review*, 5, 1977.
Vicente Cabrera, "Poetic Structure in Lorca's *La casa de Bernarda Alba*", in *Hispania*, 61, 1978.
Vicente Cabrera, "Cristo y el infierno en *La casa de Bernarda Alba*", in *Revista de estudios hispánicos*, 13, 1979.
James Dauphiné, "Le Réalisme symbolique dans *La Maison de Bernarda Alba*", in *Langues néo-Latines*, vol.73 no.4, 1979.
Isaac Rubio, "Notas sobre el realismo de *La casa de Bernarda Alba*, de García Lorca", in *Revista canadiense de estudios hispánicos*, 4, 1980.
Richard A. Seybolt, "Characterization in *la casa de Bernarda Alba*: The Case of Martirio", in *García Lorca Review*, 8, 1980.
Roberta N. Rude and Harriet S. Turner, "The Circles and Mirrors of Women's Lives in *The House of Bernarda Alba*", in *Literature in Performance*, vol.3 no.1, 1982.
Richard A. Seybolt, "*La casa de Bernarda Alba*: A Jungian Analysis", in *Kentucky Romance Quarterly*, 29, 1982.
Isabel Camara, "Vida y muerte, Eros y Thanatos: dos instintos en *La casa de Bernarda Alba*", in *García Lorca Review*, 11, 1983.
Manuel A. Arango L., "Simbolos sociales en *La casa de Bernarda Alba*, de Federico García Lorca", in *Cuadernos Americanos*, vol.43 no.5, 1984.
Austin Dias, "La dialectica escénica en *La casa de Bernarda Alba*", in *Selecta*, 5, 1984.
Bettina L. Knapp, "Federica García Lorca's *The House of Bernarda Alba*: A Hermaphroditic Matriarchate", in *Modern Drama*, 27, 1984.

The House of Bernarda Alba: Lyric Theatre, Hammersmith, London 1986

C. Brian Morris, "The 'austere abode': Lorca's *La casa de Bernarda Alba*", in *Anales de la literatura española contemporánea*, 11, 1986.

Francisco Ruiz-Ramón, "[Análisis de sociodramaturgia:] El espacio en *La casa de Bernarda Alba*", in *Gestos*, vol.1 no.1, 1986.

Stephen M. Hart, "The Bear and the Dawn: Versions of *La casa de Bernarda Alba*", in *Neophilologus*, 73, 1989.

C. Brian Morris, "Voices in a Void: Speech in *La casa de Bernarda Alba*", in *Hispania*, 72, 1989.

*   *   *

La casa de Bernarda Alba (The House of Bernarda Alba) is, like *Bodas de sangre (Blood Wedding)*, set in the Spanish countryside and tells the story of the 60-year-old Bernarda's domination of her household, including her five, spinster daughters. The beginning of Act I announces a period of eight years of mourning following the recent death of Bernarda's husband and reveals at every step Bernarda's harshness towards her servants, her mother and her daughters. Of these, the eldest, Angustias, is to marry Pepe el Romano, a circumstance which stirs up feelings of envy and resentment, particularly in the youngest and most attractive daughter, Adela, and the older and unattractive Martirio. In Act II existing tensions intensify. Adela grows more rebellious, Martirio more resentful. Her theft of Angustias's portrait of Pepe draws from the servant, la Poncia, warnings to which Bernarda responds with a demonstration of even greater

intransigence. Act III reveals that Adela has been meeting Pepe secretly at night. Her discovery by Martirio results in Bernarda attempting to shoot him as he escapes. Convinced by Martirio of Pepe's death, Adela hangs herself, and Bernarda announces a second period of mourning, for her daughter, who, others must believe, died a virgin.

Like *Blood Wedding, The House of Bernarda Alba* had its source in real life, for as a child Lorca had a next-door neighbour, "an old widow who exercises an inexorable and tyrannical watch over her spinster daughters", one of whom was said to have a lover, Pepe de la Romilla. On the other hand, there are also literary sources. The insistence which Bernarda places on the good name of the family, deeply ingrained in the Spanish temperament, had its literary antecedent in the plays of the 17th century, notably in the "honour" plays of Calderón, with which Lorca was very familiar. The obsessive concern with the good opinion of others, which drives Bernarda to incarcerate her daughters and leads finally to Adela's death, is the motive which in Calderón's *The Surgeon of Honour* (*El médico de su honra*) obliges a husband to murder an innocent wife. Another possible source was the novel *Doña Perfecta* by the 19th-century novelist Pérez Galdós, in which, in a narrow-minded, provincial town, the intolerant Doña Perfecta becomes increasingly opposed to the marriage of her daughter, Rosario, to the young liberal from Madrid, Pepe Rey. When the couple attempt to elope, she arranges Pepe's murder, after which Rosario loses her sanity. Finally, as in the case of *Blood Wedding*, the influence of Greek tragedy is very clear: the play's title suggests, a household or a lineage; Bernarda brings about, through her actions, the end she seeks to avoid; there is a powerful sense of fatality; and the final scenes are strongly cathartic. But if the literary debt is evident, the themes of the play are pure Lorca: passion and frustration, exemplified above all in Adela; passing time, personified in the ageing of all the daughters; and death, physical in Adela's case, emotional in the other girls'. Not only does the play constitute another powerful expression of his own situation, it also anticipates the divisons which would tear apart the family of Spain in the summer of 1936, only months after the play's completion.

Lorca's assertion that *The House of Bernarda Alba* is a "*documental fotográfico*" (a "photographic record"), together with his deliberate stripping-away of obviously poetic elements, has encouraged the belief that, in contrast to *Blood Wedding* and *Yerma*, this is a naturalistic play. An examination of its style and technique suggests that nothing could be further from the truth. While it is true that more of the characters have real names than is the case in the other plays—Adela, Amelia, María Josefa, la Poncia—the names of others are decidedly symbolic: Angustias and Martirio suggesting suffering incarnate, and Bernarda Alba, ironically suggestive of the illumination of dawn. Indeed, each of the characters embodies to some degree the clash of the opposites longing and denial which, concentrated in Bernarda's family, has its counterpart in other families wherever natural instinct comes into conflict with narrow-minded tradition.

Despite their apparent naturalism, the play's three settings are highly stylized, with the white walls evoking purity and virginity but also sterility and the endless monotony of imprisoned lives. Within the frame of the settings, movement and posture enhance the image: the daughters seated at the beginning of Act II, passively sewing; or later in the act the despairing Martirio, seated, head in hands. In contrast, bursts of activity suggest from time to time Adela's defiance, as does her green dress, suddenly bringing a splash of colour into the darkened house. Lighting too has a crucial role to play. In Act I the opening of a door momentarily floods the room with light, suggesting the world beyond the house. Act II sustains the idea when the girls observe the harvesters through a half-open shutter, but by Act III it is night, with Adela and Martirio engulfed by a darkness that is as much emotional, suggesting despair and mutual hate, as it is physical. The studied interplay of setting, movement, and lighting exposes the inner lives of the characters and affects the response of the audience in a way which naturalism could never do.

The language of the play, mainly in prose, is also carefully shaped, stripped of the inconsequential trivia of everyday speech. Almost every word exposes character: Bernarda's outbursts are the verbal equivalent of the stick with which she beats the ground; Adela's speech, alive with defiance, while Magdalena's is heavy with despair. When songs are introduced, on two crucial occasions, their rhythm pinpoints the importance of the moment, as in Act II when the vibrant harvester's song encapsulates a world for which Bernarda's daughters long but which they cannot reach.

The trajectory from the highly poetic *Blood Wedding* to the much more austere *The House of Bernarda Alba* is typical of Lorca's constant experimentation. But the differences between the two plays are less important than their similarity, which lies ultimately in the importance for Lorca of the poetic and the imaginative in the theatre.

—Gwynne Edwards

THE HOUSE OF BLUE LEAVES
by John Guare

First Publication: New York, 1972.
First Production: Truck and Warehouse Theater, New York, 11 February 1971.

Criticism
(For general works on the author, see *Playwrights* volume)

Articles:
Jacques Sequrd, "*The House of Blue Leaves*", in *L'Avant Scène*, January 1973.
Samuel J. Bernstein, "*The House of Blue Leaves*", in *The Strands Entwined: A New Direction in American Drama*, Boston, 1980.

*   *   *

John Guare's *The House of Blue Leaves* opens with Artie Shaughnessy performing at the El Dorado Bar Amateur Night. He fails to get the attention of either audience—neither those attending the El Dorado nor those attending Guare's play, because his tacky songs are performed to Guare's spectators, as the stage directions indicate, "*while the House Lights Are Still On, and the audience is still being seated*". He wants recognition and "a blue spotlight"; he gets neither. He needs to believe that his musical potential is his way out of a life tending animals all day at the zoo, then returning at night to tend his deranged wife, Bananas. Depressive but acute, a potent threat to his pipe dream, she can hear the blatant plagiarism of his music and is willing to say so.

On the other hand, Artie's lover, Bunny Flingus, is enthusiastically supportive of him. She knows her man is going to make it big and drag her along with him. She has claims to all sorts of special knowledge from her myriad jobs. Being a movie usher at women's weepies lets her "know these sick wives" and the way to deal with them—electric shock therapy (by virtue of her experience at Con Edison). A theatrical furniture store taught her "the score" about "casting couches"! Her conclusion is to leap onto them. She dispenses sexual pleasure with largesse but withholds her secret weapon of culinary joy in order to achieve marriage and celebrity. When Artie's old friend Billy, the Hollywood success story, breezes through, she immediately abandons Artie's cause and uses her cooking to earn a place with the famous man.

The working-class neighborhood of New York which is the setting for *The House of Blue Leaves* is called Sunnyside, yet "*the only illumination in the room is the light from the television*". Though the Pope is making his first visit ever to America, the closest Artie Shaughnessy can get his demented wife to the curative powers of the chief prelate is to have her kneel before his passing parade on the television. She obeys her husband's order to "kiss him. . . .He'll cure you! Kiss him". Even the nuns who descend from the roof down to the modest apartment kneel before this icon which glows in the dark. Of the three habited sisters, only the Little Nun escapes with her life; her last words in the play as she kisses the television are "A shrine. . .I wanted to be a Bride of Christ but I guess now I'm a gay divorcée". The Pope's broadcast is reassuring:

> We feel, too, that the entire American people is here present with its noblest and most characteristic traits: a people basing its conception of life on spiritual values, on a religious sense, on freedom, on loyalty, on work, on

The House of Blue Leaves: Truck and Warehouse Theater, New York, 1971 (first production)

the respect of duty, on family affection, on generosity and courage—

Guare's dark comedy is a brilliant and hilarious debunking of the current status of those values in a land where the book that teaches men how to live is the *Reader's Digest* and the pulpit that dispenses the word is the Johnny Carson Show. In this world the only religion that everyone bows to is fame.

Guare's commonplace people do not consider themselves fully human: "The famous ones—they're the real people". Only clerical and cinematic superstars are considered real. Artie is a zoo-keeper who turns his back on his wife and on the wonder of all the animals giving birth at once: "I've become this Dreaming Boy. I make all these Fatimas out of the future. Lourdes and Fatimas. All these shrines of the future and I keep crawling to them". Approaching the pinnacle of fame too closely cost Corrinna Stroller, Billy's girlfriend, first her hearing and then her life. Ronnie Shaughnessy, Artie's army son about to be shipped to Vietnam, will do anything to appear on the evening news, even assassinate the Pope (Guare invented this extremity; the plot on the Pope's life had not yet occurred when the play had its premiere in 1971). The Pope survives Ronnie's first attempt, but Ronnie's mother, Bananas, does have the life choked out of her before the audience's disbelieving eyes. The woman who praised his music (Bunny) gone, Artie is left with Bananas, the one who sees through it. It is necessary for Artie to shut her up; she can hear that he has no musical talent. He realizes that he will never escape Sunnyside; he will never get Hollywood recognition. He confronts his dime-a-dozen reality by choking the life out of his wife. Only now does the "*blue spotlight appear*". And who knows, even if Artie the songwriter never made it to the Academy Awards ceremony, maybe Artie the wife-killer will appear on the evening news after all. Guare's disturbing ending affirms that addiction to fame is fatal.

—Roger Sorkin

HUI-LAN JI.   See **THE CHALK CIRCLE.**

HUIS CLOS.   See **NO EXIT.**

HYDE PARK
by James Shirley

First Publication: London, 1637.
First Production: Cockpit Theatre, Drury Lane (Queen Henrietta's Men), London, 1632.

Editions

Hyde Park, edited by Edmund Gosse in *The Best Plays of James Shirley*, London, 1888.
Hyde Park, edited by Simon Trussler, London, 1987.

Criticism

(For general works on the author, see *Playwrights* volume)

Articles:
Theodore Miles, "Place Realism in a Group of Caroline Plays", in *Review of English Studies*, 18, 1942.
Richard Levin, "The Triple Plot of *Hyde Park*", in *Modern Language Review*, 62, 1967.
Albert Wertheim, "Games and Courtship in Shirley's *Hyde Park*", in *Anglia*, 93, 1975.

*   *   *

Three plots run side by side in *Hyde Park*, interweaved with one another and involving a tightly-knit group of gentry in 17th-century London. In the first plot, the gentleman Lacy marries the supposed widow, Mistress Bonavent, whose husband has been away seven years on a trading venture and is presumed dead. But Bonavent has newly returned, unrecognized by everyone, and Lacy thoughtlessly humiliates him by insisting he dance at his wedding. Bonavent has his revenge by forcing Lacy to dance publicly in the park, then reveals himself to all in the masque which closes the play. In the second plot, Mistress Bonavent's cousin, Carol, is courted by Rider, Venture, and Fairfield, but being a scoffer at love she ridicules her suitors. Fairfield eventually brings her to heel, but only after a series of strategic manoeuvres by which each tries to get the better of the other; including a ploy in which Fairfield pretends love to Julietta who (unbeknown to Carol) is really his sister. In the third plot, Julietta is herself courted by Fairfield's friend Trier, who seeks to test her affections by introducing her to the rakish Lord Bonvile as if she were a high class courtesan. His test rebounds, however, for not only does Julietta reconvert Bonvile to a proper understanding of aristocratic honour, she takes offence at the way she has been used and ends the play virtually accepting Bonvile's now chaste advances.

Hyde Park is the quintessential comedy of the Caroline world of pleasure, a dazzling and satisfying combination of romance, intrigue, and wit set in the realistically-depicted environment of fashionable London. Seizing on the potential of a three-plot design to generate a surface of apparently casual activity beneath which lies a foundation of carefully-engineered, parallel relationships, Shirley depicts a society given over to chance encounters and shifting liaisons, and interacting with a carefree grace that belies its command over the nuances of manners and of speech. His intricate structure counterpoints a social geography of relationships amongst a narrow but self-aware community (rich merchant, gentleman, complacent aristocrat) with a physical geography of closed and open spaces (drawing-room verses ballroom, garden versus park) and with a moral geography of luck which will finally and providentially separate the deserving from the undeserving, those who belong from those who do not. In this play, luck is on the side of those who can fashion themselves most nearly to the socially-sanctioned roles which their various stations demand of them. Neither the clownish Venture and Rider, nor the doubtful Trier, nor the uncivil Lacy will get their girls. Victory goes instead to men who are at ease with their breeding or who can learn to adapt their desires to the decorums of the place.

At its root, *Hyde Park* is an Elizabethan comedy which has a green world at its centre into which the characters pass from the world of everyday and re-emerge transformed. The royal park had indeed just been opened to the public when the play was written, and in the central scenes the characters move freely around its avenues, watching races, listening to the birds, and taking refreshments. In this urban Elysium, nature recolonizes and shapes the desires of a new metropolitan class: the songs of the nightingale and the cuckoo predict the winners and losers, as do the bets which are placed on the races. Yet the green world is not radically opposed to the world of the drawing-room. In both places games are forever being played, and even outside the park no one ever seems to have much business to transact. The real transactions in each environment are those which test the reality of people's protestations, whether they are promises to be faithful for seven years or promises to observe the necessary boundaries between one person's freedom and another's. For all its air of inconsequential chat, the play mounts a powerful argument for bringing everyday behaviour into line with honourable norms: its culminating episode is the scene in which Julietta disciplines the philandering aristocrat. Of course in telling Bonvile that if he wants his honour to be respected he must act like an honourable man, Julietta is not attacking the system of privilege which gives him his social prerogatives (and she has even harsher rebukes in store for her tactless lover), yet her arguments still have real political force. In trading a hierarchy of merit against a hierarchy of birth, Shirley was reflecting, however discreetly, on tensions that were actively working to transform that society for which the Drury Lane Cockpit was a principal meeting place.

The interest of the Carol / Fairfield plot centres on its significance as a midway position between the sparrings of Shakespeare's Beatrice and Benedick and the amorously-negotiating lovers of Restoration comedy. Shirley even writes a proviso scene in which Carol lists all the feminine vanities of which Fairfield must promise not to deprive her. Yet for all that there is a sisterly relationship between the three women, and however much Carol is contemptuous and suspicious of the protestations of servile lovers, a feminist writ does not really operate here. Carol's individualism is seen as "wildness" from the first and she does not so much come to an accommodation with Fairfield as allow herself to be tamed by him. Overwhelmed when she imagines Fairfield is about to commit suicide for love, she ends up happily en route for the altar and settling into submission. Here, as in so much else in this comedy, the will of the community is final.

—Martin Butler

———

THE HYPOCHONDRIAC. See **THE IMAGINARY INVALID.**

———

I, TOO, SPEAK OF THE ROSE (Yo también hablo de la rosa) by Emilio Carballido

First Publication: In *Revista de Bellas Artes*, 6, 1965.
First Production: Teatro Jimenez Rueda, Mexico City, 16 April 1966.

Translations

I, Too, Speak of the Rose, translated by William D. Oliver in *Drama and Theatre*, vol.8 no.1, 1969; also in *Voices of Change in Spanish American Theatre*, Austin, Texas, 1971.

Criticism

(For general works on the author, see *Playwrights* volume)

Articles:

R.A. Kerr, "La funcíon de la Intermediaria en *Yo también hablo de la rosa*", in *Latin American Theatre Review*, 12, 1978.

Paul C. Smith, "Simbiosis de realismo y teatralismo: *Yo también hablo de la rosa*", in *Studia hispanica in honour of Rodolfo Cardona*, edited by Néstor A. Lugones and Luis A. Romos-García, Austin, Texas, 1981.

Sandra M. Cypess, "I, Too, Speak: 'Female' Discourse in Carballido's Plays", in *Latin American Theatre Review*, 18, 1984.

David W. Foster, "*Yo también hablo de la rosa* de Emilio Carballido: Los limites del teatro brechtiano", in his *Estudios sobre teatro mexicano contemporáneo: semiología de la competencia teatral*, New York, 1984.

*   *   *

I, Too, Speak of the Rose (*Yo también hablo de la rosa*) is a play set in modern Mexico City. Throughout the play only one thing happens—two lower-class children, Toña and Polo, derail a freight train carrying food and go to jail for an unspecified (though we assume brief) period of time. The rest of the play's 21 scenes focus on the process and politics of interpretation. For the police, the incident is a criminal offense. For the scavangers picking up the food, the strewn bounty is a miracle of good fortune. The mothers blame their children's vagrancy on the absent father. The school teacher refers to Toña and Polo as truants. For the university students reading the newspaper, the event is an anarchistic, brilliant act. The bourgeois couple, reading the same paper, refer to the children as "little savages, that's what they are. All of them. They're all a bunch of savages". A Freudian psychologist expounds on the repressed libidinal component to the act. The Marxist economist interprets the destruction as the logical outburst of an oppressed class. What does the derailment mean? Whose interpretation or discourse gains authority?

While many perspectives are introduced in the play, not all of them are equal. The Intermediaria (Medium), an indigenous, or "mestizo", peasant woman, dominates the play. She appears four times, linking the episodic scenes together by telling stories that indirectly elucidate the incident involving the two children. Interestingly, however, her perspective is not valorized as correct, but as indispensible in illuminating Mexico's racial and cultural mestizage. Carballido does not suggest that she knows more than the professors, but that her source of knowledge differs from theirs. She begins the play claiming "I know many things!". As she narrates what she knows—herbs, faces, crowds, the texture of rocks, books, pages, illusions, roads, events—we come to understand that her knowledge represents a mode of perception different in kind and origin from the "scientific", objective knowledge posited by the eurocentric professors. Her epistemological framework is primarily of an oral tradition, conserved by memory, and passed on by word of mouth: "I also retain memories, memories which once belonged to my grandmother, my mother or my friends. . .many which they, in turn, heard from friends and old, old people". Her orality is both a *product of* and a *producer of* a network of communication, and establishes her central position in it as much as literacy shapes the professors. The philosophic schools which shape the professors' perception, and the literacy maintaining it, do not, by and large, form the traditions within which most Mexicans have lived, and to different degrees still continue to live. In a country like Mexico, characterized by the co-existence of literary and primary oral cultures, consciousness changes according to how people receive and store information and knowledge.

The most immediate distinction between the oral and literary cultures we see in the play lies in the relationship between knower and known. The Intermediaria's knowledge cannot be called "objective"—it is not empirically verifiable or in any way outside or disconnected from herself as knower. Unlike the professors with their methodological and causal framework, she does not aspire to the Cartesian ideal of objectification. From her first line in her first speech, the Intermediaria approaches knowledge reflexively, comparing it to her heart which, with its "canals that flow back and forth" connects her with the rest of the world. As the fluidity of her speech shows, her way of knowing is anything but isolating or reductive—each idea opens a way to another, defying the possibility of any conclusion. The Intermediaria's role demonstrates the supreme importance of the speaker in an oral culture. In contrast, the professors' way of knowing is shown as eccentric in that they stand outside and removed from the source of their knowledge and information which now, in the literate society, lies in books and newspapers. Their physical presence is gratuitous; they only read or speak what has

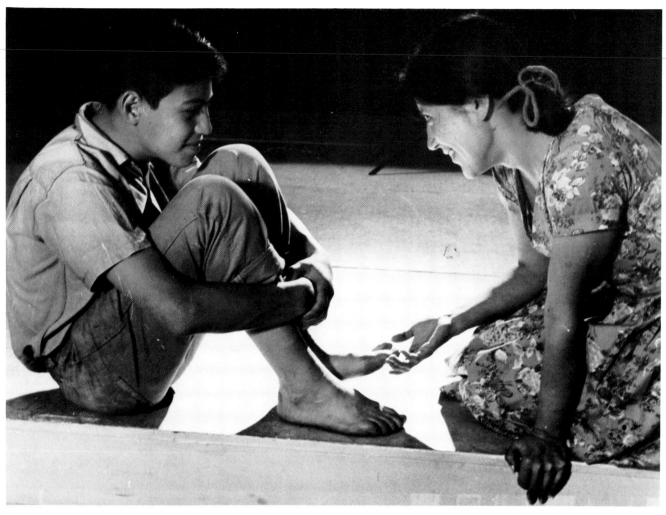

I, Too, Speak of the Rose: Mexico City, 1965 (rehearsal for first production)

already been prepared in writing. They maintain a marginal, alienated position in both the acquisition and transmission of their knowledge. Alienation, then, is not an existential given, but a product of the knower/known relationship. The separation between knower/known changes, reduces and fragments human experience. Ironically, then, while literacy allows us to know more as well as more accurately, with greater abstraction and sophistication, it simultaneously widens the gap between knower and known.

Carballido's humorous play does not condemn or endorse any one perspective. Rather, it shows all of them as co-existing simultaneously within a highly complex society. If he condemns any position whatsoever it is only the folly of those who maintain that there *is* only one correct interpretation. His ludicrous characters (such as the Announcer of the game show in which the audience is asked to identify the one "authentic" image of a rose), illustrate not only the fallacy, but the potentially inquisitorial violence, of imposing any one view at the expense of others. There is only one valid response, the Announcer asserts; the rest "should be stricken from the books so that they will be forgotten forever. And any person who divulges them should be pursued by law. All those who believe in these false images should be suppressed and isolated!".

I, Too, Speak of the Rose is a discourse about the nature of discourse. Discourses not only stem from differing traditions and create their own realities, but they also vie for explanatory power and authority. Historically, western theories have displaced Mexican and Latin American worldviews. In this play Carballido moves the marginalized experience to the very center of inquiry. This re-centering constitutes an important, liberating act for, by the same move, the eurocentric view (the professors) recedes, seen to be reduced in importance. Changing the relationship between the marginal and the dominant can change history, for as Hayden White points out in *Tropics of Discourse*, histories "are not only about events but also about the possible set of relationships that those events can be demonstrated to figure".

I, Too, Speak of the Rose is then a theatrical collage of many conflicting views of an incident and proposes a method of inquiry into the politics of perception and interpretation. Like the rose of the title, which Carballido depicts as a complicated and interconnected entity inextricable from (and inconceivable without) its multiple parts—stalk, petals, and fibers—the play too is made up of numerous, yet irreducible, interpretations.

—Diana Taylor

THE ICEMAN COMETH
by Eugene O'Neill

First Publication: New York, 1946.
First Production: Martin Beck Theatre, New York, 9 October
　　　　1946.

Criticism
(For general works on the author, see *Playwrights* volume)

Books:
Winifred L. Frazer, *Love as Death in "The Iceman Cometh":
A Modern Treatment of an Ancient Theme*, Gainesville,
Florida, 1967.
John Henry Raleigh (ed.), *Twentieth Century Interpretations
of "The Iceman Cometh"*, 1968.
Winifred L. Frazer, *E.G. and E.G.O: Emma Goldman and
"The Iceman Cometh"*, Gainesville, Florida, 1974.
Harold Bloom (ed.), *Eugene O'Neill's "The Iceman Cometh"*,
New York, 1987.
Gary Vena, *O'Neill's "The Iceman Cometh": Reconstructing
the Premiere*, Ann Arbor, Michigan, 1988.

Articles:
Sophus Winther, "*The Iceman Cometh*: A Study in Tech-
nique", in *Arizona Quarterly*, 3, 1947.
Sverre Arestad, "*The Iceman Cometh* and *The Wild Duck*", in
Scandinavian Studies, 20, 1948.
Rudolph Stamm, "A New Play by Eugene O'Neill", in *English
Studies*, 29, 1948.
Vivian C. Hopkins, "*The Iceman* Seen through *The Lower
Depths*", in *College English*, 11, 1949.
Doris Alexander, "Hugo of *The Iceman Cometh*: Realism and
O'Neill", in *American Quarterly*, 5, 1953.
Leonard Chabrowe, "Dionysius in *The Iceman Cometh*", in
Modern Drama, 4, 1962.
William Brasher, "The Wisdom of Silenus in O'Neill's *Ice-
man*", in *American Literature*, 36, 1964.
Robert J. Andreach, "O'Neill's Women in *The Iceman
Cometh*", in *Renascence*, 18, 1966.
Emil Roy, "*The Iceman Cometh* as Myth and Realism", in
Journal of Popular Culture, 2, 1968.
Robert C. Lee, "Evangelism and Anarchy in *The Iceman
Cometh*", in *Modern Drama*, 12, 1969.
James P. Quinn, "*The Iceman Cometh*: O'Neill's Long Day's
Journey into Adolescence", in *Journal of Popular Culture*,
6, 1972.
Winifred L. Frazer, "O'Neill's Iceman—Not Ice Man", in
American Literature, 44, 1973.
Nancy Reinhardt, "Formal Patterns in *The Iceman Cometh*",
in *Modern Drama*, 16, 1973.
Péter Egri, "Eugene O'Neill: *The Iceman Cometh*: An Epic
Tragi-Comedy of Illusion and Reality", in *Angol Filológiai
Tanulmányok / Hungarian Studies in English*, 11, 1977.
James G. Watson, "The Theater in *The Iceman Cometh*: Some
Modernist Implications", in *Arizona Quarterly*, 34, 1978.
Winifred L. Frazer, " 'Revolution' in *The Iceman Cometh*", in
Modern Drama, 22, 1979.
Timothy J. Wiles, "Tammanyite, Progressive, and Anarchist:
Political Communities in *The Iceman Cometh*", in *Clio*, 9,
1980.
Bette Mandl, "Absence as Presence: The Second Sex in *The
Iceman Cometh*", in *Eugene O'Neill Newsletter*, vol.6 no.2,
1982.
Thomas B. Gilmore, "*The Iceman Cometh* and the Anatomy
of Alcoholism", in *Comparative Drama*, 18, 1984.

William Hawley, "*The Iceman Cometh* and the Critics—1946,
1956, 1973", in *Eugene O'Neill Newsletter*, vol.9 no.3, 1985.
Gary Vena, "Chipping at the *Iceman*: The Text and the 1946
Theatre Guild Production", in *Eugene O'Neill Newsletter*,
vol.9 no.3, 1985.
James A. Robinson, "Convergences and Divergences: Father
and Son in *A Touch of the Poet* and *The Iceman Cometh*", in
American Literature, 59, 1987.
Normand Berlin, "O'Neill and Comedy: *The Iceman Com-
eth*", in *Eugene O'Neill Newsletter*, vol.12 no.3, 1988.
Jerome Neu, "Life-lies and Pipe Dreams: Self-Deception in
Ibsen's *The Wild Duck* and O'Neill's *The Iceman Cometh*",
in *Philosophical Forum*, 19, 1988.
Laurin R. Porter, "*The Iceman Cometh* as Crossroad in
O'Neill Long Journey", in *Modern Drama*, 31, 1988.
Yvonne Shafer, "In Ibsen's Back Room: Related Patterns in
The Iceman Cometh and *The Wild Duck*", in *Eugene O'Neill
Newsletter*, vol.12 no.3, 1988.

*　　*　　*

Written in 1939, *The Iceman Cometh* was eventually published to coincide with its world premiere in New York City on
9 October 1946. The advent of World War II apparently
discouraged the playwright's approving this play for production until world peace was restored. Under the auspices of the
Theatre Guild, which had produced numerous O'Neill successes, the play received a mixed, critical reception and played
136 performances, before touring briefly.

It was the 1956 revival at the Circle-in-the-Square in New
York City, under the direction of José Quintero, that brought
new acclaim to both play and author. Within the intimate, Off-
Broadway environment, Quintero's inspired approach
impressed audiences who, exactly ten years later, were more
responsive to the play's gloomy atmosphere, downtrodden
characters, and pessimistic themes. The ecstatic critical reaction revitalized O'Neill's waning reputation as America's
foremost playwright and prompted a new surge of interest in
his plays both in America and abroad.

The action of this play which is largely static throughout, is
set in the back room and section of Harry Hope's saloon.
Arrivals and introductions highlight a lengthy and expository
first act in which the night bartender, Rocky Pioggi, sets up the
bar for a new day while, in the back room, Larry Slade renews
acquaintance with Don Parritt and describes to him the lives of
the alcoholic lodgers sprawled at surrounding tables. Concern
is expressed that Theodore Hickman (Hickey) is unusually late
in appearing this year for Hope's birthday celebration. The
entrance of two prostitutes, Margie and Pearl, enlivens the
atmosphere. Soon the day bartender, Chuck Morello, and his
girlfriend Cora arrive and announce that they have just seen
Hickey in the neighborhood. But when Hickey makes his
grand entrance and greets Hope and his old friends, the
lodgers notice that something about him has changed.

Act II centers on Hope's surprise party, where tempers seem
highly strung and a strange uneasiness pervades the
atmosphere. The festivities are suddenly dampened when
Hickey announces that his wife, Evelyn, is dead. In the bar-
room of Act III, on the morning after the party, Hickey's
meddling interference has instigated emotional outbursts and
violent threats among the lodgers, many of whom are prepared
to leave the saloon forever to resume the lives they long ago
abandoned in the world outside. Hope himself faces the
neighborhood he has not seen in years. When Slade confronts
Hickey about Evelyn's death, Hickey reveals that she was
killed.

Act IV focuses on the lodgers, all returned to their familiar

The Iceman Cometh: Arts Theatre, London, 1958

places in the back room and drowned once again in alcoholic stupors. Sparing none of the controversial details, Hickey relates the story of his life and marriage and receives a variety of unexpected responses. Two detectives enter the saloon just in time to overhear him confess to murdering his wife. When he finishes his story, the detectives carry him away, as the lodgers return to their drinking.

O'Neill's orchestrated drama, which is deliberately circular in its arrangement of character interactions, repetitive motifs, and overall scenic design, boldly asserts the philosophical premise that man needs illusion to survive. Its deceptively simple plot achieves mythic overtones through boldly stated themes, biblical allusions, and quasi-symbolic characters. The salesman, Hickey, whose first name means "God's gift", peddles salvation to his degenerate colleagues in this "No Chance Saloon", where "booze" is freely dispensed by a proprietor ironically called Hope. Confronting his Nemesis, represented by a morbid philosopher-realist named Slade (the distorted past tense of the verb "to slay"), Hickey almost succeeds in persuading his colleagues to abandon their "pipe dreams" and begin "a new life of peace and contentment". When his cure proves too strong a medicine for them, they retreat to their illusions.

The play's title calls attention to the analogous themes of love and death which echo through the play. In contrast with the image of Christ as bridegroom who comes with a message of celebration and love, Hickey extends the cold hand of death to his drunken followers, while repeatedly sarcastic and sexual references to the mythical "iceman" harbor fatal consequences. Acknowledging his own cowardly approach towards life, Slade confesses that he is "the only real convert to death Hickey made here" and succinctly sums up the playwright's tragic thesis.

Despite its 1912 period setting, which tends to date the play in performance, *The Iceman Cometh* provides an uncompromising and realistic view of the lost humanity O'Neill himself confronted during earlier years spent in lower Manhattan's bars and flophouses. The traumas of spiritual disillusionment, alcoholism, suicide, and betrayal—all viable motifs in the play—document these experiences with an honesty and insight rarely achieved in his earlier works. That he was able to transform these characters and events into cogent, universal, theatrical metaphors at last demonstrated his unique craftsmanship. Above all it uncovered a significantly matured dimension to his playwriting and cleared the way for such biographical works as *Long Day's Journey Into Night* and *A Moon for the Misbegotten*. Constituting an unofficial trilogy, all three full-length plays were written in the same period of O'Neill's life when he was plagued with physical debilitation and psychological depression.

In terms of its literary antecedents, *The Iceman Cometh* reveals O'Neill's lifelong debt to the major continental dramatists. Critics have pointed to Ibsen's *Wild Duck* and Gorki's *Lower Depths* as important influences on the play's structure and theme. Instead of damaging the impact of *The Iceman Cometh* these comparisons have generated constructive investigations in an attempt to link O'Neill's American roots in 19th-century melodrama—where his father, James O'Neill, was an influential figure—to modern European drama. The results have strenghtened O'Neill's literary reputation and enhanced newer analyses of his work in performance. Despite the controversy that has always surrounded his work—*The Iceman Cometh* in particular—one fact remains uncontested: as one of the first American dramas to explore man's absurdist, existential dilemma, it anticipated the godless terrain explored by a post-war generation of playwrights headed by Samuel Beckett. By continually redefining itself from one literary era to another, *The Iceman Cometh* reinforces O'Neill's reputation as one of the leading theatrical innovators of the 20th Century.

—Gary Vena

THE ILLUSION.   See **THE THEATRICAL ILLUSION.**

L'ILLUSION   COMIQUE. See **THE   THEATRICAL ILLUSION.**

I'M TALKING ABOUT JERUSALEM.   See **THE WESKER TRILOGY.**

THE IMAGINARY INVALID (Le Malade imaginaire)
by Molière

First Publication: Paris, 1674.
First Production: Palais-Royal, Paris, 10 February 1673.

Editions
Le Malade imaginaire, edited by E.W. Olmsted, Boston, 1905.
Le Malade imaginaire, edited by Daniel Mornet, Paris, 1947.
Le Malade imaginaire, edited by R.P.L. Ledésert London, 1949 (with translation).
Le Malade imaginaire, edited by G. Eugène-Fasnacht, London and New York, 1961.
Le Malade imaginaire, edited by René de Messières, Paris, 1962.
Le Malade imaginaire, edited by Alphonse Bouvet, 1963.
Le Malade imaginaire, edited by Yves Hucher, Paris, 1965.
Le Malade imaginaire, edited by Peter H. Nurse, Oxford, 1965.
Le Malade imaginaire, edited by François Hinard, Paris, 1970.

Translations
The Imaginary Invalid, translated by Merritt Stone, New York, 1939.
The Would-Be Invalid, translated by Morris Bishop, New York, 1950.
The Imaginary Invalid, translated by Miles Malleson, London, 1959.
The Imaginary Invalid, in *Molière: "The Misanthrope" and Other Plays*, translated by John Wood, Harmondsworth, 1959.
The Hypochondriac, translated by H. Baker and J. Miller, in *Three Great French Plays*, edited by Vernon Loggins, 1961.
The Imaginary Invalid, translated by Bert Briscoe, Birmingham, 1967.
The Hypochondriac, translated by Alan Drury, in *Molière: Five Plays*, edited by Donald Roy, London, 1982.

Criticism
(For general works on the author, see *Playwrights* volume)

Books:
H.T. Barnwell, *Molière: "Le Malade imaginaire"*, London, 1982.

Articles:
Xavier de Courville, "Sur un intermède de Molière", in *Revue musique*, 6, 1925.
Joseph Fonsy, "La Vraie Signification du *Malade imaginaire*", in *Etudes classiques*, vol.2 no.1, 1933.
Mauriz Schuster, "Plautus und Molières Le Malade imaginaire", in *Wiener Studien*, 50, 1933.
James R. Knowlson, "*Le Malade imaginaire*: The 'invention novelle' of Cléante", in *Modern Language Review*, 58, 1963.
John T. Stoker, "Argan's Sickness in Molière's *Le Malade imaginaire*", in *Culture*, 30, 1969.
Philip R. Berk, "The Therapy of Art in *Le Malade imaginaire*", in *French Review*, 45, 1972.
Michel Albert-Fernet, "La Fiche médicale d'Argan: *Le Malade imaginaire*", in *Revue des deux mondes*, 1973.
D.J. Adams, "A Reading of *Le Malade imaginaire*", in *Modern Languages*, vol.64 no.1, 1983.
Thérèse Malachy, "La Mort en sursis dans *Le Malade imaginaire*", in *Revue d'histoire du théâtre*, vol.35 no.3, 1983.
Carol A. Mossman, "The Restitution of Paternity in Molière's *Le Malade imaginaire*", in *South Central Review*, vol.3 no.1, 1986.
Ralph Albanese Jr., "*Le Malade imaginaire*, ou le jeu de la mort et du hasard", in *Dix-septième Siècle*, 154, 1987.
Jacques L. Blais, "La Servante à la mesure de la comédie-ballet: Toinette et *Le Malade imaginaire*", in *Cahiers du Dix-septième siècle*, vol.2 no.1, 1988.

*   *   *

In Act I, Argan is a middle-aged man in vigorous good health who nonetheless believes that he needs constant medical attention. He has two daughters by his deceased wife; his second wife, Béline, is attempting to secure all of his wealth at the expense of the daughters. His elder daughter, Angélique, confides to the servant Toinette that she is in love with Cléante, who intends to ask Argan for her hand. But Argan tells her that, in order to provide for his own medical care, he has arranged for her to marry Thomas Diafoirus, a newly-certified doctor and the nephew of Argan's principal physician, M. Purgon. In Act II, Cléante, who has heard of the proposed marriage, arrives disguised as Angélique's music teacher;

The Imaginary Invalid: Engraved frontispiece, 1682

later. This macabre mingling of life and art—a sick man plays a well man who is playing sick, and dies in the process—has made it very difficult to resist the temptation to read the play as autobiography: as Molière's final testament, his farewell to the stage. Yet the temptation should be resisted: it is not likely that Molière intended to die or to make this his last play, and there is no particular reason to believe that the subject matter of the play reflects a compelling need to make a personal statement.

Molière had satirized the medical profession in earlier plays (and was not alone in doing so); here he changed the focus of the satire to the patient rather than the doctor. Argan has an obsession, and selfishly wants to marry off his daughter, and sacrifice her happiness, in order to serve that obsession; in this sense *The Imaginary Invalid* follows the formula of several of Molière's greatest plays—*Tartuffe*, *The Miser* (*l'Avare*), *The Would-Be Gentleman* (*Le Bourgeois gentilhomme*), and, changing father to mother, *Les Femmes savantes*. Of these *Le Bourgeois gentilhomme* most closely resembles *Le Malade imaginaire*, since both are *comédies-ballets* and both culminate in a delirious ballet in which the protagonist's fantasy triumphs over reality.

What is unique about the play is not the subject of health and medicine but the pervasive emphasis on rôle-playing. Cléante pretends to be a music teacher, Toinette to be a doctor, Béline to be a devoted wife; Louison feigns death to escape a whipping, Toinette feigns injury to escape a scolding. Argan is the dupe of all these deceptions; yet he also feigns death to discover what his wife and daughter think of him. The context that these peripheral deceptions provide for the central issue of Argan's hypochondria leads to the conclusion that it, too, is a form of rôle-playing, designed to manipulate those around him and to assure his place as the center of attention; and the device that ultimately reconciles Argan's needs with those of his family is yet another disguising: Argan's assumption of the costume and spurious identity of the physician. This is the perfect conclusion for Argan, since it makes him simultaneously both impostor and dupe; and it is a rôle for which he is as well qualified as the real thing.

—Roger Herzel

Thomas Diafoirus, a great fool, arrives with his father and clumsily pays his court to Angélique. Angélique and Cléante conduct a mock music lesson during which they consult in improvised song, while Argan unsuspectingly watches. But Béline has caught a glimpse of the lovers together; Argan, by threats of whipping, extracts from his little daughter, Louison, details of the interview. In Act III, Argan's brother Béralde intervenes on Cléante's behalf and also tries to persuade Argan that he does not need doctors; he succeeds to the extent that Argan postpones an enema prescribed by M. Purgon. M. Purgon arrives instantly, denounces Argan for his disobedience, threatens to punish him with disease and death, and cancels the marriage between his nephew and Angélique. Toinette impersonates a great doctor who will replace M. Purgon, then resumes her own identity and persuades Argan to feign death: Béline then reveals her greed and her contempt for her husband, and Angélique reveals her love for her father. Argan consents to her marriage with Cléante; Béralde tells his brother that, to ensure his health, he should become a doctor himself. This is immediately accomplished in a very elaborate ballet and degree ceremony that concludes the play.

Molière had been in poor health for several years when he wrote this play; while playing Argan, near the end of the fourth performance, he was fatally stricken and died a few hours

THE IMPORTANCE OF BEING EARNEST
by Oscar Wilde

First Publication: London, 1899.
First Production: St. James's Theatre, London, 14 February 1895.

Criticism
(For general works on the author, see *Playwrights* volume)

Books:

Vyvyan Holland (ed.), *The Original Four Act Version of "The Importance of Being Earnest"*, London, 1957.
W.S. Bunnell, *Oscar Wilde's "The Importance of Being Earnest"*, London, 1958.
William Tydeman (ed.), *"Lady Windermere's Fan"; "A Woman of No Importance"; "An Ideal Husband"; "The Importance of Being Earnest": A Casebook*, London, 1982.
Harold Bloom (ed.), *Oscar Wilde's "The Importance of Being Earnest"*, New York, 1988 (Modern Critical Interpretations).

The Importance of Being Earnest: Globe Theatre, London, 1939

Articles:

Otto Reinert, "Satiric Strategy in *The Importance of Being Earnest*", in *College English*, 18, 1956.

Harold E. Toliver, "Wilde and the Importance of 'Sincere and Studied Triviality' ", in *Modern Drama*, vol.5 no.4, 1963.

Robert J. Jordan, "Satire and Fantasy in Wilde's *The Importance of Being Earnest*", in *Ariel*, vol.1 no.3, 1970.

Joseph W. Donohue, "The First Production of *The Importance of Being Earnest*: A Proposal for a Reconstructive Study", in *Essays on Nineteenth Century British Theatre*, edited by Kenneth Richards and Peter Thomson, London, 1971.

L.A. Poague, "*The Importance of Being Earnest*: The Texture of Wilde's Irony", in *Modern Drama*, vol.16 nos.3–4, 1973.

David Parker, "Oscar Wilde's Great Farce: *The Importance of Being Earnest*", in *Modern Language Quarterly*, 35, 1974.

Dennis J. Spininger, "Profiles and Principles: The Sense of the Absurd in *The Importance of Being Earnest*", in *Papers on Language and Literature*, 12, 1976.

Geoffrey Stone, "Serious Bunburyism: The Logic of *The Importance of Being Earnest*", in *Essays in Criticism*, 26, 1976.

Elissa S. Guralnik and Paul M. Levitt, "Allusion and Meaning in Wilde's *The Importance of Being Earnest*", in *Eire*, vol. 13 no. 4, 1978.

Joel Fineman, "The Significance of Literature: *The Importance of Being Earnest*", in *October*, 15, 1980.

Camille A. Paglia, "Oscar Wilde and the English Epicene", in *Raritan*, vol. 4 no.3, 1985.

John Glavin, "Deadly Earnest and Earnest Revived: Wilde's Four-Act Play", in *Nineteenth Century Studies*, 1, 1987.

Walter Poznar, "Life and Play in Wilde's *The Importance of Being Earnest*", in *Midwest Quarterly*, 30, 1989.

Christopher Craft, "Alias Bunbury: Desire and Termination in *The Importance of Being Earnest*", in *Representations*, 31, 1990.

*   *   *

It is fitting that *The Importance of Being Earnest*, a play whose keynote is artifice, should have a highly patterned structure. Everything is paired: there are two young men (both pretending to be someone else) and two young ladies, who have both decided that the man they marry must be called Earnest. There are two tea parties, one in London and the other in the country, presided over by two butlers and two elderly ladies—although here the pairing diverges into a deliberately exaggerated contrast, since one of the ladies, Miss Prism, is an erstwhile romantic novelist (currently attached to the vicar) while the other, Lady Bracknell, the arch-gorgon of all prospective mothers-in-laws, stands squarely blocking the paths of both pairs of lovers.

The play was originally written in four acts, but was shortened at the request of George Alexander, who wanted to preface it by a "curtain raiser". This resulted in Wilde tightening the plot, reinforcing the parallels on which it is poised, and cutting, most notably, a lawyer, Gribsby, who arrives in the country to arrest Ernest Worthing for debt. Gribsby's notion of prison life has an extremely ironic ring when one reflects that *The Importance of Being Earnest* had only just opened when Wilde was publically disgraced and subsequently himself imprisoned: ". . .the gaol itself is fashionable and well-aired, and there are ample opportunities of taking exercise at certain stated hours of the day. In the case of a medical certificate, which is always easy to obtain, the hours can be extended".

The Importance of Being Earnest is unquestionably the funniest of Wilde's comedies of manners, all of which turn on a woman's guilty secret (Miss Prism holds the key to the mystery of Jack Worthing's parentage) and contain distinct character types—in particular a female dragon (Lady Bracknell) and a witty young man about town, a persona of Wilde himself (in this case seen in Algernon Moncrieff *and* Jack Worthing). Wilde, the flamboyant wearer of the green carnation, the man who, even at his trial, had the court laughing at his irrepressible repartee, Wilde the wit is the only voice heard in *The Importance of Being Earnest*. Where his other comedies reveal at times (and perhaps particularly for present day audiences) a tendency towards the sentimental and melodramatic, *Earnest* has no such difficulties since it is wholly and joyously artificial, with no pretensions to reality or truth:

> *Jack*: Is that clever?
> *Algernon*: It is perfectly phrased! and quite as true as any
>   observation in civilised life should be.

or:

> *Jack*: Oh, that's nonsense, Algy. You never talk any-
>   thing but nonsense.
> *Algernon*: Nobody ever does.

In *The Importance of Being Earnest* Wilde approaches the summit of witty comedy, creating a world of deliberately reversed values; to be wicked is charming in such a world and it is boring to be good. It is a brittle world, where the real is rejected for the artificial, where manners come before morals, where feelings are undignified and the aim and signature of good breeding is an expressionless face. It is a world where words are used to make brilliant patterns rather than to tell truths, and hypocrisy is a social grace. Its forte is scintillating dialogue, where paradox after paradox rings momentarily with the conviction of a maxim, evaporates (even explodes) and is replaced by the next. The play thus becomes an elaborate tissue of lies told to sound like truth, with the fragility inherent in such a situation.

The technique Wilde uses is the reversal of cliché, its force occurring through the unexpected. As Algernon says of the newly widowed Lady Harbury: "I hear her hair has turned quite gold from grief". There is no linguistic differentiation between the witty voices throughout Wilde's comedy of manners, but what sets *Earnest* apart is the omnipresence of that voice, "unclouded" (as C. J. L. Price has it) "by sincerity". It is the attitudes that delight in *Earnest*. The characters live with such style that this becomes a satisfaction in itself. Wilde, himself an artist in living, has, by banishing realism, created from his characters' behaviour a kind of art form.

Wilde called it "essentially an acting play" and Edith Evans' famous performance as Lady Bracknell (that subsequently became a cinema classic) bears this out. The timing is impeccable. Each act gains momentum from surprise entrances (Lady Bracknell's in Acts I and III and Algy's and Jack's in Act II).

The final irony in *The Importance of Being Earnest* is Jack's discovery that his life of deception has been truth all along—nature imitating art:

> *Jack*: It is a terrible thing for a man to find out suddenly
>   that all his life he has been speaking nothing but
>   the truth. Can you forgive me?
> *Gwendolen*: I can. For I feel that you are sure to change.

The play appeals to the comic side of the intellect. The idealists of Wilde's earlier comedies are mocked and his delight in absurdity is given full rein, as in the unlikely juxtaposition of ideas that he gives to Lady Bracknell when vetting her prospective son-in-law: "Now to minor matters. Are your parents living?"; or the twisted logic which has Algy eating the cucumber sandwiches ordered for Lady Bracknell because she is *his* aunt. The play is justly one of the most popular comedies in the repertoire, a magnificent puffball of word patterns and farcical action created for audience enjoyment.

—Rosemary Pountney

IN ABRAHAM'S BOSOM
by Paul Green

First Publication: In *"The Field God"* and *"In Abraham's Bosom"*, New York, 1927.
First Production: Greenwich Village Theater (Provincetown Players), New York, 30 December 1926.

Criticism
(For general works on the author, see *Playwrights* volume)

Articles:
Thomas N. Walters, "Mournful Songs and Flying Sparks: Paul Green's *In Abraham's Bosom*", in *Pembroke Magazine*, 10, 1978.

*   *   *

Abraham McCraine, a half-breed, is given the chance to rise above his slave status in the post-Civil War South of America when his white father, Colonel McCraine, offers to put him in charge of a school for his slaves. Abe's evangelical efforts fail, first through resistance from the blacks themselves, then because the white Southerners close ranks against him. Eventually he murders his white half-brother in a fit of frustrated rage and is himself shot as a criminal by the racist community.

Green's play astonished the New York theatre-going establishment when it won a Pulitzer Prize in 1927. Not only was its abrasive subject matter genuinely shocking, but its use of detailed regional dialect made it almost inaccessible to a commercially-minded audience. This was the first of Green's cycle of American folk plays, concentrating on the region round his native North Carolina. The text, as printed, related to experience as foreign to middle-class Americans as was the speech overheard in certain immigrant neighbourhoods of metropolitan America.

The Provincetown Players, who had discovered the work of Eugene O'Neill some ten years earlier, further displayed their bold initiative with Green's play by casting a group of unknown black actors, who perceived the play very much as an enactment of their own history of escape from lowly Southern origins. The production, originating in Greenwich Village, moved to the Garrick Theater, where it ran for 116 performances.

Even by later, more outspoken, standards, *In Abraham's Bosom* is explosive both in its theatricality and in its diatribe. The protagonist, while being guilty of classical, tragic *hubris*, articulates black experience as no other black protagonist was to do for the next 35 years of American drama. Even the celebrated *Porgy*, by Dubose and Dorothy Heyward (1929), could not match Green's play for expressing black anger, though ostensibly it, too, concentrates exclusively on Southern, black life. The mere fact that *Porgy* does not engage interracial conflict diminishes its authority, alongside Green's play, as a genuinely seminal contribution to black American drama. Reputed precursors of *In Abraham's Bosom* (O'Neill's *All God's Chillun Got Wings* and *The Nigger* by Edward Sheldon), undermine their intention by shallow characterisation and no real engagement with racial issues. Abe McCraine, on the other hand, takes on the issues in sustained speeches of polemical fire. Education, he insists, is the black community's only means of achieving parity in a white-dominated environment. The manically feverish way in which he preaches this gospel, which serves as his downfall, nonetheless exposes the wound irrevocably. With the advent of this play, American drama could no longer settle down with the soporific acceptance of the Black as a savage reigned-in by servitude. The desperate spoils of the Civil War had at last come to be claimed.

Such a view of the effect of a single play cannot easily be discounted when critical favour ran as highly as it did. This was not a play intended to woo anyone, certainly not the trustees of the nation's most coveted award of middlebrow acceptance— the Pulitzer Prize. Green seems almost to have set out to defy, if not to insult, critical taste by introducing a new form of theatre with an abundantly controversial theme. *In Abraham's Bosom* remains one of only a handful of truly political plays in mainstream, American drama, with Abe McCraine's precise analysis of deep-seated racial injustice extended over several five-minute-long speeches.

It could be argued, today, that the play's message has too little awareness of the difficulties inherent in the claim for equal education. Latterly, white playwrights have been criticised for even attempting to speak on behalf of blacks. What cannot be refuted is the sheer audacity of *In Abraham's Bosom* as a dramatic fact. It was produced, it was acclaimed, and American drama could no longer continue to omit its message from the agenda. The protest drama of the 1930's would have been incomplete without its clarion appeal.

—James MacDonald

IN CAMERA.   See NO EXIT.

IN DER SACHE J. ROBERT OPPENHEIMER.   See IN THE MATTER OF J. ROBERT OPPENHEIMER.

IN THE MATTER OF J. ROBERT OPPENHEIMER
(In der Sache J. Robert Oppenheimer)
by Heiner Kipphardt

First Publication: In *Theater heute*, 11, 1964; in book form, Frankfurt, 1965; revised version, in *Theaterstüke*, 1, Cologne, 1978.
First Production: Freie Volksbühne, West Berlin, and Kammerspiele, Munich, 11 October, 1964; revised version, Deutsche Schauspielhaus, Hamburg, 1977.

Translations
In the Matter of J. Robert Oppenheimer, translated by Ruth Spiers, London, 1967.

Criticism
(For general works on the author, see *Playwrights* volume)

Books:
Ferdinand van Ingen, *Heiner Kipphardt: "In der Sache J. Robert Oppenheimer"*, Frankfurt, 1978.

Articles:
Christian W. Thomsen, "Die Verantwortung des Naturwissenschaftlers in Mary Shelleys *Frankenstein* und Heiner Kipphardts *In der Sache J. Robert Oppenheimer*: Zur literarischen Gestaltung eines Problems", in *Literatur in Wissenschaft und Unterricht*, 4, 1971.
Silvia Volckmann, "Auf ideologischem Schlachtfeld: Heiner Kipphardt, *In der Sache J. Robert Oppenheimer*", in *Geshichte als Schauspiel: Deutsche Geschichtsdramen: Interpretationen*, edited by Walter Hinck, Frankfurt, 1981.
Nikolaus Miller, "Verhörprotokoll: Heiner Kipphardt, *In der Sache J. Robert Oppenheimer*", in his *Prolegomena zu einer Poetik der Dokumentarliteratur*, Munich, 1982.

* * *

In the Matter of J. Robert Oppenheimer was an immediate success, with 22 other productions within a year of its premiere in 1964. It recounts the secret hearing during Spring 1954 against Oppenheimer, the "father of the atomic bomb", for delaying development of the hydrogen bomb. Oppenheimer, in the context of McCarthyite investigations, outlines moral scruples he shared with other scientists advising on the best targets for the first atomic bombs, and defends himself against accusations of slowing down research. He refuses to divulge conversations with a former fiancée who became a communist and elicits sympathy for the vulnerability of scientists and mankind to the power of instruments such as computers that "reduce our friendships, our conversations and thoughts to scientific data". His team was chosen out of the best physicists regardless of political views. By the end of Scene 5 one of the Board concludes "no matter how extreme, the subjective views of a physicist are his own private affair as long as they don't interfere with his objective work. This dividing-line bears upon the principles of our democracy".

Whereas the first part deals with Oppenheimer's involve-

In the Matter of J. Robert Oppenheimer: Freie Volksbühne, Berlin, 1964 (first production)

ment with communist sympathisers when his team was developing the bomb, the second part concentrates on the issues, both political and personal, surrounding the bomb. His pacifist attitude is based on a belief in the limitless power of the new bomb and that an American government "would tend to *use* the weapon we were developing". Oppenheimer emerges as a sceptic, still learning from his responses to the discoveries and developments made under his joint responsibility. He also still has faith in common sense, allowing him to believe that an understanding with an enemy nuclear power is possible. Despite the evidence of the managerial Edward Teller, who was keen to gain a lead in the nuclear race in order to discredit war for ever, and Hans Bethe's insistence that no single person could be held responsible, Oppenheimer is seen to have committed "ideological treason", putting loyalty to his friends before duty to his country.

Kipphardt's plays follow documented facts more closely than do other documentary dramas. The individual's situation is portrayed accurately and then dramatized into conflict. In fact, the real Oppenheimer was later to complain to Kipphardt about this accuracy, revealing thereby his human conscience more clearly. He made his stand against the bomb too late, and by unleashing the monster he forfeited his freedom. In the play, Oppenheimer becomes victim to the authorities who will deny security clearance, for a scientist with a conscience becomes to them a threat. As Oppenheimer states: "There are people who are prepared to defend freedom until there is no more of it left". The subtext of the play also includes more basic conflicts—those between the individual and the community, between knowledge and the state, between ethics and morality. Kipphardt insisted that the text is above all intended as a "play for the theatre, not an assemblage of documentary material". He claims "to follow Hegel's advice and lay bare the core and significance of a historical event" and replace matters of secondary importance so as to highlight "the essence of the matter to appear in all its clarity" (Hegel). Only six of the original forty witnesses appear in the play in order to concentrate attention on the core issues, some characters conveying the evidence of those left out. As Kipphardt pointed out, not only was Oppenheimer a Faustian character, but his final statement is fictional, and here the play likens the work of physicists for the state as "the work of the Devil".

Kipphardt's drama comes closer than Brecht's *Life of Galileo* or Dürrenmatt's *The Physicists* to the actual relationship between scientist and state in the modern world. In all three plays the scientist is held under the "patronage" of the state, but Oppenheimer has no way out from its abuse of his potential, not even temporary escape as with Galileo abroad, or withdrawal into a madhouse as with Dürrenmatt's Möbius. Oppenheimer's way is to extend his responsibility to mankind in general, facing up to the consequences of Dürrenmatt's maxim that the implications of physics "concern all mankind".

His moral responsibility frees him from slavery to the state; simultaneously it commits him to an international struggle against nationalist interests and for peace. The central theme is thus that of the emancipation of the scientist from political manipulation towards a utopian, global society.

The two-part structure, one with six and the other with four scenes, supported by documentary and film projections, has the hallmarks of Brechtian, epic theatre. The tribunal setting encourages a dialectical approach where witnesses give differing interpretations of Oppenheimer's attitudes and actions. Much of the effect of the piece comes from the silent presence of Oppenheimer at most of the discussions. When he does speak, it is either in robust defence of his motives, or—especially in his final statement—to extend his personal involvement into an example for physicists in particular and mankind in general. There is more than a hint of ironic detachment on his part from the debate. That he is thanked at the end for his participation and afterwards rewarded by President Johnson with a special prize at the instigation of Edward Teller (as we are told by the final wall-hanging) turns the proceedings into a form of discrete history-lesson from which the politician has either learnt nothing or of which he has been kept totally ignorant.

—Brian Keith-Smith

THE INDIAN WANTS THE BRONX
by Israel Horovitz

First Publication: In *First Season*, New York, 1968.
First Production: Astor Place Theatre, New York, 17 January 1968.

*   *   *

A bus-stop is the set for this one-act play, and every design item at the start is important to the dynamics of menace that make up its central action: a telephone box, rubbish bins, and the implied outline of New York apartment blocks. Standing alone, and "visibly frightened" by the environment is Gupta, usually dressed in a turban and traditional Indian costume to accentuate his cultural displacement. The voices of two boys singing initially seem to introduce an innocent, humanising dimension to the situation, especially as when they appear they are both in their early 20's, and one is "baby-faced". Elements of playfulness recur throughout their on-stage behaviour, but from the moment that they are individualised as Murph and Joey it is clear that they also have the potential for irrational or sadistic violence. It emerges that Gupta, who speaks no English, wants to catch a bus to the Bronx, where his son lives, and the boys' response fluctuates between a pretense of being helpful or friendly and sudden eruptions of aggression; in one of the most chilling vacillations of tone, Murph actually telephones Gupta's son but then taunts him by talking about elephants, and cuts the cord before Gupta gets a chance to speak. At the end, Gupta receives a slight knife wound; but the most poignant cruelty is when he is left at the final black-out, talking his now rudimentary English into the disconnected telephone.

Although *The Indian Wants the Bronx* is among the first of Horovitz's many plays, he already had considerable dramatic experience; in 1965 he had even been the first American to be playwright-in-residence with the Royal Shakespeare Company at the Aldwych Theatre. For this reason, the parallels which critics quickly found with Pinter's "comedies of menace" and with Albee's absurdist *Zoo Story* have an obvious, though limited, validity: the boys' baiting of Gupta seems at times close to *The Caretaker*, while the play as a whole is resonant with the divorce between the individual and his environment, a central issue for Camus and the absurdists. Yet in other respects the play stands beside the 1960's work of Sam Shepard as a genuinely American indicator of the emergence of postmodernism.

Looking back at the play after a decade, Horovitz found it a dated work, essentially naturalistic in form. There is much in the play to support a naturalistic view of the boys' behaviour in particular: both their violence and their boredom are the products of environmental conditioning, and they frequently yell obscenities towards the apartment of the social worker who has recently been supervising them. One early critic argued that Horovitz had done little more than to "drag a street fight into the theater" while another observed that he had seen such boys every day in the New York streets but never before in a theatre. When the latter comment is put beside the stage direction that when the boys abuse Pussyface (their social worker) they yell across the audience, the situation verges on the metatheatrical, with the audience cast as a liberal, indulgent bourgeoisie viewing the animalism of a subspecies on stage. That situation in turn ironically reflects the attitude of the boys to Gupta, whom they bait as a Turk/turkey and generally treat as subhuman primarily because he cannot speak English. The dynamics of alienation in the play thus mobilise both social and cultural distances, and the audience is compromised and possibly indicted because—if only in language terms—it is placed on the side of the boys.

The stage Indian has a long history as a catalyst for audience racial prejudice on the English-language stage and screen, and it was a radical gesture for Horovitz to put a character speaking only Hindi on the New York stage in 1968; there are obvious parallels between Gupta and his own cultural marginalisation as an American Jew. However, if Gupta is the obvious target of the on-stage menace, there is also a pronounced phobic undertone to much of the boys' behaviour, an undertone which triggers much of their aggression. All of their bravado may be seen as a thinly-veiled expression of insecurity. The boys are obsessed with mothers, they ridicule Pussyface for trying to mother them, yet they can only yell at her when they know she is away for a holiday. The baby-faced Joey is anxious about how his mother will react if he is late home. Murph's mother is an unsuccessful prostitute, which seems to explain why he talks so much about his own sexual heroics and why he accuses Joey's mother of "humping Turkies". The swaggering masculinism of both boys is balanced by indignation at the slightest hint of homosexuality.

In the end, Gupta is defeated, not by the boys, but by the city, and his real struggle is not with human but with mechanical adversaries. Even if the boys did not appear, he would still not find his way to the Bronx because he is at the wrong bus-stop, he would not be able to ring his son because he could not explain himself to the operator. The amputated telephone cord at the end signifies not only the gratuitous aggression of a contemporary generation whose lives are purposeless but—more importantly—the severing of biological and genetic connections by the sterile city and its communication media.

—Howard McNaughton

INDIANS
by Arthur Kopit

First Publication: New York, 1969.
First Production: Aldwych Theatre, London, 4 July 1968; first US production, Arena Stage, Washington D.C., 6 May 1969.

Criticism
(For general works on the author, see *Playwrights* volume)

Articles:

John Lahr, "Arthur Kopit's *Indians*: Dramatizing National Amnesia", in his *Up Against the Fourth Wall: Essays on Modern Theater*, New York, 1970.

Vera M. Jiji, "*Indians*: A Mosaic of Memories and Methodologies", in *Players*, 47, 1972.

John B. Jones, "Impersonation and Authenticity: The Theatre as Metaphor in Kopit's *Indians*", in *Quarterly Journal of Speech*, 59, 1973.

P.D. Dubbe, "*Indians—Arthur L. Kopit*", in *Indian Scholar*, 1981.

Michael C. O'Neill, "History as Dramatic Present: Arthur L. Kopit's *Indians*", in *Theatre Journal*, 34, 1982.

Arthur Kopit's *Indians* is composed of 13 scenes which alternate between Buffalo Bill's Wild West Show and an 1886 Indian Commission hearing. In these scenes a combination of historical and non-historical figures participate in acts in the show or are involved in treaty discussions between United States government officials and Indians. Besides being hailed as one of the "best plays of 1969–70" in America it met with critical acclaim in France, Germany, Japan, and the Scandinavian countries, and was the basis for an unsuccessful film version by Robert Altman released in 1976 under the title *Buffalo Bill and the Indians: Or Sitting Bull's History Lesson*.

Kopit's underlying concept for the play dates from March 1966 when he read a statement made by General William Westmoreland, the Commander-in-Chief of American forces in Vietnam. Speaking about reports that American soldiers had killed Vietnamese civilians, Westmoreland said, "Of course innocent people have been killed. In war they always are. And of course our hearts go out to the innocent victims of this". The dramatist realized that Westmoreland's sentiment runs throughout American history, and he recalls listening to Charles Ives' *Fourth Symphony* in which two orchestras in counterpoint play opposing pieces of music based on American folk songs ("Shenandoah" and "Columbia, the Gem of the Ocean"): "you have this serene, seraphic music based on these folk songs, and then the violent opposition of a marching band

Indians: New York, 1969

drowning it out". In Kopit's mind this music was juxtaposed with Westmoreland's quote. Thus, the dramatist uses those exact words as part of Colonel Forsythe's dialogue in his comments on the massacre of a group of Indians.

Although capturing the essence of American history, Kopit has admitted that "most of the scenes in the play are based on real incidents that were distorted". The tension in the play derives from his pairing of the scenes. He uses the extravagant Wild West Show segments to illustrate American prejudices, reveal Buffalo Bill's character, and to examine a theme that has run through some of his earlier plays—the concept of mythic heroism. Opposed to the Wild West Show segments are scenes from the Indian Commission hearing that demonstrate how alien the White and Indian societies appear to each other. On the one hand the Whites do not understand why Indians do not abide by the signed treaties and do not recognize that they are innately inferior to the White race. On the other hand the Indians do not understand the concept of treaties based on land ownership, a notion which does not make sense to them because they do not believe that the land can be owned, and they also question why the Whites do not abide by the agreed-upon terms of the treaties if they are valid. Obviously neither side understands nor respects the other and therefore is unable to recognize the dignity of its opponent.

To emphasize the contrast between the basic cultural instincts of the two sides, Kopit twice incorporates into the play words that Chief Joseph uttered in 1877:

> I am tired of fighting. Our chiefs have been killed. . .the old men are all dead. It is cold and we have no blankets. The children are freezing. My people, some of them, have fled to the hills and have no food. . .no one knows where they are—perhaps frozen. I want to have time to look for my children and see how many of them I can find. Maybe I shall find them among the dead. Hear me, my chiefs. I am tired. Hy heart is sick and sad! From where the sun now stands, I will fight no more, forever.

This quotation stands in stark contrast to Westmoreland's words (cited above) and thereby epitomizes the conflict that Kopit is representing.

As demonstrated by the "Chronology for a Dreamer" that is included in the printed version of the play, it is clear that Kopit does not intend *Indians* to be taken on a literal, realistic level. This dramatic structure—an emotional Gestalt in the impressionistic, surrealistic representation of his themes through a deliberately confusing, Brechtian style—leads the audience to an awareness of the man-made nature of the historical process. For example, through the delineation of Buffalo Bill's character, combined with historical events and America's need to create heroes—which make him instrumental in destroying a people and a way of life that he admires—the dramatist shows that history is composed of human, not natural, forces, which are thus alterable.

—Steven H. Gale

THE INFANT.   See **THE MINOR.**

THE INFERNAL MACHINE (La Machine infernale)
by Jean Cocteau

First Publication: Paris, 1934.
First Production: Comédie des Champs-Elysées, 10 April 1934.

Translations
The Infernal Machine, translated by Carl Wildman, London, 1936; revised version in *International Modern Plays*, edited by Anthony Bent, 1950.
The Infernal Machine, translated by Albert Bermel, in *"The Infernal Machine" and Other Plays*, Norfolk, Connecticut, 1963.

Criticism
(For general works on the author, see *Playwrights* volume)

Articles:
Francis Fergusson, "*The Infernal Machine*: The Myth Behind the Modern City", in his *The Idea of a Theatre*, Princeton, New Jersey, 1949.
Alberta E. Feyman, "*The Infernal Machine*, Hamlet, and Ernest Jones", in *Modern Drama*, 6, 1963.
Raquel S. Zaraspe, "Sophocles' *Oedipus Rex* and Cocteau's *The Infernal Machine*: A Study on Artistic Variations of the 'Oedipus theme' ", in *Diliman Review*, 14, 1966.
José S. Lasso de la Vega, "El tema de Edipo en *La máquina infernal* de Cocteau", in his *Los temas griegos en el teatro francés contemporáneo: Cocteau, Gide, Anouilh*, Murcia, 1981.
Karelisa V. Hartigan, "Oedipus in France: Cocteau's Mythic Strategy in *La Machine infernale*", in *Classical and Modern Literature*, 6, 1986.
Sonja G. Stary, "Cosmic Disorder and the Poet in Cocteau's *La Machine infernale*", in *Romance Quarterly*, 34, 1987.
Lewis W. Leadbetter, "In Defense of Cocteau: Another View of *La Machine infernale*", in *Classical and Modern Literature*, 10, 1990.

*   *   *

The Infernal Machine (*La Machine infernale*) is a four-act dramatization of the Oedipus legend. In the first act, an ambitious young soldier seeking to conquer the Sphinx, reports a confrontation with the ghost of Laius, who wants to warn Jocasta of impending misfortune. Jocasta and the blind soothsayer Tiresias enter. Although disturbed by the murder of Laius, Jocasta is attracted to the young soldier who reminds her of Oedipus. Act II takes place simultaneously outside Thebes. Oedipus encounters the Sphinx who, appearing as a girl, reveals to him the answer to the riddle, "Which animal walks on four legs in the morning, two at noon, and three in the evening?". By exclaiming the answer "man" to Anubis, Egyptian god of death, Oedipus enjoys the delusion of triumph. He forsakes the Sphinx who becomes vindictive and, as the goddess Nemesis, executes the fate announced in the prologue. In Act III Oedipus (still unrecognised) and Jocasta are initially contented during their wedding night. Tiresias arrives to bless the marriage and, in predicting Oedipus's downfall, disturbs the bliss. Subsequently, Jocasta detects the scars that reveal Oedipus's identity. During the fourth act, seventeen years later, Oedipus and Jocasta recognize reality and accept fate. In acknowledging his acts of murder and incest, Oedipus actualizes a shame that provokes Jocasta's suicide and his self-inflicted blindness. His daughter Antigone

The Infernal Machine: Design by Jean Cocteau, c. 1934

leads him away; his brother-in-law Creon proclaims his expulsion which lifts a plague from Thebes. At the end, although Tiresias attributes to Jocasta and Oedipus a glory resulting directly and indirectly from their solving of the enigma, Creon denounces the dishonor of their actions.

Like Sophocles's Oedipus, Cocteau's protagonist struggles against destiny and, through ignorance, suffers defeat, experiences a purgation of emotions, and contends with human fallibility and vulnerability. But if the principles of Greek tragedy inform the narrative and structure of the play, Cocteau adapts ancient myth to 20th-century themes. Oedipus, like protagonists in plays by Giraudoux, Anouilh, Sartre, and Camus, acts consciously and individually. Such freedom, though, is delusory. Fate defines man's situation, and action results neither in Sophoclean heroism nor in existential self-actualization. Rather, Oedipus is entrapped in an "infernal machine" constructed by the gods for "mortal annihilation", as we are told at the start of the play. Oedipus becomes a victim who, through good intentions but disappointing decisions, comes to recognize the futility of his endeavors. Cocteau the dramatist, then, is a sort of poet–seer perceiving the nature of man's imprisonment in a destructive, diabolical world. Through dialogue and conflict of action, he reproduces a spectacle of the anxieties and meaninglessness of human existence. Two opposing pictures emerge simultaneously: the changing aspects of human struggle and the persistent presence of cosmic order. In spite of unrelenting efforts, Oedipus becomes resigned to an inevitable downfall which, in turn, enables the spectator to sense the agony of the human situation.

The confusion in the opening act results from ineffective communication. The young soldier wants to conquer the Sphinx in order to attain glory. But the Sphinx eludes him, and he encounters instead the ghost of Laius who, reminiscent of the spectre of Hamlet's father, pleads to speak to Jocasta. In spite of his attempts to tell Jocasta of disaster, he remains invisible and silent, reduced to witnessing her tripping on the scarf and her recognition of Oedipus in the young soldier. Suicide and incest are hidden but present tensions, and human inadequacies produce the circumstances of tragic downfall. In Act II, Oedipus elicits from the Sphinx the answer to the riddle and, in publicly solving the puzzle, sees himself as "more intelligent and better educated" than his fellow Thebans. Through identification of self-love with a higher love defined by the Sphinx, Oedipus misunderstands reality. In following his "star", he submits to a fatalism which, masked by fame and happiness in Act III, evolves into disgrace and despair. Reality, represented by the Sphinx, is an enigma constantly confronted and continually misconstrued. Man must act and, through his limitations, endure suffering and regret.

Through irony of action and imagery, Cocteau converts illusion into illumination. By announcing the answer to the Sphinx's riddle, Oedipus earns the privilege of marrying Jocasta and of ruling Thebes. The ascent to power and prestige, however, hides the horror of patricide and incest. Oedipus cannot efface the scars which, as an abandoned child, he incurred during a boar-attack. Self-identification shatters self-illusions; and Oedipus and Jocasta, in penetrating the veil of appearances, accept their individual realities defined by disgrace and remorse. In spite of the vicissitudes of human actions, a cosmic order remains consistent and eternal. Images denote this changing but constant setting. Laius's white beard and red blotch in Act I parallel Jocasta's white robe and red scarf in Act IV; and the ghost of Laius foreshadows the suicide of Jocasta who, stumbling on the scarf in the opening act, uses it ultimately for strangulation. Threatening supernatural forces lurk and eventually emerge to inflict pain. The Sphinx's white dress and Anubis's jackal-like head in Act II, for example, surface imagistically as white bedcovering layered with animal skin in Act III. Cocteau's characters inhabit a world which, like the creases in an unfolding robe, is a chamber for torment and grief. Love of kindred cannot prevent fated destruction; and Oedipus becomes an agent of destiny, murdering his father and driving his mother to death.

In depicting the agony of human struggle, Cocteau creates a spectacle of shock. Oedipus's recognition of his crimes instils a terror and shame which affirm the insignificance of human existence. By blinding himself with Jocasta's brooch, he attempts to eradicate recriminations and, like the sightless Tiresias, seems to attain wisdom. But Creon condemns Oedipus; and Tiresias, who has the last word, asks the spectator to decide on praise or blame. Human actions, then, are illusory and meaningless; and, for the spectator, only the presence of pain remains real in this "infernal machine" that Cocteau, in Act IV, terms "a masterpiece of horror".

—Donald Gilman

INFIDELITIES. See **THE DOUBLE INCONSTANCY.**

GL'INGANNATI. See **THE DECEIVED.**

THE INSECT PLAY (Ze života Hmyzů)
by Karel and Josef Čapek

First Publication: Prague, 1921.
First Production: Národní Divadlo [National Theatre], Brno,
　　　　　Czechoslovakia, 3 February 1922.

Translations
The Life of the Insects, translated by Paul Selver, London, 1923.
The World We Live In (*The Insect Comedy*), adapted by Owen Davis, New York, 1933.

Criticism
(For general works on the authors, see *Playwrights* volume)

Articles:
Milada Blekastad, "Probleme der Originalität in *Ze života hmyzů* der Brüder Čapek", in *Scando-Slavica*, 22, 1976.

*　　*　　*

The Insect Play is an allegorical revue rather than a play, consisting in satirical pictures of various classes and ideologies.

It has three acts, a prologue and an epilogue. In these, the Tramp—a naive observer, an "ordinary man"—asks himself: "What's it all for?"

The first act concerns the Butterflies—Clythie, Otakar, Felix, Iris and Viktor—who flirt and giggle and compose bad poetry. The Tramp is shocked by the vanity and heartlessness of this *jeunesse dorée*, especially when Iris's suitor, Victor, is gulped down by a passing bird (a natural death for a butterfly). In the second act the Tramp meets the bourgeois class, the exploiters: first, the Dung Beetle couple, who roll their precious capital around with them until it is purloined by another Dung Beetle. Then he encounters the Ichneumon Fly, busy fattening up his Larva daughter. The Crickets arrive on the scene, preoccupied with furnishing a pretty little home ready for the birth of their baby Cricket. But left alone, Mother Cricket is quickly snapped up by the Ichneumon Fly; to the horror of the Tramp—and apparently also of the Parasite, a character who tries to subvert the Tramp onto his side. The Parasite's concern turns out to be simply resentment and jealousy of the Fly's larder, and he gets his revenge and satisfaction when he munches up not only the Fly's larder, but the Larva daughter as well.

In the third act the Tramp faces a totalitarian state—the world of the Ants, where every individual action fits into a precisely formulated plan. In the interests of the common good and world peace the Ants work tirelessly to subjugate all contrary opinions. Inevitably this leads to war, and to their defeat by the Yellow Ants, who themselves claim to fight only for justice, for history, for national honour—and for commercial interests.

It is a sceptical view of the world, which is contrasted with the Tramp's wide-eyed optimism. The Tramp's hopeful spirit focuses on the Chrysalis who keeps him company, and who cries out in the desire to be born, to be alive. In the Epilogue the Tramp strikes a spark from his flint, which attracts a bevy of moths. The Chrysalis breaks from its casing and joins them; within seconds its brief life is over. The Tramp, kneeling over the body, realises that the meaning of life is simply to live; at that moment he himself falls and dies. As the sun rises, the local people—schoolchildren, a Woodcutter, a woman with a newborn child—set about the day. They stop to greet a travelling Wayfarer, who, in the Čapek's stage directions, is to be played by the same actor as the Tramp. (The authors offered an alternative ending for fainthearted theatre directors; the Tramp only dreams of death, and wakes to greet the new day himself).

The character of the Tramp and the conclusion of the play demonstrate the Čapeks' world view. It is by living that we learn to live, for we are all part of one another, of what has already been, and of what will be. The types of human being who are satirised are blinded by selfish preoccupations, and unable to respond to the gift of life. At first the Tramp is sensually attracted by the Butterflies and ashamed of his dirt and disorderly appearance. But he soon sees through this salon society, whose heartless women remind him of one who abandoned him long ago; such "love", he knows, won't last longer than the next novelty. The preoccupations of the middle classes are even less attractive. The "capital" which obsesses the Dung Beetles smells of decay. The Crickets might seem, on the surface, to be a commendable couple who give preference to a blissful and intimate domesticity. But it turns out that their cosy little nest once belonged to another cricket who was snapped up by a butcher-bird; the two of them laugh merrily at his fate. "Murder upon murder!" cries the Tramp. We human beings, he reminds himself, are not like the insect world: we work to build up something for the future; we seek a quiet and private life; we struggle resolutely to survive. However, this

The Insect Play: National Theatre, Prague, 1965 (design by Joseph Svoboda)

defence of human aspirations, he realises, is not going too well. We are all exploiters, he concludes. He himself is a good-for-nothing cockroach. There must be something greater than this—for example, a shared entirety. With this, the Čapeks introduce their vision of the scientific future in "the largest democracy", as the First Engineer describes it. "How so?" asks the Tramp. "Everyone must obey," he is told, "everyone must work. All for It". "What?" he asks. "The Entirety—the State—the Nation". At first the Tramp accommodates this to his own ideas of democracy, but eventually he sees through the pretentious slogans. How can a pitiful ant call himself Emperor of the World, when he does not even sense the wind blowing in the treetops?

The Insect Play belongs to the tradition of the small stages and the cabarets. Each scene establishes a satirical point. There is no development of character nor, although this is disguised, of action. (The Chrysalis's anticipation of its future and its brief life is merely a framework). *The Insect Play* is a didactic work which demonstrates to the public how *not* to live, and ends with a glimpse of the promise of man's life: the sun rises over the village, a woman carries a new-born child to baptism, schoolchildren are on their way to school, a woodcutter on his way to work. The Čapeks' aim is to make people aware of the essential nobility of ordinary life, of the honest labour which gives meaning to one's existence. It is a Protestant world view, in which work enables one to repudiate self-centredness, and to be responsible for one's fellowmen. The theme is also related to the "humanitist" philosophy of Tomáš Masaryk, the first president of Czechoslovakia, to whose circle the Čapeks belonged. According to Masaryk, "humanitism" had evolved from ideals of the Hussites and the Czech Brethren; nevertheless, it was cultural rather than religious, and was related to a man's awareness of himself as part of the (Czech) community. Without this awareness we may live, as the insects do, brief, meaningless lives dedicated to pleasure or profit. Humanitism was also a defence against totalitarianism; the Čapeks were concerned about the rise of fascism in post-World War I Europe. In the guise of a colourful revue, the Čapek brothers were provoking their audience to consider their own role in national life.

—Barbara Day

AN INSPECTOR CALLS
by J.B. Priestley

First Publication: London, 1947.
First Production: Opera House, Manchester, 9 September 1946.

Criticism
(For general works on the author, see *Playwrights* volume)

Articles:
Dietrich Peinert, "J.B. Priestley, *An Inspector Calls*", in *Praxis des neusprachlichen Unterrichts*, 13, 1966.
Maria Gottwald, "*An Inspector Calls*: A Problem Play or a Modern Morality?", in *Acta Universitatis Wratislaviensis*, 233, 1974.

* * *

In 1912 a family celebration in the home of factory owner Arthur Birling, to celebrate his daughter Shiela's engagement to Gerald and Birling's impending knighthood, is interrupted by an Inspector Goul, apparently investigating the suicide of an impoverished young woman, Eva Smith. The Inspector confronts each member of the party with incidents of their crass, heartless treatment of the girl: Mr. Birling's refusal to increase her meagre wage and dismissal of her for going on strike; Shiela's unjustified insistence the girl be dismissed from her shop-assistant post; Gerald's casual affair with her; brother Eric's abandonment of her when she became pregnant; and Mrs. Birling's refusal to allow her charity committee to assist Eva. When the Inspector leaves, Birling phones the police and discovers, to his relief, they know of no Inspector Goul. Moments later, the phone rings to report the suicide of a young woman.

J.B. Priestley was constantly rattling the cage of realism so that he might deal with concepts beyond the immediate moment. *An Inspector Calls* is arguably his most successful attempt at breaking the boundaries of time and space confining the conventional drawing-room drama, while still achieving an effortless bonding between form and content.

On the surface, the play appears to be a conventional drawing-room play. Certainly, the action is contained in the Birlings' sitting-room and interaction takes place through discussion. However, even with this simple setting, Priestley gently stretches the limits of the form, edging his audience to a wider, and less complacent perspective. Although the action is permanently settled in the same room, safely confined within the three walls of the permanent set, the furniture is rearranged for each act, enforcing (within the limits of the convention) a slightly different perspective, and consequently slightly unsettling a spectator.

In the same manner, Priestley employs other components of the well-made realist play to extend the limits of form and expand the possible references of the play. Setting the play in 1912 allows the audience obvious foreknowledge. Mr. Birling's arrogant assertions of his unshakable superiority, an implied moral superiority justified by a linking of wealth, position, and, apparently, intelligence, (for example, in his claims that war is not inevitable, and that the ship, the Titanic is "absolutely unsinkable") flatter the audience, make a clear ironic point, and reveal that both Mr Birling's confident position and his secure world, like his judgement, are not as unassailable as they appear.

At the height of this celebration of moral rectitude confirmed by wealth and position, the strange, uninvited, Inspector Goul arrives. So confident are the characters of their righteousness and position, they do not even ask for credentials, but rather seek to impress their credentials on him: "I was an alderman for years—and Lord Mayor two years ago—and I'm still on the bench—as I know the Bromley police officers pretty well—and I thought I'd never seen you before". Thus, the insulated, self-satisfied complacency of the Birlings' home is invaded by the larger, outside world through the Inspector. The middle-class drawing-room, that private fortress against the unstable dangers of public confusion and interaction, has become vulnerable.

As the Inspector confronts each member of the family with the abused history of Eva Smith, Priestley involves the audience on several levels at once. The members of the family reveal their attitudes towards Eva and the outside world, elaborating their concepts of their place in the world and their varying degress of callousness towards those "less fortunate" than themselves. Secondly, these perspectives and their responses to the Inspector's story set the characters against each other, creating a drama within the family. At the same time, however, the action moves beyond the personal responses of the Birlings. The "drama" of the piece cannot be contained within those three permanent, protective walls of the sitting-room. The Inspector's story, the extremities of Eva's life and the implications of the Birlings' responses render these walls transparent, exposing their inhabitants. And Eva Smith and the multitude she represents come streaming in to create metaphorically the visual and dramatic focus of the play.

In the same way that Mr. Birling's judgements on the Titanic implied more than mere personal opinion, the Birlings' attitudes toward the poor and their own relationship to the social hierarchy become more than personal attitudes. Through the story of Eva Smith, social attitude transcends mere delineation of character and becomes a platform of action with concrete consequence. So here, too, the conventional drawing-room where one might express one's opinions safely with the decorated, unchanging walls loses its magical safety. These "opinions" are revealed to be powerful instigators of action. The weight of the consequences of that action has caused them to rebound back into the cosy living-room and taint its isolated comfort.

Much of the power of the play rests in Priestley's demand, through Inspector Goul and his story, for the imaginative participation of the audience. To the function of dialogue as a means for transmitting information, Priestley has added the active function of stimulating and directing a visual and imaginative context. Without that creation in the audience's mind of the incidents of Eva's tormented story, the play loses both impact and meaning.

By the end of the play, the scenes of her despair—the strike, the department story, her love affair with Gerald, her relationship with Eric, and her desperate appeal to the charity committee and (most horrible of all), her suicide, seen from *her* point of view—outweigh the Birlings' consternation. Their denials, regrets and self-defence seem petty in comparison with the apalling struggle we have witnessed. And yet, it is the Birlings who have been onstage; Eva has been, with Priestley's help, our own construction.

Mr. and Mrs. Birling's efforts to discredit the Inspector, like Mr. Birling's prophecies, are petty, selfish, arrogant, and insignificant. Shiela's insistence on breaking off her engagement with Gerald and her genuine repentance give some hope for the future. It is a fitting irony that Mr. Birling's phone call to the police, made to discredit the Inspector, ties him to the young woman's death.

It matters less to us than to the Birlings what the true nature of the Inspector's status might be. Hopefully, we have, for the time of the play, at least, become less attached to information, fact, and material credibility and more concerned with the intangible questions of moral responsibility and emotional integrity. The process of the play is meant to detach the audience from the demands of verisimilitude. It is impossible, also, to ascertain with exactitude whether Eva Smith is really the same woman who changed her name to survive, or a series of different women. This dual possibility is not merely a clever trick to tantalize, nor only the suggestion that Eva is the representative of a multitude, but also another effort to move the drawing-room drama out of the confines of the specific and the individual to the representative and to abstract moral concepts.

Priestley has gracefully dissipated the specificity of the naturalistic stage conventions so that Eva and the Birlings emerge as representatives, creating a larger concept in which abstract concepts have weight and significance. The images of Eva's life transcend the limits of the stage. Each incident is a moral parable, an example to carry out into the street, and the Birlings' exposure becomes a fable of social ethics and moral responsibility.

The Inspector's "Sermon on the Mount" preaches basic, Christian values of charity, compassion, kindness, and, above all, the responsibility of privilege. Although the mildness of its "message", its acceptance of social hierarchy and its avoidance of the idea of social change may seem inadequate for the present day and certainly dates the play, The *Inspector Calls* merits credit and interest, not least for the skill with which Priestley fills the conventional drawing-room drama with the teeming world it is traditionally fortressed against.

—Elaine Turner

———

THE INSPECTOR GENERAL.   See **THE GOVERNMENT INSPECTOR.**

———

THE INTELLECTUAL LADIES.   See **THE PRETENTIOUS YOUNG LADIES.**

———

LOS INTERESES CREADOS.   See **BONDS OF INTEREST.**

———

THE INVESTIGATION (Die Ermittlung)
by Peter Weiss

First Publication: In *Theater heute*, August, 1965; in book form, Frankfurt, 1965.
First Production: Simultaneously, 19 October 1965, at the following theatres: Freie Volksbühne, Berlin; Deutsche Akademie der Künste, Berlin; Theater der Stadt, Cottbus; Staatstheater, Dresden; Bühnen der Stadt, Essen; Bühnen der Stadt, Gera; Städtische Bühnen, Cologne; Landestheater, Halle / Leuna; Aldwych Theatre, London (Royal Shakespeare Company); Meininger Theater; Kammerspiele, Munich; Friedrich-Wolf-Theater, Neustrelitz; Hans-Otto-Theater, Potsdam; Volkstheater, Rostock; Württembergisches Staatstheater, Stuttgart; Nationaltheater, Weimar.

Translations
The Investigation, in *The Investigation: Oratorio in 11 Cantos*, translated by Alexander Gross, London, 1966.

Criticism
(For general works on the author, see *Playwrights* volume)

Books:
Erika Salloch, *Peter Weiss: "Die Ermittlung": Zur Struktur des Dokumentartheaters*, 1972.
Gerd Weinreich, *Peter Weiss: "Die Ermittlung"*, Frankfurt, 1983.

Articles:
Wolfgang Hädecke, "Zur *Ermittlung* von Peter Weiss", in *Neue Rundschau*, 77, 1966.
R.C. Perry, "Historical Authenticity and Dramatic Form: Hochhuth's *Der Stellvertreter* and Weiss's *Die Ermittlung*", in *Modern Language Review*, 64, 1969.
Heinrich Peuckmann, "Peter Weiss: *Die Ermittlung*: Eine Unterrichtseinheit", in *Sammlung*, 3, 1980.

*   *   *

In a courtroom in West Germany nine anonymous witnesses and 18 defendants representing actual people are cross-examined by a judge, public prosecutor, and defence counsel to establish what actually happened in the concentration camp of Auschwitz in German-occupied Poland during World War II. The drama, sub-titled an *Oratorio*, presents in 11 cantos various facets of the death camps beginning with the unloading of new victims at the camp station, tracing in detail their individual and collective fates both as prisoners and as material for scientific experiments, and ending finally with their extermination in the crematoria.

19th October 1965 marks a historic date in 20th-century, German theatre. On that day 15 major theatres simultaneously premiered *The Investigation*. It was not the fame of the playwright which had caused such an unprecedented event—though Peter Weiss certainly had made a name for himself the previous year with the theatrically spectacular *Marat Sade*—nor was it the style of the play, which promised audiences the kind of sensory bombardment to which they had been exposed by the author one year previously; the 15 theatres had chosen his new play because of its subject matter. *The Investigation* deals quite unashamedly with the single most traumatic event in recent European history: the Holocaust.

The fact that it had taken a full 20 years for Peter Weiss, a Swedish citizen of German-Jewish descent, to bring himself to write about this subject, is indicative of just how deeply repressed the emotions surrounding the Holocaust actually were. And this applied not only to Weiss but to the entire German nation. A collective amnesia had befallen it. However, a 20-month-long trial of men responsible for the most notorious death camp of all, Auschwitz, began to unlock the amnesia. Weiss had personally attended the trial in Frankfurt and used his own notes as well as official transcripts of the court proceedings as the basis for his documentary play.

The choice of the documentary play as a vehicle for the presentation of such a topic is significant. Such a play prevents an audience from subconsciously divorcing the events on stage from any reality which it may be part of and feel responsible for. In a society which for 20 years had avoided any critical engagement with its recent past by hurling itself into the pursuit of material successes, a play which wished to make both a psychological and a moral impact had to present the facts of the matter starkly and without distraction.

Directors and designers have been mindful of this need too. In his acclaimed production in West Berlin, Erwin Piscator had the faces of the accused and the court officials spotlighted against a neutral set and on a semi-darkened stage. The accused were grouped as a single block in tiered rows on a platform, which formed one side of a triangular-shaped courtroom (the judge, defence, and prosecution forming another line, with the nine witnesses, seated on a bench sunk beneath the stage directly in front of the audience, completing the triangle). Such a technique highlights a further objective of Weiss's documentary approach. Seating the accused in one block emphasises the collective responsibility of the military, administrative, and scientific personnel of the camp, but the spotlighting of their faces and upper bodies compels the spectator not to forget the individual guilt either.

Indeed, Weiss's play constantly brings the universal scale of the holocaust back down to a comprehensible and believable individual, human level. It chronicles like few other contemporary works of art man's potential for suffering, man's potential for survival and, perhaps most tellingly of all, man's potential for sadism. Weiss does not paint any of these types of behaviour with broad strokes of a brush, but with a meticulous feel for detail, often to the point where the spectaor wishes to cry "stop!". And there is no doubt that Weiss, unlike Brecht, is not averse to involving an audience emotionally, for it is surely a sign of our humanity that we do have feelings and understand how to express them appropriately.

However, Weiss, as a political dramatist who had studied Brecht carefully, is only too aware of the danger of allowing the emotional forces unleashed to paralyse the intellectual responses of an audience. He has therefore structured the material and the language in a very measured, rational, and anti-dramatic manner in order to increase the spectator's ability to grasp and above all *judge* what he is following. He has not used the rhythms of everyday speech but opted instead for a rhythmically-accentuated free verse. Of its effectiveness Walter Jens, reviewing the Piscator production in West Berlin, wrote that there was no sobbing in the audience, just occasionally a burst of restrained contemptuous laughter at certain statements made by the defendants and especially by the counsel for the defence. The audience did not clap at the end, as instructed by placards, and left the theatre in almost total silence.

The one main ideological point which an audience is invited to consider is articulated by the Third Witness. He had been active in the resistance movement in the camp and had retained his socialist interpretation of the camps and their place in a fascist system. In essence he saw the concentration camps as being a microcosm of capitalist society "which allowed the exploiter / to develop his power / to a hitherto unknown degree / and the exploited / had to deliver up his own guts".

This is not the sole key to understanding *The Investigation* for it fuses many traditions of drama, modern and medieval, into one: documentary, political theatre, and passion play. Certainly in its latter role it provides the spectator with a disturbing yet unique insight into the final stations of a journey of suffering, unwillingly undertaken by millions of men, women, and children, for which there was no reason other than that we, the fortunate survivors and witnesses, might learn the lessons grotesquely magnified by Weiss and thus avoid another Auschwitz.

—Anthony Waine

L'INVITATION AU CHÂTEAU. See RING ROUND THE MOON.

IPHIGENEIA TAURICA. See **IPHIGENIA IN TAURIS.**

IPHIGENIA IN TAURUS (Iphigeneia Taurica)
by Euripides

First Production: Athens, c.414–13 B.C.

Editions
Iphigeneia in Taurica [with translation], in *Euripides, 2*, edited by Arthur S. Way, London, 1912 (Loeb Classical Library).
The Iphigenia Among the Tauri, edited by E.B. England, London, 1926.
Iphigenia in Tauris, in *Iphigenia: Two Plays*, edited by C.B. Watts, London, 1930.
Iphigenia in Tauris, edited by M. Platnauer, Oxford, 1938.
Iphigenia in Tauris, edited by David Sansone, Leipzig, 1981.

Translations
Iphigenia in Tauris, translated by Gilbert Murray, London, 1910.
Iphigenia in Tauris, translated by Witter Bynner, New York, 1915.
Iphigenia in Tauris, in *Euripides: Three Plays*, translated by Philip Vellacott, Harmondsworth, 1953; second edition, 1974.
Iphigenia in Tauris, translated by Richmond Lattimore, London, 1974.

Criticism
(For general works on the author, see *Playwrights* volume)

Articles:
R. Caldwell, "Tragedy Romanticized: The *Iphigenia Taurica*", in *Classical Journal*, 70, 1974.
D. Sansone, "The Sacrifice-Motif in Euripides' *Iphigenia Taurica*", in *Transactions of the American Philological Association* [*TAPA*], 105, 1975.
J.C.G. Strachan, "Iphigenia and Human Sacrifice in Eurpides' *Iphigenia Taurica*", in *Classical Philology*, 71, 1976.

*   *   *

The *Iphigenia in Tauris* is the type of romantic melodrama with a happy ending characteristic of the later work of Euripides. Its setting is appropriately exotic: the forecourt of a temple of Artemis on the Taurian coast in the modern Crimea. The play tells how Iphigenia, the daughter of Agamemnon, is serving as a priestess of the Taurians, having been rescued when on the point of being sacrificed at Aulis by her father, who was leading the Greeks to Troy. Her brother Orestes and his friend Pylades come to the Crimea in search of a statue of Artemis which will release Orestes from his sufferings. A report that a pair of men has been captured is brought to Iphigenia whose responsibility it is to sacrifice arrivals from Greece on the altar of Artemis. When they meet, brother and sister fail to recognise one other, but a desire on the part of Iphigenia to have a letter smuggled back to Greece leads to a realisation that the two men are Iphigenia's own brother and his companion. Now reunited, they plot an escape to Greece together with the statue, but their plan is threatened by the arrival of king Thoas who, however, is persuaded that the statue must be cleansed in the sea. Once they reach the shore, escape is achieved, but only after a fight and a most opportune

intervention by the goddess Athene. Throughout the play intense excitement is sustained by the seemingly endless twists and turns of a far from simple plot.

Iphigenia delivers a lengthy prologue of a type common in Euripides' plays. This does more than just impart basic information; it also reveals the pathos inherent in the woman's present plight. Furthermore, we learn of a dream which, ironically, is both optimistic (in depicting Iphigenia's restoration at home) and pessimistic (in seeming to anticipate the sacrifice of Orestes). It appears almost inevitable that as Iphigenia vanishes into the temple, Orestes and Pylades should take her place, busying themselves in careful examination of the blood-stained altar of Artemis. A reference to the goddess's statue and the instruction from Apollo to present it to Athens completes all we need to know in the way of information; Orestes' hesitation but Pylades' stern determination to fulfil their mission similarly complete our picture of the play's major characters.

The herdsman's account of the capture of Orestes and Pylades is certainly long, but any danger of tedium is eliminated by vivid description of an Orestes stricken by madness as he imagines himself pursued by a Fury and falls upon cattle in a belief that these too are Furies. The actual capture is almost hilarious as the herdsmen are scattered and then regroup and stone the young men into submission. The chorus finds a story so rich in detail astounding. And Iphigenia herself has another long speech in which, yet again, a heavy vein of irony is exploited: believing her brother dead Iphigenia declares her heart now to be hardened while, at the same time, delivering a pathetic account of how she came to Aulis ostensibly to be married, and then indulging in typical Euripidean philosophizing when she claims that it is men and not the gods who are evil.

The scene between Iphigenia and Orestes, who both talk vigorously but at cross-purposes, is a masterpiece of misunderstanding although it does reveal that Orestes is still alive. At every point it is expected that the full truth will come out, but it never does and our expectations are constantly frustrated. Euripides has a fondness for simple stage-props and one is then introduced: Iphigenia offers not to kill Orestes if he will carry a letter back to Argos for her, but Orestes proposes that Pylades performs the mission and proceeds to persuade his friend to do this in an exchange of an especial appeal to a Greek audience (deeply appreciative as it was of the art of rhetoric). But a complication is raised: what if Pylades' ship sinks and the letter lost but Pylades saved? The obvious solution to this dilemma is to tell Pylades the contents of the letter and this information, thus conveyed in such a way as not to strain credulity, identifies Iphigenia to the captives.

It is also quite natural that Iphigenia should delay the planning of their escape by seeking all the family news from Orestes. If Euripides drags out this episode at what initially appears inordinate length, it is done deliberately to heighten suspense. Less realistic, but again characteristic of Euripides, is the request for secrecy made to the chorus. But Thoas has still to be deceived, and Iphigenia's claim that the intended victims were unclean and so unfit for sacrifice and that Artemis's image must be purified illustrates, again surely to a Greek audience's considerable delight, its proponent's cleverness and superiority over a "barbarian". There remains one more drawn-out exposition: the messenger's description of the actual escape. In spite of their suspicions, the guards entrust the prisoners to Iphigenia; eventually they decide to investigate and find a Greek ship ready to depart and the two heroes climbing on board; both groups fight with fists in an attempt to secure Iphigenia and the Taurians are forced to fall back and use stones; the Greeks retaliate with arrows as Orestes carries his sister and statue safely aboard the ship which sails away but is then driven to the shore again by the wind. Thoas and his men make off to the shore, and it is at this point that Euripides plays his last card—the goddess Athene appears and orders Thoas to desist. The playwright has wrung an audience's every emotion and brought the most devious of plots to a happy conclusion. But Euripides adds a last detail with the obvious intention of pleasing his Athenian audience: Athene also orders the building of a sanctuary on the borders of Attica to house the statue of Artemis. The establishment of a local cult centre gives the play a special relevance to the original spectators and stresses the Athenian context of the drama.

—Peter Walcot

IRONHAND. See **GÖTZ VON BERLICHINGEN WITH THE IRON HAND.**

THE ISLAND
by Athol Fugard, John Kani, and Winston Ntshona

First Publication: In *Statements: Three Plays*, London, 1974.
First Production: As *Die Hodoshe Span*, The Space Theatre, Cape Town, 1973; as *The Island*, Royal Court Theatre, London, 2 January 1974.

Criticism
(For general works on Fugard, see *Playwrights* volume)

Books:
Deborah D. Foster, *Blood-Knot and The Islands [sic]as Anti-Tragedy*, Madison, Wisconsin, 1977.

Articles:
Patrick O'Sheel, "Athol Fugard's 'poor theatre' ", in *Journal of Commonwealth Literature*, vol. 12 no.3, 1978.
Errol Durbach, "Sophocles in South Africa: Athol Fugard's *The Island*", in *Comparative Drama*, 18, 1984.
Lauri Anderson, "The Audience as Judge in Athol Fugard's *The Island*", in *Notes on Contemporary Literature*, vol.16 no.1, 1986.
Albert Wertheim, "Political Acting and Political Action: Athol Fugard's *The Island*", in *World Literature Written in English*, 26, 1986.
Albert Wertheim, "The Prison as Theatre and the Theatre as Prison: Athol Fugard's *The Island*", in *The Theatrical Space*, Cambridge, 1987.

*   *   *

Winston and John are prisoners who have shared a cell for almost three years on Robben Island. After their gruelling day of hard and deliberately futile labour they return to their cell where John coaches Winston for his role as Antigone in their improvised drama, "The Trial and Punishment of Antigone", which they are due to present at the prison concert in six days time. Winston, however, is unenthusiastic about his role, partly because he is having trouble grasping the plot and characters but mainly because, not unjustifiably, he thinks he looks absurd playing the role of a woman in a wig and false breasts. A few days later a less than productive rehearsal is curtailed when John is ordered out of the cell, returning stunned with the news that his sentence has been commuted and he has only three more months to serve. The relationship between the two prisoners instantly changes as the implications of John's early release sink in. Winston almost cracks up as he realizes that he will have to endure day after day of his life in prison while John enjoys freedom. But he controls himself and with an enormous act of will comes to terms with his fate, and in the final scene of the play they perform their version of *Antigone* for the prison audience.

Devised through workshops by Fugard with the actors John Kani and Winston Ntshona, *The Island* works powerfully at several, related levels. It can be seen as using the theatrical medium to make a highly effective protest against the repression of political dissent in South Africa by imprisonment, and more specifically by the inhuman treatment meted out to political prisoners at South Africa's once most notorious jail. The barbarous cruelty of the punishments inflicted on the prisoners, especially by psychopathic warders such as the unseen but always menacing Hodoshe, highlights the routine abuse of human rights in South African prisons as a means of trying to deter legitimate opposition to *apartheid*. The last words of the play, uttered by Winston as Antigone, constitute a statement of defiance in the face of state terror: "Gods of our Fathers! My Land! My Home! / Time waits no longer. I go now to my living death, / because I honoured those things to which honour belongs". In the light of John's impending release, Winston's lines as Antigone assume a dreadful personal relevance. Even though he knows that he will suffer the destruction of his selfhood, and his personality will turn to the stone he hews every day in the quarry, his words as Antigone allow him to transcend the despair he experienced earlier, and to assert his refusal to renege on the political commitment which has led him to this living death.

As one might expect of a dramatist who has been preoccupied with the artist's, and especially his own, role as witness of his society, the inclusion of the "play-within-the-play" is used to focus attention on the crucial function of imagination, and particularly the theatrical imagination, in a repressive state like South Africa. The power of the imagination in the form of role-play is suggested in the first scene, when John transforms an empty mug into a telephone and asks the operator to put him through to New Brighton. For a few moments, as both men become utterly absorbed in their fantasy, they "escape" their cell and make imaginative contact with the outside world. Later, the performance of the improvised version of *Antigone* is also at one level an escape, an item of entertainment in the prison concert which may briefly take performers and audience out of their grim reality. But it also demonstrates the possibility of theatre as a means of encompassing and mastering reality, and making ethical statements of lasting significance. However amateurishly, Winston, in his role as Antigone, "witnesses" what is happening to himself and to others in contemporary South Africa, even if he and John use an ancient, Greek story to do so. John, who is presented as intellectually more sophisticated than Winston, understands some of this from the beginning; dressed as Antigone, he points out why, in the end, the audience will not laugh at their performances, in spite of the evident absurdity of their makeshift costumes and props:

Go on laughing! Why did you stop? Must I tell you why? Because behind all this rubbish is me, and you know it's me. You think those bastards out there won't know it's you? Yes, they'll laugh. But who cares about that as long as they laugh in the beginning and listen at the end. That's all we want them to do. . .listen at the end.

The truth of what is said, the imaginative truth that can be generated in performance, will eclipse the evident shortcomings of the presentation.

As well as its political and aesthetic themes, *The Island* reveals Fugard's persistent existentialism—his concern with the dramatizing of what it is like to be a conscious, sentient being in a particular place and time. And it is here that the play perhaps makes the greatest impact, especially in the theatre. With extraordinary force *The Island* conveys the experience of imprisonment and the emotions and tensions of two men who are compelled to be interdependent. For an hour or so, the audience is forced to confront something of what it is like to be confined, to be subjected to the power of others, to be struggling—through anger, humour, role-play and human solidarity with another person—to maintain the threatened sense of personal identity and meaning. The empathy between John and Winston extends to the audience's relation with both characters, the former as he faces up to the shock of his early release, the latter as he struggles to come to terms with an even greater trauma, the realization that he may never leave the island.

—Brian Crow

IT IS SO! IF YOU THINK SO. See **RIGHT YOU ARE (IF YOU THINK YOU ARE).**

AN ITALIAN STRAW HAT (Un Chapeau de paille d'Italie) by Eugène Labiche (with Marc Michel)

First Publication: Paris, 1851.
First Production: Théâtre du Palais-Royal, Paris, 14 August 1851.

Editions

Un Chapeau de paille d'Italie, edited by Stanley W. Grace, London, 1924.
Un Chapeau de paille d'Italie, in *Théâtre de Labiche, 1*, edited by Gilbert Sigaux, Paris, 1964.

Translations

A Leghorn Hat, translated by Clair Vincent Chesley, in *Poet Lore*, 28, 1917.
An Italian Straw Hat, translated by Lynn and Theodore Hoffman, in *The Modern Theatre, 3*, edited by Eric Bentley, Garden City, New York, 1955.
An Italian Straw Hat, translated and adapted by Thomas Walton, London, 1956.
The Italian Straw Hat, in *The Italian Straw Hat; The Spelling Mistake*, translated by Frederick Davies, New York and London, 1967.

* * *

Labiche's best-known play outside France recounts the adventures of a middle-class young man, Fadinard, who on his wedding day becomes involved in a complicated quest. His horse has taken a bite out of a straw hat hanging on a tree, and soon the owner of the hat, Anais, arrives with her companion, a furious military officer, to demand that Fadinard replace the hat, since the lady cannot return home to her husband without it. At the same time Fadinard's bride and in-laws arrive, insisting that it is time to leave for the marriage ceremony. The rest of the play is taken up with Fadinard's implausible experiences as he attempts to find a hat and to get married at the same time, followed constantly by the wedding party who mistake a hat shop for the city hall, a baroness's dwelling for a restaurant, and Anais's husband's apartment for that of the newly-married couple. Finally, a precise replica of the devoured hat turns up among the wedding gifts that had been present all along.

Labiche's fast-moving farce is the quintessential *vaudeville*, a form that blends the virtues of the well-made play with the light fun of farce and the appeal of songs set to popular tunes of the day. What startled Labiche's contemporaries (and almost caused his producer to reject the play) was the non-stop swiftness of the action, hurtling madly toward an (avoided) catastrophe, blended with a madcap fantasy that pre-dates some of the wild inventiveness of Ionesco. In *An Italian Straw Hat* Labiche places the chase firmly in the center of his play, thus preparing the way for the successes of the Keystone cops and other Hollywood comics of the early days. The play is built on a double chase: that of Fadinard in search of his hat (morally, if not physically, pursued by the officer and Anais who are destroying the chairs in his apartment until he returns) and that of the wedding-party who pursue Fadinard wherever he goes, and actually manage to get him married during a traffic jam. Caught between the two demands—the hat and the wedding—the young man suffers the horrors of a nightmare, and it is not the least of Labiche's accomplishments to have combined so effectively a situation of nightmarish intensity with the frivolity of the *vaudeville*. Indeed, René Char whose silent film of the play is responsible for much of its international renown, called it a *vaudeville-cauchemar*, a nightmare-vaudeville.

Like most plays of this type, *A Straw Hat* is based upon a misunderstanding (what the French call a "quiproquo"). Mistaking a frantic search for a hat for a wedding party excursion is, of course, the major mistake that underlies the entire play, but Labiche multiplies misunderstandings from scene to scene and act to act, until poor Fadinard seems like a victim caught within the cogs of a merciless machine. Going into a hat shop, he discovers that some malignant fate has decreed that its owner be a former mistress whom he had promised to marry, and subsequently abandoned. The situation requires role-playing and lies, and leads him to his next situation: an elegant reception at which the hostess mistakes him for the tenor who has come to entertain her guests. Again Fadinard is required to play a role in order to find the hat, followed always by his in-laws who seat themselves at the baroness's table and consume what they think is the wedding banquet. In the following act, he is almost crushed between the conflicting demands of the wedding guests, his own need of the hat, and the jealous husband of Anais to whom his quest has finally led him.

At last the pursuit ends where it began—at Fadinard's door, where the hat has been all the time. This senseless chase suggests the circular structure of much absurdist drama and exposes the flaws of the foolish, blind, selfish, and parsimonious characters. Like the other bourgeois who are central to Labiche's dramatic satire, they remind us of the solid realism that underlies this gaiest of all farces. If the relentless activity stopped for a moment we might reflect pessimistically on the vices of young lovers, wives, mistresses, husbands, fathers, old uncles and others, for Labiche is as steadfast an

An Italian Straw Hat: Shaftesbury Theatre, London, 1986

observer of the middle-classes as any realist or naturalist. Time and again he reminds us with precise details that we are in the world of the mid-19th-century bourgeois, a world that is materialistic, thoughtless, and superficial. Unlike most of the naturalists, however, Labiche exhibits these traits not to raise our hackles, but to force explosions of laughter. Piling trait upon trait, foolish automatic word upon word, or move on move, he reveals unthinking people who are most often victims of situations they create themselves. The well-oiled machinery of Labiche's play is a reflection of the well-oiled machinery of bourgeois society, and the pursuit which is so central to its plot mirrors the materialistic pursuit which occupied middle-class life and marriage.

An Italian Straw Hat has enjoyed frequent performances since its premiere in 1851. A none-too-faithful adaptation by Orson Welles, entitled *Horse Eats Hat*, was performed by the Federal Theatre Project in 1936 more in the style of a Marx Brothers film than a true *vaudeville*. Gaston Baty's 1938 production at the Comédie-Française was much admired, and that venerable institution revived the play once again in the 1980's.

—Leonard C. Pronko

IVANOV
by Anton Chekhov

First Publication: Moscow, 1888.
First Production: Korsch's Russian Dramatic Theatre, Moscow, 1 December 1887.

Translations

Ivanov, in *Three Plays*, translated by Elisaveta Fen, Harmondsworth, 1951.
Ivanov, in *Six Plays of Chekhov*, translated by Robert Corrigan, New York, 1962.
Ivanov, in *Chekhov: The Major Plays*, translated by Ann Dunnigan and Others, New York, 1964.
Ivanov, translated by David Magarshack, New York, 1966.
Ivanov, translated by Ariadne Nicolaeff, adapted by John Gielgud, London, 1966.
Ivanov, in *The Oxford Chekhov, 2*, edited and translated by Ronald Hingley, London, 1967.

Criticism
(For general works on the author, see *Playwrights* volume)

Articles:
Gerry Brenner, "Chekhov's Neglected Psychodrama: *Ivanov*", in *Pacific Coast Philology*, 24, 1989.

*   *   *

The play opens on a summer's evening on Ivanov's estate. It transpires that he is overwhelmed with debts, exhaustion, depression, and guilt at no longer loving his wife, a Jewess who is dying of tuberculosis. Act II is set at the Lebedevs', a neighbouring family with a young daughter, Sasha. Provincial satire evolves into character-assassination of Ivanov, who then appears. He unburdens himself to Sasha, who declares that she loves him. As they kiss, Ivanov's wife enters. In Act III Ivanov's problems close in on him, but he also attempts harder to analyse them. He tries to correct the priggish young Dr. Lvov's misinterpretation of him and he declines Sasha's offer of an "active love" that will reform him. His wife accuses him,

Ivanov: Strand Theatre, London, 1989

however, of gross deceptions and he crushes her with insults. About a year passes, during which his wife dies. Act IV is set on the day of his wedding to Sasha. She has just expressed her own doubts about the wedding to her father, when Ivanov arrives to call it off. In the confusion, Lvov challenges Ivanov to a duel. Ivanov produces a revolver, rushes off stage, and kills himself.

In the version first performed, Ivanov expired on a sofa from a heart attack amid lines reminiscent of a Chekhov vaudeville, and the play itself was sub-titled "A Comedy". This, Chekhov's first-performed and most-revised full-length play, already raises the question of what he perceived as comic. There are brilliant grotesque roles and wry portraiture, and we are clearly encouraged to see Lvov's and Sasha's "ideology" as hilariously inadequate to life. But Chekhov also claimed in *Ivanov* to be sending up the moaning, misunderstood "superfluous man" figure of recent Russian literature and attempting to "put an end to these writings". Here the tone is far less certain.

It is possible to laugh at Ivanov's early posturing in the play, what he calls his "playing at Hamlet", but he is too seriously committed to the search for the truth about himself for audiences to view every fresh self-discovery in a comic or at least ironic light. In his rewriting, in fact, Chekhov seems to have become increasingly involved in the "serious", psychological analysis of Ivanov. Partly he was reacting to criticism that Ivanov's character did not develop. He attempted to show a development in self-discovery through numerous monologues. It is possible that Ivanov attains self-understanding,

but it is largely veiled from us by the thoughtlessness of some of his actions, his chronic exhaustion, his tearfulness, and the high situational comedy of the fourth act. Despite Chekhov's avowed aim of destroying a literary type, it is clear from his letters that he himself originally conceived Ivanov somewhat as a "type" in the tradition of Russian, classical comedy. All his attempts to give Ivanov psychological development are working against that grain. As a young doctor, Chekhov was also, perhaps, over-interested in Ivanov as a clinical case. Thus to many critics Ivanov's condition has appeared less dramatic than medical.

This was the last time Chekhov attempted a full-length monodrama, and with its scenic divisions, dramatic entrances and exits, and *coup-de-théâtre* act endings, it seems very old-fashioned compared with his four "great" plays. Nevertheless, Act I is a perfect example of his genius for "atmospheric" theatre-writing, the dialogue throughout is vigorous, and the play gives an impression of remarkable assurance. It is not difficult to see, then, why it has exercised a perennial fascination.

—Patrick Miles

IZUTSU. See **WELL-CURB.**

JACOB'S WAKE
by Michael Cook

First Publication: Vancouver, 1975.
First Production: Festival Lennoxville, Lennoxville, Quebec,
11 July 1975.

Criticism
(For general works on the author, see *Playwrights* volume)

Articles:
Richard Perkyns, "*Jacob's Wake* and the European Tradition", in *Canadian Drama*, 15, 1989.

* * *

Jacob's Wake is set in a Newfoundland outport starting in the evening of Maundy Thursday. The aged Skipper, upstairs, has been bedridden for 30 years. His children are Mary, a prim teacher, and Winston, expert only at "making moonshine and cheating the Welfare". Cook has emphasized Winston as the key to his ideas: "trapped between the cultural extremes of that society—between the old sealing skipper who has been hero-worshipped because of his ability and his sons who are a rapacious ratpack with absolutely no values.. . .He's the one who is able to articulate his suffering and yet is ultimately unable to do anything about it" (in *The Work*, 1982). Winston's wife, Rosie, holds the household together. Their three sons return for Easter: Alonzo, whose way of life is shady and mysterious; the unbalanced Brad, ejected from the Church of Revelations; and Wayne, also corrupt, though a member of the provincial legislature.

The action unfolds in four scenes, ending on Good Friday afternoon. The plot turns on some scheming to send old Skipper to an institution. Winston refuses and Alonzo forges his father's signature and is exposed near the end. The family squabbles, attempts reconciliation, and revives old quarrels, while Rosie continues with her daily round of work.

Revelations from the past are significant. Brad was responsible for the death of a girl he made pregnant, and he finally goes out into the storm to die. Three events occurred 30 years earlier. The only daughter of Winston and Rosie died, and Winston still mourns. Skipper's other son, Jacob, died at the same time, ordered on to the ice by his father to join a seal-hunt as a storm was building up; Skipper took to his bed, immediately after Jacob's death. Thirdly, Skipper now believes his surviving son is Jacob. All the people in the play are shaped by the death of Jacob and are thus in his wake. Had he lived, Skipper would have had a worthy descendant and would not have given up in his prime, while the young men

would have had a fine example. As Winston is Jacob, in Skipper's eyes, the play is Winston's funeral too.

Skipper at first seems only a dying, drunken, hallucinating old man. Yet he emerges as the one with enough vision to know what the issues are, to ask vital questions. Cook insists in *The Work* that Skipper "is struggling to come to grips with his soul, with the nature of being; ultimately they will all come up with a bleak and absurdist conclusion".

A storm grows throughout the play: a literal one in which "snow and ice and hurricane combine to create a world in which nothing can live", and a metaphorical one, "a living thing, a character whose presence is always felt, if not actually heard, on the stage". A few minutes from the end fading lights suggest Skipper has died. A strange leap into unreality follows. With the corpse still in the upstairs room, Skipper—or his ghost—strides in wearing his Master's uniform, demands rum, orders Winston to the wheel and the two women below. A seal barks, and Skipper speaks the final lines: "Blood and fire and ice. A swile [seal]. A swile. I wor right, boys. They've come back. The swiles is back. Newfoundland is alive and well and roaring down the ice pack". Then "a blackout and the sound of a cosmic disaster", followed by a flash to reveal an empty stage: all are presumably dead, the house-ship swept away by the storm.

Twice in these last minutes Cook startles his audience. First, Skipper returns and takes charge, too late to save the ship (a direct allusion to Captain Shotover of Bernard Shaw's *Heartbreak House* seems intended here). Cook comments in *The Work*: "It bugs me that people have difficulty relating to ghosts. We have no trouble relating to ghosts in Newfoundland at all because everyone knows that they exist". Skipper entering through the door downstairs with his corpse still visible above must shock. Second, the storm finally sweeps all away. Cook observes that this is "pure melodrama, the universe collapsing around the characters like that.. . .I like mixing forms". The storm is also Nature hitting back. The implication of the conclusion thus ranges from the ending of the Newfoundland outports' values and way of life, through the decadence of modern society, unworthy of its ancestors, to Nature striking back at all who abuse her.

This is firstly a drama of family conflict, full of tensions, old mistrust and suspicion, with the occasional building of an alliance. The 16 hours of fictional time the play covers include the crisis of Brad's faith and the near-fulfilment of Wayne's ambitions to join the Cabinet. Cook's main subjects, however, are the state of Newfoundland, the past, and different ways of dealing with the present. Skipper has only the past, the years of the seal-hunt, and Rosie also stays in it. Brad and Mary have taken refuge in religion and Alonzo and Wayne exploit their apathetic era. With these three young men representing the present, society is spiritually bankrupt. Each generation is

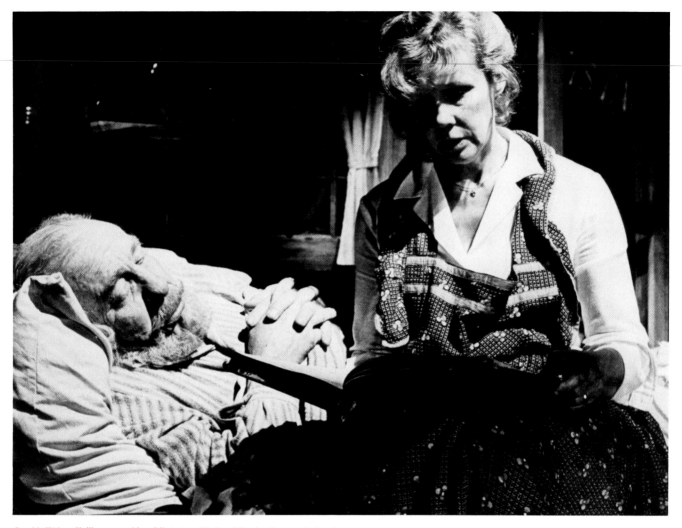

Jacob's Wake: Kollbergensemblen, Riksteatern (National Touring Company), Sweden

more alienated from nature than its predecessor. Winston expresses this bleak view: "Seems as the times was wrong. . . .Us, Rosie, us. . . .Like rats in a trap, with the Welfare as bait. I didn't know what to do, so I didn't try". Cook says: "It is a play forecasting the doom of that society. . . .I was virtually forecasting the end of Newfoundland culture as I knew it". When Skipper asks his son what he wants, Winston answers: "Nothing, Skipper. . . .A place to come and have a quiet drink, away from the women, and look out at the sea". The best of the men is indicted for passivity, as damaging to Newfoundland as the overt corruption of Wayne and Alonzo.

Thus *Jacob's Wake* ranges widely, being both portrait of a family and a study of the Newfoundland way of life in decline. Though there are comic moments, fundamentally Cook is serious, indeed close to despair. His people are destroyed internally (except perhaps Rosie) before the storm physically destroys their house. Because these people are either evil or purposeless, doom and disaster will come. While the storm dwarfs all human activity, these people deserve their fate—a sad epitaph on a once-great community.

—Malcolm Page

LE JEU DE L'AMOUR ET DU HASARD.   See **THE GAME OF LOVE AND CHANCE.**

THE JEW OF MALTA
by Christopher Marlowe

First Publication: London, 1633
First Production: London, c.1589; earliest recorded production, Lord Strange's Men, 26 February 1592.

Editions

The Jew of Malta, in *The Jew of Malta; The Massacre at Paris*, edited by H.S. Burnett, London, 1931.
The Famous Tragedy of the Rich Jew of Malta, London, 1933.
The Jew of Malta, edited by Richard W. Van Fossen, Lincoln, Nebraska 1965, (Regents Renaissance Drama Series).
The Jew of Malta, edited by T.W. Craik, London, 1966 (New Mermaid Series).
The Jew of Malta, in *Christopher Marlowe: The Complete Plays*, edited by J.B. Steane, Harmondsworth, 1969.

Christopher Marlowe's "The Jew of Malta": Text and Major Criticism, edited by Irving Ribner, New York, 1970.
The Jew of Malta, edited by N.W. Bawcutt, Manchester and Baltimore, Maryland, 1978 (Revels Plays).

Criticism
(For general works on the author, see *Playwrights* volume)

Books:
University of Illinois Department of English, *Marlowe's "The Jew of Malta": Grammar of Policy*, Urbana, Illinois, 1967.

Articles:
Arthur Swan, "The Jew That Marlowe Drew", in *Sewanee Review*, 19, 1911.
C. Reznikoff, "Story for a Dramatist: *The Jew of Malta* and *The Merchant of Venice*", in *Menorah Journal*, 28, 1940.
M.M. Mahood, "*The Jew of Malta* as Tragic Farce", in *Poetry and Humanism*, London, 1950.
Charles E. Peavy, "*The Jew of Malta* – Anti-Semitic or Anti-Catholic?", in *McNeese Review*, 11, 1959-60.
Antonio D'Andrea, "Studies on Machiavelli and His Reputation in the Sixteenth Century, 1: Marlowe's Prologue to *The Jew of Malta*", in *Medieval and Renaissance Studies*, 5, 1961.
Paul H. Kocher, "English Legal History in Marlowe's *Jew of Malta*", in *Huntington Library Quarterly*, 26, 1963.
Alfred Harbage, "Innocent Barabas", in *Tulane Drama Review*, vol. 8 no. 4, 1964.
G.K. Hunter, "The Theology of Marlowe's *The Jew of Malta*", in *Journal of the Warburg and Courtauld Institute*, 27, 1964.
Alan Warren Friedman, "The Shackling of Accidents in Marlowe's *Jew of Malta*", in *Texas Studies in Literature and Language*, 8, 1966.
Eric Rothstein, "Structure and Meaning in *The Jew of Malta*", in *Journal of English and Germanic Philology*, 65, 1966.
N.W. Bawcutt, "Machiavelli and Marlowe's *The Jew of Malta*", in *Renaissance Drama* (new series), 3, 1970.
J.L. Simmons, "Elizabethan Stage Practice and Marlowe's *The Jew of Malta*", in *Renaissance Drama* (new series), 4, 1971.
Allan C. Dessen, "The Elizabethan Stage Jew and Christian Example: Gerontus, Barabus, and Shylock", in *Modern Language Quarterly*, 35, 1974.
Soji Iwasaki, "The Fall of Barabus", in *Shakespeare Studies* (Japan), 15, 1976-77.
Catherine Minshull, "Marlowe's 'Sound Machiavel'", in *Renaissance Drama* (new series), 13, 1982.
Jean-Marie Maguin, "The *Jew of Malta*: Marlowe's Ideological Stance and the Play-World's Ethos", in *Cahiers Elisabéthains*, 27, 1985.
Arthur Humphreys, "*The Jew of Malta* and *The Merchant of Venice*: Two Readings of Life", in *Huntington Library Quarterly*, vol. 50 no. 3, 1987.
Luc Borot, "Machiavellian Diplomacy and Dramatic Developments in Marlowe's *Jew of Malta*", in *Cahiers Elisabéthains*, 33, 1988.
Sara M. Deats, "Biblical Parody in Marlowe's *The Jew of Malta*: A Re-examination", in *Christianity and Literature*, vol. 37 no. 2, 1988.
Catherine Brown Ikacz, "*The Jew of Malta* and the Pit", in *South Atlantic Review*, vol. 53, no. 2, 1988.

*   *   *

One of the most successful plays, commercially, of the late-16th Century, *The Jew of Malta* was written in 1589 or 1590. It received some of its earliest productions at the Rose theatre, a performance space we now know from archaeological evidence to have been remarkably small-scale. The leading figure, the Jew Barabas, who dominates the piece with almost half the lines, was played by Edward Alleyn, the period's most famous actor and a commanding stage presence.

The play calls to mind several of the age's most potent stereotypes and prejudices: the prevalent anti-Semitism (based on theological rather than racial grounds), the preoccupation with the subversive political opinions of Machiavelli, both genuine and attributed, and the extraordinary stage success of the Vice, a contained figure within the Morality play, but dangerously appealing in plays such as Marlowe's. This heady mix, centred on the powerful casting of Alleyn, and playing before packed audiences in a confined theatre, together with Marlowe's reputation for heterodoxy, no doubt account for the contemporary excitement the play generated. The excitement was boosted when on 7 June 1594, after much rumour and innuendo, the Jewish physician Dr. Lopez was executed on suspicion of attempting to poison the Queen. The play's after-life testifies further to its appeal: *The Merchant of Venice* and *Richard III* are indebted to it, as is Ben Jonson's *Volpone*; theatre records show performances up to the 1630's; it was probably played, in one version or another, in Germany and eastern Europe as well as England; and it has become one of the most frequently-performed Elizabethan plays on the modern stage.

To give life to his play Marlowe devised a style of theatre-writing once characterised by T.S. Eliot as "savage farce", blending the serious with the preposterous. The prologue, spoken by Machiavelli (sometimes doubled in modern performances with Barabas or, recently in Stratford-on-Avon, with the Christian, Ferneze) delightedly expounds Machiavellian guile, and claims the play as his. Barabas's long opening speech, which follows, shows him "*in his counting house, with heaps of gold before him*", eagerly enjoying the wealth he has won by trade. These motifs, guile and wealth (and with both of them, power) run through the play. Barabas becomes a preposterously resourceful intriguer, sometimes in absurd disguise (as a French musician for example), adding to the atrocities we see him commit, including poisoning a convent of nuns and strangling a Friar, such self-reported crimes as poisoning wells and killing "sick people groaning under walls". His man Ithamore, purchased as a slave, vies with him in real or fantasised villainy; he is "a shaggy tottered staring slave" with hacked face, mutilated hands and a voice that "grunts like a hog", and has a raddled courtesan, Bellamira. These grotesques between them parody Elizabethan values, including the golden world of classical myth.

Barabas is associated with Judas, and shares his name with the condemned robber who was released at the crowd's demand when Jesus was arrested and crucified. The play can be read as a bizarre essay on what happens when a Machiavellian Jew gets out of control. Yet the play's Christians, under the island's Governor, Ferneze, are no better. As greedy, guileful and corrupt as the Jew, they exploit their authority to plunder the Jew's wealth, unctuously solicit his aid when power passes to him, and cynically betray him to his death when occasion serves. The play's setting and action allude to the Turkish siege of the Christian island of Malta in 1565, though Marlowe, in the spirit of his play, changes the outcome from Turkish withdrawal to massacre of the Turkish soldiers by blatant Christian dishonesty. The single source of genuine feeling in the play is Barabas's daughter Abigail, with whom the young Christians Mathias and Lodowick (the Governor's son) are in love, and for whom Barabas himself seems to feel affection. But he manipulates the young men's

The Jew of Malta: Barbican Theatre, London, 1988 (Royal Shakespeare Company)

jealousy till they kill each other, and Abigail perishes, ironically turned Christian, in her father's poisoning of the convent she has joined to recover his wealth. Barabas himself dies in a trick prepared for the Turkish Selim Calymath, falling into a boiling cauldron—the Elizabethan emblem for the punishment of excessive ambition or usury. The tragedy thus preposterously imposes a conventional morality ending on a play in which all orthodox decency and human feeling have been outraged. Ferneze's concluding piety "let due praise be given/ Neither to fate nor fortune, but to heaven", can only be taken as a final hypocrisy.

The Jew of Malta is a strikingly original tragedy, employing vividly theatrical means of costume, language, and action in a bizarre parody of orthodox attitudes, under the auspices of Machiavelli. Marlowe's boisterous humour leaves us divided as to whether we find orthodoxy thus confirmed or violated.

—J.R. Mulryne

JOHN GABRIEL BORKMAN
by Henrik Ibsen

First Publication: Copenhagen and Stockholm, 1896.
First Production: The Swedish Theatre, Helsinki, and The Finnish Theatre, Helsinki, 10 January, 1897; first Norwegian production, at Drammen, 19 January 1897.

Translations

John Gabriel Borkman, in *Collected Works, 7*, translated by William Archer, London, 1907.
John Gabriel Borkman, in *"The Master Builder" and Other Plays*, translated by Una Ellis-Fermor, Harmondsworth, 1958
John Gabriel Borkman, translated by Norman Ginsbury, London, 1960.
John Gabriel Borkman, translated by Michael Meyer, London, 1960; corrected version, in *Ibsen: Plays Four*, London, 1980.
John Gabriel Borkman, in *The Last Plays of Ibsen*, translated by Arvid Paulsen, New York, 1962.
John Gabriel Borkman, in *Ibsen: Four Major Plays, 2*, translated by Rolf Fjelde, New York, 1965.
John Gabriel Borkman, translated by Inga Stina Ewbank and Peter Hall, London, 1975.
John Gabriel Borkman, in *The Oxford Ibsen, 8*, translated and edited by James Walter McFarlane, London, 1977.

Criticism
(For general works on the author, see *Playwrights* volume)

Articles:
Alf Kjellen, "*John Gabriel Borkman*—ensamhetens tragedi", in *Ord och Bild*, 68, 1959.
Borghild Krane, "Bergmannen og *John Gabriel Borkman*", in *Ibsen-Årbok*, 1967.
Fredrik J. Haslund, "Ibsens diktning avgir Stadig nye signaler: en struktur-analyse av *John Gabriel Borkman*", in *Forskningsnytt*, 7, 1972.

Charles R. Lyons, "The Function of Dream and Reality in *John Gabriel Borkman*", in *Scandinavian Studies*, 45, 1973.

Inga Stina Ewbank, "Ibsen's Language: Literary Text and Theatrical Context", in *Yearbook of English Studies*, 9, 1979.

Eva M. Fleck, "*John Gabriel Borkman* and the Miner of Falun", in *Scandinavian Studies*, 51, 1979.

Brian Johnston, "The Demons of *John Gabriel Borkman*", in *Comparative Drama*, 13, 1979.

Brian Johnston, "The Tragic Farce of *John Gabriel Borkman*", in *Edda*, 79, 1979.

Quay Grigg, "The Novel in *John Gabriel Borkman*: Henry James's *The Ambassadors*", in *Henry James Review*, 1, 1980.

Marie Wells, "*The Master Builder*; *John Gabriel Borkman*; *When We Dead Awaken*: Variations on a Theme or Developing Argument?", in *New Comparison*, 4, 1987.

* * *

The delaying of the entrance of the title character until the second act reflects the audacity of a major playwright in his maturity. It also allows Ibsen, in this, his second-last play, to use exposition to develop an atmosphere that is suffocating to the point that it denies intruders the right to exist—at least on their own terms. Three female power-brokers compete for control of the adult Borkman son, Erhart: his mother, his mother's twin sister, Ella (who brought him up), and Mrs Fanny Wilton (who will later be revealed as his lover). Their hostility towards each other almost totally ignores the wishes of Erhart, who is treated as a commodity, but who nevertheless generally remains polite to the extent of trying to please everyone. The second act takes us upstairs to meet Borkman who has lived there for eight years in isolation from his wife, ever since his release from prison (for embezzlement). His lack of social graces parallels his wife's. Though he is pleasant to Frida Foldal, he quickly picks a quarrel with her father, his former clerk who also lost his money but has nevertheless remained faithful to him. Foldal is sent off because he is of "no further use", and Ella enters to meet Borkman for the first time in years; it becomes clear that they were once lovers, yet Borkman surprises her by blandly admitting that he passed her on to another man to improve his business prospects. She now persuades him to allow her to adopt Erhart before her approaching death, but they are interrupted by the explosive entrance of Mrs Borkman, who has been eavesdropping. The brief third act finds the three downstairs again arguing over possession of Erhart who, summoned back from a party, surprises them with the news that he is about to elope with Mrs Wilton—who, in turn, explains that she is taking Frida along too, to provide for the day when Erhart tires of her, or she of him. In the final act the elopement has been effected, and the older generation is standing morosely outside in the snow when Foldal limps in and explains that he has been run over by Mrs Wilton's sleigh. In the finale, the scene dissolves to a mountain-top, where Borkman reiterates his dreams of a mining empire to Ella before he dies.

A summary of the action of any Ibsen play inevitably fails to do justice to the texture of poetry, symbolism, and myth, in which this play is particularly rich. If the women are basically pragmatists in their competition for Erhart, Borkman's lust for power is expressed in an obsessive but poetic affinity with the earth he has mined; he conceives of it animistically and speaks directly to it, which gives particular resonance to the final episode. Scandinavian scholars have cogently and in detail related this dimension to the folklore world of early plays like *Peer Gynt*. Beside this, though, it must also be observed that Borkman is not trying to retrieve a lost world of trolls and medieval magic; his folklore is based upon the industrial revolution, and his dreams correlate with the development of nineteenth-century capitalism. Nor is the last act a sudden shift in mode from realism to symbolism; the two have been spliced together throughout the play, and the designs of many continental productions have given cavernous, mine-like qualities to the earlier domestic interiors.

The characteristic traits of Ibsen's dramaturgy are all here: a fragmented family trying to find elements of cohesion after years of separation; revelatory meetings between people who have not talked for long periods; bankruptcy and capitalism stunting lives and invading dreams; and biological determinism (both Ella and Borkman feel they are near death). However this is also the only Ibsen play with complete unity of time, without a pause between any of the acts, and it is also unusual in that Borkman the patriarch exercises and proclaims his kingship over the domain of dreams, but the actual economic sovereignty lies in the hands of a woman, Ella, who even owns the Borkman house.

The play also accentuates the images of destructive, female strength which had developed through Rebecca West and Hedda Gabler, but here seem to be distilled, with few other passions to complicate them, so that in places Ibsen seems almost to be invading the terrain of Strindbergian misogyny. Indeed, many aspects of the play anticipate *The Dance of Death*, and it is specifically that music which Frida plays at the start of the second act. However, this play, which has been termed "elegiac" and "Ibsen's most pessimistic", also contains filaments of comedy; its action pivots on the situational mechanics of comedy rather than insuperable blows of extraneous fate, and there is much that is comic about Foldal who, as a failed tragedian, has a parodic function in relation to both Borkman's dreams and the very concept of tragedy. It was generally agreed that the one attempt to do the play essentially as a comedy—by Donald Wolfit in 1964—was a failure, but it is notable that apart from Borkman's death there are no dimensions of loss at the end: the sisters are at last united, holding hands in a final tableau, old Foldal is rapturous that his daughter has left for a better life, and—for once in Ibsen—the young survive the action, not only intact, but unscathed by parental hostilities.

—Howard McNaughton

JOHNNY JOHNSON; The Biography of a Common Man by Paul Green; music by Kurt Weill

First Publication: New York, 1937; revised edition, 1972.
First Production: 44th Street Theatre (The Group Theatre), New York, 19 November 1936.

* * *

In 1917, a typical, American town gathers to celebrate its 200th anniversary by unveiling a monument to peace sculpted by Johnny Johnson. News of war interrupts the ceremony. Johnny's girlfriend, Minnie, pleads with him to enlist while her mother teaches his wealthy rival, Anguish, how to avoid the draft. When Woodrow Wilson announces "the war to end all wars", Johnny, a simple idealist, joins up. On a mission to catch a sniper, he finds a young, wounded German in a war-torn churchyard and tends him. The latter tells him that the Germans, too, have no desire to fight. Johnny is wounded and taken to hospital where he obtains a cannister of laughing gas. He takes it to a council of war. Under the influence of the gas, the generals happily sign a cease-fire. When the gas wears off, however, they cancel their orders, and Johnny is sent to a mental institution in America. Meanwhile, Minnie has married Anguish whom the war has made prosperous. In the last scene Johnny, a street-peddler selling toys, is approached by Minnie and her son. The son rejects Johnny's toys because there are no war toys among them.

Johnny Johnson is of historical interest for a number of reasons. First, it presents an unusual contribution to the isolationist drama of America in the 1930's. Second, it offers a powerful example of American Expressionism. Third, though hardly least, it contains Kurt Weill's first musical score for the American stage. Neither a musical, nor a "play with music", the text and the score are mutually, inextricably dependent. The sentimentality of the apparently simple story is extended and commented on by Weill's dramatic score. The music also supports the expressionist elements, lending a force that allows them to transcend the mere illustration of emotional states to express personal and social irony. There is every suggestion that Green and Weill intended to offer more than an eccentric example of American isolationist drama.

Although the action begins in 1917, Green describes the setting as "a few years ago as well as now". The intention appears to be to use World War I as a transferable example, a paradigm. The play supports this view by attempting to elaborate not merely on the horrors of war, *per se*, nor the specific crisis of World War I, but to offer a view of war as a manifestation of the class struggle and the economic system.

The triangle between Johnny, Minnie, and Anguish—on the surface a knee-jerk cliché—emphasizes the profits of war. There is a constant attempt to point out the existence of elements in society for whom war is an advantage. The hapless suffering of the soldiers, the pathos of Johnny's struggle, are contrasted with the flourishing of others—the generals, for example, and Anguish. The contrast is both personal and social. Not only pathos is intended when Minnie's spoilt son rejects Johnny's toys. He is clearly being primed to enter the class for whom war offers personal advantage and is a source of economic and social power.

The presentation of war as a manifestation of the power system, and the emphasis placed on the profits of war also isolates the covert class system. Soldiers of both sides are shown to be united in their victimisation. The scene where the American and German priests simultaneously bless and encourage the troops is skilfully intercut with images of Johnny in the churchyard caring for the dying German soldier. Thus, accepted heroic and sentimental assumptions about war and religion are confronted with contrasting values. Assisted by the sharp ironies of the music, the priests' spiritual support of Patriotism becomes the extension of the arm of power sending the boys out to die.

Patriotism as an absolute value is cynically presented as a tool of power for its own gain. Minnie's romantic patriotism is set against Johnny's innocent pragmatism. In the context of her mother's materialism, itself the result of poverty, Minnie's marriage to Anguish establishes the connection between war as a source of power and profit and the cynical promotion of propagandist idealism, so ordinary people are forced into a position where they are willingly sacrificing themselves for the profit of the few.

The structure of the play is founded on the distortion of the idealistic emblems of middle America, establishing a unity of setting and action. The play begins with the image at the heart of the American Dream: the small town community gathered to celebrate its existence—and peace (as the Mayor sings: "Where each man loves his neighbour as himself / And puts his money in the bank"). However, before their monument to Peace can be revealed, war is declared and there is an about-turn justified by the same ideals. Johnny asks simply: "Are we for peace or war?". Idealized absolutes are contrasted with and undercut by the ironies of actual experience, and so Johnny's question can only be answered in the light of the growing realization that "Loving your neighbour as yourself" is in active conflict with "putting your money in the bank".

The play attempts to use war to expose the power structure of the capitalist economy, the profit motive and the slogans manipulated by the few to sustain a system for their own benefit. Thus the American and German soldiers have more in common with each other than with their leaders. Johnny's insight, that if the soldiers don't fight there will be no war, not only distorts the conventional image of war but also presents an insight into the weakness of a system which uses war to perpetuate itself. The possibility of refusal gives the soldiers power and responsibility, thus an alternative to the status quo is activated through the process of the play.

A simple, even romantic, dichotomy between "human / feeling" and "inhuman / unfeeling" is unembarrassingly used to develop an emotional attachment to the alternative perspective and to lend credance to Johnny's simple logic. Johnny's heart, humanity, and common sense deflates figures of authority and ridicules their egotism and lack of feeling. Under the influence of the gas, the generals are loveable figures of fun; restored to "normality" as calculating warmongers. This dichotomy is extended beyond human interaction. Inanimate, man-made objects prove to have more insight, depth, and feeling than the humans themselves. The Statue of Liberty, in answer to Johnny's euology, sings with compassionate despair denouncing men who swear false fealty to her. Even more moving is the "Song of the Guns" which the cannons sing to the sleeping soldiers: "We might have served a better will / But you've decreed that we must kill". Green's lyrics are bitter, and memorable. In combination with Weill's sourly nostalgic music they elicit an emotional response that transcends the simple story of Johnny himself.

The settings are visually and emotionally demanding. The open stage and quick-changing scenes set the story in an open, dangerous world. The music adds atmosphere and a critique. "The Rio Grande", for example, ironically undercuts the heroic myths of the American West; Minnie's mother's song of poverty is a reminder of the Depression still lurking beneath the American Dream; a love ballad stresses the human and emotional impulses in contrast to the dehumanizing, greed-ridden justifications behind the war. Reminiscent of Weill's work with Brecht, the music is unforgettably haunting.

Perhaps World War I was too close to 1936 to be able to serve as an informative example. For despite its originality and intelligence of vision, imagery, and sheer theatricality, the play never seems to have shaken itself free from the specifics of events in the way that, 20 years later, *Oh What a Lovely War!* was able to do, even though many of the scenes of the later work are reminiscent of *Johnny Johnson*.

—Elaine Turner

JOURNEY'S END
by R.C. Sherriff

First Publication: London, 1929.
First Production: Apollo Theatre (Incorporated Stage Society), 9 December 1928.

Criticism

Books:
I Altena, *Notes on R.C. Sherriff's "Journey's End"*, London, 1976.

Articles:
K.S. Misra, "Sherriff's *Journey's End*", in Misra's *Modern Tragedies and Aristotle's Theory*, New Delhi, 1981.

*   *   *

An infantry company of the British Army takes over in a forward position in time to face Ludendorff's offensive of May 1918. It is under the command of Captain Stanhope, aged 21, but already a survivor of three years on the Western Front and on the verge of nervous collapse. During the course of the play he loses his second-in-command—his best friend who is old enough to be his father—killed in a suicidal raid ordered by the Brigadier to discover which German unit is facing them. By the end of the play, 2nd Lieutenant Raleigh, aged 18 and formerly junior to Stanhope at school, is left alone, mortally wounded, in the dug-out they all inhabit when it receives a direct hit.

What is it that has made this play a durable minor classic, second only to the work of Owen, Graves, and Sassoon as a soldier's testimony about the World War I? The humour is sometimes abysmal, the public school idiom dated, the social assumptions rejected by late 20th-century opinion. Yet in spite of such objections the effect is entirely convincing, not least in the pathetic domesticity of the dug-out, when the play interweaves the military nightmare with memories of peace. This is, to the front-line soldier and to anyone who can make the effort to identify with him, how the war was actually experienced.

Once, in the treatment of 2nd Lieutenant Hibbert—a success theatrically but puritanically condemned by the author—does Sherriff's compassion fail him. The cook is a caricature, and so it seems is Trotter, an officer risen from the ranks. But everyone, from Colonel to private, is exactly placed in the situation, his function secured. Add to that suspense, inexorably mounting for three acts, and you can tell why the play cumulatively grips. Of the officers, Osborne is a former schoolteacher, old enough to be the father of Raleigh who is in action for the first time, innocent and enthusiastic. Public school values are the basis of their relationship; inadequate until you remember the gross mortality rate among subalterns of that class by the fourth year of the war. Hence the validity of the relationship and of the image of their judging distance from the enemy as being the width of a rugby football field.

Above and beyond these two characters is the focus on Stanhope. His leadership is shown in action from the very beginning when he learns of the outgoing unit's neglect and sets about to install proper conditions at once. A martinet, he is admired for his record and for the strategical knowledge displayed in scene after scene. On the other hand his morale is at breaking point, the private man at odds after three years of hell with the rigid efficiency of the company commander. An emotional flashpoint comes with the arrival of Raleigh, posted by family influence to the company out of some 1,800 others on

Journey's End: Savoy Theatre, London, 1929

the Western Front. Raleigh is not only a former hero-worshipper of Stanhope's at school but the brother of Stanhope's girlfriend. By now the hero is prematurely aged by too much responsibility and alcohol, anxious not to have his decline known to the girlfriend and so lose his ideal of survival and peace. Stanhope's explosive temperament, his alternations between self-control and hysteria, are explored in depth.

And yet, dominant as Stanhope is, he does not obscure the overall situation, the impending offensive which frames everything that happens, in discussion and sound effects, from early ominous silences, through mortar fire, to a final bombardment which destroys the dug-out. This scrupulously hard-nosed insistence on a wider issue, a threat to the entire army, puts the doomed company in proportion and is one explanation of *Journey's End*'s durability.

But given the dated English idiom of much of the dialogue and behaviour, what accounts for the play's global success in translation? The fact is that Sherriff hit on a valid symbol of the troglodyte nature of war in 1918: the dug-out. This means that, rather surprisingly, he joins European masters from Strindberg to Beckett who exploit the dramatic possibilities of a confined space, a cult of enclosure; it amounts to a genre of its own also cultivated by Kafka, O'Neill, and Sartre. Sherriff's masterpiece, like the work of those other writers, is ultimately about "the resistance of material to stress". Not bad for a play by an insurance assessor, composed initially for a rowing club and only reaching its West End run after an off-duty critic happened to wander one day into the try-out.

—Laurence Kitchin

JULIUS CAESAR
by William Shakespeare

First Publication: In First Folio, London, 1623.
First Production: London, 1599.

Editions

Julius Caesar, edited by H.H. Furness, Philadelphia, Pennsylvania, 1913 (New Variorum Edition).
Julius Caesar, edited by John Dover Wilson, Cambridge, 1949 (The New Shakespeare).
Julius Caesar, edited by T.S. Dorsch, London, 1955 (Arden Shakespeare).
Julius Caesar, edited by William and Barbara Rosen, New York, 1963 (Signet Classic Shakespeare).
Julius Caesar, edited by G.L. Kittredge, revised by Irving Ribner, Waltham, Massachusetts, 1966.
Julius Caesar, edited by Norman Sanders, London, 1967 (New Penguin Shakespeare).
The Tragedy of Julius Caesar, edited by Maynard Mack and Robert W. Boynton, Montclair, New Jersey, 1983.
Julius Caesar, edited by Arthur R. Humphreys, Oxford, 1984 (Oxford Shakespeare).
Julius Caesar, edited by Martin Spevack, Cambridge, 1988 (New Cambridge Shakespeare).

Bibliography

John W. Velz (ed.), *"The Tragedy of Julius Caesar": A Bibliography to Supplement the New Variorum Edition of 1913*, New York, 1977.

Criticism

(For general works on the author, see *Playwrights* volume)

Books:

Adrien Bonjour, *The Structure of "Julius Caesar"*, Liverpool, 1958.
Leonard F. Dean (ed.), *Twentieth Century Approaches to "Julius Caesar"*, Englewood Cliffs, New Jersey, 1968.
Peter Ure (ed.), *"Julius Caesar": A Casebook*, London, 1969.
David Daiches, *Shakespeare's "Julius Caesar"*, London, 1976.
S. Brad Field Jr., *Shakespeare's "Julius Caesar": A Production Collection / Comments by Eighteen Actors and Directors in Seven Different Productions*, Chicago, 1980.
John Ripley, *"Julius Caesar" on Stage in England and America, 1599–1973*, Cambridge and New York, 1980.
Ernle Bradford, *Julius Caesar: The Pursuit of Power*, London, 1984.
Harold Bloom (ed.), *William Shakespeare's "Julius Caesar"*, New York, New Haven (Connecticut) and Philadelphia, 1988 (Modern Critical Interpretations).
Mark W. Scott (ed.), *"Julius Caesar"*, in *Shakespearian Criticism, 7*, Detroit, Illinois, 1988 [anthology of criticism].

Articles:

For information on the many articles about *Julius Caesar*, see Velz's bibliography, the bibliographies listed in the *Playwrights* volume, and the annual Shakespeare Bibliography in *Shakespeare Quarterly*, published by the Folger Shakespeare Library, Washington D.C. (1950–).

*   *   *

Julius Caesar (1599) is one of three Roman tragedies written by Shakespeare (*Antony and Cleopatra* and *Coriolanus* being the others) which drew extensively from the ancient Greek biographer-historian Plutarch for its material. Julius Caesar was the subject of innumerable treatises and plays during the Renaissance—and for good reason. He excelled militarily and politically, and then in 44 B.C., just as Rome was about to hand him the Empire, Caesar was assassinated by a cadre of senators. Historical details of the assault were plentiful, and Shakespeare's aim was to shape well-known facts into entertaining theatre.

Shakespeare begins his drama with events on the eve of the killing. Julius Caesar, already one of the highest officials in Rome's hierarchy, stands one step away from being named "tyrant". But his ascension to that deific role is bitterly resisted by many in the capital. The opening scenes, their mood ominous, carefully introduce the contesting factions. Marcus Brutus, highly respected and admired by Rome, is openly disturbed by Caesar's overt ambition. Brutus's uneasiness is noticed and encouraged by Cassius, another senator. But a crucial difference separates the motives of these two key players. Brutus fears that the rule of one person in a republican system of government means the destruction of the republic; Cassius—Shakespeare makes clear—is, however, merely jealous of Caesar and wants him stopped for personal reasons.

The first two acts of *Julius Caesar* focus on Cassius's campaign to win Brutus to the conspirators' cause. Eventually Brutus is convinced, and all the conspirators meet to map strategy. Caesar is to die at the Senate the very next day—on the Ides of March. When Caesar walks to the Senate Forum the following morning, a soothsayer tries to alert him to danger, warning "Beware the Ides of March". A self-confident Caesar however mocks him and ignores the message. On cue the killers attack Caesar, stabbing him to death on the steps of the Senate. A disbelieving Caesar sees Brutus among the killers and asks, "Et tu, Brutus?". The conspirators try to keep order in Rome with speeches that rationalise their reasons for slaying Caesar. At Brutus's insistence, Mark Antony, Julius Caesar's closest companion, is also allowed to speak at Caesar's funeral. It is a mistake, for Antony ingeniously inflames the passions of the Roman citizens, turning them against the conspirators whom he repeatedly and mockingly calls "honourable men". The Roman citizens chase the assassins out of Rome, and install a triumvirate of three leaders: Antony, Octavius Caesar (Julius Caesar's nephew and adopted son), and Lepidus. The remainder of Shakespeare's drama traces the battles between the triumvirate and the former conspirators, specifically, Brutus and Cassius. Finally, the loyalists win the day, and both Cassius and Brutus take their own lives in the accepted Roman fashion for defeated warriors.

Shakespeare displays exceptional dramatic instincts with *Julius Caesar*. He faces one crucial logistical fact: because the details of the assassination were already known by his listeners, suspense was impossible. Rather than dwell on "will it happen?", the playwright emphasizes how it happens. Moreover, unlike his peers who wrote tragedies centred on single, grand figures (Tamburlaine, Faustus, etc.) Shakespeare devotes balanced attention to all the major figures involved—Brutus, Cassius, Antony, as well as Caesar. In fact, Julius Caesar is slain early in the third act and plays no major part thereafter in the action. (His ghost appears to Brutus to prophesy doom for the conspirators, but his lines are few). The murder of Caesar serves as catalyst to reveal objectively the true character of the other protagonists. Thus in Shakespeare's "history", more than the life or death of a single person is at stake. The entire empire is shown to be affected by the killing.

Lending texture and substance to Shakespeare's storytelling are dramatic strengths often encountered in his writing. Individual portraits of the main participants emerge tellingly,

Julius Caesar: Her Majesty's Theatre, London, 1898

to etch each character in the minds of playgoers. Early in Act II, Brutus struggles agonisingly with his conscience, trying to arrive at the "right" decision about Caesar. He concludes, "It must be by his death; and for my part, / I know no personal cause to spurn at him, / But for the general. He would be crown'd. / How that might change his nature, there's the question". Cassius reaches for extravagant imagery to fire Brutus's more cautious nature. Speaking of Caesar early in the play, Cassius scoffs, "Why, man, he doth bestride the narrow world / Like a Colossus, and we petty men / Walk under his huge legs and peep about / To find ourselves dishonourable graves". Yet he reveals his true nature soon afterwards when, in an aside, he declares "Well, Brutus, thou art noble; yet I see / Thy honourable mettle may be wrought / From that it is dispos'd".

The opposing faction receives no less complete a treatment in Shakespeare's hands. Mark Antony gives the impression of being wholly solicitous to the plebians when he wants their support at the funeral. He promises great things for the people in Caesar's will: "Here is the will, and under Caesar's seal. / To every Roman citizen he gives, / To every several man, seventy-five drachmas". Yet he resorts to means every bit as bloody as the conspirators' once he and the other triumvirs have control. At the opening of the fourth act, the three new rulers of Rome sit together to purge themselves of any conceivable enemies or rivals. It is a blood-chilling scene, as each agrees to the killing of kin to safeguard their alliance. Antony takes the lead. Lepidus agrees to the political slaying of his own brother on condition that Antony agree that Publius, his sister's son, also shall die. Antony responds: "He shall not live. Look, with a spot I damn him. / But, Lepidus, go you to Caesar's house. / Fetch the will hither, and we shall determine / How to cut off some charge in legacies". Both sides in the struggle for Rome are masters at manipulating others. Shakespeare appears to indicate that revolt rarely brings genuine improvement to a situation, only a different cast of characters to power.

Shakespeare employs blank verse with his usual fluidity and control, so that through language the thoughtful nature of Brutus can be differentiated from the brusque choler of Cassius. Even the speech of the same person is varied radically, depending on the context. Thus Antony, during the funeral oration, exhibits great rhetorical command as he whips the crowd into a murderous frenzy; but when relaxed with friends, his language eases into an almost prose-like rhythm.

—C.J. Gianakaris

JUMPERS
by Tom Stoppard

First Publication: London, 1972; revised edition, 1973; further revised edition, 1986.
First Production: Old Vic Theatre (National Theatre Company), London, 2 February 1972.

Criticism
(For general works on the author, see *Playwrights* volume)

Books:
Robert Gordon, *Rosencrantz and Guildenstern are Dead; Jumpers: The Real Thing*, London, 1991 (Text and Performance Series).

Articles:
Lucina P. Gabbard, "Stoppard's *Jumpers*: A Mystery Play", in *Modern Drama*, 20, 1977.
John A. Bailey, "*Jumpers* by Tom Stoppard: The Ironist as Theistic Apologist", in *Michigan Academician*, 11, 1979.
Mary R. Davidson, "Historical Homonyms: A New Way of Naming in Tom Stoppard's *Jumpers*", in *Modern Drama*, 22, 1979.
Felicia H. Londré, "Using Comic Devices to Answer the Ultimate Question: Tom Stoppard's *Jumpers* and Woody Allen's *God*", in *Comparative Drama*, 14, 1980.
Bobbi Rothstein, "The Reappearance of Public Man: Stoppard's *Jumpers* and *Professional Foul*", in *Kansas Quarterly*, vol.12 no.4, 1980.
Tim Brassell, "*Jumpers*: A Happy Marriage?", in *Gambit*, 37, 1981.
Paul Delaney, "The Flesh and the Word in *Jumpers*", in *Modern Language Quarterly*, 42, 1981.
Keir Elam, "After Magritte, After Carroll, After Wittgenstein: What Tom Stoppard's Tortoise Taught Us", in *Modern Drama*, 27, 1984.
Barbara Kreps, "How Do We Know That We Know What We Know in Tom Stoppard's *Jumpers*?", in *Twentieth Century Literature*, 32, 1986.
Neil Sammells, "The Aniseed Trail and the Metaphysical Fox: Tom Stoppard's *Jumpers*", in *Swansea Review*, 1, 1986.
Leslie Thomson, "'The Curve itself' in *Jumpers*", in *Modern Drama*, 33, 1990.

*   *   *

The play is set in the Mayfair flat of Dorothy Moore, a prematurely retired musical comedy actress, and her husband George, a Professor of Ethics. During a party held to celebrate the election victory of the Radical Liberals, a gymnast (subsequently discovered to be Duncan McFee, Professor of Logic in the same university as George) is shot. The neurotic Dotty's futile attempts to get rid of the body and obtain some solace from her husband are interwoven with George's constantly interrupted struggle to complete an academic paper, the aim of which is to prove the existence of God as a precondition for the existence of moral absolutes, to be delivered at a symposium on "Man—good, bad or indifferent?". For much of the play's action George wanders about, absent-mindedly searching for his missing pet hare, Thumper, one of the two animals (the other being a tortoise) he uses in an Aesop's fable-like demonstration of the fallacy of the standard theory of infinite series.

As Dotty becomes progressively more distressed, she is visited by Archie, who is the University Vice-Chancellor, leader of the Radical Liberal Party and her doctor, and by Inspector Bones, who has been sent to investigate the crime. Act I ends with Archie superintending his team of jumpers as they dispose of the corpse in a large plastic bag. The climax of Act II is George's discovery that he has accidentally shot his pet hare; at this moment he unwittingly steps on the pet tortoise and kills it too. As George collapses on the floor sobbing, the scene dissolves into his nightmare vision of the philosophy symposium in which the world appears to disintegrate into a totally anarchic scene of cynical, show-business gaiety where anything goes.

The eponymous jumpers are associated with the imagery of show business introduced in the play's spectacular, circus-style opening sequence. They are, in fact, professional philosophers, and their gymnastic feats become a metaphor for the philosophical relativism whose major proponent is Sir Archibald Jumper (Archie). Having accepted the impossibility of producing a logical proof for the existence of absolute moral values, the relativists consider morality as nothing more than a matter of social convention. Thus ethics is reduced to the level of technology, supplying methods for relating means to ends. Opposed to this dominant trend in philosophy and social behaviour, George Moore's own social incompetence (he behaves like the typically absent-minded professor) is a sign of the seeming illogicality of clinging to the traditionalist belief in an absolute system of morality.

Stoppard's view that "plays are events rather than texts" is brilliantly illustrated in the way that every aspect of this opposition between moral relativist and moral absolutist points of view is translated into concrete theatrical images. The play itself is constructed as a collage of seemingly unrelated literary and theatrical forms. The plot is carried forward through modes of presentation which variously resemble a montage of television images, a cabaret performance, a circus, a Cowardesque comedy of manners, a spoof detective thriller, a Whitehall farce, and a joke philosophy lecture. Not one of the play's revue-like series of gags is actually unrelated to Stoppard's central comic dialectics.

On the surface, George's dictation of his paper—a carefully detailed pastiche of a genuine academic lecture—comically illustrates the problems confronting the professional philosopher in constructing a logical proof of the existence of moral absolutes. Stoppard transforms George's vain attempts to clinch his argument into a comic *tour de force*, providing an actor with the opportunity of building up a stand-up-parody of the speech mannerisms of an eccentric university don, and then extending the joke to include moments in which George half-heartedly plays charades with the naked Dotty and is interviewed by the literal-minded Inspector Bones while in search of his missing hare. From George's point of view, most of the action constitutes a series of irrelevant intrusions of domestic life into his stream of philosophical consciousness. From Archie's perspective the action is a series of slickly executed gymnastic routines, a show-business act he has designed to mystify the other characters, allowing him at the same time to carry out his political machinations. Dotty is caught between the world of George and that of Archie, longing to gain some sense of romance or fulfilment in her relationship with George and yet carelessly falling into what appears a merely sexual liaison with Archie.

By constructing the play as a series of overlapping parodies of literary and theatrical genres, each one dramatising a particular character's view of the world, Stoppard undermines the possibility of interpreting the action through the frame of any one particular genre. The relationship between George and Dotty is expressed in a style reminiscent of Noel Coward's sophisticated comedies of manners, except that in *Jumpers* the

Jumpers: Old Vic Theatre, London, 1972 (National Theatre Company, first production)

surrounding context is so incongruous that their behaviour seems an absurd parody of the witty egoists who typically people Coward's plays. Although Dotty's persona and the chic decor of her flat evoke aspects of Coward's "cocktails and laughter" milieu, her own suggestion that her nervous breakdown was occasioned by the landing of men on the moon is so fanciful as to imply either that she is insane or that the play is an improbable farce. The fact that the lunar occurence has rendered meaningless the symbol of ideal romance in her songs about the moon in June or the blue moon etc., indicates that she is confronting another form of George's philosophical dilemma in the battle against logical positivism, the dilemma he ruefully articulates halfway through Act II in the question "How the hell does one know what to believe?". George and Dotty both intuitively feel the need for a belief in some sort of ideal which would validate their own personal existence; Dotty's is a romantic ideal, George's an ethical one.

Inspector Bones is presented as the plodding inspector of an Agatha Christie mystery. In time-honoured, show-business fashion, Bones is actually a fan of Dotty Moore; the objectivity essential to the proper conduct of his investigations is seriously undermined by his sentimental infatuation with one of the prime suspects. Although Bones's investigations constitute the major source of developing tension in the plot, as with all the other structural elements, Stoppard deliberately emphasises the most clichéd features which give the plot its banal, second-hand ring. The obvious echoes of West End thrillers and 1940's films make the point that modern life is experienced by

individuals as a social construct, expressed through the forms and images of the dominant media.

With the exception of Archie, George and Dotty, the characters in *Jumpers* behave as types in conventional dramas of their own devising. The Machiavellian Archie is a self-conscious performer, a Noel Coward dandy who never allows the potential conflicts of interest in his assumption of multifarious professional roles ("doctor of medicine, philosophy, literature and law, with diplomas in psychological medicine and P.T. including gym") to ruffle his implacably debonair image. Initially the characters of Dotty and George are treated as well-worn stage clichés (the singing star collapsing on stage from nervous exhaustion, the unworldly professor incapable of satisfying his wife's sexual needs) but they are gradually revealed as complex individuals whose personalities embrace interesting contradictions, capable of both faith and doubt, thus encouraging empathy on the part of an audience at the same time as provoking laughter at their bewilderment in the face of a rapidly expanding universe of media images.

The moment when George realizes he has killed both his pets (his concern for the pets is comically counterpointed with his lack of concern for Dotty) precipitates a nightmare vision of the philosophy symposium in which Clegthorpe, the new Archbishop of Canterbury, is shot while taking part in a gymnastic display: the same way that McFee died. Dotty at last manages to sing a version of her song, "Sentimental Journey"; George asserts that one can know through intuition that certain values are inherently good while others are bad; and

Archie delivers a cynical mock-sermon which appears to condone the most appalling injustice in the knowledge that some people at least are healthy, happy and prosperous. The implication of this ending is that while people possessed of a refined and complex moral sensibility may know how to distinguish right from wrong they appear helpless to prevent the triumph of evil.

—Robert Gordon

JUNO AND THE PAYCOCK
by Sean O'Casey

First Publication: In *Two Plays*, London, 1925.
First Production: Abbey Theatre, Dublin, 3 March 1924.

Criticism
(For general works on the author, see *Playwrights* volume)

Articles:
Errol Durbach, "Peacocks and Mothers: Theme and Dramatic Metaphor in O'Casey's *Juno and the Paycock*", in *Modern Drama*, 15, 1972.
William A. Armstrong, "The Integrity of *Juno and the Paycock*", in *Modern Drama*, 17, 1974.
Bernice Schrank, "Dialectical Configurations in *Juno and the Paycock*", in *Twentieth Century Literature*, 21, 1975.
Ronald Ayling, "*Juno and the Paycock*: A Textual Study", in *Modernist Studies: Literature & Culture 1920–1940*, 2, 1976.
Mary Papke, "*Juno and the Paycock* as a Larkinite Stage Parable", in *Sean O'Casey Review*, 3, 1977.
Leslie Thomson, "Opening the Eyes of the Audience: Visual and Verbal Imagery in *Juno and the Paycock*", in *Modern Drama*, 29, 1986.
Gary Vena, "Congruency and Coincidence in O'Casey's *Juno* and O'Neill's *Journey*", in *English Studies*, 68, 1987.

* * *

In a tenement house in Dublin during the Civil War of 1922, "Captain" Boyle's wife, Juno, struggles to support her family while her work shy husband goes "strutting about the town like a paycock" with his sycophantic crony, Joxer Daly. Their daughter, Mary, is on strike for her "principles" (learnt from her admirer, Jerry Devine, a Labour supporter) while the son, Johnny, who fought in the 1916 Easter Rising and lost his arm in the O'Connell Street fighting, broods in his room, fearful of some unnamed threat. When Boyle is told by Mary's new suitor, the English schoolteacher, Charlie Bentham, that he has been left money in a cousin's will, he proceeds to an orgy of spending on credit, displaying his new possessions, including vulgar furniture, at a party, which is cut short when a funeral procession passes. The bereaved mother, Mrs. Tancred, pauses in the doorway to lament the killing of her Republican son (once Johnny's Commandant) and to pray for an end to the murderous hate between Republicans and Free Staters. Juno repeats her words at the end of the play after everything has gone wrong for the Boyles. There will be no money, because of Bentham's careless wording of the will. Mary, whom he has made pregnant, is abandoned, and as the unpaid-for furniture is being reclaimed by removal men, Johnny is taken away by his former comrades, to be shot for betraying Tancred. Juno

goes to identify his body; she and Mary, who is now disowned by her father, leave the home, to bring up Mary's child elsewhere. The curtain falls on Boyle and Joxer groping drunkenly for the missing furniture, while the Paycock reflects grandiloquently "The whole worl's. . .in a terr. . .ible state o' chassis".

Juno and the Paycock is the second play in O'Casey's Dublin trilogy, and of the three, it was the overwhelming success. The first of the Abbey plays to have its run extended for a second week, it has remained the most popular and frequently revived of all O'Casey's plays. The vigour of the comedy intertwined with its tragedy has helped to assure this, along with the rich characterisation, which extends to minor parts like that of Mrs. Madigan as well as the great central roles. The characters are made at once larger than life and convincingly natural by language that slips easily from the colloquial into high rhetoric or lyrical minglings of the comic and nostalgic, as in the Paycock's "Them was days, Joxer, them was days. Nothin' was too hot or heavy for me then". Lady Gregory was much affected on the first night by Sara Allgood's repetition of Mrs. Tancred's prayer, "Take away our hearts o' stone. . .an' give us hearts o' flesh", telling Yeats, "This is one of the evenings at the Abbey that makes me glad to have been born".

The sense of immediacy in *Juno and the Paycock* fascinated the play's early audiences and is one cause of its continuing vitality in the theatre. O'Casey was writing remarkably, even dangerously, close to the events of the Civil War. When Mrs. Tancred's moving lines were first heard on the Abbey stage, notes Gerard Fay (in *The Abbey Theatre*, 1958), "a tremor ran through the audience unlike anything felt since the first works of Synge had burst upon Dublin". Though the political terror is off-stage, it casts a sinister shadow, from the opening line, when Mary casually reads out from the newspaper, "On a little bye-road, out beyant Finglas he was found". This first cryptic reference to the murdered Tancred gradually gathers weight and meaning as Johnny is shown reacting with desperate fear to any mention of killings or of his former Republican connections and, at the end of Act II, "seeing" Tancred's ghost kneeling by the Virgin's statue. The arrival of the gunmen creates an impression of tragic inevitability, though O'Casey has kept the audience partly in the dark about the reason for Johnny's seeming neuroticism, so increasing suspense and irony.

The comedy of *Juno and the Paycock* is one of its chief glories but presents directors with some problems. The Paycock and Joxer, if over-played for comedy, as they sometimes are, too easily dominate the play, distorting the balance of sympathy and obscuring larger issues (O'Casey thought *The Plough and the Stars* a better play because it had no such dominating figures). But the Falstaffian pair's zestful bantering provided actors like Barry Fitzgerald and F.J. McCormick, who first played them, with glorious parts: it is refreshing, in the cramped, degraded slum environment to hear the Paycock fantasising about sailing the seas and asking himself "what is the stars, what is the stars?" while Joxer fishes up the right "darlin' word" to suit his patron's mood. Juno is earth-bound in comparison, distrusting romanticists of all varieties. "You lost your best principle when you lost your arm" is her realistic view of her son's commitment to an ideal. As in the rest of the trilogy, she and the women generally are the victims of men's vanity. She does make her own mistakes (Boyle is sharper in recognising Bentham's shoddiness); but as the action moves further into tragedy, her unselfishness casts an increasingly strong light on the darker side of the Paycock's irresponsibility (Joxer is clearly a rat from the start). Boyle's reaction to Mary's pregnancy is, as Ronald Ayling says (in *Continuity and Innovation in Sean O'Casey's Drama*, 1976),

Juno and the Paycock: Aldwych Theatre, London, 1980 (Royal Shakespeare Company)

savage and "meant to sicken us". Juno is not felt to be exaggerating when she comforts Mary, upset that the child will have no father, with the brave assurance, "It'll have what's far better—it'll have two mothers".

Juno and the Paycock was written out of O'Casey's hard personal experience of tenement life. Some of its characters had real-life prototypes: Juno, notably, owes much to O'Casey's hard-working, devoted mother. A good production captures the look and feel of a Dublin tenement in the 1920's, bringing out the factors which have contributed to making the 45 year old Juno look strained and older than her years: the lack of privacy and the constant intrusions, from coal block vendors to funerals, from Joxer to debt collectors and gunmen.

The technique is not purely realistic, however. O'Casey detested the craze for "real, real life" on the stage. He creates a poetry of theatre through his poignantly musical language, and through atmospheric sound and visual effects like the votive light which goes out as Johnny's doom approaches or the telling contrast in the party scene between the melody sung with moving simplicity by Juno and Mary and Joxer's incoherent attempts to sing "in a querulous voice". Mundane realities acquire symbolic force. By the time she stands on a stage that has been stripped of home-like comforts, speaking Mrs. Tancred's lines and reproaching herself for not feeling enough pity for her when her son was found, riddled with bullets, as now her own son has been, Juno has become a figure of fate, telling the audience what they should carry into their own lives: "Ah, why didn't I remember that then he wasn't a Diehard or a Stater, but only a poor, dead son". With supreme genius, O'Casey closes his play, not on this high, emotional note, but on the comedy that has gone sour and is now seen clearly to be a factor in the tragedy. The Paycock, along with Joxer, confusedly groping for the chairs that were never paid for, mumbling drunken fantasies about "Easter Week" ("had no business to be there. . .but Captain Boyle's Captain Boyle") tells a truth greater than he knows, in his maudlin moralising: "the whole worl's. . .in a terr. . .ible state o' chassis".

—Katharine Worth

JUSTICE
by John Galsworthy

First Publication: London, 1910.
First Production: Duke of York's Theatre, London,
                 21 February 1910.

Criticism
(For general works on the author, see *Playwrights* volume)

Articles:
William B. Bache, "*Justice*: Galsworthy's Dramatic Tragedy",
  in *Modern Drama*, vol.3 no.2, 1960.
Gerhard Stilz, "Naturalistisches Drama und bürgerlich-
  reformerischer Kompromiss: John Galsworthys *Justice*", in
  *Deutsche Vierteljahrsschrift für Literaturwissenschaft und
  Geistesgeschichte*, 54, 1980.

*   *   *

John Galsworthy's *Justice* concerns the misadventures of

John Falder, a hapless clerk in a law office who falls in love with a married woman, Ruth Honeywell. She is an equally unfortunate character, a battered wife of limited intellect. They conspire to run away to South America, but are short of the necessary funds. Falder embezzles the money rather incompetently and is summarily sentenced to three years of penal servitude. Nearly driven mad by the requisite solitary confinement, upon his release Falder is unable to find either peace of mind or employment. He returns to his old law office and is about to be rehired when he learns that it is only upon the condition that he give up Ruth. Also arriving just before the final curtain is a Sergeant of Police to bring Falder back to prison for failing to report his address to the proper authorities. Shortly thereafter the overtaxed simpleton hurls himself through a convenient window and breaks his neck. He leaves behind a hushed and chastened cast of characters.

It is the play's prison scenes that originally gave the play its fame although now, since the play's sensational first production, it is the trial scene that is most riveting. Indeed it is here that Galsworthy is most successful at characterization. The dreadful *injustice* of the proceedings is graphically and tellingly represented. The judge is pompous and insensitive, the prosecutor smug and complacent, the defence attorney far too earnest and inexperienced. The characterization of Cokeson, the senior clerk in Falder's law office, is also deftly handled in the trial scene. His half-digested knowledge of courtroom procedure and fractured diction are presented realistically, and would be comic were the other men of the court not so coldly calculating. It actually seems that all the world is indeed against Falder; Ruth is made to seem little more than a slattern. Ultimately, the trial is mechanistically chilling and devoid of sentimentality.

Falder is no Jean Valjean (of Victor Hugo's novel *Les Misérables*), though it would seem that the constabulary and judiciary are populated with naught but law-enforcers like Hugo's Javert. Extenuating circumstances mean nothing: the letter of the law is writ large and its spirit is not even alluded to, although the gentler junior partner in Falder's firm "bitterly" intones "the quality of mercy is not strained" as he is taken away by the police.

The play was instrumental in influencing Winston Churchill, who was then Home Secretary, to reform the penal code. And in the United States where the play was performed six years after its 1910 premiere, John Barrymore achieved his first success as a serious actor.

When Galsworthy was asked whether he would rather have a play that would effect prison reform or one that would be a classic a hundred years hence, he charily responded, "a classic". However the play has not proven durable, but it was a tremendous sensation in its day, causing uproarious demonstrations from audiences and critics. It remains readable with crisp dialogue and fathomable characterizations, although most intriguing is the almost off-handed simplicity of Falder, the protagonist whose most powerful scene (in solitary confinement) is performed in silence.

The reality of the protagonist's colorlessness lends an overall drabness to the central character that makes his plight all the more compelling. Because the central action of the play is a conventional device of romantic melodrama, indeed even of courtly romance, the working class milieu and abject helplessness of Falder and Ruth give us a viable stage picture of complacent aristocrats lording it over their minions. What is more, Galsworthy spares not the middling social strata either, who are grittily depicted, desperate for even the pits of the plums of their betters.

Galsworthy set the stage for the play's success by launching a campaign for prison reform the year before the play was performed. Although he himself would later somewhat ruefully admit that the play's "propaganda qualities had obscured its dramatic and artistic merits and the tragic nature of its true theme". Indeed Galsworthy labeled the play "A Tragedy in Four Acts" and the petit-bourgeois status of its protagonist is in dramaturgical terms, a precursor of Arthur Miller's Willie Loman, although he lacks even the malfunctioning idealism of the American character and is therefore even closer than Miller's characters to the tragic common man that the American playwright so idealizes. The total lack of any spiritual or intellectual zest, or *elan vital*, marks Falder as truly a man of a new and disaffected age. Cooped up in an urban landscape, hemmed in by a love that would be far better off suffering in silence, Falder is a displaced spirit, restless from his first entrance, and inarticulate and strange. The sense of alienation lies heavily upon him. He is rootless, abandoned by his family; friendless, ultimately betrayed even by the woman for whom he sacrificed everything. Falder makes the headlong dive for oblivion and dies, helpless, hopeless. With the initial fire of its reformist zeal quenched, the deeper social scathing of Galsworthy's play warrants re-examination.

—Thomas F. Connolly

JUSTICE WITHOUT REVENGE (El castigo sin venganza) by Lope de Vega Carpio

First Publication: Barcelona, 1634.
First Production: Madrid, c. 3 February 1632.

Editions
El castigo sin venganza, edited by Adolfo Van Dam, Groningen, Holland, 1928.
El castigo sin venganza, edited by C.A. Jones, Oxford, 1966.
El castigo sin venganza, edited by J. Rodríguez, Zaragoza, 1966.
El castigo sin venganza, edited by J. García Aráez, Madrid, 1967.
El castigo sin venganza, in *El castigo sin venganza; La moza de cántaro*, Madrid, 1970.
El castigo sin venganza, in *El perro del hortelano; El castigo sin venganza*, edited by A.D. Kossof, Madrid, 1970.
El castigo sin venganza, in *Fuenteovejuna; El castigo sin venganza*, edited by M. Fernández Nieto, Madrid, 1982.
El castigo sin venganza, in *El villano en su rincón; El castigo sin venganza*, edited by J. García Morales, Madrid, 1986.
El castigo sin venganza, edited by José Mariá Díez Borque, Madrid, 1987.

Translations
Justice Without Revenge, in *Lope de Vega: Five Plays*, translated by Jill Booty, New York, 1961.
Justice Without Revenge, translated by Charles Davis, Warminster, 1991.

Criticism
(For general works on the author, see *Playwrights* volume)

Books:
Ricardo Doménech (ed.), *"El castigo sin venganza" y el teatro de Lope de Vega*, Madrid, 1987.

Articles:
Carlo Consiglio, "La fuente italiana de *El castigo sin venganza*", in *Mediterráneo*, 12, 1945.
T.E. May, "Lope de Vega's *El castigo sin venganza*: The Idolatry of the Duque de Ferrara", in *Bulletin of Hispanic Studies*, 37, 1960.
C.B. Morris, "Lope de Vega's *El castigo sin venganza* and Poetic Tradition", in *Bulletin of Hispanic Studies*, 40, 1963.
Charlotte Stern, "*El castigo sin venganza* and Leibniz's Theory of Possible Worlds", in *Studies in Honor of William M. McCrary*, edited by Everett W. Hesse and others, Lincoln, Nebraska, 1966.
Victor Dixon and Alexander A. Parker, "*El castigo sin venganza*: Two Lines, Two Interpretations", in *Modern Language Notes*, 85, 1970.
Victor Dixon, "*El castigo sin venganza*: The Artistry of Lope de Vega", in *Studies in Spanish Literature of the Golden Age, Presented to Edward M. Wilson*, edited by R.O. Jones, London, 1973.
Everett W. Hesse, "The Perversion of Love in Lope de Vega's *El castigo sin venganza*", in *Hispania*, 60, 1977.
Geraldine Cleardy Nichols, "The Rehabilitation of the Duke of Ferrara", in *Journal of Hispanic Philology*, 1, 1977.
Mitchell D. Traverdi, "The Source and Meaning of the Pelican Fable in *El castigo sin venganza*", in *Modern Language Notes*, 92, 1977.
William M. McCrary, "The Duke and the *Commedia*: Drama and Imitation in Lope's *El castigo sin venganza*", in *Journal of Hispanic Philology*, 2, 1978.
Frank J. Bianco, "Lope de Vega's *El castigo sin venganza* and Free Will", in *Kentucky Romance Quarterly*, 26, 1979.
Peter W. Evans, "Character and Context in *El castigo sin venganza*", in *Modern Language Review*, 74, 1979.
Jane Horowitz Murray, "Lope through the Looking-Glass: Metaphor and Meaning in *El castigo sin venganza*", in *Bulletin of Hispanic Studies*, 56, 1979.
Gwynne Edwards, "Lope and Calderón: The Tragic Pattern of *El castigo sin venganza*", in *Bulletin of the Comediantes*, vol.33 no.2, 1981.
Susan L. Fischer, "Lope's *El castigo sin venganza* and the Imagination", in *Kentucky Romance Quarterly*, vol.28 no.1, 1981.
Julio Rodríguez Puértolas, "La soledad del duque de Ferrara", in *Diálogos hispánicos de Amsterdam*, 2, 1981.
Margate A. van Antwerp, "Fearful Symmetry: The Poetic World of Lope's *El castigo sin venganza*", in *Bulletin of Hispanic Studies*, vol.58 no.3, 1981.
Currie K. Thompson, "Unstable Irony in Lope de Vega's *El castigo sin venganza*", in *Studies in Philology*, vol.78 no.3, 1983.
Donald McGrady, "Sentido y función de los cuentecillos en *El castigo sin venganza* de Lope", in *Bulletin hispanique*, vol.85, nos.1–2, 1983.
Melveena McKendrick, "Language and Silence in *El castigo sin venganza*", in *Bulletin of the Comediantes*, vol.35 no.1, 1983.
Margit Frenk, "Claves metafóricas en *El castigo sin venganza*", in *Filología*, vol.20 no.2, 1985.
David M. Gitlitz, "Ironía e imágenes en *El castigo sin venganza*", in *Revista de estudios hispánicos*, vol.14 no.1, 1986.
Dian Fox, "The Grace of Conscience in *El castigo sin venganza*", in *Studies in Honor of Bruce W. Wardropper*, edited by Dian Fox, Harry Sieber, and Robert Ter Horst, Newark, Delaware, 1989.
Bruce Golden, "The Authority of Honour in Lope's *El castigo sin venganza*", in *Shakespeare and the Dramatic Tradition*,

edited by W.R. Elton and William B. Long, Newark, Delaware, 1989.

* * *

"*Cuando Lope quiere, quiere*" ("When Lope wishes, he will"): this subtitle, added to a 1647 edition of *El castigo sin venganza* (*Justice Without Revenge*), emphasizes the carefully executed quality of this work, widely acknowledged to be one of its author's most outstanding achievements. Reputedly an instinctive artist rather than a conscientious craftsman, Lope was also capable, particularly in the later years of his extended career, of revising what he had, at first, rapidly composed. The autograph manuscript of *Justice Without Revenge* contains many corrections which confirm that even late in his career Lope was influenced by the thoughtful attitudes and meticulous techniques of his own follower Pedro Calderón.

The subject-matter of this admirably executed play, the product of scrupulous attention to unity of theme and structure, is derived from a *novella* by Bandello based on a real event in 15th-century Italian history. The play dramatizes the fatal love-relationship between Federico, bastard son of the Duke of Ferrara, and Federico's stepmother, Casandra. When the Duke discovers their adultery he determines to punish his wife and son without making public their offence and his dishonour. He persuades Federico to execute an unidentified traitor, bound and hooded, whom Federico recognizes as his stepmother and mistress only after he has committed the horrifying deed. Falsely accused by his father of having deliberately murdered Casandra in order to prevent her bearing a legitimate heir to Ferrara, Federico is then himself summarily executed by the Duke's command.

Golden Age audiences delighted in dramas of illicit love and affronted honour, and in plays with a political dimension, especially those in which rulers conflicted violently with their sons. *Justice Without Revenge* contained both such preferred elements but it was originally staged for only one day and then withdrawn for reasons which the playwright mysteriously declined to reveal, and since arousing many hypotheses among critics as to possible reasons why. Francisco de Rojas Zorrilla dramatized, likewise in the 1630's, a daring case of feminine dishonour in a work entitled *Cada cual lo que le toca* (*Each to his own Concern*). This play, in which a nobleman discovers that he has unknowingly married a woman who has already been violated by another man, was hissed at its first performance in Madrid by an audience offended by its lack of moral decorum. Casandra's blatantly immoral conduct might have provoked the first audience which attended *El castigo sin venganza* to a similarly extreme reaction of disapproval.

Described in its final lines as "tragedy", an exalted category to which Lope allocated few of his numerous plays, this complex and sombre drama has been the subject of much critical controversy. United in admiration for its artistry, scholars disagree vehemently as to its interpretation. Opinions particularly differ concerning who is the tragic hero; whether, in the final act, the Duke's professed change from libertine to faithful husband is genuine; and what meanings the drama's ambiguous title is truly intended to convey. All three principal characters are tragically blameworthy for the catastrophic denouement, though in significantly different degrees. Federico is guilty of consummating his illicit passion for Casandra. But his father's dissolutely bad example and his stepmother's seductive persuasion are decisive influences upon his behaviour, at once lessening the measure of his offence and diminishing the tragic importance of his role. Casandra is a more interestingly complex and strong-minded individual than is Federico. Married for reasons of state to a middle-aged libertine, this deeply humiliated, young woman deliberately commits adultery less from motives of love than of revenge. But the Duke is, surely, the central and most profoundly tragic figure in Lope's drama. The Duke's womanizing activities and indifference to his wife—whose bed he shares only once—impel Casandra and Federico into adultery, which, in turn (when the Duke finds out), leads inevitably to their violent deaths. The Duke discovers their crime upon his return, apparently a reformed man, from a military campaign in defence of the Pope. Some critics have judged as sincere the Duke's declared intention to change his wanton ways, though too late to prevent his wife's adultery. But had Lope intended us to believe in the Duke's reformation, he would surely have provided us with a more credible witness than his disreputable manservant, Ricardo. His declaration that his master "is now a saint" is much less convincing than the comment of a less biased figure, the wise fool Batín, that the Duke is a "false saint".

Unlike Casandra and Federico, the Duke does not die at the end. But his survival, far from reducing, instead intensifies his tragic stature as hero. A childless widower, he lives on in a torment of spiritual isolation and inwardly-acknowledged responsibility not only for the death of Casandra, but of the one person he has truly loved—his son. It is known that Lope hesitated over the title of his play. As the autograph manuscript reveals, he considered "Revenge Without Justice" before deciding upon "Justice Without Revenge". His finally chosen title confirms that the true crime for which Federico and Casandra died (their adultery) was not publicly revealed. They were punished "sin venganza" because the Duke's dishonour was never openly acknowledged nor officially avenged. More importantly, however, the title is used to signify the punishment suffered by the Duke himself, which, though bloodless and invisible (apparently "unavenging"), cruelly denies him quick release through sudden death, condemning him, instead, to imprisonment for life in the solitary confinement of guilt. A Roman-Catholic playwright, composing for religiously-minded audiences, Lope doubtless also intended his public to understand that, when he dies at last, the Duke will be punished in the hereafter for his wickedness, through the eternally just vengeance of the Lord.

—Ann L. Mackenzie

———

KASPAR
by Peter Handke

First Publication: Frankfurt, 1968.
First Production: Frankfurter Theater am Turm, Frankfurt, and Städtischen Bühnen Oberhausen, Stockholm, 11 May 1968.

Translations
Kaspar, in *"Kaspar" and Other Plays*, translated by Michael Roloff, New York, 1969.

Criticism
(For general works on the author, see *Playwrights* volume)

Books:
Peter Bekes, *Peter Handke, "Kaspar": Sprache als Folter; Entstehung, Struktur, Rezeption, Didaktik*, Paderborn, 1984.
Renate Voris, *Peter Handke: "Kaspar"*, Frankfurt, 1984.

Articles:
Rainer Taëni, "Chaos Versus Order: The Grotesque in *Kaspar* and *Marat / Sade*", in *Dimension*, 2, 1969.
Peter Handke, "Nauseated by Language: From an Interview with Arthur Joseph", in *The Drama Review*, 15, 1970.
Hans P. Franke, "*Kaspar* von Peter Handke: Versuch einer literatursoziologischen Interpretation", in *Deutschunterricht*, vol.23 no.5, 1971.
Peter Horn, "Vergewaltigung durch die Sprache: Peter Handkes *Kaspar*", in *Literatur und Kritik*, 51, 1971.
Christa Dixon, "Peter Handkes *Kaspar*: Ein Modellfall", in *German Quarterly*, 46, 1973.
Lilo Herbrandt, "Peter Handkes *Kaspar*: Ein Modell der Inhaltbezogenen Grammatik", in *Diskussion Deutsche*, 26, 1975.
Gay McAuley, "The Problem of Identity: Theme, Form and Theatrical Method in *Les Nègres*, *Kaspar* and *Old Times*", in *Southern Review*, 8, 1975.
Linda M. Hill, "Obscurantism and Verbal Resistance in Handke's *Kaspar*", in *Germanic Review*, 52, 1977.
Michael Bloom, "*Woyzeck* and *Kaspar*: The Congruities in Drama and Film", in *LFQ*, 8, 1980.
John T. Dorsey, "Plays on Words: Language in Ionesco's *La Cantatrice chauve* and Handke's *Kaspar*", in *Journal of the College of International Relations*, 2, 1981.
Rainer Nägele, "Peter Handke: The Staging of Language", in *Modern Drama*, 23, 1981.
Jeffrey Herrick, "Peter Handke's *Kaspar*: A Study of Linguistic Theory in Modern Drama", in *Philological Quarterly*, 63, 1984.

John H. Lutterbie, "The Reluctant Subject: *Kaspar* and the Frame of Representation", in *Journal of Dramatic Theory and Criticism*, vol.4 no.1, 1989.
Bettina A. Soestwohner, "*Kaspar* oder das Theater der Sprache", in *Colloquia Germanica*, 22, 1989.
Bettina L. Knapp, "Peter Handke's *Kaspar*: The Mechanics of Language—a Fractionating Schizophrenic Theatrical Event", in *Studies in Twentieth Century Literature*, 14, 1990.

*   *   *

At the beginning of the play, Kaspar can only speak one sentence: "I want to be someone like somebody else once was". Shortly after his entrance, the voices of the three Prompters begin to drone from loudspeakers, trying to persuade him to learn other, more meaningful sentences. Slowly Kaspar's resistance weakens and he learns to order his world by language, thus turning into more of a socially acceptable creature but less of an individual, as indicated by the apperance of five identical Kaspar-clones and his delivery of an elegant, conformist speech of praise about rationality and good citizenship. Now that he has mastered language, Kaspar can look at himself critically and he does not like what he sees. The only way for him to return to being an individual is to abandon everything he has learned and to return to his pre-speech condition. Amid the babbling of the surrogate Kaspars he reduces his elegant sentences to fragments and repeats Othello's cryptic words "goats and monkeys" over and over again, as the falling curtain knocks over the jabbering Kaspar clones.

The text of *Kaspar* is preceded by a listing of Kaspar's 16 developmental phases and by the poem "16 years" by Ernst Jandl that establishes a connection with the historic Kaspar Hauser, an autistic young man who appeared in Nuremberg in 1828. He could only speak one sentence ("I want to become a horseman like my father once was") and had apparently lived in complete solitude for about 16 years. In an extensive introduction Handke gives elaborate staging instructions and insists that this is not a play about how "*it really is or really was* with Kaspar Hauser", but "what is *possible* with someone". He also mentions that the play could have been entitled "speech torture", and that he does not want the audience to think of the protagonist as a clown (as suggested by the German word *Kasper*), but that he should resemble Frankenstein's monster, another tragic victim of arrogant social engineering.

Kaspar is a play about the tyranny of language and implicitly about the tyranny of society. It attempts to illustrate how society "builds" a human being. Kaspar does not only have to be conditioned but first must be *un*conditioned: his one and only sentence indicates a previous existence, however mysterious, that was not moulded by the environment into which he

Kaspar: New End Theatre, London, 1975

stumbles symbolically through a slit in the curtain. He tries to establish a foothold (Kaspar initially walks only with difficulty), but has very limited resources for success (his sentence may stand for inherited traits). These limitations are also his greatest freedom: he can define the world and his position in it on his own terms, unfettered by social and linguistic conventions.

In order to become a respected and respectable member of society he must be weaned off his sentence and taught to order his world with an ever-increasing arsenal of words and sentences. His formerly unified and simple view of the world becomes complicated and fragmented: he is not Kaspar any longer but only one of many Kaspars. He has traded individuality and freedom for security and respectability. As soon as he reaches this stage he becomes an ardent prompter himself, extolling the virtues of orderly speech and socially responsible behavior. In the end, his new cognitive-linguistic skills enable him to look critically at himself. Stunned, he realizes the "impossibility of *expressing* anything in language", and rejects what he has learned, and is, like Othello, driven to irrational speech.

In this play Handke abandons a plot as such as well as the creation of any illusion of reality. The stage props do not attempt to create any verisimilitude but serve as a symbolic reflection of the progress of the morality play in which Kaspar plays the role of Everyman. His loss of innocence is not brought about by traditional dramatic characters but by disembodied loudspeaker voices—the German word *Einsager* is usually translated as "prompters", but has a strong connota-

tion of "indoctrination". The use of the loudspeaker voices reinforces the concept of an impersonal social force rather than of an individual villain. Kaspar at first resists the attempts to educate himself out of his simple, irrational, child-like existence, but the anonymous voices are too strong and persistent. Kaspar becomes proud of his accomplishments; the growing order of his sentences is reflected in the increasing symmetry of the stage props. He is no longer unique; he becomes a member of society as evidenced by the appearance of five more identical Kaspars whom he regards with a mixture of pride and distrust and who serve as further role models for him. At the climax near the end of Act I, Kaspar has himself become a Prompter—he takes over the microphone and begins to indoctrinate the audience, potential Kaspars themselves.

Finally Kaspar realizes that all this linguistic education has only been for the benefit of society; it has not brought him any nearer to an understanding of his existential condition than did his original sentence. Reduced to Othello's agonized exclamation "goats and monkeys!" (uttered at the point in Shakespeare's play when Othello loses his reasoning faculties under the constant onslaught of Iago's sly insinuations), Kaspar now has even less than his original sentence to make sense of his life.

—Franz G. Blaha

DIE KASSETTE. See **SCENES FROM THE HEROIC LIFE OF THE MIDDLE CLASSES.**

DER KAUKASISCHE KREIDEKREIS. See **THE CAUCASIAN CHALK CIRCLE.**

KID STAKES. See **THE DOLL TRILOGY.**

KING JOHN
by William Shakespeare

First Publication: In the First Folio, 1623; some scholars believe the anonymous *The Troublesome Reign of King John*, 1591, to have been a "bad" quarto by Shakespeare.

First Production: London, probably c. 1596–97; possibly before 1590.

Editions

King John, edited by H.H. Furness, Philadelphia, Pennsylvania, 1913 (New Variorum Edition).

King John, edited by John Dover Wilson, Cambridge, 1931 (The New Shakespeare).

King John, edited by E.A.J. Honigmann, London, 1954 (Arden Shakespeare).

King John, edited by William H. Matchett, New York, 1966 (Signet Classic Shakespeare).

King John, edited by Robert L. Smallwood, Harmondsworth, 1974 (New Penguin Shakespeare).

King John, edited by A.R. Braunmuller, Oxford, 1989 (Oxford Shakespeare).

King John, edited by L.A. Beaurline, Cambridge, 1990 (New Cambridge Shakespeare).

Criticism

(For general works on the author, see *Playwrights* volume)

Books:

May Matteson, *Five Plays about King John*, Uppsala, 1977.

Francis A. Shirley (ed.), *"King John" and "King Henry VIII": Critical Essays*, New York, 1988.

Deborah T. Curren-Aquino (ed.), *"King John": New Perspectives*, Delaware, New Jersey, 1989.

Mark W. Scott and Sandra L. Williamson (eds.), *"King John"*, in *Shakespearian Criticism, 9*, Detroit, Illinois, 1989 [anthology of criticism].

Articles:

For information on articles about *King John*, see the bibliographies listed in the *Playwrights* volume and the annual Shakespeare Bibliography in *Shakespeare Quarterly*, published by the Folger Shakespeare Library, Washington D.C. (1950–).

*   *   *

The action of *The Life and Death of King John* has several strands and these do not draw together towards a common conclusion as in Shakespeare's other history plays. Here each act brings new issues into prominence.

At the start, King John has succeeded to the throne of England in accordance with the will of his deceased brother, the famed crusader Richard Coeur de Lion; but Richard's very young son, Prince Arthur, is still alive and the French king, Philip, supports his rival claim to the throne. So the two nations are drawn into war. John's mother, Eleanor, supports her son, while Constance, Arthur's mother, pursues the boy's claim with all the eloquence she can muster. Yet before this issue is brought to a climax, another has begun which is also concerned with sons and mothers: Robert Faulconbridge petitions King John for his father's lands on the grounds that his mother had conceived his elder brother, Philip, out of wedlock; Robert gets his rights, as he sees them, but Philip, the Bastard, is recognized by John as a son of Coeur de Lion, and he is knighted and taken into the king's service.

War in France follows, with the citizens of Angiers doing all that diplomacy can to save their town and their own skins. Hubert, their leader, proposes a truce based on the marriage of Lady Blanche, a Spanish princess and niece of John, to Lewis the Dauphin, son to the King of France. The treaty is concluded despite the clamorous complaints of Constance. At this point, Cardinal Pandulph, the Papal Legate, arrives to start another action by demanding that John confirm Stephen Langton as Archbishop of Canterbury: John's refusal is couched in absolute terms, which has an ironic relevance to all that has so far occurred: "What earthly name to interrogatories / Can task the free breath of a sacred king?". Pandulph replies by ordering Philip to break the peace and support Rome by fighting John. Although newly married, Lewis is eager for battle; but he loses, and John is left in possession of Arthur with whom he returns to England, leaving his own mother, Eleanor, in charge of his army of occupation. Now John complicates the action further by persuading Hubert to kill Arthur.

As the fourth act begins, still new twists of action and new issues are added. Hubert sets about blinding Arthur, but spares his life. Supported by Pandulph, Lewis invades England. John's nobles desert his side and join the French. Eleanor dies in France and Constance goes mad with grief. Arthur is reported to be alive, but is found dead, having tried to jump from his prison's high walls. John submits to Pandulph as Lewis's army approaches London. Surprisingly John's army triumphs, but he himself is murdered, poisoned by some monks; he dies believing that the battle is lost. His son, Prince Henry—of whom nothing has been heard before this time—takes command of the land and receives the submission of the surviving nobles who have returned to their first and English allegiance.

This lengthy account of the plot is necessary to show how frequently the audience's expectations are thwarted and how frequently loyalties change. Some scholars believe that the play is muddled in these respects because Shakespeare was following an earlier anonymous play, *The Troublesome Reign of King John* (published in 1591), rather than working directly from the *Chronicles* of Holinshed and Hall as was his usual practice. A few scholars believe that *King John* was a very early play, and *The Troublesome Reign* a reported or reconstructed version of it.

Not surprisingly, *King John* has always been controversial. Its plot is not at all easy to follow in performance, especially towards the end—even if the fine-drawn arguments of Pandulph are reduced in length and a number of minor incidents excised. But the play has remarkable strengths: the passion of Constance is famed in theatrical history; the vigor and rough humour of the Bastard are immediately engaging; Arthur is both brave and pathetic. The character of John is to some degree enigmatic, but can gain subtlety in performance: his grief about his mother's death wracks him physically, with scarcely a word spoken; his guilt for Arthur's murder is shown in nervous attempts at self-justification and sudden impulsive reactions; his dependence on the Bastard's stalwart support is presented with effective economy; his death is briefly courageous and affecting.

It is the Bastard who carries the play, providing an energetic response at each stage of the action. In both soliloquies and bold rejoinders, he mocks kings and nations, and men and women in peace and in war; he also mocks himself, even as he commits himself to the cause of his king and country. Through his words and presence, the audience is encouraged to see through political and moral pretensions, to understand that the play's heroes strut and fret in their brief scenes, and are only rarely true to themselves or in charge of their destinies. Thus an ironic humour seems to be the distinctive and fascinating mark of this play; it is active even in the Bastard's concluding prophecy, which has become famous out of the context which Shakespeare had created for it: "Come the three corners of the world in arms / And we shall shock them! Naught shall make us rue / If England to itself do rest but true!".

—John Russell Brown

KING LEAR
by William Shakespeare

First Publication: London, 1608 (first quarto); 1619 ("bad" second quarto); with variants, in First Folio, 1623.

First Production: London, c.1605–06; earliest recorded production, Palace at Whitehall, London, 26 December 1606/07.

Editions

King Lear, edited by H.H. Furness, Philadelphia, Pennsylvania, 1880 (New Variorum Edition).

King Lear, edited by G.L. Kittredge, New York, 1940.

King Lear, edited by G.I. Duthie, Oxford, 1949.

King Lear, edited by Kenneth Muir, London, 1952; revised edition, 1985 (Arden Shakespeare).

King Lear, edited by Alfred Harbage, Baltimore, 1958 (Pelican Shakespeare).

King Lear, edited by G.I. Duthie and John Dover Wilson, Cambridge, 1960 (The New Shakespeare).

King Lear, edited by Russell Fraser, New York, 1963 (Signet Classic Shakespeare).

King Lear, edited by G.K. Hunter, Harmondsworth, 1972 (New Penguin Shakespeare).

King Lear [First Quarto and First Folio texts] in William Shakespeare: The Complete Works, edited by Stanley Wells and Gary Taylor, Oxford, 1986.

Bibliographies

S.A. Tannenbaum, Shakespeare's "King Lear": A Concise Bibliography, New York, 1940.

Larry S. Champion, "King Lear": An Annotated Bibliography (2 vols.), New York and London, 1980 (Garland Shakespeare Bibliographies).

Criticism

(For general works on the author, see Playwrights volume)

Books:

R.W. Chambers, King Lear, Glasgow, 1940.

H. Bonheim, The King Lear Perplex, San Francisco, California, 1960.

Russell Fraser, Shakespeare's Poetics in Relation to "King Lear", London, 1962.

Nicholas Brooke, King Lear, London, 1963.

Maynard Mack, King Lear in Our Time, Berkeley, California, 1965.

William R. Elton, King Lear and the Gods, San Marino, California, 1966.

Helen Gardner, King Lear, London, 1967.

Frank Kermode (ed.), "King Lear": A Casebook, London, 1969.

Marvin Rosenberg, The Masks of "King Lear", Berkeley, California, 1972.

Rosalie L. Colie and F.T. Flahiff (eds.), Some Facets of "King Lear": Essays in Prismatic Criticism, Toronto and Buffalo, New York 1974.

Arthur G. Davis, The Royalty of Lear, Jamaica, New York, 1974.

S.L. Goldberg, An Essay on "King Lear", Cambridge, 1974.

Peter Milward, Biblical Themes in Shakespeare, Centering on "King Lear", Tokyo, 1975.

Mathilda M. Hills, Time, Space, and Structure in "King Lear", Salzburg, 1976.

Dorothy E. Nameri, Three Versions of the Story of King Lear, Studied in Relation to One Another (2 vols.), Salzburg, 1977.

Jagodish Purkayastha, The Tragic Vision of Life in "Hamlet" and "King Lear", Salzburg, 1977.

John Riebetanz, The Lear World: A Study of "King Lear" in its Dramatic Context, Toronto, and Buffalo, New York, 1977.

Janet Adelman (ed.), Twentieth Century Interpretations of "King Lear", Englewood Cliffs, New Jersey, 1978.

Peter Wensel, Die Lear-Kritik in 20 Jahrhundert: Ein Beitrag zu einer Analyse der Entwicklung der Shakespeare-Literatur, Amsterdam, 1979.

P.W.K. Stone, The Textual History of "King Lear", London, 1980.

Steven Urkowitz, Shakespeare's Revision of "King Lear", Princeton, New Jersey, 1980.

Peter W.M. Blayney, The Texts of "King Lear" and Their Origins, 1: Nicholas Oakes and the First Quarto, Cambridge, 1982.

Kenneth Muir and Stanley Wells (eds.), Aspects of "King Lear", Cambridge and New York, 1982 [articles reprinted from Shakespeare Survey].

Kenneth Muir (ed), "King Lear": Critical Essays, New York and London, 1984.

John L. Murphy, Darkness and Devils: Exorcism and "King Lear", Athens, Ohio and London, 1984.

Gāmini Salgādo, King Lear, London, 1984 (Text and Performance Series).

Joseph Wittreich, "Image of that Horror": History, Prophecy, and Apocalypse in "King Lear", San Marino, California, 1984.

Laurie Lanzen Harris and Mark W. Scott (eds.), "King Lear", in Shakespearian Criticism, 2, Detroit, Illinois, 1985 [anthology of criticism].

Harold Bloom (ed.), William Shakespeare's "King Lear", New York, New Haven, Connecticut, and Philadelphia, 1987.

William F. Martin, The Indissoluble Knot: "King Lear" as Ironic Drama, Lanham, Maryland, 1987.

King Lear: Stratford-Upon-Avon, 1982 (Royal Shakespeare Company; Anthony Sher as Fool and Michael Gambon as Lear)

William R. Elton, *King Lear and the Gods*, Lexington, Kentucky, 1988.

Alexander Leggat, *King Lear*, Boston, 1988 (Twayne's New Critical Introductions to Shakespeare).

Ann Thompson, *"King Lear": An Introduction to the Variety of Criticism*, London and Basingstoke, 1988 (The Critics Debate Series).

J.S. Bratton (ed.), *King Lear*, Bristol, 1989 (Plays in Performance Series).

Articles:

For information of the many articles about *King Lear*, see the bibliographies listed above, the bibliographies in the *Playwrights* volume, and the annual Shakespeare Bibliography in *Shakespeare Quarterly*, published by the Folger Shakespeare Library, Washington D.C. (1950–).

*   *   *

King Lear was probably written in 1605. The story already existed as folklore when, in 1136, Geoffrey of Monmouth included it in his *Historia Regum Brittaniae*, which led to its inclusion in Holinshed's *Chronicles*, one of Shakespeare's frequent sources. There was also an earlier anonymous dramatic version, *The True Chronicle History of King Leir*, staged around 1594, in which Shakespeare may possibly have acted.

Summarising a tragedy is inevitably reductive. *King Lear* deals with universal questions such as good versus evil and the necessity for self-knowledge; it also deals with kingship and with family relations. We may establish the bones of the plot on the latter level: Lear, an old man, attempts to divide his kingdom among his three daughters in proportion to their expressions of love for him. Cordelia, his youngest and favourite child, cannot bring herself to make flattering speeches like those of her sisters Goneril and Regan. Lear cuts her off and she is married to the King of France without even a dowry. Moreover Lear banishes his most loyal friend, Kent, when he protests. Lear goes to live with Goneril, but leaves when she complains that his retinue of 100 knights has disrupted her household, and goes to Regan. When Regan also refuses his followers, Lear curses both daughters and goes outside into a raging storm that echoes his anger. Overwhelmed by the realisation of his earlier folly and injustice, which has now so bitterly repaid him, Lear succumbs to a madness he had long feared.

In a subplot deftly paralleled and interwoven with the main plot, Edmund, bastard son of the Duke of Gloucester, plots to oust his legitimate brother Edgar and is adopted as an ally by Goneril and Regan. Cordelia eventually finds her father and they are reconciled, but subsequently imprisoned by Edmund. For love of Edmund, Goneril and Regan both die, and Cordelia, meanwhile, is hanged in prison. This final suffering proves too much for Lear, who dies trying to convince himself that Cordelia may still be alive.

Lear is the most far-reaching of all Shakespeare's tragedies in that an end of suffering is at first allowed (in a transcendent reconciliation scene between Lear and Cordelia); but the play is not allowed to end there. Shakespeare's other major tragedies lead inexorably to retribution and the death of the protagonist, whereas his final plays (such as *A Winter's Tale*) are allowed to culminate in reconciliation. In *Lear* alone is a moving reconciliation scene the *preliminary* to final tragedy, thus taking the play into a region of absolute suffering beyond the other tragedies.

The role of the Fool in *Lear* also distinguishes the play from Shakespeare's other tragedies. Lear has passed "fourscore years" with a very limited knowledge of either himself or his subjects. In the early scenes the Fool is the only character who can point out Lear's folly and get away with it. He is indeed "Lear's shadow" and has a major function in bringing his master to self-knowledge. It is noticeable that once Lear comes to see human life not with the distorting spectacles of kingship but as it is, the Fool, like a shadow, gradually fades away. One of the most important stages in the learning process for Lear is his encounter with Edgar, virtually naked in the storm and feigning madness, Lear asks:

> Is man no more than this? Consider him well.
> Thou owest the worm no silk, the beast no hide,
> the sheep no wool, the cat no perfume—
> Thou art the thing itself: unaccommodated man
> is no more but such a poor, bare, forked animal
> as thou art.

It is as though Lear understands human vulnerability for the first time and his response is to maintain his identity with it and try to strip himself of his pomp: "Off, off, you lendings!—come, unbutton here".

There is a similar zest to Lear's wholehearted opposition to human evil once he begins to realise the extent of it. Indeed the struggle between good and evil in the play is of especial interest. Having seen Lear's rashness when the play begins we can feel some sympathy with Goneril and Regan:

> *Goneril*: You see how full of changes his age is: the observation we have made of it hath not been little; he always loved our sister most; and with what poor judgement he hath now cast her off appears too grossly.
> *Regan*: 'Tis the infirmity of his age: yet he hath ever but slenderly known himself.

This sympathy can even be maintained over Lear's rowdy retinue; but when the women's passions are fully aroused and aggravated by jealousy over Edmund, an extraordinary violence erupts in which the natural order is overturned and evil runs rampant, feeding on itself. We can identify the point when all barriers of restraint are broken in Cornwall's horrific blinding of Gloucester, encouraged by Regan. The patterning of the subplot intensifies the action. Gloucester like Lear banishes the wrong child and it is only through intolerable suffering that he also learns to see things as they are. As he says himself: "I stumbled when I saw". Blindness becomes his teacher as madness does Lear's.

Despite Shakespeare's wonderful use of language and imagery in *King Lear*, the play is sometimes accused of verbal incoherence, as in Lear's extraordinary repetition of words such as "howl" "kill" and "never". However such repetition conveys his anger and despair more effectively than any flight of eloquence; indeed it is the domestic simplicity of his finale: "Pray you, undo this button:—thank you, sir—" that makes this perhaps the most moving line in the play. A.C. Bradley considered *King Lear* unactable, in that the full grandeur of the storm could not be conveyed in the theatre. Nonetheless no more is needed than a suggestion of thunder, wind and rain. It is the old man alone onstage battling against himself that will convey the storm to the audience. When powerfully acted this scene becomes universal; it is not only an old man struggling against madness, but the powers of good in conflict with the forces of evil. The storm indeed takes place also in the minds of the audience as they empathise with Lear and experience the catharsis of the tragedy.

—Rosemary Pountney

———

KING OEDIPUS.   See **OEDIPUS THE KING.**

———

KING UBU.   See **UBU ROI.**

———

KLOP.   See **THE BEDBUG.**

———

THE KNACK
by Ann Jellicoe

First Publication: London and New York, 1962; revised version in *The Knack; The Sport of My Mad Mother*, London, 1964.
First Production: Arts Theatre, Cambridge (The English Stage Company), 9 October 1961.

*   *   *

Nancy, a naïve young girl from the provinces, is in search of the local YWCA. She finds herself at the ground-floor window of a London house and is invited in by its three young, male occupants. She becomes the object of their sexual advances and the catalyst to their own power games. Tolen tries to demonstrate his "knack" with women in order to impress the shy and awkward Colin. Tom chooses to stay on the sidelines, encouraging Colin, deflating Tolen, and averting several nasty moments by way of funny animal stories. But the situation gets out of hand; Nancy becomes hysterical, faints, and then accuses the men of raping her while she was unconscious. The accusation soon centres on Colin who, flattered by the whole notion, chases Nancy around the room, at last impervious to Tolen's jeers. The final image is of Nancy and Colin alone, grinning at each other across the length of the bed.

The Knack is a witty, absurdist, comedy of menace that, in a light-hearted and exuberant way, examines ideas of gender, sexuality, and people's need to wield power over one another. Jellicoe's focus is character. She creates four young people, riddled with insecurities, each out to prove something. They become effective foils for each other. Tolen is a vulgar, motor-cycle-riding "smoothie", clearly the kingpin of the male trio. Tom needs his approval and Colin is in awe of his sexual prowess. He spouts the vilest of sexist attitudes:

> You must realize that women are not individuals but types. No, not even types, just women. They want to

The Knack: Royal Court Theatre, London, 1962

surrender, but they don't want the responsibility of surrendering. This is one reason why the man must dominate.. . .In this world, Colin, there are the masters and there are the servants. Very few men are real men, Colin, are real masters. Almost all women are servants. They don't want to think for themselves, they want to be dominated.

Tolen suggests to Colin, the landlord, that he evict Tom in order to accommodate Tolen's own friend Rory; these two can then share their women. They will even throw Colin the occasional bone. In action Tolen is even more repulsive, terrorizing Nancy with his belt, grabbing her, and forcing himself on her. Jellicoe makes him so dreadful so as to keep him comic. She also has Tom alleviate dangerous situations with a thoroughly entertaining story or a cup of tea, effectively emasculating Tolen into the bargain.

Tom is the voyeur, seemingly a non-participant in the sexual games (he wants to remove the bed from his room), but in fact he controls much of the action, sexual and otherwise. Colin is

Tolen's polar opposite and comic foil. He is shy, submissive to his male peers, and a total failure with women. Tolen delights in taunting him or sharing his vast experiences in a pompous lecture or a lesson in sexy walking. Nancy is hopelessly ingenuous, silly enough to get caught up in the men's games and idiotic enough to fall for Tolen's humiliating approaches. Her arrival sets the overtly sexual games in motion, but before that Jellicoe has subtly suggested the homoerotic nature of the male rivalries, their plays for dominance and control, their need to crush, please or assuage each other, and Nancy becomes a victim to these impulses as much as to Tolen's overt advances. With its complex sexual undercurrents the whole play takes on the quality of a ritualized mating-dance.

Jellicoe sets the play in male territory. It is Tom's room, emptied of most of its furniture while he paints it. All that is left are two chairs and a stepladder (used in the play to establish height, status or dominance), a chest-expander (the prop for a male strength—or ego—contest), and an all-important bed. Other beds are significant in the play. Tom wants his bed out, but finds it replaced by Colin's because the latter needs to make room for a new six-footer—as big as Tolen's. It is Colin's bed that dominates the room, taking on several functions: a cage, a prison, a safety-barrier, a push-toy, a piano. Only at the end of the play is it likely to serve a bed-like purpose.

Into this male territory comes Nancy, the female outsider, and the mating-dance already under way takes on a new dimension and urgency. Nancy is unresponsive to Colin's clumsy and more sincere overtures but is alternately attracted and terrified by Tolen's arrogance and sadistic toying with her. The ritualistic quality is reinforced by repeated action: Tolen disappearing out of the window to follow another woman and Tolen's outbursts of near-violence undercut by Tom's stories, for example. Tolen's cliché-ridden pronouncements and advances have the quality of a worn-out ritual. The language is often bizarre, and, in Nancy's case, fractured and mono-syllabic, creating a rhythmic pulse to the play, particularly in Nancy's third-act repetition of "rape" and "I've been raped".

Nancy's accusation of rape turns the tables. Perched high atop the step-ladder, drinking tea, at first quietly and then with screams of jubilation and threats of making revelations to the tabloid newspapers, she claims power over the suddenly befuddled men. For the first time she speaks in articulate sentences with a new air of confidence. Soon she decides on Colin as her assailant, which prods him into an assertion of new-found masculinity. He chases Nancy around the bed to Tolen's jeers. Tolen grabs Nancy. Colin slams the bed into the wall and tells him, "If you touch her, I'll kill you". Tolen leaves. The macho-chauvinist has been rejected.

Jellicoe exposes and ridicules male sexist attitudes. She investigates the idea of subliminal homoeroticism at work in the cult of machismo. At the same time she attacks women who submit to male dominance, women who enter the male domain on men's terms. Nancy asserts herself at the end and may claim some form of a victory, but it is at the cost of collusion. Ultimately, it is a light-hearted attack, firmly in the realm of comedy, demanding high-energy and exuberant performance. By the standards of its time, *The Knack* stands out as a provocative feminist statement.

—Elizabeth Swain

THE KNIGHT OF THE BURNING PESTLE
by Francis Beaumont

First Publication: London, 1613.
First Production: Blackfriars Theatre (Children of the Queen's Revels), London, c.1607.

Editions

The Knight of the Burning Pestle, edited by J.W. Lever, London, 1962.
The Knight of the Burning Pestle, edited by Benjamin W. Griffith Jr., Woodbury, New York, 1963.
The Knight of the Burning Pestle, edited by John Doebler, Lincoln, Nebraska, 1967 (Regents Renaissance Drama Series).
The Knight of the Burning Pestle, edited by Andrew Gurr, 1968 (Fountainwell Drama Texts).
The Knight of the Burning Pestle, edited by Michael Hattaway, London, 1969 (New Mermaid Series).
The Knight of the Burning Pestle, edited by Sheldon P. Zitner, Manchester, 1984 (Revels Plays).

Criticism
(For general works on the author, see *Playwrights* volume)

Articles:

Edwin S. Lindsay, "The Original Music for Beaumont's Play *The Knight of the Burning Pestle*", in *Studies in Philology*, 26, 1929.
Baldwin Maxwell, "'Twenty Good Nights'—*The Knight of the Burning Pestle* and Middleton's *Family of Love*", in *Modern Language Notes*, 63, 1948.
W.J. Olive, "'Twenty Good Nights'—*The Knight of the Burning Pestle, The Family of Love*, and *Romeo and Juliet*", in *Studies in Philology*, 47, 1950.
John Doebler, "Beaumont's *Knight of the Burning Pestle* and the Prodigal Son Plays", in *Studies in English Literature 1500–1900*, 5, 1956.
Inge Leimberg, "Das Spiel mit der dramatischen Illusion in Beaumont's *The Knight of the Burning Pestle*", in *Anglia*, 81, 1963.
John Doebler, "The Tone of the Jasper and Luce Scenes in Beaumont's *The Knight of the Burning Pestle*", in *English Studies*, 56, 1975.
Ronald F. Miller, "Dramatic Form and Dramatic Imagination in Beaumont's *The Knight of the Burning Pestle*", in *English Literary Renaissance*, 8, 1978.
David A. Samuelson, "The Order in Beaumont's *Knight of the Burning Pestle*", in *English Literary Renaissance*, 9, 1979.
Lee Bliss, "'Plot Me No Plots': The Life of Drama and the Drama of Life in *The Knight of the Burning Pestle*", in *Modern Language Quarterly*, vol.45 no.1, 1984.
Barbara Knight Degyansky, "A Reconsideration: George and Nell of *The Knight of the Burning Pestle*", in *English Language Notes*, vol.23 no.3, 1986.

*   *   *

The first scene is an Induction where a Prologue about to announce a play entitled *The London Merchant*, is interrupted by a citizen climbing onto the stage. The device by which the auditors in an induction comment on the play is, thus, brilliantly extended in *The Knight of the Burning Pestle* so that the citizens, George and Nell, and their apprentice, Rafe, also intervene in the action of *The London Merchant* and so transform it. George and Nell are making a rare visit to one of the private theatres where the boy players were renowned for their satirical plays. George complains of the theatre's habitually derisive attitude to the city. He and Nell demand that Rafe be given a part, that of a chivalric grocer errant to be called, in honour of their trade, the Knight of the Burning Pestle. *The London Merchant* proceeds with numerous interruptions as the citizens demand that the plot should accommodate Rafe's adventures with two other apprentices he has initiated into the ways of knighthood. Absurd elements of citizen adventure drama are thus superimposed on a basically romantic comedy. In the play proper, Venturewell, the merchant, dismisses his apprentice Jasper for presumptuously declaring his love for his daughter Luce, whom he then offers to the stupid and pusillanimous Humphrey. There is also a subplot involving Jasper's family. Old Merrythought, Jasper's father, is central to the comic life of the whole, though of slight importance to the sequence of events. His cheerful improvidence, expressed in a stream of impenitent talk and frequent outbursts of song (beginning with "Nose, nose, jolly red nose"), drives his wife to take flight with her younger son Michael and all the treasure she can assemble. Confusion abounds as Mistress Merrythought meets Rafe and his satellites and, fearful of them, drops her casket of treasure which Jasper later picks up.

The Knight of the Burning Pestle: Aldwych Theatre, London, 1981 (Royal Shakespeare Company)

Meanwhile Luce has accepted Humphrey on condition that he carries her off. They are, however, intercepted by Jasper, who beats Humphrey and elopes with Luce. An attempt on the part of Rafe to recover Luce for Humphrey ends with Rafe's discomfiture at the hands of Jasper. Then, unaccountably, Jasper tries Luce's fidelity by threatening to kill her. Luce's love for him is equal even to this and she declares her readiness to die but at this point Venturewell, Humphrey and their men arrive and rescue her, leaving Jasper in despair at his folly and the loss of his love. But all is not lost. Jasper sends what purports to be a dying man's request that the coffin containing his body shall be conveyed to Luce in token of reconciliation with her. Her father consents, Luce receives the coffin and sings a lament, and the living Jasper then rises to greet her. Luce takes his place in the coffin and is carried away while Jasper, "his face mealed", confronts Venturewell as a ghost. The merchant, driven to fear and repentance, appeases him by dismissing Humphrey and seeks forgiveness from old Merrythought for the wrongs done to him and Jasper. A happy ending is assured when Merrythought achieves his one useful action. After he has made the merchant promise to forgive the dead Jasper it is possible for the living Jasper and Luce to appear and all are reconciled. During the last act, the demands of the citizens bring about the greatest digressions from *The London Merchant*. Impatient with the boys' play, George demands "something done in honour of the city" and Rafe, as his climactic achievement, appears decked out as May Lord presiding over the annual May Day march and revels. For Nell and George, unimpressed by the argument of comedy, the

only fitting end is Rafe's death and thus he appears "with a forked arrow through his head". He delivers a ghostly valediction, recapitulating his heroic deeds before his soul flies to Grocers' Hall.

The general lack of unity and coherence in the play is exacerbated by the continual, active participation of the citizens, who keep up a running commentary on Rafe's fortunes and exploits, take sides in the Jasper–Humphrey situation (though always the wrong side) and make remarks about the actors and musicians. Beaumont burlesques the literary genres favoured by Nell and George—romance and citizen adventure drama—and gently mocks their unsophisticated response to theatrical conventions. Like Don Quixote, Rafe has some extraordinary adventures. He has an heroic encounter with a barber (Barbaroso) and brings succour to the victims of his surgical activities. (They are in fact receiving treatment for venereal disease.) At Nell's request a scene is set up in which the King of Cracovia's daughter falls in love with Rafe. The citizens are heedless of the boy actors' argument that this will offend decorum: it will be taken "ill-favoredly to have a grocer's prentice to court a King's daughter". The episode is given a further satirical twist as the staunchly patriotic and Protestant Rafe rejects the Lady who "trusts in Antichrist and false traditions", in favour of his lady in "merry England", Susan, "a cobbler's maid in Milk Street". Such displays of loyalty predictably earn the approval of Nell and George, who interrupt to give money to Rafe so that he is not beholden to the King of Cracovia.

The great success of this most enjoyable of comedies lies in the virtuosity of the language, which abounds in occasions for literary play. Rafe's rhetoric is for the most part a fine pastiche of heroic romance, but it is liable to be adulterated with plebeian talk, as when he elaborates on the tips he proposes to bestow on members of the Princess's household and adds the gift of "threepence to buy you pins at Bumbo Fair" for the Lady herself. His May-Day speech is in traditional four-teeners. The foolish Master Humphrey speaks in pompous couplets whilst the lovers' verse effectively conveys youthful affections. In contrast to these literary and mock-heroic styles is the lively prose of the citizens' commentary.

An inventive production of *The Knight of the Burning Pestle* directed by Michael Bogdanov for the Royal Shakespeare Company was staged at the Aldwych Theatre in 1981. Nell and George became contemporary small business proprietors and Rafe appeared as a skinhead, unfurling the banner of St. George during his May-Day oration. Modern audiences relish "the privy mark of irony" in the play, which nonetheless, according to Beaumont's Dedicatory Epistle, went unappreci-ated by the Jacobean audience who "utterly rejected it".

—Janet Clare

KOKUSENYA KASSEN. See **THE BATTLES OF COXINGA.**

DIE KORALLE. See **THE GAS TRILOGY.**

KRAPP'S LAST TAPE
by Samuel Beckett

First Publication: In *Evergreen Review*, Summer, 1958; in book form, in *Krapp's Last Tape; Embers*, London, 1959.
First Production: Royal Court Theatre, London, 28 October 1958.

Criticism
(For general works on the author, see *Playwrights* volume)

Books:
James Knowlson (ed.), *Samuel Beckett: "Krapp's Last Tape"*, London, 1980.

Articles:
Arthur K. Oberg, "*Krapp's Last Tape* and the Proustian Vision", in *Modern Drama*, 9, 1966.
Bernard F. Dukore, "*Krapp's Last Tape* as Tragicomedy", in *Modern Drama*, 15, 1973.
James Knowlson, "*Krapp's Last Tape*: The Evolution of a Play, 1958–75", in *Journal of Beckett Studies*, 1, 1976.
Sue Ellen Campbell, "*Krapp's Last Tape* and Critical The-ory", in *Comparative Drama*, 12, 1978.
Sighle Kennedy, " 'The famine and feasting of the ages': Samuel Beckett's Occult Endnotes to *Krapp's Last Tape*", in *Centerpoint*, vol.3 no.1, 1978.

Francis Doherty, "*Krapp's Last Tape*: The Artistry of the Last", in *Irish University Review*, 12, 1982.
Ulrike Kaiser, "Samuel Beckett, *Krapp's Last Tape*: Das Drama als dramatische Szene", in *Fremdsprachliche Unter-richt*, 16, 1982.
Mary F. Catanzaro, "The Voice of Absent Love in *Krapp's Last Tape* and *Company*", in *Modern Drama*, 32, 1989.
Lois Gordon, "*Krapp's Last Tape*: A New Reading", in *Journal of Dramatic Theory and Criticism*, vol.5 no.2, 1990.

*   *   *

The play features the 69-year-old Krapp at his birthday ritual of tape-recording the meagre events of his past year. Krapp at the outset, in an elaborate mime, shuffles round his room and unlocks desk drawers which give access to bananas and to the stored tapes that are an accounting ledger—the "retrospects" of his lonely life. He selects a tape, a post-mortem of his 39-year-old-self, and searches it obsessively for a tender, painful reminiscence of a romantic adventure. To get to that account he has to listen to several passages which record a crisis and a turning point one stormy night when he believed he had at last found access to the dark areas of his life which he determined to make the central focus of his writing. Irritably he passes back and forth over this climactic moment, which he now dismisses with mockery and contempt, to get to a memory of pleasure with a girl in a gently rocking punt in a relationship he had decided to abandon. Just as the 39-year-old mocks a younger, more eager self on a tape he had listened to, so the 69-year-old mocks the 39-year-old's sense of self-importance in an urgent dedication to a life work that evidently came to nothing. He records the meagre details of his latest year but breaks off and returns obsessively for the third time to his "farewell to love" which records the moment of tender acceptance.

This small, flawless masterpiece seems on the surface to be one of the most searching soliloquies ever recorded in drama but, because of the interaction of Krapp and the tapes of his sequent selves, it comes over almost as a dialogue. It records, like Jaques' seven ages of man speech in *As You Like It*, the ever-changing identities and roles within an individual. We absorb the poverty and shabbiness of this solitary figure in a room that is both a shelter and a prison. He starts out simply as a clown with boots, white face, and a banana-peel routine, but gradually pieces together details of a long, lonely, barren, particular life. It is a life of meagre pleasures, the artist savouring the sound of words, checking obscure ones in a dictionary, resorting for occasional solace to his drink kept hidden away in a dark hole. This is a man who has resisted temptation all his life as we see in his elegiac account of his shedding of contact with work, love, family, religion, compa-nionship, and in his estrangement even from his past selves. His life has contracted to merely casual encounters with a dog and passing figures in a park, until he is virtually marooned with his strange former life. Yet in this sparse world there is an astonishing range of tones and styles of speech from dry narrative, to flashes of passionate conviction, to lyrical memo-ries, to harsh, sardonic criticism of his former selves, to a weary disdain for the empty tedium of his present life. It is a life subjected to an excessive and meaningless sense of order, in which he can calculate the proportion of it spent in pubs with the same accuracy that his filing system of tapes summarizes his life. He started recording at 24 years of age and has nine boxes with five spools in each so that his 39th year is recorded on spool five of box five, and his last tape, at the age of 69, is recorded on spool five of box nine.

The audience sees a vivid juxtaposition of light and dark echoed relentlessly in the language of the play. Krapp exists in

Krapp's Last Tape: Max Wall as Krapp, Greenwich Theatre, London, 1975

a cone of light from which he makes occasional forays into the darkness for drinks. There is a constant attempt to bring light and dark, sense and spirit, into relationship to hold at bay death lurking in the shadows. His bleak account of his mother's death brings that shadow closer. His memories are marked by an obsessional concern with eyes, especially those of women, who confirm his existence when they gaze upon him. Especially in the case of the girl in the punt, they offer the possibility of connectedness and shared companionship. He has evidently resisted the pain and torment of love, which he calls "all that old misery", but has exchanged it merely for a bitter, half-regretful loneliness. There are powerfully touching moments—the old man in quavering voice recalling a childhood hymn, a vivid memory of Christmas eve—moments in Beckett's minimalist art which shine all the more brightly in such bleak surroundings. The autobiographical detail records, perhaps, Beckett's sense, during the many years of his artistic obscurity, of how he could have ended up making as little impact as Krapp. The record of the meagre, derisory earnings of Krapp's royalties recall Beckett's circumstances in the 1930's. At the age of 39 Beckett, too, was "at the crest of the wave" about to embark on his five most productive years, mining that dark side of his life he had "always struggled to keep under". Even with the success and fame Beckett valued so little he may, like Krapp, have considered the price paid to be excessive. When Krapp listens to the tape one final time he allows it to continue further than before and the end of his 39th-year records that he has no regrets about sacrificing the "chance of happiness", the normal life he rejected, because of his conviction that he has finally reached a renewed dedication to his art, "the fire in me now", the vision of his life's central mission. The picture of Krapp amid the ashes of that long dead fire isolated in the encroaching darkness, bleakly registering his lonely failure, is one of the most heart-rending moments in modern drama.

—Anthony Brennan

KURKA WODNA.   See **THE WATER HEN.**

L

LADY AUDLEY'S SECRET
by Colin H. Hazlewood

First Publication: In *Lacy's Acting Edition of Plays, 57,* London, 1863.
First Production: Royal Victoria Theatre, London, 25 May 1863.

Editions

Lady Audley's Secret, in *Nineteenth Century Plays,* edited by George Rowell, London, 1953; second edition, 1972.

*   *   *

Lady Audley's Secret is a melodrama in two acts. The young Lady Audley, recently married to the elderly Sir Michael, arranges a birthday celebration for her doting husband, and it is revealed that only two years ago she was a poor governess in the family. Sir Michael's nephew Robert and his friend George Talboys arrive, and George laments his separation from his young wife Helen and her death when he was in India. Lady Audley exults in her present status and wealth and tells the audience that she is the supposedly deceased Helen; as she does so she is confronted by George. He refuses to spare her and is determined to bring her to justice as a bigamist. Lady Audley pushes him down the old well and exults once more, but her deed has been witnessed by the drunken reprobate Luke Marks. In Act II, six months later, Luke begins to blackmail her, and she is challenged by Robert, who suspects that she is George's wife and murderess. Lady Audley persuades Sir Michael that Robert has been paying her unwanted attentions, and he is banished from Audley Court. However, he resolves to stay overnight in the inn kept by Luke so that he can watch and expose Lady Audley. She sets the inn on fire to destroy both Robert and Luke, but the former escapes and the latter survives long enough to denounce her. George enters in good health, having been rescued from the well by Luke. Lady Audley goes mad and dies; a "tableau of sympathy" is formed as George kneels over her.

Lady Audley's Secret was adapted from the popular novel by Mary Elizabeth Braddon, published in 1862 in *The Sixpenny Magazine.* Three stage versions of the novel were performed in 1863, but Hazlewood's became the best known because of its printing in the Lacy series of acting plays. In the novel Lady Audley is a more sympathetic person, with more justification for her bigamy than in the play, which is not surprising as the book is one of those popular novels of the 1860's, including Mrs Henry Wood's *East Lynne* and Miss Braddon's *Aurora Floyd,* which dwelt sympathetically upon the problems of middle-class women placed in extreme social and emotional difficulties. Hazlewood, however, made Lady Audley a villai-

ness, and it is here that the chief significance of the play lies, for she was the first real representative of a line of villainesses in domestic melodrama that stretched into the next century. Lady Audley acts alone, but the villainess or adventuress is often the ally of the villain. Later in the century she clothes herself, in contrast to the heroine with her simple light-coloured dress and blonde or golden hair, in showy, rich hues, with much jewellery and black hair—although the stage Lady Audley wore a red wig. She might even smoke cigarettes and drink brandy. Since Lady Audley had a dark history, she was the progenitrix of the woman with a past in the problem plays of Arthur Pinero (Paula Tanqueray in *The Second Mrs Tanqueray),* Oscar Wilde (Mrs Cheveley in *An Ideal Husband*), Henry Arthur Jones (Mrs Dane in *Mrs Dane's Defence*), and other dramatists of the 1880's and 1890's. Her origins are firmly rooted in the mid-Victorian domestic melodrama, and Lady Audley is a memorable if unusually murderous prototype.

Also of interest in *Lady Audley's Secret* is the fact that its characters well illustrate melodrama's familiar stereotypes. Despite the presence of a principal female character who is a villainess rather than a heroine—a fact that somewhat distorts the stereotypical pattern—the stock company traditions of casting are generally observed, with a hero or juvenile lead (Talboys), a walking gentleman, the hero's friend and confidant (Robert Audley), a first old man—or good old man as he was known in melodrama (Sir Michael)—, and a character actor (Luke Marks). Lady Audley would have been played by the leading lady of the company, and Alicia, Sir Michael's daughter and a minor character, was possibly undertaken by the female juvenile lead, who normally played heroines.

—Michael R. Booth

———————

THE LADY FROM THE SEA (Fruen fra havet)
by Henrik Ibsen

First Publication: Copenhagen, 1888.
First Production: Christiana Theatre, Christiana, Norway, and Hoftheater, Weimar (in German), 12 February 1889.

Translations

The Lady From the Sea, translated by F.E. Archer, in *Ibsen's Prose Dramas 5,* edited by William Archer, London 1891; revised version in *The Collected Works, 9,* edited by William Archer, London, 1907.

The Lady From the Sea, translated by Mrs. E. Marx Aveling, in *A Doll's House; The Wild Duck; The Lady From the Sea*, London, 1910.

The Lady From the Sea, in *"A Doll's House" and Other Plays*, translated by Peter Watts, Harmondsworth, 1950.

The Lady From the Sea, translated by Michael Meyer, London, 1960; corrected version, in *Ibsen: Plays, 3*, London, 1980.

The Lady From the Sea, translated by James Walter McFarlane, in *The Oxford Ibsen, 7*, edited by James Walter McFarlane, London, 1966.

The Lady From the Sea, in *Ibsen: Four Major Plays, 2*, translated by Rolf Fjelde, New York, 1970.

Criticism

(For general works on the author, see *Playwrights* volume)

Articles:

A. Le Roy Andrews, "Ibsen's *Fruen fra havet* and Molbech's *Klintekongens Brud*", in *Scandinavian Studies and Notes*, 6, 1920–21.

P. Lionel Goitein, "*The Lady From the Sea*", in *Psychoanalytical Review*, 14, 1927.

Sidonie M. Gruenberg, "*The Lady From the Sea*", in *Psyche*, 9, 1929.

Harald Beyer, "Fjell og hav som symboler hos Ibsen", in *Ibsen-Årbok*, 1953.

Pavel Fraenkl, "*Fruen Fra Havet* og nordisk folketro", in *Ibsen-Årbok*, 1954.

R. Rapheal, "Illusion and the Self in *The Wild Duck, Rosmersholm*, and *The Lady From the Sea*", in *Scandinavian Studies*, 35, 1963.

F. Fergusson, "*The Lady From the Sea*", in *Ibsen-Årboken*, 8, 1965–66.

Lorraine A. Brown, "Swan and Mermaid: *Love's Comedy* and *The Lady from the Sea*", in *Scandinavian Studies*, 47, 1975.

David Rosengarten, "*The Lady from the Sea*: Ibsen's Submerged Allegory", in *Educational Theatre Journal*, 29, 1977.

Milly S. Barranger, "*The Lady from the Sea*: Ibsen in Transition", in *Modern Drama*, 21, 1978.

Rolf Fjelde, "*The Lady from the Sea*: Ibsen's Positive World-View in a Topographic Figure", in *Modern Drama*, 21, 1978.

Lou Andreas-Salomé, "Ellida, 'the Lady from the Sea'", in *Denver Quarterly*, 13, 1979.

Kay U. Des Roches, "A Problem of Translation: Structural Patterns in the Language of Ibsen's *The Lady from the Sea*", in *Modern Drama*, 30, 1987.

Elinor Fuchs, "Marriage, Metaphysics and *The Lady From the Sea* Problem", in *Modern Drama*, 33, 1990.

*   *   *

Ellida Wangel, the second wife of a small town doctor with two daughters from his first marriage, has difficulties in feeling at home in the quiet fjord surroundings and in a family where the other members share memories which tend to exclude her. She has grown up as the daughter of a lighthouse keeper near the open sea. The main reason for her unease, however, is a strong memory of a past relationship. When she was a young girl, she had been emotionally tied to a foreign sailor who got involved in a murder case and had to flee. After her marriage she gave birth to a child, but it died after a few months. Both the pregnancy and the loss of the child afflict her mental state, and she cannot share her husband's bed. She is fond of swimming, but misses the open sea. The action starts with the arrival of Arnholm, once the teacher of the girls, sent for by the doctor in an attempt to cheer up Ellida. The tension increases, however, as the foreign sailor suddenly calls on Ellida and asks her to leave with him. In her state of mental illness she feels his strong influence, and her will is paralysed. The doctor argues desperately against her leaving, but finally understands that she must be free to choose for herself; he can force her to stay, but he can never force her mind. With this freedom Ellida's condition is dramatically changed. Suddenly the foreign sailor's power over her is gone, and she chooses to stay with her husband and respond to his love. The concluding dialogue between husband and wife can be seen in terms of a case of psychotherapy, where the cure is found more or less intuitively, the patient indicating the conditions, and the doctor fulfilling them.

In this play Ibsen reveals more openly than before his great interest in the workings of the mind, particularly the female mind. He has borrowed elements from Scandinavian folklore about mermen and mermaids, colouring the action with the sense-expanding and ambiguous quality of myth. In the importance he seems to attribute to female sexual obsessions rooted in the past (as, for example, in *Rosmersholm* and the following play, *Hedda Gabler*) he is a forerunner of Sigmund Freud.

In terms of dramatic technique *The Lady From the Sea* may seem to introduce a new stage concept in Ibsen's series of contemporary prose dramas. The first five plays, starting with *A Doll's House*, are all staged indoors, in the stifled atmosphere of upper-middle-class living-rooms, garden-rooms and the like. In this play, however, the action takes place in the open air except the fourth act which is set in Dr. Wangel's garden-room, but which contains an open glass door leading out to the veranda. The positive development of the action regarding both the mental health of the main character and the prospects for the conjugal relationship of the Wangels also might indicate an important deviation from the rather tragic kind of action we find in plays like *Ghosts* and *Rosmersholm*. And yet, on closer examination, there is no fundamental change in the way Ibsen has composed this play.

This becomes clear when we consider how the central stage metaphor emphasizing the thematic quality of extreme protection as against exposure to the harshness of life is provided this time. While this thematic function in *Ghosts* is suggested by means of the conservatory at the back part of Mrs. Alving's garden-room, and in *The Wild Duck* by means of the ingeniously constructed loft behind the sliding doors of the Ekdals' studio, in *The Lady From the Sea* it is brought out by the stagnant carp pond in the remote corner of the garden where the action takes place in Acts III and V. Corresponding stage metaphors can be spotted in all of Ibsen's contemporary dramas, but the three cases mentioned are the most conspicuous ones—the greenhouse, the menagerie, and the aquarium.

It is a common structural device linked to the underlying theme of freedom which is fundamental to Ibsen's dramatic art. In *The Lady From the Sea* this theme is quite explicit, and expressed symbolically as well, by means of a system of water metaphors on three levels. There is the carp pond, suggesting a maximum of protection and confinement, the fjord—with its brackish water only partly satisfactory, yet relatively safe if one can acclimatize—and the ocean, the dangerously attractive sphere of action of the foreign sailor, and the sphere with which Ellida's imagination is strangely obsessed until the freedom she desires is granted her by her husband. Then she settles for the medium sphere, a bourgeois existence as the wife of a fjord-town doctor. Her urge for absolute freedom, expressed by her longing for the ocean, can be seen as a symptom of her mental condition. It has been a dream and cannot be realized in practical terms.

A desire to get away from the limited, small-town existence is perceptible also in some of the minor characters. A feeling of discontent is voiced by Bolette, the elder of the two Wangel sisters, and she agrees to become Mr. Arnholm's wife since he will take her away from the small world and into a bigger one. The younger sister, Hilde, as well as the consumptive young man, Lyngstrand, seem to be content with the limitation of the carp pond, which they find "mysterious" and "thrilling", although Lyngstrand does express an ambition to go abroad and establish himself as an artist.

There is also the opposite movement, represented by Ballested, the painter, from the outer world to "our nice little town". He is a jack of all trades who has mastered the art of acclimatization. This character, well adapted without being particularly gifted, seems to represent the voice of the local community itself, being present with his comments both at the outset and at the conclusion of the play.

—Asbjørn Aarseth

LADY JULIE. See **MISS JULIE.**

THE LADY OF THE CAMELIAS (La Dame aux camélias) by Alexandre Dumas *fils*

First Publication: Paris, 1852.
First Production: Théâtre du Vaudeville, Paris, 2 February 1852.

Editions
La Dame aux camélias [with translation], edited and translated by Frederick A. Schwab, New York, 1880.

Translations
The Lady of the Camelias, translated by Edith Reynolds and Nigel Playfair, London, 1930.
Camille: The Lady of the Camelias, translated by Henriette Metcalf, London and New York, 1931.

Criticism
(For general works on the author, see *Playwrights* volume)

Articles:
Tadeusz Kowzan, "Le Mythe de *La Dame aux camélias*: Du Drame au mélodrame", in *Revue des sciences humaines*, 162, 1976.

*   *   *

Marguerite Gautier, a fashionable Paris courtesan, accepts as a lover the young Armand Duval; she is moved by his romantic idealism and, tired of the febrile artificiality of the life she has been leading, leaves with him to start a simple life in the country. Their lovers' idyll is abruptly ended when Armand's father arrives to plead with Marguerite to give up her liaison with his son for the sake of the latter's future career, and of his daughter's happiness. Persuaded by the fatality she sees as attached to her past life, and by her love for Armand, Marguerite agrees to make the sacrifice, and departs for Paris, leaving a letter telling Armand she is voluntarily returning to her former existence. In Act IV, Armand insults Marguerite in public at a reception, throwing in her face his winnings at the card-table as a settlement of his debts to her. In Act V, Marguerite is dying of consumption. Armand, having travelled the world in an attempt to forget her, and who has now received a letter from his father telling him the truth about Marguerite's sacrifice, arrives to find her on her deathbed. The lovers are reconciled, and she dies in his arms.

The Lady of the Camelias, which first saw the light of day as a novel (published in 1848, when Dumas was aged 24), was based on an episode in the author's own life: he had had a brief liaison with Marie Duplessis who had died of consumption in 1847 at the age of 23. Both novel and play were immensely popular, though the latter had to overcome objections from the censor because of the allegedly scabrous subject: the courtesan with a past who sacrifices herself for the man she loves may have been acceptable when presented in a historical context (by Victor Hugo, for instance, in *Marion de Lorme*, 1831, or *Angelo*, 1835), but was much more provocative when treated realistically in a contemporary setting. For all the realism of its portrayal of the "demi-monde", however, this play by Dumas *fils* appeals to us—and moves us—by its championing of an exceptional love which suffers at the hands of society's prejudices and constraints. Society's attitudes are expressed convincingly by Duval *père*; and the conflict between head (Duval) and heart (Marguerite) in Act III is powerfully presented in a well-balanced scene which is the pivot of the play's structure. The defence of an individual's right to passionate fulfilment may be expressed in what, taken out of context, seem to be familiar, Romantic clichés ("A woman's virginity belongs not to her first lover, but to the first man she herself loves"; or the curtain-line: "Rest in peace, Marguerite! Much will be forgiven you, for you have loved greatly!"); but there can be no doubting the emotional charge of the scenes in which Marguerite appears from Act III onwards, leading to the celebrated death-bed finale. Even before Verdi and his librettist, Piave, gave musical form to this emotion in *La traviata* (*The Fallen Woman*)—the opera was premièred at Venice in 1853—Dumas had already achieved in the play one of the most memorable artistic expressions of a theme absolutely central to the sensibility of the Romantic age: the renunciation of individual happiness in the face of society's implacable decree, the inevitable defeat of idealism by prosaic reality. *The Lady of the Camelias* has been called "morally ambiguous"; and indeed, while a modern editor can describe it as "in essence, profoundly anti-Romantic" because "social morality emerges triumphant", it was severely castigated by certain moralistic contemporaries as an attack on Christian values.

The question of the play's moral message is, however, almost irrelevant: what is of primary importance is the sense of tragic fatality, here successfully transferred from the traditional mythological or historical setting of serious drama to a milieu spectators could recognise as their own. This is a play in which the details of contemporary (or for modern spectators, period) setting have a considerable importance, as those who have seen the imaginative skill with which Franco Zeffirelli created the atmosphere of Second Empire Paris in the 1982 film of Verdi's opera will be able to judge. The five acts of Dumas's play establish an effective contrast between the glamour and opulence we associate with the fashionable, social scene of this period (Acts I and IV) and the precarious and vulnerable existence of the courtesan when left to her own devices (Act II), the pastoral retreat of the lovers in Act III,

The Lady of the Camelias: Sarah Bernhardt as Marguerite

and the simple domestic interior of the deathbed scene. The life of the kept woman is further illustrated by the juxtaposition of Marguerite's circumstances with the older Prudence, hardened into a mercenary, cold-blooded cynic, on the one hand, and on the other with the attractive role of the ingenuous young Nichette, who achieves her ambition by marrying her protector (and who speaks the play's celebrated curtain-line).

In the Preface, published in 1867, Dumas's attitudes have completely changed: the Romantic has given way to the moralist, and he is now less concerned to idealise the courtesan than to carry out a sociological investigation into the conditions which produce her kind. From this point onwards, a series of plays show him obsessed with the subject of sexual morality in an increasingly didactic manner. By the side of such "thesis plays", *The Lady of the Camelias* remains a fresh and poignant portrayal of human weakness. As such, it has appealed to many of the outstanding French actresses of the 19th and 20th centuries; and the role of Marguerite, created by Eugénie Doche at the Vaudeville Theatre, has been filled by, among others, Rose Chéri, Aimée Desclée, Aimée Tessandier, Sarah Bernhardt, Cécile Sorel, Blanche Dufrêne (who killed herself because she felt unable to do justice to the role), Ida Rubinstein, Ludmilla Pitoeff, Marie Bell, and Edwige Feuillère. In the cinema, Norma Talmadge, Yvonne Printemps and—most memorably, perhaps—Greta Garbo have played the part. The title of Garbo's film (*Camille*) derives from the hopelessly banal title given to the first American version of the play: Matilda Heron's *Camille; or, The Fate of a Coquette* (1856).

—William D. Howarth

LADY WINDERMERE'S FAN
by Oscar Wilde

First Publication: London, 1893.
First Production: St. James's Theatre, London, 20 February 1892.

Editions

Lady Windermere's Fan, edited by Vincent F. Hopper and Gerald B. Lahey, Great Neck, New York, 1960.
Lady Windermere's Fan, edited by Ian Small, London and New York, 1980 (New Mermaid Series).
Lady Windermere's Fan, London, 1985.

Criticism

(For general works on the author, see *Playwrights* volume)

Articles:

Morse Peckham, "What Did Lady Windermere Learn?", in *College English*, vol. 18 no. 1, 1956.
E.H. Mikhail, "Oscar Wilde and his First Comedy", in *Modern Drama*, 10, 1968.
David Davidson, "The Importance of Being Ernst: Lubitsch and *Lady Windermere's Fan*", in *Literature / Film Quarterly*, 11, 1983.

* * *

Lady Windermere's Fan was the play which brought Wilde his first success in the fashionable London theatre. Its opening stage direction—*Time: the Present*—implied a strategy that went beyond the choice of a modern subject. The play was to involve radical revaluation and reversal of contemporary mores. For the *Athenaeum* reviewer, it had just that effect: Wilde was, he said, "a revolutionary and an iconoclast". The ambiguous original title, *A Good Woman*, echoes Hardy's description of his "fallen" Tess as a "Pure Woman", and there are connections with Ibsen whose plays Wilde admired: he went twice to see Elizabeth Robins's as Hedda Gabler in 1891. Lady Windermere's situation has much in common with Nora's in Ibsen's *A Doll's House* (produced in London in 1889). A young wife learns to think for herself, refusing the childish role her husband has imposed on her. Wilde drew on the French boulevard drama (and English imitations such as Haddon Chambers' *The Idler*) which provided standard fare for Victorian audiences—but only to undermine those bulwarks of patriarchal morality at every turn.

Lady Windermere's Fan, produced at the St. James's Theatre in 1892, initiated a fruitful collaboration with the actor-manager, George Alexander. He and his company were skilled in an elegant, "between the lines" acting style, which, said Wilde, was "capable of producing a wonderful dramatic effect by aid of a monosyllable and two cigarettes". These skills were useful to a comedy where all the trivia are infused with irony. The scene in Act III when Lord Darlington entertains his male friends is not just a feast of comedy and repartee. The complacent witticisms about "good women" and women with a past draw a sting from the fact, unknown to the gentlemen, that Lady Windermere and Mrs. Erlynne are overhearing it all. The flippant, arrogant male conversation makes clear how ruthlessly the "double standard" of sexual morality is taken for granted, and how easily Lady Windermere could slip from the category of "good" women, simply by being discovered in Lord Darlington's rooms. Only Lord Augustus, the butt of the others' wit, seems open-minded on this question. When he maintains that "Mrs. Erlynne has a future before her", he is put down with smart repartee from Dumby—"Mrs. Erlynne has a past before her"—and replies with a disarming simplicity which probably expresses what most of the male characters secretly feel: "I prefer women with a past. They're always so demmed amusing to talk to".

The first-night audience was astonished both by the wit and the realism of the play. Scenically, it was found uncannily accurate, with its morning-room, "so like a room and so unlike a stage imitation of one" as one reviewer noted. The stage was a mirror, part flattering (no dialogue was ever so continuously witty in the real world), part distorting—or corrective, according to viewpoint. Wilde amused himself, in his first-night speech from the stage, by congratulating the audience on allowing themselves to be intellectually stretched: "your appreciation has been most intelligent".

This play with the audience was in tune with his idea of life as a play in which every individual was obliged to be a "comedian". He stylises the life of the Windermeres, the Berwicks, and the rest (as in the speeded-up "polite" rituals in the ballroom scene) to show how they are all playing, power games for the most part. Everything on the stage has at once naturalistic probability and symbolic resonance. The tableau at the close of Act III—when Mrs. Erlynne, a solitary, vulnerable figure in her *décolletée* evening dress, steps out of hiding to confront a solid phalanx of males in the safe conformity of their black tie and tails—is a silent statement about the unfair balance of power between the sexes. Wilde's acute aesthetic sensibility informs the entire scenic concept, down to details like the fan, at first a threat to the woman "of—well, more than doubtful character" and finally presented in gratitude to the same woman when she comes to be seen in a very different light.

Wilde gets vast amusement from some of the game-playing. The Duchess of Berwick, the first of his comically monstrous matriarchs, amusingly sends Lady Agatha to look at photographs and sunsets when sex is being discussed and flaunts her ignorance of outlandish places like Australia to the rich Australian she intends for her son-in-law: "Agatha has found it on the map. What a curious shape it is. Just like a large packing case". With the brutal honesty of power ("Women rule society", Wilde said), she tells him she knows his "value": "We wish there were more like you. It would make life so much easier".

Integrated with the social satire is the "psychological idea" which Wilde never lost sight of. The germ of the play was his vision of a woman discovering the maternal passion, sacrificing herself for her child, and then deciding that motherhood made her suffer too much. His portrayal of these powerful feelings in Mrs. Erlynne took him into a different dramatic convention. The emotional rhetoric of melodrama comes to the fore when she discovers her daughter Lady Windermere's letter to Lord Darlington ("The daughter must not be like the mother—that would be terrible") and pleads with her to return to her husband, pulling out all the melodrama stops: "even if he had a thousand loves you must stay with your child". Because Mrs. Erlynne is also a witty character—the master wit of the play— there is no unbelievable divide between styles. She is uninhibited and distressed in her warnings, drawn from bitter experience, about the "pit" a woman falls into once she transgresses the sexual code. But she retains intellectual control, never letting slip the secret of their relationship, and in the final scenes modulating with great finesse from tenderness for the daughter she will not undeceive, to sharp, self-protective irony against Lord Windermere whose only concern is to keep his wife in childlike ignorance of her mother's "shame".

Wilde had a modern sensitivity to the fate of society's victims. Lady Windermere's ignorance almost betrays her into the real evil of eloping with a man she does not love. Mrs. Erlynne's greatest triumph is to move her from her narrow, judgemental morality to the more humane and sensible view of the final act: "I don't think now that people can be divided into the good and the bad as if they were two separate races or creations". Wilde invited his audience to think likewise, offering them a compromise over Mrs. Erlynne which is his final stroke of realism. She is a survivor, not a tragic heroine: marriage with Lord Augustus and a discreet retreat to the Continent is what should happen, not the suicide or dreadful decline which the boulevard drama commonly ordained for its female offenders. In the midst of the intellectual glitter of ideas and repartee, at the heart of Wilde's comedy, there is psychological truth.

—Katharine Worth

THE LADY'S NOT FOR BURNING
by Christopher Fry

First Publication: London and New York, 1949; revised version, 1950; further revised version, 1958.
First Production: Arts Theatre, London, 10 March 1948.

Criticism
(For general works on the author, see *Playwrights* volume)

Articles:
John Woodbury, "The Witch and the Nun: A Study of *The Lady's Not For Burning*", in *Manitoba Arts Review*, 10, 1956.
Jacob H. Adler, "Shakespeare and Christopher Fry", in *Educational Theatre Journal*, 11, 1959.
Lewis W. Barnes, "Christopher Fry: The Chestertonian Concept of Comedy", in *Xavier University Studies*, 2, 1963.
Gunnar Urang, "The Climate is the Comedy: A Study of Christopher Fry's *The Lady's Not For Burning*", in *Christian Scholar*, 46, 1963.
S. Wiersma, "Spring and Apocalypse, Law and Prophets: A Reading of Christopher Fry's *The Lady's Not For Burning*", in *Modern Drama*, 13, 1971.
Robert Gittings, "The Smell of Sulphur: *The Lady's Not For Burning* Now", in *Encounter*, vol. 50 no.1, 1978.
Mary A.K. Davis, "The Narrow Escape in *The Lady's Not for Burning*", in *Modern Drama*, 27, 1984.

*   *   *

Thomas Mendip, a discharged but nobly born soldier, and Jennet Jourdemayne, a suspected witch, are unwelcome guests at the house of Hebble Tyson, mayor of the small market-town of Cool Clary. Mendip claims he has killed Matthew Skipps, the local rag-and-bone man, and demands to be executed. Jennet, daughter of an alchemist, is accused by the medieval mob of turning Skipps into a dog. Instead of celebrating his nephew Humphrey's marriage to sweet young Alizon Eliot, Tyson and Justice Tappercoom find themselves caught up in establishing the guilt of Mendip and Jennet. Alliances shift as Alizon falls in love with Richard, Tyson's young clerk, Humphrey and his brother Nicholas with Jennet, and Jennet and Mendip with each other. At the last minute Skipps is delivered, alive, to Tyson's house by Alizon and Richard who then elope, to be pursued by Tyson. Mendip goes free and leaves Cool Clary with Jennet. As a witch her property is forfeit to the town, but Mendip will take her off to his father's castle.

"What a wonderful thing is metaphor" exclaims the tiresomely self-dramatizing Mendip in the opening scene, and it is indeed through his metaphorical usuage that Fry distinguishes himself from the other verse dramatists (Eliot and Duncan) in the period of post-war austerity. But too often the comparisons only half-succeed. Mendip declares his father has a castle "as draughty as a tree". Castles can be draughty but neither in shape nor solidity do they resemble trees. Jennet says she has to hurry because she hears "the pickaxe voice of a cock beginning/To break up the night". The sharpness of sound may be accurate but why should dawn be like a labourer attacking a pavement? The images here are arbitrary. This imprecision particularly detracts from the force of Mendip's long speech to Richard ("I've been cast adrift on a sea of melancholy") at the beginning of Act III. He's trying to explain his self-disgust as the emotional uncertainty of a man caught between animist and scientific views of the world. This clash is, in fact, the plot, in which the superstitious Cool Clary community wants to destroy the witch/scientist Jennet. Mendip's metaphors logically progress from raft and sea to shore and pastureland. But the edge of the concrete image is blurred by abstraction—"raft of melancholy", "the little oyster-shell of this month of April", "the night's a boundless pastureland of peace". This language is not a parody of bad Edwardian verse any more than unflappable, middle-class Margaret and

The Lady's Not For Burning: Globe Theatre, London, 1949

her two wilful, puppyish sons are pastiche Forster. The turn of the century echoes throughout the play because Fry has interpolated fictional types, elaborated then (there is even a Canon Chasuble type Chaplain), into the Middle Ages.

With Jennet, however, Fry has created a contemporary figure, more current even in the 1990's than in the 1940's. She continues her father's scientific studies, lives alone, faces death, and falls in love with an accomplished mixture of rationality and passion. She is a beautiful alchemist and therefore in every sense a bewitcher. She doesn't deny her difference, but she sees men as different too. When Humphrey offers to free her if she will sleep with him she debates his offer with a freedom from hysteria unusual in the period. As she and Thomas, thrown together in Tyson's house, reveal themselves to each other, her self-knowledge and character-perception ring much truer than Mendip's rhetoric. She needs no metaphors to describe her life:

> I live alone, preferring loneliness
> To the companionable suffocation of an aunt.
> I still amuse myself with simple experiments
> In my father's laboratory. Also I speak
> French to my poodle. Then you must know
> I have a peacock which on Sundays
> Dines with me indoors.. . .

This speech echoes the tone and social range of Alexander Pope. She pricks Mendip's bombast but since love is the motive she is not satirical. Beneath his egotism she detects a fear of companionship. "You are making yourself", she remarks, "a breeding ground for love and must take the consequences"—as she herself must, which she recognises in a speech ("Sluts are only human. . .") towards the end of Act II which could have been written by a present-day feminist. Mendip is "decay and a platitude / Of flesh". He is even, "Evil, Hell, the Father of Lies". Nevertheless he can "drag upon a woman's heart" so that her rationality, which she expresses to the end, recognises its limits: "What is to be done? Something compels us into / The terrible fallacy that man is desirable / And there's no escaping into truth". Fry's Jennet may represent woman as Other, but he has her speak positively and frequently throughout the play. In her, Fry anticipated a new type of young woman—the sensuous intellectual.

—Tony Dunn

LEAR
by Edward Bond

First Publication: London and New York, 1972.
First Production: Royal Court Theatre, London, 29 September 1971.

Criticism
(For general works on the author, see *Playwrights* volume)

Books:
Horst Oppel and Sandra Christenson, *Edward Bond's "Lear" and Shakespeare's "King Lear"*, Wiesbaden, 1974.

Articles:
Gregory Dark, "Edward Bond's *Lear* at the Royal Court", in *Theatre Quarterly*, 5, 1972.

Leslie Smith, "Edward Bond's *Lear*", in *Comparative Drama*, 13, 1979.
Perry Nodelman, "Beyond Politics in Bond's *Lear*", in *Modern Drama*, 23, 1980.
Alan Sinfield, "*King Lear* Versus *Lear* at Stratford", in *Critical Quarterly*, vol.24 no.4, 1982.
Peter Fitzpatrick, "Bond's *Lear*: A Study in Conventions", in *Page to Stage: Theatre as Translation*, edited by Ortrun Zuber-Skerritt, Amsterdam, 1984.
Brean S. Hammond, "The Intertext of an Adaptation: Bond's *Lear* and *King Lear*", in *Études Anglaises*, 40, 1987.
Hubert Zapf, "Two Concepts of Society in Drama: Bertolt Brecht's *The Good Woman of Setzuan* and Edward Bond's *Lear*", in *Modern Drama*, 31, 1988.

* * *

Edward Bond's *Lear* takes as its starting-point Shakespeare's *King Lear*, but it does so with the intention of reworking Shakespeare's mythology rather than simply reproducing it in a more contemporary format. Indeed, so firm was the playwright in his intent that for a long time he considered dispensing with the figure of the King altogether, and concentrating instead on the three sisters—a possible restructuring perhaps suggested in part by his earlier translation of Chekhov's *Three Sisters*.

Bond's Lear is a despot who has enslaved his workforce to ensure that they construct a wall that he believes will guarantee his and their freedom by keeping out the enemies of the state. The ironies are apparent from the outset, and are savagely underlined in the opening scene when Lear, on a royal visit to the construction site, orders a summary execution of a worker to shake up the others into greater industry. His two daughters, Bodice and Fontenelle, rebel against him, accepting cynically arranged marriages for their political convenience with the Dukes of North and Cornwall, and wage war against their father. The mad Lear is forced to flee and finds sanctuary in the house of a gravedigger's boy, a false, pastoral idyll which is destroyed by the arrival of soldiers who kill the boy and rape his wife, whose name we only now learn is Cordelia.

It is Cordelia, with the Carpenter who kills the soldiers, who will subsequently lead the opposition to Bodice and Fontenelle. The second act moves the action into the chaos of civil war, the cruelties of Bodice and Fontenelle's forces being matched by those of a Cordelia whom the playwright has compared directly to Stalin—the inevitable tyrant thrown up by the violence of the revolution. The effects of this violence are seen on the society at large and specifically, and terrifyingly, in the scene in which Lear's eyes are removed by modern scientific methods (unlike those used to remove Gloucester's in *King Lear*).

By the beginning of the third and last act Lear has developed considerably from the earlier state of madness with which he concludes *King Lear*. He finally meets up for the last time with Cordelia and, as he resolves directly on action, any action, that is morally correct, the ghost of the gravedigger's boy (who has been haunting him) gradually fades away and finally disappears. Now, in the final scene of the play the audience sees the wall itself for the first time as, initially watched by a representative of the younger generation, Lear starts to pull down the wall with his bare hands before being shot and killed.

Bond's reputation was already high, but it was with *Lear* that he moved properly into the large-scale, epic model (which acknowledges the influence of Brecht without in any way being directly imitative) that has continued to dominate the best of his mature work. Bond wastes little time on fleshing out the narrative either chronologically or psychologically and, even

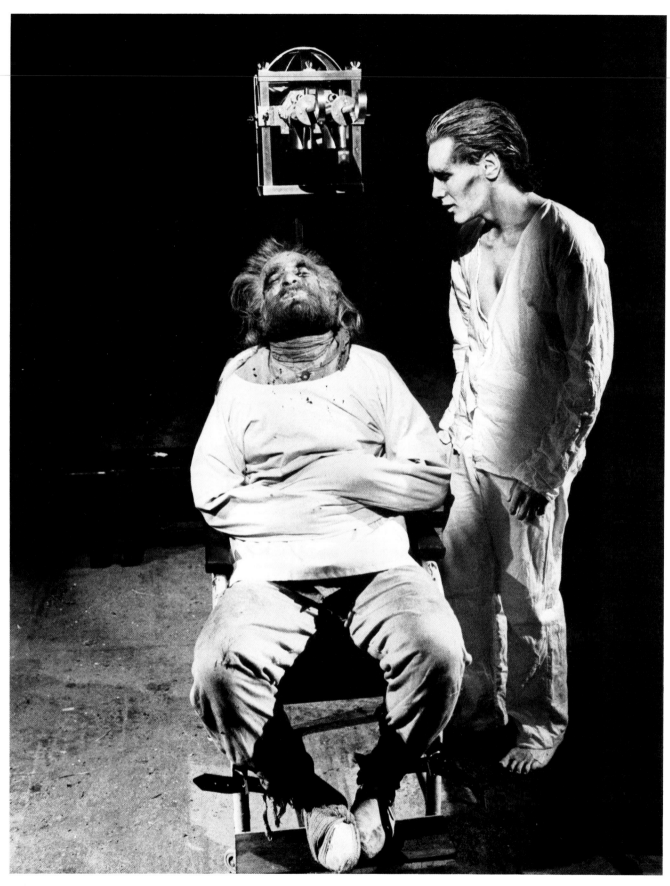

Lear: The Other Place, Stratford-Upon-Avon, 1982 (Royal Shakespeare Company)

as the action moves between the public and private worlds of action, so the impossibility of escape from the political significance of that larger, public world is stressed. In Bond's play the audience has no more space to hide from the consequences that follow on from the play's first scene than does Lear himself. It is a dense play, but not a difficult one for anyone who does not insist on there being a single, easily decodable meaning. Fed up with being, as he saw it, wilfully misunderstood in his aims as a political writer, this play saw the first of Bond's introductory prefaces printed with the published text; a preface that begins with the now famous words, "I write about violence as naturally as Jane Austen writes about manners".

This powerful play demands much of its audience both emotionally and intellectually, not least understanding that Bond's Lear has a political as well as a domestic education in his rigorous journey from political despotism, through personal madness, to a later rational comprehension of the nature of the world that he originally ruled and has latterly learned how to survive in. What Bond wants from his audiences at the end of the play is, however, something very far removed from the kind of cathartic reaction claimed by many critics on behalf of Shakespeare's *King Lear*. Tragedy in that sense is merely personal, and the political world that Bond conjures with here is always more than that. The play ends with the wall still intact but with the terms of reference that created it questioned— whether the construction be thought of specifically as the Berlin wall (as generally it was in Eastern Europe), or more loosely as a symbolic wall that divides and causes strife by isolating and promising security. *Lear* is not an optimistic play; the vision of society that it offers is that of a nightmare, the main components of which seem only too familiar to a modern audience. But it is the first of Bond's plays in which the playwright begins the long and difficult move away from a concentration on the depiction of the malaise and towards an analysis of why it is so, an analysis which must precede any attempt to change the world as it now is.

—John Bull

THE LEARNED LADIES (Les Femmes savantes)
by Molière

First Publication: Paris, 1682.
First Production: Théâtre du Palais-Royal, Paris, 11 March 1672.

Editions

Les Femmes savantes, edited by Charles A. Eggert, New York, 1911
Les Femmes savantes, edited by G. Masson, Oxford, 1939.
Les Femmes savantes, edited by R.P.L. Ledésert, London, 1947.
Les Femmes savantes, edited by Jean Cordier, London, 1959.
Les Femmes savantes, edited by Fernand Angué, Paris, 1961.
Les Femmes savantes, edited by G. Chappon, Oxford, 1968.
Les Femmes savantes, edited by Jean Cazalbou and Denise Sévely, Paris, 1971.
Les Femmes savantes, edited by Hugh Gaston Hall, Oxford, 1974.
Les Femmes savantes, edited by Michel Lagier, Paris, 1986.

Translations

The Learned Ladies, in *Molière* (2 vols.), translated by Curtis Hidden Page, New York and London, 1908.
The Blue Stockings, translated Vera Beringer and Mesley Down, London and New York, 1927.
The Learned Ladies, translated by Renée Waldinger, Great Neck, New York, 1957.
The Learned Ladies, translated by Joachim Neugroschel, New York, 1966.
The Learned Women, in *"The Misanthrope" and Other Plays*, translated by Donald Frame, New York, 1968.
The Learned Ladies, translated by Henri van Laun, New York, 1969

Criticism

(For general works on the author, see *Playwrights* volume)

Books:

J. Arnavon, *La Mise en scène des "Femmes savantes"*, Paris, 1912.
Gustave Reynier, *Les Femmes savantes*, Paris, 1937.
G. Timmermans, *"Les Femmes savantes": Analyse littéraire*, Hasselt, Belgium, 1947.
Georges Tournaire, *Causeries littéraires: "Les Femmes savantes"*, Paris, 1955.
Sylvie Chevalley, *"Les Femmes savantes": Monographie*, Paris, 1962 (Collections de la Comédie-Francaise).

Articles:

Arthur H. Upham, "English *Femmes savantes* at the End of the Seventeenth Century", in *Journal of English and Germanic Philology*, 12, 1913.
G.N. Henning, "The Denouement of *Les Femmes savantes*", in *French Review*, 13, 1939.
Jacques Morel, "La Structure de Clitandre", in *Revue d'histoire du théâtre*, 2, 1960.
Emmett J. Gossen Jr., "*Les Femmes savantes*: Métaphore et mouvement dramatique", in *French Review*, 45, 1971–72.
Judith D. Suther, "The Tricentennial of Molière's *Femmes savantes*", in *French Review*, 45 (special issue), 1972.
Olof Bratto, "Molière: *Les Femmes savantes*: Étude d'anthroponymie littéraire", in *Revue internationale d'onomastique*, 25, 1973.
Jean Molino, "Les Noeuds de la matière: L'Unité des *Femmes savantes*", in *Dix-septième Siècle*, 113, 1976.
Gérard Defaux, "Un Point de critique et d'histoire littéraire: Molière, *Les Femmes savantes*, et le florentin", in *Papers on French Seventeenth Century Literature*, 8, 1981.
James F. Gaines, "Ménage versus Salon in *Les Femmes savantes*", in *Esprit créateur*, vol.21 no.3, 1981.
Elisabeth Lapeyre, "*Les Femmes savantes*: Une Lecture aliénée", in *French Forum*, vol.6 no.2, 1981.
Betty J. Davis, "From *Précieuses* to Peasants: Names in Molière's *Les Femmes savantes*", in *Literary Onomastic Studies*, 9, 1982.
James F. Gaines, "Commentary on Roger Herzel's 'Problems in the Original Casting of *Les Femmes savantes*'", in *Actes de New Orleans*, edited by Francis L. Laurence, Paris, 1982.
Roger W. Herzel, "Problems in the Original Casting of *Les Femmes savantes*", in *Actes de New Orleans*, edited by Francis L. Laurence, Paris, 1982.
William D. Howarth, "'Une Pièce comique tout à fait achevée': Aesthetic Coherence in *Les Femmes savantes*", in *Form and Meaning: Aesthetic Coherence in Seventeenth-Century French Drama: Studies Presented to Harry Barnwell*, Amersham, 1982.

The Learned Ladies: Engraved frontispiece, 1682

David Shaw, "*Les Femmes savantes* and Feminism", in *Journal of European Studies*, vol.14 no.1, 1984.

Michael S. Koppisch, "'Bonne soupe' or 'Beau langage': Difference and Sameness in *Les Femmes savantes*", in *To Honor René Girard*, Saratoga, California, 1986.

Larry W. Riggs, "'La Raison de la plus folle est toujours la meilleure': Synthetic Language and the Hallucinations of Reason in *Les Femmes savantes*", in *Symposium*, vol.41 no.3, 1987.

*   *   *

This satirical comedy targets the intellectual aspirations of women. Chrysalde, a wealthy Parisian bourgeois, has allowed his domineering wife, Philaminte, to rule the household; but she is so obsessed with academic matters that she has lost touch with reality. Her eccentric behavior begins to have a serious impact on the household: she decides that her youngest daughter, Henriette, must marry a pretentious poet, Trissotin. Henriette, who loves Clitandre, is in despair, and the other characters are no help: her father Chrysalde is too weak to stand up to Philaminte; Trissotin is determined to have her, though he never admits that he wants her for her money. Henriette's older sister Armande is as much of an academic as her mother; she refuses to help Henriette, her main reason being that she is violently jealous because Henriette's suitor Clitandre had previously been in love with her. We witness the pretentiousness of the pedant and the "femmes savantes" in a comic scene in which atrocious poems are read and analyzed. Then salvation comes in the shape of Henriette's uncle, who tricks Trissotin into revealing that he is just after wealth by pretending that Philaminte has lost all her money. Trissotin renounces Henriette, and Philaminte graciously consents to Henriette's marriage with Clitandre. Only Armande is left dissatisfied.

The play is a sustained and consistent examination of pedantry and its disastrous impact on normal life. Each of the characters illustrates a relevant aspect. Philaminte is the full-blown bluestocking, interested in everything academic from astronomy to grammar. She also uses her obsession to get her own way and to dominate others. She is surrounded by less forceful "femmes savantes". Bélise, her sister-in-law, is an old maid, a literary romantic who lives in a dream world in which all men worship at her feet. If they seem to be avoiding her, she claims that it is through excessive respect and love. Armande, the elder daughter, strikes a more serious note. She has taken seriously the precepts of the *précieuses*, a women's movement which dominated the literary, social, and even personal lives of many society women in Molière's day. She refuses to marry on the grounds that physical love is gross and degrading. This is why her suitor, Clitandre, has turned from her in despair and found love in her younger sister.

The young couple, Henriette and Clitandre, head the group of characters who contrast with the pedants. Their views on love and marriage are presented by Molière as sensible: a woman should be a good wife, and it is not acceptable for her to reject sex and household management while concentrating on cultivating her mind. Henriette and Clitandre stand for normality, and the excesses of both the pedants and their opponents can be measured against the common sense of this youthful pair. The other non-learned characters are more extreme in their rejection of bookishness, thereby setting up a series of strong comic oppositions. The loquacious maid-servant, Martine, plumbs the depths of ignorance. When the "femmes savantes" accuse her of offending against "grammar", she replies "What's all this talk of offending Grandma and Grandpa?". Chrysalde, the so-called head of the household, is also a philistine. He rejects all learning derived from books, and claims that every book in the house should be burnt—except a copy of Plutarch, which is heavy enough for him to press his neckcloths under it. In the original production, Molière played this part; as is the case with all the roles he wrote for himself, the character is a complex one. Chrysalde is ridiculous in his attempts to stand up to his bully of a wife (played by a man in Molière's production). But his lucid awareness of his own weakness makes him touching. He fluctuates between whipping up his resolve and weakly yielding. He loves his daughter Henriette, but loves a quiet life still more. Another complex character is Armande, who is pretentious and spiteful, but whose raw feelings of jealousy and misery when she is left without a husband at the end add a dimension of psychological verisimilitude to the comedy.

The play is written in rhyming couplets. The group scenes are characterized by the symmetry in the repartee, and by a stylized formality which contrasts pleasingly with the comic effect of the dialogue, which can be outrageous. This is particularly true of the literary criticism scenes (Act III), which in many ways form the nucleus of the play since they show exactly what being a "*femme savante*" means. In these scenes, Molière uses a number of permutations of characters and effects. Most notable is a fulsome session of mutual admiration in which the poet Trissotin is congratulated for his literary talents while the women are praised for their critical acumen. An added satirical dimension is that Trissotin's ridiculous poems, so admired by the scholarly women, were the genuine work of a contemporary of Molière's, the Abbé Cotin. This scene, with its overabundance of hyperbolic flattery, is sharply contrasted with the next scene, a vitriolic verbal battle between two mediocre professional writers: Trissotin and his colleague Vadius ("He actually knows Greek! Heavens, Greek! He knows Greek, sister!", exclaims an ecstatic Philaminte to Bélise). In this scene the very poems previously admired are ripped to shreds.

Written in elegant verse and skilfully choreographed, this is the last of Molière's high comedies. Its subject-matter may seem out of tune in a feminist age: Molière's audience is encouraged to view learning with suspicion, particularly in women, and the play could be seen as a complacent celebration of intellectual mediocrity. But the material is presented with memorable wit and polish, and the play remains one of Molière's greatest comedies.

—Maya Slater

LEAVING HOME
by David French

First Publication: Toronto, 1972.
First Production: Tarragon Theatre, Toronto, 16 May 1972.

Criticism
(For general works on the author, see *Playwrights* volume)

Articles:
Ed Jewinsky, "Jacob Mercer's Lust for Victimization", in *Canadian Drama*, Spring 1976.
Chris Johnson, "Is That Us? Ray Lawler's *Summer of the Seventeenth Doll* and David French's *Leaving Home*", in *Canadian Drama*, Spring 1980.

*   *   *

The events of *Leaving Home*, set in the 1950's, tell of the breakup of a Newfoundland family that has settled in Toronto. Central to the play is the conflict between the father, Jacob, a carpenter, and his son, Ben, which causes Ben to leave home. The action of the play takes place on the eve of the shotgun wedding of the younger son, Billy, to his pregnant girlfriend, Kathy. A subsidiary theme concerns Jacob and his wife Mary who left their home in Newfoundland in 1945.

Critics of *Leaving Home* have compared it with such domestic dramas as Arthur Miller's *Death of a Salesman*, pointing especially to parallels in the relationship between Biff and Willy Loman and that between Ben and Jacob Mercer. But French's art is essentially different from Miller's; there is very little humour in *Death of a Salesman* whereas comedy is the very essence of French's play, making more striking the tragic moments in *Leaving Home*—the Oedipal struggle of *Leaving Home* is waged within situations of near farce. Jacob is an Orangeman, profoundly distrustful of Catholics, whose son is being forced to marry his pregnant fiancée, the daughter of Jacob's own former Catholic Newfoundland girlfriend, Min-

nie. The wedding represents a belated revenge acted out in Toronto. Kathy wants to get married and leave home to escape her bawdy, middle-aged mother who has brought Harold, the Toronto undertaker who embalmed her late husband, to the wedding rehearsal. This "silent stud", as French has characterized him in an interview, does not speak a single word in the play—his silence comically sets Minnie's character in higher relief and underlines the richness and volubility of speech of Newfoundlanders Jacob, Mary, and Minnie. Additionally, the contrast between Harold's professional role and the priapic role assigned him by Minnie provides a rich vein of humour. It is against this background of sexuality, story telling, dance, music, and jokes that French skilfully presents the conflict between father and son.

The conflict between Jacob and Ben rises, at one level, from a clash between older heroic values (of Newfoundland) and the mores of an urbanized society (of Toronto). Throughout *Leaving Home* Jacob challenges Ben with standards that define men—and women—back home in Newfoundland. He challenges him to drink "screech", a potent rum unique to Newfoundland; he, unlike Ben, was out "fishing on the Labrador" when he was ten; when Ben was born he went out in a blizzard for the doctor and in his absence Mary delivered the child, cut and tied the cord, herself. These are the legendary standards that define Jacob and it is Ben's refusal to join in that definition by accepting the values of "back home" that is at the heart of their struggle. The dramatic climax of the play is reached when Jacob thrashes Ben with his belt as the son prepares to leave this Newfoundland household.

While *Leaving Home* is a naturalistic play, French enriches it with symbolic and archetypal overtones. The play is framed by rites of passage—graduation, death, marriage; familial tensions unleash elemental emotions of jealousy, anger, rage, and love. Situations which at first seem simple are invested with moral complexity, as when Billy learns that Kathy has had a miscarriage and that he need not marry her. The play is lifted, finally, beyond the level of the purely naturalistic by the heightened poetic speech which French gives his Newfoundlanders. Like that cultivated by J. M. Synge in his Irish folk drama, French's speech is colloquial, racy, idiomatic and, very often, poetic. "In those days", Mary says to Jacob, "I couldn't see no further ahead than you charging down Country Road on your old white horse to whisk me away to the mainland". Such speech seems natural and totally acceptable in French's work.

Leaving Home is the first of four plays about the Mercer family. In *Of the Fields, Lately*, which was premiered in 1973, French explores more deeply the reason underlying the conflict between father and son—the scale is tipped more in favour of Jacob. The play has a moving elegiac tone as the death of Mary's sister foreshadows Jacob's. In *Salt-Water Moon*, which was first performed in 1984, French dramatizes Jacob's courtship of Mary in 1926 and reveals some of the economic and political reasons that explain Jacob's later intractability and independence of character. *1949*, which was premiered in 1988, treats the Mercer family and a number of other characters seen or mentioned in the previous Mercer plays against the historical backdrop of Newfoundland entering Canada; and more importantly, it focusses on the reason why Mary rejected Jerome McKenzie, her fiancé, to marry Jacob Mercer.

—Eugene Benson

LEBEN DES GALILEI.   See LIFE OF GALILEO.

LA LEÇON.   See THE LESSON.

A LEGHORN HAT.   See AN ITALIAN STRAW HAT.

LEI-YU.   See THUNDERSTORM.

LEIYU.   See THUNDERSTORM.

LES.   See THE FOREST.

THE LESSON (La Leçon)
by Eugène Ionesco

First Publication: Paris, 1954.
First Production: Théâtre de Poche, Paris, 20 February 1951.

Translations
The Lesson, in *Eugène Ionesco: Four Plays*, translated by
   David Allen, New York, 1958.
The Lesson, in *Eugène Ionesco: Plays, 1*, translated by Donald
   Watson, London, 1958.

Criticism
(For general works on the author, see *Playwrights* volume)

Books:
Erik M. Donnachie, *"La Leçon": An Analysis of Comic
   Disintegration*, Sydney, 1978.

Articles:
Olga and Isaak Revzine, "Expérimentation sémiotique chez
   Eugène Ionesco: *La Cantatrice chauve* et *La Leçon*", in
   Semiotica, 4, 1971.
Dietmar Fricke, "*La Leçon; Les Messes Noires de la Bonne
   Auberge*: Neue Lehrstücke für Eugène Ionescos Pub-
   likum?", in *Neusprachliche Mitteilungen aus Wissenschaft
   und Praxis*, 26, 1973.
Alexander Fischler, "The Absurd Professor in the Theater of
   the Absurd", in *Modern Drama*, 21, 1978.

*   *   *

The Lesson, Ionesco's second play, owes much of its impact
to its brevity and the simplicity of its structure. The play
comprises one single, vividly memorable image. Its one act
takes the form of a bizarre tutorial given by an elderly
professor to a young female pupil. The latter has come to the
professor's house intending to pursue research for a plethora
of doctorates. The professor therefore sets out to ascertain
what she knows. The lesson starts with arithmetic, where it
soon becomes clear that she is unable to subtract but can
perform fantastically complicated additions from memory
more accurately than her tutor. It moves on to philology,
where she fails to distinguish Spanish from neo-Spanish, which
is hardly surprising as the professor himself appears more than
a little confused about the distinction. Once the professor has
satisfied himself of his own immeasurable superiority over his
pupil, the lesson ends with his symbolic rape-killing of the girl.
This he achieves by the frenzied chanting of the word "knife",
in which he forces his pupil to join, by brandishing an
imaginary blade in her face. The action thus far may be
summarized in the words placed by Ionesco on the lips of its
third character, the professor's maid: "Arithmetic leads to
philology and philology leads to crime". The play ends with the
arrival of another pupil and potential victim, the 41st of the
day.

Plot and character, in the conventional sense, are not part of
Ionesco's theatre. But it is in the changing relationship
between the characters of *The Lesson*—their interpersonal
dynamics—that the play's principal interest lies. In the initial
conversational exchange, the pupil is voluble, self-confident,
and socially at ease. By the end of the lesson, she is confused,
in pain, incapable of coherent speech. By contrast her tutor,
who at the outset is timid and hesitant, gradually takes control
of the lesson, dominating the young woman by the sheer flow
of his discourse, and treating her as though she were a mere
child. The maid too is an interesting figure, not because she
develops in any significant way, but for her very ambiguity. On
the one hand she appears to embody a kind of peasant,
common sense, repeatedly—if ineffectually—pleading with
the professor not to proceed. But she is also a complaisant
accessary to the crime, which she signally fails to prevent. She
evinces no solicitude for the pupil, whom she never once
warns. Once the pupil has been killed, the maid helps her
employer dispose of the body without fuss, tells him how to
avoid awkward questions, and cheerfully admits his next
victim. Despite an attempt on his part to murder her, she
displays an almost maternal indulgence towards the professor
that blinds her to the fact that he is quite simply a monster.

The Lesson is not merely a telling—albeit grotesque—satire
of the pedagogical relationship. Despite its brevity, it actually
encompasses a number of Ionesco's recurrent concerns. The
first of these is language, a constant preoccupation in his early
works. Here Ionesco focusses precisely on the way in which
men pervert apparently rational discourse in the service of
their irrational impulses. There have been indications from the
beginning that the professor is not quite as he presents himself.
Outwardly correct, despite his obvious social ineptness, we are
told that from time to time a prurient gleam lights up his eye.
The lust that he feels for his young pupil is accompanied by an
aggression that is presumably rooted in his awareness of his
inadequacy. Language is the weapon that enables him to vent
these two impulses on his victim. The maid, undeceived by his
linguistic casuistry, also resists his physical assault on her with
some ease.

Ionesco's second major preoccupation in *The Lesson* is the
alienation of the individual in mass society. In conversation
with Claude Bonnefoy, the playwright has lamented the extent
to which, in modern (especially in totalitarian) societies,
people identify themselves completely with their social functions. He sees this as dehumanizing. Tellingly, the three
characters of *The Lesson* are identified only by their social
functions and the professor in particular is able to operate only

in the narrow social context provided by his profession.

Lastly Ionesco indicates fleetingly, but unequivocally, his contempt for political ideology, whether of left or right. If discourse is the chief instrument of man's hysteria and fanaticism, political doctrine provides his principal alibi. Once the deed is done the professor is encouraged by the maid to don an armband. This excuses his act as a political one and confers immunity on him. Ionesco's linking of intellectual dishonesty and political totalitarianism reflects his profound conviction that the one begets and sustains the other.

—Tim Lewis

THE LIBATION BEARERS.   See THE ORESTEIA.

THE LIFE AND DEATH OF TOM THUMB THE GREAT.   See TOM THUMB.

LIFE IS A DREAM (La vida es sueño)
by Pedro Calderón de la Barca

First Publication: Madrid, 1636.
First Production: Madrid, 1635.

Editions
La vida es sueño, edited by Milton A. Buchanan, Toronto, 1909.
La vida es sueño, edited by H.J. Chaytor, London, 1923.
La vida es sueño / Life is a Dream [with translation], edited and translated by William F. Stirling, Havana, 1942.
La vida es sueño, edited by Martin de Riquer, Barcelona, 1954.
La vida es sueño, edited by Albert E. Sloman, Manchester, 1961.
La vida es sueño, edited by Carmelo Samonà, Rome, 1966.
La vida es sueño, edited by Everett W. Hesse, Salamanca, 1978.
La vida es sueño, edited by Enrique Rull, Madrid, 1980.
La vida es sueño: Drama y Auto Sacramental, edited by José Maria Valverde, Barcelona, 1981.
La vida es sueño, edited by José María García Martín, Madrid, 1983.
La vida es sueño, edited by Ciriaco Morón, Madrid, 1983.

Translations
Life is a Dream, translated by Frank Birch and J.B. Trend, Cambridge, 1925.
Life is a Dream, translated by H. Carter, Sanderstead, 1928.
Life is a Dream, translated by William E. Colford, New York, 1958.
Life is a Dream, translated by Roy Campbell, in *The Classic Theatre, 3*, edited by Eric Bentley, New York, 1959.
Life is a Dream, translated by Edward and Elizabeth Huberman, in *Spanish Drama*, edited by Angel Flores, New York, 1962.
Life is a Dream, translated by Kathleen Raine and R.M. Nadal, London, 1968.

Life is a Dream, in *Calderón: Three Plays*, translated by Gwynne Edwards, London, 1990.

Criticism
(For general works on the author, see *Playwrights* volume)

Books:
Angel L. Cilveti, *El significado de "La vida es sueño"*, Valencia 1971.

Articles:
M.A. Buchanan, "Segismundo's Soliloquy on Liberty in Calderón's *La vida es sueño*", in *Publications of the Modern Language Association* [PMLA], 23, 1908.
M.A. Buchanan, "Calderón's *Life is a Dream*", in *Publications of the Modern Language Association* [PMLA], 47, 1933.
R. Schevill, "'Virtudes Vencan Senales' and *La vida es sueño*", in *Hispanic Review*, 1, 1933.
A.L. Risco, "El Segismundo historico de *La vida es sueño*", in *University of Buenos Aires*, 2, 1949.
P.N. Dunn, "The Horoscope Motif in *La vida es sueño*", in *Atlante*, 1, 1953.
Everett W. Hesse, "La concepción calderoniana del princípe perfecto en *La vida es sueño*", in *Clavileño*, 4, 1953.
A.E. Sloman, "The Structure of Calderón's *La vida es sueño*", in *Modern Language Review*, 48, 1953.
L.G. Crocker, "*Hamlet, Don Quixote*, and *La vida es sueño*: The Quest for Values", in *Publications of the Modern Language Association* [PMLA], 69, 1954.
William W. Whitby, "Rosaura's Role in the Structure of *La vida es sueño*", in *Hispanic Review*, 28, 1960.
Joaquin Casalduero, "Sentido y forma de *La vida es sueño*", in *Cuadernos del congreso por la libertad de la cultura*, 51, 1961.
Edwin Honig, "Reading What's in *La vida es sueño*", in *Theatre Annual*, 20, 1963.
C. Bandera, "El itinerio de Segismundo en *La vida es sueño*", in *Hispanic Review*, 35, 1967.
N.S. Maurin, "Monster, the Sepulchre and the Dark: Related Patterns of Imagery in *La vida es sueño*", in *Hispanic Review*, 35, 1967.
H.B. Hall, "Segismundo and the Rebel Soldier", in *Bulletin of Hispanic Studies*, 45, 1968.
Carroll B. Johnson, "Segismundo en Palacio: Nota sobre *La vida es sueño*, Jornada II", in *Duquesne Hispanic Review*, 8, 1969.
Ulrich Knoke, "Calderón's *La vida es sueño* und seine Kritiker", in *Romanistisches Jahrbuch*, 20, 1969.
Eugenio Suárez-Galbán, "Astolfo: La moral y su ilustración dramática en *La vida es sueño*", in *Hispanófila*, 38, 1970.
Jorge Urrutia, "Una escena de *La vida es sueño*: su organización dramática", in *Cuadernos hispanoamericanos*, 247, 1970.
C. Bandera, "Significación de Clarion en *La vida es sueño*", in *Atlantida*, 9, 1971.
J.J. Cape, "Platonic Metamorphoses of Calderón's *La vida es sueño*", in *Modern Language Notes*, 86, 1971.
Everett W. Hesse, "*La vida es sueño* and the Paradox of Violence", in *Revista de estudios hispánicos*, 5, 1971.
Alan K.G. Paterson, "The Traffic of the Stage in Calderón's *La vida es sueño*", in *Renaissance Drama*, 4, 1971.
Cesáreo Bandera, "El 'confuso abismo' de *La vida es sueño*", in *Modern Language Notes*, 87, 1972.
Francisco E. Porrata, "El sueño en *La vida es sueño*", in *Abside*, 36, 1972.
Daniel L. Heiple, "The Tradition Behind the Punishment of

Life is a Dream: The Other Place, Stratford-Upon-Avon, 1983 (Royal Shakespeare Company)

the Rebel Soldier in *La vida es sueño*", in *Bulletin of Hispanic Studies*, 50, 1973.

C.A. Merrick, "Clotaldo's Role in *La vida es sueño*", in *Bulletin of Hispanic Studies*, 50, 1973.

Angel L. Cilveti, "La fonción de la metáfora en *La vida es sueño*", in *Nueva revista de filologia hispánica* (Mexico), 22, 1973.

Gisèle Feal and Carlos Feal-Deibe, "Calderón's *Life is a Dream*: From Psychology to Myth", in *University of Hartford Studies in Literature*, 6, 1974.

Eleanor J. Martin, "Calderón's *La gran Cenobia*: Source Play for *La vida es sueño*?", in *Bulletin of the Comediantes*, 26, 1974.

Harlan G. Sturm, "From Plato's Cave to Segismundo's Prison: The Four Levels of Reality and Experience", in *Modern Language Notes*, 89, 1974.

Henry Ziomek, "Historic Implications and Dramatic Influences in Calderón's *Life is a Dream*", in *Polish Review* (New York), vol. 20 no. 1, 1975.

Ellen G. Lavroff, "Who is Rosaura? Another Look at *La vida es sueño*", in *Revue des langues vivantes* (Brussels), 42, 1976.

A. Valbuena-Briones, "La paradoja en *La vida es sueño*", in *Thesaurus*, 31, 1976.

Thomas Austin O'Connor, "*La vida es sueño*: A View From Metatheater", in *Kentucky Romance Quarterly*, 25, 1978.

Charles V. Aubrun, "*La vida es sueño*: Le Discours dramatique, sa fonction première, ses fonctions dérivées", in *Iberomania*, 14, 1981.

Clark Colahan and Alfred Rodriguez, "Hércules y Segismundo: tema y carácter senequistas de *La vida es sueño*", in *Journal of Hispanic Philology*, vol.5 no.3, 1981.

Dian Fox, "Kingship and Community in *La vida es sueño*", in *Bulletin of Hispanic Studies*, vol.58 no.3, 1981.

Ciriaco Morón Arroyo, "*La vida es sueño* y *El alcalde de Zalamea*: Para una sociologia del teatro calderoniano", in *Iberomania*, 14, 1981.

Jorge E. Sørensen, "*La vida es sueño* and Plato's Theory of Knowledge", in *Iberomania*, 14, 1981.

Angel Berenguer, "Paraluna sociologia de *La vida es sueño*", in *Nuevo hispanismo*, 1, 1982.

Raphael Lapesa, "Consideraciones sobre *La vida es sueño*", in *Boletin de la Real Academia Española*, 62, 1982.

J.B. Hall, "The Problem of Pride and the Interpretation of the Evidence in *La vida es sueño*", in *Modern Language Review*, vol.77 no.2, 1982.

Stephen H. Lipmann, "Segismundo's Fear at the End of *La vida es sueño*", in *Modern Language Notes*, vol.97 no.2, 1982.

Frederick A. de Armas, "The Serpent Star: Dream and Horoscope in Calderón's *La vida es sueño*", in *Forum for Modern Language Studies* (St. Andrews), vol.19 no.3, 1983.

Juan Ramón Resina, "Honor y razón en *La vida es sueño*", in *Cuadernos de investigación filológica*, vol. 9 nos. 1–2, 1983.

Beatriz Mariscal de Rhett, "*La vida es sueño*: Soluciones calderonianas a la crisis política e ideológica del siglio XVII", in *Bulletin of the Comediantes*, vol.37 no.2, 1985.

C. Christopher Soafas Jr., "Thinking in *La vida es sueño*", in *Publications of the Modern Language Association* [*PMLA*], vol.100 no.3, 1985.

Frederick A. De Armas, "The Apocalyptic Vision of *La vida es sueño*: Calderón and Edward Fitzgerald", in *Comparative Literature Studies*, vol.23 no.2, 1986.

Everett W. Hesse, "The Role of Deception in *La vida es sueño*", in *Renaissance and Golden Age Essays in Honor of D.W. McPheeters*, edited by Bruno M. Damiani, Potomac, Maryland, 1986.

Robert V. Piluso, "The Catalytic Role of the Dream in *La vida es sueño*", in *Renaissance and Golden Age Essays in Honor of D.W. McPheeters*, edited by Bruno M. Damiani, Potomac, Maryland, 1986.

Ruth El Saffar, "Way Stations in the Errancy of the Word: A Study of Calderón's *La vida es sueño*", in *Renaissance Drama*, 17, 1986.

Frederick A. De Armas, "Rosaura Subdued: Victorian Readings of Calderón's *La vida es sueño*", in *South Central Review*, vol.4 no.1, 1987.

J.M. Ruano de la Haza, "The Staging of Calderón's *La vida es sueño* and *La dama duende*", in *Bulletin of Hispanic Studies*, vol.64 no.1, 1987.

Donald McGrady, "Who Rules at the End of *La vida es sueño*?", in *Forum For Modern Language Studies* (St. Andrews), vol.24 no.1, 1988.

Jesús A. Ara, "Estructuras iterativas en *La vida es sueño*", in *Criticón*, 45, 1989.

Dian Fox, "In Defense of Segismundo", in *Bulletin of the Comediantes*, vol.41 no.1, 1989.

Alice Homstad, "Segismundo: The Perfect Machiavellian Prince", in *Bulletin of the Comediantes*, vol.41 no.1, 1989.

*   *   *

Life is a Dream (La vida es sueño) is the story of Segismundo, a Polish prince, imprisoned from birth by his father, King Basilio, as a result of omens and prophecies predicting disaster for the kingdom. Act I reveals that, despite Segismundo's violent behaviour, Basilio has decided, twenty years later, to give his son an opportunity to rule, and in order to do so he has him transported secretly to the palace under the influence of a powerful drug. Act II sees Segismundo awakening in the palace and, informed of his new power, proceeding to take revenge on those who have wronged him in the past or displease him in the present: his jailer, Clotaldo; his father, Basilio; a prince, Astolfo; a young woman, Rosaura; and an upstart servant. Convinced that the omens were true, Basilio imprisons his son again and instructs Clotaldo to inform him that the palace experience was merely a dream. When in Act III Segismundo is released by soldiers supporting his claims to the throne, he is unable to decide if he is dreaming or not, but feels he should behave more prudently. Confronting those people he previously saw in his "dream", he resists the impulse of the moment and, having defeated his father in battle, forgives him. The prophesy that he would see his father at his feet is fulfilled, but in a way which rejects vengeance in favour of forgiveness.

The sources of Calderón's play are many, The story of the awakened sleeper occurs in the *Arabian Nights*, as well as in the work of Spanish writers from the 14th century. The theme of the individual seeking to avoid, but merely confirming, what is foretold was also common, as in the collection of stories, *Barlaam and Josaphat*. And the idea of life as fleeting and dream-like was central to both oriental and Christian religions. But the direct source of *Life is a Dream* was Calderón's earlier play written in collaboration with Antonio Coello, *Yerros de naturaleza y aciertos de la fortuna*, in which, despite differences of detail, the basic ideas are the same: a prince who recovers his throne; a young man who, apparently unfit to rule, learns to do so, suggesting in the process that men can shape their destiny.

Life is a Dream is, however, a much more complex play. The idea that men can shape their destiny is linked now both to the process of self-discovery and to the realisation that the objects of human ambition—power, wealth and pleasure—are insubstantial in comparison with true spiritual values. Moreover, these are themes which are embodied in all the characters and incidents of the play. The affairs of Segismundo and Basilio are paralleled by the efforts of Rosaura, abandoned by Prince Astolfo, to recover her honour, which she achieves through Segismundo's recovery of his throne and his appreciation of the worth and rights of others. Basilio's initial irresponsibility towards his son has its counterpart in the self-interested behaviour of many other characters, all of whom grow wiser through disillusionment, achieving knowledge of themselves and of the world. In terms of the complex interlocking of incident and character in a meaningful and illuminating way, *Life is a Dream* is one of Calderón's most accomplished plays.

Like Don Juan, Segismundo is one of the truly memorable characters of 17th-century Spanish theatre: a man-beast initially at the mercy of his volatile emotions, subsequently bewildered by his inexplicable changes of fortune, and finally groping his way towards a greater understanding of himself and his fellow-men. But the play has other interesting characters too: Basilio, tortured by his son's predicament; Rosaura, passionate in her pursuit of honour, confused by her loss of it; Clotaldo, her father, confounded by the arrival of a child he has never seen; Astolfo, as powerful as he is insincere; and Clarion, Rosaura's servant, the self-interested seeker responsible for his own death. The gallery of brilliantly drawn characters answers the charge that Calderón was much more interested in plot than characterisation.

The characters have their counterpart in highly evocative settings, suggested, of course, by the dialogue itself. The opening scenes take place as darkness descends and they conjure up a gloomy tower, a flickering light, and a chained man dressed in skins. In total contrast the subsequent palace-scenes shimmer with silks, brocades, jewels, music and beautiful women. The effect is truly of *chiaroscuro*, splendidly dramatic, but while the changing landscapes of the play are effective backdrops, they are also reflections of the characters' emotional and mental conflicts, evoking the movements from darkness to light that in one way or another affect all the characters of the play.

Calderón's language, here as elsewhere, is highly stylised, even "operatic". Segismundo's opening soliloquy, for example, is not unlike an aria, as are other long speeches in the play. They reveal Calderón's liking for repetition, symmetry, and pattern in the structure of his verse, as well as an overall sense of musicality. The effect of such stylisation is not, however, to mute or straightjacket the emotional charge of the lines but, by channeling it into a disciplined form—lines of eight syllables in a variety of stanza form—to intensify it further. In emotional terms the language has enormous range, from the violence of Segismundo's outbursts to his lyrical praise of female beauty.

Life is a Dream, written in a strongly Catholic climate, is not a religious play, though it does, in a more general way, expound the theme of the triumph of free will, at the heart of Calderón's particular brand of Catholicism. Rather it is a play about man at any time and in any place, at the mercy of deficiencies within and without himself, and struggling to overcome them. It is this more general relevance which accounts for its lasting appeal and allows for varying interpretations that may embrace existentialism on the one hand or the efforts of postwar Poland to resist Soviet authoritarianism on the other.

—Gwynne Edwards

LIFE OF GALILEO (Leben des Galilei)
by Bertolt Brecht (with various collaborators)

First Publication: As *Galileo*, in *From the Modern Repertoire, Series 2*, edited by Eric Bentley, Bloomington, Indiana, 1953 ("American" version, translated with Charles Laughton); revised, German version, in *Versuche, 14*, Frankfurt, 1955; further revised version, in *Stücke, 2*, Frankfurt 1957.

First Production: Schauspielhaus, Zurich, 9 September 1943 (early version); Coronet Theatre, 30 July 1947 ("American" version); Cologne, April 1955 (revised, German version).

Translations

Galileo ["American" version], translated by Bertolt Brecht and Charles Laughton, in *From the Modern Repertoire, Series 2*, edited by Eric Bentley, Bloomington, Indiana, 1953.

Galileo, translated by Desmond Vesey, in *Plays, 1*, London, 1960.

Life of Galileo, translated by John Willett, London, 1980.

Criticism

(For general works on the author, see *Playwrights* volume)

Books:

Aufbau einer Rolle: Galilei, Berlin, 1956.

Werner Hecht, *Materialen zu Brechts "Leben des Galilei"*, Frankfurt, 1963; revised edition, 1981.

Werner Zimmerman, *Brechts "Leben des Galilei": Interpretation und didaktische Analyse*, Düsseldorf, 1965.

Gerhard Szcesny, *Das Leben des Galilei und der Fall Bertolt Brecht*, Frankfurt, 1966.

Karl Brinckmann, *Erläuterungen zu Bert Brechts "Leben des Galilei"*, Hollfeld, c. 1967.

Margaret Ives, *Bertolt Brecht's "Galileo": Introduction and Commentary*, New York, 1967.

Peter Beyersdorf, *Bertolt Brechts "Leben des Galilei": Zur Problematik des Stoffes*, Hollfeld, 1977.

Approches de "La Vie de Galilée" de Bertolt Brecht, Marseille, 1982.

Gerhard Szcesny, *Bertolt Brechts "Leben des Galilei": Dichtung und Wirklichkeit*, Bonn, 1986.

Roderich Grimm, *Verfremdung in Bertolt Brechts "Leben des Galilei"*, Frankfurt, 1987.

Articles:

Fritz Erpenbeck, "Verurteilung oder Mitleid? Einige Bemerkungen zur Berliner Aufführung von *Leben des Galilei*", in *Theater der Zeit*, vol.12 no.3, 1957.

Käthe Rülicke, "*Leben des Galilei*: Bemerkungen zur Schlußszene", in *Sinn und Form*, 9, 1957.

Ernst Schumacher, "Geschichte und Drama: Geschichtsdramatik, Geschichtsauffassung, Geschichtswissenschaft", in *Sinn und Form*, 11, 1959.

Ernst Schumacher, "Brechts *Galilei*: Form und Einfühlung", in *Sinn und Form*, 12, 1960.

Hans Hafen, "Bertolt Brechts *Leben des Galilei*", in *Der Deutschenunterricht*, 13, 1961.

Ernst Schumacher, "Verfremdung durch Historisierung: Bertolt Brechts *Leben des Galilei*", in *Kommunität*, 5, 1961.

Wolfgang Keisch, "Bert Brechts *Leben des Galilei*: Versuch einer Interpretation", in *Die pädagogische Provinz*, 17, 1963.

Peter Demetz, "Galileo in East Berlin: Notes on the Drama in the DDR", in *German Quarterly*, 37, 1964.

Ernst Schumacher, "Furchtbare und fruchtbare Tendenz: Brechts *Leben des Galilei* und die heutige Naturwissenschaft", in *Marxistische Blätter*, 3, 1965.

Ernst Schumacher, "*Leben des Galilei* und Leben und Werk Brechts", in *Weimarer Beiträge*, 11, 1965.

Charles R. Lyons, "*The Life of Galileo*: The Focus of Ambiguity in the Villain Hero", in *Germanic Review*, 41, 1966.

Ernst Schumacher, "The Dialectics of *Galileo*", in *Tulane Drama Review*, vol.12 no.2, 1968.

M.A. Cohen, "History and Moral in Brecht's *The Life of Galileo*", in *Contemporary Literature*, 11, 1970.

John Sidney Groseclose, "Scene Twelve of Bertolt Brecht's *Galilei*: A Structural Study", in *Monatshefte für deutschen Unterricht*, 62, 1970.

Heinrich Laidig, "Die Tragödie des Wissenschaftlers: Hinweise auf Bertolt Brechts Schauspiel *Leben des Galilei*", in *Wirklichkeit und Wahrheit*, 3, 1970.

Rainer Nägele, "Zur Struktur von Brechts *Leben des Galilei*", in *Deutschunterricht*, vol.23 no.1, 1971.

Edward M. Berckman, "Brecht's *Galileo* and the Openness of History", in *Modernist Studies*, 2, 1974.

Ann C. Fehn, "Vision and Blindness in Brecht's *Leben des Galilei*", in *Germanic Review*, 53, 1978.

George Buehler, "Brecht's *Life of Galileo*: From Hero to Anti-Hero for the Sake of Progress", in *University of Dayton Review*, vol.14 no.2, 1980.

Ellen C. Caldwell, "Poststructuring Brecht: Pluralism and Propaganda in *Galileo*", in *Communications from the International Brecht Society*, vol.17 no.2, 1988.

Friedrich Dieckmann, "*Galilei*-Komplikationen", in *Weimarer Beiträge*, 34, 1988.

Bärbel Schrader, "Brechts *Leben des Galilei*: Entstenhung und Wandlung eines Werkes für das Theater der Zeit", in *Weimarer Beiträge*, 34, 1988.

*   *   *

Bertolt Brecht's *Life of Galileo* is a dramatic biography which presents Galileo's conflict with the Papacy between 1610 and 1642 as an ideological conflict between progressive thinking and established dogma. Galileo's empirical science points the way to a new society and is taken up by the rising manufacturing classes, while the Church, in championing the discredited Ptolemaic astronomy, is actually defending the position of ruling, landowning classes. Galileo starts out as an energetic, hedonistic, and progressive if mildly rascally scholar, but is broken by being shown the instruments of torture offstage. He recants, withdrawing his discovery that the earth revolves round the sun and allowing the Church to continue to preach the fallacy that the earth is the centre of the universe. By the end of the play he loathes himself as a traitor to science and to society.

Life of Galileo was the first of the major plays Brecht was to write in exile. He wrote it in three weeks in Denmark in 1938, though he had almost certainly researched the subject earlier. It originally had the title *The Earth Moves*. In this version, which was performed in Zurich in 1943, Galileo continues his subversive research under virtual house arrest after his recantation and smuggles his findings out of Papal Italy to liberal Amsterdam. Hanns Eisler, Brecht's musical collaborator, saw the play as a demonstration, aimed at intellectuals in Nazi Germany, of how to survive in a tyranny by low cunning. An early Danish translation even shows Galileo in contact with the underground resistance. This Galileo was a positive anti-hero,

Life of Galileo: National Theatre, London, 1980

and the message was that truth, in time, would out.

When Brecht re-read *Life of Galileo* with a view to production in the USA in 1944 it struck him that where he thought he had been following history—and *Life of Galileo* is the only major Brecht play to feature an historical character and to focus on life at the top—he had somehow allowed a moral to slip in: his play implied that scientific research took precedence over social responsibility. In the 1930's he inclined to the view that scientific progress, industrialisation, and communism were interlinked aspects of the progressive materialism that would produce a prosperous, socialist future, a perspective that is reflected in Galileo's anachronistic assessments of society in 17th-century Italy. By 1944 the murderous science practised in Nazi Germany had caused him to abandon his assumption that free, scientific enquiry would automatically benefit mankind. Galileo bore the brunt of Brecht's new aversion to science, which was corroborated by the Hiroshima atomic bomb shortly after he had completed his revision of *Life of Galileo* in collaboration with Charles Laughton in California in 1945. Brecht noted, "The 'atomic' age made its debut at Hiroshima. . .Overnight the biography of the founder of the new system of physics read differently".

The California version had a redesigned Galileo. The main change is in the penultimate scene when Andrea, his former assistant, is given the *Discorsi* to take to Amsterdam, and like the earlier Brecht sees Galileo as a cunning old fox. Galileo in an outburst of self-loathing insists that if he had been less of a coward he would have defied the Church, demonstrated the social accountability of science and perhaps established a kind of Hippocratic oath for scientists, instead of which he has sold

science out to the ruling classes in what Brecht called the "original sin" of the modern, natural sciences.

Making Galileo answer for the crimes of science puts considerable strain on the characterisation. Even in the revised version he is a positive figure for the first nine scenes, firmly on the side of the individual against authority and of the peasants against the feudal landowners. He is visibly broken when the Inquisition has done with him and by the end of the play he is almost blind. He is one of Brecht's gallery of great characters, with a gargantuan appetite for life, the antithesis of the academic "stuffed shirts" at the court of Florence, and a man who is still researching and making clandestine copies of his discoveries at the end—all of which makes it hard to condemn him as Brecht wished. Charles Laughton, in the 1947 American production, seems to have been the monster Brecht intended with a combination of physical grossness and intellectual acuity—hand in pocket playing with his testicles as he ruminated. But Ernst Busch, who created the figure at the Berliner Ensemble in 1957, could not bring himself to hate Galileo even in the definitive German version which added more negative touches.

Life of Galileo is the least "epic" of Brecht's major plays. It is an indoor play with none of the rambling outdoor action that gives *Mother Courage* and *The Caucasian Chalk Circle* their characteristic, epic openness. There is no commentator and only one song. What it does have are brilliant, epic demonstrations of basic astronomy, when Galileo explains the revolutions of the earth to the boy Andrea with a chair and a washstand, and its rotation with an apple and a splinter of wood. These are theatrical inventions of the first order that set a pattern of visible experiment which runs through this play. The principles of the Ptolemaic and Copernican systems are at the heart of the intellectual argument in the play, and Brecht clarifies them at the outset in terms a child can understand, and he does so with stage images as much as words. The enrobing scene in which the Pope's attitude to his friend and colleague Galileo hardens as his person disappears under the robes of office is fine theatre and the definitive stage demonstration of the corrosive nature of power.

Galileo's journey from bright optimism to despairing cynicism under the constraints of an authoritarian regime still has the power to move an audience. It has repeatedly found issues to relate to—German rearmament in the 1950's, Vietnam in the 1960's, the American "Star Wars" defence programme in the 1980's.

—Hugh Rorrison

THE LIFE OF MAN (Zhizn Cheloveka)
by Leonid Andreyev

First Publication: In *Shipovnik* [*The Dog-Rose*], St. Petersburg, 1907; revised version in *Shipovnik*, 1908.
First Production: Vera Kommissarzhevskaya's Theatre, St. Petersburg, 22 February 1907.

Translations
The Life of Man, translated by M. Baring, in *Oxford and Cambridge Review*, Midsummer 1908.
The Life of Man, in *Savva; The Life of Man*, translated by T. Seltzer, New York, 1914.
The Life of Man, translated by C.J. Hogarth, London and New York, 1915.
The Life of Man, in *Leonid Andreyev: Two Plays*, translated by C.L. Meader and F.N. Scott, New York, 1915.
The Life of Man, translated by T.H. Dickinson, in *Continental Plays* (2 vols.), Boston, 1935.

Criticism
(For general works on the author, see *Playwrights* volume)

Articles:
James M. Woodward, "Leonid Andreyev and 'conventionalism' in the Russian Theatre", in *Modern Language Review*, 66, 1971.
Eberhard Reissner, "Andrejew: *Das Leben des Menschen*", in *Das russische Drama*, edited by Bodo Zelinsky, Düsseldorf, 1986.

*   *   *

The Life of Man was Andreyev's third play after *To the stars* (*K zvezdam*) and *Savva*. In it he turned away from the more or less traditional "realism" of his first two plays to "stylised realism", "conventionalism", or, as Andreyev himself preferred to call it, "neo-realism". In this respect he was following the general trend of Russian culture at the beginning of the 20th century. Andreyev explained his new approach in a letter to Stanislavsky before the Moscow Arts Theatre production: ". . .the stage, instead of presenting *life*, must present only a *reflection* of life" (Andreyev's italics). "The spectator must not forget for a moment that he is in a theatre watching actors depicting something".

The play (or "presentation" as it is actually called) begins with a prologue spoken "*in a firm cold voice devoid of excitement and passion*" by a "Being in Grey", presumably representing Fate, who emerges silently from the bare grey dimly lit set. "He" explains the "plot": the stages of Man's life to be presented in five pictures, as Andreyev, himself a talented artist, chose to call them, partly inspired by the paintings of Dürer and Goya. In the first picture Man is born as a candle is lit and held by the Being in Grey. In the second, "Love and Poverty", Man grows up and marries, indulging in romantic hopes and dreams. In the third, at the height of his successful career as an architect, a Grand Ball is held in his mansion. In the fourth his career fails and his son dies after being senselessly attacked by a street hooligan. This picture ends with Man hurling defiant abuse at the Being in Grey. The candle slowly burns towards extinction. In the fifth picture ("The Death of Man") Man dies, with his last breaths calling for his sword and again cursing his "Fate". The candle flickers out. The Being in Grey announces Man's death to the audience. There is a wild dance of old women followed by silence as the curtain falls.

In the letter to Stanislavsky, Andreyev emphasised that the general tone of the play was to be "like a distant and ghostly echo". The guests at the ball were to use "wooden voices and gestures". None of the characters is named and there is no indication of exactly how the rhythmic dialogue in the crowd and "chorus" scenes is to be divided between the individual actors. Andreyev appears to have been striving for an effect of mechanical inevitability. In the prologue there is reference to the "circle of iron predestination". At the same time he insisted that the play was not as negative, pessimistic, or gloomy as Meyerhold's production made it, citing Man's defiance of his Fate as evidence to the contrary. He seems to have been more satisfied with the Moscow Arts Theatre version, in which Stanislavsky used a setting mainly of black velvet. This was at least a temporary success, but Stanislavsky declared himself dissatisfied, as the "wooden voices and gestures" idea ran counter to his developing theories about acting. *The Life of Man* enjoyed a certain *succès de scandale* in tsarist Russia where in certain places, including Odessa, Kiev, and Kharkov, it was banned by the authorities, presumably for religious reasons. In the 1908 version, printed in *Shipovnik*, Andreyev modified the final scene and made other changes, introducing, for example, a "Sister of Mercy" who remains silent with closed eyes throughout the play.

If Andreyev's contemporaries were struck by the bold novelty of his approach and if he himself claimed to be ushering in a new era in the theatre, to a late 20th-century audience *The Life of Man* would undoubtedly appear unsubtle, even crude, and certainly melodramatic. The stylised dialogue, where it is intended to be satirical, as when the guests at the ball repeatedly mouth meaningless clichés, might work well for a short time, but, maintained throughout the play, would inevitably become tiresome. The obvious candle symbol might even have a comic effect. This may help to explain why *The Life of Man*, after its initial limited success, has now fallen into virtual oblivion. It is perhaps significant that Andreyev's *He Who Gets Slapped* (premiered in Moscow 1915, in Petrograd 1916) has enjoyed a greater and longer lasting success on a world scale. In that play Andreyev succeeds in blending "realism" with "conventionalism" in a more satisfyingly harmonious way and the symbolism is less crudely obtrusive.

In spite of its fairly obvious shortcomings, *The Life of Man* has an importance in the history of the Russian theatre, being a significant move against "naturalism" and so helping to stimulate developments in what is sometimes called the "Golden Age" of Russian theatre, not least in the work of Meyerhold and other less well-known directors: Evreinov, Vakhtangov, Tairov. It is also, in its way, a precursor of German expressionist drama. Andreyev also deserves credit for breaking new ground in its "multi-media" approach, his script making fairly precise provision for pictorial and lighting effects, music, sound, movement, and dance. In his initial enthusiasm for "neo-realism" Andreyev planned a grandiose cycle of plays in the same style. *The Life of Man* was to be followed by *Tsar-Hunger*, *War*, *Revolution* and, finally, *God, the Devil and Man*. Only the first two were written and *Tsar-Hunger* was never performed.

—John Goodliffe

THE LIFE OF THE INSECTS.   See **THE INSECT PLAY.**

LIGHTS OF BOHEMIA (Luces de Bohemia)
by Ramón del Valle-Inclán

First Publication: As weekly serial in *España*, 31 July–23 October, 1920; revised version, in *Opera Omnia, 19*, Madrid, 1924.
First Production: International Theatre Festival, Paris (Théâtre National Populaire—in French), 31 March 1963.

Translations
Luces de Bohemia [parallel text], edited and translated by Anthony N. Zahareas and Gerald Gillespie, Edinburgh, 1976.

Criticism
(For general works on the author, see *Playwrights* volume)

Articles:
Andrés Amorós, "Leyendo *Luces de Bohemia*", in *Cuadernos hispanoamericanos*, 67, 1966.
Gonzalo Sobejano, "*Luces de Bohemia*, elegía y satíra", in *Papeles de Son Armadans*, 43, 1966.
Frances W. Weber, "*Luces de Bohemia* and the Impossibility of Art", in *Modern Language Notes*, 82, 1967.
Hugo W. Cowes, "Indicaciones sobre estructura de *Luces de Bohemia* de Valle-Inclán", in *Razón y fábula*, 10, 1968.
Francisco Ynduráin, "*Luces de Bohemia*; variaciones: ironia y compromiso", in *Cuadernos hispanoamericanos*, 94, 1973.
Francisco Ynduráin, "Valleinclaniana: todavía sobre *Luces de Bohemia*", in *Papeles de Son Armadans*, 70, 1973.
Dru Dougherty, "*Luces de Bohemia* and Valle-Inclán's Search for Artistic Adequacy", in *Journal of Spanish Studies*, 2, 1974.
Markéta L. Freund, "La universidalidad de *Luces de Bohemia*", in *Hispanófila*, 56, 1976.
José Ortega, "*Luces de Bohemia* y [Martín Santos's] *Tiempo de silencio*: Dos concepciones del absurdo español", in *Cuadernos hispanoamericanos*, 106, 1976.
Francisco Martínez García, "El lexema 'muerte' como principio sobredeterminante en una lectura de *Luces de Bohemia*", in *Homenaje a Don Emilio Hurtado Llamas*, Léon, 1977.
Angel R. Fernández, "La literatura, signo teatral: El problema significativo de las acotaciones dramáticas: Valle-Inclán y *Luces de Bohemia*", in *La literatura como signo*, edited by José Romera Castillo, Madrid, 1981.
Rafael Osuna, "Un 'guión cinematográfico' de Valle-Inclán: *Luces de Bohemia*", in *Bulletin of Hispanic Studies*, 59, 1982.
Marta Palenque, "Los acotaciones de Valle-Inclán: *Luces de Bohemia*", in *Segismundo*, 37–38, 1983.
Maria J. Conde Guerri, "Julio Burell, el otro ministro de *Luces de Bohemia*", in *Estudios humanisticos: filologia*, 7, 1985.
Rafael Osuna, "Corporalidad y cinematografia en *Luces de Bohemia*", in *Explicación de textos literarios*, vol.14 no.2, 1985–86.
Ana P. Trapero Llobera and José Servera Baño, "Algunas consideraciones sobre el espacio en el montaje de *Luces de bohemia* del Centro Dramático National (C.D.N.)", in *Caligrama*, vol.2 nos.3–4, 1985.

* * *

The setting for this *esperpento*, or grotesque tragicomedy, is an "absurd, brilliant and starving" Madrid, around 1920. The episodic action, divided into 15 scenes, revolves around the final night in the anguished life of the impoverished blind poet Max Estrella. After suggesting a suicide pact to his wife and daughter, Max sets out on a descent into the urban hell, guided by the deceitful Don Latino de Hispalis. His journey—played against the background of workers' strikes, gunfire in the streets, and police brutality—takes him to a tavern and the streets, where he mingles with the city's seamy underside, to jail, where a Catalan anarchist correctly predicts his own assassination by the police, to the office of an effete government minister, a friend from Max's youth, and to a café frequented by modernist writers, including the famous Nicaraguan poet Rubén Darío (1867–1916). As dawn nears, Max, who has pawned his cape, dies on the street from exposure. Don Latino steals the dead man's wallet, containing money, given to him by the minister, and a winning lottery ticket. In the concluding scene, following the funeral, the news reaches the tavern that Max's desperate widow and daughter have killed themselves.

Now considered by many to be a masterpiece by Spain's greatest dramatist of the 20th century, *Bohemian Lights* was first performed in France in 1963 under the direction of Jean Vilar, almost 30 years after Valle-Inclán's death, and did not reach the Madrid stage until 1971, when José Tamayo brought it there to the Bellas Artes Theatre. The long delay may be attributed not only to the content, a bitingly satirical vision of Spanish reality, but even more so to the play's structure, more akin to Brecht and German expressionism than to the well-made play that dominated the commercial theatre of Valle-Inclán's time.

Besides requiring a cast of more than 50 characters and 11 different scene locations, the stage directions, hyper-realistic in their detail, call for a cinematic use of lights and images that was long thought to be unstageable. Moreover, many of those images and most of the characters, in keeping with Valle's aesthetic principle of systematic deformation, are to appear distorted, as if reflected by concave mirrors. The challenge of capturing this grotesque essence is compounded in foreign language productions by the difficulty of translating Valle's

The Lights of Bohemia: Madrid, 1984

highly inventive and polysemic language. The title itself is ambiguous, referring both literally to the lights in the Bohemian district and figuratively, and ironically, to the artistic luminaries. The protagonist's name suggests that he is the biggest star among them, but the unfortunate Max at times calls himself "Mala Estrella"—ill-starred. Linguistic problems notwithstanding, the French production has been followed by other foreign-language premières: English (Edinburgh Theatre Festival, 1968), German (1974), and Italian (1976).

At the urging of the director Giorgio Strehler, Lluís Pasqual, of Spain's National Drama Center, directed a revival in 1984. Although some previous directors attempted to recreate the elaborate stage directions through painted backdrops and realistic detail, Pasqual elected to evoke Valle-Inclán's grotesque dramatic world primarily through the actors. Fabiá Puigserver's design consisted of semi-opaque black screens, that could be raised or lowered to divide the stage, thus facilitating transitions. Minimal props were used to suggest the changes of locale. Mindful of the definition of the *esperpento* within the text, the stage floor was made of mirrored tiles. The emphasis on black and white, also present in the earlier Tamayo production, emphasised Valle's baroque *chiaroscuro* and recalled Goya's grotesque engravings, while also creating a photographic impression, not unrelated to the black-and-white movies of the 1920's which undoubtedly inspired the dramatist's imagery.

Bohemian Lights is a meta-theatrical work in various respects. It alludes directly and indirectly to historical events and people. The background of political unrest and violence has clear antecedents, as do many of the characters, including Max Estrella, who is based on the real Alejandro Sawa. The café conversation between Max and Rubén Darío is only one of many references to writers and literature. The pretentious modernist poets in the play generally appear inane, in contrast to the victimized proletariat, represented by the Catalan anarchist and a grieving mother whose child has been killed in the street-fighting. The blind poet and his descent into the Madrilenian hell refer, intertextually, to Homer and Dante. In the cemetery scene following Max's death, the Marqués de Bradomín, a character from Valle's early novels, expounds to Darío his concept of the *esperpento*: Spain, a deformation of Europe, is a country where great tragedies, like Shakespeare's *Hamlet*, are turned into grotesque parodies. Not surprisingly, the scene includes two gravediggers, and Bradomín's aesthetic principle of the concave mirrors alludes, self-referentially, to the play in progress.

Successful productions in Europe and Latin America have refuted the once widespread assertions that *Bohemian Lights* is unstageable and that its episodic action is disjointed. Indeed, the text is carefully structured with unifying threads that provide a cohesive framework for a heart-wrenching vision of the artist's impotence in a grotesque world.

—Phyllis Zatlin

LILIOM
by Ferenc Molnár

First Publication: Budapest, 1909.
First Production: Budapest, 1909.

Translations
Liliom, translated by Benjamin F. Glazer, London, 1921.

Criticism
(For general works on the author, see *Playwrights* volume)

Articles:
A. Battey, "*Liliom*", in *Poet-Lore*, 35, 1924.

* * *

One of the great international successes of Hungarian drama and, according to many, Ferenc Molnár's best play, *Liliom* is hard to characterize in a few words. Naturalistic in its opening scenes, the play becomes dreamlike and allegorical, with a strain of sentimentalism throughout. This blatant eclecticism clearly illustrates the secret of Molnár's popularity—his ability to offer something pleasant and attractive to all audiences, their nationality and social experience notwithstanding.

Ironically, "Liliom" is the nickname of a young barker at Budapest's amusement park who first appears as anything but lilylike in character and disposition. Being a habitual womanizer, a little petting with the teenage housemaid, Julie, on the carousel would not have meant much to him if his employer (and probably lover), the widowed carousel-owner, Mrs. Muskát, had not forbidden the young girl to appear again on her premises. Liliom defends Julie and is promptly fired. Alone in the dark park, Liliom and Julie's love unfolds and is consummated. The couple move into a shack nearby which belongs to Liliom's relatives. He does not work but spends his days loitering, playing cards, and being rude to Julie. Mrs. Muskát is willing to take Liliom back, but when he hears that Julie is pregnant, he decides to stick by her. They need money, however. Listening to the advice of a friend (a petty criminal), Liliom is involved in an ill-fated holdup. When the plan fails, Liliom is unable to face justice and stabs himself. A uniformed, celestial police judge with a long white beard condemns the unrepentant sinner to 16 years in Purgatory, at the end of which he can return to Earth for one day to show his family that he has redeemed himself. In the last act Liliom returns to Budapest and finds Julie and their daughter, Lujza, living a humble and decent existence. By telling the truth about his past failings, he manages to alienate both mother and daughter, until the latter shuts him out. Frustrated, Liliom strikes Lujza's hand. The heaven-sent detectives escort him away, leaving Lujza wondering why the blow of the uncouth vagrant did not hurt.

Liliom developed from a short prose piece entitled, *Bedtime Story* (1907). Molnár wrote the play in three weeks on the balcony of Budapest's Cafe New York, a meeting-place for writers and artists. The author's own excentricities and family problems also contributed to *Liliom*'s notoriety. On the one hand, Molnár was by then so successful that other writers, even his friends, were growing jealous of him. On the other hand, his first marriage to Margit Vészi was a shambles. Molnár was said to be a maladjusted wreck, hurting his young wife and their little daughter both emotionally and physically. According to those in favour of biographical criticism, *Liliom* was the author's statement: literary proof of the deep feelings which he was unable to reveal to his family during his own lifetime.

Liliom is, however, more than a personal confession. It is also a psychological representation of modern man and his complexes: split personality, instability, social and emotional maladjustment, with sado-masochism as compensation. Neurosis was a fashionable slogan of the time; Sigmund Freud had already published his first major works. There are also several other, more traditional and stereotyped, psychological dimensions to the play: a fight between two women over a man, a conflict between a static character (Liliom) and a dynamic one (Julie), and so on.

Furthermore, *Liliom* has also been interpreted as a legend, showing man's relationship to God and the struggle for his soul between good and evil; as a socially critical play featuring the "lower depths" of alienated city life; as an allegorical urban folk tale; and, simply, as a romantic love story. Its anthropomorphic Heaven, with its uniformed supervisors and guards who only differ from their earthly colleagues in their gentler manner, gives a naive quality to the play. The style suits its characters, situations and messages—from the poetic and metaphoric to the extremely colloquial.

Liliom was initially a failure at its Budapest and London premieres but a great triumph in Vienna (1913), Berlin (1914), and New York (1921) where Joseph Schildkraut and Eva Le Gallienne played the main roles 285 times in the Theatre Guild production. Even where success first eluded the play, it later became a popular favourite. Critical appreciation, however, has been more varied. Few modern plays inspired as many clichés as *Liliom*, ranging from ecstatic adulation ("one of the most beautiful plays") to scorn ("a tear-jerker"). While the international public liked the characters with whom it could easily identify, favourable critics were quick to point out analogies with contemporaries like Hauptmann or Hofmannsthal—one aggrandizing Hungarian reviewer even mentioned *Faust*.

Liliom was also a media success. According to a family anecdote, Puccini wanted to compose an opera score on the theme but the author declined. Two American and one French film version are known to exist. In 1945 Rodgers and Hammerstein composed a musical version, *Carousel*, another box-office hit which was brought to the screen in 1956.

—George Bisztray

THE LITTLE CLAY CART
(Mrcchakatika / Mrichchhakatika)
attributed to King Sudraka

Composition: Possibly between 1st century B.C. and 1st century A.D.; some sources suggest 5th century.

Editions
The Mrichchhakatika, edited by Rangacharya B. Raddi, Bombay, 1909.
Mrcchakatikam nama prakaranam, edited by V.G. Paranjpe, Poona, India, 1937.
The Mrichchhakatika [with translation], edited by M.R. Kále.

Translations
The Little Clay Cart, translated by Arthur William Ryder, Cambridge, Massachusetts, 1905.
The Little Clay Cart, translated by Satyendra Kumar Basa, Calcutta, 1939.

The Toy Cart, in *Great Sanskrit Plays*, translated by P. Lal, Norfolk, Connecticut, 1957.
The Little Clay Cart, translated by Barbara Stoler Miller, 1984.

Criticism

Books:
Balwant Gargi, *Theater in India*, New York, 1962.
A.B. Keith, *The Sanskrit Drama in its Origin, Development, Theory and Practice*, London, 1964.

Articles:
J. Michel, "Producing the *Little Clay Cart*", in *Asian Drama*, edited by H. Wells, 1965.
H. Wells, "Artifice and Naturalism in the East", in *Quest*, vol.1 no.1, 1965–66.

* * *

Charudatta is a Brahman so prone to generous gestures that he is now embarassed to find himself penniless. Vasantasena, a courtesan, is in love with him. She in turn is being pursued by a prince, Samsthanaka, as ridiculous in his self-regard as *Cymbeline's* Cloten. In a second plot strand that becomes central to the action in the second half of the play, an exiled prince, Aryaka, foments a rebellion against Samsthanaka's brother-in-law, the king.

At the nadir of the lovers' fortunes Samsthanaka has strangled Vasantasena and left her for dead, and Charudatta has been tried and convicted of her murder. He is saved from execution at the last moment by her reappearance. The success of Aryaka's revolt restores the fortunes of Charudatta, who aided him; establishes Vasantasena as his second wife, her social status changed by the new ruler's decreee; and brings Samsthanaka to Charudatta's feet—Charudatta, of course, forgives him. In a way admired in Sanskrit dramatic theory, only at the end are the threads knotted together.

At the midpoint of the play the scene occurs that gives the play its title. Charudatta's son plays with a little clay cart but longs for the gold cart he used to have; Vasantasena piles her jewels in his cart. The incident refers to a parable of how the gods lure man from his burning house by offering him trifles to play with. The message is not to value the things of this world, represented by the burning house. And Vasantasena declares: "Ah, mighty Fate! the destinies of men, uncertain as the water-drops which fall upon a lotus-leaf, seem to thee but play-things!". Similarly, despite the lover's final triumph, the play ends on a note of renunciation. A gambler who has turned monk, and who revived Vasantasena after Samsthanaka's attack, refuses advancement; having seen the vicissitudes of the world, he will remain a monk.

The two principal genres of Sanskrit drama are *nataka*, plays based on historical legends, and *prakarana*, plays with invented stories. *Shakuntala* is the best-known *nataka*, *The Little Clay Cart* (or *The Toy Cart*) the best-known *prakarana*. And it is, indeed, notable for the luxuriance of its invention, both in plot and verbal imagery. Scene by scene the progression is rarely linear. The author seems to delight in starting scenes with characters we have not met. Incidents fragment, vivid minor characters and even descriptions—some 1500 words, for example, cataloging the wonders of the seven courtyards of Vasantasena's palatial establishment—take possession of the stage. There are also a variety of metres in the play's verse passages, and a variety of vernacular dialects alongside the Sanskrit of the high-caste characters.

Chance seems to reign. But the seeming casualness is balanced against the author's purposeful patterns, and through them he represents the underlying purposefulness of the universe, of which the reader or spectator gradually becomes aware. Each half of this double-length play is dominated by an action that is a sequence of coincidences. In the first half a casket of jewels passes from hand to hand. In the opening scene Samsthanaka pursues Vasantasena through the night. She slips into Charudatta's house to avoid him; to cover her embarassment, she pretends she was pursued by a thief and leaves a casket of jewels in his care. Ironically, a burglar steals it. Even more ironically, he takes it to Vasantasena to purchase the freedom of her maid, whom he loves. Vasantasena takes back her jewels but frees the maid. Meanwhile, Charudatta's wife has tactfully found an excuse to give him a necklace of great worth, knowing he will use it to cover the loss of the jewels. He, in turn, makes an excuse to Vasantasena to ensure that she will accept the necklace, saying that he gambled away her jewels. She brings this exercise in mutual consideration to a close by hurrying through the night to Charudatta's (a parallel between the start and end of this half of the play that is underlined by the dance style with which such a journey would have been presented, with umbrella-bearers and others in attendance upon her) to intimate her awareness of his gesture by telling him she gambled away the necklace and showing him the casket in its place. In refinement and generosity they are a match for each other and they retire together. Thus, even the theft of the casket only returns it to the rightful owner and helps to bring Charudatta and Vasantasena's love to consummation. Furthermore, the awareness the central characters almost always have of the truth behind the stories presented to them is analogous to the sense of a meaning behind the vicissitudes of daily life.

In the second half the tone darkens and the actions advance the plot more obviously. Nevertheless, it is a confusion between two bullock-carts that delivers Vasantasena into Samsthanaka's hands, but that also allows Aryaka to escape. Thus, chance seems to doom both lovers to their deaths but leads, instead, to their triumph.

The length and variousness of *The Little Clay Cart* make as great demands on staging as its metres and dialects do on the translator. Among the most successful translations are those of Arthur William Ryder (1905) and Barbara Stoler Miller (1984).

—Anthony Graham-White

THE LITTLE FOXES
by Lillian Hellman

First Publication: New York, 1939.
First Production: National Theatre, New York, 15 February 1939.

Criticism
(For general works on the author, see *Playwrights* volume)

Articles:
Elizabeth C. Phillips, "Command of Human Destiny as Exemplified in Two Plays: Lillian Hellman's *The Little Foxes* and Lorraine Hansberry's *A Raisin in the Sun*", in *Interpretations*, 4, 1972.
James Eatman, "The Image of American Destiny: *The Little Foxes*", in *Players*, 48, 1973.

The Little Foxes: Tallulah Bankhead, New York, 1939 (first production)

Katherine Lederer, "The Foxes Were Waiting for Horace, Not Lefty: The Use of Irony in Lillian Hellman's *The Little Foxes*", in *West Virginia University Philological Papers*, 26, 1980.

*   *   *

It is 1900 and the "small town in the South" where Lillian Hellman sets *The Little Foxes* is on the brink of an unsettling future. The agrarian community is poised for the coming of industrialization. Ben Hubbard is about to realize his dream, "to bring the machine to the cotton, and not the cotton to the machine". To make this possible, he is forging a partnership with a Chicago enterprise.

Once, what he needed was to woo cotton and land. In those days, Ben and his brother Oscar were conniving shopkeepers; their own sister, Regina, threatening them with a lawsuit in front of a jury, is certain that "you couldn't find twelve men in the State you haven't cheated". Like Faulkner's Snopeses, these brothers benefited from the war between the states. They were eager to fill in the power vacuum when the aristocratic cotton barons answered the honor call to battle. Oscar married one of the baron's daughters, Birdie, and she gives birth to Leo, the crassest member of their clan. When the mother in Tennessee Williams's *Glass Menagerie* warns her daughter not to turn into one of those "little birdlike women without any nest", she is sure that marriage would protect a woman from the degradation of dependency. But Hellman depicts marriage as more terrifying than any condition of mere homelessness. All that is left for Birdie is to retreat into alcohol, music, and memories of Lionnet (where she grew up). Her romanticized vision of her childhood Eden acknowledges none of the horrors of a slave plantation: "We were good to our people. . . .Poppa used to say that *nobody* had ever lost their temper at Lionnet, and *nobody* ever would. Poppa would never let anybody be nasty spoken, or mean". Yet one cannot even accept the veracity of her version of Southern pastoral.

Regina married Horace, a righteous banker who is not cut out for the predatory capitalism that his wife's voracious appetite for power demands. Banished from his wife's bed for a decade, he has been overwhelmed by the onslaught of the new age, and his heart is giving out. He cannot survive in a Hubbard world. All they need him for is to supply the financial backing for their new venture. But he is unwilling to come across, unwilling to be a partner to their factories because he envisions their starvation wages setting mountain Whites and town Blacks at each other's throats. First the brothers scheme to steal his bonds; then his wife stares icily ahead as he suffers a fatal collapse behind her back. It is the play's most chilling *coup de théâtre*. The decent man thought he could block the feral instincts of his wife to acquire great wealth at any human cost. He clearly under-estimated her. Unaided, he struggles to save himself. All he can occupy is a tenuous moment in the present; and then he is not allowed to have even that moment.

Regina lives for the future. Thwarted as a girl—Hellman depicts her frustration at not getting what she wants in *Another Part of the Forest*—she is now fixed in her determination: "I'm going to Chicago. And when I'm settled there and know the right things to buy—because I certainly don't know now—I shall go to *Paris* and buy them". She plays her game with complete ruthlessness. The reputation of Tallulah Bankhead's portrayal of Regina since the play's first production cannot be measured, but Bette Davis's performance in the 1941 William Wyler film is indelible. Davis's great moments, such as the chilling immobility of Regina's ice-maiden death-watch, are stage images demanded by the original script.

Alexandra, Horace and Regina's daughter, finds that she cannot continue both to adore her father and respect her mother. The play is one long awakening of her independence from the grasping single-mindedness of Regina. Her father instinctively knows that Alexandra will need someone when he is gone, and he is sure that person should be Addie, the African-American servant. Addie is given great moral weight when Hellman has her deliver the words that delineate the ethical center of the play: "Well, there are people who eat the earth and eat all the people on it like in the Bible with the locusts. Then, there are people who stand around and watch them eat it. (*Softly*.) Sometimes I think it ain't right to stand and watch them do it". In the end, Alexandra pledges to stand against the Uncle Bens of American capitalism. (Uncle Ben is also the name Arthur Miller goes on to use in *Death of a Salesman*; perhaps both he and Hellman are paying sly homage to the American prophet of enterprise, Benjamin Franklin.) When Alexandra makes her vow, she acknowledges that it is from Addie that she heard about those who "ate the earth": "Well, tell him for me, Mama, I'm not going to stand around and watch you do it. Tell him I'll be fighting as hard as he'll be fighting (*Rises*. . .) some place where people don't just stand around and watch". Horace proved to be ineffective at stopping the Hubbard clan. But by the end of the play, an alliance of strength against their greed has been formed between the Shavian young woman whose eyes have been opened and the alert mammy. Uncle Oscar had already been made uneasy by Addie's penetrating gaze: "You do a lot of judging around here, Addie, eh? Judging of your white folks, I mean". Though the play abandons the genteel lady, Birdie, as a captive, the young white woman and the mature black woman get out.

Earlier, before the final breaking away, the fine-souled but passive characters of the play have the house to themselves one rainy afternoon; they have a brief respite, elderberry wine and cakes with not a Hubbard in earshot. For once, Birdie, Addie, and Horace can speak freely; Alexandra is taught to beware the model of her soft-spoken abused aunt. Alexandra's restlessness finds voice: "We sit around and try to pretend nothing's happened. . .We make believe we are just by ourselves". In the winter of 1939, America had not yet entered World War II, and Hellman was alerting her isolationist audience to the dangers of their stance. *Little Foxes* opened on 15 February 1939; Germany did not invade Poland until 1 September of that year. In Hellman's final act, Uncle Ben vividly clarifies the threat of what he represents:

> The century's turning, the world is open. Open for people like you and me. Ready for us, waiting for us. After all, this is just the beginning. There are hundreds of Hubbards sitting in rooms like this throughout the country. All their names aren't Hubbard, but they are all Hubbards and they will own this country someday. We'll get along.

Surely, he is speaking at least as much about the situation of Fascism in 1939 as he is about the situation of capitalism in 1900.

Yet Hellman's use of economics (like Ibsen's use of genetics) can be problematic. Horace recoils from the motivations of his wife's family to bring cotton mills to the South; he demands to know, is it only "to pound the bones of this town to make dividends for you to spend? You wreck the town, you and your brothers, *you* wreck the town and live on it". Whereas the Northern partner, Marshall, is indifferent to their motivations: "You want the mill here, and I want it here. It isn't my business to find out *why* you want it". Presumably, Hellman expects her audience to retreat from Marshall's commercial amorality and, instead, embrace Horace's outrage. But the depressed South desperately needed those jobs, and the audience today cannot wholeheartedly reject the opportunity to put men and women back to work. Nonetheless, Hellman's *mythos* of greed survives with glinting menace, just as melodrama itself has survived a century of pejorative connotation. *Little Foxes* provided inspiration for two forms highly adaptive to the melodramatic impulse—not only one of the best Hollywood movies, but also one of the only viable American operas, Marc Blitzstein's all-too-rarely heard *Regina. Little Foxes* deserves to regain its place on the stage.

—Roger Sorkin

LA LOCANDIERA. See **MISTRESS OF THE INN.**

LONDON ASSURANCE
by Dion Boucicault

First Publication: London, 1841.
First Production: Theatre Royal, Covent Garden, 4 March 1841.

Editions

London Assurance, in *Masterpieces of British Drama: The Nineteenth Century*, edited by Robert W. Corrigan, New York, 1967.
London Assurance, edited by Ronald Eyre, London, 1971.

* * *

Sir Harcourt Courtly, a vain elderly roué, returns after seven profligate years abroad to seal a lucrative arranged marriage to 18 year old Grace Harkaway. Unknown to him, his son Charles leads a dissipated life in London. Charles's new-found drinking companion, Richard Dazzle, is opportunely invited by Max Harkaway, Grace's uncle and guardian, to attend the wedding at Oak Hall, Gloucestershire. Pretending the country house is his, Dazzle in turn invites Charles who readily accepts to escape creditors. At Oak Hall Grace, thus far untouched by love and unimpressed by romance, accepts pragmatically her arranged betrothal, but finds her cool ruffled by Charles who, posing on arrival as Augustus Hamilton, falls for her instantly. Father inevitably meets son, both now rivals in love, but Courtly senior is persuaded despite appearances to the contrary that "Hamilton" is not his son. Ever the opportunist, Dazzle enlists the help of a neighbouring sportswoman, Lady Gay Spanker, and easily persuades Sir Harcourt to transfer his affections to Lady Gay. She playfully agrees to elope with Sir Harcourt, secure in the love of her timid husband Adolphus. As Grace suspects Charles's true identity and resents the manipulations going on around her, various tests of love are played out between her and Charles. The sudden disappearance and death of "Augustus Hamilton", his replacement by the real Charles, the anger of Adolphus at Gay's behaviour, and the plot to switch couples in the waiting elopement carriage precipitate comic confusions resulting in an aborted duel between irate husband and superannuated seducer.

Confrontation forces Sir Harcourt to admit his folly, Charles and Lady Gay to confess their deceptions, and Grace to win recognition of her independent status. Sir Harcourt duly surrenders all claims to Grace, leaving Charles to inherit both wife and property.

Often dismissed by literary critics as a pale imitation of Vanbrugh, Farquhar, Goldsmith, Sheridan, and Murphy, *London Assurance* undoubtedly exploits familiar material. Stock characters (outrageous fop, hearty squire, spirited heroine, rakes on the make) entangled in stock situations (arranged marriage, inheritance hunting, practical jokes, double wooing) illustrate stock thematic polarities (town and country, monetary calculation and true worth, deception and honesty, artifice and nature). Written hastily by a 21-year-old in collaboration with a fellow actor, and tailored for and by the Vestris–Mathews management at Covent Garden, the play openly flaunts its dramatic antecedents and revels in its borrowings from earlier successes. Anything that goes with a swing is pressed into service by Boucicault, including Shakespeare, whose *Hamlet, Twelfth Night, Macbeth,* and *Tempest* are all quoted verbally or visually.

That the play transcends these allusions is due to Boucicault's acute awareness of what will play well theatrically. Tired material is refreshed by the sheer pace of the piece, by its lively dialogue incorporating swift exchanges, risqué jokes, good talk, puns, alliterations and bright aphorisms, and by Boucicault's intuitive grasp of scene construction and rhythm, of finely judged entrances, and "peeling off" exits at act ends or before set pieces—such as the mutual testing scene between Grace and Charles in Act III, where Boucicault displays exact command of stage movement, hesitant declarations of love, wary asides, and comic misinterpretations of signals.

The first two of the five acts successfully avoid the naivety of laborious explication by relying on a series of quick-paced duologues, one of whose running jokes is a chain of mistaken identities, and reciprocal misunderstandings among characters, neatly deployed by Boucicault to anticipate and highlight cheekily the major plot improbability late in Act II when Sir Harcourt is introduced to his own son but is then persuaded that he must be mistaken in his identification. Characteristically the motif is sustained to the end through the impudent Dazzle, whose claims to be related to all the principals, thus allowing him to busy himself with every plot twist, are finally exposed when it is realised that no one has any idea who he really is.

Further instances of Boucicault's deft touch can be found in his swift establishment and delineation of characters, all of whom are generously awarded a good speech or a choice scene, and in his awareness of the importance of visual presentation of idiosyncratic or telling detail. Charles, after his night on the town, staggers home with a collection of stolen door knockers, one of them his own. Sir Harcourt favours a late levee; attired in an elegant dressing gown and tasselled nightcap, he worries over the amount of rouge he has applied, and is carefully unpacked from the fur cloak and gloves deemed necessary for the journey to deepest Gloucestershire. Comedy of manners and farce are blended with consummate ease. In short, *London Assurance* exudes Boucicault's theatrical assurance.

The young Queen Victoria attended the third performance of the original production in March 1841 and noted, "There are some good bits in it, but if it were not for the excellent actors, I hardly think it would do well". She must have been faintly amused because she saw the play four more times in the following 18 years. The play's popularity throughout the 19th century attests its vitality. Frequently revived as a certain box-office success, it was also a favourite benefit piece, since it boasted no part which an experienced actor could not make his or her own. Reputations were made or sustained in the parts of Dazzle, Sir Harcourt, Grace, Charles, and the whip-cracking Lady Gay Spanker. The smaller parts of "Dolly" Spanker, Meddle, the interfering lawyer, and Cool, a resourceful servant, were no less prized. In this century major revivals by the Royal Shakespeare Company in 1970 and the Chichester Festival Theatre in 1989 have rehabilitated *London Assurance* and confirmed its winning qualitites.

—Ronald W. Strang

THE LONDON MERCHANT; or, The History of George Barnwell
by George Lillo

First Publication: London, 1731.
First Production: Theatre Royal, Drury Lane, 1731.

Editions

When Crummles Played: Being the Full and Original Text of Lillo's Tragedy of "The London Merchant" or "George Barnwell", London, 1927.
The London Merchant, in *Plays of the Restoration and Eighteenth Century*, edited by D. MacMillan and H.M Jones, New York, 1931.
The London Merchant, in *Representative English Dramas from Dryden to Sheridan*, edited by F. and J.W. Tupper, New York, 1934.
The London Merchant, edited by Bonamy Dobrée, London, 1948.
The London Merchant, edited by William H. McBurney, Lincoln, Nebraska, 1965 (Regents Restoration Drama Series).

Criticism

(For general works on the author, see *Playwrights* volume)

Articles:

William H. Hudson, "George Lillo and *The London Merchant*", in his *A Quiet Corner in a Library*, Chicago, 1915.
Sir. Adolphus William Ward, "Introduction to Lillo's *London Merchant* and *Fatal Curiosity*", in *Collected Papers*, 4, 1921.
Reginald H. Griffith, "Early Editions of Lillo's *London Merchant*", in *Studies in English* (University of Texas), 15, 1935.
Raymond Dexter Havens, "Sentimentality in *The London Merchant*" [reply to Rodman's article], in *English Literary History*, 12, 1945.
George B. Rodman, "Sentimentality in *The London Merchant*", in *English Literary History*, 12, 1945.
Laurence M. Price, "George Barnwell Abroad", in *Comparative Literature*, 2, 1950.
Wallace Jackson, "Dryden's Emperor and Lillo's Merchant: The Relevant Bases of Action", in *Modern Language Querterly*, 26, 1965.
Michael M. Cohen, "Providence and Constraint in Two Lillo Tragedies", in *English Studies*, 52, 1971.
Frank G. Kearful, "Dramatic Rhetoric in Lillo's *London Merchant*", in *Neuphilologische Mitteilungen*, 73, 1972.

Heinz Mathias Meltzer, "Lillo's *London Merchant* als 'Conduct Play'", in *Archiv*, 213, 1976.
Robert W. Halli Jr., "This Torrent of Domestic Misery: George Lillo's *The London Merchant*", in *A Provision of Human Nature: Essays on Fielding and Others in Honor of Miriam Austin Locke*, edited by Donald Kay, Alabama, 1977.
Stephen L. Trainor Jr., "Tears Abounding: *The London Merchant* as Puritan Tragedy", in *Studies in English Literature 1500–1900*, 18, 1978.
Roberta F.S. Borkat, "The Evil of Goodness: Sentimental Morality in *The London Merchant*", in *Studies in Philology*, 76, 1979.
J. Chaouillet, "Images continentales du *Marchand de Londres*", in *Studies on Voltaire and the Eighteenth Century*, 217, 1983.
Hans-Ulrich Mohr, "Lillo's *The London Merchant*: Ein bürgerliches Trauerspiel?", in *Germanisch-Romanische Monatsschrift Grundzüge*, 36, 1986.
Clay Daniel, "The Fall of George Barnwell", in *Restoration and Eighteenth Century Theatre Research* (second series), 2, 1987.
Stephen P. Flores, "Mastering the Self: The Ideological Incorporation of Desire in Lillo's *The London Merchant*", in *Essays in Theatre*, 5, 1987.
Jones de Ritter, "A Cult of Dependence: The Social Context of *The London Merchant*", in *Comparative Drama*, vol.21 no.4, 1987.
Louis Markos, "Lillo's *The London Merchant* and the Discourse of Criminal Biography", in *Restoration and Eighteenth Century Theatre Research* (second series), vol.5 no.2, 1990.

*   *   *

Benevolence suffuses the household of the merchant Thorowgood, but one of his apprentices, George Barnwell, is seduced by a fallen woman, Millwood, in order to induce him to steal from his master. Thorowgood's daughter Maria, who silently loves Barnwell, replaces these amounts. Millwood gets Barnwell to murder his uncle, a deed so heinous her servants seek to prevent it by informing Thorowgood. The play ends with the trial and execution of the two criminals, Barnwell remorseful and believing in God's mercy, Millwood unrepentant and adding despair to her sins.

The London Merchant has been described as the first bourgeois tragedy. Several Elizabethan plays fit that description, one of which Lillo adapted, and so it could rather better be described as the first tragedy with a self-consciously mercantile philosophy. References in the opening scene give it an ostensible setting in Elizabethan England, but the spirit of the play is as 18th-century as the costumes would have been. We are not dealing with the risks to rich argosies of *The Merchant of Venice* but with interest rates at the bank of Genoa. And the play is not in verse but in prose, even if the rhythms of iambic pentameter haunt its climactic scenes.

"The method of merchandise", we are told at the midpoint of the play, "is founded in reason and the nature of things; . . .it promotes humanity, as it has opened and yet keeps up an intercourse between nations far from one another in situation, customs and religion; promoting arts, industry, peace, and plenty; by mutual benefits diffusing mutual love from pole to pole". Fortunately, "on every country heaven has bestowed some good peculiar to itself. It is the industrious merchant's business to collect the various blessings of each soil and climate, and with the product of the whole, to enrich his native country". The play is fittingly dedicated to the Sub-

Governor of the South Sea Company.

Without a conflict there would be no drama, but Barnwell's ostensible willingness to do evil is in every way diminished. First, "the powerful magic of her [Millwood's] wit and form might betray the wisest to simple dotage", Thorowgood tells us; second, Barnwell renounces Millwood after their first encounter and is only with difficulty deceived again by her tale of destitution, appealing to his compassion rather than his passion. Similarly, after undertaking to murder his uncle, he repents and throws down his weapon, an action which—ironically—alarms his uncle into drawing his sword and precipitates Barnwell's fatal stab to his uncle, which tearful cries for forgiveness, and swooning away upon his uncle's corpse cannot reverse. Fourth, he takes nothing—"nor could I, to have gained the empire of the world, have violated, by theft, his sacred corpse". Fifth, he refuses to say anything against Millwood, though confessing his own crimes. Last, he seeks solace in religion and in being an example to others. As one critic wrote: "Who can. . .forget that mawkish sweetness, that unctuous virtue, those interminable repentances?".

Even Millwood acts as she does, she claims, only in response to men's ill-treatment of her. She is allowed a scene of self-defence, in which we are meant to admire, with Thorowgood, "a mind so comprehensive, daring, and inquisitive". In 1796, some 60 years after the play's premiere in 1731, Sarah Siddons sought to play her sympathetically, a reflection perhaps of Romantic sympathies for the unfortunate.

The London Merchant chimed so well with the values of its time that it came to be played, at one or another London theatre, at Christmas, Easter, and on Lord Mayor's Day in November—those apprentices' holidays that fell within the theatre season, a tradition that was unbroken until 1819. At the same time it foreshadowed later developments in being a tragedy of an ordinary man and in using prose rather than verse (except for some moralizing tags at the ends of some scenes). Lillo justly claimed in his dedication that this was tragedy "accomodated to the generality of mankind".

Lillo's play had an influential afterlife in France and—often via French adaptations—in Germany. The difficulties its adapters had with it are a measure of its originality; on the one hand hard to accomodate to theatrical conventions—in one French version Thorowgood has become the King of Egypt, while a Viennese version added a subplot for Columbina, Hans Wurst, and Scapin—but on the other stimulating to reformers of those conventions. At least six French adaptations appeared, some with the murder prevented and a happy ending, all with some modification of Millwood. It was included in a 1755 anthology, *Théâtre bourgeois*, and helped shape the new genre of *drame bourgeois*. German versions were known to Lessing, Schiller, and Goethe.

—Anthony Graham-White

LONG DAY'S JOURNEY INTO NIGHT
by Eugene O'Neill

First Publication: New Haven, Connecticut, 1956; corrected edition, 1989.
First Production: Stockholm, 2 February 1956; first US production, Helen Hayes Theatre, New York, 2 February 1956.

Criticism
(For general works on the author, see *Playwrights* volume)

Books:
Harold Bloom (ed.), *Eugene O'Neill's "Long Day's Journey into Night"*, New York, 1987 (Modern Critical Interpretations).
Michael Hinden, *"Long Day's Journey into Night": Native Eloquence*, Boston, 1990.

Articles:
Albert Rothenberg and Eugene D. Shapiro, "The Defense of Psychoanalysis in Literature: *Long Day's Journey into Night* and *A View from the Bridge*", in *Comparative Drama*, 7, 1973.
Enrico F. Garzilli, "*Long Day's Journey into Night* (Mary) and *Streetcar Named Desire* (Blanche): An Inquiry in Compassion", in *Theatre Annual*, 33, 1977.
Judith E. Barlow, "*Long Day's Journey into Night*: From Early Notes to Finished Play", in *Modern Drama*, 22, 1979.
David McDonald, "The Phenomenology of the Glance in *Long Day's Journey into Night*", in *Theatre Journal*, 31, 1979.
Péter Egri, "The Reinterpretation of the Chekhovian Mosaic Design in O'Neill's *Long Day's Journey into Night*", in *Acta Litteraria Academiae Scientiarum Hungaricae*, 22, 1980.
Robert Einenkel, "*Long Day's Journey* Towards Separation: The Mary-Edmund Struggle", in *Eugene O'Neill Newsletter*, vol.9 no.1, 1985.
D.W. Lloyd, "Mystical Experience in *Long Day's Journey into Night*", in *Unisa English Studies*, September 1986.
Bennett Simon, "Poetry, Tragic Dialogue and the Killing of Children in Eugene O'Neill's *Long Day's Journey into Night*", in *Hebrew University Studies in Literature and the Arts*, Autumn 1986.
Jean Chothia, " 'Native eloquence': Multiple Voices in *Long Day's Journey into Night*", in *Eugene O'Neill Newsletter*, vol.12 no.3, 1988.
Bette Mandl, "Wrestling with the Angel in the House: Mary Tyrone's Long Journey", in *Eugene O'Neill Newsletter*, vol.12 no.3, 1988.
John H. Raleigh, "Communal, Familial, and Personal Memories in O'Neill's *Long Day's Journey into Night*", in *Modern Drama*, 31, 1988.

*   *   *

Long Day's Journey into Night begins at 8.30 a.m. in the Tyrone summer home in Connecticut and ends around midnight of the same, hot August day. The year is 1912. As bright daylight fades into fog-shrouded night, Mary Tyrone resumes taking morphine, dashing her family's hopes that she has been cured of her addiction. James Tyrone is an aging actor who, in the course of the play, confronts not only his family's accusations of cheapness but his own regret over wasting his talents in a popular melodrama. Their elder son, Jamie, devastated by his mother's return to drugs and by his brother Edmund's illness, tries to ease his sorrow with copious amounts of liquor and a visit to the local brothel. The youngest member of the family is Edmund, who learns that he has consumption and must enter a sanitarium. A tapestry of recriminations, regrets, apologies, and confessions, the play ends with the men sunk in a haze of alcohol and the heavily drugged Mary reliving, in her mind, the happier times of her youth.

After O'Neill completed this autobiographical work, one of his last plays, he placed it in a vault with the stipulation that it

Long Day's Journey Into Night: Globe Theatre, London, 1958

not be opened until 25 years after his death. Shortly after he died, his widow and heir, Carlotta Monterey O'Neill, removed the play and authorized its publication and production. Following the Swedish premiere it was performed in New York and earned O'Neill a posthumous fourth Pulitzer Prize. The production of *Journey* was instrumental in the resurrection of the playwright's reputation that began in the 1950's; frequent stage revivals as well as films have helped place the drama among O'Neill's most famous works.

The majority of critics consider *Journey* to be O'Neill's best play, and it is arguably one of the finest dramas created by an American. Using a form favored by American writers, the realistic family play, O'Neill has painted a searing portrait of four people caught in a web of resentment and need, anger and love. And while the Tyrone family is in many ways unique, based on O'Neill's own immediate kin, it is also a kind of "Everyfamily" writ large. Monumental as their battles may be, the Tyrones harbor grievances that are instantly recognizable: the failure of spouses and children to live up to expectations, the inevitable jealousy between siblings, the regrets and recriminations over dreams that have been shattered by time.

Except for Mary's return to drugs and the doctor's confirmation of Edmund's consumption, nothing actually happens in *Journey*; adhering to the Aristotelian Unities, O'Neill creates a drama that emphasizes character rather than plot (a fact that explains the play's appeal to a legion of fine actors). Confrontations between characters—involving accusations that are often hastily withdrawn or modified—form the building blocks of the first three acts. As the day progresses in linear fashion from early morning to night, the characters move in a circular pattern of memory through the past events that have brought them to their present plight. The emotional center of the work is Mary Tyrone, the most fully–realized female character in the O'Neill canon. Mary is the play's apostle of determinism, claiming that "none of us can help the things life has done to us", yet her constant complaints against her husband and sons reveal her belief in individual responsibility. The convent-educated Mary is trapped in a world for which she was never prepared; she retreats into reveries induced by drugs and spends the last moments of the play looking for her faith and the childhood innocence she has lost. A woman who chafes at the overwhelming familial demands placed upon her, and who imagines—albeit in a drug fantasy—a world in which she would have a story separate from that written by her male kin, Mary is one of O'Neill's most complex and theatrically compelling female creations.

The world of O'Neill's late plays is a painful one; men and women wander bewildered in a spiritual and emotional fog;

indeed they deliberately attempt to drown themselves in drugs or drink. But few of his characters wholly succeed in escaping their anguish, and the final act of *Journey* is composed of a series of confessions by the distraught Tyrone men. A self-educated immigrant whose fear of poverty conflicts with his concern for his family, Tyrone comes to understand how he has betrayed his own potential by wasting his talents in "the big money-maker" he starred in too long. Like many another O'Neill character, Jamie is a lost soul traveling on a path to self-destruction (a path O'Neill would trace more fully in his last play, *A Moon for the Misbegotten*, which focuses on Jamie). But even Jamie gains tragic stature as he confesses his attachment to his doomed mother and his jealousy of Edmund.

In a play that revolves around betrayal and blame, it is not wholly surprising to find a character accused of the crime of being born. Edmund's difficult birth was the immediate cause of his mother's addiction; he came into the world guilty of virtual matricide. In his guilt and guiltlessness, Edmund embodies O'Neill's interpretation of the concept of original sin, as well as his modern translation of the Greek sense of fate. Edmund, a young writer based on the playwright himself, is also the moral touchstone of the play. The only member of the family with the possibility for a future, he learns compassion for his less fortunate kin.

Journey is a beautifully structured play, moving inexorably through recriminations, confrontations and confessions to a stunning theatrical climax. The tragic counterpart to *Ah, Wilderness!*, O'Neill's sunny comedy of family life, *Journey* is an excoriating trip through a world where past mistakes circumscribe the present and destroy the future. But it is also, as O'Neill insisted in his dedication of *Long Day's Journey into Night* to his third wife, Carlotta, a work written "with deep pity and understanding and forgiveness for *all* the four haunted Tyrones".

—Judith E. Barlow

LOOK BACK IN ANGER
by John Osborne

First Publication: London and New York, 1957.
First Production: Royal Court Theatre, London, 8 May 1956.

Criticism
(For general works on the author, see *Playwrights* volume)

Books:
John R. Taylor (ed.), *"Look Back in Anger": A Casebook*, Nashville, Tennessee, 1970.

Articles:
Barbara Deming, "John Osborne's Man Against the Philistines", in *Hudson Review*, 11, 1959.
A.E. Dyson, *"Look Back in Anger"*, in *Critical Quarterly*, 1, 1959.
Samuel A. Weiss, "Osborne's Angry Young Play", in *Educational Theatre Journal*, 12, 1960.
Clive Barker, "*Look Back in Anger*—The Turning Point: An Assessment of the Importance of John Osborne's First Play in the Development of the British Theatre", in *Zeitschrift für Anglistik und Amerikanistik*, 14, 1966.
Dietrich Peinert, "'Bear' and 'Squirrel' in John Osborne's *Look Back in Anger*", in *Literatur in Wissenschaft und Unterricht*, 1, 1968.
Patricia Meyer Spacks, "Confrontation and Escape in Two Social Dramas", in *Modern Drama*, 11, 1968.
M.D. Faber, "The Character of Jimmy Porter: An Approach to *Look Back in Anger*", in *Modern Drama*, 13, 1970.
E.G. Bierhaus, "No World of Its Own: *Look Back in Anger* Twenty Years Later", in *Modern Drama*, 19, 1976.
John Ditsky, "Osborne's Gospel of Commitment: *Look Back in Anger*", in *Ariel*, vol.8 no.2, 1977.
Brian Murphy, "Jimmy Porter's Past: The Logic of Rage in *Look Back in Anger*", in *Midwest Quarterly*, 18, 1977.
Christine Gomez, "Bells and Trumpets, Bears and Squirrels: A Note on Some Recurring Images in *Look Back in Anger*", in *Scholar Critic*, 7–8, 1987.
Michelene Wandor, "Heroism, Crises of Manhood and the Kitchen Sink: *Look Back in Anger* and *A Patriot for Me* by John Osborne", in her *Look Back in Gender: Sexuality and the Family in Post-War British Drama*, London, 1987.
Robert G. Egan, "*Anger* and the Actor: Another Look Back", in *Modern Drama*, 32, 1989.

*   *   *

Look Back in Anger is a play dominated by its central character, Jimmy Porter. Jimmy is a product of post-war educational reform, a working-class graduate who had ideals (though these are never clearly articulated) that have been frustrated by the apparent inertia of British life in the 1950's. He marries into the upper-middle classes almost as an act of revenge and subjects his wife, Alison, to a continuous onslaught of bullying and abuse. Alison is weak, passive, and fence-sitting, and she absorbs his insults lamely, with the implication that he is emasculated by the soggy, genteel values of the English middle classes. The cramped flat in the English Midlands where they live is shared with Cliff, a mutual friend, who provides another unresponsive target for Jimmy's tirades.

In the second act, Alison's actress friend Helena arrives and encourages Alison to leave Jimmy, who is unaware that Alison is now pregnant. Helena's presence creates a new sexual dynamic. She is more able to stand up to Jimmy's abuse and her resistance to him is presented as the sexual charge that he needs to find some meaning in his life. Cliff leaves, the comfortable *ménage-à-trois* having been broken up, and Jimmy and Helena stay together for a time. However, much to Jimmy's fury, Helena is shown to believe in traditional moral values; she sees their relationship as wrongful and when Alison conveniently returns to the flat she makes way for Jimmy and Alison to be reconciled. Alison has now been through the pain of losing her baby. The experience is presented, ironically, as something positive. As she puts it, "This is what he's been longing for me to feel. . .I'm in the mud at last! I'm grovelling! I'm crawling!". Jimmy had earlier expressed the view that "anyone who's never watched someone die is suffering from a pretty bad case of virginity", he too has witnessed death, and a renewal of their relationship is now possible.

In 1956, when the play was first performed at the Royal Court Theatre in London, the character of Jimmy had a startling potency as the representative of a generation of disaffected British youth. His anger could be seen to capture a prevalent mood of the period as hopes for peace and plenty after the war faded into the drabness of the 1950's. However, part of the drabness here seems to be an inability to look back and pinpoint the cause of all the anger with any precision, or to look forward with any conviction or vision. Despite his university education, Jimmy chooses to run a sweet stall. This

Look Back in Anger: Royal Court Theatre, London, 1968 (English Stage Company)

can be understood as a gesture of protest against a society that has introduced reforms, such as wider access to education, without fundamentally altering its power base. The dominant values of society are still those of the old establishment, albeit in a state of terminal decline. This sense of social malaise was made all the more resonant, when the play was first performed in 1956, by Britain's bungling intervention in the Suez crisis that same year.

Since then, the play has been accorded an almost legendary status as a major landmark in post-war British theatre, defining the beginning of a period of writing by new, young playwrights, who often had a strong sense of social injustice. Such a view is certainly tendentious and liable to discount the work of companies like Unity Theatre Workshop who had consistently given voice to left-wing views from the 1930's onwards. Certainly, though, *Look Back in Anger* marks the emergence of the Royal Court Theatre, under the general direction of George Devine, as a major London venue for new writing. When, in 1956, an extract from the play was shown on

television, box-office takings suddenly took off and the consequent commercial success of the play (it was later made into a film with Richard Burton) showed that there was money to be made in new drama.

In retrospect the play seems fairly conventional despite the apparent newness of the subject matter, and Osborne himself admitted as much when he described it as "a formal, rather old-fashioned play". It is a three act drama written in the manner of the English well-made play. The dialogue is dominated by Jimmy, the action by naturalistic devices like ironing and reading the Sunday papers, and the location by the permanent setting of Jimmy's flat. Jimmy's marriage to Alison sets up a class conflict, but this is not really explored in any depth. It is an implicit assumption of the play that Jimmy's background makes him a person more vital and alive than Alison. By virtue of her class and gender, the latter is created as a character too weak to defend herself. Today the play has a glaring pre-feminist look to it; there is a total absence of any depth to female perspectives and Jimmy's mysogynistic views often seem suspiciously like those of Osborne himself.

In 1989 Osborne granted performance rights for the play to be revived by the English Renaissance Company in a production directed by Judi Dench, with Kenneth Branagh and Emma Thompson playing the parts of Jimmy and Alison. Critics tended to be divided about the success of the play's revival after 33 years. Jimmy was described by some as a self-pitying sentimentalist and, more heroically by Michael Billington, as "a man driven to madness by the unresponsive cool of those around him". The theme of anger and frustration had become less significant than the exploration of a power struggle between the sexes, for which a debt to Strindberg was suggested, and the influence of Eugene O'Neill was detected in the notion that pain and suffering validates human existence.

—Andy Piasecki

LORENZACCIO
by Alfred de Musset

First Publication: In *Un Spectacle dans un fauteuil, 1* (second edition), Paris, 1834.
First Production: Théâtre de la Renaissance, Paris, 3 December 1896.

Editions
Lorenzaccio, edited by Phyllis E. Crump, Manchester, 1941.
Lorenzaccio, edited by Jacques Nathan, Paris, c. 1941.
Lorenzaccio, in *Musset: Théâtre complet*, edited by Philippe van Tieghem, Paris, 1953.
Lorenzaccio, in *Musset: Théâtre complet*, edited by Maurice Allem, Paris, 1958.
La Genèse de "Lorenzaccio": Textes publiés avec introduction et notes, edited by Paul Dimoff.

Translations
Lorenzaccio, translated by E.B. Thompson, 1907.
Lorenzaccio, in *Musset: Seven Plays*, translated by Peter Meyer, New York, 1962.
Lorenzaccio, translated and adapted by John Fowles, London, 1983.

Criticism
(For general works on the author, see *Playwrights* volume)

Books:
Joachim-Claude Marmier, *Le Moment de "Lorenzaccio" dans le destin de Musset*, Athens, 1955.
Joyce Bromfield, *De Lorenzino de Medicis à Lorenzaccio: Étude d'un thème historique*, Paris, 1972.
Robert Horville, *"Lorenzaccio": Analyse critique*, Paris, 1972.
Bernard Masson, *Musset et le théâtre intérieur: Nouvelles Recherches sur "Lorenzaccio"*, Paris, 1974.
Ceri Crossley, *Musset: "Lorenzaccio"*, London, 1983.
J.-M. Thomasseau, *Alfred de Musset: "Lorenzaccio"*, Paris, 1986.
Ivan Barko and Bruce Burgess, *La Dynamique des points de vue dans le texte de théâtre: Analyses de points de vue—"Le Misanthrope"; "Le Mariage de Figaro"; "Lorenzaccio"; "En Attendant Godot"*, Paris, 1988.

Articles:

J. Ware, "Lorenzino dei Medici on the French Stage", in *Cornhill Magazine*, 66, 1929.
H.J. Hunt, "Alfred de Musset et la Révolution de Juillet: La Leçon politique de *Lorenzaccio*", in *Mercure de France*, 251, April 1934.
Joachim-Claude Merlant, "Rencontre d'une ombre d'un poète: Le *Lorenzaccio* d'Alfred de Musset", in *Bulletin de l'Université l'Aurore* (Shanghai) (third series), vol.7 no.1, 1946.
Lucien Leluc, "Le Vrai Lorenzaccio (1514–1515)", in *Le Monde Français*, vol.11 no.36, 1948.
Ettore Allodoli, "Il segreto di Lorenzino", in *Nuova antologia*, 367, 1950?
Ronald Grimsley, "The Character of Lorenzaccio", in *French Studies*, 11, 1957.
Eugene H. Falk, "Musset's *Lorenzaccio*", in *Drama Review*, 2, 1958.
Phillippe van Tieghem, "L'Évolution de Musset des débuts à *Lorenzaccio*", in *Revue d'histoire du théâtre*, 4, 1958.
André Lebois, "Analyse spectrale de *Lorenzaccio*", in *Littératures*, vol.10 no.1., 1961.
Jürgen von Stackelberg, "El *Lorenzaccio* de Alfred de Musset: Interpretación de un drama romántico", in *Finis Terrae* (Santiago, Chile), vol.10 no.38, 1963.
Robert T. Denommé, "The Motif of the *Poète maudit* in Musset's *Lorenzaccio*", in *L'Esprit créateur*, 5, 1965.
K. Hartley, "Three Lorenzacci", in *AUMLA Journal*, 28, 1967.
Pierre Nordon, "Alfred de Musset et l'Angleterre: *Lorenzaccio*", in *Lettres Romanes*, vol.21 no.3, 1967.
Steen Jansen, "L'Unité d'action dans *Andromaque* et dans *Lorenzaccio*", in *Revue Romane*, 3, 1968.
A. Callen, "The Place of *Lorenzaccio* in Musset's Theatre", in *Forum for Modern Language Studies* (St. Andrews), 5, 1969.
Bernard Dort, "Tentative de Description de Lorenzaccio", in *Travail théâtral*, 1, 1970.
L.A. Fiber, "The Masked Event in Musset's *Fantasio* and *Lorenzaccio*", in *French Review*, 45, 1972.
Jean-Marie Piemme, "*Lorenzaccio*, impasse d'une idéologie", in *Romantisme*, 1–2, 1972.
A. Callen, "Dramatic Construction in Musset's *Lorenzaccio*", in *Forum for Modern Language Studies* (St. Andrews), 9, 1973.
Raimund Rutten, "Individuum und Gesellschaft in Alfred de Mussets *Lorenzaccio*", in *Germanisch-Romanische Monatsschrift* (new series), 23, 1973.
Bernard Masson, "*Lorenzaccio* rendu au théâtre", in *L'Information littéraire*, 26, 1974.
Atle Kittang, "Action et langue dans *Lorenzaccio* d'Alfred de Musset", in *Revue romane*, vol.10 no.1, 1975.
Henning Mehnert, "Alfred de Mussets *Lorenzaccio* und die psychologisches Motivation des Dandy Dichters", in *Romantisches Jahrbuch*, 26, 1976.
Robert Abirached (ed.), "*Lorenzaccio* dans la mise-en-scène de Guy Retoré", in *L'Avant Scène* (special issue), 603, 1977.
W.J.S. Kirton, "The Importance of Family in *Lorenzaccio*", in *Trivium*, 12, 1978.
Walter Moser, "*Lorenzaccio*: Le Carnaval et le cardinal", in *Romantisme*, 19, 1978.
Jean-Jacques Thomas, "Le Vocabulaire de *Lorenzaccio*", in *Romantisme*, 19, 1978.
Marie Maclean, "The Sword and the Flower: The Sexual Symbolism of *Lorenzaccio*", in *Australian Journal of French Studies*, vol.16 no.2, 1979.

Jean Bemme, "*Lorenzaccio* entre l'histoire et le fantasme", in *Polétique*, vol.11 no.44, 1980.

Jules Bedner, "*Lorenzaccio* ou Oedipe à Florence", in *Neophilologus*, vol.67 no.1, 1983.

Barbara T. Cooper, "Staging a Revolution: Political Upheaval in *Lorenzaccio* and *Léo Burckart*", in *Romance Notes*, vol.24 no.1, 1983.

Jacqueline Machabéïs, "Propositions sur la structure de *Lorenzaccio*", in *Lettres Romanes*, vol. 38 nos. 1–2, 1984.

James F. Hamilton, "Mimetic Desire in Musset's *Lorenzaccio*", in *Kentucky Romance Quarterly*, vol.32 no.4, 1985.

Barbara T. Cooper, "Breaking Up/Down/Apart: *L'Eclatement* as a Unifying Principle in Musset's *Lorenzaccio*", in *Philological Quarterly*, vol.65 no.1, 1986.

Laurie F. Leach, "Lorenzo and the Noblest Roman: The Noble Assassins of *Lorenzaccio* and *Julius Caesar*", in *Romance Notes*, vol.28 no.3, 1988.

John W. MacInnes, "*Lorenzaccio* and the Drama of Narration", in *Text and Presentation*, edited by Karelisa Hartigan, Lanham, Maryland, 1988.

Thérèse Malachy, "*Lorenzaccio*: Du Meurtre politique au sacrifice rituel", in *Revue d'histoire du théâtre*, 40, 1988.

*　　*　　*

The plot centres on events of 1537 in Florence, when Lorenzo de Medici, known by the pejorative nickname of Lorenzaccio, assassinated the debauched and tyrannical ruler of the town, Duke Alessandro de Medici. Although resentment of Alessandro's corrupt and vicious behaviour is widespread among the noble families, the merchants, and other townspeople, Lorenzo's is a solitary act, performed for motives which remain unclear. He insinuates his way into the duke's court, becoming a despised henchman and pandering to Alessandro's lecherous excesses, in order to win the tyrant's confidence. When finally he carries out the murder, he announces it as an opportunity for the people of Florence, notably the republicans led by the Strozzi family, to replace the duke with a ruler of their choice. This does not happen. The respected Philippe Strozzi fails to rally the opposition, Cosimo de Medici is sworn in as Alessandro's successor and Lorenzo, who has been sceptical all along about the value of his act, is struck down by a bounty-hunter.

Varchi's chronicle on which the play draws was brought to Musset's attention via an adaptation by George Sand, who had used it in writing a *scène historique* typical of the vogue for historical reconstructions current among Romantics of the 1830's. Following the same pattern, that is with no intention of producing a work for the stage (he had in any case foresworn the theatre since the disastrous failure of his first play in 1830), Musset wrote what is probably the finest of French romantic dramas, and certainly the one which has best withstood the test of time. He was influenced, like many of his generation, by Shakespeare; but he is alone in creatively assimilating a dramatic method which contrasts sharply with the standard techniques passed down by French Classical tragedy. The play's loose, episodic structure embraces the whole range of Florentine society and encompasses a number of parallel subplots, integrating them into the story of Lorenzo with remarkable economy and sureness of rhythm, and especially through the achievement of a striking poetic coherence. One feature of the work's originality lies in its creation of a collective protagonist: it presents the drama of a community. The merchants are shown complaining about Alessandro's abuses of power while they are seen to be commercially tied into the regime through their trade; the bystanders jostled and scorned in the street by the aristocratic guests leaving their opulent amusements are nevertheless fascinated by the glamour of decadence; the young girls seduced in the course of the duke's nocturnal escapades become corrupt accomplices in his debauchery. Through such incidents the town as a whole is depicted as having succumbed to the baleful influence of evil. The recurring motif of Florence as a denatured mother whose feminine virtue has been perverted is mirrored in the story of the high-minded Marquise Cibo. She compromises in her resistance to Alessandro's advances in the hope that by sacrificing her honour she will gain privileged access to the Duke, thereby securing an opportunity to convince him of the need to change his ways. Needless to say he proves deaf to her pleas and she becomes a pawn in the machinations of her brother-in-law, the Cardinal Cibo, who is scheming to reassert papal authority. Against this background Musset charts the failure of the champions of republicanism: Pierre Strozzi's uprising is completely ineffectual, and the head of the family, Philippe, capitulates to despair following the murder of his daughter Louise. This aspect of the play graphically denounces the bankruptcy of liberal, humanist values in the face of brutality and violence.

The authenticity and impact of these portrayals owe a great deal to the analogy which was in Musset's mind with the failure of the revolution of July 1830 in France. There too the people had risen up against the excesses of an authoritarian regime; there too the republican movement was betrayed by the spinelessness of its leaders who allowed themselves to be outflanked by the Orleanists: the toppling of the Bourbons led only to a change of dynasty rather than the overthrow of the regime. The demoralisation this failure bred among young Romantic intellectuals is also one of the starting points for the characterization of Lorenzaccio himself, which is perhaps the play's most poignant and strikingly modern feature. Presented at the outset as something of an enigma to those around him, he appears successively as decadent, effeminate, and amoral. He is insolent, but faints at the prospect of a duel. His mother laments the waste of the great gifts he showed in his youth. But this is merely outward display, for Lorenzo has determined to adopt the mask of infamy in the pursuit of his plan to kill the duke and liberate the people of Florence. However, in ministering to Alessandro's corrupt urges, he has seen a side of humanity which has disenchanted him; he has lost his reason for acting, and the cloak of vice he originally donned as a disguise has become integral to his personality. The validity of idealistic ends pursued through cynical means is thus called into question. At the same time, the very notion of human identity becomes problematical as Lorenzo loses all sense of a consistent self within his being. The discontinuities introduced into his life by the roles he has played, and which have now become second nature to him, leave him contemplating an existential void. His planned assassination has all but lost its original motivation, though Lorenzo clings to it as the last strand linking him to his former self and his former virtue. But he can no longer be sure what drives him on: is it personal ambition, family honour, patriotic idealism, temperamental instability, warped moral sense, or the pursuit of a nihilistic notoriety? Lorenzo's anguish is explored in a series of brilliant soliloquies in Act IV which constitutes one of the play's high points and which reveals once more the debt to Shakespeare, most notably to *Hamlet*. But the writing is far from being merely derivative; these speeches show Musset's highly imaginative, psychological penetration at its most original, and effect a marked shift in the audience's perspective from neutrality, puzzlement, or antipathy in the earlier parts of the play to an intense sympathy for the tragic hero.

The play's vast dimensions—39 scenes, and a multiplicity of locations—were well beyond the staging possibilities of its time and it was over 60 years before the work was presented to a theatre audience. Sarah Bernhardt played Lorenzo in her 1896 production which adapted the text to achieve a fairly conventional format. A slightly more faithful version was performed by Mme Falconetti in 1925, exploiting the flexibility afforded by some of the most advanced set designs of the day; and in 1927 a four-tableau adaptation was put on at the Comédie-Française in Paris. It became customary in these first productions for actresses to play Lorenzo, which is in keeping with the sexual ambivalence of the character and much of the dominant imagery in the text. It was not until Gérard Philippe played the lead in 1952 that the role began to be seen as more plausibly masculine. One of the most notable productions of recent years was that of the Czech director Otomar Krejca, which was brought to Paris in 1970. The Royal Shakespeare Company mounted a Brechtian-inspired production of *The Lorenzaccio Story*, loosely based on Musset's text, in 1978; and in 1983, Michael Bogdanov, using a translation by John Fowles, staged a highly effective version at the National Theatre in London.

—David H. Walker

LOVE FOR LOVE
by William Congreve

First Publication: London, 1695.
First Production: Lincoln's Inn Fields Theatre, London, 30
    April 1695.

Editions
Love for Love, in *Comedies by William Congreve*, edited by
    Bonamy Dobrée, Oxford, 1925.
Love for Love, edited by Emmett L. Avery, Lincoln,
    Nebraska, 1966 (Regents Restoration Drama Series).
Love for Love, in *The Complete Plays of William Congreve*,
    edited by Herbert Davis, Chicago, 1967.
Love for Love, edited by M.M. Kelsall, London, 1969 (New
    Mermaid Series).
Love for Love, in *The Comedies of William Congreve*, edited
    by Anthony J. Henderson, Cambridge, 1982.
Love for Love, in *The Comedies of William Congreve*, edited
    by Eric S. Rump, Harmondsworth, 1985.

Criticism
(For general works on the author, see *Playwrights* volume)

Articles:
John B. Hodges, "The Ballad in Congreve's *Love for Love*",
    in *Publications of the Modern Language Association*
    [*PMLA*], 48, 1933.
Edward A. Norris, "A Possible Origin of Congreve's Sailor
    Ben", in *Modern Language Notes*, 49, 1934.
Arthur L. Cooke, "Two Parallels between Dryden's *Wild
    Gallant* and Congreve's *Love for Love*", in *Notes and
    Queries*, 199, 1954.
Anthony Gosse, "The Omitted Scene in Congreve's *Love for
    Love*", in *Modern Philology*, 61, 1963.
Charles R. Lyons, "Congreve's Miracle of Love", in *Criticism*,
    6, 1965.
Barry N. Olshen, "Early Nineteenth Century Revisions of
    Love for Love", in *Theatre Notebook*, 24, 1970.

Love for Love: Engraving, 1776

F.P. Jarvis, "The Philosophical Assumptions of Congreve's
    Love for Love", in *Texas Studies in Literature and Language*,
    14, 1972.
Aubrey Williams, "The 'Utmost Trial' of Virtue and Congreve's
    Love for Love", in *Tennessee Studies in Literature*,
    17, 1972.
Arthur W. Hoffman, "Allusions and the Definition of Themes
    in Congreve's *Love for Love*", in *The Author in His Work:
    Essays on a Problem in Criticism*, edited by Louis L. Martz
    and Aubrey Williams, New Haven, Connecticut, 1978.
James Thompson, "A Dance from *Love for Love*", in *Notes
    and Queries*, 25, 1978.
James Thompson, "Reading and Acting in *Love for Love*", in
    Essays in Literature, 7, 1980.
Maximillian E. Novak, "Foresight in the Stars and Scandal in
    London: Reading the Hieroglyphics in Congreve's *Love for
    Love*", in *From Renaissance to Restoration: Metamorphoses
    of the Drama*, edited by Robert Markley and Laurie Finke,
    Cleveland, Ohio, 1984.

*   *   *

The plot of *Love for Love*, as Northrop Frye pointed out, follows the comic Oedipus formula of Greek new comedy: the debt-ridden young wit, Valentine Legend, is in love with Angelica and wishes to marry her, but must overcome the opposition of his father, Sir Sampson, who plans to disinherit him in favor of his younger brother, Ben, a sailor, because of

Valentine's history of extravagant and dissolute behavior. This is, then, a distinctly late 17th–century new comedy. Sir Sampson intends to shore up the family fortunes by marrying Ben to Miss Prue, the daughter of Foresight, a wealthy neighbor and amateur astrologer. Foresight is so busy thinking about the stars that he ignores his young, second wife, leaving her to the attention of young men about town like Valentine's friend Scandal. Mrs. Foresight's sister, Mrs. Frail, has her eye on the Legend heir (whichever brother prevails), and the foppish Tattle would like to steal Angelica. Ultimately, Valentine escapes disinheritance and wins Angelica; Tattle and Mrs. Frail fall victim to their own intrigues, unwittingly marrying each other in disguise; Ben, never a willing opponent, returns to the life at sea he prefers; and Miss Prue must wait a little longer for the husband she craves.

What is especially interesting about *Love for Love*, however, is its differences from more formulaic plays. It is a play full of tricks and intrigues; they provide most of the action. But trickery invariably fails, and the successful union of the lovers comes about, instead, from the counter-plotting of the enigmatic Angelica. Valentine first tries to win her by extravagant expense. When his money runs out, he switches to tricks, most notably his plan to outwit his father and win Angelica through pretended madness: a madman cannot legally sign away his inheritance; and since his madness results from love, the object of that love must be moved to pity. But Angelica sees through the ruse, and counters with her own trick; she agrees to marry Sir Sampson and provide him with a new heir to replace his recalcitrant sons. Realising that all is lost, Valentine abandons his schemes and offers to forego his inheritance. Angelica surprises everyone by suddenly accepting the "generous Valentine" since he has passed "this utmost trial" of his "virtue". In preferring the values implicit in his title, Congreve rewrites the traditional love game of earlier comedy for the 1690's. It is Valentine's sincerity, constancy, and generosity which prove that his love is worthy of Angelica's. Even the libertine Scandal claims to be converted by her "exemplary justice in punishing an inhuman father, and rewarding a faithful lover". Relationships based on intrigue (Scandal and Mrs. Foresight) and trickery (Tattle and Mrs. Frail) on the one hand, and arranged marriages (Ben and Prue) or mercenary ones (the Foresights) on the other, offer pointed contrasts to the exemplary union between Valentine and Angelica.

Love for Love was the first production of the new company formed by Thomas Betterton with Elizabeth Barry and Anne Bracegirdle in 1695. It was an immediate success, and, despite the offense it gave to Jeremy Collier and the absence of a role that appealed to Garrick, remained Congreve's most popular play throughout the 18th century. It is Congreve's most immediately accessible play, and one that displays his major strengths as a dramatist. The characters are fine vehicles for actors: Thomas Dogget as Ben is said to have made the greatest single contribution to the success of the initial production; Valentine offered Betterton a romantic hero with abundant wit; Mrs. Bracegirdle's Angelica helped confirm her pre-eminence as the witty, chaste virgin; Elizabeth Barry was given a fine example of one of her specialities, the comic, fallen woman, Mrs. Frail. *Congreve*'s dialogue sparkles with distinctive language and figures of speech for each individual character. There is abundant wit, directed largely at the fashionable vices that are the traditional targets of high social comedy. The humorous characters are well distinguished and effectively incorporated in a well-constructed plot. Add to this an atypical (for Congreve) simplicity and clarity—due perhaps to the relative conventionality of the plot—and the contemporary popularity of *Love for Love* is not surprising.

It was first revived in the 20th century by the Stage Society in London in 1917, and has regained its place as a staple of the repertory ever since. Particularly memorable productions were staged by Tyrone Guthrie at the Old Vic, 1934, John Gielgud, 1943, and Peter Wood at the National Theatre, 1965.

—Brian Corman

LOVE'S LABOUR'S LOST
by William Shakespeare

First Publication: London, 1598.
First Production: London, c.1594?

Editions
Love's Labour's Lost (second edition), edited by H.H. Furness, Philadelphia, 1906 (New Variorum Shakespeare).
Love's Labour's Lost, edited by John Arthos, New York, 1965 (Signet Classic Shakespeare).
Love's Labour's Lost, edited by Alfred Harbage, Baltimore, Maryland, 1963; revised edition, Baltimore, Maryland, 1973 (Pelican Shakespeare).
Love's Labour's Lost, edited by R.W. David, London, 1968 (Arden Shakespeare)
Love's Labour's Lost, edited by John Kerrigan, Harmondsworth, 1982 (New Penguin Shakespeare).
Love's Labour Lost, edited by G.R. Hibbard, London, 1989.

Bibliography
Nancy Lenz Harvey and Anna Kirwan Carey (eds.), *"Love's Labour's Lost": An Annotated Bibliography*, New York, 1984 (Garland Shakespeare Bibliographies).

Criticism
(For general works on the author, see *Playwrights* volume)

Books:
Herbert A. Ellis, *Shakespeare's Lusty Punning in "Love's Labour's Lost": With Contemporary Analogues*, The Hague, 1973.
William C. Carroll, *The Great Feast of Language in "Love's Labour's Lost"*, Princeton, New Jersey, 1976.
Louis Adrian Montrose, *"Curious-Knotted Garden": The Form, Themes, and Contexts of Shakespeare's "Love's Labour's Lost"*, Salzburg, 1977.
Laurie Lanzen Harris and Mark W. Scott (eds.), *"Love's Labour's Lost"*, in *Shakespearian Criticism, 2*, Detroit, Illinois, 1985 [anthology of criticism].

Articles:
For information on the many articles about *Love's Labour's Lost*, see Harvey and Carey's bibliography, the bibliographies listed in the *Playwrights* volume, and the annual Shakespeare Bibliography in *Shakespeare Quarterly*, published by the Folger Shakespeare Library, Washington D.C. (1950–).

*   *   *

The King of Navarre and three noble companions decide to win fame by academic study. They swear to study for three

Love's Labour's Lost: Stratford-Upon-Avon, 1978 (Royal Shakespeare Company)

years under strict rules, one of which forbids them to see any woman during that time. But the prearranged visit of the Princess of France about some disputed lands means that this rule must be immediately broken. The king and princess meet, although not within the court, and agree to meet again to finish their negotiations. Meanwhile the lords and the ladies accompanying the princess have recognized each other, and the king has fallen in the love with the princess. Berowne sends a letter to his love, Rosaline. He catches his fellow votaries reciting sonnets to their loves, but is in turn betrayed when his letter is discovered. They all agree to abandon their vows and woo the women instead. After sending them favours they visit them disguised as Russians. Forewarned by Boyet, the women mask themselves and wear each other's favours, with the result that the men swear their love to the wrong partners. The women mock them for breaking their vows again, and together they watch a masque performed by the comic hangers-on. The revels are interrupted by a messenger announcing the death of the princess's father, and the play ends with the couples separated for a year. The women give the men penances which they must perform before they can claim their loves.

Love's Labour's Lost resembles Shakespeare's other comedies in some important ways. As often, the men understand themselves less well than the women; they are ready to do anything for love except take it seriously, and the women, more strong-minded and independent, will not accept them until they have learned this lesson. Shakespeare commonly allows his ignorant and humble characters to score over the educated and arrogant. In this play the "unlettered" clown, Costard, is wiser than the pedant, Holofernes, or the nobles who would be scholars; he puts down the elegant Boyet, and it is he and the dairymaid Jaquenetta who, in the name of truth, expose Berowne's hypocrisy. The pretentious soldier, Armado, is no match for the direct wit of his companion, the boy Moth. Structurally the masque of the nine worthies at the end of the play recalls the mechanicals' interlude at the end of *A Midsummer Night's Dream*. Both performances are inept, and both are mocked by a socially superior audience.

In most respects, however, *Love's Labour's Lost* stands alone. It is perhaps the most intellectual of the comedies, and it partly owes this distinction to its exceptionally slight plot, which allows Shakespeare to develop to the full his principal themes of love, language, reality, and the imagination—themes which themselves are inseparable from the question of freedom and its limits. Shakespeare increased this sense of liberty, which is one of the play's greatest delights, by refusing to tie it to a well-defined society or place. Nominally it is set in the royal court of Navarre, but there is no attempt to reproduce Navarre, and the court is more like an informal house-party. The little that we are told in fact suggests an English country house, with its "curious knotted garden", deer park, lodge, dairy, and neighbouring manor house. Social hierarchy and organization, so important in the other comedies, hardly exist in this free space. The king does not so much rule as preside over the proceedings of a club (one not unlike the Pickwick Club). He dictates the rules of the "little academe", but they are shown to be absurd, first by Berowne, and then by the "swain" Costard, who shows no respect for his betters. It is typical of this world that Armado, the "refined traveller of Spain", who has "a mint of phrases in his brain", should be hopelessly in love with the almost speechless dairymaid and finally get a child by her.

In its blithe disregard for the ties of plot and place the play can be seen as an early example of the genre of comic fantasy. Like other examples of the genre—Lewis Carroll's Alice books or the plays of Samuel Beckett—it is dominated by the idea of death. Like them, it is at once displaced and rooted in the familiar; fantastic and down-to-earth, intellectual and yet strongly physical. The intellectual clowns, for example, are both real and symbolic. Locked in their eccentricity, Nathaniel, Holofernes, and Armado are dire warnings of what the nobles might become if they kept their vows to study. At the same time, like the characters in Carroll's Wonderland, their eccentricity is utterly their own and has its own grandeur. Much of their comic effect—and in this they reflect the play as a whole—lies in the gap between their high aims and their very mundane reality. This effect is partly physical. It is best conveyed by the gestures and body language of a stage performance. Only there do the clowns (and there are six or seven of them) come into their own.

As the play begins, the nobles are free, but they do not know what to do with their freedom. Living in one fantasy world, their first impulse is to create another. They are "merely players" in the related senses of games-players and actors. The play is full of references to games: the "old infant play" of "all hid", push-pin, dicing, tennis, flapdragon, the spinning of tops. These games are governed by traditional rules. In the game of "little academe" the nobles make up their own rules, and act their parts without an audience. Wooing will be a harder game to play, for they will be faced by an opposing team who are also a critical audience. Here we encounter the play's central paradox. The women are, like a real audience, both critical and encouraging. If the men have been false to themselves in falling in love, the women have not discouraged them. As Berowne says, "Our love being yours, the error that love makes / Is likewise yours". The women make the men both false and true, and both are equally necessary. Their union is seen in the penance that Rosaline gives Berowne—to use his wit to make the dying laugh. From its first line the play has moved towards this example of fantasy tested against harsh reality.

—Roger Prior

LOVE'S LAST SHIFT; or, The Fool in Fashion
by Colley Cibber

First Publication: London, 1696.
First Production: Theatre Royal, Drury Lane, London, January 1696.

Editions

Love's Last Shift, in *Plays of the Restoration and Eighteenth Century*, edited by D. MacMillan and H.M. Jones, New York, 1931.
Love's Last Shift, in *Representative English Dramas from Dryden to Sheridan*, edited by F. and J.W. Tupper, New York, 1934.
Love's Last Shift, in *Colley Cibber: Three Sentimental Comedies*, edited by Maureen Sullivan, New Haven, Connecticut, 1973.
Love's Last Shift, in *The Plays of Colley Cibber* (2 vols.), edited by Rodney L. Hayley, New York and London, 1980.

Criticism

(For general works on the author, see *Playwrights* volume)

Articles:
Dougald MacMillan, "The Text of *Love's Last Shift*", in *Modern Language Notes*, 46, 1931.
Paul E. Parnell, "Equivocation in Cibber's *Love's Last Shift*", in *Studies in Philology*, 57, 1960.
Byrne R.S. Fone, "Colley Cibber's *Love's Last Shift* and Sentimental Comedy", in *Restoration and Eighteenth Century Theatre Research*, 7, 1968.
Byrne R.S. Fone, "*Love's Last Shift* and Sentimental Comedy", in *Restoration and Eighteenth Century Theatre Research*, 9, 1970.
Alan Roper, "Language and Action in *The Way of the World*, *Love's Last Shift*, and *The Relapse*", in *English Literary History*, 40, 1973.
Helga Drougge, "Colley Cibber's *Genteel Comedy*", in *Studia Neophilologica*, vol.54 no.1, 1982.
Derek Hughes, "Cibber and Vanbrugh: Language, Place and Social Order in *Love's Last Shift*", in *Comparative Drama*, vol.20 no.4, 1986–87.

*   *   *

The first major attack on the alleged depiction of loose and immoral behaviour in Restoration Comedy appeared in Jeremy Collier's famous *View of the Immorality and Profaneness of the English Stage* of 1698. It was not that there had not been signs of a Puritan backlash against the post-Restoration celebration of excess before this time; rather that with the accession of William and Mary, and thus the removal of the previous Stuart royal patronage, it became a less problematic, public utterance. Public taste was changing before Collier's attack created an umbrella for such change, and there is no better example of this than Colley Cibber's first play *Love's Last Shift* which received its first performances at Drury Lane two years before the *View* was published. As he was to do throughout his multi-faceted theatrical career Cibber showed from the outset an acute sense of what the audience wanted, and with this first play he offered them what was quickly heralded as the first of a new theatrical kind, the sentimental comedy; a kind that here depended more than any of its successors on the Restoration Comedy model it supposedly opposed.

Unsurprisingly this first play draws heavily from the by now well-settled machinery of the post-Restoration tradition; there is even a fop figure, Sir Novelty Fashion, who is descended in a straight line from Etherege's Sir Fopling Flutter in *The Man of Mode* and the initial plot lines seem little different from what had been on offer previously. As so often there is a double-plot—audience interest in narrative complexity by no means having lessened—each strand of which is concerned with the general theme of courtship and marriage. In the main plot Loveless decides to abandon his wife Amanda, although there are already signs of the twist in the tale when we learn that his decision is based on the modern premise that no man of honour can continue to love his wife on the instalment of a new mistress. He is the "fool in fashion" of the play's sub-title and it will be fashion and not adultery that will initiate the action. Once he has been (falsely) informed of his wife's death, he sets about acquiring a new mistress who in the last act he beds; only to have discovered to him that he has in effect been "robbing his own orchard" and that his bed-fellow is in reality the disguised and still very much alive Amanda playing the whore in "love's last shift". The deception revealed, Amanda upbraids her husband for his inhumane treatment of her and, moved (as were the first night audience) to tears, Loveless repents: "your words are utter'd with such a powerful Heart, they have awaken'd my Soul, and strike my thoughts with Horror and Remorse". His conscience awakened, Loveless ends the play with an absurdly improbable praise of married life and a diatribe against philandering.

The theme is paralleled in reverse in the other main plot in which a would-be flirt, Hillaria, receives moral instruction and respectable happiness in marriage from the worthy older man, the Elder Worthy. In both cases morality is seen to prevail over licence, but it is not difficult to observe, as many contemporaries did, that what Cibber was actually offering his audiences was in fact four acts of conventional Restoration Comedy titillation with a fifth act of moral reformation tacked somewhat awkwardly on to suit the changing tastes of the time; and certainly there can be little doubt that without the continual interventions of Sir Novelty Fashion, a satirised figure of the old order, there would be little to hold the interest.

But this deployment of the fop stereotype helps to point to what was genuinely novel about what Cibber, however cynically, was attempting. With the exception of Sir Novelty Fashion, the characters in the play do not exist as those peculiar mixtures of celebration and satire that was usually the case in earlier Restoration comedies. The resolution of both plot-strands depends upon a presentation of the characters as having gone through a process of education, and allows for their depiction at the end of the play as moral examples to be taken as role models—and as moral examples in which the sentimental qualities of compassion and fidelity are united with those of common sense and reason, a definite move away from the excesses of a court-dominated world towards the tighter confines of bourgeois conformity.

Nevertheless, the play, for all its historical significance, really did not hold together and one man in particular, the playwright Vanbrugh, remained unconvinced that the newly patched-up marriage between Loveless and Amanda would stagger very successfully into a sixth act. That same year he produced a sequel, *The Relapse*, in which Loveless does successfully commit adultery. One of the most successful features of Vanbrugh's play was the reworking of Sir Novelty Fashion (who now becomes Lord Foppington, under which guise he attempts to seduce the betrayed Amanda), and it says much about the sincerity of Cibber's original intent in *Love's Last Shift* that it was he who was so brilliantly to act the part of Lord Foppington in the sequel.

—John Bull

THE LOWER DEPTHS (Na Dne)
by Maxim Gorky

First Publication: Munich, 1903; first Russian publication, St. Petersburg, 1903.
First Production: Moscow Arts Theatre, Moscow, 18 December 1902.

Translations
The Lower Depths, translated by L. Irving, London and New York, 1912.
The Lower Depths, translated by E. Hopkins, in *Chief Contemporary Dramatists*, edited by T.H. Dickinson, Boston, 1921.
The Lower Depths, translated by J. Covan, New York, 1922.
The Lower Depths, in *Maxim Gorky: Seven Plays*, translated by A. Bakshy and Paul S. Nathan, New Haven, Connecticut, 1945; second edition, 1946.
The Lower Depths, in *Maxim Gorky: Five Plays*, translated by Margaret Wettlin, Moscow, 1956.
The Lower Depths, in *"The Storm" and Other Russian Plays*, translated by David Magarshack, New York, 1960.
The Lower Depths, translated by Kitty Hunter-Blair and Jeremy Brooks, London, 1973.

Criticism
(For general works on the author, see *Playwrights* volume)

Articles:
Charles I. Glicksberg, "The Truth of Life [*The Lower Depths*]", in his *The Ironic Vision in Modern Literature*, The Hague, 1969.
B.K. Roy, "*Lower Depths* or Dehumanised Humanity: Working Peoples and the Problems of Alienation in Gorky's Plays", in *Journal of the School of Languages*, vol. 1 no. 2, 1973–74.
Heinz Bendiks, "Einige Aspekte textsemantischer Analyse des Dramas *Na dne* von Maksim Gor'kij", in *Sowjetische Bühnenautoren: Gorkij, Rozov, Majakovskij, Amalrik*, edited by Irene Nowikowa, Hamburg, 1979.
Wolfgang Gesemann, "Seelenfänger bei Maksim Gor'kij und Ivan Klíma: Ein komparatives Theatermotiv", in *Wiener slawistischer Almanach*, vol. 28 no. 2, 1983.
Sumie Jones, "*The Lower Depths*: Gorky, Stanislavsky, and Kurosawa", in *Explorations: Essays in Comparative Literature*, edited by Makoto Ueda, Lanham, Maryland, 1986.
Carl Stief, "The Young Gor'kij and 'The Exalting Illusion' '", in *Text and Context: Essays to Honor Nils Åke Nilsson*, Stockholm, 1987.
Geir Kjetsaa, "Ambivalence in Attitude: The Character of Luka in *The Lower Depths*", in *Russian Literature*, 24, 1988.

*   *   *

Set in and around a dosshouse, run by the sanctimonious Mikhail Kostyliov and his vicious wife, Vasilisa, *The Lower Depths* depicts an assortment of derelicts struggling to survive at the very bottom of society. (The Russian title literally means "At the Bottom"). The inmates are all victims of personal misfortune or weakness (broken marriages, imprisonment, gambling, drinking, aversion to work), or of society's indifference and injustice. A glimmer of hope enters these static and sordid lives with the arrival of Luka, an enigmatic, 60-year-old palmer or pilgrim. Luka consoles the dying Anna with the promise of peace in paradise, advises the thief, Pepel, to marry Natasha (Vasilisa's sister) and start a new life in distant

The Lower Depths: Stanislavsky, centre, as Satin, Moscow Art Theatre, 1902

Siberia, supports the prostitute Nastya in her tearful fantasies about "true love", and encourages the Actor to stop drinking by promising to reveal the address of a hospital for alcoholics. Anna duly dies, comforted by Luka. Late in Act III, however, Pepel is arrested after accidentally killing Kostyliov in a violent skirmish, and Luka departs (as he has forewarned) on further wanderings.

The final act is dominated by Satin, once an educated telegraphist, now a hard-drinking cardsharp (after nearly five years in prison, for defending his sister and murdering a scoundrel). Satin denounces Luka's "consoling lie" and demeaning pity, and demands respect for "Man" in a grandiloquent, humanist hymn: "Man is the truth! . . .Everything is in Man, everything is for Man! Only Man exists, everything else is the work of his hands and his brain! Ma-an! It's magnificent! It sounds so . . . proud! . . .". Upon hearing these words the alcoholic Actor, deprived of his last hope or illusion, hurries out and hangs himself.

The Lower Depths, Gorky's most famous and most ambiguous play, was a phenomenal success when first performed at the Moscow Arts Theatre on 18 December 1902. The production, by Stanislavsky and Nemirovich-Danchenko, with sets by Simov, aspired to maximum authenticity and meticulous realism. Having already reflected his first-hand experience of tramps and vagabonds in short stories such as *Chelkash* (1895), *Konovalov* (1896) and *Byvshie lyudi* (*Ex-People*, 1897), Gorky now dramatised this "philosophic swan-song of the social outcast" (as described by Richard Hare in *Maxim Gorky*, 1962) before professing his new faith in socialism. To aid Stanislavsky, Gorky provided photographs of typical *bosyaki* (barefooted tramps); many of the characters had real-life prototypes. After exploring the dosshouses of Moscow's Khitrov Market, Stanislavsky—who had previously noted the play's special brand of "new romanticism, and pathos that bordered on both theatricality and sermonising"—perceived its "spiritual essence" as "freedom at any price!". Photographs vividly record that first Moscow production: rags and plank-beds in a sunless cellar; Moskvin's beguiling Luka, bald and bearded; Kachalov's blank-eyed Baron, bemused and buffeted; Knipper's forlorn Nastya; Stanislavsky's weary Satin, tipsily protesting.

The novelty of the play's subject-matter, and its powerfully naturalistic presentation, captivated audiences from Berlin and London to Paris and New York. The stark depiction of tramps caused some offence; one Petersburg reviewer in 1903 complained of being plunged into a "cesspit". Controversy immediately focused on the play's interpretation. Gorky was not an "objective" writer, in the Chekhovian mould; he liked to teach and preach. *The Lower Depths* was never intended as neutral reportage.

Although Gorky explained in 1928 that Satin's humanistic speeches implied a "call to insurrection", this political message was weakened by the unexpectedness of Satin's outbursts, delivered belatedly by a shadowy, inebriated character (and moreover, the censor had excised various crude expressions and outspoken phrases). Gorky realised that Satin appeared pale and unconvincing as a spokesman for revolution, and Stanislavsky felt uncomfortable in tackling the role. The issue was further clouded by Moskvin's crafty and colourful Luka, who impressed many spectators as a lovable, grandfatherly figure embodying popular wisdom, Christian charity, and compassion.

Despite its socio-political implications, the play seems essentially a philosophical one. These "naked" men, without the props of status and possessions, endlessly debate human dignity, and the merits of truth and lies, reality and illusion. Luka rejects objective "truth", responding evasively to questions about God's existence, the afterlife, and his own dubious past. He encourages Nastya's fantasies, and fabricates a hospital for alcoholics. His pity brings no salvation: Anna dies (somewhat comforted), Nastya's plight persists, and (most damningly, at the play's finale, foreshadowed by Luka's cautionary parable in Act III) the Actor commits suicide on discovering Luka's deception. It seems that, at best, Luka provides temporary consolation; at worst, he sows death and destruction. Gorky's own comments, from 1903 to 1932, condemned Luka with increasing vehemence as not only a compassionate liar, inwardly cold like Lev Tolstoy, but also a harmful rogue. Nevertheless, the central ambiguity remains, for Gorky was susceptible to the allure of religion and dream, and never fully discredited Luka within the actual play.

The Lower Depths has been aptly described by Dan Levin as "a strange, troublesome, undramatic drama; a confused sermon, a moral allegory which by its nature almost defies any form" (in *Stormy Petrel*, 1967). Chekhov's influence may be sensed in the loosening of conventional dramatic action, the ensemble orchestration, and the frequent philosophising; also, perhaps, in the basic structure, moving from arrival to departure, morning to night, with one act set out of doors. Lengthy speeches are rare; the dialogue unfolds in terse, disjointed, unfinished utterances, whose language is pungent, colloquial, and aphoristic. The characters—abusive, self-pitying, pathetic, comic—are both alive and allegorical, ranging from the cynically hopeless (Bubnov, the Baron) to the only "working man", seething with impotent fury (Kleshch). The second act brilliantly interweaves disparate motifs: games of cards and draughts, a prison-song, Luka dispensing hope and comfort. Act IV need not appear anti-climactic: it recapitulates and clarifies the main theme and milieu (Luka's effect upon the dosshouse collective). In comparison, the hierarchical "love-plot", involving Kostyliov, Vasilisa, Pepel, and Natasha, seems melodramatic and almost irrelevant, scarcely meriting a mention in the final act.

The Lower Depths remains vibrantly alive. It has been filmed twice—by Jean Renoir (*Les Bas-fonds*, 1936) and Kurosawa (1957)—and frequently staged. With its derelicts and their dilemmas (loneliness, aimlessness, waiting, hoping), it prefigures such plays as O'Neill's *The Iceman Cometh*, Beckett's *Waiting for Godot*, and Pinter's *The Caretaker*.

—Gordon McVay

LUCES DE BOHEMIA. See **THE LIGHTS OF BOHEMIA.**

LUDUS COVENTRIAE. See **N-TOWN PLAYS.**

THE LULU PLAYS
 Earth-Spirit (Der Erdgeist)
 Pandora's Box (Die Büchse der Pandora)
by Frank Wedekind

Lulu [version of both plays]
First Publication: Munich, 1913; original manuscript (the "Ur-Pandora"), entitled *Die Büchse der Pandora*, Hamburg, 1988.

Earth-Spirit (Der Erdgeist)
First Publication: Paris, Leipzig, and Munich, 1895.
First Production: Theatersaal der Krystall-Palast, Leipzig (Leipziger litterarische Gesellshcaft), 25 February 1898.

Pandora's Box (Die Büchse der Pandora)
First Publication: In *Die Insel*, vol.3 no.10, 1902 [includes acts IV and V of the "Ur-Pandora"]; revised version, Berlin, 1904; further revised version, Berlin, 1906; stage version, Munich, 1911.
First Production: Intimes Theater, Nuremberg, 1 February 1904.

Translations
Earth-Spirit, translated by S.A Eliot, New York, 1914.
Pandora's Box, translated by S.A. Eliot, New York, 1914.
Earth Spirit and *Pandora's Box*, in *Five Tragedies of Sex*, translated by Stephen Spender, London, 1952; reprinted as *The Lulu Plays and Other Sex Tragedies*, 1972.
The Lulu Plays, translated by C.R. Mueller, Greenwich, Connecticut, 1967.
Lulu, translated by C. Beck, London, 1971.

Criticism
(For general works on the author, see *Playwrights* volume)

Books:
Tilly Wedekind, *Lulu: die Rolle meines Lebens*, Munich, 1969.

Articles:
Claude Quiguer, "L'Erotisme de Frank Wedekind", in *Études germaniques*, 17, 1962.
Frank Marcus, "On Wedekind's *Lulu*", in *Gambit*, 18–19, 1971.
Francis Claudon, "*Loulou* et les limites de l'expressionisme", in *Obliques*, 6–7, 1975.
Edward P. Harris, "The Liberation of the Flesh from the Stone: Pygmalion in Frank Wedekind's *Erdgeist*", in *Germanic Review*, 52, 1977.
Patrick Besnier, "Lula et Nana: Visages de la 'femme fatale' ", in *Interferences*, 7, 1978.
Ronald Peacock, "The Ambiguity of Wedekind's *Lulu*", in *Oxford German Studies*, 9, 1978.
H. Salveson, "A Pinch of Snuff from Pandora's Box", in *Oxford German Studies*, 12, 1981.
Edson M. Chick, "Frank Wedekind and His *Lulu* Tragedy", in his *Dances of Death*, Columbia, South Carolina, 1984.
John L. Hibbert, "The Spirit of the Flesh: Wedekind's *Lulu*", in *Modern Language Review*, 79, 1984.
Jeannine Schuler-Will, "Wedekind's *Lulu*: Pandora and Pierrot, the Visual Experience of Myth", in *German Studies Review*, 7, 1984.
David Midgley, "Wedekind's *Lulu*: From *Schauertragödie* to Social Comedy", in *German Life & Letters*, 38, 1985.
Erhard Weidl, "Philologische Spurensicherung zur Erschliessung der *Lulu* Tragödie Frank Wedekinds", in *Wirkendes Wort*, 35, 1985.
Gail Finney, "Woman as Spectacle and Commodity: Wedekind's *Lulu* Plays", in her *Women in Modern Drama: Freud, Feminism, and European Theater at the Turn of the Century*, Ithaca, New York, 1989.

*   *   *

Lulu is married to the old doctor Goll who has her portrait painted by the artist Schwarz. When Goll discovers that Schwarz and Lulu are having an affair, he dies of a stroke. Lulu marries Schwarz and begins a new relationship with the journalist Dr Schön. When Schwarz discovers her unfaithfulness, *he* kills himself. Lulu becomes a dancer and is surrounded by many admirers. She persuades Dr Schön to renounce his fiancée and to choose her as his wife instead. Her new marital status is no hindrance for her to entertain amorous relationships with Schön's son, Alwa, the athlete Rodrigo Quast, the student Hugenberg, and the lesbian Countess Geschwitz. Disgusted by her behaviour, Dr. Schön hands Lulu a revolver so that she might kill herself. But Lulu turns the weapon against Dr Schön and kills the only man she ever loved. She is sentenced to prison, but, through a trick, the Countess Geschwitz manages to set her free. Lulu, accompanied by Alwa, flees to Paris. Her life in the *demi-monde* under an assumed identity is threatened by Rodrigo Quast, who seeks to blackmail her, and by the Count Casti-Piani, who tries to sell her to a brothel in Egypt. She manages to rid herself of the athlete, but the Count gives a tip-off to the police. Lulu escapes with Alwa to London, where they are joined by the Countess Geschwitz. Lulu now has to work as a street prostitute and meets Jack the Ripper, who kills her in her garret.

The history of the *Lulu* dramas is rather convoluted, and as recent productions have shown, the effect of the plays vary drastically from version to version. The first concept of the Lulu theme came to Wedekind during his Paris years, in Summer 1892, when he was working on an unpublished ballet for the Folies Bergères. The variety and circus theme was probably taken from Felicien Champsaur's *Lulu. Pantomime en 1 acte* (Paris 1888). The manuscript of the so-called "Ur-Pandora" was given to the Countess Nemethy on 21 January 1894. A second version, called *Die Büchse der Pandora. Eine Monstretragödie*, was written between September 1894 and February 1895. In 1895 he published *Der Erdgeist. Eine Tragödie*, a four-act drama which included Acts I and II of *Die Büchse der Pandora* (2nd version), a new third act, and Act III of *Die Büchse der Pandora*. In 1902 a new version of *Die Büchse der Pandora* was published in the Leipzig journal *Die Insel*. It had a new first act, followed by Acts IV and V of the *Ur-Pandora*. To avoid clashes with the censor, Wedekind prepared several stage adaptations, and in the Weimar Republic, when censorship laws had been abolished and both plays could be presented without government interference, he wrote a new five-act version combining both plays, which could be performed in one evening.

Because of the complex editorial history of the plays, each version requires a different interpretation. Themes, dramatic language, and theatrical conventions vary considerably from one edition to the next. What started off as an adultery play in the *pièce-bien-faite* tradition of boulevard theatre, mixing naturalist settings with variety theatre elements and centring the play on an archetypical *femme fatale* figure, developed into a highly allegorical and deeply philosophical drama on the conflict between human nature and the prerequisites of civilization. It is this later version that this interpretation is based on.

The Lulu Plays: Royal Court Theatre, London, 1970

Lulu appears as a representation of the principle of Nature. She is born in the reign of primeval matter (the "morass"). But as an earth*spirit* she also transcends the physical world. The pierrot costume indicates her purity and childlike innocence. The conflict between the flesh and the spirit becomes acute when she moves into civilized bourgeois society. Men try to tame her. She is fitted out with the accessories of a civilized life style. Her sexual drive is refined and she is turned into an art object (wearing fashionable clothes, altering her body design, exhibiting herself as a dancer, etc.). But Nature cannot be subjected to the rules and conventions of civilized society, so in the end Lulu turns into a tragedy of those who try to tame her. The erotic forces Lulu represents are stronger than the civilizing powers of the social figures she comes into contact with. The men she marries are therefore doomed to death. Once they have become "infected" by her animalistic qualities, they try to live out their rekindled, sexual drive under a veneer of bourgeois respectability. The incompatibility of these two urges leads to the downfall of the men. Lulu's tragedy is rooted in the same contradictions. She is corrupted by the male-dominated society and can no longer be true to herself. Her attempts to renounce her nature and to succeed in a repressive and erotophobic society have only

short-lived results. Consequently, she sinks lower and lower, and finally ends up in the slums of London and in the arms of a perverse killer.

Lulu is a personification of the "truly general", the universal human morality, which comes into conflict with the "relative morality", the historical and social circumstances of bourgeois society. Lulu is Nature in its original, uncorrupted state. She is innocent, unselfconscious, pure. She is inadvertently drawn into the perverted world of civilization. Unable to reflect on her actions and unaware of the tragic conflict that is looming, she gets more and more entangled in the destructive course of her fate. Despite her concessions to her bourgeois surroundings she manages, in the end, to keep true to her nature and even refuses to prostitute herself for money, when she most needs it. Her encounter with Jack ends as a *Liebestod*, through which the Lulu principle survives (Jack the Ripper excises her vulva and preserves it in a jar to be exhibited in the London Medical Society!).

Lulu's role and character is circumscribed by the various names and allegories that are assigned to her. As Mignon, she is the woman from the mythical South, the earthly paradise. As Lilith she is like Adam's first wife who refused to be subservient to him. She represents a positive erotic principle, an independent woman with equal status to the male world. As Helena (Nell) she is not only a personification of beauty and seduction like the figure who caused the Trojan War, but a matriarchal goddess whose name means "born out of the marshes". Also Lulu is said "to come from the water", and Schigolch calls her Melusine, a mythological figure popular with the Romantics, half reptile, half human, and living underwater. Finally, Lulu is called Eva, but Wedekind does not see her as in the biblical story of the Fall. The serpent brings mankind wisdom and through her Adam discovers his nakedness. He becomes aware of his eros, sexus, and procreative abilities. It is through the serpent that man recognizes himself and sets himself in opposition to and gains independence from God. In this liberating moment, sexus and ratio were united. But Christian dogma has called this state of self-determination and self-fulfilment sinful. Wedekind opposes this view point. What the church deems evil, he sees as being positive; what they describe as a demon, Wedekind turns into a bearer of happiness. The serpent is a symbol of wisdom; she has god-like qualities and Eva is her first disciple and apostle. Wedekind also reinterprets the Pandora myth. The deceiving beauty who brings death and destruction to mankind is seen in her original function as a fertility goddess. Drawing on Goethe's play *The Return of Pandora*, she is an unbridled spirit who brings creativity, fantasy, and imagination to mankind. Through the title *The Earth Spirit*, Lulu is linked to Mephistopheles, who in Goethe's *Faust*, is "the spirit who negates" the world order. Here, in Wedekind's play, the world is the patriarchal, bourgeois system. Lulu's rebellion is an emancipatory act against the male principle that governs the world. But Wedekind also alludes to Mephistophela in Heine's dance poem *Der Doktor Faust*, who in the end turns into a serpent (Lulu, too, is presented as a serpent in the prologue).

In the *Lulu* dramas Wedekind expressed his critique of a civilization that overemphasizes man's rational and cultural capacities to the detriment of his erotic and sensual nature. Wedekind seeks to rehabilitate man's physical and vitalistic nature in view of a social order that is characterized by its repressive conventions and moralistic codes of conduct. He operates with a Utopian vision of a new society, where a harmonious fusion of sexuality and spirituality is made possible, where the body is seen as a complement to the mind, and where man's natural disposition is being brought into accord with the requirements of social life and progress towards civilization.

—Günter Berghaus

LYSISTRATA
by Aristophanes

First Publication: Lenean Festival, Athens, 411 B.C.

Editions

Lysistrata, edited by J. van Leeuwen, London, 1903.
Lysistrata, in *The Lysistrata; The Thesmophoriazusae*, edited by Benjamin Bickley Rogers, London, 1911.
Lysistrata, edited by J. Hilton Taylor, Bryn Mawr, 1982.
Lysistrata, edited by Jeffrey Henderson, Oxford, 1987.

Translations

Lysistrata, translated by Jack Lindsay, London, 1926.
Lysistrata, translated by Gilbert Seldes, New York, 1930.
Lysistrata, translated by C.T. Murphy, in *Greek Literature in Translation*, 1944.
Lysistrata, translated by Dudley Fitts, New York, 1944.
Lysistrata, in *Two Plays: "Peace" and "Lysistrata"*, translated by Doros Alastros, London, 1953.
Lysistrata, in *Aristophanes Against War: "The Acharnians"; "The Peace"; "Lysistrata"*, Oxford, 1957.
Lysistrata, translated by Donald Sutherland, San Francisco, 1961.
Lysistrata, translated by Douglass Parker, Ann Arbor, Michigan, 1963 (Complete Greek Comedy Series).
Lysistrata, translated by Robert Henning Webb, Charlottesville, Virginia, 1963.
Lysistrata, in *The Acharnians; The Clouds; Lysistrata*, translated by Alan H. Sommerstein, Harmondsworth, 1973.

Criticism
(For general works on the author, see *Playwrights* volume)

Articles:
G.W. Elderkin, "Aphrodite and Athena in the *Lysistrata* of Aristophanes", in *Classical Philology*, 35, 1940.
A.O. Hulton, "The Women on the Acropolis: A Note on the Structure of the *Lysistrata*", in *Greece and Rome* (second series), 19, 1972
John Vaio, "The Manipulation of Theme and Action in Aristophanes' *Lysistrata*", in *Greek, Roman, and Byzantine Studies*, 14, 1973.
S.L. Radt, "Zu Aristophanes *Lysistrate*", in *Mnemosyne*, 27, 1974.

*   *   *

Appalled by male misconduct of the war with Sparta and her allies, Lysistrata ("Disbander of Armies") leads the women of Athens in a revolt, while all over Greece the enemy's wives spring the same plot. They seize the Acropolis, barricade themselves in, and, despite sore temptation, refuse all sexual contact with their husbands. Surviving frontal attack, diplomacy, personal pleading, and disaffection within, they eventually force their rampantly desperate menfolk to accept their terms for a justly negotiated peace.

Lysistrata is probably the earlier of Aristophanes' two extant comedies from 411 B.C. on the women's-conspiracy theme, and the first European comedy with a female lead. The theme quickly became an Aristophanic perennial, one he would return to a few weeks later in the *Thesmophoriazusae*, as well as in the late *Ecclesiazusae* and a number of lost plays. As early as Aeschylus's *Oresteia*, tragedy had made complex thematic and theatrical use of the Athenian segregation of women both spatially and socially; and a communal solidarity among women often takes shape in tragedies with a female lead and female chorus. But Aristophanic woman goes further, inhabiting a little-understood society within society, with its own intricate networks of communication, mutual help, and *de facto* collusion against the male. The central comic conceit in these plays is that such networks could have the force of a cabal for revolution, of the kind Athenian, political paranoia tended to see under every stone (with some justice, given that summer's oligarchic *coup*). In the Aristophanic fantasy, it is just because the women are so segregated and despised that they can hatch take-over plots without their men's suspicion.

Lysistrata herself is a complex type, owing as much to the Euripidean heroines she quotes as to conventional Old Comic heroes. Earlier Aristophanic leads share her public-spirited idealism and world-changing ingenuity and strength of will,

Lysistrata: Royal Court Theatre, London, 1957

but within an aggressively individualistic, roguishly comic, masculine mould. Unlike these male precursors, Lysistrata is not a clown, and the conventional comic desiderata of food, drink, sex, and power are delivered in the end to others. Confronted with a central ambivalence in his portrait of Athenian woman—on the one hand, intelligent, resourceful, and determined, on the other weak-willed, sensual, and morally infirm—Aristophanes resorts to a polarisation between the perilously unfunny Lysistrata herself and her more stereotypically alcoholic, sex-crazed, congenitally duplicitous inner core of lieutenants. Her debt to her real-life synonym, Lysimache ("Dissolver of Battle"), redoubtable priestess of Athena Polias on the Acropolis, has probably been exaggerated; Lysistrata's un–Aristophanic dignity and selfless-

ness owes more to the unacceptability of the alternative for Athenian male audience taste.

Formally, the play is an intricate structure of sexually coloured antagonisms and symmetries. The skene door, traditional boundary between the spaces of women (indoors) and men (outside) in tragedy, becomes the focus of storm and siege, with the repeated male attempts at penetration succeeding only when the Athenian and Spartan diplomats are admitted, side by side, to accept terms. This stage pattern of conflict and reconciliation is echoed in the orchestra, by the extraordinary device of a split chorus of men and women in confrontation and even physical combat. Metrical response reveals a remarkable use of symmetrical action and choreographed violence, before the two semi-choruses unite in harmony just as the stage action reaches its equivalent resolution. Within this larger plan, individual sketches place figures of male authority (a state official, a paterfamilias) at the mercy of women, in situations first of conflict and finally of physical abuse. And on a finer scale, and with typical, middle-Aristophanic concentration of comic theme, the language, imagery, and stage action are relentlessly sexual. The most liberated English translators are too coy, and the language itself too impoverished, to capture more than a fraction of the wall-to-wall *double entendres* in the Greek, and few productions retain full fidelity to the rampant phallic clowning indicated by the text.

But *Lysistrata* is not primarily a sex comedy. Like much Euripidean tragedy, it explores the relations between sexual and international politics, though in a more fantastic and metaphoric way than the direct connections argued by contemporary feminist analysis. Aristophanes' last extant "peace play", it argues (in surprising detail) for a cosily nostalgic Pan-

hellenism artfully equated in the play with sexual fulfilment and domestic harmony. Yet at the same time it gives space, and uncharacteristic, emotional seriousness, to the effects of war on women's lives in the real world, and the frustration of the politically neutered at the consequences of a political process outside their control. No doubt Aristophanes' overwhelmingly male audience would have slapped their thighs at the engaging, comic fantasy of their wives' entertaining a single political thought. But Aristophanes had an evident fascination for the alien lifescape of contemporary Athenian women, and it is hard to feel his obsession with the theme is purely and entirely that of a comic opportunist.

—N.J. Lowe

MACBETH
by William Shakespeare

First Publication: In First Folio, London, 1623.
First Production: London, c. 1602–06; earliest recorded production, Globe Theatre, London, 20 April 1611.

Editions
Macbeth, edited by H.H. Furness, Philadelphia, 1873 (New Variorum Shakespeare).
Macbeth, edited by John Dover Wilson, Cambridge, 1947 (New Shakespeare).
Macbeth, edited by Kenneth Muir, London, 1951 (Arden Shakespeare).
Macbeth, edited by E.M. Waith, New Haven, Connecticut, 1954 (Yale Shakespeare).
Macbeth, edited by Alfred Harbage, Baltimore, Maryland, 1956 (Pelican Shakespeare).
Macbeth, edited by Sylvan Barnet, New York, 1963 (Signet Classic Shakespeare).
Macbeth, edited by G.K. Hunter, Harmondsworth, 1967 (New Penguin Shakespeare).
Macbeth, edited by R.A. Foakes, Indianapolis, Indiana, 1968.
Macbeth, edited by Jay L. Halio, Edinburgh, 1972 (Fountainwell Drama Texts).

Criticism
(For general works on the author, see *Playwrights* volume)

Books:
Margaret Lacy, *Shakespeare and the Supernatural: A Brief Study of Folklore, Superstition, and Witchcraft in "Macbeth", "A Midsummer Night's Dream", and "The Tempest"*, 1906; reprinted, Folcroft, Pennsylvania, 1973.
Isador H. Coriat, *The Hysteria of Lady Macbeth*, New York, 1921.
David Baird, *The Thane of Cawdor: A Detective Study of "Macbeth"*, Oxford, 1937.
W.D. Sargeaunt, *"Macbeth": A New Interpretation of the Text of Shakespeare's Play*, London, 1937.
Blanche Coles, *Shakespeare Studies: "Macbeth"*, New York, 1938.
Roy Walker, *The Time is Free: A Study of "Macbeth"*, London, 1949.
Henry N. Paul, *The Royal Play of "Macbeth": When, Why, and How it was Written*, New York, 1950.
Francis Neilson, *A Study of "Macbeth" for the Stage*, New York, 1952.
G.R. Elliott, *Dramatic Providence in "Macbeth": A Study of Shakespeare's Tragic Theme of Humanity and Grace*, Princeton, New Jersey, 1958.
John Wain (ed.), *"Macbeth": A Casebook*, London, 1968.
Dennis Bartholomeusz, *"Macbeth" and the Players*, Cambridge, 1969.
Clifford Davidson, *The Primrose Way: A Study of Shakespeare's "Macbeth"*, Conesville, Iowa, 1970.
Paul A. Jorgensen, *Our Naked Frailties: Sensational Art and Meaning in "Macbeth"*, Berkeley, California, and Los Angeles, 1971.
Edgar Neis (ed.), *Erläuterungen zu Shakespeares "Macbeth"* (thirteenth edition), Hollfeld, 1972.
D.J. Murphy, *"Macbeth": A Critical Introduction*, Cork, Eire, 1973.
Terence Hawkes (ed.), *Twentieth Century Interpretations of "Macbeth"*, Englewood Cliffs, New Jersey, 1976.
Kenneth Muir and Philip Edwards (eds.), *Aspects of "Macbeth"* [articles reprinted from *Shakespeare Survey*], Cambridge, 1977.
Marvin Rosenberg, *The Masks of Macbeth*, Berkeley, California, 1978.
Angus Rose, *Close Readings: "Macbeth"*, London, 1980.
Arthur Melville Clark, *Murder under Trust of the Topical Macbeth*, Edinburgh, 1981.
Wolfgang Rudorff, *William Shakespeares "Macbeth": Grundlagen und Gedanken zum Verständnis des Dramas*, Frankfurt, 1982.
Stephen Booth, *"King Lear"; "Macbeth": Indefinition and Tragedy*, New Haven, Connecticut, 1983.
David A. Male, *"Macbeth"*, Cambridge and New York, 1984 (Shakespeare on Stage Series).
Gordon Williams, *"Macbeth"*, London, 1985 (Text and Performance Series).
James L. Calderwood, *If It Were Done: "Macbeth" and Tragic Action*, Amherst, Massachusetts, 1986.
Ann Fridén, *"Macbeth" in the Swedish Theatre, 1838–1986*, Gothenburg, Sweden, 1986.
Laurie Lanzen Harris and Mark W. Scott (eds.), *"Macbeth"*, in *Shakespearian Criticism, 3*, Detroit, Illinois, 1986 [anthology of criticism].
Harold Bloom (ed.), *Shakespeare: "Macbeth"*, New York, New Haven, Connecticut, and Philadelphia, 1987 (Modern Critical Interpretations).

Articles:
For information on the many articles about *Macbeth*, see the bibliographies listed in the *Playwrights* volume, and the annual Shakespeare Bibliography in *Shakespeare Quarterly*, published by the Folger Shakespeare Library, Washington D.C. (1950–).

* * *

449

Macbeth: Drury Lane Theatre, London, 1768 (David Garrick and Mrs Pritchard)

The Tragedy of Macbeth is the darkest and most terrible of Shakespeare's plays. At times the action is violent—a mother and her children are murdered on stage, and off-stage Macbeth is said to cleave an adversary "from the nave to th'chops"—but the play's horror lies mainly in its presentation of mental torments: "unnatural troubles" and "infected minds", the "taste of fears", guilt, insecurity, thoughts overwhelming like the "multitudinous sea", the smell of imagined blood that cannot be washed away, idiocy, emptiness, and speechlessness in the face of death. All this is conveyed with astonishingly sensitive imagery—the tyrant hero has sometimes been called a "poet" by critics trying to understand the play's hold over readers and audiences—and in quick-moving action which allows time for little relief.

Moreover, the tragic hero is not alone. Shakespeare has created so close a bond between Macbeth and Lady Macbeth that feeling is quickly communicated one to the other, as if in a separate level from the words they speak. The breaking of this bond—for each dies alone—adds to the pain which their deeds bring upon them.

The plot is comparatively simple. Macbeth becomes a national hero through prowess in battle and then, with his wife's help, murders Duncan, King of Scotland. Malcolm, the King's elder son, flees to England, and Macbeth is elected king. At once he begins to suspect the loyalty of Banquo who had been his companion in battle; he has him assassinated, and only just fails to kill his young son Fleance. Macduff, another

Thane, does not attend the coronation feast, but goes to join Malcolm in England; Macbeth thereupon murders Macduff's wife and heirs. Malcolm, with other refugees, raises an army, returns to Scotland and captures Macbeth's castle. Macduff kills Macbeth in single combat. Already Lady Macbeth, who was last seen sleepwalking in nightmare, has been reported dead. Malcolm is hailed as "King of Scotland".

The basic story is, however, complicated by the presence of three witches. The play opens with them, in thunder and lightning, planning to meet Macbeth. When they are next seen, a drum off-stage announces Macbeth's approach and they join immediately in a primitive rite. When Macbeth enters they hail him and prophesy that he shall be King of Scotland. Banquo, who attends Macbeth, is told that he, however, will beget kings, although never be one himself. The witches then vanish, and at once messengers from Duncan arrive to announce that one of the witches' minor prophecies has been fulfilled: Duncan has made Macbeth Thane of Cawdor. Later in the play, when Macbeth's triumph is threatened by his own fears and by seeing the ghost of the murdered Banquo, the witches are seen again, for Macbeth goes to them for help. They show him various apparitions, including eight heirs of Banquo, all of them crowned as kings; but they also provide further prophecies which seem to assert that Macbeth is impregnable. In the last scenes of the play, these prophecies all prove illusory because they were riddles, and each is fulfilled in Macbeth's destruction.

The nature of the witches has been much debated: do they control Macbeth's fate totally, making him an unwitting victim of their evil powers, or are they representations of his own thoughts, putting into words what he and his wife have already planned? In support of the second alternative, critics have noted that Lady Macbeth makes clear that they had talked together about murdering Duncan before her husband had seen the witches. (But is Lady Macbeth also a witch?) Moreover it is Macbeth and not the witches who uses the word "murder". Most significantly, he knows, as soon as he hears the prophecy, "If chance will have me King, why chance may crown me / Without my stir".

The witches unsettle audiences. While spectators at the first performances of the play would have been divided on whether they had power to cause harm, or prophesy, or communicate with the Devil, modern audiences are likely to believe none of this and are therefore led to question the reality of the whole play. Perhaps both reactions suit Shakespeare's purposes, because the supernatural is variously presented in this play. Macbeth also sees an airborne dagger, leading him to Duncan's bedchamber; and then he sees the ghost of Banquo sitting among the living thanes. In her sleepwalking, Lady Macbeth believes that her hands can never be washed clean of blood. All these phenomena can be readily accepted as hallucinations brought on by guilt and isolation. The porter of Macbeth's castle, on the morning after Duncan's murder, speaks as if he were keeper of hell's gates and sees ordinary sinners on their way to the "everlasting bonfire". Prodigies are reported in the skies; horses are said to be eating each other. By all these means, Shakespeare is able to show a man and woman drawn into murder and sustained in evil by a recognition that evil seems to have a power of its own.

Macbeth is a kind of nightmare: a tragedy so appalling that an audience must be led into a state of mind in which ordinary reality is not relevant. The witches are real to Macbeth and to Banquo, but their very questionable reality for the audience functions so that the later phantasmagoric horrors bring a contrasting and absolute belief.

Relieving the main thrust of the action, some characters stand up for what is good and honourable: Macduff, although he does leave his wife undefended; Malcolm, although he takes time to find confidence; the King of England, although he is remote from Scotland; a nameless Old Man who can only pray for "God's benison". Most surprisingly, in Macbeth himself, during the last scenes, a memory of good persists; he knows what he has lost:

I have lived long enough: my way of life
Is fallen into the sere, the yellow leaf;
And that which should accompany old age,
As honour, love, obedience, troops of friends,
I must not look to have. . . .

Faced by Macduff and realizing that the witches have deceived him, Macbeth confronts what he believes is certain death knowing that his "better part" is cowed and his soul "charged" with blood. The courage with which he sustains his last fight may be mere desperation, but it can also be heroic acceptance of guilt and helplessness. Malcolm, when Macbeth's bleeding head is brought on stage, speaks of "this dead butcher"; but for the audience he will always be, to varying degrees, more than that.

—John Russell Brown

LA MACHINE INFERNALE. See **THE INFERNAL MACHINE.**

DIE MACHT DER GEWOHNHEIT. See **THE FORCE OF HABIT.**

MADMEN AND SPECIALISTS
by Wole Soyinka

First Publication: London, 1971.
First Production: Playwrights' Workshop Conference, Eugene O'Neill Center, Waterford, Connecticut, 1970; revised version, University of Ibadan, Nigeria, 1971.

Criticism
(For general works on the author, see *Playwrights* volume)

Articles:
Boyd M. Berry, "On Looking at *Madmen and Specialists*", in *Pan-African Journal*, 5, 1972.
Aderemi Bamikunle, "What Is 'as'? Why 'as'? A Thematic Exegesis of Wole Soyinka's *Madmen and Specialists*", in *Work in Progress*, 2, 1973.
Barney C. McCartney, "Traditional Satire in Wole Soyinka's *Madmen and Specialists*", in *World Literature Written in English*, 14, 1975.
Chris Johnson, "Performance and Role-Playing in Soyinka's *Madmen and Specialists*", in *Journal of Commonwealth Literature*, vol. 10 no. 3, 1976.
Benedict M. Ibitokun, "Existential Struggle in Soyinka's *Madmen and Specialists*", in *Ba Shiru*, vol. 10 no. 1, 1979.
Wole Ogundele, "Irony and the Grotesque in *Madmen and Specialists*", in *World Literature Written in English*, 21, 1982.

*   *   *

The action is set in and around the surgery of Dr. Bero, who in the course of his war service has changed from being a doctor to an intelligence officer, willing and able to use his skills to torture, coerce, and accumulate power. In the process he has become the antagonist of his own father, referred to in the play as Old Man, who, in his disgust at the senseless killing and maiming, has made a symbolic protest by serving up a meal of human flesh to the officer corps, including his own son. But the plan has backfired: far from recoiling in horror, Bero and his colleagues have acquired a taste for cannibalism. The play opens with four victims of the war, the Mendicants, guarding the Old Man who has been imprisoned in the surgery, under Bero's orders. The Mendicants are former patients on a rehabilitation programme run by their prisoner, to whom they are still much attached. Instead of teaching them such conventional skills as basket-weaving, the Old Man has taught them to think, and introduced them to his cult of "As". Much of the play is taken up with the Mendicants acting out routines and exchanging banter which they have learnt from their former mentor, all of it permeated with a nihilistic black humour which comes from their partial enlightenment through him. As well as guarding Bero's father they are also charged with spying on his sister, Si Bero, and her mentors the Earth Mothers, practitioners of the traditional medicine based on knowledge of both the curative and destructive powers of plants and herbs. Bero has imprisoned his father ostensibly to save him from certain death at the hands of his fellow officers, but really to discover the secrets of the cult, which he wishes to use for his own malign purposes. But he is not successful and the play ends with Bero shooting dead the Old Man as the Earth Mothers destroy their storehouse of herbs by fire to prevent its evil use by the power-mad Bero.

Madmen and Specialists is Soyinka's theatrical response to the horrors of the Nigerian Civil War, in which his personal intervention led to imprisonment. It is also one of numerous plays in which he dramatizes the operations of the will to gain power, and the ways in which the humanist challenger may oppose, resist, and perhaps overcome them. The bleakness and despair of Soyinka's vision, deeply influenced by the trauma of the civil war, is only partly balanced by the hope implicit in the play's climax, as the forces of good successfully take defensive measures against the corrupt power of Dr. Bero and prevent the traditional wisdom and resources for healing being used for perverted and evil ends.

Central to any performance of the play must be the evocation of the brutality and savagery of war, manifest in the controlling image of cannibalism and in the presence on stage, for much of the action, of the Mendicants—Aafaa, Blindman, Goyi, and the Cripple—with their grotesque appearances, role-playing, and verbal exchanges. These are the victims not only of the organized physical violence of war but also of what the dramatist evidently conceives as a fundamental and destructive human drive—the desire to exercise power over others. The struggle for power is constantly being played out between the Mendicants in sinisterly comic form, but in deadly seriousness between Bero and his father. Bero seeks the secrets of his father's "cult", proclaimed as he blessed the "meat" served up to Bero and his fellow officers: "As Was the Beginning, As is, As Ever shall be. . .world without. . .". He repeatedly interrogates the Old Man, seeking an answer to his question, "Why As?". His questioning is yet another step on the road to perfect power, complete control over others, which ironically began with the first taste of human flesh.

The human banquet which is served to demonstrate that animals at least behave rationally in eating the flesh of other animals only in order to survive themselves has had the reverse effect on Bero, as he tells his sister:

> Afterwards I said why not? What is one flesh from another? So I tried it again, just to be sure of myself. It was the first step to power you understand. Power in its purest sense. The end of inhibitions. The conquest of the weakness of your too human flesh with all its sentiment. So again, all to myself I said Amen to his grace.

The man who tried to shock Dr. Bero and his fellow "specialists" into moral sanity dies, the sacrificial victim of his own son's violence. In killing his father, Bero carries his own logic to its end, divesting himself of the last remnant of his humanity by shedding the blood of the one who gave him life. In a balancing image, the final moments of the play insist on the ultimate sanity of nature itself, whose custodians, the Earth Mothers, prevent its potentially destructive secrets falling into Bero's evil hands. In the near despair of Soyinka's imaginative world when he wrote *Madmen and Specialists* this is the best that can be hoped for.

—Brian Crow

THE MADRAS HOUSE
by Harley Granville-Barker

First Publication: London, 1911.
First Production: Duke of York's Theatre, London, 9 March 1910.

Criticism
(For general works on the author, see *Playwrights* volume)

Articles:

Harry M. Ritchie, "Harley Granville-Barker's *The Madras House* and the Sexual Revolution", in *Modern Drama*, 15, 1972.
Heidi J. Holder, " 'The drama discouraged': Judgment and Ambivalence in *The Madras House*", in *University of Toronto Quarterly*, 58, 1988–89.

*   *   *

This is a rarely performed classic of comedy which remains as challenging in substance as it is original in form. Written by a lifelong champion of the cause of publicly subsidised theatre, it indicates the resources that only such a theatre, in 1910 or the 1970's, could certainly count upon: lengthy rehearsal time, a large cast of imaginative and accomplished actors (none of whom would have an obvious star role), an inescapable level of expenditure on settings and costumes, and an audience prepared to be intellectually engaged as well as entertained by a critique of the kind of affluence the play reflects. Yet *The Madras House* is open to creative directing as well as acting and might be tackled by a poor theatre, though never a rough one. The positive vision it moves towards is of an art which would spring from "the happiness of a whole people". Its main weakness, which makes the final scene tricky to handle, is that it becomes sententious if satire and irony eventually give way to passionate sincerity. Most effervescent in Act III, its peculiar strength lies in the combination of an undertow of sombre feeling and reflection with an exuberantly elaborate structure of wit.

The title of the play identifies a view of Edwardian England as a great shop, not the factory or workshop of the world, but a grand emporium with touches of imperialism surviving in the way it presents itself. What it sells is drapery, women's fashions. Granville Barker's analysis of the condition of England corresponds closely to Thorstein Veblen's in his classic *Theory of the Leisure Class* in the way it relates the prevailing economic system to the waste and marginalisation of women in society as surplus women, exploited women, decorative luxuries, idealised ladies. With Futurism's cult of the machine the latest fashion of 1910 and *The Stepford Wives* still a long way off, Barker's masters of society dream wistfully of replacing female flesh-and-blood with functional automata. Commerce generates its own poetry and soars away from reality into its own realm of imagination. The unconscious puns which spin off from the businessmen's dialogue cluster into images and icons of commercial art: the Madras House is subsumed in the fairytale symbol of the Crystal Palace, triumph of technological architecture for the exhibition halls of trade. Art, too, is marginalised in a high culture which is part hothouse, part museum.

Although there is a tenuous, narrative linkage between the successive acts of the play, the broad sweep of its survey is achieved by shifting the focus, act by act, to successive and contrasted social environments, different ways of life, and groups governed by different codes of behaviour. A meticulous naturalism—in character as well as in incident and ambience—provides the groundwork from which fantastic structures emerge in Act I and Act III: the comings and goings of the six unmarried Huxtable daughters are turned into a comic-grotesque, choric dance. A counterpart to this appears in the gyrations of voiceless mannequins, modelling extravagant "creations" in a sham-oriental boardroom for the benefit of an all-male directorate, setting off a rhetorical display of peacock opinions and motivating illusions. Philip Madras, a man of conscience, is on stage for almost the whole of the play, mostly as an observer and meeting-point of the sophisticated awareness of the dramatist and the audience. His detachment is threatened briefly, in Act II, by a vital, independent-minded shopgirl who, unknown to him, is pregnant by his father. In the last Act, which turns from panoramic views to look intimately at marriage, the spotlight finally settles on him. What he has seen and heard, felt and thought through the rest of the play is also at the centre of his own marriage, troubling and insistent. The playwright's strategy for uniting ideas and emotion in the last section of the play involves a withdrawal of privilege from the previously detached character. Though the views he struggles to formulate may be authorial, the personality with which they are associated is fully vulnerable to criticisms previously hinted at even while he makes the strongest claim on sympathy and understanding. The ironic effect saves the play from the stranglehold of logical conclusions, and it is open to the actor to play against the rhetorical tendencies in the dialogue, underplaying the lines to keep them reflective and slightly self-mocking.

Barker had considerable difficulty in finishing the play, writing several drafts of the ending without ever being satisfied. He and George Bernard Shaw had set out simultaneously to write new plays as companion pieces for inclusion in an experimental venture in repertory theatre to be introduced for the first time into the West End of London. (The extraordinary effect of the death of Edward VII on the British theatre was instrumental in bringing the season to a premature close, and it was many years before either the Shaw play *Misalliance*, or *The Madras House*, was re-discovered in the theatre.) The two dramatists adopted related themes and images, tried out variations on each other's styles and even on each other's characters, and introduced cross-references easily detectable by audiences going to see both plays, perhaps within the same week. Shaw went so far as to write his own mock ending to *The Madras House* in an attempt to chivvy Barker to finish the work.

As England's first director of plays in the modern sense, Granville-Barker wrote plays which made good material for the training of actors to be members of a disciplined ensemble while also developing their talents for playing more naturalistically than was usual in the theatre of the time, cultivating the art of stage speech, and giving psychological depth to the roles they played, suggesting a constantly shifting inner life. The structure of *The Madras House* uniquely favours ensemble playing. No character in it is allowed to dominate the rest for more than a scene, and every character in the play offers the actor an opportunity to develop and show his or her skills: even the maid who shows in the visitors at the start of Act I is assigned a significant piece of business with a hat and a door handle. Such constant technical care over detail is one aspect of his drama which is quite distinctive from Shaw's. Another is the close-knit quality which contrasts with Shaw's cultivation of the unpredictable effect and an almost improvisatory looseness. Whereas Shaw explodes ideas on an audience, Granville-Barker induces his audience to think through the ideas and test them as the play progresses. Act III of *The Madras House* is his most sustained imitation of Shaw's

methods in its debate around a table, featuring histrionic characters bordering on caricature, and it is notable that Constantine Madras, the star of this scene, reverts to a much more realistic and humanly flawed self when the artificial occasion breaks up. The still, sad, even bitter, music of humanity is faintly heard in the scene with his long-separated wife, as it can be heard at moments in the first two acts.

—Margery Morgan

MAGDA (Heimat)
by Hermann Sudermann

First Publication: Berlin, 1893.
First Production: Lessingtheater, Berlin, 7 January 1893.

Translations
Magda, translated by Charles Edward Amory Winslow, New York, 1899; reprinted in *Contemporary Drama: European Plays*, edited by E. B. Watson and B. Pressey, New York, 1931–34.

*   *   *

Heimat (literally "Home", but known in English by the name of its heroine, *Magda*) is a drama in four acts, set in an unidentified, Prussian, provincial town. Unity of place is preserved throughout, the action being set entirely in the living-room of Colonel Schwartze, an officer invalided out of the service some 12 years previously. The author employs the technique of analytical exposition which was familiar to his contemporaries from the work of Ibsen: the unexpected arrival of a newcomer provokes a re-examination of events long past, and a renewed confrontation with the same problems in the changed circumstances of the present. Even then no resolution is possible: the drama ends with the death of Schwartze.

The newcomer who thus disrupts the fragile stability of small-town, middle-class life is a celebrated opera singer, Maddalena dell'Orto, who has come, ostensibly, to participate in the local music festival, but who is really drawn by a mixture of homesickness and curiosity to her former home, for she is, in fact, Magda, the daughter of Colonel Schwartze. 12 years earlier she had been turned out of the house when she had refused to marry Heffterdingk, the suitor approved by her authoritarian father, and now the highly respected local pastor.

By carefully delaying the entry of the heroine until Act II, Scene 7, the author creates a high degree of expectancy and tension, as throughout the first act he builds up the picture of the stifling, provincial milieu which provoked the young Magda's revolt. In particular, a foil is created for the heroine in her passive and obedient sister, Marie, who corresponds—as the name makes clear—to the complementary female stereotype. After discussions which reveal how much the values which still dominate within the Schwartze household are opposed to those which prevail in the international, artistic circles to which the visiting *diva* is accustomed, the audience is made aware that the great opera singer is really the daughter of the house. Prevailed upon by the pastor to seek a reconciliation, Schwartze invites his daughter into the family home; old bonds of affection with sister and stepmother are renewed, as well as tensions with her aunt and, above all, with her still unyieldingly authoritarian father. It is the pastor who forces Magda to confront the past, namely the effect of her earlier behaviour on her father, who suffered a stroke which curtailed his military career shortly after his daughter left home; meanwhile Heffterdingk has patiently assisted in the slow process of partial recovery. Magda agrees to stay, but she is unwilling to assume the role of the returned prodigal, and makes it a condition that she should be asked no questions about her past. Act II therefore ends with a skilfully contrived tension which sustains the next part of the action.

After a further discussion with Heffterdingk, in which the pastor's years of self-denial are contrasted with Magda's self-assertion and fulfilment as an artist, the ghost from the past appears in the person *Regierungsrat* (Government Councillor) von Keller. Now a civil servant and a respected local figure, he had been Magda's lover during her early years of struggle in Berlin, but had abandoned her and the child she was expecting in order to further his own career; the two have an angry confrontation. Schwartze presses his daughter until she reveals the full story of her relationship with Keller, and then challenges Keller to a duel. Keller, however, is prepared to marry the wealthy and famous Magda, and paints the picture of the brilliant future that could lie before them, in which, of course, she has a subordinate role. For the sake of her sick father Magda is willing to give up her stage career, but she draws the line at renouncing her child, as Keller (its father) demands. In a final confrontation between father and daughter Magda will not give way; Schwartze now turns his pistol on her, but suffers a stroke before he can fire. He dies reaching out his hand to bless his younger daughter, but remains unforgiving towards Magda.

In the role of the heroine Sudermann created a part that was enthusiastically and successfully taken into the repertoires of the great actresses of the turn of the century: Sarah Bernhardt, Eleonora Duse, Mrs Patrick Campbell, and Adele Sandrock. From the outset the critics were cool, even hostile, seeing in this play, Sudermann's third, confirmation of the suspicions that had been voiced after his first success, *Die Ehre* (*Honour*) in 1889: namely that Sudermann was no more than a skilled but conventional technician, exploiting the themes and certain stylistic features of the newly fashionable, naturalist theatre. Such themes are certainly present in abundance: the conflict of the moral codes of two generations, the contrast of metropolis and provinces, the emancipation of women, the conflicting demands of duty to the self and duty to others, and the clash between the artist and society. The black-and-white nature of the conflict is modified only slightly in the character of the pastor, whose altruism has been asserted and maintained, despite personal disappointment, in the face of a rigid and small-minded environment; and in Magda herself, who is still emotionally bound to her family and responsive to Heffterdingk's appeal to her sense of filial duty. The most successful scenes of the play are those in which Sudermann satirises the malice and pettiness of small-town life, showing the ultimate impossibility of the reintegration of an emancipated woman. The early critics perceived rightly that the final dramatic climax does not arise from this central, thematic conflict at all; it is Magda's love of her own child that prevents her from bending entirely to her father's will. The socio-moral conflict thus gives way to a sentimental one, which is only susceptible to resolution by melodramatic means: the sudden death of the father.

—John Osborne

THE MAGISTRATE
by Arthur Wing Pinero

First Publication: London, 1892.
First Production: Royal Court Theatre, London, 21 March 1885.

Editions

The Magistrate, in *Types of Farce Comedy*, edited by R.M. Smith, New York, 1928.
The Magistrate, in *Pinero: Three Plays*, London, 1987.

Criticism
(For general works on the author, see *Playwrights* volume)

Articles:
L. Veszy-Wagner, "Pinero's Farce *The Magistrate* as an Anxiety Dream", in *American Imago*, 32, 1975.

*   *   *

On marrying Aeneas Posket, a mild and philanthropic magistrate, Agatha shaves five years off her true age, rendering Cis, her son by a previous marriage, an apparently precocious 14-year-old instead of a 19-year-old. Cis leads a double existence: at home a petted favourite, loved by his music teacher Beatie; in town a reveller and swell who keeps a room at the Hôtel des Princes. He entices a reluctant Posket there on the same night that Agatha and her visiting sister Charlotte go off on the pretext of attending a sick friend, but in reality to warn Colonel Lukyn, Cis's godfather and Posket's old schoolfriend, against revealing Agatha's age over dinner the following evening. Inevitably Lukyn too is supping at the Hôtel with Captain Horace Vale, Charlotte's spurned fiancé, in a room adjoining Cis and Posket's. Vale withdraws to a balcony, allowing Agatha a confidential meeting, but Charlotte's voracious appetite and a downpour conspire to provoke Vale's discovery. Matters worsen when police raid the hotel. Lights are extinguished and all, including Posket and Cis, conceal themselves in the same room. Father and stepson narrowly escape, but the others are arrested. Pursued by police through the night, Posket arrives dishevelled at court where first on his list are four persons involved in an affray at the hotel. In chambers Posket pompously rejects Lukyn's chivalrous plea to spare the ladies (they have given false names) and in court imposes an uncharacteristically harsh sentence before collapsing on recognising Agatha and Charlotte. A fellow magistrate later quashes the sentence on a technicality. After mutual recriminations, revelations, and reconciliations, Cis, miraculously elevated to manhood, announces his intention to marry Beatie. The magistrate, only too relieved to escape Cis's disruptive influence, readily assents.

The Magistrate, an economically plotted and deftly constructed farce brimming with ingenuity and fun, ran for 363 performances on its first appearance in 1885, and established Pinero's reputation as an accomplished farceur. Written for the Court Theatre under the management of John Clayton and Arthur Cecil, it initiated a string of highly successful farces (*Dandy Dick*, *The Schoolmistress*, *The Cabinet Minister*), and assembled the principals of Pinero's crack repertory company of Clayton, Cecil, Mrs. John Wood, Rose Norreys, and Fred Kerr.

Believing that farce should be treated "upon lines as artistic as possible" and have "as substantial and reasonable a backbone as serious plays", Pinero, master of the well-made play, inserted characters of greater than usual depth rendered

The Magistrate: Royal Court Theatre, London, 1885

believable and vulnerable by touches of revealing detail or eccentricity. Posket, for example, whose servants and milkman have all passed through his court, is normally predisposed to pass only the mildest of judgements. "Dear me", he remarks on pouring the tea, "this milk seems very poor". His sentence on his wife and his fall are all the more comic for being occasioned by a combination of punctiliousness, harassment, and guilt.

As a former actor Pinero knew the value of deploying familiar routines and set pieces. The play finds room for much comic food business, a hat-swapping sequence and, at the end of Act I when Posket is persuaded to join Cis in an "adventure", a dressing scene. Pinero repositions the soliloquy (a feature of earlier one-act farces which relied on the audiences' recognition of the leading player's "line" and personality) by giving it to Posket in Act III to relate in character the nightmare of his breathless dash across London in the small hours. In Pinero's hands such moments are always subservient to character and plot, as part of his desire for artistic integrity.

Pinero further refines the constituent elements of farce by smoothly incorporating sequences of orchestrated sounds or movements—as in the kissing scene and the multiple letter-opening of Act I, or the dark scene in the hotel—and by

building in cumulative effects and structural repetitions. The social impropriety and nuisance of cobnuts scattered on the drawing-room floor prefigure the more alarming transgressions and hazards to come. Agatha's struggling attempt to convince Lukyn of the gravity of her situation against a barrage of *doubles entendres* is echoed in Lukyn's desperate and equally misconstrued appeal to Posket to release the ladies without charge. Inventive physical comedy, stylish language, a sure control of accelerating pace, and genuinely funny tableaux contribute to the theatrical dash of the play.

Received at the time and still conventionally regarded as a thoroughly English farce, *The Magistrate* is neither free of the influence of its racier, French counterparts, nor, perhaps, quite as cheerfully innocent as it appears. A *Punch* caricature of the time depicts Pinero as a bird (a pun on his middle name) feeding his actors, crowded in a nest labelled "Court Theatre", pieces of bread inscribed with the titles of French farces and their English adaptations. The accompanying review details Pinero's many echoings of French plots and situations, not least the wholesale transfer of characters to a dubious Act II location. Like all good farces the play exploits transgressions of category boundaries, notably those separating the legal from criminal, respectable from disreputable, and domestic from exotic. Pinero also has fun with child/adult and single/married dualities. While French farceurs could openly represent the dizzying pursuit of adultery, Pinero would and could not, by virtue of inclination and censorship. A process of transcodification is therefore put in play whereby bedroom becomes supper-room, comic hunger substitutes for sexual appetite, and the degeneration and dishevelment of costume replace the shedding of clothing. Potential sexual activity is here oddly relocated in the child-like Beatie, aged 16, and Cis, ostensibly aged 14. Doubtless Victorian taste found this acceptably humorous, but a contemporary audience may bring Pinero's conscious or unconscious subtext closer to the surface.

The Magistrate has never lost its appeal nor been long absent from the British stage. The role of Posket, created by Arthur Cecil and continued by Edward Terry, Denys Blakelock and, in the 1980's at the British National Theatre, by Nigel Hawthorne, found its ideal interpreter in Alastair Sim who, at Chichester in 1969 and in London the following year, gave the best comic performance of his career.

—Ronald W. Strang

THE MAGNIFICENT CUCKOLD (Le Cocu magnifique)
by Fernand Crommelynck

First Publication: Paris, 1921.
First Production: Théâtre de La Maison de l'Oeuvre, Paris, 18 December 1920.

Criticism
(For general works on the author, see *Playwrights* volume)

Articles:
Gisèle Feal, "La Magnificence du Roi Candaule: Comparaison d'une pièce de Crommelynck", in *Romance Notes*, 13, 1971.
Alma H. Law, "Meyerhold's *The Magnanimous* [sic] *Cuckold*", in *Tulane Drama Review*, vol. 26 no. 1, 1982.
V. Renier, "Es-tu moi? La Question du *Cocu magnifique*", in *Écritures de l'imaginaire*, edited by Michel Otten, Brussels, 1985.

* * *

The Magnificent Cuckold presents with remarkable theatricality the distortions of mind and behaviour which sexual jealousy brings. Eccentric rather than surrealist, in some senses it prefigures the "Theatre of the Absurd": just as the audience accepts it as farce some grotesque or horrifying incident undermines them.

Bruno, the village scribe, is married blissfully happily to his youthful sweetheart, Stella, and they take a childish delight in one another. So delightful does Bruno find Stella, that he asks her to show Petrus, their guest, her legs. Then he himself unbuttons her bodice so Petrus may gaze on her breasts. But when he detects lust in Petrus's eye, he hits him, and turns him out of the house.

Bruno suspects Stella of infidelity with Petrus, and refuses to listen to her protestations of innocence. Unable to rid himself of his doubts about her fidelity, he decides to make himself sure of her infidelity. But when he sends her to the bedroom with Petrus, he finds he cannot believe that they have actually committed adultery. Perhaps they just say they have to placate him. He invites every man in the village to enjoy her, but can never be sure she has betrayed him, nor that she has not one genuine lover. He even disguises himself and takes her himself, but realizes she may have allowed him to enjoy her because she may have recognized him under his mask. The women of the village set upon Stella, because she is destroying their marriages; she is rescued by the cowhand, who has earlier declared his love for her. He invites her to go away with him, and eventually she accepts. But Bruno is not fooled—he knows this is just another of her loathsome pranks.

This is the nightmare logic of the jealous mind. It is a frenzied, self-induced unhappiness which seeks the impossible—absolute certainty in human affairs, exclusive possession of another human being. His fear of ridicule and his capriciousness (which shows itself with Estrugo, his friend, as much as with Stella) have a sure psychological truth, and the way he prevents Estrugo from speaking and then announces that his silence is sufficient proof of Stella's guilt demonstrates convincingly his degeneration. This is underlined by the theatrical presentation—in the second act, Bruno's "hair is ruffled, his eyes shifty, (and) his colour bilious", and in the last act he is "aged, broken and bald". Yet the time lapse is only a day or two.

Crommelynck's technique here is comparable to traditional *commedia dell'arte*. The characters are types who have a dominating trait: Bruno is the jealous lover, Stella the *ingénue*, Estrugo the faithful servant, and the Mayor a fat and sweaty bureaucrat. There are other elements of stylization from the same source: when Stella and Bruno "coo like turtledoves, the actors should improvise". At one moment, Stella, Bruno, Petrus, and the nurse all speak at once, then all fall silent. "That is all", says Bruno. The cooper weeps when told that lovers should weep, and later he and Stella sit immobile in total silence while Bruno spies on them. The play ends with a carnival, in which Bruno is masked like a *commedia* character (and it might be noted that earlier Stella also wears a mask). Related to the *commedia* elements are touches of fairy-tale fantasy. Bruno and Estrugo are as alike as twins. People cut down trees in the Forest of the Heartless Woman by night. Meanwhile, Stella and Bruno play children's games, and the people punish offenders by tying them to the back of a billy-goat. But here *commedia* has given way to melodrama, and a feeling of menace such as some absurdist plays evoke. Petrus declares he used to be frightened of travelling on the road, and Bruno appears at the end with a gun. Crommelynck said the play could be presented as either farce or tragedy, and it is never clear whether the hero should be pitied or ridiculed. The dream-like *naïveté* is charming, but subtly contaminated. Thus, at first glance, the poetry and song seem simply pleasant, but then we notice that the language contains other elements—the extensive animal imagery, for instance, which suggests Bruno is a kangaroo carrying Stella's heart in his pouch; Stella herself is a mouse capable of creeping, unseen, under doors; and Estrugo is a porcupine whose silence operates upon Bruno like poisoned quills shot at his peace of mind.

All these features help to illuminate the nature of jealousy, which is itself a spreading poison. Bruno's terrible fantasy of Stella's infidelity contains not only its own momentum, but also a kind of perverse pleasure which may echo in the subconscience: do men like the idea of exposing their women to other men's gazes? Do they like the idea of their women as impure? The play is able to reach forbidden depths, particularly of the male consciousness.

The most famous production of this play was by Meyerhold in Moscow in 1922, when he changed the title to *The*

The Magnificent Cuckhold: Meyerhold's production as *The Magnanimous Cuckhold,* Actors' Theatre, Moscow, 1922

Magnanimous Cuckold, and tried to present it as a satire on the neuroses which, he suggested, inevitably accompany the owning of property (bourgeois marriage being characterised by the husband "owning" the wife). How far this conception impinged on audiences is unclear: the fun he made at Bruno's expense seemed largely high-spirited and *commedia*-like, deriving its essential optimism from Meyerhold's belief that property-owning was a thing of the past in the USSR. The production's success made it a landmark of 20th-century theatre, though as a realization of its author's intentions it may have been less noteworthy.

—Robert Leach

THE MAID'S TRAGEDY
by Francis Beaumont and John Fletcher

First Publication: London, 1619.
First Production: London (the King's Men), c. 1608–11.

Editions

The Maid's Tragedy, in *Elizabethan Plays*, edited by Hazleton Spencer, Boston, 1933.
The Maid's Tragedy, edited by Howard B. Norland, Lincoln, Nebraska, 1968 (Regents Renaissance Drama Series).
The Maid's Tragedy, edited by T.W. Craik, Manchester, 1988 (Revels Plays).

Criticism
(For general works on the author, see *Playwrights* volume)

Articles:
A. Brouson Feldman, "The Yellow Malady: Short Studies of Five Tragedies of Jealousy", in *Literature and Psychology*, 6, 1956.
Mario Praz, "John Webster and *The Maid's Tragedy*", in *English Studies*, 37, 1956.
Robert K. Turner Jr., "The Relationship of *The Maid's Tragedy*, Q1 and Q2", in *Papers of the Bibliographical Society of America*, 51, 1957.
Michael Neill, "'The Simetry which Gives a Poem Grace': Masque Imagery and the Fancy of *The Maid's Tragedy*", in *Renaissance Drama* (new series), 3, 1970.
Barbara J. Baines, "The Complexity of Honor in *The Maid's Tragedy*", in *Journal of General Education*, 31, 1979.
Ronald Broude, "Divine Right and Divine Retribution in Beaumont and Fletcher's *The Maid's Tragedy*", in *Shakespeare and Dramatic Tradition*, edited by W.R. Elton and William B. Long, Newark, Delaware, 1989.

*   *   *

The play opens with preparations for a masque to celebrate a marriage. Melantius on his return from the wars is startled to hear that his friend Amintor has married not Aspatia, as had been expected, but his sister Evadne. An extremely elaborate masque follows, but the wedding night afterwards is a disaster, Evadne refusing to lie with her husband. Eventually she discloses to him the devastating news that she is the King's mistress and that the marriage has been arranged by the King to provide respectable cover for their liaison and a father for their children. Amintor realises that he must accept his role. They play their parts as a married pair so well that the King becomes suspicious and Amintor, stung by the King's insistence on abject compliance, tastes the full bitterness of his position. Meanwhile the deserted Aspatia, the "maid" of the title, openly laments her fate in lengthy speeches addressed to the other ladies of the court.

Melantius, detecting an unhappiness beneath Amintor's feigned contentment, asks him in the name of friendship to tell his secret, which with difficulty he does. At first, Melantius, incensed at hearing his sister described as a whore disbelieves his friend; but Amintor finally convinces him of his honesty and Melantius vows to avenge the honour of his house. The revenge plot involves Melantius in securing his own safety by demanding the surrender of the fort on the island which is in the hands of his old enemy Calianax, Aspatia's father. Calianax informs the King of this demand but, in a banquet scene of mocking double-talk and comic asides, the King—mindful of Melantius's past heroism—refuses to believe the old courtier. That night the King sends for Evadne and, following Melantius's earlier persuasion, like a triumphant figure of nemesis she kills him in his bed. The dead king's brother Lisippus is speedily proclaimed King. Fearing for his own safety, he is conciliatory towards Melantius and offers pardon. Evadne, exultant and still stained with the King's blood, comes to Amintor expecting to be taken as his wife. When he recoils with horror at her deed she kills herself as a desperate act of expiation. In the same scene Aspatia, passing herself off as her brother, provokes Amintor to fight with her and kill her. Dying, she reveals her identity when she hears Amintor speak remorsefully of his conduct towards her. Amintor then commits suicide to join Aspatia in death. Curiously, the play does not close on this tragic scene. Instead, the final focus is on Lisippus who pronounces equivocally: ". . .on lustfull Kings / unlookt for suddaine deaths from God are sent, / But curst is he that is their instrument".

The Maid's Tragedy is a work of great virtuosity rather than of moral penetration or humane insight. It is notable for the boldness of its characterisation and the theatricality of the action. Evadne encompasses extremes—insolence and defiance at the beginning of her scene with her brother, then acute awareness of her disgrace, and unshrinking resolution in the carrying out of the murder. In a period remarkable for formidable women characters in the theatre she is notable. Melantius dominates the plot, taking immense risks and succeeding through sheer force of personality, especially in the scenes with Calianax and the King. Equally extreme is Aspatia in her melancholy outpourings and her subsequent abandonment to what can only be her destruction. Action and dialogue are ingeniously controlled so that maximum effect is gained from the scenes of disclosure or recognition. This is most evident in the scene of Amintor's wedding night, where Evadne responds coolly to his bewildered questioning. When Amintor, searching for the cause of Evadne's prevarications, conjectures that she may have sworn to her companions to keep her maidenhead, Evadne replies with incredulity at Amintor's naivety: "a maidenhead Amintor at my yeares".

Once Amintor has revealed the truth to Melantius, the question of regicide becomes the focus of dramatic interest. The famous anecdote told by Thomas Fuller about the meeting of Beaumont and Fletcher in a tavern to plot a play in which Fletcher "undertook to kill the King therein" indicates the dramatists' point of departure. Censorship, however, demanded that the theme be treated with some circumspection. Only for an instant is Amintor goaded into murderous threats against the King before he withdraws, recognising the King's "divinitie" which quells his "rising passions". When

Melantius later avows "ile waken death / And hurle him on the King", Amintor refuses to join with him. But the question of regicide is never debated. Melantius's obsession with the restoration of his family honour is directed into devising stratagems to gain the fort, while urging Evadne to do the deed. The plot is so constructed that the King's murder becomes, in effect, a crime of passion rather than a political act against a tyrannical ruler. The same ideological uncertainty is present in Lisippus's appeasing words to Melantius (". . .you have lost / A noble master, which your faith, Melantius, / Some thinke might have preserved, yet you know best") and in his final speech. The playwrights would seem to be attempting to have it both ways: warnings are directed both at tyrannical rulers and at those who dare to purge the state of such rulers.

The idealism and ingenuousness of Amintor and the romantic attachment of Aspatia are seen as misplaced in the court of Rhodes, where the tone is set by the liaison of the King and Evadne to which some members of the court are privy. Evadne makes no pretence that she has become the King's mistress for any reason other than ambition. She tells him bluntly that she would forsake him if he should be thrown "from this hight". It might be argued that there is some element of redemption to counter the cynicism of the court in Melantius's desire to restore the honour of his name. He attaches much value to his friendship with Amintor, claiming even that "the name of friend is more than family", and he vows to commit suicide when his friend dies. But in the scene where Amintor reveals his grief and shame, Melantius displays little compassion, seeing his sister's conduct primarily in terms of the reputation of his family. His subsequent machinations display a similar self-interest and a capacity for survival. Beaumont and Fletcher have created a world of power games and petty rivalries which none of the characters has the integrity or strength to transcend.

—Janet Clare

THE MAIDS (Les Bonnes)
by Jean Genet

First Publication: Paris, 1948.
First Production: Théâtre de l'Athénée, Paris, 19 April 1947.

Translations
The Maids, translated by Bernard Frechtman, London, 1963.

Criticism
(For general works on the author, see Playwrights volume)

Articles:
L. Leighton, "Ecstasy Through Compulsion", in Kenyon Review, 17, 1955.
O. Pucciani, "Tragedy, Genet and The Maids", in Tulane Drama Review, vol. 7 no. 3, 1963.
Rose Zimbardo, "Genet's Black Mass", in Modern Drama, 8, 1965–66.
Renée Hubert, "The Maids as Children: A Commentary on Genet's Les Bonnes", in Romance Notes, 10, 1969.
Y. Vasseur, "Les Objets dans Les Bonnes", in Obliques, 2, 1972.
Dan Popa, "Les Bonnes de Jean Genet: L'Axe de la combinaison", in Travaux de linguistique et de littérature, vol. 14 no. 2, 1976.
M.E. Ragland-Sullivan, "The Psychology of Narcissism: Jean Genet's The Maids", in Gradiva, vol. 2 no. 1, 1979.
Sylvie D. Henning, "The Impossible Ritual of Les Bonnes", in Modern Language Studies, vol. 10 no. 2, 1980.
Sylvie D. Henning, "The Ritual Im-plications in Les Bonnes", in Boundary 2, vol. 10 no. 2, 1982.
Ellie Ragland-Sullivan, "Jacques Lacan, Literary Theory, and The Maids of Jean Genet", in Psychological Perspectives on Literature: Freudian Dissidents and Non-Freudians, edited by Joseph Natoli, Hamden, Connecticut, 1984.
Gay McAuley, "Paradigmatic Structures in Text and Performance: Movement and Gesture in Four Performances of Les Bonnes", in Kodikas / Code, 10, 1987.
Maria Paganini, "L'Inscription juridique dans Les Bonnes de Jean Genet", in Romantic Review, 80, 1989.

*   *   *

The ironically titled Les Bonnes ("une bonne" can mean a maid or a good woman) is Jean Genet's best known and most successful play. The central figures in it are two downtrodden domestic servants who have sought revenge against their mistress by denouncing her lover to the police. In the course of the play they learn that their plot has been unsuccessful. So too is a further attempt to poison Madame herself. The play ends instead with one of the two maids, Solange, poisoning her sister Claire and apparently preparing to spend the rest of her days in prison.

The play has a clear—even classical—structure, comprising five main movements. In the first of these, the two maids act out a ritualized revenge fantasy which looks set to culminate in the strangulation of their mistress, whose role is played by Claire, the younger of the pair. This denouement is forestalled by the ringing of an alarm clock, which the maids themselves have set to enable them to restore order before the actual return of Madame. The second movement deals with the relationship of mutual jealousy, hatred, and repulsion that exists between the two sisters: "I know I disgust you", Solange confesses to her sister, "And I know it because you disgust me. When slaves love one another, it's not love". Movement three is initiated by the ringing of the telephone on which Monsieur announces that he has been released and is awaiting Madame at one of their customary haunts. Threatened with exposure, the maids determine to recoup the situation by murdering Madame herself. They are prevented from doing so in Movement four by Madame's failure to drink a proffered cup of tea laced with the poison phenobarbital. After her departure they resume their revenge ritual. This time, however, it actually does end with the very real death of Claire, who instructs Solange to serve to her the tea intended for their mistress. It is at once an act of murder and of suicide.

The Maids is loosely based on a sensational real-life drama which took place in Le Mans in the 1930's. This was the murder by two sisters, Christine and Léa Papin, of the two women in whose domestic service they had been employed. Though he clearly satirizes the vacuity of the haute bourgeoisie, to which Madame belongs, Genet sardonically denies that the play is about the social plight of domestic servants. In contrast to the injustice and cruelty meted out to the Papin sisters, and although in their ritual the maids portray Madame as a sadistic tyrant, Solange and Claire are the victims at worst of their mistress's condescending patronage. "Madame adores us", intones Claire. To which Solange responds "She loves us the way she loves her armchair."

The Maids: The Pit, Barbican Centre, London, 1988 (Royal Shakespeare Company)

The Maids is essentially an examination of identity. It is a *tour de force* on Genet's part that he achieves this without resort to the conventional expedient of character. Genet declares, "I go to the theatre in order to see myself, on the stage. . .as I wouldn't be able—or wouldn't dare—to see myself, whether in reality or dream, and yet as I know myself to be. The function of the actors is therefore. . .to show me to myself".

Despite its clarity of structure and the predominance of a single theme, *The Maids* is a difficult, though perhaps not ultimately a complex work. Partly this is a matter of the different levels discernible within the play. The hatred felt by Claire and Solange towards Madame and the real tensions between the two sisters are intermingled. Both frequently surface in the same utterance, as when Claire accuses Solange: "Through her it was me you were aiming at. I'm the one who's in danger". Partly, too, the difficulty of the play stems from its ambiguity, which is compounded by the existence of no less than five versions (only three of which are extant). Superficially, the play appears to chart the failure of Claire and Solange to avenge and free themselves. But the former's death at the hands of the latter is depicted by Genet less as a catastrophe than as a consummation. The English version ends with Solange's triumphant assertion: "We are beautiful, joyous, drunk, and free!". Even in the final French version, where she silently faces the audience, hands crossed as if in handcuffs, her attitude appears to mark the completion of a ceremony and to herald her impending apotheosis.

For Genet, the assertion of identity invariably entails repudiation. This may take the form of betrayal in an action in which the traitor dramatically rejects the Other's perception of him. But an altogether more absolute and definitive repudiation is to be found in the act of murder itself. For Solange, the death of Claire is just such an assertion of identity. It confers on her the clarity of self-definition that comes with solitude. Claire is instrumental in initiating the pact which results in her death. But it is less easy to view this event positively from her perspective. It is true that she sees herself surviving beyond death in a kind of mystic union with her sister. And her espousal of suicide is no less absolute a statement than Solange's act of murder. For Genet, abnegation of self may be just as powerful a declaration of identity as repudiation of the Other. Murderers and martyrs are, after all, to be found in roughly equal numbers among the saints.

The Maids was written at the request of Louis Jouvet, who first staged it at the Théâtre de l'Athénée. Genet disliked Jouvet's production, feeling that it made too many concessions to the expectations of a contemporary bourgeois audience. These took the form of both textual cuts and naturalistic staging. Genet preferred the more violent and sexually explicit version of the text used by Tania Balachova for her 1954 revival of the play. The standard English translation, by Bernard Frechtman, is based on this version. But the production he most admired was that widely mounted by Victor Garcia, with the Nuria Espert company, between 1969 and 1971. Garcia disregarded Genet's instructions on decor, concentrating instead on acting to convey the spirit of the play and even adding scenes. Genet apparently remarked that the Argentinian director had surpassed even what he himself had sought to achieve in writing *The Maids*.

—Tim Lewis

MAJOR BARBARA
by George Bernard Shaw

First Publication: In *John Bull's Other Island; Major Barbara; How He Lied to Her Husband*, London, 1907; revised version, in *Collected Plays*, 1930.
First Production: Royal Court Theatre, London, 28 November 1905.

Criticism
(For general works on the author, see *Playwrights* volume)

Books:
Rose A. Zimbardo (ed.), *Twentieth Century Interpretations of "Major Barbara"*, Englewood Cliffs, New Jersey, 1970.
Harold Bloom (ed.), *George Bernard Shaw's "Major Barbara": Modern Critical Interpretations*, New York, 1988.

Articles:
"*Major Barbara*: Shaw's Apotheosis of Money", in *Current Literature*, 43, 1907.
C.A. Bennett, "*Major Barbara*", in *Bookman*, 63, 1926.
Joseph Frank, "*Major Barbara*: Shaw's Divine Comedy", in *Publications of the Modern Language Association* [*PMLA*], vol. 71 no. 1, 1956.
William Irvine, "*Major Barbara*", in *The Shavian*, 7, 1956.
Bernard F. Dukore, "Towards an Interpretation of *Major Barbara*", in *Shaw Review*, vol. 6 no. 2, 1963.
Sidney P. Albert, "In More Ways than One: *Major Barbara's* Debt to Gilbert Murray", in *Educational Theatre Journal*, 20, 1968.
Charles A. Berst, "The Devil and Major Barbara", in *Publications of the Modern Language Association* [*PMLA*], 83, 1968.
Barbara Bellow Watson, "Sainthood for Millionaires: *Major Barbara*", in *Modern Drama*, 11, 1968.
Sidney J. Albert, "Shaw's Advice to the Players of *Major Barbara*", in *Theatre Studies*, 10, 1969.
Daniel J. Leary, "Dialectical Action in *Major Barbara*", in *Shaw Review*, 12, 1969.
Robert J. Jordan, "Theme and Character in *Major Barbara*", in *Texas Studies in Literature and Language*, 12, 1970.
Sidney P. Albert, "The Price of Salvation: Moral Economics in *Major Barbara*", in *Modern Drama*, 14, 1971.
Raymond S. Nelson, "Responses to Poverty in *Major Barbara*", in *Arizona Quarterly*, 27, 1971.
Norman Gelber, "The *Misalliance* Theme in *Major Barbara*", in *Shaw Review*, 15, 1972.
J.L. Wisenthal, "The Underside of Undershaft: A Wagnerian Motif in *Major Barbara*", in *Shaw Review*, 15, 1972.
Bernard F. Dukore, "Revising *Major Barbara*", in *Shaw Review*, 16, 1973.
Kurt T. von Rosador, "The Natural History of *Major Barbara*", in *Modern Drama*, 17, 1974.
Stuart E. Baker, "Logic and Religion in *Major Barbara*: The Syllogism of St. Andrew Undershaft", in *Modern Drama*, 21, 1978.
W.T. Jewkes, "The Faust Theme in *Major Barbara*", in *Shaw Review*, 21, 1978.
J. Percy Smith, "Shaw's Own Problem Play: *Major Barbara*", in *English Studies in Canada*, 4, 1978.
Trevor Whittock, "*Major Barbara*: Comic Masterpiece", in *Theoria*, 51, 1978.
Thomas Noel, "Major Barbara and Her Male Generals", in *Shaw Review*, 22, 1979.

Robert G. Everding, "Fusion of Character and Setting: Artistic Strategy in *Major Barbara*", in *SHAW*, 3, 1983.

Rosanne G. Potter, "The Rhetoric of a Shavian Exposition: Act I of *Major Barbara*", in *Modern Drama*, 26, 1983.

Lisë Pedersen, "Ducats and Daughters in *The Merchant of Venice* and *Major Barbara*", in *SHAW*, 4, 1984.

* * *

Shaw wrote a number of plays concerned with wealth and its distribution, but *Major Barbara* may be the most complex in theme and the most successful as drama. Barbara Undershaft has defied upper-class conventions by becoming a major in the Salvation Army, dedicating herself to the poor of London, who, naturally enough, resist her ministrations whenever they go beyond food and shelter. Adolphus Cusins, a professor of Greek given to quoting Euripides, pretends an equal dedication in order to be near her. Her mother, Lady Britomart—the owner of one of Shaw's most resounding character names—now needs more money for her children's marriages and turns to her long-estranged husband, Andrew Undershaft, a munitions maker of low birth but noble proportions. He is "fabulously wealthy, because there is always a war going on somewhere"; but the "Undershaft inheritance", which insists that the business must be passed on to another foundling boy, has been the cause of the rupture in their marriage. Andrew Undershaft is at the opposite moral pole from Barbara, yet father and daughter are immediately fascinated with one another and strike a bargain: he will visit her shelter if she will visit his armament works. The shelter is also in financial need and is saved from ruin only by the generosity of Undershaft and a whisky distiller; Barbara, shocked that the Army will accept money from two such manufacturers of evil, loses her faith and resigns her position. But Undershaft's creed, that the worst of all possible crimes is poverty, begins to convert Cusins and Barbara, especially when they see its effects in his utopian company town. When Cusins turns out to be a foundling he is installed as the heir to the Undershaft money, gunpowder, and destruction, with Barbara by his side.

If Shaw had wished to write a simple play he would have made Undershaft an industrialist like Andrew Carnegie, someone whose labor practices may have been questionable but who made contributions to social and economic advancement. Instead Undershaft is made to be a sower of death, like Alfred Nobel, disdaining common morality and the common excuses for his trade, selling munitions to anyone who applies, revelling in the devastation his guns bring. Nobel wished to buy respectability by endowing a prize for peace; Undershaft demands that his contribution to the Salvation Army be treated anonymously. As Cusins notes continually, Undershaft is a Prince of Darkness, a Dionysus in touch with the underside of human existence. Thus the dilemma he presents to Barbara and to readers and audience is enormously complicated. If poverty is the worst of crimes, then anything that eradicates it is good, even if that thing is, itself, normally considered evil. In this extreme of cases, Shaw's play implies, the end not only justifies Undershaft's means, but his means are the only realistic ones that can achieve the end.

A powerful second act in Barbara's West Ham shelter shows that the Salvation Army is an unwitting tool of the status quo: it relieves the effects of poverty just enough to blunt the edge of social revolution, without actually altering the conditions of the classes or attempting to redistribute wealth. The violence and desperation of a bully like Bill Walker cannot be corrected by hot soup and a prayer meeting because they are caused not by moral defects but by social inequities. When Barbara loses her faith in the Army she awakens to the sentimental nature of the Christian promise of salvation; she also slowly awakens to the fact that the Army, dependent upon the largess of capitalists, is therefore part of the capitalist establishment, as much as the Parliament that Undershaft brags is in his pocket. As one of the spiritual and economic unfortunates, Walker knows this truth in his bones. After the Army has accepted Undershaft's money, Walker speaks the cruellest and most incisive line of the play, rubbing salt into Barbara's wounds: "Wot prawce selvytion nah?".

The cannon is the metaphoric heart of *Major Barbara*. From its mock-military title to its numerous references to actual battles, the play offers glimpses of the destructive impulse; the final scene is literally dominated by a huge cannon center stage. In shifting its attention from Barbara's spiritual dilemma to Undershaft's vision of an orderly universe based on gunpowder, the play seems to promote the strongman as savior, and firepower as the ultimate arbiter. Shaw's Preface, a brilliant essay on the nature of wealth, provides a less disturbing philosophic context by suggesting that public choice need not lie between poverty on the one hand and bombs on the other, since it is capitalism that sanctions both; in a more humane economy both would be eradicated. But the play itself is profoundly ambiguous in its social morality; the diabolic Undershaft is its most gripping character, and even when he is taken ironically *Major Barbara* resists neat categorizing.

Despite its disturbing theme, its theatrical vitality has been unquestioned since the first performance in 1905. Shaw wrote it for Granville Barker's Court Theatre seasons, his first play designed with a specific company of actors in mind (Barker played Cusins, a role modelled on their mutual friend Gilbert Murray, whose translations of Euripides, which Cusins quotes, were also being performed at the Court). Since its twin subjects of war and money have been the central subjects of the 20th century, it has shown little sign of losing its hold on us.

—Dennis Kennedy

LE MALADE IMAGINAIRE. See **THE IMAGINARY INVALID.**

THE MALCONTENT
by John Marston (with additions by John Webster)

First Publication: London, 1604.

First Production: Blackfriars Theatre, London (Children of the Queen's Revels), 1604.

Editions

The Malcontent, edited by G.B. Harrison, London, 1933.

The Malcontent, edited by M.L. Wine, Lincoln, Nebraska, 1964 (Regents Renaissance Drama Series).

The Malcontent, edited by Bernard Harris, London, 1967 (New Mermaid Series).

The Malcontent, in *Jacobean Tragedies*, edited by A.H. Gomme, Oxford, 1969.

The Malcontent, edited by G.K. Hunter, London, 1975 (Revels Plays).

The Malcontent, in *The Selected Plays of John Marston*, edited by MacDonald P. Jackson and Michael Neill, Cambridge, 1986.

Criticism
(For general works on the author, see *Playwrights* volume)

Articles:
E.-E. Stoll, "Shakespeare, Marston, and the Malcontent Type", in *Modern Philology*, 3, 1906.

Harold R. Walley, "The Dates of *Hamlet* and Marston's *The Malcontent*", in *Review of English Studies*, 9, 1933.

E.-E. Stoll, "The Date of *The Malcontent*: A Rejoinder", in *Review of English Studies*, 11, 1935.

Christian Kiefer, "Music and Marston's *The Malcontent*", in *Studies in Philology*, 51, 1954.

Gustav Cross, "The Date of *The Malcontent* Once More", in *Philological Quarterly*, 39, 1960.

J. Arthur Faber, "Rhetorical Strategy in John Marston's *The Malcontent*", in *Hudson Review*, 4, 1970.

Ejner Jensen, "Theme and Imagery in *The Malcontent*", in *Studies in English Literature 1500–1900*, 10, 1970.

George L. Geckle, "Fortune in Marston's *The Malcontent*", in *Publications of the Modern Language Association* [*PMLA*], 86, 1971.

R.A. Foakes, "On Marston, *The Malcontent*, and *The Revenger's Tragedy*", in *The Elizabethan Theatre*, 6, 1973.

William W.E. Slights, " 'Elder in a Deformed Church': The Function of Marston's Malcontent", in *Studies in English Literature 1500–1900*, 13, 1973.

Brownell Salomon, "The Theological Basis of Imagery and Structure in *The Malcontent*", in *Studies in English Literature 1500–1900*, 14, 1974.

T.F. Wharton, "*The Malcontent* and 'Dreams, Visions, Fantasies' ", in *Essays in Criticism*, 24, 1974.

David Greenman, "Atmosphere, Contrast, and Control in Marston's *The Malcontent*", in *Shakespeare Jahrbuch*, 3, 1975.

Donald K. Hedrick, "The Masquing Principle in Marston's *The Malcontent*", in *English Literary Renaissance*, 8, 1978.

G.W.S. Brodsky, "Fortune's Bawd: Symbolism of the Maquarelle Episode in *The Malcontent*", in *Seventeenth-Century News*, 41, 1983.

*   *   *

The play is set in the court of Genoa where the Duke, Pietro, is a usurper. The ousted duke, Altofronto, adopting the name of Malevole, has returned in disguise and plays the role of the malcontent, engaging in scurrilous talk with the disreputable members of Pietro's entourage. Malevole is the dramatist's vehicle for what has been seen as a special kind of anti-court satire of which Marston was a leading exponent. Pietro accepts him for his plain-speaking and Malevole takes full advantage, to the extent of telling him that he has been cuckolded by the villainous Mendoza. He works up Pietro's feelings with absurd ease, to splendidly comic effect. Mendoza is soon revealed as a comic villain as he congratulates himself on his good fortune in a fulsome soliloquy; but immediately afterwards his relations with the Duchess Aurelia are undermined by his rival Ferneze, who tells Aurelia that Mendoza has slighted her in favour of Emilia, a lady-in-waiting. Aurelia now vents her rage on Mendoza who is also set upon by the furious Pietro. Mendoza has no difficulty, however, in convincing Pietro that the real adulterer is Ferneze, whom he promises to kill. Ferneze is surprised leaving Aurelia's chamber and is stabbed by Mendoza, but does not die. Mendoza becomes reconciled to Aurelia, who suggests that they should murder Pietro. When Mendoza hires Malevole to do the deed, the latter discloses the plot to Pietro and provides him with a hermit's gown for disguise. Pietro's death is announced and the hermit describes his last moments; whereupon Mendoza quickly banishes Aurelia and arranges to dispose of both Malevole and the hermit by persuading each to kill the other. Malevole and the hermit promptly tell each other of these plots. Aurelia in her banishment speech expresses penitence and Pietro, now that the Duke of Florence, Aurelia's father, has disowned him, is more than ready to relinquish his dukedom for a religious life. This is an appropriate moment for Malevole to drop his disguise and a scene of forgiveness and reconciliation takes place which includes the penitent Ferneze. It remains for Mendoza to be overthrown and his downfall is achieved by Malevole, with Pietro, Ferneze, and Celso (Altofronto's faithful supporter throughout his exile) under cover of a masque designed to celebrate Mendoza's accession to the dukedom. Meanwhile Maria, Altofronto's duchess, who has been long imprisoned, has refused Mendoza's offer of marriage and nobly scorned his threats against her life. The play concludes with Mendoza's ignominious exit (he is kicked out) and the happy reunions of the couples: Altofronto with Maria, and Pietro with Aurelia.

The Malcontent displays comedy of different forms. As Mendoza's prodigious sequence of murder plots and other villainies does not lead to any fatal mishaps, his career can be seen as an entertaining, moral fable. Virtue is, of course, triumphant in the end, as is expected of a tragicomedy. A different kind of comedy is found in abundance in the often scabrous exchanges between Malevole and the ridiculous courtier Bilioso, the ladies-in-waiting, and especially Maquerelle the bawd, who is skilled in the prescription of aphrodisiacs and recipes for restoring beauty. As a representative of her profession she seems to have a recognized status in this absurdly depraved court. But there are also serious elements: Malevole, as observer, expresses moral outrage at the Court's corruption. Early in the play he tells Pietro that he comes "from the public place of much dissimulation, the church" (a comment which was judged too subversive since it was cut from some editions of the play). One of the speeches which most pungently anatomizes courtly decadence contains Malevole's often quoted lines describing the "Italian lascivious palace" where a guardianless lady is "left to the push of all allurement". Malevole speaks wildly as if half-crazed by the abuses of power he sees around him. He is first encountered producing "vilest out-of-tune" music and the effect is reinforced by his jarring opening lines. Yet Marston's virtuosity with language enables him to negotiate the transition from this level of discord with great success. Malevole's soliloquy on sleeplessness ("I cannot sleep; my eyes' ill-neighbouring lids / will hold no fellowship") is a powerful expression of melancholy. In his role as a malcontent, a social and literary type of this period, he is acting a part, but as a victim of injustice he is genuinely wounded by the state of the world. His moral preoccupations, together with the courage and steadfastness of Maria and the true repentance of Pietro, give the play an element of seriousness which is a satisfying counterpoint to the monstrous absurdities of the plot. As a combination of brilliantly theatrical artifice and basic morality play *The Malcontent* is surprisingly effective.

The play has been interpreted as carrying contemporary, political associations. In a speech present only in the third edition, Duke Altofronto dwells upon popular responses towards the ruler: princes are loved "merely for their faces / and outward shows" rather than their virtue. Yet, the Duke warns, Heaven demands that princes have virtue, however concealed, since otherwise they are liable "to forfeit their commissions". That the passage was considered ideologically questionable is suggested by the alteration in some of the editions in which the more innocuous "men" is substituted for "prince" and "kings," thus avoiding direct reference to royal authority and, more specifically, to what amounts to a legitimisation of the dethronement of monarchs.

It is generally accepted that Marston was influenced by Shakespeare's *Hamlet*. The play belongs to a category of drama in vogue at this time in which the central character is a duke in disguise, but it is dissimilar in important respects from that other, most notable example, *Measure for Measure* : in Marston's play the duke is a subversive figure. Marston, who was influenced, as Philip J. Finkelpearl has described, by "the free-spoken, irreverent, independent atmosphere of the inns of court", was, in his career as satirist, similarly subversive.

—Janet Clare

———

LE MALENTENDU.   See **CROSS PURPOSE.**

———

MAN AND SUPERMAN
by George Bernard Shaw

First Publication: London, 1903.
First Production: Royal Court Theatre, London, 21 May 1905 (without Act III); Act III produced separately as *Don Juan in Hell: A Dream*, Royal Court Theatre, 4 June 1907; complete text first performed at Lyceum Theatre, Edinburgh, 11 June 1915.

Criticism
(For general works on the author, see *Playwrights* volume)

Books:
Alan W. England, *Man and Superman*, Oxford, 1968.
Harold Bloom (ed.), *George Bernard Shaw's "Man and Superman"*, New York, 1987 (Modern Critical Interpretations).

Articles:
William Irvine, "*Man and Superman*: A Step in Shavian Disillusionment", in *Huntington Library Quarterly*, vol. 10 no. 2, 1947.
Daniel J. Leary, "Shaw's Use of Stylized Characters and Speech in *Man and Superman*", in *Modern Drama*, vol. 5 no. 4, 1963.
Frederick P.W. McDowell, "Heaven, Hell, and Turn-of-the-Century London: Reflections Upon Shaw's *Man and Superman*", in *Drama Survey*, vol. 2 no. 3, 1963.
J.L. Stamm, "Shaw's *Man and Superman*: His Struggle for Sublimation", in *American Imago*, 22, 1965.
Charles L. Holt, "Mozart, Shaw and *Man and Superman*", in *Shaw Review*, 9, 1966.
Robert L. Blanch, "The Myth of Don Juan in *Man and Superman*", in *Revue des langues vivantes*, 33, 1967.
Carl H. Mills, "*Man and Superman* and the Don Juan Legend", in *Comparative Literature*, 19, 1967.
Fred E. Stockholder, "Shaw's Drawing-Room Hell: A Reading of *Man and Superman*", in *Shaw Review*, 11, 1968.
Gene A. Barnett, "Don Juan's Hell", in *Ball State University Forum*, 11, 1970.

Gladys S. Crane, "Shaw's Comic Techniques in *Man and Superman*", in *Educational Theatre Journal*, 23, 1971.
Cyrus Hoy, "Shaw's Tragicomic Vision: From *Man and Superman* to *Heartbreak House*", in *Virginia Quarterly Review*, 47, 1971.
Carl H. Mills, "Shaw's Debt to Lester Ward in *Man and Superman*", in *Shaw Review*, 14, 1971.
J.L. Wisenthal, "The Cosmology of *Man and Superman*", in *Modern Drama*, 14, 1971.
Eric Salmon, "Shaw and the Passion of the Mind", in *Modern Drama*, 16, 1973.
Charles Carpenter, "Sex Play Shaw's Way: *Man and Superman*", in *Shaw Review*, 18, 1975.
Raymond S. Nelson, "Shaw's Heaven and Hell", in *Contemporary Review*, 226, 1975.
A.M. Gibbs, "Comedy and Philosophy in *Man and Superman*", in *Modern Drama*, 19, 1976.
T.F. Evans, "*Man and Superman*: Notes for a Stage History", in *SHAW*, 3, 1983.
Paulina S. Pollak, "Master to the Masters: Mozart's Influence on Bernard Shaw's 'Don Juan in Hell' ", in *SHAW*, 8, 1988.

*   *   *

Man and Superman: A Comedy and a Philosophy is the full title of one of Shaw's most durable plays, in which he used the traditions of romantic comedy to investigate the concept of *Übermensch*, the superior man thought by Nietzsche (in *Thus Spoke Zarathustra*) to be destined to create a superior race. At its center is John Tanner—intelligent, socially advanced, radical, disdainful of the deadly conventions of his class, and rich: in short, a Shavian superman ready to help with the ascent of humanity. But he resists marriage with all his strength, revealing a personal blindness to what the play proposes as the chief principle of life, the inescapable primacy of women and reproduction. When he is appointed the co-guardian of Ann Whitefield he must muster all his power to withstand her more vital one, the "life force", as Tanner calls it, and tries to escape her by motoring south through Europe, chauffeured at high speed by the "New Man", Henry Straker, a Cockney servant as politically aware as his master. They are detained in the Sierra Nevada by a troop of international (and socially conscious) brigands, whose literate leader, Mendoza, exiled himself from London because of love; his adored woman turns out to be Straker's sister. In a dream scene in the third act (the "Don Juan in Hell" sequence) four major characters assume roles from Mozart's *Don Giovanni*—with John Tanner as Don Juan Tenorio and Ann as Doña Ana—in a debate over eternity, gender, and the power of sexuality. In the finale, set in a garden in Granada, Tanner capitulates reluctantly and volubly to Ann's superiority.

Tanner is an upper-class Edwardian revolutionary, in the full ambiguous sense of that phrase. He has written *The Revolutionist's Handbook and Pocket Companion*, which utterly condemns him in the old-fashioned eyes of Ann's co-guardian, Roebuck Ramsden; he speaks his mind openly, even when his speech offends propriety; he is sensitively aware of the inequities of caste and politics (he signs himself "M.I.R.C."—Member of the Idle Rich Class). However he does not hesitate to live well from his privileged economic status. The automobile, a working prop central to the play's action, signifies his divided character: he delights in its modern speed and freedom but is dependent upon Straker to drive and repair it. Tanner is "*a megalomaniac, who would be lost without a sense of humour*", according to Shaw's stage direction, capable of the most incisive analysis of society and the lives of others yet ignorant of his personal relationships and

Man and Superman: National Theatre, London, 1981

desires. He is the romantic, leading man treated satirically; it is typical of Shaw's method to rely upon a Victorian dramatic convention and then turn it on its head. Tanner is the perfect "prey" for Ann because he operates from intellect, while she, though appearing to be calculating and devious, acts on instinct.

Both the play and Ann's character (which is little more than a fascinating embodiment of the mating urge) raise important and unresolved gender issues. In earlier and later works Shaw provides examples of contemporary or historical women who strike against society to redefine themselves by occupation, by change of class, or by appropriating the traditionally male virtues. In *Man and Superman*, however, women are defined in the accepted Victorian fashion, as thoroughbreds in the marital sweepstakes. In such a situation the truly vital woman, like Ann or Violet Robinson, can insure her fulfilment only by taking charge of the race herself. Here the Don Juan fable becomes particularly resonant. Both the action of the play and the debate in Act III reveal that Tanner is hopeless in the role of seducer, searching as he does for spiritual satisfaction (as Kierkegaard's Don Juan does in *Either / Or*); he is no sensualist, and too altruistic for Hell. It is Ann who is the sexual aggressor, making Tanner her ultimate conquest regardless of his protests. The new breed of supermen must be born through women's bodies, not out of men's minds.

The "philosophy" of the subtitle, dependent upon Schopenhauer and Bergson as well as Nietzsche, is inscribed in the comic action but fully visible only in the debate in Hell. Act IV thus gains a surreal dimension by adding dream characters to the existing roles, like a transparent overlay in an anatomy textbook. This turns out to be an unfortunate disability because the work, so lengthy that rarely can it be played in its entirety, is often shorn of the third act in performance. It was the last of Shaw's major plays to be written without assured production and the last to be published prior to production; its "literary" genesis has greatly affected its theatrical life. Shaw himself recognized that complete performance was possible only "under the conditions which prevail at Bayreuth and Oberammergau", and set an unfortunate precedent in its premiere by omitting Act III. Without the debate in Hell the power of *Man and Superman* is much qualified. *The Illustrated London News* said as much in 1906, about the Court Theatre performance: the play, "for all its high-sounding Nietzschean title and its Schopenhauerian philosophy, is just a very pleasant light comedy in which a charming woman is seen capturing an amusing young misogynist". To avoid this reductionist effect some productions attempt to include the essence of all four acts by severe cutting. The play's importance in the theatre, however, has rarely been questioned, and a number of the finest actors of the 20th century have played Ann or Tanner. On its own *Don Juan in Hell* has achieved a separate life as a theatre concert piece, a tradition Shaw also established.

—Dennis Kennedy

MAN AND THE MASSES. See **MASSES AND MAN.**

MAN EQUALS MAN (Mann ist Mann)
by Bertolt Brecht

First Publication: Berlin, 1926; revised version [ending at Scene 9], in *Gesammelete Werke, 1* (Malik Verlag edition), London, 1938; further revised version [Scenes 10 and 11 restored], in *Stücke*, Frankfurt, 1957.
First Production: Landestheater, Darmstadt, and Düsseldorf, 25 September 1926; revised versions, Volks-bühne, Berlin, January 1928, and Staatstheater, Berlin, 1931.

Translations
Man Equals Man [based on 1926 edition], translated by Eric Bentley, in *Seven Plays by Bertolt Brecht*, New York, 1961; adapted and retitled *A Man's a Man*, in *Baal; A Man's a Man; The Elephant Calf*, New York, 1964.
Man Equals Man, in *Man Equals Man; The Elephant Calf*, translated by Gerhard Nellhaus, London, 1979 (Collected Plays, vol. 2 no. 1).

Criticism
(For general works on the author, see *Playwrights* volume)

Books:
Carl Wege (ed.), *Brechts "Mann ist Mann": Materialien*, Frankfurt, 1982.

Articles:
Marianne Kesting, "Die Groteske vom Verlust der identität: Bertolt Brechts *Mann ist Mann*", in *Das deutsche Lustspiel*, edited by Hans Steffen, Göttingen, 1969.
J.W. Onderdelinden, "Brechts *Mann ist Mann*: Lustspiel oder Lehrstück?", in *Neophil*, 54, 1970.
Leroy R. Shaw, "The Strategy of Reassembly: Bertolt Brecht's *Mann ist Mann*", in his *The Playwright & Historical Change: Dramatic Strategies in Brecht, Hauptmann, Kaiser, & Wedekind*, Madison, Wisconsin, 1970.
Bert Cardullo, "A World in Transition: A Study of Brecht's *Mann ist Mann*", in *Germanic Review*, 59, 1984.
Desika Srinivasan, "Brechts *Mann ist Mann* im Deutschunterricht", in *German Studies in India*, 11, 1987.

*   *   *

Man Is Man (*Mann ist Mann*) is one of Brecht's most fascinating plays, partly because he worked on it for virtually the whole of his creative life, but largely because it is in this play that his characteristic, epic form becomes recognizable. The play's history reveals its formative place in his development: the premiere at Darmstadt in September 1926 saw the introduction of such typical features of Brechtian theatre as the "half-curtain", and included a jazz band on stage; the radio performance in March 1927 was responsible for introducing Kurt Weill to Brecht; and Brecht's own production of the play (with music by Weill) in Berlin in February 1931 introduced, in Peter Lorre's performance of the central role, probably the most extreme example of "epic acting".

Though there is no definitive version, all variants of the play have at least a similar plot line. The best known versions are set in a caricatured British India and concern Galy Gay, an inoffensive Irish porter, who is waylaid by three members of a machine-gun detachment. While robbing a pagoda, they have lost their fourth member, and now need Galy Gay to impersonate their friend at Bloody Five's roll call. Later, the three soldiers go to free their comrade, but he is now a captive in the pagoda. With the army leaving for the northern frontier, the three realize they will have to transform Galy Gay permanently into the fourth member of their detachment. With the help of Widow Begbick, who rejects the lustful importunings of Bloody Five, they set up a deal involving the selling of an elephant (which is really two men under a tarpaulin). Having completed the sale, Galy Gay is accused of selling regimental property, and also selling goods which are not what they seem. He is sentenced to death. In a mock ceremony he is shot, and the new fourth member of the detachment speaks the funeral oration over his coffin. During the journey towards the battle zone, Bloody Five castrates himself to subdue his lust, but when they reach their destination he wanders uselessly away. The new ferocious fourth gunner leads the bloody capture of the enemy fortress.

The play deals most obviously with problems of individuality, the sense of self, and its relationship to a wider society. It vehemently denies the existence of any essential, psychological reality ("the real me") and attempts to demonstrate how a person is formed by outside influences. Thus, Galy Gay does not resist transformation: to have done so might have lent him tragic status. When the danger of this philosophy dawned on Brecht, he added an anti-militarist bias for his 1931 production and in 1937 contemplated writing a version set in Germany, with Galy Gay's conversion being to Nazism at a Nuremberg rally.

Actually such a version would probably have negated the play's most arresting quality—the inconsistencies designed partly to undermine conventional notions of fixed, psychological truths. The soldiers veer erratically from the farcical to the brutalized; for example Widow Begbick is at one moment the soft-hearted tart and at another the flinty-hearted business-woman, sometimes the sexual provocatrice, sometimes a surrogate mother. A similar inconsistency prevails in the play's attitudes: at one moment, Brecht seems to be fascinated by imperialism, at another repelled by it. There is exoticism, crypto-racism, and comic satire in his treatment of Eastern religion, and sado-masochism and sexism in the way the soldiers are presented.

This kaleidoscope of effects is both unusual and disturbing. It results from Brecht splitting the action into individual, self-contained sections, each with its own basic "guests", or representation of meaning. This according to Brecht, "keeps the spectator out" of the action, leaving him "to make his own discoveries". Yet even while the "various phases must be separated" in this way, Brecht also insists that "everything depends on the development, on the flow". In practice this apparent paradox means that the scene of the selling of the elephant, for instance, is broken up into distinct "turns", each introduced by a sort of ringmaster ("Number One: The Elephant Deal. The MG section transfers an elephant to the man whose name must not be mentioned", and a little later: "And now for Number Two: The Elephant Auction. The man whose name must not be mentioned sells the elephant", and so on). Thus, the various phases are separated. Simultaneously, time is running extremely short, the army is packing up to leave, the artillery rolls by, then the elephants, and finally the soldiers themselves leave to board the train. These accompanying actions provide conventional dramatic suspense—will everything be completed by the time the troop trains go?

The gradual transformation of the inoffensive Galy Gay, as

Man Equals Man: Almeida Theatre, 1985, London

well as that of the murderous Bloody Five, is thus presented as a kind of "montage", a critical term associated especially with the Russian film director, Sergei Eisenstein. It is worth noting that the musician Edmund Meisel was working closely with Eisenstein to compose a score for *Battleship Potemkin* when it came to Berlin in 1926, at the same time as he was working almost equally closely with Brecht on *Man Is Man*: Brecht "sketched rough drafts of the songs that Meisel actually composed". It is reasonable to suppose, therefore, that he was aware of, and indeed influenced by, the Russian's theory. Certainly, the montage technique of breaking up the action while simultaneously giving it a dynamic flow, which was to become the hallmark of Brecht's epic theatre, makes its slightly awkward debut in this play.

—Robert Leach

A MAN FOR ALL SEASONS
by Robert Bolt

First Publication: London, 1960.
First Production: As radio play, for the British Broadcasting Corporation, 1954; on stage, Globe Theatre, London, 1 July 1960.

Criticism
(For general works on the author, see *Playwrights* volume)

Books:
Leonard Smith, *"A Man for All Seasons" by Robert Bolt*, London, 1985.

Articles:
M.W. Fosbery, *"A Man for All Seasons"*, in *English Studies in Africa*, 6, 1963.
E.E. Reynolds, "The Significance of *A Man for All Seasons*", in *Moreana*, 23, 1969.
Arthur Thomas Tees, "The Place of the Common Man: Robert Bolt's *A Man for All Seasons*", in *University Review*, 36, 1969.
Joseph R.J. McElrath, "Metaphoric Structure of *A Man for All Seasons*", in *Modern Drama*, 14, 1971.
Gilbert Storari, "From Elizabeth I to Elizabeth II: Two Popular Views of Thomas More", in *Moreana*, 30, 1971.
Klaus-Dieter Fehse, "Robert Bolt's *A Man for All Seasons*: Eine Interpretation", in *Neusprachliche Mitteilungen aus Wissenschaft und Praxis*, 26, 1973.
Barry J. Seltser, "Realists, Idealist, and Political Heroism", in *Soundings*, 68, 1985.

*　　*　　*

Robert Bolt's *A Man for all Seasons* tells the story of the conflict between Henry VIII and Sir Thomas More. It tracks their relationship back to when they were friends, when More was someone whose opinion Henry respected and sought over issues of state as well as those of conscience. It follows the controversy of Henry's divorce from Catherine of Aragon, covering its implications as regards King Charles of Spain and Henry's soul since he has married his dead brother's bride. But the play does not offer a great part to Henry. Its focus is Thomas More and how his conscience, as a Roman Catholic, cannot accept the Act of Succession which solidifies the break from Rome in stating that Anne's children are heirs to the throne. What Bolt achieves is far more than simply placing history on stage—he presents More as a man who tries to reconcile his political role as Chancellor, with his religious one as a Catholic. It vividly evokes the life More and his family must live as he maintains his ethical and religious position. It shows the plottings of Cromwell, Cranmer, and Rich to try and catch More out and prove him guilty of treason. And it is More's silence which speaks most loudly throughout the play.

Running clearly through *A Man for all Seasons* are the issues of the use of power and personal integrity which can be found throughout Bolt's work. These issues are reflected in the actual structuring of the play, which can be seen as falling into two halves—the first showing More at the height of his power, with a career going from strength to strength and in full favour with the King, and the second showing pressure mounting on More over the issue of the divorce, and the rapid loss of his material prosperity whilst, conversely, his moral integrity grows. This change in More's material and personal circumstances is firmly placed within the context of his family. The King and Parliament are there (indeed Cromwell and Cranmer have ever larger roles as the play approaches its climax), and More's relationships with them reveal him truly to be "a man for all seasons", but the affairs of state are essentially a backdrop to More's family relationships and how the workings of his conscience affects them. As they appeal to More's love, friendship, and loyalty, Bolt shows him as a man increasingly worn down by the awareness that every word could be a trap which could affect his own life, as well as that of his family.

One important point about Bolt's structuring of *A Man for all Seasons* is the part played by Rich. His development within the play clearly offers a mirror image of More himself. When More is at the height of his career, Rich is a poor hanger-on who is desperate for work, but too proud to take the teaching position More suggests for him. As More falls from favour because of the promptings of his conscience, Rich climbs ever higher, increasingly surrendering personal integrity for material gain, and only once turning to More for help, with the words "I'm adrift". Since the fortunes of the two men run side by side, illuminating each other by their contrasts, it is perfect dramatic timing that when Rich, now solicitor-general, perjures himself and sends More to his death, the future saint should be at his spiritual and moral zenith.

With so much emphasis on More's spiritual strength, the reliance upon and the respect he feels for the law must not be ignored. Bolt portrays Sir Thomas More as a man who is as adamant a lawyer as he is a Catholic, and he admits that his treatment of him is that of "treating Thomas More, a Christian saint, as a hero of selfhood". More is thrilled with his appointment as Lord Chancellor, but when Henry denies the papal supremacy of the Church, More must recognise that his involvement in the material world will only survive if he perjures his faith. So it is that he uses his training as a lawyer to try and preserve his faith—and his skin. More believes that his knowledge of the law will protect him "And whoever hunts for me. . .God, or Devil, will find me hiding in the thickets of the law!". In the end, however ambiguous Bolt's treatment of More the Lawyer *and* the Saint, it is the latter who wins the

final battle; when the law has failed him, he can give expression to his hitherto silent conscience.

This portrayal of Saint Thomas More as a man, in Bolt's words, "with an adamantine sense of his own self" risks the danger of being an unpopular depiction for the audience. Bolt is faced with the challenge of characterising a figure and dramatising a period in history which are both carefully documented, without alienating those in his audience who are familiar with the historically documented Thomas More and the progression of events leading up to his execution. The play shows Robert Bolt's *dramatization* of More; and his portrayal should be accepted as one within the canvas of the play world.

Written in 1954 and produced on stage in 1960 at the Globe Theatre, *A Man for all Seasons* was originally intended as a radio play. This genesis explains the chorus figure, the Common Man, who wanders in and out of the main action of the play; clearly a useful device for a purely oral presentation. The play was also produced as a film in 1966, which Fred Zinnemann directed. For the film, as in the first stage production, Paul Scofield played Thomas More.

—Claudia Woolgar

THE MAN FROM MUKINUPIN
by Dorothy Hewett; music by Jim Cotter

First Publication: Sydney, 1980.
First Production: Playhouse, Perth, Western Australia (The Australian National Theatre Company), 31 August 1979.

Criticism
(For general works on the author, see *Playwrights* volume)

Articles:
Lekkie Hopkins, "Language, Culture and Landscape in *The Man from Mukinupin*", in *Australasian Drama Studies*, 10, 1987.
Margaret Williams, "A Debt Repaid: The Pastoral Plays of Dorothy Hewett", in *Contemporary Australian Drama* (second edition), edited by Peter Holloway, Sydney, 1987.

*   *   *

Mukinupin, a mythical Western Australian country town, is shown during the years from 1912 to 1920 in which the outside world impinges on the isolated community, most notably through the First World War. Jack Tuesday, a local lad, goes off to the war thinking he's been turned down by the storekeeper's daughter Polly Perkins, but returns just in time to save her from a miserable marriage to an elderly travelling salesman, Cecil Brunner. Parallel to the superficial plot of commerce and courtship is a night world peopled by *doppelgängers* of the day characters (and played by the same actors), which reveals the town's dark side repressed by respectability and self-righteousness.

The play's title is something of a red herring, since the township of Mukinupin, with its disparate inhabitants and visitors, is the collective central "character" of the play. The set requires a backdrop or cyclorama suggesting the desert stretching into infinity, with the town itself evoked by cut-outs of the general store and a war memorial, the "toy" quality of the buildings underlining the fragility of White civilisation in the Australian outback. The day scenes have a deliberately naïve quality to which the alternating scenes of the night rituals add depth and significance. The night interludes expose the town's secrets; in particular the massacre of a tribe of Aborigines in the creek-bed at the instigation of the Mukinupin wives, and led by the respectable lay preacher, Eek Perkins. Jack's and Polly's traditional stage wedding is paralleled by the solemn pagan marriage between Jack's brother Harry, a war hero who is, however, the town's alcoholic outcast, and Polly's half-sister, the Aboriginal girl Touch of the Tar. The two weddings signify some possibility of reconciliation between the white and black races, and between the town's conscious and deeper, psychic levels.

The ostensible plot is almost childishly simple, and the dominant style is that of musical comedy with each of the main characters having their own musical "number", but the metaphor of show business and its deeper equivalent in primitive ritual ties the daylight world to that of the dark. The theme of performance is found at all levels throughout the play. A melodramatic travesty entitled "The Strangling of Desdemona" is enacted in the local town hall by a visiting theatrical troupe, with Othello played in an outrageous Italian accent by the leading man, Max Montebello. Jack Tuesday is "discovered" as a theatrical talent, and at the end of the play he and Polly are off to join the musical comedy world of J. C. Williamson (the major theatrical entrepreneur in Australia for the first half of this century). The finale to the play is the song "Mukinupin Carousel", performed by "the Mukinupin Glee Club of the Ladies Auxiliary of the RSL", the ultimate in amateur entertainment! The rituals of the night expose a much deeper layer of timeless, psychic forces in the "hobby horse" which frightens Polly when she goes down the "wrong end of town" looking for Jack, and the harvest mummers, disguised as "moving haystacks", whose dance begins the play. The juxtaposition of "high" and "popular" cultures is characteristic of Dorothy Hewett's work, and is found throughout the play: the Widow Tuesday, Jack's mother, for example, is an amateur elocutionist forever quoting from literary classics, and Harry and Polly's wedding recalls *A Midsummer's Night's Dream* and *The Tempest*, while by contrast the lyrics of the songs are deliberate clichés in the style of a stage musical.

The theme of *The Man from Mukinupin* is the fertilisation of a seemingly cloddish, country town by the power of the imagination through the layers of ritual, from the social and superficial to the tribal and psychic, integral to the day and night worlds. The theme is also expressed through the recurrent images of water, bringing the desert to life, and looking to the stars: Eek Perkins' brother Zeek, the town's half-"touched" seer, is a star-gazer and water-diviner, whose search for water produces nothing, but who discovers a new planet through his telescope. The theme of water runs throughout the play, in Zeek's half-ranting speeches, a pastiche of Shakespearean and Biblical evocations; while in the creek–bed near the town where her tribe was massacred, Touch of the Tar performs an ancient Aboriginal song and dance which brings longed-for thunder and rain.

Dorothy Hewett's achievement here is that, in a play which is both accessible and entertaining, the mythical town of Mukinupin is raised to the level of a metaphor for the Australian nation itself, emerging from a naïve but guilty past into a new state of awareness which embraces both the suppressed Aboriginal culture and the European literary, popular, and mythic inheritance. That the play has captured the imagination of many Australians is evident in its being

probably the most frequently revived of all recent Australian plays, regularly performed by both professional and amateur groups.

—Margaret Williams

THE MAN OF MODE; or, Sir Fopling Flutter
by Sir George Etherege

First Publication: London, 1676.
First Production: Dorset Garden Theatre, London, 11 March 1676.

Editions

The Man of Mode, in *Etherege: Dramatic Works* (2 vols.), edited by H.F.B. Brett-Smith, Oxford, 1927.
The Man of Mode, in *Plays of the Restoration and Eighteenth Century*, edited by D. MacMillan and H.M. Jones, New York, 1931.
The Man of Mode, in *Representative English Dramas from Dryden to Sheridan*, edited by F. and J.W. Tupper, New York, 1934.
The Man of Mode, edited by W.B. Carnochan, Lincoln, Nebraska, 1966 (Regents Restoration Drama Series).
The Man of Mode, in *Restoration Comedies*, edited by Dennis Davison, London, 1970.
The Man of Mode, edited by John Conaghan, Edinburgh, 1973 (Fountainwell Drama Texts).
The Man of Mode, edited by John Barnard, London, 1979 (New Mermaid Series).
The Man of Mode, in *The Plays of Sir George Etherege*, edited by Michael Cordner, Cambridge, 1982.
The Man of Mode, edited by Simon Trussler, London, 1988.

Bibliography

Nadia Rigaud, "Etherege—*The Man of Mode*: Bibliographe sélective et critique", in *Bulletin de la Societé d'Études Anglo-Américaines des XVIIe et XVIIIe siècles*, 25, 1987.

Criticism

(For general works on the author, see *Playwrights* volume)

Articles:

Arthur Sherbo, "A Note on *The Man of Mode*", in *Modern Language Notes*, 64, 1949.
Jean Auffret, "*The Man of Mode* and *The Plain Dealer*: Common Origins and Parallels", in *Études Anglaises*, 19, 1966.
Dale Underwood, "The Comic Values: *The Man of Mode*", in *Restoration Drama: Modern Essays in Criticism*, edited by John Loftis, New York, 1966.
R.S. Cox, "Richard Flecknoe and *The Man of Mode*", in *Modern Language Quarterly*, 29, 1968.
Paul C. Davies, "The State of Nature and the State of War: A Reconsideration of *The Man of Mode*", in *University of Toronto Quarterly*, 39, 1969.
John H. Hayman, "Dorimant and the Comedy of a Man of Mode", in *Modern Language Quarterly*, 30, 1969.
Daniel Krause, "The Defaced Angel: A Concept of Satanic Grace in Etherege's *The Man of Mode*", in *Drama Survey*, 7, 1969.

The Man of Mode: Stratford-Upon-Avon, 1988 (Royal Shakespeare Company)

Ronald Berman, "The Comic Passions of *The Man of Mode*", in *Studies in English Literature 1500–1900*, 10, 1970.

Robert D. Hume, "Reading and Misreading *The Man of Mode*", in *Criticism*, 14, 1972.

Dan Ford, " 'Smelling as One Does': A Comment on Time in *The Man of Mode*", in *Papers of the Arkansas Philological Association*, 2, 1976.

Brian Corman, "Interpreting and Misinterpreting *The Man of Mode*", in *Papers in Language and Literature*, 13, 1977.

The Man of Mode: Seminar Reports", in *Restoration*, 1, 1977.

Leslie H. Martin, "Part and Parody in *The Man of Mode*", in *Studies in English Literature 1500–1900*, 16, 1977.

David M. Vieth, "Divided Consciousness: The Trauma and Triumph of Restoration Culture", in *Tennessee Studies in Literature*, 22, 1977.

Albert Wertheim, "The Unrestrained and the Unconventional: Etherege's *The Man of Mode*", in *Literatur in Wissenschaft und Unterricht*, 13, 1980.

Derek Hughes, "Play and Passion in *The Man of Mode*", in *Comparative Drama*, 15, 1981.

Rose A. Zimbardo, "Of Women, Comic Imitation of Nature, and Etherege's *The Man of Mode*", in *Studies in English Literature 1500–1900*, 21, 1981.

Wilson F. Engel, "Etherege's *The Man of Mode*", in *Explicator*, 40, 1982.

James Thompson, "Lying and Dissembling in the Restoration", in *Restoration*, 6, 1982.

John Barnard, "Point of View in *The Man of Mode*", in *Essays in Criticism*, 34, 1984.

Wandalie Henshaw, "Sir Fopling Flutter, or the Key to *The Man of Mode*", in *Essays in Theatre*, 3, 1985.

Robert D. Hume, "Elizabeth Barry's First Roles and the Cast of *The Man of Mode*", in *Theatre Studies*, 5, 1985.

Jeffrey Plank, "Augustan Conversion of Pastoral: Waller, Denham, and Etherege's *The Man of Mode*", in *Essays in Literature*, 12, 1985.

Robert Wess, "Utopian Rhetoric in *The Man of Mode*", in *The Eighteenth Century*, 27, 1986.

*   *   *

The fashionable gentleman Dorimant switches his allegiance from his cast-off mistress Loveit to her friend Belinda and eventually to the rich young heiress Harriet who reciprocates his feelings but takes care to reserve herself for the state of marriage. There is a link between the central plot in which Harriet's mother, Lady Woodvil, is the only retarding influence, and the intrigue concerning the other couple to be united at the end of the comedy. Young Bellair disobeys his father's wish for him to marry Harriet and she joins him in a promise to go their different ways, Young Bellair having fallen in love with Emilia who unfortunately happens also to be the object of Old Bellair's desire. In the end, all obstacles to the Dorimant–Harriet and Young Bellair–Emilia partnerships are cleverly overcome by the two young couples. Sir Fopling Flutter, the hero that the play's title alludes to, only appears as a comic butt on the periphery of the plot's complications.

As in other plays in the genre of the comedy of manners (the pattern of which Etherege helped to fix), the plot in *The Man of Mode* does not carry too much weight. The connection between the lines of the action is neatly designed, but not substantial. The central couple (Dorimant and Harriet) contrast with the much more thinly sketched Emilia and Young Bellair. Sir Fopling Flutter's narcissistic attempts to succeed in society with his Frenchified airs do not interfere seriously with the love action. The plot's main function, typically, is to allow the playwright to establish a hierarchy among his characters based on the progression from fop to half-wit and true wit. Dorimant is placed at the top of the hierarchy that combines an essentially aristocratic *habitus* with an individualist code of cultural difference.

The action in the comedy brings out the hero's chief characteristics in a succession of revealing scenes. From the opening exchanges with servants, an orange-woman, and a shoemaker, followed by a flippant dialogue with Medley, another wit, and Young Bellair, through his two-timing conversation with Belinda and Loveit, to the witty repartees with Harriet, his penetration, disguised as Mr. Courtage, of Lady Townley's house, the brief sexual encounter with Belinda, and finally to the successful wooing of Harriet, Dorimant commands most attention and in his clever intrigues and elegant dialogue, shapes the climactic scenes of every act. Only occasionally is this perspective punctuated by Sir Fopling Flutter's intrusions on the action, providing the antithesis to Dorimant, as he is a superficial fool.

The central theme could be described as the opposition of mask and reality in social behaviour. However, when at one stage Dorimant, in one of his apparently gratuitous bursts of hostility towards his former mistress, Loveit, insists on tearing off her psychological masks to "show the passion that lies panting under", this does not signify the adoption of the satirist's role on his part, since disguising and using false pretence are among his *own* main weapons. His character resists all strategic moralization: more than almost any other Restoration rake-hero, Dorimant embodies a Hobbesian, naturalistic psychology, particularly in his unrepentant promiscuity and his *machismo* aggression deriving from the patriarchal code of courtly manners that enjoyed a brief, conspicuous flourish under Charles II. There was little doubt among Etherege's contemporaries that Dorimant was an admiring portrait of the notorious Earl of Rochester and his studied libertinism. When the neoclassicist critic John Dennis tried to vindicate *The Man of Mode* as a standard of taste in comedy half a century after its first production, he could do so only at the price of historicising Dorimant as a model of a bygone age. The historical distance robbed the play of its polemical slant against the Puritan ethic or its sentimental internalization. The hero's libertinism does not exempt him from the fate of married life in the country at the end of an extended battle of wits with Harriet Woodvil. But since the economic gains for Dorimant's heavily mortgaged estate is stressed by him as a contributing factor in this affair, and since he tries to pave the way for future meetings with Belinda in the very act of courting Harriet, there is no hint at any serious reformation of the genteel rake nor any prospect of a moralistic discourse.

In structure, *The Man of Mode* follows neoclassical rules in their demand for the unity of action, setting, and time which late-17th-century critics adopted from French and Italian models. In this respect Etherege allowed himself much less latitude than most of the other playwrights of the first generation of authors after the Restoration.

What ensured the survival of Etherege's best comedy on the British stage, albeit usually in adapted forms, was the confidence of the play's focus on its main character and the easy elegance and flexibility of a style that alternates between earthy prose and polished couplets, comic and lyrical songs, and the quotations (from Cavalier poets) uttered by the hero and his female counterpart which put them in a charmed circle all to themselves. The play increasingly became seen as so remote from real-life experience and later aesthetic standards that it was possible for Romantic critics, following Charles Lamb, to play off its fantasy content against its representational claims.

—Bernd-Peter Lange

MANDRAGOLA (La Mandragola)
by Niccolò Machiavelli

First Publication: c. 1518–24.
First Production: House of B. di Giordana, Florence, 1520.

Editions

La Mandragola, edited by Ricardo Bacchelli, Alpignano, 1960.
Mandragola, in *Machiavelli: Teatro*, edited by Guido Davico Bonino, Turin, 1964.
Mandragola, in *Niccolò Machiavelli: Il teatro e tutti gli scritti letterari*, edited by Franco Gaeta, Genoa, 1965.
Mandragola, Rome, 1977.
Mandragola, Florence, 1980.
Mandragola / The Mandrake [with translation], edited and translated by David Sices and James B. Atkinson, Hanover, New Hampshire, and London, 1985.

Translations

Mandragola, translated by Stark Young, New York, 1927.
Mandragola, translated and adapted by Ashley Dukes, London, 1940.
Mandragola, translated by Anne and Henry Paolucci, New York, 1951.
Mandragola, translated by John R. Hale, Swinford, Oxfordshire, 1956; revised version in *Machiavelli: The Literary Works*, Oxford, 1961.
Mandragola, translated by Frederick May and Eric Bentley, in *The Classic Theatre, 1*, edited by Eric Bentley, New York, 1958.
Mandragola, translated by Bruce Penman, in *Five Italian Renaissance Comedies*, edited by Bruce Penman, Harmondsworth, 1978.

Criticism

(For general works on the author, see *Playwrights* volume)

Articles:
Palmiro Togliatti, "Interpretazione di *Mandragola*", in *Rinascita*, 1953.
Natale Busetto, "*La Mandragola*: ricerche e osservazioni", in *Miscellanea crescini*, 29, 1961.
Martin Fleischer, "Trust and Deceit in Machiavelli's Comedies", in *Journal of the History of Ideas*, 27, 1966.
Robert I. Williams, "Machiavelli's *Mandragola*, Touchwood Senior, and the Comedy of Middleton's *A Chaste Maid in Cheapside*", in *Studies in English Literature 1500–1900*, 10, 1970.

Mandragola: National Theatre, London, 1984

Ezio Raimondo, "Il veleno della *Mandragola*", in his *Politica e commedia dal Beroaldo al Machiavelli*, Bologna, 1972.

Francesco Saverio Mirri, "Machiavelli *Il principe* e *La Mandragola*", in *Saggia di varia letteratura*, edited by L.B. Alberti, N. Machiavelli, A. Manzoni, and others, Florence, 1974.

Mark Hulliung, "Machiavelli's *Mandragola*: A Day and a Night in the Life of a Citizen", in *Review of Politics*, 40, 1978.

Pamela D. Stewart, "Text and Performance: The Comic Portrait in Italian Plays of the Sixteenth Century", in *Italian Studies*, 5, 1983.

Joseph A. Barber, "La Strategia linguistica di Ligurio nella *Mandragola* di Machiavelli", in *Italianistica*, 13, 1984.

Donald A. Beecher, "Machiavelli's *Mandragola* and the Emerging *Animateur*", in *Quaderni d'italianistica*, 5, 1984.

Jack D'Amico, "The *Virtù* of Women: Machiavelli's *Mandragola* and *Clizia*", in *Interpretation*, 12, 1984.

Franco Torelli, "Machiavelli's *Mandragola* and the Signs of Power", in *Drama, Sex, and Politics*, edited by James Redmond, Cambridge, 1985 (Themes in Drama Series).

*   *   *

Easily the most popular as well as the most original prose comedy of 16th-century Italy, and in some ways Machiavelli's most personal and characteristic work, *Mandragola*, in five acts, deals with a situation one finds in Ovid, Plautus, Terence, and Boccaccio. Into the treatment of this situation—a man's love for the young wife of an elderly husband and the various intrigues and machinations he has recourse to in order to obtain his end—Machiavelli injects a spirit of cynicism, coupled with pessimism, not so much concerning human nature as concerning the world, seen as full of malice, corruption and hypocrisy. Hence what is comic about the play is so only on the surface; deep down, both its subject-matter and ethos represent something which is morally sad and depressing. The play rendered Machiavelli famous at once, more than anything else he had so far written or published. Some of the implications of the play—that ends justify means, cunning prevails over trust and fidelity, cold calculation over what is spontaneously honest and straightforward—link it with Machiavelli's *The Prince* (the characters sometimes quoting maxims from *The Prince* or *The Discourses*, as for instance, when Fra Timoteo tells Lucrezia that "the end and not the means must be considered") and at the same time serve to explain its appeal to a modern spectator. But whereas in *The Prince* there is both an element of didacticism as well as an axe to grind—Machiavelli's desire to teach and influence the prince—in *Mandragola* the author accepts the world with all its corruptions, and men with all their defects and weaknessess, for what they are, thus allowing the plot of the play to unfold itself, the characters to evolve and behave as they would do without applying any *a priori* ethical criteria to their conduct, and without imposing any moralistic plan or pattern on the play. His attitude to character therefore appears objective, impersonal and detached. Hence, *Mandragola* is as far from the spirit of a satirical comedy or a morality play as a play possibly could be.

The main protagonists of the play are Dr. Nicia, a silly, elderly lawyer-husband, Lucrezia, his faithful but easily gullible wife, Callimaco, her lover, and Ligurio, the unscrupulous go-between who manipulates every other character in the play for his own ends. Francesco De Sanctis called Ligurio "odious and contemptible, and the worst type of man Machiavelli has been able to conceive in *The Prince*". If he cannot be compared with Iago, it is because Nicia cannot be compared with Othello. And if the play is decidedly a comedy rather than a tragedy, it is because it is not passions which spin the plot, but folly, intrigues, and cunning.

The title of the play (*Mandragola* means the mandrake root) has a symbolic significance. The superstitious belief that the mandrake root gave whoever ate it eternal youth and love is used by Callimaco as a stratagem. He loves Lucrezia, wife of the old and reputedly impotent lawyer Nicia and is introduced to him by Ligurio, a matchmaker and an opportunist, as a doctor who can cure his wife's sterility by giving her a potion distilled from the mandrake root. But the potion has the side-effect that any man who sleeps with her after she has taken it will die within a week. Both Callimaco and Ligurio persuade Nicia to let another man sleep with Lucrezia for the first time after she has taken the potion. He, Sostrata, (Lucrezia's mother), and Fra Timoteo (Lucrezia's confessor) all persuade the young wife to take the potion and to sleep with a stranger. Her mother argues that wisdom bids us choose the lesser of the two evils, and the greater evil is to be childless; the priest convinces her that through childbirth she will bring a soul into the divine keeping. Callimaco then disguises himself as that stranger and when he is alone with Lucrezia reveals to her his plot as well as his passionate love for her. She accepts his love and accepts him as part of her new family. Thus the play ends with everyone being happy, including Nicia who is the only character kept in the dark to the very end, and whose happiness is based on a deception of which he is so pathetically—and at the same time so blissfully—unaware.

Mandragola thus signalled a new direction and marked a new stage of development in dramatic art, drawing both its ethos and its inspiration from a detached and disinterested observation of human nature and human conduct. Irony and realism characterize Machiavelli's presentation in this play of how the profession of lofty ideals and moral principles is often made a mockery of by an unscrupulous pursuit of self-interest and self-gratification. Dramatic attention is focussed not so much on the various intrigues and conspiracies which the closely knit plot consists of, as on the natures of the protagonists and on the motives of their action and conduct—motives that are not so much analysed as seen in operation.

The society *Mandragola* depicts belonged to a certain period in Italian history—the Renaissance. But the play also portrays a world with its moral values, principles, and criteria in constant flux, and where there is an incessant interplay of laughter and tears, illusion and disillusion, mask and reality; in short, a mirror in which any age or society can, after due allowances of different customs and circumstances, find itself reflected.

—G. Singh

THE MANDRAKE. See **LA MANDRAGOLA.**

MANKIND
Anonymous

Composition: c. 1465–70.
First Production: Unknown. Possibly c. 1465–70.

Editions

Mankind, in *The Macro Plays*, edited by F.J. Furnivall and A.W. Pollard, 1904, London (The Early English Text Society Series).
Mankind, in *"Lost" Tudor Plays*, edited by J.S. Farmer, London, 1907.
Mankind, in *Chief Pre-Shakespearian Dramas*, edited by J.Q. Adams, Boston, 1924.
Mankind, in *The Macro Plays*, edited by Mark Eccles, 1969 (The Early English Text Society Series).
Mankind, in *Four Tudor Interludes*, edited by J.A.B. Somerset, London, 1976.
Mankind, in *English Moral Interludes*, edited by Glynne Wickham, London and Totowa, New Jersey, 1976.
Mankind, in *Three Late Medieval Morality Plays*, edited by G.A. Lester, London and New York, 1981.

Criticism

Books:
Mary Philippa Coogan Sr., *An Interpretation of the Moral Play "Mankind"*, Washington, D.C., 1947.
Michael R. Kelly, *Flamboyant Drama: A Study of "The Castle of Perseverance", "Mankind", and "Wisdom"*, Carbondale, Illinois, 1979.
Clifford Davidson, *Visualising the Moral Life: Medieval Iconography and the Macro Plays*, New York, 1989.

Articles:
M.M. Keiller, "The Influence of *Piers Plowman* on the Macro Play of *Mankind*", in *Publications of the Modern Language Association* [*PMLA*], 27, 1912.
Roy W. MacKenzie, "A New Source for *Mankind*", in *Publications of the Modern Language Association* [*PMLA*], 27, 1912.
W.K. Smart, "Some Notes on *Mankind*", in *Modern Philology*, 14, 1916.
W.K. Smart, "*Mankind* and the Mumming Plays", in *Modern Language Notes*, 32, 1917.
Donald C. Baker, "The Date of *Mankind*", in *Philological Quarterly*, 42, 1963.
Merle Fifield, "*Mankind*", in her *The Castle in the Circle*, Muncie, Indiana, 1967.
Paula Neuss, "Active and Idle Language: Dramatic Images in *Mankind*", in *Medieval Drama*, edited by Neville Denny, London, 1973 (Stratford-Upon-Avon Studies).
Lawrence M. Clopper, "*Mankind* and its Audience", in *Comparative Drama*, 8, 1974.
Neville Denny, "Aspects of the Staging of *Mankind*", in *Medium Aevum*, 43, 1974.
Kathleen M. Ashley, "Titivillus and the Battle of Words in *Mankind*", in *Annuale Mediaevale*, 16, 1975.
Lorraine K. Stock, "The Thematic and Structural Unity of *Mankind*", in *Studies in Philology*, 72, 1975.
Thomas J. Jambeck and Reuben R. Lee, "'Pope Pokett' and the Date of *Mankind*", in *Mediaeval Studies*, 39, 1977.
Sandra Billington, "'Suffer Fools Gladly': The Fool in Medieval England and the Play *Mankind*", in *The Fool and the Trickster: Studies in Honour of Enid Welsford*, edited by Paul V.A. Williams, Cambridge, 1979.

Lynne Diane Beene, "Language Patterns in *Mankind*", in *Language Quarterly*, 21, 1983.

W.A. Davenport, "Peter Idley and the Devil in *Mankind*", in *English Studies*, 64, 1983.

Stanton B. Garner Jr., "Theatricality in *Mankind* and *Everyman*", in *Studies in Philology*, 84, 1987.

* * *

Mankind opens with the character of Mercy delivering a monologue about the behaviour necessary for the attainment of salvation, interrupted by Mischief who mocks what he has said. Mischief is joined by three attendant vice figures, Newgyse, Nowadays, and Nought. A missing leaf in the manuscript obscures the precise progress of the plot at the point when the vices enter, but the ensuing text indicates a lot of stage business, music, dancing, a lewd audience song, and possibly acrobatics, as the vices taunt Mercy. The vices leave and Mercy turns to instructing the protagonist, Mankind, in his doctrine of labour and perseverance. Mankind, left to his own devices, is then set upon by the three attendant vices who attempt to distract him from the business of tilling his plot of ground. They fail and he repulses them, using his spade as a weapon. Once Mischief has cured them of their injuries, they devise a plot to call up the devil Titivillus to assist them. A collection is taken from the audience before the devil can appear. Making himself invisible to Mankind, Titivillus contrives the fall of the protagonist by placing a board under the earth so that it is impossible to dig, and then by sending a call of nature which makes him break off from his prayers. Thereafter the other vices take over and introduce him into a life of debauchery, which leads him into despair and ultimately into an attempt on his own life, encouraged by Mischief. Mercy, however, coming in search of his protégé, rescues and restores him at the end of the action.

A definitive "moral interlude", *Mankind* survives in only one manuscript, as one of the three "Macro Plays", assembled by the Bury St Edmunds antiquarian Cox Macro in the 18th century. The play itself—which has been dated on internal evidence to between 1465 and 1470—is of East Anglian provenance, as characters refer to place-names in Cambridgeshire and Norfolk. It shows evidence of having been written with an improvised theatrical space in mind. It requires very little scenery (a plot of ground) and few props (a spade and a coat), and condenses the potentially expansive battle between vice and virtue for the soul of the protagonist into the action of seven characters, with the possibility of doubling the parts of Mercy and Titivillus. It would have lent itself to performance by a troup of provincial touring professionals.

The protagonist is presented as an archetypal agricultural labourer, although the agrarian focus of the play can be taken too literally. As in the Bible, agricultural labour is given metaphorical force as the life of active Christian discipleship. Virtuous action is equated with persevering in the cultivation of the earth, whereas vice is anything which can distract from this labour, particularly the stock pursuits of the minor dandy—drinking, gambling, and adhering to impractical fashions of dress, as represented by Mischief's three acolytes. Mankind is armed with his spade, the weapon of his steadfast faith, and when he gives up digging the vices help him to shorten and modify his coat so that it conforms to the "new guise".

The play could be, and has been in modern reconstructions, performed both outdoors and in. The envisaged, original outdoor setting was a booth stage on the yard of an inn; but the play would also have lent itself to performance in front of the service screens in the great hall of a country house, monastery, or university college during a banquet or equivalent gathering. Modern commentators have been unable to establish one performance alternative definitively over the other. Both equally necessitate the devices which are found in the text for clearing the performance space and for introducing new characters by having them speak off-stage before they appear, devices particularly marked in the introduction of Titivillus. Circumstantial, textual details seem to favour the inn-yard, but the clear, Lenten themes of the play cast doubt on the viability of outdoor performance.

The action of the play may loosely be described as allegorical, as the characters all bear names suggesting that they personify abstract qualities. They are not, however, entirely two-dimensional in potential. Mercy, although representing an abstract quality more commonly represented as female, also advocates what he stands for and functions within the plot as the protagonist's confessor. His dialogue, although initially sanctimonious and preacherly is, towards the end of the play, increasingly charged with potential emotion. Mischief, Newgyse, Nowadays, and Nought also interact in a complex manner. In order to demonstrate complete devotion to ephemera, the three minor vices cannot be seen to do anything constructive, so Mischief is solely responsible for planning and instigating action. Nought, unable even to control his own bodily functions, is the butt of the others. Mankind, schematically, picks up on the dominant forms of diction of those by whom he is locally influenced, but this creates an impression of naïvety and gullability which is tantamount to characterisation.

The action draws heavily on the Bible for its metaphorical field, particularly on the text in Matthew's gospel, "The corn xall be sauyde, þe chaffe xall be brente", and upon the book of Job. The play's package of Lenten doctrine is directed specifically against the capital sin of sloth, and the whole movement of the play, down to details of diction, has been observed as charting the protagonist's fall into sloth and retrieval therefrom. What is more, the audience of the play is manipulated into a pattern of behaviour which anticipates and mirrors that of the protagonist, being induced first to participate in a lewd song, then to pay money to see the devil.

The devil, Titivillus, however, owes little to intellectual drama: he is not a personification but a "real" devil from the folk tradition, with, as the audience is promised, a big head. When the three minor vices are injured by Mankind, Mischief goes into a routine which is closely reminiscent of the quack doctor of the Mummers' play tradition, offering to cut off a head and set it on again as a cure for the headache. The integral collection of money is also reminiscent of the same tradition. Accordingly, although *Mankind* is generally invoked as typical of its genre, the play contains many anomalous elements which speak of an unselfconsciously mixed heritage.

—Pamela M. King

MANN IST MANN. See **MAN EQUALS MAN.**

LAS MANOS DE DIOS. See **THE HANDS OF GOD.**

MARAT/SADE (Die Verfolgung und Ermordung Jean-Paul Marats, dargestellt durch die Schauspielgruppe des Hospizes zu Charenton unter Anleitung des Herrn de Sade)
by Peter Weiss

First Publication: Frankfurt, 1964.
First Production: Schiller Theater, Berlin, 29 April 1964.

Translations

The Persecution and Assassination of Jean-Paul Marat as Performed by the Inmates of the Asylum of Charenton under the Direction of the Marquis de Sade, translated by Geoffrey Skelton, adapted by Adrian Mitchell, London, 1965.

Criticism
(For general works on the author, see *Playwrights* volume)

Books:
Karlheinz Braun (ed.), *Materialien zu Peter Weiss' "Marat/Sade"*, Frankfurt, 1967.
Gerd Weinreich, *Peter Weiss: "Marat/Sade"*, Frankfurt, 1974.
Thomas Hocke, *Artaud und Weiss: Untersuchung zur theoretischen Konzeption des "Theaters der Grausamkeit" und ihrer praktischen Wirksamkeit in Peter Weiss' "Marat/Sade"*, Frankfurt, 1978.
Sven H. Persson, *Från grymhetens till motståndets estetik: Peter Weiss tidiga författarskap och dramat "Marat/Sade"*, Gothenburg, 1979.

Articles:
Lionel Abel, "So Who's Not Mad? On *Marat/Sade* and Nihilism", in *Dissent*, 13, 1966.
E.M. Fleissner, "Revolution as Theatre: *Danton's Death* and *Marat/Sade*", in *Massachusetts Review*, 7, 1966.
Richard Schechner (ed.), "*Marat/Sade* Forum", in *Tulane Drama Review*, vol.10 no.4, 1966.
Samuel A. Weiss, "Peter Weiss's *Marat/Sade*", in *Drama Survey*, 5, 1966.
Ruby Cohn, "*Marat/Sade*: An Education in Theatre", in *Educational Theatre Journal*, 19, 1967.
William I. Oliver, "*Marat/Sade* in Santiago", in *Educational Theatre Journal*, 19, 1967.
Luc Lamberechts, "Peter Weiss' Marat-Drama: eine strukturelle Betrachtung", in *Studia Germanica Gandensia*, 10, 1968.
Rainer Taëni, "Peter Weiss' *Marat/Sade*: A Call for Liberation of Man Towards Humanism", in *Meanjin*, 27, 1968.
John J. White, "History and Cruelty in Peter Weiss's *Marat/Sade*", in *Modern Language Review*, 63, 1968.
Sybil Wuletich, "The Depraved Angel of *Marat/Sade*", in *Contemporary Literature*, 9, 1968.
Wolfram Buddecke, "Die Moritat des Herrn de Sade: zur Deutung des *Marat/Sade* von Peter Weiss", in *Geistesgeschichtliche Perspektiven*, edited by Götz Grossklaus, Bonn, 1969.
Norman James, "The Fusion of Pirandello and Brecht in *Marat/Sade* and *The Plebeians Rehearse the Uprising*", in *Educational Theatre Journal*, 21, 1969.
Summer Kirshner, "Marat or Sade? Peter Weiss and his Play in London and Rostock", in *To Find Something New: Studies in Contemporary Literature*, edited by Henry Grosshans, Pullman, Washington, 1969.
David Roberts, "Peter Weiss, *Marat/Sade* and the Revolution", in *Komos*, 2, 1969.

Rainer Taëni, "Chaos Versus Order: The Grotesque in *Kaspar* and *Marat/Sade*", in *Dimension*, 2, 1969.
Charles N. Genno, "Peter Weiss's *Marat/Sade*", in *Modern Drama*, 13, 1970.
Wesley V. Blomster and Leon J. Gilbert, "Textual Revisions in Peter Weiss's *Marat/Sade*", in *Symposium*, 25, 1971.
Karl Maurer, "Peter Weiss, *Marat/Sade*: Dichtung und Wirklichkeit", in *Poetica*, 4, 1971.
Leslie L. Miller, "Peter Weiss, Marat, and Sade: Comments on an Author's Commentary", in *Symposium*, 25, 1971.
Carl O. Enderstein, "Gestaltungsformen in Peter Weiss' *Marat/Sade*", in *Modern Language Notes*, 88, 1973.
Sidney F. Parham, "*Marat/Sade*: The Politics of Experience, or the Experience of Politics?", in *Modern Drama*, 20, 1977.
Suzanne Dieckman, "Levels of Commitment: An Approach to the Role of Weiss's Marat", in *Educational Theatre Journal*, 30, 1978.
Anke Bennholdt-Thomsen and Alfredo Guzzoni, "Peter Weiss' *Marat/Sade* und das Theaterspiel in Charenton", in *Zeitschrift für deutsche Philologie*, 102, 1983.
Mohammad Kowsar, "Analytics of Schizophrenia: A Deleuze-Guattarian Consideration of Büchner's *Danton's Death* and Weiss' *Marat/Sade*", in *Modern Drama*, 27, 1984.
Ward B. Lewis, "The American Reception of Peter Weiss' *Marat/Sade*", in *Maske und Kothurn*, 31, 1985.
John R.P. McKenzie, "Peter Weiss and the Politics of *Marat/Sade*", in *New Theatre Quarterly*, 1, 1985.
David R. Jones, "Peter Brook and *Marat/Sade*: Workshop and Production", in His *Great Directors at Work: Stanislavsky, Brecht, Kazan, Brook*, Berkeley, California, 1986.
David Roberts, "*Marat/Sade*, or the Birth of Postmodernism from the Spirit of the Avantgarde", in *New German Critique*, 38, 1986.
Roger Gross, "'*Marat/Sade*'s Missing Epilogue'", in *Journal of Dramatic Theory and Criticism*, vol.2 no.2, 1988.
Darko Suvin, "Weiss's *Marat/Sade* and Its Three Main Performance Versions", in *Modern Drama*, 31, 1988.

*   *   *

Peter Weiss's extraordinary play, *The Persecution and Assassination of Jean-Paul Marat as Performed by the Inmates of the Asylum of Charenton Under the Direction of the Marquis de Sade*, is more familiarly known within our own culture by the abbreviated title *Marat/Sade* given to its first British production, by the Royal Shakespeare Company in 1964, under the direction of Peter Brook. That relationship between dramatic and performance texts is itself an interesting one, since Brook's production, strongly influenced by Artaud, was in some ways a strategic appropriation of a play designed to hew as close to the dramaturgy of Brecht as to the theatre of cruelty.

The play consists of an imagined performance of a play about the assassination of French revolutionary hero Jean-Paul Marat, who was stabbed to death in his bath by Charlotte Corday in 1793. The play is represented as the work, in terms both of writing and production, of the Marquis de Sade, who did, in fact, write and present plays during his internment at the Asylum of Charenton from 1801 to his death in 1808. This inner play is thus performed by inmates, assisted and controlled by the asylum staff, and continually watched by de Sade as an on-stage spectator. The play scarcely has a linear narrative as such, though at the outset a "herald" offers a premonitory plot–synopsis stating that Charlotte Corday will come twice to Marat's door before making her third and fatal visit. The play

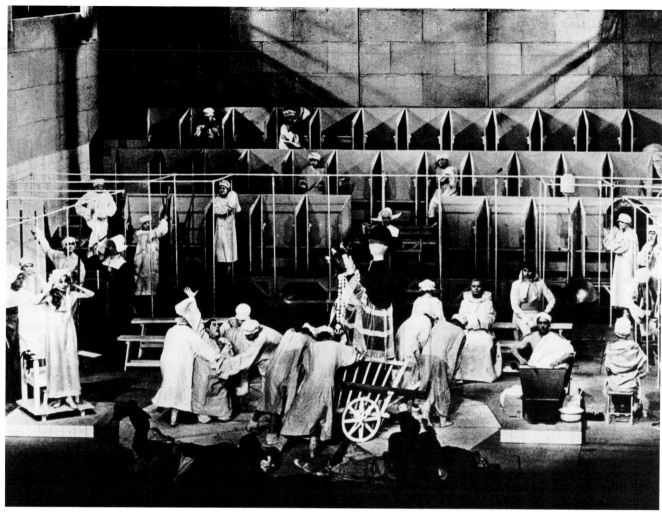

Marat/Sade: Schiller Theatre, Berlin, 1964

is divided into episodic scenes, which progress through a range of theatrical devices: formal debate, political songs, direct didactic addresses to the audience, mime, and pageant. The philosophical dialogue between the Enlightenment convictions of the revolutionary Marat, and de Sade's settled belief in the perversity and depravity of humanity, occupies a central position; but other voices are also heard. There are the voices of the fanatical priest, Roux, and the revolutionary zealot, Charlotte Corday. There is a continual defence of the status quo from Coulmier, the director of the asylum, who keeps protesting against de Sade's retention of censored cuts, and threatening to stop the play. There is the ironic commentary of the Herald, constituting a Brechtian chorus. And there are the voices of the inmates themselves, who play parts, perform the songs, and enact scenes and illustrations of what is being uttered by the main characters.

The theatrical techniques used clearly typify the strong influence on Weiss's drama of Brecht. And in many ways the play seems a classic Brechtian drama in presenting political violence and human extremity through a philosophical language and a self-reflexive, theatrical medium, and in showing a dialectical opposition of political ideas which remains unresolved in the play, but which, it is implied, should be reflected upon in the real world the audience inhabits. At the play's conclusion, Marat rises from death to deliver his final word of revolutionary faith:

As a corpse I'm not much use to you
but all the things I taught were true
and others now will carry on
the fight that I Marat begun
until one day the hour will strike
when men will share and share alike.

to be followed by a definitive statement of de Sade's scepticism: "So for me the last word can never be spoken / I am left with a question that is always open".

Peter Brook's famous production of *Marat / Sade* set out to destabilise the rationalist dialectic of epic theatre by emphasising the madness of the asylum's inmates as the basic theatrical language of the play. Each actor rehearsed a detailed study of a chosen form of insanity, and their collective display of madness proved profoundly disturbing for the theatre audience. The dramatic effect became a very un-Brechtian overwhelming of the senses with an Artaudian theatrical discourse of panic and violence; a type of "total theatre" calculated to obliterate Peter Weiss's carefully balanced dialectic of reason and emotion, sanity and madness, political conviction and cynical perversity.

—Graham Holderness

MARGARET FLEMING
by James A. Herne

First Publication: Boston, 1890.
First Production: Lynn Theatre, Lynn, Massachusetts, 1 July
1890; revised version, Chickering Hall,
Boston, 4 May 1891.

Editions

Margaret Fleming, revised by Mrs. James A. Herne, in
Representative American Plays, edited by Arthur Hobson
Quinn, New York, 1930.
Margaret Fleming, in *"The Black Crook" and Other Nine-
teenth-Century American Plays*, New York, 1967.
Margaret Fleming, in *Six Early American Plays, 1798–1900*,
edited by William Coyle and Harry G. Damaser, Columbus,
Ohio, 1968.

Criticism

(For general works on the author, see *Playwrights* volume)

Articles:
Donald Pizer, "An 1890 Account of *Margaret Fleming*", in
American Literature, 27, 1955.
Theodore Hatlen, "*Margaret Fleming* at the Boston Indepen-
dent Theatre", in *Educational Theatre Journal*, 8, 1956.
Barnard Hewitt, "*Margaret Fleming* in Chickering Hall: The
First Little Theatre in America?", in *Theatre Journal*, 34,
1982.

* * *

In *Margaret Fleming* James A. Herne dramatizes the
relationship between a dissolute husband, Philip, and his
faithful and morally superior wife, Margaret. As the play
opens, Philip, a successful manufacturer, greets a friend from
his past, Joe Fletcher, whose situation—broke, deserted by his
wife—reminds Philip of the wild oats he himself has sown. But
Philip has reformed, or so he says. "Live and let live" is his
motto. His happy-go-lucky attitude allows him no deep
feelings for Joe whom he treats in a cavalier fashion. After
Joe's departure Doctor Larkin, the moral voice of society,
brings news of a baby born to a poor mill girl—Philip's baby.
At home, Margaret is happily absorbed with her baby,
although Dr. Larkin explains that Margaret's glaucoma may
have serious consequences if she has an emotional upset. Her
maid, Maria, is worried about her unmarried sister who is
dying after giving birth. Not knowing the truth of this situation,
Margaret calls on Maria's sister and is confronted by an angry
Maria who has a letter explaining Philip's involvement. With
righteous strength, Margaret sends for Philip, complains that it
is getting dark and, in response to the crying of the child,
begins to unbutton her dress to nurse the baby. Days later, at
home, a blind but strong Margaret receives a forlorn Philip
who has wandered helplessly, afraid to return to her. The wife-
love has gone out of her, she confesses; truth killed it. Philip
wonders if there is a chance for reconciliation. As he walks
lightly toward the room where his two children wait, Margaret
smiles enigmatically.

This is the plot of *Margaret Fleming* that is available to
modern readers, the version that opened on 4 May 1891 in
Boston's Chickering Hall, with the support of that area's social
and literary elite. An earlier version had premiered on 1 July
1890 in Lynn, Massachusetts. In this version the ending was
different while still being ironically ambiguous. After the scene
of Margaret starting to nurse the baby, four years pass. The

scene is then Boston where Joe Fletcher and his wife Maria
have a five year old girl they are raising as her sister's child.
Actually, that child died, and the girl is the real daughter of
Margaret and Philip. As a blind Margaret enters the scene,
Maria confesses the identity of the child and begs Margaret to
take her. Margaret agrees but afterward lashes out at Philip in
hatred and tells him that she sold their child, as Maria gloats
over the awful revenge. Act V takes place in a police station
where the Flemings have been brought to sort out domestic
difficulties. Left alone, Margaret kindly but firmly explains to
Philip, as she takes his hand, that the "wife-heart" is gone.
Misinterpreting the situation as he returns, the police inspector
senses that they have come to an understanding. "Yes",
replies Philip, "we understand each other". "Better than we
ever did before", says Margaret.

Structurally, both versions are melodramas with several of
the embellishments common to the day, but it is the 1891 play
that attracted attention and is still described as "epoch-
marking" in consequence of the difficulty attendant upon its
production in Boston, the attitude of most of the reviewers in
1891, and the comparisons with European playwrights (Ibsen,
in particular) which have helped establish its place in the
development of American drama. The music of melodrama
appears in the song Margaret sings (Act I, scene 1) which
foreshows the action of the play. The pistol with which Maria
half-threatens Margaret in Act III suggests the necessary
violence of contemporary melodrama, and there is the letter
Maria uses in that same scene to explain the situation to
Margaret. Dr. Larkin's discussion of glaucoma is consistent
with medical knowledge of that day and representative of the
inventions and scientific discoveries of the late 19th century
with which writers of melodrama peppered their plays. Dr.
Larkin's moral declarations—particularly his speech to Philip
on the moral nature of man would have appealed to contemporary audiences, but his attitude is also clearly parallel to that of
Ibsen's Dr. Relling in *The Wild Duck* and gives substance to
Herne's basic interest in "Art for Truth's Sake in the Drama"
as he explained it in the *Arena* magazine in February 1897.

More important in determining the significance of *Margaret
Fleming* in American drama are the numerous and daring
innovations which Herne infused into his play. Philip and
Margaret are both carefully developed individuals. Philip's
light-hearted morality and superficial nature underline his
actions. When Joe admits that Maria has left him, Philip says
that he would kill himself in a similar situation. Events prove
otherwise, as Philip lies easily and never takes himself or life
seriously. However emotionally fragile Margaret appears to
be, she is the survivor, the stable force in the family, the
wronged woman who is both forgiving and forceful enough to
control both her destiny and her husband. Calling attention to
the double standard existing in society, Margaret shows that
force of woman which impressed the scholar-historian-philos-
pher Henry Adams in much of his writing and which the
popular dramatists of the day categorically denied.

The concept of social Darwinism (which Herne would
emphasize later in *Shore Acres*) is projected in the speeches of
Dr. Larkin who upbraids the wealthy and well-educated Philip
for his profligacy while accepting the idea that the less
fortunate might "go wrong" by reason of their environment.
Although only the nursing scene scandalized audiences, Herne
carefully applied the details of realism—instructions to the
cook on getting lunch and baking bread, the conversations
with Dr. Larkin, the interest in glaucoma, the symbolic use of
roses and their care, the attention to weather—in ways that
were not readily appreciated by contemporary American
audiences, (who had also been offended by a production of
Ibsen's *Ghosts* in 1889).

The play was a failure in 1891, although numerous well-known writers such as William Dean Howells and Hamlin Garland found much to praise in it. Modern critics have viewed *Margaret Fleming*, with its richness of emotion and its truth to human failings and achievements, as a play which shows the faint beginnings of modern American drama.

—Walter J. Meserve

MARIA MAGDALENA
by Friedrich Hebbel

First Publication: Hamburg, 1844.
First Production: Stadttheater, Königsberg, 13 March 1846.

Editions

Maria Magdalene, edited by Arnold Zehme, Vienna, 1912.
Maria Magdalene, edited by Ludwig Kohler, Reichenberg, 1921.
Maria Magdalene, edited by Thea Feller, Dresden, 1922.
Maria Magdalene, edited by G. Brychan Rees, Oxford, 1944.
Maria Magdalene, Berlin, 1955.
Maria Magdalene, Stuttgart, 1965; revised edition, 1980 (Reclam edition).

Translations

Maria Magdalene, translated by Paula Green, in *Poet-Lore*, 25, 1914.
Maria Magdalene, translated by Paul B. Thomas, in *The German Classics of the Nineteenth and Twentieth Centuries*, 9, New York, 1914.
Maria Magdalene, in *Hebbel: Three Plays*, translated by Barker Fairley, London, 1914.
Maria Magdalene, translated by Carl Richard Mueller, San Francisco, 1962.
Maria Magdalene [acting text], translated by Sarah Somekh, London, 1990.

Criticism

(For general works on the author, see *Playwrights* volume)

Books:
Paul Zincke, *Die Entstehungsgeschichte von Friedrich Hebbels "Maria Magdalene"*, Prague, 1910.
Reinhold Stolze, *Die wissenschaftlichen Grundlagen der Inszenierung von Hebbels "Maria Magdalene"*, Berlin, 1924 (Hebbel-Forschungen, 13).
Paul Pachaly, *Erläuterungen zu Hebbels "Maria Magdalene"*, Leipzig, 1926.
Hartwig Sievers, *Hebbels "Maria Magdalene" auf der Bühne: ein Beitrag zur Bühnengeschichte Hebbels*, Berlin and Leipzig, 1933.
Walter Fischer, *Hebbel: "Maria Magdalene"*, Frankfurt, 1958.
Karl Pörnbacher (ed.), *Friedrich Hebbel: "Maria Magdalene": Erläuterungen und Dokumente*, Stuttgart, 1970.
Ludger Lütkehaus, *Friedrich Hebbel: "Maria Magdalene"*, Munich, 1983.

Articles:
H. Brande, "Hebbels philosophisch-aesthätische Schriften und seine *Maria Magdalena*", in *Pädagogische Reform*, 37, 1913.

Flola L. Shepard, "Hebbel's *Gedanken-Lasten* in the *Maria Magdalene*", in *Journal of English and Germanic Philology*, 30, 1931.
Hartwig Sievers, "Hebbels *Maria Magdalene* in der vor- und nachmärzlichen Tageskritik", in *Archiv*, 167, 1935.
Paul Husfeldt, "Der Mythos in Hebbels Drama erläutert an *Maria Magdalene*", in *Dichtung und Volkstum*, 43, 1943.
Kurt May, "*Maria Magdalene* im Zusammenhang der jüngsten Hebbelforschung", in *Dichtung und Volkstum*, 43, 1943.
James D. Wright, "Hebbel's Klara: The Victim of a Division in Allegiance and Purpose", in *Monatshefte*, 38, 1946.
Kurt May, "Hebbels *Maria Magdalene*", in his *Form und Bedeutung: Interpretationen deutscher Dichtung des 18. und 19. Jahrhunderts*, Stuttgart, 1957.
Martin Stern, "Das zentrale Symbol in Friedrich Hebbels *Maria Magdalene*", in *Wirkendes Wort*, 9, 1959.
Georges Favier, "Lecture de Hebbel. Remarques sur le personnage de la mère dans *Maria Magdalene*", in *Études Germaniques*, 20, 1965.
Jerry H. Glenn, "The Title of Hebbel's *Maria Magdalena*", in *Papers on Language and Literature*, 3, 1967.
Erika Sterz, "Hebbel als Dramatiker für das Fernsehspiel— Rekonstrution einer Regieleistung: *Maria Magdalene*", in *Hebbel Jahrbuch*, 1967.
Joachim Müller, "Zur motivischen und dramaturgischen Struktur von Hebbels *Maria Magdalene*", in *Hebbel Jahrbuch*, 1968.
John Fetzer, "Water Imagery in *Maria Magdalene*", in *The German Quarterly*, 43, 1970.
Siegfried Streller, "*Maria Magdalene*: Die Wandlung des bürgerlichen Trauerspiels bei Friedrich Hebbel", in *Studien zur Literaturgeschichte und Literaturtheorie*, edited by Hans-Günther Thalheim and Ursula Wertheim, Berlin, 1970.
Joachim Bark, "So viel Fremdheit, so wenig Lust: Überlegungen zu Hebbel's *Maria Magdalene*", in *Wirkendes Wort*, vol. 38 no.2, 1988.

*   *   *

Klara, the daughter of a small-town joiner known as Meister Anton, becomes engaged to Leonhard, an ambitious but unprincipled town hall clerk, who had made her pregnant when he noticed her attraction to the secretary, another young man whom she knew as a boy. Her brother Karl is arrested on suspicion of theft; this is too much for their ailing mother, who suffers a fatal stroke on hearing the news. The secretary cannot forgive Klara her engagement to Leonhard, who, for his part, has second thoughts about the financial advantages of the marriage and uses the stigma of Karl's arrest to call it off. Stunned by these disasters, Klara's father threatens he will take his own life if his daughter lets him down as badly as his son. The secretary, still in love with Klara, realises what private anguish he has caused her by neglecting her, yet her stifled confession of guilt about her unborn child is too much for him. She for her part realises that her only way out is marriage to a man she loathes and who has left her. The secretary challenges Leonhard to a duel (off stage), kills him, but is himself mortally wounded. Karl, now proved innocent, plans to go to sea, but Klara, unable to conceal her pregnancy much longer, sees herself caught in a hopeless situation. Karl's request for a glass of water before Klara retires to bed provides the opportunity she needs: she throws herself into the well, leaving her father to utter his well-known curtain line, "I don't understand the world any more".

The play (in three acts) was originally to be called *Klara* after its tragic heroine; however, Hebbel decided to bring out its deeper ethical intention by calling it after the sinning Mary Magdalene in St. Luke's Gospel, whose "sins, which were many, are forgiven, for she loved much". To prevent any impression that he had dramatized an episode from scripture, he carefully subtitled it "a middle-class tragedy". Hebbel's aim (set out at length in the notable preface) was to restore dignity and a sense of high purpose to drama by focusing attention on crucial moments in the evolution of humanity. In *Maria Magdalena* he addresses what he believed was the crisis of his own day: the disparity between moral attitudes and the fundamental ethos which informs the reality of the world. Small-town society, such as he had himself known at first hand, provides both the intensely claustrophobic setting of the tragedy and the direct cause of its happening. Klara, a girl of potentially free and generous spirit, is hemmed in by her father's expectations, which reflect the conventions of a society which he has reluctantly come to accept: any brush with the law, and any moral lapse which becomes public knowledge, must inevitably bring shame on those concerned. In Klara's case matrimony alone can provide a guarantee of respectability, yet the price she is expected to pay in human terms is excessive, since it means being fettered to a man she despises and losing the man she really loves. But she is unable to resist her father's moral blackmail (powerfully exerted in Act II, scene 1); the paternalistic authority it presupposes she accepts unquestioningly, if mistakenly. Her attempt to fulfil its terms leads her in Act III, scene 2 to a remarkable dialogue in which she finds herself having to entreat Leonhard to marry her: her abject promises to put up with anything if he does, culminating in her invitation to him to remove her with rat-poison, is a powerful expression and indictment of the meekness and passivity forced on women by contemporary early Victorian, lower-middle-class attitudes and social conventions. Klara is very much her father's daughter, however; her heredity, as well as her environment, determines her reaction to the pressures to which circumstance subjects her. Father and daughter are essentially just human beings characterized by a capacity for loving and a deep sense of probity and self-respect, but their vision is narrowed by the restrictive horizons of their world, while their freedom of action and expression is curtailed by their too-ready acceptance of social norms which, in Hebbel's opinion, reflect a distorted, and therefore doomed, set of moral values. Thus the tragic conflict in *Maria Magdalena* is generated not by class conflict but by the middle class itself—here lies its true originality.

In his preface, Hebbel stated that tragic drama should confine itself to the problems underlying existence. His only realistic play is set in the contemporary world he knew at first hand, and stands at the threshold of 19th-century problem drama, as Ibsen realised. Its closely-knit structure demonstrates his command of the techniques of the well-made play. Yet he widens the play's tragic implications by the subtle use of verbal allusions (mainly biblical) and recurrent symbolism. The fact that it remained the only work of its kind by a dramatic writer of formidable creative and intellectual stature ensured its lasting success once initial moral reservations and censorship problems were overcome. Its stage life was also helped by its language which, despite the realism of the setting, avoids colloquialism and local dialect, thus enabling the play to communicate to audiences all over the German-speaking world.

In the 20th century *Maria Magdalena* became established as Hebbel's most popular play on the German-speaking stage: between 1900 and 1930 it received some 2,930 performances, and in the period 1948–67, 1,398 performances are recorded. More recently, however, changing moral attitudes have tended to diminish the appeal of a daring play set in a now largely vanished milieu of deep religious conviction and rigid, moral prejudice.

—Peter Skrine

———

MARIA MAGDALENE. See **MARIA MAGDALENA.**

———

MARIA MARTEN; or, Murder in the Red Barn
Anonymous

First Production: Unknown. Earliest version probably as *Murder in the Red Barn*, at The Royal Pavilion, Mile End (then outside London), 1828; earliest recorded production, 6 April 1840, Marylebone Theatre, London.

Editions
Maria Marten; or, Murder in the Red Barn, in a version by John Latimer, edited by Montagu Slater, London, 1928; second edition, 1971.
The Murder of Maria Marten; or, The Red Barn, edited by B. J. Burton, Birmingham, 1964.
Maria Marten, in *The Golden Age of Melodrama*, edited by Michael Kilgariff, London, 1974.

*   *   *

William Corder was executed outside Norwich Gaol on 11 August 1828 for the murder of Maria Marten. This quite commonplace crime, which took place in a Suffolk structure known locally as the Red Barn, unaccountably captured the popular imagination: Corder's gruesome relics (skull, "true confession" bound in his own skin) can still be seen in a folk museum in Bury St Edmunds; a broadside ballad purporting to relate the matter was still being sold in the 1850's, by which time it had apparently sold 1,650,000 copies; and the story passed so effectively into oral tradition that Percy Grainger recorded a version sung in Lincolnshire in 1906, 80 years after the event.

It is not surprising, then, that the touring melodrama theatres of the 1820's and onwards should have cashed in on the sensational affair; or even that *Maria Marten; or, Murder in the Red Barn* should remain one of the very few genuine 19th century melodramas to maintain a hold in the current repertoire.

At least four versions have survived. In all, as in the ballad, history has been falsified to make Maria a local byword for purity and virtue and Corder one for venal villainy, whereas the facts of the matter are that Maria had borne several, illegitimate children, (to Corder and others), had been Corder's resident mistress for some time, and was murdered, not to avoid the necessity of marriage, but in the course of a domestic quarrel when her drunken fecklessness became insupportable.

In *The Golden Age of Melodrama* (1974), Michael Kilgariff speculates that the anonymous author of the version he gives (the only one known actually to have achieved print during the 19th century) was the resident writer at the Star Theatre, Swansea. Many versions are known, however, to have been performed nationwide continuously, even from before Corder's execution.

The most commonly performed text these days is a 1960's collation by B. J. Burton. This retains the comic sub-plot of the courtship of Maria's younger sister Anne by the coarse but worthy village bumpkin Timothy, whose simple virtue is obviously to be contrasted with the gentleman-villain's deviousness. The sinister figure of Ishmael, the fortune-telling gypsy appears; he also falls victim to Corder for reasons which remain obscure, but perhaps to underline his villainy. And, of course, among much material whose essential turgidity the utmost skill can scarcely disguise, there are such undeniably effective episodes as Mrs. Marten's recurrent dream of the re-enactment of her daughter's murder and the whereabouts of her body even before her death has been confirmed; the appearance of Maria's ghost to Corder in the condemned cell; and the climactic execution.

Crude though the piece often is, it retains many theatrical qualities which a good production can draw on to enable an audience to accept the melodrama on its own terms.

—Michael Grosvenor Myer

MARIA STUART. See MARY STUART.

MARIAGE BLANC (Białe Małżeństwo)
by Tadeusz Różewicz

First Publication: In *Dialog*, 2, 1974; in book form, in *Białe małżeństwo i inne utwory sceniczne*, Cracow, 1975.
First Production: Teatr Mały, Warsaw, 24 January 1975.

Translations
Mariage Blanc [in English], in *"Mariage Blanc" and "The Hungry Artist Departs"*, translated by Adam Czerniawski, London, 1983.

Criticism
(For general works on the author, see *Playwrights* volume)

Articles:
Rhonda Blair, "*A White Marriage*: Różewicz's Feminist Drama;", in *Slavic and East European Arts*, 1985.
Allen Kuharski, "*White Marriage* and the Transcendance of Gender", in *Women in Theatre*, edited by James Redmond, Cambridge, 1989 (Themes in Drama Series).
Halina Filipowicz, "The Puzzle of Tadeusz Różewicz's *White Marriage*", in *Drama and Philosophy*, edited by James Redmond, Cambridge, 1990 (Themes in Drama Series).

*   *   *

On the country estate of a well-to-do family in the Austrian sector of partitioned Poland at the turn of the century, two pubescent girls make troubling discoveries about sexuality, while members of the older generations are tormented by their own failures to come to terms with love and lust. Engaged to the pure and gentle Benjamin, Bianca feels threatened by phallic images of male dominance; her companion Pauline has an earthy humor that enables her to accept the bodily functions as a part of daily existence. Bianca's mother, repelled by the incessant sexual demands of a husband she does not love, imagines that her daughter will find happiness in marriage and proudly enumerates the luxury items that make up the bride's trusseau. Bianca's father is driven by desire and never stops his pursuit of the buxom cook and other female servants, turning into a lustful Bull-Father, terrifying to his daughter. Even Grandfather cannot confront approaching death with dignity, but is reduced to bribing the girls with sweets so that he may pet them or treasure their stockings.

When Benjamin recites romantic verse at a social gathering, Bianca grows hysterical as she imagines she sees a huge phallus between her fiancé's legs. The onset of menstruation is another shock for Bianca, whose erotic longings are transmuted into strange poetic dreams and fantasies. The Aunt, more sensual by nature than her sister, realizes that she should have married Bianca's father. During a family picnic in a dark fairy-tale forest, the girls gather obscenely ithyphallic mushrooms and are pursued by visions of a Black Huntsman. Terrified at the thought of her coming marriage, Bianca cuts her bridal linen into pieces. At the wedding, the guests seem transformed into cackling barn-yard animals. Lying stiffly in the nuptial bed as though it were a coffin, Bianca makes Benjamin promise that theirs will be a *mariage blanc*. In the final scene the next day, Bianca looks intently at her image in the mirror, removes her clothes slowly, and throws them in the fire. Then, after cutting off her hair close to the skin, she turns to Benjamin, covers her breasts with her hands, and says, "I am your brother".

White Marriage is a poetic theatricalization in 13 tableaux of the terrors of Eros in the age of Freud and Schnitzler, seen from the point of view of two young girls in instinctive revolt against the repressive hypocrisies of a prurient, sex-ridden society. When first performed in 1975, it caused a minor scandal in Poland where critics misread the play as pornography, professing to see only a frivolous and unseemly display of the author's own sexual obsessions. The prudish and high-minded Polish literary tradition, reinforced by both Catholic and Communist puritanism, prevented the cultural establishment from recognizing the play as Różewicz's most enduring and universal work for the stage.

Following Tadeusz Minc's sensational premiere, other productions both at home and abroad (including Kazimierz Braun's in Wrocław in 1975 and Andrzej Wajda's at the Yale Repertory Theatre in 1977) revealed the play's deeper values. Young audiences throughout the world responded enthusiastically to Różewicz's sensuous imagery and compassionate yet comic probing of the crippling effects of rigid social norms and imposed gender roles on vulnerable human beings. Actors, directors, and designers found that the drama contained vividly corporeal characters, precisely rendered theatrical language and gesture, and richly detailed notation of costume and milieu.

Mariage blanc, or *White Marriage*, belongs to the European tradition of drama and fiction dealing with sexual maturing whose roots go back to the early modernist period and works such as Frank Wedekind's *Spring's Awakening*. This was the age that saw the birth of psychoanalysis, the flowering of a highly eroticized art and culture, and the first steps towards the social and sexual emancipation of women. By choosing the *fin-de-siècle* as the setting of *White Marriage*, Różewicz locates his drama of sexual sublimation and revolt within a historical context rich in artistic and literary associations. Extensive use of citation, allusion, and pastiche enables the playwright to

Mariage blanc: Wspolczesny Theatre, Wroclaw, 1975

dramatize the cultural values that are major determinants of character and action in a world where life imitates art.

In its inspiration, materials, and variety of linguistic styles, *White Marriage* is intensely literary and specifically Polish. The author himself has called the play "a kind of anthology of various languages and literary works". Ur-sources of *White Marriage* come from two emancipated Polish women writers. In a 1970 essay, "Lesbian Love in a Romantic Disguise", Różewicz revealed a long-standing interest in making a theatrical adaptation of *The Heathen Woman*, a homo-erotic novel by Narcyza Żmichowska written in 1846, but his internal censor told him it was not yet time to put lesbian love on the stage and the project was abandoned. Żmichowska's novel provided Różewicz with the names of Pauline and Benjamin, some direct citations, and the suggestion of a lesbian relationship between the two girls. Bianca's rebellion is loosely based on the tragic story of Maria Komornicka, a modernist poet who wrote under a male pseudonym and finally burned her clothes, cut her hair, and announced she was a man, only to be put in an asylum by her family. But Żmichowska and Komornicka served simply as starting points for *White Marriage*. Różewicz went to many other romantic and modernist poets and playwrights to create a dense intertextual web of reference and quotation. As the playwright himself has declared, only the most learned critic could recognize all the layers in his "layer cake", and in any case the aim of this method of compilation is the creation of a new and wholly independent work.

In the theatre Różewicz techniques of collage and pastiche produce a drama of physiologically and psychologically believable characters whose varied responses to the dilemma of human sexuality constitute the center of interest. *White Marriage* is above all a drama of the body — and of the constraints of civilization. All of the characters are doubly terrorized: by the gender roles externally imposed through social convention and by the sheer power of sexuality itself. In his declining days, Grandfather's ideals of honor and civic duty (derived from the lofty Polish tradition) are shattered against debasing carnal desires. Father is an erotic jack-in-the-box manipulated by his glands. Mother, who has had to submit to the demands of an arranged marriage with its unending burden of pregnancies and births, lacks any notion of individual fulfilment; parroting fashion magazines, cook books, and household manuals, she can only quantify domestic materialism with her menus and lists. The younger generation seeks escape from the reigning tyrannies of sex in poetry, dreams, and the playing of imagined roles. Caught up in the metaphysical anguish of the verses he declaims, Benjamin is prepared for self-sacrifice. Pauline finds a measure of freedom in ironic distancing and theatricalization. But Bianca's subjective visions are the element that gives *White Marriage* its structure as "interior theatre", which is the hallmark of Różewicz's dramaturgy. Externally realistic scenes and events run parallel to hallucinatory moments in which Bianca's imaginings are directly represented on stage. Różewicz's poetic realism penetrates to the inner realm of fear that lies hidden within the corporeality and copulative rhythm of life.

Although more linear and sequential than Różewicz's radically experimental plays, *White Marriage*, with its 13 loosely connected tableaux juxtaposing private and public, bedroom and salon, still shows characteristics of "open drama" in its refusal to be shaped by plot or conform to notions of a beginning, middle, and end. The final tableau is a powerful visual *coup de théâtre* that has been the cause of much controversy. The culmination of Bianca's rebellion is expressed by an enigmatic theatrical image that does not yield any single meaning. Is Bianca's shearing of her hair and burning of her clothes to be seen as a tragic mutilation and rejection of her own sex, or as a triumphant vanquishing of the old patriarchal order and inauguration of a new era of androgynous union? According to Różewicz, Bianca's last words are a declaration of equality transcending gender. She will no longer be defined by the trappings in which she has been encased by a society responsible for stultifying inhibitions and obsessions. In obliterating the attributes of womanhood, Bianca seeks to recover a single human identity. Through self-destruction, she affirms herself as a human being. The rebellion against her own sex is carried out in the name of the human condition. But is Bianca's act inevitably a tragic metaphysical rebellion, in that she demands an impossible oneness? That Różewicz has condensed such complex emotive and intellectual issues in the final image of *White Marriage* is a measure of the play's accomplishment.

—Daniel Gerould

LE MARIAGE DE FIGARO. See **THE MARRIAGE OF FIGARO.**

MARRIAGE (Slub)
by Witold Gombrowicz

First Publication: In *Trans-Atlantlk; Slub*, 1953.
First Production: Théâtre Récamier, Paris, 1963.

Criticism

Articles:
Michal Glowinski, "Komentarze do *Slubu*", in *Dialog*, vol.20 no.11, 1975; in English, in *Literary Studies in Poland*, 10, 1983.
Jan Kott, "On Gombrowicz", in Kott's *The Theater of Essence and Other Essays*, Evanston, Illinois, 1984.

*   *   *

Few themes recur in Polish culture of the 19th and 20th centuries with such determination as that of the wedding. As the 19th century progressed, the Polish people, divided between the Austrian, Prussian, and Russian empires, saw little likelihood of political reunification, despite two heroic but unsuccessful uprisings.

In public consciousness at the turn of the century the wedding ceremony (which can bring together two families of different classes or political positions) came to symbolise the need to foster social consensus and reinforce the sense of national identity in the face of all adversity (Stanisław Wyspiański's *Wedding* (1901) is perhaps the essential configuration of this "Polish complex"). In the decades that followed Poland's independence in 1918 the metaphor of the wedding remained an obsession with Polish writers. A powerful variation on the theme was provided by *The Marriage* (1953), a fine example of "intuitive theatricality" by Witold Gombrowicz, a writer who rarely went to the theatre.

The Marriage illustrates the core issue that dominates all of Gombrowicz's work: that of Form with a capital F. The action, as he notes in his introduction to the play, "all takes place because of Form, that is to say that people, in their inter-relationships impose on each other some or other manner of being, speaking, or action. . .and each one of us deforms others while at the same time being deformed by them. That is why this is more than anything the drama of Form itself".

Gombrowicz has left nothing to risk. He introduces the script with a three page summary of the plot of *The Marriage*, "to make the reading easier", thus underlining the low priority of performance. This preface explains the purpose of the dream-like world with its absurd actions: it is a philosophical construct which dramatically presents the idea of Form.

Henryk, a soldier fighting in France during World War II, appears to be dreaming of his return to his native country (presumably Poland). He approaches an inn with his comrade Władzio. Here he recognises the innkeepers as his parents. In the background, Henryk's fiancée, Maria, is hiding from him; confused by events that seem to be real enough, Henryk nonetheless doubts the reality of what he sees, but submits to appearances and plays along.

The entrance of a Drunk and his cronies destabilises this unexpected family reunion, especially when they begin to harass Henryk's father and call Maria a whore. The plot accelerates out of control as the characters react to all statements as irrevocable and binding: the Father suddenly declares himself "untouchable", like a king. As soon as these words are uttered everyone adopts appropriate roles as if at a royal court (though their personalities seem to remain as before). The King suggests to his son that Maria's defamed reputation can now only be restored by the sanctity of a royal marriage.

In Act II, The Drunk who is now assuming the role of Ambassador, remains a malevolent figure. Given the aristocratic behaviour of the court, The King begins to fear a plot against his person, and indeed the Ambassador encourages Henryk as heir to the throne to consider overthrowing his father. Since Henry does not actually believe in anything (the key dilemma of the work), let alone in the reality of what is happening to him, he is led through indifference into initiating a *coup d'état*, and "touches" his Father. Since he can only ultimately rely on his own being, as pointed out by the, Drunk / Ambassador, he can only truly legitimise the marriage ceremony by officiating at it himself. But The Drunk, though arrested by Henryk's guards, gives flowers and honour to Władzio and Maria as if they were already wed: "formally" he again has subverted the balance of the social relationships within the dream-drama.

Act III opens with Henryk as dictator, intending to cleanse his fiancée of all suspicion. He suggests to Władzio that he commit suicide in order to preserve the predetermined balance and allow Henryk to marry Maria without gossip spreading. As

Marriage: Polski Theatre, Wroclaw, 1976

Henryk ponders the purpose of his dream-like experiences, The Drunk enters and announces that the new king is a cuckold. To The Drunk's surprise, the courtiers separate to reveal Władzio's corpse. Though Henryk declares himself innocent of murder, he must now logically have himself arrested and imprisoned. *The Marriage* concludes with a funeral march.

Gombrowicz makes explicit reference in his preface to Shakespearean tragedy, and as the play progresses, it becomes clear that Henryk is an heir to Hamlet, unsure as to the appropriate response to the world and the events that encroach upon him: "Am I here? I am beginning to doubt whether I exist at all!". The starting point of *The Marriage* is that of a nightmare out of which there is no exit. The constantly shifting actions and motives of the other characters expose Henryk's lack of responsibility or morality, forcing the innocent him to submit to the reality into which he has been inserted.

The Marriage's characters are all utterly enslaved by words: once a word or suggestion is uttered it can redirect the chain of events. Henryk's early determination that "this is all rather unclear. I'll clear it all up" proves tragically wrong. Enmeshed in impenetrable causes, he is incapable of imposing any stable meaning to events that are propelled most decisively by the irrational suggestions of The Drunk. The combination of unreal dream and irrational motive thoroughly defeats Henryk—and he becomes the victim of his own vivid imagination. Perhaps, as he constantly repeats, "I am here alone".

Gombrowicz utilised the dramatic form of *The Marriage* in order to portray the essence of 20th-century existential despair rooted in dialogue and monologue. The depiction of the blankness of human nature in an unstable reality explains the absurdity of human existence, but does not resolve it; the self is an equally unreliable focus if it is ultimately subject to exterior forces and unable to extricate itself from its situation: "They are not people—they are just caricatures!" cries Henryk.

Despite Gombrowicz's extensive apparatus explaining the action and its implications, much of the play remains ambiguous. In tackling the theme of the wedding, Gombrowicz draws on traditional resonances for a Polish audience, but these do not hinder a universal reading of the play—indeed they give its appeal a strong foundation. *The Marriage* presents the "tyranny of Form" at its most eloquent, but without an alternative. The solution suggested by the author in his other works (for example *Trans-Atlantic*, 1953) is that of trusting in the naïve, "unformed" enthusiasm of immaturity before the young have been deformed by culture and society. By those standards, Gombrowicz's is a pessimistic vision of man's bondage to his uncontrollable dreams and aspirations, and human submissiveness to social pressure and ritual.

—Donald Pirie

MARRIAGE À-LA-MODE
by John Dryden

First Publication: London, 1673.
First Production: Lincoln's Inn Fields Theatre, c. November 1672.

Editions

Marriage à-la-Mode, in *John Dryden: Three Plays*, edited by George Saintsbury, New York, 1957 (based on earlier Mermaid edition).
Marriage à-la-Mode, in *Four Comedies; Four Tragedies* (2 vols.), edited by L.A. Beaurline and Fredson Bowers, 1967.
Marriage à-la-Mode, in *Restoration Comedies*, edited by Dennis Davison, London, 1970.
Marriage à-la-Mode, in *Dryden: A Selection*, edited by John Conaghan, 1978.
Marriage à-la-Mode, London, 1991 (New Mermaid Series).

Criticism

(For general works on the author, see *Playwrights* volume)

Articles:

Charles E. Ward, "The Dates of Two Dryden Plays", in *Publications of the Modern Language Association* [*PMLA*], 51, 1936.
Bruce King, "Dryden's *Marriage à-la-Mode*", in *Drama Survey*, 4, 1965.
Robert D. Hume, "The Date of Dryden's *Marriage à-la-Mode*", in *Harvard Library Bulletin*, 21, 1973.
Leslie Howard Martin, "The Source and Originality of Dryden's Melantha", in *Philological Quarterly*, 52, 1973.
Judith Kalitzki, "Versions of Truth: *Marriage à-la-Mode*", in *Restoration*, 4, 1980.
Derek Hughes, "The Unity of Dryden's *Marriage à-la-Mode*", in *Philological Quarterly*, 61, 1982.
Michael McKeon, "Marxist Criticism and *Marriage à-la-Mode*", in *The Eighteenth Century*, 24, 1983.
Paul Hammond, "The Prologue and Epilogue to Dryden's *Marriage à-la-Mode* and the Problem of the Covent Garden Drolery", in *Papers of the Bibliographical Society of America*, 81, 1987.

*   *   *

The Sicilian usurper Polydamas goes in search of his long-lost, only child, of whose sex he is ignorant. At first, however, he fixes on the young fisherman Leonidas and commands him to marry Amalthea, the daughter of his former partner in rebellion. Despite Amalthea's virtue and beauty, Leonidas remains loyal to his peasant sweetheart, Palmyra, whom Polydamas consequently resolves to execute. In the nick of time, however, she is identified as his true child, whereupon Leonidas returns to peasanthood and Palmyra is commanded to marry Amalthea's wicked brother, Argaleon. Leonidas then turns out to be the son of the deposed, rightful king, and therefore the rightful heir, so is sentenced to death. Divided in loyalty between her lover and her new-found father, Palmyra swoons helplessly as Leonidas is led to the scaffold, but Amalthea provokes a successful rising in his favour. Leonidas and Palmyra marry, Polydamas is forgiven, but Amalthea and Argaleon remain—despite their opposed moral characters—fixed in parallel states of painful unfulfilment.

The play's other plot—the comic plot—also depicts an imbroglio of four lovers: more obedient to paternal command than their heroic counterparts, Palamede and the scatty social climber Melantha are about to enter an arranged marriage, but nevertheless become entangled with Rhodophil and Doralice, a bored husband and wife, each man and woman coveting the other's partner. But the illicit pairs keep meeting and frustrating each others' attempts at adultery, and the men's possessive jealousy finally convinces them that fidelity is pragmatically advisable.

Both plots re-establish a legitimate status quo, and indeed Palamede and Rhodophil assist decisively in the restoration of Leonidas. But both reveal problems that survive the return to legitimacy: most notably, the problem of discovering an interior principle of selfhood amidst the forms imposed by the public world. Leonidas and Palmyra strive to maintain a consistency of self amidst bewildering and rapid shifts of social identity, while the comic lovers seek to indulge a restless instability of desire despite the rigid fixity of role imposed by marriage. Whereas Leonidas struggles to cope with his triple change of identity, Rhodophil struggles to cope with Doralice's unending sameness, indulging in sexual fantasies which successively transform her into every beautiful woman in Sicily.

Rebellion against social impositions on the self is expressed in both plots in constant attempts to gain sexual privacy, which are thwarted by the equally constant intrusion of the public world. For example, the comic lovers' final attempt at adultery is frustrated by the upheavals resulting from the discovery that Leonidas is the true king. In the end, an autonomous personal life proves unattainable, for all characters are insidiously manipulated by extrinsic influences. Even lust can be determined by public influence, Palamede and Rhodophil each starting to desire the official partner because the other does, and Melantha is an utter human chameleon, changing markedly in conduct and self-perception as she alternates between country and court. Nor can the heroic characters maintain a pure constancy of self. Like Melantha, Palmyra makes the transition from country to court, and she too undergoes a corresponding inward change, instantly acquiring love for the father who, seconds before, had decreed her death, and becoming decorously distant to her childhood sweetheart. The instability of Melantha, the comic social climber, provides an unsettling parallel to that of Palmyra, the peasant turned princess.

So vulnerable is interior life to external control that language serves less to express thought than to impose public values. In the lost, pastoral idyll of Leonidas and Palmyra, language had seemed naturally ordained to express passion: Leonidas had taught a starling to speak Palmyra's name, and had carved both their names on trees. But they now rarely converse, for language reflects the claims of their new selves: at one point, Leonidas has to silence Palmyra to stop her repudiating him, and, when Leonidas faces execution, Palmyra is so inhibited by loyalty to her father that she cannot save her lover by proclaiming his true identity. Flight from the social tyranny of language is particularly explicit among the comic lovers, whose quest for private, furtive copulation is also a desire to escape into pure, silent, inarticulate instinct: "I am now past talking", says Palamede, about (as he believes) to sleep with Doralice. The remoteness of language from interior, instinctual life is particularly illustrated by Melantha. She is so compulsive a socializer and talker that Rhodophil has never been able to sleep with her, and Palamede only manages to ensure his marriage to her by drowning her voice, in an incident which closely parallels Leonidas's silencing of Palmyra, whose language has become equally inimical to their prospects of union. It is Melantha, also, who provides the extreme illustration of language as a social convention, with no expressive relationship to the personal consciousness. In one of the play's funniest scenes, Melantha's maid reads from a paper the daily list of French words which she has chosen for her mistress's use. The words are mechanically learned and explicitly unconnected with Melantha's own experience, yet they are essential to preserve her sense of her social position. Then, in the next scene, another subordinate produces another paper, which instantly transforms Palmyra from peasant to Princess.

In portraying social identity as contingent and subject to circumstantial influence, Dryden reverses the implications of the narrative from which he derived the serious plot, the "Histoire de Sesostris et Timarete" in Madeleine de Scudéry's *Le Grand Cyrus*, which portrays the simple persistence of innate nobility throughout confusing changes of external circumstance. In Scudéry, moreover, the character corresponding to Amalthea is malevolently ambitious. In ennobling her character, and in stressing her final isolation and unhappiness, Dryden creates a morally untidy ending, suggesting that the concluding marriage of Leonidas and Palmyra preserves patterns from their old life which have been superseded by the flux and change of events and identities. If the comic lovers need the rigid loyalty of the heroic, perhaps the heroic lovers need the sexual pragmatism of their comic counterparts. Each side is inhibited by values from which the other could profit.

—Derek Hughes

THE MARRIAGE OF FIGARO
(La Folle Journée; ou, Le Mariage de Figaro)
by Pierre-Augustin Caron de Beaumarchais

First Publication: Paris, 1785.
First Production: Comédie-Française, Paris, 27 April 1784.

Editions

Le Mariage de Figaro, edited by Raymond Jean, Paris, 1951.
Le Mariage de Figaro, edited by Louis Allen, London, 1952.
Le Mariage de Figaro, edited by J. Arnould, Oxford, 1952.
Le Mariage de Figaro, edited by Annie Ubersfeld, Paris, 1956.
Le Mariage de Figaro [2 vols], edited by Louis Forestier, Paris, 1966.
Le Mariage de Figaro, edited by J.B. Ratermanis, Englewood Cliffs, New Jersey, 1968.
Le Mariage de Figaro, edited by Claude Hubert, Paris, 1971.
Le Mariage de Figaro, in *Beaumarchais: Théâtre*, edited by Jean-Pierre de Beaumarchais, Paris, 1980.

Translations

Figaro's Marriage, translated by Jacques Barzun, in *The Classic Theatre, 4*, edited by Eric Bentley, Garden City, New York, 1961.
The Marriage of Figaro, in *The Barber of Seville*; *The Marriage of Figaro*, translated by John Wood, Harmondsworth, 1964.
The Marriage of Figaro, in *The Barber of Seville*; *The Marriage of Figaro*, translated by Vincent Luciani, Great Neck, New York, 1964.
A Mad Day's Work; *or, The Marriage of Figaro*, translated by Brobury Pearce Ellis, New York, 1966.

Criticism

(For general works on the author, see *Playwrights* volume)

Books:
René Jasinski, *Le Mariage de Figaro* [3 vols.], Paris, 1947–48.
Anthony R. Pugh, *A Critical Commentary on Beaumarchais's "Le Mariage de Figaro"*, New York, 1968.
Robert Niklaus, *Beaumarchais: "Le Mariage de Figaro"*, London, 1983.
Marie Françoise Lemonnier-Delpy, *Nouvelle Étude thématique sur "Le Mariage de Figaro" de Beaumarchais*, Paris, 1987.
Ivan Barko and Bruce Burgess, *La Dynamique des points de vue dans le texte de théâtre: Analyses de points de vue—"Le Misanthrope"; "Le Mariage de Figaro"; "Lorenzaccio"; "En Attendant Godot"*, Paris, 1988.

Articles:
Henri Chantavoine, "Le Mariage de Figaro", in *Conférences de l'Odéon*, 1889–90.
Albert de Bersaucourt, "Le Mariage de Figaro et les contemporains de Beaumarchais", in *Revue des temps présents*, 2, April, 1912.
Félix Gaiffe, "Beaumarchais: *Le Mariage de Figaro*", in *Conférences de l'Odéon*, Paris, 1916.
Paul Beret, "*Le Mariage de Figaro*", in *Odéon-Magazine*, 46, 1924.
Eric Bloom, "The Literary History of Figaro", in *Musical Quarterly*, 13, 1927.
Félix Gaiffe, "Les Variantes du *Mariage de Figaro*", in *Revue de l'enseignement secondaire des jeunes filles* (new series), 17, 1930.
Eduard von Jan, "Figaro", in *Romanische Forshungen*, 56, 1942.
Jacques Scherer, "La Dramaturgie du *Mariage de Figaro*", in *L'Information littéraire*, 3, 1951.
Paul Abraham, "*Le Mariage de Figaro* de Beaumarchais", in *Annales conferencia* (new series), 44, 1954.
P. Jacques, "The Originality of *Figaro*", in *Modern Languages*, vol.38 no.4, 1957.
Jacques Vier, "*Le Mariage de Figaro*: Miroir d'un siècle, portrait d'un homme", in *Archives des lettres modernes*, 6, 1957.
Jacques Vier, "*Le Mariage de Figaro*, II: Le Mouvement dramatique et l'esprit du *Mariage à La Mère coupable*", in *Archives des lettres modernes*, 6, 1957.
Pierre Beaumarchais, "The Preface to *The Marriage of Figaro*", translated by Mary Douglas, in *Tulane Drama Review*, vol.11 no.2, 1958.
John Hampton, "Research on *Le Mariage de Figaro*", in *French Studies*, 16, 1962.
J.B. Ratermanis, "A Travers les manuscrits du *Mariage de Figaro*", in *Philological Quarterly*, 44, 1965.
W.D. Howarth, "The Recognition Scene in *Le Mariage de Figaro*", in *Modern Language Review*, 64, 1969.
Noël Musso, "Le Vocabulaire de Figaro dans *Le Mariage*", in *Études de linguistique appliquée*, April–June, 1972.
W.T. MacCary, "The Significance of a Comic Pattern in Plautus and Beaumarchais", in *Modern Language Notes*, 88, 1973.
Annie Ubersfeld, "Un Balcon sur la terreur: *Le Mariage de Figaro*", in *Europe*, April 1973.
Walter E. Rex, "Figaro's Games", in *Publications of the Modern Language Association* [*PMLA*], 89, 1974.
Hans Ludwig Scheel, "*Le Mariage de Figaro* von Beaumarchais und das Libretto der *Nozze di Figaro* von Lorenzo da Ponte", in *Die Musikforschung*, vol.8 no.2, 1975.
Maurice Descotes, "A propos du *Mariage de Figaro*: Climat politique, interprétation, accueil du public", in *Cahiers de l'Université de Pau et des Pays de l'Adour*, 4, 1978.

The Marriage of Figaro: Engraving, 1809

Francine Levy, "Une 'clef' du *Mariage de Figaro*: Le Chevalier d'Eon est-il le modèle de Marceline de Verte-Allure?", in *Association Guillaume Budé Bulletin*, 1978.

Francine Levy, "*Le Mariage de Figaro*: Essai d'interprétation", in *Studies on Voltaire and the Eighteenth Century*, 173, 1978.

François Moureau, "Une source du *Mariage de Figaro*: Le Jaloux honteux de Dufresny", in *Revue d'histoire littéraire de la France*, 82, 1982.

Pierre Testud, "Échange et change dans *Le Mariage de Figaro*, ou le cher de Chérubin", in *La Licorne*, 7, 1983.

Vivienne G. Mylne, "*Le Droit de seigneur* in *Le Mariage de Figaro*", in *French Studies Bulletin*, 11, 1984.

Ralph A. Nablow, "Beaumarchais, Figaro's Monologue and Voltaire's *Pauvre Diable*", in *Romance Notes*, vol.28 no.2, 1987.

* * *

Count Almaviva, married for three years to Rosine, now tires of her, and seeks pleasure elsewhere. The valet Figaro is to marry Suzanne, the Countess's maid, but he soon discovers that Almaviva plans to abuse feudal privilege in order to possess Suzanne himself. He plots to defend his rights, but often unsuccessfully, and he is almost forced into marriage with the importunate Marceline, who turns out to be his mother. But the Count himself fares no better. He is frequently thwarted in his schemes by the Countess and Suzanne and falls victim to a ridiculous jealousy of Cherubin, a young page in love with the Countess. In the final act the Countess, impersonating Suzanne at an assignation she has given Almaviva, confronts her husband with his infidelity and compels him to ask her forgiveness. Figaro, having been momentarily deceived also by their disguise, now looks forward to the prospect of marriage.

The comedy clearly exploits the popularity of *Le Barbier de Séville* by imagining the further adventures of familiar characters, and yet it is not just a pale continuation of the earlier play. There are significant changes in the conception of the protagonists—Figaro, the Count, and Rosine are all, in different ways, less carefree than before—but also, more importantly, in the nature of the plot. It follows the pattern of traditional intrigue comedy by having at its centre a love beset by obstacles, but, unusually, the love here is that of a servant, and the obstacles are engineered by a master. This change introduces a potentiality for satire at the expense of the Count which Beaumarchais does not miss; the rivalry becomes a battle not simply between lovers, but between servant and master.

Particularly original is the play's fertile mixture of different dramatic styles, combining *vaudeville* and *drame bourgeois*, comedy of intrigue and political satire. The plot is unashamedly improbable with its rapid changes of scene and complex interaction of different subplots—featuring Cherubin, Marceline, the Countess—around the principal intrigues of Figaro and the Count. And yet within this the dramatist seeks also to exploit other modes of theatrical expression—gestures, silences, or recurrent motifs—to suggest more than words alone might do.

In consequence, Beaumarchais creates a potent, satirical mode in which there is a fruitful interaction of different voices; the self-consciously theatrical, at times parodic, nature of the plot suggests an unnatural world into which the sharp discourse of satire, with its witty epigrams or longer tirades deriding the institutions and privileges of the old regime, bursts with renewed force. Conversely, the compelling nature of the comic action and its principal focus, a scheming servant and a ridiculous Count, does not allow the satirical voice to dominate or degenerate into sermonising.

This particular blend of tones and registers underlies, too, the presentation of characters, who are neither just satirical caricatures nor moral models, but whose significance is suggested through their fluctuating theatrical functions. The Count may partly embody the tyrannies of power, but in the Count's role of husband, Beaumarchais implies a deeper search for satisfaction and fulfilment. Figaro performs the traditional functions of the witty and resourceful valet, but to these is added, in his role as lover, a deeper awareness of life, chance, and instability. The Countess has many features of the neglected wife, typical of the *drame bourgeois*, and yet she is not simply a pathetic and innocent victim. With great delicacy and tact, through glances, *rêveries*, and the leitmotif of her ribbon—coveted and stolen by Cherubin, recovered and finally surrendered by her—Beaumarchais hints at the birth of an attraction for the young boy, discreet but persistently present. Cherubin is himself one of the most original creations in the play. He is, by turns, an agent of chaos, constantly turning up unannounced and unexpected; a catalyst, awakening the capacity for love or jealousy latent in others; and finally, in a uniquely daring way, he embodies sexual desire in its earliest and most spontaneous state, unconstrained by any form of social inhibition, but which can as yet find expression only in words.

Throughout the hectic five acts, chance is seen to play a primordial role. Figaro is often the victim of unforeseen events and he sees a similarly random disposition of rewards and punishments in existing social and political hierarchies. This sense of the chaotic emerges particularly clearly in his massive monologue of the final act, a bold piece of theatrical writing to which there is nothing comparable in either size or scope in 18th-century drama. Figaro traces the turbulent course of his life, in which he has fallen prey to the tyrannies both of man and fate, and concludes that man's very identity is no less the product of chance than the events which haphazardly befall him. Spoken at a time when Figaro believes Suzanne to be unfaithful to him, it situates him in the tradition of the ridiculous lover, prone to groundless jealousy and despair, but such is its compelling rhetoric that it gives a stark, metaphysical prominence to the comic themes of disguise and contingency so central to the development of the plot.

By the final scene, though, all turns out well. Beaumarchais does not end the play with the stern lesson provided by a reformed libertine, as would befit a *drame bourgeois*, but with songs and celebrations. Such an ending, however, does not imply that the moral problems raised by the text are forgotten, but rather, paradoxically, that they cannot be so easily neutralised by this traditional vision of virtue triumphing over vice. Instead, the audience is transported to the world of *vaudeville*, which openly acknowledges its status as theatre, but which cannot disguise the expressions of injustice, infidelity, and chance which infiltrate the songs. This self-consciously theatrical mode brings the play to an end, but it does not pretend to resolve the problems which lie at its heart.

—G. Jonathon Mallinson

MARY STUART (Maria Stuart)
by Friedrich von Schiller

First Publication: Tübingen, 1801.
First Production: Hoftheater, Weimar, 14 June 1800.

Editions

Maria Stuart, edited by Karl Breul, Cambridge, 1893; revised edition, 1897.
Maria Stuart, edited by Edward S. Joynes, Boston, 1894.
Maria Stuart, edited by C.A. Buchheim, Oxford, 1895.
Maria Stuart, edited by W.A. Hervey, New York, 1899.
Maria Stuart, edited by Charles Sheldon, New York, 1943.
Maria Stuart, edited by Werner Burkhard, Aarau, Switzerland, 1944.
Maria Stuart, edited by Gottfried Ippisch, Vienna, 1947.
Maria Stuart, Leipzig, 1959 (Reclam edition).
Maria Stuart, edited by William White, London, 1965.
Maria Stuart, Stuttgart, 1972 (Reclam edition).

Translations

Mary Stuart, translated by Günther Reinhardt, Brooklyn, New York, 1950.
Mary Stuart, translated by Sophie Wilkins, Great Neck, New York, 1959.
Mary Stuart, "freely" translated by Stephen Spender, London, 1959.
Mary Stuart, in *Classical German Drama*, translated by Theodore H. Lustig, New York, 1963.

Maria Stuart, in *Maria Stuart—A Tragedy*; *Joan of Arc—A Romantic Tragedy*, translated by Robert David MacDonald, Birmingham, 1987.

Criticism
(For general works on the author, see *Playwrights* volume)

Books:
Aloysia Cüppers, *Schillers "Maria Stuart" in ihrem Verhältnis zur Geschichte*, Schüningh, 1906.
Th. Berg, *Kommentar til Schillers "Maria Stuart"*, Copenhagen, 1924.
Oswald Woyte (ed.), *Erläuterungen zu Schillers "Maria Stuart"*, Hollfeld, 1954.
Rudolf Ibel, *Maria Stuart*, Berlin and Bonn, 1959.
Erika Swales, *Schiller: "Maria Stuart"*, London, 1988.

Articles:
Louise Veldhuis, "*Maria Stuart* bij Vondel en bij Schiller", in *Vondelkroniek*, 10, 1939.
Reinhard Buchwald, "*Maria Stuart* und *Die Jungfrau von Orleans*: Die klassische Kunstform als Träger der sittlichen Ideen und der religiösen Symbole", in *Zeitschrift für deutsche Bildung*, 17, 1941.
Adolph Beck, "*Maria Stuart*", in *Das deutsche Drama*, 1, 1958.
Roger Ayrault, "La Figure de Mortimer dans *Maria Stuart* et la conception du drame historique chez Schiller", in *Études Germaniques*, 14, 1959.
William Witte, "Zweimal *Maria Stuart* auf der englischen und schottischen Buhne", in *Maske und Kothurne*, 5, 1959.
G.W. Field, "Schiller's *Maria Stuart*", in *University of Toronto Quarterly*, 29, 1959–60.
Herbert Koch, "Zwei unbekannte Schiller-Rezensionen: eine *Don Carlos* Kritik; eine *Maria Stuart* Kritik", in *Jahrbuch der deutschen Schiller-Gesellschaft*, 6, 1962.
Alan Best, "Schiller's *Maria Stuart*: Masquerade as Tragedy", in *Modern Languages*, 53, 1972.
Jeffrey L. Sammons, "Mortimer's Conversion and Schiller's Allegiances", in *Journal of English and Germanic Philology*, 72, 1973.
Ellis Finger, "Schiller's Concept of the Sublime and its Pertinence to *Don Carlos* and *Maria Stuart*", in *Journal of English and Germanic Philology*, 79, 1980.
Anni Gutmann, "Tronchins *Maria Stuart* und Schillers *Maria Stuart*: Parallelen und Kontraste", in *Neophilologus*, vol. 67 no. 2, 1983.

*   *   *

Mary Stuart is seen by the English Queen Elizabeth as a dangerous rival for her throne and is therefore imprisoned in Fotheringay Castle. Elizabeth has had Mary tried and condemned, but is resisting pressure to have the sentence carried out. The passionate young convert Mortimer reveals to Mary a plan to free her by force, but she persuades him to join forces with Elizabeth's favourite Leicester, who is really in love with Mary. Elizabeth entrusts Mortimer with the secret killing of Mary. Leicester engineers a meeting of the queens to effect a reconciliation between them. But this meeting (a disaster) and an assassination attempt persuade Elizabeth to sign the death warrant. A letter is found in Mary's papers incriminating Leicester, who rescues his own position by unmasking Mortimer, who kills himself. The warrant, given to Davison by Elizabeth with no specific orders, is seized by Burleigh and implemented. Mary makes confession and is given the last rights by Melvil, a family friend secretly ordained for the

Mary Stuart: Greenwich Theatre, London, 1988

purpose, and is executed. Elizabeth attempts to avoid responsibility for Mary's death, but is abandoned by her advisors and Leicester, and is left to rule alone.

Classically structured in five acts, and written in blank verse, *Mary Stuart* (*Maria Stuart*) is, however, not a tragedy in the traditional sense. Schiller alternates the action of the play and the sympathy of the audience between the queens, maintaining a balance of interest between the two. In *Maria Stuart*, he portrays a struggle between two powerful, related characters, a theme much exploited by writers of the *Sturm und Drang* (Storm and Stress), movement. But, unlike Schiller's earlier *The Robbers* (*Die Räuber*), in which two brothers are in conflict, *Maria Stuart* is less a tragedy of character than a tragedy of situation. The conflict in the play is precipitated not by the characters of the protagonists as much as by the fact that the situation in which they find themselves forces each into a struggle for survival. Only one queen can survive, and then only at the expense of the other. The drama centres on the balance between the gaining and the losing of physical, political, and moral freedom.

Both of the queens are presented as being alone in a hostile, male-dominated world. Mary's only company in her confine-ment is her nurse Hannah Kennedy, who acts as a confidante, allowing Mary to confess her former life. Schiller reverses historical fact for dramatic purpose in making his Mary guilty of complicity in the murder of her husband Darnley, but innocent of any involvement in the plan to free her from Fotheringay.

Elizabeth is, by contrast, surrounded by advisors, all male, and all of whom—it would be reasonable for her to assume—eager to propose courses of action at least as much for their own advantage as for hers or the state's. They do not understand Elizabeth's ambivalent reactions to her "sister" queen. She feels for Mary's suffering as a woman, yet fears and hates her as a rival both for the throne and for the affections of the men at court. Schiller stresses the uncertain hold Elizabeth has on power, and her constant awareness of her illegitimacy.

While there is the chance of physical freedom, and as long as she seeks to uphold her innocence and justify herself, Mary remains tied to the world and its politics. It is only when she ceases to fight for earthly advantage that she begins to attain the moral freedom and integrity with which she dies. Mary's rejection of Mortimer's plan for her release and her horrified spurning of his physical advances show how far she has progressed along the path of grace. In her confession and in her famous offering of her undeserved death at the hands of Elizabeth against her unpunished involvement in her husband's death, she achieves true atonement and the moral freedom of a soul at peace. Elizabeth can only assure her own political freedom of action at the expense of her moral freedom. She can deprive Mary of her physical freedom by imprisoning her. She can have her executed, but she will have to concede the moral high ground to her. And this she is unwilling to do. It is in the third act meeting of the queens, a theatrical invention of true genius, that their relationship, until then played out by proxy, is thrown into sharpest focus. Leicester's hope in arranging the meeting was for a reconciliation—a hope shared by both Elizabeth and Mary. But he has not sufficiently prepared Elizabeth for Mary's beauty (Schiller's Mary is still 27 years old). This surprise angers Elizabeth, who goads Mary into claiming the throne and denying Elizabeth's right, as a bastard, to rule. This breakdown, followed by the assassination attempt on her during her trip back to London, convinces Elizabeth to sign the warrant. She still attempts to equivocate, however, by refusing to give Davison clear orders as to how to proceed. She still hopes to be able to avoid taking the moral responsibility for this final and decisive act in the moral game being played out between the two women. Elizabeth is all too aware of the factors conditioning her choice. But the truth comes out in the end, and she is forced to live with the political freedom she has secured for herself by the death of her only rival together with the surrender of her moral freedom.

Since its premiere in Weimar in 1800, Schiller's masterpiece *Maria Stuart* has maintained a prominent place in the German theatre repertory, as well as being performed with considerable success outside Germany.

—Anthony Meech

LA MASCHERA E IL VOLTO. See **THE MASK AND THE FACE.**

THE MASK AND THE FACE (La maschera e il volto) by Luigi Chiarelli

First Publication: Treves, 1917.
First Production: Teatro Argentina, Rome, 31 May 1916.

Translations
The Mask and the Face, translated by Noel de Vic Beamish, in *International Modern Plays*, London, 1950.

*   *   *

Count Paolo Grazia declares one evening to a gathering of his upper-middle-class friends that a husband must kill an unfaithful wife to keep his self-respect or else commit suicide. Faced with the reality of his own wife Savina's infidelity and fearing ridicule should he forgive her, he concocts a lie that he has murdered her and thrown her in Lake Como. In reality she agrees to live abroad under an assumed name. Act II opens ten months later when Paolo returns home acquitted of his wife's murder. His welcome as a hero disgusts him. He discovers how his own feelings of despair and loss contrast quite drastically with those expressed by all strata of society. There are further complications when a body is discovered in the lake. Friends claim it is Savina and demand a funeral. Coincidentally, the real Savina returns from abroad and declares that she prefers suicide to a life without him. Act III takes place the following day on the afternoon of the funeral. Paolo and Savina have spent a passionate night together and he is awakened as if for the first time to the pain of loving. When it is discovered that Savina's death was a hoax, Paolo is threatened with a prison sentence. He and Savina determine to leave behind the absurd rules of bourgeois society and wander the world incognito. The final stage image suggests a theme of resurrection. The dead body passing by off-stage is a sharp reminder of what could have happened. They embrace passionately as Chopin's Funeral March is heard.

Immediately successful in Italy and abroad, *The Mask and the Face* was hailed as the crowning achievement of the Italian grotesque movement. This movement comprised, besides Chiarelli, such authors as Luigi Antonelli, Enrico Cavicchioli, and Pier Maria Rosso di San Secondo. At the turn of the century, bourgeois theatre-goers enjoyed the theme of the wife–husband–lover triangle that French writers had popularized in the 19th century and that was taken up by Italian playwrights such as Praga, Rovetta, the Antona-Traversi, and Giacosa. While the bourgeois theatre produced self-satisfied laughter, Chiarelli used the popular triangle theme to create a fiercely ironic comment on societal values.

Some characteristics of the Italian grotesque movement found in *The Mask and the Face* are the juxtaposition of the tragic and the grotesque; the contrast between what is and what seems real, or the vision of life as illusion; and the alienation of the sensitive man from society and his anguished suffering. Chiarelli pushes the grotesque to its limits when he addresses the question of physical love, and moves, rather, into a naturalistic mode. When Paolo and Savina reunite, they reach heights of passion and carnal love undreamt of by such a staid, bourgeois couple. The character of Cirillo Zanotti explains: "You have lost a wife and have gained a lover!". Cirillo Zanotti is the most understanding character in the play. He has come to terms with life and rejects bourgeois conventions. Paolo gradually swings round to his point of view. Cirillo can be considered Chiarelli's alter ego in expressing the grotesque aesthetic: it is Cirillo who declares: "In life next to the most grotesque buffoonery burn the most terrible tragedies; the grin of the most obscene mask covers the most searing passions!".

Of the two published English translations, that of C. B. Fernald (Samuel French, 1927) is an adaptation that distorts terribly the original play. The most faithful published translation is by Noel de Vic Beamish. An unpublished translation by Somerset Maugham was used as a text for a 1933 production at the Guild Theatre, New York, which starred Humphrey Bogart and Judith Anderson.

—Jane House

MASKARAD. See **MASQUERADE.**

MASQUERADE (Maskarad)
by Mikhail Lermontov

First Publication: 1842.
First Production: Maly Theatre, Moscow, 1862.

Translations
Masquerade, translated by R.W. Phillips, in *Russian Literature Triquarterly*, Winter 1974.

Criticism
(For general works on the author, see *Playwrights* volume)

Articles:
E. Kostka, "The Influence of Schiller's Aesthetics on the Dramas of Lermontov", in *Philological Quarterly*, 30, 1951.
Simon Karlinsky, "Misanthropy and Sadism in Lermontov's Plays", in *Studies in Russian Literature in Honor of Vsevolod Setchkarev*, Columbus, Ohio, 1986.

* * *

A four-act drama in verse by the Russian poet and novelist Mikhail Lermontov, written in 1835–6. Censorship problems delayed performance until 1862 (Maly Theatre, Moscow) and 1864 (Aleksandrinsky Theatre, St Petersburg). A major performance occurred in 1917, also at the Aleksandrinsky, directed by Meyerhold with music by Glazunov and settings by Golovin. (This happened to be the last play performed before the October Revolution.) The production was revived in 1933 and 1938. The play remains in the repertory of many Soviet theatres but it has known no success abroad.

The central character of *Masquerade* is Evgeny Arbenin, a rich man-about-town, self-centred and cynical, but now ostensibly reformed, following his marriage to a beautiful young girl, Nina. However, he soon lapses into maniacal jealousy, following a masked ball during which her bracelet—which she has innocently lost—is shown to him by Prince Zvezdich who claims it as a love token. Ignoring her protestations of devotion, he murders Nina by poisoning her ice-cream. Shortly afterwards he is visited by two people, a stranger seeking revenge for a long-forgotten affront and Prince Zvezdich. The latter confirms Nina's innocence and the former gains his satisfaction by witnessing the shattered Arbenin's collapse into madness.

The play has two important antecedents in Shakespeare's *Othello*, the borrowings from which are obvious but have never been fully documented, and in Griboyedov's *Woe from Wit* (1823), a sharp satire of Moscow high society. Dealing now with St. Petersburg, *Masquerade* contains a satirical depiction of the corrupt, empty-headed, and hypocritical aristocracy so unsubtle that the censor was bound to brand the play as indecent and harmful. More importantly, the overt sarcasm

Masquerade Vakhtangov Theatre, Moscow, 1937

which replaces Griboyedov's ironical humour debases the work in artistic terms; its social criticism is now the least interesting thing about it. The more profound ideas which it attempts to explore are those encountered elsewhere in Lermontov—the problem of good and evil and the search for a meaning to life itself in a universe of apparent cruelty and absurdity. Here, too, unsubtlety is the drawback. The character of Arbenin lacks the rounded authentication of his alter ego Pechorin (in the novel *A Hero of Our Time*). His posturings and exaggerated invective place him in the ranks of melodramatic villainy. The minor characters are more successful but they are overshadowed and as underdeveloped as Arbenin is overdrawn. The construction of the play is rather lopsided with the misunderstanding and the jealous rage of the hero well established by the end of the first act; the second and fourth acts appear particularly anti-climactic.

This is a young man's drama, written when the author was about 21 years old, and its immaturity is evident. The play retains some importance, however, for a number of reasons. It has not been consigned to oblivion by the Russian theatre. It contains fluent, aphoristic and sometimes memorable poetry, the hallmark of which is variety; the lines are freely rhymed and written in varying lengths from monometer to hexameter. To a surprising degree the language, particularly in the dialogues, manages to free itself from the constraints of metre and rhyme and create an impression of elegant, conversational Russian. Most of all, this play adds something to our understanding of Lermontov himself whose desperate negativism expressed itself repeatedly through several of his literary personages. Without Arbenin this knowledge would be diminished.

—Anthony D.P. Briggs

MASSE-MENSCH. See **MASSES AND MAN.**

MASSES AND MAN (Masse-Mensch)
by Ernst Toller

First Publication: Potsdam, 1921.
First Production: Stadttheater, Nuremburg, 15 November 1920.

Translations
Masses and Man, translated by Vera Mandel, London, 1923.
Man and the Masses, translated by Louis Untermeyer, Garden City, New York, 1924.

Criticism
(For general works on the author, see *Playwrights* volume)

Articles:
S. Fishman, "Ernst Toller and the Drama of Non-Violence", in *Midwest Quarterly*, vol.7 no.1, 1965.
Malcolm Pittock, "*Masse-Mensch* and the Tragedy of Revolution", in *Forum for Modern Language Studies*, 8, 1972.
Rosemarie Altenhofer, "*Masse Mensch*", in *Masse Mensch*, by Toller, Stuttgart, 1979.

Mary K. Dahl, "*Masse Mensch*: Violence Discovered and Evaluated", in her *Political Violence in Drama: Classical Models, Contemporary Variations*, Ann Arbor, Michigan, 1987.
William R. Elwood, "Ernst Toller's *Masse-Mensch*: The Individual vs. the Collective", in *From the Bard to Broadway*, edited by Karelisa V. Hartigan, Lanham, Maryland, 1987.
Steven D. Martinson, "A Multiperspectivist Approach to the Drama of Revolution: Ernst Toller's *Masse Mensch*", in *Orbis Litterarum*, 43, 1988.

*   *   *

Written during two nights in October 1919 in Niederschönfeld prison, *Masse Mensch* (*Masses and Man*) is Ernst Toller's most interesting drama. Set during wartime, a workers' committee decides to strike to enforce peace and secure a fair society. Sonja Irene, wife of a disapproving bourgeois, has joined the committee and finds her strike call opposed by an anonymous opponent who insists that the utopia of lasting peace and social justice can only come through violent revolution. She is unable to prevent this and the shooting of an enemy soldier. In the ensuing battle she is captured, refuses help from her husband and from her anonymous former opponent because she would have to kill a warden to escape, and is executed.

An element of deliberate ambiguity in the original title, with its hyphenated form in the second version, highlights the essential dialectical purpose and form of this play set in seven scenes. Toller, in trying to reformulate his own experiences of revolution, examines the conflict between man as an individual and man as a social being, and insists that this takes place both in company and within one's inner self. The exceptional situation forces the potentially tragic dilemma that "the individual can wish for death. The masses must wish for life. And since we are men and masses at the same time we choose life and death" (Letter to Theodor Lessing, 1920).

The play is written as a vision containing "real" and "dream" scenes. The banality of real-life situations is contrasted with the utopia of a new society to come. Its diction is in free verse with extensive use of rhythm and repetition. The main character is given the extra, significant name Irene (meaning peace), and the tension within her life, as she gradually learns and accepts the personal demands of her vision, produces a further contrast. In the "real" scenes her statements are clear and decisive; in the "dream" scenes she appears through a symbolic *doppelgänger* acting out half-conscious realisations of her position. Furthermore, the issues discussed between Sonja and her *Begleiter* (Companion) in the "dream" scenes foreshadow or complement those in conflict between her and the *Namenlose* (Nameless One) in the "real" scenes. The problems of the political resolve needed for mass action are examined dialectically through the central character who is formed as a real-life person and as an abstract figure.

All the central oppositions remain unresolved. Above all the apparent, factual immediacy of revolution and counter-revolution, ably supported by use of teichoscopia in both "real" and "dream" scenes, seems to conflict with the noble ideals expressed in abstract argument. This is underscored by the banal details and sense of shame of the two women gathering Sonja's effects in the final scene while she is being shot. The Nietzschean, vitalist idealism applied to revolutionary aims is parodied in the Stock Exchange scene that presents the double standards of paternalistic capitalism and calls into question the efficacy of a peaceful outcome through strike action. Man in the mass responds to the market, which, as part of its self-defensive mechanisms, grades him even in use of the state brothel to be set up:

Three prices.
Three categories.
Brothel for officers:
Stay overnight.
Brothel for corporals:
One hour.
Other ranks' brothel:
15 minutes.

The play can be approached from many other angles. The conflict between moral principle and revolutionary expediency exemplified in the fourth scene as a vision becomes real in Scene Five, where ethical socialism clashes with applied Marxism when faced by the possibility of shooting prisoners as an act of revenge. The ideal of a state constructed as a set of relationships between mutually supportive people—a community or *Gemeinschaft*—eventually requires of Sonja an act of self-sacrifice, a form of anarchy that perpetuates an ethical ideal. The individual has to show the way, the mass can only achieve ethical freedom through an act of limited violence.

Masses and Man has many of the hallmarks of an Expressionist drama. These include the structure of its ideas; the concentration on one central figure moving through various stages (or "stations") becoming gradually aware of her private and representative fate; the use of rhythmic monologues and set tableau discussion pieces; the use of staccato language concentrating on essentials with sparse use of pronouns, articles, and even verbs; the alternation of "dream" and "real" scenes; the element of grotesque parody (in the Stock Exchange scene); the naming of only one character (the others all being representative); the anti-bourgeois stance; and the call to change and the search for a "new man" and a "new society". Despite all this, the involvement with political argument seems to suggest something beyond theoretical Expressionism. The clue lies in the final scene when Sonja corrects the priest's claim that "Man is good" with the words "Man wants to be good". *Masses and Man*, because of its dialectical structure and argument, is hostile to all forms of propaganda and ideology. Its central figure, who becomes a "new woman", combines a hard-headed understanding of her companions with a vision for the future.

—Brian Keith-Smith

———

DIE MASSNAHME. See **THE MEASURES TAKEN.**

———

THE MASTER BUILDER (Bygmester Solness)
by Henrik Ibsen

First Publication: London (in Norwegian), 1892.
First Production: Trondhjem, Norway (Petersen's Touring
　　　　　　　Company), 19 January 1893.

Translations
The Master Builder, translated by Edmund Gosse and William Archer, in *The Collected Works, 10*, edited by William Archer, 1907.

The Master Builder, translated by Eva le Gallienne, London, 1956.
The Master Builder, in *Ibsen: Three Plays*, translated by Una Ellis-Fermor, Harmondsworth, 1956.
The Master Builder, translated by Michael Meyer, London, 1961; corrected version, in *Ibsen: Plays, 1*, London, 1980.
The Master Builder, in *The Last Plays of Henrik Ibsen*, translated by Arvid Paulsen, New York, 1962.
The Master Builder, in *Ibsen: Four Major Plays, 1*, translated by Rolf Fjelde, New York, 1965.
The Master Builder, translated by James Walter McFarlane, in *The Oxford Ibsen, 7*, edited by James Walter McFarlane, London, 1966.

Criticism
(For general works on the author, see *Playwrights* volume)

Books:
Oscar Aronsohn, *Das Problem in "Bygmester Solness"*, Halle, 1911.
Aslaug G. Michaelsen, *Ibsens "Bygmester Solness" som tidsdiagnose*, Tangen, 1982.

Articles:
Frank Wedekind, "Schriftsteller Ibsen und Baumeister Solness: Ein kritischer Essay", in *Forum*, 1914; in English, in *Theater Three*, 1, 1986.
V. Schatia, "A Case of Involutional Psychosis", in *Psychoanalytic Review*, vol.33 no.2, 1940.
K. Gunvaldsen, "*The Master Builder* and *Die versunkene Glocke*", in *Monatshefte*, vol.33 no.4, 1941.
J. Riviere, "The Inner World in Ibsen's *Master Builder*", in *International Journal of Psychoanalysis*, vol.33 no.2, 1952.
Oskar Mosfjeld, "Aline Solness 'Ni deilige dukker' ", in *Ibsen-Årbok*, 1957–59.
C. Lyons, "The *Master Builder* as Drama of the Self", in *Scandinavian Studies*, 39, 1967.
H. Sehmsdorf, "Two Legends about St. Olaf, the Master Builder: A Clue to the Dramatic Structure of Henrik Ibsen's *Bygmester Solness*", in *Edda*, 67, 1967.
Bjarne Berulfsen, "Språklig Differensiering i *Bygmester Solness*", in *Maal og Minne*, 1–4, 1968.
J. Hurst, "Interpreting the *Master Builder*", in *Forum for Modern Language Studies*, 4, 1968.
Leonard Quirino, "Ibsen's Daedalus: *The Master Builder*", in *Modern Drama*, 12, 1969.
Robin Carey, "Retribution in *The Master Builder* and *Little Eyolf*", in *Research Studies* (Washington State University), 38, 1970.
Michael W. Kaufman, "Nietzsche, Georg Brandes, and Ibsen's *Master Builder*", in *Comparative Drama*, 6, 1972.
Egil Törnqvist, "The Illness Pattern in *The Master Builder*", in *Scandinavica*, 11, 1972.
Michael Hinden, "Ibsen and Nietzsche: A Reading of *The Master Builder*", in *Modern Drama*, 15, 1973.
Arne Roed, " 'Right to the Top'—?", in *Ibsen-Årbok*, 1977.
Bruce Bigley, "Praxis and Stasis in Ibsen's *Bygmester Solness*—or, Whatever Happened to Plot and Character?", in *Scandinavian Studies*, 50, 1978.
Sandra E. Saari, "Of Madness of Fame: Ibsen's *Bygmester Solness*", in *Scandinavian Studies*, 50, 1978.
Torunn Y. Sandborn, "*Bygmester Solness* og sviket mot fellesskapet", in *Vinduet*, vol.32 no.3, 1978.
Kari Elliott, "*The Master Builder*: Houses Built on Rock or Sand", in *Edda*, 79, 1979.
Thure Stenström, "Att tolka *Bygmester Solness*", in *Kungl. Humanistika Vetenskaps-samfundet i Uppsala*, Årsbok, 1979–80.

The Master Builder: Dramaten, Stockholm, 1937

Brian Crow, "Romantic Ambivalence in *The Master Builder*", in *Studies in Romanticism*, 20, 1981.

Richard Hornby, "Deconstructing Realism in Ibsen's *The Master Builder*", in *Essays in Theatre*, 2, 1983.

James L. Calderwood, "*The Master Builder* and the Failure of Symbolic Success", in *Modern Drama*, 27, 1984.

Marie Wells, "*The Master Builder*, *John Gabriel Borkman* and *When We Dead Awaken*: Variations on a Theme or Developing Argument?", in *New Comparison*, 4, 1987.

*   *   *

Two different kinds of play are interlinked in *The Master Builder*. The first introduced is a naturalistic social drama concerning a successful, middle-aged man's attempt to block the path of a potential younger rival (Ragnar Brøvik), whose father he himself displaced; working on the susceptible nature of Ragnar's fiancée, Kaia, Master-Builder Solness has created an infatuation with himself which will keep both young people, and Old Brøvik, working in his office. Still within Act I, a drama of the inner life—of fantasy, obsession, and neurosis—begins with the arrival of youth personified in Hilde Wangel and ousts the first level of the play from the centre of attention. The disturbing strangeness of the work as a whole springs from Ibsen's maintaining and interrelating the two dramatic modes to the end, so that Solness's inner renewal allows him to release

Ragnar, and his death by falling from a tower suggests a multiplicity of meanings.

A direct reflection of Strindberg's *The Father* appears in Solness's suspicion that his wife, Aline, and Dr. Herdal believe him to be insane. The Swedish playwright's example had undoubtedly encouraged Ibsen to tread more boldly in dramatic territory represented in all his plays after *The Wild Duck* (1884). This advance involves recognition that the human mind operates in stranger ways than the limited, naturalistic view that rationality admits, and that human motivation and action can have a mythic dimension. He uses the technique of intimate duologues, as developed in his social plays (especially *Ghosts*), as a method of tracing the influence of the past in the present, to explore the secret mind and the innermost nature of human relationships. One school of critics, clinging to the tenets of naturalism, interprets the play as a study in mental abnormality: Solness, Aline, and Hilde in turn qualify for the madhouse. It is more rewarding to move with the play into a more imaginatively conceived understanding of reality, not choosing between alternatives, but reaching out to encompass divergent views.

Ibsen is careful to locate Hilde in the social world: both Dr. Herdal (the confidant) and Mrs. Solness remember meeting her before, in mundane situations; it is Solness who does not recall her. She has a history outside the play: the younger daughter of Dr. Wangel of Lysanger, in *The Lady from the*

Sea, has put on years and arrived unexpectedly at the Solness house, come like the devil cheerfully on cue. To all the other characters she appears an attractive, lively, unconventional young woman, spontaneously friendly, if self-willed; to Solness, in their long solitudes *à deux*, she is an enchanting inquisitor who draws out of him all his hidden fears, desires, and sense of guilt, opens the prison of his everyday life and gives him hope. He is not troubled to verify or reject the story she tells him of their earlier meeting and her reason for seeking him out. Its fairytale quality insulates them from actuality in a world of the imagination and provides a language of metaphor in which they can talk freely. An emotionally adult woman, Hilde uses her fantasy from the past as an erotic challenge to Solness which he finds irresistible.

Although each of the three main characters recalls memories, the past that they reveal is ambiguous and unstable, as they do not verify each other's accounts. This is not the past as historical fact, but the fiction they each construct to live by. Ibsen has left it open to the actress playing Hilde to allow the character an awareness of the process that neither Solness nor Aline shares. The oddity of a mature young woman claiming a childish hero-worship of the Master Builder, and clinging to a pubertal fantasy of how, ten years before to the day, he chose her as his future princess, may be simply piquant. Solness, who spares scarcely a thought for the ruthlessness with which he treated Knut Brøvik in the pursuit of his own ambitions, and less for having failed to give his wife a love through which she might have blossomed as a woman, has attached his sense of guilt to the burning down of her home which he knows, rationally, he did not cause. Aline's is the most horrifying displacement: grieving, not for the babies who died, but for her dolls and her own lost childhood. The obsessional symbols may have a deeper truth to tell.

An unnatural arresting of time emerges as one of the play's themes through its repetition within each of the main characters: Hilde's fixation on the day, ten years ago, when Solness climbed the church tower at Lysanger; Aline, who has grown old without growing up; and Solness, intent on resisting the process of change whereby men pass from youth to age and others take over from them. The "out-of-time" quality of the duologues is entirely apt. It is also a condition of contemplation in which the play's poetic reach can be explored. As a psychological drama, *The Master Builder* testifies to the symbolic and superstitious modes of thinking sophisticated human beings still employ alongside the scientific and rational, and which poets utilise most deliberately. It is a kind of poets' thinking that passes between Solness and Hilde, and it forces its way through into the action at the end of the play.

From the play's first appearance it has been regarded as partly autobiographical, the various phases of Solness's career as a builder corresponding to the major changes in Ibsen's dramatic style from the great philosophical plays in verse onwards. Yet it has also taken its place among the supreme modern tragedies. The obvious, phallic symbolism is subsumed in the traditional tragic symbolism of the rise and fall of overweening ambition. Hilde's recollection of the master builder, high in the air, challenging some invisible power and triumphing, is matched both by Solness's terrified thought that he has called down fire from heaven and by his response to the lure of the impossible: building a new house for Aline and himself, unhappy though they are together, with three nurseries, though they neither have nor can expect to have any children, giving it a tower, and siting it vertiginously on the edge of a quarry, even though he has lost his head for heights. An impression of more than human stature attaches itself to the fault-ridden human figure, and the philosophical ideas are not far away: Aline has nothing to live by but the categorical

imperative of duty, to which Ibsen opposes *livsglede* (the joy of living); and Solness, in going beyond his nature to achieve the impossible, takes on the quality of the Nietzschean vision of man becoming superhuman. Hilde, who has goaded him out of mere idealistic dreaming (building castles in the air) and waves Aline's shawl at him in ecstasy, may be seen as his destroyer. But the Solness who takes the wreath to climb the tower is a better man than we have seen earlier in the play. He may not know that he is going to his death, but he is ready for it. The achievement is real.

—Margery Morgan

"MASTER HAROLD". . .AND THE BOYS
by Athol Fugard

First Publication: New York, 1982.
First Production: Yale Repertory Theatre, New Haven, Connecticut, 12 March 1982.

Criticism
(For general works on the author, see *Playwrights* volume)

Articles:
G. Olivier, "Notes on *Master Harold*. . .*and the Boys* at the Yale Rep", in *Standpunte*, 162, 1982.
Sheila Roberts, " 'No lessons learnt': Reading the Texts of Fugard's *A Lesson from Aloes* and *"Master Harold". . .and the Boys"*, in *English in Africa*, vol.9 no.2, 1982.
Errol Durbach, " '*Master Harold'. . .and the Boys*: Athol Fugard and the Psychopathology of Apartheid", in *Modern Drama*, 30, 1987.

*   *   *

On the face of it this is a play in which not a great deal happens. The scene is the St. George's Park Tea Room on a wet afternoon in Port Elizabeth in 1950. There are no customers, and most of the tables and chairs have been cleared and stacked to one side. Two black waiters, Sam and Willie, are on stage as the play opens, Willie mopping the floor, Sam reading one of the comic books piled on the only table laid for a meal. Willie, we learn, wants to improve his dancing, but he can't get his quickstep right and, moreover, has apparently been deserted by his partner, after beating her. Sam offers him advice, both about his dancing technique and his personal relations. Hally, the son of the owner of the tea room, enters, straight from school. He eats and talks to the two black men, with both of whom—but especially Sam—he has a close and even loving relationship. Their discussion and accompanying roleplay embraces what Hally has been learning at school about the great men of history, memories of the old Jubilee Boarding House where as a small boy he used to take shelter in Sam and Willie's room, of the kite that Sam made for him and taught him to fly, and of the fine art of ballroom dancing. In the course of their exchanges and phone conversations which Hally has with his mother, who is at the hospital where his crippled and drunken father has been under treatment for some time, it becomes apparent that when he goes home he will find his father there. Hally's emotional conflict over his father emerges; he loves him but is also deeply ashamed of him, and he wishes he would remain in the hospital. Hally's

"Master Harold"... and the Boys: National Theatre, London, 1983

mood changes. He is brutally rude to the two men who have been his best and perhaps only friends, and he insults them racially, culminating in his spitting in Sam's face. Hally leaves, and the two men dance together, to the sound of Sarah Vaughan singing the blues.

A summary such as this cannot begin to suggest the emotional intensity of *"Master Harold"*, or its potential effect on audiences in the theatre, where the play has been an outstanding critical and commercial success since its first production at the Yale Repertory Theatre in 1982. One reason for this, perhaps, is that more than any of his plays, *"Master Harold"* is deeply rooted in Fugard's personal experience. His mother owned just such a tea room, Harold is his own middle name, and as his *Notebooks* reveal Fugard had strong but troubled feelings about his father. Most important of all, Fugard in his youth was close to Sam Semela, one of his mother's employees, whom he once insulted in the street precisely as Hally does Sam in the play.

Such biographical information, however, is not needed in order for the play to make its full impact in the theatre. This is achieved primarily through an audience's empathy with the loving relationship between Hally and Sam and its violation through Hally's inability to cope with his emotional turmoil over his father, and its expression in racism. If to what extent the play manages, or even attempts, to transmute auto-biographical experience into a larger exploration or analysis of racism in South Africa is arguable; what seems quite certain is

its capacity to involve and disturb audiences everywhere.

In the final minutes of the play Sam seeks a reconciliation with Hally but he is met with a "helpless gesture" and the words: "I don't know. I don't know anything anymore". Sam responds by saying that it would be hopeless if that was indeed the case: "It would mean nothing has been learnt here this afternoon, and there was a hell of a lot of teaching going on. . .one way or the other". Although in no obvious sense a didactic play *"Master Harold"* is certainly very much about teaching and learning, both for its characters and its audiences. Most obviously, Hally takes great pride in "educating" Sam, in the sense that he shares with him some of the learning he is acquiring at school. Much in their relationship, as their debate about who qualifies as a "man of magnitude" demonstrates, is based on Hally's book-learning and Sam's admiring but humorously sceptical response to it.

But the most important teaching that goes on in the play is done by Sam, and his pupil is Hally. The image which Sam uses as his "text" is that of ballroom dancing, of which he is a skilled exponent. Early in the play Sam advises Willie that he must dance in the forthcoming competition in the Centenary Hall in New Brighton as though it were a "romance", a "love story with happy ending". Later, helping Hally with his essay on "an annual event of cultural or historical significance", he extends the image of dancing as a metaphor for personal and social relations: "There's no collisions out there, Hally. Nobody trips or stumbles or bumps into anybody else. That's what that moment is all about. To be one of those finalists on that dance floor is like. . .like being in a dream about a world in which accidents don't happen". Dancing, he continues, is beautiful "because that is what we want life to be like".

The learning, finally, extends to the audience, through empathy. Hally, we understand, may have knowledge, but it is Sam who has wisdom. Applying the image of dancing to life, we see that the young man does not yet know how to negotiate the dance-floor without bumping into others. Torn between love for his father and disgust at his crippled and alcoholic state, he loses his emotional balance and collides with Sam and Willie, his only real friends. Before Hally leaves Sam reminds him of the day he made him a kite and they flew it together from the top of a hill, which he did to give Hally something to be proud and happy about after the trauma of witnessing his drunken father being carried home on Sam's back. Hally, in his excitement, sat on a "whites only" bench and Sam had to leave him: "I reckon there's one thing you know. You don't *have* to sit up there by yourself. You know what that bench means now, and you can leave it any time you choose. All you've got to do is stand up and walk away from it". But Hally does not have the wisdom or the grace to accept the offer of reconciliation. He leaves, and the two men are left alone, dancing to the strains of Sarah Vaughan's "Little man you're crying".

—Brian Crow

MASTER PETER PATHELIN
(La Farce de Maître Pierre Pathelin)
Anonymous

First Publication: 1485.
First Production: Perhaps c.1460.

Editions
Maistre Pierre Pathelin, edited by Richard T. Holbrook, Paris, 1905; revised edition, 1937.

Translations
The Farce of Master Pierre Pathelin, translated by Richard Holbrook, Boston, 1905.
Peter Quill's Shenanigans, in *Five Comedies of Medieval France*, edited by Oscar Mandel, New York, 1970.
Master Peter Pathelin, translated by Edwin Morgan, Glasgow, 1983.

Criticism

Books:
Jean-Claude Aubailly (ed.), *"La Farce de Maistre Pierre Pathelin" et ses continuations: Le Nouveau Pathelin et le testament de Pathelin*, Paris, 1979.
Donald Maddox, *Semiotics of Deceit: The Pathelin Era*, Lewisburg, Pennsylvania, 1984.
Jean Dufournet and Michael Rouse, *Autour de "La Farce de Maître Pathelin"*, Paris, 1986.

Articles:
Alexander Fischler, "The Theme of Justice and the Structure of *La Farce de Maître Pierre Pathelin*", in *Neophilologus*, 53, 1969.

Barbara C. Bowen, "Metaphorical Obscenity in French Farce, 1460–1560", in *Comparative Drama*, 2, 1977–78.
Larry S. Crist, "Pathelinian Semiotics: Elements for an Analysis of *Maistre Pierre Pathelin*", in *L'Esprit créateur*, 18, 1978.
Donald Maddox, "The Morphology of Mischief in *Maistre Pierre Pathelin*", in *L'Esprit créateur*, 18, 1978.
Suzanne Fleischman, "Language and Deceit in the Farce of *Maistre Pathelin*", in *Tréteaux*, vol.3 no.1, 1981.
Franz Rauhut, "Erklärungsbedürftige Stellen im *Maistre Pierre Pathelin*", in *Zeitschrift für romanische Philologie*, vol.97, nos.3–4, 1981.
P.E. Bennett, "Le *Goupil*, le corbeau et les structures de *Maistre Pierre Pathelin*", in *Le Moyen Âge*, 89, 1983.
Casare Segre, "*Maistre Pathelin*: Manipulation of Topics and Epistemic Lability", in *Poetics Today* (Jerusalem), vol.5 no.3, 1984.
Carol J. Chase, "The Ideology of Deception in *La Farce de Maistre Pathelin*", in *Modern Language Studies*, vol.16 no.3, 1986.
Jean Dufournet, "Autour du 'Bée' de Pathelin", in *L'Information littéraire*, vol.38 no.5, 1986.
Eric Eigenmann, "*Pathelin* ou la fausse monnaie du discours", in *Littératures*, 16, 1987.

*   *   *

In the ten episodes of the *Farce de Maître Pierre Pathelin*, the anonymous playwright dramatizes the intrigue of the "trickster tricked". Pierre Pathelin, a lawyer with questionable credentials and ethics, assures his wife, Guillemette, that, in spite of impoverishment and lack of credit, he will acquire material for new clothes. Guillaume, the merchant, falls for Pathelin's flattery and, trusting to be paid later in gold, allows the lawyer to take away considerable cloth. When Guillaume arrives at Pathelin's house to collect his money, the lawyer fakes illness, and Guillemette attests to her husband's critical condition. Cheated, Guillaume resigns himself momentarily to loss of the material. Subsequently, Guillaume suspects his sheep have been killed; and, by taking legal action against the shepherd Thibault Aignelet for slaughter of his animals, he seeks restitution of the stolen cloth. Asking Pathelin's help, Thibault admits guilt; and Pathelin advises him to simulate idiocy. During the trial, the shepherd pronounces only one word, "Bée", ("Baa"): a pun on his name (*agneau* meaning lamb). Guillaume, obsessed with Pathelin's stealth, is enraged at seeing the lawyer in good health, and, in bringing charges, he confuses the slaughter of sheep with the theft of material. The trial is chaotic: the judge's attempts to return to the matter of the sheep are futile and absence of testimony and abundance of disorder compel him to dismiss the case. But Thibault, who had promised to pay Pathelin in gold, swindles the swindler, answering the lawyer's questions, accusations, and pleadings with "Baa". Pathelin intends to call the police. However, since the judge has stated his refusal ever again to hear litigation against Thibault, the simpleton has unexpectedly outwitted the schemer.

In late medieval France, three dramatic genres, with similar but different characteristics, emerge and develop: morality play, *sotie*, and farce. The morality play, with its allegorical representations (such as Charity, Lust, Gluttony), is invariably didactic and its plot, drawn from historical happenings or biblical episodes, recalls the spiritual conflicts of mystery or miracle plays. Like the morality play, the *sotie*, or fools' play, presents unreal or stock characters, often with fanciful names (e.g., the First Fool, Green Head, Fine Appearance).

Through slapstick skits and lively repartee, moreover, it often satirizes social conditions and political injustices. Resembling the *sotie* in its comic tone and closure, the farce provokes laughter; and, through use of engaging dialogue and natural speech of real characters placed in everyday situations, it reveals contemporary customs and conditions. Unlike the serious morality play, it is a short comedy, usually with an uncomplicated plot. Differing from the *sotie*, it employs characters who, as recognizable social types, rely upon cunning, insight, and opportunism. These features of the farce are evident in *Maître Pierre Pathelin*.

Through a subtle use of irony, the playwright injects elements of surprise which create comedies of plot, character, and language. The intrigue of the "swindler swindled" requires a logical linking of two different stories: Pathelin's deception of Guillaume and Thibault's duping of Pathelin. The presence of Pathelin and the themes of thievery and misrepresentation contribute to the cohesion and directness of a complex plot. In spite of the evils inherent in extortion and deception, the unanticipated resolution establishes an order that is absent in the opening scene. Pathelin and Guillemette use, cleverly and skillfully, their innate talents to exchange rags for robes. Thibault exists through the killing and consuming of sheep and, like Pathelin, through drawing upon his wits. Human faults and transgressions may inflict inconvenience and injustice upon Guillaume, but as an exploiter, he deserves exploitation, just as Pathelin, who depends upon his intelligence and glibness in an insensitive world, must accept the consequences of *his* actions. Evil does not end in downfall. Rather, it offers a necessary means of survival.

Pathelin's characterization is ironic. Adept in his assessment of personality, Pathelin punctures Guillaume's pretensions, thereby disclosing to the spectator the dangers of avarice and self-centeredness. But while a shepherd should be incapable of tricking a lawyer, in applying a technique taught by Pathelin, Thibault has him learn from, and pay for, his errors. Deceptions advance the plot *and* develop character delineation. In feigning illness, Pathelin mixes languages (Picard, Flemish, Norman, Breton, Lotharingian, and Latin). This gibberish convinces Guillaume that he is suffering from hallucinations. But Pathelin's blurring of illusion and reality demonstrates his uses of guile to distort the truth in order to attain particular purposes. Throughout the play Pathelin is a master of disguise and a creator of confusion, finally transforming legal principle and orderly procedure in the trial into a mayhem which, confounding Guillaume and the judge, results in Thibault's acquittal.

Exemplifying medieval French farce, *Maître Pathelin* does not convey a didactic message. Rather, by presenting middle-class characters struggling against economic and social realities, the play depicts human strengths and weaknesses that reflect life in an impersonal, materialistic world in which deceit is necessary for survival. Disguises, jokes, and an appropriate meting out of justice also enable the dramatist to ridicule certain social types. But, above all gullibility is a fallibility, and certainly spectators could readily identify within themselves and others the talents and flaws enacted on stage; in portraying vividly and vibrantly these human attributes and social settings, the dramatist creates a comic world that denotes the realistic conditions and necessary contentions of daily existence.

—Donald Gilman

THE MAYOR OF ZALAMEA (El alcalde de Zalamea)
by Pedro Calderón de la Barca

First Publication: As *El garrote más bien dado* [*The Best Garrotting Ever Done*], in *El Major de los mejores libros que ha salido de comedias nuevas*, Alcalà, 1651.
First Production: Unknown; possibly at the Royal Palace, Madrid, 12 May 1636.

Editions
El alcalde de Zalamea, edited by J. Geddes, Boston, 1918.
La vida es sueño; El alcalde de Zalamea, edited by Augusto Cortina, Madrid, 1955.
El alcalde de Zalamea; La vida es sueño, edited by Jorge Campos, Madrid, 1959.
El alcalde de Zalamea [seventh edition], edited by Gabriel Espino, Zaragoza, 1962.
La vida es sueño; El alcalde de Zalamea, edited by Sturgis E. Leavitt, New York, 1964.
El alcalde de Zalamea, edited by Peter N. Dunn, Oxford, 1966.
El alcalde de Zalamea, edited by Everett W. Hesse, Buenos Aires, 1967.
El alcalde de Zalamea; La vida es sueño; El gran teatro del mundo, edited by Amando Isasi Angulo, Barcelona, 1968.
"El alcalde de Zalamea" en las versiones de Calderón de la Barca y Lope de Vega, edited by Juan Alcina Franch, Barcelona, 1970.
El alcalde de Zalamea, edited by José Mariá Díez Borque, Madrid, 1976.
La vida es sueño; El alcalde de Zalamea, edited by Alberto Porqueras-Mayo, Madrid, 1977.

Translations
The Mayor of Zalamea, translated by William E. Colford, Woodbury, New York, 1959.
The Mayor of Zalamea, in *Calderón: Four Plays*, translated by Edwin Honig, New York, 1961.
The Mayor of Zalamea, in *Eight Spanish Plays of the Golden Age*, edited and translated by Walter Starkie, New York, 1964.
The Mayor of Zalamea; or, The Best Garrotting Ever Done, translated and adapted by Adrian Mitchell.

Bibliography
Deborah J. Hill, "*El alcalde de Zalamea*: A Chronological Annotated Bibliography", in *Hispania*, vol.66 no.1, 1983.

Criticism
(For general works on the author, see *Playwrights* volume)

Books:
P. Halkhoree, *Calderón de la Barca: "El alcalde de Zalamea"*, London, 1972.

Articles:
S. Cornejo, "Observaciones a la critica de un libro: Calderón's *El alcalde de Zalamea*", in *Revue hispanique*, 60, 1924.
A. Sloman, "Scene Division in Calderón's *El alcalde de Zalamea*", in *Hispanic Review*, 19, 1951.
Walter Küchler, "Calderóns *comedia, El alcalde de Zalamea* als Drama der Persönlichkeit", in *Archiv*, vol.190 no.4, 1954.
C. Jones, "Honor in *El alcalde de Zalamea*", in *Modern Language Review*, 50, 1955.
Sturgis E. Leavitt, "Pedro Crespo and the Captain in Calderón's *El alcalde de Zalamea*", in *Hispania*, 38, 1955.

P.N. Dunn, "Honour and the Christian Background in Calderón", in *Bulletin of Hispanic Studies*, 37, 1960.

C.A. Soons, "Caracteres y imágenes en *El alcalde de Zalamea*", in *Romanische Forschungen*, 72, 1960.

Peter D. Nunn, "Patrimonio del alma", in *Bulletin of Hispanic Studies*, 41, 1964.

Fred Abrams, "Imaginería y aspectos temáticos del *Quijote* en *El alcalde de Zalamea*", in *Duquesne Hispanic Review*, 5, 1966.

E. Honig, "Calderón's Mayor: Honor Humanized", in *Tulane Drama Review*, vol.10 no.3, 1966.

W.O. Casanova, "Honor, patrimonio del alma y opinión social, patrimonio de casta en *El alcalde de Zalamea* de Calderón", in *Hispanófila*, 33, 1968.

A.A. Parker, "The Dramatic Structure of *El alcalde de Zalamea*", Instituto de España, 1969.

José M. Aguirre, "*El alcalde de Zalamea*: ¿Venganza o justicia?", in *Estudios filológicos*, 7, 1971.

Premraj Halkhoree, "The Four Days of *El alcalde de Zalamea*", in *Romanistisches Jahrbuch*, 22, 1971.

Angel Valbuena Briones, "Una interpretación de *El alcalde de Zalamea* (el estilo en *El garrote más bien dado*)", in *Arbor*, 385, 1978.

Lewis Smith, "Calderón's Mayor", in *Romanische Forschungen*, 92, 1980.

Angel M. García Gómez, "*El alcalde de Zalamea*: Alvaro de Ataide y el capitán de Malaca", in *Iberomania*, 14, 1981.

Robert Ter Horst, "The Poetics of Honor in Calderón's *El alcalde de Zalamea*", in *Modern Language Notes*, vol.96 no.2, 1981.

Henry W. Sullivan, "*El alcalde de Zalamea* de Calderón en el teatro europeo de la segunda mitad del siglo XVIII", in *Letras de Deusto*, vol.11 no.22, 1981.

Mercedes Touron de Ruiz, "*El alcalde de Zalamea* en Lope y Calderón", in *Cuadernos hispanoamericanos*, June 1981.

Dian Fox, "'Quien tiene al padre alcalde. . .': The Conflict of Images in Calderón's *El alcalde de Zalamea*", in *Revista canadiense de estudios hispánicos*, vol.6 no.2, 1982.

John E. Varey, "Space and Time in the Staging of Calderón's *El alcalde de Zalamea*", in *Staging in the Spanish Theatre*, edited by Margaret A. Rees, Leeds, 1984.

Domingo Ynduráin, "*El alcalde de Zalamea*: Historia, ideología, literatura", in *Edad de Oro*, 5, 1986.

E.T. Aylward, "El cruce de los temas de honor y justicia en *El alcalde de Zalamea* de Calderón: Un choque de motivos estéticos y prácticos", in *Bulletin of the Comediantes*, vol.39 no.2, 1987.

*   *   *

Calderón is thought to have composed this masterly drama of peasant-honour at a relatively youthful age. Unfortunately no manuscript has survived, nor any printed version earlier than the 1651 one. Nevertheless, a date of composition later than 1644 is improbable, and almost inconceivable, for reasons connected with the subject-matter.

The play deals with an incident which supposedly took place in 1580, when a contingent of Philip II's army, which was then on its way to invade Portugal, was billeted for a short time near the border, in the village of Zalamea. That invasion was, in reality, triumphantly accomplished: Portugal was brought under Habsburg rule, and the unification of the Iberian Peninsula was achieved. The union of Portugal with Spain ended, however, during the reign of Philip IV, when in 1640, Portugal rebelled. In the period 1640–42, Calderón might have written, and Spanish audiences might still have received with pleasure, rather than dismay, a work which reminded them of the annexation. But by 1644, Spain's best efforts to reconquer Portugal had failed, and that country's permanent independence looked almost assured. Calderón would not have risked depressing his public by reminding them, through *El alcalde de Zalamea*, of the deteriorated political powers of Spain since 1580.

Calderón's vitally realistic portrayal of military life—its hardships, order and disorder; the attitudes, worthy and unworthy, of both officers and ordinary soldiers; their ribaldry, rowdiness, and loose morals—has encouraged some critics to suppose that the dramatist completed the play soon after his military service in Catalonia, 1640–42. Other factors, however, seem to indicate that the work belongs to a previous decade. After all, the playwright showed concern to dramatize military life as early as 1625, and, moreover, the play's convincingly realistic qualities are not confined to military elements, but are generally dominant in its structure, style, action and, most importantly, in its characters. *El alcalde de Zalamea* also notably resembles the earlier play *La Cisma de Inglaterra* (*Schism in England*) not only in its realism, but in the uncomplicated characteristics of its staging, indicating a work initially composed for the *corrales* (courtyard-theatres).

El alcalde de Zalamea is thus unlikely to have been written before 1630, but almost certainly completed before the inauguration in 1640 of the sumptuously appointed palace-theatre, known as *El Coliseo*—with its extraordinary variety of sets, backcloths and ramps—since the play was clearly designed to be performed in the traditional fashion on an almost bare stage, with balcony and discovery-space, but with few stage-machines and little or no scenery. Distinctive costumes, like for instance the ridiculous garb worn by Don Mendo, a figure-of-fun nobleman (*hidalgo, de figura*), assisted audiences to identify the rank, roles, and even personalities of the different characters involved. But theatre-goers were expected to use their imagination to visualize changes in scene and surroundings. A play entitled *El alcalde de Zalamea*, probably, though not definitely, Calderón's work, was performed at court on 12 May 1636, further evidence which indicates that the dramatist composed his masterpiece in the early 1630's.

Audiences liked to believe in the reality of what they saw dramatized, and official censors of plays tended to regard historical plays with particular approval as being potentially instructive rather than simply entertaining. Golden-Age playwrights, therefore, were inclined, in their concluding lines, to describe as true histories many plays which we might more accurately regard as pseudo-historical. Though Calderón insistently alludes, as he completes his play, to "this true story" ("esta historia verdadera"), the work is rather to be comprehended as a creative mixture of real circumstances (the Spanish army's march upon Portugal in 1580) with supposed or plausible happenings (the rape of a peasant girl by an army captain), and it brings together historical personages (Philip II, and his general, Don Lope de Figueroa) with largely or entirely invented people (the protagonist, Pedro Crespo, his son Juan, and daughter Isabel).

The plot, in outline, is as follows: while Spanish troops are billeted at Zalamea an unprincipled, though aristocratic captain, Don Álvaro de Ataide, rapes the virtuous daughter of Pedro Crespo, a peasant but an honourable man, and an influential member of his village-community. Rather than kill his innocently dishonoured daughter, Pedro decides to restore his good name by punishing her offender. Appointed mayor of his village, Pedro places the captain under arrest. In so doing the mayor exceeds his legal powers, for, Don Álvaro, as an officer, is not subject to civil law and ought to have been tried by a military tribunal. Pedro has asked, indeed begged, the

The Mayor of Zalamea: National Theatre, London, 1981

captain to restore Isabel's honour by marrying her. But the captain, who considers honour to be a privilege to which only the nobility are entitled, refuses to marry the daughter of a peasant. Accordingly, the mayor sentences him to death, a punishment which the army would never have imposed for his crime, because "military tribunals winked at the offences of their men, and the highest tribunal of all, the Council of War, could be relied upon to take the part of its captains" (J.H. Elliott, *Imperial Spain*, 1964). Death usually takes place off stage in the Golden-Age theatre. The captain is executed behind the scenes. Then the inner stage, or "discovery-space", is opened to display his corpse to the spectators, enabling them to verify that he has not been beheaded, with the dignity befitting his rank, but has been garrotted like a common criminal. The timely arrival of Philip II prevents the army and the villagers from engaging in violent conflict. Although Pedro has exceeded his judicial authority and violated military law, the king regards the peasant's action as morally justified, for he designates him Mayor of Zalamea in perpetuity.

El alcalde de Zalamea shows general influences from a variety of earlier plays on the theme of honour among peasants, notably Lope de Vega's *Peribáñez*, *El mejor alcalde, el rey*, and *Fuenteovejuna*. More importantly, in common with *La vida es sueño* and other key dramas on which Calderón's international reputation depends, the play is derived from a now largely forgotten source-work of inferior quality. Calderón selectively exploits the themes, action, and characteriza-

tion of his identically-named source, converting this undistinguished play by an unknown author into an individually accomplished masterpiece. The work is particularly memorable as a drama of character, owing to the psychological realism with which Pedro Crespo is portrayed, as its admirably principled yet intensely human protagonist. Other people are convincingly created: Don Lope de Figueroa, for instance, a high-ranking and impatient military man of action, yet acutely capable of perceiving, below the peasant's undistinguished exterior, Pedro's quality of mind. As for Captain Álvaro, he is egoistic and dissolute: his sexual obsession with Isabel paradoxically, but realistically enough, is composed of admiration for her mental virtues as well as passion for her beauty. Then there are Pedro's children. Isabel, for instance, after her rape, despite her innocence, is emotionally charged with shame. Equally understandably, despite her mortally injured virtue, she instinctively protects her life. So she flees from her brother, since he is impetuously disposed to kill his sister to restore his honour. And when she comes upon her father, still bound to the tree where the captain and his men have left him, she waits before releasing him until she has convinced him of her blamelessness. Only then does she surrender herself to his possibly destructive sword, trustfully allowing him to decide upon her life or death.

It is Pedro Crespo, however, uniquely distinguished by his inward sense of moral honour, who defines the structure and psychologically dominates the action of the drama. As opposed to Don Álvaro, with his high birth but base conduct, and unlike Don Mendo, a cowardly nobleman with ridiculous pretensions (and even contrasted with his own son Juan, who believes that honour can be acquired by purchasing a title of nobility), Pedro Crespo is naturally endowed with nobility of spirit and recognizes what honour truthfully is: "patrimonio del alma, / y el alma sólo es de Dios" (honour is "the patrimony of the soul, and the soul belongs to God alone"). Golden-Age plays are peopled with self-declared "honourable" men, who kill, or attempt to kill, wives, sisters, or daughters to restore their damaged reputation or self-esteem. Pedro Crespo's individual code of honour is illustrated in his exemplary decision to spare the life of his daughter, and to accomplish, instead, the judicial destruction of the man who raped her.

In the traditional sense, *El alcalde de Zalamea* is not a tragedy: wrongdoing is punished, dishonour is avenged, and dramatic conflict is resolved, finally, into order. Yet the work contains elements of underlying difficulty, emits disturbed currents of unease, and conveys insistent impressions of tragic waste. Pedro Crespo, loving father of a once happily united family, is separated conclusively from both children. His unfortunate daughter, moreover, obedient to her society's rules, enters a convent, therefore permanently losing, with her virginity, her freedom of choice to marry. Calderón has endowed his protagonist, however, with an exceptional capacity to accept adversity with fortitude. His universal quality of character has doubtless contributed to the play's enduring popularity. The work was still being performed in Madrid in 1681—the year of its author's death—in 1687, 1688, 1692, and 1696, since when it has acquired and maintained a high reputation in world theatre. Perhaps in fame and importance it does not quite equal *La vida es sueño*, but, arguably, *El alcalde de Zalamea* surpasses that poetic masterpiece through its intrinsic, dramatic qualities.

—Ann L. MacKenzie

MEASURE FOR MEASURE
by William Shakespeare

First Publication: In First Folio, London, 1623.
First Production: London, 1603–04; earliest recorded production, Palace of Whitehall, London, 26 December 1604.

Editions

Measure for Measure, edited by Arthur Quiller-Couch and John Dover Wilson, Cambridge, 1922 (The New Shakespeare).
Measure for Measure, edited by Davis Harding, New Haven, Connecticut, 1954 (Yale Shakespeare).
Measure for Measure, edited by S. Nagarajan, New York, 1964; revised edition, 1985 (Signet Classic Shakespeare).
Measure for Measure, edited by R.C. Bald, Baltimore, Maryland, 1965; revised edition, 1970 (Pelican Shakespeare).
Measure for Measure, edited by J.W. Lever, London, 1965 (Arden Shakespeare).
Measure for Measure, edited by J.M. Nosworthy, Harmondsworth, 1969 (New Penguin Shakespeare).
Measure for Measure, edited by J.G. Saunders, London, 1971.

A New Variorum Edition of Shakespeare: "Measure for Measure", edited by Mark Eccles, New York, 1980.

Criticism
(For general works on the author, see *Playwrights* volume)

Books:
Mary Lascalles, *Measure for Measure*, London, 1953.
William B. Bache, *"Measure for Measure" as Dialectical Art*, West Lafayette, Indiana, 1969.
C.K. Stead (ed.), *"Measure for Measure": A Casebook*, London, 1972.
Nigel Alexander, *Measure for Measure*, London, 1975.
Rosalind Miles, *The Problem of "Measure for Measure": A Historical Investigation*, New York, 1976.
Darryl Gless, *"Measure for Measure": The Law and the Convent*, Princeton, New Jersey, 1979.
William J. Martz, *The Place of "Measure for Measure" in Shakespeare's Universe of Comedy*, Lawrence, Kansas, 1982.
Philip Edwards, *Man Proud Man: The Debate on Authority in "Measure for Measure": A Lecture Given by Philip Edwards for the Stratford Shakespeare Festival, 1985*, Stratford, Ontario, 1985.
Lucia Folena, *The Syntax of the Gaze and the Metaphysics of Power in "Measure for Measure"*, Padua, 1985.
Laurie Lanzen Harris and Mark W. Scott (eds.), *"Measure for Measure"*, in *Shakespearian Criticism, 2*, Detroit, Illinois, 1985 [anthology of criticism].
Graham Nicholls, *Measure for Measure*, London, 1986 (Text and Performance Series).
Harriet Hawkins, *Measure for Measure*, Brighton, 1987 (Harvester New Critical Introductions to Shakespeare).

Articles:
For information on the many articles about *Measure for Measure*, see the bibliographies listed in the *Playwrights* volume, and the annual Shakespeare Bibliography in *Shakespeare Quarterly*, published by the Folger Shakespeare Library, Washington D.C. (1950–).

*   *   *

Vincentio, Duke of Vienna, hands over rule to Angelo, counting on him for strict enforcement of the law, and partly to test his austere character. The Duke adopts disguise to observe events. Claudio has made Juliet, his wife-to-be, pregnant: Angelo sentences him to death for fornication. Isabella, Claudio's sister, a novice nun, is brought to plead on his behalf. Her virtuous demeanour excites Angelo's lust, and he offers to release Claudio in return for sex. Isabella tells her brother, refusing to save him. The Duke intervenes, and through his plotting, Mariana, once betrothed to Angelo, acts as substitute bed-partner. Angelo does not thereafter pardon Claudio. The Duke now finds a substitute severed head, but tells Isabella her brother has been executed. The Duke's return to Vienna is announced. In the complex denouement, the Duke's disguise is finally removed by Lucio, a dissolute gentleman who has slandered him. Angelo surrenders to judgement: the Duke manoeuvres Isabella into pleading, with Mariana, for Angelo's life. Finally, the Duke reveals that Claudio is still alive, and in sequence marries Angelo to the formerly jilted Mariana, punishes the slanderer Lucio by obliging him to marry a woman he has acknowledged fathering a child upon, and rewards himself by proposing to Isabella. Sub-actions involve a lively group of dissolutes, and the lowest instrument of the state, Abhorson, the hangman.

Measure for Measure: Stratford-Upon-Avon, 1983 (Royal Shakespeare Company)

Shakespeare's play is a variant on the unjust judge narrative, in which a judge sexually coerces a maiden through his power to pass sentence on her brother. In most analogues the girl agrees to the Judge's coercion. Shakespeare precipitates crisis by having Isabella refuse: "Then, Isabel, live chaste, and brother, die:/More than our brother is our chastity". These lines, pointed as they were by Shakespeare with rhyme to get Isabella's decision totally clear to his audience, have never really been forgiven the character. Explanations based on Isabella's vocation cannot make the problematic quality of her decision disappear.

The play settles its action upon the concepts of remedy and redemption. The words "remedy", "redeem", and "redemption" appear more often than in any other play. Redemption is the absolute act:" Why, all the souls that were, were forfeit once,/And He that might the vantage best have took/Found out the remedy". But it can only be imitated on earth amidst the difficult moral density of society by approximations in which compromise appears. Isabella asserts "foul redemption" in what Angelo would have her do, "nothing kin" to lawful mercy. Yet she herself must refuse mercy to her brother: "Is there no remedy? None, but such a remedy as, to save a head,/To cleave a heart in twain". Isabella cannot redeem her brother: "O, were it but my life,/I'd throw it down. . .As frankly as a pin"; her generosity is too large for

the situation, irrelevant. Instead, a remedy must be concocted for Angelo's fall and her intransigence: the device of a substitute bed-partner.

The Duke's intervention in the traumatic interview between Isabella and Claudio ("to the love I have in doing good; a remedy presents itself") can been seen as the imposition on the drama of a contrived and unpersuasive compromise. To an extent the Duke has controlled the action from the start. The opening dialogue suggests how far the Duke counts on Angelo proving a severe magistrate. Our resistance to his controlling power is gratified when the pardon he complacently announces turns out to be a confirmation of sentence from Angelo, and by the ungovernable Lucio. By the fifth act, every character except Lucio has been manipulated by the Duke into words, actions, and the timing of both at his direction alone. His tendency to experiment with people, which breaks Angelo, finally claims Isabella, when she kneels to beg forgiveness for the man she believes responsible for her brother's death, on the grounds that "a due sincerity" governed Angelo's deeds "Till he did look on me". Unlike Angelo, the Duke can make Isabella compromise; he wins her from her cloister as his partner.

This play contains three of Shakespeare's finest scenes of confrontational dialogue: Isabella and Angelo's two meetings, and Isabella giving her decision to the anguished Claudio. Act

V is brilliantly contrived: attention switches from character to character, each actor gets a turn at centrality, a chance to surprise and be surprised. The poetry in which Shakespeare's drama is written (until supplanted by the prose of the scenes contrived by his proxy the Duke) is of disturbing power. As testimony to this, Dr Johnson, in old age, compounded his neurotic habit of making noises with a continued mumbling and eventually friends realised that he was locked into a sub-vocalisation of Claudio's speech to Isabella on the horror of death: "Ay, but to die, and go we know not where;/To lie in cold obstruction, and to rot. . . .".

—Roy Booth

THE MEASURES TAKEN (Die Massnahme)
by Bertolt Brecht; music by Hans Eisler

First Publication: In *Versuche, 4*, Berlin, 1931; revised version, in *Gesammelte Werke, 2*, London, 1938 (Malik-Verlag edition); further revised version, in *Stücke, 4*, Frankfurt, 1958.
First Production: Grosses Schauspielhaus, Berlin, 10 December 1930.

Translations

The Measures Taken, translated by Eric Bentley, in *Colorado Review*, vol. no.1, 1956–57; reprinted in *The Modern Theatre, 6*, edited by Eric Bentley, Garden City, New York, 1960.
The Measures Taken, translated by Stefan Brecht, in *"The Measures Taken" and Other Lehrstücke*, London, 1977.

Criticism
(For general works on the author, see *Playwrights* volume)

Books:
Werner Mittenzwei, *Bertolt Brecht: von der "Massnahme" zu "Leben des Galilei"*, Berlin, 1962.
Reiner Steinweg, *Das Lehrstück: Brechts Theorie einer politischaesthätischen Erziehung*, Stuttgart, 1972.
Reiner Steinweg, *Bertolt Brecht—"Die Massnahme": Kritische Ausgabe mit einer Spielanleitung von Reiner Steinweg*, Frankfurt, 1972; second edition, 1976.
Reiner Steinweg, *Brechts Modell der Lehrstücke: Zeugnisse, Diskussion, Erfahrungen*, Frankfurt, 1976.
Edgar Neis, *Erläuterungen zu Bertolt Brechts Lehrstücken: "Der Jasager und der Neinsager"; "Die Massnahme"; "Die Ausnahme und die Regel"; "Die Rundköpfe und die Spitzköpfe"; "Das Badener Lehrstück vom Einverständnis"*, Hollfeld, 1976.

Articles:
Werner Mittenzwei, "Grösse und Grenze des Lehrstücks: Bertolt Brechts Übergang auf die Seite der Arbeitsklasse", in *Neue deutsche Literatur*, 1960.
Herbert Schuster, "Vom Text zu Spiel: *Die Massnahme*", in *Die pädagogische Provinz*, 15, 1961.
A. Doe, "Brecht's *Lehrstücke*: Propaganda Failures", in *Educational Theatre Journal*, vol.14 no.4, 1962.

Joachim Kaiser, "Brechts *Massnahme* und die Linke Angst: Warum ein *Lehrstuck* so viel Verlegenheit und Verlogenheit provizierte", in *Neue Rundschau*, 84, 1973.
Gordon E. Nelson, "The Birth of Tragedy out of Pedagogy: Brecht's "Learning Play" *Die Massnahme*", in *German Quarterly*, 46, 1973.
Franz X. Kroetz, "Über *Die Massnahme* von Bertolt Brecht", in *Kürb*, 4, 1975.
Klaus Lazarowicz, "Die rote Messe: Liturgische Elemente in Brechts *Massnahme*", in *Literaturwissenschaftliches Jahrbuch im Auftrage der Görres-Gesellschaft*, 16, 1975.
Ina Schmidt-Ranson, "Brechts *Die Massnahme*: Ein Modell für das Theater ohne Publikum", in *Aspects de la civilisation germanique*, Saint-Etienne, 1975.
Roger Howard, "A Measure of *The Measures Taken*: Zenchiku, Brecht and Idealist Dialectics", in *Praxis*, 3, 1976.
Reinhold Grimm, "Bertolt Brecht: *Die Massnahme*: Zwischen Tragik und Ideologie", in *Das deutsche Drama vom Expressionismus bis zur Gegenwart: Interpretationen*, Bamberg, 1977.
William H. Rey, "Brechts *Massnahme*: Ein Stein des Anstosses", in *Sprachkunst*, 8, 1977.
Peter Horn, "Die Wahrheit ist konkret: Bertolt Brechts *Massnahme* und die Frage der Parteidisziplin", in *Brecht Jahrbuch*, 1978.
Hans D. Sander, "*Die Massnahme*, recht-philosophisch betrachtet: Carl Schmitt—Karl Korsch—Bertolt Brecht", in *Deutsche Studien*, 17, 1979.
Sheila Delany, "The Politics of the Signified in Bertolt Brecht's *The Measures Taken*", in *Clio*, 16, 1986.
Arlene A. Teraoka, "*Der Auftrag* and *Die Massnahme*: Models of Revolution in Heiner Müller and Bertolt Brecht", in *German Quarterly*, 59, 1986.

*   *   *

The Measures Taken, (*Die Massnahme*) also known as *The Decision*, is a short play in eight scenes. Four Communist agitators from Moscow (three men and one woman) explain to a controlling chorus why, during a mission to China to promote "the ABC of Communism" they had had to kill their guide, known in the play as the Young Comrade. In presenting their case the Agitators take it in turns (and in successive scenes) to act out the role of the dead man. They show how he had been identified by the Chinese as a infiltrator because he had given way to his personal feelings on a number of occasions. Once he had shown pity for coolies pulling rice-barges. Another time he had attacked a policeman at a factory strike. Then he had shown his contempt for a merchant by refusing to eat with him. Finally he had lost patience with the lack of progress of the mission and revealed his identity by removing his mask. (All the Agitators wore masks literally as a disguise and symbolically to erase their individuality.) To safeguard the work of the mission, and with the enemy closing in, argue the Agitators, they were forced to shoot the Young Comrade and dispose of the body in a lime-pit. In the final scene the Chorus agrees with the decision.

The Measures Taken is one of Brecht's nine *Lehrstücke* or "learning pieces", which he published under the collective title, *Versuche* (*Experiments*). They were intended as "learning experiments" for the participants rather than for the spectators and to be performed largely by schoolchildren and other non-professional performers. As Brecht put it, those involved would be "*lernend zu lehren*" ("learning in order to teach"). Hanns Eisler, the composer, collaborated in the piece, which is more a secular cantata than a conventional play. Eisler's music shows influences of various kinds: Schoenberg, Lutheran chorales, folksongs, and contemporary jazz.

The Measures Taken was originally written for the Berlin Festival of Neue Musik in 1930 but was rejected by the festival organisers because of its "artistic mediocrity of text". Six months later Brecht and Eisler organised a first performance at the Grosses Schauspielhaus with four solo actors (Helene Weigel, Ernst Busch, Granach, and Topitz) supported by the Greater Berlin Workers' Choir of 400 singers. It was not well received. At a public discussion one week later, Party members objected to the death of the Young Comrade, arguing that the most that should have happened to him was expulsion from the Party. In response Brecht modified the play to include the Young Comrade's agreement to his execution. Nevertheless, criticisms still arose. Those on the Left felt that the Party's aims were misrepresented, and the Right thought Brecht was advocating complete submission to the inhuman dictates of the Communist Party.

The Measures Taken's second performance was given in 1933 in Vienna where Eisler was in exile, but subsequent performances were banned by the collaborators. Brecht had concluded that only those who performed the role of the Young Comrade could learn anything from the play and even then only if they subsequently also experienced singing in the Control-Chorus. In 1956, he wrote in a letter that the play "was not written for an audience but exclusively for the instructions of the performers. In my experience, public performances of it inspire nothing but moral qualms, usually of the cheapest sort". The ban remained in place until 1987 when the play was performed at the Almeida Theatre in London.

At the time of writing *The Measures Taken* Brecht was much influenced by Japanese Noh Theatre. This is evident in such elements in the play as the use of masks, the importance of music and song, the direct address of the audience, the naïve representation of both narrative and characters, and even in the oriental setting. The play's power comes from the device of the four-fold playing of the victim by the Agitators: they display his character, demonstrate his behaviour, repeat his actions, and in so doing they create a dialectical relationship between, on one side, a rational debate, and, on the other, their sympathetic portrayal of their victim. A similar dialectic operates between the dialogue (rational discourse) and the songs (emotional commitment). The language of the whole piece is spare and direct and the message is clear: man must learn to deal with causes and not symptoms and avoid the temptation of seeking a short-term alleviation of individual grievances instead of long-term social change.

The essence of *The Measures Taken* is expressed in the Chorus's song: "Change the World: It Needs It", from which one line—"embrace the butcher"—was frequently selected as a stick for beating Brecht. Perhaps it was naïve of him to believe that either "side" could admit publicly that the ends can justify the means. And maybe this was why he felt only the performers could learn from the play. In terms of what we now know as Brechtian theatre, many of the elements that the writer was subsequently to re-employ and develop in his later plays are fully apparent in *The Measures Taken*: a socio-political purpose, episodic narrative, the "gestic" representation of character, the distancing effects of song, and the demonstration that powerful theatre is not dependent on naturalistic techniques.

—Margaret Eddershaw

MEDEA
by Euripides

First Production: Athens, 431 B.C.

Editions
Medea, edited by A.W. Verrall, London, 1881.
Medea, edited by Clinton E.S. Headlam, Cambridge, 1897.
Medea [with translation], in *Euripides, 4*, edited by Arthur S. Way, London, 1912.
Medea, edited by Denys L. Page, Oxford, 1938.
Medea, edited by Alan Elliott, London, 1969.

Translations
Medea, translated by Gilbert Murray, London, 1910.
Medea, in *Two Greek Plays*, translated by John Jay Chapman, Boston, 1928.
Medea, translated by R.C. Trevelyan, Cambridge, 1939.
Medea, translated by Rex Warner, London, 1944; reprinted in *Euripides, 1*, Chicago, 1955 (Complete Greek Tragedies Series).
Medea, translated by D.W. Lucas, New York and London, 1950.
Medea, in *Ten Plays by Euripides*, translated by Moses Hadas and John McLean, Toronto and London, 1960.
Medea, in *"Medea" and Other Plays*, translated by Philip Vellacott, Harmondsworth, 1963.
Medea, in *Three Greek Plays for the Theatre*, translated by Peter D. Arnott, Bloomington, Indiana, 1964.
Medea, translated by Michael Townsend, San Francisco, 1966.
Medea, translated by Jeremy Brooks, in *Euripides: Plays 1*, edited by J. Michael Walton, London, 1988.

Criticism
(For general works on the author, see *Playwrights* volume)

Articles:
L.M. Mead, "A Study in the *Medea*", in *Greece and Rome*, 12, 1943.
E.A. Thompson, "Neophron and Euripides' *Medea*", in *Classical Quarterly*, 38, 1944.
E.M. Blaiklock, "The Nautical Imagery of Euripides' *Medea*", in *Classical Philology*, 50, 1955.
R.B. Palmer, "An Apology for Jason: A Study of Euripides' *Medea*", in *Classical Journal*, 53, 1957.
G. Tarditi, "Euripide e il dramma di *Medea*", in *Revista di filologia e di instruzione classica*, 25, 1957.
T.V. Buttrey, "Accident and Design in Euripides' *Medea*", in *American Journal of Philology*, 79, 1958.
R.A. Colby, "The Sorcery of Medea", in *University of Kansas City Review*, 25, 1959.
A. Maddalena, "La *Medea* d'Euripide", in *Revista di filologia e di instruzione classica*, 91, 1963.
H. Masurillo, "Euripides' *Medea*: A Reconsideration", in *American Journal of Philology*, 87, 1966.
E. Schlesinger, "Zu Euripides' *Medea*", in *Hermes*, 94, 1966.
K.J. Reckford, "Medea's First Exit", in *Transactions and Proceedings of the American Philological Association* [*TAPA*], 99, 1968.
J.R. Dunkle, "The Aegeus Episode and the Theme of Euripides' *Medea*", in *Transactions and Proceedings of the American Philological Association* [*TAPA*], 100, 1969.
L. Golden, "Children in the *Medea*", in *Classical Bulletin*, 48, 1971.
M.D. Reeve, "Euripides, *Medea* 1021–1080", in *Classical Quarterly* (new series), 22, 1972.

H. Zuger, "The Aegeus Episode and the Poetic Structure of Euripides' *Medea*", in *Classical Bulletin*, 49, 1972.

A.P. Burnett, "*Medea* and the Tragedy of Revenge", in *Classical Philology*, 68, 1973.

W.P. MacDonald, "The Blackness of *Medea*", in *College Language Association Journal*, 19, 1975.

C. Blitxen, "The Senecan and Euripidean *Medea*: A Comparison", in *Classical Bulletin*, 52, 1976.

E.B. Bongie, "Heroic Elements in the *Medea* of Euripides", in *Transactions and Proceedings of the American Phiological Association* [*TAPA*], 107, 1977.

P.E. Easterling, "The Infanticide in Euripides' *Medea*", in *Yale Classical Studies*, 25, 1977.

B.M.W. Knox, "The *Medea* of Euripides", in *Yale Classical Studies*, 25, 1977.

P. Pucci, "Euripides: The Monument and the Sacrifice", in *Arethusa*, 10, 1977.

Rick M. Newton, "Ino in Euripides' *Medea*", in *American Journal of Philology*, 106, 1985.

Bernard Gredley, "The Place and Time of Victory: Euripides' *Medea*", in *Bulletin of the Institute of Classical Studies* (London), 34, 1987.

George Gellie, "The Character of Medea", in *Bulletin of the Institute of Classical Studies* (London), 35, 1988.

*   *   *

Medea was first performed in 431 B.C., just before the outbreak of the Peloponnesian War between Athens and Sparta. Set in Corinth the plot concentrates on the stormy relationship between Medea from Colchis beyond the Black Sea, now Georgia, and Jason, the dispossessed heir to the throne of Iolcos in Thessaly. The two had met while Jason and the crew of the Argo were attempting to carry off the Golden Fleece and bring it back to his uncle Pelias. With Medea's help the mission was successfully accomplished but instead of winning back the throne, as Jason had hoped, the two were forced into exile.

When the play opens, an old Nurse informs the audience of Jason's betrayal of Medea: he is to abandon Medea to marry the King of Corinth's daughter. Medea's entrance is delayed by the introduction of a Tutor with Medea's two children (by Jason) whom she will eventually murder before escaping in a chariot provided by the sun. This is the first of three entrances for the children, (four if you count Medea's appearance with their bodies), so that the audience can never be allowed to forget what the crime is that will stand at the centre of the play. This is necessary because of the amount of sympathy accorded to Medea by the treatment she receives from Jason and from Creon, the King. The dramatic action focuses on two main areas. The first involves her decision to kill the children. Though the original audience may have been aware in advance of Medea's reputation as a witch and as a murderess, her revenge is directed initially at Jason's new wife, a character so insignificant that she does not merit a name. The children are an instrument in the plot. She has them deliver a poisoned robe to the Princess which kills her and her father Creon. The children are therefore implicated, but in all innocence. The Chorus meanwhile, local women of Corinth, has largely acquiesced in this, shocked by the appalling callousness of Jason and Creon. Soon after, the Chorus finds itself drawn into the murder of the children at a time when it would still be possible for it to prevent it. The women fail to take action and so become accomplices.

It may seem to be in the nature of a Greek chorus to do little more than express moral indignation from time to time and reflect the position of an audience, but remain powerless to act. This is seldom the case, however, in Euripides. They offer

Medea: Sarah Bernhardt in the title role

advice in other plays; they take sides. They can deceive characters in order to promote a plot and in so doing they establish a moral viewpoint. Here in *Medea*, they serve as the audience's conscience by subscribing to the preparations for the most unnatural of all crimes, a mother's murder of her children.

This aspect is closely linked to the second dramatic focus, one which raises a host of other issues and promotes *Medea* from the level of domestic drama to that of major parable. Medea is an outsider, a foreigner who has given up home and family for Jason. She is also a woman in a man's world, who can be discarded as soon as a more convenient marriage comes along. 19th-century critics tended to treat Euripides as a misogynist for the murderous female figures he created: Hecuba, Phaedra, Medea. Given the smugness, selfishness, and sheer blindness of Jason, modern opinion would be hard-pressed not to see some justification in Medea's fury at the way she has been scorned. But Euripides' sympathies, like Brecht's, are neither easy nor obvious. If he offers the case for the defence of a matricide, he also recognises a savagery in Medea that is wholly destructive and wholly alien to the other characters. Jason may have given her a hard time but this Medea is still the sorceress who delayed the pursuit from Colchis by chopping up her brother and distributing the pieces so that their father would have to waste more time recovering the remains. Jason should hardly be surprised at what happens when he crosses her.

For an Athenian audience of 431 B.C. the play was political and social dynamite because of what it was saying about Athenian treatment of women and of their attitude to subject races. Small wonder that it was placed third of the three tragedies competing in the festival; indeed, in is surprising that it ever got on at all. The subsequent popularity of the story, in versions from that of Seneca in the 1st century A.D. to those of Anouilh and Dario Fo and Franca Rame in the 20th century, shows it has been ever-topical. The celebrated production by the Soviet director Nikolai Oklopkhov in 1962 demonstrated the breadth of the myth by drawing attention to the coincidence of Medea and Stalin both being Georgians, the one the murderer of her children, the other the scourge of the Russian people.

Of the many Greek tragedies which boast a modern ring, *Medea* has one of the strongest holds over contemporary thought. Set far from the background of war which dominates so much of the work of Aeschylus, Sophocles, and Euripides, it centres on human relationships where immorality lacks the excuse of a strategic imperative. Euripides may not exonerate or apologise for the killing of children by their mother. He does offer an account of the circumstances in which such things happen.

—J. Michael Walton

THE MEMORANDUM
by Václav Havel

First Publication: In *Dilia*, Prague, 1965 (cyclostyled edition); in *Protokoly*, Prague, 1966.
First Production: Divadlo Na zábradlí [Theatre on the Balustrade], Prague, 1965.

Translations
The Memorandum, translated by Vera Blackwell, in *Dilia*, Prague, 1965 (cyclostyled edition); then London, 1967.

Criticism
(For general works on the author, see *Playwrights* volume)

Articles:
Peter Dart, "Václav Havel's *The Memorandum*: A Study in the Terror of the Czechoslovak Bureaucratic World", in *Cimarron Review*, 6, 1968.
Paul Trensky, "Václav Havel and the Language of the Absurd", in *The Slavic and East European Journal*, 13, 1969.
James W. Flannery, "Taking Theatre to the Bureaucrats: An Experimental Production of *The Memorandum* by Václav Havel", in *Educational Theatre Journal*, 29, 1977.

*   *   *

The action of *The Memorandum* takes place in the offices of a firm whose business we never discover. The play opens as Gross, the Managing Director, is manipulated by his deputy, Balas, into committing a small infringement of the regulations. Gross is more preoccupied with an incomprehensible memo he has received; it is written in "Ptydepe", a new, bureaucratic language. He tries to insist that Balas countermand the order for the introduction of "Ptydepe", only to discover that the

"Ptydepe" personnel are so well established that, for example, the accounts department has been displaced by them into an unlit and unventilated cellar. Gross's efforts to get his memo translated take him on four perambulations from his office to the "Ptydepe" classroom and on to the translation department. By the half-way point, he has made a confession of guilt, and resigned from the post of managing director in favour of Balas.

The second half of the play shows the failure of "Ptydepe," which is far too complicated for any of the employees to learn, and the restitution of Gross in the post of managing director, with Balas demoted to Deputy. It is not, however, a simple rise and fall; Balas has learnt that power does not lie with the man on the throne, but with the man behind the throne. By his confessions Gross has hopelessly compromised himself, even when innocent, and Balas is now in a position to introduce a new language, "Chorukor".

In the twelve, short scenes, the action moves between Gross's office, the "Ptydepe" classroom, and the translation department. Each room differs from the others in the placement of the furniture, but all exude the same atmosphere. The construction of the play, whose precisely divided scenes include constant and mechanical repetitions of routine actions, reinforces the theme of the "inflexible structure". (In the first production Jan Grossman underlined the repetitiveness by setting on stage a bucket into which a drop of water fell at regular intervals throughout the performance.) The first scene of each triplet satirises the banality of office life: the secretary combs her hair and trots out for bread and rolls; a subordinate insists that orders must be properly authenticated. In the classroom, "Ptydepe", a language whose supposed purpose is to clarify communication by using a different expression for every shade of meaning, is taught by a pedantic academic. By contrast, the hedonistic staff of the translation department constantly indulge themselves in parties and idle conversation; Gross is overlooked as they hurry to the canteen, make merry in the next office, or disappear with an urgent need to relieve themselves. There are constant references to glasses of beer, goose for lunch, gingerbread, and the need for a snack-bar. Gross pleads with the staff for a cigarette, as he watches them draw on rich cigars. The atmosphere of these scenes is a reminder that Alfred Jarry's *Ubu Roi* had, since the previous year, been part of Jan Grossman's repertoire at the Theatre on the Balustrade. The relationship is even clearer when we recognise that we are in the presence of one of Alfred Jarry's "pataphysical" machines. Office life continues independently of the outside world and its procedures are self-perpetuating. The efficiency of this machine has no relevance to human activity. Similarly, the language of "Ptydepe", manufactured to simplify office procedure, is useless because it is too complicated to learn. In Jan Grossman's production, the frenzied activity of the office routine was emphasised by the lowering of a shadow curtain between scenes, against which the activity of the stage hands was silhouetted in red lighting.

The satirising of an inflexible structure which exists only for its own benefit was dangerously topical in the Communist society in which this play was first produced. Some of the passages are direct allusions to the political brainwashing which took place in the 1950's and even in the 1960's; after the first performance, Sergej Machonin wrote in *Literární noviny* that these passages sent a shiver down his back, as they reminded him of the way that people had conformed both as a whole and in their personal lives, and of the still-fresh history of the loss of feeling, reason, and character. The language of the characters was recognisably that of public rhetoric. The one character with human attributes—Marie, secretary in the translation department—is sacrificed for the expediency of

The Memorandum: Theatre on the Balustrade, Prague, 1965 (first production)

others: "No one ever spoke to me so beautifully before," she whispers at the end, after Gross has justified his reasons for endorsing her dismissal. Gross himself, whom some Western critics misunderstood to be a pleasant character, was well understood by Czech audiences. His range of language is more complex than the other characters, encompassing contemporary liberalism, pre-war "humanism", and the clichés of socialism. But his "humanism" is only superficial. His values are as banal as theirs and he fights only for his own position. He passes from a naive ignorance of the ways of the world through bewilderment and humiliation to a self-justifying acceptance of what he knows to be an unjust society, and, apparently in the role of the victim, he is an even more dangerous conformist than the others. In spite of regrets and self-criticism, he can see no alternative beyond blind submission to the system. With Gross in charge, the process of de-personalisation can continue unchallenged; as indeed it did in the real Czechoslovakia, when, four years later in 1969, all of Václav Havel's plays were banned by the authorities.

—Barbara Day

MENAECHMI. See **THE BROTHERS MENAECHMUS.**

THE MERCHANT GENTLEMAN. See **THE WOULD-BE GENTLEMAN.**

THE MERCHANT OF VENICE
by William Shakespeare

First Publication: London, 1600.
First Production: London, c. 1596–97; earliest recorded production, at Court, 10 February 1605.

Editions
The Merchant of Venice, edited by H.H. Furness, Philadelphia, 1888 (New Variorum Shakespeare).
The Merchant of Venice, edited by Arthur Quiller-Couch and John Dover Wilson, Cambridge, 1926 (The New Shakespeare).
The Merchant of Venice, edited by John Russell Brown, London, 1955 (Arden Shakespeare).
The Merchant of Venice, edited by Brents Stirling, Baltimore, Maryland, 1959; revised edition, 1970 (Pelican Shakespeare).
The Merchant of Venice, edited by Kenneth Myrick, New York, 1965 (Signet Classic Shakespeare).
The Merchant of Venice, edited by W. Moelwyn Merchant, Harmondsworth, 1967 (New Penguin Shakespeare).
The Merchant of Venice, edited by Molly M. Mahood, Cambridge, 1987 (New Cambridge Shakespeare).

Bibliographies
Samuel Tannenbaum, *"The Merchant of Venice": A Concise Bibliography*, New York, 1941.

Thomas Wheeler (ed.), *"The Merchant of Venice": An Annotated Bibliography*, New York, 1985 (Garland Shakespeare Bibliographies).

Criticism
(For general works on the author, see *Playwrights* volume)

Books:
A.D. Moody, *Shakespeare: "The Merchant of Venice"*, London, 1964.
Daniel Barnes, *The Provocative Merchant of Venice*, Silver Spring, Maryland, 1975.
Lawrence Danson, *The Harmonies of "The Merchant of Venice"*, New Haven, Connecticut, 1978.
Jeanne Heifetz, *Love Calls us to the Things of this World: The Return to Belmont in "The Merchant of Venice"*, Cambridge, Massachusetts, 1981.
Bill Overton, *"The Merchant of Venice"*, London, 1987 (Text and Performance Series).
Mark W. Scott (ed.), *"The Merchant of Venice"*, in *Shakespearian Criticism, 4*, Detroit, Illinois, 1987 [anthology of criticism].
Edward Andrew, *Shylock's Rights: A Grammar of Lockian Claims*, Toronto and Buffalo, 1988.

Articles:
For information on the many articles about *The Merchant of Venice*, see the bibliographies listed above, the bibliographies listed in the *Playwrights* volume, and the annual Shakespeare Bibliography in *Shakespeare Quarterly*, published by the Folger Shakespeare Library, Washington, D.C. (1950–).

*   *   *

The Merchant of Venice has proved to be one of the most popular of Shakespeare's comedies, delighting audiences while confounding critics. The world of the play is far from Arden or Illyria or some of the more idealised settings of Shakespearean comedy. It is a world of commerce, a vision of a youthful capitalist society in which all values are cheerfully, unselfconsciously, related to money. Within the first few lines of the opening scene, Salarino accounts for Antonio's sadness by reference to his concern about his ships and the merchandise which they carry. Antonio asserts that it is not his merchandise which makes him sad. Then, says Salanio, "you are in love". The priority given to business over love, only the second possible reason for sadness, is thematically revealing, integral to the structure of the play, leading directly to the love plot which begins to emerge later in the scene when Bassanio relates his misfortune, having squandered his own estate to his love for a lady in Belmont, "richly left" and, he adds as something of an afterthought, "she is fair, and—fairer than that word—/Of wondrous virtues. . .". Antonio offers his support and tells Bassanio to see how much money he can raise using Antonio's own credit in order to assist him to win her hand. And so we move to Belmont, to the lady of "good fortunes", Portia, who discusses with Nerissa, her waiting woman, the question of her marriage and the "lottery" which her late father has devised as a means of choosing her husband. Back in Venice, Bassanio attempts to persuade Shylock, the Jewish usurer, to lend him money. When Antonio arrives, Shylock announces his hatred for him in an aside which makes clear that any prejudice on his part is also entirely subordinate to matters of business: "I hate him for he is a Christian;/But more, for that in low simplicity/He lends out money gratis, and brings down/The rate of usance here with us in Venice".

The Merchant of Venice: Stratford-Upon-Avon, 1956 (Royal Shakespeare Company)

Shylock makes Antonio an apparently generous offer, lending him the three thousand ducats without interest, provided that Antonio signs a bond allowing Shylock one pound of his flesh should he be unable to repay him.

From here onwards, the action increases in complexity. Frequent returns to Belmont and to the lottery and the three caskets, with attempts at winning Portia's hand (made by the Prince of Morocco, the Prince of Arragon and finally and successfully, Bassanio), are counterpointed by the development of the action centered on Shylock. A subplot has been introduced (via the antics of Lancelot Gobbo), in which Jessica, Shylock's daughter, having fallen in love with a Christian, Lorenzo, flees from Shylock's house, naturally first ensuring that a supply of Shylock's jewels are in her possession—an action apparently condoned by the Christians. This only serves to fuel Shylock's bitterness, making him intent on revenge, so that he is all too eager for his pound of flesh once it becomes clear that Antonio is unable to repay his debt.

The two plots develop in opposition to each other. As Bassanio moves ever closer to winning the lottery, so Antonio's fortunes begin to plunge as the ships carrying his merchandise founder. Portia announces Bassanio's success in winning her hand in language which is suitably mercantile, wishing that for his sake she could be "trebled twenty times myself,/A thousand times more fair, ten thousand times/More rich, that only to stand high in your account/I might in virtues, beauties, livings, friends,/Exceed account".

The climax of the play is the trial scene which, in performance, can be spine chilling. In spite of the fairy tale simplicity of the court case, the audience happily accept the convention—accept that Antonio is actually about to lose a pound of flesh and that the Christians are powerless and unable to help him. Perhaps this is the real critical point of the play. Antonio's friends appear to be content to let Antonio accept his fate. It takes a woman disguised as a learned judge, Portia, no less, to put forward an argument which even the more simple-minded of the men should already have grasped. Earlier, she had told Shylock that "the quality of mercy is not strained", yet once he is defeated little mercy is shown, as he is stripped of his wealth and forced to become a Christian.

The final scenes are then given over to the resolution of the love plot and the reconciliation of the lovers. It is as if the comic structure, having collapsed during the trial scene, is being desperately re-asserted, yet it is a re-assertion which succeeds, a triumph of comic technique over matter, the play ending in confident high spirits.

Why is this play so successful in the theatre and so popular? The Christian characters in the play all appear to be prejudiced and self-seeking, including even the ever generous, noble, masochistic Antonio. Portia's main virtues are her resourcefulness and intelligence and she certainly wins sympathy, but it is Shylock who is worth all the rest, if only for his vitality, his passion, his unashamed individuality and freedom from the all-pervasive hypocrisy of the Christians—a point not lost by an actor-manager like Sir Henry Irving, who turned the play into a tragic melodrama, magnifying the role of Shylock, at the expense of the comic vision. Yet audiences identify with the Christian characters in the play. Most of us are at heart Bassanios wanting to make good marriages, or Antonios waiting for our investments to mature. It is one of the most "modern" of Shakespeare's plays, one which looks forward critically towards a new, post-Elizabethan set of values in which love, religion, justice, and friendship, become subordinate to the overriding consideration of financial profit; and yet, at once accepting and exposing, it explores these values in an elusive, ironic way. The play satisfies our group psyche, liberates our conscience, allows us to laugh with delight at our own imperfections, celebrates a good marriage and a good business deal, and as Antonio's ships return to port, richly laden, celebrates the triumph of sophistry and deception over the unpleasant bind of a legal contract.

—Brian Pearce

MERRY-GO-ROUND.   See LA RONDE.

THE MERRY WIVES OF WINDSOR
by William Shakespeare

First Publication: London, 1601 ("bad" quarto); second, "bad" quarto, 1602; revised version, in First Folio, 1623.
First Production: London, c. 1598–99; earliest recorded production, Palace of Whitehall, London, 4 November 1604.

Editions
The Merry Wives of Windsor, edited by Arthur Quiller-Couch and John Dover Wilson, Cambridge, 1921 (The New Shakespeare).
The Merry Wives of Windsor, edited by F.J. Bowers, Baltimore, Maryland, 1963 (Pelican Shakespeare).
The Merry Wives of Windsor, edited by William Green, New York, 1965 (Signet Classic Shakespeare).
The Merry Wives of Windsor, edited by H.J. Oliver, London, 1971 (Arden Shakespeare).
The Merry Wives of Windsor, edited by G.R. Hibbard, Harmondsworth, 1973 (New Penguin Shakespeare).

Criticism
(For general works on the author, see *Playwrights* volume)

Books:
William Green, *Shakespeare's "Merry Wives of Windsor"*, Princeton, New Jersey, 1972.
Jeanne Addison Roberts, *Shakespeare's English Comedy "The Merry Wives of Windsor" in Context*, Lincoln, Nebraska, 1979.
Mark W. Scott (ed.), *"The Merry Wives of Windsor"*, in *Shakespearian Criticism*, 5, Detroit, Illinois, 1987 [anthology of criticism].

Articles:
For information on the many articles about *The Merry Wives of Windsor*, see the bibliographies listed in the *Playwrights* volume, and the annual Shakespeare Bibliography in *Shakespeare Quarterly*, published by the Folger Shakespeare Library, Washington D.C. (1950–).

*   *   *

Falstaff tries to seduce the wives of Page and Ford, two citizens of Windsor, but they are outraged by his duplicity and plan to take revenge without telling their husbands. Page's daughter Anne is in love with a young gentleman, Fenton, but her father plans to marry her to the foolish Slender, while her mother favours the Frenchman, Dr. Caius.

Falstaff's intentions have been betrayed to Page and Ford by his servants, Nym and Pistol, but only the jealous Ford believes them. To test his wife he disguises himself as "Master Brook" and pays Falstaff to woo her on his behalf. The two wives set a trap for Falstaff, but they are themselves surprised by the arrival of Ford looking for Falstaff, who escapes hidden in a laundry-basket. He tells Ford of this, and that he has arranged a second meeting with his wife. Forewarned of Ford's visit, the wives disguise Falstaff as a woman, and Ford beats her out of the house. The wives arrange a final humiliation for Falstaff. Disguised as Herne the Hunter he meets them in Windsor Park at night, but is tormented by a band of supposed fairies. Meanwhile in the darkness Anne has foiled the marriage plans of her parents and has married Fenton.

There is a tradition that the play was written in a fortnight at the command of Queen Elizabeth, who was so delighted by the character of Falstaff in *Henry IV* that she wished to see him in love. Although this story is unlikely to be literally true, it does point to some important features of the play. There are several reasons for associating *Merry Wives* with the Queen, of which the most obvious is the close attention that it pays to Windsor Castle and the Order of the Garter. In such a context references to "our radiant Queen" and the "owner" of the castle must be compliments to Elizabeth. The play contains other topical references, and the most plausible explanation of some of them is Leslie Hotson's suggestion, in *Shakespeare versus Shallow*, that the play was performed in 1597 to celebrate the admission of Shakespeare's then patron, the second Lord Hunsdon, to the Order of the Garter. Hunsdon was the Queen's cousin and close friend. Moreover the tradition is correct in implying that the play was designed to capitalise on the success of the *Henry IV* plays. Besides Falstaff himself, Mistress Quickly, Bardolph, Pistol and Justice Shallow all play a necessary part in those plays, but are less well integrated into *Merry Wives*.

It is one of Shakespeare's most popular plays in the theatre, and one of the least written about by critics. It may lack the metaphysical and psychological depths of the other comedies, but it has much that they do not. It is the only "citizen" play in the canon, and the only comedy with a very specific English setting. The Garter stalls that the fairies have to clean can still be seen in St. George's Chapel; the Garter (now the Star and Garter) is still a busy Windsor inn; Falstaff could still be thrown into the Thames from "Datchet meads". Some of the characters are peculiarly English: Falstaff's companions, especially Pistol, who was much loved by Elizabethan audiences, and whose nonsense talk is almost matched by mine Host of the Garter; Mistress Quickly and her malapropisms; Shallow, the Justice from Shakespeare's own Cotswolds; and of course Falstaff himself.

Yet, as many foreign productions have shown, this play has a universal appeal. The bourgeois values on which the comedy depends are not confined to England. Windsor might be any small provincial town in which neighbours are always meeting each other by chance and husbands are likely to come home at any moment. Everyone knows everyone else's business, and social boundaries are flexible. Mistress Quickly is Dr. Caius's servant, but her social superiors constantly confide in her, and she helps to arrange Fenton's secret marriage to Anne Page. Money, not love, rules this narrow society. Page believes that Fenton will squander his daughter's fortune; his wife wants her to marry Dr. Caius because he is "well moneyed". Their attempts to control Anne's destiny are as selfish as Ford's mistrust of his wife. The most obvious threat—both sexual and financial—to this bourgeois society are the two male courtiers.

The Merry Wives of Windsor: Ada Rehan and Mrs John Drew, Philadelphia, 1885

Falstaff is after the citizens' wives and their money: Fenton is first attracted by Anne's money, and only then falls in love with her. A more serious threat, though it is never fully realised, is presented by the low-life characters among whom we may include Quickly and Falstaff, who, unconfined by social rules, spans both court and tavern. They form a truly subversive element, and it is interesting that the only successful revolt against the bourgeoisie, the secret marriage, is arranged by the Host and approved by Quickly.

The play's dramatic qualities are equally universal. It is built on a series of familiar comic stereotypes—the jealous husband, the garrulous busybody, the country simpleton, two comic foreigners who are Welsh and French and who cannot speak English properly—and one great comic creation, Falstaff. The subplots, which involve Anne's undesirable suitors, are cleverly interwoven with the main plot, and the fast-moving action culminates in a final scene in which the foolish are shown to be so, and true love triumphs. Individual scenes follow traditional comic patterns: the simpleton's absurd courtship; the non-duel between the two terrified foreigners; the deceiving of the jealous husband. But Shakespeare plays ironic variations on these themes. When the jealous Ford fails to find Falstaff in the laundry-basket all the protagonists are embarrassed and innocence is hard to tell from guilt: the wives are innocent, but afraid of appearing guilty, Ford's suspicions are correct, but proved wrong, and Falstaff is forced to hide among the dirty clothes.

Falstaff is the play's comic centre. At the simplest level his is the comedy of the man who aims too high and falls flat on his face; he tries to cuckold Ford and is left wearing the horns himself. But he is more than this. He is as spiritually excessive as he is physically; he has no regard for the laws of society or probability. He is lustful, greedy, and a liar, but he is so without being narrow-minded, limited, or mean. Much of the play's humour depends on the encounter between this embodiment of misrule and the small, closed society of Windsor.

—Roger Prior

MESYATS V DEREVNE. See **A MONTH IN THE COUNTRY.**

THE MIDDLE-CLASS GENTLEMAN. See **THE WOULD-BE GENTLEMAN.**

A MIDSUMMER NIGHT'S DREAM
by William Shakespeare

First Publication: London, 1600.
First Production: c. 1596.

Editions

A Midsummer Night's Dream, edited by Madeleine Doran, Baltimore, Maryland, 1959; revised edition, 1972 (Pelican Shakespeare).
A Midsummer Night's Dream, edited by Wolfgang Clemen, New York, 1963; revised edition, 1987 (Signet Classic Shakespeare).
A Midsummer Night's Dream, edited by Stanley Wells, Harmondsworth, 1967.
A Midsummer Night's Dream, edited by Harold F. Brooks, London, 1979 (Arden Shakespeare).
A Midsummer Night's Dream, edited by R.A. Foakes, Cambridge, 1984 (New Cambridge Shakespeare).

Bibliography

D. Allen Carroll and Gary Jay Williams (eds.), *"A Midsummer Night's Dream": An Annotated Bibliography*, New York, 1986 (Garland Shakespeare Bibliographies).

Criticism

(For general works on the author, see *Playwrights* volume)

Books:
H.B. Charlton, *A Midsummer Night's Dream*, Manchester, 1933.
Ronald Watkins and Jeremy Lemmon, *In Shakespeare's Playhouse: "A Midsummer Night's Dream"*, Newton Abbot, Devon, 1974.
Marion A. Taylor, *Bottom Thou art Translated: Political Allegory in "A Midsummer Night's Dream" and Related Literature*, Amsterdam, 1977.
Hans-Joachim Troeber, *Shakespeares "Sommernachtstraum" auf der Bühne des 20. Jahrhunderts, dargestellt an ausgewahlten Inszenierungen*, Trier, 1977.
F.W. Clayton, *The Hole in the Wall: A New Look at Shakespeare's Latin Base for "A Midsummer Night's Dream"*, Exeter, Devon, 1979.
Antony Price (ed.), *"A Midsummer Night's Dream": A Casebook*, London, 1983.
Roger Warren, *A Midsummer Night's Dream*, London, 1983 (Text and Performance Series).
Laurie Lanzen Harris and Mark W. Scott (eds.), *"A Midsummer Night's Dream"*, in *Shakespearian Criticism, 3*, Detroit, Illinois, 1986.
Harold Bloom (ed.), *William Shakespeare: "A Midsummer Night's Dream"*, New York, New Haven, Connecticut, and Philadelphia, 1987 (Modern Critical Interpretations).
Diana Akers Rhoades, *Shakespeare's Defense of Poetry: "A Midsummer Night's Dream" and "The Tempest"*, Lanham, Maryland, 1987.

Articles:
For information about the many articles on *A Midsummer Night's Dream*, see Carroll and Williams' bibliography, the bibliographies listed in the *Playwrights* volume, and the annual Shakespeare Bibliography in *Shakespeare Quarterly*, published by the Folger Shakespeare Library, Washington, D.C. (1950–).

* * *

"A Wood outside Athens" that is partly an evocation of the woods of Arden which were to the Northwest of Stratford-upon-Avon, and partly a dream-world, is the setting for most of *A Midsummer Night's Dream*, and quite as important as any character in determining the nature of this comedy. Fairies live in this wood, divided into the followers of Oberon and of Titania, their king and queen who have quarrelled over possession of a "little Indian boy" (never seen on stage). Puck also lives here, a servant of Oberon, who spends a good deal of time in playing tricks on mortals.

From Athens on Midsummer's Eve come four young lovers. First to set out are Hermia and Lysander, who are escaping from the girl's father who wishes to marry her to Demetrius; and this suitor follows shortly after, pursued by Helena who is in love with him against his will. Also from the town come Nick Bottom, a weaver, and other "rude mechanicals", "hard handed men" unused to labouring in their minds as they do now in rehearsing a play for the Duke of Athens' wedding celebrations; they have chosen to represent the doomed classical lovers, Pyramus and Thisbe. During the night, Oberon and Puck engage with both groups of Athenians. Bottom is turned into a monster with an ass's head and Titania charmed so that she dotes upon him lovingly. The young people are given a love potion so that both men declare love to an incredulous Helena; and then that muddle is sorted out in the same arbitrary way, so that Lysander still loves Hermia and Demetrius is happy with Helena.

In the morning Theseus and Hippolyta, his bride-to-be, arrive in the wood to hunt, accompanied by the "gallant chiding" of their hounds and the blare of horns. The play ends in Athens with a celebration of the marriage night of all six lovers, at which time the play of Pyramus and Thisby provides royal and hilarious entertainment.

This comedy is amazingly inventive, evocative, and mercurial. The ending is conventionally happy, but the play as a whole is as seemingly wayward as a dream. Repeatedly

A Midsummer Night's Dream: Stratford-Upon-Avon, 1970 (Royal Shakespeare Company, Peter Brook's production)

disaster threatens. In the first scene, when Theseus adjudicates between Egeus and his daughter Hermia, the accepted punishment for her refusal to marry Demetrius is death, and this is mitigated only so far as a life-time's vow of "austerity and single life". Later, in the wood, Titania's love for Bottom becomes grotesque and frightening. Titania's response to Oberon's obduracy, on their very first meeting, calls forth an image of a "mazed world" confronting a "progeny of evils". But vistas of delight and grace are also revealed: the moonlight, flowers, and morning dew of the countryside; the fantasy and transformations of the rehearsals; the delicacies with which Titania tempts the bewildered Bottom. When Titania is released from Oberon's spell, her mortal beloved stands alone in the wood, lost in the wonder of a dream that has faded; at this point, Bottom uses words taken from mystical religion: "The eye of man hath not heard, the ear of man hath not seen, man's hand is not able to taste, his tongue to conceive, nor his heart to report, what my dream was". Even the relationship of Theseus and Hippolyta, whose marriage provides the occasion for much of the action of the play, has conflicting aspects: she is an Amazonian warrior queen whom he has defeated in battle; and while Oberon equates lovers with madmen and poets who deal only in "airy nothing", she has to remind him of the "great constancy" of what the young lovers say, and of the power of their own imagination.

Oberon is, in effectiveness, the master of the comedy. He sets Puck, his "mad spirit", to work with evident pleasure, and stays to enjoy the antics of the absurdly enchanted lovers. But this "night-work" also sobers him, so that he releases Titania and is reconciled with her; he also arranges the happy conclusion for the lovers and goes with Titania and their reunited followers from the wood to Athens and Theseus's palace, there to honour and bless the bride-beds.

Evidently *A Midsummer Night's Dream* was written with great pleasure. It is light, easy, graceful, and endlessly inventive. It is intelligent, funny, evocative, sensuous, and sexual. But it is also most carefully crafted, balanced, and complicated. Its fairies are not taken from any ready-made models, but freshly created and associated with the mysteries of nature:

> I with the Morning's love have oft made sport;
> And like a forester the groves may tread,
> Even till the eastern gate, all fiery-red,
> Opening on Neptune with fair blessed beams
> Turns into yellow gold his salt green streams.

The comic conclusion, when Bottom and his fellows struggle to sustain their heroic roles in the face of light-hearted criticism and a whole string of malfunctions, is poised between many kinds of reality. It celebrates love and imagination; its characters are also actors, and those who are spectators are revealed in as clear a light as those who perform; and behind the success of this show can be seen the shadows of failure. A dance follows the hilarious conclusion of the "very tragical mirth" of *Pyramus and Thisby* and then Theseus echoes this evanescent seriousness: "The iron tongue of midnight hath told twelve. / Lovers, to bed; 'tis almost fairy time". and so does Puck, as he heralds his king's entrance: "Now the hungry lion roars, / And the wolf behowls the moon; / Whilst the heavy plowman snores, / All with weary task fordone". In some way, which it is tempting to call magic, Shakespeare has drawn into *A Midsummer Night's Dream* memories and echoes of everyday reality.

—John Russell Brown

MILES GLORIOSUS. See **THE BRAGGART SOLDIER.**

MINNA VON BARNHELM; or, The Soldier's Fortune (Minna von Barhelm; oder, Das Soldatenglück)
by Gotthold Ephraim Lessing

First Publication: Berlin, 1767.
First Production: Nationaltheater, Hamburg, 30 September 1767.

Editions
Minna von Barnhelm, edited by Ernst Hirt, Zurich, 1944.
Minna von Barnhelm, edited by Rosemarie Gruber, Munich, 1948.
Minna von Barnhelm, edited by Karl Hoppe, Bielefeld, Hannover, 1951.
Minna von Barnhelm, (revised edition), edited by Werner F. Leopold and Curt R. Goedsche, Boston, 1961.
Minna von Barnhelm, edited by Margaret S. McHaffie, London, 1962.
Minna von Barnhelm, edited by Henry B. Garland, London, Melbourne, Toronto, and New York, 1965.
"Minna von Barnhelm": Dichtung und Wirklichkeit, edited by Dieter Hildebrandt, Frankfurt, 1969.
"Minna von Barnhelm" ... mit Materialen, edited by Joachim Bark, Munich, 1979.
Minna von Barnhelm, edited by Joachim Dyck, Berlin, 1981.

Translations
Minna von Barnhelm, in *Lessing: The Dramatic Works, 2*, translated by Ernest Bell, London, 1978.
Minna von Barnhelm, translated by Patrick Maxwell, London, 1899.
Minna von Barnhelm, translated by Otto Heller, New York, 1917.
Minna von Barnhelm, translated by E.M. Uuless, London and Edinburgh, 1929.
Minna von Barnhelm, translated by Anthony Dent, in *Laocoön; Nathan the Wise; Minna von Barnhelm*, edited by William A. Steel, London, Toronto, and New York, 1930.

Criticism
(For general works on the author, see *Playwrights* volume)

Books:
Otto Spiess, *Die dramatische Handlung in Lessings "Emilia Galotti" und "Minna von Barnhelm": Ein Beitrag zur Technik des Dramas*, 1911.
Bernhart Maydorn, *Erläuterungen zu Lessings "Minna von Barnhelm"*, Paderborn, 1912.
Emil Mahler, *Lessings "Minna von Barnhelm": Erläuterungen*, Leipzig, 1913.
Oswald Woyte, *Erläuterungen zu Lessings "Minna von Barnhelm" oder Das Soldatenglück*, Hollfeld, 1956.
Walter Fischer, *Lessing: "Minna von Barnhelm"*, Frankfurt, 1960.
Dieter Hildebrandt, *G.E. Lessing: Vollständige Text. Dokumentation*, Frankfurt and Berlin, 1969.
Jürgen Hein, *"Minna von Barnhelm": Erläuterungen und Dokumente*, Stuttgart, 1970.
Horst Steinmetz (ed.), *"Minna von Barnhelm": Dokumente zur Rezeption-und Interpretationsgeschichte*, Königstein, 1979.

Simonetta Sanna, *"Minna von Barnhelm" die G.E. Lessing: Analisi del teatro teatrale*, Pisa, 1983.

Wulf Rüskamp, *Dramaturgie ohne Publikum: Lessings Dramentheorie und die zeitgenössische Rezeption von "Minna von Barnhelm" und "Emilia Galotti": Ein Beitrag zur Geschichte des deutschen Theaters und seines Publikums*, Cologne, 1984.

Robin Harrison, *Lessing: "Minna von Barnhelm"*, London, 1985.

Articles:

Robert Petsch, "Die Kunst der Charkeristik in Lessings *Minna von Barnhelm*", in *Zeitschrift für den deutschen Unterricht*, 26, 1912.

Fernand Baldensperger, "L'Original probable de la Marlinière dans la *Minna von Barnhelm* de Lessing", in *Neophilologus*, 23, Groningen, 1938.

Gerhard Fricke, "Lessings *Minna von Barnhelm*: Eine Interpretation", in *Zeitschrift für Deutschkunde*, 53, 1939.

Heinz Stolte, "Lessings *Minna von Barnhelm*", in *Zeitschrift für deutsche Bildung*, 17, 1941.

Emil Staiger, "Lessing's *Minna von Barnhelm*", in *German Life and Letters* (new series), 1, 1947–48.

Hilde D. Cohn, "Die beiden Schwierigen im deutschen Lustspiel: Lessing, *Minna von Barnhelm*; Hoffmannsthal, *Der Schwierige*", in *Monatshefte für deutschen Unterricht*, 44, 1952.

Otto Mann, "*Minna von Barnhelm*", in *Das deutsche Drama*, 1, 1958.

Harry L. Stout, "Lessing's Riccaut and Thomas Mann's Fitelberg", in *German Quarterly*, 36, 1963.

Ilse Appelbaum-Graham, "The Currency of Love: A Reading of Lessing's *Minna von Barnhelm*", in *German Life and Letters* (new series), 18, 1964.

Georg Lukács, "*Minna von Barnhelm*", in *Akzente*, 11, 1964; translated by Robert Anchor, in Lukács' *Goethe and His Age*, London, 1968.

Wolfgang F. Michael, "Tellheim eine Lustspielfigur", in *Deutsche Vierteljahrsschrift für Literaturwissenschaft und Geistesgeschichte*, 39, 1965.

Raimund Belgardt, "Minna von Barnhelm als komischer Charakter", in *Monatshefte für deutschen Unterricht*, 58, 1966.

Raimund Belgardt, "Tellheim's Honor: Flaw or Virtue?" A Reinterpretation", in *Germanic Review*, 42, 1967.

Helmut Arntzen, "Die Komödie des Individuums: Lessings *Minna von Barnhelm*", in his *Die ernste Komödie: Das deutsche Lustspiel von Lessing bis Kleist*, Munich, 1968.

Werner Schwann, "Justs Streit mit dem Wirt: Zur Frage des Lustspielbeginns und der Exposition in Lessings *Minna von Barnhelm*", in *Jahrbuch der deutschen Schiller-Gesellschaft*, 12, 1968.

Werner Rieck, "G.E. Lessings *Minna von Barnhelm*: Versuch einer Analyse", in *Deutschunterricht*, 22, 1969.

Jürgen Schröder, "Das parabolische Geschehen der *Minna von Barnhelm*", in *Deutsche Vierteljahrsschrift für Literaturwissenschaft und Geistesgeschehen*, 43, 1969.

Peter Waldeck, "Lessings *Minna von Barnhelm* und Plautus' *Amphitruo*", in *Orbis Litterarum*, 24, 1969.

Peter Weber, "Lessings *Minna von Barnhelm*: Zur Interpretation u. literahistor. Charakteristik des Wekes", in *Studien zur Literaturgeschicht und Literaturtheorie*, edited by Hans-Günther Thalheim and Ursula Wertheim, Berlin, 1970.

Leonard Wessel and Charles M. Barrack, "The Tragic Background to Lessing's Comedy *Minna von Barnhelm*", in *Lessing Yearbook*, 2, 1970.

Jürgen Schröder, "*Minna von Barnhelm*: Aesthetische Struk-

tur und 'Sprache des Herzens' ", in *Lessing Yearbook*, 3, 1971.

Bruce Duncan, "Hand, Heart, and Language in *Minna von Barnhelm*", in *Seminar*, 8, 1972.

Peter Michelsen, "Die Verbergung der Kunst: Über die Exposition in Lessings *Minna von Barnhelm*", in *Jahrbuch der deutschen Schiller-Gesellschaft*, 17, 1973.

Bert Nagel, " 'Ein unerreichbares Muster': Lessing's *Minna von Barnhelm*", in *Heidelberger Jahrbuch*, 17, 1973.

Martin Boghardt, "Zur Textgestaltung der *Minna von Barnhelm*", in *Wolfenbütteler Studien zur Aufklärung*, 2, 1975.

Alfred Hoelzel, "Truth and Honesty in *Minna von Barnhelm*", in *Lessing Yearbook*, 9, 1977.

Ulf Scramm, "Zum Verhältnis von Literatur, Gesellschaftsstruktur und Geschichte am Beispiel der Interpretation von Lessings *Minna von Barnhelm* und Ibsen's *Nora*", in *LiLi: Zeitschrift für Literaturwissenschaft und Linguistik*, 32, 1978.

Hans-Georg Werner, "Komödie der Rationalität: Zu Lessings *Minna von Barnhelm*", in *Weimarer Beiträge*, 25, 1979.

Joseph Carroll, "*Minna von Barnhelm* and *le genre sérieux*: A Reconsideration", in *Lessing Yearbook*, 8, 1981.

Ferdinand Piedmont, "*Minna von Barnhelm*, west-östlich: Zur Theaterrezeption der Lessingschen Komödie in der BRD und der DDR", in *Lessing Yearbook*, 8, 1981.

Glenn A. Guidry, "Money, Honor, and Love: The Hierarchy of Values in Lessing's *Minna von Barnhelm*", in *Lessing Yearbook*, 14, 1982.

Benjamin Bennett, "The Generic Constant in Lessing's Development of a Comedy of Institutions and Alienation", in *German Quarterly*, vol.56 no.2, 1983.

Elizabeth Boa, "*Der gute Mensch von Barnhelm*: The Female Essence and the Ensemble of Human Relations in Lessing's *Minna von Barnhelm*", in *Publications of the English Goethe Society*, 54, 1984.

Peter Christian Giese, "Riccaut und das Spiel mit Fortunata in Lessings *Minna von Barnhelm*", in *Jahrbuch der deutsche Schiller-Gesellschaft*, 28, 1984.

Mark Lehrer, "Lessing's Economic Comedy", in *Seminar*, vol.20 no.2, 1984.

G.H. Hertling, "Zur Genese des psychologischen Realismus: 'Mitleid', 'Furcht', und 'Originalität' in Lessings Denken und in *Minna von Barnhelm*", in *Text & Kontext*, vol.13 no.2, 1985.

John Whiton, "Tellheim and the Russians: Aspects of Lessing's Response to the Seven Years' War in *Minna von Barnhelm*", in *Lessing Yearbook*, 17, 1985.

Wolfgang Wittkowski, "*Minna von Barnhelm* oder die verhinderten Hausväter", in *Lessing Yearbook*, 19, 1987.

Judith P. Aiken, " 'Das klingt sehr tragisch!' : Lessing's *Minna von Barnhelm* as Embodiment of the Genre Discussion", in *Lessing Yearbook*, 20, 1988.

Osman Durrani, "Love and Money in Lessing's *Minna von Barnhelm*", in *Modern Language Review*, vol.84 no.3, 1989.

*   *   *

Minna, a Saxon, has come to Berlin in search of her fiancé Tellheim, a major, now discharged from the Prussian army. The act of generosity performed by Tellheim, (in advancing money from his own funds to cover taxes he was supposed to collect in Saxony), which won Minna's love, has been misinterpreted by the Prussian authorities as dishonourable and dishonest. Tellheim is now without funds and awaiting the outcome of an investigation into the matter. Feeling himself crippled both physically (he has been wounded in the arm), and by his slight to his honour, Tellheim rejects Minna. He is now unworthy of her. He will not owe his happiness to her. Minna contrives to convince Tellheim that she is herself penniless and threatened by her uncle, and by this ruse tricks him into declaring his love for her again. However, this is not enough for her. She feels that she must punish Tellheim further. This punishment, inflicted after Tellheim receives notification from the king that his fortune and honour are both restored, almost goes too far. The situation is redeemed by the arrival of Minna's uncle who approves the union, bringing the play to a happy conclusion.

Minna von Barnhelm was conceived in 1763 in the aftermath of the Seven Years War (in which Saxony and Prussia were enemies) and was completed in 1767, the year in which Lessing assumed his post as resident playwright and critic to the new National Theatre in Hamburg. In the play, Lessing (a Saxon working as secretary to a Prussian general) makes an impassioned plea for tolerance and reconciliation—both themes central to his writing as a whole. In his theoretical writings on the theatre Lessing calls for a national repertory for the German theatre, and in *Minna von Barnhelm* he offers a model of a truly German comedy, as much of the humour and interest in the play arises from the interaction between the vivacious and witty Saxon, Minna, and the unbending, high-principled Prussian, Tellheim.

In form the play is conventional. It is written in five acts, the scenes changing with characters' entrances. The protagonists come from the minor nobility, and their courting is mirrored in the developing relationship between Minna's pert maid Franziska and the Major's stolid sergeant-major, Werner. The play follows convention also in its observance of the classical unities of time, place, and action. Later Lessing would attack the French theatre of the day for its slavish adherence to the letter rather than to the spirit of the unities, suggesting that German theatre would be better advised to imitate the freer construction of Shakespeare's plays than those of the French. The true originality of the play lies in the freshness and contemporaneity of the characters and their concerns. The structure of the play might be reminiscent of "classical" comedy, but there is a striking quality of realism in the characterisation and settings, as well as in Lessing's rejection of verse and his choice of a supple prose for the dialogue, accurately matched to the standing of the characters. Tellheim finds himself in limbo as a discharged officer, which must have been familiar to many in the original audience. There are frequent references to both good and bad features of the recent conflict, which must have struck chords in performance. Through the character of Riccaut de la Marlinière, Lessing ridicules the fashion, prevalent in Germany at the time, and at the court of Frederick the Great, of regarding the German language as incapable of expressing the subtleties necessary for cultured conversation, and, by implication, literature. By refusing to speak in French with Riccaut, Minna (and Lessing) decisively takes sides in the argument current at the time. This, and the direct reference to the king himself in the play, led the Prussian authorities to discourage the production of *Minna von Barnhelm*, which was first performed in Hamburg, a free city beyond Prussian jurisdiction, in 1767.

The play's abiding appeal for audiences derives chiefly from the charm of the central character of Minna herself. She might with justification be seen as the first emancipated woman in German comedy. Not deterred from setting out herself in search of her fiancé, nor afraid to go on ahead of her uncle when his carriage breaks down, she is well able to defend herself against the prying questions of the landlord, and to win the hearts of the audience in her exchanges on love and romance with Franziska. Above all she is a heroine of the German bourgeoisie, embodying the virtues and standards espoused by the new theatre audience, who recognised in her self-confidence their own growing self-esteem. Despite this, however, the play owes a considerable debt to the *sächsische Typenkomödie* (the Saxon comedy of types). In this genre of comedy attempts are made to show a flawed character the unreasonableness of his behaviour, and, when reason fails, the other characters resort to intrigue. Thus it is that Minna, unable to persuade Tellheim to owe his happiness to her (his fault being his inability, as a generous man, to receive generosity), has recourse to trickery.

But here Lessing adds a new dimension to this comic form and an increased depth to the play. For Tellheim is a more complex and a more sympathetic character than the traditional butt of this type of comedy. We are shown his positive qualities in his interaction with the widow of his captain-of-horse, with Paul Werner, and with Just. We admire his honesty and sympathise with him when, after the notification from the king of the restoration of his fortune and his honour, Minna persists in deceiving him in order to teach him a lesson. Minna sees that she has taken the game too far, but Tellheim is thrown into serious confusion by Minna's dishonesty towards him, and only the arrival of Minna's uncle saves the play from an unhappy ending, Minna having lost control of the situation.

In the event *Minna von Barnhelm* was not taken as a model by the new movement of the *Sturm und Drang* (Storm and Stress) movement, whose inspiration lacked the balance necessary for the writing of comedy. But the play has retained its place in the repertory of German theatre, and is regularly performed on the stages of the German-speaking world.

—Anthony Meech

THE MINOR (Nedorosl)
by Denis Fonvizin

First Publication: St. Petersburg, 1783.
First Production: Knipper's Theatre, St. Petersburg, 24 September 1782.

Editions

Nedorosl (The Minor), edited by W. Harrison, Letchworth, Hampshire, 1965.

Translations

The Young Hopeful, translated by G.R. Noyes and G.Z. Patrick, in *Masterpieces of the Russian Drama, 1*, edited by G.R. Noyes, New York, 1933.
The Minor, translated by F.D. Reeve, in *An Anthology of Russian Plays, 1*, New York, 1961.
The Infant, in *Four Russian Plays*, translated by J. Cooper, Harmondsworth, 1972.
The Minor, in *Dramatic Works of D.I. Fonvizin*, translated by M. Kantor, Bern and Frankfurt, 1974.

Criticism

(For general works on the author, see *Playwrights* volume)

Articles:
François de Labriolle, "La Dramaturgie de Fonvizin", in *Revue des études slaves*, 46, 1967.

David Patterson, "Fonvizin's *Nedorosl* as a Russian Representative of the *genre sérieux*", in *Comparative Literature Studies*, 14, 1977.

Thomas Barran, "Rousseau and Fonvizin: *Emile* as a Source for *The Minor*", in *Ulbandus Review*, vol.2 no.2, 1982.

Vladimir E. Alexandrov, "Dialogue and Rousseau in Fonvizin's *The Minor*", in *Slavic and East European Journal*, vol.29 no.2, 1985.

Simon Karlinsky, "*The Minor*", in his *Russian Drama From Its Beginnings to the Age of Pushkin*, Berkeley, California, 1985.

*   *   *

Fonvizin's *The Minor* marks the highpoint in Russian 18th-century neo-classical comedy. It entered the repertory almost immediately and is still regularly performed on the Soviet stage; indeed it is almost the only play of its period that is. It was frequently performed at the court of Catherine the Great and her then favourite and chief minister Prince Gregory Potemkin is reported to have said to Fonvizin: "You might as well die, Denis, you'll never write anything better". The action takes place on the country estate of the meek and hen-pecked Prostakov (Mr. Simpleton). Everyone there is tyrannized by his ignorant, cruel, and domineering wife. Their 16-year-old son Mitrofan, the minor of the title, is an indolent, unintelligent, and spoiled adolescent, adored by his mother, and whose only ambition is expressed in the now proverbial words: "I don't want to study, I want to get married". Staying on the estate is a nobleman, Pravdin (Mr. Truthful), who, unbeknown to the Prostakovs, has been sent by the government to verify reports that Mrs. Prostakov has been maltreating her serfs. Mrs. Prostakov hopes to marry off her ward, the young orphan Sophia, whose estate she has illegally taken over, to her brother Skotinin (Mr. Brute), who prefers the company of pigs to that of human beings. Sophia hears that her rich uncle Starodum (Mr. Oldsense) is returning after making his fortune, and Mrs. Prostakov thinks that Sophia would now better suit her son. Sophia, though, is in love with Milon (Dear), a young army officer who soon arrives on the scene, closely followed by Starodum, who rejects as suitors for Sophia both Skotinin and Mitrofan. Mrs. Prostakov attempts to kidnap Sophia but is prevented by Milon. Pravdin announces an official order removing the Prostakovs from control over their serfs and everyone, including Miltrofan, turns on the wretched Mrs. Prostakov. Milon and Sophia are now free to marry.

Despite many attempts in Russia and the Soviet Union to make out that *The Minor* is a precursor of realism on the stage, the fact remains that it is a thorough-going, neo-classical comedy, influenced less by Molière than by Ludwig Holberg. The three unities are strictly adhered to in its five acts (the action lasts scarcely more than 24 hours and occurs in one room), violence takes place off-stage, the characters have symbolic names and represent specific human vices and virtues, there is a pair of traditional young lovers, and good conquers evil in the happy ending. Within this restricting framework Fonvizin has written a well-constructed and amusing play. The conflict between the old-fashioned, uneducated, and rough-hewn provincial gentry, and the civilized, cultured (and rich) representatives of the Enlightenment is reasonably well-balanced. Although it is clear that the positive characters have justice on their side and ultimately triumph, their speeches tend to the moralizing, didactic, and tedious, while the negative ones are far more interesting dramatically and all the real comedy in the play stems from their words and actions. Fonvizin's satire is not only directed at the grasping, narrow-minded gentry. He suggests that their faults come from a lack of education and along with his contemporaries believes that all ills will be cured once ignorance is removed. The three tutors Mrs. Prostakov employs for her son are comically incompetent and are only engaged because of the legal requirement that sons of the gentry have to receive an education. The legal bureaucracy and sycophancy at the imperial court are attacked, as are many of the abuses of serfdom. Fonvizin does not at all wish for serfdom to be abolished or for anything other than autocracy to remain the form of government, but pleads that the abuses they can engender should be eradicated. One further important theme in *The Minor* is that of duty; the duty of subjects to their monarch, of the landowners to look after their serfs, of children to respect their elders, and of all citizens to serve their country. While none of the butts of Fonvizin's satire is original (and Catherine herself had used similar targets in her own plays), it was Fonvizin's dramatic sense, his fine and apposite use of language, his ability to portray recognizable Russian life and people, and the humour of many of his characters' speeches that made *The Minor* the most popular play of its day; and it still remains very watchable and far more than the historical curios that nearly all other Russian plays of the 18th century have become.

—A. V. Knowles

MIRANDOLINA.   See MISTRESS OF THE INN.

MISALLIANCE
by George Bernard Shaw

First Publication: As *Mesallianz*, in *Frauen—Zukunft*, October 1910–March 1911 [German translation]; in book form, Berlin, 1911; English version, in *Misalliance; The Dark Lady of the Sonnets; Fanny's First Play*, London, 1914.

First Production: Duke of York's Theatre, London, 23 February 1910.

Criticism
(For general works on the author, see *Playwrights* volume)

Articles:

William L. Sharp, "*Misalliance*: An Evaluation", in *Educational Theatre Journal*, vol.8 no.1, 1956.

Gladys M. Crane, "Shaw's *Misalliance*: The Comic Journey from Rebellious Daughter to Conventional Womanhood", in *Educational Theatre Journal*, 25, 1973.

Michael J. Sidnell, "*Misalliance*: Sex, Socialism, and the Collectivist Poet", in *Modern Drama*, 17, 1974.

Frederick P.W. McDowell, "Shaw's Abrasive View of Edwardian Civilization in *Misalliance*", in *Cahiers Victoriens & Édouardiens*, 9–10, 1979.

Rodelle Weintraub, "Johnny's Dream: *Misalliance*", in *SHAW*, 7, 1987.

Robert G. Everding, "Bernard Shaw, *Misalliance*, and the Birth of British Aviation", in *SHAW*, 8, 1988.

*   *   *

Misalliance: Lyric Theatre, Hammersmith, London, 1956

Shaw wrote *Misalliance* for unbroken performance (although he gave in to management pressure to allow an interval) in what he called "the Greek form", observing the unities as he had done in the preceding play, *Getting Married*. The setting throughout is the conservatory and part of the hall of a country mansion easily accessible from London. The play opens with sunlight pouring through the glass onto a canopied, swinging seat in which young Johnny Tarleton is lounging with a novel. Such initial images introduce characters and events which keep slipping away from reality into fantasy, as in a mind on the edge of sleep. The play of ideas is combined with farce in an experimentally designed structure aping the casual and the random. Thus, Bentley Summerhayes, engaged to Johnny's sister, Hypatia, abandons conversation for kicking and screaming in a childish tantrum; he is comforted like a baby by his fiancée and her mother, while Johnny is handed an elaborate vase by a stranger (to the audience) and told to break it; the resultant crash is echoed, after an interval of various but prolonged chatter, in a greater, more cosmic crash as an aeroplane destroys the glass of an off-stage greenhouse. The family group, gathered for the weekend, is surprised by three intruders: an aviator and his androgynous passenger, and later a clerk who conceals himself in a portable, Turkish bath with the intention of shooting John Tarleton, the head of the household. The rest conspire to render the would-be assassin harmless; Hypatia chooses the airman, Joey Percival, as her mate; and the discarded Bentley summons up the courage to ascend into the skies with the divine figure who was Joey's passenger.

Written for an optimistic, West End experiment in the repertory programming of new, quality plays, *Misalliance* had achieved 11 performances when the death of King Edward VII gave the management an excuse for closing down the whole enterprise. Saddled with the reputation of failure, the play had to wait until the 1960's for some brave revivals to establish its stage-worthiness beyond question. In 1910, it was as novel and bewildering to London as the paintings of the Post-Impressionists, exposed to public obloquy in the same year. Shaw was in tune with the spirit of the new; looking back, we can relate *Misalliance* to Dada and Surrealism, to Futurism with its cult of the machine (Shaw had brought a motorcar on stage in *Man and Superman*, and here it was an aeroplane), and see that his methods of discontinuity and his rejection of logical plot-development were part of a general, European house-clearance of bourgeois order and the relics of 19th–century thinking. The introduction of farce and fantasy into the socio-political drama of ideas corresponded to the zestful buoyancy with which he set about his task.

Seeing himself as part of a group with a common purpose, Shaw took measures within his play to further the success of the Duke of York's repertory season as a whole. So as to encourage audiences to return and see other plays in the repertory programme, rather than just picking out one, he wrote his play as a variation on the principal themes, characters, and incidents of two of the others considered for presentation: Granville Barker's *The Madras House* and Gilbert Murray's version of *The Bacchae*. (In fact, the latter was not revived at this time, but Shaw had rehearsed Granville Barker's actress wife, Lillah McCarthy, in her role as the god Dionysus for the first production in 1908.) *Misalliance* certainly stands on its own, but an acquaintance with the companion plays enriches any viewing or reading of it. A few explicit cross-references link *Misalliance* and Barker's drama. More centrally, Shaw's John Tarleton, the wealthy purveyor of Tarleton's Underwear ("the soul", he puns) is allied to a brotherhood of linen drapers in *The Madras House*, while his conversational habit of citing literary references is shared with the American in Barker's play who bids for the Madras House emporium and its subsidiaries. A conservatory, actual and symbolic, figures largely in *The Madras House*, and the Turkish bath is a solid allusion to a chain of oriental imagery in that play. Leaving aside numerous other parallels between the two works, *Misalliance* and *The Madras House* are both plays about the condition of contemporary England. Barker's title sounds the note of imperialism represented by Shaw's ex-colonial governor, Lord Summerhayes, who combines extensive experience of the difficulties of controlling native populations with a mastery of *realpolitik*. As for linking with *The Bacchae*, *Misalliance* burlesques a Greek temple in its setting that contains a series of urns on pillars and has its altar for libations, a *deus ex machina*, a final judgement and apotheosis. More specifically, with comic diminution, the son of Lucinda Titmus comes, like the Stranger in Euripides' play, to avenge his mother and, emboldened by the bacchic cup, echoes the threat of destruction to Thebes: "Rome fell: Babylon fell: Hindhead's turn will come". Shaw plays about with the elements he borrows: so the clerk is captured like the Dionysian stranger, but has taken on the role of Pentheus spying on the women's orgies, as he watches Hypatia's uninhibited chase of the "brute" she desires, and the "divinity", in *Misalliance*, is the passenger from the plane, the Polish acrobat, Lina Szczepanowski.

Nothing as savage as the image of an ecstatic mother (Agave), gorged on the dismembered body of her son, appears in *Misalliance*, but it could serve as an emblem of Shaw's prevailing theme. Hypatia (whose father must have read Charles Kingsley before her christening) continually voices her frustration within the trap of family and home, constantly bombarded by talk, with nothing happening and no outlet in action. The dramatist illustrates her complaints in a chain of references to rabbits and chickens running throughout the dialogue. This culminates in the magnificent tirade, which feminist readings take to be the point towards which the whole play drives, when Lina makes her proud boast, "I am strong: I am skilful: I am brave: I am independent: I am unbought: I am all that a woman ought to be", and pours scorn on "this rrrrrrrabbit hutch" where "the eyes of all of you are sheep's eyes". Yet it was Lina who disarmed the Gunner of his pistol to enable Joey to bully him into submission and Bentley to make him drunk, before the motherly Mrs. Tarleton led him gently away to sleep off his rebellious fit. It is not at all clear that Hypatia will continue her revolt against the Victorian domestic ideal after capturing her dubious superman, left grounded when Bentley, the giant philosophic mind in a puny body (modelled on the young Bertrand Russell) defies his terror and

resolves to soar into danger, as the poet Eugene Marchbanks in *Candida*, took himself out into the night away from the temptation of domestic happiness. In this more mature play, the general air of tolerance in Tarleton's house, which can accommodate the irregularity of the old man's amours, the erotic follies of Summerhayes, and the principled sexual freedom of Lina, builds a reservation into the critique, as happens rather similarly in *Heartbreak House*.

Although Shaw described *Misalliance* as a "disquisitory play", its resemblances to the later "fantasia" *Heartbreak House* have long been recognised. The musical term "fantasia" is in keeping with the music-inspired, contrapuntal patterning of the dialogue in *Misalliance*, with its repetition, interweaving, and development of verbal motifs which constitute various applications of the idea of misalliance revealed in the play, the ultimate being between beast and god in human nature. "Fantasia" is also appropriate to the new extension of the burlesque genre which Shaw had invented in this play. There is a major risk in performance that the first half of the play, where Shaw wants a stretch of actionless dialogue to prepare for the climax of the crashing aeroplane and the subsequent frenzy of events, will in fact drag and disenchant the audience. Dispensing with an interval, as he originally intended, gives the best chance of realising the satisfying overall rhythm.

—Margery Morgan

THE MISANTHROPE (Le Misanthrope)
by Molière

First Publication: Paris, 1667.
First Production: Palais-Royal, Paris, 4 June 1666.

Editions

Le Misanthrope, edited by Ronald A. Wilson, London, 1945.
Le Misanthrope, edited by Fernand Angué, Paris, 1961.
Le Misanthrope, edited by Félix Guirand, Paris, 1962.
Le Misanthrope, edited by Edouard Lop and André Sauvage, Paris, 1963.
Le Misanthrope, edited by G. Sablayrolles, Paris, 1963.
Le Misanthrope, edited by Robert Jouanny and Georges Chappon, Paris, 1966.
Le Misanthrope, edited by Paul Gauriat, Paris, 1970.
Le Misanthrope, in *Le Misanthrope; Le Bourgeois Gentilhomme*, edited by Denis M. Calandra, Lincoln, Nebraska, 1967.
Le Misanthrope, edited by Michel Atrand, Paris, 1986.

Translations

The Misanthrope, translated by William F. Giehse, Boston and New York, 1928.
The Misanthrope, translated by Gerald E. Bentley, in *The Play's the Thing*, New York, 1936.
The Misanthrope, translated by Richard Wilbur, London and New York, 1955.
The Misanthrope, in *Molière: Eight Plays*, translated by Morris Bishop, New York, 1957.
The Misanthrope, translated by Bernard D.N. Grebanier, Great Neck, New York, 1959.
The Misanthrope, in *"The Misanthrope" and Other Plays*, translated by John Wood, Harmondsworth, 1959.

The Misanthrope, translated by Joachim Neugroschel, New York, 1966.

The Misanthrope, in *"The Misanthrope" and Other Plays*, translated by Donald Frame, New York, 1968.

The Misanthrope, translated by Tony Harrison, London, 1973; second edition, 1975.

Criticism

(For general works on the author, see *Playwrights* volume)

Books:

Henry William Gregg Markheim, *Molière and "The Misanthrope": A Lecture Delivered at the Taylor Institution, Oxford*, Oxford, 1902.

Jacques Arnavon, *L'Interprétation de la comédie classique: "Le Misanthrope": mise-en-scène, décors, représentations*, Paris, 1914.

Jole Porciani, *Sulla questione del "Misanthrope" di Molière*, Livorno, 1933.

René Doumic, *"Le Misanthrope" de Molière: Étude et analyse*, Paris, 1926.

M. Bonfantini, *Molière e il "Misanthrope"*, Milan, 1956.

Jean Pierre Vincent, *Alceste et absolutisme*, Paris, 1977.

J.H. Broome, *Molière: "L'École des femmes" and "Le Misanthrope"*, London, 1982.

Ivan Barko and Bruce Burgess, *La Dynamique des points de vue dans le texte de théâtre: Analyses de points de vue—"Le Misanthrope"; "Le Mariage de Figaro"; "Lorenzaccio"; "En Attendant Godot"*, Paris, 1988.

Articles:

C.D. Zdanowicz, "*Don Garcie* and *Le Misanthrope*", in *Modern Philology*, 16, 1918.

C.D. Zdanowicz, "From *Le Misanthrope* to *Le Malade imaginaire*", in *Modern Philology*, 19, 1921.

Luigi Sorrento, "La critica al *Misanthrope* e l'arte di Molière", in *Revista d'italia*, 26, 1923.

Georges Ascoli, "*Le Misanthrope* de Molière et la sagesse libertine", in *Revue universitaire*, vol.34 no.2, 1925.

Ernst Schmidt, "Molière's *Menschenfeind* in seiner zeitgeschichtlichen und allgemein-menschlichen Bedeutung", in *Zeitschrift für französischen und englischen Unterricht*, 24, 1925.

Fleury Rousselon, "*Le Misanthrope* de Molière", in *Chronique des lettres françaises*, 7, 1929.

Julius Schmidt, "Gedanken zu *Le Misanthrope*", in *Zeitschrift für französischen und englischen Unterricht*, 30, 1930.

Carl Appel, "*Der Misanthrope* in der neuen deutschen Molièreforschung", in *Germanisch-Romanische Monatsschrift*, 20, 1932.

Béatrice Dussane, "Trois grands roles de Molière: 3, Alceste", in *Revue hebdomadaire*, vol.93 no.5, 1934.

E.D. Sullivan, "The Actor's Alceste: Evolution of *The Misanthrope*", in *Modern Language Quarterly*, 9, 1948.

René Jasinski, "Molière et *Le Misanthrope*", in *Romanic Review*, 43, 1952.

Ulrich Leo, "Goldonis *Locandiera* und Molières *Misanthrope*: Zwei Motiv-Entwicklungen", in *Romanische Forschungen*, 70, 1958.

Quentin M. Hope, "Society in *Le Misanthrope*", in *French Review*, 32, 1958–59.

J.F. Winter, "A Forerunner of Molière's *Misanthrope*", in *Modern Language Notes*, 74, 1959.

D.J. Yarrow, "A Reconsideration of Alceste", in *French Studies*, 13, 1959.

Robert C. Elliott, "*Le Misanthrope*", in his *The Power of Satire*, Princeton, New Jersey, 1960.

Lionel Gossman, "Orgon and *Le ridicule de la nature*", in *Bucknell Review*, 10, 1961.

Hallam Walker, "Action and Illusion in *Le Misanthrope*", in *Kentucky Foreign Language Quarterly*, 9, 1962.

Marc Michel, "Alceste ou le misanthrope?", in *Nouvelle Revue Française*, 11, 1963.

Georges Lavis, "Un Fragment du *Misanthrope*", in *Cahiers d'analyse textuelle*, 7, 1965.

Seymour M. Rudin, "Molière and *Le Misanthrope*", in *Educational Theatre Journal*, 17, 1965.

Anne-Lisa Amadou, "Molière's Alceste", in *Edda*, 54, 1967.

Will G. Moore, "Reflections on *Le Misanthrope*", in *Australian Journal of French Studies*, 4, 1967.

Dorrit Cohn, "*The Misanthrope*: Molière and Hoffmansthal", in *Arcadia*, 3, 1968.

James L. Shepherd, "Arsinoé as Puppeteer", in *French Review*, 42, 1968–69.

Jules Brody, "*Don Juan* and *Le Misanthrope*, or the Esthetics of Individualism in Molière", in *Publications of the Modern Language Association* [*PMLA*], 84, 1969.

Alfred Cismaru, "*Les Sincères* (Marivaux) and *Le Misanthrope*: An Attempt to Settle the Relationship", in *French Review*, 42, 1969.

Richard Monod, "Comment parler de Célimène", in *Annales de la faculté des lettres et de sciences humaines de Nice*, 8, 1969.

Richard L. Regosin, "Ambiguity and Truth in *Le Misanthrope*", in *Romanic Review*, 60, 1969.

Artur Greive, "Molière als Verdichter: zum Alexandriner im *Misanthrope*", in *Archiv*, 207, 1970.

H. Gaston Hall, "The Literary Context of Molière's *Le Misanthrope*", in *Studi francesi*, 41, 1970.

Jean J. Smoot, "Alceste: The Incomplete Don Quixote", in *Romance Notes*, 12, 1970.

Peter Schunk, "Zur Wirkungsgeschichte des *Misanthrope*", in *Germanisch-Romanische Monatsschrift*, 21, 1971.

Elaine D. Cancalon, "L'Inversion de l'amour courtois dans trois comédies de Molière", in *Symposium*, 22, 1972.

H. Gaston Hall, "Molière's *le Misanthrope* in the Light of D'Aubignac's *Conseils d'Artiste a Célimène* and Other Contemporary Texts", in *Kentucky Romance Quarterly*, 19, 1972.

Jean Mesnard, "*Le Misanthrope*: Mise en question de l'art de plaire", in *Revue d'histoire littéraire de la France*, 72, 1972.

Richard Monod, "Un *Misanthrope* sans auto-censure et sans héros", in *Europe*, 523–24, 1972.

Paul G. Zolbrod, "Coriolanus and Alceste: A Study in Misanthropy", in *Shakespeare Quarterly*, 23, 1972.

Betty Rojtman, "Alceste dans le théâtre de Molière", in *Revue d'histoire littéraire de la France*, 73, 1973.

David C. Shaw, "*Le Misanthrope* and Classicism", in *Modern Languages*, 55, 1974.

Margareta Diot, "Alceste", in *Moderne Sprachen*, 69, 1975.

Merte Gerlach-Nielsen, "*Le Misanthrope* et l'anthropologie classique", in *Revue Romane*, 10, 1975.

Richard J. Wayne, "Contradiction in the Sonnet Scene of *Le Misanthrope*", in *L'Esprit créateur*, 15, 1975.

John Simon, "Laughter in the Soul: Molière's *Misanthrope*", in *Hudson Review*, 28, 1975.

Peter H. Nurse, "Comedy and Morality in *Le Misanthrope*", in *Modern Languages*, 58, 1977.

Larry W. Riggs, "The Optics of Power and the Hazards of Judgement in Molière's *Le Misanthrope*", in *Nottingham French Studies*, vol.18 no.2, 1979.

Elisabeth Fichet-Magnon, "La 'Maladie' d'Alceste, ou le déni de la vision tragique", in *Papers on French Seventeenth Century Litterature*, 13, 1980.

The Misanthrope: Round House, London, 1981

Roger W. Herzel, " 'Much Depends on Acting': The Original Cast of *Le Misanthrope*", in *Publications of the Modern Language Association* [*PMLA*], 95, 1980.

Jack Yashinsky, "Métaphore, language et mouvement dramatique dans *Le Misanthrope*", in *Les Lettres Romanes*, 34, 1980.

Kenneth C. Bennett, "*The Philanthropist* and *The Misanthrope*: A Study in Comic Mimesis", in *Theatre Research International*, in vol.6 no.2, 1981.

Marcel Gutwirth, "Visages d'Alceste", in *Oeuvres & critiques*, vol.6 no.1, 1981.

Rufus K. Marsh, "*Alceste: honnête homme* or *faux honnête homme*", in *Stanford French Review*, vol.5 no.1, 1981.

Albert Gérard, "Coriolan et Alceste: tragique et dérisoire de l'intégrité", in *Revue générale*, 4, 1982.

Lionel Grossman, "Molière's *Misanthrope*: Melancholy and Society in the Age of the Counter-Reformation", in *Theatre Journal*, vol.34 no.3, 1982.

Dorothy F. Jones, "Love and Friendship in *Le Misanthrope*", in *Romance Notes*, vol.23 no.2, 1982.

Simone Desmond, "Le Dénouement du *Misanthrope*: une 'source' méconnue?", in *Licorne*, vol.7, 1983.

Hans Robert Jauss, "The Paradox of the Misanthrope", in *Comparative Literature*, vol.35 no.4, 1983.

David Konstan, "A Dramatic History of Misanthropes", in *Comparative Drama*, vol.17 no.2, 1983.

Donald G. Jackson, "Gestes, déplacements et texte dans trois pièces de Molière", in *Papers on French Seventeenth Century Literature*, vol.11 no.20, 1984.

Madeleine Kernan, "Le Rôle des oppositions dans *Le Misanthrope*", in *Chimères*, vol.17 no.2, 1984.

Janet Morgan, "*Le Misanthrope* and Classical Conceptions of Character Portrayal", in *Modern Language Review*, vol.79 no.2, 1984.

Larry W. Riggs, "Context and Convergence in the Comedy of *Le Misanthrope*", in *Romance Notes*, vol.25 no.1, 1984.

Patricia Francis Cholakian, "The 'Woman Question' in Molière's *Misanthrope*", in *French Review*, vol.58 no.4, 1985.

C.J. Gossip, "The Initial Success of *Le Misanthrope*", in *French Studies*, vol.39 no.2, 1985.

Quentin M. Hope, "Philinte's *Récit* in *Le Misanthrope*", in *Papers on French Seventeenth Century Literature*, vol.12 no.23, 1985.

Patrick Henry, "Paradox in *Le Misanthrope*", in *Philological Quarterly*, vol.65 no.2, 1986.

Krzysztof Choinski, "*Le Misanthrope* de Molière: Une civilisation qui s'interroge sur elle-même", in *Kwartalnik Neofilologiczny*, vol.34 no.2, 1987.

Noel A. Peacock, "Verbal Costume in *Le Misanthrope*", in *Seventeenth Century French Studies*, 9, 1987.

Andreas Mahler, "Soziales Substrat, Komik, Satire, Komödie und ein Beispiel: Molière, *Le Misanthrope*", in *Zeitschrift für französische Sprache und Literatur*, vol.98, no.3, 1988.

Nina Ekstein, "*Le Misanthrope* and *Tartuffe*: Two Critiques of verbal Portraiture", in *Revista di letterature moderne e comparate*, vol.42 no.2, 1989.

Pierre Force, "What is a Man Worth?: Ethics and Economics in Molière and Rousseau", in *Romantic Review*, vol.80 no.1, 1989.

Norman Henfrey, "Towards a View of Molière's *Le Misanthrope*: The Sonnet Scene Reconsidered", in *Cambridge Quarterly*, vol.18 no.2, 1989.

Ingrid Heyndels, "*Le Misanthrope* dans l'intertexte philosophique de son temps", in *Papers on French Seventeenth Century Literature*, vol.16 no.30, 1989.

*   *   *

Alceste, the misanthrope of the title, opens the play by arguing with his friend Philinte about the need for complete sincerity in social intercourse. Alceste's insistence on total frankness is quickly put to the test, when he finds it difficult to criticise a sonnet read to him by its author Oronte, one of several rivals for the hand of Célimène, the young and eligible widow in whose upstairs salon the action takes place. Several of her admirers arrive in Act II, and they and she indulge in a waspish destruction of absent nonentities which effectively prevents Alceste from having the tête-à-tête with his hostess which he craves. Arsinoé, an ageing prude, arrives to demolish Célimène's reputation, but the project misfires and she is left to console herself with Alceste, to whom she promises proof of Célimène's "infidelity". The letter to a rival lover which Arsinoé passes to Alceste fails to embarrass its author Célimène, who refuses in Act V to choose between Alceste and Oronte as the object of her affections. Two marquis from among her circle of friends then produce documents in which Célimène has attacked not unseen acquaintances but the very men who have been courting her favours on stage. Alceste offers to marry her but on condition that she withdraw with him into the country near Paris, a proposal which she laughingly rejects. He, in turn is refused by her down-to-earth cousin Eliante (who will now marry Philinte) and storms off in high dudgeon.

This, the most intellectual of Molière's works, is a *grande comédie* of five acts in verse, written in the aftermath of the banning of both the first version of *Tartuffe* and of *Dom Juan*. Unlike those two controversial plays, it avoids the theme of religious belief and concentrates on the attitudes of men and women in society, specifically the behaviour of a closed set of aristocratic, salon habitués in the Paris of the young Louis XIV. The eight main characters—five male and three female—are supplemented by a host of named but absent colleagues, a device which serves to extend the range and force of Molière's satirical attack.

At the centre of this microcosm of high society is Célimène, enjoying at the age of 20 the freedom of manoeuvre conferred by premature widowhood. Conscious of her physical attractiveness, she plays the market, flirting with all and sundry but committing herself to no-one. Of her male admirers none is satisfied by this behaviour. The foppish marquises, Acaste and Clitandre, boasting of their Court connections, are as insecure as the precious poet, Oronte, whose self-indulgent reading of a hackneyed (but not disastrous) sonnet is the start of a long vendetta against its unwilling detractor, Alceste. Even allowing for the exaggeration of the defamation scene in Act II, it is clear that Molière is creating a social context of feckless hangers-on, men who fill their days with meaningless ritual and idle chatter. To that extent Alceste may seem to have targets which can justifiably be attacked. In contrast Célimène, given her youth, her position, and her sex, can be seen as a sparkling socialite, attracting male admirers like moths to a light, but enjoying the harmless fun and attention expected by a person of her condition.

Three characters, apart from Alceste, offer a necessary corrective to this scene. Célimène's cousin, Eliante, and Alceste's long-suffering friend, Philinte, provide, in the end, an example of a more conventional morality and of a relationship which will result in a stable, if—one suspects—hardly exciting marriage. The other main contrast with the salon hostess is seen in Arsinoé, a sample of what Célimène might become in middle age, a crabbed shrew of a woman, bitter at being over the hill and vulnerable to attack from all directions. Although she gets her come-uppance in the clawing match with Célimène in the centre of the play, she rebounds to prove its victor duplicitous. But this action is of no consequence, for social mores are seen not to depend on even partial honesty.

These parallels and contrasts of characters and actions are all designed to provide the misanthrope himself with a world in which he can operate. Despite Rousseau's misguided attempt to invest him with heroic, if not tragic, qualities, Alceste is the main butt for Molière's comedy. All attempts to see him as the virtuous underdog to be sided with have to be resisted strenuously. Of course, like many of the author's protagonists, he has elements in his character to be approved, even admired. Every comic character must have points of contact with reality, a norm against which his deviance can be judged. Sincerity is a good thing; absolute frankness is a social impossibility. One of the dramatic functions of Philinte is to act as *agent provocateur*, siding, for example, with Oronte in order to force Alceste into adopting ever more extreme positions. It is this exaggeration of attitude which is perhaps the main element of comedy. Allied to it is the disparity between the minor misdemeanours of society and the major attacks launched on them by a man who, in himself, displays the greatest of contradictions—a seeming abhorrence of social conventions linked to a patent inability to tear himself away from a salon setting which, by definition, thrives on insincerity. The egoistic self-righteousness and self-pity of Alceste, his anguished cries, his melodramatic entrances and exits, his rejection not of individuals but of all society, bear none of the hallmarks of true tragedy, despite some past critics' attempts to turn him into a man doomed to an unjust fate. Like the best comic heroes and heroines, Alceste brings his own discomfiture on himself. But like them too, he will not succumb. The angry retreat to a "desert" is not definitive: like Célimène after her momentary setback in Act V he will return to the salon on whose admiration he depends for his very survival. *The Misanthrope* is one of the greatest French comedies because of its skilful interlocking of numerous contrasting elements. Alceste has a point; he is admired, at least at times, by three woman as different as Célimène, Eliante, and Arsinoé; he has moments of lucidity; Philinte remains a staunch friend through thick and thin. But it is precisely these and other acceptable features which serve to bring into focus all the incongruities of language and behaviour which set him apart from the social milieu of the play. Alceste is, at heart, a loner, an outsider, a category simply not understood by 17th-century France. It is to Molière's eternal credit that he could turn what might have been a serious social issue for 1666—the perils of nonconformity—into the witty, complex comedy we can still enjoy over 300 years later.

—Christopher Gossip

THE MISER (L'Avare)
by Molière

First Publication: Paris, 1669.
First Production: Théâtre du Palais-Royal, 9 September 1668.

Editions
L'Avare, edited by Ronald A. Wilson, London, 1949.
L'Avare, edited by P.J. Yarrow, London, 1959.
The Miser [with translation], edited by H. van Laun, New
   York, 1969.
L'Avare, edited by F. Angué, Paris, 1979.
L'Avare, edited by Jacques Morel, Paris, 1986.

Translations
The Miser, adapted by Miles Malleson, London, 1950.
The Miser, in *Molière: Five Plays*, translated by John Wood,
   Harmondsworth, 1953.
The Miser, in *Molière: Six Prose Comedies*, translated by
   George Graveley, Oxford, 1956.
The Miser, translated by Wallace Fowlie, Great Neck, New
   York, 1964.
The Miser, in *"The Misanthrope" and Other Plays*, translated
   by Donald Frame, New York, 1968.
The Miser, translated by Alan Drury, in *Molière: Five Plays*,
   London, 1982.

Criticism
(For general works on the author, see *Playwrights* volume)

Books:
Sylvie and Jacques Dauvin, *"L'Avare" de Molière: Analyse
   critique*, Paris, 1979.
G.J. Mallinson, *Molière: "L'Avare"*, London, 1988.

Articles:
Judd D. Hubert, "Theme and Structure in *L'Avare*", in
   Publications of the Modern Language Association [*PMLA*],
   75, 1960.
M. Gutwirth, "Unity of Molière's *L'Avare*", in *Publications of
   the Modern Language Association* [*PMLA*], 76, 1961.
Hallam Walker, "Action and Ending of *L'Avare*", in *French
   Review*, 34, 1961.
J. Doolittle, "Bad Writing in *L'Avare*", in *L'Esprit créateur*, 6,
   1966.
William O. Goode, "The Comic Recognition Scenes in
   L'Avare", in *Romance Notes*, 14, 1972.
David J. Wells, "The Structure of Laughter in Molière's
   L'Avare", in *South Central Bulletin*, 32, 1972.
R.R. Dutton, "A Problem Play: Molière's *L'Avare*", in
   French Monographs, vol.2 no.7, 1975.
A.U. Iwara, "Molière's *L'Avare*", in *Le Français au Nigeria*,
   vol.1 no.1, 1979.
B. Zilly, "*L'Avare*: Die Struktur der Konflicte—zur Kritik der
   Bürgerlichen Gesellschaft im 17ten Jahrhundert", in
   Romanistik, 14, 1979.
Jesse Dickson, "*L'Avare*: Le rire et le jeu de l'inconsé-
   quence", in *French Forum*, 5, 1980.
Ralph Albanese, "Argent et réification dans *L'Avare*", in
   L'Esprit créateur, vol.21 no.3, 1981.
Barbara W. Alsip, "*L'Avare*: History of Scholarship", in
   Oeuvres & critiques, vol.6 no.1, 1981.
D.L. Drysdall, "*L'Avare* and 'disconvenance'", in *New
   Zealand Journal of French Studies*, vol.2 no.1, 1981.
David Shaw, "Harpagon's Monologue", in *Nottingham
   French Studies*, vol.23 no.1, 1984.

The Miser: Engraved frontispiece, 1682

N.A Peacock, "The First Two Scenes of *L'Avare*: The
   Aesthetic of Illusion", in *Quinquereme*, 8, 1985.
J. Pineau, "Harpagon ou la terre aride", in *Revue d'histoire du
   Théâtre*, vol.38 no.4, 1986.
G.J. Mallinson, "Planchon's *L'Avare* and the Expectations of
   Comedy", in *French Studies Bulletin*, 23, 1987.
Jean-Marie Apostolidès, "Molière and the Sociology of
   Exchange", in *Critical Inquiry*, vol.14 no.3, 1988.
Dorothy F. Jones, "The Treasure in the Garden: Biblical
   Imagery in *L'Avare*", in *Papers on French Seventeenth
   Century Literature*, vol.15 no.29, 1988.
Gérard R. Montbertrand, "Territoire et société dans *L'Avare*
   et *Tartuffe* de Molière", in *French Literature Series*, 15,
   1988.

*   *   *

The play is set in contemporary Paris, in the house of a rich
and autocratic miser, Harpagon. His two children, Elise and
Cléante, are completely in his power, since he holds the purse-
strings. Elise can see her suitor, Valère, only because he lives
in the house disguised as a steward. Cléante has to keep his
love for Mariane a secret from his father. Harpagon strikes
panic when he announces his decision that his children are to

marry old, rich suitors. To Cléante's horror, he announces that he himself plans to marry Mariane. Harpagon proceeds with his marriage-plans, arranging his own match with the help of Frosine, an eccentric marriage-broker, and organizing a grand, but ludicrously inexpensive, dinner for his prospective bride. Meanwhile, Cléante and Elise are desperately trying to think of a solution. Cléante tries to borrow money, but when he is confronted with the prospective money-lender it turns out to be his own father. The time comes for Mariane's visit. She is horrified to realize that the young man she loves is the son of the old man she is being forced, for financial reasons, to marry. Harpagon begins to suspect the truth about Cléante and Mariane. He tricks Cléante into revealing his love, and father and son swear undying enmity. All seems lost, but meanwhile Cléante's servant has stolen a chest full of money which Harpagon had buried in the garden. Harpagon is told that Elise's suitor, Valère, is the thief; but Cléante appears, confesses to the theft, and demands the hand of Mariane in return for the money. However, his stratagem has been unnecesary, since both the children's lovers have discovered that they are brother and sister, and that their father, Dom Thomas d'Alburcy, is alive and wealthy. He will pay for the dowries, and the young people are free to marry. Harpagon does not really mind—he rejoices in the return of his beloved treasure-chest.

The plot is not original—it is loosely based on Plautus's *Aulularia*, and the conflict between young love and aged obsession is, in any case, a common element in Molière's comedies. The originality and interest of the play lie in the portrayal of the miser. Originally played by Molière himself, Harpagon is perhaps the most extravagant of all his eccentrics. He indulges in wild excesses of avarice: he steals his own horses' oats during the night; he tells his servant: "don't dust the furniture too hard, for fear of wearing it out"; he tries to lend money at over 25-per-cent interest, forcing the borrower to accept old junk, including a lute with missing strings and a stuffed lizard, instead of cash. But the miser is not a recluse. Molière shows him in a family and a social context, and much of the play is a demonstration of how his obsession has warped him. He is convinced that his household and even his children are trying to steal his money and he is constantly rushing out to the garden to make sure that his buried treasure is safe. He cares not a jot for his children's happiness. When Elise objects to being made to marry an old man whom she cannot love, he replies simply, "no dowry": if he can marry her off without providing her with money, the fact that her suitor is unacceptable is irrelevant. As Valère puts it, "*no dowry* replaces beauty, youth, good birth, honour, wisdom and decency". And yet, Harpagon is not without affection. He is attracted to Mariane, which gives Molière scope for a new kind of comic effect. Harpagon has so far lost touch with reality that he naïvely believes the marriage-broker's assertion that Mariane prefers old men with spectacles; so he comes bespectacled to their first meeting. But his feelings for Mariane are nothing to his love for his treasure-chest. When it is stolen, he describes his loss in terms that would be better suited to the death of a mistress: "Alas! My poor money, my poor money, my dear friend! They have taken you away from me. . .I have lost my support, my consolation, my joy; everything is over for me, there is nothing more for me in the world: without you, life is impossible". In this famous soliloquy, Harpagon in the extremity of his emotion breaks through the barrier dividing the actors from the audience, and addresses them directly: "What a great gathering! Everyone I look at makes me suspicious, and everyone seems like the thief. Hey! What are you talking about, over there? About the man who stole from me? What's that noise up there? Is my thief there?. . .Isn't he

hidden over there amongst you? They are all looking at me, and they're starting to laugh".

The central figure of Harpagon is surrounded by other characters who have their own comic eccentricities—the cook-cum-coachman Maître Jacques, who swops hats whenever he changes from one of his duties to the other, or the wildly inventive marriage-broker Frosine, who "could marry the Grand Turk to the Republic of Venice" if she felt like it. And the four young people, with their straightforward needs and affections, present a sane approach to the world which contrasts sharply with Harpagon's mad one.

The whole play can be viewed as a study of the theme of avarice: what it does to human nature, how it destroys the happiness both of the miser and of his dependents. Most of the characters are obliged to be preoccupied with avarice and its effects. There is even a generous, open-handed character, Dom Thomas d'Alburcy, father to Mariane and Valère, brought in at the end to provide a salutary contrast. The miser's son, Cléante, is a spendthrift, forced to borrow at exorbitant rates to maintain a moderately decent lifestyle. Others, like Valère or Frosine, humour the miser, while Elise tries unsuccessfully to oppose him. This one man's obsession weighs heavily on all the characters in the play, leaving one the end feeling that this light-hearted farcical comedy has serious implications.

—Maya Slater

THE MISFORTUNE OF BEING CLEVER (Gore ot Uma)
by Alexander Griboyedov

First Publication: 1825 (partial version); in censored edition, 1833; complete, 1875.
First Production: St. Petersburg Theatre, May 1825 (subsequently banned); censored version, St. Petersburg, 16 January 1831; complete, Kiev Theatre, Kiev, 26 February 1831.

Editions
Gore ot Uma, edited by D.P. Costello, Oxford, 1951.

Translations
Intelligence Comes to Grief, in *Anthology of Russian Literature, 2*, edited by Leo Wiener, New York, 1902.
The Misfortune of Being Clever, translated by S. Ping, London, 1914.
The Misfortune of Being Clever, translated by B. Pares, London, 1925.
The Misfortune of Being Clever, translated by F.D. Reeve, in *Anthology of Russian Plays, 1*, New York, 1961.
Chatsky, in *Four Russian Plays*, translated by Joshua Cooper, Harmondsworth, 1972.

Criticism
(For general works on the author, see *Playwrights* volume)

Books:
Witold Kosny, "*A.S. Griboyedov: Poet and Minister: Die Zeitgenössische Rezeption seiner Komödie "Gore ot Umja" (1824-1832)*", Wiesbaden, 1985.

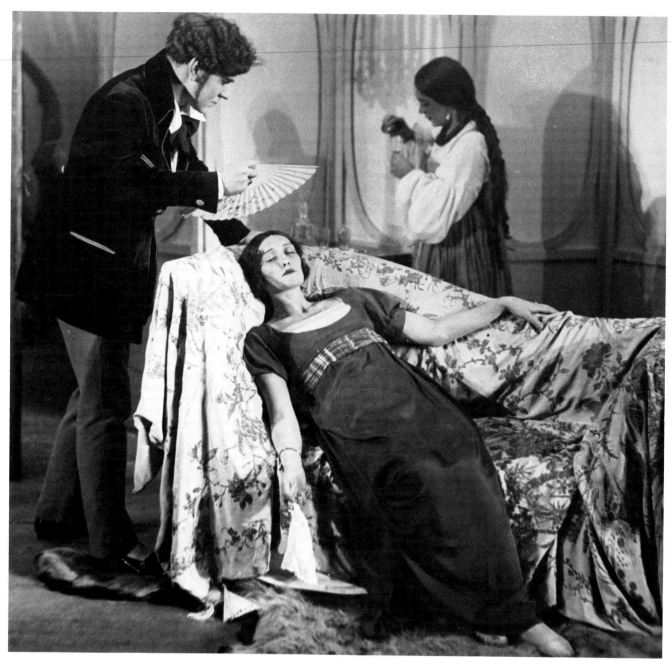

The Misfortune of Being Clever: Moscow State Theatre, 1935

Articles:

Marjorie L. Hoover, "Classic Meyerhold: *Woe to Wit* by Griboyedov", in *Russian Literature Triquarterly*, 7, 1973.

D.J. Richards, "Two Malicious Tongues: The Wit of Chatsky and Pechorin", in *New Zealand Slavonic Journal*, 11, 1973.

Gerald Janecek, "A Defense of Sof'ja in *Woe from Wit*", in *Slavic and East European Journal*, 21, 1977.

Mieczyslaw Giergielewicz, "Structural Footnotes to Griboyedov's *Woe from Wit*", in *Polish Review*, vol. 24 no. 1, 1979.

Edmund Little, "Vyazemsky, Griboyedov and *Gore ot Uma (Woe from Wit)*: A Question of Heresy", in *New Zealand Slavonic Journal*, 1984.

Witold Kosny, "A.S. Griboyedovs *Gore ot Uma*: Der Text und seine Bedeutung in der ursprünglichen Kommunikationssituation", in *Russian, Croation and Serbian, Czech and Slovak, Polish Literature* (Amsterdam), vol. 23 no. 3, 1988.

Jean Bonamour, "De Cackij à Hlestakov: Les Metamorphoses de l'esprit dans *Gore ot Uma* de Griboyedov", in *Cahiers due monde russe et soviétique*, vol. 30 nos.3-4, 1989.

Vladimir Troubetzkoy, "Griboyedov and Molière", in *Littératures*, 21, 1989.

*   *   *

Woe from Wit is the classic comedy of the Russian stage, one of the great works of Russian literature. Its hero, Chatsky, is the first and most directly political of the "superfluous men" in Russian literature of the 19th century — those heroes who, for one reason or another, are outsiders in the society of their time. The action of the play, written around 1824 by a Russian diplomat, Alexander Griboyedov, takes place on the eve of the Decembrist uprising of 1825. Russian society of the time was inundated with foreign, especially French, influences as a result of coming onto the European scene in the 18th century as a major power and, more recently, having rebuffed Napoleon's invasion. But while society went overboard for every latest European fashion, politically Russia remained a medieval autocratic state meeting the cost of keeping up with the rest of Europe by ever worsening exploitation of the serfs who made up the bulk of the population. Russia wanted the outward show of civilization but none of the enlightenment which went with it. Educated Russians of the nobility hoped the Czar would yield to reforms on constitutional lines; but even the mildest political views could only be voiced in secret societies such as started the Decembrist uprising, the failure of which ushered in an age of bleak reaction. The play portrays Moscow high society riddled with intrigue and obsessed by rank and station, where officialdom rules all, and the officer corps, so lately heroic in the Napoleonic campaign, is turning into the same repressive stagnant force as the bureaucracy.

Chatsky returns to Moscow from abroad expecting to take up again with his childhood sweetheart, Sophie, but finds that her father, Famusov, a top official, intends her to marry Skalozub, a colonel more victorious in the salon than on the field. Sophie, aided by her pert maid, Liza, is carrying on an amour with Molchalin, Famusov's poor secretary on the make, who really fancies Liza. In shock, Chatsky takes out his frustration on everyone in turn in a series of brilliant tirades. The climax comes in Act III when, at a crowded ball, Sophie spreads a rumour that Chatsky is mad, whereupon Chatsky flees Moscow and is instantly forgotten.

The play was not properly staged until 1831, after the author's untimely murder in an insurrection in Teheran, and was first treated as a comedy with a touch of burlesque in the style of the 18th century. Despite clear resemblances to Molière and Beaumarchais it is no imitative work but an original, wholly Russian creation, a striking feature of which is its rich portrayal of the social upper crust, unique in Russian literature. Not only are its members deftly caught in telling mannerisms and frozen for all time in aphorisms which have entered the language; they also give good account of themselves: beneath their vanities, pretensions, obscurantist ideas, and slavish conformity one senses the strength of the system of which they are at once the perpetuators, products, and prisoners. This was often overlooked by critics seeing the play solely in terms of Chatsky. In his magisterial 1872 study of the play, Goncharov declares: "Famusov, Molchalin, Skalozub and the others have imprinted themselves in the memory like the kings, knaves, queens of cards and everyone has formed a more or less agreed conception of all the characters with the exception of one — Chatsky . . . about Chatsky on the contrary, difference of opinion has not ceased yet and maybe will not end for a long time". These proved prophetic words as topicality faded and the play was seen in longer perspective. Chatsky is the problem character and playing him became for Russian actors like playing Hamlet in the English-speaking world. It is said that, artistically, he is a Romantic figure in a realistic setting; but the tradition of interpretation has gone through marked changes, seeing him as a tragic hero in the Byronic mould linked with Onegin (if more direct and less world-weary), or a mouthpiece of political protest. After first consigning Chatsky to the outworn category of "superfluous man" Soviet criticism rehabilitated him in the light of reappraisal of the Decembrist uprising as a forerunner of the October Revolution. In the strident black-and-white treat-

ment of the play typified by Nechkina's *Griboyedov and the Decembrists* of 1947 he towers above the other characters as leader of the "progressive camp" with history on its side. Sophie's role, too, was revised to show she still really loves Chatsky, despite the lack of evidence in the play and Griboyedov's own remark that the theme is "how a girl who is herself not stupid prefers an idiot to an intelligent man". However, not all Soviet critics have taken this simplistic approach and, since the first production of the play, criticism has been split over whether Chatsky is a political martyr or social misfit. The root cause of the problem lies in the art form, the play, which, if it be any play at all, gives if not equal rights, certainly equal life to all the characters, not just the hero — who consequently comes over in human, not symbolic terms. The first to cast doubt on the heroic stature of Chatsky was in fact Pushkin: "Everything Chatsky says is very clever, but who does he say it to? Famusov, Skalozub, Moscow ladies at the ball, Molchalin. That is unforgiveable". Nemirovich-Danchenko, producing the play at the turn of the century, declared that failure with the part of Chatsky stemmed from overloading him as a social combatant: "A young man in love is all the actor's inspiration should seek to portray and anything else is down to the devil".

There is another reason for the unique place the play holds in Russian culture. It is a masterpiece of tightly-written, succinct, and vividly expressive colloquial Russian. Griboyedov called it not a play but a "scenic poem" and its peculiar magic stems from the fact that although shot through with contemporary ideas and topical allusions, its world is encapsulated in verse and rendered into a single abstracted experience, much the way the music of an opera transcends the sometimes banal lyric. Pushkin remarked that half the play would become phrases in the language and he has been proved right. Thus the unrepeatable artistry of the play, together with the universal human situation beneath the trappings of the time in which it was written, have assured the play a lasting place in the forefront of Russian culture.

—Alan G. Waring

MISS JULIE (Fröken Julie)
by August Strindberg

First Publication: Stockholm, 1888.
First Production: Studentersamfundet [Copenhagen University Students Association], Copenhagen, 14 March 1889.

Editions
Fröken Julie, in *Fadren; Fröken Julie; Fardringsägere*, edited by Gunnar Ollén, Stockholm, 1984.
Fröken Julie, in *Fröken Julie; Mäster Olof; Fadren; Ett Drömspel*, Stockholm, 1979.

Translations
Countess Julia, translated by C. Recht, Philadelphia, 1912.
Miss Julia, in *Strindberg: Plays, 2*, translated by Edwin Björkman, New York, c.1913.
Lady Julie, in *"Lucky Peter's Travels" and Other Plays*, translated by E. Classen, C.D. Locock, Elizabeth Sprigge, and Claude Napier, London, 1931.

Miss Julie, in *Six Plays of Strindberg*, translated by Elizabeth Sprigge, Garden City, New York, 1955.

Miss Julia, in *Three Plays by August Strindberg*, translated by Peter Watts, Harmondsworth, 1958.

Miss Julie, in *"Miss Julie" and Other Plays*, translated by Max Faber, London, 1960.

Miss Julie, in *Seven Plays by August Strindberg*, translated by Arvid Paulsen, New York, 1960.

Miss Julie, in *Strindberg: Plays, 1*, translated by Michael Meyer, London, 1964; revised version, in *The Father; Miss Julie; The Ghost Sonata*, London, 1976.

Miss Julie, in *Strindberg: Five Plays*, translated by Harry G. Carlson, Berkeley, California, and London, 1983.

Criticism

(For general works on the author, see *Playwrights* volume)

Books:

Carl O. Gierow, *Documentation—évocation: Le Climat littéraire et théâtral en France des années 1880 et "Mademoiselle Julie" de Strindberg*, Stockholm. 1967.

Ulla B. Lagerroth and Göran Lindstoröm (eds), *Perspektiv på "Fröken Julie": Dokument och studier*, Stockholm. 1972.

Sven G. Edqvist and Katarina Ehnmark, *August Strindberg, "Fröken Julie":Introduktion, materialsammanställning, studieuppgifter, improvisationsövningar och förslag till instudering av centrala scener*, Stockholm, 1976.

Egil Törnqvist and Barry Jacobs, *Strindberg's "Miss Julie": A Play and Its Transpositions*, Norwich, 1988.

Articles:

C. Dahlström, "Strindberg's 'naturalistika Sorgespel' and Zola's Naturalism, 1: *Fröken Julie*: Introduction", in *Scandinavian Studies*, 17, 1943.

C. Dahlström, "Strindberg's 'naturalistika Sorgespel' and Zola's Naturalism, 2: *Fröken Julie*: Subject Matter and Sources", in *Scandinavian Studies*, 18, 1944.

C. Dahlström, "Strindberg's 'naturalistika Sorgespel' and Zola's Naturalism, 3: *Fröken Julie*, in *Scandinavian Studies*, 18, 1944.

C. Dahlström, "Strindberg's 'naturalistika Sorgespel' and Zola's Naturalism, 4: *Fröken Julie*: Situation and Plot", in *Scandinavian Studies*, 18, 1944.

C. Dahlström, "Strindberg's 'naturalistika Sorgespel' and Zola's Naturalism, 5: *Fröken Julie*: Theme, Language, Setting", in *Scandinavian Studies*, 18, 1944.

C. Dahlström, "Strindberg's 'naturalistika Sorgespel' and Zola's Naturalism, 6: *Fröken Julie*, Conclusion", in *Scandinavian Studies*, 18, 1944.

E. Ottenbacher, "A Contribution to the Origin of Strindberg's *Miss Julie*", in *Psychoanalytic Review*, vol.31 no.1, 1944.

V. Young, "The History of *Miss Julie*", in *Hudson Review*, vol.8 no.1, 1955.

Egil Törnqvist, "*Fröken Julie* och O'Neill", in *Meddelanden fran Strindbergssällskapet*, 42, 1969.

A. Cleveland Harrison, "*Miss Julie*: Essence and Anomaly of Naturalism", in *Central States Speech Journal*, 21, 1970.

Harry Bergholz, "*Miss Julia*: Strindberg's Response to J.P. Jacobsen's *Fru Marie Grubbe*", in *Scandinavica*, 11, 1972.

Stephen G. Hayes and Jules Zentner, "Strindberg's *Miss Julie*: Lilacs and Beer", in *Scandinavian Studies*, 45, 1973.

Ira Hauptmann, "Strindberg's Naturalistic Plays", in *Yale / Theater*, 3, 1974.

Margareta Mattsson, "Strindberg's *Miss Julie* in English: The Value of Literalness in Translation", in *Scandinavica*, 13, 1974.

Friedrich Dieckmann, "Diskurs über *Fräulein Julie*", in *Sinn und Form*, 27, 1975.

Harry Järv, "Den 'karaktärlösa fröken Julie'", in *Svensk Tidskrfit*, 1951; translated as "Strindberg's 'characterless Miss Julie'", in *Gradiva*, 1, 1977.

Detlef Brennecke, "Strindbergs *Fröken Julie*: Ein *plaidoyer d'un fou*", in *Skandinavistik*, 8, 1978.

Philip Dodd, "Fairy Tales, the Unconscious & Strindberg's *Miss Julie*", in *Literature and Psychology*, 28, 1978.

Manfred Karnick, "Fräulein Julie als Motivpartitur: zur musikalischen Komposition in Strindbergs 'naturalistichem Trauerspiel'", in *Poetica*, 10, 1978.

Egil Törnqvist, "Der Schluss in *Fröken Julie*", in *Skandinavistik*, 10, 1980.

Edmund A. Napieralski, "*Miss Julie*: Strindberg's Tragic Fairy Tale", in *Modern Drama*, 26, 1983.

H. Wijsbek, "Lamm och Sprinchorn om *Fröken Julie*: en argumentationsanalys", in *Tijdschrift voor Skandinavistiek*, vol.6 no.1, 1985.

John L. Greenway, "Strindberg and Suggestion in *Miss Julie*", in *South Atlantic Review*, vol.51 no.2, 1986.

Jill Timbers, "Interpreting Interpretations: *Fröken Julie*", in *Translation Review*, 21–22, 1986.

John E. Bellquist, "Rereading *Fröken Julie*: Undercurrents in Strindberg's Naturalistic Intent", in *Scandinavian Studies*, 60, 1988.

Hans G. Ekman, "Klädernas magi i *Fröken Julie*", in *Strindbergiana*, 4, 1989.

Egil Törnqvist, "Slutet i *Fröken Julie*", in *Strindbergiana*, 4, 1989.

Alice Templeton, "*Miss Julie* as 'a Naturalistic Tragedy'", in *Theatre Journal*, 42, 1990.

*   *   *

The action of *Miss Julie* takes place on Midsummer Night's Eve when Miss Julie ventures down into the castle kitchen and encounters Jean, her father's valet, and the cook Kristin, Jean's fiancée. Outside in the barn the traditional midsummer dance is in progress and Julie invites Jean to dance with her. Jean, believing or pretending to believe that she is fair game, resorts to increasingly more skilful techniques in his attempts to seduce her. In order to avoid being caught by the midsummer revellers dancing their way into the kitchen, Jean pulls Julie into his room. Julie's seduction, the first disaster which in turn will lead to another, even greater one, concludes the first, shorter part of the play.

The second part of the play is much longer. Now the extent of Jean's opportunism is rapidly revealed to us as well as to Julie. Trying to find a solution to the situation in which she has landed herself she fantasizes about eloping with Jean. But the return of the Count, her father, swiftly brings both of them back to reality. Jean reverts to being a servant again and Julie is forced to realize the degree of her degradation. Having killed her bird, Jean has already pointed the way to suicide as a possible way out. Julie leaves for the barn, razor in hand.

The French translation of *The Father* had brought Strindberg into contact with Zola and Naturalism. When, on 10 August 1888, Strindberg sent *Miss Julie* to his publisher he was "taking the liberty of submitting for publication the first naturalistic Swedish drama" and the play bears all the hallmarks of naturalistic thinking. The three unities of time, space, and character are religiously adhered to. Throughout we deal with the three characters of Jean, Julie, and to a lesser extent Kristin. The action never strays from the kitchen and the timespan required for the story to run its course on stage corresponds roughly to what it would have taken in real life.

Miss Julie: Dramaten, Stockholm, 1949

The carefully worked-out intrigue is absent and instead Strindberg offers us a slice of life, a real-life story he had heard, about a lady of noble birth who seduced her father's stable boy. Strindberg turns the stable boy into a valet and instead of the lady serving penance as a waitress at Hasselbacken, a well known restaurant in Stockholm, the eventual fate of the model for Miss Julie, he gives a more tragic ending to the story. Here he was probably influenced by the unhappy circumstances of Victoria Benedictson, the Swedish writer, who had committed suicide after a stormy relationship with the Danish literary critic George Brandes.

But in spite of his commitment to naturalism Strindberg was not altogether free from Ibsenesque symbolism. The killing of Miss Julie's greenfinch serves as a highly effective device to foreshadow her own suicide. If the intention was for the bird to escape it would have been, as was indeed pointed out to Strindberg, much more natural just to let it out of its cage. In addition to Zola, Miss Julie also owes a debt to Darwin's thoughts about the process of natural selection and survival of the fittest. Jean, who is of robust working-class origin, dreams that he is lying underneath a big tree and is longing to climb up until he reaches the top. Julie on the other hand, representing

the refined but decadent upper-classes, has a recurrent dream where she sits on top of a pillar, longing to fall down. However, at the time of writing Miss Julie Strindberg's Darwinism had been dealt a blow by his recently acquired Nietzschean ideology. While identifying with Jean, Strindberg also felt drawn to the aristocratic Julie whose hypersensitive reactions and over-charged emotions resembled his own in many respects.

Strindberg's portrayal of the battle between the classes and the sexes did, however, turn out to be too realistic for its time and at first no theatre dared produce Miss Julie. Desperate to get the play on stage, Strindberg had to resort to founding his own theatre with his wife as artistic director. But in the middle of the dress rehearsal, the police paid a visit, bringing with them the censor's ban—the result of a hate campaign that had been raging in the press against Strindberg since the publication of the play the previous autumn. The play thus received its world premiere on 14 March 1889 at the Students' Association in Copenhagen with Siri von Essen as Julie. But the press was lukewarm and real success eluded Strindberg until 1893 when André Antoine produced the play at his famous Théâtre Libre in Paris; a production which established Strindberg as a dramatist abroad. It was not until 1906 that a Swedish theatre staged *Miss Julie*. Still, the number of successful performances in Sweden (as well as in other countries) that have followed bear witness to the importance of this play, assuring it of a place in the history of modern drama.

—Gunilla Anderman

MISTERIYA-BUFF. See **MYSTERY BOUFFE.**

THE MISTRESS OF THE INN (La locandiera)
by Carlo Goldoni

First Publication: 1753.
First Production: Teatro Sant'Angelo, Venice, January 1753.

Editions

La locandiera, edited by J. Geddes Jr., Boston, New York, and Chicago, 1901.
La locandiera, in *Commedie scelte di Carlo Goldoni*, edited by M. Dazzi, Florence, 1931.
La locandiera, edited by Joseph G. Fucilla and Elton Hocking, New York, 1939.
La locandiera, in *Goldoni: Commedie*, edited by M. Lombardo Lotti, Florence, 1950.
La locandiera, edited by O. Castellino, Turin, 1950.
La locandiera, edited by G.P. Brunetta, Padua, 1967.
La locandiera, edited by Edgardo Maddalena, Florence, 1968.
La locandiera, Milan, 1976.

Translations

The Mistress of the Inn, translated by Merle Pierson, Madison, Wisconsin, 1912.
Mine Hostess, in *Four Comedies*, translated by Clifford Bax, London, 1922.
Mirandolina, adapted by Lady Gregory, London, 1924.
La Locandiera / Mistress of the Inn, translated and adapted by Helen Lohman, New York, 1926/7.
The Mistress of the Inn, translated by A. Intreglia, Pacific, Missouri, 1964.
Mirandolina, in *Four Comedies*, translated by Frederick H. Davies, Harmondsworth, 1968.

Criticism

(For general works on the author, see *Playwrights* volume)

Books:
Cristina Stevanoni (ed.), *Una tradizione neogreca inedita [della] "Locandiera" di Carlo Goldoni*, Padua, 1977.

Articles:
Ulrich Leo, "Goldonis *Locandiera* und Molières *Misanthrope*: Zwei Motiventwicklungen", in *Romanische Forschungen*, 70, 1958.
Ettore Caccia, "Le variati di *La Locandiera*", in *Annali di ca'Foscari*, 3, 1964.
Franco Fido, "Carlo Goldoni: From *La locandiera* to *Il ventaglio*", in *Italian Quarterly*, vol.8 no.29, 1964.
Patrizio Rossi, "Considerazioni sulla *Locandiera* di Carlo Goldoni", in *Studi goldoniani*, 2, 1971.

Kurt Ringger, "La Fonction dramaturgique des comédiennes dans *La locandiera*", in *Forum Italicum*, 10, 1976.
Fulvia Airoldi Namer, "I monologhi della *Locandiera*", in *Sigma*, 13, 1980.
Raffaele Morabito, "Il sistema dei personaggi nella *Locandiera*", in *L'Interpretazione goldoniana: Critica e Messinscena*, edited by Nino Borsellino, Rome, 1982.

* * *

The setting of *The Mistress of the Inn* (*La locandiera*) is a modest inn in Florence. Mirandolina, still young, attractive, and unmarried, but on her own admission now past her best, has inherited the inn from her recently deceased father and runs it with the aid of a head-servant, Fabrizio. It had been her father's wish that she should secure her reputation and respectability by marrying Fabrizio, but Mirandolina's main preoccupation is the inn, symbol of her social and economic freedom, and she employs all her charm and skill on her guests to ensure its prosperity. Two aristocrats at the inn, the impoverished Marquis of Forlimpopoli and the *nouveau riche* Count of Albafiorita, pursue her, each keen to make her his mistress. The Marquis and the Count are in perpetual warfare, the Count giving Mirandolina expensive presents, to the chagrin of the Marquis who can afford only trivial gifts. The Marquis, superior in social status to the Count, asserts the importance of rank over money and offers Mirandolina his social protection, while the Count is sceptical of the value of rank when not buttressed by money. Mirandolina manoeuvres diplomatically between them. A third aristocrat at the inn, the Baron of Ripafratta, is as impervious to Mirandolina's charms as he is to those of two actresses staying at the inn. An implacable misogynist, he despises his fellow nobles for their susceptibility to female wiles: for him Mirandolina's charm is mere hypocrisy, a way of serving her own interests. Stung by the Baron's indifference and his contempt for all womankind, Mirandolina determines to conquer him. Her stratagems of indirect flattery, mock diffidence, and apparently innocent coquettishness succeed only too well. The Baron veers from disdain to devotion, from indifference to lust, and Mirandolina can escape only by forcing him into a humiliating public denial of his feelings, and by announcing to all her intention to marry Fabrizio. The defeated Baron departs in anger, even more deeply convinced of the rightness of his misogynism, while the Marquis and Count amiably accommodate themselves to the new situation. Mirandolina herself, shaken by the unexpectedly violent outcome of what she intended to be only a joke, swears that with marriage she will reform and put off female tricks.

The plot of *La Locandiera* is of the simplest kind although Goldoni adds a number of twists. The comic action turns on Mirandolina's attempts to overcome the Baron's mysogynism. On one level the play can be seen as a series of encounters between the embodiment of female seductiveness (Mirandolina) and the epitome of masculine self-sufficiency (the Baron); in the worsting of the Baron the excesses of arrogant and unmotivated disdain and of sexual incivility are appropriately chastised, and the Baron's embittered retreat from womankind has about it the pique of the defeated, an obstinate refusal to confront and accept his own susceptibility. Such an interpretation was particularly favoured by 19th- and early 20th-century critics and performers, who emphasised the beguiling charm and delightful cunning with which Mirandolina confounded the ridiculous obtuseness of the woman-hating Baron. But although this view is persuasive, it is a decidedly partial reading of the play, and it ignores Goldoni's own stated purpose. According to the preface he wrote for the

The Mistress of the Inn: Eleanora Duse as Mirandolina

published text, a governing aim was to expose, through the behaviour of Mirandolina, the irresponsibility of certain kinds of female conduct: to demonstrate that the very flirtatiousness that makes some women attractive, and by which they seek to charm, can be dangerously misdirected to the confusion and discomfiture of others and themselves. It is true that the tone of this preface is ironic, even flippant; but what does seem clear is that Goldoni's view of Mirandolina is less than approving, and the Baron is presented in a light less than wholly alien. In fact, neither Mirandolina nor any other character is a touchstone for correct conduct. Culpability is divided, and the intricate pattern of relationships developed in the play is rich in nuance and ambiguity.

The comedy is essentially a sex contest, but that contest is clearly also a social one. Mirandolina is a woman seeking to preserve her freedom in a male-oriented world. The fact that she is the mistress of the inn is what gives her some social and economic status and ensures her personal freedom. The Baron's arrogant and dismissive treatment of her, his tendency to regard her as a mere servant, is not simply an affront to her sex; it undermines her self-respect and social dignity and calls her freedom into question; not least because that freedom is precariously based. She may be courted by the Marquis and Count, but marriage is not their intention; for all the admiration and easy familiarity, social boundaries remain absolute. Once bewitched by Mirandolina, the Baron demands her affection almost as a social right, and is ready to apply threats and violence to obtain it. A conventional ending to the play would have had Mirandolina and the Baron joined in marriage, the class impediment overcome by a *deus ex machina* "discovery", as in *La putta onorata* or *Pamela*, that Mirandolina was really of noble birth. Here, the expectations of all the aristocrats are confounded. The resolution is effected not by romantic convention, but by Mirandolina making a realistic choice. In opting for the servant Fabrizio she both asserts and secures her social and economic freedom.

—Laura Richards

THE MISUNDERSTANDING.   See **CROSS PURPOSE.**

MONEY
by Edward Bulwer-Lytton

First Publication: London, 1840.
First Production: Haymarket Theatre, London, 8 December 1840.

Editions

Money, in *Nineteenth Century Plays*, edited by George Rowell, Oxford, 1953; second edition, 1972.
Money, in *English Plays of the Nineteenth Century, 3: Comedies*, edited by Michael R. Booth, Oxford, 1973.

*   *   *

First performed at London's Haymarket Theatre on 8 December 1840, Edward Bulwer-Lytton's comedy was an immediate popular success (80 performances in its first season) and remained a staple of the 19th-century repertory in London and the provinces. It also received many productions throughout Canada and the United States.

Set in London in 1840, *Money* contrasts the high principles and moral values of Alfred Evelyn, secretary to Sir John Vesey, with those of Vesey himself and his relatives and associates. With only one or two exceptions—including his cousin Clara Douglas, with whom Evelyn is in love—Evelyn is confronted by greed, self-indulgence, and hypocrisy. Ignored until he inherits a large fortune unexpectedly, Evelyn is quickly surrounded by suppliants, strengthening his Swiftian view of humanity: "When I was poor I hated the world; now I am rich I despise it! Fools—knaves—hypocrites!". Misunderstanding Clara's rejection of him when he was still poor—she loves him, but does not want her own poverty to encumber him—he withholds further declarations of his love because he believes his wealth will now unduly influence her judgement. Falsely under the impression that Vesey's daughter Georgina has been responsible for a generous act of charity (it was actually Clara), Evelyn proposes marriage to her.

By Act III Evelyn has become implacably morose—both about the state of humanity in general and his impending marriage to a woman he does not love—and increasingly extravagant with his fortune, including frequent bouts of gambling. When he learns, however, that Georgina and her father may be in rank pursuit of his money he devises a complicated scheme to convince them that his extravagance and gambling have cost him his fortune, at which point, and after a series of comic interludes and twists of plot, Georgina renounces her engagement in favour of another suitor, (whose fortune, while smaller than Evelyn's, is less in doubt), leaving Evelyn free to marry Clara.

Money has been the object of some excessive praise. Michael Booth has quite rightly recognized its distinction as a transitional and influential play in the development of Victorian comedy. The coalescence of themes such as class antagonism with conventional, sentimental patterns of behaviour helped shape the comedies of Tom Taylor and T.W. Robertson, for example. In this regard *Money* might well be judged, as Booth suggests, "probably the most important comedy of the nineteenth century". But that it is also "one of the best," as Booth also suggests, is debatable. The play is heavily handicapped by the failure of its central character, Evelyn. As William Macready, who created the role, noted, it is an "ineffective, inferior part", shackled by sententious and tortuous speeches. In addition, the intricacies of the plot strain credulity, and the "bitter satire on Victorian commercialism" that Ernest Reynolds detects is rendered ineffectual by the constant focus on Evelyn's personal dilemma (Georgina or Clara?) rather than the vices he professes to despise. Evelyn's radicalism consists only of tempering materialism with a modest dose of charity and goodwill. Bulwer-Lytton's failure to take him beyond this keeps Evelyn a tiresome character and *Money* a less interesting play than it might have been.

George Rowell is surely right in ascribing *Money*'s contemporary success to "its novelty rather than to its achievement". Its achievement, such as it is, lies not in its satire (which is languid) or its protagonist (who is enervated and enervating), but rather in some of its minor characters. The foppish Sir Frederick Blount ("I am very fond of travelling. You'd like Wome—bad inns, but vewy fine wuins"), calculating Lady Franklin (half-sister to Vesey), and card-sharp Captain Dudley Smooth maintain our interest when others around them have forfeited it.

First published in 1840, *Money* was reprinted several times in nineteenth-century collected editions of Bulwer-Lytton's works, and has appeared in modern anthologies.

—L.W. Conolly

THE MONEY BOX. See **SCENES FROM THE HEROIC LIFE OF THE MIDDLE CLASSES.**

A MONTH IN THE COUNTRY (Mesyats v Derevne)
by Ivan Turgenev

First Publication: In *Sovremennik* [*The Contemporary*], 1855; in book form, in *Collected Works*, 1869.
First Production: Maly Theatre, Moscow, 13 January 1872.

Editions

A Month in the Country, edited by T.A. Greenan, Letchworth, Hampshire, 1971.

Translations

A Month in the Country, in *The Plays of I.S. Turgenev*, translated by M.S. Mandell, New York, 1924.
A Month in the Country, translated by G.R. Noyes, in *Masterpieces of the Russian Drama*, edited by G.R. Noyes, New York, 1933.
A Month in the Country, in *Turgenev: Three Plays*, translated by C. Garnett, London, 1934.
A Month in the Country, adapted by Emlyn Williams, London, 1943.

A Month in the Country, in *An Anthology of Russian Drama, 1*, translated by F.D. Reeve, New York, 1963.
A Month in the Country, translated by Ariadne Nicolaeff, London, 1976.
A Month in the Country, translated by Isaiah Berlin, London, 1981.

Criticism
(For general works on the author, see *Playwrights* volume)

Articles:
N. Fagin, "Turgenev's Dramatic Masterpiece", in *Hopkins Review*, vol.3 no.1, 1949.
D. Garnett, "Turgenev, Madame Viardot and *A Month in the Country*", in *Adelphi*, vol.27 no.4, 1951.
Yael Harussi, "Realism in Drama: Turgenev, Chekhov, Gorky and Their Summer Folk", in *Ulbandus Review*, vol.2 no.2, 1982.
Richard Freeborn, "Turgenev, the Dramatist", in *Transactions / Zapiski of the Association of Russian-American Scholars in the U.S.A.*, 16, 1983.
Sigrid Renaux, "Turgenev's Doctor Shpigelsky: A Prototype for Shaw's Professor Higgins", in *Shaw Review*, 1984.

*   *   *

A Month in the Country is a five-act play in prose written by the Russian novelist Ivan Turgenev in the period 1848–50.

A Month in the Country: National Theatre, London, 1981

After objections by the censors to some of its overt social criticism the play was finally passed for publication in 1855. It was performed for the first time in Moscow (at the Maly Theatre) in 1872 and assured of continuing success in the 20th century by a famous Stanislavsky production at the Moscow Arts Theatre in 1909.

The story concerns a young tutor, Aleksey Belyaev, who is hired during the summer to teach the ten year old son of the Islaevs on their country estate. Despite his own mild manner the charming Belyaev has a devastating impact on the household. Mme Islaeva (Natalia Petrovna) vies with her own young ward, Vera, for his attention. Both women fall in love with him but Vera is no match for her protectress. Natalia manoeuvres her into an arranged marriage with a ridiculous middle-aged neighbour. Belyaev departs, leaving all of the characters facing changes in their lives. In particular, Rakitin, a close friend of the family who has long been a secret admirer of Natalia, is forced to go away, suspected by her uncomprehending husband of having made advances towards her. Secondary interest, and not a little humour, arises from the down-to-earth love relationship between two middle-aged characters, Dr Shpigelsky and Lizaveta Bogdanovna.

The play has had an unusual destiny. Its author was reluctant to believe in its quality because of the negative criticism which it received. He went so far as to admit that it was not really a play, but a novel in dramatic form. In fact, a good case could be made in the opposite direction: that Turgenev, with his skill in creating atmosphere, character, and dialogue far exceeding his narrative inventiveness, might be regarded as a dramatist *manqué*. This play has not only remained in the Russian repertory, it has travelled abroad with great success, proving particularly popular on the British stage.

Its major achievement is to have introduced into Russia, half a century too early for the author's own good, a wholly new theatrical genre, the psychological drama. *A Month in the Country* is a play in which very little overt action occurs. There are arrivals and departures, one listens to conversations and gains a strong sense of hidden passions and tensions seething just below the surface of events. There are two or three moments of crisis, resolved with words rather than deeds, sufficient to raise an audience's involvement from interest to anxiety. But what is remarkable is the disparity between the radical nature of these developments and the lack of any external adventure or sensation. Ordinary people leading humdrum lives are subjected to turmoil and trauma; it is as if a whirlwind has passed through and blown away their comfortable routine, and no one saw anything happen.

Turgenev's characterization is remarkable. Not only are the 13 characters extremely realistic, they actually develop and mature during the action of the play, without ever straining credulity. Particularly poignant are the two leading female roles. For all her understated depiction, Vera approaches tragic status and cannot fail to move the spectators as they watch her rapid transformation from girlishness to womanhood, followed by her painful resignation to a hopeless future. As for Natalia, she attracts some degree of sympathy because of her boring marriage and her forceful personality, but she is despicable in her ruthless treatment of the young girl whose interests she is supposed to be protecting. Her villainy is mitigated by a sense of her powerlessness before the forces which take control of her—physical love together with a sense of panic that her youth and beauty are rapidly coming towards their end. She is complex and fascinating. Alongside these leading characters there is much else to sustain the interest: the innocence of Belyaev, the sadly amusing remoteness of Natalia's husband, the bitterness of Rakitin who only now comes to full realization of how empty his life has been. There

is a good deal of comic relief, particularly in the exchanges between Shpigelsky and Bogdanovna but also in the character of Shaaf, the German tutor, and the satirical picture of Bolshintsov, Vera's eventual husband-to-be. Productions which play upon the comedy and leave the more serious issues to speak for themselves in Turgenev's restrained manner bring out all the qualities of *A Month in the Country*, and, by keeping them nicely in balance, tend to be more successful than those which attempt to propel this complex drama explicitly in the direction of tragedy.

The question of Chekhov's debt to Turgenev has never been fully resolved. Chekhov himself denied it and claimed he had not even read *A Month in the Country* before writing his major plays. This can scarcely be true, as even a glance at the cast lists of this play and *Uncle Vanya* will reveal. Both plays (and also Balzac's *La Marâtre* from which *A Month in the Country* derives) involve groupings of characters which are anything but conventional; all three are certainly interrelated. Critics tend either to take for granted a certain influence by Turgenev, or else to deny it almost entirely. The influence seems, however, beyond question, extending as it does to setting, characterization, atmosphere, dialogue, and even perhaps to thematic interest. The outstanding success of Chekhov's psychological drama is itself a vindication of Turgenev's method, which was so unpopular in its day. What is remarkable is the early date at which Turgenev attempted to introduce the Russians to a form of drama which would sweep to popularity half a century later; *A Month in the Country* was written ten years before Chekhov was even born.

—Anthony D.P. Briggs

MÖRDER, HOFFNUNG DER FRAUEN.   See **MURDERER, HOPE OF WOMEN.**

MORTE ACCIDENTALE DI UN ANARCHICO.   See **ACCIDENTAL DEATH OF AN ANARCHIST.**

MOTHER COURAGE AND HER CHILDREN
(Mutter Courage und ihre Kinder)
by Bertolt Brecht

First Publication: In *Versuche*, 9, Berlin, 1949; revised edition, 1950.
First Production: Schauspielhaus, Zurich, 19 April 1941; revised version [corresponding to 1949 published text], Deutsches Theater, Berlin, 11 January 1949.

Translations
Mother Courage and Her Children, translated by H.R. Hays, in *New Directions*, 1941.
Mother Courage and Her Children, translated by Eric Bentley, in *The Modern Theatre*, 2, New York, 1955.
Mother Courage and Her Children, translated by John Willett, London, 1980 (Collected Plays, vol.5 no.2).

Criticism
(For general works on the author, see *Playwrights* volume)

Books:
Bertolt Brecht, *Courage-Modell 1949* [Modellbuch], Berlin, 1958.
Werner Hecht (ed.), *Materialien zu Brechts "Mutter Courage und ihre Kinder"*, Frankfurt, 1964.
Peter Leiser, *Bertolt Brecht: "Mutter Courage und ihre Kinder"; "Der kaukasische Kreidekreis"*, Hollfeld, 1973.
Dieter Thiele, *Bertolt Brecht: "Mutter Courage und ihre Kinder"*, Frankfurt, 1985.

Articles:
Herbert Blau, "Brecht's *Mother Courage*: The Rite of War and the Rhythm of Epic", in *Educational Theatre Journal*, 9, 1957.
Walter Schäfer, "War der Weg über die Lieder ein Umweg? Bert Brecht *Mutter Courage und ihre Kinder*", in *Wirkendes Wort*, 14, 1964.
Peter Palitzsch, "*Mutter Courage*, 20 Jahre danach. Arbeit an Brecht am Beispiel einer Aufführung", in *Theater heute*, 6, 1965.
Ronald Gray, "Brecht's *Mother Courage*", in *Oxford Review*, 2, 1966.
Roland Barthes, "Seven Photo Models of *Mother Courage*", in *Tulane Drama Review*, vol.12 no.1, 1967.
Walter Boeddinghaus, "Bestie Mensch in Brechts *Mutter Courage*", in *Acta Germanica*, 2, 1968.
Paul Dehem, "*Mère Courage* et l'efficacité du théâtre de Brecht", in *Langues modernes*, 64, 1970.
E. Speidel, "The Mute Person's Voice: Mother Courage and her Daughter", in *German Life and Letters*, 23, 1970.
Ronald S. Woodland, "The Danger of Empathy in *Mother Courage*", in *Modern Drama*, 15, 1972.
Helena Anders and Nikolaus Rehling, "Zum Beispiel: *Mutter Courage*", in *Alternative*, 19, 1976.
Gérard Jugan, "La réception de *Mutter Courage* en RFA.", in *Cahiers d'études germaniques*, 1978.
August Obermayer, "Die dramaturgische Funktion der Lieder in Brechts *Mutter Courage und ihre Kinder*", in *Festschrift for E.W. Herd*, edited by August Obermayer, Dunedin, New Zealand, 1980.
Klaus Bohnen, "'. . .schrieb ich mein Stück für Skandinavien': Eine historischkritische Ausgabe von *Mutter Courage* und ein auf deutsch unveröffentlicher Kommentar Brechts zu seinem Stück", in *Text & Kontext*, 9, 1981.
Sarah Bryant-Bertail, "Women, Space, Ideology: *Mutter Courage und ihre Kinder*", in *Brecht: Women and Politics*, edited by John Fuegi and others, Detroit, Michigan, 1985.
Kathleen L. Komar, "Paradigm Change: The Female Paradigm in Brecht's *Mutter Courage und ihre Kinder* and Christa Wolf's *Kassandra*", in *Euphorion*, 82, 1988.

* * *

The play chronicles the adventures during the Thirty Years' War of the canteen-woman Anna Fierling—nicknamed Mother Courage—and her three children by different fathers: bold Eilif, honest Swiss Cheese, and dumb Kattrin. She travels in her canteen wagon first with the Protestant then with the Catholic army, in order to make a living from the war for herself and her family. But the war devours her children one by one. Swiss Cheese, a regimental paymaster, is executed for not surrendering the Protestants' regimental cash-box to the victorious Catholics; Eilif continues his military exploits during a period of truce and is put to death as a common highwayman; Kattrin is shot while beating a drum in order to warn the citizens of Halle of an impending night attack. With no one left to help her, Mother Courage nevertheless carries on her trade, pulling her cart in the wake of the armies.

Loosely based on a novel by the 17th–century author Grimmelshausen, the play is set in a period with a particular resonance for German audiences: the Thirty Years' War (1616–48) was the most destructive conflict on German soil before World War II. In fact, Brecht wrote *Mother Courage and Her Children* in 1938–9, shortly before what he saw as the new impending bloodbath. An exile from Nazi Germany, he was in no position to address his countrymen directly; so the play's first production (at the Zürich Schauspielhaus on 19 April 1941) had no echo at home. Its real impact, in a somewhat amended version, only came after the war. Performed at the Deutsches Theater in Berlin on 11 January 1949, largely under Brecht's own direction, and then in a new production on 11 September 1951, *Mother Courage and Her Children* came to be regarded as the flagship of the newly founded Berliner Ensemble. Helene Weigel, Brecht's wife, who interpreted the title role with towering authority, added many touches not found in the text—such as her famous silent cry when she heard her second son being shot off-stage.

The play is a notable example of Brecht's concept of Epic Theatre. Its 12 scenes cover a part—only a part—of the Thirty Years' War, between 1624 and 1636, in a loose combination broadly comparable to a Shakespearean history. But it is history seen from the perspective of the ruled rather than of the rulers. The plot, in line with epic (i.e. narrative) principles, does not work towards any single grand climax. Ignoring the unities of time and place, the play manages to illuminate areas of social experience beyond the merely personal—as Shakespeare had done in *Henry IV*. Mother Courage is of course the heroine, or more properly the anti-heroine, of the play; but its real subject is war. Brecht wanted to drive home a number of lessons, such as that war is a continuation of business by other means; that it is not the "little" people who benefit from it; and that it so perverts human nature as to render all human virtues deadly, even for their owners. The epic treatment was designed to win the audience's rational assent to these propositions.

The Berliner Ensemble's "model" of the play—some 800 production photographs and detailed production notes—makes explicit some epic elements only implicit in the published text. Thus, the songs are not simple lyrical effusions on the part of the characters; they emphasize a point or draw a moral, however obliquely, for the benefit of the spectators. The staging method (suggestive, rather than fully executed, sets; bright white, deliberately unatmospheric lighting; the revolve which, in transporting the canteen-wagon, stresses the theatricality of the action; projected titles setting time and place and presenting the "argument"—the plot summary—at the beginning of a scene) helps to keep the spectator not so much uninvolved as capable of rational reflection.

The coolness of this method can be overstated. There is a rising curve of excitement within each scene. The penultimate one in particular, when Kattrin saves the city of Halle at the cost of her own life, is intensely dramatic in the most conventional sense. But even here, the following scene in which Mother Courage simply goes back to trading as a "hyena of the battlefield" undercuts any uncritical emotion with a chilling anti-climax.

Some commentators have claimed that the enormous success of the play is due to the artist in Brecht having got the better of the man with a message. For example, according to Martin Esslin "Brecht insisted that Mother Courage herself was a negative character. . .But the audience never fails to be

Mother Courage and Her Children: Helene Weigel, Deutsches Theater, Berlin, 1949 (Berliner Ensemble)

moved by her fate". However, this is to suggest a false antithesis between complexity and commitment. It is true that Mother Courage is as contradictory a character as, for example, Falstaff who is also amusing but morally ambiguous. It is also true that she is cynical, quick-witted, realistic, blinkered, amoral, loving, courageous, crafty, ruthless; in fact a fully rounded character; with her vitality she effortlessly dominates the stage and imposes the viewpoint of the "lower orders" on our reading of history; and at times she does make us feel for and with her. But it is wrong to conclude that we wholly indentify with her—unless indeed a particular production has bent the text to encourage such a response. Her insight into the nature of war is fitful; she damns it in Scene 6, then becomes a willing participant again. She is unregenerate.

However, what really matters is not what she, or any other characters, have learnt from their experiences; what matters is what we, the audience, take away from the play. *Mother Courage and Her Children* succeeds triumphantly in that it combines theatricality of the highest order with the most urgent lesson for our times.

—George W. Brandt

LES MOUCHES. See THE FLIES.

MOURNING BECOMES ELECTRA: A TRILOGY
Homecoming
The Hunted
The Haunted
by Eugene O'Neill

The Trilogy
First Publication: New York, 1931
First Production: Guild Theatre, New York (Theatre Guild),
                26 October 1931.

Criticism
(For general works on the author, see *Playwrights* volume)

Articles:
Horst Frenz and Martin Mueller, "More Shakespeare and Less Aeschylus in Eugene O'Neill's *Mourning Becomes Electra*", in *American Literature*, 38, 1966.
Péter Egri, "The Social and Psychological Aspects of the Conflict in Eugene O'Neill's *Mourning Becomes Electra*", in *Studies in English and American*, (Budapest) 2, 1975.
Carole and Brian McDonough, "*Mourning Becomes Electra*: A Study of the Conflict Between Puritanism and Paganism", in *English Review*, 3, 1975.
Joyce D. Kennedy, "*Pierre's* Progeny: O'Neill and the Melville Revival", in *English Studies in Canada*, 3, 1977.
Robert Feldman, "The Longing for Death in O'Neill's *Strange Interlude* and *Mourning Becomes Electra*", in *Literature & Psychology*, 31, 1981.
Marc Maufort, "The Legacy of Melville's *Pierre*: Family Relationships in *Mourning Becomes Electra*", in *Eugene O'Neill Newsletter*, vol.11 no.2, 1987.
Ronald L. Wainscott, "Exploring the Religion of the Dead: Philip Moeller Directs O'Neill's *Mourning Becomes Electra*", in *Theatre History Studies*, 7, 1987.
Richard F. Moorton, "What's in a Name? The Significance of 'Mannon' in *Mourning Becomes Electra*", in *Eugene O'Neill Newsletter*, vol.12 no.3, 1988.

*   *   *

A bald plot-summary of *Mourning Becomes Electra: A Trilogy* risks a misleading impression of melodramatic crudity at variance with title and subtitle. What might have been a three-act play with 14 successive scenes is structured as a trilogy of three, short, self-contained plays, each with either four or five acts, the whole developing a narrative line into a unified, though lengthy, dramatic presentation.

All the three plays of the trilogy are set in the New England of the American Civil War, but it is a New England defined by O'Neill as "a grim savage country of my own making". In the first, *Homecoming*, General Ezra Mannon returns to the family home to be told by his wife Christine that her love for him died with the birth of their son, Orin, now also a soldier. Their daughter, Lavinia, however, has already discovered the truth: her mother has taken as a lover the illegitimate son of Ezra's roguish brother, to whom Lavinia is also attracted. He is now a sea-captain calling himself Adam Brant, and Lavinia has forced her mother to promise to renounce him. Instead, Christine, knowing Ezra has a weak heart, confesses to him and by withholding his medicine ensures his death, but not before Lavinia has discovered what is happening.

Having resisted involvement in Ezra's murder, Brant, in the second piece, *The Hunted*, agrees to escape with Christine to an idyllic South Sea island, symbolising to him and both women innocence and freedom. Orin, returning from the war with a head-wound, is told by his sister of their mother's adultery. At Lavinia's instigation, the two watch the lovers on Brant's clipper, and then, after Christine's departure, Orin shoots Brant. Returning to the Mannon home, they confront Christine with their undetected crime as retributive justice, and she takes her own life.

Only in the third piece, *The Haunted*, do the full meaning of the title and the complexity of O'Neill's design become apparent. Orin and Lavinia return from a voyage to the South Seas. The stern black she wore in earlier scenes is now replaced by bright colours, and her manner has an open sensuality. These changes excite her sweetheart, Peter, but his sister Hazel, in love with Orin, is appalled at them and at Orin's disturbed behaviour. Like Lady Macbeth, Lavinia tries desperately but unsuccessfully to prevent her partner's guilt overwhelming him. He shoots himself, having warned Hazel to beware of Lavinia. Peter, however, is still prepared to marry her, but, inadvertently addressing him as Adam, she realises the impossibility of her position and alienates him by claiming to have had sexual relations with a South Sea islander. In the final act Lavinia reverts to her customary mourning black and accepts her destiny: disdaining suicide, she immures herself in expiation in the Mannon house, as the compliant servant Seth secures the shutters.

The trilogy is O'Neill's version of the Greek *Oresteia*. Lavinia is Electra, and the title is ironically illuminated in *The Haunted* when Peter tells her how well colours become her. Agamemnon/Ezra, Clytemnestra/Christine and Orestes/Orin are self-evident, but O'Neill also gives the theme an Oedipal dimension in the relationships between Orin and Christine, Lavinia and Ezra. Where Eliot uses the Eumenides as conventional embodiments of the nemesis that hounds the Orestes figure, O'Neill combines, more terri-

Mourning Becomes Electra: Westminster Theatre, London, 1937

fyingly, an agonised conscience and a Freudian retribution. Each of the guilty pair is helplessly but vividly taken over by the personality of the hated parent, Lavinia increasingly resembling Christine, Orin his father, until even their affection for each other verges on the incestuous.

In the detail of the descriptive stage directions even the facade of the house, as well as the face of each Mannon on first appearance, is likened to a mask, prefiguring O'Neill's later conviction that the psychological thrust might have been better served had actual masks been used. Less debatable is the role of the claustrophobically repressive Mannon house which dominates every scene but one, helping to destroy the figurative house of Mannon; as the house of Atreus, in the *Oresteia*, is finally destroyed with the death of Orestes. It becomes almost a character, like the grimly brooding farmhouse in *Desire Under the Elms*, while the merciless hounding of the Mannons anticipates, by contrast, O'Neill's eventual "deep pity and understanding and forgiveness for *all* the four haunted Tyrones" who represent his own family in *Long Day's Journey into Night*. There is no Aeschylean forgiveness or social justice in O'Neill's determinist *Oresteia*.

The trilogy was a landmark in 1931 in the establishing of O'Neill's international reputation. Its skilful blend of Freudian psychology and classical tragedy in an American context showed a powerfully imaginative command of dramatic idiom (especially irony), despite weaknesses for which it became common to criticise him. The dialogue has a stilted banality not altogether attributable to the Mannons' formally tight-lipped, mid 19th-century Puritanism, and insufficiently lifted by the recurrent island symbolism. A similarly painful awareness of the damage members of a family can do to each other is articulated with a much more convincing colloquial eloquence in *Long Day's Journey*, yet in both the theme is pressed home with remorseless cogency.

The cast-list of 20 people is uneconomical. The "chorus of types representing the town as a human background" with which each part of the trilogy opens is effective only in the last, where the locals' unsophisticated fear of ghosts in the house makes a deceptively light-hearted contrast to the real horror awaiting the characters and the audience. The overtly sexual innuendo of some of their exchanges, together with Orin's mother-fixation and sense of guilt, and his reiterated, anti-war sentiments intensified by his war-damaged personality, probably seemed daringly modern to 1930's theatre-goers, but Orin and his sister are the only characters developed with any profundity. Lavinia has the amoral dynamism and determination of a Jacobean heroine like Webster's Vittoria (in *The White Devil*), though lacking Webster's poetry to give her maximum impetus, and it is on her performance that a production stands or falls.

—Dennis Welland

MRCCHAKATICA. See **THE LITTLE CLAY CART.**

MRICHCHHAKATIKA. See **THE LITTLE CLAY CART.**

MRS. WARREN'S PROFESSION
by George Bernard Shaw

First Publication: In *Plays Unpleasant*, London, 1898.
First Production: New Lyric Club, London (Stage Society private performance), 5 January 1902; first public performance, New Haven, Connecticut, 27 October 1905.

Criticism
(For general works on the author, see *Playwrights* volume)

Articles:
Geoffrey Bullough, "Literary Relations of Shaw's Mrs. Warren", in *Philological Quarterly*, 41, 1962.
Robert Stozier, "The Undramatic Dramatist: Mrs. Warren's Shaw", in *The Shavian*, 3, 1965.
Charles A. Berst, "Propaganda and Art in *Mrs. Warren's Profession*", in *English Literary History*, 33, 1966.
Stephen Gracco, "Vivie Warren's Profession: A New Look at *Mrs. Warren's Profession*", in *Shaw Review*, 10, 1967.
Arthur C. Nethercot, "*Mrs. Warren's Profession*; *The Second Mrs. Tanqueray*", in *Shaw Review*, 13, 1970.
Raymond S. Nelson, "*Mrs. Warren's Profession* and English Prostitution", in *Journal of Modern Literature*, 2, 1971–72.
Betty F. Johnson, "Shelley's *Cenci* and *Mrs. Warren's Profession*", in *Shaw Review*, 15, 1972.
Marlie P. Wasserman, "Vivie Warren: A Psychological Study", in *Shaw Review*, 15, 1972.
William A. Dolid, "Vivie Warren and the Tripos", in *Shaw Review*, 23, 1980.
Tony J. Stafford, "*Mrs. Warren's Profession*: In the Garden of Respectability", in *SHAW*, 2, 1982.
Gladys M. Crane, "Directing Early Shaw: Acting and Meaning in *Mrs. Warren's Profession*", in *SHAW*, 3, 1983.
Mark H. Sterner, "The Changing Status of Women in Late Victorian Drama", in *Within the Dramatic Spectrum*, edited by Karelisa V. Hartigan, Lanham, Maryland, 1986.

*   *   *

Mrs. Warren's Profession, one of Shaw's *Plays Unpleasant*, begins with young Vivie Warren, a Cambridge graduate in Mathematics. She has no father and her mother is mysterious, having had little contact with her. Before taking up a career as an actuary, while looking also at law and the Stock Exchange, she amuses herself in a childish flirtation with Frank, and they play at being "babes in the wood". Her mother arrives and in a long, powerful duologue at the end of the second act Vivie discovers that her mother comes from a very poor background but has become affluent as a prostitute. "You are stronger than all England", declares Vivie. In the next act, however, Vivie finds out that her mother is still in the profession, managing a chain of brothels across Europe. Horrified, Vivie leaves at once and is seen in the final act at work in a Chancery Lane office, rejecting the friendship, and money, of both her mother and Frank. "I must be treated as a woman of business, permanently single and permanently unromantic", she says, for "life is what it is; and I am prepared to take it as it is". "Lord help the world if everybody took to doing the right thing!", laments Mrs. Warren, refusing to shake hands with Vivie. Paradoxically, Shaw shows the wages of sin as wealth, power and happiness.

There are three other characters. Crofts, Mrs. Warren's friend and partner, combines "the most brutal types of city man, sporting man, and man about town", and proposes to Vivie, confidently expecting her to accept him. Rejected, he

Mrs. Warren's Profession: New Lyric Club, London, 1902 (first production)

tells her that Frank is her half-brother, which is probably untrue. Sam, Frank's father, is a foolish clergyman; his son comments of him that he has "the irresoluteness of a sheep and the pompousness and aggressiveness of a jackass". Sam was involved with Mrs. Warren in his youth, and she still has his letters to her. Lastly, Praed is an effeminate artist, vaguely believing in Beauty.

Mrs. Warren is vulgar, sentimental, warm-hearted and energetic. Showily dressed and usually self-possessed, arguing with Vivie she descends into whining cockney, "her natural tongue—the dialect of a woman of the people". Her social position is ambiguous: working class origins, usually showing more in her clothes than in her accent; unclear marital status, as Mr. Warren has never been seen; restless, never staying more than a few weeks in one place; prosperous, yet there are suspicions about where the wealth comes from. She is a self-made woman, in fact, but these were so rare in the 1890's that some of the characters do not know how to deal with one. Crofts, secure in his title and riches, and Praed, nonconformist as an artist, can overlook these problems of status; but the clergyman, alert to propriety, cannot. Because of her resourceful triumph over adversity, we respect Mrs. Warren (despite her extraordinary assumptions about how Vivie will, in future, dutifully behave as a daughter to her). Later in the drama, we share with Vivie both the moral issue of prostitution and the unease that Mrs Warren is continuing in the business.

Shaw draws attention to the position of women; Vivie is untypical in having both money and ability. "It cant be right", complains Mrs Warren, "that there shouldnt be better opportunities for women". In her second act confrontation with her daughter she bursts out with: "The hypocrisy of the world makes me sick!". Hypocrisy is evident in the play: Sam pretends to a purity he has not practised, while Crofts is clear in his understanding of his world: "As long as you don't fly openly in the face of society, society doesn't ask any inconvenient questions".

The play is less about prostitution than about capitalism, about the pursuit of money necessarily taking precedence over principles, and about the evil of poverty, a recurring theme in Shaw's work. Shaw intends "to achieve a transference of the horror and shame conventionally associated with the sex-trade to its normally accepted and respected counterparts in the economic and social organisation of society", writes Margery Morgan (in her *The Shavian Playground*).

Shaw wrote of Vivie: "I have sought to put on the stage for the first time (as far as I know) the highly educated, capable, independent young woman of the governing class as we know her today, working, smoking, preferring the society of men to that of women simply because men talk about the questions that interest her and not about servants and babies, making no pretence of caring much about art or romance" (*Collected Letters, I*). She is, in short, a New Woman. At the beginning of the play, she is already cold, decisive, committed to earning and to a career; but she is much colder by the final act. Most find her final rejection of her mother exceedingly callous. Shaw, always striving to have his audience thinking and debating, is deliberately provocative when the young female lead, who in other plays would be clearly a heroine, acts in this way. Finally, and most importantly, Vivie is to be faulted for acceptance of life as "what it is" when her duty is to fight for change so that poor, young women will not be forced to follow the profession of Mrs. Warren.

—Malcolm Page

MUCH ADO ABOUT NOTHING
by William Shakespeare

First Publication: London, 1600.
First Production: London, c.1598–99; earliest recorded production, at Court, 1612.

Editions
Much Ado About Nothing, edited by H.H. Furness, Philadelphia, 1899 (New Variorum Shakespeare).
Much Ado About Nothing, edited by Arthur Quiller-Couch and John Dover Wilson, Cambridge, 1923 (The New Shakespeare).
Much Ado About Nothing, edited by Josephine Waters Bennett, Baltimore, Maryland, 1958; revised edition, 1974 (Pelican Shakespeare).
Much Ado About Nothing, edited by David L. Stevenson, New York, 1964 (Signet Classic Shakespeare).
Much Ado About Nothing, edited by R.A. Foakes, Harmondsworth, 1968 (New Penguin Shakespeare).
Much Ado About Nothing, edited by Arthur R. Humphreys, London, 1981 (Arden Shakespeare).
Much Ado About Nothing, edited by F.H. Mares, Cambridge, 1988 (New Cambridge Shakespeare).

Criticism
(For general works on the author, see *Playwrights* volume)

Books:
J.R. Mulryne, *Much Ado About Nothing*, London, 1965.
Walter R. Davis (ed.), *Twentieth Century Interpretations of "Much Ado About Nothing"*, Englewood Cliffs, New Jersey, 1969.
Norbert Greiner, *Studien zu "Much Ado About Nothing"*, Bern, Frankfurt, and New York, 1983.
Harold Bloom (ed.), *William Shakespeare: "Much Ado About Nothing"*, New York, New Haven, Connecticut, and Philadelphia, 1988 (Modern Critical Interpretations).
Mark W. Scott and Sandra L. Williamson (eds.), *"Much Ado About Nothing"*, in *Shakespearian Criticism*, 8, Detroit, Illinois, 1989 [anthology of criticism].

Articles:
For information on the many articles about *Much Ado About Nothing*, see the bibliographies listed in the *Playwrights* volume, and the annual Shakespeare Bibliography in *Shakespeare Quarterly*, published by the Folger Shakespeare Library, Washington D.C. (1950–).

*   *   *

Much Ado About Nothing is a comedy of love and misapprehension. A young soldier, Claudio, falls in love with a young woman, Hero. His general, Don Pedro, courts her on Claudio's behalf, and is so successful that Claudio begins to suspect betrayal. No sooner is this misconception sorted out, than the malicious Don John plots to incriminate Hero as a woman of easy virtue, leading to Claudio's accusing her at their wedding ceremony of infidelity with another man. Hero is reported dead, and the men mourn for her. Eventually through the good offices of a friar, she is restored to Claudio with her name cleared, and the marriage at last takes place. The main plot is, however, not quite the conventional romance narrative it seems to be. In performance, the play is often dominated by the subplot characters Beatrice and Benedick, whose love–hate relationship and corrosive combats of wit

Much Ado About Nothing: Stratford-Upon-Avon, 1982, (Royal Shakespeare Company)

lead to a more mature and solid relationship than the alternating idealisation and disillusionment of the romantic principals.

The play has often been interpreted as a relatively straightforward comedy of temporary misunderstanding and ultimate reconciliation. There is a running contrast between the idealised romantic affiliation of Claudio and Hero, and the cynical relationship of reciprocal banter enjoyed by Beatrice and Benedick; but these dissimilar approaches to love can be seen as mutually compatible, and need not cancel each other out. The critical moment of misunderstanding, Claudio's belief in Hero's infidelity, certainly arouses dramatic tensions; but if Claudio is seen as consistently honourable, in his love for Hero, in his indignant repudiation of her supposed betrayal, and in his eventual re-acceptance of her as his wife, then the play presents no deep artistic or ideological problems.

It is, however, more difficult to interpret the play in this straightforward way if we read it in the context of modern feminism. After all, the plot does turn on an unfounded allegation of sexual transgression against an innocent woman; and it is another woman who stands as the wronged Hero's staunchest champion. Can the play remain a straightforward comedy if we take full account of its "sexual politics"? And yet how appropriate is it for us to apply modern standards to a work of 16th-century drama? Does the play in any way question dominant Elizabethan ideas about sexual relationships and the position of women in society? When Claudio and Don Pedro are confronted with Hero's apparent death they express regret, but do not fundamentally question the correctness of their original rejection of her. Hero herself certainly

seems to have no compunction in reuniting herself with the man who publicly humiliated and abandoned her on the basis of malicious gossip and a contrived deception. Is it possible that the disquiet experienced by many at these aspects of the play has more to do with modern sensitivities about the position of women than any scruples an Elizabethan dramatist might have felt or wished to express?

The leading male characters in the play—Claudio, Don Pedro, and Don John the Bastard—are soldiers, recently returned from a military expedition. In the traditional, militaristic ideology of the feudal aristocracy, male comradeship was much more important than sexual relations with the female; women were marginalised and tightly circumscribed into the categories either of wife and breeder (to be protected), or of whore (to be used and discarded). The qualities required for the successful prosecution of a soldier's career—courage, violence, self-possession—were, in the ethical code of this particular class, bound up with notions of solidarity based on a masculine freemasonry of aristocratic honour. It would seem far more natural, to the aristocratic warrior, to defend his own honour and that of his male companions, than to invest any real trust and commitment into the keeping of a woman.

When Don John delivers to Claudio and Don Pedro his allegation of Hero's disloyalty, we see in the swift and decisive response of the men an indication of how their ideology of masculine solidarity and aristocratic honour operates. The temptation offered by Don John (which is, compared to Iago's parallel seduction of Othello, perfunctory in the extreme) works on Claudio's hypersensitive commitment to the preservation of his own honour. The men are absolutely united on what would be the appropriate course of action should Don John's accusations prove to be true: the shame and dishonour that would fall to Claudio is to be deflected back onto Hero, with the time and place carefully chosen to maximise her humiliation. As she appears for the wedding ceremony in bridal dress as the visible embodiment of female purity, the men will openly declare her corrupt and unchaste.

The immediate effect of this public denunciation is to provoke an instantaneous solidarity among all the men involved. Don Pedro feels that his own participation in the process of wooing taints his honour with the same associational guilt, and Hero's father, Leonato, shares this, sense of dishonour, immediately wishing his daughter dead. The Friar seems to stand outside this consensus, and it is he who saves the situation. But his strategy of reconciliation involves nothing less than an acknowledgement that Hero's apparent and symbolic death should be regarded, for the purposes of the moment, as real. The fact that the woman herself has been unjustly slandered and maliciously "framed" is recognised; but the affirmation of her innocence and the denunciation of her accusers seems less of a priority than the symbolic destruction of this irrevocably contaminated, female body. In fact it has been contaminated with nothing but masculine suspicion, jealousy, mistrust, and fear; nonetheless, only its total, ritual destruction can achieve the clearing of Hero's name.

Although the play's dramatic and moral crisis calls into question the whole system of patriarchal authority, Friar Francis has no wish to challenge or subvert it. This conspiracy to construct an illusion of Hero's death and rebirth leaves the male ideology that created the entire crisis virtually intact. Claudio and Don Pedro have had to admit that they made a mistake; but Claudio does not have to suffer the indignity of contact with a contaminated woman, Don Pedro does not have to witness his friend dishonoured, and neither is in any way obliged to inspect or interrogate the ludicrous premises of their own ideology.

The play thus challenges conventional notions of masculine supremacy and feminine subordination by means of a penetrating investigation of the weaknesses and contradictions in masculine-aristocratic ideology. The play's ultimate "comic" reconciliation involves such a clear disclosure and indictment of these ideological contradictions, that it can scarcely be regarded as the fulfilment of a reassuring pattern of "happy" or "festive" comedy. On the contrary, we might begin to think seriously about assigning *Much Ado About Nothing* to the category of "problem plays".

—Graham Holderness

MURDER IN THE CATHEDRAL
by T.S. Eliot

First Publication: Canterbury, 1935 (special acting edition); complete edition, London, 1935; second, edition, 1936; third edition, 1937; fourth edition, 1938.
First Production: Canterbury Cathedral, Canterbury, 10 May 1935.

Criticism
(For general works on the author, see *Playwrights* volume)

Books:
Jean Wilhelm, *T.S. Eliot's "Murder in the Cathedral"*, Adelaide, 1970.
David R. Clark (ed.), *Twentieth Century Interpretations of "Murder in the Cathedral"*, Englewood Cliffs, New Jersey, 1971.
Michael P. Gallagher, *T.S. Eliot: "Murder in the Cathedral"*, Dublin, 1977.
Paul Lapworth, *"Murder in the Cathedral", by T.S. Elliot*, London, 1988.
William Tydeman, *"Murder in the Cathedral" and "The Cocktail Party"*, London, 1988 (Text and Performance Series).

Articles:
Francis Fergusson, "Action as Passion: *Tristan* and *Murder in the Cathedral*", in *Kenyon Review*, 11, 1947.
J.T. Boulton, "The Use of Original Sources for the Development of a Theme: Eliot's *Murder in the Cathedral*", in *English*, 11, 1956.
Hans Galinsky, "T.S. Eliots *Murder in the Cathedral*: Versuch einer Interpretation", in *Die neueren Sprachen*, 7, 1958.
W.R. Mueller, "*Murder in the Cathedral*: An Imitation of Christ", in *Religion in Life*, 27, 1958.
Donna Gerstenberger, "The Saint and the Circle", in *Criticism*, 2, 1960.
Gifford W. Wingate, "*Murder in the Cathedral*: A Step Toward Articulate Theatre", in *Greyfriar*, 1960.
Wang-Rok Chang, "An Analysis of *Murder in the Cathedral*", in *English Language and Literature*, 10, 1961.
John F. Adams, "The Fourth Temptation in *Murder in the Cathedral*", in *Modern Drama*, 5, 1963.
L.R. Rehak, "On the Use of Martyrs: Tennyson, Eliot on Thomas Becket", in *University of Toronto Quarterly*, 33, 1963.
William V. Spanos, "*Murder in the Cathedral*: The Figura as Mimetic Principle", in *Drama Survey*, 3, 1963.
Robert Speaight, "With Becket in *Murder in the Cathedral*", in *Sewanee Review*, 74, 1966.
Sister M. Geraldine, "The Rhetoric of Repetition in *Murder in the Cathedral*", in *Renascence*, 19, 1967.
Robert A. Kantra, "Satiric Theme and Structure in *Murder in the Cathedral*", in *Modern Drama*, 10, 1968.
Jerry V. Pickering, "Form as Agent: Eliot's *Murder in the Cathedral*", in *Educational Theatre Journal*, 20, 1968.
Robert N. Shorter, "Becket as Job: T.S. Eliot's *Murder in the Cathedral*", in *South Atlantic Quarterly*, 67, 1968.
Kirsti Kivimaa, "Aspects of Style in T.S. Eliot's *Murder in the Cathedral*", in *Annales universitatis Turkuensis*, 1969.
John Fahy, "The Tragedy of *Murder in the Cathedral*", in *Zenith*, 1, 1971.
Allen J. Koppenhaver, "The Musical Design of T.S. Eliot's *Murder in the Cathedral*", in *Hudson Review*, 5, 1971.
Murray Krieger, "*Murder in the Cathedral*: The Limits of Drama and the Freedom of Vision", in his *The Classic Vision: The Retreat from Extremity in Modern Literature*, Baltimore, Maryland, 1971.
Edna G. Sharoni, " 'Peace' and 'Unbar the door': T.S. Eliot's *Murder in the Cathedral* and Some Stoic Forebears", in *Comparative Drama*, 6, 1972.
Pieter D. Williams, "The Function of the Chorus in Eliot's *Murder in the Cathedral*", in *American Benedictine Review*, 23, 1972.
Edith Pankow, "The 'Eternal Design' of *Murder in the Cathedral*", in *Papers on Language and Literature*, 9, 1973.
John P. Cutts, "Evidence for Ambivalence of Motives in *Murder in the Cathedral*", in *Comparative Drama*, 8, 1974.

Linda Wyman, "*Murder in the Cathedral*: The Plot of Diction", in *Modern Drama*, 19, 1976.

Michael T. Beehler, "*Murder in the Cathedral*: The Counter-sacramental Play of Signs", in *Genre*, 10, 1977.

Robert W. Ayers, "*Murder in the Cathedral*: A 'liturgy less divine'", in *Texas Studies in Literature and Language*, 20, 1978.

Francis W. Fry, "The Centrality of the Sermon in T.S. Eliot's *Murder in the Cathedral*", in *Christianity & Literature*, vol.27 no.4, 1978.

William J. McGill, "Voices in the Cathedral: The Chorus in Eliot's *Murder in the Cathedral*", in *Modern Drama*, 23, 1980.

Lionel J. Pike, "Liturgy and Time in Counterpoint: A View of T.S. Eliot's *Murder in the Cathedral*", in *Modern Drama*, 23, 1980.

Douglas G. Campbell, "Drama as Monument: Eliot's *Murder in the Cathedral*", in *Liberal & Fine Arts Review*, vol.1 no.1, 1981.

David Seed, "Eliot's Use of Tennyson in *Murder in the Cathedral*", in *Yeats Eliot Review*, 7, 1982.

Clifford Davidson, "T.S. Eliot's *Murder in the Cathedral* and the Saint's Play Tradition", in *Papers on Language & Literature*, 21, 1985.

James E. Robinson, "*Murder in the Cathedral* as Theatre of Spirit", in *Religion & Literature*, vol.18 no.2, 1986.

Kurt Tetzeli von Rosador, "Christian Historical Drama: The Exemplariness of *Murder in the Cathedral*", in *Modern Drama*, 29, 1986.

Scott Samuelson, "The Word as Sword: Power and Paradox in *Murder in the Cathedral*", in *Literature & Belief*, 7, 1987.

*   *   *

T.S. Eliot's *Murder in the Cathedral* takes place during December 1170 in Canterbury. Thomas Beckett, Archbishop of England, returns to England against the King's orders after seven years exile in France. He knows that King Henry II will have him murdered because of a continuing conflict between their strong personalities over whether church or state will be supreme in England. The play consists of two parts with an interlude. As the play opens, a Chorus of the Women of Canterbury feel drawn towards the cathedral to bear witness to the coming tragic events. Soon after his return, Beckett by himself faces four tempters representing four aspects of his personality—enjoyment of the world, enjoyment of power, compromise to achieve his ends, and, the most powerful temptation, pride in doing right for the wrong motive. The interlude is a sermon given by Beckett on Christmas morning concerning Mass as a re-enactment of the "Passion and Death of Our Lord". In the second part of the play, on 29 December, four knights threaten Beckett. Refusing to compromise with the knights or accept the advice of his priests to seek safety, he resigns himself to God's will and is killed in the cathedral. The knights then turn to the audience treating it as a jury before whom they attempt to justify themselves and the rights of the state. The play ends with the return of the chorus which claims Beckett as a martyr whose blood has enriched the earth and created a holy place at Canterbury.

Sharing in the verse and religious drama and Anglo-Catholic movements of its time, *Murder in the Cathedral* was originally written for production at the Canterbury Cathedral Festival in 1935, before it transferred to the commercial stage in London, went on various tours, and was made into a film by George Hoellering (for whom Eliot revised the play, adding additional background information at the beginning). While *Murder in the Cathedral* can be acted on a large stage, it was written for the small enclosed space available in Canterbury Cathedral and is still most theatrically effective in a church, small theatre, or theatre in the round. The effects of various entrances of the characters and the playing areas should contrast with the focus on Beckett's spiritual drama without losing a sense of the action being compressed around and within him. In reacting against realism and the seeming shapelessness of English plays, Eliot wanted a drama closer to French classicism than to Shakespearean abundance.

Murder in the Cathedral remains the finest, English, ritual drama from the period, blending modernist experimentation in non-realistic verse theatre, an anthropological view of culture, a mythic structure, and Eliot's own concern with the need for humility, faith, and obedience to divine will. The Chorus, with its allusions to the dying vegetation and passing year, creates a sense of a community threatened, a wasteland needing the sacrificial blood of martyrdom for renewal. Similarly to the knights' breaking of the theatrical frame to address the audience, the Chorus creates a continuity between play and spectators. They greet Beckett's arrival in language which often echoes biblical accounts of Christ's passion and sacrifice, an evocation strengthened by Beckett's Christmas Day sermon. Throughout the play, as in Eliot's poetry of this period, the language is rich in biblical and liturgical echoes. The Mass re-enacts the Sacrifice; the play imitates the Mass. This is in keeping with Eliot's comments that the Catholic Mass is the most intense, richest form of drama. The play thus provides a symbol of the basis of its archetype, it assumes that the origins of drama lie in myth and ritual and that drama is a secularization of religious drama. The concern with symbol, type, and figure is further brought out by such means as the Chorus (speaking of itself as "type of the common man") and the four tempters who appear before Beckett, recalling the temptations of Christ. Like Milton's *Samson Agonistes*, which is also an influence on the varied versification, formalized speeches, and portrayal of a change in will, there is little in the way of action and event; Beckett's change from pride in his forthcoming martyrdom to emptying his will so that he may accept the destiny God has ordained is, like Samson's, offered without expressionistic or realistic psychology. Any action—whether to save himself or to court martyrdom—would be a matter of pride and self-love rather than obedience to God's will. While Eliot commented that the versification was influenced by *Everyman*, *Murder in the Cathedral* might be seen as a classical foreshortening of the famous morality play: from a journey through life to the last days of a man when, still faced by temptations, he must reconcile himself to death. As in *Everyman*, the essential problem is the state of mind in which one dies. Although *Murder in the Cathedral* often shares the same mood and language as *Ash-Wednesday*, and belongs to the period when Eliot converted to the Church of England and began abandoning former worldly ambitions, the play's conflict between church and state clearly belongs to the 1930's when the Catholic revival of the previous 50 years was challenged from both the political right and left.

The usual problem with plays involving inner drama, rather than external conflict, is lack of tension and the absurdities that result from trying to externalize spiritual decisions. Eliot avoids such problems by a formality of manner, and the intensity that comes from concentration and focus on Beckett's spiritual state, the decision he must make, and the results (as celebrated by the Chorus). The internal drama is externalized in the form of the four temptations (as aspects of Beckett's own life and personality), the debate with the knights, the decision not to seek safety, and in the way the Chorus directs the audience's responses to the play's events.

While lacking in external (rather than spiritual) drama,

Murder in the Cathedral: Mercury Theatre, London, 1935

Murder in the Cathedral is highly theatrical. It has the elevation, tension, and suspense of awaiting the expected found in classical Greek tragedy. The versification is varied according to the speaker and situation. A high proportion of monosyllabic words makes for clarity while Eliot's less frequent use of unusual polysyllabics sharpens attention on themes and elevates the mood. The severely limited cast of characters, the use of the Cathedral and grounds for the scenes, the few scene changes, the many references to the threat facing Beckett, and the limiting of confrontations to those between Beckett and the tempters, three priests, and the knights create a classical intensity and concentration unusual in English drama. The play is filled with theatrical surprises ranging from the sermon to the clever, witty speeches of the four tempters; the parallelism between the four tempters and the four knights; the shock of the knights after the murder suddenly breaking the theatrical frame and addressing the audience in prose. *Murder in the Cathedral* demands the full use of the theatre's resources in any production.

—Bruce King

THE MURDER OF MARIA MARTEN. See **MARIA MARTEN.**

MURDERER, HOPE OF WOMEN
(Mörder, Hoffnung der Frauen)
by Oskar Kokoschka

First Publication: In *Der Sturm*, 1, 1910; revised version, in *O. Kokoschka: Dramen und Bilder*, Leipzig, 1913; further revised version, in *Der brennende Dornbush; Mörder Hoffnung der Frauen*, Leipzig, 1917.
First Production: Gartentheater der Kunstschau [Garden Theatre, International Art Exhibition], Vienna, 4 July 1909.

Translations

Murderer the Women's Hope, in *Anthology of German Expressionist Drama*, edited by W.H. Sokel, New York, 1963.
Murdererer Hope of Womankind, in *Seven Expressionist Plays*, edited by J.M. Ritchie and H.F. Garten, London, 1968.

Criticism
(For general works on the author, see *Playwrights* volume)

Articles:
Horst Denkler, "Die Druckfassungen der Dramen Oskar Kokoschkas", in *Deutsche Vierteljahrsschrift für Literaturwissenschaft und Geistesgeschichte*, 40, 1966.
T.J. Hines, "Collaboration of Forms in a One-Man Show: The Total Performance of *Mörder, Hoffnung der Frauen*", in *Dada*, 4, 1974.
Dorothy Pam, "Kokoschka's *Murderer, the Women's Hope*", in *The Drama Review*, vol.19 no.3, 1975.
Henry Schvey, "Oskar Kokoschka en de wederzijdse Verheldering der Kunsten", in *Forum der Letteren*, 17, 1976.
Georg Jäger, "Kokoschkas *Mörder Hoffnung der Frauen*: Die Geburt des Theater der Grausamkeit aus dem Geist der Wiener Jahrhundertwende", in *Germanisch-Romanische Monatsschrift* (new series), 63, 1982.
Bettina Knapp, "Oskar Kokoschka's *Murderer, Hope of Womankind*: An Apocalyptic Experience", in *Theatre Journal*, 35, 1983.
Peter Vergo and Yvonne Modlin, "*Murderer Hope of Women*: Expressionist Drama and Myth", in *Oskar Kokoschka 1886–1980*, London (Tate Gallery Exhibition Catalogue).

* * *

The play is set in prehistoric antiquity and presents the clash of the two elementary forces of Eros and Thanatos (Love and Death), embodied here by an archetypical Man and Woman. The stage set is dominated by symbolic representations of the male and female sex: a tower and a cage. The Man and the Woman meet in the neutral foreground and are immediately and irresistibly drawn to each other. Their emotions are reverberated in the oratorical exchanges between the two choruses of warriors and maidens accompanying the protagonists.

The Man seeks to establish his dominance over the Woman and has her branded with his sign. But the Woman breaks free and wounds him with a knife in his side. While the choruses of warriors and maidens celebrate an orgiastic nuptial, the Man is transported to the grilled tower and held captive in the cage. The Woman revels in her victory over "the wild animal I am now taming here in this cage". Lasciviously she presses her body against his, but the grill of the cage prevents their union. When she decides to open the cage and to become his wife, he no longer sees her as a lover but as a mother figure offering him peace and quiet. This role reversal evokes fear in the Woman: "You are weakening me. . .You're tying me down! I capture you—but I'm in your hold!". The Woman, once she has assumed a dominant position over the Man, loses control. He opens the gate, touches the dying Woman who has sunk to the floor, and walks away, killing everybody who stands in his way.

The play was written, as Kokoschka stated in his autobiography, as a means "to express my attitude to the world" and as "an antidote to the torpor that, for the most part, one experiences in the theatre today". Although rooted in deeply personal experiences, the play also reflects Kokoschka's interest in prehistoric cultures and the civilizatory process. He admits to having been deeply impressed by Bachofen's study on matriarchy, but there are also influences of Freud and Weininger, and the playwrights Wedekind, Strindberg, and Claudel. The play expresses Kokoschka's understanding of the "Eros and Thanatos" theme and his views "on the secret that lies beyond love and death" (*My Life*). In another autobiographical text, *Vom Erleben*, he describes the theme of the play thus: "In my first play I had offended the thoughtlessness in our patriarchal civilization by advancing the idea that man is mortal and woman immortal, and that only a murderer could attempt to revert this basic fact in the modern world".

Kokoschka's approach to the theatre was that of a painter, not a poet. Instead of using conventional dramatic language, he composes theatrical images that give visual expression to his themes and ideas. The original draft of 1907 only operated with stage pictures, and when the play was first produced in 1909 the lines spoken by the actors were only written one day before the premiere. The first edition, in *Der Sturm*, was illustrated by four woodcuts, and in all the versions the stage directions take up more space than the dialogues. The spoken lines are composed according to painterly principles. The text does not adhere to any rules of grammar or syntax. Just as a painter would arrange shapes and colours on a canvas, the dialogue places words next to each other because of their aural qualities and semantic associations. Rhythmic speech patterns clash with melodious flows of soft vowels and consonants; clusters of harsh sounds are set against songlike sentences. The choreographic treatment of gestures and movements contains similar contradictions. The kinetic qualities oscillate between angular, aggressive, and vigorous movements, and soft, flowing, solemn, or purely decorative poses.

The theme of the battle of the sexes is conveyed by means of sense impressions rather than story line or character psychology. The figures are emanations from the unconscious and express the innate contradictions within the human soul. It is therefore appropriate for the topos to be set and explored in a timeless and unlocalized sphere. The prehistoric setting fits the universal tragedy of the relations between the sexes. But the play not only deals with the clash of the male and female principle. It also shows human beings in an existentialist situation where their libidinous and vitalist forces are locked in a battle with their spiritual and cultural propensities. It is the fight of mind over matter, body over spirit, carnal desires over spiritual aspirations, which animates both protagonists.

The Woman has traits of Penthesilea, Queen of the Amazons, and a Valkyrie; yet she also appears as the Great Mother and is depicted in the poster of the 1909 production as the Virgin Mary in a *pietà* position. The Man, on the other hand, is the Warrior Prince whose Christ-like passion leads to a rebirth of his peace-harbouring proclivities. In both protagonists a struggle for predominance of their respective qualities takes place. These oppositional forces receive symbolic representation in the images of sun and moon (the active, luminous principle versus the passive, mysterious powers of darkness), and in the colours red and blue (the vitalist versus the spiritual instincts; white signifying the absence of both, i.e. death). Rather than identifying Man or Woman with the one or the other symbol, Kokoschka sees both principles as being mixed together in varying proportions in each human being.

The 1909 poster shows moon and sun in an equal position. But the backdrop for the 1917 production, in a reference to the ending of the play, reveals the sun eclipsing the moon. Here the Man is linked to the symbol of the sun, of spiritual and civilizational powers. His armour is blue, whilst the clothes of the Woman are red and her movements have strongly animalistic qualities. But this seemingly traditional distribution of sex-roles is contradicted in the poster, where the scarlet body of the dead Man is resting on the Woman's chalk-white figure. One possible interpretation is that the Man, enslaved by the powers of the flesh, must die, leaving the Woman lifeless without him. The *pietà* figuration links the Man with Christ (as the gash in his side and the crowing of the cock does in the play). After he rises from his tomb he redeems the Woman through his spiritual powers. But first she has to leave her body behind. Her physical destruction is an act of spiritual liberation. The murderer is the only hope for Woman.

Such a linear interpretation may find some justification in the first printed version of the play (which documents the first production), but not, however, in any of the subsequent editions. As Kokoschka was developing his art theory he made the meaning of the play more open and contradictory. The symbolism became more ambiguous, and no solution for the battle of the sexes is offered at the end of the play. With each version Kokoschka increased the reader's/viewer's responsibility for finding his/her own meaning of the play and for developing a personal response to the problems raised by the drama.

—Günter Berghaus

MUTTER COURAGE UND IHRE KINDER. See **MOTHER COURAGE AND HER CHILDREN.**

MYSTERY-BOUFFE (Misteriya-Buff)
by Vladimir Mayakovsky

First Publication: 1918; revised version, Moscow, 1921.
First Production: Malevich Communal Theatre, 7 November 1918; revised version, RSFSR I Theatre, Moscow, 1 May 1921.

Translations
Mystery-Bouffe, translated by G.R. Noyes and A. Kaun, in *Masterpieces of the Russian Drama, 2*, edited by G.R. Noyes, New York, 1933.
Mystery-Bouffe, in *The Complete Plays of Vladimir Mayakovsky*, translated by G. Daniels, New York, 1968.

Criticism
(For general works on the author, see *Playwrights* volume)

Articles:
Günther Wytrzens, "Lachen und Betroffenheit in den satirischen Komödien Majakovskijs", in *Maske und Kothurn*, 30, 1–2, 1984.

Robert Russell, "*Mystery-Bouffe*, and *The Bedbug* and *The Bathhouse*", in his *Russian Drama of the Revolutionary Period*, Totowa, New Jersey, 1988.

* * *

Mayakovsky described *Mystery Bouffe* as a "heroic, epic and satiric representation of our era" and it certainly succeeds in capturing the excitement so widely felt "in that dawn". It begins with the world swept by the flood of revolution and the last few survivors huddling together at the North Pole. They are the Clean (bourgeois) and the Unclean (proletariat). To save themselves, they (or rather, the Unclean) build an ark and sail away. Aboard, the Clean organise first an autocracy, then a democratic republic. When both these systems prove to be fundamentally unjust, the Unclean take over and face the future alone. Their fears are allayed by a Person from the Future, who inspires them to go forward. They harrow Hell, and Paradise as well, subdue Chaos and emerge into a Promised Land which is their home town, cleansed of exploitation and rich with promise.

Bukharin described the play as "the revolution's trumpet of Jericho". The first version, put on to celebrate the first anniversary of the revolution, included Mayakovsky himself in the cast as, among other things, the Person from the Future. The second version expanded and updated the fable, adding contemporary references and characters (an "Unclean" Red Army soldier, Lloyd George and Clemenceau as new "Clean" characters, and a highly comic Menshevik compromiser) and new scenes, including one set in the Land of Chaos and a climax glorifying the electrification of the Soviet Union.

The 1921 production was hugely successful—it was performed three times to the Comintern (in German) and received a series of productions throughout the young USSR. Revived in 1957, and several times since in the USSR, as well as abroad, it has proved its staying power.

Because it is positive and optimistic, it is easy to see *Mystery Bouffe* as naïve. In fact, its insistent allegory is Bunyanesque: the Person from the Future shows the Unclean the way as Evangelist shows Christian in *The Pilgrim's Progress*, and it is through the journey itself that the Unclean learn "the way". It leads to the end of social alienation, and this is presented as the real victory of the revolution. In the last scene, the food belongs to those who need it, the tools and machines to those who will use them. Everyone recognizes the Promised Land as "home", the worker is "at home" in the socialist revolution, while his native town—Manchester, Marseilles, Moscow, or wherever—is "home" viewed in the new way, that is, without alienation. The masses thus take possession of their heritage.

This new way of seeing familiar things depends on the Marxist conception of the international class struggle. But some of the characters are identified by their nationality (an American, for instance, and an Australian). Why should they be "Clean" rather than "Unclean"? Is there no proletariat in America or Australia? Such contradictions, often reflecting Mayakovsky's own anarchism and Bohemian irreverence, actually run through the play, making it dynamic and popular rather than theoretically sound.

This popular manner is everywhere present. The prologue, delivered in the style of a fairground barker, promises "life transformed by the theatre into a spectacle most extraordinary!", thereby immediately demystifying the drama. Spectacle is at the heart of Mayakovsky's theatre, just as it is at the heart of popular theatre, and *Mystery Bouffe* has the gaudy glitter of a popular carnival. Meyerhold's production employed banners and slogans, spilled the action into the auditorium, and presented Mayakovsky's gallery of bourgeois grotesques with

Mystery-Bouffe: Moscow Satire Theatre, 1958

a mixture of individualised buffoonery and circus-style daring, contrasting them with the solid mass of the workers, all dressed alike, often chanting their lines in unison. The play is a kaleidoscopic "montage of attractions", enabling us to delight in the theatricality of theatre.

The mystery-play framework is a powerful counterweight to the elements of bouffonade, for a mystery-play deals with legendary but important matters; here the revolution is made heroic and legendary. But *Mystery Bouffe* is a mystery-play in reverse, for the all-pervading feeling is blasphemous, not pious. Mayakovsky uses the common religious image of walking on the water to show the post-revolutionary, common man capable of this miracle. A few moments later the Sermon on the Mount is turned upside down to glorify the revolutionary fighter. And when the proletariat steal Jehovah's thunderbolts, they are seen as useless in the new materialist, socialist society: the new thunder is the roar of the steam train and the giant cargo ship.

This urgent reinterpretation of timeless imagery helps us to feel the present in relation to the past and to the future. History is shown in the making, affecting, and being affected by, common people, who are no longer the passive victims of uncontrollable forces, but are able to "move mountains"—literally in the Land of Chaos, when they hurl them out of their way.

Thus, for all its apparent ingenuousness, *Mystery Bouffe* is, as Huntley Carter noticed, "different in conception and substance" from anything that had preceded it. Significant at least for clearing the way for a new revolutionary or socialist drama, it is, in itself, an extravagant and rumbustious Aristophanic celebration.

—Robert Leach

N-TOWN PLAYS
Anonymous

Editions

Ludus Coventriae, edited by K.S. Block, 1922, Oxford (Early English Text Society Series).

The Mary Play from the N-Town Manuscript, edited by Peter Meredith, London and New York, 1987.

The Passion Play from the N-Town Manuscript, edited by Peter Meredith, London and New York, 1990.

Criticism

Books:

Esther Lydia Swenson, *An Inquiry into the Composition and Structure of "Ludus Coventriae"*, Minneapolis, Minnesota, 1914.

Articles:

John Kester Bonnell, "The Source in Art of the So-Called Prophet's Play in the *Hegge* Collection", in *Publications of the Modern Language Association* [*PMLA*], 29, 1914.

Hardin Craig, "Note on the Home of the *Ludus Coventriae*", in *University of Minnesota Studies in Language and Literature*, 1, 1914.

Madeleine H. Dodds, "The Problem of the *Ludus Coventriae*", in *Modern Language Review*, 9, 1914.

W.W. Gregg, "*Ludus Coventriae*", in *The Library* (third series), 5, 1914.

K.S. Block, "Some Notes on the Problem of the *Ludus Coventriae*", in *Modern Language Review*, 10, 1915.

Hardin Craig, "The Lincoln Cordwainer's Pageant", in *Publications of the Modern Language Association* [*PMLA*], 32, 1917.

Howard Rollin Patch, "The *Ludus Coventriae* and the Digby Massacre", in *Publications of the Modern Language Association* [*PMLA*], 35, 1920.

George Coffin Taylor, "The *Christis Redivivus* of Nicholas Grimald and the Hegge Resurrection Plays", in *Publications of the Modern Language Association* [*PMLA*], 41, 1926.

Henry W. Wells, "*Ludus Coventriae*", in *American Church Monthly*, 22, 1927.

Albert C. Baugh, "A Recent Theory of the *Ludus Coventriae*", in *Philological Quarterly*, 12, 1933.

Thomas Blake Clark, "A New Theory Concerning the Identity and History of the *Ludus Coventriae* Cycle of Mystery Plays", in *Philological Quarterly*, 12, 1933.

F.M. Salter, "The Old Testament Apocryphal Elements in Eight Plays of the *Ludus Coventriae*", in *Philological Quarterly*, 12, 1933.

Miriam J. Benkovitz, "Some Notes on the 'Prologue of Demon' of *Ludus Coventriae*", in *Modern Language Notes*, 60, 1945.

Timothy Fry, "The Unity of the *Ludus Coventriae*", in *Studies in Philology*, 48, 1951.

Joseph Allen Bryant Jr., "The Function of *Ludus Coventriae 14*", in *Journal of English and Germanic Philology*, 52, 1953.

Sister Mary Patricia Forrest, "Apocryphal Sources of St. Anne's Day Plays in the *Hegge Cycle*", in *Medievalia et Humanistica*, 17, 1966.

Sister Mary Patricia Forrest, "The Role of the Expositor Contemplacio in the St. Anne's Day Plays of the *Hegge Cycle*", in *Medieval Studies*, 28, 1966.

Kenneth Cameron and Stanley J. Kahrl, "Staging the *N-Town Cycle*", in *Theatre Notebook*, 21, 1967.

Anne C. Gay, "The 'Stage' and the Staging of the *N-Town Plays*", in *Research Opportunities in Renaissance Drama*, 10, 1967.

Jacob Bennett, "The Language and the Home of the *Ludus Coventriae*", in *Orbis Litterarum*, 22, 1973.

Martial Rose, "The Staging of the *Hegge Plays*", in *Medieval Drama*, edited by Neville Denny, London, 1973 (Stratford-Upon-Avon Studies).

Daniel P. Poteet II, "Time, Eternity, and Dramatic Form in *Ludus Coventriae: Passion Play 1*", in *Comparative Drama*, 8, 1974.

Daniel P. Poteet II, "Symbolic Character and Form in the *Ludus Coventriae: Play of Noah*", in *American Benedictine Review*, 26, 1975.

Daniel P. Poteet II, "Condition, Contrast, and Division in the *Ludus Coventriae: Woman Taken in Adultery*", in *Mediaevalia*, vol.1 no.1, 1975.

Stephen Spector, "The Composition and Development of an Eclectic Manuscript: Cotton Vespasian D VIII", in *Leeds Studies in English*, 9, 1975.

Peter Meredith, "A Reconsideration of Some Textual Problems in the *N-Town* Manuscript", in *Leeds Studies in English*, 9, 1976–77.

Theresa Coletti, "Devotional Iconography in the *N-Town Marian Plays*", in *Comparative Drama*, 11, 1977.

Gail McMurray Gibson, " 'Porta haec clausa erit': Comedy, Conception, and Ezekiel's Closed Door in the *Ludus Coventriae: Play of Joseph's Return*", in *Journal of Medieval and Renaissance Studies*, 8, 1978.

Lynn Squires, "Law and Disorder in *Ludus Coventriae*", in *Comparative Drama*, 12, 1978.

Kathleen M. Ashley, " 'Wyt' and 'Wysdam' in the *N-Town Cycle*", in *Philological Quarterly*, 58, 1979.

Theresa Coletti, "Sacrament and Sacrifice in the *N-Town Passion*", in *Mediaevalia*, 7, 1981.

Alan J. Fletcher, "The Design of the *N-Town* Play of *Mary's Deception*", in *Modern Philology*, vol.79 no.2, 1981.

Gail McMurray Gibson, "Bury St. Edmunds, Lydgate, and the *N-Town Cycle*", in *Speculum*, vol. 56 no. 1, 1981.

Alan J. Fletcher, "Layers of Revision in the *N-Town* Marian Cycle", in *Neophilologus*, vol.66 no.2, 1982.

Elizabeth J. El Itreby, "The *N-Town* Play of *The Woman Taken in Adultery*: Central to a Recapitulative 'Redemption Trilogy'", in *Forum* (Muncie, Indiana), vol.26 no.3, 1985.

Michael J. Wright, "*Ludus Coventriae Passion Play 1*: Action and Interpretation", in *Neuphilologische Mitteilungen*, vol. 86 no. 1, 1985.

John F. Plummer, "The Logomachy of the *N-Town Passion Play 1*", in *Journal of English and Germanic Philology*, vol.83 no.3, 1989.

*   *   *

The group of biblical plays now referred to as *The N-Town Plays* has been an object and a cause of confusion since it was first studied critically. For understandable reasons, the plays were long believed to constitute the fourth, intact, surviving cycle of English mystery plays. The group is comprised of 41 plays in a sequence which, like the mystery cycles, traces Christian history from the Creation and Fall of Lucifer to the Last Judgement. The first seven plays deal with Old Testament topics, plays 8 to 13 with the life of the Virgin Mary prior to the Nativity, 14 to 19 with events surrounding the Nativity of Christ, 20 to 24 with his ministry, 25 to 31 with his Passion, and the remainder with events following the Passion including the penultimate play of the Assumption of the Virgin Mary.

The similarity of this arrangement and that of the great civic cycles led to these plays being claimed for Coventry (*Ludus Coventriae*) and for Lincoln, both of which cities are among those with records of mystery playing but no complete cycle. They have also been known in their time as *The Hegge Plays*. After the first known owner of the manuscript. What modern scholarship has revealed is that this manuscript is not a cycle in the manner of those of York or Chester, but a compilation of cycle material, properly pageants, with other distinct, dramatic pieces. The whole did not belong to one town, and is not in anything like a polished, coherent form in the manuscript. Much of the marginalia indicates that the compiler (or compilers) envisaged many possibilities for extracting from the whole to produce a variety of self-sufficient productions. The *Banns*, or explanatory introductory synopses, state: "At vj of þe belle we gynne oure play/In N.town wherfore we pray/That god now be ȝoure Spede", suggesting either a touring production, which would be almost unimaginably ambitious, or a manuscript designed to be lent out for performance either in whole or part.

Nor is there consistent evidence of processional performance, but many of the plays, especially the distinct Passion sequence, show signs, both in the stage directions and the text, of performance on a big outdoor round, comparable, perhaps, with that of *The Castle of Perseverance* or the medieval Cornish plays. Particularly the manner of easy transition from one episode to the next, and directions which insist on simultaneous action in different locations, suggest scaffolds arranged in a semicircle, containing an area of ground in which some of the action might also take place. The dialect of the plays has been located to somewhere in East Anglia, an area with a comparatively wealthy, rural population and of particularly varied, dramatic activity in the 15th century.

The plays have been convincingly demonstrated to be the work of a compiler. The six plays about the early life of the Virgin are drawn from a single distinct source, imported in order to bridge the gap between Old and New Testament material, expanding on the procession of prophets which is the popular choice in the cycles. A distinct Passion play, or truly two separate plays, have also been detected buried within the sequence. The first of these, plays 25 to 27, is physically a separate booklet within the main manuscript. The two are more reminiscent of the major *Passions* of Mons or Lucerne than any surviving, native English plays. Both *The Mary Play* and *The Passion Play* have been reconstructed and published separately by Peter Meredith. The play of the Assumption of the Virgin Mary is written in a distinct hand in the manuscript and is also a physically separable importation, which shows signs of possibly having originally been designed for performance within a church building. It is the sole surviving English play which is comparable with the spectacular indoor Assumptions of the Continent and quite different from the same episode in the York cycle.

Despite the rough and ready, composite nature of the text, the *N-Town Plays* show a surprising degree of tonal evenness. The dominant modes of discourse across the whole text are those of the ceremonies of religion: prayer, liturgical chant, and sermon predominate in place of dialogue. Gesture and action, too, are as much emblematic as narrative. This is not to suggest that the plays lack the power to connect with their audience, but they do so in a distinctive manner. In, for instance, the pageant of Noah and the Flood there is none of the characteristic wrangling between Noah and his unruly wife, for here Noah's wife unites with her husband in obeying God unquestioningly and desiring to bring up their children correctly. The Noah family's plight movingly illustrates that fallen man both needs and merits redemption. Similarly, within the Mary Play, a pitch of decorous celebration is achieved when, after the Annunciation, the Virgin and Elizabeth recite the *Magnificat* together, alternating line by line, Mary in Latin, Elizabeth translating into English. Only in the *N-Town* Passion sequence is the Last Supper predominantly sacramental, focusing on transubstantiation.

Action thus constantly hovers between the historical and the allegorical. The broad unifying themes of the collection explore the nature of the central action of Redemption through examining the nature of justice and mercy, the old and new laws. The dramatist(s), therefore, imported the feudal allegory of the "four daughters of God"—Justice, Truth, Mercy, and Peace—in dramatic form at the moment when the "historical" sequence of events directly preceding the Redemption is about to begin. The *N-Town Plays* are celebratory, but not in the festive manner of the occasional cycles; their dramatic celebration of the Christian story is more removed, more conscious of a desire to give dramatic form to the ineffable. *The Mary Play* section has a commentator figure called Contemplatio who acts as mediator between play and audience, but, in line with the special emotive force of these plays, he not only explains the action to the audience but adds his voice to the intercessions and illustrates the kind of meditative, emotional response which these plays seem contrived to inspire.

—Pamela M. King

NA DNE.   See THE LOWER DEPTHS.

NAOZAMURAI.   See **SAMURAI NAO.**

NÅR VI DØDE VÅGNER. See **WHEN WE DEAD AWAKEN.**

NEDOROSL.   See **THE MINOR.**

LES NÈGRES.   See **THE BLACKS.**

NEPHELAI.   See **THE CLOUDS.**

A NEW WAY TO PAY OLD DEBTS
by Philip Massinger

First Publication: London, 1633.
First Production: Possibly by Queen Henrietta's Men, c. 1625.

Editions
A New Way to Pay Old Debts, edited by A.H. Cruikshank, Oxford, 1926.
A New Way to Pay Old Debts, in *Elizabethan Plays*, edited by H. Spencer, Boston, 1933.
A New Way to Pay Old Debts, edited by M. St. Clare Byrne, London, 1949.
A New Way to Pay Old Debts, edited by T.W. Craik, London, 1964 (New Mermaid Series).
A New Way to Pay Old Debts, in *Drama of the English Renaissance: Stuart Drama*, edited by Russell A. Fraser and Norman Rabkin, New York and London, 1976.
A New Way to Pay Old Debts, in *The Selected Plays of Philip Massinger*, edited by Colin Gibson, Cambridge, 1978.

Criticism
(For general works on the author, see *Playwrights* volume)

Books:
Robert Hamilton Ball, *The Amazing Career of Sir Giles Overreach*, Princeton, New Jersey, 1939.

Articles:
D.J. Enright, "Poetic Satire in Verse: A Consideration of Ben Jonson and Philip Massinger", in *Scrutiny*, 18, 1951.
Patricia Thomson, "The Old Way and the New Way in Dekker and Massinger", in *Modern Language Review*, 51, 1956.
Alan Gerald Cross, "Social Change and Philip Massinger", in *Studies in English Literature 1500–1900*, 7, 1967.
Frederick M. Burelbach Jr., "*A New Way to Pay Old Debts*: Jacobean Morality", in *College Language Association Journal*, 12, 1969.

R.A Fothergill, "The Dramatic Experience of Massinger's *The City Madam* and *A New Way to Pay Old Debts*", in *University of Toronto Quarterly*, 43, 1973.
Michael Neill, "Massinger's Patriarchy: The Social Vision of *A New Way to Pay Old Debts*", in *Renaissance Drama*, 10, 1979.
Albert H. Tricomi, "*A New Way to Pay Old Debts* and the Country-House Poetic Tradition", in *Medieval and Renaissance Drama in England*, 3, 1986.

*   *   *

Sir Giles Overreach, a rich and ruthless man of property, is determined to marry his daughter Margaret into the nobility. Despite her unwillingness, he pursues a match with the soldierly Lord Lovell. Alworth, Lovell's page, and stepson of the widowed Lady Alworth, loves Margaret, a love which she reciprocates, and with the connivance of his master takes his place when Overreach is prompted to arrange a secret marriage. In the past, Sir Giles deliberately ruined his nephew, the prodigal but good-hearted Welborne, to secure his lands. Welborne tricks Overreach and his lawyer Marrall into believing that he will acquire new wealth and property by marriage to Lady Alworth. In the hope of further gain, his uncle pays off his creditors, and Marrall, turning against his master, reveals that the document consigning Welborne's estate to Overreach is worthless. The discovery of Margaret's marriage to Alworth, the triumph of his enemies, and the loss of Welborne's lands drives Overreach mad, and he is committed to Bedlam. Lord Lovell and Welborne prepare to leave together on a new military campaign, but not before Lovell and Lady Alworth have also agreed on marriage.

Massinger's play is built out of traditional comic materials: the outwitting of their elders by improvident and romantically-minded younger people; a clever scheme to deceive and humiliate a wealthy and ruthlessly ambitious man; the development of natural affection between social equals; and, in the Jonsonian "humours" figure of Greedy, Overreach's tame Justice, the ridicule of moral corruption by its association with gross physical appetite. But the unusual, Nottinghamshire setting provides no dream world for the fulfilment of romance and the satisfaction of justice. Overreach and his accomplice Justice Greedy embody some of the ruthless, business practices of contemporary, real-life land-grabbers and extortioners, in particular the hated monopolist Sir Giles Mompesson and his agent Sir Francis Michell. The background of military preparations for war in the Low Countries is also authentic, and Massinger's personal experience of a great nobleman's household infuses his account of life above and below stairs in Lady Alworth's house.

One early playgoer admired the "fresh conceit" and well-crafted "mazes of the cunning plot", but Welborne's scheme to gull his uncle is a reworking of a similar intrigue in Thomas Middleton's popular play *A Trick to Catch the Old One* (1608), and Massinger actually keeps his narrative relatively uncomplicated, the lines of action clear. Massinger's skill is rather shown in the generous provision for ironic reversals which display the confusion of fools and rogues and the unstable loyalties of menials and servants, and his knitting together of a complex chain of cause and effect which culminates in the grand catastrophe that overtakes his villain-hero, Overreach.

For all its genial temper, signalled in the lenient punishments administered to all the fools and rogues but Overreach, the drama is given a disturbing edge by its author's convincing stage representation of strong, primitive emotions and the unprincipled shabbiness of much ordinary human behaviour. Marrall's servile hatred of his domineering master; Over-

A New Way to Pay Old Debts: Stratford-Upon-Avon, The Other Place, 1983 (Royal Shakespeare Company)

reach's passion for his daughter's social advancement (verging on the incestuous sexuality which surfaces in Massinger's contemporary tragedy *The Unnatural Combat*); Margaret's dignified, and finally desperate, appeals to her father's better nature; Welborne's seedy past and ready resort to outright violence against his tormentors; the Tapwells, as well as Alworth's nervous suspicion of his master's intentions towards Margaret, and Lady Alworth's servants' contemptuous hilarity over Marrall's social ignorance and awkwardness—all make for rewarding theatrical roles as well as providing a subtle and detailed analysis of pride, status, and social relationships.

In the 18th and 19th centuries, the histrionic opportunities offered by the role of Sir Giles, with its combination of obdurate villainy and violent emotions, attracted a succession of brilliant actors—John Henderson, Kemble, George Frederick Cooke, Samuel Phelps, Charles Kean, Edwin Booth, and E.L. Davenport. Edmund Kean's portrayal of Overreach turned the role into a star one, to be attempted by every aspiring actor in Great Britain and America. Overreach was played on a heroic scale that frequently brought audiences (and sometimes Kean's fellow actors) to the point of hysteria: a contemporary reviewer described the final act of his Overreach as "without doubt, the most terrific exhibition of human passion that has been witnessed on the modern stage".

Modern criticism has focused on the scheme of traditional social and moral values that underlies the action of the comedy, finding variously a simple-minded endorsement of aristocratic and patriarchal values, a defence of birth and blood against new-won riches, or an even-handed account of unscrupulous aristocrats banding together to oppose and eradicate the vigorous social and economic challenge posed by a middle-class intruder. The play certainly presents a serious, moral programme, signalled in its title, in which tradition, age, rank, order, and obligations of many kinds are weighed against innovation, youth, ambition, anarchic vitality, and egotistical satisfaction, but the dramatic presentation of these issues is not easily reduced to trite formulae (even those offered in the dialogue), and Massinger's ability to express individual personality in natural and flexible verse in a context of comic satisfactions has kept his play alive in the theatre ever since its revival by Garrick in 1748.

—Colin Gibson

THE NEW YORK IDEA
by Langdon Mitchell

First Publication: New York, 1906.
First Production: Lyric Theatre, New York, 19 November 1906.

*   *   *

Cynthia Karslake, a New York society woman divorced from her first husband, John, is about to marry stodgy judge, Philip Phillimore, who is himself recently divorced from his first wife, Vida. Cynthia, already bored by the rigid propriety of Philip's family, is unsettled by meeting John when he tries to sell one of his racehorses to Phillimore. She is further upset by a flirtation between John and Vida Phillimore and comes to realize that she is still in love with John. On impulse, she runs off to the racecourse with a sporting Englishman, Sir Wilfrid Cates-Darby. Returning in time for her wedding, Cynthia, in despair at what she takes to be an engagement between John and Vida, tries to go through with the ceremony but balks at the last minute. In the last act she pursues John to his house, where the two discover that they are still in love, and, thanks to a telephone call from John's lawyer, learn that they were never really divorced.

Following in the tradition of American social comedy dating back to Royall Tyler's *The Contrast* (1787), Langdon Mitchell satirizes the manners and mores of his contemporaries, specifically the penchant for divorce and remarriage among New York's upper class, and the resulting embarrassment when divorced couples meet one another in homes and at social gatherings. The play thus operates on two levels, as a serious indictment of lenient divorce laws and as a delightful comedy of manners in which former husbands and wives pop up at the most inconvenient moments. For modern readers and audiences the discussion of divorce may seem dated, but the vivid characterizations of Cynthia and John, the sparkling dialogue, and the farcical situations in which the various formerly-married characters find themselves remain fresh and pleasing.

Mitchell wrote *The New York Idea* with the encouragement of the distinguished actress Minnie Maddern Fiske, and the part of Cynthia Karslake was specifically tailored to Mrs. Fiske's cerebral and understated acting style. Nervous, discontented, consumed by a passion for horse-racing, Cynthia tries to negotiate the complicated social situation with dignity and grace, but an emotional exchange with John causes her to cast aside the proprieties in order to go with Sir Wilfrid to the races. This taste of freedom leads her to a greater rebellion when she jilts Philip, her "sober second choice", to return to John. John, on the other hand, has developed a cynical attitude toward marriage with which he masks his pain at losing Cynthia. He is not above using Vida Phillimore to arouse Cynthia's jealousy (while Vida uses John to encourage Sir Wilfrid to propose), but his generous and sportsmanlike attitude is clearly meant to make him sympathetic to the audience, especially in contrast to the stuffy and self-righteous Philip.

To John are given most of the humorous epigrams about marriage and divorce. He explains that "marriage is three parts love and seven parts forgiveness of sins", and "modern marriage is like a wire fence; the woman's the wire—the posts are the husbands. . .and if you cast your eye over the future, you can count them, post after post, up hill, down dale, all the way to Dakota!". Cynthia's wit lies in her ability to size up the absurdities of the other characters; thus, when Philip's priggish cousin, scandalized that Cynthia went to the racecourse on her wedding day, threatens to take back his wedding present, "an Egyptian scarab—a—a—sacred beetle, which once ornamented the person of a—eh—mummy", Cynthia replies, "It should never be absent from your pocket, Mr. Sudley".

The other characters in *The New York Idea* are drawn in broader strokes. Philip and his family are obsessed with social position and the observation of proprieties; they speak in a ludicrously stilted manner, as when Philip, in trying to persuade Cynthia to go through with the wedding, tells her, "I cannot cuculate like a wood pigeon, but—I esteem you!". Vida is a typical seductress who tries to charm every man who comes near her. And Sir Wilfrid is a stereotypical stage Englishman of the period, at home at the racecourse, completely at sea when faced with the tangled social relationships of the divorced couples, but intrigued by the "ginger" of American women.

Turn-of-the-century critics praised Mitchell for tackling what they considered to be an important social issue—the lenient divorce laws passed by some states that enabled couples to end their marriages for what were then viewed as flimsy reasons. From a modern perspective the moral issues seem quaint and dated, while Cynthia's last-minute escape from Philip, her subsequent reunion with John, and the convenient discovery that their divorce was invalid, smack of melodrama. Nevertheless, the play's depiction of American high society at the turn of the century gives it a certain historical appeal, and the lively dialogue and vivid characters have continued to make *The New York Idea* popular with readers and theatre audiences over the years.

—Margaret M. Knapp

NEXT TIME I'LL SING TO YOU
by James Saunders

First Publication: London, 1963.
First Production: Questors Theatre, London, 1962; revised version, New Arts Theatre, London, 1963.

Criticism
(For general works on the author, see *Playwrights* volume)

Articles:

Hildegard Hammerschmidt, "*Next Time I'll Sing to You*", in her *Das historische Drama in England (1956–1971): Erscheinungsformen und Entwicklungstendenzen*, Wiesbaden, 1972.

Eckhard Auberlen, "Die Nutzung des dramatischen Mediums in James Saunders' *Next Time I'll Sing to You*", in *Germanisch-Romanische Monatsschrift*, 30, 1980.

Karl K. Schäfer, "*Next Time I'll Sing to You*", in his *Hundlung im neueren britischen Drama: eine Untersuchung an Dramen der fünfziger und sechziger Jahre*, Frankfurt, 1985.

*   *   *

Prompted by the subject of Raleigh Trevelyan's *A Hermit Disclosed*, *Next Time I'll Sing to You* stages rehearsals for, and around, a play about the last 36 years in the life of Alexander James Mason, the hermit of Great Canfield. Rudge, the play's producer, is joined by Dust, Meff, and Lizzie (whose identical twin sister may or may not have participated in earlier rehearsals) together with a figure named "Hermit" (actor and role progressively merging as the play and the rehearsals advance) to "understand the purpose of existence; of one man". "We are all that man", Rudge insists: "Examine him and we shall see ourselves".

The hermit, however, is not so much a discrete "character" (as he himself becomes increasingly aware) as what he terms a "hole in the play", into which possible explanations and narratives, once rehearsed, are caused to disappear. Moreover, as Rudge very quickly concedes, "we are discussing not so much the man nor even the reason for the man but the reason for the discussion of the reason for the man". A marginalised and, he supposes, misunderstood figure, the hermit withers under the assaults of those empowered to interpret him but not before, in Rudge's words, he "identifies himself" in inviting their pity for the "grief" they grudgingly recognise. At the play's close Rudge briefly examines, then significantly departs with, the hermit's diary, hitherto deemed inadmissible evidence; future rehearsals may, in no large measure, be indebted to it for whatever illumination it may be hoped it will provide. Personal testimony (the hermit believes himself to have been a saint) has dubious authenticity in a play which shows not only the fictive nature of the expressed self—and the provisional, partisan nature of all explanation whatever—but which also stages its own procedures so persistently. The play demands we question the relationship between the reality of our solitary condition and the convivialities of the "ritual dance", be it love, conversation, or theatre. For "what is creation", Dust asks, "but part of oneself?".

Moreover, "we all", Meff declares in defence of dung-beetles, "have our parts to play". Rudge echoes Shakespeare's Jacques, "All the world's a stage", thereby staging the remark itself which he does in the course of a game of verbal cricket. Though the accusation of having "bowled a metaphor" cannot be levelled against him when he later alludes to *Macbeth* in observing that grief "signifies—nothing", it remains clear that "grief is most evident" outside the play's verbal gamesmanship—in the "silence after a joke" but also in "loneliness where there is no escape" except in the routines and rituals within which grief hides.

Next Time I'll Sing To You parades its metatheatricality in a manner which shows Saunders's debt to the drama of Ionesco and Pirandello (Kenneth Tynan dubbed the play "Actors in search of a Character") and to Beckett's *Waiting for Godot*. Saunders's underrated play persistently highlights the ubiquities of metaphor and reflection, through which reality is displaced by the creations of creatures incapable of sustaining more than an image of a putative creator. Rudge's assumption of the role of God, able dispassionately to displace himself from the world he rehearses, is quickly grounded; replications in webs and mirrors (which go some way towards accounting for Lizzie's twin sister) implicate actors and audience alike in a collective but mutually antagonistic striving for identity and understanding. Incorporating problems of evolution, determinism, individual development, and control, Meff and Dust, under Rudge's provisional direction, play out their prescribed roles in insinuating, sometimes insisting upon, identities for the hermit: "Do you want your identity", Dust asks him "in terms physical, psychological, biological, biochemical, sociological, statistical or mystical?".

But such portentousness is painfully comic. As Dust pillories the hermit, Meff pillages circumstance and opportunity for irreverent advantage. He indulges in music-hall turns, stand-up comedy, and performance routines with an audience whose own complicity he roughly exposes; meanwhile, he flirts with Lizzie whose uncomprehending common sense provides another form of scepticism in a play predicated on little else, but offering, in its gestures to what cannot be imagined and

exploited, a good deal more. *Next Time I'll Sing To You* invites us to "see ourselves" by witnessing a process of construction and dissolution and then feeling for what remains.

—James Hansford

NIEBOSKA KOMEDIA.   See **THE UNDIVINE COMEDY**.

THE NIGHT OF THE IGUANA
by Tennessee Williams

First Publication: New York, 1962.
First Production: Chicago, 1959; revised version, Royale Theatre, New York, 28 December 1961.

Criticism
(For general works on the author, see *Playwrights* volume)

Articles:
George Hendrick, "Jesus and the Osiris-Isis Myth: Lawrence's *The Man Who Died* and Williams's *The Night of the Iguana*", in *Anglia*, 84, 1966.
Ferdinand Leon, "Time, Fantasy, and Reality in *Night of the Iguana*", in *Modern Drama*, 11, 1968.
Helen E. Moritz, "Apparent Sophoclean Echoes in Tennessee Williams's *Night of the Iguana*", in *Classical and Modern Literature*, 5, 1985.

*   *   *

The "Night" of the title is a night in the summer of 1940, a "dark night of the soul" for the two principal characters of Tennessee Williams's play. At the Casa Verde, a run-down hotel on the west coast of Mexico, a busload of disenchanted, Texan schoolteachers—all female—arrive with their guide, Shannon, for what is yet another unscheduled stop. Maxine Faulk, the "rapeciously lusty" and recently widowed proprietor, is glad to see Shannon, who has "cracked up" here before and is about to do so again. Arriving slightly later that afternoon are Hannah Jelkes, a New England spinster and artist, and her "ninety-seven years young" grandfather, Nonno, a poet. He is in a wheelchair, and they are broke. The only other guests are a Nazi family of four. Shannon, a defrocked Episcopalian minister ("fornication and heresy. . .in the same week") is eyed lustfully by Maxine, who would like him to fill her dead husband's shoes, and is also frantically pursued by Charlotte, a teenager who accompanies the teachers and whom Shannon has seduced. In addition to exhaustion, he is experiencing another crisis in his religious faith which is the main cause of his imminent "crack-up". Replaced by another guide late that evening, Shannon is tied in a hammock to restrain him. That night, Hannah offers him consolation and encouragement. At her request, he cuts loose an iguana which has been caught by the Mexican houseboys and tied under the patio to be fattened for a future meal. Nonno finishes his first poem in two decades and dies a gentle death. Maxine succeeds in persuading Shannon to stay on with her, while Hannah will leave the Casa Verde the next morning.

Iguana is a play about travellers on a pilgrimage through life. It is a "hotel play", one of a genre set in lobbies, bars, and cafes, where an odd assortment of people may quite naturally assemble. Moreover, the Casa Verde is a resort hotel (hotel of last resort?) situated near the sea, "the cradle of life". A fallen Eden, it is surrounded by lush jungle in which all living forms struggle for life, with only the fittest surviving. Facing onto the verandah of the hotel are several "small cubicle bedrooms", sometimes referred to as "cells", which at night are lit from within so that each "appears as a little interior stage"—thus suggesting each character's lonely imprisonment, his "performance" in isolation.

Shannon, the focal character of the play, is facing his third "crack-up" at the Casa Verde. He views life as an operation on two levels, the real and the fantastic ("fantastic" is one of his expressions), but lately he has had to live on the fantastic and operate on the realistic—and "that's when you're spooked". Theologically, his problem involves a reconciliation of his church's view of God as "a cruel, senile delinquent" with his own personal conception of "God as Lightening and Thunder". In the most important scene of the play, Hannah offers Shannon something to believe in—not necessarily a conventional belief in God but the solace of communication between people. In return for her comfort and consolation, he gives her his gold cross, a symbol of his spiritual burden. Since by his own admission "people need human contact", the immediate resolution of his dilemma—after getting through the night with Hannah's help—is to stay on as Maxine's lover and general assistant.

Hannah, like "a Gothic cathedral image of a medieval saint", has a timeless spirituality. She is a seasoned traveller who admits she has been around the world "almost as many times as the world's been around the sun". And like Shannon, she has had her own "spook" which she calls the "blue devil". In diagnosing his problem ("the oldest one in the world—the need to believe in something or in someone"), she not only reveals her own struggles but also shares her answer. She believes in "broken gates between people so they can reach each other, even if it's just for one night only".

Maxine is, in Shannon's words, "bigger than life and twice as unnatural". If Hannah is the spiritual woman, then Maxine is the physical one. Her laugh is "a single harsh, loud bark", like a hungry seal. She is a predatory woman where Shannon is concerned; however, in the last scene of the play, she has mellowed, for she is complete in the knowledge that sexually she has found her match.

Nonno, who published his first book of poetry on "the day that President Ulysses S. Grant was inaugurated", represents the creative artist who has prevailed, temporarily, over time and nature—and is still productive. His poetry is rich in imagery and romantic in a timeless style. His recitation of the newly completed poem in the last minutes of the play is a summing up of his philosophy: courage in the face of age and death. His gentle end is a natural victory of time over the human spirit.

The happy, robust Nazi family, who gleefully listen to a shortwave radio broadcast of the Battle of Britain, are the embodiment, on one level, of German vigor and the national appetite for *lebensraum*, and, on another, of the predatory nature of man operating on an international scale. They are world devourers.

The theme of *The Night of the Iguana*, Williams has said, is "how to live beyond despair and still live". His characters are "learning to reach the point of utter despair and still go past it with courage". The iguana, according to the playwright, "doesn't stand for any particular character in the play; perhaps it stands for the human situation". Other themes include man's inability to communicate; the terror of loneliness; courage in the face of ageing, disability, and death; and the search for God and faith. Based somewhat loosely on a 1948 short story of the same title, *Iguana* is rich in poetry, characterization, symbolism, and wisdom. It is a major work of the last period of Williams's life.

—Gene A. Barnett

1913. See SCENES FROM THE HEROIC LIFE OF THE MIDDLE CLASSES.

NO EXIT (Huis clos)
by Jean-Paul Sartre

First Publication: As *Les Autres*, in *L'Arbalète*, 8, 1944; as *Huis clos*, Paris, 1945.
First Production: Théâtre du Vieux-Colombier, Paris, 27 May 1944.

Translations
No Exit, in *Sartre: Two Plays*, translated by Stuart Gilbert, London, 1946.

Criticism
(For general works on the author, see *Playwrights* volume)

Books:
Bernard Lecherbonnier, "*Huis clos*": *Analyse critique*, Paris, 1972.
Kenneth R. Dutton, *Sartre's "Huis clos": A Theatrical Approach*, North Ryde, Australia, 1973.
Peter Royle, *Sartre: L'Enfer et la liberté: Étude de "Huis clos" et des "Mouches"*, Quebec, 1973.
Thomas Bishop, "*Huis clos*" *de Jean-Paul Sartre*, Paris, 1975.

Articles:
Oreste F. Pucciani, "The Infernal Dialogue of Giraudoux and Sartre", in *Tulane Drama Review*, 3, 1959.
Ernst Loeb, "Sartre's *No Exit* and Brecht's *The Good Woman of Setzuan*", in *Modern Language Quarterly*, vol.22 no.3, 1961.
Edith Kern, "Abandon Hope All Ye. . .", in *Yale French Studies*, 30, 1962–63.
Howard L. Parson, "Existential Hell", in *Journal of Religious Thought*, vol.21 no.1, 1964–65.
Sister M. Carol Blitgen, "*No Exit*: The Satrean Idea of Hell", in *Renascence*, 19, 1967.
A. Maynor Hardee, "Garcin and Sisyphus", in *Discourse*, 12, 1969.
Eugene H. Falk, "*No Exit* and *Who's Afraid of Virginia Woolf?*: A Thematic Comparison", in *Studies in Philology*, 67, 1970.
Micheline Sakharoff, "The Polyvalence of the Theatrical Language in *No Exit*", in *Modern Drama*, vol.16 no.2, 1973.
Michael Issacharoff, "Sartre et les signes: La Dynamique spatiale de *Huis clos*", in *Travaux de linguistique et de littérature*, vol.15 no.2, 1977.

Rhiannon Goldthorpe, "*Huis clos*: An Ambiguous Thesis Play Reconsidered", in *French Studies*, 34, 1980.
Konstantin Kolenda, "The Impasse of *No Exit*", in *Philosophy and Literature*, 8, 1984.

*   *   *

Garcin, a South American pacifist writer, appears after death at the doors of hell, which, for him, is a Second Empire style drawing-room. The servant introduces two recently dead women, Garcin's companions for eternity: Inez, a lesbian who readily admits to having driven her lover to suicide and to the murder of Inez herself; and Estelle, a beautiful young woman who at first cannot understand why she is in hell. Although Garcin and Inez soon realize that they will only torment each other by talking (Estelle is slower to understand the situation), no one can keep silent. They force each other to admit the reasons for their presence in hell. Estelle killed her new-born baby and drove her younger lover to suicide. Garcin tormented his wife. What he finds much harder to face is his desertion from the army. After being captured, he was shot and died in a cowardly fashion. All three can still "see" what happens shortly after their deaths; they realize they are powerless to change the impressions of those who knew them on earth. There is little action in the play. Garcin tries to make Inez tell him he was not a coward. Inez and Garcin compete for Estelle's attention. Garcin tries to kill Inez, who points out that she is already dead. Finally they see that hell is, indeed, the relentless gaze of others upon a self that is no longer capable of change: "Hell is other people". The torment will go on. Garcin's last words are "Let us continue".

Sartre's hell is a place with none of the usual physical tortures; instead it is a series of reasonably comfortable rooms, strange only in that the light is always on, there is no way to sleep, and there are no mirrors. Garcin also notices that the servant's eyelids have atrophied. In Hell, one cannot even blink. Hell, therefore, is continually looking at others and being looked at by others, without even being able to see oneself in a mirror, in order to compose a face to present to the gaze of the world. Garcin tries the door and discovers that it would be possible to leave the room, but realizes he prefers to stay with his fellow tormentors. But there is no way to change or to escape judgement. There is "no exit" from one's past mistakes.

The characters learn, when they can no longer benefit from the lesson, that life means the ability to change, not to be confined to one's own self-image or the judgement of others; Hell is being fixed forever, incapable of deluding yourself or others about the significance of what you have done. Hell is a state that many people are willing to accept, however, as it is less fraught with anguish than living with constant awareness of one's freedom. In the terminology of Sartre's existentialism, hell is living as a "being in itself" (*être-en-soi*, an object) rather than a "being for oneself" (*être-pour-soi*, with freedom of choice). The play can be interpreted as an illustration of the psychological torture of being reduced to an "essence"; it is a call for the exercise of freedom to choose one's own values in a world without God. There is, however, no suggestion that the values one might choose are different from those of Christian morality. The reasons Garcin, Estelle, and Inez are in Hell are reasons that might be explicable in terms of traditional religion (cowardice, mistreatment of one's wife or lover, infanticide). Looked at from our later perspective, *No Exit* does not seem especially subversive of conventional moral values.

Sartre's imagination follows conventional lines in his characterizations, particularly of Inez and Estelle. Inez is a stereotypical lesbian, tough, with no sympathy for men, quick to try to seduce Estelle. Estelle is a stereotypical dumb blonde, who married for money, takes a young lover, even after death is concerned about her appearance, and tries to see back into life on earth in order to spy on the sexual behaviour of her acquaintances. Garcin's weakness in deserting from the army rather than taking a firm stand on his pacifist principles is less dramatically presented than his humiliation of his wife by bringing his mistress into the marital home. Entry into Hell then is caused by one's sexual relationships, and Hell becomes other people looking at your own sexual relationships when you can no longer change them.

While very effective theatre and a striking choice of image for the modern Hell, *No Exit* is traditional in its structure. The play conforms to the classical Unities—one set, one action, occurring within the space of a few hours. It is written in one act, divided into five scenes; the first four being very short introductions of the three characters into Hell. Almost all the drama occurs in Scene Five. It is the most tightly constructed of Sartre's plays, and gains considerable power from the economy of the situation. It is also an echo of the "well-made" play popular in France from the late-19th century: a conversation in a drawing-room in which the past is gradually revealed. But, as it is set in Hell, no changes can result from the revelation of the past. *No Exit* has power through its lack of action, lack of movement, reliance on speeches in the French classical tradition. It is effective precisely because it takes a conventional form, and, ironically, changes the drawing-room of bourgeois life into a hell.

No Exit was first produced in Paris in 1944 during the German occupation. Although it was seen as a reflection of the particular hell under which the French were then living, the play is less political in its implications than most of Sartre's work, including *The Flies* (*Les Mouches*), which was also first performed during the occupation. Garcin is a pacifist, not a fighter against tyranny. Since it was produced in the year following the publication of *Being and Nothingness* (*L'Etre et le Néant*, 1943), *No Exit* is often seen primarily in the light of Sartre's philosophical preoccupations. While the play can be explained in terms of his existentialism, it succeeds as a forceful and economical dramatization of how people define their identity in relation to others and how they torment one another.

—Adele King

NO MAN'S LAND
by Harold Pinter

First Publication: London, 1975.
First Production: Old Vic, London (National Theatre Company), 23 April 1975.

Criticism
(For general works on the author, see *Playwrights* volume)

Articles:
John B. Jones, "Stasis as Structure in Pinter's *No Man's Land*", in *Modern Drama*, 19, 1976.
Steven H. Gale, "Harold Pinter's *No Man's Land*: Life at a Standstill", in *Jewish Quarterly*, vol.24 no.4, 1976–77.
Shari Benstock, "Harold Pinter: Where the Road Ends", in *Modern British Literature*, 2, 1977.

Krystyna Napiórkowska, "Harold Pinter's *No Man's Land*: Communication in the Making", in *Studia Anglica Posnaniensia*, 9, 1977.

R.G. Collins, "Pinter and the End of Endings", in *Queen's Quarterly*, 85, 1978.

Kristen Morrison, "Pinter, Albee, and the 'Maiden in the Shark Pond' ", in *American Imago*, 35, 1978.

Thomas P. Adler, "From Flux to Fixity: Art and Death in Pinter's *No Man's Land*", in *Arizona Quarterly*, 35, 1979.

Katharine H. Burkman, "Earth and Water: The Question of Renewal in Harold Pinter's *Old Times* and *No Man's Land*", in *West Virginia University Philological Papers*, 25, 1979.

Ewa Byczkowska, "Discourse and the Pattern of Personal Relationships in Pinter's *No Man's Land*", in *Acta Universitatis Wratislaviensis*, 454, 1979.

Ruby Cohn, "Words Working Overtime: *Endgame* and *No Man's Land*", in *Yearbook of English Studies*, 9, 1979.

Therese Fischer-Seidel, "Pinter in *No Man's Land*: Selbsparodie als Mittel poetologischer Reflexion", in *Germanisch-Romanische Monatsschrift*, 29, 1979.

Anthony Suter, "The Dual Character and the Aim of the Artist in Pinter's *No Man's Land*", in *Durham University Journal*, vol.75 no.2, 1983.

Susan Melrose, "Theatre, Linguistics, and Two Productions of *No Man's Land*", in *New Theatre Quarterly*, 1, 1985.

Joachim Möller, "Erlebnisdenken als Rollenspiel in Pinters *No Man's Land*", in *Forum modernes Theater*, vol.1 no.1, 1986.

*   *   *

The plot of Harold Pinter's two-act play *No Man's Land* contains virtually no action. In a large room in his "*well but sparely furnished*" house in north-west London, Hirst, a man in his 60's, is entertaining Spooner, another man in his 60's, when the curtain rises. According to Pinter's stage directions, "*the central feature of the room is an antique cabinet, with marble top, brass gallery and open shelves, on which stands a great variety of bottles*". Apparently Hirst has invited Spooner into his home for a drink. During their conversation, the two men talk about their lives, primarily about the past—their mothers, their wives, their friends, and their professional activities. As the alcohol begins to take effect, Hirst observes that "no man's land. . .does not move. . .or change. . .or grow old. . .remains. . .forever. . .icy. . .silent". Spooner reacts to this statement with a comment reminiscent of T. S. Eliot's *The Love Song of J. Alfred Prufrock*. By the end of Act One Hirst has fallen to the floor in a drunken stupor and is led out by Briggs, one of his servants. The act ends in a black-out when Foster, another servant, turns off the light leaving Spooner standing alone in the room.

Act Two takes place the next morning. Spooner is still alone in the room. Soon Briggs enters and he and Spooner talk about Hirst. After a while Hirst reappears and talks to Spooner as though he has known him for a long time, as indicated by the details of Spooner's life that he includes in his conversation. In Act One Spooner told what may well be an apocryphal story about his seduction of Hirst's wife. In Act Two Hirst denies that that affair took place, but suggests that he may have committed adultery. Slowly the conversation dwindles and all four men in the play come to a stop both physically and intellectually. At the conclusion of the play they determine that the subject for discussion is winter, and "it'll therefore be winter forever". Spooner, referring to Hirst's description of no man's land in Act One, says, "You are in no man's land. Which never moves, which never changes, which never grows older, but which remains forever, icy and silent". Hirst replies, "I'll drink to that". The play ends with the lights slowly fading.

Despite the thin plot line, *No Man's Land* is a marvelously wrought play with an intricate structure and sustained humor. The meaning is difficult to pinpoint, but the overall image presented is clear. Hirst, who may have been a poet (though there is no evidence other than hearsay presented in the play to establish this as fact) seems to have reached a point in his life where he is essentially living a dead past, unable to function in the present, much less to move forward into the future. He lives with his memories and uses alcohol to numb himself to a world in which he no longer functions. Throughout the play, Spooner, who claims to be a poet and critic, appears to be trying to help move Hirst out of his frozen "no man's land", yet he is unsuccessful. Allusions to Eliot's *The Love Song of J. Alfred Prufrock* abound in the play, and given the thematic development within the drama and the fact that both Spooner and Hirst refer to the poem, it is obvious that the concepts of failure and paralysis are central to the meaning of *No Man's Land*. This perspective is reinforced by other allusions to paralysis from *Hamlet* and Samuel Beckett's *Endgame*. Hirst relies on his view of the past to endure in the present and it is interesting to see how references to light and shadow are incorporated in the drama to reflect this. For example, Hirst's memories involve a metaphysical combination of light, sensitivity, and change. The most striking example of this is evidenced in his description of the pictures in his photo album which link the light-and-shadow impression to memory.

On more symbolic and metaphoric levels, the play can be seen as an exploration of an individual paralyzed by the fear of old age or trapped between the fear of living and the fear of dying. Spooner may represent Death, come for Hirst (*vide* the allusion to Charon, the boatman who ferries dead souls across the River Styx, for example), and Hirst's question, "Is there a big fly in here? I hear buzzing", reverberates with overtones of death because it recalls Emily Dickinson's poem *I heard a fly buzzing where I died*. The freezing of time at the end of the drama indicates that the cycle of the seasons (i.e. life) has come to an end.

Other related interpretations can be drawn from the men's discussions of the nature of art, which in one sense is contrary to life in that it is frozen, yet in another sense is more fluid than life because every observer can interpret a work of art anew and differently, and the work lives on after the artist's death. This theme is compatible with Pinter's "memory" plays, such as *Old Times*, as there is a suggestion that the loss of the ability to manipulate the past through the creation of memories is simultaneously a loss of artistic talent and a kind of death. The concept of existentialism is apparent here, too: Hirst comments, "In my day nobody changed. A man was"; in existentialist philosophy, this situation—the cessation of a person's "becoming"—is the equivalent of death.

While not Pinter's best play, *No Man's Land* is certainly fascinating and demonstrates the masterful stagecraft that one of the most important dramatists of the 20th century can employ in expressing his thematic explorations of the nature of human life.

—Steven H. Gale

LA NOCHE DE LOS ASESINOS.   See **THE CRIMINALS.**

NORM AND AHMED
by Alexander Buzo

First Publication: In *Norm and Ahmed; Rooted; The Roy Murphy Show*, Sydney and London, 1973.
First Production: Sydney, 1974.

Criticism
(For general works on the author, see *Playwrights* volume)

Books:
Terry Sturm, *Alexander Buzo's "Rooted" and "Norm and Ahmed": A Critical Introduction*, Sydney, 1980.

* * *

Norm and Ahmed is a one-act encounter between a white middle-aged working-class "normal" Australian male and a visiting Pakistani undergraduate university student. Norm, rough and solidly built, meets the more refined Ahmed in a Sydney street on a summer night. The entire action of the play takes place in front of a construction site near a bus stop. Having already consumed a few drinks, Norm is anxious to strike up a conversation with whoever happens upon him. While waiting under a street lamp he hears Ahmed approaching. Norm requests a light for his cigarette and Ahmed reciprocates politely. Norm aggressively pursues a dialogue with Ahmed. Initially cautious, Ahmed gradually responds more freely until both characters are enthusiastically telling stories. They discuss a gamut of social and political issues such as racism, privileges of the ruling class, military life, police brutality, the role of sport in education, and the feasibility of foreign students (especially non-Caucasians) permanently settling in Australia. When the conversation reaches its conclusion, Ahmed offers his hand in friendship. Norm responds by attacking Ahmed, viciously beating him until he is unconscious. He calls Ahmed a "Fuckin' boong", and exits.

The nature of the conflict proposed by this chance meeting is illustrated by Alexander Buzo's indications for the setting. The actors are placed before an unfinished building with scaffolding—a structure suggesting danger. The construction site is an uncertain place; a temporary and transitional space. Likewise the positive interaction between Norm and Ahmed is only temporary. The public street that they cohabit becomes the scene of a territorial dispute. Norm is ultimately compelled to defend his Australian home against outsiders. In his mind, Ahmed is representative of the foreign invader.

Ahmed's provocation of Norm is unintentional. Norm is disturbed by Ahmed's eloquence and his sharp intellect. Resentment, envy, and a feeling of inferiority fuel Norm's anger. The unanticipated emotional explosion is surrounded by ambiguities. Whether the violence is premeditated or impulsive remains a point of discussion. There is no clear explanation in the text. The ironic conclusion of the play is reminiscent of the ending of Peter and Jerry's encounter in Edward Albee's *Zoo Story*. Both dramas illustrate a mysterious eruption of violence in a public setting.

The primary difference between the two characters in this play is that Norm is presented as multi-faceted while Ahmed is less complex, even two-dimensional. Norm is sometimes humorous, naïve, sympathetic, tender, absolutely hateful, and dangerous. Ahmed is relatively consistent. He is polite, idealistic, and dogmatic. He possesses a vision for change in the social structure of his own country, and potentially a vision for Australia as well. Ahmed earns our admiration for his humane ideals, yet Norm remains the more appealing person-

ality of the two. He has more humanity. When spectators see Ahmed's crushed body they are horrified and compassionate, but not moved to condemn Norm completely. Our ambivalence toward Norm is intentional. Buzo avoids a clear case of "guilty resident" versus "innocent alien". Instead he juxtaposes the fallible Norm with the diplomatic, unemotional Ahmed. The latter has all the makings of a colonial anarchist, but the audience is not sympathetic to his cause because of his flat personality. He is, quite simply, the fixed character that allows us to see the more fully-drawn character of Norm.

Despite the tragic ending and the eerie setting of the play, much of the dialogue is comic. Both characters' stories about the past and the present are written with a humor that verges upon the absurd. The audience laughs at the details recounted by Norm, spoken in a language loaded with Australian colloquialisms and slang. Ahmed, on the other hand, has an excellent command of the English language. The formality of his expression implies a superiority that is in direct contrast to the pedestrian Norm. Their contrasting uses of the English language and their different accents emphasize the gulf that separates their worlds.

When *Norm and Ahmed* was first produced the blatant confrontation with racism inspired controversy in the theatre and in the press. The text criticized the Australian establishment and brought assumed values into question and ridicule at a time when Australia was just beginning to assert itself as a country with an individual character. The controversial, "obscene" language, the surprise ending, and the extreme brevity of the play (performance time is approximately 25 minutes) shocked the Sydney audience. The play captured the shifting dynamics of the era, encapsulating the world-wide political and social unrest of 1968. *Norm and Ahmed* quickly achieved national and international recognition, and became one of the modern plays that focused attention upon Australian dramatic literature. Even in the 1990's, the play's treatment of racism and its latent violence remains pertinent and effective.

—Ludvika Popenhagen

THE NORMAN CONQUESTS
  Table Manners
  Living Together
  Round and Round the Garden
by Alan Ayckbourn

The Trilogy
First Publication: London, 1975.
First Production: Library Theatre, Scarborough, June–July 1973.

Table Manners
First Publication: In *The Norman Conquests*, London, 1975.
First Production: Library Theatre, Scarborough, 18 June 1973.

Living Together
First Publication: In *The Norman Conquests*, London, 1975.
First Production: Library Theatre, Scarborough, 25 June 1973.

Round and Round the Garden
First Publication: In *The Norman Conquests*, London, 1975.
First Production: Library Theatre, Scarborough, 9 July 1973.

Like just about all of Alan Ayckbourn's work *The Norman Conquests* started life at the Scarborough Library Theatre, before transferring to London in 1974. It is a trilogy of plays in which each makes narrative and dramatic sense separately, but when considered together, they create a vision of a world of faded middle-class gentility. In this vision, the very real laughter provoked by the events of a disastrously enforced weekend "house party" comes to take on a progressively greyer feel as the real significance of events is deciphered by the audience.

The trilogy's overall title is explained by reference to the antics of Norman, an impossible would-be Lothario who figures large in Ayckbourn's glorious catalogue of impossible male figures. Norman is a scruffy but thoroughly safe, bohemian assistant–librarian set loose in a world of estate agent husbands and charity-organising mothers. He dreams of torrid romances and heady weekends in a series of provincial scenarios that transfer rather unconvincingly from the pages of library books. The letter would need to be in large-print format to fully alert his wife, Ruth—an actively careerist woman, whose vanity prevents her from wearing the glasses that just might force her to see what really goes on in the world according to Norman.

The action in all three plays overlaps, dealing simultaneously with the consequent events of the weekend in three different locations—in *Table Manners* the dining-room of the large and run-down Victorian house in the country inhabited by the unmarried Annie and her bed-ridden and never seen mother (an off-stage ogre whose previous sexual precosity has now been converted sadly into having her daughter read her steamy romances, the contents of which are probably closer to Norman's dreams than the Romeos and other classical romancers he himself cites); in *Living Together* we learn what was happening in the sitting-room during and between-times; and finally, in *Round and Round the Garden*, the action is taken outside. In the final play there is a preface and an epilogue to events in the two internal locations.

As so often with Ayckbourn—in *Absurd Person Singular* and *How The Other Half Loves*, in particular—it was the technical invention which first attracted its contemporary audiences. Much of the audience interest is centered on observing the skill with which the playwright knits together the many complexities of a plot which is only properly revealed after three separate bites at the same story. And indeed many critics complain that the dexterity is all. Ayckbourn's many admirers would, however, cite the emotional subtext of his work—which shows that these plays are more than mechanically contrived farces, and that they are populated by characters capable of shedding real blood, as well as tears—and the increasingly dark side to his comedy; pointing in particular to the sympathetic treatment of the loneliness of women in a married world ruled over by incompetent, inadequate, and unfeeling men. That the impossible Norman should seem to offer hope not just to one but to all of the female characters in the trilogy is a measure not of his attractions as a conquering knight-errant but of the awfulness of their own situations.

The events of the weekend are initiated by Norman's plan to take his sister-in-law, the mother-burdened Annie, away for a weekend of passion; not in the Hastings which is all booked up but in the East Grinstead that is all that is available (and is, at best, only on the way to what would anyway have been a somewhat unexotic setting for library romance). To the house come Annie and Ruth's brother, Reg, and his wife Sarah to administer pills and sympathy to mother while Annie has what they believe will be a long-overdue fling with Tom, a dim and dithering vet. He has been visiting Annie for so long that she is no longer certain whether it is to prevent the need for him opening a tin of food at home, to offer her unnamed and not-much-loved cat constant medical attention, or to declare a passion for her that she is not sure she wishes to hear about. The ultra-organised Sarah worms Annie's pathetic little secret out of her in a matter of moments and immediately sets about wrecking the weekenders' plans in a mixture of moral outrage and, as it later becomes apparent when the unstoppable Norman makes her the same offer for the changed resort of Eastbourne, sexual jealousy. Add to this tangle the arrival of a Ruth intent on recovering Norman in much the same way as one might search for an overdue library book, and the stage is set for a demolition of middle-class proprieties that is Ayckbourn's special field.

In the end it is the magnificently collapsed set-pieces of social ritual that stick in the memory, disturbing in their only slightly distorted and exaggerated relationship to the world of polite discourse inhabited by the plays' audience. Two moments in particular suggest themselves for close attention. The first surrounds the desperate attempts made by Sarah to pull the family back to civilisation around a dinner-table in *Table Manners*; attempts which rapidly decline through an argument about who should sit where (as if the affair were a formal dinner engagement) into a macabre feast presided over by a manic Norman who has dressed for the occasion in the ill-fitting clothes of his dead father-in-law. The second is in *Living Together* when Reg, the estate agent and disposer of property, caught forever in the trivial escapisms of his childhood in the house, attempts to persuade the assembled company to try out his latest, home-made board-game of attempted robberies of commercial properties. Dinner-parties and party-games: these are the territories where Ayckbourn's special talents for social observation come most fully into play.

—John Bull

NOT I
by Samuel Beckett

First Publication: London, 1973.
First Production: Lincoln Center, New York, 22 November 1972.

Criticism
(For general works on the author, see *Playwrights* volume)

Articles:
Enoch Brater, "The 'I' in *Not I*", in *Twentieth Century Literature*, 20, 1974.
Enoch Brater, "Noah, *Not I*, and Beckett's 'Incomprehensibly Sublime'", in *Comparative Drama*, in 8, 1974.
Enoch Brater, "Dada, Surrealism, and the Genesis of *Not I*", in *Modern Drama*, 18, 1975.
Leonard H. Knight, "Samuel Beckett's *Not I*", in *Journal of English*, 1, 1975.
Hersh Zeifman, "Being and Non-Being: Samuel Beckett's *Not I*", in *Modern Drama*, 19, 1976.
Eileen Fischer, "'The Discourse of the Other' in *Not I*: A Confluence of Beckett and [Jacques] Lacan", in *Yale/Theater*, vol. 10 no. 3, 1979.
Katherine Kelly, "The Orphic Mouth in *Not I*", in *Journal of Beckett Studies*, 6, 1980.

Not I: Royal Court Theatre, London, 1973 (Billie Whitelaw as Mouth)

Paul Lawley, "Counterpoint, Absence and the Medium in Beckett's *Not I*", in *Modern Drama*, 26, 1983.

Alec Reid, "Impact and Parable in Beckett: A First Encounter With *Not I*", in *Hermathena*, 141, 1986.

Gerry McCarthy, "On the Meaning of Performance in Samuel Beckett's *Not I*", in *Modern Drama*, 33, 1990.

*   *   *

Beckett's *Waiting for Godot* persuaded the critic Kenneth Tynan "to re-examine the rules which have hitherto governed the drama; and having done so, to pronounce theme not elastic enough". Yet, when contrasted with the later *Not I*, the earlier play seems almost conventional. At least *Waiting for Godot* offered observable interaction between characters (albeit characters whose identities were uncertain and shifting), a division into acts and scenes, a visual context with roots—however tenuous—in stage naturalism, and a debt, in the verbal and farcical "routines", to the circus, music-hall, and silent comedy.

In *Not I*, conventional notions of plot, character, action, and rhythm—whether Aristotelian or Brechtian—are difficult to discern. In one sense, Beckett's dramatic career can be seen as a constant process of refinement and distillation, a search for a more succinct encapsulation of a reasonably consistent series of experiences and hypotheses, reaching their apotheosis in the very brief plays of the later years. *Not I* could be said to occupy a mid-way position in this process.

The stage directions specify two figures on stage. To call them "characters" would be to exaggerate; they are, rather, presences, the one primarily aural, and the other, visual. Centrally, there is Mouth—a single, seemingly detached mouth surrounded by blackness (the actress's eyes need to be covered, along with the rest of her face and body so as to seem to vanish in the darkness). To one side, there is the silent Auditor, "sex indeterminable", whose face is invisible, shrouded in a black "djellaba". The only physical action consists of Mouth's motions while speaking and "four brief movements" from the Auditor.

In contrast to this physical inactivity, there is frenetic verbal activity; although there is no plot as such, there streams forth from Mouth a frantic, fractured, repetitive narrative, supposedly about an unnamed third character, "she". The staccato phrases tell the story of an orphaned child, the recipient of "no love" (she was "spared that"), living a largely silent, uneventful life, until one day, aged 70, and searching for cowslips, she finds herself "in the dark", no longer sensing her limbs. What remains is "just the mouth ... like maddened", producing "this stream ... steady stream ... she who had never ... on the contrary ... practically speechless ... all her days".

A few events from the past are evoked—her speechless visits to the supermarket; her tears the time she "sat and watched them dry" on Croker's Acres; the occasions, "once or twice a year", usually on Winter evenings, when she had an urge to talk and would "then rush out stop the first she saw ... nearest lavatory ... start pouring it out ... steady stream ... mad stuff".

Clearly the narrative is autobiography rather than biography; but Mouth will not, or cannot, accept the story as being her own. At four points Mouth pauses, asks "what? ... who?" before emphatically shouting "no! ... she!", as the silent

Auditor gestures, seemingly attempting to persuade her to change from third to first-person narrative. Yet mouth never says "I".

This short play is capable of interpretation on a number of discrete levels. It can be viewed as a psychological study, in expressionistic mode, of a disturbed state of mind: the events of the narrative could suggest a woman of low mental age, suffering from a disorder akin to autism, with the corresponding inability to enter into normal social communication. From this perspective, the two presences on stage become the body and mouth of the same person represented expressionistically, unable to become whole, to constitute a normal individual, an "I".

From a theological or metaphysical viewpoint, *Not I* can be seen as a further examination by Beckett of his own particular sense of the after-life as a kind of purgatorial wilderness, in which, while bodies are trapped or immobilised, mental processes of self analysis are engaged in attempts to rationalise, inadequately, yet endlessly, past existence. In the earlier *Play*, three characters, encased in urns, are made to repeat their banal story of a suburban love-triangle to the promptings of a spotlight, the "unique inquisitor". In Beckett's theatre, light and darkness are key symbols. Although their precise associations vary, light suggests, in a broad sense, life, the life of the mind, rational thought, and the urge towards definition and self-definition, while dark suggests loss of self, sensual experience, sleep, possibly death. In Beckett's purgatorial settings, while the figures are enveloped in darkness, that darkness serves to accentuate the piercing light. In *Play*, while the light is external, it can be interpreted as the internal urge to analyse. In *Not I* the light exists largely through verbal reference, and is more obviously symbolic—"the beam ... flickering on and off" in the "skull" is related to Mouth's outpourings.

If this is the afterlife, it is a cruelly ironic one. Mouth reports:

> her first thought was ... oh long after ... sudden flash ... brought up as she had been to believe ... with the other waifs ... in a merciful ... (*Brief laugh*) ... God ... (*Good laugh*) ... first thought was ... oh long after ... sudden flash ... she was being punished ... for her sins ...

Yet, the realisation that she is in no physical pain also brings the possibility of no release from the present limbo. Beckett's purgatory posits the possibility of bodily disintegration yet an undiminished cerebral activity, becoming a torture in itself: "all part of the same wish to ... torment" as Mouth describes the "beam".

On yet another level, *Not I* can be viewed as another paradoxical expression by Beckett of his scepticism about language as a vehicle of definition, and therefore about the expressibility of self and experience. Given an urge to define, any attempt to do so can only be crudely approximate given the conventional and codified nature of language which is the tool, not only of speech, but of thought. Much of Beckett's work approaches the question of whether perception can exist outside linguistic convention. *Not I* thus evokes not only a traditional Cartesian dichotomy of mind and body (through the references in the text—the body becomes "the machine"—and the separation of Mouth as source of language from the Auditor on stage), but fractures identity further by suggesting a split *within* the mental processes. While it is the brain providing the mixture of confusion and insight which Mouth pours forth, there is also "something begging in the brain ... begging the mouth to stop"—perhaps some undefined sense of being, pre-existant to language. From this perspective, Mouth ceases to be warped or disturbed, but becomes a universal metaphor, caught in the treadmill of attempting selfhood through language yet refusing to allow language to be acceptable as an adequate definition of "I".

The play remains, however, more than any of these interpretations individually or combined, for it is typical of Beckett's work that it operates on both the most directly evocative and emotional level, as well as on the sophisticated, intellectual one. While available for literary study and textual analysis, Beckett's plays, *Not I* included, are articulated in bold, theatrical images which are both concrete and abstract. The evocation of an individual life here runs parallel with the metaphorical resonance, and, whether through an imaginative reading or through watching a performance, the sheer theatrical *experience* of confronting the play imparts a profound poignancy. And that poignancy—which reduced Billie Whitelaw to tears on her first reading—is every bit as much of the "meaning" of the play, and part of Beckett's strategy, as whatever textual analysis can unearth.

Billie Whitelaw played Mouth both in the 1973 Royal Court production, and in the televised version of 1977. In the latter, the camera focused solely on Mouth, excluding the Auditor completely, and can be considered an adaptation of the original play. The ability of the camera to concentrate on the mouth does make for a mesmeric experience, intensifying the impression of involuntary verbal discharge, as incessant as it is disordered and incomplete.

—Mark Hawkins-Dady

NUBES. See **THE CLOUDS.**

O

OBERAMMERGAU PASSION PLAY (Oberammergauer Passionspiel)
by Othmar Weis (and others)

Composition: Original version (based on the *Augsburg Passion Play*), c. 1633/34; continually revised and rewritten in 18th Century; present text based largely on 1810 version.
First Production: Oberammergau, Bavaria, 1634.

Criticism

Books:

August Hartmann, *Das "Oberammergauer Passionspiel" in seiner ältesten Gestalt zum ersten Male*, Leipzig, 1880.
Janet H. McKelvey Swift, *"The Passion Play of Oberammergau": Its History and Significance*, New York, 1930.

*   *   *

The *Oberammergau Passion Play* is not just an interesting historical survival. It is a dramatic presentation of Christ's betrayal, crucifixion, and resurrection which, thanks largely to its reliance on the gospel narratives, has long had the power to move Catholics and Protestants alike, rarely leaving even professed sceptics indifferent. Furthermore, as it has changed over more than three and a half centuries, it has reflected new religious, social, and theatrical conceptions in ways which would themselves make a fascinating study.

In the course of the Thirty Years War the little Bavarian village of Oberammergau, some 60 miles south-west of Munich, was visited by the plague. In 1633 the inhabitants, in their affliction, made a vow that if their Catholic community was spared they would for ever afterwards perform a passion play at periodic intervals. At that time there was nothing particularly unusual in such a response to a crisis of this sort, and modern epidemiology would not necessarily see a miracle in a striking drop in cases of fatal infection. What is most remarkable is that the villagers have fulfilled their vow ever since the initial performance in 1634. For that first Passion play an old text, already the subject of some revision, was used, and this takes us back to the end of the Middle Ages. The basis was a Passion play which had originally been written by the monks of the Augsburg monastery of St. Ulrich and St. Afra in the 15th century and revised in the 16th century by the Meistersinger Sebastian Wild. The fact that the people of Oberammergau, led by their priest, were able to turn to such a source is some indication of the tradition of performing Passion plays in Bavaria, and the pattern of borrowing and adapting is typical of popular religious drama throughout Western Europe in the late Middle Ages.

By the early 18th century the people of Oberammergau began to look for changes in what was, essentially, a medieval play, complete with its crude, knock-about, farcical interludes between the simple scenes portraying the gospel narrative, and they turned for help to the nearby monasteries of Ettal and Rotenbuch. Anselm Manhardt attempted to improve the tone of the play by making the devils allegorical figures, and in 1740 Clemens Prasser, who had been parish priest at Oberammergau, rewrote several scenes, emphasising moral aspects. For the 1750 performance the text was largely rewritten by Ferdinand Rosner, but his style was regarded as too mannered and literary, and Magnus Knipfelberger was called on to make simplifications for subsequent productions up to 1800–1. For the 1810 production Othmar Weis, provided a text drawn in almost every detail from Scripture, and this, with periodic revisions (most notably by Joseph Daisenberger in 1860 and 1870) has remained in use to the present day. Weis did retain from Rosner's play the striking feature of punctuating the dramatisation of the Passion with a score of tableaux from the Old Testament which serve to place Christ's suffering in the perspective of a providential plan unfolding from the beginning of time.

In 1770, supporting the Catholic hierarchy which was suspicious of popular, religious events, Maximilian Joseph, Prince-Elector of Bavaria, decreed the banning of all passion plays in his domains, but the people of Oberammergau were successful, unlike some of their fellow-countrymen, in resisting the injunction. A threat of a different sort emerged as tourists began to flock to Oberammergau. It is said that 10,000 visitors were expected to witness the 1770 performance, but in the mid-19th century there was an enormous increase in numbers and they have remained high ever since. Whenever the time comes round for a new production it is feared that the tone of the event will be changed because the audience has grown too large. In fact this seems not to happen, in part because many tourists treat the event as a sort of pilgrimage and also because the amateur actors of Oberammergau continue to regard performing the *Passion Play* as a religious observance.

The first *Oberammergau Passion Play* was performed in the village church, and later productions took place on knock-down stages in the open air. In 1890 the architect Ludwig Lang and Karl Lautenschläger, from the Munich Court Theatre, following traditional lines, designed the permanent stage which, with some simplification of the ornamentation, remains to the present. With its central opening under a severe pediment and flanked by semi-circular arches the effect is perhaps more neo-Grecian than medieval, but there is ample space for the marshalling of a huge cast in the crowd scenes that are a major feature of the play and for the presentation, in the central section of the stage, of the spectacular scenes from both the Passion and the Old Testament tableaux. There is an

THE ODD COUPLE   561

orchestra pit, the music being a revision by Eugen Papst of compositions by Rochus Dedler (1779–1822), and the audience, numbering some 6,000, now sits, not outside in the Passion Meadow as once it did, but in a vast, somewhat uncomfortable, auditorium which opens out onto the stage which itself is still bathed in daylight. Performances begin early in the morning and last some five and half hours, with a long luncheon interval. The productions, whose general style is historically realistic, are meticulously planned and magnificently costumed, with colours carefully co-ordinated (if less bright in 1990 than formerly). Thanks to good acoustics the words can be heard clearly. The cast is made up of local people, amateurs who train for their taxing roles by taking part in other plays in Oberammergau; the selection of actors for the various parts is in the hands of a local committee and is always a matter of intense concern for the inhabitants of the village.

In recent years perceived anti-Semitic elements in the *Passion Play* have been the object of some controversy, resulting in further revisions of the text. Such changes may be taken as further evidence of that characteristic of the *Oberammergau Passion Play* over the centuries, its capacity for evolving while somehow retaining an essential strength which is no doubt derived both from the basic religious drama that is enacted and from the commitment of the Oberammergau community which performs it.

—Christopher Smith

OBERAMMERGAUER PASSIONSPIEL.   See **OBERAMMERGAU PASSION PLAY.**

THE ODD COUPLE
by Neil Simon

First Publication: New York, 1966.
First Production: Plymouth Theatre, New York, 10 March 1965.

*   *   *

A realistic, three-act comedy, *The Odd Couple* is set in the Manhattan apartment of Oscar Madison, a divorced sportswriter who is successful but nevertheless disorganized, lazy, and sloppy. Friends at a regularly scheduled poker game share concern for the whereabouts of missing player Felix Ungar, whose wife reportedly has that day thrown him out. A distraught Felix arrives and tearfully confirms this, whereupon Oscar offers to let Felix share his apartment. The two men soon come to grate on each other's nerves, for directly opposite to carefree Oscar is Felix, compulsively neat, organized, fond of cleaning and perfectly planned meals, and a hypochondriac. Friction intensifies. On a later poker night, Felix's regime of cleanliness and finicky food preparation disrupts the customarily relaxed game and hastens the players' departure. Soon after, both to satisfy his need and to offer Felix a chance for normal behavior, Oscar arranges a double date with two English sisters named Pigeon. Felix insists on preparing a gourmet meal, which is subsequently ruined when Oscar is thoughtlessly late. The party mood is further spoiled by Felix's eliciting tearful sympathy from the sisters as he

dwells on the pain of his separation and unhappiness. Oscar hopes the evening may still be saved by accepting the Pigeons' invitation to their apartment, but the hope is dashed when Felix refuses. Still fuming the next evening, Oscar reaches the end of his patience and orders Felix to leave. The poker players arrive to find Felix gone and Oscar remorseful, fearing Felix's suicide. But Felix returns, accompanied by the Pigeon sisters, to collect his things because they, having taken pity on him, have offered to share their apartment. Oscar and friends are surprised but relieved, and the two men part amicably.

This play is the best known of Neil Simon's realistic comedies, most of which deal with recognizable, American, middle-class persons trying to cope with the complications of middle-class mores in employment, parenthood, marriage, and divorce. Furthermore, the play effects a characteristic Simon pattern which, dependent less on carefully structured plot than on character and situation, frequently throws together two people of disparate natures and gives them a stormy relationship at the end of which they have influenced each other, whatever the resolution. The incompatible brothers in *Come Blow Your Horn* and the newlyweds in *Barefoot in the Park* are predecessors of Oscar and Felix, in a pattern employing a basic ingredient of comedy: incongruity.

Oscar and Felix are an incongruous pair of misfits, refugees from marriages which have failed due to their personal idiosyncrasies. Oscar is slovenly and careless. Felix is compulsively fastidious and self-pitying. The poker buddies serve as witnesses to and commentators on the two characters and their behavior. Oscar and Felix enter into a domestic arrangement which proves their incompatibility and demonstrates why their wives refused to put up with them. While both men admit shortcomings and engage in self-criticism, neither believes at bottom that his unpleasant qualities outweigh the good, or that he is entirely to blame for marital failure. At heart self-loving, they refuse to, and are incapable of, change.

Much of the humor stems from the situation in which two heterosexual men dwelling together can come to sound and behave like a married couple, duplicating such common marital incidents as being reprimanded for messiness, being late for dinner without notifying the cook, and being scolded with such lines as "Where were you?" and "Do you know what time it is?". An additional source of humor is provided as the audience observes the collapse of the relationship while two selfish and opposing personalities increasingly irritate one another. Dramatically it is Felix, however, who generates the greatest irritation, highlighted in Act II when he unwittingly destroys the relaxed informality of the poker game by unceasing ministrations of refreshments and demands for tidiness, and when he morosely upsets the gaiety of a double date and then refuses the women's invitation to join them upstairs. For Oscar the double-date fiasco is the last straw. While Act III does not match the previous comic level, it amusingly resolves the "trial marriage ending in divorce" by fulfilling another characteristic pattern of the author. In Felix's seeking out and accepting the Pigeon sisters' refuge, he has acted in an uncharacteristically humble way that suggests at least a tentative change of character. At the same time, Oscar reveals some behavioral change by reprimanding the poker friends for sloppiness, protesting, "Watch your cigarettes, will you? This is my house, not a pig sty". At the play's end, both men acknowledge that they have helped each other. Oscar says Felix should thank him for doing two things—taking him in and throwing him out—and Felix agrees. The two shake hands, remaining friends while parting. Simon seems to project the view that incompatible persons can accommodate one another in durable friendship if not forced into impossible proximity unsustainable in daily living.

The Odd Couple, with its distinctive creation of two, misfit, male title characters and its humorous lines, continues to enjoy a lasting stage career, and is regarded by many critics as Simon's most successful comedy. The critically and commercially successful 1965 Broadway production featuring Walter Matthau and Art Carney was followed by a motion picture version and was subsequently the basis of a durable television series with Jack Klugman and Tony Randall. The play remains a staple of community and regional theatres in the United States and abroad. So great was the play's acceptance by audiences that Simon wrote a female version presented on Broadway in 1985 which achieved considerable regional popularity.

—Christian H. Moe

OEDIPUS
by Seneca

Composition: 1st Century A.D.

Editions
Oedipus, in *L. Annaei Senecae Tragoediae* (3 vols.) edited by Humbertus Moricca, Turin, 1917–23; second edition, 1947.
Oedipus [with translation], in *Seneca: Tragedies*, translated by F.J. Miller, London, 1960 (Loeb Classical Library).
Oedipus, in *L. Annaei Senecae Tragoediae* (2 vols.), edited by G.C. Giardina, Bologna, 1966.
Oedipus, in *L. Annaei Senecae Tragoediae*, edited by Otto Zwierlein, Oxford, 1986.
Oedipus, edited by Bruno W. Häuptli, Frauenfelde, 1983.

Translations
Oedipus, in *Seneca: Tragedies*, translated by Ella I. Harris, London and New York, 1904.
Oedipus, in *Seneca: Tragedies*, translated by Frank J. Miller, Chicago, 1907.
Oedipus, in *The Complete Roman Drama*, edited by George E. Duckworth, New York, 1942.
Oedipus, translated by Moses Hadas, New York, 1956.
Oedipus, in *Seneca: Four Tragedies and "Octavia"*, translated by E.F. Watling, Harmondsworth, 1966.

Criticism
(For general works on the author, see *Playwrights* volume)

Articles:
G. Miller, "Seneca's *Oedipus* and Drama", in *Hermes*, 81, 1953.
E. Paratore, "La poesia nell' *Oedipus* di Seneca", in *Giornale italiano di filologia*, 9, 1956.
W. Schetter, "Die Prologszene zu Senecas *Oedipus*", in *Der altsprachliche Unterricht*, 11, 1968.
Ian Scott-Kilvert, "Seneca or Scenario", in *Arion*, 7, 1968.
Donald J. Mastronarde, "Seneca's *Oedipus*: The Drama in the Word", in *Transactions and Proceedings of the American Philological Association* [*TAPA*], 101, 1970.
J. Hind, "The Death of Agrippina and the Finale of the *Oedipus* of Seneca", in *AUMLA Journal*, 38, 1972.

* * *

Although it is not known whether *Oedipus* was ever produced in an ancient theatre, we no longer consider Seneca's tragedies as simply rhetorical exercises or expositions of Stoic philosophy which exploit a dramatic form for the sake of convenience alone, and a greater sympathy for a play such as *Oedipus* is to be seen in Ted Hughes's poetic translation *The Oedipus of Seneca*, or, more generally, in the work of Edward Bond. The model for Seneca's *Oedipus* was Sophocles's *Oedipus Rex*, but that model was not rigidly followed and the inclusion, for example, of two scenes of divination and necromancy very much reflects a contemporary, Roman interest. The relative closeness of *Oedipus Rex* and *Oedipus* is suggested by a comparison of the two lists of dramatis personae: the only Senecan addition is that of Manto, the daughter of Tiresias the prophet. But pace of action is very different: in Sophocle's play the truth—that Oedipus has killed his father and married his mother and so caused the plague at Thebes—is slowly but inevitably revealed, whereas the action in Seneca's version is swift and devastating. The centrepiece of the play is provided by a speech delivered by the ghost of Laius, itself incorporated into a very long, messenger-type speech from Creon where the supernatural and the occult, already anticipated by the scene in which Oedipus consults Tiresias and Manto, loom large.

In fact a fundamental difference in dramatic technique is marked at the very beginning of the Senecan play when Oedipus reveals the prophecy that he was fated to kill his father and marry his mother and tells how he, as a result left Corinth. Deferred in Sophocles until after the Tiresias and the Creon scene, this oracle is introduced immediately so that the twin horrors of parricide and incest can thrill the audience from the outset. Seneca's characterization of Oedipus is different too: he is wretched rather than magnificently defiant; as a Stoic hero, Oedipus can be allowed no free-will but must accept the dictates of fate. Oedipus alone is untouched by the plague afflicting Thebes, and this is not the isolation of the Sophoclean hero but another horror element—it can only mean that Oedipus is reserved for a yet worse punishment. The description of plague given by Oedipus is lurid enough but in no way compares with what is shortly to be described by the Chorus, in what is quite clearly a set-piece exposition which has antecedents going back to the Greek historian Thucydides.

Sophocles's separate Creon and Tiresias scenes are, in this play, combined, but they hardly illustrate Oedipus's harsh temper, concentrating rather on activity on stage as a sacrifice is performed and its course described to blind Tiresias by Manto. The climax is an unnatural birth—a foetus in a virgin heifer's womb—the commonest type of Roman portent. But neither this combined scene, nor the subsequent invocation of the spirit of the dead Laius, really advances the action. The latter owes nothing to Sophocles, and Creon's speech of over 150 lines represents pure declamation and has a distinct literary flavour. If it has any Greek equivalent it is in the *Odyssey* Book 11 when Odysseus visits the underworld; in Seneca we have described in turn a dark, overgrown grove reminiscent of a Roman sacred grove; invocation of the dead; a series of rhetorical questions before the spirits appear; the spirits themselves, personifications such as Plague, Horror, Fury, Sorrow, Sickness, and Age which underline the literary quality of the speech; an extended simile; a catalogue of spirits; and finally, Laius himself with a gruesome indictment of his son.

Then Seneca reverts to his Greek source, and Oedipus suspects conspiracy. At the same time Stoic sentiments—"endure your fate", Creon tells Oedipus—are expressed, and Roman touches—as when Creon mentions the friends that attend upon his house—are introduced. The Chorus quotes more mythology and lists even stranger prodigies. More exciting, however, are the two final scenes which comprise Acts IV and V, although much of the tension created by Sophocles is lost as events are telescoped together. In the first scene the shepherd Phorbas reveals how he exposed the baby Oedipus, while the second is made up of two elements: a long messenger speech relates how Oedipus gouged out his own eyes and there is a further appearance of Jocasta who has yet to commit suicide. The Queen has appeared for a brief moment at the beginning of Act IV and now she reappears as the tragedy concludes. Why does Seneca abandon Sophocles at this point? It is difficult to resist the thought that Seneca wanted a crazed woman on stage and a woman who can kill herself in full view of an audience—ordering her hand, in a climactic and very rhetorical flourish, to "strike at this teeming womb which gave me sons and husbands"—a gesture also associated with the death of Nero's mother, Agrippina, and an appropriately theatrical ending to a melodrama which illustrates throughout the playwright's near obsession with destructive passions.

—Peter Walcot

OEDIPUS AT COLONUS (Oedipus Coloneus)
by Sophocles

First Production: Athens, 401 B.C.

Editions

Oedipus Coloneus [with translation], edited and translated by Sir Richard Jebb, London, 1886; second edition, 1890; third edition, 1900.

Oedipus Coloneus, in *Sophoclis Fabulae*, edited by A.C. Pearson, Oxford, 1928.

Oedipus Coloneus, in *Sophoclis Fabulae, 2*, edited by A. Colunna, Turin, 1978.

Oedipus Coloneus, in *Sophoclis Tragediae, 2*, edited by R.D. Dawe, Leipzig, 1979.

Oedipus Coloneus, in *Sophoclis: Fabulae*, edited by H. Lloyd-Jones and N.G. Wilson, Oxford, 1990.

Translations

Oedipus at Colonus, translated by Robert Fitzgerald, New York, 1941.

Oedipus at Colonus, translated by Gilbert Murray, London and New York, 1941.

Oedipus at Colonus, translated by R.C. Trevelyan, Cambridge, 1946.

Oedipus at Colonus, in *The Theban Plays*, translated by E.F. Watling, Harmondsworth, 1947.

Oedipus at Colonus, in *Three Theban Plays*, translated by Theodore Howard Banks, New York, and London, 1956.

Oedipus at Colonus, in *The Oedipus Plays*, translated by Paul Roche, New York, 1958.

Oedipus at Colonus, in *The Three Theban Plays*, translated by Robert Fagles, London, 1982.

Oedipus at Colonus, in *The Three Theban Plays*, translated by Don Taylor, London, 1986.

Oedipus at Colonus, in *The Three Theban Plays*, translated by C.A. Trypanis, Warminster, Wiltshire, 1986.

Oedipus at Colonus, in *Oedipus*, translated by Christopher Stace, Birmingham, 1987.

Criticism
(For general works on the author, see *Playwrights* volume)

Books:

J.C. Kamerbeek, *The Plays of Sophocles: Commentaries, 7: The "Oedipus Coloneus"*, Leiden, 1984.

Articles:

I.M. Linforth, "Religion and Drama in *Oedipus at Colonus*", in *University of California Publications in Classical Philology*, 14, 1951.

S.M. Adams, "Unity of Plot in the *Oedipus Coloneus*", in *Phoenix*, 7, 1953.

R.P. Winnington Ingram, "A Religious Function of Greek Tragedy: A Study of the *Oedipus Coloneus* and the *Oresteia*", in *Journal of Hellenic Studies*, 74, 1954.

H.G. Shields, "Sight and Blindness Imagery in *Oedipus Coloneus*", in *Phoenix*, 15, 1961.

N. Heiman, "*Oedipus at Colonus*: A Study of Old Age and Death", in *American Imago*, 19, 1962.

T.P. Howe, "Taboo in the Oedipus Theme", in *Transactions and Proceedings of the American Philological Association* [*TAPA*], 93, 1962.

C. Rado, "*Oedipus at Colonus*: An Interpretation", in *American Imago*, 19, 1962.

P.E. Esterling, "Oedipus and Polynices", in *Proceedings of the Cambridge Philological Society*, 193, 1967.

D. Grene, "*Oedipus at Colonus*", in his *Reality and the Heroic Pattern: Last Plays of Ibsen, Shakespeare and Sophocles*, Chicago, 1967.

Heinz Politzer, "*Oedipus auf Kolonos*: Versuch über eine Gemeinsamkeit von Psychoanalyse und Literaturkritik", in *Psyche*, 26, 1972.

Bernd Seidensticker, "Beziehungen zwischen den beiden Oidipusdramen des Sophokles", in *Hermes*, 100, 1972.

P. Burian, "Suppliant and Saviour: *Oedipus at Colonus*", in *Phoenix*, 28, 1974.

R. Forrer, "*Oedipus at Colonus*: A Crisis in the Greek Notion of Deity", in *Comparative Drama*, 8, 1974–75.

D.A. Hester, "To Help One's Friends and Harm One's Enemies: A Study in the *Oedipus at Colonus*", in *Antichthon*, 11, 1977.

*   *   *

The events of *Oedipus Tyrannus* now in the past, Oedipus, accompanied by his daughter Antigone, arrives at Colonus, near Athens, seeking protection. Despite attempts to persuade him to return to Thebes, Oedipus recognises Colonus as his final resting-place. The play ends with his death.

Aristotle in the *Poetics* refers several times to *Oedipus the King* (*Oedipus Tyrannus*) but does not mention *Oedipus at Colonus*. Regarding plot as the most important element in a play, he might not have had much time for *Oedipus at Colonus* which eschews plot in favour of a series of incidents. Sophocles' last play, it was produced posthumously but there is no suggestion that the unusual form is the result of lack of application or revision. Nowadays it seems an appropriate climax to a rich career.

The setting of *Oedipus at Colonus* is a grove, sacred to the Furies, near Athens. The arrival of Oedipus seems to the chorus of locals to represent a threat to the sanctity of the place but Theseus, King of Athens, hears Oedipus's plea for protection and offers him sanctuary. In a series of episodes Oedipus proceeds to finalise his account with members of his family and it begins to become evident that there is something more to him than the pathetic victim of fate which he first appeared. His other daughter, Ismene, tells him of an oracle bestowing benefits on the country which houses his body after death. Creon, both uncle and brother-in-law, tries to force him back to Thebes by kidnapping his daughters, but is thwarted by Theseus. Oedipus's son, Polyneices, arrives, also wanting something from the old man: his support in the battle for the throne of Thebes. Oedipus sends him away, a father's curse ringing in his ears. The sound of thunder warns Oedipus that the end of his life is near. He leads his daughters and Theseus out of the grove. A Messenger reports his passing and Antigone and Ismene return to mourn him.

What no recitation of the sequence of scenes can do is give any impression of how powerful and strange the play can be. Oedipus is initially a broken man, blind, helpless, weighed down by the burden of his past. An object of revulsion when he identifies himself to the Chorus, it seems that there is nothing left for him but the support offered by Antigone. The physical blindness which he inflicted on himself at the end of *Oedipus Tyrannus*, no longer wanting to see the light of the sun, offers no compensation of understanding or inner peace. Not yet, that is; but Oedipus does sense that this sacred place may be the haven for which he has been searching.

Oedipus Tyrannus and *Oedipus at Colonus* were not written as companion pieces. *Antigone*, which might be expected to form a trilogy with them, dates from the early 440's B.C.. *Oedipus Tyrannus* comes next, over 20 years before the last play. But the two Oedipus plays do have links and are often presented in tandem. The contrast between physical and spiritual blindness, in the persons of Tiresias and Oedipus in the first play, has its counterpart in the second, during the course of which the physically frail old man gradually acquires a stature. Neither repentant nor likeable, he nevertheless begins to transcend the burden of his earthly fate.

The moment that demonstrates this for an audience is when Zeus's thunder roars and Oedipus recognises it as a summons. After having to be led throughout the play, Oedipus now assumes the role of leader, striding confidently off-stage, Theseus, Antigone, and Ismene in his wake. This transformation offers a powerful enough moment but the description of Oedipus's end suggests something more mystical. Only Theseus is allowed to witness what happens to Oedipus, and Theseus is unwilling, or unable, to describe what he saw. Oedipus has no ordinary death as he had no ordinary life. The sense of a journey completed gives the play an autobiographical dimension found in so many final works. Sophocles was born in Colonus and the ode in celebration of Colonus is one of the most beautiful he wrote.

Oedipus at Colonus is not a tragedy according to any accepted formula, Aristotelian or otherwise. Oedipus, who in *Oedipus Tyrannus* makes at least some contribution to his own fate, is seen in *Oedipus at Colonus* as a victim whose cruel life somehow entitles him to a privileged status in death. The appeal of the play may reside here. Alexis Minotis of the Greek National Theatre has directed it on no fewer than ten occasions. The play inspired T. S. Eliot to write *The Elder Statesman* (1958) while Lee Breuer's *Gospel at Colonus* (1983) was a rock gospel theatre piece which used a considerable amount of the Sophoclean text in translation.

As the final play that Sophocles created, *Oedipus at Colonus*, despite its highly individual construction, has clear thematic links to his previous work. Oedipus displays all the single-mindedness of Electra, where other characters are defined by their response to the central figure. The stubbornness of Antigone or Ajax is set in stone in the unyielding Oedipus. Heroes at the far extremity of physical pain, Heracles and Philoctetes, look forward to Oedipus, a man who has faced the worst the gods can throw at him and who has

found relief at the far end of suffering. A play of memorable scenes, *Oedipus at Colonus* offers a suitable finale to the golden age of Greek tragedy.

—J. Michael Walton

OEDIPUS COLONEUS.   See OEDIPUS AT COLONUS.

OEDIPUS THE KING (Oedipus Tyrannus / Oedipus Rex) by Sophocles

First Production: Athens, after 430 B.C.

Editions

Oedipus Tyrannus, edited by Sir Richard Jebb, Cambridge, 1883; second edition, 1893.
Oedipus Tyrannus [with translation], edited and translated by J.T. Sheppard, Cambridge and New York, 1920.
Oedipus Rex, edited by R.D. Dawe, Cambridge, 1982.

Translations

Oedipus the King, translated by Gilbert Murray, London and New York, 1911.
Oedipus the King, in *Three Greek Tragedies*, translated by David Grene, Chicago, 1942.
King Oedipus, in *The Theban Plays*, translated by E.F. Watling, Harmondsworth, 1947.
Oedipus Rex, translated by Dudley Fitts and Robert Fitzgerald, New York, 1949.
Oedipus the King, in *Three Theban Plays*, translated by Theodore Howard Banks, New York and London, 1956.
Oedipus the King, in *The Oedipus Plays*, translated by Paul Roche, New York, 1958.
Oedipus the King, translated by Bernard M.W. Knox, 1959.
Oedipus the King, in *Oedipus the King; Antigone*, translated by Peter Arnott, London and New York, 1962.
Oedipus the King, in *Three Tragedies*, translated by H.D.F. Kitto, London and New York, 1962.
Oedipus the King, translated by Stephen Berg and Dukin Clay, Oxford and New York, 1978.
Oedipus the King, in *The Three Theban Plays*, translated by Robert Fagles, London, 1982.
King Oedipus, in *The Three Theban Plays*, translated by C.A. Trypanis, Warminster, Wilts, 1986.
Oedipus the King, in *The Theban Plays*, translated by Don Taylor, London, 1986.
Oedipus the King, in *Oedipus*, translated by Christopher Stace, Birmingham, 1987.

Criticism

(For general works on the author, see *Playwrights* volume)

Books:
Albert Cook (ed.), "*Oedipus Rex*": *A Mirror For Greek Tragedy*, 1963.
J.C. Kamerbeek, *The Plays of Sophocles: Commentaries, 4: The "Oedipus Tyrannus"*, Leiden, 1967.
Alister Cameron, *The Identity of Oedipus the King*, New York, 1968.

Michael J. O'Brien (ed.), *Twentieth Century Interpretations of "Oedipus Rex"*, Englewood Cliffs, New Jersey, 1968.

P.H. Vellacott, *Sophocles and Oedipus: A Study of "Oedipus Tyrannus", With a New Translation*, London, 1971.

Articles:

E.R. Dodds, "On Misunderstanding the *Oedipus Rex*", in *Greece and Rome*, 13, 1906.

W. Ax, "Die Parados des *Oedipus Tyrannos*", in *Hermes*, 67, 1932.

J.P. Carroll, "Some Remarks on the Questions in the *Oedipus Tyrannus*", in *Classical Journal*, 32, 1937.

E.T. Owen, "Drama in Sophocles' *Oedipus Tyrannus*", in *University of Toronto Quarterly*, 10, 1940.

L. Deubner, "Oedipusprobleme", in *Abhandlung der preuss-ischen Akademie der Wissenschaft*, 1943.

J. Frierman and S. Gassel, "The Chorus in Sophocles' *Oedipus Tyrannus*", in *Psychoanalytic Quarterly*, 19, 1950.

W.C. Helmbold, "Paradox of the *Oedipus Tyrannus*", in *American Journal of Philology*, 72, 1951.

B.M.W. Knox, "Why is Oedipus called 'Tyrannus'?", in *Classical Journal*, 50, 1954.

Philip Whaley Harsh, "Implicit and Explicit in the *Oedipus Tyrannus*", in *American Journal of Philology*, 79, 1958.

Richmond Yancey Hathorn, "The Existential Oedipus", in *Classical Journal*, 53, 1958.

W.M. Calder III, "The Blinding, *Oedipus Tyrannus*", in *American Journal of Philology*, 80, 1959.

W.M. Calder III, "*Oedipus Tyrannus*", in *Classical Philology*, 57, 1962.

T.P. Howe, "Taboo in the Oedipus Theme", in *Transactions and Proceedings of the American Philological Association* [*TAPA*], 93, 1962.

A. Paolucci, "The Oracles are Dumb or Cheat: A Study of the Meaning of *Oedipus Rex*", in *Classical Journal*, 58, 1963.

G.H. Gellie, "Second Stasimon of the *Oedipus Tyrannus*", in *American Journal of Philology*, 85, 1964.

W.H. Hewitt, "The *Oedipus Tyrannus*: Sophocles and Mr. Vellacott", in *Theoria*, 23, 1964.

P.H. Vellacott, "The Guilt of Oedipus", in *Greece and Rome* (second series), 11, 1964.

Thomas Gould, "Innocence of Oedipus: The Philosophers on *Oedipus the King*", in *Arion*, 4 & 5, 1965–66.

Frances Atkins, "The Social Meaning of the Oedipus Myth", in *Journal of Individual Psychology*, 22, 1966.

Simon O. Lesser, "*Oedipus the King*: The Two Dramas, the Two Conflicts", in *College English*, 29, 1967.

P.H. Vellacott, "The Chorus in *Oedipus Tyrannus*", in *Greece and Rome* (second series), 14, 1967.

Melvin D. Faber, "Self-Destruction in *Oedipus Rex*", in *American Imago*, 27, 1970.

Bernd Seidensticker, "Beziehungen zwischen den beiden Oidipusdramen des Sophokles", in *Hermes*, 100, 1972.

M. Dyson, "Oracle, Edict and Curse in *Oedipus Tyrannus*", in *Classical Quarterly* (new series), 23, 1973.

Emil Staiger, "Sophokles: *König Oedipus*", in *Scheidewege: Vierteljahrsschrift für skeptisches Denken*, 3, 1973.

J.-P. Vernant, "Ambiguity and Reversal: On the Enigmatic Structure of *Oedipus Rex*", in *New Literary History*, vol.9, no.3, 1978.

David Bain, "A Misunderstood Scene in Sophokles' *Oidipous*", in *Greece and Rome* (second series), vol.26 no.2, 1979.

* * *

Oedipus Rex, or *Oedipus the King*, is distinguished by a total concentration on its hero, Oedipus the monarch of Thebes. A plague is afflicting Thebes and an oracle from the god Apollo reveals that the murderer of the previous king, Laius, must be found and punished, and Oedipus curses the murderer; then the truth is slowly uncovered: Oedipus himself is the criminal, and he has not only murdered his father but also married his mother, Jocasta. Appalled by her recognition of the deed, Jocasta commits suicide and Oedipus tears out his eyes. The play ends with a blind but still defiant Oedipus, who has at last fulfilled Apollo's command to "know thyself", expelled from the city. What is dramatic throughout is the rapid change in purpose and mood of the king as the truth is painfully prised out, and the exploitation of irony at a variety of levels: on the verbal level—as Oedipus inadvertently curses himself—and on the non-verbal level—as Jocasta comforts Oedipus, offering consolation as a mother consoles a recalcitrant child, or as the playwright contrasts the sighted but ignorant Oedipus and the blind but all-knowing prophet of Apollo, Tiresias.

It has been argued that Sophocles, famed in antiquity for his piety, was a devout believer in the gods and justified them in this play: the gods cannot intervene but they possess a knowledge denied to man and can predict, and so the oracles in *Oedipus Rex* prove to be true. All the characters, it is claimed, deserve their fate: Jocasta because she is sceptical and impious, though only a single passage in which she seems to claim that everything is governed by chance really supports such an interpretation (in fact this is another example of Sophoclean irony and offers a neat piece of pre-Freudian psychology as the Queen goes on to say, "Many a man before you, in his dreams, has shared his mother's bed"); Oedipus accepts oracles but he is hot-tempered (in arguing with Tiresias), suspicious (in accusing his brother-in-law, Creon, of conspiring against him), and brutal (in maltreating the old shepherd), and has the excessive confidence of the self-made man. But Oedipus falls not because of a defect of character but because of an intellectual failing—he miscalculates and misunderstands at every stage of his investigations; he unwittingly does something absolutely horrific and blinds himself not as a punishment but as an escape, to avoid the world. Without his eyes he "sees" so much more. Oedipus is the great hero, especially in disaster, and his magnificence is heightened by his isolation and thrown into sharper focus by the contrast with Creon, who is moderate, cautious, and quite colourless.

Oedipus dominates: as the drama begins. He speaks first, is addressed in prayer by priest and citizens, and has already taken action by sending Creon to consult Apollo at Delphi. He becomes impatient at the delay in Creon's return and when the latter arrives, reacts strongly to his announcement that Laius was murdered by "a whole band" and only one person escaped, by delivering the "Great Curse". With typical irony Oedipus says he will fight on behalf of Laius "as if he were my father" and lists the ancestors of Laius—you need just to append the name of Oedipus himself and the list is complete—to stress the legitimacy of his own reign. Tiresias next appears but is reluctant to speak. Oedipus loses his temper and accuses Tiresias of being in league with a treacherous Creon; then, at this early stage, Tiresias reveals the truth and the impending fate of Oedipus, who however, believing himself to be the son of the Corinthian King and Queen, simply cannot understand. The "prophet scene" has come very early and, the truth having been revealed, Sophocles must rely on a succession of further "twists" to sustain the plot.

A very reasonable Creon attempts to defend himself against Oedipus's accusations, but it is left to Jocasta to settle this quarrel and it is now that oracles come fast and thick—oracles, she claims, are useless as Laius was killed by robbers when death at the hands of his son was predicted. Learning that

Laius was killed where three roads meet, Oedipus becomes anxious and reveals how he went to Delphi to establish the truth of his parentage and, on being told he would kill his father and sleep with his mother, fled Corinth and killed an old man. Has he actually cursed himself? It all depends on the number—one or several—who attacked Laius. The solitary survivor is hastily summoned.

Then the excitement mounts even more: we expect the survivor to arrive but it is in fact a messenger from Corinth who relates how Oedipus is no Corinthian but was received as a baby from a shepherd of Laius. Jocasta realises the truth and dashes from the stage. By a staggering coincidence, but one of which an audience is not conscious, the solitary survivor and the shepherd of Laius are one and the same person so that the question "who killed Laius?" can be dropped and replaced by the yet more urgent "what happened to Laius's son?".

There is still one final shock and one final surprise: the shock is provided by the terrifying description of Oedipus's self-mutilation, and the surprise by the reappearance of the blind Oedipus—one expects lamentation between hero and Chorus but Oedipus remains in command, displaying a pride once again contrasted with the pettiness of Creon. The introduction of his two daughters to be Oedipus's guides adds a note of pathos which does not detract from an overwhelming impression of a hero who converts disaster into triumph.

—Peter Walcot

OEDIPUS REX.   See **OEDIPUS THE KING.**

OEDIPUS TYRANNUS.   See **OEDIPUS THE KING.**

OFFENDING THE AUDIENCE (Publikumsbeschimpfung) by Peter Handke

First Publication: Frankfurt, 1966.
First Production: Theater am Turm, Frankfurt, 8 June 1966.

Translations
Tongue-Lashing, translated by A. Leslie Willson, in *Dimension*, vol. 1 no. 1, 1968.
Offending the Audience, in *"Kaspar" and Other Plays*, translated by Michael Roloff, New York, 1969.

Criticism
(For general works on the author, see *Playwrights* volume)

Articles:
Helmut Heissenbüttel, "Peter Handke: *Publikumsbeschimpfung*", in *Text und Kritik*, 24, 1969; in English, in *Universitas*, 12, 1970.
Johannes Vanderath, "Peter Handkes *Publikumsbeschimpfung*: Ende des aristotelischen Theaters?", in *German Quarterly*, 43, 1970.
Arno G. Preller, "Handke's *Publikumsbeschimpfung*: A New Concept of Language and Theatre", in *Proceedings, Pacific Northwest Conference on Foreign Languages*, 23, 1972.
Marcello Soffritti, "Innovation und Virtuosismus in der *Publikumsbeschimpfung*", in *Quaderni di filologia germanica della Facoltà di Lettere e Filosofia dell'Università di Bologna*, 1, 1980.
Timothy J. Wiles, "*Offending the Audience* and Embracing It", in his *The Theater Event: Modern Theories of Performance*, Chicago, 1980.
Johannes Vandenrath, "*Outrage au public* de Peter Handke: Fin du théâtre aristotélicien?", in *Austriaca*, 16, 1983.
Georg Behse, "Über Peter Handkes Erfolgsstück *Publikumsbeschimpfung*", in *Wege der Literaturwissenschaft*, edited by Jutta Kolkenbrock-Netz and others, Bonn, 1985.

*   *   *

After conventional signals that a performance is about to begin—a rustled curtain, the shuffling of feet, gradually dimmed lights, etc.—four speakers appear on stage who warm up using disconnected phrases from the play, then deliver well over 500 short lines. As the play states, "*The order in which they speak is immaterial. The speakers have roughly the same amount of work to do*". Houselights come up along with the stage lights so that the speakers and the audience "*form a unit*". The uttered sentences form an acoustic space in which to contemplate the "world within the words" rather than the worlds to which they might refer. The first lines directed at the audience are: "You are welcome. This piece is a prologue". What follows is a running commentary on and argument with the phenomenon of theatre, sometimes descriptive, sometimes exploratory; sometimes cajoling the audience, but in the end hostile towards them. The typically stylized last lines of the play drip with sarcasm: "You ladies and gents you, you celebrities of public and cultural life you, you who are present you, you brothers and sisters you, you comrades you, you worthy listeners you, you fellow humans you. You were welcome here. We thank you. Good night". A piped-in roar of applause and wild whistling continue until the audience begin to leave. Then the curtain closes.

Offending the Audience is one of a group of early plays which Handke referred to as *Sprechstücke* ("speech plays"), whose substance and subject is language. The precise *locus* for the exploration of language in *Offending the Audience* is the extended set of signs which constitute the communicative system(s) of theatre. The play is also an elaborate gag, which depends for full effect on an unsuspecting audience. A disappointment of the usual expectations is part of the experience. That this proved not to be possible after the notoriety of early productions, may have been one of the reasons Handke withdrew performance rights.

None of the paraphernalia familiar from other types of drama is present: no characters, plots, settings. The speakers chip away at the "fourth wall", breaking from the conventional actor/audience arrangement, referred to once by Handke as "geometrically this right angled relationship, in which people on the stage speak to one another, while others look at them". Though Handke was not the first to experiment with performances which aggressively attack the theatrical status quo, the style of his purely verbal assault is unique. The speakers disavow any affinity with previous theatrical experience. In the old style theatre, they say,

Always something lay in ambush between the words, gestures, props and sought to mean something to you. . .Not a play, reality was played. Since time was played, reality was played. The theatre played tribunal. The theatre played arena. The theatre played moral institution. The theatre played dreams. The theatre played tribal rites. The theatre played mirrors for you. The play exceeded the play. It hinted at reality. It became impure. It meant.

"Time is for real here", says one of the speakers, highlighting the moment of audience reception. In a typical sequence the speakers begin by fixing attention on physical details. "You become aware that you are sitting in a theatre. . .of raising your eyebrows. . .of sweating under your armpits. . ." and so on. Next, the lesson shifts to another amusing form of awareness—education. "Try not to blink your eyelids. . .not to sweat. . .not to shift in your seat. . .". These repetitions lead to the chant-like series "Why, you are breathing. Why, you are salivating. . .Why, how terribly self-conscious you are". The sequence ends with four words: "Swallow. Salivate. Blink. Breathe".

The "rules for actors" which precede the play urge performers to heighten their own awareness by listening to litanies in churches, cheers at football matches, chants at demonstrations. (Whimsical notes also suggest they do such things as watch llamas spitting at the zoo.) Relentless sequences such as the one described above might of course be amusing, annoying, perhaps even nauseating in their repetitions of words and phrases. This depends on the style of presentation and the degree of attention of individuals in the audience. The rules for the actors and the references in the script to "acoustic patterns", however, do make it clear that Handke hopes at some points to create the illusion of sheer sound out of the babble of the speakers' syllables, to have the words become performative material, emptying and filling with meaning in an imprecisely predictable manner.

What Handke does for the here-and-now physical experience of an audience in a theatre he also does for other aspects of theatre: its history, its bags of performance tricks, its significance as an art form and as a part of the "world theatre" of politics. In production, the actors have abundant opportunity to explore Handke's verbal technique in the languages of theatre. For instance, a pause could easily be taken between one line—"We make no artificial pauses"—and the next—"Our pauses are natural pauses".

The insults for which the play became infamous in the mid-1960's would seem to be goading the audience on to some kind of active response, to fight back, shout back, or maybe just walk out on the speakers (such occurrences were further reason for the author to ban subsequent performance). This would bring the theatre event full circle, to the point where a receptive audience exchanges its apparently passive role for an active one. Several minutes of "you butchers, you buggers, you bullshitters, you bullies, you rabbits, you fuck-offs, you farts" even if carefully stylized at intervals into forms such as "O you cancer victims, O you haemorrhoid sufferers, etc.", seems calculated to stretch the patience, even if an active intervention is not desired.

Offending the Audience begins by announcing itself as a prologue. It might serve to make audiences more precisely aware of their involvement, and thus be a prologue to future experiences in the theatre. It is also certainly a prologue to the rest of Handke's work, especially to the brilliant *Kaspar* in which the eponymous hero faces the world armed with a single sentence.

—Denis Calandra

OH DAD, POOR DAD, MAMMA'S HUNG YOU IN THE CLOSET AND I'M FEELIN' SO SAD
by Arthur Kopit

First Publication: New York, 1960.
First Production: Harvard University, Cambridge, Massachusetts, 1960; professionally, at Agassiz Theatre, Cambridge, Massachusetts, 1960.

Criticism
(For general works on the author, see *Playwrights* volume)

Articles:
Zoltá Szilassy, "Yankee Burlesque or Metaphysical Farce? Kopit's *Oh Dad, Poor Dad. . .* Reconsidered", in *Hungarian Studies in English*, 11, 1977.

*   *   *

The setting is a lavish suite in a Caribbean hotel, where Madame Rosepettle, her son Jonathan, and her dead husband (in a coffin) as well as their very large, carnivorous plants and assorted treasure, have ensconced themselves. Entering their restricted quarters is Commodore Roseabove, who attempts to court Madame Rosepettle, followed by Rosalie, who seduces and tries to free the imprisoned Jonathan from his mother. In addition to this collection of characters, there are a platoon of bellboys as well as Rosalinda, the rare (and talking) goldfish, which apparently eats cats voraciously. This peculiar, not to say zany, ménage has intimations of something more, and in the 1960's it seemed very avant-garde to some scholars and no doubt to much of its Broadway audience. A number of writers put the play into the absurdist camp, and perhaps it belongs there still, but for all those dark implications it seems to have settled into being accepted simply as a "farce in three scenes", which is all that Mr. Kopit claims for it.

Jonathan, a stuttering, frightened young man, lives out his meager life by looking out at the world through binoculars, and he sees a world, into which his mother has forbidden him to venture. And then Rosalie enters: vamp and liberator who comes over to flirt and eventually lure Jonathan into bed in the very room where Dad is stuffed in the closet. The goofy actions of the beginning of the play in time give way to both long monologues and to some serious (or at least gruesome) goings on. The plants, for example, must not be put "close together. . .they fight". Jonathan is terrified, it would seem with good reason, of everything and everyone. especially of Mother, the indomitable Madame. Exaggeration, of course, is the manner in which the play is cast, but at its heart there is a reality which is both recognizable and horrifying.

Jonathan tries to avoid this reality by constantly having "so much to do". There is here, it seems, an echo of Tennessee Williams's *The Glass Menagerie* and of its pathetic Laura. Instead of a unicorn to keep him from truly experiencing life, Jonathan has his stamps, his plants to feed, his coins to examine, and above all his spying on Rosalie, the baby-sitter across the street. He will do almost anything to avoid facing the facts of his closed world. When he is asked why he never goes out, he responds, "Because Mother locks the door".

Not surprisingly, Rosalie notices that "there's something very strange here". This is not a normal family by any standard, and the farce challenges the concept of "normality" and effectively exposes major eccentricities which may be funny to the outsider but terribly destructive to the intimates. Madame Rosepettle philosophizes that, in any event, "life is a lie" and that one must be very careful, for life" isn't what it seems"—implicating both the shenanigans on stage and in the audience's world in her comment.

Audiences today may find the play nothing more than an undergraduate prank by Arthur Kopit, who has since moved on to more serious theatre writing. But *Oh Dad, Poor Dad*, remains a funny, sometimes surprising and startling reaction by a young writer against parental domination. "True love" in the form of the alluring Rosalie, who may be an innocent or may be a slut, liberates the young Jonathan (perhaps, by extension, all youngsters) from the mad, material restrictions of his mother. When the outraged Madame Rosepettle discovers the seduction of her son, she announces that "this place is a madhouse" and she is quite right. By the end of the play Jonathan, the sweet *naif*, has destroyed the plants, the goldfish, his own hopes for liberation, *and* poor Rosalie, leaving Madame Rosepettle asking: "What is the meaning of all this?".

—Arthur Ballet

OH LES BEAUX JOURS.   See **HAPPY DAYS.**

L'OISEAU BLEU.   See **THE BLUE BIRD.**

OLD CANTANKEROUS.   See **THE BAD-TEMPERED OLD MAN.**

OLD TIMES
by Harold Pinter

First Publication: London and New York, 1971.
First Production: Aldwych Theatre, London (Royal Shakespeare Company), 1 June 1971.

Criticism
(For general works on the author, see *Playwrights* volume)

Articles:

Anthony M. Aylwin, "The Memory of All That: Pinter's *Old Times*", in *English*, 22, 1973.
Stephen Martineau, "Pinter's *Old Times*: The Memory Game", in *Modern Drama*, 16, 1973.
Stanley Kauffmann, "Pinter and Sexuality: Notes, Mostly on *Old Times*", in *American Poetry Review*, vol. 3. no. 3, 1974.
Peter Brigg, "*Old Times*: Beyond Pinter's Naturalism", in *English Studies in Canada*, 1, 1975.
Lawrence I. Eilenberg, "Rehearsal as Critical Method: Pinter's *Old Times*", in *Modern Drama*, 18, 1975.
Gay McAuley, "The Problem of Identity: Theme, Form and Theatrical Method in *Les Nègres, Kaspar* and *Old Times*", in *Southern Review* (Adelaide), 8, 1975.
Ewa Byczkowska, "Pinter's Treatment of Time in *Old Times*", in *Acta Universitatis Wratislaviensis*, 360, 1977.
Rainer Lengeler, "Erinnerte Gegenwart: Pinters Drama *Old Times*", in *Literatur in Wissenschaft und Unterricht*, 10, 1977.
A.R. Braunmuller, "A World of Words in Pinter's *Old Times*", in *Modern Language Quarterly*, 40, 1979.
Katherine H. Burkman, "Earth and Water: The Question of Renewal in Harold Pinter's *Old Times* and *No Man's Land*", in *West Virginia University Philological Papers*, 25, 1979.
Christopher C. Hudgins, "Inside Out: Filmic Techniques and the Theatrical Depiction of a Consciousness in Harold Pinter's *Old Times*", in *Genre*, 13, 1980.
David Savran, "The Girardian Economy of Desire: *Old Times* Recaptured", in *Theatre Journal*, 34, 1982.
Art Borreca, "*Old Times*: Pinter's Drama of the Invisible", in *Before His Eyes: Essays in Honor of Stanley Kauffmann*, edited by Bert Cardullo, Lanham, Maryland, 1986.
J.A. De Reuck, "*Old Times* and Pinter's Dramatic Method", in *English Studies in Africa*, 29, 1986.
Steven H. Gale, "Observations on Two Productions of Harold Pinter's *Old Times*", in *Pinter Review*, 1, 1987.

*   *   *

The play is set in a country home in England, which contains Kate and from which her husband Deeley ranges abroad in his work. At the outset husband and wife discuss the imminent arrival of Anna, a friend of Kate's from many years before, who shared a flat with her when they were secretaries in London. Anna, the object of Deeley's insecure speculations and inquiries, is on stage from the outset and, though she has no part in the initial conversation, she steps into it without any preparatory transition. The unreality of this suggests, symbolically, that Anna is always an unspoken presence in the marriage or that we are observing action that is a dream or has the texture of a dream. Much of the action has the abrupt disjointedness of dreams with sudden digressions into the past unheralded by any appropriate transition. A large part of the play is a recall of conflicting versions of past events in which Deeley and Anna struggle to assert their control of, influence over, and possession of Kate. In their duel, the two use their wits and memories to try to shut each other out, Deeley asserting his continuing rights to Kate, Anna trying to repossess her. There are revealed quite different versions of first meetings in a cinema, of parties they attended, and of attempts at sexual conquest. Neither can attain dominance because, though Kate is present for much of their competitive story-telling, she neither affirms nor denies their varying accounts. Kate, in the end, crushes them both by indicating that she has never yielded full allegiance to either of them.

We can never resolve the ambiguity of the action for it induces in us the uncertainty that is the defining quality of the two competitors for Kate. It may be a real, slightly disordered, visit of an old friend, or it may be Deeley's nightmare about his insecure control of his wife which an imminent visit by her friend further threatens. Kate's seeming indifference to her past and her enigmatic silence is used as a weapon in face of the desperate search of the other two for certainty. She is a withdrawn figure with a puritan distaste for dirt and sex, registered in her ritual, cleansing bath. She is said to be a parson's daughter with "a good deal of the Brontë about her"; she is, in fact, a characteristic Pinter figure, retaining power through silence against voluble companions whose competitive babbling makes them ever more deeply vulnerable. In spite of their insecurity and competition they talk about her conspiratorially as though she were not present and even swap lines of pop songs in attempts to characterize her and assert possession of her.

Deeley is tormented by a fear that, in the past, Anna achieved a greater closeness to Kate than he has ever managed with her, and that she might displace him by reasserting her hold. When he hears of quite a different Kate prior to his marriage to her, he evidently fears that she will awaken from the passivity he has found and accepted in her to become a more demanding, independent woman rather than a compliant, domestic companion. His version of his first meeting with Kate in a cinema showing *Odd Man Out* is challenged by Anna who strives, as in a later account of his sexual advances to her in a room the women shared, to make Deeley the odd man out. Anna's account of her past with Kate is full of specific and vivid detail of their shared excitement in their busy London life which is in total contrast to Kate's current rural life in abeyance punctuated only by occasional, solitary walks. Anna speaks also of her own successful life, her wealthy husband and Mediterranean villa, as if to indicate how much better a life she has than the one Deeley has offered Kate. At times she and Kate regress into that youthful life which effectively excludes Deeley. On such occasions, however, it seems to be Kate who is the one eager for adventure and Anna the shy stay-at-home, jealous perhaps, as Deeley still is, of losing her. Kate has evidently been able to maintain power over both by making them woo her and resisting their efforts to control her. The more Deeley babbles, especially in his claims—to compete with Anna's exotic life-style—that he is a successful globe-trotting film-maker, the weaker he becomes. While Kate is absent taking a bath, it seems, in their struggle to stake territorial rights, that Deeley may have first pursued Anna and that his sexual success with Kate may have lost Anna her friendship. In that case Anna's visit could be an attempt to take revenge for his original displacing of her.

Kate's return from her bath establishes her control. For much of the play she has spoken only brief phrases in response to the reminiscences of the others but finally she launches into her own lengthy, detailed account of the past. As a secretive, repressed figure she may have tried, as a young woman, to live by proxy through Anna. We never find out if there was any sexual relation between Anna and Deeley but, in any case, in disdain for the dirtiness of sex Kate indicates that they both became dead to her. In punishment she symbolically buried them by smearing them with dirt and achieved a vengeful ascendancy by abandoning Anna and marrying Deeley. The final tableau presents the two women on single beds, Deeley the odd man out in an armchair between them, a sobbing figure who re-enacts the scene of sexual frustration that he had first experienced with the two young secretaries in their London flat. Kate remains as untouchable and unavailable as she has always been.

—Anthony Brennan

THE OLD WIVES TALE
by George Peele

First Publication: London, 1595.
First Production: London (The Queen's Men?), c. 1588–94.

Editions

The Old Wives Tale, in *Five Elizabethan Comedies*, edited by A.K. McIlwraith, London, 1934.

The Old Wives Tale, in *The Dramatic Works of George Peele*, 2, edited by C.T. Prouty, New Haven, Connecticut, 1961.

The Old Wives Tale, in *The Old Wives Tale; The Blacking Man*, edited by Robert Leach, London, 1978.

The Old Wives Tale, edited by Patricia Binnie, Manchester, 1980 (Revels Plays).

The Old Wives Tale, in *Three Sixteenth-Century Comedies*, edited by Charles W. Whitworth Jr., London, 1984 (New Mermaid Series).

Criticism

(For general works on the author, see *Playwrights* volume)

Articles:

Herbert Gladstone, "Interplay in Peele's *The Old Wives Tale*", in *Boston University Studies in English*, 4, 1960.

M.C. Bradbrook, "Peele's *Old Wives Tale*: A Play of Enchantment", in *English Studies*, 43, 1962.

Mark Gelber, "The Unity of George Peele's *The Old Wives Tale*", in *New York-Pennsylvania MLA Newsletter*, 2, 1969.

Laurilyn J. Rockey, "*The Old Wives Tale* as Dramatic Satire", in *Educational Theatre Journal*, 22, 1970.

John Doebler, "The Tone of George Peele's *The Old Wives Tale*", in *English Studies*, 53, 1972.

John D. Cox, "Homely Matter and Multiple Plots in Peele's *Old Wives Tale*", in *Texas Studies in Literature and Language*, 20, 1978.

Thomas N. Grove, "Some Observations on the 'Marvellous' *Old Wives Tale*", in *Studia Anglia Posnaniensia*, 11, 1979.

Joan C. Marx, "'Soft, Who Have We Here?': The Dramatic Technique of *The Old Wives Tale*", in *Renaissance Drama*, 12, 1981.

Roger de V. Renwick, "The Mummers Play and *The Old Wives Tale*", in *Journal of American Folklore*, 91, 1981.

Susan T. Viguers, "The Hearth and the Cell: Art in *The Old Wives Tale*", in *Studies in English Literature 1500–1900*, 21, 1981.

Jackson G. Cope, "Peele's *Old Wives Tale*: Folk Stuff into Ritual Form", in *English Literary History*, 49, 1982.

Mary G. Free, "Audience Within Audience in *The Old Wives Tale*", in *Renaissance Papers*, 1983.

Leanore Lieblein, "Doubling as a Language of Transformation: The Case of *The Old Wives Tale*", in *Du Texte à la scène: Languages du théâtre*, Paris, 1983.

Paul Werstine, "Provenance and Printing History in Two Revels Editions", in *Medieval and Renaissance Drama in England*, 1, 1984.

*   *   *

"Once upon a time there was a king or a lord or a duke that had a fair daughter, the fairest that ever was. . .''; so commences the old wives' tale of the title. The entertainment of two young pages who have been found wandering, lost, in the woods with "a merry winter's tale" told by Madge, wife of Clunch the smith, provides the dramatic "frame" for the tale itself which is mysteriously enacted before them as she begins to speak. Characters from folk-tales, and conventional "types" from romance literature, fill the stage, and in an innovative, theatrical move, Peele relegates Madge and her two listeners to the status of observers and commentators.

Madge's particular qualities as a story-teller appear throughout the action of this secondary drama: the imprecision in the opening lines (above) manifests itself in numerous small inconsistencies, and her trite formulae provide the foundation for a conventionally romantic fiction. The fair princess, Delia, is "as white as snow and as red as blood", and she has been "stolen away" by a conjurer "who could do anything, and he turned himself into a great dragon, and carried [her] away in his mouth to a castle that he made of stone, and there he kept her I know not how long".

Besides this plot about Delia and the wicked sorcerer, Sacrapant, Madge's story presents a bewildering array of characters with unusual problems: Erestus, another victim of Sacrapant's magic, is "a bear in the night and a man in the day"—a state of affairs which has, not surprisingly, driven his "lady", Venelia, mad; Lampriscus is a man afflicted by two daughters, the one good-looking but bad-tempered, and the other so ugly that no dowry could be great enough to tempt a suitor; Huanebango is a ranting braggart who claims to be more than a match for Sacrapant and, like his side-kick, Corebus (sometimes called Booby), seeks the love of fair Delia; and Eumenides is a poverty-stricken Wandering Knight who is in love with Delia too.

As the tale progresses, the audience becomes aware both of the alarming arbitrariness of the romantic mode, and of the comforting predictability of its narrative structures. The unexpected always turns out to have its place in the action, whether it be the pot of honey brought in by Lampriscus, which makes an excellent gift for the bear/man Erestus, or the sudden eruption of singing reapers: "But soft, who comes here? O, these are the harvest-men; ten to one they sing a song of mowing". The definite article alone is their passport into the tale: they are included in Madge's scheme of events even if their function is far from obvious to us.

Each strand of the story is woven into the final pattern by the interventions of Erestus who, Merlin-like, provides a network of prophetic advice which, when followed, secures appropriate results for all. Eumenides, who gives "more than all" to pay for the burial of Jack, a poor man, is rewarded by the dead man's ghost with a purse of gold, and wins Delia. The father of the two, ineligible daughters is advised to send them to the well of "the water of life" where, as a result of their different reactions to two heads which rise magically from the water, the shrewish daughter gains Huanebango (now deaf), and the kind, but ugly, daughter gains Corebus (now blind) and a shower of gold. The justice of this distribution has been prepared for by the two men's earlier dealings with Erestus: Corebus had offered him cake, while Huanebango arrogantly refused to give him alms. Delia's two brothers, encouraged by rhyming instructions from Erestus, are brave and steadfast in the pursuit of Sacrapant, the ghostly Jack is responsible for his death, and Venelia fulfills a prophecy by being (although her exact qualifications are not explained) "neither wife, widow nor maid" and hence able to put out the magic light which sustains Sacrapant's power. As a result, Delia is freed, the two brothers are rescued from enchantment, Erestus is saved from nights of bearhood, and Venelia herself is restored to sanity.

There is no record of a contemporary performance which might help to give the play a context: it is attributed to the Queen's Men, a public theatre company, on its title page (1595), but the number of locations required by the action suggests the need for simultaneous staging, more often a feature of court entertainments. The play also defies categorization. It can be viewed as a carefully-observed attempt to dramatize the characteristics of the folk-tale, specifically in the motifs of the Grateful Dead (Jack) and the Heads in the Well, and there is a gesture towards classical comedy in the portrayal of the swaggering Huanebango. But by far the most important elements are those of romance, like the story of the Wandering Knight, the strange transformations wrought by Sacrapant's magic, and the conflict between love and friendship which emerges as an issue when Jack asks Eumenides for half of Delia since they have vowed to share their fortunes. A satirical

intention is evident in such episodes as this last one, and in the extraordinary range of imitated, literary styles, from the high-flown blustering of Huanebango and Sacrapant's mighty lines to the colloquial prose of Madge and Jack's neighbours. But this rich mixture of music, magic, and spectacle amounts to something more than satire. A strong emphasis on the virtue of generosity compels sympathetic attention, and the on-stage audience's earnest attempts to follow the story gives the fiction a theatrical "reality" which is not jeopardised by ridicule. The skilful use of an apparently artless, internal narrator ensures a complex response to a rare blend of sophisticated and simple pleasures.

—Joanna Udall

ON BAILE'S STRAND
by W.B. Yeats

First Publication: In *In the Seven Woods*, Dundrum, Ireland, 1903.
First Production: Abbey Theatre, Dublin, 27 December 1904; revised version, Oxford, 1905.

Criticism
(For general works on the author, see *Playwrights* volume)

Articles:
Patrick A. McCarthy, "Talent and Tradition in Yeats' *On Baile's Strand*", in *Eire*, vol.11 no.1, 1976.
Rita T. Schmidt, "W.B. Yeats' Ideal of Lyrical Drama: Myth and Ritual in *On Baile's Strand*", in *Estudos anglo-americanos*, 12–13, 1988–89.

*   *   *

On Baile's Strand is one of five plays by Yeats based on the life of Cuchulain, hero of the Ulster saga, *The Tain*. Cuchulain is a sort of Achilles figure, half-god, half-man, destined to achieve great fame and die young. The extant stories make it hard to pin any simple character on the hero (the sagas are not novels, and the folk imagination has also had its way with him). Yeats adds to the complexity by allowing him to grow old in this play. He generally avoids the eccentricities of the old stories, Cuchulain's grotesque "warp spasm", and the fact that his son, who easily overcomes the mature Ulster warriors, is only a child of six or so (Cuchulain was killing men at the same age). Nevertheless he holds on to the supernatural element and modifies it to his own tastes.

The subject is very powerful. The hero has no children by his wife, Emer; but during his early training as a warrior he has impregnated a Scottish warrior Queen, Aoife. Although he had given the Queen instructions to send the boy to him when he grew up, all versions allow him to have forgotten this. Yeats shows extraordinary skill in dramatising this material. He lets the plot unfold through two characters that he always uses well (Lady Gregory helped him with the dialogue for these): the Blind Man and the Fool. The latter is greedy and curious, the former wily and well informed. Neither is heroic. The Blind Man gulls the Fool by spinning him yarns while he gets to eat the stolen chicken. Yeats uses them elsewhere in plays and poems to good effect because he makes them embody the materialist, wily side of Irish life that was at war with his own high ambitions. The Blind Man distracts the Fool from the cooking chicken by feeding him gossip about what is going on among the heroes—that a young man has arrived from Scotland, that he has some connection with Cuchulain.

This sets up the main part of the drama which is at first a battle of wills between Conchubar, the High King, and Cuchulain. The latter is the guardian of Ulster, but personally unruly. Conchubar wants an oath of subordination to be sure that Cuchulain will be a willing servant of Conchubar's unwarlike children; his main point being that the hero must serve the state. His chief taunt is that Cuchulain has no children and is becoming an irresponsible middle-aged man. It is a curious bit of writing, brilliant in Yeats's having learnt so much from Shakespeare, dubious in that it always has an air of intelligent pastiche. It is all in more or less iambic blank verse, and when it is good it is good Shakespeare rather than a modern play. Shakespeare was able to treat Roman heroes like living Elizabethans; Yeats doesn't persuade us that the problems he dramatises are immediate although they may be perennial.

When the young kings urge Cuchulain to take the oath of allegiance, he accepts. Then his son suddenly appears, sworn not to give his name. In the first part Yeats has established Cuchulain's memories of Aoife in a whole complex of images of war: love is as "a brief forgiveness between opposites". It obviously has some connection with frustrated love for Maude Gonne, "that high, laughing, turbulent head of hers". He emphasises a pale skin and red hair for Aoife. Although Yeats has apparently dropped the traditional madness of Cuchulain from his scenario, he retains or invents his own symbolism of witches in the Blind Man's talk, in Conor's accusations. At first Cuchulain is drawn to the turbulent young man, obviously welcoming him as the son he never had and relishing his resemblance to Aoife, his ideal lover. But in a rather arbitrary dramatic moment, when he pushes the High King aside to defend the boy, he is shocked by his own action and agrees that he must have been enchanted. Nevertheless what happens is very touching, because Yeats has set up a strong affection between boy and father.

All the violent action takes place off stage, reported by the Fool. Cuchulain kills his son, then he comes in and is gradually, tormentingly, informed by the Blind Man of what he has done. Yeats hits off some brilliant effects here that totally justify his oblique approach. The Blind Man complains that the bench is shaking, and we don't need the Fool to tell us that Cuchulain is reacting. He rushes out and the Fool reports his fight with the waves. He wants to kill Conchubar, but the witches of the air displace his anger towards the sea. Yeats sinks this heroic grief further by allowing the Blind Man to say: "There will be nobody in the houses. Come this way; come quickly! The ovens will be full. We will put our hands into the ovens". The language isn't quite right, but the idea is terrific, and that seems to encapsulate Yeats the dramatist at his best.

—James Simmons

ONCE IN A LIFETIME
by George Kaufman and Moss Hart

First Publication: New York, 1930.
First Production: Music Box Theatre, New York, 24 September 1930.

A third-rate New York vaudeville team down on their luck—cynical May, would-be entrepreneur Jerry, and simple literal-minded George—go to Hollywood to cash in on the new talkies. In a Hollywood overrun with money and totally lacking in sense, Jerry and May start an elocution school while George falls in love with hopeful *ingénue* Susan and is haplessly made a production supervisor. The school becomes a Hollywood casualty. Jerry, besotted with wheeling and dealing, becomes estranged from May, and she starts back to New York. George's blatantly terrible film becomes a critical success. However, confused by being continually hired and fired for his idiotic decisions, and lonely, George begs May to return. The trio are united and are soon on their way to fortune.

Once in a Lifetime is the first of the long and hugely successful collaboration between George S. Kaufman and Moss Hart and is, arguably, their most good-natured and least acerbic piece. The play's good-hearted innocence and slightly chaotic sense of good humour endears us to the characters because of their faults rather than despite them.

Even in the 1930's, these characters would have been stereotypes, and film stereotypes at that. May's hard-bitten cover to a heart of fondant; Jerry's self-absorbed ambition; even George's kindly stupidity—all become positive qualities in a Hollywood where even personal characteristics are stripped in the grapple for profit and fame.

To our eyes, their spoof on Hollywood may seem mild and familiar, although it still retains the humour of the sheer extremity and banality of it all. Perhaps one of the reasons the play retains its humour lies in the simple, clear-sighted morality at its base. Hollywood and the antics of its movie-making inhabitants are hilarious and appalling in their gross, unrelenting waste. Having no moral or artistic criteria, the movie moguls grope for fortune with arbitrariness and greed. Their vacuous stupidity, bereft of taste, integrity, or sense, makes George's ingenuous stupidity positively endearing. Even though the trio are in Hollywood to feed off it and get rich quick, and their endeavour is based on fraud, their bonding sets them apart from others. George's love for Susan, who is the epitome of harmless stupidity, gains for her admittance to this sacred circle of those who have retained some human feeling.

The humour of the play is firmly based in the American tradition: the wisecrack; aggressive sarcasm designed to establish superiority over the butt of the joke; and the standard one-liner inherited from burlesque which is arguably the foundation of American comedy. Kaufman and Hart's use of these techniques, however, is polished and sophisticated. Rather than relying on verbal slapstick, their dialogue is infused with a modicum of wit (a commodity at a premium in American comedy) emphasising word play. They also flatter their audience with jokes and references based on the assumption of knowledge and education, such as references to the work of Noël Coward and Eugene O'Neill.

Kaufman and Hart also have one more string to their bow. Possibly their strongest and most lasting source of humour lies in their ability to create, through the dialogue, images of visual humour, enlisting the audience to create pictures beyond the stage action. These imagined pictures of ridiculous disproportion remain in the mind and are capable of producing a chuckle long after the play is over; the long, empty corridors of the studio where writers, bought in bulk, waste away through neglect; the writer's sanatorium where, together, they recover from their Hollywood-induced nervous breakdowns; George's purchase of 2,000 aircraft (so he can get one free!). These images create a whole world of bizarre, unimaginable waste and chaos which establishes the context for the play. When

Once in a Lifetime: Piccadilly Theatre, London, 1980

George, now an executive producer, continues his habit of cracking and consuming Indian nuts even during the showing of his film, a critic writes:

> The audience was puzzled by a constant knocking, and it seemed to many of us that something might be wrong with the sound aparatus. Then suddenly, we realized that what was being done was what Eugene O'Neill did with the constant beating of the tom-tom in "The Emperor Jones". It was the beat of hail on the roof. It is another of the masterly touches brought to the picture by the new genius of the film, Dr. George Lewis.

Two emperors—the film makers and the critics—have been shown to have no clothes, and all accomplished through a small eccentricity established humbly in the beginning of the play. This remarkably scrupulous structuring and the adherence to detail are typical of the Kaufman–Hart style.

The drama and its morality work on a simple basis. The brittle, pointless, self-gratifying artificiality of the film industry is set, on the one hand, against the down-to-earth simplicity of George who is flatly incapable of dissembling (indeed, barely capable of putting one foot in front of the other), and, on the other hand, against the writer, Laurence Vail, quite possibly talented, intelligent, and with genuine integrity. He leaves Hollywood because, although they are paying him, they are not asking him to write. George's literalness provides a handy platform for play with language. Vail provides an intelligent and understanding listener for May's verbal ironies.

A simply dichotomy is set up between human care and warmth on one side, and the lustful grapple for wealth and fame on the other. George's simple concern for Susan exonerates her from the consequences of her stupidity. May's concern for Jerry and George, and her insight into the world they have adopted, distance her from it and exonerate her from the dubious nature of her and Jerry's venture in opening a school they are unqualified to teach in. The "love story" between Jerry and May is obligatory Broadway, but Jerry's story is also a little morality tale of a Faust saved in the nick of time from signing away his soul.

Safe in the knowledge that George's pure literalism will prevent them all from a serious lack of integrity, the audience can leave the theatre confirmed in their intelligence and their superiority (after all, they have been seeing a *play*, not attending a film!). Well structured, skilfully written, and peppered with verbal sophistication, the play, however, never really bites all that deeply. Part of its pleasure is having the illusion of satire without the danger.

—Elaine Turner

OP HOOP VAN ZEGEN.   See **THE GOOD HOPE.**

ORESTE
by Vittorio Alfieri

First Publication: 1784.
First Production: Teatro di Foligno, Rome, 1781.

Editions
Oreste, edited by A.C. Clapin, London, 1889.
Oreste, in *Alfieri: Tragedie, 1*, edited by Nicola Bruscoli, Bari, 1946.
Oreste, edited by R. de Bello, 1967.
Oreste, in *Alfieri: Tragedie e scritti scelti*, edited by Pietro Cazzani, Brescia, 1975.

Translations
Oreste, in *Alfieri: The Tagedies* [3 vols.], translated by Charles Lloyd Baldwin, 1815; augmented edition [2 vols.], edited by E.A. Bowring, 1876.

* * *

The play is concerned with the tragic fate of the family of the Atrides, and follows on from Alfieri's own tragedy, *Agamemnone*. Ten years have passed since the tragic events which led Clytemnestra to seduce Aegisthus and arrange the death of her husband, King Agamemnon, after he had earned her remorseless hatred by making a blood sacrifice of their daughter, Iphigenia. But although Aegisthus is now firmly established on the throne of Argos, all is far from well: Aegisthus is plagued by unknown fears, Clytemnestra is racked with guilt, Electra, daughter of Clytemnestra and Agamemnon, harbours revenge, and Orestes, her brother, grows to manhood, doomed to avenge his father's murder. As Orestes and his faithful friend, Pylades, wend their way towards Argos and the destiny of the Atrides, Clytemnestra, Aegisthus, and Electra seem locked in an endless round of accusation and recrimination. Electra's prayers for the return of Orestes are now answered, for he arrives at the palace determined to avenge his father's murder. He and Pylades pretend to be messengers sent by the King of Phocis to advise Aegisthus of Orestes' death. They encounter Electra about to visit her father's tomb, and after talking together Orestes and Electra discover they are brother and sister. But when Orestes eventually meets his mother, he tells her that Orestes is dead, and he explains in detail to Aegisthus exactly how Orestes came to meet his death in a chariot race. But Aegisthus's suspicions are aroused and he gives orders for Orestes and Pylades to be arrested and imprisoned. Electra's concern convinces him that at last he has his enemy, Orestes, as a prisoner, and he decides to kill Electra, then Pylades, then Orestes. But in a busy final act the people of Argos denounce Aegisthus and proclaim Orestes their king. Aegisthus and Clytemnestra flee, battle is joined, and Orestes kills Aegisthus; but in his rage and by accident he kills his mother too. He is stunned and bewildered by his crime, as the Furies begin to assemble about the new victim of fate.

In his *Vita*, Alfieri says that the play was conceived at Pisa after reading Seneca's rather nondescript *Agamemnon*, but composition was temporarily halted when the poet discovered Voltaire had written a tragedy on the same subject. His hesitations were later overcome, however, and the play was eventually completed. In addition to the Senecan version, Aeschylus's *Choephori* (*Libation Bearers*) contributed, and possibly other versions of the story. Few would make great claims for Alfieri as a dramatist, and the limitations of his plays in general are those of *Oreste* in particular. It tends to be static and too heavily rhetorical, and the characters are more like formally devised emblematic stage figures than persuasive fictional representations of human beings. Alfieri was, too, rather dangerously attracted to dramatic material and situations which in one way or another reflected his own particular interest in the noble rebel, the lone hero impelled to a tragic act that even further isolates him from the world of ordinary men. The climate of Alfieri's plays is excessively rarefied; his characters cannot speak the language of ordinary men, so their discourse is always immersed in profundities. Like most of the Romantic poets who turned their hands to drama, Alfieri could not manage a dialogue both poetically elevated and persuasively colloquial.

But *Oreste* won early praise for its nobility and intensity, the outcome of the most careful composition on Alfieri's part. The subject-matter was of a kind to which Alfieri responded positively, not least in that it is a play with the conflict between a tyrant and an anti-tyrant at its centre; the former brought to destruction notwithstanding the sacrifice required of the anti-tyrant to achieve it. These were materials particularly pertinent to Alfieri's own passionately held political views with their curious love–hate relationship for the authoritarian ruler. Some have argued also that no less highly personal to Alfieri was the theme of matricide, for Alfieri's own relations with his mother were strained and a major preoccupation; this, however, is to reach too much for a Freudian gloss, when the dramatic situation, in all its essentials, has been determined rather by the source materials. Even where the fictional incident is more peculiar to Alfieri—as in the detail of Orestes murdering his mother while in a trance-like state—it would be hazardous to conclude much of personal pertinence, for the detail could as easily be explained by the purely theatrical appeal of the action.

Oreste was not only successful in its own age, but was performed later by many of the greatest Italian actors of the 19th century, like Gustavo Modena, Ernesto Rossi, and Tommaso Salvini; while in this century it has occasionally been given impressive stagings, as when Luchino Visconti directed it in Rome in 1949. And the great actor Vittorio Gassman played the lead throughout Italy and at the Théâtre des Nations, in Paris, in 1957. It cannot be said, however, that *Oreste* has entered the European repertory, for Alfieri's work does not translate well, and is rarely performed by other than Italian actors.

—Laura Richards

THE ORESTEIA
   Agamemnon
   The Libation Bearers (Choephori / Choephoroi)
   The Furies (Eumenides)
by Aeschylus

The Trilogy
First Production: Athens, 458 B.C.

Editions
The Oresteia [with translation], edited and translated by George Thomson, Cambridge, 1938; revised edition, Amsterdam, 1966.
The Oresteia, [with translation], edited and translated by J.T. Sheppard, Cambridge, 1939.

Translations

The Oresteia, translated by R.C. Trevelyan, Cambridge, 1920.

Agamemnon; Choephoroe; Eumenides, translated by C. M. Cookson, London, 1924.

The Oresteia, translated by Gilbert Murray, 1928.

Aeschylus, 1: The "Oresteia", translated by Richmond Lattimore, Chicago, 1953 (Complete Greek Tragedies Series).

The Oresteia Trilogy, translated by Philip Vellacott, Harmondsworth, 1956.

The Orestes Plays of Aeschylus, translated by Paul Roche, New York, 1962.

The Oresteia [2 vols.], translated by Peter D. Arnott, New York, 1964.

The Oresteia Trilogy and "Prometheus Bound", translated by Michael Townsend, San Francisco, 1966.

The Oresteia, translated by Hugh Lloyd-Jones, Englewood Cliffs, 1970.

The Oresteia, translated by Douglas Young, Norman, Oklahoma, 1974.

The Oresteia, translated by Robert Fagles, London, 1976.

The Oresteia, translated by Robert Lowell, New York, 1978.

The Oresteia, translated by David Grene and Wendy Doninger O'Flaherty, Chicago and London, 1989.

Agamemnon

Editions

Agamemnon, edited by A. Sidgewick, Oxford, 1881; sixth edition, 1939.

The "Agamemnon" of Aeschylus [with translation], edited by A.W, Verrall, London, 1889; second edition, 1904.

Agamemnon, edited by F.H.M. Blaydes, London, 1898.

The "Agamemnon" of Aeschylus [with translation], edited by A.C Pearson, Cambridge, 1910.

The "Agamemnon" of Aeschylus [with translation], edited by J.C. Lawson, Cambridge, 1932.

The "Agamemnon" of Aeschylus: A Revised Text, edited by A.Y. Campbell, Liverpool, 1936.

Agamemnon [with translation and commentary; 3 vols.], edited by Eduard Fraenkel, Oxford, 1950.

Agamemnon, edited by John Dewar Denniston and Denys Page, Oxford, 1957.

The "Agamemnon" of Aeschylus [with translation], edited by Raymond Postgate, Cambridge, 1969.

Translations

The Agamemnon, translated by A.W. Verrall, London and New York, 1904.

The Agamemnon, translated by John Connington, Oxford, 1907.

The Agamemnon, translated by Rushworth Kennard Davis, Oxford, 1919.

The "Agamemnon" of Aeschylus, translated by Gilbert Murray, London, 1920.

The Agamemnon, translated by T.G. Tucker, Melbourne and London, 1935.

The Agamemnon, translated by Louis MacNeice, London, 1936.

The Agamemnon, translated by Archibal Y. Campbell, Liverpool and London, 1940.

The Agamemnon, translated by Anthony Holden, Cambridge, 1969.

Agamemnon, translated by Hugh Lloyd-Jones, Englewood Cliffs, New Jersey, 1970.

The Libation Bearers (Choephori / Choephoroe)

Editions

Choephori (2 vols.), edited by A. Sidgewick, Oxford, 1884; revised edition, 1924.

Aeschyli "Choephoroi", edited by F.H.M. Blaydes, London, 1899.

The "Choephori" [with translation], edited and translated by T.G. Tucker, Cambridge, 1901.

Choephori, edited by A.F. Garvie, Oxford, 1986.

Choephori, edited by A. Bowen, Bristol, 1986.

Translations

The Choephoroe (The Libation Bearers), translated by Gilbert Murray, London, 1923.

The "Choephoroe" of Aeschylus, translated by A.S. [sic], Winchester, 1938.

The Libation Bearers, translated by Hugh Lloyd-Jones, Englewood Cliffs, New Jersey, 1970.

The Furies (Eumenides)

Editions

The Eumenides, edited by F.A. Paley, Cambridge, 1880.

Aeschylus: "Eumenides" (2 vols.), edited by A. Sidgewick, Oxford, 1887; second edition, 1895; third edition, 1927.

The Eumenides, edited by Lionel D. Barnett, London, 1901.

Aeschyli "Eumenides" [3 vols; with translation], edited by T.R. Mills, translated by F.G. Plaistowe, London, 1901.

Eumenides [with translation], edited and translated by A.W. Verrall, London, 1908.

Eumenides [with translation], edited and translated by Anthony J. Podlecki, Warminster, Wiltshire, 1989.

Eumenides, edited by Alan H. Sommerstein, Cambridge, 1989.

Translations

The Eumenides, translated by A.W. Verrall, Cambridge, 1885.

The "Eumenides" (The "Furies") of Aeschylus, translated by Gilbert Murray, London, 1925.

The "Eumenides" of Aeschylus, translated by A.S. [sic], Winchester, 1939.

The Eumenides, translated by Hugh Lloyd-Jones, Englewood Cliffs, New Jersey, 1970.

Criticism

(For general works on the author, see *Playwrights* volume)

Books:

F. Fletcher, *Notes to the "Agamemnon" of Aeschylus*, Oxford, 1949.

Anne Lebeck, *Image and Idea of the "Agamemnon" of Aeschylus*, New York, 1964.

Anne Lebeck, *The "Oresteia": A Study in Language and Structure*, Washington D.C., 1971.

Simon Goldhill, *Language, Sexuality, Narrative: The "Oresteia"*, Cambridge, 1984.

Deborah H. Roberts, *Apollo and His Oracle in the "Oresteia"* Göttingen, 1984.

Philip Vellacott, *The Logic of Tragedy, Moral, and Integrity in Aeschylus' "Oresteia"*, Durham, North Carolina, 1984.

A.J.N.W. Prag, *The "Oresteia": Iconographic and Narrative Tradition*, Chicago, 1985.

D.J. Conacher, *Aeschylus' "Oresteia": A Literary Commentary*, Toronto, 1987.

Articles:

R.W. Livingstone, "The Problem of the *Eumenides*", in *Journal of Hellenic Studies*, 35, 1925.

F.M.B. Anderson, "The Character of Clytemnestra in the *Choephoroe* and the *Eumenides*", in *American Journal of Philology*, 53, 1932.

W. Schadewaldt, "Der *kommos* in Aischylos *Cheophoren*", in *Hermes*, 67, 1932.

G. Thomson, "Mystical Allusions in the *Oresteia*", in *American Journal of Philology*, 53, 1933, and 55, 1935.

R.P. Winnington-Ingram, "The Role of Apollo in the *Oresteia*", in *Classical Review*, 47, 1933.

G. Thomson, "Notes on *Oresteia*", in *Classical Quarterly*, 28, 1934.

A.Z. Campbell, "*Agamemnon*", in *Classical Quarterly*, 29, 1935.

W.C. Greene, "Dramatic and Ethical Motives in the *Agamemnon*", in *Harvard Studies in Classical Philology*, 54, 1943.

P.B.R. Forbes, "Law and Politics in *The Oresteia*", in *Classical Review*, 62, 1948.

R.P. Winnington-Ingram, "Clytemnestra and the Vote of Athens", in *Journal of the Hellenic Society*, 68, 1948.

F.R. Earp, "Studies in Character: Agamemnon", in *Greece and Rome*, 19, 1950.

K. Burke, "Form and Persecution in the *Oresteia*", in *Sewanee Review*, 60, 1952.

B.M.W. Knox, "The Lion in the House", in *Classical Philology*, 47, 1952.

R.F. Goheen, "Aspects of Dramatic Symbolism: Three Studies in the *Oresteia*", in *American Journal of Philology*, 76, 1955.

K.J. Dover, "The Political Aspects of Aeschylus' *Eumenides*", in *Journal of the Hellenic Society*, 77, 1957.

Oskar Seidlin, "The *Oresteia* Today: A Myth Dehumanized", in *Thought*, 34, 1959.

E.P. Dodds, "Morals and Politics in the *Oresteia*", in *Proceedings of the Cambridge Philological Society*, 6, 1960.

C.H. Reeves, "The Parados of the *Agamemnon*", in *Classical Journal*, 55, 1960.

J.S. Kenna, "The Return of Orestes", in *Journal of Hellenic Studies*, 81, 1961.

H. Lloyd-Jones, "Some Alleged Interpolations in Aeschylus' *Choephoroi* and Euripides' *Electra*", in *Classical Quarterly* (new series), 11, 1961.

H. Lloyd-Jones, "The Guilt of Agamemnon", in *Classical Quarterly*, 12, 1962.

G. Rousseau, "Dream and Vision in Aeschylus' *Oresteia*", in *Arion*, 2, 1963.

J.J. Peradotto, "Some Patterns of Nature Imagery in the *Oresteia*", in *American Journal of Philology*, 85, 1964.

J. Quincy, "Orestes and the Argive Alliance", in *Classical Quarterly* (new series), 14, 1964.

William Whallon, "Maenadism in the *Oresteia*", in *Harvard Studies in Classical Philology*, 68, 1964.

D.C.C. Young, "Gentler Medicines in the *Agamemnon*", in *Classical Quarterly* (new series), 14, 1964.

N.G.L. Hammond, "Personal Freedom and Its Limitations in the *Oresteia*", in *Journal of Hellenic Studies*, 85, 1965.

Harry L. Levy, "*The Oresteia* of Aeschylus", in *Drama Survey*, 4, 1965.

F.I. Zeitlin, "The Motif of the Corrupted Sacrifice in Aeschylus' *Oresteia*", in *Transactions and Proceedings of the American Philological Association* [*TAPA*], 96, 1965.

W.C. Scott, "Wind Imagery in the *Oresteia*", in *Transactions and Proceedings of the American Philological Association* [*TAPA*], 97, 1966.

L. Bergson, "The Hymn to Zeus in Aeschylus' *Agamemnon*", in *Eranos*, 65, 1967.

F. Solmsen, "Electra and Orestes: Three Recognitions in Greek Tragedy", in *Medelingen de koninklijke Nederlanse Akademie van Wetenschappen Afd Letterkunde*, 30, 1967.

J.T Hooker, "The Sacrifice of Iphigenia in the *Agamemnon*", in *Agon*, 2, 1968.

A.F. Garvie, "The Opening of the *Choephori*", in *Bulletin of the Institute of Classical Studies* (London), 17, 1970.

J. Fontenrose, "Gods and Men in the *Oresteia*", in *Transactions and Proceedings of the American Philological Association* [*TAPA*], 102, 1971.

Michael Simpson, "Why Does Agamemnon Yield?", in *La parola del passato, Revista di studi Antichi*, 137, 1971.

D.C.C. Young, "Readings in Aeschylus' *Choephori* and *Eumenides*", in *Greek, Roman and Byzantine Studies*, Autumn, 1971.

J. Wilma Counts, "Cassandra: An Approach to Aeschylus' *Agamemnon*", in *English Journal*, 62, 1973.

K.J. Dover, "Some Neglected Aspects of Agamemnon's Dilemma", in *Journal of Hellenic Studies*, 93, 1973.

Ole Langwitz Smith, "Once Again: The Guilt of Agamemnon", in *Eranos*, 71, 1973.

D.J. Conacher, "Interaction Between Chorus and Characters in the *Oresteia*", in *American Journal of Philology*, 95, 1974.

I. Lallot, "*Xumbola Kranai*: Reflections sur la fonction du symbolon dans *L'Agamemnon* d'Eschyle", in *Cahiers internationaux du symbolisme*, 26, 1974.

W.F. Lanahan, "Levels of Symbolism in the Red Carpet Scene of *Agamemnon*", in *Classical Bulletin*, 51, 1974.

D.M. Leahy, "The Representation of the Trojan War in Aeschylus' *Agamemnon*", in *American Journal of Philology*, 95. 1974.

M. Pope, "Merciful Heavens? A Question in Aeschylus' *Agamemnon*", in *Journal of Hellenic Studies*, 94, 1974.

M. Ewans, "Agamemnon at Aulis: A Study in the *Oresteia*", in *Ramus*, 4, 1975.

M. Gagarin, "The Vote of Athena", in *American Journal of Philology*, 96, 1975.

L. Mendelsohn, "Seven Characters in Search of Roles: Conflict in Aeschylus' *Agamemnon*", in *Adam*, 391–393, 1975.

Stuart E. Laurence, "Artemis in the *Agamemnon*", in *American Journal of Philology*, 97, 1976.

J.R. Cole, "The *Oresteia* and Cimon", in *Harvard Studies in Classical Philology*, 81, 1977.

T.J. Fleming, "The Musical Nomos in Aeschylus' *Oresteia*", in *Classical Journal*, 72, 1977.

T.N. Gantz, "Fires of the *Oresteia*", in *Journal of the Hellenic Society*, 97, 1977.

W.E. Higgins, "Double-Dealing Ares in the *Oresteia*", in *Classical Philology*, 73, 1978.

David Sider, "Stagecraft in the *Oresteia*", in *American Journal of Philology*, 99, 1978.

F. Zeitlin, "Dynamics of Misogyny in the *Oresteia*", in *Arethusa*, 11, 1978.

T.C.W. Stinton, "The First Stasimon of Aeschylus's *Choephori*", in *Classical Quarterly* (new series), 29, 1979.

M.L. West, "The Parados of the *Agamemnon*", in *Classical Quarterly* (new series), vol. 29, 1979.

Alan H. Sommerstein, "Notes on the *Oresteia*", in *Bulletin of the Institute of Classical Studies* (London), 27, 1980.

R.M. Harriott, "The Argive Elders, the Discerning Shepherd and the Fawning Dog: Misleading Communication in the *Agamemnon*", in *Classical Quarterly*, vol. 32 no. 1, 1982.

The Oresteia: National Theatre, London, 1981

C.W. Macleod, "Politics and the *Oresteia*", in *Journal of Hellenic Studies*, 102, 1982.

R. Seaford, "The Last Bath of Agamemnon", in *Classical Quarterly* (new series), 34, 1982.

A.L. Brown, "The *Erinyes* and the *Oresteia*: Real Life, the Supernatural and the Stage", in *Journal of Hellenic Studies*, 103, 1983.

Timothy Ganz, "The Chorus of Aeschylus' *Agamemnon*", in *Harvard Studies in Classical Philology*, 87, 1983.

William Scott, "The Splitting of Choral Lyric in Aeschylus' *Oresteia*", in *American Journal of Philology*, 105, 1984.

David Armstrong and Elizabeth A. Ratchford, "Iphigenia's Veil: Aeschylus, *Agamemnon*, 228–48", in *Bulletin of the Institute of Classical Studies* (London), 32, 1985.

William D. Furley, "Motivation in the Parados of Aeschylus' *Agamemnon*", in *Classical Philology*, 81, 1986.

M. Davies, "Aeschylus' Clytemnestra: Sword or Axe?" in *Classical Quarterly* (new series), vol. 37 1987.

D. Kovacs, "The Way of a God With a Maid in Aeschylus' *Agamemnon*", in *Classical Philology*, 82, 1987.

R. Meridor, "Aeschylus' *Agamemnon* 944–57: Why Does Agamemnon Give in?", in *Classical Philology*, 82, 1987.

David Wiles, "The Staging of the Recognition Scene in the *Choephoroi*", in *Classical Quarterly* (new series), vol. 38, 1988.

*   *   *

The only surviving Greek, tragic trilogy, the *Oresteia* begins with the *Agamemnon* which depicts the return of Agamemnon, King of Argos, following the ten-year-long Trojan war.

Clytemnestra, Agamemnon's queen, who in his absence has been seduced by his cousin, Aegisthus, greets him as he arrives in his chariot and persuades him to enter the palace by walking upon a rich carpet laid out before it. Once inside, she murders him and Cassandra, Apollo's priestess—King Priam of Troy's daughter—whom Agamemnon had carried off as a concubine.

In the second play, the *Libation Bearers*, several years have passed when Orestes, exiled son of Agamemnon, returns to Argos under orders from the god Apollo, to avenge his father. He is reunited at the dead King's tomb with his sister, Electra, and together they evoke Agamemnon's ghost to assist them in taking vengeance. In subsequent scenes they bring about the deaths first of Aegisthus and then of Clytemnestra, who pleads in vain to Orestes for mercy. The play ends with the sudden departure of Orestes, pursued by unseen Furies, come to avenge the death of his mother.

The third play, the *Eumenides*, begins at Apollo's temple at Delphi, where Orestes has sought refuge from the Furies. He is sent by Apollo on to Athens to have his case judged. The ghost of Clytemnestra urges the Furies to follow him, and the scene shifts to Athens where Orestes desperately calls for Athena's aid. The goddess decrees a proper trial, and institutes a court of Athenian citizens, the Areopagus, to hear the case. Orestes is condemned by the Furies, but defended by Apollo. The jury's vote is equal; Athena resolves it in Orestes' favour, and then eventually persuades the resentful Furies to become benevolent and remain at Athens as its future guardians.

The *Oresteia* is one of the greatest works in all of theatrical history. In it, Aeschylus reveals a mastery of dramatic construction and theatrical technique, in the service of a work of outstanding poetic beauty and philosophical power. His consummate stagecraft is most strikingly evident in his use of the *skene*, or scene building (which in 458 B.C. was probably a recent innovation in the Athenian theatre) in the *Agamemnon* and *Libation Bearers*. Representing the cursed House of Atreus—blighted by a cycle of murder and revenge—its physical presence dominates these plays, and controls their actions, as characters enter and exit through it; its doors alternatively concealing and revealing information to the Chorus and audience. The visually stunning device of the crimson carpet leads Agamemnon, a victim, into its maw; a little later Cassandra utters semi-hysterical prophecies about the horrors contained within, before slowly entering it herself. The Chorus and audience first hear the death cries from within, and then, when the doors open, see displayed before them the bodies—the consequence of Clytemnestra's deceit and revenge. In the second play a similar pattern is followed as Clytemnestra—who, dog-like, has controlled access to the house—surrenders it to Orestes, and with it control of the play's action. The subsequent tableau displaying her body and that of Aegisthus together with the net in which Agamemnon was snared and killed, mirrors the powerful image that concluded the first play, and thus emphasises the relentless pattern of murder endlessly repeating itself.

The Chorus, too, is employed to great effect to condense and convey much of the meaning of the trilogy, in the course of which it assumes an increasingly active role. From the beginning of the *Agamemnon* the old men of Argos who comprise the Chorus create suspense through their own deep anxiety and foreboding. This is greatly increased later when they fail to understand the awful visions of Cassandra, and as the murders are heard taking place, disintegrate from a single unit into confused and frightened individuals, disagreeing and impotent to intervene. In the *Libation Bearers* the Chorus conspires with Electra and Orestes, and actively assists in the plot to deceive Aegisthus. The greatest of all choral effects in Greek drama is achieved in the *Eumenides* through Aeschylus's use of a dynamic chorus of hideous furies simultaneously incorporating and enacting the ancestral curse and Clytemnestra's lust for vegeance. Similarly, their subsequent transformation at the conclusion of the trilogy graphically represents the final triumph of reason and justice.

The three plays also include a great many highly effective and carefully crafted scenes between individuals, such as the process by which Clytemnestra tempts Agamemnon to the fatal act of *hubris* in treading upon the carpet; the extended recognition scene between Orestes and Electra; and the emotional confrontation of mother and son, when Clytemnestra begs for her life. The latter is resolved by the unexpected intervention of Orestes' friend, Pylades who (in his only line in the entire play) breaks the moral dead-lock by evoking Apollo's command.

In addition to these, and a great many other, theatrical highpoints, the *Oresteia* is suffused with potent imagery, such as the contrast between light and darkness, the net of entrapment, and the concept of prey being hunted down. This imagery is conveyed through Aeschylus's majestic language (notoriously difficult to convey in translation), which enables the meaning and ideas of the work to function and resonate on several levels simultaneously. In the end, this earliest masterpiece of Western drama transcends the story of Orestes and his fate to distil a more universal meaning, celebrating a triumph of hope over despair, reason over superstition, and justice over brutality.

—Richard C. Beacham

ORNITHES. See **THE BIRDS.**

OROONOKO
by Thomas Southerne

First Publication: London, 1696.
First Production: Theatre Royal, Drury Lane, London, c. November 1695.

Editions
Oroonoko, edited by Maximillian E. Novak and David Stuart Rodes, Lincoln, Nebraska, 1976 (Regents Restoration Drama Series).
Oroonoko, in *The Works of Thomas Southerne*, edited by Robert Jordan and Harold Love, Oxford, 1988.

Criticism
(For general works on the author, see *Playwrights* volume)

Articles:
Michael M. Cohen, " 'Mirth and Grief Together': Plot Unity in Southerne's *Oroonoko*", in *Xavier Review* (New Orleans), 11, 1972.
Julia A. Rich, "Heroic Tragedy in Southerne's *Oroonoko* (1695): An Approach to a Split Plot Tragicomedy", in *Philological Quarterly*, 62, 1983.

*   *   *

The play deals with Oroonoko, an African prince who has been treacherously seized and sold into slavery in Surinam, a Dutch colony. Here he discovers his wife, Imoinda, who has also been enslaved, through the jealousy of his father. A few of the colonists respond to Oroonoko's nobility, but many fear him, and the lieutenant-governor, infatuated with Imoinda, hopes for his ruin. Aboan, Oroonoko's faithful servant, finally persuades him to take up arms to recover his freedom, but the revolt fails through the cowardice of their fellow slaves, and the Prince surrenders upon honourable terms. These, however, are promptly violated by his captors. Forseeing only suffering and humiliation, Oroonoko, in an extended and lyrical scene, kills Imoinda and commits suicide. In a comic subplot, interspersed with this tragedy, two impecunious young adventuresses from London carry out an elaborate deception of the crude and domineering widow of a plantation owner. As a result of this they are able to make successful marriages, one to the rich and half-witted son of the widow.

A dazzling success on its first production, *Oroonoko* remained one of the most frequently produced plays of the 18th century, rivalling Shakespeare for much of this period. Critics of the time were a little cooler, usually putting Southerne firmly below Otway in their esteem, but still treating the work with considerable respect. For his play Southerne took Mrs. Behn's novel, *Oroonoko; or, The Royal Slave*, and stripped away many of the features most likely to appeal to a modern audience, such as the author's romantic delight in the exotic and the primitive. Southerne's Oroonoko is a much less particularised and much more Europeanised noble savage than Mrs. Behn's. A model of heroic rectitude and decorous nobility, he stalks through the play with the measured dignity of a neoclassic Roman. This dignity, however, is coupled with a powerful infusion of pathos, a pathos that comes from his vulnerability, which in turn derives

Oroonoko: Engraving, 1776

change may also provide is a heroine with whom white women in the audience could more readily identify. The 1690's were alive to the box-office importance of female theatre-goers, and on several occasions Southerne had portrayed himself as a particular servant of the ladies. The glib generalisations of the time had it that the men preferred comedy and the women tragedy, particularly tragedy in the style Southerne had chosen to write in—heavy with pathos and sentiment.

If Southerne has shaped his main plot with half an eye to pleasing the ladies, then his subplot may look like a calculated attempt to throw a sop to the men. Here we have the cynical libertinism, and the merciless deception and exploitation of fools, that are features of much Restoration comedy, though the world depicted is as close to that of rogue literature as of the Restoration comic theatre. This violent juxtaposition of heroic idealism and libertine cynicism, through the use of double plots, is a feature of much Restoration tragicomedy. Efforts to justify the combination in *Oroonoko*, by finding thematic parallels between the two stories, have been only moderately successful, and Southerne himself (in the Epistle Dedicatory to his previous play) claimed to be providing comic subplots merely because the audience wanted them. In spite of this dismissiveness, the subplot of *Oroonoko* is not without its value in helping to build up a picture of the feverish, unstable, and brutal world of Surinam. It is a society whose Europeans are of dubious social backgrounds, with the normal class structures and patterns of class control weak and vulnerable, and with greed and insecurity the dominant instincts. As such, it provides the strongest possible contrast to the calm, moral certitude and dignity of Oroonoko, as well as a suitably nightmarish background for his suffering and death.

—Robert Jordan

from those very qualities which Southerne uses to characterise him as a noble primitive: his guilelessness, his high idealism, and his tender love for his wife. These qualities are shown as admirable, but, in the corrupt world of Surinam, they not only make him vulnerable to treachery, they also hinder him from action. Oroonoko may be the great warrior and mighty prince, but time and again Aboan or Imoinda have to stir him out of an immobility which comes from scrupulous high-mindedness or his delicate feelings for his wife. Ultimately these qualities of primitive innocence lead to his destruction.

While the late 18th century frequently saw the play in terms of the anti-slavery debate, Southerne's concern is clearly with the tragedy and pathos of a great prince enslaved, not with the evils of slavery as a system. Oroonoko himself, in his days of power, had taken slaves; he accepts the planters' property rights over those they own; and when his fellow slaves prove cowardly and fall away from his attempted revolt, he scorns them as fit only for enslavement. It is the inappropriateness of slavery for the heroic and well-born that is Southerne's premise. For the naturally servile it is quite acceptable.

In Mrs. Behn's version, Imoinda is, like Oroonoko, a black African. Southerne makes her the daughter of a European general serving with Oroonoko's father. The change elicited some wry comments at the time, but seems to be part of the process of minimising the alien quality of the hero. Not only is Oroonoko sufficiently personable to win the total love of a white woman, but also (in striking contrast to one of Southerne's models, *Othello*) no one in the play, however base, reacts to the marriage as offensive or unnatural. What the

OTHELLO, THE MOOR OF VENICE
by William Shakespeare

First Publication: London, 1622 (First Quarto); with variants, in the First Folio, London, 1623.
First Production: London, c.1602–03; earliest recorded production: by the Kings Men, at Whitehall, November 1604.

Editions

"Othello": Paralleldruck der ersten Quarto und der ersten Folio, Heidelberg, 1949.
Othello, edited by Alice Walker and John Dover Wilson, Cambridge, 1957 (The New Shakespeare).
Othello, edited by M.R. Ridley, London, 1958 (Arden Shakespeare).
Othello, edited by A. Kernan, New York, 1963; revised edition, 1987 (Signet Classic Shakespeare).
Othello, edited by Kenneth Muir, Harmondsworth, 1968 (New Penguin Shakespeare).
Othello, edited by Norman Sanders, Cambridge, 1984 (New Cambridge Shakespeare).

Bibliography

John Hazel Smith (ed.), *Shakespeare's "Othello": A Bibliography*, New York, 1988 (AMS Studies in the Renaissance).

Othello: Savoy Theatre, London, 1930 (Paul Robeson and Peggy Ashcroft)

Criticism
(For general works on the author, see *Playwrights* volume)

Books:

E.-E. Stoll, *"Othello": An Historical and Comparative Study*, Minneapolis, Minnesota, 1915.

James H.E. Brock, *Iago and Some Shakespearian Villains*, Cambridge, 1937.

Konstantin Stanislavsky, *Stanislavski Produces "Othello"*, translated by H. Nowak, London, 1948.

L.F. Dean (ed.), *A Casebook on "Othello"*, New York, 1961.

Kenneth Tynan, *"Othello": The National Theatre Production*, New York, 1966.

G.K. Hunter, *Othello and Colour Prejudice*, London, 1969.

Stanley Edgar Hyman, *Iago: Some Approaches to the Illusion of his Motivation*, London, 1970.

Juliet McLauchlan, *Shakespeare: "Othello"*, London, 1971.

John Wain (ed.), *"Othello": A Casebook*, London, 1971.

Kenneth Geach, *"Othello" Unexpurgated: A Critical Essay*, Weybridge, Surrey, 1972.

Gino J. Matteo, *Shakespeare's "Othello": The Study and the Stage, 1604–1904*, Salzburg, 1974.

Rosa Maria Colombo, *Le utopie e la storia: saggio sull' "Othello" di Shakespeare*, Bari, 1975.

Peter Bettinger, *Shakespeare's "Othello" im Spiegel der literarischen Kritik*, Frankfurt, 1977.

Kenneth Muir and Philip Edwards (eds.), *Aspects of "Othello"*, Cambridge, 1977 [articles reprinted from *Shakespeare Survey*].

Marion B. Smith, *Casque to Cushion: A Study of "Othello" and "Coriolanus"*, Ottawa, 1979.

Jane Adamson, *"Othello" as Tragedy*, Cambridge, 1980.

Martin L. Wine, *Othello*, London, 1984 (Text and Performance Series).

Daniel Amneus, *The Three Othellos*, Alhambra, California, 1986.

Harold Bloom (ed.), *William Shakespeare's "Othello"*, New York, New Haven, and Philadelphia, 1987 (Modern Critical Interpretations Series).

Julie Hankey (ed.), *Othello*, Bristol, 1987 (Plays in Performance Series).

Mark W. Scott (ed.), "*Othello*", in *Shakespearian Criticism, 4*, Detroit, Illinois, 1987 [anthology of criticism].

Peter Davison, *"Othello": An Introduction to the Variety of Criticism*, London, 1988 (Critics Debate Series).

Martin Elliott, *Shakespeare's Invention of Othello: A Study of Early Modern English*, New York, 1988.

Susan Snyder (ed.), *"Othello": Critical Essays*, New York and London, 1988.

Articles:

For information on the many articles about *Othello*, see Smith's bibliography (listed above), the bibliographies listed in the *Playwrights* volume, and the annual Shakespeare Bibliography in *Shakespeare Quarterly*, published by the Folger Shakespeare Library, Washington D.C. (1950-).

*   *   *

Much sought-after, young Desdemona falls in love with Othello, a Moorish warrior in the service of Venice, and marries him against her father's wishes. Iago, whom he mistakenly believes to be a loyal, honest, plain-speaking soldier, hates Othello and plots his downfall. Iago tells Othello that women are always unfaithful. He arranges a drunken scene for which the handsome Cassio is blamed and demoted in rank by Othello. Iago persuades Cassio to seek Desdemona's intercession with her husband. When Cassio speaks with Desdemona, Othello looks on jealously from a distance. Iago's wife steals a much treasured handkerchief that Othello has given to Desdemona. Iago puts it among the belongings of Cassio. Seeing Cassio with the handkerchief and a courtesan appears proof to Othello of Desdemona's unfaithfulness. Maddened with jealousy Othello kills Desdemona; learning that Iago has deceived him with a series of lies, he then kills himself.

Othello is a study in jealousy. Suspicion of his wife's unfaithfulness becomes an obsession, turning Othello into the murderer of what he loves. Iago is envious of Othello's winning Desdemona, envious of Cassio being made lieutenant instead of himself, and imagines that Othello and Cassio may have slept with his wife Emilia. *Othello* is an ambivalent study of an outsider, an alien easily enraged and made victim. He is a warrior uneasy in society, a Black among Whites, a Moor (probably African) among Europeans, a convert to Christianity, and also an older man newly married to a strong-willed, young woman. His naïvety is paralleled by that of Roderigo, a Venetian gentleman who, desiring Desdemona, wastes his fortune in the expectation that Iago will procure her for him. Desdemona and Cassio also trust Iago, believing that his gruff, satiric "honesty" of speech proves his actual honesty. Iago often tells Othello what he is doing but in such a way that the Moor thinks the warnings are against others. Like the traditional Vice character of the older Morality Plays, Iago is engagingly gleeful in his evil and clever deceit. Unlike the traditional Vice he is given a complex psychology; we never know exactly what motivates him. Like most malcontents of Jacobean drama he is envious, satirical, cynical, mocking of the hypocrisies and simplicities of others, and a creator of a plot to revenge himself for some earlier wrong.

Othello concerns illusion and reality, words and truth, different kinds of honesty. Evil in disguise is unlikely to be discovered before it has done its damage. As is shown by the elaborate evidence which Iago manufactures of Desdemona's supposed infidelity, our eyes and common sense often deceive us. We cannot know why others act. There are many unexplained subtexts. Why does Desdemona reject the courtship of her peers? Why does she press Cassio's case when it bothers her husband? She is as unknowable as Iago. The question of identity, how we are seen, how we see ourselves, and the unspoken basis of our actions, is linked to the shifting meanings of "honest". Is Iago honest when he tells the truth to mislead? Is honesty to be self-interested and deceive for advantage? Such honesty assumes a world of dog eat dog as seen in Iago's habitual imagery of life in terms of animals, insects, and brutal sex. It becomes the angry vision of jealous Othello ("Goats and monkeys"; "a cistern for foul toads / to knot and gender in!"). There is an analogy between theatre and the drama that is plotted, directed, staged, and acted in by Iago. Numerous passages allude to theatre or acting ("Were it my cue to fight, I should have known it / Without a prompter"; " 'Tis a pageant / To keep us in false gaze"); while they thicken the texture of the play by creating a world of self-reflecting mirrors, they seem to imply both that the theatre of the world is an illusion based on deceptions and misunderstandings and that art itself is deceitful and morally dangerous. We enjoy Iago's punning, cunning, and plotting, willingly let him take us into his confidence. Part of the theatricality of the play and our own enjoyment of excitement, suspense, fear, and pity, requires temporary complicity with evil.

Is there an essential Othello? Early in the play he seems assured, maturely in control of his emotions; but at that stage he has an established place in his world. Marriage, the move to Cyprus, command of the island, and Iago's deceptions bring out a different person—insecure, emotionally unstable, unjust, inept. Othello himself fears an inner chaos. The three women offer three different versions of femininity—Bianca is the courtesan, Emilia is on the border between loyalty and dishonesty according to circumstance and price, while Desdemona remains loyal to her husband even while she is dying. Just as Iago increasingly seems a devil, so Desdemona proclaims "I am a Christian", believes she "shall be sav'd" and asks Heaven's forgiveness for herself and others, including those who do her harm. Within this intermittent allegory Othello rejects seeing himself as a Job being tried with "affliction" and needing "patience".

The compression of action into a few days, the shift in the location to Cyprus where the main characters are isolated from a wider society, the way our perspective is often that of either Iago or Othello, the awareness that Othello may not have had time to consummate his marriage, all create an emotional intensity. But this is a play in which the public and domestic are intertwined. Othello is commander of the forces, and in effect governs Cyprus; he is also Desdemona's "lord", so should govern his own emotions. There is, however, disorder from the first, when Desdemona marries against her father's wishes. Disorder increases as Othello, for a time, will do whatever Desdemona wants and as he lets himself be governed by Iago. The increasing disorder and injustice is shown by the trial scenes. Othello is given a fair trial in Venice for eloping with Desdemona. In Cyprus, however, Othello hastily and wrongly condemns Cassio without a trial and we later learn he has been influenced in his verdict by the standing of Montano, whom Cassio insulted. Othello judges and kills Desdemona without any trial. He claims to administer "justice" but he also speaks of "revenge". The occurrence of such words as "mercy", "merciful", "sacrifice", "heaven", and "love" bring Christian values into opposition with those of the law, especially as the latter is administered by those blinded by deceit, personal interest, and the desire for revenge.

—Bruce King

OTHER TIMES.   See **THE DOLL TRILOGY.**

OUR TOWN
by Thornton Wilder

First Publication: New York, 1938.
First Production: McCarter Theatre, Princeton, New Jersey,
22 January 1938.

Criticism
(For general works on the author, see *Playwrights* volume)

Books:
Donald C. Haberman, *"Our Town": An American Play*,
Boston, 1989.

Articles:
Walter J. Engler, "A Project on *Our Town* for Communica-
tion Classes", in *College English*, 14, 1952.
W.T. Scott, "*Our Town* and the Golden Veil", in *Virginia
Quarterly Review*, 29, 1953.
George D. Stevens, "*Our Town*—Great American Trag-
edy?", in *Modern Drama*, 1, 1958.
Rudolf Haas, "Thornton Wilders *Our Town*: Gedanken zur
wissenschaftlichen und unterreichlichen Erschliessung eines
modernen amerikanischen Dramas", in *Mitteilungsblatt des
allgemeinen deutschen Neuphilologenverbandes*, 14, 1961.
Thomas E. Porter, "A Green Corner of the Universe: *Our
Town*", in his *Myth and Modern American Drama*, Detroit,
1969.
Berthold Schik, "Problematisierung des Banalen: Thornton
Wilders *Our Town* als Standardlektüre im Englischunterricht der Oberstufe?", in *Neueren Sprachen*, 5, 1975.
Joseph C. Schöpp, "Thornton Wilders *Our Town*: The-
oretischer Anspruch und künstlerische Realisierung", in
Amerikanisches Drama und Theater im 20. Jahrhundert,
edited by Alfred Weber and Siegfried Neuweiler, Göt-
tingen, 1975.
Sang-Kyong Lee, "Zur Rezeption ostasiatischer Theater-
tradition in Thornton Wilders *Our Town*", in *Arcadia*, 22,
1987.
Mariana Net, "The Way We Come Back into *Our Town*", in
Cahiers roumains d'études littéraires, 1, 1988.

*   *   *

One of the most successful American plays of the 20th
century, Thornton Wilder's *Our Town* owes its fame chiefly to
the skill with which its author dramatizes the age-old theme of
the importance of ordinary day-to-day human existence:
namely, by means of a daring rearrangement of conventional
stagecraft. To depict the supreme worth of savoring life fully
while we possess it, Wilder drew upon such classic models as
Homer's *Odyssey* and Dante's *Purgatorio*, both of which offer
poignant contrasts between the fleeting beauty of the living
and the dreary permanence of the dead, as in Achilles's dour
comment in Hades that he would rather be a living slave than a
dead king. In *Our Town*, Wilder converted the universal
message implicit in this scene into an allegory involving birth,
marriage, and death in the United States of the 1930's. By his
bold methods of staging his drama, his artful manipulation of
time and place, he related the here and now of an insignificant
New England village to the timeless concerns of human nature
everywhere. His aim, he wrote, was "an attempt to find a value

above all price for the smallest events in our daily life. I have
made the claim as preposterous as possible, for I have set the
village against the largest dimensions of time and place".

Wilder's two major innovations enabling him to fulfill his
aim were the use of a bare stage and a centralizing character,
the Stage Manager, a throwback to both the Chorus in classic
Greek drama and the Property Man in Chinese theatre. As a
stand-in for author and director, he not only arranges stage
props, but also initiates, controls, and interprets setting and
action, explaining directly to the audience from the outset that
they are going to witness a play about life in an ordinary little
town in New Hampshire, Grover's Corners, beginning just
before dawn on 7 May 1901. After pointing to some of its
notable imaginary features, including the cemetery, he gives a
brief history of the town, identifies some of its leading citizens,
focusing on several members of the two neighboring families,
the Webbs and the Gibbses, whose interrelationships will
dominate the action from there on. As the Stage Manager
develops their typical encounters with one another that day
throughout Act I, he also offers further commentary, from
time to time, which illustrates the commonplaceness of routine
in the Webb and Gibbs households, but also suggests its
broader, metaphysical significance. The blessed tie that binds
Grover's Corners to the Universe and the mind of God is then
circuitously expressed in the colloquy between young George
Gibbs and his sister Rebecca at the end of the first act.

Similar techniques are employed in the second and third acts
to strengthen and clarify the union of theme and action. In Act
II, which deals with the courtship and marriage of George
Gibbs and Emily Webb three years later, the Stage Manager
serves as both the minister who weds them and the commentator who disparages the glamour of the ceremony, which, he
says, is interesting only "once in a thousand times". Nevertheless, as he muses on the fact that millions of folk since the dawn
of time have celebrated such marriage rites as these, it
becomes clear that the wedding of this particular young
couple, however commonplace it appears, symbolizes a universal "fusion of nature's physical and spiritual purposes".

Again, in Act III, Wilder boldly extends his basic analogy by
literally juxtaposing life and death on the stage. Nine more
years have elapsed, and some of the town's recent dead who
were alive in Act II are now seated on chairs representing their
graves in the cemetery, where they are witnessing the burial of
Emily, who has just died in childbirth. As she joins them in the
vacant chair next to her mother-in-law, she becomes the
catalyst for the swift evocation of Wilder's deepest meaning.
The granting of her desire to relive just a single day of her
former life, her 12th birthday, leads to her discovery that the
living can neither appreciate nor understand the beauty of life
till they have lost it. Crying "Oh, earth you're too wonderful
for anybody to realize you", she is ready to return to the
passionless Dead, whom the Stage Manager had described at
the opening of the act as "waitin' for something they feel is
comin'. Something important and great". The action has built
up steadily throughout the play toward the dramatic revelation
that human life, however painful, dreary, or inconsequential
its quotidian events, is both a precious gift in itself as well as
part of a mysterious plan that rests in the "Mind of God".

—Eugene Current-Garcia

OVER ÆVNE, I-II.   See **BEYOND HUMAN POWER.**

A PAIR OF DRAWERS. See **SCENES FROM THE HEROIC LIFE OF THE MIDDLE CLASSES.**

THE PALACE OF ETERNAL YOUTH (Changsheng dian / Ch'ang-sheng tien)
by Hong Sheng

Composition: 1679–1688.
First Production: Early 1680's.

*   *   *

The Palace of Eternal Youth (*Changsheng dian* or *Ch'ang-sheng tien*) by Hong Sheng (1645–1704) concerns the famous Emperor Minghuang (reigned 712–56) of the Tang dynasty and his love for his favourite concubine, Yang Guifei. The rebellion of An Lushan breaks out, forcing Minghuang and Yang Guifei to flee the capital. At Mawei Post Station Minghuang's soldiers mutiny; they kill the Prime Minister, Yang Guozhong (the cousin of Yang Guifei) holding him responsible for the rebellion. They then demand the death of Yang Guifei as well. The Emperor agrees after a short hesitation, and she hangs herself with her own silk belt. Later, however, they are reunited in the moon. Like many Chinese dramas, this one is partly based on history, though in reality Yang Guifei was killed by a powerful eunuch.

The core theme is the love between the two central characters. Much of the play's libretto is a refined and deeply felt lyric to love. One of the main scenes, and the one which gives the drama its title, is "The Disk Dance", in which the Emperor gives his beloved a birthday banquet in the Palace of Eternal Youth, as part of which she performs a dance on a green disk. However, what separates this drama from most in the Chinese tradition is the combination of love and court politics, set against one of the most famous and important rebellions in Chinese history. The sordidness of intrigue is starkly contrasted with the tenderness of the love theme. The drama also contrasts the lives of ordinary people with those at court. The scene before "The Disk Dance", entitled "The Lychee Fruit", deals with the tribute several regions distant from the capital pay by bringing lychees to the court especially for Yang Guifei. A blind man is trampled to death as one of the envoys taking these lychees gallops past.

The characterization of the main characters is well drawn. Minghuang is shown with all the weaknesses, as well as the irrational power, of his position. The opening lines of the prologue, and thus of the drama, praise him as a rarity: "Since ancient times how few lovers have really remained constant to

the end". Yet during the core mutiny scene, "Death at the Post Station", he does not need much persuasion to accept that Yang Guifei should commit suicide. He is shown as tender and doting on Yang Guifei, and expresses heart-felt remorse at his own weakness after her death, but when out of sorts, following a quarrel with her, is quite easy about inflicting 100 lashes on several eunuchs for no crime.

Yang Guifei herself is shown as jealous and ill-tempered with her sisters, whom she regards as rivals for the affection of the Emperor. But she is suitably submissive to the Emperor and though taken by surprise at the soldiers' mutiny and her cousin's death, immediately puts forward an "earnest wish" that the Emperor give her up at once and allow her to commit suicide in order to save him.

The drama gives a good reflection of the inferior position of women in traditional, Chinese society, but the playwright appears more strongly on their side than the standard Confucian official would have been. In Chinese history the story of Yang Guifei is often regarded as showing that the female sex should take the blame when a disaster such as a rebellion befalls the empire. But in "Death at the Post Station" Hong Sheng clearly has the soldiers blame Yang Guozhong for treason; they demand Yang Guifei's death as well because of her family connection with the traitor, even though they know perfectly well she is innocent. There is no suggestion that they want her to accept the blame as a woman.

The role of tragedy in Chinese drama has been a matter of controversy. In general the Chinese prefer the happy end, and the main division is between civilian and military, not between tragedy and comedy. Not surprisingly, the Greek notion of tragedy is totally lacking in Chinese drama. In *The Palace of Eternal Youth*, there is a clear thread throughout of personal tragedy for both the leading characters and most others as well. Yang Guifei's many appearances as a spirit mostly show her as a tragic figure, while the Emperor is frequently led to muse on his sufferings, grief, and loneliness because of the early death of his love. The happy end of the drama, with the lovers' reunion in the moon, is not in the dominant mood.

To a modern reader one weakness of *The Palace of Eternal Youth* is that the linchpin of the action from a dramatic point of view, Yang Guifei's suicide, takes place about half way through the drama. There is very little action in the second half. However, it is necessary to remember that fiction, drama, and story-telling in traditional China were episodic. The idea of laying the seeds of a plot, increasing the dramatic tension, and then rising to a climax and denouement, is not part of Chinese drama.

The Palace of Eternal Youth is exceedingly long and took several days to perform in full. Over time it has become practice to select only specific scenes for performance, and this accords with the episodic approach to fiction and drama. To this day some of the main scenes are still performed and popular in a variety of different regional styles.

Like most dramatic works in the Chinese tradition, *The Palace of Eternal Youth* combines sung lyrics with musical accompaniment and prose spoken in a stylized manner, and it has won great praise for the excellent weaving together of prose and poetry. The romantic story is among the most popular in all Chinese history and literature, and the characterization is subtle and convincing.

—Colin Mackerras

PANDORA'S BOX. See **THE LULU PLAYS.**

PARTAGE DE MIDI. See **BREAK OF NOON.**

IL PASTOR FIDO. See **THE FAITHFUL SHEPHERD.**

PASTOR SANG. See **BEYOND HUMAN POWER.**

PAUL SCHIPPEL ESQ. See **SCENES FROM THE HEROIC LIFE OF THE MIDDLE CLASSES.**

PEACH BLOSSOM FAN (Taohua shan / T'ao-hua shan) by Kong Shangren [K'ung Shan-Jen]

First Publication: 1699.

Criticism

Articles:
David Hawkes, "The Decline of Dynasty", in *Times Literary Supplement*, 15 May 1891

* * *

Peach Blossom Fan (Taohua shan or *T'ao-hua shan)* by Kong Shangren (1648–1718) is about the love between the scholar Hou Fangyu and Li Xiangjun (Fragrant Princess Li) against the background of the Manchu conquest of the Ming dynasty in southern China in the mid-1640's. The painter Yang Wencong, Hou Fangyu's friend introduces the lovers. They marry, but are soon parted when Yang advises Hou to flee in order to avoid arrest at the behest of a political enemy, Ruan Dacheng. The lovers do not meet again until the very end of the play, but are then torn apart by a Daoist priest, Zhang Wei, and persuaded to enter the monastic life, Hou sent to the southernmost part of China, Fragrant Princess to the north.

The title comes from the fan which Hou gave his beloved as a gift of betrothal. After the parting, a senior minister seeks her for himself, but this makes her so angry that that she knocks her head against the ground, and the blood stains the fan. Yang Wencong paints leaves and twigs around the blood stains to resemble peach blossoms. In the end Zhang Wei shreds the fan.

The events in this drama are based quite closely on history. All the main characters are historical figures, including the corrupt Ruan Dacheng (1587?–1646), and the painter Yang Wencong (1597–1646). The liaison between scholar Hou Fangyu (1618–55) and the beautiful singing-girl Li Xiangjun is a historical fact. Each scene is dated to the month and in chronological order going from the second lunar month of 1643 to the seventh of 1645. The actual events associated with the Manchu conquest are mentioned and depicted many times in the drama. There is considerable focus on the Revival Club, of which Hou was an active member. This was a political organization attempting to revive the Ming dynasty, in the teeth of opposition not only of the Manchus but also of the corrupt Ming remnant court of Nanjing, of which a chief supporter was Ruan Dacheng.

The title shows the core theme of the drama—the love between Hou and Fragrant Princess. This is also a highly political drama. By selecting Hou Fangyu as his hero, the author shows himself very anti-Manchu. What is striking is that he was writing under Manchu control only a few decades after the events which are central to the drama. Perhaps it is not surprising that he was dismissed from office very soon after the completion of the drama. Yet there is a clear suggestion in the drama that the Ming remnants had themselves to blame for their defeat. Ruan is shown as selfish, corrupt and opportunistic, ready to sacrifice anybody for his own ends. The man was probably as bad in real life as in the drama.

This is an enormously long play with a very complicated plot and a large cast. There are many threads in it, including the destruction of the Revival Club by Ruan Dacheng and the consequent arrest and imprisonment of Hou Fangyu and others. But it retains its excitement throughout as a combination of love and politics. Both main characters are impressively drawn as courageous, honest and loving. Hou is shown as politically principled and tender in his love for Fragrant Princess, while she is depicted as headstrong and determined in her love for him. Of the two she is portrayed as the stronger and more devoted, which is not surprising given the Chinese society of the seventeenth century. However, one serious weakness in the drama is at the moment when Zhang Wei declares angrily that they must go their separate ways into the monastic life. Hou puts up a token resistance, in prose not poetry so that it loses dramatic impact, but Fragrant Princess accepts without demur. Told she must go to the north "to cultivate the Way", all she has to say is: "I go. All is illusion; I know not that man before me". Given the intensity of her longing throughout the drama, expressed so passionately in many places, and given that the lovers have not seen each other for so long, the dramatist could surely have managed a better reason for her.

This drama combines the basic dichotomy of Chinese drama, that between civilian and military life. Although most of the play is clearly civilian, including the major themes, there are also important battle scenes and several important military characters. Zhang Wei, the Daoist priest, begins as a commander of the Imperial Guard in Beijing. It is definitely tragic in feeling. Although neither hero nor heroine is killed, the dramatist clearly regards it is as tragedy for them to live isolated in monasteries. Hou is defeated politically and, although the villains of the piece—the corrupt Ming remnants—also suffer defeat, the victory of the Manchus is a cause for sorrow, not rejoicing.

The language of *Peach Blossom Fan* is highly literary, complicated, and full of classical illusions. It was originally written for a style of drama called *Kunqu*, which only the educated appreciated. However the integration of poetry and prose, and the manner in which this contributes to the characterization and to the contrast between civilian and military life, has won praise from contemporary Chinese critics.

Peach Blossom Fan is much too long for performance in one session, and even when it was given over several days, members of the audience attended selectively. The practice later was to focus only on individual scenes. The drama is never performed exactly in its original form nowadays, but it has been adapted into various traditional Chinese regional drama styles and also made into a spoken drama and a film.

—Colin Mackerras

PEER GYNT
by Henrik Ibsen

First Publication: Copenhagen, 1867.
First Production: Christiana Theatre, Christiana, 24 February 1876.

Editions
Peer Gynt, Oslo, 1978.

Translations
Peer Gynt, translated by William and Charles Arthur, London, 1892; revised version in *The Collected Works*, 5, London, 1907.
Peer Gynt, translated by R. Farquaharson-Sharp, London, 1921.
Peer Gynt, translated by Norman Ginsbury, 1946.
Peer Gynt, translated by Peter Watts, Harmondsworth, 1950.
Peer Gynt, translated by Paul Green, 1952.
Peer Gynt, translated and condensed by Michael Meyer, London, 1963; corrected version, in *Ibsen: Plays*, 6, London, 1987.
Peer Gynt, translated by Rolf Fjelde, New York, 1965.
Peer Gynt, translated by Kay Jurgensen and Robert Schankkon, 1967.
Peer Gynt, in a version by Christopher Fry, based on literal translation by Johan Fillinger, in *The Oxford Ibsen*, 3, edited by James Walter McFarlane, London, 1972.
Peer Gynt, translated and adapted by Kenneth McLeish, London, 1990.

Criticism
(For general works on the author, see *Playwrights* volume)

Books:
H. Logeman, *A Commentary, Critical and Explanatory, on the Norwegian Text of Henrik Ibsen's "Peer Gynt", Its Language, Literary Associations and Folklore*, The Hague, 1917.
Francis Bull, *Henrik Ibsen's "Peer Gynt"*, Oslo, 1947.
Daniel Haakonsen, *Henrik Ibsens "Peer Gynt"*, Oslo, 1967.

Otto Hageberg (ed.), *Omkring "Peer Gynt"*, Oslo, 1967 (anthology of criticism).
Finn Thorn, *Henrik Ibsens "Peer Gynt": Et Drama om kristen identitet*, Oslo, 1971.
Bjørn Hemmer, *"Brand", "Kongsemnerne", "Peer Gynt": En Studie i Ibsens romantiske diktning*, Oslo, 1972.
Erik Overås, *"Peer Gynt": Eit Foredrag for ungdom*, Stange, 1974.
Asbjørn Aarseth, *Dyret i mennesket: Et Bidrag til tolkning av Henrik Ibsens "Peer Gynt"*, Oslo, 1975.
Helmer Lång, *Ibsen, "Peer Gynt" och trollen: Essäer om en symbol*, Viken, 1976.
Olav Bo, *Folketradisjonens "Peer Gynt"*, Vinstra, 1978.
Trygve Brynjulvsrud, *"Peer Gynt" under Bibelens lupe*, Oslo, 1980?
Rolf Fjelde (ed.), *Peer Gynt*, Minneapolis, 1980.
Asbjørn Aarseth, *"Peer Gynt" and "Ghosts": Text and Performance*, London, 1989.

Articles:
J.D. Stone, "*Peer Gynt*: An Interpretation", in *Poet-Lore*, 18, 1907.
W.S. Bishop, "Ibsen's *Peer Gynt*: A Philosophy of Life", in *Sewanee Review*, 17, 1909.
A. le Roy Andrews, "Ibsen's *Peer Gynt* and Goethe's *Faust*", in *Journal of English and Germanic Philology*, 13, 1914.
A. le Roy Andrews, "Further Influences upon Ibsen's *Peer Gynt*", in *Journal of English and Germanic Philology*, 13, 1915.
H. Logeman, "The 'Caprices' in Henrik Ibsen's *Peer Gynt*", in *Edda*, 17, 1917.
Trevor H. Davies, "The Ignominy of Half-Heartedness: *Peer Gynt*", in his *Spiritual Voices in Modern Literature*, New York, 1919.
Julius E. Olsen, "Phases of Ibsen's Authorship: 1—Subconscious Elements in the Composition of *Peer Gynt*", in *Scandinavian Studies and Notes*, 7, 1921.
G.P. Dilla, "*Peer Gynt*", in *English Journal* (Chicago), 11, 1922.
L. Konner, "Psychiatric Study of Ibsen's *Peer Gynt*", in *Journal of Abnormal Psychology*, 19, 1925.
Jacob W. Richardson, "*Peer Gynt*: Study and Exposition", in *Holborn Review*, July 1928.
H. Steinhauer, "*Faust* and *Peer Gynt*", in *Queen's Quarterly*, 35, 1928.
A. Anstensen, "Notes on the Text of Ibsen's *Peer Gynt*", in *Journal of English and Germanic Philology*, 29, 1930.
Einar Haugen, "On Translating *Peer Gynt*", in *Scandinavian Studies*, vol.14 no.8, 1937.
Arne Lidén, "Peer Gynt i Egypten", in *Edda*, 40, 1940.
A. Zucker, "Goethe and Ibsen's Button Moulder", in *Publications of the Modern Language Association* [*PMLA*], 57, 1942.
John Horton, "Ibsen, Grieg, and *Peer Gynt*", in *Music and Letters*, April 1945.
T. Guthrie, "Some Afterthoughts on *Peer Gynt*", in *Norseman*, 5, 1949.
F.J. Schöningh, "Der unbekannte Ibsen: Bemerkungen zu *Peer Gynt*", in *Hochland* (Munich), 44, 1950–51.
F.W. Kaufmann, "Ibsen's Search for the Authentic Self", in *Monatshefte*, 45, 1953.
Leif Tjersland, "'Den fremmede passager' i *Peer Gynt*", in *Ibsen-Årbok*, 1953.
D. Haakonsen, "Genre-problemet i *Peer Gynt*", in *Vinduet*, 8, 1954.
Sverre Arestad, "*Peer Gynt* and the Idea of Self", in *Modern Drama*, 3, 1960.

Peer Gynt: Stockholm, 1927

Milada Blekastad, "Speculum og analogi i *Peer Gynt*", in *Tradisjon og fornyelse: Festkrift til A.H. Winsnes*, Oslo, 1960.

R. Williams, "Ibsen's Non-Theatrical Plays: *Brand* and *Peer Gynt*", in *Ibsen-Årboken*, 1960–62.

James R. Hurt, "Fantastic Scenes in *Peer Gynt*", in *Modern Drama*, 5, 1962.

O. Anderson, "Before the Century of *Peer Gynt*", in *World Theatre*, 12, 1963–64.

H. Jeffreys, "Some Points in the Interpretation of *Peer Gynt*", in *Scandinavica*, 3, 1964.

Mrs. L.R. Edwards, "Structural Analysis of *Peer Gynt*", in *Modern Drama*, 8, 1965.

Ronald Gaskell, "Symbol and Reality in *Peer Gynt*", in *Drama Survey*, 4, 1965.

Rolf Fjelde and Sverre Arestad, "Translating *Peer Gynt*", in *Modern Drama*, 10, 1967.

Daniel Haakonsen, "Prestens tale i *Peer Gynt*", in *Ibsenforbundet: Årbok*, 1967.

Gunhild Ramm, "Solveigskikkelsen i *Peer Gynt*", in *Ibsen-Årbok*, 1967.

Harald L. Tveterås, "Botten-Hansens *Huldrebrylluppet* og Ibsens Peer Gynt", in *Edda*, 67, 1967.

Rolf Fjelde, "Peer Gynt, Naturalism, and the Dissolving Self", in *Tulane Drama Review*, vol.13 no.2, 1968.

Ole Koppang, "Har *Peer Gynt* et positivt budskap?", in *Kirke og Kultur*, 73, 1968.

Harald Noreng, "Litt om dyresymbolikken i *Peer Gynt*", in *Norsk Litteraer Årbok*, 1968.

Harry Bergholz, "Peer Gynt's Redemption", in *Edda*, 69, 1969.

John Simon, "*Peer Gynt*", in *Hudson Review*, 22, 1970.

Denzell Smith, "The Relationship of Setting and Idea in *Peer Gynt*", in *Modern Drama*, 13, 1970.

Jules Zentner, "Peer Gynt: The Quest for Shine and the Giving Way of a Loop", in *Scandinavica*, 9, 1970.

Marilyn A. Anderson, "Norse Trolls and Ghosts in Ibsen", in *Journal of Popular Culture*, 5, 1971.

Harald Engberg, "*Peer Gynt* udsat for grappeteatret", in *Ibsenforbundet: Årbok*, 1972.

Svend E. Larsen, "Symbol og fiktion i Ibsens *Peer Gynt*", in *Exil*, 6, 1972.

Jules Zentner, "Figures of Estrangement: Peer Gynt's Other Selves", in *Edda*, 73, 1973.

Richard Bark, "Gå udenom, Peer Gynt!", in *Edda*, 76, 1976.

Hans Lund, "Fra Toppen og till Roden: Relasjonen mellom topografi og livsverdi i Henrik Ibsens *Peer Gynt*", in *Edda*, 76, 1976.

Ensaf Thune, "The Paradox of the Boyg: A Study of Peer Gynt's Humanization", in *Modern Drama*, 19, 1976.

Bjorn J. Tysdahl, "Byron, Norway and Ibsen's *Peer Gynt*", in *English Studies*, 56, 1976.

Klaus Neiiendam, "The Second Staging of *Peer Gynt*, 1886", in *Theatre Research International*, 2, 1977.

Knut Brynhildsvoll, "Über Rolle und Identität und ihr gegenseitiges Verhältnis in *Peer Gynt*", in *Edda*, 1978.

Dagne G. Myhren, "Hverken eller og Enten eller: Et Bidrag til belysning av personlighetsproblematikken i Henrik Ibsens *Peer Gynt*", in *Edda*, 79, 1979.

Olav Lysberg, "*Peer Gynt*—eit anti-romantisk drama?", in *Kirke og Kultur*, 85, 1980.

Samuel G. McLellan, "The Problem of Genre in Ibsen's *Peer Gynt*: The Search for a Contemporary Model", in *Journal of English and Germanic Philology*, 80, 1981.

Patricia Merivale, "*Peer Gynt*: Ibsen's *Faustiad*", in *Comparative Literature*, 35, 1983.

Henk Schouwvlieger, "*Peer Gynt*: De Anamnese van een geval van alcoholisme", in *Tijdschrift voor Skandinavistiek*, vol.4 no.1, 1983.

Horst Bien, "Ideelle und ästhetische Aspekte in Ibsens *Peer Gynt*", in *Nordeuropa*, 18, 1984.

Joseph and Lanayre Liggera, "Going Roundabout: Similar Images of Pilgrimage in Ibsen's *Peer Gynt* and Bergman's *The Seventh Seal*", in *West Virginia University Philological Papers*, 35, 1989.

*   *   *

Unlike the central character of *Brand*, Peer Gynt is a character whose actions are dictated by a wish to avoid commitments of any kind. He is constantly on the move, running away or trying to impress those around him. His mother is temporarily fooled by his tall-tale inventiveness. As an intruder at a wedding, he escapes with the bride, an offence for which he is outlawed by the community. A young girl, the innocent Solveig, loves him, and is willing to share his conditions. Peer's search for power and glory as well as his frivolous lustfulness constantly bring him into situations where he is either nearly annihilated, or fooled. While the first three acts show Peer as a young man—a native of the Gudbrandsdal region in Eastern Norway—in various confrontations with people of the valley as well as with mythical beings residing in the mountains, the fourth act is staged in North Africa with Peer as a middle-aged gentleman, and in the fifth act he is an old man, on his way back to his native region. The action involves a constant change of appearance on his part, whether he is on the run or trying to establish himself as a prince, a businessman, a prophet, or a scholar. Yet the main focus of interest throughout the text is the moral question of identity, basically the same theme as in *Brand*. The Dovre-Master has taught Peer that the motto of the human race, as opposed to the trolls, is "to thine own self be true". He does not grasp the meaning of these words, yet keeps quoting them as his guiding star. As an old man he is made to understand that he in fact has been led by the troll motto: "To thine own self be—all-sufficient!". Acknowledging his moral failure, he is finally ready to meet Solveig, and is welcomed by her on Whitsunday morning. The Buttonmoulder, sent to collect Peer in his casting ladle to melt him down, is near, but Solveig promises that she will protect him.

The central character of *Peer Gynt*, originally a local hero of the folklore of Eastern Norway, is transformed into an anti-hero by Ibsen. The text is a dramatic poem in five acts and in rhymed verse, like *Brand*. The two poems are counterparts, variations on the Romantic theme of human identity. While Brand is trying to live according to the ideals of his conviction, and paying a high price for it, Peer is concerned with self-indulgence and worldly success. There is also a difference in kind between the two dramas. *Brand* deals with regularly human characters in a fjord community, while *Peer Gynt* includes fantastic figures of Norwegian folklore in addition to a large number of human characters, more than in any other drama by Ibsen. The great variety of beings facing Peer under different circumstances and the frequent references to philosophical and moral issues in the dialogue indicate the extent to which this work is open to an allegorical reading. The text abounds with proverbs, quotations (and misquotations) from various literary sources, references to historical incidents and public figures of past or contemporary Scandinavia, as well as extremely complex imagery. The literary tradition to which this dramatic poem belongs includes late medieval moralities like *Everyman*, and Romantic drama like Goethe's *Faust*. The story of Peer Gynt and his wandering through the world can be read as an idealist allegory of the ego erring between its lower instincts and its divine core.

Solveig, whose appearance has an almost ethereal quality compared to that of other and more sensuous girls whom Peer comes across, stands as an image of the higher self—that spiritual potential of Peer which is there all the time, ready to realize itself, even though he is not at all faithful to her. Solveig is connected with various religious symbols, like the hymn book, her recent confirmation, and church-going. The lower self is represented by Peer's intellectual and moral shortcomings, his futile day-dreaming, his lack of spiritual depth and consistency, and also by the large number of animal motifs and imagery connected with his experiences and his way of expressing himself. Altogether about 60 different species of animals are referred to in the text. Peer's association with these creatures and with a number of mythical beings combining human and animal attributes, such as the trolls (with the cow's tail as their distinguishing mark), the Boyg, and the Sphinx, emphasizes his bestial qualities, his soulless mind, and his lack of true, human identity. Many of the proverbs and metaphors involving animal motifs in the original Norwegian tend to lose this significance when they are translated.

At the end of Act III Peer has made up his mind to leave his country for America. In Act IV, however, the action takes place in different parts of North Africa. This change of scene enables Ibsen to fit elements of Hegelian philosophy into his poem, particularly in the Egyptian scenes. In his *Aesthetics* Hegel discusses the abundant use of animals and of figures partly human and partly bestial in ancient, Egyptian art and religion. In *Peer Gynt*, the statue of Memnon, the Sphinx, and various inmates of the mad-house in Cairo testify to a certain Hegelian influence. The German Professor Begriffenfeldt, who is a somewhat confused director of the lunatic asylum is clearly an ironic portrait of Hegel, although Ibsen generally held this philosopher in high esteem.

The allegorical sense of the end of the drama, with Peer at last approaching Solveig in front of her hut, is the unity of the higher and the lower self to form a complete human being. For this to happen, Peer has been made to understand, through a series of shocking encounters in Act V, that he is, in fact, without human identity; he is "no one", and his life without Solveig has been a waste of energy. She is the divine essence of his being, or, metaphorically, the core that he could not find when he was peeling the onion.

—Asbjørn Aarseth

PÉLLEAS AND MÉLISANDE (Pelléas et Mélisande)
by Maurice Maeterlinck

First Publication: Brussels, 1892.
First Production: Bouffes-Parisiennes, Paris, 17 May 1893.

Editions
Pelléas et Mélisande, 1956 (Fasquelle edition).

Translations
Pelléas and Mélisande, in *Maeterlinck: The Plays, 2*, translated by Richard Hovey, Chicago, 1896 [reprinted in various anthologies].
Pelléas and Mélisande, in *"A Miracle of St. Antony" and Five Other Plays*, New York, 1917.

Criticism
(For general works on the author, see *Playwrights* volume)

Books:
René Terrasson, *Pelléas et Mélisande, ou, L'initiation*, Paris, 1982.
Daniel Blampain and Maryse Descamps (eds.), *Maurice Maeterlinck: "Pelléas et Mélisande"*, Brussels, 1986.

Articles:
Joan P. Kosove, "Maeterlinck's *Pelléas et Mélisande*", in *French Review*, 40, 1967.
Pierre Maillard, "Musique et poésie, à propos de *Pelléas*", in *Points et contrepoints*, 88, 1968.
René Leibowitz, "*Pelléas et Mélisande*, ou les fantômes de la réalité", in *Temps modernes*, 27, 1971.
Ch. Lutaud, "La Musique de *Pelléas et Mélisande* à Debussy", in *Annales Maeterlinck*, 23, 1977.
Stéphane Doreau, "Étude d'un drame lyrique: *Pelléas et Mélisande* (Debussy et Maeterlinck)", in *Mythes, rites, symboles dans les littératures Françaises et étrangères de la fin du XIXe siècle à 1970*, Angers, 1982.
Catherine Soulier, "*Pelléas et Mélisande*: Problème de mise en scène", in *Hommages à Jacques Petit*, Paris, 1985.
Michel Sapanet, "A la découverte du *Pelléas* de Maeterlinck: Les Impressions d'un jeune étudiant, il y a cinquante ans", in *D'Eschyle à Genet: Hommage à Francis Pruner*, Dijon, 1986.

*   *   *

The symbolist nature of the drama is signalled in the opening scene at the gate of the castle: housemaids demand that the porter open the heavy, rusty-hinged door so that they can scrub the threshhold. The scene changes to a deep wood. Prince Golaud, heir to the kingdom of Allemonde, has lost his way while following a wounded stag. He comes upon a beautiful young woman, Mélisande, weeping beside a pool. A crown sparkles in the water, but she will not let Golaud retrieve it for her. In Scene 3, six months later, the royal family reads a letter from Golaud, announcing his imminent return with the mysterious child-woman he has married. Golaud's half-brother Pelléas begs permission to travel to visit a friend who is mortally ill, but his mother Geneviève insists that he stay to welcome Golaud and his bride, Mélisande. In the gloomy environment of the castle, Mélisande is drawn to Pelléas, for the two of them share a childlike innocence of soul. While playing with him at the Fountain of the Blind, Mélisande loses her wedding ring in its depths. A third innocent is the child Yniold, Golaud's son by a previous marriage. Yniold senses something between his stepmother and uncle that he cannot verbalize other than to react to external events like the sight of swans being chased by dogs. Pelléas has decided to go to his dying friend; when he comes to say goodbye, Mélisande is combing her hair at a tower window. She leans dangerously far out the window to touch his hand and her long hair tumbles down, envelopping him. This is the lyrical peak of the play; the normally spare dialogue blossoms with sensuous imagery as Pelléas luxuriates in Mélisande's tresses. The innocent yet sexually-charged love scene is cut short by the appearance of Golaud. In the next scene, Golaud is showing Pelléas the subterranean vaults beneath the castle, and Pelléas narrowly misses falling into the void; Golaud's unspoken death wish for Pelléas is palpable. Golaud later interrogates Yniold about Pelléas and Mélisande, but the child's half-formed responses only fuel his jealousy. Mélisande's innocent beauty incites Golaud to violence: he forces her to her knees and pulls on her

Pélleas and Mélisande: Vaudeville Theatre, London, 1904 (Sarah Bernhardt and Mrs Patrick Campbell)

hair as if it were the reins on a horse. Late at night, on the eve of Pelléas's departure, Mélisande meets him at the Fountain of the Blind. No sooner have they breathlessly declared their love for each other than they hear the castle gates being closed and locked for the night. Their fear turns tentatively to rejoicing until they realize that Golaud is watching from the shadows. They embrace passionately. Golaud strikes Pelléas dead and chases Mélisande into the woods. The fifth act finds Mélisande on her deathbed. She has borne a daughter as frail as herself. Golaud begs her forgiveness, questions her again about her relations with Pelléas, but finds no solace in the simple honesty of her reply. The door to the chamber has been left open. The housemaids enter and fall to their knees at the quiet passing of Mélisande's soul.

The invisible presence of death pervades the play; it is conveyed in the shadowy atmosphere, in specific references like Golaud's talk of the smell of death in the vaults beneath the castle, and in symbolic stage images like beggars dying of hunger and sheep being driven to the slaughterhouse. Pelléas seems drawn inescapably toward death—to that of his friend or, when he does not go to the latter, his own. The gate, the door, and the threshhold function as symbols of the boundary between life and death, just as they do in Maeterlinck's other plays like *L'Intruse* (*The Intruder*) or *La Mort de Tintagiles* (*The Death of Tintagiles*). Some of the play's myriad symbols

are specific (such as the lost wedding ring); some are evocative, like the flight of doves when Mélisande lets down her hair; others are multivalent like the effects of various kinds of light and dark on Pelléas and Mélisande.

In its stage action and scenic atmosphere, *Pelléas et Mélisande* shows the influence of Richard Wagner's *Tristan und Isolde* as well as of Shakespeare's *Macbeth*, *Othello*, and *The Winter's Tale*. Maeterlinck's originality lay in his understatement. Since his characters are not fully fleshed out, they emerge as archetypes. By leaving much unsaid in the dialogue, Maeterlinck exploited the power of suggestion and provoked the reader or spectator's imaginative participation. One of the primary aims of symbolist theatre was to restore to the stage the evocative power of poetry, both verbal and visual. Maeterlinck succeeded in that, and in achieving a musicality of dramatic form that he was able to sustain for five acts, so that *Pelléas et Mélisande* remains the most successful, full-length drama in the symbolist mode.

Pelléas et Mélisande was first produced during a transitional phase in Parisian symbolist theatre, between the closure of Paul Fort's Théâtre d'Art and the opening of Lugné-Poë's Théâtre de l'Oeuvre. Lugné-Poë, who also played Golaud, staged the play's acclaimed single performance in Paris. Toured to Brussels in July 1893, the production elicited a mixed response from the critics. In the 20th century, the work has been most frequently performed in its operatic version by Claude Debussy, which opened on 30 April 1902 at the Opéra-Comique in Paris. The opera was first performed in the United States on 19 February 1908 at the Manhattan Opera House, and in England on 21 May 1909 at Covent Garden.

—Felicia Hardison Londré

PENTHESILEA
by Heinrich von Kleist

First Publication: Tübingen, 1808.
First Production: Königliches Schauspielhaus, Berlin, 25 April 1876.

Editions
Penthesilea, Frankfurt, 1980.
Penthesilea, Berlin, 1983.

Translations
Penthesilea, translated by H. Trevelyan, in *The Classic Theatre, 2*, edited by Eric Bentley, Garden City, New York.
Penthesilea, in *Heinrich von Kleist: Five Plays*, translated by Martin Greenberg, New Haven, and London, 1988.

Criticism
(For general works on the author, see *Playwrights* volume)

Books:
H.M. Brown, *Kleist and the Tragic Ideal: A Study of "Penthesilea" and Its Relationship to Kleist's Personal and Literary Development, 1806–1808*, Bern, 1978.

Articles:
Joseph Mersand, "Kleist's Penthesilea: A Modern Tragic Heroine", in *Germanic Review*, 12, 1937.
Siegfried Streller, "Zur Problematik von Kleist's *Penthesilea*", in *Weimarer Beiträge*, 1959.

Penthesilea: Staatstheater, Stuttgart, 1935

Denys Dyer, "The Imagery in Kleist's *Penthesilea*", in *Publications of the English Goethe Society*, 31, 1961.

P.B. Salmon, " 'Hellenistic' Diction in Kleist's *Penthesilea*", in *German Life and Letters*, 15, 1961.

D. Crosby, "Kleist's 'Oak Image' ", in *German Quarterly*, 38, 1965.

H. Schrimpf, "Tragedy and Comedy in Kleist", in *Monatshefte*, 58, 1966.

Kurt Adel, "Grillparzer's Hero-Drama and Kleist's *Penthesilea*", in *Jahrbuch der Grillparzer-Gesellschaft*, 7, 1967.

Ronald Gray, " 'Jenseits von Sinn und Unsinn': Kleist's *Penthesilea* and Its Critics", in *Publications of the English Goethe Society*, 37, 1967.

S. Hardy, "Kleist: Portrait of a Mannerist", in *Studies in Romanticism*, 6, 1967.

H. Salinger, "Heinrich von Kleist's *Penthesilea*: Amazon or Bluestocking?", in *Comparative Drama*, 1, 1967–68.

Donald H. Crosby, "Psychological Realism in the Works of Kleist: *Penthesilea* and *Die Marquise von O. . .*", in *Literature and Psychology*, 19, 1969.

V.C. Hubbs, "The Plus and Minus of *Penthesilea* and *Katchen*", in *Seminar*, 6, 1970.

Hilda Brown, "Penthesilea: Nightingale and Amazon", in *Oxford German Studies*, 7, 1972–73.

Paul Whitaker, "*Penthesilea* and the Problem of Bad Faith", in *Colloquia Germanica*, 6, 1972.

Manfred Durzak, "Das Gesetz der Athene und das Gesetz der Tanais: Zur Funktion des Mythischen in Kleists *Penthesilea*", in *Jahrbuch des freien deutschen Hochstifts*, 1973.

Luanne T. Frank, "Kleist's Achilles: *Hilfskonstruktion* or Hero?", in *Husbanding the Golden Grain: Studies in Honor of Henry W. Nordringer*, Michigan, 1973.

Luanne T. Frank, " 'The Strangest Love Scene in World Literature' (The Dismemberment of Achilles in Kleist's *Penthesilea*) Reassessed", in *Proceedings: Pacific Northwest Conference on Foreign Languages*, 25, edited by Walter C. Kraft, Washington D.C., 1974.

R. St. Leon, "The Question of Guilt in Kleist's *Penthesilea*", in *Seminar*, 10, 1974.

Peter Horn, "*Penthesilea*: The Revival of a Greek Myth as an Endorsement of Kleist's Social and Political Ideals", in *English Studies in Africa*, 18, 1975.

Luanne T. Frank, "Der Gott der Erde in Kleists *Penthesilea*: Ein Schlüssel zum Werk?", in *Jahrbuch für internationale Germanistik*, 2, 1976.

Gerhard Kaiser, "Mythos und Person in Kleists *Penthesilea*", in *Geist und Zeichen: Festschrift für Arthur Henkel*, Heidelberg, 1977.

Peter Goldammer, "Heinrich von Kleists *Penthesilea*: Kritik der Rezeptionsgeschichte als Beitrag zur Rezeption", in *Impulse: Aufsätze, Quellen, Berichte zur deutschen Klassik und Romantik*, 1978–79.

Ursula R. Mahlendorf, "The Wounded Self: Kleist's *Penthesilea*", in *German Quarterly*, 52, 1979.

E.M. Oppenheimer, "On the Shape of Kleist's *Penthesilea*", in *Carleton Germanic Papers*, 7, 1979.

Linda Hoff-Purviance, "The Form of Kleist's *Penthesilea* and the *Iliad*", in *German Quarterly*, 55, 1982.

Robert Raiser, "Heinrich von Kleist's *Penthesilea*: Eine Uraufführung?", in *Neue deutsche Hefte*, 29, 1982.

Françoise Derre, "De Phèdre à Penthesilea: Une Filiation possible", in *Recherches germaniques*, 13, 1983.

Roger Paulin, "Kleist's Metamorphoses: Some Remarks on the Use of Mythology in *Penthesilea*", in *Oxford German Studies*, 14, 1983.

Peter Michelsen, "Der Imperativ des Unmöglichen: Über Heinrich von Kleists *Penthesilea*", in *Antike Tradition und Neuere Philologien*, edited by Hans Joachim Zimmermann, Heidelberg, 1984.

Maurice Regnaut, "*Penthésilée* et l'agonie originelle", in *Littérature*, 53, 1984.

Barbara Belhalfaoui, "Kleist's *Penthesilea* in heilgeschichtlicher Sicht: Eine Interpretation", in *Études germaniques*, 40, 1985.

Manfred Fuhrmann, "Christa Wolf über *Penthesilea*", in *Kleist-Jahrbuch*, 1986.

Ulrich Fülleborn, "'Der Gang der Zeit von Anfang': Frauenherrschaft als literarischer Mythos bei Kleist, Brentano und Grillparzer", in *Kleist-Jahrbuch*, 1986.

Hasso Hofmann, "Individuum und allgemeines Gesetz: Zur Dialektik in Kleist's *Penthesilea* und *Prinz Friedrich von Homburg*", in *Carleton Germanic Papers*, 14, 1986.

Falk Horst, "Kleist's *Penthesilea* oder die Unfähigkeit, aus Liebe zu kämpfen", in *Germanisch-Romanische Monatsheft*, 36, 1986.

Renate Rolle, "Amazonen in der archäologischen Realität", in *Kleist-Jahrbuch*, 1986.

Gerhart Pickerodt, "*Penthesilea* und Kleist: Tragödie der Leidenschaft und Leidenschaft der Tragödie", in *Germanisch-Romanische Monatsheft*, 37, 1987.

Chris Cullens and Dorothea von Mücke, "Love in Kleist's *Penthesilea* and *Katchen von Heilbronn*", in *Deutsche Vierteljahrsschrift für Literaturwissenschaft und Geistesgeschichte*, 63, 1989.

* * *

In *Penthesilea*, a one-act, 3,000-line tragedy in blank verse with 24 scenes, Penthesilea, Queen of the Amazons, is bound by the law of Tanais with her subjects only to marry those they have defeated in battle. Mars, their particular god, chooses potential enemies who become their mates at the Rose Festival after each battle. Penthesilea explains all this to Achilles, who—together with other Greeks and Trojans—cannot understand the Amazons' desperate attack. She further narrates how her dying mother had forecast Achilles would become her future mate. In selecting a particular victim she extends her mother's earlier transgression of Amazon law, for both mother and daughter have usurped Mars's rights, the Amazon state depending on strict observance of impersonal love. Penthesilea's "crime" is intensified when her admiration for Achilles as a hero grows into love when she first meets him. After a successful battle with enough prisoners taken to celebrate a Rose Festival, she insists on a further attack to capture Achilles, but she is at first thwarted by unexpected weakness—presumably intervention by Mars—and then is defeated by Achilles and faints. Believing she has captured him, she reveals all, only to be silenced when he announces she is his prisoner. Eventually she renews hostilities in a state of frenzy, savagely slaughters an almost unarmed Achilles, using the great bow—emblem of the Amazon state—and tears him apart limb from limb in cannibalistic fury. When she recovers, to be confronted with his corpse decked out with roses for burial, she renounces the "law of women" and stabs herself to death in order to follow him.

In *Penthesilea*, Kleist pits the single-mindedness of Penthesilea against the Amazon law. Penthesilea does not comprehend the concept of love, and expresses this in her obsession to conquer Achilles in battle. Achilles' challenge to her to fight unleashes in her an all-consuming passion whose expression is seen in extremes of love and hatred. Amazon law is based on the suppression of feeling, so that the basic, instinctive function of womanhood is denied and replaced by an unnatural system of government devised on reason. As Queen of the Amazons, Penthesilea is the repository of this law and feels herself responsible for it. As a woman she is, like all Kleist's major figures, totally sincere. The play shows her gradual realisation of the conflict within her as woman and as queen. She is at first incapable of understanding the significance of Achilles' challenge, but worse, she cannot at this point choose to avoid it and is bound to accept a fate apparently out of her control. It is probably significant that when Kleist first planned *Penthesilea* in 1800 he was reading both Kant and Rousseau just before his so-called "Kantian crisis" in March 1801. Kleist hoped that Goethe would support a production in Weimar, but the play's excesses and, in places, near travesties of classical form made Goethe turn it down, and the play was only first performed, in a three-act version, in 1876.

Penthesilea appears as the tragedy of human passion driven by Kleist to excess and exacerbated by Achilles's incompatibility with Penthesilea's nature. Their disjunction cannot find reconciliation in this life—only in his death at her hands and in her demise do they come close to understanding. Her way to full self-realisation is complicated by the varying levels of language she must use as queen and as woman, also by the deception she experiences on awakening from her swoon that she has conquered Achilles.

In reality the story of her passion illuminates the underlying problem of the consequences of a clash between a law artificially abstracted and formulated by the state and "natural" motivations and needs in the individual human being. The closer Penthesilea approaches self-satisfaction, the more dangerous she is to the stability of the state personified in her as its queen. Kleist makes it impossible for her to settle for either—she must either sacrifice herself or her central role in her community. He then forces the issue by bringing her face to face with her admired and loved Achilles. From that moment on the two poles within her being are in deadly inner conflict. Her identification with both extremes shows—in typical Kleistian terms—just how uncompromisingly she is bound to her fate. Penthesilea's bipolar existence—for Kleist especially typical of a woman's fate—lies at the heart of this tragedy. While she is still responsive to the law of Tanais, this polarity afflicts her and she, as queen, must fight Achilles. Once she reacts to him as a woman, her suppressed passions are released. The quasi-religious responsibilities of her role as queen imply a way of life extreme in its purity. Once that is questioned and found wanting, her commitment to love for Achilles is total. Her surrender of role and discovery of self is, however, no easy adjustment, especially when she feels herself defeated and despised by Achilles. Indeed, the tearing apart of her inner core renders her incapable of independent decision and action, so that she is reduced to uncoordinated reaction, to irrational behaviour. Walter Müller-Seidel (writing in 1929) showed how this central, absolute problem fits into a basic Kleistian pattern of conflict between pure feeling and reflection. One is tempted to interpret Penthesilea's tragedy as an example of a struggle towards a new stage of innocence after the pattern of Kleist's essay on puppets (*Über das Marionettentheater*). This does not take full account however of the fateful role played by Achilles' demonstration of love, necessarily interpreted by Penthesilea as derision. Her self-appointed death can represent the eventual triumph of her feelings over the state, despair, loss of Achilles, or need for self-identity. It can also be seen as the inevitable outcome of a totally split consciousness, as Mars' revenge, and as a sign of the collapse of the Amazon state already foreshadowed by the destruction of the bow which Penthesilea drops when she emerges from her trance.

The play is remarkable for the double level of Penthesilea's language corresponding to the bipolarity of her being. Alongside her reasoned, formal pronouncements as queen emerge utterances from a more elemental level of consciousness, an apparent contradiction that reinforces the impression of her final loneliness both as queen and as lover. The loneliness is partly chosen, partly imposed, and against it she has the one weapon—to fight on regardless. This takes the form of actual martial conflict but also, on a subtler level, of a search for the telling image. Image-seeking becomes her lifeline; its use also offers the necessary link needed to resolve her bipolarity. From the moment she realises Achilles has defeated her she feels more isolated and her imagery is restricted to that of destruction. Only the sight of his corpse brings back her powers of imagery, and it is left to her companion Prothoe to sum up her fate in Kleist's favourite imagery of the oak-tree. Ultimately this tragedy of uncertainty of gender-identity and over–awareness of the potentials of language to define and expand the bounds of the self becomes a mirror to Kleist's own sense of inadequacy.

—Brian Keith-Smith

PERIBÁÑEZ AND THE COMENDADOR OF OCAÑA
(Peribáñez y el comendador de Ocaña)
by Lope de Vega Carpio

First Publication: In *Doze comedias de Lope de Vega, 4*, Madrid, 1614.
First Production: Unknown.

Editions
Peribáñez y el comendador de Ocaña, edited by Bonilla San Martín, Madrid, 1916.
Peribáñez y el comendador de Ocaña, edited by Panceira, Buenos Aires, 1938.
Peribáñez y el comendador de Ocaña, edited by Henríquez Ureña, Buenos Aires, 1938.
Peribáñez y el comendador de Ocaña, in *Fuenteovejuna; Peribáñez y el comendador de Ocaña*, edited by F. Garcia Pavon, Madrid, 1965.
Peribáñez y el comendador de Ocaña, edited by Juan María Marín, Madrid, 1979.
Peribáñez y el comendador de Ocaña, edited by J.M. Ruano and J.E. Varey, London, 1980.

Peribáñez y el comendador de Ocaña, edited by Alberto Blecua, Madrid, 1981.
Peribáñez y el comendador de Ocaña, edited by Felipe Pedraza Jiménez, Madrid, 1985; second edition, 1986.
Peribáñez y el comendador de Ocaña, edited by Alonso Zamora Vicente, Madrid, 1987.

Translations
Peribáñez, translated by Eva R. Price, Redlands, California, 1936.
Peribáñez, in *Lope de Vega: Five Plays*, translated by Jill Booty, New York, 1961.
Peribáñez and the comendador of Ocaña, in *Eight Spanish Plays of the Golden Age*, translated by Walter Starkie, New York, 1964.
Peribáñez and the comendador de Ocaña, translated by James Lloyd, Warminster, Wiltshire, 1980.

Criticism
(For general works on the author, see *Playwrights* volume)

Articles:
Otis H. Green, "The Date of *Peribáñez y el comendador de Ocaña*", in *Modern Language Notes*, 46, 1931.
Charles Philip Wagner, "The Date of *Peribáñez*", in *Hispanic Review*, 15, 1947.
Courtney Bruerton, "More on the Date of *Peribáñez*", in *Hispanic Review*, 17, 1949.
Juan Loveluck, "La fecha de *Peribáñez y el comendador de Ocaña*", in *Atenea* (Concepción, Chile), 30, 1953.
Gustavo Correa, "El doble aspecto de la honra en *Peribáñez y el comendador de Ocaña*", in *Hispanic Review*, 26, 1958.
Victor Dixon, "The Symbolism of *Peribáñez*", in *Bulletin of Hispanic Studies*, 43, 1966.
Alison Turner, "The Dramatic Function of Imagery and Symbolism in *Peribáñez* and *El castellero de Olmedo*", in *Symposium*, vol.20 no.2, 1966.
Guillermo Araya, "Paralelismo antitético en *Peribáñez y el comendador de Ocaña*", in *Estudios filológicos*, 5, 1969.
Georges Güntert, "Relección del *Peribáñez*", in *Revista de filología espagñola*, 54, 1971–72.
Thomas E. Case, "El papal de Inés en *Peribáñez*", in *Romanische Forschungen*, 84, 1972.
Mary G. Randel, "The Portrait and the Creation of *Peribáñez*", in *Romanische Forschungen*, 85, 1973.
J.E. Varey, "The Essential Ambiguity in Lope de Vega's *Peribáñez*: Theme and Staging", in *Theatre Research International*, 1, 1976.
John Bryans, "Providence or Discretion in *Peribáñez*", in *Journal of Hispanic Philology*, 2, 1978.
P.R.K. Halkhoree, "The Dramatic Use of Place in Lope de Vega's *Peribáñez*", in *Bulletin of the Comediantes*, 30, 1978.
Loren L. Zeller, "The Dramatic Function of Comic Relief in Lope de Vega's 'Tragicomedia' *Peribáñez*", in *Philological Quarterly*, 57, 1978.
Ciriaco Morón Arroyo, "Axiomática: *Peribáñez* y *La vida es sueño*: Estudio de los signos básicos en torno a los cuales se organiza un texto", in *Dieciocho*, vol.4 no.1, 1981.
Clark Colahan and Alfred Rodríguez, "La fusión barroca de las artes en *Peribáñez*", in *Neophilologus*, vol.66 no.2, 1982.
Peter Evans, "*Peribáñez* and Ways of Looking at Golden Age Dramatic Characters", in *Romanic Review*, vol.74 no.2, 1983.
Kathleen L. Kirk, "Image as Revealer of Truth in Two Plays by Lope de Vega", in *Ariel* (University of Kentucky), vol.1 no.1, 1983.
José M. Ruano de la Haza, "An Early Rehash of Lope's

Peribáñez", in *Bulletin of the Comediantes*, vol. 35 no.1, 1983.

Robin Carter, "*Peribáñez*: Disorder Restored", in *What's Past is Past: A Collection of Essays in Honour of L.J. Woodward*, edited by Salvador Bacarisse and others, Edinburgh, 1984.

José M. Ruano de la Haza, "Malicia compensina y la ambigüedad essencial de *Peribáñez y el comendador de Ocaña* de Lope de Vega", in *Hispanófila*, vol.28 no.3, 1985.

Manuel Delgado-Morales, "Iconología de *Peribáñez y el comendador de Ocaña* de Lope de Vega", in *Anales de literatura española*, 5, 1986–87.

*   *   *

In the *Arte nuevo de hacer comedias en este tiempo* (*The New Art of Composing Plays in our Time*) of 1609, Lope de Vega declared his special interest in a notably dramatic theme: "Los casos de la honra son mejores, / porque mueven con fuerza a toda gente" ("cases of honour are best, because everybody is extremely moved by them"). Among Lope's most memorably dramatized "cases of honour", *Fuenteovejuna*, *El mejor alcalde, el rey*, and *Peribáñez y el comendador de Ocaña* (*Peribáñez and the Comendador of Ocaña*) form almost a trilogy, since all three are plays of peasant honour, in which base overlords are destroyed by nobly-minded peasants whose conduct is ultimately approved or forgiven by right-thinking Spanish monarchs. These are all plays in which Lope extols the unsophisticated pleasures of country life, contrasts naturally authentic love with destructively sexual passion, condemns the abuse of political power and social privilege, and distinguishes between surface-honour (the immediate prerogative of high birth and rank) and the superior quality of inner honour, to which every man, regardless of his class, is entitled to aspire. Though its exact date of composition is unknown, internal evidence (preferred verse-forms, etc.) indicate that *Peribáñez* was written earlier than the other two dramas, and probably in the period 1605–08. Audiences in Madrid must have received the play with enthusiastic approbation, for its fame evidently soon inspired an unknown author to compose a burlesque version, entitled *El comendador de Ocaña*, which entertainingly parodies the Comendador's lascivious interest in his vassal's wife and Peribáñez's jealously offended reactions. Some decades later Lope's drama was reworked—and retitled *La mujer de Peribáñez*—by three anonymous imitators of Calderón. Theatre documents record that *Peribáñez*—perhaps this inferior adaptation, however, rather than the original masterpiece—was staged in Valladolid in 1691, and was still being performed in Madrid, at the royal palace in 1684, and at the *corrales* (public theatres) in 1689 and 1695.

The drama is set in the reign of Enrique III of Castile (1390–1406), a turbulent period of campaigns against the Moors and conflicts with powerful noblemen opposed to the king's authority. The play opens with a *boda de villanos*, as the village of Ocaña celebrates the wedding of a prosperous and respected, young peasant to Casilda, his extremely virtuous and extraordinarily beautiful bride. Their overlord, the Comendador Don Fadrique, injured during a bullfight which forms part of the festivities, is tended by Casilda with whom he falls passionately in love. At first he attempts to seduce Casilda and render her husband complaisant through flattery and gifts; but when persuasion fails he resorts to extreme measures of deceit and violence. Apparently he honours and ennobles Peribáñez by appointing him captain over 100 peasant-soldiers, but the honour which is intended, as the Comendador reveals to his servant, Leonardo, is "honra aforrada en infamia" ("honour wrapped in ignominy"). Don Fadrique's evil purpose is to separate the jealously protective husband from his devoted

wife. Peribáñez is sent, at the head of his soldiers, to join the king in his campaign against the Moors. The Comendador enters the peasant's house prepared to rape Casilda if she resists him. But Peribáñez, aware of his lord's ignoble passion and suspecting his intention, returns home as Casilda struggles to oppose her aggressor. Peribáñez protects his wife's virtue and defends his own honour by killing the Comendador. Peribáñez almost pays with his life for the death of his overlord. Having heard the true facts, however, King Enrique is finally persuaded to pardon, even reward him. His noble rank of captain is confirmed and, a peasant no longer, Peribáñez embarks upon a career in the king's army, to serve in the war against the Moorish kingdom of Granada.

Despite the convincing authenticity of its medieval setting, and the presence among its characters of an impressively historical, Spanish monarch, *Peribáñez* differs notably from *Fuenteovejuna* and *El mejor alcalde, el rey*, in that the main elements of its plot were not derived from chronicle-sources. The play was essentially developed from its author's imagination, uniquely stimulated to creativity by the sentiments of a traditional song:

> más quiero yo a Peribáñez
> con su capa la pardilla
> que al Comendador de Ocaña
> con la suya guarnecida.

> I love Peribáñez
> with his plain brown cloak
> more than the Comendador of Ocaña
> with his cloak so richly adorned.

This song is worked into the dramatic centre of the action, where, in Act II, it forms part of the key speech which Casilda delivers, as she addresses Don Fadrique from the safety of a window in her locked room,—the speech through which she rejects the aristocratic Comendador's dishonourably sexual advances and demonstrates her virtuous devotion to her honourable peasant-husband. The song also dramatically inspired Lope's symbolic use of contrasted costumes and differently visual effects. Peribáñez usually appears dressed as a peasant in plain brown cloak, though he acquires a less humble costume, a sword, and even a plumed hat after the Comendador has appointed him to the rank of captain. Significantly, however, Peribáñez reverts to his peasant's plain cloak when he appears before the king to explain honestly and justify the death of the Comendador. As for Don Fadrique, in contrast to Peribáñez, he is always splendidly attired, which indicates not only his status but his vanity and arrogance. His dress is also used suggestively to prepare us for his violent death. Throughout the play he wears a tunic decorated with a blood-red cross, the insignia of the military order to which he proudly belongs. That same tunic, together with the red cloak which, ominously, he chooses to wear during his final visit to Peribáñez's house, will be fatally stained in the crimson reality of his own blood, ironically shed by a vassal whom he has personally armed.

Lope thoughtfully manages symbolism and imagery to motivate the central conflict and prepare us for its outcome. In the first scene the bull, through its horned presence at the wedding festivities, symbolizes sexual aggression, signifying that danger already threatens Peribáñez's honour and marital happiness. Still more significantly, the almost fatal injury which Don Fadrique sustains in his encounter with that animal leads us to expect that the violent passion which he immediately conceives for Casilda will ultimately destroy the Comendador himself. Another remarkable aspect of Lope's achievement is his lyricism—as illustrated by the poems in which Peribáñez and Casilda respectively recite their "ABC's" of love, listing the qualities which each considers essential in a wife or husband. Equally noteworthy is Lope's sympathetic, yet realistically detailed, representation of country life: Peribáñez harvests his crops, tends his animals, embraces his wife in the stables; and their evening meal, bubbling in the pot, is seasoned with onions and garlic.

Lope also offers convincingly vital portrayals of the main characters. Casilda is less profoundly individualized than her husband or the Comendador. Nevertheless, besides extraordinary beauty and exceptional virtue, she is acceptably endowed with more ordinary qualities, such as good sense and quick wits, and she displays some naturally feminine weaknesses, occasionally indulging her fondness for pretty clothes and frivoluos pleasures. Her husband is distinguished by a more interestingly ambiguous personality. To an extent he is happily active within the peasant community. Yet there are other still unsatisfied ambitions and undeveloped abilities in this man, which cause him to give up his humble occupation with alacrity when he is offered a notably different profession with distinctly elevated social status. The Comendador is an even more memorably complex individual. Far from being simply an evil-minded overlord, he is also a nobleman possessed of courage, intelligence, and self-perception. Moreover, the love which he conceives for Casilda is passionately genuine. He longs to be her husband and the father of her children. These longings, however, are impossible to realize because of her already married state and her impossibly inferior social rank. Consequently his love, from its more exalted aspects, degenerates violently to levels of ultimately self-destructive lust.

In the final moments of life the Comendador recognizes, courageously and with dignity, that the fatal punishment administered by Peribáñez is justified, so that we are moved to appreciate his human qualities and to regret his death. At this point we are almost inclined to accord him the lofty status of tragic hero. However, since the action is not yet concluded, the impression made upon us by Don Fadrique's death soon diminishes when his accomplices—Inés and Luján—are also killed by Peribáñez. The latter's success in protecting his wife's virtue attracts our principal attention and holds our admiration, while his elevation in rank gains our lasting approval as an appropriate reward for his noble attitudes and honourable conduct. In its last lines Lope alludes to the play as a "*tragicomedia*" ("tragicomedy"), which is an entirely accurate description. With its combination of sad and happy events and its finally optimistic conclusion, *Peribáñez* fulfils the main purpose of drama—as Lope understood it—by reflecting the variety in the reality of human experience.

—Ann L. MacKenzie

PERIBAÑEZ Y EL COMENDADOR DE OCAÑA. See **PERIBAÑEZ AND THE COMENDADOR OF OCAÑA.**

PERICLES, PRINCE OF TYRE
by William Shakespeare (possibly with George Wilkins)

First Publication: London, 1609 ("bad" quarto).
First Production: Unknown; possibly 1608?

Editions
Pericles, Prince of Tyre, edited by J.C. Maxwell, Cambridge, 1956 (New Shakespeare).
Pericles, edited by R.D. Hoeniger, London, 1963 (Arden Shakespeare).
Pericles, Prince of Tyre, edited by Ernest Schanzer, New York, 1965; revised version, in *Pericles, Prince of Tyre; Cymbeline; The Winter's Tale*, 1988.
Pericles, Prince of Tyre, edited by Philip Edwards, Harmondsworth, 1976 (New Penguin Shakespeare).

Bibliography
Nancy N. Michael (ed.), *"Pericles": An Annotated Bibliography*, New York, 1987 (Garland Shakespeare Bibliographies).

Criticism
(For general works on the author, see *Playwrights* volume)

Books:
A.H. Smyth, *Shakespeare's "Pericles" and Apollonius of Tyre*, Philadelphia, 1898.
George Wilkins, *The Painful Adventures of Pericles Prince of Tyre*, edited by Kenneth Muir, Liverpool, 1953 [a 1608 prose narrative, possibly based on the play].
Jürgen Beneke, *Metaphorik im Drama: Dargestellt an Shakespeares "Pericles" und "Cymbeline"*, Bonn, 1975.
Maqbool H. Khan, *Shakespeare's "Pericles" and Other Studies*, Aligarth, 1986.

Articles:
For information on articles about *Pericles*, see Michael's bibliography, the bibliographies listed in the *Playwrights* volume, and the annual Shakespeare Bibliography in *Shakespeare Quarterly*, published by the Folger Shakespeare Library, Washington D.C. (1950–).

*   *   *

To win the daughter of King Antiochus, Pericles, ruler of Tyre, must solve a riddle; if he fails, he will lose his life. Pericles solves the riddle, but its answer reveals that Antiochus is guilty of incest with his daughter. Afraid for his life, Pericles embarks on a voyage. He relieves a famine at Tharsus, but, hearing that Antiochus seeks to murder him, leaves Tharsus and is shipwrecked. Thrown ashore at Pentapolis he finds in a fisherman's net the armour that his father left to him. Wearing it he enters a jousting contest held in honour of Thaisa, the daughter of King Simonides. Though ignorant of Pericles's true rank, Simonides agrees to his marriage to Thaisa. His identity is revealed when news comes of the death of Antiochus and of discontent in Tyre. The couple take ship for Tyre, but Thaisa dies giving birth during a storm. The chest that contains her body comes ashore at Ephesus, and she is restored to life by Lord Cerimon. She becomes a votaress of Diana. Pericles leaves the baby Marina at Tharsus and returns to Tyre. 14 years pass. The governor's wife envies Marina and arranges to have her killed, but she is rescued by pirates who sell her to a brothel in Mytilene, where her virtue converts the customers, including the governor, Lysimachus. Believing Marina dead, Pericles wears sackcloth and refuses to speak. Driven by the wind to Mytilene he is cured of his melancholy by Marina and identifies her as his daughter. The goddess Diana tells him in a vision to go to Ephesus. He is reunited with Thaisa, and Marina is betrothed to Lysimachus.

Pericles has an unusual place in Shakespeare's work. It was not included in the 1623 Folio edition of his collected plays, but it was long ago accepted into the canon and is the only such addition to be universally agreed. Nevertheless, problems remain. Acts I–II are markedly inferior to Acts III–V, and this has usually been explained by assuming that Shakespeare did not write them. Another theory suggests that they are the result of incompetent reporting. Recent studies, however, favour the second author, and the most popular candidate is George Wilkins, a minor dramatist and pamphleteer who was also an innkeeper and associate of prostitutes. He wrote for Shakespeare's company, and the two men had friends in common. Shakespeare probably re-wrote an original version by Wilkins, leaving untouched Gower's choruses and most of Acts I–II. Although well educated, Wilkins led a dissolute life, and it is interesting that he should be the origin of a play which deals with the overcoming of corruption and it itself of a mysterious beauty.

Pericles is the first of the four Romance plays that Shakespeare wrote in the last years of his life and which resemble each other in their themes and their disregard for realistic conventions. *Pericles* is particularly close to *The Winter's Tale* and *The Tempest*. All three plays deal with meaningless evil, loss, and rebirth. In all three, time and the sea are agents of both destruction and healing. At the centre of each is a father-daughter relationship in which the child redeems her parent.

The first two acts of *Pericles*, despite the ineptness of much of the verse, are extremely powerful, and it is easy to see why Shakespeare added little to them. They use the incest taboo to create a situation which is explicitly compared to the Fall of Man, but which has a disturbing resonance all its own. Pericles believes that in Antiochus's daughter he has found perfection, but in reality she is the opposite—total corruption. Moreover, he too is tainted, since he has committed his life to her. He is her father's partner in evil, since both of them desire the same woman and share the same secret. It is not surprising that he begins to suffer from sleeplessness and "dull-eyed melancholy"; his faith in life has been destroyed. His decision to travel is prudent, but it is also an evasion of responsibility, as the Tyrian nobles recognize when they mutiny. But his travels also provide opportunities for him to win back his self-respect, first by relieving the famine at Tharsus and then by his victory in the joust. The sea itself is a teacher. Although it takes everything else, it saves what he has abandoned—his life, and, as a sign that the parent-child relationship may have value, the armour that his father bequeathed him. The sea will again take all and yet give life when Marina is born and Thaisa is thrown overboard. Thaisa, like Pericles, will be washed ashore and brought back to life. Good and evil ebb and flow like the sea. Cleon and Dionyza care for Marina as a child, only for Dionyza to order her death when she grows up. About to be killed on the sea-shore, she is saved by pirates (rescuers from the sea) only to be carried off and sold into the brothel.

All these events are carefully patterned. For example, while Thaisa worships Diana in a temple, her virginal daughter prays to her in a brothel, and Pericles will later see her in a vision. The play derives much of its power from such parallels, of which that between Antiochus and Pericles is one of the most evocative, largely because it cannot be "explained" or translated into other terms. Not only are the two men accomplices; both have daughters who metaphorically kill their mothers and give life to their fathers. Pericles' famous description of Marina—"Thou that begetst him that did thee beget"—echoes the words of the riddle: "I mother, wife, and yet his child". The relationships are mirror-images: one is destructive, the other restorative. Marina is the daughter of Antiochus in reverse. The latter is passive, and almost speechless; she is a nameless object to be desired. Marina, by contrast, is active and eloquent. She wins her freedom from the brothel by her

accomplishments in music, dancing and needlework, and by her skill in persuasion. She can rescue her passive and silent father because she is his opposite. She is the great redemptive force in the play, and, like the sea after which she is named, she destroys as well as revives. Her birth in effect kills her mother, implying that life depends on loss. It is this that she teaches Pericles.

—Roger Prior

PERSAE.   See THE PERSIANS.

PERSAI.   See THE PERSIANS.

THE PERSECUTION AND ASSASSINATION OF JEAN-PAUL MARAT....   See MARAT/SADE.

THE PERSIANS (Persae / Persai)
by Aeschylus

First Production: Athens, 472 B.C.

Editions
Persae, edited by A. Sidgewick, Oxford, 1903.
Persae, edited by H.D. Broadhead, Cambridge, 1960.

Translations
Persians, in *Four Plays of Aeschylus*, translated by G.M. Cookson, Oxford, 1922.
Persians, translated by T.G. Tucker, Melbourne and London, 1935.
Persians, translated by Gilbert Murray, London, 1939.
Persians, translated by S.G. Benardete, in *Aeschylus, 2*, Chicago and London, 1956 (Complete Greek Tragedies Series).
The Persians, in *Prometheus Bound; The Suppliants; Seven Against Thebes; The Persians*, translated by Philip Vellacott, Harmondsworth, 1961.
Persians, translated by Anthony J. Podlecki, Englewood Cliffs, New Jersey, 1970.
Persians, translated by Janet Lembke and C.J. Herington, Oxford and New York, 1981.

Criticism
(For general works on the author, see *Playwrights* volume)

Books:
P. Keiper, *"Die Perser" des Aischylos als Quelle für altpersische Altertamskunde*, Erlangen, 1877.
J. Stavridès, *Quelques remarques sur les "Perses" d'Eschyle*, Paris, 1890.

Articles:
P. Pedrizet, "Le Témoignage d'Eschyle sur le sac d'Athènes par les Perses", in *Revue des études grecques*, 34, 1921.

E. Cohen, "Sur quelques traits du récit de Salamis", in *Revue des études anciennes*, 1924.

J.D. Craig, "The Interpretation of Aeschylus' *Persae*", in *Classical Review*, 38, 1924.

S. Eitrem, "The Necromancy of the *Persae* of Aeschylus", in *Symbolae Osloenses*, 6, 1926.

A.S.F. Gow, "Notes on the *Persae* of Aeschylus", in *Journal of Hellenic Studies*, 48, 1928.

A.M. Harmon, "Scene of the *Persae* of Aeschylus", in *Transactions and Proceedings of the American Philological Association* [*TAPA*] 1932.

Richmond Lattimore, "The Evocation of Darius", in *Classical Quarterly*, 28, 1934.

Richmond Lattimore, "Aeschylus on the Defeat of Xerxes", in *Classical Studies in Honor of W.A. Oldfather*, Urbana, Illinois, 1943.

G. Clifton, "The Mood of the *Persai* of Aeschylus", in *Greece and Rome* (second series), 10, 1963.

M. Anderson, "The Imagery of the *Persians*", in *Greece and Rome* (second series), 19, 1972.

S. Ireland, "Dramatic Structure in the *Persae* and *Prometheus Bound* of Aeschylus", in *Greece and Rome*, 20, 1973.

R.P. Winnington-Ingram, "Zeus in the *Persae*", in *Journal of Hellenic Studies*, 93, 1973.

William G. Thalmann, "Xerxes' Rags: Some Problems in Aeschylus' *Persians*", in *American Journal of Philology*, 101, 1980.

*   *   *

Persian Elders await with foreboding the return of the invasion that Xerxes, their king, has led from Asia into Europe. The Queen Mother approaches them and recounts a dream she has had presaging some disaster for the royal house. They counsel her to offer libations to her dead husband, Darius. A messenger arrives to tell of the destruction of the Persians in Greece. The Queen Mother and Elders invoke the spirit of Darius, who rises from his tomb. The former King bemoans his son's abuse of power and, before returning to his grave, predicts there will be a further loss to the nation. The Queen Mother leaves to prepare for her son's return. Xerxes, his royal robes in shreds, arrives to face the reproaches and distress of the Elders. He unites them in a processional lament which he then leads towards the Palace.

The *Persai* is the earliest tragedy we possess and is unique among the texts to survive in that its subject is taken from contemporary events rather than mythology. First performed eight years after the battle of Salamis, the messenger's description of that naval engagement is an eyewitness account of a battle in which Aeschylus and many of the spectators had fought. The events of the drama take place after that encounter but before the Dorian victory at Plataea which is foretold by Darius and portrayed as a divine punishment for the destruction of temples and shrines (a destruction of which some signs must still have been visible above the theatre where the first audience sat).

However, the play is not a chauvinist celebration nor an accurate historical dramatisation. It attempts to see events from the point of view of the defeated enemy and laments *their* loss and suffering. No Greek is mentioned by name, though catalogues of Persian heroes are honoured. Marathon is only cursorily invoked, while Darius is idealised and his westward expansion ignored; the importance of the engagement on the island of Psyttaleia is exaggerated and the death of survivors on the melting surface of a frozen river Strymon is invented. The creation of this image of disaster on a "natural" bridge of ice—mirroring that actual but "unnatural" bridge of rafts which Xerxes built across the Bosphorus in his bid to bind Europe to Asia—indicates something of Aeschylus's intentions. By stressing ecological disturbance, he conveys a sense of inevitable compensation for the encroachments of a human desire for mastery. Aeschylus reshapes the recent experiences of his community to lead its thoughts and feelings towards a recognition of the collective pain that flows from individual *hubris* and tyranny. In doing this, he addresses, implicitly, the developing, political structures of Athens and the young Delian League.

The play opens with the entry of the Chorus of Elders. Through recitative, song, and dance, they portray the extent of the invasion and establish, by repetition, the fateful importance of the "yoking" of the Hellespont, stressing Xerxes' culpable "god-like" confidence in attacking both by land and sea. They articulate the fear of divine retribution and show how every family in Asia is affected by their leader's actions. (This emphasis on "parents and wives" is a constant feature in the play. It is heightened by the focus on the Queen as mother and wife and on Darius as father, so that by the end the royal house stands for familial loss as well as imperial loss, which allows—in the long delayed entry of Xerxes—for the return of the son to be discerned amid the tatters of the tyrant.) When Atossa (the Queen) enters, she furthers the theme of "yoking" in her dream of two women harnessed to her son's chariot. In the questions she asks of the Chorus, she draws attention to the related theme of authority and government. These themes merge as the Messenger bears witness to the consequences of irreligious excess and abuse of power, and Atossa's reappearance, carrying libations "to soothe and calm the dead", embodies the underlying lesson (her simple dress and solitary entry contrasts with the pomp and luxury of her first appearance in a chariot and with a retinue). It is left to the ghost of Darius to expound fully on the divine and the human aspects of his son's rashness in seeking to harness the flow of the sea. Then, and only then, Xerxes appears, unaccommodated, to engage with the Chorus in a sustained, threnodic dialogue, a lyric exploration of a community coming to terms with the flood and disturbance unleashed.

A common criticism of this drama is that it lacks development and is too static, but performance proves this to be a superficial perception. As in the plays of Racine and Beckett, economy of plot intensifies the slightest incident or signifier and generates resonant stage-images. However, comparison with these playwrights shows how varied and energetic are the expressive means that Aeschylus employs. *Rheseis* and lyrics embrace both the communication of complex ideas and the charting of inarticulate cries from the dark (of which the "woe" and "alas" of many a translation is not an equivalent). It is easy, when reading the text, to appreciate the spectacle and excitement of the raising of Darius but more difficult to imagine the affective progression of the concluding stasimon and kommos which together comprise more than a fifth of the script and towards which the entire action is crafted. The nostalgic joy of the Elders contrasts with the divisive anger and despair that follows and the slow reintegration painfully achieved in the formation of the procession which Xerxes leads off. The facile solidarity of the stasimon, with its ironic allusion to the liberation of Ionia begun at Mykale, precedes a truer cohesion born of the necessity to face the loss and waste, "to begin from what has happened", and to move on. This fusion of thought, feeling, and motion is an illuminating example of the distinctive choreographic and musical quality of Greek tragedy.

—Leslie du S. Read

PETER PAN
by J.M. Barrie

First Publication: In *Collected Plays*, London, 1928.
First Production: Duke of York's Theatre, London, 22
        December 1904.

Criticism

(For general works on the author, see *Playwrights* volume)

Articles:

Lionel Stevenson, "A Source for Barrie's *Peter Pan*", in
        Philological Quarterly, 8, 1929.
Marietta Karpe, "The Origins of Peter Pan", in *Psychoana-
        lytic Review*, 43, 1956.
Stanford Sternlicht, "A Source for Golding's *Lord of the Flies*:
        Peter Pan", in *The English Record*, 14, 1963.
Frederick L. Meisel, "The Myth of Peter Pan", in *The
        Psychoanalytic Study of the Child*, 32, 1977.
John Griffith, "Making Wishes Innocent: *Peter Pan*", in *Lion
        & the Unicorn*, vol.3 no.1, 1979.
Lynette Hunter, "J.M. Barrie's Islands of Fantasy", in
        Modern Drama, 23, 1980.
Michael Egan, "The Neverland of Id: Barrie, *Peter Pan* and
        Freud", in *Children's Literature*, 10, 1982.

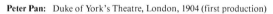

*   *   *

The curtain rises on the night nursery of the Darling
children—Michael, John, and Wendy. Their secure life under
the control of loving parents and dog-nurse Nana is invaded by
Peter Pan, the sprite child who never grows up. He takes them
to his own realm, the Never Land, after teaching them to fly.
There, Wendy becomes the story-teller and mother to the Lost

Boys and a series of adventures is played out according to the
free laws of the childish imagination. A more adult line is
introduced via the various determined assaults mounted on
Peter's sexual innocence by the fairy wiles of Tinker Bell, the
open flirtations of the piccaninny Tiger Lily, and Wendy's
maternal pleadings. But the central battle lies between Pirates
(led by the pale, cadaverous Hook) and Boys (led by Peter).
Hook is finally consumed by a crocodile; Wendy leads a return
to Bloomsbury and the Darling family. The Lost Boys are
adopted but Peter returns to the Never Land. There, in the
most commonly known version, he is rejoined by Wendy a
year later for spring-cleaning. Clearly, time is drawing them
apart and the ageing Wendy already thinks that a younger girl
should take her place.

Criticism of *Peter Pan* centres around a number of ironies
and paradoxes. Theatrically, this was Barrie's greatest commercial success. It ran every year in London over the
Christmas period from 1904 (Peter: Nina Boucicault; Hook:
Gerald du Maurier) until 1938 (Peter: Jean Forbes-Robertson;
Hook: Seymour Hicks). The leading parts became the equivalent of yearly Oscars while only the finest juveniles (Noël
Coward was one) aspired to be Lost Boys. Yet the author so
feared the failure of this pantomime-ballet-musical that he
offered the "safer" *Alice Sit-By-The-Fire* as an inducement to
any producer daring enough to take on his "Dream". This is
not surprising. Apart from its unusual generic definition, *Peter
Pan* (in its original form) needed five expensive sets and a cast
of over 50 people. Its many ambitious technical effects
included some so dangerous that the leading players had to
take out personal insurance and relied on "doubles" in a few of
the more demanding scenes. Now an emblem of theatrical
cosiness, it was in its own day so radical and eccentric that
Beerbohm Tree saw it as proof that Barrie had, at last, "gone
out of his mind".

The second paradox concerns the audience. In one sense,

Peter Pan: Duke of York's Theatre, London, 1904 (first production)

Peter Pan addresses everyone. It is splendid children's entertainment. Barrie knew the importance of quickly gaining a child's confidence and attention. The appearance of a world ruled by youthful imagination and dominated by a dog standing on its hind legs performing the roles of mother and nanny achieves both. He also understood the need to cope with shorter attention span and so moves from adventure to adventure with speed, introducing new characters and effects the while. It is not surprising that *Peter Pan* proved much more popular with children than Shaw's *Androcles and the Lion*; its author had not set aside childish things. Yet, in another sense, it addresses and finds no answer to the ultimate questions of origin, time, and power in an age whose comforting Christian beliefs had been upset by Nietzsche and Darwin. A subtle restructuring of the romance form favoured by Shakespeare in *The Tempest* and followed by Barrie in other works such as *Quality Street* and *The Admirable Crichton* permits Barrie to address at once the world as child and the world as the age of the Superman, as foreseen by his artist-hero Tommy Sandys in *Sentimental Tommy*.

Ironically, most criticism stresses only the personal and psychological line in the play. Certainly, this is present. Barrie admits that the adventures are based on actual games played with the Llewelyn Davies boys to whom he wittily grants co-authorship in the Dedication. One of his personal tragedies was a failure to come to grips with the world of adult sexuality and so, in that sense, he may be said never to have "grown up" himself. The obsession with motherhood, likewise, is fairly related to the power over him of his own mother, Margaret Ogilvy. Yet the play which is his most personal, *Peter Pan*, is also his most universal. Theorists agree that the nature of myth conjoins the two. In three other senses at least the very same evidence points to a man whose vision, far from being childish, is at once complex and uncompromisingly adult. Interest in himself is justified from a literary/philosophical viewpoint by the fact that, consistently, Barrie was a perspectivist, aware that his view on life could change many times before lunchtime (*Sentimental Tommy, Tommy and Grizel*). Further, as creation myth, *Peter Pan* develops the thesis of *The Little White Bird*, that there is a rivalry between the artist's power of creative imagination and the mother's ability to give birth. Finally, the presumption that Pan is the major figure within the play runs counter to various lines of evidence. The earlier drafts certainly did not highlight the boy-god; the recursive structure is a mirror of the Russian-box mind of Wendy and it is Wendy who both decides that they will go to the Never Land and initiates the return.

Most crucially of all, the play which was a culmination of all Barrie's careful theatrical apprenticeship has an end but no conclusion. That is the point of the author's order that it should never be revived but kept on a single, never-ending run; that is the point of the constant revisions, each producing variations on the final scene but never offering optimism or simplicity where compromise and irresolution reign; that is the point of a text which comments as much on the inadequacy of the codes of communication (the pipes of Pan; the bell-language of Tink; the tales of Wendy; the literary soliloquys of Hook) as on the loss of Dantesque certainty. It is no coincidence that the major tableau in this world of battle converts Pan into Napoleon, first of Nietzsche's heroes in the dark struggle for survival of the species.

—R.D.S. Jack

PETER QUILL'S SHENANIGANS. See **MASTER PETER PATHELIN.**

THE PETRIFIED FOREST
by Robert Sherwood

First Publication: New York, 1935.
First Production: Broadhurst Theatre, New York, 7 January 1935.

Criticism
(For general works on the author, see *Playwrights* volume)

Articles:
A.N. Lausch, "Robert Sherwood's 'Heartbreak Houses'", in *Shaw Review*, 6, 1963.
Richard Wattenberg, "America Redeemed: The Shape of History in Robert E. Sherwood's *The Petrified Forest* and *Abe Lincoln in Illinois*", in *Historical Drama*, edited by James Redmond, Cambridge, 1986 (Themes in Drama Series).

* * *

It is 1934—the Depression in America—and in the lunchroom of the Black Mesa Filling Station and Bar-B-Q, located in eastern Arizona near the petrified forest, Gabby (Gabrielle) explains her dreams of visiting France, the home of her mother, as she waits on a customer, Alan Squier. A disillusioned eastern writer, hitching-hiking west, Squier is looking for something worth living for—or dying for. Although Squier soon gets a ride with a rich couple, they are forced to return by Duke Mantee, a gangster-killer who has evaded a police dragnet and chosen this lunchroom to meet his girlfriend. As they wait, Squier compares himself with Mantee—both individuals, both part of a vanishing race—and suggests that they be buried in the petrified forest. In a moment of romantic idealism, Squier signs over his life insurance to Gabby who has impressed him with her dreams and asks Mantee to shoot him before he leaves. As the sheriff's posse closes in, Mantee obliges and escapes; Gabby cradles the dying Squier and promises to bury him in the petrified forest.

At this time in America's history, people wanted something to dream about, and they found great appeal in this romantic linking of the gunman and the poet. On stage the play was a brilliant theatrical success and almost immediately became a popular movie. In terms of dramatic structure Sherwood simply accumulated a number of lost and dissatisfied people and let them complain. Jason, Gabby's father, wants to go to Los Angeles; Boze, the young football player who thinks mainly of Gabby, is worried about his future; Gramps is a somewhat delightful, if macabre, individual who lives in the past; Squier has lost faith in himself; Mrs. Childress, the wife of the rich man, has not lived the life that she imagined. Gabby lives mainly through the romantic poetry of François Villon.

And why have these characters lost their illusions and abandoned their ideals? Because people are not free, truth is not spoken, emotions are not expressed. Man is shown now living in a "world of outmoded ideas". It is a changed world where the ideals of Platonism, patriotism, Christianity, Adam Smith, and individuality are gone. The idealists are condemned; only the fittest survive. Into this thoughtful situation

The Petrified Forest: Globe Theatre, 1942

Sherwood introduces Duke Mantee, who stimulates a few people to think and to act.

In this world of "outmoded ideas" both Mantee and Squier are condemned—but not for the romantic argument expressed by Squier, the major character in the play, and the only one who makes a discovery in the Aristotelian sense. Through Gabby, Squier feels that he can believe in himself. It is clear that Sherwood sensed the garbled expression of his thoughts, although he probably did not feel that his major characters were unequal to the task he assigned them. In point of fact, neither Squier nor Mantee is seemingly fit to survive: neither is heroic, and each dies for a woman, neither worthy of the sacrifice. Mantee's girlfriend betrays him, and Gabby, with her extremely rough language, hardly seems to be one in whom the hopes for the future should rest. Although in Squier's statement that he belongs to a "vanishing race" Sherwood attempted to show his own disillusionment as well as that of his age, it is his hasty perusal of this and other ideas that make his play ineffective as a thesis drama. Basically, it becomes simply spectacle and fast-moving melodrama with an apparently serious idea that is never developed. In fact, Sherwood admitted that he lost control of his theme. He liked the first act, he once confessed, but could find no conclusive way to end his play. This was a problem Sherwood had with his playwriting in general: he would find a serious point that he wanted to dramatize but would then undercut it in his writing, either intentionally or by default.

Amidst the confusions and disillusionments of the present, where does one go? Sherwood made a suggestion: to the petrified forest as "Homo Semi-Americanus—a specimen of the in-between age!". In this play, however, Sherwood lacked a penetrating and unified approach and, as he obliquely admitted, had to resort to an artificial and romantic conclusion. Sherwood was not a philosopher, but, in *The Petrified Forest* he nevertheless offered evident food for thought.

—Walter J. Meserve

PHAEDRA
by Seneca

Composition: 1st century A.D.

Editions

Phaedra, in *L. Annaei Senecae Tragoediae* (3 vols.), edited by
    Humbertus Moricca, Turin, 1917–23; second edition, 1947.
Phaedra [with translation], in *Seneca: Tragedies*, translated by
    F.J. Miller, London, 1960.
Phaedra, edited by P. Grimal, Paris, 1965.
Phaedra, in *L. Annaei Senecae Tragoediae* (2 vols.), edited by
    G.C. Giardina, Bologna, 1966.
Phaedra, in *L. Annaei Senecae Tragoediae*, edited by Otto
    Zwierlein, Oxford, 1986.
Seneca's "Phaedra" [with translation], edited by A.J. Boyle,
    Liverpool, 1987.
Phaedra, edited by Michael Coffey and Roland Mayer,
    Cambridge, 1990.

Translations

Phaedra, in *Seneca: Tragedies*, translated by Ella T. Harris,
    London and New York, 1904.
Phaedra, in *Seneca: Tragedies*, translated by Frank J. Miller,
    Chicago, 1907.
Phaedra, in *The Complete Roman Drama*, edited by George
    E. Duckworth, New York, 1942.
Phaedra, in *Seneca: Four Tragedies and "Octavia"*, translated
    by E.F. Watling, Harmondsworth, 1966.

Criticism
(For general works on the author, see *Playwrights* volume)

Books:

Charles Segal, *Language and Desire in Seneca's "Phaedra"*,
    Princeton, New Jersey, 1986.

Articles:

S.G. Flygt, "Treatment of Character in Euripides and Seneca:
    The Hippolytus", in *Classical Journal*, 29, 1934.
E. Paratore, "Sulla *Phaedra* di Seneca", in *Dioniso* (new
    series), 15, 1952.
M. Ruch, "La Langue de la psychologie amoureuse dans la
    Phèdre de Sénèque", in *L'Information littéraire*, 16, 1964.
D. Henry and P. Walker, "Phantasmagoria and Idyll: An
    Element of Seneca's *Phaedra*", in *Greece and Rome* (second
    series), 13, 1966.
Konrad Heldmann, "Seneca's *Phaedra* und ihre griechischen
    Vorbilder", in *Hermes*, 96, 1968.

*   *   *

Theseus has long been absent from Athens, and his wife
Phaedra is convinced that he is dead. She now harbours an
overpowering passion for the chaste Hippolytus, her stepson.
She confesses her lust to her nurse, threatening to commit
suicide. The nurse at length agrees to talk with Hippolytus, and
does so, trying to soften his hatred and rejection of all women.
Hippolytus is unmoved, whereupon Phaedra herself tells him
of her love, and throwing herself upon him, begs him to
reciprocate. Horrified, he draws his sword to slay her, but
decides instead to flee, leaving the sword behind. The nurse
then falsely raises the alarm, claiming that Hippolytus has
violated Phaedra. At this point Theseus returns, and Phaedra
denounces his son to him, claiming Hippolytus has raped her,
and offering the abandoned sword as evidence. Theseus is

enraged. Having been granted three wishes by the sea god,
Neptune, he now calls for the death of his son. After a short
choral interlude, a messenger enters to relate how Hippolytus,
riding in his chariot along the shore, has been confronted by a
terrible sea monster. Caught in the reins and dragged along by
his terrified horses, Hippolytus died horribly, torn to pieces.
His remains are brought on stage piece by piece. Acknowledging her crime, but vowing still to pursue Hippolytus through
Hades, Phaedra kills herself. Theseus is consumed with guilt
and on the point of taking his own life. The Chorus persuades
him to change his mind, and the play ends as, cursing Phaedra,
he reassembles the grisly remnants of Hippolytus for funeral
rites.

Phaedra displays the characteristic defects and virtues of
Senecan drama. The stage action is limited and somewhat
static. It is dominated by rhetorical set pieces which sometimes
descend into overheated bombast. There is a marked emphasis
on the evocation of direst woe and catastrophe, and on
sensational violence both of emotional expression by the
characters and in lurid descriptions of events reported as
taking place off stage. Seneca aims not for a subtle (nor always
consistent) character delineation, but for immediate, verbal
impact and the excitement of raw emotion supported and
extended by complex systems of imagery. Despite its limitations, *Phaedra* rises from time to time to moments of genuine
pathos, poetic beauty, and thrilling drama.

The emphasis throughout is upon the character of Phaedra
herself, to whom the other characters (with the partial
exception of Hippolytus) are little more than props. Unlike
Euripides, who in his *Hippolytus* frames and locates the play
within a conflict between the jealous goddesses Aphrodite and
Artemis, Seneca concentrates his drama entirely in the conflict
within Phaedra herself, and this compels and focuses the
reader's attention. Phaedra's is a morbid personality,
darkened and debilitated by guilt and embarrassment, while at
the same time motivated by its fixation upon her stepson and its
lust to possess him. This imbues the drama with a pervasive
sense of tension and anxiety and, particularly as intimated by
the choral odes, the threat of imminent catastrophe.

Seneca adds to his Euripidean model a scene of confrontation and confession between Phaedra and Hippolytus that
allows the fullest expression and exposure of the queen's
divided personality, and serves further to stress the psychological basis of the tragedy. Together with much else in the play it
invites and supports a psycho-sexual interpretation. Phaedra
sees in her stepson a younger incarnation of her absent
husband, and when rejected, longs for him to plunge his sword
within her—the sword that Hippolytus leaves behind as
"polluted" and which subsequently is used to incriminate him
with his father, as Phaedra recites to him her fantasy account of
the ravishment which, though wished for, never took place.

The messenger's gruesome account of Hippolytus's death at
the hands of the loathsome creature from the sea depicts an
external incarnation of Phaedra's monstrous state of mind, as
well as its effective agent. His description of Hippolytus's
ghastly mutilation is particularly poignant in the light of the
earlier choral ode that celebrated his vibrant youth and fragile
beauty. Phaedra's consequent guilt at the sight of the gruesome result of her crime is joined to fury that the broken object
of her passion has escaped into death. She turns her anger
briefly and cruelly upon Theseus, as with truly pathological
hatred she blames him for the catastrophe that she claims he
caused by his homecoming. She then destroys herself in a
deliberate *Liebestod*. Her final determination to hound Hippolytus even in Hell is literally the last word in maniacal love as
she welcomes the sword finally into her breast.

Although *Phaedra* poses difficulties to anyone attempting to stage it (as opposed to presenting the work as a dramatic reading, or as a radio drama), they are not insurmountable, particularly as audiences have grown accustomed to various modes of non-realistic presentation that can readily be applied to Senecan drama, and with very good results. The bleak mental landscapes in which his plays are set and the psychic horrors that inform them are analogous to material comprising much modern drama. The anti-naturalistic settings through which such drama is realised on stage may also suggest an appropriate setting for Seneca's nightmare imagery.

—Richard C. Beacham

PHAEDRA (Phèdre)
by Jean Racine

First Publication: Paris, 1677.
First Production: Théâtre de l'Hôtel de Bourgogne, Paris, 1 January 1677.

Editions

Phèdre, edited by H.R. Loach, London, 1950.
Phaedra, edited by Henri P. Salomon, Paris, 1966.
Phèdre, edited by Jean Salles, Paris, 1970.
Phaedra [with translation], edited and translated by R.C. Knight, Austin, Texas, 1971.
Phèdre, edited by Alain Viala, Paris, 1985.
Théâtre et mise en scène: "Phèdre", Paris, 1986.

Translations

Phaedra, translated by R. Henderson, in *Six Plays by Corneille and Racine*, edited by Paul Landis, New York, 1931.
Phaedra, translated by John Cairncross, Geneva, 1958; reprinted in *Iphegenia; Phaedra; Athaliah*, translated by John Cairncross, Harmondsworth, 1963.
Phaedra, translated by Agnes Tobin, San Francisco, 1958.
Phaedra, translated by Oreste F. Pucciani, New York, 1959.
Phèdre, in *Jean Racine: Five Plays*, translated by Kenneth Muir, London, 1960.
Phaedra, in *Three Plays*, translated by George Dillon, Chicago, 1961.
Phaedra, in *Phaedra; Figaro*, translated by Robert Lowell, New York, 1961.
Phèdre, translated by Margaret Rawlings, London, 1961.
Phaedra, translated by Wallace Fowlie, in *Classical French Drama*, New York, 1962.
Phaedra, translated by Richard Wilbur, New York, 1968.
Phaedra, in *Britannicus; Phaedra; Athaliah*, translated by C.H. Sisson, Oxford, 1987.

Criticism

(For general works on the author, see *Playwrights* volume)

Books:
Thierry Maulnier, *Lecture de "Phèdre"*, Paris, 1943.
Jean-Louis Barrault, *Mise en scène de "Phèdre"*, Paris, 1946.
Charles Dédeyon, *La "Phèdre" de Racine*, Paris, 1956; second edition, as *Racine et sa "Phèdre"*, Paris, 1978.
Vittorio Luglio, *Interpretazioni di "Phèdre"*, Bologna, 1958.
Charles Mauron, *Phèdre*, 1968.
Roger Mathé, *Phèdre*, Paris, 1973.
J.P. Short, *Racine: "Phèdre"*, London, 1983.

Articles:
H. Joubert, "L'Inceste dans *Phèdre*", in *Revue d'histoire du théâtre*, 1931.
Tanqueray, "Le Jansénisme de *Phèdre*", in *Revue des cours et conférences*, 1932.
J. Cousin, "Phèdre n'est point janséniste", in *Revue d'histoire littéraire de la France*, 1933?
G.H. Gifford, "L'Inceste dans *Phèdre*", in *Revue d'histoire littéraire de la France*, 39, 1933.
E.-E. Stoll, "*Phèdre*", in *Revue anglo-américaine*, 12, 1934.
R. Jones, "Racine's *Phèdre* and D'Annunzio's *Fedra*", in *Comparative Literature Studies* [Cardiff], 6–7. 1942.
R. Knight, "Hippolyte and Hippolytes", in *Modern Language Review*, 39, 1944.
C. Lyons, "A Defense of the *Récit de Théramène*", in *Modern Language Notes*, 59, 1944.
John C. Lapp, "Hippolyte, Phèdre and the *Récit de Théramène*", in *University of Toronto Quarterly*, 19, 1950.
Roger Pons, "*Phèdre* ou le vertige de l'âme", in *L'Anneau d'Or*, January–February, 1954.
J. Dedieu, "Ambiguité de *Phèdre* de Racine: Tragédie antique ou drame Chrétien?", in *Humanitas*, 2, 1955.
Walter Mönch, "Racines *Phèdre*: Eine literatur- und geistesgeschichtliche Betrachtung", in *Zeitschrift für französische Sprache und Literatur*, 66, 1956.
P.J. Yarrow, "*Un Temple sacré*: A Note on Racine's *Phèdre*", in *Modern Language Notes*, 72, 1957.
André Blanchet, "Phèdre entre le soleil et la nuit", in *Études*, October 1958.
N. Edelman, "The Motion of *Phèdre* from Act III to Act IV: An Alternative Reading", in *Romanic Review*, 50, 1959.
Abraham C. Keller, "Error and Invitation in Racine: *Phèdre*, IV, 2", in *Romanic Review*, 50, 1959.
Jean-Pierre Jouve, "La Leçon de *Phèdre*", in *Mercure de France*, February 1960.
Jean Pommier, "A Propos de *Phèdre*", in *Mercure de France*, May, 1960.
Roger Pons, "Explication française: L'Angoisse de la damnation", in *L'Information littéraire*, September–October 1960.
G. Couton, "Le Mariage d'Hippolyte et d'Aricie, ou Racine entre Pausanias et le droit canon", in *Revue des sciences humaines*, July–September, 1962.
Carlo Francois, "Phèdre et les dieux", in *French Review*, 35, 1962.
Norbert Gutermann, "Faut-il Retraduire Phèdre?", in *La Nouvelle Revue française*, September 1962.
Abraham C. Keller, "Death and Passion in Racine's *Phèdre*", in *Symposium*, vol.16 no.2, 1962.
Herman Prins Salomon, "*Phèdre*: Pièce Janséniste?", in *Cahiers Raciniens*, 15, 1964.
D. Levin, "Phèdre and Oenone", in *Rice University Studies*, 51, 1965.
J. White, "Racine's *Phèdre*: A Sophoclean and Senecan Tragedy", in *Revue de littérature comparée*, vol.39 no.4, 1965.
C. Nelson, "Politics and Passion in *Phèdre*", in *French Review*, 39, 1965–66.
H. Neumann, "Phèdre's Death in Euripides and Racine: Moral Responsibility in Closed and Open Societies", in *Cithara*, vol.6 no.2, 1967.
Julian White, "Phèdre is not Incestuous", in *Romance Notes*, 9, 1967.
Patrick Cruttwell, "Six Phaedras in Search of One *Phèdre*", in *Delos: A Journal On and Of Translation*, 2, 1968.
Rupert T. Pickens, "Hippolyte's Horses: A Study of a Metaphorical Action in Racine's *Phèdre*", in *Romanic Review*, 9, 1968.

Phèdre: Rachel as Phèdre, 1855

Phillip Koch, "Innocent Hippolyte", in *French Review*, 43, 1970.

Genevieve Sutton, "Phèdre et Thérèse Desqueyroux: Une Communante du destin", in *French Review*, 43, 1970.

Christian Delmas, "La Mythologie dans la *Phèdre* de Racine", in *Revue d'histoire du théâtre*, 1, 1971.

Pierre Han, "Vénus and Neptune: Baroque Music in *Phèdre*", in *Romance Notes*, 13, 1971.

Roger Caillois, "*Phèdre* et la mythologie", in *Nouvelle Revue française*, 234, 1972.

Donald Gilman, "The River of Death: Motif and Metaphor in Racine's *Phèdre*", in *Romance Notes*, 14, 1972.

J. Hoyt Rogers, "The Symmetry of *Phèdre* and the Role of Aricie", in *French Review* [special issue], 45, 1972.

Lance K. Donaldson-Evans, "The *Récit de Théramène* Reconsidered", in *Romance Notes*, 14, 1972–73.

William L. Crane, "A Problem in Racine's *Phèdre*: Whose Murderous Hand?", in *Romance Notes*, 14, 1973.

Pierre Han, "The Symbolism of *Lieu* in Racine's *Phèdre*", in *South Atlantic Bulletin*, 38, 1973.

E. Méron, "De *Hippolyte* d'Euripide à la *Phèdre* de Racine: Deux Conceptions du tragique", in *Dix-septième Siècle*, 100, 1973.

T.G. Pavel, "*Phèdre*: Outline of a Narrative Grammar", in *Language Sciences*, 28, 1973.

Michelle Coquillat, "*Phèdre*, ou la liberté dans l'acte héroïque", in *French Review*, 47, 1974.

Joseph M. Duffy, "Subject and Structure as Cosmology in Racine's *Phèdre*", in *Mosaic*, 7, 1974.

Pierre Han, "A Baroque Marriage: Phèdre's *Déclaration* and Théramène's *Récit*", in *South Atlantic Bulletin*, 39, 1974.

Monique Pasternak, "Racine: Le Probleme de la responsabilité de *Phèdre*", in *Revue de l'Université d'Ottawa*, 44, 1974.

Pierre Han, "Thésée: An Anti-Baroque Man in a Baroque World", in *Romance Notes*, 16, 1975.

K. Alfons Knauth, "Racines *Phèdre* auf dem Hintergrund von Emblematik und Mythenallegorese", in *Germanisch-Romanische Monatsschrift*, 25, 1975.

Gretchen R. Besser, "The Monster Metaphor in *Phèdre*", in *Hebrew University Studies in Literature*, 4, 1976.

Jean-Pierre Dens, "La Parole de Phèdre", in *Revue Romane*, 11, 1976.

R.L. Myers, "The *Récit de Théramène*: A Semantic View", in *Revue de l'Université d'Ottawa*, 46, 1976.

R.L. Myers, "Mythic Reality in Racine's *Phèdre*", in *Revue de l'Université d'Ottawa*, 46, 1976.

Timothy J. Reiss, "Of Time and Eternity: From *Phèdre* to History", in *Australian Journal of French Studies*, 13, 1976.

Lionel P. Honoré, "Othello and Phèdre: The Protagonist as Deluded Victim", in *College Language Association Journal*, 21, 1978.

Michael J. Pretina, "*Phèdre*: Levels of Comprehension", in *Studi francesi*, 68, 1979.

Ph. Sellier, "De la tragédie considérée comme une liturgie funèbre", in *L'Information littéraire*, January–February 1979.

D.C. Shaw, "The Ambiguity of *Phèdre*", in *Nottingham French Studies*, vol.19, no.1, 1980.

J.-M. Pelous, "Métaphores et figures de l'amour dans *Phèdre*", in *Travaux de linguistique et de littérature*, 2, 1981.

Anne Ubersfeld, "The Space of *Phèdre*", in *Poetics Today*, vol.2 no.3, 1981.

Elizabeth L. Berg, "Impossible Representation: A Reading of *Phèdre*", in *Romanic Review*, vol.73 no.4, 1982.

Peter France, "Myth and Modernity: Racine's *Phèdre*", in *Myth and Legend in French Literature*, edited by Keith

Apsley, David Bellos, and Peter Sharratt, London, 1982.

Hugh Gaston Hall, "A Propos de *Phèdre*: Quatre Schémas mythologiques", in *La Mythologie au XVIIIe siècle*, Marseille, 1982.

K.J. Phillips, "Enclosing Designs in Racine's *Phèdre*", in *Romanic Review*, vol.73 no.4, 1982.

A.G. Branan, "*Dramatis Res* and *Couleur mythologique* in Racine's *Phèdre*", in *Romance Notes*, vol.23 no.1, 1983.

Pierre Han, "Terme fatal: Accouchement comme métaphore ironique dans *Phèdre*", in *Revue Belge de philologie et d'histoire*, 3, 1983.

Martine Reid, "Tout *Phèdre*, une histoire d'enfants", in *Papers on French Seventeenth-Century Literature*, vol.11 no.21, 1984.

Ade Ojo, "Le Théâtre de Racine et le public contemporain: L'Example de *Phèdre*", in *Revue d'histoire du théâtre*, vol.37 no.3, 1985.

Claude Abraham, "Une Aventure théâtrale en classe: *Phèdre*", in *French Review*, vol.60 no.2, 1986.

Maria L. Assad, "Une Réponse classique à la crise de la culture: *Phèdre*", in *Papers on French Seventeenth-Century Literature*, vol.13 no.25, 1986.

Harriet A. Stone, "The Seduction of the Father in *Phèdre* and *Athalie*", in *Actes de Baton Rouge*, edited by Selma A. Zebouni, Paris, 1986.

Françoise Siguret, "'Le Ciel avec horreur voit ce monstre sauvage': Genèse de textes et d'images", in *Papers on French Seventeenth-Century Literature*, vol.14 no.26, 1987.

Norman Burford, "Liturgical Structures in Racine's *Phèdre*", in *Papers on French Seventeenth-Century Literature*, vol.15 no.29, 1988.

Laurence de Looze, "*Dire, Devoir*, and the Conditional Mode of Discourse in Racine's *Phèdre*", in *French Forum*, vol.13 no.3, 1988.

Alain Liepitz, "*Phèdre*: Identification d'un crime", in *Temps modernes*, 43, 1988.

William Franklin Panici, "Le Champ élargissant de *Phèdre*", in *Papers on French Seventeenth-Century Literature*, vol.15 no.28, 1988.

Constant Venesoen, "Genèse mythologique du *Récit de Théramène*", in *Papers on French Seventeenth-Century Literature*, vol.16 no.30, 1989.

*   *   *

Racine's masterpiece, inspired by Euripides' play *Hippolytus*, is a recreation of an episode late in the life of the legendary Theseus. Theseus has travelled far from his kingdom of Troezen, leaving his wife, Phaedra, in charge. She is the daughter of Minos and Pasiphae, the ill-fated King and Queen of Crete. Her whole family was cursed by Venus, various members being condemned to experience a monstrous love (Phaedra's mother, Pasiphae, suffered an unnatural passion for a bull and gave birth to the Minotaur). Phaedra reveals to her old nurse, Oenone, that she too is tainted by the curse: she is incestuously in love with her own stepson, Hippolytus—Theseus's son by the Amazon Queen Hippolyta—who is a youth renowned for his valour as a hunter and for his farouche indifference to women. News comes that Theseus has died during his travels; Oenone renews Phaedra's hopes: "your passion is now a normal love". Phaedra makes a declaration of love to Hippolytus. The young prince is horrified, doubly so because he is secretly in love with a captive princess, Aricia. The moment the declaration is made, when it is too late to retract, the news comes that far from being dead, Theseus has returned; it is as though the gods have timed events to confound Phaedra. Neither she nor Hippolytus can conceal their distress when they meet Theseus. Oenone takes over; she persuades Phaedra that Hippolytus will betray her incestuous passion unless he is forestalled by an accusation that it was he who was attempting to rape Phaedra. Oenone speaks to Theseus, who believes her story. Phaedra however is shamed and remorseful at what has been done, and Oenone takes her own life. Phaedra is planning to confess the truth when she learns that Hippolytus and Aricia are in love. Consumed by jealousy, she abandons Hippolytus to his fate, which is swift to strike. Theseus invokes Neptune, and urges the god to destroy his son. The youth is brutally crushed to death by his own bolting horses. Phaedra poisons herself, and comes, dying, to Theseus to tell him the truth.

The fascination of the play lies in the complex interaction between legend and psychology. The characters believe in the supernatural and in the gods: Phaedra is even afraid to kill herself because the ghost of her own father, Minos, will confront her as the judge in the underworld. Convinced that her passion is inflicted on her by Venus, she describes her first sight of Hippolytus as follows: "I felt my body freeze and burn; / I recognized Venus and her fearful fires, / The inescapable torment of those she pursues". Since she feels she is the goddess's victim, she sees herself as passive, incapable of resisting her passion. But all this does not absolve her from experiencing guilt. Her sufferings are intense, and vividly portrayed, so that she oscillates between uncontrollable passion and violent remorse.

The themes of love and guilt, together with the atmosphere of divine intervention, are interwoven throughout the play, affecting the lives of all the characters. The mutual love of Hippolytus and the innocent Aricia contrasts with the violent, guilty passion of Phaedra; but Hippolytus's love is also guilty, since Theseus has explicitly ordered that no man should love Aricia, an enemy princess. The gods seem to have singled out Phaedra as a victim; but other characters can also be seen as their targets. Theseus invokes Neptune, who kills his son according to his instructions, but the god, if he exists, makes sure that the death is reported to Theseus at the very moment that he begins to suspect that Hippolytus was innocent. Each character is destroyed through love; even the nurse Oenone is finally driven to suicide because her excessive love for Phaedra had led her to wrongdoing. Theseus suffers for having been a womanizer in the past. Now he is faced with the humiliating spectacle of his wife, who has, of all women, at last fixed his emotions, writhing in the throes of a monstrous passion for his own son.

The subtlety of the play lies in the fact that although the characters are convinced that the gods exist, Racine leaves room for doubt. Could it be that it is all in the mind, that Phaedra's helpless inability to resist her destructive passion is her own fault? The impression is of an enigmatic world in which the powers above, if they exist, seek only to destroy. Racine draws heavily on Euripides and Seneca for his tragedy, but there are crucial differences. First, he is writing for a Christian audience, which explains his ambivalent approach to Greek legend. Secondly, he emphasizes the impact of love on the personality. To do this, he adds to the individuality of the characters, and examines their reactions to love. This new emphasis also serves to increase the psychological complexity of the play. For example, he invents a new character to enrich the legend, the princess Aricia. Her presence in turn transforms Hippolytus from a cold, unloving worshipper of Diana (or Artemis: the goddess of chastity and hunting) as he is shown in the classical versions, into a further instance of the impact of love on the personality. This aspect also provides a much more complex relationship between stepmother and stepson, since both have experienced passion. Further, it enables Racine to introduce the theme of sexual jealousy when Phaedra discovers that she has a rival, and lastly it gives further colour and importance to Hippolytus, who can now be seen as the centre of his own love tangle.

One of the most admired features of this play is its style. Written in rhyming couplets (like all Racine's tragedies), the language conveys the powerful emotions in simple, pared-down, conventional words. The imagery is understated, but builds up an obsessive power through the reiterated allusions to the flames and torment of love, or to the pitiless light of day that glares down on Phaedra and her shame—light that recalls the sun-god, her ancestor. The formal rules of French, classical versification confine the violent emotions within strict parameters which serve only to emphasize their strength. The characters seem to be struggling to break through the barriers of conventional language in their attempts to free themselves from their horrible, claustrophobic predicament. The final impression is of a starkly pessimistic play.

—Maya Slater

PHÈDRE. See PHAEDRA.

PHILADELPHIA, HERE I COME!
by Brian Friel

First Publication: London, 1965.
First Production: Gate Theatre, Dublin, 28 September 1964.

*   *   *

On the eve of his emigration to Philadelphia, where he has been offered a home by his childless aunt, 25 year-old Gareth O'Donnell of Ballybeg, County Donegal, takes leave of his past with feelings that swing between euphoria and nostalgic regret at leaving the place and people of his childhood. He is represented on stage by two personae, "Public Gar" and "Private Gar". The latter provides a running commentary on Public Gar's behaviour and that of the people in his life, most importantly, his dourly uncommunicative father and the shrewd housekeeper, Madge, the linchpin of the motherless household. Visits from friends and local worthies such as the conventional Canon demonstrate the deadly sameness of Ballybeg life, and flashbacks re-enact Gar's key memories. His romantic passion for Katie Doogan is shown ending in humiliation as she accepts her parents' wish for her to marry someone with better social prospects than Gar's (in his ill-paid, dead-end job as assistant to his grocer father). He re-enacts the meeting with his aunt, when his excitement at her offer of a more opulent, American future alternates with shrinking from her vulgarity. In the final scene, which takes place in the small hours, Gar and his father express, but not to each other, memories of happy moments they shared in Gar's childhood. Madge alone sees how much father and son feel for each other and how they are too inhibited to communicate. The curtain falls on Gar resolving to register every detail of the scene he knows he will carry with him and which will run in his mind, like a film, "over and over again".

This was the play which established Brian Friel's reputation as a leading Irish playwright. Earlier plays like *The Enemy*

Within had been found interesting, but *Philadelphia, Here I Come!* made a powerful impact on those who saw the first production and has remained one of Friel's most frequently revived plays.

Various reasons can be suggested for its special appeal. The play explored a topic of vital interest to the general public—the new wave of emigration sweeping Ireland during a period of depression. It struck a common chord by identifying some of the social reasons for this phenomenon: the stagnation of small-town society; the narrow moral attitudes and sexual inhibition encouraged by an ultra-conservative Church; the lack of career opportunities—or even ordinary social excitement—for young men. Gar has no hope of winning Katie Doogan, although she is seen responding to him emotionally in an excited love episode, because he has neither money nor prospects—he admits to cheating his father on egg sales to make a miserable extra for himself. The Church's grip even on rebellious members of the community is shown in the rosary scene when Gar automatically contributes, as required, to the "monotonous, somnolent drone" while his mind enjoys Walter Mitty type fantasies of sexual adventures in America. He blames the cosy, "arid" Canon for not trying to "translate all this loneliness, this groping, this dreadful bloody buffoonery, into Christian terms that will make life bearable for us all". The schoolmaster who once had aspirations to poetry and learning is a pathetic alcoholic and the noisy "Boys", who swagger in to take leave of Gar, are similarly frustrated; their great show of *macho* devilry, he reflects sadly, will amount to no more than taking an "odd, furtive look" at the English-women sitting knitting in the lounge of the local hotel.

Theatrically, the play offered a new experience by using two actors to represent on stage two different views of one man. Public Gar, the only persona the rest of the characters ever see or hear, is aware of his other self and occasionally talks to him. Friel specifies that he never look at him: Private Gar is "the unseen man, the man within, the conscience, the alter ego, the secret thoughts, the id", and "one cannot look at one's alter ego". Private Gar conducts the ebullient, role-playing fantasies ("Let's git packin', boy. Let's git that li'l ole saddle bag opened and let's git packin' "), which add lively amusement to the play. He is also sardonic, angry (often with himself), and deeply nostalgic. He broods on the beautiful young mother, with her wild, free, peasant ways, whom her son never knew, and obsessively repeats Edmund Burke's lines about Marie Antoinette: "It is now sixteen or seventeen years since I saw the Queen of France, then the Dauphiness, at Versailles". Though he never gets further with the quotation than "and surely never lighted on this orb", the incomplete, vicarious memory adds to an impression of beauty's poignant brevity which could be seen as the strongest single theme in the play. Some have taken the oblique allusion to one of Ireland's greatest orators as strengthening the layer of political concern, with the meanness of the present being compared with past glories.

The use of the "private" persona also allows Friel to interweave, often very amusingly, remarks Gar makes aloud with those his subversive, inner self "thinks". Public Gar says only "aye" when his father asks if he set a rat trap in the store, while Private Gar mocks the dreary repetitiveness of his father's routine, giving him orders—"Repeat slowly after me. Another day over"—which he obeys unwittingly, following ingrained habit. The two selves have a tense debate over the question of whether to accept Aunt Lizzie's offer to make Gar her son. Private shrinks from the vulgarity of her style, Public resists ("Her grammar? Shut up!"). The tension is never resolved between Gar's dislike for American lack of reserve and the plethora of that quality in Ballybeg.

Friel was generally thought to have found his true voice in this play which reflects, in subtle ways, his experience of life in Londonderry, where he was born and brought up in the Catholic minority. He transfers some of the more depressing aspects of that experience to his imagined Ballybeg, fusing them, as Seamus Deane has pointed out (in *A Short History of Irish Literature*, 1986), with impressions of Donegal, the region just across the border, and equally poor, but full of wild beauty. In Gar's mind Ballybeg always has this double aspect. It is the scene of many frustrations, and also of some rare, ecstatic memories. Even the low-level hell-raising with the "Boys" had its joyous side, Private Gar reflects, and his unsatisfactory relationship with his father pains him all the more because he recalls an episode of pure happiness with him during a fishing expedition in his childhood. Much of the play's appeal is due to the affectionate understanding bestowed on all the characters, despite the irritating effect they have on Gar in his critical mood. The play ends on a tender as well as ironic note when Gar and his father, unable to sleep in the last hours before the former's departure for America, recall golden moments, although not the same ones: the divide remains. Madge sees across the gulf of inhibition to the likeness underneath: the father was once "the very same" as the son, "leppin, and eejitin' about an' actin' the clown; as like as two peas". As she goes to bed, the inner self of Gar reminds the other to watch "every movement, every gesture, every little peculiarity", for the memory of the last night at home that he will play "over and over again". Friel leaves them as uncertain as they were at the start: Public Gar still cannot answer his own question, "God, boy, why do you have to leave? Why? Why?". The play has moved behind public issues into the private consciousness, faced with insoluble problems of time, memory, and the hard struggle to communicate with others on the deepest level.

—Katharine Worth

THE PHILADELPHIA STORY
by Philip Barry

First Publication: New York, 1939.
First Production: Shubert Theatre, New York (Theatre Guild), 28 March 1939.

Criticism
(For general works on the author, see *Playwrights* volume)

Articles:
Gary L. Green, "The Author Behind the Author: George Cukor and the Adaptation of *The Philadelphia Story*", in *Film and Literature: A Comparative Approach to Adaptation*, edited by Michael Schoenecke and Wendell Aycock, Lubbock, Texas, 1988.

*   *   *

Philip Barry's social comedy in three acts is set in the house of a rich, high-society Philadelphia family in the 1930's. Tracy Lord, the mercurial, oldest daughter of the family's separated parents, is a divorcee who will, on the morrow, embark on a second marriage to a stuffy, self-made millionaire named George Kittredge. Puritanical about the frailties of others, Tracy has recently divorced a childhood friend, Dexter Haven, for his past alcoholic weakness, and holds no sympathy for her

The Philadephia Story: Duchess Theatre, London, 1949

father, whose escapades with a dancer are to be made the feature of a popular magazine. To avoid public disclosure of a family scandal, Tracy's brother has persuaded the magazine's editor to suppress the story in return for letting two reporters do an inside story on Tracy's wedding. The journalists soon arrive: Mike Connor, an idealistic writer unafraid of venting disapproval of mainline society, and a young woman journalist clearly in love with her colleague. To render their observations harmless, Tracy assumes a deceptive facade and falsely identifies her uncle as her father, whom she has not asked to the wedding. Equilibrium tumbles when the father arrives along with her uninvited first husband, Dexter. When both men are reprimanded by Tracy for showing up, each accuses her of being coldly unforgiving of others' frailties. Disturbed by the accusation, the heroine gives way to a mutually shared attraction with Mike, leading to a kiss and a champagne-inebriated, midnight swim without suits. In realizing that she too is capable of lapses which demonstrate warm, human feelings, Tracy gains a truer measure of herself and a larger tolerance of others. Her bridegroom-to-be learns of the incident, suspects the worst, and demands an explanation on the wedding morning. Fully recognizing his pompousness, Tracy breaks off the engagement and happily accepts Dexter's offer of remarriage, and the wedding takes place with a new bridegroom.

One of Barry's most accomplished works, *The Philadelphia Story* belongs to a small group of his social comedies, *Holiday* among them, dealing with the nature of marriage and the life of the upper classes—the stratum of society from which the author sprang and which he knew well. These refined comedies represent the most successful category of Barry's work, departing from his larger group of plays treating serious religious, moral, and psychological questions often developed in symbolic or fantastic form as in *Hotel Universe*. However, moral concerns remain essential ingredients in his comedies, including *The Philadelphia Story*.

Underlying the wittily and elegantly presented portrait of Philadelphia's mainline society, there is a theme which questions class mores and conventional ideas about marriage, advocating the value of tolerance. Tracy, the focal character, only has the possibility of self-fulfillment and hope for a happy marriage if she fully realizes that her nature is humanly frail and her lack of tolerance (and that in others) reprehensible. Having been quick to condemn the human frailties of her former husband and her father, she is shaken when told by them individually that her intolerance of weakness renders her a cold "Virgin Goddess" whose sinless high standards only spur on transgressions by others. When, however, she recalls her affectionately intoxicated, unrestrained "skinny-dipping" escapade with Mike on the eve of the wedding, from which she had emerged chaste owing only to Mike's gentlemanly behavior, she learns that she too is capable of the same lively, hedonistic impulses she has condemned in others.

Embodying the thematic thrust of the play, Tracy's growth forms the spine of the action. The intolerant heroine is surrounded by several people committed to their prejudices and a refusal to accept ideas or behavior that differ from their own. Together with her class and family, she shares a suspicion and dislike of reporters, whom she sees, initially, as spying intruders with no manners or sensitivity until she realizes Mike's dimension as a writer and human being. Yet Mike, who like her fiancé George is her social inferior, has the inverted snobbery of the proletarian intellectual who perceives the rich as non-productive, social parasites. George is a parvenu who has embraced the restrictive conventionality of the moneyed, upper class to which he aspires, and he expects the unconventional Tracy to fit his image of a wife. Upon discovering his fiancée's behavior with Mike, and shocked by it, his nasty reaction and demand for explanation reveal him to Tracy as the stuffed shirt he is. She then breaks off the engagement and kindly rejects a marriage proposal from Mike to accept that of Dexter, her tolerant first husband who has always understood and loved her. Her final decision reflects the central character's culmination of a journey toward self-understanding, tolerance, and humanity.

A fine example of its genre, *The Philadelphia Story* demonstrates its author's skilled craftsmanship in creating the milieu of high society peopled by three-dimensional, interesting characters within a well-structured and highly polished comic plot. The plot, whose humorous action arises from an attempt to keep a private scandal from exposure by the press, richly provides comic complications, confrontations, and revelations typical of an effective comedy of manners. In terms of characterization, the figure of Tracy Lord (which was written for, and was the springboard to fame for, Katharine Hepburn, both in the original and successful Broadway production and the subsequent motion picture version) remains a stunning portrait of an intelligent young woman who discovers tolerance and humanity. Reversing a typical pattern of the genre, the author shows in George Kittredge a man risen from the ranks who turns out to be a prig, and in Dexter Haven a man from society's upper crust who proves himself to be gallant and understanding. Also interestingly drawn are such characters as reporter Mike Connor, Tracy's unpredictable and hoydenish younger sister, and an uncle fond of pinching ladies' bottoms.

A successful 1980 Broadway revival gave proof of the play's

durability, as have its frequent productions in regional theatre. With *The Philadelphia Story*, Barry has earned a firm place in American letters as an elegant writer of social comedy.

—Christian H. Moe

THE PHILANTHROPIST
by Christopher Hampton

First Publication: London, 1970.
First Production: Royal Court Theatre, London, 3 August 1970.

Criticism
(For general works on the author, see *Playwrights* volume)

Articles:
Douglas Colby, " 'An Act of suicide': *The Philanthropist* by Christopher Hampton", in his *As the Curtain Rises: On Contemporary British Drama 1966–1976*, Rutherford, New Jersey, 1978.
Ruth M. Schneider, "A Comedy of Manners in a World Gone Mad: Christopher Hampton's *The Philanthropist*", in *Horizontes*, 43, 1978.
Günther Blaicher, "Die Komödie im permissiven Zeitalter: zur Normenproblematik in Christopher Hamptons *The Philanthropist* (1970)", in *Germanisch-Romanische Monatsschrift*, 35, 1985.

* * *

The Philanthropist (1970), Christopher Hampton's witty and elegant satire of English life, opens with a man literally blowing his brains out—a definite *coup de théâtre*, but an event that appears to have nothing to do with the scenes that follow. Hampton creates this seeming disjunction deliberately; in the Oxbridge circle so brilliantly anatomized in this "Bourgeois Comedy" (the play's subtitle), all the violence and perversity swirling around it in the "external" world is simply ignored. And that external world is *drenched* in violence: the Prime Minister and most of the Cabinet have been assassinated by a retired lieutenant-colonel masquerading as an innocuous granny; a disillusioned student sets fire to his college; and a lunatic group called F.A.T.A.L.—Fellowship of Allied Terrorists Against Literature—is poised to murder 25 of the most eminent English writers. With the exception of the opening-scene bloodbath, however, the "external" violence in the play is all narrated rather than directly enacted—and rightly so, for this gaggle of academics seem to view the world outside their cosy college rooms as a kind of fiction, a tall tale that is never really permitted to impinge on their own egocentric concerns.

Hampton's central character, the philanthropist of the title (appropriately named *Phil*ip), is a lover not only of humanity but also of words (he lectures in philology). During the course of the play, all of which is set in Philip's room at college, his philanthropy manages, paradoxically, to alienate almost everyone he encounters: the aspiring student dramatist, John; the crudely obnoxious, right-wing novelist, Braham Head; Araminta, "quickest drawers in the faculty", who cajoles Philip into bed with disastrous results; and, most crucially of all, his fiancée, Celia, who breaks off their engagement because of Philip's weakness ("I haven't even got the courage

of my lack of convictions", Philip confesses). At the play's close, this lover of humanity is left utterly alone on stage with a pistol in his hand and, as he informs his colleague Don on the telephone, "about to do something terrible". He then turns the pistol towards him and pulls the trigger—an event that brings the play full circle. But Philip doesn't blow his brains out; instead, "a small flame springs from the hammer", with which Philip lights a cigarette. This is the "something terrible" this reformed smoker has warned of—a suitably bland "suicide" for such a nonentity.

As a satire both of bourgeois decadence and of a desire to please so profound that it becomes a crippling liability, *The Philanthropist* works wonderfully as a self-contained comedy. But the play becomes infinitely richer when seen as a sardonic riposte to Molière's 17th-century masterpiece, *Le Misanthrope*. Hampton cunningly provides a number of subtle clues to his play's French "parentage": thus all of his seven characters have specific counterparts in Molière, and sometimes similar names (Celia, for example, is an updated Célimène); and Braham at one point tells of encountering an American tourist at the Comédie-Française who plaintively asks him what the play they are watching is about: "So I said, 'Well, madam, it's about a man who hates humanity so much that he would undoubtedly refuse to explain the plot of a world-famous play to an ignorant tourist' ".

Like *The Misanthrope*, *The Philanthropist* satirizes a corrupt, hermetic, monstrously vain and bitchy world in which hypocrisy and back-stabbing exist under a shell of clever repartee. And like an inverted Alceste, Molière's misanthrope, it is the philanthropist Philip who acts as primary satiric agent: his guilelessness and essential sweetness unconsciously expose the moral bankruptcy of the others (Hampton has stated that he conceived of each of his characters as embodying one of the seven deadly sins). But Hampton's satire, again like Molière's, is a double-edged sword: like Alceste, Philip is both agent and *victim* of the satire. Alceste's punctilious honesty, while clearly exposing the duplicitousness of his society, is so rigid and inflexible that it too begins to strike us as a flaw; and the same can be said of Philip's virtues. On one level, of course, the two protagonists are at opposite extremes, but like all opposites they ultimately begin to merge. Philip's philanthropy is as foolish, in its own way, as Alceste's misanthropy: bred not out of genuine love for humanity but out of a profound loneliness, a desire to be liked so intense that Philip refers to it as a "terror". This compulsion to please forces him to suppress his own ego so ruthlessly that finally there is no real "self" left. Philip's refusal to engage in critical judgment in order to embrace everybody is thus ironically parallel to, and equally absurd as, Alceste's refusal to suspend critical judgment in order to embrace nobody: both characters end up as emotional hermits.

For all its lightness of wit, *The Philanthropist* is, in some ways, an even "darker" comedy than *The Misanthrope*. All that violence in the play's background, however humorously treated, inevitably begins to "bleed" into the foreground: whereas social tension in Molière leads only to endless litigation, in Hampton it results in murder (literal assassination rather than simply character assassination). Equally grim is Hampton's handling of his counterpart's to Molière's *raisonneurs*, Philinte and Eliante, those exemplars of sense and moderation in a corrupt world; Hampton's Philinte (Don) is utterly cynical and apathetic, while his Eliante (Liz), in the single scene in which she appears, is totally silent: in Hampton's mordant satire, goodness no longer has a voice. Finally, and most ironically, the tone is considerably darkened with the switch in title character from misanthropist to philanthropist. "I wanted to create a character", Hampton has noted, "who was exactly the opposite of Molière's—but exactly the same things happen to him, which shows how times have changed. A different kind of man is unpopular now". Molière's characters understandably became angry when faced with Alceste's constant carping and criticism; Hampton's characters, by contrast, become angry when faced with Philip's gentleness and lack of guile, assuming there *must* be a hidden "knife" somewhere.

—Hersh Zeifman

PHILASTER; or, Love Lies A-Bleeding
by Francis Beaumont and John Fletcher

First Publication: London, 1620.
First Production: Globe Theatre, London (King's Men), c. 1608–10.

Editions

Philaster, edited by F.S. Boas, London, 1898.
Philaster, in *Philaster; The Maid's Tragedy*, edited by Ashley H. Thorndike, Boston, 1906.
Philaster, in *Elizabethan Plays*, edited by Hazelton Spencer, Boston, 1933.
Philaster, edited by Andrew Gurr, London, 1969 (Revels Plays).
Philaster, edited by Dora Jean Ashe, Lincoln, Nebraska, 1974 (Regents Renaissance Drama Series).

Criticism
(For general works on the authors, see *Playwrights* volume)

Articles:
J.H. Schutt, "*Philaster* considered as a Work of Literary Art", in *English Studies*, 6, 1924.
Mary G.M. Adkins, "The Citizens in *Philaster*: Their Function and Significance", in *Studies in Philology*, 43, 1946.
James E. Savage, "Beaumont and Fletcher's *Philaster* and Sidney's *Arcadia*", in *English Literary History*, 14, 1947.
James E. Savage, "The 'Gaping Wounds' in the Text of *Philaster*", in *Philological Quarterly*, 28, 1949.
Harold A. Wilson, "*Philaster* and *Cymbeline*", in *English Institute Essays*, 1951.
Peter Davison, "The Serious Concerns of *Philaster*", in *English Literary History*, 30, 1963.
D. Jerry White, "Irony and the Three Temptations in *Philaster*", in *Thoth: Syracuse University Graduate Studies in English*, 15, 1975.
Lee Bliss, "Three Plays in One: Shakespeare and *Philaster*", in *Medieval and Renaissance Drama in England*, 2, 1985.
Nicholas F. Radel, " 'Then Thus I Turne My Language to You': The Transformation of Theatrical Language in *Philaster*", in *Medieval and Renaissance Drama in England*, 3, 1986.

*   *   *

The King of Calabria has usurped the throne of Sicily even though the true heir, Philaster, lives, beloved of the people. To strengthen his position, the King intends to marry his daughter, Arethusa, to the braggart Spanish prince Pharamond. Arethusa, however, loves Philaster, who returns her love, in

Philaster: Woodcut from frontispiece, 1620 edition

token of which he places in her service his loyal and affectionate page, Bellario. When Pharamond and the lustful, court lady Megra are discovered in bed together, Megra, in revenge, accuses Arethusa of a sexual liaison with Bellario. Lord Dion, desiring Philaster to lead an uprising and regain his throne, tells him of Arethusa's supposed fornication. Philaster is torn between anger and despair but finally believes the falsehood despite Bellario's protestations of innocence. The court goes hunting; Arethusa, Bellario, and Philaster, each despairing and desiring death, wander through the woods, where they variously encounter and misunderstand one another. Philaster wounds Arethusa and then Bellario to make it appear that the page has stabbed the princess, but when Bellario tries to save him from his pursuers, Philaster repents and admits his guilt. In prison Philaster is forgiven by Bellario and Arethusa, and she then marries him. The King is forced to accept the marriage when the citizens rise in Philaster's defence and capture Pharamond. In the last scene Megra again accuses Arethusa and Bellario of fornication. About to be tortured to tell the truth, Bellario reveals that he is, in fact, Lord Dion's daughter, Euphrasia, who, out of love for Philaster, disguised herself as a boy to be near him. Arethusa's innocence is thus proven beyond a doubt, and the play, formally at least, ends happily.

Philaster combines pseudo-history and pastoral romance with situations drawn from Shakespeare's *Hamlet, Othello*, and *Twelfth Night*. Beaumont wrote much the greater portion of *Philaster*, though the play's design follows the pattern of Guarinian tragicomedy that Fletcher established in *The Faithful Shepherdess* and defined in his preface to the earlier play. *Philaster* typifies Guarinian–Fletcherian tragicomedy in several ways: it deals with noble characters engaged in private actions (the political plot serves primarily as a frame for the characters' personal concerns); it mingles high-born and humble, serious and comic characters; and it introduces the danger of death but allows no one to die. Through clues (that Bellario is really a girl, for example) and through the careful manipulation of emotional effects, the dramatists lead us to expect a happy ending. Though Beaumont and Fletcher engage our sympathy for Philaster, Arethusa, and Bellario, they also moderate our response to the characters' suffering by undercutting comically the serious episodes and by their overt use of artifice both in the management of the plot and in the rhetorical expression of emotion.

Philaster, himself, perfectly illustrates the dramatists' tragi-comic techniques. Melancholy, dispossessed, and grieving for his dead father, he has initially the tragic aura of a Hamlet, but his extreme and sudden shifts of mood, his rhetorical hyperbole, and his offers to kill, variously, Bellario, Arethusa, and himself make it impossible to take him entirely seriously and so distance us from his misery. The following speech, for example, illustrates the comic potential of Philaster's wild emotional shifts. He has just decided to be calm and ask Arethusa the truth, when he comes across Bellario bending over the princess, who has fainted. Instantly he misconstrues the situation: "I will be temperate / In speaking, and as just in hearing.— / Oh monstrous! Tempt me not, you gods, good gods / Tempt not a fraile man". Though Philaster expresses his agony here, the juxtaposition of his determination to keep his temper with the instant loss of it is comic in its incongruity. Furthermore, the speech's carefully deployed rhetoric—balanced phrases, chiasmus—also serves to disengage the audience from Philaster's suffering by drawing attention to its own virtuosity.

The scene in which this episode occurs also illustrates the subject matter and handling of perspective that are typical of Beaumont and Fletcher's tragicomedies. Their chief topic is sexuality, which the plays' genre connects to both death and laughter. In Act IV, Scene 5, after first seeking death himself, Philaster provides the danger of death required by Fletcherian tragicomedy by stabbing Arethusa (and in the next scene Bellario). Psychologically, his act is obviously a symbolic fulfillment of his own frustrated sexuality. Arethusa, too, shares this view of death as sexual consummation: "If my fortune be so good, to let me fall / Upon thy hand, I shall have peace in death". The morbid view of sex and the tragic tone of the scene are relieved, however, by the intrusion of a country fellow, who rescues Arethusa and provides a common-sense perspective on Philaster's cowardly behaviour. Beaumont and Fletcher offer an ironic critique of their protagonists' absurdity and also of their own tragicomic construct in Arethusa's strained rebuke to the Country Fellow—"What ill-bred man art thou, to intrude thy selfe / Upon our private sports, our recreations"—and in his inability to understand the "rethoricke"—of his social superiors. The combination of the painful and the ridiculous in the lovers' confused experience of sexuality helps to make them recognizable human beings with whom we can sympathize, despite their extraordinary behaviour. At the same time the overt artifice in the dramatists' handling of tragicomic perspective makes bearable a painful situation and reassures us of the play's overall comic design.

Beaumont and Fletcher's skilful manipulation of plot—the citizens' rising, the discovery of Bellario's identity—brings the characters out of their difficulties. But though Philaster is restored to his kingdom and happily married to Arethusa, the continued presence in the royal household of the lovelorn Euphrasia contributes a disquieting note to the play's final harmony. The play's integrity lies in its refusal to tie up loose ends. *Philaster* is tragicomic to the end.

—Verna A. Foster

PHILOCTETES (Philoktetes)
by Sophocles

First Production: Athens, 409 B.C.

Editions
Philoctetes, edited by Frederick H.M. Blaydes, London, 1870.
Philoctetes [with translation], edited and translated by Sir Richard Jebb, Cambridge, 1890; abridged edition (Greek only), 1923.
Philoctetes, in *Sophoclis Fabulae*, edited by A.C. Pearson, Cambridge, 1924.
Philoctetes, edited by T.B.L. Webster, Cambridge, 1970.
Philoctetes [with translation], edited by R.G. Ussher, Warminster, Wiltshire, 1990.
Philoctetes, in *Sophoclis Fabulae*, edited by Hugh Lloyd-Jones and N.G. Wilson, Oxford, 1990 (Oxford Classical Texts).

Translations
Philoctetes, in *"Electra" and Other Plays*, translated by E.F. Walting, Harmondsworth, 1953.
Philoctetes, translated by Kathleen Freeman, in *Ten Greek Plays*, edited by L.R. Lind, Boston, 1957.
Philoctetes, in *Philoctetes; The Women of Trachis*, Boston, 1966.
Philoctetes, in *Electra; Antigone; Philoctetes*, translated by Kenneth McLeish, Cambridge, 1979.

Criticism
(For general works on the author, see *Playwrights* volume)

Books:
I.M. Linforth, *Philoctetes: The Play and the Man*, Berkeley, California, 1956 (University of California Publications in Classical Philology).
J.P. Poe, *Heroism and Divine Justice in Sophocles' "Philoctetes"*, Leiden, 1974.
J.C. Kamerbeek, *The Plays of Sophocles: Commentaries, 6: The "Philoctetes"*, Leiden, 1980.

Articles:
W.J. Woodhouse, "The Scenic Arrangements of the *Philoctetes* of Sophocles", in *Journal of the Hellenic Society*, 32, 1912.
A.R. Bellinger, "Achilles' Son and Achilles", in *Yale Classical Studies*, 6, 1939.
E. Wilson, "*Philoctetes*: The Wound and the Bow", in his *The Wound and the Bow: Seven Studies in Literature*, New York, 1941.
J.P. Kieffer, "Philoctetes and Arete", in *Classical Philology*, 37, 1942.
N.T. Pratt, "Sophoclean Orthodoxy in the *Philoctetes*", in *American Journal of Philology*", 70, 1949.
M.H. Jameson, "Politics and the *Philoctetes*", in *Classical Philology*, 51, 1956.
Philip W. Harsh, "The Role of the Bow in the *Philoctetes* of Sophocles", in *American Journal of Philology*, 81, 1960.
Lilian Feder, "The Symbol of the Desert Island in Sophocles' *Philoctetes*", in *Drama Survey*, 3, 1963.
B.M.W. Knox, "*Philoctetes*", in *Arion*, 3, 1964.
Penelope Biggs, "The Disease Theme in Sophocles' *Ajax, Philoctetes*, and *Trachinae*", in *Classical Philology*, 61, 1966.
D. Grene, "*Philoctetes*", in his *Reality and the Heroic Pattern: Last Plays of Ibsen, Shakespeare and Sophocles*, Chicago, 1967.
A.E. Hinds, "The Prophecy of Helenus in Sophocles' *Philoktetes*", in *Classical Quarterly* (new series), 17, 1967.
G. Huxley, "Thersites in Sophokles' *Philoktetes*", in *Greek, Roman and Byzantine Studies*, 1, 1967.
A. Cook, "The Patterning of Effect in Sophocles' *Philoctetes*", in *Arethusa*, 1, 1968.

Philoctetes: National Theatre, London, 1964

R. Skloot, "*Philoctetes*: Wound and Bow Revisited", in *Drama Survey*, 6, 1968.

D.R. Robinson, "Topics in Sophocles' *Philoctetes*", in *Classical Quarterly* (new series), 19, 1969.

C.R. Beye, "Sophocles' *Philoctetes* and the Homeric Embassy", in *Transactions and Proceedings of the American Philological Association* [*TAPA*] 101, 1970.

W.M. Calder III, "Sophoclean Apologia: *Philoctetes*", in *Greek, Roman and Byzantine Studies*, 12, 1971.

Oliver Taplin, "Significant Actions in Sophocles' *Philoctetes*", in *Greek, Roman and Byzantine Studies*, 12, 1971.

D. Seale, "The Element of Surprise in Sophocles' *Philoctetes*", in *Bulletin of the Institute of Classical Studies* (London), 19, 1972.

S.C. Schucard, "Some Developments in Sophocles' Late Plays of Intrigue", in *Classical Journal*, 69, 1973.

C. Fuqua, "Studies in the Use of Myth in Sophocles' *Philoctetes* and the *Orestes* of Euripides", in *Traditio*, 32, 1976.

C. Segal, "Philoctetes and the Imperishable Piety", in *Hermes*, 105, 1977.

Christopher Gill, "Bow, Oracle, and Epiphany in Sophocles' *Philoctetes*", in *Greece and Rome*, vol.27 no.2, 1980.

Oliver Taplin, "The Mapping of Sophocles' *Philoctetes*", in *Bulletin of the Institute of Classical Studies* (London), 34, 1987.

*   *   *

On the way to Troy, the Greek hero, Philoctetes, received a snake-bite in the foot. The wound festered and his comrades abandoned him on the island of Lemnos with only his bow to help him survive—a miraculous bow given to him by Heracles. After several years of an unsuccessful campaign at Troy, the Greeks discover that they will never capture the city without the bow. When *Philoctetes* opens, Odysseus and Neoptolemus (son of the dead hero Achilles) have arrived on Lemnos to try and persuade Philoctetes to return with them to Troy. Aware that Philoctetes will never willingly help the Greeks who marooned him, Odysseus decides to use guile. He reckons without the scruples of Neoptolemus who befriends the cripple and ultimately decides to take him home. Only the arrival of Heracles, *ex machina*, persuades Philoctetes and Neoptolemus that their destiny does demand that they go to Troy.

The title role is a massive and a gruelling one. Philoctetes is in constant pain from the gangrenous foot. Despite this, he demonstrates an integrity and honesty honed by years of isolation. So forceful are these elements in his character that the young Neoptolemus, initially content to serve Odysseus, comes to question his own motives and ultimately sides with Philoctetes. The conversion is neither easy nor abrupt. It does provide a powerful focus for the play's balancing of expediency against humanity.

Odysseus, in Sophocles' *Ajax* a pillar of rectitude, is cast in *Philoctetes*, a much later play, as the villain. He spends much of the first scene lurking on the fringe of the action while Neoptolemus takes the risks, investigating Philoctetes' cave, outside of which the action takes place. Later Odysseus contrives a plan which involves a trader in disguise with a counterfeit message. Later still, he stays offstage apparently while calling out to Neoptolemus, too afraid of Philoctetes' bow to risk getting in range. Odysseus' devotion to trickery is positively compulsive.

Neoptolemus, by contrast, emerges as one of the purest characters in Sophocles, lacking even that tiny streak of jealousy in the presence of the man who possesses his father's armour that contrives Deianira's downfall in *Women of Trachis*. Goodness is never an easy quality to portray on stage but in *Philoctetes* Neoptolemus is always seen in contrast to either the go-getting, mealy-mouthed Odysseus or to the self-absorbed, granite-chip Philoctetes. Philoctetes may be the title character and the centre of the play but this is no monodrama.

Though a late piece in Sophocles' career, *Philoctetes* possesses no more than three characters of note and there is no female character. Heracles arrives at the end in a scene which appears strongly influenced by Euripides. The dramatic argument over whether or not Philoctetes should go to Troy is manipulated with skill. Sympathies vary as head vies with heart. Always at the back of the audience's mind is the knowledge that the one thing that the playwright cannot change is a Greek victory against the Trojans. If that could only be achieved with Philoctetes and his bow at Troy, then that is how the play has to end, whatever the playwright contrives in the interim.

The Euripidean factor is that everything in the play seems to be resolved, yet appears to be heading for the "wrong" ending, with Philoctetes and Neoptolemus about to leave for home. Only the arrival of Heracles, translated to the status of demigod, can convince them that the will of Zeus is that they shall go to Troy. Philoctetes has mastered both the guile of Odysseus and the argument of Neoptolemus. Only the hero who awarded him the bow can prevail over him. As in several plays of Euripides, such an ending is not a confession of weakness by the playwright but a hugely effective means of putting into perspective all the main actions of the play.

The presence of the bow as an object of significance gives a visual dimension to the series of stage conflicts. The person who is holding the bow holds the key to what will happen next, and the tension generated when Philoctetes decides—at that time, unwisely—that he can trust Neoptolemus with it is almost tangible. Philoctetes' island is a place where he has had to survive with the minimum of physical resources and the play points to this in a series of contrasts: his bow and his bandages, his status and the cave where he lives, the physical prowess of Achilles's son compared with a castaway's limp. *Philoctetes* is a play of extremes.

The shape of the piece shows how far Greek tragedy had developed from the time when Sophocles first began to present plays and Aeschylus was his living rival, to the last decade of the fifth century B.C. nearly 60 years later, when he and Euripides were the grand old men of the Athenian stage. All three tragedians wrote a *Philoctetes*. Sadly the other versions have not survived. The storyline might at first sight seem to

offer limited dramatic possibilities but Sophocles demonstrates with some clarity the links between physical and emotional pain which no one can hope fully to escape.

—J. Michael Walton

———

PHILOKTETES. See **PHILOCTETES.**

———

PHORMIO
by Terence

First Production: Rome, c. 161 B.C.

Editions
The "Phormio" of Terence, edited by W.C. Laming, London, 1902.
Phormio, in The Comedies of Terence, edited by Sidney G. Ashmore, New York, 1908.
Phormio [with translation], in Terence, 2, edited and translated by John Sargeaunt, London and New York, 1912 (Loeb Classical Library).
Phormio, in Terenti Afri Comoediae, edited by Robert Kauer and Wallace M. Lindsay, Oxford, 1926.
Phormio, edited by R.H. Martin, Letchworth, Hampshire, 1959; corrected edition, 1964.

Translations
Phormio, translated by Barrett H. Clark, New York, 1915.
Phormio, in The Plays of Terence, translated by William Ritchie, London, 1927.
The "Phormio" of Terence, translated by F. Perry, London, 1929.
Phormio, in The Complete Roman Drama, edited by George Duckworth, New York, 1942.
Phormio, translated by Frank O. Copley, New York, 1958.
Phormio, in Roman Drama, translated by Samuel L. Liebermann, New York, 1964.
Phormio, in "Phormio" and Other Plays, translated by Betty Radice, Harmondsworth, 1967; revised version, in Terence: The Comedies, Harmondsworth, 1976.
Phormio, in The Complete Comedies of Terence, translated by Palmer Bovie, Constance Carrier, and Douglass Parker, edited by Palmer Bovie, New Brunswick, New Jersey, 1974.

Criticism
(For general works on the author, see *Playwrights* volume)

Articles:
W.G. Arnott, "Phormio Parasitus: A Study in Dramatic Methods of Characterization", in Greece and Rome (second series), 17, 1970.
R.K. Bohm, "Money Matters in Phormio", in Classical World, 70, 1976.

*   *   *

While the elderly brothers Chremes and Demipho are away in Lemnos, their respective sons Phaedria and Antipho both fall in love: Phaedria with the expensive slave Pamphila, Antipho with the penniless orphan Phanium, who, unknown to all, is really Chremes' own daughter by a bigamous marriage in Lemnos. Geta, Antipho's resourceful slave, enlists the help of the professional freeloader Phormio, who brings a bogus suit under Athenian law to force Antipho to marry Phanium; by arrangement Antipho throws the defence, and the marriage goes ahead. On their return, the outraged Demipho and Chremes pay Phormio to dissolve Antipho's marriage and marry Phanium himself. Phormio, who has no intention of complying, promptly hands the cash to Phaedria, who uses it to buy Pamphila. Too late, Chremes discovers that his nephew's wife is his own missing daughter, and tries to recover the cash; but Phormio, far from obliging, now exploits Chremes' bigamous secret by exposing it to Chremes' legitimate wife Nausistrata, and all but the weaselly Chremes get their wishes.

No summary can capture the bizarre convolutions of this supremely Terentian plot, adapted with more than his usual fidelity from the lost Greek *Epidikazomenos* of Apollodorus of Carystus. The intricate ironic symmetries are typical: contrasted pairs of fathers, sons, girls, houses, with complementary love-plots intertwining around the pairs. With elegant perversity, each cousin finds himself jealous of the other's predicament—Antipho envies Phaedria's freedom of action, while Phaedria covets Antipho's having and holding. Typical, too, are the gleefully paradoxical coincidences. Chremes travels to Lemnos in search of his family, and with the intention of marrying his secret daughter to Antipho—only to miss them because they have left for Athens in search of him, and to return to find that his very absence has resulted in the couple's meeting and marrying by pure chance. And meanwhile, the courtroom bluffs that Phanium is a freeborn Athenian and Antipho her kinsman turn out to be nothing less than the truth.

Terence slyly claims to have changed the title to highlight the flamboyant Phormio. In fact the change owes more to the Greek title's reference to the obscure (to Romans) Athenian law of *epidikasia*, under which orphaned heiresses had to be married to their nearest, eligible male kin, or else provided with a dowry by the same. Terence's other interventions are structurally minimal, though he seems to have increased the plot's demands on the audience by boldly suppressing any early exposition of the truth of Chremes' bigamy. He also, characteristically, takes the opportunity to layer in extra local ironic complications with the addition of fourth characters in the intricate scenes 606 ff. and 990 ff. The latter, especially, is perhaps the most astonishingly crafted display of human clockwork anywhere in ancient drama, dizzily showcasing Terence's unparalleled gift for rapidly intercut dialogue in three or more voices.

Terence had learned a good deal from the recent triumph of his *Eunuch*, his first compromise attempt at a broader, more Plautine comic style than the austerely brilliant abstractions of his early plots. Thus *Phormio* features a wily slave, an amoral pimp, and even a *parasitus* hero in the mould of Plautus's *Curculio*. But the veneer of farce is this time laid over a complex human comedy of citizen values, exploring Terence's favoured terrain of love, law, authority, and the family, and the labyrinthine codes of responsibility that bind the characters within each. As generally in Terence, the citizen love-plot comes to dominate the play's interest, with the more spirited Phaedria's purely pecuniary romantic difficulties driven progressively offstage. Even the master of intrigue Phormio, an inspired and deservedly influential creation, is a citizen hero barely recognisable as a descendant of the marginalised, Plautine sponger, and quite against the grain of the subversive, Plautine slave: a manipulator of the institutions of free society such as law, dowries, and betrothal, and a virtuoso leading player in his own impersonations. Only the parasite's free-floating detachment from visible family or home, the roots of citizen identity in New Comedy, remain from the stereotype to authorise Phormio's free hand in the interests of others.

In a sense, though, the real centre of the plot is not Phormio but his elusive antagonist, the hapless Chremes—whose 15 years' guilty secret haunts both the man and his household, and who finally pays by seeing his arch-enemy Phormio admitted by his wife to the family table. Chremes' crime, within the codes of New Comedy, is more against the family than against the direct victim, the woman he raped and then married in Lemnos 15 years before the play starts, and has since supported by diverting revenue from his wife's dowry estates. The genre's notoriously casual view of premarital rape cannot tolerate Chremes' offence, unparalleled elsewhere, of rape by a married man, and so Chremes' personal, financial, and domestic humiliation are a necessary consequence of his lapse. Yet it is Chremes who gets perhaps the play's best line: informed that his daughter has married Antipho, whom Chremes still believes married to an unidentified orphan stranger, the bigamous Chremes blurts "What? *He's* got two wives?". Few lines in Terence better sum up the playwright's delight in psychology, irony, and the preposterous moment.

—N.J. Lowe

THE PHYSICISTS (Die Physiker)
by Friedrich Dürrenmatt

First Publication: Zurich, 1962; revised version in *Werkausgaber*, 1962.
First Production: Schauspielhaus, Zurich, 20 February 1962.

Criticism
(For general works on the author, see *Playwrights* volume)

Books:
Oskar Keller, *Friedrich Dürrenmatt: "Die Physiker": Interpretation*, Munich, 1970.
Volker Schüler, *Dürrenmatt: "Der Richter und sein Henker"; "Die Physiker": Dichterbiographie und Interpretation*, Hollfeld, 1976.
Gerhard P. Knapp, *Friedrich Dürrenmatt: "Die Physiker"*, Frankfurt, 1979.

Articles:
Herbert Lehnert, "Fiktionale Struktur und physikalische Realität in Dürrenmatts *Die Physiker*", in *Rice University Studies*, vol.55 no.3, 1969.
Kurt J. Fickert, "The Curtain Speech in Dürrenmatt's *The Physicists*", in *Modern Drama*, 13, 1970.
George C. Forest, "The 'Cosmonauts' Song' in Dürrenmatt's *Physicists*", in *Hartford Studies in Literature*, 2, 1970.
Brian Murdoch, "Dürrenmatt's *Physicists* and the Tragic Tradition", in *Modern Drama*, 13, 1970.
Michael Morley, "Dürrenmatt's Dialogue with Brecht: A Thematic Analysis of *Die Physiker*", in *Modern Drama*, 14, 1971.
Robert W. Corrigan, "Dürrenmatt's *The Physicists* and the Grotesque", in his *The Theatre in Search of a Fix*, New York, 1973.

The Physicists: Schauspielhaus, Zurich, 1962 (first production)

Manfred Durzak, "Die Travestie der Tragödie in Dürrenmatts *Der Besuch der alten Dame* und *Die Physiker*", in *Deutschunterricht*, vol.28 no.6, 1976.

Neville E. Alexander, "Friedrich Dürrenmatt: *Die Physiker*: Die Verantwortung des Forschers", in *Denken und Umdenken: Zu Werk und Wirkung von Werner Heisenberg*, edited by Heinrich Pfeiffer, Munich, 1977.

Sylvia S. Weiss, "Dürrenmatt's *The Physicists*: The Moebius Strip as Structural Analogue", in *STTH: Science / Technology & the Humanities*, 3, 1980.

Gerhard P. Knapp, "Dürrenmatt's *Physicists* as a Turning-Point for the Dramatist and His Concept of History", in *Play Dürrenmatt*, edited by Moshe Lazar, Malibu, California, 1983.

Robert P. Reno, "Science and Prophets in Dürrenmatt's *The Physicists*", in *Renascence*, 37, 1984.

*   *   *

The Physicists, which was completed in 1961, given its first performance in Zurich in 1962 and revised to some degree, (to improve its literary aspect, as opposed to its dramatic qualities) when it was included in Friedrich Dürrenmatt's collective *Werkausgabe*, is an amusing, clever and uncompromisingly disturbing play about the potentially destructive folly of modern science. The everyday drawing-room setting, the patent banalities of the investigation of a murder in a petty-bourgeois environment, the solid construction of a play which respects the Aristotelean unities of time, place, and action—all show up, by contrast, the absurdity of the warping of the human personality and of inter-personal relationships which is the product of the hyper-intellectualisation that may well turn the discoveries of modern physics into the nightmare of an indiscriminate, nuclear holocaust.

In a neat, modern, humane and obviously very expensive, private sanitorium for the mentally sick—to call it a lunatic asylum would give a wholly false impression of the attitudes towards the inmates and suggest something quite different from the ambiance of "Les Crérisiers"—Inspector Voss is conducting, in the time-honoured police style, a murder enquiry; the second, in fact, in three months. The head of the institution, Mathilde von Zahnd, unmarried, rich, and as highly qualified as she is highly regarded in the world of psychiatric medicine, gives very little away. Her patients, she reveals however, are scientists of the highest order, and her policy is always to treat them with kindness and consideration, respecting even their delusions. After all, does it really matter so very much if Ernest Heinrich Ernesti thinks of himself as

Einstein when the only apparent practical consequence is that he likes nothing better than to pass the time playing classical sonatas on the violin? Herbert Georg Beutler's self-identification with Sir Isaac Newton causes even less bother. There is something eerie, it is true, about Beutler's statement that he has, however, assumed the role of the great English scientist only in order to conceal the fact that really it is he who is Einstein—because revealing that piece of information would be bound to upset Ernesti. Still, we let that pass in this odd sanitorium where, as we learn, the nurses are the proud holders of judo and wrestling titles, which, we may note with some consternation, makes it odd that two of their number could not protect themselves better when attacked.

Gradually attention focuses not on the two men who take the names of famous physicists but on another scientist, Johann Wilhelm Möbius. His alienation from the everyday world is brought out in a bizarre episode when his former wife Rose comes, along with her three children and her new husband, a psalm-spouting missionary, to say goodbye. Rose recalls the sacrifices she has made over the years to support Möbius as he devoted himself to the pursuit of scientific truth, but he shows little interest in all this and seems not to care much for his children either. On the departure of his visitors, one of the nurses, Monika, approaches him. She has watched him carefully and knows that he is not really mad. All she asks is that the two should go away together, and she will help him to continue his scientific career which, she is sure, will be a glorious success. His immediate response is to strangle her.

Act Two opens with a distorted replay of Act One. Voss is once again making murder enquiries, and the audience, of course, knows who committed the crime. The attitudes of the director of the sanitorium have, however, undergone a change, though we cannot quite see why. Gradually, through layer upon layer of overlapping deception and confusion, it emerges that Möbius is a physicist who made an enormously important, but potentially utterly destructive discovery. Rather than publish it, he has feigned madness, and he has just killed Monika precisely because she has discovered he was sane and would have revealed his secret to the world. As for the other two "madmen", they are the agents of two great powers, sent to spy on Möbius and steal his discovery. Before they get any further, the true character of Dr Zahnd is shown. Her sanitorium is a prison, complete with iron grilles at the windows and a team of erstwhile pugilists to maintain order. She has, moreover, succeeded in foiling Möbius by ensuring that a photocopy of his thesis, which he had naturally tried to destroy, has been preserved. Powerless to prevent the disasters they foresee, Möbius, Ernesti, and Beutler conclude that they can offer no solutions to the dilemmas they have helped create. It is best, they decide, to retreat once more into the personalities they had adopted earlier. That makes a sombre ending to a comedy that has a lot of laughter and good deal of inventive stage business.

The "Twenty-One Points" about *The Physicists* which Dürrenmatt provided by way of appendix to the play in the collected volume of his *Komödien* in 1962, are cryptic comments that seem to concentrate more on the dramatist's working practices than on his ideology. He begins: "I don't start out from a thesis but rather from a story", and that, he implies, means there has to be an ending. He goes on to state that "a story has been thought through to its end when it has taken its worst possible turn", adding that chance must be allowed its due role in coming to the denouement. Making a comparison with *Œdipus Rex* he stresses the way in which chance hits hardest those very people who lay the most careful plans, with results that are grotesque, but not absurd in the sense of being illogical. On the role of physics in modern

society he insists on the paradoxicality of their endeavours, reminding his readers that though the content of physics is properly the concern of scientists, the consequences of their discoveries and actions concern us all.

—Christopher Smith

DIE PHYSIKER.   See **THE PHYSICISTS.**

DIE PICCOLOMINI.   See **WALLENSTEIN.**

THE PICCOLOMINI .   See **WALLENSTEIN.**

PICNIC
by William Inge

First Publication: New York, 1953.
First Production: Music Box Theatre, New York, 19 February 1953.

Criticism
(For general works on the author, see *Playwrights* volume)

Articles:
Philip M. Armato, "The Bum as Scapegoat in William Inge's *Picnic*", in *Western American Literature*, 10, 1976.
Robert K. Donovan, "The Dionysiac Dance in William Inge's *Picnic*", in *Dance Chronicle*, 7, 1985.
Jane W. Lange, " 'Forces get loose': Social Prophecy in William Inge's *Picnic*", in *Kansas Quarterly*, vol.18 no.4, 1986.
Michael Wentworth, "The Convergence of Fairy Tale and Myth in William Inge's *Picnic*", in *Kansas Quarterly*, vol.18 no.4, 1986.
Eleanor A. Gobrecht, "William Inge's *Picnic*: The Impact of Individualism", in *Tsuda Review*, 32, 1987.

*   *   *

"Women are gettin desperate," says the hunky, unintelligent and unsophisticated Hal Carter to his old college friend, Seymour, and that statement sums up the situation in *Picnic*. William Inge set his Pulitzer Prize-winning drama in a small, Kansas town, the sort of place in which he had himself grown up, with the typical sun-baked landscape of the Midwest with its grain elevator, a great silo, and a railway that seems to be the only link between the endless prairie and the world outside. As in classical drama that respects the unity of place, there is a single setting, a realistic one showing "the porches and the yards of two small houses", and this helps to create a sense of a closed community which receives a stranger into its midst and from which some will want to escape while others realize they cannot. There is also something not unlike the unity of time, the action beginning early one day and finishing a few hours later the following morning, and, still in classical style, the scantiness of action, the most spectacular portions of which occur off-stage, is more than made up for by the great force of psychological tensions as past, present, and future come into sharp focus in the lives of two sets of essentially similar but also sharply differentiated characters. The play takes place on Labor Day, the first Monday in September, which marks the end of the summer and the start of the difficulties of autumn and winter. The irony of it is that this holiday will, as often happens when there is a break from work, be a fraught time of self-questioning and even downright unhappiness; as for the traditional picnic, not only does it, of course, mean extra work for the women, but it is also an occasion when human values will be questioned. This is indeed a Labor Day to remember, but not for the customary reasons.

The two modest houses shown on stage are inhabited by women. The first of them that we see is Mrs Helen Potts, described in the first stage-direction as a "merry, dumpy little woman close to sixty", but we realize before long we should not let ourselves be deceived by appearances. Her life is still largely controlled by her imperious, bed-ridden mother who, years back, had intervened to have her daughter's marriage annulled, and we ask ourselves if it is simply kind-heartedness that impels Helen not to turn away "bums" like Hal when they turn up on her doorstep offering to do odd jobs in return for a bite to eat. Her neighbour, Flo Owens, also has no husband any longer. He had been affectionate enough at the time of the birth of Madge, their first daughter, but was already seeking his pleasure elsewhere when Millie was born a couple of years later on, and soon after he went his way. 18-year-old Madge is "unusually beautiful", and though, according to Inge's stage direction she "seems to take her beauty very much for granted", she puts some effort into making herself attractive, shampooing her hair, painting her nails and so on. Her mother is not slow to point out the need to capitalize on good looks to ensure a comfortable future with a grateful husband. Millie, on the other hand, is more intellectual, a girl who won a scholarship to the local school and likes reading; it is she who says most clearly that she wants a more exciting future than a small town in Kansas can promise. "Anyone mind if an old-maid schoolteacher joins their company?", is the entry line of Rosemary Sydney, who is rooming in Flo's house. She is a miniature masterpiece of characterization, its seemingly resigned self-depreciation paradoxically high-lighting what is really a cry of enraged frustration. The irony becomes perhaps a little too blatant when she is joined by two other spinster representatives of the teaching profession, one of whom specializes in the subject of Feminine Hygiene.

The four male characters are all, in a sense, intruders into this world of women. Bomber, the newpaper boy, makes only brief appearances, but Millie's readiness to quarrel with him is significant of her desire for more than he can ever provide. As for Alan Seymour, he is Madge's beau, a nice enough college lad with some prospects in business in the small town, but he is shy and uncharismatic. His deficiencies of physique and personality are shown up in a most unflattering light by Hal. Anything but economically prosperous, Hal arrives in T-shirt, dungarees, and cowboy boots, ready to undertake menial tasks to assuage his hunger and thirst, but there is no denying the physical attractions of this young man who was able, for a time, to hold down a footballing scholarship at the college Seymour attended. It is true he has not got a lot of brains, and whenever he dreams of the future he talks of a most banal existence. This lack of imagination, like his social gaucheness, does not seem to matter when he appears stripped to the waist, the image of healthy, West Coast manhood. His relationship with Madge is essentially sexual; it is brief too. By the end of the play we realize, however, that though he has played a vital role in her emancipation, he cannot provide her with all that she will need if she is to develop fully. The link between Rosemary and Howard, a middle-aged man in business as a haberdasher, offers a somewhat less serious parallel to the main action of the play as the man who hitherto had been quite content simply to be a steady, if somewhat uninspiring admirer is cajoled into taking the step of at last agreeing to marry her.

Picnic is a powerful play, its homely realism as a portrayal of the life of ordinary people in the Midwest being given a cutting edge as Inge develops his theme with great, psychological insight. Occasionally the contrivance may appear a little too obvious, as is the symbolism too, but in the detail, as in the style of the dialogue, there is much that has the ring of authenticity. All the craftsmanship and observation that make up this very American play are put to the service of a vision of life whose disabused bleakness is redeemed by a breath of a vital optimism that, in the last analysis, refuses to be gainsaid.

In 1955 a filmed version of *Picnic* was released, directed by Joshua Logan. It appears, however, that in the long run, the very success of the film has led to an unjustifiable neglect of *Picnic* as a piece of writing for the stage that is as skilful as it is powerful.

—Christopher Smith

THE PILLARS OF SOCIETY (Samfundets støtter) by Henrik Ibsen

First Publication: Copenhagen, 1877.
First Production: Møllergaten Theatre (in Swedish), Christiana, 6 November 1878; in Norwegian, Bergen, 30 November, 1879.

Translations

The Pillars of Society, translated by William Archer, in *"The Pillars of Society" and Other Plays*, London, 1888; revised version, in *Ibsen: The Collected Works, 6*, edited by William Archer, London, 1906.
The Pillars of Society, in *The Pretenders; Pillars of Society; Rosmersholm*, translated by R. Farquharson Sharp, London, 1913.
The Pillars of the Community, in *Ibsen: Three Plays*, translated by Una Ellis-Fermor, Harmondsworth, 1950.
Pillars of Society, in *The Oxford Ibsen, 5*, edited and translated by James Walter McFarlane, London, 1961.
The Pillars of Society, translated by Michael Meyer, London, 1963; corrected version, in *Ibsen: Plays, 4*, London, 1980.
The Pillars of Society, in *Ibsen: The Complete Prose Plays*, translated by Rolf Fjelde, New York, 1970.

Criticism
(For general works on the author, see *Playwrights* volume)

Articles:
Inga Stina Ewbank, "Drama and Society in Ibsen's *Pillars of the Community*", in *Drama and Society*, edited by James Redmond, Cambridge, 1979 (Themes in Drama Series).

*　　*　　*

Like the later *Enemy of the People*, this play hinges on the conflict between private profit and public good, between bosses and workers. Karsten Bernick, the big businessman and community leader, is "the richest and most powerful man in town". But despite his claims of setting a high moral tone and despite the activities of his wife and her friends in sewing busily for "fallen women", Bernick is living a lie. His initial wealth was dishonestly kept, in that creditors were held at bay while a rumour of theft was spread abroad, and the blame put on his brother-in-law (who left for America); Bernick now makes his money by insuring ships which are unsound. Ibsen is dealing with the contemporary scandal of the "coffin ships" which were sent to sea in deliberately unseaworthy state. Bernick asks for repairs to be done with impossible speed, then arranges for the trade unions to be blamed for bad workmanship and "going slow" as a gesture against the introduction of machinery which is putting men out of work. Bernick is no stranger to sharp practice. During the 1870's—a decade when strenuous efforts were being made to extend Norway's inadequate railway system—he is buying up the land on which the railway was to have been built, because the railway would have competed with his shipping. Bernick may be hedging his bets, because if the railway does come he will make a killing. Pretending to be protecting the area from development, Bernick is setting out to buy up all the forests, all the minerals, all the water-power, in order to create a monopoly.

1875 was the year the Plimsoll Line was introduced for British shipping, with inspection and codification of sea-going vessels. Shipping was a lucrative Norwegian industry: servant girls used to buy shares in boats and cargoes with their savings. But Norway was under pressure, because, though it could produce wooden sailing ships easily enough from local timber and with local craftsmen, it could not compete with the iron steamers which it had neither the ores for, the coal to work, nor the skills to build. Thus the drama turns on a problem of economic development as well as private morality.

Yet while this play holds our attention as a drama of conscience and social observation, it is also highly symbolic, as many critics have pointed out. The coffin ships are crucial to the action and also symbolise the greed and corruption of the shipping companies and the rottenness of the society in which they are enmeshed. Only the workman, Aune—carpenter, craftsman, salt of the earth—resists corruption. Aune is introduced in the opening lines, and is immediately threatened for organising the workforce as a unionist. Yet even Aune is browbeaten into performing hasty and inadequate repairs. He redeems himself at the end, however, by stopping the ship from sailing when circumstances dictate. We find here narrow puritanical morality, based on hypocrisy, and a fundamental conflict he was to develop more fully later. Against this provincial morality is set the urge for freedom, here represented by America and voyages to it. Ibsen anticipated Freud in seeing civilisation as repressive, while recognising at the same time the danger of uncontrolled passion.

Pillars of Society has the potential for tragedy. "The Indian Girl" is to sail with inadequate repairs, a doomed "coffin ship". Bernick's son Olaf runs away from home and stows away on her, and is missed in the nick of time. When he is finally discovered in the hold so Aune takes it upon himself to delay the sailing. The "free spirit" is Lona Hessel, half-sister to Mrs. Bernick, the girl who loved Bernick but whom he did not marry. Emancipated, she has cut her hair short and scandalises the community by wearing men's boots in wet weather. She holds letters which incriminate Bernick, but out of love tears them up. This act of generosity, together with the recovery of his only son, unfreezes Bernick's heart so that at a presentation by the townsfolk he makes a full confession and all ends happily. There is a less interesting subplot concerning the love of the brother-in-law for Dina Dorf, a rebellious orphan. Indeed, there are various supernumary characters, which the mature Ibsen would learn to prune: sisters and brothers and a cousin, Hilmar Tönnesen, whose only function is to be rich and idle, with fantasies of violent action; the doctor's wife and daughter, the postmaster's wife and daughter. Later Ibsen would represent society and its forces more economically.

—Valerie Grosvenor Myer

THE PLAIN DEALER
by William Wycherley

First Publication: London, 1677.
First Production: Theatre Royal, Drury Lane, 11 December 1676.

Editions

The Plain Dealer, in *The Plays of William Wycherley*, edited by Arthur Friedman, Oxford, 1979.
The Plain Dealer, edited by James L. Smith, London, 1979 (New Mermaid Series).
The Plain Dealer, in *The Plays of William Wycherley*, edited by Peter Holland, Cambridge, 1981.
The Plain Dealer, edited by Simon Trussler, London, 1988.

Criticism
(For general works on the author, see *Playwrights* volume)

Articles:
Emmett L. Avery, "*The Plain Dealer* in the Eighteenth Century", in *Research Studies of the State College of Washington*, 11, 1943.
Katharine M. Rogers, "Fatal Inconsistency: Wycherley and *The Plain Dealer*", in *English Literary History*, 25, 1961.
Rose A. Zimbardo, "The Satiric Design in *The Plain Dealer*", in *Studies in English Literature 1500–1900*, 1, 1961.
James L. Shepherd, "Molière and Wycherley's *Plain Dealer*: Further Observations", in *South Central Bulletin*, 23, 1963.
J.M. Auffret, "*The Man of Mode* and *The Plain Dealer*: Common Origin and Parallels", in *Études anglaises*, 19, 1966.
Ian Donaldson, "The 'Tables Turned': *The Plain Dealer*", in *Essays in Criticism*, 17, 1967.
Anthony M. Friedson, "Wycherley and Molière: Satirical Points of View in *The Plain Dealer*", in *Modern Philology*, 64, 1967.
B. Eugene McCarthy, "Wycherley's *The Plain Dealer* and the Limits of Wit", in *English Miscellany*, 22, 1977.
Anthony Kaufmann, "Idealization, Disillusion, and Narcissistic Rage in Wycherley's *The Plain Dealer*", in *Criticism*, 21, 1979.
W. Gerald Marshall, "Wycherley's Drama of Madness: *The Plain Dealer*", in *Philological Quarterly*, 59, 1980.
H. Gaston Hall, "From *Le Misanthrope* to *Le Prude* via *The Plain Dealer*", in *Papers on French Seventeenth Century Literature*, 10, 1983.
Ronald Berman, "Wycherley's Unheroic Society", in *English Literary History*, 51, 1984.
Robert Markley, "Drama, Character, and Irony: Kierkegaard and Wycherley's *The Plain Dealer*", in *Kierkegaard and*

Literature: Irony, Repetition, and Criticism, edited by Ronald Schliefer and Robert Markley, Oklahoma, 1984.

Richard Brauerman, "Libertines and Parasites", in *Restoration*, 11, 1987.

Derek Cohen, "The Alternating Styles of *The Plain Dealer*", in *Restoration and Eighteenth Century Theatre Research* (second series), 2, 1987.

Robert F. Bode, "A Rape and No Rape: Olivia's Bedroom Revisited", in *Restoration*, 12, 1988.

Laura Morrow, "Phenomenological Psychology and the Comic Form in *The Plain Dealer*", in *Restoration and Eighteenth Century Theatre Research* (second series), 3, 1988.

Robert F. Bode, "'Try me, at Least': The Dispensing of Justice in *The Plain Dealer*", in *Restoration and Eighteenth Century Theatre Research* (second series), 4, 1989.

*   *   *

At the opening of Act I, Captain Manly, who has just returned to London from a sea voyage to the Indies, is engaged in an argument with Lord Plausible (a fop who is indiscriminately polite and obliging) about whether the manners of polite society are necessary or are merely forms of affectation and dishonesty. In some respects, *The Plain Dealer* is constructed as a satirical, five-act demonstration of Manly's view that the sophistication of apparently civilised people is, in fact, a vicious form of conventionalised hypocrisy.

As if to prove Manly's point, a dazzling succession of contemporary social ceremonies and types of behaviour is paraded across the stage. During the action a running argument is conducted by Manly and his Lieutenant Freeman; although Freeman shares Manly's awareness of the selfishness and duplicity which is the norm of behaviour in this society, he is "a complier with the age", perhaps as a consequence of being "a gentleman, well-educated, but of a broken fortune". Their disagreement provokes a reflection on the most appropriate way of responding to the realities of social existence. Manly believes that "plain-dealing is a jewel", and refuses to compromise his integrity at all, behaving rudely and aggressively in every social encounter. Freeman's acceptance of the fact that a degree of hypocrisy is the way of the world leads him to adopt the conventional strategy of the witty rake of a typical Restoration comedy of manners: he unashamedly exploits the double standard of society to achieve his own selfish ends. Towards the end of Act I, the illustration of the nature of social relationships is amplified by the introduction of Olivia's cousin, Widow Blackacre, who demands Manly's presence as a witness in a court hearing. In this way, a connection is established between the hypocritical nature of social life and the corrupt legal system which underpins it.

In striking contrast to Act I, a scene of upper-class manners provides the focus of Act II. The lodging of Manly's mistress, Olivia, is the setting for Wycherley's brilliant pastiche of the typically Etheregean scene in which a series of mental combats is played out by witty male and female rakes and fops in such a way as to test the judgment of a spectator, who must distinguish truly witty characters from fashionable fools and hypocrites. Wycherley transforms Etherege's battle of wits into a series of darkly ironic exposures whereby Olivia and the two fops, Novel and Plausible, condemn themselves out of their own mouths as shallow and malicious hypocrites.

In Act III, set in the legal precinct of Westminster Hall, Wycherley's direct and scathing attack on social vice is transformed into a complex and disturbing observation of human psychology. Manly's satirical attack is subverted by Wycherley's portrayal of his naïvety in continuing to love Olivia in spite of his awareness that she embodies all the traits of social affectation and hypocrisy he has so vehemently criticised in others. This naïvety is savagely exposed in the grotesquely comic scene (Act V, Scene 2) where he recounts to his friend Vernish the revenge he has taken on Olivia; Vernish has in fact been secretly married to Olivia and, like her, is ironically an exemplar of the vicious and sophisticated dishonesty which Manly despises. By the end of Act III, Manly's naïvety manifests itself in a more sinister way as an inability to recognise the enormous contradiction between thought and feeling, between the conscious and unconscious aspects of his identity.

Viewed in conjunction with the equivocal behaviour of Olivia and Vernish, Manly's contradictory responses suggest as an inescapable fact of human psychology that people's instincts inevitably compel them to betray their professed social or moral principles. Like Olivia and Vernish, most people are aware of the contradiction between instinct and moral principle, and therefore hypocritically deny their true motives in public while privately acknowledging them; Manly is unusual in at first refusing to believe that he is capable of duplicity or hypocrisy, yet he becomes as ruthlessly determined to pursue his instinctual desire under the guise of moral principle as anyone else in the play.

By contrast, Freeman, in openly accepting the selfish and competitive instincts of his own human nature, at least acts intelligently in accordance with the new rationalistic norms of social behaviour established after the Restoration of the monarchy in 1660. Whereas Freeman overtly attempts to woo the litigious and self-repressed Widow Blackacre, openly manipulating her son Terry in order to gain control over her fortune, Manly sends Fidelia (the young woman who, having followed him to sea disguised as a man, has fallen in love with him) to Olivia in order, in his own words, to "pimp" for him: "Go flatter, lie, kneel, promise, anything to get her for me. I cannot live unless I have her".

At this point, Manly is more blindly a hypocrite than any other character in the play. Various kinds of awareness (both conscious and subconscious) are being brought into play here. An audience is acutely aware that Fidelia is infatuated with Manly, who is infatuated with Olivia, who, in turn, is sexually attracted to the boy she takes Fidelia to be. Wycherley deliberately echoes the ambiguous relation of desire and voyeurism explored in the Viola–Orsino–Olivia triangle in Shakespeare's *Twelfth Night*; but in *The Plain Dealer* feelings of impotence in the face of rejection are immediately experienced as a sado-masochistic drive towards the betrayal of a lover, self-torture, or rape as revenge upon the unattainable object of desire. In Act IV, Scene 2, the status of Manly's attack on society is further called into question as Wycherley parallels Manly's hypocrisy with that of Vernish and Olivia, in a debased form of intrigue comedy that contrives to unmask as a complete sham each character's pretence at upholding even the most basic moral principles. In the dark, all three reveal themselves to be motivated by the crudest form of lust.

Act V, Scene 3 brings the improbable series of unmaskings to a fantastic climax when Fidelia pulls off her peruke to reveal to Manly that she is a woman, who, conveniently (as it turns out) is an heiress with an income of £2,000 a year. The play ends with Manly's somewhat absurd promise of marriage to Fidelia and his glib verse rationalisation of what has happened: "I will believe there are now in the world / Good-natured friends who are not prostitutes, / And handsome women worthy to be friends".

An account of the play's main love intrigue in itself indicates the baroque complications characterising Wycherley's moral and theatrical perspective. Is an audience to take the plot

The Plain Dealer: 18th-century engraving

seriously as an accurate depiction of social behaviour in the period? How much of the play is a burlesque of the artifice inherent in contemporary conventions of both tragedy and comedy? What is an audience to make of the bewildering series of volte-faces which the character of Manly seems easily able to comprehend? What significance can be given to the fact that Eliza (Olivia's cousin) and Freeman (the only two characters who might in any comedy of manners of the period be expected to form a romantic alliance) remain noticeably unattached? Is the denial of this appropriate pairing intended as a cynical reflection on the irony that, after all, Manly and Fidelia are so blind to their own selfishness that they can truly be said to deserve each other?

While generally in agreement about the originality of Wycherley's alternation of a style of savage, Jonsonian satire with a witty, Etheregean presentation of social mores, critics have achieved no consensus on the meaning of this highly self-conscious intermingling of English dramatic traditions. Certainly, the ending of the play seems open to endless possible interpretation. On the evidence of his earlier *The Country Wife*, it seems clear that Wycherley's decision to conclude the play in this way was a conscious, artistic choice. Whether or not one could (or should even try to) determine the playwright's point of view, Wycherley seems to have intended to confound the easy expectations of a Restoration audience at a tragedy or a comedy, in refusing to allow either the strictly moral and unrealistic justice of an heroic tragedy ending, or the amoral and realistic justice of a comic ending.

Instead the artifice of the play is exaggerated to create a grotesque parody of wish-fulfilment fantasy. The villains remain free to pursue their lives of selfish dishonesty, while the naïve are rewarded for having hypocritically followed the dictates of their own corrupted natures. The two characters who are both realistic about the world and honest about themselves remain single. It could be argued that in refusing the easy closure which the conventions of either tragedy or comedy might have supplied, Wycherley throws the responsibility for interpretation upon the audience. This would imply the recognisably modern attitude which insists that the responsibility for interpretation lies with the audience or reader rather than the author.

A comparison of the play with Molière's *Le Misanthrope* or Shakespeare's *Twelfth Night*, the two most obvious sources for *The Plain Dealer*, will serve to emphasise the baroque nature of the aesthetic determining Wycherley's conscious artifice in the dramatic structure and the disturbing scepticism which motivates the presentation of character. *The Plain Dealer* offers a view of life utterly devoid of the romantic idealism of Shakespeare's love comedies or the bourgeois respect for a rational mean of behaviour apparent in plays of Molière.

—Robert Gordon

PLAY
by Samuel Beckett

First Publication: As *Spiel* (German translation), in *Theater heute*, July 1963; as *Play*, in *"Play" and Two Short Pieces for Radio*, London, 1964.
First Production: As *Spiel* (in German), Ulmer Theater, Ulm-Donau, 14 June 1963; as *Play*, Cherry Lane Theatre, New York, 1964.

Criticism
(For general works on the author, see *Playwrights* volume)

Articles:
Renée R. Hubert, "Beckett's *Play* Between Poetry and Performance", in *Modern Drama*, 9, 1966.
Shoshana Avigal, "Beckett's *Play*: The Circular Line of Existence", in *Modern Drama*, 18, 1975.
Rosemary Pountney, "Samuel Beckett's Interest in Form: Structural Patterning in *Play*", in *Modern Drama*, 19, 1976.
Walter D. Asmus, "Beckett inszeniert sein *Spiel*: Proben-Tagebuch", in *Theatre Heute*, vol. 19 no.12, 1978.
Maurice Blackman, "The Shaping of a Beckett Text: *Play*", in *Journal of Beckett Studies*, 10, 1985.
Karen Laughlin, "Beckett's Three Dimensions: Narration, Dialogue, and the Role of the Reader in *Play*", in *Modern Drama*, 28, 1985.
W.B. Worthen, "Playing *Play*", in *Theatre Journal*, 37, 1985.
Kenneth Gaburo, "The Music in Beckett's *Play*", in *Review of Contemporary Fiction*, vol. 7 no.2, 1987.
Lori H. Burghardt, "Talking Heads: Samuel Beckett's *Play* as a Metaphor for the Schopenhauerian Will", in *Comparatist*, 12, 1988.

* * *

Play was written in 1962–3. Each voice was written separately and the three resulting monologues were interleaved. The dramatic image is of three heads (a man and two women,

W1 and W2) emerging from funerary urns. When light is focused on a head, it must speak. All three heads recount details of a past love affair—their own (as it emerges), though none has any idea that the two other members of the triangle occupy adjacent urns. The reminiscences of the three progress to a consideration of their current situation, which they are unable to change. This becomes evident when the play is repeated in its entirety and is beginning again for a third time when the curtain finally falls—giving the effect of a vicious circle from which no exit is possible. Indeed the play is often played in conjunction with Sartre's *No Exit* (*Huis clos*) or Yeats's *Purgatory*, two plays also dealing with the afterlife.

Beckett's dramatic technique in *Play* is extremely daring: it is a theatrical commonplace that dialogue between two or more characters is spoken on stage and that stage movement is required to hold audience attention and prevent the play becoming static. Beckett, however, disregards these conventions, imprisoning his characters in urns, so that their heads (made up "to seem almost part of urns") face "undeviatingly front throughout". Moreover their voices are "toneless except where an expression is indicated" and there is no dialogue as such at all. However, in an innovatory masterstroke, light provides the necessary stage movement as it "provokes" speech from each urn—so that, despite the extreme reduction from conventional staging, the stage picture is hauntingly full of interest. As Beckett pointed out in the manuscript of another play, *That Time*, "less = more". Reduction produces an intensification of dramatic impact. Light becomes a character in the action: when it focuses on all three urns, the heads speak in chorus; when it focuses on a single urn, it appears as an inquisitor, eliciting speech from its victim.

Dramatic tension builds and tightens as the play is repeated in full and the audience gradually realises the characters are stuck in a time loop, unable either to progress or to cease their recital. The play begins in comedy as each woman reflects on her rival and W1 displays cat-like jealousy, delivered like rifle shot: "Pudding face, puffy, spots, blubber mouth, jowls, no neck, dugs you could . . . Calves like a flunkey—". The comedy increases until the man, exhausted, pants: "I simply could no longer—"; at this point a blackout intervenes in the text and when it resumes light is at "half previous strength" and the voices are "proportionately lower", which also has the effect of increasing audience concentration and lowering the comic tone. Light remains at this strength until the first run of the text ends, but when the "repeat" begins light must return to its original strength and the volume of voices must increase as before. Thus when the blackout intervention is repeated and the voices are again reduced, the vicious circle becomes apparent to the audience, and is confirmed when the play ends at the beginning of a third cycle.

There is an interesting comparison here with Yeats's drama: Yeats believed it was a human spirit's destiny to "dream back" over its life from the point of death, gradually unwinding its experience until returning to the state of innocence it was born with. Should the spirit encounter any unresolved earthly experience during this process, it would be held there until the knot was unravelled. The possibility of eventual resolution or release for the spirit remains open (although not yet achieved) in plays such as Yeats's *Purgatory* and *The Dreaming of the Bones*, whereas Beckett generally closes the door upon any such possibility. Nonetheless in a Paris production in 1964 that Beckett was involved in, he allowed a weakening of light to continue during the repeat, so that a dwindling effect of both light and voices was apparent throughout the play. But when the present writer enquired whether this notion had become a preferred alternative, Beckett's response was: "Exact repeat preferred".

By the end of the play it seems as though light is playing an on/off game with the three characters (the play is, after all, entitled *Play*) provoking speech in an arbitrary fashion, with no interest in the responses it elicits. Far from suggesting implications of purgatory (which generally occur to audiences with a background knowledge of Christianity) the idea of a light with no controlling intelligence behind it, one that simply goes on and off since that is its function, is terrifying and raises universal questions about human existence and the nature of life and death. A controlling intelligence would imply meaning—that both light and heads are there for a purpose, in search of "some truth" perhaps, as M reflects at the end of the play. But he concludes with a chilling alternative: "Mere eye. No mind. Opening and shutting on me. / Am I as much—/ Am I as much as. . .being seen?". If light is merely an arbitrary force, with no interest in M's current predicament (is indeed in a similar predicament—also unable to change its situation), its existence is meaningless and, by extension, so is human hope. The notion of an intelligent inquirer or listener (represented by the light) degenerates into a blind torture; light is not even conscious that it offers a glimpse of possible mercy (by reducing to half strength) only to snatch it away anew each time the play begins again and it returns once more to normal strength. A no-exit situation indeed. Yet it should always be remembered that Beckett allows ambiguity to permeate even the most pessimistic of his plays, and *Play* is no exception. Thus Beckett's assertion that "the key word in my plays is 'perhaps' " is especially salutary here.

—Rosemary Pountney

THE PLAYBOY OF SEVILLE. See **THE TRICKSTER OF SEVILLE.**

THE PLAYBOY OF THE WESTERN WORLD
by John Millington Synge

First Publication: Dublin and London, 1910.
First Production: Abbey Theatre, Dublin, 26 January 1907.

Criticism
(For general works on the author, see *Playwrights* volume)

Books:
Susan Solomont, *The Comic Effect of "The Playboy of the Western World" by John Millington Synge*, Bangor, Wales, 1962.
Alan Price, *Riders to the Sea; The Playboy of the Western World*, Oxford, 1969.
Thomas R. Whitaker (ed.), *Twentieth Century Interpretations of "The Playboy of the Western World"*, Englewood Cliffs, New Jersey, 1969.
James Kilroy, *The Playboy Riots*, Dublin, 1970.
Harold Bloom (ed.), *John Millington Synge's "The Playboy of the Western World"*, New York, 1988 (Modern Critical Interpretations Series).

Articles:
W.B. Yeats, "The Controversy over *The Playboy*", in *The Arrow*, 1, 1907.

The Playboy of the Western World: Riverside Studios, London, 1984

Percival Presland Howe, "The *Playboy* in the Theatre", in *Oxford and Cambridge Review*, 21, 1912.

Sidney Wentworth Caroll, "*The Playboy of the Western World*", in his *Some Dramatic Opinions*, London, 1923.

Herbert Farjeon, "The Birth of *The Playboy*", in *Theatre Arts*, 16, 1933.

David H. Greene, "*The Playboy* and Irish Nationalism", in *Journal of English and Germanic Philology*, 46, 1947.

Norman Podhoretz, "Synge's *Playboy*: Morality and the Hero", in *Essays in Criticism*, 3, 1953.

William Blisset, "Synge's *Playboy*", in *Adam International Review*, 1954.

Hugh H. Maclean, "The Hero as Playboy", in *University of Kansas City Review*, 21, 1954.

Daniel J. Murphy, "The Reception of Synge's *Playboy* in Ireland and America, 1907–12", in *Bulletin of the New York Public Library*, 64, 1960.

Cyril Cusack, "A Player's Reflections on *Playboy*", in *Modern Drama*, 4, 1961.

Patricia Meyer Spacks, "The Making of *The Playboy*", in *Modern Drama*, 4, 1961.

Howard D. Pearce, "Synge's Playboy as Mock-Christ", in *Modern Drama*, 8, 1965.

M.J. Sidnell, "Synge's Playboy and the Champion of Ulster", in *Dalhousie Review*, 45, 1965.

Richard M. Kain, "A Scrapbook of the 'Playboy Riots'", in *Emory University Quarterly*, 22, 1966.

Wallace H. Johnson, "The Pagan Setting of Synge's *Playboy*", in *Renascence*, 19, 1967.

R. Reed Sanderlin, "Synge's Playboy and the Ironic Hero", in *Southern Quarterly*, 6, 1968.

Harry W. Smith, "Synge's *Playboy* and the Proximity of Violence", in *Quarterly Journal of Speech*, 55, 1969.

Stanley Sultan, "A Joycean Look at *The Playboy of the Western World*", in *The Celtic Master: Contributions to the First James Joyce Symposium Held in Dublin, 1967*, Dublin, 1969.

Eric Salmon, "J.M. Synge's *Playboy*: A Necessary Reassessment", in *Modern Drama*, 13, 1970.

E.H. Mikhail, "Two Aspects of Synge's *Playboy*", in *Colby Library Quarterly*, 9, 1971.

Leslie D. Foster, "Heroic Strivings in *The Playboy of the Western World*", in *Eire*, vol.8 no.1, 1973.

Bernard L. Edwards, "The Vision of J.M. Synge: A Study of *The Playboy of the Western World*", in *English Literature in Transition, 1880–1920*, 17, 1974.

Donald Gutierrez, "Coming of Age in Mayo: Synge's *Playboy of the Western World* as a Rite of Passage", in *Hartford Studies in Literature*, 6, 1974.

Malcolm Kelsall, "The *Playboy* Before the Riots", in *Theatre Research International*, 1, 1975.

Paul M. Levitt, "The Two Act Structure of *The Playboy of the Western World*", in *Colby Library Quarterly*, 11, 1975.

Michel Bariou, "Margaret Flaherty: The Awakening and Failure of Love in *The Playboy of the Western World*", in *Cahiers de l'Association Internationale des Études Françaises*, 2, 1977.

Bruce Bigley, "*The Playboy of the Western World* as Anti-drama", in *Modern Drama*, 20, 1977.

Gérard Leblanc, "The Three Deaths of the Father in *The Playboy of the Western World*", in *Cahiers du centre d'études anglo-irlandaises*, 2, 1977.

Mark Mortimer, "Stagecraft in *The Playboy*", in *Cahiers du centre d'études anglo-irlandaises*, 2, 1977.

Arthur H. Nethercot, "The *Playboy* of the Western World", in *Eire*, vol.13 no.2, 1978.

René Agostini, "A Reading of John Millington Synge's *The Playboy of the Western World*: The Problem of Identity", in *Cahiers Victoriens & Édouardiens*, 9–10, 1979.

Warren Akin, "'I just riz the loy': The Oedipal Dimension of *The Playboy of the Western World*", in *South Atlantic Bulletin*, vol.45 no.4, 1980.

Michael J. Collins, "Christy's Binary Vision in *The Playboy of the Western World*", in *Canadian Journal of Irish Studies*, vol.7 no.2, 1981.

Gulshan R. Kataria, "Role of the Feminine in Christy Mahon's Development: A Jungian Reappraisal of *The Playboy of the Western World*", in *Punjab University Research Bulletin: Arts*, 12, 1981.

René Fréchet, "Synge and Ireland: The Solitude of the Artist in *The Playboy of the Western World*", in *Threshold*, 33, 1983.

Randolph Parker, "Gaming in the Gap: Language and Liminality in *Playboy of the Western World*", in *Theatre Journal*, 37, 1985.

Heidi J. Holder, "Between Fiction and Reality: Synge's *Playboy* and Its Audience", in *Journal of Modern Literature*, 14, 1988.

Jane M. Lindskold, "Synge's Christy: Mayo's Diminutized Christ", in *Eire*, vol.23 no.3, 1988.

Una Chaudhuri, "The Dramaturgy of the Other: Diegetic Patterns in Synge's *The Playboy of the Western World*", in *Modern Drama*, 32, 1989.

*   *   *

The play, in three acts, takes place in a country pub in Mayo (the Wild West of Ireland) with no particular emphasis on time, but obviously pretelevision and post Penal Laws. The power of the Catholic Church is established. The daughter of the house, Pegeen Mike, is to be married to Shawn Keogh, pious and pusillanimous. The drunken father of the house is going off to a funeral, Shawn feels it might be immoral to be left alone with his fiancée. Christy Mahon, a distraught and travel-worn young man, comes in and quickly reveals that he has killed his father and is on the run. The company is more curious than horrified, and Pegeen Mike thinks him a more glamorous figure than her intended: "I've heard all times it's the poets are your like fine, fiery fellows with great rages when their temper's roused". Christy, who has been brow-beaten by his father, flowers under Pegeen's admiration and reveals a tender and poetic, if very immature, soul. Shawn has alerted The Widow Quin, who interrupts the young couple and shows some amorous interest in Christy (she has killed her own husband). Pegeen hunts her off.

In the second act Christy is further flattered by some local girls. When he is disposed to flirt with them, Pegeen revenges herself on him by reminding him that he will probably hang for his crime. In the quarrel and reconciliation they discover that both have been timid and lonely all their lives. Shawn tries to bribe Christy to leave and Widow Quin tries to woo him, but he is constant. Suddenly Christy's father arrives, bleeding from the wound that had only stunned him. The widow misdirects him on and Christy goes out to join in the sports on the strand.

The third act cogently resolves these threads. Christy turns out to be a considerable sportsman, made confident by admiration. But his father has come back and confronts him in his triumph. They fight and Christy wins; but the company is less impressed by an actual struggle than by Christy's account of his distant deed. As Pegeen now says, "he after doing nothing but hitting a soft blow and chasing Northward in a sweat of fear". The whole company, including Pegeen, turns against him, but he and his father frighten them off and leave. He is cured of his feeling for Pegeen, but retains his new violent mastery, the father his servant. When they are gone Pegeen laments her loss and reveals her lack of understanding, "I've lost the only Playboy of the Western World".

It is obviously a very strong plot and Synge has the true dramatic poet's strength of finding language to point up the significance. There have been many attempts to re-establish poetic drama in the 20th century; no one seems to have done it in verse, but Synge and Beckett managed it in heightened prose. Synge had been a bad symbolist poet when Yeats met him in Paris and encouraged him to come home and write about Irish peasants. Synge in fact knew Irish and was already sympathetic to Nationalism, being guilty about his ancestors' misuse of their Irish tenants. He was also reacting against the guilt-ridden Protestant religion of his family. Living with the peasants on the remote island of Aran, he found himself in touch with a less cerebral life, and in listening to them he found a more concrete and emotional language than is normal to middle-class life. In his famous preface he pays tribute to the speech he heard "from herds and fishermen along the coast from Kerry to Mayo or from beggar-women and ballad-singers near Dublin". He imagined himself privileged to be in touch with a "rich and living" language, as he imagined Shakespeare had been. Like Yeats himself (to a lesser degree) and so many composers of the time he fed on "the folk-imagination".

However, since no one has done it so well since, the main tribute must go to Synge's own intelligence and talent. He created a resonant parable of Irish life, and something more universal. The young people are betrayed by their elders, drunken or materialistic or priest-ridden. By the realistic accidents of the first act Christy discovers both self-confidence and the tenderness of love; but this is precariously based on a mistake, both as to his actual deed and its implications. He is not the wild man of Pegeen's imagination; he is something better. The climax is not liberating, but sad (if not tragic). In realising the ugliness of her admiration for violence (although the young do need to be liberated from something), she turns against her liberator, who inspired love in her; and he goes off, loveless but genuinely violent, to face the world. The old men welcome peace for their drinking.

In fact Synge's language is a very mannered version of Irish speech in English, and sometimes it deserves the contempt Joyce shows for it in *Ulysses*, "Synge-song"; but it rises to lyric heights at key moments to express the wonder of love, and continually accommodates the rich ironies of Synge's agile, observing mind:

> *Pegeen*: *with blank amazement*: Is it killed your father?
> *Christy*: *subsiding*: With the help of God I did, surely. . . .

Apart from the unwelcome moral that scandalised the first audiences, and the friendly mockery of confused moral stances, and the subtext of anti-clericalism, the play has a marvellously rich texture, true to Irish life, that has kept it at the centre of the Irish repertory to this day.

—James Simmons

THE PLEBEIANS REHEARSE THE UPRISING
(Die Plebejer proben den Aufstand)
by Günter Grass

First Publication: Neuwied, 1966.
First Production: Schiller-Theater, Berlin, 15 January 1966.

Translations
The Plebeians Rehearse the Uprising, translated by Ralph Mannheim, New York, 1966.

Criticism
(For general works on the author, see *Playwrights* volume)

Articles:
Karl Stocker, "Günter Grass: *Die Plebejer proben den Aufstand*: Ein Diskussionsbeitrag zu einem umstrittenen Stücke", in *Blätter für den Deutschlehrer*, 11, 1967.
Norman James, "The Fusion of Pirandello and Brecht in *Marat / Sade* and *The Plebeians Rehearse the Uprising*", in *Educational Theatre Journal*, 21, 1969.
Jürgen Kuczynski, "Günter Grass: *Die Plebejer proben den Aufstand*—oder: Der Kleinbürger versucht die Macht abzugeben", in *Gestalten und Werke: Soziologische Studien zur deutschen Literatur*, Berlin, 1969.
Noel L. Thomas, "Shakespeare's *Coriolanus* and Grass's *Die Plebejer proben den Aufstand*: A Comparison", in *New German Studies*, 5, 1977.

Gertrud B. Pickar, "*Silberpappeln* and *Saatkartoffeln*: The Interaction of Art and Reality in Grass' *Die Plebejer proben den Aufstand*", in *Theatrum mundi: Essays on German Drama and German Literature*, Munich, 1980.

*   *   *

The play is set in East Berlin on the occasion of the workers' rebellion of 17 June 1953. The entire action takes place in the theatre of the Boss, a dramatist of international repute, where the rehearsal of his adaptation of Shakespeare's *Coriolanus* is interrupted by striking workers intent on securing his active support for their cause. Instead, the Boss uses their intervention for his theatrical purposes by inducing them to act out on stage the beginnings of the uprising. Despite repeated pleas both from the workers and from members of his company the Boss remains aloof until he is finally won over by the emotional appeal of an idealistic young hairdresser—too late, however, for by now the Russian tanks have crushed the revolt. Approached by the government representative, Kosanke, for a declaration of support and fearing for the future of his theatre should he refuse, the Boss formulates an ambiguous statement before wearily resolving to abandon his production of *Coriolanus* and devote himself henceforth to the writing of poetry.

In a speech given in 1964 and entitled "The Prehistory and Posthistory of the Tragedy of *Coriolanus* from Livy and Plutarch via Shakespeare down to Brecht and Myself", in which he sketched out the basic plot of his as yet unwritten play, Grass had been extremely critical of Brecht's Marxist

The Plebeians Rehearse the Uprising: Aldwych Theatre, London, 1970

interpretation of *Coriolanus*. That speech, plus the 1960's vogue in West Germany for documentary theatre, help explain the charge frequently levelled at Grass that in his first full-length drama he had delivered a savage indictment of Brecht's conduct at the time of the East German uprising, much in the same personalised way as four years earlier Hochhuth had lambasted Pope Pius XII in *The Representative*. While nowhere in the play is Brecht explicitly mentioned by name, the liberal use made of his artistic and political utterances, together with the many obvious parallels with historical figures (the character of Volumnia is clearly modelled on Brecht's wife, Helene Weigel; that of Kosanke on the party hack, Kurt Bartel, etc.), result in there being precious little mystery as to the identity of the play's principal character.

Moreover, since—as was well known—Brecht's actual behaviour in 1953 differed in several significant respects from that of the Boss (crucially Brecht did not cocoon himself away in the theatre on the day in question), Grass was also accused of falsifying history. His response was to deny any documentary or polemical intent, insisting on the representative nature of the Boss who was to be seen as "a model of the poet and intellectual who does not come to grips with the political reality he has so often invoked". If such were indeed his ambitions, then arguably Grass's purpose would have been better served by an unambiguously fictional character caught up in less historically specific circumstances.

Indicted in the main protagonist then is the figure of the ideologically committed writer who takes refuge in the sphere of politicised art as a surrogate for the real world of activist politics, and it is the illusory nature of this posture that by the end of the play the Boss is compelled to recognise. Far from helping the workers' cause by functioning as a vehicle of instruction, his theatre serves only to deflect them from their original, political design, and the Boss's decision to cancel further work on *Coriolanus* is born out of his insight that "we cannot change Shakespeare as long as we do not change ourselves". The plural form here is significant—and is repeated in the play's final line, the Boss's impassioned outcry to the departed rebels—"Bowed down with guilt I accuse you!"—for, in truth, the play apportions blame on all sides. Despite the fundamentally flawed aesthetic he preaches, the Boss's hard-nosed analysis of the actual, political reality is repeatedly shown to be superior to that of the naive workers, whose immature spontaneity ensures that their uprising will indeed remain a mere rehearsal, an improvised revolt enacted by lay-revolutionaries. Similarly, the solidarity with the strikers displayed by members of the Boss's ensemble proves to be somewhat fragile and Volumnia, who is quick to chastise the Boss for his vacillation during the uprising, is the first to exhort him to sign Kosanke's manifesto once it is learnt that the revolt has failed. Contrasted with such opportunism the Boss's indecisiveness begins to acquire the virtue of consistency.

The broader context Grass wished to address is also indicated by his designation of the play as "Ein deutsches Trauerspiel" ("A German Tragedy"), a subtitle which *The Plebeians* shares with Hebbel's *Agnes Bernauer*, and which Grass seeks to justify at the formal level through his adherence to the classical unities and the occasional use of elevated, iambic pentameters. The tragedy Grass alludes to resides at three different levels: in the tragic dilemma any political intellectual (and not just Brecht) might find himself/herself confronted with; in the "tragedy of theory" (Volker Klotz) manifest in what Grass regards as the peculiarly German failure to harmonise theory and practice; and in the repeated tragedy of Germany's failed revolutions (of 1848, 1918, and 1953).

Meanwhile history has added an ironic epilogue to the play, for in the real-life drama played out almost a quarter of a century later, Grass's scenario was turned on its head: the successful East German revolution of 1989 was not betrayed, but initiated, by the intellectuals (of New Forum). However, their aspirations towards the creation of a truly democratic but still independent East German state were quickly jettisoned by a populace intent on German unification—an objective which, since the mid-1960s, the author of *The Plebeians* has consistently and passionately opposed.

—Rob Burns

DIE PLEBEJER PROBEN DEN AUFSTAND. See **THE PLEBEIANS REHEARSE THE UPRISING.**

PLENTY
by David Hare

First Publication: London, 1978.
First Production: National Theatre, London, 7 April 1978.

Criticism
(For general works on the author, see *Playwrights* volume)

Articles:
Steven H. Gale, "Sex and Politics: David Hare's *Plenty*", in *Drama, Sex and Politics* edited by James Redmond Cambridge, 1985 (Themes in Drama Series).
Colin Chambers and Mike Prior, "David Hare: *Plenty* and the Politics of Despair", in their *Playwrights' Progress: Patterns of Postwar British Drama*, Oxford, 1987.

*   *   *

In 12 scenes spaced over 20 years, *Plenty* charts the development of Susan Traherne from her dangerous wartime work as a courier in occupied France in 1943 to her loss of sanity and abandonment of her husband in 1962. Through focusing on her disappointments after the war, the play offers a critique of the economic and ideological decline of post-war British society, and what Hare sees as the betrayal of the democratic ideals which accompanied the defeat of Fascism in 1945. Never after the war does Susan regain the certainty of purpose which she possessed during the 1940's when she knew what she was fighting for and believed in a better world to come; her marriage to a civil servant at the foreign office takes her into a world of lies and hypocrisy, where belief in the pre-war values of the British Empire has remained largely unchanged. In 1956, the British attitudes towards Suez and the deceit practised by the government drive her close to insanity. After leaving her husband, she makes a desperate attempt to recapture the past through a relationship with a fellow wartime resistance fighter in whom she has invested her idealism, only to find that he too has been dragged into a predictably pedestrian and suburban life. "I want to believe in you. So tell me nothing. That's best", she urges him, desperate to keep her dream alive; but he leaves her drugged and unconscious in a

Blackpool hotel room, to return to his routine existence. The final scene backtracks to 1944—though it also represents Susan's dream in the hotel in 1962—to show her admiring the French landscape under a glorious August sun, and confidently promising her French companion that "there will be days and days and days like this". It is this vision and confidence which subsequent events have betrayed.

Plenty is an episodic play which focuses on particular moments in Susan's life, partly as a way of exploring developments in the society of post-war Britain; however, because so few moments are dramatised, and because scenes are often honed down to the barest bones of understatement, we are offered a fragmentary and sometimes tantalising perspective rather than a whole view, an avowedly ambiguous and complex perspective rather than a reductive explanation. It is even possible to misread the play as being without social comment and entirely about Susan and her struggles in a world which is inevitably futile; but in Hare's view the futility is specific to the society portrayed, and it is the gap between wartime idealism and post-war developments which represents the play's focal point. Yet because the details of Susan's life seem so personal, and because she herself can be destructive and obsessively self-indulgent, we respond to her on an individual level with both irritation and sympathy, rather than to someone who symbolises the legitimate disappointments of an entire generation. Furthermore, the world we see is based largely around Knightsbridge, and contains no sense of a wider society or a schematic analysis of Britain in the 1950's. Susan's descent to madness may indicate how individuals are destroyed by a society lacking morals, for Hare has commented that "people go clinically mad if what they believe bears no relation to how they live"; but though her character is created by the way in which political events impinge on her, the play's focus is on Susan rather than the events. Generally, the political elements seem submerged in the personal, the public world in the private. Hare has also described the play as being "about the cost of spending your whole life in dissent": while in part *Plenty* is clearly an historical play presenting an alternative perspective on the recent past, perhaps Susan's confident vision and subsequent disappointment with a society which did not become more just and democratic also reflects some of Hare's own expectations and disillusionment with regard to the Harold Wilson government of 1964, which doomed so many left-wing playwrights to spending their lives in dissent.

Theatrically, the play's strengths are the depth of the ideas and characterisation, and the moments of surprise it springs on an audience. Some characters appear only briefly, or with gaps of many years between appearances, yet they never seem mere shorthand devices or ciphers representing particular viewpoints; one believes in them all as real people with a full history and lives which continue offstage. For an audience, each scene requires careful attention in order to work out where it takes place both geographically and chronologically, who the characters are, and how they may have changed since their previous appearance. By dramatising only 12 moments from a period covering nearly 20 years, Hare is able to highlight key images which create strong theatrical effects: the bare room and the naked man with which the play opens; the scene on the Embankment where, to the sound of a cello, Susan invites a virtual stranger to father her child in return for a deal involving 500 cheese graters; a night-time parachute landing in occupied France; the door of a hotel bedroom which opens to reveal not a corridor, but a French hillside under a brilliant August sun. On a first viewing, such isolated images may dominate one's response, for Hare's play is always complex and ambiguous, and it is only with repeated viewings or readings that the implications become apparent and the play's "hidden" theme

of the decline of idealism in post-war British society begins to emerge.

Although *Plenty* enjoyed reasonable success in Britain, it was in New York that it received particular acclaim; in 1985 Hare substantially adapted the script for a commercially successful film, starring Meryl Streep.

—Steve Nicholson

PLODY PROSVESHCHENIYA. See **THE FRUITS OF ENLIGHTENMENT.**

THE PLOUGH AND THE STARS
by Sean O'Casey

First Publication: London and New York, 1926.
First Production: Abbey Theatre, Dublin, 8 February 1926.

Criticism
(For general works on the author, see *Playwrights* volume)

Books:
Robert G. Lowery (ed.), *A Whirlwind in Dublin: The "Plough and the Stars" Riots*, Westport, Connecticut, 1984.
Ronald Ayling (ed.), *The Dublin Trilogy: "The Shadow of a Gunman"; "Juno and the Paycock"; "The Plough and the Stars": A Casebook*, London, 1985.
Patrick Murray, *Companion to "The Plough and the Stars"*, Dublin, 1988.

Articles:
G. Vernon, "*The Plough and the Stars*", in *Commonweal*, 21, 1934.
W.A. Anthony, "The Sources and Themes of *The Plough and the Stars*", in *Modern Drama*, 4, 1961.
Ronald G. Rollins, "Form and Content in Sean O'Casey's Dublin Trilogy", in *Modern Drama*, 8, 1966.
Bobby L. Smith, "Satire in *The Plough and the Stars: A Tragedy in Four Acts*", in *Ball State University Forum*, vol.10 no.3, 1969.
Michael W. Kaufman, "The Position of *The Plough and the Stars* in O'Casey's Dublin Tilogy", in *James Joyce Quarterly*, 8, 1970.
Edward E. Pixley, "*The Plough and the Stars*: The Destructive Consequences of Human Folly", in *Educational Theatre Journal*, 23, 1971.
Ronald Ayling, "Ideas and Ideology in *The Plough and the Stars*", in *Sean O'Casey Review*, 2, 1976.
Michael J. Durkan, "The First American Production of *The Plough and the Stars*", in *Sean O'Casey Review*, 3, 1976.
Jack Lindsay, "*The Plough and the Stars* Reconsidered", in *Sean O'Casey Review*, 2, 1976.
Ronald Ayling, "History and Artistry in *The Plough and the Stars*", in *Ariel*, vol.8 no.1, 1977.
Bernice Schrank, "'Little ignorant Yahoo': The Theme of Human Limitation in O'Casey's *The Plough and the Stars*", in *Études irlandaises*, 6, 1981.
Bernice Schrank, "Between Anarchy and Incarceration: The

Struggle for Freedom in Sean O'Casey's *The Plough and the Stars*", in *Literatur in Wissenschaft und Unterricht*, 18, 1985.

Bernice Schrank, " 'There's nothin' derogatory in th' use o' th' word': A Study in the Use of Language in *The Plough and the Stars*", in *Irish University Review*, 15, 1985.

Bernice Schrank, "Language and Silence in *The Plough and the Stars*", in *Moderna Språk*, 80, 1986.

Bernice Schrank, "Anatomizing an Insurrection: Sean O'Casey's *The Plough and the Stars*", in *Modern Drama*, 29, 1986.

Shaun Richards, " 'A Question of Location': Theatrical Space and Political Choice in *The Plough and the Stars*", in *Theatre Research International*, 15, 1990.

*   *   *

The play deals with the Irish Rising during Easter Week 1916, but looks at the event not so much from the perspective of the insurgents as from that of the Dublin slum-dwellers, who remain largely aloof from it. Three of the four acts are set inside or outside one tenement whose herded residents form the staple cast of the play. The richly diverse individuality of these "ordinary" people is a notable political and artistic triumph, disposing, as it does, with the crude assumption, still widely held in the 1920's, that the working class or the lumpenproletariat form an undifferentiated mass of amorphous beings. O'Casey treats these people—their quarrelsome and egoistic dispositions, their confusions and veering moods, but also their slumbering energies, their courage and devotion—with a mixture of sympathy and satire deriving from a deep-seated humanism. The title's reference to the flag of the Irish Citizen Army, the working-class organisation behind the Rising (as opposed to its middle-class ally, the Irish Volunteers), also underlines this particular social focus.

There is, then, not one middle- or upper-class character in the play, but neither does any one of the tenement dwellers serve as a central figure or mouthpiece of the author. If the play has a protagonist, it is, ironically, the collective anti-hero of the non-combatants. For, despite an earlier pompous display of support for Irish independence, only one out of their midst eventually joins in the fighting, and that against the desperate pleadings of his wife. But however passively or indifferently the others may follow the actual Rising, they are all ineluctably drawn into it, as the British troops—and with them the tragedy—close in on them. And in one of those deadly ironies common in every war situation, it is the fiercest opponent of the insurrection among them, Bessie Burgess, a Protestant and Loyalist with a soldier son fighting in Flanders for King and Country, who is accidentally killed by a British bullet.

Throughout the action the dramatic tension grows out of the intertwining and contrasting of the backstage uprising with the foregrounded lives of the ordinary folk. In Act II, for example, the fervent nationalist rhetoric of an unseen orator addressing a Republican street meeting is called in question by the parallel pub-brawls in which one character after another gets embroiled over trifling matters, at a moment when popular unity appears sorely needed. But the debunking works both ways. The discrepancy between the high-flying ideals voiced off stage and the wild boozing in the foreground, between the ranting and the babbling, is—much like the shoplooting incident in Act III—an indictment both of the isolation of the rebels from the masses, and of the inability of those self-same masses to rise to the historic occasion and turn out in support of the cause of Irish independence. This distance between the real and the ideal, the contingently actual and the historically possible, is again hinted at by the image of the title.

Yet exposure of the failures and shortcomings is not the whole story, and the critique never deteriorates into cynicism. Several characters, far from being crushed, emerge strongly resilient from the onslaught of the warfare. Fluther Good, so much the talker and drinker who is seemingly incapable of sustained action, awakes to active solidarity in the face of suffering and death. Again, Bessie Burgess, a foul-mouthed and cantankerous hag for three-quarters of the play, in an unexpected revelation of her human potential, which yet has nothing implausible about it, develops into a caring and generous neighbour ready to aid the helpless. Not quite on the same level, though adding to the general picture of unpredictable human behaviour and inexhaustible human resources, is Jack Clitheroe's courageous fighting and dying: driven into the ranks of the insurgents by ambition and vanity, his weaknesses are partly redeemed by his actions, and the refusal to fire at the civilian looters. Even the sectarian Marxist Covey, so often given to mere phrase-mongering, parries with the British corporal who evacuates the tenement in an exchange over the duty of a socialist.

Beneath the scum surface of social degradation and political immaturity lie then, in O'Casey's view, resources of hope and dignity—a diagnosis carried further by the vitality of the language, and the rowdy humour amid the horror.

Given the temporal proximity of an event which in the Nationalist consciousness had fast become mythologised, it was, of course, the more directly unglorifying and deprecatory political insinuations of the play that wreaked havoc. The surprise is perhaps not that there should have been violent protests when *The Plough* was first staged at the Abbey Theatre, Dublin, but that it took four nights for the ructions to flare up. The scandal, which was reminiscent of the stormy reception of Synge's *The Playboy of the Western World* two decades earlier, continued in the Irish press well after the play's run. The whole affair left more than a taste of bitterness in O'Casey's mind, and played no small part in his decision to quit Ireland.

—H. Gustav Klaus

THE POHUTUKAWA TREE
by Bruce Mason

First Publication: Wellington, New Zealand, 1960; second edition, 1963.
First Production: New Zealand Players' Theatre Workshop, Wellington, 1957.

Criticism
(For general works on the author, see *Playwrights* volume)

Articles:
Don Mcara, "Bruce Mason's *The Pohutukawa Tree*: A Director's Log", in *Landfall*, 147, 1983.

*   *   *

The play is set in New Zealand in the 1950's. Aroha Mataira is a Maori matriarch of chiefly lineage, the last of her tribe still to live on the ancestral land, but profoundly set apart from both them and from the local *pakeha* (non-Maori European) community by a rigid Old Testament Protestantism. Her isolation grows as her daughter rebels and becomes pregnant by an itinerant *pakeha* barman, her son desecrates the local church, and her minister urges her to sell her land—the tribe's spiritual home—to the neighbouring orchardist. Forced to choose between Christian submission to inexorable *pakeha* encroachment or traditional warrior defiance, she wills her own death, unrepentant.

Prior to *The Pohutukawa Tree* any theatrical appearance of Maori in New Zealand tended to be for stereotypically comic or exotic interest. Bruce Mason was, in this play, presenting the first serious and substantial dramatic treatment of the biracial nature of the society. Furthermore, the play was immediately recognized as a major theatrical and literary achievement. Within a few years it had received many productions (including BBC television in 1959) and become the first New Zealand play to appear on the school syllabus.

The opening stage direction specifies that "*a large pohutukawa tree in bloom hangs over the porch*". The blood-red flowers of this tree, which blooms just before Christmas, make the pohutukawa a potent Christian symbol (it is some-times known as the New Zealand Christmas Tree). The old tree in the play is the last pohutukawa left on Aroha's land, and droops lower over the house as the action progresses, clearly associated with the ageing and inevitable fall of Aroha herself. As in *The Cherry Orchard*, the developers will destroy the old tree and the old life. For Aroha herself, however, the symbolism is double: her grandfather planted the tree on the site of a great battle with the British, "that its red flowers might be a sign of blood between Maori and pakeha for ever".

Aroha's dilemma is also visually evident from the two pictures over the fireplace, Holman Hunt's "The Light of the World" and a framed photograph of the fierce tatooed face of her grandfather. Her Christianity is imbued with a stern warrior spirit and a determination to retain her sacred land. She quotes her grandfather's words to the British colonists: "God made this land for us. It cannot be sliced. If it were a whale, it could be sliced. Do you return to your own country which was made by God for you."

Her attempt to reconcile warrior pride with Christian humility is as doomed as her attempt to keep her children away from dancing and enjoyment, or the land sacrosanct from developers. These themes emerge from traditionally well-made plotting and dialogue. For instance, the daughter Queenie's seduction by the young drifter Roy is motivated by her mother's puritan refusal to allow her to meet any young men. Her pregnancy, and Roy's refusal to marry a Maori, result in Queenie being banished into exile and in her brother Johnny going on a wild drinking spree. His attack with his great grandfather's *taiaha* (spear) on the figure of Christ in the church's stained glass window is in his eyes both a romantic Robin Hood continuation of the fight against the colonial oppressor, and a rejection of his mother's impossibly high Christian demands: ". . .the glass roared and the face disap-peared for ever! Dark, all dark. I had put out the Light of the World! And I shouted with joy, yes with joy, Ma. (*AROHA'S wail is now a thin thread of sound.*) Ma. You're too big. The world can't hold you. . .you tried to make me as big as you. I tried, Ma. But me: I'm not big. . .I had to show you that, Ma." Here as elsewhere the detail of plotting combines with the symbolism to focus on the central figure of Aroha.

Criticism of the play has partly been on grounds of cultural sensitivity; Mason has been charged with creating Maori characters who react in ways that are utterly contrary to Maori values (e.g., Aroha striking her daughter in the face, the most sacred part of her body; or sending a pregnant daughter away from the home). Mason defended himself by reading the play at a Maori leaders' conference, which "regarded Aroha as wrong but authentic". Even so, the power of the play lies in the fact that Aroha is a figure of such authority as to be representative of her race in the thematic clash of cultures. To then defend non-representative behaviour on the grounds that she is atypical—that is, an unusual individual—is to argue against the strength of the dramaturgy. Critical charges of patronising the Maori by stereotyping can also be directed at the description of the remainder of the tribe (only ever reported on in the play) as happy-go-lucky types playing guitars, "swilling beer and going to seed". The play is, in fact, a *pakeha* view of race relations, and Mason's good intentions do not always do justice to complex Maori values relating to family, tribe, ancestors, and the land.

The other major criticism has been that the play is melo-dramatic and romantic. Melodrama, however, implies action that relies principally on incident and excitement, a clear polarity of good and evil, and simple unchanging characters. None of this is true of *The Pohutukawa Tree*, in which plot and theme are centrally concerned with a complex moral debate, and in which even the secondary roles are fully developed (this is nowhere better seen than in the comic-satiric-dramatic episode of the typical Kiwi wedding of the orchardist's daughter).

Romantic it is, however, in its theme of the clash of great civilizations and beliefs, in the musical heightening of emotion (as, for instance, in the keening that continues under Johnny's speech quoted above, or the stage direction for the end of Scene 1: "*There comes a faint throbbing in the air of a rhythmic and barbaric Maori chant*"), and in the larger-than-life charac-terization of Aroha. This is also the explanation of the play's success on stage, where Maori rhetoric and music support a central acting role of operatic grandeur. The play's stance is also romantic in its concern with Aroha's personal response to the crisis, rather than dealing in any substantial way with the continuing post-colonial dynamics of one society dispossessing another of land, language, and culture. Within these limits, however, Aroha's refusal to submit to the inevitable loss of land and of Maori spiritual values is defiant, noble, and close to tragic.

—David Carnegie

THE POST OFFICE (Dakghar)
by Rabindranath Tagore

First Publication: As *Dakghar* (in Bengali), 1912; as *The Post Office*, London, 1914.

Criticism
(For general works on the author, see *Playwrights* volume)

Articles:
D.V.S.R. Murty, "The Message of Tagore's *Post Office*", in *The Modern Review*, vol. 119 no.1, 1966.
Krishnanand Joshi and B. Syamala Rao, "Tagore the Drama-tist: An Appreciation of *Chitra, The King of the Dark Chamber*, and *The Post Office*", in *Studies in Indo-Anglian Literature*, Bara Bazaar, 197?

S.K. Desai, *"The Post Office"*, in *Perspectives on Indian Drama in English*, edited by M.K. Naik and S. Mokashi-Punekar, Madras, 1977.

O.P. Mathur, "'Love's Lotus': A Study of the Protagonist in Tagore's Major Plays", in *Indo-European Literature: A Collection of Critical Essays*, edited by K.K. Sharma, Ghaziabad, India, 1977.

Yeong Yoo, "On Tagore's Drama", in *Immun Kwahak: The Journal of Humanities*, vol.48 no.2, 1982 (with English summary).

*   *   *

One of Rabindranath Tagore's best known and, in some respects, most characteristic prose plays, *The Post Office*, was published in Bengali under the title *Dakghar* in 1912 and in English in 1914. In the 1918 version of the play some songs were added. The play was widely staged both in India and abroad—chiefly in Berlin and Paris. Tagore himself liked it; in fact, it was his favourite play. Written in three or four days at a time when he was also writing *Gitanjali*—his most famous book of lyrics—the play deals with the yearnings of a young child confined because of illness to a room from where he wistfully watches the world go by and the people around him live their lives, while he cannot go out, as the doctor has ordered him not to. The play, with its rich symbolic and poetic undertones, dramatically enacts what Tagore called "a truthful evocation of his own lonely and yearning childhood". That is why he denied that the play had an allegorical character, and regarded it as something very real and concrete. Nevertheless the sick child Amal's longing to escape his confinement and walk out into the world at large and experience all those things he can merely daydream about has a certain symbolism about it: representing, for instance, the soul wanting to escape the trammels of the flesh or, as Yeats would say, the tatters of "its mortal dress", a freedom that only death can give.

"All the organs of his little body", we are told, "are at loggerheads with each other" and the only way to save his life is to keep him out of the autumn wind and sun. But such restrictions, together with his bodily ailment, fire his imagination and fuel his curiosity all the more. In his desire to escape, the child identifies himself imaginatively with whatever moves about freely: "the squirrel. . .sitting with his tail up and with his wee hands. . .picking up the broken grains of lentils and crunching them"; a labourer with "a bamboo staff on his shoulder with a small bundle at the top, and a brass pot in his left hand, and an old pair of shoes on. . .going out to seek work", the dairyman selling curds; women in red saris filling their pitchers from the river and carrying them on their heads; the watchman on his rounds, who sounds his gong only when it is time to tell people that "time waits for none, but goes on for ever". The less the sick child knows where he wants to go and why, the more poignant is his longing to escape—"to fly with the time", he tells us, striking a note of dramatic irony, "to that land of which no one knows anything". It is, however, not the doctor, but one greater than him, the watchman tells Amal, who will come and set him free. From his conversation with the watchman Amal gets glimpses of the world outside: he learns that the big house with a flag flying, that he sees from his room, is His Majesty's new post office; and he starts daydreaming about his receiving a letter from the King when he is beguiled by the watchman into believing that the King sends tiny notes to little boys. There rises before his "inward eye" the image of the postman with a round gilt badge on his chest delivering letters from house to house, "rain or sunshine, rich or poor". The village headman is another man from whose conversation Amal learns that he will certainly get the letter the King has

sent him. Sudha, a flower-seller's young daughter, is another interlocutor who Amal talks to about gathering flowers. But all Amal knows about the flowers is what he has learnt from the fairy-tale of Champa—also the name of a flower—and his six brothers. "If only they let me", he longingly tells Sudha, "I'll go right into the dense forest where you can't find your way. And where the honey-sipping humming-bird rocks himself on the end of the thinnest branch, I will blossom into a *champa*".

But like everyone else, much though Amal would like her to stay talking to him, Sudha too has to go, though she promises that on her way back home she'll call again. Amal then sees a troop of boys going off to play, and he stops some of them and gives them his toys with the pathetically valid excuse: "I can't play alone. They are getting dirty and are of no use to me". There is also a fakir who helps Amal while away his time, telling him about many of the lands he has visited, and especially about the Parrot's Isle, a haunt of birds: "No men are there; and they neither speak nor walk, they simply sing and they fly". All this is music to Amal's ears, but it also intensifies his longing to be free, to wander, to discover for himself what he only knows through hearsay.

But what Amal loses out on on the plane of reality, he more than makes up for on the plane of fantasy. The doctor may prevent him from stepping out of his room, but he cannot prevent his fancy—"deceiving elf"—from conjuring up before his eyes so many tantalizing visions; as, for instance, the road "winding through the trees which you can follow to the end of the forest when the sky is quite clear after the rain"; his "lovely little bride with a pair of pearl drops in her ears and dressed in a lovely red sari", milking with her own hands the black cow and feeding him "with warm milk with foam on it from a brand-new earthen cruse"; the King's postman coming down the hillside alone, a lantern in his left hand and on his back a bag of letters ("I can feel him coming nearer and nearer", says Amal, "and my heart becomes glad"). But in the cruel world of facts, the expected letter doesn't arrive. However, the expectation itself and the symbolic significance that the post office has come to assume for Amal end up engendering in him a mood of philosophical resignation. "When they shut me here," he observes, "I felt the day was so long. Since the King's post office was put there I like more and more being indoors, and as I think I shall get a letter one day, I feel quite happy and then I don't mind being quiet and alone. I wonder if I shall make out what'll be in the King's letter?".

The subtle delicacy of poetic symbolism with which Tagore brings to a close not only Amal's life and his oppressively circumscribed world, but also the world that the sick child has created in his own mind—the intensity of his yearnings in a way giving a body and a substance to what he yearns for—is the work of a genius in whom the claims of poetry and the claims of drama had found a happy resolution. "Everything seems like a dream", says the half-dreaming, half-delirious Amal, "I long to be quiet. I don't feel like talking at all. Won't the King's letter come? Suppose this room melts away all of a sudden, suppose"—what melts away is not the room itself, but the intensely throbbing world of yearning and imagination, of dreams and longings that were never to be realized but which kept the fire of hope and faith burning within him. When the oil-lamp is blown out and the starlight streams in, the end of Amal's life comes like a gentle sleep, eventually giving him the liberation he had longed for all his poignantly brief life.

Thus in *The Post Office*, as in some other plays by Tagore (*The King of the Dark Chamber, The Cycle of Spring*, and *Red Oleanders*, for instance) the principle of an invincible though visible force—the force of human personality—working triumphantly against all kinds of odds, physical or mechanical, social or political, constitutes the moral backbone; even though such a force is conveyed through what W. B. Yeats called "an emotion of gentleness and peace" which pervades this "perfectly constructed" play from first to last.

—G. Singh

THE POWER OF DARKNESS; or, If a Claw is Caught the Bird is Lost
(Vlast Tmy, Ili "Kogotok Uvayaz, Vsey Ptichke Propast'") by Leo Tolstoy

First Publication: Moscow, 1887.
First Production: Théâtre Libre, Paris, 2 February 1888 (in French); first Russian production, at the Alexandrinsky Theatre, St. Petersburg, 18 October 1895.

Editions

The Power of Darkness, in *Leo Tolstoy: Plays*, translated by Louise and Aylmer Maude, London, 1905 (revised edition of the *Works*)
The Power of Darkness, translated by G.R. Noyes and G. Patrick, in *Masterpieces of the Russian Drama*, edited by G.R. Noyes, New York and London, 1933.
The Power of Darkness, in *"The Storm" and Other Russian Plays*, translated by David Magarshack, New York, 1960.
The Power of Darkness, translated by A. Clark, London, 1989.

Criticism
(For general works on the author, see *Playwrights* volume)

Articles:
Simon Jeune, "Une 'première' mondiale du théâtre russe à Paris: *La Puissance des ténèbres* (*Vlas t'my*) de Léon Tolstoi", in *Actes du Ve congrès de l'Association internationale de littérature comparée*, edited by Nikola Banasevic, Amsterdam, 1969.
Andrew Donskov, "Tolstoj's Use of Proverbs in *The Power of Darkness*", in *Russian Literature*, 9, 1975.
Andrew Donskov, "Dialect and Non-Standard Speech in the Peasant Plays of L.N. Tolstoj", in *Poetica Slavica: Studies in Honour of Zbigniew Folejewski*, edited by J. Douglas Clayton, Ottawa, 1981.
David Matual, "Shaw's *The Shewing-Up of Blanco Posnet* and Tolstoy's *The Power of Darkness*: Dramatic Kinship and Theological Opposition", in *Shaw Review*, 1, 1981.
Neil Carruthers, "The Paris Première of Tolstoy's *Vlast' t'my (The Power of Darkness)*", in *New Zealand Slavonic Journal*, 1, 1987.

*   *   *

Tolstoy's *The Power of Darkness*, in both method and feeling, is closer to the late 19th-century European realism of Zola and Hauptmann than it is to the Russian tradition embodied by Gogol, Ostrovsky and others.

The story centres on the weak, self-indulgent, sentimental Nikita, a farm labourer, who at the start of the play is embroiled in a sexual relationship with Anisya, wife of his employer. Akim, his father, wants him to marry Marina, a local girl whom he has also seduced, but his mother, Matriona,

seeing he might acquire the farm if he married Anisya, encourages her to poison her husband. She does so, and marries Nikita, but, to Akim's disgust and Anisya's despair, Nikita now takes up with Akulina, the old man's slow-witted daughter by his first marriage. She becomes pregnant. To cover the scandal, Anisya, with Matriona's backing and Nikita's feeble connivance, plans to get her married off. But first they must get rid of the baby, who is born during a visit from the matchmaker. Anisya fetches it, throws it at the protesting Nikita, who crushes it to death under a board he sits on. He is horrified by his own act.

At Akulina's marriage, Nikita, supported by his father, confesses his sins and begs forgiveness of Marina for seducing her, of Akulina for poisoning her father, for seducing her, and for murdering their baby, and of Akim for flouting him. He is apprehended and tied up, and the wedding halted.

The play is based on a real event which Tolstoy had come across. It provided him with an uncomplicated vehicle for his religious fervour and was written in three weeks in October 1886. It was initially intended for the popular fairground theatre, wherein peasant farces and satires were presented: hence the inclusion of none but peasant characters. But Tolstoy aimed to raise the tone of such entertainments, partly at least by providing truth of both language and setting.

Actually, when the play was read aloud to a group of peasants by an actor friend of Tolstoy's, they simply failed to understand what it was about. Tolstoy then had it published, and meanwhile the actor friend read it to an audience which included the tsar and tsarina, as well as noblemen and ministers. They understood the play, and the tsar was highly enthusiastic about it. However, his enthusiasm was soon dampened by his former tutor, Konstantin Pobedonostsev, by then procurator of the Holy Synod and extremely powerful. Sensing sedition, he persuaded the tsar to ban the play, which remained unperformed in Russia until 1895. Then, however, it was a sensation, acclaimed by all, to such a degree that some members of the first night audience, finding Tolstoy was not in the theatre, rushed to his home after the curtain, and roared their approbation outside his front door.

The play often betrays its author's background as a novelist rather than a dramatist, and this is the first source of the European realism mentioned above. Its structure as drama is weak, and there is awkwardness of plotting (for instance, in the feeble excuse to bring Marina on for the denouement in the last act). Nevertheless, the overall effect is extremely gripping.

The excitement derives, in the first instance, from the total lack of compromise either in conception or execution. It is extremely brutal and frank at all times, and achieves an intensity of horror in the scene of the murder of the baby almost equal to the putting out of Gloucester's eyes in *King Lear*. The intensity also springs partly from Tolstoy's own inner psychology—his personal disgust with his own sexuality and his simultaneous inability to abstain. The honesty with which he confronts these problems informs every scene, and we are baffled by the inextricable and remorseless drives for personal, animal pleasure, for power over others, and for searing self-flagellation. This in turn gives Nikita's final Christian conversation a conviction which almost removes one's suspicions of schematic plotting. It is not seen as an evasion.

The credibility is also enhanced by the vividness with which Tolstoy presents his characters (another typical feature of realism). Anisya, for instance, is utterly unscrupulous when pursuing her own ends, which are all ultimately to do with sensual gratification. Nikita's parents are a clever contrast: the stuttering but idealistic father, Akim, with his scheming, smooth-talking, but actually cowardly wife, Matriona.

The Power of Darkness: Moscow Arts Theatre, 1902

Characters who behave "believably" are more commonly found in novels than in plays, of course. A structure built on the inexorable logic of a "chain of events" is a novelist's technique, too: certainly *The Power of Darkness* relies on this, and the fact that its scenes supposedly happen months apart helps to give the feeling of fidelity to life. Yet the fact that Akim is so good and his wife so bad might give us pause to wonder just what kind of fidelity this is. And perhaps the ending does not jar because not only is it short, it is also completely overshadowed by the power of what has gone before. Because that is so absorbing, the conversion at the end is simply not very interesting. Indeed, spectators seem frequently to forget the reversal of the last scene and remember only the bitterness of the onward march of corruption: as a picture of corruption this play is virtually unmatched.

Since its first performance the play has retained its place in the Russian, and to some extent the international, repertory. Of a number of adaptations, possibly the best was Henry Livings's *This Jockey Drives Late Nights* (1970), wherein the action was transferred from a Russian peasant's farm to a London taxi cab firm: the horror and brutality were just as forceful.

—Robert Leach

PRAVDA
by Howard Brenton and David Hare

First Publication: London, 1985; revised version, 1986.
First Production: National Theatre, London, 2 May 1985;
revised version, National Theatre, London,
2 May 1986.

Criticism
(For general works on the authors, see *Playwrights* volume)

Articles:
Robert Wilcher, "*Pravda*: A Morality for the 1980s", in
Modern Drama, 33, 1990.

*   *   *

Pravda is a political satire centred on Fleet Street, about a
rich South African business man who purchases two daily
British National newspapers—an up-market "quality" paper
and a down-market popular paper. In controlling their output,
Lambert Le Roux then hires and fires staff at will, always
remaining several steps ahead of the many people whom he
upsets and who seek revenge. Most obviously, the play attacks
the nature of a press which is entirely compliant to a right-wing
government, suppressing opposition and helping to impose its
ideology even while professing to be free. The focal point
occurs when the editor of the quality paper obtains a leaked
document proving that a senior government minister has been
lying, and is sacked by Le Roux before he can print it. By the
end of the play, Le Roux is in a position of absolute power, and
even the sacked editor sacrifices his principles by begging for
his job back, accepting with delight the editorship of the down-
market paper.

Like Richard III, the more evil and manipulative Le Roux
becomes, the more he is also attractive and enjoyable for an
audience. This is a double irony since the play focuses not just
on Le Roux himself, but on why he is allowed to succeed. As
Brenton asks: "How can we all convince ourselves that brutal
ugliness is charming, witty and intelligent?". Written when the
Left in Britain felt that newspapers were becoming
increasingly concentrated in the hands of fewer and fewer
wealthy proprietors, and the use of government briefings and
contrived leaks allowed their cynical manipulation by the
Government, the title refers ironically to the nature of the
"truth" peddled throughout the British press. It implicitly
invites comparison with newspapers of the Eastern Bloc which
more *obviously* reproduce the Government line, asking why it
is that if our press has more freedom it remains similarly
subservient. The word "*Pravda*" is used sarcastically by a
journalist after his carefully researched account of police
breaking up a Scottish peace camp is re-written by a deputy
editor ("Peace on this paper is always in inverted
commas. . .call it a peace—inverted commas—squat. . .")
and the play ends with Le Roux welcoming us "to the factory of
lies". Even the first scenes of the play, in the office of a small
provincial newspaper, have shown journalists forging readers'
letters, and refusing to print apologies for errors because it is
vital that the public trust without question what they read. Le
Roux, supporting the political status quo, introduces his South
African formula, commenting on the pointlessness of producing good newspapers when bad ones sell better:

Page one, a nice picture of the Prime Minister. Page
two, something about actors. Page three, gossip. . .a
rail crash if you're lucky. Four, high technology. Five,
sex, sex crimes, court cases. . .Then letters. All pleas-

ingly like-minded, all from Kent. . .Then six pages of
sport. Back page, a lot of weather and something nasty
about the Opposition.

However, *Pravda* is not just about the press. Le Roux, who
delights in frightening people by exaggerating rather than
hiding high unemployment figures, epitomises the rampant
and aggressive confidence of the New Right which had (in the
1980's) replaced in government the benevolent paternalism of
an older tradition of Conservatism. He breaks into the British
establishment against the opposition of such Conservatives
who find him not "a proper person", through arrogance,
money, and the weakness of opposition. Le Roux succeeds
because he knows exactly what he wants, and is contemptuous
both of those who get trodden underfoot and of the very notion
of morality. For Le Roux, making money is "a natural thing"
and moral feelings to be compared only to feelings of
indigestion which pass overnight. By contrast, those who
oppose him are hopelessly woolly and vague in their beliefs, as
no one realises better than Le Roux himself: "You are all weak
because you don't know what you believe", he tells his sacked
editor, contemptuously dismissing the irrelevance of attacks
carried on through letters to newspapers, books which don't
sell, and even questions in the House. He alone recognises that
only strength, even violence, can defeat him: "You should hit a
man in the face to make his face disappear. . .I don't know
why they don't have the manhood to shoot me".

The only other character who understands the futile naïvety
of the opposition to Le Roux is Rebecca, who offers an
alternative to both the childish plotting for revenge and the
violence which Le Roux suggests. She argues vehemently for
the need to fight the ideas of the Right with genuine ideas from
the Left, and although within the play she is alone and
powerless, it is she, significantly the play's only prominent
female character, who carries all the weight of possibilities for
positive change in the future.

Theatrically, *Pravda* delighted in striking images, drawing
on the facilities and technology of the theatre for which it was
written; it demanded a large cast and luxuriated in the
opportunity to shift scenes between newspaper offices, an
English garden, a Frankfurt Exhibition Hall, the Irving Club, a
greyhound track, the Yorkshire Moors, and a Japanese
bungalow in Weybridge complete with water garden. The
play's considerable success during its year-long run at
London's National Theatre was probably due to its visual and
verbal wit as much as to its politics, and also to the monstrous
central role it created for Anthony Hopkins. Though some
critics thought its humour crudely undergraduate, others
found it Jonsonian, and the writers themselves characterised
the play as a "comedy of excess". *Pravda* is without doubt a
genuinely funny play, which offers an unusual mix of broad
satire and scathing political attack.

—Steve Nicholson

———

LES PRÉCIEUSES RIDICULES. See **THE PRETENTIOUS
YOUNG LADIES.**

———

THE PRECIOUS DAMSELS. See **THE PRETENTIOUS
YOUNG LADIES.**

———

THE PRETENTIOUS YOUNG LADIES
(Les Précieuses ridicules)
by Molière

First Publication: Paris, 1660.
First Production: Théâtre du Petit-Bourbon, Paris, 18 November 1659.

Editions
Les Précieuses ridicules, edited by H. Ashton, Toronto, 1924.
Les Précieuses ridicules [second edition], edited by Andrew Lang, Oxford, 1926.
Les Précieuses ridicules, edited by R.P.L. Ledésert, London, 1948.
Les Précieuses ridicules, in *Les Précieuses ridicules*; *l'Impromptu de Versailles*, Paris, 1959.
Les Précieuses ridicules, in *Les Précieuses ridicules*; *La Jalousie de Barbouillé*; *Sganarelle, ou, Le Cocu imaginaire*, edited by Fernand Angué, Paris, 1962.
Les Précieuses ridicules, edited by Félix Guirand and Pierre Dussange, Paris, 1962.
Les Précieuses ridicules, edited by Jean Balcou, Paris, 1965.
Les Précieuses ridicules, edited by Hubert Carrier, Paris, 1969.
Les Précieuses ridicules, edited by Micheline Cuénin, Geneva, 1973.

Translations
The Affected Young Ladies, translated by Barrett H. Clark, New York, 1915.
The Precious Damsels, in *Molière: Eight Plays*, translated by Morris Bishop, New York, 1957.
The Pretentious Young Ladies, translated by Herma Briffault, Woodbury, New York, c. 1959.
The Pretentious Young Ladies, translated by Renée Waldringer, Great Neck, New York, 1959.
The Intellectual Ladies, translated by Wallace Fowlie, in *Classical French Drama*, edited by Wallace Fowlie, New York, 1962.
The Ridiculous Précieuses, in *"Tartuffe" and Other Plays*, translated by Donald M. Frame, New York, 1967.

Criticism
(For general works on the author, see *Playwrights* volume)

Books:
Francesco Gianasso, *La Précosité et Molière: Étude littéraire*, Turin, 1920.
Bonnie Treloar, *Molière: "Les Précieuses ridicules"*, London, 1970.
Pol Gaillard, *Les Précieuses ridicules*; *Les Femmes savantes*, Paris, 1979.

Articles:
Hobart C. Chatfield-Taylor, "First Modern Comedy", in *World Today* [New York], 11, 1906.
Abel Lefranc, "La Troupe de Monsieur au Petit-Bourbon; la représentation des *Précieuses*; les Précieuses avant Molière; la société des Précieuses; Molière et la précosité", in *Revue des cours et conférences*, vol.15 no.2, 1906–07.
Henri Potez, "Que vous Enseigne Molière dans *Les Précieuses ridicules* et *Les Femmes savantes*?", in *Revue pédagogique*, 57, 1910.
Francesco Picco, "Des Précieuses de l'Hôtel de Rambouillet aux *Précieuses ridicules* de Molière", in *Nouvelle Revue d'Italie*, vol.19 no.2, 1922.
Gustave Reynier, "La Crise de la précosité et *Les Précieuses ridicules*", in his *La Femme au XVIIe. siècle*, Paris, 1929.
Antoine Adam, "Le Genèse des *Précieuses ridicules*", in *Revue d'histoire de la philosophie et d'histoire générale de la civilisation*, 7, 1939.
René Pintard, "Pour le Tricentenaire des *Précieuses ridicules*: Précosité et classicisme", in *Dix-septième Siècle*, 50–51, 1961.
Spire Pitou, "A Precious Note: Molière and Meunier", in *Romance Notes*, 6, 1965.
Harold Weinrich, "Zur Szene XI des *Précieuses ridicules*", in *Romanische Forschungen*, 79, 1967.
Quentin M. Hope, "Dramatic Techniques in *Les Précieuses ridicules*", in *Renaissance and Other Studies in Honor of W.L. Wyley*, edited by George B. Daniel, Chapel Hill, North Carolina, 1968.
Odette de Morgues, "Molière et le comique de la precosité", in *Mélanges offerts à Georges Couton*, edited Jean Jehasse, Claude Martin, Pierre Rétat, and others, Lyons, 1981.
Marcel Gutwirth, "Molière and the Woman Question: *Les Précieuses ridicules*; *L'École des femmes*; *Les Femmes savantes*", in *Theatre Journal*, vol.34 no.3, 1982.
Martha M. Houle, "Plots and Plausibilities in *Les Précieuses ridicules*", in *Cahiers du Dix-septième Siècle*, vol.2 no.1, 1988.

*   *   *

A pair of empty-headed young women, Magdelon and Cathos, newly arrived from the provinces with a smattering of fashionable ideas, aim to impress Parisian high society with their refinement. Their vanity and self-delusion make them easily taken in by Mascarille and Jodelet, two valets disguised as noblemen, who have been sent by their masters to avenge themselves for having been spurned by the *précieuses*.

This one-act sketch, Molière's third play, but the first to be performed in Paris, marked the appearance of comic devices that were to become the hallmarks of Molière's comedy. One is his pursuit of comic effect through character and situation, rather than in an intricate plot, as was the case with the prevailing type of literary comedy of the time. The play's sources lie rather in the stock masks and situations (such as the *burla*) of *commedia dell'arte* and traditional French farce. At the same time, however, Molière injects new life into popular traditions by locating the action in a recognisable contemporary social milieu, giving the comedy a double focus. As well as ridiculing universal human foibles, such as pretentiousness and gullibility, it draws its comic effects from a topical satire of manners.

The play is often said to have been an attack on particular individuals, though Molière regularly denied the charge. In fact, no-one has succeeded in demonstrating that his satire was directed against identifiable people rather than social types. The *précieuses* of the title refer to a phenomenon in polite society existing between the 1630's and the 1650's when literary salons, such as those of Mme. de Rambouillet and Mlle. de Scudéry, held sway. "Preciosity", itself, involved a movement which sought to introduce greater refinement into language, manners, and relations between the sexes. As such it was an inoffensive expression of an increasingly sophisticated, urban society, but it attracted some silly imitators in whom delicacy degenerated into affectation and hyper-refinement. It is these pale followers of fashion, rather than the originators of the movement, that Molière attacks. The basic joke is not that they are refined but that they unerringly mistake vulgar affectation for genuine sophistication. Magdelon and Cathos, their heads full of romanesque fiction and platonic notions, are against marriage and sex. Molière shows them denying all heighten the comic contrast with the aspirations of the *précieuses*. La Grange and Du Croisy complete the social spectrum within the play and introduce a norm, that of polite society, against which the more deviant characters are highlighted.

A deceptively simple sketch with the flimsiest of story lines and no literary pretentions, the play is essentially a performance piece. As such, it reveals a playwright who already possessed a remarkably sure command of the resources of his art. The structure derives from Molière's habitual formula of postulating an irrational attitude to the world, then testing that attitude in friction with the real world. Starting from a basically plausible and recognisable situation, Molière progressively heightens the fantasy until it implodes under its own contradictions. Its abrupt collapse brings comic discomfiture in the form of humiliation for the *précieuses* and the traditional beating of farce for the impersonators. This painful return to reality is both an implicit lesson and a satisfying, artistic resolution of the action.

Les Précieuses ridicules represents a landmark in the development of French, comic drama. It was originally presented as a curtain-raiser for the company's production of Corneille's *Cinna*. The decision to write it may have been a professional expedient, dictated by the dearth of original, comic texts and the need to furnish material to exploit the talents of his fellow-actors. But it proved a decisive event. The play's box-office popularity, exceptional by the standards of the day, and its success at Court transformed Molière from a struggling actor-manager into the most popular and controversial entertainer of his time. And the original formula, combining farce with provocative satire of contemporary manners, marked the appearance of a wholly new type of comedy and established the basic pattern for Molière's later masterpieces. It cannot claim to have the depth of vision of *Tartuffe* or *The Misanthrope* but its directness, simplicity, and vigour make it perennially effective.

—David Whitton

The Pretentious Young Ladies: Engraved frontispiece, 1682

reality and living in a fantasy world which collapses in ruins with their public exposure to ridicule in the play's farcical ending.

No less ridiculous than the women are the two pseudo-aristocrats. Mascarille, although played without a mask by Molière, is a direct descendent of the *commedia dell'arte* mask of the quick-witted valet, adept at assuming disguises. Onto this traditional role Molière grafts a piquant caricature of the affected courtier with his exuberant display of dress and artificial manners and language. He is complemented by Jodelet, a less complex but equally vigorous role created to capitalise on the talents of a recent recruit to the company, Julien Bedeau. Under his stage name, Jodelet, he was famous for his portrayal of stock characters of native, Gallic farce. He was characterised by a face covered in flour and a nasal delivery. As an old soldier ineptly impersonating the military aristocracy, Jodelet provides the perfect dull-witted foil to Mascarille's extravagant posturing.

The supporting characters are lightly sketched and serve largely to point up the central comedy. Gorgibus is a variation on another *commedia dell'arte* role, that of the irascible, bourgeois father. His low-brow vulgarity, like the uneducated speech of the servant, Marotte, is exaggerated by Molière to

PRINCE FRIEDRICH OF HOMBURG.   See **THE PRINCE OF HOMBURG.**

PRINZ FRIEDRICH VON HOMBURG.   See **THE PRINCE OF HOMBURG.**

THE PRINCE OF HOMBURG (Prinz Friedrich von Homburg) by Heinrich von Kleist

First Publication: In *Hinterlassene Schriften*, Berlin, 1821.
First Production: As *Die Schlacht von Fehrbellin*, Burgtheater, Vienna, 3 October 1821.

Editions
Prinz Friedrich von Homburg, edited by G.F. Bridge, London, 1898.
Prinz Friedrich von Homburg, edited by G.M. Baker, New York, 1914.

The Prince of Homburg: National Theatre, London, 1982

Prinz Friedrich von Homburg, edited by Richard Samuel, London, 1957.

Prinz Friedrich von Homburg, edited by Richard Samuel, Berlin, 1964.

Prinz Friedrich von Homburg: Text, Kontexte, Kommentar, edited by Klaus Kanzog, Munich and Vienna, 1977.

Translations

The Prince of Homburg, translated by Charles E. Passage, New York, 1956.

The Prince of Homburg, translated by James Kirkup, in *The Classic Theatre, 2*, edited by Eric Bentley, New York, 1959.

Prince Friedrich of Homburg, in *Heinrich von Kleist: Five Plays*, translated by Martin Greenberg, New Haven, Connecticut, and London, 1988.

Criticism

(For general works on the author, see *Playwrights* volume)

Books:

Mary Garland, *Kleist's "Prinz Friedrich von Homburg": An Interpretation Through Word Patterns*, The Hague and Paris, 1968.

Karl Schweizer, *Heinrich von Kleist: "Prinz Friedrich von Homburg": Interpretation*, Munich, 1968.

J.M. Ellis, *Kleist: "Prinz von Homburg": A Critical Study*, Berkeley, California, 1970.

Fritz Hackert, *Heinrich von Kleist: "Prinz Friedrich von Homburg": Erlaüterungen und Dokumente*, Stuttgart, 1979.

Articles:

J.C. Blakenagel, "*Prinz Friedrich von Homburg* and Freedom of Initiative", in *Modern Language Notes*, 52, 1937.

A.E. Zucker, "Biographical Elements in Homburg's Todesfurchtsszene", in *Studies in Philology*, 34, 1937.

Hans M. Wolff, "Rotrous *Venceslas* und Kleists *Prinz Friedrich von Homburg*", in *Modern Philology*, 37, 1939.

W. Silz, "On *Homburg* and the Death of Kleist", in *Monatsschrift*, vol.32 no.7, 1940.

Sten Flygt, "Kleist's Struggle with the Problem of Feeling", in *Publications of the Modern Language Association* [*PMLA*], 58, 1943.

E. Furstenheim, "The Sources of Kleist's *Prinz Friedrich von Homburg*", in *German Life and Letters*, vol.8 no.2, 1955.

G. Mathieu, "The Struggle for a Man's Mind: A Modern View of Kleist's *Prinz von Homburg*", in *German Life and Letters*, 13, 1960.

Peter Salm, "'Confidence' and the 'Miraculous' in Kleist's *Prinz Friedrich von Homburg*", in *German Quarterly*, 34, 1961.

Wolfgang Wittkowski, "Absolutes Gefuhl und absolute Kunst in Kleists *Prinz Friedrich von Homburg*", in *Deutschunterricht*, 8, 1961.

Arthur Henkel, "Traum und Gesetz in Kleists *Prinz von Homburg*", in *Neue Rundschau*, 73, 1962.

V.C. Hubbs, "Heinrich von Kleist and the Symbol of the Wise Man", in *Symposium*, 1962.

S. Burchhardt, "*Egmont* and *Prinz Friedrich von Homburg*", in *German Quarterly*, 36, 1963.

A. Henschel, "The Primacy of Free Will in the Mind of Kleist and in *Prinz Friedrich von Homburg*", in *German Life and Letters*, vol.17 no.2, 1964.

J.M. Benson, "Kleist's *Prinz Friedrich von Homburg*", in *Modern Languages*, 46, 1965.

Hans-Günther Thalheim, "Kleists *Prinz Friedrich von Homburg*", in *Weimarer Beiträge*, 1965.

J. Parker, "A Motif and Certain Peculiarities of Style in Heinrich von Kleist's *Prinz Friedrich von Homburg*", in *AUMLA Journal*, 23, 1965.

J. Ellis, "The Heidelberg ms. of Kleist's *Prinz Friedrich von Homburg*", in *Euphorion*, 60, 1966.

E.W. Herd, "Form and Intention in Kleist's *Prinz Friedrich von Homburg*", in *Seminar: A Journal of Germanic Studies*, 2, 1966.

John J. Parker, "Kleists Schauspiel *Prinz von Homburg*: Ein in Jeder Hinsicht politisches Werk?", in *Germanisch-Romanische Monatsschrift*, 16, 1966.

G. Baumgartel, "Zur Frage der Wandlung in Kleists *Prinz Friedrich von Homburg*", in *Germanisch-Romanische Monatsschrift*, 16, 1966.

John Gearey, "Character and Idea in *Prinz Friedrich von Homburg*", in *Germanic Review*, 42, 1967.

Helmut Sembdner, "Noch einmal zur Manuskript-Lage des *Prinz von Homburg*", in *Euphorion*, 61, 1967.

Peter U. Hohendahl, "Der Pass des Graten Horn: Ein Aspekt des Politischen in *Prinz Friedrich von Homburg*", in *German Quarterly*, 41, 1968.

Donald Crosby, "Kleist's *Prinz von Homburg*—An Intensified *Egmont*?", in *German Life and Letters*, 23, 1970.

Heinz Politizer, "Kleists Trauerspiel von Traum: *Prinz Friedrich von Homburg*", in *Euphorion*, 64, 1970.

Wolfgang Nehring, "Kleists *Prinz von Homburg*: Die Marionette auf dem Weg zum Gott", in *Germanic Quarterly*, 44, 1971.

Rolf N. Linn, "Die prästabilierte Harmonie in Heinrich von Kleists *Prinz von Homburg*", in *Modern Language Notes*, 88, 1973.

Fritz Hackert, "Kleists *Prinz Friedrich von Homburg* in der Nachkriegsinterpretationen, 1947–1972: Ein Literaturbericht", in *LiLi: Zeitschrift für Literaturwissenschaft und Linguistik*, 12, 1973.

Marie M. Tatar, "Psychology and Poetics: J.C. Reil and Kleist's *Prinz Friedrich von Homburg*", in *Germanic Review*, 48, 1973.

Gerhard Bauer, "Absicht, Wirksamkeit und Kunst von Kleists Dialog im *Homburg*: Beitrag zur Kritik an der 'Poetik' des Dialogs", in *Beiträge zur Poetic des Dramas*, edited by Werner Keller, Darmstadt, 1976.

Stuart Atkins, "Taught by Success: Kleist's *Prince of Homburg*", in *German Quarterly*, 50, 1977.

Raimund Belgardt, "*Prinz Friedrich von Homburg*'s neues Wissen", in *Neophilologus*, 61, 1977.

E.M. Oppenheimer, "How Prince Friedrich von Homburg Learned to Write", in *Carleton Germanic Papers*, 5, 1977.

Marion Faber, "The Tragic Impulse: *Prinz Friedrich von Homburg* and *Der Besuch der alten Dame*", in *Language Quarterly*, 17, 1978.

Richard Samuel, "A Final Word Regarding the Manuscripts of *Prinz Friedrich von Homburg*", in *German Life and Letters*, 33, 1979.

Dirk Grathoff, "Zur frühen Rezeptionsgeschichte von Kleists Schauspiel *Prinz Friedrich von Homburg*", in *Germanisch-Romansiche Monatsschrift*, 30, 1980.

John G. Mulligan, "Kleist's *Friedrich von Homburg*: Prince Without a Choice", in *Forum for Modern Language Studies*, 16, 1980.

Roland Heine, " 'Ein Traum, was sonst?': Zum Verhältnis von Traum und Wirklichkeit in Kleist's *Prinz Friedrich von Homburg*", in *Literaturwissenschaft und Geistesgeschichte: Festschrift für Richard Brinkman*, edited by Jürgen Brummack and others, Tübingen, 1981.

Klaus Kanzog, "Geschichtlicher Stoff und geschichtlicher Code: Heinrich von Kleists *Prinz Friedrich von Homburg*", in *Geschichte als Schauspiel: Deutsche Geschichtsdramen: Interpretationen*, Frankfurt, 1981.

W.C. Reeve, "An Unsung Villain: The Role of Hohenzollern in Kleist's *Prinz Friedrich von Homburg*", in *Germanic Review*, 1981.

Valentine C. Hubbs, "Die Ambiguität in Kleist's *Prinz Friedrich von Homburg*", in *Kleist-Jahrbuch*, 1981–82.

Helmut Sembdner, "Schauspieler interpretieren Kleists *Prinz Friedrich von Homburg*", in *Sameln und Sichten: Festschrift für Oscar Fambach zum 80. Geburtstag*, Bonn, 1982.

Erika Swales, "Configurations of Irony: Kleist's *Prinz Friedrich von Homburg*", in *Deutsche Vierteljahrsschrift für Literaturwissenschaft und Geistesgeschichte*, 56, 1982.

G.A. Wells, "Der Kurfurst gegen den Prinzen: Recht und Unrecht in Kleists Schauspiel *Prinz Friedrich von Homburg*", in *Wirkendes Wort*, 5, 1983.

Klaus Lüderssen, "Recht als Verständigung unter gleichen in Kleists *Prinz Friedrich von Homburg*: Ein aristokratisches oder ein demokratisches Prinzip?", in *Kleist-Jahrbuch*, 1985.

Roger A. Nicholls, "*Schlug meiner Leiden letzte Stunde*: The Problems of the Resolution of Kleist's *Prinz Friedrich von Homburg*", in *Carleton Germanic Papers*, 14, 1986.

Rosemarie Zeller, "Kleists *Prinz Friedrich von Homburg* auf dem Hintergrund der literarischen Tradition", in *Jahrbuch der deutschen Schiller-Gesellschaft*, 30, 1986.

*   *   *

Prince Friedrich of Homburg is centred upon events associated with the Battle of Fehrbellin of 1675, in which the "Great Elector", Friedrich Wilhelm of Brandenburg, decisively defeated the Swedish army. The eponymous Prince Friedrich, the Elector's nephew, is a senior officer in the Brandenburg army. While the orders for battle are being given, the Prince, distracted by his love for Natalie, Princess of Orange, fails to listen. Consequently, during the battle he leads a cavalry charge that is strictly against the Elector's orders. The Prince's charge actually wins the battle for the Brandenburg army, but the Prince himself is condemned to death for disobeying orders. He pleads with Natalie to intercede with the Elector. The Elector is prepared to pardon the Prince if he (the Prince) considers that the sentence is unjust, but the Prince, acknowledging the pre-eminence of law, effectively signs his own death warrant by accepting the justice of the sentence. Catastrophe is averted at the last moment and Friedrich is given Natalie's hand in marriage. War against the Swedes resumes.

There can be few plays in the German language that have aroused so much critical controversy as *Prince Friedrich of Homburg*. In a recent study of the play, over 270 different readings are noted. The reasons for the interest aroused by the play are not difficult to find. For a start the main action of the play is framed by two puzzling episodes, both of which take place at night-time in the palace garden at Fehrbellin. In the opening scene Prince Friedrich is seen sleepwalking, in which state he reveals his love for Natalie, his filial feelings for the Elector and his desire to win glory. Natalie and the Elector with his court observe this and the Elector tantalizingly offers Friedrich the symbols of success in love and war only to withdraw them again. At the end of the play, the staging of this scene is re-enacted with Friedrich blindfold, thinking he is about to be shot. Instead he is given the hand of Natalie and the glory, imagined in the opening scene, is fulfilled.

A further reason why the play has created such interest is the uncertainty as to the attitude expressed by Kleist toward Prussian militarism. Kleist had been born into a military family and had tried to make his career both in the Prussian army and in the civil service. His failures as a soldier, as a civil servant, and as a writer all contributed toward his suicide that occurred soon after the completion of *Prince Friedrich of Homburg*. Not surprisingly, therefore, the play can be seen to express Kleist's irreconcilably divided response to the society that produced and rejected him.

At the risk of oversimplification, most critical interpretations of the play are biased toward one side of the dramatic conflict at the expense of the other. Accordingly, if the Elector is favoured as the play's point of gravity, *Prince Friedrich of Homburg* might be regarded as a dramatic equivalent of the *Bildungsroman*, in which the young hero is initiated into the ways of the world and accepts his position within it. If, however, the Prince is considered to be the central character, an argument that is possibly corroborated by both the title and the structure of the action, then the play can appear to be primarily an attack upon the rigid discipline that was so characteristic of the Prussian army. Certainly the latter interpretation makes for a more complex drama, as therefore the Prince does not have to appear as a spotless paragon, while the Elector, symbol of Prussian authority, is revealed as being equally fallible. Both men thus grow toward a more mature understanding of the world.

The Prince achieves greater wisdom primarily through realising the imminence of death in all his undertakings. On his way from prison to plead with Natalie to intercede with the Elector, he sees his grave already dug. This results in the famous "*Todesfurchtszene*" ("fear of death scene"), in which he totally abases himself and renounces all privileges in life as long as he is allowed to survive. Natalie assuages his terror by insisting that "the grave that has been opened to receive you / . . .is no more terrible and no wider / Than the grave that always waited for you on the field of battle". Friedrich's recognition of this fact and his acceptance of the inviolability of the law are crucial steps toward his maturation. At the end of the play, it can be argued that he has earned the rewards of which previously he had only dreamed.

The Elector is a more questionable figure. An unsympathetic interpretation of him will make him out to be an ageing, potential tyrant who is jealous of younger men aspiring to his military glory and, possibly, to his political power. Certainly, his conduct at the battle of Fehrbellin is irresponsible in the extreme, for he is constantly in the middle of the fighting and, during the crucial final phase, is actually thought by his army to be dead. His later intransigence toward Friedrich also causes Natalie to exploit her position as commander-in-chief of a regiment in a manner that brings the army close to open mutiny. Ultimately the Elector appears to be persuaded by arguments that if he does not allow some freedom of action to his soldiers he will have an army that is so cowed it will be useless. But a more compelling, though unspoken, reason for his final grant of clemency to Friedrich might well be his recognition that he has been acting toward the young man from motives of personal jealousy.

Like most of Kleist's dramas, it was several years before *Prince Friedrich of Homburg* found a stage. In particular, his contemporaries found the "*Todesfurchtszene*" to be distasteful and Kleist's insistence that it be retained contributed significantly to the play's rejection. In fact, it is only in the 20th century that this great play has received full recognition and come to occupy a central position in the repertory. Kleist's verse is leaner and is more suited to the creation of dramatic momentum than is Schiller's comparatively more ponderous verse, which is still perhaps the standard idiom of German, classical drama. Furthermore, in contrast to Schiller, Kleist's characters are not ideal creations. Although a successful staging of the play may well require all the detailed stage-spectacle that was characteristic of much early 19th-century theatre, ultimately a successful performance depends upon the completeness of the realization of the radical, and often destructive, contradictions that tear apart Kleist's characters and the society of which they are representative.

—Simon Williams

PRIVATE LIVES
by Noël Coward

First Publication: London, 1930.
First Production: King's Theatre, Edinburgh, 18 August 1930.

* * *

Noel Coward's quarrelsome quartet—Elyot, Amanda, Sibyl, and Victor—inhabits the play that is most closely associated with the Coward milieu. The brickbat is tossed as effortlessly as the *bon mot*, marriage vows are broken, old flames rekindled and no one seems to care about anything significant or important. The play opens at a Riviera hotel, the adjoining terraces of a particularly smart set of suites revealing two couples on their respective honeymoons. Marital bliss proves fleeting however when we learn that Amanda was once married to Sibyl's new husband, Elyot. The once-wedded pair happen to meet, rapidly convince themselves that their divorce was a mistake, and run off to Paris together. As far as the plot goes, that is really about it. The second act is taken up with billing and cooing alternating with wrestling bouts, the curtain coming down on the entrance of the avenging spouses, Sibyl and Victor. The final act is a brittle and stunning "morning after", during which Elyot and Amanda once again realize that they are inseparable. They quietly exit, leaving Victor and Sibyl to their own nettlesome devices.

The play is celebrated for such lines as "certain women should be struck regularly, like gongs". There is though, beneath the shimmer of Coward's *badinage*, a coherent world view that enables his comic world to function. In Act I Amanda speaks the words which give the play its title:

> I think very few people are completely normal really, deep down in their private lives. It all depends upon a combination of circumstances. If all the various cosmic thingummys fuse at the same moment, and the right spark is struck, there's no telling what one mightn't do. . .

Indeed, for Coward, "complete normality" is often a superficial excuse for the cut and parry of his comic interplay. In Act II when the telephone rings, interrupting their extra-marital idyll, Amanda and Elyot are momentarily discomposed, fearing it may be Sibyl and Victor. They quickly recover themselves though, by determining to "behave exquisitely".

The humor of the third act depends entirely upon the audience recognizing along with Elyot that: "this situation is entirely without precedent. We have no prescribed etiquette to fall back on". By stating bluntly the basic premise of the comedy of manners—the existence of "prescribed etiquette"—Coward perfectly positions himself to subvert etiquette's prescriptions. The small talk and "polite conversation" that Amanda attempts to make are juxtaposed with Victor's attempts at fisticuffs with Elyot—both are, after all, traditional ways of dealing with unwanted situations. However, Victor's choice of violence is easily overcome by Elyot's level-headed lightheartedness, and Amanda is reduced to muffled silence when Elyot's frivolous reply to her drivelling disquisition on the wonders of travel causes her to choke on a croissant.

Throughout his career, Coward attempted to give the play its dramaturgical due. In his introduction to it in *Play Parade, 1* he candidly appraises the quality of the love scene between Amanda and Elyot in the first act, describing it as being "well-written", and claims that there is a "certain amount of sound sex psychology underlying the quarrel scenes" in the second act. Later in his life Coward described the play as: "the lightest of light comedies, based upon a serious situation which is two people who love each other too much. I wouldn't say it's a tragedy, but there's a sadness below it".

Elyot indeed has a rather low moment in the third act when he bemoans his fate and declares that no one would care in the slightest if he dropped dead at that very instant. Of course, Victor sees this as Elyot's relentless flippancy asserting itself. And the objective of Elyot's gloom is not so much to make him appear suddenly serious, as it is an enabling device that keeps him within the audiences's sympathies. The situation is almost getting "serious", the legally married couples are on the verge of possibly patching things up. This would totally undo everything that the audience has been led to expect and, more importantly, what Coward has directed it to desire.

One of Coward's especial skills as a dramatist is his ability to keep his audience fascinated by his characters. The virtual plotlessness of *Private Lives* demands that we continue to be interested in what the characters say, precisely because there is so little for them to do.

Frequently acknowledged as Coward's masterpiece, *Private Lives* endures because it is so peculiarly mannered that it transcends manners *per se*; it explains itself so carefully as it goes along that the glittering society that it reflects need not be understood by the audience. The Great Depression wiped out that society forever a few years after the play's premiere anyway. Thus *Private Lives* is a mirror not so much held up to nature, as it is beyond nature, reflecting not a particular society but rather more primal social impulses.

—Thomas F. Connolly

PROCESSIONAL
by John Howard Lawson

First Publication: New York, 1925.
First Production: Garrick Theatre, New York (Theatre Guild), 12 January 1925.

Criticism
(For general works on the author, see *Playwrights* volume)

Articles:
M.J. Mendelsohn, "The Social Critics on Stage", in *Modern Drama*, 6, 1963.
Kurt Müller, "John Howard Lawsons *Processional* als Vorläufer der New-Playwright-Inszenierungen", in his *Konventionen und Tendenzen der Gesellschaftskritik im expressionistischen amerikanischen Drama der zwanziger Jahre*, Frankfurt, 1977.

*   *   *

Subtitled "a jazz symphony of American life", this drama employs elements of jazz and vaudeville to make a sardonic statement about social struggle. In four acts, the action occurs in a West Virginia coal mining community during a 1920's strike. In Act I a musical band of striking miners march into town on Independence Day, warning that soldiers are arriving to break the strike and intimidate sympathizers. The antagonists are led by two caricatured figures of capitalistic authority: the Man in a Silk Hat (representing Big Business) and his henchman, the Sheriff. In the crowd are Sadie Cohen, a store owner's daughter, Phillpotts, a city reporter, and Psinski, a miner and Communist agitator. As the anti-labor leaders arrive, the townspeople and miners disperse in confusion.

Dynamite Jim Flimmins, a hard-drinking, brawling, lustful coal miner, is the play's protagonist. Acts II and III find him jailed for having drunkenly torn an American flag when taunted by soldiers; escaping from jail and hiding in first one place and then another as he is relentlessly pursued by the Sheriff, soldiers, and Ku Klux Klan; then being caught again and blinded by the man-hunting posse. Before his capture, he encounters Sadie and makes love to her. In Act IV, Sadie has gone to live with Flimmins's mother as she awaits the birth of his child, who to her is prophecy of a free mankind. Blind Jim returns and is united with Sadie in marriage, with the whole town forming a wedding procession. To the amazement of labor-agitator Psinski, the Man in the Silk Hat declares the strike settled and the strikers pardoned. The Klan is disbanded, and a telegram from Calvin Coolidge proclaims that "all men are brothers".

Processional evidences two major characteristics of John Howard Lawson's work: a political commitment to social protest and a bent for theatrical experimentation. Stylistically, the drama encompasses theatrical devices which are nowadays associated with musical comedy. In his preface, Lawson stresses his wish to "express the American scene in native idiom" by using a method, removed from realism, that is essentially vaudeville in character. Many vaudeville or melodrama stereotypes are used: for example, the Jewish low comedian (Sadie Cohen's father), the Negro comedian (a black miner named Rastus), the smart city slicker/brash reporter (Phillpotts), the hard-nosed officer of the law (Sheriff), and the callous business tycoon (Man in a Silk Hat). Jim Flimmins is the image of the tough, courageous proletarian hero (who initially combines traits of the "Dumb Swede" and "Drunken Irishman") and Sadie, the naïve, rural girl deserving a better life beyond her circumstances. Like olio acts, the scenes are identified by descriptive captions: "On the Fourth of July", "Dynamite Jim", "What Happened to Sadie", "The Jazz Wedding", etc. Mordecai Gorelik's scenic designs for the original 1925 production emphasized the cartoon quality of the locales and action. Throughout the melodramatic action, a jazz march called "Yankee Doodle Blues" and the music of the miners, each with his own instrument, create a background.

Serious emotion is ameliorated by scenes breaking up into song-and-dance or tumbling acts of physical action in chase-and-fight sequences. The constant intrusion of music into the action is also vaudevillian.

The ills of American society, particularly as they relate to the struggle of labor, are accented by the force of exaggeration and a theatrical, cartoon style. Moreover, a number of sacred cows of the Right and the Left are discredited: capital, labor, radical agitators, the press, the military, motherhood, the presidency, and the flag. While the story of the strike and the young lovers seemingly ends on a happy note, the final image of blind Jim and pregnant Sadie, who are left alone on stage as the wedding procession exits through the audience, makes a wry, solitary comment on the Presidential telegram that "all men are brothers".

A characteristic Lawson theme is drawn upon in the pattern of a dynamic protagonist achieving regeneration and revelation through an ordeal of solitude and suffering brought on by confinement. Indeed, the root concept of Lawson's dramatic theory, expressed in his *Theory and Technique of Playwriting and Screenwriting*, is that of "the conscious will" (an idea borrowed from French theorist Ferdinand Brunetière), whereby the protagonist must strive to understand the world in order to be able to choose consciously his course of action. Dynamite Jim is initially a physical animal, a politically unaware drinker and brawler. Yet he develops social and personal awareness through a series of revelations generated by confinement in such restricted spaces as a jail, a coffin, a cellar, a mine shaft. Each confinement triggers an arousal of emotion—be it fear, frustration, rage, lust, or loss of filial love—which culminates in the ultimate confinement: the solitude of blindness. From these experiences of confinement, in which Jim often hears "voices" (an expressionistic device) serving to objectify those forces leading him toward mental regeneration, he is borne forth, ultimately converted from being a lustful, drunken brawler into a kind of inchoate political anarchist. A similar pattern can be found in the development of other Lawson protagonists, such as the title character of *Roger Bloomer*, a predecessor of Jim Flimmins.

While dated in its material and approach, *Processional* remains an excellent, interesting example of American protest drama of the 1920's and of the utilization of a highly theatrical style. It is a major work by its author.

—Christian H. Moe

PROFESSOR TARANNE
by Arthur Adamov

First Publication: In *Théâtre, 1*, Paris, 1953.
First Production: Théâtre de la Comédie, Lyon, 18 March 1953.

Criticism
(For general works on the author, see *Playwrights* volume)

Articles:
Renée Geen, "A Propos du *Professeur Taranne*", in *Essays in French Literature*, 7, 1970.
Michèle Blin, "La Fonction de la répétition dans *Le Professeur Taranne*: Essai d'approche sémio-analytique d'une pièce d'Adamov", in *Revue de Pacifique*, 2, 1976.
Linda K. Stillman, "*Le Professeur Taranne*: A Marxist Critique", in *French Literary Criticism*, Columbia, South Carolina, 1977.

*   *   *

In a style that draws on both Strindberg and Kafka, *Professor Taranne* shows a character who is unable to convince the people around him that he is who he claims to be. Gradually he is overwhelmed by a sense of guilt and failure until, at the end of the play, the audience sees his character disintegrate. The play opens in a police station, where Taranne seems to be accused of indecent exposure, though formal charges are never brought against him. At first he appears to have an alibi, but this is thrown into doubt by the fact that the people he encounters, and whom he claims to know, fail to recognise him; worse, they accuse him of aping the mannerisms of another well-known professor. His claims are undermined by a series of further revelations, the last of which comes in the form of a letter from a Belgian university where he had previously been invited to lecture, accusing him of outright plagiarism. He turns slowly to the wall and begins to undress, committing the act that he perhaps secretly desired to all along, or that has perhaps been forced upon him by the accusations he has been unable to counter.

The resemblance of this plot to one of Strindberg's dream plays is not incidental: it is the faithful transcription of one of Adamov's own dreams. In his original dream he struggled in vain to assert that he was the author of *The Parody* (his first play, written in 1947); for the play he changed only the profession of the central character, making him a professor rather than an author. His name, Taranne, is borrowed from the discreetly respectable hotel that faces you as you sit on the terrace of the *Deux Magots* café on the Boulevard St. Germain in Paris.

The play's autobiographical origins are evident in the fact that the only character of any consistency is Taranne himself. All the others have functional roles in relation to the drama of his unfolding neurosis. It is successful as a dream play because it respects reality and observes the paradox that dreams are most frightening when they are most real. Kafka's stylistic device of presenting his character's situations through a narrative apparently emanating from a third person, but which turns out to have its origin in the character's own thoughts, here finds an equivalent dramatic form. At first, the audience is drawn into seeing the situation entirely from the point of view of Taranne, but the revelations and comments of the other characters gradually cast doubt on his claims. As the play continues, these claims develop self-contradictory aspects: to counter the accusation of exposure, he claims he always uses a bathing cabin; but to counter a later accusation of leaving litter in the bathing cabins, he claims never to have used one. The audience experiences a shift, from initial identification with Taranne, through a stage of doubting the truth of his statements, to the point where they once more identify with his struggle against his all-engulfing doubts. These doubts, that had at first appeared only on the professional level (could he maintain his claim to professional respectability; was he really the author of the notebook he claimed as his, but which turned out to be full of blank pages?), then move onto a more personal plane, as the setting shifts from the police station to a hotel foyer, and the threatening policemen are replaced by the more subtly treacherous figure of Taranne's own sister.

Despite its brevity (it runs for about an hour in performance), *Professor Taranne* is generally considered to be Adamov's masterpiece, and occupies a special place in his *oeuvre*. This is partly because it was his first play to be premiered not in Paris but in Lyon, by Roger Planchon, soon to become the leader of the Brechtian school of theatre directors in France; but also because it was the first of his plays in which he managed to reconcile Surrealist fantasy with everyday reality. It was the only one of his early plays that he did not reject during his "political phase" (1956–66). The importance of the play for its author probably lay in the fact that here, for the first time, he found an adequate dramatic image for his extreme insecurity about his own identity. *Professor Taranne* embodies the dilemma of the confessional writer, driven to expose himself in public, but whose very identity is put in question by this act: if the public does not recognise and reward him by according him the status of recognised author, he risks being completely unmade by his act of exposure.

—David Bradby

PROMETHEUS BOUND (Prometheus Vinctus / Prometheus Desmotes)
by Aeschylus?

First Production: c.466–59 B.C.

Editions

The Prometheus Chained, edited by F.A. Paley, Cambridge, 1875.

The "Prometheus Bound" of Aeschylus, edited by H. Rackham, Cambridge, 1899; second edition, 1903.

The "Prometheus Vinctus" of Aeschylus, edited by C.E. Laurence, London, 1901.

The "Prometheus Bound" [with translation], edited and translated by George Thomson, Cambridge, 1932.

Prometheus Bound, edited by Mark Griffith, Cambridge, 1983.

Translations

Prometheus Bound, translated by Robert Whitelaw, Oxford, 1907.

The "Prometheus Bound" of Aeschylus, translated by Edward George Harmon, London, 1920.

Prometheus Bound, in *Four Plays of Aeschylus*, translated by G.M. Cookson, Oxford, 1922.

Prometheus Bound, translated by Gilbert Murray, London, 1931.

Prometheus Bound, translated by T.G. Tucker, Melbourne and London, 1935.

Prometheus Bound, translated by R.C. Trevelyan, Cambridge, 1939.

Prometheus Bound, in *Three Greek Tragedies*, translated by David Grene, New York, 1942.

Prometheus Bound, translated by Rex Warner, London, 1947.

Prometheus Bound, in *Prometheus Bound; The Suppliants; Seven Against Thebes; The Persians*, translated by Philip Vellacott, Harmondsworth, 1961.

Prometheus Bound, translated by Warren B. Anderson, New York, 1963.

Prometheus Bound, translated by Paul Roche, New York, 1964.

Prometheus Bound, in *"The Oresteia Trilogy" and "Prometheus Bound"*, translated by Michael Townsend, San Francisco, 1966.

Prometheus Bound, in *Seven Against Thebes; Prometheus Bound*, translated by Peter Arnott, London and New York, 1968.

Prometheus Bound, in *"The Frogs" and Other Plays*, translated by Kenneth McLeish, 1970.

Prometheus Bound, translated by James Scully and C.J. Herington, Oxford and New York, 1975.

Criticism
(For general works on the author, see *Playwrights* volume)

Books:

E. Vandvik, *Prometheus of Hesiod and Aeschylus*, Oslo, 1943.

Christian Kreutz, *Die zentrale Funktion des äschyleischen Prometheus im Denken Samuel Taylor Coleridges*, 1963.

L. Golden, *In Praise of Prometheus*, Chapel Hill, North Carolina, 1966.

C.J. Herington, *The Author of the "Prometheus Bound"*, Austin, Texas, 1970.

M. Griffith, *The Authenticity of "Prometheus Bound"*, Cambridge, 1977.

D.J. Conacher, *Aeschylus' "Prometheus Bound": A Literary Commentary*, Toronto, 1980.

Articles:

F.H. Gile, "Prometheus Bound and Unbound", in *Arena*, 39, 1908.

A.K. Thomson, "Religious Background of the *Prometheus Vinctus*", in *Harvard Studies in Classical Philology*, 31, 1920.

O.J. Todd, "Character of Zeus in Aeschylus' *Prometheus Bound*", in *Classical Quarterly*, 19, 1925.

H.W. Smyth, "Commentary on Aeschylus' *Prometheus* in the Codex Neapolitanus", in *Harvard Studies in Classical Philology*, 32, 1921.

S.M. Adams, "Four Elements in the *Prometheus Vinctus*", in *Classical Philology*, 28, 1933.

L.R. Farnell, "The Paradox of the *Prometheus Vinctus*", in *Journal of Hellenic Studies*, 53, 1933.

D. Grene, "*Prometheus Bound*", in *Classical Philology*, 35, 1940.

J.M. Robertson, "Aeschylus and the Messianic Idea: A Re-Reading of *Prometheus Bound*", in *London Quarterly and Holborn Review*, 168, 1937.

J. Davison, "The Date of the *Prometheia*", in *Transactions and Proceedings of the American Philological Association* [*TAPA*], 80, 1949.

B. Weaver, "*Prometheus Bound* and *Prometheus Unbound*", in *Publications of the Modern Language Association* [*PMLA*], 64, 1949.

D.S. Robertson, "Prometheus and Chiron", in *Journal of Hellenic Studies*, 71, 1951.

E.G. Ballard, "The Unbinding of Prometheus", in *Classical Journal*, 50, 1955.

B.H. Fowler, "The Imagery of the *Prometheus*", in *American Journal of Philology*, 78, 1957.

H.S. Long, "Notes on Aeschylus' *Prometheus Bound*", in *Proceedings of the American Philosophical Society*, 102, 1958.

A.D. Fitton-Brown, "*Promethia*", in *Journal of Hellenic Studies*, 79, 1959.

G. Whalley, "Coleridge on the *Prometheus* of Aeschylus", in *Royal Society of Canada Proceedings and Transactions* (third series), vol.54 no.2, 1960.

F. Will, "*Prometheus* and the Question of Self-Awareness in Greek Literature", in *American Journal of Philology*, 83, 1962.

C.J. Herington, "A Study in the *Promethia*: Part 1: The Elements in the Trilogy", in *Phoenix*, 17, 1963.

C.J. Herington, "A Study in the *Promethia*: Part 2: Birds and *Promethia*", in *Phoenix*, 17, 1963.

L. Gunderson, "The Human Situation and Its Religious Implications in the *Gilgamesh* Epic and *Prometheus Bound*", in *Discourse*, vol.7 no.4, 1964.

F. Duysinx, "Les Passages lyriques dans le *Prométhée enchaîné* d'Eschyle", in *L'Antiquité classique*, 1, 1965.

A. Garzya, "Le Tragique du *Prométhée enchaîné* d'Eschyle", in *Mnemosyne: Bibliotheca Classica Batava*, 18, 1965.

A.J. Podlecki, "Reciprocity in the *Prometheus*", in *Greek, Roman and Byzantine Studies*, 10, 1969.

A.C. Yu, "New Gods and Old: Tragic Theology in the *Prometheus Bound*", in *Journal of the American Academy of Religion*, 39, 1971.

S. Ireland, "Dramatic Structure in the *Persae* and *Prometheus* of Aeschylus", in *Greece and Rome* (second series), 20, 1973.

C.J. Herington, "Introduction to the *Prometheus Bound*", in *Arion* (new series), 1, 1973–74.

D.J. Conacher, "Prometheus as Founder of the Arts", in *Greek, Roman and Byzantine Studies*, 18, 1977.

M. Ewans, "*Prometheus Bound*", in *Ramus*, 6, 1977.

D. Konstan, "Ocean Episode in the *Prometheus Bound*", in *Hispanic Review*, 17, 1977.

M.L. West, "The Prometheus Trilogy", in *Journal of Hellenic Studies*, 99, 1979.

M. Griffith, "The Vocabulary of *Prometheus Bound*", in *Classical Quarterly* (new series), vol.34 no.2, 1984.

*   *   *

The Titan Prometheus is nailed to a remote crag by Zeus's uneasy agents, in punishment for his theft of fire from the gods to give to humans. As a succession of fantastic visitors come his way (the minor deities Ocean and his daughters, the half-human Io), it gradually emerges that Prometheus has a potential hold over Zeus: he knows the identity of the goddess who is destined to bear a son mightier than his father, and whose offspring by Zeus will one day overthrow the tyrant. Alarmed, Zeus sends Hermes to wrest the secret from Prometheus, under threat of far greater torment. Prometheus refuses, and the aeons of nightmare begin.

We know less about this resonant play than was once supposed. Author, date, trilogy, and relation to the lost *Unbound* have in the last 60 years become topics of heated and still-unresolved debate. In the dispute over these external problems, the dramatic reputation of the Romantics' favourite tragedy has itself become caught up in the struggle, with aspects of the play's intellectual and dramatic construction criticised—in an age less receptive to this kind of cosmic baroque—as unworthy of Aeschylus.

In Britain, Aeschylean authorship is overwhelmingly dis-believed (though generally accepted for the *Unbound*); elsewhere, a consensus is still emerging. In ascending order of weight, the main arguments against are: (i) the tyrannical Zeus, at odds with Aeschylean "theology" elsewhere; (ii) unparalleled number of spectacular and mechanical effects, and other perceived lapses from Aeschylean theatrical practice; (iii) shambling episodic structure; (iv) heavy apparent sophistic influence on thought, language, and expression; (v) linguistic anomalies, particularly in the range of vocabulary and particles; (vi) metrical anomalies in iambic dialogue, choral lyrics, and anapaests. Those who cling to Aeschylean authorship argue for a very late date, certainly post-*Oresteia* (458) and so probably written during the playwright's final visit to Sicily, where he died in 456. Sicilian production has sometimes been claimed to explain some of the theatrical oddities; and other novelties of style and technique have been attributed to the growing influence of Sophocles, whose heroes' truculent integrity is certainly anticipated in the figure of Prometheus. But neither excuse carries much persuasion, and at present the case against authenticity is much better documented than the case for. The next move will need to come from computer stylometrics, currently awaiting an acceptable measure of statistical significance for the relatively small Aeschylean textual corpus.

A Prometheus trilogy is not directly attested, but the scholia refer to a sequel in which Prometheus is freed, and such a play is known from the comparatively generous fragments of the *Prometheus Lyomenos*—in which Prometheus revealed his prophecy in time to prevent Zeus's union with Thetis, and was released by Heracles. The third play has been variously identified: Aeschylus wrote a *Prometheus Pyrphoros*, the *Firebringer*, but the theft of fire is so fully related in our play that an earlier instalment seems redundant. A popular, if highly speculative, view, sees the *Firebringer* as the *third* play after *Bound* and *Unbound*, in which Zeus and Prometheus are reconciled and the fire-festival of the Prometheia instituted at Athens (whence the title). But others dispute whether *Firebringer* was a tragedy at all, or whether there ever was a trilogic *Prometheia* in the first place.

What is agreed is that *Prometheus Bound*, if not by Aeschylus, is at the very least eminently Aeschylean—to the extent that opponents of authenticity have suggested one of Aeschylus's own relatives as the author, or even a posthumous collaboration on an unfinished text. Even without the bizarre mechanical contrivances suggested by an earlier generation of scholars—a giant hollow dummy for the Titan hero, a dozen flying chariots on the machine for the choral entry, an aerial arrival for Oceanus on winged horseback, and final earthquake in which the entire cast vanish down a trapdoor in the orchestra—bravura theatrical effects abound (some would say to excess). There are few plays that require their lead actor to hold 15,000 people silent and spellbound while remaining nailed to a rock, unable to move a muscle, for the entire duration of the play (or two plays, if the *Unbound* followed). The device is more startling yet in the masked Greek theatre, where body movement was the only means of expression other than the voice; but such immobility was a notorious Aeschylean trademark, and the strong sense of tableau throughout is characteristic. Aristotle, indeed, cites the play as a prime example of a tragedy whose main impact is visual.

A second, even more striking respect in which *Prometheus* seems determined to out-Aeschylus the master is its bold, political overlay, remaking the Hesiodic culture-myth in an almost transparent allegory of mid-century domestic politics. Aeschylus's own links to the radical, democrat reformers go back at least to the young Pericles' sponsorship of the *Persians* in 472, and the *Eumenides* deliberately invokes echoes of their recent, political struggles. It would be preposterous to say that Prometheus "is" Ephialtes, Zeus the Attic aristocracy, humanity the newly-enfranchised, Athenian *demos*, and fire the devolution of political power; but associations like these are undeniably one stratum of the play's meaning, and it is typical of Aeschylus to assimilate patterns of myth and contemporary history in cosmic structures that transcend both.

But there is far more to *Prometheus* than the rich exploration of the paradoxes of political and intellectual power that have made the play such a central text in the West's definitions of itself. It is also, supremely, a play about suffering—about the willing choice of superhuman agonies, and the moral power of pity for the guiltless victim. The one Aeschylean play to place the emotional experience and moral will of the individual at its dramatic centre, its last two words define the agenda for the tortured, agnostic tragedy of Aeschylus's successors: suffering, without justice. If Aeschylus's sequel did try to repair this intolerable fact of existence, our own culture at least may ironically have gained something from its loss.

—N.J. Lowe

PROMETHEUS DESMOTES.   See **PROMETHEUS BOUND.**

PROMETHEUS VINCTUS.   See **PROMETHEUS BOUND.**

THE PROPER GENTLEMAN.   See **THE WOULD-BE GENTLEMAN.**

THE PROVOKED WIFE
by John Vanbrugh

First Publication: London, 1697.
First Production: Lincoln's Inn Fields Theatre, London, c. May 1697.

Editions
The Provoked Wife, edited by Curt Zimansky, Lincoln, Nebraska, 1969 (Regents Restoration Drama Series).
The Provoked Wife, edited by Antony Coleman, Manchester, 1982 (Revels Plays Series).
The Provoked Wife, in *John Vanbrugh: Four Comedies*, edited by Michael Cordner, Harmondsworth, 1989.

Criticism
(For general works on the author, see *Playwrights* volume)

Articles:
Frank M. Patterson, "The Revised Scenes of *The Provok'd Wife*", in *English Language Notes*, 4, 1966.
Anthony Coleman, "Sir John Brute on the Eighteenth-Century Stage", in *Restoration and Eighteenth Century Theatre Research*, 8, 1969.
Jean-François Camé, "Vanbrugh's *The Provok'd Wife* and Milton's *Comus*", in *Cahiers études*, 19, 1981.

*   *   *

Lady Brute, the provoked wife of the title, has married Sir John Brute for his estate. Two years after their marriage, the play finds them in a state of cordial and unresolvable hostility, civil divorce being legally impossible. Sir John seeks solace in the drunken company of the rakes of the town; Lady Brute entertains the notion of adultery with Constant without ever

quite committing herself to that action. Heartfree, Constant's companion and ally, is enamoured of Lady Brute's niece Bellinda, who finally agrees to marry him, hoping to eschew the permanent chagrin which mars the Brutes' misalliance.

The plot of *The Provoked Wife* is sparse. The action of the play proceeds at a leisurely pace, in a series of loosely connected episodes. In part this is because the play was evidently written over an extended period of time, and so lacks the cohesiveness we should expect of a play written in a single burst of inspiration. Partly, too, Vanbrugh is simply not interested in the intricacies of plot. His skills lie instead in the creation of convincing character, the evocation of realistic situations, and in the writing of natural dialogue.

Vanbrugh's dialogue may be contrasted with Congreve's. No less epigrammatic in structure, it lacks Congreve's brilliant finish and musicality, but then the script does not read as if the author had searched his copybook, in Wildean fashion, for clever maxims with which to salt his characters' conversations. Vanbrugh's characters sound, instead, altogether more natural: they have the air of speaking much as, one imagines, persons of their time and status really did talk. This talk, wrote Colly Cibber, was "so catching to the ear, so easy to the memory" that actors found Vanbrugh's lines the easiest to learn. In the hectic repertory of the late 17th-century theatre, that must have seemed a considerable virtue indeed.

This gift for dialogue, moreover, coupled with the leisurely plot, creates space in the play for the protracted discussion of its central issues. The result is something like a Shavian problem play. The problem, in this case, is that of the difficulty of achieving a harmonious and prosperous marriage. Lady Brute has married Sir John for his money, thinking that this alone will be enough for her; Sir John for his part has married for physical pleasure, since Lady Brute would not otherwise sleep with him. Each has frustrated the other's expectations. Divorce is inconceivable, and Vanbrugh is too "wise about follies" to invent a "fairytale" resolution, such as Farquhar provided in *The Beaux' Stratagem*, in order to dissolve the similarly unpleasant marriage of the Sullens. During the play, Lady Brute creeps nebulously towards a relationship with Constant. By the end her desire for that alliance has been demonstrated, but she still has not acted on it; the fifth act thus leaves her in the same marital limbo as the first.

Bellinda tries to profit from the dispiriting example of her aunt. Her decision to marry Heartfree is cautious but not cynical, affectionate but not heartfelt. She would not marry him under any circumstance whatsoever—she is wise enough to avoid living in a cell upon "love and bread and butter"; she has sufficient fortune to eschew that meagre estate. She settles for an income smaller than her aunt's, in the hope that her marriage to Heartfree will be blessed by greater warmth and affection than the Brutes enjoy. This is the only form of marital happiness—so limited and conditional—that the play is prepared to endorse.

Like Shaw, Vanbrugh leavens his dialectics with spirited bursts of farcical action, most notably in the scenes "on the town" where Sir John carouses with Lord Rake, seeking the solace of raucous male conviviality. Sir John is a great comic role; since the first performance, actors have revelled in the sequence where Sir John accosts a tailor and steals a bundle of clothes, subsequently appearing shamefaced before a judge, dressed either as a bishop (in the original) or as a woman (in the revised version). This was one of Garrick's great comic "turns".

Garrick's acting version was an emasculated version of the 1697 text. Vanbrugh was attacked in Jeremy Collier's *Short View of the Immorality and Profaneness of the English Stage*, for encouraging immoral behavior by presenting it on stage;

The Provoked Wife: David Garrick as Sir John Bute, 1768

the play was eventually amended in response to Collier's critique. Vanbrugh's response was characteristic. He replied to Collier with his own *Short Vindication of the Relapse and The Provoked Wife, from Immorality and Prophaneness*. Here he reasonably enough claims not to have invented adultery nor unhappy marriages. There are Brutes in life; he has simply put them on stage. Their failings are not approved but rather gently reproved by this play, which manages to be compassionate, witty, and wise about its characters. This combination, for a modern audience, makes it one of the most attractive of Restoration plays.

—Mark Anthony Houlahan

PUBLIKUMSBESCHIMPFUNG. See **OFFENDING THE AUDIENCE.**

LA PUCE À L'OREILLE. See **A FLEA IN HER EAR.**

THE PUPPET SHOW (Balaganchik)
by Alexander Blok

First Publication: In *Torches* [an anthology], 1906.
First Production: Kommissarzhevskaya Theatre, St. Petersburg, 30 December 1906.

Translations
The Puppet Show, translated by M. Kriger and G. Struve, in *Slavonic Review*, 28, 1949–50.

Criticism
(For general works on the author, see *Playwrights* volume)

Articles:
Virginia Bennett, "Russian *Pagliacci*: Symbols of Profaned Love in *The Puppet Show*", in *Drama and Symbolism*, edited by James Redmond, Cambridge, 1982 (Themes in Drama Series).

*   *   *

The Puppet Show (also known as *The Fairground Booth* and *Farce*) was Alexander Blok's first play, an astounding demolition of romantic symbolism by Russia's leading romantic symbolist poet. Its perfection as a piece was perhaps, as Blok's

English biographer notes, "beginner's luck", but its content, based on its author's contorted triangular relationship with his wife and his friend and fellow poet, Andre Bely, set among the pretensions of pseudo-intellectual Petersburg and Moscow at the beginning of the century, was deeply felt and personal. Blok's success in distancing and objectifying this remains a remarkable achievement.

The Puppet Show is extremely short. It opens with a group of fashionable mystics awaiting the "Last Things", with Pierrot in the place of a kind of court jester, awaiting his beloved Columbine. A statuesque lady arrives; her braided hair is mistaken by the mystics for the ineffectual scythe of Death, but Pierrot recognizes her as Columbine. After ineffectual protests from The Author, who complains that his drama is being misrepresented, the earthy, energetic Harlequin intervenes, and whirls Columbine away. The scene dissolves into a masked ball where Pierrot describes how Harlequin took Columbine out in a sledge, but she, being cardboard, fell out. Pierrot joined Harlequin's rejoicing and they celebrated together. Several couples of masquers pass until a clown supervenes: his head is cut off with a cardboard sword and he sprawls over the footlights protesting that he is bleeding cranberry juice. A torchlight procession is led in by Harlequin, but when he jumps out of the window, Death arrives. The revellers run away, but Pierrot approaches her. It is Columbine. The Author reappears to unite the lovers, but the scenery suddenly flies away and Pierrot is left alone. "I'm very sad", he says. "Do you think it's funny?".

The play is elegant, cool, amused. It is that rare phenomenon, a genuinely lyrical drama—that is, one which expresses a mood, or an emotion, rather than a conventional dramatic conflict. It seems to concern poisoned innocence, and is suffused with a kind of bashful irony: the tantalizing vagueness is entirely typical of Russian Symbolism of the early years of the twentieth century. Beyond the personal and private connotations it had for Blok, its resonances have conjured several different interpretations, none of them completely satisfactory. The nearest Blok came to defining a meaning remained generalized: "In the embraces of a jester and puppet-master", he said, "the old world grows prettier, younger, and its eyes become transparent, fathomless".

It may be about Russia between the 1905 and 1917 revolutions, which was, Blok suggested in 1913, "breaking away from one revolution, and staring avidly into the eyes of another, perhaps a far more terrible one". The mystics awaiting death could then represent tsarism; Harlequin and Columbine the lower classes whose love and energy sweep the mystics into the "dustbin of history"; and Pierrot the intelligentsia who, like Blok, were against the old order but not precisely on the side of the revolution. More obviously the play reflects on love, togetherness and loneliness, the nature of dominance and submission in love, love consummated and love idealized. These reflections are aroused especially by the series of swift scenes which juxtapose contrasting pairs of lovers and set them in a context beside the eternal triangle of Harlequin, Columbine, and Pierrot. Thus, the play works through a densely woven sequence of highly theatrical images, each with its own suggestiveness, and each modifying the response to the other images.

The Puppet Show was first produced in Petersburg by Vsevolod Meyerhold, who himself played the role of Pierrot with memorable brilliance. It was greeted clamorously—half the audience booed and catcalled, the other half cheered and clapped. Blok seemed to have succeeded in his aim to "smash through all the dead stuff". He dedicated the published text to Meyerhold in gratitude for the production. What Meyerhold had achieved was actually to find a further dimension of meaning not in the original script (though present in all subsequent published versions), in which the other levels of meaning could meet and find expression. This was the level of theatricality. In a sense, Meyerhold made *The Puppet Show* a play about theatricality, so that the ambiguities and ambivalences of Blok's text dissolved in the essential ambiguity of the theatre. Blok seems unclear whether his characters are essences or concrete beings, fantasies or symbols; Meyerhold made them theatrical roles, so that the relationship between reality and non-reality was preserved and indeed heightened. Thus, the mystics sat solemnly in cardboard frockcoats. Harlequin hurled himself through the window, and the blue sky outside turned out to be paper which Harlequin tore as he fell through it. As Pierrot approached Columbine, the stage decorations and scenery suddenly flew away. The clown bled real cranberry juice (which, to be fair, was Blok's idea from his earlier poem, also called *The Puppet Show*). The production was also marked by static tableaux, with slightly grotesque poses and groupings. Each character had his or her typical, faintly exaggerated gestures. The stage itself was decked in blue throughout and in the centre was a puppet booth with its own stage, its own curtain, and so on, to form a visual succession of mirrored images. Thus was created, by Meyerhold and Blok together, perhaps the first example of theatrical demystification in a modernist sense. Later practitioners (and Meyerhold himself) went further with the process, but all took their cue, consciously or not, from this delicate confection.

—Robert Leach

PURGATORY
by W.B. Yeats

First Publication: In *Last Poems and Two Plays*, Dublin, 1939.
First Production: Abbey Theatre, Dublin, 10 August 1938.

Criticism
(For general works on the author, see *Playwrights* volume)

Articles:
Una Ellis-Fermor, "Dramatic Notes: The Abbey Theatre Festival (7–20 August, 1938)", in *English*, 2, 1938.
Donald R. Pearce, "Yeats' Last Plays: An Interpretation", in *English Literary History*, 18, 1951.
Ronald Gaskell, "*Purgatory*", in *Modern Drama*, 4, 1961.
John Rees Moore, "An Old Man's Tragedy: Yeats' *Purgatory*", in *Modern Drama*, 5, 1963.
Marjorie J. Lightfoot, "*Purgatory* and *The Family Reunion*: In Pursuit of Prosodic Description", in *Modern Drama*, 7, 1964.
Sidney Warschansky, "Yeats' Purgatorial Plays", in *Modern Drama*, 7, 1964.
Frederick S. Lapisardi, "A Most Conscious Craftsman: A Study of Yeats' *Purgatory* as the Culmination of his Expressed Dramatic Theories", in *Eire*, vol.2 no.4, 1967.
Marilyn G. Rose, "The Purgatory Metaphor of Yeats and Beckett", in *London Magazine*, vol.7 no.5, 1967.
Douglas B. Kurdys, "The Dance Plays and *Purgatory*", in his *Form in the Modern Verse Drama*, Salzburg, 1972.

Natalie C. Schmitt, "Curing Oneself of the Work of Time: W.B. Yeats's *Purgatory*", in *Comparative Drama*, 7, 1973.

Uma Bhowani-Sethi and Lewis T. Cetta, "The Theme of Reincarnation in Yeats's *Purgatory*", in *Theatre Annual*, 30, 1974.

David L. Vanderwerken, "*Purgatory*: Yeats's Modern Tragedy", in *Colby Library Quarterly*, 5, 1974.

Jacqueline Genet, "W.B. Yeats: *Purgatory*", in *Poétique(s): Domaine anglais*, Lyon, 1983.

W.J. McCormack, "On *Purgatory*", in McCormack's *Ascendancy and Tradition in Anglo-Irish Literary History from 1789 to 1939*, Oxford, 1985.

Margaret S. Breen, "The Feminine Position of Auditor in Yeats's *Purgatory*", in *Colby Library Quarterly*, 25, 1989.

* * *

When thinking of *Purgatory* towards the end of his life, Yeats described it as "a scene of tragic intensity". The action concerns an old man drawn back to a ruined house that is haunted by his mother's ghost. An aristocrat, she had married beneath her and died bringing the old man into the world. At the age of 16 the old man had killed his father (who was burning their house down in a drunken stupor). When the play opens the old man has become a pedlar, with a son of his own (begotten "upon a tinker's daughter in a ditch") but has returned to his old home on his parent's wedding anniversary. He tries to interest his son in his heritage, but without success; the boy only wants to steal from his father and the old man finally kills him—on the principle of destroying his posterity. Nonetheless since it was his mother's original act that began the chain of circumstances, she must await her own release; the old man cannot take her sin upon himself and realises at the end of the play that he is "twice a murderer and all for nothing".

The play is heavily symbolic and political in outlook and it is necessary to know something of the Japanese Noh Theatre and Yeats's own changing political perspective in order to appreciate its resonances. Ezra Pound introduced Yeats to the Noh Theatre, and the possibilities inherent in its stylization and its capacity to convey different levels of meaning to an audience immediately appealed to the poet. He began to see how he could use this form to explore ideas about Ireland that had preoccupied him—in particular political ideas, since falling under the spell of Maud Gonne, the prominent Irish nationalist, for whom he had written two early and openly propagandist plays (*The Countess Cathleen* and *Cathleen ni Houlihan*).

Purgatory, however, written at the end of his life (1939), reveals a change in his political perspective and comprises what he then considered "his own conviction about this world and the next". In order to understand what he meant it is helpful to examine *Purgatory* in connection with his *The Dreaming of the Bones* in which Yeats follows the Japanese tradition more closely than in any other play, by transposing a Noh ghost play, *Nishikigi*, to Ireland. *Nishikigi* tells the story of a young man who, scorned by the girl he loved, dies of a broken heart. Afterwards she too dies—of remorse—but, in death, their situations are reversed and she is condemned to love him unrequitedly until both spirits are united by an itinerant priest, to whom they tell their story. In *The Dreaming of the Bones* Yeats makes his spirits Diarmuid and Devorgilla. King Diarmuid has eloped with Devorgilla, another man's wife. When her husband begins to win the subsequent battle Diarmuid brings in English aid, thus initiating the yoke from which Ireland was still suffering. Yeats set the play in 1916, just after the Easter Rising against English rule and made the Young Man to whom the spirits tell their story a Nationalist on

the run. Naturally he is unable to forgive the spirits and thus release them from their guilt, so they must remain in limbo.

The theme of guilt persisting in death is echoed in *Purgatory*. Yeats believed that a human spirit "dreamed back" through its life from the moment of death, until reaching the state of innocence it was born with. If, in the course of this process, the spirit encountered an unresolved situation (such as a guilty action) it was obliged to remain at that point of its human experience, until achieving a resolution. Thus Diarmuid and Devorgilla have waited seven centuries for forgiveness, but are still in bondage to their guilt. Similarly, the Old Man's mother in *Purgatory* remains in limbo. She embodies the cultural values of the old Ireland; values which nationalist revolutionaries have disregarded in their zeal for change. Throwing (as it were) the baby out with the bath water, they have destroyed their Irish cultural heritage, in burning and pillaging ancestral homes. Ireland itself is the ruined house, haunted by its past.

The Old Man himself represents a split between the old Ireland and the new. He has inherited his mother's values, but he has also inherited from his father (the destroyer of the house) a belief in violence as a solution. Thus in killing his father, the new order stabs the old in the back. His own son inherits only material values: "What's right and wrong? My grand-dad got the girl and the money". In the space of a generation the son's grandmother's values have become meaningless and the Old Man kills the boy in order not to pass "pollution on". In emphasising the age of 16 when the murders occur, Yeats again returns to the violence of the 1916 Easter Rising. Although the Old Man can sever the cycle of heredity, his mother remains locked in the fervour of the blind passion that led to her marriage with a groom. At the end of the play the tree gleams white "like a purified soul" as though the Old Man had managed to purge his mother's sin by the second murder. But the sound of hoofs returns. His mother must relive the sensuality of her marriage bed and all her consequent remorse until such time as the old Ireland and the new become reconciled and she can be released from purgatory. The power and economy of the ending make this a highly effective play; it is interesting also to observe the change in Yeats's political outlook, from the idealistic nationalism of his youth to the angry realism of his old age.

—Rosemary Pountney

PUSS IN BOOTS (Der gestiefelte Kater)
by Ludwig Tieck

First Publication: In *Volksmärchen*, 2, Berlin, 1797.
First Production: Berlin, 20 April 1844.

Editions
Der gestiefelte Kater, in *Ludwig Tieck: Werke, 2*, edited by Marianne Thalmann, Munich, 1964.
Der gestiefelte Kater [with translation], edited and translated by G. Gillespie, Edinburgh, 1974.

Translations
Puss in Boots, translated by Lillie Winter, in *The German Classics of the Nineteenth and Twentieth Centuries, 4*, edited by Kuno Francke and W.G. Howard, New York, 1914.

Criticism
(For general works on the author, see *Playwrights* volume)

Articles:

R. Immerwahr, "The Esthetic Intent of Tieck's Fantastic Comedies", in *Washington Studies in Language and Literature*, 22, 1953.

Karl Pestalozzi, "Tieck: *Der gestiefelte Kater*", in *Die deutsche Komödie: Vom Mittelalter bis zur Gegenwart*, edited by Walter Hinck, Düsseldorf, 1977.

Patricia R. Paulsell, "Ludwig Tieck's *Der gestiefelte Kater* and the English Burlesque Drama Tradition", in *Michigan German Studies*, 11, 1985.

*   *   *

Puss in Boots is described by Tieck as a fairy-tale (*Kindermärchen*) in three acts, with interludes, a prologue, and an epilogue. The fairy-tale elements are quite simple. One strand tells of a king who seeks an appropriate husband for his daughter, but the princess finds none of her suitors to her liking. A second strand shows how a clever talking cat, Hinze, who wears boots, manipulates events so that his "master" (Gottlieb), is passed off as the highly eligible Count of Carabas and wins the daughter's hand in marriage.

Although the stories are simple, their telling is complicated by not only the direct involvement on stage of the supposed author, stage-hands, and an audience (among which are vociferous critics), but also because Tieck plays fast and loose with dramatic illusion. For example, at the beginning of the third act, the author appears on stage with a stage machinist. The latter protests that the author demands too much: "to have all this, completely improvised, put into operation in such a hurry". The author complains that the machinist is joining a general conspiracy against him: "The second act has already closed in a way quite different from how it reads in my manuscript". Members of the audience comment, "Does that [the exchange between author and machinist] belong to the play?"; the king can be heard from behind the scenery refusing to go on because he is being laughed at; the author begs him to make his entry as there is "absolutely nothing we can do about it"; and the clown, Jackpudding, says he'll try his luck and, to comments from the audience, offers "to deliver a few words which actually don't belong to the play", and so forth. Throughout the play, reality and illusion blur one with another so that a genuine audience of *Puss in Boots* must oscillate between wonder, confusion, uncertainty, and delight. Bugbear, representing the Law, changes momentarily into a rhinoceros (to terrify a poor peasant), a mouse (so as not to frighten an official offering a bribe), a lion, and back into a mouse, only to be chased off stage by Hinze, the cat, who returns crying, "Freedom is equality! The Law is devoured! Now indeed will the third estate, Gottlieb, assume the government" (these transformations all taking place in a mere 70 lines). The stage audience hisses but one critic realises "it's a revolutionary play—people shouldn't stamp", but stamp they do. The play concludes with a variation on Mozart's *The Magic Flute* (written six years earlier). Gottlieb, to the accompaniment of "Within These Sacred Halls", passes tests of fire and water. Thus a commoner will ascend the throne.

It is impossible to represent fairly in brief extracts the rich variety—and the fun—of *Puss in Boots*, but a brief reference to a passage in Act III might show how Tieck combines satire of royalty, the idealisation of nature, and the alleged power of the imagination. On arriving at what he takes to be the border of his own country, the king remarks on looking at the neighbouring lands: "But I always thought that this land would have to look quite different when I came over the border, just as it does on the map". He climbs a tree because he loves "free prospects of beautiful nature" but regrets his view is limited: "if it weren't for the cursed mountains, one would see still further". When he complains of the bugs in the tree, the princess explains there are bugs because "this is nature which has not yet been idealized; imagination must first ennoble it".

It can be seen that *Puss in Boots* is far more than a dramatised fairy-tale. It is revolutionary in content and technique, quite astonishingly so for its date of composition (1797). Nor is it artistically confused. It fiercely satirises authority—autocratic rule by a king who is so ignorant he does not know that bread is baked from wheat—, the law, drama critics (especially Karl August Böttiger, thinly disguised as Bötticher), rationalism, and the false idealisation of nature. It is hardly surprising that Tieck's play was not performed until 1844 and rarely since, although two important productions took place in Berlin in 1921 and 1963.

Despite its irregular productions, *Puss in Boots* speaks pointedly across the years and has been disproportionately influential. It is impossible to be sure which sources influenced Tieck. He was singularly well-informed about 16th- and 17th-century English drama: he translated Jonson's *Volpone* and *Epicoene*, and when at Göttingen University (1792) read plays by Jonson, Fletcher, and Massinger. Fielding's plays were available in Göttingen Library and there he could have read *Pasquin* and *The Author's Farce*, the last of which features a cat and an author-within-the-play, the aptly named Luckless. What is certain is that Tieck created something fresh and original out of whatever sources he drew upon.

Just as it is difficult to pinpoint the origins of *Puss in Boots*, so is it impossible to be dogmatic about what has been influenced by Tieck's play. However, there can be little doubt that *Puss in Boots* was an important influence on Pirandello's *Six Characters in Search of an Author*, and Brecht's "Alienation effect" owes something, directly or indirectly, to Tieck's play. It is surprising to read critical accounts of contemporary English plays such as Stoppard's *The Real Inspector Hound* or Frayn's *Look, Look* which reveal no awareness of what the sometimes-disparaged Tieck achieved two centuries earlier.

—Peter Davison

PYGMALION
by George Bernard Shaw

First Publication: In German translation, Berlin, 1913; in English in serial form, in *Everybody's* Magazine, New York, 1914; in book form, in *Androcles and the Lion; Overruled; Pygmalion*, London, 1916; revised version, 1941 ("Standard edition").

First Production: Hofburg Theater, Vienna, 16 October 1913 (in German); first English production, His Majesty's Theatre, London, 11 April 1914.

Criticism
(For general works on the author, see *Playwrights* volume)

Books:

Nigel Alexander, *A Critical Commentary on Bernard Shaw's "Arms and the Man" and "Pygmalion"*, London, 1968.

Harold Bloom (ed.), *George Bernard Shaw's "Pygmalion"*, New York, 1988 (Modern Critical Interpretations).

Articles:

Bertrand M. Wainger, "Henry Sweet: Shaw's Pygmalion", in *Studies in Philology*, 21, 1930.

Milton Crane, "*Pygmalion*: Bernard Shaw's Dramatic Theory and Practice", in *Publications of the Modern Language Association* [*PMLA*], 66, 1951.

Norbert F. O'Donnell, "On the Unpleasantness of *Pygmalion*", in *Shaw Bulletin*, 1, 1955.

Alan J. Lerner, "*Pygmalion* and *My Fair Lady*", in *Shaw Bulletin*, 1, 1956.

Myron Mathew, "Will Higgins Marry Eliza?" in *The Shavian*, 12, 1958.

Myron Mathew, "The Denouement of *Pygmalion*", in *Modern Drama*, 1, 1958.

Paul Lauter, "*Candida* and *Pygmalion*: Shaw's Subversion of Stereotypes", in *Shaw Review*, 3, 1960.

J. Kennen, "Rond *Pygmalion* van G.B. Shaw", in *Dietsche Warande en Belfort*, 106, 1961.

S.J. Solomon, "The Ending of *Pygmalion*: A Structural View", in *Educational Theatre Journal*, 16, 1964.

Renate Bühler, "Drei Lustspiele im Unterricht: Aristophanes *Die Frösche*, Plautus *Amphitryon*, Shaw *Pygmalion*", in *Deutschunterricht*, 18, 1966.

Louis Crompton, "Improving *Pygmalion*", in *Prairie Schooner*, 41, 1967.

Diderik Roll-Hansen, "Shaw's *Pygmalion*: The Two Versions of 1916 and 1941", in *Review of English Literature*, vol.8 no.3, 1967.

Robert C. Harvey, "How Shavian Is the *Pygmalion* We Teach?", in *English Journal*, 59, 1970.

Trude Jackson, "*My Fair Lady*: Analyse eines literarischen Musicals", in *English Miscellany*, 21, 1970.

Emil Roy, "Pygmalion Revisited", in *Ball State University Forum*, vol.11 no.2, 1970.

Horia Hulban, "Notes on Style and Substance in Shaw's *Pygmalion*", in *Analele Stiintifice ale Universitatii. . .Iasi*, 18, 1972.

H. Appia, "A Propos de *Pygmalion*: George Bernard Shaw phonéticien", in *Études anglaises*, 27, 1974.

Hugo Baetens Beardsmore, "A Sociolinguistic Interpretation of *Pygmalion*", in *English Studies*, 60, 1979.

Michael K. Goldberg, "Shaw's *Pygmalion*: The Reworking of *Great Expectations*", in *Shaw Review*, 22, 1979.

Bernard F. Dukore, "The Director as Interpreter: Shaw's *Pygmalion*", in *SHAW*, 3, 1983.

Richard Hornby, "Beyond the Verbal in *Pygmalion*", in *SHAW*, 3, 1983.

Martin Quinn, "The Informing Presence of Charles Dickens in Bernard Shaw's *Pygmalion*", in *Dickensian*, 404, 1984.

*   *   *

The central plot-device is a bet between two students of language that one of them can use his science to turn a guttersnipe into a duchess. Henry Higgins, phonetician, and Colonel Pickering, student of Indian languages, meet as part of a crowd sheltering from a rainstorm under the columned porch of St. Paul's Church, Covent Garden, in the late evening. Among the crowd, drawn from all levels of society, is Eliza Doolittle, a Cockney flower seller, part of the audience for Higgins' Sherlock Holmes-like deductions about his companions on the basis of hearing them speak. Having heard him boast of the transformations he can work through speech training, and enriched by the money he throws at her, in Act II

Pygmalion: His Majesty's Theatre, London, 1914 (first English production)

Eliza turns up at his house to demand elocution lessons. The rest of the play presents stages in her evolution, culminating after the winning of the bet, when she comes to full, independent life and turns against her puppet-master.

Language is the theme which unifies the various elements in the play. Two experiments demonstrate the possibility of upward mobility in the stratified society of Edwardian England: a woman makes the shift through "purity" of upper-class speech, aided by beauty and conventional good manners; but Eliza's father, a dustman, is promoted from "undeserving poverty" to middle-class respectability through his natural mastery of language, the piquant articulacy with which he challenges received middle-class ideas. This brings him a much larger windfall than that which started Eliza's progress. (Although the dialogue focuses on language, the action of the play quietly indicates the importance of money.) Shaw's presentation of language as an instrument or force of social regulations in the scene of Mrs. Higgins' "At Home", Eliza's first public rehearsal (Act III), is the climax of Shaw's treatment of the theme in this play. Not only does it demonstrate the differences and comic inconsistencies of linguistic register which subdivide society (the language of the streets and of the drawing-room, the language of men and that of women, formal or technical language, and the empty small talk of polite conversation), it shows a link between language and inhibition, the relation of language to freedom. The most famous moment in the play, when the beautifully dressed, carefully enunciating Eliza comes out with "Not bloody likely!", broke a taboo for the first audiences. Although Shaw's comic build-up to the line remains effective, it now takes historical imagination to recapture the sense of danger which infected the cast, or the shock and release expressed in the record-breaking laughter of the first audiences. It was a revolutionary instant, half-mischievously turned aside by Higgins's promotion of demotic speech as a new upper-class fashion.

The title of the play invokes Ovid's legend of a sculptor who scorned living women to create a statue of his ideal, with which he then fell in love. In answer to his prayers, Venus brought the statue to life so that Pygmalion was able to marry the perfect woman of his imagination. More recent treatments had transmitted the story to Shaw's contemporaries: Burne-Jones had painted a series of pictures on the Pygmalion theme, and W. S. Gilbert had turned it into a burlesque. So Shaw was setting up some expectation of a conventional happy ending, and he strengthened this with more generally recognisable reminders of the rags-to-riches fairytale of Cinderella. He subtitled his text "A Romance", and coloured the relationship between Eliza and Higgins with mutual attraction, kept fresh, lively, and amusing by their continual sparring. Yet the conflict in *Pygmalion* runs deeper as the play proceeds. Indeed the high tension of the piece arises from Shaw's determined working against the structures he has set up. There is too much realism in character and emotion for the wish-fulfilling fantasy to prevail. Higgins is no Prince Charming, and not simply because he is much older than Eliza. As well as being Holmes to Pickering's Watson, he has affinities with more sinister figures: Svengali (first played on the stage by Beerbohm Tree who was also the first Higgins in England), Frankenstein, and Faust the practitioner of black arts and seducer of Gretchen. Some ten years later, Shaw returned to Pygmalion, bringing him into the last part of *Back to Methuselah* as a scientist who makes human automata in his laboratory and dies from the bite of a female doll that evolves out of his control. Eliza merely wishes she were dead and is glad to have "wounded" Higgins "to the heart".

Two aspects of the expressive structure of the play are reminders of Shaw's admiration for, and study of, Henrik Ibsen: the interruption of the main action at two points by a character (Alfred Doolittle here, Ulrik Brendel in Ibsen's *Rosmersholm*) who takes the centre of the stage, this character's state being radically changed at his second appearance. (Shaw had previously used this device in the first of his plays to be staged, with Lickcheese in *Widowers' Houses*.) From *A Doll's House* he learnt to prolong his play beyond the point where a conventional treatment of the plot would have ended, in order to explore more deeply the thematic and emotional implications of the previous action. It is significant that the scene of Eliza's public triumph is left to the audience's imagination (Shaw gave way for the film); the dramatist has more serious business: to bring out between Eliza and Higgins the issues of sexual politics which stand in the way of any marriage between them. Shaw is dialectically engaging the idealist Pygmalion–Cinderella theme with contemporary social reality. Earlier scenes of the play have prepared for this development: the very women who provide Higgins with the order, comfort, and emotional security that has enabled him to concentrate on the profession which is also his chief passion, have urged consideration of the consequences for Eliza of the game the two male babies are playing with their doll; and Doolittle's arrival, in Act II, to claim compensation for the taking-over of his property in his daughter by two gentlemen whose intentions may well be vicious, is calculated to raise feminist hackles.

Shaw had to struggle against his public, as against actors and directors, to keep matters unresolved at the close. Keeping the options open for Eliza and Higgins creates a brilliant dramatic effect, enabling the play to end on a note of hopeful expectation, yet not compromising the recognition that head and heart are at odds. It helps keep the work for ever alive with the zest of its author's almost-passionate involvement with the actress (Mrs. Patrick Campbell) for whom he wrote the part of Eliza.

Few modern plays have so successfully bridged the gulf between popular and sophisticated, intellectual, art. This success extended to a wider public when *Pygmalion* became the basis of the musical, *My Fair Lady*.

—Margery Morgan

THE QUARE FELLOW
by Brendan Behan

First Publication: London and New York, 1956.
First Production: Pike Theatre, Dublin, 19 November 1954;
     revised version, Theatre Royal Stratford
     East, London (Theatre Workshop), 24 May
     1956.

Criticism
(For general works on the author, see *Playwrights* volume)

Articles:
Seán McMahon, "*The Quare Fellow*", in *Eire*, 4, 1969.
Patrick C. Hogan, "Class Heroism in *The Quare Fellow*", in
    Études irlandaises, 2, 1986.

*   *   *

The action of Behan's first three-act play occupies less than
24 hours, and is set entirely in a city prison: the first act in a
corridor and the rest in the yard, where the prisoners exercise
and dig a grave for the non-appearing title character. Dunlavin, an old prisoner, tells the rest that a gentlemanly wife-
murderer has been reprieved, and that another murderer, the
"quare fellow", who butchered his victim with a meat chopper,
is to be hanged. Dunlavin dominates the first act, leading the
discussion about who will occupy the vacant cell, giving clinical
detail of the hanging process, and slyly drinking the methy-
lated spirits with which a warder is massaging his rheumatic
legs. The tone of the second act becomes more serious, as the
prisoners exercise and finish digging the grave; but in the third
act there is a startling reversal of perspective, as the guards
take over the stage. They have gradually been individualised to
a much greater extent: Regan, the vaguely religious humanist;
Donelly, a thoroughly unpleasant careerist; and Crimmin, a
young warder, obviously unnerved by the experience. In the
brief last scene, it is morning, and four prisoners are marched
on to fill in the grave and carve the hanged prisoner's name on a
stone. They carve E777 because the right number is too
difficult to carve, and the play ends with them arguing about
who will get the quare fellow's last letters to sell to a
newspaper.

The Quare Fellow commands attention as a seminal work in
the new British movement of neo-naturalism (which would
leap to prominence two years later with Osborne's *Look Back
in Anger*), and as the first major English-language work in the
sub-genre of prison plays which would achieve a vogue on the
British stage in the 1960's and after. Even more importantly,
the play brought an idiosyncratic new voice to an Irish theatre
which had been losing momentum since the work of Yeats and
O'Casey in the 1920's.

Behan's self-taught naturalism echoes that of Zola in its
essentials. Animalism pervades the dialogue, from the first act,
where the prisoners see themselves as "dirty beasts" and the
doctor as a "vet", to the collective dynamics of the last scene,
where the unseen inmates' response to the hanging is just a
"ferocious howling", powerfully suggestive of a pack. Such a
self-image inevitably determines much of their behaviour, and
the same correlation is also evident in the situation of the
guards. At the end of the first act, Regan startles Holy Healey,
from the Department of Justice, by suggesting that they
collude in the system of incarceration and execution. The
description of the hanging itself is strongly suggestive of a
slaughterhouse, an irony because the condemned man, a pork
butcher, had killed his brother like a pig, and the process of
execution is complicated because the hangman has drunk
himself into oblivion.

The prison, where people are reduced to the status of caged
animals, is an ideal laboratory for a naturalistic vision of
humanity. Behan does not use the prison play, as later
playwrights would, to advance a particular thesis about prisons
as schools of crime. However, he does implicitly present the
conditioning effects of the prison environment as a force which
questions and possibly negates the concepts of responsibility
and culpability. The prisoners are the product of a sustained
manufacturing process which has reduced their goals and their
appetites to a rudimentary level, so that they may explode into
predatory behaviour over simple issues such as food. Moreover, the audience is denied the consolation of viewing the
warders as answerable for the system, because their vulnerability is at least as apparent as the prisoners'. This is
registered with considerable emphasis in the final scene, when
the audience sees an empty grave and expect a burial of the
executed man, but instead two warders appear carrying
Crimmin, whom the prisoner chose for company because he is
"a young lad, not yet practised in badness", but who has
fainted as the trap was sprung. In as much as a judgement is to
be passed on the prison system, blame is to be placed not on the
warders but on the society which sanctions the institution.

Behan's play has inescapably serious undertones, which
some critics have extended macroscopically to find an implicit
commentary on humanity at large. However, the play is
subtitled "A Comedy-Drama", and much of its tone may be
seen as the peculiarly Irish laughter "at the gate of the grave",
which O'Casey had articulated as an essential survival technique for an Ireland that was continuously on the brink of
tragedy. In this sense, Dunlavin approximates to an O'Casey
picaro, using a slyly flexible morality to survive in the context
of an unbearable reality. However, the ironies of the play are
more expansive than this, particularly in the way that biblical
parallels with Christ, the thieves, Pontius Pilate, and the
Antichrist permeate the dialogue. The prisoners' tone is often
sardonic, as in the references to cells as "flowery dells" and

"Hell's gates", but there is no trace of humour in Holy Healey's habit of distributing holy pictures in the cells. To an extent, the prisoners satirise him in their sometimes floridly religious allusions, but there is a coherence to the biblical parallels which admits a reading as a contemporary passion play, with New Testament archetypes inverted to suggest the fate of a Gaelic messiah confronted with a barbarous imperialism.

—Howard McNaughton

QUEEN AFTER DEATH (La Reine morte; ou, Comment on tue les femmes)
by Henry de Montherlant

First Publication: Paris, 1942.
First Production: Comédie-Française, Paris, 8 December 1942.

Translations
Queen after Death, in *"The Master of Santiago" and Four Other Plays*, translated by J. Griffin, New York, 1951.

Criticism
(For general works on the author, see *Playwrights* volume)

Books:
André Blanc, *"La Reine morte": Analyse critique*, Paris, 1970.
Maurice Bruézière, *"La Reine Morte" d'Henry de Montherlant*, Paris, 1973.

Articles:
Robert B. Johnson, "The Ferrante Image in Montherlant's *La Reine morte*", in *French Review*, 36, 1963.
David L. Gobert, "Structural Identity of *La Reine morte* and *Le Maître de Santiago*", in *French Review*, 38, 1964.
Clayde H. Frèches, "Le Personnage d'Inès de Castro chez Ferreira, Vélez de Guevara et Montherlant", in *Arquivos do Centro Cultural Português*, 3, 1971.
Merril A. Rosenberg, "Montherlant and the Critics of the French Resistance", in *French Review*, 44, 1971.
Laurence W. Cor, "*La Reine morte* and *Reinar después de morir*", in *Romance Notes*, 13, 1972.
Geoffrey A. Carpenter, "Le Roi, seul, meurt dans *La Reine morte*: Pourqui on tue les femmes?", in *Revue de l'Université de Moncton*, vol.6 no.3, 1973.
D.B. Edney, "Two Stage Versions of Montherlant's *La Reine morte*", in *Modern Drama*, 16, 1973.
Isolina C. Wakerley, "*La Reine morte*, ou, 'un anachronisme volontaire'", in *Revue de littérature comparée*, 47, 1973.
Laurence W. Cor, "Reflectors in Two Plays by Montherlant", in *Romance Notes*, 17, 1977.
Manuel Sito Alba, "Diatopía y diachronía de un titulo teatral: De la *Castro* de Ferreira a *La Reine morte* de Montherlant", in *Spicilegio moderno*, 9, 1978.
Mary F. Crabtree, "El parantesco de *Reinar después de morir* de Luis Vélez de Guevara y *La Reine morte* de Henry de Montherlant: Una comparación", in *Hispanófila*, 65, 1979.
Jean Foyard, "En relisant encore *La Reine morte*", in *D'Eschyle à Genet: Hommage à Francis Pruner*, Dijon, 1986.

* * *

Henry de Montherlant's *La Reine morte* was one of the most successful plays to be performed in France during the German occupation of the country in World War II. Although the Germans could deprive the French of their political independence, their food, warmth, and national dignity, they could not take away from them their literature and language. Between 1940 and 1944, there was a great renaissance of theatrical activity marked by the success of plays by Anouilh, Giraudoux as well as by those of Montherlant and Claudel. Why did *La Reine morte*, a drama set in 16th-century Portugal, occupy so eminent a place in this extraordinary flowering of talent?

The first answer lies in the permanent appeal to the French of their own national tradition in the theatre. Racine defined this in 1669 as "une action simple chargée de peu de matire" ("a simple, uncomplicated plot") and *La Reine morte* corresponds exactly to that idea. Ferrante, King of Portugal, wishes to unite his country with Spain by having his son Pedro marry the Infanta of Navarre. But Pedro is secretly married to Inès de Castro, who is expecting his child. For motives which vary from anger at seeing his plans frustrated, determination to avoid what he sees as the political catastrophe of having his son reign with a woman originally born out of wedlock as his queen, despair at the impossibility of bringing order to an imperfect universe, to a kind of horror at the idea that life will continue after his approaching death, Ferrante has Dona Inès killed. He is then so stricken with despair that he dies himself, and the play ends with everyone, including the page who had previously been devoted to him, leaving his body to lie in state alone as they all follow the example of Pedro and go to kneel around the coffin of the dead Queen.

The French classical tradition is one of purity and elegance of diction. Montherlant was one of the greatest stylists of his generation, and the prose of *La Reine morte* reassured the French that their language had remained as unaffected by military defeat as had their gift for psychological analysis. In the French, classical tradition, what happens on stage has relatively little importance. Indeed, *les bienséances* (formal decencies of classical tragedy) required all physical events to take place in the wings. Montherlant respects this tradition, and his theatre is essentially a verbal one. French audiences, even after the impact of the absurdist drama of Adamov, Beckett, and Ionesco, still go to the theatre to listen, and *La Reine morte* is still regularly performed at the *Comédie-Française*, as well as in the commercial theatre both in France and abroad. The solidity of its dramatic construction, like the tension of the dialogue and the variety of its characterisation, have shown that it can outlive the unusual circumstances surrounding its original success.

This success can be interpreted, according to the preferences of the critic, in two contrasting and even mutually incompatible ways: as proof that the audiences in occupied Paris were looking for high-class escapism; as a tribute to Montherlant's ability to write a play whose themes awoke all kinds of echoes in the recent historical experience of the French. The setting of the action in 16th-century Portugal offered a marked contrast to the moral and physical dinginess of the France of the 1940's. The characters in *La Reine morte* wore splendid costumes and expressed elevated sentiments in noble language. In the streets outside, the French police collaborated with the Gestapo in rounding up Jews for the gas chambers, the black market flourished, and politicians plotted as to whom they should next betray. Montherlant had always centered his work on the need to restore moral values to France, and had written with great sympathy of the virile, chevalric virtues traditionally associated with Spain. In that respect, *La Reine morte* provided a perfect opportunity for a moral escapism to nobler climes. But at the same time, the total disillusionment with politics expressed by King Ferrante, like the advice given to him by his corrupt Prime Minister, Egas Coelho, to sacrifice the innocent and beautiful Inès de Castro to the needs of the state, and the Machiavellian atmosphere of the Court all recalled the Vichy regime at its turning point: the moment in 1942 at which any idea that Pétain's "National Revolution" might give new life to France had given way to power seeking and time-serving collaboration with the increasingly brutal, German authorities. In 1944, Jean Anouilh was to present in his *Antigone* another legend in which a disillusioned ruler, Créon, was to sacrifice youthful idealism to *realpolitik*. Montherlant's was a more subtle, less obviously didactic and sentimental play than Anouilh's. It nevertheless confirmed the view, frequently expressed by commentators in the revival of classical themes in mid-20th century, French theatre, that the most effective way of talking about the immediate problems of one's own society was to present a situation which had taken place several centuries earlier.

—Philip Thody

A RAISIN IN THE SUN
by Lorraine Hansberry

First Publication: New York, 1959.
First Production: Ethel Barrymore Theatre, New York, 11 March 1959.

Criticism
(For general works on the author, see *Playwrights* volume)

Articles:

Elizabeth C. Phillips, "Command of Human Destiny as Exemplified in Two Plays: Lillian Hellman's *The Little Foxes* and Lorraine Hansberry's *A Raisin in the Sun*", in *Interpretations*, 4, 1972.

Lloyd W. Brown, "Lorraine Hansberry as Ironist: A Reappraisal of *A Raisin in the Sun*", in *Journal of Black Studies*, 4, 1974.

Anthony Barthelemy, "Mother, Sister, Wife: A Dramatic Perspective", in *Southern Review*, 21, 1985.

Margaret B. Wilkerson, "*A Raisin in the Sun*: Anniversary of an American Classic", in *Theatre Journal*, 38, 1986.

J. Charles Washington, "*A Raisin in the Sun* Revisited", in *Black American Literature Forum*, 22, 1988.

*   *   *

Lorraine Hansberry was 28 when *A Raisin in the Sun* opened at the Ethel Barrymore Theatre in 1959. She was the first black woman to have her work produced on Broadway, and Lloyd Richards, the director, was the first black man to direct a play for the Broadway stage. The play won the New York Critics' Circle Award, and Hansberry also became the first black writer and the first woman to receive that prize.

The title of the play, a line from Langston Hughes's poem "Dream Deferred", refers to both the subject and plot of the drama: the Younger family, trapped in poverty and over-crowded housing conditions, await the arrival of an insurance policy cheque for $10,000, following the death of the father. Act I deals with the family's situation and attitudes towards their condition and in a series of confrontations, members of the family reveal their different dreams in relation to the insurance cheque. The central tensions between Mama's dream and that of her son, Walter, provide the axis and ultimately the action of the play. Walter proposes investing the money in a liquor-store business, which he believes to be the only way to break the cycle of servitude and poverty in which the family is trapped. His dream offers the potential to regain his pride and dignity, which has been eroded by his work as a chauffeur for a white man: "I open and close car doors all day long. I drive a man around in his limousine and I say, 'Yes, sir;

no, sir; very good, sir; shall I take the Drive, sir?' Mama, that ain't no kind of job. . .that ain't nothing at all".

Mama begins to fulfil her dream in Act II when she announces that she has put a payment down on a house for the family, a place where she hopes the three generations of Youngers can thrive. The house is located in a white suburb, and this adds fuel to Walter's bitterness as his hope of opening a store fades. He articulates his anger in terms of his dream: "So you butchered up a dream of mine—you—who always talking 'bout your children's dreams". Fearful that his bitterness will destroy him, Mama entrusts the remainder of the $10,000 to Walter. Walter is duped by a friend who, instead of using the money to open the liquor store, steals it and disappears.

In Act III Walter, diminished and beaten as much by his failure of judgement as by the loss of the money, proposes to accept a lucrative bribe offered by a white man in an effort to keep the Youngers out of the white suburb where Mama has chosen their house. Walter plays out for the horrified family the full portrait of his humiliation, which is couched in terms of the social degradation to which black Americans are subjected and the roles which Whites expect them to play. Finally, Walter finds the strength and pride to reject the bribe, and the play ends with the Youngers moving out of their cramped apartment, on their way to their new home in the suburbs. An earlier draft of the play ended with the Youngers in their new home, preparing to face racial attack and, for some, the absence of a clear recognition of this future confrontation within the final draft of the play undermines the note of hope on which *A Raisin in the Sun* ends.

Interest in the play, at the time of its first performance, was undoubtedly fuelled by the unusual experience, for a Broadway audience, of watching a play in which all but one character was black. Furthermore, the tone of the play was not didactic. Its values were familiar, even if its characters and setting were not, and to some extent audiences and critics, both predominantly white, must have felt some relief that the protest implicit in the play was not belligerent. One of the dilemmas confronting black playwrights attempting to gain access to Broadway in 1959, was that their audiences were both the consumers and the object of the black writer's protest, and there is certainly, within the play, an acceptance of some of the myths inherent in the American dream and a lack of critical scrutiny of the values embedded in those aspirations. This led later critics to regard the play as middle-class and assimilationist. Opinions continue to differ as to whether it is a play of social protest or a soap opera. But, in 1959, the central tenet of the Civil Rights policy was to demand access to such aspirations, rather than to challenge them and, in this sense, *A Raisin in the Sun* is true to its cultural and political environment.

In form, the play is conventionally naturalistic, a three-act play within a single set. Dialogue and action are gently, even

A Raisin in the Sun: Roundabout Theatre Company, New York, 1986

humorously, home-spun. The characters, whilst being affectionately drawn, are familiar types, only occasionally rising above the stock. There are, however, some fine moments of realisation and self-confrontation in the play, particularly when the aspirations of individuals encounter the constraints of social reality. The focus of the play centres on the characters' struggle to make choices of value, despite social constraints, and out of those choices to retain integrity. This may place *A Raisin in the Sun* within the tradition of Miller's *Death of a Salesman*, to which Hansberry acknowledged her debt, but the Younger family's search for dignity has a specific and inevitable resonance in relation to the political struggle current in black America in 1959.

—Glendyr Sacks

RALPH ROISTER DOISTER
by Nicholas Udall

First Publication: London, c. 1566–67.
First Production: Probably at Windsor Castle, Windsor, c. September 1552.

Editions

Ralph Roister Doister, in *Representative English Comedies from the Beginnings to Shakespeare*, edited by Charles Mills Gayley, 1903.
Ralph Roister Doister, edited by H. Williams and P.A. Robin, London, 1911.
Ralph Roister Doister, in *Chief Pre-Shakespearean Dramas*, edited by Joseph Quincey Adams, London, 1924.
Ralph Roister Doister, in *Five Pre-Shakespearean Comedies*, edited by F.S. Boas, 1934.
Roister Doister, edited by W.W. Greg, Oxford, 1935.
Ralph Roister Doister, edited by G. Scheurweghs, Louvain, 1939.
Roister Doister, in *Three Sixteenth-Century Comedies*, edited by Charles W. Whitworth Jr., London and New York, 1984 (New Mermaid Series).

Roister Doister, in *Four Tudor Comedies*, edited by William Tydeman, Harmondsworth, 1984.

Criticism

(For general works on the author, see *Playwrights* volume)

Articles:
L. Maulsky, "The Relations Between *Roister Doister* and the Comedies of Plautus and Terence", in *Englische Studien*, 38, 1907.
J.S. Hinton, "The Source of *Roister Doister*", in *Modern Philology*, 11, 1913–14.
A.W. Reed, "Nicholas Udall and Thomas Wilson", in *Review of English Studies*, 1, 1925.
T.W. Linthicum Baldwin and M. Chenning, "The Date— *Ralph Roister Doister*", in *Philological Quarterly*, 6, 1927.
Edwin Shepherd Miller, "Roister Doister's 'Funeralls' ", in *Studies in Philology*, 43, 1946.
William Peery, "The Prayer for the Queen in *Roister Doister*", in *University of Texas Studies in English*, 27, 1948.
Catherine H. Wheat, "*A Pore Hope, Ralph Roister Doister* and *Three Laws*", in *Philological Quarterly*, 28, 1949.
A.W. Plumstead, "Satirical Parody in *Roister Doister*", in *Studies in Philology*, 60, 1963.
Catherine A. Hebert, "Udall's *Ralph Roister Doister*", in *Explicator*, 37, 1979.
Philip Dust and William D. Wolf, "Recent Studies in Early Tudor Drama: *Gorboduc, Ralph Roister Doister, Gammer Gurton's Needle*, and *Cambises*", in *English Literary Renaissance*, 8, 1978 [bibliographical survey].

*   *   *

Ralph Roister Doister has the distinction of being the first "regular" comedy to be written in English. Based on the *Eunuchus* and *Phormio* of Terence, and the *Miles Gloriosus* of Plautus, it localizes type characters from Roman comedy, fusing them with native counterparts, to produce a play which has much more than just its historical status to recommend it.

The story is a simple one: the virtuous widow, Christian Custance, is wooed by the vain braggart, Ralph Roister Doister, with the pretended help of the versatile Mathew Merygreke. Custance is already promised to Gawyn Goodluck, and wards off Roister Doister's advances with some fortitude, eventually waging a pitched battle against him with the help of her servants who wield kitchen implements. She and her "knightesses" win outright after Roister Doister's cowardly retreat, but all are forgiven and the story ends in reconciliation.

Written for performance by children, and undoubtedly framed with their capacities in mind, the play nevertheless has much to offer adult audiences in the way of acute observation of human behaviour and an ironic stance which verges on the parodic. Merygreke communicates the chief characteristics of Roister Doister (including his tendency to fall in love and strike romantic attitudes) to the audience before he appears, and then commentates in an "I-told-you-so" tone on Roister Doister's opening lines, which has the effect of reducing his pretensions from the outset, making his desires look preposterous, if not pathetic. The ambiguous presentation of Merygreke himself prevents this from being a purely pedagogical intervention. Merygreke, whose ancestors are the parasite of Roman comedy and the Vice of English morality plays, describes himself as both "merry and wise"; he is living off his wits and, on this occasion, exploiting Roister Doister for his capacity to keep him in food and drink. He boasts of his ability to manipulate his patron's moods and manner of speech, and

proceeds to make good his claims. He encourages Roister Doister's worst vanities for the audience's benefit, and even teaches him how to stand when presenting himself as a wooer ("Up with that snout, man. . .So, that is somewhat like").

A major function of Merygreke is to provide an ironic critique of the trappings of chivalry and romance which have clearly influenced Roister Doister's attitudes. He knows that a lover is supposed to die of unrequited love, but it turns out that he cannot remember the name of his beloved, and has to be prompted. Merygreke's technique is almost Swiftian, and exceeds the source material in exaggeration, as in the bravura speech in which he imitates the voices of a number of women whom, he claims, have asked after Roister Doister with a view to liaisons with him. Each, he says, compared Roister Doister either to Sir Lancelot, or Guy of Warwick, Hector of Troy, or Alexander the Great, or Charlemagne; the list becomes outrageous and the presence of Roister Doister with his obvious inadequacies undoubtedly makes excellent comedy. The mock-heroic tone is also present when Merygreke fabricates a list of Roister Doister's exploits, which include killing "the blue spider in Blanchepowder land", plucking a tusk from a passing elephant, and conquering all the towns from Rome to Naples in one day.

Roister Doister is a character of substance, but the substance is all ego: "Why did God make me such a goodly person?", he asks himself, and his arrogance in the face of Custance's continued rejection exposes the Petrarchan lover's habitual position: "Yes, dame, I will have you whether ye will or no!/I command you to love me! Wherefore should ye not?/Is not my love to you chafing and burning hot?". Merygreke encourages him in these outrageous ambitions, and we are shown how infantile desires may turn into something more sinister. Roister Doister sets out to burn Custance's home and kill her and her servants, maintaining that she is to blame for his agression: she has forced him to fight against his will! The emblematic assault on the "castle" of a woman's virtue is presented here ironically, and not without a hint of real menace.

Besides the battle, there are a number of other set-pieces of comic action: a mock funeral with intoned Latin, a debate with Custance's maidservants about kissing, and a scene in which Merygreke pretends to think that the object of Roister Doister's affections is really Custance's old nurse, Madge Mumblecrust. The most well-known of the play's ingredients, however, is an ambiguous letter which was quoted in the third edition of Thomas Wilson's *Rule of Reason* (1553) as an example of the effect of punctuation on meaning. (The letter's attribution to Udall is the only means of identifying the play as his, since the title-page of the only extant copy is missing and there is no author's name in the Stationers' Register entry of 1566.) At 35 lines, the letter is no mean accomplishment, being equally convincing in each of its two renderings, one highly complimentary, the other very offensive. It is also, as Wilson (an old pupil of Udall) had recognized, an excellent educational tool, and one of several aspects of the play which reminds us of Udall as the humanist schoolmaster writing for schoolboys (most probably, in this case, the children of the Chapel Royal at Windsor). However amusing, the letter points towards important issues about the social power of language and its inherent instability, and Udall seems keen to stress the wider consequences of other apparently trivial activities too— the acceptance of gifts, for example, and gossip—although never at the expense of wit and humour.

—Joanna Udall

RANAE. See **THE FROGS.**

DIE RÄUBER. See **THE ROBBERS.**

THE REAL THING
by Tom Stoppard

First Publication: London, 1982; revised edition, 1983; further revised edition, 1984.
First Production: Strand Theatre, London, 16 November 1982.

Criticism
(For general works on the author, see *Playwrights* volume)

Articles:
Mimi Kramer, "No Time for Comedy", in *New Criterion*, 1, 1983.
Hersh Zeifman, "Comedy of Ambush: Tom Stoppard's *The Real Thing*", in *Modern Drama*, 26, 1983.
Paul Delaney, "Cricket Bats and Commitment: The Real Thing in Art and Life", in *Critical Quarterly*, vol.27 no.1, 1985.
Susan Rusinko, "The Last Romantic: Henry Boot, Alias Tom Stoppard", in *World Literature Today*, 59, 1985.

Leslie Thomson, "The Subtext of *The Real Thing*: It's 'All Right' ", in *Modern Drama*, 30, 1987.

* * *

When we first meet Henry, the playwright-hero of Tom Stoppard's *The Real Thing*, he is married to an actress, Charlotte, but having an affair with another actress, Annie. Annie is herself married, to Max, an actor co-starring with Charlotte in Henry's latest play, *House of Cards*. By Scene 4, Henry and Annie have ditched their respective mates and are now living together. Can their love, however, survive Annie's subsequent affair with a younger actor, Billy, or her political involvement with the young soldier, Brodie? Brodie is currently in jail for committing criminal acts during an anti-nuclear protest, and has written an autobiographical television play which Annie hopes Henry will "cut and shape". (Henry, we quickly discover, is unsympathetic both to Brodie's politics and to his playwriting.) Is their love, in other words, "the real thing"? What *is* "the real thing" when it comes to love? Stoppard's play is an attempt to answer these questions—as well as a number of related ones. For if love holds centre stage here (and, for Henry and Annie, successfully so—their love *does* survive, though constantly tested and examined and redefined), there are many other aspects of the play which prompt the same sort of questioning and which parallel and enrich the central theme: "real" music versus sham, for example; "real" sex versus mere biology; the "real" self versus various masks; the "real" motivations behind political commitment; and, most significant of all, "real" writing versus trash.

The Real Thing: Strand Theatre, London, 1982 (first production)

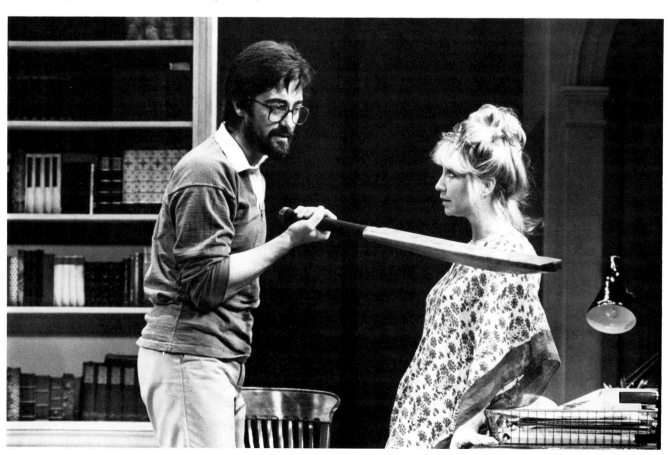

In a sense, all of Stoppard's major plays are about defining "the real thing": the only element that varies from play to play is the nature of the particular reality under debate: philosophy, art, political freedom, journalism. And yet *The Real Thing* appears to mark, at first glance, a significant departure for Stoppard. On the one hand, it is much more "realistic" than his previous drama—less tricky structurally, less profligate and ostentatious in its theatricality. And, on the other hand, Stoppard has never before written about so "personal", so *emotional* a topic as love. His previous plays were generally viewed as being clever, "cool", and intellectually detached; *The Real Thing*, by contrast, is, surprisingly, far more "auto-biographical" in tone: more emotionally open, more naked in its vulnerability, more willing to explore its characters' (and its author's?) pain. Stoppard has himself acknowledged this "new departure" in his playwriting: "For better or worse", he has commented, "I've been aware of the process that's lasted 25 years, of shedding inhibitions about self-revelation".

As is so often the case with Stoppard's plays, however, that first glance is somewhat deceptive: for all its apparent realism and emotionally frank dramaturgy, *The Real Thing* is still a recognizably Stoppardian play, stuffed to the brim with the master's comic trademarks: scintillating repartee, witty puns, hilarious misunderstandings and, especially, the clever "ambushes" of an audience's perceptions for which Stoppard has become celebrated. In the play's opening scene, for example, there is a dialogue about infidelity between a husband and wife. Halfway through the play's second scene, however, the ground shifts beneath our feet; what we *thought* we were seeing in the first scene turns out to be an "illusion", a scene from Henry's play *House of Cards*. Stoppard is deliberately shaking his audience up, like Max's miniature Alp in a glass bowl which, when shaken, creates a snowstorm—a snowstorm that, at the end of Scene 1, according to the stage-direction, *"envelops the stage"*. When the snow settles, we discover we have been tricked; just when we think we have latched on to "the real thing", the reality alters. Thus, Stoppard involves his audience in the "debate" formula of his plays not just intellectually but viscerally. The very structure of *The Real Thing* dramatizes the difficulty inherent in determining precisely what "the real thing" is; as always, the *form* of a Stoppard play mirrors its theme.

This "debate formula" is not simply Stoppard's way of sitting on the fence when it comes to examining love. We can usually tell where Stoppard stands in his plays, but that's not really the point: rather, an audience is encouraged to question its own values and feelings, to guard against smugness by acknowledging the genuine complexities of a profoundly complex issue. Different characters in the play hold different views on love, *embody* different views. For Henry's teenage daughter Debbie, for example, love has nothing to do with sexual fidelity: "Exclusive rights isn't love", she asserts, "it's colonization". And Debbie's perspective is only one among many with which Henry (and the audience) is required to grapple.

Stoppard explores this conundrum further through yet another series of comic ambushes, deliberately juxtaposing the "real life" love scense between Henry and Annie with love scenes from specific plays. Scenes from Ford's *'Tis Pity She's a Whore*, Strindberg's *Miss Julie*, and Henry's own *House of Cards*, all carefully interpolated into the text of *The Real Thing*, thus function, structurally, as self-consciously theatrical, "artificial" models against which we are meant to judge the "real" love of Stoppard's central characters. But is the love expressed in stage plays, however artificial they may appear, necessarily less "real" than the love in "real life"? (That's an especially intriguing question, if for no other reason than that

the "real life" so truthfully dramatized in Stoppard's play, and so carefully counterpointed with the "artificiality" of theatre, is itself, of course, part of a play!) Stoppard's ambushes never cease: *The Real Thing* keeps circling endlessly back on itself, constantly reminding us that love speaks in many different tongues, with many different accents.

—Hersh Zeifman

THE RECRUITING OFFICER
by George Farquhar

First Publication: London, 1706; corrected edition, 1706.
First Production: Theatre Royal, Drury Lane, London, 8 April 1706.

Editions

The Recruiting Officer, in *George Farquhar*, edited by William Archer, London, 1906 (Mermaid Series).
The Recruiting Officer, in *A Discourse Upon Comedy; The Recruiting Officer; The Beaux' Stratagem*, edited by Louis B. Strauss, Boston, 1914.
The Recruiting Officer, edited by Michael Shugrue, Lincoln, Nebraska, 1977 (Regents Restoration Drama Series).
The Recruiting Officer, edited by John Ross, London, 1977 (New Mermaid Series).
The Recruiting Officer, edited by Peter Dixon, Manchester, 1986.

Criticism
(For general works on the author, see *Playwrights* volume)

Books:
Raymond A. Anselment (ed.), *"The Recruiting Officer" and "The Beaux' Stratagem": A Casebook*, London, 1977.

Articles:
William J. Lawrence, "The Mystery of the Stage Coach", in *Modern Language Review*, 27, 1932.
Sybil Rosenfeld, "Notes on *The Recruiting Officer*", in *Theatre Notebook*, 18, 1963/64.
Albert Wertheim, "Bertolt Brecht and George Farquhar's *The Recruiting Officer*", in *Comparative Drama*, 7, 1973.
J.C. Ross, "Some Notes on *The Recruiting Officer*", in *Notes & Queries* (new series), 18, 1981.

*   *   *

Although George Farquhar's play was first produced at Drury Lane in 1706, the basic components of its plot structure are drawn from the familiar territory of post-Restoration comedy. After a series of adventures involving forged letters, invitations to a duel, masked assignations, disguise, and the deployment of a crooked fortune-teller, two sets of lovers are eventually united in marriage and in fortune. Mr. Worthy, a character whose name as so often in the comedy-of-manners tradition allows an audience to anticipate his ultimate fate, has latterly attempted to gain the fair Melinda, now a "lady of fortune", as his wife, having formerly sought to buy her as a mistress in her then impoverished state. His friend, Captain Plume, passing through town in pursuit of recruits for the army, eventually wins the hand, as he has already won the heart, of Silvia, daughter of Justice Balance. The marriages are held back by the actions of the two ladies, each intent on ensuring that the proposed husbands are capable of proving themselves not part of the world of rakes, debauchers, and bounty-hunters that their roles would have made them in earlier comedies. And herein lies a major distinction between this play and its earlier models. Farquhar may be drawing heavily from the *matter* of Restoration comedy, but he draws scarcely at all from the *manner*. Mr. Worthy does nothing that will besmirch the promise of a name that owes more to the post-Collier expectations of the sentimental comedy than the adulturous excesses of the comedy of Etherege, Wycherley, and Congreve; whilst, for all his bluster and sexual bravado, Captain Plume not only preserves the willingly-offered honour of Rose—described as a "country girl" with all that was then understood to mean—but even refuses money for the release of his beloved Silvia from the army, having mistakenly recruited her in the disguised role in which she spends most of the play.

Farquhar's stress on the role of the women in organising affairs does much to move the sexual balance of power away from that of the earlier comedies: as well as the key initiatives of the strongly-drawn Melinda and Silvia, the action is developed significantly by the attempts of Melinda's maid Lucy to get both a settlement and a husband; and even Rose has more vitality than her earth-bound brother, Bullock, one of Plume's easiest new recruits. Generally, for all the early boastings of the unmarried, male characters, there is less emphasis than before on the idea of the men as hunters and the women as the hunted; although Farquhar has Plume admit to an illegitimate offspring at the opening, he is also careful to have him make arrangements for the well-being of both mother and child, and nothing of this order intrudes into the plot itself. Indeed, there is not a single character in the play who is not capable of doing the decent thing. Even Plume's rival recruiting officer, Brazen, eventually belies his name sufficiently to behave honourably; and thus moves away from the kind of easy stereotype he appears to be initially.

There are other, novel features to this play. Just as Farquhar's final play, *The Beaux' Stratagem* of the following year, would be set in Lichfield, so *The Recruiting Officer* is set not in the fashionable West End of London—the most usual location for the sexual romps and intrigues of earlier Restoration comedy—but in Shrewsbury, a provincial setting that the playwright succeeds in evoking well. This is not social realism but nevertheless the strong sense of locale and the interaction of the social classes is depicted in this play in a way that is unmatched by any previous comedy of the post-Restoration period. Before he realises that his latest recruit is the disguised Silvia, Plume acknowledges the information that the new "soldier" is heir to £12,000 a year with the laconic "I am very glad to hear it—for I wanted but a man of that quality to make my company a perfect representative of the whole commons of England"; and certainly, with a comparatively small cast, Farquhar succeeds quite brilliantly in depicting the range of society in middle England from farm-workers to Justices of the Peace. It was a feature of the play that needed no special emphasis to be quite apparent in Max Stafford-Clark's highly successful revival of the play at the Royal Court Theatre, London, in the 1980's, and was something that evidently attracted the attention of Bertolt Brecht whose *Trumpet and Drums*, one of the two plays presented in the Berliner Ensemble's first visit to Britain in 1956, was an adaptation of Farquhar's play.

What Farquhar offered in the way of social analysis has arguably come to seem more revolutionary than was originally intended. The role of money is not restricted to its use as a marriage condition for those at the top of the tree, and Rose's pathetic attempt to sell her "chickens" at the going rate in the market-place provides a potentially savage counterpart. And it is Farquhar's deliberate deployment of a humanistic slant to the familiar material that makes such a reading of the play possible. Interestingly, many contemporaries saw in the depiction of the free-hearted Captain Plume a portrait of the playwright; whether that be true or not, Farquhar is certainly drawing from his own experiences. After marrying a lady who proved not to be the rich widow he had been led to believe (itself a stock component of Restoration comedy plots) financial pressure led to him becoming a lieutenant in the army, and to a period spent recruiting in Shropshire just before he started work on the play. Where Farquhar and his contemporaries would have seen the tricks and deceptions of recruitment as a part of the general comic business of the piece, later generations have increasingly seen how the play offers a view of the world in which the life of the Justices of the Peace and the other town worthies is ultimately unaffected by the attempts to recruit for an army they rightly see as fighting for their particular class interests, whilst the poor and the dispossessed are forced into service in order to survive. The paraphenalia of law and order and its social functioning begin to take on an increasingly modern feel far removed from any easy celebration of social unity, and it is this, rather than the conventional wit and banter, that makes the play stand out from the rest of Farquhar's work for the stage.

—John Bull

THE REHEARSAL
by George Villiers, Duke of Buckingham, and others

First Publication: London, 1672; revised version, 1675.
First Production: Theatre Royal, Drury Lane, London, 7 December 1671.

Editions

The Rehearsal, edited by Montague Summers, Stratford-Upon-Avon, 1914.
The Rehearsal, in *"The Rehearsal" by George Villiers and "The Critic" by Richard Brinsley Sheridan*, edited by A.G. Barnes, London, 1927.
The Rehearsal, in *George, Duke of Buckingham: "The Rehearsal", and Richard Brinsley Sheridan: "The Critic"*, edited by C. Gale, New York, 1960.
The Rehearsal, edited by D.E.L. Crane, Durham, 1976.

Criticism

Articles:

Emmett L. Avery, "The Stage Popularity of *The Rehearsal*, 1671–1777", in *Research Studies of the State College of Washington*, 7, 1939.
S.L. Macey, "Fielding's *Tom Thumb* as the Heir to Buckingham's *Rehearsal*", in *Texas Studies in Literature and Language*, 10, 1968–69.
Peter Lewis, "*The Rehearsal*: A Study of Its Satirical Methods", in *Durham University Journal* (new series), vol.31 no.2, 1970.

*   *   *

The Rehearsal: Theatre Royal, London, 1777

The Rehearsal is a farce in the long line of English plays about the staging of plays. In it, Johnson, a London gentleman, and Smith, a gentleman from the country, meet Bayes, a playwright who is just supervising the rehearsal of his new play by a company of players in a London theatre. Together they watch scenes from the play being rehearsed and discuss their literary merit as well as problems of play-writing in general. Their dialogue alternates with short scenes from the heroic play that Bayes is having staged, called *The Two Kings of Brentford*. The rehearsal remains incomplete, because both the audience and the players themselves soon lose interest in the play and finally make their exit to the nearest tavern.

The play was a collaborative work in progress that could easily be adapted to changing circumstances after its first (unperformed) version appeared in 1665. Its main author was unquestionably George Villiers, second Duke of Buckingham, but research has identified at least three co-authors in Thomas Spratt, Samuel Butler, and Martin Clifford, with the likelihood of even more contributors. For the first production in 1671 the name and characterization of the hero were revised to make Bayes an unmistakeable portrait of the poet John Dryden, who was currently enjoying great popularity with his heroic play *The Conquest of Granada*, produced in the same theatre as Buckingham's burlesque.

Although obvious elements of personal satire are in the play, it yet transcends the immediate occasion of its polemic and becomes a witty document in the debate about standards of taste in the widening public sphere of the late 17th-century literary scene. The extracts from Bayes' (Dryden's) heroic play

The Two Kings of Brentford highlight some of the peculiarities of the fashionable genre that had been enjoying a first flowering after 1660 in plays by Dryden's brother-in-law, Sir Robert Howard, and Sir William Davenant, the original target of Buckingham's ridicule in 1665. The play-within-the-play about a quite imaginary rivalry between two kings in the small borough of Brentford features, in grossly exaggerated but very funny form, parodies the literary weaknesses that contemporary literary criticism singled out in heroic plays: their heroes' rant; the absence of unified plots and their replacement by mere historical narrative; the improbabilities of the action; their rhetorical bombast; and other characteristics that were subsumed under their main function of creating melodramatic effect. The main charge directed against Bayes' new play is ironically put into his own mouth: by giving free reign to poetic fancy the play has deviated from nature and violated all decorum and probability. In resorting to conventional rhetoric on the well-worn themes of love and honour—as in a hilarious monologue by Volscius, one of the characters in Bayes' heroic drama—the genre it belongs to is deflated by the incompatibility between expression and its referent: Volscius manages to express the opposition of love and honour—familiar to Restoration audiences through translations of the contemporary French *tragédie classique*—in imagery derived from the decision about which of his boots to put on first.

The dramatic texture of Buckingham's burlesque is shaped by the roles of Johnson and Smith as mediators between the audience on the one hand, and Bayes as satiric butt and his literary creation on the other. While Smith and Johnson are initially slightly differentiated from each other as town and country dwellers, their main function requires no individualization as it consists in providing a kind of epic commentary on the proceedings. They represent a reasonable court of appeal and offer accessible standards of taste as bulwarks against Bayes' poetic fancy and lurid sensationalism. The orientation they allow does not need to be emphasized too much, since the burlesque and obvious comedy of the character of Bayes and his play speak for themselves in most of the short scenes of the five acts. Some of Bayes' literary shortcomings are seen as natural; others are blamed on a wilful transgression of classical norms (which the play's mouthpieces, Smith and Johnson, legitimize as so much plain, common sense): decorum, an overall aesthetic design, and a distaste for mere novelty. At the end the audience and even the players turn against the playwright and force him into an isolated railing against the Town's taste, especially its insistence on "sound and sense".

The Rehearsal certainly does less than justice to the target of its burlesque. Its deconstruction of the heroic mode in plays vacillates between serious and trivial characteristics of the new literary fashion, between personal satire and freewheeling fun. Yet the play succeeds in exposing the difficulty of a dramatic form that chooses an elevated setting but relies on operatic and melodramatic effect, with an audience appeal that does not presuppose the higher types of literacy or classical learning. The contradiction between the exalted setting in Bayes' new play (as in most heroic drama) and the fact that its debunking was instigated by the Court wits around Charles II was only an apparent one. It can be regarded as an attempt by the Court libertines to reassert a hegemony in matters of taste in the civilized discourse of the public sphere that was endangered by the classes newly enfranchised. The reception accorded to *The Rehearsal* was proof of its success; for some time the vogue for heroic drama and its burlesque caricature ran side by side. But eventually the stage success of the burlesque copy surpassed that of its model. It also survived it. In the century after its first production on the London stage, followed by its first printed edition in 1672, there were nearly 300 performances of *The*

Rehearsal, and both Fielding and Sheridan adopted Buckingham's structural device of a playwright and some friends arguing about a play in rehearsal in their own work.

—Bernd-Peter Lange

REIGEN. See **LA RONDE.**

LA REINE MORTE. See **QUEEN AFTER DEATH.**

THE RELAPSE; or, Virtue in Danger
by John Vanbrugh

First Publication: London, 1696.
First Production: Theatre Royal, Drury Lane, 21 November 1696.

Editions

The Relapse, in *British Dramatists From Dryden to Sheridan*, edited by G.H. Nettleton and A.E. Case, Boston, 1935.
The Relapse, in *Sir John Vanbrugh*, edited by A.E.H. Swaen, London, 1935 (Mermaid Series).
The Relapse, introduced by Cyril Ritchard, London, 1948.
The Relapse, edited by Curt A. Zimansky, Lincoln, Nebraska, 1970 (Regents Restoration Drama Series).
The Relapse, edited by Bernard Harris, London, 1971 (New Mermaid Series).
The Relapse, in *John Vanbrugh: Four Comedies*, edited by Michael Cordner, Harmondsworth, 1989.

Criticism

(For general works on the author, see *Playwrights* volume)

Articles:
Pieter Jan Van Niel, "*The Relapse*—Into Death and Damnation", in *Educational Theatre Journal*, 21, 1969.
C.R. Kropf, "*The Relapse* and the Sentimental Mark", in *Journal of Narrative Technique*, 1, 1971.
Jack D. Durant, "*The Relapse*, Shakespeare's *Romeo*, and Otway's *Marius*", in *Restoration and Eighteenth Century Theatre Research*, 12, 1973.
Alan Roper, "Language and Action in. . .*The Relapse*", in *English Literary History*, 40, 1973.
Irma Z. Sherwood, "Vanbrugh's *Romeo and Juliet*: A Note on *The Relapse*", in *Restoration and Eighteenth Century Theatre Research*, 12, 1973.
Carolyn Chiappelli, "The Single-Plot Structure of Vanbrugh's *The Relapse*", in *English Miscellany*, 1979–80.
James S. Malek, "Comic Irony in Vanbrugh's *The Relapse*", in *College Language Association Journal*, 26, 1983.
Michael Cordner, "Time, the Churches, and Vanbrugh's Lord Foppington", in *Durham University Journal*, 77, 1984.
Frank McCormick, "Vanbrugh's *The Relapse* Reconsidered", in *Studia Neophilologica*, 7, 1985.
Margaret D. Bauer, "Parallel Scenes in *Othello* and *The Relapse*", in *Comparative Drama*, vol.21 no.4, 1987.

The main plot of the comedy concerns the central couple, Amanda and Loveless (or Lovelace), who have to face the temptation of extra-marital affairs. Loveless soon succumbs to the charms of Amanda's cousin Berinthia, while Amanda resists all ploys to get her involved with Worthy, Amanda's former lover. A subplot concerns Young Fashion's attempts, as an impoverished younger son, to be revenged on his miserly, coxcomb brother, Lord Foppington, who has recently been elevated to the peerage. He succeeds in his plot by marrying the naïve Miss Hoyden whom her father, Sir Tunbelly Clumsey, had promised to Lord Foppington. In the denouement the two strands of the play's action are juxtaposed: Young Fashion manages to retain possession of his rich heiress, while the marital crisis of Amanda and Loveless remains unresolved.

In *The Relapse*, as in Vanbrugh's other comedies focusing upon a marriage in crisis, he engages polemically with Colley Cibber's concessions to the changing taste of late-17th century audiences. The comedy is a sequel to Cibber's *Love's Last Shift* (1696) and starts off from the final situation of that play in which Amanda and Loveless, having been reconciled with each other through the fifth-act reformation of the formerly rakish Loveless, are determined to retire to a peaceful life in the country. In *Love's Last Shift* a fairly conventional comedy of manners had, as Vanbrugh saw it, lapsed into a sentimental reconciliation of the Restoration "gay couple" within the institution of marriage. If there is one dominant theme in *The Relapse*, it is the demonstration that a man like Loveless can too easily be drawn away from marital bliss with his wife and from a peaceful country house life to the lure of the metropolis where most scenes of the comedy are set.

Most of the main plot in *The Relapse* is geared to test both partners' morality in a stereotypical role distribution: Loveless soon pursues the tempting young widow, Berinthia, and seduces her almost under Amanda's nose, while Amanda successfully repulses the advances of the seasoned rake (ironically called Worthy). The sub-plot, only rather thinly connected with the main one and concerning Cibber's Sir Novelty Fashion (now Lord Foppington), is also taken from *Love's Last Shift* and was later re-adopted for another comedy by Cibber in a rare kind of running dramatic dialogue between two playwrights. This dialogic writing process hints at a common basis between the two authors. While Vanbrugh stops short of the sentimental affirmation of bourgeois virtues in the post-1689 movement for the reformation of manners, he is equally out of tune with the predatory libertinism of some of the first generation of Restoration dramatists. Loveless's hedonism is of a furtive kind and signals the interiorization of middle-class morality. It seems devoid of all aggressive traits and of the freebooting demonstrativeness with which earlier rakes covered the underlying insecurity of their social position. Even so, Vanbrugh's main character did not escape the (undeserved) prominence of being singled out as a negative example in Collier's invective against late-17th-century comedy, *A Short View of the Immorality and Profaneness of the English Stage* (1698).

The Relapse recycles most of the character types of the Restoration comedy of manners. There is the hierarchy based on wit, comprising rakes (Loveless, Worthy, Young Fashion), a country squire (Sir Tunbelly Clumsey), a resplendently narcissistic fop (Lord Foppington), the "natural" Miss Hoyden—a delightful successor to the equally naïvely hedonistic Margery Pinchwife in Wycherley's *The Country Wife*—and a young widow as the standard projection of female cupidity. It is in the "gay couple" that the change-over to a bourgeois type of comedy registers most conspicuously. What is epitomised in Congreve's mastery of an urbane public code of expression in comedies, dissolved, in other dramatists, into a pattern consonant with the interiorization of a stricter, and often repressive, private morality: a libidinous husband who cannot live up to his moral resolves and a wife who perpetuates the double standards of morality by upholding those virtues. Significantly, this conflict is, in this play, left unresolved and gets relegated to the background of the action. In the juxtaposition of Amanda's final assertion of a non-repressive, personal morality that can resist the temptations which her husband succumbs to with some of the traditional zest of earlier Restoration rakes, there is an apt expression of a transient compromise between libertinism and the benevolent morality of 18th-century, English comedy.

The early scenes of *The Relapse* alternate in setting between Loveless's country house and the fashionable life around St. James and Whitehall, epitomised by the brothers Fashion. Only in the second act, in a perfunctory (and of course unsuccessful) pass Lord Foppington makes at Amanda, and then again in the final act in the *omnium gatherum*, is there more than a vague thematic connection between the two plots. Their respective climaxes in Acts III and IV consist in the successful wooing of two willing victims of male lust: Berinthia, whom her cousin Amanda had unwittingly invited into her own household, and the natural simpleton Miss Hoyden, who is a similarly easy prey to, first, Young Fashion's designs, then the claims of his richer and older brother, and finally to Young Fashion again who reasserts his previous clandestine marriage. He had brought about this marriage with the help of two devious intermediaries: Chaplain Bull, and Coupler—an early portrait of a homosexual man in English comedy. While the outcome of these lines of action is never seriously in doubt, Vanbrugh develops their parallels very elegantly. The play nowhere resorts to the strident breaking of social taboos like many earlier Restoration comedies. Its wit is so much toned down that Collier's invective in 1698, to which Vanbrugh replied in a pamphlet, could only hit on side issues like blasphemy and the satirical portrait of the clergy in Chaplain Bull. It certainly did not prevent Vanbrugh from standing his comic ground in his plays that followed *The Relapse*, nor did it prevent this play from becoming a minor classic of the British theatrical repertory into the 20th century.

—Bernd-Peter Lange

THE REMOVALISTS
by David Williamson

First Publication: Sydney, 1972.
First Production: Café La Mama, Melbourne, 22 July 1971.

Criticism
(For general works on the author, see *Playwrights* volume)

Articles:
David Williamson, "*The Removalists*: A Conjunction of Limitations", in *Meanjin*, 33, 1974.

* * *

A realistic play in two acts, *The Removalists* opens in a small, slovenly-kept police sub-station in Melbourne. Sergeant Simmonds, a cynical policeman in his 50's, explains to Constable Ross, an enthusiastic 20-year-old rookie arriving for his first day of duty, the essence of police work: to do as little as possible while always maintaining the balance of authority. Eager to prove his competence, Ross's idealistic concept of his new role is cunningly broken down by his superior, who denigrates his family background and religion, and undermines his belief in proper police procedures. Two, good-looking sisters arrive to complain of an assault against the younger of the two, Fiona, by her husband. Simmonds treats the complaint with mock seriousness and insists on slowly examining, with lecherous relish, the bruises on Fiona's thigh to her embarrassment and her older sister Kate's enjoyment. Plainly dominating Fiona, Kate, a middle-class dentist's wife, insists that her sister leave her wife-bashing, working-class husband. The prurient Simmonds, hoping for future sexual favors from Kate, offers his and Ross's assistance to a removalist (i.e., a furniture-mover) whom Kate has engaged for the next evening to move her sister's belongings to a new address. The women accept and leave, and, uneasily, Ross agrees to accompany his superior.

Act II occurs in the drab flat of Fiona and Kenny Carter. Kenny has not chosen to go to the pub that night despite his wife's urging. Kate arrives with one removalist, soon followed by the two policemen. When a surprised Kenny becomes abusive at seeing much of his furniture removed, he is handcuffed to the door and repeatedly punched by Simmonds. Distressed by this, the women leave, offering no encouragement to the police. Siding with the latter, the removalist is single-mindedly bent on finishing his job, and departs after doing so. The spirited and foulmouthed Kenny storms at the policemen to the point where the inexperienced Ross, finding himself the butt of demeaning insults by both Simmonds and Kenny, uncontrollably attacks the husband, causing him fatal concussion. Now panic-stricken, Ross forces Simmonds to share the blame. As the play closes, the two fiercely pummel each other, hoping their bruises will be attributed to Kenny.

An Australian writer given to exploring his own society, David Williamson examines the violent behavior inherent in the male's concept of authority and his self-image as a forceful fighter and lover. This concern is embodied in the interplay of the three major male characters. Sergeant Simmonds possesses an uneasy self-esteem dependent upon his self-image as a tough, authoritative cop. Anyone challenging his authority challenges his private concept of himself. Consequently, he strives to dominate the rookie Ross through humiliation and false paternalism, a process initiated in Act I and intensified in Act II. When the frustration of his salacious expectations is augmented by Kenny's refusal to accept his authority, Simmonds is prodded to irrational anger. He hypocritically vilifies Kate, exposed as being tempted by infidelity, brutalizes the husband, and goads his young partner to fatal violence. Constable Ross's idealized self-image of professional competence begins to be shattered when he is continually taunted by his superior's domineering authoritarianism. Moreover, he abandons his initially fair treatment of Kenny when the latter joins Simmonds in ridiculing him. After the ensuing, senseless manslaughter, and the brawl between the two policemen at the play's end, the unplanned violence has run its course. With his self-esteem proved to be as precarious as the sergeant's, Ross has descended to the brutish level of his superior. In relation to the policemen, Kenny is a feisty working man whose image of himself as a great lover and fighter makes him a counterpart to Simmonds. He chauvinistically thinks it acceptable to thump a wife periodically to keep her in line, and feels unjustly betrayed by her desertion. Surprised and outraged at the invasion of his home, he resists aggressively, provoking repeated beatings by Simmonds by hurling foulmouthed insults at the women and the police. His irreverence toward

The Removalists: Royal Court Theatre, London, 1973

authority and his assertion of sexual prowess unleash a repressed sexuality and demand for dominance in Simmonds, and a fear of incompetence in Ross. The eruption of the policemen's repressed frustrations causes Kenny to become a sacrificial scapegoat. Representing the public indifference to violence is the removalist Rob, who gratefully accepts the police's brutal removal of a work-obstructing husband. The two women regret having been catalysts of such brutality and flee it.

Not an anti-police play, by the author's own admission, *The Removalists* resembles a modern allegory accenting the pervasive presence and consequences of violence in human beings in general, and in male-dominated Australian society in particular. In a society which vicariously relishes violence in sport, the media, and elsewhere, Williamson questions whether there is any way to end its arousal and acceptance. He diagnoses the disease of violence but does not prescribe a cure.

Characteristically, Williamson here places three dimensional, credible, characters in ordinary settings, and provides them with forceful dialogue and well-constructed, flowing action to make a salient commentary on human nature. While doing so, he maintains a balance between the comic and the serious, despite the severity of the play's climax and denouement. The vulnerabilities and the often colorful vernacular of the characters are interlaced with a dark humor. The briskly-paced dialogue—filled with insults, obscenity, and sexual innuendos—reflects the underlying capacity for violence, Simmonds warns Kenny he will "crack" his "bloody skull";

women are called "bitches" and "tarts". Language and character clearly embody the theme.

—Christian H. Moe

THE REPRESENTATIVE (Der Stellvertreter)
by Rolf Hochhuth

First Publication: Reinbek, 1963.
First Production: Freie Volksbühne, Berlin, 29 February 1963.

Translations
The Representative, translated by Robert David MacDonald, London, 1963.
The Deputy, translated by Richard and Clara Winston, New York, 1964.

Criticism
(For general works on the author, see *Playwrights* volume)

Books:
Der Streit um Hochhuths "Stellvertreter", Stuttgart, 1963 [various contributors].

Eric Bentley (ed.), *The Storm over "The Deputy"*, New York, 1964.

Paul Rassinier, *Operation "Stellvertreter"*, Munich, 1966.

Edgar Neis, *Erlauterungen zu Rolf Hochhuth: "Der Stellvertreter"; "Soldaten"*, Hollfeld, 1974.

Jan Berg, *Hochhuths "Stellvertreter" und die "Stellvertreter"-Debatte: "Vergangenheitsbewältigung" in Theater und Presse der sechziger Jahre*, Kronberg, 1977.

Bernd Balzer, *Rolf Hochhuth: "Der Stellvertreter"*, Frankfurt, 1986.

Articles:

Robert A. Hall, "Fogazzaro's *Il santo* and Hochhuth's *Der Stellvertreter*", in *Italian Quarterly*, vol.10 no.1, 1966.

Susan Sontag, "Reflections on *The Deputy*" [1964 essay], in her *Against Interpretation, and Other Essays*, New York, 1966.

Leonidas E. Hill, "History and Rolf Hochhuth's *The Deputy*", in *Mosaic*, vol.1 no.1, 1967.

R.C. Perry, "Historical Authenticity and Dramatic Form: Hochhuth's *Der Stellvertreter* and Weiss's *Die Ermittlung*", in *Modern Language Review*, 64, 1969.

Rolf Hochhuth and Robert David MacDonald, "Eine Dokumentation zum *Stellvertreter*, Programmheft *Stellvertreter*", 1972 [for the Swiss Touring Theatre].

Sidney F. Parham, "Editing Hochhuth for the Stage: A Look at the Major Productions of *The Deputy*", in *Educational Theatre Journal*, 28, 1976.

John Simon, "*The Deputy* and Its Metamorphoses" [1964 essay], in his *Singularities: Essays on the Theater, 1964–1973*, New York, 1976.

Otto F. Riewoldt, "'Nimm ein Brechmittel, du, der du dies lieserst': Die katholische Reaktion auf Hochhuths *Stellvertreter*", in *Text und Kritik*, 58, 1978.

E. Elaine Murdaugh, "The Apostate Ethic: The Alternative to Faith in Hochhuth's *Der Stellvertreter*", in *Seminar*, 15, 1979.

Jerry Glen, "Faith, Love, and the Tragic Conflict in Hochhuth's *Der Stellvertreter*", in *German Studies Review*, 7, 1984.

Peter Epp, "*Der Stellvertreter*", in his *Die Darstellung des Nationalsozialismus in der Literatur*, Frankfurt, 1985.

Larry D. Bouchard, "Rolf Hochhuth: Vocation and Silence", in his *Tragic Method and Tragic Theology: Evil in Contemporary Drama and Religious Thought*, University Park, Pennsylvania, 1989.

* * *

The action takes place in 1942 and 1943—the time of the Holocaust. In Berlin, Italian Jesuit, Riccardo Fontana, learns from Kurt Gerstein, a Christian resistance fighter who has infiltrated Hitler's S.S., about the full horror of the genocide of Jews currently in progress. Fontana returns to Rome and attempts—unsuccessfully—to influence a cardinal to persuade Pope Pius XII to speak out against Nazi mass murder. At last Fontana appeals personally to Pius; but the Pope refuses to go beyond mere non-committal generalities. Fontana, who identifies with the Jews to the point of wearing the Yellow Star, is himself shipped to Auschwitz. There, confronted by a diabolical camp doctor, he is first made to work in the crematoria and then murdered. Gerstein, exposed by the doctor as an anti-Nazi activist, is also killed.

The Representative, by the then unknown playwright Rolf Hochhuth, caused a tremendous stir when veteran left-wing director Erwin Piscator first staged it in Berlin in 1963. This play, far from innovative in its form, broke a double taboo.

Not only did it spell out explicitly Nazi, wartime atrocities—it accused Pius XII of having failed to live up to his moral responsibilities.

The Berlin production was followed by performances elsewhere in Germany as well as abroad—in Stockholm, Paris, London, New York. Everywhere the play triggered off heated debates and, in some places, hostile demonstrations. Some Catholic apologists focused on what they claimed was a misrepresentation of Pius XII. However, this was by no means the only point, or even the main point Hochhuth was making. *The Representative* investigated *any* individual's responsibility in matters of moral choice.

The Representative's subtitle must be taken seriously. This "Christian tragedy" asserts that even in an age of impersonal mass manipulation choices are still open to us. Side by side with the ethical obtuseness of most of the characters in the play, we are shown right and wrong conduct at their polar extremes: saintliness in the persons of Fontana (modelled on the Polish priest, Maximilian Kolbe) and Gerstein (the latter a real, historical character); total evil in the doctor (inspired by the notorious Joseph Mengele) whose Mephistophelian nature exudes metaphysical horror. The "representative" of the title is not only the Pope as the vicar of Christ, but also Fontana, who assumes a voluntary martyrdom, becoming a self-chosen representative.

The message emerges clearly enough from the printed text; it may not be equally apparent in production. The vastly over-written script, which would require some seven hours to perform in its entirety, has invariably been staged in one of several, trimmed-down versions. Piscator's omission of five of its 11 scenes, including the whole of the Auschwitz act, has been adopted by many other directors. This makes the Pope's "Gran Rifiuto" more of a dramatic climax than the author had had in mind. The script's excessive length may have reflected Hochhuth's lack of theatrical experiences; it also signalled a personal obsession. The *Historical Sidelights* appended to the text are evidence of the extensive, background research he had undertaken over a period of years; so are his editorialising stage directions.

In spite of the large cast of characters and the editorial comments on them, *The Representative* remains concerned not so much with individual psychology as with individual ethics. Ordinary characterisation is jettisoned most conspicuously in the case of the doctor, a devil figure all but incomprehensible in other than religious terms.

What the play does exhibit is a full spectrum of corrupt *social* attitudes, expressed in apparently naturalistic, though to some extent stylised, dialogue. Laid out as verse, this frequently falls into iambic pentameters. Some lines of shattering brutality are spoken in dialect, which gives them an uncannily homey or even comical texture. This tension between realism and stylisation goes beyond the dialogue. The first four acts, by and large, follow the conventions of naturalistic staging. But the last act, set in Auschwitz, makes a decisive formal break. In it, the machinery of mass murder is symbolised by a red spotlight and the sound of a cement mixer. As Hochhuth puts it in his stage directions: "*documentary realism is no longer any sort of stylistic principle. . .The stage setting throughout is ghostly, dreamlike, even if "reality" is technically possible*".

The play's polemical success is not in doubt. It put on the public agenda questions studiously ignored before. Its artistic success is somewhat more ambiguous. Hochhuth may well have been justified in largely avoiding experimentation which might have weakened the directness of his message. But the novel-like sweep of the action seems almost to defy staging requirements. This is a potential pitfall, for the scenes, however over-long, are not arbitrary in their sequence—they illuminate one another: characters interlock, themes are varied and resolved. To do justice to the play's structure in production, it is essential not to cut any scenes as such but to trim them internally. The sensational impact of *The Representative* in its first performances is not likely to be repeated in future; but suitably edited it deserves to keep an honourable place in the world repertory.

—George W. Brandt

—————

THE RESISTABLE RISE OF ARTURO UI
(Der aufhaltsame Aufstieg des Arturo Ui)
by Bertolt Brecht

First Publication: In *Sinn und Form: Zweites Sonderheft Bertolt Brecht*, 1957; in book form, in *Stücke, 9*, Frankfurt, 1957.
First Production: Stuttgart, 10 November 1958.

Translations
The Resistable Rise of Arturo Ui, translated by Ralph Mannheim, London, 1976 (vol.6 no.2 of *Collected Plays*).

Criticism
(For general works on the author, see *Playwrights* volume)

Books:
Raimund Gerz, *Bertolt Brecht und der Faschismus: In den Parabelstücken "Die Rundküpfe un die Sptitzköpfe", "Der aufhaltsame Aufstieg des Arturo Ui", und "Turandot oder der Kongress der Weisswascher": Rekonstruktion einer Versuchsreihe*, Bonn, 1983.

Articles:
Joachim Tenschert, "Mit *Arturo Ui* in Westdeutschland: Aus dem Tournee-Tagebuch des Berliner Ensemble", in *Theater der Zeit*, 15, 1965.
Edouard Pfrimmer, "Brecht et la parodie: *Arturo Ui*", in *Études germaniques*, 26, 1971.
Livio Sichirollo, "'Die tollen Zwanzigerjahre': Parole introduttive ad un dibattito sull' *Arturo Ui* di Brecht", in *Studi urbinati di storia, filosofia e litteratura*, 45, 1971.
Richard C. Beacham, "Brecht's *Arturo Ui*: The Dramatization of Contemporary History", in *Theatre Annual*, 29, 1973.
Ernst Schürer, "Revolution from the Right: Bertolt Brecht's American Gangster Play *The Resistable Rise of Arturo Ui*", in *Perspectives on Contemporary Literature*, 2, 1976.
Bernhard Keller, "Die Auseinandersetzung mit dem Nationalsozialismus im Drama: Vergleichende Analyse von Zuckmayers *Des Teufels General* und Brechts *Arturo Ui*", in *Sammlung: Jahrbuch für antifaschistische Literatur und Kunst*, 1, 1978.
M.E. Humble, "The Stylisation of History in Bertolt Brecht's *Der aufhaltsame Aufstieg des Arturo Ui*", in *Forum for Modern Language Studies*, 16, 1980.
Luis Feijoo Inglesias, "La actualidad del *Arturo Ui* de Brecht", in *Cuadernos hispanoamericanos*, 361–362, 1980.
Jean Philippon, "*Arturo Ui* et l'affaire Röhm: Réflexions sur la conscience politique de l'homme moderne", in *Actes du groupe de recherches sur l'expression littéraire et les sciences humaines*, Paris, 1983.
Peter Epp, "*Der aufhaltsame Aufstieg des Arturo Ui*", in his

Die Darstellung des Nationalsozialismus in der Literatur, Frankfurt, 1985.
Hans W. Nieschmidt, "Glorifizierung oder Preisgabe des politischen Gegners? Zum Geisterauftritt in Brechts *Arturo Ui*", in *Seminar*, 22, 1986.
Anthony Grenville, "Idealism versus Materialism in the Representation of History in Literature: The Dictator Figure in Thomas Mann's *Mario und der Zauberer* and Brecht's *Der aufhaltsame Aufstieg des Arturo Ui*", in *Journal of European Studies*, 17, 1987.
Robert Atkins, "'Und es ist Kein Gott ausser Adolf Hitler': The Biblical Motifs in Brecht's *Arturo Ui* and Related Works as Political Counter-Propaganda", in *Modern Language Review*, 85, 1990.

*   *   *

A small-time crook takes control of the cauliflower business in Chicago and then extends his protection racket to neighbouring Cicero. In *The Resistable Rise of Arturo Ui* Brecht combines stock incidents from the Hollywood gangster films of the 1930's with classical verse dialogue to form what he himself once defined as a historical farce. The farce is also a parable because the gangster's career is a trenchant parody of the rise of Hitler from the 1929 depression to the annexation of Austria in 1938.

When he was in New York in 1935 for a production of *The Mother* Brecht was fascinated by gangster films, and indeed by the whole subject of gangsterdom. He saw in the career of Dutch Schulz, whose killing made headlines at the time, the elements of the Hitler story as he had experienced it in Germany: police corruption, tie-ups with legitimate business, venal politicians rigging the law to suit the gangsters, and finally the ability of thugs to operate in open defiance of the authorities. In the biography of Al Capone Brecht discovered intriguing parallels to the rise of the Nazis and this provided the plot of *The Resistable Rise of Arturo Ui*.

The gangster action is a montage of self-contained scenes, after each of which Brecht projects a text naming the historical event to which the scene alludes. So the role of the tycoons, and of the hitherto incorruptible politician, Dogsborough, in Ui's rise from cheap hoodlum to city boss stand for the roles of the Ruhr industrialists and President Hindenburg in the rise of Hitler to the German Chancellorship. The rigged, slapstick trial in which the hapless and drugged Fish is framed for the warehouse fire which Ui's men themselves started, corresponds to the trial in Leipzig of the unemployed Dutchman, Van der Lübbe, for burning down the Reichstag. Ui's murder of Roma, which is based on the St. Valentine's Day Massacre when Capone wiped out a rival bootlegging gang, alludes to Hitler's elimination, in 1934, of head storm-trooper Ernst Röhm and his lieutenants, who had helped Hitler to power and then become a political embarrassment. Givola, who, like the Chicago gangster O'Banion, had a limp, stands for Goebbels, and Giri (who collects his victims' hats) stands for Goering. The murder of Dullfeet corresponds to the assassination of the Austrian Chancellor, Dollfuss, in 1935, and Ui's designs on Cicero correspond to the annexation of Austria in 1938.

All this is done with a light touch. The play is written in verse, using broken hexameters which parody the high style of German historical drama. The deliberate mismatching of elevated metre with low-life subject cuts the criminals down to size. Brecht's intention was to expose Hitler as a perpetrator of great political crimes rather than as a great political criminal, and to demolish any possibility of the kind of posthumous respect usually accorded to historical figures of his scale. There are nice moments of literary parody which further undermine

The Resistable Rise of Arturo Ui: Saville Theatre, London, 1969

Ui/Hitler, such as Ui's meeting with Dullfeet in Givola's flower shop, which, with its ambulatory dialogue composed of intercalated, single, rhyming lines is a formal reprise of the seduction of Gretchen in Martha's garden from Goethe's *Faust*. Ui's abrupt approach to Dullfeet's widow is a parody of Gloucester's wooing of Lady Anne in *Richard III*, and the apparition of Roma after his murder could be derived from either *Richard III* or *Julius Caesar*. Brecht makes Ui take a lesson in voice and movement from an actor, just as Hitler is supposed to have done, and Ui haltingly masters Mark Antony's subtly modulated obituary from *Julius Caesar*, rising to a final rhetorical flourish that is undercut by his pose, both hands placed firmly over his genitals.

Ui is a bravura role, as Ekkehard Schall amply demonstrated at the Berliner Ensemble in 1959. On that occasion the gangsters wore shabby raincoats and had green and white make-up to give them the appropriate touch of menace. In 1987, at the height of the controversy about Austrian Chancellor Kurt Waldheim's supposed Nazi involvement, Alfred Kirchner directed a production at the Vienna Burgtheater in which the gangsters wore loden coats and Tyrolean hats, proving that the play can still have a topical effect.

German critics tend to quibble that Brecht gives a partial and partisan version of Nazism, exposing Hitler's capitalist backers but ignoring his support among the unemployed proletariat and failing to mention the Jews. This assumes the play is a definitive analysis of the rise of Hitler, a tall order in 1941. The British view of Hitler is more detached, and the play is accepted on its own terms as an effective warning against corruption and tyranny—and with a fine leading role in which Leonard Rossiter and Nicol Williamson have starred.

Brecht wrote *The Resistable Rise of Arturo Ui* in three weeks in 1941 while waiting in Finland for an immigrant visa for the United States. He thought it would go down well there, but an America that was about to enter the war was not the place for a spoof on Hitler, and the American stage was, anyway, to take some 20 years to accept Brecht's epic theatre. The play was never produced in his lifetime. After 1945 the Germans had problems in coming to terms with their past. They have always had problems with comedy, and Brecht, especially after he resettled in East Berlin in 1948, could see that a farcical treatment of the Nazis invited criticism from many quarters. He suggested that, to achieve the right balance, the play should be produced in tandem with *Fear and Misery of the Third Reich* which gives a factual treatment of life in Nazi Germany in short naturalistic episodes.

—Hugh Rorrison

THE REVENGER'S TRAGEDY
by Thomas Middleton or Cyril Tourneur

First Publication: London, 1607.
First Production: London (King's Men), c.1606–07.

Editions

The Revenger's Tragedy, edited by G.B. Harrison, London, 1934.
The Revenger's Tragedy, edited by R.A. Foakes, London, 1965 (Revels Plays Series).
The Revenger's Tragedy, edited by Lawrence J. Ross, Lincoln, Nebraska, 1966 (Regents Renaissance Drama Series).
The Revenger's Tragedy, edited by Brian Gibbons, London, 1967; second edition, 1990 (New Mermaid Series).
The Revenger's Tragedy, in *Jacobean Tragedies*, edited by A.H. Gomme, Oxford, 1969.
The Revenger's Tragedy, in *The Plays of Cyril Tourneur*, edited by George Parfitt, Cambridge, 1978.
The Revenger's Tragedy, in *Thomas Middleton: Five Plays*, edited by Bryan Loughrey and Neil Taylor, Harmondsworth, 1988.

Criticism
(For general works on the author, see *Playwrights* volume)

Books:
Daniel J, Jacobson, *The Language of "The Revenger's Tragedy"*, Salzburg, 1974 (Jacobean Drama Studies, 38).
Philip J. Ayres, *Tourneur: "The Revenger's Tragedy"*, London, 1977.
Robert C. Jones, *Engagement With Knavery: Point of View in "Richard III", "The Jew of Malta", "Volpone", and "The Revenger's Tragedy"*, Durham, North Carolina, 1986.

Articles:
E.C. Oliphant, "The Authorship of *The Revenger's Tragedy*", in *Studies in Philology*, 23, 1926.
W.D. Dunkel, "The Authorship of *The Revenger's Tragedy*", in *Publications of the Modern Language Association* [*PMLA*], 46, 1931.
Una M. Ellis-Fermor, "The Imagery of *The Revenger's Tragedy* and *The Atheist's Tragedy*", in *Modern Language Review*, 30, 1935.
L.G. Salingar, "*The Revenger's Tragedy* and the Morality Tradition", in *Scrutiny*, 6, 1938.
Marco K. Mincoff, "The Authorship of *The Revenger's Tragedy*", in *Studia-Historico-Philologica-Serdicensia*, 2, 1939.
Richard H. Barker, "The Authorship of *The Second Maiden's Tragedy* and *The Revenger's Tragedy*", in *South Atlantic Bulletin*, 20, 1945.
Henry Hitch Adams, "Cyril Tourneur on Revenge", in *Journal of English and Germanic Philology*, 48, 1949.
R.A. Foakes, "On the Authorship of *The Revenger's Tragedy*", in *Modern Language Review*, 48, 1953.
Robert Ornstein, "The Ethical Design of *The Revenger's Tragedy*", in *English Literary History*, 21, 1954.
Samuel Schoenbaum, "*The Revenger's Tragedy*: Jacobean Dance of Death", in *Modern Language Quarterly*, 15, 1954.
Peter Lisca, "*The Revenger's Tragedy*: A Study in Irony", in *Philological Quarterly*, 38, 1959.
Inga-Stina Ewbank, "An Approach to Tourneur's Imagery", in *Modern Language Review*, 54, 1959.
Inga-Stina Ewbank, "On the Authorship of *The Revenger's Tragedy*", in *English Studies*, 41, 1960.

George M. Price, "The Authorship and Bibliography of *The Revenger's Tragedy*", in *Library* (fifth series), 15, 1960.
L.G. Salingar, "*The Revenger's Tragedy*: Some Possible Sources", in *Modern Language Review*, 60, 1965.
Louis Charles Stagg, "Figurative Imagery in Revenge Tragedies by Three Seventeenth-Century Contemporaries of Shakespeare", in *South Central Bulletin*, vol.26 no.4, 1966.
Sanford Sternlicht, "Tourneur's Imagery and *The Revenger's Tragedy*", in *Papers on Language and Literature*, 6, 1970.
R.A. Foakes, "The Art of Cruelty: Hamlet and Vindice", in *Shakespeare Survey*, 26, 1973.
George Geckle, "Justice in *The Revenger's Tragedy*", in *Renaissance Papers*, 1973.
B.J. Layman, "Tourneur's Artificial Noon: The Design of *The Revenger's Tragedy*", in *Modern Language Quarterly*, 34, 1973.
Leslie Sanders, "*The Revenger's Tragedy*: A Play on the Revenge Play", in *Renaissance and Reformation*, 10, 1974.
Larry S. Champion, "Tourneur's *The Revenger's Tragedy* and the Jacobean Comic Perspective", in *Studies in Philology*, 72, 1975.
Stanley Wells, "*The Revenger's Tragedy* Revived", in *Elizabethan Theatre*, 6, 1975.
Stephen Wigler, "If Looks Could Kill: Fathers and Sons in *The Revenger's Tragedy*", in *Comparative Drama*, 9, 1975.
Nancy G. Wilds, "'Of Rare Fire Compact': Image and Rhetoric in *The Revenger's Tragedy*", in *Texas Studies in Literature and Language*, 17, 1975.
John Mark Huemann, "Death Culture and the World of *The Revenger's Tragedy*", in *Gradiva*, 1, 1976.
Lillian Wilds, "The Revenger as Dramatist: A Study of the Character-as-Dramatist in *The Revenger's Tragedy*", in *Rocky Mountain Review*, 3, 1976.
Peter Arnold, "*The Revenger's Tragedy*: The Dramatic Significance of Sex", in *North Dakota Quarterly*, 45, 1977.
Ronald Huebert, "*The Revenger's Tragedy* and the Fallacy of the Excluded Middle", in *University of Toronto Quarterly*, 48, 1978.
Shyamel Bagchee, "'To be Honest is not to be i' the World': Defining a Perspective on *The Revenger's Tragedy*", in *Journal of English* (San'a University), 7, 1980.
Jonathon Dollimore, "Two Concepts of Mimesis: Renaissance Literary Theory and *The Revenger's Tragedy*", in *Drama and Mimesis*, edited by James Redmond, Cambridge, 1980 (Themes in Drama Series).
Mitsuru Kamachi, "Vindice Vindicatus: The Hidden Trickster in *The Revenger's Tragedy*", in *Shakespeare Studies* (Japan), 16, 1980.
Larry S. Champion, "Fantasies of Violence: Hamlet and *The Revenger's Tragedy*", in *Studies in English Literature 1500–1900*, 21, 1981.
Peter Hyland, "The Disguised Revenger and *The Revenger's Tragedy*", in *Southern Review* (Adelaide), 15, 1981.
Michael E. Mooney, "'This Luxurious Circle': *Figurenposition* in *The Revenger's Tragedy*", in *English Literary Renaissance*, 13, 1983.
William L. Stall, "'This Metamorphosde Tragoedie': Thomas Kyd, Cyril Tourneur, and the Jacobean Theatre of Cruelty", in *Ariel*, 14, 1983.
Laurie A. Finke, "Painting Women: Images of Femininity in Jacobean Tragedy", in *Theatre Journal*, vol.36 no.3, 1984.
Scott McMillin, "Acting and Violence: *The Revenger's Tragedy* and its Departures from *Hamlet*", in *Studies in English Literature 1500–1900*, vol.24 no.2, 1984.
Robert C. Evans, "Women and the Meaning of *The Revenger's Tragedy*", in *Postscript*, 4, 1987.
M.W.A. Smith, "*The Revenger's Tragedy*: The Derivation and

Interpretation of Statistical Results for Resolving Disputed Authorship", in *Computers and the Humanities*, vol.21 no.1, 1987.

Peter Stallybrass, "Reading the Body: *The Revenger's Tragedy* and the Jacobean Theatre of Consumption", in *Renaissance Drama*, 18, 1987.

*   *   *

Vindice, the revenger, is a poor gentleman on the fringes of a depraved ducal court. His mistress was poisoned by the Duke, and in pursuit of vengeance he infiltrates the web of plots and counter-plots which constitutes the social life of the ruling family, all of whose members are obsessively lecherous, or obsessively ambitious, or both. He is fantastically successful, eventually murdering both the Duke and his heir by means which are at once spectacular, appropriate, and secret. The rest of the ducal family slaughter each other in farcical sequences of greed and misunderstanding. The dynasty having been wiped out, the dukedom is handed to a virtuous old gentleman named Antonio. However, in a final ironic twist, Vindice casually reveals his multiple murders, and Antonio instantly has him executed. This lightning denouement (Vindice's confession comes only 30 lines before the end of the play) is perhaps a purely formal concession to the genre, since the revenger has until this point been coasting towards a highly unorthodox happy ending. But it could also be a serious stroke of poetic justice, whereby Vindice is punished for having come to resemble the monsters he has exterminated; or again, it could be a cynical note to the effect that no old gentleman is too virtuous to adopt Machiavellian principles on attaining power. The moment is typical of the play's unique texture, not only in its ambivalence, but equally in its speed.

Both kinds of distinctiveness are found above all in the language: a rapid and fractured blank verse, at once colloquial and gaudy, judgmental yet self-mocking. The uncertainty about who wrote the play is still unresolved partly because neither of the most popular candidates—Cyril Tourneur and Thomas Middleton—writes quite like this anywhere else:

> Now 'tis full sea abed over the world.
> There's juggling of all sides. Some that were maids
> E'en at sunset are now perhaps i' the toll-book;
> This woman in immodest thin apparel
> Lets in her friend by water, here a dame
> Cunning, nails leather hinges to a door
> To avoid proclamation.
> Now cuckolds are a-coining, apace, apace, apace, apace!
> And careful sisters spin that thread i' the night
> That does maintain them and their bawds i' the day.

The impression of breakneck pace comes partly from the rhetorical insistence on the present as, throughout the play, everything is happening *here* and *now*; the verse here seems intoxicated by its own contemporaneity. It also has to do with the jump-cutting between images: characteristically, the panorama of the whole darkened world is succeeded by close-ups of a woman's clothes, the hinges of a door. But still more, the sense of speed comes from a sort of overload in the associations of the words. "Full sea" means high tide, suggesting climax, and "juggling" amplifies the orgasmic implication with a physical effect of rocking. In that sense, the line seems to be imagining sexual acts in many separate beds. But then "sea abed" is very close to "sea-bed", and the immediately following phrase "*over* the world" fuses with that to offer a picture of the whole world at the bottom of the sea—a sea

which is both a paranoiac version of nightfall and, in the same moment, an inundation of lust. With all that half-consciously in the background, the image, a couple of lines later, of the woman who "lets in her friend by water", has an obscure perversity which the immediate details don't justify. Or, again, if we take a different route, "juggling" also means swindling, and so sets off a sequence of economic associations, through "toll-book" and "coining" to the mock-Puritan emblem of female industriousness in the last two lines. Fiercely moralistic, the writing is none the less complicit with the excesses it evokes through its own voluptuous, semantic promiscuity. In a tease which is directly thematised when Vindice, in disguise, attempts to seduce his own sister on behalf of the Duke's son, the satiric discourse teeters along the dangerous boundary between denunciation and incitement.

When, in the 1960's, the play was rediscovered for the theatre as well as the library, it turned out to be characterised on the stage by this same feverish overdetermination of the images. Take the famous scene of the Duke's murder. An old lecher, he is introduced to what he takes to be a masked prostitute. He kisses her, and discovers that the mask hides the skull of Vindice's mistress. Its mouth has been smeared with a poison which eats his lips away before he dies. What kind of theatre is this? In a way, it's an extreme of allegory. Whores are, as Webster put it, sweetmeats that rot the eater; beneath the brief attraction of the flesh there is always the reality of the bone; and so on—moral commonplaces are being acted out with startling literalness, as if in an animated emblem-book. But then it's also clear that this enactment, with its scenic lavishness, its intimate physicality, and its orgiastic cruelty, is Vindice's fantasy. If the emblems are part of a punitive moralism, they are equally part of a perverse eroticism of murder. What the avenger gets out of his vengeance, with scandalous explicitness, is pleasure. Moreover, these unconformable elements are negotiated by an alarming humour: the device is, among other things, a practical joke, and Vindice is never too immersed in either his justice or his *jouissance* to laugh. And yet another signification is introduced by the preface to the vengeance, when Vindice, looking at the skull, reflects in verse of gorgeous melancholy on the nothingness of all life and love when it is brought to such a measure; the symbolism of his revenge negates the very passions which motivated it. This joke, a sad one, is on him. Thus, in performance, the text's naive moralism is compromised in several ways at once. There is the promise of the most rigid kind of metaphysical closure, but the promise is betrayed, as its allegorical signifiers come to mean at once much more and much less than they should.

One important solvent of the rigidity is money. From the opening speech, when Vindice's dead mistress is recalled as able to have "made a usurer's son / Melt all his patrimony in a kiss", the codes of expenditure and sexuality are blended together with inexhaustible flexibility, and their literal meeting point—prostitution—is arguably the play's controlling model of both sexual and economic relations. Vindice sees, in manic, historical shorthand, "fruit fields turned into bastards": the text regards both physical and financial liquidity with the same expression of fascinated disgust. This is perhaps the underside of the play's nervy and exciting modishness: on the obverse of its preoccupation with "now" is inscribed an arcadian image of "then", a time when wealth, and rank, and faces, and significations, were all stable and real. But the inscription is so faint that the appeal to it is mocking, almost camp. The form of the play has adapted brilliantly to the social mobility that its content continues to rage against. Positive values within the text adhere to abstract *sententiae* and chaste women; both, like the phenomenologically innocent world before money, guarantee their integrity by being dead. *Now* there is only prostitution or starvation, and the deviser of this lurid and startlingly modern entertainment has already made his choice.

—Peter Womack

REVIZOR. See **THE GOVERNMENT INSPECTOR.**

RHINOCEROS (Rhinocéros)
by Eugène Ionesco

First Publication: Paris, 1959.
First Production: Schauspielhaus, Düsseldorf, 31 October 1959; first production in France, at the Odéon-Théâtre de France, Paris, 22 January, 1960.

Translations

Rhinoceros, translated by Derek Prouse, in *Rhinoceros; The Leader; The Future in Eggs*, London, 1960.

Criticism

(For general works on the author, see *Playwrights* volume)

Books:
Etienne Frois, *"Rhinocéros": Analyse critique*, Paris, 1970.
C.E.J. Dolamore, *Ionesco: "Rhinocéros"*, London, 1984.

Articles:
Ecaterina Cleynen-Serghiev, *"Rhinocéros* d'Eugène Ionesco en Roumanie", in *Revue des sciences humaines*, 36, 1971.
Dorothy Knowles, "Ionesco's Rhinoceroses: Their Romanian Origin and Their Western Fortunes", in *French Studies*, 28, 1974.
George Martin, "Bérenger and his Counterpart in *La Photo du colonel*", in *Modern Drama*, 17, 1974.
David B. Parsell, "A Reading of Ionesco's *Rhinocéros*", in *Furman Studies*, vol.21 no.1, 1974.
Ionesco: "Rhinocéros", in *Cahiers Renaud-Barrault*, 97, 1978 [essays by Jean-Louis Barrault and others].
G. Richard Danner, "Bérenger's Dubious Defense of Humanity in *Rhinocéros*", in *French Review*, 53, 1979.
Eliza M. Ghil, "Ideological Parody in Eugène Ionesco's *Rhinocéros* and in *A Lost Letter* by I.L. Caragiale", in *Yearbook of Romanian Studies*, 7, 1982.
Robert L. Tener, "Scenic Metaphors: A Study of Ionesco's Geometrical Vision of Human Relationships in the Bérenger Plays", in *Papers on Language and Literature*, 23, 1987.
Ulrich Schoeter, "Deutschland im Denken und Wirken von Eugène Ionesco oder die Parabel über den Hässlichen Deutschen: *Rhinocéros*", in *Grenzgänge: Kulturelle Begegnungen zwischen Deutschland und Frankreich*, edited by Hans T. Siepe, Essen, 1988.

*   *   *

A political parable told in the mythical mode of a fable, *Rhinoceros* takes place in a small town in France which witnesses first the appearance of a rhinoceros which might have escaped from a circus or a zoo, and then of a growing number of rhinos. These animals are actually former human beings who have suffered a metamorphosis. This disease is a strange disease ("rhinoceritis") which can afflict anyone who is not immune: it is the malady of conformity. Ionesco's anti-hero, Bérenger, retains his humanity to the end, but sees all his acquaintances, friends, and even the woman he loves transformed into these brutal beasts. Ionesco's fable was inspired by the growing wave of fascism in Romania and elsewhere in Europe on the eve of *World War II*, but it could easily also be about a mindless kind of Communism. For Ionesco there are various forms of this epidemic: anyone who walks in step to any kind of anthem, who shouts slogans, tramples over the bodies of his fellow men, and never thinks for himself, is a rhinoceros. *Rhinoceros* shows how a well-meaning average man manages to retain his modest humanity in the face of horror.

Ionesco's play opens in the pleasant square of a small provincial town. Women are going about their morning grocery shopping while men are sipping their noon-time apéritif sitting at the *terrasse* of a cheerful café. The sky is postcard blue on this typical Sunday morning.

Two friends, Jean and Bérenger meet on the *terrasse* of a café: Jean is carefully groomed, while Bérenger is unshaven, dishevelled, tired-looking, and Jean begins to berate his friend for his drinking habit and unkempt appearance. He lectures him with growing rage, ordering him to cultivate himself methodically by going to museums and theatres. Bérenger endures this attack with equanimity and even promises to mend his ways. By way of an apology he ventures an explanation: "Life in a small town is so boring. I'm not cut out for office work".

The dominical peace of the little square is suddenly shattered by a loud noise, the heavy stomping and breathing of a huge animal. Invisible to the audience, but clearly perceived by the characters on the stage, the first rhinoceros fills the characters with horror and dismay. Bérenger would prefer to dismiss the incident, particularly since Daisy, the pretty secretary from his office, is walking in the direction of their table. At this very moment a rhinoceros is heard again. This time the wild beast runs over the cat of one of the shoppers. Once again this happening is out of the audience's line of vision. Among the characters on the stage a pedantic controversy arises over whether this is the same rhino or another, in which Jean and Bérenger argue with each other, Jean revealing, in the course of this, his racist prejudices.

The first scene of Act II takes place in Bérenger's office, a publishing concern specializing in law books. The various employees discuss the strange phenomenon they have heard about. Some believe that rhinos were seen in the streets of their town, others refuse to give credence to the story. Boeuf (the name means ox), one of the office workers, has not come in yet. His wife rushes in, shouting that a rhinoceros has been chasing her down the street. A crash and wild trumpeting are heard. The stage fills with plaster dust, and as Madame Boeuf looks down the broken stairs, she recognizes her husband in the animal below. Her loyalty undented, she jumps out of the window, lands on the animal's back, and apparently gallops off.

In the next scene—the core of the play—Bérenger is shown paying a sick call on Jean. The latter is bed-ridden, felled by some kind of strange malaise. He keeps on clearing his throat and complains of pain in the middle of his forehead. When Bérenger suggests that he ought to see a doctor, Jean states that he has confidence only in veterinarians. It becomes obvious that his malady is rhinoceritis. He is undergoing a

Rhinoceros: Royal Court Theatre, London, 1960

metamorphosis which becomes increasingly clear in the course of his numerous trips to the bathroom. Each time he emerges, he looks less and less human: a bump in the middle of his forehead grows into a fully-fledged horn. Nor is this transformation a surprise for the audience which was shown a man full of proud self-assurance and moralistic indignation. In Jean-Louis Barrault's famous production, this effect was achieved by the use of partial masks. Ionesco favored this approach which lent his comedy the character of a mythical fable. This is also the only scene in the play in which the audience watches the process of metamorphosis, sees how a person turns into a monster. As Bérenger flees from Jean's room, he realizes that the streets are now crowded with rhinos. They have taken over.

In Act III we see the anti-hero confined to his own small room. He now lives in constant fear of turning into a wild beast, like all the others. He is visited by his office mate, Dudard, a former lawyer. Later, Daisy, now his fiancée, joins him. Dudard is endorsing the rhinoceros cause while preaching impartiality. His logic and misplaced broad-mindedness lead him to posit the following question: "What could be more natural than a rhinoceros?". He is not ready to agree with Bérenger's sensible retort, "Yes, but for a man to turn into a rhinoceros is abnormal beyond question". A cultured, intelligent man, Dudard has lost any sense of what is normal or abnormal. In conversation, Ionesco says that he thought of Jean-Paul Sartre when he created the character of Dudard.

As for Daisy, she is loving at first, but she, too, begins to turn against Bérenger. The short scene between them ranges over a whole, married lifetime. The tender fiancée becomes, gradually, her husband's scolding mother ("Have you been good today? You haven't had any brandy?"). The couple's privacy is interrupted by the ringing of the telephone. Trumpeting is heard coming from the receiver when Daisy picks it up. Indeed the presence of the brutal beasts is all-pervasive, and this begins to poison the happy couple's life. The rhinos have taken over the radio station, and "the authorities have joined them". As the whole apartment house shakes, and plaster falls from the ceiling Daisy begins to express doubts: "Perhaps it's all our own fault". From that moment on she is, to Bérenger clearly lost. She claims to feel ashamed of what her husband calls love: "this morbid feeling, this male weakness. And female, too. It just doesn't compare with the ardour and the tremendous energy emanating from all these creatures around us". Daisy has begun to see a kind of beauty in the thick skin of the rhinos; their hoarse shouts sound to her like singing. She exclaims: "They're like gods". Bérenger knows he is defeated: "In the space of a few minutes we've gone through 25 years of married life". Indeed, it is Ionesco's feat as a playwright to encapsulate these years in a brief, tragic exchange. Daisy runs out of the conjugal apartment to join the throng of monstrous creatures outside.

Alone, Bérenger considers what has occurred in a moving soliloquy. He voices his own doubts about his choice. Perhaps he ought not to have retained his humanity, but it is now too late to turn back. The monologue ends on a note of defiance: "I'm the last man left, and I'm staying that way until the end. I'm not capitulating!".

What type of man is Ionesco's Bérenger? What did the dramatist have in mind when he created him? First, it is a self-portrait. Bérenger is a loner, a romantic, seemingly passive, yet able to withstand social pressures, to remain uninvolved in ideological struggle. He is what Ionesco calls in *Man with Bags* "a specialist in survival". Above all, he is a humanist, albeit a comical one.

Rhinoceros may not be Ionesco's greatest comic drama, but it is the one that has ensured his international reputation. First heard as a BBC Third Program broadcast, it was presented at the Odéon in January 1960—directed by Jean-Louis Barrault, who also played Bérenger. In April of the same year, it was shown in London at the Royal Court Theatre, with Laurence Olivier as the heroic anti-hero, and in January 1961, it opened in New York, with Eli Wallach as Bérenger, Ann Jackson as Daisy, and Zero Mostel as Jean.

—Rosette C. Lamont

RICHARD II
by William Shakespeare

First Publication: 1597 (first quarto); complete in First Folio, London, 1623.
First Production: The Theatre?, London, c. 1595.

Editions
Richard II, edited by John Dover Wilson, Cambridge, 1939 (New Shakespeare).
Richard II, edited by Mathew Black, Philadelphia, 1955 (New Variorum Shakespeare).
Richard II, edited by Peter Ure, London, 1956; revised edition 1966 (Arden Shakespeare).
Richard II, edited by Mathew W. Black, Baltimore, Maryland, 1957 (Pelican Shakespeare).
Richard II, edited by Kenneth Muir, New York, 1963 (Signet Classic Shakespeare).
Richard II, edited by Stanley Wells, Harmondsworth, 1969 (New Penguin Shakespeare).
Richard II, edited by Andrew Gurr, Cambridge, 1984 (New Cambridge Shakespeare).

Bibliographies
Mathew W. Black and G. Harold Metz (eds.), *"The Life and Death of King Richard II": A Bibliography to Supplement the New Variorum Edition of 1955*, New York, 1977.
Josephine A. Roberts (ed.), *"Richard II": An Annotated Bibliography* (2 vols.), New York, 1988 (Garland Shakespeare Bibliographies).

Criticism
(For general works on the author, see *Playwrights* volume)

Books:
A.R. Humphreys, *Richard II*, London, 1967.
Edwart Weber, *John Gowers "Cronica Tripertita" und William Shakespeares "Richard II"*, The Hague, 1970.

James L. Calderwood, *Shakespeare's Metadrama: The Argument of the Play in "Titus Andronicus", "Love's Labours Lost", "Romeo and Juliet", "A Midsummer Night's Dream", and "Richard II"*, Minneapolis, 1971.
Paul M. Cubeta (ed.), *Twentieth Century Interpretations of "Richard II"*, Englewood Cliffs, New Jersey, 1971.
Nicholas Brooke (ed.), *"Richard II": A Casebook*, London, 1973.
G.A. Wilkes, *Image and Pattern: Shakespeare's "Richard II"*, Sydney, 1974.
James L. Calderwood, *Metadrama in Shakespeare's Henriad: "Richard II" to "Henry V"*, Berkeley, California, 1979.
Jeanne T. Newlin (ed.), *"Richard II": Critical Essays*, New York and London, 1984 [anthology of Criticism].
Malcolm Page, *Richard II*, London, 1986 (Text and Performance Series)
Mark W. Scott and Sandra L. Williamson (eds.), *"Richard II"*, in *Shakespearian Criticism, 6*, Detroit, Illinois, 1987 [anthology of criticism].

Articles:
For information on the many articles about *Richard II*, see the bibliographies listed above, the bibliographies listed in the *Playwrights* volume, and the annual Shakespeare Bibliography in *Shakespeare Quarterly*, published by the Folger Shakespeare Library, Washington D.C., (1950–).

*   *   *

The story-line of *Richard II* is simple. Richard is shown to rule weakly and through favourites. His authority is tested, indirectly, in the first scene of the play when Bolingbroke challenges Mowbray. Richard manipulates events so that their trial by tournament is aborted at the last moment and both contestants are banished. Richard is then warned by John of Gaunt of the folly of his ways but this advice is spurned. When Gaunt dies, Richard seizes all "whereof our uncle Gaunt did stand possessed" to finance a campaign against the "rugheaded kerns" of Ireland, so dispossessing the banished Bolingbroke. The Duke of York's protest is a key to understanding the play:

> Take Herford's [Bolingbroke's] rights away, and take from time
> His charters, and his customary rights;
> Let not tomorrow then ensue today:
> Be not thyself. For how art thou a king
> But by fair sequence and succession?

Bolingbroke, though banished, returns ostensibly to claim his inheritance. He forces Richard's abdication and himself assumes the crown as Henry IV. Richard is murdered at Henry's wish (if not by his direct command) and the order he seemed to promise England in place of Richard's misrule does not materialise. The play ends with reports of a series of insurrections and of Henry's own son's unruly behaviour, and, finally with the presentation on stage of the coffin bearing the murdered king's body.

This factual outline, which roughly accords with the historical events (though Gaunt was far from being a fatherly protector) gives only one dimension of the play's development. A striking image of *Richard II* is that of two buckets in a deep well (representing the "golden crown"): one empty, aloft, "ever dancing in the air"; the other "down, unseen, and full of water". The rise and fall of the buckets is obviously symbolic—the empty Bolingbroke; the tearful Richard—but only represents the relationship of king and usurper superficially. It is, perhaps, simplest to explore this relationship first through Bolingbroke.

When the play opens, Bolingbroke is shown as a man of his word. No fewer than five times in less than 75 lines does he maintain that what he says he will prove true; his words and actions will correspond exactly, precisely. In the third scene he refuses to admit things can be other than they are. Then Bolingbroke is shown from Richard's point of view. Richard describes how Bolingbroke woos "poor craftsmen with the craft of smiles, doffs his hat to an oyster-wench, and bends his knee to draymen". This may strike a modern audience as democratic, but in the play's world, due order and decorum are being subverted. In Act II, Scene 3, Bolingbroke's relationship of words and meaning begins to slip. He justifies his illegal return by arguing that he was banished as Herford but returns as Lancaster (owing to the death of his father, Gaunt). In Act III he orders the execution of Bushy and Greene, so assuming regal power: he is now acting as a usurper but he still maintains that he owes Richard allegiance and comes but to have his banishment repealed and his lands restored. As late as Act III, Scene 3 he still protests his "true service shall deserve your love", though Richard is effectively his prisoner. Ironically, in the great deposition scene, Richard exerts a measure of control, refusing to be "stage-managed" by Northumberland (and the play makes much use of stage imagery), whereas Bolingbroke, as Richard notes, is silent. At the end of the play, when the state is in turmoil despite Bolingbroke's promise of firm government, Bolingbroke resorts to prevarication when presented with Richard's murdered body: "Though I did wish him dead, / I hate the murderer, love him murdered", and this despite the murderer's claim, "from your own mouth, my lord, did I this deed".

Thus, paradoxically, as Bolingbroke gains power, he declines morally. Richard, on the other hand, starts off as pathetically self-indulgent, but, after his fall, he gains in moral stature. His complex speech in Act V, Scene 5 and his exchange with the loyal groom in that scene reveal a human depth lacking in Bolingbroke. It is commonly said that Richard falls because he is a poet-manqué. This is to confuse the language of a poetic drama with characterisation. Richard fails as a king because he contravenes the very process by which he became king. His other failings contribute to his fall, especially his self-centredness (revealingly shown in his farewell to his queen in Act V). Yet he can inspire love and loyalty in others, something never apparent in Bolingbroke. There is a very curious link between the characters of Richard II and the future Henry V which simultaneously suggests what Richard lacks and what Hal must avoid. In *Richard II*, Henry IV describes his son as a "young wanton, and effeminate boy"; one of the play's sources, Daniel's poem *The Civil Wars* (1595), describes Richard as "this wanton young effeminate". Both descriptions use "effeminate" (probably to mean "self-indulgent") in the same, unusual sense.

The language of *Richard II* is particularly rich in images— pallor, blood, blushing; blots and stains; earth, land, garden (especially Gaunt in Act II, Scene 1 and the symbolic "Garden Scene" in Act III, the verse of which suggests that this is no ordinary, common gardener); sickness and wounds; weeping, breath, and words; and the theatre itself. These images form a complex pattern—hence the play's "symphonic imagery". Further, as emotion is intensified, so the language becomes increasingly complex.

One of Shakespeare's techniques in *Richard II* is to bring members of the audience into the centre of the conflict through the characters of York and his son, Aumerle. Both face, in different ways, the dilemma posed by the conflict of loyalties. Both would remain loyal to the "true king". York makes a

timely switch to the usurper; his son remains loyal to Richard just too long, only to be dubbed a traitor by his own father—so much for family loyalty.

Richard II is a moving historical tragedy that has rightly maintained its place in the repertory. It moves us partly because of its human conflict, partly because of its dramatisation of a crucial moment of historical change: the shift from the medieval to the modern, and in particular, the exercise of authority, an issue of abiding concern.

—Peter Davison

RICHARD III
by William Shakespeare

First Publication: London, 1597 (first quarto); with variants and additions, in First Folio, London, 1623.
First Production: London, c.1592–93.

Editions
Richard III, edited by John Dover Wilson, Cambridge, 1954 (New Shakespeare).
Richard III, edited by G. Blakemore Evans, Baltimore, Maryland, 1959 (Pelican Shakespeare).
Richard III, edited by Mark Eccles, New York, 1964 (Signet Classic Shakespeare).
Richard III, edited by E.A.J. Honigmann, Harmondsworth, 1968 (New Penguin Shakespeare).
"The Tragedy of King Richard III": Parallel Texts of the First Quarto and the First Folio with Variants of the Early Quarto, edited by Kristian Smidt, Oslo, 1969.
Richard III, edited by Antony Hammond, London, 1981 (Arden Shakespeare).

Bibliography
James A. Moore (ed.), *"Richard III": An Annotated Bibliography*, New York, 1986 (Garland Shakespeare Bibliographies).

Criticism
(For general works on the author, see *Playwrights* volume)

Books:
Sidney Thomas, *The Antic Hamlet and Richard III*, New York, 1943.
Paul Murray Kendall, *Richard the Third*, New York, 1956.
Wolfgang H. Clemen, *Kommentar zu Shakespeares "Richard III"*, Göttingen, 1957; translated by J. Bonheim as *A Commentary Upon Shakespeare's "Richard III"*, London, 1968.
Paul Haeffner, *A Critical Commentary on Shakespeare's "Richard III"*, London, 1966.
Robert J. Lordi and James E. Robinson, *"Richard III": A Scene by Scene Analysis with Critical Commentary*, New York, 1966.
Kristian Smidt, *Memorial Transmission and Quarto Copy in "Richard III": A Reassessment*, Oslo, 1970.
D.C. Gunby, *Richard III*, London, 1980.
Julie Hankey (ed.), *Richard III*, London, 1981 (Plays in Performance Series).

Richard III: Laurence Olivier as Richard, New Theatre, London, 1944

Bettina Gessner, *Der Machtkampf in Shakespeares "King Richard III" als Konflikt zweier Weltbilder*, Essen, 1985.

Robert C. Jones, *Engagement with Knavery: Point of View in "Richard III", "The Jew of Malta", "Volpone", and "The Revenger's Tragedy"*, Durham, North Carolina, 1986.

Chris. R. Hassel, *Songs of Death: Performance, Interpretation and the Text of "Richard III"*, Lincoln, Nebraska and London, 1987.

Mark W. Scott and Sandra L. Williamson (eds.), *"Richard III"*, in *Shakespearian Criticism, 8*, Detroit, Illinois, 1989 [anthology of criticism].

Articles:

For information on the many articles about *Richard III*, see Moore's Bibliography, the bibliographies listed in the *Playwrights* volume, and the annual Shakespeare Bibliography in *Shakespeare Quarterly*, published by the Folger Shakespeare Library, Washington D.C. (1950–).

*　　*　　*

Shakespeare's *Richard III* forms a sequel to his three history plays about the reign of Henry VI. This final part of the tetralogy brings the story of the Wars of the Roses to a close. After the usurpation of Richard II in 1399, England was thrown into a period of crisis during which the royal houses of Lancaster and York disputed the rights of succession and vied with each other for power. The crisis came to a head in the mid-15th century, in the reign of the weak King Henry V1, who was succeeded by Richard III. Richard was himself overthrown at the Battle of Bosworth, by Henry, Earl of Richmond.

The play is one of Shakespeare's earliest, probably written sometime around 1593. Another work entitled *The True Tragedy of Richard III* existed at this time and the question as to which of the two came first is a matter of dispute amongst scholars. The direct influence of the partial pro-Tudor accounts of Richard provided by the historians Edward Hall and Raphael Holinshed is less contentious. Shakespeare drew on these sources to create a character of monstrous villainy who ruthlessly annihilates all who stand in his way to becoming King of England. Once in supreme power, though, his fortunes rapidly change and the final scenes of the play depict his defeat and demise at the hands of the benevolent Richmond, who finally succeeds to the throne. Strict historical accuracy was less important to Shakespeare than political pragmatism; as Richmond was the grandfather of Elizabeth I it was natural that Shakespeare should portray him as the rightful King of England and Richard as an evil usurper.

No other play of Shakespeare's is so totally dominated by one central character, and the role of Richard has had a magnetic appeal for actors and audiences alike ever since the part was originally performed by Richard Burbage. Six versions of the play existed by 1622. Between 1700 and the late 19th century it was the adaptation by the theatrical entrepreneur and actor Colley Cibber that was usually performed. This abbreviated version of the play, with a proportionately enlarged role for the actor playing Richard, proved to be a strong commercial proposition for actor-managers, from Garrick onwards, looking for suitable tragic roles wit which to promote their own careers. In 1877 Henry Irving made some attempt to restore Shakespeare's words but even his playing text was heavily cut. The most famous of all interpretations of the role of Richard is that by Laurence Olivier in his London stage performances during the 1940's and his film version of 1955 (upon which the influence of Cibber is still evident). More recently it has become fashionable to perform *Richard III* in conjuction with its companion plays, the three parts of Henry VI. These productions have tended to stress historical process and this has tended to diminish the stature of Richard himself by bringing to the fore the context of the prolonged period of violent and bloody history during Henry VI's reign.

No matter how the play is interpreted, Richard remains one of the great roles in English drama. He is, above all, a performer with an outrageous histrionic audacity and a mercurial wit which enable him to outshine by far all his political opponents, and he seems to have no equal in the play until the arrival of Richmond who, insipid as he may be, is shown to have the force of God on his side. Richard's speech is playful, self-consciously theatrical, and often addressed directly to the audience. Though physically crippled he plays a variety of energetic parts, including that of the lover when he woos Lady Anne (while the corpse of her husband lies on stage). This demonic act of persuasion and seduction is achieved through the use of a formal, stichomythic style of speech borrowed from Senecan drama, a device which provides a kind of joke for the audience about the rhetorical tricks of the playwright's craft. The development of the action is ritualistic and a baleful choric commentary is provided by the isolated figure of old Queen Margaret, widow of Henry VI. Bold techniques of medieval staging are borrowed—notably for the final scenes at Bosworth, for which the stage space is divided into two halves by the tents of Richmond and Richard: good on one side, and evil on the other. Here the ghosts of Richard's victims return one by one to torment him and to encourage Richmond to exact righteous revenge.

Richard's character can be seen as a development of the medieval vice figure who lures the audience into complicity in evil through his attractive and dynamic stage personality, in order to illustrate the fallibility and weakness of human nature. His charismatic persona is also shaped by the Elizabethans' corrupted view of Machiavelli. He is the "murderous machiavel" who attains power through cruel and bloody deeds; he has the attraction of Renaissance humanism at its most aggressive. Like Marlowe's Tamburlaine he displays a superhuman strength and for much of the play he can conquer all obstacles of fortune through wit, vigour, subtle scheming, and an unyielding force of will.

It is possible to read the play as a moral history in which Richard is seen as an agent of Nemesis, an avenging angel sent by God to punish England for her disobedience, and who is, himself, destroyed when his task is completed. But this interpretation ignores the play's foregrounding of new and challenging ideas in the Renaissance about man's ability to influence and control his own destiny; ideas which, in the context of this play, challenged the notion of the divine right of kings and were radical, if not actually dangerous, in the England of the 1590's. It could be argued that Richard's demise in the play is more a matter of political necessity than theatrical logic. Two opposing views of history come together here: one in which the past is used "to show the ways of God to men" and to reveal a pattern of divine providence, and one in which events from the past are used to illustrate the art of politics. History plays were, after all, one of the few ways in which Elizabethans could learn not just about their past but also about issues relating to power and politics in their own day.

—Andy Piasecki

RIDERS TO THE SEA
by John Millington Synge

First Publication: In *Samhain*, September 1903; in book form,
in *"The Shadow of the Glen" and "Riders to
the Sea"*, London, 1905.
First Production: Molesworth Hall, Dublin (Irish National
Theatre Society), 25 February 1904.

Criticism
(For general works on the author, see *Playwrights* volume)

Books:

Alan Price, *Riders to the Sea; The Playboy of the Western
World*, Oxford, 1969.
David R. Clark (ed.), *Riders to the Sea*, Columbus, Ohio, 1970
[collection of essays].

Articles:

R.L. Collins, "The Distinction of *Riders to the Sea*", in
University of Kansas City Review, 13, 1946–47.
Denis Donoghue, "Synge: *Riders to the Sea*: A Study", in
University Review (Dublin), 1, 1955.
Thomas F. van Laan, "Form as Agent in Synge's *Riders to the
Sea*", in *Drama Survey*, 3, 1964.
William W. Coombs, "J.M. Synge's *Riders to the Sea*: A
Reading and Some Generalizations", in *Papers of the
Michigan Academy of Science, Arts, and Letters*, 1965.
Ryder Hector Currie and Martin Bryan, "*Riders to the Sea*:
Reappraised", in *Texas Quarterly*, vol.11, no.4, 1968.
Malcolm Pittock, "*Riders to the Sea*", in *English Studies*, 49,
1968.
Paul M. Leavitt, "The Whole Analysis: *Riders to the Sea*", in *A
Structural Approach to the Analysis of Drama*, The Hague,
1971.
Daniel J. Casey, "An Aran Requiem: Setting in *Riders to the
Sea*", in *Antigonish Review*, 9, 1972.
Errol Durbach, "Synge's Tragic Vision of the Old Mother and
the Sea", in *Modern Drama*, vol.14 no.4, 1972.
William J. Free, "Structural Dynamics in *Riders to the Sea*", in
Colby Library Quarterly, 11, 1975.
Almire Martin, "On Synge's *Riders to the Sea*: Maurya's
Passion", in *Cahiers du Centre d'Etudes Anglo-Irlandaises*,
2, 1977.
Carlo Bigazzi, "*Riders to the Sea*: Problemi di traduzione", in
English Miscellany, 26–27, 1977–78.
Leslie D. Foster, "Maurya: Tragic Error and Limited Tran-
scendance in *Riders to the Sea*", in *Eire / Ireland*, vol.16
no.3, 1981.
Bert Cardullo, "*Riders to the Sea*: A New View", in *Canadian
Journal of Irish Studies*, vol.10 no.1, 1984.
D.S. Neff, "Synge's Stoic Tragedy in *Riders to the Sea*", *Eire*,
vol.23 no.3, 1988.
D.S. Neff, "Bartley's Fall: Pyrolatreia and *Riders to the Sea*",
in *Notes on Modern Irish Literature*, 1, 1989.
Judith R. Leder, "Synge's *Riders to the Sea*: Island as Cultural
Battleground", in *Twentieth Century Literature*, 36, 1990.

*   *   *

The plot of this brief tragedy concerns Maurya, an old
woman, who hopes that the body of her son, Michael, drowned
nine days earlier, will be washed ashore. She has already lost
four other sons, her husband, and her father-in-law. The play
opens as her two daughters, Cathleen and Nora, receive
clothes from the body of a drowned man, and as Bartley, the
last and youngest son, prepares for a journey from his home on
the Aran Islands to the mainland. Despite his mother's
entreaties he sets off. The clothes are identified as Michael's,
and Bartley is drowned. In the last third of the play Maurya
presides over the funeral rites for Michael and Bartley and
invokes mercy on all the living and dead.

The bleakness of Synge's vision in *Riders to the Sea* is
exemplified in the irony of Maurya's remark early in the play
that the young priest will dissuade Bartley from going to the
mainland; for Nora has already told Cathleen that the priest
feels no need to stop him because God would not be so cruel as
to take her only remaining son. The dramatic irony here
reinforces a recurring theme in Synge's work—the opposition
of pagan and Christian belief. The young priest, the play
suggests, is powerless in the face of the eternal, malignant sea.

When the daughters identify the clothes of the drowned man
as Michael's, because of four dropped stitches, Synge works
skilfully on two levels, directing attention both to Michael's
death and Bartley's imminent demise. No sooner is Michael's
death established than Maurya enters keening because she
claims to have seen Michael riding a grey horse by the sea. The
reversal which Synge achieves here—in apparent contradiction to the literal truth which is that Michael is dead—is linked
to the recognition by all three that Bartley will die. Aristotle
claimed that in Sophocles' *Oeidipus Rex* the finest kind of
recognition (*anagnorisis*) is accompanied by simultaneous
reversal (*peripeteia*), which is what Synge achieves here in one
of his finest, theatrical strokes. The grey horse, of course,
suggests the "pale horse" of the Apocalypse ("his name that
sat on him was Death").

The remainder of the play is an extended threnody in which
the mother intones the names of her dead sons. As Maurya,
mater dolorosa, remembers Bartley as a baby on her knees, his
body is brought into the house. The imagery of Maurya's last
speeches suggests that death is not negative. Birth is hard, life a
bitterness to be endured, death a deliverance. "No man can be
living for ever", she states, "and we must be satisfied". The
passivity of the characters in *Riders to the Sea*, and the
inevitability of the men's tragic end, reinforce Synge's conviction that suffering has no redemptive or liberating role. The
women of the play may mourn the death of the men, but they
are also portrayed as destined to preside over their deaths.
They are—although the equation is not an exact one—Irish
equivalents of the Greek Fates, Clotho, Lachesis, and
Atropos, who were supposed to preside over birth, marriage,
and death. Clotho spun the thread of life, Lachesis measured
its length, Atropos cut it. When *Riders to the Sea* opens,
Cathleen's rapid spinning is interrupted by Nora's news that
they must identify the drowned man's clothes. Cathleen stops
her wheel "with a rapid movement". Later she cuts the string
tying the clothes with a sharp knife and Nora identifies them.
The mother withholds the bread from Bartley, a puzzling
gesture made clear by the fact she is aware his allotted time has
come to an end. The tragic inevitability of Bartley's fate is
established even as he leaves the house. "He's gone now, God
spare us", Maurya says, "and we'll not see him again".

In W. B. Yeats' play *Cathleen Ni Houlihan* the old woman
calls the young men of Ireland to their deaths, but she also
promises them immortality: "They shall be remembered for
ever". But Synge is no last Romantic; he is modern in his
disbelief, in his cynicism, and in his alienation. In *Riders to the
Sea* he projects his own obsessively tragic view of life onto the
Aran islanders, ignoring their deep-rooted Catholicism which,
presumably, offered strength in times of sorrow and death.

Synge's visits to the Aran Islands gave him not only a
number of themes but also a style. As he became more fluent in
Gaelic he married the languor and ornateness of the *fin de
siècle* English he employed in the 1899 prose piece *Étude*

Morbide with the vigour of peasant colloquialism (speech "as fully flavoured as a nut or apple"), Gaelic syntax and rhythms, and the prodigality of the Irish folk imagination: "Ah, Nora, isn't it a bitter thing to think of him floating that way to the far north, and no one to keen him but the black hags that do be flying on the sea?". T.S. Eliot in his essay, "Poetry and Drama", argued that Synge's plays formed a special case because their language was based on the idiom of a peasantry whose speech was "naturally poetic, both in imagery and in rhythm". This is largely true, but what also must be insisted on is Synge's genius in modifying that folk language and idiom to convey the highest reaches of tragedy (as in *Riders to the Sea*), or of comedy (as in *The Playboy of the Western World*).

—Eugene Benson

THE RIDICULOUS PRÉCIEUSES. See **THE PRETENTIOUS YOUNG LADIES.**

RIEL. See **THE RIEL TRILOGY.**

THE RIEL TRILOGY
    Riel
    The Crime of Louis Riel
    The Trial of Louis Riel
by John Coulter

Riel
First Publication: Toronto, 1962.
First Production: Royal Ontario Museum Theatre (New Play Society), Toronto, 17 February 1950.

The Crime of Louis Riel
First Publication: Toronto, 1976.
First Production: Dominion Drama Festival, London, Ontario, 1966.

The Trial of Louis Riel
First Publication: Ottawa, 1968.
First Production: Regina, Saskatchewan, 14 June 1967.

Criticism
(For general works on the author, see *Playwrights* volume)

Articles:

Geraldine Anthony, "Similarities to Brechtian Technique in John Coulter's Play *Louis Riel*", in *Canadian Drama*, 2, 1976.
Margaret Gail Osachoff, "*Riel* on Stage", in *Canadian Drama*, vol.8 no.2, 1982.
Geraldine Anthony, "Coulter's *Riel*: A Reappraisal", in *Canadian Drama*, 11, 1985.
Kathleen Garay, "John Coulter's *Riel*: The Shaping of 'A Myth for Canada'", in *Canadian Drama*, 11, 1985.

*   *   *

The Riel trilogy dramatizes events in the life of Louis Riel, the Métis leader who was the founding father of the province of Manitoba (an area of Canada known then as the Northwest Territories). Driven to desperation by British incursions on Métis land, Riel rebelled against the Canadian government, first in the rebellion of 1869–70, and again in 1885. He was tried for high treason, found guilty, and hanged on 16 November 1885.

Riel is the most ambitious of the three Riel plays in which Coulter successfully fuses legend, myth, history, and epic in a manner which was to influence profoundly later playwrights like James Reaney (in the Donnelly trilogy) and Sharon Pollock in her historical plays (like *Walsh*). The structure of *Riel* is episodic and flowing, the action moving fluidly between Western Canada and Ottawa. Coulter's stage directions call for "presentation in the Elizabethan manner: a continuous flow of scenes on a bare stage with the aid of no more than indicative settings and properties and modern stage lighting". The multiple incidents of Parts I and II are given coherence by the analogies evoked between the execution (by Riel's provincial government) of the Orangeman Thomas Scott and the execution (by the government of Canada) of the Métis Riel.

In his autobiography, *In My Day*, Coulter described *Riel* as "A Myth for Canada". Sensitized to intolerance and bigotry by his Irish background, Coulter saw Riel's story as embodying the quintessential, Canadian myth. He makes Riel a heroic and mythic figure, at once leader, victim, and martyr. Riel represents the just grievances of Canada's native peoples (he is part Indian); he represents the oppressed Catholic and Canadian French as opposed to the Protestant English; he represents the young West as against the manipulative bureaucracy of the East (Riel's naivety and integrity act as foil to Prime Minister Sir John A. Macdonald's guile and political expediency). Throughout the play Riel's stature is enhanced by allusions to David (who defeated Goliath) and to Joan of Arc. The trial scene gave Coulter great difficulty and to help him he read Shaw's *Saint Joan*. Obviously he had in mind similarities between Shaw's protagonist and his own—Joan and Riel represent the French against the English; they are both accused of being proto-Protestants; they both claim to be divinely inspired; they are both executed. But if Coulter drew upon Shaw he drew more heavily on the New Testament, especially in the trial scene of Part II, to suggest analogies between Christ in his trial, condemnation, and death, and Riel's. "I've been thinking we know a little more now, of the considerations Pilate had to weigh", the police surgeon at the trial states, "in a case with, shall we say, certain parallels". Critics of the play have complained that the trial scene is anticlimactic; certainly this scene is too long and too "talky" and Coulter bridles Riel's passion with a rather bland reasonableness. Despite this fault the final scenes of the play retain their power to shock, gathering emotional resonance as 19th century quarrels over language and nationhood still threaten to divide Canada.

The Crime of Louis Riel was written for theatre companies which lacked the resources to mount the full scale *Riel*. While *The Crime of Louis Riel* draws heavily on the latter play there are significant differences. In the foreword to the first published edition Coulter wrote that he wanted to illustrate how Riel and the rebellions he led were precursors of later uprisings, especially those in the Third World. To simplify and focus more clearly on the historical events associated with Riel, Coulter also omitted mention of the first rebellion, concentrating only on that of 1885.

The Trial of Louis Riel is a one-act documentary—"an editing of transcriptions of evidence given at the actual trial at Regina in 1885", according to Coulter. Commissioned by the

Regina Chamber of Commerce to play as a tourist attraction, the play is offered annually for a summer-season run in a courtroom-theatre built to resemble the original courtroom. Actors in period costume mingle with present-day audiences as the trial, complete with counsel, witnesses, a jury, judges, and Riel in the dock, commences. Such verisimilitude makes for extraordinarily effective theatre.

—Eugene Benson

RIGHT YOU ARE! (IF YOU THINK SO).   See **RIGHT YOU ARE (IF YOU THINK YOU ARE).**

RIGHT YOU ARE (IF YOU THINK YOU ARE)
(Così è (si vi pare))
by Luigi Pirandello

First Publication: In *La nuova antologia*, June, 1918; in book form, Milan, 1918.
First Production: Teatro Olimpia, Milan (Talli Company), 18 June 1917.

Translations
It is So! If You Think So, translated by Arthur Livingston, in *Luigi Pirandello: Three Plays*, New York, 1922.
"Right You Are": A Stage Version, translated by Eric Bentley, New York, 1954.
Right You Are! (If You Think So), translated by Frederick May, in *"Right You Are! (If You Think So)" and Other Plays*, edited by E. Martin Browne, Harmondsworth, 1962.
Right You Are! (If You Think You Are), translated by Bruce Penman, in *Luigi Pirandello: Collected Plays, 1*, edited by Robert Rietty, London, 1987.

Criticism
(For general works on the author, see *Playwrights* volume)

Articles:
J. Crawford, "*Così è (si vi pare)*", in *Drama* (New York), 1925.
P.L. Goiten, "*Così è (si vi pare)*", in *Psychoanalytic Review*, 16, 1929.
E. Finci, "Il laboratorio drammatico di Pirandello: *Così è (si vi pare)*", in *Pregled*, 14, 1938.
Sandro Sticca, "The Drama of Being and Seeming in Schnitzler's *Anatol* and Pirandello's *Così è, si vi pare*", in *Journal of the International Arthur Schnitzler Research Association*, vol.5 no.2, 1966.
Robert S. Dombroski, "Laudisi's Laughter and the Social Dimension of *Right You Are (If You Think So)*", in *Modern Drama*, 16, 1973.
Albert R. Ascoli, "Mirror and Veil: *Così è (si vi pare)* and the Drama of Interpretation", in *Stanford Italian Review*, 7, 1987.

*   *   *

As its title suggests, the theme of *Right You Are* is centred on the relativity of truth, the plot basically consisting of the efforts of a group of provincials in a small town to discover the "real facts" about the apparently mysterious relationship between a certain Signor Ponza and his mother-in-law, Signora Frola. Act I is mainly exposition of the mystery. Following an earthquake in his own village, which razed buildings to the ground and destroyed everything, a government official, Signor Ponza, has recently arrived in town to take up a minor administrative post. He has brought with him his wife, and her mother, Signora Frola. A group of upper-middle-class inhabitants of the town (the Neighbours), led by Signor Ponza's superior, Councillor Agazzi, and several members of his family, are intrigued by Ponza's behaviour, thinking he treats his mother-in-law with extreme cruelty by not allowing her access to her daughter. But when questioned by the Neighbours, Signora Frola adamantly defends her son-in-law's behaviour, insisting that the arrangement is mutually convenient.

Dissatisfied with her explanation, the Neighbours decide to investigate further in order to determine the "truth" of the situation. They talk to Signor Ponza, and he seems to give them a plausible version of the truth: his mother-in-law, he explains, became mad on the death of her daughter, his first wife; he has since remarried, however, and finds himself in an awkward position, for Signora Frola is firmly convinced that his second wife is her daughter; in kindness he has been obliged to maintain this pretence in order not to shatter her illusion. No sooner are the Neighbours content they have unearthed the truth, than their hopes are dashed with the return of Signora Frola, for she presents them with an alternative explanation: it is not she but Signor Ponza who is mad, for so desperately in love is he with her daughter that he keeps the latter shut up and refuses to let her see anyone. The first act thus ends with the "truth" of the Ponza–Frola relationship more elusive than ever.

Act II, like most of Act III, centres on the Neighbours' continuing quest to discover the "truth". But this turns out to be a futile task, for such bureaucratic or administrative evidence as might once have existed about the Frola family and Signor Ponza's marriage has been destroyed by the earthquake. Finally, in a last, desperate attempt to discover the "truth", the Neighbours decide to confront the third party of the situation, Signora Ponza. Right at the end of the play she appears veiled before them, and reveals that she is not only Signora Frola's daughter, but also Signor Ponza's second wife. Questioned by the Neighbours she explains, "for myself, I am whoever you think me to be". Thus the play concludes with the Neighbours no closer to uncovering the "truth" of the Ponza–Frola situation than they were at the beginning.

The play was composed in six days, and from the moment he completed it, Pirandello recognised it to be something unusual, describing it in a letter to his son of 3 April 1917 as "a great devilry that could be highly successful". Many critics think it a turning-point in his career as a dramatist: it marks his abandonment of realism in the theatre, and contains many of the essential themes which were to characterise his later and most important work. Critical interpretation has been various, recent commentary tending to point up the variety of Pirandellian ideas treated in the play. *Right You Are* is subtitled "a parable in three acts", and being a parable, it inevitably has a moralist: he appears in the guise of a certain Laudisi, a mocking, sceptical Neighbour who acts throughout as a commentator on the action. Although not the protagonist, Laudisi is a key figure, present on stage for much of the action and ironically symbolising the futility of the search for absolute truth. Through him Pirandello points up the profounder philosophical issues lying beneath the comic surface of his play: the relativity of truth, the instability of individual identity, and the need of the individual to seek a definition (a mask) behind which to hide his existential nakedness.

From the very beginning Laudisi sees the pointlessness of the Neighbours' quest, and in an attempt to demonstrate this to them uses two of the Neighbours—the Sirellis—to prove how impossible it is to establish objective truth. He intervenes in the argument between this husband and wife to point out that every individual is entitled to believe in whatever he wishes, but must also respect what others believe, even though it be the very opposite to his own perception. Throughout the play each time the Neighbours fail to verify the "truth", or seem to unearth a new version of it, Laudisi's loud, mocking laughter exposes the hollowness and futility of their quest. As a result, the Neighbours become ever more dogmatic, determined to hound out the facts of the Ponza–Frola relationship; and the more damagingly insistent their enquiry, the more Laudisi is transformed from a ridiculing commentator to an engaged humanitarian: thus he attempts to help the persecuted family by asking the Prefect to concoct administrative data that will suffice as a version of the truth to satisfy the Neighbours. The importance of Laudisi's role is reflected in the structure of the play, its circular movement being underlined by the fact that he speaks the opening and closing lines, and that he points, at the beginning and at the end, to the futility of seeking absolute truth. One of his most important speeches is to his reflection in the mirror. He emphasises the mask/face dichotomy: the multi-personalities of each human being, which differ according to every person he meets and which are always different from the image of himself he creates in his own mind.

The predicament of the protagonists, Signor Ponza, Signora Ponza, and Signora Frola, is clearly defined by their costume: they are dressed in black, which sets them apart physically from the rest of the characters. Their dialogue too has a dark, quasi-tragic cast to it, distinguishing it from the more humorous discourse of the Neighbours. They are outcasts, forced to play out their various roles before the Neighbours like actors playing to an audience; and by so doing their actions reflect the stage/life dichotomy. Signora Ponza, who makes only a brief appearance at the end of the play, has been seen by many critics to be the very symbol of truth itself. With her famous enigmatic words, "I am she whom you believe me to be", she emphasises the idea that the self cannot have direct knowledge of itself, but can only know itself as it is reflected through the perception of another. By this same token she could equally represent the incarnation of life, illusion, or the mask. In this Pirandellian world madness is as subjective as truth, as we see in the conflicting stories of Signor Ponza and Signora Frola: the Ponza–Frola family have found a bizarre kind of personal and domestic stability, and in doing so have achieved a certain kind of happiness, albeit illusory. Their mystery is only a means of coping with overwhelming distress, of making life bearable; what "truth" lies in it is relative to their particular situation.

Yet the play is not elusively philosophical, not just a broad dramatic treatment of abstract ideas. As a group, the Neighbours provide a convincing study of a social unit and the effect upon it of social conventions, and their attitudes and actions throughout reflect the power and the subtle operations of the class structure. Amalia and Dina typify the bourgeoisie who, determined to satisfy their own curiosity, exploit forms and conventions in an attempt to uncover the mystery of Signora Frola's private life. The Neighbours assume their elevated position in society confers on them the automatic right to probe into the private life of anyone lower in the social scale. Signor Ponza, accordingly, is subjected to the whims of his social superiors, and must passively accept their interference in his affairs in order to retain his position.

One of Pirandello's most cogent Anglo-Saxon critics, Eric Bentley, in his introduction to a collection of the Italian

dramatist's plays, *Naked Masks*, neatly summed up one motive of *Right You Are* when he described it as "the most famous statement of Pirandello's relativism". And indeed it is, for by the end of the play Pirandello has wittily demonstrated not only that truth is relative, but that personal privacy is relative to social position, personality is relative to situation, and, perhaps most important of all, that happiness is relative to illusion.

—Francesca H.A. Richards

RING ROUND THE MOON (L'Invitation au château) by Jean Anouilh

First Publication: In *Pièces brillantes*, Paris, 1951.
First Production: Théâtre de l'Atelier, Paris, 5 November 1947.

Translations
Ring Round the Moon, translated and adapted by Christopher Fry, London and New York, 1950.

*   *   *

It is to be a glittering social occasion: a ball at the country home of Madame Desmermortes to announce the engagement of her nephew Frédéric to Diana Messerschmann, daughter of the richest man in the world. But between the luncheon before the ball and daybreak the following morning, events at the Château de Saint-Flour become extremely, extravagantly, complicated. For one thing, the timid, diffident Frédéric has an identical twin brother, Horace, who plans to intervene, partly because he doubts the sincerity of Diana's love and the wisdom of Frédéric's choice, and partly because—rich, debonair, reckless—he simply decides to challenge the established order of society and human destiny. So he arranges an invitation to the ball for Isabelle, one of the *corps de ballet* at the Paris Opéra, so that her grace and beauty will deflect Frédéric's attention from Diana. The scheme works extremely well—for about ten minutes, but then complications occur: Isabelle's mother turns out to have studied music at the same provincial conservatoire as Madame Desmermortes' companion, Capulat; and the totally eccentric Lady Dorothy India, supposedly M. Messerschmann's mistress, appears to be having an affair with his private secretary, Patrice Bombelles. From one hilarious disaster to the next, the pace quickens and the precipice approaches—until, like some kindly fairy godmother in her wheelchair, Madame Desmermortes takes over from Horace the role of puppeteer and disentangles the imbroglio, but not before Anouilh has treated his audience to an unforgettable tango, a western saloon brawl (between Isabelle and Diana!), a near duel, and an even nearer suicide by drowning (except that the water in the lake is only about two feet deep!). So, thanks to Madame Desmermortes' magic wand, the ball ends happily with not one engagement, but two.

L'Invitation au château is a dazzling example of Anouilh's outstanding comic verve and technical virtuosity. It has the perfectly-timed comic pace of his early *pièces roses*, their comic flair and fantasy, yet is unobtrusively laced with the more serious themes of the *pièces noires*; so that, far from presenting his audience, as some critics believe, with frivolity and froth, Anouilh offers us a finely-cut glass filled with vintage cham-

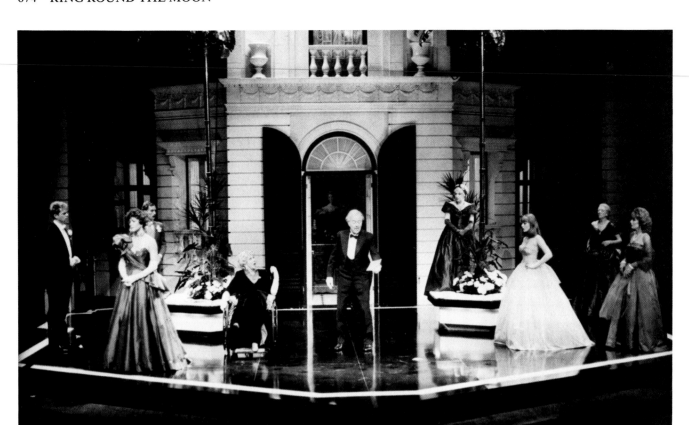

Ring Round the Moon   National Theatre, London, 1988

pagne. The plot is as intricate as any by Beaumarchais or Feydeau; the music of the orchestra in the central three acts provides both texture and commentary; the dialogue dances and the speeches sparkle with comic inventiveness and ingenuity. And yet, barely concealed by the surface glitter, a glimpse of familiar images such as ugliness and stray dogs, and of familiar themes such as love and friendship, childhood and happiness, social distinctions and money, should convince us that Anouilh is being serious—perhaps never more serious than when he is being, apparently, frivolous.

For all its sparkle, *L'Invitation* is a key work in Anouilh's theatre. Never again does he quite recapture its light-hearted, gay, extravagantly playful mood. Indeed, there is already a slender hint of the more bitter, brutal, and sardonic tone to come, behind the gentle teasing and kindly mockery that characterise the revels at Saint-Flour: mockery of French theatre, for example, when the two overgrown music students break into the alexandrine verse-form of neo-Romantic French drama; mockery of his audience as Anouilh challenges them to enjoy his revitalisations of such a stock subject as the Cinderella story and such a stock theatrical device as identical twins; and mockery even of himself in the reappearance of such stock Anouilh characters as the fairy godmother with grey hair whom we have already met in the guise of Lady Hurf and the Duchess Dupont-Dufort, or Josué, the crumbling butler, who takes his place in a long lineage of domestic staff whose function is to provide the audience with a worm's eye-view of events, as seen by a typically blinkered, conventional, and snobbish worm.

It is this self-mockery that invites us to see *L'Invitation* as an important stage in Anouilh's personal and theatrical evolution. Accustomed to heroines and heroes who, like Thérèse Tarde and Antigone, reject mediocre happiness and even life

itself, we are hardly surprised to find the theme of revolt echoed in this play; but here the revolt is carefree and unsuccessful. The characters' defiance falters. Isabelle refuses to be bribed by Messerschmann's wealth; she even uses the same attack on reason that Anouilh's Antigone had used, but probably marries the elder twin and so inherits the château; Horace plans to denounce all social pretence, but capitulates and resigns himself to marrying Diana's wealth; and even Messerschmann, whose diet has, for years, been limited to noodles without butter and without salt, is moved to a paroxysm of joy that enables him, at the final curtain, to say a "yes"—exceptionally—to noodles with just a taste of salt.

Of all Anouilh's many plays to be performed in England, *L'Invitation* is one of the most popular. Christopher Fry's quite remarkable adaptation, *Ring Round the Moon*, was aptly subtitled "a charade with music", for one permanent theme of Anouilh's work is the theatricality of life, which appears not simply in the condemnation of socialite sham nor the conversion of Saint-Flour into a theatre for a one-night, unrepeatable performance, but in the total pretence of life. As in earlier plays like the *Rendez-vous de Senlis*, the utter improbability of the happy ending underlines the very elusiveness of the happiness it appears to promise. "Vanity, vanity. . .", quotes Horace at one stage in the proceedings. There are other references to religion which Anouilh examines more fully in the later *L'Alouette* and *Becket*; and references to politics which will reappear at the core of *Poor Bitos*.

—Colin Radford

THE RIVALS
by Richard Brinsley Sheridan

First Publication: London, 1775.
First Production: Theatre Royal, Covent Garden, London, 17 January 1775.

Editions

The Rivals, in *The Dramatic Works of Richard Brinsley Sheridan* (2 vols.), edited by Cecil Price, Oxford, 1957.

The Rivals, edited by Vincent F. Hopper and Gerald B. Lahey, Woodbury, New York, 1958.

The Rivals, in *Sheridan's Plays*, edited by Cecil Price, London, 1975.

The Rivals, edited by Elizabeth Duthie, London, 1979 (New Mermaid Series).

The Rivals, edited by Susan Macklin, Harlow, Essex, 1985.

The Rivals, in *"The School for Scandal" and Other Plays*, edited by Eric D. Rump, Harmondsworth, 1988.

Criticism

(For general works on the author, see *Playwrights* volume)

Articles:

W.D. Armes, "The Source of Sheridan's *Rivals*", in *Transactions and Proceedings of the American Philological Association* [*TAPA*], 34, 1903.

J.Q. Adams, "The Text of Sheridan's *The Rivals*", in *Modern Language Notes*, 25, 1910.

Miriam Gabriel and Paul Mueschke, "Two Contemporary Sources of Sheridan's *The Rivals*, Garrick's *Miss in her Teens* and Coleman's *Deuce is in Him*", in *Publications of the Modern Language Association* [*PMLA*], 43, 1928.

P. Fijn van Draat, "Sheridan's *Rivals* and Ben Jonson's *Every Man in His Humour*", in *Neophilologus*, 1932.

Richard B. O'Connel, "Gorostiza's *Contigo, pan y cepolla* and Sheridan's *The Rivals*", in *Hispania*, 43, 1960.

Sailendra Kumar Sen, "Sheridan's Literary Debt: *The Rivals* and *Humphrey Clinker*", in *Modern Language Quarterly*, 21, 1960.

James Trainer, "Tieck's Translation of *The Rivals*", in *Modern Language Quarterly*, 21, 1960.

James K. Stonks, "*The Rivals* as a Possible Source for *Walden*", in *Thoreau Society Bulletin*, Spring 1966.

Cecil Price, "The First Prologue to *The Rivals*", in *Review of English Studies*, 20, 1969.

Jack D. Durant, "Sheridan's 'Royal Sanctuary': A Key to *The Rivals*", in *Ball State University Forum*, 14, 1973.

Mark S. Auburn, "The Pleasures of Sheridan's *The Rivals*: A Critical Study in the Light of Stage History", in *Modern Language Philology*, 72, 1975.

James S. Malek, "Julia as a Comic Character in *The Rivals*", in *Studies in the Humanities*, 7, 1978.

H.M. Williams, "The Other Rivals: A New Look at Julia and Faulkland in Sheridan's Play", in *Journal of English* (Sana'a University), 11, 1983.

Anne Parker, "Absolute Sense in Sheridan's *The Rivals*", in *Ball State University Forum*, 27, 1986.

*   *   *

Sheridan's first play, *The Rivals*, is now solidly established in the repertory as a prime example of the very kind of theatre, the sentimental comedy, that it originally set out to satirise. The plot concerns the courtship of Captain Absolute who is being compelled by his father, Sir Anthony, to make a suitable match with the woman that he is already intent on marrying, Lydia Languish. This most sentimental of heroines, whose knowledge of love is drawn from the pages of books from the lending library, has decided that she must marry beneath her, and so the Captain has become an Ensign in order to woo her. Their amorous entanglements are paralleled by those of Lydia's contrastingly level-headed and sensible friend, Julia Melville, who has to struggle through the maddening jealousies of her man, Faulkland, so that the play ends with a double wedding. The tortuous path towards wedded bliss is made the more so by the interference of Lydia's aunt, the infamous Mrs. Malaprop, and by the many bravados of the indomitable Sir Lucius O'Trigger.

The play is set in the spa resort of Bath, a location for leisured activity in which only the ruling-class and its servants are to be found. In such a society—at least as it was depicted on the contemporary stage—the main energies are naturally to be devoted towards the various relationships between the sexes; and although non-marital variants are occasionally given an airing, the emphasis is always on the inevitability of marriage as the resolution of the plot. At the outset Lydia is forced to hide her romantic novels, but we soon learn that her aunt, from whom they are to be hidden, is herself carrying out an amorous correspondence through the agency of the same maid who introduced Lydia to the romances.

The characters all communicate in a brisk line of wit which stands somewhere between Sir George Etherege and Oscar Wilde, linguistically and historically; but the overall feeling is one of cosiness, a cosiness that continues to appeal to audiences for whom the original terms of reference—marriage as a serious contractual arrangement involving the disposal of property and capital—now have little, real meaning. But then, as now, much of the popular comic appeal came from Mrs. Malaprop's delightful mismanagement of language, her inability to use the right word mirroring her inability to match her moral protestations to the reality of her behaviour were she able to defy age and convention. The audience savours her efforts to keep control of a language whose meaning constantly eludes her; but often the humour is given an extra edge by our realisation that, accidently, she speaks more sense than even she pretends to. In her reply to Sir Anthony Absolute's question about the desirable limits of a woman's knowledge, for instance, her reply not only tells us much about her but also raises more important questions about the limitations placed on the education of women in general:

I would send her, at nine years old, to a boarding-school, in order to learn a little ingenuity and artifice. Then, sir, she should have a supercilious knowledge in accounts;—and as she grew up, I would have her instructed in geometry, that she might know something of the contagious countries;—but above all, Sir Anthony, she should be mistress of orthodoxy, that she might not mis-spell, and mis-pronounce words so shamelessly as girls usually do.

The play may set out to satirise the values of the sentimental comedy, but much of its apparently timeless appeal derives from the young playwright's quite cheerful use conventional devices to push the plot along to its necessary, happy ending. Thus, the patient and long-suffering Julia is eventually won over by the creakiest of plot movers, the mock dual—the thrill of romance and the fear of blood overcoming all scruples on the part of the sensible heroine.

Similarly, there can be doubt about the ultimate coming together of Lydia and her Captain, even when it is finally revealed to her that he is not the Ensign Beverly she takes him for. He appeals to her to "lay aside some of our romance—a little wealth and comfort may be endured after all", and tells her that the lawyers will procure the necessary licence. Lydia's riposte, "licence—I hate licence", is acutely ironic. The heroine loves licence only too well; the licence to dream, however, and not the paper one to marry with. But like Polly Peachum in John Gay's *Beggar's Opera*—another near-contemporary, satirised, sentimental heroine—the audience is only too happy to accept her on her own terms. She has had her romantic fling, and now has the satisfaction of knowing that she is marrying the man that she loves, and the match is satisfactory in economic terms. Sheridan was no radical—he was later to declare in the Houses of Parliament that politics had no place in the theatre—and certainly was not about to raise real questions about the role of women in this society. Julia is allowed her doubts and Lydia her dreams, but ultimately even the mildly satirical impulses which started the piece off give way to the understanding of the need for a happy ending.

—John Bull

THE RIVERS OF CHINA
by Alma de Groen

First Publication: Paddington, New South Wales, 1988.
First Production: Wharf Theatre, Sydney, 9 September 1987.

Criticism
(For general works on the author, see *Playwrights* volume)

Articles:
Elizabeth Perkins, "Form and Transformation in the Plays of Alma de Groen", in *Australasian Drama Studies*, 11, 1987.

* * *

Rivers of China interweaves two complementary narratives. One story is of the last three months of the writer Katherine Mansfield's life. The other, set in Sydney, Australia, in the present time (although presented here as a dystopia dominated by women) concerns a young man who is brought back from the brink of death (probably a suicide attempt), given plastic surgery and, through hypnosis, a new, female mind—that of Katherine Mansfield.

Probably De Groen's most successful play to date, *Rivers of China* comes close to achieving her often-stated ambition to fuse form and content—in other words, to have the audience experience directly, through the play's form, the thematic concerns of the play. De Groen proposes a feminist notion that women have no history—or, more accurately, that their history has been suppressed with the result that their concept of themselves is only a reflection of men's concept of women.

In the first narrative, Katherine Mansfield checks into Gurdjieff's Institute for the Harmonious Development of Man at Fontainebleau in the hope that she will be cured of her tuberculosis through his strict regimen of diet and physical and spiritual exercises. At the same time she is looking for enlightenment, or "the Truth", as she puts it. Gurdjieff's philosophy, however, pictures women as existing on a lower plane than men. Men and women have different roles and it is men who have the vocation to create and to undertake physical and spiritual journeys. Lidia, one of Gurdjieff's ostensible disciples (in fact, she confesses to Katherine that she stayed with him only because he could get her out of Russia) explains that, according to him, "for women there must be two people; that for a woman to progress in the work, she must have a man beside her". Katherine is not cured and is ultimately negated by Gurdjieff, her own uniquely feminine aesthetic ignored. This narrative is discontinuous, using flashbacks and extracts from journals and letters. In the end, Katherine records her own death and the two narratives come together.

The second narrative works in an ironic relationship to the first. In the dystopia of this narrative, it is the men who have no history. When the injured man is brought into the hospital, a young wardsman, Wayne, takes an interest in him. Wayne writes poetry. This is illegal for a man and, in fact, the work of past male authors has been suppressed. Wayne goes around singing Keats' line "Much have I travelled in the realms of gold", thinking it only a piece of graffiti.

The audience, then, is being asked to experience the world as feminist ideology would have us believe women do. In conversation with the Man, Wayne says he can understand the latter wanting to go home. "I can understand that", he says. "I live in a room—and it isn't home. I live on earth—and it isn't home".

But the female doctor charged with looking after the Man uses hypnosis (also illegal in the new society), both to hasten the healing process and to perform an experiment—to change the Man's identity by imbuing him with a female spirit, specifically the character and memory of Katherine Mansfield. The doctor explains to Wayne: "I made him. Or what you think is him. You can give anybody a history that never happened and they'll believe it".

Giving the Man Mansfield's memory, though, also gives him a history. He is able to tell Wayne that what he thinks is graffiti was actually written by a man, John Keats. At the same time, it is the Man who is able to articulate Mansfield's artistic persona. "While I am writing I am engulfed. Possessed. Anyone who comes near me is my enemy. It takes the place of religion for me". However, the doctor finally balks at her experiment—an experiment to create a man "who could be an equal without being a danger". She faces the choice of stripping the Man of his new identity or letting him die. When she asks Wayne, he says "kill him" rather than destroy the identity Wayne has come to revere.

Rivers of China is a feminist play. But De Groen is a sceptical feminist who does not allow her feminist, ideological explorations to detract from the aesthetic potential of the play, and so the play is, formally and temperamentally, an ironic work: ironic in its wit and scepticism. The new female society is a dystopia, after all. De Groen actually welcomes a society without the extremes either of patriarchy or matriarchy, and makes fun of the suppression of male literature. The play is also ironical in the way it juxtaposes scenes from the two narratives, successfully preventing the audience too readily accepting one version of reality as the "true" one.

Through its formal irony and through its fragmentary structure—its *bricollage*—the play attempts to create a genuinely feminist theatre in which the audience experiences the world through the female sensibility in two ways: firstly, in the sense that it is a history-less, male-constructed, non-identity, and secondly, in the more positive sense, that the world has a whole new potential when perceived through a liberated, female perspective. Katherine Mansfield and her art of the short story are held up by De Groen as exemplifying this ideal.

—Paul McGillick

THE ROAD
by Wole Soyinka

First Publication: In *Gambit*, 1965; in book form, London, 1965.
First Production: Theatre Royal, Stratford East, London (Stage Sixty Company), October 1965.

Criticism
(For general works on the author, see *Playwrights* volume)

Articles:

S. Phaniso C. Moyo, "*The Road*: A Slice of the Yoruba Pantheon", in *Ba Shiru: A Journal of African Languages and Literatures*, vol.2, nos.1–2, 1971.

Theo Vincent, "The Modern Inheritance: Studies in J.P. Clark's *The Raft* and Soyinka's *The Road*", in *Òdumá*, vol.2 no.1, 1974.

D.S. Izevbaye, "Language and Meaning in Soyinka's *The Road*", in *African Literature Today*, 8, 1976.

Elaine F. Fido, "*The Road* and Theatre of the Absurd", in *Caribbean Journal of African Studies*, 1, 1978.

R.N.C Okafor, "Wole Soyinka's *The Road* and the Faustian Dimension", in *Présence africain*, 111, 1979.

Jeanne N. Dingome, "Soyinka's *The Road* as Ritual Drama", in *Kunapipi* (Aarhus, Norway), vol.2 no.1, 1980.

Robert M. Wren, "The Last Bridge on *The Road*: Soyinka's Rage and Compassion", in *Research in African Literature*, 13, 1982.

Denise Coussy, "Metaphors of Life and Death in *The Road*", in *Commonwealth*, vol.7 no.1, 1984.

Biodun Jeyifo, "The Hidden Class War in *The Road*", in Biodun's *The Truthful Lie: Essays in a Sociology of African Drama*, London, 1985.

A.P. Vithal, "Ambivalence in Wole Soyinka's *The Road*", in *Indian Readings in Commonwealth Literature*, edited by G.S. Amur and others, New Delhi, 1985.

Simon O. Umukoro, "Structure as Meaning in Wole Soyinka's *The Road*", in *Literary Half-Yearly*, vol.27 no.2, 1986.

Akpofure Oduaran, "Linguistic Function and Literary Style: An Inquiry into the Language of Wole Soyinka's *The Road*", in *Research in African Literatures*, 19, 1988.

K.J. Phillips, "Exorcising Faustus from Africa: Wole Soyinka's *The Road*", in *Comparative Literature Studies*, 27, 1990.

*   *   *

Formerly a Christian lay-reader, the Professor was expelled from his church for misappropriating funds. He lives as a forger, especially of licences, and by selling second-hand parts from cars involved in accidents that he himself causes by removing road signs. His store, where the Professor holds his own religious services, is a meeting place for layabouts, thugs, truck drivers, and corrupt police. There is little linear narrative and much of the play consists of recounting memories and of dramatized flashbacks of the past. The main revelation concerns Kotonu, a truck driver who hit a masquerader in an Egungun festival. Kotonu hid the masquerader in his truck, put on the mask himself, and danced all night until he could make his escape. Brought by Kotonu to the Professor, the wounded masquerader, Murano, apparently recovers but has become mute. At the end of the play, during the evening's ceremony at the shop, Murano, who has become the Professor's servant, puts on his Egungun mask, starts dancing, and becomes possessed. A fight breaks out and Say Tokyo Kid, a driver and leader of the thugs, stabs the Professor with a knife

and is, himself, killed by Murano. The Professor dies saying "Be even like the road itself. . .Be the road".

Although the Professor is an amusing fraud he is representative of those caught between old and new, and of the general condition of modern Nigeria in which Christianity, Americanization, modern transportation, and the problems of urbanization exist side by side with ritual festivals, tribal beliefs, and various syncretisms of the past and present. Soyinka's concern, however, is not with the problems of biculturalism—he seems to take delight in the incogruities of social change and the meeting of cultures—but in establishing his own version of a Yoruba world-view. Although it is possible to interpret *The Road* in relation to the Western Region crisis of the early 1960's when the thugs in the play would have been working for politicians, or to see the play in Marxist terms as a study of a capitalist class that has developed in the large cities of the post-colonial Third World, its main significance is pointed to by Soyinka's note "For the Producer". He explains that Agemo is "a religious cult of flesh dissolution" and the dance is "the movement of transition" which is used in his play as a "visual suspension of death—in much the same way as Murano, the mute, is a dramatic embodiment of this suspension". Murano hit by a lorry when in masquerade was in "the passage of transition from the human to the divine essence (as in the festival of Ogun in this play)".

Although Soyinka may have been influenced by European notions of ritual drama, he sees the relationship of acting to religious masquerade as more contemporary and less distant in origin. His actors are expected to treat the play as a moment of ritual, a participation in a divine drama in which the actor's self is temporarily dissolved and undergoes a period of chaos or transition between life and death. *The Road* embodies a spiritual mystery which cannot be expressed in words. It is a moment of union between Murano and the divine; an illumination which the Professor seeks but cannot find because it cannot be discovered through rational understanding. The play expresses this distinction by contrasting the experience central to the Egungun ritual with the Professor's failure to find the truth he calls the "Word". The "Word", thus, is a metaphor with various meanings, but essentially refers to the inability of language, including the language of the play, to express the inexpressible, although drama can symbolise it visually.

The title, *The Road*, alludes to Ogun, a Yoruba deity. Ogun is the god of travellers and drivers. Road journeys re-enact Ogun's original descent from the spirit world through primordial chaos to establish a link between the gods and man, thus creating the Yoruba world in which their ancestors and gods live near them (rather than in a distant heaven, as in the Christian world view). But only in death, or in the possession by the gods during a masquerade, can the mystery be experienced. Murano is mute because having been hit by a lorry while possessed he is held in a state between life and death, between human and divine. He cannot communicate his knowledge, unlike the Professor who is clever with words but who seeks an impossible communion—impossible because the experience is available only to those who undertake a journey between the two worlds, such as the ritual masquerader or the artist.

The Road uses comedy, incongruity, repetition, fragmentation, and parody to suggest paradox and the lack of continuity between different kinds of reality. The Professor is adept in the ways of his society and its corruptions; while amusing he is understood to represent contemporary Nigeria. The comic discrepancy in the play between uniforms and employment is part of the portrayal of a syncretic culture, but it is also symbolic of the discrepancy between words and the "Word".

The Professor is proud of his learning and concerned with money and status; he is dishonest, neither a Christian nor part of tribal society. His quest is for psychic harmony, a lost unity, which he mistakenly assumes he can find through study and literacy, rather than in participation and experience. When he is killed, the Professor has, for the first time, come close to (and perhaps experiences) the "Word". As the conclusion shows, the quest is necessary to give life meaning. The Professor is a comic Everyman of modern urban Africa, someone whose quest for meaning in his life consists of confused ideas, mixed cultural notions, and words.

—Bruce King

THE ROAD TO DAMASCUS. See **TO DAMASCUS.**

THE ROBBERS (Die Räuber)
Friedrich von Schiller

First Publication: Stuttgart [title page wrongly indicates Frankfurt and Leipzig], 1781.
First Production: Nationaltheater, Mannheim, 13 January 1782.

Editions
Die Räuber, edited by L.A. Willoughby, Oxford, 1922; revised edition, co-edited with C.P. Magill, 1949.
"Die Räuber": Mit Materialen, edited by Dietrich Steinbach, Stuttgart, 1979.

Translations
The Robbers, in *"The Robbers" and "Wallenstein"*, translated by F.J. Lamport, Harmondsworth, 1979.
The Robbers, 1792, Oxford, 1989 (facsimile).

Criticism
(For general works on the author, see *Playwrights* volume)

Books:
Willhelm Rullmann, *Die Bearbeitungen, Forsetzungen und Nachahmungen von Schillers " Räubern" (1782–1802)*, Berlin, 1910.
Rudolf Ibel, *Schiller: "Die Räuber": Bearbeitung* Frankfurt, 1964.
Herbert Kraft, *"Die Räuber": Texte und Zeugnisse zur Entstehungs- und Wirkungsgeschichte*, Frankfurt, 1967.
Manfred Wacker, *Schillers "Räuber" und der Sturm und Drang: Stilkritische und typologische Überprüfung eines Epochen begriffs*, Göppingen, 1973.
Oswald Woyte, *Erläuterungen zu Schillers Jugenddrama "Die Räuber"*, Hollfeld, 1973.
Michael Mann, *Sturm-und-Drang-Drama: Studien und Vorstudien zu Schillers "Räubern"*, Bern and Munich, 1974.
Das Räuberbuch: Die Rolle der Literaturwissenschaft in des deutschen Bürgertums am Beispiel von Schillers "Die Räuber", Frankfurt, 1974.
P. Michelsen, *Der Bruch mit der Vaterwelt: Studien zu Schillers "Räubern"*, Stuttgart, 1979.

Articles:
W. Kurrelmeyer, "A Contemporary Critique of Schiller's *Räuber*", in *Journal of English and Germanic Philology*, 18, 1919.
L.A. Willoughby, "English Translations and Adaptations of Schiller's *Robbers*", in *Modern Language Review*, 16, 1921.
Wilhelm Martin Becker, "Das Urbild des alten Moor in Schillers *Räubern*", in *Zeitschrift für Geschichte des Oberrheins*, 43, 1929.
G. Waterhouse, "Schiller's *Räuber* in England Before 1800", in *Modern Language Review*, 30, 1935.
H. Glaesener, "Une Source historique des *Brigands* de Schiller", in *Revue germanique*, 29, 1938.
Elisabeth Blochmann, "Das Motiv vom verlorenen Sohn in Schillers Räuberdrama", in *Deutsche Vierteljahrsschrift für Literaturwissenschaft und Geistesgeschichte*, 25, 1951.
Israel J. Stamm, "The Religious Aspect of *Die Räuber*", in *Germanic Review*, 27, 1952.
S. Wilcox, "Schiller's Influence on Lermontov's *The Two Brothers*", in *Philological Quarterly*, 35, 1956.
D. Milburn, "The First English Translation of *Die Räuber*", in *Monatshefte*, 59, 1957.
Wilhelm Greuzmann, "Schillers frühe Dramen: *Die Räuber* und *Kabale und Liebe*: Eine Analyse", in *Doits Bungaku*, 23, 1959.
Heinz Rieder, "Schillers *Räuber*: Eine Tragödie des Weltgerichts", in *Stimmen der Zeit*, 165, 1959.
Max Rouché, "Nature de la liberté légitime de l'insurrection dans *Les Brigands* et *Guillaume Tell*", in *Études germaniques*, 14, 1959.
Hans Schwerte, "Schillers *Räuber*", in *Deutschunterricht*, 12, 1960.
Douglas Milburn, "The First English Translation of *Die Räuber*: French Bards and Scottish Translators", in *Monatshefte*, vol.59 no.1, 1961.
Peter Michelsen, "Studien zu Schillers *Räubern*", in *Jahrbuch der deutschen Schiller-Gesellschaft*, 1964.
Karl S. Guthke, "Räuber Moors Glück und Ende", in *German Quarterly*, 39, 1966.
Robert R. Heitner, "Luise Milbrin and the Shock Motif in Schiller's Early Dramas", in *Germanic Review*, 41, 1966.
Wolfgang Nehring, "Dramatische Funktionalität und epische Breite in Schillers *Räubern*", in *Aquila: Chestnut Hill Studies in Modern Languages and Literatures*, 1, The Hague, 1968.
Philipp F. Veit, "The Strange Case of Moritz Spiegelberg", in *Germanic Review*, 44, 1969.
Gero von Wilcke, "Genealogische Hintergründe zu Schillers Dramen *Die Räubern* und *Kabale und Liebe*", in *Genealogie: Deutsche Zeitschrift für Familienkund*, 10, 1970.
Hans Mayer, "Der weise Nathan und der Räuber Spiegelberg: Antinomie der jüdischen Emanzipation in Deutschland", in *Jahrbuch der deutschen Schiller-Gesellschaft*, 1973.
Philipp F. Veit, "Moritz Spiegelberg: Eine Charakterstudie zu Schillers *Räubern*", in *Jahrbuch der deutschen Schiller-Gesellschaft*, 17, 1973.
Heinrich Huesmann, "*Räuber* Inszenierungen an den Reinhardt-Bühnen", in *Études germaniques*, 29, 1974.
Gerhard Kluge, "Zwischen Seelenmechanik und Gefühlspathos: Umrisse zum Verständnis der Gestalt in *Die Räuber*: Analyse der Szene I, 3", in *Jahrbuch der deutschen Schiller-Gesellschaft*, 20, 1976.
Regine Otto, "Schiller als Kommentator und Kritiker seiner Dichtungen von den *Räubern* bis zum *Don Carlos*", in *Weimarer Beiträge*, 22, 1976.
Lowell A. Bangerter, "*Die Räuber*: Friedrich Schiller and E.T.A Hoffmann", in *Germanic Review*, 52, 1977.

The Robbers: Staatstheater, Berlin, 1926

Roland Dressler, "Erwin Piscator's *Räuber*-Inszenierung von 1926", in *Weimarer Beiträge*, 26, 1980.

Hans-Jürgen Schings, "Philosophie der Liebe und Tragödie des Universalhasses: *Die Räuber* im Kontext von Schillers Jugendphilosophie", in *Jahrbuch des wiener Goethe Vereins*, 84–85, 1980–81.

A. Mahennet, "Schiller and the 'Germanico-Terrific' Romance", in *Publications of the English Goethe Society*, 51, 1981.

Gert Mattenklott, "Schiller's *Räuber* in der Frühgeschichte des Anarchismus", in *Text & Kontext*, 9, 1981.

Dietrich Steinbach, "Das Interesse an Franz Moor oder Lese Proxesse als Erkenntnisprozesse: Anmerkungen zur literarischen Hermeneutik", in *Deutschunterricht*, 33, 1981.

Waltroud Linder-Beroud, " 'Das Theater glich einem Irrenhause': 200 Jahre Rezeptionsgeschichte der *Räuber* und des *Räuberliedes*", in *Jahrbuch für Volksliedforschung*, 27–28, 1982–83.

Klaus R. Scherpe, "Schillers *Räuber*: Theatralisch", in *Deutschunterricht*, 35, 1983.

Jurgen E. Schlunk, "Vertrauern als Ursache und Überwindung tragischer Verstickung in Schillers *Räuber*: Zum Verständnis Karl Moors", in *Jahrbuch der deutschen Schiller-Gesellschaft*, 27, 1983.

Detlej Brennecke, "Schön wie Engel, voll Walhallas Wonne': Altnordisches bei Schiller", in *Germanisch-Romanische Monatsschrift*, 35, 1985.

Richard Koc, "Fathers and Sons: Ambivalence Doubled in Schiller's *Räuber*", in *Germanic Review*, 61, 1986.

Alan C. Leidner, " 'Fremde Menschen fielen einander schluchzend in die Arme': *Die Räuber* and the Communal Response", in *Goethe Yearbook*, 3, 1986.

Arnd Bohm, "Possessive Individualism in Schiller's *Die Räuber*", in *Mosaic*, 20, 1987.

Stephanie Barbé Hammer, "The Sublime Crime: Fascination and Failure in Schiller's *Die Räuber* and Laclos' *Les Liaisons dangereuses*", in *Comparatist*, 11, 1987.

Denis Jonnes, "Pattern of Power: Family and State in Schiller's Early Drama", in *Colloquia Germanica*, 20, 1987.

Jörg Heininger, "Schiller: Die Kanaille Franz, die ästhetische Erziehung und die Theorie der Komödie", in *Weimarer Beiträge*, 34, 1988.

Gudrun Schulz, "Werbung für ein Trauerspiel: Ein Beitrag zu Schillers *Räuber*", in *Gutenberg-Jahrbuch*, 63, 1988.

Klaus Weimar, "Vom Leben in Texten: Zu Schillers *Räuber*", in *Merkur*, 42, 1988.

*   *   *

Karl Moor, banished from his family by a mendacious letter written by his jealous younger brother, Franz (but purporting to be from his father), abandons his studies out of disillusionment with his father and mankind in general, and joins fellow students in a life of brigandry in Bohemia. Franz becomes master at home after—so it seems—killing his father by concocting a tale of Karl's death in battle. Karl, pining for his fiancée, Amalia, returns home in disguise, to learn the full extent of Franz's treachery. He stumbles across his father—weak, confused, but miraculously alive—who is being secretly fed in his dungeon by a retainer. Karl sends his men to bring Franz, but Franz evades justice by strangling himself.

Tormented by guilt for all the suffering his brigandry has caused, Karl now deliberately kills his father by revealing that he, Karl, is leader of a band of robbers. Amalia, recognizes him at last and despite everything wants to be united with him; but now the robbers reclaim him as their own: he had sworn a solemn oath of loyalty to them in Bohemia. Forced to choose between them and Amalia, Karl kills her and gives himself up to the authorities. He realizes the futility of trying to set the world to rights by lawlessness.

This is a summary of the earliest text of *The Robbers*, subtitled "A Drama", though the text of the first production ("The Mannheim Version") has several important changes; a further acting version, dating from 1782, is subtitled "A Tragedy". *The Robbers* enjoyed probably the most sensational première in German theatrical history. One eye-witness reports that "the theatre resembled a madhouse—rolling eyes, clenched fists, stamping feet, and hoarse cries from the audience. Total strangers fell weeping into one another's arms; women, practically fainting, tottered towards the exit". The 22-year-old's debut was a highly charged, melodramatic piece he had written in secret during his final year at the military academy at Stuttgart. It is an original reworking of the parable of the Prodigal Son, where the son's return proves fatal to his father. Both brothers are, in effect, guilty of parricide, while the father himself can also be viewed as a prodigal because of his invincible favouritism towards Karl: "I have sinned against Heaven and against you. I am not worthy to be called your father". Two plays of 1776, *Julius von Tarent* by J.A. Leisewitz and *The Twins* by F.M. Klinger, show a murderous rivalry between two brothers over a woman. For Schiller, however, this theme is secondary to the relationship of each brother to his father, which gives the whole play its dynamism.

Franz, the younger brother, rails against this accident of birth and his physical ugliness. To compensate for these disadvantages he employs an amoral logic to achieve Karl's banishment and then remove his father. In his soliloquies, normal pieties, such as love for one's blood relations, are subjected to a corrosive analysis far more radical than anything the outlaw Karl says. Unable at the end to still the voice of conscience, Franz earns a certain admiration by his desperate defiance.

Karl is, in E.J. Hobsbawm's terms, a noble bandit who is launched on his anti-social career by Franz's treachery and pursues it in the style of Robin Hood. Though his associates commit some horrible excesses, Karl remains honourable. No revolutionary at heart, his basic desire is to rejoin his family—hence his anguish on learning that Franz's letter went far beyond his father's actual wishes, and that he had not earned his father's curse. At the end, Karl calmly gives himself up to the authorities. This certainly puzzled republicans in France, who took the play's motto "*In tirannos*" seriously, unaware that these words were an addition by the publisher.

The play is an uneven work, but one already bearing the imprint of the lion's paw. It suffers from a surfeit of intrigue, with its attendant dissembling and disguise. For this to be sustained, the major characters display a gullibility that sometimes stretches belief. Thus, Amalia accepts as genuine the sword with messages written in blood on its blade, which Franz says comes from Karl and "proves" his death. The play's violent language is matched by violent, exaggerated gesture which verges on the ridiculous. Schiller often uses pauses to establish a tableau, and large groups—the robbers themselves—to intensify a dominant emotion. Such features, as has been persuasively argued, derive from the world of opera and ballet, which figured largely in Schiller's early, theatrical experience. Schiller is, here, a long way from both Lessing's rational realism and Goethe's developing classicism. The high, emotional temperature of the play links it with the *Sturm und Drang* movement, but its visionary, nightmare quality foreshadows later developments. A stern critic of his own work, Schiller claimed (in his unpublished preface to the first edition) that *The Robbers* is more of a dramatized novel than a truly theatrical drama. However, the play's shortcomings are those of youth's impatient ambition rather than literary weakness.

—M.A. Levene

THE ROGUE OF SEVILLE. See **THE TRICKSTER OF SEVILLE.**

ROISTER DOISTER. See **RALPH ROISTER DOISTER.**

THE ROMANS IN BRITAIN
by Howard Brenton

First Publication: London, 1980; revised edition, 1981.
First Production: National Theatre, London, 16 October 1980.

Criticism
(For general works on the author, see *Playwrights* volume)

Articles:
Philip Roberts, "Howard Brenton's Romans", in *Critical Quarterly*, vol.23 no.3, 1981.

* * *

The first production of *The Romans in Britain* at the National Theatre in 1980 created a furore which culminated in the trial of its director, Michael Bogdanov, on the charge of "procuring an act of gross indecency". The "act" was a simulated buggery performed by the actors in one scene of the play. When Brenton spoke of his play as one which enters "fights over political issues", the issues raised by the trial—important though they are—were not the ones he had in mind. *The Romans in Britain* is a "history play for now" which centres on "the great wrong of England in Ireland". "What my play says", Brenton explained, "is that all empire is bad. The Republican cause is just. The border is a crime. But bald statements are no good. To convince an audience of the truth of my arguments, I find myself writing about Britain in 54 B.C. and a British officer going off his head in an Irish cornfield today. . .".

The play is epic in both the loose sense (it's big and deals with history) and in the specifically Brechtian one. It is concerned to manipulate parallels between imperialisms of different epochs. Part 1 ("Caesar's Tooth") is set in a single day in August 54 B.C.. It dramatizes the effect of the Roman invasion of Britain on a tribe living just north of the River Thames. The matriarch of the tribe publicly rejects as liars and political tricksters the envoys of a neighbouring tribe who come to warn her of the Roman advance. Privately she admits awareness of the threat, but refuses resistance because of traditional bonds with a group of families which has arrived at an "agreement" ("the Romans took five hundred hostages") with the invaders. The devastation of her tribe, its land, and its culture is represented not by large-scale destruction but by the

wanton killing of two foster-brothers and the homosexual rape of a third, the trainee druid priest, Marban, by three off-duty Roman soldiers. We see Julius Caesar himself, official historian in tow, organizing this military expedition to "the edge of the world" with ruthless efficiency. He has Marban released, but the youth kills himself, having first voiced the need for resistance in a desperate vision. Through the main action is threaded the progress towards an illusionary freedom of the escaped Irish criminal, Conlag. He is killed by the stone-wielding, female slave who has accompanied him. But when she herself is finally killed, it is not by the Romans but by the Roman army advancing "in British Army uniforms and with the equipment of the late 1970's". Historical parallel has given way to identification.

If Part 1 is (in the playwright's own words) "violent, dynamic and tragic", Part 2 ("Arthur's Grave") is "elegiac, still and flooded with an hysterical, light hearted, comic spirit". The historical parallel is this time an explicit one. Actions set in Ireland in A.D. 1980 and in Britain (again just north of the Thames) in A.D. 515 run concurrently through alternating scenes. But the *location*, "*a field, harvested, the corn in sheaves*", is the same for each, and a visual and aural overlap between periods is insisted upon throughout. The dual action spans a single day. In 1980 the British Army captain, Thomas Chichester, working undercover on an Irish farm, becomes increasingly unhinged by liberal doubt and self-hatred ("I am the great wrong in Ireland") as he waits to "contact" and assassinate an IRA "target". He deliberately reveals his identity to his victim, but just before he himself is "executed" he gives utterance to a vision of imperialist violence and suffering which seems to encompass all three of the play's "periods". In A.D. 515 the daughters of a veteran, pagan Saxon-fighter kill him when he refuses to acknowledge the reality of the threat of advancing Saxon forces. Eventually they join up with two comic cooks ("I'm meat and he's vegetables") from the household of "the Last Roman Lady" Adona, who, dying of the "yellow plague", has been finished off by the opportunistic survivor who is her steward and lover. The play ends as the cooks are inventing the legend of King Arthur. . .

Brenton's work on Brecht (his translation of *Galileo*, 1980) had an evident impact on this play. The ancient, Celtic stone-thrower killed by the modern British Army; Chichester lying on stage asleep throughout the A.D. 515 scenes, and his dead body lying on stage during the final scene; the cooks in A.D. 515 eating wheat from the sheaves stacked by Chichester in 1980; the cries of the dying Adona heard by Chichester in 1980: all these combine to effect a *strangeness* in our sense of the play's fictional worlds that we recognize as one of the aims of Brechtian dramaturgy. The uniform contemporaneity of the language ("Where the fuck are we?" is the first line in 54 B.C.) works in a similar way—to enforce likeness through strange dislocations. Yet Brenton's dramaturgy, as distinct from Brecht's, is characterized by image rather than debate, provocation rather than logic. His is a figural imagination, which expresses itself through sudden, often sensational, juxtapositions and an almost oppressive physicality. Political meanings in this play are registered upon the body: imperialist penetration is imaged in the rape of Marban, Caesar's attitude towards Britain in the peremptory extraction of an aching tooth, and the incurable decadence of Roman society in 6th-century Britain in the plague which marks the last Roman lady: "What do you expect when civilization dies? Good health?".

It is hard not to feel, even whilst sympathizing with the play's political aims, that its force is occasionally vitiated by the sensational emphasis and stridency of tone that its dramatic style encourages, and by the unargued parallels that its formal layout proposes. Yet an important part of Brenton's political intention is to dramatize the "culture shock" felt when "two worlds touch", and in this he is notably successful. In Part 1, especially, Celtic culture (matriarchal, ritualistic, custombound, familial, rural, local, religious) is opposed to Roman (patriarchal, militaristic, expediency-oriented, rhetoricbound, economic, linear, expansionist) without being sentimentalized. The Celts have their customs involving the ritual murder of strangers, their brutality towards slaves, their rooted, internecine prejudices. And they are no more able to articulate the nature of the invading army ("a ship of horror. . .they are one huge thing") than the Romans are inclined to understand this "filthy backwater of humanity, somewhere near the edge of the world". (Similarly, for the British soldier of A.D. 1980, the Irish countryside "is the surface of the moon".)

The experiences of geographical displacement and cultural disorientation brought about by imperialist invasion repeatedly generate in the play's characters a mythopoeic impulse. "The old Gods are dead", Caesar tells Marban. But if the search for new ones produces utopian chimeras, it also yields a story, in the last scene, that will serve as a basis for resistance, a story about a "golden age" not just lost but "yet to come". In "the Making of Arthur", Brenton ends with a satisfyingly witty balance between dramatic quality and political commitment.

—Paul Lawley

ROMEO AND JULIET
by William Shakespeare

First Publication: London, 1597 ("bad" first quarto); with variants, 1599 (second, "good" quarto).
First Production: London, c.1591–96.

Editions

Romeo and Juliet, edited by H. H. Furness, Philadelphia, 1871 (New Variorum Shakespeare).
The Tragedy of Romeo and Juliet [revised edition], edited by Richard Hosley, New Haven, Connecticut, 1954 (Yale Shakespeare).
Romeo and Juliet, edited by John Dover Wilson and George Ian Duthie, Cambridge, 1955 (New Shakespeare).
Romeo and Juliet, edited by T.J.B. Spencer, Harmondsworth, 1967 (New Penguin Shakespeare).
Romeo and Juliet, edited by Brian Gibbons, London, 1980 (Arden Shakespeare).
Romeo and Juliet, edited by G. Blakemore Evans, Cambridge, 1984 (New Cambridge Shakespeare).

Criticism
(For general works on the author, see *Playwrights* volume)

Books:
H.B. Charlton, *"Romeo and Juliet" as an Experimental Tragedy*, London, 1939.
Harry R. Hope, *The Bad Quarto of "Romeo and Juliet": A Bibliographical and Textual Study*, Ithaca, New York, 1948.
Olin H. Moore, *The Legend of Romeo and Juliet*, Columbus, Ohio, 1950.
Robert O. Evans, *The Osier Cage: Rhetorical Devices in "Romeo and Juliet"*, Lexington, Kentucky, 1966.

Inge Leimberg, *Shakespeares "Romeo and Juliet": Von der Sonettdichtung zur Liebestragödie*, Munich, 1968.
Douglas Cole (ed.), *Twentieth Century Interpretations of "Romeo and Juliet"*, Englewood Cliffs, New Jersey, 1970.
James L. Calderwood, *Shakespeare's Metadrama: The Argument of the Play in "Titus Andronicus", "Love's Labours Lost", "Romeo and Juliet", "A Midsummer Night's Dream", and "Richard II"*, Minneapolis, 1971.
James H. Seward, *Tragic Vision in "Romeo and Juliet"*, Washington D.C., 1973.
Luis Capecchi, *"Romeo and Juliet": La expansión del tema*, Zaragoza, 1982.
L. Levenson, *Romeo and Juliet*, Manchester, 1987 (Shakespeare in Performance Series).

Articles:
For information on the many articles about *Romeo and Juliet*, see the bibliographies listed in the *Playwrights* volume and the annual Shakespeare Bibliography in *Shakespeare Quarterly*, published by the Folger Shakespeare Library, Washington D.C. (1950–).

*   *   *

Romeo and Juliet is a "separation-romance" concerned with the relationship of young lovers who belong respectively to mutually antagonistic families, the Montagues and Capulets of Verona. Romeo and Juliet fall in love, meet and marry secretly, but are separated when Romeo is banished for the killing of Juliet's cousin Tybalt in an inter-family street brawl. An attempted resolution of the problem by a friar leads to tragic consequences: Juliet takes a drug which produces the symptoms of apparent death, and is laid in her family vault; but the message intended for Romeo explaining the plot never reaches him. Believing Juliet is dead, he kills himself in her tomb. She wakes to find him dead, and commits suicide to join him in death.

The action of the play is introduced by the Chorus, a figure of prescient wisdom like a narrator, who stands both inside and outside the action of the play, and is therefore better able to deliver a judgement on the meaning of its dramatized events. At the play's opening the Chorus lays the basis for the story by outlining the feud between the two great houses, a quarrel rooted in inveterate enmity ("ancient grudge"), and now breaking out into re-opened hostilities ("new mutiny"). The significance of the relationship between Romeo and Juliet is placed by the Chorus firmly within the context of the feud: he calls them "a pair of star-crossed lovers", doomed to undergo a tragedy fated in their fortunes, written in their stars. The Chorus then makes it clear that this tragedy does, however, entail positive consequences, since the tragic deaths of Romeo and Juliet will bring their parents to a new understanding, will reconcile their deep-rooted familial enmity, and pacify their habitual violence. The Chorus's speech stresses this aspect particularly strongly, repeating the claim by emphasising that nothing else but the deaths of their children could have healed the civil breach: he speaks of ". . .their parents' rage, / Which, but their children's end, nought could remove. . .".

The Prologue is in a sense a blue-print for the action of the play, a model in miniature of its artistic and emotional structure. There is the feud, then there are the lovers whose passion transcends it; there is the paradoxical denouement in which the feuding families destroy the lovers, but are then redeemed by the example of their love. There is, of course, an element of contradiction in this structure: the love of Romeo and Juliet is the only good thing produced by the feud, yet it must be destroyed if the feud is to be reconciled. This

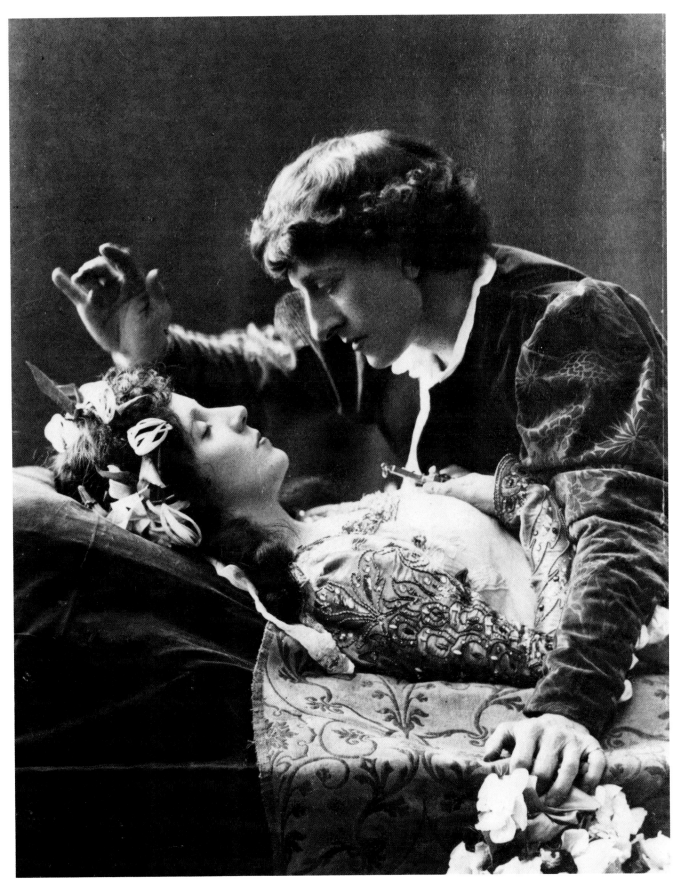

Romeo and Juliet: Lyceum Theatre, London, 1895 (Mrs Patrick Campbell and Johnston Forbes-Robertson)

contradictory structure represents a highly problematic aspect of *Romeo and Juliet*. Most interpretations agree in taking a positive view of the lovers themselves, in regarding their love as a healthy and therapeutic challenge to the casual hostility and routine violence of a divided society, and in taking a negative view both of the feud and of the families who sustain it. Other interpretations question whether the sacrificial deaths of the two lovers can be regarded as having a decisively beneficial effect on their society.

The play's conclusion is, in this respect, highly ambiguous:

> *Capulet*: O brother Montague, give me thy hand.
> This is my daughter's jointure, for no more
> Can I demand.
>
> *Montague*: But I can give thee more.
> For I will raise her statue in pure gold,
> That whiles Verona by that name is known,
> There shall no figure at such rate be set
> As that of true and faithful Juliet.
>
> *Capulet*: As rich shall Romeo's by his lady lie,
> Poor sacrifices of our enmity!

Of course these lines can be interpreted sympathetically, as indicative of a genuine change of heart in the leaders of both the families. We can infer that their strongest, shared emotion is a sense of loss, and that they are very much aware of the poverty and bitterness of all that is left to them—two old men shaking hands, planning a memorial tribute to their slaughtered children; a poor substitute for the marriage alliance they might have mutually enjoyed.

At the same time, we might take a different view. The lovers are here envisaged as transformed from the shameful and piteous image of their stabbed and poisoned corpses into decorative, artistic objects, expressive of both aesthetic and material value. This combined emphasis on wealth and prettiness operates to conceal the brutal and uncomfortable truths the play has disclosed. Capulet admits that the lovers are "*poor* sacrifices": but both families are eager to change them back into something "rich". Both Montague and Capulet here speak a language of commercial transaction, sealing a parodic marriage-contract in which the principals, being dead, are symbolically eliminated from their parents' financial preoccupations. If Montague does give Capulet his hand (the text does not indicate whether or not this is meant to occur) it may be more in the spirit of a bargain struck than a gesture of amity. Furthermore, the exchange is conducted as a kind of competition ("I can give thee more". . ."as rich. . ."), as if the two houses are still vying with one another for pre-eminence in wealth and status.

There seems to be, in the play, no acknowledgement at all that Romeo and Juliet have been made victims of the families' competitive emulation (the feud, through which Romeo kills Tybalt) and of their hunger for status and power (the arranged marriage between Juliet and Paris), rather than of some abstract and inexplicable "enmity". In a play which continually sets love as a challenging value against the mercenary ethics of profit, competition, property marriage, there is surely something odd about the final reconciliation being formulated in precisely those terms; as if the two families are closing ranks very much in the old way, having expelled the unassimilable element of an inter-family relationship.

—Graham Holderness

LA RONDE (Reigen)
by Arthur Schnitzler

First Publication: Vienna, 1900 (private printing); Vienna, 1903.
First Production: Akademisch-Dramatischer Verein, Munich, 25 June 1903 (Scenes 4, 5, and 6 only); complete, at the Kleines Schauspielhaus, Berlin, 23 December, 1920.

Translations

Hands Around, translated by L.D. Edwards and F.L. Glaser, New York, 1920.
Couples, translated by Lily Wolfe and E.W. Titus, Paris, 1927.
Hands Around, translated by Keene Wallis, New York, 1929.
La Ronde, translated by Eric Bentley, in *From the Modern Repertoire*, edited by Eric Bentley, 1954.
Merry-Go-Round, translated by Frank and Jacqueline Marcus, London, 1953; retitled as *La Ronde*, 1959.
La Ronde, translated by H. Weigert and P. Newhall, New York, 1962.
La Ronde, translated by Sue Davies, adapted by John Barton, Harmondsworth, 1982.
The Round Dance, in *"The Round Dance" and Other Plays*, translated by Charles Osborne, Manchester, 1982.

Criticism
(For general works on the author, see *Playwrights* volume)

Books:
Wolfgang Heine, *Der Kampf um den "Reigen": Vollständiger Bericht über die sechstägige Verhandlung gegen Direktion und Darsteller des Kleinen Schauspielhauses Berlin*, Berlin, 1922.

Articles:
Fritz Dehnow, "Der Prozess um den *Reigen*", in *Zeitschrift für Sexualwissenschaft*, 9, 1922.
Otto P. Schinnerer, "The History of Schnitzler's *Reigen*", in *Publications of the Modern Language Association* [*PMLA*], vol.46 no.3, 1931.
A. Feldmann, "The Pattern of Promiscuity Seen in Schnitzler's *Round Dance*", in *Psychoanalytic Review*, 47, 1960.
Hunter G. Hannum, " 'Killing Time': Aspects of Schnitzler's *Reigen*", in *Germanic Review*, 37, 1962.
Ludwig Marcuse, "Der *Reigen* Prozess: Sex, Politik und Kunst 1920 in Berlin", in *Der Monat*, 14, 1962.
H. Politzer, "Arthur Schnitzler: The Poetry of Psychology", in *Modern Language Notes*, 1963.
Friedbert Aspetsberger, "Der Prozess gegen die Berliner Aufführung des *Reigen* 1922", in *Akzente*, 12, 1965.
John B. Sanders, "Arthur Schnitzler's *Reigen*: Lost Romanticism", in *Modern Austrian Literature*, vol. 1 no.4, 1968.
Lotte S. Couch, "*Der Reigen*: Schnitzler and Sigmund Freud", in *Österreich in Geschichte und Literatur*, 16, 1972.
Erna Neuse, "Die Funktion von Motiven und stereotypen Wendung in Schnitzlers *Reigen*", in *Monatshefte*, 64, 1972.
Reinhard Urbach (ed.), "Ihre liebenswürdige Anfrage zu beantworten: Brief zum *Reigen*", in *Ver Sacrum*, 5, 1974.
Annette Delius, "Schnitzlers *Reigen* und der *Reigen*-Prozess: Verständliche und manipulierte Missverständnisse in der Rezeption", in *Deutschunterricht*, vol.28 no.2, 1976.
Anna K. Kuhn, "The Romanticization of Arthur Schnitzler: Max Ophuls' Adaptations of *Libelei* and *Reigen*", in *Probleme der Moderne: Studien zur deutschen Literatur von*

La Ronde: Aldwych Theatre, London, 1982 (Royal Shakespeare Company)

Nietzsche bis Brecht, edited by Benjamin Bennett and Others, Tübingen, 1983.

Helga Schiffer, "Arthur Schnitzlers *Reigen*", in *Text & Kontext*, 11, 1983.

Johanna Bossinade, " 'Wenn es aber. . .bei mir anders wäre': Die Frage der Geschlechterbeziehungen in Arthur Schnitzlers *Reigen*", in *Amsterdamer Beiträge zur neueren Germanistik*, 18, 1984.

Gail Finney, "Female Sexuality and Schnitzler's *La Ronde*", in her *Women in Modern Drama: Freud, Feminism, and European Theater at the Turn of the Century*, Ithaca, New York, 1989.

*   *   *

The play consists of ten, self-contained scenes, depicting the erotic encounters between five men and five women. Each of the characters appears twice, in the context of two different relationships. The first scene shows a soldier and a prostitute having furtive and hasty sex on the banks of the Danube. The second dialogue takes place in the Prater park near a dance hall, where the soldier persuades a housemaid to have sex with him. In Scene Three we witness the maid at work being seduced by a young gentleman, who in the following scene has a rendezvous with a married woman in a flat rented for this purpose. After this clandestine and illicit encounter we witness the woman in her respectable, bourgeois surroundings. Her husband gives her a lesson on marital morality, which in Scene Six he himself contradicts when he meets a "sweet young thing" from the suburbs in a *chambre séparée*. Next we see the girl flirting with a pompous poet, who delights himself in the girl's simplicity and lack of culture. Scene Eight takes place in the country in a hotel room, where the poet serves as a plaything to a well-known actress. In Scene Nine the actress receives a morning visit from a Count whose social etiquette and personal disposition forbids "early morning sex". But in the end also he succumbs to the situation. The last scene, which returns to the starting point of the cycle, shows the Count awakening from a drunken stupor in the room of the prostitute from scene one. He vaguely remembers the girl from the evening before, but does not recall making love to her.

Instead of a usual plot development, *La Ronde* offers ten variations on the theme of sex. Every scene is built around the physical act. But instead of showing copulation itself, the play offers insights into the behaviour before and after intercourse. The play reveals typical attitudes to sex in a representative cross section of society. The characters are not shown as individuals, but representatives of the social classes they come from. Their treatment of the sexual act is typical of the kind of education they have received and the moral codes prevalent in their social environment. All of them profess to loving their partner. But as each following scene reveals, the romantic concept of love has no real basis in the character's actual lives. Although society still clings to an idealized notion of love and shuns any recognition of sex, people's behaviour is in opposition to the official moral code of the period. Schnitzler focuses on this loss of romantic ideals and on the contradiction between public morale and private activity.

La Ronde was written in Vienna in 1896/7, when Sigmund Freud began his psychoanalytic career in the same city. He later recognized in Schnitzler a *doppelgänger* and acknowledged in a letter to the playwright "the extensive concurrence which exists between your views and mine regarding some psychoanalytic and erotic problems". Indeed, *La Ronde* seems to exemplify Freud's dictum that human beings "choose a never-ending series of ersatz objects, none of which are ever fully satisfying". Each of the play's characters is propelled to change partner in the following scene because his/her desires have not been fulfilled. The hope that the next encounter may lead to the desired satisfaction forces the protagonists to carry on with the "round dance".

It has been suggested that the play deals with the theme of sexuality as a levelling force that abolishes all social differences. But Schnitzler is not interested in the *homo sexualis per se*. He explores, like Freud, the psychological framework of sexual behaviour. But for Schnitzler psychology and sexuality also have a social basis. The play offers minute observations on how sex is determined by social status and how it is used in the relationships between people of different social backgrounds. The social dimension accounts for the fact that men have to be on a superior social level to perform successfully. When, like the Young Gentleman, they find a woman of equal social standing, they prove to be impotent. Schnitzler makes us aware that women are always the victims of this socially determined sexual order. Even when they, like the actress, emancipate themselves and control their own sexuality, they lose out in the end, for when they act like the men of the time, they have to suffer the same emotional depravations as they do.

—Günter Berghaus

ROOTS.   See **THE WESKER TRILOGY.**

THE ROPE (Rudens)
by Titus Maccius Plautus

First Production: Possibly 189 B.C.

Editions

Rudens, edited by Edward A. Sonnenschein, Oxford, 1901.

The Rope [with translation], in *Plautus, 4*, edited and translated by Paul Nixon, Cambridge, Massachusetts and London, 1932 (Loeb Classical Library).

Plautus: "Rudens": Text und Kommentar, by Friedrich Marx, Amsterdam, 1959.

Translations

Slip-Knot, in *Plautus: Three Plays*, translated by Frederick A. Wright and H. Lionel Rogers, London and New York, 1925.

The Rope, translated by Frank O. Copley, New York, 1956.

The Rope, in *Plautus: Six Plays*, translated by Lionel Casson, Garden City, New York, 1963.

The Rope, in *"The Rope" and Other Plays*, translated by E.F. Watling, Harmondsworth, 1964.

The Rope, in *Roman Drama*, translated by Samuel Lieberman, New York, 1964.

Rudens, in *Rudens; Curculio; Casina*, translated by Christopher Stace, Cambridge, 1981.

Criticism

(For general works on the author, see *Playwrights* volume)

Articles:

C.C. Coulter, "The Composition of the *Rudens* of Plautus", in *Classical Philology*, 8, 1913.

E. Fraenkel, "Stars in the Prologue of the *Rudens*", in *Classical Quarterly*, 36, 1942.

G. Highet, "Shipwrecked Slaves in Plautus' *Rudens*", in *American Journal of Philology*, 63, 1942.

E.W. Leach, "Plautus' *Rudens*: Venus Born From a Shell", in *Texas Studies in Literature and Language*, 15, 1974.

*   *   *

Plautus's play is preceded by a prologue presented by Arcturus, a star, who relates the background to the story which is set on the lonely seacoast of North Africa. Here the Athenian, Daemones, having earlier lost a fortune through his generous nature, lives frugally together with his wife in a small cottage adjacent to a temple of Venus. His daughter, Palaestra, was stolen as a child and sold to a pimp, Labrax, who later brought her to this same remote spot on the African shore. A young man, Plesidippus, has fallen in love with the girl, and had agreed to buy her, but Labrax broke their contract and slipped away thinking to get a higher price in Sicily. His ship has, however, just been wrecked in a storm (conveniently raised by Arcturus), and as the play begins, one by one the survivors reach shore: first Palaestra and another slave girl Ampelisca, who take refuge in the shrine to Venus; then Labrax and his friend Charmides. Learning from a slave of Daemones where the girls are, the pimp goes to seize them. He is seen however, by Trachalio, the slave of Plesidippus, who fetches Daemones to rescue and protect the girls. Plesidippus soon arrives and takes Labrax away to be prosecuted for his fraud. A trunk bound with rope is fished up from the sea by Daemones' slave, Gripus. It belongs to Labrax and is discovered to contain items from Palaestra's childhood that identify her, and allow her a joyful reunion with her father, Daemones, as well as the right to marry Plesidippus. Daemones uses money negotiated from Labrax for finding the trunk to purchase Ampelisca's freedom, agrees to free Gripus as well, and all ends happily.

Rudens is a somewhat uncharacteristic play, frequently cited as amongst Plautus's best works by those who prefer it to the robust slapstick and farce that prevail in most of his other plays. There is little buffoonery; irrelevant jokes and diversions from the plot are kept to a minimum; and a general atmosphere of romance and noble sentiment is much in evidence. The innocent girls, the kindly father, the unlikely reunion, the triumph of love and justice over greed and corruption—all of these place the work on a loftier plane than that occupied by the bawdy and ribald pieces more typical of Plautus. The playwright, himself, was evidently well aware of this, and is unable to resist inserting a wry, theatrically self-conscious joke from time to time to undercut his high-minded material. Even the location of the play in an exotic seaside spot is distant from the urban settings and street scenes generally favoured by Plautus and his Greek predecessors.

As well as eschewing his usual tone and comic style, Plautus has modified his dramaturgy too: there is little intrigue, and no clever slave planning the plot (and outwitting his master) as it goes along. Instead, the god Arcturus has determined the course of the action and its outcome. Despite being punctuated by moments of humour and some extended, comic business, the plot is essentially a serious one, albeit far-fetched and romantic; indeed its tone and some of its details are frequently compared to later romances, including the late plays of Shakespeare. The desperate attempt of the two girls to escape from their captor; his villainous attempt to repossess them; the timely aid of Daemones; and of course, the reunion of father, daughter, and lover: such actions are both moving and dramatically engaging. Although the characters conform in a general way to those which were recycled throughout Plautus's works, they are less obviously "stock", and more carefully and sympathetically drawn than elsewhere. Even the bad-tempered and greedy slave, Gripus, is deftly individualised and allowed, finally, to have his freedom, while the mean-spirited pimp, Labrax, is invited to join in with the general mood of forgiveness and celebration at the end of the play.

The play takes its title from the rope with which, after the play is two-thirds over, Gripus hauls the mysterious trunk from the sea—the object that will bring about the drama's happy denouement. The subsequent struggle for its possession between Gripus and Trachalio (Plesidippus' slave), has often been dismissed as diverting, but dramatically unnecessary. In fact, it helps reveal and clarify a deeper significance in the work. Daemones honourably refuses to support Gripus's claim of "finders keepers", insisting instead that the trunk must go to its rightful owner. In undertaking to determine who that might be, he discovers the identity of his long-lost daughter: in the very act of seeking to behave justly, he in turn is rewarded with justice. A little later he explicitly underscores the moral to Gripus; the wise man avoids greed and always trys to act fairly and with integrity. In showing this principle at work—and the benefits it brings to those who follow it—in a place removed from civilization, Plautus raises it from an abstraction or a mere expediency to a universal ideal. The play, thereby, aptly demonstrates the assertion made by Arcturus in the prologue: that Jupiter watches over men's affairs, and intervenes to promote justice: "I therefore urge you who are good men, and lead honourable and righteous lives: hold steadfast to your course, that happiness may thereafter be yours".

—Richard C. Beacham

ROSENCRANTZ AND GUILDENSTERN ARE DEAD
by Tom Stoppard

First Publication: London and New York, 1967; revised edition, 1968.

First Production: Cranston Street Hall, Edinburgh, 24 August 1966 (abbreviated version); Old Vic Theatre (National Theatre Company), London, 11 April 1967.

Criticism
(For general works on the author, see *Playwrights* volume)

Books:

Anja Easterling, *Shakespearean Parallels and Affinities With the Theatre of the Absurd in Tom Stoppard's "Rosencrantz and Guildenstern are Dead"*, Umeå, Sweden, 1982.

T. Bareham (ed.), *"Rosencrantz and Guildenstern Are Dead"*; *"Jumpers"*; *"Travesties"*: A Casebook, London, 1990.

Robert Gordon, *Rosencrantz and Guildenstern Are Dead; Jumpers; The Real Thing*, London, 1991 (Text and Performance Series).

Articles:

C.J. Gianakaris, "Absurdism Altered: *Rosencrantz and Guildenstern Are Dead*", in *Drama Survey*, 7, 1968–69.

Walter D. Asmus, "*Rosencrantz and Guildenstern Are Dead*", in *Deutsche Shakespeare-Gesellschaft West: Jahrbuch*, 1970.

Rosencrantz and Guildenstern Are Dead: Young Vic Theatre, London, 1975

Peter Carroll, "They Have Their Entrances and Exits: *Rosencrantz and Guildenstern Are Dead*", in *Teaching of English*, 20, 1971.

Normand Berlin, "*Rosencrantz and Guildenstern Are Dead*: Theater of Criticism", in *Modern Drama*, 16, 1973.

Susan Bassnett-McGuire, "Textual Understructures in Jean-Louis Barrault's *Rabelais* and Tom Stoppard's *Rosencrantz and Guildenstern Are Dead*", in *Comparison*, 1, 1975.

Helene Keyssar-Franke, "The Strategy of *Rosencrantz and Guildenstern Are Dead*", in *Educational Theatre Journal*, 27, 1975.

Christian W. Thomsen, "Tom Stoppard: *Rosencrantz and Guildenstern Are Dead*: Spiel vom Sterbe, Spiel vom Tod, Spiel vom Tod in Leben", in *Maske und Kothurn*, 24, 1978.

Heinz Zimmerman, "T. Stoppards Publikumsverwirrung: Zu Rezeption und Sinn von *Rosencrantz and Guildenstern Are Dead*", in *Deutsche Shakespeare-Gesellschaft West: Jahrbuch*, 1978–79.

Robert Egan, "A Thin Beam of Light: The Purpose of Playing in *Rosencrantz and Guildenstern Are Dead*", in *Theatre Journal*, 31, 1979.

Borbara Rajahn-Dejk, "Tod ohne Verklärung: Zur Todesthematik in Tom Stoppards *Rosencrantz and Guildenstern Are Dead*", in *Anglistik & Englischunterricht*, 7, 1979.

Richard Corballis, "Extending the Audience: The Structure of *Rosencrantz and Guildenstern Are Dead*", in *Ariel*, vol.11 no.2, 1980.

J.C. Nitzsche, "McLuhan's Message and Stoppard's Medium in *Rosencrantz and Guildenstern Are Dead*", in *Dutch Quarterly Review of Anglo-American Letters*, 10, 1980.

Simon Varey, "Nobody Special: On *Rosencrantz and Guildenstern Are Dead*", in *Dutch Quarterly Review of Anglo-American Letters*, 10, 1980.

Rosandra Janisch, "The Vision of the Beyond-Absurd in Tom Stoppard's *Rosencrantz and Guildenstern Are Dead*", in *CRUX*, vol.15 no.3, 1981.

Judith Zivanovic, "Meeting Death Already There; The Failure to Choose in Stoppard's *Rosencrantz and Guildenstern Are Dead*", in *Liberal and Fine Arts Review*, 1981.

William E. Gruber, "'Wheels Within Wheels, Etcetera': Artistic Design in *Rosencrantz and Guildenstern Are Dead*", in *Comparative Drama*, 15, 1981–82.

Margarete Holubetz, "A Mocking of Theatrical Conventions: The Fake Death Scenes in *The White Devil* and *Rosencrantz and Guildenstern Are Dead*", in *English Studies*, 63, 1982.

John M. Perlette, "Theatre at the Limit: *Rosencrantz and Guildenstern Are Dead*", in *Modern Drama*, 28, 1985.

N. Eakambaram, "Tradition and the Individual Talent in Tom Stoppard's *Rosencrantz and Guildenstern Are Dead*", in *Osmania Journal of English Studies*, 22, 1986.

*   *   *

In *Rosencrantz and Guildenstern Are Dead* Tom Stoppard constructed a play both comic and absurd around the independent lives of two marginal characters in Shakespeare's *Hamlet*. In Shakespeare's play, Rosencrantz and Guildenstern are little people, continually made to seem irrelevant and unimportant. Their very presence is a consequence of their subordination: the King and Queen have sent for them to spy on Hamlet. This they do very badly, and Hamlet continually makes fools of them. They almost always appear together, and their characters are almost indistinguishable. They try to manipulate Hamlet, but Hamlet manipulates them. The King sends them to take Hamlet to England, with a message to the English King

requiring that the prince be executed. Hamlet changes the letter so that Rosencrantz and Guildenstern are executed in his place.

Stoppard puts these two marginal characters into the foreground of his play: they are its "heroes". The same things happen to them as happen in Shakespeare's *Hamlet*: they have no autonomy, being pushed and pulled here and there by other people; they have no individuality—no one remembers which of them is which; they are made fools of by Hamlet; and the play ends with their execution, contrived almost as a practical joke. The difference is that in Stoppard's play, the main concern is with the "private" lives of Rosencrantz and Guildenstern: with what they do when they are not on stage, when they are waiting "in the wings" for their appearances in Shakespeare's play. So the interest and sympathy of the audience lies with *them*, not with the major characters of *Hamlet*.

The main dramatic and thematic business of the Shakespeare play—the appearance of the ghost, Hamlet's task of revenge, the hero's tortured and divided personality—are all marginalised in Stoppard's play. We see Hamlet in this play in exactly the same way as Rosencrantz and Guildenstern see him: as a man who comes in and talks in an extraordinary language, behaves in ridiculous ways without any obvious reason, and fools and humiliates Rosencrantz and Guildenstern who are helpless victims of his practical jokes. The King and Queen also talk in this mysterious fashion (one of the play's characteristics is the movement from ordinary, modern conversation to Elizabethan blank verse) and give Rosencrantz and Guildenstern absurd commands, without explanation, manipulating and humiliating them unmercifully.

Most contemporary reviewers saw *Rosencrantz and Guildenstern Are Dead* as a drama of the "Absurd", similar to Beckett's *Waiting For Godot*. John Russell Taylor voiced this majority opinion in his book *The Second Wave*: "We know from Beckett that Godot will not come, nothing will ever change, the two figures will remain waiting in the wings of life for the rest of their lives, never quite grasping what is happening centre-stage of life". In this interpretation, the action of the play is a simple parable of the nature of human existence; a demonstration of life's essential meaninglessness, its absence of choice or purpose, its lack of any direction or significance. Ronald Hayman concurs with this view of the play as an absurdist metaphor for the futility of life, but simultaneously proposes a radically different approach: "The theatrical situation is used as an image of the human condition. Birth, growth and death come to seem like the fatalistic web of text that holds the actor stuck". It is one thing to be trapped by a human condition, quite another to be trapped by a *text*, which is after all quite obviously a man-made construction. If the dramatic narrative of the play enacts not a general human condition, but the subjection of human beings to particular social and ideological forces, then it is perhaps closer to Brecht than to Beckett. If the point of Beckett's plays is to say that life is absurd and uncontrollable, the point of Brecht's plays is to say that we, the audience, have the power to change our lives and to make them less absurd, more meaningful.

If we ask what it is that in this play limits and constrains human freedom, the answer is not a universal condition, but a specific cultural object—a play (*the* play) by Shakespeare. *Rosencrantz and Guildenstern Are Dead* can be read as a play about Shakespeare, and about the ways in which culture can become a powerful ideological force helping to oppress and determine our lives. The play *Hamlet* is shown by Stoppard to be exactly such an enormously potent, cultural token, forcing compliance with its ideological hegemony. At many points in the play Rosencrantz and Guildenstern try to act spontaneously, try to escape from the determining pressures of the *Hamlet*-play. They attempt to intervene, to change things, to acquire some control over the process they are caught in. But their actions are never free. At one point one of them shouts into the wings, "I forbid anyone to enter!". Immediately the entire Danish court sweeps onto the stage. Whenever they try to do something spontaneous, they find that it fits into the predetermined pattern of the *Hamlet*-play. "If we just began to suspect", Guildenstern ominously suggests, "that our spontaneity was part of their order, we'd be finished". As indeed, of course, they are.

Rosencrantz and Guildenstern are Dead is not necessarily then, an absurdist drama, for the force which determines and shapes the lives of the characters is not some mysterious, alien power, never seen and never understood; it is nothing more than a play, but the most celebrated play of our most famous national playwright. Whatever power that play, as a cultural token, may possess, it cannot be regarded as invincible or impervious to change.

—Graham Holderness

ROSMERSHOLM
by Henrik Ibsen

First Publication: Copenhagen, 1886.
First Production: Norske Theatre, Bergen, Norway, 17 January 1887.

Translations

Rosmersholm, translated by Charles Archer, in *Ibsen's Prose Dramas, 5*, edited by William Archer, London, 1891; revised version, in *Collected Works, 9*, London, 1907.
Rosmersholm, in *The Pretenders; Pillars of Society; Rosmersholm*, translated by R. Farquharson Sharp, London, 1913.
Rosmersholm, in *Ibsen: Six Plays*, translated by Eva Le Gallienne, New York, 1957.
Rosmersholm, in *"The Master Builder" and Other Plays*, translated by Una Ellis-Fermor, Harmondsworth, 1958.
Rosmersholm, in *The Oxford Ibsen, 6*, edited and translated by James Walter McFarlane, London, 1960.
Rosmersholm, translated by Michael Meyer, London, 1966; corrected version in *Ibsen: Plays, 3*, London, 1980.

Criticism
(For general works on the author, see *Playwrights* volume)

Books:
Ingjald Nissen, *Vildanden; Rosmersholm; Hedda Gabler*, Oslo, 1973 [revision of part of his *Sjelige kriser i menneskets liv*, 1931].

Articles:
N. Willey, "Ibsen's Mollefoss", in *Scandinavian Studies*, 18, 1944.
Cleanth Brooks and Robert B. Heilman, "*Rosmersholm*", in their *Understanding Drama*, New York, 1945.
K. Reichert, "Tragedy of Idealism: Henrik Ibsen", in *Tragic Themes in Western Literature*, edited by Cleanth Brooks, New Haven, Connecticut and London, 1955.
A. Gustafson, "Some Notes on Theme, Character and Symbol in *Rosmersholm*", in *Carleton Drama Review*, 1, 1955–56.

L. Fraiberg, "Freud's Writings on Art", in *Literature and Psychology*, 6, 1956.
J.W. McFarlane, "A Note on Ibsen's Draft Mss. to *Vildanden* and *Rosmersholm*", in *Modern Language Review*, 54, 1959.
M. Brunsdale, "*Rosmersholm*: A Study in Duality", in *Discourse*, 6, 1963.
John D. Hurrell, "*Rosmersholm*: The Existential Drama and the Dilemma of Modern Tragedy", in *Educational Theatre Journal*, 15, 1963.
Robert Raphael, "Illusion and the Self in *The Wild Duck*, *Rosmersholm*, and *The Lady From the Sea*", in *Scandinavian Studies*, 35, 1963.
Thomas F. van Laan, "Art and Structure in *Rosmersholm*", in *Modern Drama*, 6, 1963.
Horst Frenz, "Eugene O'Neill's *Desire Under the Elms* and Henrik Ibsen's *Rosmersholm*", in *Jahrbuch für Amerikastudien*, 9, 1964.
J. Northam, "Dividing Worlds: Shakespeare's *Tempest* and Ibsen's *Rosmersholm*", in *Kristiansand Museum Pamphlets*, 2, 1965.
Brian Johnston, "The Dialectic of *Rosmersholm*", in *Drama Survey*, 6, 1967.
Ensaf Thune, "Tragedy and Myth in *Rosmersholm*", in *Scandinavian Studies*, 40, 1968.
John R. Northam, "A Note on the Language of *Rosmersholm*", in *Ibsen-Årbok*, 1968–69.
Kari Sylngstad, "Skyld, psyke og skjebne: En analyse av fortidsperspektivet i *Rosmersholm*", in *Ibsen-Årbok*, 1968–69.
Jon R. Farris, "The Evolution of the Dramatic Functions of the Secondary Characters in *Rosmersholm*", in *Educational Theatre Journal*, 21, 1969.
Sigmund Freud, "Those Wrecked by Success", in *The Great Playwrights: Twenty Five Plays With Commentaries by Critics and Scholars*, edited by Eric Bentley, New York, 1970.
Marvin Carlson, "Patterns of Structure and Character in Ibsen's *Rosmersholm*", in *Modern Drama*, 17, 1974.
Hohn S. Chamberlain, "Tragic Heroism in *Rosmersholm*", in *Modern Drama*, 17, 1974.
Errol Durbach, "Temptation to Err: The Denouement of *Rosmersholm*", in *Educational Theatre Journal*, 29, 1977.
Anni Carlsson, "*Rosmersholm*: Ein Beitrag zur Psychologie des Verbrechens Ibsens 'Schuld und Sühne'", in *Deutsche Vierteljahrsschrift für Literaturwissenschaft und Geistesgeschichte*, 53, 1979.
Sigmund Freud, "Henrik Ibsens *Rosmersholm*", translated by Bjørn Braaten, *Vinduet*, vol.36 no.1, 1982.
Frantisek Deák, "Ibsen's *Rosmersholm* at the Théâtre de l'Oeuvre", in *Drama Review*, vol.28 no.1, 1984.
Carl F. Engelstad, "*Rosmersholm*: Et Forvekslingsdrama om skyfølelse", in *Skriften mellom linjene: Sju bidrag om psykoanalyse og litteratur*, edited by Irene Engelstad, Oslo, 1985.
Errol Durbach, "*Antony and Cleopatra* and *Rosmersholm*: 'Third Empire' Love Tragedies", in *Comparative Drama*, 20, 1986.

*   *   *

This is the last of Ibsen's plays on a political theme. Johannes Rosmer, encouraged by Rebekka West (who was brought into the household by his late wife, Beata) has given up his religious orders and his belief in God, as well as his political conservatism, but retains a sense of vocation, a liberal idealism. On announcing his changed beliefs, he finds himself attacked by his old friends and yet something of an embarrassment to the radicals. The attacks focus on his relationship with Rebekka, formerly accepted as "innocent" while he was believed to be a man of God, and on the motives which led Beata to drown herself in the mill-race. Using his now-familiar device of the intimate conversation which moves forward the action by exploring the past, Ibsen shows Rosmer losing all certainty as Rebekka confesses to him and his brother-in-law, Kroll, the part she has played in freeing him from a nightmare marriage at the same time as she nurtured his new, progressive ideas. Hoping that she has lifted the burden of guilt from him, she prepares to leave Rosmersholm. Late at night, Rosmer's further questioning leads her to explain how his values have influenced her: how she passed from having a mere manipulative intention to having an equally-concealed sexual passion for him, then gradually into the calm of a deep, selfless love which has ended by breaking her own will to power. Their final reconciliation takes the form of a spiritual marriage and expiatory death in the mill-race. This is the playwright's symbolic answer to the philosophical question he has pursued through the play: whether human nature, without hope of divine intervention, is capable of the moral improvement necessary to sustain a democracy for the good of the people.

The house itself (Rosmersholm) has a prevailing character which sums up the emotionally repressed, high minded, Christian tradition that Rebekka, even in the flowers she has introduced, opposes with a robust, free-thinking happiness. The family has produced, alternately, priests and soldiers, the aristocracy of the district. So the expectation to lead or guide others is laid upon Rosmer. Yet he is no heroic figure, but timid, indecisive; and the vagueness and impracticality of his political programme—that he should go from house to house ennobling souls—recalls Gregers Werle presenting the claims of the ideal in *The Wild Duck*. Kroll's low opinion of his judgement of men and affairs goes unopposed by Rebekka. Rosmer is guilt-ridden, like the culture he represents, but does not face up to his past actions and attitudes which might be rational causes of guilt: his treatment of Peter Mortensgaard, and the destructive force that let loose on society; his horrified rejection of Beata's sexual passion.

For the most part, Ibsen undermines his characters through small details and casual remarks by others, but in this play he also employs a major structural feature to the same end. Act I and Act IV have their steady advance cut across by an interruption apparently inessential to the plot, a diversion which calls for a virtuoso performance in a Dickensian-style satirically comic role. Ulrik Brendel, whose arrival is unanticipated each time, fits into the naturalistic scheme of the play. He is Rosmer's old tutor, a radical driven away by his martinet employer and since gone to the dogs; but the old tramp, with his inflated rhetoric and intellectual pretensions, announcing his plan of public lectures, is essentially a parody of Rosmer. Whether Rosmer perceives this or not, Brendel, in Act I, gives him time to reach his own decision to declare himself and enter the political fray. In Act IV, Brendel projects himself as the bankrupt idealist, a hollow man who found he had nothing to say. The strangeness of this second appearance is deepened by the fact that neither Rosmer nor Rebekka makes any comment when he leaves—almost as though he had not been there. Yet his sinister metaphors and the notion of sacrificial disfigurement he leaves behind not only point toward the ending of the play in death; they re-emerge in the morbid fascination, like some interior devil, that drives Rosmer to ask for the proof that will restore his faith: that Rebekka will gladly go the way that Beata went.

Much of the dispute over the interpretation of this play has arisen from the tension Ibsen has set up between satire and idealist (or romantic) tragedy. (At one extreme it has been judged utterly bleak, ending in despair and the mutual destruction of the two main characters.) Although Rebekka is a strong character, her deviousness is as evident in the course of the play as in the history of plotting and contrivance she confesses; and her readiness to lie denies any priveleged certainty to the reader or audience, and to Rosmer within the play. Undoubtedly, Ibsen has presented his two protagonists as, in Nietzsche's phrase, "human, all-too-human". About Rebekka, indeed, there are imputations of illegitimacy, incest (more explicit in the first version), the lure of a *femme fatale*, as well as the crime of psychological murder to which she admits. Uncertainty can work both ways, however, and what is shown in Act III is an impulse of redemptive love, taking *all* the blame upon itself. The character who speaks the final word upon the *liebestod* at the end is the housekeeper, Mrs. Helseth, reacting to what she sees through the window: a white apparition in the darkness; an embrace she finds "sinful"; then the fall into the mill-race, interpreted as the working of a primitive vengeance—"the dead woman has taken them". Although she has contributed her share of humanising warmth and sympathy to Rosmersholm, Mrs. Helseth is too simple and superstitious for her verdict to carry absolute weight. What she sees as vengeance has been directly presented as voluntary atonement, the humanists' judgment executed upon themselves, an alternative view. She misses, too, the culmination of the play's second theme, of equality between the sexes in this spiritual marriage.

Mrs. Helseth's belief in superstition gave the naturalistic dramatist his warrant for introducing a range of images drawn from folklore and legend into the dialogue, starting in the first moments with the white horses which supplied the title for his first draft of the play. The general effect of such images is to endow his prose with a mysterious poetry, leading the imagination on, enabling the play to range beyond the world of Kroll into a realm of transcendental values. Wagner's practice of drawing on folk legend in his attempt to nurture the soul of the German people is comparable.

—Margery Morgan

THE ROUND DANCE. See **LA RONDE.**

THE ROVER; or, The Banished Cavaliers, Parts One and Two by Aphra Behn

Part One
First Publication: London, 1677.
First Production: Duke's House, Dorset Gardens, London, 24 March 1677.

Part Two
First Publication: London, 1681.
First Production: Duke's Theatre, Dorset Gardens, London, c. 1680–81.

Editions
The Rover, in *The Works of Aphra Behn* (6 vols.), edited by Montague Summers, London, 1915.

The Rover, edited by Frederick M. Link, Lincoln, Nebraska, 1967 (Regents Restoration Drama Series).
The Rover, Part One, in *Aphra Behn: Five Plays*, edited by Maureen Duffy, London, 1990.

Criticism

(For general works on the author, see *Playwrights* volume)

Articles:

Herschel Baker, "Mrs. Behn Forgets", in *University of Texas Studies in English*, 22, 1942.
Edward A. Langhans, "Three Early Eighteenth Century Promptbooks", in *Theatre Notebook*, 20, 1966.
Joseph F. Musser Jr., "'Imposing Nought but Constancy in Love': Aphra Behn Shares *The Rover*", in *Restoration*, 3, 1979.
Jones DeRitter, "The Gipsey, The Rover, and The Wanderer: Aphra Behn's Revision of Thomas Killigrew", in *Restoration*, 10, 1986.
Elin Diamond, "Gestus and Signature in Aphra Behn's *The Rover*", in *English Literary History*, 56, 1989.

*   *   *

The source for Aphra Behn's play *The Rover* is Thomas Killigrew's lengthy closet drama *Thomaso; or, The Wanderer*, written in the 1650's and published in 1664. *Thomaso* needed extensive cutting and recasting to fit it for the stage, and though Behn used many of its incidents and some of its dialogue, the overall shape and controlling tone of the play are her own. She uses the conventions of Spanish intrigue comedy with great skill, producing a tightly patterned, fastmoving plot, with contrasting pairs of lovers, multiple tricks, disguises and mistakes, and conflicts between love and honour, often leading to duels. First played in March 1677, *The Rover* soon became one of Behn's most popular works. It was very frequently performed up to the 1740's, and revived in the 1750's, but afterwards disappeared from the stage until very recently, when it has become one of the few Behn plays (others include *The Feigned Courtesans* and *The Lucky Chance*) to be given a 20th-century performance.

It must have originally delighted royalist taste as a nostalgic glimpse of an idealised, cavalier past. Set in Naples during the Interregnum, it follows the adventures of a group of "Banished Cavaliers" whose loyalty to their king has robbed them not only of estate and fortune but also the responsibilities that go with them. For the moment it is by thoroughly enjoying themselves that they can best prove their allegiance to the future Charles II, now, like Behn's hero, "a rover of fortune", though still "a prince aboard his little wooden world". Its appeal was not just topical. It is set at Carnival time in Naples, and many of comedy's enduring, carnivalesque delights are brought into play. Hellena's father is away, and with his authority temporarily withdrawn she and her companions only have to contend with a rather easily-fooled brother in order to join the festivities and find lovers. Hierarchies are reversed and a fool gets his come-uppance when the "jilting wench", Lucetta, entices the silly, country gentleman Blunt into her chamber, drops him through a trapdoor into a sewer, and robs him. The old Spanish general is dead, and his mistress Angellica Bianca has the money and freedom to choose a lover for herself.

The 1670's saw the flourishing of the most licentious of Restoration comedies. Wycherley's *The Country-Wife* (1675) and Etherege's *The Man of Mode* (1676) both celebrate, if somewhat ambivalently, the rake-hero: successful seducer, wit, and controller of plots. Behn is partly using this pattern with her rover, Willmore, who first wins his way into Angellica's bed—she even gives him money instead of charging her usual, exorbitant fee—then discards her in favour of Hellena, a rich and marriageable virgin. Willmore, however, is no clever schemer, being much more likely to ruin his friend Belvile's plots by mistake than to think up any of his own. The women play a more active role than he does, and many of the scenes focus on their point of view. Witty Hellena and her sober sister, Florinda, are both plotting to avoid unwanted destinies planned by men: in Florinda's case, a forced marriage to Antonio, in Hellena's, imprisonment in a nunnery. Angellica is treated with a sympathy most unusual in Restoration comedy's handling of a rejected mistress: her choice of love and desire over financial gain is taken seriously, as is her disappointment. Women's vulnerability in love is shown differently in Florinda, whose attempts to find her true love, Belvile, nearly end in disaster. She is mistaken for a whore and is in danger of being raped by Blunt and even by the supposedly likeable Frederick and Willmore; briefly, the play shows a dark underside to its holiday humour.

The heroine Hellena, however, is determined not to share her sister's vulnerability. Hellena is Behn's creation: the character called Helena in Killigrew's play is an old blind prostitute humiliated by the other characters. Behn takes the name and creates a new character. Killigrew's hero marries a virginal heroine, a woman who is all virtue, helplessness and submission. In *The Rover* her role is split between Hellena and Florinda. Florinda gets all the victimization, Hellena gets the hero. The latter is active, and disguises herself as a gipsy and then as a boy to get what she wants. Her skill with words gives her the power to evade her brother's control and negotiate an acceptable relationship with her lover. She is an inventive interpreter of others' words: when Florinda dutifully tells Don Pedro "I shall strive to do as shall become your sister", Hellena glosses this as "that is, to be as resolved your way as he is his"— a radical re-reading of the brother-sister relationship, and an assertion of the importance of woman's will which is central to the play. Hellena represents an attempt on Behn's part to create a female counterpart to the rake, equally careless and free. She names herself "Hellena the Inconstant", and Willmore, marrying her, promises not to bother about her honour; at one point she is even addressed by his epithet of "rover".

However, we are kept aware that Hellena's victory is at Angellica's expense, and Behn was perhaps dissatisfied with it for that reason. In her sequel *The Second Part of The Rover* (1681), she coolly dispatches Hellena to an early grave, and then re-runs the contest between a courtesan and a rich virgin for possession of Willmore. This time the courtesan, La Nuche, wins.

—Jane Spencer

———————

THE ROYAL HUNT OF THE SUN
by Peter Shaffer

First Publication: London, 1964.
First Production: Chichester Festival Theatre (National Theatre Company), 7 July 1964.

Criticism

(For general works on the author, see *Playwrights* volume)

Articles:

Jules Glenn, "Twins in Disguise: A Psychoanalytic Essay on *Sleuth* and *Royal Hunt of the Sun*", in *Psychoanalytic Quarterly*, vol.43 no. 2, 1974.

James R. Stacy, "The Sun and the Horse: Peter Shaffer's Search for Worship", in *Educational Theatre Journal*, 28, 1976.

Joan F. Dean, "Peter Shaffer's Recurrent Character Type", in *Modern Drama*, 21, 1978.

Barbara Lounsberry, " 'God-Hunting': The Chaos of Worship in Peter Shaffer's *Equus* and *Royal Hunt of the Sun*", in *Modern Drama*, 21, 1978.

Gene A. Plunka, "Roles, Rites, and Rituals: Peter Shaffer's *The Royal Hunt of the Sun*", in *Ball State University Forum*, vol.27 no.3, 1986.

*   *   *

The Royal Hunt of the Sun (1964) is Peter Shaffer's first and most overt drama based on his favourite theme of man's seeking for a god to lend order to the universe. Shaffer ingeniously frames his search motif within historical accounts of the pillage, then dismemberment of the Inca civilisation in Peru by the Spanish conquistadors early in the 1500's. Pizarro becomes the play's god-seeker in Act I, "The Hunt", when, during his drive to seize the Incas' gold in the New World, he hears of the supernatural powers held by their sun-god, Athahuallpa. The first half of the drama shows the Spaniards being recruited in their homeland for the unknown adventure in the Americas. Gold is their incentive for making the highly dangerous expedition, though the Church, wholly attuned to political needs, declares the purpose is to convert New World heathens to Christ. Once in South America, the conquistadors undertake impossible treks across snow-peaked mountains (in Scene Eight, "The Mime of the Great Ascent"), driven on by thirst for gold. They finally encounter Atahuallpa and his 3,000 unarmed men, promptly seizing the king for ransom while slaying all the others. Act II, "The Kill", concerns Pizarro's gradual conversion to Atahuallpa's transcendental world system—that is, a religion based on nature. As the Incas collect gold to ransom their god-monarch, Pizarro becomes Atahuallpa's most ardent defender, because the king offers godhead. In Pizarro's words, "I've gone god-hunting and caught one. A being who can renew his life over and over . . . .". Atahuallpa and Pizarro end up "bond brothers" who believe Inca metaphysics allow for transcending mankind's mortality. The drama concludes with Atahuallpa, although confident that he cannot be killed, none the less garotted by the conquistadors who act against Pizarro's injunctions. Atahuallpa does not arise from the dead as he promised, and an angered Pizarro is left to lament bitterly over the godless universe.

Shaffer follows the overall historical contour in his plot. Pizarro in fact did lead a Spanish militia into Peru to gain gold by any means necessary; Atahuallpa was captured by the invaders, held for ransom, and killed when the gold ransom was paid. But the entire god-search element was Shaffer's own interpolation. *Royal Hunt* emerges as a historical tale with several levels of meanings superimposed on top of it. Shaffer peoples his play with historical participants in the Peruvian events, including Pizarro, Atahuallpa, Hernando de Soto, and Friars Vincente de Valverde and Marcos de Nizza. Moreover, he sets his scenes in historically accurate Peruvian sites. By building on W. H. Prescott's classic account (*The History of the Conquest of Peru*), Shaffer had amazing events at hand with which to work: Pizarro with his 167 Spanish warriors was able, through stealth and guile, to vanquish 6,000,000 natives ruled

The Royal Hunt of the Sun: National Theatre, London, 1964

by Atahuallpa. On another level, Shaffer presents the happenings not simply as a battle of soldiers against one another but of entire civilisations in collision—the jaded, cynical, European culture versus the ancient and innocent, native world. On yet another, fictional level, the author transforms the historical Pizarro into a spiritual pilgrim. The "hunt" of the play's title mirrors both the search for gold and Pizarro's seeking a benevolent deity to offer order to the universe. In both cases, Atahuallpa serves as the goal: the conquistadors obtain their gold as ransom for Atahuallpa, and for a brief time the sunking provides Pizarro with a promise of godhead on earth.

Even a brief scan of *Royal Hunt* suggests its complex structure which involves several layers of meaning flowing into one other; the actions furthermore require nearly three dozen performers, adding to the difficult logistics of performance. Peter Shaffer was ready, however, to implement a variety of daring stage techniques to make his moral fable "work". *Royal Hunt* incorporates methods derived in part from epic theatre and total theatre. Brecht's notions of displaying plot events episodically was intended to drive a wedge between the illusion of the story and the reality of the audience. Adding to the disruption of illusion was Brecht's conception of a stage narrator who addresses playgoers directly. Shaffer creates such a character in Martin. Seen in the present, he is a grizzled, middle-aged soldier looking back on earlier times when he was Pizarro's protégé and aide; for episodes from the past, another, much younger version of the Martin character plays an active role in the story proper. Antonin Artaud's ideas of "total theatre" enter Shaffer's drama as well. Again anti-illusionary, Artaud emphasizes the necessity of appealing to all the senses of the audience. To reach the ritualistic basis of human behaviour—another facet of Artaud's writings—Shaffer combines eerie masks, worn by the Incas, with suggestive, symbolic, sounds and images. *Royal Hunt* is therefore replete with strange bird calls, Indian chants, bells, and nature sounds. Highly stylised gestures and body movements characterise the Indians in the play, while the Spaniards' cross-mountain treks are depicted in stylised mime. The massacre scene concluding the first act remains one of the most thrilling—and chilling—in theatre history. In it, the Spanish forces are choreographed in slow motion, moving around the stage, slashing at the unarmed natives. The scene ends with a giant red cloth billowing across the play area, denoting the sea of blood from the mass killing.

Finally, to consolidate the varying theatrical methods used, Shaffer draws on his exceptional command of language. Audiences are mesmerised by memorable lines such as Pizarro's upon discovering Atahuallpa has actually died. The Spaniard's last desperate hope for a meaningful world is destroyed, and his cry of agony against the dead chief speaks for anyone living in bewildering times: "Cheat! You've cheated me! Cheat!. . .God's just a name on your nail; and naming begins cries and cruelties. But to live without hope of after, and make whatever God there is, oh, that's some immortal business surely!".

—C.J. Gianakaris

———————

RUDENS.   See THE ROPE.

———————

THE RULING CLASS
by Peter Barnes

First Publication: London and New York, 1969.
First Production: Playhouse, Nottingham, 6 November 1968.

*   *   *

The Ruling Class is a large-cast, epic, state-of-England play, resembling others of the 1960's and early 1970's, such as *The Workhouse Donkey*, by John Arden, and *Brassneck*, by Howard Brenton and David Hare. It is in 27 scenes, with prologue and epilogue, and opens with the 13th Earl of Gurney delivering a speech praising England, parodying Shakespeare's *Richard II*: "this teeming womb of privilege, this feudal state. . .this ancient land of ritual", followed by the National Anthem. An abrupt switch follows the first of many: the Earl returns home to Tucker, his faithful old butler, and speaks, with the rich language typical of Barnes' work, of passing the death sentence (for he is a judge, too): "If you've once put on the black cap, everything else tastes like wax fruit". Then the Earl disconcertingly puts on a cocked hat and ballet skirt, climbs a step-ladder, puts his head in a silk noose, swings and accidentally kicks over the steps and hangs himself.

The Earl's funeral is conducted by a "magnificently dressed" Bishop, who then disrobes on stage and changes into "a small, bald-headed, asthmatic old man". The will is read and Tucker is left £20,000. He breaks into the Edwardian music hall song: "I'm Gilbert the Filbert the Knut with a 'K'"; Barnes continues using songs for contrast and surprise.

The heir, the 14th Earl, appears, dressed as a Franciscan monk. He believes he is God, explaining this with the brilliant line: "When I pray to Him I find I'm talking to myself", adding "What a beautiful day I've made". Shocked, his family decide to have him marry, and—as soon as he has fathered an heir—he is declared insane. He is convinced he is already married to the Lady of the Camelias, so Grace, his uncle's mistress, is dressed as Marguerite Gautier and makes a stunning entrance singing *La traviata*. The Earl arrives for his wedding night on a unicycle. In the continuing series of theatrical coups, a psychiatrist brings together the Earl and a Scotsman who also believes he is God, and the shock to the Earl is expressed by an eight-foot beast "dressed incongruously in high Victorian fashion", wrestling with him.

In the second half of the play the Earl changes to a stern, authoritarian, judgemental man, thinking he lives in the Victorian era. The Master of Lunacy, brought in to certify him, will not, for they are both Old Etonians. The Earl comes to believe that he is Jack the Ripper—an impression reinforced by the setting of "*a dark huddle of filthy houses. . .an impression of dark alleys*". He murders his sister-in-law and lets Tucker be arrested for it, and Tucker reveals that secretly he is a Communist. The Earl, now seen as "normal" by his circle, goes to the House of Lords, represented very strikingly on stage by "*tiers of mouldering dummies. . .covered with cobwebs*". Here he speaks as the Old Testament God, in favour of stern punishment, and finally he is seen stabbing the loving Grace.

Barnes wrote in a programme note, never reprinted:

In a playhouse. . .we can use vivid colours, studied effects, slapstick, slang, songs, dances and blasphemies to conjure up men, monsters and ghosts. We can also raid mystery plays, puppet shows, Shakespeare (damn his eyes!) and demagogy to create a comic theatre of conflicting moods and opposites where everything is simultaneously tragic and ridiculous. This comedy is about the withdrawal of light from the world, the obstinacy of defeat, and asks again the question, is God a 10,000 foot tall, pink jelly bean?

The two acts of the play contrast the ideas of a loving God and a vengeful one and show that society is ruled by the latter concept. Along the way are satirical swipes at many aspects of British life: mockery of bishops, members of parliament, the House of Lords, the aristocracy, psychiatrists. Some of this is high-spirited, yet Barnes insists that this is a serious commentary on what was wrong with Britain: "I cared about the abuses and vices I was attacking. So much so that I was full of hate for them. . .I was taking the ruling classes as a symbol of what I was really attacking, which was something deeper than just blood sports".

This long play has a Jacobean richness (Barnes later adapted several of Ben Jonson's plays for stage and radio) in language, incident, and variety. It is also varied, surprising, and hugely theatrical. *The Ruling Class* anticipates aspects of the political debate of the 1980's: what were "Victorian values", and were they a good thing?

—Malcolm Page

———————

R.U.R. (RUR)
by Karel Čapek

First Publication: Prague, 1920.
First Production: Narodni divadlo [National Theatre],
        Prague, 25 January 1921.

Translations
R.U.R., translated by Paul Selver, Oxford, 1923.

Criticism
(For general works on the author, see *Playwrights* volume)

Articles:
R. Pletnev, "The Concept of Time and Space in *R.U.R.* by
    Karel Čapek", in *Études slaves et est-européenes*, 12, 1967.
Mary A. Fox, "Lost in Translation: The Ending of Čapek's
    R.U.R.", in *ICarbS* (University of Southern Illinois), 4,
    1981.
Barbara Bengels, " 'Read History': Dehumanization in Karel
    Čapek's *R.U.R.*", in *The Mechanical God: Machines in
    Science Fiction*, edited by Thomas P. Dunn and Richard D.
    Erlich, Westport, Connecticut, 1982.
James D. Naughton, "Futurology and Robots: Karel Čapek's
    R.U.R.", in *Renaissance and Modern Studies*, 28, 1984.

Sharon D. King, "A Better Eve: Women and Robots in
    Čapek's *R.U.R.* and Pavlovsky's *El robot*", in *Women in
    Theatre*, edited by James Redmond, Cambridge, 1989
    (Themes in Drama Series).

*   *   *

The dystopian play *R.U.R.* has three acts and a prelude. Ten
years pass between the action of the prelude and that of the
play itself. The setting is an island, the site of a factory which
makes and exports humanoids which can be manufactured by
the thousand to relieve men of the need to work. During the
prelude, the general manager of the factory, Harry Domin,
refers back to 1920 as the date when "old Rossum", as a young
apprentice, sets out on his lifetime's work. He is outlining the
history of robot manufacture to Helena Glory—campaigner
for the emancipation of robots. Domin explains and demonstrates the nature of their physiology. He and his team of
managers fall in love with Helena; she marries Domin, and the
first two acts take place in her drawing-room. When the first act
opens, Domin and his managers are preparing for the tenth
anniversary of Helena's arrival, and trying to keep from her
the fact that all is not well; no news has come from the outside
world for over a month. It becomes clear that the robots have
already conquered the rest of the world. Domin and his

R.U.R: Set design by Bedrich Feuerstein for first production, National Theatre, Prague, 1921

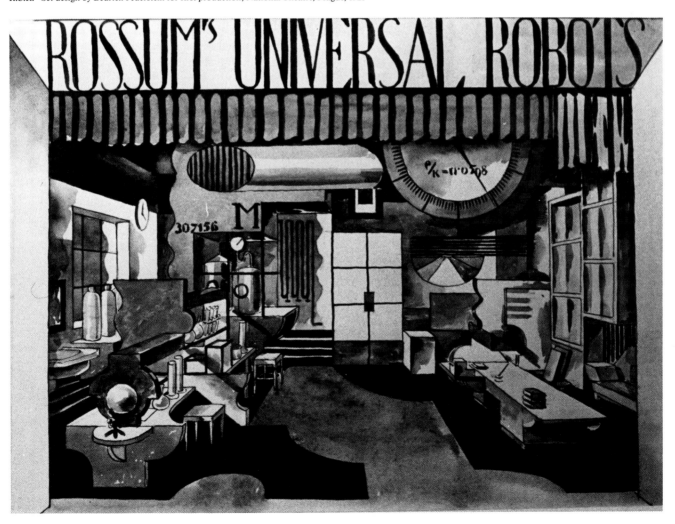

managers hold the one treasure which gives them dominance over the robots; the formula for their manufacture. Helena reveals that she has burnt it.

When the second act opens, the managers' quarters are under siege. The men wonder how the robots have acquired the human characteristics which enable them to revolt; it turns out that Helena once prevailed on Dr. Gall to add the ingredient necessary to create "souls" to the manufacturing formula. One by one the managers are killed, and their quarters are occupied by the robots. In the third act, which takes place in a laboratory, only the construction manager, Dr. Alquist, survives, because he is the only man who still works with his hands. The robots want him to rediscover the formula, but he is incapable of that. The human beings are dead, and the robots are unable to propagate. It seems that life on earth will perish; until Alquist makes the discovery that two of the robots, significantly named Primus and Helena (after Miss Glory), have fallen in love.

R.U.R. was the first Czech play to achieve international popularity; it was performed all over the world, from Paris to Tokyo. The noun "robot", coined by Karel's brother Josef from a word for toil and drudgery, entered the international vocabulary. The play's popularity stemmed from its topicality: the potential of 20th-century technology, and technological utopianism. It owed something to the influence of Georg Kaiser's *Gas* plays, with their images of an ever-accelerating technology which takes civilization with it to destruction. There were, however, similar concerns in the works of contemporary Czech writers. Feuerstein's original designs were markedly Expressionist, although muted in the National Theatre's realisation.

The characters are not so much individuals as types, who embody the preoccupations of the society of that time. Harry Domin (his name means "Lord") is characterised as the practical, energetic man, not an intellectual nor even as capable as his colleagues, but able to get what he wants. Helena Glory has a privileged background and is autocratic in her actions. She is, however, idealistic in her ambitions for the robots. The Anglo-Saxon/Latin combination of both their names has an exotic flavour. Consul Busman, the commercial director, is a Jew, able at any time to reel off figures of expenditure and production. When the robots surround the factory, his concern is to balance the accounts, and he proposes to use the manufacturing formula to make a deal with the robots. Dr. Gall, who has the scientific skills to make changes in the physiology of the robots, and the understanding to realise what is happening in the outside world, acts under the orders, first, of Domin and, later, of Helena. He is the sensitive scientist. Together with Fabry, Hallemeier, and Alquist (whose names suggest Hungary, Germany, and Scandinavia) they are representatives of contemporary Europe.

Čapek wrote about *R.U.R.*:

I confess that what led me to the writing of this play was its action; and especially the two acts where a handful of people are awaiting their doom with heads held high. The idea of man's heroism is a favourite of mine, and that was what drew me towards this material. . .which isn't about robots at all, but about people. Yes, I desperately wanted the audience to feel, at the moment the robots launch their attack, that something immeasurably great and priceless is at stake; that is, humanity—man—we ourselves.

—Barbara Day

RUY BLAS
by Victor Hugo

First Publication: Leipzig, 1838 (with variants and misprints); in *Oeuvres complètes*, 7, Paris, 1838.
First Production: Théâtre de la Renaissance, Paris, 8 November 1838.

Editions
Ruy Blas, edited by H.L. Hutton, Oxford, 1919.
Ruy Blas, edited by H.F. Collins, New York, 1966.
Ruy Blas, edited by Anne Ubersfeld (2 vols., with *Documents*), Paris, 1971–72.
Ruy Blas, in *Victor Hugo: Théâtre, 2*, edited by R. Pouilliart, Paris, 1979.

Translations
Ruy Blas, translated by W.D.S. Alexander, London, 1890.
Ruy Blas, in *The Dramas of Victor Hugo* (4 vols.), translated by I.G. Burnham, 1895.
Ruy Blas, translated by N. Crosland, in *Great Plays (French and German)*, edited by B. Mathews, New York, 1901.
Ruy Blas, translated by Brian Hooker, New York, 1931.

Criticism
(For general works on the author, see *Playwrights* volume)

Articles:
Anne Ubersfeld, "*Ruy Blas*: Genèse et structure", in *Revue d'histoire littéraire de la France*, 70, 1970.
Constance L. Lyons, "Tragedy and the Grotesque: Act IV of *Ruy Blas*", in *French Review* (special issue 4), 45, 1972.
Ruy Blas ou le miroir aux alouettes", in *Studi francesi*, January–April, 1981.
Jean-Michel Charles Lanskin, "*Ruy Blas*: Héros romantique ou amant courteois?", in *Studies in Medievalism*, vol.2 no.2, 1983.
Jean-Marie Thomasseau, "Le Jeu des écritures dans *Ruy Blas*", in *Revue des lettres modernes*, 693–697, 1984.
Jean-Marie Thomasseau, "Pour une Analyse du para-texte théâtral: Quelques éléments du para-texte hugolien", in *Littérature*, 33, 1984.

*   *   *

The action occurs in Madrid in the 1690's, during the reign of the ineffective Carlos II, when government corruption was causing Spain's rapid decline from its Golden-Age brilliance. Although the plot is fictional, Hugo was proud of the authenticity of his historical background and details of local color. The five-act Romantic drama mingles romance, intrigue, political commentary, and comedy, and contains some of Hugo's finest dramatic poetry. Ruy Blas, a commoner with high ideals and a strong sense of honor, burns with selfless love for the lonely, German-born Queen, who is ignored by her husband and hemmed in by the restrictive court etiquette. Suffering because it is his lot to serve as a valet, Ruy Blas describes himself as "an earthworm in love with a star". His master, Don Salluste, seizes an opportunity to use Ruy Blas as an unwitting tool of revenge against the Queen, who has ordered Don Salluste's banishment to punish his refusal to marry the lady-in-waiting he seduced. Don Salluste charges Ruy Blas to assume the identity of Don César, whom Don Salluste has secretly kidnapped and deported. As Don César, Ruy Blas rises to prominence at court through the Queen's recognition of his integrity and devotion. His famous speech,

Ruy Blas: Sarah Bernhardt as the Queen, c. 1870

"O ministres intègres!", in Act 3, excoriates the highly-placed officials who enrich themselves at their country's expense. Ruy Blas's moment of sublime happiness—the Queen's declaration of her love for him—is followed instantly by a reversal of fortune: the return of Don Salluste in disguise. While Don Salluste is drawing the net around his victims, a comic interlude centers upon the return of the real Don César, a scapegrace adventurer, who stumbles into Don Salluste's preparations, but ironically helps to move events toward the tragic denouement. The Queen is tricked into leaving the palace to meet Ruy Blas alone in a room, at night. Having failed to avert her being placed in this compromising situation, Ruy Blas reveals his true identity, kills Don Salluste, and drinks poison. He dies, happy in the knowledge that the Queen loves him even as a valet.

In his preface to the play, Hugo described the several audience appeals he was trying to build into *Ruy Blas*. According to Hugo, the general public wants action to provoke sensations—for them he wrote melodrama; women prefer passion to arouse the emotions—their genre is tragedy; thinkers are drawn to character studies that will give them something to reflect upon—humanity is best depicted in comedy. By combining these elements, Hugo intended *Ruy Blas* to gratify the theatregoer's eyes, heart, and mind all at once. He achieved a fusion of moods within what is generally acknowledged as his most skilful dramatic construction. In a remarkable harmony of checks and balances, the low-born Ruy Blas embodies the nobility of the tragic hero while the nobly-born Don César is a delightful ruffian; Ruy Blas brings honor to Don César's name, although the source of his greatness of heart is an unthinkably audacious forbidden love; the same setting provides for both Don César's comic entrance down the chimney and Ruy Blas's tragic end. Hugo's treatment of the subject occurs on three levels simultaneously: in philosophical terms, the play is about common man striving to better himself; in human terms, a man loves a woman; in dramatic terms, a lackey loves a queen.

The original production, starring Frédérick Lemaître in the title role, won enthusiastic audiences, although the critical response was decidedly mixed. A parody entitled *Ruy Blas* appeared in 1838, followed by Dumanoir and Dennery's long-popular sequel, *Don César de Bazan*, in 1844. *Ruy Blas* was banned for its populist sentiments during the Second Empire, but the Odéon put together a production that was performed in Brussels in 1867. Sarah Bernhardt played the Queen in the successful 1872 Paris revival at the Odéon. A centenary production at the Comédie-Française pushed the interpretation toward comic opera, but the 1954 version, starring Gérard Philippe, at the Théâtre National Populaire revealed anew the full beauty and power of the work.

—Felicia Hardison Londré

S

SABATO, DOMENICO E LUNEDI. See **SATURDAY, SUNDAY, MONDAY.**

LA SAGOUINE
by Antonine Maillet

First Publication: Montreal, 1971; expanded version, 1974.
First Production: As radio serial for Moncton Radio, 1969; first professional stage production, at Théâtre du Rideau Vert, Montreal, 9 October 1972.

Translations
La Sagouine, translated by Luis de Céspedes, Toronto, 1979.

Criticism
(For general works on the author, see *Playwrights* volume)

Articles:
Denis Saint-Jacques, "*La Sagouine* d'Antonine Maillet", in *Voix et images de pays: Littérature québécoise*, 8, 1974.
Antonine Maillet, "Interview d'Antonine Maillet sur *La Sagouine*", in *Canadian Drama*, 2, 1976.
Douglas Mance, "Acadjen, eh? On Translating Acadian Literature", in *Canadian Drama*, 2, 1976.
Antonine Maillet, "A Propos de *La Sagouine*: Entretien avec Jean-Michel Lacroix . . .", in *Études canadiennes*, 3, 1977.
Karolyn Waterson, "L'Envergure des revendications de *La Sagouine*", in *Atlantic Provinces Colloquium Papers*, Saint John, 1977.
Stéphane Sarkany, "Bibliologie poétique de *La Sagouine* d'Antonine Maillet", in his *Québec Canada France: Le Canada littéraire à la croisée des cultures*, Aix-en-Provence, 1985.
Phyllis Wrenn, "Le Transcodage d'une parlure en texte: *La Sagouine* et le mythe du dialecte", in *Francofonia*, 8, 1985.
Paulette Collet, "La Sagouine: Un Regard perçant et lucide, source d'espoir", in *Canadian Drama*, 13, 1987.

*   *   *

In a monodrama comprising 16 monologues, with transitions demarcated only by lighting effects, La Sagouine—an elderly Acadian woman, wife and daughter of fishermen, former prostitute, now an urban charlady—recounts her experiences in life. In the archaic, Acadian dialect she comments on her people and the injustices they have suffered since the deportation of the 1750's.

La Sagouine was the first play to bring national and international fame to its author, who is now recognized as the foremost artistic voice of Acadia (a territory formerly comprising the Maritime Provinces of Atlantic Canada). The play initially aroused interest because of its exclusive use of the Acadian dialect—archaic-sounding, but quite comprehensible to all educated francophones. But audiences soon realized that the quaint speech of the illiterate woman offered a penetrating analysis of her society and her times, in subtly nuanced, verbal portraits and anecdotes that arouse universal interest and sympathy.

72-years-old, La Sagouine (this untranslatable nickname suggests physical, but not moral uncleanliness; her proper name is not given), indomitable in spirit and irreverent in outlook, describes her life—first as a fisherman's daughter on Prince Edward Island, then as the wife of a fisherman on New Brunswick's coast, where her people have eked out a marginal existence in a harsh and demanding climate. Mother of a dozen children (only three have survived infancy), she has had to turn to prostitution to feed them and, as that option disappeared with age, to the menial, urban labour which is her present lot. Through anecdote and commentary she describes the economic and social hardship she and the Acadians have suffered, the political injustices, the hypocrisy of the church, illiteracy, ignorance, and superstition. But she also speaks poignantly of universal themes: youth and love; friendship and generosity; war, conscription, and violence; bureaucracy and the insolence of officials; disease, ageing, and death. The strength, originality, humour, and wisdom of the character are communicated directly by the monologue form, ideally suited to the author's intentions. Each 15-minute segment turns on one topic ("Youth"; "Christmas"; "The Lottery"; The Priests"; "The War"; "The Spring"; "The Risurrection" [*sic*]; "The Census"; "Death", etc.), but these divisions are not rigid, and the only close connection between them is the narrator's tone and personality. Memorable characters are portrayed, notably La Sagouine's husband, Gapi, and many of them reappear in the fascinating universe of Maillet's numerous other plays and novels.

The political dimension of this work is essential to the author's purpose: *La Sagouine* is intended to replace the eponymous heroine of Longfellow's *Evangeline*, too long a symbol of Acadia—tragic, barren, and passive. Maillet's contemporary anti-Evangeline, on the other hand, is active, sanguine, resourceful, and determined—despite age and illness—to endure. La Sagouine is not bitter or vengeful, although she appears to have every right to be: her anger and indignation are tempered by naïve humility and by her own profound knowledge of human weakness and suffering. Sincere in her simple faith, but confused and disillusioned by the Church's commendation of the poor, and by its toadying to the rich and powerful, she exerts a strong spiritual presence. Deprived of material necessities all her life, she is generous and forgiving in spirit towards those responsible for her and her people's deprivation. Old and ailing herself, she speaks with vigour and hope of the future of her tiny nation. As interpreted by the Acadian actress Viola Léger, who has become virtually inseparable from the fictive character she portrays, the performances in Canada and abroad, on radio, television, and stage have unfailingly stirred the deepest emotions.

—Leonard E. Doucette

SAINT JOAN
by George Bernard Shaw

First Publication: In German translation as *Die heilige Johanna*, in *Neue Rundschau*, June–September, 1924; English version, London, 1924.
First Production: Garrick Theatre, New York (Theatre Guild), 28 December 1923.

Criticism
(For general works on the author, see *Playwrights* volume)

Books:
Stanley Weintraub (ed.), *"Saint Joan" Fifty Years After: 1923/24–1973/74*, Baton Rouge, Louisiana, 1973.
Brian Tyson, *The Story of Shaw's "Saint Joan"*, Kingston, Ontario, 1982.
Holly Hill, *Playing Joan: Actresses on the Challenge of Shaw's Saint Joan: 26 Interviews*, New York, 1987.

Articles:
J.C. Blankenagel, "Shaw's *St. Joan* and Schiller's *Jungfrau von Orleans*", in *Journal of English and Germanic Philology*, 25, 1926.
C. Hollis, "Some Notes on Mr. Shaw's *St. Joan*", in *Dublin Review*, 182, 1928.
Frederick S. Boas, "Joan of Arc in Shakespeare, Schiller and Shaw", in *Shakespeare Quarterly*, vol.2, no.1, 1951.
E.J. West, "*St. Joan*: A Modern Classic Reconsidered", in *Quarterly Journal of Speech*, 40, 1954.
John Rosselli, "The Right Joan and the Wrong One", in *Twentieth Century*, 157, 1955.
Hans Stoppel, "Shaw and Sainthood", in *English Studies*, vol.36 no.2, 1955.
Helmut Papajewski, "Bernard Shaw's Chronicle Play *St. Joan*", in *Germanisch-Romanische Monatsschrift* (new series), 6, 1956.
John Fielden, "Shaw's *Saint Joan* as Tragedy", in *Twentieth Century Literature*, vol.3 no.2, 1957.
Clarinda Lane, "Saint Joan Through the Eyes of Saint Bernard", in *Western Speech*, vol.22 no.2, 1958.
W.W., "Shaw and Shakespeare on Saint Joan", in *Independent Shavian*, vol.2 no.1, 1963.
Irving McKee, "Shaw's *St. Joan* and the American Critics", in *Shavian*, 2, 1964.
Stanley Solomon, "*Saint Joan* as Epic Tragedy", in *Modern Drama*, vol.6 no.4, 1964.
J.L. Gribben, "Shaw's *St. Joan*: A Tragic Heroine", in *Thought*, 40, 1965.
Alok Bhalla, "An Obstinate Margin in Tragedy: Shaw's *Saint Joan*", in *Quest*, 54, 1967.

S. John Macksoud and Ross Altman, "Voices in Opposition: A Burkeian Rhetoric of *Saint Joan*", in *Quarterly Journal of Speech*, 57, 1971.
William Searle, "Shaw's St. Joan as Protestant", in *Shaw Review*, 15, 1972.
Kurt Tetzeli von Rosador, "Shaws *St. Joan* und die Historiker", in *Germanisch-Romanische Monatsschrift* (new series), 23, 1973.
John R. Dolis, "Bernard Shaw's *St. Joan*: Language is not Enough", in *Massachusetts Studies in English*, 4, 1974.
Helmut Slogsnat, "G.B. Shaw: *Saint Joan*: Ein Idealfall des Literaturunterrichts", in *Anglistik und Englischunterricht*, 9, 1979.
John A. Bertolini, "Imagining *Saint Joan*", in *SHAW*, 3, 1983.
Stephen Watt, "Shaw's *Saint Joan* and the Modern History Play", in *Comparative Drama*, 19, 1985.
Bernard F. Dukore, "[Barnes'] *Red Noses* and *Saint Joan*", in *Modern Drama*, 30, 1987.
Carl Woodring, "Ricketts and *Saint Joan*", in *Columbia Library Columns*, vol. 37 no.3, 1988.

* * *

Shaw's play analyses the remarkable events in the life of Joan of Arc, the peasant girl who commanded an army against the English who were over-running her native France, crowned the weak and vacillating Dauphin King of France, and was eventually tried for heresy and witchcraft. The historical Joan had relied on what she was convinced were the voices of the saints Catherine and Margaret for justification. When she recanted, the sentence of burning was commuted to life imprisonment. Impulsively she tore up her recantation and declared that her voices had lied: she preferred death to confinement. Being burnt alive, she begged for a cross to hold and an English soldier made two pieces of wood into a rough cross and gave it to her. 20 years after her death, she was rehabilitated and her judges vilified.

Shaw sets out to show in his play that the judges, far from giving her a drumhead court-martial, were honourable and scrupulous according to their lights, and that Joan was crushed between the mills of Church and State. He has to make characters anachronistically coin the expressions Protestantism and Nationalism to explain the historical forces operating at the time, and makes them improbably analytical about the nature of feudalism. He represents Joan's social class and her illiteracy by making her speak in a sort of Mummerset Yorkshire.

But non of this matters: *Saint Joan* is a powerful and moving play, and arguably Shaw's greatest achievement. It is inseparable from its brilliant preface, a lucid essay in historical philosophy, argued with dazzling clarity and drive (apart from a sideswipe at vaccination, which seemed to Shaw a totalitarian measure). The preface sets out to demolish false images of Joan: the scurrilous (Shakespeare's *Henry VI*); the burlesqued (Voltaire); and the romanticised (Schiller, Mark Twain, and Andrew Lang, the last two "equally determined to make Joan a beautiful and most ladylike Victorian"). Shaw points out that she was a bossy, managing female who wore men's clothes for severely practical reasons.

Shaw has succeeded in his objective, that of wiping the slate of history clean of alternative images of Joan: since his day, the play has been seen by and taught to generations for whom his picture is all they know of her. The strength of Shaw's play, presented as a chronicle, is that it illuminates "Christendom and the Catholic Church and the Holy Roman Empire and the Feudal System": far from isolating Joan from the environment which made her astonishing achievement possible (and then

Saint Joan: Sybil Thorndike as Joan, New Theatre, London, 1924

killed her for it), Shaw offers a diagrammatic, political analysis. Shaw the Irishman cannot resist a dig at the English, who within the play are represented by the crafty and urbane Earl of Warwick, and the bumbling de Stogumber: the Englishman, seen through Irish eyes, is either treacherous or stupid. But within the play, de Stogumber provides comic relief, and his tears of shame, after he has seen Joan executed, are genuinely moving and foreshadow her later rehabilitation.

Shaw, though an Irish Protestant, goes out of his way to be fair to the Catholic church, which acted according to what seemed, at the time, God-given authority, and he points out that, unlike the English who wanted to get rid of her by fair means or foul, the ecclesiastics tried hard to save Joan from the consequences of her own "superbity," the arrogant belief that she knew best. The Inquisitor in the play says, "I am accustomed to the fire: it is soon over. But it is a terrible thing to see a young and innocent creature crushed between these mighty forces, the Church and the Law". The Bishop of Beauvais, Peter Cauchon, replies in astonishment, "You call her innocent!", and the Inquisitor responds, "Oh, quite innocent. What does she know of the Church and the Law? She did not understand a word we were saying. . . .".

The epilogue has been criticised as unnecessary, extra-dramatic, and impossible. But the Dauphin's dream, in which he is visited by the martyr's ghost, exists to dramatise Shaw's main thrust: that Joan was, like Socrates and Christ, impeccably virtuous but too disturbing to authority to be tolerated: it was the natural superiority of such figures, their greater, ethical wisdom, which was seen as a threat, and led to the inevitable executions of all three. As Shaw is at pains to point out, 20th-century history shows no decline in either superstition or cruelty. The final words are Joan's: "Oh God that madest this beautiful earth, when will it be ready to receive Thy saints? How long, O Lord, how long?".

—Valerie Grosvenor Myer

UNE SAISON AU CONGO.   See A SEASON IN THE CONGO.

SAKUNTALA.   See SHAKUNTALA.

SAKURA HIME AZUMA BUNSHO.   See THE SCARLET PRINCESS OF EDO.

SALOMÉ
by Oscar Wilde

First Publication: Paris and London, 1893 [in French].
First Production: Théâtre de l'Oeuvre, Paris, 11 February 1896 [in French]; first production in English, at Bijou Theatre, London, 10 May 1905.

Editions
Salomé [in French], in *"Salomé" and "A Florentine Tragedy"*, introduced by Robert Ross, London, 1908.

Translations
Salomé, translated by Lord Alfred Douglas, London and Boston, 1896.

Criticism
(For general works on the author, see *Playwrights* volume)

Articles:
E.P. Bendz, "A Propos de la *Salomé* de Oscar Wilde", in *English Studies*, 51, 1917.
Edmund Bergler, "*Salomé* and the Turning Point in the Life of Oscar Wilde", in *Psychoanalytic Review*, vol.43 no.1, 1956.
Z. Raafat, "The Literary Indebtedness of Wilde's *Salomé* to Sardou's *Théodora*", in *Revue de littérature comparée*, 40, 1966.
Marilyn Gaddis Rose, "The Daughters of Herodias in *Herodiade*, *Salomé*, and *A Full Moon in March*", in *Comparative Drama*, 1, 1967.
Richard C. Beacham, "Sex and the Uncensored *Salomé*", in *Yale / Theater*, 3, 1968.
Richard Ellmann, "Overtures to Wilde's *Salomé*", in *Yearbook of Comparative and General Literature*, 1968.
Nicholas Joost and Franklin E. Court, "*Salomé*, the Moon, and Oscar Wilde's Aesthetics: A Reading of the Play", in *Papers on Language and Literature*, 8 (supplement), 1972.
D. Radha Krishnayya, "Wilde's *Salomé*: Deviations from the Biblical Episode", in *Commonwealth Quarterly*, 2, 1978.
Graham Good, "Early Productions of Oscar Wilde's *Salomé*", in *Nineteenth Century Theatre Research*, 11, 1983.
Pierre Han, "Wilde's *Salomé*: Survival in a Hothouse", in *Journal of Comparative Literature and Aesthetics*, 7, 1984.
Laurence Senelick, "*Salomé* in Russia", in *Nineteenth Century Theatre Research*, 12, 1984.
Robert C. Schweik, "Oscar Wilde's *Salomé*, the Salome Theme in Late European Art, and a Problem of Method in Cultural History", in *Twilight of Dawn: Studies in English Literature in Translation*, edited by O.M. Brack, Tucson, Arizona, 1987.
Gail Finney, "The (Wo)man in the Moon: Wilde's *Salomé*", in her *Women in Modern Drama: Freud, Feminism, and European Theater at the Turn of the Century*, Ithaca, New York, 1989.
Anthony Pym, "The Importance of Salomé: Approaches to a *fin de siècle* Theme", in *French Forum*, 14, 1989.

*   *   *

Salomé was conceived and written in French between 1890 and 1892. Wilde had cherished the idea of staging the play in London with Sarah Bernhardt in the title role, but it was banned by the censor in 1892, a measure which ironically confirmed its implicit challenge to Victorian philistinism. The work originated in Wilde's fascination with the biblical character of Salome, as represented in painting and literature through the ages. Wilde was familiar with many representations of the Princess of Judea, who dances for her stepfather King Herod and who demands as her reward the head of his captive, John the Baptist. The theme was, however, particularly favoured by the French-inspired Symbolist and aesthetic movements in which Wilde was immersed. Among his sources were Flaubert's novel *Salammbô*, Mallarmé's unfinished but well-known poem "Hérodiade" as it was later called, and J.C. Heywood's dramatic poem *Salome*, reviewed

Salomé: Bijou Theatre, London, 1905

by Wilde in the *Pall Mall Gazette* (February 1888). The most important model, however, was probably the lyrical description in Chapter Five of J.-K. Huysmans' *A Rebours* (*Against Nature*) of two paintings of Salome by Gustave Moreau. Huysmans called her "the symbolic incarnation of undying Lust, the goddess of immortal Hysteria" and described her as "poisoning, like the Helen of ancient myth, everything that she touches".

Why did Salome became a decadent heroine for writers such as Huysmans and Wilde? In the biblical accounts, her role in events is not dwelt upon; she is presented as the mere instrument of her mother Herodias's machinations for power, rather than being motivated, as in Wilde's play, by her own amorous desire for the prophet. None the less her story lent itself to the intensification of that pathological strain in Romanticism which eroticised pain and suffering through the figure of the fatal woman. Wilde saw Salome as embodying both uncontrollable sensuality and virginal purity, a paradoxical combination which he thought of as definitively aesthetic. The dance (through which she wreaks destruction) was often invoked as an analogy for the ideal unity of form and meaning, sense and spirit incarnated in the poetic symbol.

Salomé is a dramatized reverie concentrated on a single episode which is made to resonate with all the play's meanings. Action and dialogue are stylized and anti-naturalist; the dream-like, hieratic repetition of words and images make the play seem to aspire to the status of a static, visual object or icon. Wilde's language mingles biblical cadences with long passages of decorative indulgence, such as the catalogue of precious gems offered to Salomé by Herod. The cluster of associations (moon–death–princess–dancer) which begins the play goes through a number of balletic permutations, grouping and regrouping with other images, as it is employed by different characters, but remains part of a closed, hermetic system. Conventional plot is replaced by the dance of language, a languorous, auto-erotic, circular movement which desires an eternal present and rejects historical sequence.

Though Salomé's power to compel the gaze of the young Syrian captain and of Herod is the engine of destruction in the play, all the major characters, except Iokanaan, are ultimately in love with themselves; the young captain, for example, adores Salomé, but when he is dead we learn that "he had much joy to gaze at himself in the river". The quality in Iokanaan which attracts Salomé is an inorganic hardness, purity, and remoteness which is a mirror image of herself. "How wasted he is!" she says. "He is like a thin ivory statue. He is like an image of silver. I am sure he is chaste, as the moon is. He is like a moonbeam, like a shaft of silver. His flesh must be very cold, cold as ivory. . .". The desire for sexual possession is seen as essentially voyeuristic and fatally destructive, an unnatural doubling of the self.

Yet the world of the play is not autonomous but internally threatened by forces it cannot yet understand. Beneath the effeminate, sensualist court the prophet of a virile, ascetic, new religion calls down divine wrath on the incestuous union of the Tetrarch with Herodias; Salomé, the most refined expression of a decadent culture, perversely desires its apocalyptic opposite. She tries to seduce Iokanaan by profanely hymning his physical beauty in erotic imagery drawn from the Song of Songs, but he refuses to look at her and thus remains outside the ritual circulation of narcissistic desire mirrored in language. His metaphors do not court exquisite sensations, as those of the other characters do, but convey a vision beyond language, a figural or typological meaning derived from a biblical design.

A moral ambivalence about "art for art's sake" is therefore built into this key text of the aesthetic movement. Richard

Ellmann argues that Salomé and Iokanaan correspond to the conflicting influences of Ruskin, who insisted on the morality of art, and Pater, who emphasised a hedonistic, aesthetic "sensibility" over narrowly moral or doctrinal concerns. Wilde identifies, to some extent, with the character of Herod, who is responsive to the claims of both, and ends by destroying both.

—Christina Britzolakis

SAMFUNDETS STØTTER. See **THE PILLARS OF SOCIETY**.

SAMOUBIITSA. See **THE SUICIDE**.

SAMURAI NAO (Naozamurai)
by Kawatake Mokuami

First Production: Shintomi Theatre, Tokyo, 1881.

Translations
Naozamurai (*Kumo ni Magō Ueno no Hatsuhana*), in *The Art of Kabuki: Famous Plays in Performance*, translated by Samuel L. Leiter, Berkeley, California, 1979.

* * *

Naozamurai (*Samurai Nao*) is a Kabuki play in two acts. It is the second half of a longer play known commonly as *Kōchiyama* and *Naozamurai*, but whose formal title is *Kumo ni Magō Ueno no Hatsuhana* (*The First Cherry Blossoms of Ueno Appearing as if They Were Heavenly Clouds*). The category of the play is *Shiranami-mono* (Bandit Play) or *Kizewa-momo* (True Domestic Play). Its source is a piece from *kōshaku* (a kind of traditional popular form of storytelling art), titled *Tempō Rokkasen* (Six Notorieties of the Tempō Era), by Shōrin Haku'en, who was known as "Thief" Haku'en due to his specialization in stories of thieves. Mokuami, himself, was known as a *Shiranami* playwright for his fondness for writing a number of masterpieces dealing with notorious criminals.

Act I, "The Soba Shop Scene", is set on a snowy, April night. Two police spies are eating soba (long noodles served in a hot broth) in a shop. After the two men leave, accompanied by the "snow fall" drum beat, Naozamurai appears, chilled to the bone, and drops in the shop. His full name is Kataoka Naojirō, but he is called Nao, or Naozamurai at times, because he is a fallen samurai (warrior) now, and a member of the gang headed by Kōchiyama (thus "Nao-Zamurai": Samurai Nao). He is on the run to avoid an intensified pursuit by the police, but he plans to see his girl, Michitose, a courtesan, once more before taking off. He learns in the shop that Michitose is staying in a nearby hostel, lovesick from pining for him. Before Nao reaches the hostel, he is stopped by Ushimatsu, a close fellow gang member, and both agree that it is time to flee elsewhere. After parting, Ushimatsu conceives the idea that he can save himself from the police if he can put them on the trail of Naojirō, so he follows him.

Act II is the "Ōguchi Hostel Scene". In deepening snow, Naojirō arrives at the hostel and is invited in, being watched stealthily by Ushimatsu, who then proceeds to inform the police. Naojirō is busy warming himself by the brazier when Michitose enters. She assures Nao that she feels much better since he is with her now. Naojirō reveals that he is a fleeing common criminal. To his surprise, Michitose informs him that she has known his true identity and implores him to take her with him on his escape. Throughout this love scene, Kiyomoto samisen music (known for its lyricism and high-pitched, sensual chanting, which is accompanied by three-stringed instruments) is performed in the guise of a neighbor rehearsing. The combination of the music and intimate lover's quarrel creates one of the most famous, tender, and moving scenes to be found in domestic plays of Kabuki, and is performed as a mimed dance.

The lovers are interrupted by the unexpected visit of Kaneko Ichinojō, who is a client of Michitose. He intends to ransom her and take her away with him. After a heated argument between the two men, Ichinojō leaves the two, flinging a packet at their feet. In it Michitose finds some money, a paper to release her from the brothel, and a letter stating that he is really her brother and wishes she would save herself from the misery of being associated with Naozamurai. Before they can devise their getaway, the police burst into the room and Naojirō only just escapes. Michitose, left behind, calls out his name desperately, as she stands on the step watching his flight.

Of all traditional Japanese theatre forms, a *Sewa-mono* play most nearly approaches a realistic acting style, but *Kize-wa-mono* extends that tendency one step further. However, this is all in a relative sense. There remains, still, a number of stylized expressions, mixed intricately with realistic touches. In the Noodle Eating Scene, the two spies chew their food quietly, indicating that they are country folk, in contrast to Naojirō's slurping and sucking in true "Edokko" fashion (the children of Edo). To simulate falling snow, many pieces of shredded paper are used; piled-up snow is indicated with cotton. As Naozamurai approaches the hostel gate and strikes the bamboo clapper on the gateway to signal his arrival, a hidden stage assistant in the wings pulls a string, causing a pile of "snow" to fall heavily onto Nao's shoulders from the eaves—a delightful touch. The dance-mime love scene is known as *kudoki* (lover's lamentation). Even an expression of intense love has to be tempered and put into a certain patterned motion to be an acceptable element of Kabuki acting. It cannot be a wildly uncontrolled act of passion.

Mokuami was clever and skillful in his presentation of interesting, criminal characters. They are not, however, vicious, murderous, or cruel killers. On the contrary, they are often sympathetic to the oppressed, and willingly render them assistance. But Mokuami stayed safely within the guidelines of the government of the Meiji period (after 1868), always providing a last scene to show how the ruffians are caught for eventual execution in accordance with the principle of *Kanzen Chōaku* (Promote good and punish evil).

—Andrew T. Tsubaki

THE SATIN SLIPPER; or, The Worst is not the Surest
(Le Soulier de satin; ou, Le Pire n'est pas toujours sûr)
by Paul Claudel

First Publication: Paris, 1925 ("*Première Journée*" only); complete, Paris 1928–29 (4 vols); stage version, Paris, 1944.
First Production: Comédie-Française, Paris, 27 November 1943.

Translations
The Satin Slipper, translated by Fr. John O'Connor [with the collaboration of Claudel], London and New Haven, Connecticut, 1931.

Criticism
(For general works on the author, see *Playwrights* volume)

Books:
Jacques Petit, *Pour une Explication du "Soulier de satin"* (second edition), Paris, 1972.
Joan S. Freilich, *Paul Claudel's "Le Soulier de satin": A Stylistic, Structuralist, and Psychoanalytic Interpretation*, Toronto, 1973.
Michael Autrand, *Le Dramaturge et ses personnages dans "Le Soulier de satin" de Paul Claudel*, Paris, 1987.
Michael Autrand, *"Le Soulier de satin": Étude dramaturgique*, Paris, 1987.
Jacques Houriez, *La Bible et le sacré dans "Le Soulier de satin" de Paul Claudel*, Paris, 1987.

Articles:
Barbara Selna, "Paul Claudel: Prison and the *Satin Slipper*", in *Renascence*, 7, 1955.
Sister Fidelia Maria Cox, "Prayer and Sacrifice; Claudel's *Satin Slipper*", in *Renascence*, 13, 1961.
Anne M. Mazzega, "Une Parabole historique: *Le Soulier de satin*", in *Revue des lettres modernes*, 150–52, 1967.
W.N. Ince, "The Unity of Claudel's *Soulier de satin*", in *Symposium*, 22, 1968.
Jean N. Segrestaa, "Regards sur la composition du *Soulier de satin*", in *Revue des lettres modernes*, 180–82, 1968.
Michael Wood, "The Theme of the Prison in *Le Soulier de satin*", in *French Studies*, 22, 1968.
Alain Baudot, "*Le Soulier de satin*: Est-il une Anti-tragédie", in *Études françaises*, 5, 1969.
Michio Kurimura, "*Le Soulier de satin*: Drame de la solidarité universelle des âmes", in *Études de langue et littérature de la France*, 14, 1969.
Randi M. Birn, "The Comedy of Disrespect in Claudel's *Soulier de satin*", in *French Review*, vol.63 (special issue), 1970.
Václav Cerny, "Le 'Baroquisme' du *Soulier de satin*", in *Revue de littérature comparée*, 44, 1970.
Lorraine D. Burghardt, "Paul Claudel's *Soulier de Satin* as a Baroque Drama", in *Modern Drama*, 14, 1971.
Michel Brethenoux, "L'Espace dans *Le Soulier de satin*", in *Revue des lettres modernes*, 1972.
Joan S. Freilich, "*Le Soulier de satin*: Four Levels Through Imagery", in *Claudel Studies*, 1, 1972.
Jacques Henriot, "Le Thème de la quête dans *Le Soulier de satin*", in *Revue des lettres modernes*, 310–14, 1972.
Jean N. Landry, "Chronologie et temps dans *Le Soulier de satin*", in *Revue des lettres modernes*, 310–14, 1972.
Jacques Petit, "Les Jeux du Double dans *Le Soulier de satin*", in *Revue des lettres modernes*, 310–14, 1972.

Harold Watson, "Fire and Water, Love and Death in *Le Soulier de satin*", in *French Review*, 45, 1972.

John W. Erwin, "Hero as Audience: *Antony and Cleopatra* and *Le Soulier de satin*", in *Modern Language Studies*, 4, 1974.

Michel Malicet, "La Peur de la femme dans *Le Soulier de satin*", in *Revue des lettres modernes*, 391–97, 1974.

Jacques Petit and Others, "Les Images dans *Le Soulier de satin*", in *Revue des lettres modernes*, 391–97, 1974.

Elsie M. Wiedner, "Philosophies and Stagings: Notes on Three Productions of 'la quatrième journée' of Paul Claudel's *Le Soulier de satin*", in *Claudel Studies*, vol.1 no.4, 1974.

Antoinette Wakker, "Quelques remarques sur le texte et sur le manuscrit du *Soulier de satin*", in *Revue des lettres modernes*, 510–515, 1977.

Marie F. Mathion Cavigioli, "Figuration scènique et symbolisme cosmique dans le théâtre du *Soulier de satin* (III, 8)", in *Saggi e ricerche di letteratura francese*, 18, 1978.

André Courribet, "Résonances mystiques dans *Le Soulier de satin* de Paul Claudel", in *Queste: Estudios de lengua y literatura francesas*, 1, 1984.

Colette Bottin-Fourchotte, "Le Jeu de cartes à icône dans *Le Soulier de satin* de Paul Claudel", in *Hommage à Jean Richer*, Paris, 1985.

Michel Lioure, "Ordre et désordre dans *Le Soulier de satin*", in *Littératures*, 17, 1987.

Antonio Linage, "Christopher Columbus in *Le Soulier de satin*", in *Claudel Studies*, vol.15 no.2, 1988.

*　　*　　*

This epic work, divided into four "days", opens with the prayer of a drowning Jesuit that his brother, Rodrigue, should come to God even through evil and disorder. Dom Pélage entrusts his wife, Prouhèze, to the care of Dom Balthazar, while he arranges the marriage of his kinswoman Musique. Prouhèze refuses to run away with Dom Camille to North Africa, yet warns Balthazar that she will try to escape him to join Rodrigue, the man she loves. She asks Balthazar to guard her closely, and as a symbol of her desire to keep herself from sin, places her satin slipper in the hands of a statue of the Virgin. Meanwhile Rodrigue, chosen as Viceroy of the Indies by the King, is injured and taken to his mother's house. Musique escapes and comes to the inn where Prouhèze has been brought. Prouhèze escapes to join Rodrigue. Soldiers searching for Musique attack the inn and Balthazar is killed.

On the Second Day, Pélage transmits to Prouhèze the King's order that she go alone to Africa to defend Mogador and restrain the activities of the renegade Camille. The King sends Rodrigue to Mogador with letters for Prouhèze. They do not meet and Prouhèze refuses to return. Meanwhile, Musique is shipwrecked and meets the Viceroy of Naples she has predicted she will marry. In the ten-year interval between the Second and Third Days, Prouhèze's husband dies and she writes to Rodrigue, but her letter does not reach him in time, and she is obliged to marry Camille. In a dream she is made to understand that she is the bait by which Rodrigue may be brought to God. Rodrigue at last receives her letter and departs. They finally meet off the coast of the besieged Mogador, when Prouhèze comes as an envoy to Rodrigue's ship. She entrusts her daughter to his care, but insists on returning to Camille and certain death.

On the Fourth Day, Rodrigue, having lost a leg and having been imprisoned in Japan, has returned in disgrace to the Balearic Isles. Prouhèze's daughter, Seven Swords, loves Musique's son, Dom Juan, who is about to lead a campaign against the Turks. Rodrigue is persuaded by an actress impersonating Mary Queen of Scots to accept the governorship of England; but he is arrested as a traitor, and given to a common soldier to be sold. He is comforted by the priest who married Prouhèze to Camille, and finally understands that death is impossible in spiritual terms. A mendicant sister begging for rubbish is persuaded to take him, and the play ends with the signal that Seven Swords is safe aboard Dom Juan's ship.

The initial idea for *The Satin Slipper* occurred to Claudel in 1919. This was for a "nautical festival" and from it emerged the whole of the Fourth Day. The play was finally completed in Japan in 1924, after the manuscript of the Third Day had been destroyed in a fire and rewritten. It has been considered by many, including its author, as the pinnacle of his art and the synthesis of all his previous experience. On a personal level, the origins of *The Satin Slipper* are the same as those of *The Break of Noon*, but rather than the torment of the original crisis, this later work traces the suffering of the ensuing 20 years with the intention of illustrating the Augustinian doctrine that everything co-operates for good. Thus the main difference lies in the fact that it is through acceptance of eternal separation that Prouhèze and Rodrigue attain supernatural joy.

In *The Satin Slipper*, the story of the chief protagonists is set against a synthesis of over 100 years of Spanish history, from the conquest and colonization of the Americas to the defeat of the Armada. Claudel is not, however, concerned with creating local colour or with a meticulous adherence to historical truth—time is telescoped and the order of events rearranged so that he can use the facts to serve his drama. Even so, the play is an eloquent portrait of Spanish political and religious preoccupations during the Counter-Reformation.

More than any other of Claudel's works, *The Satin Slipper* was written with performance in mind. Despite its length, the author attempted to avoid fatiguing the spectators by eliminating long speeches and ensuring that the stage picture is constantly varied by changes of scene, the use of cinema projections, and a perpetual succession of characters, including allegorical and religious figures. Also, although still written in Claudelian free verse, the extreme lyricism of his earlier works has been abandoned, so that the language is far more conversational, and frequently even comic. This introduction of comedy into what is essentially a tragic subject is one of the most striking features of *The Satin Slipper*. It is done chiefly by having characters such as the Announcer, the Irrepressible One, and the Actress break the illusion to reveal theatrical truth. According to Claudel's instructions in the preface, theatrical mechanisms should also be obvious in the play's presentation, with stage-hands changing scenery and putting the final touches to the set in full view of the audience. Claudel called this "theatre in the process of being born", but did not intend the overall effect to be one of chaos. Indeed, the balance between organization and chaos is a feature of *The Satin Slipper* as a whole, with seemingly haphazard scenes being in fact carefully juxtaposed, and the apparently disparate characters being linked by an elaborate network of social, familial, and sentimental relationships. The same is true of the *mise en scène*, where apparently impromtu interruptions and deviations are, in fact, meticulously regulated.

The Satin Slipper was first produced at the Comédie-Française in 1943, directed by Jean-Louis Barrault—who also played Rodrigue—with Marie Bell as Prouhèze. The play was reduced to two three-hour performances, omitting many of the philosophical and comic digressions and all but the last scene of the Fourth Day. Its success in the face of the difficult circumstances of occupied France, ranging from electricity cuts and air-raids, to censorship and the hostility of the Occupation newspapers, was in no little part due to the fact that the realization of such a spectacle was seen as a striking affirmation of French national genius. Barrault directed the play again in 1958 and in 1963, when certain scenes were reintroduced. In 1972, the Fourth Day was first performed separately by Barrault's company, directed by Jean-Pierre Granval; but it was not until 1980, when Barrault's 1963 production was combined with that of Granval, that *The Satin Slipper* was first produced in its entirety.

—Janet Clarke

A SATIRE OF THE THREE ESTATES
by Sir David Lindsay

Composition: 1539–54.
First Publication: Edinburgh, 1602.
First Production: Possibly in an early version at Linlithgow Palace, Scotland, 1540; some scholars prefer later performance at Cupar, Fife, Scotland, 7 June 1552; with variants, at the Greenside, Edinburgh, 12 August 1554.

Editions

The Satire of the Three Estates: The Edinburgh Festival Version, edited by Robert Kemp, London, 1951.
Ane Satyre of the Thrie Estaits, edited by James Kingsley, London, 1954.
A Satire of the Three Estates, adapted by Matthew McDiarmid from Kemp's version, London, 1967.
Ane Satire of the Thrie Estates in *Four Morality Plays*, edited by Peter Happé, Harmondsworth, 1979.

Criticism

(For general works on the author, see *Playwrights* volume)

Books:
Ruth Mohl, *The Three Estates in Medieval and Renaissance Literature*, New York, 1933.
Joanne S. Kantrowitz, *Dramatic Allegory: Lindsay's "Ane Satyre of the Thrie Estaitis"*, Lincoln, Nebraska, 1975.

Articles:
Anna J. Mill, "The Influence of the Continental Drama on Lyndsay's *Satyre of the Thrie Estaitis*", in *Modern Language Review*, 25, 1930.
Anna J. Mill, "Representations of Lyndsay's *Satyre of the Thrie Estaitis*", in *Publications of the Modern Language Association* [*PMLA*], 47–48, 1932–33.
Raymond A. Houk, "Versions of Lindsay's *Satire of the Three Estates*", in *Publications of the Modern Language Association* [*PMLA*], 55, 1940.
Allan H. MacLaine, "'Christis Kirk on the Grene' and Sir David Lindsay's *Satyre of the Thrie Estaits*", in *Journal of English and Germanic Philology*, 56, 1957.
Alan C. Dessen, "The Estates Morality Play", in *Studies in Philology*, 62, 1965.
John MacQueen, "*Ane Satyre of the Thrie Estaitis*", in *Studies in Scottish Literature*, vol.3, 1965–66.

Anna J. Mill, "The Original Version of Lindsay's *Satyre of the Thrie Estaitis*", in *Studies in Scottish Literature* (University of South Carolina), vol.3, 1968–69.
Joanne S. Kantrowitz, "Encore: Lindsay's *Thrie Estaitis*: Date and New Evidence", in *Studies in Scottish Literature* (University of South Carolina), 10, 1972.
Claude Graf, "Sottie et folie dans la *Satire des trois états*", in *Recherches anglaises et américaines*, 3, 1974.
Claude Graf, "Theatre and Politics: Lindsay's *Satyre of the Thrie Estaitis*", in *Bards and Makers: Scottish Language and Literature: Medieval and Renaissance*, edited by Adam J. Aitken, Mathew P. McDiarmid, and Derek Thomson, Glasgow, 1977.
R.S. Lyall, "The Linlithgow Interlude of 1540", in *Actes du deuxième Colloque de langue et de littérature*, edited by J.-J. Blanchot and C. Graf, Strasbourg, 1978.
Claude Graf, "Audience Involvement in Lindsay's *Satyre of the Thrie Estaitis*", in *Scottish Studies* (Frankfurt), 4, 1984.
J. Derrick McClure, "A Comparison of the Bannatyne MS and the Quarto Texts of Lyndsay's *Ane Satyre of the Thrie Estaitis*", in *Scottish Studies* (Frankfurt), 4, 1984.
David Reid, "Rule and Misrule in Lindsay's *Thrie Estaitis* and Pitcairne's *Assembly*", in *Scottish Literary Journal*, vol.11 no.2, 1984.

*   *   *

Sir David Lindsay's morality drama begins with a sermon of Christian doctrine from a doctor (Diligence) and ends with a sermon of chaos from Folie. The principles of order and disorder thus frame a long, elaborate play, dealing with that theme in theological, moral, and political contexts. The first part focuses mainly on the figure of King Humanitie. Although anxious for reform, he proves susceptible to the wiles of Sensualitie and is led to accept the rule of the Vices representing duplicity. In this world-upside-down, Chastitie is appropriately placed in the stocks beside Veritie. The arrival of Diligence announces the reform of the King and prepares us for the transition to reform of the Estates. Prior to this, an interlude, in which the Pauper speaks from among the audience, draws us into the action. His alliance with Johne the Common-weill strengthens the immediate political bias of the allegory. The satire in Part Two begins by attacking all three Estates but soon concentrates on the Clergy alone. A long list of reforms having been agreed, order appears to have been established fully, from king to country. Only the arrival of Folie opens up the question once more.

Despite evidence that Scotland enjoyed both a Miracle cycle and a morality-play tradition, David Lindsay's play is practically the only remaining Scottish text within these traditions. The long and troubled reigns of successive monarchs and the increasingly hostile attitude of the reformers towards drama contributed to this situation. Fortunately, *Ane Satyre* is not only unique in status but in nature and is agreed by critics to be of a very high, literary quality. In length and in the ambitiousness of presentation, it invites parallels with *The Castle of Perseverance*; in its theological, moral, and political focus, it belongs to the later period of the morality drama not only chronologically but thematically. *Magnyfycens* (*Magnificence*) would be a fair analogue from this point of view.

Sir David Lindsay of the Mount has a deserved reputation as the finest Scottish poet of the mid 16th-century. The concerns voiced in his play had earlier been conveyed poetically in long poems, notably *The Dreme* and *The Complaynt*. A man of considerable culture and influence, he became Lord Lyon, King of Arms, and spent much of his political life in France and the Netherlands. Theologically, he was on the side of the reformers but took a studiously liberal and humane viewpoint in contrast to any extremist tendencies within that movement.

Three early performances are relevant to the history of his play. Documents prove that a work bearing notable similarities to *Ane Satyre* was performed before James V and Mary of Lorraine at Linlithgow Palace in 1540, but critics divide on whether this is the earliest performance of the play or the description of a different, though analogous, drama. Surviving texts relate either to the Cupar production of 1552 or an Edinburgh presentation in 1554. The troupes adapted their material for the different open-air settings and added local references. Well-known personalities within the Cupar area, for example, are made a butt of particular satire in the earlier text.

The Scottish flavour continues in the nature of some of the reforms proposed and, somewhat paradoxically, in the play's reliance on French as well as English models. Politically (through the old alliance), Scotland and France had frequently stood together, and this closeness is mirrored in much medieval and early Renaissance Scots writing. Estates satire is, in itself, a form primarily associated with French literature. The overall structure of *Ane Satyre* combines the most favoured of French dramatic forms—the *moralité*, the farce, and the *sottie*. The final sermon of Folie, especially, cannot be understood without seeing that it is a fullblown *sermon joyeux*. Nowhere in English morality drama do we find such a sermon. Occasionally, too, the pro-French bias becomes part of the dialogue: "Quhat cummer have ye had in Scotland Be our auld enemies of England? Had nocht bene the support of France, We had bene brocht to great mischance".

Lindsay does show a keen theatrical awareness. He changes tone frequently and, with the exception of the lengthy list of reforms in the second part, prevents drama from becoming homily. He also uses visual effects regularly. Characters such as Pauper and Johne the Common-weill are skilfully introduced to bridge the distinction between audience and action, artifice and actuality, both in terms of argument and setting. The Vices become successful sources of comedy without losing their moral darkness, both definitions being implicit in the medieval view of error as amusement and moral and theological blindness.

Unfortunately, although courtly performances for coterie audiences grew in popularity and sophistication in Scotland throughout the Renaissance, the religious climate made it increasingly difficult for satiral drama of this sort to find suitable auspices under which to be performed. The later 16th century in Scotland can only match the great wealth of Elizabethan drama with the turgid Senecan dramas of Sir William Alexander and a single anonymous comedy, *Philotus*. Other texts, doubtless, were lost or destroyed, but it was a thin tradition which suffered diminution. Centuries were to pass before another Scottish dramatist could claim to have achieved the high standards reached by Lindsay in *Ane Satyre*.

—R.D.S. Jack

SATURDAY, SUNDAY, MONDAY
(Sabato, domenico e lunedi)
by Eduardo De Filippo

First Publication: Turin, 1960.
First Publication: Teatro Quirino, Rome, 6 November 1959.

Translations
Saturday, Sunday, Monday, adapted by Keith Waterhouse and Willis Hall, London, 1974.

* * *

The action is set in Naples, in the house of Peppino Priore and his wife, Rosa. The prosperous owners of a men's clothing shop, they have been married for 30 years, and have three children, two of whom, Rocco and Giulianella, are still at home, while the third, though married, lives nearby and returns home regularly for Sunday lunch. Other members of the family in residence include Rosa's eccentric father, Antonio, and Peppino's sister, the equally eccentric Meme. Yet other characters, either relatives or neighbours, drift in and out during the course of the action, which takes place over three days, from Saturday afternoon to Monday morning.

In Act I we encounter Rosa and her maid preparing *ragu* for the Sunday lunch. As they talk it becomes clear that beneath the surface of domestic life there are many tensions: all is not well between Peppino and Rosa, and relations between parents and children are strained; the children too have their own problems, Rocco being dissatisfied because he wants to start a shop of his own, but is getting no support from his father, and Giulianella because she has the chance to work in television, yet her boyfriend opposes her doing so. The tensions come to a head during Sunday lunch. This lunch makes up Act II and is the centre-piece of the play: for lunch is a kind of domestic and social ceremony, to which not only relatives, but neighbours, too, are invited. All the accumulated resentments and irritations in the family, some of which also embrace the neighbours, gradually come to a head. Finally Peppino explodes, and we learn the reason for his recent, peculiar behaviour: he thinks Rosa has been having an affair with one of the neighbours. But on Monday (Act III) all is sorted out: problems are resolved or come to terms with, various, small enmities are settled, and those who have quarrelled are eventually reconciled.

A comedy in the Neapolitan dialect, there is little here in the way of plot in the more conventional sense of the word; rather, the play provides us with a glimpse into a not-untypical weekend in the Priore household. De Filippo's comedy of local observation is lively and naturalistic, and exploits the humorous possibilities in domestic situations and the vivid, colloquial richness of Neapolitan dialogue. It has a strong bias towards the farcical, and is clearly the work of an actor-dramatist: the parts are nearly all created for the regular actors of the De Filippo company, roles like Meme's pampered son or the maidservant's brute of a brother being comic vignettes crafted expressly for performance. The main strength of the piece, indeed, lies in the rich character roles sketched out by the dialogue for players to bring alive in performance. Yet the play also has a more serious side. It raises a number of broad, domestic issues: changing social and sexual attitudes and the ways in which these affect personal relationships; the inescapable contrasts and conflicts which always emerge in families between the young and the old. The values affirmed are the usual De Filippo imperatives: the need for honesty in personal affairs and openness between people, the civilising role of the family, the importance of the local community, and the need for a sense of engagement with, and concern for, others. Other prominent motifs include the need for the old to trust in the right judgement of the young, and how imperative it is, for social cohesiveness, to come to terms with remorselessly changing times. One may note too how, through the figure of Meme—who claims to have found her own freedom in life by openly and sincerely telling her husband of her love for

Saturday, Sunday, Monday: Old Vic Theatre, London, 1973 (National Theatre Company)

another man—the play touches, however undeliberately, on the emerging issue of female independence; it must be said, though, that as a social and moral point this is rather undercut by the presentation of Meme as a comic figure. The fact is that ultimately De Filippo never really confronts the more serious implications of many of the issues he raises, and *Saturday, Sunday, Monday* remains, finally, a rather thin piece, verbally undistinguished, tentative in its handling of its subject-matter, a little short on comic "business" arising directly from, and thus thematically pertinent to, its major concerns, and overly dependent on the skills of actors to bring it alive. But for all that, evident here is De Filippo's fine touch with domestic dialogue and incident and his ability to charge the action of his plays with an air of the spontaneous. In the theatre, and in the hands of accomplished players, the piece is undeniably engaging: hence its very considerable popularity not only in Naples, and more widely in Italy, but with theatre audiences throughout Europe and North America. It is one of the comparatively few Eduardo plays to have broken free of its regional ties and to have found a substantial non-Italian following.

—Laura Richards

***

SAVED
by Edward Bond

First Publication: London and New York, 1966; corrected version, in *Bond: Plays, 1*, London, 1977.
First Production: Royal Court Theatre, London, 3 November 1965.

Criticism
(For general works on the author, see *Playwrights* volume)

Articles:
Urs H. Mehlin, "Die Behandlung von Liebe und Aggression in Shakespeares *Romeo and Juliet* und in Edward Bonds *Saved*", in *Deutsche Shakespeare-Gesellschaft West: Jahrbuch*, 1970.
Errol Durbach, "Herod in the Welfare State: *Kindermord* in the Plays of Edward Bond", in *Educational Theatre Journal*, 27, 1975.
Ruth von Ledebur, "The Adaptation and Reception in Germany of Edward Bond's *Saved*", in *The Play Out of Context: Transferring Plays From Culture to Culture*, edited by Hanna Scolnicov and Peter Holland, Cambridge, 1989.

*   *   *

Controversy surrounded the first production of *Saved* at the Royal Court Theatre in 1965: there were demonstrations, visits to the theatre by the police, letters to the press, a prosecution brought against the theatre, and theatre censorship debated in parliament. The reason for all this was the play's coolly graphic depiction of violence in everyday surroundings.

The play traces the relationship of a young working-class couple, Pam and Len. What starts as a casual pick-up quickly turns into something more as Len moves into the south London house of Pam's parents, Harry and Mary. Pam loses interest in Len, and when she has a baby she assumes that the father is Len's friend Fred, whom she now prefers and sees regularly. She neglects the baby, and when she leaves it in the local park after an argument with Fred (who is no longer interested in her), he and the gang of youths of which he is the leader stone it to death in its pram. Fred alone is imprisoned for the killing. Pam grows increasingly frantic at his absence, blaming everything on Len, who nevertheless doggedly sticks by both her and Fred. Meanwhile the living death of Pam's parents' marriage is galvanized into momentary domestic violence, Mary having sexually compromised the willing Len in the presence of Harry. Yet when Len finally decides to leave the house, it is Harry who persuades him to stay and help make the best of their lives. In the almost-wordless final scene, Len addresses himself to the task of mending a chair broken in the earlier family quarrel, whilst Harry, Mary, and Pam sit in the silence of stalemate.

This summary suggests a busy plot, but the effect is quite the opposite. Bond dramatizes his story in a sequence of 13 scenes, each carefully shaped so as to claim a measure of rhythmic self-sufficiency. Because the focus is on the minutiae of interrelation between characters rather than on events, the effect is of a narrative *edged* along rather than freely flowing. The underlying concern of the play—environmental determinism—is that of classic Naturalism, as is the rhetoric of linguistic authenticity in the phonetic rendering of a version of London working-class speech, with its grim, elliptical reserve. However, the precision and economy of the dramaturgical demands and the ability to extract an entirely unsentimental lyricism from a rich orchestration of dialogue and sound are features that—though entirely characteristic of Bond—evoke Pinter's drama. And the effect of the scenic form, on a stage "as bare as possible", is decidedly post-Brechtian. We are invited to scrutinize rather than identify. In this way Bond's declared aim to teach "moral scepticism and analysis, and not faith" is inscribed within the very form of *Saved*. Even so, the play would never have been controversial were it not for its sudden power to compel the strongest feelings at those points where events *are* dramatized: the family argument and, above all, the stoning of the baby.

In a 1981 interview, Bond pointed out that his earlier plays were concerned not with solutions but with the presentation of problems. The problem in *Saved* is environment, social and domestic. It is seen as a trap, and every place seems palled in a kind of deadness. In the house, each individual impinges constantly and irritatingly on the living space of the others, and the blaring television is used to drown out the crying baby. The café is likewise dominated by a desensitizing, electronic medium, the juke-box. The quiet park is a place of lingering threat and explosive violence: a wartime bomb there killed Harry's and Mary's first baby, and now their daughter's child is the victim of the wanton, eruptive violence of the youths

Saved: Royal Court Theatre, London, 1969

("might as well enjoy ourselves"). All three places are always *cold*. Everyday living in and around them generates a repressed fury which is constantly seeking outlet. Harry's memory of the war aptly describes the rhythm of present experience: "Once or twice the 'ole lot blew up. Not more. Then it went quiet. Everythin' still". Under these circumstances moral life degenerates into varieties of childishness: melodramatic petulance, sulky brooding, egotism, and ethical myopia.

In the world of *Saved*, reserve is a terminal symptom. Characters are afflicted not with inarticulateness so much as by an *unwillingness* to articulate. (We may recall one of William Blake's "Proverbs of Hell": "Sooner murder an infant in its cradle than nurse unacted desires".) This is why Len's constant curiosity is vitally important. His very obtuseness is part of his strength, enabling him as it does to *irritate* others into expression. At various times he presses Pam about her parents, Fred about what killing the baby was like, and Harry about Mary's sexual responsiveness and (again) killing in wartime. The preoccupations are, as Bond himself has pointed out, morbid or prurient (and Len tells Fred that he secretly observed the baby-killing). Yet this seems to be a necessary stage in Len's experience. A similar ambiguity must surround his ability to catalyse argument within the dead marriage of Pam's parents. The release of repressed anger and resentment "clears the air", but the energy provoked is manifested in violence: Mary hits Harry with a teapot and he wields a breadknife.

The last two scenes of the play carry a pivotal significance, but the ambiguity concerning positives extends to them also. In the strange, even ghostly, nocturnal encounter between Len and Harry in Scene 12, the men finally make meaningful contact across the generation gap when Harry speaks about his marital and war experiences and assures Len that "yer fit in now. It'll settle down". Yet the male bond that constitutes their "*shared* victory" (the author's own phrase) is achieved at the expense of, and in spite of, the women. "Don't speak to 'em at all", counsels Harry, "It saves a lot a misunderstandin'". The chill choreography of the final scene makes it amply apparent that this is no solution to the impasse which occasions Len's frustration: "I don't give a damn if they don't talk, but they don't even listen t'yer". "He lives with people at their worst and most hopeless. . .and does not turn away from them", says the author's note of this scene. Yet to speak—as Bond goes on to—of Len's heroic optimism does as little justice to the play as his implicitly political comment of 1981, that at the end the characters "are still fighting, still resisting". The unsentimental poise of *Saved* disdains this kind of uplift, as indeed it resists the seductions of despair. The play's title is problematic, but not ironic.

—Paul Lawley

SAVERIO EL CRUEL
by Roberto Arlt

First Publication: In *Saverio el cruel; El fabricante de fantasmas; La isla desierta; 300 millones*, Buenos Aires, 1950.
First Production: Teatro del Pueblo, Buenos Aires, 4 September 1936.

Criticism
(For general works on the author, see *Playwrights* volume)

Articles:

Naomi Lindstrom, "The World's Illogic in Two Plays by Argentine Expressionists", in *Latin American Literary Review*, vol. 4 no.8, 1976.
James Troiano, "The Grotesque Tradition and Interplay of Fantasy and Reality in the Plays of Roberto Arlt", in *Latin American Literary Review*, 8, 1976.
Gerardo Luzuriaga, "Las máscaras de la crueldad en el teatro de Roberto Arlt", in *Texto crítico*, 10, 1978.

* * *

Saverio el cruel (1936) by Roberto Arlt foregrounds the rupture between the real and the illusory world through gameplaying. A complex series of embedded and selfconsuming games produces a communicative act that demands attention, at often contradictory levels, from the audience. The play begins with a group of bored wealthy people deciding that for their next party they will create a game in which they hope that Saverio, the dairyman, will play the role of a colonel. The purpose of the role, as told to Saverio, is to save the hostess, Susana, from her delusion that she is a queen robbed of her kingdom. Though at first hesitant, Saverio soon enters into the game, adopting all too seriously his role as colonel, confusing reality and illusion. Towards the end of the play, he appears to return to lucidity as he confronts Susana, accusing her of trying to make him appear a fool. Susana tries to convince Saverio to continue the game, and when she is rebuffed, she shoots him, causing both the characters and the audience to question whether her gameplaying was a reality that occurred because she was mad all along, or whether the illusion worked because Saverio believed in it as reality. Within the play there is a constant fluctuation between reality and illusion, between sanity and madness. The disjunction occurs through a series of Pirandellian plays-within-plays, which are all part of a larger game.

There is the "real world" of all the characters which is unknown to Saverio but known to Susana, her friends, and the audience all along. Saverio is duped into a game that he ends up accepting as real. There is also the world of Susana's madness in which everyone—Saverio, her friends, and even the audience—has been manipulated, and she seems to be in total control.

Saverio is roped into the game because he believes that playing the role of colonel will actually make him powerful, more like the authoritarian despot he would like to be. He sees only his chance to remake history as he believes it should be. As the play unfolds, Saverio becomes more and more involved in the part of the colonel; he acquires a uniform complete with sword, brings a guillotine into his room, and in general adopts the characteristics of a despotic authoritarian. In a series of dream sequences in which Saverio becomes more assertive, the audience perceives how he has become so immersed in the fiction of playing the colonel that it totally obfuscates reality for him. In his immersion in the "role" of colonel, Saverio has gone directly to the nightmarish core of brutality that is engendered by war. His innate cruelty surfaces when the reality of day-to-day living is obliterated through the opportunity to play *at* being cruel. Saverio has created for himself a world whose laws parallel those of his everyday existence. In his illusory world, however, he is in control; in everyday life, he is *not*. While his cruelty seems improbable, it follows established patterns and rules in the fiction he has created.

Susana plays a double game in which she has altered the rules for her own purposes, and has kept the knowledge of these new rules from the others, so that while they appear to be playing along with her, she is, in fact, playing *with* them and with Saverio. When Susana–Queen Bragatiana first enters in the play within the play, the setting is rustic, wild, and frenetic. In contrast, Act III opens in an elaborately-decorated ballroom with the invited guests dressed in 18th-century costumes, much in the style of Marie Antoinette. In the first scene, the focus is on establishing Susana's insanity; Saverio was an onlooker and not a participant. In the last act, Saverio is expected by all to be a participant; all, of course except Susana, who has her own intentions.

The audience sees the games as they are unfolding, games which reflect, metaphorically, aspects of the modern world, where the significant "game" is one of oppression and intimidation. The audience is involved, trapped within each set of successive games, enjoying the whimsical and farcical elements of Susana's and her friends' plots. When Susana then kills Saverio, the audience is forced to share in the grotesque vision of the world, because it too has seen logic and reality displaced. The total effect of these puzzling devices is to prevent the audience from discovering an orderly overall design in the work which permits a coherent reading arriving at closure. Whatever may be the realities of the "real world", in the "play" world those realities take on the character of a game. Each character wears multiple masks which appear to be mirrors reflecting the reverse sides of what the masks really are.

Saverio's difficulty in understanding Susana stems from believing that what is said and what is meant coincide in her language, thereby eliminating double meaning. The other characters swear that he is the colonel, thus affirming something that does not exist. His language as colonel is also based on something that does not exist. That language is marked by multiple meanings but interpreted as if it were unequivocal, and thus points to the paradoxical structure of meaning itself.

Until the end of the play, the audience believes in the line which separates the pretense from the reality, what it intrinsically accepts as lie versus truth. When Susana kills Saverio at the end, everything is twisted around so that the truth is erased. Susana manipulates everyone into believing that she is pretending to be insane, when she is, in fact sane.

The games force the audience to attempt to solve the enigma. The most disturbing aspect of the outcome is the recognition that the grounds for meaning and coherency have been placed within the insane world of Susana's delusions/illusions. By making strange the conventional world through the essence of madness, Arlt stretches the relative concepts of reality, forcing the audience to accept a reading that is fragmented and which reflects the world's thoroughgoing illogicality.

—Lynn Carbón Gorell

SAVERIO THE CRUEL. See **SAVERIO EL CRUEL.**

THE SCARLET PRINCESS OF EDO
(Sakura Hime Azuma Bunshō)
by Tsuruya Nanboku IV, with Sakurada Jisuke II and possibly Tsuchii Genshichi

First Production: Kawarazaki Theatre, Edo (Tokyo), March 1817.

Translations

The Scarlet Princess of Edo, in *Kabuki: Five Classic Plays*, translated by James Brandon, Cambridge, Massachusetts, 1975.

*   *   *

Sakura Hime Azuma Bunshō (literally translated, *The Story of Princess Cherry Blossom of Edo*) is a Kabuki Play in seven Acts, by Tsuruya Nanboku IV (1755–1829), Chief Playwright, assisted by Sakurada Jisuke II (1768–1829) and Tsuchii Genshichi (?). Nanboku is credited with writing Acts II (with Genshichi), III, IV, V, and the Finale. The category of the Play is *Jidai-Sewa-Mono* ("history-domestic play"). The first performance of this play took place in March, 1817, at the Kawarazaki Theatre in Edo (Tokyo). In modern days, several performances of the play have been staged, but most significant was the Japanese National Theatre production in 1967, since it revived most of the original scenes.

There are three major sources for the play. The earliest was a puppet play called *Seigen Sakurahime*. First staged in 1762, in Kyoto, the play provides the basic storyline of Priest Seigen of the Kiyomizu Temple being consumed by his one-sided love affair with Princess Sakura, and eventually being killed because of it. The second relates to the struggle for succession within the Yoshida Clan, commonly referred to as the Sumida River World because the bank of the river of that name provided the venue for the murder scene of the Clan Lord. The third source is an incident in which a prostitute named Okoto, in Shinagawa, near Edo, was punished by the authorities for claiming that she was the daughter of a courtier, Hino no Chūnagon. She was reported to have appeared in courtly attire and given a poem to a client signing it as a lady of the court. This incident took place in 1807, and Nanboku utilized it in his play ten years later by changing Princess Sakura into a prostitute nicknamed "Fūrin Ohime" (Princess Windbell) because of her temple bell tatoo, which was so tiny it resembled a windbell.

Following the oft-practiced, thinly disguised device of setting the time reference in a far earlier period of Kamakura (1192–1333) and thus avoiding government censorship of his unfavorable treatment of the warrior's conflict, Nanboku placed Princess Cherry Blossom (referred to as the Scarlet Princess in Brandon's translation) at the core of the play. In the Prologue, the Princess appears in her former incarnation as a temple page, Shiragiku, a nicely featured boy of 12 or 13, who sacrifices his life by joining in an act of double suicide with Priest Seigen in order to achieve the eventual union of their love in the other world. Seigen, however, hesitates and fails to complete the act.

17 years later, Princess Sakura, the daughter of Lord Yoshida, is found in Act I with a crippled left hand. This has caused a number of rejections from prospective suitors for marriage, most recently Iruma Akugorō, a high-ranking retainer of the Lord Yoshida. Despite her incomparable beauty, the Princess is burdened not only with the misfortune of her hand, but also the loss of her father and the scroll of Miyakodori (a gull), a precious heirloom. She is now determined to escape the misery of this world by placing herself in service to the Buddha, and she comes to ask the help of Seigen, now chief abbot of the New Kiyomizu Temple. As he and other priests pray for her, her left hand opens miraculously, revealing the lid of a crushed incense box with the name of "Kiyoharu" in Chinese characters (could also be read as "Seigen"), which was held in Shiragiku's hand when he jumped off the cliff. This discovery puts Seigen's future in complete disarray. With revived passion for the Princess (the

former Shiragiku in his mind), Seigen abandons all for which he has toiled—position, security and peace of mind. Meanwhile, the Princess is violated by Gonsuke (actually the villainous fallen samurai, Shinobu no Sōta), who was a tool of Akugorō's in killing her father, stealing the heirloom, murdering her brother and later selling her to the brothel, and eventually is slain by her when all his secrets spill from his mouth in drunken confusion.

Seigen follows the wandering Princess around as she cares for the baby she bore from her association with Gonsuke. The Princess shows no interest in Seigen and finally kills him to terminate his persistent suit for union. Seigen's undiminished desire appears nightly as a ghost, tormenting the Princess even when she is with clients. This ruins her popularity as the Princess Windbell, who has developed a unique style combining her courtly upbringing with the earthy language and attitude she has acquired as a prostitute, presenting an irresistable charm to many clients.

All falls into place in the Epilogue, in which the Princess is surrounded by captors but rescued by loyal retainers of the Yoshida Clan, who enter to protect the Princess and announce their intention of marching to the House of Yoshida to present the regained heirloom and to expose the wrongdoings of Akugorō.

After Kabuki theatre had developed and enriched itself, particularly through interchange with the puppet theatre, it reached the apex of its prosperity. It was Nanboku who opened up a new phase of the Kabuki world by introducing bloody situations tainted with murder, cruelty, indecency and black humor, often resulting in masterpieces dealing with ghosts and presenting bizarre excitement. To provide a number of intricate, quick-change scenes for capable actors of the time, Nanboku perfected this technique. In one scene of this play, Gonsuke's face appears to merge with that of Seigen. Such a moment can be realized only through precision quick-change techniques. *Sakura Hime Azuma Bunshō* successfully embodies all the qualities that distinguish Nanboku's works.

—Andrew T. Tsubaki

THE SCAVENGERS. See **THE VULTURES.**

THE SCENARIOS OF FLAMINIO SCALA
(Il teatro dell favole rappresentative)
by Flaminio Scala

First Publication: Venice, 1611.

Editions
La Commedia dell'arte: Storia, Technica, Scenari, edited by Enzo Petraccone, Naples, 1927 [contains the following scenarii: *Il marito; Il ritratto; I tappeti alessandrini; L'Alvida; La forsennata principessa*].
Il teatro delle favole rappresentative (2 vols.), edited by Ferrucio Marotti, Milan, 1976.

Translations
Scenarios of the Commedia dell'Arte, translated by Henry F. Salerno, New York, 1976.

Criticism
(For general works on the author, see *Playwrights* volume)

Books:
Kenneth and Laura Richards, *The Commedia dell'Arte: A Documentary History*, Oxford, 1990.

Articles:
Winifred Smith, "A Comic Version of *Romeo and Juliet*", in *Modern Philology*, 7, 1909.
Allardyce Nicoll, "The Comedy of Skill", in his *The World of Harlequin*, Cambridge, 1963.
Ferrucio Marotti, "Il *Teatro dell favole rappresentative*: Un progetto utopico", in *Biblioteca teatrale*, 15–16, 1976.

*   *   *

Italian *Commedia dell'arte* players for the most part did not work with scripted texts, but improvised many of the plays they performed on the basis of brief scenarios. About 800 of these *scenarii* (also called *soggetti* or *cannovacci*) have survived, most of them in manuscript collections formed in the 17th and 18th centuries. Basically guides for actors, they are a useful source of information about improvised performance, indicating something of the ways in which players might, through improvisation, compose a play. Scenarios may have been pinned up backstage to serve as action mnemonics for the players, and they can be helpful in indicating something of the pattern of exits and entrances, of appearances at windows and aloft (which were features of the comic action), and in some instances they point to specific "business" and scene changes; but they present many interpretative difficulties. Most of those extant can be dated only approximately, and by no means all were scripted or performed by professionals, for not only they, but amateurs too, practised play-making by improvisation. The utility of the scenarios as guides to stage practice is variable, for some provide very general, technical indications, others much more specific ones, of what actors might do at particular moments in the action of a play. Although they usually contain fairly clear indications of plot lines, they are not simply plot synopses, and for that reason too they present interpretative difficulties. Finally, when attempting to draw conclusions about stage practice from the scenarios, it is essential to remember that they are not plays in miniature, and even more than is the case with a play text, any given *scenario* could be radically different in the hands of different groups of players.

Many of the extant collections of scenarios were probably gathered in random fashion, eventually finding their way into libraries in the late-17th and 18th centuries, like the Corsini collection now in the Accademia dei Lincei in Rome. Some, like the Adriani collection in the Biblioteca Comunale in Perugia, contain not only scenarios, but a range of performance materials, like *lazzi* and set speeches. An important early collection of scenarios, and the only one published during the great period of the *commedia dell'arte* (from the mid-16th through to the mid-18th centuries) is Flaminio Scala's *Il teatro delle favole rappresentative* (Venice, 1611). Scala (1547–1621) was a major figure in the history of the professional companies, but undoubtedly he is most important as a collector of scenarios. Whether those he published were of his own composition is not absolutely certain, but it seems highly likely, from the comments of contemporaries and early historians, and from his own remarks in the prologue to his comedy *Il finto marito* (1619) which claimed authorship for most, if not all of them. Scala was indeed a versatile man of the theatre, for in addition to composing plays, he was an actor and probably a company director. He acted under the stage name of Flavio, playing lovers' roles, and was no doubt a capable performer, although there are few references to his skills as a player. It seems highly likely he directed companies for a time, including the Confidenti troupe, and it was perhaps in both capacities, as player and as manager, that he won his reputation for contributing substantially to the artistic organisation and refinement of the professional drama: the 18th-century commentator Bartoli refers to him as "the first to organise the *commedia dell'arte improvviso* in a systematic way, and to formulate all the exact rules for it".

Scala's collection reflects his brilliant dramaturgical gifts, theatrical flair, and eye for detail: "Their structure is slight", said the 18th-century troupe manager, Luigi Riccoboni, "but [Scala] possessed skilful invention, and so was praised by the best poets of his time: their verses preface his book and they held him in the very highest regard for having produced the finest drama seen up to that time". The Prologue Scala wrote to his *Il finto marito*, shows how aware he was of the importance of the actor as creator, for he attempted to advance a reasoned and coherent aesthetic for actor-devised drama. His collection of scenarios indicates the range of genres encompassed by the improvising players, for it includes comedy, tragicomedy, tragedy, pastoral, and historical and mythological spectacle, and it provides useful information about characteristic properties, stage appurtenances, and decorations. We can see from Scala scenarios that the late 16th- and early 17th-century comedians were accustomed to perform before comparatively simple settings, the invariable *locus* of these action mnemonics being a street or *piazza* backed by two or three houses or an inn (although some, like one of the finest in Scala, *The Jealous Old Man*, have rather more diverse settings).

Scala's collection was possibly organised to be read on a *giornate* basis, rather like Boccaccio's *novelle*. In preparing it for readers he probably clarified the content and paid particular attention to matters of literary style; thus exactly how much he modified his stage materials for publication remains open to conjecture, and must leave some doubt as to the kind of evidence we can extract from the collection about actual stage practice. We can note, however, that the plot lines are richly various, that comedy dominates, and that many of the type figures and stock materials of classical and Renaissance scripted drama recur: the *dramatis personae* is invariably made up mainly of *senes*, *servi*, and young lovers; servants scheme against masters, young lovers are frustrated by the plans of old parents, experienced women are deceived and seek revenge, boasting pedants or military men are invariably worsted; trickery, disguise, and mistaken identity abound; and there are as many confusions, deceptions, and love pursuits in the scenarios as are to be found in the popular *novelle*. As the only early printed collection of scenarios, Scala's *Il teatro delle favole rappresentative* was highly influential and probably conditioned the written form of many later professional scenarios; although by the later 17th and the early 18th centuries, its content may have been seen as old-fashioned, as the Italian improvised drama, including the comedy, (as Luigi Riccoboni's extant early-18th-century Comedie Italienne *scenarii* indicate) came increasingly to exploit more scenery and machines than are called for in Scala.

—Kenneth Richards

SCENES FROM THE HEROIC LIFE OF THE MIDDLE CLASSES
(Aus dem bürgerlichen Heldenleben)

> The Bloomers (Die Hose)
> The Money Box (Die Kassette)
> Paul Schippel Esq. (Bürger Schippel)
> The Snob (Der Snob)
> 1913
> The Fossil (Die Fossil)

by Carl Sternheim

The Bloomers (Die Hose)
First Publication: Leipzig, 1911.
First Production: As *Der Reise*, Kammerspiele des Deutsches Theater, Berlin, 25 February 1911.

The Money Box (Die Kassette)
First Publication: Leipzig, 1912.
First Production: Kammerspiele des Deutsches Theater, Berlin, 24 November 1911.

Paul Schippel Esq. (Bürger Schippel)
First Publication: Leipzig, 1913.
First Production: Kammerspiele des Deutsches Theater, Berlin, 5 March 1913.

The Snob (Der Snob)
First Publication: Leipzig, 1914.
First Production: Kammerspiele des Deutsches Theater, Berlin, 2 February 1914.

1913
First Publication: Leipzig, 1915.
First Production: Schauspielhaus, Frankfurt am Main, 23 January 1919.

The Fossil (Das Fossil)
First Publication: In *Die Aktion*, vol.13; in book form, Potsdam, 1925.
First Production: Kammerspiele, Hamburg, 6 November 1923.

Translations
A Pair of Drawers [translation of *Die Hose*], in *Translation* (Paris), 6–9, 1927.
A Place in the World [translation of *Der Snob*], translated by B. Clark and W. Katzin, in *Eight European Plays*, edited by W. Katzin, New York, 1927.
The Snob, translated by Eric Bentley, in *From the Modern Repertoire* (series 1), edited by Eric Bentley, Denver, Colorado, 1949.
The Underpants, in *The Modern Theatre, 6*, edited and translated by Eric Bentley, Garden City, NY, 1960.
The Money Box, translated by Maurice Edwards and Valerie Reich, in *An Anthology of German Expressionist Drama*, edited by W.H. Sokel, New York, 1963.
Carl Sternheim Plays [contains *Paul Schippel Esq.*, translated by M.A.L. Brown; *The Bloomers*, translated by M.A. McHaffie; *The Snob*, translated by J.M. Ritchie and J.D. Stowell; *1913*, translated by J.M. Ritchie; *The Fossil*, translated by J.M. Ritchie], London, 1970.

Scenes from the Heroic Life of the Middle Classes: The Snob,   Kammerspiele, Berlin, 1914 (first production)

Criticism

(For general works on the author, see *Playwrights* volume)

Books:

Winifred Freund, *Die Bürgerkomödien Carl Sternheims*, Munich, 1976.

Eckehard Czucka, *Idiom der Entstellung: Auffaltung des Satirischen in Carl Sternheims "Aus dem bürgerlichen Heldenleben"*, Münster, 1982.

Articles:

Paul Rilla, "Sternheims Bürgerkomödien", in his *Literatur, Kritik und Polemik*, Berlin, 1950.

Edson M. Chick, "Sternheim's *1913* as Satire: Fantasy and Fashion", in *Studies in the German Drama: A Festschrift in Honor of Walter Silz*, edited by Donald H. Crosby and George C. Schoolfield, Chapel Hill, North Carolina, 1974.

Rainer Rumold, "Carl Sternheims Komödie *Die Hose*: Sprachkritik, Sprachsatire und der Verfremdungseffekt vor Brecht", in *Michigan Germanic Studies*, vol. 4 no.1, 1978.

Heinrich Siefkin, "'Ein ganzes Arsenal nichtssagender Floskeln': Sternheim's Comedy *Bürger Schippel*", in *Forum for Modern Language Studies*, 15, 1979.

Jean Favrat, "Dialogue et langage théâtral dans la comédie de Carl Sternheim: *Bürger Schippel*", in *Essais sur le dialogue*, edited by Jean Lavédrine, Grenoble, 1980.

Günter Scholdt, "Gegenentwürfe: Zu Sternheims *Bürgerlichen Heldenzyklus* und seinem Verhältnis zu Molière", in *Jahrbuch der deutschen Schiller-Gesellschaft*, 26, 1982.

Helmut Arntzen, "Komödien des Irrtums: Zur heutigen Rezeption von Sternheims Stücken *Aus dem bürgerlichen Heldenleben*", in his *Zur Sprachen kommen*, Münster, 1983.

Edson M. Chick, "Carl Sternheim's *1913*: Obsessed by Prestige", in his *Dances of Death: Wedekind, Brecht, Dürrenmatt, and the Satiric Tradition*, Columbia, South Carolina, 1984.

Hildegard Nabbe, "Parodie und literarische Satire in Carl Sternheims *Die Hose*", in *Neophilologus*, 68, 1984.

Theo Buck, "Sternheim oder das Ende des Dialogs: zur Dramaturgie in den Stücken *Aus dem bürgerlichen Heldenleben*", in *Text und Kritik*, vol. 87, 1985.

Eckehard Czucka, "Schimären des Tatsächlichen: die Maske-Tetralogie in Carl Sternheims *Aus dem bürgerlichen Heldenleben*", in *Neophilologus*, vol. 72, 1988.

*   *   *

Carl Sternheim's *Scenes from the Heroic Life* is generally considered to include six dramas, although *The Bloomers* (*Die Hose*), *The Snob*, (*Der Snob*), and *Paul Schippel Esq.* (*Bürger Schippel*) are the most usually performed and read. *The Bloomers*, written 1909–10, is the first of four dramas about a typical, Wilhelmine, bourgeois family before World War I, successful economically and socially because of its combination of apparent respectability and extravagant life-style. Luise, the attractive young wife of Theobald Maske, a petty but ambitious civil servant, has brought the Emperor's procession to a halt when the fastening of her knickers snaps—she had been daydreaming when she put them on, and now they come down at the exciting moment when the Emperor is about to pass. Theobald is seen at the start beating his wife because he feels her "misdemeanour" will cost him his job. Instead, it brings them fortune through two witnesses who come to rent a room: Mandelstam, a barber, and Scarron, a struggling poet. They give up their aim of seducing Luise, Theobald realizing their intentions, exploiting their wishes, and overcharging them. Luise feels she has a right to seek love elsewhere, her

husband proving so brutal, and resolves to develop a romantic passion for Scarron whom fate has delivered to her. In this plan she is supported by their neighbour, Fräulein Deuter, whose frustrated sexual desires are transferred vicariously when she fantasizes with Luise in preparing a new pair of frilly knickers for the latter's first night with Scarron. However, Scarron proves to be incapable of fulfilling his projected romantic role, and Luise is reduced to trying to inflame the passions of Mandelstam, whom she had rejected previously as an obstacle between her and Scarron. Mandelstam rejects her advances, and she is forced to return to her husband. While she is confessing her sins in church, Fräulein Deuter comes to deliver the finished underwear and, Theobald happening to be present, he exploits the opportunity to take her off to the bedroom.

Theobald exploits every opportunity and protects number one. He knows, well-nigh instinctively, just how far he can go, often mimicking others in the process. Technically the play is a masterpiece in the controlled use of surprise turns, all of which serve to remind the audience of the scandalous knickers. Indeed, they almost attain the significance of a hidden character, determining the actions and fate of all the real characters. All start the play with definite, idealized aims, which have totally unexpected outcomes. The result is a study on different levels of social irony—however farcical Sternheim's situations may seem to be, they all reflect back on or hint at the continuous presence of the needs of society at large.

Theobald can rightly claim that the extra financial security he now has through rents will enable him and Luise to raise a family (money that has come through her moment of inattention), yet at the same time he can ensure that his affair with Fräulein Deuter will continue on a weekly basis. Thanks to his ruthlessness, imperturbability, and self-seeking qualities, he emerges alarmingly as an all-too successful character in contrast with the insipid creatures who surround him. Paradoxically, it is the evil character who exercises most attraction and hence affords an albeit cynical grandiloquence, only to show up the pettiness of the average man and woman, unable to surpass themselves. The underlying theme of the triumph of the foolish husband over his rivals satirizes a long tradition in bourgeois comedy, for by sticking closely to his bourgeois values and masking his true motives Theobald can present a facade of simple self-assurance and win all he wants. The characters are like figures out of a fairy-tale, their antics close to farce, their behaviour bordering on melodrama of a vulgar kind. Yet their apparently grotesque behaviour turns into all-too human responses when faced with unexpected situations. Sternheim thus passes off the playful and superficial as sharp comments on social mores and contemporary bourgeois life with all its artificiality.

The shamelessly embarrassing opening of *The Bloomers* has been all but forgotten by the opening of *The Snob* where the central character, Christian Maske (son of Luise and Theobald) is arranging to marry the daughter of Count Palen and achieve acceptance into a higher social sphere, when his father returns unexpectedly from Switzerland. Christian fears he will lose everything when it is discovered he comes from a humble background, only to find that it is fashionable; he is all the more acceptable in his self-identification with the nobility. His status as a self-made man (who can pay off his former, caring girlfriend with five per cent interest) now leads him to boast of something for which he is not responsible. His success turns his head, so that on his wedding night, enjoying the triumph of his rise up the social ladder, he remembers the story of his mother's earlier unfortunate episode and turns this to his profit by narrating how—as he puts it—his parents were walking in the Bois de Boulogne, when his mother's knickers fell down just as the artist Renoir was passing. Renoir, enchanted by the episode, offered to paint her as he first saw her and introduced her to a French viscount; all this happening about a year before Christian was born. As his mother has just died, he can produce a painting by Renoir to "prove" the story. He talks of the family country estate, apparently recently repurchased by him, thus showing that he too is finally persuaded of the false validity of his fable. Christian, as a bourgeois, has needed to act out a lie to get to the top, and in the end forfeits his own integrity and real identity in doing so. He *becomes* the mask he has put on.

In *Paul Schippel Esq.* three members of a successful vocal quartet are left with an awkward problem when their fourth member dies just before an important competition. The only possible replacement is a local worker, Schippel, whose remarkable singing talent overcomes their bourgeois pride, so he joins the group. Schippel realizes he is indispensable and asks Thekla, Hicketier's sister, to marry him. She has recently lost her virginity to the local prince, so Hicketier finds his proposal convenient, although he declares his sister no longer socially acceptable. Schippel then refuses to allow his new-found dignity to be compromised by such a woman and casts doubt on her to Krey, who has proposed to her and been accepted. Insulted, Krey challenges Schippel to a duel, and the latter (trembling with fear) manages to wound him. Honour now satisfied, Hicketier welcomes Schippel as a full-blown bourgeois. Both Schippel and Hicketier fall foul of their actions, and the irony is laid on thick—especially in the duel scene and in Schippel's final acceptance. Sternheim's art of interleaving primary and secondary plots here reaches its peak, for in addition to the satire in *Die Hose* and the ironic ending of *Der Snob*, here he parodies a whole literary and musical world aped by amateur connoisseurs of bourgeois culture.

—Brian Keith-Smith

SCHERZ, SATIRE, IRONIE, UND TIEFERE BEDEUTUNG. See **COMEDY, SATIRE, IRONY AND DEEPER MEANING.**

THE SCHOOL FOR SCANDAL
by Richard Brinsley Sheridan

First Publication: Dublin, 1780 ("bad", private printing); first "good" text, Dublin, 1799; with revisions, in *Collected Works*, 1821.
First Production: Theatre Royal, Drury Lane, 8 May 1777.

Editions

The School for Scandal, in *Sheridan: Six Plays*, edited by Lewis Gibbs, London, 1906.
The School for Scandal, in *The Dramatic Works of Richard Brinsley Sheridan* (2 vols.), edited by Cecil Price, Oxford, 1957.
The School for Scandal, edited by Vincent F. Hopper and Gerald B. Lahey, Woodbury, New York, 1958.
The School for Scandal, in *Sheridan's Plays*, edited by Cecil Price, London, 1975.

The School for Scandal, edited by F.W. Bateson, London, 1979 (New Mermaid Series).
The School for Scandal, in *"The School for Scandal" and Other Plays*, edited by Eric D. Rump, Harmondsworth, 1988.

Criticism
(For general works on the author, see *Playwrights* volume)

Articles:
John R. Dolman, "Laugh Analysis of *The School for Scandal*", in *Quarterly Journal of Speech*, 16, 1930.
Andrew Schiller, "*The School for Scandal*: The Restoration Unrestored", in *Publications of the Modern Language Association* [*PMLA*], 62, 1956.
J.R. de J. Jackson, "The Importance of Witty Dialogue in *The School for Scandal*", in *Modern Language Notes*, 76, 1961.
Christian Deelman, "The Original Cast of *The School for Scandal*", in *Review of English Studies*, 13, 1962.
Arthur Sprague, "In Defence of a Masterpiece: *The School for Scandal* Re-examined", in *English Studies Today*, edited by George I. Duthie, 1964.
Kenneth S. Rothwell, "*The School for Scandal*: The Comic Spirit in Sheridan and Rowlandson", in *The School for Scandal: Thomas Rowlandson's London*, Lawrence, Kansas, 1967.
Leonard J. Leff, "The Disguise Motif in *The School for Scandal*", in *Educational Theatre Journal*, 22, 1970.
Jack Durant, "The Moral Focus of *The School for Scandal*", in *South Atlantic Bulletin*, vol.37 no.4, 1972.
Jack Durant, "Prudence, Providence and the Direct Road of Wrong: *The School for Scandal* and Sheridan's Westminister Hall Speech", in *Studies of Burke and His Time*, 15, 1974.
F.W. Bateson, "The Application of Thought to an Eighteenth Century Text: *The School for Scandal*", in *Evidence in Literary Scholarship: Essays in Memory of James Maxwell Osborn*, edited by René Wellek and Alvaro Ribeiro, Oxford, 1979.
B.S. Pathania, "*The School for Scandal*: A Re-evaluation", in *Journal of the Department of English* (Calcutta University), 17, 1981–82.
Ernest W.B. Hess-Lüttich, "Maxims of Maliciousness: Sheridan's School for Conversation", in *Poetics*, 11, 1982.
Jack D. Durant, "Sheridan's Picture-Auction Scene: A Study in Contexts", in *Eighteenth Century Life*, 11, 1987.

* * *

A "college" of scandalmongers meets in Lady Sneerwell's house to murder people's reputations. Sneerwell is attracted to Charles, the profligate brother of Joseph Surface. Joseph, who assumes the guise of "a man of sentiment", pursues Maria, who is in love with Charles. Sir Peter Teazel has married a woman much younger then himself. Lady Teazel encourages Joseph's pretended interest in her, but Joseph is using her to insinuate himself with Maria. Sir Oliver Surface, Charles and Joseph's uncle and benefactor, returns from India. To test Charles he visits him disguised as a moneylender and is scandalized when the former sells him the family portraits. Charles disarms him, however, by refusing to part with Sir Oliver's portrait. He also shows compassion for a poor relation, Mr. Stanley.

Lady Teazel visits Joseph and hides behind a screen when Sir Peter appears. Sir Peter exposes Joseph's interest in Maria and his own concern for his wife, with Lady Teazel listening in. Charles arrives, and, when Joseph briefly leaves the room, knocks down the screen to reveal Lady Teazel, who denounces

The School for Scandal: Theatre Royal, Drury Lane, London, 1777 (first production)

the hypocritical Joseph and, touched by her husband's concern, promises a reformed relationship with him. Joseph is further disgraced when Sir Oliver appears to him disguised as Mr. Stanley to test his generosity—and Joseph proves heartless. Despite a last-ditch attempt by Lady Sneerwell to compromise Charles, he is able to discredit her and her accomplice, Joseph, and is united with Maria.

When Sheridan combined his two preliminary sketches—the first exposing the excesses of a group of inveterate scandalmongers, and the second the misfortunes of the relationship between Sir Peter and Lady Teazel—into *The School for Scandal*, he achieved what would prove to be the most popular English comedy of the 18th century. The play revived the witty dialogue of Restoration comedy; Sheridan gathered aphorisms and elegant phrases, sometimes insinuating them into the mouths of inappropriate characters. The result earned him the title of "the modern Congreve".

As with the comedies of Congreve, the play owed much of its success to the skill with which Sheridan accommodated the roles to the actors at his disposal. *The School for Scandal* is an actor's play, offering, in even the smallest parts, superb opportunities for comic acting. Joseph Surface was perfectly adapted to the abilities of "Plausible Jack" Palmer, of whom Charles Lamb wrote: "Jack had two voices—both plausible, hypocritical, and insinuating; but his secondary or supplemental voice still more decisively histrionic than his common one. . .the sentiments in Joseph Surface, were thus marked out in a sort of italics to the audience". William "Gentleman"

Smith played Charles; William King played Sir Peter Teazel; and Lady Teazel perfectly suited the "comic archness and vitality" of Frances Abingdon. The role combines two propensities: the "naturalness" that springs from Lady Teazel's country origins, and the sophistication from her experience in town. Frances Abingdon, *The London Magazine* observed in May 1777, brought to the performance "more of the town, than country coquette". Later Mrs. Jordan would demonstrate in the role "all the natural ingenuousness of an artless unsullied mind". The variety of possible interpretations and emphases contributes to the play's reputation as a superb vehicle for actors.

The comparison with Congreve, however, serves also to underline the extent to which Sheridan's play differed from the great Caroline comedies. It is distinguished by a domestic morality, a belief in innate human goodness, which is quite at odds with the comedy of the earlier period. Thus, Charles Surface differs from Valentine in Congreve's *Love for Love* (1695) by possessing a benevolence that will not allow him to sell Sir Oliver's portrait, and expresses itself in his concern for the unfortunate Stanley. Lady Teazel proves impervious to Joseph's attempted seduction and is touched to the quick by Sir Peter's concern for her well-being. A comparison between Lady Teazel and Margery Pinchwife in Wycherley's *The Country Wife* (1675) reveals the differences between these two characters. Sir Peter makes it clear on his first entrance that he loves his wife in spite of her vexatiousness ("Yet the worst of it is. . .I love her, or I should never bear all this"): he is a world removed from the brutal oppressiveness of Pinchwife in Wycherley's play.

The wit of Lady Sneerwell and her "college" is sustained by malice ("The malice of a good thing is the barb that makes it stick", Lady Sneerwell asserts) and is marked by artfulness and complexity. Mrs. Clackitt, as a scandalmonger, is inferior to Lady Sneerwell for, we are told, "She wants that delicacy of hint and mellowness of sneer which distinguishes your ladyship's scandal". Complexity also characterizes the actions of the aberrant characters. "So close at last", Durant observes (in his article "The Moral Focus of *The School for Scandal*"), "is the correlation between complexity and evil that complexity, as an agent of evil, becomes a force apart from the character generating it".

The truly virtuous are ingenuous and straightforward, as is evident, for instance, in the directness with which Charles confesses to his financial embarrassment ("I am an extravagant young fellow who wants to borrow money, you I take to be a prudent old fellow, who have got money to lend") or in the candour with which Lady Teazel counters the devious arguments of Joseph in the screen scene. The two, contradictory impulses, towards brittle cynicism on the one hand, and sentimentality on the other, may seem, at times, to threaten the unity of the whole; but they are a fruitful source of irony and dramatic contradiction. The play is finally resolved, however, in terms of human benevolence. Indeed, the charm of *The School for Scandal* and the reason for its enduring popularity lie in its ability to persuade us of the essential goodness of human nature.

—Colin Wills Visser

THE SCHOOL FOR WIVES (L'École des femmes)
by Molière

First Publication: Paris, 1663.
First Production: Théâtre du Palais-Royal, Paris, 26 December 1662.

Editions
L'École des femmes, edited by A. Nockels, London, 1956.
L'École des femmes, edited by P. Cabanis, Paris, 1963.
"*L'École des femmes*" with "*La Critique de L'École des femmes*", edited by W.D. Howarth, Oxford, 1963.
L'École des femmes, edited by G. Sablayrolles, Paris, 1965.
L'École des femmes, edited by Alfred Simon and Hubert Gignoux, Paris, 1970.
"*L'École des femmes*" suivi de la "*Critique de L'École des femmes*", edited by Rosalyne Laplace, Paris, 1983.

Translations
The School for Wives, in *Molière: Eight Plays*, edited and translated by Morris Bishop, New York, 1957.
The School for Wives, in "*Tartuffe*" and Other Plays, translated by Donald Frame, New York, 1967.
The School for Wives, adapted by Eric M. Steel, New York, 1971.
The School for Wives, translated by Richard Wilbur, New York, 1971.
The School for Wives, translated by Robert David MacDonald, Birmingham, 1987.

Criticism
(For general works on the author, see *Playwrights* volume)

Books:
Jacques Arnavon, *L'Interpretation de la comédie classique: "L'École des femmes" de Molière*, Paris, 1936.
J.H. Broome, *Molière: "L'École des femmes" and "Le Misanthrope"*, London, 1982.
Noël Peacock, *Molière: "L'École des femmes"*, Glasgow, 1988.

Articles:
Napoléon Maurice Bernardin, "Le Théâtre de Molière: *L'École des femmes*; Conférence à l'Odeon", in *Revue des cours et conférences*, vol. 12 no.1, 1903–04
Judd D. Hubert, "*L'École des femmes*: Tragédie burlesque?", in *Revue des sciences humaines*, 97, 1960.
P.H. Nurse, "The Role of Chrysalde in *L'École des femmes*", in *Modern Language Review*, 56, 1961.
Alfred Cismaru, "Agnès and Arnolphe: An Attempt to Settle the Relationship", in *French Review*, 35, 1962.
Jacques Ehrmann, "Notes sur *L'École des femmes*", in *Revue des sciences humaines*, no.97, 1963.
W.D. Howarth, "The Source of *L'École des femmes*", in *Modern Language Review*, 58, 1963.
W. Beck, "Arnolphe ou Monsieur de la Souche", in *French Review*, 42, 1968–69.
H.D. Porter, "Comic Rhythm in *L'École des femmes*", in *Forum for Modern Language Studies*, 5, 1969.
Robert N. Nicolich, "Door, Window, and Balcony in *L'École des femmes*", in *Romance Notes*, 12, 1971.
Bernard Magné, "*L'École des femmes* ou la conquête de la parole", in *Revue des sciences humaines*, 145, 1972.
R. Picard, "Molière comique ou tragique? Le Cas Arnolphe", in *Revue d'histoire de la littérature française*, 1972.
Edith Kern, "*L'École des femmes* and the Spirit of Farce", in *L'Esprit créateur*, 13, 1973.
B. Weinberg, "Plot and Thesis in *L'École des femmes*", in *Romance Notes*, 15, supplement 1, 1973.
Myrna K. Zwillenberg, "Arnolphe, Fate's Fool", in *Modern Language Review*, 68, 1973.
Ralph Albanese Jr., "Pédagogie et didactisme dans *L'École des femmes*", in *Romance Notes*, 16, 1974.
Renate Baader, "Religion und Preziosität in der *École des femmes*", in *Germanisch-Romanische Monatsschrift*, 26, 1976.
Robert McBride, "La Question du raisonneur dans les *Écoles* de Molière", in *Dix-septième Siècle*, 113, 1976.
Gabriel Conesa, "Remarques sur la structure dramatique de *L'École des femmes*", in *Revue d'histoire du théâtre*, 30, 1978.
Elisabeth Schulze-Witzenrath, "Sprachhandlung und hohe Komödie in Molières *École des femmes*", in *Poetica*, 10, 1978.
J.T. Letts, "*L'École des femmes* ou la défaite de la parole inauthentique", in *Modern Language Notes*, 95, 1980.
James F. Gaines, "*L'École des femmes*: Usurpation, Dominance, and Social Closure", in *Papers on French Seventeenth Century Literature*, vol. 9 no.17, 1982.
Peter Hampshire, "Introduction to Molière's *L'École des femmes*", in *Modern Languages*, vol. 63 no.4, 1982.
Nina C. Ekstein, "The Functions of the *Récit* in *L'École des femmes*", in *Kentucky Romance Quarterly*, vol. 30 no.3, 1983.
Henri Bonnard, "Étude de langue et du style d'un passage de *L'École des femmes*", in *L'Information grammaticale*, 23, 1984.

Micheline Bourbeau-Walker, "L'Échec d'Arnolphe: Loi du genre ou faille intérieure?", in *Papers on French Seventeenth Century Literature*, vol.11 no.20, 1984.

N.A. Peacock, "Verbal Costume in *L'École des femmes*", in *Modern Language Review*, vol.79 no.3, 1984

Françoise Berlan, "L'Ingénuité d'Agnes: Étude d'un champ lexical dans *L'École des femmes*", in *L'Information grammaticale*, 24, 1985.

Thomas Braga, "The *Le-là* Conflict and *Les* Contract in *L'École des femmes*", in *French Studies in Honor of Philip A. Wadsworth*, edited by Donald W. Tappon, Birmingham, Alabama, 1985.

Patrick Dandrey, "Structures et espaces de communication dans *L'École des femmes*", in *Littérature*, 63, 1986.

Jocelyn Powell, "Making Faces: Character and Physiognomy in *L'École des femmes* and *L'Avare*", in *Seventeenth Century French Studies*, 9, 1987.

William J. Beck, "La Métamorphose avortée d'Arnolphe", in *Revue d'histoire du théâtre*, vol.40 no.3, 1988.

David Clarke, "*L'École des femmes*: Plotting and Significance in a *Machine à rire*", in *Seventeenth Century French Studies*, 11, 1989.

*   *   *

This is the earliest of the five-act verse comedies of manners for which Molière is chiefly remembered today. Molière himself took the main role, that of Arnolphe, a respected bourgeois of Paris, who has an obsessive fear of being cuckolded. He has adopted a four-year-old orphan, Agnes, and has had her brought up in complete ignorance, planning to make her his wife. He believes that her naivety will preserve her virtue. When the play begins, he is 42 and she is 18. He returns from a trip and runs into Horace, the son of an old friend. Horace is new to Paris, but has already fallen in love with Agnes. He fails to connect Arnolphe with the absent M. de la Souche, Agnes's amorous guardian: he is not to know that Arnolphe has recently changed his name to M. de la Souche for snobbish reasons, so he innocently tells Arnolphe every detail of his new romance.

Arnolphe conceals his true interest in these events, resolving to outwit Horace by marrying Agnes himself immediately. Horace continues to pay court to Agnes, and to make Arnolphe his confidant. Arnolphe is thus able to forestall all Horace's plans for outwitting "M. de la Souche". However, it soon becomes clear that Agnes has fallen in love with Horace. Despite her ignorance, she manages to outwit her guardian, and to elope with Horace. The young man hands her over to his friend Arnolphe for safekeeping, and leaves. Arnolphe unmasks himself and confronts her. She defies him, but is powerless to save her love. Horace arrives with his father, who is in Paris to arrange the marriage of his son to an unknown woman. To Horace's dismay, Arnolphe urges the father to force his son to go through with this arranged marriage despite his love for Agnes. When Arnolphe is referred to as "M. de la Souche", the truth finally dawns on the naive, young man. All seems lost, but a final, improbable twist brings about a happy ending: Agnes is not an orphan after all, but is the very same girl whom the father destined for Horace.

The play's principal theme is innocence versus experience. Arnolphe, knowing and worldly-wise, represents experience, pitted against a group of innocents. Even the two comic servants supposed to be guarding Agnes are ludicrously naïve. Horace is feather-brained, never asking himself how his secret plans are somehow forestalled by his rival. Agnes starts out as a figure of fun—she thinks children come out of people's ears. But she is also intelligent and honest. She gradually comes to realize that she has been brought up a fool, and her intellectual and emotional awakening, which gives the play its title, is moving to watch.

By far the most important character, however, is Arnolphe. His is the longest and most taxing of all of the roles that Molière wrote for himself. The character has a strong farcical side: fear of cuckoldry was a source of ribald mirth in the theatre in Molière's day, and Arnolphe was a traditional name for a stage cuckold. Arnolphe is frequently the butt of farcical stage action. He is pushed around by his own servants; forced to laugh uproariously while Horace tells him how successfully he is outwitting "M. de la Souche"; repeatedly made so furious that he is in a lather, or longing to tear out half his hair. Yet Arnolphe has admirable qualities too: he is generous to Horace, respected by his friends, and above all, his passion for Agnes is real and moving. His feelings for her grow, even as she grows in wisdom. He begins by regarding her as putty in his hands, but by the end is willing to allow her every freedom if only she will stay with him. Molière himself wrote of the character: "it is not inconsistent for a man to be worthy in some respects and ridiculous in others". The role has complex implications, and has been interpreted in a number of ways, from the farcical to the sombre. From contemporary accounts, we learn that Molière favoured a light-hearted rendering.

Despite its ludicrous plot, the play has a satirical edge. Arnolphe's fear of cuckoldry is founded on a disenchanted view of contemporary society, in which complaisant husbands allow their wives to fritter fortunes away on cards and fripperies, even turning a blind eye to their infidelities. Arnolphe advocates an alternative ideal of marriage in which the wife is the drudge of her lord and master, and should not even be permitted to write letters. This, too, is a satire of the practices of excessively devout Catholics: Molière was violently attacked for mocking these ideals in the play. It is difficult to establish where the playwright actually stands in this debate about marriage. The character of the "raisonneur", Chrysalde (Arnolphe's friend), maintains that the important thing is to be a civilized Parisian, and to avoid scandal. If one's wife chooses to misbehave, one should at least have the consolation of keeping up appearances. This view might seem over-cynical; it has even been argued that Chrysalde was exaggerating in order to tease his friend. On the other hand, the sincerity of the formulation does seem to argue some considerable degree of conviction on the author's part.

Modern productions have tended to concentrate on the implications for women of Arnolphe's treatment of Agnes and of her fight to liberate herself. Yet this controversial play presents a real challenge for the director; there are different ways of making sense of it, and it remains among the most performed of Molière's comedies.

—Maya Slater

DER SCHWIERIGE. See **THE DIFFICULT MAN.**

THE SEA GULL. See **THE SEAGULL.**

THE SEAGULL (Chaika / Chayka)
by Anton Chekhov

First Publication: In *Russkaya Mysl* [*The Russian Idea*], December 1896; in book form, in *Chekhov: Plays*, St. Petersburg, 1897; revised version, in *Collected Works, 7*, 1901.
First Production: Alexandrinsky Theatre, St. Petersburg, 17 October 1896.

Translations

The Seagull, translated by Julius West, London, 1915.
The Sea Gull, in *"The Cherry Orchard" and Other Plays*, translated by Constance Garnett, London, 1923.
The Seagull, translated by Stark Young, New York, 1939.
The Seagull, [with production score by Stanislavsky], translated by David Magarshack, London, 1952.
The Seagull, in *"The Seagull" and Other Plays*, translated by Elisaveta Fen, Harmondsworth, 1953/54.
The Sea Gull, in *Six Plays of Chekhov*, translated by Robert Corrigan, New York, 1962.
The Sea Gull, in *Chekhov: The Major Plays*, translated by Ann Dunnigan, New York, 1964.
The Seagull, in *The Oxford Chekhov, 2*, edited and translated by Ronald Hingley, Oxford, 1967.
The Gull, translated by Bernerd W. Sznyer, New York, 1967.
The Seagull, in *Anton Chekhov, Selected Works, 2: Plays*, translated by Ivy Litvinov and Kathleen Cook, Moscow, 1973.
The Seagull, in *The Cherry Orchard; The Seagull*, translated by Laurence Senelick, Arlington Heights, Illinois, 1977.
The Seagull, translated by Tania Alexander and Charles Sturridge, Oxford, 1985.
The Seagull, translated by Michael Frayn, London, 1986.

Criticism

(For general works on the author, see *Playwrights* volume)

Articles:

T.G. Winner, "Chekhov's *Seagull* and Shakespeare's *Hamlet*: A Study of Dramatic Device", in *American Slavic Review*, 15, 1956.
T.A. Stroud, "Hamlet and *The Seagull*", in *Shakespeare Quarterly*, 9, 1958.
Dorothy U. Seyler, "*The Sea Gull* and *The Wild Duck*: Birds of a Feather?", in *Modern Drama*, 8, 1965.
Dorothea Krook, "Tragic and Comic: *The Seagull* and *The Cherry Orchard*", in her *Elements of Tragedy*, New Haven, Connecticut, 1969.
Burton S. Kendle, "The Elusive Horses in *The Seagull* and Maupassant's *Sur L'Eau*", in *Modern Drama*, 13, 1970.
Jacob H. Adler, "Two Hamlet Plays: *The Wild Duck* and *The Seagull*", in *Journal of Modern Literature*, 1, 1970–71.
James M. Curtis, "Spatial Form in Drama: *The Sea Gull*", in *Canadian-American Slavic Studies*, 6, 1972.
Keith Sagar, "Chekhov's Magic Lake: A Reading of *The Seagull*", in *Modern Drama*, 15, 1973.
W.G. Jones, "*The Sea Gull*: Second Symbolist Play-Within-the-Play", in *Slavonic and East European Review*, 53, 1975.
Laurence Senelick, "The Lake-Shore of Bohemia: *The Seagull*'s Theatrical Context", in *Educational Theatre Journal*, 29, 1977.
Virginia Scott, "Life in Art: A Reading of *The Seagull*", in *Educational Theatre Journal*, 30, 1978.
A. Colin Wright, "Translating Chekhov for Performance", in *Canadian Review of Comparative Literature*, 7, 1980.

Vladimir Nabokov, "Notes on *The Seagull*", in his *Lectures on Russian Literature*, edited by Fredson Bowers, New York, 1981.
Carol Strongin, "Irony and Theatricality in Chekhov's *The Sea Gull*", in *Comparative Drama*, 15, 1981–82.
Eugene K. Bristow, "Let's Hear it for the Losers; Or, Chekhov, Komissarzhevskaya, and *The Sea Gull* at St. Petersburg in 1896", in *Theatre Survey*, 2, 1982.
James M. Curtis, "Ephebes and Precursors in Chekhov's *The Seagull*", in *Slavic Review*, 44, 1985.
David R. Jones, "Konstantin Stanislavsky and *The Seagull*: The Paper Stage", in his *Great Directors at Work*, Berkeley, California, 1986.
Laurence Senelick, "Stuffed Seagulls: Parody and the Reception of Chekhov's Plays", in *Poetics Today*, 8, 1987.
Eli Rozik, "The Interpretive Function of the 'Seagull' Motif in *The Seagull*", in *Assaph*, 4, 1988.

* * *

Any comedy where the young hero destroys his life's work and then himself, where the heroine is abandoned pregnant and unhinged, while the survivors bask on in their own egotism, must be considered highly innovatory. Apart from its black comedy, however, Chekhov's *The Seagull* has many other modern features. It is full of "intertextuality", incorporating or alluding to a great deal of *Hamlet*, to *Faust*, to Guy de Maupassant and to Chekhov's own prose. It was also "interactive" theatre: many characters, incidents, props, and lines were taken from Chekhov's own life and his social circle and he took some care to see that they experienced the full impact of this fictionalisation by being invited to the first performance. It is "deconstructive", since it is a play about the futility of the theatre, in which the old art (Trigorin) and the new art (Trepliov) fight out the battle of naturalism and symbolism, and the old theatre (Arkadina) and the new theatre (Nina Zarechnaya) fight out the conflict between histrionics and expressionist acting.

The Seagull is a total anomaly in Chekhov's work. Nowhere else does he have the writer as hero or blatantly exploit autobiographical material. Even the symbolic title—a parody of Ibsen's *Wild Duck*—is utterly out of keeping with his reluctance to advertise a play's intentions. Written in 1895, it was performed in 1896 in St. Petersburg with unscripted and catastrophic results that equalled the disasters of the drama itself. It must be seen as an attack on the conventional theatre, designed to embarrass and disable actors and audience. At the same time, so many lines of Chekhov's own fiction and letters, as well as his fishing rods, self-evaluation, and compulsions are attributed to Trigorin, that it appears to be a work of intense self-parody—a product of an inner crisis in which both old and new forms of writing and behaving seem trite.

The Seagull was written after six years' virtual abstention from writing plays. Apart from Ibsen, other Nordic reading seems to have suggested the new directions Chekhov's dramaturgy now took. As in Strindberg, a female oligarchy takes control of the action, the males—whether the writers, the old brother Sorin, or doctor Sorin, the objective bystander—being unable to resist their ruthless atavism. The eroticism of the play, however, is uniquely Chekhovian: the middle-aged Arkadina and Polina pursue their lovers, Trigorin and Dr. Dorn, with unrelenting passion; the male characters are locked into a ludicrous chain of unrequited love: Medvedenko loves Masha who loves Trepliov who loves Nina who loves Trigorin.

The experimental absurdity is deliberate, as Chekhov's letters show: "I am writing it with some pleasure, although I do awful things to the laws of the stage. . .not much action and

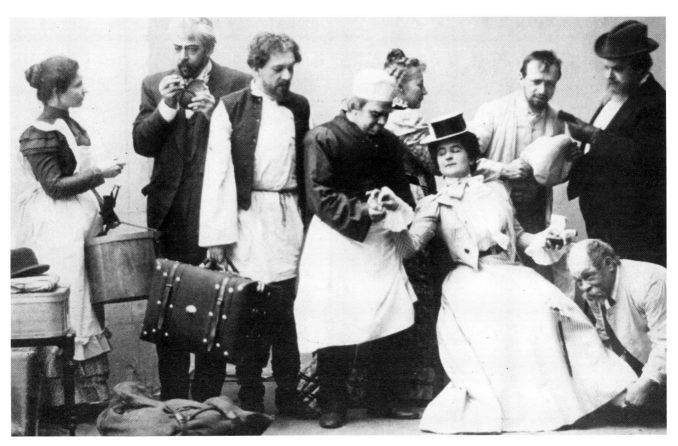

The Seagull: Moscow Art Theatre, 1898 (Olga Knipper as Arkadina, seated centre)

two hundredweight of love". Many of the preoccupations of his short stories surface here in dramatic form: the idea of Hamlet as a naturalized Russian citizen is reinforced in the semi-incestuous quarrelling between Trepliov and his mother and in the playlet he stages in Act I to provoke her anger; Nina Zarechnaya and Arkadina, both examples of womanhood destroyed by acting, are the culmination of the unhappy Katya of *A Dreary Story*. An adoration of Maupassant as the workmanlike writer's writer saturates Chekhov's prose: *The Seagull*'s opening lines, "Why are you wearing black?—Because I am in mourning for my life"—are lifted straight from Maupassant's *Bel-Ami*. The futility of medicine and contemplation, which Chekhov expressed in his bitter *Ward No. 6*, reaches its climax in the cruel refusal of Dr. Dorn to treat "old age".

But Chekhov also incorporated farce and vaudeville techniques into *The Seagull*. When Arkadina successively rows with her brother, her son, and her lover, it is with all the speed of a music-hall sketch. Usually quoted by the mordently ironic Dr. Dorn, popular song and snatches of operetta—though their import is lost on today's audience—only remind the other characters of how commonplace their predicament is.

The play functioned primarily as a purgative both for Chekhov's creativity and for the contemporary theatre—all the more surprising is its importance as the first of the truly Chekhovian later plays and as the emblem of Stanislavsky's Moscow Arts Theatre. As with *The Cherry Orchard* the subtitle, "Comedy", provides an insistent tempo-marking to override any temptation to dwell on the tragic possibilities; the setting, remote from Moscow or St. Petersburg, imbues a spirit of exile in those characters who will never leave; powerful forces off stage hold the cast in thrall and prevent them from acting on their motivation; phrases pass from character to character putting them under a disabling spell: Chekhov appears to have invented a new dramatic genre simply by demolishing the old.

Although Stanislavsky's theatre, with its totalitarian control over the actors, redeemed the play from the oblivion that otherwise threatened it, *The Seagull* remains the most ambiguous of all Chekhov's plays. Is Trepliov's playlet about the end of the world a parody of symbolist drama still to be written, or is it—as its echoes of Chekhov's narrative landscapes suggest—a serious attempt to convey what a new poetic drama might sound like? Is Nina, drenched and raving in Act IV, an Ophelia-like victim of ruthless and self-obsessed males, or is she an example of female indestructibility, just an Arkadina at a more decorative phase? Perhaps the play's real intent is buried in the allusion it nearly makes: in Act II, Arkadina takes over from Dorn the reading of Maupassant's travelogue *Sur l'eau* and shuts the book in annoyance. The passage she cannot stomach reads: "As soon as [a woman] sees [a writer] softened, moved, won over by constant flattery, she isolates him, cuts bit by bit all his links". Chekhov is one of the few male writers who can be seen both as misogynist and feminist: he knew well that the seagull is as predatory as it is vulnerable and the play, for all its "throw-away" symbolism, explores both the danger and the appeal of love for the artist.

—Donald Rayfield

THE SEASON AT SARSAPARILLA
by Patrick White

First Publication: In *Patrick White: Four Plays*, London, 1965.

First Production: Adelaide University, Adelaide, 14 September 1962.

Criticism
(For general works on the author, see *Playwrights* volume)

Articles:

J.F. Burrows, "Patrick White's Four Plays", in *Australian Literary Studies*, 2, 1966.

Douglas Dennis, "Influence and Individuality: The Indebtedness of Patrick White's *The Ham Funeral* and *The Season at Sarsaparilla* to Strindberg and the German Expressionist Movement", in *Bards, Bohemians, and Bookmen: Essays in Australian Literature*, edited by Leon Cantrell, St. Lucia, Queensland, 1976.

*   *   *

The set for White's "charade of suburbia" requires three platforms, on each of which is represented the kitchen and yard of a very ordinary middle-class family. The "season" of the title refers to the period in which a bitch is on heat, a motif which gives the play much of its total coherence: it starts with the sound of barking, it contains recurrent references in the dialogue to the way every dog in the district is plaguing the bitch, and it ends when the bitch's season is over. Within this frame, the women of two of the families represented act out parts of the reproductive cycle. The childless and middle-aged Nola Boyle allows herself to be seduced by her husband's wartime mate; the younger Mavis Knott, pregnant when the play begins, is later taken off to hospital with labour pains. Also related to this theme are the details that the adolescent girl in the third household (in the centre of the stage) eventually makes a choice between the two men who have shown an interest in her, and that a glamorous model (not related to any of the families) finds herself pregnant by a politician and commits suicide. The charade thus represents the animal cycle of intimacy, copulation, conception, pregnancy, labour, and child-birth.

However, White also dramatises two other characters whose function is to interpret the charade from their own perspectives. Pippy, an energetic and enquiring little girl, becomes interested in the dogs when Mrs. Boyle explains the physiological facts. But when Pippy reads Gibbon's account of the Roman imperial line and sees Mrs. Boyle acting like a daughter of Augustus, she draws an easy parallel between canine and human behaviour; she loses her innocent enthusiasm for life, and her outlook merges with that of her puritanical mother. The second interpreter is Roy Child, a schoolteacher on holiday who is related to the Knotts. Roy is also built into the story, if only in an inconsequential subplot; however, at times he is released into the role of a Brechtian commentator to the audience, and is not infrequently accompanied by expressionistic lighting and sound effects, as well as scripted changes in acting style. Roy is attracted to two women: Judy, Pippy's violin-playing, older sister, and Julia, the model. Each of these women is attended by another man as well: Julia by Erbage the politician, and Judy by Ron Suddards, a post-office worker who emerges triumphant. Apart from the way that the complexity of these relationships reflects the promiscuity of the dogs, they construct an obvious symmetry in the play which verges on contrivance when the suicide gives the ending a climax that is not available from any of the other resources.

White's fictitious Sydney suburb of Sarsaparilla had been the location of his 1961 novel *Riders in the Chariot*, but the play was written in anger at responses to the première of his *The Ham Funeral*, and reflects Australian suburban life as even more aridly irredeemable than does the novel. In both cases, however, the depiction echoes his perception of "the Great Australian Emptiness" on returning as "the prodigal son" after the War. He stated his writing purpose as being to probe that emptiness: "I wanted to discover the extraordinary behind the ordinary, the mystery and the poetry which alone could make bearable the lives of such people, and incidentally, my own life since my return". Later plays like *A Cheery Soul* would successfully penetrate that emptiness through a psycho-expressionistic portrayal of the vitality inside characters that the rest of society would like to avoid. *The Season at Sarsaparilla*, however, is a socio-expressionistic depiction of the broad surfaces of society, an excellent vehicle for the satire which has made it the most frequently revived of White's early plays. There is a great deal of poignancy in the hopelessness of the adults' position, and in the erosion of the young people's dreams; but there is no redemptive dimension to the sometimes vatic, but more often cynical, stylised outbursts that punctuate the dialogue.

Roy delivers three large choric passages, each of which introduces an expressionistic tableau dominated by the "razzle-dazzle", a lighting device to express the effect of "those twin dazzlers, time and motion". The theme of his meditations is the box-like existence of suburbia, which institutionalises mediocrity; but he also has a fatalistic acceptance that he too is trapped within this Procrustean state. When the "razzle-dazzle" occurs (for several pages), all three families are engaged in a miniature of suburban routine, moving like animated automata and talking inconsequential trivia. At other times also characters move into stylisation, as when the women—in separate houses—go through a ritual of dusting and sweeping while speaking a choric passage in unison. Whenever parallel activity occurs in all three houses, the effect is of an oppressive sense of sameness. This is obviously why White chose to use so many characters: not because of an inability to create psychological depth (as he had done in numerous novels and in *The Ham Funeral*), but because fully-engaging characters would distract audiences from his social panorama.

Other characters address the audience in a manner similar to Roy's. Ern Boyle describes the sight of the bitch in the street in a style that a stage direction says "might be the messenger's speech from a Greek tragedy", a posture supported by his reminiscences of desert warfare. At other times, characters drift into separate dreamlike planes: the Boyles move into "a kind of double soliloquy", and later into "a short reverie. . .as if from an inescapable nightmare". Despite White's intentions, such situations recall the haunting separateness of *The Tree of Man*: "Two people do not lose themselves at the identical moment, or else they might find each other, and be saved. It is not as simple as that". *The Season at Sarsaparilla*, however popular its satirical veneer, makes the same statement about 14 people, whose hopes, dreams, and even growth are hermetically sealed, and stunted by society's barriers.

—Howard McNaughton

A SEASON IN THE CONGO (Une Saison au Congo)
by Aimé Césaire

First Publication: Paris, 1966.
First Production: By Compagnie du Théâtre Vivant, Brussels, 20 March 1966.

Translations
A Season in the Congo, translated by Ralph Mannheim, New York, 1968.

Criticism
(For general works on the author, see *Playwrights* volume)

Articles:

Frédérique Dutoit, "Quand le Congo ne sera qu'une saison que le sang assaisonne", in *Présence africain*, 64, 1967.

Pierre Laville, "Aimé Césaire et Jean-Marie Serreau: Un Acte politique et poétique: *La Tragédie du Roi Christophe* et *Une Saison au Congo*", in *Les Voies de la création théâtrale*, 2, 1971.

Robert P. Smith, "Aimé Césaire, Playwright, Portrays Patrice Lumumba, *Man of Africa*", in *College Language Association Journal*, 14, 1971.

Lilian Pestre de Almeida, "Le Bestaire symbolique dans *Une Saison au Congo*: Analyse stylistique des images zoomorphes dans la pièce de Césaire", in *Présence francophone*, 13, 1976.

Premduth Benimadhu, "*Une Saison au Congo*: Problématique de la décolinisation", in *Indian Cultural Review* (Port Louis), 1980.

David L. Dunn and Aimé Césaire, "Interview With Aimé Césaire on a New Approach to *La Tragédie du Roi Christophe* and *Une Saison au Congo*", in *Cahiers Césairiens*, 4, 1980.

Ernstpeter Ruhe, "Aimé Césaires Bearbeitungen von *Une Saison au Congo*", in *Romanische Literaturbeziehungen im 19. und 20. Jahrhundert*, Tübingen, 1985.

*   *   *

Like his other works for the theatre, *Et Les Chiens se taisaient* (1956), *La Tragédie du Roi Christophe* (1963) and *Une Tempete* (1969), Aimé Césaire's third play, *Une saison au Congo* (*A Season in the Congo*), has been described as a "*tragédie de la décolonisation*". Césaire's theatrical style actually tends rather more to Brechtian epic, but *A Season in the Congo* is a play that the unfolding of history itself continues to make tragic. Césaire takes as his subject the real-life drama of the attainment of independence by that country (now Zaïre) in 1960 and the martyrdom of its first post-independence prime minister, Patrice Lumumba. There are in fact two tragedies in this play. Firstly, the personal fate of the visionary and uncompromising Lumumba has long made him a mythic figure in the black consciousness. But the more enduring tragedy (as Lumumba, himself a convinced pan-Africanist, courageously observed in his last letter to his wife) is the public one of Africa herself, politically independent in name, but unable to shake off her economic thraldom to the neo-imperialist powers. This, more than anything, gives the play an enduring resonance, despite its being so firmly anchored in a specific historical situation.

The first of the play's three acts sketches Lumumba's rise to prominence and the birth of the independent Congo, at the end of June 1960. Its *pièce de résistance* is the lyrical assertion of freedom with which — at the independence ceremony itself — Lumumba responds to the patronizing banalities of the departing King of the Belgians. The remaining scenes chart the new state's turbulent first month. This was marked, first of all, by a mutiny in the Congolese army and worse still, by the imperialist-inspired secession of the richest Congolese province, Katanga. This Césaire depicts through the machinations of a group of five anonymous bankers. These events provided the Belgian government with a ready pretext for armed intervention, an act of aggression which Lumumba seeks to counter by securing the assistance of a United Nations peacekeeping force. For Lumumba and the Congo, the UN troops prove a Trojan horse. Their ostensible role is to defend the newly independent state. But they also serve the ulterior purpose of protecting the interests of the neo-imperialists from a leader whom some in the West see as unstable, inflammatory, and pro-Communist. Thus Césaire concludes Act I with a minatory "word to the wise" from the representative of those interests, the Ambassador of the Grand Occident.

Act II covers the period up to the middle of September 1960. It takes place against the background of the civil war sparked off by the Congolese army's attempt to put down the secessionists in Katanga and Kasai. In Scene 5, the Congolese cabinet learns of a massacre of tribes-people, which has provoked accusations of genocide at the United Nations. Lumumba's reaction to this is ambivalently depicted. On the one hand he expresses passing regret for the fate of the murdered Balubas. On the other he celebrates the capture of Bakwanga, the provincial capital, by dancing publicly with a woman of the rival Lulua tribe. The gesture is a provocative one, aimed at the colonialists whom he blames for pitting the two peoples against each other. His rejection of the hypocrisy of the West is wholly understandable, but the manner in which he does so is perhaps injudicious. This is followed by a key scene in which the elderly Congolese president Kala Lubu (Césaire's thinly veiled counterpart of the real-life Joseph Kasavubu) bemoans the impulsiveness of Lumumba, as he sits down to write a speech revoking the latter's prime-ministership. Whatever we may think of his subsequent behaviour, Kala's assessment here of his younger colleague's qualities seems fair. It coincides with that attributed by Césaire to Dag Hammarskjöld, the UN Secretary-General, who also appears in the play; and it is illustrated by a subsequent episode in which Lumumba is prevented from broadcasting to the Congolese people by a Ghanaian officer in the service of the UN. This scene is historically grounded and Lumumba's anger at the role of the UN is again justified. But his treatment of the Ghanaian as an individual seems petulant and his pan-Africanism momentarily degenerates into bullying, as he uses the name of his friend Kwame Nkrumah in an attempt to intimidate his interlocutor. Characteristically, he redeems himself almost immediately by a display of cool courage, as the outraged colonel threatens him with a pistol. This is another key scene, displaying African solidarity being rent apart by pressures emanating from the institutions of the so-called civilized world. In the eleventh and final scene of Act II, Lumumba is visited by Mokutu, the Chief of Staff of the Congolese Army, who has mounted a military takeover "to restore order". Historically, this coup was carried out on 14 September 1960 by Colonel Joseph Mobutu, the present ruler of Zaïre.

The first two scenes of Act III seem to be based on a conflation of two historical events. These are Lumumba's brief escape from house arrest in Leopoldville at the end of November 1960 and a prison mutiny which occurred at Thysville, where he was afterwards held, on 13 January 1961. On the first occasion Lumumba was greeted by enthusiastic crowds not as a fugitive, but as the nation's duly elected prime minister. On the second, rank and file soldiers defied their officers and left open the cells of Lumumba and his companions. The offer of a cabinet post made by Kala to Lumumba at the end of Scene 2 is again historically accurate. But Césaire also uses these scenes to depict both Lumumba's strengths and his weaknesses: in the words of his most loyal of friends, Maurice Mpolo, "You march ahead and proclaim the future. That's your strength and your weakness"; and in those attributed to his wife Pauline, "You've always been stubborn and intractable. A regular mule". Against this perspective should be set the historical fact that it was precisely Lumumba's devotion to his wife and to his youngest son, Roland, which led to his recapture in November 1960. Another of Lumumba's character traits was clearly his fearlessness, both physical and intellectual. It is perhaps a moot point whether this is a weakness or a strength. But Lumumba displays remarkable self-awareness in taking as his symbolic sign not the ferocious leopard's skin, or the holy man's stole, but the wings of the ibis. He is, above all, the messenger of the new Africa.

The play ends with Lumumba's death at the hands of the Katangese rebels and their white mercenaries, to whom Mokutu has agreed to hand over his troublesome prisoner. It is a *tour de force*, in which Césaire combines factual accuracy with an accomplished epic staging. Once Lumumba is dead, those who mourn him and those guilty of complicity in his death (these are not wholly separate groups) have the opportunity first to voice their sorrow then to make their excuses. The result is a consciously bathetic scene in which highly charged elegy gives way to mendacity and evasion. The scene concludes with an equally sardonic epilogue, of which there are a number of versions. Mokutu, presiding over Independence Day celebrations in Kinshasa (formerly Leopoldville) plays tribute to the man at whose murder he has connived, while donning the leopard skin Lumumba had eschewed. But there are still some members of the crowd bold enough to greet the symbolic coffins, around which Mokutu's ceremony centres, with cries of "Uhuru Lumumba!". In the 1973 French version of the text, which may perhaps be regarded as definitive, an enraged and contemptuous Mokutu orders that the crowd be machine-gunned, killing in the process the sanza player who acts throughout as Césaire's sometimes lyrical, sometimes ironic commentator. There is a sense in which the death of this Zaïrean Everyman is as sad as that of the protagonist himself.

—Tim Lewis

THE SECOND MRS. TANQUERAY
by Arthur Wing Pinero

First Publication: London, 1895.
First Production: St. James's Theatre, 27 May 1893.

Editions

The Second Mrs. Tanqueray, in *Arthur Wing Pinero: Three Plays*, London, 1985.
The Second Mrs. Tanqueray, in *Arthur Wing Pinero: Plays*, edited by George Rowell, Cambridge, 1986.

Criticism

(For general works on the author, see *Playwrights* volume)

Articles:
William H. Rideing, "Some Women of Pinero's", in *North American Review*, 188, 1908.

Winifred Burns, "Certain Women Characters of Pinero's Serious Dramas", in *Poet-Lore*, 54, 1948.
Alexander Leggatt, "Pinero: From Farce to Social Drama", in *Modern Drama*, 17, 1974.
John Dawick, "The First *Mrs. Tanqueray*", in *Theatre Quarterly*, 35, 1979.
Simon M. Elliott, "A Second Look at Pinero's *The Second Mrs. Tanqueray*", in *Journal of the Eighteen-Nineties Society*, 12–13, 1981–82.
Götz Schmitz, "Pineros kleines Welttheater: Raum, Zeit und Figur in *The Second Mrs. Tanqueray*", in *Anglistentag: 1983, Konstanz*, Giessen, 1984.
Austin E. Quigley, "*The Second Mrs. Tanqueray*", in his *The Modern Stage and Other Worlds*, New York, 1985.
Mark H. Sterner, "The Changing Status of Women in Late Victorian Drama", in *Within the Dramatic Spectrum*, edited by Karelisa V. Hartigan, Lanham, Maryland, 1986.
Simon M. Elliott, "Arthur Wing Pinero's *The Second Mrs. Tanqueray*: A Reappraisal", in *Ball State University Forum*, vol.28 no.1, 1987.

*   *   *

The Second Mrs. Tanqueray, usually described as a "problem play", is concerned with the marriage of Aubrey Tanqueray, a middle-aged member of respectable London society and a widower, to Paula Ray, a young woman whose dubious moral reputation has kept her outside that society. Both hope that eventually their marriage will be accepted; but the action of the play demonstrates that this cannot be. When Aubrey's daughter Ellean, not knowing of the second marriage, returns from a convent to live with him, he begins to see Paula as a dangerous influence on the innocent girl, while Paula becomes jealous of Aubrey's love for Ellean, and of Ellean's innocence. The marriage withers, too, in the atmosphere of social isolation. Against Aubrey's wishes, Paula invites another couple, the Orreyeds (who have married in similar circumstances) to stay with them. But the tense, unsatisfactory nature of the Orreyeds' marriage only serves to show Paula what her own future might hold. Meanwhile Aubrey, persuaded that Ellean should experience life outside the home and convent, sends her in the company of an older woman to Paris, where she meets a young army officer; when they return, with the intention of marrying, Paula learns that the officer is a man with whom she had a liaison several years before. She confesses this to Aubrey, who forbids the marriage. In despair at her failure to escape her past, and unable to envision any happiness in her future, Paula kills herself.

Pinero's first play had been staged in 1877, and he was already warmly esteemed for a succession of farces and comedies. But it was not until 1893 that his reputation as a serious dramatist was established by the enthusiastic reception of *The Second Mrs. Tanqueray*. Pinero had met with considerable difficulty in finding a theatre to take the play, mainly because its subject-matter was considered sordid and depressing, and several actresses had refused the leading role of Paula before Mrs. Patrick Campbell accepted, launching what was to become one of the most brilliant acting careers of the period. Despite its theatrical success, however, critical controversy over the play's merits has continued to the present day.

At one extreme (that of Bernard Shaw) *The Second Mrs. Tanqueray* has been seen as merely a late manifestation of the French "well made play", and dismissed as a shallow, contrived attempt to exploit the then current vogue for Ibsen without really providing the intellectual depth and range of Ibsen's work. At the other extreme it has been cited as the finest English play of the late 19th century, an "epoch-making"

The Second Mrs. Tanqueray: St James's Theatre, London, 1893 (Mrs Patrick Campbell and George Alexander, first production)

work. Pinero was, indeed, a master of theatrical techniques (which are more evident and intrusive to a reader than to a viewer of the play), and he never claimed to be a great thinker. But he had a keen sense of how individuals were affected by current social issues and a powerful instinct for those details of character and action which create an aura of reality.

Pinero once wrote that "the beginning of a play to me is a little world of people. I live with them, get familiar with them, and *they* tell me the story". The story in *The Second Mrs. Tanqueray* is that of people from *two* "little worlds": the narrow, snobbish, bigoted, hypocritical world of respectable society, and the marginalized world of that society's outcasts and casualties like Paula Ray. We observe the posturing, self-deception, mixed motivation, and suffering of these people; but Pinero neither asks us to take sides nor suggests that there is a simple solution to their problems. Rather, the credibility and dramatic force of the play are greatly enhanced by the complexities that he provides for his characters.

This is not a play which pits the abstraction "society" against individual characters. Instead, their conflicts come from within. Aubrey Tanqueray's idealistic pursuit of purity has led him to a disastrous first marriage with a woman whose innocence turns out to be coldness; after her death he searches for warmth and finds it in Paula. His idealism reasserting itself, he offers her marriage, assuming that this action will challenge society to lay aside its judgements and be more compassionate. When Ellean comes to live with them, he finds Paula's easy-

going ways both repugnant and a dangerous influence on the girl, so Ellean replaces Paula in his affections. It might be argued that Aubrey's preoccupation with innocence is a Victorian social flaw which causes his crisis; but the problem for Aubrey is personal: he tries to live in two different worlds at the same time, but cannot.

Similarly, Paula has always wanted to be a free spirit, but she has also wanted social approval of her actions. Before meeting Aubrey she had hoped for marriage from the men with whom she had "kept house"; once married to Aubrey she becomes bored. Anxious for social approval, she is also jealous of her husband's daughter and terrified of ageing. Paula's suicide is neither improbable nor unprepared for. In the first act of the play, she tells Aubrey that if he had not married her she would have killed herself, and she makes a similar statement later. Even more important, she is portrayed throughout the play as a woman suffering from a total and long-established dissatisfaction with her life. Hers is an existential anguish, not a social one, and she takes the only exit that is open to her. Whether the final suicide makes this play a tragedy rather than a "problem play" is a question which will depend on one's definition of tragedy. Given the power of the play as Pinero conceived it, perhaps the question is irrelevant.

—John D. Hurrell

THE SECOND SHEPHERDS' PLAY. See **THE TOWNELEY PLAYS.**

SEI PERSONAGGI IN CERCA D'AUTORE. See **SIX CHARACTERS IN SEARCH OF AN AUTHOR.**

SEJANUS HIS FALL
by Ben Jonson

First Publication: London, 1605.
First Production: London (King's Men), 1603.

Editions

Sejanus His Fall, edited by Jonas A. Barish, New Haven, Connecticut, 1965 (Yale Ben Jonson).
Sejanus His Fall, edited by W.F. Bolton, London, 1966 (New Mermaid Series).
Sejanus His Fall, in *The Complete Plays of Ben Jonson, 2*, edited by G.A. Wilkes, Oxford, 1981.
Sejanus His Fall, in *The Selected Plays of Ben Jonson, 1*, edited by Johanna Procter, Cambridge, 1989.
Sejanus His Fall, edited by P.J. Ayres, Manchester, 1990 (Revels Plays).

Criticism

(For general works on the author, see *Playwrights* volume)

Articles:
Evelyn Mary Simpson, "The Folio Text of Ben Jonson's *Sejanus*", in *Anglia*, 61, 1937.
Joseph Allan Bryant Jr., "The Nature of the Conflict in Jonson's *Sejanus*", in *Vanderbilt Studies in Humanities*, 1, 1951.
Edwin Honig, "*Sejanus* and *Coriolanus*: A Study in Alienation", in *Modern Language Quarterly*, 12, 1951.
W.J. Olive, "*Sejanus* and *Hamlet*", in *A Tribute to George Goffin Taylor*, edited by Arnold Williams, Chapel Hill, North Carolina, 1952.
Allan Gilbert, "The Eavesdroppers in Jonson's *Sejanus*", in *Modern Language Notes*, 69, 1954.
Siegfried Kominger, "Zu Ben Jonson's Römmedrama *Sejanus*", in *Innsbrucker Beiträge zur Kulturwissenschaft*, 4, 1955–56.
Daniel C. Boughner, "Jonson's Use of Lipsius in *Sejanus*", in *Modern Language Notes*, 73, 1958.
Daniel C. Boughner, "Juvenal, Horace, and *Sejanus*", in *Modern Language Notes*, 75, 1960.
Daniel C. Boughner, "*Sejanus* and Machiavelli", in *Studies in English Literature 1500–1900*, 1, 1961.
Christopher Ricks, "*Sejanus* and Dismemberment", in *Modern Language Notes*, 76, 1961.
Jacob J. de Villiers, "Ben Jonson's Tragedies", in *English Studies*, 45, 1964.
Barbara N. Lindsay, "The Structure of Tragedy in *Sejanus*", in *English Studies* (Anglo-American Supplement), 1969.
Lawrence L. Levin, "Justice and Society in *Sejanus* and *Volpone*", in *Discourse*, 13, 1970.
Arthur F. Marotti, "The Self-Reflexive Art of Ben Jonson's *Sejanus*", in *Texas Studies in Literature and Language*, 12, 1970.

K.W. Evans, "*Sejanus* and the Ideal Prince Tradition", in *Studies in English Literature 1500–1900*, 11, 1971.
Gary D. Hamilton, "Irony and Fortune in *Sejanus*", in *Studies in English Literature 1500–1900*, 11, 1971.
J.W. Lever, "Roman Tragedy: *Sejanus*; *Caesar and Pompey*", in his *Tragedy of State*, London, 1971.
Marvin L. Vawter, "The Seeds of Virtue: Political Imperatives in Jonson's *Sejanus*", in *Studies in the Literary Imagination*, 6, 1973
Frederick Kiefer, "Pretense in Ben Jonson's *Sejanus*", in *Essays in Literature*, 4, 1977.
Wildon F. Engel III, "The Iron World of *Sejanus*: History in the Crucible of Art", in *Renaissance Drama*, 11, 1980.
Wilson F. Engel III, "Jonson and the Analytical Mythographers: *Sejanus*", in *Classical and Modern Literature*, 1, 1981.
Russ McDonald, "Jonsonian Comedy and the Value of *Sejanus*", in *Studies in English Literature 1500–1900*, 21, 1981.
John G. Sweeney III, "*Sejanus* and the People's Beastly Rage", in *English Literary History*, 48, 1981.
Annabel Patterson, " 'Roman-Cast Similitude': Ben Jonson and the English Use of Roman History", in *Rome in the Renaissance: The City and the Myth*, Binghampton, 1982.
Philip J. Ayres, "Drusus or Germanicus?: A Twentieth-Century Problem in *Sejanus*", in *English Language Notes*, 20, 1983.
Philip J. Ayres, "Jonson, Northampton, and the 'Treason' in *Sejanus*", in *Modern Philology*, 80, 1983.
Danielle Bonneau, "Monstrueux, monstres et prodiges dans une tragédie élisabéthaine: *Sejanus* de Jonson", in *Le Monstrueux dans la littérature et la pensée anglaises*, edited by Nadia J. Rigaud, Aix-en-Provence, 1985.
Philip J. Ayres, "The Nature of Jonson's Roman History", in *English Literary Renaissance*, 16, 1986.
John Jowett, " 'Fall Before This Booke': The 1605 Quarto of *Sejanus*", in *Text*, 4, 1988.

*   *   *

Sejanus is the favourite of the Emperor Tiberius at an absolutist Roman court where the only effective motives are self-interest, appetite, and terror. An opposition faction, loyal to the memory and family of the Emperor's dead nephew, Germanicus, is shown as principled, intelligent, and courageous, but wholly ineffective. The virtuous characters merely watch and comment on the main plot, which concerns Sejanus's ruthless moves against potential rivals for his power: the Emperor's son, the sons of Germanicus, and the Germanicans themselves. Such is the favourite's ascendancy that even the Emperor's own position is threatened. However, Tiberius observes this, and initiates countermoves against Sejanus, first by setting another court careerist, the equally unscrupulous Macro, to work against him under cover, and then by writing a long, equivocal letter to the Senate which effectively deprives him of imperial support. As cynical senators desert Sejanus in panic, Macro steps in to condemn him. The fallen favourite is executed and torn to pieces by the populace. The Emperor's authority is regenerated, but it is explicitly predicted that Macro will be as bad as his predecessor.

The play is formally and self-consciously a tragedy: the protagonist, who is at the height of his prosperity when the action begins, hubristically seeks to rise still further, and so sets in motion the train of events which ultimately annihilates him. In the unity of that conception, and the sustained gravity of language and situation, the text shows Jonson as the dissident classicist, choosing an unpopular Aristotelian purity against the eclecticism and baroque metatheatricality of his own theatre's tragic modes. But for a number of reasons the outcome is both less pure and more interesting than the intention.

First of all, there's the fact that the source of nemesis is, unmistakably, Tiberius. Despite one portentous scene in which the goddess Fortuna averts her face from Sejanus, it is really only as the Emperor's favourite that he rises so high, and only when he loses that favour that he falls. Tiberius is in this formal sense divine; especially in the last two acts, when he has withdrawn to Capreae and is rebuilding his mystery by issuing contradictory messages. Absent and absolute, rumoured to be living in luxurious caves and indulging in unnamable pleasures, he leaves the on-stage characters to guess at his intentions amid a terrifying paucity of evidence. The letter to the Senate which licenses the destruction of Sejanus is delphic, not only in its ambiguity, but also in its prose irruption into a blank verse scene, and in its shocking disclosure of power (like a sacred text, it can be interpreted but not questioned, because its author can't be reached). In these ways the Emperor appears, with a decorum both Jacobean and classical, as a god. But on the other hand, his non-divinity is insisted on at every level: he himself weightily vetoes a proposal to deify him; he is shown experiencing doubt and fear; and most importantly, his manoeuvres against Sejanus are explicitly Machiavellian—that is, he is plotting against his courtiers according to the very code which informs their plotting against each other. He wins because he is more powerful and devious than his opponent; there's no transcendence; the tragic structure is drastically politicised and deprived of absolute value.

Moreover, Jonson's classicism ironically disrupts itself in the sense that his concern with tragic form is in tension with his concern for historical accuracy. As the annotated text of 1616 shows, the play is minutely documented from the annalists of Imperial Rome and their Renaissance commentators: it is a work of Latin scholarship as Shakespeare's Roman plays, for example, are not. As modern editors have pointed out, this procedure doesn't necessarily produce historiographical accuracy; nevertheless, it does produce a dramaturgy in which many rituals, phrases, and characters are introduced primarily on the basis that they are authentic. Tragedy is hybridised with something that might be called documentary drama. Among the effects of this fidelity is a multiplication of minor roles which amounts to the representation of a *system*. For example, the Germanican group are dogged by seven or eight assorted informers, prosecutors, cynical instruments of the regime. A single-mindedly "tragic" dramatic economy could easily reduce this number to one or two. By not doing that—by according these functionaries the impersonal and fragmentary presence which they have in historical narrative—Jonson enacts their subordination to the network of power and information which they serve. Informing appears as a regular trade, and the experience of being spied on as a daily routine. Gallus—a tiny part—seems at first to be a Germanican; then some sycophantic contributions to a Senate debate apparently reveal that he's a double agent; then a casual comment shows that Tiberius sees him as an opponent who is protecting himself by flattery. We never discover what the truth is: the sharp little detail is typical of the general texture of insecurity and deception. This level of political realism further undermines the authority of the catastrophe: the terror and pity of Sejanus's fall can't be read as a cleansing or renewal of the body politic when the corruption has been so minutely realised as endemic. Sejanus becomes a scapegoat, certainly, but the play doesn't perform that ritual: it only represents it, with sceptical detachment.

The third factor which complicates the tragic programme is the formal didacticism of the dramaturgy. As in the comical satires which Jonson had just been writing, scene after scene splits its cast into amoral participants and ethical observers. Arruntius, for example, the most voluble of the Germanicans, has no involvement in the plot at all: as Sejanus brutally puts it, "he only talks". His role, which is one of the largest in the play, is to keep up a running commentary on the actions of everyone else. The generic affiliation of the device is not tragedy but satire: having staged the Rome of Horace in *Poetaster* (1601), Jonson is, in this respect, here staging that of Juvenal. The effect of this insistent dualism is that the action seems not to claim full significance in its own right: despite the outsize passions and high political stakes, the actors are denied tragic grandeur by being seen always as the object of the hostile and disenchanted knowledge of the free minds on the sidelines.

In all these ways, tragedy loses much of its contact with the sacred, and expresses instead, when combined with the other classical discourses Jonson is working in, a complicated secular and ethical humanism. At the end, there is a clear move to recuperate this critical heterogeneity. With great tragic propriety, the destruction of Sejanus is related by two successive messengers, and interpreted as an instance of the irresistible might of the gods. This belated depoliticising turn is accompanied by the appearance, for the first time in the play, of the anti-populist *topos* of the "many-headed monster" which is so insistent in Shakespeare's Roman plays: interestingly, the reinstatement of the tragic goes hand in hand with the demonisation of the masses. This highlights, in retrospect, how thoroughly the stoical humanism of the rest of the play has had, as its political aspect, an oligarchic republicanism directed against the evils of absolute power. Jonson was questioned by the Privy Council over *Sejanus*, someone—Jonson thought it was Henry Howard, the recently created and blatantly opportunistic Earl of Northampton—having accused him, and it, of popery and treason. Scholars continue to speculate, in the absence of conclusive evidence, on what lay behind this charge; but clearly the aspiring favourites of the new Jacobean court were right to hear in the play a conservative, élitist, but fiercely oppositional voice.

—Peter Womack

SEPARATE TABLES
Table by the Window
Table Number Seven
by Terence Rattigan

First Publication: London, 1955.
First Production: St. James's Theatre, 22 September 1954.

*   *   *

Separate Tables consists of two, one-act plays—*Table by the Window* and *Table Number Seven*—which share a common location and supporting characters, as well as complementary themes. The action takes place in a residential hotel in Bournemouth. In a period of post-war austerity and entrenchment, keeping up appearances is paramount.

In *Table by the Window*, the ordered, empty lives of the residents are disrupted by the mysterious and glamorous Anne Shankland. A fading beauty of slender means, she is twice divorced and unable to face the loneliness of middle age. Her first husband resides at the hotel, under an assumed name. He served a prison sentence for assault and ruined his career as a promising Member of Parliament. Anne persuades him that their reunion is coincidental. After she has charmed him once more, he discovers that she deliberately tracked him down, not for himself, but because she feels she has no other options. Yet they decide to try again. "You realise, don't you, that we don't have very much hope together?" he says. She replies, "Have we all that much apart?".

Table Number Seven allows the two leading actors to transform themselves into Sybil, a repressed spinster, and Major Pollock, a man who has invented for himself a socially acceptable and successful past. When he is convicted of indecent assault at a local cinema, his life is revealed as a lie. The response of the residents forces Sybil to take a stand against her overbearing mother, emblematic of a parsimonious and hypocritical society. Nevertheless, the ending is muted. Life is not transformed, it merely resumes.

Indices of respectability alter. It is easy to mock the secrets and revelations which galvanise the plots of *Separate Tables*. We are no longer much shocked by divorce nor (by and large) impressed by the "right" schools and regiments. Anne Shankland's view of herself and her lack of options is unlikely to attract sympathy or empathy in a post-feminist age, as also is Sybil's privileged ability to stay at home and tremble. But though the surface of the play has dated, the power of the piece remains, deriving from the tensions between what is seen and what must be hidden.

What is forced below the well-modulated surface of middle-class society, and why, is the theme to which Rattigan returns in play after play. *Separate Tables* is no exception. Behind the facade of the well-made, middle-brow play, *Separate Tables* dissects loneliness and despair. Beneath the urbane exterior of the successful playwright burns the tormented artist, creating four central characters obliged, in different ways, to create a public face to mask the private self, unacceptable to themselves or others.

As Edward Bond has noted, "Most of our lives are spent reacting to events". In *Separate Tables*, the leading characters' lives are shaped by events long ago or off stage. This is in keeping with the seemly traditions of Greek tragedy and French classical drama, both antecedents of the well-made play. But it is also perfect for Rattigan's central themes: it is precisely because the surface is tranquil, even banal, that when the hidden breaks through, the impact is all the more powerful. The form is therefore appropriate to the content, a point that Rattigan's detractors overlook.

Much criticism naïvely assumes that Rattigan endorses the values of the world he depicts. This is not the case. *Table by the Window* and *Table Number Seven*, apart and together, are chamber pieces. Themes dovetail and echo. All the characters are, in some way or another, lonely, failed, living on dreams. It is as if the Bowery bar in O'Neill's *The Iceman Cometh* had been given a small annuity and social aspirations and sent to live in Bournemouth.

Separate Tables may operate within a narrow social stratum, but Rattigan offers a consistent and agonised view of a world where passion, expressed or denied, is equally destructive. The image of separate tables is an apt one for a play where the possibility of genuine communion is denied and isolation is seen as the inevitable human condition.

—Joss Bennathan

SEPTEM CONTRA THEBAS. See **SEVEN AGAINST THEBES.**

SERJEANT MUSGRAVE'S DANCE
by John Arden

First Publication: London, 1959; revised edition, 1972.
First Production: Royal Court Theatre, London, 22 October 1959.

Criticism
(For general works on the author, see *Playwrights* volume)

Articles:
Malcolm Page, "The Motives of Pacifists: John Arden's *Serjeant Musgrave's Dance*", in *Drama Survey*, 6, 1967.
John Mills, "Love and Anarchy in *Serjeant Musgrave's Dance*", in *Drama Survey*, 1968–69.
R.J. Jordan, "Serjeant Musgrave's Problem", in *Modern Drama*, 13, 1970.
Mary B. O'Connell, "Ritual Elements in John Arden's *Serjeant Musgrave's Dance*", in *Modern Drama*, 13, 1971.
Barry Thorne, "*Serjeant Musgrave's Dance*: Form and Meaning", in *Queen's Quarterly*, 78, 1971.
Thomas P. Adler, "Ritual and Religion in John Arden's *Serjeant Musgrave's Dance*", in *Modern Drama*, 16, 1973.
Grant E. McMillan, "The Bargee in *Serjeant Musgrave's Dance*", in *Educational Theatre Journal*, 25, 1973.
Malcolm Page, "Some Sources of Arden's *Serjeant Musgrave's Dance*", in *Mélanges de science religieuse*, 67, 1973.
M.W. Steinberg, "Violence in *Serjeant Musgrave's Dance*: A Study in Tragic Antithesis", in *Dalhousie Review*, 57, 1977.
Ishwar Dutt, "The Rebel and the Tyrant: An Analysis of Violence in *Serjeant Musgrave's Dance*", in *Punjab University Research Bulletin: Arts*, 14, 1983.
Helena Forsås-Scott, "Life and Love and Serjeant Musgrave: An Approach to Arden's Play", in *Modern Drama*, 26, 1983.
Mary K. Dahl, "*Serjeant Musgrave's Dance*: The Priest Adrift", in her *Political Violence in Drama: Classical Models, Contemporary Variations*, Ann Arbor, Michigan, 1987.

*   *   *

Serjeant Musgrave's Dance is set in a northern mining town, (resembling Barnsley, Arden's home town), in a cold winter of about 1880. Musgrave arrives with three soldiers: disillusioned old Attercliffe and two young men, one tough and the other joking to conceal fear. Ostensibly they are a recruiting party. In the town they find a bitter conflict, with striking miners, led by Walsh, facing three authority figures: the mayor—also the mine-owner—the parson, and the constable. The soldiers lodge at the inn, where Mrs. Hitchcock is the landlady, hardboiled but kindly, and Annie, strange and withdrawn, the barmaid. The remaining character, the bargee, crooked Joe Bludgeon, takes the soldiers to town. Constantly whistling "Michael Finnegan", he always schemes to be on the winning side.

Through scenes at the inn, a churchyard (where Musgrave plots melodramatically), and a stable, we gradually realise that the soldiers have been involved in a colonial atrocity and want to bring the message—and "wild-wood madness"—back to England. But their purposes are confused: Attercliffe is a

Serjeant Musgrave's Dance: Royal Court Theatre, London, 1959 (first production)

complete pacifist, the second soldier believes that "it's time we did our *own* killing", and the third mourns his dead friend. Musgrave is against colonial wars, relying on God to guide him when the time comes, for "the new, deserter's duty" is "God's dance on this earth".

One soldier is accidentally killed in a drunken fight before Musgrave calls his recruitment meeting. Here he switches abruptly from praising army life to telling of its horrors, then dances and chants as a skeleton of a youth from the town (who had left after making Annie pregnant) is hoisted in the air. Musgrave announces that by his logic 25 people from the town must be killed (or possibly taken as hostages); dragoons then enter, shooting one soldier, and arresting the two survivors. Beer is served; the colliers' leader decides "We're back where we were"; spring is coming and everyone joins in a round dance.

The final scene has Musgrave and Attercliffe in prison awaiting execution, visited by Mrs. Hitchcock, who brings grog. Attercliffe offers an explicit moral, "You can't cure the pox by further whoring": you can't end violence by violence. Attercliffe's wife had left him for a greengrocer, who "sold good green apples and. . .fed the people"—more useful than soldiering, and Attercliffe's curtain-line is: "D'you reckon we can start an orchard?".

Arden's language is often vivid and unusual, and he frequently uses fragments of 19th-century songs. He also requires stage colour: red versus black and white, writing: "In the ballads the colours are primary. Black is for death, and for the coal mines. Red is for murder, and for the soldier's coat the collier puts on to escape from his black". He continues that if social criticism is "expressed within the framework of the traditional poetic truths it can have a weight and an impact derived from something more than contemporary documentary facility". Arden subtitles his work "an un-historical parable", set in plausible past time, but not based on an actual event; he observes that he succeeded in creating an "ambiance of English lower-class life in the Victorian period".

The subject of *Musgrave* is violence and the response to it—more violence or turning the other cheek? Originally the reference was to the British occupation of Cyprus, but Arden is anxious to transcend the specific: "I wrote a play attacking the complacency with which the British public was prepared to regard actions undertaken by the British Army in foreign parts. The play becomes famous. . .and the British Army continues to do exactly the same things in Ireland, and has been doing so for ten years". Arden explores both the necessity of non-violence and the mixed and inadequate motivations of those who try to pursue it. He asserts a preference for simple individual goodness over all abstractions. He speaks up powerfully for life and love—sought eagerly and pathetically by Annie—and anarchy: people should scribble on the book of rules of Musgrave, the parson and the constable.

—Malcolm Page

THE SERVANT OF TWO MASTERS
(Il servitore di due padroni)
by Carlo Goldoni

First Publication: In *Commedie, 3*, Florence, 1753.
First Production: Estate dell'Anno, c. 1746.

Editions

Arlecchino servitore di due padroni, in *Carlo Goldoni: Commedie* (4 vols.), edited by Kurt Ringger, Turin, 1972.
Arlecchino servitore di due padroni, Milan, 1979 (Biblioteca universale Rozzoli).

Translations

The Servant of Two Masters, translated by Edward J. Dent, 1928; second edition, 1952.
The Servant of Two Masters, adapted by David Turner and Paul Lapworth, London, 1973.
Servant of Two Masters, in a version by Tom Cone, London and New York, 1980.

Criticism

(For general works on the author, see *Playwrights* volume)

Articles:
Odette Aslan, "L'*Arlequin serviteur de deux maîtres*", in *Le Masque: Du Rite au théâtre*, edited by Odette Aslan, Paris, 1985.

*   *   *

The Servant of Two Masters (*Il servitore di due padroni*) is closest of all Goldoni's extant comedies to the scenarios he devised at the beginning of his career in the theatre, being originally prepared as one in 1745 for the *commedia dell'arte* actor Antonio Sacchi, and later (in the 1750's) fully written out by the dramatist from this scenario as it had been developed in performance by Sacchi and his fellow players. The text that has come down to us is, then, as Goldoni himself acknowledged, both his own play and, in a sense, Sacchi's; for the dramatist incorporated many of the comic embellishments supplied by the improvising performers as he shaped, developed, and refined it into a fully scripted comedy, by introducing the tricks and set-pieces (*lazzi*) and extended passages of stage-business (*burle*) which were characteristic of the performance of stage *arlecchini*.

The play's plot is justly celebrated as one of the most ingeniously organised in comic drama, at once dazzlingly intricate and consistently lucid. Clarice, the daughter of Pantalone, has been promised by her father to one Federigo Rasponi of Turin, but when he is reported killed in a duel with a certain Florindo Aretusi, Clarice appears to be free to marry the man she really loves, Silvio. Unfortunately, on the very day of their formal betrothal Beatrice Rasponi, sister of Federigo

and in love with Florindo, turns up in Venice dressed in male attire, passing herself off as her brother, and hot in pursuit of her lover who has fled to Venice. As no one in Venice has actually met Federigo, save for the inn-keeper Brighella, Beatrice is accepted as her brother, and it is assumed that this Federigo has prior claim over Silvio for the hand of Clarice. Silvio and his father, Dottore Lombardi, are livid at this turn of events, and (convinced the law is on their side) they exit, vowing revenge. Brighella, however, has recognised Beatrice, and when they are alone together, and Beatrice has explained the reason for her disguise, he agrees to keep her secret, and offers to accommodate her at his inn. This inn duly becomes the scene of hilarious complications and misunderstandings, for Florindo, who has now arrived in Venice, also puts up there. Beatrice's servant unwittingly confuses the situation even more by offering to become Florindo's servant as well as Beatrice's: by being the servant of these two masters he hopes, with a little dexterity, to eat and be paid wages twice over. His scheme generates a host of comic imbroglios, the most sustained of which is a long scene in which the servant triumphantly succeeds in serving dinner to both masters.

The Servant of Two Masters is particularly interesting in being both a literary work and a product of performers' theatre; the most substantial contribution of the latter to the text later prepared by Goldoni being found in this lead part of the servant, originally played by Sacchi, and carrying his stage-name, Truffaldino. The original scenario has not survived, but in the extant scripted version it is not difficult to calculate Goldoni's indebtedness to it, and to perceive the extent to which he has fleshed-out a skeleton plot that was formerly an actors' brief. The highly complicated plot-line turns on what were stock motifs in the Italian improvised comedy: mistaken identity, misunderstandings, and disguise. The movement of scenes is rapid, focus is upon exchanges between two or three characters, scenic linkage is often made by soliloquies directly addressed to the audience, and there are frequent shifts of tempo to ensure lively and engaging stage action. The characters are recognisably of the stock types: separated lovers, hostile parents, and an agile-minded, well-intentioned, but at times inept comic servant who compounds the confusions. Further, though a written comedy, the play is verbally economic and is still very much a script for actors to expand in performance. In general we shall be disappointed if we look in it for those marks which often distinguish a comic play as dramatic literature, like brilliant and witty phrasing and epigrams, complex diction, evocative image, or, indeed, any profound view of men and manners. These are rarely characteristics of Goldonian comedy, and in this play, in particular, Goldoni is pre-eminently the creative theatrical craftsman, furnishing a play whose quality lies in its latent performance possibilities.

Goldoni's achievement in *The Servant of Two Masters* was to refine the materials of the *commedia dell'arte* as he found them, by eliminating crudities, individualising within the world of the play the traditional mask stereo-types, and developing *lazzi* and *burle* as integral elements in the plot rather than as extraneous set-pieces: they emerge from and contribute to the plot, and do not provide licence for comic entertainers to improvise at the expense of dramatic structure and balance. While the stage figures are the familiar types, there is a perceptible attempt to individualise them and to locate them within a particular environment. This is notable in Goldoni's handling of the *vecchi* (old men), Pantalone and the Dottore, who even in an early play such as this are seen to have shed the cruder characteristics of their mask stereotypes and to have taken on many of the qualities and defects of the Venetian middle class. The play is, indeed, one of the earliest examples of the *embourgeoisement* of Italian comedy that later became a distinctive feature of many of Goldoni's scripted plays.

—Laura Richards

———————

IL SERVATORE DI DUE PADRONI.   See **THE SERVANT OF TWO MASTERS.**

———————

SEVEN AGAINST THEBES
   (Septem Contra Thebas / Hepti epi Thebas)
by Aeschylus

First Production: Athens, 467 BC.

Editions
The Seven Against Thebes [with translation], edited and translated by A.W. Verrall, London, 1887.
Septem Contra Thebas, edited by A. Sidgewick, Oxford, 1903.
Seven Against Thebes [with translation], edited and translated by T.G. Tucker, Cambridge, 1908.
Septem Contra Thebas, edited by G.O. Hutchinson, Oxford, 1985.

Translations
Seven Against Thebes, in *Four Plays of Aeschylus*, translated by G.M. Cookson, Oxford, 1922.
The Seven Against Thebes, translated by Gilbert Murray, London, 1935.
Seven Against Thebes, translated by David Grene, in *Aeschylus, 2*, Chicago, 1956 (Complete Greek Tragedies Series).
Seven Against Thebes, in *Prometheus Bound; The Suppliants; Seven Against Thebes; The Persians*, Harmondsworth, 1961.
Seven Against Thebes, in *Seven Against Thebes; Prometheus Bound*, translated by Peter Arnott, London and New York, 1968.
The Seven Against Thebes, translated by Christopher M. Dawson, Englewood Cliffs, New Jersey, 1970.
The Seven Against Thebes, translated by Anthony Hecht and Helen H. Bacon, New York and London, 1973.

Criticism
(For general works on the author, see *Playwrights* volume)

Books:
H.D. Cameron, *Studies on the "Seven Against Thebes" of Aeschylus*, The Hague and Paris, 1971.
William G. Thalmann, *Dramatic Art in Aeschylus' "Seven Against Thebes"*, New Haven, Connecticut, 1978.

Articles:
M. Wundt, "Die Schlußszene der *Sieben gegen Theben*", in *Philologus*, 65, 1906.
J.T. Sheppard, "The Plot of the *Septem Contra Thebas*", in *Classical Quarterly*, 7, 1913.
O. Klotz, "Zu Aischylos thebanischer Tetralogie", in *Rheinisches Museum für Philologie*, 72, 1917–18.
O. Regenbogen, "Bemerkungen zu dem *Sieben* des Aischylos", in *Hermes*, 68, 1933.

F. Solmsen, "The Erinys in Aischylos' *Septem*", in *Transactions and Proceedings of the American Philological Association* [*TAPA*], 68, 1937.
H. Patzel, "Die dramatische Handlung der *Sieben gegen Theben*", in *Harvard Studies in Classical Philology*, 63, 1958.
E. Wolff, "Die Entscheidung Eteokles in den *Sieben gegen Theben*", in *Harvard Studies in Classical Philology*, 63, 1958.
H. Lloyd-Jones, "The End of *Seven Against Thebes*", in *Classical Quarterly* (new series), 9, 1959.
B. Otis, "The Unity of *Seven Against Thebes*", in *Greek, Roman and Byzantine Studies*, 3, 1960.
Albin Lesky, "Eteokles in den *Sieben gegen Theben*", in *Studien: Wiener Zeitschrift für klassische Philologie*, 74, 1961.
T. Rosenmayer, "*Seven Against Thebes*: The Tragedy of War", in *Arion*, 1, 1962.
H.H. Bacon, "The Shield Of Eteocles", in *Arion*, 3, 1964.
H.D Cameron, "The Debt to Earth in the *Seven Against Thebes*", in *Transactions and Proceedings of the American Philological Association* [*TAPA*], 95, 1964.
H. Erbse, "Interpretationsprobleme in den *Septem* des Aischylos", in *Hermes*, 92, 1964.
E. Fraenkel, "Zum Schluss der *Sieben gegen Theben*", in *Museum Helveticum*, 21, 1964.
E. Fraenkel, "Die sieben Redepaare im Thebanerdrama des Aeschylus", in *Kleine Beiträge zur klassischen Philologie*, 1, 1964.
L. Golden, "The Character of Eteocles and the Meaning of the *Septem*", in *Classical Philology*, 59, 1964.
A.J Podlecki, "The Character of Eteocles in Aeschylus' *Septem*", in *Transactions and Proceedings of the American Philological Association* [*TAPA*], 95, 1964.
R.D. Dawe, "The End of *Seven Against Thebes*", in *Classical Quarterly* (new series), 17, 1967.
H.D. Cameron, "'Epigoni' and the Law of Inheritance in Aeschylus' *Septem*", in *Greek, Roman and Byzantine Studies*, 9, 1968.
B.H. Fowler, "The Imagery of the *Seven Against Thebes*", in *Symbolae Osloenses*, 45, 1970.
Anne P. Burnett, "Curse and Dream in Aeschylus' *Septem*", in *Greek, Roman, and Byzantine Studies*, 14, 1973.
R. Caldwell, "The Misogyny of Eteocles", in *Arethusa*, 6, 1973.
A.L. Brown, "Eteocles and the Chorus in the *Seven Against Thebes*", in *Phoenix*, 31, 1977.
R.P. Winnington-Ingram, "*Septem Contra Thebas*", in *Yale Classical Studies*, 25, 1977.

*   *   *

Eteocles speaks of his responsibility as king to protect the city of Thebes which has been under siege for some time. He tells the citizens that they also have a responsibility to defend the community, and that augury indicates a major attack will be mounted by the enemy that very night. A messenger brings news that seven heroes are drawing lots to determine which of the seven gates of Thebes each will attack. The women of Thebes (the Chorus), frightened by the terrors of the assault, panic. They are admonished by Eteocles. He advises them to pray for victory while he goes off to prepare defences. The women envisage the pain and waste of a ransacked city, then see the messenger and Eteocles returning from opposite directions. The messenger has discovered what the lots have determined. As he names each hero, his demeanour, the emblem on his shield, and the gate he is to attack, so Eteocles interprets these signs, and names a matching champion. At the last gate the enemy is his brother—Polyneices—and Eteocles names himself as the fit adversary. The women try to persuade him not to go, but he leaves to defend the seventh gate. Alone, they recall the history of Laius and Oedipus, and the curse that hangs over the third generation. The messenger returns to tell them that the city is safe, the enemy defeated, but that the sons of Oedipus have died by each other's swords. As their corpses are borne on, the women lament and form a funeral procession.

Originally this *kommos* probably concluded the tragedy. The ending which survives in the text is thought to be a later revision by actors, making use of the *kommos* and of material suggested by Sophocles' handling of the Theban story. Antigone and Ismene appear. They lament their dead brothers and, when a herald pronounces that Eteocles will be buried with honour and Polyneices will be left unburied, Antigone challenges the decree. The women of Thebes divide behind the two sisters who lead separate processions out of the theatre. This ending introduces elements that are not anticipated in the rest of the play and works against Aeschylus's stress both on the termination of the House of Laius in the third generation and on the continuation of the *polis* of Thebes.

First performed five years after *The Persians*, *Seven Against Thebes* is the second of Aeschylus's tragedies to survive relatively intact and, like the earlier text, its formal, cumulative structure challenges many an assumption of what makes a good tragedy. However it is easier than *The Persians* to re-interpret according to later aesthetic notions and interests because there is a single hero throughout, who dominates the play and in the end dies, and is mourned. Many a critic has felt this to be an "advance" on the static quality of the former work, but this concentration on the psychological unity of character (which has led to diametrically-opposed views of Eteocles' personality) is mistaken and misleading; not that Aeschylus is uninterested in Eteocles's psychology, but it is the pattern of interpretation and consequence which is important, especially as it affects the well-being of the community. It is not just that action reveals character, but that there is an instability and ambiguity in the notion of character in relation to both the cosmos and society. Heraclitus's maxim on the volatility of *ethos*—"character is daemon (daemon character)"—is literally enacted in Eteocles's "possession" of the seventh gate. His blind rejection of the Chorus's advice not to let his rage for the inevitable make him realize his father's curse, is among the most vivid of the ironic mirror-images and reversals that stud the play like so many reflecting jewels. It contrasts with his clear-sighted advice to the same women, earlier in the play, not to allow their fear of destruction bring that very destruction on themselves and the city. Wish-fulfilment and a magical bond between naming and creating are a constant concern of the tragedy, which ends with the destruction of the royal line but *not* the destruction of the community.

Seven Against Thebes is the concluding play of what appears to have been a connected trilogy (the three parts corresponding to the three generations of the house of Laius). With the loss of the first two parts, specific details in Aeschylus's handling of the myth are missing (allowing considerable scope for debate). In the crucial exchange with the women of Thebes, Eteocles mentions a dream in which a stranger figures. This dream seems to have been important earlier in the trilogy and was possibly misinterpreted. In the choral ode that follows this exchange the dream becomes central, and the stranger is seen not to have been a human mediator from Scythia but the "hammered steel" produced in that area: steel which divides and brings death. This symbol is further elaborated in the final *kommos* but we can only guess as to the dream's precise

relationship to Oedipus's curse or to the "guilt", "fate", "conscious self-sacrifice", or "choice" of Eteocles. Controversy is fuelled by uncertainty concerning the staging envisaged in the central scene (which accounts for a third of the playing time). Has Eteocles already chosen, even posted, his champions? Or does he bring them on with him and then despatch them one by one during the scene, according to the way he interprets the emblems on the shields of the adversaries? If the latter, has he brought on six champions and determined in advance that he will fight at one of the seven gates? If so, why is the messenger so surprised by Eteocles' "decision"? It is ironic that a play which so clearly explores the pitfalls of interpretation should become so much a playground for critical debate.

—Leslie du S. Read

SHADOW AND SUBSTANCE
by Paul Vincent Carroll

First Publication: New York, 1937.
First Production: Abbey Theatre, Dublin, 1937.

Criticism
(For general works on the author, see *Playwrights* volume)

Articles:
John D. Conway, "Paul Vincent Carroll's Major Dramatic Triumphs", in *Connecticut Review*, vol.6 no.2, 1973.

*   *   *

The Very Reverend Thomas Canon Skerritt is a priest more at home with his grandee friends in Spain than with clod-hopping curates and obsequious parishioners in an Irish country town. Proud and classical in his tastes, scathing in his criticism of the vulgarity that surrounds him, his only friend is his 20-year-old housekeeper, Brigid. In her innocence Brigid loves both the Canon and the anti-clerical schoolmaster, Dermot O'Flingsley. She claims to be instructed by visions of her patron saint, St. Brigid, to reconcile the two adversaries in a spirit of mutual love. O'Flingsley declares he does not believe in love. He has written a book under a pseudonym attacking the whole system of Church domination of the educational system and, by implication, the Canon himself. But, fearful of poverty, he cannot wrench himself free from the Canon's autocratic rule. To the Canon Brigid's belief in her visions is an example of the vulgar emotionalism that he considers the curse of Irish Catholicism. She is ill. She must be sent for a holiday, and he will call on one of his parishioners, the toadying Jemima Cooney, to take her place. When the authorship of O'Flingsley's book is revealed, the Canon dismisses him and appoints Miss Cooney's sheepish nephew, Francis O'Connor, in his place. This is insufficient for the outraged parishioners. Led by the Canon's curates, Fathers Corr and Kirwan, a mob converges on the schoolmaster's house, determined to beat him up. In an attempt to save him Brigid is hit by a stone, her face lacerated as was the face of St. Brigid herself. O'Flingsley carries her back to the Canon's house and, whilst he and the Canon stand on each side of her couch, she dies. O'Flingsley spurns the Canon's plea to stay with him and walks out, a free

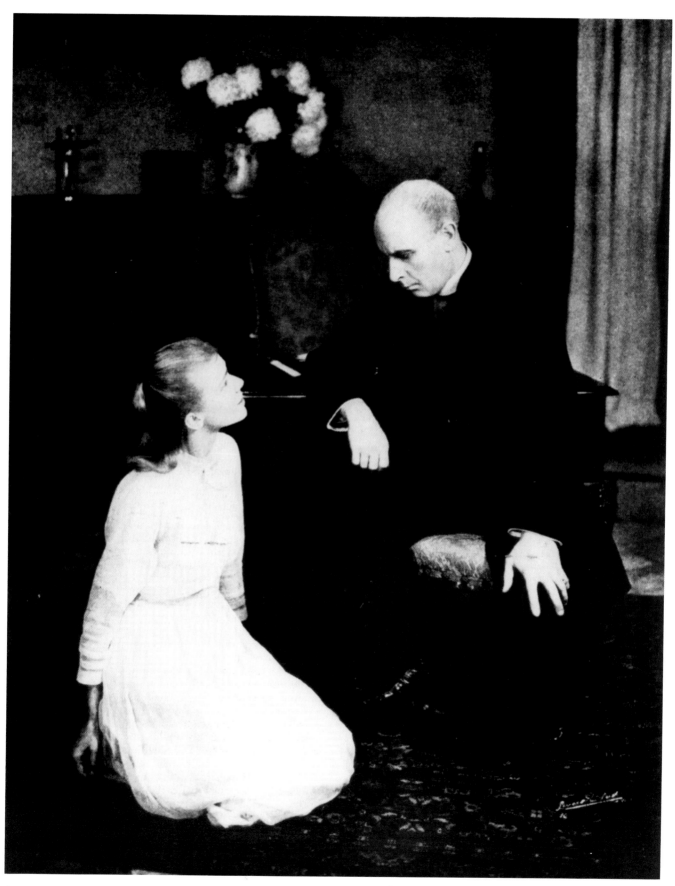

Shadow and Substance: Golden Theatre, New York, 1938 (Cedric Hardwicke and Julie Haydon)

man at last, leaving his adversary alone to face the question of whether he was right in refusing to accept Brigid's visions.

With considerable skill, Carroll drives the play's two major issues in tandem. Their tragic conclusion is reached with Brigid's death. But the serious purpose of the plot is relieved by the humourous characters, though these come close to caricature. The Canon's awful niece, Thomasina, "given to giggling and eternally sucking sweetmeats"; Jemima Cooney and her obsequious Irish-speaking nephew; Martin Mullahone, the local publican and football referee, and his wife, Rosey Violet, of whom the Canon remarks "if my recollection is correct, she is neither rosy nor a violet"; the ill-educated curates who "prescribe cures for old ladies' rheumatics and various diseases in horses and cows", and join the football club to entice the men into the Sacred Heart Confraternity—all provide an easy target for the Canon's sardonic humour.

Carroll has been criticised for failing to face up to the tensions engendered in his plays: Brigid dies before the miracle she predicts is put to the proof; the schoolmaster's condemnation of the Canon's autocratic rule is left unanswered. Carroll neither affirms nor denies the reality of miracles; he condemns the credulity of "a whole world of spiritual rowdies willing to sell themselves to anything that can produce signs and wonders to please their vanity". The reality of Brigid's "visions" lies in the message of humility and reconciliation that is rejected by both the Canon and the schoolmaster. It could be argued that the schoolmaster's criticism of clerical control of the education system is left unsolved. Carroll, a schoolmaster himself, chose to pursue his career in Glasgow rather than submit to clerical domination in his native Dundalk. O'Flingsley is no "clerical handyman"; he refers to the Irish Free State's education system as "the sewer of European culture". When he is dismissed and told he will be replaced by the sycophantic Francis O'Connor, his challenge demands an answer:

> *O'Flingsley*: As a scholar who knows what he won't publicly admit, you loathe and detest the whole miserable fabric of things here. You detest that disgraceful apology for a school down there, even more than I do. . .Why then do you deliberately prepare to perpetuate it throughthat poor spineless imbecile there beside you?
>
> *Francis* (*Outraged*): Canon! He's insultin' me. I'd make him take that back.
>
> (*The Canon's eyes meet O'Flingsley's challengingly, in a silent tense duel. Pause.*)
>
> *Canon* (*tensely*): That will be all, O'Flingsley.

To the critic this may appear as the failure of the dramatist to resolve the issue, but to the actor playing the part of the Canon no other response is possible. The success of *Shadow and Substance* in New York where it received the Critics' Award for the best foreign play of the year, as well as its favourable reception in London and on the Continent, was largely due to the superb acting part of Canon Skerritt and to the appeal of Brigid's steadfast faith.

—Hugh Hunt

SHAKUNTALA (Abhijnanasakuntala)
by Kalidasa

Composition: Date unknown; possibly 5th century A.D.

Translations

Shakuntala, translated by Sir William Jones, London, 1789.

Shakuntala, in *Translations of "Shakuntala" and Other Works*, translated by A.W. Ryder, London, 1912.

Shakuntala, in *Great Sanskrit Plays*, translated by P. Lal, New York, 1957.

Sakuntala, in *Theater of Memory: The Plays of Kalidasa*, translated by Barbara Stoler Miller, Edwin Gerow, and David Gitomer, New York, 1984.

Criticism
(For general works on the author, see *Playwrights* volume)

Books:

Mandakranta Bose, *Supernatural Intervention in "The Tempest" and "Sakuntala"*, Salzburg, 1980.

Articles:

P. Lal, "On Translating *Shakuntala*", in his *Transcreation: Two Essays*, Calcutta, 1972.

H.H. Annich Gowda, "*The Tempest* and *Sakuntala*: Retribution and Reconciliation", in *Literary Half-Yearly*, vol.15 no.2, 1974.

P.P. Sharma, "Kalidasa's *Shakuntala*: Some Sidelights", in *Indian Literature*, vol.22 no.3, 1979.

Garland Cannon, "Eighteenth-Century Sanskrit Studies: The British Reception of Sir William Jones' Translation of the *Sakuntala*", in *South Asian Review*, vol.6 no.3, 1982.

Charles W. Nuckolls, "Causal Thinking in *Sakuntala*: A Schema-Theoretic Approach to a Classical Sanskrit Drama", in *Philosophy East and West*, vol.37 no.3, 1987.

*   *   *

Goethe's delight in reading George Förster's German translation of Kalidasa's *Shakuntala* was expressed in his well-known lines on the drama: "Would'st thou the young year's blossoms and the fruits of its decline / And all by which the soul is charmed, enraptured, feasted, fed? / Would'st thou the Earth and Heaven itself in one sole name combine? / I name thee O Sakoontala! and all at once is said". His words indicate the fame and prestige the Sanskrit drama was to enjoy with Western readers. The great Indian poet and philosopher, Sri Aurobindo, was to say of *Shakuntala* that it was one of the best plays "not only in Sanskrit literature, but in the literature of the world", largely by virtue of which Kalidasa "stands not only unsurpassed but even unrivalled".

Kalidasa borrowed the story for his seven-act play from the epic poem *Mahabharata*, but he altered it in some important respects as well as adding to it some new characters and incidents. The story relates how King Dushyanta, arriving at the hermitage of the great sage Kanva, who has gone out, meets his daughter Shakuntala with whom he falls in love. He proposes to her. Shakuntala agrees on condition that if she has a son, he will be the King's heir. The King accepts the condition and marries her. But soon after he is summoned to the court for important state business; Shakuntala is left behind—unhappy and dejected. In this mood she shows some discourtesy to an old irascible sage, Durvasas, who is visiting her father's hermitage. He is so provoked that he pronounces a curse upon her, to the effect that Dushyanta will forget his bride. Later on he relents a little saying that whether the King remembers her or not will depend on her keeping safe the ring he has given her. But it so happens that, while bathing in the river, she loses the ring and becomes even more desperate to join the King. So, while she is expecting his child, Shakuntala goes to the court. But the King refuses to recognize her and sends her away. Through some miraculous intervention she is carried to the mountain retreat of another sage, Kashyapa, and his wife Aditi, where a son is born to her and is named Bharata. In the meantime, a fisherman finds the lost ring in the belly of a fish, which brings back the King's memory. And by another coincidence Dushyanta, who has been asked by the god Indra to wage a war against the demons, arrives in the vicinity of Kashyapa's hermitage, where he sees his son—but without recognising him. Eventually, however, this all leads to Dushyanta's reunion with his wife and his son.

In the hands of Kalidasa the dramatic features of the play are indistinguishable from the poetic qualities in which it is so rich. First of all the characterization of Shakuntala and Dushyanta itself owes a good deal to Kalidasa's poetic intuition and his imaginative grasp of human psychology, both in its realistic and idealistic dimensions. Secondly, Kalidasa's treatment of the theme of love is that of a poet as well as that of a dramatist; combining, as it does, lyric fervour, moral sympathy, and impassioned involvement in handling the lovers' emotions— the ecstasy of falling in love, the pangs of separation, the feelings of remorse, the yearning for the object of love—and elevating of them, to quote Sri Aurobindo, "from the sphere of physical beauty to the eternal heaven of moral beauty". Thirdly, and perhaps most importantly, Kalidasa's treatment of external nature is that of a poet, with his deep sympathy with what he depicts, his keen powers of observation, and his intimate knowledge of the multiple aspects of the Indian landscape in its haunting beauty as well as its throbbing vitality. The grandest as well as the minutest aspects of nature are described with such subtlety and delicacy of touch, and with such evocative vividness, that they are seen as part of the emotions and vicissitudes of the protagonists.

While the play has no religious significance or undertone, the code of conduct that the actions, thought, and principles of the characters embody, and the ethical thread that binds them all, represent the very essence of Hindu philosophy, religion, and morality rolled into what is called the *Dhrama*, of which Kalidasa had a profoundly erudite knowledge and with which he was both instinctively and intellectually in sympathy. Combined with this, we have Kalidasa's extraordinary dramatic skill and imaginative depth and richness. In drawing Shakuntala's character, for instance, the poet and the dramatist, the psychologist and the moralist in Kalidasa are all fully engaged, which enables him to delineate with the same subtlety and delicacy of touch her virgin innocence as well as her "intoxicating sense of youth", her bashfulness as well as her strong assertion of her personality, and to bring out her emotional turmoil as well as her inner calm and self-mastery. Hence if her sense of personal purity and innocence makes her feel wrong so deeply, she puts up with it with such calm bravery that she is both endearing and impressive in her real, as well as ideal, character and personality.

This play, therefore, not only constitutes Kalidasa's masterpiece and one of the masterpieces of world drama but is also a monument to the best that Indian civilization and culture had achieved during the Gupta period (400 to 500 A.D.), fulfilling, as it does supremely well, what T.S. Eliot considered to be the ultimate function of art; namely, "to bring us to a condition of serenity, stillness and reconciliation".

—G. Singh

THE SHAUGHRAUN
by Dion Boucicault

First Publication: London, c. 1883.
First Production: Wallack's Theatre, New York, 14 November 1874.

Editions
The Shaughraun, in *The Dolmen Boucicault*, edited by David Krause, Dublin, 1964.
The Shaughraun, in *The Plays of Dion Boucicault*, edited by Peter Thomson, Cambridge, 1984.

*   *   *

Robert Ffolliott has been convicted for his Fenian activities and sent to Australia. The play opens behind an Irish coastal cottage where his sister Claire and his fiancée Arte are visited by Molineux, an English officer searching for an escaped Fenian who has been landed on the coast, Kinchela, an exploitative landlord who is betraying his role as trustee of the Ffolliott estate by victimising the women, and Father Dolan, the other trustee, whose honesty is a fulcrum to the whole melodrama. The appearance of Robert in the second scene confirms that he is the escapee, and he has an ironically convivial meeting with Molineux, who admits that he is in love with Claire. The third scene contains the delayed entrance of the last of the major characters, Conn the Shaughraun, the hero who will engineer most of the central action through his energy, resourcefulness, likeable roguery, and elastic morality. This action consists of a network of stratagems and counter-stratagems, mainly to do with the arrest and contrived escape of Robert, but expanded through extensive dramatic ironies, the duplicity of the villain Kinchela (particularly in concealing news of Robert's pardon), the apparent murder of Conn, the kidnapping of several of the women, and the uncompromising honesty of the priest. After Boucicault's characteristic sensation scene, and a show-down scene in which all is revealed to all, there is a melodramatic resolution involving the predictable romantic matches.

The Shaugraun represents the mature development of Boucicault's Irish melodrama, an idiosyncratic invention of his own which he had evolved partly because of a shortage in the 19th-century dramatic repertory of major roles for actors with broad Irish accents; he himself created on stage, and toured extensively, the part of Conn. Complexity of action, defying unravelling, was a virtue in melodrama, and the abductions, mistaken identities, misdirected communications, and varieties of deviousness which make up the bulk of this play contribute to its status as a classic of the genre. Boucicault was a prodigious innovator in both theatrical and dramaturgical terms, and his most celebrated structural invention was the "sensation scene", in which acting would briefly take second place to an often cataclysmic display of Victorian production virtuosity. The second act of this play ends in a ruined abbey, where Kinchela and his men are ambushing Robert. Arte yells a warning to Robert, but the villains gun him down with two shots, inadvertently signalling the lighting of a beacon so that a rescue ship will send a boat. In spite of this, the figure of Robert is then seen swimming out to the ship, and the corpse is turned over to reveal Conn, who has acted as decoy. Moonlight streams through the abbey window, picking out the figure of St. Bridget, extending her arms over the martyred shaughraun. All of these details were represented on the stage, at a date long before electricity would make moonbeams among the most manageable of stage properties.

The Shaughraun: Dion Boucicault as Conn

Conn is a marvellous complicator of the action, in both serious and comic terms. His death in the abbey is a pretense, but he manages to extend it through much of the final act—to the extent of lying in state at his own wake, slyly drinking much of the supplies—before moving off to apprehend the villains while walking round the stage in a barrel. Such prominence had never been accorded to a comic in melodrama before Boucicault. Yet Conn's role as complicator is even more conspicuous in dialogue: the whole play is peppered with his yarns, in which he valorises his own turpitude with an amazingly resourceful and captivating rhetoric. The focus of the play thus intermittently tightens to become, briefly, a one-man show. But the characterisation of Conn is, in itself, a challenge to one of the cornerstones of melodrama, the moral polarisation of characters as epitomising either virtue or villainy. That Conn is, ethically, a bridging figure, straddling both moral extremities, is an indicator of the death of Victorian melodrama and the birth in the 20th century of what has loosely been termed the picaresque anti-hero. Sean O'Casey, whose admiration of Boucicault was profound, generated such characters in his early plays as the only viable antidote to an "Irish problem", the reality of which was too severe to confront on any other terms. The signification of Boucicault's shrine, ruined abbey, and statue of a saint is strongly anticipatory of O'Casey, not only of *The Silver Tassie* but also of *Juno and the Paycock* (especially as Conn's grieving mother clearly parallels Juno).

The Irishness of Boucicault's play is itself a suggestion of the collapse of melodrama, especially as Boucicault was arguably the first playwright consciously to address a cosmopolitan audience, through his quick awareness of the touring potential of the recently developed steamer and railway services. Melodrama had always pivoted on the exploitation of audience prejudice, whether on a nationalistic, racial, patriotic, or class-related plane. Boucicault, however, did not celebrate Irish values before an Irish audience; instead, his plays may be read as a popularising of Irishness as a survival technique in a world of exploitation and victimisation. That the play was, in virtually unmodified form, an outstanding success in both hemispheres demonstrates that Boucicault had transcended the provincialism that was endemic to earlier melodrama, though he himself never assessed his achievement in such portentous terms.

—Howard McNaughton

SHE STOOPS TO CONQUER; or, The Mistakes of a Night by Oliver Goldsmith

First Publication: London, 1773.
First Production: Theatre Royal, Covent Garden, 15 March 1773.

Editions
She Stoops to Conquer, in *Poems and Plays of Oliver Goldsmith*, introduced by Austin Dobson, London, 1910; second edition, revised by Tom Davis, 1975.
She Stoops to Conquer, edited by Katharine C. Balderston, New York, 1951.
She Stoops to Conquer, edited by Vincent F. Hopper and Gerald B. Lahey, Woodbury, New York, 1958.
She Stoops to Conquer, edited by Arthur Friedman, Oxford, 1968.
She Stoops to Conquer, edited by Tom Davis, London, 1979 (New Mermaid Series).

Criticism
(For general works on the author, see *Playwrights* volume)

Books:
Alexander N. Jeffares, *A Critical Commentary on "She Stoops to Conquer"*, London, 1966.

Articles:
Robert S. Forsythe, "Shadwell's Contribution to *She Stoops to Conquer* and to *The Tender Husband*", in *Journal of English and Germanic Philology*, 11, 1912.

She Stoops to Conquer Theatre Royal, Covent Garden, 1773 (first production)

Gertrude Ingalls, "Some Sources of Goldsmith's *She Stoops to Conquer*", in *Publications of the Modern Language Association* [*PMLA*], 44, 1929.

Maurice Baudin, "Une Source de *She Stoops to Conquer*", in *Publications of the Modern Language Association* [*PMLA*], 48, 1933.

Katharine C. Balderston, "A Manuscript Version of *She Stoops to Conquer*", in *Modern Language Notes*, 45, 1930.

Coleman O. Parsons, "Textual Variations in a Manuscript of *She Stoops to Conquer*", in *Modern Philology*, 40, 1942.

John H. Smith, "Tony Lumpkin and the Country Booby Type in Antecedant English Comedy", in *Publications of the Modern Language Association* [*PMLA*], 58, 1944.

John Hennig, "The Auerbachs Keller Scene and *She Stoops to Conquer*", in *Comparative Literature*, vol.7 no.3, 1955.

B. Eugene McCarthy, "The Theme of Liberty in *She Stoops to Conquer*", in *University of Windoor Review*, 7, 1971.

Jack D. Durant, "Laughter and Hubris in *She Stoops to Conquer*: The Role of Young Marlowe", in *Southern Speech Journal*, 37, 1972.

Margaret Hassert, "Appraisals: The Plays of Oliver Goldsmith", in *Journal of Irish Literature*, vol.3 no.3, 1974.

Tom Davis and Susan Hamlyn, "What Do We Do When Two Texts Differ? *She Stoops to Conquer* and Textual Crit-
icism", in *Evidence in Literary Scholarship: Essays in Memory of James Marshall Osborn*, edited by René Wellek and Alvaro Ribeiro, Oxford, 1979.

Vicki Wheeler, "The Education of Charles Marlow in *She Stoops to Conquer*", in *Publications of the Missouri Philological Association*, 8, 1983.

Richard B. Taylor, "A Source for Goldsmith's Tony Lumpkin in *The Connoisseur*", in *English Language Notes*, 26, 1989.

*   *   *

Hastings and Marlow come up from London into the country, the first in search of Constance Neville, the second despatched by his father to seek the hand of Kate Hardcastle, cousin to Miss Neville. The men are tricked by Tony Lumpkin, Mrs. Hardcastle's son by her first marriage, into thinking the Hardcastle estate is an inn. Accordingly at first they treat Mr. Hardcastle peremptorily as an innkeeper rather than as their host. Marlow, notoriously shy with well-born ladies, greets Kate with stammering modesty; but when she reappears as a maid of the Hardcastle "Inn" his address towards her becomes provocatively direct. Finally she contrives to have him demonstrate this forthrightness before their fathers; his true feelings revealed, Marlow is free to marry Kate. Meanwhile, after a night spent wandering, lost in her own garden, and trying to save Constance (and her jewels) from falling into Hastings' hands, Mrs. Hardcastle relents. Constance's jewels are placed at her own disposal, and she is thereby freed to betroth herself to Hastings.

Critical debate has still not settled the question of exactly how *She Stoops* sets about reforming sentimental comedy by leavening it with laughing comedy; nor whether that blend was entirely successful. Those controversies, which the prologue for the first performance initiated, look likely to continue indefinitely. The first audience was much less equivocal in its response, thus setting the pattern for audiences ever since. The play was a great success and continues to be one of the most popular of English plays.

Like Farquhar before him, Goldsmith effected a flight on stage from the London scene, though Goldsmith himself briskly enacted in his own life the part of the quintessential London gadfly. As did Farquhar in *The Beaux' Strategem*, Goldsmith sets two young men-about-town in a rural setting, to seek their fortunes. Like Farquhar's Archer, Marlow falls for the barmaid that Kate pretends to be (in self-conscious homage to Farquhar's Cherry, the innkeeper's daughter). Goldsmith goes one better by giving us not one but two inns—one real, the Three Pigeons; the other the "inn" projected onto Hardcastle's estate by Hastings and Marlow, as they reify Lumpkin's initial joke.

Lumpkin is the play's Puck. He epitomises puckishness, in his penchant for jokes of this kind and in his irrepressible boyishness. More importantly, he accidentally stumbles upon some of Puck's transformational magic. As Hastings and Marlow make his jest real, the play shifts ground from the earthy realism of *The Beaux' Stratagem* to the poetic fantasy of *A Midsummer Night's Dream*. Like the latter, *She Stoops* chronicles the mistakes of a night, ends by blessing the union of two young couples, and the climax of its farce action takes place in a wood—in this case the bottom of Hardcastle's garden, where Hastings, Constance, Tony, and Mrs. Hardcastle spend the first part of Act V, in varying states of confusion. The successful conclusion of these wanderings in a dark wood triumphantly demonstrates the capacity of belief to pattern reality in its own image. Kate's instinctive grasp of this principle enables her, finally, to trap Marlow into a public declaration of his true feelings.

When they first meet, Kate treats him to an ironic and accomplished display of courting language, as if to demonstrate that, like her author, she has been attentively studying the plays of Etherege, Congreve, and Vanbrugh—which for both function as a primer of such language. Without having set foot in Covent Garden, Kate has full command of the urbane syntax of the metropolis.

For his part, Marlow persists in being tongue-tied before a well-bred lady. Later in the evening, however, when he meets Kate dressed as a servant, his approach is eloquently sexual. Kate's dilemma is then a double indemnity: she must somehow merge the two Marlows, while persuading this new Marlow to love, in one guise, the one "true" Kate. She is of course, more than equal to the task. As the play's title promises, her stooping leads to the conquest of Marlow. In her resourcefulness she is thus a descendant of Shakespeare's energetic comic heroines, Rosalind and Viola.

The climax of Kate's scheme fulfils also Goldsmith's agenda of laughing into absurdity the excesses of sentimentalism. Disguised still as the maid, she attempts to refuse Marlow's hand in marriage, on the ground that she is too low for him: he must not, she protests, stoop to conquer her. This forces from Marlow a frank declaration of his feelings. In his address he uses the familiar tropes of sentimentalism, rescued from bathos by the hilarity of his address to the "wrong" woman, by Kate's scarcely suppressed humour at his mistake, and by the astonished commentary of Hardcastle and Sir Charles Marlow.

The scene thus stands as a fitting emblem for Goldsmith's design in the whole. He invigorates the clichés of sentiment by placing them in an absurdly contrived and complex setting—the mistaken lovers, the perplexed, observing patriarchs—and then, through a touch of genial magic, he grants the wishes of young lovers and parents alike. As his prologue promises, Goldsmith effects a rescue of the comic muse; the which, in his hands, contrives to be satirical, comical, amorous, and rural all at once.

—Mark Anthony Houlahan

SHE WOULD IF SHE COULD
by Sir George Etherege

First Publication: London, 1668.
First Production: Lincoln's Inn Fields, London (Duke's Company), 6 February 1668.

Editions

She Would if She Could, in *Sir George Etherege: Dramatic Works*, edited by H.F.B. Brett-Smith, Oxford, 1927.
She Would if She Could, in *Restoration Comedies*, edited by Dennis Davison, London, 1970.
She Would if She Could, edited by Charlene M. Taylor, Lincoln, Nebraska, 1971 (Regents Restoration Drama Series).
She Would if She Could, in *Restoration Comedies* (4 vols.), edited by Norman A. Jeffares, London, 1974.
She Would if She Could, in *The Plays of Sir George Etherege*, edited by Michael Cordner, Cambridge, 1982.

Criticism
(For general works on the author, see *Playwrights* volume)

Articles:
C. Harry Bruder, "Women in the Comedies of Sir George Etherege", in *Publications of the Arkansas Philological Assiciation*, 10, 1984.

*   *   *

Frank Freeman and Ned Courtall, "two honest gentlemen of the town", are contemplating another dreary day with their old mistresses, until they learn of the arrival in town of two country knights, Sir Joslin Jolley and Sir Oliver Cockwood, together with Lady Cockwood and Sir Joslin's young nieces, Ariana and Gatty, a pair of witty and pretty heiresses. In a series of amusing episodes, the gallants try to gain access to the girls while Courtall holds off the lecherous Lady Cockwood, and encourages both Sir Joslin's drunken debauchery and Sir Oliver's search for a mistress, though knowing he is, in fact, both henpecked and impotent. First, they encounter the nieces in Mulberry Garden, promising to see no other women until they meet again—only to be introduced to them hours later back at Sir Oliver's. Next morning Courtall holds off Lady

Cockwood at the New Exchange and takes the ladies off to The Bear, while Sir Joslin persuades Sir Oliver, now dressed in his penitential suit for getting drunk last night, to meet Madam Rampant and her whores—also at The Bear. Both parties collide at the tavern, and dance together in masquerade, but when their identities are revealed, Lady Cockwood takes the offensive and forces Sir Oliver to beg for pardon, while Sir Joslin secretly arranges a second rendezvous with the whores later that day at Spring Garden, Lady Cockwood, realising Courtall's true motives, resolves on revenge and sends both the gallants letters as if from the girls, appointing a meeting— at Spring Garden. Here the young lovers meet and quarrel, but when the knights arrive, and Sir Oliver supposes Courtall is seducing his wife, swords are drawn. Back at Sir Oliver's, Etherege contrives to hide both gallants in a closet where they overhear the girls innocently confess their love; once discovered, Courtall again talks his way out of trouble, and brings Lady Cockwood to accept the situation. All are reconciled, and the girls take the gallants as husbands—on a month's probation.

She Would if She Could was Etherege's second play and a unique achievement. He abandons the heroic plot in rhymed couplets of his first comedy, *Love in a Tub; or, The Comical Revenge* (1664), and offers instead a "talking play" which reproduces with casual ease the wit and grace of polished, conversational prose. Low-life characters like the pimp Rakehell and Madam Rampant are now thrust to the play's periphery or kept off stage, and the broad humour of the farcical, country squires is discreetly curtailed. The play's bawdy element is, in fact, restricted to Sir Joslin Jolley's airy songs; Sir Oliver lacks the stamina to commit adultery, and Lady Cockwood is ridiculed as a domestic tyrant whose self-deceiving and absurd pretensions to "honour" are exploited by Courtall to prevent the fruition of her desires. Our laughter, however, remains more sympathetic than satiric; these clowns and dupes are blessed with a kind of boisterous innocence, and fail not because they have immoral longings in them, but because they lack the intelligence and social skill to accomplish their wishes—compare Lady Cockwood's disastrous efforts to conceal unwanted visitors in Act V with Courtall's suave success in a similar predicament in the play's opening scene. His initial conversation with Freeman establishes that both are libertines, sceptical of conventional morality, shrewd, worldly, "honest" with friends and equals, wary of marriage, and seeking only the fresh gratification of their appetites. Their attempts at the seduction of Gatty and Ariana turn into courtship when they realise the girls share their scepticism but will not take their pleasure outside of matrimony. The meetings of this quartet form the core of Etherege's "talking play", while its open-ended resolution, in which Courtall's confidence in the future marriage is balanced by Freeman's doubt of such a "dangerous trial" as a month's probation, anticipates a pattern for the "gay couples" in many later comedies of this period.

—James L. Smith

THE SHOEMAKER'S HOLIDAY: or, The Gentle Craft
by Thomas Dekker

First Publication: London, 1600.
First Production: At Court, London, 1 January 1600.

Editions

The Shoemaker's Holiday, in *Thomas Dekker*, edited by Ernest Rhys, London, 1894 (Mermaid Series).
The Shoemaker's Holiday, in *Early Seventeenth Century Drama*, edited by Robert G. Lawrence, London, 1963.
The Shoemaker's Holiday, edited by J.B. Steane, Cambridge, 1965.
The Shoemaker's Holiday, edited by P.C. Davies, Edinburgh, 1968.
The Shoemaker's Holiday, edited by D.J. Palmer, London, 1975 (New Mermaid Series).
The Shoemaker's Holiday, edited by Merritt E. Lawliss, Woodbury, New York, 1979.
The Shoemaker's Holiday, edited by R.L. Smallwood and Stanley Wells, Manchester, 1979 (Revels Plays).

Criticism
(For general works on the author, see *Playwrights* volume)

Articles:

Robert Adger Law, "*The Shoemaker's Holiday* and *Romeo and Juliet*", in *Studies in Philology*, 21, 1924.
W.K. Chandler, "The Topography of *The Shoemaker's Holiday*", in *Modern Philology*, 27, 1929.
W.L. Halstead, "New Source Influence on *The Shoemaker's Holiday*", in *Modern Language Notes*, vol.56 no.2, 1941.
Norman Hidden, "*Julius Caesar* and *The Shoemaker's Holiday*", in *Modern Language Review*, vol.48 no.2, 1953.
Patricia Thomson, "The Old Way and the New Way in Dekker and Massinger", in *Modern Language Review*, vol.51 no.2, 1956.
David Novarr, "Dekker's Gentle Craft and the Lord Mayor of London", in *Modern Philology*, vol.57 no.4, 1960.
H.E. Toliver, "*The Shoemaker's Holiday*: Theme and Image", in *Boston University Studies in English*, 5, 1961.
Frederick M. Burelbach Jr., "War and Peace in *The Shoemaker's Holiday*", in *Tennessee Studies in Literature*, 13, 1968.
J.H. Kaplan, "Virtue's Holiday: Thomas Dekker and Simon Eyre", in *Renaissance Drama* (new series), 2, 1969.
Michael Mannheim, "The Construction of *The Shoemaker's Holiday*", in *Studies in English Literature 1500–1900*, 10, 1970.
Arthur F. Kinney, "Thomas Dekker's *Twelfth Night*", in *University of Toronto Quarterly*, 41, 1971.
Richard France, "*The Shoemaker's Holiday* at the Mercury Theatre", in *Theatre Survey*, 16, 1975.
Peter Mortenson, "The Economics of *The Shoemaker's Holiday*", in *Studies in English Literature*, 16, 1976.
Eril Barnett Hughes, "The Tradition of the Fool in Thomas Dekker's *The Shoemaker's Holiday*", in *Publications of the Arkansas Philological Association*, 8, 1982.
David Scott Kartan, "Workshop and/as Playhouse: Comedy and Commerce in *The Shoemaker's Holiday*", in *Studies in Philology*, 84, 1987.
Heather Henderson, "Re-Creating Dekker's Aesthetics of Mirth", in *Theater*, 19, 1988.

*   *   *

Lacy, a kinsman of the Earl of Lincoln, is in love with Rose, the daughter of Sir Roger Oatley, the Mayor of London, but their marriage is prevented. Worried by the implications of the match, Lincoln sends Lacy to the French wars. This does not curb Lacy's ardour, however; he manages to return to London, to marry Rose, and to be pardoned. Accompanying this romantic plot are scenes which centre upon Simon Eyre, the

The Shoemaker's Holiday: National Theatre, London, 1981

shoemaker, and his social rise. When he returns from the wars, Ralph, Eyre's journeyman, is forced to fight for Jane, his wife, who has become the object of the attentions of Hammon, a gentleman. The King in the final scene successfully brings about reconciliations and participates in the holiday festivities.

Social mobility and class rivalry shape the action of *The Shoemaker's Holiday* and contribute to its mood of boisterousness and vitality. The courtship of Lacy and Rose provokes a bitter enmity between Lincoln and Oatley and constitutes one of several challenges in the play to the Elizabethan class structure. A shrewd business acumen permits Eyre to impersonate an alderman, to secure the lucrative cargo of a ship, and to promote himself into the ranks of the city authorities. While Eyre insists that sovereignty is not dependent upon high birth, he is hesitant to admit to the deception he has practised; and his success undermines one of the principles he espouses, that hard work is the only means to ensure social advancement.

Without money Eyre and the members of his household are powerless and incapable of resisting a system built upon prejudice and privilege. The conscription scene shows Eyre in an unfavourable light; despite his promises, he is unable to persuade the officers to free Ralph and to discharge him from his military obligations. Only money will release Ralph, but Eyre, at this point, is not in a position to bribe or to pay the sum that will deliver his journeyman from a fate involving masterlessness, dispossession, and physical disablement.

Insensitively used, money in *The Shoemaker's Holiday* reinforces social divisions and fosters class hostility and injustice. One of the temptations offered by Hammon to Ralph for Jane is a gift of 20 pounds, but his proposal is rejected. In place of money, the values of generosity and hospitality are emphasized. Food takes over from money at the end and is presented as a healthy alternative which encourages harmony and contentment. The shoemakers are the prime dispensers of hospitality, and Dekker's treatment of them advances an approving attitude towards the social importance of the guilds and city corporations.

This would suggest that *The Shoemaker's Holiday* is essentially a light-hearted and buoyant drama which endorses mirth, fellowship, and conviviality. Such a reading can be supported, but other aspects of the play point to a preoccupation with a darker underside and with questions of pride, deprivation, and impoverishment. Waiting for news of Eyre's promotion, Margery, his wife, ignores Ralph, who has returned lame from the wars, and indulges in insensitive speculation about her personal appearance. The abandoned Ralph has no choice but to depart. A sequence of songs enhances the sombre tone, and musical references to cuckoos and nightingales bring to mind the consideration elsewhere of infidelity, separation, and the uncertainty of marital relations. The play ends with a song about the wind and the rain which chastens the mood, modulating the final scene from the festive to the reflective.

The alternating between contrasting moods is matched by a variety and inventiveness of linguistic style. Competing dramatic genres are juxtaposed, and characters move in and out of prose and verse with nimble ingenuity. Rose speaks in a lyrical vein and expresses a pastoral lament about the misfortunes of love. On another occasion, she joins Hammon in a witty antiphony of rhyming couplets. At one moment, the false, pidgin English of Lacy, disguised as a Dutch shoemaker, dominates; at another, attention focuses upon Hammon's creamy courtesies and romantic hyperboles.

Most adept in linguistic ability is Eyre himself. His prose is an excited and exciting mixture of extravagant asseverations, commonplace proverbs, classical allusions, abusive colloquialisms, apostrophic utterances, and expansive, rhetorical, declarations. His vigorous, exclamatory style of speaking (a combination of compound phrases, idiosyncratic idioms, and gusty pronouncements) is compelling and powerful: it enables him to rule his household efficiently, to solve labour disputes, to humble the ambitious, and to persuade the King to grant to the shoemakers a new set of trading privileges.

As Eyre's language meshes together and reflects upon itself, so the play's structure unites the various strands of the narrative. The episodic dramatic form allows Dekker to move rapidly between different locations and to examine recurrent issues from a multiplicity of perspectives. Lacy's courtship of Rose is initially described and then contrasted with the situation of Ralph and Jane, newly married. A range of servants is explored; Eyre's foreman and journeymen are set against Dodger, the parasite, who is in turn compared to Sybil, Rose's bawdy maid. Ideas suggested in word-play are taken up in the action, and the hunting scene demonstrates, in its stage business, a fresh approach to the themes of flight, pursuit, and capture. All of the plots coalesce at the end; although the echoes of war sound in the distance and recall problems still to be confronted, arguments are settled, a banquet heals divisions, generosity is affirmed and social mobility, if morally justified, is given royal approval.

—Mark Thornton Burnett

SHOPPING FOR AN UMBRELLA.   See **SUEHIOGARI.**

THE SIAMESE TWINS.   See **LOS SIAMESES.**

LOS SIAMESES
by Griselda Gambaro

First Publication: Buenos Aires, 1967.
First Production: Di Tella Institute, Buenos Aires, 25 August
          1967.

Criticism
(For general works on the author, see *Playwrights* volume)

Articles:
David Muxó, "La violencia del doble: *Los siameses* de
    Griselda Gambaro", in *Prismal*, 2, 1978.
David W. Foster, "El lenguaje como vehículo espiritual en
    Los siameses de Griselda Gambaro", in *Escritura: Teoría y
    crítica literarias*, 8, 1979.
Miguel Angel Giella, "El victimario como víctima en *Los
    siameses* de Griselda Gambaro: Notas para el análisis", in
    Gestos, 3, 1987.

*   *   *

Los siameses portrays Argentina's escalating fratricidal violence of the 1960's through the depiction of a love–hate relationship between two brothers, Lorenzo and Ignacio. Ostensibly, the bone of contention between the brothers is the parental home they inherited, a small room with two cots and a few sticks of furniture. Lorenzo and Ignacio, though adults, seem unable to leave home. Ignacio explicitly expresses his desire to be autonomous, to lead his own life, marry, and bring his wife to live in "my house. My parent's house". Yet, he feels morally and financially responsible for Lorenzo, who appears to be the weaker of the two. Lorenzo, on the other hand, claims the home belongs to him, and he alternates between the need to separate from and cling to his brother.

When the play begins, the room is empty. Lorenzo runs in frantically, locking the door behind him. He and Ignacio have been out in the street and Lorenzo has just thrown a stone at a child. The child's father runs after him, but Lorenzo succeeds in getting back to the room before his brother. As Ignacio beats on the door and begs Lorenzo to open it, Lorenzo dawdles and asks him questions as to the whereabouts of his pursuer until the father finally catches up with Ignacio and beats him senseless. Thus begins the drama of victimization whereby Lorenzo establishes himself as master of the territory and casts himself as the innocent and endangered self, while forcing Ignacio into the role of the dangerous other, the criminal, to be eliminated at all costs. In the effort to free himself permanently from Ignacio, Lorenzo conceives and directs the drama that Ignacio dies by; he engineers events so that Ignacio will be rejected by his girlfriend, arrested by the police, and killed while in custody.

The metaphor of the Siamese twins reflects the problematic symbiosis between self / other that, the play suggests, lies at the heart of victimization. The image captures not only the violent and grotesque unity of the two men joined into one. It also reflects the opposite: the "one" entity violently struggling to become two autonomous beings. When Lorenzo locks Ignacio out, at the same time he mirrors Ignacio's movements down to the last detail. Lorenzo imitates Ignacio's prostrate position, his thrashings, his groans. This mirroring suggests a shared identity between the two men, a deeper identification than simple mimicry in so far as Lorenzo, peering through the keyhole, has a very limited vision of Ignacio. Although Lorenzo leaves Ignacio's battered body outside all night, when he finally allows him in the next day he fantasizes that they are one being. He now wants to incorporate his twin. He lies next to him on the cot; he insists on walking together around the room for exercise, leg-to-leg, as if they were joined at the hip. Lorenzo also claims that they are *one* in the eyes of the world, maintaining that outsiders cannot tell them apart: "But who is capable of distinguishing between us? I can't. We're the same. That's our tragedy. We're so similar that our actions become confused". He almost convinces himself that Ignacio, rather than himself, was the one who threw the stone. Whether we accept Lorenzo's version that the Siamese twins were separated at birth by means of an operation, or Ignacio's perception of them as still joined in his repeated longings to "cut the cord", the unity, presented as an ironic *ideal* in Lorenzo's aforementioned fantasy, is concurrently perceived by both brothers as a life-threatening liability.

The image of the Siamese twins is especially apt in the depiction of the violence associated with Argentina's deep-seated fascism because it combines the violent symbiosis of self / other with the myth of unity (oneness), with its fictions of shared origins, history, and destiny characteristic of fascist discourse. (Fascism, etymologically, means "uniting".) Lorenzo is unable to allow the slightest distance between himself and his brother but, rather, incessantly intrudes on

Ignacio's plans, his privacy, and his person. In the manner of a fascist leader, Lorenzo belabors myths of their shared birth, past, and future, particularly in times of trouble, when Ignacio gets angry with him and threatens to separate. The myths are as potent as they are dangerous. Ignacio repeatedly succumbs to them against his better judgment, and they cost him his life. And since the 1930's, Argentines have found it difficult to resist fascistic fantasies. Gambaro's use of the biological metaphor of monstrous unity highlights the socio-political and psychological dangers of creating ficticious unities and ficticious differences: both work for the extinction of the other. Lorenzo's refusal to accept his brother's autonomy makes necessary the life-threatening "operation" to separate two unnaturally joined human-beings—Siamese twins. Lorenzo's description of the operation that supposedly separated the two characters bespeaks the dangerous politics of enforced differentiation associated with Argentina's civil conflict: "What happens, in operations like these, is that they can't save them both. One of them is ruined. In order to leave one of them in perfect condition, they have to ruin the other. They have to".

Siameses is a representation of victimization stripped down to the core. There is no race, gender, or class dimension to complicate the process. Although, unlike most Latin American countries, Argentina's population consists predominantly of white European immigrants (the indigenous population was almost completely exterminated by the mid-19th century), Gambaro is not suggesting that there is no significant racist, misogynist, or class-related violence in Argentina. However, in *Siameses* she stresses that perceivable *difference* (race, gender, class) is not necessary for victimization to occur. Even societies that are basically homogeneous are vulnerable to violence. Victimization, this play shows, invents difference, and fabricates an enemy "other" even when that "other" is identical, even inseparable, from self.

—Diana Taylor

———————

THE SILENT WOMAN.   See EPICOENE.

———————

THE SILVER KING
by Henry Arthur Jones

First Publication: London, 1907.
First Production: Princess's Theatre, London, 16 November 1882.

Editions
The Silver King, in *Plays by Henry Arthur Jones*, edited by Russell Jackson, Cambridge, 1982.

*   *   *

Wilfred Denver, a good man but a gambler, becomes accidentally involved in the machinations of Captain "Spider" Skinner and is tricked into believing himself guilty of a murder committed by the latter. He flees in disguise and jumps from a train which afterwards crashes, leading to a general belief that he has perished. He makes his way abroad where he amasses a fortune, becoming "the silver king". Meanwhile his wife,

Nelly, falls upon hard times. Denver returns, ameliorates his family's condition as an anonymous benefactor, and rewards his faithful retainer. In a complicated last act he unmasks Skinner and resolves the plot.

The play, although in many ways only a modest achievement, might nevertheless be thought to signal a turning-point in Victorian drama, and is worth noting not least as a first major success for Jones who, together with Pinero, went on to dominate the English commercial theatre of the 1890's. Commissioned by Wilson Barrett, whose management of the Princess's Theatre was notable for its emphasis on melodrama, it owed something of its structure to a collaborator, Henry Herman, who later claimed co-authorship. Jones, characteristically combative, went to arbitration almost a decade later and was pronounced substantive author by a panel of distinguished theatre practitioners. There is no doubt that the play reveals many of the traits that helped to distinguish Jones from other contemporary dramatists. Although he remained throughout his career deeply mistrustful of the avant-garde, he was a diligent reformer, and early drafts show him striving to refine essentially melodramatic material, introducing a colloquial naturalness to much of the dialogue, controlling a complex plot, inventing theatrically effective incident, and above all attempting originality within a popular form. However, despite substantial revision, the conventionally melodramatic nature of the play remains clear. The plot is lurid and episodic and the characterization broad and unsubtle. Music cues abound. Among the time-honoured devices are a drunkard's downfall and remorse, an unrelenting landlord, the eviction on a winter's night of heroine and sick child, comic lovers, a tearful reunion. Aside and soliloquy are frequent. Moreover there are many echoes of established melodramas; the opening scene in a tavern and the recurrent presence of Baxter, the detective, recall Taylor's *The Ticket of Leave Man*, and the hero's speech as he remembers his supposed victim is strongly reminiscent of Mathias's mesmerised horror in Lewis's *The Bells*.

One must ask, then, wherein lay the originality? For it is clear from reviews of the time that the play was widely perceived to be fresh and innovative. First, Jones was determined to keep the plot before the audience and not to obscure it with spectacle and incident. His apprenticeship as a writer of one-act plays had sharpened his skill as a story-teller, and the basic struggle between Denver and the "Spider" is kept in sharp focus. A large cast of characters is clearly delineated and controlled. Violence is not gratuitous and is sparingly employed. The sometimes elaborate staging is made to serve as a background to human activity. If one compares Act II, Scene 2, set in a railway station, with a similar episode from a popular earlier melodrama, *London by Night* (sometimes attributed to Selby), it is clear that in the latter the setting was seen as important in itself, dwarfing the action; Jones uses his setting to make genuine dramatic effect, having a newspaper boy call our attention to the plight of the hunted Denver ("Winner of the Derby, sir! Murder in Hatton Garden last night") and involving his hero in a tantalising encounter with a tipsy passenger. Such enhancing of the melodrama by setting it against an everyday ordinariness is a device that Jones employs with considerable skill, as Hitchcock was to do many years later, and it demonstrates a higher standard of dramatic workmanship than was the norm in the popular theatre of his day.

Another source of the play's reputation for originality was its literary style. Mathew Arnold wrote: ". . .diction and sentiments do not overstep the modesty of nature. . .Instead of giving the audience transpontine diction and sentiments, Messrs Jones and Herman give them literature". It seems clear that his commendation was earned by the overall restraint of the dialogue, for he also criticised as superfluous a piece of "fine writing"—Denver's elaborately rhetorical description of a dream—of a kind that Jones was habitually drawn to. But as well as such purple patches, and the wealth of soliloquy and histrionics and attitudinising that Jones inherited with the form he was employing, there is sufficient evidence of *flair* for spare and effective dialogue and an accurately-observed presentation of class speech habits to explain Arnold's enthusiasm.

Another reason for the play's enthusiastic reception by discerning critics is suggested by a review in *The Times* commending the plot for being "thoroughly home-made". There was considerable sensitivity at the time about the intrusiveness of the French drama into the London theatre and Jones provided an "Englishness", almost certainly at Wilson Barrett's request, which was very welcome. He knew provincial and rural life well, both from his own upbringing and from his early employment as a commercial traveller, and the many scenes exhibiting this knowledge have the ring of authenticity.

Finally a note of caution is necessary. Many histories and surveys of the drama suggest that *The Silver King* is an early example of the problem play, possibly because Allardyce Nicoll so describes it. Nicoll observes that the play best represents Jones's early work, but goes on to write that it also "presents a desire to treat social problems seriously" (*History of the English Drama, 5*, 1946). Not so, for Jones's source was an adventure story, *Dead in the Desert*, and he remained true to its spirit. To find Jones deliberately trafficking in social ideas we have to look to much later work; *The Silver King*, perhaps the most frequently revived of any of his plays, owes its success and its small but secure place in the history of English drama to its author's sure instinct for what a public increasingly impatient with imported, aped, and outmoded fare wanted from the theatre, and a grasp of dramatic structure and theatrical narrative firm enough to bring it to them.

—Robert Silvester

THE SILVER TASSIE
by Sean O'Casey

First Publication: London, 1928.
First Production: Apollo Theatre, London, 11 October 1929.

Criticism
(For general works on the author, see *Playwrights* volume)

Articles:
Ronald G. Rollins, "O'Casey, O'Neill and Expressionism in *The Silver Tassie*", in *Bucknell Review*, 10, 1962.
Jacqueline Doyle, "Liturgical Imagery in Sean O'Casey's *The Silver Tassie*", in *Modern Drama*, 21, 1978.
Elisabeth Freundlich, "*The Silver Tassie* and the Cold War", in *Southern Review*, 4, 1978.
Marguerite Harkness, "*The Silver Tassie*: No Light in the Darkness", in *Southern Review*, 4, 1978.
Carol Kleiman, "*The Silver Tassie* and Others: A Re-Evaluation in the Light of the Absurd", in *Southern Review*, 4, 1978.
Heinz Kosok, "The Revision of *The Silver Tassie*", in *Southern Review*, 5, 1978.
John O'Riordan, "The Garlanded Horror of War: Reflections on *The Silver Tassie*", in *Southern Review*, 4, 1978.
Richard F. Peterson, "Polishing up the *Silver Tassie* Controversy: Some Lady Gregory and W.B. Yeats Letters to Lennox Robinson", in *Southern Review*, 4, 1978.
Simon Williams, "The Unity of *The Silver Tassie*", in *Southern Review*, 4, 1978.
Barbara Kreps, "The Meaning of Structure and Images in Sean O'Casey's *The Silver Tassie*", in *Studi dell'Instituto Linguistico*, 2, 1979.
Ronald G. Rollins and Llewellyn Rabby, "*The Silver Tassie*: The Post-World-War-I Legacy", in *Modern Drama*, 22, 1979.
Heinz Kosok, "*The Silver Tassie* and British Plays of the First World War", in *Arbeiten aus Anglistik und Amerikanstik*, 10, 1985.
Bernice Schrank, "O'Casey's *The Silver Tassie*: From Manuscripts to Published Texts", in *Bulletin of Research in the Humanities*, 87, 1986-87.
Violet M. O'Valle, "Deliberate Distortions of Grail Motifs, Solar Myth, and Bird Metaphor in Sean O'Casey's *The Silver Tassie*", in *Eire / Ireland*, vol.22 no.3, 1987.

*   *   *

The Silver Tassie is "a Tragi-Comedy in Four Acts" with a large cast, set at the time of World War I. The title refers to a cup that the Dublin football hero, Harry Hegan, brings home triumphantly in the first act, and the Burns song that he sings in celebration. The women are keen to get the young men off to the war transport vessel. Slapstick comedy is provided by two old men, Sylvester and Simon. Susie and Jessie are in love with Harry.

The famous second act is totally formal, with chanting and echoes of the Mass. It is a comprehensive portrayal of the comedy and misery and confusion of life in the trenches. Individual characters are submerged in the war machine. The third act is set in a hospital where, for reasons never explained, the civilian comedians, Simon and Sylvester, are reluctantly occupying beds beside the wounded soldiers. The style is knockabout comedy, the language somewhat overblown poetic in Harry's speeches. His legs have been paralysed in action. Susie, who was religious in the first act, has become a nurse who flirts with the doctor. Jessie is now indifferent to the man she used to worship. Harry is very bitter: "I'll make my chair a Juggernaut, and wheel it over the neck and spine of every daffodil that looks at me, and strew them dead to manifest the mercy of God and the justice of man". Act IV takes place at a dance given by the football club. By now Harry is in a wheelchair and Teddy Foran is blind: the act confirms what has happened in Act III. These two ruined soldiers are passed by in the gay dance of life, and Harry has lost the attentions of both Susie (to his surgeon) and Jessie (to his friend, Barney).

This is the play that Yeats turned down for the Abbey Theatre, which led to O'Casey moving to England for the rest of his life. It shows a proper desire to go beyond personal experience and experiment with new styles. The second act is generally taken to be a success. It is a great challenge to the set designer, with its ruined church, guns, barbed wire, and a soldier being punished, lashed to a large wheel, (Augustus John designed the first set). However, O'Casey is not a poet, and when he ignores his good ear for common speech the language becomes inflated or grotesque. He has a weakness for heavy handed alliteration, as when Mrs. Foran says: "Every little bit of china I had in the house is lyin' above in a mad an' muddled heap like the flotsum and jetsum of the seashore".

There is great energy in the first act which manages to suggest that these burly football heroes are really not in control

The Silver Tassie: Aldwych Theatre, London, 1969 (Royal Shakespeare Company)

of their lives, but at the mercy of a government that needs their strength for war, and wives and mothers who need their money. When the men are in the middle of their drunken song of celebration, a ship's siren is heard. The old men and women speak together, "You must go back", and they are echoed by a crowd outside. The civilians drape the young men in their military gear and hustle them off. It is not a realistic crowd: "Come on from your home to the boat; / Carry on from the boat to the camp. / From the camp up the line to the trenches". It certainly makes a point, but how are actors meant to speak such lines?

The third act is an uneasy mixture of melodrama and farce, although the crudeness helps to rub our noses in the misery of these simple men with their broken bodies. The final act is more successful. We are spared the cavortings of Simon and Sylvester and brutally exposed to the contrast between the ruined veterans, bitter and jealous, and the mindless, jolly dancers, as O'Casey (admittedly rather awkwardly) has the surgeon sing:

> Swing into the dance,
> Take joy when it comes, ere it go;
> For the full flavour of life
> Is either a kiss or a blow,
> He to whom joy is a foe,
> Let him wrap himself up in his woe;
> For he is a life on the ebb,
> We a full life on the flow.

It is noticeable that there are no memorable characters, just broadly presented types. Similarly, the two comedians are not integrated into the action and are more stupid than funny; pale imitations of previous successes. It may be that O'Casey was happier working from life, that he was an observer rather than an imaginer.

—James Simmons

THE SISTERS-IN-LAW (Les Belles-Soeurs)
by Michel Tremblay

First Publication: Montreal, 1968.
First Production: Théâtre du Rideau Vert, Montreal, 28 August 1968.

Translations
The Sisters-in-Law, translated by Bill Glassco and John van Burek, Vancouver, 1974.

Criticism
(For general works on the author, see *Playwrights* volume)

Articles:
André Turcotte, "Les 'Belles-Soeurs' en révolte", in *Voix et images du pays: Littérature québécoise*, 3, 1970.
Jean P. Ryngaert, "Du Réalisme à la théâtricalité: La Dramaturgie de Michel Tremblay dans *Les Belles-Soeurs* et *A toi, pour toujours, ta Marie-Lou*", in *Livres et auteurs québécois*, 1971.
Lise Duquette-Perrier, "Langage et paraître: Analyse sémiotique des *Belles-Soeurs*", in *Journal canadien de recherche sémiotique*, Autumn 1974.

Catherin McQuaid, "Michel Tremblay's Seduction of the 'Other Solitude' ", in *Canadian Drama*, Autumn, 1976.

Micheline Herz, "Le Froid et le chaud dans *les Belles-Soeurs* de Michel Tremblay", in *Société des professeurs français en Amérique: Bulletin*, 1976–77.

René Juéry, "Michel Tremblay: Une Interprétation psycho-analytique des *Belles-Soeurs*", in *Études littéraires*, December 1978.

Jutta Lietz, "Huis clos in Montréal: Zu *Belles-Soeurs* von Michel Tremblay", in *Romanistisches Jahrbuch*, 31, 1980.

Elain F. Nardoccio, "*Les Belles-Soeurs* et la révolution tranquille", in *Action nationale*, 70, 1980.

Jayne H. Abrate, "Le Thème de l'inconscience dans *Les Beaux Dimanches* et *Les Belles-Soeurs*", in *Présence francophone*, 24, 1982.

Jeannine Hiester, "La Structure classique des *Belles-Soeurs* de Michel Tremblay", in *Incidences*, vol.6 nos.1–2, 1982.

Pierre P. Karch, "Analyse d'un condition du comique appliquée aux *Belles-Soeurs* de Michel Tremblay: La Distanciation", in *Thalia*, vol.8 no.1, 1985.

Alvina Ruprecht, "Effets sonores et signification dans *Les Belles-Soeurs* de Michel Tremblay", in *Voix et images*, 36, 1987.

Michel Tremblay, " 'Par la Porte d'en avant. . .': Entretien avec Michel Tremblay", in *Jeu*, 47, 1988.

*   *   *

In *Les Belles-Soeurs*, Germaine, a middle-aged, working-class, Montreal housewife, has just won a million trading stamps in a contest. She has invited 14 women—sisters, sister-in-law, daughter, friends—to help her paste the stamps in booklets. Their exchanges, in dialogue, chorus, and stylized monologue, create a depressing mosaic of urban economic, cultural, and emotional destitution. Separate incidents weave into a social tableau rather than a plot. As their bickering progresses, the women, envious, begin to steal Germaine's booklets. As the curtain falls to the singing of "O Canada" she is left alone and bereft on stage.

Completed in 1965, this play found no one willing to stage it for three years, primarily because of the language it uses: *joual*, the impoverished, heavily anglicized French of working-class Montreal, previously considered unfit for public exposure except in burlesque. Critics, misled by its depressing atmosphere, have frequently labelled the work "naturalistic", a term that is here decidedly imprecise. Each of the 15 female characters is entirely credible, and drawn largely from people the author knew. But their depiction by Tremblay is purposely distanced through unrealistic, lyrical monologues heightened by spotlights and recorded sound, by stylized choruses, and by a surrealist ending in what is in fact an intensely poetic, incantatory work.

These women represent three generations, all similarly victimized by heredity and environment, unaware of the cultural and spiritual deprivation which is the real cause of their condition. Capitalist economics, the patriarchal society of Quebec in the 1960's, the Roman Catholic religion, and the marginal status of francophones in Canada, have conspired to entrap them in lives of daily futility and inevitable, future despair. The situation of 93-year-old Olivine Dubuc, senile and brutalized by daughter-in-law responsible for her care, is as deplorable as that of Germaine's 20-year-old daughter, Linda, who is pregnant and unwed. Those who have sought to break away from this oppressive environment, like Germaine's youngest sister Pierrette or the middle-aged spinster Angéline, are rejected and despised by the others and, conditioned irredeemably by their past, are at least as miserable.

The repressed despair which is central to each of these 15 lives is expressed differently: fear of the men in their lives (husbands, sons, lovers, priests—all physically absent here but ever-present in their conversation); fear of poverty, ageing, solitude, disease, death, and what they believe lies beyond. But this despair, for Tremblay, is endemic to the working-class, francophone, proletariat of Montreal: only the prospect of sudden material enrichment in a contest or lottery appears, at the beginning of the play, to offer some faint hope. That hope is, of course, destroyed by the closing scene. As each of the 15 takes the spotlight, the cumulative effect of their intimate revelations becomes incantatory; and this effect is intensified by recurrent "choruses" (such as "This Stupid Rotten Life"; "Goddamn Johnny!"; "Ode to Bingo";), building towards a frenetic closing sequence where the women, screaming, throw booklets at each other while old Olivine, wheelchair-bound, intones an ironic "O Canada", and the anthem is taken up by the others—even by Germaine, who is left on stage, alone, "standing at attention, with tears in her eyes". Then "a rain of stamps falls slowly from the ceiling". Sudden material improvement will make no qualitative difference in these barren lives.

Before 1968 Quebec's distinctive brand of French had been heard on stage only from the mouths of comic, subservient, or marginal characters. This fact was perceived by Tremblay, of working-class origin himself, as a betrayal of his cultural identity. In *Les Belles-Soeurs* he set out to confront that bias, to expose the deplorable conditions he had seen and experienced and, by poetic exorcism, contribute towards changing them. Proof of the author's at least partial success is that *joual* is now considered entirely acceptable, even in traditionalist theatres. The battle over language and "official" culture occasioned by its first performances obscured for a time the work's striking originality and its universal appeal. It was a watershed in Quebec dramaturgy, and is now a standard of the Canadian repertory in both languages.

—Leonard E. Doucette

SIX CHARACTERS IN SEARCH OF AN AUTHOR
(Sei personaggi in cerca d'autore)
by Luigi Pirandello

First Publication: In *Maschere nude, 3* (second edition), Florence, 1921; revised version, 1925.
First Production: Teatro Valle, Rome, 10 May 1921.

Translations
Six Characters in Search of an Author, in *Luigi Pirandello: Three Plays*, London, 1921.
Six Characters in Search of an Author, translated by Frederick May, London, 1954.
Six Characters in Search of an Author, translated by John Lindstrum, London, 1979.

Criticism
(For general works on the author, see *Playwrights* volume)

Books:
Doug Thompson, *An Introduction to Pirandello's "Sei personaggi in cerca d'autore"*, Hull, 1985.

Six Characters in Search of an Author: National Theatre, London, 1987

Anna Vaglio, *Comme leggere: "Sei personaggi in cerca d'autore" di Luigi Pirandello*, Milan, 1989.

Articles:

L. Ongley, "Pirandello Confesses: Why and How he Wrote *Six Characters in Search of an Author*", in *Virginia Quarterly Review*, 1, 1925.

F. Montana, "La tragedia dei *Sei personaggi*", in *Studium*, 55, 1959.

C.K. Kligerman, "A Psychoanalytic Study of Pirandello's *Six Characters in Search of an Author*", in *Journal of the American Psychoanalysis Association*, 10, 1962.

A. Richard Sogliuzzo, "The Uses of the Mask in *The Great God Brown* and *Six Characters in Search of an Author*", in *Educational Theatre Journal*, 18, 1966.

Antonio Illiano, "Pirandello's *Six Characters in Search of an Author*: A Comedy in the Making", in *Italica*, 44, 1967.

Jørn Moestrup, "Le correzioni ai *Sei personaggi* e il Castelvetro di Pirandello", in *Revue romane*, 2, 1967.

Eric Bentley, "Father's Day: In Search of Six Characters in Search of an Author", in *Tulane Drama Review*, 13, 1968.

Maryse Meynaud-Jeuland, "A Propos des didascalies des *Sei personaggi in cerca d'autore*", in *Revue des études italiennes*, 14, 1968.

David Nolan, "Theory in Action: Pirandello's *Sei personaggi*", in *Forum for Modern Language Studies*, 4, 1968.

Andrew K. Kennedy, "*Six Characters*: Pirandello's Last Tape", in *Modern Drama*, 12, 1969.

Wlodzimierz Krysínski, "*Six Personnages en quête d'auteur*: Remise d'une question du théâtre traditionnel à illusion scènique", in *Zagadnienia Rodzajów Literackich*, 12, 1969.

Gaspare Giudice, "L'ambiguità nei *Sei personaggi in cerca d'autore*", in *Quaderni del teatro stabile della città di Torino*, 24, 1972.

Jan B. Gordon, "*Sei personaggi in cerca d'autore*: Myth, Ritual, and Pirandello's Anti-Symbolist Theatre", in *Forum Italicum*, 6, 1972.

Sei personaggi in cerca d'autore: Studi e documentazioni", in *Quaderni del teatro stabile della città di Torino*, 24, 1972 [reviews and essays].

Claudio Vicentini, "I *Sei personaggi in cerca d'autore* e la nascita del teatro nuovo", in *Quaderni del teatro stabile della città di Torino*, 24, 1972.

Mario Apollonio, "Prologo ai *Sei personaggi*", in *Istituto di studi Pirandelliani, Quaderni*, 1, 1973.

David McDonald, "Derrida and Pirandello: A Post Structuralist Analysis of *Six Characters in Search of an Author*", in *Modern Drama*, 20, 1977.

Alan Roland and Gino Rizzo, "Psychoanalysis in Search of Pirandello: *Six Characters* and *Henry IV*", in *Psychoanalytic Review*, 64, 1977.

J.L. Styan, "Pirandellian Theatre Games: Spectator as Victim", in *Modern Drama*, 23, 1980.

Robert Bigazzi, "I *Sei personaggi* e l'autore", in *Modern Language Notes*, 97, 1982.

Jennifer Lorch, "The 1925 text of *Sei personaggi in cerca d'autore* and Pitoëff's Production of 1923", in *Yearbook of the British Pirandello Society*, 2, 1982.

Alessandro Tinterri, "Two Flights of Steps and a Stage Direction: Pirandello's Staging of *Six Characters in Search of an Author* in 1925", in *Yearbook of the British Pirandello Society*, 3, 1983.

Franco Ferrucci, "Pirandello e il palcoscenico della mente", in *Lettere italiane*, 36, 1984.

Tim Fitzpatrick, "Strategies of Antithesis: The Opening of *Sei personaggi in cerca d'autore*", in *Yearbook of the British Pirandello Society*, 5, 1985.

Manfredi Piccolomini, "Sull'episodio di 'Madama Pace' nei *Sei personaggi* di Pirandello", in *Revista di studi italiani*, vol.3 no.1, 1985.

Olga Ragusa, "Teaching *Six Characters*", in *Teaching Language Through Literature*, vol.24, no.2, 1985.

Adelin C. Fiorato, "Les *Six personnages* de Pirandello et le 'mal' du théâtre", in *Acta Universitatis Wratislaviensis*, 895, 1986.

Grazia Sotis, "Gioco come improvisazione nel' *Il gott con gli stivali* e *Sei personaggi in cerca d'autore*: Un'ipotesi", in *Forum Italicum*, 20, 1986.

Doug Thompson, "Pirandello's *Inferno*: Time and Punishment in *Sei personaggi in cerca d'autore*", in *Perspectives on Contemporary Literature*, 12, 1986.

Mary A.F. Witt, "*Six Characters in Search of an Author* and the Battle of the Lexis", in *Modern Drama*, 30, 1987.

*   *   *

This is the play that established Pirandello's international reputation as a playwright. Already well-known in Italy as a prose writer, critic, and poet, he had begun to write for the theatre shortly before World War I, increasing his output rapidly after 1918. *Six Characters* caused a scandal when it first appeared, and the first night ended with a riot, due to the taboo subject-matter of the play: incestuous desire.

Six Characters is the first of three plays known as the "theatre-in-the-theatre" triology, because the action involves the attempted staging of a play within another play. A rehearsal of a Pirandello play is supposedly taking place in an Italian theatre, but is interrupted by the arrival of six people, who claim to be characters looking for a playwright to tell their story. That story then gradually unfolds, told principally by the Father and the Stepdaughter. At some point in the past, the Father and the Mother have separated, and the Mother has gone to live with another man by whom she has had children. She is accompanied on stage by the Son and by two smaller children, the Boy and the Little Girl. Relations between the characters are strained: the Stepdaughter detests the Son and the Boy, the Son has a grudge against the Mother, and the Father is an outsider altogether. The Father claims to have always loved the Mother and her children, but the Stepdaughter depicts him as a debauched elderly man who used to spy on her when she was a child.

In the second act, the Characters summon up a seventh person, Madame Pace, the owner of a seedy milliner's shop that serves as a brothel, where the Stepdaughter was working and where the Father met her when he came looking for a girl. The incestuous encounter between the Father and the Stepdaughter is interrupted by the Mother's cry. In the last act, the Mother tries to win over her sullen, resentful Son, but while her attention is distracted, the Little Girl drowns in a fountain and the Boy shoots himself. The Stepdaughter runs away and the Father, Mother, and Son are left, prisoners of their own despair. The boundary between fiction and reality has completely broken down, the Director and the other Actors are left bewildered by what has happened, and the play ends.

Pirandello uses ingenious devices to mark the passage from one act to another, and manages to preserve the shape of the well-made play while simultaneously deconstructing it as a form. The text of the play was modified considerably after the famous Pitoëff production in 1923, when the appearance of the Six Characters, one of the great moments of theatre magic, was heightened by having them arrive on stage in a huge elevator. In the preface that he added to the second version of the play, Pirandello explains the function of the Characters in relation to his own creative process. He was constantly concerned with the problem of the vital, moving process that constitutes life, in contrast to the rigid fixity of art, and *Six Characters* explores that duality. The Characters are fixed in their tragic story, unmovably, for as Pirandello says, they are created out of "unvarying fantasy". Ironically, although the Characters are fictitious, Pirandello argues that they appear more real than the Actors with their "changeable naturalness". Art, for Pirandello, can seem more real than life, and this is the paradox he seeks to expose.

What Pirandello does in *Six Characters* is to strip the play down to its bones, offering the audience the basic tools—the Actors, the Characters, a story—but leaving the final inter-pretation open. The play thus becomes an investigation of the processes of artistic creation; it is a play about playing that uses the device of play-making as its central, structural principle.

After the initial shock at the subject-matter of the play, *Six Characters* became a huge success, both in Italy and around the world. It has since come to be regarded as a classic experimen-tal play that prefigured many later developments in the theatre. The work of Brecht and Piscator in exposing the theatricality of theatre finds its parallel in it, while the relativity of truth that means there is no single, straightforward solution to the story of the Six Characters, foreshadows the "Theatre of the Absurd".

Six Characters has remained one of Pirandello's most popular and best-known plays. It continues to be performed throughout the world and has been televised, filmed, and, (in 1959) turned into an opera. Although the subject-matter no longer causes feelings of outrage, the ingenious structure of the play continues to raise important questions about the nature of stage illusion and its relationship to life.

—Susan Bassnett

SIZWE BANSI IS DEAD
by Athol Fugard, John Kani, and Winston Ntshona

First Publication: In *Statements*, Oxford and New York, 1974.
First Production: The Space, Cape Town, 8 October 1972.

Criticism
(For general works on the author, see *Playwrights* volume)

Articles:
Patrick O'Sheel, "Athol Fugard's 'Poor Theatre'", in *Journal of Commonwealth Literature*, vol.12, no.3, 1978.
Hilary Seymour, "*Sizwe Bansi is Dead*: A Study of Artistic Ambivalence", in *Race and Class*, 21, 1980.

*   *   *

The play is set in the South African township of New Brighton, Port Elizabeth, in a photographic studio owned by Styles. Styles reminisces about his life as a worker in the Ford car factory and tells of his decision to set up his own business as a photographer, establishing his "strong-room of dreams". Into the studio comes a man calling himself Robert Zwelinzima. This is the newly-assumed name of Sizwe Bansi, a worker from outside the city, who has evaded police harass-ment as an illegal resident by taking on the identity of the murdered Zwelinzima. In a series of flashbacks, with Styles playing Sizwe's friend Buntu, Sizwe Bansi's experiences are played out. The photograph Styles is taking is to be sent to Sizwe's wife to reassure her of his safety and "success" in the city. The play centres upon the desperate existence of the black migrant worker trying to make a living in the face of constant regulation and persecution by the white authorities.

The play (together with *The Island*, 1973) was devised by Fugard and the two actors, John Kani and Winston Ntshona,

Sizwe Bansi is Dead: Royal Court Theatre, London, 1973

who were in the original production. The piece grew out of their experiences as black South Africans, and their performance of the play earned them worldwide praise. The text as printed offers the kernel of the piece as seen by the audiences for whom Kani and Ntshona played, but they elaborated upon the text in performance, relating to their mainly white audiences in a way that first delighted them and then turned upon them to face them with their shared responsibility for the plight of blacks in South Africa's apartheid society. The roles played by the two actors in this many-peopled drama were extended to place audience members in their own roles. This improvisation added a dynamic dimension to the play in performance and raises the question as to whether, in the hands of other actors, the play can be quite the "real" thing. The original image (a studio photograph and the cast of a man with a cigarette in one hand and a pipe in the other) formed the starting-point for the process of devising undertaken by the writer/director and the actors. Kani and Ntshona brought to the process their direct experience of the realities of life for black South Africans.

The tone of the play is initially amusing, with Styles describing the visit of Mr. Henry Ford the Second to the car plant where he had previously been employed. Styles relates how he had offered "free" translations of the foreman's instructions to the workers on their behaviour in front of Mr. Ford. As audience we laugh with Styles at the way he has made a fool of the foreman, but the joke is on us, as the point is made that Styles represents a world into which we have little real access. In this section the actor addresses the audience directly, but the style and the mood of the play change as Styles' customer, Sizwe Bansi, in the alias of Robert Zwelinzima, enters to have his photograph taken.

From this point the play develops through what Dennis Walder has described as "a complex web of monologues" (in *Athol Fugard*, 1984) to look back at the circumstances that have brought Sizwe Bansi to this moment. We retrace his arrival in the city seeking work but without a permit, his attempts to evade the police and to avoid deportation to his home 150 miles away, and the moment when, coming across the murdered body of Zwelinzima, he is faced with the choice of assuming his identity and his legal status as a permit-holding "work-seeker", or continuing with his precarious existence in the city. Sizwe Bansi's eventual decision to become Robert Zwelinzima, despite his despair at the loss of his own name, is justified by his friend Buntu:

> Look, brother, Robert Zwelinzima, that poor bastard out there in the alleyway, if there *are* ghosts, he is smiling tonight. He is here, with us, and he's saying: "Good luck, Sizwe! I hope it works." He's a brother, man.

The play protests about the condition of the black working class in South Africa. But despite its undoubted success in these terms some critics argued that, though it describes graphically the conditions in which the blacks have to live, it does nothing to articulate action to destroy the oppressive system; it is inhibited by "liberal" instincts when it should be calling for revolution. With events in South Africa moving towards at least the possibility of a non-racial democracy, the play may have lost some of its edge, but it remains one of the most theatrically powerful statements to have emerged from South Africa in recent years.

—Martin Banham

THE SKIN OF OUR TEETH
by Thornton Wilder

First Publication: New York, 1942.
First Production: Plymouth Theatre, New York, 18 November 1942.

Criticism
(For general works on the author, see *Playwrights* volume)

Articles:
Gerald Rabkin, "*The Skin of Our Teeth* and the Theatre of Thornton Wilder", in *The Forties: Fiction, Poetry, Drama*, edited by Warren French, Deland, Florida, 1969.
Charles H. Helmetag, "Mother Courage and her American Cousins in *The Skin of Our Teeth*", in *Modern Language Studies*, vol.8 no.3, 1978.
Paul Hernadi, "The Face Value of the Actor's Mask: *The Skin of Our Teeth* and *Marat/Sade*", in his *Interpreting Events: Tragicomedies of History on the Modern Stage*, Ithaca, New York, 1985.
Jared Lobdell, "Thornton Wilder as Fantasist and the Science-Fiction Anti-Paradism: The Evidence of *The Skin of Our Teeth*", in *Patterns of the Fantastic, 2*, Mercer Island, Western Australia, 1985.

*   *   *

The Antrobus family of suburban New Jersey are having a difficult time keeping up their life-style while dealing with the Ice Age. Mr. Antrobus has just achieved fame through his invention of the wheel and the alphabet. In the second act, he is elected president of the Mammals Society, is seduced by the maid, Sabina, and is just about to leave his wife when activity is interrupted by the onslaught of the Deluge and he is called on to get all the animals into the Ark. The next time we see them, they have just come through the Napoleonic Wars—"by the skin of our teeth". All the while, the actors step out of character, having a difficult time getting through the play, what with scenes that might be upsetting, a bout of food poisoning, and several temperamental outbursts. Finally, Mr. Antrobus confesses to his uninterested wife his thoughts on the genuine problems of existence, delivered in the words of famous philosophers like Spinoza, Plato, and Aristotle.

Thornton Wilder's disgust for the middle-class, drawing-room plays of his day was profound. His exasperation at the failure of the theatre of his time to utilize "the theatre's power to raise the exhibited individual action into the realm of idea and type and universal" because it insisted on "squeezing it into that removed showcase" of the box set formed the basic motive behind most of his plays. The misinterpretation of *Our Town* as a realistic eulogy to small-town America inspired the even more radical, overt attack of *Skin of Our Teeth*, a literal illustration of how, in his own words, "the middle class devitalized the theatre". The theatre, Wilder insisted, "is a work of pretense". Discussing Chinese theatre, he cited two basic elements: "the collaborative activity of the spectator's imagination" and "raising the action from the specific to the general". Middle-class realism, he pointed out, does exactly the opposite; dispensing with the imagination altogether, it reduces even the most phenomenal to the trivia of ordinary domesticity.

Skin of our Teeth is usually treated as a rather off-beat romp. However, though it might, now, seem somewhat dated, the play has a good set of fairly sharp incisors and means to bite more deeply. The attacks on box-set conventions are obvious enough. Sabina's exposition directly lampoons clumsy introductory expositions (much as Stoppard later did in *The Real Inspector Hound*): "Oh! oh! oh! Six o'clock and the master not home yet. Pray God nothing has happened to him crossing the Hudson River". To further call attention to the artificiality of the stage drama, Wilder has Sabina effortlessly slip into clichés of serving maids and of stylized melodrama.

These barbs, however, are merely the more readily available surface of the attack. The conventions and form of middle-class drama are shown to be the products of middle-class consciousness, a set of priorities, values, and self definitions. It is these Wilder is gunning for.

One tactic is to detach his audience from the play. Ridicule of form and the constant interruption so the actors, notably Sabina, can have their say, destroys the comfort of a transferable reality. The usual devices of missing cues, commenting on the play, talking to the audience, call attention to the theatrical act itself. The scene where Sabina takes it on herself to tell the audience the plot so she can skip the scene, highlights the assumption that a play is merely a story in dialogue by taking it literally. In the third act, the cast and Stage Manager burst on stage announcing that several actors have been taken to hospital with food poisoning. They then proceed to have a "top and tail" rehearsal with their "volunteer understudies" for a later scene. More is going on here than merely removing the "mystique" of theatre. The actors are being presented as fallible individuals, ordinary persons doing a job of work, and we watch them going about the business of preparing a performance in a clumsy, self-conscious, unromantic manner.

The play being performed, *The Skin of our Teeth*, is made into a separate entity, detached not only from the audience but from the actors as well. "The action", says Wilder, "takes place both in historical times and in 20th century suburban New Jersey at once". Actually, the play is not taking place in either the Ice Age or New Jersey, but *on* stage. The stage itself (and its relationship to the audience) is the focus of the play. Nor can the characters "live" in either place. The confines of theatrical convention annihilate any credibility, however, peripheral. Since not even the most Promethean "suspension of disbelief" could bridge this gap, the conventions, values, and assumptions of both the theatre and 20th-century suburban New Jersey become isolated and held up for evaluation. The language and references are so modern that the apparent setting makes the desperate attempts of the Antrobus family to behave as "average suburbanites" completely bizarre.

The mismatch between setting and content is the central device. Set precariously in the Ice Age, the middle-class family have dinosaurs and mammoths for pets (both played by actors), listen to the news on the radio, drive cars, go to High School—even though Mr. Antrobus has just invented the wheel and the alphabet. The petty concerns of everyday life and their values—comfort, wealth, personal neurosis, good manners—are preposterous responses to events like the Ice Age, the Flood, and the Napoleonic Wars.

The image of self-satisfied suburban America reflected reassuringly back from drawing-room dramatic realism is not only mocked for its superficial smugness but bitterly pilloried for its untruthfulness. Following the usual conventions, everyone is ascribed a middle-class consciousness. Thus Mrs. Antrobus advises the Telegram Boy on dealing with the Ice Age: "Just keep as warm as you can and don't let your wife and children see you're worried". Sabina refuses to play the scene where she seduces Mr. Antrobus away from his wife because she has a friend in the audience who has had a similar experience and might be upset: "I don't think the theatre is a place where people's feelings ought to be hurt". When the down-and-outs from the streets of New York appear to shelter from the ice, Sabina reassures the audience: "Most people really have enough to eat and a roof over their heads. Nobody actually starves—besides they're only savages. Savages don't love their families—not like we do!".

The conventions of suburban realism lead on to the assumption that people are, and have always been, the same, regardless of different historical periods or situations. Thus well-made, "historical" plays confidently reassured audiences that, say, Mary Queen of Scots, felt and acted exactly as they would. Wilder has merely driven this assumption to its ultimate absurdity. In presenting "the events of our homely daily life depicted against the vast dimensions of time and space" he exposes these underlying assumptions in all their pernicious ludicrousness. A fundamental concern with personal trivia leads to an inability to establish priorities, to distinguish between major upheaval and momentary crisis. The powerful speeches of the philosophers regale the audience with fundamental questions that might more justifiably concern the theatre: what is the purpose of life? How does one choose rulers? What is good government? What is man's relationship with God? After an evening of hilarious and shameless trivia, their speeches are a powerful and moving contrast.

—Elaine Turner

THE SLEEP OF REASON (El sueño de la razón) by Antonio Buero Vallejo

First Publication: In *Primer acto*, 117, February 1970; in book form, Madrid, 1970; revised edition, Barcelona, 1985.
First Publication: Teatro Reina Victoria, Madrid, 6 February 1970.

Translations
The Sleep of Reason, in *Antonio Buero-Vallejo: Three Plays*, translated by Marion Peter Holt, San Antonio, Texas, 1985.

Criticism
(For general works on the author, see *Playwrights* volume)

Articles:
Antonio Buero Vallejo, "Sobre *El sueño de la razón*: Una conversación con Antonio Buero Vallejo", in *Primer acto*, 117, 1970.
Ricardo Doménech, "Notas sobre *El sueño de la razón*", in *Primer acto*, 117, 1970.
John Dowling, "Introducción", in *El sueño de la razón*, by Antonio Buero Vallejo, Philadelphia, 1971.
Martha T. Halsey, "Goya in the Theater: Buero Vallejo's *El sueño de la razón*", in *Kentucky Romance Quarterly*, vol.18 no.2, 1971.
John Dowling, "Buero Vallejo's Interpretation of Goya's Black Art", in *Hispania*, vol.56 no.2, 1973.
David K. Herzberger, "The Painterly Vision of Buero Vallejo's *El sueño de la razón*", in *Symposium*, 39, 1985.
Peter Ashworth, "Silence and Self-Portraits: The Artist as Young Girl, Old Man and Scapegoat in [Victor Erice's film] *El espíritu de la colmena* and *El sueño de la razón*", in *Estreno*, vol.12 no.3, 1986.

*   *   *

The Sleep of Reason: Gorki Art Theatre, Moscow 1973

The action takes place over a period of a few days in December 1823, in Madrid, and in the nearby country house of the painter Francisco de Goya. In an opening framing scene, the autocratic King Fernando VII slyly discusses the successful repression of the liberal opposition with his minister Calomarde, and is shown an intercepted letter in which the ageing painter has criticised the king. The action shifts to Goya's house, where he has covered the walls with the dark and phantasmagoric "Black Paintings". Rather than being seen as fixed, scenic reproductions, these are projected singly, and in orchestrated combinations, throughout the play, providing a continuous visual commentary. Goya's young mistress and companion, Leocadia Weiss, suspects that he may be on the verge of madness and summons his personal physician, Arrieta, to examine him. Both the doctor and Leocadia have learned sign language to communicate with the totally deaf painter, and when Goya is on stage, the audience hears no dialogue except Goya's reactions to their signing and to their silently-mouthed words. But the audience *does* hear the disembodied voices and animal sounds that Goya imagines he hears—as well as the amplified heartbeats that convey his increasing apprehension. Father Duaso, a friend of Goya's, but also the King's appointed censor for the arts, pays a visit. In response to the priest's written questions, Goya asserts his opposition to the autocratic Fernando and eloquently describes for Duaso the surreal world of a person imprisoned in deafness for 30 years and the effects of repression on creativity. At the end of the first act, a threatening message is hurled through the window, and the increasing volume of the heartbeats signals the old man's terror.

In the second act, following another brief introductory scene in which the King questions Duaso about Goya's recalcitrance and craftily determines the exact time of Duaso's next visit, the suspicious painter accuses his mistress of flirting with a sergeant of the royal volunteers stationed nearby. Dr. Arrieta and Father Duaso express their concern for Goya's welfare, and Duaso suddenly realizes that he has been tricked by the king. They hasten to reach Goya before he suffers possible physical harm. Meanwhile, the painter falls asleep at his desk and experiences a nightmare which essentially replicates the etching ("The sleep of reason produces monsters") from which the play draws its title. He is awakened by heavy pounding on the door; the sergeant and two other members of the royal volunteers enter, put a heretic's hood on the helpless Goya, and violate his mistress before his very eyes, Arrieta and Duaso arriving too late to prevent the outrage. Goya's resistance is broken by the horror he has witnessed, and he agrees to take refuge in a friend's house before his flight to France. The final action is played against a projection of "The Witches' Sabbath" as a chorus of echoing voices repeats the line: "If it dawns, we will go"—suggesting an eventual awakening from Spain's political nightmare.

First staged in Spain only a few years before the end of the Franco regime, *The Sleep of Reason* was recognized not only as a remarkable exploration of the effects of repression on the creative process but also as an eloquent, albeit oblique, protest against the very censorship that had almost prevented the play's initial production. It soon became the most frequently performed work of post-Lorcan Spanish theatre, as it was translated into more than a dozen languages and staged in Eastern Europe, Scandinavia and, more than a decade after its premiere, in the United States. Productions by such internationally renowned directors as Liviu Ciulei (1972) and Andrzej Wajda (1974) aroused additional interest in Buero's theatre.

Arguably, this multi-media exploration of the effects of terror and intimidation on the creative mind is Buero Vallejo's finest play. Certainly it is the work which illustrates most effectively his concepts of total theatre, incorporating visual elements and non-verbal sounds as equal to, or complementary with, dialogue in furthering the dramatic action and in achieving a more intense audience involvement. The only prominent technique in Buerian theatre that is missing in *The Sleep of Reason* is the use of musical themes or motifs, which are replaced by sound motifs such as amplified heartbeats, animal cries, or the spoken titles of certain of Goya's etchings for the purpose of triggering a visual association.

Shortly after the first production of the play, the Spanish critic Ricardo Doménech published a study in which he coined the term "*efectos de inmersión*", or "immersion effects", to describe the various scenic devices employed in Buero's theatre to intensify the physical or psychological identification of viewer with character; Buero himself had already referred to his approach to audience participation as "*interiorización*". In 1823, the time of the play, Goya had already endured the agony of total deafness for many years, and Buero employs sound and the absence of sound in the way he had used light and darkness in two earlier plays dealing with the blind. None of the words spoken in the deaf man's presence are audible to the audience, and complementary visual actions—such as the silent ringing of a small bell—underscore the painter's isolation. The demands on the actor portraying Goya are enormous: not only must he react to the silently-mouthed dialogue and sign language of the other characters, he must also interact with the projections of the Black Paintings and the nagging inner voices, while seeking to maintain a vocal tone suitable for a man who has long been locked in silence. Set designs which do not facilitate the interaction of actor with the paintings would violate the playwright's intent and make an authentic performance of the play virtually impossible.

Critics have suggested the influences of the grotesque *esperpentos* of Valle-Inclán and Artaud's "Theatre of Cruelty" on Buero's mature dramas. He himself has acknowledged his familiarity with Artaud's theories and his greater admiration for Pirandello's innovations, while maintaining that his own concepts of total theatre took form before his encounters with Artaud or practitioners of audience participation such as The Living Theatre (which performed in Spain in the 1960's). In the final analysis, the play provides a masterly demonstration of techniques that are unmistakably Buerian and reveals a definable progression both aesthetically and thematically from the Spanish playwright's earlier dramas.

—Marion Peter Holt

SLUB. See **MARRIAGE.**

THE SNOB. See **SCENES FROM THE HEROIC LIFE OF THE MIDDLE CLASSES.**

DER SOHN
by Walter Hasenclever

First Publication: In *Die weissen Blätter*, 1, nos.8–10, 1914; in book form, Leipzig, 1914.
First Production: Deutsche Landestheater, Prague, 30 September 1916.

Criticism
(For general works on the author, see *Playwrights* volume)

Articles:
Richard C. Helt and Eric Muirhead, "The Necessity to Create in Hasenclever's *Der Sohn*: Nietzsche and German Expressionism", in *South Central Bulletin*, 39, 1979.

*   *   *

This five-act play depicts the rebellion of a 20-year-old son against his tyrannical father; this rebellion, characterized by obviously adolescent traits—the son deliberately fails his final high-school examination, contemplates suicide, is physically attracted to his governess—leads him to incite his generation to unite against the world and to bring down the existing authoritarian system. After the death of his father the son emerges as a mature young man free to pursue his mission.

Following its publication, but especially after the performance on 8 October 1916 at the Alberttheater, Dresden, *Der Sohn* (*The Son*) was hailed as the first successful expressionist play, ironically, for features which were later criticised as the main weaknesses of expressionist drama: the unbearably exalted style and emotions which—in Hasenclever's case—border on the violent, and the eccentricity of the author's vision. The dialogue is interrupted by long, hymnic outbursts, and the dramatic style is reminiscent of both Wedekind and Goethe. In fact, the Son's monologue in which he at first contemplates suicide but rejects it in favor of a future life filled with women, cars, money and—above all—success is obviously indebted to Faust's famous speech in his study, although it lacks the dramatic power of the original. Hasenclever even has the Friend acknowledge the reference to Goethe: "You owe your life to a plagiarism from Faust". The Friend, himself, is a composite character, resembling at times a Mephistophelean figure, at other times Wedekind's affirmative *Vermummter Herr* (in *Spring's Awakening*). However, in 1916, in war-torn Germany, a disillusioned young generation acclaimed Hasenclever's call for revolution against the establishment. The enthusiastic response to the play was also due to Ernst Deutsch's interpretation of the role of the Son. His ecstatic and eloquent pathos (according to contemporary accounts), combined with utter precision of speech, were so overwhelming in representing the Son's fierce struggle for freedom that most of the spectators identified themselves with the protagonist. Hasenclever had by then declared *Der Sohn* to be a political document, a "rebellion of the spirit against reality" and "a call to all mankind" to remember that "we are more than sons: we are brothers".

Rebellion against an overbearing authority and the break with tradition, became favoured themes of expressionist plays. They depict the restrictive physical and spiritual reality experienced by many contemporaries of the young authors; parricide became the symbolic expression of their desire to rid themselves of authority and clear the path for self-determination. Hasenclever is one of the most outspoken advocate of the new generation's futuristic vision: "We must abolish the tyranny of the family, this medieval pest boil, this black sabbath and sulphurous torture chamber! Let's quash the laws and re-establish freedom, the greatest good of mankind".

It is not surprising that the play's fame peaked during the war years. Although the Dresden performance remained the only one until 1918 (since the play was censored because of Hasenclever's pacifist attitude), the 1918/19 season saw more than 40 performances of *Der Sohn*, all but one with Ernst Deutsch in the lead. The play was again offered during the next season. But with the establishment of the Weimar Republic the play's message seemed to become less relevant. Furthermore, the rise of Ernst Toller and Georg Kaiser overshadowed Hasenclever who himself had begun to explore a different kind of drama.

In its portrayal of the father figure *Der Sohn* is without doubt the most authentic of Expressionist *Bekenntnis-Drama* ("confession drama"). Hasenclever reveals a great number of intensely private and autobiographical details from his brutal life under his own father. In this, the play goes far beyond the depiction of the traditional father/son conflict and can be considered almost as a psychological act of liberation from the mental and physical abuse inflicted on Hasenclever until he fled his home. The Father and Son of the play reveal a deadly hatred of each other and of the era to which each belongs, mirroring an unbridgeable generation gap which finally leaves room only for one of them. With the help of the Friend, the Son undergoes a transformation from an obedient, imprisoned youth to a liberated self-confident leader of a revolution—a transformation dramatically heightened when the actors intone the "Marseillaise". This unbloody revolution is to result in mankind's spiritual and ethical renewal. Hasenclever has the Son, in this particular scene, go in front of the curtain and address the audience directly in order to convey the universality of his message. The ending of *Der Sohn* may appear disappointing, in that the Father dies moments before the Son is to shoot him. However, this is more in line with the ethical aspect of the play's message, which would be flawed by a murder.

The action of *Der Sohn* is the most realistic, and its structure the most traditional, of German plays of the Expressionist period. However, as in August Strindberg's *To Damascus*, Reinhard Sorge's *Der Bettler* (*The Beggar*), and Ernst Toller's *Die Wandlung* (*Transfiguration*), the play is written from the protagonist's perspective; the action and characters—who are nameless types—should be understood as projections of the Son's mind. This was best demonstrated in Richard Weichert's 1918 production in Mannheim, in which the Son, in a cone of light, held centre-stage in an otherwise darkened room; the other characters were brought to life through spotlighting and disappeared into the dark again, thus underlining that they were mere creations of the protagonist. This status is particularly true of the character of the Friend, who can be considered as the Son's mature alter ego; when the Son reaches maturity the Friend feels no longer needed and commits suicide. But this suicide also indicates that the Son must follow his destiny alone, and at the same time hints at the underlying nihilism displayed in Hasenclever's early works. Weichert's production underlined the Son's essential loneliness; because the characters are often at cross purposes, their conversations take on the character of monologues. In this regard *Der Sohn* anticipates similar usage in the plays of Ionesco and Beckett.

—Renate Benson

DIE SOLDATEN.   See **THE SOLDIERS.**

———————

A SOLDIER'S PLAY
by Charles Fuller

First Publication: New York, 1982.
First Production: New York (Negro Ensemble Company),
          1981.

Criticism
(For general works on the author, see *Playwrights* volume)

Articles:
Linda K. Hughes and Howard Faulkner, "The Role of
   Detection in *A Soldier's Play*", in *Clues*, vol.7 no.2, 1986.
William W. Demastes, "Charles Fuller and *A Soldier's Play*:
   Attacking Prejudice, Challenging Form", in *Studies in
   American Drama, 1945–the Present*, 2, 1987.

*   *   *

Vernon Waters, a non-commissioned officer in a black army
unit in Louisiana, is murdered in 1944. Members of his outfit
suspect the Ku Klux Klan, but the murder does not bear
distinguishing Klan features. Racial tension mounts as Captain
Davenport, one of the unit's few black commissioned officers
and a lawyer by profession, is brought in to investigate.
Captain Taylor, his white colleague, objects, ostensibly on the
grounds that Davenport will get nowhere questioning the
white Southern locals. In fact, Taylor resents having to defer to
Davenport. As one by one the enlisted men are questioned,
the hatred between them and Waters emerges. He had driven
one of them to suicide, and his murder was an act of revenge. It
will go down in history as just another "Cain and Abel story of
the week" in the black press.

Charles Fuller's Pulitzer Prize drama was staged by the
Negro Ensemble Company of New York and has since toured
the country. Ibsenesque in structure, working in flashback to
discover inner corruption, it also owes something to the early
plays of Amiri Baraka (LeRoi Jones), specifically in its
depiction of internecine venom within the black community.
The murdered sergeant's hatred is based on his contempt for
the "clown in blackface" image he sees his men adopting.
Freedom, he insists, will come only when they succeed in
achieving parity with Whites. Their immediate opportunity is
to win the regional service baseball championship enabling
them to play the New York Yankees in an exhibition game.
Waters' tormenting of the team's leading hitter is intended to
toughen this resolve.

The men, for their part, see Waters merely as sadistic
("Stone-Ass", they call him). They cannot see his long-term
ambitions, and in fact his behaviour in the early scenes does
appear self-negating.

Given the integrally hierachical nature of army life, it is
surprising that black playwrights in general have neglected this
as a focus of black drama. Racial tension in the police, too, has
been largely the preserve of television—significantly scripted
by white writers, who necessarily soften the perspective to
placate white advertisers.

Fuller is defter in his characterisation of Whites than are
James Baldwin and Ed Bullins, further suggesting that the
army is ideal for dramatic debate of racial issues. The
American military, like professional sport, was not desegre-
gated until after World War II. The origins of this desegrega-

tion process are identified in this play in the relationship
between Davenport and Taylor. "Captain", the lawyer says
with perfect self-possession, "like it or not, I'm all you've got.
I've been ordered to look into Sergeant Waters's death, and I
intend to do exactly that". In congratulating Davenport at the
end, Taylor concedes, "I was wrong—about the bars—the
uniform—about Negroes being in charge. I guess I'll *have* to
get used to it". Such acceptance, again, has featured for 20
years in television police soaps, which have also braved the
frontier of portraying police corruption among Blacks. Playwrights, for the most part, have confined themselves to
exploring indigenous black experience.

The conferring of national recognition on a play that
attempts to combine a picture of black life with a drama of
inter-race relations (Whites here occupying something of the
token position which Blacks have elsewhere done) invites a re-
examination of the problem today. In this context, it has to be
seen as a serious omission that Baraka's best work, anticipating Fuller's by almost 20 years, was simultaneously hailed and
confined to the "underground", and has yet to be given a place
in mainstream American culture.

—James MacDonald

———————

THE SOLDIERS (Die Soldaten)
by Jakob Michael Reinhold Lenz

First Publication: 1776.
First Production: In adaptation by Edward von Bauernfeld,
          Burgtheater, Vienna, 1863.

Editions
Die Soldaten, Cambridge, 1950 (Cambridge Plain Texts
   Series).
Die Soldaten, in *Die Soldaten; Der Hofmeister*, Munich,
   c.1971.
"Die Soldaten": Text, Materialen, Kommentar, edited by
   Edward McInnes, Munich, 1977.

Translations
The Soldiers, in *The Tutor; The Soldiers*, translated by William
   E. Yuill, Chicago and London, 1972.

Criticism
(For general works on the author, see *Playwrights* volume)

Books:
Herbert Haffner, *Lenz: "Der Hofmeister"; "Die Soldaten";
   mit Brecht's Hofmeister—Bearbeitung und Materialen*,
   Munich, 1979.

Articles:
Brian Duncan, "The Comic Structure of Lenz's *Soldaten*", in
   Modern Language Notes, 91, 1976.
Helga Stipa Madland, "J.M.R. Lenz's *Soldaten*: The Lan-
   guage of Realism: A Collision of Codes", in *Selecta*, 3, 1982.
Helga Stipa Madland, "Gesture as Evidence of Language
   Skepticism in Lenz's *Der Hofmeister* and *Die Soldaten*", in
   German Quarterly, vol.57 no.4, 1984.
David Hill, " 'Das Politische' in *Die Soldaten*", in *Orbis
   Litterarum*, vol.43 no.4, 1988.

The Soldiers: Deutsches Theater, Berlin, 1916

Lenz's play *The Soldiers* (*Die Soldaten*) tells the story of the fall of a pretty, young, middle-class girl, corrupted by social ambition and romantic yearning, and driven to her ruin by the sexual aggression of the aristocratic officers of the local garrison. Superficially it is a *pièce à thèse*, addressed to a specific problem—the law which prohibited the officers of the Prussian army from marrying. This was, in fact, a subject on which Lenz wrote a treatise in 1776, with the intention of submitting it to the Duke of Weimar. The play ends with a proposed solution, namely that the state should protect society by employing women who would minister to the sexual needs of the soldiery in state-run brothels.

In its form *The Soldiers* is far from being an orthodox problem play. It consists of five acts with a total of 35 short scenes, bursting with vitality, which defy the conventions of the unities of time, place, and action, and which swing violently from the farcical to the tragic, and include the satirical and the sentimental. The inspiration was Shakespeare, as understood by the young German dramatists of the *Sturm und Drang* movement; and Lenz's heir was his admirer Büchner.

The play opens in Lille in the house of the haberdasher, Wesener, and shows his daughter, Marie (Mariane in the manuscript version and in newer critical editions of Lenz's works) in correspondence with a loyal admirer from her own social class, the young cloth-merchant, Stolzius in Armentières. Tension and jealousy between Marie and her plainer sister, Charlotte, emphasise the constriction and pettiness of the girls' environment, and also point to a way out for Marie as the more attractive of the two. With the arrival of the officer, Desportes, Marie becomes a willing victim to his flattery. Defying parental authority, she accepts an invitation to the theatre, but so excited is her response to this imaginative glimpse into a new world that she cannot maintain the deception and confides in her father. With great insight Lenz now undermines the traditional image of the middle-class father in domestic tragedy as the stern upholder of authority and morality, and shows him, too, corrupted by the hope that his daughter might cross the class barrier and become a baroness. Without firm guidance, Marie is lost: she is easily seduced on the basis of the slenderest of promises. But Wesener, himself, is not significantly less naive, thinking that Desportes' written promise of marriage will be regarded as binding by his parents. The only moral resistance comes from an aristocratic observer, the Gräfin von la Roche, who attempts to reform Marie by teaching her reason; but neither father nor daughter is to be halted on the road to ruin. Wesener neglects his business and takes responsibility for the debts of Desportes, after the latter has abandoned his daughter; but far from achieving his aim of maintaining a hold on the suitor, he bankrupts himself. Marie enters into a relationship with one soldier after another, and becomes a prostitute begging from her own father in a powerful scene which might well have made a more suitable ending than the unrealistic marriage proposal with which the play does conclude.

The linear central plot, developed elliptically in a series of briefly-sketched scenes, is punctuated by a number of disconnected episodes devoted to the wild and irresponsible social life of the officers, in which all females are fair game and those who succumb are branded as whores. These scenes, which provide a context for the fall of Marie, are linked to the main plot by explicit discussion of the Weseners' fate and by the involvement of certain characters in both strands of the play. The principal commentator on the action is the military chaplain, Eisenhardt, who leads the enlightened criticism of the soldiers' conduct and sees the girls as victims. On the level of the action, resistance is concentrated on the initially pathetic figure of Marie's bourgeois suitor, Stolzius, whom Lenz invests with considerable dignity as he, too, abandons his business and enlists in order to be near Marie, and ultimately to pursue a slow and patient vengeance, eventually poisoning her seducer.

The Soldiers brings together a full range of finely and economically drawn characters, such as Stolzius, this antecedent of Büchner's Woyzeck, downtrodden into almost total insignificance and arrogantly overlooked by the officers who have wronged him and yet still preserving a final assertive spark; or Marie, too lively and spirited ever to be happy with the restricted existence society offers her; or even the soldiers, whose carefully differentiated styles of almost manic activity—from high to low spirits—stamp them as victims of circumstances: they cannot control events and do not fully understand. It is in the characterisation that the value of the play resides, rather than in its shallow response to the problem identified explicitly in its first and last acts, about which Lenz himself seems to have had second thoughts.

Unorthodox in form, and shocking in some of its substance, *The Soldiers* did not enjoy any success in the theatre until the 20th century. In 1968 the dramatist Heinar Kipphardt published an adaptation, which is less radical than Brecht's adaptation of Lenz's earlier play *The Tutor*, but follows Brecht in making Lenz's social-critical implications more explicit and his subtleties more crude. In 1965 Bernd Alois Zimmermann composed an opera based on Lenz's play; this work of pacifist tendency has been highly acclaimed as a masterpiece of modern opera and, despite enormous technical difficulties, has received memorable productions by a number of major directors in several countries.

—John Osborne

LOS SOLES TRUNCOS
by René Marqués

First Publication: In *Marqués: Teatro*, 1959; second edition, 1974.
First Production: First Theater Festival, San Juan, Puerto Rico, 1958.

Criticism
(For general works on the author, see *Playwrights* volume)

Articles:
Charles Pilditch, "La escena puertorriqueña—*Los soles truncos*", in *Asomante*, vol.17 no.2, 1961.
Howard M. Fraser, "Theatricality in *The Fanlights* and [Dias Gomes'] *Payment as Pledged*", in *American Hispanist*, 10, 1977.
Margot Arce de Vázquez, "*Los soles truncos*: comedia trágica de René Marqués", in *Sin nombre*, vol.10 no.3, 1979.
José J. Beauchamp, "La tragedia de la negación, la resistencia y la recuperación en el universo clausurado de René Marqués: aproximación sociológica a *Los soles truncos*", in *Revista de estudios hispánicos*, 11, 1984.

* * *

This play, based on Marqués's short story, *Purificación en la Calle del Cristo*, dramatizes the story of the three Burkhart sisters, of German and Spanish descent, whose parents had been wealthy landowners during the period of Spanish colonialism in Puerto Rico after Spain's ceding of the island to the United States. We encounter two of the sisters, Inés and Emilia, now elderly spinsters, living in the family house in old San Juan, at the moment of the third sister, Hortensia's, death. Throughout the play, we find the sisters embroiled not only in an external conflict with the materialistic world which surrounds their family house, but also in an internal conflict between themselves, revealed through the appearance of the dead sister. They are unable to confront the changing outside reality, as they are victims of the socio-political conditions existing in Puerto Rico. The world on the outside constantly threatens to bring an end to the one which they have created within, so that at the end of the play, they make the decision to destroy the house and themselves by fire as an ironic solution to giving meaning to their inevitable destruction.

The play integrates space and time in such a way that past, present, and future coexist on stage. The spectator or reader's attention is drawn towards the underlying crisis at the center of the play's development; a crisis brought on by the characters' refusal, or perhaps inability, to act in the face of the invasion of Puerto Rico by the United States and the destruction (by time and their own lack of action) of the only world the sisters have known. The play presents an anachronistic reality in which the sisters live with evocations of an illusory past of Strasbourg, Germany, and the Toa Alta plantation in Puerto Rico, while at the same time secrets of each of the sisters, which have been the real motives for their withdrawal from life, are brought to the surface. The offstage world immediately beyond the house denotes the "outside" world.

Contrasting these worlds becomes a dramatic technique throughout the course of the play that serves not only to move the action forward but also to depict the constant threat of violation of the sisters' world. The stage setting fuses and at the same time separates the play's several realms, further enhancing lines of tension between play and audience.

The house, various props, sound, light and color, serve double purposes as they represent the passage of time and also unite, for brief moments, two or more of the spatial/temporal realms. The house serves first a very practical purpose as the dwelling place of the play's antagonists, and second it divides the sisters' world from the outside world. The absence of any direct physical connection on stage with the outside world maintains an ever-present tension between those two spaces. Thirdly, seen in its stage of deterioration and shadow, the house serves as a visual representation of the state of the sisters' decaying world.

Various props also provide a point of contact between the two interior spaces. One of the more obvious is the candelabra which in Act I is either lit or extinguished before each of Hortensia's two appearances. Inés' extinguishing of the candle mysteriously signals Hortensia's first entrance and the transference of action to the level of the evoked past. Extinguishing the candle sets off a chain reaction which breaks the bounds of logic and creates the illusion that the passage of time is suspended as the scene now occupies the somewhat different space of the past.

In addition, voices and music coming from the offstage area serve to enhance our perception of the tension between the various realms. At the beginning of both acts, the voice of the Street Vendor penetrates the house from the outside world. As various scenes move toward or into the dream-like sequences, music comes from an offstage orchestra or a piano, neither seen nor acknowledged in any way by the play's characters: the music corresponds to the action in much the same way as music functions in the cinema.

Light and color are intricately linked to each of the spatial/temporal realms. In Act I, the elements of light and color are the very first to be set out in the stage directions which draw attention to the sun shining through the semi-circular crystals of red, blue, and yellow. The sun's light from the outside gives shape to the interior of the house and thus to the audience's perception of the sisters' inner world. The sun itself also becomes a symbol of the passage of time. The yellow becomes associated with the immediate, outside world and the sun's light. Except for the dream-like sequences, in which Hortensia appears and all "natural" light is extinguished, it is constantly present as a reminder of that exterior world and of the threat it poses to the sisters' interior world. The color blue is linked to the illusory past as seen in Hortensia's three stage appearances; in each of these scenes, the blue light accompanies Hortensia, and at the end of the play it illuminates her deathbed. It also indicates that normal time has ceased flowing while the past controls the scene. Red dominates the play's final scene as the flames of the fire spread throughout the house. The color intensifies as the volume of the music increases, creating a cinematographic effect. The red appears gradually until it overpowers the blue light, and until the exterior light is extinguished.

The final scenes integrate the play's exterior reality, the world inside the house, and the illusory past evoked within the house. As the Burkharts sever the ties, and thus the threat, with the outside world, they definitively bring an end to that incompatible world's penetration into their own.

—Bonnie Hildebrand Reynolds

THE SON.   See **DER SOHN.**

LE SOULIER DE SATIN.   See **THE SATIN SLIPPER.**

THE SPANISH BAWD.   See **CELESTINA.**

THE SPANISH TRAGEDY
by Thomas Kyd

First Publication: London, 1592; with "additions", 1602.
First Production: London, c.1582–92; first recorded performance, by Lord Strange's Men, 23 February 1592.

Editions
The Spanish Tragedy, edited by J. Schick, London, 1898.
The Spanish Tragedy, in *Five Elizabethan Tragedies*, edited by A.K. McIlwraith, Oxford, 1938.

The Spanish Tragedy: National Theatre, London, 1982

The Spanish Tragedy, edited by Philip Edwards, London, 1959 (Revels Plays).

The First Part of Hieronimo and The Spanish Tragedy, edited by Andrew S. Cairncross, Lincoln, Nebraska, 1967 (Regents Renaissance Drama Series).

The Spanish Tragedy, edited by T.W. Ross, Berkeley, California, 1968 (Fountainwell Drama Texts).

The Spanish Tragedy, edited by J.R. Mulryne, London, 1970; second edition, 1989 (New Mermaid Series).

Criticism

(For general works on the author, see *Playwrights* volume)

Books:

Howard Baker, *Induction to Tragedy: A Study in the Development of Form in "Gorboduc", "The Spanish Tragedy", and "Titus Andronicus"*, Baton Rouge, Louisiana, 1939.

Frank R. Ardolino, *Thomas Kyd's Mystery Play: Myth and Ritual in "The Spanish Tragedy"*, New York, Bern, and Frankfurt, 1985.

Articles:

Howard Baker, "Ghosts and Guides: Kyd's *Spanish Tragedy* and the Medieval Tragedy", in *Modern Philology*, 32, 1935.

William Empson, "*The Spanish Tragedy*", in *Nimbus*, 3, 1956.

John D. Ratliff, "Hieronimo Explains Himself", in *Studies in Philology*, 54, 1957.

C.K. Cannon, "The Relation of the Addition of *The Spanish Tragedy* to the Original Play", in *Studies in English Literature 1500–1900*, 2, 1962.

Ernst de Chikera, "Divine Justice and Private Revenge in *The Spanish Tragedy*", in *Modern Language Review*, 57, 1962.

S.F. Johnson, "*The Spanish Tragedy*, or Babylon Revisited", in *Essays on Shakespeare and Elizabethan Drama in Honour of Hardin Craig*, edited by Richard Hosley, London, 1963.

Michael Henry Levin, "'Vindicta Mihi!': Meaning, Morality, and Motivation in *The Spanish Tragedy*", in *Studies in English Literature 1500–1900*, 4, 1964.

G.K. Hunter, "Ironies of Justice in *The Spanish Tragedy*", in *Renaissance Drama*, 8, 1965.

Ejner J. Jensen, "Kyd's *Spanish Tragedy*: The Play Explains Itself", in *Journal of English and Germanic Philology*, 64, 1965.

David Laird, "Hieronimo's Dilemma", in *Studies in Philology*, 62, 1965.

Jonas A. Barish, "*The Spanish Tragedy*, or The Pleasures and Perils of Rhetoric", in *Elizabethan Theatre*, edited by John Russell Brown and B.A. Harris, London, 1966 (Stratford-Upon-Avon Studies).

Ken C. Burrows, "The Dramatic and Structural Significance of the Portuguese Subplot in *The Spanish Tragedy*", in *Renaissance Philology*, 1968.

Herbert R. Coursen Jr., "The Unity of *The Spanish Tragedy*", in *Studies in Philology*, 65, 1968.

Barry B. Adams, "The Audiences of *The Spanish Tragedy*", in *Journal of English and Germanic Philology*, 68, 1969.

Sacvan Bercovitch, "Love and Strife in Kyd's *Spanish Tragedy*", in *Studies in English Literature 1500–1900*, 9, 1969.

Siegfried Wyler, "'Death' in Thomas Kyd's *Spanish Tragedy*: A Study of a Semantic Field", in *Festschrift Rudolf Stamm*, Bern, 1969.

M.D. Faber and Carol Skinner, "*The Spanish Tragedy*: Act IV", in *Philological Quarterly*, 48, 1970.

Ronald Broude, "Time, Truth, and Right in *The Spanish Tragedy*", in *Studies in Philology*, 68, 1971.

David P. Willburn, "Thomas Kyd's *Spanish Tragedy*: A Study of a Semantic Field", in *American Imago*, 28, 1971.

Scott McMillin, "The Figure of Silence in *The Spanish Tragedy*", in *English Literary History*, 39, 1972.

Arthur L. Kistner and M.K. Kistner, "The Senecan Background of Despair in *The Spanish Tragedy* and *Titus Andronicus*", in *Shakespeare Survey*, 7, 1974.

Scott McMillin, "The Book of Seneca in *The Spanish Tragedy*", in *Studies in English Literature 1500–1900*, 14, 1974.

Margaret Lamb, "Beyond Revenge: *The Spanish Tragedy*", in *Mosaic*, 9, 1975.

Deborah Rubin, "Justice, Revenge and Villainy in Kyd's *Spanish Tragedy*", in *Thoth: Syracuse University Graduate Studies in English*, 16, 1976.

Frank Ardolino, "The Hangman's Noose and the Empty Box: Kyd's Use of Dramatic and Mythological Sources in *The Spanish Tragedy*", in *Renaissance Quarterly*, 30, 1977.

Frank R. Ardolino, "'Veritas Filia Temporis': Time, Perspective and Justice in *The Spanish Tragedy*", in *Studies in Iconography*, 3, 1977.

Charles A. Hallett, "Andrea, Andragio and King Hamlet: The Ghost as Spirit of Revenge", in *Philological Quarterly*, 56, 1977.

Rebecca M. Howard, "The Ironic Consolation of *The Spanish Tragedy*", in *Selected Papers From the West Virginia Shakespeare and Renaissance Association*, 4, 1979.

Frank R. Ardolino, "'Sit We Down to see the Mystery': Detection and Allegory in Kyd and Shakespeare", in *Allegorica*, 5, 1980.

Barbara J. Baines, "Kyd's Silenus Box and the Limits of Perception", in *Journal of Medieval and Renaissance Studies*, 10, 1980.

Pierre Spriet, "Antisocial Behaviour and the Code of Love in Kyd's *The Spanish Tragedy*", in *Cahiers études*, 17, 1980.

Stephen Watt, "Emblematic Tradition and Audience Response to Kyd's *The Spanish Tragedy*", in *Studies in Iconography*, 6, 1980.

John S. Weld, "*The Spanish Tragedy* as the Fall of Babylon", in *Mediaevalia*, 6, 1980.

Thelma N. Greenfield, "*The Spanish Tragedy*: Revengers and Andrea's Kindred", in *Pacific Coast Philology*, 16, 1981.

Charles Stein, "Justice and Revenge in *The Spanish Tragedy*", in *Iowa State Journal of Research*, 56, 1981.

Peter Sachs, "Where Words Prevail Not: Grief, Revenge, and Language in Kyd and Shakespeare", in *English Literary History*, 49, 1982.

Elizabeth Maslen, "The Dynamics of Kyd's *Spanish Tragedy*", in *English*, 32, 1983.

Richard Proudfoot, "Kyd's *Spanish Tragedy*", in *Cambridge Quarterly*, 25, 1983.

Frank R. Ardolino, "*Corrida* of Blood in *The Spanish Tragedy*: Kyd's Use of Revenge as National Destiny", in *Medieval and Renaissance Drama in England*, 1, 1984.

Eugene D. Hill, "Senecan and Vergilian Perspectives in *The Spanish Tragedy*", in *English Literary Renaissance*, 15, 1985.

Wolfgang G. Müller, "Dissimulation as a Theme and Rhetorical Device in Kyd's *Spanish Tragedy*", in *Arbeiten aus Anglistik und Amerikanistik*, 10, 1985.

Joost Daalder, "The Role of 'Senex' in Kyd's *The Spanish Tragedy*", in *Comparative Drama*, 20, 1986.

Mark Kobernick, "The Phenomenology of Time in *The Spanish Tragedy*", in *Journal of English* (San'a University), 14, 1986.

Richard C. Kohler, "Kyd's Ordered Spectacle: 'Behold. . ./ What 'tis to be Subject to Destiny'", in *Medieval and Renaissance Drama in England*, 3, 1986.

Richard Horwich, "The Settings of *The Spanish Tragedy*", in *College English Association Critic*, 49, 1986–87.

Geoffrey Aggeler, "The Eschatological Crux in *The Spanish Tragedy*", in *Journal of English and Germanic Philology*, 86, 1987.

Roslyn L. Knutson, "The Influence of the Repertory System on the Revival and Revision of *The Spanish Tragedy* and *Dr. Faustus*", in *English Literary Renaissaince*, 18, 1988.

*   *   *

The opening speech of *The Spanish Tragedy* is delivered by the ghost of Don Andrea, a Spanish courtier killed in battle against the Portuguese. With him is the personification of Revenge, who promises him that he will see his killer (Prince Balthazar of Portugal) "depriv'd of life" by his mistress, Bel-imperia. The two sit down to watch the proceedings, and "serve for Chorus in this tragedy".

The chain of events which they witness, leading up to the inevitable carnage of the last scene, is ingeniously structured to keep the audience, and the ghost, guessing. The greater part of the action concerns not the promised attack on Balthazar, but the revenge of Hieronimo, Knight Marshal of Spain, for the murder of his son Horatio. In the war with Portugal, Horatio had won honour by defeating Balthazar, but Lorenzo, son to the Duke of Castile (the King of Spain's brother), is a rival for that honour, claiming Balthazar as his captive. He and Balthazar align themselves, as fellow princes, against Horatio, a mere commoner, and have him murdered when it is proved that he has won the love of Bel-imperia, Lorenzo's sister, whom Balthazar wants for himself. After Horatio's death, the play becomes, primarily, Hieronimo's story: his attempts to gain justice from the King are thwarted by Lorenzo (who is trying to protect himself), and he begins to show signs of madness. Having discovered the impossibility of legal redress, he debates the matter and chooses to undertake revenge.

Although the rhetorical methods deployed in some of the play's most dramatic moments are far from subtle, the play is remarkably sophisticated, both in the degree of self-referentiality provided by the comments of the ghost and Revenge as on-stage audience, and in the number of ways in which it eschews the obvious in its delineation of character and action. There are no simple heroes or villains: Lorenzo is motivated, in part, by a plausible sense of aristocratic superiority to Horatio, and Balthazar by a grand passion for Bel-imperia. Although it is implied that Balthazar's killing of Don Andrea was dishonourable, the deed took place on the battlefield and was not an act of private malice. Hieronimo's position as a revenger similarly avoids a simple moral response: the play's vision of a classical pagan underworld actively promoting revenge is curiously at odds with his expressions of doubt which are supported by biblical quotation. Hieronimo is made to act in a space created between the two ideologies, and in a period which has been left historically undefined.

The play also qualifies its presentation of the romantic and the sentimental. Bel-imperia woos Horatio with a coolly divided purpose to be both lover (to Horatio) and avenger (for Don Andrea), and her calculation works against the romantic tone of their scene in the bower. Strong emotional outbursts, like Hieronimo's lament for Horatio, or his poignant encounter with an old man whose son has also been murdered, are balanced by scenes of wickedly ironic, black comedy. The servant Pedringano, a tool in the murder of Horatio, jokes his way to the gallows, convinced that his pardon is about to be produced; Hieronimo's play of "Soliman and Perseda" is cunningly cast so that avengers can easily encounter their victims, and his theatrical coup is the grisly revelation to his courtly audience that art and life (or, rather, death) have, for once, completely coincided:

> Haply you think, but bootless are your thoughts,
> That this is fabulously counterfeit,
> And that we do as all tragedians do:
> To die today, for fashioning our scene,
> The death of Ajax, or some Roman peer,
> And in a minute starting up again,
> Revive to please tomorrow's audience.
> No, princes,.. . .

The real audience can obtain gleeful satisfaction from the acts of revenge, and rejoice with the ghost of Andrea as he foresees bliss in the Elysian fields for his friends, and a variety of endless tortures for his enemies.

The Spanish Tragedy was one of the most popular plays of the Elizabethan period, and subsequently much parodied and imitated. Its earliest known performances were at the Rose Theatre on London's Bankside, and it may be assumed that it continued to flourish on the stage during the period of the ten printed editions between 1592 and 1633. Ben Jonson was paid for additions to the play in 1601 and 1602, and "additions" probably earlier than Jonson's (which seem not to have survived) appear in the fourth quarto (1602). These testify to a continuing stage life, although there is no specific record of performance after October 1597. Its influence on English tragedy was considerable. Numerous progeny expanded variously on its scenes of irony, horror, and emotional intensity, and Lorenzo became the prototype of a generation of Machiavellian schemers. Shakespeare's *Hamlet* has several notable similarities—the ghost, the madness of the revenger, the play-within-the-play—and both plays share an ironic approach to the dramatic structure of the revenge play. In *Hamlet*, the Prince himself provides critical distance as he questions, in soliloquy, the progress of the action and his own involvement in it. Kyd gives such reflections to the ghost of Andrea and Revenge who, as observers rather than participants, mirror the audience and seem to anticipate its possible critical reactions. Revenge advises Andrea to be patient: "The sickle comes not till the corn be ripe", and his authoritative tone, as assured as that of a playwright who already knows the outcome, gives the audience an ironic perspective on Hieronimo's attempts to shape his own destiny. At the National Theatre's Cottesloe auditorium (London) in 1982, this apparently modern emphasis on the status of the play as play was one of many compelling aspects of the tragedy which helped to explain its original success, and the durability of its theatrical reputation.

—Joanna Udall

SPÖKSONATEN.   See **THE GHOST SONATA.**

THE SPOOK SONATA.   See **THE GHOST SONATA.**

SPRING'S AWAKENING (Frühlings Erwachen)
by Frank Wedekind

First Publication: Zürich, 1891.
First Production: In a censored version, Kammerspiele des
                 Deutsches Theater, Berlin, 20 November
                 1906.

Editions
Frühlings Erwachen, edited by Hugh Rank, London, 1976.

Translations
The Awakening of Spring, translated by F.J. Ziegler, Philadelphia, 1909.
Spring's Awakening, in *Tragedies of Sex*, translated by S.A. Eliot, New York and London, 1923.
Spring's Awakening, in *Five Tragedies of Sex*, translated by F. Fawcett and Stephen Spender, London, 1952.
Spring's Awakening, translated by Eric Bentley, in *The Modern Theatre, 6*, Garden City, New York, 1960.
Spring Awakening, translated by Tom Osborn, London, 1969.
Spring's Awakening, translated by Edward Bond, London, 1980.

Criticism
(For general works on the author, see *Playwrights* volume)

Articles:
Friedrich Rothe, "*Frühlings Erwachen*: Zum Verhältnis von sexueller und sozialer Emazipation bei Frank Wedekind", in *Studi Germanici*, 7, 1969.
Leroy R. Shaw, "The Strategy of Reformulation: Frank Wedekind's *Frühlings Erwachen*", in his *The Playwright and Historical Change*, Madison, Wisconsin, 1970.
Keith Bullivant, "The Notion of Morality in Wedekind's *Frühlings Erwachen*", in *New German Studies*, 1, 1973.
Ulrich Vohland, "Wider die falsche Erziehung: Zu Wedekinds *Frühlings Erwachen*", in *Diskussion deutsch*, 45, 1979.
J.L. Hibberd, "Imaginary Numbers and 'Humor': On Wedekind's *Frühlings Erwachen*", in *Modern Language Review*, 74, 1979.
Gordon Birrell, "The *Wollen-Sollen* Equation in Wedekind's *Frühlings Erwachen*", in *Germanic Review*, 57, 1982.
Leroy R. Shaw, "Frank Wedekind's *Spring's Awakening*", in *Alogical Modern Drama*, edited by Kenneth S. White, Amsterdam, 1982.
Peter Jelavich, "Wedekind's *Spring Awakening*: The Path to Expressionist Drama", in *Passion and Rebellion: The Expressionist Heritage*, edited by Stephen E. Bronner and Douglas Kellner, New York, 1983.
U. Henry Gerlach, "Wer is der 'vermummte Herr' in Wedekinds *Frühlings Erwachen*", in *Maske und Kothurn*, 31, 1985.
Adrian del Caro, "The Beast in the Child: Wedekind as the Psychologist of Morals", in *Germanic Notes*, 20, 1989.
Nancy S. Rabinowitz, "Constructing Desire: Sexual Politics in Frank Wedekind's *Spring Awakening*", in *Theater Three*, 7, 1989.

*   *   *

Melchior Gabor, his schoolfriend Moritz Stiefel, and Wendla Bergmann, three sensitive middle-class teenagers, awaken to their own sexuality and to the emotional demands it rouses in them. Moritz, a timid, introverted boy, opts out of his problems at home, at school, and in himself by committing suicide; Wendla, pregnant by Melchior though without realizing it, dies prematurely, the victim of an abortion arranged by her mother to avoid embarrassment and social disapproval. Melchior, expelled from school for his "dirty" behaviour, is sent to a reformatory. Will he survive to grow up into a normal balanced adult? There is hope: in the last scene, set symbolically in the churchyard where Wendla is buried, the dead Moritz tries to lure his friend to his death, but a masked gentleman unexpectedly appears and coaxes him back to life in the grown-up world.

Spring Awakening earned Wedekind notoriety as a provocative and controversial playwright. Its premiere at the Berlin Kammerspiele, a newly-opened experimental theatre, in a production by Max Reinhardt which made imaginative use of the most up-to-date stage techniques (revolving stage, no "realistic" sets, gauzes), set a precedent for later productions of a play soon regarded in German-speaking countries as the pioneer for a new concept of drama. It ran for 351 performances, demonstrating that the new and controversial could appeal to an audience receptive to new ideas. Reinhardt's backing proved influential: *Spring Awakening* went on to achieve the highest production and performance figures of any German play this century. It is significant, however, that stagings tended to tail off in the 1960's, perhaps because increasing permissiveness had dulled the play's impact: this would be a vindication of Wedekind's reforming purpose in writing it. Basing the play on his boyhood experiences, he deliberately broke a 19th-century taboo by writing a play about sex. With it, the adolescent came of age as a figure of dramatic interest.

Caught between the late Victorian image of childhood and the stark realities of the world of their stuffy elders and so-called betters, Wedekind's teenagers experience joys and suffering appropriate to the phase they are going through, but none the less intense and cruel. The evasiveness of their parents and teachers drives them into a world of make-believe: for Wendla the facts of life are suppressed; Moritz cannot face up to them; but Melchior accepts them, thanks to his juvenile philosophy that selfishness is the prime motive of human behaviour. The masked gentleman, a part Wedekind liked to act himself, teaches him that the morality of the real adult world is the product of two imaginary quantities: what one ought to do and what one wants to do. Wedekind's "immoral" play is the work of a moralist in disguise.

Spring Awakening is often interpreted as the tragedy of natural healthy adolescence repressed and destroyed by the disapproval of conventional middle-class society, but this is to oversimplify it. To contemporaries it gave daring dramatic expression to matters that were on people's minds, and exposed the hypocrisy of double standards in sexual behaviour and morality. Now it can be seen as the prelude to Wedekind's lifelong exploration of the forces and impulses which shape the lives of human beings and dictate their actions and interactions. The alternation of naturalistic social realism with elements of fantasy and the grotesque emphasizes the fact that the audience is watching a piece of theatre about a real world which is seldom straightforward. A satirical strain is also often present, reminding the spectator or reader that this is an "unpleasant" play with a deliberate purpose.

—Peter Skrine

THE ST. NICHOLAS HOTEL. See **THE DONNELLY PLAYS.**

STALLERHOF. See **FARMYARD.**

DER STELLVERTRETER. See **THE REPRESENTATIVE.**

STICKS AND STONES. See **THE DONNELLY PLAYS.**

THE STORM (Groza)
by Alexander Ostrovsky

First Publication: In *Biblioteka dlya chteniya* [*Readers' Library*], January, 1860.
First Production: Maly Theatre, Moscow, 16 November 1859.

Editions

Groza, in *Groza; Les; Bespridannitsa*, edited by E. Kalmanovskogo, Leningrad, 1977.
Groza, edited by A.V. Knowles, Oxford, 1988.

Translations

The Thunderstorm, in *World Drama, 2*, edited by G.R. Noyes and B.H. Clarke, New York, 1956.
The Storm, in *"The Storm" and Other Russian Plays*, translated by David Magarshack, New York, 1960.
The Storm, in *Five Plays of Alexander Ostrovsky*, translated by E.K. Bristow, New York, 1969.
Thunder, in *Four Russian Plays*, translated by Joshua Cooper, Harmondsworth, 1972.
The Storm, translated by Margaret Wettlin, in *Ostrovsky: Plays*, Moscow, 1974.

Criticism

(For general works on the author, see *Playwrights* volume)

Articles:

Irene Zohrab, "Problems of Style in the Plays of A.N. Ostrovsky", in *Melbourne Slavonic Studies*, 12, 1977.
Irene Zohrab, "Problems of Translation: The Plays of A.N. Ostrovsky in English", in *Melbourne Slavonic Studies*, 16, 1982.
R.A. Peace, "A.N. Ostrovsky's *The Thunderstorm*: The Dramatization of Conceptual Ambivalence", in *Modern Language Review*, vol.84 no.1, 1989.

*   *   *

The Storm, written by Alexander Ostrovsky in 1859 and produced in both Moscow and St. Petersburg before its publication in the following January, is his most successful and enduring play. It is set in the fictitious town of Kalinov on the banks of the river Volga, although it is clearly based on similar small towns, notably Torzhok and Tver, that Ostrovsky had seen and whose customs he had observed on a visit to the Upper Volga area in 1856.

The heroine, Katerina, is married to Tikhon, a man she does not love, and both their lives are ruled by her tyrannical mother-in-law, Kabanova, or Kabanikha (the name derives from the Russian for a wild boar). Katerina is in love with Boris who is in as much terror of his uncle, Dikoy, as is Katerina of Kabanova. Tikhon escapes his mother's clutches through a business trip, but refuses to take Katerina with him, as that would upset his plans for a drinking spree. Tikhon's sister, Varvara, is unmarried and free to meet her friend Kudryash. She steals a key to enable herself and Katerina to see Kudryash and Boris secretly, and encourages Katerina to take the opportunity. Katerina and Boris become lovers (which caused contemporary audiences to hiss their disapproval of the former's immorality); but Katerina is also immediately beset by feelings of guilt and confusion, which rapidly develop into hopeless despair. Tikhon returns home earlier than expected and Katerina reveals to him and his mother her love for Boris. Tikhon does not know what to do, mainly from fear of his mother's reaction. Boris is forced by Dikoy to leave for the furthest frontiers of Asia, Varvara and Kudryash elope, and Katerina is left alone. Guilt, shame, deep unhappiness, the cruel attitude of Kabanova, Dikoy, and the other townspeople all combine to force Katerina to feel there can be no happy solution to her problems. After long contemplation of death she finally commits suicide by throwing herself into the Volga.

The natural setting and the physical environment both play their part in the action, and the time of day and the summer's weather are used to good effect—particularly the impending storm, which heightens the tension throughout. Nearly all the scenes in the five acts are placed out of doors: the first and last acts are set in a public park high above the Volga; the first part of Act III takes place in a street in the town, where the passers-by can also be seen as a form of chorus; the second part, romantically, takes place in a ravine at night; and Act IV is in a frescoed gallery which overlooks the river. The only scenes set indoors, in Kabanikha's house, underline the stifling, oppressive, and dark atmosphere of the play as a whole. The Volga itself is all but a character and has a dual role to play, first as a symbol of the freedom that some of the characters so ardently desire, with its distant views and fast-flowing current, and second as a threat, with its silent, hidden depths and gathering storm. Ostrovsky also introduces songs and music, both as a means of commenting on the action and as a lightening of the mood (and Janáček's opera *Katya Kabanova* of 1921, based on the play, has been criticized for not using the songs already there).

First and foremost, though, *The Storm* is about contrasts and conflicts. The most obvious ones are those between the petty, wilful tyrant and the rest of society, between unbending authority and the quest for freedom. There are also those between old and young, conservatism and innovation, love and duty; and those between the arts and beauty on the one hand, and staleness and stagnation on the other. The negative aspects are portrayed most obviously in the frightful Kabanova and in Dikoy, both of whom personify injustice, ignorance, cruelty, and intolerance; while the positive side is embodied in Varvara, Kudryash, Kuligin and, in some respects, even in Boris and Tikhon. All of them, in their various ways, try to oppose the awfulness of their lives but there is little they can do when faced with the iron will of those who control them. For Ostrovsky, good does not necessarily overcome evil and the picture he presents is far from a happy one. The most hapless of the characters, though, is Katerina whose only release is in death. From the first appearance of the play there has been much controversy about the motives for her suicide. Can it be

The Storm: Moscow Art Theatre (Nemirovich-Danchenko's production)

seen as a protest against unbearable conditions, or as a plea for change, or does it stem rather from her own character traits? Religious (even mystical), unsophisticated, honest, and yearning for happiness and freedom, yet possessed of a sense of sin, Katerina cannot cope with a situation that is hardly within her own control. She cannot work things out intellectually; she is ruled as much by her emotions as by Kabanova. Her tragedy might have its social causes, but is it not equally the result of the inadequacies of her own character? Such questions have led to various interpretations of her personality and provide actresses with a superb, albeit demanding, role.

The Storm has become a classic of the Russian stage on account of its vivid characters and clear dramatic conflict, its lively, idiomatic language, its realistic depiction of a section of Russian provincial society where the past lives on victoriously side by side with the present, its combination of comedy and tragedy, the prosaic and the lyrical, and with its exposure of social malpractice as the setting for profound, human problems.

—A. V. Knowles

THE STORY OF PRINCESS CHERRY BLOSSOM OF EDO. See **THE SCARLET PRINCESS OF EDO.**

STREET SCENE
by Elmer Rice

First Publication: New York, 1929.
First Production: Playhouse Theatre, New York, 10 January 1929.

*   *   *

The setting for *Street Scene* is the "exterior of a 'walk-up' apartment house in a mean quarter of New York" on an evening in June and on the morning and afternoon of the following day, presumably contemporary with the play's first production (1929). The play focuses on the lives of 21 tenants of the apartment building—a collection of lower-middle-class people of various ancestry, religions, political beliefs, and occupations. The central action, into which many smaller strains are woven, concerns the Maurrant family. Frank Maurrant, who works as a stagehand, is a gruff, unyielding patriarch. Anna, his wife, longs for gentleness and a kind word, and finds it difficult to control their son Willie, "*a disorderly boy of twelve*", who runs wild in the streets. Their daughter, Rose, "*a pretty girl of twenty*", is the only one to understand her mother's search for some beauty in her life. Mrs. Maurrant's unhappiness has led her into an extra-marital affair with Steve Sankey, a collector for the milk company, and the liaison is a favorite topic of gossip and innuendo for all the neighbors. In the second act, Frank Maurrant, who is supposed to be out of town and has been drinking, returns unexpectedly, finds Sankey with his wife, and kills them both. Act III depicts the aftermath of the shooting, Maurrant's capture, and Rose's attempt to cope with her changed circumstances and begin a new life.

While the dramatic through-line of *Street Scene* is the sensational story of marital infidelity and its consequences, the major thrust of the play is its depiction of the ebb and flow of life in the urban environment. Unlike Rice's earlier work, *The Adding Machine* (1923), which experimented with expressionism, the style of *Street Scene* is minutely realistic. To a great extent the action is organized and directed by the "ugly brownstone" setting which is painstakingly described in the stage directions; indeed, the play was first called "Landscape with Figures". Rice carefully choreographs the movements of his characters in and out of the building, their appearances in the various apartment windows, their gatherings on the stoop. He specifies the constant intrusion of urban noise and periodically sends carefully described passers-by moving through the stage picture in an attempt to capture on stage the visual and aural texture of the city.

The play presents a bleak picture of lower-middle-class life in New York. While there are some instances of kindness and moments of simple pleasure, the emphasis is on the oppressiveness of the environment and the pettiness, intolerance, and inflexibility of the characters. The collection of tenants includes an Italian music teacher and his German wife, the Swedish janitor, the Maurrants, who are of Irish extraction, and the Kaplans, a Jewish family headed by a committed Marxist who constantly preaches the necessity for social revolution. The other neighbors often band together for anti-Semitic remarks about the Kaplans, to warn against "Bolshevism" and the current state of moral degeneration, or to level judgment against the erring Anna Maurrant. Tired of their sniping and arguing, Anna suggests, "People ought to be able to live together in peace and quiet, without making each other miserable". She defends her transgression of traditional morality to Rose in light of her own colorless existence: "What's the good of being alive if you can't get a little something out of life? You might just as well be dead".

In a major subplot, Rose Maurrant finds friendship and support from Sam Kaplan, a sensitive and intelligent student who is deeply in love with her. Their conversations provide two opposing approaches to the life they see around them. Sam's is the voice of pessimism; at the cry of an upstairs neighbor in childbirth, he observes: "That's all there is in life—nothing but pain. From before we're born, until we die! Everywhere you look, oppression and cruelty! If it doesn't come from Nature, it comes from humanity—humanity trampling on itself, and tearing at its own throat". In contrast, Rose finds great enjoyment in small pleasures. She is the voice of hope in the play, rejecting, in the end, both the romantic plans of Sam to run away together and the offer of a well-to-do co-worker who proposes financial help in return for sexual favors. She chooses, instead, independence and an uncertain future: "I don't think people ought to belong to anybody but themselves. I was thinking, that if my mother had really belonged to herself, and that if my father had really belonged to himself, it never would have happened. It was only because they were always depending on somebody else, for what they ought to have had inside themselves". Rose understands the negative influence of the city environment on the quality of life, and believes things "might be different if you only had a chance to breathe and spread out a little". At the close of the play, she leaves the apartment house to forge a new life with her brother in a different place, while the neighbors return to their characteristic gossip.

As the most sympathetic figure in the play, Rose carries the author's message of support for tolerance and independent action in the face of narrow-minded and oppressive society.

The character's sweetness and rather self-conscious simplicity of expression, however, are problematic for a modern audience, and *Street Scene* is, in general, a difficult play to produce due to its large cast and demanding set requirements. The strengths of the play are Rice's colorful, yet economical, characterizations and his careful construction as he intertwines the various strands of the characters' lives. The aggregate effect of all the production elements in building the urban milieu still make this Pulitzer Prize-winning play a fascinating example of realism for the stage.

—Kathy Fletcher

A STREETCAR NAMED DESIRE
by Tennessee Williams

First Publication: New York, 1947.
First Production: Ethel Barrymore Theatre, New York, 3 December 1947.

Bibliography
S. Alan, "*A Streetcar Named Desire*: Twenty-Five Years of Criticism", in *Notes on Mississippi Writers*, 7, 1974.

Criticism
(For general works on the author, see *Playwrights* volume)

Books:
Jordan Y. Miller (ed.), *Twentieth Century Interpretations of "A Streetcar Named Desire"*, Englewood Cliffs, New Jersey, 1971.
Harold Bloom (ed.), *Tennessee Williams's "A Streetcar Named Desire"*, New York, 1988 [anthology of criticism].
Thomas P. Adler, "*A Streetcar Named Desire*": *The Moth and the Lantern*, Boston, 1990.

Articles:
Joseph N. Riddell, "*A Streetcar Named Desire*: Nietzsche Descending", in *Modern Drama*, 1963.
Thomas E. Porter, "The Passing of the Old South: *A Streetcar Named Desire*", in his *Myth and Modern American Drama*, Detroit, Illinois, 1969.
Mary A. Corrigan, "Realism and Theatricalism in *A Streetcar Named Desire*", in *Modern Drama*, 19, 1976.
Joan Templeton, "*A Streetcar Named Desire*: Blanche Dubois and the Old South", in *Trames: Travaux et mémoires de l'Université de Limoges . . . Collection anglaise*, 2, 1979.
Roxanna Stuart, "The Southernmost *Desire*", in *Tennessee Williams Newsletter*, vol.1 no.2, 1979 and vol.2 no.1, 1980.
Ellen Dowling and Nancy Pride, "Three Approaches to Directing *A Streetcar Named Desire*", in *Tennessee Williams Newsletter*, vol.2 no.2, 1980.
Henry I. Schvey, "Madonna at the Poker Night: Pictorial Elements in Tennessee Williams' *A Streetcar Named Desire*", in *From Cooper to Philip Roth: Essays on American Literature*, edited by J. Bakker and D.R.M. Williamson, Amsterdam, 1980.
Milly S. Barranger, "New Orleans as Theatrical Image in Plays by Tennessee Williams", in *Southern Quarterly*, vol.23 no.2, 1985.
Ana L.A. Gazolla, "*A Streetcar Named Desire*: Myth, Ritual and Ideology", in *Ritual in the United States: Acts and*

A Streetcar Named Desire: Aldwych Theatre, London, 1949

Representations, edited by Don Harkness, Tampa, Florida, 1985.

June Schlueter, "Imitating an Icon: John Erman's Remake of Tennessee Williams's *A Streetcar Named Desire*", in *Modern Drama*, 28, 1985.

Pamela A. Hanks, "Must We Acknowledge What We Mean? The Viewer's Role in Filmed Versions of *A Streetcar Named Desire*", in *Journal of Popular Film and Television*, vol. 14 no.3, 1986.

David R. Jones, "Elia Kazan and *A Streetcar Named Desire*", in his *Great Directors at Work*, Berkeley, California, 1986.

Anca Vlasopolos, "Authorizing History: Victimization in *A Streetcar Named Desire*", in *Theatre Journal*, 38, 1986.

Susan Spector, "Alternative Visions of Blanche Dubois: Uta Hagen and Jessica Tandy in *A Streetcar Named Desire*", in *Modern drama*, 32, 1989.

Philip C. Kohn (ed.), "*A Streetcar Named Desire*: A Playwrights' Forum", in *Michigan Quarterly Review*, 29, 1990.

*   *   *

The plot of *A Streetcar Named Desire* is deceptively simple. Stanley and Stella Kowalski live in a poor section of New Orleans. Stanley, a northerner of Polish descent, has recently returned from fighting in World War II. He is between 28 and 30 years old. Stella is a "*gentle young woman*" of about 25. She was raised in genteel surroundings on Belle Reeve, a former plantation in Mississippi. Blanche, Stella's older sister, comes to visit. During her visit, it becomes apparent that Blanche's refined bearing is objectionable to Stanley, and his animalistic crudity is offensive to her. It is soon revealed that Stella is pregnant, but she has not told Stanley because she is not sure how he will react. In the meantime, Mitch, a friend of Stanley's, becomes romantically interested in Blanche. It is also revealed that Blanche has been married and feels guilty for the suicide of her young husband who took his own life when she confronted him with her knowledge of his homosexuality. Stanley learns of this incident along with the fact that Blanche has been fired in her home town as a schoolteacher because of her sexual escapades with young men. As a result of this knowledge, Stanley declares that he does not want Blanche to have any more contact with Mitch.

Soon afterwards Stella goes to the hospital to have the baby. While his wife is giving birth, Stanley rapes Blanche. In the play's final scene, which takes place some weeks later, it is apparent that Blanche has suffered a nervous breakdown because of the incident. As Stanley and his friends are engaged in a poker game, he, Stella, and Eunice watch a doctor and a nurse arrive to take Blanche to a mental institution. As the curtain falls, the card game continues and Stanley caresses Stella.

At least part of the reason for the immense success of the play must lie in the casting for the premiere production, directed by Elia Kazan, which featured Marlon Brando in the role of Stanley (and established his star status), along with Kim Hunter as Stella, Karl Malden as Mitch, and Jessica Tandy as Blanche. Four years later, in 1951, a multi-Oscar-winning film version of *Streetcar* was released. Directed by Kazan, the cinematic adaptation starred Brando, Hunter, and Malden, with Vivien Leigh replacing Tandy.

The initial appearance of Stanley (indeed the first words in the play) set the tone for what is to follow. Dressed as a blue-collar laborer and carrying a blood-stained package from the butcher's, Stanley bellows, "Hey, there! Stella, Baby!". The image produced is that of the male warrior returning home from the hunt with meat for his mate. Throughout the drama Stanley's animalistic nature is emphasized: he is uncouth, rough, and blunt. Physical comfort seems to be one of his prime considerations; he is uninhibited and does not give a second thought to appearing in public wearing a T-shirt.

Given Stanley's crude nature, it is difficult for some to understand how the refined, cultured, sophisticated Stella could find him attractive—let alone marry him and bear his child. As the play develops, however, it is apparent that these characteristics are part of his appeal for Stella. George Bernard Shaw posited the existence of a "life force": the most vital men and women were attracted to one another and the result was that they would ultimately produce a race of supermen which combined the best aspects of the mother and father. Shaw also indicated that he did not think that social class was a determining factor, (and frequently his heroes and heroines were from disparate classes). Stella's actions make sense if they are seen as analogous to this concept. It is clear that Stella represents the best of her society, the *ante bellum* South; even though that civilization no longer exists and what is left has degenerated considerably. Stanley, on the other hand, is alive in the fullest sense of that word. The strength and power that he exudes, therefore, is a magnet that draws Stella to him. When Stanley mistreats Stella it is not because he does not love her. And, Stella, who loves Stanley, recognizes this. Their love is based on the mutual attraction of the two strongest characters in the play.

Blanche is a representative of the same civilization that produced Stella, but her character has become perverted by the destruction of that civilization. The homosexuality of her dead young husband, and the music of the "rapid, feverish polka tune", the "Varsouviana", exemplify the old South that she grew up in and is unable to escape. Her pursuit of young men was, ironically, an attempt to recapture the innocence of her youth and the past. When that old South is finally, absolutely, lost to her—when Belle Reeve has been sold and all of the family connections have been severed—she has no one to turn to but her younger sister. Stanley immediately understands the threat that Blanche represents to his relationship with Stella. For her own survival Blanche must supplant Stanley in Stella's affections. The resultant conflict can only bring the destruction of one or the other of these two characters.

The garish, ruthless, sensual world of *Streetcar* is captured in one of the primary scenes of the play, the poker night. Interestingly, Williams had originally titled this drama *The Poker Night* (and the importance of this scene is underscored by Thomas Hart Benton's painting of the poker game to represent the play). Besides demonstrating the essence of the lower-class New Orleans culture in which *Streetcar* takes place, the poker game also functions metaphorically, for it represents the concept of game playing that runs throughout the play (particularly in Blanche's actions); the melting-pot concept of America; the male bonding and camaraderie that epitomize Stanley's nature; and the exclusion of the outsider. Blanche had had the strength to keep Belle Reeve together for a long time, but when it was lost the source of her strength was also removed; yet Stanley senses her underlying strength of character and the family ties that bind her and Stella together. To defeat his adversary he must employ his attributes represented metaphorically by the poker night.

Stanley knows therefore that he must expel Blanche, the intruder, in order to save his marriage. Whether from animal cunning or intelligence or a combination of both, he also knows that he must do this in such a way that Stella participates in the expulsion. His rape of Blanche is brutal, ruthless, callous, and premeditated. He knows that Blanche will tell Stella about the attack; he knows that Stella *cannot* believe Blanche or she will have to give him up. And he is right. Stella *chooses* to believe that Blanche has tried to seduce Stanley. Since Stella participates in rejecting her sister, she will not be able to bring her back. Blanche is not capable of handling this rejection. Ironically, Blanche, for whom family was the most important thing, is reduced to uttering the most poignant statement in the entire drama with her last words: "I have always depended on the kindness of strangers".

Blanche's concluding statement makes this play terribly bleak and depressing. There is hope, however, at the end. Stanley and Stella are together, and they end where they began, with their relationship reconfirmed. While there is a lack of concern for what has had to be rejected in order to insure survival of their relationship, the baby remains as the ultimate symbol of hope. Stanley and Stella's child can be interpreted as a combination of the best of both cultures.

Some interpretations of *Streetcar* add a further symbolic dimension. If Stanley is seen as a representative of the North in American society and Stella is seen as representing the South, the play is a metaphor for a specific period in American history. The harsh, raw, realistic, insensitive, masculine, new, industrial part of the nation is brought into contact with the old, feminine, romantic, agrarian, cultured part of the nation, and the blending of the two produces a vital new nation.

Williams's craftsmanship allowed him to create realistic characters, place them in a significant situation, and bring together layers of emotional, intellectual, and historical meaning in ways that make this play his masterpiece. Whatever interpretation or combination of interpretations is accepted, *A Streetcar Named Desire* remains a landmark in the American theatre.

—Steven H. Gale

A STRETCH OF THE IMAGINATION
by Jack Hibberd

First Publication: Sydney, 1973.
First Production: The Pram Factory, Melbourne (Australian Performing Group), 8 March 1972.

Criticism
(For general works on the author, see *Playwrights* volume)

Articles:
Carla Dente Baschiera, "Allusioni/illusioni: *A Stretch of the Imagination* di Jack Hibberd", in *Quaderni di anglistica*, 4, 1986.

*   *   *

A Stretch of the Imagination takes place over one day, from dawn to dusk. It is a day in the life of Monk O'Neill, described by the author as "a self-willed exile and part-time misanthrope wrestling obsessively with his own imminent death". This day may be typical in Monk's life or it may be his last. But things are certainly getting worse with Monk's legs and bladder seizing up. Nothing overtly significant actually happens during the play. Monk gets up on a frosty, outback morning, does some chores, eats lunch, has a siesta, gets up again and finally goes to bed at sundown.

When *Stretch* was published it was described in its introduction as "the first unmistakable Australian theatrical classic". It is one of the most performed Australian plays in Australia and

its ability to speak to people everywhere is attested by the number of productions elsewhere in the world.

A play becomes a classic presumably because it is a deep and rich mine of theatrical possibilities, always open to reinterpretation and engaging audiences regardless of time or place. How this most Australian of plays does this lies not so much in its themes as in its theatrical imagination. It is Hibberd's first mature play and it still represents one of his most successful attempts to fuse form and content. In it, Hibberd for the first time uses the theatre as a metaphor for life itself. Always fascinated by the way communities fashion an identity for themselves through the collective play of the theatrical experience, Hibberd here explores the theatre of the individual: *Stretch* is a monodrama—a dramatic recreation by a character of his own life, an acting-out of his own personal mythology with one voice sounding for the many that intrude into a single life, and one person playing the roles of many.

Monk represents his exile from civilisation as voluntary. However, it becomes clear that he has practically always been a sociopath. His life has been typical of the itinerant and it may be that Monk finally had nowhere left to go but here, to One Tree Hill, living in a corrugated iron hut somewhere in the distant outback of Australia.

Sociopath or not, Monk uses his isolation to explore his own identity. He does this by theatricalising his life—reliving past events and dramatising such current trivia as trying to urinate, eating a meat pie, sweeping the ground in front of the hut, and going to sleep. In short, his life is a performance for himself and we can only assume that the events he re-enacts—supposed visits by old mates, past love affairs, scaling Mount Kosciusko with the boxer, Les Darcy, visiting Paris—change every time as he tests out different possibilities.

What matters in the play is not whether the events are truthfully re-enacted or whether the things he says are true. The issue is *why* he does and says these things. Hibberd explores the "why" by using the theatre as a metaphor. The theatre is a place where the games of life and death are ritualised, where reality is tested, and where the mystery of life is objectified. It is a communal activity in which a society entertains itself by testing definitions of reality. But before any of us get into a theatre, we live out our own theatre, both in the personal scripts which govern our lives and by the way we all have to perform social roles. Therefore, when Monk acts out his past, we recognise the activity—if only because we all talk to ourselves and entertain ourselves. Also like us, Monk is a flawed individual struggling to understand why he did what he did and wrestling with the big issue of "what's it all about".

In many ways he is a thoroughly nasty person: he is selfcentred and oblivious of the rights and needs of others; he saves his urine now—his "nitrogenous waste"—because he wants to atone for chopping down the only tree on One Tree Hill; he is a bully and a braggart; and he is aggressive, vulgar, foul-mouthed, and uneducated (though with considerable pretensions to cultivation). Yet Monk touches us because he is on a quest. However dimly conscious he may be of it, he has set out to find himself, to learn how to be alone, to become an honest and autonomous human being. He wants to understand the process by which we all construct that performance we call life.

Ironically, Monk realises that—on what may be the last day of his life—the aloneness he values so much only has value within the frame of others. He realises, having alienated himself from the world, that he can only be himself in interaction with others. So, there is a quiet despair to Monk and beneath his pornographic reminiscences of women and violent relations with other men, a genuine love shows through—a love which Monk was then unable to express and which he disguised behind aggression. Ultimately, he is life-affirming.

The play has many dimensions to it which contribute to its "classic" character. It is, for example, an acute portrait of the "ocker", that typically Australian male who hides his lack of self-esteem behind violence, misogyny, and philistinism. At the same time, Hibberd uses vernacular so that the play's poetic power belies the often coarse language of its protagonist. The play is also a metaphor for people's relationship to their environment; specifically, Monk's tenuous occupation of One Tree Hill is a metaphor for European civilisation in Australia, or indeed in any post-colonial country.

—Paul McGillick

* * *

STRIFE
by John Galsworthy

First Publication: London, 1910.
First Production: Duke of York's Theatre, 9 March 1909.

Criticism
(For general works on the author, see *Playwrights* volume)

Articles:
Philip E. Smith, "Galsworthy's *Strife*: The Dramatic Art of Ethical Naturalism", in *Studies in the Humanites*, vol.6 no.1, 1977.
Non Worral, "Introduction" in *Strife*, by John Galsworthy, London, 1984.

* * *

A strike in a Welsh tinplate factory is in its fifth month, and the continuing deadlock has led to overt bitterness on both sides, but also to growing dissension within each camp. The board of directors, disgruntled by the loss of dividends and fall in the company's shares, are unhappy with their chairman's intransigent handling of the dispute. The strikers have reached the point of exhaustion and near-starvation, and would go back on previously offered terms, were it not for the dogged perseverance of their leader.

It is a classical capital versus labour issue, sharpened by a singularly class-conscious and uncompromising protagonist on each side. Antony represents the old-style, autocratic employer who prides himself on having defeated, during his 30-year control of the company, strikes on several previous occasions; whereas Roberts, "not one of these 'ere ordinary 'armless Socialists" (Act III), stands for a similarly principled working-class militancy. His is a vision of a future classless society beyond the immediate struggle, which is only an episode in the long march to progress. Antony, by contrast, is an essentially backward-looking man to whom the idea of a social policy, let alone a democratic society, is anathema, opening the gates as he sees it, to "the black waters of confusion", and to "mob government" (Act III). The two diehards agree on one point only: namely that, in Antony's words, to argue "that masters and men are equal" is just as much "cant" as to assert "that Capital and Labour have the same interests" (Act III).

Galsworthy's own position falls exactly between the two extremes. He takes a seemingly neutral approach to the conflict by perfectly balancing the social forces, settings, arguments, and characters. The resultant, impartial stance enables him to drive home all the more credibly his underlying message of class reconciliation and peaceful co-existence. Several minor characters speak the voice of reason and compromise, among them Harness, the representative of a union which has not supported the strike, and Edgar, Antony's son. Both are instrumental in finally reaching a settlement, though not until irreparable damage has been done.

It is a mark of Galsworthy's successful empathy that, according to one of his biographers, H. V. Marrot, both middle- and working-class audiences could feel vindicated. The play certainly also has a stage history in the workers' theatre movement of the inter-war period. In fact, so naturalistically convincing is the author's reproduction of both the bourgeois scene and the proletarian milieu that it becomes a matter of debate, and of choice and emphasis for a theatre director, whether it is the gulf between the two classes, or the final good-willed bridging of it, which achieves the more lasting impression. This impression is partly due to the weight and character of the two main antagonists. But several minor incidents add to the general picture of two mutually exclusive and ultimately irreconcilable worlds. The *borné* thinking of the capitalists is illustrated when even their most humane representative, Edgar, can only impute personal vengeance to Robert's strong-willed opposition; as if a strike leader driven by mere self-interest would have shared out the 700 pounds he had received from the company for an invention from which it made hundreds of thousands. The ideological class barriers extend to the women. Enid, Antony's daughter, is at a loss to understand why Roberts's ailing wife, her former maid, refuses to accept her food parcels; and in another telling incident, the working-class wives, in bitter argument over Robert's role only a moment earlier, instinctively close ranks against the well-wishing middle-class intruder.

If this powerful evocation of class entrenchment runs counter to the author's central intention, his commiseration with the workers' plight (and especially that of their families) is sincere and deeply felt, thereby undermining the outwardly objective stance. For what is the preoccupation of one board member with taking his wife to Spain the next day compared to a striker's wavering loyalty because of devotion to his sweetheart? What is the uninviting prospect for a city magnate of facing another dinner at that "dreadful" provincial hotel compared to the lack of food among the locals? What is the 20 pounds another magnate graciously donates to a welfare fund when contrasted with Robert's wholesale parting with his savings? A balancing of such stark contrasts would have been a violation of all sense of justice.

However, Galsworthy's anger against the rich and privileged remains firmly subordinated to his controlled vision of social harmony and moderation. Hence, despite the greater sympathy for the suffering and misery of the working-class community, Roberts's radicalism must be shown to be as mistaken and disastrous as Antony's obstinacy, and it is the moderates who carry the day and end the dispute. Isolated and overruled, the two hotheads dumbly bow to each other in mutual defeat when the curtain falls in what Galsworthy later regarded "the best moment in any of my plays", though again Robert's tragedy is the greater, since he has not only lost the struggle and the leadership but also his wife.

Strife, written contemporaneously with Robert Tressell's famous working-class novel *The Ragged Trousered Philanthropists*, was completed two years prior to its first production. It is one of the earliest British attempts to bring industrial conflict to the stage and ranks, through its presentation of the partly impersonal forces of class antagonism, with Hauptmann's *The*

Strife: Comedy Theatre, London, 1913

Weavers as one of the more successful social dramas of the turn of the century.

—H. Gustav Klaus

SUEHIROGARI
probably by Priest Genne-Hōin

First Publication: Early 17th Century

*   *   *

Shopping for an Umbrella (*Suehirogari*), a Kyōgen play, is in the category "*Kahō-mono*" (Play of a Well-to-do-Person) in the division of a "*Waki-Kyōgen*" (Plays of Congratulatory Nature), placed following the Waki-Nō in a day's program. (a Waki-Nō play starts off the program). The early Kyōgen plays were transmitted orally. Hence, most plays were put together collectively by actors throughout years of performance. The first known Kyōgen anthology is the *Tenshō-Kyōgen-bon*, 1578, but what was recorded in this work are essentially rough storylines of plays. A full-fledged anthology of Kyōgen texts was compiled in the Keichō period (1596–1614) by the Izumi School. The book is known as *Tenri-bon*. The other celebrated anthology, by the Ōkura School, was compiled in 1642 and called *Torá aki-bon*, crediting the famed Kyōgen master, Ōkura Torá aki, as the compiler.

In this play a well-to-do Master sends his servant, Tarōkaja, to the capital (Kyoto) to purchase several *suehirogari* (a kind of folding fan which spreads out toward the tip of the fan) so that he can present them as a gift to each of the main guests at his New Year's party. Realizing his ignorance of what *suehirogari* is, Tarōkaja calls out in the middle of a capital street, following the example of some merchants, "Is there anyone who sells *suehirogari*?" Shortly he catches the attention of a clever Swindler who decides to unload an old umbrella on Tarōkaja, assuring him that an umbrella is indeed a *suehirogari*. After receiving proper answers to all the specifications the Master wanted on the item, Tarōkaja is quite pleased and purchases it at a considerable price.

The Swindler compliments Tarokaja on his buying acumen and offers to teach him how to humor his master in case he does not appreciate what Tarōkaja brings back. Tarōkaja obliges and returns home. The master, however, was not in the least pleased by Tarōkaja's grave mistake. His clever explanation taught by the Swindler provides an answer to each of the Master's specifications, but it only helps to fuel the Master's anger, and he eventually drives Tarōkaja away.

Remembering what he was taught by the Swindler, Tarōkaja starts chanting and dancing outside to humor the Master. Soon the instrumental music accompanies Tarōkaja, and the Master finds it difficult to resist the music and Tarōkaja's singing. The Master, too, joins in the dancing with hearty laughter. The play ends while the two are enjoying singing and dancing together.

The great master of the Nō theatre, Zeami, said, "Of all the effects the art of performance can give, most importantly we can identify a softening of the feelings of man, of moving emotionally people of all classes and, in the end, of increasing the possibility of being happy and of providing a means to prolong life". The art of performance in medieval Japan emphasized the overall nature of the play to contribute to an ideal atmosphere of blissfulness. This comedy was most frequently performed during the Edo period (1603–1867), when the major patrons of the art, Samurai warriors, were in their peaceful reign of Japan. Even after the Restoration of the Meiji in 1968, the play was often performed to entertain guests attending a wedding reception. In the period prior to World War II, this play was included in a nationally standardized Japanese reader for the elementary school system, hence, it became the most well-known Kyōgen play to the general public.

The humor in the first half of the play, created by the situation of Tarōkaja, a simple country rustic, being tricked into buying a mere old umbrella at an exorbitant price, is heightened by the clever answers of an urban chiseler, who manages to contrive an appropriate and humorous explanation to each and all specifications the Master listed for Tarōkaja. In the second half, the anticipating audience sees how the Master's anger dissolves into an uncontrollable burst of laughter after he hears and sees Tarōkaja's song and dance routine, learned from the Swindler. The fact that because of this unexpected pleasurable routine the Master came to forgive the servant enhances the ability of the comedy to bring about a blissful atmosphere to the audience: the duly expected function of the "congratulatory play".

From a structural point of view, Tarōkaja is the main character (*shite*), but traditionally the role of the Master is given that distinction due to the considerable demand for delicate acting which is placed on him, as he is gradually and humorously drawn into the song and dance routine presented by Tarōkaja. It is rather rare to see the full component of four instrumental musicians playing music for a song and dance routine (known as *hayashimono*) which constitutes the important moments of the concluding scene of a Kyōgen play. Having such accompanying music is intended to add weight to the significance of the play.

—Andrew T. Tsubaki

EL SUEÑO DE LA RAZÓN.   See **THE SLEEP OF REASON.**

THE SUICIDE (Samoubiytsa)
by Nikolai Erdman

Composition: 1928.
First Publication: In English translation, in *Russian Literature Triquarterly*, 7, 1973; in Russian, in *Novyi Zhurnal* [*New Journal*], New York, 112–114, 1973–74.
First Production: Sweden, 1969; first Soviet production, at The Moscow Theatre of Satire, Moscow, 1982.

Translations
The Suicide, in *Russian Triquarterly*, 7, 1973; subsequently in *The Mandate; The Suicide*, translated by George Genereux Jr. and Jacob Volkov, Ann Arbor, Michigan, 1975.
The Suicide, translated by Peter Tegel, London, 1979.

Criticism
(For general works on the author, see *Playwrights* volume)

The Suicide: Aldwych Theatre, London, 1980 (Royal Shakespeare Company)

Articles:

Marjorie Hoover, "Nikolai Erdman: A Soviet Dramatist Rediscovered", in *Russian Literature Triquarterly*, 2, 1972.

John Freedman, "Nikolai Erdman: An Overview", in *Slavic and East European Journal*, 28, 1984.

Eberhard Reissner, "Erdman: *Der Selbstmörder*", in *Das russische Drama*, edited by Bodo Zelinsky, Bagel, 1986.

*   *   *

Erdman's *The Suicide* was written and banned during "the golden" age of Soviet drama, the 1920's. Put into rehearsal both by Meyerhold and by Stanislavsky at their respective theatres, it was refused a licence by Stalin's henchman, Kaganovich, and remained suppressed and almost invisible for decades. When finally it did burst upon the stage in the late-20th century, especially in productions in Sweden, and in London (by the Royal Shakespeare Company), it was hailed as a most unexpected masterpiece.

This history causes some problems. It was first published after its author's death and in a foreign language (English) in 1973. It had apparently circulated in manuscript surreptitiously in the four decades before that, but because Erdman did not oversee the publication it may be wondered how exactly the version we have reflects his original conception. *Samizdat* manuscripts are known sometimes to have been tampered with, and it may be wondered why, if it was as anti-Soviet as it is sometimes now supposed to be, Stalin was only mildly opposed to it, and why, indeed, the paranoid dictator did not execute this author as he did so many others.

Set in the Soviet Russia of the New Economic Policy (1921–8), it concerns the socially inadequate Semyon Semyonovich Podsekalnikov, who is drifting towards suicidal despair because he cannot find a job. Ashamed that he is forced to live off his wife's earnings, he swears that if he could only learn the tuba, he could earn good money from giving concerts. But when he acquires a tuba, he discovers that learning to play it is not so simple. For one thing you need a piano! He is visited by a series of disaffected ne'er-do-wells who have been told of his despair by his next door neighbour. Each begs him to put his suicide down to his or her special cause. They give him a farewell banquet, but he lacks the nerve to commit suicide after it. Instead, he gets drunk and lies down in his coffin to sleep it off. Of course, everyone imagines he is dead; they conduct a funeral service for him and take him to the graveyard for burial. Here, he finally jumps out of the coffin, and declares himself for life.

The story does not in itself seem particularly anti-Soviet, most of the political sideswipes coming in odd remarks through the play. Indeed, Erdman clearly presents Semyon as largely contemptible: he is self-centred, pompous, and cowardly, though among the vultures and spivs who hover around him he sometimes seems more human. Moreover, any central character must be interesting, and it is only a short step from interest to sympathy. Furthermore, all the other characters are hopeless drop-outs and fantasists, who are incorrigibly anti-Soviet. They are opportunistic scoundrels who have no interest in helping Semyon. Even his family, whom some critics have tried to see as figures of moral worth, are in truth bumbling and sometimes vicious, as when Serafima tells a series of jokes whose humour relies on cruelty and anti-Semitism. These characters, not what they oppose, are the objects of the satire; though it must be added that the positives of socialism or the new Soviet way of life are nowhere to be seen in the play.

In this milieu, it is not difficult to present Semyon in the theatre as sympathetic, even almost-tragic, by relying on naturalistic techniques. But the play was actually written for Meyerhold, whose production of Erdman's earlier *The Mandate* had provoked Stanislavsky's envy and the desire to present an Erdman play for himself. Meyerhold's "circusization" of theatre and deployment of his system of gymnastic biomechanics is what the play needs, as the protests of several characters tell us: "We can't go on like this, Semyon", says his wife. "It'll do for a circus act, but it's no way to live". The hopeless poet, Viktor Viktorovich, complains: "I want to be Tolstoy, not a circus performer".

The style Erdman is seeking is properly known as "eccentrism", whereby serious matters are heightened in grotesque and comic ways, and significances may be undercut by unexpected twist of meaning or attention. When Semyon's family and neighbours seek to prevent him committing suicide in the lavatory, they tiptoe over in an idiotic, exaggerated line. When Semyon becomes increasingly desperate as he seeks answers to the hardest of questions about life and death, he shakes and shakes his interlocutor, demanding reassurance, but the boy turns out to be deaf and dumb. This is pure clowning, which however sets up fathomless reverberations.

Structurally, *The Suicide* begins as domestic and homely, and through a simple misunderstanding, soars to exorbitant heights. Like the best farces, it crackles with excellent jokes ("Stop beating about the bush, Alexander Petrovich", his jealous mistress shrieks, "what slut have you taken up with now?"; "Only with you, Margarita Ivanovna", he replies timidly); but they exist in a dark atmosphere suffused with foreboding. It deals with the specifics of life in the Soviet Union during the NEP period, but rises from that to discuss larger themes of life and death, the individual and society. It is in fact no surprise that having finally been reclaimed by the theatre, *The Suicide* is now a standard in the repertories of theatres East and West.

—Robert Leach

SUMMER OF THE SEVENTEENTH DOLL. See THE DOLL TRILOGY.

SUMMERFOLK (Dachniki / Dachniky)
by Maxim Gorky

First Publication: Berlin, 1904.
First Production: Kommissarzhevskaya Theatre, St. Petersburg, November 1904.

Translations
Scenes From a Life, translated by A. Delano, in *Poet-Lore*, vol.16 no.3, 1905.
Summer Folk, translated by Margaret Wettlin, in *Gorky: Five Plays*, Moscow, 1956.
Summerfolk, in *Maxim Gorky: Five Plays*, translated by Kitty Hunter-Blair and Jeremy Brooks, edited by Edward Braun, London, 1988.

Criticism
(For general works on the author, see *Playwrights* volume)

Articles:
Yael Harussi, "Realism in Drama: Turgenev, Chekhov, Gorky and Their Summer Folk", in *Ulbandus Review*, vol.2 no.2, 1982.

*   *   *

The play was conceived by Gorky when he and his wife were staying in a country cottage (*dacha*) near Nizhni-Novgorod (Gorky's birthplace and the town subsequently named after him). The countryside was littered with rubbish from previous holiday-makers and Gorky wrote: "the summer visitor is the most useless and perhaps the most harmful individual on earth; he descends on a *dacha*, fouls it up with rubbish and then leaves"—a comment relevant to a central theme of the play which criticises the bourgeoisie and the intellectuals.

The Russian intellectuals are presented in the play partly through the conventional method of amorous love triangles (reminiscent of Turgenev's *A Month in the Country* and Chekhov's *The Seagull*). Varvara, the heroine, turns to the writer Shalimov (reminiscent of Trigorin in *The Seagull*) out of disillusionment with her husband, but Shalimov—like her husband—has also given up and lost most of his ideals. Varvara, in turn, has an ardent suitor, Ryumin, but she is unresponsive to both his love and his philosophising. His subsequent attempt to kill himself fails (again, there are parallels with *The Seagull* and Trepliov's first suicide attempt). A different variation on relationships in the play consists of Varvara's brother, Vlas, who loves the doctor, Maria Lvovna—but she considers her work and duty more important than love. It is Maria Lvovna who recognises the gulf between the intellectuals and the ordinary masses of the people, and the need to educate the latter. As she says in Act II:

> We are the children of cooks and washerwomen and decent working people—we should be different. This country's never before had an educated class with direct blood ties to the people. Surely this blood relationship ought to have nourished in us a burning desire to bring some light and meaning into the lives of our own people? . . .They sent us ahead to seek out a road that would lead them to a better life, and we left them behind, went on and lost our way and created a lonely wilderness for ourselves.

Gorky condemned the intelligentsia for its indecisiveness, cowardice, and alienation from the people, and considered it an obligation of the writer to use literary and dramatic skills to aid the people in their struggle for change. This pre-revolutionary play demonstrates Gorky's view of the intellectuals and liberals as little more than "windbags", unprepared to struggle or to make a sacrifice for an ideal. Again to quote Varvara:

> We are mere transients and summer folk in our own country. We live on this earth as strangers and we are not the sort of useful creatures life really needs. . .it seems to me that soon—perhaps tomorrow—other men, strong and bold, will arrive and mop us up as so much muck.

These were indeed prophetic words, and it is here that one may see Gorky's association of several of his characters with "rubbish". Writing in anger and characteristic passion about the realities of life for the ordinary people—hunger, unem-

Summerfolk: Aldwych Theatre, London, 1973 (Royal Shakespeare Company)

ployment, and repression by the authorities—Gorky, impatient with the intellectuals' endless debates (the play uses extensive monologues), considered that the intelligentsia should commit itself actively to the cause of the common people. Varvara's husband, Bassov, for example consistently states his belief in the need to change Russia but actually does nothing.

The response from the Moscow Arts Theatre when Gorky sent them the play was lukewarm: neither Stanislavsky nor Nemirovich-Danchenko were enthusiastic about it. After subsequent revision, Gorky then gave the play to the actress Vera Komissarzhevskaya who had started a new company in St. Petersburg. The first performance of the play was in November 1904 (the year of Chekhov's *The Cherry Orchard*) at Komissarzhevskaya's Passage Theatre. Although Gorky was dissatisfied with the production, the play created considerable controversy and debate amongst audience and critics alike, and views were polarised between those who violently disliked it and those passionately in sympathy with the play. Lunacharsky (the Bolshevik critic who became Commissar of Culture after the 1917 Revolution) wrote a critique in the newspaper *Pravda* praising *Summerfolk* as a work of art, while the poet Alexander Blok, writing in the journal *Golden Fleece*, stated that "Gorky loses his grip". The debate delighted Gorky and he wrote to his fellow-writer Leonid Andreev: "Needless to say, I have not revised my opinion of *Summerfolk* in the light of these events".

Gorky's characterisation is often unsubtle, and the passionate conviction with which he wrote about contemporary social life sometimes results in a lack of objectivity. But in writing *Summerfolk* Gorky was clearly influenced by Chekhov's dramatic style and mood. There is an interesting parallel with Chekhov in the use of outdoor settings, and the relationship between music and sound effects, and mood or atmosphere. The mood of the play is gloomy: nothing is changing, despite a great need for change, and the characters' disillusionment remains. Like Chekhov's *The Cherry Orchard* there is little, external, dramatic action, but unlike Chekhov's comedy, the atmosphere of *Summerfolk* is that of despair, impotence, and failure. As Varvara puts it in Act IV:

> We are just the summer folk of this country—people who have just dropped by from somewhere else. We bustle about looking for comfortable little nests for ourselves. . .and do nothing else but talk a ridiculous amount. . .we hide our spiritual bankruptcy from each other by dressing ourselves up in fine phrases and the tattered remnants of second hand wisdom and we go on about how tragic life is without ever having experienced it.

The play received a memorable production by Peter Stein at the Schaubühne Theatre, West Berlin, in 1974, and was also successfully produced by the Royal Shakespeare Company, directed by David Jones, in 1973.

—Irene Slatter

THE SUPPLIANT WOMEN. See THE SUPPLIANTS.

THE SUPPLIANTS (Supplices)
by Aeschylus

First Production: Athens, c.463 BC.

Editions

The "Supplices" of Aeschylus [with translation], edited by T.G. Tucker, London, 1889.

The Suppliants [with translation and commentary], edited by H. Friis Johansen, Copenhagen, 1970.

Translations

The Suppliants, in *Four Plays of Aeschylus*, translated by G.M. Cookson, Oxford, 1922.

The Suppliant Women, translated by Gilbert Murray, London, 1930.

The Suppliant Maidens, translated by Seth G. Bernadete, in *Aeschylus, 2*, Chicago, 1956 (Complete Greek Tragedies Series).

The Suppliants, translated by L.R. Lind, in *Ten Greek Plays in Contemporary Translation*, edited by L. R. Lind, Boston, 1957.

The Suppliants, in *Prometheus Bound; The Suppliants; Seven Against Thebes; The Persians*, translated by Philip Vellacott, Harmondsworth, 1961.

The Suppliants, translated by Janet Lembke, London and New York, 1975.

Criticism

(For general works on the author, see *Playwrights* volume)

Books:

Robert D. Murray, *The Motif of Io in Aeschylus's "Suppliants"*, Princeton, New Jersey, 1958.

Alexander F. Garvie, *Aeschylus's "Supplices": Play and Trilogy*, Cambridge, 1969.

Articles:

K. von Fritz, "Die Danaiden Trilogie des Aeschylus", in *Philologus*, 91, 1936.

Richard Livingstone, "Rights of the Weak: A Modern Problem in Ancient Dress: *The Suppliants* of Aeschylus", in *Hibbert Journal*, 39, 1940.

Grace Harriet Macurdy, "Had the Danaid Trilogy a Social Problem?", in *Classical Philology*, 39, 1944.

A. Diamantopoulos, "The Danaid Trilogy of Aeschylus", in *Journal of the Hellenic Society*, 77, 1957.

R.P. Winnington-Ingram, "The Danaid Trilogy of Aeschylus", in *Journal of the Hellenic Society*, 81, 1961.

H. Spier, "The Motive for the Suppliants' Flight", in *Classical Journal*, 57, 1962.

A.J. Podlecki, "Politics in Aeschylus' *Supplices*", in *Classical Folia*, 26, 1972.

J. Lembke, "Aeschylus' *Suppliants*: Design in a Beholder's Eye", in *Arion* (new series), 1, 1973–74.

R.S. Caldwell, "The Psychology of Aeschylus' *Supplices*", in *Arethusa*, 7, 1974.

M. McCall, "The Secondary Choruses in Aeschylus' *Supplices*", in *California Studies in Classical Antiquity*, 9, 1976.

A.H. Sommerstein, "Notes on Aeschylus' *Suppliants*", in *Bulletin of the Institute of Classical Studies* (London), 24, 1977.

*   *   *

Fleeing Egypt and the threat of forced marriage to the 50

sons of Aegyptus, the 50 daughters of Danaus escape with their father to their ancestral Greek city of Argos, to claim sanctuary in a grove outside the city gates under the Greek institution of suppliancy, or religious asylum. King Pelasgus of Argos considers their case and, after consultation with the people, undertakes to guarantee the refugees' safety. But Aegyptus and his sons are in pursuit, an armada at their backs. A herald demands that Pelasgus surrender the fugitives; Pelasgus refuses, and the suppliants are transferred to the protection of the city. For now they are safe; but Aegyptus is unlikely to be deterred for long.

Until 1952, few doubted that this play was the earliest European drama we possess. The static stage action, severely minimal plot, rudimentary use of the second actor, and (above all) the central role assigned to the chorus: all these seemed primitive features within our comfortably linear evolutionary picture of the early Greek stage, arguing for a date close to the start of Aeschylus's career in the 490's. 36 letters on a postage-stamp scrap of papyrus have torn that neat picture to tatters. The *Suppliants* is one of Aeschylus's very last plays, winning first prize against Sophocles no earlier than 466, with 463 marginally the likeliest date. Forced to reappraise this play as a work of Aeschylus's maturity, scholars have found in hindsight all manner of reasons to have suspected better all along, and, more importantly, have come to recognise artistic choice rather than historical necessity in its chief dramatic decisions.

The play was apparently the first of a connected tetralogy. In the traditional sequel, the Danaids were eventually married off to the sons of Aegyptus, but on their wedding night took their revenge in a gruesome conspiracy, all but one (Hypermnestra) murdering their husbands in their marriage-beds. Our only substantial clue as to how Aeschylus treated the story is an astonishing fragment of the final tragedy, *Danaids*, spoken by Aphrodite, goddess of sex, describing how her power extends to the natural world as a force for universal generation. An influential view imagines the murder (at the end of play two, or between two and three) followed by an *Oresteia*-style, divine trial scene, in which Aphrodite bears witness to the cosmic implications of the bond of marriage violated in the myth. These are enjoyable fantasies, but we are still stranded with what is effectively the first act of a monumental work whose main punch was apparently in its last.

Even so, what we have is impressive, often dazzling, choral theatre—even without the old theory, inspired by a witlessly literal-minded ancient commentator, that the 50 Danaids were played by a chorus of 50 with a supplementary chorus of 50 handmaidens. The dominant tableau is a classic and characteristic Aeschylean stroke of minimalist spectacular: the chorus flocking around the stage altar in the orchestra (there was probably no stage building at this time), framed by the unmoving images of the gods as their pursuers draw nearer to this last desperate refuge. Such suppliant scenes were much imitated in later tragedy, particularly by Euripides; they remained one of the boldest, most highly-charged patterns of large-scale action available to the Greek theatre.

The dramatic transformations of this tableau are patterned, as in other Aeschylus plays earlier than the *Oresteia*, around the movements of the two solo actors, and the epic off-stage action they mediate to the visible play. The respective arrivals of the Argive chariots and the Egyptian armada are each watched and narrated to the chorus, and audience, by Danaus; the city's decision on the suppliants is relayed by Pelasgus and Danaus from the (cheerfully anachronistic) democratic assembly; and these two mighty off-stage multitudes, balanced carefully against one another by an elaborate series of visual and situational echoes, come finally into direct conflict through the on-stage clash of the city's agent Pelasgus with the Egyptians' herald. The stage and chorus become the eye of a dramatic hurricane that sucks in whole nations as they helplessly watch and react, modulating from suicidal desperation to ecstatic hope, from panic and terror to joy. Only with the closing lines are the suppliants crucially allowed to transfer at last from the religious sanctuary, and the care of the gods, to the city of Argos itself, and the protection of the community.

Throughout all this, and with typically Aeschylean, metaphoric layering, the religious and political tensions are steeped in the language of sexual and military violence, the threatened mass rape of the Danaids escalating to the possible violation of the religious and communal codes of the *polis*. Already, as the stakes rise, there are intimations of the developments to come; unfortunately, we cannot trace their treatment in detail. But the play remains the most ambitious essay we have in that most extraordinary and alien Greek performance resource, the tragic chorus. If we know less about its early form than we once thought, there have been plenty of compensating lessons to occupy us instead.

—N.J. Lowe

SUPPLICES.   See THE SUPPLIANTS.

THE SWAGGERING SOLDIER.   See THE BRAGGART SOLDIER.

T

TABLE BY THE WINDOW.   See **SEPARATE TABLES.**

TABLE NUMBER SEVEN.   See **SEPARATE TABLES.**

TALES FROM THE VIENNA WOODS
(Geschichten aus dem Wiener Wald)
by Ödön von Horváth

First Publication: Berlin, 1931.
First Production: Deutsches Theater, Berlin, 2 November
   1931.

Translations
Tales from the Vienna Woods, translated by Christopher
   Hampton, London, 1977.

Criticism
(For general works on the author, see *Playwrights* volume)

Books:
Traugott Krischke (ed.), *Materialien zu Ödön von Horváths
   "Geschichten aus dem Wiener Wald"*, Frankfurt, 1972.
Traugott Krischke (ed.), *Horváths "Geschichten aus dem
   Wiener Wald"*, Frankfurt, 1983.

Articles:
Peter Handke, "Totenstille beim Heurigen", in edition of
   Geschichten aus dem Wiener Wald, Frankfurt, 1971.
Charles N. Genno, "'Kitsch' Elements in Horváth's
   Geschichten aus dem Wiener Wald", in *German Quarterly*,
   45, 1972.
Peter Stenberg, "The Last of the Magicians. . .: Horváth's
   Zauberkönig and His Ancestors", in *German Life & Letters*,
   28, 1975.
Hans U. Lindken, "Illusion und Wirklichkeit in Ödön von
   Horváths Volksstück *Geschichten aus dem Wiener Wald*", in
   Modern Austrian Literature, vol.9 no.1, 1976.
Dirk Bruns, "Horváth's Renewal of the Folk Play and the
   Decline of the Weimar Republic", in *New German Critique*,
   18, 1979.
Herbert Kaiser, "Unterrichtsreihe: Zur Deformation sozialer
   Vernunft: Das Problem von Fremd- und Selbstbestimmung
   in bürgerlicher Literatur des 19. und 20. Jahrhunderts", in
   Literatur für Leser, 2, 1979.
Peter Wapnewski, "Ödön von Horváth und seine *Geschichten
aus dem Wiener Wald*: Dem Andenken Peter Szondis
gewidmet", in his *Zumutungen: Essays zur Literatur des 20.
Jahrhunderts*, Düsseldorf, 1979.
Helmut Arntzen, "Komödie mit Musik: Ödön von Horváth:
   Geschichten aus dem Wiener Wald", in his *Zur Sprache
   kommen*, Münster, 1983.
Russell E. Brown, "The Death of Baby Leopold: Hostility to
   Children in Horváth's *Geschichten aus dem Wiener Wald*",
   in *German Life & Letters*, 40, 1987.
Hans Richter, "Eine moderne Gretchentragödie? Ödön von
   Horváths *Geschichten aus dem Wiener Wald*", in his *Ver-
   wandeltes Dasein: Über deutschsprachige Literatur von
   Hauptmann bis heute*, Berlin, 1987.

*   *   *

Ödön von Horváth's most successful play, *Tales from the
Vienna Woods* (1931), self-consciously derives from the traditional genre of Viennese Popular Theatre (*The Magic Flute* by
Schikaneder and Mozart is an early example), yet it represents
an ironic, modern altercation with that tradition. In terms of its
subject-matter and treatment, it is a tragicomedy, but one
which employs a deliberately trivial, conventional plot which
serves as an artifice through which the subtler social and
political drama is explored. Horváth works with a finely
gauged combination of realism and stylization, in which the
use of musical quotation pointedly and ironically underscores
the text.

The action is set in the drab suburbs of petit-bourgeois
Vienna and involves a naïve, pious young girl who falls for an
indifferent loafer by whom she has a child. Rejected by her
father, jilted by her lover, and without any material support,
she becomes a stripper in a nightclub, where she is convicted of
theft. On her release, she finds that her child, who had been
entrusted to her lover's malevolent grandmother, has died. In
dumb defeat she sinks into the brutish arms of her original
fiancé, the butcher next door, to the sentimental strains of the
titular waltz by Strauss.

The contrast and interplay between kitsch and convention,
the brutal and the sentimental, the menacing and the banal,
serve both an historical and a dramatic purpose: they are sharp
reflections of the unwholesome ideology of Viennese society in
the early 1930's, and they inform the dialogue with that
subversive irony and perspicacity which signals the pervasive
critical intelligence of the playwright. This more muted drama
of latent tensions consists of a sequence of skilfully orchestrated dialogues which constitute the three "parts" of the play.
There is no dramatic build-up to a climax; on the contrary,
Horváth prefers to use the device of repetition (through
recurrent motifs, snatches of dialogue and tunes) so as to
intensify a helpless sense of stagnation, passivity, and the
conservative rut.

The 21 characters, all of them unqualified mediocrities, are clearly stereotyped; each is a recognizable Viennese type, stamped by the limitations imposed by class, profession, and social schooling. Only the North German student, Erich, with his militant fascism, and the Mister from New York, as the unctuous vessel of Viennese nostalgia, are seen as extraneous contrasts. The retired cavalry captain, the "Zauberkönig", like the so-called "Baronin" (in reality a procuress) are the shabby representatives of "the old school", remnants of a society that uses titles to disguise the sorry truth. All Horváth's characters engage in a relaxed, conventional, semi-educated form of speech which is laced with cliché, popular sayings, or literary allusion; all intended to lend an air of sophistication. Yet it is the playwright's ironic design to "unmask the consciousness" of the speaker (Horváth's own phrase) by betraying hidden thoughts and disguised intentions. Such use of language goes further: it lays bare the very mentality or ideological basis beneath. The device is assisted by the strategic interpolation of momentary silence which serves to heighten awareness of the implicit. One might call this original approach to pacing dialogue the "drama of pregnant silences": the text persistently challenges the critical attention of the audience.

Each scene is set in, or around, the city of Vienna, and the copious stage directions are both a precise guide to actors and a commentary. They allude to visual, aural, and atmospheric elements as well as offering clear indications as to gesture, movement, tone, or mood. The setting alternates from the Wachau to a "quiet street in the eighth District", to the Vienna Woods, then to the banks of the Danube, and back again to the eighth district. The specified milieu and its attendant clichéd associations of class and lifestyle are exploited with a distinctive mixture of realism and critical irony. The opening domestic scene has a sinister undercurrent of ill-disguised egotism and avarice, as Alfred the wastrel tries to wheedle money out of his suspicious and cunning granny. The courteous, public manners of the staid inhabitants of suburbia contrast starkly with their vulgar and brutal outbursts whenever they drop their guard. The picnic excursion to celebrate Alfred and Marianne's betrothal turns into a minor scandal, as infidelity is exposed to the leering delight of the guests.

The second part consists of seven, compact, contrasting scenes which variously explore the predicament of the penniless couple and their attempts to find a way out. The last, entitled "In St. Stephen's Cathedral" (which shows Marianne in the confessional) is a stark, moving recollection of that other penitent, Gretchen, in the cathedral scene of Goethe's *Faust*. The drunken revelry of the scene at Maxim's nightclub is a brutal exposure of the baser impulses in the human species, once bourgeois respectability has been discarded; animal imagery abounds in this grotesque social bestiary where vulgarity and brutishness all but stifle the comedy. The invidious menace of every kind of human nastiness lurks beneath the most "innocent" gesture in Horváth's play, from Alfred's suspicious glare at his mother as he clutches his knife in the opening scene, to the grandmother's fiendish jingling of the dead baby's toy at the end.

The importance of mime, studied gesture, and expressive pauses between spoken lines give the play that vivid theatricality which is so characteristic of the tradition of Austrian theatre from Grillparzer, Schnitzler, and Hofmannsthal to Hochwälder, Handke, and Bernhard. Unlike Brecht, with whom he is often contrasted, Horváth's theatre is not didactic, and neither does it attempt to show that the world may be changed; it represents, rather, a subtle form of social and psychological realism imbued with its own subversive irony. In this respect especially (yet in others too), Horváth stands

closer to Chekhov, as one emphatic self-avowal indicates: "For me there is but one law and that is truth".

—Alexander Stillmark

TAMBURLAINE THE GREAT
Tamburlaine the Great, Part One
Tamburlaine the Great, Part Two
by Christopher Marlowe

Tamburlaine the Great (both parts)
First Publication: London, 1590.

Tamburlaine the Great, Part One
First Production: London, c.1587–88; earliest recorded production, by the Admiral's Men, London, 30 August 1594.

Tamburlaine the Great, Part Two
First Production: London, c.1587–88; earliest recorded production, by the Admiral's Men, 19 December 1594.

Editions

Tamburlaine the Great, in *Tamburlaine the Great; Dr. Faustus*, edited by Allan Neilson, London, 1924.
Tamburlaine the Great, edited by Una Ellis-Fermor, London, 1931; revised edition, 1951.
Tamburlaine the Great, edited by Tatiana M. Wolf, London, 1964.
Tamburlaine the Great, edited by John D. Jump, Lincoln (Nebraska) and London, 1967 (Regents Renaissance Drama Series).
Tamburlaine the Great, in *Christopher Marlowe: The Complete Plays*, edited by J.B. Steane, Harmondsworth, 1969.
Tamburlaine the Great, edited by J.W. Harper, London, 1971.
"Tamburlaine the Great": Part One and Part Two: Text and Major Criticism, edited by Irving Ribner, New York, 1974.
Tamburlaine the Great, edited by J.S. Cunningham, Manchester and Baltimore, Maryland, 1981.

Criticism
(For general works on the author, see *Playwrights* volume)

Books:
Roy W. Battenhouse, *Marlowe's "Tamburlaine": A Study in Renaissance Moral Philosophy*, Nashville, Tennessee, 1941.
Frank B. Fieler, *"Tamburlaine, Part I" and Its Audience*, Gainesville, Florida, 1962.
Siegfried Wyler, *Der Begriff der Macht in Christopher Marlowes "Tamburlaine I"*, Zurich and St. Gallen, 1965.
William A. Armstrong, *Marlowe's "Tamburlaine": The Image and the Stage*, Hull, 1966.
Lawrence M. Bemquist, *The Tripartite Structure of Christopher Marlowe's "Tamburlaine" Plays and "Edward II"*, Salzburg, 1975.
James Robinson Whitworth, *Marlowe, Tamburlaine, and Magic*, Athens, Ohio, 1976.
George L. Geckle, *"Tamburlaine" and "Edward II"*, London, 1988 (Text and Performance Series).

Articles:

Leslie Spence, "The Influence of Marlowe's Sources on *Tamburlaine I*", in *Modern Philology*, 24, 1926.

Leslie Spence, "Tamburlaine and Marlowe", in *Publications of the Modern Language Association* [*PMLA*], 42, 1927.

Carrol Camden Jr., "Tamburlaine: The Choleric Man", in *Modern Language Notes*, 44, 1929.

Willard Thorp, "The Ethical Problem in Marlowe's *Tamburlaine*", in *Journal of English and Germanic Philology*, 29, 1930.

Roy W. Battenhouse, "Tamburlaine, the Scourge of God", in *Publications of the Modern Language Association* [*PMLA*], 56, 1941.

Helen L. Gardner, "The Second Part of *Tamburlaine the Great*", in *Modern Language Review*, 37, 1942.

Thomas C. Izard, "The Principal Source for Marlowe's *Tamburlaine*", in *Modern Language Notes*, 58, 1943.

Johnstone Parr, "Tamburlaine's Malady", in *Publications of the Modern Language Association* [*PMLA*], 59, 1944.

T.M. Pearce, "Tamburlaine's 'Discipline to his Three Sonnes': An Interpretation of *Tamburlaine, Part II*", in *Modern Language Quarterly*, 15, 1945.

Hallett Smith, "*Tamburlaine* and the Renaissance", in *Elizabethan Studies and Other Essays: In Honor of George F. Reynolds*, Boulder, Colorado, 1945.

Johnstone Parr, "The Horoscope of Mycetes in Marlowe's *Tamburlaine I*", in *Philological Quarterly*, 25, 1946.

Hugh Dick, "*Tamburlaine* Sources Once More", in *Studies in Philology*, 46, 1949.

Jean Jacquot, "La Pensée de Marlowe dans *Tamburlaine the Great*", in *Études anglaises*, 6, 1953.

Irving Ribner, "The Idea of History in Marlowe's *Tamburlaine*", in *English Literary History*, 20, 1954.

Mary Ellen Rickey, "Astronomical Imagery in *Tamburlaine*", in *Renaissance Papers*, 1954.

Katherine Lever, "The Image of Man in *Tamburlaine, Part I*", in *Philological Quarterly*, 35, 1956.

Charles Brooks, "*Tamburlaine* and Attitudes Toward Women", in *English Literary History*, 24, 1957.

Donald Peet, "The Rhetoric of *Tamburlaine*", in *English Literary History*, 26, 1959.

Michael Quinn, "The Freedom of Tamburlaine", in *Modern Language Quarterly*, 21, 1960.

Robert Kimbrough, "*Tamburlaine*: A Speaking Picture in Tragic Glass", in *Renaissance Drama*, 7, 1964.

Clifford Leech, "The Structure of *Tamburlaine*", in *Tulane Drama Review*, 8, 1964.

Peter V. Lepage, "The Search for Godhead in Marlowe's *Tamburlaine*", in *College English*, 26, 1965.

Susan Richards, "Marlowe's *Tamburlaine II*: A Drama of Death", in *Modern Language Quarterly*, 26, 1965.

G.I. Duthie, "The Dramatic Structure of Marlowe's *Tamburlaine the Great: Parts One and Two*", in *Archiv*, 203, 1966.

John P. Cutts, "Tamburlaine: As Fierce Achilles was", in *Comparative Drama*, 1, 1967.

Robert Cockcroft, "Emblematic Irony: Some Possible Significances of Tamburlaine's Chariot", in *Renaissance and Modern Studies*, 12, 1968.

David Daiches, "Language and Action in Marlowe's *Tamburlaine*", in *More Literary Essays*, Edinburgh, 1968.

Marion B. Smith, "The Structure of Meaning in *Tamburlaine, Part I*", in *Studies in Philology*, 67, 1970.

Nancy J. Leslie, "Tamburlaine in the Theatre: Tartar, Grand Guignol, or Janus?", in *Renaissance Drama*, 1971.

Kenneth Friedenreich, "'Huge Greatness Overthrown': The Fall of Empire in Marlowe's *Tamburlaine* Plays", in *Clio*, 1, 1972.

Roy W. Battenhouse, "Protestant Apologetics and the Sub-Plot of *2 Tamburlaine*", in *English Literary Renaissance*, 3, 1973.

Helen Watson-Williams, "The Power of Words: A Reading of *Tamburlaine the Great, Part One*", in *English*, 22, 1973.

Roy W. Battenhouse, "The Relation of *Henry V* to *Tamburlaine*", in *Shakespeare Survey*, 27, 1974.

Claude J. Summers, "Tamburlaine's Opponents and Machiavelli's *Prince*", in *English Language Notes*, 11, 1974.

James Maloon, "From Beast to Mad Beast: A Further Look at Tyrone Guthrie's *Tamburlaine*", in *Theatre Survey*, 18, 1977.

J.S. Cunningham and Roger Warren, "*Tamburlaine the Great* Rediscovered", in *Shakespeare Survey*, 31, 1978.

George L. Geckle, "The National Theatre Production of *Tamburlaine*", in *Educational Theatre Journal*, 30, 1978.

Richard A. Martin, "Marlowe's *Tamburlaine* and the Language of Romance", in *Publications of the Modern Language Association* [*PMLA*], 93, 1978.

R.B. Reed, "Christopher Marlowe's *Tamburlaine*: Its Topicality and Its Tone", in *Cithara*, 17, 1978.

Samuel Schuman, "Minor Characters and the Thematic Structure of Marlowe's *Tamburlaine II*", in *Modern Language Studies*, 8, 1978.

Sibyl Truchet, "*Tamburlaine* on the Modern Stage", in *Cahiers études*, 13, 1978.

Michael J.B. Allen, "Tamburlaine and Plato: A Colon, a Crux", in *Research Opportunities in Renaissance Drama*, 23, 1980.

Audrey Ekdahl Davidson and Clifford Davidson, "The Function of Rhetoric, Marlowe's *Tamburlaine*, and 'Reciprical Illumination'" in *Ball State University Forum*, 22, 1981.

Peter Berek, "Tamburlaine's Weak Sons: Imitation as Interpretation Before 1593", in *Renaissance Drama*, 13, 1982.

Frances J. Chivers, "Marlowe's *Tamburlaine*: Ironic Portrait of Fortune's Fool", in *Selected Papers from the West Virginia Shakespeare and Renaissance Association*, 7, 1982.

Thomas McAllindon, "*Tamburlaine the Great* and *The Spanish Tragedy*: The Genesis of a Tradition", in *Huntington Library Quarterly*, 45, 1982.

Johannes H. Birringer, "Marlowe's Violent Stage: 'Mirrors' of Honor in *Tamburlaine*", in *English Literary History*, 51, 1984.

Richard Levin, "The Contemporary Perception of Marlowe's *Tamburlaine*", in *Medieval and Renaissance Drama in England*, 1, 1984.

Ian Gaskell, "*2 Tamburlaine*: Marlowe's 'War Against the Gods'", in *English Studies in Canada*, 11, 1985.

Herbert B. Rothschild Jr., "The Conqueror-Hero, the Beseiged City, and the Development of an Elizabethan Protagonist", in *South Central Review*, 3, 1986.

Mark Thornton Burnett, "*Tamburlaine* and the Renaissance Concept of Honour", in *Studia Neophilologica*, 59, 1987.

Mark Thornton Burnett, "Tamburlaine: An Elizabethan Vagabond", in *Studies in Philology*, 84, 1987.

Mathew N. Proser, "*Tamburlaine* and the Art of Destruction", in *University of Hartford Studies in Literature*, 20, 1988.

Anthony Brian Taylor, "Tamburlaine's Doctrine of Strife and John Calvin", in *English Language Notes*, 27, 1989.

David R. Thurn, "Sights of Power in *Tamburlaine*", in *English Literary Renaissance*, 19, 1989.

* * *

Tamburlaine, a humble shepherd, helps Cosroe to win the Persian crown from Mycetes, Cosroe's brother. After defeating Cosroe and securing the crown for himself, Tamburlaine vanquishes Bajazeth, Emperor of the Turks, and captures Damascus. Only the Soldan of Egypt escapes death, as he is the father of Zenocrate with whom Tamburlaine has fallen in love. *Part Two* dramatizes the decline of Tamburlaine's bloody empire. The violence continues (captive kings are forced to pull Tamburlaine's chariot), but Zenocrate dies, and increasingly powerful enemies emerge. The death of Tamburlaine concludes the play; but Marlowe does not make clear if the hero's demise is a result of divine punishment.

In terms of their linguistic ability, the enemies ranged against Tamburlaine are weak and inadequate. Feeble puns and touchy expostulations mark Mycetes' speech, and he elects others to communicate his petty requests. In contrast, Tamburlaine is indisputably the master of language; he commands through words, he seduces with his lofty claims, he demands acknowledgement when he delivers his captivating declarations. A bold, iambic stress and a strongly alliterative emphasis characterize Marlowe's verse, and they lend the drama a muscularity of metre, an innovation of utterance, and a vigour of poetic announcement.

Marlowe's language in this play is also capable of a variety of dramatic effects; it is by no means uniform or unchanging, as has sometimes been claimed. The mood can shift abruptly, as when Tamburlaine contemplates, in elevated vocabulary, his love for Zenocrate, and then asks if Bajazeth is fed and securely caged. Verse can give way to prose with startling, unsettling results—Zabina responds to her husband's death by braining herself, and her speech collapses into staccato, fragmented, prosaic phrases. The versatility and flexibility of the metre facilitate changes of pace, too; for example, Tamburlaine, to come to terms with Zenocrate's death, schools his sons in the art of war, and his instructions are rushed, breathless, and frantically articulated.

Featuring prominently among the play's images are crowns. The object of Tamburlaine's restless lust for dominion is "the sweet fruition of an earthly crown" which perfectly accords with his need to subdue opponents and to bring kingdoms under his rule. Crowns connote identity in *Tamburlaine the Great*, and references to them often accompany catalogues of names and titles. In wearing crowns, Tamburlaine is adopting and fashioning for himself new, respectable identities, concealing the fact of his low origins, and attempting to obscure his status as a social upstart. With crowns there are invariably geographical and cosmic allusions, granting to the play a vastness of scope, a grandeur of stature, a spaciousness of subject.

The foregoing discussion might suggest that the appeal of *Tamburlaine the Great* is merely stylistic. But the drama is simultaneously rich in visual impact and draws much of its power from elaborate tableaux and stage spectacles. The first entrance of the hero shows his soldiers weighed down with plundered treasure; it is a compelling image of Tamburlaine's dedication to brigandage and conquest. Tamburlaine himself wears violently contrasting colours (which signify his mood) during the course of his campaigns; white, red, and black. At the end of *Part One* the bodies of Bajazeth and Zabina litter the stage, and their presence questions Tamburlaine's expression of heroic aspirations. The actor who plays Tamburlaine also needs to impress visually as there are repeated references to his grim countenance and awesome appearance.

Despite the spectacles, there is not a wealth of action or movement; the play is essentially static, and the focus of attention is upon the rhetoric and the formalized groupings of characters and events. The drama is structured in terms of Tamburlaine's ever more daring achievements and the steadily increasing powers of his enemies. Mycetes is a sorry monarch, but those who come after (Bajazeth, the Soldan of Eygyt, and Callapine) exhibit qualities of leadership and eloquence that invite comparison with Tamburlaine himself. Symmetrical pairings are the basis of Marlowe's structural technique: he frequently places together speeches of equal length in which characters join to express the same opinion or argue to assert their own, wilful convictions.

The stylistic range and the spectacular character of *Tamburlaine the Great* are testimony to its unprecedented importance. Indeed, Marlowe declares his departure from established dramatic norms when he betrays his contempt for contemporary playwrights in the prologue, labelling them disparagingly as "rhyming mother-wits". It is, then, an audacious play, and chief among its challenges is Tamburlaine, the Marlovian overreacher. A particularly difficult problem for an audience is how to judge the protagonist: although he is clearly a tyrant who appals and terrifies, he is, at the same time, an exciting figure who insists upon admiration and urges participation in the proud display of a heightened poetic sensibility.

A political radicalism informs Marlowe's play as well as a dramatic inventiveness. Tamburlaine's enemies are the voices of orthodoxy (they accuse him of being a thief, an *arriviste*, and a threat to the social order), but they are also fools and hypocrites who deserve the humiliating fates visited upon them. Tamburlaine destroys these forces of opposition with a callous indifference, ignoring pleas for clemency and warnings of divine retribution. When, in a final display of hubris, he burns the Koran, he is afflicted with a fatal illness. His consequent death may be related to his irreverence, or may be coincidental. In encouraging both responses to Tamburlaine, Marlowe espouses official points of view even as he subjects them to critical scrutiny.

—Mark Thornton Burnett

THE TAMING OF THE SHREW
by William Shakespeare

First Publication: As *The Taming of a Shrew*, London, 1594 [possibly a "memorial reconstruction"]; as *The Taming of the Shrew*, in the First Folio, London, 1623 [with variants, and missing later Christopher Sly episodes].

First Production: Probably before 1592; earliest recorded production, at Newington Butts Theatre, 11 June 1594.

Editions
The Taming of the Shrew, edited by Sir Arthur Quiller-Couch and John Dover Wilson, Cambridge, 1928 (The New Shakespeare).
The Taming of the Shrew, edited by Richard Hosley, Baltimore, Maryland, 1964.
The Taming of the Shrew, edited by Robert Heilman, New York, 1965 (Signet Classic Shakespeare).
The Taming of the Shrew, edited by G.R. Hibbard, Harmondsworth, 1968 (New Penguin Shakespeare).
The Taming of the Shrew, edited by Brian Morris, London, 1981 (Arden Shakespeare).

The Taming of the Shrew: Stratford-Upon-Avon, 1982 (Royal Shakespeare Company)

The Taming of the Shrew, edited by H.J. Oliver, Oxford, 1982 (Oxford Shakespeare).
The Taming of the Shrew, edited by Ann Thompson, Cambridge, 1984 (New Cambridge Shakespeare).

Criticism
(For general works on the author, see *Playwrights* volume)

Books:
Tori Haring-Smith, *From Farce to Metadrama: A Stage History of "The Taming of the Shrew", 1594–1983*, Westport, Connecticut, 1985.
Harold Bloom (ed.), *Shakespeare's "The Taming of the Shrew"*, New York, New Haven (Connecticut), and Philadelphia, 1988 (Modern Critical Interpretations).
Mark W. Scott and Sandra L. Williamson, *"The Taming of the Shrew"*, in *Shakespearian Criticism, 9*, Detroit, Illinois, 1989 [anthology of criticism].

Articles:
For information on the many articles about *The Taming of the Shrew*, see the bibliographies listed in the *Playwrights* volume and the annual Shakespeare Bibliography in *Shakespeare Quarterly*, published by the Folger Shakespeare Library, Washington D.C. (1950–).

*   *   *

The central action of this play can, in terms of bare events, easily be summarised. Petruchio arrives in Padua to seek his fortune by marrying money. With that ambition he is prepared to take on a woman, Katherina, universally condemned as a "shrew". He is not, however, content to leave her in her shrewishness, but insists on "taming" her unruly and anti-social behaviour. This he accomplishes, producing her at the end of the play as a reformed model wife, prepared not only to obey her husband, but also to preach to other women the value of obedience.

Within this simple plot the possibilities of interpretation seem to be enormously wide. Is Petruchio really an unscrupulous fortune-hunter, or does he conceal a deeper, more sensitive, personality beneath his crudely mercenary behaviour? Is Katherina depicted simply as a stock type, a "shrew", or as a woman caught in the throes of a psychological illness? Do Katherina and Petruchio actually (as many productions try to suggest) fall in love with one another immediately, so that the rest of the action is truly an elaborate game? Is Petruchio's "taming" of Kate a sophisticated technique of psychotherapy, or a mixture of terrorism and torture? Does Kate deliver her final speech of submission seriously, as a tribute to the patriarchal power that has delivered her? Or, is that speech rather an ironic offer of love to Petruchio merely designed to "give her man what he wants"? Is it a statement Kate has been brainwashed or terrorised into providing, or an imposed task that the woman is obliged to perform, though obviously resenting every minute of her public humiliation?

All these interpretations are to be found in criticism of *The Taming of the Shrew*, and in its stage history. One of the reasons for this complexity of response may be that the play actually has a rather complex organisation. It is often played as if the main plot, the taming story, stood alone (one of the best-known versions of the play, the film directed by Franco Zeffirelli starring Richard Burton and Elizabeth Taylor, virtually excludes everything else). For many years the most popular version was an adaptation by David Garrick called, simply, *Catherine and Petruchio*. But in Shakespeare's play—

text the story of Katherina and Petruchio does not stand alone: it contains a "sub-plot", and is *contained by* a framing device constructed around the figure of Christopher Sly, a drunken tinker who is fooled into believing that he is a lord, and that the play is being privately performed in his honour. The Sly-frame is often cut or its impact minimalised, with the effect of turning the play into a naturalistic comedy (with varying degrees of farce) in which issues of marriage and sexual politics are dramatised (with more or less seriousness) by actors presenting themselves as real characters within a convincingly realistic, social and domestic setting.

Retention of the Sly-frame, however, creates an entirely different dramatic medium: for the "inner play" is designated by that frame as an elaborate hoax—part of a series of tricks calculated to fool a poor man into a temporary illusion of riches and power; a contrived fantasy designed (unsuccessfully, as it proves) to keep a drowsy itinerant awake. Kept entire, the Sly-frame confronts the audience with a continual, *unforgettable* reminder that the actors of the *Shrew* play are a fortuitously gathered bunch of travelling players capriciously engaged to enact a whimsical nobleman's practical joke.

As the servants and players constitute Christopher Sly's reality—his awareness of his poverty, his geographical orientation, his expulsion at the hands of the hostess—as "abject lowly dreams", the spectators may begin to ask themselves if the play is not similarly suppressing and occluding their own reality and replacing it with a persuasive fantasy, structurally similar to the fantasies of masculine wish-fulfilment offered to the intoxicated, on-stage, surrogate spectator.

If the Sly-frame is incorporated, the *Shrew* becomes a play with three separable centres of action, or three interwoven plots: the gulling of Christopher Sly, the wooing/taming of Katherina by Petruchio, and the courtship romance built around the figure of Bianca, Katherina's sister. The Bianca plot allows for a sustained contrast between the characters and actions of the two sisters, which becomes at certain points (especially with the rather arbitrary introduction of Hortensio's widow) a deployment and interplaying of different modes of feminine behaviour. In more naturalistic productions much can be made of the manifest and violent sibling rivalry between the two sisters; while more feminist productions need the presence of other women, either to indicate that Katherina's history is no isolated eccentricity but a general condition; or as a means of establishing and evaluating female reactions to Katherina's "shrewishness" and to her "taming".

The most important function of the Bianca-plot lies, however, in its emphasis on disguise and illusion; a thematic strategy which operates both at the narrative level of romance and comic, courtship disguises, and at the psychological level of complicating an audience's perspective on Bianca (does she prove the verier shrew of the two?) and on Katherina and Petruchio (are they truly what they seem?). The thematic context of pretence, dissimulation, and illusion broached by the Sly-frame is thus played with at various different levels. The travelling players assume the disguises of Bianca, Katherina, and Petruchio, whose roles may themselves mask "true identity" behind a facade of deceptive conformity or outrageously unconventional behaviour. Modern actors assume the roles of Elizabethan actors who assume roles like Lucentio and Hortensio, which then require further levels of duplicitous disguising as they assume the identities of Cambio and Litio. A focus on the Bianca-plot can thus disclose in the *Shrew* a dramatic structure of some intricacy: not in terms of delicately interwoven tissues of metaphor or of elaborate psychological counterpointing of character, but in terms of a vertiginously Pirandellian interaction of theatrical illusion and dramatic "reality". In such a dramatic context, no simple ideology of male supremacy and female subordination is likely to survive for very long.

In terms of its production history, *The Taming of the Shrew* demonstrates these internal conflicts and ambiguities in the form of widely differing ways of representing the Katherina–Petruchio relationship. Throughout the 18th and 19th centuries the emphasis was on broad comedy and farce, with the "taming" idea either accepted as bluff, manly humour or treated as a harmless and good-humoured game. Underpinning such interpretations lie certain assumptions—that the behaviour displayed by Katherina is not acceptable in women, and that a man may legitimately go to considerable lengths of persuasion and force to exact marital obedience—which became increasingly questionable. New views on the position of women and on the nature of marriage enabled new readings and stagings of *The Taming of the Shrew*: Katherina's virago fierceness was increasingly regarded as an admirable type of female strength, and Petruchio's treatment of her—particularly the later scenes at his house, where he deprives her of food, sleep, and liberty—seen as a brutalising form of torture.

—Graham Holderness

TANGO
by Sławomir Mrożek

First Publication: In *Dialog*, 11, 1964; in book form, in *Utwory Sceniczne, 2*, Warsaw, 1973.
First Production: Wspolczesny Theatre, Warsaw, 1964.

Translations
Tango, translated by Ralph Mannheim and Teresa Dzieduscycka, London and New York, 1968.

Criticism
(For general works on the author, see *Playwrights* volume)

Articles:
John Lahr, "Sławomir Mrożek: The Mask of Irony", in *Evergreen Review*, 67, 1969.
C.J. Gianakaris, "Mrożek's *Tango* and Other Savage Comedies", in *Savage Comedy: Structures of Humor*, edited by Kenneth White, Amsterdam, 1978.
Boleslaw Taborski, "Mrożek's *Tango*", in *Slavic and East European Arts*, vol.3 no.1, 1985.

*   *   *

Tango is set in the living-room of the Stomil family, cluttered with mementos of times past. Arthur has returned home from university to find his family in a state of moral and intellectual dissipation. He is determined to restore morality and order, even though Stomil (his father) and Eleanor (his mother) point out that their generation has sacrificed much to overthrow all moral and artistic conventions. Arthur, however, considers his parents' nonconformism as only a new kind of conformism: in order to preserve his right to rebel against previous generations' values, he will become a doctor, marry his fiancée, Ala, in a traditional wedding, and establish a new set of rules of behavior, forcing his family at gunpoint to obey him. But the young man discovers, to his dismay, that a return to the values of the past is impossible: his father refuses to kill the servant Eddie for having an affair with Eleanor; Ala is attracted to the idea of a traditional wedding only because she likes to dress in white; and his grandmother prefers to die rather than be a part of Arthur's world of coerced, traditional morality. The young man himself is not cut out to be a tyrant, unlike Eddie, who kills Arthur when the latter tries to assert his authority and forces the family to dance to his tune as the play ends.

Tango alludes to the political and social history of Poland by using Shakespeare's *Hamlet* as a paradigm for the modern Polish intellectual. Like Hamlet, Arthur is a cerebral young man, faced with a world out of joint which he feels called upon to set right. But, like all intellectuals, he is disposed more towards philosophical speculation than vigorous action. He constantly berates himself for his indecision; instead of actively establishing a new regime he dreams nostalgically of the old order and deludes himself into believing that restoring old forms and ceremonies will also restore traditional values. Arthur, a product of the upheavals of the Western world after World War I, longs for a new order, a structure that would give him moral and political guidance. Tragically, he has nothing to put up against this lack of order but abstract philosophy and empty formality.

Eddie, the former servant and anti-intellectual man of action, steps into the power vacuum and assumes command. He establishes his brand of order, which is autocratic and based on the force of arms, and the rest of the family meekly assents to his rule; old hangers-on like Eugene do so enthusiastically. Paradoxically, the tune they will dance to at Eddie's command is the tango, the dance that symbolized the breaking of all moral traditions to Stomil and his generation.

The literary analogy mirrors an obvious political theme. Poland and the Western world is likened to the Stomil household: Eugene and Eugenia, the grandparents, are senile remnants of *fin de siècle* hedonism; Stomil and Eleanor are the representatives of the amoral and nihilistic generation produced by two world wars; and like many contemporary young people, Ala, Arthur's fiancée, drifts dully and dazed in a society which provides neither stimulation nor support for her. Eddie, the proletarian of simple tastes, and unburdened by traditions and conventional restraints, can, and will, act from simple, egoistical motives, and eventually fill the power vacuum left by a decadent bourgeoisie and an intelligentsia paralyzed by its own values and its incapacity to do more than talk. This is the reason, Mrożek shows, for Hitler's rise to power, for the ascendancy of Stalin in Russia, and for the existence of other communist tyrants in Poland and Eastern Europe. Mrożek's lesson is that unless we forcefully create new values from the chaos of the 20th century, values that will go beyond re-establishing the old, outdated, forms and ceremonies of Western civilization, we will be led a merry dance by the likes of Eddie.

Contrary to Mrożek's earlier plays, *Tango* makes little use of the formal devices of the "theatre of the absurd". The play conforms fully to the conventions of the "well-made" play by adhering strictly to the unities of time, place, and action, and by its traditional organization into introduction, complication, and resolution. Another conventional device, absent from Mrożek's early plays, is the use of proper names for his characters. Still, *Tango* is not a psychological play in which the dramatic interest concentrates on the motivations of the characters. The Stomil household is composed of allegorical figures that mirror contemporary European types. In this sense, *Tango* can be viewed as a modern morality play. Beyond the political allegory, there is the existential level: Arthur is a modern Everyman trying to come to grips with an essentially godless world.

Tango: Wybrzeze Theatre, Sopot, Poland, 1980

Although *Tango* is Mrożek's most conventional play, it contains elements of the modern, anti-illusionist drama—most obviously the catafalque on which Arthur forces Eugenia to lie as a punishment for her violation of his house rules. This exemplifies Arthur's attempt to bury the past. An additional device from the "theatre of the absurd" is the experimental play Stomil puts on at the end of Act II. To a degree it parallels the play-within-the-play from *Hamlet*, but it also demonstrates that, like the tearing down of all social and moral conventions by Stomil's generation, the tearing down of all theatrical conventions by the dramatists of the "theatre of the absurd" has left an uneasy void.

—Franz G. Blaha

TARTUFFE; or, The Imposter (Le Tartuffe; ou, L'Imposteur) by Molière

First Publication: Paris, 1669 [five-act version].
First Production: Versailles, 12 May 1664 [three-act version];
in five-act version, Théâtre du Palais-Royal,
Paris, 5 August 1667.

Editions

Le Tartuffe, edited by H. Ashton, Oxford, 1946.
Le Tartuffe, edited by R.P.L. Ledésert, London, 1949.
Le Tartuffe, edited by Henry Poulaill, Paris, 1951.
"Tartuffe": Mise en scene de Fernand Ledoux, Paris, 1953 (Editions du Seuil).
Le Tartuffe, edited by Pierre Clarac, Paris, 1962.
Le Tartuffe, edited by Jacques Guicharnaud, New York, 1962.
Le Tartuffe, edited by Hugh Gaston Hall, London, 1963.
Le Tartuffe, edited by Raymond Bernex, Paris, 1963.
Le Tartuffe, edited by H.P. Salomon, Paris, 1965.
Le Tartuffe, edited by Hallam Walker, Englewood Cliffs, New Jersey, 1969.
Le Tartuffe, edited by J.-P. Caput, Paris, 1971.
Le Tartuffe, edited by Emile Lavielle, Paris, 1970.
Le Tartuffe, in *Le Tartuffe; Dom Juan; Le Misanthrope*, edited by Georges Couton, Paris, 1973.
Le Tartuffe, edited by J.-P. Collinet, Paris, 1985.

Translations

Tartuffe, translated by Curtis Hidden Page, Leipzig, 1930.
Tartuffe, in *Molière: Eight Plays*, translated by Morris Bishop, New York, 1957.
Tartuffe, translated by Haskell M. Block, New York, 1958.
Tartuffe, translated by Renée Waldinger, New York, 1959.
Tartuffe, in *"The Misanthrope" and Other Plays*, translated by John Wood, Harmondsworth, 1959.
Tartuffe, translated by James L. Rosenberg, San Francisco, 1962.

Tartuffe: The Pit, Barbican Centre, London, 1983 (Royal Shakespeare Company)

Tartuffe, translated by Richard Wilbur, New York, 1963.
Tartuffe, translated by Robert W. Hartle, Indianapolis, 1965.
Tartuffe, in *"Tartuffe" and Other Plays*, translated by Donald M. Frame, New York, 1967.
Tartuffe, translated by Christopher Hampton, London, 1984.

Criticism
(For general works on the author, see *Playwrights* volume)

Books:
Paul Emard, *Tartuffe: Sa Vie, son milieu, et la comédie de Molière*, Paris, 1932.
Henri D'Alméras, *"Le Tartuffe" de Molière*, Paris, 1946.
Hugh Gaston Hall, *Molière: "Tartuffe"*, London, 1960.
Herman P. Salomon, *"Tartuffe" devant l'opinion française*, Paris, 1962.
Jacques Scherer, *Structure de "Tartuffe"*, Paris, 1967; revised edition, 1974.
Robert Horville, *"Le Tartuffe" de Molière*, Paris, 1973.
Jerry Lewis Kasparek, *Molière's "Tartuffe" and the Traditions of Roman Satire*, Chapel Hill, North Carolina, 1977.
Gérard Ferreyrolles, *Molière: "Tartuffe"*, Paris, 1987.

Articles:
Gustave Charlier, "Le Premier *Tartuffe*", in *Acadèmire de Bruxelles*, 2, 1923.
W.G. Moore, "*Tartuffe* and the Comic Principle", in *Modern Language Review*, January 1948.
W.D. Howarth, "The Theme of *Tartuffe* in 18th Century Comedy", in *French Studies*, 4, 1950.
L. Gossman, "Alceste, Orgon, and *Le Ridicule de la vertu*", in *Bucknell Review*, vol.10 no.1, 1961.
Odaric O.F.M. Bouffard, "Tartuffe: Faux Monnayeur en dévotion?", in *Culture*, 23, 1962.
E. Chill, "*Tartuffe*, Religion, and Courtly Culture", in *French Historical Studies*, vol.3 no.2, 1963.
K. Hartley, "Pietro Aretino and Molière", in *AUMLA Journal*, 20, 1963.
R. Mazzara, "Unmasking the Imposter: *Les Lettres provinciales* and *Tartuffe*", in *French Review*, vol.37 no.6, 1964.
A. Cismaru, "Molière's *Tartuffe* in Marivaux's Words", in *Foreign Language Quarterly*, vol.12 no.3, 1965.
Bernard Dupriez, "Tartuffe et la sincérité", in *Études françaises*, vol.1 no.1, 1965.
V. Torpokov, "Stanislavsky Works With *Tartuffe*" [translated by James B. Woodward], in *Drama Survey*, vol.5 no.1, 1966.
Georges Pholien, "Une Défense du *Tartuffe*", in *Marche romane*, 17, 1967.
Gifford P. Orwin, "*Tartuffe* Reconsidered", in *French Review*, 41, 1968.
P.F. Butler, "*Tartuffe* et la direction spirituelle au XVIIe. siècle", in *Modern Miscellany Presented to Eugène Vinaver by Pupils, Colleagues, and Friends*, edited by T.E. Lawrenson, F.E. Sutcliffe, and G.F.A. Gadoffre, Manchester and New York, 1969.
Georges Couton, "Quand Hippocrate colabre avec Molière", in *AUMLA Journal*, 31, 1969.
Georges Couton, "Réflexions sur *Tartuffe* et le péché d'hypocrise, cas-réservé", in *Revue d'histoire littéraire de la France*, 69, 1969.
Lionel Gossman, "Molière and *Tartuffe*: Law and Order in the Seventeenth Century", in *French Review*, 43, 1970.
G.N. Boiadjiev, "*Tartuffe* sur la scène soviétique" [translated by Claude Dossat], in *Europe*, 523–24, 1972.
John Cairncross, "*Tartuffe*, ou Molière hypocrite", in *Revue d'histoire littéraire de la France*, 72, 1972.

Edward D. Montgomery, "Tartuffe: The History and Sense of a Name", in *Modern Language Notes*, May 1973.
Hugh Gaston Hall, "Some Background to Molière's *Tartuffe*", in *Australian Journal of French Studies*, 10, 1973.
Quentin M. Hope, "Place and Setting in *Tartuffe*", in *Publications of the Modern Language Association* [*PMLA*], 89, 1974.
Marcel Gutwirth, "*Tartuffe* and the Mysteries", in *Publications of the Modern Language Association* [*PMLA*], 92, 1977.
P. Muñoz Simonds, "Molière's Satiric Use of the *deus ex machina* in *Tartuffe*", in *Educational Theatre Journal*, 29, 1977.
William J. Beck, "More on Molière's *Tartuffe*", in *Papers on Language and Literature*, 16, 1980.
Rosette Lamont, "Lyubimov's *Tartuffe*", in *Theater*, vol.11 no.3, 1980.
Brian Nicholas, "Is Tartuffe a Comic Character?", in *Modern Language Review*, 75, 1980.
Thérèse Goyet, "Tartuffe parle-t-il chrétien? Essai sur l'emploi des 'termes consacrés' à la scène", in *Mélanges offerts à Georges Couton*, edited by Jean Jehasse and others, Lyons, 1981.
William Jaynes, "Critical Opinion of Cléante in *Tartuffe*", in *Oeuvres & critiques*, vol.6 no.1, 1981.
William John Beck, "Tartuffe: La Fouine de Séville ou simplement une belette de La Fontaine", in *Revue d'histoire du théâtre*, vol.34, no.3, 1982.
Marie-France Hilgar, "*Tartuffe, Tartuffe* toujours recommencé: Les Mises en scène de 1980", in *Papers on French Seventeenth Century Literature*, vol.9 no.16, 1982.
Marie-France Hilgar, "Modern and Post-Modern Interpretations of *Tartuffe*", in *Theatre Journal*, vol.34, no.2, 1982.
Jean-Denis Marzi, "Rupture and Bonding in *Le Tartuffe*", in *Language Quarterly*, vol.22, nos.3–4, 1984.
Michael Spingler, "The King's Play: Censorship and the Politics of Performance in Molière's *Tartuffe*", in *Comparative Drama*, vol.19, no.3, 1985.
Ronald W. Tobin, "*Tartuffe*, texte sacré", in *Dramaturgies: Langages dramatiques*, edited by Jacqueline de Jomaron, Paris, 1986
Andrew J. McKenna, "*Tartuffe*, Representation and Difference", in *Papers on French Seventeenth Century Literature*, vol.16, no.30, 1989.
Peter H. Nurse, "*Tartuffe*, Comedy or Drama?", in *Modern Languages*, vol.70, no.2, 1989.
Henry Phillips, "Molière and *Tartuffe*: Recrimination and Reconciliation", in *French Review*, vol.62, no.5, 1989.

*　　*　　*

Tartuffe was first presented in 1664, in a three-act version which traced the seduction of a wife by a hypocritical priest; it was rapidly banned. It was only in 1669, after a series of re-writings and fruitless attempts to re-establish the play in the repertory, that the ban was finally lifted. In its final five-act form, Tartuffe, a crook and libertine, engineers his way into the household of the credulous Orgon under a guise of piety. Orgon, in spite of the opposition of his brother-in-law, wife, and son, plans to marry his daughter to Tartuffe, and even makes over the whole of his property to him. His eyes are only finally opened when his wife arranges for him to witness the impostor's attempted seduction of her. Meanwhile, Tartuffe has become the owner of Orgon's house, and orders him out of it, contriving even to have him arrested. In the final scene, the King intervenes, defeats the fraud, and Tartuffe is taken to prison.

This is the first of Molière's comedies to focus on a household and to explore in this domestic context the destabilising effects of an obsession. The plot is potentially disturbing, but the dramatist maintains, throughout, a clear comic perspective: Marianne, the dutiful daughter, exists only at the level of stylised theatrical exclamations which give little cause for alarm; Dorine, the pert servant, in her refusal to take seriously the threats posed by either Orgon or Tartuffe, encourages the audience's emotional detachment; and Elmire, Orgon's wife, is as wily as the impostor who seeks to seduce her, and has her husband's interests at heart. Molière borrows characters, themes, and situations from the world of farce—dupe and deceiver, the unpopular marriage, the threat of cuckoldry—but he invests them with a more sophisticated comic effect and significance. By reducing Orgon, for instance, to the level of an automaton, whose responses are as inappropriate as they are inflexible, he suggests both the social abnormality of Orgon's behaviour and the intellectual limitations of his position. This skill is seen too in the dramatist's conception of entire scenes. Orgon's long delay in his hiding-place under the table, as his wife lures Tartuffe ever further into self-disclosure, provides the immediate impact of farce; but it also captures and expresses in a memorable comic image the complex, three-way relationship of husband, wife, and impostor on the shared grounds of cunning and self-deception.

The importance of the play lies not simply in its comic techniques, however, but in Molière's bold and dangerous step to take as his central preoccupation the very sensitive subject of devotion. Tartuffe himself is a particularly original creation, in whom there is a clear discrepancy between his claims to austere piety and his more sensual, selfish, and ambitious nature. In the course of the play, Cleante, Orgon's brother-in-law, openly attacks such displays of holiness which are mere show, and comic effects are derived from those moments when Tartuffe's true nature becomes apparent beneath the facade. However, it is one of the subtleties of Molière's presentation that Tartuffe's language of piety serves not simply to conceal his true self, but also, paradoxically, to reveal it; and his protestations of devotion are shown to have a double purpose—simultaneously to gratify and to justify his desires and designs. At this level, the character's cynical manipulation of language is given a sharp satirical force and he echoes in many respects the biting caricature of the casuistical Jesuit who dominated Pascal's *Lettres provinciales*.

And yet the implications of Molière's portrayal extend further than the exposure of a hypocrite. Tartuffe is comic not simply because he is seen to play a part, but because, in Orgon's household, he does not need to pretend very hard. The comedy is as much about Orgon, the dupe, as it is about Tartuffe, the hypocrite; as much about the nature of credulity as it is about belief. Deceived by Tartuffe, Orgon clings resolutely to his faith in this image of him, and in so doing loses all common sense, all control over his own language, and all understanding of others. Indeed, such is the extent of his obsession that even Tartuffe's open and apt condemnation of himself as a worthless villain is interpreted by Orgon as evidence of his virtue.

The interaction of these two characters is at the core of the play's significance. At one level, they suggest equally extreme views with regard to religion, Tartuffe demonstrating too much compromise with its principles, and Orgon too little; both attitudes are presented as equally untenable and ridiculous. And through this pair, the comedy explores the nature of power and the way it may be manipulated or disguised; Tartuffe uses piety to deceive and control Orgon; Orgon uses piety to dominate—or to try to dominate—his household.

Like all great comedy, *Tartuffe* does not provide simple moral lessons, but offers matter for reflection. The ending in which the King administers punishment to the villain may appear to reaffirm order, and yet, as so often in Molière, this denouement leaves problems unresolved. Tartuffe does not fail because his influence is naturally flawed, but because he is faced with a superior power. There is something essentially flattering and symbolic in the association of royal might with the control of vice, but its awesome intrusion has all the self-conscious unexpectedness and magnificence of the *deus ex machina*. As a consequence, the comedy situates the moral order as much in the world of theatrical tradition as it does in the solid, bourgeois world where the action has taken place. Control over the hypocrite may be possible in comedy; in life there can be less certainty.

—G. Jonathan Mallinson

A TASTE OF HONEY
by Shelagh Delaney

First Publication: London and New York, 1959.
First Production: Theatre Royal, Stratford East, London, 27 May 1958.

Criticism
(For general works on the author, see *Playwrights* volume)

Articles:
J. Noel, "Some Aspects of Shelagh Delaney's Use of Language in *A Taste of Honey*", in *Revue des langues vivantes*, 26, 1960.
A.K. Oberg, "*A Taste of Honey* and the Popular Play", in *Wisconsin Studies in Contemporary Literature*, 7, 1966.
Alessandra Tong, "*A Taste of Honey*: fra modelli e metafore della solitudine", in *Spicilegio moderno*, 1, 1972.

*   *   *

The play opens as Helen, a "semi-whore", and her teenage schoolgirl daughter, Josephine, are moving into a shabby flat in a slum area of Manchester. Soon Helen becomes engaged to her latest boyfriend Peter, a "brash car-salesman" who is ten years her junior. Left to fend for herself even before Helen is married, Jo invites her boyfriend Jimmy, a black naval rating, to stay with her over Christmas. The first act closes with Helen departing to get married, leaving Jo alone in the flat. In the second act Jo invites Geoff, a young homosexual art-student who has been thrown out by his landlady, to move in with her. When he discovers that Jo is pregnant and that her boyfriend has returned to sea, Geoff adopts the role of surrogate mother. He is however ejected rudely by Helen who, after Peter has left her for a "bit of crumpet", returns to her daughter's side.

A summary of the plot of *A Taste of Honey* conveys nothing of its contemporary impact and significance. It was written by a 19-year-old working-class girl from Lancashire, directed by Joan Littlewood, and opened at the Theatre Royal, Stratford East, in May 1958. A play written by one woman and directed by another was still a somewhat unusual circumstance even in the "new" British theatre of the 1950's. Although *A Taste of Honey* is basically realistic in approach and accorded with the current fashion for seedy locations and regional settings and accents, in production the fourth wall convention was abandoned and, during the first act, Helen occasionally addressed comments directly to the audience in the manner of a music-hall entertainer. In addition a live jazz-band played during the scene changes.

More significant than these stylistic devices was, however, the fact that the action of the play was seen solely from the viewpoint of women. Untypically for the theatre of the period the male characters are not the focus of the plot but are introduced when necessary to contribute to the play's exploration of the meaning of motherhood, a theme in itself uncharacteristic of a theatre dominated almost exclusively by male concerns. Centring upon this subject, the play constantly questions and re-evaluates social roles and assumptions. In the opening minutes of Act I Helen asserts that children owe a debt to their parents but later, when she is about to leave for a holiday with her boyfriend Peter, she absolves herself from the need to reciprocate by denying ever having "laid claim to being a proper mother". In one way or another each of the play's relationships is linked with motherhood and even Peter, with his one eye and his fondness for older women, is identified with Oedipus. Jo herself is set to become a mother in consequence of the Christmas spent alone with her boyfriend, but her initial response to pregnancy is that she wants to be neither a mother nor even a woman. She realises that, whatever Helen says to the contrary, mothers do have a responsibility for their children's upbringing, and contends that some women are so irresponsible that they should not be allowed to have any children at all. Indeed, underpinning this examination of motherhood is a belief, expressed repeatedly by Jo, in the sanctity of the individual, and a recognition that the role of mother is not one which all women necessarily find natural. In one of the play's characteristic reversals of role assumptions Geoffrey, in fact, proves to be far more supportive to Jo than was her biological mother, Helen.

Delaney's sympathetic portrayal of such social "outsiders" as gays or blacks differed markedly from their normally comic or patronising treatment by the contemporary British theatre. That is not to say however that homosexuality or race are explored in their own right. Indeed it is significant that, although Jo questions Geoff about what he does with other men, no reference is made to his lovers and he is kept away from any sexual activity during the action of the play. Jo's black lover is presented predominantly as a figure of fantasy—Prince Ossini—an escape from loneliness. "It was only a dream I had", Jo later admits to Geoff. Nevertheless, in contrast to the caricatured figure of Peter, both Geoff and Jimmy are presented as sensitive and caring human beings; a fact which, in itself, must be seen as a positive feature uncharacteristic of the period.

The play was well-received by both critics and the public and transferred in February 1959 to Wyndham's Theatre in London's West End. It was acknowledged as an unsentimental, honest, and vital expression of contemporary relationships: Kenneth Tynan applauded it in the *Observer* for its "smell of living" and called Shelagh Delaney, in retrospect rather prematurely, "a portent". The play offers no explicit message, and the absence of any wider reference to the world outside the flat serves to lead the audience's attention away from ideas and instead focuses it upon the interrelationship between the characters. The play's conclusion, although by no means a resolution of the problematic relationship between Jo and Helen (which one assumes will continue to be dominated by Helen's sexuality and their constant bickering), nevertheless does leave Jo with the understanding and confidence to carry on, and perhaps in time become a better mother than

Helen. "For the first time in my life I feel really important", she tells her mother towards the end of the play, "I feel as though I could take care of you, too!". The play has moved full circle from the uneasy relationship between the two women, through the ultimately unsatisfactory experiences with men, back to the unsentimental recognition that, however fraught it may occasionally be, there is some comfort in the shared bonds of blood and gender.

—D. Keith Peacock

TAOHUA SHAN.   See PEACH BLOSSOM FAN.

TEAHOUSE (Chaguan / Ch'a-kuan)
by Lao She (Shu Sheh-yu)

First Publication: Peking, 1958.
First Production: People's Art Theatre, Peking [Beijing], 29 March 1958.

Translations
Teahouse, translated by John Howard Gibbon, Beijing, 1980.

Criticism

Articles:
Uwe Kräuter, "Opening the Door to a Strange World: *Teahouse* in Europe", in *Chinese Literature*, 3, 1981.
Ying Ruocheng, "Lao She and his *Teahouse*", in *Westerly*, vol.26 no.3, 1981.

*   *   *

Teahouse, (*Chaguan or Ch'a-kuan*) by Lao She takes place in the Yutai Teahouse in Beijing (Peking) during three specific periods: just after the collapse of the reform movement of 1898, soon after the death of President Yuan Shikai in 1916, and not long before the Chinese Communist Party seized power in Peking in 1949. The whole drama is set in the teahouse. The proprietor is Wang Lifa, who commits suicide at the end of the play because he is compelled to surrender the teahouse to a corrupt government official and brothel-owner.

Teahouse belongs to a form of drama which the Chinese designate as *huaju*, or spoken drama. The principal feature is that the dialogue is carried on entirely or almost entirely in speech, not song as in traditional Chinese drama. The form is an import from the West through Japan and did not take root in China until the first decade of the 20th century.

Lao She knew Peking intimately, a fact crucial to his ability to write *Teahouse*, which is really a dramatized documentary of Peking society over the half-century before the Communists came to power. He himself saw the teahouses as "a microcosm of society as a whole". His aim was less to tell a story than to paint the decline and collapse of the corrupt and oppressive old Peking society.

Using the same setting at three widely separated time-periods allows the audience to see the physical changes in one particular institution and the social changes of which it is a part. The play is not only unique, but outstanding in Chinese theatre in the way the idea is put into effect. The disadvantage of the concept is that there are very few characters who appear in all three acts, thus making it difficult to trace through a developing drama as it affects the participants, or to show character development.

One of the characters who does appear in all three acts is the proprietor of Yutai Teahouse, Wang Lifa, and the dramatist has indeed developed his character well from the young, tough, and ambitious youth of the first act, through the hardened and cynical businessman of the second act, to the embittered and worn out old man of the last act.

A much smaller but still dramatically important role which appears in all three acts is that of Kang Shunzi, who first enters as a 15-year-old peasant girl to be sold as a wife to a eunuch. Act I climaxes with her fainting with horror when she sees her husband. She reappears in Act II with the news that the eunuch was allowed by his nephews to starve to death and she herself was thrown out without even a blanket. She has with her a small boy whom the eunuch bought as a son when only one year old. The peasant girl has developed into a bitter but courageous woman, who refuses to be overcome by the hardships which afflict her, and Wang Lifa employs her in the teahouse. But in Act III he is forced, for financial reasons, to let her go. She has developed into a defiant but dignified character, but she accepts that it is not Wang Lifa's fault that disaster has struck and harbours no ill feelings towards him.

Apart from the personality development of Wang Lifa and Kang Shunzi, Lao She's device for maintaining dramatic intensity is to let the son of one period's character appear in the next act. Pockface Liu is "a cruel and treacherous flesh merchant" in his thirties in Act I; it is he who is responsible for the sale of Kang Shunzi to the eunuch. Liu's son, Little Pockface Liu, who is a similar but, if anything, even more ruthless kind of person than his father, appears in Act III. One of his first announcements, made almost proudly, is that his father, who "didn't really amount to much", had been seized and had his head chopped off right on the street outside the teahouse. No reason is given for this injustice. Little Pockface Liu's role in the drama is to arrange for the sale of the Yutai Teahouse, thus leading to Wang Lifa's suicide.

In the sense that it revolves around the disintegration of the old society, this drama is clearly political and supportive of the Chinese Communist Party. It is strongly implied in Act III that Kang Shunzi's bought son has joined the Communists. On the other hand, they do not loom large in the dialogue and are rarely mentioned.

Lao She quite deliberately uses the language of old Peking in the play. It follows that the various characters adopt the language which he had heard people of a similar class and calling use. The dialogue is full of Peking colloquialisms. A related characteristic of *Teahouse* is the incorporation of elements of traditional Chinese drama and balladry, as in the introductions to each of the three acts and the epilogue to the play, all of which use the style of the traditional Peking clapper-ballads. These interludes help to give the play a highly local flavour.

Teahouse is the most distinguished drama to emerge from the People's Republic of China. This is because of the originality of the concept which underlies it, the richness of the language, and the understanding the playwright shows of the vanished society of old Peking.

—Colin Mackerras

IL TEATRO DELLE FAVOLE RAPPRESENTATIVE.   See **THE SCENARIOS OF FLAMINIO SCALA.**

TEETH 'N' SMILES
by David Hare; music and lyrics by Tony Bicât

First Publication: London, 1976.
First Production: Royal Court Theatre, London, 2 September 1975.

Criticism
(For general works on the author, see *Playwrights* volume)

Articles:
Michelene Wandor, "Satire, Creativity and Annihilation: *Slag* and *Teeth 'n' Smiles* by David Hare", in her *Look Back in Gender: Sexuality and the Family in Post-War British Drama*, London, 1987.

*   *   *

As the play begins, a young roadie, thick in leather and jewellery, is building a great stack of amplifiers. The lights dim; he completes his task and addresses no one and everyone: "Right. Let's smash the place up". It is 9 June 1969. Class warfare hits Cambridge University as a disintegrating rock band plays the annual May Ball at Jesus College. They are joined on their long night of disaster by Arthur—ex-student of the college, song-writer for the group, and erstwhile lover of the lead singer (Maggie) who is set on a course of alchoholic self-destruction—and by Seraffian, their manager from the old days of non-subversive British rock. He has arrived to sack the disruptive and unwanted Maggie from the group. After a bad start, things rapidly get worse. After Maggie has drunkenly sabotaged their second appearance, the group is busted by the police and prohibited from performing their final set. In the furore of sex, drugs, and looting that follows, Maggie sets fire to a marquee and the group makes a rapid exit leaving everything essentially unaltered.

The play, first performed in 1975 with Helen Mirren as Maggie, is a conscious look back at the contradictions of 1960's counter-culture. It is, as always with David Hare's work, a very witty play, full of incisive one-liners; but it is, at the same time, a very sad play, full of the disappointment following youthful hopes and aspirations. It was seen by Hare as one of a series of what he has described as "history plays", plays which place individual despair and disillusionment within the larger context of the dismal unrolling of post-1939 British history. The dating of the action, just one year after the Paris Spring of 1968, is deliberate, as is the use of the rock group—and in particular its still idealistic song-writer Arthur—to contemplate the possibility of a popular culture with a real radical edge to it. "Would you say the ideas expressed in popular music have had the desired effect of changing society in any way?" asks Anson, the diffident medical student responsible for booking them, and Maggie's response is to take him off and screw him. Not much is to be expected from a group that is uncertain whether it is playing in Cambridge or Canterbury; and the first scene of the play is dominated by a demarcation dispute about whose job it is to fix the one plug that stands between the group and the politicisation of its public.

In contrast, the old world of the college remains invulnerably elastic in its ability to assimilate the cultural shock-troops of the new. The group set out to smash up the place, but succeed only in smashing up themselves: in a post-action projection we learn that the bass player, the chief exponent of drug excess, died by inhaling his own vomit in 1973. The college and what it represents may change peripherally, but the power will remain where it always has. This is a truth only too bitterly apparent to Arthur; he is an ex-student of the establishment and, as he is forced to acknowledge, never more than a fellow-traveller in the alternative society: "One day it's a revolution to say fuck on the bus. Next day it's the only way to get a ticket. That's how the system works".

But if Arthur's is the failure of an idealism that sought change through individual efforts in the radical-culture-market, the studied aggression represented by the group will fare no better. Blocked off by a sea of drugs and alcohol from the unreality they would confront, the band's wildest attempts at anarchic destruction are met with indifference or containment. Even Maggie's final act of defiance, the firing of the tent, is assimilated; as Arthur tells her: "They all love it you know. Dashing about in the smoke. They're hoping to make it an annual event".

The economic context of the new world of the market is provided by Seraffian, who is perfectly happy to deal with a world of class privilege from which he had been traditionally excluded by his own social origins—"me a boy from Tottenham whose dad ran a spieler in his own back room". The manager's commercial cynicism—seeing music only as a product to be marketed—is in contrast to the frustration of Arthur's hopes for music as a radical tool, and to Maggie's vision of it as a vehicle for her personal pain. As the smoke clears from the burning marquee towards the end of the play Seraffian makes the link between past and present with a long anecdote about being in the Café de Paris when it was bombed in 1941. Then, after the initial shock, he had come to in time to observe a looter removing the ring from his finger, business going on as usual; an image of capitalist hope for him, but one which provokes only anger from Maggie—an anger, however, that will remain internalised, without any public manifestation. That Arthur ends the play with vestiges of his idealistic optimism still intact is as nothing compared to the ability of the old order and the new commerce to come to terms with, rather than yield to, change. The bombed ball-room in the Café de Paris had been a perfect reproduction of that in the *Titanic*, and the final song in Hare's play is Maggie's rendition of "Last Orders on the Titanic": but if the nation, symbolised by these institutions, has been steadily sinking, it is clear that the top deck is still populated much as it always has been.

—John Bull

THE TEMPEST
by William Shakespeare

First Publication: In First Folio, London, 1623.
First Production: c. 1610–11; earliest recorded production, at the Banqueting House, Whitehall, London, 1 November 1611.

Editions
The Tempest, edited by H.H. Furness, Philadelphia, 1892 (New Variorum Shakespeare).

The Tempest, edited by John Dover Wilson, Cambridge, 1921 (The New Shakespeare).
The Tempest, edited by Frank Kermode, London, 1954 (Arden Shakespeare).
The Tempest, edited by Robert Langbaum, New York, 1964 (Signet Classic Shakespeare).
The Tempest, edited by Anne Barton, Harmondsworth, 1968 (New Penguin Shakespeare).
The Tempest, edited by Stephen Orgel, Oxford, 1987 (Oxford Shakespeare).

Criticism
(For general works on the author, see *Playwrights* volume)

Books:
Colin Stil, *Shakespeare's Mystery Play: A Study of "The Tempest"*, London, 1921; revised as *The Timeless Theme*, London, 1936.
D.G. James, *The Dream of Prospero*, Oxford, 1967.
A.D. Nuttall, *Two Concepts of Allegory: A Study of Shakespeare's "The Tempest" and the Logic of Allegorical Expression*, London, 1967.
D.J. Palmer (ed.), *"The Tempest": A Casebook*, London, 1968.
John Russell Brown, *The Tempest*, London, 1972.
Max Dorsinville, *Caliban Without Prospero*, Toronto, 1974.
William J. Martz, *The Place of "The Tempest" in Shakespeare's Universe of Comedy*, Lawrence, Kansas, 1978.
Harold F. Brooks, *"The Tempest": What Sort of Play?*, London, 1980.
David Lucking, *The Artifice of Eternity: An Essay on "The Tempest"*, Lecce, Italy, 1983.
David L. Hirst, *The Tempest*, London, 1984 (Text and Performance Series).
Michael Srigley, *Images of Recreation: A Study of Shakespeare's "The Tempest" and Its Cultural Background*, Uppsala, Sweden, 1985.
Harold Bloom (ed.), *Shakespeare's "The Tempest"*, New York, New Haven (Connecticut), and Philadelphia, 1988 (Modern Critical Interpretations).
Mark W. Scott and Sandra L. Williamson (eds.), *"The Tempest"*, in *Shakespearian Criticism, 8*, Detroit, Illinois, 1989 [anthology of criticism].

Articles:
For information on the many articles about *The Tempest*, see the bibliographies listed in the *Playwrights* volume, and the annual Shakespeare Bibliography in *Shakespeare Quarterly*, published by the Folger Shakespeare Library, Washington D.C. (1950-).

*   *   *

The background to the action of *The Tempest* is that Prospero, the rightful Duke of Milan, has been deposed by his brother Antonio who, needing help from Alonso, King of Naples, has made Milan subservient to Naples. Prospero escaped to an island where for the past 12 years he has educated his daughter Miranda. His study of magic has enabled him to rule over the island's creatures, Ariel "an airy spirit", and Caliban, "a savage and deformed slave" associated with the physical world.

The play begins with Antonio, Alonso, and others from Milan and Naples being shipwrecked during a storm. This is an illusion created by Ariel. Although no one is drowned, the travellers become separated into different groups on the island where they come ashore. Ferdinand, the son of the King of

The Tempest: Derek Jacobi as Prospero, Stratford-Upon-Avon, 1982-3 (Royal Shakespeare Company)

Naples, meets and falls in love with Miranda. His love is tested in various trials by Prospero who, satisfied, celebrates the coming nuptials between the two royal families with an elaborate masque of spirits. Two drunkards among the shipwrecked are mistaken by Caliban for gods whom he worships and urges to usurp and kill Prospero. The play ends in reconciliation as the wrongdoers are brought before Prospero, confess their guilt, and admit his authority. Prospero gives his restored Dukedom to the young lovers, renounces his magic powers, and announces that after retiring to Milan he will prepare himself for death.

The Tempest is Shakespeare's last complete play. It is intricately plotted—a love story set in an exotic foreign place filled with spirits and amazing spectacles, a tale of long separation, reconciliation, and restoration with a happy ending and the passing of power from the old to the young. Whether or not we regard Prospero's renunciation of magic as alluding to Shakespeare's decision to give up writing for the stage, there is an analogy between Prospero the magician and a writer for the stage. Prospero designs a complicated plot which, through his magic, is enacted as the play. He has power over the others, like an author over his characters. The action covers about three hours, the actual time of performing the play. Prospero uses his power to create several scenes, the opening tempest and the nuptial masque, as well as directing the actors through Ariel, and acting himself. He is playwright, director, actor, while Ariel is the spirit world of imagination which Prospero controls through his magic. In a related series of symbolic associations, Ariel is air or spirit, while Caliban is earth or the natural physical world of matter without moral purpose. Mankind is between the two and needs to control both the imagination and body. Without Caliban's labour and knowledge of the island's fresh water and edible fruits, Prospero and Miranda would have perished. Ariel does not appear interested in sex or procreation; Caliban attempted to rape Miranda and would populate the island with little Calibans. Prospero's task as father is to oversee Miranda's moral education so that she is pure, can rightly judge, and loves the man she will marry.

In this multi-layered play with its various hierarchies of characters, symbols, and values, order and control are central themes. It is a conservative, patriarchial, monarchial vision. In *The Tempest*, as in much theatre associated with the Court of James I, power and order radiate from the monarch—father of the nation—downward through society. If there is disorder, injustice, or weakness at the top, such faults spread through all other aspects of life. Prospero devoted too much time to study, "neglecting worldly ends, all dedicated / To closeness and the bettering of my mind", and "awak'd an evil nature" in his brother Antonio who, seeing the power vacuum, became ambitious and usurped him. Prospero now knows he must be actively engaged with his world and use his power as ruler of the island and as head of the family. Either man controls his instincts or they usurp the rational. Without such control, through Ariel, Prospero cannot bring all the activity on the island together to a successful conclusion and the righting of past wrongs. Nor, following the analogy between the theatre of the world and the play, can he, as "dramatist", bring all the actions to resolution within the playing time unless he has control over the airy spirit of the imagination.

In another analogy suggested by the play, Prospero is God-like (and a suffering Christ-like figure—"one of their kind"), the play is a figure for the providential scheme, and "the hour's now come" for final judgement. This is the "sixth hour", symbolic of the sixth age, when "lies at my mercy all mine enemies". Prospero's role as spiritual mentor is to bring the evildoers to repentance. Alonso must confess his evil, be penitent, and restore what he has wrongfully gained if he is to be forgiven. This he does: "Thy dukedom I resign, and do entreat / Thou pardon me my wrongs". But Prospero on his island is like God who foresees and shapes what appears to be human choice: ". . .and require / My dukedom of thee, which perforce I know / Thou must restore". In this house of analogy the father is a figure of the king who is a figure of God. Caliban is the world without revelation, the body without soul, fallen mankind without the New Law. At the play's conclusion he admits "I'll be wise hereafter / And seek for grace". *The Tempest* offers a series of analogies and mirrors which reflect on each other and allude to the religious, political, and moral. Caliban is Earth and the "savage" of the New World (the island is associated with the Bermudas), the colonised race, who protests: "You taught me language, and my profit on't / is, I know how to curse". At the play's last judgement with its symbolism of a new heaven and earth ("O brave new world"), when nature which has fallen with man is restored, Caliban is set free and promised pardon.

Within this play of hierarchies there is also a hierarchy of styles of poetry and prose, ranging from the miniature masque within the play celebrating the forthcoming marriage in rhymed formal rhythms with it's blend of biblical and classical allusions ("Honor riches, marriage-blessing, / Long continuance, and increasing"), to Ariel's airy songs and Caliban's curses, and to the prose of drunken Stephano and Trinculo.

—Bruce King

THE THEATRICAL ILLUSION (L'Illusion comique) by Pierre Corneille

First Publication: Paris, 1639.
First Production: Théâtre du Marais, Paris, 1635 or 1636.

Editions
L'Illusion comique, edited by Pierre Melese, Paris, c. 1937.
L'Illusion comique, edited by R. Bizot, Paris, 1938.
L'Illusion comique, edited by J. Marks, Manchester, 1944; second edition, 1969.
L'Illusion comique, edited by Robert Garapon, Paris, 1957, revised editions, 1965, 1970, and 1985.
L'Illusion comique, Paris, 1966 (Collection Théâtre Nationale Populaire)
L'Illusion comique, edited by Colette Cosnier, Paris and Montreal, 1971.
L'Illusion comique, in *Théâtre choisi de Corneille*, edited by Maurice Rat, Paris, 1974.
L'Illusion comique, edited by Georges Forestier, Paris, 1987.

Translations
The Theatrical Illusion, in *The Cid; Cinna; The Theatrical Illusion*, translated by John Cairncross, Harmondsworth, 1975.
The Illusion, in *The Liar; The Illusion*, translated and adapted by Ranjit Bolt, Bath, 1989.

Criticism
(For general works on the author, see *Playwrights* volume)

Books:
Annie Richard, *"L'Illusion comique" de Corneille et le baroque: Étude d'une oeuvre dans son milieu*, Paris, 1972.

The Theatrical Illusion: Engraving, 1877

Articles:

R. Nelson, "Pierre Corneille's *L'Illusion comique:* The Play as Magic", in *Publications of the Modern Language Association* [*PMLA*], 1956.

A. Sellstrom, "*L'Illusion comique:* The Tragic Scenes of Act V", in *Modern Language Notes*, 73, 1958.

A. Sellstrom, "Sources of Corneille's *L'Illusion comique*", in *Modern Language Notes*, 76, 1961.

Hans Sckommodau, "Die Grotte der *Illusion comique*", in *Wort und Text: Festschrift für Fritz Schalk*, Frankfurt, 1963.

C. Cherpack, "The Captive Audience in *L'Illusion comique*", in *Modern Language Notes*, 81, 1966.

Marc Fumaroli, "Rhétorique et dramaturgie dans *L'Illusion comique* de Corneille", in *Dix-septième siècle*, 80–81, 1968.

Gordon Walters Jr., "Society and the Theatre in Corneille's *L'Illusion comique*", in *Romance notes*, 10, 1969.

François-Xavier Cuche, "Les Trois Illusions de *L'Illusion comique*", in *Travaux de linguistique et de littérature* (Strasbourg), vol.9 no.2, 1971.

Colette Cosnier, "Un Étrange monstre: *L'Illusion comique*", in *Europe*, 540–41, 1974.

Madeleine Alcover, "Les Lieux et les temps dans *L'Illusion comique*", in *French Studies* 30, 1976.

David L. Rubin, "The Hierarchy of Illusions and the Structure of *L'Illusion comique*", in *La Cohérence intérieure: Études sur la littérature française du dix-septième siècle présentées en hommage à Judd D. Hubert*, Paris, 1977.

H.T. Barnwell, "*L'Illusion comique:* A Dramatic Anticipation of Corneille's Critical Analyses of his Art", in *Theatre Research International*, vol.8 no.2, 1983.

André Blanc, "A Propos de *L'Illusion comique* ou sur quelques hauts secrets de Pierre Corneille", in *Revue d'histoire du théâtre*, vol.36 no.2, 1984.

Marc Fumaroli, "Illusion et illumination: Corneille poète 'métaphysique' dans *L'Illusion comique*", in *Théâtre en Europe*, October 1984.

Marie-Joséphine Whitaker, "*L'Illusion comique*, ou l'école des pères", in *Revue d'histoire littéraire de la France*, vol.85 no.5, 1985.

G.J. Mallinson, "Strehler, Corneille, and *L'Illusion*: A Play in Retrospect", in *French Studies Bulletin*, 17, 1985–86.

Hamdi Hemaidi, "Écriture/Charme dans *L'Illusion comique*", in *Actes du Colloque Corneille à Tunis*, edited by Alya Baccar and Georges Couton, Paris, 1986.

Colette Scherer, "La Tragédie du 5ème acte de *L'Illusion comique* et le théâtre du temps", in *Dramaturgies: Languages dramatiques*, edited by Jacqueline Jomaron, Paris, 1986.

Harriet Ray Allentuch, "Reading *L'Illusion comique* Psychologically", in *Romanic Review*, vol.78 no.1, 1987.

Cynthia B. Kerr, "Rencontre autour d'une *Illusion:* Pierre Corneille et Giorgio Strehler", in *Travaux de littérature*, 1, 1988.

Claude Abraham, "'From Page to Stage': More than an Illusion", in *Seventeenth Century French Studies*, 11, 1989.

Tomotoshi Katagi, "*L'Illusion comique* de Corneille et les problèmes de la repésentation", in *L'Information littéraire*, vol.41 no.3, 1989.

John Trethewey, "Structures of *L'Illusion comique*", in *Seventeenth Century French Studies*, 11, 1989.

*   *   *

The bourgeois Pridamant, seeking his runaway son, Clindor, comes to the grotto of the magician Alcandre, who promises to reveal Clindor's whereabouts, and as a preliminary shows Pridamant scenes illustrating his son's activities since he left home. He is employed as servant to the braggart soldier Matamore, who pays court to Isabelle, daughter of the bourgeois Géronte, as does another suitor, Adraste; it is, however, Clindor whose love Isabelle secretly returns, though he is also amusing himself with her servant Lyse. Clindor is attacked by Adraste and a band of cut-throats, but manages to kill Adraste before he is overpowered. In prison, he laments his lot; but the gaoler is suborned by Lyse, and they flee, together with Isabelle. In Act V, Clindor and Isabelle enjoy a much enhanced rank and fortune; however Clindor, who has been having an adulterous affair with the wife of his benefactor Prince Florilame, is ambushed and killed. Pridamant is grief-stricken at his son's death, but a curtain is drawn aside, showing Clindor and the other participants in this "tragedy" to be actors, counting their takings now the play is over. Pridamant, mortified that his son has sunk so low as to become an actor, is persuaded by Alcandre of the respectability of the theatre and the glorious prospects of those who work in it.

Produced at short notice for Montdory and his company at the *Théâtre du Marais* (including the new recruit Bellemore, a specialist in the role of braggart soldier), Corneille's eighth play is an unashamed apologia for the theatre, a demonstration of the range of styles available to the dramatist practising in the 1630's, and a vindication of the theatrical profession in the face of prejudice on moral grounds. Montdory himself had, like Clindor (the role he played), left a good home and scandalised his family by becoming an actor; so that the whole play, and not just Alcandre's homily in Act V, should be seen as a justification of the *métiers* of playwright and performer. Its structure—that of a play-within-a-play within a play—shows a highly inventive and skilful handling of the interplay of various levels of illusion, typical of the baroque imagination in France (as well as elsewhere in Europe) in this period just before the general acceptance of the more disciplined and coherent formulas imposed by neo-classical dramatic theory, as well as by the more streamlined staging practice of the single perspective set. Produced in a simplified version of the older convention of multiple décor, deriving from medieval staging tradition, *L'Illusion comique* nevertheless possesses its own overall unity. Not the least pleasing feature of this attractive play is that while, from one point of view, we are offered an episodic display of contrasting styles—various registers of comic writing, from the mimetic realism of the lovers' conversation to the extravagant verbal fantasy of Matamore; the elegiac pathos of Clindor in prison; and the rather more elevated dialogue of the Act V "tragedy"—at the same time the whole is controlled by the presence of Alcandre, conjuring up these visions in the single location of his cave and according to the most rigorous interpretation of the unity of time. Alcandre, then, is the surrogate playwright, showing us the magical quality of theatrical illusion (*l'illusion comique*); while Pridamant, in turn surprised, apprehensive, and grief-stricken represents the ideal spectator. Standing in for the naïve spectator in the genuine audience, he reacts in these various ways to the successive demonstrations of the dramatist's skill, and is completely taken in (as Corneille hopes his real spectators will be) by the deceptive links of character and plot between Acts IV and V.

The relationships between Isabelle, her father, and her lovers in Acts II–IV could be said to reproduce the style and tone of the series of comedies Corneille had written in the years leading up to 1635; Lyse is a spirited development of the "*suivante*" figure; while Clindor illustrates the theme of inconstancy in love which runs through these earlier plays. It is Matamore who stands out in contrast: a character, as the author himself admits, who "exists only in the imagination". Derived from a long line of braggart soldiers going back to Plautus, Matamore's speeches, whether he is boasting of his warlike prowess or his amorous exploits, rarely descend from the level of extravagant hyperbole, backed up by mythological fantasy. If Alcandre is the surrogate playwright, there is in Matamore something of the surrogate poet; and it has been well said that his vainglorious rhetoric is that of Corneille's genuine warrior-heroes, unsupported by their real achievements.

Popular for a generation or so after its first appearance, *L'Illusion comique* fell out of favour in the French theatre for nearly 200 years; and when it was revived at the Comédie-Française in the mid-19th century, it was extensively adapted by the omission of Act IV and the substitution of other Corneille material for the inset play of Act V. André Antoine directed the play at the Odéon in 1895, but in a production whose characteristically naturalistic approach failed to do justice to the qualities of fantasy and poetry which are so distinctive in Corneille's text. In 1937 Louis Jouvet directed a revival at the Comédie-Française, designed by Christian Bérard, which won considerable acclaim; however, this production made the mistake of sacrificing the surprise effect of Act V—on which the aesthetic unity of the play, as well as the detail of the plot, surely depend—by playing the tragedy on an inset stage built for the purpose. Contemporary interest in *L'Illusion comique* as one of the most stageworthy of Corneille's plays was shown by the 1965 production at the *Théâtre National Populaire* at Avignon (directed by George Wilson,

who himself played Matamore), and, in Britain, by the Old Vic production (in translation as *The Illusion*) in 1990.

—William D. Howarth

THÉRÈSE RAQUIN
by Émile Zola

First Publication: As novel, Paris, 1867; as play, Paris, 1873.
First Production: Théâtre de la Renaissance, Paris, 11 July 1873.

Translations
Thérèse Raquin, translated by Kathleen Boutall, in *From the Modern Repertoire, 3*, edited by Eric Bentley, Bloomington, Indiana, 1956; reprinted in *The Seeds of Modern Drama*, edited by Norris Houghton, New York, 1963.
Thérèse Raquin, translated by Pip Broughton, Bath, 1989.

Criticism
(For general works on the author, see *Playwrights* volume)

Articles:
T. Hatlen, "Darwinism in the Theater", in *Western Speech*, 24, 1960.
James B. Sanders, "Antoine, Zola, et le théâtre", in *Les Cahiers naturalistes*, 17, 1971.
James B. Sanders, "Antoine et Zola", in *Les Cahiers naturalistes*, vol.22 no.50, 1976.

*   *   *

Émile Zola's *Thérèse Raquin* (1873) is a hauntingly powerful psychological study, "a steamy story of sexual passion plumbing the murky depths of murder, revenge and retribution". The long-suffering Thérèse is married to Mme. Raquin's sickly son Camille. She is seduced by her husband's best friend, the untalented painter Laurent, and together the lovers murder Camille. Married with the blessing of Mme. Raquin, they become haunted by Camille's ghost. Their earlier all-consuming passion turns to loathing; their lives are dominated by terror and mutual hatred. When Mme. Raquin learns the truth about her son's death, on the murderers' wedding night, she has a stroke which leaves her paralysed and unable to speak. The final catastrophe, the criminals' suicide pact, is accomplished under the eyes of a jubilant mother who has suddenly regained her faculties. The bleakness of the action is relieved by the comic figures of old Grivet and Michaud, who visit the Raquins every Thursday evening to play dominoes, and by a charming love story told by Suzanne, Michaud's niece.

Zola's aim was to put a "slice of life" on the stage with scientific precision in order to help the theatre in its attempts at realizing an art made of "truth and scientific exactitude". But rather than write an original play, he adapted his novel (published in 1867) as a response to critics who dared him to put "such filth" on the stage. The strength of *Thérèse Raquin* lies primarily in "the interior struggles of the characters". Unfortunately these "struggles" are better suited to the novel, where each character's state of mind, his every change of mood, his hopes and fears, can be subtly analysed. One can only concur with the judgement of the most enlightened critic of the first night who wrote: "The subject which, in itself, is so profoundly dramatic, is unfortunately anti-theatrical".

The deliberately ordinary setting, bordering on the sordid, shocked the 19th-century audiences. But Zola, not satisfied with flying in the face of convention, highlights his offending background by giving his characters plenty of trivial activities to perform, stage business not in keeping with the unfolding of a tragedy, thus destroying the idea of how a tragic character should behave. The Raquins' room is a multi-purpose space: it combines Thérèse's bedroom, the dining-room, and sitting-room, and has several entrances (the staircase to the shop, doors to the kitchen, to Mme. Raquin's room, and to the small corridor leading directly into the passage). The room is dirty and black, badly in need of decoration. Artificial flowers and some photographs are the only derisory embellishment. A single window opens onto a dark wall, thereby increasing the feeling of oppression and imprisonment. Respecting the classical unity of space, the stage is so cluttered with furniture that there is hardly any room for the characters to move. Zola was concerned with creating the impression of witnessing "real" people living their everyday lives, unaware of the presence of a viewer. The illusion of reality should be total.

The first performance of *Thérèse Raquin* took place in Paris on Friday 11 July 1873, at the *Théâtre de la Renaissance*. Its director, Hippolyte Hostein, had courageously agreed to stage a play that many more-prestigious theatres had turned down. The *mise en scène* and the actors were generally praised; the play attracted more critical attention than any other production that season, and the press was not so negative as many commentators have made out (Henri Mitterand includes a wide-ranging critical panorama in his edition of the *Oeuvres complètes*). The run of nine performances was short, but still respectable. It was regularly revived until the start of World War II. The Théâtre de l'Odéon (the second national theatre of France) staged it with great success in 1905 and 1910. It was taken on national tour in 1912 and, in 1920, it was put on in two different Parisian theatres. More recently, however, when French directors are attracted to *Thérèse Raquin*, they tend to write their own adaptation of the novel rather than put on Zola's playtext. Jacques Feyder adapted the novel for the silent screen, but Marcel Carné's film of 1953 (with Simone Signoret and Raf Vallone in the leading roles) retains only the broad outlines of the plot: it is set in Lyon, and Vallone is an Italian lorry driver.

The Independent Theatre staged *Thérèse Raquin* in an English translation by A. Texeira de Mattos, directed by H. de Lange, at the Royalty Theatre, London, on 9 October 1891. As in Paris 18 years earlier, the play was damned for having no literary merit, the set condemned, but the actors applauded for creating memorable characters, although the Raquins were described as "vulgar plebeians". The critics objected to the "terrible realism", though some were fascinated by that "nightmare of horrors, that ghastly picture of human depravity and human weakness". It was faulted for its undiluted romanticism, for its melodrama, for its insistence on naturalist details. *Thérèse Raquin* was revived in 1983 at the Liverpool Playhouse (translated and adapted by Pip Broughton), and in 1990 at the Chichester Minerva Studio (translated by Nicholas Wright and directed by David Leveaux).

Despite being overshadowed by the novel, *Thérèse Raquin* remains the prototype of the naturalist play and no discussion of naturalism in the theatre can afford to ignore it.

—Claude Schumacher

THEY KNEW WHAT THEY WANTED
by Sidney Howard

First Publication: Garden City, New York, 1925.
First Production: Garrick Theatre, New York, 24 November 1924.

Criticism
(For general works on the author, see *Playwrights* volume)

Articles:
Walter J. Meserve, "Sidney Howard and the Social Drama of the Twenties", in *Modern Drama*, 6, 1963.

*   *   *

Tony, a 60-year-old Italian winegrower living in the Napa Valley of California has met, and fallen in love with, Amy, a lonely San Francisco waitress. Having seen her only once, he woos and wins her through letters and the photograph of his handsome young helper, Joe. On their wedding day, when Tony is seriously injured in a car accident, Joe meets Amy who is at first attracted to him and then furious when she discovers the deception; but she finally decides to stay. That evening, more sympathetic toward Tony, yet weary with the shock and tension of her experience, Amy succumbs to Joe's careless emotions. Three months later she discovers that she is pregnant; Amy's shame and misery, Tony's anger, his struggle with his pride and his final acceptance and triumph, as well as the happy resolution of the problem for all three characters, comprise the heart of the play. Each gets what he or she wants.

Much has been written about this play as a modern version of the Paolo–Francesca love story, but comparisons are worth making only in general terms. No characters in the ancient and modern stories bear close comparison, and the plots have only a vague resemblance at one or two points. There is, for example, a very different approach toward *honor* in Howard's play, where characters are less concerned with egos and revenge than with a reasoned solution to their problems. According to Tony, Amy committed a "mistake in da head, not in da heart. . .Mistake in da head is no matter", but he is also interpreting her act in an expedient and Christian manner. Amy was not using her head any more than she was her heart, but Tony employs both very wisely in his decision. He knows what he wants without being burdened by traditions, ritualistic behavior patterns, or unnecesary pride. As a balanced American in the modern world, Tony understands Alexander Pope's admonition to "know thyself" and follows the preachings of Ralph Waldo Emerson, with the result that he sees life more in terms of a comic spirit than a tragic muse and can become "the most happy fella" that Frank Loesser makes him in the popular musical of 1956.

Never an experimenter in dramatic styles or forms, Sidney Howard once stated that he was content to "get a kind of glamor around reality". At the opening of Act 1 the audience sees a cluttered room decorated with a portrait of George Washington draped with the flag of Italy and a picture of Garibaldi swathed in an American flag. Ah Gee, the Chinese helper, is on a ladder decorating the porch; Joe is singing as he opens a packing crate. It is a festive scene into which Father McKee intrudes with the cautious concern of the clergy on such an occasion. Everything is bright and real, even the extravagantly attired Tony with his purple suit, his oriental waistcoat and great gold watch, a green tie, a derby, and patent leather shoes. Contradicting his florid exuberance, Tony projects the inner turbulence of a very nervous groom. In these expository scenes Howard carefully and clearly reviews the situation, contrasting visually and through dialogue the realistic balance of humor and seriousness that shapes the lives of these people.

To enhance the realism Howard deftly entangles comedy and melodrama. An empty stage in the middle of Act 1 prepares for the entrance of Amy, whose constant attention to Joe clearly shows her lack of knowledge. She is gracious and sweet; she is impressed by everything and by everyone; all approve of her and never mention the absent Tony. Alone together, Joe and Amy have a beautifully constructed scene which builds slowly to a climax at her recognition of the mistaken identity. Immediately, the news of Tony's accident and his sudden appearance interrupt Amy's reaction. Then there is silence, distress, and anger, as Amy, sufficiently shaken to consider leaving the house, thinks again and, seeing Joe's picture, pushes it away and makes her decision: she will "stick". Howard knew well how to manipulate the emotions of his characters with scenes imbued with appropriate atmosphere and the controlled rhythm of excellent melodrama. He could be preachy, as writers of realistic melodrama frequently are, with Joe's polemics on individual freedom and Father McKee's warnings, but everything supports his development of characters and the flowing lines of his plot. More importantly, in *They Knew What They Wanted* he added to conventional melodrama a carefully contrived and entertaining play that is significant for its sense of humanity and its insight into social morality.

Distinguished by its modern point of view, *They Knew What They Wanted* identifies a positive individualism in social drama quite different from that which appeared previously in American drama or which followed. Prior to World War I plays generally emphasized the force of social custom. Before *Nice People* in 1921 and *Expressing Willie* in 1924 Rachael Crothers did not allow her characters to assert themselves beyond social acceptability. They might question, but they did not act. Nor did Jessie Lynch Williams's *Why Marry?* of 1917 suggest anything beyond the acceptance of social custom. Drama during the 1930's, on the other hand, frequently presented man as representative of a social class and sometimes victimized by the social structure, although the individualism of the 1920's did not disappear. Through its title, *They Knew What They Wanted* epitomizes the thought of a decade—of Clark Storey in S. N. Berhman's *The Second Man*, 1927; of Mary and Jim Hutton in Philip Barry's *Paris Bound*, 1927, as well as Johnny Case in *Holiday*, 1928, and Maxwell Anderson's *Saturday's Children*, 1927, or Jane in Owen Davis' *Icebound*, 1923, or the characters in Elmer Rice's *The Adding Machine*, 1923. There are other plays, of course, that do not fit the pattern, but Howard should be given credit for putting his finger on an idea which helps define the social drama of the 1920's in America.

—Walter J. Meserve

THE THREE SISTERS (Tri Sestry)
by Anton Chekhov

First Publication: In *Russkaya Mysl*, 2 [*The Russian Idea*, 2] 1901; in book form, 1901; revised version, as supplement to *Collected Works*, 7, 1902.
First Production: Moscow Arts Theatre, Moscow, 31 January 1901.

Translations
The Three Sisters, in *Plays by Anton Tchekoff: Second Series*, translated by Julius West, London, 1916.
The Three Sisters, translated by Constance Garnett and Theodore Komisarjevsky, London, 1926.
The Three Sisters, translated by Stark Young, New York, 1941.
The Three Sisters, in *Anton Chekhov: Three Plays*, translated by Elisaveta Fen, Harmondsworth, 1951.
The Three Sisters, in *Six Plays of Chekhov*, translated by Robert Corrigan, New York, 1962.
The Three Sisters, in *Chekhov: The Major Plays*, translated by Ann Dunnigan, New York, 1964.
The Three Sisters, in *The Oxford Chekhov, 3*, translated by Ronald Hingley, Oxford, 1964.
The Three Sisters, translated by Randall Jarrell, New York, 1969.
The Three Sisters, in *Anton Chekhov: Four Plays*, translated by David Magarshack, London, 1969.
The Three Sisters, translated by Moura Budberg, London, 1971.
The Three Sisters, in *Anton Chekhov's Plays*, edited and translated by Eugene K. Bristow, New York, 1977 (Norton Critical Edition).
The Three Sisters, translated by Michael Frayn, London, 1983.

Criticism
(For general works on the author, see *Playwrights* volume)

Books:
Louis V. Talento, *Anton Chekhov: "The Three Sisters", "The Cherry Orchard"*, New York, 1970.

Articles:
M. Walton, "If Only We Knew", in *New Theatre Magazine*, vol.8 no.1, 1967.
G. Tovstonogov, "Chekhov's *Three Sisters* at the Gorky Theatre", in *Tulane Drama Review*, vol.13 no.2, 1968.
John L. Bennett, "An Examination of Chekhov's Presentation of Characters and Themes in Act I of *Three Sisters*", in *Proceedings, Pacific Northwest Conference on Foreign Languages*, 20, 1969.
Beverly Hahn, "Chekhov: *The Three Sisters*", in *Critical Review*, 15, 1972.
Albert Bermel, "The Society as Mosaic: *Three Sisters*", in his *Contradictory Characters: An Interpretation of the Modern Theatre*, New York, 1973.
William Babula, "*Three Sisters*, Time, and the Audience", in *Modern Drama*, 18, 1975.
Liam Purdon, "Time and Space in Chekhov's *The Three Sisters*", in *Publications of the Arkansas Philological Association*, vol.2 no.2, 1976.
Howard Moss, "*Three Sisters*", in *Hudson Review*, 30, 1977–78.
David Parker, "Three Men in Chekhov's *Three Sisters*", in *Critical Review*, 21, 1979.
Timothy J. Wiles, "*The Three Sisters*: Stanislavski's Tragedy, Chekhov's Vaudeville", in his *The Theater Event: Modern Theories of Performance*, Chicago, 1980.
Ulrich Busch, "Zur literarischen Kompetenz des Literaturwissenschaftlers und des Laienlesers: am Beispiel von Anton Cechovs *Drei Schwestern*", in *Poetica*, 16, 1984.
Charles J. Rzepka, "Chekhov's *The Three Sisters*, Lear's Daughters, and the Weird Sisters: The Arcana of Archetypal Influence", in *Modern Language Studies*, vol.14 no.4, 1984.
Harai Golomb, "Communicating Relationships in Chekhov's *Three Sisters*", in *Russian Language Journal*, 132–34, 1985.

The Three Sisters: Moscow Art Theatre, 1901 (first production)

C.J.G. Turner, "Time in Chekhov's *Tri sestry*", in *Canadian Slavonic Papers*, 28, 1986.

Victor Emeljanow, "Komisarjevsky's *Three Sisters:* The Prompt Book", in *Theatre Notebook*, 41, 1987.

*   *   *

Set in a provincial town with 100,000 inhabitants, *The Three Sisters* depicts the lives and aspirations of the Prozorov family (three sisters and a brother) and their assorted friends (mainly military). Frustrated and dissatisfied with their present existence, the Prozorovs recall past happiness in Moscow, which they left 11 years before the play begins, and long to return there to attain future happiness. Olga, the eldest sister (aged 28), a conscientious but harassed schoolteacher, yearns to be married; Masha, the middle sister, loathes her pedantic, kindly husband, the Latin teacher, Kulygin; Irina, the youngest (aged 20), seeks fulfilment in work and love. As daughters of a recently deceased general, the sisters have high expectations of life, and their brother, Andrei, dreams of becoming professor at Moscow University.

In the course of four acts, spanning several years, happiness proves elusive. Olga becomes a reluctant headmistress while remaining unmarried; Masha has an affair with Lieutenant-Colonel Vershinin, and is grief-stricken when he departs; Irina, disheartened by prosaic routine work, agrees to marry the ugly Baron Tusenbach—yet he is killed the day before their wedding. Andrei marries a local girl, Natasha, who is unfaithful and domineering, gradually expelling the Prozorovs from their family home. Despite these disappointments, however, the sisters do not despair. In a final tableau, while the drunken doctor, Chebutykin, expresses his customary nihilistic indif-

ference, the three sisters stand together, determined to live, to work, and to discover the meaning of their suffering.

Chekhov's richest and greatest play has inspired a bewildering variety of interpretations since its premiere at the Moscow Arts Theatre on 31 January 1901. *The Three Sisters* has been viewed as tragedy or comedy, as a poignant testimony to the eternal yearning for love, happiness, beauty, and meaning, or as a devastating indictment of the folly of inert gentility and vacuous day-dreaming. Its characters have been deemed worthy embodiments of the universal "human condition", keenly experiencing hope, disappointment, frustration, loneliness, and the passage of time—or passive products of pre-revolutionary Russian privilege, remnants fit only for the scrap-heap of history.

Chekhov himself, modestly undogmatic, aspired to "objectivity" in his writing, allowing his readers the role of "jury". Nevertheless, a careful study of his personality, life, letters, and art strongly suggests that he sympathised with the fundamental dispositions and ideals of Olga, Masha, Irina, Andrei, Vershinin, and Tusenbach. These individuals, although comically ineffectual at times and touchingly vulnerable, avoid most of the negative characteristics which Chekhov abhorred. They are *not* petty, cruel, drunken, crude, ignorant, self-satisfied, and hypocritical. Whereas Natasha is unutterably vulgar, and aesthetically and morally barbarous, the three sisters and their closest friends strive for spiritual, non-materialistic goals and long for a happier, more beautiful, more meaningful life.

Such tenuous aims will not impress the self-assertive mind, which prides itself on being energetic, competitive, successful, and illusion-free. "Active" people often condemn the Prozorovs as weak-willed, fatalistic, and supine, and sneakingly admire the odious Natasha. Anatoly Lunacharsky in 1903 scolded "these stupid three sisters who were given everything but could not regulate their lives": "They moan and weep for a quite unfathomable reason. Would you believe it, they want to go to Moscow! Heavens above, go to Moscow then, who on earth is stopping you?". Desmond MacCarthy in 1938 understood Chekhov's play:

> In common with all genuine works of art *The Three Sisters* is addressed to the contemplative, not the practical mind. To the practical the spectacle of failure in any shape is merely depressing; not necessarily to the contemplative, who, whether religious or sceptical, have down the ages found wisdom and even a beauty in the lessons of frustration. . .Chekhov is the dramatist of good-byes. . .good-byes to hopes, possessions and ambitions, good-byes to love. . .Yet out of this conception of life, which the practical optimist would label "depressing", and the Communist regard as sociologically symptomatic, Chekov makes a work of art which exalts like a beautiful piece of music. It is not in a mood of depression one leaves the theatre after seeing *The Three Sisters*, the best of all his plays. . .

Although Chekhov's underlying sympathies are discernible, the subtle delicacy of his writing precludes any single, "correct" interpretation. Stanislavsky recalls Chekhov's anger at the initial Arts Theatre response—"he had written a happy comedy and all of us had considered the play a tragedy and even wept over it". *The Three Sisters* is, indeed, permeated with humour, producing a characteristic blend of triviality and profundity, "relevance" and "irrelevance". Serious themes—such as loneliness and unhappiness, the inexorable passing of time, the non-achievement of goals, frustration in love and work—are punctuated with laughter, for nothing could be further from Chekhov's art than unrelieved earnestness and unsmiling solemnity. Vershinin and Tusenbach are comically self-repeating, while opening up vast philosophical vistas.

The alleged "plotlessness" of *The Three Sisters* yields an abundance of internal action; its complex emotional interrelationships demand meticulous direction and ensemble playing. The greatest Chekhovian productions balance every element, like a symphonic orchestration. At the Queen's Theatre, London, in 1938, Michel Saint-Denis blended acting, costumes and scenery, sound effects and lighting in rare perfection, highlighting the play's cycle of the seasons (Spring, Winter, Summer, Autumn) and times of day or night (midday, 8.15 p.m., 2 a.m., midday).

After interweaving the strands of pessimism and optimism, irony and indifference, there remains an unanswered but indomitable yearning. In Act 2, Masha remarks: "It seems to me that man must have faith or seek faith, for otherwise life is empty, empty. . .Either you know why you live, or everything's pointless, mere straw in the wind". Portraying ordinary people in everyday circumstances, *The Three Sisters* captures the beauty and the brevity of human life, the blessing and the bewilderment. In her closing lines, Olga declares: "Time will pass, and we shall depart for ever, people will forget us, forget our faces, voices, and how many of us there were. . ." But they are *not* forgotten. The three sisters and their friends have transcended time, class, and country, and—without a trace of pretentiousness—have become hauntingly universal, symbols of undying aspiration.

—Gordon McVay

THE THREEPENNY OPERA (Die Dreigroschenoper)
by Bertolt Brecht (with Elizabeth Hauptmann); music by Kurt Weill

First Publication: Vienna, 1929; in *Versuche, 3*, 1931.
First Production: Theater am Schiffbauerdamm, Berlin, 31 August 1928.

Translations

The Threepenny Opera, in *From the Modern Repertoire, 1*, translated by D. Vesey and Eric Bentley, Denver, Colorado, 1949; revised version in *Bertolt Brecht: Plays, 1*, London, 1960.
The Threepenny Opera, translated by Hugh McDiarmid, London, 1973.
The Threepenny Opera, translated by Ralph Mannheim and John Willett, London, 1979 (*The Collected Plays*, vol. 2, part 2).

Criticism
(For general works on the author, see *Playwrights* volume)

Books:
Siegfried Unseld (ed.), *Bertolt Brecht's Dreigroschenbuch: Texte, Materialen, Dokumente*, Frankfurt, 1960.

Articles:
Werner Hecht, "Bearbeitung oder Umgestaltung: Über die *Dreigroschenoper* und ihr Urbild", in *Theater der Zeit*, 13, 1958.
Boris Singermann, "Brechts *Dreigroschenoper*: Zur Ästhetik der Montage", in *Brecht Jahrbuck*, 1976.
R.C. Speirs, "A Note on the First Published Version of *Die Dreigroschenoper* and Its Relation to the Standard Text", in *Forum for Modern Language Studies*, 13, 1977.
Renée R. Hubert, "The Encounter of Bertolt Brecht and François Villon: A Commentary on *The Threepenny Opera*", in *Comparatist*, 5, 1981.
Richard J. Salmon, "Two Operas for Beggars: A Political Reading", in *Theoria*, 57, 1981.
Frank D. Kievitt, "Three Times *Three Penny*: Brecht's Adaptations of *The Beggar's Opera*", in *Mid-Hudson Language Studies*, 7, 1984.
Fritz Hennenberg, "Weill, Brecht und die *Dreigroschenoper*: Neue Materialien zur Entstehung und Uraufführung", in *Österreichische Musikzeitschrift*, 40, 1985.
John Fuegi, "Most Unpleasant Things with *The Threepenny Opera*: Weill, Brecht, and Money", in *A New Orpheus: Essays on Kurt Weill*, edited by Kim H. Kowalke, New Haven, Connecticut, 1986.
Ulrich Weisstein, "Brecht's Victorian Version of Gay: Imitation and Originality in the *Dreigroschenoper*", in his *Links und links gesellt sich night: Gesammelte Aufsätze zum Werk Heinrich Manns und Bertolt Brechts*, New York, 1986.

*   *   *

The Threepenny Opera is set in Victorian London. Peachum, king of London's beggars, learns to his horror that his daughter Polly has eloped with underworld gang leader Macheath, known as Mac the Knife. With stolen goods for wedding gifts, Polly Peachum and Mac get married in a stable, in the presence of London's police chief Tiger Brown, an old army pal of Mac's. Peachum denounces Mac to the authorities but Polly tips off her husband in time; he flees and makes over the crime syndicate to her in his absence. In fact he merely goes

The Threepenny Opera: Sadlers Wells Theatre, London, 1976

to his regular brothel; the police easily catch him there, betrayed by the whores. In prison he runs across one of his many mistresses—Lucy, Tiger Brown's daughter. After a jealous confrontation with Polly, Lucy helps him to break out of gaol. Tiger Brown, reluctant to have him recaptured, is blackmailed into doing so by Peachum who threatens to spoil the Queen's coronation by a mass turn-out of London's beggars. So Mac, once again back at the whorehouse, is nabbed once again; but when he is about to be hanged, Brown arrives on horseback with the Queen's pardon, and Mac is knighted, given an annual pension and a country house.

This adaptation by Brecht, with music by Kurt Weill, of John Gay's *The Beggar's Opera* was first performed at the *Theater am Schiffbauerdamm* in Berlin on 31 August 1928. In spite of disastrous rehearsals and a general expectation of failure, it proved an enormous popular success, putting Brecht on the map as a major theatrical talent. Indeed, *The Three-penny Opera* became a key play in the brief golden age of Weimar theatre. Banned under the Nazis, it was revived in Germany shortly after the end of World War II; since then it has been produced around the whole world with great *éclat*.

In what ways did the 1928 Brecht–Weill version change Gay's original ballad opera of 1728? Basically Brecht moderni-sed what had been a satire aimed both at the conventions of Handelian opera and the cabals of Whig politics. Actually, he did not alter the storyline of *The Beggar's Opera* all that much: the new and exciting ingredient was the language. Gay's diction had been genteel; Brecht's was cynical, vulgar, hip in the 1920's manner, full of underworld slang. It was particularly the hard-boiled lyricism of the play's 19 songs, some of them borrowed from François Villon, that seized the popular imagination. Brecht's satirical butt was significantly different from Gay's. Both authors poked fun at the high style in opera, the sort of entertainment Brecht dismissed as "culinary". But whilst Gay, in pointing out the "similitude of manners in high and low life", had attacked the corrupt values of the aristoc-racy, Brecht satirised the hypocrisies—indeed the crimes—of the bourgeoisie. His own politics were developing in a Marxist direction without quite having arrived at that destination yet. In Brecht's version, Gay's dashing highwayman Macheath has become an entrepreneur of crime, an exponent of market forces; Lockit, the Newgate prison chief in *The Beggar's Opera*, appears in the guise of a corrupt chief of police, Tiger Brown; and Peachum, instead of being a receiver of stolen goods, systematically milks the public's squeamishness about poverty. The exploited, who had been totally invisible in Gay's universe, here turn up in the form of beggars, strictly organised into a mafia of scrofulous misery.

Ironic in tone and structure, *The Threepenny Opera* has had a stage history itself riddled with ironies. This satire on the "Establishment" was enthusiastically received by the very middle classes it lampooned. Much of this success was due to its ambiguity; it was actually less dead on target than *The Beggar's Opera* had been in its day. Brecht's picture of London was far more fantasticated than Gay's; for example, the vaguely late-Victorian ambiance is incompatible with a Queen's coronation (1837?). The play's fancy-dress appearance made it more picturesque than incisive: Peachum's beggars hardly provided an adequate theatrical correlative for the industrial proletariat of the 1920's.

Ironically enough, the music which was a major reason for the play's appeal, nearly didn't happen. The theatre manager E. J. Aufricht preferred the original *Beggar's Opera* score by Pepusch and meant to block Brecht's intention of having the songs set by Kurt Weill. But without Weill's score—a harsh, impudent, thinly orchestrated blend of folk, jazz, and avant-garde music—*The Threepenny Opera* would have been a different and infinitely less memorable play.

Erich Engel's pseudo-naïve production, with Caspar Neher's "incomplete" sets and with explanatory placards dropped in from the flies, laid the groundwork for what was later to become typical Brechtian staging. Even the "alienation effect" (*Verfremdungseffekt*) originated here: songs were clearly distinguished from the rest of the action by special lighting; actors reminded the audience that they were acting, not "being".

What has *The Threepenny Opera* to say to contemporary audiences? Brecht complained that the commercial theatre had a way of "theatring down" whatever was new in drama. And indeed *The Threepenny Opera* has been "theatred down" in post-World-War II productions. But then it is probably impossible to recapture that first fine rapture of the 1920's. Just the same, *The Threepenny Opera* remains eminently stageworthy—less for the (now questionable) sharpness of its social insights than for the sheer impudence of its engagement with the audience, its joyous aggressiveness, and the bitter-sweet, gutter lyricism of its songs.

—George W. Brandt

THUNDER.   See THE STORM.

**THUNDERSTORM (Leiyu / Lei-yü)
by Cao Yu (Ts'ao Yü)**

First Publication: c. 1933.
First Production: Shanghai, 1936.

Translations
Thunderstorm, translated by A.C. Barnes, Peking [Beijing], 1958.

Criticism
(For general works on the author, see *Playwrights* volume)

Articles:
Uwe Kräuter, "In the Limelight Again: Introducing China's Leading Dramatist Cao Yu", in *Chinese Literature*, 11, 1980.
Lewis S. Robinson, "On the Sources and Motives Behind Ts'ao Yü's *Thunderstorm*: A Qualitative Analysis", in *Tamkang Review*, vol.16 no.2, 1985.

*   *   *

Mine-director, Zhou Puyuan, has had three sons. The first two were by a woman called Shiping, and the elder of them, Ping, still lives with Zhou. 27 years before, Zhou drove away Shiping and their younger son, Dahai, and he thinks that she drowned at that time. He lives with his second wife, Fanyi, their son Chong, and Ping. Zhou doesn't know that Fanyi has had a love-affair with Ping, nor that their manservant, Lu Gui, is the third husband of Shiping—actually still alive—while their maidservant, Sifeng, is none other than a daughter of Zhou's born to Shiping after she departed.

As the play starts, all are unaware of the relationships between the Zhou and Lu families. Dahai, now a workers' representative in Zhou's mines, is in violent dispute with Zhou. Ping is now having a love affair with Sifeng. Shiping comes to the house. She encounters Zhou, and the various relationships are exposed. When she knows that the child she's expecting has been fathered by her own half-brother, Sifeng runs horrified from the house. She accidentally blunders into a faulty electrical cable. Chong tries to save her, but both are electrocuted. Dahai comes to the house to make trouble, but, although Zhou now feels drawn to him as his father, Dahai is chased out by servants. Ping commits suicide by shooting himself, and Zhou and Fanyi are left wailing and utterly distraught.

A study of the plot-summary, a reading of the play itself, and even a watching of a stage or filmed performance of this play will inevitably fail to explain to an uninitiated Westerner why *Thunderstorm* has held the position of prime importance in Chinese, Western-style drama these last 50 years and more. For all the copious dramatic writing of these years—interrupted and virtually annihilated, it is true, for the so-called Cultural Revolution era of 1966–76—no other "spoken-drama play" (*huaju*) has matched its general theatrical reputation and audience appeal. Even during the 1950's, when official policy was heavily on the side of promoting more recent, more ideological plays, Chinese audiences preferred *Thunderstorm* and other plays by Cao Yu. The first reaction of the Westerner may be lukewarm to say the least, cooled by the multiplicity of prominent roles, the unusually elaborate network of unusual relationships among the characters, the seemingly over-intense sequence of startling events, the hyper-laconic, psychological—too often truncated—dialogue, the frequent use of apparent sentimentality, the unfinished feel of the denouement, the pack-of-cards deaths, the possibly simplistic encapsulation of social and economic clash, and above all the whole power of the paternalistic family that underlies much of the tension.

A closer investigation, however, reveals a number of clues as to the Chinese enthusiasm for this work. Some of these are intimately related to major political trends and events, and thus, debatably, outside the strict confines of theatrical value judgements; or partly so, for the borderlines between political impetus and popular affection are not always easy to disentangle, especially in 20th-century China. It was in many ways a "first" when it appeared, establishing the shaky *huaju* genre in Chinese affection as no other play had done before. It had exotic appeal, difficult for a Westerner to appreciate since the source of the exoticism was the West itself. Maybe we can begin to intellectualise the effect it had on Chinese playgoers through comparisons with our own fascinations for chinoiserie and the "mysterious East". The influences from Ibsen and O'Neill were strong, and the predominance of speech (instead of the singing which is the forte of traditional styles of Chinese drama), the use of realistic costume and scenery, the very contemporaneity of the topic, and the "tragic" ending would all still have an exciting freshness for those Chinese—mainly at first the new-style, Western-orientated, politically-minded, urban intellectuals—who turned from the age-old stage, the Peking Opera, and other forms towards the new unrhythmic, unallusive, unadorned, speech-drama.

Above all perhaps, we must reason ourselves into the social and ethical situations of China as far back as the 1930's, acknowledging a temporal as well as spatial dislocation in our respective, intuitive reactions. In the 1930's in China, the family counted immensely as a cohesive and controlling unit. No civilisation has a more powerful and conscious ethos of family than that of China with its principal abiding system of thought, Confucianism—which in no uncertain terms proclaims the family as the bedrock of the nation and world peace and harmony. By "family", the extended, not the nuclear, is here intended. As China moved (or tumbled) rapidly towards the modern and Western world, a violent conflict arose between the concepts of family on the one hand, and mobile labour, individual freedom, individual social choice, and involvement on the other. This conflict, often manifested between the generations, was no mere neurotic drawing-room squabble, but a red-blooded and bloody war, still unresolved in intellectual terms and possibly not rationally soluble. It was the very stuff of the titanic combat between old and new, involved thousands of suicides, and was at the heart of all the major changes. What might seem *passé* to a Westerner was not and remains nothing of the sort in China.

It is in the light of the above considerations that we should view the incest, deaths, suicide, and high-strung emotionality of the play and judge the dramatic validity of it in its home environment. The electricity cable is no commonplace prop, but a symbol of modernity.

—William Dolby

THE THUNDERSTORM (Ostrovsky).   See **THE STORM.**

THE TICKET-OF-LEAVE MAN
by Tom Taylor

First Publication: In *Lacy's Acting Edition, 59*, London, 1863.
First Production: Olympic Theatre, London, 27 May 1863.

Editions

The Ticket-of-Leave Man, in *Nineteenth Century Plays*, edited by George Rowell, Oxford, 1953; second edition, 1972.
The Ticket-of-Leave Man, in *English Plays of the Nineteenth Century, 2*, edited by Michael R. Booth, Oxford, 1973.
The Ticket-of-Leave Man, introduced by John Russell Brown, London, 1981.
The Ticket-of-Leave Man, in *Plays by Tom Taylor*, edited by Martin Banham, Cambridge, 1985.

Criticism

(For general works on the author, see *Playwrights* volume)

Articles:
David Mayer, "*The Ticket-of-Leave Man* in Context", in *Essays in Theatre*, vol.6 no.1, 1987.

*   *   *

A traditional, yet in many ways out-of-the ordinary English melodrama, Tom Taylor's *Ticket-of-Leave Man*, first per-

The Ticket-of-Leave Man: Olympic Theatre, London, 1863 (first production)

formed in 1863 retained its popularity well into the 20th century. Adapted from *Léonard; ou, Le Retour de Mélun* by Edouard Brisebarre and Eugène Nus (performed in Paris in 1862), *The Ticket-of-Leave Man* concerns the trials and tribulations of a young Lancashire man, Robert Brierly. Attempting to make a living in London, Brierly becomes embroiled with criminals and alcohol and is arrested and imprisoned for passing off, albeit unwittingly, a counterfeit banknote. During three years in prison he is sustained by the love of a woman (May Edwards) he befriended before his arrest. Once destitute, she now lives comfortably from her needlework. Released early from prison for good behaviour on parole (a ticket-of-leave) Brierly, thoroughly cured of his earlier refractory ways, gets a job with a London brokerage firm, and plans to marry May. He has not, however, revealed his prison record to his employer, and when his former criminal associates stumble, by chance, upon his situation, they betray him and he is dismissed. By informing prospective employers of Brierly's past, they contrive to thwart his attempts to find a job. Apparently resigned to resuming a dissolute and criminal life, Brierly plots with his oppressors to rob the brokerage where he once worked, but with the help of Hawkshaw, the plain-clothed detective who initially arrested him, he hoodwinks the robbers and proves to everyone his worthiness.

Although the action of the play is predictable (and far too dependent on coincidence) and its moral underpinnings transparent, it breaks free from the restraints of its genre in a number of ways. There is, for example, an unusual richness of language, ranging from the Mistress Quickly-like loquaciousness of Mrs. Willoughby (May's landlady), to the colloquialism of Brierly ("thee looks welly clemmed", he tells the pallid May on their first meeting), to the criminal and police slang of Hawkshaw and his adversaries ("I have the beautifullest lot of Bank of England flimsies [banknotes] that ever came out of Birmingham"; "I had the darbies [handcuffs] open under the desk"; "By the by, lend me your barker [pistol]"). Authenticity surrenders to tendentiousness in the final act when Brierly must sermonize—"you may hold out your hand—you may cry for help—you may struggle hard—but the quicksands are under your foot—and you sink down, down, till they close over your head", he warns the wayward Sam Willoughby—but it is the jauntiness of language in the earlier acts that makes the greater impression.

The aspect of *The Ticket-of-Leave Man* that has attracted greatest critical attention, however, is its treatment of the parole or ticket-of-leave system in Victorian England; an issue about which there was, as David Mayer has shown, considerable public concern in the 1850's and 1860's, parolees being held responsible in the House of Commons and in the press for increases in violent crime in London. This attitude contrasts with the humane spirit of Taylor's play. Brierly serves his time and emerges from prison determined to live an honest and honourable life. Employer after employer, however, rejects him as soon as he is identified as a ticket-of-leave man. Society, it seems, is not prepared to give Brierly a second chance; his ticket of leave is really only a ticket back to crime. In highlighting this injustice, *The Ticket-of-Leave Man*, Mayer argues, "functions as energetic polemic in a specific, identifiable social and political process".

Mayer is right to emphasize this facet of the play, but both the energy and the polemic are compromised by Taylor's presentation of Brierly and his situation. Brierly is not so much the victim of systemic discrimination against parolees, but rather the dupe of circumstance and his own character failings. He is naïve more than he is criminal when, drunk, he negotiates the counterfeit banknote; he is foolish not to tell his first (and extremely benevolent) employer that he is on parole; he is unlucky that he encounters again his criminal confrères, who are set upon destroying him; and he is unfortunate in that bankers and navvies alike judge him for what he was rather than what he is. Brierly, then, hardly seems to be a representative ticket-of-leave man. What we have in *The Ticket-of-Leave Man* is an engaging case study, but not a compelling indictment of the ticket-of-leave system as such.

The Ticket-of-Leave Man is also notable for one of the earliest (perhaps *the* earliest) presentations of the English plainclothed detective in drama—the ubiquitous Hawkshaw. Another sensitive contemporary issue, the introduction of plainclothed police in 1842 aroused public suspicion and mistrust. This is reflected in the early scenes of the play when Hawkshaw and his surveillance colleagues succeed only in arresting the artless Brierly, while the hardened criminals escape. Ultimately, however, Hawkshaw collaborates with Brierly to see that justice is done. Any criticism Taylor intended of plainclothes detectives is extremely muted, while as a character, Hawkshaw lacks colour and vitality.

Tom Taylor, says Michael Booth in the introduction to his edition of the play, "was no reformer". In characterization, plot, and morality he acquiesced to melodramatic convention. None the less, Booth fittingly concludes, in *The Ticket-of-Leave Man* Taylor "shaped a drama refreshingly different in spirit and humanity from the mass of its contemporaries".

—L. W. Connolly

TIGER AT THE GATES. See **THE TROJAN WAR WILL NOT TAKE PLACE.**

TILL DAMASKUS, I-III. See **TO DAMASCUS.**

THE TIME IS NOT YET RIPE
by Louis Esson

First Publication: Melbourne, 1912; revised edition, Sydney, 1973.
First Production: Athenaeum Hall, Melbourne, 23 July 1912.

Criticism
(For general works on the author, see *Playwrights* volume)

Articles:
Philip Parsons, "Introduction", in *The Time is Not Yet Ripe*, by Louis Esson, Sydney, 1973.

*   *   *

The first of the play's four acts, located in the drawing-room of the Australian Conservative Prime Minister, Sir Joseph Quiverton, quickly defines its mode and theatrical lineage, and economically sets in motion the range of personal and political conflicts which are the focus of the satire. Doris, Sir Joseph's daughter, is in love with Sydney Barrett, who improbably reconciles his large land-holdings with revolutionary socialism. An election is shortly to be held, and among the interested parties are the fusty Anglophiles Sir Henry and Lady Pillsbury, the entrepreneurial American John K. Hill, and Miss Perkins, secretary of the Anti-Socialist League and resolute defender of the purity of the home; to that group will shortly be added some unionists and hard-liners from the Socialist Club, Violet Faulkner, an earnest feminist, and her fiancé Bertie Wainwright, a particularly thin-witted cricketer. All of them appear to be in conflict with Barrett's devil-may-care brand of socialist aestheticism, and most of them are concerned to court the support of Doris and her considerable charm for their cause. Doris stands against Sydney, in the event, and despite her humorous scepticism about all things political (and her significant absence from the street rally which occupies all of the third act) is duly returned for the electorate of Wombat. She resigns immediately, however, bequeathing her seat to Miss Perkins and joyously embracing Barrett; while Sir Joseph acknowledges the triumphant return of his party by an electorate which has decided once again that the time is not yet ripe for change, Doris and Barrett look forward to travelling overseas, and leaving behind a stultified Australia as a world well lost for love.

Esson commented before the publication of *The Time Is Not Yet Ripe* that it seemed already five years out of date, and he came increasingly to dislike and disown the play that, ironically, may have done more than any other to establish his contemporary reputation in the Australian theatre; and that has certainly, through several successful professional revivals in the 1970's, done most to maintain it. His rejection of this stylish political satire was no doubt partly the product of a conviction that it was not only derivative, but derivative from the wrong models. By 1912 Esson had become convinced that the development of a strong indigenous theatre was dependent on the dramatization of distinctive cultural myths, and his work characteristically reflects that view in its treatments of the archetypal conflicts of the outback and the urban world of "larrikin" workers and petty criminals. The playful urbanity of *The Time Is Not Yet Ripe*, with its drawing-room sets and its obvious indebtedness to the satiric style and debate structure of Shaw, seems at odds with the serious sense of mission that marked Esson's career in the theatre.

But the play has more to offer than a polished imitation of English manners. In part it is directly concerned to expose just that kind of cultural deference; the absurdities of the Conservatives in the play, from the pompous Sir Joseph down to the vacuous Bertie, are defined very much in terms of their derivativeness. Doris defines the conversational agenda, and her mischievous intelligence is quick to recognize and to unmask all forms of sham. At the same time, though, her scepticism makes for an anarchic mode of satire which is inclined to view all ideas and beliefs as varieties of affectation; the one commitment which she does not find silly is her own, to Sydney and to romance. Esson's reservations about the play may partly reflect an unease with the dominance of a character who, like Shaw's Candida (though with more wit), debunks most human aspirations on very dubious grounds. It ensures a quality of youthful freshness in the comedy, but allows the prospect of domestic bliss to be the only form of millennialism to escape mockery.

Doris's absence from the street rally is significant in that her role in deflating all pretension passes to the hecklers in the crowd, whose sense of political realities is thereby exempted from her wit. In this sequence the political aspirants are, in turn, subjected to the scepticism of the "common man", who proves just as astute in dealing with the egoism that underlies Barrett's demagoguery as he is in seeing through the more obvious posturings of Sir Joseph. Here, out of the drawing-room, Esson's own socialism finds some room in which to express itself; while Esson's ideas, as presented in *The Socialist* and elsewhere, bear some resemblance to those of Barrett, the third act suggests a degree of faith in the intelligence of ordinary people which qualifies the spirit of disillusioned irony that marks the end of the play, and which, perhaps, offers some terms for a critique of the attitudes of its likeable lovers. Doris and Sydney turn their backs on their culture at the end, but they are giving up a game in which neither has played as more than a dilettante. The spirit of their departure from the play ("Yes, we are alone in the world") is perhaps placed within a wider ironic framework by the presence in the play of the supposedly powerless classes; the rather fashionable disillusionment of the lovers may be seen from that perspective not as the end of a journey to maturity, but as a fairly early station on that road. They are, ironically, planning to go to England; so did the playwright who created them, a few years later, but for all his ambivalence about Australian culture he returned to persist in the task of giving it dramatic life. *The Time Is Not Yet Ripe* provides some terms, in its depiction of the larrikins and its consciousness of cultural imperialism from a number of directions, for understanding Esson's own attitudes to Australian life and politics, and for recognizing a complexity in its satirical impulse which makes it much more than the lightweight imitation for which the playwright came to feel such shame.

—Peter Fitzpatrick

THE TIME OF YOUR LIFE
by William Saroyan

First Publication: New York, 1939.
First Production: Booth Theatre, New York, 25 October, 1939.

Criticism
(For general works on the author, see *Playwrights* volume)

Articles:
James H. Justus, "William Saroyan and the Theatre of Transformation", in *The Thirties: Fiction, Poetry, Drama*, edited by Warren French, Deland, Florida, 1967.
Thelma J. Shinn, "William Saroyan: Romantic Existentialist", in *Modern Drama*, 15, 1972.
Kenneth W. Rhoads, "Joe as Christ-Type in Saroyan's *The Time of Your Life*", in *Essays in Literature*, 3, 1976.
John A. Mills, "'What. What-not.' Absurdity in Saroyan's *The Time of Your Life*", in *Midwest Quarterly*, 26, 1985.

*   *   *

The Time of Your Life is set in Nick's Pacific Street Saloon, Restaurant, and Entertainment Palace in San Francisco, during an afternoon and night of a day in October, 1939. An assortment of colorful and eccentric characters gather in the honky tonk. Joe, "a young loafer with money and a good heart", sits at his table drinking champagne, ordering toys and various other items for study, and carefully observing the people around him. He facilitates the play's most sustained action as he brings together Tom, his simple but compassionate errand boy, and Kitty Duval, a street-walker who remembers and yearns for her more innocent past. Nick, the bar's benevolent proprietor, is a gruff-speaking Italian who serves and converses with regular customers and curious visitors. He hires Wesley, a young black man, as a piano player, and Harry, an aspiring comedian who makes no one laugh, as a dancer. Dudley R. Bostwick furiously pursues his great love, Elsie Mandelspiegel, over the phone, and an old man who looks like Kit Carson staggers into the bar with tall tales of strange love affairs, hurricanes, Indian fights, and herding cattle on a bicycle.

Into the collection of basically sympathetic characters comes Blick, a mean-spirited and violent cop, who interrupts the friendly comfort of the bar, and, in the final scene, forces Kitty to begin a striptease, punches Kit Carson, and beats up Wesley. After Joe has hustled Kitty and Tom off to marriage in San Diego, he attempts to shoot Blick, but finds that the old revolver Tom has procured for him will not fire. Shortly after being pushed out of the bar, Blick is shot by an unknown assailant, Kit Carson re-enters with the story that he has killed Blick, and Joe slowly exits, after suggesting that he probably will not return.

The public setting of *The Time of Your Life* allows Saroyan to introduce a wide variety of characters, suggesting a cross-section of American society with differing racial, cultural, and socio-economic backgrounds; and the play's rapidly shifting focus as these people interact, pursue their dreams, or tell of broken hopes, creates a play about the general human condition rather than individuals. A master of creation and variation of mood, Saroyan manipulates piano music, harmonica playing, waltz music from the phonograph, Wesley's dancing, and other aural as well as visual elements to unify the work in the absence of a traditional cause-to-effect structure of events. The feeling of warmth and ease which Saroyan calls for reinforces Nick's perception that people gather at the honky tonk because "they can't feel at home anywhere else"; the bar is a haven out of time and place, but the unpleasant reality of the world outside keeps impinging on its comfort. There is the repeated suggestion of a society on the verge of violence and chaos, from Harry's would-be comic monologues about Hitler, hunger, and poverty to the pronouncements of a nihilistic Arab philosopher: "No foundation. All the way down the line". When the long-awaited Elsie finally arrives for Dudley, she consents to go off with him, even though she despairs of being able to sustain a love in the face of harsh reality: "Come on. The time for the new pathetic war has come. Let's hurry, before they dress you, stand you in line, hand you a gun, and have you kill and be killed". In the final scene of the play, labor unrest erupts into violence on the docks outside as Blick, the personification of evil, brings destruction from the outer world along with him into the bar.

To a great extent, the character Joe provides an anchor to the play's diverse action and voices many of the playwright's important ideas. Joe has assumed his largely stationary position in order to reject meaningless activity and take advantage of his "time of living": "I've been trying for three years to find out if it's possible to live what I think is a civilized life. I mean a life that can't hurt any other life". Joe sees in human beings a basic goodness, a fragile beauty of spirit, and the pain caused when circumstances force the abandonment of cherished dreams. He sees the inner self of Kitty Duval, and acts as her guardian angel, moving her from a cheap room to a high-class hotel, buying her expensive clothes, attempting to take her away from the world which hurts her. Joe recognizes the darker side of life as well, and interprets the Arab's cryptic statement, "What. What-not", as meaning "this side, that side. Inhale, exhale. What: birth. What-not: death. The inevitable, the astounding, the magnificent seed of growth and decay in all things. Beginning, and end".

Even though the evil Blick is neutralized and Tom and Kitty are shipped off to potential bliss, the play's final moments are ambiguous. When Joe takes on the responsibility to kill, he is powerless to do so, and while Kit Carson claims to be Blick's murderer, doubt is cast on his veracity by his earlier behavior. It is impossible to know the truth in the end, and once the outer world has invaded the bar, Joe leaves, seemingly in despair, with no explanation of what the future will bring. Much of *The Time of Your Life* is comic; the quirkiness of character often provides humor and a celebration of human diversity and eccentricity. The play's reaffirmation of the basic goodness of human nature, however, is matched by mourning for lost innocence in a world which has somehow gone out of control, sadness over the inevitability of the coming war, and regret at the inability of good people to live in the world without suffering emotional and physical pain.

—Kathy Fletcher

TIMON OF ATHENS
by William Shakespeare

First Publication: In First Folio, London, 1623.
First Production: c. 1604–05.

Editions

The Life of Timon of Athens, edited by J.C. Maxwell, Cambridge, 1957 (The New Shakespeare).

Timon of Athens, edited by H.J. Oliver, London, 1963 (Arden Shakespeare).

The Life of Timon of Athens, edited by Charlton Hinman, Baltimore, Maryland, 1964 (Pelican Shakespeare).

Timon of Athens, edited by Maurice Charney, New York, 1965 (Signet Classic Shakespeare).

Timon of Athens, edited by G.R. Hibbard, Harmondsworth, 1970 (New Penguin Shakespeare).

Bibliography

John K. Ruskiewicz, *"Timon of Athens": An Annotated Bibliography*, New York, 1986 (Garland Shakespeare Bibliographies).

Criticism

(For general works on the author, see *Playwrights* volume)

Books:

Francelia Butler, *The Strange Critical Fortunes of Shakespeare's "Timon of Athens"*, Ames, Iowa, 1966.

Rolf Soellner, *"Timon of Athens": Shakespeare's Pessimistic Tragedy, with a Stage History by Gary Jay Williams*, Columbus, Ohio, 1979.

Laurie Lanzen Harris and Mark W. Scott, *"Timon of Athens"*, in *Shakespearian Criticism, 1*, Detroit, Illinois, 1984 [anthology of criticism].

A.D. Nuttall, *Timon of Athens*, New York, London, etc., 1989 (Harvester New Critical Introductions to Shakespeare).

Articles:

For information on articles about *Timon of Athens*, see Ruskiewicz's bibliography, the bibliographies listed in the *Playwrights* volume, and the annual Shakespeare Bibliography in *Shakespeare Quarterly*, published by the Folger Shakespeare Library, Washington D.C. (1950–).

* * *

Like *Coriolanus*, *Timon of Athens* is a play in which a virtue comes under scrutiny. Timon is generous: he gives all he had to others indiscriminately, whether they are people in need or artists seeking his patronage. The economic structure within which he lives means that bankruptcy is the inevitable result. Timon is shown not to be the apex of a pyramid of patronage as he had first appeared, but part of a wider, flatter economic topography in which his generosity causes him to be in debt to others. When his faithful steward manages to persuade him of the seriousness of his position, Timon has no hesitation in sending him to those whom he has helped in the past, expecting similar open-handedness on their part. When his requests are rejected, Timon gives a final dinner-party at which he offers his guests stones in warm water to eat, and then leaves Athens, full of hatred for the city and the whole of mankind, to live in the woods outside the walls.

The second part of the play, although it follows a pattern familiar from *As You Like It* and *King Lear*, for example, is no "pastoral" respite. Timon is as much visited there as he was in the city, and nature offers little either to enlighten or restore him. In fact, nature's sense of irony is similar to Timon's: while grubbing for roots to eat, Timon finds not stones, but gold, a substance of no value outside the commercial network of the city. If absence of wealth was Timon's original problem, then its restoration should signal that all is well and that he can return. Timon's decision utterly to repudiate the world in which wealth circulates is both exhilarating and disconcerting. Timon has turned his back on materialism, but also on the whole human race.

Timon of Athens: Engraved frontispiece from Nicholas Rowe's 1709 edition

Timon hath made his everlasting mansion
Upon the beached verge of the salt flood,
Who once a day with his embossed froth
The turbulent surge shall cover.

Alcibiades' attempt to interpret Timon's final gesture is doomed to failure. That Timon intended the sea ("Neptune") to weep for ever on his grave, "on faults forgiven", is too fanciful, and reflects Alcibiades' compromising humanity and not Timon's uncompromising rage.

The play is often treated as an unfinished work, and commentators note the irregular versification, confusion of character names, and some apparently loose ends in the plot to support this view. Investigations into the printing of the First Folio (1623), the only early text of the play, have suggested that Timon was printed to fill a gap which arose when the copy for *Troilus and Cressida* was temporarily unavailable. It is possible that the play might not have been printed at all but for this accident, although, since a copy was obviously to hand, it might be argued that it was intended for inclusion elsewhere in the volume.

There has been much speculation that another author besides Shakespeare was involved in its composition, and recent studies favour Thomas Middleton as the collaborator—although whether he worked with Shakespeare, or acted as a reviser, is not ascertainable. Analysis has indicated that Middleton's likely contributions were mainly, although not exclusively, in the first part of the play, the scenes in Athens; and it is noticeable that much of the sharp, ironic analysis of citizen behaviour, so typical of Middleton's comedies, is situated here.

The success of the Royal Shakespeare Company's production in 1980, with Richard Pasco as Timon, indicates that, in the theatre at least, the play feels complete enough to offer a satisfying dramatic experience; but its consistency shows many marked differences from other Shakespeare plays. Human relationships are frequently presented by means of a series of repeated actions, as in a parable, or a folktale: responses to the steward's requests for money to help Timon give little access to "character", but provide telling examples of that much-used social formula, the excuse. The play is also unusual in the extreme and unremitting negativity of its central character. The audience is not given the satisfaction of knowing that Timon has learned anything from experience, or even moderated his views; it is left, like Alcibiades, to interpret Timon's story as best it can.

—Joanna Udall

A parallel to Timon's situation is to be found in that of the soldier, Alcibiades, who has been banished from Athens after failing in his plea to the senators to spare the life of a friend accused of manslaughter. All he has previously done for the city carries no weight in his argument. The scene with the senators has uneasy echoes of that in *Henry IV, Part Two* in which Davy pleads for the life of a villain, expecting his own "credit" with Justice Shallow to count against the crime of the accused. Alcibiades expects leniency on account both of his own and his friend's military service, and of the balance between unacceptable special pleading and reasonable desert is delicately poised. Alcibiades, sharing Timon's disgust with Athens, leads troops against it, but unlike Timon, he is persuaded to make allowances because "All have not offended", and he relents. Timon had been prepared to admit the existence of "one honest man", his steward, but his vision of mankind as irredeemably corrupt remained intact. Invective and irony are all he directs against Athens, and ultimately he obliterates himself, not the city. Timon's death is mysterious, not least from the point of view of staging. A series of epitaphs, one spoken by him, the other two found—apparently in different languages—on his "tomb", replace him as he is absorbed into the landscape:

TINY ALICE
by Edward Albee

First Publication: New York, 1965.
First Production: Billy Rose Theatre, New York, 13 October
      1962.

Criticism
(For general works on the author, see *Playwrights* volume)

Articles:
Edward Albee and John Gielgud, "Edward Albee and John
      Gielgud Talk About Theater", in *Atlantic Monthly*, 1965.

Leighton M. Ballew, "Who's Afraid of *Tiny Alice?*", in *Georgia Review*, 20, 1966.

Robert M. Post, "Albee's *Alice*", in *Western Speech*, 31, 1967.

Mardi Valgemae, "Albee's Great God Alice", in *Modern Drama*, 10, 1967.

Mary E. Campbell, "The Statement of Edward Albee's *Tiny Alice*", in *Papers on Language and Literature*, 4, 1968.

Richard A. Davison, "Edward Albee's *Tiny Alice:* A Note of Re-Examination", in *Modern Drama*, 11, 1968.

Herbert M. Simpson, "*Tiny Alice:* Limited Affirmation in a Conflict Between Theatre and Drama", in *Forum* (Houston), 6, 1968.

Ryder H. Curry and Michael Porte, "The Surprising Unconscious of Edward Albee", in *Drama Survey*, 7, 1968–69.

William F. Lucey, "Albee's *Tiny Alice:* Truth and Appearance", in *Renascence*, 21, 1969.

William E. Willeford, "The Mouse in the Model", in *Modern Drama*, 12 1969.

Dorothy D. Tolpegin, "The Two-Petaled Flower: A Commentary on Edward Albee's Play *Tiny Alice*", in *Cimarron Review*, 14 1971.

James E. White, "Albee's *Tiny Alice:* An Exploration of Paradox", in *Literatur in Wissenschaft und Unterricht*, 6, 1973.

Jules Glenn, "The Adoption Theme in Edward Albee's *Tiny Alice* and *The American Dream*", in *Psychoanalytic Study of the Child*, 29, 1974.

Richard M. Coe, "Beyond Absurdity: Albee's Awareness of Audience in *Tiny Alice*", in *Modern Drama*, 18, 1975.

Kristin Morrison, "Pinter, Albee, and 'the Maiden in the Shark Pond'", in *American Imago*, 35, 1978.

Harry N. Langdon, "Ritual Form: One Key to Albee's *Tiny Alice*", in *Theatre Annual*, 35, 1980.

Dennis Grunes, "God and Albee: *Tiny Alice*", in *Studies in American Drama 1945-Present*, 1, 1986.

*   *   *

In the opening scene the Lawyer, on behalf of his client Miss Alice, formally offers to the Cardinal a two-billion-dollar grant for the Church. Julian, a lay brother, is sent by the Cardinal to arrange the details. The vast, strange castle he enters, peopled by the beautiful Miss Alice, the Lawyer, and a butler named Butler, is one of illusion and complex meaning. The library is dominated by an enormous scale model of the castle which seems to respond to events in the real castle by having lights go on and off inside it as people move from room to room and by having its chapel catch fire when the real one does. Julian, who has previously spent time in an asylum due to a loss of faith caused by his grief at the fashion in which people create self-serving images of God, is drawn into a love affair with Miss Alice, and is torn by the complex interplay between sacrificing his vow of chastity and fulfilling his task of serving as requested to assure the grant. After he has married Miss. Alice the full horror of the situation unfolds as the Lawyer, the Butler, and Miss. Alice explain that Miss. Alice is only a fleshly analogue for Alice, a presence who presumably exists within the model and for whom the others are only trapped servants. The Lawyer then shoots Julian in the stomach, all abandon him, and at the close he dies backed up against the model with arms outflung as in a crucifixion while Tiny Alice, a "great shadow or darkening, fills the stage" to the accompaniment of slow, powerful breathing and menacing heartbeats.

No summation of the events of this play can even begin to approximate its sense of puzzle and mystery or the anguished, emotional pavane of Julian, struggling for a sense of personal and religious meaning in the centre of its distorting mirror of dimensions and circuitous betrayal. Albee has undertaken to conflate a number of concepts in a single play, and attempts to unravel the strands are bound to weaken the metaphoric compression of the actual stage images.

On one level this is a play about religious faith and sacrifice. Julian is tested on all levels of his faith and obedience. He sees the Cardinal marry him to Miss. Alice and then abandon him to carry the contract for the "grant" away. He struggles with his own desire to be a servant and with the problem of being conscious of the very pride which is inherent in knowing one is suitably humble. And finally, in a puzzling parody of the central Christian sacrifice he cries out: "Alice? ALICE? MY GOD, WHY HAST THOU FORSAKEN ME?"

On another plane this play is a fantasia about a malevolent Platonic reality, a world of forms and their embodiments. Central to this is the Miss Alice / (Tiny) Alice paradox, a fleshly Miss Alice who tells Julian that he has married the Alice of the doll's-house model and that she has served only as the conduit for this event. The attitudes of the Butler, the Lawyer, and Miss Alice as they leave the dying Julian are clearly those of people forced to perform for some greater force and who expect to be doomed to go on repeating their actions. The audience's solid sense of reality—in the characters and scenes of the play—becomes inverted and finally overwhelmed by the great pulsing, breathing shadow which dominates the conclusion.

Albee might have seen the Miss Alice / Tiny Alice image as an envisioning of the psychic relationship between the woman and the inner force of the overwhelming mother, eternal and possessive and destructive. Or he may have seen it as the epitome of the conflict between the flesh and the ideal and the confusions into which one is led by the reality of incarnation. There is no clear or simple meaning, only a powerful metaphoric paradox.

The play is a triumph of Albee's skill in unnerving an audience. It is as full of the switches in emotional balance which were achieved in *Who's Afraid of Virginia Woolf?*, but here they are more psychologically shocking because they are stylized without the rationalization of game playing. Thus, in Scene 1 the Cardinal meets the Lawyer in a formal visit which suddenly degenerates through ironic comedy into a vicious and naked power struggle as both men, completely out of their professional roles, tear at one another in a hate born in their schooldays and which reveals depraved greed and lust for dominance in both. Julian moves through the central scenes confused and buffeted, as the audience begins to grasp that some horrible and mysterious event is unfolding, and the other characters by turns treat him normally at the level of wit and logic, and then with cryptic emotional deviousness.

When, in the puzzling and powerful ending, the dying Julian cries out to God, in words from the Psalms and the Crucifixion, he is crying for Alice at the same time. The exotic and surreal emotional reality which Albee has engineered does not suddenly release its secrets in this sacrificial denouement. Rather, this powerful and enigmatic play remains an image burnt in the minds of the audience, a dark and forceful psychological puzzle that can neither be forgotten nor rationally dismissed.

—Peter Brigg

'TIS PITY SHE'S A WHORE
by John Ford

First Publication: London, 1633.
First Production: Phoenix Theatre, London (Queens Company), c. 1629–33.

Editions

'Tis Pity She's a Whore, in *'Tis Pity She's a Whore; The Broken Heart*, edited by S.P. Sherman, Boston and London, 1915.
'Tis Pity She's a Whore, in *Five Stuart Tragedies*, edited by A.K. McIlwraith, Oxford, 1953.
'Tis Pity She's a Whore, edited by N.W. Bawcutt, Lincoln (Nebraska) and London, 1966 (Regents Renaissance Drama Series).
'Tis Pity She's a Whore, edited by Brian Morris, London, 1968 (New Mermaid Series).
'Tis Pity She's a Whore, edited by Derek Roper, Manchester, 1975 (Revels Plays Series).
'Tis Pity She's a Whore, in *The Selected Plays of John Ford*, edited by Colin Gibson, Cambridge, 1986.

Bibliography

Georges Bas, "John Ford: *'Tis Pity She's a Whore*: Bibliographie sélective et critique", in *Bulletin de la Societé d'études anglo-américaines des XVIIe et XVIIIe siècles*, 5, 1977.

Criticism

(For general works on the author, see *Playwrights* volume)

Articles:

G. Bauer, "*Dommage qu'elle soit une prostituée:* Critique", in *Annales politiques et littéraires*, 1934.
Cyrus Hoy, "Ignorance in Knowledge: Marlowe's Faustus and Ford's Giovanni", in *Modern Philology*, 57, 1960.
R.J. Kaufmann, "Ford's Tragic Perspective", in *Texas Studies in Literature and Language*, 1, 1960.
Irving Ribner, "By Nature's Light: The Morality of *'Tis Pity She's a Whore*", in *Tulane Studies in English*, 10, 1960.
Donald K. Anderson, "The Heart and the Banquet: Imagery in Ford's *'Tis Pity She's a Whore* and *The Broken Heart*", in *Studies in English Literature 1500–1900*, 2, 1962.
Sidney R. Homan, "Shakespeare and Dekker as Keys to Ford's *'Tis Pity She's a Whore*", in *Studies in English Literature 1500–1900*, 7, 1967.
Kenneth A. Requa, "Music in the Ear: Giovanni as Tragic Hero in Ford's *'Tis Pity She's a Whore*", in *Papers on Language and Literature*, 7, 1971.
Lucette Andriev, "*Dommage qu'elle soit une prostituée* de John Ford: Vitalité et devenir scenique de la tragédie", in *Cahiers élisabéthans*, 3, 1973.
Kenneth A. Requa, "Music in the Ear: Giovanni as Tragic Hero in Ford's *'Tis Pity She's a Whore*", in *Comparative Drama*, 8, 1974.
Carol C. Rosen, "The Language of Cruelty in Ford's *'Tis Pity She's a Whore*", in *Comparative Drama*, 8, 1974–75.
Larry A. Champion, "Ford's *'Tis Pity She's a Whore* and the Jacobean Tragic Perspective", in *Publications of the Modern Language Association* [PMLA], 90, 1975.
Fernand Lagarde, "L'Italie de *'Tis Pity She's a Whore*", in *Hommage à Emile Gasquet, 1920–1977*, with a foreword by Pierre Marainbaud, Paris, 1978.
Claudine Defaye, "Annabella's Unborn Baby: The Heart in the Womb in *'Tis Pity She's a Whore*", in *Cahiers études*, 15, 1979.

Gulles D. Monsarrat, "The Unity of John Ford: *'Tis Pity She's a Whore* and *Christ's Bloody Sweat*", in *Studies in Philology*, 77, 1980.
Jean-Pierre Macquelot, "*'Tis Pity She's a Whore:* La Justice divine comme élément de l'esthétique baroque", in *Société française Shakespeare: Actes du congrès 1980*, edited by Marie-Thérèse Jones-Davies, Paris, 1981.
R.L. Smallwood, "*'Tis Pity She's a Whore* and *Romeo and Juliet*", in *Cahiers études*, 20, 1981.
Simone Dorangeon, "Harmonie rompue et esthétique dans *'Tis Pity She's a Whore*", in *Visages de l'harmonie dans la littérature anglo-américaine*, Reims, 1982.
Bruce Boehrer, "'Nice Philosophy': *'Tis Pity She's a Whore* and the Two Books of God", in *Studies in English Literature 1500–1900*, 24, 1984.
Zia Hasan, "Incest Over the Ages: A Comparison Between *'Tis Pity She's a Whore* and *The Alexandria Quartet*", in *Literary Criticism*, 20, 1985.
Rick Bowers, "John Ford and the Sleep of Death", in *Texas Studies in Literature and Language*, 28, 1986.
Denis Gauer, "Heart and Blood: Nature and Culture in *'Tis Pity She's a Whore*", in *Cahiers études*, 31, 1987.
Christine Gomez, "Profaning the Sacred: The Juxtaposition of Incest and Marriage in Ford, Ibsen, and Osborne", in *Aligarh Critical Miscellany*, 2, 1989.

*　　*　　*

A brilliant young student, Giovanni, falls in love with his sister, Annabella. The couple conceal their sexual relationship from their father Florio, a merchant of Parma, and Annabella rejects offers of marriage from a wealthy simpleton, Berghetto; an arrogant Roman soldier, Grimaldi; and Soranzo, a rich young nobleman. However, when she falls pregnant she confesses her situation to Giovanni's tutor, Friar Bonaventura, and on his advice marries Soranzo. Her husband discovers her condition but fails to force from her the name of the child's father; that is wormed out of Annabella's accomplice, her nurse Putana, by Soranzo's servant, Vasques. Soranzo invites Annabella's brother and father to his birthday feast, intending to have Giovanni killed. Despite warnings from his lover and tutor, Giovanni accepts the invitation, and takes the opportunity for a last meeting with his sister whom he stabs to death. He enters the feasting place with her heart on his dagger, and manages to kill Soranzo before Vasques despatches him. His father, Florio, dies of shock and grief.

In a subplot, Hippolita, a woman Soranzo has seduced, and her husband Richardetto separately seek vengeance against Soranzo; but Vasques makes Hippolita drink the poison she intended for Soranzo. Berghetto, who has fallen in love with Richardetto's niece, Philotis, is mistaken for Soranzo and murdered by Grimaldi (ironically, at Richardetto's instigation).

Although several other Jacobean and Caroline authors wrote plays dealing with incestuous desire, the directness of Ford's treatment of the subject and the sympathy declared in the title of his tragedy kept *'Tis Pity She's a Whore* off the stage until the present century. Now its place in the contemporary theatre seems assured, with 32 British productions alone since 1950.

No single source for the play has been discovered. Ford may have used a narrative in Francois de Rosset's *Tragic Stories of our Time* (1615) as the basis for his own, but in dramatising it he drew on scenes and situations in Beaumont and Fletcher's *A King and No King*, Chapman's *Bussy D'Ambois*, Middleton's

Women Beware Women, and Webster's *Duchess of Malfi*. Shakespeare's *Romeo and Juliet* offered a general model for a tragedy of secret love in a warring world, though Ford replaces public, family feuding with private, sexual rivalry and revenge.

The central conception of the play is tragic in a larger sense than that implied by the violent deaths of Giovanni, Annabella and others, including Hippolita. The lovers are the extraordinary protagonists of high tragedy, with an intense inner life and spiritual values that set them apart from the ordinary citizens around them. Giovanni is "a miracle of wit", the wonder of his age, educated to so strong a commitment to the noblest love he can conceive of that he is willing to defy and rationalise his rejection of social convention and divine law. Annabella responds to him with equal ardour and innocence of spirit, emphasised by the earthy excitement of her old nurse. The young couple invest each other with divinity and declare an absolute affection: "love me or kill me". Ford charts their downward trajectory through self-congratulating cleverness, defiant adultery, fear, and remorse, to a state of egotistical frenzy in which Giovanni boasts the slaughter of his sister and demands that the heart on his dagger point be read as an icon of true love and exultant revenge.

The dramatist's skill in counterpointing the secret life of the lovers with the bustle of an ignorant world pursuing marriage or murder, in devising richly symbolic stage images and patterns of obsessive imagery, in finding an eloquent simplicity of language and gesture to express intensity of being, makes for a compelling account of the gradual corruption of a love which at the beginning at least has a special kind of intensity and integrity.

Ford's Parma, the city setting of the play, is not a world of great public affairs and important people; it provides a mundane, almost domestic context for a tragic passion, an ordinary urban community whose busy activities (from gossip at the barber's shop to civilised marriage negotiations between two fathers) are focused on life in the streets, and the dwellings of Florio, Soranzo, and Friar Bonaventura. Ford is careful to suggest a balance of harmonious prosperity and casual disorder giving way to more sinister violence: Berghetto is first pushed into the gutter by a swaggering passer-by, then later murdered in a dark street by an assassin.

Generous intention, kindliness, and comically innocent pleasure in life are to be found among the inhabitants of Parma, but Ford also displays striking instances of folly, outrageous injustice, moral cowardice, and vicious cruelty which both highlight the essential innocence of Giovanni and Annabella's love and help explain its final destruction. The murderer Grimaldi's protection from the law by the Papal Nuncio, Richardetto's part in the organisation of the crime and his self-righteous delight in the agonising death of his wife, Bonaventura's flight on the eve of disaster, Vasques's sadism, and Soranzo's brazen double-dealing make it impossible for the audience to align themselves with any of the representatives of conventional morality.

Ford's tragic vision is not of any kind of legal justice dispensed by the corrupt civic and religious authorities of Parma, nor of wild justice achieved through the blind rage of his private revengers, but an altogether darker justice visited in the terrible and pitiful end of his two young lovers, brought about both by their special circumstances and the human flaws inherent in their finest qualities.

—Colin Gibson

TIT-COQ
by Gratien Gélinas

First Publication: Montreal, 1950.
First Production: Monument National Theatre, Montreal, 22 May 1948.

Translations
Tit-Coq, Toronto and Vancouver, 1967.

Criticism
(For general works on the author, see *Playwrights* volume)

Articles:
Jean C. Godin, "Orphelins ou bâtards: *Fridolin, Tit-Coq, Bousille*", in *Le Théâtre québécois: Introduction à dix dramaturges contemporains*, by Godin and Laurent Mailhot, Montreal, 1970.
Bernard Julien, "*Tit-Coq* et [Dumas's] *Antony*: Analogies des structures, des personnages et des destins", in *Mélanges de civilisations canadienne-française offerts au professeur Paul Wyczynski*, Ottawa, 1977.

*   *   *

An illegitimate orphan, Arthur Saint-Jean nicknamed "Tit-Coq" ("Little Rooster") because of his temperament, falls in love with Marie-Ange, the sister of an army chum. They become engaged before he is sent overseas, but in his absence she marries another. On his return, he confronts her and persuades her to run away with him. But a Catholic chaplin convinces him he will be recreating the very illegitimacy and lack of identity he seeks to avoid in marriage. Tit-Coq and Marie-Ange, disconsolate, go their separate ways.

From its very first performances, *Tit-Coq* was seen by critics as the most important milestone in the evolution of an indigenous, French-Canadian, dramatic tradition and an apogee of dramatic art. Historians have since refined that perception—the play is now seen as somewhat outmoded, its French-Canadian diction unconvincing (it was more audible in stage and film versions than visible in the printed text), its treatment of illegitimacy and divorce no longer controversial, its resolution predictable and conventional—but have not radically altered it. At the time, Quebec audiences tended to see in this simple but compelling depiction of a foundling's search for identity a parallel with the situation of their own nation, orphaned before maturity and never comfortable in its bicultural Canadian status. The acute self-awareness Quebec has experienced since its Quiet Revolution of the 1960's no longer accommodates that identification.

Theatre historians have also pointed out that the play, far from being revolutionary, is, in fact, a natural outgrowth of Quebec's long theatrical tradition. Gélinas, at the time of *Tit-Coq*'s composition, was already one of the best-known performers and dramatists in the province, primarily because of his annual satirical revues, *Fridolinons* (named after their central character, Fridolin, played by the author). Fridolin, a sort of Québécois Everyman with whose irrepressible verve and good humour French Canadians easily identified, is visible in the personality of Tit-Coq, and two of the sketches from these revues are the germ and the basis for the play. The title-role of the play was acted by Gélinas in the French and English stage versions, as in the film; and that fact also explains in good part the warm reception the work received at home. A brusque, awkward, but empathic character, an outsider in his conservative society, Tit-Coq is capable of great loyalty and affection, but is insecure, suspicious, and possessed of a hot temper and mordant tongue.

Obsessed by his illegitimacy (he has been brought up in a foundlings' home) he is drawn to Marie-Ange primarily, as the final scene proves, because she is the product of a large, long-established, and well-adjusted (if somewhat stereotypical) Quebec family. He sees her as his passport to social legitimacy, but unwisely insists on waiting until the war's end before they marry. Marie-Ange, immature and susceptible to family pressures during his long absence, marries another—a fact that Tit-Coq learns only after the event. In an effective climactic scene, she is forced by Tit-Coq to meet with him and explain her actions. The Chaplain who had been indirectly responsible for their meeting, and who had accompanied Tit-Coq overseas, has heard of this confrontation and insists on being present, much to the latter's discomfort. Tit-Coq has little difficulty convincing Marie-Ange to renounce her marriage vows, abandon her husband, and leave with him; but the Chaplain reminds both that their union would always remain illegal (divorce did not exist in Quebec before the 1960's) and their children would be bastards—like the protagonist himself. The latter's yearning for legitimacy is stronger than his love: sadly, he departs, in the only sort of denouement that was possible in a play staged publicly in conservative, Catholic French Canada at the time.

Tit-Coq is now rarely performed, although it is widely read in schools and universities in French and English Canada and continues to elicit much attention from cultural historians. Its powerful impact on audiences throughout Canada in the 1940's and 1950's has been overbalanced by hypercritical assessment since the 1960's. Its true place, as a modest drama that succeeded in capturing something of Quebec's mood and aspirations in the difficult years following World War II, now seems deservedly secure.

—Leonard E. Doucette

TITUS ANDRONICUS
by William Shakespeare

First Publication: London, 1594 ("good" first quarto); with variants and Act III, Scene 2 in First Folio, 1623.
First Production: London, c.1592–94.

Editions

Titus Andronicus, edited by John Dover Wilson, Cambridge, 1948 (The New Shakespeare).
Titus Andronicus, edited by J.C. Maxwell, London, 1953; third edition, 1961 (Arden Shakespeare).
Titus Andronicus, edited by Sylvan Barnet, New York, 1964 (Signet Classic Shakespeare).
Titus Andronicus, edited by Gustav Cross, Baltimore, Maryland, 1967 (Pelican Shakespeare).
Titus Andronicus, edited by Eugene M. Waith, Oxford, 1984 (Oxford Shakespeare).

Criticism

(For general works on the author, see *Playwrights* volume)

Books:
Howard Baker, *Induction to Tragedy: A Study in the Develop-* *ment of Form in "Gorboduc", "The Spanish Tragedy", and "Titus Andronicus"*, Baton Rouge, Louisiana, 1939.
James L. Calderwood, *Shakespeare's Metadrama: The Argument of the Play in "Titus Andronicus", "Love's Labours Lost", "Romeo and Juliet", "A Midsummer Night's Dream", and "Richard II"*, Minneapolis, 1971.
Mark W. Scott (ed.), *"Titus Andronicus"*, in *Shakespearian Criticism, 4*, Detroit, Illinois, 1987 [anthology of criticism].
Alan C. Dessen, *Titus Andronicus*, Manchester, 1989.
Maurice Charney, *Titus Andronicus*, New York, London, etc., 1990 (Harvester New Critical Introductions to Shakespeare).

Articles:
For information on articles about *Titus Andronicus*, see the bibliographies listed in the *Playwrights* volume, and the annual Shakespeare Bibliography in *Shakespeare Quarterly*, published by the Folger Shakespeare Library, Washington D.C. (1950–).

* * *

The most sensational of Shakespeare's plays, *The Most Lamentable Roman Tragedy of Titus Andronicus*, starts at the hustings for election of a new Emperor: Saturninus argues that he is the eldest son of the previous ruler; Bassianus that he is not dishonourable like his brother. But the people of Rome have chosen Titus Andronicus, the general victorious against the neighbouring Goths. All this is managed with good order and dignity, and the disputants file off stage together. But then Titus returns to Rome at the head of a long procession of mourners, soldiers, and captives, and the mood changes. Titus weeps for joy at his homecoming and solemnly buries the body of a son killed in battle, the 21st of his sons killed in this way. He also orders Alarbus, eldest son of Tamora, Queen of the Goths, to be killed for a sacrifice; and he is deaf to the mother's cries for mercy. At this point, the other characters return, and again the mood changes, and expectations are overturned. Quickly, in a strange mixture of barbarism and noble sentiment, Titus refuses the crown and asks that it should be given to Saturninus; he gives the new Emperor as bride his only daughter Lavinia, who is already betrothed to Bassianus.

When his remaining four sons try to prevent this, Titus kills one of them and forbids his honourable burial. Meanwhile, however, Saturninus has asked Tamora to be his Empress and has freed all the remaining prisoners. The long first scene ends with the re-entry of Saturninus and Tamora, and of Bassianus and Lavinia, both pairs newly married. Apparently all is at peace, but in a long aside Tamora tells her new lord that she will "massacre" all the Andronici. Everyone leaves the stage except Aaron, a Moor, who in a soliloquy reveals that he is Tamora's lover and promises the destruction of Saturninus and all the Romans.

After these sweeping changes of fortune, the pace hardly slackens. Bassianus is murdered. Lavinia is raped, her hands cut off, and her tongue cut out. Titus is tricked into having his own hand cut off by Aaron in order to save the lives of two of his sons, whose decapitated heads are then delivered to him. At this centre-point in the play, Titus vows revenge, and Lucius, his one remaining son, leaves Rome to raise an army of Goths to be revenged on Saturninus. Titus—his "heart all mad with misery"—kills the two remaining sons of Tamora and bakes them in a pie. Lavinia helps her father as best she can. Aaron protects Tamora by killing the midwife who assisted at the birth of her black child; he then escapes with his infant son, only to be captured by Lucius's army.

Titus Andronicus: Stratford-Upon-Avon, 1981 (Royal Shakespeare Company)

In a final crowded scene—brutal, frenzied, grotesque, and complicated—Lucius returns to Rome; Titus, dressed like a cook, kills Lavinia, so that her shame dies too, and then serves Tamora with the flesh of her sons; thereupon Titus kills Tamora; Saturninus kills Titus, and Lucius murders Saturninus. Lucius becomes Emperor and gives order that the still-defiant Aaron shall be tortured to death.

Reprints of the first edition of *Titus Andronicus* are testimony to its early popularity, and an adaptation was staged after the Restoration. But until Hereward Price's work for the Variorum edition of the play (which began to be published as a study of its language, in an article of 1935), few critics gave it serious attention. Despite all the external evidence, it was commonly said to be too outrageous and clumsy to have been written by Shakespeare and many different authors were suggested for the "worst" parts of it, George Peele being the favourite candidate. It was the rarest of Shakespeare's to be staged.

However, Price had revealed its careful structure, its originality, and imaginative unity, and in 1955 Peter Brook staged a memorable production with Laurence Olivier as Titus, Anthony Quayle as Aaron, and Alan Webb as the one temperate voice, Marcus, the brother of Titus. The horrors were staged carefully and with restraint: blood flowing from Lavinia's wrists were broad bands of red ribbon, and the grisly humor of the last scene was strictly censored. Olivier acted Titus's long rhetorical speeches so that the verbal images were vivid and sensitive, and they struck deep into his audience's minds.

Shakespeare's imitation of Seneca's revenge tragedies and of Ovid's most fanciful style are nowhere more obvious, nor his power to shock and bewilder an audience. But during the last 50 years, critics and playgoers have been able to recognize the play's other qualities: its bold structure, bitter humour, strong passions, cutting moments of pathos. Shakespeare has presented in this early tragedy a series of images of a political jungle: ". . .Rome is but a wilderness of tigers;/Tigers must prey, and Rome affords no prey/But me and mine". As Titus struggles to vindicate himself, his sanity is precarious and his strength challenged:

> For now I stand as one upon a rock,
> Environed with a wilderness of sea,
> Who marks the waxing tide grow wave by wave,
> Expecting ever when some envious surge
> Will in his brinish bowels swallow him.

Imaginatively, *Titus Andronicus* was Shakespeare's preparation for later, more subtle, and more deeply sustained studies of men of power and conscience—Richard II, Hamlet, Lear, Timon—each isolated in a world he cannot control and can begin to understand only by withstanding its cruelty.

In some productions and some readings, Aaron almost usurps attention from the hero. Like Iago (*Othello*), Edmund (*King Lear*), and Caliban (*The Tempest*), he is alien to the other characters from the very start of the action. By daring to stand alone, he maintains an egotism and ambition that demand respect, and almost unsettle the established world.

Titus is more than a dark and vicious horror-drama: at the heart of an appalling image of cruelty and suffering, Shakespeare's quick and truthful intelligence is at work.

—John Russell Brown

TO DAMASCUS (Till Damaskus)
  To Damascus, I (Till Damaskus, I)
  To Damascus, II (Till Damaskus, II)
  To Damascus, III (Till Damaskus, III)
by August Strindberg

To Damascus, I (Till Damaskus, I)
First Publication: With *Till Damaskus, II*, 1898.
First Production: Dramaten [Royal Dramatic Theatre], Stockholm, 19 November 1900.

To Damascus, II (Till Damaskus, II)
First Publication: With *Till Damaskus, I*, 1898.
First Production: Lorensbergsteatern, Gothenburg, Sweden, 9 December 1924.

To Damascus, III (Till Damaskus, III)
First Publication: 1904.
First Production: Lorensbergsteatern, Gothenburg, Sweden, 16 November 1922.

Editions
Till Damaskus, edited by G. Lindström, 1964.

Translation
To Damascus, translated by Sam E. Davidson, Boston, 1913.
To Damascus, translated by Graham Rawson, London, 1939.
To Damascus, Part One, translated by Evert Sprinchorn, in *The Genius of the Scandinavian Theater*, edited by Evert Sprinchorn, New York, 1964.
To Damascus, I, II, and III", in *Strindberg: Eight Expressionist Plays*, translated by Arvid Paulsen, New York, 1965.
To Damascus [Parts I, II, and III] in *Strindberg: Plays, 2*, translated by Michael Meyer, London, 1975.
Plays of Confession and Therapy: "To Damascus I, II, and III", translated by Walter Johnson, Seattle and London, 1979 (Washington Strindberg).

Criticism
(For general works on the author, see *Playwrights* volume)

Articles:
Carl E.W.L. Dahlström, "Situation and Character in *Till Damaskus*", in *Publications of the Modern Language Association [PMLA]*, 53, 1939.
D. Scanlon, "*The Road to Damascus, Part One*: A Skeptic's Everyman", in *Modern Drama*, vol.5 no.3, 1962.
Sister M. Vincentia, "Wagnerism in Strindberg's *The Road to Damascus*", in *Modern Drama*, vol.5 no.3, 1962.
Sven M. Kristensen, "Strindberg's Damascus", in *Orbis Litterarum*, 22, 1967.
Ernest Ferlita, "*The Road to Damascus*", in his *The Theatre of Pilgrimage*, New York, 1971.
Ted Frank, "Strindberg's *Damascus* Plays: The Pilgrimage of an Uneasy Rider", in *Southern Speech Communication Journal*, 39, 1973.
Kurt Klinger, "August Strindbergs Trilogie *Nach Damaskus*", in his *Konfrontationen: Theateressays*, Vienna, 1973.
Mary G. Hamilton, "Strindberg's Alchemical Way of the Cross", in *Mosaic*, vol.7 no.4, 1974.
Henning Thies, "Archetypische Namenmagie: Strindberg, *Nach Damaskus*", in his *Namen in Kontext von Dramen: Studien zur Funktion von Personennamen im englischen, amerikanischen und deutschen Drama*, Frankfurt, 1978.
Jocelyn Powell, "Demons That Live in Sunlight: Problems in Staging Strindberg", in *Yearbook of English Studies*, 9, 1979.

To Damascus: Dramaten, Stockholm, 1900 (first production)

Winnie de Wit, "Strindbergs *Naar Damaskus:* Een publiek-sonderzoek", in *Tijdschrift voor Skandinavistiek*, vol.4 no.1, 1983.

Diane Filby Gillespie, "Strindberg's *To Damascus:* Archetypal Autobiography", in *Modern Drama*, 26, 1983.

Carole J. Lambert, "Strindberg's Medievalism: Depth Psychology in *To Damascus I*", in *Selecta*, 5, 1984.

Natalie Sandler, "*To Damascus I:* Reading the Set", in *Modern Drama*, 28, 1985.

*   *   *

Part One follows the pilgrimage of the Stranger (the Unknown One) through stages of suffering and spiritual growth. The Stranger, alienated and haunted by guilt, takes the Lady away from her husband, the Doctor, and visits her family. In an asylum, images from the past torment him, and the Confessor reads a ritualistic curse. The Stranger receives help from the Lady's mother in approaching his "road to Damascus". Reunited with the Lady and reconciled with the Doctor, the Stranger discovers that apprehension about a letter was unfounded. Spiritually healed yet skeptical, he agrees to enter but not stay in the church.

In *Part Two* the Stranger cannot trust the Lady, now his wife. Still arrogant and self-centered, he takes no pleasure in their child, being more concerned about gaining destructive power through experiments with electricity and alchemy. The Stranger is invited to an elaborate banquet, which turns grotesque. Confronting again figures from his past, he undergoes emotional trials and spiritual lessons.

In *Part Three* the Stranger approaches a monastery on a mountain top. After bidding farewell to his daughter, he finds a pool where syphilis patients, including his son, are bathing. They blame the Stranger for corrupting them with his liberal morality. Seeing the Lady transformed into his mother, the Stranger approaches in hope of reconciliation with humanity, but the image disappears. The Lady next represents his third wife. After a beautiful wedding dinner the couple quarrel, and the Stranger abandons hope of happiness with a woman. Withdrawing to the monastery, he submits to instruction and ritual burial, anticipating salvation and rebirth.

Despite the broad scope of action and multiplicity of details, the dramatic action in the *To Damascus* trilogy has a unity centered on the anguish and penitence of the Stranger as he learns humility and submits to God or the higher powers. Although he compares himself to Saul (Paul), the Stranger does not undergo the same dramatic and definitive conversion; rather, he vacillates and resists as he progresses toward the peace of the monastery.

Strindberg drew from his experiences and expressed his own spiritual anguish when writing the trilogy. He had survived the depression of the Inferno (1894–7). Using incidents from the marriage to his second wife, Frida Uhl, his stay in a hospital in Paris, treatment by Dr. Anders Eliasson in Ystad, and experimentation with alchemy, Strindberg revealed his sense of persecution and how he found the way back to religious faith. Although Strindberg used real people and intensely personal episodes as material, he gave *To Damascus* universal significance comparable to that of *Faust*. The Stranger is related to heroic figures from the Bible, mythology, and world history, and his life-journey is an archetype of human experience.

Critical analysis of *To Damascus* usually concentrates on *Part One*. Its structure is symmetrical, with 17 scenes progressing from one location to the next until the focal scene in the asylum, then reversing the sequence of locations with a circular effect. Influenced by medievalism, Strindberg creates a modern Everyman, who encounters figures reminding him that he is accountable for his moral choices. Strindberg draws upon musical inspiration, both by using actual compositions, such as Mendelssohn's funeral march, and by creating a contrapuntal pattern of verbal and visual motifs in a Wagnerian manner. Numerous recurring images and themes are interwoven into the complex structure of the play—the Rose Chamber, colors, death, the Garden of Eden, the hollowness of fame, the mill, and many more.

Characters have an identity of their own, yet are doubles of the Stranger or projections of aspects of his personality. The Beggar is the most obvious *Doppelgänger*: well-educated, an outcast, bearing a scar on his forehead just like the Stranger's. Even the Lady mirrors the Stranger's thoughts. She has an important function in the trilogy as a symbol of love and redemption, but also of sin and disenchantment. When beautiful and inspiring, she comforts the Stranger and asks him thoughtful questions. After reading about his first marriage, she feels sullied and turns destructive, plotting against him as Laura did against her husband in *The Father*. He then sees her as one of the Fates weaving his life into her crocheting, a tangle like the network of nerves in the human brain. It is difficult for both the Lady and the Stranger to reconcile conflicting impulses and rise above their sense of original sin. Although the Lady has some individuality, she is present primarily to represent all women.

To Damascus is significant for its theatricality. Calling for dynamic acting, vivid costuming and scenery, and cinematic effects, Strindberg presented a challenge to theatre artists. *Part One* has often been produced independently, starting at Dramaten in Stockholm in 1900 when Harriet Bosse, who would become Strindberg's third wife, played the Lady. Notable productions presenting an adaptation or condensation of the trilogy have included Per Lindberg's in 1935 (Nationaltheatret, Oslo), Olof Molander's in 1965 (Stockholm stadsteaters studio), and Ingmar Bergman's in 1974 (Dramaten).

Strindberg referred to *To Damascus* as a dream play; yet it seems not to present a continous dream but to alternate between reality and the mystifying atmosphere of a nightmare. The nightmare effect may be seen in the corpse-like people at the asylum and the transformation from the formal testimonial dinner to an ugly tavern where the Stranger is taunted because he cannot pay for the meal. Egil Törnqvist describes the play as "half-reality", Evert Sprinchorn as "an artfully arranged nightmare", and other critics as a dramatization of "inner reality". However described, it was a milestone in the development of Expressionism.

—Carla Waal

TOM THUMB
by Henry Fielding

First Publication: London, 1730; revised version, as *The Tragedy of Tragedies; or, The Life and Death of Tom Thumb the Great*, 1731.
First Production: Little Theatre in the Haymarket, London, 24 April 1730; revised version (*The Tragedy of Tragedies*), Little Theatre in the Haymarket, 24 March, 1731.

Editions

The Life and Death of Tom Thumb the Great, in *"The Life and Death of Tom Thumb the Great" and Some Miscellaneous Writings*, London, 1902.
The Tragedy of Tragedies, edited by James T. Hillhouse, New Haven, Connecticut, 1918.
The Tragedy of Tragedies, in *Eighteenth Century Comedy*, edited by W.D. Taylor, Oxford, 1929.
Tom Thumb [1730 version], in *Burlesque Plays of the Eighteenth Century*, edited by Simon Trussler, London, 1969.

Criticism
(For general works on the author, see *Playwrights* volume)

Articles:
Nancy A. Mace, "Fielding, Theobald, and *The Tragedy of Tragedies*", in *Philological Quarterly*, 66, 1987.

*   *   *

During his short theatrical career between 1728 and 1737, Fielding made an important contribution to English drama, but his plays are not widely known today, except for the much-anthologized *Tom Thumb*, an uproariously funny burlesque of contemporary tragedy. As a two-act afterpiece this so-called "tragedy" was first staged in 1730 along with Fielding's very recent dramatic satire *The Author's Farce*. The immediate success of *Tom Thumb* encouraged Fielding to improve and extend it, and the revised second version, with a witty preface making fun of Colley Cibber's prose style, was published as the work of Scriblerus Secundus. By choosing this name, Fielding was laying claim to be the successor to the first Scriblerians, including Gay, Pope, and Swift.

In the following theatrical season, a brief satirical play about the appointment of Cibber as Poet Laureate, *The Battle of the Poets; or, The Contention for the Laurel*, was incorporated into some productions of the second *Tom Thumb*, although it was not by Fielding. Published under the name of Scriblerus Tertius, the playlet has usually been attributed to Thomas Cooke. After this, Fielding revised *Tom Thumb* again, this time in a more thoroughgoing manner. He expanded the play substantially into three acts, changed the title to *The Tragedy of Tragedies; or, The Life and Death of Tom Thumb the Great*, and for the published version provided a completely new and elaborate framework in place of the preface, prologue, and epilogue of the second edition.

Fielding possessed a prodigious gift for burlesque and parody, and a number of his plays, especially his best, are at least partly burlesque, but *Tom Thumb* (in all its versions) is the purest example. It is a worthy successor to Buckingham's *The Rehearsal* (1671) and Gay's *The What D'Ye Call It* (1715), the two finest dramatic burlesques of heroic drama and tragedy during the previous 70 years. For Fielding, as for his predecessors, burlesque was a form of creative criticism, diagnosing the condition of contemporary tragedy by parodic imitation in

Tom Thumb: Young Vic Theatre, London, 1974

order to clarify the decline of great dramatic poetry and true tragedy (associated, in particular, with Shakespeare) into pretentious sensationalism and factitious bombast. In *The Author's Farce* Fielding has some fun at the expense of contemporary tragedy, but without indulging in extended burlesque. *Tom Thumb*, on the other hand, is a miniature mock tragedy in which Fielding systematically burlesques Restoration and Augustan tragedy, including the rhymed heroic play. At least 42 plays written since the reopening of the theatres in 1660 are parodied, many from the late 17th rather than the 18th century. It may seem surprising that Fielding alludes more frequently to Dryden, Otway, Lee, and Banks than to his contemporaries Dennis, Rowe, Addison, Thomson, and Young, but the plays of the older dramatists still held the stage and were at least as popular as many of the more recent tragedies. Some of Fielding's targets are similar to those of earlier burlesquers, but his imaginative method of adapting a children's story to a heroic tragedy is entirely original and succeeds brilliantly.

The setting is King Arthur's Court and the action is ostensibly heroic, but all the characters are travesties of heroic figures, as their nonsense names suggest, and the result is a zany burlesque. Arthur is partial to giantesses and afraid of his wife, Dollallolla, who is attracted to midgets and fond of alcohol. The "tragic heroine" Huncamunca has a gargantuan appetite but yearns for something more than food. Fielding's treatment of Tom Thumb is different in that it depends on diminution rather than exaggeration. In every way except physical size, Tom Thumb is the typical hero of tragedy. A "man" of unimpeachable honour, he is boastful, completely self-confident, able to conquer any enemy with little effort, including an army of giants, and prepared to put an immediate end to anyone who affronts him or his friends. Yet despite Dollallolla's description of him as "a Godlike Creature", Tom Thumb is a dwarf, seen through the wrong end of a telescope, and his fate is to be ignominiously swallowed by a cow. The burlesque incongruity between Tom Thumb's dimensions and his actions and speeches are fully established in the text, but must have been even more effective and hilarious on stage, especially as he was usually played by child actors, sometimes girls and sometimes aged as young as five.

Although *Tom Thumb* is to a considerable extent constructed from parodies of single lines and short passages, Fielding welds these together so invisibly that the resulting mock tragedy is completely coherent, the specific parodies being transmuted into a general burlesque. The plot, in which the all-conquering hero becomes tangled in a web of passions and antagonisms, is fairly typical of heroic tragedies. By placing his mock-heroic figures in a conventional heroic framework, Fielding presents the stock situations of contemporary tragedy in a ridiculous light, and caricatures the complex amorous relationships, the unbearable torments of envy and jealousy, and the conflicts between love and honour that are central in many tragedies of the period. The denouement reaches its climax with six murders and a suicide in eight lines. Yet inventive as Fielding's burlesque situations are, it is above all the language of the play that makes it an evergreen classic of its genre. Fielding could have modelled his mock play on the standard situations of heroic tragedy without providing all the extended burlesque similes that add so much to the comic effect. Abuse of the simile is one of the most striking weaknesses of the Restoration and Augustan tragic style, and Fielding's burlesque similes are a major weapon in his mockery of the rhetorical excesses of contemporary dramatic poetry.

Tom Thumb is a masterpiece of dramatic burlesque, but in its final published form as *The Tragedy of Tragedies* it is also a masterpiece of ironic literature. The appearance of Pope's *The Dunciad Variorum* (1729), containing the Martinus Scriblerus Prolegomena and notes, almost certainly gave Fielding the idea of presenting his burlesque in a "scholarly edition", designed to satirize the pedantry of contemporary scholars and critics. Fielding achieves this by creating a mock editor, H. Scriblerus Secundus, who presents the play as a major tragedy of the Elizabethan period, possibly even by Shakespeare, and provides an extremely learned preface and copious annotations. The mock preface follows the usual pattern of scholarly introductions to acknowledged classics, but the "editor", who regards "Bathos" and "Doggrel" as words of commendation, is a perfect example of a Swiftian "Modern". He has no difficulty in proving that the nonsensical plot is an excellent example of neoclassical regularity and uniformity, and, by reference to Aristotle, that there is nothing incongruous in a tragic hero of minute proportions. To justify his claims for the play's greatness and influence, H. Scriblerus Secundus cites in his footnotes the many passages that Restoration and Augustan dramatists have supposedly derived or borrowed from *The Tragedy of Tragedies*. Fielding thus reverses the actual writing process and presents his parodies as the sources of many "sublime" speeches in contemporary tragedy. For the reader, the editorial framework and the burlesque text enhance each other to produce a superb Augustan satire.

—Peter Lewis

TONGUE-LASHING.   See OFFENDING THE AUDIENCE.

TOO TRUE TO BE GOOD
by George Bernard Shaw

First Publication: In *Three Plays: "Too True to Be Good"*, *"Village Wooing"* and *"On the Rocks*, London and New York, 1934.
First Production: National Theatre, Boston, 29 February 1932; first British production, at the Malvern Festival Theatre, Malvern, Worcestershire, 6 August 1932.

Criticism
(For general works on the author, see *Playwrights* volume)

Articles:
Frederick P. McDowell, "The 'Pentecostal Flame' and the 'Lower Centers': *Too True to be Good*", in *Shaw Review*, 2, 1959.
Albert H. Silverman, "Bernard Shaw's Political Extravaganzas", in *Drama Survey*, 5, 1966–67.
Alison L. Hopwood, "*Too True to be Good:* Prologue to Shaw's Later Plays", in *Shaw Review*, 11, 1968.
Arthur E. Regan, "The Fantastic Reality of Bernard Shaw: A Look at *Augustus* and *Too True*", in *Shaw Review*, 11, 1968.
Anne Wright, "Shaw's Burglars: *Heartbreak House* and *Too True to Be Good*", in *Shaw Review*, 23, 1980.
W.R. Martin, "GBS, DHL, and TEL: Mainly *Lady Chatterly* and *Too True*", in *SHAW*, 4, 1984.

*   *   *

It is just possible to describe this play in terms of a coherent action. In Act I, a Nurse and her boyfriend, the Burglar, attempt to steal a pearl necklace from an invalid who regains her health in defending her property. The three agree to go off together, sell the necklace, and enjoy life on the proceeds, which may be swelled by a ransom for the supposedly kidnapped Patient. Act II reveals them disguised, frustrated and bored, on the beach of some tropical territory where there is a British military presence. Act III, set on another part of the beach, introduces the Burglar's father and the Sergeant, the latest man to take the Nurse's fancy, occupying adjacent caves; the Patient's mother arrives in search of her daughter, but so enrages the Colonel that he strikes her, thus unexpectedly making her sane; disguises now abandoned, most of the characters go on their way, some in pairs; but the play does not end, as the erstwhile Burglar continues talking—though invisible in clouds of mist—until the auditorium is empty and, perhaps, afterwards.

This is the furthest Shaw ever went in fracturing dramatic structure, though his impatience with conventional forms is traceable back to his youthful apprenticeship to freely digressive novels in the 18th-century tradition. His preference for spontaneous liveliness over tight organisation was particularly suited, in this instance, to his chosen theme of general cultural breakdown: the loss of Victorian certainties in science as in religion, the breakdown of morality during and after World War I, and abandonment of the sovereignty of reason to the powerful impulses of the unconscious. The dramatic principles he adopts include unpredictability, discontinuity, instability of character, variety of tone, and the liberation of an anarchic humour which observes no distinctions of high and low, intellect and foolishness, but throws in farce and fantasy, brilliance of wit and the silliest of bad jokes indiscriminately. Shaw classified *Too True to be Good* as an extravaganza, lifting the term from the early 19th-century prolific writer of burlesques, J. R. Planché (father of the Christmas pantomime), who defined it as "the whimsical treatment of a poetical subject" in contrast to parody of a literary or dramatic work. It is the miscellaneous variety of Shakespearian comedy which is the ultimate precedent for extravaganza in the English dramatic tradition.

As Shakespeare was free to introduce a Puck, or an Ariel, among his human characters, so Shaw presents his Microbe in Act I, apparently invisible but not always totally inaudible to the other characters. (It seems likely that the recent success of *The Insect Play* by the Čapek brothers, in London, encouraged him.) Once admitted, and aided by an actor's acrobatic

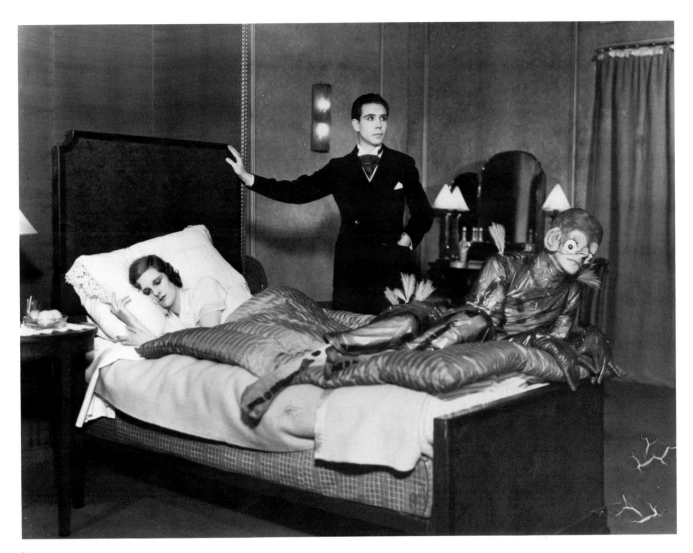

Too True to be Good: New Theatre, London, 1932 (first production)

training, he makes a sprightly and useful chorus, making play of theatrical illusion, at the end of the act, by warning the audience that there is nothing but interminable discussion to follow. Shaw sometimes gave similar warnings in press interviews, preparing audiences psychologically by taking up a critical charge often laid against him and, in the event, mixing in much more entertainment than he had led them to expect: here the changes of scene, the disguises, the unannounced introduction of new characters in each act, the absurd skirmish with off-stage natives in Act II, the disruptive machine-gun noise of the motorbike ridden by Private Meek, the Figaresque factotum who is the real master of the situation (a character-parody of Lawrence of Arabia), and the encounter between the Colonel and Mrs. Mopply which ends with her metaphorical unmasking and restoration to her "real" self.

   These obvious devices would count for little if there was nothing else to the play. To the audience at the Malvern Festival in 1932 Shaw explained: "When people have laughed for an hour, they want to be serio-comically entertained for the next hour; and when that is over they are so tired of not being wholly serious that they can bear nothing but a torrent of sermons. My play is arranged accordingly". The first of the "sermons", relatively brief, comes towards the end of Act I, and is directed against the concepts of "safety first" and national security. So the plot is anchored to an idea of the

world as "a field for the adventures of the life everlasting". The tone in which the serious reflections are delivered in Act II is not always grave, but a degree of thoughtful intensity touches a succession of themes: the public conspiracy of lying, the power of unconscious drives, a case for sexual promiscuity, the temptation to use destructive weapons, the immorality of war. In Act III, first the Sergeant, then the Elder, and finally his son Aubrey (the Burglar) deliver sermons of steadily increasing length and considerable passion. This is not in itself new in Shaw's plays: the "Don Juan in Hell" act of *Man and Superman* used a similar form very successfully; *Back to Methuselah* reverted to it, particularly in the "Elderly Gentleman" section. The dramatist's personal experience as an orator doubtless sustained his belief in the power of a tirade to hold an audience spellbound; but its effectiveness depends on the technical virtuosity of the speaker or, in this case, the actor. There is plentiful testimony from Shaw and others that the author liked to cast his plays according to the vocal timbre he wanted for the individual roles and their place in the vocal ensemble ("I thought I heard the old trombone", is Aubrey's greeting to his father). Not the inclusion of actual music, but a prose equivalent of operatic singing seems to have been his aim, achievable only with actors of great vocal flexibility and skill in phrasing, prepared to rehearse as rigorously as professional singers. It is worth observing that the actor

(Kenneth Haigh) who played the Burglar in the 1965 production, which revolutionised critical evaluation of the play, had cut his teeth on Jimmy Porter's tirades in the first production of John Osborne's *Look Back in Anger*.

Since that production, by Frank Dunlop, with an outstandingly talented cast, *Too True to be Good*, which bewildered and irritated early audiences and was read as proof of Shaw's decline, has been ranked among his major plays. It was unknown Shaw, with little trace of Victorian positivism, acknowledging Freud and D. H. Lawrence, saluting the sisterhood of women, revelling in the breakdown of institutions, and stressing the horror and futility of war, future as well as past: in tune with mid-1960's consciousness. Moreover, the theatre had caught up with such anarchic black comedy through familiarity with examples of a later drama of the absurd.

—Margery Morgan

THE TOOTH OF CRIME
by Sam Shepard

First Publication: In *The Tooth of Crime*; *Geography of a Horse*, New York and London, 1974.
First Production: Open Space Theatre, London, 17 July 1972.

Criticism
(For general works on the author, see *Playwrights* volume)

Articles:
Richard Schechner, "Drama, Script, Theatre, and Performance", in *Tulane Drama Review*, vol. 17 no.3, 1973.
Stefan Brecht, "Schechner contro Shepard: *The Tooth of Crime*", in his *Nuovo teatro americano 1968–1973*, Rome, 1974.
Herbert Grabes, "Metadrama and the History of Taste: Sam Shepard, *The Tooth of Crime*", in *Studien zur Ästhetik des Gegenwartstheaters*, edited by Christian W. Thomsen, Heidelberg, 1985.
Leonard Wilcox, "Modernism vs. Postmodernism: Shepard's *The Tooth of Crime* and the Discourses of Popular Culture", in *Modern Drama*, 30, 1987.
Leonard Mustazza, "'In the old style': The Tragic Vision in Sam Shepard's *The Tooth of Crime*" in *Text and Performance Quarterly*, 9, 1989.

*   *   *

Sam Shepard, probably the most highly regarded American playwright of the 1970's, brings to *The Tooth of Crime* his background as a drummer for the "rockabilly" band Holy Moly Rounders. The play, actually "a sort of talking opera" about the violent paranoia experienced by rock stars at the top, is the work of a musician whose playwrighting has endured far beyond his music-making. Using an inventive hip lingo of the future (in the manner of the Anthony Burgess novel *Clockwork Orange*), Shepard places at the heart of *Tooth of Crime* the ritualized musical battle between an older style of performance, one with its roots deeply embedded in the African-American blues, and a newer threat to that style, one that is brittle, androgynous, heartless. As the reigning star, Hoss, is

challenged by the rising star, Crow, the threatening language often involves the hardware of combat; the central showdown is a musical *agon*, but the battle to the death is performed with microphones, not knives. The contest is over the heart of the culture: will it be represented by music with a soul or will it be taken over by a harsher brand of punk, where the essence is in the body moves and not in the sound, where the content is "nothin' but flash"?

The people of the not-so-distant future who inhabit Shepard's dramatic space are *aficionados*, not only of the nuances between blues and rock entertainers of different decades and different styles—Ma Rainey vs. Mongo Santamaria, Keith Richards vs. Keith Moon, Bob Dylan vs. The Velvet Underground—but also they are *aficionados* of a range of hard drugs, gleaming weaponry ("really beautiful and clean"), Italian racing cars. An entourage satisfies the immediate craving for exhilaration, whether that excitement is provided by speed shot intravenously or experienced on the interstate highways; astrological and sexual comforts are available at the snap of a finger. In a Sam Shepard play, there are inevitable evocations of the old West, of gangster shoot-outs, of teenage class combat in southern California. A young woman presents the struggle of a date rape where she plays both the abuser and the abused; she must both protect herself from exposure and also rip off her own psychic and material layers of protection.

Act I is devoted to Hoss fixated on impending doom. Uneasy lies the head that wears this bopper's crown. He knows that the sharp edge of his art is losing its visionary gleam: "We ain't flyin' in the eye of contempt. We've become respectable and safe. Soft, mushy, chewable. . .What's happened to our killer heart? . . .We were warriors once". What popular art aims for is to "knock 'em dead", to "make a killing". Shepard picks up on this aggressive showbiz terminology, takes it a step further, turns his musicians into "warriors". Hoss surely is named to invoke the cowboy West; Crow to suggest the eaters of carrion, the cleansers who dispose of road kill. In the grandeur of his perch at the top of the charts, "lonely as an ocean", Hoss hunches over, brooding about who will come to challenge his authority. He recognizes his former self in the potential challenger: "I can smell blood. It's right. The time is right! I'm fallin' behind". Act I ends with the announcement that the *Doppelgänger* has arrived: "He's my brother and I gotta kill him. He's gotta kill me".

Act II is the musical *agon*. Inevitably the reigning monarch loses. Though Euripides and Shakespeare did not have basketball referees overseeing the combat and cheerleaders mooning the audience, *Tooth of Crime* is open to comparisons with dramas of the past: Dionysus will outsmart his cousin Pentheus; Bolingbroke will outmaneuver his cousin Richard; Crow will overwhelm his blues brother Hoss.

At the height of his power, this youthful playwright was already obsessed with being corrupted by success, with selling out to a dehumanized system. Just off stage are "the keepers", who exact obedience and threaten liquidation if the artist does not strictly follow their system of "points" and "penalties"; does not strictly adhere to their "code" of rules. The play explicitly celebrates the martyrs of recent popular and high culture, Jimmy Dean, Jackson Pollock, Duane Allman. There is a strong sense of the ephemeral nature of an artistic career: "Sure you'll have a few moments of global glow, maybe even an interplanetary flash. But it won't last, Hoss, it won't last".

—Roger Sorkin

THE TOOTHBRUSH.   See EL CEPILLO DE DIENTES.

TOP GIRLS
by Caryl Churchill

First Publication: London, 1982; revised edition, 1984.
First Production: Royal Court Theatre, 28 August 1982.

Criticism
(For general works on the author, see *Playwrights* volume)

Articles:
Joseph Marohl, "De-realised Women: Performance and Identity in *Top Girls*", in *Modern Drama*, 30, 1987.

*   *   *

For a writer who considers herself, as Caryl Churchill does, "both a socialist and a feminist", the phenomenon of Margaret Thatcher poses a problem. The most successful woman politician in British history, the dominant political figure of a whole decade, is a radical—and openly ideological—Conservative. *Top Girls* is Churchill's first response to Thatcherism. It is a play which explores the relation between female success and political positions. In dramatic terms it does so by enacting a *peripeteia:* Churchill wanted the play to seem at first "to be celebrating the extraordinary achievements of women. Then it

would cut another way and say that this sort of movement is useless if you don't have a socialist perspective on it".

The long first scene appears, technically and narratively, to be almost self-contained. In it, the dynamic Marlene hosts a party to celebrate her promotion to the managing directorship of the "Top Girls" employment agency. However, the guests are not her immediate friends and colleagues but successful women from history or legend. The personal stories of Victorian traveller Isabella Bird, of Lady Nijo (the 13th-century Japanese Emperor's concubine and Buddhist nun), and of Pope Joan, are interwoven in a rich counterpoint which touches upon the themes of fathers, religion, lovers, and turning-points in life. When Patient Griselda arrives (late) the talk turns to child-bearing, husbands, and personal loss. As the increasingly intoxicated gathering brings up memories of dissent and rebellion against male power, the hitherto mono-syllabic Dull Gret (from the painting) delivers a climactic account of how she led her Flemish women in the harrowing of Brueghel's surreal (though politicized) Hell.

The remainder of the play's action is split between two locations and involves an important time-shift. At the employment agency itself (in London), we see Marlene and her colleagues talking among themselves and interviewing a number of women clients—all different, but all representative types. Marlene's niece Angie, who at 16 is physically and psychologically underdeveloped (if not actually backward), and who idolizes her aunt, turns up unannounced at the agency and looks on in admiration as Marlene rebuffs the irate and harrassed wife of her former rival for the big post. The final scene takes place "a year earlier" in the house of Marlene's sister Joyce, who has stayed in the country and struggled to

Top Girls: Royal Court Theatre, London, 1982 (first production)

bring Angie up there. This long scene balances the opening one by developing an argument between the sisters which invites consideration of the success of women in the context of the political climate of the 1980's. The argument is polarized: Marlene is a Thatcherite whose ultimate point of reference is Reaganite America; Joyce has inherited the entrenched left-wing views of her father. Marlene has left home and become successful; Joyce has stayed and stagnated. When it is revealed that Angie is actually Marlene's daughter (Joyce has been married, but is childless), the final irony takes shape: the ethic of acquisitive individualism which has been the foundation for Marlene's success is one that would condemn her own pathetic child to a life of deprivation and wretchedness. As Marlene says, Angie is "not going to make it".

Churchill's minute concern for speech rhythms and her large-scale use of precisely-notated overlap in dialogue seem together to imply a scrupulously naturalistic intention. Yet the effect in the opening scene is somewhat abstract, musical—a kind of fugue for voices. More generally, a species of *Verfremdungseffekt*, a "making-strange", is achieved through various strategies of discontinuity: historical, in the gathering of famous women for Marlene's party; theatrical, in the space opened up between actor and role by the specified doubling of roles (inviting cross-referencing of characters) and by having Angie and her 12 year old friend Kit played by adults; narratival, in the chronological shift of the final scene. Such strategies invite an awareness in the audience of the play's status as artifact, thereby encouraging scrutiny and debate rather than identification. We are always aware of a group of women playing a script.

The dramatic debate hinges, to a large extent, on the way the first and last scenes engage with one another. The central office-scenes evoke the culture for which Marlene is spokesperson—one within which a woman can succeed if she subscribes to an ethic of competitive individualism, whereby the shape of society is seen to be determined by individual energy and initiative, with little or no reference being made to constraints of class or culture. By contrast, both Joyce's life and her arguments bear witness to determining forces of class and culture. For her, Marlene's challenge is merely to a superstructure rather than to a prevailing social base. How, then, does the opening scene enter the debate?

The great women who gather at Marlene's party have all, in their different ways, been "top girls" within male-fashioned and male-dominated cultures. The remarkable sustained energy and tenacity of each of them would seem to stand as an endorsement of Marlene's position. Yet it is less their resemblances that make for the scene's richness of texture and passing comic disharmonies than the extent to which they *differ* from one another. Each has her concerns or obsessions—Isabella her illnesses, her sister, and her Victorian, moral muscularity; Nijo her "thin silks"; Joan her theological disquisition; Gret her sensory instincts (potatoes, cake, and big cocks). These are not just personal idiosyncracies but indelible marks of *cultural* identity. For Marlene their shared gender is the overriding factor, but each of the women is firmly embedded within the culture of her origin. It is precisely because the scene rejects any sentimental idea of an automatic sisterhood (with the concomitant implied narrative, in which a series of heroic individual women, all just like Mrs. Thatcher, are seen to prefigure a triumphant "post-feminist" present) that its climax, at which each of the women comes to realize the perniciousness of her position within her culture, is so powerful and so convincing.

In this way the debate of *Top Girls* is dramatized rather than merely stated. The case for subsuming concerns of gender within larger radical politics is made not through a mouthpiece

(despite the presence of Joyce), not in a polemic against the "bad dream" of Thatcherism, but in the densely orchestrated realization of a particular cultural situation.

—Paul Lawley

TORCH SONG TRILOGY
by Harvey Fierstein

First Publication: New York, 1981.
First Production: Richard Allen Center, New York, October 1981.

Criticism
(For general works on the author, see *Playwrights* volume)

Articles:
William Green, "*Torch Song Trilogy:* A Gay Comedy with a Dying Fall", in *Maske und Kothurn*, 30, 1984.

*   *   *

Torch Song Trilogy comprises three plays so different in style that at first sight they seem totally self-contained; only the central character, a professional drag queen named Arnold, providing a nominal link. However, the stylistic differences are important to the whole concept in that they comment on and enrich one another in complex ways.

The first play, *The International Stud*, opens with Arnold in full warpaint in the eponymous gay bar and charts the ups and downs of his relationship with his lover, Ed, a man uncertain about his sexuality, his willingness to come out of the closet, and his commitment to Arnold. The second, *Fugue in a Nursery*, takes place one year later. Ed is now married and Arnold has a new lover. The two couples meet at Ed's upstate farmhouse and discover cross-currents of desire, jealousy, and insecurity running between them. Ed sleeps with Alan, finds that he is still drawn to Arnold, and finally marries Laurel, while Alan and Arnold arrange a wedding of their own. The final play, *Widows and Children First!* takes place five years later. Alan has been brutally murdered. Arnold is fostering a gay teenage boy, David, a project he originally undertook with Alan, and it is clear that the centre of his life is now the father–son relationship he soon hopes to make official. He is visited by Ed, estranged from Laurel, and his own mother. In the course of the play he tries to make his mother come to terms not just with his sexuality but his feelings as Alan's "widow" and David's father. Meanwhile David does some strenuous matchmaking between Arnold and Ed.

The movement of the whole trilogy is towards the values of commitment and a reinterpreted ideal of the family, symbolised by the changing on-stage patterns created by the characters. *The International Stud* consists almost entirely of soliloquies. Arnold addresses us, Ed addresses an unseen Arnold, Arnold makes love to an anonymous figure in the backroom of the bar, again unseen. Arnold and Ed speak on the phone, both visible to us but not to each other. It is in fact only in the last scene that they are both present in each other's space on stage, in what starts out as Ed's farewell visit to Arnold's dressing room and becomes some kind of reconciliation. The play explores the tension between Arnold's two kinds of desire for love: one the urge for a relationship stronger and more meaningful that the joyless one-night stands of the back room; the other springing from an insatiable desire for security. This tension removes the play from the territory of easy answers, because one desire is never entirely untouched by the other. Fierstein, writing before the AIDS crisis changed American gay life beyond recognition, allows the limited freedom of the bar its place in the scheme of things, and in his dedication wishes its *habitués* "the courage to leave it when they can, and the good sense to come back to it when they must". Arnold clear-sightedly recognises that his search for secure love is both his curse and part of his vulnerable charm; he says of Ed, "Maybe I use him to give me that tragic torch-singer status I admire so in others".

Fugue in a Nursery follows logically by exploring love in a wider community. Its setting has a surreal edge: the action takes place in a bed which represents all the rooms in Ed's house. The effect is multi-layered. First, the bed stresses the erotic groundbase of all the relationships in the play. All the characters are to some extent romantics, in that they have not fully relinquished the ideal of a single, lasting, sexual love. Secondly, it creates an atmosphere of intimacy that makes credible the four-cornered rapport, the confidences flying thick and fast. Thirdly, it adds an element of stylisation which emphasises that this play is ultimately a comedy of manners. As Arnold points out, however, in the world of the new sexual mores, manners have to be improvised as you go along. "You were wrong to do what you did! . . .Though I know why you did. . .And Laurel was wrong to use what you two did! . . .Though I know why she did. And I was wrong to do everything I did! But I did. I don't know, maybe it all evens out. . .".

Widows and Children First! takes Arnold away from the circle of lovers into a wider world: of families, of the law of the land. Reminders of how the latter has failed the gay community are ever present in the frequent allusions to Alan's fate; the family we have to judge for ourselves—but here Fierstein shows his optimism by his chosen style, that of sitcom, the form created specifically to exalt family values. Arnold's wisecracking mother, the farcical misunderstandings when she assumes David is Arnold's lover, her ridiculous rabbit slippers and her home cooking—all belong to sitcom; but while the play never questions the status of the family as the vital unit in society, it suggests that one can construct a "family" to suit one's individual needs and desires. The success of *Torch Song Trilogy* is perhaps owed to the fact that it does not simply celebrate gay life but the right of the individual, straight or gay, to create the family unit in which that individuality can be expressed.

—Frances Gray

TOT KTO POLYUCHAYET POSCHECHINY. See **HE WHO GETS SLAPPED.**

THE TOWNELEY PLAYS
Anonymous

Composition: c. late-15th Century or 16th Century.
First Production: Probably West Yorkshire, 16th Century.

Editions

The Towneley Plays, edited by George England and Alfred W. Pollard, London, 1897 (Early English Texts Society Series).
The Wakefield Pageants in the Towneley Cycle, edited by A.C. Cawley, Manchester, 1958.
The Wakefield Mystery Plays, edited by Martial Rose, London, 1961.
Three Towneley Plays [*The Killing of Abel*; *Noah and His Sons*; *The First Shepherds' Play*], edited by Dennis Hamley, London, 1962.
The Complete Plays of the Wakefield Master, in a version by John Russell Brown, London, 1983.
The Wakefield's Shepherd's Play, edited by David Self, London, 1983.

Criticism
(For general works on the author, see *Playwrights* volume)

Books:
Marie Caroline Lyle, *The Original Identity of the York and Towneley Cycles*, Minneapolis, Minnesota, 1919.
Millicent Carey, *The Wakefield Group in the Towneley Cycle*, Göttingen and Baltimore, Maryland, 1930.
Walter E. Myers, *A Figure Given Typology in the Wakefield Plays*, Pittsburgh, 1970.
John E.G. Gardner, *The Construction of the Wakefield Cycle*, Carbondale (Illinois) and London, 1974.
Dieter M. Schmidt, *Die Kunst des Dialogs in den Wakefield-Spielen*, Frankfurt and Cirencester, 1980.
Jeffrey Helterman, *Symbolic Action in the Plays of the Wakefield Master*, Athens, Georgia, c.1981.

Articles:
Frank W. Cady, "Liturgical Basis of the Towneley Mysteries", in *Publications of the Modern Language Association* [*PMLA*], 25, 1909.
Frank W. Cady, "The Wakefield Group in Towneley", in *Journal of English and Germanic Philology*, 11, 1912.
Frank W. Cady, "The Passion Group in Towneley", in *Modern Philology*, 10, 1913.
Albert C. Baugh, "Parallels to the Mak Story", in *Modern Philology*, 15, 1918.
Louis Wann, "The Influence of French Farce on the Towneley Cycle of Mystery Plays", in *Transactions of the Wisconsin Academy of Sciences, Arts, and Letters*, 19, 1918.
Oscar Cargill, "The Authorship of the *Secunda Pastorum*", in *Publications of the Modern Language Association* [*PMLA*], 41, 1926.
Frank W. Cady, "The Maker of Mak", in *University of California Chronicle*, 29, 1927.
Louis Wann, "A New Examination of the Manuscript of the Towneley Plays", in *Publications of the Modern Language Association* [*PMLA*], 43, 1928.
Grace Frank, "On the Relation Between the York and Towneley Plays", in *Publications of the Modern Language Association* [*PMLA*], 44, 1929.
Curtis G. Chester, "The York and Towneley Plays on the Harrowing of Hell", in *Studies in Philology*, 30, 1933.
Mendall G. Frampton, "The Date of the Flourishing of the Wakefield Master", in *Publications of the Modern Language Association* [*PMLA*], 50, 1935.
Mendall G. Frampton, "The Date of the Wakefield Master: Biographical Evidence", in *Publications of the Modern Language Association* [*PMLA*], 53, 1938.
Edward Murray Clarke, "Liturgical Influences in the Towneley Plays", in *Orate Fratres*, 16, 1941.

Mendall G. Frampton, "The Towneley *Harrowing of Hell*", in *Publications of the Modern Language Association* [*PMLA*], 56, 1941.

Anna Jean Mill, "Noah's Wife Again", in *Publications of the Modern Language Association* [*PMLA*], 56, 1941.

Mendall G. Frampton, "Towneley XX: The *Conspiracio (et Capcio)*", in *Publications of the Modern Language Association* [*PMLA*], 58, 1943.

Mendall G. Frampton, "The *Processus Talentorum* (Towneley XXIV)", in *Publications of the Modern Language Association* [*PMLA*], 59, 1944.

Robert C. Cosbey, "The Mak Story and Its Folklore Analogues", in *Speculum*, 20, 1945.

J. Speirs, "The Mystery Cycle, 1: Some Towneley Plays", in *Scrutiny*, 18, 1951.

Eugene E. Zumwalt, "Irony in the Towneley Shepherds' Plays", in *Research Studies of the State College of Washington*, 26, 1958.

Catherina E. Dunn, "The Medieval Cycle as History Play: An Approach to the Wakefield Plays", in *Studies in the Renaissance*, 7, 1960.

Donald F. Peel, "The Allegory in *Secunda Pastorum*", in *Northwest Missouri State College Studies*, 24, 1960.

Catherina E. Dunn, "Lyrical Form and the Prophetic Principle in the Towneley Plays", in *Medieval Studies*, 23, 1961.

Howard H. Schless, "The Comic Element in the Wakefield *Noah*", in *Studies in Medieval Literature*, 17, 1961.

Alan H. Nelson, " 'Sacred' and 'Secular' Currents in the Towneley Play of Noah", in *Drama Survey*, 3, 1964.

H.-J. Diller, "The Craftsmanship of the Wakefield Master", in *Anglia*, 83, 1965.

John Gardner, "Theme and Irony in the Wakefield *Mactacio Abel*", in *Publications of the Modern Language Association* [*PMLA*], 80, 1965.

Eugen B. Cantelupe and Richard Griffith, "The Gifts of the Shepherds in the Wakefield *Secunda Pastorum*: An Iconographical Interpretation", in *Medieval Studies*, 28, 1966.

Martin Stevens, "The Dramatic Setting of the Wakefield *Annunciation*", in *Publications of the Modern Language Association* [*PMLA*], 81, 1966.

Clifford Davidson, "The Unity of the Wakefield *Mactacio Abel*", in *Traditio*, 23, 1967.

Lawrence Ross, "Symbol and Structure in the *Secunda Pastorum*", in *Comparative Drama*, 1, 1967.

John Gardner, "Imagery and Allusion in the Wakefield *Noah* Play", in *Papers on Language and Literature*, 4, 1968.

William F. Munson, "Typology and the Towneley Isaac", in *Research Opportunities in Renaissance Drama*, 11, 1968.

Clifford Davidson, "An Interpretation of the Wakefield *Judicium*", in *Annuale Medievale*, 10, 1969.

James W. Earl, "The Shape of Old Testament History in the Towneley Plays", in *Studies in Philology*, 69, 1972.

Linda E. Marshall, " 'Sacral Parody' in the *Secunda Pastorum*", in *Speculum*, 47, 1972.

Michael Paull, "The Figure of Mahomet in the Towneley Cycle", in *Comparative Drama*, 6, 1972.

Joseph L. Baird and Amy Cassidy, "Humility and the Towneley *Annunciation*", in *Philological Quarterly*, 52, 1973.

Martin Stevens, "The Manuscript of the Towneley Plays: Its History and Editions", in *Papers of the Bibliographical Society of America*, 67, 1973.

Jane P. Campbell, "The Idea of Order in the Wakefield *Noah*", in *Chaucer Review*, 10, 1975.

Thomas J. Jambeck, "The Dramatic Implications of Anselmian Affective Piety in the Towneley Play of the Crucifixion", in *Annuale Mediaevale*, 16, 1975.

Jennifer Strauss, "Grace Enacted: The *Secunda Pastorum*", in *Parergon*, 14, 1976.

Cynthia H. Tyson, "Property Requirements of *Purificacio Marie*: Evidence for Stationary Production of the Towneley Cycle", in *Studies in Medieval Culture*, 8–9, 1976.

Robert B. Bennett, "Homiletic Design in the Towneley *Abraham*", in *Modern Language Studies*, 7, 1977.

Bennett A. Brockman, "Comic and Tragic Counterpoint in the Medieval Drama: The Wakefield *Mactacio Abel*", in *Medieval Studies*, 39, 1977.

John M. Cleland, "*Second Shepherds' Play* and *Homecoming*: Two Dramatic Imitations of Life", in *Faith and Reason*, vol.3 no.2, 1977.

Dorrel T. Hanks Jr., "The *Mactacio Abel* and the Wakefield Cycle: A Study in Context", in *Southern Quarterly*, 16, 1977.

Jeanne S. Martin, "History and Paradigm in the Towneley Cycle", in *Medievalia et Humanistica*, 8, 1977.

Alicia K. Nitecki, "The Sacred Elements of the Secular Feast in *Prima Pastorum*", in *Mediaevalia*, 3, 1977.

Martin Stevens, "Language as Theme in the Wakefield Plays", in *Speculum*, 52, 1977.

George A. West, "An Analysis of the Towneley Play of *Lazarus*", in *Philological Quarterly*, 56, 1977.

Thomas P. Campbell, "Why do the Shepherds Prophesy?", in *Comparative Drama*, 12, 1978.

Cherrell Guilfoyle, " 'The Riddle Song' and the Shepherds' Gifts in *Secunda Pastorum* with a Note on the 'Tre Callyd Persidis' ", in *Yearbook of English Studies*, 8, 1978.

Thomas J. Jambeck, "The Canvas-Tossing Allusion in the *Secunda Pastorum*", in *Modern Philology*, 76, 1978.

Maynard Mack Jr., "The *Second Shepherds' Play*: A Reconsideration", in *Publications of the Modern Language Association* [*PMLA*], 93, 1978.

Rose A. Zimbardo, "Comic Mockery of the Sacred: *The Frogs* and *The Second Shepherds' Play*", in *Educational Theatre Journal*, 30, 1978.

Theresa Coletti, "Theology and Politics in the Towneley *Play of the Talents*", in *Medievalia et Humanistica*, 9, 1979.

F.P. and S.J. Manion, "A Reinterpretation of *The Second Shepherds' Play*", in *American Benedictine Review*, 30, 1979.

Edmund Reiss, "The Symbolic Plow and Plowman and the Wakefield *Mactacio Abel*", in *Studies in Iconography*, 5, 1979.

Edmund M. Taft, "Surprised by Love: The Dramatic Structure and Popular Appeal of the Wakefield *Second Shepherds' Pageant*", in *Journal of Popular Culture*, 14, 1980.

Míceál Vaughan, "The Three Advents in *Secunda Pastorum*", in *Speculum*, 55, 1980.

Donna Smith Vintner, "Didactic Characterization: The Towneley Abraham", in *Comparative Drama*, 14, 1980.

Wendy Clein, "The Towneley *Magnus Herodes* and the Comedy of Redemption", in *Renascence*, vol.38 no.1, 1982.

Clifford Davidson, "Jest and Earnest: Comedy in the Work of the Wakefield Master", in *Annuale Mediaevale*, 22, 1982.

Robert E. Jungman, "Mak and the Seven Names of God", in *Lore and Language*, 3, 1982.

M.F. Vaughan, "Mak and the Proportions of the *Second Shepherds' Play*", in *Papers on Language and Literature*, vol.18 no.4, 1982.

Laureen Lepow, "Drama of Communion: The Life of Christ in the Towneley Cycle", in *Philological Quarterly*, vol. 62 no.3, 1983.

J.W. Robinson, "Form in the *Second Shepherds' Play*", in *Proceedings of the PMR Conference*, 8, 1983.

Lois Roney, "The Wakefield *First* and *Second Shepherds'*

Plays as Complements in Psychology and Parody", in *Speculum*, vol.58 no.3, 1983.

Shearle Furnish, "Technique Versus Feeling in the Wakefield Master's *Magnus Herodes*", in *Kentucky Philological Association Bulletin*, 1984.

Martin Stevens, "*Processus Torontoniensis:* A Performance of the Wakefield Cycle", in *Research Opportunities in Renaissance Drama*, 28, 1985.

David Mills, "'The Towneley Plays' or 'The Towneley Cycle'?", in *Leeds Studies in English*, 17, 1986.

Maris G. Fiondella, "Framing and Ideology in the Towneley Creation Play", in *Exemplaria*, vol.1 no.2, 1987.

Barbara Palmer, "Towneley Plays or Wakefield Cycle Revisited", in *Comparative Drama*, 21, 1987–88.

Harry S. Anderson and Leonore Lieblein, "Staging Symbolic Action in the Medieval Cycle Drama: The York/Towneley *Harrowing of Hell*", in *Fifteenth-Century Studies*, 13, 1988.

Kathleen M. Ashley, "An Autobiographical Approach to the Cycle Drama: The Shepherds' as Sacred Clowns", in *Fifteenth-Century Studies*, 13, 1988.

Barbara A. Miliares, "The Politics of Religion and the Heretical Left in Northern England: Interaction Between Theatre and Audience in the Towneley Cycle", in *Fifteenth-Century Studies*, 13, 1988.

J.W. Robinson, "The Wakefield Master as a 'Master': Speculations on the Influences and Imitations", in *Acta*, 12, 1988.

Rose A. Zimbardo, "A Generic Approach to the *First* and *Second Shepherds' Plays* of the Wakefield Cycle", in *Fifteenth-Century Studies*, 13, 1988.

*   *   *

The entire Creation to Doom series of mystery plays in the Towneley Manuscript (dated 16th century) has sometimes been associated with the town of Wakefield in West Yorkshire; but only some of these plays have verifiable Wakefield connections. The most important are the plays which have been linked with the so-called "Wakefield Master". The Towneley Manuscript may be a West Yorkshire anthology from which plays were chosen for performance, perhaps some of them at Wakefield, but we cannot be certain of either places or dates.

The Towneley Manuscript contains 32 plays, not all of them complete, which follow the course of history from the Creation (Play 1) to Doomsday (30), with two plays out of order at the end of the manuscript: *Lazarus* and the incomplete *Suspencio Jude* (the hanging of Judas). Five plays are borrowed directly from the York cycle: *Pharoah*, *The Doctors* (recounting the story of Jesus in the temple at age 12), *Extraccio animarum* (Harrowing of Hell), *Resurreccio Domini* (Resurrection), and the incomplete *Judicium* (a section of the manuscript, including the beginning of this Doomsday play, has been torn out, and the drama also has elaborate dialogue among the devils added by the Wakefield Master). Very similar to York pageants are the *Conspiracy* (the betrayal of Jesus in the garden) and *Peregrinus* (the Emmaus story), both of which have additions by the Wakefield Master, as well as *Suspencio Jude*.

The Wakefield Master is the author of the *Mactacio Abel* (the sacrifice of Cain and Abel and the killing of Abel), *Processus Noe cum Filiis* (the story of Noah and the flood, with comic domestic violence involving Noah's wife), *Prima Pastorum* or the First Shepherds' Play, *Secunda Pastorum* or the Second Shepherds' Play, *Magnus Herodes* (Herod and the slaughter of the Innocents), and *Coliphizacio* (the buffeting of Christ during his Passion). Of the remainder, the following also have portions which have been assigned to the Wakefield

Master: *Flagellacio* (the scourging of Christ during his Passion), *Processus crucis* (the carrying of the cross to the place of crucifixion), *Processus talentorum* (the conclusion of the crucifixion), and *Ascensio Domini* (Ascension of Christ). All the plays are written in the Yorkshire dialect, which is most pronounced in the plays and portions of plays written by the Wakefield Master.

The name of the town of Wakefield appears in the manuscript to suggest a connection of at least some of the plays with either the manor or town of Wakefield, but the identification of the entire Towneley Manuscript as a cycle from this West Yorkshire town actually rested on the accounts included in the Wakefield Burgess Court Rolls as published by J. W. Walker, the Wakefield antiquarian. Recent scholarship has demonstrated that only three references to the Corpus Christi play at Wakefield are authentic, and that these are dated between 1556 and 1576. That Wakefield, an unincorporated town, had some sort of Corpus Christi play in the 16th century when it had grown to a population size that could support pageants (though probably—with a population of 2,000 adults in 1548—not a full cycle) does not prove that the plays in the Towneley Manuscript must all of them have comprised *the* Wakefield cycle. Indeed, the guild ascriptions that appear with some of the plays do not match with guilds known to have existed in Wakefield. Perhaps more positive location of the plays may be possible once the dramatic records of West Yorkshire are fully collected.

Nevertheless, the Towneley plays, especially those written by the Wakefield Master, are of a very high quality, and are recognized as some of the finest English plays before Shakespeare. The Wakefield Master is known for his effective comic scenes. The claim that the Wakefield Master pre-dated the introduction of French farce into England cannot, however, be proven, since all attempts to date his work must remain, for the time being, tentative, with the most informed guess being late-15th century at the earliest. The Towneley manuscript itself has been dated variously between 1500 and 1575.

The Wakefield Master's additions to the Towneley collection of plays are characterized by a unique stanza form that is displayed as made up of nine lines in all modern editions. These stanzas are very skilfully constructed and adjusted to the speaker, whether he be a sinner or saint. For example, Herod blusters, the executioners who torture Christ show appropriate (and terrifying) evidence of callousness as they go about their "work", and Mak in the *Secunda Pastorum* speaks with an accent that mimics the southern speech that was so disliked in Yorkshire, while Christ, as the Lamb being taken to slaughter, shows in his speech the patience that is required of him in the biblical and apocryphal texts.

Hugh of St. Victor had said that the sight of the ugly and grotesque should influence people to desire the good and the beautiful, and this progression is precisely what is suggested by these plays. For example, the foreigner Mak, who attempts to steal sheep, is not only the antithesis of the Good Shepherd but also an alien with whom the viewer is not invited to empathize; while Noah's recalcitrant wife serves as a symbol of a world-upside-down because of her lack of the grace and the intellectual illumination that, historically, will be brought by Christianity.

Controversy surrounds the staging of the Towneley plays; they suggest performance using fixed scaffolds rather than on pageant wagons. The use of scaffolds was apparently more widespread in late medieval England than wagons, and another complete cycle of plays—the *N-town* compilation from East Anglia—calls for such staging. The plays in the Towneley Manuscript seem to demand a "place and scaffold" arrangement in which the ground level (*platea*, or place) before the scaffolds also might be used for some of the action. Thus the shepherds in the *Secunda Pastorum* might use the *platea* for their entrance, for much of the action connected with their meeting with the thief Mak, and also for their vision of the angel who announces the birth of Christ. The angel, however, would have appeared on a Heaven scaffold. Two additional scaffolds would also be required for Mak's house and the stable of the Nativity, which are set over against each other in a way that foreshadows the division into good souls and bad souls at Doomsday, when the damned are relegated to Christ's lower left, and the saved are taken up into Heaven (above right).

Like the York Cycle, the Towneley Plays have been revived in the second half of the 20th century, with a very successful complete outdoor production produced as part of the Wakefield Festival in 1980. However, the *Secunda Pastorum* has for a considerable time been a favorite among college and amateur groups.

—Clifford Davidson

THE TOY CART.   See THE LITTLE CLAY CART.

TRACHINIAE.   See THE WOMEN OF TRACHIS.

THE TRAGEDY OF MAN (Az Ember Tragédiája)
by Imre Madách

First Publication: In *Drámai Koltemény*, Pest [now in Budapest], 1861; corrected edition, 1963.
First Production: Budapest, 21 September 1883.

Editions
Az Ember Tragédiája, edited by Alexander B. Második, Budapest, 1909.
Az Ember Tragédiája, edited by Alexander Bernát, Budapest, 1921.
Az Ember Tragédiája, edited by Károly Kardeván, Budapest, 1942.
Az Ember Tragédiája, edited by József Waldapfel, Budapest, 1954.

Translations
The Tragedy of Man, translated by William N. Loew, New York, 1909.
The Tragedy of Man, translated by C. P. Sanger, London, 1933.
The Tragedy of Man, translated by J.C.W. Horne, Budapest, 1963.
The Tragedy of Man, translated by George Szirtes, Budapest, 1988.

Criticism
(For general works on the author, see *Playwrights* volume)

Books:
László Juhász, *Un Disciple du romantisme français: Madách et "La Tragédie de l'homme"*, Szeged, Hungary, 1930.

Articles:
Alexander Hevesi, "Madách and *The Tragedy of Man*", in *Slavonic and East European Review*, December 1930.
C. Wojastsek, "The Philosophical and Ethical Concept of the *Tragedy of Man*", in *Slavic and East European Studies*, vol.6 no.3, 1961–62.
I. Soter, "Imre Madách's *Tragedy of Man*", in *New Hungarian Quarterly*, vol.5 no.16, 1964.
A. Faj, "Probable Byzantine and Hungarian Models of *Ulysses* and *Finnegan's Wake*", in *Arcadia*, 1968.
Dezsö Keresztury, "Über Madách's *Die Tragödie des Menschen*", in *Lenau Forum*, vol.3 nos. 3–4, 1971.
Günther Mahal, "Bemerkungen zum 'ungarischen *Faust*': Die *Tragödie des Menschen* von Imre Madách", in *Ansichten zu "Faust": Karl Theens zum 70. Geburtstag*, edited by Günther Mahal, Stuttgart, 1973.
Thomas R. Mark, "*The Tragedy of Man*: Salvation or Tragedy?", in *Acta Litteraria Academiae Scientorum Hungaricae*, 15, 1973.
József Mezei, "La Tragédie chrétienne", in *Acta Litteraria Academiae Scientorum Hungaricae*, 15, 1973.
Mihály Szegedy-Maszák, "Life-Conception and Structure in *The Tragedy of Man*", in *Acta Litteraria Academiae Scientorum Hungaricae*, 15, 1973.
György M. Vajda, "L'Élément européen et hongrois dans *La Tragédie de l'homme*", in *Acta Litteraria Academiae Scientorum Hungaricae*, 15, 1973.
Thomas R. Mark, "Madách Revisited: Towards a New Translation of *Tragedy of Man*", in *Canadian-American Review of Hungarian Studies*, 4, 1977.
Esther H. Lesér, "A Hungarian View of the World, Expressed in a Faustian Legend", in *Canadian-American Review of Hungarian Studies*
Dieter P. Lotze, "Madách's *Tragedy of Man* and the Tradition of the 'Poème d'humanité' in European Literature", in *Neohelicon*, vol.6 no.1, 1978.
Kálmán Kalocsay, "*La Tregedio de l'homo*, kaj Imre Madách", in *Literatura foiro*, vol.15, no.83, 1984.
Dieter P. Lotze, "Les Fondements philosophiques de *La Tragedie de l'homme* de Madách", in *Revue de littérature comparée*, 60, 1986.
Massimo Corsinovi, "*L'umana tragedia* di Imre Madách", in *Città di vita*, vol.44 no.5, 1989.

*   *   *

Madách's *magnum opus* has an ambitious universal perspective inasmuch as it encompasses both the religious and historical story of mankind. While an omnipotent, omniscient God has to see his creation challenged by Lucifer's successful temptation of the first man and woman, he allows the spirit of negation to compete for Man's soul. In order to prove the meaninglessness of existence, Lucifer induces a deep dream in this first couple, then guides them down through history: ancient Egypt, Greece, Rome, medieval Byzantium, renaissance Prague (seat of the Holy Roman Empire), revolutionary Paris, enterprising 19th-century London. Then they look into the future. Provisions on Earth are dwindling, and only an inhuman Communist egalitarianism can, for some time, provide the necessities of mankind. In despair, Adam wants to find a new world in the universe, but the force of Earth pulls him back. 4,000 years pass and mankind, having relapsed into a vegetating existence, faces extinction from a global cooling of the Earth's atmosphere. Having awakened from his nightmare, Adam decides to commit suicide in order to cancel history. Eve, who accompanied Adam and Lucifer, also awakens and tells Adam that she is pregnant—therefore the human race will survive. "You defeated me, Lord!" exclaims Adam falling on his knees—actually, the defeat is Lucifer's.

The Tragedy of Man has been the most discussed drama of Hungarian literature. Four problematic areas have crystallized during the controversy since its publication: Lucifer's role; Eve's role; the interpretation of the concluding message; and the place of *The Tragedy* in world literature, with special reference to Goethe's *Faust*.

Different from the great diabolical figures of world literature (such as Milton's Satan or Goethe's Mephisto), Lucifer represents the intellect that challenges the unquestioning, spontaneous thrust of life. The more man knows, the more he recognizes his limitations and the futility of his existence. Lucifer shares neither the resignation to the laws of existence that science advocates, nor the self-annihilating despair that almost drives Adam to suicide. Rather, he wants mankind to continue to exist as proof of the absurdity and futility of God's creation. One may recognize here something of the defiance of Sisyphus in Albert Camus' essay written decades later—and this is not the only trace of 20th-century existentialism in *The Tragedy*.

No less complex than Lucifer's role is Eve's. Adam usually appears as the representative of the governing ideas of various historical time periods: the Pharaoh, Miltiades, Tancred, Kepler, and Danton. Eve, on the other hand, represents different faces of human existence. She is a suffering slave in Egypt, Miltiades's devoted and Kepler's vain wife, a cunning bourgeois girl in London selling herself to matrimony—and in Paris, she appears both as an aristocratic woman to be beheaded and as a Jacobine slut. She supports and betrays man, guides or perplexes him, but in all circumstances complements the one-dimensional male character with her spontaneous earthiness and attraction.

The message of the drama is partly derivable from its structure, partly from the conclusion. Individual historical scenes are based on Hegelian dialectics: Adam represents an ideal, becomes disenchanted, and grabs at the promise of a future ideal. Together, however, the historical and futuristic scenes of the drama (scenes 4–14) make up a great and seemingly pessimistic Spenglerian cycle. Until the French Revolution, history manifests new ideals that man feels are worth fighting for—after that, he becomes a victim of his own greed and stupidity, wasting the natural resources of the Earth and overpopulating the globe. Some critics have argued, however, that this image of history was not necessarily shared by the writer, since Madách probably wanted to show what a biased interpretation Lucifer would give of the future in order to win Adam over to his side. Acting as a frame for the historical spectacle, the first three and the last scenes dwell on the meaning of Creation and human life—both being failures in Lucifer's eyes. Eventually it is belief in God's will, overcoming absurdity through hope, and the self-perpetuating, constructive forces of an otherwise unfathomable Nature, that save mankind and defeat the spirit of negation.

In the history of European theatre, Madách is regarded as an author in the tradition of universal drama. Paradoxically, *The Tragedy of Man* has been staged only in a handful of countries, such as Austria, Germany, and Czechoslovakia. Perhaps the critical tradition of the German-speaking countries accounts for the numerous attempts to compare *The Tragedy* to Goethe's *Faust*. Tendentiously or not, some of these comparisons in Austrian and German criticism were unfavourable to Madách, portraying him as a Goethe epigone. While this bias had some bearing on Madách's compatriots, Hungarian criticism, as a whole, lined up well-considered arguments in defence of Madách's originality. For example, the director and critic, Sándor Hevesi, listed four distinct points of difference:

In Goethe the hero was a male; the woman was just an episodic figure; Mephisto was an incarnation of hedonistic empiricism; and the milieu was unimportant since *Faust* was a book drama. On the other hand, Madách's heroes were a man and a woman appearing against the background of humankind; the woman played a central role; Lucifer was the spirit of negation who still contributed to the motivation of man's action; and *The Tragedy* was written for the stage with carefully designed scenes. It is unfortunate that the international stage history of the play does not provide a sufficient verification of Hevesi's last thesis.

—George Bisztray

THE TRAGEDY OF TRAGEDIES.   See **TOM THUMB.**

LA TRAGICOMEDIA DE CALISTO Y MELIBEA.   See **CELESTINA.**

TRANSLATIONS
by Brian Friel

First Publication: London, 1981.
First Production: Guildhall, Londonderry, Northern Ireland,
       23 September 1980.

Criticism
(For general works on the author, see *Playwrights* volume)

Articles:
Ronald Rollins, "Friel's *Translations:* The Ritual of Naming", in *Canadian Journal of Irish Studies*, vol.11 no.1, 1985.
Anthony Roche, "A Bit Off the Map: Brian Friel's *Translations* and Shakespeare's *Henry IV*", in *Literary Interrelations: Ireland, England and the World*, edited by Wolfgang Zach and Heinz Kosok, Tübingen, 1987.
Catherine Wiley, "Recreating Ballybeg: Two Translations by Brian Friel", in *Journal of Dramatic Theory and Criticism*, vol.1 no.2, 1987.
Csilla Bertha, "Tragedies of National Fate: A Comparison Between Brian Friel's *Translations* and Its Hungarian Counterpart, András Süto's *A szuzai menyegzo*", in *Irish University Review*, 17, 1987.
F.C. McGrath, "Irish Babel: Brian Friel's *Translations* and George Steiner's *After Babel*", in *Comparative Drama*, 23, 1989.

*   *   *

Set "in the townland of Baile Beag/Ballybeg, an Irish-speaking community in County Donegal" in the summer of 1833, *Translations* tells the story of how British army engineers carried out their assignment to remap and rename all of Ireland after its integration into the United Kingdom. Friel shows the effects of this geographic and linguistic dislocation

Translations: Hampstead Theatre, London, 1981

on a small community of rural Irish who are "invaded" by a detachment of English officers accompanied by Owen, a former citizen of the town. Owen's father Hugh is the master of the tiny hedge-school where people congregate in the evening to learn, for a tiny fee, such subjects as Latin, Greek, and mathematics. After Lieutenant Yolland falls in love with Marie, a local farm woman, and then mysteriously disappears, the English commander, suspecting murder, orders his army to destroy the entire village and evict the people if the Lieutenant isn't found. The play concludes quietly showing Hugh, Marie, and filthy Jimmy, another member of the "community", awaiting the threatened conflagration, and with the two old men, well-liquored, rhapsodizing multilingually about past civilizations' glory and how they fell.

Translations is a wonderful example of how a playwright can take a political issue and dramatize it for maximum theatrical effect. According to Seamus Deane, Friel's colleague in the founding of Field Day Theatre in 1980 (for which *Translations* was first produced), the play is a "tragedy of English imperialism as well as of Irish nationalism", played out in terms of language. In performance, the audience is asked to *hear* an assortment of competing languages in the same play, underscoring the theme of how failing to protect the language of a culture inevitably leads to the destruction of all of that culture. There are, in fact, two distinct ways of speaking and hearing the English language in the performance of the play, each contrasting with the other to dramatize and press home Friel's political statement. At one moment in Act II, Scene I, Hugh speaks English-accented English to Yolland (who doesn't understand Irish), Irish-accented English to Owen (to conceal his words from the Lieutenant), and precedes both with a quotation in Latin from Ovid. Thus, the dynamic *use* of language by the characters speaking differently-accented English (as well as classical Greek, Latin, and Irish) to each other, creates both the image of one culture overtaking another and the pressure on the inhabitants of this community to confront and deal with the socio-political conflict at the center of their lives.

The most moving yet trenchant scene (Act II, Scene 2) describes how Yolland and Marie manage to fall in love without knowing each other's language until finally, frustrated by their mutual incomprehension and incomprehensibility, they discard language entirely and allow their bodies to "talk" for them. They declare love for the "sound" of each other's speech, but must learn to set aside its literal meaning which, in personal and political circumstances says Friel, is open to constant misinterpretation. (At the play's conclusion, Yolland's disappearance, because it is intended to serve only as the pretext for raising these themes, is neither solved nor even remembered.)

The lovers' sentimental interlude is but the soft underside of a steely political vision concerning how language gives power to the person who speaks it, reads and writes it, and who finally insists on its dominance above all others. (The first action of the play shows Sarah, a woman with a severe speech defect, learning to speak her name for the first time.) In an astonishing turn from the previously benign events of the geographical "renaming", the ordinance survey's Captain Lancey returns in the third act to announce publicly the names of the places he will destroy in his search for his English comrade. As Lancey reads the landscape's newly assigned names, Owen speaks them in their Irish original, and the inevitable clash between cultures is powerfully *sounded*.

As imperialism's loutish and destructive power lays waste to a way of life and thought, we come to feel the brutal effect of how (in Deane's words) "divorcing power from eloquence" can lead to cultural impoverishment and/or quaint but useless

romantic fantasy in a subjugated people. (Another response is armed resistance, implied by Owen's final departure to look for his comrades, and although we do not see the results of his meeting, insurrection is, historically speaking, a definite option.) As one of the helpless folk, unable to withstand the verbal and martial onslaught of the vigorous, pragmatic English, the schoolmaster Hugh articulates one reason for his failure: "a civilization can be imprisoned in a linguistic contour which no longer matches the landscape of. . .fact" (Act II, Scene 1).

Truly, the success of a production of *Translations* lies in how forcefully it demands we *listen* to it. Most of us have visited "foreign" countries, including those "at home", and we know the discomfiture of both not understanding another's language and our need to "translate" the language into one we can comprehend. Around the world, terrible cultural disputes among communities and nations flare into fatal violence. In the universities, debate is intense and prolific concerning the nature of language (linguistics and philosophy), the meaning of language (semiotics and literary criticism), and the politics of language (anthropology, sociology, multicultural education, and law). *Translations* contributes to the full range of these discussions by dramatizing them with passionate, voluble theatricality. The number of personal and geographical analogies we can make to the situation in Baile Beag/Ballybeg in 1830 is only one reason to applaud the way this play "loses nothing in translation".

—Robert Skloot

TRAVELLING NORTH
by David Williamson

First Publication: Sydney, 1980.
First Production: Nimrod Theatre, Sydney, 22 August 1979.

Criticism
(For general works on the author, see *Playwrights* volume)

Articles:
Philip Parsons, "This World and the Next: *Travelling North*", in *London Magazine*, vol.20 nos. 8–9, 1980.

*   *   *

Comprised of 33 scenes in two acts, the episodic action of David Williamson's *Travelling North* moves between Melbourne in temperate southern Australia and a remote tropical area in northern Queensland. The plot focuses on the autumnal relationship of Frances, a middle-aged divorcee with two married daughters, and Frank, a retired widower of 70 years whose opinionated nature forbids his relating to people easily. A failed parent, he is estranged from his adult son and only tolerated by his daughter. Frances falls in love with the apparently vigorous Frank and agrees to share unwedded life in a cottage in the north's perpetual sunshine. Guiltily believing that she had failed to give her children a good home, Frances now hopes to find a measure of fulfillment with her lover away from urban Melbourne and burdensome family concerns. Soon, however, Frank falls prey to a degenerative heart ailment demanding that Frances serve as his nurse.

Refusing to accept the truth of his illness, Frances' ageing lover becomes increasingly crotchety, making her feel entrapped in a now strained relationship. Wishing not to repeat her earlier domestic irresponsibility, Frances unshirkingly cares for him until her patience breaks and she retreats to her urban life in the south. Left alone, Frank realizes his necessary dependence on others, and arrives at the discovery that while he has "always loved mankind in general" he has been ungenerous to those closest to him. He puts aside his anti-conventional prejudices, and he and Frances are reconciled and marry in the north before his death. She achieves a more defined, guilt-free, concept of herself and determines, in widowhood, not to return again to her past. She will go "travelling further north".

Employing a cinematically naturalistic style, *Travelling North* is a bittersweet comedy reflecting themes that both examine and celebrate the human condition. Both central characters are involved in an odyssey toward self-discovery in a bewildering world of conflicting duties and expectations. In one respect they are subjects for Williamson's concern with the exploration of the clash between moral duty and the self. Frances, the protagonist, is a sensitive, emotional, insecure person with conventional standards whose nature is antithetical to that of Frank, an atheist and disillusioned ex-Communist assertively governed by his own rationality. Both have failed with offspring and prior marriage partners. Frances recalls her distracted mothering of her children and feels guilty about their present domestic unhappiness arising from failed marriages. The daughters, wanting their mother's emotional support, are distressed by her going off to northern isolation with an older man who may eventually require her as a nurse.

Illness does strike Frank. He becomes so intolerable that Frances abandons her commitment as loving nurse and returns to Melbourne. There she watches her daughters heading for marital catastrophe and realizes, as rationally as would Frank, that they are responsible for their own lives. Her departure forces Frank to contemplate his own life: he needs her and has, despite an intellectualized love of mankind, withheld concern for persons in the particular. In their ensuing reconciliation, the lovers resolve their individual conflicts of obligation and self, and achieve fulfillment. Frances leaves guilt behind as she returns north, where a long-denied marriage becomes possible. After Frank's death, she celebrates his life with champagne according to his wishes. Now blessed with greater self-assurance, she foregoes further domestic duty to "travel north" independently.

A thematic concern of Williamson's implicit in the play is confrontation with the ironic unpredictability of life which refuses to reduce itself to a rational pattern. In Frank's eventual acquiescence in the face of the inevitable, he accepts that life is a mystery and cannot be measured by slide-rule rationality. That the couple's reconciliation and reunion, even in final suffering, is celebratory—marked by marriage, physical love, and mutual fulfillment—represents a reaffirmation of the human spirit.

The author's thematic intent is developed in several ways. The double setting of the play suggests the opposing forces of Winter and Spring. The wintry grayness of the urban south represents the world of business, domestic failures and obligations, and the complications of the workaday world that threaten happiness. Juxtaposed with this world is the warm, paradisal north, which is associated with rejuvenation—even if such spring-like renewal comes from the sacrifice of life. The current of the play flows through the two polarities, from unrealized life to fullness of life. Additionally, Williamson establishes classical music as a love shared by both central characters which overrides time, place, and circumstance. The stage directions provide explicit instructions for the use of specific compositions, as well as lighting, which underscore emotional atmosphere and thematic intent.

In *Travelling North*, Williamson's effective theatrical craftsmanship, manifesting a talent for characterization and dialogue, has created a fluent play, free of sentimentality, with credible characters. Scenes are well constructed, with individual conflicts and climaxes interwoven to accumulate emotional tension and drive the action forward. The play's cinematic realism lent itself well to a motion-picture version written by the author, effectively highlighting the work's intended comic tone.

Williamson is an Australian dramatist noted for creating an accurate social and personal world composed of his country's urban society, yet in *Travelling North* the author goes beyond national boundaries to examine more universal questions. One may deduce that Frank and Frances, being the masculine and feminine forms of the same name (with the former sounding more hard and rational than the latter), represent the south and north, the yin and yang of the human individual, constantly torn by contradictions and spurred to search for fulfillment and answers to life's larger questions. *Travelling North* stands as its author's most universal play to date.

—Christian H. Moe

TRAVESTIES
by Tom Stoppard

First Publication: London, 1975.
First Production: Aldwych Theatre, London (Royal Shakespeare Company), 10 June 1974.

Criticism
(For general works on the author, see *Playwrights* volume)

Articles:
Margaret Gold, "Who are the Dadas of *Travesties?*", in *Modern Drama*, 21, 1978.
Coppélia Kahn, "*Travesties* and the Importance of Being Stoppard", in *New York Literary Forum*, 1, 1978.
Armin Geraths, "Geschichte und Geschichtskritik in Tom Stoppards 'Ideen-Komödie' *Travesties*", in *Anglistik & Englischunterricht*, 7, 1979.
Howard D. Pearce, "Stage as Mirror: Tom Stoppard's *Travesties*", in *Modern Language Notes*, 94, 1979.
Carol Billman, "The Art of History in Tom Stoppard's *Travesties*", in *Kansas Quarterly*, vol.12 no.4, 1980.
C.J. Gianakaris, "Tom Stoppard as Master Game Player: *Travesties* and After", in *Perpectives on Contemporary Literature*, 6, 1980.
Neil Sammells, "Earning Liberties: *Travesties* and the *The Importance of Being Earnest*", in *Modern Drama*, 29, 1986.
Werner Wolf, "Geschichtsfiktion im Kontext dekonstruktivistischer Tendenzen in neuerer Historik und literarischer Postmoderne: Tom Stoppards *Travesties*", in *Poetica*, 18, 1986.

*   *   *

In an interview with the editors of *Theatre Quarterly* in 1974, Stoppard confessed to having "enormous difficulty in working

Travesties: Aldwych Theatre, London, 1974 (Royal Shakespeare Company; first production)

out plots". Thus a major reason for his using another play for a basic structure is that it takes off " a lot of pressure". It is a method of composition that he shares with other dramatists, not least Shakespeare. Nevertheless, Stoppard enjoys bursting out of whichever text is his chosen frame in a stream of paradox, building up extraordinary juxtapositions like a verbal collage, so that it is not surprising for his sharp wit to have been likened to Wilde's even before he thought of using *The Importance of Being Earnest* as a basic structure for *Travesties*.

In *Travesties*, Stoppard created from some seeds of fact (that James Joyce, Tristan Tzara and Lenin all spent time in Zurich in the 1914–18 war and that Joyce organised a production of *The Importance of Being Earnest*—in which a minor consular official, Henry Carr, played the role of Algernon Moncrieff and subsequently quarrelled with Joyce over the reimbursement of his expenses) a "faction" in which fiction is paramount and fact travestied in a wonderful embroidery of wit. Stoppard indeed described his technique in similar terms in an interview with Ronald Hayman:

> . . .there's more than one point of origin for a play, and the only useful metaphor I can think of for the way I think I write my plays is convergences of different threads. Perhaps carpet-making would suggest something similar.

Events in *Travesties* are seen through distorting spectacles, the unreliable memory of an old man. Henry Carr, in old age, taking his cue from his leading role in Wilde's play, sets himself centre-stage in history; forgetting his minor role in consular affairs, he relegates the actual consul (General Bennett) to the status of manservant, making Bennett into Lane, butler to his Algernon, and regaling the audience with "memories" of Joyce, Tzara, and Lenin.

The opening of *Travesties*, in which Joyce is dictating *Ulysses*, Tzara is cutting up a poem and reading the result drawn (Dada-fashion) from his hat, and Lenin is discussing revolution in Russian with his wife, Nadya, leaves a non-Russian speaking audience unable to understand anything for several minutes! It is a theatrical masterstroke—in itself revolutionary, reflecting the fundamental changes under discussion: Joyce breaking the mould of the traditional novel, Tzara introducing the world to new possibilities in art, and Lenin laying the groundwork for the Russian revolution. Nonetheless in emphasising the creative brilliance that conjured this extraordinary synthesis of different threads as it were from a Wildean hat, we must not assume that Stoppard had worked out the whole scheme in advance. Indeed in the Ronald Hayman interview, he stressed the role of "lucky accident" in the creation of his plays, even though they may "seem to hinge around carefully thought out structural pivots".

A major thread in *Travesties* is a debate on the value of art which Stoppard first introduced in *Artist Descending A Staircase* (1972) and continued in almost identical form in *Travesties*. Indeed Stoppard refers to Joyce's justification of his art as "the most important speech in the play". It was not present in the original text, but added when Peter Wood, Stoppard's director, said some clarification of ideas was necessary. The speech is elicited from Joyce, in the role of Aunt Augusta (a name Joyce was in fact christened with, in mistake for Augustine) quizzing Jack Worthing (in this case Tristan Tzara) not, as in Wilde, about his matrimonial qualifications, but about the nature of art: "What now of the Trojan War if it had been passed over by the artist's touch? Dust". The speech ends in the precise cadence of Lady Bracknell: "I would strongly advise you to try to acquire some genius. . .before the season is quite over". Joyce's scepticism as to Tzara's artistic ability echoes earlier discussion about the meaning of Dada between Carr and Tzara (Algy and Jack):

> *Tzara*: Nowadays an artist is someone who makes art mean the things he does. A man may be an artist by exhibiting his hindquarters. He may be a poet by drawing words out of a hat. . .
> *Carr*: But that is simply to change the meaning of the word Art.
> *Tzara*: I see I have made myself clear.
> *Carr*: . . .Don't you see my dear Tristan you are simply asking me to accept that the word Art means whatever you wish it to mean;

When accused of overbalancing *Travesties* with Cecily's "lecture" in Act II, Stoppard replied that after the "lengthy exposition of Dada" in Act 1, he wanted "a corresponding exposition" in political terms in Act II of how Lenin got to Zurich. He felt it was impossible to "integrate the Lenins into the *Importance* scheme". Lenin castigates the frivolity of the arts, thus laying down a gauntlet to which Stoppard the dramatist responds by introducing the even greater frivolity of the Gallagher and Shean routines. Stoppard referred to this riposte as "the architectural thing I was after". Nonetheless the surprise generated by Cecily's lecture and Lenin's subsequent oration on art creates a change of tone that largely dominates Act II, despite the manic activity of the interspersing Gallagher and Shean routines. Perhaps it is not too fanciful to see in the dying out of the laughter in the second act and Lenin's takeover of Stoppard's play, a foretaste of a joyless totalitarian regime, such as Stoppard deals with in subsequent plays.

—Rosemary Pountney

TRI SESTRY. See **THE THREE SISTERS.**

THE TRIAL OF LOUIS RIEL. See **THE RIEL TRILOGY.**

THE TRICKSTER OF SEVILLE AND THE GUEST OF STONE
(El burlador de Sevilla y convidado de piedra)
by Tirso de Molina

First Publication: In *Doce comedias nuevas de Lope de Vega y otros autores*, Barcelona, 1630.
First Production: Teatro San Bartolomeo, Naples, 22 December 1625.

Editions

El burlador de Sevilla, edited by Joaquim Casalduero, Madrid, 1977.

El burlador de Sevilla, edited by Manuel Carreras Díaz, Aubi, 1978.

El Burlador de Sevilla, edited by Gerald E. Wade and Everett W. Hesse, Salamanca, 1978.

El burlador de Sevilla, Madrid, 1980 (Clasicos comentados Playor)

El burlador de Sevilla, edited by Xavier A. Fernandez, Madrid, 1982.

The Trickster of Seville and the Stone Guest [with translation], edited and translated by Gwynne Edwards, Warminster, Wiltshire, c.1986.

"El Burlador de Sevilla": Andrés de Claramonte atribuído tradicionalmente a Tirso de Molina, edited by Alfredo Rodríguez López-Vázquez, Kassel, 1987.

Translations

The Love-Rogue, translated by Harry Kemp, New York, 1923.

The Trickster of Seville and the Guest of Stone, translated by Roy Campbell, in *Masterpieces of the Golden Age*, edited by Angel Flores, New York, 1957.

The Rogue of Seville, translated by Robert O'Brien, in *Spanish Drama*, edited by Angel Flores, New York, 1962.

The Playboy of Seville, in *Eight Spanish Plays of the Golden Age*, translated and edited by Walter Starkie, New York, 1964.

Criticism

(For general works on the author, see *Playwrights* volume)

Books:

Daniel Rogers, *Tirso de Molina: "El burlador de Sevilla"*, London, 1977.

Alfredo Rodríguez López-Vázquez, *Andrés de Claramonte y "El burlador de Sevilla"*, Kassel, 1987.

Articles:

E. Templin, "The *Burla* in the Plays of Tirso de Molina", in *Hispanic Review*, 8, 1940.

E. Templin, "Possible Reminiscences of La Senora Cornelia in *El burlador de Sevilla*", in *Modern Language Forum*, 33, 1948

A. Marni, "Did Tirso Employ Counterpassion in his *Burlador de Sevilla?*", in *Hispanic Review*, 20, 1952.

F. Sedgwick, "Mozart's Sources for *Don Giovanni*", in *Hispania*, 37, 1954.

F. Sedgwick, "*El burlador*, Don Giovanni, and the Popular Concept of Don Juan", in *Hispania*, 38, 1955.

B. Wardropper, "*El burlador de Sevilla:* A Tragedy of Errors", in *Philological Quarterly*, 36, 1957.

D. Pratt, "The Don Juan Myth", in *American Imago*, vol. 17 no.3, 1960.

A. Singer, "Chaucer and Don Juan", in *West Virginia University Bulletin: Philological Papers*, 13, 1961.

A. Morris, "Metaphor in *El burlador de Sevilla*", in *Romanic Review*, 55, 1964.

D. Rogers, "Fearful Symmetry: The Ending of *El burlador de Sevilla*", in *Bulletin of Hispanic Studies*, 41, 1964.

G. Wade, "*El burlador de Sevilla:* Some Annotations", in *Hispania*, 47, 1964.

A. Sloman, "The Two Versions of *El burlador de Sevilla*", in *Bulletin of Hispanic Studies*, 42, 1965.

G. Wade, "*El burlador de Sevilla:* The Tenorios and the Ulloas", in *Symposium*, vol.19, no. 3, 1965.

The Trickster of Seville: Teatro Espanol, Madrid, 1966

G. Wade, "Further Notes on *El burlador de Sevilla*", in *Bulletin of the Comediantes*, 18, 1966.

R. McDowell, "Tirso, Byron, and the Don Juan Tradition", in *Arlington Quarterly*, 1, 1967.

C. Mills, "*Man and Superman* and the Don Juan Legend", in *Comparative Literature*, 19, 1967.

G. Wade, "The Authorship and Date of Composition of *El burlador de Sevilla*", in *Hispanofíla*, 32, 1968.

Jon Aghnesa and Henry Sullivan, "The Unholy Martyr: Don Juan's Misuse of Intelligence", in *Romanische Forschungen*, 81, 1969.

Rosina D. Navarrete, "Don Juan: El impulso destructor", in *Bulletin of the Comediantes*, 20, 1969.

Francisco Fernández-Turienzo, "*El burlador:* Mito y realidad", in *Romanische Forschungen*, 86, 1974.

Gerald E. Wade, "Hacia una compresión del tema de Don Juan y *El burlador*", in *Revista de archivos, bibliotecas y museos*, 77, 1974.

Carlos Feal Diebe, "*El burlador* de Tirso y la mujer", in *Symposium*, 29, 1975.

Ruth Lundelius, "Tirso's View of Women in *El burlador de Sevilla*", in *Bulletin of the Comediantes*, 27, 1975.

Joseph H. Silverman, "Anti-Semitism in Tirso de Molina's *Burlador de Sevilla*", in *Studies in the Literature of Spain: Sixteenth and Seventeenth Centuries*, edited by Michael J. Ruggerio, Brockport, New York, 1977.

J.E. Varey, "Social Criticism in *El burlador de Sevilla*", in *Theatre Research International*, 2, 1977.

Alfred Rodríguez, "Tirso's Don Juan as Social Rebel", in *Bulletin of the Comediantes*, 30, 1978.

Gerald E. Wade, "The Character of Tirso's Don Juan of *El burlador de Sevilla:* A Psychoanalytical Study", in *Bulletin of the Comediantes*, 31, 1979.

Dorothy Clotelle Clarke, "Tirso's Don Juan and Juan Ruiz's Don Amor", in *Folio*, 12, 1980.

Eleanor Jean Martin, "A Consideration of the Role of Honor in Tirso de Molina's *El burlador de Sevilla*", in *Kentucky Romance Quarterly*, 27, 1980.

Georges Parain, "La Pastorale dans le *Don Juan* de Tirso", in *Le Genre pastoral en Europe du XVe au XVIIe siècle*, edited by Claude Longeon, Saint-Étienne, 1980.

D.W. Cruikshank, "The First Edition of *El burlador de Sevilla*", in *Hispanic Review*, vol.49 no. 4, 1981.

Everett W. Hesse, "Tirso's Don Juan and the Opposing Self", in *Bulletin of the Comediantes*, vol.33 no. 1, 1981.

Armand E. Singer, "Don Juan's Women in *El burlador de Sevilla*", in *Bulletin of the Comediantes*, vol.33 no.1, 1981.

Silvana De Vicentis, "Metamorfosi di Don Giovanni: Da Tirso a Shaw", in *Lingua e stile*, vol.17 no. 2, 1982.

Ruth P. Weintraub, "In Defense of Don Juan: Deceit and Hypocrisy in Tirso de Molina, Molière, Mozart, and G.B. Shaw", in *Romanic Review*, vol.74 no. 4, 1983.

Elizabeth Teresa Howe, "Hell or Heaven? Providence and Don Juan", in *Renascence*, vol.37 no. 4, 1985.

Peter W. Evans, "The Roots of Desire in *El burlador de Sevilla*", in *Forum for Modern Language Studies*, vol.22 no. 3, 1986.

Gerald E. Wade, "*El burlador de Sevilla* as Metaphor", in *Studies in Honor of William C. McCrary*, edited by Robert Fiore and others, Lincoln, Nebraska, 1986.

Alfredo Rodríguez López-Vázquez, "Apportaciones críticas a la autoría de *El burlador de Sevilla*", in *Criticón*, 40, 1987.

James Mandrell, "Language and Seduction in *El burlador de Sevilla*", in *Bulletin of the Comediantes*, vol.40 no.2, 1988.

Antonio Gómez-Moriana, "Pragmática del y reciprocidad de perspectivas: Sobre las promesas de Don Juan y el desenlace del *Burlador*", in *Gesto*, vol.4 no. 7, 1989.

The action of *The Trickster of Seville* is built around the elements of disguise, seduction, and flight. The term *burlador* (and its related forms, *burlar* and *burla*) designates deceits or "tricks" of different types. The first are the disguises Don Juan adopts in order to carry out his seductions; second are the seductions or sexual "deceits" themselves; finally there are the moral deceits insofar as Don Juan believes he will not be called to account for his actions. Don Juan seduces four women in Tirso's play, and each seduction occurs in a different place. Two of the women (the Duchess Isabela and Doña Ana) are nobles, two (Tisbea and Aminta) are from the common ranks of society.

The principal themes of the work are introduced in Act I, with the seduction of the Duchess Isabela in the palace in Naples. Isabella is deceived in part because Don Juan has artfully disguised himself as the Duke Octavio, but also because she has committed herself to a prearranged nocturnal encounter with the Duke. After Don Juan is recognized as an impostor, he flees to Spain, where he and his aide, Catalinón, land on the coast of Tarragona; there Don Juan attempts to seduce a fisherwoman, Tisbea. Unlike the other women in the play, Tisbea claims to be strong enough to resist his advances, yet she too eventually falls.

In Act II Don Juan disguises himself as the Marqués de la Mota, and in an attempt to seduce a cousin of the Marqués, the noblewoman Ana de Ulloa, he kills her father, Don Gonzalo de Ulloa, in a duel. In Act III Don Juan interrupts the wedding celebration of the peasant couple, Aminta and Batricio, and steals the bride away. At the close of Act III Don Gonzalo returns from the dead and, as the "Stone Guest", challenges Don Juan to accept a dinner invitation. Once Don Juan is dragged down into Hell by the Stone Guest the other couples in the play are happily married off.

The Trickster of Seville thus has what may be regarded as two conclusions—or a conclusion in two parts. The first, where Don Juan meets the Stone Guest, is tragic in tone. The second allows for the reconciliation of those members of society who have been dishonored by Don Juan, and is comic in the dramatic sense. The first conclusion enacts the near sacrificial elimination of the tyrant of seduction in the form of a banquet; this ritual elimination in turn permits accession to civil society or social life.

The action of *The Trickster of Seville* is set within a larger, theological framework that demands (and produces) divine retribution for Don Juan's actions. Throughout the play his aide Catalinón advises him to mend his ways and repent, but Don Juan refuses, always insisting that he has plenty of time to repent ("¡*Que largo me lo fiáis!*"). At one level, Catalinón is simply cowardly and Don Juan defiant; Don Juan has heroic aspirations, however misguided his actions may be. But on another level, Tirso's play is a late example of the drama of the Counter-Reformation in Spain; the insistent moral overtones of the work serve as a warning of the powers of divine justice and retribution regulating earthly life.

It has been said that the artistry of Tirso's play lies in its internal pace, its dramatic rhythm, and its language, rather than in its detailed psychological characterizations. *The Trickster of Seville* is, to be sure, a formulaic work; yet it has, built into its formulae, a greater degree of psychological complexity than often is recognized. On the one hand Tirso seems to have understood the psychology of the seducer, and to have recognized the mobile sense of selfhood required to sustain a life of disguise and deceit. Such mobility demands of the trickster the ability to imagine himself in the role of others and also the negative capability for the absorption of alien roles as his own. As a result of this process, Don Juan has a vacillating, almost vacant identity; indeed, he defines himself from the beginning of the play as "A man with no name" ("*Un hombre sin nombre*"). On the other hand, Tirso seems to have comprehended the psychology of those who exhibit the desire *for* seduction. This is where the distinctiveness of the play is to be found. Don Juan seduces women of all social ranks, and has a social-levelling effect; as a result, the motives of the different strata of society are reduced to their common denominator in desire.

Linguistically and thematically, *The Trickster of Seville* has been seen as an example of Mannerism or of the Baroque in Spain, and may be compared to the art of El Greco. In its rapid movement, violent changes of scene, its poetic use of visual perspectives, its elaborately constructed metaphors and figures of speech, and in its consciousness of time and space the play is, indeed, baroque. On the one hand, Don Juan is acutely aware of time: time is, for him, the intensity of the moment; yet on the other hand Tirso reminds his audience of the pressures of theological time—the time for justice, when Don Juan will be forced to account for his actions.

When viewed in social terms, *The Trickster of Seville* represents a moment of the decline of the nobility in Spain. As Aminta says, "Shame itself has become the knighthood of Spain" ("*La desvergüenza en España / Se ha hecho caballería*"). Don Juan is the anti-type of the typical hero of the Spanish Golden-Age theatre, on whom the values of honor are so often staked. Whereas the prototypical hero upholds the standards of society by remaining faithful to the values of honor, Don Juan seeks, by transgressing social norms, to undermine the order of society itself. If the typical heroes of the theatre of Golden-Age Spain are characteristically the proponents of a conservative ideology, then Don Juan is both socially subversive and threateningly modern.

The figure of the "trickster" derives in part from legend, in part from Spanish ballads, and partly from the seducing courtier or *galán* of the Spanish theatre, with his real-life counterpart in the degenerate nobility. Tirso's play is none the less the first full-blown example of the Don Juan legend in literature and art, and has served as the source for countless works since, including, most prominently, Molière's *Dom Juan*, Mozart and da Ponte's *Don Giovanni*, Zorilla's *Don Juan Tenorio*, Kierkegaard's *Either / Or* (in the figure of the Seducer), and George Bernard Shaw's *Man and Superman*.

—Anthony J. Cascardi

TROADES. See THE TROJAN WOMEN.

TROILUS AND CRESSIDA
by William Shakespeare

First Publication: London, 1609; with variants, in First Folio, 1623.
First Production: London, c.1602–03.

Editions
Troilus and Cressida, edited by H.N. Hillebrand (supplemented by T.W. Baldwin), Philadelphia, 1953 (New Variorum Shakespeare).

Troilus and Cressida, edited by Alice Walker, Cambridge, 1957 (The New Shakespeare).
The History of Troilus and Cressida, edited by Virgil K. Whitaker, Baltimore, Maryland, 1958 (Pelican Shakespeare).
The History of Troilus and Cressida, edited by Daniel Seltzer, New York, 1963 (Signet Classic Shakespeare).
Troilus and Cressida, edited by Kenneth Muir, Oxford, 1982 (Oxford Shakespeare).
Troilus and Cressida, edited by Kenneth Palmer, London and New York, 1982 (Arden Shakespeare).
Troilus and Cressida, edited by R.A. Foakes, Harmondsworth, 1987.

Criticism
(For general works on the author, see *Playwrights* volume)

Books:
O.J. Campbell, *Comicall Satyre and Shakespeare's "Troilus and Cressida"*, San Marino, California, 1938.
Robert K. Presson, *Shakespeare's "Troilus and Cressida" and the Legends of Troy*, 1953.
Robert Kimbrough, *Shakespeare's "Troilus and Cressida" and Its Setting*, 1964.
Astrid Kirchheim, *Tragik und Komik in Shakespeare's "Troilus and Cressida", "Measure for Measure", und "All's Well That Ends Well"*, Frankfurt, 1971.
Laurie Lanzen Harris and Mark W. Scott (eds.), *"Troilus and Cressida"*, in *Shakespearian Criticism, 3*, Detroit, Illinois, 1986 [anthology of criticism].
Janet Adamson, *Troilus and Cressida*, Brighton, 1987 (Harvester New Critical Introductions to Shakespeare).

Articles:
For information on the many articles about *Troilus and Cressida*, see the bibliographies listed in the *Playwrights* volume, and the annual Shakespeare Bibliography published by the Folger Shakespeare Library, Washington D.C. (1950–).

*   *   *

Critics have tended to apologise for *Troilus and Cressida*, using words like "satire", not so much to assign the play to a genre as to explain a perceived incoherence. Its performance history, or rather lack of it, is often used to imply that it has been, from the beginning, a box-office flop.

As the play begins, the Trojan war has gone on for seven years; morale is low and Achilles has withdrawn from the fight despite various strategies to persuade him back. The Trojans regret their involvement in the war but cannot bring themselves to return Helen, the cause of it, to her husband. The Trojan Prince Troilus falls in love with Cressida, whose father has gone over to the Greek side. Egged on by her uncle, Pandarus, they commence a love affair which is interrupted when the Greeks offer to exchange a Trojan prisoner for Cressida. She betrays Troilus who witnesses this in the company of Ulysses. Achilles returns to the war to avenge the death of his friend, Patroclus, and brutally joins with his troops to kill Hector, the noblest of the Trojan princes. Troilus rushes into battle to avenge Hector and kill Cressida's new lover, Diomed. A cynical speech by Pandarus closes the play on this inconclusive note.

From a summary alone one might well deduce a lack of definition: is the play a story about two lovers, or about the Trojan war? If the former, why are we not shown the end of their story, familiar to Shakespeare's audience—death for

Troilus and Cressida: Engraving published by Boydell, 1800

Troilus, leprosy for Cressida? If the latter, why conclude the story in mid-war and in mid-battle? However, if one abandons certain preconceptions, a focus becomes apparent: that of the limits of real individual power in areas like love and enmity which might be seen as prime sites of individualism. This focus is at its sharpest in the characterisation of Cressida herself, and perhaps one of the main reasons why critics deny coherence to the play is their wilful insistence on reading her as the proud and faithless whore of Elizabethan tradition. This, in turn, enforces a reading of Troilus as tragic hero with a dramatic right to a death scene, perhaps one which reflects the existential agony of his betrayal-speech, "The bonds of heaven are slipped, dissolved and loosed". The world Shakespeare portrays, however, is one in which personal courage, chivalry, or love have no real power to change the situation, and any individual who, like Troilus, attempts to ground his or her existence in the consistency of human nature is in for a rude shock.

Cressida is a hostage in Troy. Her value to both sides is not determined by her personal qualities, her "self", but by her market price as the daughter of Calchas, the defector. At the beginning of the play she seems to have some power of choice, symbolised by the parade of princes across the stage; while Pandarus urges her to have eyes for Troilus alone, the dazzling procession suggests that here is a girl who might take her pick of the best. In Act IV an ironic parallel parade reveals the truth about her powers of self-determination: Cressida was received into the Greek camp with a courteous kiss from Agamemnon; Ulysses turns this into a crude ceremony in which she is kissed by all the assembled generals, a rite over which Cressida attempts to gain some measure of control by acting flirtatiously; this Ulysses takes to be evidence of her promiscuity and proclaims her "a daughter of the game", a reading which critics have been all too eager to adopt. If one looks at the scene with a visual memory of Act I, where she is placed in a commanding position *vis-à-vis* potential lovers, it is clear that the point stressed here is her vulnerability: a woman passed like a parcel down a line of fully armed top brass, a hostage traded by her lover's kinsmen for someone strategically more valuable, is hardly in a position to refuse a kiss, or the chance of a male protector like Diomed.

Cressida herself knows that a woman's value is not intrinsic but fluctuates on a patriarchal stock market; clear sightedly she recognises at the outset that to yield to Troilus is to risk being devalued in his eyes. Her gamble is justified on the individual, erotic level, but both lovers have, by loving, rendered themselves politically vulnerable. It is in the Greek interest both to destroy her relationship with a Trojan and to ensure the demoralisation of Troilus by making him witness her attachment to Diomed.

In Shakespeare's comedies, women often articulate most clearly the play's commitment to certain values—life, joy, fertility. They do this as the characters in whom those values manifest themselves most clearly. In a play where the question most often posited is "What's aught but as 'tis valued?", Cressida articulates the position of all those trapped by a war over which they can have no control: she speaks for Helen, for the women of both camps, for those whose blood will be shed because others have determined whether a war is still worth fighting.

—Frances Gray

THE TROJAN WAR WILL NOT TAKE PLACE
(La Guerre de Troie n'aura pas lieu)
by Jean Giraudoux

First Publication: Paris, 1935.
First Production: Théâtre de l'Athénée, Paris, 21 November 1935.

Translations
Tiger at the Gates, translated by Christopher Fry, London and New York, 1955; reprinted as *The Trojan War Will Not Take Place*, London, 1983.

Criticism
(For general works on the author, see *Playwrights* volume)

Books:
Henri Baudin (ed.), *La Guerre de Troie n'aura pas lieu*, Paris, 1970.
Étienne Frois, *"La Guerre de Troie n'aura pas lieu": Analyse critique*, Paris, 1971.
Roy Lewis, *Giraudoux: "La Guerre de Troie n'aura pas lieu"*, London, 1971.
Michel Raimond, *Sur trois pièces de Giraudoux: "La Guerre de Troie n'aura pas lieu", "Electre", "Ondine"*, Paris, 1982.

Articles:
Günter Schweig, "Jean Giraudoux: *La Guerre de Troie n'aura pas lieu*", in *Die neueren Sprachen* (new series), 1966.
R.H. Desroches, "Reality Behind the Myth in Giraudoux's *La Guerre de Troie n'aura pas lieu*", in *Revue des langues vivantes*, 34, 1968.
Neal Oxenhandler, "Dialectic and Rhetoric in *La Guerre de Troie n'aura pas lieu*", in *Esprit créateur*, 9, 1969.
Roy Lewis, "Giraudoux: *La Guerre de Troie n'aura pas lieu*", in *Studies in French Literature*, 19, 1971.
T. Jefferson Kline, "The Crisis of Language in Giraudoux's Theater", in *Romanic Review*, 67, 1976.
Alan J. Singerman, "Helen and Troïlus: War and Allegory in Giraudoux's *La Guerre de Troie n'aura pas lieu*", in *French Review*, 49, 1976.
Gunnar Graumann, "Les Allusions politiques dans *La Guerre de Troie n'aura pas lieu*", in *Cahiers Jean Giraudoux*, 7, 1978.
G. Macklin, "*La Guerre de Troie n'aura pas lieu* and the Limitations of Man", in *Humanitas: Studies in French Literature Presented to Henri Godin*, edited by R. Leslie Davis and others, Coleraine, 1984.

*   *   *

This two-act play in prose is set in the hours immediately preceding the outbreak of the Trojan War. Paris has abducted Helen, and the Greek ambassador, Ulysses, is on his way to demand her return. If he is rebuffed then war will necessarily ensue. King Priam and the old men of Troy, represented by the poet Demokos, dote on Helen and will not give her up, but the army is weary of war, and its general, Hector, insists that she should be returned. Hector confronts Helen, who appears indifferent both to Paris and to the fate of Troy. Nevertheless, she accedes to Hector's wish that she should return to Greece. The Trojans ceremonially close the Gates of War as a sign of their desire for peace; but Hector's wife, Andromache, believing war to be increasingly inevitable, appeals to Helen to give it some meaning by truly loving Paris. There follows, a series of narrowly-averted occasions for the declaration of war:

Hector is insulted by the Greek Oiax; Demokos tries to avenge him but is prevented; and Hector and Paris's comic attempt to pretend that Helen is untouched is interrupted by an inconclusive message from the gods. Finally, Hector and Ulysses meet face to face and the respective merits of themselves and their countries are weighed in the balance. Despite Hector's efforts, he imagines the scales tipping in favour of the Greeks. Yet Ulysses, too, agrees to co-operate by taking Helen back. Hector's resolve is tested once more when the drunken Oiax embraces his wife, and finally Hector stabs Demokos to silence his last attempt to rally the Trojans. The dying and vengeful poet, however, accuses Oiax, and, as the Gates of War swing open, the curtain falls on the certainty of the forthcoming conflict.

The title, taken from the first line of the play, spoken by Andromache to her sister-in-law, the tragic prophetess Cassandra, is an admirable example of Giraudoux's gift for dramatic irony. As such, it is also the means of instigating in the audience the reflection on an issue of major importance that Giraudoux believed to be the main purpose of theatre. Like Hector, we are well aware that all his attempts to avert the Trojan War are doomed to failure, no matter how improbably successful they may appear. Thus we are led to question the point and value of his struggle, and to consider how far we would go in similar circumstances, as we see the hero accepting insults to his family, to himself, and to his wife, and even committing murder in the interests of peace.

One of Giraudoux's main preoccupations, and a recurrent theme in his work, is the reconciliation of the different concepts of civilisation he saw represented by France and Germany. Indeed, he believed the cause of peace between the two countries to be the major question of his age. As a distinguished diplomat, however, he was only too aware in 1935, at the time of the composition of *The Trojan War Will Not Take Place*, that World War I had not, in fact, been the "war to end all wars", and that, like Hector and his returning army, the young men of Europe would soon be facing another campaign at the instigation of the politicians and propagandists. As a diplomat, too, he was aware that despite calls to arms in the name of patriotism, heroism, woman, or beauty, the causes of war are almost always economic and social (when they are not, quite simply, absurd). Thus, Ulysses cites both the Greeks envy of the richness of Troy, as well as their need of "lebensraum" as contributing, though not necessarily deciding, factors in their desire for war. Ulysses, too, refers to his meeting with Hector in terms reminiscent of all those ultimately futile diplomatic summits held on the eve of war, the most recent of which had taken place at Stresa, on Lake Maggiore, in April 1935. When asked by a journalist if his play was alluding directly to the current political situation, however, Giraudoux replied that there was no direct allusion but that it was simply "a question of war and peace".

The composition of *The Trojan War Will Not Take Place* was also influenced by Giraudoux's experience as a soldier. Despite his love of Germany, the author distinguished himself in the war of 1914–18 —he was mentioned twice in despatches and was awarded the *Légion d'honneur*. In Hector, therefore, we probably see something of the ambivalence of Giraudoux's own attitude in the former enjoyment of war now turned to hatred, in his love of his enemy, and his refusal to romanticize combat and glorify the fallen.

The characters of *The Trojan War Will Not Take Place* are familiar to us from Homer, Shakespeare, and others, and an interesting feature of Giraudoux's play is the way in which he uses and often subverts this familiarity. Thus, Hector is the valiant warrior who hates war, and Andromache is the faithful wife who describes the lack of harmony between herself and her husband. Above all, we are presented not with a noble royal house but with the members of an ordinary family in crisis: the kind but patronising Priam; the sharp-tongued virago, Hecuba; the embittered spinster, Cassandra; and the playboy black-sheep, Paris. It is in his treatment of Helen, however, that Giraudoux's novelty is most striking, for this legendary symbol of beauty is presented as a childlike but unfeeling, fickle *femme fatale*. Her depiction is not entirely unsympathetic though; endowed by Giraudoux with clairvoyance, she refrains from telling Hector the worst of her premonitions, and is as lacking in pity for herself as she is for her fellow men. Ulysses explains her detachment by saying that she is merely the instrument of destiny. She sees herself as one of the world's stars, necessary to give meaning to the lives of those such as the old men of Troy. Her appeal is not, however, restricted to the aged, and in her two scenes with Troilus, we see the force of the sex and glamour she personifies on both the young man and the town he represents.

The often anachronistic reduction of the myth to a domestic human level is also apparent in the treatment of the divine, for the gods are no more able to influence the outcome of the events than men. It is also reflected in the variety of tones employed, ranging from the somewhat precious beauty of the descriptions of Troy at peace, through the strength of Hector's "Speech to the Dead", the burlesque of the follies of the old men of Troy, and the comic sexual innuendo of the account of Paris and Helen's return, to the crudity of Hecuba's description of the face of war. Thus Giraudoux, with tenderness and often amusement, presents us with the whole panorama of the human condition, but above all with the dignity of a knowingly doomed struggle against the greatest of all evils—war.

—Janet Clarke

THE TROJAN WOMEN (Troades)
by Euripides

First Production: Athens, 415 B.C.

Editions

The Trojan Women, edited by F.A. Paley, Cambridge, 1881.
Troades (revised edition), edited by Robert Yelverton Tyrrell, London, 1882; revised edition, 1897.
The Daughters of Troy, in *Euripides, I* [with translation], edited by Arthur S. Way, London, 1912 (Loeb Classical Library)
Troades, edited by K.H. Lee, Basingstoke and London, 1976.
The Trojan Women [with translation], edited and translated by Shirley A. Barlow, Warminster, Wiltshire, 1986.

Translations

The Trojan Women, translated by Gilbert Murray, London, 1905.
The Trojan Women, in *Three Greek Plays*, translated by Edith Hamilton, New York, 1937.
The Trojan Women, translated by Richmond Lattimore, in *Greek Plays in Modern Translation*, edited by Dudley Fitts, New York, 1947.
The Trojan Women, in a version by F. Kinchin Smith, London, 1951.
The Trojan Women, translated by Neil Curry, Old Woking, Surrey, 1964; revised edition, London, 1966.

The Trojan Women: In *The Greeks* cycle, Aldwych Theatre, 1980 (Royal Shakespeare Company)

The Women of Troy, in *Euripides: The War Plays*, translated by Don Taylor, London, 1990.

Criticism
(For general works on the author, see *Playwrights* volume)

Articles:
L.M. Mead, "The *Troades* of Euripides", in *Greece and Rome*, 8, 1939.
E. O'Neill, "The Prologue of the *Troades* of Euripides", in *Transactions and Proceedings of the American Philological Association* [*TAPA*], 72, 1941.
H. Westlake, "Euripides' *Troades* 205–229", in *Mnemosyne*, vol. 6 no. 3, 1953.
Rheby, "The Daughters of Troy", in *Greece and Rome* (second series), vol. 2 no.1, 1955.
P. Mason, "Kassandra", in *Journal of Hellenic Studies*, 79, 1959.
J. Fontenrose, "Poseidon in the *Troades*", in *Agon*, 1, 1967.
J. Wilson, "An Interpretation in the Prologue of Euripides' *Troades*", in *Greek, Roman and Byzantine Studies*, vol. 8 no.3, 1967.
J. Wilson, "The Etymology in Euripides' *Troades*", in *American Journal of Philology*, 89, 1968.
K. Gilmartin, "Talthybius in the *Trojan Women*", in *American Journal of Philology*, 91, 1970.
C.A.E. Luschnig, "Euripides' *Trojan Women*: All is Vanity", in *Classical Weekly*, 65, September 1971.

A. Poole, "Total Disaster: Euripides' *The Trojan Women*", in *Arion* (new series), 3, 1976.

*   *   *

The play depicts events immediately following the fall of Troy to the Greeks, concluding the bitter war which has lasted ten years. Following a prologue, presented by the gods Poseidon and Athena, the play continues with Hecuba, Queen of Troy, alone on stage lamenting the catastrophe that has befallen the Trojans. She is joined by the chorus of Trojan women, all waiting to learn what the victorious Greeks have determined to do with them. A Greek herald, Talthybius, enters to announce that Hecuba's daughter, the prophetess Cassandra, is to be King Agamemnon's concubine; Andromache, the wife of Hercuba's dead son Hector, has been given to Achilles's son, Neoptolemus; and Hecuba herself will be slave to the deceitful Odysseus. After a scene in which Cassandra frantically forecasts the future travails of Odysseus, Andromache enters upon a wagon loaded with plunder, clutching her little son, Astyanax. The herald returns to announce with shame that the boy is to be thrown to his death from Troy's walls. Andromache frantically resists, but the boy is taken from her arms, and she herself is then led away. Hecuba confronts Menelaus, King of Sparta, encouraging him to take immediate revenge upon Helen, who caused the war. Helen forcefully defends her conduct to her husband, who in the end decides to delay the punishment until after he returns home. The herald returns once more, bearing Astyanax's broken body on Hector's shield. Andromache has asked Hecuba to bury her grandchild. As Hecuba and the Chorus mourn, the herald gives orders for Troy to be burned. The women are led away into slavery.

The *Trojan Women* is one of the most powerful anti-war dramas ever written, and despite its overwhelmingly desolate vision of unrelieved human suffering, highly effective theatre. For both of these reasons, it is the most frequently performed of Euripides' works. The playwright's consummate stagecraft redeems what would otherwise be merely depressing and monotonous, to create an intensely moving and involving drama. There is little detailed characterisation. Very little happens. No real conflict arises, since the most painful reality of the women's situation that Euripides depicts is their powerlessness to effect what, passively, they have to endure. All the usual theatrical devices of suspense, reversal, and surprise are almost entirely absent. The plot itself is little more than a series of episodes, without complication or subtlety. These however, as one horror succeeds another, stretch and refine our emotions, and at the same time communicate such powerful insights into human behaviour that the result is a masterpiece of theatrical art.

Hecuba begins the play, literally prostrate, and in the course of it, one thing after another is taken from her, loss following loss; grief piled upon grief. The audience witness this process physically enacted before them, most graphically when Astyanax is pulled from his mother's arms to reappear at the end of the play—a pitiful, battered corpse, lying on his dead father's shield. At the play's conclusion *nothing* at all remains, as the women depart and Troy itself collapses into oblivion.

The utter absurdity and futility of all this suffering is unwittingly expressed by Menelaus when he reveals his intention to kill Helen, for which noble act and privilege the war was fought. And yet, even here Euripides introduces his characteristic ambiguity and scepticism. Helen in one sense, powerfully asserted by Hecuba, is indeed the cause of all this woe. And yet, in another—as Helen herself argues in a speech of alternating irony, sophistry, and keen intelligence—she too, together with everyone else (indeed, all of suffering humanity) has been a victim, subject to powerful and mysterious forces: "the gods are to blame, not I".

In the course of this bleak play, something redemptive takes place, and the appearance and defense of Helen helps to highlight it. As the women suffer one degradation after another, their moral stature steadily grows. The victorious Greeks by contrast are incrementally revealed to be ever more contemptible, because in their arrogance they fail to recognise the human condition—the vulnerability and suffering—that they share with the Trojans. But the audience, by contrast, have been made keenly aware of this, and it colours their perception of everything that happens or is said in the play. In the prologue, Athena, who had supported the Greeks, announces that she is now withdrawing her favour, offended that the Greeks have violated her temple. Moreover, with the aid of the sea-god, Poseidon, she will have her revenge: the Greeks will endure a terrible home-coming. The victorious Greeks, having triumphed over Troy, will now themselves experience dreadful suffering. This knowledge abides with the audience throughout the play, and it serves to lend the work a universal meaning in its arousal of pity and compassion for pain uselessly endured and anger at the spectacle of men's ignorance and cruelty; nowhere so dismally evident as in the ultimate folly of war.

—Richard C. Beacham

TRUE WEST
by Sam Shepard

First Publication: London, 1971.
First Production: Magic Theatre, San Francisco, 10 July 1980.

Criticism
(For general works on the author, see *Playwrights* volume)

Articles:
John Dark (ed), "The *True West* Interviews", in *West Coast Plays*, 9, 1981.

Tucker Orbison, "Mythic Levels in Shepard's *True West*", in *Modern Drama*, 27, 1984.

James D. Riemer, "Integrating the Psyche of the American Male: Conflicting Ideals of Manhood in Sam Shepard's *True West*", in *University of Dayton Review*, vol. 18 no.2, 1986–87.

Jeffrey D. Mason, "Farcical Laughter in *True West*", in *Theatre Annual*, 42, 1987.

Michael Tager, "Sam Shepard's Pastoral Dilemmas", in *Studies in the Humanities*, 14, 1987.

Molly Smith, "Beckettian Symbolic Structure in Sam Shepard's *True West*: A Jungian Reading", in *Journal of Evolutionary Psychology*, 10, 1989.

Richard Wattenberg, "'The Frontier Myth' on Stage: From the Nineteenth Century to Sam Shepard's *True West*", in *Western American Literature*, 24, 1989.

*   *   *

Austin, a college-educated screenwriter, is working in his mother's Los Angeles home while she is in Alaska on vacation; but he is distracted by his older brother Lee, a petty thief and drifter, who has arrived after three months of living in the desert. Austin has a family up north, but is in town for conferences with Saul Kimmer, a Hollywood producer, about his script. Lee "crashes" a meeting, pitches Saul a story of his own, and gets him interested over a golf game. When Austin refuses to script Lee's "authentic" Western story, Saul drops Austin's project altogether. This steps up conflict between the brothers and hastens an "interchange" of identities: Austin goes on a drunken toaster-stealing spree and Lee attempts to type up a script on his own. Eventually Austin agrees to help him in exchange for Lee taking him to live in the desert. The mother returns from Alaska to find her home in a shambles and leaves for a motel. The truce between the brothers then collapses; Austin half-strangles Lee with a telephone cord, but Lee tricks him and breaks free. There is a brief deadlocked tableau; the stage direction is: "the figures of the brothers appear to be caught in a vast, desert-like landscape, they are very still but watchful for the next move. . .".

True West marked a change in style in Sam Shepard's writing for the theatre. Whereas the earlier plays employed verbal "arias", surreal inscapes of the characters' minds which fractured the "outer" action, *True West* fuses striking images with a greater representationalism. The creative process was rigorous, especially with selectivity of language. Shepard told Bernard Weiner "I constantly peeled back the language to where I wanted it", and that he didn't want "the tangents and garrulousness" associated with the earlier plays. He also implied that this selectivity enabled actors to do more with the subtext: "It seems tighter in the script, which gives the actors more room" (*San Francisco Chronicle*, 12 April, 1981).

The changes in Shepard's style and the careful design of the play, not to mention the place of *True West* in the Shepard

True West: Cherry Lane Theatre, New York, 1982

canon, were obscured at first by the furore over the first New York production: the director (Robert Woodruff) resigned and Shepard disowned the production. Two years later the play was vindicated in New York by a long-running revival from Chicago's Steppenwolf Theatre Company, which emphasised the comic potential of the play. This production was notable for John Malkovitch's performance as Lee, which Stanley Crouch hailed as having the "emotional syncopation that pleasurably shocks in the way a great jazzman does".

Shepard himself described his thematic intention in the play, and the point of the ambiguous resolution, in an interview with Robert Coe: "I wanted to write a play about double nature, one that wouldn't be symbolic or metaphorical or any of that stuff. I just wanted to give a taste of what it feels like to be two-sided. It's a real thing, double nature. I think we're split in a much more devastating way than psychology can ever reveal. . .It's something we've got to live with" (*New York Times Magazine*, 23 November, 1980). William Kleb, in a searching essay-review ("Worse Than Being Homeless", in Bonnie Marranca's *American Dreams*) related this to the larger arena of the schizoid condition of modern man, as posited in R. D. Laing's *The Divided Self*—people are forever alienated from themselves and others and trapped in a sense of impermanence. A major achievement of the play, however, is that the characterization of the brothers is complex, not transparently schematic. Austin's remarks about his writing a "project" and a "simple love story", for instance, are surely not meant to be taken as literal evidence of his shallowness—as some commentators have interpreted them—but as a deprecatory means of negotiating with Lee, to try to share some ground with him.

Kleb mentions two other major Shepard themes revisited in the play. First there is the exploration of the significance of the ethos of the West. The "true" West of history is inaccessible behind romantic myths similar to Lee's concocted story: while the "true" West of the present is found to be elusive and evanescent in a plastic, suburban California. Austin describes his own alienation from the very neighborhood he grew up in, in which he thinks he recognises streets he once knew, only to find himself mistaken: "streets I can't tell if I lived on or saw in a postcard. Fields that don't even exist anymore".

The other major theme is that of the compromise and destruction of art through commerce, a theme that Shepard has dealt with elsewhere, notably in *Angel City*, and which is here epitomised in the sleazy, prevaricating Saul Kimmer. But Shepard also deals with the reluctance of people working at an art to even declare themselves as artists. *True West* is meta-theatrical in that it concerns the process and the difficulty of artistic creation, and the attendant bug-bear of commercial "communicability"; and it ends with the art-work aborted.

—Dennis Carroll

TURANDOT
by Carlo Gozzi

First Publication: In *Carlo Gozzi: Opere*, Venice, 1772.
First Production: Teatro San Samuele, Venice (Company of Antonio Sacchi), 22 January 1762.

Editions
Turandot, in *Carlo Gozzi: Fiabe teatrali*, edited by P. Bosisio, Rome, 1984.

Translations
Turandot, Princess of China, translated by Jethro Bithel from the German version by Karl Vollmoeller, London and New York, 1913.
Turandot, translated by Jonathan Levey, in *The Genius of the Italian Theatre*, edited by Eric Bentley, New York, 1964.
Turandot, in *Carlo Gozzi: "The Love of Three Oranges", "Turandot", and "The Snake Lady"*, edited by John Louis Di Gaetani, New York and London, 1988.
Turandot, in *Carlo Gozzi: Five Tales for the Theatre*, edited by Ted Amery and Albert Bermel, translated by Albert Bermel, Chicago, 1989.

Criticism
(For general works on the author, see *Playwrights* volume)

Articles:
Kurt Ringger, "Carlo Gozzi's *Fiabe teatrali*: Wirklichkeit und romantischer Mythos", in *Germanisch-Romanische Monatsschrift* (new series), 18, 1968.
David Nicholson, "Gozzi's *Turandot*: A Tragicomic Fairy Tale", in *Theatre Journal*, 31, 1979.
Jacques Joly, "La *Turandot* de Carlo Gozzi: Récit, fantasmes, allégorie", in *Les voies de la création théâtrale*, 8, edited by Elie Konigson, Paris, 1980.

*   *   *

Turandot tells the fairy-tale of the dazzlingly beautiful, but maliciously intelligent, wilful, perverse, and self-regarding Princess Turandot, whose hand is sought in marriage by numerous eligible princes, but who is so hostile to men and unwilling to marry that she will only accept a husband able to answer the three riddles she puts to him. Attracted by her beauty, and the possibility of winning not only her hand in marriage, but all the lands of China as her dowry, numerous suitors try their luck, but without success. Those who lose are beheaded, and their heads set to decorate the Peking city gates as a warning to further potential suitors.

The young prince Calaf, son of the King of Tartary, who has been banished from his lands by the evil Sultan of Carizmano, after many adventures, has arrived at Peking intending to offer the Emperor his services as a soldier. Unfortunately, despite the earnest warnings of those who wish him well, by accident he catches sight of a picture of Turandot, and like many luckless princes before him, bewitched by her extraordinary beauty, presents himself instead as a suitor. When he appears before her, Turandot is strangely attracted to him, but insists he take the trial, and the more successful he is in solving the riddles she puts to him, the more her fury rises. When he succeeds in solving all three riddles, far from being delighted that an appropriate suitor has now met her challenge, Turandot feels worsted by the defeat and refuses to abide by the rules she herself has laid down. All the courtiers are taken aback at her duplicity and arrogance, and none more so than her father, whose insistence that she keep her word underscores the stubborn wilfulness of her personality.

Calaf, however, observes her wish and provides her with a further opportunity to avoid marriage by setting her the riddle of discovering his name and parentage. Unfortunately, a certain Adelma, profoundly in love with him, knows both, and reveals the secrets to Turandot, who in triumph declares herself the victor and Calaf the vanquished. Overwhelmed at the thought of losing her, Calaf is about to commit suicide when Turandot intervenes, stays his dagger, and declares her love for him. All ends happily. Turandot renounces her hatred of men and marries Calaf; Calaf's long-suffering father is restored to his throne; and even Adelma, treacherous only because she is so desperately in love with Calaf, is restored to her kingdom and provided with a husband.

One of two *fiabe* Gozzi wrote for the 1762 Carnival, the other being *Il Re Cervo* (*The King Stag*), *Turandot* is a romantic story ultimately of oriental derivation, but taken by Gozzi from a French version of *The Thousand and One Nights*. By any measure it is a superb tale, rich in implication, and Gozzi tells it with considerable theatrical flair, his own embellishments adding suspense and details of fanciful characterisation to the material he took from the *novella*—for he treated the tale very freely, and it is shot through with incidents and "business" wholly of his own devising, or matter he drew from the popular traditions of the Italian improvised stage comedy.

Unlike those *fiabe* more characteristic of Gozzi's work, like *La donna serpente* (*The Serpent Woman*, 1762), or *L'augellino bel verde* (*The Green Monster*, 1765), the plot of *Turandot* does not have recourse to spells, incantations, and magic potions, nor does it make use of supernatural beings or wonderful transformations. Indeed, for all its exotic setting and trafficking in the matter of high romance, the play's main focus is on character psychology explored in the context of an exceptional place and circumstance: its success in performance depends very much on appropriate casting, for the drama turns essentially on the conflict between two protagonists, Turandot and Calaf, of charismatic romantic appeal but radically differing psychology. Calaf is uncomplicated, the epitome of the young and handsome, generous and considerate, warrior hero. His very stereotypicality sets him sharply in opposition to Turandot, a complex and enigmatic figure who is the embodiment of bewitching beauty and treacherous evil and a wholly desirable but wickedly destructive *femme fatale*, the mystery of whose contrary personality is the more powerful for being ultimately inexplicable. Some have been tempted to read into Turandot's hostility to men and marriage a quasi-feminist gesture for independence of male domination and patriarchal pressure; but while this is clearly a motive, it does not wholly, or indeed substantially, account for either her actions or the complexity of the relations between the characters.

Simple though the play is in its story-line, it is powerfully affecting in its blending of romance, comedy, and stage spectacle. Gozzi's attempt to revive the traditional masks and improvised comic playing of the actors of the *commedia dell'arte*—a reactionary gesture by a writer artistically conservative and socially aristocratic against the bourgeois values in the comedy of Carlo Goldoni—enjoyed a great vogue in the Venetian theatre of the 1760's, and one can appreciate from this play how effective was his blend of the traditional and the novel. Certainly it was a master-stroke of comic fantasy to have translated the familiar masked stage figures to the court of the Emperor of China. They contribute little to the romantic tale itself, notwithstanding that Pantalone and Tartaglia are court ministers involved in the marriage trials, Brighella a senior court servant, and Truffaldino, an outrageously camp chief eunuch of the seraglio. But even more than setting and costumes, the antics of these comic stage types help to establish the extravagantly fantastic mood of the whole. Like most of Gozzi's *fiabe*, *Turandot* lends itself to stage orchestration with its exotic settings in the divan and the seraglio of the Peking court, its curious stage figures, like the troupe of royal eunuchs, and its touches of gruesome "business", like that of the blood-stained executioner staking the Prince of Samarkand's head on a pike at the city gate. Rich too in pageantic processions and opportunities for the improvised comedy of professional clowns, it is a piece for actors to bring alive on stage and must have well merited its great success.

Turandot continued to exercise great appeal long after the particular occasion of the play's success had passed, notably for writers of the Romantic movement and their successors: it was adapted by a number of dramatists, including Schiller, and was set to music by several composers, notably Puccini. The revival of interest in the *commedia dell'arte* at the end of the 19th century not only accounts (in part) for Puccini taking up the story, but also for some memorable revivals of the play itself in the early years of the 20th century—notably a celebrated Russian theatre production by Vakhtangov mounted at the Studio Theatre of the Moscow Art Theatre in 1922.

—Kenneth Richards

TURCARET
by Alain-René Lesage

First Publication: Paris, 1709; revised version, in *Recueil des pièces mises au théâtre français par M. Le Sage*, Paris, 1739.
First Production: Comédie-Française, Paris, 14 February 1709.

Editions

Turcaret, edited by A, Hamilton Thompson, Cambridge, 1918.
Turcaret, edited by Edgar Ewing Brandon and Maurice Baudin, New York and Oxford, 1927.
Turcaret, in *Lesage: Théâtre*, edited by M. Bardon, Paris, 1948.
Turcaret, edited by T.E. Lawrenson, London, 1969.
Turcaret, edited by B. Blanc, Paris, 1970.
Turcaret, edited by E. Lavielle, Paris, 1970.
Turcaret, in *Théâtre du XVIIIe. siècle, 1*, edited by J. Truchet, Paris, 1971.

Translations

Turcaret; or, The Financier, in *French Comedies of the Eighteenth Century*, translated by Richard Aldington, London, 1923.
Turcaret, translated and adapted by John Norman, Bath, 1989.

Criticism

(For general works on the author, see *Playwrights* volume)

Books:
George Evans, *"Crispin rival de son maître" and "Turcaret"*, London, 1987.

Articles:
François-Xavier Cuche, "La formule dramatique de *Turcaret* ou le rythme et le jeu", in *Travaux de linguistique et de littérature*, vol. 10 no.2, 1972.
J. Dunkley, *"Turcaret* and the Techniques of Satire", in *British Journal for Eighteenth-Century Studies*, 2, 1979.
Richard Parish, " 'Marie chassée': A Reconsideration of the Dramatic Structure of Lesage's *Turcaret*", in *"En Marge du Classicisme": Essays on the French Theatre From the Renaissance to the Enlightenment*, edited by Alan Howe and Richard Waller, Liverpool, 1987.

Joseph G. Reish, "Lesage's Dramatization of a Social Cycle: The Ups and Downs of the Likes of Turcaret", in *French Literature Series*, 15, 1988.

*   *   *

Turcaret, perhaps the most unsparing satire of the 18th century, was a great success at its creation in 1709, but was then mysteriously withdrawn after seven performances. At its centre is Turcaret, a self-seeking *financier* (tax-farmer) whose financial astuteness is exceeded only by his vanity. He is easily duped by a fortune-hunting *baronne*, and she is herself exploited by a *chevalier*, who thus indirectly milks the *financier*. The play traces the slow but inevitable downfall of Turcaret, as his past begins to emerge and engulf him. A *marquis* tells the *baronne* that Turcaret is an unscrupulous usuror, and that, in addition, he used to be a servant before acquiring his great fortune; it turns out that the impecunious Mme. Jacob is his sister, whom he cruelly leaves in penury, and that his wife, neglected and kept well away from Paris, has returned to the capital in need of money. In the final act, sister and wife come together to embarass the *financier*, before the last blow is delivered: news that he has been duped by one of his accountants, and that he is now bankrupt. The *baronne* and the *chevalier* are themselves exploited by their servants, Frontin and Lisette, and by the end of the play these two are revealed as the great survivors, having taken advantage of the day's events to make something in excess of 40,000 francs.

This is very much a play of its time, a comedy of manners which depicts both a milieu and a man. It reflects a world in which distinctions of class become blurred in the widespread pursuit of wealth and it portrays the extremes, at once criminal and comic, to which this pursuit may lead. Tax-collectors are not unknown in comedy before this, but none is given the prominence or acute critical scrutiny given here to Turcaret. Such biting satire was particularly daring at a time when financiers were powerful social (and political) figures, and it is often suggested that this influential body was instrumental in having the comedy removed from the repertory.

Turcaret's background is evoked in considerable detail—his humble origins as a *laquais*, his marriage to the daughter of a *patissier*, his shady financial dealings. He may recall in different ways Molière's *bourgeois gentilhomme* with his vain claims to good taste, his literary pretensions, his ponderous methods of courtship, and his credulity; however, unlike M. Jourdain, who is essentially inoffensive, Turcaret is presented in a much less sympathetic light. His belief that wealth can buy whatever his (non-existent) natural charm cannot acquire inspires scorn rather than amusement in those around him, and he is openly mocked by the *baronne* and the *chevalier*. But not only is he tasteless, he is also corrupt and unpleasant. His wealth has been acquired by all kinds of trickery and his cynical exploitation of others is reflected in the ill-treatment of his sister and wife. Such is his ruthless self-interest that he inspires no sympathy in the process of his demise.

Significantly, though, the presentation of the other characters is no more favourable; they, like their victim, are seen to be possessed of a deep desire to further their own ends as they operate around him, greedy and unscrupulous. The *chevalier* is a duplicitous schemer and libertine; the *baronne* is weak, coquettish, and unprincipled; the *marquis* is a dissolute, if elegant, aristocrat; Mme. Jacob a wily go-between; and even Madame Turcaret has none of the pathetic qualities of the abandoned wife, but is as pretentious and self-seeking as everyone else. Of all such characters, the most original and disturbing is the servant, Frontin. As surely as Turcaret falls, because of the inexorable mechanism of self-destruction built

into his very success, so Frontin rises, as he takes full advantage of events. He may make us think of Beaumarchais's Figaro, insofar as he is an intellectually agile and independent servant; and yet such similarities are superficial. Unlike Figaro, Frontin does not act simply to defend his rights as an individual; he seeks to dislodge those with power and wealth in order to appropriate it for himself. As a character, he lacks the buoyant, self-conscious energy of Beaumarchais's hero; instead, Lesage gives him a cold, inscrutable efficiency which both punishes and embodies the corruption around him.

Originally written for, and performed by, the Comédie-Française, this play has many features of French classical comedy. Its simple episodic structure offers the pleasures of a traditional comedy of intrigue with its succession of comic situations and encounters; it sets out to characterise a social type in a series of incidents which reveal different aspects of his nature; and it seeks to combine physical gestures of comedy with sharp exchanges of wit. What distinguishes it, though, from so much earlier comedy is, above all, the complete absence of any sense of moral justice. It may mete out apt punishment on a corrupt *financier*, but it also witnesses the success of Frontin, whose financial astuteness and humble origins offer an ominous echo of Turcaret's own; the social and moral evil is not defeated, it is simply replaced. Lesage depicts a society in which money is power, but the comedy offers no hope of changing it; within this traditional form, the dramatist expresses a cynical vision that is unparalleled in comedy before him.

—G. Jonathan Mallinson

THE TUTOR
(Der Hofmeister; oder, Der Vorteile die Privaterziehung) by Jakob Michael Reinhold Lenz

First Publication: Leipzig, 1774.
First Production: In an adaptation by Friedrich Ludwig Schröder, Hamburg, 22 April 1778.

Editions
Der Hofmeister, with afterword by Karl S. Guthke, Stuttgart, 1963.
Der Hofmeister, in *Die Soldaten; Der Hofmeister*, Munich, c.1971.
Der Hofmeister, edited by Michael Kohlenbach, Basle, 1986.

Translations
The Tutor, in *The Tutor; The Soldiers*, translated by William E. Yuill, Chicago and London, 1972.

Criticism
(For general works on the author, see *Playwrights* volume)

Books:
M.A. Brown, "Lenz's *Hofmeister* and the Drama of Storm and Stress", in *Periods in German Literature, 2: Texts and Kontexts*, London and Chester Springs, Pennsylvania, 1970.
Ford B. Parkes, *Epische Elemente in Jakob Michael Reinhold Lenzens Drama "Der Hofmeister"*, Göppingen, 1973.
Herbert Haffner, *Lenz: "Der Hofmeister"; "Die Soldaten"; mit Brecht's "Hofmeister"—Bearbeitung und Materialen*, Munich, 1979.

The Tutor: Old Vic Theatre, London, 1988

Franz Werner, *Soziale Unfreiheit und bürgerliche Intelligenz im 18. Jahrhundert: Der organisierende Gesichtspunkt in J.M.R. Lenzens Drama "Der Hofmeister oder Vorteile der Privaterziehung"*, Frankfurt, 1981.

Friedrich Voit (ed.), *Jakob Michael Reinhold Lenz: "Der Hofmeister oder Vorteile der Privaterziehung": Erläuterungen und Dokumente*, Stuttgart, 1986.

Articles:

Edward P. Harris, "Structural Unity in J.M.R. Lenz's *Der Hofmeister:* A Revaluation", in *Seminar*, 8, 1972.

Karl Eibl, "'Realismus' als Widerlegung von Literatur: Dargestellt am Beispiel von Lenz' *Hofmeister*", in *Poetica*, 6, 1974.

G.M. Martin, "A Note on the Major Plays of J.M.R. Lenz", in *German Life and Letters*, 31, 1977.

Michael Butler, "Character and Paradox in Lenz's *Der Hofmeister*", in *German Life and Letters*, 32, 1979.

Andreas Huyssen, "Gesellschaftsgeschichte und literarische Form: J.M.R. Lenz's Komödie *Der Hofmeister*", in *Monatshefte*, 71, 1979.

Claus O. Lappe, "Wer hat Gustchens Kind gezugt? Zeitstruktur und Rollenspiel in Lenz' *Hofmeister*", in *Deutsche Vierteljahrsschrift für Literaturwissenschaft und Geistesgeschichte*, 54, 1980.

Helga Stipa Madland, "Gesture as Evidence of Language Skepticism in Lenz's *Der Hofmeister* and *Die Soldaten*", in *German Quarterly*, vol. 57 no. 4, 1984.

Monika Wiessmeyer, "Gesellschaftskritik in der Tragikomödie: *Der Hofmeister* (1774) und *Die Soldaten* (1776) von J.M.R. Lenz", in *New German Review*, 2, 1986.

Klaus Bohnen, "Irrtum als dramatische Sprachfigur: Sozialzerfall und Erziehungsdebatte in J.M.R. Lenz' *Hofmeister*", in *Orbis Litterarum*, vol. 42 nos. 3–4, 1987.

Helga Stipa Madland, "A Question of Norms: The Stage reception of Lenz's *Hofmeister*", in *Seminar*, vol. 23 no. 2, 1987.

Claudia Albert, "Verziehungen, Heiraten, Lotterien: Der Schluss der Lenzeschen *Hofmeister*", in *Wirkendes Wort*, vol. 39 no. 1, 1989.

*   *   *

Subtitled "The advantages of private education", Lenz's play is focused on Läuffer, a young graduate who is taken on as a private tutor to the children of Major von Berg in Insterburg, a small place in what was then East Prussia. When her cousin, Fritz, goes up to university, an attachment begins to develop between Gustchen (Major von Berg's daughter, Auguste) and her tutor. Scandal threatens. In Act III they both run away; Läuffer finds shelter with an eccentric village schoolmaster, Gustchen in old Martha's woodland cottage, where her child is born. She attempts to kill herself by drowning, but is saved by her adoring father. When Läuffer recognises the child as his, he castrates himself. Meanwhile Fritz von Berg has become a student at Leipzig University, and is initiated into undergraduate life. The action ends happily when Läuffer marries Lise, a village girl, who prefers educated men and has no wish to have children. Gustchen and her cousin Fritz von Berg renew their attachment.

Lenz's play is a work rich in paradoxes. Written in 1772, and published at Goethe's instigation, it created a sensation with the reading public and was favourably received by most German writers and critics. Contemporaries hailed it as a remarkably authentic depiction of the world as they knew it and praised the accuracy of its author's observations. Lenz himself, writing in 1775, expressed his view that "comedy is a picture of human society, and when society turns serious, the picture cannot be a funny one". He also made the point that in comedy characters are there for the sake of the plot, whereas in tragedy the plot is generated by the tragic protagonist. In this sense *The Tutor* is indeed a comedy, albeit a drastic one; its main purpose is to highlight (and not just expose to ridicule) the plight of private tutors in later 18th-century society: impecunious young men, aiming for careers in the Church, were expected to demonstrate due respect and humility towards their employers; after years of exploitation and social and intellectual isolation, their reward might be a living in their employer's gift. Based partly on personal experience, the play treated a subject which was of great concern to the new generation of young intellectuals whose leaders formed the *Sturm und Drang* movement. An often indignant critical tone was clearly audible in their works, and Lenz's play is no exception. It also exemplifies the "loose" construction favoured by the *Sturm und Drang* writers in contrast to the stylized formality associated with regular 18th-century drama.

The play's authentic portrayal of a vanished age has been much admired; this is evident not least in its language, which runs the whole gamut of contemporary speech registers. Equally striking is the satirical sharpness of its characterisation and its intellectually vibrant dialogue. The plot brings out the further implications of the play's subject: Läuffer's self-castration literally symbolizes the impotence of a sizeable section of educated German society, while his ultimate preference for Lise, the village beauty, suggests that the intelligentsia should ally itself with the common people rather than with the aristocracy. Like the plays of Beaumarchais, *The Tutor* is a vital document of the *ancien régime* in Europe. Brecht, who (like Georg Büchner) admired the play enormously, described Läuffer as Germany's answer to Figaro. But the central theme—namely the undervaluation of tutors and teachers by a society whose values they do not share and which regards them as socially inferior—has not lost relevance, as Brecht realised when he adapted the play for production in 1950.

—Peter Skrine

TWELFTH NIGHT; or, What You Will
by William Shakespeare

First Publication: In First Folio, London, 1623.
First Production: London, c. 1601–02.

Editions

Twelfth Night, edited by H.H. Furness, Philadelphia, 1901 (New Variorum Shakespeare).

Twelfth Night, edited by Arthur Quiller-Couch and John Dover Wilson, Cambridge, 1930; revised edition, 1949 (The New Shakespeare).

Twelfth Night, edited by C.T. Prouty, Baltimore, Maryland, 1958 (Pelican Shakespeare).

Twelfth Night, edited by Baker Herschel, New York, 1965; revised edition [with updated bibliography], 1985 (Signet Classic Shakespeare).

Twelfth Night, edited by M.M. Mahood, Harmondsworth, 1968 (New Penguin Shakespeare).

Twelfth Night, edited by J.M. Lothian and T.W. Craik, London, 1975 (Arden Shakespeare).

Twelfth Night, edited by Elizabeth Donno, Cambridge, 1985 (New Cambridge Shakespeare).

Bibliography

William C. McAvoy, *"Twelfth Night, or What You Will": A Bibliography to Supplement the New Variorum Edition of 1901*, New York, 1984.

Criticism

(For general works on the author, see *Playwrights* volume)

Books:

J.W. Draper, *The "Twelfth Night" of Shakespeare's Audience*, New York, 1950.

Leslie Hotson, *The First Night of "Twelfth Night"*, New York, 1954.

Clifford Leech, *"Twelfth Night" and Shakespearian Comedy*, Toronto, 1965.

Walter N. King (ed.), *Twentieth Century Interpretations of "Twelfth Night"*, Englewood Cliffs, New Jersey, 1968.

D.J. Palmer (ed.), *"Twelfth Night": A Casebook*, London, 1972.

J.M. Gregson, *Shakespeare: "Twelfth Night"*, London, 1980.

Laurie Lanzen Harris and Mark W. Scott (eds.), *"Twelfth Night"*, in *Shakespearian Criticism, 1*, Detroit, Illinois, 1984 [anthology of criticism].

Roy Fuller, *"Twelfth Night": A Personal View*, Edinburgh, 1985 [limited edition].

Lois Potter, *Twelfth Night*, London, 1985 (Text and Performance Series).

Stanley Wells (ed.), *"Twelfth Night": Critical Essays*, New York and London, 1986 (Shakespeare Criticism Series).

Harold Bloom (ed.), *William Shakespeare's "Twelfth Night"*, New York, New Haven (Connecticut), and Philadelphia, 1987 (Modern Critical Interpretations).

Articles:

For information on the many articles about *Twelfth Night*, see McAvoy's bibliography, the bibliographies listed in the *Playwrights* volume, and the annual Shakespeare Bibliography in *Shakespeare Quarterly*, published by the Folger Shakespeare Library, Washington D.C. (1950–).

*　*　*

Like all of Shakespeare's romantic comedies, the chief theme of *Twelfth Night* concerns love in some of its limitless varieties. And like all of Shakespeare's plays, *Twelfth Night* uses an amalgam of differing dramatic elements.

The story is complicated. Viola, a highborn young lady, has been shipwrecked on the coastline of Illyria. Fearful for her safety alone in a strange land and believing her twin brother, Sebastian, dead from the same shipwreck, Viola takes on the disguise of a young man called Cesario. While she decides her next move, as Cesario she goes to Duke Orsino's court in

Twelfth Night: Stratford-Upon-Avon, 1983 (Royal Shakespeare Company)

search of temporary employment. Meanwhile Orsino continues his fruitless attempts to woo the noblewoman Olivia. Cesario is made welcome in the court and is immediately sent to win over Olivia on behalf of Orsino. Viola as Cesario gets Olivia's attention, but not in the manner expected: Olivia begins to fall in love with her. Much of the rest of the main plot centres on Olivia's attempts to woo Cesario, while Cesario (Viola) fends off the noblewoman and tries to deflect the latter's love toward Orsino. Yet, Viola has fallen in love with the duke and so has misgivings about serving him as go-between with Olivia.

Sebastian also survived the ship tragedy and lands in Illyria accompanied by a sea-captain friend, Antonio. Olivia accidentally encounters Sebastian, and thinks it is Cesario because the twins so resemble each other. Sebastian and Olivia get along so well that her proposal of marriage is accepted by the puzzled but willing newcomer in town. Eventually, in a grand resolution scene, the mistaken identities are exposed, allowing Olivia to marry Sebastian, and Orsino to marry Viola (now undisguised).

A second plot concerns Olivia's arrogant steward Malvolio (his name is a give-away—"ill will") who is tricked by others in her household into believing Olivia secretly loves him. Malvolio's excessive pride allows him to delude himself long enough for the others (Olivia's uncle Sir Toby Belch, her maid Maria, and a pesky suitor, Sir Andrew Aguecheek) to derive many laughs from his bizarre behavior. In a correlated resolution, Malvolio is disabused of his delusions, and Sir Toby marries Maria for the cleverness of her schemes against Malvolio.

Shakespeare's sources for *Twelfth Night* appear to be several but most significantly Barnabe Riche's *Farewell to Militarie Profession* (1581) and the anonymous Italian play *Gl'Ingannati* (*The Deceived Ones*) published in 1537. But the idea of confusion caused by misidentification of twins reaches back at least to Plautus and *The Menaechmi*, a work Shakespeare had already used as source for his *Comedy of Errors*. Whatever the sources, in *Twelfth Night* there are examples of several misidentifications: Viola purposely disguises herself as the boy Cesario; Sebastian is misidentified as Cesario by Olivia and Sir Toby; and Feste, the clown, disguises himself as the curate, Sir Topas, to trick Malvolio. In each instance, comedy ensues.

The play's secondary plot also concerns love but on another level altogether. Sir Toby Belch, though Olivia's uncle, exhibits no gentlemanly qualities but seems more a harmless parasite on her household. Maria, Olivia's lady-in-waiting or maid (she's listed simply as Olivia's "woman"), allies herself with Sir Toby and the pallid Sir Andrew to gain comic revenge against the aloof spoil-sport Malvolio. Their trap to humiliate and humble Malvolio remains one of the brightest devices in English dramatic literature. Maria forges the handwriting of Olivia to write a note addressed to Malvolio. In it, he is invited to make advances openly to Olivia since she secretly loves him. The letter urges on Malvolio with such statements as "be not afraid of greatness: some are born great, some achieve greatness and some have greatness thrust upon 'em". Malvolio is not surprised that she should favour him and promptly dresses in an eccentric fashion (which Olivia detests) and behaves more stupidly than usual in her presence. As a result, Olivia believes her usually staid steward has gone mad, and she has him confined for mental treatment.

Shakespeare uses other comic devices in *Twelfth Night* which had great popularity with Elizabethan audiences at the time. Ben Jonson had popularised a form of comedy which emphasized the "humours" that dominated in some persons—that is, a dominant trait or idiosyncracy in one's personality. Shakespeare, like Jonson, knew how dramatically to feature a character's odd conduct to elicit laughter. Sir Toby for example enjoys his drink and so is ready for tricks and sports on a moment's notice. His companion is Sir Andrew Aguecheek whose name—like Belch's—gives away his "humour". Aguecheek is as tall, sallow, and gaunt as Belch is pudgy, round, and merry. Together, they constitute the original "odd couple". Malvolio is serenely enamoured of himself. Olivia accuses him of excessive pride, and Maria deems him a Puritan, a pejorative term in that period. Shakespeare instructs that Malvolio be dressed in black or dark sombre colours and that he play the kill-joy at every opportunity.

Nor in fact does Shakespeare limit his mocking of eccentric conduct to non-nobility. Orsino, ruler of Illyria, opens the play with the lines of a love-sick puppy: "If music be the food of love, play on;/Give me excess of it, that, surfeiting,/The appetite may sicken, and so die". Olivia, too, shows herself a flirt when Viola as Cesario comes to court for Orsino; and her claim to be in mourning for seven years over her father's and brother's deaths is a mere dodge to fend off Orsino's courtship. Her instantaneous love for Cesario offers another dimension of gentle laughter. Adding yet more lightness and gaiety are the clowns' songs which Shakespeare sprinkles throughout *Twelfth Night*.

Shakespeare wraps up *Twelfth Night* in traditional fashion. Multiple marriages are announced for Olivia and Sebastian, Viola and Orsino, and Maria and Sir Toby. The subtitle for *Twelfth Night*—"What You Will"—precisely captures the tone of this playful, merry comedy.

—C.J. Gianakaris

THE TWINS.   See **THE BROTHERS MENAECHMUS.**

THE TWO GENTLEMEN OF VERONA
by William Shakespeare

First Publication: In First Folio, London, 1623.
First Production: London, c. 1592–98

Editions
The Two Gentlemen of Verona, edited by Berners A.W. Jackson, Baltimore, Maryland, 1964 (Pelican Shakespeare).
The Two Gentlemen of Verona, edited by Bertrand Evans, New York, 1964 (Signet Classic Shakespeare).
The Two Gentlemen of Verona, edited by Norman Sanders, Harmondsworth, 1968 (New Penguin Shakespeare).
The Two Gentlemen of Verona, edited by Clifford Leech, London, 1969 (Arden Shakespeare).
The Two Gentlemen of Verona, edited by J. Schleuter, Cambridge, 1990 (New Cambridge Shakespeare).

Bibliography
D'Orsay W. Pearson, *"The Two Gentlemen of Verona": An Annotated Bibliography*, New York and London, 1988 (Garland Shakespeare Bibliographies).

Criticism
(For general works on the author, see *Playwrights* volume)

Books:
Mark W. Scott and Sandra L. Williamson (eds.), "*The Two Gentlemen of Verona*", in *Shakespearian Criticism, 6*, Detroit, Illinois, 1987 [anthology of criticism].

Articles:
For information on articles about *The Two Gentlemen of Verona*, see Pearson's bibliography, the bibliographies listed in the *Playwrights* volume, and the annual Shakespeare Bibliography in *Shakespeare Quarterly*, published by the Folger Shakespeare Library, Washington D.C. (1950–).

* * *

The Two Gentlemen of Verona is almost certainly Shakespeare's earliest comedy, possibly his first play, but it is possible only to state that it was written at some time between 1587 and 1589. Nor do we know by whom it was first performed: probably by Strange's Men, later by the Chamberlain's Men.

As in many of the comedies, the action is structured around pairs of characters. The two gentleman of the title are two friends, the magnanimous Valentine and the inconstant and treacherous Proteus. Valentine has a witty page called Speed, and Proteus a clownish servant called Launce, both "naturals" who set in perspective the vapourings of the courtly lovers. Proteus is in love with and is loved by Julia. Valentine, who at first eschews love, departs for Milan, where he promptly falls in love with Silvia, daughter to the Duke of the city. Proteus too is sent abroad, having exchanged pledges of faith with Julia. When he arrives in Milan, he too falls in love with Silvia, and, in an attempt to obtain her favour, betrays both Julia and his friend—the latter by revealing to the Duke Valentine's plan to elope with Silvia. The Duke banishes Valentine who is adopted by a band of outlaws as their captain. Julia disguises herself as a boy, comes to Milan, and is engaged as his page. Silvia leaves Milan in order to avoid marriage with Thurio, who is favoured by her father, but she is captured by robbers and rescued by Proteus. He is on the brink of raping her when Valentine appears. Proteus is so stricken with shame and guilt that Valentine gives him Silvia—his greatest sacrifice. Julia, the disguised page, swoons then reveals herself. Proteus recognizes both her and her virtue and turns back to his former love.

The play is built out of the games and commonplaces of courtly romance: heroes who venture to a "comic world" abroad, and a heroine who, with the help of Sir Eglamour her champion, redeems her fortunes by taking on a man's role. Much of the play is familiar to students of comedy: droll servants, rings, rope-ladders, letters, badinage concerning folly and wit, and fine discourses concerning love and the deceptiveness of appearances that are similar to passages in the plays of John Lyly. The play is also indebted to classical comedy with its story of a heroine rescued from her father's authority, a caricatured unsuitable lover, Sir Thurio, and with its plot that depends upon the "errors" caused by fortune or disguise. The sagacious Launce is given a celebrated set-piece where he rebukes his dog, Crab, for not joining in the miseries caused in his family by his departure for "the Imperial's court". In the theatre the dog, who cannot "act", sets off the "natural" whose performance depends upon a cluster of the comedian's skills. The text sometimes rejoices in its spasms of lyricism and preciosity:

For Orpheus' lute was strung with poet's sinews
Whose golden touch could soften steel and stones,
Make tigers tame, and huge leviathans
Forsake unsounded deeps to dance on sands.

However, in other parts of the play, Shakespeare is perhaps beginning to question the distortions imposed upon the romantic experience of men—and even more on that of women—by the language of Petrarchan courtship.

There are many inconsistencies in the plot, but these are far more apparent in the study than on the stage. However, the ending, seemingly contrived and reductively schematic—and disappointing from the point of view of its language—points to the serious concerns that underlie this divertissement. What is the nature of "the woman's part" in a world of masculine perjury? Can love withstand fortune? How might the competing claims of love and friendship be accommodated? The play is in fact related to a tradition of "friendship literature" that includes its main source, a French translation (1578) from the Portuguese of J. de Montemayor's prose pastoral romance *Diana*, Chaucer's "Knight's Tale", and one of Shakespeare's last plays, written in collaboration with Fletcher, *The Two Noble Kinsmen*. The obvious artifice of the play, which disturbed earlier critics, has, more recently, been related to a tradition of metadrama, and Proteus has been read as a figure of the "theatrical self". It is also possible to read the play as a satire on courtly life—an index of this is the portrait of the knight-errant, Sir Eglamour—a reading which tends to turn Valentine into a fool.

There are no performances known before 1762 when an adaptation by Benjamin Victor was performed under the management of David Garrick. An operatic version by Frederick Reynolds, which featured a pageant of the four seasons and added various mythological characters as well as Cleopatra in her barge, was performed at Convent Garden in 1821, and later versions have also added to the musical content of the play. There were notable revivals by Denis Carey at the Old Vic in 1952 and by Robin Philips at Stratford in 1970 who offered a modern adaptation: a set that centred on a swimming pool, the favoured place of resort of a group of gilded youth.

—Michael Hattaway

THE TWO NOBLE KINSMEN
by William Shakespeare and John Fletcher

First Publication: London, 1634.
First Production: London, c.1613.

Editions
The Two Noble Kinsmen, edited by H. Littledale, London, 1874–75.
The Two Noble Kinsmen, edited by Clifford Leech, New York, 1966 (Signet Classic Shakespeare).
The Two Noble Kinsmen, edited by G.R. Proudfoot, Lincoln (Nebraska) and London, 1970 (Regents Renaissance Drama Series).
The Two Noble Kinsmen, edited by N.W. Bawcutt, Harmondsworth, 1977 (New Penguin Shakespeare).
The Two Noble Kinsmen, edited by E.M. Waith, Oxford, 1989 (Oxford Shakespeare).

Criticism

(For general works on the author, see *Playwrights* volume)

Books:

Paul Bertram, *Shakespeare and "The Two Noble Kinsmen"*, New Brunswick, New Jersey, 1965.

Mark W. Scott and Sandra L. Williamson (eds.), *"The Two Noble Kinsmen"*, in *Shakespearian Criticism, 9*, Detroit, Illinois, 1989 [anthology of criticism].

Articles:

For information on articles about *The Two Noble Kinsmen*, see the bibliographies listed in the *Playwrights* volume, and the annual Shakespeare Bibliography in *Shakespeare Quarterly*, published by the Folger Shakespeare Library, Washington D.C. (1950–).

*   *   *

The question of the possible Shakespearean authorship of *The Two Noble Kinsmen* has largely overshadowed the questions posed by the play itself. The most interesting of these is implicit in the title. What, precisely, are we to understand by the term "nobility"? Palamon and Arcite, prisoners of Duke Theseus, fall in love with the same girl, Emilia. Their apparently impossible situation changes: Arcite is set free and Palamon escapes with the help of his gaoler's daughter; thus they are free to act upon their desires. As neither can renounce Emilia, their only option, Theseus decrees, is single combat, the loser to be beheaded. Arcite wins, but falls from his horse, and with his dying breath gives Emilia to Palamon. Meanwhile the gaoler's daughter has run mad for Palamon's love but accepts another lover disguised as him.

For a play in which at least three characters are passionately in love (not to mention Theseus and Hippolyta, who, as in *A Midsummer Night's Dream*, are celebrating their wedding day) there is an amazing paucity of love scenes. Love here, however, is less a passion to be explored dramatically than a trigger for an analysis of "nobility". There is, however, considerable ambiguity as to whether nobility is a virtue to be cultivated or a class attribute to be cherished. Indeed we first meet Palamon and Arcite debating this point: they are aware that they inhabit a decadent world which Arcite feels can only corrupt them; when, however, war is declared on their tyrant ruler, Creon, they agree that "to be neutral to him were dishonour, / Rebellious to oppose", and fight on his side until captured by a Theseus profoundly admiring of their chivalry.

The same chivalry is found in their preparations for single combat, arming each other with care lest a strap slip or a corslet pinch. "I would have nothing hurt thee but my sword", explains Palamon, "a bruise would be dishonour". This courtesy accords oddly with the moral nub of the dispute as seen by Palamon—"I saw her first", he claims, and Arcite with his dying breath repentantly acknowledges that this does, in fact, validate Palamon's claim to Emilia.

Does the "nobility" of the kinsmen reside more in their dislike of Creon's corruption; in their willingness to fight for his regime; in loving; or in their inability to resolve love's dilemmas by any other way than in an elaborately orchestrated brawl? Only if we assume the play is an exercise in nostalgia for some chivalric fantasy world is it possible to see "nobility" as a single attribute comprising both social status and fidelity to *noblesse oblige*. The roles of the women, however, suggest that the play is interrogating this simplistic concept. Central to the action is Emilia's refusal to take sides. This has often been interpreted as mere dithering—"What a sweet face has Arcite! . . .Palamon, thou art alone / And only beautiful. . ." But she does not merely attempt to weigh up their attractions; she struggles for other solutions, such as banishment; she prays to Diana to resolve matters; and she refuses finally, against all chivalric convention, to be present at the combat. Her response to Arcite's victory is not that of the queen of a tournament, but that of a moral human being: "Is this winning?".

Her refusal to choose between two men for whom she has political and moral rather than sexual sympathy is illuminatingly counterpointed by the story of the gaoler's daughter. She—unlike both Emilia and her father—can distinguish effortlessly between the two prisoners. Palamon owes her his freedom; he might have acted in a fairy-tale tradition and married her; he might, in a more practical Jacobean spirit, have lamented that class differences kept her from her deserved reward. But he does not even think of it. The ease with which he accepts his freedom at considerable risk to her, and his subsequent gung-ho sexual reminiscences with Arcite, leave us wondering whether the rigidly codified chivalric world can achieve the quality of love attained by the gaoler's daughter or the young lover who will accept his role of Palamon-substitute rather than lose her.

—Frances Gray

UBU REX. See **UBU ROI**.

UBU ROI
by Alfred Jarry

First Publication: Paris, 1896.
First Production: Théâtre de l'Oeuvre, 10 December 1896.

Editions

Ubu Roi, in *Ubu*, edited by Noël Arnaud and Henri Bordillon, Paris, 1978.
Ubu Roi [with chronology, bibliography, notes, and criticism], edited by Jean C. Dinguirand and Paul Gayot, Paris, 1986.

Translations

Ubu Roi, translated by Barbara Wright, London, 1951.
King Turd, in *The Ubu Plays*, translated by B. Keith and G. Leyman, New York, 1953.
King Ubu, in *Modern French Theatre*, edited and translated by Michael Benedikt and George E. Wellwarth, New York, 1964.
Ubu Rex, translated by Cyril Connolly and Simon Watson Taylor, in *The Ubu Plays*, edited by Simon Watson Taylor, London, 1968.

Criticism

(For general works on the author, see *Playwrights* volume)

Books:
Judith Cooper, *"Ubu Roi": An Analytic Study*, New Orleans, 1974.
Gérard Damerval, *"Ubu Roi": La Bombe comique de 1896*, Paris, 1984.
Keith Beaumont, *Jarry: "Ubu Roi"*, London, 1987.

Articles:
R. York, "*Ubu* Revisited: The Reprise of 1922", in *French Review*, vol.35 no.3, 1962.
D. Church, "Père Ubu: The Creation of a Literary Type", in *Drama Survey*, vol.4 no.3, 1965.
V. Gassler, "The Legend of Ubu", in *Bard Review*, vol.2 no.4, 1967.
Brian E. Rainey, "Alfred Jarry and Ubu: The 'fin de siècle' in France", in *Wascana Review*, vol.4 no.1, 1969.
John Erickson, "The Gyres of *Ubu Roi*", in *Dada*, 4, 1974.
Rosette C. Lamont, "*Ubu Roi*: A Collage", in *Dada*, 4, 1974.
John M. Lipski, "Jarry's Ubu: A Study in Multiple Associa-

tion", in *Zeitschrift für Französische Sprache und Literatur*, vol.85 no.1, 1975.
John M. Lipski, "Pronominal Code-Switching in *Ubu Roi*", in *Romance Notes*, 16, 1975.
Linda K. Stillman, "The Morphophonetic Universe of Ubu", in *French Review*, 50, 1977.
Luigi de Nardis, "Solitudine di Ubu", in *Linguistica e Letteratura*, 4, 1979.
Kenneth S. White, "Through Metamorphosis, Theater Loses Rationality as *sina qua non:* Jarry's *King Ubu*", in his *Man's New Shapes: French Avant-Garde Drama's Metamorphoses*, Lanham, Maryland, 1979.
David Jeffery, "The Challenge of *Ubu Roi* as Archetypal Student Drama", in *Modern Languages*, 67, 1986.
Clare Tufts, "Languages in Jarry's *Ubu Roi:* 'Mise en signes' of the mise en scène", in *Approches de l'opéra*, edited by André Helbo, Paris, 1986.
Renée R. Hubert, "*Ubu Roi* and the Surrealist *Livre de peintre*", in *Word & Image*, vol.3 no.4, 1987.
Patrick Lobert, "*Ubu Roi*, Jarry's Satire of Naturalism", in *French Literature Series*, 14, 1987.
Ben Fisher, "Jarry and Florian: Ubu's Debt to Harlequin", in *Nottingham French Studies*, vol.27 no.12, 1988.
Anne Greenfeld, "Jarry, Ubu and *Humour noir*", in *Romance Notes*, 28, 1988.

* * *

In this five-act satirical farce, Jarry adapts the serious story of seizure of power to the comic aims of ridicule and relief. Mère Ubu, playing upon her husband's bestial instincts, urges him to overthrow Wenceslas, King of Poland. After enlisting Bordure's assistance, Ubu usurps the throne in the second act, murdering the ruler and his two sons. Bourgelas, one of the King's sons, escapes with his mother. Meanwhile, in order to placate the Poles and satisfy his greed, Ubu offers the people gold that he reclaims through taxation. In the third act, Ubu assumes authority, liquidating the nobility and magistrates and confiscating national wealth. He also condemns Bordure who, taking refuge in Russia, requests Czar Alexis to help restore order and justice. Alexis attacks, and Mère convinces Ubu of the necessary recourse to war.

In Act IV, while Ubu battles against the Russians, his wife plunders the treasures of Poland. Ubu kills Bordure, but the decimation of his army compels him and his two Palotins to retreat. In fending off a rapacious bear, the Palotins perceive their leader's cowardice and abandon him. In the final act, Ubu's wife flees Bourgelas's avenging army, arriving at the cave where Ubu is sleeping. Darkness enables her to impersonate the angel Gabriel which, in turn, impels him to confess his wrongdoings. The light of daybreak, though, reveals her identity, and Ubu reverts to his former ways. Bourgelas

Ubu Roi: Young Vic Theatre, London 1978

attacks, and the Ubus, along with the Palotins who return, sail home with nostalgia for Poland.

Ubu's grotesqueness evokes caricature and disbelief. His rotund body and pear-shaped head seem ludicrous and fantastical, and the opening trite insults between Mère and Père suggest a slapstick show or a puppet-play. Like the closing scenes in farce, a comic resolution dispels danger as husband and wife return home, physically secure and morally unchanged. Lack of development of character excludes introspection: throughout the play, Ubu remains stupid, indolent, and totally egocentric; his wife stays avaricious, complaining, and domineering. Through incongruities and inversions, Jarry employs irony to elicit surprise and to induce absurdity. Besides his ridiculous appearance, Ubu swears meaningless oaths ("by my green candle", "shittr"), exaggerates the ordinary (his feast becomes a two-day orgy), and misconstrues reality (a bear is a "little bow-wow"). By exploiting the unexpected, Jarry has this Falstaff-like personage debunk the solemn and dignify the preposterous: his stepping on Wenceslas's toe incites revolution; unlike the agile Czar, he jumps over a trench; and, seated safely on a rock, he recites a *paternoster* during the Palotins' struggle with the bear. Jarry also uses dramatic parody: like Macbeth urged to depose Duncan, Ubu yields to his wife's goadings, but his clumsiness, moral blindness, and inanities turn potential pathos into rollicking burlesque. Disparities of language and action heighten the ridiculous. During deliberations and battles, Ubu blends religious and literary references with nonsensical statements, thereby reducing the serious and dignified to the trivial and foolish. And, in the dream-sequence that recalls epic conventions, medieval allegories, and Renaissance romances, Mère convinces Père that her ugliness is comparable to Aphrodite's beauty and her depravities to saintly accomplishments.

The deceptions and distortions, though, present a superficial enjoyment that obscures the horrors of human bestiality and bourgeois shallowness. Ubu's self-absorption and obsession with material wealth and sensual gratification explain his callous disregard and vicious abuse of others; and, prodded by his unbridled instincts, he acts irrationally and erratically. In depicting this primal nature devoid of reason and discipline, Jarry converts innocuous horseplay into actions provoking appalling disgust. For example, Ubu's attack on his guests with bison-ribs provokes amusement; but his subsequent serving of human excrement at table replaces laughter with repugnance. Mère's duplicity punctures pleasure. By injecting false courage into Ubu's cowardly character, she yields to her insatiable greed for wealth and power, manipulating her husband to commit pillage and genocide.

As caricatures, they resemble cartoon animations; but their self-interest, insensitiveness, and indignities reflect the values and evils in bourgeois society. Exemplifying the ethos of this post-Darwinian era, Ubu disregards spiritual values; religion lacks belief, and Ubu facilely recites prayers to escape danger and death. He is a survivor whose instincts endure, and whose bestial superiorities destroy the weak and unfortunate. If Ubu is Everyman, he is also, paradoxically, Nobody, with his prosperity encasing a spiritual void. Instead, Ubu's obesity suggests a material gluttony that assures an aggression necessary for success and stature.

In neglecting the unities of time, place, and action, Jarry constructs a series of scenes resembling a montage of inconsistent happenings and absurd characterizations. Ubu's ludicrous appearance, irrational behavior, and vile words demonstrate a rejection of the established principles of verisimilitude and decorum; and at the first performance, the audience, expecting entertaining farce, was stunned and outraged. But by shattering the illusions that often, paradoxically, define reality, Jarry reveals the potential evils inherent in the subconscious. Through the humor, resulting from fantasy and foolishness, Jarry attacks the materialism, egocentricism, and superficialities which, embodied by Ubu, reflect bourgeois aims and attitudes. Ubu's jokes are meaningless, insensitive utterances, and his unscrupulous deeds become unconscionable crimes. Satire, moreover, evolves into a probing of the dynamics of human impulses. Time and place dissolve, and Ubu emerges as an emblem of man's primal nature. Futility and absurdity characterize Ubu's endeavors: his actions end at the beginning; speech is claptrap; his uncontrolled affections and merciless, unrelenting aggressions destroy order and civlization. Jarry goes beyond a renunciation of conventional dramatic practice and accepted social standards. By creating a drama that suggests the later theories and plays of Artaud, Beckett, Genet, and Ionesco, he forces the spectator to confront, through Ubu, the savagery, isolation, and pain of human existence.

—Donald Gilman

UNCLE VANYA (Dyadya Vanya / Diadia Vania)
by Anton Chekhov

First Publication: In *Anton Chekhov: Plays*, 1897.
First Production: In the Russian provinces, 1897; first Moscow production, at the Moscow Arts Theatre, Moscow, 26 October 1899.

Translations

Uncle Vanya, translated by Jennie Covan, New York, 1922.
Uncle Vanya, in *"The Cherry Orchard" and Other Plays*, translated by Constance Garnett, London, 1923.
Uncle Vanya, translated by Rose Caylor, New York, 1930.
Uncle Vanya, in *"The Seagull" and Other Plays*, translated by Elisaveta Fen, Harmondsworth, 1953.
Uncle Vanya, translated by Stark Young, New York, 1956.
Uncle Vanya, in *"The Storm" and Other Russian Plays*, translated by David Magarshack, New York, 1960.
Uncle Vanya, in *Six Plays of Chekhov*, translated by Robert Corrigan, New York, 1962.
Uncle Vanya, in *Chekhov: The Major Plays*, translated by Ann Dunnigan, New York, 1964.
Uncle Vanya, in *The Oxford Chekhov, 3*, edited and translated by Ronald Hingley, London, 1964.
Uncle Vanya, in *Anton Chekhov's Plays*, translated by Eugene K. Bristow, New York, 1977.
Uncle Vanya, translated by Michael Frayn, London, 1987.

Criticism
(For general works on the author, see *Playwrights* volume)

Articles:
Eric Bentley, "Craftsmanship in Uncle Vanya", in his *In Search of Theater*, 1953.
Philip Bordinat, "Dramatic Structure in Chekhov's *Uncle Vanya*", in *Slavic and East European Journal*, 16, 1958.
Ian M. Matley, "Chekhov and Geography", in *Russian Review*, 31, 1972.
Ieva Vitins, "Uncle Vanya's Predicament", in *Slavic and Eastern European Journal*, 22, 1978.

Uncle Vanya: Hampstead Theatre, London, 1979

Péter Egri, "A Touch of the Story-Teller: The Dramatic
Function of the Short Story Model in Chekhov's *Uncle
Vanya* and O'Neill's *A Touch of the Poet*", in *Hungarian
Studies in English*, 13, 1980.

Pierre Lavoie, "L'Idiot de la famille. . .: *Oncle Vania*: Trois
productions", in *Jeu*, 28, 1983.

A.G.F. van Holk, "Thematic Composition in Russian Drama:
The Theme of Envy in Pushkin's *Mozart and Salieri*,
Turgenev's *A Month in the Country* and Chekhov's *Uncle
Vanya*", in *Essays in Poetics*, vol.8 no.1, 1983.

Stewart A. Kingsbury, "Name Symbolism in Chekhov's *Uncle
Vanya*", in *Festschrift in Honor of Virgil J. Vogel*, edited by
Edward Callary, DeKalb, Illinois, 1985.

*   *   *

Uncle Vanya (*Diadia Vania*) can be seen as the last of
Chekhov's earlier plays, all based on a problematic, male anti-
hero. It was published in 1897 and first performed in 1899, after
The Seagull, and was written, or reconstituted, out of the
wreck of *The Wood Demon*, between 1892 and 1896. It is thus,
also, the second of Chekhov's mature plays, its acts not broken
into scenes, its Act IV an anti-climax of embarrassed departure, its tone hovering between cruel comedy and pathos. The
basic plot, two thirds of the text, and the characters are carried
over from *The Wood Demon*: comparing the two plays is a
lesson on how a flop may be turned into a great play.

The core of both plays is the arrival of the professor and his
young second wife, disrupting the life, and threatening the
livelihood, of his daughter Sonya and of Uncle Vanya. The
differences in *Uncle Vanya* are, firstly, that the Uncle turns the
gun against the professor, not himself, but farcically fails to
alter anything; secondly, that a new Act IV makes a mockery
of reconciliation and instead leaves the old professor in full
charge while the remaining characters are abandoned to their
desolate future; and thirdly, that the catalyst of the action—the
ecological idealist, the doctor—is also a lecherous alcoholic.
Thus the inverted principles of Chekhovian comedy are
established: age triumphs over youth, the servants rule their
masters, and the normal world has crumbled. The subtitle—
Scenes from Country Life—is deliberately ironic.

Like many other Chekhov plays, *Uncle Vanya* incorporates
material from his stories which certainly would have guided a
contemporary audience's interpretation. Dr. Astrov's impassioned (though comically pedantic) laments for the ravaged
environment recapitulate the lyrical complaints of the story
Panpipes (*Svirel*) of 1887; the professor, terrified of death and
torturing his wife and daughter with his hypochondria through
a stormy summer night, is parodying the impressive professor,
the narrator of *A Dreary Story* (*Skuchnaia istoriia*) of 1889.
But once this material is in a dramatic framework, comic
absurdity evaporates the authorial presence; the residual

lyricism is to be found in the non-verbal elements—the storm winds, the nightwatchman's banging of a rail, the reproachfully silent piano, Telegin's tentative strumming of a guitar, Marina's knitting, or the starling in a cage.

The play was first offered to the state Maly theatre in Moscow. After the failure of *The Seagull* the Maly prevaricated and Chekhov ceded *Uncle Vanya* to the Moscow Arts Theatre, which had made a success of *The Seagull*. Stanislavsky was persuaded to take the role of Dr. Astrov under Nemirovich-Danchenko's direction. As always, Stanislavsky saw social comment and pathos in the ruin of the sensitive provincials, Uncle Vanya and Astrov, by the ruthless professorial careerist from the capital; Chekhov's laconic comments, however, stressed the dry comedy. Nevertheless, *Uncle Vanya* has a little of the autobiographical input that made *The Seagull* so shocking a play: the self-sacrificing Sonya, doomed to spinsterhood, was clearly recognisable as Chekhov's sister Marya, while the play's impoverished and diseased landscape was specified as the Serpukhov district around Chekhov's estate, Melikhovo.

By 1900 *Uncle Vanya* was acclaimed: for the first time Chekhov could consider himself a playwright by vocation and not renounce the theatre, although the play's success embarrassed him as much as earlier plays' failures: literati and their wives wept, while country doctors saw it as an expression of their grievances. Russian critics felt it was "an exercise in thought, in working out life and finding a way out".

The one resistant spectator was Tolstoy: "I went to see *Uncle Vanya* and I was appalled. . .Where's the drama? The play treads water". In fact, in refusing to let actions have their usual dramatic consequences—nobody arrests Uncle Vanya for firing at the professor—Chekhov shows his genius for unprecedented dramatic compression. Yelena doesn't have to compare herself to a caged bird: the starling is there in its cage. The forests don't catch fire (as they do in *The Wood Demon*): Astrov looks at the map of Africa and remarks how hot it must be there. The clothes are vestimentary markers of the character's neuroses: the professor in his galoshes and overcoat, Uncle Vanya in his flashy tie. The climaxes are built up as carefully as Ibsen's: Act III's announcement of the professor's plan to appropriate the entire estate for himself starts a long crescendo that culminates in gunshots. But the tension is constantly broken by apparent parody: Uncle Vanya goes over the top, claiming he "could have been Dostoevsky or Schopenhauer", reverting to infantile tantrums at his mother's knee. A modern audience reacts as Chekhov intended—they cannot weep at farce, but take their lead from Marina, the imperturbable servant, for whom all this row is "ganders cackling".

The key to *Uncle Vanya*, as to *The Cherry Orchard*, is in the doomed trees. Astrov's passionate defence of them is comic because it bores and puzzles his listener, Yelena; but it switches the audience's concern from the disrupted family to nature off-stage, which desperately signals its distress to the uncaring characters. Uncle Vanya, unlike Platonov or Ivanov in earlier plays, is thus out of focus, for all his eponymous status: his irrelevance makes him, in the last analysis, comic. What Chekhov shows happening to the Voinitsky family is only a symptom of a more fatal convulsion in the outside world—among the epidemics and dried-up rivers of the Russian landscape.

—Donald Rayfield

UNDER THE GASLIGHT
by Augustin Daly

First Publication: New York, 1867.
First Production: New York Theatre, New York, 13 August 1867; revised version, 1881.

Editions

Under the Gaslight, in *Hiss the Villain: Six English and American Melodramas*, edited by Michael R. Booth, New York, 1964.

*   *   *

The Cortland cousins, Laura and Pearl, are spending New Year's Eve at home in their elegantly furnished New York City residence, accompanied by Ray Trafford, Laura's fiancé. A one-armed Civil War veteran, Snorky, appears at the door with a bouquet and a billet-doux signed by the villainous Byke. Byke's visit, soon after, forces Pearl to reveal to Ray that Laura, as a child, was a pickpocket whom the Cortland family adopted and educated overseas. Once Ray finds out the truth about Laura, he writes a letter to her stating his reservations about their impending marriage; this letter is accidentally discovered by Mrs. Van Dam and her society blue-bloods, who threaten to expose and expel Laura. Laura takes refuge in a squalid basement apartment with Peachblossom, a former member of Byke's gang, whom she has befriended; but Byke and his cohort, Old Judas, trace Laura and drag her off to the Tombs Police Court. There, Byke is legally declared Laura's real father. He and Judas take Laura to Pier 30 where Snorky, his young accomplice Bermudas, and Ray Trafford succeed in rescuing Laura.

Act IV finds Laura at the Cortland Long Branch residence; but because of her lowered social standing, she has arranged for Ray to marry Pearl. Peachblossom follows Laura there and Laura realizes she is no longer safe because her whereabouts might be discovered. The climactic scene of the play occurs when Laura, locked in a shed at the railroad station, preparing to wait until the morning when the train back to the city will arrive, overhears Byke tie the hapless Snorky to the railroad track. Laura manages to axe her way out of the shed and rescue Snorky just before the train rumbles by. In Act V Byke is caught by Snorky and Bermudas in the act of stealing Pearl's valuable jewellery and reveals that Pearl and Laura were switched in their cradles and Pearl is really the child of obscurity. Laura is now free to marry Ray; Snorky makes plans to marry Peachblossom. Byke exits hurriedly.

Augustin Daly knew how to please an audience. A man involved in almost every aspect of theatre, from criticism to theatre management, Daly created in this, his first original play, a domestic melodrama that uses the traditional aspects of the melodramatic form to present a terrifying vision of 19th-century American urban life to an audience hungry for the lurid details of "Life and Love in These Times".

The melodramatic world here is a simple one of stark contrasts. Characters are either good or evil; rich or poor; cowardly or courageous. Daly exploits this polarity by creating two separate and distinct environments within the world of his play. The action helps to delineate each environment, moving back and forth between elegant boudoirs and crowded basements, Delmonico's Restaurant and Pier 30. At the top of this social stratification is the world of Ray Trafford, the Cortlands, Mrs. Van Dam, and assorted other blue-bloods. In this world there is lounging on settees, empty conversation, and forced laughter. Those who live here are superficial and humorless.

Ray is cowardly; Mrs. Van Dam is bigoted. They live dull, empty lives that lack spontaneity and richness of spirit.

Underneath this world lies the other one; one even more populous, inhabited by immigrants, have-nots, and assorted misfits. This is the world of Snorky, Peachblossom, Bermudas, Byke, Old Judas, and, most recently, Laura. Some, like Snorky (who is denied a pension from the government for his Civil War service), are victims of society. Some, like Laura, try to work within society's legal and moral structures. Others, like Byke and Old Judas, prey on society. They are all survivors whose ingenuity helps them to carve out an existence where little is possible. They live in the shadows, in cramped, rat-infested spaces. To the patrons of Delmonico's, they are terrifying creatures who steal, kidnap, and murder. No home is secure. Yet, even within a society that neither recognizes nor understands them, they manage to forge their own destinies and create their own moralities.

Under The Gaslight has all the characteristics of the well-made melodrama: a heroine and a villain; a simplistic view of life; characterization subordinated to plot development; an accident to advance the plot; stage devices of the day to create spectacle; and a happy ending. Yet Daly surprises and excites by embellishing standard melodramatic elements. His heroine, Laura, is not the weak-willed victim of more traditional melodramas. She is self-determining, unafraid, and able to act on her impulses. Also, for the first time in the history of the form, a victim is tied to the railroad track. It is the train that represents Daly's real villain: the upper society bearing down on the lower.

Finally, while Daly's surprise revelation of cradle-switching sets up a happy ending for Laura and Ray, he leaves a couple of loose ends. Because of her lowered social status, Pearl remains uncoupled, at least temporarily. More importantly, Byke, who has been the major antagonist during most of the play, manages to escape retribution by making a very hasty exit. The play, while ending happily, does not necessarily end justly, for Byke is free to terrorize again.

—Marcia K. Morrison

THE UNDERPANTS.   See SCENES FROM THE HEROIC LIFE OF THE MIDDLE CLASSES.

**THE UNDIVINE COMEDY (Nieboska Komedia)
by Zygmunt Krasiński**

First Publication: Paris, 1835.
First Production: Cracow, 29 November 1902.

Editions
Nie-boska Komedyja, edited by Juliusz Kleiner, Cracow, 1921.

Translations
The Undivine Comedy, in *"The Undivine Comedy" and Other Poems*, translated by M.W. Cook, Philadelphia, 1875.
The Undivine Comedy, translated by H.E. Kennedy and Z. Uminska, London, 1924.
The Undivine Comedy, in *Polish Romantic Drama*, translated by Harold B. Segel, Ithaca, New York, 1977.

Criticism
(For general works on the author, see *Playwrights* volume)

Articles:
A Wagner, "*Undivine Comedy:* Zygmunt Krasiński and German Expressionism", in *American Slavic and East European Review*, 6, 1947.
S. Moser, "Zur Frage der Übertragung von Werken der polnischen Romantik am Beispiel der *Ungöttlichen Komödie*", in *Zeitschrift für Slawistik*, 20, 1975.
Malgorzata Sugiera, "La *Non-Divine Comédie* de Krasiński dans la lecture littéraire et théâtrale", in *Le Texte dramatique: La Lecture et la scène*, edited by Józef Heistein, Wroclaw, 1986.

*   *   *

Zygmunt Krasiński's play (published anonymously in Paris in 1835, first performed in Kraków in 1902) is a conscious parody of Dante's *Divine Comedy*, but can be understood on many levels, most notably as a pessimistic prognosis of the future course of human history, and as a morality play demonstrating the workings of divine Providence.

The Un-Divine Comedy oscillates between poetic rhapsody and dramatic conflict in a manner typical of the Polish Romantic imagination. In a letter to his friend Konstanty Gaszyński, Krasiński wrote that he intended it to be a "drama that deals with the crucial issue of our era: that of the struggle of two principles, aristocracy and democracy". The play was written a year after the Lyon weavers' uprising of 1832, a rebellion which Krasiński maintained was the consequence of the French Revolution and the Terror, and presaged the approach of the apocalypse. The 20-year-old artistocrat identified this with the imminent collapse of the rule of his own class, preordained by God himself.

The Un-Divine Comedy is perfectly balanced between the personal feelings of Henryk the lover, husband, and father, and the public duties he must perform as leader of the aristocrats. The vast social conflict that dominates the last two acts of the "drama" is thus preceded by two acts that present the private world of the ambiguous protagonist, Count Henryk.

Henryk is the parody of a Romantic hero, and is portrayed as a self-conscious Romantic poseur, who desperately wants to be considered a poet. He is torn between the sentimental satisfactions of family life with his new wife and the tempting charms of Beauty, Fame, and Eden, respectively—symbolic incarnations of various Romantic myths (individualism, emotional authenticity, and natural purity). Seduced by these ideals, he is almost led to suicide, but protected from the abyss by his Guardian Angel. Henryk is "heartless", however, and though his Guardian warns that "you are inventing a drama", his lack of interest in his family causes his wife to lose her mind and curse him at her death. Their son, Orcio is born blind, but according to the dying wish of his mother, becomes a true visionary "poet", providing Henryk with yet another opportunity for self-sacrifice that he does not take, wrapped as he is in his own selfish dreams. The Guardian Angel reveals to Henryk that only "the love of one's neighbour" can offer true redemption, but his words fail to convince (and to save) the doomed Count.

At the beginning of the third act, Henryk appears as the leader of the aristocratic knights committed to defending the honour and integrity of their world against the masses of the rebellious poor. Having retreated to their last refuge on the crags of the Castle of the Holy Trinity, his peers reveal themselves to be decadent, cowardly snobs bent on survival

The Undivine Comedy: Dramatic Theatre, Plock, Poland, 1985

and caring little for the honour of their ancestors. The world's poor collect at the foot of the Castle and utter defeat faces the aristocrats. Henryk visits the camp of the bloodthirsty hordes at the foot of the crags in disguise and comprehends that his last stand will not be able to resist the masses' desire for bread and revenge.

A confrontation between Henryk and Pankracy, the wily leader of the horde, only reveals that they are both equally arrogant and disparaging of their followers. When the final onslaught overwhelms the aristocrats' defences and turns the Castle into a bloodbath, Orcio is shot, and Henryk commits suicide by jumping off the Holy Trinity's battlements shouting

"Damn you, Poetry!". But the drama does not end there: in his moment of ecstatic victory, Pankracy has an intense vision of Christ's Second Coming and he dies of terror screaming "Galilaee vicisti!" (You have won, Christ!).

However much his contemporaries disagreed with the politics of *The Un-Divine Comedy*, no one could deny the extraordinary power of the work and most particularly its climax, which Adam Mickiewicz considered unequalled in Polish literature. Ironically, the drama was written to counteract the "heretical" Christian-socialist tendencies of such writers as Mickiewicz, as well as to denounce the dangers of liberal and revolutionary ideas that threatened the feudal social order to which Krasiński belonged.

The Un-Divine Comedy, still largely unknown to the English-speaking world, can be seen as more than an enactment of the universal confrontation of good and evil; it reveals itself to be a multi-layered work that unmasks the shallowness and hopelessness of a whole range of ideas: it is as critical of aristocratic traditions as it is of social radicalism; it attacks selfish individualism as much as ignorant populism. Only Christian revelation shines through the course of events and Krasiński's apocalyptic ending makes clear that man's puny achievements are insignificant in the face of divine Providence. While Henryk and Pankracy profess to search for meaning and truth in the world and themselves, in fact they cannot perceive the eternal values of God's will because of their earthly arrogance.

Of all Polish Romantic dramas, the *Comedy* is the most exactly composed and visually striking in its evocation of frenetic passions and horrors. Conceived independently of the issue of the Polish struggle for freedom, Krasiński's sublime morality play is at the same time a universal tragedy that prophetically tears away the masks of propaganda, ideology, and ritual that hide corruption and cynicism. Its cinematic evocation of a holocaust of humanity as a whole seems terrifyingly prophetic of the events of the mid-20th century. As Krasiński himself wrote, "I know that our civilisation is doomed to die".

—Donald Pirie

UTINOI OKHOTY.   See DUCK HUNTING.

THE VENETIAN WOMAN.   See **LA VENEXIANA.**

LA VENEXIANA
Anonymous

Composition: 16th Century.
First Publication: Bologna, 1928.

Editions
La Venexiana, edited by L. Lovarini, Bologna, 1928.
La Venexiana [with translation], edited and translated by
    Matilde Valente Pfeiffer, New York, 1950.
La Venexiana, edited by Ludovico Zorzi, Turin, 1965.
La Venexiana, edited by G. Padoan, Padova, 1974.

Translations
La Venexiana [with translation], edited and translated by
    Matilde Valente Pfeiffer, New York, 1950

Criticism
(For general works on the author, see *Playwrights* volume)

Books:
G. Padoan, *Momenti del Rinascimento veneto*, Padova, 1978.
G. Padoan, *La commedia rinascimentale veneta*, Vicenza,
    1982.

Articles:
Ireneo Sanesi, "*La Venexiana*", in *Nuova antologia*, 64, 1929.
A. Mortier, "Une Comédie vénitienne de la Renaissance", in
    Études italiennes (new series), 11, 1932.
E. Lovarini, "Una commedia in cerca d'autore", in *Nuova
    antologia*, 81, 1946.
A. Momo, "*La Venexiana:* La Commedia di Venezia", in
    Angelus Novus, 5–6, 1965.
B.L.O. Richter, "*La Venexiana* in Recent Criticism", in *The
    Drama of the Renaissance: Essays for Leicester Bradner*,
    edited by E.M. Blistein, Providence, Rhode Island, 1970.

*   *   *

La Venexiana deals with the love adventures of Giulio, a
young man from Milan, with Anzola and Valiera, two
Venetian gentlewomen, variously assisted by their maidens,
Nena and Oria, and a porter, Bernardo. Plot and characters
recall traditional situations and figures familiar from Italian
short stories (from Boccaccio's *Decameron* on) and Renaissance comedies (such as Machiavelli's *Mandragola*); but the
play, written in 1535–6, also conveys a close reflection of
contemporary reality. The two ladies have been identified with
real persons whom the contemporary public could easily
recognize. They belonged to the same family: the middle-aged
Anzola Valier, widow of a member of the aristocracy (Marco
Barbarigo) who died in 1535; the young Valiera Valier, who
married in the same year a less noble man, Giacomo Semi-
tecolo, much older than she. *La Venexiana* is, therefore, a very
interesting case because it tried to bring onto the stage a love
story which was, presumably, the subject of rumours and
gossip in Venice at the time—and perhaps because of that it
may have never been actually performed. It should be seen in
relation more to the realistic dialect plays, such as those by
Ruzzante, which were popular in the Venetian area at the time
(the four female characters use Venetian dialect; Bernardo,
the porter from Bergamo, the dialect from his city; while
Giulio, a "foreigner" from Milan, speaks Italian) than to the
formal Italian Renaissance comedies which derived their
inspiration mostly from the classical theatre.

The most interesting aspect of *La Venexiana* lies in its
structure. Rather than counting on plot complications and
tricks, or on the comic aspects of language and situation in
order to attract the attention of the public, the play aims to
portray its protagonists from a psychological point of view—
indeed, there is very little to laugh at in this comedy, which
more resembles a modern drama.

Giulio, a young man in his late teens or early twenties, is a
cold and indifferent lover who hides with his courtesy and
politeness towards the ladies his egotism and his intention to
use the women for mere pleasure and, possibly, financial help.
At the beginning he courts Valiera and even plans to marry her
(being unaware that she is already married) only because of
her beauty, nobility, and dowry; when fortune throws him into
the arms of the older Anzola, her passionate sensuality, and
gifts of a golden chain and an emerald ring, are enough to
convince him to forget the first lady and to settle for the
second; but his strong sexual drive and the desire to experience
the beautiful and younger Valiera do not permit him to miss
the chance he is given to spend one night with her.

The two women are even more clearly defined, in their
forceful urges for erotic satisfaction, in their jealousy of each
other, and their fears of being betrayed by their lover. As the
author states in the prologue, the play seems to have been
written as a confirmation of what love can lead women (not
only men) to feel and to do. The scene in the first act, in which
Anzola, in bed with Nena, tells her to curse and to speak the
dirty words used by men in a whorehouse, so that, closing her
eyes, she may pretend to be in the arms of Giulio, rates among
the most effective presentations of female sensuality (and
without indulging in any form of parody or satire, as was
common practice in Medieval and Renaissance literature).

La Venexiana follows the classical pattern of the division

854

into five acts, but applies freely the three Aristotelian unities. The action takes place within four days and three nights, rather than 24 hours, and the scene changes from the street near the inn where Giulio is lodged to various rooms in the houses of Anzola and Valiera—however, the locations are very close to one another. In the third act, two consecutive scenes occur in the same room, but there is a lapse of time between them, since the author could not possibly have Giulio and Anzola performing a sexual act in front of the audience. As for the unity of action, both ladies share the role of protagonist; this ambiguity is reflected in the title, to be interpreted as either "the Venetian woman" or as "the story which takes place in Venice".

In any case the play has no conclusion. Giulio repeats twice a statement well known from *Decameron* love tales: it is impossible for one man to satisfy the sexual drives of two women. The public is left to wonder whether he will continue his relation with Valiera, abandoning Anzola for good, or will go back to the latter forgetting the former. In either case *La Venexiana*, rather than celebrating the joyous triumph of sensuality, leaves the audience with the melancholic feeling of its transience and bitter aftertaste.

—Antonio Franceschetti

VENICE PRESERVED; or, A Plot Discovered
by Thomas Otway

First Publication: London, 1682.
First Production: Dorset Garden Theatre (Duke's Company), London, 9 February 1682.

Editions

Venice Preserved, in *"The Orphan" and "Venice Preserved"*, edited by C.F. McClumpha, Boston and London, 1908.
Venice Preserved, edited by Malcolm Kelsall, Lincoln, Nebraska, 1969 (Regents Restoration Drama Series).

Criticism

(For general works on the author, see *Playwrights* volume)

Articles:
J.R. Moore, "Contemporary Satire in Otway's *Venice Preserved*", in *Publications of the Modern Language Association [PMLA]*, 43, 1928.
Aline McKenzie, "*Venice Preserved* Reconsidered", in *Tulane Studies in English*, 1, 1949.
D.R. Hansen, "Otway Preserved: Theme and Form in *Venice Preserved*", in *Studies in Philology*, 55, 1958.
William H. McBurney, "Otway's Tragic Muse Debauched: Sensuality in *Venice Preserved*", in *Journal of English and Germanic Philology*, 58, 1959.
W. van Voris, "Tragedy Through Restoration Eyes: *Venice Preserved* in its own Theatre", in *Hermathena*, 99, 1964.
H.R. Kleinberger, "Otway's *Venice Preserved* and Hofmannsthal's *Das gerettete Venedig*", in *Modern Language Review*, 62, 1967.
Gordon Williams, "The Sex-Death Motive in Otway's *Venice Preserv'd*", in *Trivium*, 2, 1967.
Ronald Berman, "Nature in *Venice Preserved*", in *English Literary History*, 36, 1969.
Robert Pasquarelle, "On the Nicky-Nacky Scene of *Venice Preserved*", in *Restoration and Eighteenth Century Theatre Research*, 8, 1969.
Derek Hughes, "A New Look at *Venice Preserved*", in *Studies in English Literature 1500–1900*, 11, 1971.
Bessie Proffitt, "Religious Symbolism in Otway's *Venice Preserved*", in *Papers on Language and Literature*, 7, 1971.
Jack D. Durant, "'Honour's Toughest Task': Family and State in *Venice Preserved*", in *Studies in Philology*", 71, 1974.
Gerald D. Parker, "The Image of Rebellion in Thomas Otway's *Venice Preserved* and Edward Young's *Busiris*", in *Studies in English Literature 1500–1900*, 21, 1981.
Michael de Porte, "Otway and the Straits of Venice", in *Papers on Language and Literature*, 18, 1982.
David Bywaters, "Venice, Its Senate, and Its Plot in Otway's *Venice Preserved*", in *Modern Philology*, 80, 1983.
Katherine Rogers, "Masculine and Feminine Values in Restoration Drama: The Distinctive Power of *Venice Preserved*", in *Texas Studies in Literature and Language*, 27, 1985.
Harry M. Solomon, "The Rhetoric of Redressing Grievances: Court Propaganda as the Hermeneutical Key to *Venice Preserved*", in *English Literary History*, 53, 1986.
Philip Harth, "Political Interpretations of *Venice Preserved*", in *Modern Philology*, 85, 1988.
Candy B.K. Schille, "Reappraising Pathetic Tragedies: *Venice Preserved* and *The Massacre at Paris*", in *Restoration*, 12, 1988.

*   *   *

Jaffeir has married Belvidera against the will of her father Priuli, a senator of the Venetian Republic, in recompense for which Priuli bankrupts Jaffeir. Jaffeir turns for solace to his close friend Pierre who is plotting a revolt against the Republic. Jaffeir joins the rebel cadre, offering his wife as a token of his belief in the cause. The rebel leader Renault betrays this trust: he attempts to rape Belvidera. In anguish, Belvidera and Jaffeir betray the plot to the Senate, which sentences the rebels to death. On the scaffold Jaffeir is reconciled with Pierre, whom he stabs, thereby freeing him from the ignominy of execution. Jaffeir then stabs himself. In response to these deaths, Belvidera finally succumbs to fits of erotic madness, and herself dies, leaving Priuli to curse the fate of cruel patriarchs like himself.

Venice Preserved remains the most spectacular tragedy of the Restoration. Together with Dryden's *Absolom and Achitophel*, it remains the most elaborate literary "sign" of the trauma inflicted by the Popish Plot of the late 1670's on the cultural life of London.

The play was first performed in February 1682, several months after the fall of the Whig leader, Shaftesbury, and the collapse of his campaign to supplant the Catholic Duke of York as heir to the throne. The acclamation which greeted that first performance, together with the prologue and epilogue suggests that it was initially read as a pro-monarchical, pro-Tory play. Modern readers have been less ready to allegorise the play in support of fixed critical positions.

Shaftesbury is caricatured not once but twice: as the masochistic, senile, and corrupt Senator Antonio, whose "nicky nacky" scenes with the whore Aquilina are the most notorious as well as the most sordidly hilarious in the play; and as Renault, the leader of the rebels, who longs for a Venetian apocalypse as bloody as that dreamt of by the conspirators in *Julius Caesar*. The rebellion is compromised by Renault's rhetorical as well as sexual excesses. Murkier still, however, is the Venetian Republic itself, which is governed by impulses no

Venice Preserved: David Garrick as Jaffeir and Mrs. Cibber as Belvidera, 1764

less sordid than those of the rebels, to judge by Antonio's grubby sexuality and hypocrisy, and Priuli's vengeful callousness towards his daughter as well as his son-in-law.

The play thus frustrates direct and simplistic perceptions of forces of "good" and "evil". Instead Otway evokes the exotic hysteria of the Popish Plot, driven by the extreme paranoic thoughts of Catholic invasions habitually evoked in the minds of late 17th-century English protestants. Otway dramatises the "headstrong, moody, murmuring race" of Londoners, London being the vortex of the plot.

Venice Preserved frequently uses that vortex as background for the story, more personal than directly political, it wishes to enact. The three main characters have no counterpart either in the events of the Plot or in the history of Venice which provided Otway with his framing narrative. Nevertheless there is an emotional lability which marks the shifting relationships between those three, who are warped by the fetid politics in which they find themselves immersed.

Jaffeir is the focus of this instability. His erotic power, which dominates Belvidera (and in which their relationship parallels that between Othello and Desdemona) is transferred to Pierre, where it is transformed into submission. Jaffeir's sexual ambivalence is confirmed by his remarkable speech at the end of Act II, where he imagines himself coming "like a panting

turtle" (dove) both to Pierre's and Belvidera's breasts; it is confirmed visually by the stage business of the dagger, which passes from rebel to husband to wife so suggestively that it becomes both an overtly erotic as well as an overtly political metaphor. At the end of Act IV Jaffeir repeatedly offers to stab Belvidera, to repay her for betraying Pierre; but then he relents and embraces her instead. Perhaps his true affections are realised in the famous climax to Act V, where Jaffeir embraces Pierre on the scaffold, stabs his friend and kills himself, with the same dagger: achieving a consummation in death with his friend, finally realising the demands of honour and the homoerotic attraction which electrifies his encounters with Pierre.

Restoration dramatists are notorious for their reconstructions of Shakespeare in the interests of perfect decorum and just closure. *Venice Preserved* does not seek to do this but, in many respects, Otway is the most "Shakespearean" of Restoration playwrights. *Venice Preserved* is suffused with recollections of *Othello* and *Julius Caesar*. His characters are aligned with symmetrical precision, but they address each other in a blank verse remarkable for its emotional force. The opening confrontation between Priuli and Jaffeir is direct, compelling, and, in this respect at least, highly Shakespearean.

The action of the play develops moreover with a dreamlike

fluidity reminiscent of action on the open Elizabethan stage. In Act V, Antonio abases himself at the feet of Aquilina, staging his own death. There is no indication that he then leaves the stage, in which case his "corpse" would ironically be present during the deaths of Pierre, Jaffeir, and Belvidera. This further suggests a stage eventually littered with bodies during Priuli's closing speech: an illogical and poetic effect, evocative of the Elizabethan penchant for using the body as prop.

Tonally the play recalls the sardonic Jacobean revenge tragedies of Tourneur, Webster, and Middleton. Pierre self-consciously represents himself as a warped, revenging malcontent, as if he too had studied to excess the parts of Tourneur's Vindice or Marston's Antonio. The play is marked also by "horrid laughter", a grim amusement at the corruption of the Republic: this too seems Jacobean. Otway uses his understanding of his forebears to persuade us that, though Venice is indeed preserved at the end of the play, there remains "something rotten in the state".

—Mark Anthony Houlahan

DIE VERFOLGUNG UND ERMORDUNG JEAN-PAUL MARATS ....   See MARAT/SADE.

THE VERGE
by Susan Glaspell

First Publication: Boston, 1922.
First Production: Provincetown Playhouse, New York, 14 November 1921.

Criticism
(For general works on the author, see *Playwrights* volume)

Articles:
Arthur E. Waterman, "Susan Glaspell's *The Verge:* An Experiment in Feminism", in *Great Lakes Review*, vol.6 no.1, 1979.

*   *   *

Claire Archer wants to break with conventional life and achieve "integrity in otherness", both in her experimental greenhouse (the set used as a striking visual symbol) dedicated to producing plants that are not better or prettier, but radically different from previous ones—and in her personal life. Surrounded by men named Tom (lover), Dick (friend), and Harry (husband), she finds little support for, and less understanding of, her endeavor. She retreats alternately to the greenhouse and to her twisted tower (another piece of symbolic décor), "like some masonry that hasn't been". When the laboriously bred "Edge Vine" fails to reproduce, although it seems to "go outside what it was", Claire brutally uproots it. She is equally ruthless with her daughter, Elizabeth, whom she sees as an automation of social conformity. A second experimental plant, "Breath of Life", shows itself capable of reproduction, and Tom Edgeworthy (the symbolic names *are* heavy-handed) of spiritual companionship. He finally understands that

Claire's experiments are seeking "a door on the far side of destruction". But even the possibility of Tom's support threatens to suffocate Claire. Afraid she will stop creating new life by enjoying what she has, in a final embrace she strangles her lover, then whispers almost madly: "Nearer, Nearer—my God. To Thee, Nearer—to Thee", as the curtain falls.

No play of Glaspell's justified better Isaac Goldberg's early recognition that she "leans toward the rebellious woman. . .", and is "largely the playwright of woman's selfhood". *The Verge* is the strongest example of the dramatist's rule breaking, and her most overt treatment of the feminist theme. In it, she not only embraces the concept of women's liberation from encrusted social shackles, but also explores the dangers in making that position (and by implication, any radicalism) absolute. This is also Glaspell's most innovative script with its jarring use of language that often seems to belong to the human potential movement of the 1960's, and with its extreme demands on the scene designer and on the leading actress. Contemporaries as well as recent critics have shown both bewilderment toward and appreciation of the play, seeing it as an imperfect but remarkable work of art.

—Robert K. Sarlós

LE VERRE D'EAU.   See THE GLASS OF WATER.

VESTIDO DE NOIVA.   See WEDDING DRESS.

VICTORY: CHOICES IN REACTION
by Howard Barker

First Publication: London and New York, 1983.
First Production: Gardner Centre, Brighton, Sussex (Joint Stock Theatre Company), 17 February 1983.

*   *   *

Victory opens in a field that seems initially as historically unlocatable as the play's first words. A man enters: "I know I swore. I know I promised. On the Bible. And because I can take or leave the Bible, got your child in and told me put my two hands on her cheeks and looking in her eyes say I would not disclose this place". The displacement—with its mixture of archaicisms and contemporary slang—is deliberate and important because, although the play is set in the England of the post-Restoration period, it is quite aggressively not another costume drama; it refuses to become a part of a sentimental nostalgia. Barker's creation of a gloriously ahistorical language, borrowing from past and present, is itself a part of the conscious intent to create both connections and disconnections between that past and present. The events and the contexts in which those events occur in *Victory* are better thought of as having a parallel, rather than a separate, existence to our own.

The man speaking at the opening is Scrope, who has been secretary to the man whose buried body he has promised to protect, Bradshaw—a once-influential regicide and revolutionary writer. Characteristically, given the play's subtitle, he immediately points out the exact location of the grave to the soldiers who will exhume the body, dismember it, and scatter its various parts about the kingdom in a grisly monarchist revenge. The main narrative thread of the play will be concerned with what happens to Bradshaw's widow, Susan, in her path of survival through the nightmare world of lechery, greed, and corruption that sees the birth of Western capitalism. Willing to do anything in order to survive—for, in this unbrave world, mere survival has taken over as an ambition from the egalitarian ideals of the Commonwealth generation—she possesses but one further ambition: to re-unite the various parts of her dead husband's body—a past that must be properly laid to rest, no longer able to haunt the present and the graspable future. Hers is a long journey towards the achievement of her goal and the acquisition of a self-knowledge that comes only from the bitter realities of lived, rather than theoretical, experience; and it is marked by a series of confrontations with the likes of King Charles and the poet John Milton.

Although the narrative is loosely organised around Susan's journey, there is no sense in which she represents a conventional heroine-figure with whose scrapes and adventures an audience is intended to become emotionally involved, or whose conclusions necessarily convey the meaning of the play. Barker is no idealogue: he is concerned with debate and not with conclusions. Neither Susan nor any other figure in the play can be assumed to possess the status of a consistently reliable, central protagonist—a point that is crucial when considering the role played by Milton.

Given Barker's uncompromising hostility to the values of capitalist society—represented in this play by the new order of bankers who would curb the worst libidinous excesses of the King and his court because it disturbs their market—we would expect Milton's words, as those of a revolutionary in his own time, to carry considerable weight. But he concludes Act II, Scene 2, with a lecture on the nature of revolution that is as impressive in its rhetoric as it is inconsistent in its thesis, arguing both for the permanent revolution ("Every civil war must be the parent of another") and for the revolution to end all revolutions ("Next time, should we start there must be no finish"). Trust the words of no one, perhaps least of all those of the writer who would be taken as prophet!

But equally the monarchy, in the shape of Charles II, provides no easy scapegoat. In this play, the King may look to have victory over yesterday's Commonwealth men, but the future no more belongs to him than it does to Milton. His is a sad lechery, a private enactment of failing powers that mirrors the hollowness of the public rituals of a political power that no longer really rests with him. In the interlude at the end of the first half of the play we are taken for the first time into the vaults of the newly created Bank of England; here Charles and the audience are re-educated into understanding just whose "victory" it has been. The exporter, Undy, lays it on the line: "I thought we had a civil war to get this straight. I spent four years on horseback chasing over garden fences to sort this out. Four years! And now you want to take your gold home and rip up the floorboards. *I have a wound five inches long in my groin says England's got to have a bank!*".

At moments like these the gap between past and present narrows. These are more than connections being made; this is where our own history started—not, as Barker could easily (and dishonestly optimistically) have chosen to locate it, in the Civil War itself, but in its aftermath. Thus he shows the defeat of one new order, revolution, and the triumph not of the old order, but of another new one, of the world of the banker and

of the speculator. The "choices in reaction" are ours as much as they are those of the characters in Barker's magnificently disturbing play.

—John Bull

LA VIDA ES SUEÑO.   See **LIFE IS A DREAM.**

A VIEW FROM THE BRIDGE
by Arthur Miller

First Publication: In *"A View from the Bridge": Two One-Act Plays*, New York, 1955; two-act version, 1957.
First Production: Coronet Theatre, New York, 29 September 1955 [one-act version]; two-act version, Comedy Theatre, London, 11 October 1956.

Criticism
(For general works on the author, see *Playwrights* volume)

Articles:
A.D. Epstein, "A Look at *A View from the Bridge*", in *Texas Studies in Literature and Language*, 7, 1965.
Albert Rothenberg and Eugene D. Shapiro, "The Defense of Psychoanalysis in Literature: *Long Day's Journey into Night* and *A View from the Bridge*", in *Comparative Drama*, 7, 1973.
Karin Helwig, "Die komparative Strategie der Charaktere, die Grammatik der Handlung im Stück *A View from the Bridge* von Arthur Miller und dem entsprechenden Librett von Renzo Rossellini", in *Cahiers de linguistique théorique et appliquée*, 11, 1974.
Steven R. Centola, "Compromise as Bad Faith: Arthur Miller's *A View from the Bridge* and William Inge's *Come Back, Little Sheba*", in *Midwest Quarterly*, 28, 1986.

*   *   *

A neighborhood lawyer, Alfieri, recounts the story of one of his clients, Eddie Carbone, a Brooklyn longshoreman. Eddie is extremely possessive of his niece, Catherine, whom he and his wife, Bea, have raised since childhood. Into their life enter two illegal immigrants, Beatrice's distant relatives from Sicily, whom Eddie has agreed to protect. A crisis develops when Catherine falls in love with the younger immigrant, Rodolpho. Torn between his more-than-familial love for Catherine and his loyalty to his immigrant relatives, Eddie is driven by passions he cannot control. Going against his own code of honor as well the code of his local ethnic community, Eddie informs against the immigrants. Unable to live with his act of betrayal, yet refusing to acknowledge his guilt, Eddie challenges the elder immigrant, Marco, to a mortal combat, in which Eddie is killed.

In *A View from the Bridge*, Arthur Miller seeks to imbue a contemporary action with the quality of ancient myth. Through a narrator-chorus in the figure of the lawyer, Alfieri,

A View from the Bridge: Ambassador Theatre, New York, 1982

Miller evokes the spirit and values of ancient Sicily and Carthage as a pervasive ambience for the inherently naturalistic drama of Eddie Carbone. Eddie's tragic action may thus be viewed not only with reference to his immediate situation and environment (the Italian-American Brooklyn waterfront), but also in relation to universal and fated passions rooted in antiquity.

In his original, more self-consciously poetic, starker version of the play, Miller employed a loose verse format for many of Alfieri's speeches, compressed the action into one extended act, and limited the exploration of psychological complications. The ambience of universality and antiquity was also heightened by the original stage design (Boris Aronson's), which was obviously based on Miller's vision: a backdrop of the open sea, and an overtly abstract, open-platform setting, with Greek columns representing the doorway of Eddie's building. Negative critical response led to Miller's revised version, which eliminated the verse, developed additional psychological, domestic touches (e.g., Eddie's marital and sexual problems), and expanded the action to two acts.

In performance, the integration of Alfieri's narration and chorus-like comment with the action recalled from the past is effective. Alfieri is not a completely detached observer: he interacts directly with Eddie in two critical scenes from the past, which reveal clearly the implications of Eddie's anguished state and the disastrous, but seemingly inevitable, course he is set on. Moreover, the alternation of the relatively brief Alfieri scenes with the main body of the past action provides a variety of rhythm for the total stage action of the play. In the mainstream scenes of the past, Miller creates a well-textured sense of working-class reality: the idiom, the allusions, the stage business, and the use of props are all authentic, as is the delineation of the characters' unrefined but vivid sensibilities. Only in the relationship of Rodolpho and Catherine is there some degree of contrivance and even triteness.

Miller's feeling for the spatial and visual stage life of the play is evident in his blending of interior and exterior scenes, in the carefully selected use of minor but functional characters to reinforce the impact of certain scenes (especially in the climactic, fatal encounter of Marco and Eddie), and in confrontations whose power is not based on words at all—such as the tableau ending of the first act when Marco wordlessly warns Eddie by looming above him with a chair held aloft in one hand.

The thematic core of the play in both versions concerns

issues of ethical choice and integrity, thus sustaining a focus found in Miller's earlier *All My Sons*, *Death of a Salesman*, and *The Crucible*. Questions of one's sense of self, one's name, one's living by a code of values become paramount. Eddie is consumed by inner forces he cannot understand, much less control, but he acquires tragic dimensions (at least in Miller's eyes) by his refusal to submit to the loss of his core of identity. "I want my name!" becomes his repeated, agonized cry of frustration, a frustration intensified by his guilty knowledge of what he has done: by informing on the immigrants he has not only betrayed them but also his tightknit community, and—most crucially—he has betrayed and violated his own self-image as a decent, loyal, honorable person.

The fact that Eddie's choices and actions are primarily instinctual and irrational may weaken the play for some; but it can strengthen it for others. Eddie's sudden surges of passion, revealing unconscious incestuous and homosexual drives, come as a shock on stage; they reveal dark layers of motivation that are unusual for Miller. The figure of Alfieri partially provides a perspective on these events: not a rational analysis or explanation, but a suggestive distancing of Eddie's raw urges that associates them with their ancestral, mythic roots. Miller's judgement on Eddie may be inferred from Alfieri's final comment: "I confess that something perversely pure calls to me from his memory—not purely good but himself purely, for he allowed himself to be wholly known and for that I think I will love him more than all my sensible clients".

On another, less visceral level, the ethical spine of the drama can be related to the era in which the play was written: the early and middle 1950's, the so-called "McCarthy era", when questions of loyalty, honor, and betrayal were vivid, painful realities, not theoretical speculations. But it must be emphasized that *A View from the Bridge* is far from a thesis play; Eddie's crisis exists in the form of dramatic action, not rhetorical discussion.

—Jarka M. Burian

VILDANDEN.   See THE WILD DUCK.

THE VIRTUOSO
by Thomas Shadwell

First Publication: London, 1676.
First Production: Dorset Garden Theatre (Duke's Company), 25 May 1676.

Editions
The Virtuoso, edited by Marjorie Hope Nicholson and David Stuart Rhodes, Lincoln, Nebraska, 1966 (Regents Restoration Drama Series).

Criticism
(For general works on the author, see *Playwrights* volume)

Articles:
Claude Lloyd, "Shadwell and the Virtuosi", in *Publications of the Modern Language Association* [*PMLA*], 44, 1929.

G. Blakemore Evans, "The Source of Shadwell's Character of Sir Formal Trifle in *The Virtuoso*", in *Modern Language Review*, vol.35 no.2, 1940.
Everett L. Jones, "Robert Hooke and *The Virtuoso*", in *Modern Language Review*, 66, 1951.
Joseph M. Gilde, "Shadwell and the Royal Society: Satire in *The Virtuoso*", in *Studies in English Literature 1500–1900*, 10, 1970.
Stephen D. Cox, "Public Virtue and Private Vitality in Shadwell's Comedies", in *Restoration and Eighteenth Century Theatre Research*, 16, 1977.
Brian Corman, "Thomas Shadwell and the Jonsonian Comedy of the Restoration", in *From Renaissance to Restoration: Metamorphoses of the Drama*, edited by Robert Markley, 1984.

*   *   *

Bruce and Longvil, courting the nieces of Sir Nicholas Gimcrack, feign an interest in his outlandish scientific experiments to gain access to his house. His lustful wife promptly pursues the young men, who are easily tempted, but saved by timely interruptions. In a series of farcical scenes the amorous designs of various fools in the play are likewise frustrated. Sir Nicholas's wife, in masquerade, then seduces the young men, afterwards persuading each that his masked lover was the other's beloved. In resolving this confusion they discover that each girl really loves the other's wooer, and so they promptly change partners. The Gimcracks, squabbling over their separate infidelities, agree to separate. News then arrives that Sir Nicholas's estates have been seized for debts incurred by his scientific experiments. His friends desert him, leaving him to contemplate the folly of devoting himself to speculative science instead of the study of man.

By 1676 Shadwell, who eight years earlier was protesting at the tendency towards plays of wit, bawdy, and libertinism, had succumbed to the fashion and was writing a play structured around the sexual adventures of two libertines and a variety of fools, with a *frisson* provided by the depiction of an aged masochist being caned by his whore, and by the spectacle of one fool attempting to rape another who is disguised as a woman. The libertine credentials of his heroes, moreover, are established in the play's first moments, when they proclaim their devotion to Epicurus. It was a direction he had begun to take as early as 1671, and his detractors were not impressed, sneering at the lack of real polish in his witty gentlemen. Indeed his four young lovers speak sturdy, rather than elegant, prose, and show a disconcerting taste for crude horseplay, buffetting, and manhandling the fools as well as mocking them. It was no help to this side of the play that it was first performed only a few weeks after the quintessential comedy of wit and manners, Etherege's *The Man of Mode*.

Shadwell's conversion to wit and libertinism, however, is relatively superficial. His two rakes may begin by eulogising Lucretius and discussing the previous night's drunken debauch, but their conversations have relatively little of the cynicism, the sexual innuendo, and the sneers at priests, marriage, and virtue, that are the stock-in-trade of the full-blown theatrical libertine. Indeed their principal objects of scorn are the wild and debauched young men about town. There is an unanalysed distinction between these "fools" and the "wits" (such as Longvil and Bruce themselves) but their attacks look much like those Shadwell himself was delivering on the witty rakes of Dryden and others eight years before. Certainly, Bruce and Longvil are sexually susceptible, but this is viewed more as a physiological imperative (the heat of young blood) than as the consequences of wild company and the reading of atheistic authors. It is something that Shadwell was to look benignly upon even in such calculatedly moral plays as *The Squire of Alsatia*.

In spite of these concessions to audience taste, Shadwell nailed his colours firmly to the mast in the play's preface, continuing his ongoing battle with Dryden by proclaiming that not wit, but "humours" (or obsessive character types), were central to comedy, and trumpeting *The Virtuoso*'s success in providing four brand new humours figures based on observation of society. Shadwell's enthusiasm seems to have been echoed in the reception of the play, for it was these four—Sir Nicholas the "virtuoso", Sir Formal the rhetorician, Sir Samuel the boisterous lover of masquerade and sexual intrigue, and Snarl, the aged masochist—who were remembered and praised. For a generation or more the names Sir Nicholas Gimcrack and Sir Formal Trifle became short-hand terms for the character types they embodied.

For a modern reader the play's major attraction is undoubtedly that devotee of science, Sir Nicholas. He provides the play's finest comic scene, in which he attempts to learn swimming, scientifically, by lying on a table and imitating the actions of a frog placed in a bowl of water; but beyond that he gives rise to the play's most interesting topic: Restoration responses to the emerging age of science. Shadwell's attitude is simple: applied science, producing useful inventions, is good; pure science is a ludicrous waste of time. Shadwell is hardly concerned to do justice to the attitudes of contemporary scientists, nor is his position always consistent. Accuracy will always be sacrificed for a joke. But out of such simplifications come the energies of comedy.

As on previous occasions, Shadwell, in his prologue, claimed that his plays satirised general social types, not specific individuals. Not everyone was persuaded. Sir Nicholas's experiments are nearly all parodies of ones conducted by English virtuosi, and Shadwell's text appropriates entire passages from their published accounts. One such plagiarised scientist was Robert Hook, and he had no doubt that he was the original of Sir Nicholas: "With Godfrey and Tompion at Play. . .Damned Doggs. *Vindica me Deus*. People almost pointed", he wrote in his diary, later reporting that friends "floutingly smiled" upon him. Even if it was not a satire on individuals, it could readily be construed as one on the Royal Society, despite the fact that Gimcrack had explicitly been rejected by that organisation.

Shadwell's yoking of two comic genres has its problems. The plot line is created by the sexual manoeuvres of the comedy of wit, and while Sir Samuel's amorous intrigue and Snarl's masochism integrate with this, Sir Nicholas and Sir Formal must reveal their humours as set-piece displays marginal to the action. To involve them in the plotting, Shadwell gives them both sexual appetites, but these are inadequately developed as character traits, only sporadically manifest, and unrelated to their humours. In consequence the play's two most powerful creations falter and decline in impact as the play progresses, though Sir Nicholas makes something of a rally in the last few minutes.

—Robert Jordan

VISHNEVY SAD. See THE CHERRY ORCHARD.

THE VISIT (Der Besuch der alten Dame)
by Friedrich Dürrenmatt

First Publication: Zurich, 1956.
First Production: Schauspielhaus, Zurich, 29 January 1956.

Translations
The Visit, translated by Maurice Valency and Friedrich Dürrenmatt, New York, 1958.
The Visit, translated by Patrick Bowles, New York, 1962.

Criticism
(For general works on the author, see *Playwrights* volume)

Books:
Michael P. Loeffler, *Friedrich Dürrenmatts "Der Besuch der alten Dame" in New York: ein Kapitel aus der Rezeptionsgeschichte der neuren Schweizer Dramatik*, Basel, 1976.
Sigrid Mayer, *Friedrich Dürrenmatt: "Der Besuch der alten Dame"*, Frankfurt, 1981.

Articles:
Melvin W. Askew, "Dürrenmatt's *The Visit of the Old Lady*", in *Tulane Drama Review*, 5, 1961.
Ian C. Loram, "*Der Besuch der alten Dame*: On *The Visit*", in *Monatshefte*, 53, 1961.
Hans P. Guth, "Dürrenmatt's *Visit:* The Play Behind the Play", in *Symposium*, 16, 1962.
Jenny C. Hortenbach, "Biblical Echoes in Dürrenmatt's *Der Besuch der alten Dame*", in *Monatshefte*, 57, 1965.
Ernst S. Dick, "Dürrenmatt's *Der Besuch der alten Dame*: Welttheater und Ritualspiel", in *Zeitschrift für deutsche Philologie*, 87, 1968.
Eli Pfefferkorn, "Dürrenmatt's Mass Play", in *Modern Drama*, 12, 1969.
Donald G. Daviau and Harvey I. Dunkle, "Friedrich Dürrenmatt's *Der Besuch der alten Dame*: A Parable of Western Society in Transition", in *Modern Language Quarterly*, 35, 1974.
E. Speidel, " 'Aristotelian' and 'Non Aristotelian' Elements in Dürrenmatt's *Der Besuch der alten Dame*", in *German Life & Letters*, 28, 1974.
Roman S. Struc, "Sinn und Sinnlosigkeit des Opfers: Gotthelfs *Die schwarze Spinne* und Dürrenmatts *Der Besuch der alten Dame*", in *Proceedings, Pacific Northwest Conference on Foreign Languages*, 25, 1974.
Erna K. Neuse, "Das Rhetorische in Dürrenmatts *Der Besuch der alten Dame*: Zur Funktion des Dialogs im Drama", in *Seminar: A Journal of Germanic Studies*, 11, 1975.
Hugo Dittberner, "Dürrenmatt, der Geschichtenerzähler: Ein 50-Dollar-Missverständnis zum *Besuch der alten Dame*", in *Text und Kritik*, 50–51, 1976.
Manfred Durzak, "Die Travestie der Tragödie in Dürrenmatts *Der Besuch der alten Dame* und *Die Physiker*", in *Deutschunterricht*, vol.28 no.6, 1976.
Edward R. McDonald, "Friedrich Dürrenmatt's *The Visit:* Comedy or Tragedy? Avant-Garde or Traditional Theater?", in *Maske und Kothurn*, vol.23 no.2, 1977.
Alkis Kontos, "The Dialectics of Domination: An Interpretation of Friedrich Dürrenmatt's *The Visit*", in *Powers, Possessions and Freedom: Essays in Honour of C.B. Macpherson*, edited by Kontos, Toronto, 1979.
Mario Andreotti, "Die kollektivierte Figur: Dürrenmatts *Besuch der alten Dame* als moderner Text", in *Sprachkunst*, 15, 1984.

The Visit: Schauspielhaus, Zurich 1956 (first production)

Kirsten Arnvig, "Dialogtypen in Dürrenmatts *Der Besuch der alten Dame*", in *Text & Kontext*, 11, 1985.

William E. Gruber, "Comedy, Community, and the Anonymous Audience: Dürrenmatt's *Der Besuch der alten Dame*", in his *Comic Theaters: Studies in Performance and Audience Response*, Athens, Georgia, 1986.

Jamie Rankin, "Re-Visiting *Der Besuch der alten Dame*: Strategies for Interpretation and Interaction at the Intermediate Level", in *Unterrichtspraxis for the Teaching of German*, 22, 1989.

* * *

Claire Zachanassian, a 62-year-old multi-millionnairess, revisits her native Swiss town of Güllen. There, 45 years previously, she had become pregnant and, because the real father had denied his responsibility, she had been forced to leave the town in disgrace. While working as a whore in a Hamburg brothel she met her first husband, an oil and shipping magnate, from whom she inherited her wealth. Meanwhile the town of Güllen has fallen on hard times so the townsfolk await her arrival with particularly high hopes. They are not to be disappointed. She promises them a billion, but on one condition: the townsfolk must kill Alfred Ill, her former lover and father of the child she had borne. Slowly but surely Alfred's fellow Gülleners turn against him, as their standard of living, paid for on credit, rises and the necessity for meeting Claire's condition becomes unavoidable.

The German-speaking theatre of the post-war period is particularly indebted to the Swiss dramatists Friedrich Dürrenmatt and Max Frisch. They breathed new life into an institution which had been a victim of Hitler's ill-fated designs for revitalising the German national community. Indeed, it is possible to interpret *The Visit* itself as a parable about how an economically run-down society (such as Weimar Germany was in the early 1930's) is at the mercy of powerful leader-figures promising salvation and economic revival. Just as the Jews were sent to their slaughter as part of the bargain struck between Hitler and the Germans, so Ill falls victim to the deal made between Claire and his all too opportunistic fellow citizens.

Without doubt the play evokes historical associations of this kind. But it would be one-sided to emphasise parallels only to past epochs. As Kenneth Tynan observed after its first performance in Britain: "I seriously doubt whether any theatrical text more wickedly subversive of the Western way of life has ever been staged in London". In other words the play is about our own society, about the here and now. It tells us that in our pursuit of the good life, as defined by material possessions, leisure, and pleasure, we are ready to become the accomplices of the forces of evil. The play compels us, like few other modern dramas, to think in terms of our collective behaviour and our shared responsibilities.

Some believe that *The Visit*'s main achievement lies in the unmasking of a community (in Swiss German the town's name means "liquid manure"), and that it is the social collective which actually forms the main "character". Certainly directors have been at pains to reinforce this view. Thus one review of Oskar Wälterlin's Zurich premiere commented on how "the citizens of Güllen appear as a collective unit in sometimes extremely stylised arrangements", while of Peter Brook's New York production it was said that he "stages strongly choreographed ensemble scenes (partly with musical accompaniment)". Dürrenmatt undoubtedly encourages directors to think along these lines by having all of the large cast, with the exception of Claire and Alfred, characterised by their professions, status, or merely by numbers.

Claire Zachanassian's and Alfred Ill's individualised identities, on the other hand, place them apart from the anonymous collective and invite our interest and, at times, even pity. However calculating and *schadenfroh* Claire may appear, she has been made to suffer a great deal of emotional pain, especially at the hands of men. Used and betrayed by Ill, cast out from her native community, she was forced to turn to prostitution. So, when she states: "The world turned me into a whore and I'm turning it into a brothel", we may be shocked by the grotesque scale of her lust for revenge, but we do understand the rationale. Indeed, behind the rather macabre facade of a vengeful, super-powerful old lady, there is still visible the spirited young girl she once was, and her return to Güllen can also be seen as a search for this other (more human) identity.

Claire needs the counterweight of a male antagonist in order that she is seen in this light and not just as a mere catalyst for the community's metamorphosis. Her former lover, Alfred, is perfectly cast for this role. From his initial illusory belief in himself as the town's local hero by dint of his earlier liaison with Claire, through the chilling sense of his growing isolation in Güllen and the realisation of his inevitable doom to the admission of his guilt and the final acceptance of the consequences, Alfred Ill grows in tragic stature and imbues the play with a moral, even religious, significance. Ill reminds the audience, if not his fellow citizens who blindly conform to the dictates of the affluent society, that individual existence is about suffering, responsibility, and true self-awareness as well.

Perhaps in a paradoxical sense, this was also part of Claire's mission. On the one hand, she forces a community to show its true (anti-humanitarian) colours while also compelling one individual to reveal his essential humanity. Though this may make Dürrenmatt appear like a moralising evangelist, the play never thrusts didactic designs into the foreground. He tells a story, partly funny, partly serious, employs overtly colourful symbolism, integrates cabaret-style elements into the dramatic situations, juxtaposes lyrical passages with grotesquely comical ones, and parades before us a panoply of both surreal and very real human types.

—Anthony Waine

VLAST TMY "KOGOTOK UVAYAZ, VSEY PTICHKE PROPAST". See **THE POWER OF DARKNESS.**

THE VOICE OF THE TURTLE
by John Van Druten

First Publication: New York, 1944.
First Production: Morosco Theatre, New York, 8 December 1943.

* * *

Sally Middleton, 22-year-old unemployed actress, sublets a small flat in midtown Manhattan and rehearses "Juliet" with her friend Olive between engagements. She finds herself acting as stand-in for Olive over a wartime weekend with serviceman Bill Page. Sally is concerned about the label "promiscuous" after too many ill-fated love affairs, and only gradually succumbs to what both she and the jilted soldier hope will be a lasting romance.

English playwright John Van Druten marked his permanent move to the United States with this long-running comedy of manners which opened on Broadway in 1943 and ran for 1,557 performances, and which starred Margaret Sullivan and Elliot Nugent. It has since become a perennial favourite with "little theatre" companies and stands as Van Druten's most enduring original script.

Although this was not the first American play to feature illicit sex, it was perhaps the first to do so sympathetically, and it stood as a salutary antidote to more "wholesome" pictures of wartime romance, like Norman Krasna's *John Loves Mary* and Joseph Field's *The Doughgirls*. In its depiction of ingenuous female emancipation, it was a harbinger of such "sophisticated" American successes as *The Moon is Blue*, *The Seven-Year Itch*, and *Two for the Seesaw*, which consolidated the type of the off-beat single girl on her own in the big city. Van Druten later developed the characterisation in his adaptation of Christopher Isherwood's Sally Bowles in *I Am a Camera*.

His own Sally Middleton breaks fresh ground not only in her frank discussion of extra-marital sex but also in the fact that, in the third-act resolution, it is she, rather than the man, who initially favours an affair to the more binding attachment Page has in mind. "We must keep this gay", she warns him. And while her stance is later revealed to be self-protective, this reversal of conventional sexual assumptions without condemnation retains its boldness, despite the commonplace nature of casual sex in more recent American drama. Sally is given the option to have sex or not and to make it as serious as she wishes: privileges not granted by many male playwrights to women characters from the provinces. More frequently, feminist playwrights have had to claim these rights for themselves.

Van Druten's play also stands as a landmark among "two-character" plays, though, strictly speaking, it cheats with the appearance of Olive briefly in Acts I and III. The author described his use of the third character at length. It is to his credit as a craftsman that the small cast seems perfectly integral to his story rather than as a novelty in its own right. He is able to sustain the action, moreover, with virtual unity of time, unlike those plays which sustain a duologue over a matter of months (*Two for the Seesaw; The Owl and the Pussycat*) or years (*The Fourposter; Same Time, Next Year*).

This no doubt is the result of expert character delineation. Van Druten later identified as a handicap his inability to plot, but in this case at least it is a measure of sheer dramaturgy that he has only to remain with the basic situation to hold continually the audience's attention. He pays tribute to his schooling in the text itself when Sally describes how she and Olive resort to Stanislavskian character-building when rehearsing by "never playing a part as it is written". A standing joke in the play, this nonetheless highlights Van Druten's creation of Sally, whose innocence is filtered through several fascinating, "life-like" contradictions. Without a qualm for her virtue, she goes off to rehearse alone with a noted womaniser, neither childishly coy nor belligerent. Her attractiveness, too, is achieved without mannered hyperbole. Her "patter" runs to nothing more eccentric than saying she likes to "cuddle up with a salad" on her evenings in. Such lines are arresting but stop short of transforming her into a freak.

Van Druten always insisted on Sally's ordinariness, and her strength lies precisely in the fact that she is representative and fully-rounded at the same time. Unfortunately, the play as a whole pays a severe price. It remains a one-character portrait rather than the anatomy of a relationship, however timely the situation may be. Van Druten fully acknowledged this, too,

when he later said that Bill Page was conceptually no more than a "straight man". He is by way of being a blank Page without Sally, and it is a sorry commentary on Ronald Reagan's acting career that the former President could cite his portrayal of Page in the 1947 film version of the play as the only instance where he "got the girl".

—James MacDonald

VOLPONE; or, The Fox
by Ben Jonson

First Publication: London, 1607; with variants, in *Works*, 1616.
First Production: Globe Theatre, London, c.February–March 1606.

Editions

Volpone, edited by H.B. Wilkins, Oxford, 1906.
Volpone, edited by John D. Rea, New Haven, Connecticut, 1919.
Volpone, edited by Alvin B. Kernan, New Haven, Connecticut 1962 (Yale Ben Jonson).
Volpone, edited by David Cook, London, 1967.
Volpone, edited by Philip Brockbank, London, 1968 (New Mermaid Series).
Volpone, edited by John W. Creaser, London, 1978.
Volpone, in *Complete Plays of Ben Jonson, 3*, edited by G.A. Wilkes, Oxford, 1982.
Volpone, edited by R.B. Parker, Manchester, 1983 (Revels Plays).
Volpone, in *Ben Jonson: Selected Plays, 1*, edited by Johanna Procter, Cambridge, 1984.

Criticism
(For general works on the author, see *Playwrights* volume)

Books:

Jonas A. Barish (ed.), *"Volpone": A Casebook*, London, 1972.
Derek de Silva, *Jonson: Wit and the Moral Sense in "Volpone" and the Major Comedies*, 1972.
Harold Bloom (ed.), *Ben Jonson's "Volpone; or, The Fox"*, New York, 1988 (Modern Critical Interpretations).

Articles:

R.G. Noyes, "'Volpone': The Evolution of a Nickname", in *Harvard Studies and Notes in Philology*, 16, 1934.
Richard H. Perkinson, "*Volpone* and the Reputation of Venetian Justice", in *Modern Language Review*, 35, 1940.
Ralph Nash, "The Comic Intent of *Volpone*", in *Studies in Philology*, 44, 1947.
Gloria E. Newton, "Dramatic Imagery in *Volpone*", in *Manitoba Arts Review*, 8, 1952.
Jonas A. Barish, "The Double Plot in *Volpone*", in *Modern Philology*, 51, 1953.
John S. Weld, "Christian Comedy: *Volpone*", in *Studies in Philology*, 51, 1954.
S.L. Goldberg, "Folly into Crime: The Catastrophe of *Volpone*", in *Modern Language Quarterly*, 20, 1959.

Annabelle Cloudsley, "*Volpone* in Germany", in *Twentieth Century*, 168, 1960.

Rainer Pineas, "The Morality of Vice in *Volpone*", in *Discourse*, 5, 1961–62.

P.H. Davison, "*Volpone* and the Old Comedy", in *Modern Language Quarterly*, 24, 1963.

Tinsley Helton, "Theme as a Shaping Factor in *Volpone* and *The Alchemist*", in *English Review*, 13, 1963.

Alan C. Dessen, "*Volpone* and the Late Morality Tradition", in *Modern Language Quarterly*, 25, 1964.

Judd Arnold, "The Double Plot in *Volpone*: A Note on Jonsonian Dramatic Structure", in *Seventeenth-Century News*, 23, 1965.

Malcolm H. South, "Animal Imagery in *Volpone*", in *Tennessee Studies in Literature*, 10, 1965.

Ian Donaldson, "Jonson's Tortoise", in *Review of English Studies*, 19, 1968.

C.J. Gianakaris, "Identifying Ethical Values in *Volpone*", in *Huntington Library Quarterly*, 32, 1968.

Harriet Hawkins, "Folly, Incurable Disease, and *Volpone*", in *Studies in English Literature 1500–1900*, 8, 1968.

William Empson, "*Volpone*", in *Hudson Review*, 21, 1968–69.

Alexander Leggatt, "The Suicide of Volpone", in *University of Toronto Quarterly*, 39, 1969.

Dorothy E. Litt, "Unity of Theme in *Volpone*", in *Bulletin of the New York Public Library*, 73, 1969.

Douglas Duncan, "Audience Manipulation in *Volpone*", in *Wascana Review*, 5, 1970.

Charles A. Hallett, "The Satanic Nature of Volpone", in *Philological Quarterly*, 49, 1970.

Pierre Han, "'Taberine' in Ben Jonson's *Volpone*", in *Seventeenth-Century News*, 28, 1970.

Ian Donaldson, "*Volpone*: Quicke and Dead", in *Essays in Criticism*, 21, 1971.

Charles A. Hallett, "Jonson's Celia: A Reinterpretation of *Volpone*", in *Studies in Philology*, 68, 1971.

Frank N. Clary Jr., "The 'Vol' and the 'Pone': A Reconsideration of Jonson's *Volpone*", in *English Language Notes*, 10, 1972.

Gerard H. Cox III, "Celia, Bonario, and Jonson's Indebtedness to the Medieval Cycles", in *Études anglaises*, 25, 1972.

Ian Donaldson, "*Volpone*" in *Essays in Criticism*, 22, 1972.

W. Speed Hill, "Biography, Autobiography, and *Volpone*", in *Studies in English Literature*, 12, 1972.

James Tulip, "Comedy as Equivocation: An Approach to the Reference of *Volpone*", in *Southern Review*, 5, 1972.

L.A. Beaurline, "Volpone and the Power of Gorgeous Speech", in *Studies in the Literary Imagination*, 6, 1973.

J.V. Crewe, "Death in Venice: A Study of *Othello* and *Volpone*", in *University of Cape Town Studies in English*, 4, 1973.

David McPherson, "Rough Beast into Tame Fox: The Adaptations of *Volpone*", in *Studies in the Literary Imagination*, 6, 1973.

Richard A. Dutton, "*Volpone* and *The Alchemist*: A Comparison in Satiric Techniques", in *Renaissance and Modern Studies*, 18, 1974.

C.J. Gianakaris, "Jonson's Use of *Avocatori* in *Volpone*", in *English Language Notes*, 12, 1974.

George A.E. Parfitt, "Notes on the Classical Borrowings in *Volpone*", in *English Studies*, 55, 1974.

Robert Westcott, "Volpone? Or the Fox?", in *Critical Review*, 17, 1974.

Mark A. Anderson, "Structure and Response in *Volpone*", in *Renaissance and Modern Studies*, 19, 1975.

John Creaser, "*Volpone*: The Mortifying of the Fox", in *Essays in Criticism*, 25, 1975.

John Creaser, "Vindication of Sir Politic Would-Be", in *English Studies*, 25, 1975.

John Creaser, "The Popularity of Jonson's Tortoise", in *Review of English Studies*, 57, 1976.

Donald Gertmenian, "Volpone's Mortification", in *Essays in Criticism*, 26, 1976.

Stephen J. Greenblatt, "The False Ending in *Volpone*", in *Journal of English and Germanic Philology*, 75, 1976.

R.B. Parker, "*Volpone* and *Reynard the Fox*", in *Renaissance Drama*, 1976.

R.B. Parker, "Wolfit's Fox: An Interpretation of *Volpone*", in *University of Toronto Quarterly*, 45, 1976.

Kenneth Friedenreich, "*Volpone* and the *Confessio Amantis*", in *South Central Bulletin*, 37, 1977.

Donald Gertmenian, "Comic Experience in *Volpone* and *The Alchemist*", in *Studies in English Literature 1500–1900*, 17, 1977.

A.K. Nardo, "The Transmigration of Folly: Volpone's Innocent Grotesques", in *English Studies*, 58, 1977.

George A.E. Parfitt, "*Volpone*", in *Essays in Criticism*, 21, 1977.

Ralph A. Cohen, "The Setting of *Volpone*", in *Renaissance Papers*, 1978.

Ronald Broude, "Volpone and the Triumph of Truth: Some Antecedents and Analogues of the Main Plot in *Volpone*", in *Studies in Philology*, 77, 1980.

Carol A. Carr, "Volpone and Mosca: Two Types of Roguery", in *College Literature*, 8, 1981.

Ben Hardman, "The Magnifico and the Unmoved Mover: The Nature of Power in *Volpone*", in *Selected Papers from the West Virginia Shakespeare and Renaissance Association*, 6, 1981.

B.A. Park, "*Volpone* and Old Comedy", in *English Language Notes*, 19, 1981.

James A. Riddel, "*Volpone's* Fare", in *Studies in English Literature 1500–1900*, 21, 1981.

Yumiko Yamada, "*Volpone* and *The Devil is an Ass*: Damnation and Salvation Through Metamorphoses", in *Studies in English Literature* (Tokyo), 58, 1981.

Martin R. Orkin, "Languages of Deception in *Volpone*", in *Theoria*, 59, 1982.

R.E.R. Madelaine, "Parasites and 'Politicians': Some Comic Stage Images in *Volpone*", in *AUMLA Journal*, 58, 1982.

John Sweeney, "*Volpone* and the Theater of Self-Interest", in *English Literature Review*, 12, 1982.

Myles Hurd, "Between Crime and Punishment in Jonson's *Volpone*", in *College Literature*, 10, 1983.

Ronald St. Pierre, "'So Rare a Musique Out of Discordes?': Chaos and Order in Ben Jonson's *Volpone*", in *Shoin Literary Review*, 17, 1983.

Anne Burley, "The Influence of Ben Jonson's First Two Masques on the Dramatic Environment of *Volpone*", in *Selected Papers of the West Virginia Shakespeare and Renaissance Association*, 9, 1984.

Don Beecher, "The Progress of Trickster in Ben Jonson's *Volpone*", in *Cahiers études*, 27, 1985.

William W.E. Slights, "The Play of Conspiracies in *Volpone*", in *Texas Studies in Literature and Language*, 27, 1985.

David M. Bergeron, "'Lend Me Your Dwarf': Romance in *Volpone*", in *Medieval and Renaissance Drama in England*, 3, 1986.

Frances Dolan, "'We Must Here be Fixed?': Discovering a Self Behind the Mask in *Volpone*", in *Iowa State Journal of Research*, 60, 1986.

Geraldo U. de Sousa, "Boundaries of Genre in Ben Jonson's *Volpone* and *The Alchemist*", in *Essays in Theatre*, 4, 1986.

Earl V. Bryant, "Jonson's Corvino and the Scriptural Pearl

Merchant", in *American Benedictine Review*, 38, 1987.
Robert C. Evans, "Thomas Sutton: Ben Jonson's Volpone?", in *Philological Quarterly*, 68, 1989.

*   *   *

Volpone is an "old magnifico" and "brave clarissimo" (grandee) of Venice. He has no heir to whom to leave his fortune and seems to allow himself to be prey to those who, by lavishing gifts upon him, would persuade him to leave his wealth to them (a transference to the early-17th century of the Roman practice of *captatio*). But Volpone, aided by his parasite, Mosca (fly), plots to deceive them out of their wealth instead. Voltore (vulture), a lawyer, Corbaccio (carrion crow), an old miser himself near to death, and Corvino (raven), a rich, foolish merchant, visit and re-visit Volpone in turn, offering gift upon gift. Corvino, a fiercely jealous husband, is even persuaded to offer his "fair and proper wife" for Volpone's enjoyment; she is only rescued at the last—melodramatic—moment by Corbaccio's honest son, the aptly-named Bonario.

Volpone is also visited (and tormented) by Lady Politic-Would-Be, a woman with an "everlasting voice" who is obsessed by fashion. Her husband, Sir Politic (Sir Pol—parrot), is a foolish English knight who pretends to more wit than he possesses. He keeps a diary crammed with his foolish projects and tells a young and sensible English visitor, Peregrine (hawk), that he knows how to sell Venice to the Turks. In a series of actions (rather than a plot), each character seeking Volpone's riches is tricked out of his own wealth and Sir and Lady Politic are shamed. However, in tricking others, Volpone overreaches himself. He fakes his own death and is outwitted by Mosca. The principal victims then make common cause and though each suffers public ignominy, Volpone is imprisoned and has all his goods confiscated to the benefit of a hospital for the incurable. Mosca, not being a gentleman, is even more savagely treated; he is whipped and sentenced to a life in the galleys.

Jonson wrote at a time when it seemed to some that "old values" were being replaced by acquisitiveness and entrepreneurialism. The activities of merchant venturers, the growth of monopolies, legalisation of usury (so that capital might be raised to finance commerce) had aspects that were beneficial to society but also characteristics to be deplored. This shift interested Jonson, and his comedy is marked by repugnance at man's voraciousness. This is seen fiercely and effectively in *Volpone* and *The Alchemist*, the former the more harshly because of the ultimate fate of Volpone and Mosca. Acquisitiveness is shown by Jonson to debase man, and *Volpone* makes much use of the symbolic crossing of the line that divides man from beast. Not only are so many of the characters given names that point to their beastliness (and contrast Bonario and Celia: names that evokes goodness and heavenliness)—but the blurring of man's natural functions is epitomised in Volpone's servants: Nano, the dwarf; Castrone, the eunuch; and Andogyno, the hermaphrodite. When these three present their anti-masque we should feel a sense of revulsion that should prime us to the true nature of the characters in the principal actions. Whether this works is another matter. It is perhaps too erudite a device, a fault to which Jonson was prone, as his notes to some of his masques demonstrate. Nevertheless, we are being warned that what may make us laugh may be "no laughing matter". To Jonson, man too readily debases himself, sinks to the bestial, and behaves like a bird of prey. This is particularly so when he performs the "unnatural act" of making money breed money: procreation is for the animate not the inanimate.

The key to what Jonson is about in *Volpone* is provided by an understanding of its genre. Genre can be dismissed as mere pigeon-holing, but for certain plays it provides a vital clue to their nature. Northrop Frye regarded *Volpone* as exceptional in being a kind of comic imitation of a tragedy, with the point of Volpone's *hubris* carefully marked (*The Anatomy of Criticism*). Jonson himself described his *Every Man Out of His Humour* as "somewhat like *Vetus Comoedia*" (Old Comedy) and in his address to the reader of *Poetaster* he links "the salt of the old comedy", "bold satire", "scalding rage", and Aristophanes. Here Jonson gives clues to *Volpone's* genre. It was to be distinguished from "New" or "Romantic Comedy" (*Twelfth Night, As You Like It*); it was a kind of comedy that gave effect to Puttenham's 1589 view that comedy was "for the good amendment of man by discipline and example".

The public shaming of Voltore, Corvino, and Corbaccio, and the losses they suffer, are punishment enough for them but Jonson gives his play an added twist. Whereas for most of the play, Volpone and Mosca exploit and expose others, Volpone overreaches himself and is exploited by his parasite. Volpone tempts Providence with his imposture of a lover and then of death. He survives his attempt to seduce Celia, and it is her rescuer, Bonario, whom we are tempted to find ridiculous when, leaping from his hiding place, he cries out, "Forbear, foul ravisher! libidinous swine!/ Free the forc'd lady, or thou diest, imposter". Our laughter here is that which is "a fault in Comedy" for we become party to Volpone's malpractice. The significant word here is "imposter"; in Greek this is *alazon*, and the overreaching of the *alazon*, *alazoneia*, is directly equatable with the hubris of the tragic hero. When Volpone takes on the imposture of death, he shifts fatally from exposer of the follies of others to imposter. He is then at Mosca's mercy and it is his turn to be exposed.

Old Comedy does not end in feasting and marriage but in dismissal and punishment. For all that, and for all its didacticism, it is also very funny, actions are often hilarious (Volpone peeping over the screen), and the language is brilliantly witty. The opening speech is not unlike that in Marlowe's *Dr. Faustus* in that the audience, which is being primed to perceive the truth, can easily be seduced into accepting Volpone's point of view. The confusion of the material and the sacred (like that of man with beast) is expertly carried through in the language. Note the blasphemy in "thou son of Sol" (gold) being kissed in adoration as if it were a religious relic; in "Riches, the dumb god, that giv'st all men tongues" as if gold were Pentecostal fire; and in gold equated with "the price of souls"; above all, in "hell, with thee to boot,/ Is made worth heaven". Volpone's rhetoric, like that of Faustus, may win us over initially, but both are shown from the first to be flawed. Such use of language is not restricted to Volpone. Corvino, for example, as he tries to make Celia yield to Volpone, not only disgusts us by the way he abuses his wife (so that allowing the decrepit Volpone to paw her is no different from handling a commodity—"What is my gold/ The worse for touching, clothes for being look'd on") but describes her prostitution in terms which should shock even a secular age: as "a pious work", "mere charity"; she will be martyred for not acquiescing; and Celia "mayest redeem all yet".

—Peter Davison

VON MORGENS BIS MITTERNACHTS. See **FROM MORNING TO MIDNIGHT.**

VOR SONNENAUFGANG.   See **BEFORE DAWN.**

THE VOYSEY INHERITANCE
by Harley Granville-Barker

First Publication: London, 1909; revised edition, 1938.
First Production: (Royal) Court Theatre, London, 7 November 1905.

Criticism
(For general works on the author, see *Playwrights* volume)

Articles:
Sheila Stowell, " 'A quaint and comical dismay': The Dramatic Strategies of Granville Barker's *The Voysey Inheritance*", in *Essays in Theatre*, 5, 1987.

*   *   *

Edward Voysey, a conscience-ridden liberal (or Fabian socialist) and junior partner to a prosperous and respected solicitor, has the true state of the firm's affairs revealed to him by his father: their finances and the comfort of the Voysey family depend upon speculation with clients' trust funds. Family life at the Chislehurst home is presented as background to Edward's reluctant decision to stay with the firm, on condition that an attempt is made quietly to put things right. Edward loses his second chance of freedom in Act III when, after old Mr. Voysey's funeral, he breaks the news to the family that there is no money to pay the bequests in his father's will, only to have them persuade him to carry on as before; the more enlightened argument of Alice, whom he loves, that there is no useful alternative, ensures his capitulation. At the

office, having dealt with the conniving clerk, Peacey, he is confronted by the severest threat of exposure when Voysey's old friend, George Booth, decides to withdraw all his business from the firm. Over Christmas at Chislehurst, George Booth and the rector lay down harsh conditions for not prosecuting: Edward is to restore their lost assets first. As mitigation of what may be a life-sentence to his hated office desk, he has the prospect of a marriage with Alice.

This is Granville Barker's most immediately accessible play. It was written specially for the programme of new plays he put on at the Court Theatre, with J. E. Vedrenne as his business manager, to show the quality of work a national theatre might offer, and it proposes questions of national interest. The Voyseys represent the prosperous English middle class at the end of the Victorian period. The plot is a comic parable of capitalist economics sustained by the methods of the confidence trickster. Edward is the naïve man of goodwill whose eyes are opened to the realities of a system with which a largely parasitic society conspires. His attempt to live honestly in a corrupt world is not easy to distinguish from unresisting participation.

Old Mr. Voysey's children are a disappointment to him. He thinks Edward weak, but there seems little behind his own irritating, bullying, and opinionated manner; Hugh, the self-doubting artist, cannot make a living from his work; Honor, the eldest daughter, is taken for granted, an unpaid servant-companion, used up in domestic duties. The youngest daughter, Ethel, spoilt and sprightly, dies with the child she conceives, in the course of the play (though only a manner of speaking about her conveys the fact). The third generation is limited to Booth's two children. The 1905 text of the play indicates that the family mirrors a society in decline from high imperialism. The author's rewriting of Hugh's diatribe against an empire that kills creativity, and cannot even keep its streets clean, makes the point more forcibly yet, ironically, with considerable exhilaration.

Irony pervades the play. It is there in the naming of Honor

The Voysey Inheritance: Kingsway Theatre, London, 1912

and, on a larger scale, in the essentially comic pattern of successive anti-climaxes, in which a crash is threatened but does not occur, leaving the play marking time on the spot—an anti-drama to match an anti-hero. It works through the different methods of presenting the two central characters and the ambiguous division of sympathies they evoke. Edward is the moral centre of the dramatic structure and the focus of empathy, too. His father is much more charismatic and genial, attracting admiration, amusement, and curiosity. His presence haunts the play after his death, provoking interpretation and reinterpretation, teasing the imagination to the end and graspable only by affection. He presents himself histrionically, but cannot be played only rhetorically, for the mask may be true and there is certainly a complex human being behind it. Edward tries to explain to George Booth that his father could both love him and rob him because he did not value money in itself. That Edward has come to understand this is a measure of his own growth; but it is not enough to suppress the unspoken question that hovers over the contrasted characters: whether the old adventurer's cavalier mastery of the system was not more life-enhancing than Edward's scrupulously responsible slavery to it.

The commentary, loosely called "stage directions", included in the published text was intended, on the advice of Bernard Shaw and following the example of his practice, to make the play easily readable for a public accustomed to reading novels. The amount of realistic detail in the play proper, and the constant feeding in of fresh scraps of information, not always easy to reconcile with what is already known about characters or the history of the family, creates a sense of richness and depth more frequently seen in the realistic novel than in drama. The life of the Voyseys seems to sprawl outside the artistic frame. A notable example of this *trompe-l'oeil* effect is the brief introduction of the disinherited eldest son, Trenchard, the absence of any development from it, and the tantalisingly little we are told about his quarrel with his father. Trenchard seems as strong a character as old Voysey was, and the dramatist has certainly introduced him in order to reject him as the kind of hero he wants for his play. If the making of this point adds another possible indication of old Voysey's psychological make-up which may help an actor give to his portrait the kaleidoscopic quality of actual personality, that is so much artistic gain.

Barker had himself begun life as an actor and went on to become a leading director. Although he did not visit Russia to observe Stanislavsky at work until 1914, he had long been using similar methods, encouraging his actors to build up the inner lives of their roles to give richness and truth to naturalistic drama and, later, to Shakespeare's plays. Working surrounded by a commercial theatre in which star performance was all, and the rest of the cast was expected merely to support it, he set out to build up a company that excelled in ensemble work. In *The Voysey Inheritance* he provided for them an opportunity to show what they could do, reliant as the play is on skilled and creative interpretation from every player, so that a complex group portrait emerges: it is a drama of *milieu*.

The ending is disappointingly trite, even sentimental. Alice's cool blandness is not enough. "If I had developed her more", the author wrote to his German translator, "it would have been in the direction of making her considerably more like old Voysey in unscrupulousness". A production in which the actress took this hint to heart would give the play a whole new dimension.

—Margery Morgan

THE VULTURES (Les Corbeaux)
by Henry Becque

First Publication: Paris, 1882.
First Production: Comédie-Française, Paris, 14 September 1882.

Editions
Les Corbeaux, edited by I. Lockerbie, London, 1962.

Translations
The Crows, translated by Benedict Papot, in *The Drama*, 5 February 1912.
The Vultures, in *The Vultures; The Woman of Paris; The Merry-go-Round*, translated by Freeman Tilden, New York, 1913.
The Scavengers, translated by David H. Walker, Blairgowrie, Scotland, 1986.

Criticism
(For general works on the author, see *Playwrights* volume)

Articles:
C. Wooton, "*The Vultures*: Becque's Realistic Comedy of Manners", in *Modern Drama*, vol.4 no.1, 1961–62.
Norman Araujo, "The Role of Death in Becque's *Les Corbeaux*", in *Revue des langues vivantes*, 36, 1970.
Philippe Chardin, "Quelques problèmes idéologiques posés par *Les Corbeaux* d'Henry Becque", in *Cahiers naturalistes*, 53, 1979.
René Saurel, "Corbeaux et tourterelles: De la belle ouvrage", in *Temps modernes*, 434, 1982.
Philippe Senart, "Henry Becque: *Les Corbeaux*", in *Revue des deux mondes*, 10, 1982.
Norman Arujo, "The Language of Business and the Business of Language in Becque's *Les Corbeaux*", in *French Review*, 63, 1989.

*   *   *

M. Vigneron manages a small factory which has enabled him to raise himself and his family—wife, son, and three daughters—from modest beginnings to the brink of wealth and financial security. With some misgivings he has agreed a marriage contract between his youngest daughter and the penniless son of a widow with aristocratic pretensions. In Act I the Vignerons are preparing a dinner to mark the occasion. As the guests are arriving it is announced that M. Vigneron has suffered a stroke and died. The following three acts trace the inexorable expropriation of the wealth of Mme. Vigneron and her daughters by M. Vigneron's predatory business associates, chiefly his partner Teissier, an elderly banker, and Bourdon, the lawyer. The women are forced to leave their home and in the final resort the middle daughter, the only one who has shown any capacity to cope with the machinations of the businessmen, decides to accept an offer of marriage from Teissier in order to spare her family further misery.

On the basis of fairly commonplace observations about the rapacity and lack of scruples that characterized 19th-century commerce, Henry Becque's play scorns the sentimentality and facile moralising that were the standard treatments by much French theatre of the era. At the same time it ignores the customary devices of the well-made play, eschewing gratuitously witty dialogue and complex manipulation of plot. With one or two exceptions, the dialogue is sober, faithful to everyday speech, accurately reflecting the standing and temperament of the characters; but in the playing it offers insights into the unspoken tensions between victims and scavengers and among the vultures themselves as they jostle for the pickings. In this respect the play explores territory that was to become familiar as Ibsen's work began to have an impact. Moreover, there are premonitions of Chekhov in the work's manipulation of mood rather than event. One daughter is pursued then abandoned by a lecherous music-teacher; a second is cajoled and destroyed by the ruthless mother of her husband-to-be who breaks off the marriage plans when the Vigneron fortune is revealed as inadequate; the third resists, then resolves to accommodate the attentions of the wily Teissier: these dramas are enacted in a pattern of restrained but intense two-handed scenes interspersed with set-pieces in which the women's interests are brushed aside as the scavengers squabble among themselves under the very noses of their victims. The dramatic texture is completed by "choral" scenes in which the women, left alone, muse wearily over their increasingly inescapable fate.

The strong narrative line sustaining this modulation of moods brings no unexpected developments: on the contrary, the grip it exerts on the spectator derives from the hopelessness of the women's plight as they vainly try one avenue of escape after another. In this respect the play possesses a classical simplicity of line, its impact being due to the way Becque ruthlessly prunes inessentials. After the garish opulence and densely peopled stage of the opening act—a measure of Vigneron's standing as one who earns money but has not yet acquired respectable substance—Becque excludes the peripheral hangers-on, consigns the son to a military posting, drops one of the servants, paring down the household to its desolate, claustrophobic core of women at bay before the encroaching forces of greed.

It is not altogether surprising that the play's first reviewers found it a lugubrious piece. Affected by its bleak portrayal of human nature, many put this down to the work's supposed naturalistic ambitions, though in fact it was written in the early 1870's, before the resounding polemical campaigns of Zola and quite independently of any concerted artistic movement. What best characterizes the play is its unnerving objectivity,

the sense it conveys of a detached, controlling intelligence presiding over the proceedings. And, despite the bitter irony with which it is suffused, the play is extremely funny. The Chekhovian device of comedy in tears is adumbrated in Act II as Mme. Vigneron's thrice-repeated lamentations on her husband's death are greeted at every turn by an embarrassed silence and an inconsequential rejoinder. Not for nothing did the play appeal to Alan Ayckbourn, a connoisseur of black comedy, who adapted it for the Stephen Joseph Theatre, Scarborough, in 1989. Becque extracts telling comedy from the portrayal of rogues and scoundrels so wrapped up in their devious schemes and the pursuit of their selfish interests that their responses to the women's distress are incongruous and inappropriate. In all of this, Becque's play can be seen as a precursor of the tragi-comic mode which has been so important in modern drama. While clearly concerned to highlight the vulnerability of women whom society and convention have kept apart from the workings of the world, Becque does not explicitly take sides. He is as severe on the folly of the victims as he is on the scheming of the scoundrels.

The play was so far in advance of its time that it had to wait some seven years before it found a director willing to take it on. Even then, certain features offended against the canons of good taste and had to be cut. The young Gaston's Act I party-piece, poking fun at his father just before the announcement of the latter's death, was declared unseemly. The final scene in which Teissier, as the new head of the household, oversees the dismissal of a crooked creditor was deemed to be redundant after the announcement of his marriage to Mlle. Vigneron—a move conventional conclusion. Hence the first full production which the play received can be said to be not the première at the Comédie-Française but a revival in 1897 at the Odéon in Paris, which consecrated it as the masterpiece of French dramatic realism.

—David H. Walker

WAITING FOR GODOT (En Attendant Godot)
by Samuel Beckett

First Publication: As *En Attendant Godot* [in French], Paris, 1952; as *Waiting for Godot*, London, 1955.
First Production: As *En Attendant Godot*, Théâtre de Babylone, Paris, 15 January 1953; as *Waiting for Godot*, Arts Theatre Club, London, 3 August 1955.

Criticism
(For general works on the author, see *Playwrights* volume)

Books:
Ruby Cohn (ed), *"Waiting for Godot": A Casebook*, New York, 1967, revised edition, London, 1987.
Dan O. Via, *Samuel Beckett's "Waiting for Godot"*, New York, 1968.
Bernard Lalande, *"En Attendant Godot": Analyse critique*, Paris, 1970.
Ursula Dreysse (ed), *Materialien zu Samuel Becketts "Warten auf Godot"*, Frankfurt, 1973.
Fränzi Maierhöfer, *Samuel Beckett, "Warten auf Godot": Interpretation*, Munich, 1973.
Maria C. Coco Davani, *Godot: Il crack del codice*, Palermo, 1977.
Bert O. States, *The Shape of Paradox: An Essay on "Waiting for Godot"*, Berkeley, California, 1978.
Hartmut Engelhardt and Dieter Mettler (eds), *Materialien zu Samuel Becketts "Warten auf Godot", II*, Frankfurt, 1979.
Frederick A. Busi, *The Transformation of Godot*, Lexington, Kentucky, 1980.
J.P. Little, *"En attendant Godot" and "Fin de partie"*, London, 1981.
K. Alfons Knauth, *Invarianz und Variabilität literarischer Texte: Baudelaires "Spleen IV" und Becketts "En Attendant Godot"*, Amsterdam, 1981.
Harold Bloom (ed), *"Waiting for Godot": Modern Critical Views*, New York, 1987.
Lawrence Graver, *Samuel Beckett: "Waiting for Godot"*, Cambridge, 1989.
Thomas Cousineau, *"Waiting for Godot": Form in Movement*, Boston, 1990.
Katharine Worth, *"Waiting for Godot" and "Happy Days"*, London, 1990 (Text and Performance Series).

Articles:
Bernard Dort, "*En Attendant Godot*, pièce de Samuel Beckett", in *Les Temps modernes*, 8, 1953.
Edith Kern, "Drama Stripped for Inaction: Beckett's *Godot*", in *Yale French Studies*, 14, 1954–55.

Daniel Chaucer, "*Waiting for Godot*", in *Shenandoah*, 1955.
Jeremy Beckett, "Compte rendu de *Waiting for Godot*", in *Meanjin*, 15, 1956.
Alan Levy, "The Long Wait for Godot", in *Theatre Arts*, 40, 1956.
Ronald Gray, "*Waiting for Godot*: A Christian Approach", in *Listener*, 57, 1957.
Charles S. McCoy, "*Waiting for Godot:* A Biblical Appraisal", in *Religion in Life*, 28, 1959.
R. Champigny, "Interprétation d'*En Attendant Godot*", in *Publications of the Modern Language Association [PMLA]*, 75, 1960.
Ruby Cohn, "Waiting is All", in *Modern Drama*, 3, 1960.
C. Chadwick, "*Waiting for Godot*: A Logical Approach", in *Symposium*, 14, 1960.
Ethelbert Flood, "A Reading of Beckett's *Godot*", in *Culture*, 12, 1961.
Jerome Ashmore, "Philosophical Aspects of *Godot*", in *Symposium*, 16, 1962.
Harry L. Buther, "Balzac and Godeau, Beckett and Godot: A Curious Parallel", in *Romance Notes*, 3, 1962.
Bernard F. Dukore, "Gogo, Didi and the Absent Godot", in *Drama Survey*, 1, 1962.
Bernard F. Dukore, "Controversy: A Non-Interpretation of *Godot*", in *Drama Survey*, 3, 1963.
S.A. Rhodes, "From Godeau to Godot", in *French Review*, 36, 1963.
Robert S. Cohen, "Parallels and the Possibility of Influence Between Simone Weill's *Waiting for God* and Samuel Beckett's *Waiting for Godot*", in *Modern Drama*, 6, 1964.
Ruby Cohn, "The Absurdly Absurd: Avators of Godot", in *Comparative Literature Studies*, 2, 1965.
Curtis M. Brooks, "The Mythic Pattern in *Waiting for Godot*", in *Modern Drama*, 9, 1966.
Gábor Mihályi, "Beckett's *Godot* and the Myth of Alienation", in *Modern Drama*, 9, 1966.
Anselm Atkins, "Lucky's Speech in Beckett's *Waiting for Godot:* A Punctuated Sense-Line Arrangement", in *Educational Theatre Journal*, 19, 1967.
V.A. Kolve, "Religious Language in *Waiting for Godot*", in *Centennial Review*, 11, 1967.
Karl Schwarz, "Die Zeitproblematik in Samuel Becketts *En Attendant Godot*", in *Neueren Sprachen*, 66, 1967.
Dennis Douglas, "The Drama of Evasion in *Waiting for Godot*", in *Komos*, 1, 1968.
Konrad Schoell, "The Chain and the Circle: A Structural Comparison of *Waiting for Godot* and *Endgame*", in *Modern Drama*, 11, 1968.
Hélène Webner, "*Waiting for Godot* and the New Theology", in *Renascence*, 21, 1968.
Bernard F. Dukore, "The *Other* Pair in *Waiting for Godot*", in *Drama Survey*, 7, 1968–69.

Franz Blaha, "Jack Gelbers *The Connection* und Samuel Becketts *Waiting for Godot:* Eine vergleichende Studie zum Theater des Absurden in Europa und den U.S.A.", in *Moderne Sprachen*, vol.13 no.1, 1969.

Roger Bodart, "*En Attendant Godot*", in *Bulletin de l'Académie Royale de Langue et Littérature Françaises*, 47, 1969.

Robert R. Findlay, "A Confrontation in Waiting: *Godot* and the Wakefield Play", in *Renascence*, 21, 1969.

Betty de Wet, "*Waiting for Godot* by Samuel Beckett", in *Unisa English Studies*, vol.2 no.2, 1969.

Errol Durbach, "The Formal Pattern of *Waiting for Godot*", in *English Studies in Africa*, 13, 1970.

Horst Breuer, "Ordnung und Chaos in Luckys 'Think': Zu Samuel Becketts *Warten auf Godot*", in *Germanisch-Romanische Monatsschrift*, 21, 1971.

Yves Bridel, "Sur le temps et l'espace dans le théâtre de S. Beckett: *En attendant Godot—Oh les beaux jours*", in *Études et lettres*, vol.6 no.2, 1973.

Ishrat Lindblad, "Towards Understanding 'Pozzo'", in *Tidskrift för litteraturvetenskap*, 3, 1973–74.

Isabel García Manzano, "*En Attendant Godot:* communication ou incommunication? Une étude du language de Beckett", in *Estudios escénicos*, 20, 1974.

Louisa Jones, "Narrative Salvation in *Waiting for Godot*", in *Modern Drama*, 17, 1974.

Stephani P. Smith, "Between Pozzo and Godot: Existence as Dilemma", in *French Review*, 47, 1974.

Walter D. Asmus, "Beckett Directs *Godot*", in *Theatre Quarterly*, 19, 1975.

K. Alfons Knauth, "Luckys und Bonaventuras unglückliche Weltansichten: Ein Vergleich von Becketts *En attendant Godot* mit den Nachtwachen von Bonaventura", in *Romanistisches Jahrbuch*, 26, 1975.

Giuseppina Restivo, "'Pozzo! Does that name mean nothing to you?'", in *Paragone*, 306, 1975.

H.L. Sutcliffe, "Maeterlinck's *Les Aveugles* and Beckett's *En Attendant Godot*", in *Essays in French Literature*, 12, 1975.

George Watson, "Beckett's *Waiting for Godot:* A Reappraisal", in *Maynooth Review*, vol.1 no.1, 1975.

Axel Kruse, "Tragicomedy and Tragic Burlesque: *Waiting for Godot* and *Rosencrantz and Guildenstern Are Dead*", in *Sydney Studies in English*, 1, 1975–76.

Rolf Breuer, "The Solution as Problem: Beckett's *Waiting for Godot*", in *Modern Drama*, 19, 1976.

Jacques Le Marinel, "Le Thème du clochard dans *En attendant Godot* et dans *Le Gardien*", in *Revue d'histoire du théâtre*, 28, 1976.

Ishrat Lindblad, "*Waiting for Godot:* Translation or Revision?", in *Studia Neophilologica*, 48, 1976.

Robert J. Nelson, "Three Orders in *En Attendant Godot* and *Fin de partie*: A Pascalian Interpretation of Beckett", in *French Forum*, 1, 1976.

Anna Hargreaves, "Five Themes in *Waiting for Godot*", in *Studia Romanica et Anglica Zagrabiensia*, 44, 1977.

George Martin, "'Pozzo and Lucky': A Key to *Godot*", in *American Benedictine Review*, 28, 1977.

Henning Mehnert, "Samuel Becketts Neuinszenierung als Deutungshilfe für *En Attendant Godot*", in *Archiv*, 214, 1977.

Hersh Zeifman, "The Alterable Whey of Words: The Texts of *Waiting for Godot*", in *Educational Theatre Journal*, 29, 1977.

Michael B. Kline, "*Waiting for Godot* as Entropic Myth", in *Michigan Academician*, 10, 1978.

Dina Sherzer, "De-Construction in *Waiting for Godot*", in *The Reversible World: Symbolic Inversion in Art and Society*, edited by Barbara A. Babcock, Ithaca, New York, 1978.

Cedric Watts, "The Ambushes of Beckett's *Waiting for Godot:* A Lecture in a Series on Tragedy", in *Kwartalnik Neofilologiczny*, 25, 1978.

Lewis Elton, "On a Possible Source of *En Attendant Godot*", in *Quinquereme*, 2, 1979.

Martha O'Nan, "Names in Samuel Beckett's *Waiting for Godot*", in *Literary Onomastic Studies*, 6, 1979.

Daniela Roventa, "Le fonctionnement du dialogue dans le théâtre de l'absurde: Beckett *En attendant Godot*", in *Revue roumaine de linguistique*, 24, 1979.

Judwiga Dudkiewicz, "The Problem of Time in Samuel Beckett's *Waiting for Godot*", in *Acta Universitatis Lodziensis*, 66, 1980.

Jerry A. Flieger, "Blanchot and Beckett: *En attendant Godot* as 'Discontinuous' Play", in *French Forum*, 5, 1980.

Lois A. Cuddy, "Beckett's 'dead voices' in *Waiting for Godot*: New Inhabitants of Dante's *Inferno*", in *Modern Language Studies*, vol.12 no.2, 1982.

Aspasia Velissariou, "Language in *Waiting for Godot*", in *Journal of Beckett Studies*, 8, 1982.

Egon Werlich, "'Go and see is he hurt': On the Meaning of 'Godot' in Beckett's *Waiting for Godot*", in *Festschrift für Karl Schneider*, edited by Ernst S. Dick and Kurt R. Jankowsky Amsterdam, 1982.

Larry W. Riggs, "Slouching Toward Consciousness: Destruction of Spectator-Role in *En attendant Godot* and *Fin de partie*", in *Degré Second*, 7, 1983.

Manuela Corfariu and Daniela Roventa-Frumusani, "Absurd Dialogue and Speech Acts: Beckett's *En attendant Godot*", in *Poetics*, 13, 1984.

Katherine H. Burkman, "Initiation Rites in Samuel Beckett's *Waiting for Godot*", in *Papers in Comparative Studies*, 3, 1984.

A. Petitjean, "Analyse des conversations dans *En Attendant Godot* de Samuel Beckett", in *Verbum*, 2–3, 1985.

James L. Calderwood, "Ways of Waiting in *Waiting for Godot*", in *Modern Drama*, 29, 1986.

Mary F. Catanzaro, "The Psychic Structure of the Couple in *Waiting for Godot*", in *Journal of Dramatic Theory and Criticism*, vol.1 no.1, 1986.

Ewa Hryniewicz, "*Waiting for Godot:* Beckett's *homo ludens*", in *Arizona Quarterly*, 42, 1986.

Kripa K. Gautam and Manjula Sharma, "Dialogue in *Waiting for Godot* and Grice's Concept of Implicature", in *Modern Drama*, 29, 1986.

Gale Schricker, "The Antinomic Quest of *Waiting for Godot*", in *CEA Critic*, vol.49 nos 2–4, 1986–87.

Wolfgang Iser, "Counter-Sensical Comedy and Audience Response in Beckett's *Waiting for Godot*", in *Gestos*, 4, 1987.

David McCandless, "Beckett and Tillich: Courage and Existence in *Waiting for Godot*", in *Philosophy & Literature*, 12, 1988.

Jeffrey Nealon, "Samuel Beckett and the Postmodern: Language Games, Play and *Waiting for Godot*", in *Modern Drama*, 31, 1988.

Phyllis Toy, "Theatrical Design as Thematic Gesture in Beckett's *Waiting for Godot*", in *West Virginia University Philological Papers*, 35, 1989.

*   *   *

On a country road at evening Vladimir and Estragon (nicknamed Didi and Gogo) meet by a solitary tree for a rendezvous with a Mr. Godot whom neither has seen. Vladimir, however, claims to have had instructions from him and assures Estragon that when he comes they will be "saved".

Waiting for Godot: Arts Theatre Club, London, 1955

They fill in the time with reminiscences, complaints, reflections, and many varieties of witty "blathering". A diversion is created when a second pair arrives, en route for a fair, where Pozzo intends to sell his slave, Lucky, whom he drives by a rope round his neck. Lucky is made to dance by Pozzo, and then "think"; his tirade of thinking is brought to a stop when Vladimir follows Pozzo's advice to remove his hat. When the Pozzo/Lucky pair return in Act II, Pozzo has gone blind and Lucky dumb, but they continue relentlessly on their way. At the end of each act, a moon rises and a boy appears with a message from Godot: he is not coming, but will come the next day. Vladimir and Estragon contemplate hanging themselves, using the tree (which has astonishingly leafed in Act II) and the rope that holds up Estragon's trousers. The attempt ends in farce, with Estragon's trousers round his feet and, as in Act I, him saying "Let's go"—and neither moving.

Waiting for Godot is the play above all others which changed the face of modern drama. First performed in its original French at the tiny Théâtre de Babylone, directed by Roger Blin, it demolished all conventional expectations of what theatre should be. Rhythms of ordinary life were suspended. Beckett advised Peter Hall, who directed the first British production, to lengthen the many pauses and bore the audience more, implying that he wanted them drawn more fully into the bafflement, uncertainty, and boredom the characters experience in the course of waiting for Godot: "Nothing happens, nobody comes, nobody goes, it's awful".

Deliberate rejection of obvious suspense was one of the play's liberating aspects. Another was the minimal set, a stage bare except for a single tree (given distinctively slender, stylised form by Giacometti in a production of 1961). Beckett later added a stone to which earth-bound Estragon gravitates whenever he can. The country road where the hypothetical meeting is to take place reflects, in dream-like form, the journey during the war made by Beckett and his wife, members of the Resistance, into the French countryside, travelling by night to avoid notice from the Gestapo. The road also serves as a theatre space where the characters pass the time with a great variety of "turns", from the conversational "canters" of Vladimir and Estragon to Lucky's spectacularly fractured "think". In another aspect the empty stage is the road into the "void" along which the Boy comes, at twilight, bearing tantalising messages from Godot.

The abandonment of a conventional plot-structure was an important element in the play's liberating influence. The structure (often described as musical) is circular rather than linear. Variations are played on a cluster of powerful themes ("We're waiting for Godot", "why will you never let me sleep?", "Nothing to be done"). Everything repeats itself, changing just enough to suggest that bigger changes are possible. These seem to happen in Act II, the briefer and more sombre of the two acts: the tree has leafed, Lucky has been struck dumb and Pozzo is "blind as Fortune". But change may be an illusion, for memory cannot be relied on. From one act (or evening) to the next, Estragon forgets about Lucky, despite having been bitten by him, and the Boy denies having spoken with Vladimir before, though we saw him doing so. And in both acts the end is the same: Estragon says "Let's go" and the pair do not move. "Being there" is their role and they cannot escape it.

The metatheatrical trend in modern drama and theatre was given an enormous boost by Beckett's artful play with the idea of play in *Waiting for Godot*. All the characters perform (Pozzo needs an audience to support his unstable identity) and Didi and Gogo slyly display their awareness of being in a theatre. Estragon directs Vladimir to the Gents ("End of the corridor on the left") and declares to the auditorium, "Charming spot. . . .Inspiring prospects". In the 1984 production by the San Quentin Company (partly directed by Beckett) Larry Held's Estragon looked out to the auditorium on the line "Where are all these corpses from?", a gesture in tune with the company's belief that Beckett wanted to "smash that fourth wall".

Jean Anouilh summed up the play's extraordinary mix of knockabout, banter, and philosophical reflection when he called it "a music-hall sketch of Pascal's *Pensées* played by the Fratellini clowns". Roger Blin, who shared Beckett's fondness for silent comedians like Laurel and Hardy, cast a music-hall comedian, Lucien Raimbourg, as Vladimir, and Alan Schneider directed the first American production with Bert Lahr as Estragon. When Beckett directed his play in 1975 at the Schiller-Theater in West Berlin, the physical contrast between Stefan Wigger's tall, thin Vladimir and Horst Bollmann's dumpy Estragon highlighted the presentation of character as a matter of complementary opposites. Everything is in balance: Vladimir suffers from urinary trouble, Estragon from bad feet (his trouble with his boots is a major leitmotif). Vladimir the reasoner needs Estragon the dreamer and vice versa, while Pozzo and Lucky are equally interdependent in their complex sado-masochistic relationship. Links between the unlike pairs, suggesting a universal human likeness, are hinted at in comic routines like the hat swapping (derived from the Marx Brothers' film *Duck Soup*) and Pozzo's fall, which results in the collapse of all four.

Waiting for Godot made an enormous impact on the collective unconscious. Godot has commonly been equated with God but has also been seen simply as the unknown future. Vladimir's preoccupation with the gospel story of the thieves crucified with Christ ("one of the four says one of the two was saved") has encouraged interpretation along Christian lines, while Godot's failure to appear has been taken as evidence for a nihilistic view. The play has received an astonishing number of different explanations. It has been seen as a mystical search for a *deus absconditus*, a Cartesian probe into the body / mind divide, a Buddhist "journey", an existentialist drama, and in many other ways. The diversity and passion of the critical reaction shows what a deep vein of imagination Beckett has struck with his haunting image of the two friends, waiting in the void in the hope of being saved. . .

Beckett's production notebook, the basis for the revised edition published after his death, illuminates the cryptic text. Lucky's "think" proves, like so much else in the play, to be a lamentation for humanity. Uncertainty may be the ruling principle of the action ("Nothing is certain") but one or two certainties emerge all the same. Vladimir and Estragon will remain "faithful" even if Godot never comes. And Vladimir will respond, if erratically, to the cries for help which have been seen by some as the real meaning of the play. It is one of the most searching as well as poignant moments in all theatre when the nightmare-ridden Estragon falls asleep and Vladimir puts his coat over him, reflecting as he does so, "Was I sleeping while the others suffered? Am I sleeping now?".

—Katharine Worth

WAITING FOR LEFTY
by Clifford Odets

First Publication: In *Three Plays by Clifford Odets*, New York, 1935.
First Production: Civic Repertory Theatre, New York, 5 January 1935.

Criticism:
(For general works on the author, see *Playwrights* volume)

Articles:
Albert Hunt, "Only Soft Centered Left: Odets and Social Theatre", in *Encore*, vol. 8 no. 3, 1961.
R. Baird Shuman, "*Waiting for Lefty*: A Problem of Structure", in *Revue des langues vivantes*, vol. 28 no. 6, 1962.
Susanne Vietta, "Formen der Sozialkritik in Elmer Rices *The Adding Machine* und Clifford Odets *Waiting for Lefty*", in Karl Schubert and Ursula Müller-Richter (eds), *Geschichte und Gesellschaft in der amerikanischen Literatur*, Heidelberg, 1973.
Herbert Grabes, "Über die Wirkungsstrategie des agitatorischen Dramas: Clifford Odets *Waiting for Lefty*", in *Neueren Sprachen*, 24, 1975.
Lori Seward and David Barbour, "*Waiting for Lefty*", in *Drama Review*, vol. 28 no. 4, 1984.

*   *   *

The play takes place in 1930's USA, and concerns a newly formed trade union. As members wait agitatedly for the arrival of their leader, Lefty, so they can vote on unprecedented strike action, personal stories are told of how some of them came to join the union. When news comes of Lefty's murder, the meeting unanimously agrees to strike.

The plot is minimal. The "message", on the surface, unmistakable and singular: solidarity of the workers in active strike. However, even the terms of its delivery suggest a hidden complexity: the terminology of individuality is used as the motivation and justification of group action. The "American Rights" of "Life, liberty, and the pursuit of happiness" demand unified action against the bosses and the powerful, exclusive, monied elite. The play owes much of its power to its roots in 1930's street theatre: Agitprop and the Living Newspaper. Its confrontational style both gives *Waiting for Lefty* a raw, unsettling edge and forces participational judgement on its audience. More than simply agitprop, it still flaunts its agitprop style.

In the context of a trade union meeting, the play presents a series of personalized vignettes offering the fabric of human emotion and personalization that signifies "reality" and thus "seriousness" in conventional American realism. These glimpses into individual struggles and passions are set firmly in the larger context: the political meeting. To reinforce this context, Odets brings each personal story to a climax of desperation whose resolution (either stated or implied) lies in one single action: to strike.

The play begins with a bare stage on which the strike committee wait for "Lefty" to arrive. A gunman lounges menacingly against the proscenium. Although Odets has assumed the conventional proscenium stage for the play, the bareness of the setting breaks the convention of stage realism. Fatt's opening speech is made directly to the audience. Amongst its other functions, this speech sets the tone of immediacy and urgency of the entire play: "You're so wrong, I ain't laughing. Any guy with eyes to see knows it. Look at the textile strike...". The audience thus becomes both participant and arbitrator.

The stories themselves centre on the small, helpless, isolated individual oppressed by impersonal, powerful forces. These apparent opposites are ultimately synthesized through the strike. By joining together to solve their personal problems, the separate individuals become a larger force empowered by a common aim. The progress of the play stresses the common denominator in their personal stories by stripping away the individual details to expose the common oppression by the bosses for profit. The play is thus constructed so that the strike is seen to be not only viable but essential to ensure the God-given "rights" of individual "freedom".

In this process, Odets jibes at the knee-jerk American phobia about "the Left". First, he delineates a clear opposition between the workers and the monied elite, the bosses, across a front wide enough to include cabbies, industrial chemists, and doctors. Second, he works from the opposite direction, reducing the dichotomy between "reds" and "true Americans" until those in control are themselves seen as "unAmerican" and the God-given rights of the American citizen can only be obtained by striking. In this context, the Russian workers are seen, not as a threat because of their "communism" but as allies, because they are workers, "comrades" who share a common plight.

In the first vignette, Joe, a mild-mannered cabbie, is confronted by his wife Edna's sudden militancy when she threatens to leave him for another man if he doesn't take action to save his dwindling wage. The strike committee interrupt: "She will ... she will ... it happens that way", directing the audience perspective and response, reminding them of the larger drama within which this private crisis is taking place. When Joe protests that one man can do little, Edna replies: "I don't say one man! I say a hundred, a thousand ... start in your own union. Get those hack boys together ...".

The industrial lab assistant discovers that his "promotion" involves not only dealing with deadly poison but also an obligation to spy on his superior for the management, so he loses his job and finds political consciousness: "Plenty of hard feelings! Enough to want to bust you and all your kind square in the mouth!". It's handkerchiefs all round when Florence and her cab-driver fiancé, Sid, deeply in love, are forced by poverty to part:

Florence:	Something wants us to be lonely like that - crawling alone in the dark.
Sid:	Sure, the big shot money men want us like that.
Florence:	Highly insulting us.

Sid:	Keeping us in the dark about what is wrong with us in the money sense. They know if they give in just an inch, all the dogs like us will be down on them together ...

When the "worker" introduced to confirm the uselessness of the strike is exposed as a management spy by his own brother, the audience bond in solidarity with the workers. From this point, Odets can proceed to more theoretically elevated social levels where the Jewish surgeon is replaced by an incompetent doctor who "just happens" to be a Senator's nephew. Racism is thus linked with economic repression, and human rights with social consciousness when the "charity case" the new doctor has treated dies. The departing doctor aligns the informing intentions of the Russian revolution with the "American way": "I wanted to go to Russia ... the wonderful opportunities to do good work in their socialized medicine ... No! our work's here - America ... Fight! Maybe get killed but goddam! We'll go ahead!".

The necessity, indeed the moral obligation, to take communal action against the repression of human rights by the economic system is established across the board. When news comes of Lefty's murder, the characters and the hearts and minds of the audience are driven through emotional and moral obligation towards "strike!": "We're stormbirds of the working class. Workers of the world ... And when we die they'll know what we did to make a new world."

Despite its apparent emotional and thematic simplicity, *Waiting For Lefty* makes complex use of the theatre: a brazenly confrontational style incorporates a sentimental personalisation and turns the comfortable proscenium theatre from a place of passive entertainment into an urgent and immediate crisis in which the audience is directly involved. At the very least, the alternative view becomes, if only for those few moments, plausible and viable. At the same time, Odets chips gently away at unquestioned definitions and assumptions. *Waiting For Lefty* owes much of its power and immediacy less to its objective subject-matter than to its courageous use of the theatre and the subtler workings of its form.

—Elaine Turner

WAITING FOR THE PARADE
by John Murrell

First Publication: Vancouver, 1980.
First Production: Alberta Theatre Projects, Calgary, Alberta, 4 February 1977.

*   *   *

Since its premiere in Calgary, Alberta, in February 1977, John Murrell's play has had numerous productions within Canada as well as productions in London in 1979 and in New York in 1981. It was also broadcast by the CBC as a radio play in 1981, and on CBC television in 1984.

Set in Calgary, *Waiting for the Parade* illuminates the lives of five women and their attitudes towards the times they live in, the years of World War II. Through pantomime, dialogue, monologue, song, and dance, Murrell conveys the frustrations, fears, and strengths of these women as they try to cope with forces over which they have no control. Although there are never any men on stage, their presence and control over the women are demonstrated through the women's self-definitions and the presentation of these definitions to the audience.

Only through their men—either son, husband, father, lover—and, in a complementary effect, the war, do the women achieve any significance. Margaret, for example, is the self-sacrificing widow and mother. Janet embodies the strong, dependable wife whose sense of self is so enmeshed with her husband's that she takes on his burdens in an effort to restore her pride in the family unit. Marta personifies the dutiful daughter, while Eve is the eternal child, moulded into womanhood by the paternal figure of her older husband. With Catherine, Murrell draws the familiar portrait of a woman of tarnished morals but with a heart of gold.

The women are identified, both by themselves and by the audience, as complements to a male standard, a standard they accept as defining their femininity. Mother, wife, daughter, child, and whore, each character takes her place on stage and acts out the identity assigned her. With no men on stage to enforce the restrictions of these definitions, the women do a remarkable job of keeping themselves in line. They come together over the 25 scenes that comprise the play yet never form an alliance that could collectively challenge the restrictive nature of their existence.

This lack of real intimacy between the women is reflected by their never calling each other by name. The effect of this is to distort any effort on the spectator's part to identify any character as a distinct individual. A distancing effect is created that demands that the spectator categorize each woman in the stereotype she has herself created. The audience can understand the characters only through their dialogue and actions, and since all dialogue and action revolve around the men in their lives, all understanding evolves through their men.

The lack of a distinctive individuality for the characters, while sometimes perceived as a weakness, is a deliberate strategy on Murrell's part and, in fact, constitutes an attractive strength of the play. Leading Canadian actresses continue to perform the roles, and audiences to enjoy them, in part at least because the play's restrictive definition of femininity allows the actors to suggest deeper levels to the characterization that contrast effectively with the obvious surface level. Murrell has spoken of the mystery and unavailability that he likes to instil in his characters. In *Waiting for the Parade* five women present what is expected of them, but the audience continues to be intrigued by what is behind the veil, what they are hiding.

The duality of what is present and what is hidden is underlined by the duality inherent in the theatre: what hides behind the veil of the character is the actor. Murrell's play illustrates the contrast between the women's definition of self and their authentic self by giving it the context of the authentic actor hidden behind the performed character. This approach, which grants the actresses who perform his characters enormous freedom of interpretation, is one of the major contributing factors to the play's popularity.

—Mary Pat Mombourquette

THE WAKEFIELD PLAYS. See **THE TOWNELEY PLAYS.**

WALLENSTEIN
Wallenstein's Camp (Wallensteins Lager)
The Piccolominis (Die Piccolomini)
Wallenstein's Death (Wallensteins Tod)
by Freidrich von Schiller

Wallenstein [the trilogy]
First Publication: Tübingen, 1800.
First Production: Hoftheater, Weimar, 15–20 April 1799.

Wallenstein's Camp (Wallensteins Lager)
First Production: Hoftheater, Weimar, 12 October 1798.

The Piccolominis (Die Piccolomini)
First Production: Hoftheater, Weimar, 30 January 1799.

Wallenstein's Death (Wallensteins Tod)
First Production: Hoftheater, Weimar, 20 April 1799.

Editions
Wallensteins Tod, edited by A.J. Ulrich, 1894.
Wallenstein, edited by Karl Breul, 1896; second edition, Cambridge, 1937.
Wallenstein, edited by William Witte, Oxford, 1952.
Wallenstein [2 vols.], Stuttgart, 1959 (Reclam edition).
Wallensteins Lager; Die Piccolomini, edited by Werner Burkhard, Aarau, 1960.
Wallensteins Lager; Die Piccolomini; Wallensteins Tod, edited by Gerhard Storz, Reinbek, 1961.

Translations
Wallenstein, translated by Samuel Taylor Coleridge, London, 1800.
The Piccolomini, translated by W.R. Walkington, London, 1862.
Wallenstein's Camp, translated by Sir Theodore Martin, 1894.
Wallenstein, translated by Max Winkler, New York, 1901.
Wallenstein, translated by A.F. Murison, London, 1931.
Wallenstein, translated by Charles E. Passage, London, 1958.

Criticism
(For general works on the author, see *Playwrights* volume)

Books:
Rudolf Ibel, *Wallenstein*, Frankfurt, Berlin, and Bonn, 1961 (Grundlagen und Gedanken zum Verständnis klassischer Dramen).
Friedrich K. Blocher, *Schillers "Wallenstein" als dramatisches Gedicht*, Stuttgart, 1963.
Horst Hartmann, *"Wallenstein": Geschichte und Dichtung*, Berlin, 1970.
Lars F.H. Hermodsson, *Kommentar zu Schillers "Wallensteins Tod"*, 1973.
Barbara Lange, *Die Sprache von Schillers "Wallenstein"*, Berlin, 1973.
Alfons Glück, *Schillers "Wallenstein"*, Munich, 1976.
Fritz Hauer and Werner Keller (eds.), *Schiller's "Wallenstein"*, Darmstadt, 1977.
Walter Hinderer, *Der Mensch in der Geschichte: Ein Versuch über Schillers Wallenstein*, Königstein, 1980.
Gisela N. Burns, *Greek Antiquity in Schiller's "Wallenstein"*, Chapel Hill, North Carolina, 1985.
Dieter Borchmeyer, *Macht und Melancholie: Schillers "Wallenstein"*, Frankfurt, 1988.

Articles:

J.C. Blankenagel, "*Wallenstein* and *Prinz Friedrich von Homburg*", in *Germanic Review*, 2, 1927.

Valentin Veit, "*Wallenstein* After Three Centuries", in *Slavonic Review*, 14, 1935.

John Rothman, "Octavio and Buttler in Schiller's *Wallenstein*", in *German Quarterly*, 27, 1954.

R. Marleyn, "*Wallenstein* and the Structure of Schiller's Tragedies", in *Germanic Review*, 32, 1957.

Karl S. Guthke, "Die Sinnstruktur des *Wallenstein*", in *Neophilologus*, 42, 1958.

Hans Jürgen Geerdts, "Theorie und Praxis in Schillers Schaffen, dargestellt am *Wallenstein*", in *Weimarer Beiträge*, 5, 1959.

Rolf N. Linn, "Wallenstein's Innocence", in *Germanic Review*, 34, 1959.

Herbert Meyer, "Heinrich IV. von Frankreich im Werk Schillers: Ein Beitrag zum Verständnis der Wallensteinfigur", in *Jahrbuch der deutschen Schillergesellschaft*, 3, 1959.

Siegfried Seidel, "Neue Positionen in der Theorie Schillers während der Arbeit am *Wallenstein*", in *Weimarer Beiträge*, 5, 1959.

Herbert Singer, "Dem Fürsten Piccolomini", in *Euphorion*, 53, 1959.

Siegfried Streller, "Entwurf und Gestaltung in Schillers *Wallenstein*", in *Weimarer Beiträge*, 6, 1960.

Wolfgang Wittkowski, "Octavio Piccolomini: Zur Schaffensweise des *Wallenstein*-Dichters", in *Jahrbuch der deutschen Schillergesellschaft*, 5, 1961.

Werner Spanner, "Schillers *Wallenstein*: Ein Beiträge zur Gestaltinterpretation", in *Wirkendes Wort*, 13, 1963.

Werner Spanner, "Schillers *Wallenstein* in Unterprima", in *Wirkendes Wort*, 13, 1963.

Horst Hartmann, "Schiller's *Wallenstein*: Eine Analyse", in *Weimarer Beiträge*, 1965.

Michael Mann, "Zur Charakterologie in Schiller's *Wallenstein*", in *Euphorion*, 63, 1969.

G.A. Wells, "Astrology in Schiller's *Wallenstein*", in *Journal of English and Germanic Philology*, 68, 1969.

Jeffrey Barnouw, "Das 'Problem der Aktion' und *Wallenstein*", in *Jahrbuch der deutschen Schillergesellschaft*, 16, 1972.

Klaus Berghahn, "'Doch eine Sprache braucht das Herz': Beobachtungen zu den Libesdialogen in Schillers *Wallenstein*", in *Monatshefte*, 64, 1972.

Klaus F. Gille, "Das astrologische Motiv in Schillers *Wallenstein*", in *Amsterdamer Beiträge zur neueren Germanistik*, 1, 1972.

John Neubauer, "The Idea of History in Schiller's *Wallenstein*", in *Neophilologus*, 56, 1972.

Herbert Meyer, "Schillers *Wallenstein* auf der Mannheimer Bühne 1807–1960", in *Jahrbuch der deutschen Schillergesellschaft*, 17, 1973.

Harold Jantz, "Schiller's *Wallenstein*-Brief vom 1. März 1799: Seine Beziehungen zu Böttinger", in *Jahrbuch der deutschen Schillergesellschaft*, 18, 1974.

Harold C. Hill, "Astrology and Friendship: The Net of Commitment in *Wallenstein*", in *Modern Language Notes*, 91, 1976.

Helmut K. Krause, "Die Schwägerin: Marginalien zu Schiller's *Wallenstein*", in *Modern Language Notes*, 85, 1976.

Walter Müller-Seidel, "Episches im Theater der deutschen Klassik: Eine Betrachtung über Schillers *Wallenstein*", in *Jahrbuch der deutschen Schillergesellschaft*, 20, 1976.

Hartmut Reinhardt, "Schiller's *Wallenstein* and Aristoteles", in *Jahrbuch der deutschen Schillergesellschaft*, 20, 1976.

Klaus Köhuke, "Max Piccolomini und die Ethik des Herzens", in *Acta Germanica*, 11, 1979.

Roberta M. Glassey, "The Concept of Freedom in Schiller's *Wallenstein*", in *Journal of European Studies*, 10, 1980.

Wolfgang Wittkowski, "Theodizee oder Nemesistragödie? Schillers *Wallenstein* zwischen Hegel und politischer Ethik", in *Jahrbuch des freien deutschen Hochstifts*, 1980.

David B. Richards, "The Problem of Knowledge in *Wallenstein*", in *Goethezeit: Studien zur Erkenntnis und Rezeptions Goethes und seiner Zeitgenossen*, edited by Gerhart Hoffmeister, Bern, 1981.

Eugene Montreux, "The Betrayal of Friendship in Schiller's *Wallenstein* and in History: Wallenstein's Antagonists Ferdinand, Octavio, and Buttler", in *Colloquia Germanica*, vol.15 no.3, 1982.

Eugene Montreux, "*Wallenstein*: Guilty and Innocent", in *Germanic Review*, vol.57 no.1, 1982.

Karl S. Guthke, "Der Partieren Gunst und Hass in Hamburg: Schillers Bühnenfassung des *Wallenstein*", in *Zeitschrift für deutsche Philologie*, vol.102, no.2, 1983.

Barbara Belhalfaoui, "*Wallensteins Tod*: Die Tragödie als Theodizee", in *Recherches germaniques*, 14, 1984.

Joyce Crick, "Some Editorial and Stylistic Observations on Coleridge's Translation of Schiller's *Wallenstein*", in *Publications of the English Goethe Society*, 54, 1984

Walter Hinderer, "Die Damen des Hauses: Eine Perspektive von Schillers *Wallenstein*", in *Monatshefte*, vol.77 no.4, 1985.

Gisela N. Burns, "Greek Archetypes in the Poetic Fabric of Schiller's *Wallenstein*", in *Archiv*, vol.223 no.2, 1986.

Joyce Crick, "Coleridge's *Wallenstein*: Two Legends". in *Modern Language Review*, vol.83 no.1, 1988.

Dennis F, Mahoney, "The Thematic Significance of Astrology in Schiller's *Wallenstein*", in *Journal of European Studies*, vol.10 nos.3–4, 1989.

*   *   *

The Trilogy is set in 1634 during the Thirty Years War. Parts II and III (which together form one vast blank-verse tragedy) are introduced by *Wallenstein's Camp*, a lively prologue in rhyming couplets which evokes the spirit and vitality of Wallenstein's cosmopolitan troops, united in their trusting devotion to their commander-in-chief.

In Part II (*The Piccolominis*) Wallenstein's relationships to his lieutenant Ottavio Piccolomini and the latter's (fictitious) son Max are developed in contrapuntal relationship to the great affairs of state and war in which Wallenstein is involved and the love which blossoms between his (fictitious) daughter, Thekla, and his protégé Max. Wallenstein's secret plans to desert the Emperor and go over to the apparently victorious Swedes with his army, and thus to hold the nation to ransom, are fuelled by his ambition to be the arbitrator between the warring parties and by his unquestioning dependence on his astrologer, Seni. His officers organise a demonstration of loyalty to him in a memorably handled scene of drunken carousing underscored by sombre intrigue. Meanwhile Ottavio reveals to his son that he is secretly planning to pre-empt Wallenstein's betrayal by organising a counterplot.

In Part III (*Wallenstein's Death*), after prolonged deliberation and hesitation, Wallenstein finally makes his decision; but it is foiled by Ottavio, his would-be successor. The army mutinies and deserts him, and he withdraws with his few loyal supporters from Pilsen to Eger, while Max, disillusioned with his hero, invites death in a rash cavalry charge against the Swedes. Cornered, Wallenstein is finally murdered at the

Wallenstein: Wallenstein's Camp Engraving of first production, Weimar, 1798

instigation of Colonel Buttler who, to settle a personal slight, becomes the instrument of destiny.

Wallenstein occupies a central position in Schiller's dramatic *oeuvre*. It was the fifth of his nine completed plays. It may also be said to occupy the high ground of German historical drama, for in it the author, at the height of his powers, achieved a masterly fusion of imaginative breadth and intellectual power. The expansive, epic quality of *Wallenstein's Camp*, with its rumbustious down-to-earth *joie de vivre* shot through with heroism and apocalytic foreboding, acts as a theatrically effective curtain-raiser to the subtly controlled unfolding of a vast dramatic action which embraces the ringing ardour and youthful idealism of the Max–Thekla love intrigue, the probing complexities of Wallenstein's intense, almost paternal, relationship with the promising young officer, and his day-to-day dealings with his general staff, in which popularity and loyalty, though apparently firm, are gradually shown to depend on other factors such as outward success and inner self-confidence. Schiller's high-ranking officers in this largely male play (there are only three female roles) are differentiated from one another by his accurate eye for individual mannerisms and motivations. Together and individually they reflect the diversity of their commanding officer's enigmatic personality.

The hero's character dominates the action of the drama and has been the subject of debate ever since the earliest performances. Wallenstein's complexity arises from his multiple motivations and apparently conflicting qualities and shortcomings such as his strategic clear-sightedness and sheer good luck,

yet fatalistic acceptance of occult forces whose symbolism permeates the poetic text. In a good performance (for example, Gustav Gründgens' in the 1950's), the role can create a remarkable sense of rounded personality while at the same time reflecting the paradoxes of the man and his age in theatrical terms. From start to finish the action unfolds in the chiaroscuro of the age of Rembrandt. Himself a professor of history at Jena University and an authority on the Thirty Years War, Schiller knew a great deal about the world he was imaginatively recreating and the issues he was dramatizing. Owing something to *Macbeth*, *Julius Caesar*, and to *Oedipus Rex*, too, the trilogy explores the interrelated themes of authority and loyalty, duplicity and treason, bringing them into close association with the central issue: leadership, and the processes of decision-making which are essential to it. Wallenstein's indecision—that is, his prudent reluctance to hazard a decision until he is in full possession of all the facets and implications of his political situation—is both humanly understandable, historically plausible, and tragically self-destructive. Such themes, set in the context of what amounted to a German civil war of almost pan-European proportions, accounts in large measure for the fascination and relevance this grandiose play holds as Germany's most penetrating and haunting historical drama.

—Peter Skrine

WALLENSTEIN'S CAMP.   See **WALLENSTEIN.**

WALLENSTEIN'S DEATH.   See **WALLENSTEIN.**

WALLENSTEINS LAGER.   See **WALLENSTEIN.**

WALLENSTEINS TOD.   See **WALLENSTEIN.**

THE WATER HEN (Kurka Wodna)
by Stanisław Ignacy Witkiewicz

First Publication: In *Witkiewicz: Dramaty, 2*, Warsaw, 1962.
First Production: Slowacki Theatre, Cracow, 1922.

Translations
The Water Hen, in *The Madman and the Nun*, translated by
Daniel Gerould and C.S. Durer, New York, 1989.

Criticism
(For general works on the author, see *Playwrights* volume)

Articles:
Daniel Gerould, "*The Water Hen:* Creation and Revolution",
in *First Stage*, vol.6 no.2, 1967.
Jan Kott, "Mrożek's Family", in his *Theatre Notebook 1947–
67*, translated by Boleslaw Taborski, London, 1968.
Daniel C. Gerould, "A-causality and the Strangeness of
Existence in the Theatre of Witkiewicz", in *Dada*, 3, 1973.
Bettina L. Knapp, "Stanisław Ignacy Witkiewicz's *Kurda
Wodna:* 'Perform no operation till all be made of water' ", in
Symposium, 33, 1979.
Felicia H. Londré, "Witkiewicz and Lorca: A Creative
Congruency", in *Slavic and East European Arts*, vol.3 no.1,
1985.

*   *   *

Standing in her chemise beneath a street lamp in an open
field by the seashore, at dusk, the Water Hen incites Edgar to
kill her since only by such an irrevocable act can Edgar achieve
greatness and overcome his lack of self-definition. Dressed in
an 18th-century costume and armed with a blunderbuss, Edgar
reluctantly shoots the Water Hen through the heart; but her
death is delayed until they finish their conversation. Suddenly,
out of nowhere, a precocious ten-year-old child, Tadzio,
appears, claiming Edgar as his father. Gradually the previously empty landscape becomes enclosed and peopled by an
entire world of relationships that limit and imprison the hero,
but fail to give him an identity. Edgar's father, a jaunty sea
captain, insists that Edgar become an artist, despite his lack of
vocation, and provides him with a wife in Alice, Duchess of
Nevermore, who arrives accompanied by her accordion-
playing lover and her three business partners in the Theosophical Jam Company.

Now Edgar has a synthetic family and lives in Nevermore
Palace mired in everyday reality. The Water Hen returns alive
and well, as though the murder had never taken place.
Everything is repeatable. To justify his existence by doing
penance, Edgar climbs into a torture box from the Duchess's
museum, but his suffering is as artificial and inauthentic as the
rest of his life. Ten years pass. Tadzio, under pressure from
Edgar to study mathematics so that he can become someone,
carries on a flirtation with the Water Hen who has not aged.
Violent revolution breaks out in the streets, and in the ensuing
turmoil Tadzio plans to make it to the top. Donning his
theatrical costume, Edgar shoots the Water Hen for a second
time and blows his own brains out as the old world disinte-
grates. During the social upheaval, the sea captain and three
businessmen play cards and try to drink away three abortive
generations. As grenades explode, the last word of the play is
"pass".

A dream play making use of startling juxtapositions and
bizarre images, *The Water Hen* presents a large canvas,
painted in bright colors, of a once-secure world of leisure and
privilege, now out of control and hurtling toward catastrophe.
In its apocalyptic sensibility and techniques of distortion, this
"Spherical Tragedy" (its subtitle) has affinities with Expressionism, but totally eschews the abstract and ecstatic solemnity of
the German movement. By exploring the pictorial dimensions
of the unconscious, Witkiewicz anticipates the Surrealists.
Ultimately the author's playful eclecticism, parodic humor,
and self-irony give the drama a texture and tonality that belong
less to the 1920's than to the postmodern era. After the 1922
premiere (a prosaic staging as though of Ibsen), *The Water Hen*
did not reappear in the theatre until Wanda Laskowska's
ebullient Warsaw production in 1964 and Tadeusz Kantor's
highly personal version at Cricot II in 1967, which was seen at
avant-garde festivals throughout the world.

The Water Hen unites disparate realms of thought and
experience in a satisfying aesthetic whole. Rejecting the
psychological characterization and sequential plot that are the
basis of realism, Witkiewicz creates a formal composition out
of the basic elements of his art, as would a modern painter or
musician. In *The Water Hen*, more than elsewhere in his work,
the playwright has succeeded in giving balanced form to a
drama about the dissolution of forms.

Theatrical rather than discursive in the presentation of its
philosophy, *The Water Hen* is both a metaphysical speculation
on the dualities of birth and death, creation and destruction,
and an existential confrontation between the solitary individual and an alien cosmos. It is also a study of the "social
spheres", a play about roles and identities, growing up and
falling to pieces, the loss of self and the fabrication of artificial
people. *The Water Hen* offers a history of man entrapped in
concentric circles of universe, society, family, and self. Caught
in a web of public and private constrictions, threatened by
usurping doubles, in constant danger of being swallowed by his
own nothingness, the bewildered anti-hero Edgar must at
every moment re-invent himself.

Using as his microcosm three generations in the life of a
family with two interlocked pairs of fathers and sons (Edgar is
the middle term), Witkiewicz traces the social and cultural
history of late-19th and early 20th-century Europe from *fin-de-
siècle* dalliance and despair to Bolshevik collectivization.
Subject to radical discontinuities and disjunctions, "family
drama" in Witkiewicz's hands begins as domestic Oedipal
rebellion against patriarchal authority, but soon becomes a
broader register of social and ideological change that signals
the end of old hierarchies. First insecurities and tensions within
society are played out in the sexual domain; then the erotic is
politicized.

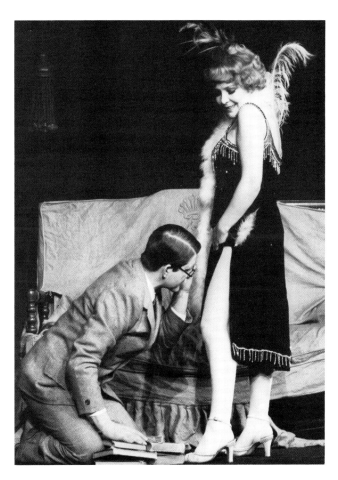

The Water Hen: Wspolczesny Theatre, Warsaw, 1985

Parody is a controlling principle in *The Water Hen*. The characters, like the playwright himself, strive to create new forms out of the fragmentation and dismemberment of old roles and genres. The breakdown of communal bonds has produced an over-theatricalized society in which the adoption of poses and the making of gestures proliferate. Edgar is like an actor trying out different ways of playing his part, but he is not sure for which role he has been cast or even in what sort of a play he is appearing. The failure of authority means that there are no genuine models, only a plurality of conflicting styles and modes. Plunged into a world that is not his own after separation from a lost unity of being, the youthful "newborn" Tadzio must create a mother and father and contrive his own reality. In a disintegrating culture heading for the abyss, the individual's quest for self-identity is doomed to failure. A play of masks, an aesthetics of inauthenticity, reigns in this provisional world of the makeshift and ersatz.

Edgar can thus only repeat old gestures and borrow lines from other literary and dramatic texts. The stage of his life is littered with leftover costumes and ideas, old props taken out of the theatrical storeroom, scraps of words already spoken, feelings many times felt, reducing his performance to that of a puppet. In *The Water Hen* Witkiewicz presents culture as refuse, the detritus from previous ages, a heterogeneous mass of shards and fragments that no longer coalesce. Unable to find its identity in a time of crumbling social structures, mankind rushes headlong into violence; the war of son against father takes to the streets. At the end of the play revolution, unplanned and unforeseen, erupts as an act of spontaneous combustion as inevitable as it is surprising. But even revolution

produces repetition, not rebirth. The sea captain will become a revolutionary admiral, and Tadzio, awakening for the third and final time from his dream, is "born" as an adult—which means as scoundrel.

Matter is constantly in motion in Witkiewicz's "Spherical Tragedy". Spinning selves and worlds collide and disintegrate; out of the debris new clusters and constellations of individual traits and social classes are formed. At each moment unexpected perspectives and possibilities revolve briefly before our eyes and then dissolve. The play's dynamics are generated by such strange malleability and mutability. Witkiewicz brings *The Water Hen* into the world of modern physics and mathematics by applying principles of relativity, complementarity, and uncertainty to dramatic action. Time and space are no longer universal and pre-existing categories inhabited by all, but subjective constructs capable of expansion, contraction, and conversion, one into the other. The Water Hen's death takes place in slow motion, while Tadzio's concurrent birth and growing up are radically accelerated.

In *The Water Hen* Witkiewicz subverts the traditional priorities of realistic dramaturgy and creates artful formal structures by the destruction of causality and displacement of plot fragments (much as Picasso and the Cubists displaced body parts in their paintings). The play opens with a climax, as hero shoots heroine. The finality of the denouement is undercut by the ongoing card game and the abrupt anticlimax of the final word, "Pass". The parallel shootings of the Water Hen in Acts I and III, each time following the appearance of an enigmatic lamplighter, heighten the feeling that events happen all by themselves and that the characters are marionettes manipulated by inscrutable forces. Randomness is also invoked as a compositional element. By a process of free association a word or phrase in *The Water Hen* calls forth a person or event as in a dream. Imagery of birds weaves its way erratically through the play, less as a system of symbols than a potpourri of buried recollections, jokes, and accidental connections. The title, *Water Hen* (which in Polish contains a hidden anagram for whore), takes aim at such famous plays as *The Wild Duck*, *The Seagull*, and Maeterlinck's *Blue Bird*. Alice, Duchess of Nevermore, derives her title and estate from the refrain of Edgar Allan Poe's Raven, a large black bird paired off against the smaller "Water Hen". In the complex structure of *The Water Hen* borrowings from other literary works play a germinal and enriching role. The relatively stable worlds of Ibsen, Chekhov, and Strindberg appear as shattered but brilliant pieces of a mosaic in disarray within the problematic reality of the play.

—Daniel Gerould

THE WAY OF THE WORLD
by William Congreve

First Publication: London, 1700.
First Production: Lincoln's Inn Fields, London, March 1700.

Editions

The Way of the World, in *Comedies by William Congreve*, edited by Bonamy Dobrée, London, 1925.
The Way of the World, edited by Joseph Wood Krutch, New York, 1927.

The Way of the World: Engraving, 1776

The Way of the World, edited by A.R. Middleton Todd, London, 1928.

The Way of the World, edited by W.P. Barnett, London, 1933.

The Way of the World, edited by Henry T.E. Perry, 1951.

The Way of the World, edited by Vincent F. Hopper and Gerald B. Lahey, Great Neck, New York, 1958.

The Way of the World, edited by Kathleen M. Lynch, Lincoln, Nebraska, 1965 (Regents Restoration Drama Series).

The Way of the World, in *Incognita; The Way of the World*, edited by Norman Jeffares, London, 1966.

The Way of the World, edited by Gerald Weales, San Francisco, 1966.

The Way of the World, in *The Complete Plays of William Congreve*, edited by Herbert Davis, Chicago, 1967.

The Way of the World, edited by Brian Gibbons, London, 1971 (New Mermaid Series).

The Way of the World, in *The Comedies of William Congreve*, edited by Anthony G. Henderson, Cambridge, 1982.

The Way of the World, in *The Comedies of William Congreve*, edited by Eric S. Rump, Harmondsworth, 1985.

Criticism

(For general works on the author, see *Playwrights* volume)

Books:

Paul and Miriam Mueschke, *A New View of Congreve's "Way of the World"*, Michigan, 1958.

Articles:

William van Voris, "Congreve's Gilded Carousel", in *Educational Theatre Journal*, vol.10 no.3, 1958.

Paul T. Nolan, "Congreve's Moment of Truth", in *Southern Speech Journal*, vol.25 no.2, 1959.

C. Leech, "Congreve and the Century's End", in *Philological Quarterly*, 41, 1962.

Paul T. Nolan, "Congreve's Lovers: Art and the Critic", in *Drama Survey*, 1, 1962.

Jean E. Gayen, "Congreve's Mirabell and the Ideal of the Gentleman," in *Publications of the Modern Language Association [PMLA]*, vol.79 no.4, 1964.

Paul J. Hurley, "Law and the Dramatic Rhetoric of *The Way of the World*", in *South Atlantic Quarterly*, 70, 1971.

H. Jeyssandier, "Congreve's *Way of the World:* Decorum and Morality", in *English Studies* (Amsterdam), 52, 1971.

Charles K. Lyons, "Disguise, Identity, and Personal Value in *The Way of the World*", in *Educational Theatre Journal*, 23, 1971.

David S. Zeidberg, "Fainall and Marwood: Vicious Characters and the Limits of Comedy", in *Thoth*, vol.12 no.1, 1971.

Anthony Kaufman, "Language and Character in Congreve's *The Way of the World*", in *Texas Studies in Literature and Language*, 15, 1973.

Alan Roper, "Language and Action in *The Way of the World, Love's Last Shift*, and *The Relapse*", in *English Literary History*, 40, 1973.

Robert A. Erickson, "Lady Wishfort and the Will of the World", in *Modern Language Quarterly*, 45, 1984.

James E. Neufeld, "The Indigestion of Widow-Hood: Blood, Jonson, and *The Way of the World*", in *Modern Philology*, 81, 1984.

Richard Braverman, "Capital Relations and *The Way of the World*", in *English Literary History*, 52, 1985.

Richard W.F. Kroll, "Discourse and Power in *The Way of the World*", in *English Literary History*, 53, 1986.

Elizabeth Kraft, "Why Didn't Mirabell Marry the Widow Languish?", in *Restoration*, 13, 1989.

Alvin Snider, "Professing a Libertine in *The Way of the World*", in *Papers on Language and Literature*, 25, 1989.

* * *

The couple dominating the comedy, Millamant and Mirabell, succeed in skilfully and elegantly removing all obstacles to their eventual union in a marriage based on affection. Before this conventional ending is reached in the play's final act, they have to counter the intrigues of Fainall (husband of one of Mirabell's cast-off mistresses), Lady Wishfort, who plans a match between Millamant (who is her niece and ward) and the country squire Sir Wilful Witwoud, and Mrs. Marwood who is frustrated in her efforts to win Mirabell's favour. These female antagonists are supported by the designs of the schemer Fainall who, under the guise of being Mirabell's friend, tries at one stroke to get rid of his unloved wife and deprive both Mrs. Fainall and Millamant of their fortunes, attempting to enlist Lady Wishfort on his side. His schemes are foiled in the nick of time.

As in Congreve's earlier comedies, the plot focuses on a family circle, and its exasperating complexities show both the divisive forces of rivalry, envy, and aggression between most characters and the final reconciliation of the central couple with the institution of marriage. The five acts spell out the difficulties that have to be overcome for the final re-affirmation of a social world. More than once the antagonisms between the members of the Wishfort family circle threaten to disrupt the comic pattern altogether. The play's protagonists have to resort to counter-intrigues little more dignified than their adversaries' to survive, and their final triumph can only be achieved by their resorting to legal niceties (for which Congreve drew on his legal training) and the threat to expose Lady Wishfort's overhasty willingness to marry Mirabell's servant Waitwell, disguised as Sir Rowland. It is only through falling in with the "way of the world", justifiably stressed by the comedy's title, that the fine couple can negotiate a viable position for themselves in society and even in their own relationship.

The tone for the action is set in a subtle first scene between Mirabell and Fainall at cards, in which their submerged rivalry is hinted at in a way which reverberates through the play. The contest for Millamant's person and her fortune, the politely veiled hatred of the ill-matched couple (the Fainalls), and Lady Wishfort's egoistically motivated attempts to marry off her niece Millamant to Sir Wilful Witwoud, impart a dynamic to the dramatic action that blends disruptive individualism with what looks like a fairly stereotypical comedy-of-manners plot of a libertine chasing after body and money of a desirable and witty heroine.

On this conventional level Congreve redefines the received hierarchy of wit involving the rakes (Mirabell, Fainall), a "gay couple" of lovers exchanging brilliant repartees, fops in fashionable upper-class London society (the inimitable quarrelling friends Witwould and Petulant), a country squire out of tune with the sophistication of metropolitan life (Sir Wilful Witwoud), a middle-aged lady of well-preserved amorous appetites, and various intelligent servants as intermediaries in the action's framework (Waitwell, Betty). Urbanity as the normative virtue is reflected in Congreve's choice of settings in London's West End (St. James Park, a chocolate house, and Lady Wishfort's house). The settings are fitting background for the scintillating dialogues, particularly pithily concentrated in Millamant's exchanges with her school of admirers. The conversational style and the apparant flippancy do not, however, conceal the seriousness of the comedy's dominant themes. To mediate them, Congreve manipulates the stock figures and situational clichés of Restoration Comedy in the teeth of mounting opposition after 1689 to what, from the viewpoint of the ascendant ideology of the Protestant work ethic, could only be regarded as frivolity, immorality, and gross materialism.

For Congreve, the privileged discourse of the charmed circle of the Restoration gentry was a means of dealing with significant wider issues. In the famous "proviso scene" Mirabell and Millament playfully draw up a sketch of a marriage contract in which, despite Millamant's coquettish exaggerations and the superficiality of some of the provisions, the independence of the male upper-class role is claimed by the heroine in an attempt to save her liberty from imprisonment in patriarchal domesticity. Similarly, Mirabell's materialistic insistence in gaining not only Millamant's person, but also her considerable fortune, signifies, among other things, a protest against the encroaching split between the public and the private spheres in the vogue of sentimentality engendered by the campaign for the reformation of manners. In Jeremy Collier's pamphlet against the "immorality and profaneness" of the contemporary stage, Congreve's plays were singled out as targets. Against such opposition it mattered little that generic libertinism is muted in Congreve's comedy and loses its predatory aggressiveness in the sexual politics of the play. Mirabell becomes a genuine friend of his former mistress Mrs. Fainall, and while he scorns the reformation that other heroes of the comedies of manners in his period were subjected to, the final agreement between Mirabell and Millament carries more than just strategic weight.

The lukewarm reception of the first production of *The Way of the World* precipitated Congreve's departure from the stage and his absorption in upper-class life that was later to horrify Voltaire. But from the early 18th century onwards, Congreve's last comedy has held the English stage as part of its classical heritage, receiving a host of excellent productions.

—Bernd-Peter Lange

THE WEAVERS (Die Weber)
by Gerhart Hauptmann

First Publication: As *Da Waber* [dialect version], Berlin, 1892; as *Die Weber*, Berlin, 1892.
First Production: Freie Bühne, Berlin, 26 February 1893.

Editions
Die Weber, Cambridge, 1951 (Cambridge Plain Texts Series).
Die Weber, edited by M. Boulby, London, 1962.

Translations
The Weavers, translated by Mary Morrison, London, 1899; reprinted in *A Treasury of the Theatre*, 2, edited by John Gassner, New York, 1951.
The Weavers, in *Gerhart Hauptmann: Five Plays*, translated by Theodore H. Lustig, New York, 1961.
The Weavers, translated by Frank Marcus, London, 1980.

Criticism
(For general works on the author, see *Playwrights* volume)

Books:
Helmut Praschek (ed.), *Gerhart Hauptmanns "Weber": Eine Dokumentation*, Berlin, 1981.
Barbara Schumann, *Untersuchungen zur Inszenierungs- und Wirkungsgeschichte von Gerhart Hauptmanns Schauspiel "Die Weber"*, Düsseldorf, 1982.
Reiner Poppe, *Gerhart Hauptmann, "Die Weber"*, Hollfeld, 1984.

Articles:
J. Blankenagel, "The Early Reception of Hauptmann's *Die Weber* in the United States", in *Modern Language Notes*, 68, 1953.
C. Moore, "A Hearing on *Germinal* and *Die Weber*", in *Germanic Review*, 33, 1958.
Evsej M. Mandel, "Gerhart Hauptmanns *Weber* in Russland", in *Zeitschrift für Slawistik*, 12, 1967.
Ann B. Dobie, "Riot, Revolution and *The Weavers*", in *Modern Drama*, 12, 1969.
Józef Kozlowski, "Gerhart Hauptmanns *Weber* im Dienste der Sache der Arbeiterklasse in Polen während der Zeit der Teilungen", in *Zeitschrift für Slawistik*, 25, 1980.
Brian Holbeche, "Naturalist Set and Social Conflict in Hauptmann's *Die Weber*", in *AUMLA Journal*, 56, 1981.
William H. Rey, "Der offene Schluss der *Weber*: Zur Aktualität Gerhart Hauptmanns in unserer Zeit", in *German Quarterly*, 55, 1982.
Christine Heiss, "Gerhart Hauptmanns *Weber* auf deutschen Bühnen der USA im neunzehnten Jahrhundert", in *German Quarterly*, 59, 1986.

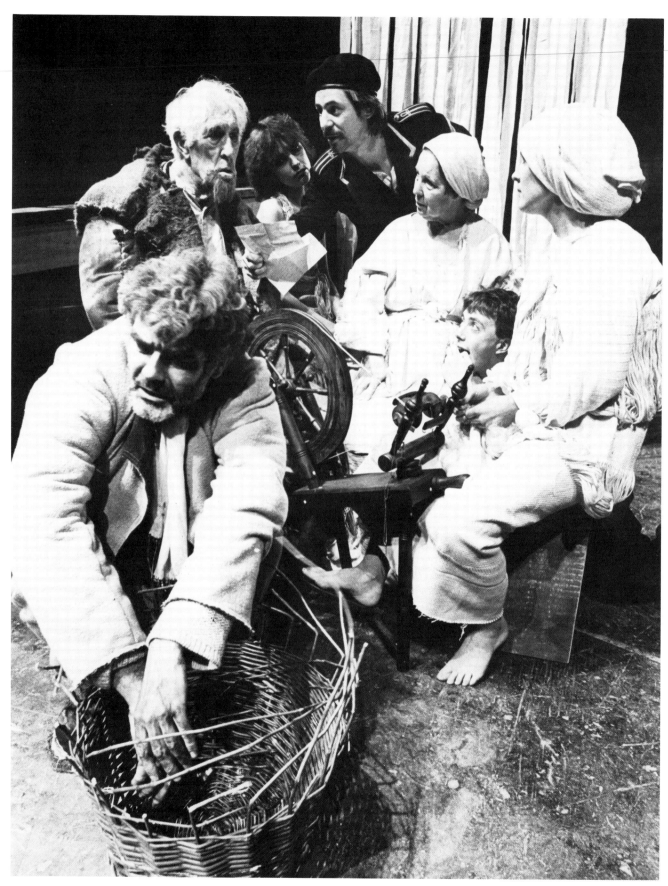

The Weavers: The Round House, London, 1980

Piotr Knapik, "Ein neues literarisches Vorbild für Gerhart Hauptmanns Drama *Die Weber?*", in *Text & Kontext*, 15, 1987.

* * *

The Weavers, based closely on historical and contemporary accounts, is a dramatic rendering of the weavers' revolt which took place in Gerhart Hauptmann's native Silesia in 1844. The five acts are relatively self-contained: each has a different setting and focuses on a different group of characters, with the fifth moving on to a different community, showing the revolt spreading from Peterswaldau to Langenbielau.

The action opens in the house of the manufacturer, Dreissiger, where the weavers, who operate on the cottage industry principle, are bringing in finished cloth for payment. Their passive dependence is immediately captured as they wait patiently, submitting to the contempt of Dreissiger's employees. In extensive and detailed stage directions Hauptmann emphasises their poverty and under-nourishment; the dialogue which accompanies the process of inspection and payment confirms this. An element of tension is introduced by the arrival of Bäcker, an insolent younger weaver who, it emerges, had been involved in a demonstration outside Dreissiger's house the previous evening. Attention is diverted from his confrontation with the manufacturer by the collapse of a starving child. The act concludes with Dreissiger offering to take more weavers onto his payroll; but the announcement—after his exit—that this will be done at lower rates of pay provokes increased murmuring among the weavers.

This pattern of a relatively quiet beginning, with tension mounting to an increasingly threatening conclusion is repeated in the following three acts. Act II, set in a weaver's cottage, focuses on the situation of the Baumert family. As in the previous act the arrival of a younger man, Moritz Jäger, returning home after a spell of military service, introduces an element of active protest; continuity is provided by the singing of several verses of the weavers' song, which Bäcker had mentioned in Act I. Along with the setting, the point of view changes once again in the third act which takes place in the village inn. New perspectives are introduced as the situation is explained to a traveller; and here Hauptmann demonstrates the skill which sets him apart from the majority of naturalist dramatists in his precise and individual delineation of a range of typical characters, and in using the contrasts of temperament and attitude to transform the description of situation into fully dramatic, interpersonal conflict. Again the act ends with the weavers' song, sung now by a growing number, as they threateningly set out from the inn for Dreissiger's house.

The fourth act begins quietly, but the underlying tension immediately surfaces as the children's tutor speaks out—albeit moderately—in defence of the weavers, and is dismissed, brutally, on the spot. As the rioters arrive Jäger is arrested and brought into the house, only to be freed by the crowd as he is taken away by the police. Dreissiger and his family escape, the crowd breaks in and begins to destroy the house, prior to moving on to destroy the mechanical looms in neighbouring Langenbielau.

The scene now changes to the house of a weaving family where, for the first time, resistance to the revolt comes from within, from the person of a quietist and patriarchical old weaver, Hilse, who defends the view that social protest is sinful, but does so in a way that reveals the same bitter hatred of his oppressors as is felt by his fellow weavers and by the powerful figure of his daughter-in-law, Luise, who joins the men in the revolt. In view of this it is difficult to see in the conclusion of the play, in which Hilse is shot by a stray bullet as the forces of law and order begin to come into action, anything more than an open ending, signifying continuity rather than closure.

The Weavers is Hauptmann's finest play and the masterpiece of German naturalism, although in certain respects it is untypical, most notably in its abandonment of the middle-class setting and the articulate discussion of moral problems which had been adopted from the social dramas of Ibsen. The play is written in Silesian dialect and is dominated by characters from the lower end of the social scale who are barely able to express their problems, and have very little understanding of the forces which govern their lives. Nor is there in the play any character who claims to possess such understanding. The revolt is neither politically led nor politically inspired; Hauptmann himself always insisted that it was a social drama, but not a socialist one. Such distinctions were, however, lost on the authorities in Wilhelmine Germany, and lengthy struggles were pursued through the courts before the play was finally free for unhindered public performance.

In formal respects it is a bolder and more innovatory work than any other German drama of its time, with its episodic structure and the absence of any identifiable hero. Certain of its positive features were preserved in Hauptmann's later naturalist dramas: the Silesian setting, the passively suffering characters moved to ineffective violent action by frustration; but for Hauptmann, as for naturalism in Germany, it marks both a high point and a turning point, after which there was to be a significant diversification into poetic drama with a strongly subjective flavour.

—John Osborne

DIE WEBER.   See THE WEAVERS.

THE WEDDING (Wesele)
by Stanisław Wyspiański

First Publication: 1901.
First Production: Teatr Slowackiego [Slowacki Theatre], Cracow, 1901.

Translations
The Wedding, translated by F. Sobieniowski and H. Pearson, New Haven, Connecticut [for Yale University production], 1933.

Criticism
(For general works on the author, see *Playwrights* volume)

Articles:
Malgorzata Pruska-Munk, "Wyspiański's *The Wedding* and Witkiewicz's *The Shoemakers*: From Polish to Universal Question", in *Polish Review*, vol.22 no.4, 1977.
Gerard T. Kapolka, "The Three Major Transformations of Wyspiański's *Wesele*", in *Polish Review*, vol.28 no.1, 1983.

* * *

The Wedding (*Wesele*), by Stanisław Wyspiański, when shown in Cracow in 1901 became a turning-point in the

The Wedding: Teatr Slowackiego, Cracow, 1974

development of modern Polish theatre. This innovative play in three acts appeared at the time of militant modernism when theories of "art for art's sake" were to become undermined by the national commitment of Wyspiański's otherwise experimental drama.

It originated in an event of November 1900. Wyspiański was then present at a wedding party given by his friend, Lucjan Rydel, a popular poet, who married a peasant girl. The party, which took place on the outskirts of Cracow, gathered together peasants, the friends and relatives of the bride, as well as guests from the city, members of the local intelligentsia, and, predominantly, artists. The unusual union between a gentleman and an uneducated country girl was symptomatic of a new

trend in the Galician culture: the idealization of the peasantry and the simple rural life by those writers and painters who were looking for fresh ideas around the time of the *fin de siècle*.

Wyspiański's play combines a realistic, factual report of the wedding with modern dramatic poetry. On the one hand his characters, taken from the actual event, were easily recognizable to their contemporaries. So was the setting, faithfully recreating its real counterpart. Correspondingly the dialogue often refers to actual facts of the time and consists of colloquial language, including peasant dialect and even some vulgar words. The feeling of direct observation is intensified by the structure of the story, the simple flow of interrupted dialogue, accompanied by music and dancing. Some critics compared this technique to a puppet show; others to the smooth movement of ballet or film. The colours and sumptuousness of folk costumes, worn by the peasants, and the scenery, somewhere between a village hut and a nobleman's cottage, make up an impressive spectacle, described in detail by the author in his stage directions.

Nevertheless, Wyspiański went much further than colourful pageantry and in the second act lifted the tone and transformed the wedding party into a symbol of Poland. The reportage technique of the first act, aimed at realistic typicality, diminishes; the next two acts are dominated by fairy-tale imagery with poetic generalizations and symbolism: the demarcation line between real and unreal is blurred. In the second act the wedding guests are confronted by symbolic figures, usually representing historical persons from the past. Their ghost-like appearance is rather confusing, because actually they are not supernatural creatures but literary devices enabling the author to make his point, as is the introduced legend about a national uprising, initiated by a message delivered by an old bard from the past.

Wyspiański's lesson is complex, ambiguous, and subject to various interpretations. He certainly probes the unity of Polish society and its readiness for action. The realistic stratum is the initial step before the symbolic expansion of meaning. It forms a pattern of repeated acts, gestures and expressions, leitmotifs and key-words, centred upon major problems. The basic one involves a split within society, where peasants and gentlemen or masters (*panowie*) form two separate camps, divided by their views and ways of life. The lack of mutual understanding, seen in the opening scene and then shown repeatedly, demonstrates that contacts between the two groups hardly penetrate the superficial. The artists admired living folklore, but from a perspective alien to the practical realism of the peasants. When the Groom revels in effusive talk about the beauty of his exotic Bride, her matter-of-fact remark "my shoes are a little too tight" cools the mood and makes a comic counterpoint; this technique of counterpoint is common in this play.

The idea of unity and national power appears to be an illusion, a myth, which Wyspiański attempts to unmask. Keywords, appearing throughout the play, indicate that a state of langour, inhibiting any action, has overpowered the represented world. Such words as "sleep", "dream", "drowsiness", "intoxication" are often repeated, occasionally accompanied by "grave" and "death". Those signals of inertia are seen in the intelligentsia, which make up the main target of the attack. They are regarded as a group of unproductive dreamers, inducing inaction throughout the nation. The most conspicuous among them are so-called "peasant-lovers" (*chłopomani*), for whom the country folk usually represent nothing more than a colourful spectacle. The Groom is portrayed with exceptional irony: as a poet he indulges himself in a purely aesthetic approach to life and attempts to escape from its complexities into a simple world of music, costumes, and fairy-tales. The more mature form of "love for peasantry" is represented by the Host, who creates a myth of national unity and regeneration, where robust peasants play the central roles. Fully aware of the mythopoetic power of artistic imagery is the poet, but he openly enjoys the very act of make-believe, so far as it allows him to overstep the mediocrity of everyday existence. His attempts at heroic poetry, however, are bound to be futile; spiritual emptiness can breed only similar offspring, in the vicious circle of a degenerating mythology.

The heroic mythology of the past has been animated and actually invades the wedding at the end of the Act II. This event is preceded by an ironic self-examination of the national conscience, carried out by the symbolic phantoms who appear before some guests and point out their shortcomings or remind them about ill-concealed cracks in relations between the peasants and the nobility. The last of the strangers, Wernyhora, has a completely different function however. The historical Ukrainian bard of the 18th century frequently present in Polish literature and painting, he incarnates the spirit of patriotic and prophetic poetry, in all its positive and negative aspects. His call for a national uprising contains both the greatness and the misleading appeal of the old patriotic ideology. In accordance with the Romantic tradition, it has a visionary power, centred on a messianic leader-liberator and a great miraculous event which will bring freedom and justice. His appearance before the Host seems to explore the latter's ability to turn his desires into real actions. This test of will proves fatal both for the message and for its supposed carriers. The members of the intelligentsia are unable to act patriotically and to guide the aroused but disoriented peasants. In the third act the artists are reluctant to leave their enchanted circle. On the other hand, when eventually they feel better disposed towards the insurrection, they are misled by Wernyhora's request to them to wait passively for his signal—which never comes. The myth turns into a fairy-tale, founded on fantasy and self-deception. Created by artists and intellectuals, it has misled the peasants, active and energetic, but still immature.

As a result the drama ends in an impressive pantomime where, under the impact of uselessly waiting for miracles, the wedding guests fall into a motionless trance. This turns later into dancing, where all the couples, still unconscious, move slowly around the table. The music is played by the most enigmatic, symbolic character, the "Chochol". He is in fact nothing more than a bundle of straw which protects roses against frost in winter; but thanks to the poetic whim of Rachela, a female admirer of literary imagery, he has been brought to life and invited to the wedding party. Nothing in the drama seem to prove better that vivid imagination is able to create fairylands out of nothing. As a result, the wedding guests follow the tunes coming from a fairy-tale creature: the evidence of artistic power and its deception in an alluring musician who is really nothing more than straw.

—Stanislaw Eile

WEDDING BAND; A Love/Hate Story in Black and White by Alice Childress

First Publication: New York, 1974.
First Production: University of Michigan, Ann Arbor, Michigan, December 1966.

Criticism
(For general works on the author, see *Playwrights* volume)

Articles:
Rosemary Curb, "An Unfashionable Tragedy of American Racism: Alice Childress's *Wedding Band*", in *MELUS*, vol.7 no.4, 1980.
John Dillon, "Alice Childress's *Wedding Band* at the Milwaukee Repertory Theater: A Photo Essay", in *Studies in American Drama 1945–Present*, 4, 1989.

Subtitled *A Love / Hate Story in Black and White*, *Wedding Band* is set in South Carolina during the summer of 1918. At the centre of the play is the love affair between a black woman, Julia Augustine, and a white man, Herman. State laws prohibit interracial marriages and social codes virtually prohibit any inter-racial relationships; yet the couple have survived ten years together. They imagine the freedom they might achieve by moving to New York City (where such laws do not prevail), but are prevented from leaving first by Herman's sense of familial responsibility to his mother and sister, and then, at the end of the play, by his death from influenza.

Wedding Band is not a typical Childress play, nor has it always been well received. Her choice of an inter-racial relationship makes it unlike her other works which have only black protagonists, and the relationship itself has provoked censure from both black and white critics. The premiere performance of *Wedding Band* on the New York stage, as well as its later transmission on ABC television, broke a taboo in both media about representing inter-racial relationships, and this gave Childress's text an immediate notoriety. Black critics felt that *Wedding Band* should have concentrated on a black couple or that, at least, Julia should have rejected Herman. As *Wedding Band* demonstrates, however, Childress is more interested in staging the world which so many people experience than in offering an idealized portrayal of positive role models and their successes. White critics of the play felt that Herman should have left South Carolina, that he should have been strong enough to reject the claims of his mother and sister. Both types of criticism neglect Childress's ability to look with compassion at both black and white poor in the context of Julia and Herman's culturally unacceptable love. The play suggests the possibility, despite immense economic hardship, not only of survival, but of survival in loving relationships. With the death of Herman, however, it is evident that while the characters are, for the most part, survivors, they are always and especially vulnerable.

The play's opening set indicates the naturalism of Childress's dramatic method. The scene is three houses in a backyard, and Julia is the new tenant in the middle house. In this setting, we see the problems which dominate the everyday actions of working-class Blacks and the pressures these place on familial and community relations. As well as being physically situated in the middle, Julia is also in the middle culturally. While she cannot be acknowledged by her lover's racial group, she is also distanced from fellow Blacks by that alliance. Her history is, as she says, one of constant moving in an attempt to avoid the apparently inevitable disapproval.

Through the presentation of the landlady and other tenants, as well as through Julia, Childress demonstrates the economic conditions and cultural values which inform and shape the experience of working-class Blacks. Another tenant, Mattie, has an absent husband and her attempts to survive as a single parent are juxtaposed with Julia's economically easier, but socially impossible, situation with Herman. While both Julia and Mattie react to their circumstances with a persistent and determined dignity, events show that to be black and to be a woman is to be doubly disadvantaged. Yet Herman, white and male, is not portrayed as the play's villain.

Herman is trapped by his bakery store which he feels obliged to maintain in order to repay an earlier loan from his mother. While Herman's procrastinations might seem to be the direct cause of Julia's troubles, Childress points out that Herman's endeavours to fulfill class, race, and gender norms leave him as much a victim as Julia. At the end of Act I, Herman falls sick at Julia's home and the tension that having a white man stay in the black neighbourhood provokes is signalled by the act's stark closing line: the landlady makes the social unacceptability and, indeed, the risk of such an action all too apparent in her simple command to Julia: "Get him out of my yard".

In the second act, Herman's mother and sister arrive to take him back and much of the action centres on schemes to move him discreetly out of Julia's home. As the neighbours function as representatives of black social values, so Herman's mother and sister provide stereotypic white responses. In many ways the intolerance shown to Julia and Herman's relationship by both communities stems from those people's sense of the difficulty in simply surviving, let alone with the extra burden of dealing with the claustrophobia of a society so rigidly divided on grounds of class, race, and gender.

The wedding band of the title that Herman gives to Julia (significantly to wear on a chain around her neck rather than on her finger) in celebration of their ten years "together" signifies survival despite racial prejudice. But what *all* the characters fight against is economic oppression. The black couple (Mattie and her absent husband), evidently as much "in love" as Julia and Herman, struggle endlessly and painfully like the latter to avoid destruction at the hands of class-determined economics. Moreover, Herman's mother describes her own life as putting up with a man who breathed stale whiskey in her face every night and enduring the birth of seven babies, five stillborn. For Annabelle, Herman's sister, the chance to marry for love depends on Herman's agreeing to marry Celestine, his mother's choice.

Although based on a true story and on common circumstance, Julia and Herman's relationship is perhaps less than convincing. Nonetheless, for the audience / reader who responds not only to the central couple but to all the characters Childress draws, *Wedding Band* underscores the dependence of everyone's individual happiness on prevailing social and political conditions.

—Susan Bennett

WEDDING DRESS (Vestido de noiva)
by Nelson Rodrigues

First Publication: In *Nelson Rodrigues: Teatro, 1*, Rio de Janeiro, 1959.
First Production: Municipal Theatre, Rio de Janeiro, 28 December 1943.

Translations
Wedding Dress, translated by Fred M. Clark, Valencia, 1980.

Criticism
(For general works on the author, see *Playwrights* volume)

Articles:
Paul B. Dixon, "Scenic Space and Psychic Space in Nelson Rodrigues' *Vestido de noiva* and René Marqués' *El apartamiento*", in *Papers on Romance Literary Relations*, 1983.
David George, "Os Comediantes and *Bridal Gown*", in *Latin American Theatre Review*, 21, 1987.

*   *   *

The action of Nelson Rodrigues's three-act play *Vestido de noiva* (*Wedding Gown*) unfolds in the mind of Alaíde, the protagonist. She has suffered an automobile accident and she lies, near death, on an operating table. The plot alternates between three planes—hallucination, memory, and reality—and the puzzle of the young woman's life is gradually pieced together and her secrets revealed: her fascination with a murdered prostitute who appears in hallucinations, the elegant Madame Clessy, and the brutal love triangle she shares with her husband, Pedro, and her sister, Lúcia. The last scene of the play takes place after the protagonist's death. During Pedro and Lúcia's wedding, Alaíde's ghost reaches out with a bridal bouquet toward her sister and widowed husband. Before the blackout, moonlight falls on the dead woman's grave.

Critics frequently make the claim that *Wedding Gown* is Brazil's first modern play and that it revolutionized that nation's theatre. (It would be more accurate to say that the first modern playtext is Oswald de Andrade's 1937 *O Rei da vela* (*The Candle King*), but this play was not staged until 1967.) Because Nelson Rodrigues's play fell into the hands of a director, polish emigré Zbigniev Ziembinski, and a theatre company, Os Comediantes, up to the task of innovation, *Wedding Gown* was the first modern Brazilian play to receive a performance worthy of its revolutionary structure and themes. The playtext and its 1944 performance thus constitute the beginning of the modern Brazilian stage and helped to overturn the 19th-century conventions which dominated that nation's theatre well into this century.

Rodrigues broke with tradition in creating a play that tears away the conscious mind's veil of censorship, drawing the reader/spectator into a realm of forbidden desires and archetypal symbols, and in presenting the first female protagonist in Brazilian drama to revolt against the strictures of patriarchal society. Alaíde expresses her defiance in her secret obsession with the prostitute Clessy. The protagonist discovers the madame in a old diary and enters her world and takes on her identity during the death-bed hallucinations. Alaíde's quest in the play is thus to express that part of herself which a male-dominated society has repressed. Clessy serves as Alaíde's inner voice and forces her to unravel, through the plane of memory, the enigma of her short life: her frustrated revolt against conventions that destroy her, and the murderous love triangle with her sister and Pedro. Clessy, the phantom temptress, beckons Alaíde to violate taboos and to lay bare the crumbling façade of middle-class respectability, the social entrapment of marriage.

The wedding gown and ritual provide an ironic, metaphoric structure. The play depicts marriage not as a sacred union but as an archaic institution that kills desire and impedes liberation. The wedding ritual leads to destructive relationships instead of recreating the eternal bond. The playwright transforms the white gown, a symbol of purity and innocence, into a death shroud, Alaíde's post-mortem costume, a mask that hides the violence and repression of a patriarchal society.

Vestido de Noiva's ritual and archetypal machinery result in plot fragmentation, in simultaneous actions in different time planes on its three levels of perception (hallucination, memory, and reality) and allow Rodrigues to overturn the dramatic convention of focusing action in a linear time matrix in which a protagonist must confront, overcome (or be defeated by), an obstacle. In *Wedding Gown* Alaíde's death is both the beginning and end of the action. The temporal matrix becomes ritual time, and the plot moves in circular patterns and in flashbacks and flashforwards in the mind of the protagonist. External action is thus relegated to a minor role.

All of the innovations in Rodrigues' script would have come to nought had it not been for the Os Comediantes's production. Particularly important were the contributions of the director and designer, who were able to fulfill the potential of the playwright's stage directions. The set design, by painter Tomás Santa Rosa, ran counter to the usual drawing-room sets of the day, and created varied and flexible spaces for multiple and rapid scene changes. Ziembinski's lighting design gave life to Santa Rosa's poetic set and increased the flexibility of the scenic space. The use of microphones and loudspeakers was also innovative for the period, suggesting the playwright's scenic conception may have been influenced by the cinema. No Brazilian stage production had ever featured an elaborate "sound track". Ziembinski also brought to the production, and to the Brazilian stage, new conceptions of acting and blocking. His ensemble approach was a total departure from the actor/impresario-based star system of the old professional companies. If the latter relied on improvisation and slap-dash methods, the Polish director choreographed every moment with precise timing and trained his actors in a variety of styles, including the expressionistic and Stanislavskian methods.

Os Comediantes's production of *Wedding Gown* was an immediate and resounding success, in spite of a storm of protest from the traditional companies and the critics who supported them. Another group of younger critics belonging to a new generation open to aesthetic renewal, as well as writers and artists from the modernist generation (who had given up on what Oswald de Andrade called the "gangrenous corpse" of the Brazilian stage) grasped immediately the upheaval taking place before their eyes. Many of them hit the mark by declaring that Ziembinski's staging of Nelson Rodrigues's play *Vestido de Noiva* was a milestone that would bring the national theatre into the modern era.

—David George

WELL-CURB (Izutsu)
by Kanze Zeami Motokiyo

First Production: Unknown; earliest recorded production, 30 March 1595.

Translations

Izutsu (*Well-Curb*), in *The Noh Drama: Ten Plays from the Japanese*, translated by Nippon Gakajutsu Shinkokai, Tokyo, 1960.

*   *   *

The category of the Play is III, *Onna-mono* (Women's Plays) or also *Kazura-mono* (Wig Pieces). There is no record of any performance before March 30, 1595 (*The Record of Lord Genkyo*). Its source is Chapter XXIII of *Ise Monogatari* (*The Tales of Ise*), written sometime in the early Heian Period, 794–930. The same poems exchanged between the two lovers and a prefatory note to the poems are also contained in Volume XV of the *Kokin Wakashu* (*Imperial Anthology of the Poems*, 905), which states explicitly that Narihira married Aritsune's daughter.

In *Izutsu* a Buddhist priest on pilgrimage from province to province comes to the Ariwara Temple in Yamato (province of present day Nara). He is ready to offer a religious rite for the souls of Narihira, a poet, and his wife when he sees a village woman drawing water from a well (*izutsu*, placed on the stage as a stage property) for flowers and offering them to a grass-covered mound. In response to the priest's question, she tells him that she is praying for Ariwara-no-Narihira's salvation. She goes on to talk about Narihira, who married the daughter of Ki-no-Aritsune, and the poetry exchanged between them by the side of this well:

Standing against the well-curb,
As children we compared our heights,
But I have grown much taller
Since last I saw you. (Narihira)

The hair I parted
When by the well-curb we compared our heights
Now loose flows down my back.
For whom but you should it again be tied? (The daughter)

Before she fades away, the woman reveals the fact that she, herself, is that daughter, and appears here because of her strong yearning for Narihira.

The Man of the Place appears, answers the Priest's questions and tells the couple's story. The main character makes her second appearance as the ghost of the daughter, this time wearing Narihira's ceremonial hat and robe. She dances a slow-paced "Jo-no-mai" and looks into the well, reminiscing fondly of the time she did so with Narihira in their youth. But as the sky turns grey, the ghost of the lady evaporates. The priest is awakened from his dream as he hears the temple bell tolling.

The primary value of the play lies in its lyrical handling of the sentiment of love. Against the background of an old temple in an autumn setting, the story of a woman's intense longing for her man unfolds. Famous poems were woven into the text of the play and chanted in turn by the priest, the woman, and the chorus, with appropriate musical accompaniment of two hand-drums and a flute. Some of the movements, such as the woman's contemplation of the sheaf of *susuki* grass which is attached to the well-curb and of the old mound by it, the "Jo" dance, and the ghost's gaze into the well, are very memorable and accentuate the romantically tinged, poetic mood.

The play very effectively conveys the aesthetic quality of *yugen* (beauty of elegance) characteristic of the Women's Play category. This quality was deeply appreciated by the audience and emphasized as the most important quality of the Nō drama by Zeami, who is credited with formulating the essential characteristics of the Nō drama, which are still preserved and admired by today's audiences.

The structure of this play typifies the format of the Nō drama. A travelling priest (a representative of the audience) encounters a local person in a place known for some incident. This person is well acquainted with the legend but disappears before the priest has a chance to ask more questions. Another local resident enters and tells what he knows about the famous events. Although this may appear to be a redundant scene, it is a useful device to allow time for the main character to change his costume while the general audience is given a run-down on the plot, delivered in a stylized common vernacular which must have been useful to those members of the audience who were not educated enough to be familiar with the chanting and with all the quotations of famous poems or literature. The last part of the play actually regresses in time, as the true identity of the main character is revealed: in the case of *Izutsu*, this is the ghost of the woman who longs for her husband, reliving her past in the dream of the priest.

The Nō drama is believed to have its origin in the Buddhist rite of appeasing the dissatisfied soul of a deceased person who met his or her death either with too strong an emotion (like this wife) or in an untimely or brutal way (as in other stories). The priest's prayer or his promise for a special rite satisfies the ghost, and it disappears in the twilight of dawn.

Some plays, including this one, use a minimalist approach to suggest the environment, limiting both the number and size of stage property pieces to items such as a pine tree, hut, carriage or, as in this instance, a well-curb. This is a reflection of the influence of Zen Buddhism.

—Andrew T. Tsubaki

WESELE.   See THE WEDDING.

THE WESKER TRILOGY
  Chicken Soup with Barley
  Roots
  I'm Talking About Jerusalem
by Arnold Wesker

The Wesker Trilogy
First Publication: London, 1960.
First Production: Royal Court Theatre, London, June–July 1960.

Chicken Soup With Barley
First Publication: In *New English Dramatists, 1*, Harmondsworth, 1959.
First Production: Belgrade Theatre, Coventry, 7 July 1958.

Roots
First Publication: Harmondsworth, 1959.
First Production: Belgrade Theatre, Coventry, 25 May 1959.

I'm Talking About Jerusalem
First Publication: Harmondsworth 1960.
First Production: Belgrade Theatre, Coventry, 4 April 1960.

Criticism
(For general works on the author, see *Playwrights* volume)

Articles:
John Mander, "Arnold Wesker's *Roots*", in his *The Writer and Commitment*, London, 1961.
Jacqueline Latham, "*Roots*: A Reassessment", in *Modern Drama*, 8, 1965.
John Kershaw, "*Roots*: Arnold Wesker, the Determined Missionary", in *The Present Stage*, London, 1966.
Robert Kleinberg, "Seriocomedy in *The Wesker Trilogy*", in *Educational Theatre Journal*, 21, 1969.
Dietrich Peinert, "*Chicken Soup With Barley*: Untersuchungen zu Dramentechnik Arnold Weskers", in *Literatur in Wissenschaft und Unterricht*, 3, 1970.
D. Bonneau, "*The Trilogy*: Arnold Wesker and Commitment", in *Annales de l'Université du Bénin, Togo: Lettres*, vol.2 no.2, 1975.
Hermann J. Weiand, "The Chicken Soup Trilogy: *Roots*", in his *Insight IV: Analyses of Modern British and American Drama*, Frankfurt, 1975.

The Wesker Trilogy: Roots, Royal Court Theatre, London, 1960

Thomas P. Adler, "*The Wesker Trilogy* Revisited: Games to Compensate for the Inadequacy of Words", in *Quarterly Journal of Speech*, 65, 1979.

Colin Chambers and Mike Prior, "Arnold Wesker: The Trilogy and the Spirit of Socialism", in their *Playwrights Progress: Patterns of Postwar British Drama*, Oxford, 1987.

A.A. Mutalik-Desai, "*The Wesker Trilogy:* Propaganda or Allegory?", in *Indian Journal of English Studies*, 26, 1987.

* * *

Arnold Wesker audaciously began his playwriting career in his twenties with this trilogy. *Chicken Soup With Barley* introduces the Kahn family in the East End of London. The parents are Hungarian-born Jews and Communists—energetic Sarah and timid Harry—with two children, teenage Ada and the child Ronnie. In the first act, in October 1936, the Kahns and friends take part in successfully breaking up a Fascist march and a youth asserts: "There's no turning back now— nothing can stop the workers now". The mood in Act II, ten years later, is more of post-war exhaustion than hope, and Harry has a stroke on stage. The third act moves on to 1955–6 and again incorporates the decline of the family and the decline

of the hopes of the Left. Monty, active in the 1930's, visits and says: "There's nothing I can do any more. I'm too small; who can I trust?". With the truth about Stalin revealed and the suppression of the rising in Hungary, even Ronnie is disillusioned. Yet the curtain-line—always important for Wesker—is Sarah's: "If you don't care, you'll die", and the image of the title is of caring: a neighbour brought chicken soup for young Ada when she was ill.

Roots is the most admired play of the three (partly because of Joan Plowright's success in the first production). The East-Enders of *Chicken Soup* are contrasted here with a farming family in Norfolk that is wholly unpolitical. Beatie, the daughter, has escaped to work in kitchens in Norwich and London, where she has fallen in love with Ronnie Kahn. She returns home for two weeks and Wesker riskily communicates the boredom of rural life. Ronnie does not appear (so is ingeniously created through Beatie's quotations and imitations), but writes near the end to break off their engagement. After tears and a quarrel with her mother, Beatie finds her own voice, no longer quoting Ronnie: "We don't fight for anything, we're so mentally lazy we might as well be dead. . .The whole stinkin' commercial world insults us and we don't care a damn". Though the family ignores her, she grasps the fact that she is now thinking and feeling for herself: "It does work, it's happening to me, I can feel it's happened, I'm beginning, on my own two feet—I'm beginning". Though this is a breakthrough only for Beatie, Wesker has commented on the others, "everyone of them could have been a Beatie". Some critics have perversely refused to identify with Beatie, preferring the uneducated, unambitious locals. Yet Beatie's final breakthrough is exciting, theatrical, and convincing.

I'm Talking About Jerusalem is the story of Ada and her husband, Dave, from 1946 to 1959. Dave has fought in the Spanish Civil War and then in the Far East in World War II. They are living in a cottage deep in the country, and Dave is making furniture there, attempting to integrate his home and his working life. But few can afford his expensive work and his apprentice chooses to earn more in a factory. So, at the end, they move to London; but Dave does not see this as a defeat, and Ronnie closes the play with: "We must be bloody mad to cry". Wesker makes fuller use of the possibilities of the stage in *Jerusalem* than previously: the singing of Yiddish folk songs and dancing a Zanny Hora; a silent scene in which Dave apologises to Ada by doing homage to her; Dave as "Mr Life" putting "the fire of life" into his child with a "touch of magic and of clowning".

Wesker's programme note (never reprinted) for the first staging of the full trilogy at the Royal Court in 1960 states:

Basically it is a family; on another level it is a play about human relationships; and on a third, and most important level, it is a story of people moved by political ideas in a particular social time. There are many theories about socialism. *Chicken Soup With Barley* handles the Communist aspect. *Roots* handles the personal aspect, that is, Ronnie feels you can only teach by example. *I'm Talking About Jerusalem* is a sort of study in a William Morris kind of socialism. If you like, the three plays are three aspects of socialism, played out through the lives of a Jewish family".

Wesker acknowledges the strong autobiographical element in the plays, with only the cynical visitor in *Jerusalem* entirely his creation.

Wesker shows the joys, miseries, richness, complexity, changeability of working-class family life. He sketches in, equally, a history of socialism from idealism in the 1930's to withdrawal or disenchantment at the end of the 1950's (the last scene of *Jerusalem* is the day after the Conservatives win the election). Yet in different ways Sarah, Ada, Dave, Ronnie, and Beatie are keeping the faith or finding their way to new ones.

—Malcolm Page

THE WEST INDIAN
by Richard Cumberland

First Publication: London, 1771.
First Production: Theatre Royal, Drury Lane, London, 19 January 1771.

Editions

The West Indian, in *Plays of the Eighteenth Century*, edited by Ernest Rhys, London and New York, 1928.

The West Indian, in *The Plays of Richard Cumberland* (6 vols.), edited by Roberta F.S. Borkat, New York and London, 1982.

Criticism
(For general works on the author, see *Playwrights* volume)

Articles:
Stanley J. Williams, "Richard Cumberland's *West Indian*", in *Modern Language Notes*, 35, 1920.
Wylie Sypher, "The West-Indian as a 'Character' in the Eighteenth Century", in *Studies in Philology*, 36, 1939.
Robert J. Detisch, "The Synthesis of Laughing and Sentimental Comedy in *The West Indian*", in *Educational Theatre Journal*, 22, 1970.
Wolfgang Zach, "Richard Cumberland: *The West Indian*", in *Transactions of the Fourth International Congress on the Enlightenment*, Oxford, 1976.
Elizabeth M. Yearling, "Victims of Society in Three Plays by Cumberland", in *Durham University Journal*, vol.74 no.1, 1981.

*   *   *

Belcour, Cumberland's title character, is, at the start of the play, visiting England for the first time. He is unaware that Stockwell, a benevolent London merchant who is closely observing his movements, is, in fact, his father. Stockwell's concern is to scrutinise the character of the son he has never known, particularly in the management of his considerable wealth, until the time seems appropriate to acknowledge their relationship. Belcour's moral nobility, however, is paired with a total naïvety about city life, and for most of the central action he is exploited and duped in both financial and amatory terms. The philanthropy of Stockwell pervades most of the characters to a degree, but is polarised against the hypocritical puritanism of the old Lady Rusport, who invokes Locke in support of her miserly abnegation of her stepdaughter Charlotte, her nephew Charles Dudley, Dudley's father, and sister Louisa. In the course of the action, matches are established between Charlotte and Charles, and between Louisa and Belcour, thwarted for some time by the counter-stratagems of Lady Rusport and Mrs. Fulmer, the Dudleys' landlady, who anticipates the female heavy of 19th-century melodrama. The comic resolution is in terms of marriage, revelation of Belcour's paternity, and a redistribution of wealth precipitated by the production of a hitherto-unknown family will. The agent of much of this is the good-natured but not overly intelligent Major O'Flaherty, progenitor of the "stage Irishman" of Boucicault and O'Casey.

The West Indian has traditionally been analysed as a sentimental comedy combining hackneyed plot elements with a more innovative perspective on late 18th-century issues such as the status of the middle classes, the distribution of wealth, the residual impact of puritanism and its related family structures, philosophies of nature, and notions of virtue and honour. All of these are developed in a depth that is remarkable for a play which had considerable success on the popular stage—an illuminating reflection on the values of David Garrick, who championed the script from its first draft.

In the era of colonial and post-colonial theorising, however, *The West Indian* stands out as a play with a scope that is almost unique for its period. Certainly, there is little that is culturally specific about the figure of Belcour, who could almost as easily be Anglo-Indian as West Indian. Also, in a play that is resonant with various humanistic dimensions there seems to be a curious evasion of the issues of slavery and imperialism. But

Belcour is, more generically, an embryonic stereotype of the rough-and-ready, pioneering white settler, whose frankness, fairness, and pragmatism serve as instruments for the satirical overhauling of the pretension, exploitation, and deceit that pass for urbanity in London society. Belcour's colonising energy has thus been turned back on his "parent culture", epitomised by his arrival in London, which he finds "as full of defiles as the Island of Corsica", leading to a street brawl with "the whole tribe of custom-house extortioners" and refuge in a pub. By the end of the play, Stockwell can tell Belcour that he is "no match for the cunning and contrivances of this intriguing town" and explain to Louisa that "his manners, passions, and opinions are not as yet assimilated to this climate; he comes amongst you a new character, an inhabitant of a new world". The correlation between climate and behaviour is frequently asserted, as when Charlotte says, "O blessed be the torrid zone for ever, whose rapid vegetation quickens nature into such benignity! These latitudes are made for politics and philosophy; friendship has no root in this soil". Yet the play's development has, to a degree, belied the assertions of both Charlotte and Stockwell: Belcour does help friendship to find a root in London, and, whatever other reassertions of London normality may be implied in the resolution, Belcour's prospects of "assimilation" seem, fortunately, remote.

Belcour's ethic represents, throughout the play, the voice of a severely marginalised counter-discourse which continually challenges audience norms. But he is not alone in bringing types of colonising energy to focus on London. The Fulmers are shamelessly engaged in exploitation, having come from Boulogne in search of London as "a second Eldorado, rivers of gold and rocks of diamonds". However, it is O'Flaherty who most closely parallels the function of Belcour—though he finally chooses repatriation in Ireland, from which he has been absent for 30 years. Like Belcour's, O'Flaherty's behaviour is certainly not beyond reproach, but he too has an instinctive generosity, automatically championing the exploited even to his own considerable disadvantage. In his early scenes, O'Flaherty has an obvious interest in Lady Rusport's wealth, and seems prepared to trade his own vestigial dignity for a stake in it. In this respect, his commodity thinking might seem parallel to that of Mrs. Fulmer, who suggests a career of prostitution for Louisa. But when Lady Rusport reveals that she has refused to relieve the Dudleys' poverty, O'Flaherty leaves her house immediately, telling her she is "as hard-hearted as a hyena" and the most "savage" animal "in the whole creation". Stockwell, similarly, will come to describe some London customs as "savage"—a striking inversion of the colonial gaze.

—Howard McNaughton

WHAT PRICE GLORY?
by Maxwell Anderson and Laurence Stallings

First Publication: In *Three American Plays*, New York, 1926.
First Production: Plymouth Theatre, 5 September 1924.

*   *   *

A group of American marines are using a French farmhouse as their headquarters towards the end of World War I. In particular, Kiper, the long-term career soldier, brags about his womanising, but the subject turns to the imminent leave of Captain Flagg, their company commander, and the expected arrival of a new sergeant. The latter materialises in the form of Quirt, another old-timer whose extensive service has involved constant animosity and rivalry with Flagg. The predominantly comic tone of the first act is most clear in the mutually unexpected meeting of the two; then Flagg says farewell to his lover Charmaine and departs, leaving Quirt to begin seducing the French girl. In the second scene, Flagg returns from a leave that has been mostly spent in a military lock-up after a brawl, and is confronted by Charmaine's father who is intent on restoring his daughter's honour; Quirt seems all but manipulated into marriage when the company is ordered to advance in 20 minutes.

The second act is much more sombre, set in a cellar at the front line, where the wounded are treated and strategy is rethought. Again, however, there is personal interaction between sergeant and captain, when Quirt is wounded just seriously enough to justify return to the town of the first act. The final act is set in Charmaine's father's tavern, where Flagg and Quirt engage in various forms of contest over the woman. It ends comically, with both men responding to an order—incredible after the ordeals of Act II—for the batallion to return to the front: a triumph of military instinct over the amorous.

What Price Glory? is unusual for a jointly authored work in that, whereas both writers collaborated in the final draft, initially Stallings wrote the second act while Anderson wrote the other two. This accounts for the fluctuation in tone and type of action between these two areas of the play, and also for the writing style: Stallings' stage directions in particular have a documentary brutality, consistent with the fact that their author had lost a leg in precisely such circumstances. Anderson's attitude to war developed somewhat during his long writing career, and this, his first published play, reflects cynicism about war but does not articulate his earlier overt pacifism.

As what was felt to be a new high-water mark in terms of realism on the American stage, *What Price Glory?* shocked its first audiences through the language of its servicemen and through the precisely scripted scenes of warfare in the second act. Neither of these dimensions retains such an impact in the 1990's, when audiences would be more likely to register disgust at the coarse commodity thinking of the central characters, particularly in their attitudes to women. In fact, the play's pervasive comedy is indulgent towards—if not celebratory of—a variety of masculine stereotyping that is not fundamentally different from that of R. C. Sherriff's *Journey's End*. If warfare is not exactly portrayed as "boys' games", the survival skills of the career servicemen who are the main characters certainly come across as an antidote to the grotesquerie of their present circumstances, an antidote which is both escapist and exploitative, abusive of the dignity of other men and women (the captain's lover is even referred to as his "meat"). As such, the play offers a strong contrast with other dramatic treatments of World War I, including O'Casey's *Silver Tassie* and Kubrick's *Paths of Glory*.

Two factors in the play still command particular attention. Initially, it was frequently termed "naturalistic", but—at a time when even O'Neill had difficulty distinguishing between naturalism and realism—the application of the term should not be stretched. However, the second act in particular does graphically represent the degradation and animalism of life at the front, and the conditioning effect of the war suggests that people who have to live like this cannot afford too much morality. This intermittently explodes in startling vignettes, such as an early episode of xenophobia in an attack on a soldier from Cincinnati with a German name. The tension, however, is defused by Quirt "planting one squarely" on the chin of the drunk Irish bully, leaving Charmaine "smiling at her wonderful hero with the powerful punch". As happens not infrequently in this play, a situation is thus interestingly problematised but then trivialised by dissolving into coyness or cliché.

In addition, there is considerable subtlety in the character explication, and this extends through all three acts. Flagg, it is revealed, is a reconstituted puritan who was once "straight as a mast, muscled like a gorilla, Christian as hell. Good deal of liquor has flowed under his belt since then". He now adopts a diametrically opposite stance, referring to headquarters as "a stinking theosophical society for ethical culture and the Bible-backing uplift". When the General calls his men "a bunch of tramps", Flagg insists that they should be called "individualists". In the central act, Flagg tells a horribly wounded officer that he can commit suicide if he likes ("Go ahead. It's your affair"), and then turns to a lieutenant who has broken down, while uttering: "rising quickly as though he might kill the man, and then putting his arm around the chap. . .with a gentility never before revealed". In the third act, he can be "suddenly apathetic", but earlier he has described himself as "the sinkhole and cesspool of this regiment. . .I corrupt youth and lead little boys astray into the black shadows between the lines of hell. . .I take chocolate soldiers and make dead heroes out of them. I did not send for you, Mister. . .". Flagg thus epitomises a perspective on character development which is also discernible in secondary figures—that war imposes roles on people which fit uncomfortably, so that there is always the possibility of breaking roles and exposing what the German Expressionist playwrights of the same war had called "nude spirits".

—Howard McNaughton

WHAT THE BUTLER SAW
by Joe Orton

First Publication: London, 1969.
First Production: Queen's Theatre, London, 5 March 1969.

Criticism
(For general works on the author, see *Playwrights* volume)

Articles:
Ronald W. Strange, "*What the Butler Saw*", in *Insight IV: Analyses of Modern British and American Drama*, edited by Hermann J. Weiand, Frankfurt, 1975.
Maurice Charney, "What Did the Butler See in Orton's *What the Butler Saw?*", in *Modern Drama*, 25, 1982.
Margaret MacIntyre and David Buchbinder, "Having It Both Ways: Cross-Dressing in Orton's *What the Butler Saw* and Churchill's *Cloud Nine*", in *Journal of Dramatic Theory and Criticism*, vol.2 no.1, 1987.
William Hutchings, "Joe Orton's Jacobean Assimilations in *What the Butler Saw*", in *Farce*, edited by James Redmond, Cambridge, 1988 (Themes in Drama Series).

*   *   *

What the Butler Saw turned out to be Joe Orton's final play, a

magnificently comic celebration of excess that for the first time properly, or perhaps improperly, united his interest in the comic potential of language with his wonderment at the absurdities of the physical manifestations of behaviour. It is not only quite easily his best play, it heralds the arrival of what would have been one of the major post-war playwrights.

The plot is not readily summarised, its many and intricate complications being themselves a major part of the play's concern with the way in which rationalising words are ultimately always betrayed by the stronger imperatives of the body. Suitably enough the play is set in an asylum presided over by a psychiatrist, Dr. Prentice, whose intended sexual adventures and his continual attempts to lie his way out of the frustrated consequences are themselves a part of the tension between the desire for liberation and the protective retreat into repression which lies at the heart of the play.

At the outset Prentice is interviewing a candidate for a secretarial position, an interview which inevitably concludes with a demand that the girl, Geraldine, undress for a complete physical examination. Surprised by the unexpected arrival of Prentice's wife, the naked girl is first hidden and then easily persuaded to borrow the clothes of Nicholas, a porter from the Station Hotel who has arrived bearing Mrs. Prentice's luggage.

Add to this initial sexual confusion the potential for chaos afforded by the introduction of, first, Rance, a visiting psychiatrist intent on examining the suitability of Prentice and his clinic for the treatment of the insane, and then a Sergeant Match in pursuit of anything remotely illegal—which covers just about everything that subsequently occurs to the characters or is revealed about their pasts—and one has a fair idea of the kind of revelations to follow. Incest is added to adultery and tranvestisism when it transpires that Geraldine and Nicholas are, unknown to all parties concerned, the twin children of the Prentices, conceived in the linen cupboard of the Station Hotel—Orton's equivalent of Oscar Wilde's abandoned handbag in *The Importance of Being Earnest*.

It is obvious that the further the plot proceeds, the less Orton is concerned with anything like a moral evaluation of the characters' actions or motivations. Farce here is more than a technique; it is a way of life. On his first entrance Dr. Rance asks, "Why are there so many doors? Was the house designed by a lunatic?". It is a question that not only emphasises the function of the psychiatric clinic—a madhouse with openings for all tastes—but also recalls the play's epigram, from Tourneur's *The Revenger's Tragedy*: "Surely we're all mad people, and they whom we think, are not". Orton's redefinition of farce allowed for a complete abandonment of the naturalistic trappings of plot and character in favour of a world in which the repressions and sublimations of life are allowed a fully-articulated play.

The world of *What the Butler Saw* is a true Freudian nightmare of unleashed sexual repression. It is civilisation without its clothes. Indeed it is Dr. Prentice's inability to admit to the only comparatively straightforward heterosexual act in the entire play that sets things in motion. The wife he would deceive has just returned from a meeting of a club "primarily for lesbians", during the proceedings of which she has availed herself of the body of the young porter Nick, who has actually arrived at the asylum intent on demanding money for the photographs taken during the event; and Nick himself spent a large part of the previous evening sexually harrassing an entire corridor of schoolgirls.

Normality is never the norm in this play; as in the brothel in Genet's *The Balcony*, the asylum converts dreamed fantasy into actable reality. "Marriage excuses no-one the freaks' roll-call", Sergeant Match assures Prentice when he attempts to protest his absolute innocence. What follows is a sort of sexual

Bartholemew Fair in which clothing is first removed and then redistributed in a confusion of sexual roles—the whole business being observed and interpreted by the lunatic inspector Rance, who offers a succession of psychoanalytical explanations of the characters' behaviour, the unlikelihood of which is only surpassed by the truths of the various cases.

It is a flawed play. It needs, and would certainly have received, considerable rewriting—in particular, the tedious running gag about the lost penis from the statue of Winston Churchill, which is eventually used to bring proceedings to a close, is a part of an interest in the over-facile shooting of sacred cows that characterised his earliest work, and could easily be removed. However, what it promises is a redefinition of farce, a complete liberation of libido in a glorious celebration of chaos and *fin-de-civilisation*. "'It's the only way to smash the wretched civilisation', I said, making a mental note to hot-up *What the Butler Saw* when I came to rewrite. . .Yes. Sex is the only way to infuriate them. Much more fucking and they'll be screaming hysterics in no time", noted Orton.

But sex is both the subject of the play and the vehicle which suggests potentially more serious matters. The tradition of farce inherited by Orton was diluted and trivial, confirming rather than questioning the assumptions of its audience. His awareness of the proximity of farce and tragedy—as seen, for instance, in the scene of the mad King Lear and the blind Gloucester on the beach at Dover—both as theatrical modes and as mirrors of psychological reaction to chaos, points to what he was really attempting. While the plays of those such as Tourneur and Webster move easily from farce to tragedy, the presentation of chaos counterpointed by the articulation of a sense of a moral order, in this play there is no possibility of a transition to a tragic definition of farce. The characters end the play bloodied but unbowed; the ending is, however, purely mechanical. As Orton argued, farce had become an escapist medium, on the run from precisely that which it had originally presented—the disturbing manifestation of the human consciousness which threatens the stability of the social order.

Orton has frequently been compared to Oscar Wilde, and in this play in particular it is a useful comparison. But here more than ever there is a key distinction. Where Wilde invites us to look beyond the brittle and studied brilliance of his characters' dialogue to the hollowness underneath, Orton presents all his cards directly to the audience. What we are being shown *is* the underneath. What Orton was moving towards was the presentation of a pre-civilised world in which the awakened subconscious, at large in a decadent society, makes everyone a "minority group". Had he lived, his redefinition of the boundaries of comedy would have been a major feature of the modern theatre.

—John Bull

WHEN WE DEAD AWAKEN (Når vi døde vågner)
by Henrik Ibsen

First Publication: Copenhagen, 1899.
First Production: Hoftheater, Stuttgart, 26 January 1900; first Norwegian Production, at the National Theatre, Christiana, 6 February 1900.

Translations
When We Dead Awaken, translated by William Archer, in

Ibsen: Collected Works, 11, edited by William Archer, London, 1907.
When We Dead Wake, in *"Ghosts" and Other Plays*, translated by Peter Watts, Harmondsworth, 1964.
When We Dead Awaken, translated by Michael Meyer, London, 1960; corrected version, in *Ibsen: Plays, 4*, London, 1980.
When We Dead Awaken, in *The Last Plays of Henrik Ibsen*, translated by Arvid Paulsen, New York, 1962.
When We Dead Awaken, in *The Oxford Ibsen, 8*, edited and translated by James Walter McFarlane, Oxford, 1977.
When We Dead Awaken, in *Ibsen: The Complete Major Prose Plays*, translated by Rolf Fjelde, New York, 1978.

Criticism
(For general works on the author, see *Playwrights* volume)

Articles:
Paul Henry Grumman, "Ibsen's Symbolism in *The Master Builder* and *When We Dead Awaken*", in *Nebraska University Studies*, 10, 1910.
Herman Anker, "*Når vi døde vågner*: Ibsen's dramatische epilog", in *Edda*, 56, 1956.
S. Arestad, "*When We Dead Awaken* Reconsidered", in *Scandinavian Studies*, 30, 1958.
S. Arestad, "Ibsen's Portrait of the Artist", in *Edda*, 60, 1960.
Erik Østerud, "*Når vi døde vågner* på mytologisk bakgrunn", in *Ibsen-Årbok*, 1963–64.
Amiya Dev, "The Artist in Ibsen's *When We Dead Awaken* and Joyce's *Exiles*", in *Jadavpur Journal of Comparative Literature*, 7, 1967.
Pavel Fraenkl, "Tabu og drama i *Når vi døde vågner*: Et Bidrag till den etnologiske dramaturgi", in *Nordisk Tidskrift för vetenskap, konst och industri*, 43, 1967.
Yngvar Ustvedt, "Professor Rubek og Henrik Ibsen", in *Edda*, 67, 1967.
Gudrun H. Gvåle, "Henrik Ibsen: *Når vi døde vågner*: Ein Epilog til eit livsverk", in *Ibsen-Årbok*, 1968–69.
Edvard Beyer, "*When We Dead Awaken*", in *Ibsen-Årbok*, 11, 1970–71.
Milly S. Barranger, "Ibsen's Endgame: A Reconsideration of *When We Dead Awaken*", in *Modern Drama*, 17, 1974.
David Thomas, "All the Glory of the World: Reality and Myth in *When We Dead Awaken*, in *Scandinavica*, 18, 1979.
Mary G. Wilson, "Edvard Munch's *Woman in Three Stages*: A Source of Inspiration for Henrik Ibsen's *When We Dead Awaken*", in *Centennial Review*, 24, 1980.
Marie Wells, "*The Master Builder, John Gabriel Borkman*, and *When We Dead Awaken*: Variations on a Theme or Developing Argument", in *New Comparison*, 4, 1987.

*   *   *

Ibsen's last play was given the subtitle *A Dramatic Epilogue in Three Acts*, not because he intended it to be his final work, but because it concluded the series of contemporary prose dramas beginning with *A Doll's House*. Thus the stage concept and the dialogue is basically of the same kind as in the rest of the series. All three acts are set in the open air, but on different levels. The first act takes place outside a spa hotel with a view of the fjord in the background. An elderly, well established sculptor, Professor Rubek, and his youthful wife, Maja, are discussing the reasons for the rather insipid character of their relationship and the not very exciting status of his later art. A squire and bear-hunter, Ulfheim, talks about the healthy life in the mountains, urging Maja to come with him. Rubek meets Irene, the model from his earlier days as artist; she reproaches him for taking away her soul, leaving her dead. The second act takes place in the mountains, near a sanatorium. The couple are drifting further apart, as they are drawn each to their own separate objects of fascination. Maja decides to go bear-hunting with Ulfheim, while Rubek and Irene, in an effort to retrieve the life they once replaced with art, want to experience a summer night on the mountain together. The last act is set higher up in the mountains, in wild precipitous surroundings, near the ruin of an old cottage. Ulfheim and Maja on their way down, escaping the approaching storm, meet Rubek and Irene climbing to the top. The heavy weather releases an avalanche, killing the two climbers, while the couple descending are safe.

In terms of dramatic events, the action of Ibsen's last play is simple. It consists of a series of dialogues, mostly between a man and a woman. The theme can be seen as a quest for revitalization. Traditionally the play has been regarded as the elderly dramatist's own judgement on the way he had spent his life. "When we dead awaken", Irene says at the end of Act II, "We see that we have never lived". The path chosen by the artist has been too much dominated by art, and a full life in earthly terms has been neglected.

The opposite view can also find support, however. In his dialogues with Irene, Rubek blames himself for not being sufficiently concerned with his calling as an artist. He has yielded to popular demand by creating portrait busts, being well paid, but lacking fulfilment as an artist. The masterpiece of his youth, "The Day of Resurrection", to which the model Irene, when a young woman, contributed so much, has been altered in later years, indicating a spirit of compromise, a betrayal of the very idea of art. Rubek is restless and displeased at the outset. His situation is spelled out in the dialogue with Maja, and suggested through the stage symbolism in the first-act stage directions: "*Open park-like space with a fountain, groups of tall old trees and shrubs. Left, a little pavilion, almost overgrown with ivy and wild vine. . . .It is a still, hot, summer's morning*". The set can be said to accentuate a quality of stagnation, life come to a standstill. In the opening lines the Rubeks talk about hearing the stillness. The feeling of unhealthy passivity is further underlined by the spa hotel on the right hand side. The effect has parallels with, for example, the openings of *Ghosts*, *Rosmersholm*, *Hedda Gabler*, and *John Gabriel Borkman*. The need for change is strongly felt; the gradual change of scenery in *When We Dead Awaken* is thus an important aspect of the dramatic development.

The relations between the characters are also stated through symbolical properties. Ulfheim (a family name meaning the home of a wolf) is a sprightly fellow with a peculiar taste for hunting: "Bears for preference, ma'am. But I'm happy to take any kind of game that offers itself—eagles, wolves, women, elk, reindeer. . . .Anything that's got life and vigour and warm blood. . .". His straightforward, brutal manner seems both attractive and repulsive to Maja. His symbolic opposite is Irene (the name is the Greek word for peace), dressed in white and talking about herself being dead. While Ulfheim is generally accompanied by his servant and his gluttonous hunting dogs, Irene is looked after by a nun-like figure, suggesting that her mental health is not stable. While Maja is thus attracted to an existence on a simple level in the company of a bearded faun and his animals, Rubek is drawn in the opposite direction of artistic idealism, the beautiful but perilous heights of snowcapped mountains. To Rubek, there is something ethereal about Irene. She is the symbolic mother of his masterpiece "The Day of Resurrection". Her ideal beauty is symbolically linked to chastity, purity, and the chill of death. And yet he is also clearly attracted to her as a woman.

The sculptor is situated between the demands of his artistic calling and his inclinations for life on practical terms, in the lowlands. It is not difficult for him to choose between Maja and Irene. His artistic ambition drives him to climb to the heights with his ideal love, to regain what was lost. Life on this level, however, is impossible.

In his last play Ibsen is taking the "analytical" drama to its limits. The stage effect of *When We Dead Awaken* obviously does not rely solely on the developing plot. Dramatic qualities are inherent in the symbolic relations connecting expressions of full-blooded vitalism and the death wish, artistic idealism and zest for life. The use of natural scenery and mythological references add to the complex web of the dialogue, probing into the past and the liberation from the entanglements of the present.

—Asbjørn Aarseth

THE WHITE DEVIL
by John Webster

First Publication: London, 1612.
First Production: Red Bull Theatre, London (Queen's Men), c. 1612.

Editions
The White Devil, edited by G.B. Harrison, London, 1933.
The White Devil, edited by John Russell Brown, London, 1960; revised edition, 1966 (Revels Plays).
The White Devil, edited by Elizabeth M. Brennan, London, 1966 (New Mermaid Series).
The White Devil, edited by J.R. Mulryne, Lincoln, Nebraska, 1970 (Regents Renaissance Drama Series).
The White Devil, in *John Webster: Three Plays*, edited by D.C. Gunby, Harmondsworth, 1972.
The White Devil, edited by Clive Hart, Edinburgh, 1972 (Fountainwell Drama Texts).
The White Devil, in *Selected Plays of John Webster*, edited by Jonathon Dollimore and Alan Sinfield, Cambridge, 1983.
The White Devil, edited by Stephen White, London, 1987.

Criticism
(For general works on the author, see *Playwrights* volume)

Books:
G. Boklund, *The Sources of "The White Devil"*, Uppsala, Sweden, 1957.
D.C. Gunby, *The White Devil*, London, 1971.
Anders Dallby, *The Anatomy of Evil: A Study of John Webster's "The White Devil"*, Lund, The Netherlands, 1974.
Roger V. Holdsworth (ed.) *"The White Devil" and "The Duchess of Malfi": A Casebook*, London, 1975.
Frederick O. Waage, *The White Devil Discover'd: Backgrounds and Foregrounds to Webster's Tragedy*, New York, 1984.
Richard Allen Cave, *"The White Devil" and "The Duchess of Malfi"*, London, 1988 (Text and Performance Series).

Articles:
Hazleton Spencer, "Nahum Tate and *The White Devil*", in *English Literary History*, 1, 1934.
John Russell Brown, "On the Dating of Webster's *The White Devil* and *The Duchess of Malfi*", in *Philological Quarterly*, 31, 1952.

B.J. Layman, "The Equilibrium of Opposites in *The White Devil*: A Reinterpretation", in *Publications of the Modern Language Association* [*PMLA*], 74, 1959.

H. Bruce Franklin, "The Trial Scene of Webster's *The White Devil* Examined in Terms of Renaissance Rhetoric", in *Studies in English Literature*, 1, 1961.

James R. Hunt, "Inverted Rituals in John Webster's *The White Devil*", in *Journal of English and Germanic Philology*, 61, 1962.

Roma Gill, " 'Quaintly Done': A Reading of *The White Devil*", in *Essays and Studies (by Members of the English Association)*, 19, 1964.

E.B. Benjamin, "Patterns of Morality in *The White Devil*" in *English Studies*, 46, 1965.

George Sensbaugh, "Tragic Effect in Webster's *The White Devil*", in *Studies in English Literature 1500-1900*, 5, 1965.

Thomas B. Stroup, "Flamineo and the 'Comfortable Words'", in *Renaissance Papers*, 1965.

Robert W. Dent, "The White Devil or Vittoria Corombona?", in *Renaissance Drama*, 9, 1966.

George Holland, "The Function of the Minor Characters in *The White Devil*," in *Philological Quarterly*, 52, 1973.

Norma Kroll, "The Democritean Universe in Webster's *The White Devil*", in *Comparative Drama*, 7, 1973.

Larry S. Champion, "Webster's *The White Devil* and the Jacobean Tragic Perspective", in *Texas Studies in Literature and Language*, 16, 1974.

S.W. Sullivan, "The Tendency to Rationalize in *The White Devil* and *The Duchess of Malfi*", in *Yearbook of English Studies*, 4, 1974.

James T. Henke, "John Webster's Motif of 'Consuming': An Approach to the Dramatic Unity and Tragic Vision of *The White Devil* and *The Duchess of Malfi*", in *Neuphilologische Mitteilungen*, 76, 1975.

John F. McElroy, "*The White Devil*, *Women Beware Women*, and the Limits of Rationalist Criticism", in *Studies in English Literature 1500-1900*, 19, 1979.

Susan H. McLeod, "Duality in *The White Devil*", in *Studies in English Literature 1500-1900*, 20, 1980.

Rupin W. Desai, " 'Spectacles Fashioned with such Perspective Art': A Phenomenological Reading of Webster's *The White Devil*", in *Medieval and Renaissance Drama in England*, 1, 1984.

Ewa Elandt-Jankowska, "John Webster's *The White Devil*: A Study in Black Humour and Laughter as Audience Response", in *Studia Anglia Posnaniensa*, 17, 1984.

A.L. and M.K. Kistner, "Traditional Structures in *The White Devil*", in *Essays in Literature* (Macomb, Illinois), vol. 12 no. 2, 1985.

Ann Rosalind Jones, "Italians and Others: Venice and the Irish in *Coryat's Crudities* and *The White Devil*", in *Renaissance Drama*, 18, 1987.

*   *   *

The White Devil is based on the career of Vittoria Accoramboni, between 1580 and 1585 the mistress of, and subsequently wife to, Paulo Giordano Orsini, Duke of Bracciano. In Webster's version of events, Vittoria and her brother Flamineo, a malcontented gentleman in the Duke's service, are first seen capitalizing on their relationship with Bracciano, despite the resistance of their mother, Cornelia. Bracciano offends Francisco, the Duke of Florence, and his ally the cardinal Monticelso, by refusing a reconciliation with his wife, Isabella, sister to Francisco. Instead, he arranges for Isabella's murder, and for the murder of Vittoria's husband, Camillo. Subsequently Francisco and Monticelso have Vittoria

arraigned for a whore and sent to a house of convertites, but their justice is clearly compromised by the political rivalry between Francisco and Bracciano; then Flamineo quarrels with Lodovico, a follower of Isabella's, formerly banished, who has returned with news of Isabella's death. Monticelso is elected Pope; Francisco recruits Lodovico to a party against Bracciano; and tensions erupt between the lovers.

In the final act, the revengers, disguised as Capuchins (and led for a while by Francisco himself, disguised as a moor), arrive at Bracciano's court. They poison Bracciano's armour, and strangle him under cover of administering extreme unction. Meanwhile, Vittoria's family is falling apart. Cornelia runs mad, and in a desperate final scene Flamineo and Vittoria try to outreach one another, only to be overtaken by Lodovico and his agents. In the closing moments, Bracciano's young son arrests the revengers and takes over his father's government.

Violent, poetic, and macabre, *The White Devil* is the archetypal Italianate tragedy, that brings together a torrid sexuality and a philosophic scepticism within a setting of cynical and ruthless statecraft. Regarded at one time as a lurid and sensational melodrama, the tragedy is now more often seen as a compelling portrayal of a society in which ideals have been overwhelmed by the naked enforcement of power, and which echoes the anxieties of an age conscious that it was undergoing traumatic and corrosive transformations. Webster's distinction is the relentlessness with which he confronts the collision between individual desire and the brutalities of political necessity. His characters—endowed with an incandescent and densely concrete language—live with a special intensity: it is the very violence of the desires which impel them that burn them up (Flamineo will compare his death to a "spent taper" that recovers for a flash and then instantly goes out). Yet they inhabit a perplexing, comfortless maze from which there is no escape and which puzzles their futile attempts to control their own destinies. The survivors in this world (Francisco and Monticelso) will be the men who are most dispassionate and calculating.

Formally, the play is a revenge tragedy: the vengeance of Francisco and Lodovico on Bracciano and Vittoria answers the crimes they had committed against Isabella and Camillo. Yet the outcome gives little cause for reassurance, as the agents of retribution are scarcely different from their victims: Lodovico is a cut-throat, Francisco is a calculating Machiavel, Monticelso is an intelligencing Pope who uses excommunication for political ends. Furthermore, Webster's plotting sprawls (the fifth act alone is twice the length it ought to be) and suggestions of an emerging design are undermined by the fragmentary dramaturgy which he employs. His construction advances by way of shocking juxtapositions of tone: farce against murder, litigation against madness, pious exhortation against sensual encounters. The play's architecture seems to be monumental but shattered, and it articulates a torrential chaos, populated by aristocrats who are cruel and sordid, yet who are invested with a glamour that evokes powerfully divided responses from the spectator. The play's title, which refers specifically to Vittoria, at one and the same time vixen and victim, whore and wronged woman, signals more broadly the quality of openly paradoxical ambivalence which hangs over the world of the play as a whole.

Not surprisingly, the evaluation of Vittoria and Flamineo is beset with problems; obviously compromised as individuals, their plight is rendered understandable by the oppressiveness of the world to which they belong. They certainly are unpleasant people, opportunists and pragmatists who sell their integrity for the sake of getting on and they end up tearing each other apart. Yet, as members of a gentry family whose fortunes are in decline, they are rendered vulnerable by the gap between their expectations and their circumstances. Flamineo is presented as a frustrated intellectual for whom the only way to preferment is by quiescently forwarding the desires of the great. Vittoria is a woman whose beauty is her fortune, yet who cannot advance herself without forfeiting her public respect and who finds herself distrusted and blamed even by Bracciano, for whom she has sacrificed everything. She may be the whore that Francisco and Monticelso, in the justly famous arraignment scene, try to demonstrate her to be; yet her response powerfully exposes the hidden bias in their charade. In countercharging that her judge and accuser are the same person, Vittoria steals the moral high ground and proves the process of law which condems her to be little better than a judicial rape.

On the other hand, it has to be stressed that Webster does not sentimentalize or idealize Vittoria and Flamineo. There are no heroes or heroines in this world, and even people whose suffering entitles them to the audience's sympathy are denied the luxury of heroic transcendence: Vittoria and Flamineo die regretting their errors but are unable to recover enough faith in themselves to do more than drift towards a perpetual silence. The play ends with a kind of tough flippancy, in which Vittoria's exhaustion is counterpointed against Flamineo's contempt for the "glorious villains" who murder him, and both die "in a mist", overwhelmed not only by the violence of their antagonists but by the absence of any form of consolation which might make their deaths bearable. The banal moral tags to which they finally cling hardly add up to an effective ethical counterbalance to the wild and brutal world which they have exploited but which now destroys them.

—Martin Butler

**THE WHITE GEESE (Au Retour des oies blanches)
by Marcel Dubé**

First Publication: Montreal, 1969.
First Production: Comédie-Canadienne, Montreal, 21 October, 1966.

Translations
The White Geese, translated by Jean Remple, Toronto, 1972.

Criticism
(For general works on the author, see *Playwrights* volume)

Articles:
André Vanasse, "*Au Retour des oies blanches*", in *Dictionnaire des oeuvres littéraires du Québec, 4*, Montreal, 1984.

*   *   *

Late one afternoon the members of a well-to-do family are assembled in Quebec City's Upper Town: Achille, a disgraced middle-aged politician desperately seeking to return to favour in the new provincial cabinet; his mother, Amélie; his wife, Elizabeth; their two adult children, Robert and Geneviève, who have each invited a friend for the weekend; and Achille's step-brother Thomas, younger than him and important to the action, although he never appears on stage. Apart from his doting, protective mother, Achille's family is united only in its scorn and detestation of him. As the play progresses, his hypocrisy, duplicity, and moral bankruptcy are revealed, culminating in the revelation, within an effective play-within-play, that Laure, the friend his daughter has invited, was violated by Achille while he was in government.

Geneviève and her mother share a curious bond: they have each, at different times, been drawn to Achille's step-brother. When the daughter learns that Thomas, the uncle-lover with whom she had gone goose hunting the previous autumn, is in fact her father from a similar brief and illicit liaison with Elizabeth, she commits suicide. As the stricken family prepares to dissolve definitively, the arrival of Thomas is announced.

Consciously classical in form (the structure is simple—two acts, four scenes—and the action takes place in one house, in a space of some 12 hours), in inspiration (explicit and implicit references to the legend of the Atreus family are numerous), and tragic atmosphere, this intensely sombre portrayal of a troubled family in crisis is generally considered the best of the 40-odd plays composed by Dubé, the dominant playwright of French Canada in the 1950's and 1960's. Freudian overtones are striking, particularly in the many skilful allusions to the Electra complex. Less obvious to the present-day reader or spectator are allusions to the political situation in Quebec at the time the play was first produced. These, however, are not vital for appreciation of this work.

The focal character, Achille, is one of Dubé's most memorable creations. The contradictions in his personality are entirely credible: domineering but weak, he despises all weakness in others; narcissistic but insecure, he fears and loathes the step-brother whose birth destroyed his own privileged relationship with his mother (her unquestioning devotion to him is the source of much of his psychological burden, since her expectations of him go far beyond his moral capabilities); outwardly conformist, law-abiding, and self-righteous, he is capable of the lowest actions in private and public life, notably during his term as minister in the provincial cabinet. When his daughter arranges the parlour game that is central to the action, a ferocious *jeu de la vérité* or "Truth and Consequences", her intent is to make him confront, once and for all, the vile contradictions in his past actions, and their present consequences. Her game is only too successful; as in Sophocles, truths that were better masked come to light and their spin-off effects destroy, literally or figuratively, all those present.

None of the members of this family is above reproach—either their own, or others'. Elizabeth, unfaithful spouse and ineffectual mother, bears a personal guilt made heavier by the lucidity she seeks to dull with drink. Robert, suffocated like his father by maternal attention and repelled by the father he has known, is haunted by his homosexual inclinations in an intensely homophobic society (here Freud's now-suspect theories of gender identification are apparent). Geneviève, catalyst of the action and its principal victim, is drawn fatefully towards her uncle because he seems to incarnate all the virtues she finds lacking in her presumed father. Her pregnancy by Thomas and the subsequent illegal abortion she procured are a burden rendered unbearable by the revelations her "game" provokes.

The white geese of the title provide a powerful, unifying, and obsessive symbol: the play opens with a brace of geese, left inside the door in a hunting-bag as a presage of Thomas's return. The call of migrating geese is heard at intervals (most strikingly at the very moment of Geneviève's suicide), and they evoke the two fateful hunting excursions with Thomas: one, some 20 years earlier, which resulted in Geneviève's conception; and one the previous autumn, when Geneviève too had conceived and subsequently procured an abortion. In fact, mother and daughter have both been merely trophies for

Thomas, the liberated, insouciant hunter of wild geese (in French, *une oie blanche* also means a naïve, innocent woman) whose attraction for them derives mainly from his dissimilarity to Achille.

The Wild Geese almost immediately became part of the canon of Quebec drama, and remains so today. Theatre historians have also seen this play as a significant turning-point in the career of Marcel Dubé, whose previous works had presented young working-class characters in characteristically tawdry settings, pursuing vestiges of tawdry ideals. Although social class, age, and setting are distinctly different here, the values of the characters portrayed in this play prove to be just as ineffectual and their ideals just as tawdry.

—Leonard E. Doucette

THE WHITE GUARD (Dni Turbinykh)
by Mikhail Bulgakov

First Publication: With Pushkin's *Poslednie dni*, 1955.
First Production: Moscow Art Theatre, Moscow, 5 October 1926.

Translations
The Days of the Turbins, in *Six Soviet Plays*, translated by Eugene Lyons, London, 1935.
The White Guard, translated by Michael Glenny, London, 1979.

Criticism
(For general works on the author, see *Playwrights* volume)

Articles:
Volker Levin, "*Belj dom*—eine Parodie auf M.A. Bulgakovs Drama *Dni Turbinych:* Ein Beitrag zur sowjetischen Bulgakov-Rezeption der zwanziger Jahre", in *Welt der Slawen*, 26, 1981.
Gail Lenhoff, "Chronological Error and Irony in Bulgakov's *Days of the Turbins*", in *Russian Literature and American Critics*, edited by Kenneth N. Brostrom, Ann Arbor, Michigan, 1984.
A. Smeljanski, "Bulgakows *Tage der Turbins* am Moskauer Künstlertheater", in *Kunst und Literatur*, vol.34 no.1, 1986.
Robert Russell, "Bulgakov's *The White Guard* and *Flight*", in his *Russian Drama of the Revolutionary Period*, Totowa, New Jersey, 1988.

*   *   *

In 1918 Colonel Alexei Turbin of the Russian Imperial Army is in Kiev to protect the "legitimate" Ukrainian ruler, the Hetman (who in reality is a puppet of the occupying German army), against the unruly Ukrainian nationalist partisans of Petliura and the Bolshevik Red Army, which is advancing from the North. In the first act Talberg, liaison officer with the Germans, and married to Alexei's sister Elena, leaves his wife behind by joining the German withdrawal. The Hetman too deserts for Berlin, as Petliura's partisans enter the city. Thus the White Russian forces are left isolated and without purpose. Alexei tells his brigade of cadets to discard their uniforms and hide. However, when Petliura's cossacks

arrive, Alexei himself is killed and young Nikolai Turbin is wounded. As the city falls, several Guards officers take refuge with Elena in the Turbins' house. In the last act the Red Army finally arrives to drive out the cossacks, and the Whites prepare to reconcile themselves to their revolutionary fellow-countrymen—apart from Captain Studinsky, who intends to join the royalists still fighting in the South under General Danikin.

Based on his novel, *The White Guard* (*Belaya Gvardiya*, 1924), Bulgakov's dramatisation was written at the instigation of the Moscow Art Theatre, and was presented, under the title *The Days of the Turbins* (*Dni Turbinykh*), on 5 October 1926. The change of title reflects the problems the theatre had in getting the play past the censorship of the *Glavrepertkom*, as a civil war story presented from the point of view of the royalist Whites; there was particular controversy over the singing of the Tsarist national anthem in the first act. Nor did it go unnoticed that this was the first new Russian play to be presented by the Art Theatre since the 1917 revolution. As Stanislavski wrote, the theatre was reluctant to mount simplistic revolutionary propaganda, and "was not interested in watching people marching with red banners, but in getting a real insight into the revolutionary soul of our country".

In fact the play, like the novel, was a genuine attempt to reconcile conservatives to the inevitability of permanent change, and was also a plea to the triumphant Bolsheviks to accept the "fellow-travelling" credentials of the liberal intelligentsia. Bulgakov's attitude was shared by many Muscovites who attended the first performances, as well as by the directors of the Art Theatre. Commissar for Art, Anatoli Lunacharsky, considered the play "ideologically inconsistent" but found that the Art Theatre's production revealed "its true value". This lay in the realistic representation of the decent and bewildered Turbin family, who remain loyal to each other and to their humane principles while their whole world is being destroyed, significantly, not by the Bolsheviks, but by the duplicity of the Germans and their puppet Hetman, and by the thuggery of Petliura's nationalists. Nevertheless, the critics, striving to demonstrate their own political orthodoxy, attacked the play's "bourgeois" qualities, and not only ensured the banning of Bulgakov's next play, *Flight* (*Beg*), but the removal of *The Days of the Turbins* from the repertory, despite its continuing popularity with audiences. However, in 1932 the production was revived—apparently Stalin so enjoyed the play that he had seen it 15 times during its first run.

In its form and style the play owes much to the Moscow Art's naturalistic tradition of Chekhov and Gorky, and, apart from the rather melodramatic exaggeration of the pompous Hetman suddenly realising his allies have all deserted him, and the swaggering ruthlessness of Petliura's "banditti", the scenes in the Turbins' cluttered appartment have something of the strained jocularity in the face of catastrophe to be found in *The Three Sisters*. Particularly effective are the characters of Shervinsky, the romantic braggart who eventually wins the affections of Elena (who has been deserted by the worthless Talberg), and the clumsy young cousin, Lariosik, who turns up at just the wrong moment, hoping to get into Kiev university. The comedy provided by these two characters undercuts the panic and pathos of the more overtly emotional scenes, and this helped audiences identify with the "reactionary" Whites, seeing them as ordinary people caught up in the conflicting loyalties of the Civil War. The Turbins themselves, Alexei, Elena, and Nikolai, appear rather flat on the page, but the original actors must have brought some of the complexity of the novel to their character-interpretations; according to Victor Nekrasov, their personalities lived on in his imagination for over 40 years.

The Days of the Turbins was the first play Norris Houghton

The White Guard: Moscow Art Theatre, 1926 (first production, as *Days of the Turbins*)

saw at the Moscow Art Theatre, when he arrived in Russia to study theatre in 1934, and he was particularly impressed by the authenticity of the ensemble playing:

> Actors talk to each other in the tones of natural conversation. . .On this stage no actor is better than any other; there is complete give and take. One finds oneself interested in the family, in the whole group of people, not in each character separately. . .When at the end of the play the bands of the victorious invading troops are heard playing in the distant street, and the Turbins stand quietly at the window listening to the strains of music that herald a new order and a new day, we know that life for them is over, and it seems a hard thing.

—George Taylor

WHITE MARRIAGE. See **MARIAGE BLANC.**

WHO'S AFRAID OF VIRGINIA WOOLF?
by Edward Albee

First Publication: New York, 1962.
First Production: Billy Rose Theatre, 13 October 1962.

Criticism
(For general works on the author, see *Playwrights* volume)

Articles:
Allan Lewis, "The Fun and Games of Edward Albee", in *Educational Theatre Journal*, 1964.
Pierre Dommergues, "La Conscience magique d'Edward Albee", in *Cahiers Renaud-Barrault*, 63, 1967.
Arthur Evans, "Love, History and Edward Albee", in *Renascence*, 19, 1967.
Joy Flasch, "Games People Play in *Who's Afraid of Virginia Woolf?*", in *Modern Drama*, 10, 1967.
Louis Paul, "A Game Analysis of Albee's *Who's Afraid of Virginia Woolf?: The Core of Grief*", in *Literature and Psychology*, 17, 1967.
Ruth Meyer, "Language: Truth and Illusion in *Who's Afraid of Virginia Woolf?*", in *Educational Theatre Journal*, 20, 1968.
Terry Otten, "Ibsen and Albee's Spurious Children", in *Comparative Drama*, 2, 1968.
Richard J. Dozier, "Adultery and Disappointment in *Who's Afraid of Virginia Woolf*", in *Modern Drama*, 11, 1969.
Thomas E. Porter, "Fun and Games in Suburbia: *Who's Afraid of Virginia Woolf?*", in his *Myth and Modern American Drama*, Detroit, Michigan, 1969.
Rictor C. Norton, "Folklore and Myth in *Who's Afraid of Virginia Woolf?*", in *Renascence*, 23, 1971.
S.M. Agnihotri, "Child Symbol and Imagery in Edward Albee's *Who's Afraid of Virginia Woolf?*", in *Panjab University Research Bulletin: Arts*, vol.3 no.4, 1972.
John A. Byars, "*Taming of the Shrew* and *Who's Afraid of Virginia Woolf?*", in *Cimarron Review*, 21, 1972.

Rachel B. Duplessis, "In the Bosom of the Family: Evasions in Edward Albee", in *Recherches anglaises et américains*, 5, 1972.
Thomas P. Adler, "Albee's *Who's Afraid of Virginia Woolf?*: A Long Night's Journey into Day", in *Educational Theatre Journal*, 25, 1973.
Duane R. Carr, "St. George and the Snapdragons: The Influence of Unamuno on *Who's Afraid of Virginia Woolf?*", in *Arizona Quarterly*, 29, 1973.
John Dollard, "The Hidden Meaning of *Who's Afraid. . .*", in *Connecticut Review*, vol.7 no.1, 1973.
Orley I. Holtan, "*Who's Afraid of Virginia Woolf?* and the Patterns of History", in *Educational Theatre Journal*, 25, 1973.
Richard Martin, "One v. One, or Two Against All? A Note on Edward Albee's *Who's Afraid of Virginia Woolf?*", in *Neueren Sprachen*, 72, 1973.
James P. Quinn, "Myth and Romance in Albee's *Who's Afraid of Virginia Woolf*", in *Arizona Quarterly*, 30, 1974.
Grace S. Wurster, "Albee's Festival Chant: *Who's Afraid of Virginia Woolf?*", in *Michigan Academician*, 9, 1976.
Alina Nowacka, "The Hybrid Structure in Albee's Plays", in *Acta Universitatis Wratislaviensis*, 360, 1977.
Terry Otten, "'Played to the Finish': Coward and Albee", in *Studies in the Humanities*, vol.6 no.1, 1977.
Alison Hopwood, "'Hey what's that from?': Edward Albee's *Who's Afraid of Virginia Woolf?*", in *Atlantis*, 3, 1978.
M. Thomas Inge, "Edward Albee's Love Story of the Age of the Absurd", in *Notes on Contemporary Literature*, vol.8 no.5, 1978.
Steven H. Gale, "Breakers of Illusion: George in Edward Albee's *Who's Afraid of Virginia Woolf?* and Richard in Harold Pinter's *The Lover*", in *Vision*, vol.1 no.1, 1979.
Dan Ducker, "'Pow!' 'Snap!' 'Pouf!': The Modes of Communication in *Who's Afraid of Virginia Woolf?*", in *CLA Journal*, 26, 1982.
Terry Otten, "*Who's Afraid of Virginia Woolf*", in his *After Innocence: Visions of the Fall in Modern Literature*, Pittsburgh, Pennsylvania, 1982.
Jeffrey B. Loomis, "After the Acts: Destructive Illusion or Restorative Allusion in *Who's Afraid of Virginia Woolf?*", in *Notes on Contemporary Literature*, vol.14 no.1, 1984.
James L. Kastely, "Some Things Are Sad, Though: Accident in *Who's Afraid of Virginia Woolf?*", in *Essays in Theatre*, 7, 1988.

*   *   *

The action of the play takes place late one evening in the New England campus home of a childless, middle-aged couple. George has an impressive record of academic mediocrity teaching in the history department of the college where, in spite of having married the principal's daughter early in his career, he has failed to fulfil the overpowering expectations of his wife and her father. George's personal failings and lack of professional ambition have provided abundant ammunition for the vitriolic war of attrition waged by Martha against him. However, the years of abuse have enabled George to develop his own verbal arsenal and sharpen an acerbic wit, equally skilled in offensive as well as defensive capability. The domestic battleground has become entrenched with its own strategies and rules of engagement, complicated by the invention of a non-existent son, who inhabits the most private quarter of their game-playing province. The chief rule is that under no circumstances should the boy be mentioned to anyone.

Into this arena, Martha invites a new appointee to the

Who's Afraid of Virginia Woolf?: National Theatre, London, 1981

college, the handsome young biologist Nick, and his wife Honey, to continue an inaugural party hosted on campus earlier in the evening. The liberal quantities of liquor and the arrival of the younger couple, who in many ways mirror the sterility of George and Martha's own marriage, provoke an explosive confrontation with the realities of past and present. Nick confesses his material motives for marrying the once hysterically pregnant Honey. She, in turn, reveals her fear of bearing a child. The exorcism of the illusory aspects of all their lives is symbolically achieved when George, prompted by Martha's forbidden disclosure of the "fact" of their son's forthcoming 21st birthday and then sickened by her attempted sexual liaison with an incapable Nick, announces the death of the boy in an automobile accident.

The appearance of *Who's Afraid of Virginia Woolf?* on Broadway in 1962 briefly established Edward Albee's reputation as the inheritor of a predominantly naturalistic post-War American playwriting tradition. Yet Albee's subsequent plays were to baffle critical and popular audiences alike, with their marked and uncompromising departure from a familiar realism. It is possible to see that while *Who's Afraid of Virginia Woolf?* may appear to be essentially naturalistic, several features serve to undermine the conventional domestic situation of the "battle-of-the-sexes" kind that Strindberg and Ibsen were dramatising decades earlier. Albee creates a confining theatrical space within which the role-play of private disputation assumes a larger, public significance. In spite of the success of the film version of the play with Richard Burton and Elizabeth Taylor, its adaptation for the screen sacrificed the self-consciousness, the illusory and ephemeral nature of the medium of the theatre for which it was written and for which it is so appropriate.

The historical resonance with the Washingtons is clearly not meant to go unnoticed, as George and Martha's relationship to Western cultural values and the edifice of dreams and self-deceptions that New World mythology has long cherished becomes apparent. The character of Nick might be seen as one of these dreams made flesh, the blond-haired, blue-eyed quarterback with a promise of a genetically engineered future who proves to be such an attractive sexual lure for Martha. (Such a figure appears as the Young Man in another of Albee's plays from the same period, *The American Dream* of 1962). Yet Nick's impotence in this adulterous encounter suggests a deeper relevance: the hollow ring of an empty vessel. These symbolic undercurrents run beneath a dramatic setting which enables Albee to juxtapose representatives from the intellectual worlds of scientific objectivity and historical inevitability through the campus meeting of the younger and older man.

George's history is ambiguous. Is he, in part at least, the subject of his own story of the boy who accidentally shot his mother and a year later saw his father killed in a car crash? Was it an autobiographical narrative in the book ridiculed by Martha and her father? Such an explanation might account for motivations in a naturalistic sense, but we need not have the facts of this history verified in order to experience an intensification of the characters' sense of loss through this metaphorical tale. Edward Albee's preoccupation with the gaping wound of missing parents and lost children must be rooted in his own experience of having been abandoned by his mother and father in the late 1920's and subsequently adopted. Central to the play is the notion of absence: the child whose painful absence has been filled with an imagined presence; the absence of love in a marriage which has had its unconfronted truths veneered.

Who's Afraid of Virginia Woolf? is a raw, moving, emotionally exhausting play to witness in performance. Albee has constructed, through the characters of George and Martha, two of the most demanding roles in modern dramatic writing. The deadly struggle between them unleashes a chain of events which pursues its inevitable course of destruction. Yet there is renewal in this tragedy of loss, epitomized by the rising light in the darkened sky at the play's conclusion, when night begins to turn to dawn. Here there is at last affirmation of the strength gained from mutual support, the promise of courage through reconciliation, and the final abandonment of an unsustainable lie.

—Chris Banfield

THE WILD DUCK (Vildanden)
by Henrik Ibsen

First Publication: Copenhagen, 1884.
First Production: Bergen, Norway, 9 January 1885.

Translations

The Wild Duck, translated by Mrs. F.E. Archer, in *Ibsen's Prose Dramas, 2*, edited by William Archer, 1890; revised version in *Ibsen: Collected Works, 8*, edited by William Archer, London, 1907.

The Wild Duck, translated by Mrs. E. Marx-Aveling, in *The Prose Dramas of Henrik Ibsen, 2*, edited by William Case, London, 1890.

The Wild Duck, in *Henrik Ibsen: Three Plays*, translated by Una Ellis-Fermor, Harmondsworth, 1956.

The Wild Duck, translated by Max Faber, London, 1958.

The Wild Duck, translated by Michael Meyer, London, 1962; corrected version, in *Ibsen: Plays, 1*, translated by Michael Meyer, London, 1980.

The Wild Duck, in *Ibsen: Four Major Plays, 1*, translated by Rolf Fjelde, New York, 1965.

The Wild Duck, translated by Christopher Hampton, London, 1980.

The Wild Duck, in *John Gabriel Borkman; The Wild Duck*, translated by Inga-Stina Ewbank and Peter Hall, Bath, 1990.

Criticism
(For general works on the author, see *Playwrights* volume)

Books:

Erik M. Christensen and Lars Nilsson, *Om Ibsens "Vildanden"*, Odense, Denmark, 1969.

Ingjald Nissen, *Vildanden; Rosmersholm; Hedda Gabler*, Oslo, 1973.

Olav Stokland, *Hjalmar Ekdal og andre essays*, Oslo, 1977.

Peter Kramer, *"Ein Volksfiend und "Die Wildente": Die Wandlung der dramatischen Anlage und des Persönlichkeitsbildes in ihrer Bedeutung für Erziehung und Unterricht*, Bern, 1985.

Articles:

M. Kelly, "*The Wild Duck*: A Study", in *Welsh Review*, vol.5 no.4, 1946.

S. Arestad, "*The Iceman Cometh* and *The Wild Duck*", in *Scandinavian Studies*, 20, 1948.

O. Reinert, "Sight Imagery in *The Wild Duck*", in *Journal of English and Germanic Philology*, 55, 1956.

L. Compton, "The 'Demonic' in *The Wild Duck*", in *Tulane Drama Review*, vol.4 no.1, 1959.

R. Raphael, "The Illusion and the Self in *The Wild Duck, Rosmersholm*, and *The Lady From the Sea*", in *Scandinavian Studies*, vol.35 no.1, 1963.

B. Johnston, "The Metaphoric Structure of *The Wild Duck*", in *Ibsen-Årbok*, 8, 1965–66.

D. Seyler, "*The Sea Gull* and *The Wild Duck*: Birds of a Feather", in *Modern Drama*, 8, 1965–66.

Francis Bull, "*Vildanden*", in *Vildanden og andre essays*, Oslo, 1966.

Ole Koppang, "*Vildanden* av Henrik Ibsen", in *Kirke og kultur*, 73, 1968.

J. Mueller, "Ibsen's *Wild Duck*", in *Modern Drama*, vol.11 no.4, 1969.

Martha T. Halsey, "Reality Versus Illusion: Ibsen's *The Wild Duck* and Buero Vallejo's *En la ardiente oscuridad*", in *Contemporary Literature*, 11, 1970.

Ruth Harmer, "Character, Conflict, and Meaning in *The Wild Duck*", in *Modern Drama*, 12, 1970.

Erwin R. Steinberg, "Gregers Werle as Loki", in *Papers on Language and Literature*, 6, 1970.

Alberta B. Szalita, "Some Questions for Psychoanalysts: Reflections on Ibsen's *The Wild Duck*", in *Psychoanalytic Review*, 57, 1970.

Jacob H. Adler, "Two Hamlet Plays: *The Wild Duck* and *The Sea Gull*", in *Journal of Modern Literature*, 1, 1970–71.

C.T. Watts, "The Unseen Catastrophe in Ibsen's *Vildanden*", in *Scandinavica*, 12, 1973.

Errol Durbach, "Sacrifice and Absurdity in *The Wild Duck*", in *Mosaic*, vol.7 no.4, 1974.

Yomas F. Van Laan, "Language in *Vildanden*", in *Ibsen-Årbok*, 1974.

Charles A. Hallett, "*The Wild Duck* and Critical Cliché", in *Papers on Language and Literature*, 11, 1975.

Anni Carlsson, "Andersenspuren in Ibsens *Vildanden*", in *Ibsen-Årbok*, 1977.

Joan Carr, " 'The Forest's Revenge': Subconscious Motivation in *The Wild Duck*", in *Modern Language Review*, 72, 1977.

D. Brian McCredie, "Falcons and Ducks: A Possible Source of Ibsen's Wild Duck Symbol", in *Modern Language Notes*, 93, 1978.

Marvin Carlson, "Ibsen's *Vildanden* (*The Wild Duck*) in Translation", in *Yearbook of Comparative and General Literature*, 30, 1981.

Daniel Haakonsen, "*Vildanden* og fire russike romaner", in *Ibsen-Årbok*, 1981–82.

Albert Bermel, "Hedvig's Suicide: A Re-Examination of *The Wild Duck*", in *Theater Three*, 1, 1986.

Thomas F. van Laan, "The Novelty of *The Wild Duck*: The Author's Absence", in *Journal of Dramatic Theory and Criticism*, vol.1 no.1, 1986.

Errol Durbach, "Playing the Fool to Sorrow: 'Life-Lies' and 'Life-Truths' in *King Lear* and *The Wild Duck*", in *Essays in Theatre*, 6, 1987.

Thomas Bredsdorff, "The Sins of the Fathers: Bergman, Ronconi, and Ibsen's *Wild Duck*", in *New Theatre Quarterly*, 14, 1988.

Ingard Hauge, "*Vildanden*, welhaven og den romantiske symboltradisjon", in *Edda*, 88, 1988.

The Wild Duck: National Theatre, London, 1979

Neu Jerome, "Life-Lies and Pipe Dreams: Self-Deception in Ibsen's *The Wild Duck* and O'Neill's *The Iceman Cometh*", in *Philosophical Forum*, 19, 1988.

Malcolm Pittock, "*The Wild Duck*: A Revaluation", in *Cambridge Quarterly*, 19, 1990.

* * *

In the five-act play *The Wild Duck*, Ibsen develops further the kind of drama he created with *A Doll's House* and *Ghosts*, the analytical dialogue probing into the past to throw light on the characters in the present. The first act takes place at the rich widower Haakon Werle's residence, where a dinner is given in honour of the home-coming son; while the rest of the play is staged in the modest flat of the Ekdal family, in the photographic studio of Hjalmar Ekdal. Werle's son Gregers, a school friend of Hjalmar's, is an idealist not unlike Brand. He does not approve of the way his father is treating old Ekdal, a one time his business companion. He discovers that Hjalmar's wife, Gina is identical to the girl who was his father's maid, and that his father has helped the couple in starting their photographer's business. The eyesight of their daughter, Hedvig, 14 years old, is declining, just like that of old Werle. Gregers confronts his father, accusing him of a cover-up.

The Ekdals take pleasure in keeping a wild duck and other animals in a sham forest they have created in a loft. Gregers sees it as his mission to purge the house of this and other illusions. His real opponent is Dr. Relling, who wants to protect the family, particularly Hedvig, from the effects of disclosing the secret about her parentage. Hjalmar is informed by his zealous friend of Gina's past relationship with old Werle, and he directs his resentment against the child. Hedvig is desperate to regain his affection, and agrees to Gregers' proposal of shooting the duck as a token of her love for Hjalmar, but shoots herself, misunderstanding Hjalmar's theatrical outburst heard through the wall.

The Wild Duck is a masterpiece of plot construction and stage symbolism. The playwright uses a part of the stage, the loft behind the sliding doors, as a metaphor of the kind of artificial, protected existence of the family he is focusing on. The loft with pigeons, rabbits, hens, and a wild duck among the recesses and stove-pipes is a scenic parallel to the conservatory of Mrs. Alving's garden room in *Ghosts*, another play about the tragic effect of protection, illusion, and exposure. The loft is a lot more conspicuous than the conservatory, however. It is in itself a theatre on the stage, with characters of its own and an elaborate setting.

Into this stagnant world of the Ekdal family Gregers Werle brings his claim of the ideal. Coming from the forests where old Ekdal used to go hunting in his prime, he represents the inexorable world of the outside, of truth. As in the majority of Ibsen's prose plays there is in *The Wild Duck* a marked contrast between inside and outside. This structural device, emphasized by the loft, where the animals are kept under artificial conditions, is also noticeable in the introductory act with the dinner party. An element to be noted in this act is the special title used for the gentlemen who are Mr. Werle's guests: they are more or less all of them referred to individually as *kammerherre*, "chamberlain". This word is used 17 times. In the literal sense a chamberlain is a man connected with a chamber, traditionally a servant at court or to rich families. In the case of the late Mr. Alving in *Ghosts* and the dinner guests in *The Wild Duck* the title suggests both the unhealthy life of indoor parties, drinking, smoking cigars, etc., and the inclination for a secretive and promiscuous bedchamber existence. The dinner guests certainly have the appearance of unwholesome habits—three of them are referred to as a "fat gentleman", a "balding gentleman", and a "short-sighted gentleman", and Mrs. Sørby compares them to grapes: their quality depends on the amount of sunshine they get.

The loft in the Ekdal flat is not merely a menagerie where Hjalmar and his father can go hunting. Hedvig is very much attracted to the place. To her it is as if time has come to a standstill between the curious old books and things packed away in there. The duck, wounded during a real hunt by Mr. Werle's gunshot and given to the Ekdals to recover, is Hedvig's special treasure. It can be seen as a symbol, meaning different things to the different characters. To Hedvig it suggests the vital need for protection, having been exposed to the dangers of the outdoor existence. To Hjalmar it represents a challenge to which he can apply his genius as an inventor. To old Ekdal it is part of the illusion that he is still a hunter. To Gregers Werle it is an obstacle which must be removed to help the Ekdal family reconstruct a relationship based on the truth.

Gregers' purpose is to found a true marriage between Hjalmar and Gina. He wants to heal what is unhealthy, and the remedy is truth. In Dr. Relling's opinion, Gregers is a quack—he is demanding too much of people who are not strong enough to stand the shock of revelation, people who need to keep their "life-lie" going. Hedvig's suicide indicates that the doctor was justified in his warning, but the ending may suggest the possibility of a new start between the parents: "*Now* she's as much yours as mine, isn't she?" Gina says to her husband. The concluding dialogue between Gregers and Dr. Relling, however, leaves open the question as to whether the death of Hedvig will have a lasting effect on Hjalmar.

—Asbjørn Aarseth

WILD OATS; or, The Strolling Gentleman
by John O'Keeffe

First Publication: Dublin, 1791.
First Production: Theatre Royal, Covent Garden, London, 16 April 1791.

Editions

Wild Oats, prepared by Clifford Williams, London, 1977.
Wild Oats, in *The Plays of John O'Keefe*, edited by Frederick M. Link, New York and London, 1981.

Criticism

(For general works on the author, see *Playwrights* volume)

Articles:
Desmond Rushe, "*Wild Oats*", in *Eire*, vol.13 no.1, 1978.

The plot of *Wild Oats*, John O'Keeffe's 1791 comedy, is complex and highly resistant to brief summation which, in any case, can hardly do justice to a very rich and, until 1976, a much neglected play. Much that is important happens before the curtain goes up on Act I. Sometime in the last decades of the 18th century, George Thunder "tricked" the woman he loved, Amelia Banks, into a "sham marriage" under an assumed name. He then broke her heart by going to sea. Later, "forc'd to it" by his father, he married another lady who had a "great fortin" and who subsequently died, leaving him with a son, Harry. That first "sham marriage" had been arranged by Thunder's then boatswain, John Dory, now his "valet-de-Shamber". However, Dory had, in fact, tricked his captain by arranging for the ceremony to be performed by a bona fide clergyman, who was the bride's brother. This first marriage, unknown to Thunder, is entirely legal and binding.

The action of the play begins 19 years later, when Sir George, now a retired naval officer in pursuit of three deserters, stops for refreshment at a country house in Hampshire which, unknown to him, is now the home of his niece, Lady Maria Amaranth Thunder, who has recently inherited it from a Quaker relative with the proviso that she become, and remain, a Quaker. In the intricately plotted five acts and 13 scenes of the play, O'Keeffe cleverly brings together under Lady Amaranth's roof, in addition to uncle and niece, four more principals, including Jack Rover, the hero, and a good number of supporting characters. Harry Thunder, Sir George's only known heir, has, without his father's knowledge and permission, precipitously left the naval academy at Portsmouth and, as "Dick Buskin", joined a troupe of travelling players. When Sir George discovers his beautiful and now-wealthy young niece, Amaranth, he decides to encourage a match between the two cousins who have not seen each other in 12 years. Harry's recently acquired young friend, Rover, is a professional actor who knows neither his father nor his mother. After a friendly parting of the two young men, Rover meets and immediately falls in love with Lady Amaranth, who is equally smitten with him. Miss Amelia, Sir George's first and true wife, lives in the neighborhood in very reduced circumstances with her brother, Banks, the retired naval chaplain who performed her marriage to Sir George. Farmer Gammon, who also lives nearby, wishes to marry Miss Amelia, and when she resists, he resorts to underhand means to gain her consent.

The outcome of all this—though not O'Keeffe's complicated plotting to arrive at it—might easily be guessed. The capture of the three deserters acts as a catalyst for bringing all the characters together in Lady Amaranth's mansion. In this final confrontational scene, Amelia and Sir George joyfully recognize in each other their long-lost spouses. On being questioned by Sir George, Jack Rover reveals enough of his background for Amelia to discover in him her long-lost son, Charles, separated from her in his infancy, and now, of course, the true heir of Sir George. Lady Amaranth immediately claims Charles/Rover as a husband, but on the generous condition that Harry be designated heir to the Thunder lands and fortune ("mine is sufficient for us"). Harry, of course, has happily found not only a brother in Rover but also a sister-in-law-to-be in his beautiful cousin. That evening, a planned performance of Shakespeare's *As You Like It* (O'Keeffe's favorite) is to be offered up for the entertainment not only of the reunited family, some of whom will be acting in it, but also for the guests at Lady Amaranth's housewarming.

The plot of *Wild Oats* depends heavily on many of the classic devices first used by the Latin playwrights, Plautus and Terence, and, later and better, by Shakespeare: a false marriage, a lost child, an abandoned wife, a young man of unknown (but actually of aristocratic) birth, good friends who discover they are brothers, lovers who discover they are cousins, an heiress with a condition attached to her inheritance, and, most importantly, several characters who, knowingly or unknowingly, are in some form of disguise. In a play which is replete with the playwright's love of acting and the theater, it is not surprising that there are several characters who conceal their identities and/or their true natures or who are misidentified by others. Most characters in this play are, in some way, "playing a role".

Jack Rover is a professional actor in search of a "real-life" role—an identity, his parents, a heritage. He is unique in that one of his several disguises is verbal: in his conversation he frequently employs quotations from roles he has played. An important example is a line from *The Rehearsal* (by George Villiers, Duke of Buckingham): "I am the bold Thunder". A good deal of confusion results from the fact that the surname of Villiers' character is also the surname of Harry and Sir George. Clifford Williams, who directed the celebrated Royal Shakespeare Company revival in 1976, found that a major problem of the play was identifying the numerous quotations and deciding how to play them. Many are garbled, perhaps intentionally, or because O'Keeffe was relying on memory, or because he was using (as with Shakespeare) an 18th-century adaptation.

These quotations are merely one of several speech types used in the play. Sir George and John Dory depend heavily on nautical terms and expressions. Lady Amaranth and her Quaker servants use "thees" and "thous". Farmer Gammon and his two children speak in colorful rural accents. Such linguistic variety adds considerably to the richness of the play. In addition, there is frequent use of the aside, common in English drama of that period. In the background, there are hints of the poverty, violence, and injustice common in the 18th century, which add a note of realism to the play. Above all, there is the vitality, good humour, and general optimism of the playwright, all of which allows *Wild Oats* to stand comparison with the best work of the period. William Hazlitt, in an oft-quoted line, referred to O'Keeffe as an "English Molière". This is going too far (and in any case, O'Keeffe was Irish); but he and *Wild Oats* deserve to be much better known.

—Gene A. Barnett

THE WINTER'S TALE
by William Shakespeare

First Publication: In First Folio, London, 1623.
First Production: London, c.1611; earliest recorded production, at the Globe Theatre, London, 15 May 1611.

Editions
The Winter's Tale, edited by H.H. Furness, Philadelphia, 1898 (New Variorum Shakespeare).
The Winter's Tale, edited by Sir Arthur Quiller-Couch and John Dover Wilson, Cambridge, 1931 (The New Shakespeare).
The Winter's Tale, edited by Frank Kermode, New York, 1963 (Signet Classic Shakespeare).

The Winter's Tale, edited by J.H.P. Pafford, London, 1963 (Arden Shakespeare).
The Winter's Tale, edited by Ernest Schanzer, Harmondsworth, 1969 (New Penguin Shakespeare).

Criticism
(For general works on the author, see *Playwrights* volume)

Books:
A.D. Nuttall, *William Shakespeare: "The Winter's Tale"*, London, 1966.
S.L. Bethell, *"The Winter's Tale": A Study*, London, 1947.
Geoffrey Percival Fox, *The Winter's Tale*, Oxford, 1967.
John Anthony Williams, *The Natural Work of Art: The Experience of Romance in Shakespeare's "The Winter's Tale"*, Cambridge, Massachusetts, 1967.
Kenneth Muir (ed.), *"The Winter's Tale": A Casebook*, London, 1968.
Fitzroy Pyle, *"The Winter's Tale": A Commentary on the Structure*, New York, 1968.
Friedrich Oberklager, *"Das Wintermärchen" von William Shakespeare: Eine geisteswissenschaftliche Studie*, Stuttgart, 1976.
Charles Frey, *Shakespeare's Vast Romance: A Study of "The Winter's Tale"*, Columbia, Missouri, 1980.
Dennis Bartholemeusz, *"The Winter's Tale" in Performance in England and America, 1611–1976*, Cambridge and New York, 1982.
Richard Pilgrim, *You Precious Winners All: A Study of Shakespeare's "The Winter's Tale"*, Oxford, 1983.
Soji Iwasaki, *Nature Triumphant: Approach to "The Winter's Tale"*, Tokyo, 1984.
David A. Male, *The Winter's Tale*, Cambridge and New York, 1984 (Shakespeare on Stage Series).
R.P. Draper, *The Winter's Tale*, London, 1985 (Text and Performance Series).
Harold Bloom, *William Shakespeare's "The Winter's Tale"*, New York, New Haven (Connecticut), and Pennsylvania, 1987 (Modern Critical Interpretations).
Wilbur Sanders, *The Winter's Tale*, Boston, 1987 (Twayne's New Critical Introductions to Shakespeare).
Mark W. Scott and Sandra L. Williamson (eds.), *"The Winter's Tale"*, in *Shakespearian Criticism*, 7, Detroit, Illinois, 1988.

Articles:
For information on the many articles about *The Winter's Tale*, see the bibliographies listed in the *Playwrights* volume, and the annual Shakespeare Bibliography in *Shakespeare Quarterly*, published by the Folger Shakespeare Library, Washington D.C. (1950–).

*   *   *

The Winter's Tale, one of Shakespeare's "romances" produced near the end of his career, is believed to have been written early in 1611 for presentation at the private Blackfriars Theatre in London, but a production at the Globe Theatre was reported by Simon Forman on 15 May of that year in his notebook. It was a popular play, and the King's Men presented it on 14 February 1613 at the festivities for the wedding of Princess Elizabeth and also in 1633 at the Whitehall Banqueting House. Based on Robert Greene's *Pandosto*, a prose romance, *The Winter's Tale* is a play in two parts; the first presenting the friendship of Leontes, King of Sicily, and Polixenes, King of Bohemia—a friendship which will be violated on account of the irrational jealousy of Leontes, who

The Winter's Tale: Stratford-Upon-Avon, 1986 (Royal Shakespeare Company)

fears that his queen Hermione is being unfaithful to him with his friend. Tragically, his son Mamillius dies, and his wife (following her swooning during her trial for adultery) is reported to have died; furthermore, his daughter also is lost to him: she is brought to the coast of Bohemia by the loyal Antigonus, who is attacked by a bear and killed off stage. The infant Perdita, however, is rescued by a shepherd. Leontes, recognizing too late that he has wrongfully accused Hermione and apparently destroyed his family, repents.

The second part of the play opens with figure of Time as chorus announcing a "wide gap" having passed—16 years, enough to allow the daughter Perdita to develop into an innocent and highly attractive young girl who is identified as "now grown in grace / Equal with wond'ring". Though raised in the family of a simple shepherd, she attracts the son of Polixenes, the prince Florizel, who chooses her above the courtly ladies he has known. His father Polixenes, who has arrived in disguise, angrily forbids their marriage. The young lovers flee to Sicily, where the true identity of the young woman is discovered: she is the missing princess, long presumed dead. But the wonder elicited by the final "resurrection" scene depends on an even more spectacular marvel, as a purported statue of Hermione by the Italian painter Julio Romano reveals itself to be more than life-like since it is actually the living queen herself—a revelation which affirms the comic structure of Shakespeare's romance.

The Winter's Tale is Shakespeare's treatment of the pastoralism that in England had been best represented by Sidney's *Arcadia* and Book VI of Spenser's *Faerie Queene*. Because Shakespeare's play adopts a complexity of tone and of subject-

matter, it is a far more satisfactory drama than such examples of Italian pastoral tragicomedy as Tasso's *Aminta* and Guarini's *Il pastor fido*. On one level *The Winter's Tale* remains an esoteric drama in the tradition of pastoral tragic-comedy, therefore, and works out the motif *temporis filia veritas* ("Truth is the daughter of Time") which had formed the motto on the title page of *Pandosto*. But the play also, and more enduringly, delivers a spectacle which vividly probes jealousy, abuse of human rights, class distinctions, and those loyalties which bring out the best in persons. Friendship, the direct opposite of the envy and jealousy which is held up as a unifying force at the opening of the play, is clearly the ideal that provides a touchstone for the subsequent violations of it. This great Renaissance ideal provides a moral resting point at the end of the play, though it is there broadened to include the friendship of men and women as well as purely masculine friendship. Thus the pattern of trust and love is re-established in the play not only between the two monarchs but also in the kingdom and the families of the rulers. The play is in a sense the reverse of *Othello*, in which tragedy in the end overwhelms and destroys, and in which friendship and love are permanently violated. *Othello* concludes with the depiction of the hero's despair and suicide, *The Winter's Tale* with hope. Indeed, hope has sustained and preserved Hermione until she might see her daughter once more, and now there is hope for the future through the promise of family and dynastic succession. This ending stands in direct contrast to the tragic conclusion of *Pandosto*.

The Winter's Tale nevertheless avoids sentimentality in its resolution, partly because of the realism with which a character like Autolycus, an irresponsible and yet delightful cheat and minstrel, has been presented. Almost a thorough-going Vice figure, Autolycus maintains an aesthetic that is essentially exploitative and represents economic principles at their most unscrupulous; yet his singing and entertaining are pure delight—a subversive element found in rural Bohemia to undercut the neatness of the world inherited by Shakespeare from the pastoral dramatists and writers.

The ultimate effect of *The Winter's Tale* as a drama is very different from earlier comedies and tragedies by Shakespeare which addressed similar themes. For example, Leontes' jealousy is as quickly roused as King Lear's anger—and with a similar lack of attention to motivation—but it is also very quickly overcome; while the love of Perdita and Florizel must overcome seemingly rather conventional obstacles placed in the way of young love—obstacles that, as in *The Tempest*, will only serve to strengthen their attachment to each other. *The Winter's Tale*, when compared with the ornamented style of such early plays as *Richard II* or the rich imagery of the great tragedies, utilizes verbal images sparingly and carefully. Nevertheless, the play is carefully planned from a visual standpoint, and concludes with the tableau in which Hermione seems to come to life—a scene of reconciliation and renewal that has led numerous critics to interpret the play in terms of an affirmation of Christian values.

From both a literary and a theatrical point of view, Shakespeare's last plays, including *The Winter's Tale*, are sometimes considered inferior. Certainly they are attuned to a new taste—a taste also for the court masque, of which Ben Jonson and Inigo Jones had proved themselves masters following the production of *The Masque of Blackness* in 1605. But the success of *The Winter's Tale* on stage, though not so great as *The Tempest*, has been substantial. Harley Granville-Barker's production of 1912 was the first in modern times to return, at least in part, to the thrust stage, where the action of the play is allowed to move out as if into the audience—a very significant break with 19th-century staging, as George Bernard Shaw observed: "To the imagination it looks as if he had invented a new heaven and a new earth. Instead of the theatre being a huge auditorium, with a picture frame at one end of it, the theatre is now a stage with some unnoticed spectators round it".

—Clifford Davidson

WINTERSET
by Maxwell Anderson

First Publication: Washington D.C., 1935.
First Production: Martin Beck Theatre, New York, 25 September 1935.

Criticism
(For general works on the author, see *Playwrights* volume)

Articles:

Winston Weathers, "*Winterset*: The Archetypal Stage", in his *The Archetype and the Psyche: Essays in World Literature*, Tulsa, Oklahoma, 1968.

Robert L. Gilbert, "Mio Romagna: A New View of Maxwell Anderson's *Winterset*", in *North Dakota Quarterly*, vol.38 no.1, 1970.

Douglas B. Kurdys, "*Winterset*, by Maxwell Anderson: An Ambivalent Play of Theme", in his *Form in the Modern Verse Drama*, Salzburg, 1972.

Arthur T. Tees, "*Winterset*: Four Influences on Mio", in *Modern Drama*, 14, 1972.

John B. Jones, "Shakespeare as Myth and the Structure of *Winterset*", in *Educational Theatre Journal*, 25, 1973.

Robert B. Pearsall, "Maxwell Anderson's *Winterset* and the Social-Justice Dramas of the Nineteen-Thirties", in *Amerikanisches Drama und Theater im 20. Jahrhundert*, edited by Alfred Weber and Siegfried Newweiler, Göttingen, 1975.

N.S. Sahu "*Winterset*: A Tragedy by a Gifted Technician", in *Commonwealth Quarterly*, 13, 1980.

*   *   *

Some years after the execution for murder of Bartolomeo Romagna, a West Coast academic writes an article about the case, drawing attention to a possible witness for the defence who was never called to testify at Romagna's trial: Garth Esdras. In response to the article, three men come to New York City to seek Garth, for different reasons. For Mio Romagna, the dead man's son, it is the evidence which will finally clear his father's name—and allow him to rebuild his own shattered life—that he seeks. For Judge Gaunt, presiding judge at Romagna's trial and the man who ordered his execution, it is confirmation of Romagna's guilt that he seeks: a guilt that will confirm and revalidate that hard judgement which now haunts him, unbalancing his mind. For Trock Estrella, gang leader and possibly the real murderer in the Romagna case, it is Garth's silence that is required: voluntary, or enforced and permanent, if necessary. Mio and the Judge learn the truth of Romagna's innocence; but instead of publicising it as he had intended, Mio finds himself caught between the indifference of the authorities and the likelihood of harm being caused to his newly beloved Miriamne, Garth's young sister, by such a revelation. But to Trock, their knowledge is a threat and a challenge; he kills both Mio and Miriamne, bereaving Garth and his father, and doubtless guaranteeing their continued, frightened silence.

Maxwell Anderson's 1935 verse tragedy takes as its source a celebrated murder case of the 1920's, popularly known as the Sacco and Vanzetti case. Two Italians, Nicola Sacco and Bartolomeo Vanzetti, were arrested for the murder of a paymaster and payroll guard during a robbery in Massachusetts. Despite their protests of innocence, the flimsiness of the circumstantial evidence against them, and the testimony of convicted criminal Celestino Madeiros as to his own involvement in the robbery and their innocence, the two men were convicted, and later executed, having been refused clemency by the State Governor. It is believed that the real reason for their conviction lay in the politics espoused by both men as self-confessed anarchists, and the upsurge of patriotic and anti-radical feeling in America, in the wake of the Russian Revolution (a number of Italian immigrants in the industrial areas of the country had been imprisoned or deported for political activities).

Commercially produced on Broadway, where it was both a box-office and a critical success, winning the first New York Drama Critics Circle award, *Winterset* was Anderson's first attempt at a modern verse tragedy. It was a rarity for him, his other work having eschewed contemporary American settings, choosing instead the historically and/or geographically distanced settings of Tudor England or the American past in which to trace his perennial—and universal—themes: the nobility and resilience of the enduring human spirit, and the positive values of human society, such as love and justice. In this respect, both Anderson and *Winterset* were somewhat out of step with the prevailing ethos of American theatre, which invoked detailed stage realism as a means of engaging with

Winterset: University of Oregon, 1950

immediate socio-political and economic concerns in the wake of the 1929 Wall Street Crash, the Depression, Prohibition, and the advent of the new Roosevelt administration. The times, characterised by Ernest Hemingway as "non-tragic", revealed, and to some extent also perpetuated, a loss of national and individual confidence, and gave rise to a perception that personal engagement was both absurd and potentially dangerous. Dominant stage images were of claustrophobic environments: cages, machines, urban streets and tenements, and dramatic action showed characters under vast, continual pressure, alienated from the spiritual and human securities of earlier (happier) times.

For Anderson, the sense of social and moral disintegration around him was ill-served by the "journalism" of social-realist drama; he also found it fairly pessimistic in tone. As both a pacifist and an eternal optimist about the nobility of the human spirit, Anderson created for his plays an elevated poetic language derived from Shakespearean pastiche and blended with the reductive slang of contemporary street argot. In *Winterset*, this linguistic mixture is further crossed with patches of prose, creating an uneasy idiom; at times, the arias of the principal characters do reach a poignant and beautiful height, though they do not advance the dramatic action (rather, they impede it). However, the attempt to elevate the banality of everyday conversation frequently fails, producing not pathos, but bathos.

Anderson's plotting has also been criticised; Mio's abrupt shift from his obsessive quest for justice to a somewhat queasy, romanticised compromise which leaves Trock victorious, was felt variously to be unbelievable, politically suspect, or morally unsound. The 1939 film version rewrote the ending, Mio and Miriamne being saved by police who come to arrest them for playing the hurdy-gurdy, banned from use in an earlier scene. This rewriting was necessitated by the demands of the Screen Production Code, which forbade depictions of evil triumphing over good. Possibly the alteration was also due to a rejection of the play's tragic status; unlike its classical Greek and Shakespearean models, *Winterset*'s plot, characters, and language do not really achieve such status. It is more properly a melodrama, with gothic overtones.

Yet that is not to denigrate the play. It does have a certain emotional power, and Mio and Miriamne a naïve charm, whilst Trock is a villain in the mould of Brecht's Arturo Ui—though, unlike Ui, he is not comic. In part, the interest resides in moments of linguistic richness, but also in the evocative setting Anderson contrived and designer Jo Mielziner realized: a river front bridgehead, the vaulting arch of the bridge span seeming to break the proscenium; counterpointed by an outcrop of rock, lit by a streetlamp and the glimmer of apartment lights. The setting confers upon the play a grandeur and meaning, a juxtaposition of modernity and tradition, transience and endurance, which seems to achieve the transcendence Anderson sought.

—Val Taylor

THE WITCH OF EDMONTON
by Thomas Dekker, John Ford, and William Rowley

First Publication: London, 1658.
First Production: Cockpit Theatre, London, 1621.

Editions
The Witch of Edmonton, in *Stuart Plays, 2*, edited by A.H. Nethercot, C.R. Baskervill, and V.B. Heltzel, 1934.
"The Witch of Edmonton": A Critical Edition, edited by Etta S. Onat, New York, 1980.
The Witch of Edmonton, with commentary by Simon Trussler, and notes by Jacqui Russell, London, 1983 (Methuen Student Editions).
The Witch of Edmonton, in *Three Jacobean Witchcraft Plays*, edited by Peter Corbin and Douglas Sedge, Manchester, 1986 (Revels Plays).

Criticism
(For general works on the authors, see *Playwrights* volume)

Articles:
Edward Sackville West, "The Significance of *The Witch of Edmonton*", in *Criterion*, 17, 1937.
J.W. Ashton, "Dekker's Use of Folklore in *Old Fortunatus, If This be Not a Good Play*, and *The Witch of Edmonton*", in *Philological Quarterly*, vol. 41 no. 1, 1962.
L.L. Brodwin, "The Domestic Tragedy of Frank Thorney in *The Witch of Edmonton*", in *Studies in English Literature 1500-1900*, 7, 1967.
A. Harris, "Instruments of Mischief", in *Night's Black Agents: Witchcraft and Magic in Seventeenth-Century English Drama*, Manchester, 1980.
Simon Trussler, "Commentary", in *The Witch of Edmonton*, by John Ford, Thomas Dekker, and William Rowley, London, 1983.
Michael Hattaway, "Women and Witchcraft: The Case of *The Witch of Edmonton*", in *Trivium*, 20, 1985.
Nadia J. Rigaud, "Cuddy Banks: Une Trez Longue Mémoire: L'Attitude de Rowley envers une mentalité dans *The Witch of Edmonton*", in *Mythes, croyances et religions dans le monde anglo-saxon*, 6, 1988.
Viviana Comensoli, "Witchcraft and Domestic Tragedy in *The Witch of Edmonton*", in *The Politics of Gender in Early Modern Europe*, edited by Jean R. Brink, Alison P. Coudert, and Maryanne C. Horowitz, Kirksville, Missouri, 1989.

* * *

The play dramatizes two stories, centring on individuals who are both guilty and not guilty of heinous crimes. In that which opens the play, Frank Thorney has married his fellow servant Winnifride unbeknownst to his father, a gentleman whose fortunes are in decline, and against his father's will. Winnifride is with child, but the text does not make clear whether it is Frank's or that of their employer, Sir Arthur Clarington, who has been taking advantage of his maid. In order to stave off disinheritance, Frank, at his father's bidding, marries Susan Carter, daughter of a rich yeoman whose dowry will restore the fortunes of the Thorneys.

Elizabeth Sawyer, an old, poor, and lonely woman has been hounded by her neighbours, especially Old Banks and his son Cuddy, and, in order to be revenged, sells her soul to the Devil who appears in the play in the guise of a familiar spirit, a dog. Frank, in desperation and dogged by the devil, murders Susan, and attempts to lay the guilt on her two rejected suitors. Mother Sawyer has the devil perform various acts of malefice and with his help sends a neighbour who has been persecuting her, Anne Ratcliffe, into madness and death. Frank's guilt is discovered by Susan's virtuous sister Katherine, Mother Sawyer is seized after the community has "tried" her by firing the thatch of her cottage to see if she comes running out. The last scene shows both Thorney and Sawyer repentant but being taken off to execution.

This play offers an exploration of the issues aroused by the notorious contemporary trial and execution of Elizabeth Sawyer in April of the year in which the play was performed. The authors offer a far more tolerant view of the case than does their source, a moralistic pamphlet by the minister Henry Goodcole who visited the old woman in Newgate and participated in the lubricious searches of her person for the "devil's mark". They suggest, in the case of both protagonists, that the true devils of the world are "beggary and want", and show how Mother Sawyer, reviled by the world because she is "poor, deformed, and ignorant", grows to become the image of her constructed by the community. (The play was written and performed just after the peak number of witchcraft trials had passed and the proportion of acquittals was rising.) She detests her persecutor, Old Banks, promising to "go out of" herself, "so I might work / Revenge upon this miser, this black cur / That barks and bites, and sucks the very blood / Of me and of my credit. 'Tis all one / To be a witch as to be counted one".

Likewise the authors make strong suggestions concerning double sexual standards: Winnifride confesses to her seducer, Sir Arthur, that it was her "lewdness" which generated the "waste of his virtue", and although Clarington confesses to his abuse of Winnifride and Frank, he is let off with a fine.

In contrast to the stresses and social fissures in the "real" world of Edmonton, the authors set the play in an idealized, timeless community incarnated in the band of Morris dancers led by Cuddy Banks. This milieu may offer supporting evidence to those who argue that accusations of witchcraft were a function of the decline of neighbourliness and the rise of a more individualistic community. Although the text offers a good sense of the hierarchies and divisions in Edmonton society, its members pride themselves on retaining the old friendly ways of the country in contrast with rapacious and mercantile values associated with the city.

There have been several revivals of the play this century, most recently at the Mermaid Theatre in London in 1962 and at The Other Place by the Royal Shakespeare Company in September 1981. The director of the last, Barry Kyle, took great pains to establish, through detail, the precarious nature of the economy of Edmonton and the ambivalent nature of the Dog-Devil, at once frightening and engaging.

—Michael Hattaway

The Witch of Edmonton: The Other Place, Stratford-Upon-Avon, 1981

WOE FROM WIT.   See **THE MISFORTUNE OF BEING CLEVER.**

A WOMAN KILLED WITH KINDNESS
by Thomas Heywood

First Publication: London, 1607.
First Production: London (Worcester's Men), 1607.

Editions

A Woman Killed With Kindness, in *"A Woman Killed With Kindness" and "Fair Maid of the West"*, edited by Katherine Lee Bates, 1917.

A Woman Killed With Kindness, in *Elizabethan Tragedy*, edited by G. Rylands, 1933.

A Woman Killed With Kindness, in *Elizabethan Plays*, edited by H. Spencer, 1933.

A Woman Killed With Kindness, in *Elizabethan and Stuart Plays*, edited by C.R. Baskervill, V.B. Heltzel, and A.H. Nethercott, 1934.

A Woman Killed With Kindness, in *Five Elizabethan Tragedies*, edited by A.K. McIlwraith, Oxford, 1938.

A Woman Killed With Kindness, in *Four English Tragedies of the 16th and 17th Centuries*, edited by J.M. Morell, 1953.

A Woman Killed With Kindness, edited by R.W. van Fossen, London, 1959 (Revels Plays).

A Woman Killed With Kindness, in *Early Seventeenth Century Drama*, edited by Robert G. Lawrence, London and New York, 1963.

A Woman Killed With Kindness, in *Three Elizabethan Domestic Tragedies*, edited by Keith Sturgess, Harmondsworth, 1969.

A Woman Killed With Kindness, edited by Brian W.M. Scobie, London, 1985 (New Mermaid Series).

Criticism
(For general works on the author, see *Playwrights* volume)

Articles:

McEvoy Patterson, "The Origin of the Main Plot of *A Woman Killed With Kindness*", in *University of Texas Studies in English*, 17, 1937.

Hallett Smith, "*A Woman Killed With Kindness*", in *Publications of the Modern Language Association* [*PMLA*], 53, 1939.

Freda L. Townsend, "The Artistry of Thomas Heywood's Double Plots", in *Philological Quarterly*, 25, 1946.

P. Ure, "Marriage and Domestic Drama in Heywood and Ford", in *English Studies*, 32, 1951.

Patricia Meyer Spacks, "Honor and Perception in *A Woman Killed With Kindness*", in *Modern Language Quarterly*, 20, 1959.

A.G. Hooper, "Heywood's *A Woman Killed With Kindness*", in *English Studies in Africa*, 4, 1961.

Lloyd E. Berry, "A Note on Heywood's *A Woman Killed With Kindness*", in *Modern Language Review*, 58, 1963.

David Cook, "*A Woman Killed With Kindness*: An Un-Shakespearian Tragedy", in *English Studies*, 45, 1964.

Herbert R. Coursen, Jr., "The Subplot of *A Woman Killed With Kindness*", in *English Language Notes*, 2, 1965.

John J. McDermott, "Henryson's *Testament of Cresseid* and Heywood's *A Woman Killed With Kindness*", in *Renaissance Quarterly*, 20, 1967.

John Canuteson, "The Theme of Forgiveness in the Plot and Sub-Plot of *A Woman Killed With Kindness*", in *Renaissance Drama*, 2, 1969.

K.M. Sturgess, "The Early Quartos of Heywood's *A Woman Killed With Kindness*", in *Library*, 1970.

Margaret Bryan, "Food Symbolism in *A Woman Killed With Kindness*", in *Renaissance Papers*, 1973.

Cecile Williamson Cary, "'Go Break This Lute': Music in Heywood's *A Woman Killed With Kindness*", in *Huntington Library Quarterly*, 37, 1974.

Robert Ornstein, "Bourgeois Morality and Dramatic Convention in *A Woman Killed With Kindness*", in *English Renaissance Drama: Essays in Honor of Madeleine Doran and Mark Eccles*, edited by Standish Henning and others, Carbondale, Illinois, 1976.

Leanore Lieblein, "The Context of Murder in English Domestic Plays, 1590–1610", in *Studies in English Literature 1500–1900*, 23, 1983.

Gerald W. Morton, "The Two Faces of Eve: Thomas Heywood's Anne Frankford and Mrs. Wincott", in *Bulletin of the West Virginia Association of College English Teachers*, 8, 1983.

Peter L. Rudnytsky, "*A Woman Killed With Kindness* as Subtext for *Othello*", in *Renaissance Drama*, 14, 1983.

Rick Bowers, "*A Woman Killed With Kindness*: Plausibility on a Smaller Scale", in *Studies in English Literature 1500–1900*, 24, 1984.

Harry Garlick, "Anne Frankford's Fall: A Complementary Perspective", in *AUMLA Journal*, 61, 1984.

Laura G. Bromley, "Domestic Conduct in *A Woman Killed With Kindness*", in *Studies in English Literature 1500–1900*, 26, 1986.

Diana E. Henderson, "Many Mansions: Reconstructing *A Woman Killed With Kindness*", in *Studies in English Literature 1500–1900*, 26, 1986.

Frederick Kiefer, "Heywood as Moralist in *A Woman Killed With Kindness*", in *Medieval and Renaissance Drama in England*, 3, 1986.

David Atkinson, "An Approach to the Main Plot of Thomas Heywood's *A Woman Killed With Kindness*", in *English Studies*, 70, 1989.

Nancy A. Guterrez, "The Irresolution of Melodrama: The Meaning of Adultery in *A Woman Killed With Kindness*", in *Exemplaria*, 1, 1989.

*   *   *

The play gives a lively picture of contemporary country life and relates an unusual end to a tale of adultery. A gentleman (Wendoll) "of a good house, somewhat press'd by want" is befriended and taken into the household of a well-to-do, newly married young couple (John and Anne Frankford). It is not long before he repays such generosity by seducing his host's wife. The husband, informed of their affair by a loyal servant, but unwilling to believe in his friend's disloyalty and his wife's infidelity, arranges to leave home temporarily but secretly returns at midnight and surprises the errant pair "close in each other's arms and fast asleep" in the marital bed. Rousing the household, during which mêlée the lover escapes, the husband, after due deliberation, punishes his wife by obliterating all reminders of her from his house and banishing her to one of his distant manors, never to see him or their two children more. By now full of remorse and truly penitent, the estranged wife starves herself to death; but at the 11th hour she is visited by her husband and re-united with him as she dies. The husband closes the play by declaring that on her tomb he will engrave in golden letters: "Here lies she whom her husband killed with kindness". Interwoven with the main plot is an active subplot too detailed to relate here, but which is commented on below.

The play belongs to a genre known as "domestic tragedy" akin to such plays as *The Yorkshire Tragedy* and *Arden of Faversham*, but unlike these, the main plot contains no violence. It is a Christian moral tale with a structure of sin, repentance, atonement, and forgiveness. Domestic drama is distinguished from contemporary tragedy in that it deals with domestic matters in the middle classes, is usually set in the provinces, and is plainly told—whereas a typical tragedy deals with affairs of state involving people in high places, at court or in cities, and is expressed in heightened language. The prologue to the play warns "Look for no glorious state. . ." and, like *Arden of Faversham*, insists that "simple truth is gracious enough" without the need for "glozing stuff". The language of the play is therefore generally unembellished, written in a mixture of prose, blank verse, and rhymed couplets. The rhymed couplets to a modern ear smack of sentiment and too pat a construction; but the prose sections nicely capture the "below-stairs" and rural aspect of the piece. The bulk of the play, written in blank verse, is effective rather than memorable, though there are a number of noteworthy passages.

Domestic tragedies were written as exemplars. Both the main plot and subplot of this play offer portraits of people who succumb to acts in the "heat of the blood", violating both virtue and honour, and for which they are later penitent. Main plot and subplot complement each other in that the faithless wife and unprincipled nature of the lover are contrasted with the chaste and highly principled brother and sister Sir Charles and Susan Mountford. The husband's action, in not publicly denouncing and physically injuring his unfaithful wife, is unusual in contemporary terms and adds to the interest of the play. There are strong religious overtones in much of the dialogue: the lover is referred to as the Devil, the husband refers to the Great Judge of Heaven, and the wife speaks of her zeal towards Heaven and her tears having washed her "black soul white".

The plot narrative proceeds swiftly, belying the actual passage of time which covers several years; so much so that one is surprised to learn that the Frankfords have managed in the course of the play to produce two children. Perhaps because of this celerity of plot, the volte-face of the guilty characters seems largely unexplored; and certainly in the subplot (which most critics have difficulty in fully accepting) the reversals in feeling occur abruptly. Nevertheless the portrait of Frankford is admirably drawn and the fallen woman, after she has succumbed to Wendoll's persistance, is convincing in her ensuing regret. There is effective cameo-writing in the role of Cranwell, another of Frankford's house-guests—a man of few words, who, in the absence of his host, and when the wife and lover are clearly becoming amorous in public, hastily excuses himself with: "I am on the sudden grown exceeding ill / And would be spar'd from supper. . .". There is also a theatrically telling scene reminiscent of one in Middleton's *Women Beware Women*, though in this instance the game is cards and not chess, in which the dialogue throughout is stiff with double meaning.

An unusually large number of explicit stage directions informative of Elizabethan theatre practice, but also rich in reference to contemporary domestic life, appear in the play. Carpets, for instance, are not for the floor but for the table (to facilitate the playing of cards); hawking and hunting are blood sports seriously and freely indulged in; prison existence is vividly conveyed by means of bare feet, garments in tatters, and limbs heavily fettered in gyves. In its stage directions the

play makes clear the costume difference between a shift and a night-gown, between ordinary clothes and *"gentlemanlike"* clothes, and the importance of boots (which signify the undertaking of a journey). The play is full of subtle detail such as carters who whistle as they convey the wife and her chattels to another home, and references to tablecloth, napkins, voider, wooden knife, bread, trenchers, and salt in the preparation and clearing away of a six o'clock supper.

There have been several revivals of the play in the 20th century, notably that of Jacques Copeau who opened his Vieux-Colombier theatre with it in 1913 (though he cut the subplot). The play has met with a varied critical reception and may not be wholly to the taste of a modern audience; but, in the hands of a sensitive cast and director, there is enough good writing, especially in the main plot, to accomplish an agreeable production. T. S. Eliot has perhaps the last word on the play: "Only moderately poetical but very highly dramatic".

—Philip S. Cook

WOMEN BEWARE WOMEN
by Thomas Middleton

First Publication: London, 1653.
First Production: London, c.1625–27.

Editions

Women Beware Women, edited by Roma Gill, London, 1968.
Women Beware Women, in *Jacobean Tragedies*, edited by A.H. Gomme, London, 1969.
Women Beware Women, in *Thomas Middleton: Three Plays*, edited by Kenneth Muir, London, 1975.
Women Beware Women, edited by J.R. Mulryne, London, 1975.
Women Beware Women, in *Selected Plays of Thomas Middleton*, edited by David L. Frost, Cambridge, 1978.
Women Beware Women, in *Thomas Middleton: Five Plays*, edited by Bryan Loughrey and Neil Taylor, Harmondsworth, 1988.

Criticism
(For general works on the author, see *Playwrights* volume)

Articles:
P. Simpson, "Thomas Middleton's *Women Beware Women*", in *Modern Language Review*, 33, 1938.
D. Dodson, "Middleton's Livia", in *Philological Quarterly*, 27, 1948.
Irving Ribner, "Middleton's *Women Beware Women*: Poetic Imagery and the Moral Vision", in *Tulane Studies in English*, 9, 1959.
Jackson C. Cope, "The Date of Middleton's *Women Beware Women*", in *Modern Language Notes*, 76, 1961.
C. Ricks, "Word-Play in *Women Beware Women*", in *Review of English Studies*, 12, 1961.
E. Engelberg, "Tragic Blindness in *The Changeling* and *Women Beware Women*", in *Modern Language Quarterly*, 23, 1962.
Dorothea Krook, "Tragedy and Satire: Middleton's *Women Beware Women*", in *Scripta Hierosolymitana*, 17, 1966.
George Core, "The Canker and the Muse: Imagery in *Women Beware Women*", in *Renaissance Papers*, 1968.

Inga-Stina Ewbank, "Realism and Morality in *Women Beware Women*", in *Essays and Studies by Members of the English Association*, 22, 1969.

J.B. Batchelor, "The Pattern of *Women Beware Women*", in *Yearbook of English Studies*, 2, 1972.

Charles A. Hallett, "The Psychological Drama in *Women Beware Women*", in *Studies in English Literature 1500–1900*, 12, 1972.

J.R. Mulryne, "The French Source for the Sub-Plot of Middleton's *Women Beware Women*", in *Review of English Studies*, 25, 1974.

J.R. Mulryne, "Manuscript Source-Material for the Main Plot of Thomas Middleton's *Women Beware Women*", in *Yearbook of English Studies*, 5, 1975.

Larry S. Champion, "Tragic Vision in *Women Beware Women*", in *English Studies*, 57, 1976.

Huston Hallahan, "The Thematic Juxtaposition of the Representational and the Sensational in Middleton's *Women Beware Women*", in *Studies in Iconography*, 2, 1976.

A.L. and M.K. Kistner, "Will, Fate, and the Social Order in *Women Beware Women*", in *Essays in Literature*, 3, 1976.

Marjorie S. Lancaster, "Middleton's Use of the Upper Stage in *Women Beware Women*", in *Tulane Studies in English*, 22, 1977.

Verna Ann Foster, "The Deed's Creature: The Tragedy of Bianca in *Women Beware Women*", in *Journal of English and Germanic Philology*, 18, 1979.

John McElroy, "*The White Devil, Women Beware Women* and the Limitations of Rationalistic Criticism", in *Studies in English Literature 1500–1900*, 19, 1979.

A.L. and M.K. Kistner, "Thomas Middleton's Symbolic Action", in *Ariel*, 11, 1980.

Kenneth Muir, "The Role of Livia in *Women Beware Women*", in *Poetry and Drama, 1570–1700: Essays in Honour of Harold F. Brooks*, edited by Antony Coleman, Antony Hammond, and Arthur Johnston, London, 1981.

Jennifer Strauss, "Dance in Thomas Middleton's *Women Beware Women*", in *Parergon*, 29, 1981.

John Potter, "'In Time of Sports': Masques and Masking in Middleton's *Women Beware Women*", in *Papers on Language and Literature*, 18, 1982.

Izumi Kadono, "The Inserted Masque in *Women Beware Women*", in *Sophia English Studies*, 9, 1984.

Nadia J. Rigaud, "La Modification de l'implicité du mariage forcé dans *Women Beware Women* de Middleton", in her *L'Implicité dans la littérature et la pensée anglaises*, Aix-en-Provence, 1984.

Neil Taylor and Brian Loughrey, "Middleton's Chess Strategies in *Women Beware Women*", in *Studies in English Literature 1500–1900*, 24, 1984.

G.B. Shand, "The Stagecraft of *Women Beware Women*", in *Research Opportunities in Renaissance Drama*, 28, 1985.

A.A. Bromham, "The Tragedy of Peace: Political Meaning in *Women Beware Women*", in *Studies in English Literature 1500–1900*, 26, 1986.

Laura Severt King, "Violence and the Masque: A Ritual Sabotaged in Middleton's *Women Beware Women*", in *Pacific Coast Philology*, 21, 1986.

Leslie Thomson, "'Enter Above': The Staging of *Women Beware Women*", in *Studies in English Literature 1500–1900*, 26, 1986.

Anthony B. Dawson, "*Women Beware Women* and the Economy of Rape", in *Studies in English Literature 1500–1900*, 27, 1987.

William Hutchings, "'Creative Vandalism': Or a Tragedy Transformed: Howard Barker's 'Collaboration' with Thomas Middleton on the 1986 Version of *Women Beware Women*", in *Text and Presentation*, edited by Karelisa Hartigan, Lanham, Maryland, 1988.

Albert H. Tricomi, "Middleton's *Women Beware Women* and Anti-Court Drama", in *Modern Language Studies*, 19, 1989.

*   *   *

Leantio, a merchant's clerk, marries Bianca, a gentlewoman from a good family. The Duke of Florence spies her in an open window and decides to make her his mistress. With the help of Livia, a widow (who detains Leantio's mother at chess), the Duke successfully executes his seduction. An estrangement ensues: Bianca is taken on by the Duke as a mistress while Leantio becomes Livia's paid lover. When the Lord Cardinal, the Duke's brother, discovers the corrupt state of affairs, a masque is arranged in which all of the major characters are killed. A subplot dramatizes the plight of Isabella who, to conceal her passion for her uncle, Hippolito, marries a foolish young heir.

Women Beware Women has a topical contemporary resonance as it brings into focus debates about the institution of marriage, male anxieties about dominant women and disempowerment, questions about sexual ideals, and protests against the inhibiting patriarchal structures that enforce obedience. Many of these issues are broached in the opening scene which delineates a homecoming; Leantio is returning home to visit his mother and to introduce her to his new bride. Immediately, however, doubts are raised about the stability of the marriage. A dark undercurrent runs beneath the scene: in a jaunty and uxorious vein, Leantio describes his wife as his property, and there are gloomy references to death, sin, and adultery. Throughout, Bianca's silence and the allusions to locks and keys (Leantio wishes to imprison his wife's sexuality) are troubling and call into question the scene's celebratory aspirations.

The first scene is part of an extended five-part movement that takes up the main sections of the play. It finds its second stage in Leantio's departure for a week of employment. The second homecoming constitutes the third stage and marks the beginning of Leantio and Bianca's disaffection. Unctuously self-congratulatory and prim, Leantio imagines his voraciously sexual wife waiting to embrace him; but he is cruelly disappointed. The domestic idyll that he has erected for himself is built on sand and soon crumbles into debris.

A reunion of sorts between husband and wife (the fourth stage of the play's movement) takes place when they meet and comment upon the change in their social fortunes. A new tone of refined courtesy and specious *politesse* characterizes the occasion: both unused to the splendour of the court, Bianca and Leantio attempt to come to terms with striking changes in their environment. While drawn to each other's leisured lifestyle, they are forced to admit that they thrive best apart.

With the proposed wedding of the Duke and Bianca (after the murder of Leantio) the play's movements conclude. A wedding functions as a framing device which begins and ends the dramatic narrative. The Duke maintains that he will be legitimizing his relationship with Bianca but he is unconvincing: another marriage is being constructed on unstable soil, on deception, vice, and intrigue.

What is revealed in the play's movement is Middleton's representation of various attempts to establish female independence. All of the women in *Women Beware Women* are struggling to throw off the restraints of patriarchy, to resist male rule, to realize autonomous selves, and to become individual subjects. Bianca inveighs against the morality that has shackled her to a stultifying decorum and respectability; Isabella is dissatisfied with the order that endeavours to mould

Women Beware Women: Royal Court Theatre, London, 1986

her in an allotted social niche; Livia indicts the injustice of a paternalistic system that operates to control women and to match them with unsuitable marriage partners. Women are victims; but they also victimize the society that seeks to inflict upon them models of virtuous conduct.

Connected with themes of emancipation are male fears about women who seem to be transgressive and uncontrollable. For instance, the crude doggerel of Sordido, the young heir's servant, suggests an attempt to manage women through degradation and abuse. His anxieties are reproduced in the behaviour of the Duke, who cannot tolerate the way in which Livia uses her status as a widow to act as she pleases; he suggests marriage as a means of taming her wilful and fiery spirit.

Images of food and drink are frequently employed, not surprising in a play preoccupied with forms of sexual consumption and appetitiveness. Puns abound in references to cates, cordials, and sweetmeats, and characters make use of this language to issue sexual invitations while preserving an illusion of decency and politeness.

Locks and treasure are among the other images of the drama and are linked incrementally to the exploration of physical passion and lust. Most galling for Leantio is that the locks of his house-prison should be broken, that his "jewel" should be removed, and that Bianca should reject the home, the traditional *locus* of masculine authority.

Middleton's dramatic strategies are best exemplified in Act II, Scene 1, the chess scene. While Livia and the mother play at chess, Bianca is seduced. But Livia also seduces the mother, lifting her fluttering anxieties with a show of genial gossip and good neighbourliness, relaxing her so that the Duke can begin his smooth-faced courtship unhindered. The chess game is the play's most potent metaphor for sexual manoeuvring and confrontation, and the Duke's honeyed compliments and references to rooks, queens, and monuments all carry a clear erotic charge. The scene is a masterly exposition of the play's concerns, seamlessly constructed, bristling with innuendo, carefully modulated and inflected.

A masque precipitates the deaths that take place in the final scene. The title of the play is suggested in Bianca's condemnation of the "deadly snares / That women set for women", but her moralizing seems inadequate as Middleton demonstrates that women need to guard against men as well as the members of their own sex. As the play ends, questions of responsibility and contemporary sexual attitudes are still being debated.

—Mark Thornton Burnett

THE WOMEN OF TRACHIS (Trachiniae)
by Sophocles

First Production: Athens, c. 420–430 B.C.

Editions
Trachiniae, edited by Frederick H.M. Blaydes, London, 1871.
Trachiniae, edited by Sir Richard Jebb, Cambridge, 1892.
Trachiniae, edited by P.E. Easterling, Cambridge, 1982.

Translations
The Wife of Hercules, translated by Gilbert Murray, London, 1948.
Women of Trachis, in *"Electra" and Other Plays*, translated by E.F. Watling, Harmondsworth, 1953.
Women of Trachis, translated by Ezra Pound, London, 1956.
The Women of Trachis, translated by Michael Jameson, in *Sophocles, 2*, Chicago, 1957 (Complete Greek Tragedies Series).
Women of Trachis, in *Sophocles: Four Plays*, translated by Theodore Howard Banks, London and New York, 1966.
Women of Trachis, in *Women of Trachis; Philoctetes*, translated by Robert Torrance, Boston, 1966.
Women of Trachis, translated by C.K. Williams and Gregory W. Dickerson, New York, 1978.
The Women of Trachis, translated by J. Michael Walton, in *Sophocles: Plays, 2*, London, 1990.

Criticism
(For general works on the author, see *Playwrights* volume)

Books:
I. Linforth, *The Pyre on Mount Oeta in Sophocles' "Trachiniae"*, Berkeley, California, 1952.

Articles:
H.D.F. Kitto, "Sophocles, Statistics and the *Trachiniae*", in *American Journal of Philology*, 60, 1939.
G. Kirkwood, "The Dramatic Unity of Sophocles's *Trachiniae*", in *Transactions and Proceedings of the American Philological Association* [*TAPA*], 72, 1941.
A.Y. Campbell, "Sophocles' *Trachiniae*: Discussions of Some Textual Problems", in *Classical Quarterly* (new series), vol.8 no.2, 1959.
H. Musarillo, "Fortune's Wheel: The Symbolism of Sophocles's *Women of Trachis*", in *Transactions and Proceedings of the American Philological Association* [*TAPA*], 92, 1961.
H. Mason, "*The Women of Trachis*", in *Arion*, vol.2 nos.1–2, 1963.
T. Hoey, "Presentational Imagery in the *Trachiniae* of Sophocles", in *Harvard Studies in Classical Philology*, 68, 1964.
P. Biggs, "The Disease Theme in Sophocles's *Ajax, Philoctetes*, and *Trachiniae*", in *Classical Philology*, 61, 1966.
P. Easterling, "Sophocles: *Trachiniae*", in *Bulletin of the Institute of Classical Studies* (London), 15, 1968.
T.F. Hoey, "The *Trachiniae* and the Unity of a Hero", in *Arethusa*, 3, 1970.
T.F. Hoey, "Sun Symbolism in the Parodos of the *Trachiniae*", in *Arethusa*, 5, 1972.
M. McCall, "The *Trachiniae*: Structure, Focus, and Herakles", in *American Journal of Philology*, 43, 1972.
D. Wender, "The Will of the Beast: Sexual Imagery in the *Trachinae*", in *Ramus*, 3, 1974.
C.P. Segal, "Sophocles' *Trachiniae*: Myth, Poetry, and Heroic Values", in *Yale Classical Studies*, 25, 1977.
C.E. Sorem, "Monsters and the Family: The Exodes of Sophocles *Trachiniae*", in *Greek, Roman and Byzantine Studies*, 19, 1978.

*   *   *

Heracles has been absent from his home for several years. News is brought to his wife, Deianira, that he is at last about to return, but among the captured slaves he has sent on ahead she discovers there is a princess whom he intends to install as his second wife. Deianira anoints a robe with what she believes is a love-charm, but it turns out to be a lethal poison which burns into Heracles' skin. Appalled at what she has unwittingly done, Deianira commits suicide. Heracles is carried in close to death and is finally convinced by their son Hyllus of Deianira's innocence. The play ends with Heracles planning his own cremation.

Why *Women of Trachis* should have been relegated to the sidelines of Sophocles' work is a mystery. Only seven Sophocles plays survive from the large number he wrote during his long life. These seven might not be the ones the playwright would have chosen to represent him best to posterity, but anyone reading all seven should be in little doubt that *Women of Trachis* is an important work. It complements the other plays while providing its own special insights into Sophocles' theatrical craft.

It is undeniable that Sophocles takes a number of risks in the play's structure. Prime among them is the relationship between Deianira and Heracles. Their marriage is the focus of the play. It has been Deianira's whole life from the time that Heracles rescued her from an even more terrifying suitor, through her husband's regular absences performing the mighty feats with which his name is associated. Yet on stage the two never share a scene. By the time that Heracles makes his entrance, in agony from the fatal robe, Deianira is already dead. Though she dies before Heracles' entrance, she is undoubtedly the most interesting character, a victim of circumstances and of her beauty. Despite her husband's past and present infidelities, she is so without malice as to demand that his latest love be treated with kindness and respect.

The cause of Deianira's personal tragedy is her own gullible nature. When newly married, she had been assaulted by a centaur who was ferrying her across a river. When she cried out for help Heracles fired an arrow, fatally wounding the man-horse. With his dying breath the centaur bequeathed her a vial of the blood from his wound, claiming that it would rekindle Heracles' love, should he ever start looking elsewhere. Only the most naïve would have taken the creature at its word. But Deianira does believe him and, in all innocence, destroys Heracles. The fate of the innately gentle in a savage world is a wonderfully suitable theme for the drama of any age, but far from easy to handle.

As in several of his other plays, Sophocles builds his ideas dramatically by means of contrast. Heracles is the strongest man who ever lived. The play is steeped in his exploits. Deianira excuses his failings by suggesting that in such a hero what might seem moral faults are an inevitable complement to the man. But by the time that Heracles is seen, he is prostrate on a litter hardly able to bear his pain. Responsible for his diminished state are the centaur, a monster which has been dead for years, and a woman who loved him.

The manner in which Deianira discovers the truth about the captive princess is also contrived by dramatic contrast between the suave herald, Lichas, to whom lying comes naturally, and the down-to-earth Messenger who reveals the truth. Unfortunately it is honesty, not deceit, that provokes disaster. Hyllus witnesses his father putting on the infected robe and what happens when it sticks to his skin. He accuses his mother of trying to murder his father and only discovers the truth when she has reacted by killing herself. Hyllus is then faced with first convincing Heracles that Deianira was innocent, then with trying to get out of killing his own father who has demanded to be burnt while still alive.

Women of Trachis received its greatest notoriety through a free adaptation by Ezra Pound, published in 1954. The hickory-smoked dialogue left Sophocles seeming more a purveyor of folk-wisdom than of the traditional classical ideals. A more stringent criticism of Pound's version was that the argument of the play had been lost in the camp-fire rhetoric. Sophocles' play functions most powerfully as a dramatic examination of the destructive potential of love.

This theme, explored by Euripides in plays like *Medea* and *Hippolytus*, acquires from Sophocles a sense of desperation at the calamity which can result from the best of intentions. In *Women of Trachis* there is no destructive witch, transformed to goddess-status, as in *Medea*, nor warring extremes of chastity and lust, as in the Artemis and Aphrodite of *Hippolytus*. Instead, Sophocles offers in Deianira the destructive force of a love that is long-suffering and unconditional. The poisoned robe is the perfect symbol of a love which clings to the hero and will not release him until it has burned his body through and through. Heracles' love for the princess proves, by contrast, to be doubly destructive, corrupting his judgement and provoking a response from Deianira which even his celebrated physical strength cannot match. If this is minor Sophocles, it is still formidable drama.

—J. Michael Walton

THE WOMEN OF TROY. See **THE TROJAN WOMEN.**

THE WORKHOUSE DONKEY: A VULGAR MELODRAMA
by John Arden

First Publication: London, 1964.
First Production: Chichester Festival Theatre, 8 July 1963.

Criticism
(For general works on the author, see *Playwrights* volume)

Articles:
John R. Brown, "John Arden: Artificial Theatre: *Serjeant Musgrave's Dance, The Workhouse Donkey* and *The Hero Rises Up*", in his *Theatre Language: A Study of Arden, Osborne, Pinter and Webster*, New York, 1972.

*   *   *

The Workhouse Donkey may be the 20th century's most Jonsonian play. The title refers to Alderman Charlie Butterthwaite, nine times mayor of an anonymous Yorkshire industrial town and Labour Party boss (known as "the Napoleon of the North") who is happy to coexist with a powerless Tory party in a corrupt, but mutually beneficial, torpor. The greatest controversy concerns the opening of a municipal art gallery. When a new Chief Constable is appointed, and

Butterthwaite and his cronies are caught drinking after hours, Butterthwaite suspects that the appointee is in the pocket of the Tories. He lays wild and unsubstantiable allegations against the Copacabana Club, owned by Tory leader Alderman Sweetman, as a sort of challenge to Chief Constable Feng.

Meanwhile Dr. Blomax, his easy-virtued "fixer", is getting him into his power by lending him money with which to back horses. When Blomax's daughter is courted by Sweetman's son, Blomax is persuaded to call in these debts. Butterthwaite's only recourse is to rob the Town Hall, which he does with Blomax's connivance. However, the utterly upright Feng has himself fallen for Wellesley Blomax, so that when the doctor desires to "shop" Butterthwaite (thereby implicating himself, too), Feng refuses his evidence. The Council still strips Butterthwaite of his committee chairmanships, whereupon he leads his drinking partners, the riff-raff of the town, on a march against the opening of the new Sweetman art gallery, where Feng, Blomax, even the Labour councillors, are foregathered. He disrupts the event before being carted off, by which time Feng has resigned, Wellesley has promised herself to young Sweetman, and Blomax has become accepted into Tory society. Of course, the town is left under Labour's control.

The play initially baffled the critics, who were unable to grasp the structure, the overt theatricality, or the author's standpoint. To them it seemed, as one put it, a "muck-up". Today the play, though clearly demanding, in no way presents the "difficulties" it held then. The first element which Arden "mucked up" was the critics' belief that all plays must expose a central character to a searing emotional experience. Instead, he took some incidents in the downfall of Charlie Butterthwaite, and presented them one after another in a series of vivid dramatic miniatures. The style resembles that of a ballad, with Dionysian overtones. On the one hand it provides a sequence of close-ups, which we must interpret. On the other hand, the lack of detailed psychological penetration is compensated for by Butterthwaite's enormous theatrical vigour. He may be corrupt, even loathesome, but he is certainly fun to watch.

Much the same is true of the groups of characters. Rather than accepting a static array of admirable or blameworthy persons whom we can easily label, we must sort out the shifting patterns for ourselves. Boocock is tempted to desert Butterthwaite; Superintendent Wiper's attitude to Colonel Feng is suddenly deliberately ambivalent; Blomax tries to turn Queen's Evidence. Again as in a ballad, we are presented not with a gradually developing crisis, but with a series of turning points which affect not just predictable groups, Labour and Tory, but also individuals within groups and individuals of different groups (and of no group at all).

The changing fortunes and attitudes of the characters lead to an apparent obscurity in the author's moral stance. Actually, Arden is interested here in telling a tale rather than pronouncing a moral judgment. It is hard to take any of the characters' sides: the most attractive personage is undoubtedly the workhouse donkey himself because he is most honest with himself. Yet we have already noticed his loathesomeness. Such a paradox should give warning to those who would have drama resort to moralising.

More pertinent is the effect gained by Arden's extravagant mix of styles. The play is a "melo-drama"; that is, it uses a good deal of music and song, mostly in popular idioms such as music hall or folk song, but there is also plenty of background music to specific scenes. Melodrama also requires speed of performance, and the author insists that "the action be allowed to flow from one scene into the next with the least possible delay".

The turning points which the scenes depict are presented almost as turns. There is, for instance, the scene when each Labour councillor enters to tell, in virtually the same words, how Charlie Butterthwaite has tried to borrow money from him; or the final scene when Butterthwaite disrupts the opening of the art gallery and dresses fantastically in a table-cloth, with a paper chain round his neck, and a wreath of flowers on his head. Blomax comes out in a song-and-dance shuffle at unexpected moments. Each character speaks an idiosyncratic variation of the rich, distinctive language Arden uses, based on Yorkshire vernacular but forged with the skill of a word-drunk poet. It may be free verse, rhyme or prose, but it never "droops into casual flaccidities", in the author's words. Finally, there are the characters, whose names give them away: Labour councillors such as Boocock, Hopefast, and Hardnutt, the Tory Sweetman, Chief Constable Feng, and his officers Wiper and Lumber.

Arden himself ironically remarks that in all this he has not exceeded "the limits of extravagance normally adhered to by the artists of seaside picture postcards", and this indeed encapsulates the style. It has literary affinities with Dickens, Wycherley, Jonson, and medieval dramatists. But equally it has non-literary affinities with pantomimes, Punch and Judy, and popular mummings. It is consciously theatrical: "realist, not naturalist" Arden says.

Thus Arden achieves in this play a dramatic method which is highly unusual in this century, though perhaps commoner in earlier periods when theatre did not have to compete with films and television for a "popular" audience. Its hallmark is a luxurious theatricality which "grants pride of place to the old essential attributes of Dionysus: noise, disorder, drunkenness, lasciviousness, nudity, generosity, corruption, fertility and ease".

—Robert Leach

THE WORLD WE LIVE IN (THE INSECT COMEDY). See **THE INSECT PLAY.**

THE WOULD-BE GENTLEMAN
(Le Bourgeois Gentilhomme)
by Molière

First Publication: Paris, 1671.
First Production: Château de Chambord, 13 October 1670.

Editions
Le Bourgeois Gentilhomme, edited by René Vaubourdolle, Paris, 1935.
Le Bourgeois Gentilhomme, in *Les Comédies-Ballets de Molière*, edited by Jacques Copeau, Lyons, 1942.
Le Bourgeois Gentilhomme, edited by Ronald A. Wilson, Oxford, 1954.
Le Bourgeois Gentilhomme, edited by Louis M. Moriarty, London and New York, 1962.
Le Bourgeois Gentilhomme, edited by Jean Thoraval, Paris, 1963.
Le Bourgeois Gentilhomme, edited by A.C. Clapin, Cambridge, 1963.

Le Bourgeois Gentilhomme, edited by Yves Hucher, Paris, 1965.
Le Bourgeois Gentilhomme, edited by H. Gaston Hall, London, 1966.
Le Bourgeois Gentilhomme, edited by Claude K. Abraham, Englewood Cliffs, New Jersey, 1966.
Le Bourgeois Gentilhomme, edited by René Jouanny and Georges Chappon, Paris, 1966.
Le Bourgeois Gentilhomme, edited by Fernand Angué, Paris, 1967.
Le Bourgeois Gentilhomme, edited by Yves Brunswick and Paul Ginestier, Paris, 1968.
Le Bourgeois Gentilhomme, edited by Jacques Morel, Paris, 1985.

Translations
The Merchant Gentleman, translated by Margaret Baker, New York and London, 1915.
The Prodigious Snob, translated and adapted by Miles Malleson, London, 1952.
The Would-Be Gentleman, in *Molière: Five Plays*, translated by John Wood, Harmondsworth, 1953.
The Self-Made Gentleman, in Six Prose Comedies of *Molière*, translated by George Graveley, London, 1956.
The Middle-Class Gentleman, translated by Herma Briffault, Great Neck, New York, 1957.
The Would-Be Gentleman, translated by J.S. Dugdale, Bath, 1963.
The Proper Gent, translated and adapted by Henry S. Taylor, London, 1966.
The Bourgeois Gentleman, in "The Bourgeois Gentleman" and "The Doctor in Spite of Himself", translated by Albert Bermel, New York, 1987.

Criticism
(For general works on the author, see *Playwrights* volume)

Books:
Sylvie Chevalley, *Les Dossiers Molière: "Le Bourgeois Gentilhomme"*, Geneva, 1975.
Salwa Mishriky, *Le Costume de déguisement et la théâtralité dans "Le Bourgeois Gentilhomme"*, Paris, 1983

Articles:
R. Talamon, "La Marquise du *Bourgeois Gentilhomme*", in *Modern Language Notes*, 50, 1935.
E. Miller, "The Real M. Jourdain of the *Bourgeois Gentilhomme*", in *Studies in Philology*, 56, 1959.
E. Falk, "Molière the Indignant Satirist: *Le Bourgeois Gentilhomme*", in *Tulane Drama Review*, vol.5 no.1, 1960.
Hallam Walker, "Strength and Style in *Le Bourgeois Gentilhomme*", in *French Review*, vol.37 no.3, 1964.
C.D. Rouillard, "The Background of the Turkish Ceremony in Molière's *Le Bourgeois Gentilhomme*", in *University of Toronto Quarterly*, 39, 1969.
J.T. Stoker, "*Le Bourgeis Gentilhomme*, 1670–1970", in *Culture*, 31, 1970.
Richard E. Wood, "The Lingua Franca in Molière's *Le Bourgeois Gentilhomme*", in *Language Quarterly*, vol.10, nos.1–2, 1971.
Jean-Louis Barrault, "*Le Bourgeois Gentilhomme* ou la poésie du rire", in *Modern Drama*, 16, 1973.
Nathan Gross, "Values in *Le Bourgeois Gentilhomme*", in *Esprit créateur*, 15, 1975.
Gérard Defaux, "Rêve et réalité dans *Le Bourgeois Gentilhomme*", in *Dix-septième siècle*, 117, 1977.

The Would-Be Gentleman: Engraved frontispiece, 1682

Jesse Dickson, "Non-sens et sens dans *Le Bourgeois Gentilhomme*", in *French Review*, 51, 1978.

Larry W. Riggs, "Language and Art as Merchandise in *Le Bourgeois Gentilhomme*", in *Language Quarterly*, vol.17 nos.1–2, 1978.

María Dolores Olivares Vaquero, "Quelques aspects sociologiques dans *Le Bourgeois Gentilhomme* et dans *Les Femmes savantes*", in *Senara*, 1, 1979.

David Shaw, "*Le Bourgeois Gentilhomme* and the 17th Century Social Revolution", in *Modern Languages*, 60, 1979.

Helen M.C. Purkis, "Monsieur Jourdain, Dorante and the *Ballet des Nations*", in *Studi francesi*, 24, 1980.

Anthony A. Ciccione, "Metalanguage and Knowledge in Molière's *Le Bourgeois Gentilhomme*", in *Degré second*, 6, 1982.

Robert McBride, "The Triumph of Ballet in *Le Bourgeois Gentilhomme*", in *Form and Meaning: Aesthetic Coherence in Seventeenth Century French Drama: Studies Presented to Harry Barnwell*, Amersham, 1982.

Dietmar Fricke, "*Le Bourgeois Gentilhomme* im Französisch-unterricht: Die *Comédie-Ballet* Molières und Lullys als Einführung in die Literatur der französischen Klassik", in *Die neueren Sprachen*, vol.83 no.6, 1984.

Ronald W. Tobin, "Fusion and Diffusion in *Le Bourgeois Gentilhomme*", in *French Review*, vol.59 no.2, 1985.

P.J. Yarrow, "M. Jourdain and Colbert", in *Seventeenth Century French Studies*, 9, 1987.

Claude Abraham, "Farce and Ballet: *Le Bourgeois Gentilhomme* Revisited", in *Cahiers du dix-septième*, vol.2 no.1, 1988.

*   *   *

A comedy of character and manners presented in the form of a comedy-ballet, the play centres on the aristocratic pretensions of a wealthy bourgeois. It shows Monsieur Jourdain's hilariously inept attempts to give himself the trappings of nobility, and the havoc he wreaks on his family and entourage in the process. The conventional plot involves his determination to acquire an aristocratic son-in-law and his opposition to the marriage of his daughter Lucile to her suitor Cléonte. A secondary intrigue, where M. Jourdain is cast incongruously as a lover, shows his fleecing at the hands of the Marquise whom he is courting and an impecunious young aristocrat. Recognising that the only way to circumvent such an intractable obsession is to work with it, not against it, the young people organise an outlandish Turkish charade where M. Jourdain is duped into believing he is being initiated into the noble rank of "Mamamouchi". With the would-be gentleman in a state of blissful delusion, the way is then open for Lucile to marry the fictitious son of the Grand Turk (in reality, Cléonte in disguise). The traditional comic ending is followed by a final celebratory ballet.

The Would-Be Gentleman was Molière's tenth comedy-ballet, and the consummate example of this especially seductive genre. Commissioned by Louis XIV for a court entertainment at the Château de Chambord, it has remained one of Molière's most popular works thanks to its near-perfect blend of spectacle, music, and irresistible comic effect. *Comédie-ballet*, a genre invented by Molière and developed in partnership with the court musician Lully, represented an attempt within the context of French classicism to create a total art form appealing to all the senses. Its generic origins can be traced to the court ballet of the period, but its true inspiration probably lies as much in Molière's own taste for song, music, and spectacle.

The original *Would-Be Gentleman* was an elaborate multimedia entertainment devised jointly by Molière, Lully, and the royal ballet-master Beauchamp. That spectacle, mounted with all the lavish resources of royal patronage, has never been performed in its entirety since 1670, though a scaled-down version had a highly successfully run in Molière's public theatre in Paris. Nor was *The Would-Be Gentleman* considered by Molière's contemporaries to be a play accompanied by ballet, but rather a court ballet which included comedy. Ironically, the five-act play which we now think of as Molière's *Would-Be Gentleman* has suffered over the centuries from a converse tendency to be read and performed as a straightforward comedy, with the music and dance as optional embellishments. Fortunately that tendency has now been reversed, and the play is again performed with integral ballet elements, albeit on a reduced scale.

As a play it has been criticised for its weak structure. It is true that the action, spread fitfully between five acts of unequal length, is irregular by the standards of classical drama. But its real coherence is that of a comedy-ballet, and as such it is unrivalled. Molière here achieves a total unification of all the performance arts. Rather than being grafted on to the action, the music and ballet arise naturally out of the action itself. What the spectator perceives is a single continuous action in which the various media—dialogue, music, song, and dance—are skilfully orchestrated into a unified theatrical experience. Moreover, the ballet and the drama are structurally interdependent, with the balletic interludes providing the real climaxes to the action. Each phase of the action builds by degrees to a climax which is crowned by a ballet, each one more spectacular than the last.

Although the comedy's outstanding qualities as entertainment have never been disputed, it has long suffered from a tendency to treat comedy-ballet as a secondary facet of Molière's art. Ultimately, it is felt, a play where comic realism gives way to riotous fantasy and sheer fun must belong to a lower order of comedy than, say, Tartuffe or The Misanthrope. If, however, one allows that comic fantasy is not an escape from reality but reality transposed to a higher plane, then The Would-Be Gentleman can be recognised as the culmination of a particular comic vision. Allowing eccentricity to run its course, and substituting an indulgent carnivalesque aura for critical judgment, the comedy-ballet provides a poetic medium for the simple but infinitely rich proposition to which all Molière's comedies are dedicated; namely, the infinite variety of human irrationality.

As well as heightening our awareness of the irrational, the comedy explores the socially disruptive consequences of a consuming obsession. Molière traces its source to a fundamental egocentricity in man but supplies no solution because none is realistically possible. In the play the immediate problem is resolved to the satisfaction of all parties, but one is well aware that this is a theatrically contrived denouement. In real life the problems created by selfish behaviour admit of no simple solutions. Molière implicitly recognises this by presenting M. Jourdain's condition as incurable.

As a court entertainment in which the oddities of the mercantile class are viewed with bemused indulgence, the play seems at first to take for granted the natural superiority of aristocratic taste over middle-class vulgarity. Yet within a predominantly courtly framework, aristocratic values are not entirely spared from satire. If M. Jourdain is comically vulgar, the culture he envies is shown as comically artificial or comically over-precious. Molière's ultimate perspective seems rather to be that of a detached observer of life, interested in the foibles of people of all classes and conditions.

Above all, The Would-Be Gentleman is an exhilarating explosion of fun whose immediate appeal arises from its serene good humour and infectious carnivalesque mood. Less moralising than some of Molière's plays, it casts an indulgent eye on human folly. The comedy projects the inner world of an incorrigible dreamer. Reason would require M. Jourdain's selfish obsession to be corrected. Instead, every significant stage of the action marks a further retreat of prosaic realism. Rather than forcing him into line with reason, the action serves to bring the world into line with his imagination. Prosaic judgment may find this contrary to morality, but it is a logical and deeply satisfying outcome. Instead of provoking the laughter of disapproval, it invites the liberating laughter which comes with recognition of the absurd.

—David Whitton

WOYZECK
by Georg Büchner

Composition: c. 1836–7.
First Publication: A version in Georg Büchner: Sämtliche Werke und handschriftlicher Nachlass; Frankfurt, 1879; first accurate version in Georg Büchner: Sämtliche Werke und Briefe (2 vols.), edited by Werner R. Lehmann, Hamburg, 1967–71.
First Production: Kammerspiele, Munich, 8 November 1913.

Editions
Woyzeck, in "Dantons Tod" and "Woyzeck", edited by Margaret Jacobs, Manchester, 1954; second edition, 1963; third edition, 1971.
"Woyzeck": Vollständiger Text und Paralipomena, Dokumentation, edited by Hans Meyer, Frankfurt, 1963.
Woyzeck, edited by Egon Krause, Frankfurt, 1969.
Woyzeck: Fassungen und Wandlungen, edited by Wilfried Buch, Dortmund, 1970.
Woyzeck, edited by John Guthrie, Oxford, 1988.

Translations
Woyzeck, in The Plays of Georg Büchner, translated by Geoffrey Dunlop, London, 1927.
Woyzeck, translated by John Holstrum, in Three German Plays, edited by Martin Esslin, 1963.
Woyzeck, in Danton's Death; Leonce and Lena; Woyzeck, translated by Victor Price, Oxford, 1971.
Woyzeck, in Leonce and Lena; Lenz; Woyzeck, translated by Michael Hamburger, Chicago and London, 1972.
Woyzeck, translated by John MacKendrick, London, 1979; also in George Büchner: The Complete Plays, edited by Michael Patterson, London, 1987.
"Woyzeck": Translation and Theatrical Commentary, translated by Michael Ewans, New York, Bern, Frankfurt, and Paris, 1989.

Criticism
(For general works on the author, see Playwrights volume)

Books:
Bo Ullman, Die sozialkritische Thematik im Werk Georg Büchners und ihre Entfaltung im "Woyzeck", 1970.
Lothar Bornscheuer, "Woyzeck": Kritische Lese—und Arbeitsausgabe, Stuttgart, 1972.
David G. Richards, Georg Büchners "Woyzeck": Interpretation und Textgestaltung, Bonn, 1975.
Rainer Poppe, Georg Büchner: "Dantons Tod"; "Lenz"; "Woyzeck": Darstellungen und Interpretationen, Hollfeld, 1976.
Mario Regina, Struttura e significato del "Woyzeck" di Georg Büchner, Bari, 1976.
Wolfgang Salzmann, Stundenblätter "Woyzeck": Eine literatursoziologische Analyse, Stuttgart, 1978
Albert Meier, Georg Büchner: "Woyzeck", Munich, 1980.

Articles:
Hermann van Dam, "Zu Georg Büchners Woyzeck", in Akzente, 1, 1954.
Wolfgang Martens, "Der Barbier in Büchners Woyzeck", in Zeitschrift für deutsche Philologie, 79, 1960.
Franz H. Mautner, "Wortgewebe, Sinngefüge und "Idee" in Büchners Woyzeck", in Deutsche Vierteljahrsschrift für Literaturwissenswchaft und Geistesgeschichte, 4, 1961.

Woyzeck: Lyric Theatre, Hammersmith, London, 1980 (Foco Novo production)

Ursula Paulus, "Georg Büchner's *Woyzeck*: Eine kritische Betrachtung zu der Edition Fritz Bergemanns", in *Jarbuch der deutschen Schillergesellschaft*, 8, 1964.

Werner R. Lehmann, "Repliken: Beiträge zu einem Streitgespräch über den *Woyzeck*", in *Eurphorion*, 65, 1971.

A.P. Messenger, "Barefoot into Hell: Clothing Imagery in *Woyzeck*", in *Modern Drama*, 13, 1971.

David G. Richards, "Zur Textgestaltung von Büchners *Woyzeck*", in *Euphorion*, 65, 1971.

Luc Lambrechts, "Zur Struktur von Büchners *Woyzeck*: Mit einer Darstellung des dramaturgischen Verhaltnisses Büchner-Brecht", in *Amsterdamer Beiträge zur neueren Germanistik*, 1, 1972.

Jack M. Stein, "From *Woyzeck* to *Wozzeck*: Alban Berg's Adaptation of Büchner", in *Germanic Review*, 47, 1972.

Klaus Kanzog, "*Wozzeck*, Woyzeck und kein Ende: Zur Standortbestimmung der Editionsphilologie", in *Deutsche Vierteljahrsschrift für Literaturwissenschaft und Geistesgeschichte*, 47, 1973.

J.H. Stodder, "The Influences of *Othello* on Büchner's *Woyzeck*", in *Modern Language Review*, 69, 1974.

Ingeborg Baumgartner, "Ambiguity in Büchner's *Woyzeck*", in *Michigan Germanic Studies*, 1, 1975.

John A. McCarthy, "Some Aspects of Imagery in Büchner's *Woyzeck*", in *Modern Language Notes*, 91, 1976.

Leo Treitler, "*Wozzeck* and the Apocalypse: An Essay in Historical Criticism", in *Critical Inquiry*, 3, 1976.

Luciano Zagori, "Segni apocalittici e critica delle ideologie nel *Woyzeck* di Büchner", in *Annal Instituto Orientale, Napoli, senzione germanica studi tedeschi*, vol.19 no.2, 1976.

John M. Grandin, "Woyzeck and the Last Judgement", in *German Life and Letters*, 31, 1978.

Terry Otten, "*Woyzeck* and *Othello*: The Dimensions of Melodrama", in *Comparative Drama*, 12, 1978.

Benno von Wiese, "Der 'arme' Woyzeck: Ein Beitrag zur Umwertung des Heldenideals im 19. Jahrhundert", in *Perspektiven, 2*, Berlin, 1978.

Michael Patterson, "Contradictions Concerning Time in Büchner's *Woyzeck*", in *German Life and Letters*, 32, 1979.

Wolfgang Martens, "Über Georg Büchners *Woyzeck*", in *Jahrbuch des Wiener Goethe-Vereins*, 84–85, 1980–81.

Heinz Wetzel, "Die Entwicklung Woyzecks in Büchner's Entwürfen", in *Euphorion*, 74, 1980.

Karl Eibl, "*Ergo todtgeschlagen*: Erkenntnisgrenzen und Gewalt in Büchners *Dantons Tod* und *Woyzeck*", in *Euphorion*, 75, 1981.

Mathias Langhoff, "Die Sehnsucht nach einem Theater des

Azozialen:. . .Büchners *Woyzeck*", in *Theater heute*, vol.22 no.1, 1981.

Hans G. Werner, "Dichtungssprache als Analyseobject: Büchners *Woyzeck*", in *Weimarer Beiträge*, 27, 1981; reprinted in his *Text und Dichtung: Analyse und Interpretation*, Berlin, 1984.

Svend E. Larsen, "Genre et dialogue: La Sémiologie du théâtre à propos de G. Büchner: *Woyzeck*", in *Degrés*, 30, 1982.

Heinz D. Kittsteiner and Helmut Lethen, "Ich-Losigkeit, Entbürgerlichung und Zeiterfahrung: Über die Gleichgültigkeit zur 'Geschichte' in Büchners *Woyzeck*", in *Georg Büchner Jahrbuch*, 3, 1983.

Günter Oesterle, "Das Komischwerden der Philosophie in der Poesie: Literatur-, philosophie- und gesellschaftsgeschichtliche Konsequenzen der "voie physiologique" in Georg Büchners *Woyzeck*", in *Georg Büchner Jahrbuch*, 3, 1983.

Günter Oesterle, "Verbale Präsenz und poetische Rücknahme des literarischen Schauers: Nachweise zur ästhetischen Vermittelheit des Fatalismusproblems in Georg Büchners *Woyzeck*", in *Georg Büchner Jahrbuch*, 3, 1983.

Alfons Glück, "Militär und Justiz in Georg Büchners *Woyzeck*", in *Georg Büchner Jahrbuch*, 4, 1984.

Alfons Glück, "Der 'ökonomische Tod': Armut und Arbeit in Georg Büchners *Woyzeck*", in *Georg Büchner Jahrbuch*, 4, 1984.

Alfons Glück, " 'Herrschende Ideen': Die Rolle der Ideologie, Indoktrination und Desorientierung in Georg Büchners *Woyzeck*", in *Georg Büchner Jahrbuch*, 5, 1985.

Svend E. Larsen, "The Symbol of the Knife in Büchner's *Woyzeck*", in *Orbis Litterarum*, 40, 1985.

Norbert Abels, "Die Ästhetik des Pathologischen: Zu Georg Büchners *Woyzeck*", in *Diskussion deutsch*, 92, 1986.

Julie D. Prandi, "Point of View and the Possibility of Empathy: *Woyzeck*", in *Literature/Film Quarterly*, 13, 1986.

William C. Reeve, "Büchner's *Woyzeck* on the English-Canadian Stage", in *Theatre History in Canada*, 8, 1987.

Heidi E. Faletti, "The Storm-and-Stress Idiom of Elegiacal Madness in Goethe's *Gretchen Tragedy* and Büchner's *Woyzeck*", in *Euphorion*, 82, 1988.

Richard Grey, "The Dialectic of Enlightenment in Büchner's *Woyzeck*", in *German Quarterly*, 61, 1988.

Günter Hartung, "Woyzecks Wahn", in *Weimarer Beiträge*, 34, 1988.

Ken Mills, "Moon, Madness and Murder: The Motivation of Woyzeck's Killing of Marie", in *German Life and Letters*, 41, 1988.

*   *   *

The plot of the play can be summed up as follows: the soldier Woyzeck lives with Marie, whom he cannot marry for lack of money, although they have a child together. In order to top up his insufficient pay he serves his captain as a batman and works as an experimental guinea-pig for the doctor of the town by eating only peas. As he is becoming too busy, feeble, and impotent for her, Marie falls in love and betrays him with the drum major of the company. Woyzeck finds out, becomes even more melancholic and delirious, buys a knife from a Jew, and in a field, at night, stabs her to death. He then commits suicide or, in an alternative version, is apprehended as the murderer.

As the possibility of different versions of the plot shows, Georg Büchner's last and most influential play *Woyzeck*, which he wrote shortly before his early death in 1836, is very problematic as a text. Büchner left several drafts in manuscript form and there is no authoritative choice or sequence of the fragmentary scenes that we have. As the play was not published or performed in his life-time the "text" of *Woyzeck* is even more than usual a product and construct of the time of its reception. The first edition, by Karl Emil Franzos in 1879, used a process of making the manuscripts readable which made them even more illegible for the later editors. A very much improved edition was published in 1922 by Fritz Bergemann, but editions that satisfy modern expectations of accuracy were only published as recently as 1967, 1969, and 1972, and the more recent English translations are based on these. There is still no generally acknowledged authentic text. What makes the fragments that we have so influential and fascinating is their openness to different interpretations. In fact, all the modern developments in drama have claimed Büchner's *Woyzeck* as their early predecessor: naturalistic and expressionistic drama as well as epic, absurd, or documentary theatre. It is also seen as the first tragedy with a working-class hero, long before Arthur Miller's *Death of a Salesman*. The fact that this hero cannot express himself serves only as an additional reason for his suffering.

The fragmentary nature of the text may also have added to the contradictory possibilities in the interpretation of the title character. Woyzeck is seen variously as either egocentric, jealous and brutish, or as atheistic, reasoning, and grotesque, or as God fearing and Christ-like. Büchner based the character and the story on a notorious court case of the time, which led to a legal controversy and discussion about the responsibility of mentally disturbed persons for their crimes.

That the plot can be seen as a documentary of the real-life case is not what makes the drama original, although the documentary forms of theatre as well as the naturalistic theatre revolution of the latter part of the 19th-century claimed *Woyzeck* as a predecessor. What makes the play so intriguing and revolutionary is the form in which this plot is related. Sparse, very small scenes are juxtaposed, and the reader or spectator has to piece the bits together, like those of a puzzle, in order to arrive at a kind of panoramic view of social life in a 19th-century garrison town, or a psychological landscape of the soul of a murderer, or a view of the human condition in a materialistic, scientific, and Darwinistically competitive world.

Only the lower-class characters in the play have names; the representatives of the ruling class are only identified by their professions: for example, the Captain represents the military order, the Doctor embodies the scientific profession, or the Jew who worships money. In fact, the stereotyping of the Jew in an obvious Shakespearian tradition is perhaps one of the few features of the play that would make a modern public uneasy.

The language of the working-class characters is borrowed from the Bible and from folklore, and quite a few folk-songs are interspersed in the text. The upper-classes speak in an awkward and mannered way, reflecting their bookish learning. In fact, the process of civilization is made thematic in the play in scenes where animals are made to perform or when Woyzeck is likened to an animal, because he cannot hold his urine as the Doctor wants him to do. The "civilized" city is also juxtaposed throughout the play with the natural settings of the fields outside.

In view of its radical cultural criticism the play has been interpreted as a secularized baroque martyr-tragedy or as a materialist critique of a capitalist society, and was an important influence on such diverse modern dramatic theorists as Artaud, and Brecht (whose notion that one can only afford morals if one has money is already expressed here).

With his play Büchner reverses the historical trial of society versus Woyzeck, conducting his own trial of a society that causes individuals like Woyzeck to become what they are. Woyzeck is not presented just as an individual psychological case, but as an extreme form of the typical exploitation of the people at the time. In this way Büchner attacks the ideology and reality of 19th-century Germany, where the political, social, and economic revolutions which had taken place around it were suppressed, which in turn led to explosive consequences in the 20th century.

The drama also plays an important role in the history of modern opera. Alban Berg used the text for his opera *Wozzeck* in 1922, which still preserves the faulty spelling of the early editions and also changes the open form of the drama into a more traditional tragedy with four acts. In the 1970's, theatre innovators like Charles Marowitz used the text for experimental performances on the British stage and it was filmed by Werner Herzog, one of the outstanding directors of the New German cinema. *Woyzeck* has provided a dramatic text for the experimental avant-garde until the present day and may well continue to do so in the future.

—Peter Falckenberg

YERMA
by Federico García Lorca

First Publication: Buenos Aires, 1937.
First Production: Teatro Espagñol, Madrid, 29 December 1934.

Translations
Yerma, in *Three Tragedies of Federico García Lorca*, translated by Sue Bradbury, London, 1947.
Yerma, in *Three Tragedies of Federico García Lorca*, translated by James Graham-Luján and Richard L. O'Connell, New York, 1947.
Yerma, translated by Peter Luke, in *Federico García Lorca: Three Plays*, introduced by Gwynne Edwards, London, 1987.
Yerma, translated by Ian MacPherson and Jacqueline Minett, Warminster, Wiltshire, 1987.
Yerma, in *"Yerma" and "The Love of Don Perlimplin for Belisa in the Garden"*, translated by David Johnston, London, 1990.

Criticism
(For general works on the author, see *Playwrights* volume)

Books:
Rupert C. Allen, *Psyche and Symbol in the Theater of Federico García Lorca: "Perlimplín"; "Yerma"; Blood Wedding"*, Austin, Texas, 1974.

Articles:
C. Cannon, "Imagery of Lorca's *Yerma*", in *Modern Language Quarterly*, 21, 1960.
Rafael Vázquez Zamora, "García Lorca en el eslava: *Yerma*", in *Insula*, 15, 1962.
Gustavo Correa, "Honor, Blood and Poetry in *Yerma*", in *Tulane Drama Review*, 7, 1962–63.
Robert E. Lott, "*Yerma*: The Tragedy of Unjust Barrenness", in *Modern Drama*, 8, 1965.
Robert Skloot, "Theme and Image in Lorca's *Yerma*", in *Drama Survey*, 5, 1966.
John V. Falconieri, "Tragic Hero in Search of a Role: *Yerma's* Juan", in *Revista de Estudios Hispánicos*, vol.1 no.1, 1967.
Serge Salaün, "Essai de (nouvelle) critique: *Yerma*", in *Langues Néo-Latines*, 194, 1970.
James A. Parr, "La escena final de *Yerma*", in *Duquesne Hispanic Review*, 10, 1971.
C.B. Morris, "Lorca's *Yerma*: Wife Without an Anchor", in *Neophiloligus*, 56, 1972.
Patricia L. Sullivan, "The Mythic Tragedy of *Yerma*", in *Bulletin of Hispanic Studies*, 49, 1972.

Patricia Pinto V., "El símbolo del agua y el motivo de la sed en *Yerma*", in *Boletín de filologia, Universidad de Chile*, 23–24, 1972–73.
Murray Baumgarten, "'Body's image': *Yerma*, [Yeats's] *The Player Queen*, and the Upright Posture", in *Comparative Drama*, 8, 1974.
Frank Benitez, "Tensíon poética en *Yerma* de García Lorca", in *Explicación de Textos Literarios*, 4, 1975.
Francisco Olmos García, "*Yerma*, tragedia de la esterilidad?", in *Revista de la Universidad Complutense*, 108, 1977.
Dennis A. Klein, "Christological Imagery in Lorca's *Yerma*", in *García Lorca Review*, 6, 1978.
Mario Hernández, "Cronología y estreno de *Yerma*, poema trágico, de García Lorca", in *Revista de archivos, bibliotecas y museos*, 82, 1979.
María L. Alvarez Harvey, "Lorca's Yerma: Frigid. . .or Mismatched?", in *CLA Journal*, 23, 1980.
C. Brian Morris, "Lorca's *Yerma* and the 'beso sabroso'", in *Mester*, 142, 1981.
Reed Anderson, "The Idea of Tragedy in García Lorca's *Yerma*", in *Hispanófila*, 74, 1982.
Francie Cate, "Los motivos de la espera y la esperanza en *Yerma* y *Doña Rosita la soltera*", in *García Lorca Review*, 10, 1982.
Lloyd Halliburton, "An Aristotelian Analysis of *Yerma*", in *García Lorca Review*, 11, 1983.
Marcia D. Yarmus, "Federico García Lorca's *Yerma* and John Steinbeck's *Burning Bright*: A Comparative Study", in *García Lorca Review*, 11, 1983.
Luis Fernández-Cifuentes, "*Yerma*: anatomía de una transgresión", in *Modern Language Notes*, 99, 1984.
Eutimio Martín, "*Yerma* o 'la imperfecta casada' de García Lorca", in *Cahiers d'etudes romanes*, 9, 1984.
Bettina L. Knapp, "Federico García Lorca's *Yerma*: A Woman's Mystery", in her *Women in Twentieth-Century Literature: A Jungian View*, University Park, Pennsylvania, 1987.
Guadalupe Martínez Lacalle, "*Yerma*: 'una tragedia pura y simplemente'", in *Neophilologus*, 72, 1988.

*   *   *

Yerma is one of Lorca's last plays and was first performed less than two years before his death. The essence of this tragedy is indicated by the name of the protagonist, Yerma, which means barren. But it is not so much Yerma herself who is barren as the relationship with her husband Juan. He has no interest in children, thinks only of work and making money from his farm, and looks on marriage as a convenient opportunity for occasional sex. Yerma, by contrast, is overwhelmed by a passionate desire to fulfill herself through procreation. She is very much a victim of an oppressive

Yerma: National Theatre, London, 1987

Spanish code of honour, which dictates the terms of female fulfilment not just as the creation of children but, more specifically, as the creation of sons, and leads Yerma to accept that "a woman who doesn't bear children is as useless as a bunch of thistles—something fit for God's rubbish heap". Furthermore the honour code is shown to frustate Yerma's natural instincts since once married she feels herself doomed to remain faithful to her husband, despite her overwhelming sexual attraction to the shepherd Victor. Tormented by feelings of failure and entrapment she is finally driven to despair and murders her husband in a climactic frenzy, thereby destroying the son she longs for.

As in so much of Lorca's writing a strong antithesis is set up between intense natural desire and a crushing concept of honour that demands suffering and self-denial. This subject of repression was understood well by Lorca as it was quite impossible for him to be open about his own homosexuality in the Spain of the 1930's. In such a machismo society the only way in which the tragedy of sexual repression could be expressed was through female suffering in a heterosexual world. Yerma, then, can also be seen as an represenation of homosexual frustration in a homophobic society.

Compression of time, a sense of inevitable disaster and the choral interludes of peasant women give this tragedy a classical feel; yet, despite the universal yearnings in the theme and the form, the play is steeped in the atmosphere of rural, Andalucian Spain. Yerma's solitary suffering is played out against a natural landscape where life is struggling to burst forth all around her. The story unfolds with deceptive simplicity despite Lorca's use of a varied dramatic language that illustrates his receptivity to the ideas of theatrical innovators like Appia and Craig. In characteristic Lorca fashion, poetic dialogue, song, dance, movement and lighting effects combine to create a highly visual and theatrical representation of peasant life. Simple but bold theatrical images are used to powerful dramatic effect. At the start of the play a shepherd enters the stage leading a small boy dressed in white up to the sleeping Yerma. After a moment of silence they depart and the lighting changes from a "weird dreamlike" state to sunny morning as Yerma wakes from her dream. Thus, Yerma's subconscious yearnings, which will eventually destroy her, are immediately conveyed. There is a rhythmic momentum to the play that builds inexorably towards the final disaster. Yerma's murder of her husband Juan is presented as a cruelly orgasmic finale as she throttles him to the accompaniment, offstage, of a pagan fertility rite, an event which involves the whole village and in which two masked dancers, representing male and female sexuality, perform a celebratory and ritualistic version of the sexual act.

The role of Yerma demands a degree of passion that does not come easily to all actresses. The most famous production of the play to date is that by Nuria Espert's company, directed by Victor Garcia, which was performed at London's Aldwych Theatre in 1973 and revived for the Edinburgh Festival in 1986. The set was dominated by a huge trampoline symbolically depicting desert, mountain, or barren womb. However, while this device worked well to stress the hostile and unyielding elements in the play, and provide an opportunity for athletic performances, it did so at the expense of the fecund, life-giving forces in the play, forces that accentuate the cruelty of Yerma's fate.

—Andy Piasecki

YO TAMBIÉN HABLO DE LA ROSA. See **I, TOO, SPEAK OF THE ROSE.**

THE YORK CYCLE
By various authors

Composition: Late 14th Century and 15th Century.
First Production: After c. 1470.

Editions
A Rosary of Mystery Plays: Fifteen Plays Selected From the York Cycle. . ., edited by Margaret S. Mahoney, Albany, New York, 1915.
The York Cycle of Mystery Plays: A Complete Version, edited by J.S. Purvis, London, 1957.
The York Plays, edited by Richard Beadle, London, 1982.
The York Mystery Plays: A Selection in Modern Spelling, edited by Richard Beadle and Pamela M. King, Oxford, 1984.
"The Death, Assumption, and Coronation of the Virgin" from the York Cycle, edited by John McKinnell, Lancaster, 1988.

Criticism
(For general works on the author, see *Playwrights* volume)

Books:
Marire Caroline Lyle, *The Original Identity of the York and Towneley Cycles*, Minneapolis, Minnesota, 1919.
Clifford Davidson, *From Creation to Doom: The York Cycle of Mystery Plays*, New York, 1984.

Articles:
F. O'Neill, "Blessed Virgin in the York Cycle of Mystery Plays", in *American Catholic Quarterly Review*, 34, 1909.
P.R. Wallis, "The Miracle Plays of *Crucifixio Christi* in the York Cycle", in *Modern Language Review*, 12, 1917.
Frances H. Miller, "The Northern Passion and the Mysteries", in *Modern Language Notes*, 34, 1919.
Eleanor G. Clark, "The York Plays and the *Gospel of Nicodemus*", in *Publications of the Modern Language Association* [*PMLA*], 43, 1928.
Grace Frank, "On the Relation Between the York and Towneley Plays", in *Publications of the Modern Language Association* [*PMLA*], 44, 1929.
Marie C. Lyle, "The Original Identity of the York and Towneley Cycles: A Rejoinder", in *Publications of the Modern Language Association* [*PMLA*], 44, 1929.
Effie MacKinnon, "Notes on the Dramatic Structure of the York Cycle", in *Studies in Philology*, 28, 1931.
Chester G. Curtiss, "The York Play of the Pater Noster", in *Speculum*, 7, 1932.
Margaret Trussler, "The York *Sacrificium Cayme and Abell*", in *Publications of the Modern Language Association* [*PMLA*], 49, 1934.
Mendall G. Frampton, "The York Play of *Christ Led up to Calvary* (Play XXXIV)", in *Philological Quarterly*, 20, 1941.
Anna J. Mill, "The York Plays of the Dying, Assumption, and Coronation of Our Lady", in *Publications of the Modern Language Association* [*PMLA*], 65, 1950.
Anna J. Mill, "The Stations of the York Corpus Christi Play", in *Yorkshire Archeological Journal*, 37, 1951.

Jesse Byers Reese, "Alliterative Verse in the York Cycle", in *Studies in Philology*, 48, 1951.

J.W. Robinson, "The Art of the York Realist", in *Modern Philology*, 60, 1963.

Mary Claridge, "Blessed Margaret Clitherow and the York Plays", in *Month*, 31, 1964.

Peter S. Macauley, "The Play of the *Harrowing of Hell* as a Climax in the English Mystery Cycles", in *Studia Germanica Gandensia*, 8, 1966.

M. James Young, "The York Pageant Wagon", in *Speech Monographs*, 33, 1967.

Margaret Dorrell, "The Mayor of York and the Coronation Pageant", in *Leeds Studies in English*, 5, 1971.

Alexandra F. Johnson and Margaret Dorrell, "The Doomsday Pageant of the York Mercers, 1433", in *Leeds Studies in English*, 5, 1971.

Robert A. Brawer, "The Characterization of Pilate in the York Play Cycle", in *Studies in Philology*, 69, 1972.

Margaret Dorrell, "Two Studies of the York Corpus Christi Play", in *Leeds Studies in English*, 6, 1972.

Alexandra F. Johnston and Margaret Dorrell, "The York Mercers and Their Pageant of Doomsday, 1433–1526", in *Leeds Studies in English*, 6, 1972.

Martin Stevens, "The York Cycle: From Procession to Play", in *Leeds Studies in English*, 6, 1972.

James F. Hoy, "The Staging Time of the York Cycle of Corpus Christi Plays", in *Emporia State Research Studies*, vol.21 no.3, 1973.

Alexandra F. Johnston, "The Procession and Play of Corpus Christi in York after 1426", in *Leeds Studies in English*, 7, 1973–74.

Thomas N. Grove, "Light in Darkness: The Comedy of the York *Harrowing of Hell* as Seen Against the Backdrop of the Chester *Harrowing of Hell*", in *Neuphilologishe Mitteilungen*, 75, 1974.

Clifford Davidson, "After the Fall: Design in the Old Testament Plays in the York Cycle", in *Mediaevalia*, vol.1 no.1, 1975.

Clifford Davidson, "The Realism of the York Realist and the York Passion", in *Speculum*, 50, 1975.

Alexandra F. Johnston, "The Plays of the Religious Guilds of York: The Creed Play and The Pater Noster Play", in *Speculum*, 50, 1975.

Richard J. Collier, "The Action of Fulfillment in the York Corpus Christi Play", in *Pacific Coast Philology*, 11, 1976.

Douglas Cowling, "The Liturgical Celebration of Corpus Christi in Medieval York", in *Records of Early English Drama Newsletter*, 2, 1976.

Clifford Davidson and Nona Mason, "Staging the York *Creation* and *Fall of Lucifer*", in *Theatre Survey*, 17, 1976.

Alexandra F. Johnston, "The Guild of Corpus Christi and the Procession of Corpus Christi in York", in *Medieval Studies*, 38, 1976.

Clifford Davidson, "From *Tristia* to *Gaudium*: Iconography and the York-Towneley *Harrowing of Hell*", in *American Benedictine Review*, 28, 1977.

Alexandra F. Johnston, "The York Cycle: 1977", in *University of Toronto Quarterly*, 48, 1978.

Margaret Rogerson, "The York Corpus Christi Play: Some Practical Details", in *Leeds Studies in English*, 10, 1978.

Paula Ložar, "Time in the Corpus Christi Cycles: 'Aesthetic' and 'Realistic' Models", in *Papers on Language and Literature*, 14, 1978.

Meg Twycross, " 'Places to Hear the Play': Pageant Stations at York, 1398–1572", in *Records of Early English Drama Newsletter*, 2, 1978.

Alan D. Justice, "Trade Symbolism in the York Cycle", in *Theatre Journal*, 31, 1979.

Edmund Reiss, "The Tradition of Moses in the Underworld and the York Plays of the Transfiguration and Harrowing", in *Mediaevalia*, 5, 1979.

Peter Holding, "Stagecraft in the York Cycle", in *Theatre Notebook*, vol.34 no.2, 1980.

Peter Meredith, "The *Ordo Paginarum* and the Development of the York Tilemakers' Pageant", in *Leeds Studies in English*, 11, 1980.

Sally Mussetter, "The York Pilate and the Seven Deadly Sins", in *Neuphilologische Mitteilungen*, 81, 1980.

A.K. Reed, " 'A Thing Like a Love Affair': A Study of the Passion of Obedience in the York Play of *Abraham and Isaac*", in *Christianity and Literature*, vol.29 no.2, 1980.

Charles Beadle, "The Origins of Abraham's Preamble in the York Play of *Abraham and Isaac*", in *Yearbook of English Studies*, 11, 1981.

Richard L. Homan, "Ritual Aspects of the York Cycle", in *Theatre Journal*, vol.33 no.3, 1981.

D. Levey, " 'Nowe is Ful fillid all for-oght': A Study of Comedy, Satire, and Didacticism in the York Cycle", in *English Studies in Africa*, vol.24 no.2, 1981.

Alicia Korzeniowska Nitecki, "The Dramatic Impact of the Didactic Voice in the York Cycle of Mystery Plays", in *Annuale Mediaevale*, 21, 1981.

Ellen White, "The Tenants at the Common Hall Gates: The Manor's Station for the Corpus Christi Play in York", in *Records of Early English Drama Newsletter*, 2, 1982.

Jean Q. Seaton, "Source of Order or Sovereign Lord: God and the Pattern of Relationships in Two Middle English *Fall of Lucifer* Plays", in *Comparative Drama*, vol.18 no.3, 1984.

Paul Willis, "The Weight of Sin in the York *Crucifixio*", in *Leeds Studies in English*, 15, 1984.

Elza C. Tiner, "Classical Invention in the York Trial Plays", in *Florilegium*, 8, 1986.

R.H. Nicholson, "The Trial of Christ the Sorcerer in the York Cycle", in *Journal of Medieval and Renaissance Studies*, vol.16 no.2, 1986.

Martin Stevens, "The York Cycle as Carnival", in *Fifteenth-Century Studies*, 13, 1988.

Lee Jobling, "The Pilate of the York Mystery Plays", in *Words and Wordsmiths: A Volume for H.L. Rogers*, edited by John Gunn and Others, Sydney, 1989.

*   *   *

The York Cycle is a cycle of plays produced on pageant wagons at various locations along a route through the streets of York from the late-14th century. It was frequently revised, and survived until suppressed in 1580. In recent years, it has been revived, in abbreviated form, on a fixed stage in the ruins of St. Mary's Abbey, York, in 1951.

The York cycle in the unique manuscript in the British Library (c. 1470, with later additions) contains 47 short plays beginning with the *Creation and Fall of Lucifer*, followed by the *Creation and Fall of Man*, as well as the stories of Cain and Abel, Noah, Abraham and Isaac, and Pharaoh and Moses. But major emphasis is on the Nativity and Passion of Christ, along with the events of Christ's life after the Resurrection and the matter of the Assumption and Coronation of the Virgin. The final play of the cycle is *Doomsday*, sponsored by the prestigious Mercers guild.

These vernacular plays did not appear as developments out of the earlier Latin liturgical music-drama, nor are they mere dramatizations of the Bible stories, for they are richly interwoven with medieval legend and unique iconographic features. For example, the York Tilethatchers guild's *Nativity* is

The York Cycle: The Abbey ruins, York, 1988

based on the emotionally charged way of visualizing the birth of Jesus derived from a vision of St. Bridget of Sweden while she was on a pilgrimage to the Holy Land in 1370; the York text was, however, rewritten at some date after 1477 when the cast of characters listed in a revised *Ordo paginarum* included midwives, who are not required in the extant play. The visual dimension of these plays in production thus is shown to have had much in common with the visual arts, and not surprisingly the English dramatic records note payments to artists such as painters for preparing the sets and for painting masks, costumes, and banners.

Revision of the York cycle in the 15th century resulted in the pageants written by the York Realist, the anonymous playwright mainly responsible for the present text of the Passion sequence in the manuscript. The York Realist's principal achievements have been held to be his mastery of Middle English alliterative verse—the verse form that had also been used in *Piers Plowman*—and his exactitude in presenting details, a characteristic he shared with the visual artists of the period. Like the nominalist philosophers of that time, he apparently saw reality as inhering in particulars rather than in universals. The plays also are enlivened by the tendency to stress Christ's *humanity*—a tendency that had been apparent in the Franciscan *Meditations on the Life of Christ*, a book which was one of the York Realist's direct or indirect sources.

Allowing for revisions of the text and changes in the sets, the York plays probably had one of the longest runs in English theater history (the longest would have been the *Visit to the Sepulchre—Visitatio Sepulchri*—for Easter Sunday, done as a dramatic expansion of the liturgy from c. 980 to the Reforma-

tion in some monasteries and churches). The York plays, sponsored by the city corporation and produced by the various craft guilds, are first noted in the civic records in 1376, though they are probably older. They were produced at the time of the feast of Corpus Christi nearly every summer, and hence are sometimes known as Corpus Christi plays. Eventually their Catholic content caused them to be suppressed in spite of considerable enthusiasm for drama on the part of the citizens of York, who had traditionally spent great sums of money on their plays. Similar civic cycles of plays were suppressed at Coventry and Chester.

The motives behind the plays were mixed. They were ostensibly produced for the glory of God, but they were also a tourist attraction, bringing business to the municipality; they also gave people an outlet for devotional experiences in an age when religious pilgrimages were popular. While it is commonly believed that the plays were didactic in intent, this aspect is not particularly prominent; they are often entertaining and are not cumbersomely "religious" in their treatment of sacred history. Some insight into the audience response that was expected by the producers may be gauged by the reports of the reception of the play of *Fergus*, which featured a Jew who attempted to overturn the bier of the Virgin Mary during her funeral procession. The guild sponsors of this play complained that it did not encourage devotion but rather found persons in the audience rowdy and irreverent—perhaps signs of the anti-Semitism of the times. The producers and the city officials who oversaw the entire production were anxious that the entire cycle should be presented in a manner which would reflect well on the "honor" of the city.

The pageant wagons that were used in presenting this cycle are known only through the dramatic records, which preserve a Mercers' indenture of 1433 and also an inventory dated 1526 for the new *Doomsday* pageant of the early-16th century. The 1433 indenture specifies a wagon with four wheels, a hell mouth, masks, puppet angels, a rainbow for Christ to sit upon and machinery for his descent as Judge, and costumes, including garb (presumably white leather body stockings) for the good and bad souls who rise out of their graves—souls who were given a separate pageant in 1463.

After their suppression, the plays were not performed again until 1951, when an abridged version of the text of the cycle, prepared by Canon J. S. Purvis, was presented, using a set based on a drawing of the Valenciennes stage of 1547; the producer was E. Martin Browne. Though at first there was considerable nervousness on account of stage censorship which prohibited God from appearing as a character in a play, the York plays have been frequently and successfully staged more recently, most notably in the mid-1970's at Leeds (36 plays; produced by Jane Oakshott) and Toronto (complete text; under the aegis of the Poculi Ludi Societas) using amateur actors playing on wagons. In the mid-1980's, the National Theatre's *Mysteries*, using Tony Harrison's adaptation of the York text (with additions from other English mystery plays), was a highly experimental presentation which, however, many found to be iconographically inconsistent in spite of its linguistic vitality.

—Clifford Davidson

THE YORK MYSTERY PLAYS.   See THE YORK CYCLE.

YOU CAN'T TAKE IT WITH YOU
by George Kaufman and Moss Hart

First Publication: New York, 1937.
First Production: Booth Theatre, New York, 14 December 1936.

Criticism
(For general works on the author, see *Playwrights* volume)

Articles:
Charles Kaplan, "Two Depression Plays and Broadway's Popular Idealism", in *American Quarterly*, vol.15 no.4, 1963.

*   *   *

You Can't Take It With You is a comedy of characters: the Vanderhof–Sycamore families are living through the Depression in New York City, coping with life and doing it with grace and humor. The stories involving each of the family members and their friends are interwoven into a coherent whole with subplots aplenty and action galore. Essentially, though, it is a play about wonderfully innocent, eccentric, and extraordinary people. One must remember the dreary Depression years and place the work in that context. The family joyously endures and triumphs at a time when most people felt defeated and

were without hope. The play was a distraction from everyday woes and a dollop of good sense for weary society.

Kaufman and Hart were craftsmen such as we seldom have had in commercial theater, for here they richly blend the love of Alice and Tony (poor girl, rich boy) with a pack of lurking federal agents trying to get Grandpa Vanderhof for income tax evasion, and then they toss in a quirky, hungry Russian Grand Duchess and an exuberant ballet master. The skill with which Kaufman and Hart mix the ingredients is a delight and lesson in playmaking, and the result is not a throw-away confection, but rather a sweet and touching portrait of endurance and good humor.

In fact, it is the craftsmanship that shines most gloriously throughout the play; there are no wasted words or characters, no subplot unexplored, and no planted gag left unexploded. If all this is contrived and plugged in too neatly, at least it pays off in delivering the laugh, developing a character or the plot, and even sending out some thought-provoking signals.

Nowadays, critics might ask for greater motivation of the characters, but the playwrights are so superb at their job that the audience never stops to ask why the mother, Penny, is writing a play; we accept her statement that she does so because "eight years earlier a typewriter was delivered. . .". Or why does Essie assume she is capable of becoming a ballerina? The characters are all dreamers, and we, the audience, believe their dreams.

Today, a black and sassy maid, Rheba, and her boyfriend Ed, would seem stereotypes; but they work splendidly on stage, providing wry counterpoint and common sense. Ed, for example, is a minor figure in the play but he has one of the best lines when he says that he doesn't much like being on relief because picking up his welfare check "breaks up my week". The whole crew of characters is unmotivated psychologically, but that does not matter: they appear and do their stuff because Kaufman and Hart call them up.

You Can't Take It With You opened in New York at the end of 1936 and became an instant commercial hit, and within four years, high schools across America were staging it. It has remained in the repertory, professional and amateur, ever since. Constantly revived and "rediscovered", it actually was never lost, for audiences love its gentle humor, its kindness, its ease, and even its neatness and clarity. Moreover, it is loved because it is truly "family fare", echoing a far less frantic age, a time when people may have been poor but they were confident and loving. It has been much imitated, particularly in television situation comedies: urban or country, black or white, middle class or poor or filthy rich, the family comedy is a constant staple, and almost all such shows can be traced back to the influences of *You Can't Take It With You*. The formula seems to be engraved on writers: a slightly goofy but lovable family which gets into bizarre scrapes and emerges victoriously over all obstacles.

What is original is the way in which the characters are brought together around the central figure, Grandpa Vanderhof, who is a philosopher in a low key. Kaufman and Hart are geniuses at creating such pivotal eccentrics (another example is Sheridan Whiteside in *The Man Who Came to Dinner*). Incredibly, Grandpa has not paid his income taxes in 30 years, although he "wouldn't mind paying if [the money] went for something sensible".

In fact, the playwrights wonderfully blend comedy and wise observations which remain current through the years. Grandpa, for example, might have been a rich man, "but it took too much time. . .Life is kind of beautiful if you let it come to you". How sweet those thoughts are in an age of take-overs and leveraged buy-outs and greed, and how old-fashioned it would seem to modern audiences, were it not for

You Can't Take It With You: National Theatre, London, 1983

the enveloping innocence of the characters and for the audience's longing that such notions could indeed be true.

The ending is, of course, contrived, as love is seen to conquer all after a series of calamities and hilarities. But it is brilliantly contrived, and as sure-fire as this kind of comedy, verging on raging farce, can be when it works. And it is a rare production that does not work.

Leave it to Grandpa to sum up the play as he says grace before the family dinner: "All we ask is to just go along and be happy in our own sort of way. . .[and we] leave the rest to you". Not a small order; but in a dark era, a prayer for all people. *You Can't Take It With You* is a placebo which the audience happily accepts because it hopes that joy is more important than money. The play endures because it is not only well-made but because it is what we want, and perhaps even need to see, in the theater.

—Arthur Ballet

—————

THE YOUNG HOPEFUL.   See **THE MINOR.**

—————

ZAÏRE
by Voltaire

First Publication: Paris, 1733.
First Production: Comédie-Française, Paris, 13 August 1732.

Editions
Zaïre, edited by M.M. Léger, 1899.
Zaïre, edited by Marc Ceppi, London, 1913.
Zaïre, edited by Eva Jacobs, London, 1975.

Translations
Zaïre, translated by Albany Wallace, Worthington, 1854.
Zaïre, in *The Chief Rivals of Corneille and Racine*, translated by Lacy Lockert, Nashville, Tennessee, 1956.

Criticism
(For general works on the author, see *Playwrights* volume)

Articles:
Theodore E.D. Braun, "Subject, Substance and Structure in *Zaïre* and *Alzire*", in *Studies on Voltaire and the Eighteenth Century*, 87, 1972.

*   *   *

The play is set in 13th-century Jerusalem, where French Crusader knights are held captive by the proud but liberal-minded sultan, Orosmane. He is in love with Zaïre, a palace slave-girl who has grown up a Muslim unaware of her Christian parentage and whom he now proposes, in defiance of custom, to make his sole wife. The action is set in motion by the return of the knight, Nérestan, with ransom money for the release of ten of his companions, a number augmented by Orosmane's characteristic magnanimity to 100 including, at Zaïre's plea, their valiant former commander, Lusignan. In a melo-dramatically affecting recognition scene Nérestan and Zaïre are revealed as the surviving children of the aged Lusignan, who makes Zaïre vow to re-embrace Christianity but swears her to secrecy.

Pressed by Nérestan to console her dying father by receiving baptism without delay, a distraught Zaïre begs Orosmane to defer their nuptials and compounds his bewilderment by professing ardent love for him while refusing to explain the reasons for her hesitation. The interception of a letter from Nérestan summoning Zaïre to a secret rendezvous that night—in reality for her baptism—appears to confirm the sultan's suspicion that she has betrayed him with this young rival and leads to the passionate violence of the concluding scenes, in which Orosmane, surprising Zaïre on her way to the nocturnal assignation, stabs her in a fit of jealous rage; then, overcome by remorse on discovering the truth, orders the release of all Christian prisoners, entrusts Nérestan with his sister's body for safe return to Europe, and finally kills himself with the same blood-stained dagger.

Voltaire's dramatic output, though prolific and fashionable in its day, is no longer highly esteemed; thus *Zaïre* is largely of historical value, as a token of his energetic campaign to revitalize French neo-classical tragedy while remaining true to its essential conventions. Already in his first play, *Œdipe* (1718), he had reintroduced a chorus of Thebans in the Greek manner; but *Zaïre*'s innovations are more ambitious and, at least in intention, more organic. To begin with, he situates the action within a specific episode from French history, the seventh crusade of Louis IX, and reinforces the sense of period by incorporating actual historical incidents and associated family names from the French aristocracy (Lusignan, Châtillon) among his dramatis personae. Admittedly, Volt-aire's chronology is scarcely precise: events from the seventh crusade mingle with earlier encounters, and his historical personages tend to be composite or representative characters. Similarly, the Palestinian local colour is merely skin-deep, despite his declared intention of portraying "Turkish manners in opposition to Christian manners" and the provision of five custom-made "*habits à la turque*", furs, and satin-covered footwear for its first performance. Voltaire's purpose is simply to create an acceptable socio-historical atmosphere, to evoke a moment in time capable of informing the tragedy. Even so, this represents a significant departure from the timeless landscape of classical mythology customarily favoured by his predeces-sors, and reminds us that *Zaïre* was written shortly after Voltaire's return from a three-year exile in England where he had been impressed by the exploitation of indigenous history as subject-matter for drama.

The emotional relationship at the heart of the play also marks something of a departure for Voltaire. Having deplored the dependence of French tragedy on "long conversations of love", he had been reproached for excluding love interest altogether from his own work, and with *Zaïre* he seems to have set out deliberately to over-compensate by fashioning an egregiously tender story of love, calculated to appeal to the growing sensibility of the age and a pronounced taste for sentimental, tearful fare among contemporary theatre-goers. Here, too, a possible debt to his familiarity with English drama is discernible: the superficial resemblance to Shakespeare's pairing of Othello and Desdemona is striking, and though the thrust of the two plays is fundamentally different the idea of physical and cultural miscegenation adds a particular dimen-sion to the tragic outcome.

While yielding to audience expectations on this score, Voltaire none the less clung resolutely to his conviction that the renewal of French tragedy could best be achieved through the espousal of what he called "*grands intérêts*", and *Zaïre* is an early example of his confronting, in dramatic terms, an issue that was to preoccupy him throughout his life: fanaticism and religious intolerance. In fact it enjoys the perhaps unique distinction of having been considered both a Christian and an anti-Christian play. In some scenes Voltaire does allow his Christian characters to speak spiritedly and persuasively about their faith and he even observed that *Zaïre* came to rival Corneille's *Polyeucte* as an appropriate pre-Easter offering at the Comédie-Française; yet several critics saw an irreligious intent in the depth of Zaïre's passion for a Muslim and the play's apparent imperviousness to Divine Grace, and in the depiction of Orosmane as more sympathetic and far less bigoted than his Christian counterparts. Moreover, the rationalist voice of Voltaire himself is plainly heard in Zaïre's lengthy speech in Act I about the relativity of all religious beliefs and values, and the ultimate effect of the play is to underline the tragic waste and destruction perpetrated in the name of religion.

Zaïre remains interesting by virtue of Voltaire's attempt to combine its three main innovations into a compelling dramatic nexus: his choice of a critical historical episode serves as the pre-condition for a display of mutual religious hostility which must, in turn, destroy the two protagonists. Unfortunately this is also responsible for the play's many improbabilities of plot and characterization and the contrived misunderstanding upon which the final catastrophe hinges. The result is less tragedy than pathos and melodrama, and helps to explain why *Zaïre* has failed to live up to the success it initially enjoyed at the Comédie-Française in 1732 (and at Drury Lane in Aaron Hill's adaptation, *Zara*, four years later); though its popularity survived well into the 19th century, it has not now been performed since 1936 and any revival would need to find a suitable convention of performance to render it acceptable to modern audiences.

—Donald Roy

DER ZERBROCHENE KRUG. See **THE BROKEN JUG.**

ZHIZN CHELOVEKA. See **THE LIFE OF MAN.**

ZIMMERSCHALCHT. See **HOME FRONT.**

ZE ŽIVOTA HMYZU. See **THE INSECT PLAY.**

THE ZOO STORY
by Edward Albee

First Publication: In *The Zoo Story; The Death of Bessie Smith; The Sandbox*, New York, 1960.
First Production: Schillertheater Werkstatt, Berlin, 28 September 1959; first US production, Provincetown Playhouse, New York, 14 January 1960.

Criticism
(For general works on the author, see *Playwrights* volume)

Articles:
Rose A. Zimbardo, "Symbolism and Naturalism in Edward Albee's *The Zoo Story*", in *Twentieth-Century Literature*, 1962.
Keith Wilson, "Social and Moral Conflicts in Edward Albee's *The Zoo Story*", in *Osmania Journal of English Studies*, vol.5 no.2, 1966.
Linda L. Woods, "Isolation and the Barrier of Language in *The Zoo Story*", in *Research Studies*, 36, 1968.
Sigrid P.M.L.S. Renaux, "The Opposing Forces in Albee's *The Zoo Story*", in *Letras*, 20, 1972.
Mary M. Nilan, "Albee's *The Zoo Story:* Alienated Man and the Nature of Love", in *Modern Drama*, 16, 1973.
Carol A. Sykes, "Albee's Beast Fables: *The Zoo Story* and *A Delicate Balance*", in *Educational Theatre Journal*, 25, 1973.
Robert S. Wallace, "*The Zoo Story:* Albee's Attack on Fiction", in *Modern Drama*, 16, 1973.
Lucina P. Gabbard, "At the Zoo: From O'Neill to Albee", in *Modern Drama*, 19, 1976.
Robert B. Bennett, "Tragic Vision in *The Zoo Story*", in *Modern Drama*, 20, 1977.
Alina Nowacka, "The Hybrid Structure in Albee's Plays", in *Acta Universitatis Wratislaviensis*, 360, 1977.
Shanta Acharya, "*The Zoo Story:* Alienation and Love", in *Literary Criterion*, vol.13 no.2, 1978.
Shanta Acharya, "*The Zoo Story* and the Myth of the Garden Setting", in *Rajasthan Journal of English Studies*, 7–8, 1978.
John Ditsky, "Albee's Parabolic Christ: *The Zoo Story*", in his *The Onstage Christ: Studies in the Persistence of a Theme*, London, 1980.
Cynthia Thomiszer, "Child's Play: Games in *The Zoo Story*", in *College Literature*, vol.9 no.2, 1982.
Fred D. White, "Albee's Hunger Artist: *The Zoo Story* as a Parable of the Writer vs. Society", in *Arizona Quarterly*, 39, 1983.
Chakradhar P. Singh, "The Human Isolation: A Study in Edward Albee's *The Zoo Story*", in *Journal of Literature and Aesthetics*, vol.4 no.1, 1984.
P.D. Dubbe, "Edward Albee's *The Zoo Story*", in *Scholar Critic*, 7–8, 1987.

*   *   *

The Zoo Story is a short one-acter in a single scene—a mere 30 pages—and its story is, superficially, slight. The setting is Central Park, New York. Peter, who works for a publisher, is in his late forties though his "*dress and manner would suggest a man younger*" than one moving into middle age. He is sitting, reading, on one of two park benches when Jerry enters. Jerry, in his late thirties, not poorly but carelessly dressed and showing "*great weariness*", has been to the zoo. He imposes himself on Peter, insisting on talking to him. He extracts from Peter details of his life. He is married, has two daughters, cats—and two parakeets: it is almost as if it is Peter who lives in a zoo.

Jerry describes his life in a sordid rooming-house—his neighbours, his possessions, his appalling landlady (who approaches him with "sweaty lust"), and her truly awful dog, which regularly attacks him. He describes in a long monologue—almost a quarter of the play's length—his relationship with this dog, his attempt at poisoning it, and the common understanding they have achieved. From this he has learned that "neither kindness nor cruelty by themselves. . .creates any effect beyond themselves. . .[but] the two combined, together, at the same time, are the teaching emotion". At last Jerry starts to tell Peter about the zoo; as he does so, constantly moving, shoving, punching Peter along "his" bench, he gradually dispossesses him, to Peter's impotent fury. Jerry tries to make Peter fight him and throws a flick-knife. Peter reluctantly holds this away from him, defensively, but Jerry rushes at him, impaling himself on the knife to Peter's horror. As Jerry told him at the start of the scene, he would see it on TV that night and read about it in the papers the next day. Peter returns, distraught, to his "zoo", leaving the stage, and both benches, to the dead Jerry.

Though the play is so brief, it is remarkably packed with incident, actual and implied, and its often comic language is dramatically at variance with the play's disturbing undertones. It is, indeed, one of the outstanding short plays of the 20th century, standing comparison with Synge's *Riders to the Sea*. Part of Albee's skill lies in the way he undercuts our responses. The standpoint of the average member of the audience is likely to be represented by Peter; Jerry might well represent a freer-spirit, untrammelled by *passé* conventions, yet uncertain and rootless. However, neither will receive the audience's unqualified and continuous support. The quarrel over the park bench is but the climax of a number of incidents and responses calculated to discommode the audience. Jerry, for all his easy-goingness, plainly bullies Peter; but Peter obviously lays claim to what is not his—"my bench"—and that offends a member of the established property-owning class. The audience's allegiances are challenged and there is calculated uncertainty whether to laugh at the absurdity of the situation or be exasperated by the pettiness of the two characters.

The play is marked by a very high standard of language. In the first part of the play there are wry turns of phrase, skilful use of colloquialism, inventive dialogue, and wit. There is a very well-judged moment when Peter's attempt at humour just fails to come off, exposing his personality to us. Jerry has accused him of patronising him. Peter replies, "I. . .I don't express myself too well, sometimes. (*He attempts a joke on himself.*) I'm in publishing not writing". There is a frequent imaginativeness that is telling and delightful. When Peter alludes to Jerry's parents, he explains that "good old Mom and good old Pop are dead. . .That particular vaudeville act is playing the cloud circuit now, so I don't see how I can look at them, all neat and framed".

A second feature of the language is the brilliant monologue which Jerry introduces "as if reading from a huge billboard": "THE STORY OF JERRY AND THE DOG!". Peter reacts from time to time as this lengthy tale unfolds but says nothing. The effect is that of a vaudeville monologue (Albee's grandfather ran an important vaudeville booking agency) or "stump speech". In the tradition of vaudeville and music-hall monologues (and a characteristic found in Shakespeare), there are "asides" within the monologue. A hint of this technique, and of the combination of social observation, the comic, and the cruel, can be found in this extract:

> When I bought the hamburger I asked the man not to bother with the roll, all I wanted was the meat. I expected some reaction from him, like: we don't sell no hamburgers without rolls; or, wha' d'ya wanna do, eat it out' a ya han's? But no; he smiled benignly, wrapped up the hamburger in waxed paper, and said: A bite for ya pussy-cat? I wanted to say: No, not really; it's part of a plan to poison a dog I know. But you can't say "a dog I know" without sounding funny; so I said, a little too loud I'm afraid, and too formally: YES, A BITE FOR MY PUSSY-CAT.

Later, in *Who's Afraid of Virginia Woolf?*, Albee used the technique of marrying the comic and the cruel extensively, but its foundations can be seen deployed with great economy in *The Zoo Story*. Thus, when the dog has eaten the poisoned meat, "THE BEAST WAS DEATHLY ILL":

> I knew this because he no longer attended me, and because the landlady sobered up. She stopped me in the hall the same evening of the attempted murder and confided the information that God had struck her puppy-dog a surely fatal blow. She had forgotten her bewildered lust, and her eyes were wide open for the first time. They looked like the dog's eyes.

In the monologue, as in the play as a whole, the audience is uncertain how to respond—in the crudest terms, whether to laugh or cry. The overall effect is that at the end of the play, the audience, in a curious way, becomes party to Peter's "act" in killing Jerry, even though that "act" was no more than a defensive reaction. The effect for an audience, if the play is well acted, is surprisingly draining.

The socio-political lessons which may be drawn from this short play are many, but in some ways it is Albee's dramatic technique in forcing his audience to confront those lessons that is most interesting. Albee seems to be showing us that in the human zoo, inaction can be even more dangerous than action, and can have as violent an outcome. By his manipulation of the audience's expectations, Albee shocks the audience from amusement to a confrontation with its own reluctance to become emotionally involved in the concerns of others—with its reluctance, more generally, to shift from observation to participation.

—Peter Davison

NOTES ON ADVISERS AND CONTRIBUTORS

AARSETH, Asbjørn. Professor of Scandinavian Literature, University of Bergen, Norway. Formerly editor of *Edda: Scandinavian Journal of Literary Research*, 1986–90. Author of *Peer Gynt*, 1975, *"Peer Gynt" and "Ghosts"* (Text and Performance Series), 1989, and of books in Norwegian on the Bergen National Theatre (1901–31), 1969, applied narratology, 1976, realism in Norwegian literary history, 1981, and Romanticism in Scandinavian literary history, 1985. **Essays:** Beyond Human Power; Brand; The Lady from the Sea; Peer Gynt; When We Dead Awaken; The Wild Duck.

ANDERMAN, Gunilla. Director of Centre for Translation and Language Studies and Head of Swedish, University of Surrey. Author of play reviews, articles on translation theory, and on theatre. Translator of *The Changing Roles of Men and Women*, 1967, *Swedish Literature in the Post-War Period*, 1979, and plays by P.-O. Enqvist, S.-O. Ericsson, and Lars Norén. **Essays:** A Dream Play; Miss Julie.

ANDREWS, Richard. Professor of Italian, University of Leeds. Author of articles on Ariosto, Calvino, Italian Renaissance comedy, community theatre in Tuscany, and a forthcoming book on 16th-century Italian comedy. **Essay:** The Deceived.

ARDOLINO, Frank. Associate Professor of English at the University of Hawaii, Manoa. Author of *Thomas Kyd's Mystery Play: Myth and Ritual in "The Spanish Tragedy"*, 1985, and articles on Kyd, Shakespeare, Gascoigne, Browne, Dekker, Greene, and Marlowe. **Essay:** Cymbeline.

BALLET, Arthur. Professor Emeritus of Theatre, University of Minnesota. Advisory Editor, *New Theatre Quarterly*. Formerly: Program Director (Theatre), National Endowment for the Arts; Executive Director, Office for Advanced Drama Research, Minneapolis; dramaturg at the Guthrie Theatre, Minneapolis, and at the American Conservatory Theatre, San Francisco. Editor of *Playwrights for Tomorrow*, volumes 1–13. **Essays:** Come Back Little Sheba; The Crucible, Oh Dad, Poor Dad, Mamma's Hung You in the Closet and I'm Feelin' So Sad; You Can't Take It With You.

BANFIELD, Chris. Lecturer in Theatre Arts, University of Birmingham. **Essay:** Who's Afraid of Virginia Woolf?

BANHAM, Martin. Professor of Drama and Theatre Studies, University of Leeds. Author of *Osborne*, 1969, *African Theatre Today*, 1976. Editor of *Plays by Tom Taylor*, 1985, *The Cambridge Guide to World Theatre*, 1988. Co-editor (with John Hodgson) of three volumes of *Drama in Education*, 1972, 1973, and 1975. **Essay:** Sizwe Bansi is Dead.

BARLOW, Judith E. Associate Professor of English and Women's Studies, State University of New York, Albany. Author of *Final Acts: The Creation of Three Late O'Neill Plays*, 1985, and many theatre reviews and articles on O'Neill, Crothers, Tina Howe, and American drama. Editor of *Plays by American Women (1900–30)*, 1981, and O'Neill centennial issue of *Theatre Survey*, 1988. **Essays:** He and She; Long Day's Journey Into Night.

BARNETT, Gene A. Professor of English and Comparative Literature, Fairleigh Dickinson University, Teaneck, New Jersey. Author of *Denis Johnston*, 1978, *Lanford Wilson*, 1987, and articles on modern drama and American literature. **Essays:** Da; The Death and Resurrection of Mr. Roche; The Night of the Iguana; Wild Oats.

BASSNETT, Susan. Reader and Head of Graduate School of Comparative Literary Theory and Translation Studies, University of Warwick. Formerly lecturer in English Literature, University of Rome. Author of a number of books, including *Luigi Pirandello*, 1983, *Magdalena: Experimental Women's Theatre*, 1988, the forthcoming *Shakespeare: The Elizabethan Plays*, and articles on theatre semiotics and women's theatre history. Co-author of *Bernhardt, Terry, Duse: The Actress in Her Time*, 1988. Compiler of *File on Pirandello*, 1989. Translator of plays, poems, and novels. **Essays:** Francesca da Rimini (D'Annunzio); Henry IV (Pirandello); Six Characters in Search of an Author.

BEACHAM, Richard C. Senior Lecturer in Theatre Studies, University of Warwick. Author of *Adolphe Appia: Theatre Artist*, 1987, *Adolphe Appia: Essays, Scenarios and Designs*, 1989, *The Roman Theatre and its Audience*, 1991, and articles on theatre history in *Theater*, *Theatre Research International*, *Maske und Kothurn*, *Opera Quarterly*, and *New Theatre Quarterly*. Editor of the video series *Ancient Theatre and its Legacy*. Translator of Roman comedies. **Essays:** Antigone (Sophocles); The Brothers; Hippolytus; The Oresteia; Phaedra (Seneca); The Rope; The Trojan Women.

BENNATHON, Joss. Freelance writer, drama teacher, actor, and community theatre worker. Contributor of articles to *Contemporary Dramatists*, 1988. **Essays:** The Green Pastures; Separate Tables.

BENNETT, Susan. Assistant Professor of English, University of Calgary, Canada. Author of *Theatre Audiences: A Theory of Production and Reception*, 1990, and articles on contemporary British, Canadian, and American drama. **Essay:** Wedding Band.

BENSON, Eugene. Professor of English, University of Guelph, Ontario; editor of the journal *Canadian Drama*. Former Chairman of the Writers' Union of Canada, 1983–4. Author of the plays *Joan of Arc's Violin*, 1972, *The Gunners' Rope*, 1973; the novels *The Bulls of Ronda*, 1976, *Power Game*, 1980; and the critical monograph, *J.M. Synge*, 1980. librettist of operas *Heloise and Abelard*, 1973, *Everyman*, 1974, and *Psycho Red*, 1980. Co-editor (with L.W. Connolly) of *English-Canadian Theatre*, 1980, and *The Oxford Companion to Canadian Theatre*, 1989. **Essays:** Leaving Home; Riders to the Sea; The Riel Trilogy.

BENSON, Renate. Professor of German, University of Guelph, Ontario. Author of *Erich Kästner: Studien zu seinem Werk*, 1973, *German Expressionist Drama: Ernst Toller and Georg Kaiser*, 1985, and articles on Toller and Anne Hébert. Translator of Louis-H. Frechette's *Papineau*, 1982, M. Lescarbot's *The Theatre of Neptune*, 1982, E. Paquin's *Riel*, and three plays by Anne Hébert. **Essays:** The Beggar; Der Sohn; From Morning to Midnight; Hoppla!

BERGHAUS, Günter. Lecturer in Drama, University of Bristol. Author of *Nestroy's Revolutionspossen*, 1978, *Gryphius' "Carolus Stuarolus"*, 1984, *The Reception of the English Revolution*, 1989, *Theatre and Film in Exile*, 1989, and articles on Italian Renaissance drama, German Baroque theatre, Austrian popular drama, and 20th Century avant-garde performance. **Essays:** The Lulu Plays; Murderer Hope of Women; La Ronde.

BERTIN, Michael. Freelance Writer and Teacher. Formerly Assistant Professor at Temple University, Philadelphia;

Washington Correspondent for *Plays International*, 1985–86; theatre critic for *New Haven Journal Courier*, 1979–81. Editor of *The Play and its Critic: Essays for Eric Bentley*, 1986. **Essays:** Fences; Fool for Love.

BILLINGTON, Michael. Theatre Critic for *The Guardian* since 1971, and London Correspondent for *New York Times* since 1978; author and broadcaster. Formerly theatre, film, and television critic for *The Times*, 1965–71. Author of *The Modern Actor*, 1973, *How Tickled I Am*, 1977, *Alan Ayckbourn*, 1983, *Tom Stoppard: Playwright*, 1987; *Peggy Ashcroft*, 1988. Editor of *The Performing Arts*, 1980, *The Guinness Book of Theatre Facts and Feats*, 1982, and *Director's Shakespeare: "Twelfth Night"*, 1990. **Essay:** Absurd Person Singular.

BISZTRAY, George. Professor of Hungarian Studies, University of Toronto, and Editor of *Hungarian Studies Review*. Author of *Marxist Models of Literary Criticism*, 1978, *Hungarian-Canadian Literature*, 1987, and numerous articles on Hungarian, Scandinavian, and comparative literature. Associate editor, *National Theatre in Northern and Eastern Europe (1746–1900)*, 1991. **Essays:** Liliom; The Tragedy of Man.

BLAHA, Franz G. Professor of English, University of Nebraska, Lincoln. Author of essays on Ludwig Anzengruber, Giraudoux, Beckett, Jack Gelber, Hammett, Parker, Leonard Sciascia, and popular literature. Translator of various works, including Peter Handke's *Kaspar*, 1969. **Essays:** The Force of Habit; Kaspar; Tango.

BOOTH, Michael R. Professor and Chairman of the Department of Theatre, University of Victoria, British Columbia. Author of *Victorian Spectacular Theatre*, 1981, *Prefaces to English Nineteenth Century Theatre*, 1981, *Victorian Theatrical Trades*, 1981. Editor of *Hiss The Villain*, 1964, *English Melodrama*, 1965, *English Plays of The Nineteenth Century* (5 vols.), 1969–76. **Essays:** The Bells; The Factory Lad; Lady Audley's Secret.

BOOTH, Roy. Lecturer in English, Royal Holloway and Bedford New College, University of London. Author of articles on John Donne and Webster in *English*. **Essays:** Arden of Faversham; Endimion; Measure for Measure.

BRADBY, David. Professor of Drama and Theatre Studies, Royal Holloway and Bedford New College, University of London. Formerly Reader in French Theatre Studies, University of Kent, Canterbury. Author of *Modern French Drama*, 1984 (revised 1991), *The Theatre of Robert Planchon* (Theatre in Focus Series), and various articles on French theatre. Co-author (with John McCormick) of *People's Theatre*, 1978, and (with David Williams) *Director's Theatre*, 1988. Editor of *Landmarks of French Classical Drama*, 1991. Co-editor (with Claude Schumacher) of *New French Plays*, 1989. Compiler of the bibliography *Adamov*, 1975. **Essay:** Professor Taranne.

BRANDON, James. Professor of Theatre, University of Hawaii, Honolulu. Previously taught at Michigan State University, East Lancing, 1961-68. Author of *Theatre in Southeast Asia*, 1967 and *Brandon's Guide to Theater in Asia*, 1976. Advisory editor of *The Cambridge Guide to World Theatre*, 1988. Editor of *On Thrones of Gold: Three Javanese Shadow Plays*, 1970, *The Performing Arts in Asia*, 1971, *Traditional Asian Plays*, 1972, *Chushingura: Studies in Kabuki and the Puppet Theater*, 1982. Co-editor (with Tamako Niwa) of *Kabuki Plays*, 1966, and (with Rachel Baumer) *Sanskrit* *Drama in Performance*, 1981. Translator of *Kabuki: Five Classic Plays*, 1975.

BRANDT, George W. Freelance writer and lecturer. Former Professor of Radio, Film and Television Studies, Drama Department, University of Bristol. Author of *British Television Drama*, 1981, and articles on theatre, film, radio and television for *Cassell's Encyclopaedia of World Literature*, 1953, *The Cambridge Guide to World Theatre*, 1988, and various periodicals. Translator of Hans Sachs' *The Wandering Scholar in Paradise* and Lope de Rueda's *The Troublesome Olives* (both in *Medieval Interludes*, 1972), and Calderón's *The Great Stage of the World*, 1976. **Essays:** At the Hawk's Well; Mother Courage and Her Children; The Representative; The Threepenny Opera.

BRENNAN, Anthony. Professor of English, McMaster University, Hamilton, Ontario. Author of the novels *The Carbon Copy*, 1973, and *The Crazy House*, 1976, the critical works *Shakespeare's Dramatic Structures*, 1983, *Onstage and Offstage Worlds in Shakespeare's Plays*, 1989, and numerous articles on Shakespeare, modern drama, and Canadian fiction for a variety of journals. **Essays:** All's Well That Ends Well; Antony and Cleopatra; As You Like It; Krapp's Last Tape; Old Times.

BRIGG, Peter. Associate Professor of English, University of Guelph, Ontario. Author of *J.G. Ballard*, 1985, *Shanghai Year*, 1987, and essays on Pinter, the New Birmingham Repertory Theatre, Canadian drama, and other subjects. **Essay:** Tiny Alice.

BRIGGS, Anthony D.P. Professor of Russian Language and Literature, University of Birmingham. Author of *Mayakovsky: A Tragedy*, 1979, *Alexander Pushkin: A Critical Study*, 1983, *A Comparative Study of Pushkin's "The Bronze Horseman", Nekrasov's "Red-nosed Frost" and Blok's "The Twelve"*, 1990, and the forthcoming *Eugene Onegin*. Co-author of *A Wicked Story: The Rhetoric of "A Hero of our Time"*, 1989. **Essays:** Boris Godunov; Masquerade; A Month in the Country.

BRITZOLAKIS, Christina. Research Fellow in English Literature, St. Hilda's College, University of Oxford. Author of articles on the poetry of Ezra Pound, Eliot, and Yeats in *English Studies in Africa*, 1989, and on the literature of the 1930's in *C.I.E.F.L. Bulletin*, 1989. **Essays:** The Ascent of F6; The Cocktail Party; Salomé.

BROWN, John Russell. Professor of Theatre, University of Michigan, since 1985. Formerly: Head of Drama, University of Birmingham, 1964–71; Professor of English, University of Sussex, 1971–82; Literary Manager and Associate of the National Theatre of Great Britain, 1973–88. Author of *Shakespeare and His Comedies*, 1957, *Shakespeare's "Macbeth"*, 1963, *Shakespeare's Plays in Performance*, 1966, *Effective Theatre*, 1969, *Shakespeare's "The Tempest"*, 1969, *Shakespeare's Dramatic Style*, 1970, *Theatre Language: A Study of Arden, Osborne, Pinter, Wesker*, 1972, *Free Shakespeare*, 1974, *Shakespeare in Performance*, 1976, *Discovering Shakespeare*, 1981, *Shakespeare and His Theatre*, 1982, and *Shakespeares*, 1991. General Editor of the Stratford-Upon-Avon Studies, 1960–67, and Theatre Production Studies. Editor of Shakespeare's *The Merchant of Venice*, 1955, Webster's *The White Devil*, 1960, *The Duchess of Malfi*, 1965, and Shakespeare's *Henry V*, 1965. **Essays:** The Duchess of Malfi;

Hamlet; Henry V; King John; Macbeth; A Midsummer Night's Dream; Titus Andronicus.

BROWN, Molly. Actress, freelance writer, and editor of Womens Writers' Network Newsletter. Formerly, contributing-editor with various arts magazines and newsletters. Regular writer for *The Annual Obituary* and *Matrix*, a science-fiction newsletter. Has written, directed and performed for fringe theatre groups in Britain and the USA. **Essay:** East.

BULL, John. Lecturer in English Literature and Drama, University of Sheffield. Author of *New British Political Dramatists*, 1984, *Stage Right: The Recovery of the Mainstream*, 1988, and articles on modern British drama. Editor of *Howard Brenton: Three Plays*, 1988, and *The Penguin Book of Pastoral Verse*, 1988. **Essays:** The Churchill Play; Entertaining Mr. Sloane; Lear; Love's Last Shift; The Norman Conquests; The Recruiting Officer; The Rivals; Teeth 'n' Smiles; Victory: Choices in Reaction; What the Butler Saw.

BURIAN, Jarka M. Professor of Theatre, State University of New York at Albany. Author of *The Scenography of Josef Svoboda*, 1971, *Svoboda: Wagner*, 1983, and many articles on scenography, design, and Czechoslovakian theatre for *Theatre Journal*, *Theater Crafts*, *Drama Review*, *Modern Drama*, *American Theater*, and other journals. Contributor to *Contemporary Designers*, 1984, *Contemporary Dramatists* (fourth edition), 1988, and *The Cambridge Guide to World Theatre*, 1988. **Essays:** The Glass Menagerie; A View From the Bridge.

BURNETT, Mark Thornton. Lecturer in English Literature, Queen's University, Belfast. Author of essays on Marlowe, Marston and Renaissance literature for various publications, including *Studies in Philology*, 1987, *CIEFL Bulletin*, 1989, *L'Artiste Témoin de Son Temps*, 1990, and *Criticism*, 1991. **Essays:** The Fair Maid of the West, Parts I & II; The Shoemaker's Holiday; Tamburlaine the Great, Parts I & II; Women Beware Women.

BURNS, Rob. Senior Lecturer in German, University of Warwick. Author of articles on Wedekind, Heinrich Böll, Hiessenbüttel, Wellershoff and Nazi culture. Co-author (with Wilfried Van der Will) of *Die Arbeiterkulturbewegung in der Weimar Republik*, 1982, and *Protest and Democracy in West Germany*, 1988. **Essay:** The Plebeians Rehearse the Uprising.

BUTLER, Martin. Lecturer in English, University of Leeds. Author of *Theatre and Crisis (1632–42)*, 1984, *"Volpone": A Critical Study*, 1987, and various articles on Tudor and Stuart theatre. Co-editor of *The Selected Plays of Ben Jonson, 2*, 1989. **Essays:** Hyde Park; The White Devil.

CALANDRA, Denis. Professor of Theatre, University of South Florida, Tampa; playwright and theatre director. Formerly, Senior Lecturer in Drama, Middlesex Polytechnic, London, and lecturer in English and Drama at the University of Regensburg, West Germany. Author of *New German Dramatists*, 1983, and of articles on performance history, theory and dramatic literature for *Theatre Quarterly*, *The Drama Review*, and *Modern Drama*. Translator and editor of *Rainer Werner Fassbinder: Plays*, 1985. **Essays:** Farmyard; Offending the Audience.

CARLSON, Marvin A. Sidney E. Cohn Professor of Theatre, Graduate School, City University of New York. Formerly taught at Cornell University, Ithaca, New York, 1961–79, and at Indiana University, Bloomington. Author of *The*

Theatre of the French Revolution, 1966, *The French Stage in the Nineteenth Century*, 1972, *The German Stage in the Nineteenth Century*, 1972, *Goethe and the Weimar Theatre*, 1978, *The Italian Stage in the Nineteenth Century*, 1980, *Theories of the Theatre: A Historical and Critical Survey From the Greeks to the Present*, 1984, *The Italian Shakespearians: Performances by Ristori, Salvini, and Rossi in England and America*, 1985, *Places of Performance: The Semiotics of Theatre Architecture*, 1989, and articles on theatre and drama in *Comparative Literature*, *Modern Drama*, *Educational Theatre Journal*, and other periodicals. Translator of *André Antoine's Memories of the Théâtre-Libre*, 1964.

CARNEGIE, David. Senior Lecturer in Theatre and Film, Victoria University of Wellington, New Zealand. Author of articles on New Zealand theatre and Renaissance drama for various publications, including *Landfall*, *Australasian Drama Studies*, and *The Oxford Companion to the Theatre*. Editor of Shakespeare's *Henry IV Part 1*, 1970, Thomas Goffe's *The Raging Turke and The Courageous Turk*, 1974, and a forthcoming edition of the works of John Webster. **Essays:** Foreskin's Lament; The Pohutukawa Tree.

CARROLL, Dennis. Professor of Theatre, University of Hawaii at Manoa. Author of *Australian Contemporary Drama (1909–82): A Critical Introduction*, 1985, *David Mamet*, 1987, and articles on Australian and American theatre for *Modern Drama*, *Theatre Journal*, and essays collections. **Essays:** The Basic Training of Pavlo Hummel; True West.

CASCARDI, Anthony J. Associate Professor of Comparative Literature, Rhetoric, and Spanish, University of California, Berkeley. Author of *The Limits of Illusion: A Critical Study of Calderón*, 1984, *The Bounds of Reason: Cervantes, Dostoevsky, Flaubert*, 1986, and many essays on Lope de Vega, Tirso de Molina, Calderón de la Barca, Cervantes, and literary theory, in *New Literary History*, *Modern Language Notes*, *Cervantes*, *The Review of Metaphysics*, and other publications. Editor of *Literature and the Question of Philosophy*, 1987. **Essays:** Fuenteovejuna; The Great Theatre of the World; The Trickster of Seville.

CLARE, Janet. Lecturer in English, Bath College of Higher Education; tutor for the Open University. Author of *"Art made Tongue-tied by Authority": Elizabethan and Jacobean Dramatic Censorship*, 1990, and articles and book reviews on Renaissance theatre, Shakespeare, and censorship, for *Review of English Studies*, *Renaissance Drama Newsletter*, *Shakespeare Studies*, and other periodicals. **Essays:** Bussy D'Ambois; Edward II; The Knight of the Burning Pestle; The Maid's Tragedy; The Malcontent.

CLARKE, Janet. Part-time Lecturer, University of Lancaster. Formerly, lecturer at the University of Exeter. Author of articles on the Evénégaud Theatre for *17th Century French Studies*, and editor of Thomas Corneille's *Circé*, 1989. **Essays:** Berenice; Break of Noon; Coelina; The Satin Slipper; The Trojan War Will Not Take Place.

COCKIN, Katharine. Part-time lecturer in English, Nene College, Northampton, and part-time tutorial assistant in English, Leicester University. Author of articles on the Victorian and Edwardian Age (1837–1913) for *Victorian Periodicals Review*, 1990, and on Edith Craig for *Theatre Notebook*, 1991. **Essay:** The Good Hope.

COHN, Ruby. Professor of Comparative Drama, University of California, Davis; on the editorial board of *Modern Drama, Theatre Journal,* and *Cambridge Guide to World Drama.* Author of *Samuel Beckett: The Comic Gamut,* 1962, *Currents in Contemporary Drama,* 1969, *Edward Albee,* 1969, *Dialogue in American Drama,* 1971, *Back to Beckett,* 1971, *Modern Shakespeare Offshoots,* 1976, *Just Play: Beckett's Theatre,* 1980, *From Desire to Godot,* 1987, *New American Dramatists 1960–1990,* 1991.

CONNOLLY, L.W. Associate Vice-President Academic, and Professor of Drama, University of Guelph, Ontario; Co-editor and co-founder of *Nineteenth-Century Theatre Research* and *Essays in Theatre.* Author of *The Censorship of the English Drama (1737–1824),* 1976. Co-author of *English-Canadian Theatre,* 1987. Editor of *Theatrical Touring and Funding in North America,* 1982, and *Canadian Drama and the Critics,* 1987. Co-editor of *English Drama and Theatre (1800–1900): A Guide to Information Sources,* 1978, and *The Oxford Companion to Canadian Theatre,* 1989. **Essays:** Caste; Money; The Ticket-of-Leave Man.

CONNOLLY, Thomas F. Senior Lecturer in English, Suffolk University, Boston, Massachusetts. **Essays:** Hay Fever; Justice; Private Lives.

COOK, Philip S. Lecturer in Drama, University of Manchester. Author of *How to Enjoy Theatre,* 1983, and of articles and reviews on contemporary theatre productions in Manchester. Director of Medieval, Renaissance and Classical plays, including two major productions of *The Castle of Perseverance.* **Essays:** The Atheist's Tragedy; The Castle of Perseverance; Gorboduc; A Woman Killed With Kindness.

CORMAN, Brian. Associate Professor and Director of Graduate Studies in English, University of Toronto. Author of articles on Congreve, Etherege, Fielding, Shadwell, Samuel Johnson, Otway, Pope, Swift, Nahum Tate, and on genre theory and the history of drama and the novel (1660–1800). **Essays:** The Double Dealer; Love for Love.

COUPE, W.A. Professor of German, University of Reading. Formerly Professor of German, University of Southampton. Publications include *The German Illustrated Broadsheet in the 17th Century* (2 vols.), 1966–67, *A 16th Century German Reader,* 1972, *German Political Satires (1918–45),* 1985, *Germany Through the Looking Glass: A Cartoon Chronicle of the Federal Republic,* 1986, *German Political Satire (1849–1918)* (2 vols.), 1987, and various articles on German literature and the history of German cartoons. Co-author of *The Continental Renaissance,* 1971. **Essay:** Comedy, Satire, Irony, and Deeper Meaning.

CRONACHER, Karen. Member of the School of Drama, University of Washington, Seattle. Currently engaged in research on Ntozake Shange. **Essay:** For Coloured Girls Who Have Considered Suicide When the Rainbow is Enuf.

CROW, Brian. Lecturer in Drama and Theatre Arts, University of Birmingham. Previously taught drama at Ahmadu Bello University, Nigeria, and the University of Western Australia. Author of *Studying Drama,* 1983, and of articles on Ibsen, Soyinka, and African theatre for periodicals, including *Studies in Romanticism, The Journal of Commonwealth Literature, Theatre Research International,* and *Australasian Drama Studies.* **Essay:** The Alchemist; Boesman and Lena; Death and

the King's Horseman; The Island; Madmen and Specialists; "Master Harold". . . and the Boys.

CURRENT-GARCIA, Eugene. Hargis Professor Emeritus of American Literature, Auburn University, Alabama; editor of *Southern Humanities Review,* 1967–79. Author of *O. Henry (W.S. Porter): A Critical Study,* 1965, and *The American Short Story Before 1850,* 1985. Editor (with Walton R. Patrick) of *American Short Stories,* 1952 (4th edition 1982), *What Is the Short Story?,* 1961, *Realism and Romanticism in Fiction,* 1962, and *Short Stories of the Western World,* 1969, and of *Shem, Ham, and Japheth: The Papers of W.O. Tuggle,* 1973. **Essay:** Our Town.

DACE, Tish. Professor of English, Southeastern Massachusetts University, North Dartmouth; contributor to *Plays International, Plays and Players, Theater Week, Theatre Crafts, Other Stages, Village Voice,* New York *Times, American Theatre, Playbill,* and other periodicals. Author of *LeRoi Jones (Imamu Amiri Baraka): A Checklist of Works by and about Him,* 1971, *The Theatre Student: Modern Theatre and Drama,* 1973, and *Langston Hughes: Early Critical Responses,* 1991. **Essay:** Caritas.

DAVIDSON, Clifford. Professor of English and Medieval Studies, Western Michigan University, Kalamazoo; executive editor of *Early Drama, Art and Music,* and co-editor of *Comparative Drama.* Author of *The Primrose Way: A Study of Shakespeare's "Macbeth",* 1970, *Drama and Art,* 1977, *From Creation to Doom,* 1984, *The Guild Chapel Wall Paintings at Stratford-upon-Avon,* 1988, *Vizualising the Moral Life,* 1989, and many articles and reviews on drama, literature, and art for a variety of periodicals. Co-author (with David O'Connor) of *York Art,* 1978. Editor of *A Middle English Treatise on the on the Playing of Miracles,* 1981, *The Saint Play in Medieval Europe,* 1986. Co-editor (with C.J. Gianakaris and John H. Stroupe) of *Drama in the Middle Ages,* 1982, and *Drama in the Twentieth Century,* 1984, (with Jennifer Alexander) *The Early Art of Coventry, Stratford-Upon-Avon, Warwick, and Lesser Sites in Warwickshire,* (with Thomas Campbell) *The Fleury Playbook: Essays and Studies,* 1985, (with C.J. Gianakaris and John H. Stroupe) *Drama in the Renaissance,* 1986, (with Ann E. Nichols) *Iconoclasm vs. Art and Drama,* 1989. **Essays:** Everyman; The Towneley Plays; The Winter's Tale; The York Cycle.

DAVISON, Peter. President of the Bibliographical Society. Former Professor of English, St. David's University College, Lampeter, and Professor of English & American Literature, University of Kent. Author of *Songs of the British Music Hall: A Critical Study,* 1971, *Popular Appeal in British Drama to 1850,* 1982, *Contemporary Drama and the Popular Dramatic Tradition in England,* 1983, *Hamlet* (Text and Performance Series), 1985, *"Henry V": Masterguide,* 1987, *"Othello": The Critical Debate,* 1988. Editor of *The Fair Maid of the Exchange,* 1963, Shakespeare's *Richard II,* 1964, *The Merchant of Venice,* 1967, *Henry IV, Part 1,* 1968, and *Henry IV, Part 2,* 1977, Marston's *The Dutch Courtesan,* 1968, *Facsimile of the Manuscript of Nineteen Eighty-Four,* 1984, *Sheridan: A Casebook,* 1986, *The Works of George Orwell* (vols. 1–9), 1986–1987 [vols 10–20, forthcoming], and the forthcoming *The Word Encompassed: Studies for the Centenary of the Bibliographical Society, 1892–1992.* Contributing editor of *Theatrum Revivum,* 1972, *Literary Taste, Culture, and Mass Communication,* 1978–80, and *Year's Work in English Studies,* 1984–5, and has also contributed articles and reviews on bibliography, drama, and literature & society to many other periodicals. **Essays:** The Adding Machine; Black Eyed Susan; Death of a Salesman; Doctor Faustus; The Donnelly Plays; Henry IV, Parts I & II; Puss in Boots; Richard II; Volpone; The Zoo Story.

DAY, Barbara. Freelance writer and translator; Secretary of the Jan Hus Educational Foundation. Author of articles and contributor to essay-collections on Czech theatre. Translator of Ivan Klíma's *Games* (produced 1990). **Essays:** The Insect Play; The Memorandum; R.U.R.

DOLBY, William Lecturer in Chinese Studies, University of Edinburgh. Formerly, Lecturer in Chinese, University of Malaysia, Kuala Lumpur. Author of *A History of Chinese Drama*, 1976, *Eight Chinese Plays*, 1978, and many other works on Chinese literature and theatre. **Essays:** The Chalk Circle; Thunderstorm.

DOUCETTE, Leonard E. Professor of French, University of Toronto. Co-editor of *Theatre History in Canada*. Former Editor of *University of Toronto Quarterly*, and former Vice-President of the Association for Canadian Theatre History. Author of *Emery Bigot*, 1970, *Theatre in French Canada*, 1984, and many articles on French and French-Canadian theatre history, including major contributions to *The Oxford Companion to Canadian Theatre*, *The Canadian Encyclopaedia*, *The Cambridge Guide to World Theatre*, *The Oxford Companion to Canadian Literature*, and *The Dictionary of Literary Biography*. **Essays:** La Sagouine; The Sisters-in-Law; Tit-Coq; The White Geese.

DUNN, Tony. Senior Lecturer in Literature and Drama, Portsmouth Polytechnic; editor of the theatre journal *Gambit*. Author of articles on Howard Barker, Howard Brenton, and modern British theatre and society for various periodicals, including *Plays and Players*, *English-Amerikanische Studien*, *Toneel Teatraal*, and *Tribune*. **Essays:** After Haggerty; Bingo; The Family Reunion; Home; The Lady's Not For Burning.

EDDERSHAW, Margaret. Senior Lecturer in Theatre Studies, University of Lancaster. Author of *Grand Fashionable Nights: Kendal Theatre (1575–1985)*, 1989, articles on Brecht and Stanislavsky for *Brecht in Perspective*, 1982, and on Brecht's *Mother Courage* for *New Theatre Quarterly*, 1991. **Essay:** The Measures Taken.

EDWARDS, Gwynne. Professor of Spanish, University College of Wales, Aberystwyth. Author of *Lorca: The Theatre Beneath the Sand*, 1980, *The Discreet Art of Luis Buñuel*, 1982, *Dramatists in Perspective: Spanish Theatre in the Twentieth Century*, 1985, and many articles on Spanish dramatists of the 17th and 20th centuries. Editor of *Lorca: Plays 1*, 1987, *Lorca: Plays 2*, 1990, *Lorca: Plays 3*, 1991, *Calderón: Plays 1*, 1991. Translator of plays by Lorca for productions at the Bristol Old Vic, Battersea Arts Theatre, and the Edinburgh Festival. **Essays:** Blood Wedding; The House of Bernarda Alba; Life is a Dream.

EILE, Stanislaw. Senior Lecturer in Polish, University of London. Formerly Associate Professor, University of Cracow, and visiting Professor, University of Michigan. Author of the following books in Polish: a biography of Stefan Zeromski, 1961, *The Legend of Zeromski*, 1965, and *The Semantics of the Novel*, 1973, and of articles in English on Polish drama and literature for journals including *New Literary History*, *Soviet Jewish Affairs*, and the collection *Perspectives on Literature*

and Society in Eastern and Western Europe, 1989. **Essays:** Forefathers' Eve; The Wedding.

FALCKENBERG, Peter. Lecturer in German, University of Canterbury, New Zealand. **Essay:** Woyzeck.

FITZPATRICK, Peter. Senior Lecturer in English, Monash University. Author of *After the Doll: Australian Drama Since 1955*, 1979, *Williamson*, 1987, and articles on Australian drama. **Essay:** The Time is Not Yet Ripe.

FLETCHER, Kathy. Visiting Assistant Professor of Theatre, University of Nebraska, Lincoln. Author of the play *Necessities*, and of many articles on Planché, pantomime, and Victorian popular theatre for *Women's Studies Encyclopaedia*, *Nineteenth Century Theatre*, *Victorian Britain: An Encyclopaedia*, *Theatre Studies*, and other publications. **Essays:** American Buffalo; Children of a Lesser God; Street Scene; The Time of Your Life.

FOSTER, Verna A. Professor of English, Loyola University, Chicago. Author of essays on Ford, Middleton, Fletcher, and Shakespeare for various journals including *Renaissance Drama*, *Renaissance Tragi-comedy*, *Modern Language Quarterly*, and *Studies in English Literature*. **Essay:** Philaster.

FOULKES, Richard. Lecturer, Department of Adult Education, University of Leicester. Author of *The Shakespeare Tercentenary of 1864*, 1984, and articles on Samuel Phelp's *A Midsummer Night's Dream*, Helen Faucet, Ellen Terry, Terence Rattigan, The Royal Dramatic College, Charles Calvert's *Henry V*, and other topics for publications including *Theatre Notebook*, *Modern Drama*, *Theatrefile*, and *Shakespeare Survey*. Editor of *Shakespeare and the Victorian Stage*, 1986. **Essay:** The Browning Version.

FRANCESCHETTI, Antonio. Professor of Italian, University of Toronto; Co-president of Internazionale per gli Studi di Lingua e Letteratura Italiana; Editor of *Quaderni d'italianistica*. Former President, Canadian Society for Italian Studies. Author of *L'Orlando innamorato e le sue componenti tematiche e strutturali*, 1975, and articles on Italian literature from the Middle Ages to the 19th Century, and on Italian-Canadian literature and culture. Editor of *Letteratura italiana e arti figurative* (3 vols.), 1988. **Essays:** The Chest; La Venexiana.

GALE, Steven H. University Endowed Professor in Humanities, Kentucky State University. Formerly director of honours program, Missouri Southern State College, and Fulbright Professor of British and American Literature and Drama. Author of *Butter's Going Up*, 1977, *S.J. Perelman: A Critical Study*, 1987. Compiler of *Harold Pinter: An Annotated Bibliography*, 1978, *S.J. Perelman: An Annotated Bibliography*, 1985. Editor of *Harold Pinter: Critical Approaches*, 1986, *Encyclopaedia of American Humorists*, 1988, *Critical Essays on Harold Pinter*, 1990, the forthcoming *S.J. Perelman: Critical Essays* and *Encyclopaedia of British Humorists*, and of many articles on modern British and American dramatists, Elizabethan and 19th-century theatre, poetry, and film. **Essays:** Butley, Indians, No Man's Land, A Streetcar Named Desire.

GEORGE, David. Professor in the Department of Foreign Languages, Lake Forest College, Illinois. Author of *Teatro e antropofagia*, 1985, *Grupo Macunaíma: Carnavalização e Mito*, 1990, and of several articles on Brazilian theatre and fiction in *Theatre Research International, Latin American Theatre Review, Suplemento literário de Minas Gerais*. Translator of Marcelo Rubens Paiva's autobiography *Happy Old Year*, 1991, and Edla Van Steens' *A Bag of Stories* and *Village of the Ghost Bells*, 1991. **Essay:** Wedding Dress.

GEROULD, Daniel. Lucille Lortel Distinguished Professor of Theatre and Comparative Literature, Graduate School, City University of New York. Author of *Witkacy: Stanislaw Ignacy Witkiewicz as an Imaginitive Writer*, 1981, and *Guillotine*, 1991. Co-author of *A Life of Solitude: Stanislaw Przybyszewska*, 1989. Editor and translator of *Twentieth Century Polish Avant-Garde Drama*, 1977, *Gallant and Libertine: Divertissements & Parades of 18th Century France*, 1983, *Doubles, Demons and Dreamers: An International Collection of Symbolist Drama*, 1985, and *A Witkiewicz Reader*, 1991. **Essays:** Mariage Blanc; The Water Hen.

GIANAKARIS, C.J. Professor of English and Theatre, Western Michigan University, Kalamazoo. Co-founder and former co-editor of *Comparative Drama*, from 1966. Formerly Associate Dean, College of Arts and Sciences, Western Michigan University. Author of *Plutarch*, 1970, and *Foundations of Drama*, 1975. Editor of *Antony and Cleopatra*, 1969. Co-editor (with Clifford Davidson and John H. Stroupe) of *Drama in the Middle Ages*, 1984, *Drama in the Twentieth Century*, 1985, and *Drama of the Renaissance*, 1986. Author of many essays for *Modern Drama, Drama Studies, Opera News, Theatre Journal, Comparative Drama, Theatre Week*, and other journals. **Essays:** Epicoene; Equus; Julius Caesar; The Royal Hunt of the Sun; Twelfth Night.

GIBSON, Colin. Donald Collie Professor of English, University of Otago, Dunedin, New Zealand. Author of numerous articles on Massinger, Jonson, Ford, and Elizabethan drama for *Notes & Queries, Modern Language Review*, and *AUMLA Journal*. Editor of Shakespeare's *As You Like It*, 1965, *The Selected Plays of Philip Massinger*, 1978, *The Selected Plays of John Ford*, 1986, *Art and Society in the Victorian Novel: Essays on Dickens and His Contemporaries*, 1989, and *Witts Recreation (1640)*, 1989. **Essays:** The Broken Heart; A New Way to Pay Old Debts; 'Tis Pity She's a Whore.

GIDEZ, Richard B. Associate Professor of English and American Studies, Pennsylvania State University. Author of *P.D. James*, 1986, articles on Emlyn Williams, Enid Bagnold, and Ronald Harwood for *The Dictionary of Literary Biography*, 1982, on John P. Marquand for *Research Guide to Biography and Criticism: Literature*, 1986, and on Emlyn Williams for *Critical Survey of Drama*, 1986. **Essay:** Brighton Beach Memoirs.

GILMAN, Donald. Professor and Co-ordinator of French, Ball State University, Muncie, Indiana. Author of numerous articles in US and European journals on Ronsard, the theory of Renaissance dialogue, the moral play, Racine, Maeterlinck, Cocteau, Anouilh, and Mauriac. Editor of *Everyman and Company: Essays on the Theme and Structure of the European Moral Plays*, 1989. Co-Editor of *Dialogues of Louis Le Caron*, 1986. **Essay:** The Infernal Machine; Master Peter Pathelin; Ubu Roi.

GONTARSKI, S.E. Professor of English, Florida State University; Editor of *The Journal of Beckett Studies*. Formerly, Visiting Distinguished Professor of Comparative Literature, California State University, and Visiting Associate

Professor of English, University of California, Riverside. Author of *The Intent of Undoing in Samuel Beckett's Dramatic Texts*, 1985. Editor of *Happy Days*, 1977, *On Beckett: Essays and Criticism*, 1986, *The Theatrical Notebooks of Samuel Beckett: "Endgame"*, 1991. Co-editor (with Morris Beja and Pierre Astier) of *Samuel Beckett: Humanistic Perspectives*, 1983, and (with John Calder) *The Surrealist Reader*, 1991. Guest Editor of *Modern Fiction Studies*, 1983. **Essay:** The Empire Builders.

GOODLIFFE, John. Senior Lecturer in Russian, University of Canterbury, Christchurch, New Zealand. **Essay:** The Life of Man.

GORDON, Robert. Senior Lecturer in Drama, Goldsmith's College, University of London; co-director of Magna Carta Productions (theatre company). Formerly, Lecturer in Drama and Theatre Studies, Royal Holloway College, University of London. Author of the plays *Red Earth*, (produced) 1985, and *Waterloo Road* (produced 1987), the critical study *Rosecrantz and Guildenstern Are Dead; Jumpers; The Real Thing* (Text and Performance Series) 1991, and articles on Simon Gray and the beginnings of the Avante-Garde. **Essays:** Jumpers; The Plain Dealer.

GORELL, Lynn Carbón. Assistant Professor and Curriculum Supervisor, Department of Spanish, Italian and Portuguese, Pennsylvania State University, University Park. Former Editorial Assistant for *Latin-American Theatre Review*, and President, Mid-American Association of Luso-Brazilianists. Author of *De lector a escritor: Desarrollo de la comunicación personal*, 1991, and articles on literature and foreign language study for *Modern Language Journal* and *Language Learning*. **Essay:** The Criminals; Saverio El Cruel.

GOSSIP, Christopher. Professor of French, University of New England, Armidale, New South Wales. Formerly Senior Lecturer, University College of Swansea, and Lecturer, University of Aberdeen. Author of *An Introduction to French Classical Tragedy*, 1981, and many articles on 17th-century French theatre. Editor of Thomas Corneille's *Stilicon*, 1974, and Cyrano de Bergerac's *La Mort d'Agrippine*, 1982. **Essays:** Andromache; Cinna; Horatius; The Misanthrope.

GOTTLIEB, Vera. Professor of Drama, Goldsmith's College, University of London; co-director of Magna Carta Productions (theatre company). Author of *Chekhov and the Vaudeville*, 1982, *Chekhov in Performance in Russia and Soviet Russia* (Theatre in Focus Series), and articles on contemporary theatre, Chekhov, and farce for *Themes in Drama, New Theatre Quarterly*, and other periodicals. Translator and adaptor of *Chekhov Quartet* (produced London, Yalta, and Moscow, 1989). Co-director of *Red Earth* and *Waterloo Road*.

GRAHAM-WHITE, Anthony. Professor of Theatre, University of Illinois at Chicago. Former editor of *Educational Theatre Journal* (now *Theatre Journal*), 1972–5. Author of *The Drama of Black Africa*, 1974, and articles on traditional theatre, ritual in contemporary theatre, and Shakespeare's *Richard III* for *Yale Theatre, Journal of Dramatic Theory and Criticism*, and other publications. **Essays:** The Candle Bearer; Dingo; Eastward Ho!; Friar Bacon and Friar Bungay; Gammer Gurton's Needle; The Little Clay Cart; The London Merchant.

GRAY, Frances. Lecturer in Drama, University of Sheffield.

Author of *John Arden*, 1982, *Noël Coward*, 1987, radio plays including *Mary*, 1983, *Neverland*, 1985, and *Dawnhorse*, 1991, and articles on radio drama, modern theatre, and women in comedy. Editor of *Second Wave at the Albany*. **Essays:** Comedians; The Corn is Green; Design for Living; Torch Song Trilogy; Troilus and Cressida; The Two Noble Kinsmen.

GROSENOR MYER, Michael. Writer and Critic. Former British Council Lecturer, Beijing Language Institute. Author of theatre and book reviews for various periodicals, including *The Times Educational Supplement* and *Plays and Players*. Contributor to *Folk Music in School*, 1978, *The Cambridge Guide to Literature in English*, 1988. **Essay:** Maria Marten.

GROSVENOR MYER, Valerie. Lecturer in English, University of Sierra Leone. Author of *Margaret Drabble: Puritanism and Permissiveness*, 1974, *Jane Austin*, 1980, *Charlotte Brontë: Truculent Spirit*, 1987, *Culture Shock* (a novel), 1988, *A Victorian Lady in Africa: The Story of Mary Kingsley*, 1989, *Ten Great English Novelists*, 1990, *Margaret Drabble: A Reader's Guide*, 1991, and theatre and book reviews for *The Stage* and *Notes & Queries*. Editor of *Laurence Sterne: Riddles and Mysteries*, 1984, and *Samuel Richardson: Passion and Prudence*, 1986. **Essays:** The Pillars of Society, Saint Joan.

HANSFORD, James. Teacher of English, Royal Grammar School, Guildford; tutor in literature, Open University; tutor in literature, Surrey University Extra-Mural Department. Author of essays on Beckett for *The Journal of Beckett Studies* and *Studies in Short Fiction*, on Conrad for *The Conradian* and *Conradiana*, on Gabriel Josipovici and Alan Burns in *Prospice*, and a pamphlet on Post-War British drama for the English Association. **Essay:** Next Time I'll Sing to You.

HATTAWAY, Michael. Professor of English Literature, University of Sheffield. Formerly, Senior Lecturer in English, University of Kent. Author of *Elizabethan Popular Theatre*, 1982, *Hamlet: The Critics Debate*, 1987. Editor of Jonson's *The New Inn*, 1985, Shakespeare's *Henry VI (Parts 1 and 2)*, 1990–1. Co-editor (with A.R. Braunmuller) of *The Cambridge Companion to English Renaissance Drama*, 1990. **Essays:** Coriolanus; The Two Gentlemen of Verona; The Witch of Edmonton.

HAWKINS-DADY, Mark. Editor of the *International Dictionary of Theatre*. **Essay:** Not I.

HERZEL, Roger W. Professor and Director of Graduate Studies, Department of Theatre and Drama, Indiana University, Bloomington. Author of studies and articles on Molière and French theatre. **Essays:** Don Juan; The Game of Love and Chance; The Imaginary Invalid.

HIDALGO CIUDAD, Juan Carlos. Research Fellow, University of Seville, Spain. Author of article on London Fringe theatre in the 1980's for *Nuevos mitos en la literatura Anglosajona*, 1990. **Essay:** [with Rafael Portillo] The Conscious Lovers.

HOLDERNESS, Graham. Head of Drama, Roehampton Institute of Higher Education, London. Formerly Lecturer in English, University College, Swansea. Author of *D.H. Lawrence: History, Ideology and Fiction*, 1982, *Shakespeare's History*, 1985, *Shakespeare in Performance: "The Taming of the Shrew"*, 1989, the forthcoming *Shakespeare Recycled: The Making of Historical Drama*, and many articles on Renaissance and modern literature and theatre. Co-author of *Shakespeare: The Play of History*, 1988, and *Shakespeare out of Court*, 1990. Editor of *The Shakespeare Myth*, 1988, and *The Politics of Theatre and Drama*, 1991. **Essays:** Hedda Gabler; Marat/Sade; Much Ado About Nothing; Romeo and Juliet; Rosencrantz and Guildenstern Are Dead; The Taming of the Shrew.

HOLLAND, Peter. Judith E. Watson University Lecturer in Drama, Faculty of English, University of Cambridge. Author of *The Ornament of Action: Text and Performance in Restoration Comedy*, and of articles on Shakespeare, Chekhov, and contemporary theatre in *Shakespeare Survey*, *New Theatre Quarterly*, *Themes in Drama*, and other journals. Editor of *The Plays of Wycherley*, 1981. Co-editor (with Hanna Scolnicov) of *The Play out of Context*, 1988, and *Reading Plays*, 1991.

HOLT, Marion Peter. Professor of Theatre, City University of New York. Author of *The Contemporary Spanish Theatre: 1949–1972*, 1975, and numerous articles on modern Spanish drama and performance. Editor and translator of *Antonio Buero-Vallejo: Three Plays*, 1985, and Buero's *Las Meninas*, 1987. Editor of *Drama Contemporary: Spain*, 1985. **Essay:** The Sleep of Reason.

HOULAHAN, Mark Anthony. Assistant Professor of English, University of Waterloo, Ontario. **Essays:** The Clandestine Marriage; The Provoked Wife; She Stoops to Conquer; Venice Preserved.

HOUSE, Jane. Assistant Professor of Educational Theatre, New York University and Department of Drama, Vassar College. Formerly actress, and Director of the Institute on Western Europe Theatre Project, Columbia University, 1985–90. Author of articles on Italian theatre and translations for *Western European Theatre*, *LMDA Review*, and *Italian Journal*. Editor of *Political Theatre Today*, 1988. **Essays:** Corruption in the Palace of Justice; The Mask and the Face.

HOWARTH, William D. Emeritus Professor of French, University of Bristol. Formerly Fellow and Tutor in Modern Languages, Jesus College, University of Oxford, 1948–66; Professor of Classical French Literature, Bristol University, 1966–88. Author of *Life and Letters in France: The Seventeenth Century*, 1965, *Sublime and Grotesque: A Study of French Romantic Drama*, 1975, *Molière: A Playwright and his Audience*, 1982, *Anouilh: "Antigone"*, 1983, *Corneille: "Le Cid"*, 1988, and many articles on French literature and theatre. Editor of *Comic Drama: The European Heritage*, 1978, and editions of works by Anouilh, Molière, La Chaussée, and Voltaire. Co-editor of *Molière: Stage and Study*, 1973. Member of the editorial board for the series *A Documentary History of the European Theatre* (15 vols.), 1989–. **Essays:** Antony; Chatterton; Cyrano de Bergerac; Hernani; The Lady of the Camelias; The Theatrical Illusion.

HUGHES, Derek. Senior Lecturer in English, University of Warwick. Former Lecturer in English, Brock University, Ontario. Author of *Dryden's Heroic Plays*, 1981, and articles on Restoration drama in various journals, including *English Literary History*, *Modern Language Review*, *Modern Language Quarterly*, and *Comparative Drama*. **Essay:** Marriage à-la-Mode.

HUNT, Hugh. Emeritus Professor of Drama, Manchester University. Formerly Producer, Abbey Theatre, Dublin, 1935–38; Director, Bristol Old Vic, 1945–9; Artistic Director,

Old Vic Company, London, 1949–53; Executive Director, Australian Elizabethan Trust, 1955–60; Professor of Drama, Manchester University, 1961–73; Artistic Director, Abbey Theatre Dublin, 1969–71. Made Commander of the British Empire, 1971. Author of *Old Vic Prefaces*, 1954, *The Director in the Theatre*, 1954, *The Making of Australian Theatre*, 1960, *The Living Theatre*, 1961, *The Abbey: Ireland's National Theatre*, 1979, *Sean O'Casey*, 1980, various articles and contributions to collections of essays, and several plays, including *The Invincibles* and *In the Train*. **Essay:** Shadow and Substance.

HURRELL, John D. Emeritus Professor of English, University of Minnesota, Minneapolis; Advisory Editor, *Comparative Drama*, since 1966. Formerly, editor of *Drama Survey*, 1961–68, Associate Dean, College of Liberal Arts, 1964–68, and Associate Chair, English Department, at the University of Minnesota, 1981–84. Author of articles on Shakespeare, Ibsen, Chekhov, Whiting, Medieval drama, and farce for various periodicals, including *Quarterly Journal of Speech*, *Educational Theatre Journal*, *College English*, and *Modern Drama*. Editor of *Two Modern American Tragedies*, 1961. **Essay:** The Second Mrs. Tanqueray.

INNES, Christopher. Professor of English, York University, North York, Ontario; general editor of the "Directors in Perspective" series for Cambridge University Press. Author of *Erwin Piscator's Political Theatre*, 1972, *Modern German Drama*, 1979, *Holy Theatre: Ritual and the Avant Garde*, 1981, *Edward Gordon Craig*, 1983, and articles on drama and theatre.

JACK, R.D.S. Professor of Scottish and Medieval Literature, University of Edinburgh. Former Visiting Professor, University of Virginia, Charlottesville. Author of *The Italian Influence on Scottish Literature*, 1972, *Alexander Montgomerie*, 1985, *Scotland's Literary Debt to Italy*, 1986, *Patterns of Divine Comedy in Medieval Drama*, 1989, *Structured Thought: The Road to Never Land*, 1990, and of many articles and reviews on Scottish literature for *Studies in Scottish literature*, *Comparative Literature*, *Review of English Studies*, *Modern Language Review*, *Scottish Literary Journal*, and other periodicals. Editor of *Scottish Prose (1550–1700)*, 1971, *A Choice of Scottish Verse (1550–1660)*, 1978, *The History of Scottish Literature: Volume 1, Origins to 1660*, 1988. Co-editor of *Robert Maclellan's "Jamie the Saxt"*, 1971, *The Art of Robert Burns*, 1982, *Sir Thomas Urquhart, "The Jewel"*, 1984, and *Leopardi: A Scottis Quair*, 1987. **Essays:** The Admirable Crichton; Peter Pan; A Satire of the Three Estates.

JORDAN, Robert. Professor of Theatre Studies, University of New South Wales, Australia. Formerly, Foundation Professor of Drama, University of Newcastle, Australia, and Reader in English, University of Queensland. Author of articles on Restoration theatre and society, Jacobean, early 20th-century British, and Australian theatre and drama. Co-editor (with H.H.R. Love) of *The Works of Thomas Southerne* (2 vols.), 1988. **Essays:** Oroonoko; The Virtuoso.

KEITH-SMITH, Brian. Senior Lecturer in German, University of Bristol. Author of *Johannes Bobrowski*, 1970, *Lothar Schreyer*, 1990, and essays on 20th-century writers, chiefly Hoffmansthal and Schreyer. Editor of *Essays on Contemporary German Literature*, 1966, *Anthologie neuerer deutscher Prosaerzählungen*, 1971, *German Men of Letters, 6*, 1972, *Martin Luther*, 1983, *Das expressionistische Werk Lothar Schreyers*, 1985, *German Expressionism in the United Kingdon*

and Ireland, 1986, *Büchner in Britain*, 1987, *Georg Büchner: Tradition and Innovation*, 1990, *Bristol Austrian Studies*, 1990. **Essays:** The Captain of Köpenick; The Gas Trilogy; In the Matter of J. Robert Oppenheimer; Masses and Man; Penthesilea; Scenes From the Heroic Life of the Middle Classes.

KELLY, Veronica. Senior Lecturer in English, University of Queensland, Brisbane; Co-editor of *Australasian Drama Studies*. Author of *Louis Nowra*, 1987, and articles on contemporary Australian drama for *Australasian Drama Studies*, *Kunapipi*, *Southerly*, and other periodicals. Editor of Garnet Walch's *Australia Felix; or, Harlequin, Laughing Jackass and the Magic Bat* 1988. **Essay:** The Golden Age.

KENNEDY, Dennis. Professor of Theatre Studies, University of Pittsburgh; general editor of the series "Pittsburgh Studies in Theatre and Culture." Author of *Granville Barker and the Dream of Theatre*, 1985, *Looking at Shakespeare*, 1991, a number of plays, and essays on Shakespeare in performance and modern playwrights, including Shaw and Barker. Editor of *Plays by Harley Granville Barker*, 1987. **Essays:** Major Barbara; Man and Superman.

KING, Adele. Professor of French, Ball State University, Muncie, Indiana. Former Reader in French, Ahmadu Bello University, Nigeria; lecturer in French, universities of Lagos and Ibadan, Nigeria. Author of *Camus*, 1964, *Proust*, 1968, *Paul Nizan: Ecrivain*, 1976, *The Writings of Camara Laye*, 1980, *French Women Novelists: Defining a Female Style*, 1989, and articles on women writers in France and the Third World, African literature in French, Camus, and study guides on Camus, Camara Laye, Hemingway, Graham Greene and Ibsen. Editor of the forthcoming *Camus's "L'Etranger": Fifty Years On*. **Essays:** Caligula; Ghosts; No Exit.

KING, Bruce. Visiting Professor of English, University of Paris 7; general editor of the series "Modern Dramatists" and "English Dramatists". Formerly Professor and Visiting Professor of English at universities in the United States, Canada, Scotland, France, Israel, Nigeria, and New Zealand. Author of *Dryden's Major Plays*, 1966, *Marvell's Allegorical Poetry*, 1977, *The New English Literatures: Cultural Nationalism in a Changing World*, 1980, *History of Seventeenth Century English Literature*, 1988, *Modern Indian Poetry in English*, 1987/1989, *Coriolanus*, 1989, *Three Indian Poets: Ezekiel, Ramanujan and Moraes*, 1991. Editor of *Twentieth Century Interpretations of "All for Love"*, 1968, *Dryden's Mind and Art*, 1969, *Introduction to Nigerian Literature*, 1971, *Literatures of the World in English*, 1974, *A Celebration of Black and African Writing*, 1976, *West Indian Literature*, 1979, *Contemporary American Theatre*, 1991, *The Commonwealth Novel Since 1960*, 1991. **Essays:** All for Love; Dream on Monkey Mountain; Murder in the Cathederal; Othello; The Road; The Tempest.

KING, Pamela M. Senior Lecturer in English, and Director of the Centre for Medieval Studies, Queen Mary and Westfield College, University of London. Editor of *Church Monuments Society Newsletter*, 1985–88. Author of essays on Medieval drama and culture for various publications, including *Medieval English Theatre*, *Drama and Philosophy* (Themes in Drama Series), *Studies in Scottish Literature*, as well as reviews for *The Times Higher Education Supplement*, *Theatre Notebook*, and *Medieval Theatre*. Co-editor (with Richard Beadle) of *York Mystery Plays: A Selection in Modern Spelling*, 1984. **Essays:** The Chester Cycle; Mankind; N-Town Plays.

KITCHIN, Laurence. Former Professor of Liberal Arts, City University of New York, and Visiting Professor of Drama, Stanford University. Author of *Mid-Century Drama*, 1960, *Drama in the Sixties*, 1966, and numerous articles on drama for *The Times*, 1956–62. **Essays:** For Services Rendered; Journey's End.

KLAUS, H. Gustav. Part-time Professor of English, University of Osnabrück, Germany. Former Visiting Professor, University of Queensland and University of Edinburgh. Author of *Caldwell in Kontext*, 1978, and *The Literature of Labour*, 1985. Editor of *The Socialist Novel in Britain*, 1982, *The Rise of Socialist Fiction 1880–1914*, 1987, and *Tramps, Workmates and Revolutionaries*, 1991. Author of articles for *Contemporary Novelists*, 1986, *Contemporary Dramatists*, 1988, and *London Magazine*, 1989. **Essays:** The Plough and the Stars; Strife.

KNAPP, Margaret M. Associate Professor of Theatre, Arizona State University. Co-author of *"The Ancient and Famous Cittie": David Rogers and the Chester Mystery Plays*, and author of articles on Minnie Maddern Fiske for *Journal of American Drama and Theatre*, on Agnes Morgan, Irene and Alice Lewisohn for *Notable Women in American Theatre: A Biographical Dictionary*, and on musical theatre for *The Cambridge Guide to World Theatre*. **Essay:** The New York Idea.

KNOWLES, A.V. Senior Lecturer in Russian and Soviet Studies, and Assistant Director of Combined Honours (Arts), University of Liverpool. Author of *Turgenev*, 1988. Co-author of *Anglescina za vsakogar*, 1962. Editor of *Tolstoy: The Critical Heritage*, 1978, *Turgenev's Letters*, 1983, Ostrovsky's *The Storm*, 1988, and author of articles on Russian literature, history and drama. **Essays:** The Forest; The Minor; The Storm.

KREMER, Manfred K. Professor of German and Chair of Department of Languages and Literatures, University of Guelph, Ontario. Author of *Die Satire bei Johann Beer*, 1964, and articles on Günter Grass, Lessing, Thelens, Christian Weis, and satire for various publications including *German Quarterly*, *Lessing and the Enlightenment*, 1986, *Der moderne deutsche Schelmenroman*, 1986, *Absurda Comica*, 1988, and *Simpliciana*. Editor of Johann Beer's *Der Kurtzweilige Bruder Blau-Mantel*, 1979. **Essay:** Danton's Death.

LAMONT, Rosette C. Professor of French and Comparative Literature, Queen's College and at the Graduate School of the City University of New York. Author of *The Life and Works of Boris Pasternak*, 1964, *De Vive Voix*, 1971, *Ionesco*, 1973, *The Two Faces of Ionesco*, 1978, and various articles. Contributing Editor for *Performing Arts Journal* and *Centrepoint*. **Essays:** The Bald Prima Donna; Rhinoceros.

LANGE, Bernd-Peter. Professor of English, University of Oldenburg, Germany. Former Editor of *Gulliver* and *German-English Yearbook*. Author of *Charles Dickens*, 1969, *George Orwell*, 1975, *The Theory of Genres*, 1979, *Orwell, "1984"*, 1982, *Cultural Studies*, 1984, *The Spanish Civil War in British and American Literature*, 1988, *Classics in Cultural Criticism 1: Britain*, 1990, and essays on Edward Bond, Steve Gooch, George Orwell, and William Beckford. **Essays:** Cloud Nine; The Conquest of Granada; The Country Wife; The Man of Mode; The Rehearsal; The Relapse; The Way of the World.

LAWLEY, Paul. Senior Lecturer in English, Polytechnic South West. Author of essays and reviews for *Contemporary Dramatists*, 1982 (and the fourth edition, 1988), *The Journal of Beckett Studies*, *Modern Drama*, *Modern Fiction Studies*, *Theatre Journal*, *Modern Language Review*, and the collection *"Make Sense Who May": Essays on Samuel Beckett's Later Works*, 1988. **Essays:** The Caretaker; Glengarry Glen Ross; Happy Days; The Homecoming; The Romans in Britain; Saved; Top Girls.

LAYERA, Ramon. Professor in the Department of Spanish and Portuguese, Miami University, Oxford, Ohio. **Essay:** El Gesticulador.

LEACH, Robert. Lecturer in Drama and Theatre Arts, University of Birmingham. Former Director of Cannon Hill Community Theatre, Birmingham. Author of *Theatre For Youth*, 1970, *The Wellsbourne Tree: A Musical Documentary Play*, 1975, *How to Make a Documentary Play*, 1975, *Theatre Workshop Series*, 1977–83, *The Punch and Judy Show*, 1985, and *Vsevelod Meyerhold*, 1989. **Essays:** The Bedbug; The Dragon; The Government Inspector; The Magnificent Cuckold; Man Equals Man; Mystery Bouffe; The Power of Darkness; The Puppet Show; The Suicide; The Workhouse Donkey.

LEVENE, M.A. Lecturer in German, University of Bristol. **Essay:** The Robbers.

LEWIS, Peter. Reader in English, University of Durham. Author of *John Gay: "The Beggar's Opera"*, 1976, *Orwell: The Road to 1984*, 1984, *John Le Carré*, 1985, *Fielding's Burlesque Drama*, 1987, *Eric Ambler*, 1990, and many articles on Restoration and 18th-century drama, and contemporary literature. Editor of *The Beggar's Opera*, 1973, *Poems '74*, 1974, *Papers of the Radio Literature Conference 1977*, 1978, and *Radio Drama*, 1981. Co-editor (with Nigel Wood) of *John Gay and the Scriblerians*, 1988. **Essays:** The Beggar's Opera; Tom Thumb.

LEWIS, Tim. Lecturer in French, Queen Mary and Westfield College, University of London. Author of essay on André Malraux and the art of propaganda for *Art, Literature and the Spanish Civil War*, 1988. **Essays:** The Balcony; The Blacks; The Chairs; The Lesson; The Maids; A Season in the Congo.

LONDRÉ, Felicia Hardison. Curators' Professor of Theatre, University of Missouri, Kansas City; Dramaturg for Missouri Repertory Theatre. Author of *Tennessee Williams*, 1979, *Tom Stoppard*, 1981, *Federico García Lorca*, 1984, *The History of World Theatre, 2*, 1991, and articles on continental European and American theatre history for essay-collections, casebooks, and various journals including *Theatre Research International*, *Theatre History Studies*, *Theatre Journal*, *Theater Week*, *Slavic and East European Arts*, *Studies in Popular Culture*, *Comparative Drama*. **Essays:** Pelleas and Melisande; Ruy Blas.

LOWE, N.J. Lecturer in Classics, Queen Mary and Westfield College, University of London. Author of the forthcoming *The Classical Plot*, and articles on Greek and Latin literature, especially comedy, for various journals, including *Themes in Drama*, *Bulletin of the Institute of Classical Studies*, and *Classical Quarterly*. **Essays:** The Braggart Soldier; The Frogs; Lysistrata; Phormio; Prometheus Bound; The Suppliants.

MacDONALD, James. Fellow in Drama, University of Exeter, and Play-reader for Northcott Theatre, Exeter. Formerly

Associate Editor of *The Freethinker*. Reviewer and author of articles on humanism and the arts for *The Freethinker*, 1977–81. **Essays:** The Children's Hour; Dead End; In Abraham's Bosom; A Soldier's Play; The Voice of the Turtle.

MacKENZIE, Ann L. Senior Lecturer in Hispanic Studies, University of Liverpool; editor of *Bulletin of Hispanic Studies*. Former Visiting Professor of Golden Age Literature, University of Chicago, Illinois, 1990. Author of *La escuela de Calderón: Estudios y ensayos*, 1991, and numerous articles on Spanish drama in *Ibero-romania*, *Dieciocho*, and other journals and collections. Co-author (with Kenneth Muir) of *Calderón: Four Comedies*, 1980, *Calderón: Three Comedies*, 1985, and *Calderón: "La cisma de Inglaterra" / The Schism in England*, 1990. Editor of *The Eighteenth Century in Spain: Essays in Honour of I.L. McLelland*, 1991. **Essays:** Justice Without Revenge; The Mayor of Zalamea; Peribañez and the Comendador of Ocaña.

MACKERRAS, Colin. Professor and Director, Key Centre for Asian Language Studies, Griffith University, Brisbane. Formerly Chairman, School of Modern Asian Studies, Griffith University, 1979–85, and Foreign Expert, Beijing Institute of Foreign Languages, 1964–1966, 1986, and 1990. Author of *The Rise of Peking Opera*, 1972, *The Chinese Theatre in Modern Times*, 1975, *The Performing Arts in Contemporary China*, 1981, and numerous articles on China and Chinese theatre. Editor of *Chinese Theater From its Origins to the Present Day*, 1983, and *Chinese Drama: A Historical Perspective*, 1990. **Essays:** The Palace of Eternal Youth; Peach Blossom Fan; Teahouse.

MALLINSON, G. Jonathon. Lecturer in French and Fellow of Trinity College, University of Oxford. Formerly Fellow and Director of French Studies, Pembroke College, University of Cambridge. Author of *The Comedies of Corneille: Experiments in the Comic*, 1984, *Molière: "L'Avare"*, 1988, and articles on French 17th and 18th-century theatre and prose fiction. **Essays:** The Cid; The Double Inconstancy; The Marriage of Figaro; Tartuffe; Turcaret.

MARKER, Frederick J. Professor of English, University College, University of Toronto. Author of articles for *The Revels History of Drama in English, 1750–1880*, 1975, *Ibsen and the Theatre*, 1980, *Ibsen Yearbook*, *Theatre Survey*, *Theatre Notebook*, *Scandinavian Review*, *Modern Drama*, and other publications. Co-author (with Lise-Lone Marker) of *The Scandinavian Theatre: A Short History*, 1975, *Edward Gordon Craig and "The Pretenders": A Production Revisited*, 1981, *Ingmar Bergman: Four Decades in the Theater*, 1982. Editor of *The Heibergs*, 1971, and Hans Christian Anderson's *Den nye Barselstue*, 1975. Co-editor and translator of *Ingmar Bergman: A Project for the Theatre*, 1983.

MARTINUS, Eivor. Writer and Translator. Author of five novels in Swedish, 1971–78, the plays *You* (produced 1974), *The Misogynist* (produced 1984), *Behind a Dream* (produced 1989), and of critical articles for *Swedish Book Review*, *Scandinavica*, and *Adam International Review*. Translator of Swedish films, plays, television documentaries, and the following Strindberg plays: *Motherly Love; The First Warning; Pariah*, 1987, *Thunder in the Air*, 1989, *The Great Highway*, 1990, and *Five Chamber Plays: The Father; The Pelican; After the Fire; The Ghost Sonata; The Black Glove*, 1991. **Essay:** The Dance of Death, Parts I & II.

McGILLICK, Paul. Lecturer in Applied Linguistics, University of Sydney; Theatre Critic for *Australian Financial Review*. Formerly Editor of *New Theatre Australia*. Author of *Hack Hibberd*, 1988, and numerous monographs and articles on theatre and the visual arts. **Essays:** The Rivers of China; A Stretch of the Imagination.

McNAUGHTON, Howard. Reader in English, University of Canterbury, Christchurch, New Zealand. Author of *Bruce Mason*, 1976, *New Zealand Drama*, 1981, and the section on the novel in *The Oxford History of New Zealand Literature* (forthcoming). Editor of *Contemporary New Zealand Plays*, 1976, and *James K. Baxter: Collected Plays*, 1982. **Essays:** After the Fall; Cato; Cock-a-Doodle Dandy; An Enemy of the People; The Front Page; Funnyhouse of a Negro; The Indian Wants the Bronx; John Gabriel Borkman; The Quare Fellow; The Season at Sarsaparilla; The Shaughraun; The West Indian; What Price Glory?

McVAY, Gordon. Reader in Russian, University of Bristol. Author of *Esenin: A Life*, 1976, *Isadora and Esenin*, 1980, and of articles on Sergei Esenin, Chekhov, the peasant poets, and the Imaginists for journals, and play reviews for *Plays and Players*. **Essays:** The Lower Depths; The Three Sisters.

MEECH, Anthony. Lecturer in Drama, University of Hull. Author of articles on German theatre (especially East German), and a forthcoming history of German theatre for Cambridge University Press. **Essays:** Baal; The Good Person of Setzuan; Götz von Berlichingen with the Iron Hand; Mary Stuart; Minna von Barnhelm.

MESERVE, Walter J. Distinguished Professor of Theatre and English, Graduate School, City University of New York; Co-editor of *Journal of American Drama and Theatre*. Formerly Professor of Theatre and Drama and Director of the Institute for American Studies, Indiana University, Bloomington. Author of *An Outline History of American Drama*, 1965, *Robert Sherwood: Reluctant Moralist*, 1970, *An Emerging Entertainment: The Drama of the American People to 1828*, 1977, *American Drama* (vol. 8 of the Revels History), with others, 1977, *American Drama to 1900: A Guide to Reference Sources*, 1980, and *Heralds of Promise: The Drama of the American People During the Age of Jackson 1829–1849*, 1986. Editor of *The Complete Plays of William Dean Howells*, 1960, *Discussions of Modern American Drama*, 1966, *American Satiric Comedies*, 1969, *Modern Drama from Communist China*, 1970, *The Rise of Silas Lapham by Howells*, 1971, *Studies in Death of a Salesman*, 1972, and *Modern Literature from China*, 1974. Compiler of *Who's Where in the American Theatre*, 1990. **Essays:** Fashion; Francesca da Rimini (Boker); Margaret Fleming; The Petrified Forest; They Knew What They Wanted.

MILES, Patrick. Senior Research Associate, Gonville and Caius College, University of Cambridge. Formerly Russian literary consultant and translator, National Theatre of Great Britain, 1977–80, and director of the Cambridge Young Chekhov Company, 1974–77. Author of *Chekhov on the British Stage, 1909–1987*, 1987. Translator (with Harvey Pitcher) of *Chekhov: The Early Stories, 1883–87*. **Essays:** Duck Hunting; Ivanov.

MOE, Christian H. Professor of Theatre, Southern Illinois University, Carbondale; member of the Dramatists Guild. Previously taught at Flinders University, South Australia, and Vita International Center, Luxembourg. Author of articles on dramatists and children's writers for *Twentieth-Century Chil-*

dren's Writers, 1989, *Encyclopedia of Literary Characters*, 1990, *Twentieth-Century Romance and Historical Writers*, 1990, *Contemporary Dramatists*, 1988, and in various journals. Co-author of *Creating Historical Drama*, 1965, *The Strolling Players*, 1971, *When Santa Claus Came to Simpson's Crossing*, 1975, *Three Rabbits White*, 1979, *Tom Sawyer: An Adaptation*, 1979. Co-editor of *Six New Plays for Children*, 1971. **Essays:** The Floating World; The Glass of Water; The Odd Couple; The Philadelphia Story; Processional; The Removalists; Travelling North.

MOMBOURQUETTE, Mary Pat. Member of the University of Guelph, Ontario. **Essays:** Blood Relations; Waiting for the Parade.

MORGAN, Margery. Emeritus Reader in English and Theatre Studies, University of Lancaster. Formerly, Lecturer in English, Royal Holloway College (University of London), and Reader in English, Monash University, Australia. Author of *A Drama of Political Man: A Study of the Plays of Harley Granville Barker*, 1961, *The Shavian Playground*, 1972, *York Notes on "Pygmalion"*, 1980, *Bernard Shaw* (Writers and their Work), 1982, *John Galsworthy* (Writers and their Work), 1982, *York Notes on "Major Barbara"*, 1982, *August Strindberg*, 1985, *York Handbook on Drama*, 1987, and articles on Granville-Barker, Shaw, Wesker, Gregan McMahon, and other topics. Editor of Granville-Barker's *The Madras House*, 1977, and Shaw's *The Doctor's Dilemma*, 1981. Compiler of *File on Shaw*, 1989, and *File on Wilde*, 1990. **Essays:** Back to Methuselah; The Ghost Sonata; The Madras House; The Master Builder; Misalliance; Pygmalion; Rosmersholm; Too True to be Good; The Voysey Inheritance.

MORRISON, Marcia K. Assistant Professor of Theatre, State University of New York at Albany. Formerly, associate artistic director of a professional melodrama theatre; freelance director, acting coach, and new play reader in Los Angeles, New York and Boston. Author of reviews. Co-author of *Anton and Olga*, a dramatization of the correspondence between Anton Chekhov and Olga Knipper. **Essay:** Under the Gaslight.

MULRYNE, J.R. Professor of English and Comparative Literary Studies, and Chairman of the Graduate School of Renaissance Studies, University of Warwick. Former Reader in English Literature, University of Edinburgh, 1962–77. Author of essays on Middleton, Kyd, Shakespeare, Webster, Sir Thomas Browne, and W.B. Yeats. Editor of Middleton's *Women Beware Women*, Webster's *The White Devil*, Kyd's *The Spanish Tragedy*, and *An Honoured Guest: New Essays on W.B. Yeats*. Co-editor of *War Literature and the Arts in Sixteenth Century Europe*; *English and Italian Theatre of the Renaissance*; *Italian Renaissance Festival and its European Influence*; *Theatre and Government under the Early Stuarts*. Joint editor, compiler, and publisher (with Margaret Shewring) of *This Golden Round: The Royal Shakespeare Company at the Swan*. **Essays:** Bartholemew Fair; The Jew of Malta.

NICHOLSON, Steve. Lecturer in The Workshop Theatre, University of Leeds. Author of two articles on British political theatre for *New Theatre Quarterly*. **Essays:** The Cheviot, the Stag, and the Black, Black Oil; Destiny; Plenty; Pravda.

NIGRO, Kirsten F. Associate Professor of Spanish, University of Cincinnati; Member of editorial board of *Latin American Theatre Review*; Editor, *Studies in Latin American*

Chicano and U.S. Latino Theatre. Former Associate Professor, Arizona State University and Assistant Provost, Washburn University of Topeka. Author of articles on modern Latin American theatre and literature, women writers and feminist theory, José Triana, Vicente Leñero, Griselda Gambaro, Luisa Josefina Hernández, Carlos Fuentes, José Ignacio Cabrujas, and Rosario Castellanos for *Latin American Theatre Review*, *Hispania*, *Revista de estudios hispánicos*, *Theatre Journal*, *Theatre Annual*, and other journals. **Essays:** El cepillo de dientes; The Hands of God.

OSBORNE, John. Professor of German, University of Warwick. Formerly, Alexander von Humboldt Research Fellow, University of Göttingen, 1972–73, and 1975–76; Visiting Professor, University of Metz, 1985–86. Author of *The Naturalist Drama in Germany*, 1971, *J.M.R. Lenz: The Renunciation of Heroism*, 1975, *Die Meininger: Texte zur Rezeption*, 1980, *The Meiningen Court Theatre (1866–90)*, 1988, and articles on German drama and theatre of the 18th and 19th Centuries. **Essays:** Magda; The Soldiers; The Weavers.

PAGE, Malcolm. Professor of English, Simon Fraser University, Burnaby, British Columbia. author of *John Arden*, 1984, and *Richard II*, 1987. Editor of *File on Arden*, 1985, *File on Stoppard*, 1986, *File on Shaffer*, 1987, *File on Osborne*, 1988, *File on Ayckbourn*, 1989, *File on Hare*, 1990. Co-editor (with Simon Trussler) of *File on Edgar*, 1991. **Essays:** Heartbreak House; Jacob's Wake; Mrs. Warren's Profession; The Ruling Class; Serjeant Musgrave's Dance; The Wesker Trilogy.

PATTERSON, Michael. Senior Lecturer in Theatre Studies, University of Ulster, Coleraine, since 1987. Formerly, Lecturer in German, Queens University of Belfast, 1965–70; Lecturer in Drama, University College of North Wales, Bangor, 1970–74; Senior Lecturer in Drama and Theatre Arts, University of Leeds, 1974–87. Author of *German Theatre Today*, 1976, *The Revolution in German Theatre, 1900–1933*, 1981, *Peter Stein*, 1981. Editor of *Büchner: The Complete Plays*, 1987.

PEACOCK, D. Keith. Lecturer in Drama, University of Hull. Author of the forthcoming *Radical Stages: Alternative History in Modern British Drama*, and of articles on European theatre and critical theory. **Essays:** The Devils; A Taste of Honey.

PEARCE, Brian. Tutor and researcher in Drama, Royal Holloway and Bedford New College, University of London; formerly, Lecturer in Drama, Rhodes University, Grahamstown, South Africa. **Essays:** The Father; The Merchant of Venice.

PIASECKI, Andy. Freelance writer; formerly Lecturer in Drama, Royal Holloway and Bedford New College, University of London, 1981–90. Author of articles on Elizabethan theatre for *The Shakespeare Handbook*, 1987, and on modern British drama for *The Bloomsbury Guide to English Literature*, 1989. Compiler of *File on Lorca*, 1991. Contributor to *Plays International*. **Essays:** Look Back in Anger; Richard III; Yerma.

PIRIE, Donald. Stepek Lecturer in Polish Language and Literature, University of Glasgow, since 1984. Author of articles on Polish writers for *Great Foreign Language Writers*, 1984, *Contemporary Foreign Language Writers*, 1984, and on

Stalinist and contemporary Polish poetry. Editor of *Polish Realities: The Arts in Poland, 1980–1989*, 1990, and a forthcoming anthology of contemporary Polish poetry. **Essays:** Marriage; The Undivine Comedy.

POPENHAGEN, Ludvika. Researcher and teacher of acting, University of California, Santa Barbara; also professional actress. Has previously taught acting in Australia, Lithuania, and France. **Essays:** Norm and Ahmed.

PORTILLO, Raphael. Lecturer in English, University of Seville. Author of many articles on the theory of drama, Medieval and Renaissance English theatre, and contemporary playwrights. Co-author (with Jesús Casado) of *English-Spanish, Spanish-English Dictionary of Theatre Terms*, 1986, and *Abecedario del teatro*, 1988. Co-author (with P. Hidalgo, A. Usandizaga and B. Dietz) of *Historia crítica del teatro inglés*, 1988. Editor of *Estudios literarios ingleses: Shakespeare y el teatro de su epoca*, 1987. **Essay:** [with Juan Carlos Hidalgo Cuidad] The Conscious Lovers.

POUNTNEY, Rosemary. Lecturer in English, Jesus College, University of Oxford, and Senior Lecturer in Drama, King Alfred's College, Winchester. Formerly a professional actress. Author of *Notes on "Waiting for Godot"*, 1981, *Theatre of Shadows: Samuel Beckett's Drama, 1956–76*, 1988, and articles and reviews on Beckett and contemporary theatre. **Essays:** The Birthday Party; The Changeling; A Doll's House; The Importance of Being Earnest; King Lear; Play; Purgatory; Travesties.

PRESTON, Jennifer. Member of the University of Guelph, Ontario. **Essay:** The Ecstasy of Rita Joe.

PRIOR, Roger. Senior Lecturer in English, Queen's University of Belfast. Author of articles on George Wilkins, Shakespeare, and Jews in Tudor England for *Shakespeare Quarterly*, *Shakespeare Survey*, *Jewish Historical Studies*, and *Musical Quarterly*. **Essays:** Love's Labour's Lost; The Merry Wives of Windsor; Pericles.

PRONKO, Leonard C. Professor of Theatre, Claremont College, Pomona, California. Author of *The World of Jean Anouilh*, 1961, *Avant-Garde*, 1962, *Eugène Ionesco*, 1965, *Theatre East and West*, 1967, *Guide to Japanese Drama*, 1973, *Georges Feydeau*, 1975, *Eugène Labiche and Georges Feydeau*, 1982, and articles for many journals including *Tulane Drama Review*, *Bucknell Review*, *Educational Theatre Journal*, *Comparative Drama*, and *Japan Quarterly*. **Essays:** A Flea in Her Ear; The Italian Straw Hat.

RADFORD, Colin. Professor of French, Queen's University of Belfast, and Director of the School of Modern and Medieval Languages. Author of several books, articles and reviews. **Essays:** Antigone (Anouilh); The Flies; Ring Around the Moon.

RANALD, Margaret Loftus. Professor of English, Queen's College, City University of New York. Author of *The Eugene O'Neill Companion*, 1984, *Shakespeare and His Social Context: Essays in Osmotic Knowledge and Literary Interpretation*, 1987, *John Webster*, 1989, and numerous articles and reviews on Shakespeare, Webster, O'Neill, research methodology, computer applications, historiography, bibliography, biography, and theatre history. Associate Editor of *International Bibliography of Theatre*, 1982–85. **Essay:** Desire Under the Elms.

RAYFIELD, Donald. Professor of Russian, Queen Mary and Westfield College, University of London. Author of *Chekhov: The Evolution of His Art*, 1975, *Nikolay Przhevalsky: Explorer of Central Asia*, 1976, and many articles on Russian literature and theatre. **Essays:** The Seagull; Uncle Vanya.

READ, Leslie du S. Lecturer in Drama, University of Exeter, Devon. Contributor to *The Cambridge Guide to World Theatre*, 1988, *The Cambridge Encyclopaedia*, 1990, and to the forthcoming *Literature and Criticism: A New Century Guide*. **Essays:** Henry VI, Parts I, II, & III; The Persians; Seven Against Thebes.

REYNOLDS, Bonnie Hildebrand. Professor of Latin American Literature, University of Louisville, Kentucky. Author of *Space, Time and Crisis: The Theatre of René Marqués*, 1988, and of articles on Marqués, Roberto-Ramos-Perea, and Latin American theatre. **Essay:** Los soles truncos.

RICHARDS, Francesca H.A. Freelance lecturer, writer, and translator; formerly lecturer at universities in Sardinia and Paris, 1986–89. **Essay:** Right You Are (If Your Think You Are).

RICHARDS, Kenneth. Professor of Drama and Director of University Theatre, University of Manchester; previously taught at universities of Ljubljana (Yugoslavia), Trondheim (Norway), and Uppsala, and has been a Fellow of the Folger Shakespeare Library, Washington D.C., and the Huntington Library, California. Author of *Comedy*, 1977, many articles on drama and theatre for *The Oxford Companion to the Theatre*, *The Cambridge Guide to World Theatre*, 1988, and various journals. Co-author (with Laura Richards) of *The Commedia dell'arte: A Documentary History*, 1991. Editor of *Nineteenth Century British Theatre*. Co-editor (with Peter Thomson) of *The Eighteenth Century English Stage*, 1973, and (with David Meyer) *Western Popular Theatre*, 1978. **Essays:** Hindle Wakes; The Scenarios of Flaminio Scala; Turandot.

RICHARDS, Laura. Lecturer in the Department of Modern Languages, University of Salford. Co-author (with Kenneth Richards) of *Commedia dell'arte: A Documentary History*, 1991. **Essays:** Accidental Death of an Anarchist; The Mistress of the Inn; Oreste; Saturday, Sunday, Monday; The Servant of Two Masters.

RORRISON, Hugh. Senior Lecturer in German, University of Leeds. Author of *Erwin Piscator: Politics on the Stage in the Weimar Republic*, 1987, play reviews for *Plays and Players*, *Drama*, and *Plays International*, and articles on Peter Handke, Wolfgang Bauer, Heiner Müller, Botho Strauss, Ernst Stern, Ibsen, and the Berliner Schaubühne. Editor of plays by Brecht, including *Mother Courage and her Children*, 1983, *The Caucasian Chalk Circle*, 1984, and *Life of Galileo*, 1986. Translator of Piscator's *The Political Theatre*, 1978, Pavel Kohout's *The Maple Tree Game* (produced 1990), and Wedekind's *The Lulu Plays* (produced 1991). **Essays:** The Caucasian Chalk Circle; Life of Galileo; The Resistable Rise of Arturo Ui.

ROUND, Nicholas. Stevenson Professor of Hispanic Studies, University of Glasgow. Author of articles on *Celestina* in *Studies in Honour of P.E. Russell*, 1980, the journal *Celestinesca*, 1987, and the forthcoming *Celestina: A Critical Guide*. Translator of Buero Vallejo's *The Cards Face Down* (BBC radio, 1973), Perez Galdós' *In Real Life* (BBC radio, 1975), Rivas's *Don Alvero* (Scottish Opera, 1990), and Almeida

Garrett's *Frei Luís de Sousa* (produced 1991). Editor and translator of Tirso de Molina's *Damned for Despair*, 1986. **Essay:** Celestina.

ROY, Donald. Profesor of Drama, University of Hull; formerly lecturer in French, at the Universities of Glasgow and St. Andrews. Author of articles on 17th and 18th-Century French theatre and 19th-Century British theatre. Editor of *Molière: Five Plays*, 1982, and *Plays by James Robinson Planché*, 1986. **Essays:** The Barber of Seville; Zaïre.

SACKS, Glendyr. Lecturer in Drama, University of Exeter. **Essay:** A Raisin in the Sun.

SARLÓS, Robert K. Professor of Dramatic Art, University of California at Davis. Author of *Jig Cook and the Provincetown Players: Theatre in Ferment*, 1982, and of many articles on O'Neill, the Provincetown Players, and European and American theatre history. **Essays:** The Emperor Jones; The Hairy Ape; The Verge.

SENELICK, Laurence. Fletcher Professor of Drama, Tufts University, Medford, Massachusetts. Formerly: member of the US-Soviet Commission on Theatre and Dance Studies; Fellow, Wissenschaftskolleg zu Berlin; Fellow, John Simon Guggenheim Foundation. Author of *Gordon Craig's Moscow Hamlet*, 1982, *Serf Actor: The Life and Art of Mikhail Shchepkin*, 1984, *Anton Chekhov*, 1985, *The Age and Stage of George L. Fox*, 1988, and *The Prestige of Evil: The Murderer as Romantic Hero*. Editor of *British Music-Hall, 1840–1923: A Bibliography*, 1981, *Russian Dramatic Theory from Pushkin to the Symbolists*, 1981, *Russian Satiric Comedy*, 1983, *Cabaret Performance in Europe, 1890–1920*, 1989, *National Theatre in Northern and Eastern Europe, 1743–1900*, 1991.

SCHUMACHER, Claude. Reader in Theatre Studies, University of Glasgow; editor of *Theatre Research International*. Author of *Jarry and Apollinaire*, 1984, and articles on Dürrenmatt, Frisch, Appia, Zola, the theatre of the absurd, and other aspects of literature and theatre. Editor of *40 Years of Mise en Scène*, 1986, *Marivaux: Plays*, 1988, and *Artaud on Theatre*, 1990. Co-editor (with David Bradby) of *New French Plays*, 1989. **Essay:** Thérèse Raquin.

SCOBBIE, Irene. Reader and Head of Department of Scandinavian Studies, University of Aberdeen. Author of *Pär Lagerkvist: An Introduction*, Stockholm, 1962, *Sweden: Nation of the Modern World*, 1972, *Pär Lagerkvist: Gäst hos verkligheten*, 1974, and many articles on Lakerkvist, Strindberg, and Swedish drama and literature. Editor of *Essays on Swedish Literature: From 1880 to the Present Day*, 1979, *An Anthology of Swedish Poetry From 1880 to the Present Day*, 1980, *Aspects of Modern Swedish Literature*, 1988, *Proceedings of the 8th Biennial Conference of Teachers of Scandinavian Studies*, Edinburgh, 1989. Translator of Stig Claesson's *Ancient Monuments*, 1980, and (with Susan Davies) B. Henriksson's *Not For Sale*, 1983. **Essay:** The Hangman.

SHARPE, Lesley. Lecturer in German, University of Exeter. Author of *Schiller and the Historical Character*, 1982, *Friedrich Schiller: Drama, Thought and Politics*, and articles on Goethe and Schiller for *Modern Language Review*, *German Life and Letters*, *German History*, and other periodicals. **Essay:** Faust

SILVESTER, Robert. Visiting Professor, University of Southern Maine, and freelance researcher; formerly Head of Drama, King Alfred's College, Winchester. Compiler of a forthcoming bibliography of American drama, published by Motley Press. **Essay:** The Silver King.

SIMMONS, James. Writer in Residence, Queen's University of Belfast; formerly, Senior Lecturer in Drama and Anglo-Irish Literature, University of Ulster, 1968–84. Author of seven volumes of poetry, 1956–86, *Sean O'Casey*, 1982. Founding editor of *The Honest Ulsterman*, 1968. Has made several recordings of songs. **Essays:** The Death of Cuchulain; On Baile's Strand; Playboy of the Western World; The Silver Tassie.

SINGH, G. Professor of Italian, Queen's University of Belfast. Formerly, Reader in English, Bocconi University, Milan, and Lecturer in English, Muslim University, Aligarh, India. Author of *Leopardi and the Theory of Poetry*, 1964, *Leopardi e L'Inghilterra*, 1968, *Poesie di Thomas Hardy*, 1968, *Eugenio Montale: A Critical Study*, 1973, *Ezra Pound*, 1979, *T.S. Eliot: Poeta, drammaturgo e critico*, 1985, and articles in various English and Italian journals and magazines. Translator (with Ezra Pound) of *Poesie di Kabir*, 1966. **Essays:** Aminta; The Faithful Shepherd; Mandragola; The Post Office; Shakuntala.

SKLOOT, Robert. Professor of Theatre and Drama, University of Wisconsin, Madison. Formerly Fulbright Professor of American Drama in Israel, 1980–81, and Vienna, 1988–89. Author of *The Darkness We Carry: The Drama of the Holocaust*, 1988. Editor of *The Theatre of the Holocaust*, 1982. **Essays:** Cat on a Hot Tin Roof; Translations.

SKRINE, Peter. Professor of German and Head of Department, University of Bristol. Formerly, Senior Lecturer in German, University of Manchester. Author of *The Baroque*, 1978, *Hauptmann, Wedekind and Schnitzler*, 1989, and numerous articles on German and European drama in *Modern Language Review*, *German Life and Letters*, *Jahrbuch für internationale Germanistik*, *Wolfenbütteler Arbeiten zur Barockforschung*, and *Bristol Austrian Studies*. Co-author (with Lilian Furst) of *Naturalism*, 1971. **Essays:** Before Dawn; Maria Magdalena; Spring's Awakening; The Tutor; Wallenstein.

SLATER, Maya. Senior Lecturer in French, Queen Mary and Westfield College, University of London. Author of *Humour in the Works of Proust*, 1979, and articles on Molière and Racine for *Themes in Drama*, 1988 and 1989, and for *Reading Plays: Interpretation and Reception*, 1991. **Essays:** Britannicus; The Learned Ladies; The Miser; Phaedra (Racine); The School for Wives.

SLATTER, Irene. Tutor in Russian, University of Durham; formerly Head of Russian at Central Foundation Girls School and tutor at Newcastle Polytechnic. Author of *Simple Etiquette in Russian*, 1990, and *Very Simple Russian*, 1991. **Essays:** The Cherry Orchard; The Fruits of Enlightenment; Summerfolk.

SMITH, Christopher. Senior Lecturer in French and Comparative Literature, University of East Anglia. Author of *Jean Anouilh: Life Work and Criticism*; *Alabaster, Bikinis and Calvados*, 1985; and numerous articles on drama and translation. Editor of Jean de Taille's *Dramatic Works*, Jacques de la Taille's *Alexandre*, A. Montchrestien's *Two Tragedies*, and of the journal *Seventeenth-Century French Studies*. **Essays:** The Broken Jug; Endgame; The Oberammergau Passion Play; Picnic; The Physicists.

SMITH, James L. Senior Lecturer in English, University of Southampton. Author of *Melodrama*, 1973, and articles on Kyd, Marlowe, Wycherley and other topics. Editor of Vanbrugh's *The Provoked Wife*, 1974, *Victorian Melodramas*, 1976, Wycherley's *The Plain Dealer*, 1979, and Boucicault's *London Assurance*, 1984. **Essay:** She Would if She Could.

SORKIN, Roger. Associate Professor of English, Southeastern Massachusetts University; formerly teacher at Beijing University. **Essays:** Awake and Sing!; A Delicate Balance; The House of Blue Leaves; Little Foxes; The Tooth of Crime.

SOULE, Lesley Anne. Writer and researcher in drama and theatre. **Essay:** The Hostage.

SPENCER, Jane. Lecturer in English Literature, University of Exeter, Devon. Author of *The Rise of the Woman Novelist: From Aphra Behn to Jane-Austen*, 1986. **Essay:** The Rover.

STILLMARK, Alexander. Reader in German, University of London. Author of articles in *German Life and Letters*, *Forum for Modern Language Studies*, *London German Studies*, *New Comparison*, *Publications of the English Goethe Society*, and various essay collections. Co-editor of *Adalbert Stifter heute*, 1985, *Deutsche Romantik und das 20. Jahrhundert*, 1986, *Grillparzer und die europäische Tradition*, 1987, *Erbe und Umbruch in der neueren deutschsprachigen Komödie*, 1990. **Essay:** Tales From the Vienna Woods.

STRANG, Ronald W. Lecturer in Drama and Theatre Studies, University of Kent, Canterbury. Formerly, Lecturer in Drama, University College of North Wales, Bangor. Author of articles on Orton and British theatre, and reviewer of books for *Theatre Research International* and *Notes & Queries*. **Essays:** Forty Years On; London Assurance; The Magistrate.

SWAIN, Elizabeth. Associate Professor of Theatre, Barnard College, New York, and professional actress. Has also taught at New York University and City College, New York. Author of *David Edgar: Playwright and Politician*, 1984, *Notable Women in American Theatre*, 1989, and articles for *Contemporary Dramatists*, 1988, and for various US publications. **Essays:** The Contractor; The Knack.

TAYLOR, Diana. Associate Professor of Spanish and Comparative Literature, Dartmouth College. Author of *Theatre of Crisis: Drama and Politics in Latin America*, 1990, and of numerous articles on modern theatre, especially that of Latin America, for *Theatre Journal*, *Performing Arts Journal*, *Latin American Theatre Review*, *Gestos*, and other journals. Editor of anthologies on Fernando Arrabal, and Griselda Gambaro and José Triana. **Essays:** I, Too, Speak of the Rose; Los Siameses.

TAYLOR, George. Lecturer in Drama, University of Manchester. Author of *Henry Irving and the Lyceum*, 1980, and *Players and Performances in the Victorian Theatre*, 1990. Editor of *Plays of Samuel Foote and Arthur Murphy*, 1984. **Essay:** The White Guard.

TAYLOR, Val. Lecturer in Drama, Roehampton Institute of Higher Education, London; freelance theatre director. Contributor to the forthcoming collection *The Politics of Theatre and Drama*, and has written on Timberlake Wertenbaker's *Our Country's Good* and Britain's National Theatre for *Critical Survey*. **Essays:** Dutchman; Winterset.

THODY, Philip. Professor of French Literature, University of Leeds. Past positions include Visiting Professorships at the universities of Western Ontario, California (at Berkeley), Harvard, Adelaide, Canterbury (New Zealand), Western Australia, and Virginia. Author of *Albert Camus*, 1957, *Jean-Paul Sartre*, 1960, *Albert Camus*, *1913–1960*, 1961, *Jean Anouilh*, 1968, *Jean Genet*, 1968, *Jean-Paul Sartre*, 1971, *Aldous Huxley*, 1973, *A True Life Reader for Children and Parents*, 1977, *Dog Days in Babel*, 1979, *Faux Amis and Keywords*, 1985, *Marcel Proust*, 1987, *Albert Camus*, 1989, *French Caesarism from Napoleon to Charles de Gaulle*, the forthcoming *Jean-Paul Sartre, Novelist*, many articles on French language and literature, and a series of teaching tapes on French authors. Editor of Sartre's *Les Séquestrés d'Altona*, 1965, Camus' *Caligula*, 1973, Christiane Rochefort's *Les Petits Enfants du siècle*, London, 1982. Translator of works by Camus, Orwell, Lucien Goldmann, Jacqueline de Romilly. **Essays:** The Doll Trilogy; Queen After Death.

THOMSON, Peter. Professor of Drama, University of Exeter. Author of *Shakespeare's Theatre*, 1983, *Shakespeare's Professional Career*, 1991, and articles on Shakespeare, 19th-century theatre, and other topics. Co-author (with Jan Needle) of *Brecht*, and (with Gāmini Salgādo) *The Everyman Companion to the Theatre*, 1985. Editor of Shakespeare's *Julius Caesar*, 1970, Malcolm Elwin's *Lord Byron's Family*, 1975, and *Plays by Dion Boucicault*, 1984. Co-editor (with Kenneth Richards) of *Nineteenth Century British Theatre*, 1971, and *The Eighteenth Century English Stage*, 1973.

TSUBAKI, Andrew T. Professor of Theatre, Film, East Asian Languages and Cultures, and Director of International Theatre Studies Centre, University of Kansas. Area Editor for *Asian Theatre Journal*. Former Chairman, East Asian languages and Cultures, University of Kansas, and Chairman, Asian Theatre Program of American Theatre Association. Author of articles on Japanese theatre for *The Journal of Aesthetics and Art Criticism*, 1971, and *Educational Theatre Journal*, 1977. Co-author of article for *Indian Theatre: Traditions and Performance*, 1990. Contributing editor for the Asian section of *Theatre Companies of the World*, 1986. Has directed many productions of Japanese, Classical Greek, and Shakespearian plays. **Essays:** The Battles of Coxinga; Benkei in the Boat; Samurai Nao; The Scarlet Princess of Edo; Suehirogari; Well-Curb.

TURNER, Elaine. Lecturer in Drama, University of Warwick; also teaches at Central School of Speech and Drama and the British American Drama Academy; Member of the editorial board of *New Theatre Quarterly*. Author of articles for *Contemporary Dramatists*, 1988. **Essays:** The Dybbuk; The Entertainer; The Great God Brown; He Who Gets Slapped; Johnny Johnson; An Inspector Calls; Once in a Lifetime; The Skin of Our Teeth; Waiting for Lefty.

TWYCROSS, Meg. Reader in English Studies, Lancaster University; Co-editor of *Medieval English Theatre*, and its associated playtext and monograph series. Author of *The Medieval Anadyomene: A Study in Chaucer's Mythography*, 1972. Editor of *"Purification, "Antichrist", and "Noah"*, 1983, and *That Girl From Andros*, 1989. Author of articles on Medieval theatre, acting, costume and masks. Director of productions of Tudor and Medieval plays in original settings. **Essays:** Fulgens and Lucrece.

UDALL, Joanna. Specialist in Renaissance drama. Has lectured for Kings College and Royal Holloway and Bedford

New College (both University of London), Lawrence University, University of Connecticut, and St. Lawrence University. Author of commentaries on *The Comedy of Errors* and *Cymbeline* for the forthcoming Oxford University Press Annotated Shakespeare. Editor of a forthcoming edition of *The Birth of Merlin*. **Essays:** The Comedy of Errors; The Old Wives Tale; Ralph Roister Doister; The Spanish Tragedy; Timon of Athens.

VENA, Gary. Associate Professor of English and World Literature, Manhattan College. Author of *O'Neill's "The Iceman Cometh": Reconstructing the Première*, 1988, and *How to Read and Write about Drama*, 1988. Advisory Editor for the *Eugene O'Neill Review*. **Essay:** The Iceman Cometh.

VISSER, Colin Wills. Professor and Associate Chairman, English Department, and Director of Graduate Center for the Study of Drama, University of Toronto. Former Director, University College Drama Programme. Author of articles on Restoration and 18th-century theatre for *Theatre Survey*, *Theatre Notebook*, and *Theatre Research International*. Contributor to *The London Theatre World*, 1980. **Essays:** The Critic; The Fair Penitent; The School for Scandal.

WAAL, Carla. Professor of Theatre, University of Missouri, Columbia. Formerly, Associate Professor of Theatre, University of Georgia, Athens. Author of *Johanne Dybwad: Norwegian Actress*, 1967, *Harriet Bosse: Strindberg's Muse and Interpreter*, 1990, and articles Ibsen, and Scandinavian and American theatre, for publications including *Southern Speech Communication*, *Educational Theatre Journal*, *Theatre History Studies*, *Encyclopaedia of World Literature in the Twentieth Century*, and *Theatre Companies of the World*. Translator of some of Bjørg Vik's writings for *Scandinavian Studies*, *Scandinavian Review*, and the anthologies *An Everyday Story*, 1984, and *Scandinavian Women Writers*, 1987. **Essay:** To Damascus.

WAINE, Anthony. Lecturer in German Studies, Lancaster University. Author of *Martin Walser: The Development as Dramatist (1950–70)*, 1978, *Martin Walser*, 1980. Co-editor (with Graham Bartram) of *Brecht in Perspective*, 1982, and *Culture and Society in the German Democratic Republic*, 1984. **Essays:** The Fireraisers; Home Front; The Investigation; The Visit.

WALCOT, Peter. Professor in the School of History and Archaeology, University College of Wales, Cardiff; Joint editor of the journal *Greece and Rome*. Formerly Visiting Professor, University of California, 1982, and Webster Lecturer, Stanford University, 1991. Author of *Hesiod and the Near East*, 1966, *Greek Peasants, Ancient and Modern*, 1970, *Greek Drama in its Theatrical and Social Context*, 1976, *Envy and the Greeks, A Study of Human Behaviour*, 1978, and articles and reviews on Greek, Roman, and Near Eastern literature and culture for various periodicals, including *Journal of Hellenic Studies*, *Classical Quarterly*, *Times Literary Supplement*, *Classical Review*. **Essays:** The Bad-Tempered Old Man; The Birds; The Clouds; Electra (Euripides); Iphigenia in Tauris; Oedipus (Seneca); Oedipus the King.

WALKER, David H. Professor of French and Head of the Department of Modern Languages, University of Keele. Former Assistant Editor, *Theatre Research International*. Author of *André Gide*, 1990, and essays on Camus, Gide, Robbe-Grillet, and John Fowles. Editor of Genet's *Le Balcon*, 1982. Translator of French drama for BBC radio, and of Henry

Becque's *The Scavengers*, 1986. **Essays:** Cross Purpose; Lorenzaccio; The Vultures.

WALTON, J. Michael. Reader in Theatre History, University of Hull; general editor, Methuen Classical Texts in Translation. Author of *Greek Theatre Practice*, 1980, *The Greek Sense of Theatre: Tragedy Reviewed*, 1984, *Living Greek Theatre: A Handbook of Classical Performance and Modern Production*, 1987, and of articles for *Theatre Research International*, *New Theatre Magazine*, *Asian Theatre Bulletin*, *Plays and Players* and other periodicals. Editor of *Craig on Theatre*, 1983, *Euripides: Plays, 1* (also translator of *The Bacchae*), and *Sophocles: Plays, 2* (also translator of *Women of Trachis*). **Essays:** Ajax; Alcestis; The Bacchae; The Brothers Menaechmus; Electra (Sophocles); Medea; Oedipus at Colonus; Philoctetes; The Women of Trachis.

WARING, Alan G. Head of Department of Russian and Slavonic Studies, University of Sheffield. Author of *Science Russian Grammar*, 1967, *Comprehensive Russian*, 1985, and articles on Slavonic language and literature. Translator of works by Griboyedov and Mayakovsky. **Essay:** The Misfortune of Being Clever.

WATERMEIER, Daniel J. Professor of Theatre and Drama, University of Toledo, Ohio. Formerly, Visiting Professor of Drama, University of Southern California, Los Angeles. Author of articles and reviews on 19th-century actors, American drama, and Shakespearian production for *Theatre History Studies*, *Theatre Research International*, *Shakespeare Quarterly*, and *The Cambridge Guide to World Theatre*, 1988. Editor of *Between Actor and Critic: Selected Letters of Edwin Booth to William Winter*, 1971, *Edwin Booth's Performances: The Mary Isabella Stone Commentaries*, 1990. Associate editor of *Shakespeare Around the Globe: A Guide to Notable Postwar Revivals*, 1986. **Essays:** Burn This; The Great Divide.

WELLAND, Dennis. Emeritus Professor, University of Manchester, and Chairman of Contact Theatre Company (since 1984). Formerly Professor of American Literature, University of Manchester, 1965–83, and founder-editor of *Journal of American Studies*, 1967. Author of *Wilfred Owen: A Critical Study*, 1960 (revised, 1978), *Arthur Miller*, 1961 (several subsequent revisions); *Mark Twain in England*, 1978, and numerous articles on English and American literature. Editor of *The U.S.A.: A Companion to American Studies*, 1974 (revised 1977 and 1987). **Essay:** Mourning Becomes Electra.

WELLS, Stanley. Professor of Shakespeare Studies, and Director of the Shakespeare Institute, University of Birmingham, since 1988; general editor (with Gary Taylor) of "The Oxford Shakespeare" series; editor of *Shakespeare Survey*, since 1981. Formerly, Reader in English, University of Birmingham, 1962–77; Senior Research Fellow, Balliol College, Oxford, 1980–88. Author of *Literature and Drama*, *Royal Shakespeare*, 1977, *Shakespeare: An Illustrated Dictionary*, 1978, *Shakespeare: The Writer and His Work*, 1978, and many articles on Shakespeare and Renaissance drama. Editor of *Thomas Nashe: Selected Writings*, 1964, Shakespeare's *A Midsummer Night's Dream*, 1967, *Richard II*, 1969, *Shakespeare: A Reading Guide*, 1969, *The Comedy of Errors*, 1972, the Select Bibliographical Guides *Shakespeare*, 1973 (revised as *Shakespeare: A Bibliographical Guide*, 1990) and *English Drama Excluding Shakespeare*, 1975, *The Cambridge Companion to Shakespeare Studies*, 1986, *The Oxford Anthology of Shakespeare*, 1987. General editor, with Gary Taylor, of *The Complete Oxford Shakespeare*, 1986. Co-editor (with R.L.

Smallwood) of Dekker's *The Shoemaker's Holiday*, 1979, and (with others) *William Shakespeare: A Textual Companion*, 1987.

WELLWARTH, George E. Professor of Theatre and Comparative Literature, State University of New York, Binghampton, since 1970; co-editor, *Modern International Drama*, since 1967. Author of *The Theatre of Protest and Paradox*, 1964, *Modern Drama and the Death of God*, 1986. Editor of *The New Wave Spanish Drama*, 1970, *German Drama Between the Wars*, 1972, *Themes of Drama*, 1972, *Spanish Underground Drama*, 1972, *New Generation Spanish Drama*, 1974, *Three Catalan Dramatists*, 1974. Co-editor of *Modern French Theatre*, 1964, *Modern Spanish Theatre*, 1968. Translator of *Concise Encyclopedia of the Modern Drama*, 1964.

WHITTON, David. Lecturer in French, University of Lancaster. Author of *Stage Directors in Modern France*, 1987, *Molière: "Le Bourgeois Gentilhomme*, 1991, *Molière: "Le Misanthrope"*, 1991, and articles on French playwrights and directors for *Theatre Research International*, *Forum for Modern Language Studies*, *Nottingham French Studies*, and other journals. **Essays:** The Architect and Emperor of Assyria; The Pretentious Young Ladies; The Would-Be Gentleman.

WILLIAMS, Margaret. Senior Lecturer in Theatre Studies, University of New South Wales, Kensington, Australia. Author of *Drama* (Writers and Their Work Series), *Australia on the Popular Stage, 1829–1929*, 1983, and many articles on Australian drama for *Contemporary Australian Drama*, 1981, *The Cambridge Guide to World Theatre*, 1988, and various periodicals. **Essays:** The Chapel Perilous; The Man From Mukinupin.

WILLIAMS, Simon. Professor of Dramatic Art, University of California at Santa Barbara. Previously taught at universities in Sweden, Austria, Libya, Iran, and, in the USA, at the University of Regina, University of Alberta, and Cornell University. Author of *German Actors of the Eighteenth and Nineteenth Centuries: Idealism, Romanticism and Realism*, 1985, *Shakespeare on the German Stage, 1587–1914*, 1990, and articles on Irish theatre, 18th and 19th-century theatre, acting, and opera, in various periodicals. **Essays:** Emilia Galotti; The Prince of Homburg.

WOMACK, Peter. Lecturer in English, University of East Anglia, Norwich. Author of *Ben Jonson*, 1986, *Improvement and Romance: Constructing the Myth of the Highlands*, 1989, and articles on Renaissance and modern drama. **Essays:** The Beaux' Stratagem; Everyman in His Humour; Henry VIII; The Revenger's Tragedy; Sejanus His Fall.

WOODYARD, George. Professor of Spanish, University of Kansas, Lawrence; editor of *Latin American Theater Review*. Author of articles on Latin American theatre. Editor of *The Modern Stage in Latin America: Six Plays*, 1971. Co-editor (with Leon F. Lyday) of *Dramatists in Revolt: The New Latin American Theatre*, 1976, and *A Bibliography of Latin American Theatre Criticism, 1940–1974*, 1976.

WOOLGAR, Claudia. Freelance theatre critic and journalist. Author of articles and reviews for various US and British newspapers and periodicals. Co-editor of the forthcoming *World Encyclopaedia of Contemporary Theatre*. **Essays:** Candida; A Chaste Maid in Cheapside; A Man for All Seasons.

WORTH, Katharine. Emeritus Professor, University of London, and Visiting Professor at King's College, University of London. Formerly Professor of Drama and Theatre Studies, Royal Holloway and Bedford New College until 1987. Author of *Revolutions in Modern English Drama*, 1973, *The Irish Drama from Yeats to Beckett*, 1978, *Oscar Wilde*, 1983, *Maeterlinck's Plays in Performance*, 1985, *"Waiting for Godot" and "Happy Days"* (Text in Performance Series), 1990, and many articles on Beckett, Yeats, Irish and Noh drama for collections and periodicals. Has co-directed (with David Clark) television versions of Beckett's *Eh Joe*, *Words and Music*, *Embers*, *Cascando*, and made an award-winning adaptation of Beckett's *Company* for the stage in 1987. **Essays:** The Blue Bird; Juno and the Paycock; Lady Windermere's Fan; Philadelphia, Here I Come!; Waiting for Godot.

YATES, W.E. Professor of German, University of Exeter. Formerly Deputy Vice-Chancellor, University of Exeter, 1986–89, and Germanic editor for *Modern Language Review*, 1981–88. Author of *Grillparzer: A Critical Introduction*, 1972, *Nestroy: Satire and Parody in Popular Viennese Comedy*, 1972, *Humanity in Weimar and Vienna: The Continuity of an Ideal*, 1973, *Tradition in the German Sonnet*, 1981, and various articles on Viennese cultural and theatrical history, German literature and lyric poetry. Editor of Hofmannsthal's *Der Schwierige*, 1966, Grillparzer's *Der Traum ein Leben*, 1968, and five volumes of Nestroy's works, 1981–91. Co-editor of *Viennese Popular Theatre*, 1985, and *Grillparzer und die europäische Tradition*, 1987. **Essay:** The Difficult Man.

ZATLIN, Phyllis. Professor of Spanish, State University of New Jersey, Rutgers. Author of *Elena Quirogs*, 1977, *Victor Ruiz Iriarte*, 1980, *Jaime Salom*, 1982, and numerous articles on contemporary Spanish theatre. Co-author of *Lengua y lectura: Un repaso y una continuación*, 1970. Editor of Francisco Ayala's *El rapto*, 1971, Iriarte's *El landó de seis caballos*, 1979, Salom's *La piel del limón*, 1980, Antonio Gala's *Noviembre y un poco de yerba; Petra Regalada*, 1981, Francisco Nieva's *Combate de Opalos y Tasia; Sombra y quimera de Larra; La magosta*, 1990. Co-editor (with Martha T. Halsey) of *The Contemporary Spanish Theatre: A Collection of Critical Essays*, 1988. Translator of French and Spanish plays and short stories. **Essays:** Bonds of Interest; Lights of Bohemia.

ZEIFMAN, Hersh. Associate Professor of English, York University, Toronto; Co-editor of *Modern Drama;* President of the Samuel Beckett Society. Author of numerous articles on Beckett and aspects of modern drama. Editor of the forthcoming *David Hare: A Casebook*, and *Contemporary British Drama*. **Essays:** All My Sons; A Day in the Death of Joe Egg; The Philanthropist; The Real Thing.

PICTURE ACKNOWLEDGEMENTS

Australian Overseas Information Service, London: The Doll Trilogy

The British Library, London: The Double-Dealer (1777 edition, frontispiece); The Marriage of Figaro (P.A. Caron de Beaumarchais: *Les Oeuvres completes,* Paris 1809); The Merry Wives of Windsor (G.H.H. Paul and G. Gebbie: *The Stage and Its Stars*, Vol I, Philadelphia, 1885): Philaster (1620 edition frontispiece); The Imaginary Invalid; The Learned Ladies; The Miser; The Pretentious Young Ladies; The Would-Be Gentlman (all from *Les Oeuvres de M. Molière*, Paris, 1682)

J.M. Burian: The Insect Play (photo Jaromir Svoboda); The Memorandum; R.U.R

Centralna Agencja Fotograficzna, Warsaw; Forefathers' Eve; Mariage blanc; The Marriage; Tango; The Undivine Comedy; The Water Hen; The Wedding

Emilio Carballido; I, Too, Speak of the Rose

Jean-Loup Charmet, Paris; El Cid; The Infernal Machine; The Theatrical Illusion

Compania Nacional de Teatro Clasico, Madrid: Celestina (photo Ros Ribas)

Michael Cook: Jacob's Wake

© **Donald Cooper, London:** All My Sons; All's Well That Ends Well; American Buffalo; Andromache; Antigone (Sophocles); Antony and Cleopatra; The Architect and Emperor of Assyria; The Balcony; The Birthday Party; Blood Wedding; Boesman and Lena; The Broken Jug; The Caretaker; The Changeling; The Cherry Orchard; The Churchill Play; The Comedy of Errors; Coriolanus; The Crucible; Danton's Death; Death of a Salesman; The Devils; Doctor Faustus; The Duchess of Malfi; The Dybbuk; Eastward Ho!; Edward II; Electra (Sophocles); Endgame; Entertaining Mr. Sloane; A Flea in her Ear; Fool For Love; The Forest; Fuenteovejuna; The Game of Love and Chance; Ghosts; Glengarry Glen Ross; The Good Person of Setzuan; The Government Inspector; The Hairy Ape; Hamlet; Happy Days; Hedda Gabler; Henry IV (Pirandello); Henry IV, Part Two; Home; The Homecoming; The House of Bernarda Alba; An Italian Straw Hat; Ivanov; The Jew of Malta; Jumpers; Juno and the Paycock; Kaspar; King Lear; The Knight of the Burning Pestle; Krapp's Last Tape; Lear; Life of Galileo; Life is a Dream; Love's Labour's Lost; The Lulu Plays; The Maids; Man and Superman; Man Equals Man; The Man of Mode; Mandragola; Mary Stuart; "Master Harold"... and the Boys; The Mayor of Zalamea; Measure for Measure; A Midsummer Night's Dream; The Misanthrope; A Month in the Country; Much Ado About Nothing; A New Way to Pay Old Debts; Not I; Once in a Lifetime; The Oresteia; The Playboy of the Western World; The Plebians Rehearse The Uprising; The Prince of Homburg; The Real Thing; The Removalists; The Resistable Rise of Arturo Ui; La Ronde; Rosencrantz and Guildenstern Are Dead; Saturday, Sunday, Monday; Saved; The Shoemaker's Holiday; The Silver Tassie; Six Characters in Search of an Author; Sizwe Bansi is Dead; The Spanish Tragedy; The Suicide; Summerfolk; The Taming of the Shrew; Tartuffe; The Tempest; The Threepenny Opera; Titus Andronicus; Top Girls; Translations; Travesties; The Trojan Women; The Tutor; Twelfth Night; Ubu Roi; Uncle Vanya; The Weavers; Who's Afraid of Virginia Woolf?; The Wild Duck; The Winter's Tale; The Witch of Edmonton; Women Beware Women; Woyzeck; Yerma; The York Cycle; You Can't Take It With You

© **Zoë Dominic, London:** The Bacchae; The Captain of Köpenick; Cat on a Hot Tin Roof; A Day in the Death of Joe Egg; Equus; Look Back in Anger; Lysistrata; Philoctetes; Rhinoceros; Ring Round the Moon

Drottningholms teatermuseum, Stockholm: A Doll's House; A Dream Play; The Ghost Sonata; The Hangman; The Master Builder; Peer Gynt

Gwynne Edwards: The Trickster of Seville (photo courtesy Centro nacional de documentacion teatral, Madrid)

M.P. Holt; Lights of Bohemia; The Sleep of Reason

Hulton-Deutsch Collection, London: Bartholomew Fair; The Beaux' Stratagem; The Bells; The Blue Bird; Caste; The Critic; Every Man in his Humour; The Fair Penitent; Francesca da Rimini (Boker); Henry V; Love for Love; Medea; Richard III

Lippische Landesbibliothek Detmold, Grabbe-Archiv; Comedy, Satire, Irony and Deeper Meaning

The Mander and Mitchenson Theatre Collection: The Admirable Crichton; The Ascent of F6; Back To Methuselah; The Beggar's Opera; Black-Eyed Susan; The Browning Version; Candida; Cato; The Cocktail Party; The Corn is Green; Da; The Emperor Jones; For Services Rendered; The Glass Menagerie; The Green Pastures; Heartbreak House; Hindle Wakes; The Hostage; The Iceman Cometh; The Importance of Being Earnest; Journey's End; The Lady's Not For Burning; The Little Foxes; Long Day's Journey Into Night; The Magistrate; Misalliance; The Mistress of the Inn; Mourning Becomes Electra; Mrs. Warren's Profession; Murder in the Cathedral; Othello; The Petrified Forest; The Philadelphia Story; Pygmalion; The Royal Hunt of the Sun; Ruy Blas; Saint Joan; Salomé; The Second Mrs Tanqueray; Serjeant Musgrave's Dance; Shadow and Substance; A Streetcar Named Desire; Strife; The Ticket-of-Leave Man; Tom Thumb; Too True to be Good; The Voysey Inheritance; Waiting for Godot; The Wesker Trilogy

The Mansell Collection, London; As You Like It; Troilus and Cressida

Roger Mayne: The Knack

James Reaney: The Donnelly Plays (photo Robert A. Barnett)

Society for Cultural Relations with the USSR: The Bedbug; The Fruits of Enlightenment; The Lower Depths; Masquerade; The Misfortune of Being Clever; Mystery Bouffe; The Power of Darkness; The Seagull; The Storm; The Three Sisters; The White Guard

Stadtarchiv Zürich: The Fire Raisers; The Physicists; The Visit

Martha Swope Photography Inc., New York: Burn This; Children of a Lesser God; For Colored Girls...; The House of Blue Leaves; Indians; A Raisin in the Sun; True West; A View from the Bridge

Theatermuseum der Universität zu Köln: The Gas Trilogy; Götz von Berlichingen; Hoppla, wir leben!; In The Matter of J. Robert Oppenheimer; Mother Courage and her Children; The Robbers; Scenes from the Heroic Life....; The Soldiers; Wallenstein

University of Bristol Theatre Collection: All For Love; At the Hawk's Well; Break of Noon; The Country Wife; Cyrano de Bergerac; Dead End; The Father; The Great Theatre of the World; The Magnificent Cuckold; Marat/Sade; The Merchant of Venice; Miss Julie; Oroonoko; Penthesilea; To Damascus; Winterset

Victoria and Albert Museum, London: (courtesy of the Board of Trustees of the V&A): The Alchemist; Chatterton; The Clandestine Marriage; Cymbeline; The Family Reunion; Faust; Hay Fever; Julius Caesar; The Lady of the Camelias; Macbeth; Pélleas and Mélisande; Peter Pan; Phèdre; The Plain Dealer; The Provoked Wife; The Rehearsal; Romeo and Juliet; The School for Scandal; The Shaughraun; She Stoops to Conquer; Timon of Athens; Venice Preserved; The Way of the World